BANKRUPTCY CODE, RULES, AND OFFICIAL FORMS

2015 Law School Edition

WEST ACADEMIC PUBLISHING

The publisher is not engaged in rendering legal or other professional advice, and this publication is not a substitute for the advice of an attorney. If you require legal or other expert advice, you should seek the services of a competent attorney or other professional.

© 2013 Thomson Reuters
© 2014 LEG, Inc. d/b/a West Academic
© 2015 LEG, Inc. d/b/a West Academic

    444 Cedar Street, Suite 700
    St. Paul, MN 55101
    1-877-888-1330

Printed in the United States of America

ISBN: 978-1-63459-593-3

[No claim of copyright is made for official U.S. government statutes, rules or regulations.]

PREFACE

This publication contains the current Bankruptcy Code (11 U.S.C.) and related provisions of United States Code Titles 18 and 28, as amended through Pub.L. 113–295, approved December 19, 2014. Dollar amounts listed in the Code have been adjusted, pursuant to 11 U.S.C. § 104, to reflect the amounts published by the Judicial Conference of the United States on Feb. 21, 2013, 78 F.R. 12089-01, effective as of Apr. 1, 2013.

The current bankruptcy court fee schedule, including changes effective in June 2014, appears following 28 U.S.C. § 1930.

THE PUBLISHER

April 2015

TABLE OF CONTENTS

		Page
BANKRUPTCY CODE		1
Chapter		
1.	General Provisions	1
3.	Case Administration	51
5.	Creditors, the Debtor, and the Estate	117
7.	Liquidation	221
9.	Adjustment of Debts of a Municipality	269
11.	Reorganization	281
12.	Adjustment of Debts of a Family Farmer or Fisherman With Regular Annual Income	339
13.	Adjustment of Debts of an Individual With Regular Income	359
15.	Ancillary and Other Cross-Border Cases	385
RELATED PROVISIONS OF U.S. CODE TITLES 18 AND 28		399
	Title 18, Crimes and Criminal Procedure	401
	Title 28, Judiciary and Judicial Procedure	423
	Bankruptcy Fees	481
FEDERAL RULES OF BANKRUPTCY PROCEDURE		491
Part		
I.	Commencement of Case: Proceedings Relating to Petition and Order for Relief	493
II.	Officers and Administration; Notices; Meetings; Examination; Elections; Attorneys and Accountants	533
III.	Claims and Distribution to Creditors and Equity Interest Holders; Plans	587
IV.	The Debtor: Duties and Benefits	627
V.	Bankruptcy Courts and Clerks	647
VI.	Collection and Liquidation of the Estate	663
VII.	Adversary Proceedings	677
VIII.	Appeals to District Court or Bankruptcy Appellate Panel	707
IX.	General Provisions	745
X.	United States Trustees [Abrogated]	787
OFFICIAL BANKRUPTCY FORMS		789
RELATED UNIFORM LAWS		1005
	Uniform Voidable Transactions Act	1005
	Uniform Fraudulent Transfer Act	1013
	Uniform Commercial Code	1019

TABLE OF CONTENTS

FEDERAL TAX LIEN STATUTES—INTERNAL REVENUE CODE 1037
INDEX 1047

BANKRUPTCY CODE, RULES, AND OFFICIAL FORMS

2015 Law School Edition

THE CODE OF THE LAWS OF THE UNITED STATES OF AMERICA

TITLE 11

BANKRUPTCY CODE

Chapter		Section
1.	General Provisions	101
3.	Case Administration	301
5.	Creditors, the Debtor, and the Estate	501
7.	Liquidation	701
9.	Adjustment of Debts of a Municipality	901
11.	Reorganization	1101
12.	Adjustments of Debts of a Family Farmer or Family Fisherman with Regular Annual Income[1]	1201
13.	Adjustment of Debts of an Individual with Regular Income	1301
15.	Ancillary and Other Cross-Border Cases	1501

CHAPTER 1—GENERAL PROVISIONS

Sec.
101. Definitions.
102. Rules of construction.
103. Applicability of chapters.
104. Adjustment of dollar amounts.
105. Power of court.
106. Waiver of sovereign immunity.
107. Public access to papers.
108. Extension of time.
109. Who may be a debtor.
110. Penalty for persons who negligently or fraudulently prepare bankruptcy petitions.
111. Nonprofit budget and credit counseling agencies; financial management instructional courses.
112. Prohibition on disclosure of name of minor children.

§ 101. Definitions

In this title the following definitions shall apply:

(1) The term "accountant" means accountant authorized under applicable law to practice public accounting, and includes professional accounting association, corporation, or partnership, if so authorized.

(2) The term "affiliate" means—

(A) entity that directly or indirectly owns, controls, or holds with power to vote, 20 percent or more of the outstanding voting securities of the debtor, other than an entity that holds such securities—

(i) in a fiduciary or agency capacity without sole discretionary power to vote such securities; or

(ii) solely to secure a debt, if such entity has not in fact exercised such power to vote;

(B) corporation 20 percent or more of whose outstanding voting securities are directly or indirectly owned, controlled, or held with power to vote, by the debtor, or by an entity that

---

[1] So in original. Does not conform to chapter heading.

directly or indirectly owns, controls, or holds with power to vote, 20 percent or more of the outstanding voting securities of the debtor, other than an entity that holds such securities—

 (i) in a fiduciary or agency capacity without sole discretionary power to vote such securities; or

 (ii) solely to secure a debt, if such entity has not in fact exercised such power to vote;

(C) person whose business is operated under a lease or operating agreement by a debtor, or person substantially all of whose property is operated under an operating agreement with the debtor; or

(D) entity that operates the business or substantially all of the property of the debtor under a lease or operating agreement.

(3) The term "assisted person" means any person whose debts consist primarily of consumer debts and the value of whose nonexempt property is less than $186,825[1].

(4) The term "attorney" means attorney, professional law association, corporation, or partnership, authorized under applicable law to practice law.

(4A) The term "bankruptcy assistance" means any goods or services sold or otherwise provided to an assisted person with the express or implied purpose of providing information, advice, counsel, document preparation, or filing, or attendance at a creditors' meeting or appearing in a case or proceeding on behalf of another or providing legal representation with respect to a case or proceeding under this title.

(5) The term "claim" means—

(A) right to payment, whether or not such right is reduced to judgment, liquidated, unliquidated, fixed, contingent, matured, unmatured, disputed, undisputed, legal, equitable, secured, or unsecured; or

(B) right to an equitable remedy for breach of performance if such breach gives rise to a right to payment, whether or not such right to an equitable remedy is reduced to judgment, fixed, contingent, matured, unmatured, disputed, undisputed, secured, or unsecured.

(6) The term "commodity broker" means futures commission merchant, foreign futures commission merchant, clearing organization, leverage transaction merchant, or commodity options dealer, as defined in section 761 of this title, with respect to which there is a customer, as defined in section 761 of this title.

(7) The term "community claim" means claim that arose before the commencement of the case concerning the debtor for which property of the kind specified in section 541(a)(2) of this title is liable, whether or not there is any such property at the time of the commencement of the case.

(7A) The term "commercial fishing operation" means—

(A) the catching or harvesting of fish, shrimp, lobsters, urchins, seaweed, shellfish, or other aquatic species or products of such species; or

(B) for purposes of section 109 and chapter 12, aquaculture activities consisting of raising for market any species or product described in subparagraph (A).

(7B) The term "commercial fishing vessel" means a vessel used by a family fisherman to carry out a commercial fishing operation.

(8) The term "consumer debt" means debt incurred by an individual primarily for a personal, family, or household purpose.

(9) The term "corporation"—

(A) includes—

---

[1] Dollar amount as adjusted by the Judicial Conference of the United States. See Adjustment of Dollar Amounts notes set out under this section and 11 U.S.C.A. § 104.

(i) association having a power or privilege that a private corporation, but not an individual or a partnership, possesses;

(ii) partnership association organized under a law that makes only the capital subscribed responsible for the debts of such association;

(iii) joint-stock company;

(iv) unincorporated company or association; or

(v) business trust; but

(B) does not include limited partnership.

(10) The term "creditor" means—

(A) entity that has a claim against the debtor that arose at the time of or before the order for relief concerning the debtor;

(B) entity that has a claim against the estate of a kind specified in section 348(d), 502(f), 502(g), 502(h) or 502(i) of this title; or

(C) entity that has a community claim.

(10A) The term "current monthly income"—

(A) means the average monthly income from all sources that the debtor receives (or in a joint case the debtor and the debtor's spouse receive) without regard to whether such income is taxable income, derived during the 6-month period ending on—

(i) the last day of the calendar month immediately preceding the date of the commencement of the case if the debtor files the schedule of current income required by section 521(a)(1)(B)(ii); or

(ii) the date on which current income is determined by the court for purposes of this title if the debtor does not file the schedule of current income required by section 521(a)(1)(B)(ii); and

(B) includes any amount paid by any entity other than the debtor (or in a joint case the debtor and the debtor's spouse), on a regular basis for the household expenses of the debtor or the debtor's dependents (and in a joint case the debtor's spouse if not otherwise a dependent), but excludes benefits received under the Social Security Act, payments to victims of war crimes or crimes against humanity on account of their status as victims of such crimes, and payments to victims of international terrorism (as defined in section 2331 of title 18) or domestic terrorism (as defined in section 2331 of title 18) on account of their status as victims of such terrorism.

(11) The term "custodian" means—

(A) receiver or trustee of any of the property of the debtor, appointed in a case or proceeding not under this title;

(B) assignee under a general assignment for the benefit of the debtor's creditors; or

(C) trustee, receiver, or agent under applicable law, or under a contract, that is appointed or authorized to take charge of property of the debtor for the purpose of enforcing a lien against such property, or for the purpose of general administration of such property for the benefit of the debtor's creditors.

(12) The term "debt" means liability on a claim.

(12A) The term "debt relief agency" means any person who provides any bankruptcy assistance to an assisted person in return for the payment of money or other valuable consideration, or who is a bankruptcy petition preparer under section 110, but does not include—

(A) any person who is an officer, director, employee, or agent of a person who provides such assistance or of the bankruptcy petition preparer;

(B) a nonprofit organization that is exempt from taxation under section 501(c)(3) of the Internal Revenue Code of 1986;

(C) a creditor of such assisted person, to the extent that the creditor is assisting such assisted person to restructure any debt owed by such assisted person to the creditor;

(D) a depository institution (as defined in section 3 of the Federal Deposit Insurance Act) or any Federal credit union or State credit union (as those terms are defined in section 101 of the Federal Credit Union Act), or any affiliate or subsidiary of such depository institution or credit union; or

(E) an author, publisher, distributor, or seller of works subject to copyright protection under title 17, when acting in such capacity.

(13) The term "debtor" means person or municipality concerning which a case under this title has been commenced.

(13A) The term "debtor's principal residence"—

(A) means a residential structure if used as the principal residence by the debtor, including incidental property, without regard to whether that structure is attached to real property; and

(B) includes an individual condominium or cooperative unit, a mobile or manufactured home, or trailer if used as the principal residence by the debtor.

(14) The term "disinterested person" means a person that—

(A) is not a creditor, an equity security holder, or an insider;

(B) is not and was not, within 2 years before the date of the filing of the petition, a director, officer, or employee of the debtor; and

(C) does not have an interest materially adverse to the interest of the estate or of any class of creditors or equity security holders, by reason of any direct or indirect relationship to, connection with, or interest in, the debtor, or for any other reason.

(14A) The term "domestic support obligation" means a debt that accrues before, on, or after the date of the order for relief in a case under this title, including interest that accrues on that debt as provided under applicable nonbankruptcy law notwithstanding any other provision of this title, that is—

(A) owed to or recoverable by—

(i) a spouse, former spouse, or child of the debtor or such child's parent, legal guardian, or responsible relative; or

(ii) a governmental unit;

(B) in the nature of alimony, maintenance, or support (including assistance provided by a governmental unit) of such spouse, former spouse, or child of the debtor or such child's parent, without regard to whether such debt is expressly so designated;

(C) established or subject to establishment before, on, or after the date of the order for relief in a case under this title, by reason of applicable provisions of—

(i) a separation agreement, divorce decree, or property settlement agreement;

(ii) an order of a court of record; or

(iii) a determination made in accordance with applicable nonbankruptcy law by a governmental unit; and

(D) not assigned to a nongovernmental entity, unless that obligation is assigned voluntarily by the spouse, former spouse, child of the debtor, or such child's parent, legal guardian, or responsible relative for the purpose of collecting the debt.

(15) The term "entity" includes person, estate, trust, governmental unit, and United States trustee.

(16) The term "equity security" means—

(A) share in a corporation, whether or not transferable or denominated "stock", or similar security;

(B) interest of a limited partner in a limited partnership; or

(C) warrant or right, other than a right to convert, to purchase, sell, or subscribe to a share, security, or interest of a kind specified in subparagraph (A) or (B) of this paragraph.

(17) The term "equity security holder" means holder of an equity security of the debtor.

(18) The term "family farmer" means—

(A) individual or individual and spouse engaged in a farming operation whose aggregate debts do not exceed $4,031,575[1] and not less than 50 percent of whose aggregate noncontingent, liquidated debts (excluding a debt for the principal residence of such individual or such individual and spouse unless such debt arises out of a farming operation), on the date the case is filed, arise out of a farming operation owned or operated by such individual or such individual and spouse, and such individual or such individual and spouse receive from such farming operation more than 50 percent of such individual's or such individual and spouse's gross income for—

(i) the taxable year preceding; or

(ii) each of the 2d and 3d taxable years preceding;

the taxable year in which the case concerning such individual or such individual and spouse was filed; or

(B) corporation or partnership in which more than 50 percent of the outstanding stock or equity is held by one family, or by one family and the relatives of the members of such family, and such family or such relatives conduct the farming operation, and

(i) more than 80 percent of the value of its assets consists of assets related to the farming operation;

(ii) its aggregate debts do not exceed $4,031,575[1] and not less than 50 percent of its aggregate noncontingent, liquidated debts (excluding a debt for one dwelling which is owned by such corporation or partnership and which a shareholder or partner maintains as a principal residence, unless such debt arises out of a farming operation), on the date the case is filed, arise out of the farming operation owned or operated by such corporation or such partnership; and

(iii) if such corporation issues stock, such stock is not publicly traded.

(19) The term "family farmer with regular annual income" means family farmer whose annual income is sufficiently stable and regular to enable such family farmer to make payments under a plan under chapter 12 of this title.

(19A) The term "family fisherman" means—

(A) an individual or individual and spouse engaged in a commercial fishing operation—

(i) whose aggregate debts do not exceed $1,868,200[1] and not less than 80 percent of whose aggregate noncontingent, liquidated debts (excluding a debt for the principal residence of such individual or such individual and spouse, unless such debt arises out of a commercial fishing operation), on the date the case is filed, arise out of a commercial fishing operation owned or operated by such individual or such individual and spouse; and

(ii) who receive from such commercial fishing operation more than 50 percent of such individual's or such individual's and spouse's gross income for the taxable year

---

[1] Dollar amount as adjusted by the Judicial Conference of the United States. See Adjustment of Dollar Amounts notes set out under this section and 11 U.S.C.A. § 104.

preceding the taxable year in which the case concerning such individual or such individual and spouse was filed; or

(B) a corporation or partnership—

(i) in which more than 50 percent of the outstanding stock or equity is held by—

(I) 1 family that conducts the commercial fishing operation; or

(II) 1 family and the relatives of the members of such family, and such family or such relatives conduct the commercial fishing operation; and

(ii)(I) more than 80 percent of the value of its assets consists of assets related to the commercial fishing operation;

(II) its aggregate debts do not exceed $1,868,200[1] and not less than 80 percent of its aggregate noncontingent, liquidated debts (excluding a debt for 1 dwelling which is owned by such corporation or partnership and which a shareholder or partner maintains as a principal residence, unless such debt arises out of a commercial fishing operation), on the date the case is filed, arise out of a commercial fishing operation owned or operated by such corporation or such partnership; and

(III) if such corporation issues stock, such stock is not publicly traded.

(19B) The term "family fisherman with regular annual income" means a family fisherman whose annual income is sufficiently stable and regular to enable such family fisherman to make payments under a plan under chapter 12 of this title.

(20) The term "farmer" means (except when such term appears in the term "family farmer") person that received more than 80 percent of such person's gross income during the taxable year of such person immediately preceding the taxable year of such person during which the case under this title concerning such person was commenced from a farming operation owned or operated by such person.

(21) The term "farming operation" includes farming, tillage of the soil, dairy farming, ranching, production or raising of crops, poultry, or livestock, and production of poultry or livestock products in an unmanufactured state.

(21A) The term "farmout agreement" means a written agreement in which—

(A) the owner of a right to drill, produce, or operate liquid or gaseous hydrocarbons on property agrees or has agreed to transfer or assign all or a part of such right to another entity; and

(B) such other entity (either directly or through its agents or its assigns), as consideration, agrees to perform drilling, reworking, recompleting, testing, or similar or related operations, to develop or produce liquid or gaseous hydrocarbons on the property.

(21B) The term "Federal depository institutions regulatory agency" means—

(A) with respect to an insured depository institution (as defined in section 3(c)(2) of the Federal Deposit Insurance Act) for which no conservator or receiver has been appointed, the appropriate Federal banking agency (as defined in section 3(q) of such Act);

(B) with respect to an insured credit union (including an insured credit union for which the National Credit Union Administration has been appointed conservator or liquidating agent), the National Credit Union Administration;

(C) with respect to any insured depository institution for which the Resolution Trust Corporation has been appointed conservator or receiver, the Resolution Trust Corporation; and

(D) with respect to any insured depository institution for which the Federal Deposit Insurance Corporation has been appointed conservator or receiver, the Federal Deposit Insurance Corporation.

---

[1] Dollar amount as adjusted by the Judicial Conference of the United States. See Adjustment of Dollar Amounts notes set out under this section and 11 U.S.C.A. § 104.

(22) The term "financial institution" means—

　(A) a Federal reserve bank, or an entity that is a commercial or savings bank, industrial savings bank, savings and loan association, trust company, federally-insured credit union, or receiver, liquidating agent, or conservator for such entity and, when any such Federal reserve bank, receiver, liquidating agent, conservator or entity is acting as agent or custodian for a customer (whether or not a "customer", as defined in section 741) in connection with a securities contract (as defined in section 741) such customer; or

　(B) in connection with a securities contract (as defined in section 741) an investment company registered under the Investment Company Act of 1940.

(22A) The term "financial participant" means—

　(A) an entity that, at the time it enters into a securities contract, commodity contract, swap agreement, repurchase agreement, or forward contract, or at the time of the date of the filing of the petition, has one or more agreements or transactions described in paragraph (1), (2), (3), (4), (5), or (6) of section 561(a) with the debtor or any other entity (other than an affiliate) of a total gross dollar value of not less than $1,000,000,000 in notional or actual principal amount outstanding (aggregated across counterparties) at such time or on any day during the 15-month period preceding the date of the filing of the petition, or has gross mark-to-market positions of not less than $100,000,000 (aggregated across counterparties) in one or more such agreements or transactions with the debtor or any other entity (other than an affiliate) at such time or on any day during the 15-month period preceding the date of the filing of the petition; or

　(B) a clearing organization (as defined in section 402 of the Federal Deposit Insurance Corporation Improvement Act of 1991).

(23) The term "foreign proceeding" means a collective judicial or administrative proceeding in a foreign country, including an interim proceeding, under a law relating to insolvency or adjustment of debt in which proceeding the assets and affairs of the debtor are subject to control or supervision by a foreign court, for the purpose of reorganization or liquidation.

(24) The term "foreign representative" means a person or body, including a person or body appointed on an interim basis, authorized in a foreign proceeding to administer the reorganization or the liquidation of the debtor's assets or affairs or to act as a representative of such foreign proceeding.

(25) The term "forward contract" means—

　(A) a contract (other than a commodity contract, as defined in section 761) for the purchase, sale, or transfer of a commodity, as defined in section 761(8) of this title, or any similar good, article, service, right, or interest which is presently or in the future becomes the subject of dealing in the forward contract trade, or product or byproduct thereof, with a maturity date more than two days after the date the contract is entered into, including, but not limited to, a repurchase or reverse repurchase transaction (whether or not such repurchase or reverse repurchase transaction is a "repurchase agreement", as defined in this section)[2] consignment, lease, swap, hedge transaction, deposit, loan, option, allocated transaction, unallocated transaction, or any other similar agreement;

　(B) any combination of agreements or transactions referred to in subparagraphs (A) and (C);

　(C) any option to enter into an agreement or transaction referred to in subparagraph (A) or (B);

　(D) a master agreement that provides for an agreement or transaction referred to in subparagraph (A), (B), or (C), together with all supplements to any such master agreement, without regard to whether such master agreement provides for an agreement or transaction that is not a forward contract under this paragraph, except that such master agreement shall be considered to be a forward contract under this paragraph only with respect to each

---

[2] So in original. A comma should probably appear.

agreement or transaction under such master agreement that is referred to in subparagraph (A), (B), or (C); or

(E) any security agreement or arrangement, or other credit enhancement related to any agreement or transaction referred to in subparagraph (A), (B), (C), or (D), including any guarantee or reimbursement obligation by or to a forward contract merchant or financial participant in connection with any agreement or transaction referred to in any such subparagraph, but not to exceed the damages in connection with any such agreement or transaction, measured in accordance with section 562.

(26) The term "forward contract merchant" means a Federal reserve bank, or an entity the business of which consists in whole or in part of entering into forward contracts as or with merchants in a commodity (as defined in section 761) or any similar good, article, service, right, or interest which is presently or in the future becomes the subject of dealing in the forward contract trade.

(27) The term "governmental unit" means United States; State; Commonwealth; District; Territory; municipality; foreign state; department, agency, or instrumentality of the United States (but not a United States trustee while serving as a trustee in a case under this title), a State, a Commonwealth, a District, a Territory, a municipality, or a foreign state; or other foreign or domestic government.

(27A) The term "health care business"—

(A) means any public or private entity (without regard to whether that entity is organized for profit or not for profit) that is primarily engaged in offering to the general public facilities and services for—

(i) the diagnosis or treatment of injury, deformity, or disease; and

(ii) surgical, drug treatment, psychiatric, or obstetric care; and

(B) includes—

(i) any—

(I) general or specialized hospital;

(II) ancillary ambulatory, emergency, or surgical treatment facility;

(III) hospice;

(IV) home health agency; and

(V) other health care institution that is similar to an entity referred to in subclause (I), (II), (III), or (IV); and

(ii) any long-term care facility, including any—

(I) skilled nursing facility;

(II) intermediate care facility;

(III) assisted living facility;

(IV) home for the aged;

(V) domiciliary care facility; and

(VI) health care institution that is related to a facility referred to in subclause (I), (II), (III), (IV), or (V), if that institution is primarily engaged in offering room, board, laundry, or personal assistance with activities of daily living and incidentals to activities of daily living.

(27B) The term "incidental property" means, with respect to a debtor's principal residence—

(A) property commonly conveyed with a principal residence in the area where the real property is located;

(B) all easements, rights, appurtenances, fixtures, rents, royalties, mineral rights, oil or gas rights or profits, water rights, escrow funds, or insurance proceeds; and

(C) all replacements or additions.

(28) The term "indenture" means mortgage, deed of trust, or indenture, under which there is outstanding a security, other than a voting-trust certificate, constituting a claim against the debtor, a claim secured by a lien on any of the debtor's property, or an equity security of the debtor.

(29) The term "indenture trustee" means trustee under an indenture.

(30) The term "individual with regular income" means individual whose income is sufficiently stable and regular to enable such individual to make payments under a plan under chapter 13 of this title, other than a stockbroker or a commodity broker.

(31) The term "insider" includes—

(A) if the debtor is an individual—

(i) relative of the debtor or of a general partner of the debtor;

(ii) partnership in which the debtor is a general partner;

(iii) general partner of the debtor; or

(iv) corporation of which the debtor is a director, officer, or person in control;

(B) if the debtor is a corporation—

(i) director of the debtor;

(ii) officer of the debtor;

(iii) person in control of the debtor;

(iv) partnership in which the debtor is a general partner;

(v) general partner of the debtor; or

(vi) relative of a general partner, director, officer, or person in control of the debtor;

(C) if the debtor is a partnership—

(i) general partner in the debtor;

(ii) relative of a general partner in, general partner of, or person in control of the debtor;

(iii) partnership in which the debtor is a general partner;

(iv) general partner of the debtor; or

(v) person in control of the debtor;

(D) if the debtor is a municipality, elected official of the debtor or relative of an elected official of the debtor;

(E) affiliate, or insider of an affiliate as if such affiliate were the debtor; and

(F) managing agent of the debtor.

(32) The term "insolvent" means—

(A) with reference to an entity other than a partnership and a municipality, financial condition such that the sum of such entity's debts is greater than all of such entity's property, at a fair valuation, exclusive of—

(i) property transferred, concealed, or removed with intent to hinder, delay, or defraud such entity's creditors; and

(ii) property that may be exempted from property of the estate under section 522 of this title;

(B) with reference to a partnership, financial condition such that the sum of such partnership's debts is greater than the aggregate of, at a fair valuation—

(i) all of such partnership's property, exclusive of property of the kind specified in subparagraph (A)(i) of this paragraph; and

(ii) the sum of the excess of the value of each general partner's nonpartnership property, exclusive of property of the kind specified in subparagraph (A) of this paragraph, over such partner's nonpartnership debts; and

(C) with reference to a municipality, financial condition such that the municipality is—

(i) generally not paying its debts as they become due unless such debts are the subject of a bona fide dispute; or

(ii) unable to pay its debts as they become due.

(33) The term "institution-affiliated party"—

(A) with respect to an insured depository institution (as defined in section 3(c)(2) of the Federal Deposit Insurance Act), has the meaning given it in section 3(u) of the Federal Deposit Insurance Act; and

(B) with respect to an insured credit union, has the meaning given it in section 206(r) of the Federal Credit Union Act.

(34) The term "insured credit union" has the meaning given it in section 101(7) of the Federal Credit Union Act.

(35) The term "insured depository institution"—

(A) has the meaning given it in section 3(c)(2) of the Federal Deposit Insurance Act; and

(B) includes an insured credit union (except in the case of paragraphs (21B) and (33)(A) of this subsection).

(35A) The term "intellectual property" means—

(A) trade secret;

(B) invention, process, design, or plant protected under title 35;

(C) patent application;

(D) plant variety;

(E) work of authorship protected under title 17; or

(F) mask work protected under chapter 9 of title 17;

to the extent protected by applicable nonbankruptcy law.

(36) The term "judicial lien" means lien obtained by judgment, levy, sequestration, or other legal or equitable process or proceeding.

(37) The term "lien" means charge against or interest in property to secure payment of a debt or performance of an obligation.

(38) The term "margin payment" means, for purposes of the forward contract provisions of this title, payment or deposit of cash, a security or other property, that is commonly known in the forward contract trade as original margin, initial margin, maintenance margin, or variation margin, including mark-to-market payments, or variation payments.

(38A) The term "master netting agreement"—

(A) means an agreement providing for the exercise of rights, including rights of netting, setoff, liquidation, termination, acceleration, or close out, under or in connection with one or more contracts that are described in any one or more of paragraphs (1) through (5) of section 561(a), or any security agreement or arrangement or other credit enhancement related to one or more of the foregoing, including any guarantee or reimbursement obligation related to 1 or more of the foregoing; and

(B) if the agreement contains provisions relating to agreements or transactions that are not contracts described in paragraphs (1) through (5) of section 561(a), shall be deemed to be a master netting agreement only with respect to those agreements or transactions that are described in any one or more of paragraphs (1) through (5) of section 561(a).

(38B) The term "master netting agreement participant" means an entity that, at any time before the date of the filing of the petition, is a party to an outstanding master netting agreement with the debtor.

(39) The term "mask work" has the meaning given it in section 901(a)(2) of title 17.

(39A) The term "median family income" means for any year—

(A) the median family income both calculated and reported by the Bureau of the Census in the then most recent year; and

(B) if not so calculated and reported in the then current year, adjusted annually after such most recent year until the next year in which median family income is both calculated and reported by the Bureau of the Census, to reflect the percentage change in the Consumer Price Index for All Urban Consumers during the period of years occurring after such most recent year and before such current year.

(40) The term "municipality" means political subdivision or public agency or instrumentality of a State.

(40A) The term "patient" means any individual who obtains or receives services from a health care business.

(40B) The term "patient records" means any record relating to a patient, including a written document or a record recorded in a magnetic, optical, or other form of electronic medium.

(41) The term "person" includes individual, partnership, and corporation, but does not include governmental unit, except that a governmental unit that—

(A) acquires an asset from a person—

(i) as a result of the operation of a loan guarantee agreement; or

(ii) as receiver or liquidating agent of a person;

(B) is a guarantor of a pension benefit payable by or on behalf of the debtor or an affiliate of the debtor; or

(C) is the legal or beneficial owner of an asset of—

(i) an employee pension benefit plan that is a governmental plan, as defined in section 414(d) of the Internal Revenue Code of 1986; or

(ii) an eligible deferred compensation plan, as defined in section 457(b) of the Internal Revenue Code of 1986;

shall be considered, for purposes of section 1102 of this title, to be a person with respect to such asset or such benefit.

(41A) The term "personally identifiable information" means—

(A) if provided by an individual to the debtor in connection with obtaining a product or a service from the debtor primarily for personal, family, or household purposes—

(i) the first name (or initial) and last name of such individual, whether given at birth or time of adoption, or resulting from a lawful change of name;

(ii) the geographical address of a physical place of residence of such individual;

(iii) an electronic address (including an e-mail address) of such individual;

(iv) a telephone number dedicated to contacting such individual at such physical place of residence;

(v) a social security account number issued to such individual; or

(vi) the account number of a credit card issued to such individual; or

(B) if identified in connection with 1 or more of the items of information specified in subparagraph (A)—

(i) a birth date, the number of a certificate of birth or adoption, or a place of birth; or

(ii) any other information concerning an identified individual that, if disclosed, will result in contacting or identifying such individual physically or electronically.

(42) The term "petition" means petition filed under section 301, 302, 303 and[3] 1504 of this title, as the case may be, commencing a case under this title.

(42A) The term "production payment" means a term overriding royalty satisfiable in cash or in kind—

(A) contingent on the production of a liquid or gaseous hydrocarbon from particular real property; and

(B) from a specified volume, or a specified value, from the liquid or gaseous hydrocarbon produced from such property, and determined without regard to production costs.

(43) The term "purchaser" means transferee of a voluntary transfer, and includes immediate or mediate transferee of such a transferee.

(44) The term "railroad" means common carrier by railroad engaged in the transportation of individuals or property or owner of trackage facilities leased by such a common carrier.

(45) The term "relative" means individual related by affinity or consanguinity within the third degree as determined by the common law, or individual in a step or adoptive relationship within such third degree.

(46) The term "repo participant" means an entity that, at any time before the filing of the petition, has an outstanding repurchase agreement with the debtor.

(47) The term "repurchase agreement" (which definition also applies to a reverse repurchase agreement)—

(A) means—

(i) an agreement, including related terms, which provides for the transfer of one or more certificates of deposit, mortgage related securities (as defined in section 3 of the Securities Exchange Act of 1934), mortgage loans, interests in mortgage related securities or mortgage loans, eligible bankers' acceptances, qualified foreign government securities (defined as a security that is a direct obligation of, or that is fully guaranteed by, the central government of a member of the Organization for Economic Cooperation and Development), or securities that are direct obligations of, or that are fully guaranteed by, the United States or any agency of the United States against the transfer of funds by the transferee of such certificates of deposit, eligible bankers' acceptances, securities, mortgage loans, or interests, with a simultaneous agreement by such transferee to transfer to the transferor thereof certificates of deposit, eligible bankers' acceptance, securities, mortgage loans, or interests of the kind described in this clause, at a date certain not later than 1 year after such transfer or on demand, against the transfer of funds;

(ii) any combination of agreements or transactions referred to in clauses (i) and (iii);

---

[3] So in original. Probably should be "or". See 2010 Amendments note set out under this section.

(iii) an option to enter into an agreement or transaction referred to in clause (i) or (ii);

(iv) a master agreement that provides for an agreement or transaction referred to in clause (i), (ii), or (iii), together with all supplements to any such master agreement, without regard to whether such master agreement provides for an agreement or transaction that is not a repurchase agreement under this paragraph, except that such master agreement shall be considered to be a repurchase agreement under this paragraph only with respect to each agreement or transaction under the master agreement that is referred to in clause (i), (ii), or (iii); or

(v) any security agreement or arrangement or other credit enhancement related to any agreement or transaction referred to in clause (i), (ii), (iii), or (iv), including any guarantee or reimbursement obligation by or to a repo participant or financial participant in connection with any agreement or transaction referred to in any such clause, but not to exceed the damages in connection with any such agreement or transaction, measured in accordance with section 562 of this title; and

(B) does not include a repurchase obligation under a participation in a commercial mortgage loan.

(48) The term "securities clearing agency" means person that is registered as a clearing agency under section 17A of the Securities Exchange Act of 1934, or exempt from such registration under such section pursuant to an order of the Securities and Exchange Commission, or whose business is confined to the performance of functions of a clearing agency with respect to exempted securities, as defined in section 3(a)(12) of such Act for the purposes of such section 17A.

(48A) The term "securities self regulatory organization" means either a securities association registered with the Securities and Exchange Commission under section 15A of the Securities Exchange Act of 1934 or a national securities exchange registered with the Securities and Exchange Commission under section 6 of the Securities Exchange Act of 1934.

(49) The term "security"—

(A) includes—

(i) note;

(ii) stock;

(iii) treasury stock;

(iv) bond;

(v) debenture;

(vi) collateral trust certificate;

(vii) pre-organization certificate or subscription;

(viii) transferable share;

(ix) voting-trust certificate;

(x) certificate of deposit;

(xi) certificate of deposit for security;

(xii) investment contract or certificate of interest or participation in a profit-sharing agreement or in an oil, gas, or mineral royalty or lease, if such contract or interest is required to be the subject of a registration statement filed with the Securities and Exchange Commission under the provisions of the Securities Act of 1933, or is exempt under section 3(b) of such Act from the requirement to file such a statement;

(xiii) interest of a limited partner in a limited partnership;

(xiv) other claim or interest commonly known as "security"; and

(xv) certificate of interest or participation in, temporary or interim certificate for, receipt for, or warrant or right to subscribe to or purchase or sell, a security; but

(B) does not include—

(i) currency, check, draft, bill of exchange, or bank letter of credit;

(ii) leverage transaction, as defined in section 761 of this title;

(iii) commodity futures contract or forward contract;

(iv) option, warrant, or right to subscribe to or purchase or sell a commodity futures contract;

(v) option to purchase or sell a commodity;

(vi) contract or certificate of a kind specified in subparagraph (A)(xii) of this paragraph that is not required to be the subject of a registration statement filed with the Securities and Exchange Commission and is not exempt under section 3(b) of the Securities Act of 1933 from the requirement to file such a statement; or

(vii) debt or evidence of indebtedness for goods sold and delivered or services rendered.

(50) The term "security agreement" means agreement that creates or provides for a security interest.

(51) The term "security interest" means lien created by an agreement.

(51A) The term "settlement payment" means, for purposes of the forward contract provisions of this title, a preliminary settlement payment, a partial settlement payment, an interim settlement payment, a settlement payment on account, a final settlement payment, a net settlement payment, or any other similar payment commonly used in the forward contract trade.

(51B) The term "single asset real estate" means real property constituting a single property or project, other than residential real property with fewer than 4 residential units, which generates substantially all of the gross income of a debtor who is not a family farmer and on which no substantial business is being conducted by a debtor other than the business of operating the real property and activities incidental thereto.

(51C) The term "small business case" means a case filed under chapter 11 of this title in which the debtor is a small business debtor.

(51D) The term "small business debtor"—

(A) subject to subparagraph (B), means a person engaged in commercial or business activities (including any affiliate of such person that is also a debtor under this title and excluding a person whose primary activity is the business of owning or operating real property or activities incidental thereto) that has aggregate noncontingent liquidated secured and unsecured debts as of the date of the filing of the petition or the date of the order for relief in an amount not more than $2,490,925[1] (excluding debts owed to 1 or more affiliates or insiders) for a case in which the United States trustee has not appointed under section 1102(a)(1) a committee of unsecured creditors or where the court has determined that the committee of unsecured creditors is not sufficiently active and representative to provide effective oversight of the debtor; and

(B) does not include any member of a group of affiliated debtors that has aggregate noncontingent liquidated secured and unsecured debts in an amount greater than $2,490,925[1] (excluding debt owed to 1 or more affiliates or insiders).

(52) The term "State" includes the District of Columbia and Puerto Rico, except for the purpose of defining who may be a debtor under chapter 9 of this title.

---

[1] Dollar amount as adjusted by the Judicial Conference of the United States. See Adjustment of Dollar Amounts notes set out under this section and 11 U.S.C.A. § 104.

(53) The term "statutory lien" means lien arising solely by force of a statute on specified circumstances or conditions, or lien of distress for rent, whether or not statutory, but does not include security interest or judicial lien, whether or not such interest or lien is provided by or is dependent on a statute and whether or not such interest or lien is made fully effective by statute.

(53A) The term "stockbroker" means person—

    (A) with respect to which there is a customer, as defined in section 741 of this title; and

    (B) that is engaged in the business of effecting transactions in securities—

        (i) for the account of others; or

        (ii) with members of the general public, from or for such person's own account.

(53B) The term "swap agreement"—

    (A) means—

        (i) any agreement, including the terms and conditions incorporated by reference in such agreement, which is—

            (I) an interest rate swap, option, future, or forward agreement, including a rate floor, rate cap, rate collar, cross-currency rate swap, and basis swap;

            (II) a spot, same day-tomorrow, tomorrow-next, forward, or other foreign exchange, precious metals, or other commodity agreement;

            (III) a currency swap, option, future, or forward agreement;

            (IV) an equity index or equity swap, option, future, or forward agreement;

            (V) a debt index or debt swap, option, future, or forward agreement;

            (VI) a total return, credit spread or credit swap, option, future, or forward agreement;

            (VII) a commodity index or a commodity swap, option, future, or forward agreement;

            (VIII) a weather swap, option, future, or forward agreement;

            (IX) an emissions swap, option, future, or forward agreement; or

            (X) an inflation swap, option, future, or forward agreement;

        (ii) any agreement or transaction that is similar to any other agreement or transaction referred to in this paragraph and that—

            (I) is of a type that has been, is presently, or in the future becomes, the subject of recurrent dealings in the swap or other derivatives markets (including terms and conditions incorporated by reference therein); and

            (II) is a forward, swap, future, option, or spot transaction on one or more rates, currencies, commodities, equity securities, or other equity instruments, debt securities or other debt instruments, quantitative measures associated with an occurrence, extent of an occurrence, or contingency associated with a financial, commercial, or economic consequence, or economic or financial indices or measures of economic or financial risk or value;

        (iii) any combination of agreements or transactions referred to in this subparagraph;

        (iv) any option to enter into an agreement or transaction referred to in this subparagraph;

        (v) a master agreement that provides for an agreement or transaction referred to in clause (i), (ii), (iii), or (iv), together with all supplements to any such master agreement, and without regard to whether the master agreement contains an agreement or transaction that is not a swap agreement under this paragraph, except that the master agreement shall be considered to be a swap agreement under this paragraph only with respect to each agreement or transaction under the master agreement that is referred to in clause (i), (ii), (iii), or (iv); or

(vi) any security agreement or arrangement or other credit enhancement related to any agreements or transactions referred to in clause (i) through (v), including any guarantee or reimbursement obligation by or to a swap participant or financial participant in connection with any agreement or transaction referred to in any such clause, but not to exceed the damages in connection with any such agreement or transaction, measured in accordance with section 562; and

(B) is applicable for purposes of this title only, and shall not be construed or applied so as to challenge or affect the characterization, definition, or treatment of any swap agreement under any other statute, regulation, or rule, including the Gramm-Leach-Bliley Act, the Legal Certainty for Bank Products Act of 2000, the securities laws (as such term is defined in section 3(a)(47) of the Securities Exchange Act of 1934) and the Commodity Exchange Act.

(53C) The term "swap participant" means an entity that, at any time before the filing of the petition, has an outstanding swap agreement with the debtor.

(56A)[4] The term "term overriding royalty" means an interest in liquid or gaseous hydrocarbons in place or to be produced from particular real property that entitles the owner thereof to a share of production, or the value thereof, for a term limited by time, quantity, or value realized.

(53D) The term "timeshare plan" means and shall include that interest purchased in any arrangement, plan, scheme, or similar device, but not including exchange programs, whether by membership, agreement, tenancy in common, sale, lease, deed, rental agreement, license, right to use agreement, or by any other means, whereby a purchaser, in exchange for consideration, receives a right to use accommodations, facilities, or recreational sites, whether improved or unimproved, for a specific period of time less than a full year during any given year, but not necessarily for consecutive years, and which extends for a period of more than three years. A "timeshare interest" is that interest purchased in a timeshare plan which grants the purchaser the right to use and occupy accommodations, facilities, or recreational sites, whether improved or unimproved, pursuant to a timeshare plan.

(54) The term "transfer" means—

   (A) the creation of a lien;

   (B) the retention of title as a security interest;

   (C) the foreclosure of a debtor's equity of redemption; or

   (D) each mode, direct or indirect, absolute or conditional, voluntary or involuntary, of disposing of or parting with—

      (i) property; or

      (ii) an interest in property.

(54A) The term "uninsured State member bank" means a State member bank (as defined in section 3 of the Federal Deposit Insurance Act) the deposits of which are not insured by the Federal Deposit Insurance Corporation.

(55) The term "United States", when used in a geographical sense, includes all locations where the judicial jurisdiction of the United States extends, including territories and possessions of the United States.

(Pub.L. 95–598, Nov. 6, 1978, 92 Stat. 2549; Pub.L. 97–222, § 1, July 27, 1982, 96 Stat. 235; Pub.L. 98–353, Title III, §§ 391, 401, 421, July 10, 1984, 98 Stat. 364, 366, 367; Pub.L. 99–554, Title II, §§ 201, 251, 283(a), Oct. 27, 1986, 100 Stat. 3097, 3104, 3116; Pub.L. 100–506, § 1(a), Oct. 18, 1988, 102 Stat. 2538; Pub.L. 100–597, § 1, Nov. 3, 1988, 102 Stat. 3028; Pub.L. 101–311, Title I, § 101, Title II, § 201, June 25, 1990, 104 Stat. 267, 268; Pub.L. 101–647, Title XXV, § 2522(e), Nov. 29, 1990, 104 Stat. 4867; Pub.L. 102–

---

[4] So in original. Par. (56A) was inserted between pars. (53C) and (53D).

Title 11 GENERAL PROVISIONS 11 § 101

486, Title XXX, § 3017(a), Oct. 24, 1992, 106 Stat. 3130; Pub.L. 103–394, Title I, § 106, Title II, §§ 208(a), 215, 217(a), 218(a), Title III, § 304(a), Title V, § 501(a), (b)(1), (d)(1), Oct. 22, 1994, 108 Stat. 4111, 4124, 4126–4128, 4132, 4141–4143; Pub.L. 106–554, § 1(a)(5) [Title I, § 112(c)(3), (4)], Dec. 21, 2000, 114 Stat. 2763, 2763A–393; Pub.L. 109–8, Title I, § 102(b), (k), Title II, §§ 211, 226(a), 231(b), Title III, § 306(c), Title IV, §§ 401(a), 414, 432(a), Title VIII, § 802(b), Title IX, § 907(a)(1), (b), (c), Title X, §§ 1004, 1005, 1007(a), Title XI, § 1101(a), (b), Title XII, § 1201, Apr. 20, 2005, 119 Stat. 32, 35, 50, 66, 73, 80, 104, 107, 110, 145, 170, 175, 186, 187, 189, 192; Pub.L. 109–390, § 5(a)(1), Dec. 12, 2006, 120 Stat. 2695; Pub.L. 111–327, § 2(a)(1), Dec. 22, 2010, 124 Stat. 3557.)

HISTORICAL AND STATUTORY NOTES

References in Text

The Social Security Act, referred to in par. (10A)(B), is Act Aug. 14, 1935, c. 531, 49 Stat. 620, as amended, which is classified generally to chapter 7 of Title 42, 42 U.S.C.A. § 301 et seq.

Section 501(c)(3) of the Internal Revenue Code of 1986, referred to in par. (12A)(B), is classified to 26 U.S.C.A. § 501(c)(3).

Section 3 of the Federal Deposit Insurance Act, referred to in pars. (12A)(D), (21B)(A), (33)(A), (35)(A), and (54A) is Act Sept. 21, 1950, c. 967, § 2 [3], 64 Stat. 873, which is classified to 12 U.S.C.A. § 1813.

Section 101 of the Federal Credit Union Act, referred to in pars. (12A)(D), (34), is Act June 26, 1934, c. 750, Title I, § 101, formerly § 2, 48 Stat. 1216, as amended, which is classified to 12 U.S.C.A. § 1752.

The Investment Company Act of 1940, referred to in par. (22)(B), is Act Aug. 22, 1940, c. 686, Title I, 54 Stat. 789, as amended, which is classified principally to subchapter 1 of chapter 2D of title 15, 15 U.S.C.A. § 80a–1 et seq. For complete classification, see Short Title set out as 15 U.S.C.A. § 80a–51 and Tables.

Section 402 of the Federal Deposit Insurance Corporation Improvement Act of 1991, referred to in par. (22A)(B), is Pub.L. 102–242, Title IV, § 402, Dec. 19, 1991, 105 Stat. 2372, which is classified to 12 U.S.C.A. § 4402.

Section 206 of the Federal Credit Union Act, referred to in par. (33)(B), is section 206 of Act June 26, 1934, c. 750, Title II, as added Oct. 19, 1970, Pub.L. 91–468, § 1(3), 84 Stat. 1003, which is classified to section 1786 of Title 12.

Sections 414(d) and 457(b) of the Internal Revenue Code of 1986, referred to in par. (41)(C), are sections 414(d) and 457(b), respectively, of Title 26, Internal Revenue Code.

Section 3 of the Securities and Exchange Act of 1934, referred to in par. (47), is Act June 6, 1934, c. 404, Title I, § 3, 48 Stat. 882, which is classified to 15 U.S.C.A. § 78c.

Section 17A of the Securities and Exchange Act of 1934, referred to in par. (48), is section 17A of Act June 6, 1934, c. 404, Title I, as added June 4, 1975, Pub.L. 94–29, § 15, 89 Stat. 141, which is classified to section 78q–1 of Title 15, Commerce and Trade.

Section 3(a)(12) of such Act, referred to in par. (48), is Section 3 of the Securities and Exchange Act of 1934, Act June 6, 1934, c. 404, Title I, 48 Stat. 882, which is classified to 15 U.S.C.A. § 78c(a)(12).

Section 15A of the Securities Exchange Act of 1934, referred to in par. (48A), is June 6, 1934, c. 404, Title I, § 15A, as added June 25, 1938, c. 677, § 1, 52 Stat. 1070, and amended which is classified to 15 U.S.C.A. § 78o–3.

Section 6 of the Securities Exchange Act of 1934, referred to in par. (48A), is June 6, 1934, c. 404, Title I, § 6, 48 Stat. 885, as amended, which is classified to 15 U.S.C.A. § 78c.

The Securities Act of 1933, referred to in par. (49)(A)(xii), is Act May 27, 1933, c. 38, Title I, 48 Stat. 74, as amended, which is classified generally to subchapter I (section 77a et seq.) of chapter 2A of Title 15, Commerce and Trade. For complete classification of this Act to the Code, see section 77a of Title 15 and Tables.

Section 3 of the Securities Act of 1933, referred to in pars. (49)(A)(xii) and (B)(vi), is section 3 of Act May 27, 1933, c. 38, Title I, 48 Stat. 75, which is classified to section 77c of Title 15.

The Securities Exchange Act of 1934, referred to in par. (53B)(B), is Act June 6, 1934, c. 404, 48 Stat. 881, as amended, which is classified principally to chapter 2B of Title 15, 15 U.S.C.A. § 78a et seq. Section

3(a)(47) of the Act, as amended, is classified to 15 U.S.C.A. § 78c(a)(47). For complete classification, see Short Title set out as 15 U.S.C.A. § 78a and Tables.

The Commodity Exchange Act, referred to in par. (53B), is Act Sept. 21, 1922, c. 369, 42 Stat. 998, as amended, which is classified principally to chapter 1 of Title 7, 7 U.S.C.A. § 1 et seq. For complete classification, see Short Title set out as 7 U.S.C.A. § 1 and Tables.

The Gramm-Leach-Bliley Act, referred to in par. (53B), is Pub.L. 106–102, Nov. 12, 1999, 113 Stat. 1338, also known as the Financial Services Modernization Act of 1999, which principally enacted chapters 93, 94 and 95 of Title 15, 15 U.S.C.A. § 6701 et seq., 15 U.S.C.A. § 6801 et seq., and 15 U.S.C.A. § 6901 et seq., respectively, and amended chapters 16 and 17 of Title 12, 12 U.S.C.A. § 1811 et seq., and 12 U.S.C.A. § 1841 et seq. For complete classification, see Tables.

The Legal Certainty for Bank Products Act of 2000, referred to in par. (53B), is Pub.L. 106–554, § 1(a)(5) [Title IV, §§ 401 to 408], Dec. 21, 2000, 114 Stat. 2763, 2763A–457, which enacted 7 U.S.C.A. §§ 27 and 27a to 27f. For complete classification, see Short Title set out as a note under 7 U.S.C.A. § 1 and Tables.

Amendments

2010 Amendments.

Par. (13A)(A). Pub.L. 111–327, § 2(a)(1)(A)(i), inserted "if used as the principal residence by the debtor" following "residential structure".

Par. (13A)(B). Pub.L. 111–327, § 2(a)(1)(A)(ii), inserted "if used as the principal residence by the debtor" following "or trailer".

Par. (35)(B). Pub.L. 111–327, § 2(a)(1)(B), struck out "(23) and (35)" and inserted "(21B) and (33)(A)".

Par. (40B). Pub.L. 111–327, § 2(a)(1)(C), struck out "written document relating to a patient or a" and inserted "record relating to a patient, including a written document or a".

Par. (42). Pub.L. 111–327, § 2(a)(1)(D), which directed the substitution of "303 and 1504" for "303, and 304", was executed by making the substitution for "303, or 304" to reflect the probable intent of Congress.

Par. (51B). Pub.L. 111–327, § 2(a)(1)(E), inserted "thereto" before the period at the end.

Par. (51D)(A). Pub.L. 111–327, § 2(a)(1)(F), inserted "of the filing" following "debts as of the date".

2006 Amendments. Par. (22)(A). Pub.L. 109–390, § 5(a)(1)(A)(i), struck out "(domestic or foreign)" after "an entity".

Pub.L. 109–390, § 5(a)(1)(A)(ii), inserted "(whether or not a 'customer', as defined in section 741)" after "custodian for a customer".

Par. (22A)(A). Pub.L. 109–390, § 5(a)(1)(B)(i), struck out "on any day during the previous 15-month period" following "actual principal amount outstanding" and following "(other than an affiliate)" and inserted "at such time or on any day during the 15-month period preceding the date of the filing of the petition".

Pub.L. 109–390, § 5(a)(1)(B)(ii), inserted "(aggregated across counterparties)" after "principal amount outstanding".

Par. (25)(A). Pub.L. 109–390, § 5(a)(1)(C)(i), inserted ", as defined in section 761" after "commodity contract".

Pub.L. 109–390, § 5(a)(1)(C)(ii), struck out "repurchase transaction, reverse repurchase transaction," following "but not limited to, a" and inserted "repurchase or reverse repurchase transaction (whether or not such repurchase or reverse repurchase transaction is a 'repurchase agreement', as defined in this section)".

Par. (53B)(A)(i)(II). Pub.L. 109–390, § 5(a)(1)(D)(i)(I), struck out "or precious metals" following "or other foreign exchange" and inserted ", precious metals, or other commodity".

Par. (53B)(A)(i)(VII). Pub.L. 109–390, § 5(a)(1)(D)(i)(II), struck out "or" at the end.

Par. (53B)(A)(i)(VIII). Pub.L. 109–390, § 5(a)(1)(D)(i)(III), struck out "weather derivative, or weather option" following "weather swap," and inserted "option, future, or forward agreement".

Par. (53B)(A)(i)(IX). Pub.L. 109–390, § 5(a)(1)(D)(i)(IV), added subcl. (IX).

Par. (53B)(A)(i)(X). Pub.L. 109–390, § 5(a)(1)(D)(i)(IV), added subcl. (X).

Par. (53B)(A)(ii)(I). Pub.L. 109–390, § 5(a)(1)(D)(ii)(I), inserted "or other derivatives" after "dealings in the swap".

Par. (53B)(A)(ii)(II). Pub.L. 109–390, § 5(a)(1)(D)(ii)(II), struck out "future, or option" following "is a forward, swap," and inserted "future, option, or spot transaction".

Par. (53B)(B). Pub.L. 109–390, § 5(a)(1)(E), struck out "the Securities Act of 1933, the Securities Exchange Act of 1934, the Public Utility Holding Company Act of 1935, the Trust Indenture Act of 1939, the Investment Company Act of 1940, the Investment Advisers Act of 1940, the Securities Investor Protection Act of 1970, the Commodity Exchange Act, the Gramm-Leach-Bliley Act, and the Legal Certainty for Bank Products Act of 2000" following "or rule, including" and inserted "the Gramm-Leach-Bliley Act, the Legal Certainty for Bank Products Act of 2000, the securities laws (as such term is defined in section 3(a)(47) of the Securities Exchange Act of 1934) and the Commodity Exchange Act".

2005 Amendments. Pub.L. 109–8, § 1201(1), in the matter preceding par. (1), struck out "In this title—" and inserted "In this title the following definitions shall apply:".

Pars. (1), (2). Pub.L. 109–8, § 1201(2), (8), inserted "The term" after the paragraph designations and substituted a period for a semicolon at the end of each paragraph.

Par. (3). Pub.L. 109–8, § 226(a)(1), added par. (3).

Pub.L. 109–8, § 1201(2), (8), inserted "The term" after the paragraph designation and substituted a period for a semicolon at the end.

Par. (4). Pub.L. 109–8, § 1201(2), (8), inserted "The term" after the paragraph designation and substituted a period for a semicolon at the end.

Par. (4A). Pub.L. 109–8, § 226(a)(2), added par. (4A).

Pub.L. 109–8, § 1201(2), (8), inserted "The term" after the paragraph designation and substituted a period for a semicolon at the end.

Pars. (5) to (7). Pub.L. 109–8, § 1201(2), (8), inserted "The term" after the paragraph designations and substituted a period for a semicolon at the end of each paragraph.

Par. (7A). Pub.L. 109–8, § 1007(a)(1), added par. (7A).

Pub.L. 109–8, § 1201(2), (8), inserted "The term" after the paragraph designation and substituted a period for a semicolon at the end.

Par. (7B). Pub.L. 109–8, § 1007(a)(1), added par. (7B).

Pub.L. 109–8, § 1201(2), (8), inserted "The term" after the paragraph designation and substituted a period for a semicolon at the end.

Pars. (8) to (10). Pub.L. 109–8, § 1201(2), (8), inserted "The term" after the paragraph designations and substituted a period for a semicolon at the end of each paragraph.

Par. (10A). Pub.L. 109–8, § 102(b), added par. (10A).

Pub.L. 109–8, § 1201(2), (8), inserted "The term" after the paragraph designation and substituted a period for a semicolon at the end.

Pars. (11), (12). Pub.L. 109–8, § 1201(2), (8), inserted "The term" after the paragraph designations and substituted a period for a semicolon at the end of each paragraph.

Par. (12A). Pub.L. 109–8, § 211(1), struck out par. (12A), which formerly read: " 'debt for child support' means a debt of a kind specified in section 523(a)(5) of this title for maintenance or support of a child of the debtor;".

Pub.L. 109–8, § 1201(2), inserted "The term" after the paragraph designation.

Pub.L. 109–8, § 1201(8), which directed the substitution of a period for a semicolon at the end, could not be executed because par. (12A) ended in a period after amendment by Pub.L. 109–8, § 226(a)(3). See below.

Pub.L. 109–8, § 226(a)(3), added par. (12A) relating to "debt relief agency".

Par. (13). Pub.L. 109–8, § 1201(2), (8), inserted "The term" after the paragraph designation and substituted a period for a semicolon at the end.

Par. (13A). Pub.L. 109–8, § 306(c)(1), added par. (13A).

Pub.L. 109–8, § 1201(2), (8), inserted "The term" after the paragraph designation and substituted a period for a semicolon at the end.

Par. (14). Pub.L. 109–8, § 414, rewrote par. (14), which formerly read:

"**(14)** "disinterested person" means person that—

"**(A)** is not a creditor, an equity security holder, or an insider;

"**(B)** is not and was not an investment banker for any outstanding security of the debtor;

"**(C)** has not been, within three years before the date of the filing of the petition, an investment banker for a security of the debtor, or an attorney for such an investment banker in connection with the offer, sale, or issuance of a security of the debtor;

"**(D)** is not and was not, within two years before the date of the filing of the petition, a director, officer, or employee of the debtor or of an investment banker specified in subparagraph (B) or (C) of this paragraph; and

"**(E)** does not have an interest materially adverse to the interest of the estate or of any class of creditors or equity security holders, by reason of any direct or indirect relationship to, connection with, or interest in, the debtor or an investment banker specified in subparagraph (B) or (C) of this paragraph, or for any other reason;".

Par. (14). Pub.L. 109–8, § 1201(2), (8), inserted "The term" after the paragraph designation and substituted a period for a semicolon at the end.

Par. (14A). Pub.L. 109–8, § 211(2), added par. (14A).

Pub.L. 109–8, § 1201(2), (8), inserted "The term" after the paragraph designation and substituted a period for a semicolon at the end.

Pars. (15) to (17). Pub.L. 109–8, § 1201(2), (8), inserted "The term" after the paragraph designations and substituted a period for a semicolon at the end of each paragraph.

Par. (18). Pub.L. 109–8, § 1201(2), (8), inserted "The term" after the paragraph designation and substituted a period for a semicolon at the end.

Par. (18)(A). Pub.L. 109–8, §§ 1004(1), 1005, struck out "$1,500,000" and inserted "$3,237,000", struck out "80" and inserted "50", and struck out "for the taxable year preceding the taxable year" and inserted the following:

"for—

"**(i)** the taxable year preceding; or

"**(ii)** each of the 2d and 3d taxable years preceding; the taxable year".

Par. (18)(B)(ii). Pub.L. 109–8, § 1004(2), struck out "$1,500,000" and inserted "$3,237,000" and struck out "80" and inserted "50".

Par. (19). Pub.L. 109–8, § 1201(2), (8), inserted "The term" after the paragraph designation and substituted a period for a semicolon at the end.

Par. (19A). Pub.L. 109–8, § 1007(a)(2), added par. (19A).

Pub.L. 109–8, § 1201(2), (8), inserted "The term" after the paragraph designation and substituted a period for a semicolon at the end.

Par. (19B). Pub.L. 109–8, § 1007(a)(2), added par. (19B).

Pub.L. 109–8, § 1201(2), (8), inserted "The term" after the paragraph designation and substituted a period for a semicolon at the end.

Pars. (20) to (21B). Pub.L. 109–8, § 1201(2), (8), inserted "The term" after the paragraph designations and substituted a period for a semicolon at the end of each paragraph.

Par. (22). Pub.L. 109–8, § 907(b)(1), rewrote par. (22), which formerly read:

"(22) the term 'financial institution'—

"(A) means—

"(i) a Federal reserve bank or an entity (domestic or foreign) that is a commercial or savings bank, industrial savings bank, savings and loan association, trust company, or receiver or conservator for such entity and, when any such Federal reserve bank, receiver, conservator, or entity is acting as agent or custodian for a customer in connection with a securities contract, as defined in section 741 of this title, the customer; or

"(ii) in connection with a securities contract, as defined in section 741 of this title, an investment company registered under the Investment Company Act of 1940; and

"(B) includes any person described in subparagraph (A) which operates, or operates as, a multilateral clearing organization pursuant to section 409 of the Federal Deposit Insurance Corporation Improvement Act of 1991;".

Pub.L. 109–8, § 1201(2), (8), inserted "The term" after the paragraph designation and substituted a period for a semicolon at the end.

Par. (22A). Pub.L. 109–8, § 907(b)(2), added par. (22A).

Pub.L. 109–8, § 1201(2), (8), inserted "The term" after the paragraph designation and substituted a period for a semicolon at the end.

Par. (23). Pub.L. 109–8, § 802(b), rewrote par. (23), which formerly read: " 'foreign proceeding' means proceeding, whether judicial or administrative and whether or not under bankruptcy law, in a foreign country in which the debtor's domicile, residence, principal place of business, or principal assets were located at the commencement of such proceeding, for the purpose of liquidating an estate, adjusting debts by composition, extension, or discharge, or effecting a reorganization;".

Pub.L. 109–8, § 1201(2), (8), inserted "The term" after the paragraph designation and substituted a period for a semicolon at the end.

Par. (24). Pub.L. 109–8, § 802(b), rewrote par. (24), which formerly read: " 'foreign representative' means duly selected trustee, administrator, or other representative of an estate in a foreign proceeding;".

Pub.L. 109–8, § 1201(2), (8), inserted "The term" after the paragraph designation and substituted a period for a semicolon at the end.

Par. (25). Pub.L. 109–8, § 907(a)(1)(A)(i), (ii), struck out "means a contract" and inserted "means— "(A) a contract"; and struck out ", or any combination thereof or option thereon;" and inserted ", or any other similar agreement;".

Pub.L. 109–8, § 1201(2), (8), inserted "The term" after the paragraph designation and substituted a period for a semicolon at the end.

Par. (25)(B). Pub.L. 109–8, § 907(a)(1)(A)(iii), added subpar. (B).

Par. (25)(C). Pub.L. 109–8, § 907(a)(1)(A)(iii), added subpar. (C).

Par. (25)(D). Pub.L. 109–8, § 907(a)(1)(A)(iii), added subpar. (D).

Par. (25)(E). Pub.L. 109–8, § 907(a)(1)(A)(iii), added subpar. (E).

Par. (26). Pub.L. 109–8, § 907(b)(3), rewrote par. (26), which formerly read: " 'forward contract merchant' means a person whose business consists in whole or in part of entering into forward contracts as or with merchants in a commodity, as defined in section 761(8) of this title, or any similar good, article, service, right, or interest which is presently or in the future becomes the subject of dealing in the forward contract trade;".

Pub.L. 109–8, § 1201(2), (8), inserted "The term" after the paragraph designation and substituted a period for a semicolon at the end.

Par. (27). Pub.L. 109–8, § 1201(2), (8), inserted "The term" after the paragraph designation and substituted a period for a semicolon at the end.

Par. (27A). Pub.L. 109–8, § 306(c)(2), added par. (27A) relating to "incidental property".

Pub.L. 109–8, § 1201(2), (8), inserted "The term" after the paragraph designation and substituted a period for a semicolon at the end.

Pub.L. 109–8, § 1101(a), redesignated par. (27A) relating to "incidental property" as par. (27B), and added a new par. (27A) relating to "health care business".

Par. (27B). Pub.L. 109–8, § 1101(a)(1), redesignated par. (27A) relating to "incidental property" as par. (27B).

Pub.L. 109–8, § 1201(2), (8), inserted "The term" after the paragraph designation and substituted a period for a semicolon at the end.

Pars. (28) to (34). Pub.L. 109–8, § 1201(2), (8), inserted "The term" after the paragraph designations and substituted a period for a semicolon at the end of each paragraph.

Par. (35). Pub.L. 109–8, § 1201(2), (8), inserted "The term" after the paragraph designation and substituted a period for a semicolon at the end.

Par. (35)(B). Pub.L. 109–8, § 1201(3), struck out "paragraphs (21B) and (33)(A)" and inserted "paragraphs (23) and (35)".

Par. (35A). Pub.L. 109–8, § 1201(4), struck out "; and" at the end and inserted a period.

Pars. (36), (37). Pub.L. 109–8, § 1201(2), (8), inserted "The term" after the paragraph designations and substituted a period for a semicolon at the end of each paragraph.

Par. (38). Pub.L. 109–8, § 1201(2), (4), inserted "The term" after the paragraph designation and substituted a period for "; and" at the end.

Par. (38A). Pub.L. 109–8, § 907(c), added par. (38A).

Pub.L. 109–8, § 1201(2), (8), inserted "The term" after the paragraph designation and substituted a period for a semicolon at the end.

Par. (38B). Pub.L. 109–8, § 907(c), added par. (38B).

Pub.L. 109–8, § 1201(2), (8), inserted "The term" after the paragraph designation and substituted a period for a semicolon at the end.

Par. (39). Pub.L. 109–8, § 1201(2), inserted "The term" after the paragraph designation.

Par. (39A). Pub.L. 109–8, § 102(k), added par. (39A).

Pub.L. 109–8, § 1201(2), (8), inserted "The term" after the paragraph designation and substituted a period for a semicolon at the end.

Par. (40). Pub.L. 109–8, § 1201(2), (8), inserted "The term" after the paragraph designation and substituted a period for a semicolon at the end.

Par. (40A). Pub.L. 109–8, § 1101(b), added par. (40A).

Pub.L. 109–8, § 1201(2), (8), inserted "The term" after the paragraph designation and substituted a period for a semicolon at the end.

Par. (40B). Pub.L. 109–8, § 1101(b), added par. (40B).

Pub.L. 109–8, § 1201(2), (8), inserted "The term" after the paragraph designation and substituted a period for a semicolon at the end.

Par. (41). Pub.L. 109–8, § 1201(2), (8), inserted "The term" after the paragraph designation and substituted a period for a semicolon at the end.

Par. (41A). Pub.L. 109–8, § 231(b), added par. (41A).

Pub.L. 109–8, § 1201(2), (8), inserted "The term" after the paragraph designation and substituted a period for a semicolon at the end.

Pars. (42) to (45). Pub.L. 109–8, § 1201(2), (8), inserted "The term" after the paragraph designations and substituted a period for a semicolon at the end of each paragraph.

Par. (46). Pub.L. 109–8, § 907(a)(1)(B), struck out "on any day during the period beginning 90 days before the date of" and inserted "at any time before".

Pub.L. 109–8, § 1201(2), (8), inserted "The term" after the paragraph designation and substituted a period for a semicolon at the end.

Par. (47). Pub.L. 109–8, § 907(a)(1)(C), rewrote par. (47), which formerly read: "'repurchase agreement' (which definition also applies to a reverse repurchase agreement) means an agreement, including related terms, which provides for the transfer of certificates of deposit, eligible bankers' acceptances, or securities that are direct obligations of, or that are fully guaranteed as to principal and interest by, the United States or any agency of the United States against the transfer of funds by the transferee of such certificates of deposit, eligible bankers' acceptances, or securities with a simultaneous agreement by such transferee to transfer to the transferor thereof certificates of deposit, eligible bankers' acceptances, or securities as described above, at a date certain not later than one year after such transfers or on demand, against the transfer of funds;".

Pub.L. 109–8, § 1201(2), (8), inserted "The term" after the paragraph designation and substituted a period for a semicolon at the end.

Par. (48). Pub.L. 109–8, § 907(a)(1)(D), inserted ", or exempt from such registration under such section pursuant to an order of the Securities and Exchange Commission," after "1934".

Pub.L. 109–8, § 1201(2), (8), inserted "The term" after the paragraph designation and substituted a period for a semicolon at the end.

Par. (48A). Pub.L. 109–8, § 401(a), added par. (48A).

Pub.L. 109–8, § 1201(2), (8), inserted "The term" after the paragraph designation and substituted a period for a semicolon at the end.

Pars. (49) to (51A). Pub.L. 109–8, § 1201(2), (8), inserted "The term" after the paragraph designations and substituted a period for a semicolon at the end of each paragraph.

Par. (51B). Pub.L. 109–8, § 1201(2), (5), (8), inserted "The term" after the paragraph designation, inserted "who is not a family farmer" after "debtor" the first place it appeared, and struck out "thereto having aggregate noncontingent, liquidated secured debts in an amount no more than $4,000,000." and inserted a period.

Par. (51C). Pub.L. 109–8, § 432(a), struck out par. (51C), which formerly read: "'small business' means a person engaged in commercial or business activities (but does not include a person whose primary activity is the business of owning or operating real property and activities incidental thereto) whose aggregate noncontingent liquidated secured and unsecured debts as of the date of the petition do not exceed $2,000,000;"; and added new par. (51C).

Pub.L. 109–8, § 1201(2), (8), inserted "The term" after the paragraph designation and substituted a period for a semicolon at the end.

Par. (51D). Pub.L. 109–8, § 432(a), added par. (51D).

Pub.L. 109–8, § 1201(2), (8), inserted "The term" after the paragraph designation and substituted a period for a semicolon at the end.

Pars. (52) to (53A). Pub.L. 109–8, § 1201(2), (8), inserted "The term" after the paragraph designations and substituted a period for a semicolon at the end of each paragraph.

Par. (53B). Pub.L. 109–8, § 907(a)(1)(E), rewrote par. (53B), which formerly read:

"**(53B)** 'swap agreement' means—

"**(A)** an agreement (including terms and conditions incorporated by reference therein) which is a rate swap agreement, basis swap, forward rate agreement, commodity swap, interest rate option, forward foreign exchange agreement, spot foreign exchange agreement, rate cap agreement, rate floor agreement, rate collar agreement, currency swap agreement, cross-currency rate swap agreement, currency option, any other similar agreement (including any option to enter into any of the foregoing);

"**(B)** any combination of the foregoing; or

"**(C)** a master agreement for any of the foregoing together with all supplements;".

Pub.L. 109–8, § 1201(2), (8), inserted "The term" after the paragraph designation and substituted a period for a semicolon at the end.

Pars. (53C), (53D). Pub.L. 109–8, § 1201(2), (8), inserted "The term" after the paragraph designations and substituted a period for a semicolon at the end of each paragraph.

Par. (54). Pub.L. 109–8, § 1201(2), inserted "The term" after the paragraph designation.

Pub.L. 109–8, § 1201(6), rewrote par. (54), which formerly read: " 'transfer' means every mode, direct or indirect, absolute or conditional, voluntary or involuntary, of disposing of or parting with property or with an interest in property, including retention of title as a security interest and foreclosure of the debtor's equity of redemption;".

Pub.L. 109–8, § 1201(8), substituted a period for a semicolon at the end.

Par. (54A). Pub.L. 109–8, § 1201(4), (7), struck out "; and" at the end and inserted a period, struck out "the term" and inserted "The term", and indented the left margin 2 ems to the right, requiring no change in text.

Pub.L. 109–8, § 1201(8), which directed the substitution of a period for a semicolon at the end, could not be executed because par. (54A) ended in a period after amendment by Pub.L. 109–8, § 1201(4). § See below.

Par. (55). Pub.L. 109–8, § 1201(2), (8), inserted "The term" after the paragraph designation and substituted a period for a semicolon at the end.

Par. (56A). Pub.L. 109–8, § 1201(2), inserted "The term" after the paragraph designation.

Pub.L. 109–8, § 1201(8), which directed the substitution of a period for a semicolon "in each of paragraphs (40) through (55)" at end, was executed to par. (56A), to reflect the probable intent of Congress, because par. (56A) follows par. (53C) in text.

2000 Amendments. Par. (22). Pub.L. 106–554, § 1(a)(5) [Title I, § 112(c)(3)], rewrote par. (22), which formerly read: " 'financial institution' means a person that is a commercial or savings bank, industrial savings bank, savings and loan association, or trust company and, when any such person is acting as agent or custodian for a customer in connection with a securities contract, as defined in section 741 of this title, such customer;".

Par. (54A). Pub.L. 106–554, § 1(a)(5) [Title I, § 112(c)(4)], added par. (54A).

1994 Amendments. Par. (3). Pub.L. 103–394, § 501(a)(1), redesignated former par. (3) as (21B).

Par. (6). Pub.L. 103–394, § 501(b)(1)(A), substituted "761" for "761(9)".

Par. (12A). Pub.L. 103–394, § 304(a), added par. (12A).

Par. (21B). Pub.L. 103–394, § 501(a)(1), redesignated former par. (3) as (21B).

Par. (22). Pub.L. 103–394, § 501(b)(1)(B), substituted "741" for "741(7)".

Par. (33)(A). Pub.L. 103–394, § 501(d)(1)(A)(i), struck out "(12 U.S.C. 1813(u))" following "section 3(u) of the Federal Deposit Insurance Act".

Par. (33)(B). Pub.L. 103–394, § 501(d)(1)(A)(ii), struck out "(12 U.S.C. 1786(r))" following "Federal Credit Union Act".

Par. (34). Pub.L. 103–394, § 501(d)(1)(B), struck out "(12 U.S.C. 1752(7))" following "Federal Credit Union Act".

Par. (35)(A). Pub.L. 103–394, § 501(d)(1)(C), struck out "(12 U.S.C. 1813(c)(2))" following "Federal Deposit Insurance Act".

Par. (35)(B). Pub.L 103–394, § 501(b)(1)(C), substituted "paragraphs (21B)" for " paragraphs (3)".

Par. (35A). Pub.L. 103–394, § 501(a)(4), redesignated former par. (56), defining "intellectual property", as (35A).

Par. (39). Pub.L. 103–394, § 501(a)(2), redesignated former par. (39) as (51A).

Pub.L. 103–394, § 501(a)(5), redesignated former par. (57), defining "mask work", as (39).

Par. (41). Pub.L. 103–394, § 106, added par. (41) and struck out former par. (41) which read as follows: " 'person' includes individual, partnership, and corporation, but does not include governmental unit, *Provided, however,* That any governmental unit that acquires an asset from a person as a result of operation of a loan guarantee agreement, or as receiver or liquidating agent of a person, will be considered a person for purposes of section 1102 of this title."

Par. (42A). Pub.L. 103–394, § 208(a)(1), added par. (42A).

Par. (48). Pub.L. 103–394, § 501(d)(1)(D), struck out "(15 U.S.C. 78q-1)" following "Securities Exchange Act of 1934", and "(15 U.S.C. 78c(12))" following "section 3(a)(12) of such Act".

Par. (49)(A)(xii). Pub.L. 103–394, § 501(d)(1)(E)(i), struck out "(15 U.S.C. 77a et seq.)" following "Securities Act of 1933", and "(15 U.S.C. 77c(b))" following "section 3(b) of such Act".

Par. (49)(B)(ii). Pub.L. 103–394, § 501(b)(1)(D), substituted "section 761" for "section 761(13)".

Par. (49)(B)(vi). Pub.L. 103–394, § 501(d)(1)(E)(ii), struck out "(15 U.S.C. 77c(b))" following "Securities Act of 1933".

Par. (51A). Pub.L. 103–394, § 501(a)(2), redesignated former par. (39) as (51A).

Par. (51B). Pub.L. 103–394, § 218(a), added par. (51B).

Par. (51C). Pub.L. 103–394, § 217(a), added par. (51C).

Par. (53A)(A). Pub.L. 103–394, § 501(b)(1)(E), substituted "section 741" for "section 741(2)".

Par. (53A). Pub.L. 103–394, § 501(a)(3), redesignated former par. (54), defining "stockbroker", as (53A).

Par. (53B). Pub.L. 103–394, § 501(a)(3), redesignated former par. (55), defining "swap agreement", as (53B).

Par. (53C). Pub.L. 103–394, § 501(a)(3), redesignated former par. (56), defining "swap participant", as (53C).

Par. (53D). Pub.L. 103–394, § 501(a)(3), redesignated former par. (57), defining "timeshare plan", as (53D).

Pub.L. 103–394, § 501(d)(1)(F), substituted "timeshare plan;" for "timeshare plan.".

Par. (54). Pub.L. 103–394, § 501(a)(3), redesignated former par. (54), defining "stockbroker", as (53A).

Par. (55)(A). Pub.L. 103–394, § 215, in par. (55) relating to swap agreement, included agreement which is a spot foreign exchange agreement within definition.

Par. (55). Pub.L. 103–394, § 501(a)(3), redesignated former par. (55), defining "swap agreement", as (53B).

Par. (56). Pub.L. 103–394, § 501(a)(3), redesignated former par. (56), defining "swap participant", as (53C).

Pub.L. 103–394, § 501(a)(4), redesignated former par. (56), defining "intellectual property", as (35A).

Par. (56A). Pub.L. 103–394, § 208(a)(2), added par. (56A), following par. (56) relating to "swap participant".

Par. (57). Pub.L. 103–394, § 501(a)(3), redesignated former par. (57), defining "timeshare plan", as (53D).

Pub.L. 103–394, § 501(a)(5), redesignated former par. (57), defining "mask work", as (39).

1992 Amendments. Par. (21A). Pub.L. 102–486, § 3017(a), added par. (21A).

1990 Amendments. Par. (3). Pub.L. 101–647, § 2522(e)(4), added par. (3). Former par. (3) redesignated (4).

Pars. (4) to (23). Pub.L. 101–647, § 2522(e)(3), redesignated pars. (3) to (22) as (4) to (23). Former par. (23) redesignated (24).

Par. (24). Pub.L. 101–647, § 2522(e)(3), redesignated par. (23) as (24). Former par. (24) redesignated (25).

Pub.L. 101–311, § 201(1), added provisions relating to section 761(8) of this title and similar goods, articles, etc., which are or will be the subject of dealing in a forward contract trade, and provisions relating to repurchase transactions, reverse repurchase transactions, etc.

Par. (25). Pub.L. 101–647, § 2522(e)(3), redesignated par. (24) as (25). Former par. (25) redesignated (26).

11 § 101   **BANKRUPTCY CODE**   **Title 11**

Pub.L. 101–311, § 201(2), substituted "a commodity, as defined in section 761(8) of this title, or any similar good, article, service, right, or interest which is presently or in the future becomes the subject of dealing in the forward contract trade" for "commodities".

Par. (26) to (32). Pub.L. 101–647, § 2522(e)(3), redesignated pars. (25) to (31) as (26) to (32), respectively. Former par. (32) redesignated (36).

Par. (33). Pub.L. 101–647, § 2522(e)(2), added par. (33). Former par. (33) redesignated (37).

Par. (34). Pub.L. 101–647, § 2522(e)(2), added par. (34). Former par. (34) redesignated (38).

Pub.L. 101–311, § 201(4), added par. (34). Former par. (34) redesignated (36).

Par. (35). Pub.L. 101–647, § 2522(e)(2), added par. (35). Former par. (35) redesignated (39).

Pub.L. 101–311, § 201(4), added par. (35). Former par. (35) redesignated (37).

Par. (36). Pub.L. 101–647, § 2522(e)(1), redesignated par. (32) as (36). Former par. (36) redesignated (40).

Pub.L. 101–311, § 201(3), redesignated par. (34) as (36). Former par. (36) redesignated (38).

Pars. (37) to (48). Pub.L. 101–647, § 2522(e)(1), redesignated pars. (33) to (44) as (37) to (48), respectively. Former pars. (37) to (48) redesignated (41) to (52), respectively.

Pub.L. 101–311, § 201(3), redesignated former pars. (35) through (48) as (37) through (50), respectively. Former pars. (37) to (48) redesignated (39) to (50), respectively.

Pars. (49), (50). Pub.L. 101–647, § 2522(e)(1), redesignated former pars. (45) and (46) as (49) and (50), respectively. Former pars. (49) and (50) redesignated (53) and (54), both respectively defining "stockbroker".

Pub.L. 101–311, § 201(3), redesignated pars. (47) and (48) as (49) and (50), respectively. Former pars. (49) and (50) redesignated as (51) and (52), respectively.

Pub.L. 101–311, § 101, added pars. (49) and (50). Former pars. (49) and (50) redesignated as (51) and (52), respectively.

Par. (51). Pub.L. 101–647, § 2522(e)(1), redesignated par. (47) as (51). Former par. (51) redesignated as (55) defining "swap agreement".

Pub.L. 101–311, § 201(3), redesignated par. (49) as (51). Former par. (51) redesignated as (53).

Pub.L. 101–311, § 101(1), redesignated par. (49) as (51). Former par. (51) redesignated as (53).

Par. (52). Pub.L. 101–647, § 2522(e)(1), redesignated par. (48) as (52). Former par. (52) redesignated as (56) defining "swap participant".

Pub.L. 101–311, § 201(3), redesignated par. (50) as (52). Former par. (52) redesignated as (54) defining "transfer".

Pub.L. 101–311, § 101(1), redesignated par. (50) as (52). Former par. (52) redesignated as (54).

Par. (53). Pub.L. 101–647, § 2522(e)(1), redesignated par. (49) as (53). Former par. (53) redesignated as (57) defining "timeshare plan".

Pub.L. 101–311, § 201(3), redesignated par. (51) as (53). Former par. (53) redesignated as (55) defining "United States".

Pub.L. 101–311, § 101(1), redesignated par. (51) as (53). Former par. (53) redesignated as (55).

Par. (54). Pub.L. 101–647, § 2522(e)(1), redesignated par. (50) as (54) defining "stockbroker".

Pub.L. 101–311, § 201(3), redesignated par. (52) as (54) defining "transfer". Former par. (54) redesignated as (56) defining "intellectual property").

Pub.L. 101–311, § 101(1), redesignated par. (52) as (54).

Par. (55). Pub.L. 101–647, § 2522(e)(1), redesignated par. (51) as (55) defining "swap agreement".

Pub.L. 101–311, § 201(3), redesignated par. (53) as (55). Former par. (55) redesignated as (57) defining "mask work".

Pub.L. 101–311, § 101(1), redesignated par. (53) as (55).

Par. (56). Pub.L. 101–647, § 2522(e)(1), redesignated par. (52) as (56) defining "swap participant".

Pub.L. 101–311, § 201(3), redesignated par. (54) as (56) defining "intellectual property".

Par. (57). Pub.L. 101–647, § 2522(e)(1), redesignated par. (53) as (57) defining "timeshare plan".

Pub.L. 101–311, § 201(3), redesignated par. (55) as (57) defining "mask work".

1988 Amendments. Par. (31). Pub.L. 100–597, § 1, inserted in subpar. (A) "and a municipality" after "partnership" and added subpar. (C).

Pars. (52), (53). Pub.L. 100–506, § 1(a), added pars. (52) and (53).

1986 Amendments. Par. (14). Pub.L. 99–554, § 201(1), substituted "trust, governmental unit, and United States trustee" for "trust, and governmental unit".

Par. (17), (18). Pub.L. 99–554, § 251(2), (3), and added pars. (17) and (18) redesignated former pars. (17) and (18) as (19) and (20), respectively.

Par. (19). Pub.L. 99–554, § 251(1), (2), redesignated former par. (17) as (19) and inserted "(except when such term appears in the term 'family farmer')" following "means". Former par. (19) was redesignated (21).

Pars. (20) to (25). Pub.L. 99–554, § 251(2), redesignated former pars. (18) to (23) as (20) to (25), respectively. Former pars. (20) to (25) were redesignated as (22) to (27), respectively.

Par. (26). Pub.L. 99–554, § 201(2), substituted "of the United States (but not a United States trustee while serving as a trustee in a case under this title), a State" for "of the United States, a State".

Pub.L. 99–554, § 251(2), redesignated former par. (24) as (26). Former par. (26) was redesignated (28).

Pars. (27) to (42). Pub.L. 99–554, § 251(2), redesignated former pars. (25) to (40) as (27) to (42), respectively. Former pars. (27) to (42) were redesignated (29) to (44), respectively.

Par. (43). Pub.L. 99–554, § 251(2), redesignated former par. (41) as (43). Former par. (43) was redesignated (45).

Par. (43)(A)(xv). Pub.L. 99–554, § 283(a)(1), substituted "security" for "secuity".

Pars. (44) to (50). Pub.L. 99–554, § 251(2), redesignated former pars. (42) to (48) as (44) to (50), respectively. Former pars. (44) to (49) were redesignated (46) to (51), respectively.

Par. (51). Pub.L. 99–554, § 283(a)(2), substituted "States." for "States;".

Pub.L. 99–554, § 251(2), redesignated former par. (49) as (51).

1984 Amendments. Par. (2)(D). Pub.L. 98–353, § 421(a), struck out "or all" after "business".

Par. (8)(B). Pub.L. 98–353, § 421(b), substituted a semicolon for the colon at the end of subpar. (B).

Par. (9)(B). Pub.L. 98–353, § 421(c), added "348(d)" after "section".

Par. (14). Pub.L. 98–353, § 421(d), added "and" after "trust,".

Par. (19). Pub.L. 98–353, § 421(j)(4), added par. (19). Former par. (19) was redesignated as (20).

Pars. (20), (21). Pub.L. 98–353, § 421(j)(3), redesignated pars. (19)) (20) and (21) as (20), (21) and (24) respectively.

Par. (22). Pub.L. 98–353, § 421(j)(5), added par. (22). Former par. (22) was redesignated as (25).

Par. (23). Pub.L. 98–353, § 421(j)(5), added par. (23). Former par. (23) was redesignated as (26).

Par. (24). Pub.L. 98–353, § 421(j)(2), redesignated former par. (21) as (24). Former par. (24) was redesignated as (27).

Par. (25). Pub.L. 98–353, § 421(j)(2), redesignated former par. (22) as (25). Former par. (25) was redesignated as (28).

Par. (26). Pub.L. 98–353, § 421(j)(2), redesignated former par. (23) as (26). Former par. (26) was redesignated as (29).

Par. (27). Pub.L. 98–353, § 421(e), (j)(2), redesignated former par. (24) as (27) and substituted "stockbroker" for "stock broker". Former par. (27) was redesignated as (30).

Par. (28). Pub.L. 98–353, § 421(j)(2), redesignated former par. (25) as (28). Former par. (28) was redesignated as (31).

Par. (29). Pub.L. 98–353, § 421(f), (j)(2), redesignated former par. (26) as (29) and, in subpar. (B)(ii), substituted "nonpartnership" and "(A)" for "separate" and "(A)(ii)", respectively, wherever appearing. Former par. (29) was redesignated as (32).

Par. (30). Pub.L. 98–353, § 421(j)(2), redesignated former par. (27) as (30). Former par. (30) was redesignated as (33).

Par. (31). Pub.L. 98–353, § 421(j)(2), redesignated former par. (28) as (31). Former par. (31) was redesignated as (34).

Par. (32). Pub.L. 98–353, § 421(j)(2), redesignated former par. (29) as (32). Former par. (32) was redesignated as (35).

Par. (33). Pub.L. 98–353, § 421(g), (j)(2), redesignated former par. (30) as (33) and added proviso relating to consideration of certain governmental units as persons for purposes of section 1102 of this title. Former par. (33) was redesignated as (36).

Par. (34). Pub.L. 98–353, § 421(j)(2), redesignated former par. (31) as (34). Former par. (34) redesignated (37).

Pars. (35), (36). Pub.L. 98–353, § 421(j)(2), redesignated former pars. (32) and (33) as (35) and (36), respectively. Former pars. (35) and (36), as added by Pub.L. 98–353, § 391(2), redesignated (38) and (39), respectively.

Pub.L. 98–353, § 391, added pars. (35) and (36), and redesignated former pars. (35) and (36) as (37) and (38) which were again redesignated as (40) and (41), respectively.

Par. (37). Pub.L. 98–353, § 421(j)(2), redesignated former par. (34) as (37). Former par. (37) redesignated successively as (39) and again as (42).

Par. (38). Pub.L. 98–353, §§ 391(2), 421(j)(2), added par. (35) and redesignated such par. (35) as (38). Former par. (38) redesignated successively as (40) and again as (43).

Par. (39). Pub.L. 98–353, §§ 391(2), 421(j)(2), added par. (36) and redesignated such par. (36) as (39). Former par. (39) redesignated successively as (41) and again as (45).

Par. (40). Pub.L. 98–353, §§ 391(1), 421(j)(2), redesignated successively former par. (35) as (37) and again as (40). Former par. (40) redesignated successively as (42) and again as (46).

Par. (41). Pub.L. 98–353, §§ 391(1), 401(1), 421(h), (j)(2), redesignated successively former par. (36) as (38) and again as (41), and, in subpar. (B)(vi), substituted "certificate of a kind specified in subparagraph (A)(xii)" for "certificate specified in clause (xii) of subparagraph (A)" and substituted "required to be the subject of a registration statement" for "the subject of such registration statement". Former par. (41) redesignated successively as (43), again as (44), and again as (48).

Par. (42). Pub.L. 98–353, §§ 391(1), 421(j)(2), redesignated successively former par. (37) as (39) and again as (42).

Par. (43). Pub.L. 98–353, §§ 391(1), 421(j)(2), redesignated successively former par. (38) as (40) and again as (43).

Pub.L. 98–353, § 401, redesignated former par. (43), originally par. (41), as (44), and added another par. (43) which was redesignated (47).

Par. (44). Pub.L. 98–353, § 421(j)(6), added par. (44). Former par. (44) originally was par. (41) and was redesignated successively as (43), again as (44), and again as (48).

Pars. (45), (46). Pub.L. 98–353, §§ 391(1), 421(j)(1), redesignated successively former pars. (39) and (40) as (41) and (42), and again as (45) and (46), respectively.

Par. (47). Pub.L. 98–353, §§ 401(2), 421(j)(1), added par. (43) and redesignated such par. (43) as (47).

Par. (48). Pub.L. 98–353, §§ 391(1), 401(1), 421(i), (j)(1), redesignated successively former par. (41) as (43), again as (44), and again as (48), and substituted "and foreclosure of the debtor's equity of redemption; and" for the period at the end.

Par. (49). Pub.L. 98–353, § 421(j)(7), added par. (49).

1982 Amendments. Par. (35). Pub.L. 97–222, § 1(a) (2), added par. (35). Former par. (35) was redesignated (36).

Par. (36). Pub.L. 97–222, § 1(a) (1), (b), (c), redesignated par. (35) as (36) and in par. (36) as so redesignated, substituted "is required to be the subject of a registration statement" for "is the subject of a registration statement" in subpar. (A) (xii) and substituted "forward contract" for "forward commodity contract" in subpar. (B) (iii). Former par. (36) was redesignated (37).

Pars. (37) to (39). Pub.L. 97–222, § 1(a)(1), redesignated pars. (36) to (38) as (37) to (39), respectively. Former pars. (37) to (39) were redesignated (38) to (40), respectively.

Par. (40). Pub.L. 97–222, § 1(a)(1), (d), redesignated par. (39) as (40) and in par. (40) as so redesignated restructured its provisions by dividing the former introductory provisions into subpars. (A) and (B) and by redesignating former subpars. (A) and (B) as cls. (i) and (ii), respectively, of subpar. (B). Former par. (40) was redesignated (41).

Par. (41). Pub.L. 97–222, § 1(a)(1), redesignated par. (40) as (41).

Adjustment of Dollar Amounts

For adjustment of dollar amounts specified in pars. (3), (18), (19A), (51D) of this section by the Judicial Conference of the United States, see note set out under 11 U.S.C.A. § 104 of this title.

§ 102. Rules of construction

In this title—

  (1) "after notice and a hearing", or a similar phrase—

   (A) means after such notice as is appropriate in the particular circumstances, and such opportunity for a hearing as is appropriate in the particular circumstances; but

   (B) authorizes an act without an actual hearing if such notice is given properly and if—

     (i) such a hearing is not requested timely by a party in interest; or

     (ii) there is insufficient time for a hearing to be commenced before such act must be done, and the court authorizes such act;

  (2) "claim against the debtor" includes claim against property of the debtor;

  (3) "includes" and "including" are not limiting;

  (4) "may not" is prohibitive, and not permissive;

  (5) "or" is not exclusive;

  (6) "order for relief" means entry of an order for relief;

  (7) the singular includes the plural;

  (8) a definition, contained in a section of this title that refers to another section of this title, does not, for the purpose of such reference, affect the meaning of a term used in such other section; and

  (9) "United States trustee" includes a designee of the United States trustee.

(Pub.L. 95–598, Nov. 6, 1978, 92 Stat. 2554; Pub.L. 98–353, Title III, § 422, July 10, 1984, 98 Stat. 369; Pub.L. 99–554, Title II, § 202, Oct. 27, 1986, 100 Stat. 3097.)

HISTORICAL AND STATUTORY NOTES

Amendments

1986 Amendments. Par. (9). Pub.L. 99–554, § 202, added par. (9).

1984 Amendments. Par. (8). Pub.L. 98–353 substituted "contained" for "continued".

§ 103. Applicability of chapters

(a) Except as provided in section 1161 of this title, chapters 1, 3, and 5 of this title apply in a case under chapter 7, 11, 12, or 13 of this title, and this chapter, sections 307, 362(o), 555 through 557, and 559 through 562 apply in a case under chapter 15.

(b) Subchapters I and II of chapter 7 of this title apply only in a case under such chapter.

(c) Subchapter III of chapter 7 of this title applies only in a case under such chapter concerning a stockbroker.

(d) Subchapter IV of chapter 7 of this title applies only in a case under such chapter concerning a commodity broker.

(e) **Scope of application.**—Subchapter V of chapter 7 of this title shall apply only in a case under such chapter concerning the liquidation of an uninsured State member bank, or a corporation organized under section 25A of the Federal Reserve Act, which operates, or operates as, a multilateral clearing organization pursuant to section 409 of the Federal Deposit Insurance Corporation Improvement Act of 1991.

(f) Except as provided in section 901 of this title, only chapters 1 and 9 of this title apply in a case under such chapter 9.

(g) Except as provided in section 901 of this title, subchapters I, II, and III of chapter 11 of this title apply only in a case under such chapter.

(h) Subchapter IV of chapter 11 of this title applies only in a case under such chapter concerning a railroad.

(i) Chapter 13 of this title applies only in a case under such chapter.

(j) Chapter 12 of this title applies only in a case under such chapter.

(k) Chapter 15 applies only in a case under such chapter, except that—

  (1) sections 1505, 1513, and 1514 apply in all cases under this title; and

  (2) section 1509 applies whether or not a case under this title is pending.

(Pub.L. 95–598, Nov. 6, 1978, 92 Stat. 2555; Pub.L. 97–222, § 2, July 27, 1982, 96 Stat. 235; Pub.L. 98–353, Title III, § 423, July 10, 1984, 98 Stat. 369; Pub.L. 99–554, Title II, § 252, Oct. 27, 1986, 100 Stat. 3104; Pub.L. 106–554, § 1(a)(5) [Title I, § 112(c)(5)(A)], Dec. 21, 2000, 114 Stat. 2763, 2763A–394; Pub.L. 109–8, Title VIII, § 802(a), Apr. 20, 2005, 119 Stat. 145; Pub.L. 111–327, § 2(a)(2), Dec. 22, 2010, 124 Stat. 3557.)

HISTORICAL AND STATUTORY NOTES

References in Text

Section 25A of the Federal Reserve Act, referred to in subsec. (e), is Dec. 23, 1913, c. 6, § 25A, formerly § 25(a), as added Dec. 24, 1919, c. 18, 41 Stat. 378, as amended, which is classified to subchapter II of chapter 6 of Title 12, 12 U.S.C.A. § 611 et seq.

Section 409 of the Federal Deposit Insurance Corporation Improvement Act of 1991, referred to in subsec. (e), is Pub.L. 102–242, Title IV, § 409, as added by Pub.L. 106–554, § 1(a)(5) [Title I, § 112(a)(3)], Dec. 21, 2000, 114 Stat. 2763, 2763A–394, which is classified as 12 U.S.C.A. § 4422.

Amendments

2010 Amendments. Subsec. (a). Pub.L. 111–327, § 2(a)(2), struck out "362(n)" and inserted "362(o)".

2005 Amendments. Subsec. (a). Pub.L. 109–8, § 802(a)(1), inserted the following: ", and this chapter, sections 307, 362(n), 555 through 557, and 559 through 562 apply in a case under chapter 15" before the period at the end.

Subsec. (k). Pub.L. 109–8, § 802(a)(2), added subsec. (k).

2000 Amendments. Subsecs. (e) to (j). Pub.L. 106–554, § 1(a)(5) [Title I, § 112(c)(5)(A)], added subsec. (e), and redesignated former subsecs. (e) through (i) as (f) through (j), respectively.

1986 Amendments. Subsec. (a). Pub.L. 99–554, § 252(1), added reference to chapter 12.

Subsec. (i). Pub.L. 99–554, § 252(2), added subsec. (i).

1984 Amendments. Subsec. (c). Pub.L. 98–353 substituted "stockbroker" for "stockholder".

1982 Amendments. Subsec. (d). Pub.L. 97–222 struck out "except with respect to section 746(c) which applies to margin payments made by any debtor to a commodity broker or forward contract merchant" following "concerning a commodity broker".

CROSS REFERENCES

Applicability of other sections to Chapter 9, see 11 USCA § 901.

§ 104. Adjustment of dollar amounts

(a) On April 1, 1998, and at each 3-year interval ending on April 1 thereafter, each dollar amount in effect under sections 101(3), 101(18), 101(19A), 101(51D), 109(e), 303(b), 507(a), 522(d), 522(f)(3) and 522(f)(4), 522(n), 522(p), 522(q), 523(a)(2)(C), 541(b), 547(c)(9), 707(b), 1322(d), 1325(b), and 1326(b)(3) of this title and section 1409(b) of title 28 immediately before such April 1 shall be adjusted—

    (1) to reflect the change in the Consumer Price Index for All Urban Consumers, published by the Department of Labor, for the most recent 3-year period ending immediately before January 1 preceding such April 1, and

    (2) to round to the nearest $25 the dollar amount that represents such change.

(b) Not later than March 1, 1998, and at each 3-year interval ending on March 1 thereafter, the Judicial Conference of the United States shall publish in the Federal Register the dollar amounts that will become effective on such April 1 under sections 101(3), 101(18), 101(19A), 101(51D), 109(e), 303(b), 507(a), 522(d), 522(f)(3) and 522(f)(4), 522(n), 522(p), 522(q), 523(a)(2)(C), 541(b), 547(c)(9), 707(b), 1322(d), 1325(b), and 1326(b)(3) of this title and section 1409(b) of title 28.

(c) Adjustments made in accordance with subsection (a) shall not apply with respect to cases commenced before the date of such adjustments.

(Pub.L. 95–598, Nov. 6, 1978, 92 Stat. 2555; Pub.L. 103–394, Title I, § 108(e), Oct. 22, 1994, 108 Stat. 4112; Pub.L. 109–8, Title I, § 102(j), Title II, §§ 224(e)(2), 226(b), Title III, § 322(b), Title IV, § 432(c), Title X, § 1002, Title XII, § 1202, Apr. 20, 2005, 119 Stat. 35, 65, 67, 97, 110, 186, 193; Pub.L. 110–406, § 7, Oct. 13, 2008, 122 Stat. 4293.)

HISTORICAL AND STATUTORY NOTES

Amendments

2008 Amendments. Subsec. (a). Pub.L. 110–406, § 7(1), (2) struck out former subsec. (a) and redesignated former subsec. (b)(1) as subsec. (a). Prior to deletion, subsec. (a) read:

"(a) The Judicial Conference of the United States shall transmit to the Congress and to the President before May 1, 1985, and before May 1 of every sixth year after May 1, 1985, a recommendation for the uniform percentage adjustment of each dollar amount in this title and in section 1930 of title 28."

Subsec. (b)(1). Pub.L. 110–406, § 7(2), redesignated subsec. (b)(1) as subsec. (a) and subpars. (A) and (B) of that subsection as pars. (1) and (2), respectively.

Subsec. (b)(2). Pub.L. 110–406, § 7(3), redesignated subsec. (b)(2) as subsec. (b).

Subsec. (b)(3). Pub.L. 110–406, § 7(4), redesignated subsec. (b)(3) as subsec. (c).

Subsec. (c). Pub.L. 110–406, § 7(4), (5), redesignated subsec. (b)(3) as subsec. (c); and, in subsec. (c), as so redesignated, struck out "paragraph (1)" and inserted "subsection (a)".

2005 Amendments. Subsec. (b)(1). Pub.L. 109–8, § 1202(1)–(4), in introductory provisions, inserted "101(19A)," after "101(18),", "522(f)(3) and 522(f)(4)," after "522(d),", and "541(b), 547(c)(9)," after "523(a)(2)(C)," and substituted "1322(d), 1325(b), and 1326(b)(3) of this title and section 1409(b) of title 28" for "and 1325(b)(3)".

Pub.L. 109–8, § 1002, inserted "101(18)," after "101(3)," in introductory provisions.

Pub.L. 109–8, § 432(c), inserted "101(51D)," after "101(3)," in introductory provisions.

Pub.L. 109–8, § 322(b), inserted "522(p), 522(q)," after "522(n)," in introductory provisions.

Pub.L. 109–8, § 226(b), inserted "101(3)," after "sections" in introductory provisions.

Pub.L. 109–8, § 224(e)(2), inserted "522(n)," after "522(d)," in introductory provisions.

Pub.L. 109–8, § 102(j), substituted "523(a)(2)(C), 707(b), and 1325(b)(3)" for "and 523(a)(2)(C)" in introductory provisions.

Subsec. (b)(2). Pub.L. 109–8, § 1202(1)–(3), (5), inserted "101(19A)," after "101(18),", "522(f)(3) and 522(f)(4)," after "522(d),", and "541(b), 547(c)(9)," after "523(a)(2)(C)," and substituted "1322(d), 1325(b), and 1326(b)(3) of this title and section 1409(b) of title 28" for "and 1325(b)(3) of this title".

Pub.L. 109–8, § 1002, inserted "101(18)," after "101(3),".

Pub.L. 109–8, § 432(c), inserted "101(51D)," after "101(3),".

Pub. L. 109–8, § 322(b), inserted "522(p), 522(q)," after "522(n),".

Pub.L. 109–8, § 226(b), inserted "101(3)," after "sections".

Pub.L. 109–8, § 224(e)(2), inserted "522(n)," after "522(d),".

Pub.L. 109–8, § 102(j), substituted "523(a)(2)(C), 707(b), and 1325(b)(3)" for "and 523(a)(2)(C)".

1994 Amendments. Subsec. (a). Pub.L. 103–394, § 108(e)(1), designated existing provisions as subsec. (a).

Subsec. (b). Pub.L. 103–394, § 108(e)(2), added subsec. (b).

Adjustment of Dollar Amounts

By notice published Feb. 21, 2013, 78 F.R. 12089, the Judicial Conference of the United States increased the dollar amounts in provisions specified in subsec. (b) of this section, effective Apr. 1, 2013, and provided also that these increases do not apply to cases commenced before the effective date of the adjustments, *i.e.*, April 1, 2013.

Previous adjustments of the dollar amounts in provisions specified in subsec. (b) of this section were contained in the following:

Notice published Feb. 25, 2010, 75 F.R. 8747, effective Apr. 1, 2010.

Notice published Feb. 14, 2007, 72 F.R. 7082, modified Mar. 30, 2007, 72 F.R. 15162, effective Apr. 1, 2007.

Notice published Feb. 18, 2004, 69 F.R. 8482, effective Apr. 1, 2004.

Notice published Feb. 20, 2001, 66 F.R. 10910, effective Apr. 1, 2001.

Notice published Feb. 3, 1998, 63 F.R. 7179, effective Apr. 1, 1998.

The most recent dollar amount adjustments have been as follows:

Code Provision	Dollar Amount			
	April 1, 2004 (or enactment) to March 31, 2007	April 1, 2007 to March 31, 2010	April 1 2010 to March 31 2013	April 1, 2013 to current
Title 11				
§ 101(3)	$150,000	$164,250	$175,750	$186,825
§ 101(18)	$3,237,000	$3,544,525	$3,792,650	$4,031,575
§ 101(19A)	$1,500,000	$1,642,500	$1,757,475	$1,868,200
§ 101(51D)	$2,000,000	$2,190,000	$2,343,300	$2,490,925

Title 11 GENERAL PROVISIONS 11 § 104

Code Provision	Dollar Amount			
	April 1, 2004 (or enactment) to March 31, 2007	April 1, 2007 to March 31, 2010	April 1 2010 to March 31 2013	April 1, 2013 to current
§ 109(e)	$307,675	$336,900	$360,475	$383,175
	$922,975	$1,010,6650	$1,081,400	$1,149,525
§ 303(b)(1)	$12,300	$13,475	$14,425	$15,325
§ 303(b)(2)	$12,300	$13,475	$14,425	$15,325
§ 507(a)(4)	$10,000	$10,950	$11,725	$12,475
§ 507(a)(5)	$10,000	$10,950	$11,725	$12,475
§ 507(a)(6)	$4,925	$5,400	$5,775	$6,150
§ 507(a)(7)	$2,225	$2,425	$2,600	$2,775
§ 522(d)(1)	$18,450	$20,200	$21,625	$22,975
§ 522(d)(2)	$2,950	$3,225	$3,450	$3,675
§ 522(d)(3)	$475	$525	$550	$575
	$9,850	$10,775	$11,525	$12,250
§ 522(d)(4)	$1,225	$1,350	$1,450	$1,550
§ 522(d)(5)	$975	$1,075	$1,150	$1,225
	$9,250	$10,125	$10,825	$11,500
§ 522(d)(6)	$1,850	$2,025	$2,175	$2,300
§ 522(d)(8)	$9,850	$10,775	$11,525	$12,250
§ 522(d)(11)(D)	$18,450	$20,200	$21,625	$22,975
§ 522(f)(3)	$5,000	$5,475	$5,850	$6,225
§ 522(f)(4)	$500	$550	$600	$650
§ 522(n)	$1,000,000	$1,095,000	$1,171,650	$1,245,475
§ 522(p)	$125,000	$136,875	$146,450	$155,675
§ 522(q)	$125,000	$136,875	$146,450	$155,675
§ 523(a)(2)(C)(i)(I)	$500	$550	$600	$650
§ 523(a)(2)(C)(i)(II)	$750	$825	$875	$925
§ 541(b)(5)(C)	$5,000	$5,475	$5,850	$6,225
§ 541(b)(6)(C)	$5,000	$5,475	$5,850	$6,225
§ 547(c)(9)	$5,000	$5,475	$5,850	$6,225
§ 707(b)(2)(A)(i)(I)	$6,000	$6,575	$7,025	$7,475
§ 707(b)(2)(A)(i)(II)	$10,000	$10,950	$11,725	$12,475
§ 707(b)(2)(A)(ii)(IV)	$1,500	$1,650	$1,775	$1,875
§ 707(b)(2)(B)(iv)(I)	$6,000	$6,575	$7,025	$7,475
§ 707(b)(2)(B)(iv)(II)	$10,000	$10,950	$11,725	$12,475
§ 707(b)(5)(B)	$1,000	$1,100	$1,175	$1,250
§ 707(b)(6)(C)	$525	$575	$625	$675

Code Provision	Dollar Amount			
	April 1, 2004 (or enactment) to March 31, 2007	April 1, 2007 to March 31, 2010	April 1 2010 to March 31 2013	April 1, 2013 to current
§ 707(b)(7)(A)(iii)	$525	$575	$625	$675
§ 1322(d)	$525	$575	$625	$675
§ 1325(b)	$525	$575	$625	$675
§ 1326(b)(3)	$25	$25	$25	$25
Title 28				
§ 1409(b)	$1,000	$1,100	$1,175	$1,250
	$15,000	$16,425	$17,575	$18,675
	$10,000	$10,950	$11,725	$12,475

§ 105. Power of court

(a) The court may issue any order, process, or judgment that is necessary or appropriate to carry out the provisions of this title. No provision of this title providing for the raising of an issue by a party in interest shall be construed to preclude the court from, sua sponte, taking any action or making any determination necessary or appropriate to enforce or implement court orders or rules, or to prevent an abuse of process.

(b) Notwithstanding subsection (a) of this section, a court may not appoint a receiver in a case under this title.

(c) The ability of any district judge or other officer or employee of a district court to exercise any of the authority or responsibilities conferred upon the court under this title shall be determined by reference to the provisions relating to such judge, officer, or employee set forth in title 28. This subsection shall not be interpreted to exclude bankruptcy judges and other officers or employees appointed pursuant to chapter 6 of title 28 from its operation.

(d) The court, on its own motion or on the request of a party in interest—

(1) shall hold such status conferences as are necessary to further the expeditious and economical resolution of the case; and

(2) unless inconsistent with another provision of this title or with applicable Federal Rules of Bankruptcy Procedure, may issue an order at any such conference prescribing such limitations and conditions as the court deems appropriate to ensure that the case is handled expeditiously and economically, including an order that—

(A) sets the date by which the trustee must assume or reject an executory contract or unexpired lease; or

(B) in a case under chapter 11 of this title—

(i) sets a date by which the debtor, or trustee if one has been appointed, shall file a disclosure statement and plan;

(ii) sets a date by which the debtor, or trustee if one has been appointed, shall solicit acceptances of a plan;

(iii) sets the date by which a party in interest other than a debtor may file a plan;

(iv) sets a date by which a proponent of a plan, other than the debtor, shall solicit acceptances of such plan;

(v) fixes the scope and format of the notice to be provided regarding the hearing on approval of the disclosure statement; or

(vi) provides that the hearing on approval of the disclosure statement may be combined with the hearing on confirmation of the plan.

(Pub.L. 95–598, Nov. 6, 1978, 92 Stat. 2555; Pub.L. 98–353, Title I, § 118, July 10, 1984, 98 Stat. 344; Pub.L. 99–554, Title II, § 203, Oct. 27, 1986, 100 Stat. 3097; Pub.L. 103–394, Title I, § 104(a), Oct. 22, 1994, 108 Stat. 4108; Pub.L. 109–8, Title IV, § 440, Apr. 20, 2005, 119 Stat. 114; Pub.L. 111–327, § 2(a)(3), Dec. 22, 2010, 124 Stat. 3557.)

HISTORICAL AND STATUTORY NOTES

Amendments

2010 Amendments. Subsec. (d)(2). Pub.L. 111–327, § 2(a)(3), inserted "may" following "Procedure,".

2005 Amendments. Subsec. (d). Pub.L. 109–8, § 440(1), struck ", may" following "party in interest" in the matter preceding par. (1).

Subsec. (d)(1). Pub.L. 109–8, § 440(2), rewrote par. (1), which formerly read:

"(1) hold a status conference regarding any case or proceeding under this title after notice to the parties in interest; and".

1994 Amendments. Subsec. (d). Pub.L. 103–394, § 104(a), added subsec. (d).

1986 Amendments. Subsec. (a). Pub.L. 99–554, § 203, added "No provision of this title providing for the raising of an issue by a party in interest shall be construed to preclude the court from, sua sponte, taking any action or making any determination necessary or appropriate to enforce or implement court orders or rules, or to prevent an abuse of process" following "of this title".

1984 Amendments. Subsec. (a). Pub.L. 98–353, § 118(1), struck out "bankruptcy" preceding "court".

Subsec. (b). Pub.L. 98–353, § 118(1), struck out "bankruptcy" preceding "court".

Subsec. (c). Pub.L. 98–353, § 118(2), added subsec. (c).

§ 106. Waiver of sovereign immunity

(a) Notwithstanding an assertion of sovereign immunity, sovereign immunity is abrogated as to a governmental unit to the extent set forth in this section with respect to the following:

(1) Sections 105, 106, 107, 108, 303, 346, 362, 363, 364, 365, 366, 502, 503, 505, 506, 510, 522, 523, 524, 525, 542, 543, 544, 545, 546, 547, 548, 549, 550, 551, 552, 553, 722, 724, 726, 744, 749, 764, 901, 922, 926, 928, 929, 944, 1107, 1141, 1142, 1143, 1146, 1201, 1203, 1205, 1206, 1227, 1231, 1301, 1303, 1305, and 1327 of this title.

(2) The court may hear and determine any issue arising with respect to the application of such sections to governmental units.

(3) The court may issue against a governmental unit an order, process, or judgment under such sections or the Federal Rules of Bankruptcy Procedure, including an order or judgment awarding a money recovery, but not including an award of punitive damages. Such order or judgment for costs or fees under this title or the Federal Rules of Bankruptcy Procedure against any governmental unit shall be consistent with the provisions and limitations of section 2412(d)(2)(A) of title 28.

(4) The enforcement of any such order, process, or judgment against any governmental unit shall be consistent with appropriate nonbankruptcy law applicable to such governmental unit and, in the case of a money judgment against the United States, shall be paid as if it is a judgment rendered by a district court of the United States.

(5) Nothing in this section shall create any substantive claim for relief or cause of action not otherwise existing under this title, the Federal Rules of Bankruptcy Procedure, or nonbankruptcy law.

(b) A governmental unit that has filed a proof of claim in the case is deemed to have waived sovereign immunity with respect to a claim against such governmental unit that is property of the estate and that arose out of the same transaction or occurrence out of which the claim of such governmental unit arose.

(c) Notwithstanding any assertion of sovereign immunity by a governmental unit, there shall be offset against a claim or interest of a governmental unit any claim against such governmental unit that is property of the estate.

(Pub.L. 95–598, Nov. 6, 1978, 92 Stat. 2555; Pub.L. 103–394, Title I, § 113, Oct. 22, 1994, 108 Stat. 4117; Pub.L. 111–327, § 2(a)(4), Dec. 22, 2010, 124 Stat. 3557.)

HISTORICAL AND STATUTORY NOTES

Amendments

2010 Amendments. Subsec. (a)(1). Pub.L. 111–327, § 2(a)(4), struck out "728," following "726,".

1994 Amendments. Subsecs. (a) to (c). Pub.L. 103–394, § 113, amended subsecs. (a) to (c) generally. Prior to amendment, subsecs. (a) to (c) read as follows:

"**(a)** A governmental unit is deemed to have waived sovereign immunity with respect to any claim against such governmental unit that is property of the estate and that arose out of the same transaction or occurrence out of which such governmental unit's claim arose.

"**(b)** There shall be offset against an allowed claim or interest of a governmental unit any claim against such governmental unit that is property of the estate.

"**(c)** Except as provided in subsections (a) and (b) of this section and notwithstanding any assertion of sovereign immunity—

"**(1)** a provision of this title that contains 'creditor', 'entity', or 'governmental unit' applies to governmental units; and

"**(2)** a determination by the court of an issue arising under such a provision binds governmental units."

§ 107. Public access to papers

(a) Except as provided in subsections (b) and (c) and subject to section 112, a paper filed in a case under this title and the dockets of a bankruptcy court are public records and open to examination by an entity at reasonable times without charge.

(b) On request of a party in interest, the bankruptcy court shall, and on the bankruptcy court's own motion, the bankruptcy court may—

(1) protect an entity with respect to a trade secret or confidential research, development, or commercial information; or

(2) protect a person with respect to scandalous or defamatory matter contained in a paper filed in a case under this title.

(c)(1) The bankruptcy court, for cause, may protect an individual, with respect to the following types of information to the extent the court finds that disclosure of such information would create undue risk of identity theft or other unlawful injury to the individual or the individual's property:

(A) Any means of identification (as defined in section 1028(d) of title 18) contained in a paper filed, or to be filed, in a case under this title.

(B) Other information contained in a paper described in subparagraph (A).

(2) Upon ex parte application demonstrating cause, the court shall provide access to information protected pursuant to paragraph (1) to an entity acting pursuant to the police or regulatory power of a domestic governmental unit.

(3) The United States trustee, bankruptcy administrator, trustee, and any auditor serving under section 586(f) of title 28—

(A) shall have full access to all information contained in any paper filed or submitted in a case under this title; and

(B) shall not disclose information specifically protected by the court under this title.

(Pub.L. 95–598, Nov. 6, 1978, 92 Stat. 2556; Pub.L. 109–8, Title II, §§ 233(c), 234(a), (c), Apr. 20, 2005, 119 Stat. 74, 75; Pub.L. 111–327, § 2(a)(5), Dec. 22, 2010, 124 Stat. 3557.)

HISTORICAL AND STATUTORY NOTES

Amendments

2010 Amendments. Subsection (a). Pub.L. 111–327, § 2(a)(5), struck out "subsection (b) of this section" and inserted "subsections (b) and (c)".

2005 Amendments. Subsec. (a). Pub.L. 109–8, § 233(c), inserted "and subject to section 112" after "section".

Pub.L. 109–8, § 234(c), which directed that subsec. (a) is amended by striking "subsection (b)," and inserting "subsections (b) and (c)," was incapable of execution.

Subsec. (c). Pub.L. 109–8, § 234(a), added subsec. (c).

§ 108. Extension of time

(a) If applicable nonbankruptcy law, an order entered in a nonbankruptcy proceeding, or an agreement fixes a period within which the debtor may commence an action, and such period has not expired before the date of the filing of the petition, the trustee may commence such action only before the later of—

(1) the end of such period, including any suspension of such period occurring on or after the commencement of the case; or

(2) two years after the order for relief.

(b) Except as provided in subsection (a) of this section, if applicable nonbankruptcy law, an order entered in a nonbankruptcy proceeding, or an agreement fixes a period within which the debtor or an individual protected under section 1201 or 1301 of this title may file any pleading, demand, notice, or proof of claim or loss, cure a default, or perform any other similar act, and such period has not expired before the date of the filing of the petition, the trustee may only file, cure, or perform, as the case may be, before the later of—

(1) the end of such period, including any suspension of such period occurring on or after the commencement of the case; or

(2) 60 days after the order for relief.

(c) Except as provided in section 524 of this title, if applicable nonbankruptcy law, an order entered in a nonbankruptcy proceeding, or an agreement fixes a period for commencing or continuing a civil action in a court other than a bankruptcy court on a claim against the debtor, or against an individual with respect to which such individual is protected under section 1201 or 1301 of this title, and such period has not expired before the date of the filing of the petition, then such period does not expire until the later of—

(1) the end of such period, including any suspension of such period occurring on or after the commencement of the case; or

(2) 30 days after notice of the termination or expiration of the stay under section 362, 922, 1201, or 1301 of this title, as the case may be, with respect to such claim.

(Pub.L. 95–598, Nov. 6, 1978, 92 Stat. 2556; Pub.L. 98–353, Title III, § 424, July 10, 1984, 98 Stat. 369; Pub.L. 99–554, Title II, § 257(b), Oct. 27, 1986, 100 Stat. 3114; Pub.L. 109–8, Title XII, § 1203, Apr. 20, 2005, 119 Stat. 193.)

HISTORICAL AND STATUTORY NOTES

Codifications

Amendment by Pub.L. 99–554, § 257(b)(2)(B), which directed amendment of subsec. (c)(2) by inserting "1201," after "722," was incapable of execution.

Amendments

2005 Amendments. Subsec. (c)(2). Pub.L. 109–8, § 1203, substituted "922, 1201, or" for "922, or".

1986 Amendments. Subsec. (b). Pub.L. 99–554, § 257(b)(1), inserted "1201 or" preceding "1301".

Subsec. (c). Pub.L. 99–554, § 257(b)(2)(A), in the matter preceding par. (1) struck out "section 1301" and inserted "section 1201 or 1301".

Subsec. (c)(2). Pub.L. 99–554, § 257(b)(2)(B), which directed the amendment of subsec. (c) by inserting "1201," after "722," could not be executed because "722," did not appear in text.

1984 Amendments. Subsec. (a). Pub.L. 98–353, § 424(b), added "nonbankruptcy" after "applicable" and "entered in a" in provisions preceding par. (1).

Subsec. (a)(1). Pub.L. 98–353, § 424(a), substituted "or" for "and" after the semicolon.

Subsec. (b). Pub.L. 98–353, § 424(b), added "nonbankruptcy" after "applicable" and "entered in a" in provisions preceding par. (1).

Subsec. (b)(1). Pub.L. 98–353, § 424(a), substituted "or" for "and" after the semicolon.

Subsec. (c). Pub.L. 98–353, § 424(b), added "nonbankruptcy" after "applicable" and "entered in a" in provisions preceding par. (1).

Subsec. (c)(1). Pub.L. 98–353, § 424(a), substituted "or" for "and" after the semicolon.

§ 109. Who may be a debtor

(a) Notwithstanding any other provision of this section, only a person that resides or has a domicile, a place of business, or property in the United States, or a municipality, may be a debtor under this title.

(b) A person may be a debtor under chapter 7 of this title only if such person is not—

   (1) a railroad;

   (2) a domestic insurance company, bank, savings bank, cooperative bank, savings and loan association, building and loan association, homestead association, a New Markets Venture Capital company as defined in section 351 of the Small Business Investment Act of 1958, a small business investment company licensed by the Small Business Administration under section 301 of the Small Business Investment Act of 1958, credit union, or industrial bank or similar institution which is an insured bank as defined in section 3(h) of the Federal Deposit Insurance Act, except that an uninsured State member bank, or a corporation organized under section 25A of the Federal Reserve Act, which operates, or operates as, a multilateral clearing organization pursuant to section 409 of the Federal Deposit Insurance Corporation Improvement Act of 1991 may be a debtor if a petition is filed at the direction of the Board of Governors of the Federal Reserve System; or

   (3)(A) a foreign insurance company, engaged in such business in the United States; or

   (B) a foreign bank, savings bank, cooperative bank, savings and loan association, building and loan association, or credit union, that has a branch or agency (as defined in section 1(b) of the International Banking Act of 1978) in the United States.

(c) An entity may be a debtor under chapter 9 of this title if and only if such entity—

   (1) is a municipality;

   (2) is specifically authorized, in its capacity as a municipality or by name, to be a debtor under such chapter by State law, or by a governmental officer or organization empowered by State law to authorize such entity to be a debtor under such chapter;

(3) is insolvent;

(4) desires to effect a plan to adjust such debts; and

(5)(A) has obtained the agreement of creditors holding at least a majority in amount of the claims of each class that such entity intends to impair under a plan in a case under such chapter;

(B) has negotiated in good faith with creditors and has failed to obtain the agreement of creditors holding at least a majority in amount of the claims of each class that such entity intends to impair under a plan in a case under such chapter;

(C) is unable to negotiate with creditors because such negotiation is impracticable; or

(D) reasonably believes that a creditor may attempt to obtain a transfer that is avoidable under section 547 of this title.

(d) Only a railroad, a person that may be a debtor under chapter 7 of this title (except a stockbroker or a commodity broker), and an uninsured State member bank, or a corporation organized under section 25A of the Federal Reserve Act, which operates, or operates as, a multilateral clearing organization pursuant to section 409 of the Federal Deposit Insurance Corporation Improvement Act of 1991 may be a debtor under chapter 11 of this title.

(e) Only an individual with regular income that owes, on the date of the filing of the petition, noncontingent, liquidated, unsecured debts of less than $383,175[1] and noncontingent, liquidated, secured debts of less than $1,149,525[1], or an individual with regular income and such individual's spouse, except a stockbroker or a commodity broker, that owe, on the date of the filing of the petition, noncontingent, liquidated, unsecured debts that aggregate less than $383,175[1] and noncontingent, liquidated, secured debts of less than $1,149,525[1] may be a debtor under chapter 13 of this title.

(f) Only a family farmer or family fisherman with regular annual income may be a debtor under chapter 12 of this title.

(g) Notwithstanding any other provision of this section, no individual or family farmer may be a debtor under this title who has been a debtor in a case pending under this title at any time in the preceding 180 days if—

(1) the case was dismissed by the court for willful failure of the debtor to abide by orders of the court, or to appear before the court in proper prosecution of the case; or

(2) the debtor requested and obtained the voluntary dismissal of the case following the filing of a request for relief from the automatic stay provided by section 362 of this title.

(h)(1) Subject to paragraphs (2) and (3), and notwithstanding any other provision of this section other than paragraph (4) of this subsection, an individual may not be a debtor under this title unless such individual has, during the 180-day period ending on the date of filing of the petition by such individual, received from an approved nonprofit budget and credit counseling agency described in section 111(a) an individual or group briefing (including a briefing conducted by telephone or on the Internet) that outlined the opportunities for available credit counseling and assisted such individual in performing a related budget analysis.

(2)(A) Paragraph (1) shall not apply with respect to a debtor who resides in a district for which the United States trustee (or the bankruptcy administrator, if any) determines that the approved nonprofit budget and credit counseling agencies for such district are not reasonably able to provide adequate services to the additional individuals who would otherwise seek credit counseling from such agencies by reason of the requirements of paragraph (1).

(B) The United States trustee (or the bankruptcy administrator, if any) who makes a determination described in subparagraph (A) shall review such determination not later than 1 year after the date of such determination, and not less frequently than annually thereafter.

---

[1] Dollar amount as adjusted by the Judicial Conference of the United States. See Adjustment of Dollar Amounts notes set out under this section and 11 U.S.C.A. § 104.

Notwithstanding the preceding sentence, a nonprofit budget and credit counseling agency may be disapproved by the United States trustee (or the bankruptcy administrator, if any) at any time.

(3)(A) Subject to subparagraph (B), the requirements of paragraph (1) shall not apply with respect to a debtor who submits to the court a certification that—

    (i) describes exigent circumstances that merit a waiver of the requirements of paragraph (1);

    (ii) states that the debtor requested credit counseling services from an approved nonprofit budget and credit counseling agency, but was unable to obtain the services referred to in paragraph (1) during the 7-day period beginning on the date on which the debtor made that request; and

    (iii) is satisfactory to the court.

(B) With respect to a debtor, an exemption under subparagraph (A) shall cease to apply to that debtor on the date on which the debtor meets the requirements of paragraph (1), but in no case may the exemption apply to that debtor after the date that is 30 days after the debtor files a petition, except that the court, for cause, may order an additional 15 days.

(4) The requirements of paragraph (1) shall not apply with respect to a debtor whom the court determines, after notice and hearing, is unable to complete those requirements because of incapacity, disability, or active military duty in a military combat zone. For the purposes of this paragraph, incapacity means that the debtor is impaired by reason of mental illness or mental deficiency so that he is incapable of realizing and making rational decisions with respect to his financial responsibilities; and "disability" means that the debtor is so physically impaired as to be unable, after reasonable effort, to participate in an in person, telephone, or Internet briefing required under paragraph (1).

(Pub.L. 95–598, Nov. 6, 1978, 92 Stat. 2557; Pub.L. 97–320, Title VII, § 703(d), Oct. 15, 1982, 96 Stat. 1539; Pub.L. 98–353, Title III, §§ 301, 425, July 10, 1984, 98 Stat. 352, 369; Pub.L. 99–554, Title II, § 253, Oct. 27, 1986, 100 Stat. 3105; Pub.L. 100–597, § 2, Nov. 3, 1988, 102 Stat. 3028; Pub.L. 103–394, Title I, § 108(a), Title II, § 220, Title IV, § 402, Title V, § 501(d)(2), Oct. 22, 1994, 108 Stat. 4111, 4129, 4141, 4143; Pub.L. 106–554, § 1(a)(5) [Title I, § 112(c)(1), (2)], (8) [§ 1(e)], Dec. 21, 2000, 114 Stat. 2763, 2763A–393, 2763A–665; Pub.L. 109–8, Title I, § 106(a), Title VIII, § 802(d)(1), Title X, § 1007(b), Title XII, § 1204(1), Apr. 20, 2005, 119 Stat. 37, 146, 188, 193; Pub.L. 111–16, § 2(1), May 7, 2009, 123 Stat. 1607; Pub.L. 111–327, § 2(a)(6), Dec. 22, 2010, 124 Stat. 3557.)

HISTORICAL AND STATUTORY NOTES

References in Text

    Section 351 of the Small Business Investment Act of 1958, referred to in subsec. (b)(2), is section 351 of Pub.L. 85–699, which is classified to 15 U.S.C.A. § 689.

    Subsection (c) or (d) of section 301 of the Small Business Investment Act of 1958, referred to in subsec. (b)(2), is subsection (c) or (d) of section 301 of Pub.L. 85–699, Title III, Aug. 21, 1958, which is classified to 15 U.S.C.A. § 681(c) or (d). Subsection (d) of section 301 was repealed by Pub.L. 104–208, Div. D, Title II, § 208(b)(3)(A), Sept. 30, 1996, 110 Stat. 3009–742.

    Section 3 of the Federal Deposit Insurance Act, referred to in subsec. (b)(2), is section 2[3] of Act Sept. 21, 1950, c. 967, 64 Stat. 873, which is classified to 12 U.S.C.A. § 1813.

    Section 25A of the Federal Reserve Act, referred to in subsecs. (b)(2) and (d), is Dec. 23, 1913, c. 6, § 25A, formerly § 25(a), as added Dec. 24, 1919, c. 18, 41 Stat. 378, as amended, which is classified to subchapter II of chapter 6 of Title 12 (12 U.S.C.A. § 611 et seq.).

    Section 409 of the Federal Deposit Insurance Corporation Improvement Act of 1991, referred to in subsecs. (b)(2) and (d), is Pub.L. 102–242, Title IV, § 409, as added by Pub.L. 106–554, § 1(a)(5) [Title I, § 112(a)(3)], Dec. 21, 2000, 114 Stat. 2763, 2763A–391, which is classified as 12 U.S.C.A. § 4422.

    Section 1(b) of the International Banking Act of 1978, referred to in subsec. (b)(3)(B), is Pub.L. 95–369, § 1(b), Sept. 17, 1978, 92 Stat. 607, as amended, which is classified to 12 U.S.C.A. § 3101.

Title 11   GENERAL PROVISIONS   11 § 109

Amendments

2010 Amendments. Subsec. (b)(3)(B). Pub.L. 111–327, § 2(a)(6)(A), struck out "1978" and inserted "1978)".

Subsec. (h)(1). Pub.L. 111–327, § 2(a)(6)(B), inserted "other than paragraph (4) of this subsection" following "this section", and struck out "preceding" and inserted "ending on".

2009 Amendments. Subsec. (h)(3)(A)(ii). Pub.L. 111–16, § 2(1), struck out "5-day" and inserted "7-day".

2005 Amendments. Subsec. (b)(2). Pub.L. 109–8, § 1204(1), struck out "subsection (c) or (d) of" preceding "section 301 of the Small Business Investment Act of 1958".

Subsec. (b)(3). Pub.L. 109–8, § 802(d)(1), rewrote par. (3), which formerly read: **"(3)** a foreign insurance company, bank, savings bank, cooperative bank, savings and loan association, building and loan association, homestead association, or credit union, engaged in such business in the United States."

Subsec. (f). Pub.L. 109–8, § 1007(b), inserted "or family fisherman" after "family farmer".

Subsec. (h). Pub.L. 109–8, § 106(a), added subsec. (h).

2000 Amendments. Subsec. (b)(2). Pub.L. 106–554, § 1(a)(8)[§ 1(e)], inserted "a New Markets Venture Capital company as defined in section 351 of the Small Business Investment Act of 1958,," after "homestead association".

Pub.L. 106–554, § 1(a)(5) [Title I, § 112(c)(1)], struck "; or" and inserted the following: ", except that an uninsured State member bank, or a corporation organized under section 25A of the Federal Reserve Act, which operates, or operates as, a multilateral clearing organization pursuant to section 409 of the Federal Deposit Insurance Corporation Improvement Act of 1991 may be a debtor if a petition is filed at the direction of the Board of Governors of the Federal Reserve System; or".

Subsec. (d). Pub.L. 106–554, § 1(a)(5) [Title I, § 112(c)(2)], revised subsec. (d). Prior to revision, subsec. (d) read as follows:

"(d) Only a person that may be a debtor under chapter 7 of this title, except a stockbroker or a commodity broker, and a railroad may be a debtor under chapter 11 of this title."

1994 Amendments. Subsec. (b)(2). Pub.L. 103–394, § 220, added a small business investment company licensed by the Small Business Administration under subsection (c) or (d) of section 301 of the Small Business Investment Act of 1958 to the list of institutions which may not be debtors under chapter 7 of this title.

Pub.L. 103–394, § 501(d)(2), struck out "(12 U.S.C. 1813(h))" following "Federal Deposit Insurance Act".

Subsec. (c)(2). Pub.L. 103–394, § 402, substituted "specifically authorized, in its capacity as a municipality or by name," for "generally authorized".

Subsec. (e). Pub.L. 103–394, § 108(a), substituted "$250,000" for "$100,000", wherever appearing, and substituted "$750,000" for "$350,000", wherever appearing.

1988 Amendments. Subsec. (c)(3). Pub.L. 100–597 deleted from definition of debtor an entity "unable to meet such entity's debts as such debts mature".

1986 Amendments. Subsec. (f). Pub.L. 99–554, § 253(1)(B), (2), added subsec. (f). Former subsec. (f) was redesignated (g).

Subsec. (g). Pub.L. 99–554, § 253(1), redesignated former subsec. (f) as (g) and, as so redesignated, added reference to family farmer.

1984 Amendments. Subsec. (a). Pub.L. 98–353, § 425(a), struck out "in the United States," after "only a person that resides".

Subsec. (c)(5)(D). Pub.L. 98–353, § 425(b), substituted "transfer that is avoidable under section 547 of this title" for "preference".

Subsec. (d). Pub.L. 98–353, § 425(c), substituted "stockbroker" for "stockholder".

Subsec. (f). Pub.L. 98–353, § 301, added subsec. (f).

1982 Amendments. Subsec. (b)(2). Pub.L. 97–320 inserted reference to industrial banks or similar institutions which are insured banks as defined in section 3(h) of the Federal Deposit Insurance Act (12 U.S.C. 1813(h)).

Adjustment of Dollar Amounts

For adjustment of dollar amounts specified in subsec. (e) of this section by the Judicial Conference of the United States, see note set out under 11 U.S.C.A. § 104.

CROSS REFERENCES

Filing of Chapter 9 petition by certain unincorporated tax or special assessment districts notwithstanding provisions under this section, see 11 USCA § 921.

§ 110. Penalty for persons who negligently or fraudulently prepare bankruptcy petitions

(a) In this section—

(1) "bankruptcy petition preparer" means a person, other than an attorney for the debtor or an employee of such attorney under the direct supervision of such attorney, who prepares for compensation a document for filing; and

(2) "document for filing" means a petition or any other document prepared for filing by a debtor in a United States bankruptcy court or a United States district court in connection with a case under this title.

(b)(1) A bankruptcy petition preparer who prepares a document for filing shall sign the document and print on the document the preparer's name and address. If a bankruptcy petition preparer is not an individual, then an officer, principal, responsible person, or partner of the bankruptcy petition preparer shall be required to—

(A) sign the document for filing; and

(B) print on the document the name and address of that officer, principal, responsible person, or partner.

(2)(A) Before preparing any document for filing or accepting any fees from or on behalf of a debtor, the bankruptcy petition preparer shall provide to the debtor a written notice which shall be on an official form prescribed by the Judicial Conference of the United States in accordance with rule 9009 of the Federal Rules of Bankruptcy Procedure.

(B) The notice under subparagraph (A)—

(i) shall inform the debtor in simple language that a bankruptcy petition preparer is not an attorney and may not practice law or give legal advice;

(ii) may contain a description of examples of legal advice that a bankruptcy petition preparer is not authorized to give, in addition to any advice that the preparer may not give by reason of subsection (e)(2); and

(iii) shall—

(I) be signed by the debtor and, under penalty of perjury, by the bankruptcy petition preparer; and

(II) be filed with any document for filing.

(c)(1) A bankruptcy petition preparer who prepares a document for filing shall place on the document, after the preparer's signature, an identifying number that identifies individuals who prepared the document.

(2)(A) Subject to subparagraph (B), for purposes of this section, the identifying number of a bankruptcy petition preparer shall be the Social Security account number of each individual who prepared the document or assisted in its preparation.

(B) If a bankruptcy petition preparer is not an individual, the identifying number of the bankruptcy petition preparer shall be the Social Security account number of the officer, principal, responsible person, or partner of the bankruptcy petition preparer.

(3) [Repealed. Pub.L. 109–8, Title II, § 221(3)(B), Apr. 20, 2005, 119 Stat. 60]

(d) A bankruptcy petition preparer shall, not later than the time at which a document for filing is presented for the debtor's signature, furnish to the debtor a copy of the document.

(e)(1) A bankruptcy petition preparer shall not execute any document on behalf of a debtor.

(2)(A) A bankruptcy petition preparer may not offer a potential bankruptcy debtor any legal advice, including any legal advice described in subparagraph (B).

(B) The legal advice referred to in subparagraph (A) includes advising the debtor—

  (i) whether—

   (I) to file a petition under this title; or

   (II) commencing a case under chapter 7, 11, 12, or 13 is appropriate;

  (ii) whether the debtor's debts will be discharged in a case under this title;

  (iii) whether the debtor will be able to retain the debtor's home, car, or other property after commencing a case under this title;

  (iv) concerning—

   (I) the tax consequences of a case brought under this title; or

   (II) the dischargeability of tax claims;

  (v) whether the debtor may or should promise to repay debts to a creditor or enter into a reaffirmation agreement with a creditor to reaffirm a debt;

  (vi) concerning how to characterize the nature of the debtor's interests in property or the debtor's debts; or

  (vii) concerning bankruptcy procedures and rights.

(f) A bankruptcy petition preparer shall not use the word "legal" or any similar term in any advertisements, or advertise under any category that includes the word "legal" or any similar term.

(g) A bankruptcy petition preparer shall not collect or receive any payment from the debtor or on behalf of the debtor for the court fees in connection with filing the petition.

(h)(1) The Supreme Court may promulgate rules under section 2075 of title 28, or the Judicial Conference of the United States may prescribe guidelines, for setting a maximum allowable fee chargeable by a bankruptcy petition preparer. A bankruptcy petition preparer shall notify the debtor of any such maximum amount before preparing any document for filing for the debtor or accepting any fee from or on behalf of the debtor.

(2) A declaration under penalty of perjury by the bankruptcy petition preparer shall be filed together with the petition, disclosing any fee received from or on behalf of the debtor within 12 months immediately prior to the filing of the case, and any unpaid fee charged to the debtor. If rules or guidelines setting a maximum fee for services have been promulgated or prescribed under paragraph (1), the declaration under this paragraph shall include a certification that the bankruptcy petition preparer complied with the notification requirement under paragraph (1).

(3)(A) The court shall disallow and order the immediate turnover to the bankruptcy trustee any fee referred to in paragraph (2)—

  (i) found to be in excess of the value of any services rendered by the bankruptcy petition preparer during the 12-month period immediately preceding the date of the filing of the petition; or

  (ii) found to be in violation of any rule or guideline promulgated or prescribed under paragraph (1).

(B) All fees charged by a bankruptcy petition preparer may be forfeited in any case in which the bankruptcy petition preparer fails to comply with this subsection or subsection (b), (c), (d), (e), (f), or (g).

(C) An individual may exempt any funds recovered under this paragraph under section 522(b).

(4) The debtor, the trustee, a creditor, the United States trustee (or the bankruptcy administrator, if any) or the court, on the initiative of the court, may file a motion for an order under paragraph (3).

(5) A bankruptcy petition preparer shall be fined not more than $500 for each failure to comply with a court order to turn over funds within 30 days of service of such order.

(i)(1) If a bankruptcy petition preparer violates this section or commits any act that the court finds to be fraudulent, unfair, or deceptive, on the motion of the debtor, trustee, United States trustee (or the bankruptcy administrator, if any), and after notice and a hearing, the court shall order the bankruptcy petition preparer to pay to the debtor—

(A) the debtor's actual damages;

(B) the greater of—

(i) $2,000; or

(ii) twice the amount paid by the debtor to the bankruptcy petition preparer for the preparer's services; and

(C) reasonable attorneys' fees and costs in moving for damages under this subsection.

(2) If the trustee or creditor moves for damages on behalf of the debtor under this subsection, the bankruptcy petition preparer shall be ordered to pay the movant the additional amount of $1,000 plus reasonable attorneys' fees and costs incurred.

(j)(1) A debtor for whom a bankruptcy petition preparer has prepared a document for filing, the trustee, a creditor, or the United States trustee in the district in which the bankruptcy petition preparer resides, has conducted business, or the United States trustee in any other district in which the debtor resides may bring a civil action to enjoin a bankruptcy petition preparer from engaging in any conduct in violation of this section or from further acting as a bankruptcy petition preparer.

(2)(A) In an action under paragraph (1), if the court finds that—

(i) a bankruptcy petition preparer has—

(I) engaged in conduct in violation of this section or of any provision of this title;

(II) misrepresented the preparer's experience or education as a bankruptcy petition preparer; or

(III) engaged in any other fraudulent, unfair, or deceptive conduct; and

(ii) injunctive relief is appropriate to prevent the recurrence of such conduct,

the court may enjoin the bankruptcy petition preparer from engaging in such conduct.

(B) If the court finds that a bankruptcy petition preparer has continually engaged in conduct described in subclause (I), (II), or (III) of clause (i) and that an injunction prohibiting such conduct would not be sufficient to prevent such person's interference with the proper administration of this title, has not paid a penalty imposed under this section, or failed to disgorge all fees ordered by the court the court may enjoin the person from acting as a bankruptcy petition preparer.

(3) The court, as part of its contempt power, may enjoin a bankruptcy petition preparer that has failed to comply with a previous order issued under this section. The injunction under this paragraph may be issued on the motion of the court, the trustee, or the United States trustee (or the bankruptcy administrator, if any).

(4) The court shall award to a debtor, trustee, or creditor that brings a successful action under this subsection reasonable attorneys' fees and costs of the action, to be paid by the bankruptcy petition preparer.

(k) Nothing in this section shall be construed to permit activities that are otherwise prohibited by law, including rules and laws that prohibit the unauthorized practice of law.

(l)(1) A bankruptcy petition preparer who fails to comply with any provision of subsection (b), (c), (d), (e), (f), (g), or (h) may be fined not more than $500 for each such failure.

(2) The court shall triple the amount of a fine assessed under paragraph (1) in any case in which the court finds that a bankruptcy petition preparer—

(A) advised the debtor to exclude assets or income that should have been included on applicable schedules;

(B) advised the debtor to use a false Social Security account number;

(C) failed to inform the debtor that the debtor was filing for relief under this title; or

(D) prepared a document for filing in a manner that failed to disclose the identity of the bankruptcy petition preparer.

(3) A debtor, trustee, creditor, or United States trustee (or the bankruptcy administrator, if any) may file a motion for an order imposing a fine on the bankruptcy petition preparer for any violation of this section.

(4)(A) Fines imposed under this subsection in judicial districts served by United States trustees shall be paid to the United States trustees, who shall deposit an amount equal to such fines in the United States Trustee Fund.

(B) Fines imposed under this subsection in judicial districts served by bankruptcy administrators shall be deposited as offsetting receipts to the fund established under section 1931 of title 28, and shall remain available until expended to reimburse any appropriation for the amount paid out of such appropriation for expenses of the operation and maintenance of the courts of the United States.

(Added Pub.L. 103–394, Title III, § 308(a), Oct. 22, 1994, 108 Stat. 4135; amended Pub.L. 109–8, Title II, § 221, Title XII, § 1205, Apr. 20, 2005, 119 Stat. 59, 194; Pub.L. 110–161, Div. B, Title II, § 212(b), Dec. 26, 2007, 121 Stat. 1914; Pub.L. 111–327, § 2(a)(7), Dec. 22, 2010, 124 Stat. 3558.)

HISTORICAL AND STATUTORY NOTES

References in Text

Paragraph (2), referred to in subsec. (h)(4), was redesignated as par. (3) and repealed and a new par. (3) was added by Pub.L. 109–8, Title II, § 221(8)(A), (D), Apr. 20, 2005, 119 Stat. 59. The new par. (3) provides for court orders similar to those provided for in former par. (2).

Amendments

2010 Amendments. Subsec. (b)(2)(A). Pub.L. 111–327, § 2(a)(7)(A), inserted "or on behalf of" following "from".

Subsec. (h)(1). Pub.L. 111–327, § 2(a)(7)(B)(i), struck out "a debtor" and inserted "the debtor", and inserted "or on behalf of" following "from".

Subsec. (h)(3)(A). Pub.L. 111–327, § 2(a)(7)(B)(ii)(I), struck out "found to be in excess of the value of any services" following "paragraph (2)".

Subsec. (h)(3)(A)(i). Pub.L. 111–327, § 2(a)(7)(B)(ii)(II), inserted "found to be in excess of the value of any services" following "(i)".

Subsec. (h)(4). Pub.L. 111–327, § 2(a)(7)(B)(iii), struck out "paragraph (2)" and inserted " paragraph (3)".

2007 Amendments. Subsec. (l)(4)(A). Pub.L. 110–161, Div. B, § 212(b), rewrote subpar. (A), which formerly read: "Fines imposed under this subsection in judicial districts served by United States trustees shall be paid to the United States trustee, who shall deposit an amount equal to such fines in a special account of the United States Trustee System Fund referred to in section 586(e)(2) of title 28. Amounts deposited under this subparagraph shall be available to fund the enforcement of this section on a national basis."

2005 Amendments. Subsec. (a)(1). Pub.L. 109–8, § 221(1), substituted "for the debtor or an employee of such attorney under the direct supervision of such attorney" for "or an employee of an attorney".

Subsec. (b)(1). Pub.L. 109–8, § 221(2)(A), added at the end of par. (1) the following:

"If a bankruptcy petition preparer is not an individual, then an officer, principal, responsible person, or partner of the bankruptcy petition preparer shall be required to—

"**(A)** sign the document for filing; and

"**(B)** print on the document the name and address of that officer, principal, responsible person, or partner."

Subsec. (b)(2). Pub.L. 109–8, § 221(2)(B), rewrote par. (2), which formerly read: "A bankruptcy petition preparer who fails to comply with paragraph (1) may be fined not more than $500 for each such failure unless the failure is due to reasonable cause."

Subsec. (c)(2). Pub.L. 109–8, § 221(3)(A), substituted "(2)(A) Subject to subparagraph (B), for purposes" for "(2) For purposes" and added subpar. (B).

Subsec. (c)(3). Pub.L. 109–8, § 221(3)(B), struck out former par. (3), which read: "A bankruptcy petition preparer who fails to comply with paragraph (1) may be fined not more than $500 for each such failure unless the failure is due to reasonable cause."

Subsec. (d)(1), (2). Pub.L. 109–8, § 221(4), redesignated par. (1) as subsec. (d) and struck out former par. (2), which read: "A bankruptcy petition preparer who fails to comply with paragraph (1) may be fined not more than $500 for each such failure unless the failure is due to reasonable cause."

Subsec. (e)(2). Pub.L. 109–8, § 221(5), rewrote par. (2), which formerly read: "A bankruptcy petition preparer may be fined not more than $500 for each document executed in violation of paragraph (1)."

Subsec. (f)(1), (2). Pub.L. 109–8, § 221(6), redesignated par. (1) as subsec. (f) and struck out par. (2), which formerly read: "A bankruptcy petition preparer shall be fined not more than $500 for each violation of paragraph (1)."

Subsec. (g)(1), (2). Pub.L. 109–8, § 221(7), redesignated par. (1) as subsec. (g) and struck out par. (2), which formerly read: "A bankruptcy petition preparer shall be fined not more than $500 for each violation of paragraph (1)."

Subsec. (h)(1). Pub.L. 109–8, § 221(8)(A),(B), redesignated former par. (1) as par. (2) and inserted a new par. (1).

Subsec. (h)(2). Pub.L. 109–8, § 221(8)(A), (C), redesignated former par. (1) as par. (2). Former par. (2) redesignated par. (3).

Pub.L. 109–8, § 221(8)(C), in redesignated par. (2), substituted "A" for "Within 10 days after the date of the filing of a petition, a bankruptcy petition preparer shall file a", inserted "by the bankruptcy petition preparer shall be filed together with the petition," after "perjury", and added the following at the end: "If rules or guidelines setting a maximum fee for services have been promulgated or prescribed under paragraph (1), the declaration under this paragraph shall include a certification that the bankruptcy petition preparer complied with the notification requirement under paragraph (1)."

Subsec. (h)(3). Pub.L. 109–8, § 221(8)(A), redesignated former par. (2) as par. (3). Former par. (3) redesignated par. (4).

Pub.L. 109–8, § 221(8)(D), inserted a new par. (3) and struck out redesignated par. (3), which read: "The court shall disallow and order the immediate turnover to the bankruptcy trustee of any fee referred to in paragraph (1) found to be in excess of the value of services rendered for the documents prepared. An individual debtor may exempt any funds so recovered under section 522(b)."

Subsec. (h)(4). Pub.L. 109–8, § 221(8)(A), redesignated former par. (3) as par. (4). Former par. (4) redesignated par. (5).

Pub.L. 109–8, § 221(8)(E), in redesignated par. (4), substituted "the United States trustee (or the bankruptcy administrator, if any) or the court, on the initiative of the court," for "or the United States trustee".

Subsec. (h)(5). Pub.L. 109–8, § 221(8)(A), redesignated former par. (4) as par. (5).

Subsec. (i)(1). Pub.L. 109–8, § 221(9), rewrote the matter preceding subpar. (a), which formerly read: "If a bankruptcy case or related proceeding is dismissed because of the failure to file bankruptcy papers, including papers specified in section 521(1) of this title, the negligence or intentional disregard of this title or the Federal Rules of Bankruptcy Procedure by a bankruptcy petition preparer, or if a bankruptcy petition preparer violates this section or commits any fraudulent, unfair, or deceptive act, the bankruptcy court shall certify that fact to the district court, and the district court, on motion of the debtor, the trustee, or a creditor and after a hearing, shall order the bankruptcy petition preparer to pay to the debtor—".

Subsec. (j)(2)(A)(i)(I). Pub.L. 109–8, § 221(10)(A)(i), struck out "a violation of which subjects a person to criminal penalty" after "provision of this title".

Subsec. (j)(2)(B). Pub.L. 109–8, § 221(10)(A)(ii)(I), substituted "has not paid a penalty" for "or has not paid a penalty".

Pub.L. 109–8, § 221(10)(A)(ii)(II), inserted "or failed to disgorge all fees ordered by the court" after "a penalty imposed under this section,".

Subsec. (j)(3). Pub.L. 109–8, § 221(10)(B), (C), inserted a new par. (3) and redesignated former par. (3) as par. (4).

Subsec. (j)(4). Pub.L. 109–8, § 221(10)(B), redesignated former par. (3) as par. (4).

Pub.L. 109–8, § 1205, in redesignated par. (4), struck out "attorney's" and inserted "attorneys'".

Subsec. (l). Pub.L. 109–8, § 221(11), added subsec. (l).

§ 111. Nonprofit budget and credit counseling agencies; financial management instructional courses

(a) The clerk shall maintain a publicly available list of—

   (1) nonprofit budget and credit counseling agencies that provide 1 or more services described in section 109(h) currently approved by the United States trustee (or the bankruptcy administrator, if any); and

   (2) instructional courses concerning personal financial management currently approved by the United States trustee (or the bankruptcy administrator, if any), as applicable.

(b) The United States trustee (or bankruptcy administrator, if any) shall only approve a nonprofit budget and credit counseling agency or an instructional course concerning personal financial management as follows:

   (1) The United States trustee (or bankruptcy administrator, if any) shall have thoroughly reviewed the qualifications of the nonprofit budget and credit counseling agency or of the provider of the instructional course under the standards set forth in this section, and the services or instructional courses that will be offered by such agency or such provider, and may require such agency or such provider that has sought approval to provide information with respect to such review.

   (2) The United States trustee (or bankruptcy administrator, if any) shall have determined that such agency or such instructional course fully satisfies the applicable standards set forth in this section.

   (3) If a nonprofit budget and credit counseling agency or instructional course did not appear on the approved list for the district under subsection (a) immediately before approval under this section, approval under this subsection of such agency or such instructional course shall be for a probationary period not to exceed 6 months.

   (4) At the conclusion of the applicable probationary period under paragraph (3), the United States trustee (or bankruptcy administrator, if any) may only approve for an additional

1-year period, and for successive 1-year periods thereafter, an agency or instructional course that has demonstrated during the probationary or applicable subsequent period of approval that such agency or instructional course—

    (A) has met the standards set forth under this section during such period; and

    (B) can satisfy such standards in the future.

  (5) Not later than 30 days after any final decision under paragraph (4), an interested person may seek judicial review of such decision in the appropriate district court of the United States.

(c)(1) The United States trustee (or the bankruptcy administrator, if any) shall only approve a nonprofit budget and credit counseling agency that demonstrates that it will provide qualified counselors, maintain adequate provision for safekeeping and payment of client funds, provide adequate counseling with respect to client credit problems, and deal responsibly and effectively with other matters relating to the quality, effectiveness, and financial security of the services it provides.

  (2) To be approved by the United States trustee (or the bankruptcy administrator, if any), a nonprofit budget and credit counseling agency shall, at a minimum—

    (A) have a board of directors the majority of which—

      (i) are not employed by such agency; and

      (ii) will not directly or indirectly benefit financially from the outcome of the counseling services provided by such agency;

    (B) if a fee is charged for counseling services, charge a reasonable fee, and provide services without regard to ability to pay the fee;

    (C) provide for safekeeping and payment of client funds, including an annual audit of the trust accounts and appropriate employee bonding;

    (D) provide full disclosures to a client, including funding sources, counselor qualifications, possible impact on credit reports, and any costs of such program that will be paid by such client and how such costs will be paid;

    (E) provide adequate counseling with respect to a client's credit problems that includes an analysis of such client's current financial condition, factors that caused such financial condition, and how such client can develop a plan to respond to the problems without incurring negative amortization of debt;

    (F) provide trained counselors who receive no commissions or bonuses based on the outcome of the counseling services provided by such agency, and who have adequate experience, and have been adequately trained to provide counseling services to individuals in financial difficulty, including the matters described in subparagraph (E);

    (G) demonstrate adequate experience and background in providing credit counseling; and

    (H) have adequate financial resources to provide continuing support services for budgeting plans over the life of any repayment plan.

(d) The United States trustee (or the bankruptcy administrator, if any) shall only approve an instructional course concerning personal financial management—

  (1) for an initial probationary period under subsection (b)(3) if the course will provide at a minimum—

    (A) trained personnel with adequate experience and training in providing effective instruction and services;

    (B) learning materials and teaching methodologies designed to assist debtors in understanding personal financial management and that are consistent with stated objectives directly related to the goals of such instructional course;

(C) adequate facilities situated in reasonably convenient locations at which such instructional course is offered, except that such facilities may include the provision of such instructional course by telephone or through the Internet, if such instructional course is effective;

(D) the preparation and retention of reasonable records (which shall include the debtor's bankruptcy case number) to permit evaluation of the effectiveness of such instructional course, including any evaluation of satisfaction of instructional course requirements for each debtor attending such instructional course, which shall be available for inspection and evaluation by the Executive Office for United States Trustees, the United States trustee (or the bankruptcy administrator, if any), or the chief bankruptcy judge for the district in which such instructional course is offered; and

(E) if a fee is charged for the instructional course, charge a reasonable fee, and provide services without regard to ability to pay the fee; and

(2) for any 1-year period if the provider thereof has demonstrated that the course meets the standards of paragraph (1) and, in addition—

(A) has been effective in assisting a substantial number of debtors to understand personal financial management; and

(B) is otherwise likely to increase substantially the debtor's understanding of personal financial management.

(e) The district court may, at any time, investigate the qualifications of a nonprofit budget and credit counseling agency referred to in subsection (a), and request production of documents to ensure the integrity and effectiveness of such agency. The district court may, at any time, remove from the approved list under subsection (a) a nonprofit budget and credit counseling agency upon finding such agency does not meet the qualifications of subsection (b).

(f) The United States trustee (or the bankruptcy administrator, if any) shall notify the clerk that a nonprofit budget and credit counseling agency or an instructional course is no longer approved, in which case the clerk shall remove it from the list maintained under subsection (a).

(g)(1) No nonprofit budget and credit counseling agency may provide to a credit reporting agency information concerning whether a debtor has received or sought instruction concerning personal financial management from such agency.

(2) A nonprofit budget and credit counseling agency that willfully or negligently fails to comply with any requirement under this title with respect to a debtor shall be liable for damages in an amount equal to the sum of—

(A) any actual damages sustained by the debtor as a result of the violation; and

(B) any court costs or reasonable attorneys' fees (as determined by the court) incurred in an action to recover those damages.

(Added Pub.L. 109–8, Title I, § 106(e)(1), Apr. 20, 2005, 119 Stat. 39; amended Pub.L. 111–327, § 2(a)(8), Dec. 22, 2010, 124 Stat. 3558.)

HISTORICAL AND STATUTORY NOTES

Amendments

2010 Amendments. Subsec. (d)(1)(E). Pub.L. 111–327, § 2(a)(8)(A), struck out the period at the end and inserted "; and".

Pub.L. 111–327, § 2(a)(8)(B), made technical corrections requiring no change in text.

Debtor Financial Management Training Test Program

Pub.L. 109–8, Title I, § 105, Apr. 20, 2005, 119 Stat. 36, provided that:

"**(a) Development of financial management and training curriculum and materials.**—The Director of the Executive Office for United States Trustees (in this section referred to as the 'Director') shall consult with a wide range of individuals who are experts in the field of debtor education, including trustees who serve in cases under chapter 13 of title 11, United States Code [11 U.S.C.A. § 1301 et seq.], and who operate financial management education programs for debtors, and shall develop a financial management training curriculum and materials that can be used to educate debtors who are individuals on how to better manage their finances.

"(b) Test.—

"(1) Selection of districts.—The Director shall select 6 judicial districts of the United States in which to test the effectiveness of the financial management training curriculum and materials developed under subsection (a) [of this note].

"(2) Use.—For an 18-month period beginning not later than 270 days after the date of the enactment of this Act [April 20, 2005], such curriculum and materials shall be, for the 6 judicial districts selected under paragraph (1), used as the instructional course concerning personal financial management for purposes of section 111 of title 11, United States Code.

"(c) Evaluation.—

"(1) In general.—During the 18-month period referred to in subsection (b) [of this note], the Director shall evaluate the effectiveness of—

"(A) the financial management training curriculum and materials developed under subsection (a) [of this note]; and

"(B) a sample of existing consumer education programs such as those described in the Report of the National Bankruptcy Review Commission (October 20, 1997) that are representative of consumer education programs carried out by the credit industry, by trustees serving under chapter 13 of title 11, United States Code [11 U.S.C.A. § 1301 et seq.], and by consumer counseling groups.

"(2) Report.—Not later than 3 months after concluding such evaluation, the Director shall submit a report to the Speaker of the House of Representatives and the President pro tempore of the Senate, for referral to the appropriate committees of the Congress, containing the findings of the Director regarding the effectiveness of such curriculum, such materials, and such programs and their costs."

[Amendments by Pub.L. 109–8 effective, except as otherwise provided, 180 days after April 20, 2005, and inapplicable with respect to cases commenced under Title 11 before the effective date, see Pub.L. 109–8, § 1501, set out as a note under 11 U.S.C.A. § 101.]

§ 112. Prohibition on disclosure of name of minor children

The debtor may be required to provide information regarding a minor child involved in matters under this title but may not be required to disclose in the public records in the case the name of such minor child. The debtor may be required to disclose the name of such minor child in a nonpublic record that is maintained by the court and made available by the court for examination by the United States trustee, the trustee, and the auditor (if any) serving under section 586(f) of title 28, in the case. The court, the United States trustee, the trustee, and such auditor shall not disclose the name of such minor child maintained in such nonpublic record.

(Added Pub.L. 109–8, Title II, § 233(a), Apr. 20, 2005, 119 Stat. 74.)

CHAPTER 3—CASE ADMINISTRATION

SUBCHAPTER I—COMMENCEMENT OF A CASE

Sec.
301. Voluntary cases.
302. Joint cases.
303. Involuntary cases.
304. [Repealed.]
305. Abstention.
306. Limited appearance.
307. United States trustee.
308. Debtor reporting requirements.

SUBCHAPTER II—OFFICERS

321. Eligibility to serve as trustee.
322. Qualification of trustee.
323. Role and capacity of trustee.
324. Removal of trustee or examiner.
325. Effect of vacancy.
326. Limitation on compensation of trustee.
327. Employment of professional persons.
328. Limitation on compensation of professional persons.
329. Debtor's transactions with attorneys.
330. Compensation of officers.
331. Interim compensation.
332. Consumer privacy ombudsman.
333. Appointment of patient care ombudsman.

SUBCHAPTER III—ADMINISTRATION

341. Meetings of creditors and equity security holders.
342. Notice.
343. Examination of the debtor.
344. Self-incrimination; immunity.
345. Money of estates.
346. Special provisions related to the treatment of State and local taxes.
347. Unclaimed property.
348. Effect of conversion.
349. Effect of dismissal.
350. Closing and reopening cases.
351. Disposal of patient records.

SUBCHAPTER IV—ADMINISTRATIVE POWERS

361. Adequate protection.
362. Automatic stay.
363. Use, sale, or lease of property.
364. Obtaining credit.
365. Executory contracts and unexpired leases.
366. Utility service.

CROSS REFERENCES

Applicability of this chapter to—

Cases under Chapters 7, 11, 12, or 13 of this title, see 11 USCA § 103.

Investor protection liquidation proceedings, see 15 USCA § 78fff.

SUBCHAPTER I—COMMENCEMENT OF A CASE

§ 301. Voluntary cases

(a) A voluntary case under a chapter of this title is commenced by the filing with the bankruptcy court of a petition under such chapter by an entity that may be a debtor under such chapter.

(b) The commencement of a voluntary case under a chapter of this title constitutes an order for relief under such chapter.

(Pub.L. 95–598, Nov. 6, 1978, 92 Stat. 2558; Pub.L. 109–8, Title V, § 501(b), Apr. 20, 2005, 119 Stat. 118.)

HISTORICAL AND STATUTORY NOTES

Amendments

2005 Amendments. Subsec. (a). Pub.L. 109–8, § 501(b)(1), inserted "**(a)**" before "A voluntary" and struck the last sentence, which read: "The commencement of a voluntary case under a chapter of this title constitutes an order for relief under such chapter."

Subsec. (b). Pub.L. 109–8, § 501(b)(2), inserted subsec. (b).

CROSS REFERENCES

Applicability of this section in Chapter 9 cases, see 11 USCA § 901.

"Petition" defined, see 11 USCA § 101.

§ 302. Joint cases

(a) A joint case under a chapter of this title is commenced by the filing with the bankruptcy court of a single petition under such chapter by an individual that may be a debtor under such chapter and such individual's spouse. The commencement of a joint case under a chapter of this title constitutes an order for relief under such chapter.

(b) After the commencement of a joint case, the court shall determine the extent, if any, to which the debtors' estates shall be consolidated.

(Pub.L. 95–598, Nov. 6, 1978, 92 Stat. 2558.)

CROSS REFERENCES

"Petition" defined, see 11 USCA § 101.

§ 303. Involuntary cases

(a) An involuntary case may be commenced only under chapter 7 or 11 of this title, and only against a person, except a farmer, family farmer, or a corporation that is not a moneyed, business, or commercial corporation, that may be a debtor under the chapter under which such case is commenced.

(b) An involuntary case against a person is commenced by the filing with the bankruptcy court of a petition under chapter 7 or 11 of this title—

(1) by three or more entities, each of which is either a holder of a claim against such person that is not contingent as to liability or the subject of a bona fide dispute as to liability or amount, or an indenture trustee representing such a holder, if such noncontingent, undisputed

claims aggregate at least $15,325[1] more than the value of any lien on property of the debtor securing such claims held by the holders of such claims;

(2) if there are fewer than 12 such holders, excluding any employee or insider of such person and any transferee of a transfer that is voidable under section 544, 545, 547, 548, 549, or 724(a) of this title, by one or more of such holders that hold in the aggregate at least $15,325[1] of such claims;

(3) if such person is a partnership—

(A) by fewer than all of the general partners in such partnership; or

(B) if relief has been ordered under this title with respect to all of the general partners in such partnership, by a general partner in such partnership, the trustee of such a general partner, or a holder of a claim against such partnership; or

(4) by a foreign representative of the estate in a foreign proceeding concerning such person.

(c) After the filing of a petition under this section but before the case is dismissed or relief is ordered, a creditor holding an unsecured claim that is not contingent, other than a creditor filing under subsection (b) of this section, may join in the petition with the same effect as if such joining creditor were a petitioning creditor under subsection (b) of this section.

(d) The debtor, or a general partner in a partnership debtor that did not join in the petition, may file an answer to a petition under this section.

(e) After notice and a hearing, and for cause, the court may require the petitioners under this section to file a bond to indemnify the debtor for such amounts as the court may later allow under subsection (i) of this section.

(f) Notwithstanding section 363 of this title, except to the extent that the court orders otherwise, and until an order for relief in the case, any business of the debtor may continue to operate, and the debtor may continue to use, acquire, or dispose of property as if an involuntary case concerning the debtor had not been commenced.

(g) At any time after the commencement of an involuntary case under chapter 7 of this title but before an order for relief in the case, the court, on request of a party in interest, after notice to the debtor and a hearing, and if necessary to preserve the property of the estate or to prevent loss to the estate, may order the United States trustee to appoint an interim trustee under section 701 of this title to take possession of the property of the estate and to operate any business of the debtor. Before an order for relief, the debtor may regain possession of property in the possession of a trustee ordered appointed under this subsection if the debtor files such bond as the court requires, conditioned on the debtor's accounting for and delivering to the trustee, if there is an order for relief in the case, such property, or the value, as of the date the debtor regains possession, of such property.

(h) If the petition is not timely controverted, the court shall order relief against the debtor in an involuntary case under the chapter under which the petition was filed. Otherwise, after trial, the court shall order relief against the debtor in an involuntary case under the chapter under which the petition was filed, only if—

(1) the debtor is generally not paying such debtor's debts as such debts become due unless such debts are the subject of a bona fide dispute as to liability or amount; or

(2) within 120 days before the date of the filing of the petition, a custodian, other than a trustee, receiver, or agent appointed or authorized to take charge of less than substantially all of the property of the debtor for the purpose of enforcing a lien against such property, was appointed or took possession.

---

[1] Dollar amount as adjusted by the Judicial Conference of the United States. See Adjustment of Dollar Amounts notes set out under this section and 11 U.S.C.A. § 104.

(i) If the court dismisses a petition under this section other than on consent of all petitioners and the debtor, and if the debtor does not waive the right to judgment under this subsection, the court may grant judgment—

    (1) against the petitioners and in favor of the debtor for—

        (A) costs; or

        (B) a reasonable attorney's fee; or

    (2) against any petitioner that filed the petition in bad faith, for—

        (A) any damages proximately caused by such filing; or

        (B) punitive damages.

(j) Only after notice to all creditors and a hearing may the court dismiss a petition filed under this section—

    (1) on the motion of a petitioner;

    (2) on consent of all petitioners and the debtor; or

    (3) for want of prosecution.

(k)(1) If—

    (A) the petition under this section is false or contains any materially false, fictitious, or fraudulent statement;

    (B) the debtor is an individual; and

    (C) the court dismisses such petition,

the court, upon the motion of the debtor, shall seal all the records of the court relating to such petition, and all references to such petition.

(2) If the debtor is an individual and the court dismisses a petition under this section, the court may enter an order prohibiting all consumer reporting agencies (as defined in section 603(f) of the Fair Credit Reporting Act (15 U.S.C. 1681a(f))) from making any consumer report (as defined in section 603(d) of that Act) that contains any information relating to such petition or to the case commenced by the filing of such petition.

(3) Upon the expiration of the statute of limitations described in section 3282 of title 18, for a violation of section 152 or 157 of such title, the court, upon the motion of the debtor and for good cause, may expunge any records relating to a petition filed under this section.

[(l)] Redesignated (k)]

(Pub.L. 95–598, Nov. 6, 1978, 92 Stat. 2559; Pub. L. 98–353, Title III, §§ 426, 427, July 10, 1984, 98 Stat. 369; Pub.L. 99–554, Title II, §§ 204, 254, 283(b), Oct. 27, 1986, 100 Stat. 3097, 3105, 3116; Pub.L. 103–394, Title I, § 108(b), Oct. 22, 1994, 108 Stat. 4112; Pub.L. 109–8, Title III, § 332(b), Title VIII, § 802(d)(2), Title XII, § 1234(a), Apr. 20, 2005, 119 Stat. 103, 146, 204; Pub.L. 111–327, § 2(a)(9), Dec. 22, 2010, 124 Stat. 3558.)

HISTORICAL AND STATUTORY NOTES

References in Text

Section 603 of the Fair Credit Reporting Act, referred to in subsec. (k)(2), is Pub.L. 90–321, Title VI, § 603, as added Pub.L. 91–508, Title IV, § 601, Oct. 26, 1970, 84 Stat. 1128, and amended, which is classified to 15 U.S.C.A. § 1681a.

Amendments

2010 Amendments. Subsec. (k). Pub.L. 111–327, § 2(a)(9), redesignated former subsec. (l) as (k).

Subsec. (l). Pub.L. 111–327, § 2(a)(9), redesignated former subsec. (l) as (k).

2005 Amendments. Subsec. (b)(1). Pub.L. 109–8, § 1234(a)(1)(A), inserted "as to liability or amount" after "bona fide dispute".

Pub.L. 109–8, § 1234(a)(1)(B), struck "if such claims" and inserted "if such noncontingent, undisputed claims".

Subsec. (h)(1). Pub.L. 109–8, § 1234(a)(2), inserted "as to liability or amount" before the semicolon at the end.

Subsec. (k). Pub.L. 109–8, § 802(d)(2), struck out subsec. (k), which formerly read: **"(k)** Notwithstanding subsection (a) of this section, an involuntary case may be commenced against a foreign bank that is not engaged in such business in the United States only under chapter 7 of this title and only if a foreign proceeding concerning such bank is pending."

Subsec. (l). Pub.L. 109–8, § 332(b), added subsec. (l).

1994 Amendments. Subsec. (b)(1). Pub.L. 103–394, § 108(b)(1), substituted "if such claims aggregate at least $10,000 more than the value of any lien" for "if such claims aggregate at least $5,000 more than the value of any lien".

Subsec. (b)(2). Pub.L. 103–394, § 108(b)(2), substituted "hold in the aggregate at least $10,000 of such claims" for "hold in the aggregate at least $5,000 of such claims".

1986 Amendments. Subsec. (a). Pub.L. 99–554, § 254, added reference to family farmer.

Subsec. (b). Pub.L. 99–554, § 283(b)(1), substituted "subject of" for "subject on".

Subsec. (g). Pub.L. 99–554, § 204(1), substituted "may order the United States trustee to appoint" for "may appoint".

Subsec. (h)(1). Pub.L. 99–554, § 283(b)(2), substituted "are the" for "that are the".

Subsec. (i)(1)(A). Pub.L. 99–554, § 204(2), substituted "costs; or" for "costs;".

Subsec. (i)(1)(C). Pub.L. 99–554, § 204(2), struck out "(C) any damages proximately caused by the taking of possession of the debtor's property by a trustee appointed under subsection (g) of this section or section 1104 of this title; or".

1984 Amendments. Subsec. (b). Pub.L. 98–353, § 426(a), added "against a person" after "involuntary case".

Subsec. (b)(1). Pub.L. 98–353, § 426(b)(1), added "or the subject of a bona fide dispute," after "liability".

Subsec. (h)(1). Pub.L. 98–353, § 426(b)(2), added "unless such debts that are the subject of a bona fide dispute" after "due".

Subsec. (j)(2). Pub.L. 98–353, § 427, substituted "debtor" for "debtors".

Adjustment of Dollar Amounts

For adjustment of dollar amounts specified in subsec. (b)(1), (2) of this section by the Judicial Conference of the United States, see note set out under 11 U.S.C.A. § 104.

CROSS REFERENCES

Allowance of administrative expenses incurred by creditor filing involuntary petition, see 11 USCA § 503.

"Petition" defined, see 11 USCA § 101.

[§ 304. Repealed. Pub.L. 109–8, Title VIII, § 802(d)(3), Apr. 20, 2005, 119 Stat. 146]

§ 305. Abstention

(a) The court, after notice and a hearing, may dismiss a case under this title, or may suspend all proceedings in a case under this title, at any time if—

    (1) the interests of creditors and the debtor would be better served by such dismissal or suspension; or

(2)(A) a petition under section 1515 for recognition of a foreign proceeding has been granted; and

(B) the purposes of chapter 15 of this title would be best served by such dismissal or suspension.

(b) A foreign representative may seek dismissal or suspension under subsection (a)(2) of this section.

(c) An order under subsection (a) of this section dismissing a case or suspending all proceedings in a case, or a decision not so to dismiss or suspend, is not reviewable by appeal or otherwise by the court of appeals under section 158(d), 1291, or 1292 of title 28 or by the Supreme Court of the United States under section 1254 of title 28.

(Pub.L. 95–598, Nov. 6, 1978, 92 Stat. 2561; Pub.L. 101–650, Title III, § 309(a), Dec. 1, 1990, 104 Stat. 5113; Pub.L. 102–198, § 5, Dec. 9, 1991, 105 Stat. 1623; Pub.L. 109–8, Title VIII, § 802(d)(6), Apr. 20, 2005, 119 Stat. 146.)

HISTORICAL AND STATUTORY NOTES

Amendments

2005 Amendments. Subsec. (a)(2). Pub.L. 109–8, § 802(d)(6), rewrote par. (2), which formerly read:

"**(2)(A)** there is pending a foreign proceeding; and

"**(B)** the factors specified in section 304(c) of this title warrant such dismissal or suspension."

1991 Amendments. Subsec. (c). Pub.L. 102–198 substituted "title 28" for "this title", wherever appearing.

1990 Amendments. Subsec. (c). Pub.L. 101–650 declared abstention determinations in bankruptcy cases nonreviewable by the court of appeals or by the Supreme Court.

§ 306. Limited appearance

An appearance in a bankruptcy court by a foreign representative in connection with a petition or request under section 303 or 305 of this title does not submit such foreign representative to the jurisdiction of any court in the United States for any other purpose, but the bankruptcy court may condition any order under section 303 or 305 of this title on compliance by such foreign representative with the orders of such bankruptcy court.

(Pub.L. 95–598, Nov. 6, 1978, 92 Stat. 2561; Pub.L. 109–8, Title VIII, § 802(d)(5), Apr. 20, 2005, 119 Stat. 146.)

HISTORICAL AND STATUTORY NOTES

Amendments

2005 Amendments. Section. Pub.L. 109–8, § 802(d)(5), struck out ", 304," following "under section 303" twice.

§ 307. United States trustee

The United States trustee may raise and may appear and be heard on any issue in any case or proceeding under this title but may not file a plan pursuant to section 1121(c) of this title.

(Added Pub.L. 99–554, Title II, § 205(a), Oct. 27, 1986, 100 Stat. 3098.)

HISTORICAL AND STATUTORY NOTES

Standing and Authority of Bankruptcy Administrator

Pub.L. 101–650, Title III, § 317(b), Dec. 1, 1990, 104 Stat. 5115, provided that: "A bankruptcy administrator may raise and may appear and be heard on any issue in any case under title 11, United States Code, but may not file a plan pursuant to section 1121(c) of such title."

§ 308. Debtor reporting requirements

(a) For purposes of this section, the term "profitability" means, with respect to a debtor, the amount of money that the debtor has earned or lost during current and recent fiscal periods.

(b) A debtor in a small business case shall file periodic financial and other reports containing information including—

(1) the debtor's profitability;

(2) reasonable approximations of the debtor's projected cash receipts and cash disbursements over a reasonable period;

(3) comparisons of actual cash receipts and disbursements with projections in prior reports;

(4) whether the debtor is—

(A) in compliance in all material respects with postpetition requirements imposed by this title and the Federal Rules of Bankruptcy Procedure; and

(B) timely filing tax returns and other required government filings and paying taxes and other administrative expenses when due;

(5) if the debtor is not in compliance with the requirements referred to in paragraph (4)(A) or filing tax returns and other required government filings and making the payments referred to in paragraph (4)(B), what the failures are and how, at what cost, and when the debtor intends to remedy such failures; and

(6) such other matters as are in the best interests of the debtor and creditors, and in the public interest in fair and efficient procedures under chapter 11 of this title.

(Added Pub.L. 109–8, Title IV, § 434(a)(1), Apr. 20, 2005, 119 Stat. 111; amended Pub.L. 111–327, § 2(a)(10), Dec. 22, 2010, 124 Stat. 3558.)

HISTORICAL AND STATUTORY NOTES

Amendments

2010 Amendments. Subsec. (b). Pub.L. 111–327, § 2(a)(10)(A), struck out "small business debtor" and inserted "debtor in a small business case".

Subsec. (b)(4). Pub.L. 111–327, § 2(a)(10)(B), redesignated former par. (4)(A) as par. (4) and therein redesignated former cls. (i) and (ii) as subpars. (A) and (B), respectively; redesignated former par. (4)(B) as par. (5), and therein struck out "subparagraph (A)(i)" and inserted "paragraph (4)(A)", and struck out "subparagraph (A)(ii)" and inserted "paragraph (4)(B)"; and redesignated former par. (4)(C) as par. (6).

Subsec. (b)(5). Pub.L. 111–327, § 2(a)(10)(B)(ii), redesignated former par. (4)(B) as par. (5), and therein struck out "subparagraph (A)(i)" and inserted "paragraph (4)(A)", and struck out "subparagraph (A)(ii)" and inserted "paragraph (4)(B)".

Subsec. (b)(6). Pub.L. 111–327, § 2(a)(10)(B)(iii), redesignated former par. (4)(C) as par. (6).

SUBCHAPTER II—OFFICERS

§ 321. Eligibility to serve as trustee

(a) A person may serve as trustee in a case under this title only if such person is—

(1) an individual that is competent to perform the duties of trustee and, in a case under chapter 7, 12, or 13 of this title, resides or has an office in the judicial district within which the case is pending, or in any judicial district adjacent to such district; or

(2) a corporation authorized by such corporation's charter or bylaws to act as trustee, and, in a case under chapter 7, 12, or 13 of this title, having an office in at least one of such districts.

(b) A person that has served as an examiner in the case may not serve as trustee in the case.

(c) The United States trustee for the judicial district in which the case is pending is eligible to serve as trustee in the case if necessary.

(Pub.L. 95–598, Nov. 6, 1978, 92 Stat. 2561; Pub. L. 98–353, Title III, § 428, July 10, 1984, 98 Stat. 369; Pub.L. 99–554, Title II, §§ 206, 257(c), Oct. 27, 1986, 100 Stat. 3098, 3114.)

HISTORICAL AND STATUTORY NOTES

Amendments

1986 Amendments. Subsec. (a). Pub.L. 99–554, § 257(c), added references to chapter 12 in two places.

Subsec. (c). Pub.L. 99–554, § 206, added subsec. (c).

1984 Amendments. Subsec. (b). Pub.L. 98–353 substituted "the case" for "a case" after "an examiner in".

§ 322. Qualification of trustee

(a) Except as provided in subsection (b)(1), a person selected under section 701, 702, 703, 1104, 1163, 1202, or 1302 of this title to serve as trustee in a case under this title qualifies if before seven days after such selection, and before beginning official duties, such person has filed with the court a bond in favor of the United States conditioned on the faithful performance of such official duties.

(b)(1) The United States trustee qualifies wherever such trustee serves as trustee in a case under this title.

(2) The United States trustee shall determine—

(A) the amount of a bond required to be filed under subsection (a) of this section; and

(B) the sufficiency of the surety on such bond.

(c) A trustee is not liable personally or on such trustee's bond in favor of the United States for any penalty or forfeiture incurred by the debtor.

(d) A proceeding on a trustee's bond may not be commenced after two years after the date on which such trustee was discharged.

(Pub.L. 95–598, Nov. 6, 1978, 92 Stat. 2562; Pub. L. 98–353, Title III, § 429, July 10, 1984, 98 Stat. 369; Pub.L. 99–554, Title II, §§ 207, 257(d), Oct. 27, 1986, 100 Stat. 3098, 3114; Pub.L. 103–394, Title V, § 501(d)(3), Oct. 22, 1994, 108 Stat. 4143; Pub.L. 111–16, § 2(2), May 7, 2009, 123 Stat. 1607.)

HISTORICAL AND STATUTORY NOTES

Amendments

2009 Amendments. Subsec. (a). Pub.L. 111–16, § 2(2), struck out "five days" and inserted "seven days".

1994 Amendments. Subsec. (a). Pub.L. 103–394, § 501(d)(3), substituted "1202, or 1302" for "1302, or 1202".

1986 Amendments. Subsec. (a). Pub.L. 99–554, § 207(1), substituted "Except as provided in subsection (b)(1), a person" for "A person".

Pub.L. 99–554, § 257(d), added reference to section 1202 of this title.

Subsec. (b). Pub.L. 99–554, § 207(2), added par. (1), designated existing provisions as par. (2), and, as so designated, substituted "The United States trustee" for "The court", "(A) the amount" for "(1) the amount", and "(B) the sufficiency" for "(2) the sufficiency".

1984 Amendments. Subsec. (b)(1). Pub.L. 98–353 added "required to be" after "bond".

CROSS REFERENCES

Appointment of trustee or examiner upon failure to qualify, see 11 USCA § 1104.

Certain customer transactions affected before qualification of trustee, see 11 USCA § 746.

"Debtor in possession" defined as debtor except when qualified person is serving as trustee under this section, see 11 USCA § 1101.

Interim trustee, see 11 USCA § 701.

Qualification of trustee and attorney in investor protection liquidation proceedings, see 15 USCA § 78eee.

Standing trustee—

    Chapter 12 cases, see 11 USCA § 1202.

    Chapter 13 cases, see 11 USCA § 1302.

Successor trustee, see 11 USCA § 703.

§ 323. Role and capacity of trustee

(a) The trustee in a case under this title is the representative of the estate.

(b) The trustee in a case under this title has capacity to sue and be sued.

(Pub.L. 95–598, Nov. 6, 1978, 92 Stat. 2562.)

§ 324. Removal of trustee or examiner

(a) The court, after notice and a hearing, may remove a trustee, other than the United States trustee, or an examiner, for cause.

(b) Whenever the court removes a trustee or examiner under subsection (a) in a case under this title, such trustee or examiner shall thereby be removed in all other cases under this title in which such trustee or examiner is then serving unless the court orders otherwise.

(Pub.L. 95–598, Nov. 6, 1978, 92 Stat. 2562; Pub.L. 99–554, Title II, § 208, Oct. 27, 1986, 100 Stat. 3098.)

HISTORICAL AND STATUTORY NOTES

Amendments

1986 Amendments. Pub.L. 99–554, § 208, designated existing provisions as subsec. (a), and, as so designated, substituted "a trustee, other than the United States trustee, or an examiner" for "a trustee or an examiner", and added subsec. (b).

CROSS REFERENCES

Adverse interest and conduct of officers of estate, see 18 USCA § 154.

Appointment of trustee or examiner upon removal, see 11 USCA § 1104.

Authority of Attorney General to investigate trustees, see 28 USCA § 526.

Embezzlement by trustee, see 18 USCA § 153.

Successor trustee, see 11 USCA § 703.

§ 325. Effect of vacancy

A vacancy in the office of trustee during a case does not abate any pending action or proceeding, and the successor trustee shall be substituted as a party in such action or proceeding.

(Pub.L. 95–598, Nov. 6, 1978, 92 Stat. 2562.)

§ 326. Limitation on compensation of trustee

(a) In a case under chapter 7 or 11, the court may allow reasonable compensation under section 330 of this title of the trustee for the trustee's services, payable after the trustee renders such services, not to exceed 25 percent on the first $5,000 or less, 10 percent on any amount in excess of $5,000 but not in excess of $50,000, 5 percent on any amount in excess of $50,000 but not in excess of $1,000,000, and reasonable compensation not to exceed 3 percent of such moneys in excess of $1,000,000, upon all moneys disbursed or turned over in the case by the trustee to parties in interest, excluding the debtor, but including holders of secured claims.

(b) In a case under chapter 12 or 13 of this title, the court may not allow compensation for services or reimbursement of expenses of the United States trustee or of a standing trustee appointed under section 586(b) of title 28, but may allow reasonable compensation under section 330 of this title of a trustee appointed under section 1202(a) or 1302(a) of this title for the trustee's services, payable after the trustee renders such services, not to exceed five percent upon all payments under the plan.

(c) If more than one person serves as trustee in the case, the aggregate compensation of such persons for such service may not exceed the maximum compensation prescribed for a single trustee by subsection (a) or (b) of this section, as the case may be.

(d) The court may deny allowance of compensation for services or reimbursement of expenses of the trustee if the trustee failed to make diligent inquiry into facts that would permit denial of allowance under section 328(c) of this title or, with knowledge of such facts, employed a professional person under section 327 of this title.

(Pub.L. 95–598, Nov. 6, 1978, 92 Stat. 2562; Pub. L. 98–353, Title III, § 430(a), (b), July 10, 1984, 98 Stat. 369; Pub.L. 99–554, Title II, § 209, Oct. 27, 1986, 100 Stat. 3098; Pub.L. 103–394, Title I, § 107, Oct. 22, 1994, 108 Stat. 4111.)

HISTORICAL AND STATUTORY NOTES

Amendments

1994 Amendments. Subsec. (a). Pub.L. 103–394, § 107, substituted "25 percent on the first $5,000 or less, 10 percent on any amount in excess of $5,000 but not in excess of $50,000, 5 percent on any amount in excess of $50,000 but not in excess of $1,000,000, and reasonable compensation not to exceed 3 percent of such moneys in excess of $1,000,000" for "fifteen percent of the first $1,000 or less, six percent on any amount in excess of $1,000 but not in excess of $3,000, and three percent on any amount in excess of $3,000".

1986 Amendments. Subsec. (b). Pub.L. 99–554, § 209, substituted "under chapter 12 or 13 of this title" for "under chapter 13 of this title", "expenses of the United States trustee or of a standing trustee appointed under section 586(b) of title 28" for "expenses of a standing trustee appointed under section 1302(d) of this title", and "under section 1202(a) or 1302(a) of this title" for "under section 1302(a) of this title".

1984 Amendments. Subsec. (a). Pub.L. 98–353, § 430(a), substituted "and three percent on any amount in excess of $3000" for "three percent on any amount in excess of $3,000 but not in excess of $20,000, two percent on any amount in excess of $20,000 but not in excess of $50,000, and one percent on any amount in excess of $50,000".

Subsec. (d). Pub.L. 98–353, § 430(b), substituted "(d) The court may deny allowance of compensation for services or reimbursement of expenses of the trustee if the trustee failed to make diligent inquiry into facts that would permit denial of allowance under section 328(c) of this title or, with knowledge of such facts, employed a professional person under section 327 of this title." for "(d) The court may deny allowance of compensation for services and reimbursement of expenses of the trustee if the trustee—

"(1) failed to make diligent inquiry into facts that would permit denial of allowance under section 328(c) of this title; or

"(2) with knowledge of such facts, employed a professional person under section 327 of this title."

§ 327. Employment of professional persons

(a) Except as otherwise provided in this section, the trustee, with the court's approval, may employ one or more attorneys, accountants, appraisers, auctioneers, or other professional persons, that do not hold or represent an interest adverse to the estate, and that are disinterested persons, to represent or assist the trustee in carrying out the trustee's duties under this title.

(b) If the trustee is authorized to operate the business of the debtor under section 721, 1202, or 1108 of this title, and if the debtor has regularly employed attorneys, accountants, or other professional persons on salary, the trustee may retain or replace such professional persons if necessary in the operation of such business.

(c) In a case under chapter 7, 12, or 11 of this title, a person is not disqualified for employment under this section solely because of such person's employment by or representation of a creditor, unless there is objection by another creditor or the United States trustee, in which case the court shall disapprove such employment if there is an actual conflict of interest.

(d) The court may authorize the trustee to act as attorney or accountant for the estate if such authorization is in the best interest of the estate.

(e) The trustee, with the court's approval, may employ, for a specified special purpose, other than to represent the trustee in conducting the case, an attorney that has represented the debtor, if in the best interest of the estate, and if such attorney does not represent or hold any interest adverse to the debtor or to the estate with respect to the matter on which such attorney is to be employed.

(f) The trustee may not employ a person that has served as an examiner in the case.

(Pub.L. 95–598, Nov. 6, 1978, 92 Stat. 2563; Pub. L. 98–353, Title III, § 430(c), July 10, 1984, 98 Stat. 370; Pub.L. 99–554, Title II, §§ 210, 257(e), Oct. 27, 1986, 100 Stat. 3099, 3114.)

HISTORICAL AND STATUTORY NOTES

Codifications

Amendment by Pub.L. 99–554, § 257(e)(1), has been executed to text following "section 721" as the probable intent of Congress, notwithstanding directory language which required amendment to be executed following "section 721,".

Amendment by Pub.L. 99–554, § 257(e)(2), has been executed to text following "chapter 7" as the probable intent of Congress, notwithstanding directory language which required amendment to be executed following "section 7".

Amendments

1986 Amendments. Subsec. (b). Pub.L. 99–554, § 257(e)(1), added reference to section 1202 of this title. See, also Codifications note under this section.

Subsec. (c). Pub.L. 99–554, § 210, substituted "another creditor or the United States trustee, in which case" for "another creditor, in which case".

Pub.L. 99–554, § 257(e)(2), added reference to chapter 12. See Codifications note under this section.

1984 Amendments. Subsec. (c). Pub.L. 98–353 substituted "In a case under chapter 7 or 11 of this title, a person is not disqualified for employment under this section solely because of such person's employment by or representation of a creditor, unless there is objection by another creditor, in which case the court shall disapprove such employment if there is an actual conflict of interest." for "In a case under chapter 7 or 11 of this title, a person is not disqualified for employment under this section solely because of such person's employment by or representation of a creditor, but may not, while employed by the trustee, represent, in connection with the case, a creditor.".

CROSS REFERENCES

Duty of United States trustee to monitor applications, see 28 USCA § 586.

Qualification for employment by debtor in possession despite prior employment or representation, see 11 USCA § 1107.

§ 328. Limitation on compensation of professional persons

(a) The trustee, or a committee appointed under section 1102 of this title, with the court's approval, may employ or authorize the employment of a professional person under section 327 or 1103 of this title, as the case may be, on any reasonable terms and conditions of employment, including on a retainer, on an hourly basis, on a fixed or percentage fee basis, or on a contingent fee basis. Notwithstanding such terms and conditions, the court may allow compensation different from the compensation provided under such terms and conditions after the conclusion of such employment, if such terms and conditions prove to have been improvident in light of developments not capable of being anticipated at the time of the fixing of such terms and conditions.

(b) If the court has authorized a trustee to serve as an attorney or accountant for the estate under section 327(d) of this title, the court may allow compensation for the trustee's services as such attorney or accountant only to the extent that the trustee performed services as attorney or accountant for the estate and not for performance of any of the trustee's duties that are generally performed by a trustee without the assistance of an attorney or accountant for the estate.

(c) Except as provided in section 327(c), 327(e), or 1107(b) of this title, the court may deny allowance of compensation for services and reimbursement of expenses of a professional person employed under section 327 or 1103 of this title if, at any time during such professional person's employment under section 327 or 1103 of this title, such professional person is not a disinterested person, or represents or holds an interest adverse to the interest of the estate with respect to the matter on which such professional person is employed.

(Pub.L. 95–598, Nov. 6, 1978, 92 Stat. 2563; amended Pub. L. 98–353, Title III, § 431, July 10, 1984, 98 Stat. 370; Pub.L. 109–8, Title XII, § 1206, Apr. 20, 2005, 119 Stat. 194.)

HISTORICAL AND STATUTORY NOTES

Amendments

2005 Amendments. Subsec. (a). Pub.L. 109–8, § 1206, inserted "on a fixed or percentage fee basis," after "hourly basis,".

1984 Amendments. Subsec. (a). Pub.L. 98–353 substituted "not capable of being anticipated" for "unanticipatable".

§ 329. Debtor's transactions with attorneys

(a) Any attorney representing a debtor in a case under this title, or in connection with such a case, whether or not such attorney applies for compensation under this title, shall file with the court a statement of the compensation paid or agreed to be paid, if such payment or agreement was made after one year before the date of the filing of the petition, for services rendered or to be rendered in contemplation of or in connection with the case by such attorney, and the source of such compensation.

(b) If such compensation exceeds the reasonable value of any such services, the court may cancel any such agreement, or order the return of any such payment, to the extent excessive, to—

    (1) the estate, if the property transferred—

        (A) would have been property of the estate; or

        (B) was to be paid by or on behalf of the debtor under a plan under chapter 11, 12, or 13 of this title; or

    (2) the entity that made such payment.

(Pub.L. 95–598, Nov. 6, 1978, 92 Stat. 2564; Pub. L. 98–353, Title III, § 432, July 10, 1984, 98 Stat. 370; Pub.L. 99–554, Title II, § 257(c), Oct. 27, 1986, 100 Stat. 3114.)

HISTORICAL AND STATUTORY NOTES

Amendments

1986 Amendments. Subsec. (b)(1)(B). Pub.L. 99–554, § 257(c), added reference to chapter 12.

1984 Amendments. Subsec. (a). Pub.L. 98–353, § 432(a), substituted "or" for "and" after "in contemplation of".

Subsec. (b)(1). Pub.L. 98–353, § 432(b), substituted "estate" for "trustee".

CROSS REFERENCES

Disclosure of compensation, debtor's attorney, see Fed.Rules Bankr.Proc. Form B 203, 11 USCA.

Fee agreements, see 18 USCA § 155.

§ 330. Compensation of officers

(a)(1) After notice to the parties in interest and the United States Trustee and a hearing, and subject to sections 326, 328, and 329, the court may award to a trustee, a consumer privacy ombudsman appointed under section 332, an examiner, an ombudsman appointed under section 333, or a professional person employed under section 327 or 1103—

   (A) reasonable compensation for actual, necessary services rendered by the trustee, examiner, ombudsman, professional person, or attorney and by any paraprofessional person employed by any such person; and

   (B) reimbursement for actual, necessary expenses.

(2) The court may, on its own motion or on the motion of the United States Trustee, the United States Trustee for the District or Region, the trustee for the estate, or any other party in interest, award compensation that is less than the amount of compensation that is requested.

(3) In determining the amount of reasonable compensation to be awarded to an examiner, trustee under chapter 11, or professional person, the court shall consider the nature, the extent, and the value of such services, taking into account all relevant factors, including—

   (A) the time spent on such services;

   (B) the rates charged for such services;

   (C) whether the services were necessary to the administration of, or beneficial at the time at which the service was rendered toward the completion of, a case under this title;

   (D) whether the services were performed within a reasonable amount of time commensurate with the complexity, importance, and nature of the problem, issue, or task addressed;

   (E) with respect to a professional person, whether the person is board certified or otherwise has demonstrated skill and experience in the bankruptcy field; and

   (F) whether the compensation is reasonable based on the customary compensation charged by comparably skilled practitioners in cases other than cases under this title.

(4)(A) Except as provided in subparagraph (B), the court shall not allow compensation for—

   (i) unnecessary duplication of services; or

   (ii) services that were not—

      (I) reasonably likely to benefit the debtor's estate; or

      (II) necessary to the administration of the case.

(B) In a chapter 12 or chapter 13 case in which the debtor is an individual, the court may allow reasonable compensation to the debtor's attorney for representing the interests of the debtor in connection with the bankruptcy case based on a consideration of the benefit and necessity of such services to the debtor and the other factors set forth in this section.

(5) The court shall reduce the amount of compensation awarded under this section by the amount of any interim compensation awarded under section 331, and, if the amount of such interim compensation exceeds the amount of compensation awarded under this section, may order the return of the excess to the estate.

(6) Any compensation awarded for the preparation of a fee application shall be based on the level and skill reasonably required to prepare the application.

(7) In determining the amount of reasonable compensation to be awarded to a trustee, the court shall treat such compensation as a commission, based on section 326.

(b)(1) There shall be paid from the filing fee in a case under chapter 7 of this title $45 to the trustee serving in such case, after such trustee's services are rendered.

(2) The Judicial Conference of the United States—

(A) shall prescribe additional fees of the same kind as prescribed under section 1914(b) of title 28; and

(B) may prescribe notice of appearance fees and fees charged against distributions in cases under this title;

to pay $15 to trustees serving in cases after such trustees' services are rendered. Beginning 1 year after the date of the enactment of the Bankruptcy Reform Act of 1994, such $15 shall be paid in addition to the amount paid under paragraph (1).

(c) Unless the court orders otherwise, in a case under chapter 12 or 13 of this title the compensation paid to the trustee serving in the case shall not be less than $5 per month from any distribution under the plan during the administration of the plan.

(d) In a case in which the United States trustee serves as trustee, the compensation of the trustee under this section shall be paid to the clerk of the bankruptcy court and deposited by the clerk into the United States Trustee System Fund established by section 589a of title 28.

(Pub.L. 95–598, Nov. 6, 1978, 92 Stat. 2564; Pub.L. 98–353, Title III, §§ 433, 434, July 10, 1984, 98 Stat. 370; Pub.L. 99–554, Title II, §§ 211, 257(f), Oct. 27, 1986, 100 Stat. 3099, 3114; Pub.L. 103–394, Title I, § 117, Title II, § 224(b), Oct. 22, 1994, 108 Stat. 4119, 4130; Pub.L. 109–8, Title II, § 232(b), Title IV, §§ 407, 415, Title XI, 1104(b), Apr. 20, 2005, 119 Stat. 74, 106, 107, 192.)

HISTORICAL AND STATUTORY NOTES

Amendments

2005 Amendments. Subsec. (a)(1). Pub.L. 109–8, § 232(b), in the matter preceding subparagraph (A), inserted "a consumer privacy ombudsman appointed under section 332," before "an examiner".

Pub.L. 109–8, § 1104(b), inserted "an ombudsman appointed under section 333, or" before "a professional person" in the matter preceding subparagraph (A), and inserted "ombudsman," before "professional person" in subparagraph (A).

Subsec. (a)(3). Pub.L. 109–8, § 407(1), struck "(A) In" and inserted "In" and inserted "to an examiner, trustee under chapter 11, or professional person" after "awarded".

Subsec. (a)(3)(D). Pub.L. 109–8, § 415(1), struck "and" at the end of subpar. (D).

Subsec. (a)(3)(E). Pub.L. 109–8, § 415(2), (3), redesignated subparagraph (E) as subparagraph (F), and added a new subpar. (E).

Subsec. (a)(3)(F). Pub.L. 109–8, § 415(2), redesignated subparagraph (E) as subparagraph (F).

Subsec. (a)(7). Pub.L. 109–8, § 407(2), added par. (7).

1994 Amendments. Subsec. (a). Pub.L. 103–394, § 224(b), completely revised subsec. (a). Prior to revision, subsec. (a) read as follows:

"(a) After notice to any parties in interest and to the United States trustee and a hearing, and subject to sections 326, 328, and 329 of this title, the court may award to a trustee, to an examiner, to a professional person employed under section 327 or 1103 of this title, or to the debtor's attorney—

"(1) reasonable compensation for actual, necessary services rendered by such trustee, examiner, professional person, or attorney, as the case may be, and by any paraprofessional persons employed by such trustee, professional person, or attorney, as the case may be, based on the nature, the extent, and the value of such services, the time spent on such services, and the cost of comparable services other than in a case under this title; and

"(2) reimbursement for actual, necessary expenses."

Subsec. (b)(1). Pub.L. 103–394, § 117(1), designated existing provisions as par. (1).

Subsec. (b)(2). Pub.L. 103–394, § 117(2), added par. (2).

1986 Amendments. Subsec. (a). Pub.L. 99–554, § 211(1), substituted "notice to any parties in interest and to the United States trustee and a hearing" for "notice and a hearing".

Subsec. (c). Pub.L. 99–554, § 257(f), added reference to chapter 12.

Subsec. (d). Pub.L. 99–554, § 211(2), added subsec. (d).

1984 Amendments. Subsec. (a). Pub.L. 98–353, § 433(1), struck out "to any parties in interest and to the United States trustee" after "After notice".

Subsec. (a)(1). Pub.L. 98–353, § 433(2), substituted "nature, the extent, and the value of such services, the time spent on such services" for "time, the nature, the extent, and the value of such services".

Subsec. (b). Pub.L. 98–353, § 434(a), substituted "$45" for "$20".

Subsec. (c). Pub.L. 98–353, § 434(b), added subsec. (c).

CROSS REFERENCES

Adverse interest and conduct of officers of estate, see 18 USCA § 154.

Allowances to trustee and trustee's attorney in investor protection liquidation proceedings, see 15 USCA § 78eee.

Approval of Securities and Exchange Commission for payment of fees, expenses and remuneration in cases involving holding companies under this title, see 15 USCA § 79k.

Debtor in possession's right of compensation—

Chapter 11 cases, see 11 USCA § 1107.

Chapter 12 cases, see 11 USCA § 1203.

Guidelines for reviewing applications for compensation and reimbursement of expenses, see Fed.Rules Bankr.Proc. Rule 2016, 11 USCA.

Officers' compensation as administrative expense, see 11 USCA § 503.

Supervision by Attorney General, see 28 USCA § 586.

United States Trustee System Fund establishment and purpose, see 28 USCA § 589a.

§ 331. Interim compensation

A trustee, an examiner, a debtor's attorney, or any professional person employed under section 327 or 1103 of this title may apply to the court not more than once every 120 days after an order for relief in a case under this title, or more often if the court permits, for such compensation for services rendered before the date of such an application or reimbursement for expenses incurred before such date as is provided under section 330 of this title. After notice and a hearing, the court may allow and disburse to such applicant such compensation or reimbursement.

(Pub.L. 95–598, Nov. 6, 1978, 92 Stat. 2564.)

§ 332. Consumer privacy ombudsman

(a) If a hearing is required under section 363(b)(1)(B), the court shall order the United States trustee to appoint, not later than 7 days before the commencement of the hearing, 1 disinterested person (other than the United States trustee) to serve as the consumer privacy ombudsman in the case and shall require that notice of such hearing be timely given to such ombudsman.

(b) The consumer privacy ombudsman may appear and be heard at such hearing and shall provide to the court information to assist the court in its consideration of the facts, circumstances, and conditions of the proposed sale or lease of personally identifiable information under section 363(b)(1)(B). Such information may include presentation of—

(1) the debtor's privacy policy;

(2) the potential losses or gains of privacy to consumers if such sale or such lease is approved by the court;

(3) the potential costs or benefits to consumers if such sale or such lease is approved by the court; and

(4) the potential alternatives that would mitigate potential privacy losses or potential costs to consumers.

(c) A consumer privacy ombudsman shall not disclose any personally identifiable information obtained by the ombudsman under this title.

(Added Pub.L. 109–8, Title II, § 232(a), Apr. 20, 2005, 119 Stat. 73; amended Pub.L. 111–16, § 2(3), May 7, 2009, 123 Stat. 1607.)

HISTORICAL AND STATUTORY NOTES

Amendments

2009 Amendments. Subsec. (a). Pub.L. 111–16, § 2(3), struck out "5 days" and inserted "7 days".

§ 333. Appointment of patient care ombudsman

(a)(1) If the debtor in a case under chapter 7, 9, or 11 is a health care business, the court shall order, not later than 30 days after the commencement of the case, the appointment of an ombudsman to monitor the quality of patient care and to represent the interests of the patients of the health care business unless the court finds that the appointment of such ombudsman is not necessary for the protection of patients under the specific facts of the case.

(2)(A) If the court orders the appointment of an ombudsman under paragraph (1), the United States trustee shall appoint 1 disinterested person (other than the United States trustee) to serve as such ombudsman.

(B) If the debtor is a health care business that provides long-term care, then the United States trustee may appoint the State Long-Term Care Ombudsman appointed under the Older Americans Act of 1965 for the State in which the case is pending to serve as the ombudsman required by paragraph (1).

(C) If the United States trustee does not appoint a State Long-Term Care Ombudsman under subparagraph (B), the court shall notify the State Long-Term Care Ombudsman appointed under the Older Americans Act of 1965 for the State in which the case is pending, of the name and address of the person who is appointed under subparagraph (A).

(b) An ombudsman appointed under subsection (a) shall—

(1) monitor the quality of patient care provided to patients of the debtor, to the extent necessary under the circumstances, including interviewing patients and physicians;

(2) not later than 60 days after the date of appointment, and not less frequently than at 60-day intervals thereafter, report to the court after notice to the parties in interest, at a

hearing or in writing, regarding the quality of patient care provided to patients of the debtor; and

(3) if such ombudsman determines that the quality of patient care provided to patients of the debtor is declining significantly or is otherwise being materially compromised, file with the court a motion or a written report, with notice to the parties in interest immediately upon making such determination.

(c)(1) An ombudsman appointed under subsection (a) shall maintain any information obtained by such ombudsman under this section that relates to patients (including information relating to patient records) as confidential information. Such ombudsman may not review confidential patient records unless the court approves such review in advance and imposes restrictions on such ombudsman to protect the confidentiality of such records.

(2) An ombudsman appointed under subsection (a)(2)(B) shall have access to patient records consistent with authority of such ombudsman under the Older Americans Act of 1965 and under non-Federal laws governing the State Long-Term Care Ombudsman program.

(Added Pub.L. 109–8, Title XI, § 1104(a)(1), Apr. 20, 2005, 119 Stat. 191.)

HISTORICAL AND STATUTORY NOTES

References in Text

The Older Americans Act of 1965, referred to in subsecs. (a)(2)(B), (C) and (c)(2), is Pub.L. 89–73, July 14, 1965, 79 Stat. 218, as amended, which is classified principally to chapter 35 of Title 42, 42 U.S.C.A. § 3001 et seq. For complete classification, see Short Title note set out under 42 U.S.C.A. § 3001 and Tables.

SUBCHAPTER III—ADMINISTRATION

§ 341. Meetings of creditors and equity security holders

(a) Within a reasonable time after the order for relief in a case under this title, the United States trustee shall convene and preside at a meeting of creditors.

(b) The United States trustee may convene a meeting of any equity security holders.

(c) The court may not preside at, and may not attend, any meeting under this section including any final meeting of creditors. Notwithstanding any local court rule, provision of a State constitution, any otherwise applicable nonbankruptcy law, or any other requirement that representation at the meeting of creditors under subsection (a) be by an attorney, a creditor holding a consumer debt or any representative of the creditor (which may include an entity or an employee of an entity and may be a representative for more than 1 creditor) shall be permitted to appear at and participate in the meeting of creditors in a case under chapter 7 or 13, either alone or in conjunction with an attorney for the creditor. Nothing in this subsection shall be construed to require any creditor to be represented by an attorney at any meeting of creditors.

(d) Prior to the conclusion of the meeting of creditors or equity security holders, the trustee shall orally examine the debtor to ensure that the debtor in a case under chapter 7 of this title is aware of—

(1) the potential consequences of seeking a discharge in bankruptcy, including the effects on credit history;

(2) the debtor's ability to file a petition under a different chapter of this title;

(3) the effect of receiving a discharge of debts under this title; and

(4) the effect of reaffirming a debt, including the debtor's knowledge of the provisions of section 524(d) of this title.

(e) Notwithstanding subsections (a) and (b), the court, on the request of a party in interest and after notice and a hearing, for cause may order that the United States trustee not convene a meeting of creditors or equity security holders if the debtor has filed a plan as to which the debtor solicited acceptances prior to the commencement of the case.

(Pub.L. 95–598, Nov. 6, 1978, 92 Stat. 2564; Pub.L. 99–554, Title II, § 212, Oct. 27, 1986, 100 Stat. 3099; Pub.L. 103–394, Title I, § 115, Oct. 22, 1994, 108 Stat. 4118; Pub.L. 109–8, Title IV, §§ 402, 413, Apr. 20, 2005, 119 Stat. 104, 107.)

HISTORICAL AND STATUTORY NOTES

Amendments

2005 Amendments. Subsec. (c). Pub.L. 109–8, § 413, inserted at the end the following: "Notwithstanding any local court rule, provision of a State constitution, any otherwise applicable nonbankruptcy law, or any other requirement that representation at the meeting of creditors under subsection (a) be by an attorney, a creditor holding a consumer debt or any representative of the creditor (which may include an entity or an employee of an entity and may be a representative for more than 1 creditor) shall be permitted to appear at and participate in the meeting of creditors in a case under chapter 7 or 13, either alone or in conjunction with an attorney for the creditor. Nothing in this subsection shall be construed to require any creditor to be represented by an attorney at any meeting of creditors.".

Subsec. (e). Pub.L. 109–8, § 402, added subsec. (e).

1994 Amendments. Subsec. (d). Pub.L. 103–394, § 115, added subsec. (d).

1986 Amendments. Subsec. (a). Pub.L. 99–554, § 212(1), substituted "this title, the United States trustee shall convene and preside at a meeting of creditors" for "this title, there shall be a meeting of creditors".

Subsec. (b). Pub.L. 99–554, § 212(2), substituted "The United States trustee may convene a meeting" for "The court may order a meeting".

Subsec. (c). Pub.L. 99–554, § 212(3), substituted "this section including any final meeting of creditors." for "this section.".

Participation by Bankruptcy Administrator at Meetings of Creditors and Equity Security Holders

Section 105 of Pub.L. 103–394 provided that:

"(a) Presiding officer.—A bankruptcy administrator appointed under section 302(d)(3)(I) of the Bankruptcy Judges, United States Trustees, and Family Farmer Bankruptcy Act of 1986 (28 U.S.C. 581 note; Public Law 99–554; 100 Stat. 3123), as amended by section 317(a) of the Federal Courts Study Committee Implementation Act of 1990 (Public Law 101–650; 104 Stat. 5115), or the bankruptcy administrator's designee may preside at the meeting of creditors convened under section 341(a) of title 11, United States Code [subsec. (a) of this section]. The bankruptcy administrator or the bankruptcy administrator's designee may preside at any meeting of equity security holders convened under section 341(b) of title 11, United States Code [subsec. (b) of this section].

"(b) Examination of the debtor.—The bankruptcy administrator or the bankruptcy administrator's designee may examine the debtor at the meeting of creditors and may administer the oath required under section 343 of title 11, United States Code [section 343 of this title]."

CROSS REFERENCES

Election of—

    Creditors' committee, see 11 USCA § 705.

    Trustee, see 11 USCA § 702.

Inapplicability of this section in railroad reorganization cases, see 11 USCA § 1161.

§ 342. Notice

(a) There shall be given such notice as is appropriate, including notice to any holder of a community claim, of an order for relief in a case under this title.

(b) Before the commencement of a case under this title by an individual whose debts are primarily consumer debts, the clerk shall give to such individual written notice containing—

  (1) a brief description of—

   (A) chapters 7, 11, 12, and 13 and the general purpose, benefits, and costs of proceeding under each of those chapters; and

   (B) the types of services available from credit counseling agencies; and

  (2) statements specifying that—

   (A) a person who knowingly and fraudulently conceals assets or makes a false oath or statement under penalty of perjury in connection with a case under this title shall be subject to fine, imprisonment, or both; and

   (B) all information supplied by a debtor in connection with a case under this title is subject to examination by the Attorney General.

(c)(1) If notice is required to be given by the debtor to a creditor under this title, any rule, any applicable law, or any order of the court, such notice shall contain the name, address, and last 4 digits of the taxpayer identification number of the debtor. If the notice concerns an amendment that adds a creditor to the schedules of assets and liabilities, the debtor shall include the full taxpayer identification number in the notice sent to that creditor, but the debtor shall include only the last 4 digits of the taxpayer identification number in the copy of the notice filed with the court.

(2)(A) If, within the 90 days before the commencement of a voluntary case, a creditor supplies the debtor in at least 2 communications sent to the debtor with the current account number of the debtor and the address at which such creditor requests to receive correspondence, then any notice required by this title to be sent by the debtor to such creditor shall be sent to such address and shall include such account number.

(B) If a creditor would be in violation of applicable nonbankruptcy law by sending any such communication within such 90-day period and if such creditor supplies the debtor in the last 2 communications with the current account number of the debtor and the address at which such creditor requests to receive correspondence, then any notice required by this title to be sent by the debtor to such creditor shall be sent to such address and shall include such account number.

(d) In a case under chapter 7 of this title in which the debtor is an individual and in which the presumption of abuse arises under section 707(b), the clerk shall give written notice to all creditors not later than 10 days after the date of the filing of the petition that the presumption of abuse has arisen.

(e)(1) In a case under chapter 7 or 13 of this title of a debtor who is an individual, a creditor at any time may both file with the court and serve on the debtor a notice of address to be used to provide notice in such case to such creditor.

(2) Any notice in such case required to be provided to such creditor by the debtor or the court later than 7 days after the court and the debtor receive such creditor's notice of address, shall be provided to such address.

(f)(1) An entity may file with any bankruptcy court a notice of address to be used by all the bankruptcy courts or by particular bankruptcy courts, as so specified by such entity at the time such notice is filed, to provide notice to such entity in all cases under chapters 7 and 13 pending in the courts with respect to which such notice is filed, in which such entity is a creditor.

(2) In any case filed under chapter 7 or 13, any notice required to be provided by a court with respect to which a notice is filed under paragraph (1), to such entity later than 30 days after the filing of such notice under paragraph (1) shall be provided to such address unless with respect to a particular case a different address is specified in a notice filed and served in accordance with subsection (e).

(3) A notice filed under paragraph (1) may be withdrawn by such entity.

(g)(1) Notice provided to a creditor by the debtor or the court other than in accordance with this section (excluding this subsection) shall not be effective notice until such notice is brought to the attention of such creditor. If such creditor designates a person or an organizational subdivision of such creditor to be responsible for receiving notices under this title and establishes reasonable procedures so that such notices receivable by such creditor are to be delivered to such person or such subdivision, then a notice provided to such creditor other than in accordance with this section (excluding this subsection) shall not be considered to have been brought to the attention of such creditor until such notice is received by such person or such subdivision.

(2) A monetary penalty may not be imposed on a creditor for a violation of a stay in effect under section 362(a) (including a monetary penalty imposed under section 362(k)) or for failure to comply with section 542 or 543 unless the conduct that is the basis of such violation or of such failure occurs after such creditor receives notice effective under this section of the order for relief.

(Pub.L. 95–598, Nov. 6, 1978, 92 Stat. 2565; Pub.L. 98–353, Title III, §§ 302, 435, July 10, 1984, 98 Stat. 352, 370; Pub.L. 103–394, Title II, § 225, Oct. 22, 1994, 108 Stat. 4131; Pub.L. 109–8, Title I, §§ 102(d), 104, Title II, § 234(b), Title III, § 315(a), Apr. 20, 2005, 119 Stat. 33, 35, 75, 88; Pub.L. 111–16, § 2(4), May 7, 2009, 123 Stat. 1607.)

HISTORICAL AND STATUTORY NOTES

Amendments

2009 Amendments. Subsec. (e)(2). Pub.L. 111–16, § 2(4), struck out "5 days" and inserted "7 days".

2005 Amendments. Subsec. (b). Pub.L. 109–8, § 104, rewrote subsec. (b), which formerly read:

"**(b)** Prior to the commencement of a case under this title by an individual whose debts are primarily consumer debts, the clerk shall give written notice to such individual that indicates each chapter of this title under which such individual may proceed."

Subsec. (c). Pub.L. 109–8, § 234(b), inserted "last 4 digits of the" before "taxpayer identification number", and added "If the notice concerns an amendment that adds a creditor to the schedules of assets and liabilities, the debtor shall include the full taxpayer identification number in the notice sent to that creditor, but the debtor shall include only the last 4 digits of the taxpayer identification number in the copy of the notice filed with the court." at the end.

Subsec. (c)(1). Pub.L. 109–8, § 315(a)(1)(A), (B), inserted "(1)" after "(c)" and struck out ", but the failure of such notice to contain such information shall not invalidate the legal effect of such notice" following "taxpayer identification number of the debtor".

Subsec. (c)(2). Pub.L. 109–8, § 315(a)(1)(C), added par. (2).

Subsec. (d). Pub.L. 109–8, § 102(d), added subsec. (d).

Subsecs. (e) to (g). Pub.L. 109–8, § 315(a)(2), added subsecs. (e), (f), and (g).

1994 Amendments. Subsec. (c). Pub.L. 103–394, § 225, added subsec. (c).

1984 Amendments. Subsec. (a). Pub.L. 98–353, § 302(1), designated existing provisions as subsec. (a).

Pub.L. 98–353, § 435, added requirement respecting notice to any holder of a community claim.

Subsec. (b). Pub.L. 98–353, § 302(2), added subsec. (b).

CROSS REFERENCES

Instructions in notice to customers, see 11 USCA § 765.

"Net equity" defined in relation to payments made by customers to trustee within 60 days after notice, see 11 USCA § 741.

Notice in—

   Commodity broker liquidation cases, see 11 USCA § 762.

   Investor protection liquidation proceedings, see 15 USCA § 78fff–2.

   Stockbroker liquidation cases, see 11 USCA § 743.

§ 343. Examination of the debtor

The debtor shall appear and submit to examination under oath at the meeting of creditors under section 341(a) of this title. Creditors, any indenture trustee, any trustee or examiner in the case, or the United States trustee may examine the debtor. The United States trustee may administer the oath required under this section.

(Pub.L. 95–598, Nov. 6, 1978, 92 Stat. 2565; Pub.L. 98–353, Title III, § 436, July 10, 1984, 98 Stat. 370; Pub.L. 99–554, Title II, § 213, Oct. 27, 1986, 100 Stat. 3099.)

HISTORICAL AND STATUTORY NOTES

Amendments

1986 Amendments. Pub.L. 99–554, § 213, substituted "Creditors, any indenture trustee, any trustee or examiner in the case, or the United States trustee may examine the debtor. The United States trustee may administer the oath required under this section." for "Creditors, any indenture trustee, or any trustee or examiner in the case may examine the debtor.".

1984 Amendments. Pub.L. 98–353 substituted "examine" for "examiner".

Participation by Bankruptcy Administrator at Meetings of Creditors and Equity Security Holders

The bankruptcy administrator or the bankruptcy's designee may examine the debtor at the meeting of the creditors and may administer the oath required by this section, see section 105 of Pub.L. 103–394, set out as a note under section 341 of this title.

CROSS REFERENCES

Concealment of assets deemed continuing offense, see 18 USCA § 3284.

Concealment of assets; false oaths and claims, see 18 USCA § 152.

Inapplicability of this section in railroad reorganization cases, see 11 USCA § 1161.

§ 344. Self-incrimination; immunity

Immunity for persons required to submit to examination, to testify, or to provide information in a case under this title may be granted under part V of title 18.

(Pub.L. 95–598, Nov. 6, 1978, 92 Stat. 2565.)

CROSS REFERENCES

Applicability of this section in chapter 9 cases, see 11 USCA § 901.

Debtor's duty to surrender records despite grant of immunity under this section, see 11 USCA § 521.

§ 345. Money of estates

(a) A trustee in a case under this title may make such deposit or investment of the money of the estate for which such trustee serves as will yield the maximum reasonable net return on such money, taking into account the safety of such deposit or investment.

(b) Except with respect to a deposit or investment that is insured or guaranteed by the United States or by a department, agency, or instrumentality of the United States or backed by the full faith and credit of the United States, the trustee shall require from an entity with which such money is deposited or invested—

　(1) a bond—

　　(A) in favor of the United States;

　　(B) secured by the undertaking of a corporate surety approved by the United States trustee for the district in which the case is pending; and

(C) conditioned on—

(i) a proper accounting for all money so deposited or invested and for any return on such money;

(ii) prompt repayment of such money and return; and

(iii) faithful performance of duties as a depository; or

(2) the deposit of securities of the kind specified in section 9303 of title 31;

unless the court for cause orders otherwise.

(c) An entity with which such moneys are deposited or invested is authorized to deposit or invest such moneys as may be required under this section.

(Pub.L. 95–598, Nov. 6, 1978, 92 Stat. 2565; Pub.L. 97–258, § 3(c), Sept. 13, 1982, 96 Stat. 1064; Pub.L. 98–353, Title III, § 437, July 10, 1984, 98 Stat. 370; Pub.L. 99–554, Title II, § 214, Oct. 27, 1986, 100 Stat. 3099; Pub.L. 103–394, Title II, § 210, Oct. 22, 1994, 108 Stat. 4125.)

HISTORICAL AND STATUTORY NOTES

Amendments

1994 Amendments. Subsec. (b). Pub.L. 103–394, § 210(2), added provisions authorizing court for cause to order an alternative to bond or securities requirement.

1986 Amendments. Subsec. (b)(1)(B). Pub.L. 99–554, § 214, substituted "approved by the United States trustee for the district" for "approved by the court for the district".

1984 Amendments. Subsec. (c). Pub.L. 98–353 added subsec. (c).

1982 Amendments. Subsec. (b)(2). Pub.L. 97–258 substituted "9303 of title 31" for "15 of title 6".

CROSS REFERENCES

Adverse interest and conduct of officers of estate, see 18 USCA § 154.

Duty of United States trustee to deposit or invest money, see 28 USCA § 586.

Embezzlement by trustee, see 18 USCA § 153.

§ 346. Special provisions related to the treatment of State and local taxes

(a) Whenever the Internal Revenue Code of 1986 provides that a separate taxable estate or entity is created in a case concerning a debtor under this title, and the income, gain, loss, deductions, and credits of such estate shall be taxed to or claimed by the estate, a separate taxable estate is also created for purposes of any State and local law imposing a tax on or measured by income and such income, gain, loss, deductions, and credits shall be taxed to or claimed by the estate and may not be taxed to or claimed by the debtor. The preceding sentence shall not apply if the case is dismissed. The trustee shall make tax returns of income required under any such State or local law.

(b) Whenever the Internal Revenue Code of 1986 provides that no separate taxable estate shall be created in a case concerning a debtor under this title, and the income, gain, loss, deductions, and credits of an estate shall be taxed to or claimed by the debtor, such income, gain, loss, deductions, and credits shall be taxed to or claimed by the debtor under a State or local law imposing a tax on or measured by income and may not be taxed to or claimed by the estate. The trustee shall make such tax returns of income of corporations and of partnerships as are required under any State or local law, but with respect to partnerships, shall make such returns only to the extent such returns are also required to be made under such Code. The estate shall be liable for any tax imposed on such corporation or partnership, but not for any tax imposed on partners or members.

(c) With respect to a partnership or any entity treated as a partnership under a State or local law imposing a tax on or measured by income that is a debtor in a case under this title, any gain or loss resulting from a distribution of property from such partnership, or any distributive share of any income, gain, loss, deduction, or credit of a partner or member that is distributed, or considered distributed, from such partnership, after the commencement of the case, is gain, loss, income, deduction, or credit, as the case may be, of the partner or member, and if such partner or member is a debtor in a case under this title, shall be subject to tax in accordance with subsection (a) or (b).

(d) For purposes of any State or local law imposing a tax on or measured by income, the taxable period of a debtor in a case under this title shall terminate only if and to the extent that the taxable period of such debtor terminates under the Internal Revenue Code of 1986.

(e) The estate in any case described in subsection (a) shall use the same accounting method as the debtor used immediately before the commencement of the case, if such method of accounting complies with applicable nonbankruptcy tax law.

(f) For purposes of any State or local law imposing a tax on or measured by income, a transfer of property from the debtor to the estate or from the estate to the debtor shall not be treated as a disposition for purposes of any provision assigning tax consequences to a disposition, except to the extent that such transfer is treated as a disposition under the Internal Revenue Code of 1986.

(g) Whenever a tax is imposed pursuant to a State or local law imposing a tax on or measured by income pursuant to subsection (a) or (b), such tax shall be imposed at rates generally applicable to the same types of entities under such State or local law.

(h) The trustee shall withhold from any payment of claims for wages, salaries, commissions, dividends, interest, or other payments, or collect, any amount required to be withheld or collected under applicable State or local tax law, and shall pay such withheld or collected amount to the appropriate governmental unit at the time and in the manner required by such tax law, and with the same priority as the claim from which such amount was withheld or collected was paid.

(i)(1) To the extent that any State or local law imposing a tax on or measured by income provides for the carryover of any tax attribute from one taxable period to a subsequent taxable period, the estate shall succeed to such tax attribute in any case in which such estate is subject to tax under subsection (a).

(2) After such a case is closed or dismissed, the debtor shall succeed to any tax attribute to which the estate succeeded under paragraph (1) to the extent consistent with the Internal Revenue Code of 1986.

(3) The estate may carry back any loss or tax attribute to a taxable period of the debtor that ended before the date of the order for relief under this title to the extent that—

(A) applicable State or local tax law provides for a carryback in the case of the debtor; and

(B) the same or a similar tax attribute may be carried back by the estate to such a taxable period of the debtor under the Internal Revenue Code of 1986.

(j)(1) For purposes of any State or local law imposing a tax on or measured by income, income is not realized by the estate, the debtor, or a successor to the debtor by reason of discharge of indebtedness in a case under this title, except to the extent, if any, that such income is subject to tax under the Internal Revenue Code of 1986.

(2) Whenever the Internal Revenue Code of 1986 provides that the amount excluded from gross income in respect of the discharge of indebtedness in a case under this title shall be applied to reduce the tax attributes of the debtor or the estate, a similar reduction shall be made under any State or local law imposing a tax on or measured by income to the extent such State or local law recognizes such attributes. Such State or local law may also provide for the reduction of other attributes to the extent that the full amount of income from the discharge of indebtedness has not been applied.

(k)(1) Except as provided in this section and section 505, the time and manner of filing tax returns and the items of income, gain, loss, deduction, and credit of any taxpayer shall be determined under applicable nonbankruptcy law.

(2) For Federal tax purposes, the provisions of this section are subject to the Internal Revenue Code of 1986 and other applicable Federal nonbankruptcy law.

(Pub.L. 95–598, Nov. 6, 1978, 92 Stat. 2565; Pub.L. 98–353, Title III, § 438, July 10, 1984, 98 Stat. 370; Pub.L. 99–554, Title II, §§ 257(g), 283(c), Oct. 27, 1986, 100 Stat. 3114, 3116; Pub.L. 103–394, Title V, § 501(d)(4), Oct. 22, 1994, 108 Stat. 4143; Pub.L. 109–8, Title VII, § 719(a)(1), Apr. 20, 2005, 119 Stat. 131.)

HISTORICAL AND STATUTORY NOTES

References in Text

The Internal Revenue Code of 1986, referred to in text, is classified to Title 26 of the Code.

Amendments

2005 Amendments. Section. Pub.L. 109–8, § 719(a)(1), rewrote this section, which formerly read:

" **§ 346. Special tax provisions**

"**(a)** Except to the extent otherwise provided in this section, subsections (b), (c), (d), (e), (g), (h), (i), and (j) of this section apply notwithstanding any State or local law imposing a tax, but subject to the Internal Revenue Code of 1986.

"**(b)(1)** In a case under chapter 7, 12, or 11 of this title concerning an individual, any income of the estate may be taxed under a State or local law imposing a tax on or measured by income only to the estate, and may not be taxed to such individual. Except as provided in section 728 of this title, if such individual is a partner in a partnership, any gain or loss resulting from a distribution of property from such partnership, or any distributive share of income, gain, loss, deduction, or credit of such individual that is distributed, or considered distributed, from such partnership, after the commencement of the case is gain, loss, income, deduction, or credit, as the case may be, of the estate.

"**(2)** Except as otherwise provided in this section and in section 728 of this title, any income of the estate in such a case, and any State or local tax on or measured by such income, shall be computed in the same manner as the income and the tax of an estate.

"**(3)** The estate in such a case shall use the same accounting method as the debtor used immediately before the commencement of the case.

"**(c)(1)** The commencement of a case under this title concerning a corporation or a partnership does not effect a change in the status of such corporation or partnership for the purposes of any State or local law imposing a tax on or measured by income. Except as otherwise provided in this section and in section 728 of this title, any income of the estate in such case may be taxed only as though such case had not been commenced.

"**(2)** In such a case, except as provided in section 728 of this title, the trustee shall make any tax return otherwise required by State or local law to be filed by or on behalf of such corporation or partnership in the same manner and form as such corporation or partnership, as the case may be, is required to make such return.

"**(d)** In a case under chapter 13 of this title, any income of the estate or the debtor may be taxed under a State or local law imposing a tax on or measured by income only to the debtor, and may not be taxed to the estate.

"**(e)** A claim allowed under section 502(f) or 503 of this title, other than a claim for a tax that is not otherwise deductible or a capital expenditure that is not otherwise deductible, is deductible by the entity to which income of the estate is taxed unless such claim was deducted by another entity, and a deduction for such a claim is deemed to be a deduction attributable to a business.

"**(f)** The trustee shall withhold from any payment of claims for wages, salaries, commissions, dividends, interest, or other payments, or collect, any amount required to be withheld or collected under applicable State or local tax law, and shall pay such withheld or collected amount to the appropriate governmental unit at the time and in the manner required by such tax law, and with the same priority as the claim from which such amount was withheld was paid.

"**(g)(1)** Neither gain nor loss shall be recognized on a transfer—

"**(A)** by operation of law, of property to the estate;

"(B) other than a sale, of property from the estate to the debtor; or

"(C) in a case under chapter 11 or 12 of this title concerning a corporation, of property from the estate to a corporation that is an affiliate participating in a joint plan with the debtor, or that is a successor to the debtor under the plan, except that gain or loss may be recognized to the same extent that such transfer results in the recognition of gain or loss under section 371 of the Internal Revenue Code of 1986.

"(2) The transferee of a transfer of a kind specified in this subsection shall take the property transferred with the same character, and with the transferor's basis, as adjusted under subsection (j)(5) of this section, and holding period.

"(h) Notwithstanding sections 728(a) and 1146(a) of this title, for the purpose of determining the number of taxable periods during which the debtor or the estate may use a loss carryover or a loss carryback, the taxable period of the debtor during which the case is commenced is deemed not to have been terminated by such commencement.

"(i)(1) In a case under chapter 7, 12, or 11 of this title concerning an individual, the estate shall succeed to the debtor's tax attributes, including—

"(A) any investment credit carryover;

"(B) any recovery exclusion;

"(C) any loss carryover;

"(D) any foreign tax credit carryover;

"(E) any capital loss carryover; and

"(F) any claim of right.

"(2) After such a case is closed or dismissed, the debtor shall succeed to any tax attribute to which the estate succeeded under paragraph (1) of this subsection but that was not utilized by the estate. The debtor may utilize such tax attributes as though any applicable time limitations on such utilization by the debtor were suspended during the time during which the case was pending.

"(3) In such a case, the estate may carry back any loss of the estate to a taxable period of the debtor that ended before the order for relief under such chapter the same as the debtor could have carried back such loss had the debtor incurred such loss and the case under this title had not been commenced, but the debtor may not carry back any loss of the debtor from a taxable period that ends after such order to any taxable period of the debtor that ended before such order until after the case is closed.

"(j)(1) Except as otherwise provided in this subsection, income is not realized by the estate, the debtor, or a successor to the debtor by reason of forgiveness or discharge of indebtedness in a case under this title.

"(2) For the purposes of any State or local law imposing a tax on or measured by income, a deduction with respect to a liability may not be allowed for any taxable period during or after which such liability is forgiven or discharged under this title. In this paragraph, 'a deduction with respect to a liability' includes a capital loss incurred on the disposition of a capital asset with respect to a liability that was incurred in connection with the acquisition of such asset.

"(3) Except as provided in paragraph (4) of this subsection, for the purpose of any State or local law imposing a tax on or measured by income, any net operating loss of an individual or corporate debtor, including a net operating loss carryover to such debtor, shall be reduced by the amount of indebtedness forgiven or discharged in a case under this title, except to the extent that such forgiveness or discharge resulted in a disallowance under paragraph (2) of this subsection.

"(4) A reduction of a net operating loss or a net operating loss carryover under paragraph (3) of this subsection or of basis under paragraph (5) of this subsection is not required to the extent that the indebtedness of an individual or corporate debtor forgiven or discharged—

"(A) consisted of items of a deductible nature that were not deducted by such debtor; or

"(B) resulted in an expired net operating loss carryover or other deduction that—

"(i) did not offset income for any taxable period; and

"(ii) did not contribute to a net operating loss in or a net operating loss carryover to the taxable period during or after which such indebtedness was discharged.

"(5) For the purposes of a State or local law imposing a tax on or measured by income, the basis of the debtor's property or of property transferred to an entity required to use the debtor's basis in whole or in part shall be reduced by the lesser of—

"(A)(i) the amount by which the indebtedness of the debtor has been forgiven or discharged in a case under this title; minus

"(ii) the total amount of adjustments made under paragraphs (2) and (3) of this subsection; and

"(B) the amount by which the total basis of the debtor's assets that were property of the estate before such forgiveness or discharge exceeds the debtor's total liabilities that were liabilities both before and after such forgiveness or discharge.

"(6) Notwithstanding paragraph (5) of this subsection, basis is not required to be reduced to the extent that the debtor elects to treat as taxable income, of the taxable period in which indebtedness is forgiven or discharged, the amount of indebtedness forgiven or discharged that otherwise would be applied in reduction of basis under paragraph (5) of this subsection.

"(7) For the purposes of this subsection, indebtedness with respect to which an equity security, other than an interest of a limited partner in a limited partnership, is issued to the creditor to whom such indebtedness was owed, or that is forgiven as a contribution to capital by an equity security holder other than a limited partner in the debtor, is not forgiven or discharged in a case under this title—

"(A) to any extent that such indebtedness did not consist of items of a deductible nature; or

"(B) if the issuance of such equity security has the same consequences under a law imposing a tax on or measured by income to such creditor as a payment in cash to such creditor in an amount equal to the fair market value of such equity security, then to the lesser of—

"(i) the extent that such issuance has the same such consequences; and

"(ii) the extent of such fair market value."

1994 Amendments. Subsec. (a). Pub.L. 103–394, § 501(d)(4)(A), substituted "Internal Revenue Code of 1986" for "Internal Revenue Code of 1954 (26 U.S.C. 1 et seq.)".

Subsec. (g)(1)(C). Pub.L. 103–394, § 501(d)(4)(B), substituted "Internal Revenue Code of 1986" for "Internal Revenue Code of 1954 (26 U.S.C. 371)".

1986 Amendments. Subsec. (a). Pub.L. 99–514, § 2, substituted "Internal Revenue Code of 1986" for "Internal Revenue Code of 1954".

Subsec. (b)(1). Pub.L. 99–554, § 257(g)(1), added reference to chapter 12.

Subsec. (g)(1)(C). Pub.L. 99–554, § 257(g)(2), added reference to chapter 12.

Pub.L. 99–514, § 2, substituted "Internal Revenue Code of 1986" for "Internal Revenue Code of 1954".

Subsec. (i)(1). Pub.L. 99–554, § 257(g)(3), added reference to chapter 12.

Subsec. (j)(7). Pub.L. 99–554, § 283(c), substituted "owed" for "owned".

1984 Amendments. Subsec. (c)(2). Pub.L. 98–353 substituted "corporation" for "operation".

CROSS REFERENCES

Request for determination of tax effects of—

Chapter 12 plan, see 11 USCA § 1231.

Reorganization plan, see 11 USCA § 1146.

§ 347. Unclaimed property

(a) Ninety days after the final distribution under section 726, 1226, or 1326 of this title in a case under chapter 7, 12, or 13 of this title, as the case may be, the trustee shall stop payment on any check remaining unpaid, and any remaining property of the estate shall be paid into the court and disposed of under chapter 129 of title 28.

(b) Any security, money, or other property remaining unclaimed at the expiration of the time allowed in a case under chapter 9, 11, or 12 of this title for the presentation of a security or the performance of any other act as a condition to participation in the distribution under any plan confirmed under section 943(b), 1129, 1173, or 1225 of this title, as the case may be, becomes the property of the debtor or of the entity acquiring the assets of the debtor under the plan, as the case may be.

(Pub.L. 95–598, Nov. 6, 1978, 92 Stat. 2568; Pub.L. 99–554, Title II, § 257(h), Oct. 27, 1986, 100 Stat. 3114.)

HISTORICAL AND STATUTORY NOTES

Amendments

1986 Amendments. Subsec. (a). Pub.L. 99–554, § 257(h)(1), added references to section 1226 and chapter 12 of this title.

Subsec. (b). Pub.L. 99–554, § 257(h)(2), added references to chapter 12 and section 1225 of this title.

CROSS REFERENCES

Applicability of this section in Chapter 9 cases, see 11 USCA § 901.

§ 348. Effect of conversion

(a) Conversion of a case from a case under one chapter of this title to a case under another chapter of this title constitutes an order for relief under the chapter to which the case is converted, but, except as provided in subsections (b) and (c) of this section, does not effect a change in the date of the filing of the petition, the commencement of the case, or the order for relief.

(b) Unless the court for cause orders otherwise, in sections 701(a), 727(a)(10), 727(b), 1102(a), 1110(a)(1), 1121(b), 1121(c), 1141(d)(4), 1201(a), 1221, 1228(a), 1301(a), and 1305(a) of this title, "the order for relief under this chapter" in a chapter to which a case has been converted under section 706, 1112, 1208, or 1307 of this title means the conversion of such case to such chapter.

(c) Sections 342 and 365(d) of this title apply in a case that has been converted under section 706, 1112, 1208, or 1307 of this title, as if the conversion order were the order for relief.

(d) A claim against the estate or the debtor that arises after the order for relief but before conversion in a case that is converted under section 1112, 1208, or 1307 of this title, other than a claim specified in section 503(b) of this title, shall be treated for all purposes as if such claim had arisen immediately before the date of the filing of the petition.

(e) Conversion of a case under section 706, 1112, 1208, or 1307 of this title terminates the service of any trustee or examiner that is serving in the case before such conversion.

(f)(1) Except as provided in paragraph (2), when a case under chapter 13 of this title is converted to a case under another chapter under this title—

(A) property of the estate in the converted case shall consist of property of the estate, as of the date of filing of the petition, that remains in the possession of or is under the control of the debtor on the date of conversion;

(B) valuations of property and of allowed secured claims in the chapter 13 case shall apply only in a case converted to a case under chapter 11 or 12, but not in a case converted to a case under chapter 7, with allowed secured claims in cases under chapters 11 and 12 reduced to the extent that they have been paid in accordance with the chapter 13 plan; and

(C) with respect to cases converted from chapter 13—

(i) the claim of any creditor holding security as of the date of the filing of the petition shall continue to be secured by that security unless the full amount of such claim determined under applicable nonbankruptcy law has been paid in full as of the date of conversion, notwithstanding any valuation or determination of the amount of an allowed secured claim made for the purposes of the case under chapter 13; and

(ii) unless a prebankruptcy default has been fully cured under the plan at the time of conversion, in any proceeding under this title or otherwise, the default shall have the effect given under applicable nonbankruptcy law.

(2) If the debtor converts a case under chapter 13 of this title to a case under another chapter under this title in bad faith, the property of the estate in the converted case shall consist of the property of the estate as of the date of conversion.

(Pub.L. 95–598, Nov. 6, 1978, 92 Stat. 2568; Pub.L. 99–554, Title II, § 257(i), Oct. 27, 1986, 100 Stat. 3115; Pub.L. 103–394, Title III, § 311, Title V, § 501(d)(5), Oct. 22, 1994, 108 Stat. 4138, 4144; Pub.L. 109–8, Title III, § 309(a), Title XII, § 1207, Apr. 20, 2005, 119 Stat. 82, 194; Pub.L. 111–327, § 2(a)(11), Dec. 22, 2010, 124 Stat. 3558.)

HISTORICAL AND STATUTORY NOTES

Amendments

2010 Amendments. Subsec. (b). Pub.L. 111–327, § 2(a)(11)(A), struck out "728(a), 728(b)," following "727(b),", and struck out "1146(a), 1146(b),"following "1141(d)(4),".

Subsec. (f)(1)(C)(i). Pub.L. 111–327, § 2(a)(11)(B), inserted "of the filing" following "security as of the date".

2005 Amendments. Subsec. (f)(1)(A). Pub.L. 109–8, § 309(a)(1), struck out "and" at the end of subpar. (A).

Subsec. (f)(1)(B). Pub.L. 109–8, § 309(a)(2)(A), struck out "in the converted case, with allowed secured claims" and inserted "only in a case converted to a case under chapter 11 or 12, but not in a case converted to a case under chapter 7, with allowed secured claims in cases under chapters 11 and 12".

Pub.L. 109–8, § 309(a)(2)(B), struck out the period and inserted "; and" at the end of subpar. (B).

Subsec. (f)(1)(C). Pub.L. 109–8, § 309(a)(3), added subpar. (C).

Subsec. (f)(2). Pub.L. 109–8, § 1207, inserted "of the estate" after "bad faith, the property".

1994 Amendments. Subsec. (b). Pub.L. 103–394, § 501(d)(5), substituted "1201(a), 1221, 1228(a), 1301(a), and 1305(a)" for "1301(a), 1305(a), 1201(a), 1221, and 1228(a)", and substituted "1208, or 1307" for "1307, or 1208".

Subsec. (c). Pub.L. 103–394, § 501(d)(5)(B), substituted "1208, or 1307" for "1307, or 1208".

Subsec. (d). Pub.L. 103–394, § 501(d)(5)(B), substituted "1208, or 1307" for "1307, or 1208".

Subsec. (e). Pub.L. 103–394, § 501(d)(5)(B), substituted "1208, or 1307" for "1307, or 1208".

Subsec. (f). Pub.L. 103–394, § 311, added subsec. (f).

1986 Amendments. Subsec. (b). Pub.L. 99–554, § 257(i)(1), substituted references to sections 1201(a), 1221, and 1228(a) of this title for reference to section 1328(a) of this title, and added reference to section 1208 of this title.

Subsec. (c). Pub.L. 99–554, § 257(i)(2), added reference to section 1208 of this title.

Subsec. (d). Pub.L. 99–554, § 257(i)(3), added reference to section 1208 of this title.

Subsec. (e). Pub.L. 99–554, § 257(i)(2), added reference to section 1208 of this title.

§ 349. Effect of dismissal

(a) Unless the court, for cause, orders otherwise, the dismissal of a case under this title does not bar the discharge, in a later case under this title, of debts that were dischargeable in the case dismissed; nor does the dismissal of a case under this title prejudice the debtor with regard to the filing of a subsequent petition under this title, except as provided in section 109(g) of this title.

(b) Unless the court, for cause, orders otherwise, a dismissal of a case other than under section 742 of this title—

> **(1)** reinstates—
>> **(A)** any proceeding or custodianship superseded under section 543 of this title;
>> **(B)** any transfer avoided under section 522, 544, 545, 547, 548, 549, or 724(a) of this title, or preserved under section 510(c)(2), 522(i)(2), or 551 of this title; and
>> **(C)** any lien voided under section 506(d) of this title;
>
> **(2)** vacates any order, judgment, or transfer ordered, under section 522(i)(1), 542, 550, or 553 of this title; and
>
> **(3)** revests the property of the estate in the entity in which such property was vested immediately before the commencement of the case under this title.

(Pub.L. 95–598, Nov. 6, 1978, 92 Stat. 2569; Pub.L. 98–353, Title III, § 303, July 10, 1984, 98 Stat. 352; Pub.L. 103–394, Title V, § 501(d)(6), Oct. 22, 1994, 108 Stat. 4144.)

HISTORICAL AND STATUTORY NOTES

Amendments

1994 Amendments. Subsec. (a). Pub.L. 103–394, § 501(d)(6), substituted "109(g)" for "109(f)".

1984 Amendments. Subsec. (a). Pub.L. 98–353 added "; nor does the dismissal of a case under this title prejudice the debtor with regard to the filing of a subsequent petition under this title, except as provided in section 109(f) of this title" before the period.

§ 350. Closing and reopening cases

(a) After an estate is fully administered and the court has discharged the trustee, the court shall close the case.

(b) A case may be reopened in the court in which such case was closed to administer assets, to accord relief to the debtor, or for other cause.

(Pub.L. 95–598, Nov. 6, 1978, 92 Stat. 2569; Pub.L. 98–353, Title III, § 439, July 10, 1984, 98 Stat. 370.)

HISTORICAL AND STATUTORY NOTES

Amendments

1984 Amendments. Subsec. (b). Pub.L. 98–353 substituted "A" for "a".

CROSS REFERENCES

Applicability of subsec. (b) of this section in Chapter 9 cases, see 11 USCA § 901.

Scheduled property deemed abandoned, see 11 USCA § 554.

Successor trustee, see 11 USCA § 703.

§ 351. Disposal of patient records

If a health care business commences a case under chapter 7, 9, or 11, and the trustee does not have a sufficient amount of funds to pay for the storage of patient records in the manner required under applicable Federal or State law, the following requirements shall apply:

(1) The trustee shall—

(A) promptly publish notice, in 1 or more appropriate newspapers, that if patient records are not claimed by the patient or an insurance provider (if applicable law permits the insurance provider to make that claim) by the date that is 365 days after the date of that notification, the trustee will destroy the patient records; and

(B) during the first 180 days of the 365-day period described in subparagraph (A), promptly attempt to notify directly each patient that is the subject of the patient records and appropriate insurance carrier concerning the patient records by mailing to the most recent known address of that patient, or a family member or contact person for that patient, and to the appropriate insurance carrier an appropriate notice regarding the claiming or disposing of patient records.

(2) If, after providing the notification under paragraph (1), patient records are not claimed during the 365-day period described under that paragraph, the trustee shall mail, by certified mail, at the end of such 365-day period a written request to each appropriate Federal agency to request permission from that agency to deposit the patient records with that agency, except that no Federal agency is required to accept patient records under this paragraph.

(3) If, following the 365-day period described in paragraph (2) and after providing the notification under paragraph (1), patient records are not claimed by a patient or insurance provider, or request is not granted by a Federal agency to deposit such records with that agency, the trustee shall destroy those records by—

(A) if the records are written, shredding or burning the records; or

(B) if the records are magnetic, optical, or other electronic records, by otherwise destroying those records so that those records cannot be retrieved.

(Added Pub.L. 109–8, Title XI, § 1102(a), Apr. 20, 2005, 119 Stat. 189.)

SUBCHAPTER IV—ADMINISTRATIVE POWERS

§ 361. Adequate protection

When adequate protection is required under section 362, 363, or 364 of this title of an interest of an entity in property, such adequate protection may be provided by—

(1) requiring the trustee to make a cash payment or periodic cash payments to such entity, to the extent that the stay under section 362 of this title, use, sale, or lease under section 363 of this title, or any grant of a lien under section 364 of this title results in a decrease in the value of such entity's interest in such property;

(2) providing to such entity an additional or replacement lien to the extent that such stay, use, sale, lease, or grant results in a decrease in the value of such entity's interest in such property; or

(3) granting such other relief, other than entitling such entity to compensation allowable under section 503(b)(1) of this title as an administrative expense, as will result in the realization by such entity of the indubitable equivalent of such entity's interest in such property.

(Pub.L. 95–598, Nov. 6, 1978, 92 Stat. 2569; Pub.L. 98–353, Title III, § 440, July 10, 1984, 98 Stat. 370.)

HISTORICAL AND STATUTORY NOTES

Amendments

1984 Amendments. Par. (1). Pub.L. 98–353 added "a cash payment or" after "make".

CROSS REFERENCES

Applicability of this section in Chapter 9 cases, see 11 USCA § 901.

Inapplicability of this section in Chapter 12 cases, see 11 USCA § 1205.

§ 362. Automatic stay

(a) Except as provided in subsection (b) of this section, a petition filed under section 301, 302, or 303 of this title, or an application filed under section 5(a)(3) of the Securities Investor Protection Act of 1970, operates as a stay, applicable to all entities, of—

(1) the commencement or continuation, including the issuance or employment of process, of a judicial, administrative, or other action or proceeding against the debtor that was or could have been commenced before the commencement of the case under this title, or to recover a claim against the debtor that arose before the commencement of the case under this title;

(2) the enforcement, against the debtor or against property of the estate, of a judgment obtained before the commencement of the case under this title;

(3) any act to obtain possession of property of the estate or of property from the estate or to exercise control over property of the estate;

(4) any act to create, perfect, or enforce any lien against property of the estate;

(5) any act to create, perfect, or enforce against property of the debtor any lien to the extent that such lien secures a claim that arose before the commencement of the case under this title;

(6) any act to collect, assess, or recover a claim against the debtor that arose before the commencement of the case under this title;

(7) the setoff of any debt owing to the debtor that arose before the commencement of the case under this title against any claim against the debtor; and

(8) the commencement or continuation of a proceeding before the United States Tax Court concerning a tax liability of a debtor that is a corporation for a taxable period the bankruptcy court may determine or concerning the tax liability of a debtor who is an individual for a taxable period ending before the date of the order for relief under this title.

(b) The filing of a petition under section 301, 302, or 303 of this title, or of an application under section 5(a)(3) of the Securities Investor Protection Act of 1970, does not operate as a stay—

(1) under subsection (a) of this section, of the commencement or continuation of a criminal action or proceeding against the debtor;

(2) under subsection (a)—

(A) of the commencement or continuation of a civil action or proceeding—

(i) for the establishment of paternity;

(ii) for the establishment or modification of an order for domestic support obligations;

(iii) concerning child custody or visitation;

(iv) for the dissolution of a marriage, except to the extent that such proceeding seeks to determine the division of property that is property of the estate; or

(v) regarding domestic violence;

(B) of the collection of a domestic support obligation from property that is not property of the estate;

(C) with respect to the withholding of income that is property of the estate or property of the debtor for payment of a domestic support obligation under a judicial or administrative order or a statute;

(D) of the withholding, suspension, or restriction of a driver's license, a professional or occupational license, or a recreational license, under State law, as specified in section 466(a)(16) of the Social Security Act;

(E) of the reporting of overdue support owed by a parent to any consumer reporting agency as specified in section 466(a)(7) of the Social Security Act;

(F) of the interception of a tax refund, as specified in sections 464 and 466(a)(3) of the Social Security Act or under an analogous State law; or

(G) of the enforcement of a medical obligation, as specified under title IV of the Social Security Act;

(3) under subsection (a) of this section, of any act to perfect, or to maintain or continue the perfection of, an interest in property to the extent that the trustee's rights and powers are subject to such perfection under section 546(b) of this title or to the extent that such act is accomplished within the period provided under section 547(e)(2)(A) of this title;

(4) under paragraph (1), (2), (3), or (6) of subsection (a) of this section, of the commencement or continuation of an action or proceeding by a governmental unit or any organization exercising authority under the Convention on the Prohibition of the Development, Production, Stockpiling and Use of Chemical Weapons and on Their Destruction, opened for signature on January 13, 1993, to enforce such governmental unit's or organization's police and regulatory power, including the enforcement of a judgment other than a money judgment, obtained in an action or proceeding by the governmental unit to enforce such governmental unit's or organization's police or regulatory power;

[**(5) Repealed.** Pub.L. 105–277, Div. I, Title VI, § 603(1), Oct. 21, 1998, 112 Stat. 2681–886]

(6) under subsection (a) of this section, of the exercise by a commodity broker, forward contract merchant, stockbroker, financial institution, financial participant, or securities clearing agency of any contractual right (as defined in section 555 or 556) under any security agreement or arrangement or other credit enhancement forming a part of or related to any commodity contract, forward contract or securities contract, or of any contractual right (as defined in section 555 or 556) to offset or net out any termination value, payment amount, or other transfer obligation arising under or in connection with 1 or more such contracts, including any master agreement for such contracts;

(7) under subsection (a) of this section, of the exercise by a repo participant or financial participant of any contractual right (as defined in section 559) under any security agreement or arrangement or other credit enhancement forming a part of or related to any repurchase agreement, or of any contractual right (as defined in section 559) to offset or net out any termination value, payment amount, or other transfer obligation arising under or in connection with 1 or more such agreements, including any master agreement for such agreements;

(8) under subsection (a) of this section, of the commencement of any action by the Secretary of Housing and Urban Development to foreclose a mortgage or deed of trust in any case in which the mortgage or deed of trust held by the Secretary is insured or was formerly insured under the National Housing Act and covers property, or combinations of property, consisting of five or more living units;

(9) under subsection (a), of—

(A) an audit by a governmental unit to determine tax liability;

(B) the issuance to the debtor by a governmental unit of a notice of tax deficiency;

(C) a demand for tax returns; or

(D) the making of an assessment for any tax and issuance of a notice and demand for payment of such an assessment (but any tax lien that would otherwise attach to property of the estate by reason of such an assessment shall not take effect unless such tax is a debt of the debtor that will not be discharged in the case and such property or its proceeds are transferred out of the estate to, or otherwise revested in, the debtor).

(10) under subsection (a) of this section, of any act by a lessor to the debtor under a lease of nonresidential real property that has terminated by the expiration of the stated term of the lease before the commencement of or during a case under this title to obtain possession of such property;

(11) under subsection (a) of this section, of the presentment of a negotiable instrument and the giving of notice of and protesting dishonor of such an instrument;

(12) under subsection (a) of this section, after the date which is 90 days after the filing of such petition, of the commencement or continuation, and conclusion to the entry of final judgment, of an action which involves a debtor subject to reorganization pursuant to chapter 11 of this title and which was brought by the Secretary of Transportation under section 31325 of title 46 (including distribution of any proceeds of sale) to foreclose a preferred ship or fleet mortgage, or a security interest in or relating to a vessel or vessel under construction, held by the Secretary of Transportation under chapter 537 of title 46 or section 109(h) of title 49, or under applicable State law;

(13) under subsection (a) of this section, after the date which is 90 days after the filing of such petition, of the commencement or continuation, and conclusion to the entry of final judgment, of an action which involves a debtor subject to reorganization pursuant to chapter 11 of this title and which was brought by the Secretary of Commerce under section 31325 of title 46 (including distribution of any proceeds of sale) to foreclose a preferred ship or fleet mortgage in a vessel or a mortgage, deed of trust, or other security interest in a fishing facility held by the Secretary of Commerce under chapter 537 of title 46;

(14) under subsection (a) of this section, of any action by an accrediting agency regarding the accreditation status of the debtor as an educational institution;

(15) under subsection (a) of this section, of any action by a State licensing body regarding the licensure of the debtor as an educational institution;

(16) under subsection (a) of this section, of any action by a guaranty agency, as defined in section 435(j) of the Higher Education Act of 1965 or the Secretary of Education regarding the eligibility of the debtor to participate in programs authorized under such Act;

(17) under subsection (a) of this section, of the exercise by a swap participant or financial participant of any contractual right (as defined in section 560) under any security agreement or arrangement or other credit enhancement forming a part of or related to any swap agreement, or of any contractual right (as defined in section 560) to offset or net out any termination value, payment amount, or other transfer obligation arising under or in connection with 1 or more such agreements, including any master agreement for such agreements;

(18) under subsection (a) of the creation or perfection of a statutory lien for an ad valorem property tax, or a special tax or special assessment on real property whether or not ad valorem, imposed by a governmental unit, if such tax or assessment comes due after the date of the filing of the petition;

(19) under subsection (a), of withholding of income from a debtor's wages and collection of amounts withheld, under the debtor's agreement authorizing that withholding and collection for the benefit of a pension, profit-sharing, stock bonus, or other plan established under section 401, 403, 408, 408A, 414, 457, or 501(c) of the Internal Revenue Code of 1986, that is sponsored by the employer of the debtor, or an affiliate, successor, or predecessor of such employer—

(A) to the extent that the amounts withheld and collected are used solely for payments relating to a loan from a plan under section 408(b)(1) of the Employee

Retirement Income Security Act of 1974 or is subject to section 72(p) of the Internal Revenue Code of 1986; or

   (B) a loan from a thrift savings plan permitted under subchapter III of chapter 84 of title 5, that satisfies the requirements of section 8433(g) of such title;

but nothing in this paragraph may be construed to provide that any loan made under a governmental plan under section 414(d), or a contract or account under section 403(b), of the Internal Revenue Code of 1986 constitutes a claim or a debt under this title;

   (20) under subsection (a), of any act to enforce any lien against or security interest in real property following entry of the order under subsection (d)(4) as to such real property in any prior case under this title, for a period of 2 years after the date of the entry of such an order, except that the debtor, in a subsequent case under this title, may move for relief from such order based upon changed circumstances or for other good cause shown, after notice and a hearing;

   (21) under subsection (a), of any act to enforce any lien against or security interest in real property—

   (A) if the debtor is ineligible under section 109(g) to be a debtor in a case under this title; or

   (B) if the case under this title was filed in violation of a bankruptcy court order in a prior case under this title prohibiting the debtor from being a debtor in another case under this title;

   (22) subject to subsection (l), under subsection (a)(3), of the continuation of any eviction, unlawful detainer action, or similar proceeding by a lessor against a debtor involving residential property in which the debtor resides as a tenant under a lease or rental agreement and with respect to which the lessor has obtained before the date of the filing of the bankruptcy petition, a judgment for possession of such property against the debtor;

   (23) subject to subsection (m), under subsection (a)(3), of an eviction action that seeks possession of the residential property in which the debtor resides as a tenant under a lease or rental agreement based on endangerment of such property or the illegal use of controlled substances on such property, but only if the lessor files with the court, and serves upon the debtor, a certification under penalty of perjury that such an eviction action has been filed, or that the debtor, during the 30-day period preceding the date of the filing of the certification, has endangered property or illegally used or allowed to be used a controlled substance on the property;

   (24) under subsection (a), of any transfer that is not avoidable under section 544 and that is not avoidable under section 549;

   (25) under subsection (a), of—

   (A) the commencement or continuation of an investigation or action by a securities self regulatory organization to enforce such organization's regulatory power;

   (B) the enforcement of an order or decision, other than for monetary sanctions, obtained in an action by such securities self regulatory organization to enforce such organization's regulatory power; or

   (C) any act taken by such securities self regulatory organization to delist, delete, or refuse to permit quotation of any stock that does not meet applicable regulatory requirements;

   (26) under subsection (a), of the setoff under applicable nonbankruptcy law of an income tax refund, by a governmental unit, with respect to a taxable period that ended before the date of the order for relief against an income tax liability for a taxable period that also ended before the date of the order for relief, except that in any case in which the setoff of an income tax refund is not permitted under applicable nonbankruptcy law because of a pending action to determine the amount or legality of a tax liability, the governmental unit may hold the refund pending the resolution of the action, unless the court, on the motion of the trustee and after

notice and a hearing, grants the taxing authority adequate protection (within the meaning of section 361) for the secured claim of such authority in the setoff under section 506(a);

(27) under subsection (a) of this section, of the exercise by a master netting agreement participant of any contractual right (as defined in section 555, 556, 559, or 560) under any security agreement or arrangement or other credit enhancement forming a part of or related to any master netting agreement, or of any contractual right (as defined in section 555, 556, 559, or 560) to offset or net out any termination value, payment amount, or other transfer obligation arising under or in connection with 1 or more such master netting agreements to the extent that such participant is eligible to exercise such rights under paragraph (6), (7), or (17) for each individual contract covered by the master netting agreement in issue; and

(28) under subsection (a), of the exclusion by the Secretary of Health and Human Services of the debtor from participation in the medicare program or any other Federal health care program (as defined in section 1128B(f) of the Social Security Act pursuant to title XI or XVIII of such Act).

The provisions of paragraphs (12) and (13) of this subsection shall apply with respect to any such petition filed on or before December 31, 1989.

(c) Except as provided in subsections (d), (e), (f), and (h) of this section—

(1) the stay of an act against property of the estate under subsection (a) of this section continues until such property is no longer property of the estate;

(2) the stay of any other act under subsection (a) of this section continues until the earliest of—

(A) the time the case is closed;

(B) the time the case is dismissed; or

(C) if the case is a case under chapter 7 of this title concerning an individual or a case under chapter 9, 11, 12, or 13 of this title, the time a discharge is granted or denied;

(3) if a single or joint case is filed by or against a debtor who is an individual in a case under chapter 7, 11, or 13, and if a single or joint case of the debtor was pending within the preceding 1-year period but was dismissed, other than a case refiled under a chapter other than chapter 7 after dismissal under section 707(b)—

(A) the stay under subsection (a) with respect to any action taken with respect to a debt or property securing such debt or with respect to any lease shall terminate with respect to the debtor on the 30th day after the filing of the later case;

(B) on the motion of a party in interest for continuation of the automatic stay and upon notice and a hearing, the court may extend the stay in particular cases as to any or all creditors (subject to such conditions or limitations as the court may then impose) after notice and a hearing completed before the expiration of the 30-day period only if the party in interest demonstrates that the filing of the later case is in good faith as to the creditors to be stayed; and

(C) for purposes of subparagraph (B), a case is presumptively filed not in good faith (but such presumption may be rebutted by clear and convincing evidence to the contrary)—

(i) as to all creditors, if—

(I) more than 1 previous case under any of chapters 7, 11, and 13 in which the individual was a debtor was pending within the preceding 1-year period;

(II) a previous case under any of chapters 7, 11, and 13 in which the individual was a debtor was dismissed within such 1-year period, after the debtor failed to—

(aa) file or amend the petition or other documents as required by this title or the court without substantial excuse (but mere inadvertence or negligence shall not be a substantial excuse unless the dismissal was caused by the negligence of the debtor's attorney);

(bb) provide adequate protection as ordered by the court; or

(cc) perform the terms of a plan confirmed by the court; or

(III) there has not been a substantial change in the financial or personal affairs of the debtor since the dismissal of the next most previous case under chapter 7, 11, or 13 or any other reason to conclude that the later case will be concluded—

(aa) if a case under chapter 7, with a discharge; or

(bb) if a case under chapter 11 or 13, with a confirmed plan that will be fully performed; and

(ii) as to any creditor that commenced an action under subsection (d) in a previous case in which the individual was a debtor if, as of the date of dismissal of such case, that action was still pending or had been resolved by terminating, conditioning, or limiting the stay as to actions of such creditor; and

(4)(A)(i) if a single or joint case is filed by or against a debtor who is an individual under this title, and if 2 or more single or joint cases of the debtor were pending within the previous year but were dismissed, other than a case refiled under a chapter other than chapter 7 after dismissal under section 707(b), the stay under subsection (a) shall not go into effect upon the filing of the later case; and

(ii) on request of a party in interest, the court shall promptly enter an order confirming that no stay is in effect;

(B) if, within 30 days after the filing of the later case, a party in interest requests the court may order the stay to take effect in the case as to any or all creditors (subject to such conditions or limitations as the court may impose), after notice and a hearing, only if the party in interest demonstrates that the filing of the later case is in good faith as to the creditors to be stayed;

(C) a stay imposed under subparagraph (B) shall be effective on the date of the entry of the order allowing the stay to go into effect; and

(D) for purposes of subparagraph (B), a case is presumptively filed not in good faith (but such presumption may be rebutted by clear and convincing evidence to the contrary)—

(i) as to all creditors if—

(I) 2 or more previous cases under this title in which the individual was a debtor were pending within the 1-year period;

(II) a previous case under this title in which the individual was a debtor was dismissed within the time period stated in this paragraph after the debtor failed to file or amend the petition or other documents as required by this title or the court without substantial excuse (but mere inadvertence or negligence shall not be substantial excuse unless the dismissal was caused by the negligence of the debtor's attorney), failed to provide adequate protection as ordered by the court, or failed to perform the terms of a plan confirmed by the court; or

(III) there has not been a substantial change in the financial or personal affairs of the debtor since the dismissal of the next most previous case under this title, or any other reason to conclude that the later case will not be concluded, if a case under chapter 7, with a discharge, and if a case under chapter 11 or 13, with a confirmed plan that will be fully performed; or

(ii) as to any creditor that commenced an action under subsection (d) in a previous case in which the individual was a debtor if, as of the date of dismissal of such case, such action was still pending or had been resolved by terminating, conditioning, or limiting the stay as to such action of such creditor.

(d) On request of a party in interest and after notice and a hearing, the court shall grant relief from the stay provided under subsection (a) of this section, such as by terminating, annulling, modifying, or conditioning such stay—

(1) for cause, including the lack of adequate protection of an interest in property of such party in interest;

(2) with respect to a stay of an act against property under subsection (a) of this section, if—

(A) the debtor does not have an equity in such property; and

(B) such property is not necessary to an effective reorganization;

(3) with respect to a stay of an act against single asset real estate under subsection (a), by a creditor whose claim is secured by an interest in such real estate, unless, not later than the date that is 90 days after the entry of the order for relief (or such later date as the court may determine for cause by order entered within that 90-day period) or 30 days after the court determines that the debtor is subject to this paragraph, whichever is later—

(A) the debtor has filed a plan of reorganization that has a reasonable possibility of being confirmed within a reasonable time; or

(B) the debtor has commenced monthly payments that—

(i) may, in the debtor's sole discretion, notwithstanding section 363(c)(2), be made from rents or other income generated before, on, or after the date of the commencement of the case by or from the property to each creditor whose claim is secured by such real estate (other than a claim secured by a judgment lien or by an unmatured statutory lien); and

(ii) are in an amount equal to interest at the then applicable nondefault contract rate of interest on the value of the creditor's interest in the real estate; or

(4) with respect to a stay of an act against real property under subsection (a), by a creditor whose claim is secured by an interest in such real property, if the court finds that the filing of the petition was part of a scheme to delay, hinder, or defraud creditors that involved either—

(A) transfer of all or part ownership of, or other interest in, such real property without the consent of the secured creditor or court approval; or

(B) multiple bankruptcy filings affecting such real property.

If recorded in compliance with applicable State laws governing notices of interests or liens in real property, an order entered under paragraph (4) shall be binding in any other case under this title purporting to affect such real property filed not later than 2 years after the date of the entry of such order by the court, except that a debtor in a subsequent case under this title may move for relief from such order based upon changed circumstances or for good cause shown, after notice and a hearing. Any Federal, State, or local governmental unit that accepts notices of interests or liens in real property shall accept any certified copy of an order described in this subsection for indexing and recording.

(e)(1) Thirty days after a request under subsection (d) of this section for relief from the stay of any act against property of the estate under subsection (a) of this section, such stay is terminated with respect to the party in interest making such request, unless the court, after notice and a hearing, orders such stay continued in effect pending the conclusion of, or as a result of, a final hearing and determination under subsection (d) of this section. A hearing under this subsection may be a preliminary hearing, or may be consolidated with the final hearing under subsection (d) of this section. The court shall order such stay continued in effect pending the conclusion of the final hearing under subsection (d) of this section if there is a reasonable likelihood that the party opposing relief from such stay will prevail at the conclusion of such final hearing. If the hearing under this subsection is a preliminary hearing, then such final hearing shall be concluded not later than thirty days after the conclusion of such preliminary hearing, unless the 30-day period is extended with the consent of the parties in interest or for a specific time which the court finds is required by compelling circumstances.

(2) Notwithstanding paragraph (1), in a case under chapter 7, 11, or 13 in which the debtor is an individual, the stay under subsection (a) shall terminate on the date that is 60 days after a request is made by a party in interest under subsection (d), unless—

(A) a final decision is rendered by the court during the 60-day period beginning on the date of the request; or

(B) such 60-day period is extended—

(i) by agreement of all parties in interest; or

(ii) by the court for such specific period of time as the court finds is required for good cause, as described in findings made by the court.

(f) Upon request of a party in interest, the court, with or without a hearing, shall grant such relief from the stay provided under subsection (a) of this section as is necessary to prevent irreparable damage to the interest of an entity in property, if such interest will suffer such damage before there is an opportunity for notice and a hearing under subsection (d) or (e) of this section.

(g) In any hearing under subsection (d) or (e) of this section concerning relief from the stay of any act under subsection (a) of this section—

(1) the party requesting such relief has the burden of proof on the issue of the debtor's equity in property; and

(2) the party opposing such relief has the burden of proof on all other issues.

(h)(1) In a case in which the debtor is an individual, the stay provided by subsection (a) is terminated with respect to personal property of the estate or of the debtor securing in whole or in part a claim, or subject to an unexpired lease, and such personal property shall no longer be property of the estate if the debtor fails within the applicable time set by section 521(a)(2)—

(A) to file timely any statement of intention required under section 521(a)(2) with respect to such personal property or to indicate in such statement that the debtor will either surrender such personal property or retain it and, if retaining such personal property, either redeem such personal property pursuant to section 722, enter into an agreement of the kind specified in section 524(c) applicable to the debt secured by such personal property, or assume such unexpired lease pursuant to section 365(p) if the trustee does not do so, as applicable; and

(B) to take timely the action specified in such statement, as it may be amended before expiration of the period for taking action, unless such statement specifies the debtor's intention to reaffirm such debt on the original contract terms and the creditor refuses to agree to the reaffirmation on such terms.

(2) Paragraph (1) does not apply if the court determines, on the motion of the trustee filed before the expiration of the applicable time set by section 521(a)(2), after notice and a hearing, that such personal property is of consequential value or benefit to the estate, and orders appropriate adequate protection of the creditor's interest, and orders the debtor to deliver any collateral in the debtor's possession to the trustee. If the court does not so determine, the stay provided by subsection (a) shall terminate upon the conclusion of the hearing on the motion.

(i) If a case commenced under chapter 7, 11, or 13 is dismissed due to the creation of a debt repayment plan, for purposes of subsection (c)(3), any subsequent case commenced by the debtor under any such chapter shall not be presumed to be filed not in good faith.

(j) On request of a party in interest, the court shall issue an order under subsection (c) confirming that the automatic stay has been terminated.

(k)(1) Except as provided in paragraph (2), an individual injured by any willful violation of a stay provided by this section shall recover actual damages, including costs and attorneys' fees, and, in appropriate circumstances, may recover punitive damages.

(2) If such violation is based on an action taken by an entity in the good faith belief that subsection (h) applies to the debtor, the recovery under paragraph (1) of this subsection against such entity shall be limited to actual damages.

(l)(1) Except as otherwise provided in this subsection, subsection (b) (22) shall apply on the date that is 30 days after the date on which the bankruptcy petition is filed, if the debtor files with the petition and serves upon the lessor a certification under penalty of perjury that—

    (A) under nonbankruptcy law applicable in the jurisdiction, there are circumstances under which the debtor would be permitted to cure the entire monetary default that gave rise to the judgment for possession, after that judgment for possession was entered; and

    (B) the debtor (or an adult dependent of the debtor) has deposited with the clerk of the court, any rent that would become due during the 30-day period after the filing of the bankruptcy petition.

(2) If, within the 30-day period after the filing of the bankruptcy petition, the debtor (or an adult dependent of the debtor) complies with paragraph (1) and files with the court and serves upon the lessor a further certification under penalty of perjury that the debtor (or an adult dependent of the debtor) has cured, under nonbankruptcy law applicable in the jurisdiction, the entire monetary default that gave rise to the judgment under which possession is sought by the lessor, subsection (b)(22) shall not apply, unless ordered to apply by the court under paragraph (3).

(3)(A) If the lessor files an objection to any certification filed by the debtor under paragraph (1) or (2), and serves such objection upon the debtor, the court shall hold a hearing within 10 days after the filing and service of such objection to determine if the certification filed by the debtor under paragraph (1) or (2) is true.

    (B) If the court upholds the objection of the lessor filed under subparagraph (A)—

        (i) subsection (b)(22) shall apply immediately and relief from the stay provided under subsection (a)(3) shall not be required to enable the lessor to complete the process to recover full possession of the property; and

        (ii) the clerk of the court shall immediately serve upon the lessor and the debtor a certified copy of the court's order upholding the lessor's objection.

(4) If a debtor, in accordance with paragraph (5), indicates on the petition that there was a judgment for possession of the residential rental property in which the debtor resides and does not file a certification under paragraph (1) or (2)—

    (A) subsection (b)(22) shall apply immediately upon failure to file such certification, and relief from the stay provided under subsection (a)(3) shall not be required to enable the lessor to complete the process to recover full possession of the property; and

    (B) the clerk of the court shall immediately serve upon the lessor and the debtor a certified copy of the docket indicating the absence of a filed certification and the applicability of the exception to the stay under subsection (b)(22).

(5)(A) Where a judgment for possession of residential property in which the debtor resides as a tenant under a lease or rental agreement has been obtained by the lessor, the debtor shall so indicate on the bankruptcy petition and shall provide the name and address of the lessor that obtained that pre-petition judgment on the petition and on any certification filed under this subsection.

    (B) The form of certification filed with the petition, as specified in this subsection, shall provide for the debtor to certify, and the debtor shall certify—

        (i) whether a judgment for possession of residential rental housing in which the debtor resides has been obtained against the debtor before the date of the filing of the petition; and

(ii) whether the debtor is claiming under paragraph (1) that under nonbankruptcy law applicable in the jurisdiction, there are circumstances under which the debtor would be permitted to cure the entire monetary default that gave rise to the judgment for possession, after that judgment of possession was entered, and has made the appropriate deposit with the court.

(C) The standard forms (electronic and otherwise) used in a bankruptcy proceeding shall be amended to reflect the requirements of this subsection.

(D) The clerk of the court shall arrange for the prompt transmittal of the rent deposited in accordance with paragraph (1)(B) to the lessor.

(m)(1) Except as otherwise provided in this subsection, subsection (b) (23) shall apply on the date that is 15 days after the date on which the lessor files and serves a certification described in subsection (b)(23).

(2)(A) If the debtor files with the court an objection to the truth or legal sufficiency of the certification described in subsection (b)(23) and serves such objection upon the lessor, subsection (b)(23) shall not apply, unless ordered to apply by the court under this subsection.

(B) If the debtor files and serves the objection under subparagraph (A), the court shall hold a hearing within 10 days after the filing and service of such objection to determine if the situation giving rise to the lessor's certification under paragraph (1) existed or has been remedied.

(C) If the debtor can demonstrate to the satisfaction of the court that the situation giving rise to the lessor's certification under paragraph (1) did not exist or has been remedied, the stay provided under subsection (a)(3) shall remain in effect until the termination of the stay under this section.

(D) If the debtor cannot demonstrate to the satisfaction of the court that the situation giving rise to the lessor's certification under paragraph (1) did not exist or has been remedied—

(i) relief from the stay provided under subsection (a)(3) shall not be required to enable the lessor to proceed with the eviction; and

(ii) the clerk of the court shall immediately serve upon the lessor and the debtor a certified copy of the court's order upholding the lessor's certification.

(3) If the debtor fails to file, within 15 days, an objection under paragraph (2)(A)—

(A) subsection (b)(23) shall apply immediately upon such failure and relief from the stay provided under subsection (a)(3) shall not be required to enable the lessor to complete the process to recover full possession of the property; and

(B) the clerk of the court shall immediately serve upon the lessor and the debtor a certified copy of the docket indicating such failure.

(n)(1) Except as provided in paragraph (2), subsection (a) does not apply in a case in which the debtor—

(A) is a debtor in a small business case pending at the time the petition is filed;

(B) was a debtor in a small business case that was dismissed for any reason by an order that became final in the 2-year period ending on the date of the order for relief entered with respect to the petition;

(C) was a debtor in a small business case in which a plan was confirmed in the 2-year period ending on the date of the order for relief entered with respect to the petition; or

(D) is an entity that has acquired substantially all of the assets or business of a small business debtor described in subparagraph (A), (B), or (C), unless such entity establishes by a preponderance of the evidence that such entity acquired substantially all of the assets or business of such small business debtor in good faith and not for the purpose of evading this paragraph.

(2) Paragraph (1) does not apply—

(A) to an involuntary case involving no collusion by the debtor with creditors; or

(B) to the filing of a petition if—

(i) the debtor proves by a preponderance of the evidence that the filing of the petition resulted from circumstances beyond the control of the debtor not foreseeable at the time the case then pending was filed; and

(ii) it is more likely than not that the court will confirm a feasible plan, but not a liquidating plan, within a reasonable period of time.

(o) The exercise of rights not subject to the stay arising under subsection (a) pursuant to paragraph (6), (7), (17), or (27) of subsection (b) shall not be stayed by any order of a court or administrative agency in any proceeding under this title.

(Pub.L. 95–598, Nov. 6, 1978, 92 Stat. 2570; Pub.L. 97–222, § 3, July 27, 1982, 96 Stat. 235; Pub.L. 98–353, Title III, §§ 304, 363(b), 392, 441, July 10, 1984, 98 Stat. 352, 363, 365, 371; Pub.L. 99–509, Title V, § 5001(a), Oct. 21, 1986, 100 Stat. 1911; Pub.L. 99–554, Title II, §§ 257(j), 283(d), Oct. 27, 1986, 100 Stat. 3115, 3116; Pub.L. 101–311, Title I, § 102, Title II, § 202, June 25, 1990, 104 Stat. 267, 269; Pub.L. 101–508, Title III, § 3007(a)(1), Nov. 5, 1990, 104 Stat. 1388–28; Pub.L. 103–394, Title I, §§ 101, 116, Title II, §§ 204(a), 218(b), Title III, § 304(b), Title IV, § 401, Title V, § 501(b)(2), (d)(7), Oct. 22, 1994, 108 Stat. 4107, 4119, 4122, 4128, 4132, 4141, 4142, 4144; Pub.L. 105–277, Div. I, Title VI, § 603, Oct. 21, 1998, 112 Stat. 2681–886; Pub.L. 109–8, Title I, § 106(f), Title II, §§ 214, 224(b), Title III, §§ 302, 303, 305(1), 311, 320, Title IV, §§ 401(b), 441, 444, Title VII, §§ 709, 718, Title IX, § 907(d), (o)(1), (2), Title XI, § 1106, Title XII, § 1225, Apr. 20, 2005, 119 Stat. 41, 54, 64, 75, 77, 79, 84, 94, 104, 114, 117, 127, 131, 176, 181, 182, 192, 199; Pub.L. 109–304, § 17(b)(1), Oct. 6, 2006, 120 Stat. 1706; Pub.L. 109–390, § 5(a)(2), Dec. 12, 2006, 120 Stat. 2696; Pub.L. 111–327, § 2(a)(12), Dec. 22, 2010, 124 Stat. 3558.)

HISTORICAL AND STATUTORY NOTES

References in Text

Section 5(a)(3) of the Securities Investor Protection Act of 1970, referred to in subsecs. (a) and (b), is section 5(a)(3) of Pub.L. 91–598, Dec. 30, 1970, 84 Stat. 1644, which is classified to section 78eee of Title 15, Commerce and Trade.

Section 466 of the Social Security Act, referred to in subsec. (b)(2)(D) to (F), is Act Aug. 14, 1935, c. 531, Title IV, § 466, as added Aug. 16, 1984, Pub.L. 98–378, § 3(b), 98 Stat. 1306, and amended, which is classified to 42 U.S.C.A. § 666.

Section 464 of the Social Security Act, referred to in subsec. (b)(2)(F), is Act Aug. 14, 1935, c. 531, Title IV, § 464, as added Aug. 13, 1981, Pub.L. 97–35, Title XXIII, § 2331(a), 95 Stat. 860, and amended, which is classified to 42 U.S.C.A. § 664.

Title IV of the Social Security Act, referred to in subsec. (b)(2)(G), is Act Aug. 14, 1935, c. 531, Title IV, § 401 et seq., as added Aug. 22, 1996, Pub.L. 104–193, Title I, § 103(a)(1), 110 Stat. 2113, and amended, which is classified principally to subchapter IV of chapter 7 of Title 42, 42 U.S.C.A. § 601 et seq. For complete classification, see Tables.

The National Housing Act, referred to in subsec. (b)(8), is Act June 27, 1934, c. 847, 48 Stat. 1246, as amended, which is classified principally to chapter 13 (section 1701 et seq.) of Title 12, Banks and Banking. For complete classification of this Act to the Code, see section 1701 of Title 12 and Tables.

Chapter 537 of title 46, referred to in subsecs. (b)(12) and (13), is Loans and Guarantees, 46 U.S.C.A. § 53701 et seq.

The Higher Education Act of 1965, including such Act, referred to in subsec. (b)(16), is Pub.L. 89–329, Nov. 8, 1965, 79 Stat. 1219, as amended, which is classified principally to chapter 28 (§ 1001 et seq.) of Title 20, Education. Section 435(j) of the Act is classified to section 1085(j) of Title 20. For complete classification of this Act to the Code, see Short Title note set out under section 1001 of Title 20 and Tables.

Section 401, 403, 408, 408A, 414, 457, or 501(c) of the Internal Revenue Code of 1986, referred to in subsec. (b)(19), is classified to 26 U.S.C.A. § 401, 403, 408, 408A, 414, 457, or 501(c).

Section 414(d) or section 403(b) of the Internal Revenue Code, referred to in subsec. (b)(19), is classified to 26 U.S.C.A. § 414(d) or 26 U.S.C.A. § 403(b).

Section 408(b)(1) of the Employee Retirement Income Security Act of 1974, referred to in subsec. (b)(19)(A), is Pub.L. 93–406, Title I, § 408(b)(1), Sept. 2, 1974, 88 Stat. 883, as amended, which is classified to 29 U.S.C.A. § 1108(b)(1).

Section 72(p) of the Internal Revenue Code of 1986, referred to in subsec. (b)(19)(A), is classified to 26 U.S.C.A. § 72(p).

Subchapter III of chapter 84 of title 5, referred to in subsec. (b)(19)(B), is 5 U.S.C.A. § 8431 et seq.

Section 1128B(f) of the Social Security Act, referred to in subsec. (b)(28), is Act Aug. 14, 1935, c. 531, Title XI, § 1128B, formerly Title XVIII, § 1877(d), and Title XIX, § 1909, as added and amended Oct. 30, 1972, Pub.L. 92–603, Title II, §§ 242(c), 278(b)(9), 86 Stat. 1419, 1454, which is classified to 42 U.S.C.A. § 1320a–7b(f).

Title XI of such Act, referred to in subsec. (b)(28), means title XI of the Social Security Act, Act Aug. 14, 1935, c. 531, Title XI, § 1101 et seq., 49 Stat. 647, as amended, which is classified principally to subchapter XI of chapter 7 of Title 42, 42 U.S.C.A. § 1301 et seq.

Title XVIII of such Act, referred to in subsec. (b)(28), means title XVIII of the Social Security Act, Act Aug. 14, 1935, c. 531, Title XVIII, § 1801 et seq., as added July 30, 1965, Pub.L. 89–97, Title I, § 102(a), 79 Stat. 291, and amended, which is classified principally to subchapter XVIII of chapter 7 of Title 42, 42 U.S.C.A. § 1395 et seq.

Codifications

Renumbering and conforming amendments by Pub.L. 101–508 failed to take into consideration prior renumbering and conforming amendments by Pub.L. 101–311, thereby resulting in two pars. numbered "(14)". To accommodate such duplication, the renumbering reflects changes by Pub.L. 101–311 set out first, and by Pub.L. 101–508 set out second, but does not reflect the minor conforming amendments.

Amendments

2010 Amendments. Subsec. (a)(8). Pub.L. 111–327, § 2(a)(12)(A), struck out "concerning a corporate debtor's tax liability" and inserted "concerning a tax liability of a debtor that is a corporation".

Subsec. (c)(3). Pub.L. 111–327, § 2(a)(12)(B)(i), inserted "a" following "against".

Subsec. (c)(4)(A)(i). Pub.L. 111–327, § 2(a)(12)(B)(ii), inserted "under a chapter other than chapter 7 after dismissal" following "refiled".

Subsec. (d)(4). Pub.L. 111–327, § 2(a)(12)(C), struck out "hinder, and" and inserted "hinder, or".

Subsec. (l)(2). Pub.L. 111–327, § 2(a)(12)(D), struck out "nonbankrupcty" and inserted "nonbankruptcy".

2006 Amendments. Subsec. (b)(6). Pub.L. 109–390, § 5(a)(2)(A), rewrote par. (6), which formerly read: "**(6)** under subsection (a) of this section, of the setoff by a commodity broker, forward contract merchant, stockbroker, financial institution, financial participant, or securities clearing agency of any mutual debt and claim under or in connection with commodity contracts, as defined in section 761 of this title, forward contracts, or securities contracts, as defined in section 741 of this title, that constitutes the setoff of a claim against the debtor for a margin payment, as defined in section 101, 741, or 761 of this title, or settlement payment, as defined in section 101 or 741 of this title, arising out of commodity contracts, forward contracts, or securities contracts against cash, securities, or other property held by, pledged to, under the control of, or due from such commodity broker, forward contract merchant, stockbroker, financial institution, financial participant, or securities clearing agency to margin, guarantee, secure, or settle commodity contracts, forward contracts, or securities contracts;".

Subsec. (b)(7). Pub.L. 109–390, § 5(a)(2)(A), rewrote par. (7), which formerly read: "**(7)** under subsection (a) of this section, of the setoff by a repo participant or financial participant, of any mutual debt and claim under or in connection with repurchase agreements that constitutes the setoff of a claim against the debtor for a margin payment, as defined in section 741 or 761 of this title, or settlement payment, as defined in section 741 of this title, arising out of repurchase agreements against cash, securities, or other property held by, pledged to, under the control of, or due from such repo participant or financial participant to margin, guarantee, secure or settle repurchase agreements;".

Subsec. (b)(12). Pub.L. 109–304, § 17(b)(1)(A), struck out "section 207 or title XI of the Merchant Marine Act, 1936" and inserted "chapter 537 of title 46 or section 109(h) of title 49".

Subsec. (b)(13). Pub.L. 109–304, § 17(b)(1)(B), struck out "section 207 or title XI of the Merchant Marine Act, 1936" and inserted "chapter 537 of title 46".

Subsec. (b)(17). Pub.L. 109–390, § 5(a)(2)(B), rewrote par. (17),, which formerly read: "**(17)** under subsection (a), of the setoff by a swap participant or financial participant of a mutual debt and claim under or in connection with one or more swap agreements that constitutes the setoff of a claim against the debtor for any payment or other transfer of property due from the debtor under or in connection with any swap agreement against any payment due to the debtor from the swap participant or financial participant under or in connection with any swap agreement or against cash, securities, or other property held by, pledged to, under the control of, or due from such swap participant or financial participant to margin, guarantee, secure, or settle any swap agreement;".

Subsec. (b)(27). Pub.L. 109–390, § 5(a)(2)(C), rewrote par. (27), which formerly read: "**(27)** under subsection (a), of the setoff by a master netting agreement participant of a mutual debt and claim under or in connection with one or more master netting agreements or any contract or agreement subject to such agreements that constitutes the setoff of a claim against the debtor for any payment or other transfer of property due from the debtor under or in connection with such agreements or any contract or agreement subject to such agreements against any payment due to the debtor from such master netting agreement participant under or in connection with such agreements or any contract or agreement subject to such agreements or against cash, securities, or other property held by, pledged to, under the control of, or due from such master netting agreement participant to margin, guarantee, secure, or settle such agreements or any contract or agreement subject to such agreements, to the extent that such participant is eligible to exercise such offset rights under paragraph (6), (7), or (17) for each individual contract covered by the master netting agreement in issue; and".

2005 Amendments. Subsec. (a)(8). Pub.L. 109–8, § 709, struck out "the debtor" and inserted "a corporate debtor's tax liability for a taxable period the bankruptcy court may determine or concerning the tax liability of a debtor who is an individual for a taxable period ending before the date of the order for relief under this title".

Subsec. (b)(2). Pub.L. 109–8, § 214, rewrote par. (2), which formerly read: "under subsection (a) of this section—

"**(A)** of the commencement or continuation of an action or proceeding for—

"**(i)** the establishment of paternity; or

"**(ii)** the establishment or modification of an order for alimony, maintenance, or support; or

"**(B)** of the collection of alimony, maintenance, or support from property that is not property of the estate;".

Subsec. (b)(6). Pub.L. 109–8, § 907(d)(1)(A), inserted ", pledged to, under the control of," after "held by".

Pub.L. 109–8, § 907(o)(1), substituted "financial institution, financial participant," for "financial institutions," each place such term appeared.

Subsec. (b)(7). Pub.L. 109–8, § 907(d)(1)(B), inserted ", pledged to, under the control of," after "held by".

Pub.L. 109–8, § 907(o)(2), inserted "or financial participant" after "repo participant" each place such term appeared.

Subsec. (b)(17). Pub.L. 109–8, § 224(b)(1), struck out "or" at the end of par. (17).

Pub.L. 109–8, § 907(d)(1)(C), rewrote par. (17), which formerly read: "under subsection (a) of this section, of the setoff by a swap participant, of any mutual debt and claim under or in connection with any swap agreement that constitutes the setoff of a claim against the debtor for any payment due from the debtor under or in connection with any swap agreement against any payment due to the debtor from the swap participant under or in connection with any swap agreement or against cash, securities, or other property of the debtor held by or due from such swap participant to guarantee, secure or settle any swap agreement;"

Subsec. (b)(18). Pub.L. 109–8, § 224(b)(2), substituted a semicolon for the period at the end of par. (18).

Pub.L.109–8, § 1225, rewrote par. (18), which formerly read: "under subsection (a) of the creation or perfection of a statutory lien for an ad valorem property tax imposed by the District of Columbia, or a political subdivision of a State, if such tax comes due after the filing of the petition;"

Subsec. (b)(19). Pub.L. 109–8, § 224(b)(3), added par. (19).

Subsec. (b)(20), (21). Pub.L. 109–8, § 303(b), added pars. (20) and (21).

Subsec. (b)(22) to (24). Pub.L. 109–8, § 311(a), added pars. (22) to (24).

Subsec. (b)(25). Pub.L. 109–8, § 401(b), added par. (25).

Subsec. (b)(26). Pub.L. 109–8, § 718, added par. (26).

Subsec. (b)(27). Pub.L. 109–8, § 907(d)(1)(D), added par. (27).

Subsec. (b)(28). Pub.L. 109–8, § 1106, added par. (28).

Subsec. (c). Pub.L. 109–8, § 305(1)(A), in the text preceding par. (1), struck out "(e), and (f)" and inserted "(e), (f), and (h)".

Subsec. (c)(1). Pub.L. 109–8, § 302(1), struck out "and" at the end of par. (1).

Subsec. (c)(2). Pub.L. 109–8, § 302(2), struck out the period at the end of par. (2) and inserted a semicolon.

Subsec. (c)(3), (4). Pub.L. 109–8, § 302(3), added pars. (3) and (4).

Subsec. (d)(2). Pub.L. 109–8, § 303(a)(1), struck out "or" at the end of par. (2).

Subsec. (d)(3). Pub.L. 109–8, § 303(a)(2), struck out the period at the end of par. (3) and inserted "; or".

Pub.L. 109–8, § 444(1), inserted "or 30 days after the court determines that the debtor is subject to this paragraph, whichever is later" after "90-day period".

Subsec. (d)(3)(B). Pub.L. 109–8, § 444(2), rewrote subpar. (B), which formerly read:

"**(B)** the debtor has commenced monthly payments to each creditor whose claim is secured by such real estate (other than a claim secured by a judgment lien or by an unmatured statutory lien), which payments are in an amount equal to interest at a current fair market rate on the value of the creditor's interest in the real estate; or"

Subsec. (d)(4). Pub.L. 109–8, § 303(a)(3), added par. (4) and concluding provisions.

Subsec. (e)(1). Pub.L. 109–8, § 320(1), inserted "(1)" after "(e)".

Subsec. (e)(2). Pub.L. 109–8, § 320(2), added par. (2).

Subsec. (h). Pub.L. 109–8, § 305(1)(B),(C), redesignated former subsec. (h) as subsec. (k), and inserted a new subsec. (h).

Subsec. (i). Pub.L. 109–8, § 106(f), added subsec. (i).

Subsec. (j). Pub.L. 109–8, § 106(f), added subsec. (j).

Subsec. (k). Pub.L. 109–8, § 305(1)(B), redesignated former subsec. (h) as subsec. (k).

Subsec. (k)(1). Pub.L. 109–8, § 441(1)(A), in subsec. (k) as so redesignated, struck out "An" and inserted **"(1)** Except as provided in paragraph (2), an".

Subsec. (k)(2). Pub.L. 109–8, § 441(1)(B), added par. (2).

Subsecs. (l) and (m). Pub.L. 109–8, § 311(b), added subsecs. (l) and (m).

Subsec. (n). Pub.L. 109–8, § 441(2), added subsec. (n).

Subsec. (o). Pub.L. 109–8, § 907(d)(2), inserted subsec. (o).

1998 Amendments. Subsec. (b)(4). Pub.L. 105–277, § 603, rewrote par. (4), which formerly read: "under subsection (a)(1) of this section, of the commencement or continuation of an action or proceeding by a governmental unit to enforce such governmental unit's police or regulatory power;".

Subsec. (b)(5). Pub.L. 105–277, § 603(1), struck out par. (5), which formerly read: "under subsection (a)(2) of this section, of the enforcement of a judgment, other than a money judgment, obtained in an action or proceeding by a governmental unit to enforce such governmental unit's police or regulatory power;".

1994 Amendments. Subsec. (a). Pub.L. 103–394, § 501(d)(7)(A), struck out "(15 U.S.C. 78eee(a)(3))" following "Securities Investor Protection Act of 1970".

Subsec. (b)(2). Pub.L. 103–394, § 304(b), completely revised par. (2). Prior to revision, par. (2) read as follows:

"under subsection (a) of this section, of the collection of alimony, maintenance, or support from property that is not property of the estate;"

Subsec. (b)(3). Pub.L. 103–394, § 204(a), substituted "of any act to perfect, or to maintain or continue the perfection of, an interest in property" for "of any act to perfect an interest in property".

Subsec. (b)(6). Pub.L. 103–394, § 501(b)(2)(A), substituted "section 761" for "section 761(4)", "section 741" for "section 741(7)", "section 101, 741, or 761" for "section 101(34), 741(5), or 761(15)", and "section 101 or 741" for "section 101(35) or 741(8)".

Subsec. (b)(7). Pub.L. 103–394, § 501(b)(2)(B), substituted "section 741 or 761" for "741(5) or 761(15)", and "section 741" for "section 741(8)".

Subsec. (b)(9). Pub.L. 103–394, § 116, designated a portion of former par. (9) as subpar. (B), and added subpars. (A), (C), and (D).

Subsec. (b)(10). Pub.L. 103–394, § 501(d)(7)(B)(ii), struck out "or" following "possession of such property;".

Subsec. (b)(12). Pub.L. 103–394, § 501(d)(7)(B)(iii), substituted "section 31325 of title 46" for "the Ship Mortgage Act, 1920 (46 App. U.S.C. 911 et seq.)", and struck out "(46 App. U.S.C. 1117 and 1271 et seq., respectively)" following "Merchant Marine Act, 1936".

Subsec. (b)(13). Pub.L. 103–394, § 501(d)(7)(B)(iv), substituted "section 31325 of title 46" for "the Ship Mortgage Act, 1920 (46 App. U.S.C. 911 et seq.)", struck out "(46 App. U.S.C. 1117 and 1271 et seq., respectively)" following "Merchant Marine Act, 1936", and struck out "or" following ";".

Subsec. (b)(14). Pub.L. 103–394, § 501(d)(7)(B)(vii)(I), substituted "swap agreement; or" for "swap agreement.".

Pub.L. 103–394, § 501(d)(7)(B)(vii)(II), redesignated former par. (14), relating to setoff by a swap participant of any mutual debt and claim under or in connection with a swap agreement, as par. (17).

Subsec. (b)(15). Pub.L. 103–394, § 501(d)(7)(B)(v), struck out "or" after "educational institution;".

Subsec. (b)(16). Pub.L. 103–394, § 501(d)(7)(B)(vi), substituted "such Act; " for "such Act." and struck out "(20 U.S.C. 1001 et seq.)" following "Higher Education Act of 1965".

Subsec. (b)(17). Pub.L. 103–394, § 501(d)(7)(B)(vii)(II), (III), redesignated former par. (14), relating to setoff by a swap participant of any mutual debt and claim under or in connection with a swap agreement, as par. (17).

Subsec. (b)(18). Pub.L. 103–394, § 401, added par. (18).

Subsec. (b). Pub.L. 103–394, § 501(d)(7)(B)(i), struck out "(15 U.S.C. 78eee(a)(3))" following "Securities Investor Protection Act of 1970".

Subsec. (d)(3). Pub.L. 103–394, § 218(b), added par. (3).

Subsec. (e). Pub.L. 103–394, § 101, substituted "If the hearing under this subsection is a preliminary hearing, then such final hearing shall be concluded not later than thirty days after the conclusion of such preliminary hearing, unless the 30-day period is extended with the consent of the parties in interest or for a specific time which the court finds is required by compelling circumstances.", for "If the hearing under this subsection is a preliminary hearing, then such final hearing shall be commenced not later than thirty days after the conclusion of such preliminary hearing."

1990 Amendments. Subsec. (b)(6). Pub.L. 101–311, § 202, added provisions referring to sections 101(34) and 101(35) of this title.

Subsec. (b)(12). Pub.L. 101—508, §§ 3007(a)(1)(A), 3008, which temporarily directed the striking of "or" after "State law;", could not be executed because of a prior amendment by Pub.L. 101—311. See amendment note for section 102(1) of Pub.L. 101–311, immediately following. See also Effective and Applicability Provisions note under this section.

Pub.L. 101—311, § 102(1), struck out "or" after "State law".

Subsec. (b)(13). Pub.L. 101—508, §§ 3007(a)(1)(B), 3008, which temporarily directed the substitution of a semicolon for a period at end thereof, could not be executed because of a prior amendment by Pub.L. 101—311. See amendment note for section 102(2) of Pub.L. 101–311, immediately following. See also Effective and Applicability Provisions note under this section.

Pub.L. 101—311, § 102(2), substituted "; or" for period at end.

Subsec. (b)(14) to (16). Pub.L. 101—508, §§ 3007(a)(1)(C), 3008, temporarily added pars. (14) to (16). Notwithstanding directory language adding pars. (14) to (16) immediately following par. (13), pars. (14) to (16) were added after par. (14), as added by Pub.L. 101–311, to reflect the probable intent of Congress. See Effective and Applicability Provisions note under this section.

Pub.L. 101—311, § 102(3), added par. (14) relating to the setoff by a swap participant of any mutual debt and claim under or in connection with a swap agreement. Notwithstanding directory language adding par. (14) at end of subsec. (b), par. (14) was added after par.(13) to reflect the probable intent of Congress.

1986 Amendments. Subsec. (b). Pub.L. 99–509, § 5001(a), inserted undesignated provision, following numbered pars., that the provisions of pars. (12) and (13) of this subsection shall apply with respect to any such petition filed on or before December 31, 1989.

Subsec. (b)(6). Pub.L. 99–554, § 283(d)(1), substituted ", financial institutions" for "financial institution," wherever appearing.

Subsec. (b)(9). Pub.L. 99–554, § 283(d)(2), (3), struck out "or" at end of first par. (9) and redesignated as par. (10) the second par. (9) relating to leases of nonresidential property, which was added by section 363(b) of Pub.L. 98–353.

Subsec. (b)(10). Pub.L. 99–554, § 283(d)(3), (4), redesignated par. (9), as added by Pub.L. 98–353, § 363(b), as par. (10), and, in par. (10), as so redesignated, substituted "property; or" for "property.". Former par. (10) was redesignated (11).

Subsec. (b)(11). Pub.L. 99–554, § 283(d)(3), redesignated former par. (10) as (11).

Subsec. (b)(12), (13). Pub.L. 99–509, § 5001(a), added pars. (12) and (13).

Subsec. (c)(2)(C). Pub.L. 99–554, § 257(j), added reference to chapter 12 of this title.

1984 Amendments. Subsec. (a)(1). Pub.L. 98–353, § 441(a)(1), added "action or" after "other".

Subsec. (a)(3). Pub.L. 98–353, § 441(a)(2), added "or to exercise control over property of the estate" after "estate".

Subsec. (b)(3). Pub.L. 98–353, § 441(b)(1), added "or to the extent that such act is accomplished within the period provided under section 547(e)(2)(A) of this title" after "title".

Subsec. (b)(6). Pub.L. 98–353, § 441(b)(2)(A), added "or due from" after "held by".

Pub.L. 98–353, § 441(b)(2)(B), added "Financial institution," after "stockbroker" wherever appearing and substituted "secure, or settle commodity contracts" for "or secure commodity contracts".

Subsec. (b)(7). Pub.L. 98–353, § 392(b), added par. (7). Former par. (7) was redesignated as (8).

Subsec. (b)(8). Pub.L. 98–353, § 392(a), redesignated former par. (7) as (8). Former par. (8) was redesignated as (9).

Pub.L. 98–353, § 441(b)(3)(A), substituted "the" for "said".

Pub.L. 98–353, § 441(b)(3)(B), struck out "or" after "units;".

Subsec. (b)(9). Pub.L. 98–353, § 363(b), added par. (9), relating to leases of nonresidential real property, which resulted in two pars. designated "(9)" in view of renumbering of former par. (8) as (9) by Pub.L. 98–353, § 392(a).

Pub.L. 98–353, § 392(a), redesignated former par. (8) as (9). See note under this section relating to subsec. (b)(8).

Pub.L. 98–353, § 441(b)(4), substituted a semicolon for the period at the end of par. (9).

Subsec. (b)(10). Pub.L. 98–353, § 441(b)(5), added par. (10).

Subsec. (c)(2)(B). Pub.L. 98–353, § 441(c), substituted "or" for "and".

Subsec. (d)(2). Pub.L. 98–353, § 441(d), added "under subsection (a) of this section" after "property".

Subsec. (e). Pub.L. 98–353, § 441(e), added "the conclusion of" after "pending" and substituted "The court shall order such stay continued in effect pending the conclusion of the final hearing under subsection (d) of this section if there is a reasonable likelihood that the party opposing relief from such stay will prevail at the conclusion of such final hearing. If the hearing under this subsection is a preliminary hearing, then such final hearing shall be commenced not later than thirty days after the conclusion of such preliminary hearing." for "If the hearing under this subsection is a preliminary hearing—

"(1) the court shall order such stay so continued if there is a reasonable likelihood that the party opposing relief from such stay will prevail at the final hearing under subsection (d) of this section; and

"(2) such final hearing shall be commenced within thirty days after such preliminary hearing."

Subsec. (f). Pub.L. 98–353, § 441(f), substituted "Upon request of a party in interest, the court, with or" for "The court,".

Subsec. (h). Pub.L. 98–353, § 304, added subsec. (h).

1982 Amendments. Subsec. (a). Pub.L. 97–222, § 3(a), inserted ", or an application filed under section 5(a)(3) of the Securities Investor Protection Act of 1970 (15 U.S.C. 78eee(a)(3))," following "this title" in the provisions preceding par. (1).

Subsec. (b). Pub.L. 97–222, § 3(b), inserted ", or of an application under section 5(a)(3) of the Securities Investor Protection Act of 1970 (15 U.S.C. 78eee(a)(3))," following "this title" in the provisions preceding par. (1).

Subsec. (b)(6). Pub.L. 97–222, § 3(c), substituted provisions that the filing of a bankruptcy petition would not operate as a stay, under subsec. (a) of this section, of the setoff by a commodity broker, forward contract merchant, stockbroker, or securities clearing agency of any mutual debt and claim under or in connection with commodity, forward, or securities contracts that constitutes the setoff of a claim against the debtor for a margin or settlement payment arising out of commodity, forward, or securities contracts against cash, securities, or other property held by any of the above agents to margin, guarantee, or secure commodity, forward, or securities contracts, for provisions that such filing would not operate as a stay under subsection (a)(7) of this section, of the setoff of any mutual debt and claim that are commodity futures contracts, forward commodity contracts, leverage transactions, options, warrants, rights to purchase or sell commodity futures contracts or securities, or options to purchase or sell commodities or securities.

CROSS REFERENCES

Abstention of district court from hearing a proceeding based upon State law as cause of action, provision as not limiting applicability of stay under this section, see 28 USCA § 1334.

Adequate protection in Chapter 12 cases, method of obtaining, see 11 USCA § 1205.

Applicability of this section in Chapter 9 cases, see 11 USCA § 901.

Assessment of taxes against estate, see 11 USCA § 505.

Denial of debtor status to debtor who obtained voluntary dismissal following filing of relief from provisions of this section, see 11 USCA § 109(g).

Effect of this section on subchapter III of Chapter 7, see 11 USCA § 742.

Enforcement of claims against debtor in Chapter 9 cases, automatic stay of, see 11 USCA § 922.

Extension of time, see 11 USCA § 108.

Grain storage facility bankruptcies, expedited determinations, see 11 USCA § 557.

Right of possession of party with security interest in—

Aircraft equipment and vessel, see 11 USCA § 1110.

Rolling stock equipment, see 11 USCA § 1168.

Secretary of Commerce or Transportation as mortgagee, see 46 USCA § 31308.

Setoff, see 11 USCA § 553.

Turnover of property to estate, see 11 USCA § 542.

§ 363. Use, sale, or lease of property

(a) In this section, "cash collateral" means cash, negotiable instruments, documents of title, securities, deposit accounts, or other cash equivalents whenever acquired in which the estate and an entity other than the estate have an interest and includes the proceeds, products, offspring, rents, or profits of property and the fees, charges, accounts or other payments for the use or occupancy of rooms and other public facilities in hotels, motels, or other lodging properties subject to a security interest as provided in section 552(b) of this title, whether existing before or after the commencement of a case under this title.

(b)(1) The trustee, after notice and a hearing, may use, sell, or lease, other than in the ordinary course of business, property of the estate, except that if the debtor in connection with offering a product or a service discloses to an individual a policy prohibiting the transfer of personally identifiable information about individuals to persons that are not affiliated with the debtor and if such policy is in effect on the date of the commencement of the case, then the trustee may not sell or lease personally identifiable information to any person unless—

(A) such sale or such lease is consistent with such policy; or

(B) after appointment of a consumer privacy ombudsman in accordance with section 332, and after notice and a hearing, the court approves such sale or such lease—

(i) giving due consideration to the facts, circumstances, and conditions of such sale or such lease; and

(ii) finding that no showing was made that such sale or such lease would violate applicable nonbankruptcy law.

(2) If notification is required under subsection (a) of section 7A of the Clayton Act in the case of a transaction under this subsection, then—

(A) notwithstanding subsection (a) of such section, the notification required by such subsection to be given by the debtor shall be given by the trustee; and

(B) notwithstanding subsection (b) of such section, the required waiting period shall end on the 15th day after the date of the receipt, by the Federal Trade Commission and the Assistant Attorney General in charge of the Antitrust Division of the Department of Justice, of the notification required under such subsection (a), unless such waiting period is extended—

(i) pursuant to subsection (e)(2) of such section, in the same manner as such subsection (e)(2) applies to a cash tender offer;

(ii) pursuant to subsection (g)(2) of such section; or

(iii) by the court after notice and a hearing.

(c)(1) If the business of the debtor is authorized to be operated under section 721, 1108, 1203, 1204, or 1304 of this title and unless the court orders otherwise, the trustee may enter into transactions, including the sale or lease of property of the estate, in the ordinary course of business, without notice or a hearing, and may use property of the estate in the ordinary course of business without notice or a hearing.

(2) The trustee may not use, sell, or lease cash collateral under paragraph (1) of this subsection unless—

(A) each entity that has an interest in such cash collateral consents; or

(B) the court, after notice and a hearing, authorizes such use, sale, or lease in accordance with the provisions of this section.

(3) Any hearing under paragraph (2)(B) of this subsection may be a preliminary hearing or may be consolidated with a hearing under subsection (e) of this section, but shall be scheduled in accordance with the needs of the debtor. If the hearing under paragraph (2)(B) of this subsection is a preliminary hearing, the court may authorize such use, sale, or lease only if there is a reasonable likelihood that the trustee will prevail at the final hearing under subsection (e) of this section. The court shall act promptly on any request for authorization under paragraph (2)(B) of this subsection.

(4) Except as provided in paragraph (2) of this subsection, the trustee shall segregate and account for any cash collateral in the trustee's possession, custody, or control.

(d) The trustee may use, sell, or lease property under subsection (b) or (c) of this section—

(1) in the case of a debtor that is a corporation or trust that is not a moneyed business, commercial corporation, or trust, only in accordance with nonbankruptcy law applicable to the transfer of property by a debtor that is such a corporation or trust; and

(2) only to the extent not inconsistent with any relief granted under subsection (c), (d), (e), or (f) of section 362.

(e) Notwithstanding any other provision of this section, at any time, on request of an entity that has an interest in property used, sold, or leased, or proposed to be used, sold, or leased, by the trustee, the court, with or without a hearing, shall prohibit or condition such use, sale, or lease as is necessary to provide adequate protection of such interest. This subsection also applies to property that is subject to any unexpired lease of personal property (to the exclusion of such property being subject to an order to grant relief from the stay under section 362).

(f) The trustee may sell property under subsection (b) or (c) of this section free and clear of any interest in such property of an entity other than the estate, only if—

(1) applicable nonbankruptcy law permits sale of such property free and clear of such interest;

(2) such entity consents;

(3) such interest is a lien and the price at which such property is to be sold is greater than the aggregate value of all liens on such property;

(4) such interest is in bona fide dispute; or

(5) such entity could be compelled, in a legal or equitable proceeding, to accept a money satisfaction of such interest.

(g) Notwithstanding subsection (f) of this section, the trustee may sell property under subsection (b) or (c) of this section free and clear of any vested or contingent right in the nature of dower or curtesy.

(h) Notwithstanding subsection (f) of this section, the trustee may sell both the estate's interest, under subsection (b) or (c) of this section, and the interest of any co-owner in property in which the debtor had, at the time of the commencement of the case, an undivided interest as a tenant in common, joint tenant, or tenant by the entirety, only if—

(1) partition in kind of such property among the estate and such co-owners is impracticable;

(2) sale of the estate's undivided interest in such property would realize significantly less for the estate than sale of such property free of the interests of such co-owners;

(3) the benefit to the estate of a sale of such property free of the interests of co-owners outweighs the detriment, if any, to such co-owners; and

(4) such property is not used in the production, transmission, or distribution, for sale, of electric energy or of natural or synthetic gas for heat, light, or power.

(i) Before the consummation of a sale of property to which subsection (g) or (h) of this section applies, or of property of the estate that was community property of the debtor and the debtor's spouse immediately before the commencement of the case, the debtor's spouse, or a co-owner of such property, as the case may be, may purchase such property at the price at which such sale is to be consummated.

(j) After a sale of property to which subsection (g) or (h) of this section applies, the trustee shall distribute to the debtor's spouse or the co-owners of such property, as the case may be, and to the estate, the proceeds of such sale, less the costs and expenses, not including any compensation of the trustee, of such sale, according to the interests of such spouse or co-owners, and of the estate.

(k) At a sale under subsection (b) of this section of property that is subject to a lien that secures an allowed claim, unless the court for cause orders otherwise the holder of such claim may bid at such sale, and, if the holder of such claim purchases such property, such holder may offset such claim against the purchase price of such property.

(l) Subject to the provisions of section 365, the trustee may use, sell, or lease property under subsection (b) or (c) of this section, or a plan under chapter 11, 12, or 13 of this title may provide for the use, sale, or lease of property, notwithstanding any provision in a contract, a lease, or applicable law that is conditioned on the insolvency or financial condition of the debtor, on the commencement of a case under this title concerning the debtor, or on the appointment of or the taking possession by a trustee in a case under this title or a custodian, and that effects, or gives an option to effect, a forfeiture, modification, or termination of the debtor's interest in such property.

(m) The reversal or modification on appeal of an authorization under subsection (b) or (c) of this section of a sale or lease of property does not affect the validity of a sale or lease under such authorization to an entity that purchased or leased such property in good faith, whether or not such entity knew of the pendency of the appeal, unless such authorization and such sale or lease were stayed pending appeal.

(n) The trustee may avoid a sale under this section if the sale price was controlled by an agreement among potential bidders at such sale, or may recover from a party to such agreement any amount by which the value of the property sold exceeds the price at which such sale was consummated, and may recover any costs, attorneys' fees, or expenses incurred in avoiding such sale or recovering such amount. In addition to any recovery under the preceding sentence, the court may grant judgment for punitive damages in favor of the estate and against any such party that entered into such an agreement in willful disregard of this subsection.

(o) Notwithstanding subsection (f), if a person purchases any interest in a consumer credit transaction that is subject to the Truth in Lending Act or any interest in a consumer credit contract (as defined in section 433.1 of title 16 of the Code of Federal Regulations (January 1, 2004), as amended from time to time), and if such interest is purchased through a sale under this section, then such person shall remain subject to all claims and defenses that are related to such consumer credit transaction or such consumer credit contract, to the same extent as such person would be subject to such claims and defenses of the consumer had such interest been purchased at a sale not under this section.

(p) In any hearing under this section—

(1) the trustee has the burden of proof on the issue of adequate protection; and

(2) the entity asserting an interest in property has the burden of proof on the issue of the validity, priority, or extent of such interest.

(Pub.L. 95–598, Nov. 6, 1978, 92 Stat. 2572; Pub.L. 98–353, Title III, § 442, July 10, 1984, 98 Stat. 371; Pub.L. 99–554, Title II, § 257(k), Oct. 27, 1986, 100 Stat. 3115; Pub.L. 103–394, Title I, § 109, Title II, §§ 214(b), 219(c), Title V, § 501(d)(8), Oct. 22, 1994, 108 Stat. 4113, 4126, 4129, 4144; Pub.L. 109–8, Title II, §§ 204, 231(a), Title XII, § 1221(a), Apr. 20, 2005, 119 Stat. 49, 72, 195; Pub.L. 111–327, § 2(a)(13), Dec. 22, 2010, 124 Stat. 3559.)

HISTORICAL AND STATUTORY NOTES

References in Text

Section 7A of the Clayton Act, referred to in subsec. (b)(2), is section 7A of Act Oct. 15, 1914, c. 323, as added Sept. 30, 1976, Pub.L. 94–435, Title II, § 201, 90 Stat. 1390, which is classified to section 18a of Title 15, Commerce and Trade.

The Truth in Lending Act, referred to in subsec. (o), is Title I of Pub.L. 90–321, May 29, 1968, 82 Stat. 146, as amended, also known as TILA, which is classified principally to subchapter I of chapter 41 of Title 15, 15 U.S.C.A. § 1601 et seq. For complete classification, see Short Title note set out under 15 U.S.C.A. § 1601 and Tables.

Amendments

2010 Amendments. Subsec. (d). Pub.L. 111–327, § 2(a)(13)(A), struck out "only" following "of this section".

Subsec. (d)(1). Pub.L. 111–327, § 2(a)(13)(B), rewrote par. (1), which formerly read: "**(1)** in accordance with applicable nonbankruptcy law that governs the transfer of property by a corporation or trust that is not a moneyed, business, or commercial corporation or trust; and".

Subsec. (d)(2). Pub.L. 111–327, § 2(a)(13)(C), inserted "only" after "(2)".

2005 Amendments. Subsec. (b)(1). Pub.L. 109–8, § 231(a), struck out the period at the end and inserted the following:

", except that if the debtor in connection with offering a product or a service discloses to an individual a policy prohibiting the transfer of personally identifiable information about individuals to persons that are not affiliated with the debtor and if such policy is in effect on the date of the commencement of the case, then the trustee may not sell or lease personally identifiable information to any person unless—

"**(A)** such sale or such lease is consistent with such policy; or

"**(B)** after appointment of a consumer privacy ombudsman in accordance with section 332, and after notice and a hearing, the court approves such sale or such lease—

"**(i)** giving due consideration to the facts, circumstances, and conditions of such sale or such lease; and

"**(ii)** finding that no showing was made that such sale or such lease would violate applicable nonbankruptcy law."

Subsec. (d). Pub.L.109–8, § 1221(a), struck out "only to the extent not inconsistent with any relief granted under section 362(c), 362(d), 362(e), or 362(f) of this title" at the end of the subsection and inserted "only—

"**(1)** in accordance with applicable nonbankruptcy law that governs the transfer of property by a corporation or trust that is not a moneyed, business, or commercial corporation or trust; and

"**(2)** to the extent not inconsistent with any relief granted under subsection (c), (d), (e), or (f) of section 362."

Subsec. (o). Pub.L. 109–8, § 204(1), (2), added a new subsec. (o) and redesignated former subsec. (o) as subsec. (p).

Subsec. (p). Pub.L. 109–8, § 204(1), redesignated former subsec. (o) as subsec. (p).

1994 Amendments. Subsec. (a). Pub.L. 103–394, § 214(b), added provisions stating that "cash collateral" includes the fees, charges, accounts or other payments for the use or occupancy of rooms and other public facilities in hotels, motels, or other lodging properties.

Subsec. (b)(2). Pub.L. 103–394, § 501(d)(8)(A), struck out "(15 U.S.C. 18a)" following "section 7A of the Clayton Act".

Subsec. (b)(2)(A), (B). Pub.L. 103–394, § 109, completely revised subpars. (A) and (B). Prior to revision, subpars. (A) and (B) read as follows:

"**(A)** notwithstanding subsection (a) of such section, such notification shall be given by the trustee; and

"(B) notwithstanding subsection (b) of such section, the required waiting period shall end on the tenth day after the date of the receipt of such notification, unless the court, after notice and hearing, orders otherwise."

Subsec. (c)(1). Pub.L. 103–394, § 501(d)(8)(B), substituted "1203, 1204, or 1304" for "1304, 1203, or 1204".

Subsec. (e). Pub.L. 103–394, § 219(c), added sentence directing that subsec. (e) applies to property that is subject to any unexpired lease of personal property.

1986 Amendments. Subsec. (c)(1). Pub.L. 99–554, § 257(k)(1), added reference to sections 1203 and 1204 of this title.

Subsec. (l). Pub.L. 99–554, § 257(k)(2), added reference to chapter 12.

1984 Amendments. Subsec. (a). Pub.L. 98–353, § 442(a), added "whenever acquired" after "equivalents" and added "and includes the proceeds, products, offspring, rents, or profits of property subject to a security interest as provided in section 552(b) of this title, whether existing before or after the commencement of a case under this title" after "interest".

Subsec. (b). Pub.L. 98–353, § 442(b), designated existing provisions as par. (1) and added par. (2).

Subsec. (e). Pub.L. 98–353, § 442(c), added ", with or without a hearing," after "court" and struck out "In any hearing under this section, the trustee has the burden of proof on the issue of adequate protection".

Subsec. (f)(3). Pub.L. 98–353, § 442(d), substituted "all liens on such property" for "such interest".

Subsec. (h). Pub.L. 98–353, § 442(e), substituted "at the time of" for "immediately before".

Subsec. (j). Pub.L. 98–353, § 442(f), substituted "compensation" for "compenation".

Subsec. (k). Pub.L. 98–353, § 442(g), substituted "unless the court for cause orders otherwise the holder of such claim may bid at such sale, and, if the holder" for "if the holder".

Subsec. (l). Pub.L. 98–353, § 442(h), substituted "Subject to the provisions of section 365, the trustee" for "The trustee", "condition" for "conditions", "or the taking" for "a taking", and "interest" for "interests".

Subsec. (n). Pub.L. 98–353, § 442(i), substituted "avoid" for "void", "avoiding" for "voiding", and "In addition to any recovery under the preceding sentence, the court may grant judgment for punitive damages in favor of the estate and against any such party that entered into such an agreement in willful disregard of this subsection." for "The court may grant judgment in favor of the estate and against any such party that entered into such agreement in willful disregard of this subsection for punitive damages in addition to any recovery under the preceding sentence.".

Subsec. (o). Pub.L. 98–353, § 442(j), added subsec. (o).

CROSS REFERENCES

Adequate protection in chapter 12 cases, method of obtaining, see 11 USCA § 1205.

Adverse interest and conduct of officers of estate, see 18 USCA § 154.

Confirmation of plan, see 11 USCA § 1129.

Continuity of business operation and use, acquisition or disposition of property by debtor, see 11 USCA § 303.

Grain storage facility bankruptcies, expedited determinations, see 11 USCA § 557.

Identical rights and powers of debtor in Chapter 13 cases, see 11 USCA § 1303.

Postpetition effect of security interest, see 11 USCA § 552.

Priorities, see 11 USCA § 507.

Property of estate, see 11 USCA § 541.

Right of possession of party with security interest in—

    Aircraft equipment and vessels, see 11 USCA § 1110.

Rolling stock equipment, see 11 USCA § 1168.

Rights and powers of debtor engaged in business, see 11 USCA § 1304.

Sale of property as affecting allowance of claim secured by lien on property of estate, see 11 USCA § 1111.

Sales free of interests, see 11 USCA § 1206.

Setoff, see 11 USCA § 553.

Turnover of property to estate, see 11 USCA § 542.

§ 364. Obtaining credit

(a) If the trustee is authorized to operate the business of the debtor under section 721, 1108, 1203, 1204, or 1304 of this title, unless the court orders otherwise, the trustee may obtain unsecured credit and incur unsecured debt in the ordinary course of business allowable under section 503(b)(1) of this title as an administrative expense.

(b) The court, after notice and a hearing, may authorize the trustee to obtain unsecured credit or to incur unsecured debt other than under subsection (a) of this section, allowable under section 503(b)(1) of this title as an administrative expense.

(c) If the trustee is unable to obtain unsecured credit allowable under section 503(b)(1) of this title as an administrative expense, the court, after notice and a hearing, may authorize the obtaining of credit or the incurring of debt—

(1) with priority over any or all administrative expenses of the kind specified in section 503(b) or 507(b) of this title;

(2) secured by a lien on property of the estate that is not otherwise subject to a lien; or

(3) secured by a junior lien on property of the estate that is subject to a lien.

(d)(1) The court, after notice and a hearing, may authorize the obtaining of credit or the incurring of debt secured by a senior or equal lien on property of the estate that is subject to a lien only if—

(A) the trustee is unable to obtain such credit otherwise; and

(B) there is adequate protection of the interest of the holder of the lien on the property of the estate on which such senior or equal lien is proposed to be granted.

(2) In any hearing under this subsection, the trustee has the burden of proof on the issue of adequate protection.

(e) The reversal or modification on appeal of an authorization under this section to obtain credit or incur debt, or of a grant under this section of a priority or a lien, does not affect the validity of any debt so incurred, or any priority or lien so granted, to an entity that extended such credit in good faith, whether or not such entity knew of the pendency of the appeal, unless such authorization and the incurring of such debt, or the granting of such priority or lien, were stayed pending appeal.

(f) Except with respect to an entity that is an underwriter as defined in section 1145(b) of this title, section 5 of the Securities Act of 1933, the Trust Indenture Act of 1939, and any State or local law requiring registration for offer or sale of a security or registration or licensing of an issuer of, underwriter of, or broker or dealer in, a security does not apply to the offer or sale under this section of a security that is not an equity security.

(Pub.L. 95–598, Nov. 6, 1978, 92 Stat. 2574; Pub.L. 99–554, Title II, § 257(l), Oct. 27, 1986, 100 Stat. 3115; Pub.L. 103–394, Title V, § 501(d)(9), Oct. 22, 1994, 108 Stat. 4144.)

HISTORICAL AND STATUTORY NOTES

References in Text

Section 5 of the Securities Act of 1933, referred to in subsec. (f), is section 5 of Act May 27, 1933, c. 38, Title I, 48 Stat. 77, which is classified to section 77e of Title 15, Commerce and Trade.

The Trust Indenture Act of 1939, referred to in subsec. (f), is Title III of Act May 27, 1933, c. 38, as added Aug. 3, 1939, c. 411, 53 Stat. 1149, as amended, which is classified generally to subchapter III (§ 77aaa et seq.) of chapter 2A of Title 15, Commerce and Trade. For complete classification of this Act to the Code, see section 77aaa of Title 15 and Tables.

Amendments

1994 Amendments. Subsec. (a). Pub.L. 103–394, § 501(d)(9)(A), substituted "1203, 1204, or 1304" for "1304, 1203, or 1204".

Subsec. (f). Pub.L. 103–394, § 501(d)(9)(B), struck out "(15 U.S.C. 77e)" following "Securities Act of 1933", and struck out "(15 U.S.C. 77aaa et seq.)" following "Trust Indenture Act of 1939".

1986 Amendments. Subsec. (a). Pub.L. 99–554 added reference to sections 1203 and 1204 of this title.

CROSS REFERENCES

Adequate protection in Chapter 12 cases, method of obtaining, see 11 USCA § 1205.

Applicability of subsecs. (c) to (f) of this section in Chapter 9 cases, see 11 USCA § 901.

Enforcement of claims against debtor in Chapter 9 cases, automatic stay of, see 11 USCA § 922.

Priorities, see 11 USCA § 507.

Reversal on appeal of finding of jurisdiction as affecting validity of debt incurred, see 11 USCA § 921.

Rights and powers of debtor engaged in business, see 11 USCA § 1304.

§ 365. Executory contracts and unexpired leases

(a) Except as provided in sections 765 and 766 of this title and in subsections (b), (c), and (d) of this section, the trustee, subject to the court's approval, may assume or reject any executory contract or unexpired lease of the debtor.

(b)(1) If there has been a default in an executory contract or unexpired lease of the debtor, the trustee may not assume such contract or lease unless, at the time of assumption of such contract or lease, the trustee—

(A) cures, or provides adequate assurance that the trustee will promptly cure, such default other than a default that is a breach of a provision relating to the satisfaction of any provision (other than a penalty rate or penalty provision) relating to a default arising from any failure to perform nonmonetary obligations under an unexpired lease of real property, if it is impossible for the trustee to cure such default by performing nonmonetary acts at and after the time of assumption, except that if such default arises from a failure to operate in accordance with a nonresidential real property lease, then such default shall be cured by performance at and after the time of assumption in accordance with such lease, and pecuniary losses resulting from such default shall be compensated in accordance with the provisions of this paragraph;

(B) compensates, or provides adequate assurance that the trustee will promptly compensate, a party other than the debtor to such contract or lease, for any actual pecuniary loss to such party resulting from such default; and

(C) provides adequate assurance of future performance under such contract or lease.

(2) Paragraph (1) of this subsection does not apply to a default that is a breach of a provision relating to—

Title 11   CASE ADMINISTRATION   11 § 365

(A) the insolvency or financial condition of the debtor at any time before the closing of the case;

(B) the commencement of a case under this title;

(C) the appointment of or taking possession by a trustee in a case under this title or a custodian before such commencement; or

(D) the satisfaction of any penalty rate or penalty provision relating to a default arising from any failure by the debtor to perform nonmonetary obligations under the executory contract or unexpired lease.

(3) For the purposes of paragraph (1) of this subsection and paragraph (2)(B) of subsection (f), adequate assurance of future performance of a lease of real property in a shopping center includes adequate assurance—

(A) of the source of rent and other consideration due under such lease, and in the case of an assignment, that the financial condition and operating performance of the proposed assignee and its guarantors, if any, shall be similar to the financial condition and operating performance of the debtor and its guarantors, if any, as of the time the debtor became the lessee under the lease;

(B) that any percentage rent due under such lease will not decline substantially;

(C) that assumption or assignment of such lease is subject to all the provisions thereof, including (but not limited to) provisions such as a radius, location, use, or exclusivity provision, and will not breach any such provision contained in any other lease, financing agreement, or master agreement relating to such shopping center; and

(D) that assumption or assignment of such lease will not disrupt any tenant mix or balance in such shopping center.

(4) Notwithstanding any other provision of this section, if there has been a default in an unexpired lease of the debtor, other than a default of a kind specified in paragraph (2) of this subsection, the trustee may not require a lessor to provide services or supplies incidental to such lease before assumption of such lease unless the lessor is compensated under the terms of such lease for any services and supplies provided under such lease before assumption of such lease.

(c) The trustee may not assume or assign any executory contract or unexpired lease of the debtor, whether or not such contract or lease prohibits or restricts assignment of rights or delegation of duties, if—

(1)(A) applicable law excuses a party, other than the debtor, to such contract or lease from accepting performance from or rendering performance to an entity other than the debtor or the debtor in possession, whether or not such contract or lease prohibits or restricts assignment of rights or delegation of duties; and

(B) such party does not consent to such assumption or assignment; or

(2) such contract is a contract to make a loan, or extend other debt financing or financial accommodations, to or for the benefit of the debtor, or to issue a security of the debtor; or

(3) such lease is of nonresidential real property and has been terminated under applicable nonbankruptcy law prior to the order for relief.

[(4) Repealed. Pub.L. 109–8, Title III, § 328(a)(2)(C), Apr. 20, 2005, 119 Stat. 100]

(d)(1) In a case under chapter 7 of this title, if the trustee does not assume or reject an executory contract or unexpired lease of residential real property or of personal property of the debtor within 60 days after the order for relief, or within such additional time as the court, for cause, within such 60-day period, fixes, then such contract or lease is deemed rejected.

(2) In a case under chapter 9, 11, 12, or 13 of this title, the trustee may assume or reject an executory contract or unexpired lease of residential real property or of personal property of the debtor at any time before the confirmation of a plan but the court, on the request of any party to

such contract or lease, may order the trustee to determine within a specified period of time whether to assume or reject such contract or lease.

(3) The trustee shall timely perform all the obligations of the debtor, except those specified in section 365(b)(2), arising from and after the order for relief under any unexpired lease of nonresidential real property, until such lease is assumed or rejected, notwithstanding section 503(b)(1) of this title. The court may extend, for cause, the time for performance of any such obligation that arises within 60 days after the date of the order for relief, but the time for performance shall not be extended beyond such 60-day period. This subsection shall not be deemed to affect the trustee's obligations under the provisions of subsection (b) or (f) of this section. Acceptance of any such performance does not constitute waiver or relinquishment of the lessor's rights under such lease or under this title.

(4)(A) Subject to subparagraph (B), an unexpired lease of nonresidential real property under which the debtor is the lessee shall be deemed rejected, and the trustee shall immediately surrender that nonresidential real property to the lessor, if the trustee does not assume or reject the unexpired lease by the earlier of—

 (i) the date that is 120 days after the date of the order for relief; or

 (ii) the date of the entry of an order confirming a plan.

(B)(i) The court may extend the period determined under subparagraph (A), prior to the expiration of the 120-day period, for 90 days on the motion of the trustee or lessor for cause.

 (ii) If the court grants an extension under clause (i), the court may grant a subsequent extension only upon prior written consent of the lessor in each instance.

(5) The trustee shall timely perform all of the obligations of the debtor, except those specified in section 365(b)(2), first arising from or after 60 days after the order for relief in a case under chapter 11 of this title under an unexpired lease of personal property (other than personal property leased to an individual primarily for personal, family, or household purposes), until such lease is assumed or rejected notwithstanding section 503(b)(1) of this title, unless the court, after notice and a hearing and based on the equities of the case, orders otherwise with respect to the obligations or timely performance thereof. This subsection shall not be deemed to affect the trustee's obligations under the provisions of subsection (b) or (f). Acceptance of any such performance does not constitute waiver or relinquishment of the lessor's rights under such lease or under this title.

[(6) to (9)] Repealed. Pub.L. 109–8, Title III, § 328(a)(3)(A), Apr. 20, 2005, 119 Stat. 100]

[(10) Redesignated (5)]

(e)(1) Notwithstanding a provision in an executory contract or unexpired lease, or in applicable law, an executory contract or unexpired lease of the debtor may not be terminated or modified, and any right or obligation under such contract or lease may not be terminated or modified, at any time after the commencement of the case solely because of a provision in such contract or lease that is conditioned on—

 (A) the insolvency or financial condition of the debtor at any time before the closing of the case;

 (B) the commencement of a case under this title; or

 (C) the appointment of or taking possession by a trustee in a case under this title or a custodian before such commencement.

(2) Paragraph (1) of this subsection does not apply to an executory contract or unexpired lease of the debtor, whether or not such contract or lease prohibits or restricts assignment of rights or delegation of duties, if—

 (A)(i) applicable law excuses a party, other than the debtor, to such contract or lease from accepting performance from or rendering performance to the trustee or to an assignee of such contract or lease, whether or not such contract or lease prohibits or restricts assignment of rights or delegation of duties; and

 (ii) such party does not consent to such assumption or assignment; or

(B) such contract is a contract to make a loan, or extend other debt financing or financial accommodations, to or for the benefit of the debtor, or to issue a security of the debtor.

(f)(1) Except as provided in subsections (b) and (c) of this section, notwithstanding a provision in an executory contract or unexpired lease of the debtor, or in applicable law, that prohibits, restricts, or conditions the assignment of such contract or lease, the trustee may assign such contract or lease under paragraph (2) of this subsection.

(2) The trustee may assign an executory contract or unexpired lease of the debtor only if—

(A) the trustee assumes such contract or lease in accordance with the provisions of this section; and

(B) adequate assurance of future performance by the assignee of such contract or lease is provided, whether or not there has been a default in such contract or lease.

(3) Notwithstanding a provision in an executory contract or unexpired lease of the debtor, or in applicable law that terminates or modifies, or permits a party other than the debtor to terminate or modify, such contract or lease or a right or obligation under such contract or lease on account of an assignment of such contract or lease, such contract, lease, right, or obligation may not be terminated or modified under such provision because of the assumption or assignment of such contract or lease by the trustee.

(g) Except as provided in subsections (h)(2) and (i)(2) of this section, the rejection of an executory contract or unexpired lease of the debtor constitutes a breach of such contract or lease—

(1) if such contract or lease has not been assumed under this section or under a plan confirmed under chapter 9, 11, 12, or 13 of this title, immediately before the date of the filing of the petition; or

(2) if such contract or lease has been assumed under this section or under a plan confirmed under chapter 9, 11, 12, or 13 of this title—

(A) if before such rejection the case has not been converted under section 1112, 1208, or 1307 of this title, at the time of such rejection; or

(B) if before such rejection the case has been converted under section 1112, 1208, or 1307 of this title—

(i) immediately before the date of such conversion, if such contract or lease was assumed before such conversion; or

(ii) at the time of such rejection, if such contract or lease was assumed after such conversion.

(h)(1)(A) If the trustee rejects an unexpired lease of real property under which the debtor is the lessor and—

(i) if the rejection by the trustee amounts to such a breach as would entitle the lessee to treat such lease as terminated by virtue of its terms, applicable nonbankruptcy law, or any agreement made by the lessee, then the lessee under such lease may treat such lease as terminated by the rejection; or

(ii) if the term of such lease has commenced, the lessee may retain its rights under such lease (including rights such as those relating to the amount and timing of payment of rent and other amounts payable by the lessee and any right of use, possession, quiet enjoyment, subletting, assignment, or hypothecation) that are in or appurtenant to the real property for the balance of the term of such lease and for any renewal or extension of such rights to the extent that such rights are enforceable under applicable nonbankruptcy law.

(B) If the lessee retains its rights under subparagraph (A)(ii), the lessee may offset against the rent reserved under such lease for the balance of the term after the date of the rejection of such lease and for the term of any renewal or extension of such lease, the value of any damage caused by the nonperformance after the date of such rejection, of any obligation of the debtor under such lease, but the lessee shall not have any other right against the estate or the debtor on account of any damage occurring after such date caused by such nonperformance.

(C) The rejection of a lease of real property in a shopping center with respect to which the lessee elects to retain its rights under subparagraph (A)(ii) does not affect the enforceability under applicable nonbankruptcy law of any provision in the lease pertaining to radius, location, use, exclusivity, or tenant mix or balance.

(D) In this paragraph, "lessee" includes any successor, assign, or mortgagee permitted under the terms of such lease.

(2)(A) If the trustee rejects a timeshare interest under a timeshare plan under which the debtor is the timeshare interest seller and—

(i) if the rejection amounts to such a breach as would entitle the timeshare interest purchaser to treat the timeshare plan as terminated under its terms, applicable nonbankruptcy law, or any agreement made by timeshare interest purchaser, the timeshare interest purchaser under the timeshare plan may treat the timeshare plan as terminated by such rejection; or

(ii) if the term of such timeshare interest has commenced, then the timeshare interest purchaser may retain its rights in such timeshare interest for the balance of such term and for any term of renewal or extension of such timeshare interest to the extent that such rights are enforceable under applicable nonbankruptcy law.

(B) If the timeshare interest purchaser retains its rights under subparagraph (A), such timeshare interest purchaser may offset against the moneys due for such timeshare interest for the balance of the term after the date of the rejection of such timeshare interest, and the term of any renewal or extension of such timeshare interest, the value of any damage caused by the nonperformance after the date of such rejection, of any obligation of the debtor under such timeshare plan, but the timeshare interest purchaser shall not have any right against the estate or the debtor on account of any damage occurring after such date caused by such nonperformance.

(i)(1) If the trustee rejects an executory contract of the debtor for the sale of real property or for the sale of a timeshare interest under a timeshare plan, under which the purchaser is in possession, such purchaser may treat such contract as terminated, or, in the alternative, may remain in possession of such real property or timeshare interest.

(2) If such purchaser remains in possession—

(A) such purchaser shall continue to make all payments due under such contract, but may,[1] offset against such payments any damages occurring after the date of the rejection of such contract caused by the nonperformance of any obligation of the debtor after such date, but such purchaser does not have any rights against the estate on account of any damages arising after such date from such rejection, other than such offset; and

(B) the trustee shall deliver title to such purchaser in accordance with the provisions of such contract, but is relieved of all other obligations to perform under such contract.

(j) A purchaser that treats an executory contract as terminated under subsection (i) of this section, or a party whose executory contract to purchase real property from the debtor is rejected and under which such party is not in possession, has a lien on the interest of the debtor in such property for the recovery of any portion of the purchase price that such purchaser or party has paid.

(k) Assignment by the trustee to an entity of a contract or lease assumed under this section relieves the trustee and the estate from any liability for any breach of such contract or lease occurring after such assignment.

(l) If an unexpired lease under which the debtor is the lessee is assigned pursuant to this section, the lessor of the property may require a deposit or other security for the performance of the debtor's obligations under the lease substantially the same as would have been required by the landlord upon the initial leasing to a similar tenant.

(m) For purposes of this section 365 and sections 541(b)(2) and 362(b)(10), leases of real property shall include any rental agreement to use real property.

---

[1] So in orginal. The comma probably should not appear.

(n)(1) If the trustee rejects an executory contract under which the debtor is a licensor of a right to intellectual property, the licensee under such contract may elect—

   (A) to treat such contract as terminated by such rejection if such rejection by the trustee amounts to such a breach as would entitle the licensee to treat such contract as terminated by virtue of its own terms, applicable nonbankruptcy law, or an agreement made by the licensee with another entity; or

   (B) to retain its rights (including a right to enforce any exclusivity provision of such contract, but excluding any other right under applicable nonbankruptcy law to specific performance of such contract) under such contract and under any agreement supplementary to such contract, to such intellectual property (including any embodiment of such intellectual property to the extent protected by applicable nonbankruptcy law), as such rights existed immediately before the case commenced, for—

      (i) the duration of such contract; and

      (ii) any period for which such contract may be extended by the licensee as of right under applicable nonbankruptcy law.

(2) If the licensee elects to retain its rights, as described in paragraph (1)(B) of this subsection, under such contract—

   (A) the trustee shall allow the licensee to exercise such rights;

   (B) the licensee shall make all royalty payments due under such contract for the duration of such contract and for any period described in paragraph (1)(B) of this subsection for which the licensee extends such contract; and

   (C) the licensee shall be deemed to waive—

      (i) any right of setoff it may have with respect to such contract under this title or applicable nonbankruptcy law; and

      (ii) any claim allowable under section 503(b) of this title arising from the performance of such contract.

(3) If the licensee elects to retain its rights, as described in paragraph (1)(B) of this subsection, then on the written request of the licensee the trustee shall—

   (A) to the extent provided in such contract, or any agreement supplementary to such contract, provide to the licensee any intellectual property (including such embodiment) held by the trustee; and

   (B) not interfere with the rights of the licensee as provided in such contract, or any agreement supplementary to such contract, to such intellectual property (including such embodiment) including any right to obtain such intellectual property (or such embodiment) from another entity.

(4) Unless and until the trustee rejects such contract, on the written request of the licensee the trustee shall—

   (A) to the extent provided in such contract or any agreement supplementary to such contract—

      (i) perform such contract; or

      (ii) provide to the licensee such intellectual property (including any embodiment of such intellectual property to the extent protected by applicable nonbankruptcy law) held by the trustee; and

   (B) not interfere with the rights of the licensee as provided in such contract, or any agreement supplementary to such contract, to such intellectual property (including such embodiment), including any right to obtain such intellectual property (or such embodiment) from another entity.

(o) In a case under chapter 11 of this title, the trustee shall be deemed to have assumed (consistent with the debtor's other obligations under section 507), and shall immediately cure any deficit under, any commitment by the debtor to a Federal depository institutions regulatory agency (or predecessor to such agency) to maintain the capital of an insured depository institution, and any claim for a subsequent breach of the obligations thereunder shall be entitled to priority under section 507. This subsection shall not extend any commitment that would otherwise be terminated by any act of such an agency.

(p)(1) If a lease of personal property is rejected or not timely assumed by the trustee under subsection (d), the leased property is no longer property of the estate and the stay under section 362(a) is automatically terminated.

(2)(A) If the debtor in a case under chapter 7 is an individual, the debtor may notify the creditor in writing that the debtor desires to assume the lease. Upon being so notified, the creditor may, at its option, notify the debtor that it is willing to have the lease assumed by the debtor and may condition such assumption on cure of any outstanding default on terms set by the contract.

(B) If, not later than 30 days after notice is provided under subparagraph (A), the debtor notifies the lessor in writing that the lease is assumed, the liability under the lease will be assumed by the debtor and not by the estate.

(C) The stay under section 362 and the injunction under section 524(a) (2) shall not be violated by notification of the debtor and negotiation of cure under this subsection.

(3) In a case under chapter 11 in which the debtor is an individual and in a case under chapter 13, if the debtor is the lessee with respect to personal property and the lease is not assumed in the plan confirmed by the court, the lease is deemed rejected as of the conclusion of the hearing on confirmation. If the lease is rejected, the stay under section 362 and any stay under section 1301 is automatically terminated with respect to the property subject to the lease.

(Pub.L. 95–598, Nov. 6, 1978, 92 Stat. 2574; Pub.L. 98–353, Title III, §§ 362, 402–404, July 10, 1984, 98 Stat. 361, 367; Pub.L. 99–554, Title II, §§ 257(j), (m), 283(e), Oct. 27, 1986, 100 Stat. 3115, 3117; Pub.L. 100–506, § 1(b), Oct. 18, 1988, 102 Stat. 2538; Pub.L. 101–647, Title XXV, § 2522(c), Nov. 29, 1990, 104 Stat. 4866; Pub.L. 102–365, § 19(b)–(e), Sept. 3, 1992, 106 Stat. 982–984; Pub.L. 103–394, Title II, §§ 205(a), 219(a), (b), Title V, § 501(d)(10), Oct. 22, 1994, 108 Stat. 4122, 4128, 4145; Pub.L. 103–429, § 1, Oct. 31, 1994, 108 Stat. 4377; Pub.L. 109–8, Title III, §§ 309(b), 328(a), Title IV, § 404, Apr. 20, 2005, 119 Stat. 82, 100, 104.)

HISTORICAL AND STATUTORY NOTES

Codifications

Amendment to subsec. (c)(1)(A) by Pub.L. 99–554, § 283(e)(1)(1), struck out "or an assignee of such contract or lease" as the probable intent of Congress, notwithstanding directory language requiring "or and assignee of such contract or lease" be struck out.

Amendment by section 501(d)(10)(A) of Pub.L. 103–394, purporting to amend subsec. (d)(6)(C) of this section by substituting "section 40102 of title 49" for "the Federal Aviation Act of 1958 (49 U.S.C. 1301)", could not be executed, as the latter phrase did not appear in text.

Amendment by section 1(2) of Pub.L. 103–429, purporting to amend subsec. (p) of this section by substituting "section 40102(a) of title 49" for "section 101(3) of the Federal Aviation Act of 1958", could not be executed, as subsec. (p) had already been stricken out pursuant to section 510(d)(10)(E) of Pub.L. 103–394.

Amendments

2005 Amendments. Subsec. (b)(1)(A). Pub.L. 109–8, § 328(a)(1)(A), struck out the semicolon at the end of subpar. (A) and inserted the following: "other than a default that is a breach of a provision relating to the satisfaction of any provision (other than a penalty rate or penalty provision) relating to a default arising from any failure to perform nonmonetary obligations under an unexpired lease of real property, if it is impossible for the trustee to cure such default by performing nonmonetary acts at and after the time of assumption, except that if such default arises from a failure to operate in accordance with a nonresidential real property lease, then such default shall be cured by performance at and after the time of assumption in accordance with such lease, and pecuniary losses resulting from such default shall be compensated in accordance with the provisions of this paragraph;".

Subsec. (b)(2)(D). Pub.L. 109–8, § 328(a)(1)(B), struck out "penalty rate or provision" and inserted "penalty rate or penalty provision".

Subsec. (c)(2). Pub.L. 109–8, § 328(a)(2)(A), inserted "or" at the end of par. (2).

Subsec. (c)(3). Pub.L. 109–8, § 328(a)(2)(B), struck out "; or" at the end of par. (3) and inserted a period.

Subsec. (c)(4). Pub.L. 109–8, § 328(a)(2)(C), struck out par. (4), which formerly read:

"(4) such lease is of nonresidential real property under which the debtor is the lessee of an aircraft terminal or aircraft gate at an airport at which the debtor is the lessee under one or more additional nonresidential leases of an aircraft terminal or aircraft gate and the trustee, in connection with such assumption or assignment, does not assume all such leases or does not assume and assign all of such leases to the same person, except that the trustee may assume or assign less than all of such leases with the airport operator's written consent."

Subsec. (d)(4). Pub.L. 109–8, § 404(a), rewrote par. (4), which formerly read:

"(4) Notwithstanding paragraphs (1) and (2), in a case under any chapter of this title, if the trustee does not assume or reject an unexpired lease of nonresidential real property under which the debtor is the lessee within 60 days after the date of the order for relief, or within such additional time as the court, for cause, within such 60-day period, fixes, then such lease is deemed rejected, and the trustee shall immediately surrender such nonresidential real property to the lessor."

Subsec. (d)(5). Pub.L. 109–8, § 328(a)(3), struck out par. (5) and redesignated par. (10) as par. (5). Prior to striking, par. (5) formerly read:

"(5) Notwithstanding paragraphs (1) and (4) of this subsection, in a case under any chapter of this title, if the trustee does not assume or reject an unexpired lease of nonresidential real property under which the debtor is an affected air carrier that is the lessee of an aircraft terminal or aircraft gate before the occurrence of a termination event, then (unless the court orders the trustee to assume such unexpired leases within 5 days after the termination event), at the option of the airport operator, such lease is deemed rejected 5 days after the occurrence of a termination event and the trustee shall immediately surrender possession of the premises to the airport operator; except that the lease shall not be deemed to be rejected unless the airport operator first waives the right to damages related to the rejection. In the event that the lease is deemed to be rejected under this paragraph, the airport operator shall provide the affected air carrier adequate opportunity after the surrender of the premises to remove the fixtures and equipment installed by the affected air carrier."

Subsec. (d)(6). Pub.L. 109–8, § 328(a)(3)(A), struck out par. (6), which formerly read:

"(6) For the purpose of paragraph (5) of this subsection and paragraph (f)(1) of this section, the occurrence of a termination event means, with respect to a debtor which is an affected air carrier that is the lessee of an aircraft terminal or aircraft gate—

"(A) the entry under section 301 or 302 of this title of an order for relief under chapter 7 of this title;

"(B) the conversion of a case under any chapter of this title to a case under chapter 7 of this title; or

"(C) the granting of relief from the stay provided under section 362(a) of this title with respect to aircraft, aircraft engines, propellers, appliances, or spare parts, as defined in section 40102(a) of title 49, except for property of the debtor found by the court not to be necessary to an effective reorganization."

Subsec. (d)(7). Pub.L. 109–8, § 328(a)(3)(A), struck out par. (7), which formerly read:

"(7) Any order entered by the court pursuant to paragraph (4) extending the period within which the trustee of an affected air carrier must assume or reject an unexpired lease of nonresidential real property shall be without prejudice to—

"(A) the right of the trustee to seek further extensions within such additional time period granted by the court pursuant to paragraph (4); and

"**(B)** the right of any lessor or any other party in interest to request, at any time, a shortening or termination of the period within which the trustee must assume or reject an unexpired lease of nonresidential real property."

Subsec. (d)(8). Pub.L. 109–8, § 328(a)(3)(A), struck out par. (8), which formerly read: "**(8)** The burden of proof for establishing cause for an extension by an affected air carrier under paragraph (4) or the maintenance of a previously granted extension under paragraph (7)(A) and (B) shall at all times remain with the trustee."

Subsec. (d)(9). Pub.L. 109–8, § 328(a)(3)(A), struck out par. (9), which formerly read: "**(9)** For purposes of determining cause under paragraph (7) with respect to an unexpired lease of nonresidential real property between the debtor that is an affected air carrier and an airport operator under which such debtor is the lessee of an airport terminal or an airport gate, the court shall consider, among other relevant factors, whether substantial harm will result to the airport operator or airline passengers as a result of the extension or the maintenance of a previously granted extension. In making the determination of substantial harm, the court shall consider, among other relevant factors, the level of actual use of the terminals or gates which are the subject of the lease, the public interest in actual use of such terminals or gates, the existence of competing demands for the use of such terminals or gates, the effect of the court's extension or termination of the period of time to assume or reject the lease on such debtor's ability to successfully reorganize under chapter 11 of this title, and whether the trustee of the affected air carrier is capable of continuing to comply with its obligations under section 365(d)(3) of this title."

Subsec. (d)(10). Pub.L. 109–8, § 328(a)(3)(B), redesignated former par. (10) as par. (5).

Subsec. (f)(1). Pub.L. 109–8, § 328(a)(4), struck out "; except that the trustee may not assign an unexpired lease of nonresidential real property under which the debtor is an affected air carrier that is the lessee of an aircraft terminal or aircraft gate if there has occurred a termination event." and inserted a period at the end.

Pub.L. 109–8, § 404(b), struck out "subsection (c)" following "Except as provided in" and inserted "subsections (b) and (c)".

Subsec. (p). Pub.L. 109–8, § 309(b), added subsec. (p).

1994 Amendments. Subsec. (b)(2)(D). Pub.L. 103–394, § 219(a), added subpar. (D).

Subsec. (d)(6)(C). Pub.L. 103–429, § 1(1), substituted "section 40102(a) of title 49" for "section 101 of the Federal Aviation Act of 1958 (49 App. U.S.C. 1301)".

Pub.L. 103–394, § 501(d)(10)(A), substituted "section 40102 of title 49" for "the Federal Aviation Act of 1958 (49 U.S.C. 1301)", which could not be executed to text. See Codification note under this section.

Subsec. (d)(10). Pub.L. 103–394, § 219(b), added par. (10).

Subsec. (g)(2)(A), (B). Pub.L. 103–394, § 501(d)(10)(B), substituted "1208, or 1307" for "1307, or 1208", wherever appearing.

Subsec. (h). Pub.L. 103–394, § 205(a), reorganized text, retaining par. (1) and (2) designations, in par. (1) as so reorganized added subpar. (A) and (B) and subpar. (A), cl. (i) and (ii) designations, and added subpars. (C) and (D), and in par. (2) as reorganized added subpar. (A) and (B) and subpar. (A), cl. (i) and (ii) designations.

Subsec. (n)(1)(B). Pub.L. 103–394, § 501(d)(10)(C), substituted "a right to enforce" for "a right to enforce".

Subsec. (o). Pub.L. 103–394, § 501(d)(10)(D), substituted provisions directing that trustee shall be deemed to have assumed any commitment by debtor to a Federal depository institutions regulatory agency (or predecessor to such agency), for provisions directing that trustee shall be deemed to have assumed any commitment by debtor to particular institutions, or to predecessors or successors.

Subsec. (p). Pub.L. 103–429, § 1(2), substituted "section 40102(a) of title 49" for "section 101(3) of the Federal Aviation Act of 1958".

Pub.L. 103–394, § 501(d)(10)(E), struck out subsec. (p), relating to affected air carriers.

1992 Amendments. Subsec. (c)(4). Pub.L. 102–365, § 19(c), added par. (4).

Subsec. (d)(5)–(9). Pub.L. 102–365, § 19(b), added pars. (5) through (9).

Subsec. (f)(1). Pub.L. 102–365, § 19(d), inserted provisions prohibiting the trustee from assigning an unexpired lease of nonresidential real property under which the debtor is an affected air carrier that is the lessee of an aircraft terminal or gate if a termination event has occurred.

Subsec. (p). Pub.L. 102–365, § 19(e), added subsec. (p).

1990 Amendments. Subsec. (o). Pub.L. 101–647 added subsec. (o).

1988 Amendments. Subsec. (n). Pub.L. 100–506, § 1(b), added subsec. (n).

1986 Amendments. Subsec. (c)(1)(A). Pub.L. 99–554, § 283(e)(1)(1), struck out "or an assignee of such contract or lease" following "debtor in possession". See Codifications note set out under this section.

Subsec. (c)(3). Pub.L. 99–554, § 283(e)(1)(2), inserted "is" following "lease" and "and" following "property".

Subsec. (d)(2). Pub.L. 99–554, § 257(j), added reference to chapter 12.

Subsec. (g)(1). Pub.L. 99–554, § 257(m)(1), added reference to chapter 12.

Subsec. (g)(2). Pub.L. 99–554, § 257(m)(2), added references to chapter 12 and section 1208 of this title.

Subsec. (h)(1). Pub.L. 99–554, § 283(e)(2), inserted "or timeshare plan" following "to treat such lease".

Subsec. (m). Pub.L. 99–554, § 283(e)(3), substituted "362(b)(10)" for "362(b)(9)".

1984 Amendments. Subsec. (a). Pub.L. 98–353, § 362(a), substantially reenacted provisions with minor changes in phraseology.

Subsec. (b)(3). Pub.L. 98–353, § 362(a), added reference to par. (2)(B) of subsec. (f) of this section in provisions preceding subpar. (A).

Subsec. (b)(3)(A). Pub.L. 98–353, § 362(a), added provisions relating to financial condition and operating performance in the case of an assignment.

Subsec. (b)(3)(C). Pub.L. 98–353, § 362(a), substituted "that assumption or assignment of such lease is subject to all the provisions thereof, including (but not limited to) provisions such as a radius, location, use, or exclusivity provision, and will not breach any such provision contained in any other lease, financing agreement, or master agreement relating to such shopping center; and" for "that assumption or assignment of such lease will not breach substantially any provision, such as a radius, location, use, or exclusivity provision, in any other lease, financing agreement, or master agreement relating to such shopping center; and".

Subsec. (c)(1)(A). Pub.L. 98–353, § 362(a), substituted "applicable law excuses a party, other than the debtor, to such contract or lease from accepting performance from or rendering performance to an entity other than the debtor or the debtor in possession or an assignee of such contract or lease, whether or not such contract or lease prohibits or restricts assignment of rights or delegation of duties; and" for "applicable law excuses a party, other than the debtor, to such contract or lease from accepting performance from or rendering performance to the trustee or an assignee of such contract or lease, whether or not such contract or lease prohibits or restricts assignment of rights or delegation of duties; and".

Subsec. (c)(3). Pub.L. 98–353, § 362(a), added par. (3).

Subsec. (d)(1). Pub.L. 98–353, § 362(a), added reference to residential real property or personal property of the debtor.

Subsec. (d)(2). Pub.L. 98–353, § 362(a), added reference to residential real property or personal property of the debtor.

Subsec. (d)(3), (4). Pub.L. 98–353, § 362(a), added pars. (3) and (4).

Subsec. (h)(1). Pub.L. 98–353, § 402, substituted "If the trustee rejects an unexpired lease of real property of the debtor under which the debtor is the lessor, or a timeshare interest under a timeshare plan under which the debtor is the timeshare interest seller, the lessee or timeshare interest purchaser under such lease or timeshare plan may treat such lease or timeshare plan as terminated by such rejection, where the disaffirmance by the trustee amounts to such a breach as would entitle the lessee or timeshare interest purchaser to treat such lease as terminated by virtue of its own terms, applicable nonbankruptcy law, or other agreements the lessee or timeshare interest purchaser has made with other parties; or, in the alternative, the lessee or timeshare interest purchaser may remain in possession of the leasehold or timeshare interest under any lease or timeshare plan the term of which has commenced for the balance of such term and for any renewal or extension of such term that is enforceable by such lessee or timeshare interest purchaser under applicable nonbankruptcy law." for "If the trustee rejects an unexpired lease of real property of the debtor under which the debtor is the lessor, the lessee under such lease may treat the lease as terminated by such rejection, or, in the alternative, may remain in possession for the balance of the term of such lease and any renewal or extension of such term that is enforceable by such lessee under applicable nonbankruptcy law.".

Subsec. (h)(2). Pub.L. 98–353, § 403, substituted "If such lessee or timeshare interest purchaser remains in possession as provided in paragraph (1) of this subsection, such lessee or timeshare interest purchaser may offset against the rent reserved under such lease or moneys due for such timeshare interest for the balance of the term after the date of the rejection of such lease or timeshare interest, and any such renewal or extension thereof, any damages occurring after such date caused by the nonperformance of any obligation of the debtor under such lease or timeshare plan after such date, but such lessee or timeshare interest purchaser does not have any rights against the estate on account of any damages arising after such date from such rejection, other than such offset." for "If such lessee remains in possession, such lessee may offset against the rent reserved under such lease for the balance of the term after the date of the rejection of such lease, and any such renewal or extension, any damages occurring after such date caused by the nonperformance of any obligation of the debtor after such date, but such lessee does not have any rights against the estate on account of any damages arising after such date from such rejection, other than such offset.".

Subsec. (i)(1). Pub.L. 98–353, § 404, added provisions relating to timeshare interests under timeshare plans.

Subsecs. (l), (m). Pub.L. 98–353, § 362(b), added subsecs. (l) and (m).

CROSS REFERENCES

Allowance of claims, see 11 USCA § 502.

Applicability of this section in Chapter 9 cases, see 11 USCA § 901.

Assumption or rejection of certain executory contracts within reasonable time after order for relief, see 11 USCA § 744.

Collective bargaining agreements, see 11 USCA § 1167.

Contents of plan, see 11 USCA § 1222.

Contractual right to liquidate—

Commodities contract or forward contract, see 11 USCA § 556.

Repurchase agreement, see 11 USCA § 559.

Securities contract, see 11 USCA § 555.

Contractual right to terminate a swap agreement, see 11 USCA § 560.

Effect of—

Conversion, see 11 USCA § 348.

Rejection of lease of railroad line, see 11 USCA § 1169.

Grain storage facility bankruptcies, expedited determinations, see 11 USCA § 557.

Impairment of claims or interests by plans which cure certain defaults, see 11 USCA § 1124.

Municipal leases, see 11 USCA § 929.

Provisions in plan for assumption or rejection of certain executory contracts or unexpired leases, see 11 USCA §§ 1123 and 1322.

Right of possession of party with security interest as affected by default—

Aircraft equipment and vessels, see 11 USCA § 1110.

Rolling stock equipment, see 11 USCA § 1168.

Setoff, see 11 USCA § 553.

§ 366. Utility service

(a) Except as provided in subsections (b) and (c) of this section, a utility may not alter, refuse, or discontinue service to, or discriminate against, the trustee or the debtor solely on the basis of the commencement of a case under this title or that a debt owed by the debtor to such utility for service rendered before the order for relief was not paid when due.

(b) Such utility may alter, refuse, or discontinue service if neither the trustee nor the debtor, within 20 days after the date of the order for relief, furnishes adequate assurance of payment, in the form of a deposit or other security, for service after such date. On request of a party in interest and after notice and a hearing, the court may order reasonable modification of the amount of the deposit or other security necessary to provide adequate assurance of payment.

(c)(1)(A) For purposes of this subsection, the term "assurance of payment" means—

(i) a cash deposit;

(ii) a letter of credit;

(iii) a certificate of deposit;

(iv) a surety bond;

(v) a prepayment of utility consumption; or

(vi) another form of security that is mutually agreed on between the utility and the debtor or the trustee.

(B) For purposes of this subsection an administrative expense priority shall not constitute an assurance of payment.

(2) Subject to paragraphs (3) and (4), with respect to a case filed under chapter 11, a utility referred to in subsection (a) may alter, refuse, or discontinue utility service, if during the 30-day period beginning on the date of the filing of the petition, the utility does not receive from the debtor or the trustee adequate assurance of payment for utility service that is satisfactory to the utility.

(3)(A) On request of a party in interest and after notice and a hearing, the court may order modification of the amount of an assurance of payment under paragraph (2).

(B) In making a determination under this paragraph whether an assurance of payment is adequate, the court may not consider—

(i) the absence of security before the date of the filing of the petition;

(ii) the payment by the debtor of charges for utility service in a timely manner before the date of the filing of the petition; or

(iii) the availability of an administrative expense priority.

(4) Notwithstanding any other provision of law, with respect to a case subject to this subsection, a utility may recover or set off against a security deposit provided to the utility by the debtor before the date of the filing of the petition without notice or order of the court.

(Pub.L. 95–598, Nov. 6, 1978, 92 Stat. 2578; Pub.L. 98–353, Title III, § 443, July 10, 1984, 98 Stat. 373; Pub.L. 109–8, Title IV, § 417, Apr. 20, 2005, 119 Stat. 108.)

HISTORICAL AND STATUTORY NOTES

Amendments

2005 Amendments. Subsec. (a). Pub.L. 109–8, § 417(1), struck out "subsection (b)" and inserted "subsections (b) and (c)".

Subsec. (c). Pub.L. 109–8, § 417(2), added subsec. (c).

1984 Amendments. Subsec. (a). Pub.L. 98–353 added "of the commencement of a case under this title or" after "basis".

CROSS REFERENCES

Applicability of this section in Chapter 9 cases, see 11 USCA § 901.

CHAPTER 5—CREDITORS, THE DEBTOR, AND THE ESTATE

SUBCHAPTER I—CREDITORS AND CLAIMS

Sec.
501. Filing of proofs of claims or interests.
502. Allowance of claims or interests.
503. Allowance of administrative expenses.
504. Sharing of compensation.
505. Determination of tax liability.
506. Determination of secured status.
507. Priorities.
508. Effect of distribution other than under this title.
509. Claims of codebtors.
510. Subordination.
511. Rate of interest on tax claims.

SUBCHAPTER II—DEBTOR'S DUTIES AND BENEFITS

521. Debtor's duties.
522. Exemptions.
523. Exceptions to discharge.
524. Effect of discharge.
525. Protection against discriminatory treatment.
526. Restrictions on debt relief agencies.
527. Disclosures.
528. Requirements for debt relief agencies.

SUBCHAPTER III—THE ESTATE

541. Property of the estate.
542. Turnover of property to the estate.
543. Turnover of property by a custodian.
544. Trustee as lien creditor and as successor to certain creditors and purchasers.
545. Statutory liens.
546. Limitations on avoiding powers.
547. Preferences.
548. Fraudulent transfers and obligations.
549. Postpetition transactions.
550. Liability of transferee of avoided transfer.
551. Automatic preservation of avoided transfer.
552. Postpetition effect of security interest.
553. Setoff.
554. Abandonment of property of the estate.
555. Contractual right to liquidate, terminate, or accelerate a securities contract.
556. Contractual right to liquidate, terminate, or accelerate a commodities contract or forward contract.
557. Expedited determination of interests in, and abandonment or other disposition of grain assets.
558. Defenses of the estate.
559. Contractual right to liquidate, terminate, or accelerate a repurchase agreement.
560. Contractual right to liquidate, terminate, or accelerate a swap agreement.
561. Contractual right to terminate, liquidate, accelerate, or offset under a master netting agreement and across contracts; proceedings under chapter 15.
562. Timing of damage measure in connection with swap agreements, securities contracts, forward contracts, commodity contracts, repurchase agreements, and master netting agreements.

HISTORICAL AND STATUTORY NOTES

Amendments

2010 Amendments. Pub.L. 111–327, § 2(a)(50), Dec. 22. 2010, 124 Stat. 3562, rewrote item 562 which formerly read: "562. Timing of damage measure in connection with swap agreements, securities contracts, forward contracts, commodity contracts, repurchase agreements, or master netting agreements".

2005 Amendments. Pub.L. 109–8, Title VII, § 704(b), Apr. 20, 2005, 119 Stat. 126, added item 511.

Pub.L. 109–8, Title II, § 227(b), April 20, 2005, 119 Stat. 69, added item 526.

Pub.L. 109–8, Title II, § 228(b), April 20, 2005, 119 Stat. 71, added item 527.

Pub.L. 109–8, Title II, § 229(b), April 20, 2005, 119 Stat. 72, added item 528.

Pub.L. 109–8, Title IX, § 907(p)(1), Apr. 20, 2005, 119 Stat. 182, rewrote items 555, 556, 559, and 560, which formerly read:

"555. Contractual right to liquidate a securities contract.

"556. Contractual right to liquidate a commodity contract or forward contract."

"559. Contractual right to liquidate a repurchase agreement.

"560. Contractual right to terminate a swap agreement."

Pub.L. 109–8, Title IX, § 907(k)(2), Apr. 20, 2005, 119 Stat. 181, added item 561.

Pub.L. 109–8, Title IX, § 910(a)(2), Apr. 20, 2005, 119 Stat. 184, added item 562.

1990 Amendments. Pub.L. 101–311, Title I, § 106(b), June 25, 1990, 104 Stat. 268, added item 560.

1986 Amendments. Pub.L. 99–554, Title II, § 283(q), Oct. 27, 1986, 100 Stat. 3118, in item 557, substituted in it "557. Expedited determination of interests in, and abandonment or other disposition of grain assets" for "557. Expedited determination of interests in and disposition of grain", and reenacted items 558 and 559 without change.

1984 Amendments. Pub.L. 98–353, Title III, § 352(b), July 10, 1984, 98 Stat. 361, added item 557.

Pub.L. 98–353, Title III, § 396(b), July 10, 1984, 98 Stat. 366, added item 559.

Pub.L. 98–353, Title III, § 470(b), July 10, 1984, 98 Stat. 380, added item 558.

1982 Amendments. Pub.L. 97–222, § 6(b), July 27, 1982, 96 Stat. 237, added items 555 and 556.

CROSS REFERENCES

Applicability of this chapter to—

    Cases under Chapter 7, 11, 12, or 13 of this title, see 11 USCA § 103.

    Investor protection liquidation proceedings, see 15 USCA § 78fff.

SUBCHAPTER I—CREDITORS AND CLAIMS

§ 501. Filing of proofs of claims or interests

(a) A creditor or an indenture trustee may file a proof of claim. An equity security holder may file a proof of interest.

(b) If a creditor does not timely file a proof of such creditor's claim, an entity that is liable to such creditor with the debtor, or that has secured such creditor, may file a proof of such claim.

(c) If a creditor does not timely file a proof of such creditor's claim, the debtor or the trustee may file a proof of such claim.

(d) A claim of a kind specified in section 502(e)(2), 502(f), 502(g), 502(h) or 502(i) of this title may be filed under subsection (a), (b), or (c) of this section the same as if such claim were a claim against the debtor and had arisen before the date of the filing of the petition.

(e) A claim arising from the liability of a debtor for fuel use tax assessed consistent with the requirements of section 31705 of title 49 may be filed by the base jurisdiction designated pursuant to the International Fuel Tax Agreement (as defined in section 31701 of title 49) and, if so filed, shall be allowed as a single claim.

(Pub.L. 95–598, Nov. 6, 1978, 92 Stat. 2578; Pub.L. 98–353, Title III, § 444, July 10, 1984, 98 Stat. 373; Pub.L. 109–8, Title VII, § 702, Apr. 20, 2005, 119 Stat. 125.)

HISTORICAL AND STATUTORY NOTES

Amendments

2005 Amendments. Subsec. (e). Pub.L. 109–8, § 702, added subsec. (e).

1984 Amendments. Subsec. (d). Pub.L. 98–353 added "502(e)(2)," preceding "502(f)".

Child Support Creditors or Their Representatives; Appearance Before Court

Pub.L. 103–394, Title IV, § 304(g), Oct. 22, 1994, 108 Stat. 4134, provided that: "Child support creditors or their representatives shall be permitted to appear and intervene without charge, and without meeting any special local court rule requirement for attorney appearances, in any bankruptcy case or proceeding in any bankruptcy court or district court of the United States if such creditors or representatives file a form in such court that contains information detailing the child support debt, its status, and other characteristics."

CROSS REFERENCES

Applicability of this section in Chapter 9 cases, see 11 USCA § 901.

Binding effect of confirmation whether or not claim is filed or deemed filed, see 11 USCA § 944.

Discharge of—

    Debtor after confirmation of plan, see 11 USCA § 1141.

    Liabilities on claims whether or not filed, see 11 USCA § 727.

Distribution of property of estate, see 11 USCA § 726.

False oaths and claims, see 18 USCA § 152.

Proof of claim deemed filed in—

    Chapter 11 cases, see 11 USCA § 1111.

    Chapter 9 cases, see 11 USCA § 925.

§ 502. Allowance of claims or interests

(a) A claim or interest, proof of which is filed under section 501 of this title, is deemed allowed, unless a party in interest, including a creditor of a general partner in a partnership that is a debtor in a case under chapter 7 of this title, objects.

(b) Except as provided in subsections (e)(2), (f), (g), (h) and (i) of this section, if such objection to a claim is made, the court, after notice and a hearing, shall determine the amount of such claim in lawful currency of the United States as of the date of the filing of the petition, and shall allow such claim in such amount, except to the extent that—

    (1) such claim is unenforceable against the debtor and property of the debtor, under any agreement or applicable law for a reason other than because such claim is contingent or unmatured;

    (2) such claim is for unmatured interest;

    (3) if such claim is for a tax assessed against property of the estate, such claim exceeds the value of the interest of the estate in such property;

    (4) if such claim is for services of an insider or attorney of the debtor, such claim exceeds the reasonable value of such services;

    (5) such claim is for a debt that is unmatured on the date of the filing of the petition and that is excepted from discharge under section 523(a)(5) of this title;

    (6) if such claim is the claim of a lessor for damages resulting from the termination of a lease of real property, such claim exceeds—

(A) the rent reserved by such lease, without acceleration, for the greater of one year, or 15 percent, not to exceed three years, of the remaining term of such lease, following the earlier of—

(i) the date of the filing of the petition; and

(ii) the date on which such lessor repossessed, or the lessee surrendered, the leased property; plus

(B) any unpaid rent due under such lease, without acceleration, on the earlier of such dates;

(7) if such claim is the claim of an employee for damages resulting from the termination of an employment contract, such claim exceeds—

(A) the compensation provided by such contract, without acceleration, for one year following the earlier of—

(i) the date of the filing of the petition; or

(ii) the date on which the employer directed the employee to terminate, or such employee terminated, performance under such contract; plus

(B) any unpaid compensation due under such contract, without acceleration, on the earlier of such dates;

(8) such claim results from a reduction, due to late payment, in the amount of an otherwise applicable credit available to the debtor in connection with an employment tax on wages, salaries, or commissions earned from the debtor; or

(9) proof of such claim is not timely filed, except to the extent tardily filed as permitted under paragraph (1), (2), or (3) of section 726(a) of this title or under the Federal Rules of Bankruptcy Procedure, except that a claim of a governmental unit shall be timely filed if it is filed before 180 days after the date of the order for relief or such later time as the Federal Rules of Bankruptcy Procedure may provide, and except that in a case under chapter 13, a claim of a governmental unit for a tax with respect to a return filed under section 1308 shall be timely if the claim is filed on or before the date that is 60 days after the date on which such return was filed as required.

(c) There shall be estimated for purpose of allowance under this section—

(1) any contingent or unliquidated claim, the fixing or liquidation of which, as the case may be, would unduly delay the administration of the case; or

(2) any right to payment arising from a right to an equitable remedy for breach of performance.

(d) Notwithstanding subsections (a) and (b) of this section, the court shall disallow any claim of any entity from which property is recoverable under section 542, 543, 550, or 553 of this title or that is a transferee of a transfer avoidable under section 522(f), 522(h), 544, 545, 547, 548, 549, or 724(a) of this title, unless such entity or transferee has paid the amount, or turned over any such property, for which such entity or transferee is liable under section 522(i), 542, 543, 550, or 553 of this title.

(e)(1) Notwithstanding subsections (a), (b), and (c) of this section and paragraph (2) of this subsection, the court shall disallow any claim for reimbursement or contribution of an entity that is liable with the debtor on or has secured the claim of a creditor, to the extent that—

(A) such creditor's claim against the estate is disallowed;

(B) such claim for reimbursement or contribution is contingent as of the time of allowance or disallowance of such claim for reimbursement or contribution; or

(C) such entity asserts a right of subrogation to the rights of such creditor under section 509 of this title.

(2) A claim for reimbursement or contribution of such an entity that becomes fixed after the commencement of the case shall be determined, and shall be allowed under subsection (a), (b), or (c) of this section, or disallowed under subsection (d) of this section, the same as if such claim had become fixed before the date of the filing of the petition.

(f) In an involuntary case, a claim arising in the ordinary course of the debtor's business or financial affairs after the commencement of the case but before the earlier of the appointment of a trustee and the order for relief shall be determined as of the date such claim arises, and shall be allowed under subsection (a), (b), or (c) of this section or disallowed under subsection (d) or (e) of this section, the same as if such claim had arisen before the date of the filing of the petition.

(g)(1) A claim arising from the rejection, under section 365 of this title or under a plan under chapter 9, 11, 12, or 13 of this title, of an executory contract or unexpired lease of the debtor that has not been assumed shall be determined, and shall be allowed under subsection (a), (b), or (c) of this section or disallowed under subsection (d) or (e) of this section, the same as if such claim had arisen before the date of the filing of the petition.

(2) A claim for damages calculated in accordance with section 562 shall be allowed under subsection (a), (b), or (c), or disallowed under subsection (d) or (e), as if such claim had arisen before the date of the filing of the petition.

(h) A claim arising from the recovery of property under section 522, 550, or 553 of this title shall be determined, and shall be allowed under subsection (a), (b), or (c) of this section, or disallowed under subsection (d) or (e) of this section, the same as if such claim had arisen before the date of the filing of the petition.

(i) A claim that does not arise until after the commencement of the case for a tax entitled to priority under section 507(a)(8) of this title shall be determined, and shall be allowed under subsection (a), (b), or (c) of this section, or disallowed under subsection (d) or (e) of this section, the same as if such claim had arisen before the date of the filing of the petition.

(j) A claim that has been allowed or disallowed may be reconsidered for cause. A reconsidered claim may be allowed or disallowed according to the equities of the case. Reconsideration of a claim under this subsection does not affect the validity of any payment or transfer from the estate made to a holder of an allowed claim on account of such allowed claim that is not reconsidered, but if a reconsidered claim is allowed and is of the same class as such holder's claim, such holder may not receive any additional payment or transfer from the estate on account of such holder's allowed claim until the holder of such reconsidered and allowed claim receives payment on account of such claim proportionate in value to that already received by such other holder. This subsection does not alter or modify the trustee's right to recover from a creditor any excess payment or transfer made to such creditor.

(k)(1) The court, on the motion of the debtor and after a hearing, may reduce a claim filed under this section based in whole on an unsecured consumer debt by not more than 20 percent of the claim, if—

(A) the claim was filed by a creditor who unreasonably refused to negotiate a reasonable alternative repayment schedule proposed on behalf of the debtor by an approved nonprofit budget and credit counseling agency described in section 111;

(B) the offer of the debtor under subparagraph (A)—

(i) was made at least 60 days before the date of the filing of the petition; and

(ii) provided for payment of at least 60 percent of the amount of the debt over a period not to exceed the repayment period of the loan, or a reasonable extension thereof; and

(C) no part of the debt under the alternative repayment schedule is nondischargeable.

(2) The debtor shall have the burden of proving, by clear and convincing evidence, that—

(A) the creditor unreasonably refused to consider the debtor's proposal; and

(B) the proposed alternative repayment schedule was made prior to expiration of the 60-day period specified in paragraph (1)(B)(i).

(Pub.L. 95–598, Nov. 6, 1978, 92 Stat. 2579; Pub.L. 98–353, Title III, § 445, July 10, 1984, 98 Stat. 373; Pub.L. 99–554, Title II, §§ 257(j), 283(f), Oct. 27, 1986, 100 Stat. 3115, 3117; Pub.L. 103–394, Title II, § 213(a), Title III, § 304(h)(1), Oct. 22, 1994, 108 Stat. 4125, 4134; Pub.L. 109–8, Title II, § 201(a), Title VII, § 716(d), Title IX, § 910(b), Apr. 20, 2005, 119 Stat. 42, 130. 184.)

HISTORICAL AND STATUTORY NOTES

Amendments

2005 Amendments. Subsec. (b)(9). Pub.L. 109–8, § 716(d), inserted ", and except that in a case under chapter 13, a claim of a governmental unit for a tax with respect to a return filed under section 1308 shall be timely if the claim is filed on or before the date that is 60 days after the date on which such return was filed as required" before the period at the end of par. (9).

Subsec. (g)(1), (2). Pub.L. 109–8, § 910(b), designated existing text in subsec. (g) as par. (1) and added par. (2).

Subsec. (k). Pub.L. 109–8, § 201(a), added subsec. (k).

1994 Amendments. Subsec. (b)(9). Pub.L. 103–394, § 213(a), added par. (9).

Subsec. (i). Pub.L. 103–394, § 304(h)(1), substituted "section 507(a)(8)" for "section 507(a)(7)".

1986 Amendments. Subsec. (b)(6)(A)(ii). Pub.L. 99–554, § 283(f)(1), substituted "repossessed" for "reposessed".

Subsec. (g). Pub.L. 99–554, § 257(j), added reference to chapter 12.

Subsec. (i). Pub.L. 99–554, § 283(f)(2), substituted "507(a)(7)" for "507(a)(6)".

1984 Amendments. Subsec. (a). Pub.L. 98–353, § 445(a), added "general" before "partner".

Subsec. (b). Pub.L. 98–353, § 445(b)(1)(2), in provisions preceding par. (1), added "(e)(2)," after "subsections" and "in lawful currency of the United States" after "claim" the second place such word appeared.

Subsec. (b)(1). Pub.L. 98–353, § 445(b)(3), substituted "and" for ", and unenforceable against".

Subsec. (b)(3). Pub.L. 98–353, § 445(b)(4), redesignated former par. (4) as (3), and struck out former par. (3), which read "such claim may be offset under section 553 of this title against a debt owing to the debtor;".

Pub.L. 98–353, § 445(b)(5), in par. (3), as so redesignated, added "the" after "exceeds".

Subsec. (b)(4). Pub.L. 98–353, § 445(b)(4), redesignated former par. (5) as (4). Former par. (4) was redesignated as (3).

Subsec. (b)(5). Pub.L. 98–353, § 445(b)(4), redesignated former par. (6) as (5). Former par. (5) was redesignated as (4).

Pub.L. 98–353, § 445(b)(6), in par. (5), as so redesignated, substituted "such claim" for "the claim" and struck out the comma after "petition".

Subsec. (b)(6). Pub.L. 98–353, § 445(b)(4), redesignated former par. (7) as (6). Former par. (6) was redesignated as (5).

Subsec. (b)(7). Pub.L. 98–353, § 445(b)(4), redesignated former par. (8) as (7). Former par. (7) was redesignated as (6).

Pub.L. 98–353, § 445(b)(7)(A), in par. (7), as so redesignated, added "the claim of an employee" before "for damages".

Subsec. (b)(7)(A)(i). Pub.L. 98–353, § 445(b)(7)(B), substituted "or" for "and".

Subsec. (b)(7)(B). Pub.L. 98–353, § 445(b)(7)(C), (D), substituted "any" for "the" and substituted "contract, without" for "contract without".

Subsec. (b)(8). Pub.L. 98–353, § 445(b)(4), redesignated former par. (9) as (8). Former par. (8) was redesignated as (7).

Subsec. (b)(9). Pub.L. 98–353, § 445(b)(4), redesignated former par. (9) as (8).

Subsec. (c)(1). Pub.L. 98–353, § 445(c)(1), added "the" before "fixing" and substituted "administration" for "closing".

Subsec. (c)(2). Pub.L. 98–353, § 445(c)(2), added "right to payment arising from a" after "any" and struck out "if such breach gives rise to a right to payment" after "breach of performance".

Subsec. (e)(1). Pub.L. 98–353, § 445(d)(1), (2), substituted ", (b), and (c)" for "and (b)" and substituted "or has secured" for ", or has secured,".

Subsec. (e)(1)(B). Pub.L. 98–353, § 445(d)(3), added "or disallowance" after "allowance".

Subsec. (e)(1)(C). Pub.L. 98–353, § 445(d)(4), substituted "asserts a right of subrogation to the rights of such creditor" for "requests subrogation" and struck out "to the rights of such creditor" after "of this title".

Subsec. (h). Pub.L. 98–353, § 445(e), substituted "522" for "522(i)".

Subsec. (j). Pub.L. 98–353, § 445(f), added provisions relating to reconsideration of a disallowed claim, and provisions relating to reconsideration of a claim under this subsection.

CROSS REFERENCES

Acceptance of plan by holders of claims or interests, see 11 USCA § 1126.

Applicability of this section in Chapter 9 cases, see 11 USCA § 901.

Certain claims for which partner and partnership are liable, see 11 USCA § 723.

Claims secured by lien on property of estate, see 11 USCA § 1111.

Creditor as meaning entity having certain claims specified in this section, see 11 USCA § 101.

Deductibility of allowed claim, see 11 USCA § 346.

Discharge of liabilities on claims in—

    Chapter 7 cases, see 11 USCA § 727.

    Chapter 13 cases, see 11 USCA § 1328.

    Chapter 12 cases, see 11 USCA § 1228.

Effect of confirmation in—

    Chapter 11 cases, see 11 USCA § 1141.

    Chapter 9 cases, see 11 USCA § 944.

Filing and allowance of postpetition claims, see 11 USCA § 1305.

Liability of exempted property for debtor's debt, see 11 USCA § 522.

Municipal leases, see 11 USCA § 929.

Payment of insurance benefits to retired employees, see 11 USCA § 1114.

Setoff, see 11 USCA § 553.

Trustee as lien creditor and as successor to certain creditors and purchasers, see 11 USCA § 544.

§ 503. Allowance of administrative expenses

(a) An entity may timely file a request for payment of an administrative expense, or may tardily file such request if permitted by the court for cause.

(b) After notice and a hearing, there shall be allowed administrative expenses, other than claims allowed under section 502(f) of this title, including—

    (1)(A) the actual, necessary costs and expenses of preserving the estate including—

(i) wages, salaries, and commissions for services rendered after the commencement of the case; and

(ii) wages and benefits awarded pursuant to a judicial proceeding or a proceeding of the National Labor Relations Board as back pay attributable to any period of time occurring after commencement of the case under this title, as a result of a violation of Federal or State law by the debtor, without regard to the time of the occurrence of unlawful conduct on which such award is based or to whether any services were rendered, if the court determines that payment of wages and benefits by reason of the operation of this clause will not substantially increase the probability of layoff or termination of current employees, or of nonpayment of domestic support obligations, during the case under this title;

(B) any tax—

(i) incurred by the estate, whether secured or unsecured, including property taxes for which liability is in rem, in personam, or both, except a tax of a kind specified in section 507(a)(8) of this title; or

(ii) attributable to an excessive allowance of a tentative carryback adjustment that the estate received, whether the taxable year to which such adjustment relates ended before or after the commencement of the case;

(C) any fine, penalty, or reduction in credit relating to a tax of a kind specified in subparagraph (B) of this paragraph; and

(D) notwithstanding the requirements of subsection (a), a governmental unit shall not be required to file a request for the payment of an expense described in subparagraph (B) or (C), as a condition of its being an allowed administrative expense;

(2) compensation and reimbursement awarded under section 330(a) of this title;

(3) the actual, necessary expenses, other than compensation and reimbursement specified in paragraph (4) of this subsection, incurred by—

(A) a creditor that files a petition under section 303 of this title;

(B) a creditor that recovers, after the court's approval, for the benefit of the estate any property transferred or concealed by the debtor;

(C) a creditor in connection with the prosecution of a criminal offense relating to the case or to the business or property of the debtor;

(D) a creditor, an indenture trustee, an equity security holder, or a committee representing creditors or equity security holders other than a committee appointed under section 1102 of this title, in making a substantial contribution in a case under chapter 9 or 11 of this title;

(E) a custodian superseded under section 543 of this title, and compensation for the services of such custodian; or

(F) a member of a committee appointed under section 1102 of this title, if such expenses are incurred in the performance of the duties of such committee;

(4) reasonable compensation for professional services rendered by an attorney or an accountant of an entity whose expense is allowable under subparagraph (A), (B), (C), (D), or (E) of paragraph (3) of this subsection, based on the time, the nature, the extent, and the value of such services, and the cost of comparable services other than in a case under this title, and reimbursement for actual, necessary expenses incurred by such attorney or accountant;

(5) reasonable compensation for services rendered by an indenture trustee in making a substantial contribution in a case under chapter 9 or 11 of this title, based on the time, the nature, the extent, and the value of such services, and the cost of comparable services other than in a case under this title;

(6) the fees and mileage payable under chapter 119 of title 28;

(7) with respect to a nonresidential real property lease previously assumed under section 365, and subsequently rejected, a sum equal to all monetary obligations due, excluding those arising from or relating to a failure to operate or a penalty provision, for the period of 2 years following the later of the rejection date or the date of actual turnover of the premises, without reduction or setoff for any reason whatsoever except for sums actually received or to be received from an entity other than the debtor, and the claim for remaining sums due for the balance of the term of the lease shall be a claim under section 502(b)(6);

(8) the actual, necessary costs and expenses of closing a health care business incurred by a trustee or by a Federal agency (as defined in section 551(1) of title 5) or a department or agency of a State or political subdivision thereof, including any cost or expense incurred—

(A) in disposing of patient records in accordance with section 351; or

(B) in connection with transferring patients from the health care business that is in the process of being closed to another health care business; and

(9) the value of any goods received by the debtor within 20 days before the date of commencement of a case under this title in which the goods have been sold to the debtor in the ordinary course of such debtor's business.

(c) Notwithstanding subsection (b), there shall neither be allowed, nor paid—

(1) a transfer made to, or an obligation incurred for the benefit of, an insider of the debtor for the purpose of inducing such person to remain with the debtor's business, absent a finding by the court based on evidence in the record that—

(A) the transfer or obligation is essential to retention of the person because the individual has a bona fide job offer from another business at the same or greater rate of compensation;

(B) the services provided by the person are essential to the survival of the business; and

(C) either—

(i) the amount of the transfer made to, or obligation incurred for the benefit of, the person is not greater than an amount equal to 10 times the amount of the mean transfer or obligation of a similar kind given to nonmanagement employees for any purpose during the calendar year in which the transfer is made or the obligation is incurred; or

(ii) if no such similar transfers were made to, or obligations were incurred for the benefit of, such nonmanagement employees during such calendar year, the amount of the transfer or obligation is not greater than an amount equal to 25 percent of the amount of any similar transfer or obligation made to or incurred for the benefit of such insider for any purpose during the calendar year before the year in which such transfer is made or obligation is incurred;

(2) a severance payment to an insider of the debtor, unless—

(A) the payment is part of a program that is generally applicable to all full-time employees; and

(B) the amount of the payment is not greater than 10 times the amount of the mean severance pay given to nonmanagement employees during the calendar year in which the payment is made; or

(3) other transfers or obligations that are outside the ordinary course of business and not justified by the facts and circumstances of the case, including transfers made to, or obligations incurred for the benefit of, officers, managers, or consultants hired after the date of the filing of the petition.

(Pub.L. 95–598, Nov. 6, 1978, 92 Stat. 2581; Pub.L. 98–353, Title III, § 446, July 10, 1984, 98 Stat. 374; Pub.L. 99–554, Title II, § 283(g), Oct. 27, 1986, 100 Stat. 3117; Pub.L. 103–394, Title I, § 110, Title II, § 213(c), Title III, § 304(h)(2), Oct. 22, 1994, 108 Stat. 4113, 4126, 4134; Pub.L. 109–8, Title III, §§ 329,

331, Title IV, § 445, Title VII, § 712(b), (c), Title XI, § 1103, Title XII, §§ 1208, 1227(b), Apr. 20, 2005, 119 Stat. 101, 102, 117, 128, 190, 194, 200.)

HISTORICAL AND STATUTORY NOTES

Amendments

2005 Amendments. Subsec. (b)(1)(A). Pub.L. 109–8, § 329, rewrote subpar. (A), which formerly read: **"(1)(A)** the actual, necessary costs and expenses of preserving the estate, including wages, salaries, or commissions for services rendered after the commencement of the case;".

Subsec. (b)(1)(B). Pub.L. 109–8, § 712(c)(1), struck out "and" at the end of subpar. (B).

Subsec. (b)(1)(B)(i). Pub.L. 109–8, § 712(b), inserted "whether secured or unsecured, including property taxes for which liability is in rem, in personam, or both," before "except".

Subsec. (b)(1)(C). Pub.L. 109–8, § 712(c)(2), added "and" at the end of subpar. (C).

Subsec. (b)(1)(D). Pub.L. 109–8, § 712(c)(3), added subpar. (D).

Subsec. (b)(4). Pub.L. 109–8, § 1208, inserted "subparagraph (A), (B), (C), (D), or (E) of" before "paragraph (3)".

Subsec. (b)(5). Pub.L. 109–8, § 445(1), struck out "and" at the end of par. (5).

Subsec. (b)(6). Pub.L. 109–8, § 445(2), struck out the period at the end of par. (6) and inserted a semicolon.

Subsec. (b)(7). Pub.L. 109–8, § 445(3), added par. (7).

Subsec. (b)(8). Pub.L. 109–8, § 1103, added par. (8).

Subsec. (b)(9). Pub.L.109–8, § 1227(b), added par. (9).

Subsec. (c). Pub.L. 109–8, § 331, added subsec. (c).

1994 Amendments. Subsec. (a). Pub.L. 103–394, § 213(c), substituted "An entity may timely file a request for payment of an administrative expense, or may tardily file such request if permitted by the court for cause." for "An entity may file a request for payment of an administrative expense."

Subsec. (b)(1)(B)(i). Pub.L. 103–394, § 304(h)(2), substituted "section 507(a)(8)" for "section 507(a)(7)".

Subsec. (b)(3)(F). Pub.L. 103–394, § 110, added subpar. (F).

1986 Amendments. Subsec. (b)(1)(B)(i). Pub.L. 99–554, § 283(g)(1), substituted "507(a)(7)" for "507(a)(6)".

Subsec. (b)(5). Pub.L. 99–554, § 283(g)(2), inserted "and" following "title;".

Subsec. (b)(6). Pub.L. 99–554, § 283(g)(3), substituted "28." for "28; and".

1984 Amendments. Subsec. (b). Pub.L. 98–353, § 446(1), struck out the comma after "be allowed" in provisions preceding par. (1).

Subsec. (b)(1)(C). Pub.L. 98–353, § 446(2), struck out the comma after "credit".

Subsec. (b)(2). Pub.L. 98–353, § 446(3), added "(a)" after "330".

Subsec. (b)(3). Pub.L. 98–353, § 446(4), added a comma after "paragraph (4) of this subsection".

Subsec. (b)(3)(C). Pub.L. 98–353, § 446(5), struck out the comma after "case".

Subsec. (b)(5). Pub.L. 98–353, § 446(6), struck out "and" following "title;".

Subsec. (b)(6). Pub.L. 98–353, § 446(7), substituted "; and" for the period at the end of par. (6).

CROSS REFERENCES

Adequate protection, other than granting certain administrative expenses, see 11 USCA § 361.

Applicability of this section in Chapter 9 cases, see 11 USCA § 901.

Claims arising from automatic stay, see 11 USCA § 922.

Discharge of liabilities on claims in Chapter 12 cases, see 11 USCA § 1228.

Deductibility of allowed claim, see 11 USCA § 346.

Deduction of administrative expenses for income tax purposes, see 26 USCA § 1398.

Deduction of administrative expenses from payments received by trustee if plan not confirmed in—

> Chapter 13 cases, see 11 USCA § 1326.
>
> Chapter 12 cases, see 11 USCA § 1226.

Distribution of property of estate, see 11 USCA § 726.

Effect of conversion, see 11 USCA § 348.

Grain storage facility bankruptcies, expedited determinations, see 11 USCA § 557.

Method of obtaining adequate protection in Chapter 12 case, see 11 USCA § 1205.

Payment of insurance benefits to retired employees, see 11 USCA § 1114.

Performance of obligations under executory contracts and unexpired leases notwithstanding subsec. (b)(1) of this section, see 11 USCA § 365.

Proof of claim, see Official Bankr. Form 10, 11 USCA.

Unsecured debt as administrative expense or having priority over certain administrative expenses, see 11 USCA § 364.

§ 504. Sharing of compensation

(a) Except as provided in subsection (b) of this section, a person receiving compensation or reimbursement under section 503(b)(2) or 503(b)(4) of this title may not share or agree to share—

(1) any such compensation or reimbursement with another person; or

(2) any compensation or reimbursement received by another person under such sections.

(b)(1) A member, partner, or regular associate in a professional association, corporation, or partnership may share compensation or reimbursement received under section 503(b)(2) or 503(b)(4) of this title with another member, partner, or regular associate in such association, corporation, or partnership, and may share in any compensation or reimbursement received under such sections by another member, partner, or regular associate in such association, corporation, or partnership.

(2) An attorney for a creditor that files a petition under section 303 of this title may share compensation and reimbursement received under section 503(b)(4) of this title with any other attorney contributing to the services rendered or expenses incurred by such creditor's attorney.

(c) This section shall not apply with respect to sharing, or agreeing to share, compensation with a bona fide public service attorney referral program that operates in accordance with non-Federal law regulating attorney referral services and with rules of professional responsibility applicable to attorney acceptance of referrals.

(Pub.L. 95–598, Nov. 6, 1978, 92 Stat. 2582; Pub.L. 109–8, Title III, § 326, Apr. 20, 2005, 119 Stat. 99.)

HISTORICAL AND STATUTORY NOTES

Amendments

2005 Amendments. Subsec. (c). Pub.L. 109–8, § 326, added subsec. (c).

CROSS REFERENCES

Applicability of restrictions on sharing of compensation to allowances in investor protection liquidation proceedings, see 15 USCA § 78eee.

Applicability of this section in Chapter 9 cases, see 11 USCA § 901.

§ 505. Determination of tax liability

(a)(1) Except as provided in paragraph (2) of this subsection, the court may determine the amount or legality of any tax, any fine or penalty relating to a tax, or any addition to tax, whether or not previously assessed, whether or not paid, and whether or not contested before and adjudicated by a judicial or administrative tribunal of competent jurisdiction.

(2) The court may not so determine—

(A) the amount or legality of a tax, fine, penalty, or addition to tax if such amount or legality was contested before and adjudicated by a judicial or administrative tribunal of competent jurisdiction before the commencement of the case under this title;

(B) any right of the estate to a tax refund, before the earlier of—

(i) 120 days after the trustee properly requests such refund from the governmental unit from which such refund is claimed; or

(ii) a determination by such governmental unit of such request; or

(C) the amount or legality of any amount arising in connection with an ad valorem tax on real or personal property of the estate, if the applicable period for contesting or redetermining that amount under applicable nonbankruptcy law has expired.

(b)(1)(A) The clerk shall maintain a list under which a Federal, State, or local governmental unit responsible for the collection of taxes within the district may—

(i) designate an address for service of requests under this subsection; and

(ii) describe where further information concerning additional requirements for filing such requests may be found.

(B) If such governmental unit does not designate an address and provide such address to the clerk under subparagraph (A), any request made under this subsection may be served at the address for the filing of a tax return or protest with the appropriate taxing authority of such governmental unit.

(2) A trustee may request a determination of any unpaid liability of the estate for any tax incurred during the administration of the case by submitting a tax return for such tax and a request for such a determination to the governmental unit charged with responsibility for collection or determination of such tax at the address and in the manner designated in paragraph (1). Unless such return is fraudulent, or contains a material misrepresentation, the estate, the trustee, the debtor, and any successor to the debtor are discharged from any liability for such tax—

(A) upon payment of the tax shown on such return, if—

(i) such governmental unit does not notify the trustee, within 60 days after such request, that such return has been selected for examination; or

(ii) such governmental unit does not complete such an examination and notify the trustee of any tax due, within 180 days after such request or within such additional time as the court, for cause, permits;

(B) upon payment of the tax determined by the court, after notice and a hearing, after completion by such governmental unit of such examination; or

(C) upon payment of the tax determined by such governmental unit to be due.

(c) Notwithstanding section 362 of this title, after determination by the court of a tax under this section, the governmental unit charged with responsibility for collection of such tax may assess such tax against the estate, the debtor, or a successor to the debtor, as the case may be, subject to any otherwise applicable law.

(Pub.L. 95–598, Nov. 6, 1978, 92 Stat. 2582; Pub.L. 98–353, Title III, § 447, July 10, 1984, 98 Stat. 374; Pub.L. 109–8, Title VII, §§ 701(b), 703, 715, Apr. 20, 2005, 119 Stat. 124, 125, 129; Pub.L. 111–327, § 2(a)(14), Dec. 22, 2010, 124 Stat. 3559.)

Title 11 CREDITORS, THE DEBTOR, AND THE ESTATE 11 § 506

HISTORICAL AND STATUTORY NOTES

Amendments

2010 Amendments. Subsec. (a)(2)(C). Pub.L. 111–327, § 2(a)(14), struck out "any law (other than a bankruptcy law)" and inserted "applicable nonbankruptcy law".

2005 Amendments. Subsec. (a)(2)(A). Pub.L. 109–8, § 701(b)(1), struck out "or" at the end of subpar. (A).

Subsec. (a)(2)(B). Pub.L. 109–8, § 701(b)(2), struck out the period at the end of subpar. (B) and inserted "; or".

Subsec. (a)(2)(C). Pub.L. 109–8, § 701(b)(3), added subpar. (C).

Subsec. (b). Pub.L. 109–8, §§ 703, 715, rewrote subsec. (b), which formerly read:

"(b) A trustee may request a determination of any unpaid liability of the estate for any tax incurred during the administration of the case by submitting a tax return for such tax and a request for such a determination to the governmental unit charged with responsibility for collection or determination of such tax. Unless such return is fraudulent, or contains a material misrepresentation, the trustee, the debtor, and any successor to the debtor are discharged from any liability for such tax—

"(1) upon payment of the tax shown on such return, if—

"(A) such governmental unit does not notify the trustee, within 60 days after such request, that such return has been selected for examination; or

"(B) such governmental unit does not complete such an examination and notify the trustee of any tax due, within 180 days after such request or within such additional time as the court, for cause, permits;

"(2) upon payment of the tax determined by the court, after notice and a hearing, after completion by such governmental unit of such examination; or

"(3) upon payment of the tax determined by such governmental unit to be due."

1984 Amendments. Subsec. (a)(2)(B)(i). Pub.L. 98–353 substituted "or" for "and".

CROSS REFERENCES

Declaratory judgments, see 28 USCA § 2201.

§ 506. Determination of secured status

(a)(1) An allowed claim of a creditor secured by a lien on property in which the estate has an interest, or that is subject to setoff under section 553 of this title, is a secured claim to the extent of the value of such creditor's interest in the estate's interest in such property, or to the extent of the amount subject to setoff, as the case may be, and is an unsecured claim to the extent that the value of such creditor's interest or the amount so subject to setoff is less than the amount of such allowed claim. Such value shall be determined in light of the purpose of the valuation and of the proposed disposition or use of such property, and in conjunction with any hearing on such disposition or use or on a plan affecting such creditor's interest.

(2) If the debtor is an individual in a case under chapter 7 or 13, such value with respect to personal property securing an allowed claim shall be determined based on the replacement value of such property as of the date of the filing of the petition without deduction for costs of sale or marketing. With respect to property acquired for personal, family, or household purposes, replacement value shall mean the price a retail merchant would charge for property of that kind considering the age and condition of the property at the time value is determined.

(b) To the extent that an allowed secured claim is secured by property the value of which, after any recovery under subsection (c) of this section, is greater than the amount of such claim, there shall be allowed to the holder of such claim, interest on such claim, and any reasonable fees, costs, or charges provided for under the agreement or State statute under which such claim arose.

(c) The trustee may recover from property securing an allowed secured claim the reasonable, necessary costs and expenses of preserving, or disposing of, such property to the extent of any benefit to the holder of such claim, including the payment of all ad valorem property taxes with respect to the property.

(d) To the extent that a lien secures a claim against the debtor that is not an allowed secured claim, such lien is void, unless—

(1) such claim was disallowed only under section 502(b)(5) or 502(e) of this title; or

(2) such claim is not an allowed secured claim due only to the failure of any entity to file a proof of such claim under section 501 of this title.

(Pub.L. 95–598, Nov. 6, 1978, 92 Stat. 2583; Pub.L. 98–353, Title III, § 448, July 10, 1984, 98 Stat. 374; Pub.L. 109–8, Title III, § 327, Title VII, § 712(d), Apr. 20, 2005, 119 Stat. 99, 128.)

HISTORICAL AND STATUTORY NOTES

Amendments

2005 Amendments. Subsec. (a)(1). Pub.L. 109–8, § 327(1), inserted "(1)" after "(a)".

Subsec. (a)(2). Pub.L. 109–8, § 327(2), added par. (2).

Subsec. (b). Pub.L. 109–8, § 712(d)(1), inserted "or State statute" after "agreement".

Subsec. (c). Pub.L. 109–8, § 712(d)(2), inserted ", including the payment of all ad valorem property taxes with respect to the property" before the period at the end.

1984 Amendments. Subsec. (b). Pub.L. 98–353, § 448(a), added "for" after "provided".

Subsec. (d)(1). Pub.L. 98–353, § 448(b), substituted "such claim was disallowed only under section 502(b)(5) or 502(e) of this title; or" for "a party in interest has not requested that the court determine and allow or disallow such claim under section 502 of this title; or".

Subsec. (d)(2). Pub.L. 98–353, § 448(b), substituted "such claim is not an allowed secured claim due only to the failure of any entity to file a proof of such claim under section 501 of this title." for "such claim was disallowed only under section 502(e) of this title.".

CROSS REFERENCES

Applicability of this section in Chapter 9 cases, see 11 USCA § 901.

Automatic preservation of avoided transfer, see 11 USCA § 551.

Claims secured by lien on property of estate, see 11 USCA § 1111.

Contents of plan and interest on interest, see 11 USCA §§ 1123, 1222 and 1322.

Effect of dismissal, see 11 USCA § 349.

Liability of exempted property for debtor's debt, see 11 USCA § 522.

Postpetition effect of security interest, see 11 USCA § 552.

§ 507. Priorities

(a) The following expenses and claims have priority in the following order:

(1) First:

(A) Allowed unsecured claims for domestic support obligations that, as of the date of the filing of the petition in a case under this title, are owed to or recoverable by a spouse, former spouse, or child of the debtor, or such child's parent, legal guardian, or responsible relative, without regard to whether the claim is filed by such person or is filed by a governmental unit on behalf of such person, on the condition that funds received under this paragraph by a governmental unit under this title after the date of the filing of the petition shall be applied and distributed in accordance with applicable nonbankruptcy law.

(B) Subject to claims under subparagraph (A), allowed unsecured claims for domestic support obligations that, as of the date of the filing of the petition, are assigned by a spouse, former spouse, child of the debtor, or such child's parent, legal guardian, or responsible relative to a governmental unit (unless such obligation is assigned voluntarily by the spouse, former spouse, child, parent, legal guardian, or responsible relative of the child for the purpose of collecting the debt) or are owed directly to or recoverable by a governmental unit under applicable nonbankruptcy law, on the condition that funds received under this paragraph by a governmental unit under this title after the date of the filing of the petition be applied and distributed in accordance with applicable nonbankruptcy law.

(C) If a trustee is appointed or elected under section 701, 702, 703, 1104, 1202, or 1302, the administrative expenses of the trustee allowed under paragraphs (1)(A), (2), and (6) of section 503(b) shall be paid before payment of claims under subparagraphs (A) and (B), to the extent that the trustee administers assets that are otherwise available for the payment of such claims.

(2) Second, administrative expenses allowed under section 503(b) of this title, unsecured claims of any Federal reserve bank related to loans made through programs or facilities authorized under section 13(3) of the Federal Reserve Act (12 U.S.C. 343), and any fees and charges assessed against the estate under chapter 123 of title 28.

(3) Third, unsecured claims allowed under section 502(f) of this title.

(4) Fourth, allowed unsecured claims, but only to the extent of $12,475[1] for each individual or corporation, as the case may be, earned within 180 days before the date of the filing of the petition or the date of the cessation of the debtor's business, whichever occurs first, for—

(A) wages, salaries, or commissions, including vacation, severance, and sick leave pay earned by an individual; or

(B) sales commissions earned by an individual or by a corporation with only 1 employee, acting as an independent contractor in the sale of goods or services for the debtor in the ordinary course of the debtor's business if, and only if, during the 12 months preceding that date, at least 75 percent of the amount that the individual or corporation earned by acting as an independent contractor in the sale of goods or services was earned from the debtor.

(5) Fifth, allowed unsecured claims for contributions to an employee benefit plan—

(A) arising from services rendered within 180 days before the date of the filing of the petition or the date of the cessation of the debtor's business, whichever occurs first; but only

(B) for each such plan, to the extent of—

(i) the number of employees covered by each such plan multiplied by $12,475[1]; less

(ii) the aggregate amount paid to such employees under paragraph (4) of this subsection, plus the aggregate amount paid by the estate on behalf of such employees to any other employee benefit plan.

(6) Sixth, allowed unsecured claims of persons—

(A) engaged in the production or raising of grain, as defined in section 557(b) of this title, against a debtor who owns or operates a grain storage facility, as defined in section 557(b) of this title, for grain or the proceeds of grain, or

---

[1] Dollar amount as adjusted by the Judicial Conference of the United States. See Adjustment of Dollar Amounts notes set out under this section and 11 U.S.C.A. § 104.

(B) engaged as a United States fisherman against a debtor who has acquired fish or fish produce from a fisherman through a sale or conversion, and who is engaged in operating a fish produce storage or processing facility—

but only to the extent of $6,150[1] for each such individual.

(7) Seventh, allowed unsecured claims of individuals, to the extent of $2,775[1] for each such individual, arising from the deposit, before the commencement of the case, of money in connection with the purchase, lease, or rental of property, or the purchase of services, for the personal, family, or household use of such individuals, that were not delivered or provided.

(8) Eighth, allowed unsecured claims of governmental units, only to the extent that such claims are for—

(A) a tax on or measured by income or gross receipts for a taxable year ending on or before the date of the filing of the petition—

(i) for which a return, if required, is last due, including extensions, after three years before the date of the filing of the petition;

(ii) assessed within 240 days before the date of the filing of the petition, exclusive of—

(I) any time during which an offer in compromise with respect to that tax was pending or in effect during that 240-day period, plus 30 days; and

(II) any time during which a stay of proceedings against collections was in effect in a prior case under this title during that 240-day period, plus 90 days; or

(iii) other than a tax of a kind specified in section 523(a)(1)(B) or 523(a)(1)(C) of this title, not assessed before, but assessable, under applicable law or by agreement, after, the commencement of the case;

(B) a property tax incurred before the commencement of the case and last payable without penalty after one year before the date of the filing of the petition;

(C) a tax required to be collected or withheld and for which the debtor is liable in whatever capacity;

(D) an employment tax on a wage, salary, or commission of a kind specified in paragraph (4) of this subsection earned from the debtor before the date of the filing of the petition, whether or not actually paid before such date, for which a return is last due, under applicable law or under any extension, after three years before the date of the filing of the petition;

(E) an excise tax on—

(i) a transaction occurring before the date of the filing of the petition for which a return, if required, is last due, under applicable law or under any extension, after three years before the date of the filing of the petition; or

(ii) if a return is not required, a transaction occurring during the three years immediately preceding the date of the filing of the petition;

(F) a customs duty arising out of the importation of merchandise—

(i) entered for consumption within one year before the date of the filing of the petition;

(ii) covered by an entry liquidated or reliquidated within one year before the date of the filing of the petition; or

---

[1] Dollar amount as adjusted by the Judicial Conference of the United States. See Adjustment of Dollar Amounts notes set out under this section and 11 U.S.C.A. § 104.

(iii) entered for consumption within four years before the date of the filing of the petition but unliquidated on such date, if the Secretary of the Treasury certifies that failure to liquidate such entry was due to an investigation pending on such date into assessment of antidumping or countervailing duties or fraud, or if information needed for the proper appraisement or classification of such merchandise was not available to the appropriate customs officer before such date; or

(G) a penalty related to a claim of a kind specified in this paragraph and in compensation for actual pecuniary loss.

An otherwise applicable time period specified in this paragraph shall be suspended for any period during which a governmental unit is prohibited under applicable nonbankruptcy law from collecting a tax as a result of a request by the debtor for a hearing and an appeal of any collection action taken or proposed against the debtor, plus 90 days; plus any time during which the stay of proceedings was in effect in a prior case under this title or during which collection was precluded by the existence of 1 or more confirmed plans under this title, plus 90 days.

(9) Ninth, allowed unsecured claims based upon any commitment by the debtor to a Federal depository institutions regulatory agency (or predecessor to such agency) to maintain the capital of an insured depository institution.

(10) Tenth, allowed claims for death or personal injury resulting from the operation of a motor vehicle or vessel if such operation was unlawful because the debtor was intoxicated from using alcohol, a drug, or another substance.

(b) If the trustee, under section 362, 363, or 364 of this title, provides adequate protection of the interest of a holder of a claim secured by a lien on property of the debtor and if, notwithstanding such protection, such creditor has a claim allowable under subsection (a)(2) of this section arising from the stay of action against such property under section 362 of this title, from the use, sale, or lease of such property under section 363 of this title, or from the granting of a lien under section 364(d) of this title, then such creditor's claim under such subsection shall have priority over every other claim allowable under such subsection.

(c) For the purpose of subsection (a) of this section, a claim of a governmental unit arising from an erroneous refund or credit of a tax has the same priority as a claim for the tax to which such refund or credit relates.

(d) An entity that is subrogated to the rights of a holder of a claim of a kind specified in subsection (a)(1), (a)(4), (a)(5), (a)(6), (a)(7), (a)(8), or (a)(9) of this section is not subrogated to the right of the holder of such claim to priority under such subsection.

(Pub.L. 95–598, Nov. 6, 1978, 92 Stat. 2583; Pub.L. 98–353, Title III, §§ 350, 449, July 10, 1984, 98 Stat. 358, 374; Pub.L. 101–647, Title XXV, § 2522(d), Nov. 29, 1990, 104 Stat. 4867; Pub.L. 103–394, Title I, § 108(c), Title II, § 207, Title III, § 304(c), Title V, § 501(b)(3), (d)(11), Oct. 22, 1994, 108 Stat. 4112, 4123, 4132, 4142, 4145; Pub.L. 109–8, Title II, §§ 212, 223, Title VII, §§ 705, 706, Title XIV, § 1401, Title XV, § 1502(a)(1), Apr. 20, 2005, 119 Stat. 51, 62, 126, 214, 216; Pub.L. 111–203, Title XI, § 1101(b), July 21, 2010, 124 Stat. 2115; Pub.L. 111–327, § 2(a)(15), Dec. 22, 2010, 124 Stat. 3559.)

HISTORICAL AND STATUTORY NOTES

References in Text

The Federal Reserve Act, referred to in subsec. (a)(2), is Act Dec. 23, 1913, c. 6, 38 Stat. 251, as amended, which is classified principally to chapter 3 of Title 12, 12 U.S.C.A. § 221 et seq. Section 13(3) of such Act is classified to 12 U.S.C.A. § 343. For complete classification, see References in Text note set out under 12 U.S.C.A. § 226 and Tables.

Codifications

Amendments by Pub.L. 109–8, § 1401, to pars. (4) and (5) of subsec. (a) of this section, as amended by section 212 of Pub.L. 109–8, were made to pars. (3) and (4) of subsec. (a) of this section, as the probable intent of Congress. The redesignation of pars. (3) and (4) as pars. (4) and (5) by section 212 of Pub.L. 109–8 does not take effect until 180 days after April 20, 2005.

Amendments

2010 Amendments. Subsec. (a)(2). Pub.L. 111–203, § 1101(b), inserted "unsecured claims of any Federal reserve bank related to loans made through programs or facilities authorized under section 13(3) of the Federal Reserve Act (12 U.S.C. 343)," after "this title,".

Subsec. (a)(8)(A)(ii)(II). Pub.L. 111–327, § 2(a)(15), struck out the period at the end and inserted "; or".

2005 Amendments. Subsec. (a)(1). Pub.L. 109–8, § 212(2), (9), redesignated former par. (1) as par. (2) and inserted a new par. (1).

Subsec. (a)(2). Pub.L. 109–8, § 212(2), (3), redesignated former par. (1) as par. (2) and, in par. (2) as redesignated, substituted "Second" for "First". Former par. (2) redesignated par. (3).

Subsec. (a)(3). Pub.L. 109–8, § 212(2), (4), redesignated former par. (2) as par. (3) and, in par. (3) as redesignated, substituted "Third" for "Second". Former par. (3) redesignated par. (4).

Subsec. (a)(4). Pub.L. 109–8, § 212(2), (5), redesignated former par. (3) as par. (4) and, in par. (4) as redesignated, substituted "Fourth" for "Third" and substituted a period for the semicolon at the end. Former par. (4) redesignated par. (5).

Pub.L. 109–8, § 1401, struck out "90" and inserted "180", and struck out "$4,000", which had been adjusted by the Judicial Conference to "$4,925", and inserted "$10,000", in par. (3) before redesignation as par. (4) by Pub.L. 109–8, § 212(2) took effect 180 days after April 20, 2005. See Codifications note set out under this section.

Subsec. (a)(5). Pub.L. 109–8, § 212(2), (6), redesignated former par. (4) as par. (5) and, in par. (5) as redesignated, substituted "Fifth" for "Fourth". Former par. (5) redesignated par. (6).

Pub.L. 109–8, § 1401(2), struck out "$4,000", which had been adjusted by the Judicial Conference to "$4,925", and inserted "$10,000", in par. (4) before redesignation as par. (5) by Pub.L. 109–8, § 212(2) took effect 180 days after April 20, 2005. See Codifications note set out under this section.

Subsec. (a)(5)(B)(ii). Pub.L. 109–8, § 1502(a)(1)(A)(i), struck out "paragraph (3)" and inserted "paragraph (4)".

Subsec. (a)(6). Pub.L. 109–8, § 212(2), (7), redesignated former par. (5) as par. (6) and, in par. (6) as redesignated, substituted "Sixth" for "Fifth". Former par. (6) redesignated par. (7).

Subsec. (a)(7). Pub.L. 109–8, § 212(1), (2), (8), redesignated former par. (6) as par. (7), substituted "Seventh" for "Sixth" in redesignated par. (7), and struck out former par. (7) which read: "Seventh, allowed claims for debts to a spouse, former spouse, or child of the debtor, for alimony to, maintenance for, or support of such spouse or child, in connection with a separation agreement, divorce decree or other order of a court of record, determination made in accordance with State or territorial law by a governmental unit, or property settlement agreement, but not to the extent that such debt—

"(A) is assigned to another entity, voluntarily, by operation of law, or otherwise; or

"(B) includes a liability designated as alimony, maintenance, or support, unless such liability is actually in the nature of alimony, maintenance or support."

Subsec. (a)(8). Pub.L. 109–8, § 705(2), added "An otherwise applicable time period specified in this paragraph shall be suspended for any period during which a governmental unit is prohibited under applicable nonbankruptcy law from collecting a tax as a result of a request by the debtor for a hearing and an appeal of any collection action taken or proposed against the debtor, plus 90 days; plus any time during which the stay of proceedings was in effect in a prior case under this title or during which collection was precluded by the existence of 1 or more confirmed plans under this title, plus 90 days." to the end of par. (8).

Subsec. (a)(8)(A). Pub.L. 109–8, § 705(1)(A), in the matter preceding cl. (i), inserted "for a taxable year ending on or before the date of the filing of the petition" after "gross receipts".

Subsec. (a)(8)(A)(i). Pub.L. 109–8, § 705(1)(B), struck out "for a taxable year ending on or before the date of the filing of the petition" before "for which a return, if required, is last due".

Subsec. (a)(8)(A)(ii). Pub.L. 109–8, § 705(1)(C), rewrote cl. (ii), which formerly read: **"(ii)** assessed within 240 days, plus any time plus 30 days during which an offer in compromise with respect to such tax that was made within 240 days after such assessment was pending, before the date of the filing of the petition; or"

Subsec. (a)(8)(B). Pub.L. 109–8, § 706, struck out "assessed" and inserted "incurred".

Subsec. (a)(8)(D). Pub.L. 109–8, § 1502(a)(1)(A)(ii), struck out "paragraph (3)" and inserted "paragraph (4)".

Subsec. (a)(10). Pub.L. 109–8, § 223, inserted par. (10).

Subsec. (b). Pub.L. 109–8, § 1502(a)(1)(B), struck out "subsection (a)(1)" and inserted "subsection (a)(2)".

Subsec. (d). Pub.L. 109–8, § 1502(a)(1)(C), struck out "subsection (a)(3)" and inserted "subsection (a)(1)".

1994 Amendments. Subsec. (a)(3). Pub.L. 103–394, § 207, completely revised par. (3). Prior to revision, par. (3) read as follows:

"(3) Third, allowed unsecured claims for wages, salaries, or commissions, including vacation, severance, and sick leave pay—

"(A) earned by an individual within 90 days before the date of the filing of the petition or the date of the cessation of the debtor's business, whichever occurs first; but only

"(B) to the extent of $2,000 for each such individual."

Subsec. (a)(4)(B)(i). Pub.L. 103–394, § 108(c)(1), substituted "multiplied by $4,000" for "multiplied by $2,000".

Subsec. (a)(5)(A). Pub.L. 103–394, § 501(b)(3), substituted "section 557(b)" for "section 557(b)(1)", and "section 557(b)" for "section 557(b)(2)".

Subsec. (a)(5). Pub.L. 103–394, § 108(c)(2), substituted "but only to the extent of $4,000 for each such individual." for "but only to the extent of $2,000 for each such individual.".

Subsec. (a)(6). Pub.L. 103–394, § 108(c)(3), substituted "allowed unsecured claims of individuals, to the extent of $1,800 for each such individual," for "allowed unsecured claims of individuals, to the extent of $900 for each such individual,".

Subsec. (a)(7). Pub.L. 103–394, § 304(c)(2), (3), added par. (7). Former par. (7) redesignated (8).

Subsec. (a)(8). Pub.L. 103–394, § 304(c)(1), (2), redesignated former par. (7) as (8). Former par. (8) redesignated (9).

Subsec. (a)(9). Pub.L. 103–394, § 304(c)(1), redesignated former par. (8) as (9).

Pub.L. 103–394, § 501(d)(11)(A), substituted "a Federal depository institutions regulatory agency (or predecessor to such agency)" for "the Federal Deposit Insurance Corporation, the Resolution Trust Corporation, the Director of the Office of Thrift Supervision, the Comptroller of the Currency, or the Board of Governors of the Federal Reserve System, or their predecessors or successors,".

Subsec. (d). Pub.L. 103–394, § 501(d)(11)(B), inserted reference to (a)(7), (a)(8), or (a)(9), following reference to (a)(6).

1990 Amendments. Subsec. (a)(8). Pub.L. 101–647 added par. (8).

1984 Amendments. Subsec. (a)(3). Pub.L. 98–353, § 449(a)(1), added a comma following "severance".

Subsec. (a)(4). Pub.L. 98–353, § 449(a)(2), substituted "an employee benefit plan" for "employee benefit plans" in provisions preceding Subpar. (A).

Subsec. (a)(4)(B)(i). Pub.L. 98–353, § 449(a)(3), added "each" following "covered by".

Subsec. (a)(5). Pub.L. 98–353, § 350(3), added par. (5). Former par. (5) was redesignated as (6).

Subsec. (a)(6). Pub.L. 98–353, § 350(1), redesignated former par. (5) as (6) and, as so redesignated, substituted "Sixth" for "Fifth". Former par. (6) was redesignated as (7).

Subsec. (a)(7). Pub.L. 98–353, § 350(2), redesignated former par. (6) as (7) and, as so redesignated, substituted "Seventh" for "Sixth".

11 § 508 BANKRUPTCY CODE Title 11

Pub.L. 98–353, § 449(a)(4), added "only" following "units,".

Subsec. (c). Pub.L. 98–353, § 449(b), substituted "has the same priority" for "shall be treated the same".

Adjustment of Dollar Amounts

For adjustment of dollar amounts specified in subsec. (a)(4), (5), (6), (7) of this section by the Judicial Conference of the United States, see note set out under 11 U.S.C.A. § 104.

CROSS REFERENCES

Applicability of subsec. (a)(1) of this section in Chapter 9 cases, see 11 USCA § 901.

Confirmation upon payment of administrative expenses, fees, and charges, see 11 USCA § 943.

Contents of plan in—

    Chapter 13 cases, see 11 USCA § 1322.

    Chapter 12 cases, see 11 USCA § 1222.

Designation by plan of classes of claims, see 11 USCA § 1123.

Distribution of—

    Certain estate property subject to liens, see 11 USCA § 724.

    Customer property in commodity broker liquidation cases, see 11 USCA § 766.

    Customer property in stockbroker liquidation cases, see 11 USCA § 752.

    Property of estate, see 11 USCA § 726.

Executory contracts and unexpired leases, see 11 USCA § 365.

Involuntary cases future adjustments, see 11 USCA § 104.

Proof of claim, see Official Bankr. Form 10, 11 USCA.

Recoupment of funds advanced by Securities Investor Protection Corporation as priority administrative expense, see 15 USCA § 78fff.

Tax or customs duty excepted from discharge, see 11 USCA § 523.

Time of payment of administrative expenses, fees and charges in—

    Chapter 13 cases, see 11 USCA § 1326.

    Chapter 12 cases, see 11 USCA § 1226.

Treatment of certain claims as affecting confirmation of plan, see 11 USCA § 1129.

Unsecured debt having priority over certain administrative expenses, see 11 USCA § 364.

Unsecured priority claims, see Official Bankr. Form 6, 11 USCA.

§ 508. Effect of distribution other than under this title

If a creditor of a partnership debtor receives, from a general partner that is not a debtor in a case under chapter 7 of this title, payment of, or a transfer of property on account of, a claim that is allowed under this title and that is not secured by a lien on property of such partner, such creditor may not receive any payment under this title on account of such claim until each of the other holders of claims on account of which such holders are entitled to share equally with such creditor under this title has received payment under this title equal in value to the consideration received by such creditor from such general partner.

(Pub.L. 95–598, Nov. 6, 1978, 92 Stat. 2585; Pub.L. 109–8, Title VIII, § 802(d)(7), Apr. 20, 2005, 119 Stat. 146.)

HISTORICAL AND STATUTORY NOTES

Amendments

2005 Amendments. Subsec. (a). Pub.L. 109–8, § 802(d)(7)(A), struck out subsec. (a), which formerly read: **"(a)** If a creditor receives, in a foreign proceeding, payment of, or a transfer of property on account of, a claim that is allowed under this title, such creditor may not receive any payment under this title on account of such claim until each of the other holders of claims on account of which such holders are entitled to share equally with such creditor under this title has received payment under this title equal in value to the consideration received by such creditor in such foreign proceeding."

Subsec. (b). Pub.L. 109–8, § 802(d)(7)(B), struck out "**(b)**".

§ 509. Claims of codebtors

(a) Except as provided in subsection (b) or (c) of this section, an entity that is liable with the debtor on, or that has secured, a claim of a creditor against the debtor, and that pays such claim, is subrogated to the rights of such creditor to the extent of such payment.

(b) Such entity is not subrogated to the rights of such creditor to the extent that—

  (1) a claim of such entity for reimbursement or contribution on account of such payment of such creditor's claim is—

  (A) allowed under section 502 of this title;

  (B) disallowed other than under section 502(e) of this title; or

  (C) subordinated under section 510 of this title; or

  (2) as between the debtor and such entity, such entity received the consideration for the claim held by such creditor.

(c) The court shall subordinate to the claim of a creditor and for the benefit of such creditor an allowed claim, by way of subrogation under this section, or for reimbursement or contribution, of an entity that is liable with the debtor on, or that has secured, such creditor's claim, until such creditor's claim is paid in full, either through payments under this title or otherwise.

(Pub.L. 95–598, Nov. 6, 1978, 92 Stat. 2585; Pub.L. 98–353, Title III, § 450, July 10, 1984, 98 Stat. 375.)

HISTORICAL AND STATUTORY NOTES

Amendments

1984 Amendments. Subsec. (a). Pub.L. 98–353, § 450(a)(1), substituted "subsection (b) or" for "subsections (b) and".

Pub.L. 98–353, § 450(a)(2), added, "against the debtor" following "a creditor".

Subsec. (b)(1). Pub.L. 98–353, § 450(b), substituted "of such" for "of a" following "account".

Subsec. (c). Pub.L. 98–353, § 450(c) substituted "this section" for "section 509 of this title".

CROSS REFERENCES

Applicability of this section in Chapter 9 cases, see 11 USCA § 901.

§ 510. Subordination

(a) A subordination agreement is enforceable in a case under this title to the same extent that such agreement is enforceable under applicable nonbankruptcy law.

(b) For the purpose of distribution under this title, a claim arising from rescission of a purchase or sale of a security of the debtor or of an affiliate of the debtor, for damages arising from the purchase or sale of such a security, or for reimbursement or contribution allowed under section 502 on account of such a claim, shall be subordinated to all claims or interests that are senior to or equal the claim or interest represented by such security, except that if such security is common stock, such claim has the same priority as common stock.

(c) Notwithstanding subsections (a) and (b) of this section, after notice and a hearing, the court may—

(1) under principles of equitable subordination, subordinate for purposes of distribution all or part of an allowed claim to all or part of another allowed claim or all or part of an allowed interest to all or part of another allowed interest; or

(2) order that any lien securing such a subordinated claim be transferred to the estate.

(Pub.L. 95–598, Nov. 6, 1978, 92 Stat. 2586; Pub.L. 98–353, Title III, § 451, July 10, 1984, 98 Stat. 375.)

HISTORICAL AND STATUTORY NOTES

Amendments

1984 Amendments. Subsec. (b). Pub.L. 98–353 substituted "For the purpose of distribution under this title, a claim arising from rescission of a purchase or sale of a security of the debtor or of an affiliate of the debtor, for damages arising from the purchase or sale of such a security, or for reimbursement or contribution allowed under section 502 on account of such a claim, shall be subordinated to all claims or interests that are senior to or equal the claim or interest represented by such security, except that if such security is common stock, such claim has the same priority as common stock." for "Any claim for recission of a purchase or sale of a security of the debtor or of an affiliate or for damages arising from the purchase or sale of such a security shall be subordinated for purposes of distribution to all claims and interests that are senior or equal to the claim or interest represented by such security.".

CROSS REFERENCES

Applicability of this section in Chapter 9 cases, see 11 USCA § 901.

Certain customer claims in stockbroker liquidation proceedings, see 11 USCA § 747.

Confirmation of plan, see 11 USCA § 1129.

Distribution of—

    Customer property, see 11 USCA § 752.

    Property of estate, see 11 USCA § 726.

Effect of dismissal, see 11 USCA § 349.

Property of estate, see 11 USCA § 541.

Property recoverable by trustee as exempt, see 11 USCA § 522.

Unpaid portion of certain claims as entitled to distribution, see 11 USCA § 766.

§ 511. Rate of interest on tax claims

(a) If any provision of this title requires the payment of interest on a tax claim or on an administrative expense tax, or the payment of interest to enable a creditor to receive the present value of the allowed amount of a tax claim, the rate of interest shall be the rate determined under applicable nonbankruptcy law.

(b) In the case of taxes paid under a confirmed plan under this title, the rate of interest shall be determined as of the calendar month in which the plan is confirmed.

(Added Pub.L. 109–8, Title VII, § 704(a), Apr. 20, 2005, 119 Stat. 125.)

Title 11   CREDITORS, THE DEBTOR, AND THE ESTATE   11 § 521

SUBCHAPTER II—DEBTOR'S DUTIES AND BENEFITS

§ 521. Debtor's duties

(a) The debtor shall—

   (1) file—

      (A) a list of creditors; and

      (B) unless the court orders otherwise—

         (i) a schedule of assets and liabilities;

         (ii) a schedule of current income and current expenditures;

         (iii) a statement of the debtor's financial affairs and, if section 342(b) applies, a certificate—

            (I) of an attorney whose name is indicated on the petition as the attorney for the debtor, or a bankruptcy petition preparer signing the petition under section 110(b)(1), indicating that such attorney or the bankruptcy petition preparer delivered to the debtor the notice required by section 342(b); or

            (II) if no attorney is so indicated, and no bankruptcy petition preparer signed the petition, of the debtor that such notice was received and read by the debtor;

         (iv) copies of all payment advices or other evidence of payment received within 60 days before the date of the filing of the petition, by the debtor from any employer of the debtor;

         (v) a statement of the amount of monthly net income, itemized to show how the amount is calculated; and

         (vi) a statement disclosing any reasonably anticipated increase in income or expenditures over the 12-month period following the date of the filing of the petition;

   (2) if an individual debtor's schedule of assets and liabilities includes debts which are secured by property of the estate—

      (A) within thirty days after the date of the filing of a petition under chapter 7 of this title or on or before the date of the meeting of creditors, whichever is earlier, or within such additional time as the court, for cause, within such period fixes, file with the clerk a statement of his intention with respect to the retention or surrender of such property and, if applicable, specifying that such property is claimed as exempt, that the debtor intends to redeem such property, or that the debtor intends to reaffirm debts secured by such property; and

      (B) within 30 days after the first date set for the meeting of creditors under section 341(a), or within such additional time as the court, for cause, within such 30-day period fixes, perform his intention with respect to such property, as specified by subparagraph (A) of this paragraph;

except that nothing in subparagraphs (A) and (B) of this paragraph shall alter the debtor's or the trustee's rights with regard to such property under this title, except as provided in section 362(h);

   (3) if a trustee is serving in the case or an auditor is serving under section 586(f) of title 28, cooperate with the trustee as necessary to enable the trustee to perform the trustee's duties under this title;

   (4) if a trustee is serving in the case or an auditor is serving under section 586(f) of title 28, surrender to the trustee all property of the estate and any recorded information, including

books, documents, records, and papers, relating to property of the estate, whether or not immunity is granted under section 344 of this title;

(5) appear at the hearing required under section 524(d) of this title;

(6) in a case under chapter 7 of this title in which the debtor is an individual, not retain possession of personal property as to which a creditor has an allowed claim for the purchase price secured in whole or in part by an interest in such personal property unless the debtor, not later than 45 days after the first meeting of creditors under section 341(a), either—

   (A) enters into an agreement with the creditor pursuant to section 524(c) with respect to the claim secured by such property; or

   (B) redeems such property from the security interest pursuant to section 722; and

(7) unless a trustee is serving in the case, continue to perform the obligations required of the administrator (as defined in section 3 of the Employee Retirement Income Security Act of 1974) of an employee benefit plan if at the time of the commencement of the case the debtor (or any entity designated by the debtor) served as such administrator.

If the debtor fails to so act within the 45-day period referred to in paragraph (6), the stay under section 362(a) is terminated with respect to the personal property of the estate or of the debtor which is affected, such property shall no longer be property of the estate, and the creditor may take whatever action as to such property as is permitted by applicable nonbankruptcy law, unless the court determines on the motion of the trustee filed before the expiration of such 45-day period, and after notice and a hearing, that such property is of consequential value or benefit to the estate, orders appropriate adequate protection of the creditor's interest, and orders the debtor to deliver any collateral in the debtor's possession to the trustee.

(b) In addition to the requirements under subsection (a), a debtor who is an individual shall file with the court—

(1) a certificate from the approved nonprofit budget and credit counseling agency that provided the debtor services under section 109(h) describing the services provided to the debtor; and

(2) a copy of the debt repayment plan, if any, developed under section 109(h) through the approved nonprofit budget and credit counseling agency referred to in paragraph (1).

(c) In addition to meeting the requirements under subsection (a), a debtor shall file with the court a record of any interest that a debtor has in an education individual retirement account (as defined in section 530(b)(1) of the Internal Revenue Code of 1986), an interest in an account in a qualified ABLE program (as defined in section 529A(b) of such Code, or under a qualified State tuition program (as defined in section 529(b)(1) of such Code).

(d) If the debtor fails timely to take the action specified in subsection (a)(6) of this section, or in paragraphs (1) and (2) of section 362(h), with respect to property which a lessor or bailor owns and has leased, rented, or bailed to the debtor or as to which a creditor holds a security interest not otherwise voidable under section 522(f), 544, 545, 547, 548, or 549, nothing in this title shall prevent or limit the operation of a provision in the underlying lease or agreement that has the effect of placing the debtor in default under such lease or agreement by reason of the occurrence, pendency, or existence of a proceeding under this title or the insolvency of the debtor. Nothing in this subsection shall be deemed to justify limiting such a provision in any other circumstance.

(e)(1) If the debtor in a case under chapter 7 or 13 is an individual and if a creditor files with the court at any time a request to receive a copy of the petition, schedules, and statement of financial affairs filed by the debtor, then the court shall make such petition, such schedules, and such statement available to such creditor.

(2)(A) The debtor shall provide—

   (i) not later than 7 days before the date first set for the first meeting of creditors, to the trustee a copy of the Federal income tax return required under applicable law (or at the election of the debtor, a transcript of such return) for the most recent tax year ending immediately before the commencement of the case and for which a Federal income tax return was filed; and

(ii) at the same time the debtor complies with clause (i), a copy of such return (or if elected under clause (i), such transcript) to any creditor that timely requests such copy.

(B) If the debtor fails to comply with clause (i) or (ii) of subparagraph (A), the court shall dismiss the case unless the debtor demonstrates that the failure to so comply is due to circumstances beyond the control of the debtor.

(C) If a creditor requests a copy of such tax return or such transcript and if the debtor fails to provide a copy of such tax return or such transcript to such creditor at the time the debtor provides such tax return or such transcript to the trustee, then the court shall dismiss the case unless the debtor demonstrates that the failure to provide a copy of such tax return or such transcript is due to circumstances beyond the control of the debtor.

(3) If a creditor in a case under chapter 13 files with the court at any time a request to receive a copy of the plan filed by the debtor, then the court shall make available to such creditor a copy of the plan—

(A) at a reasonable cost; and

(B) not later than 7 days after such request is filed.

(f) At the request of the court, the United States trustee, or any party in interest in a case under chapter 7, 11, or 13, a debtor who is an individual shall file with the court—

(1) at the same time filed with the taxing authority, a copy of each Federal income tax return required under applicable law (or at the election of the debtor, a transcript of such tax return) with respect to each tax year of the debtor ending while the case is pending under such chapter;

(2) at the same time filed with the taxing authority, each Federal income tax return required under applicable law (or at the election of the debtor, a transcript of such tax return) that had not been filed with such authority as of the date of the commencement of the case and that was subsequently filed for any tax year of the debtor ending in the 3-year period ending on the date of the commencement of the case;

(3) a copy of each amendment to any Federal income tax return or transcript filed with the court under paragraph (1) or (2); and

(4) in a case under chapter 13—

(A) on the date that is either 90 days after the end of such tax year or 1 year after the date of the commencement of the case, whichever is later, if a plan is not confirmed before such later date; and

(B) annually after the plan is confirmed and until the case is closed, not later than the date that is 45 days before the anniversary of the confirmation of the plan;

a statement, under penalty of perjury, of the income and expenditures of the debtor during the tax year of the debtor most recently concluded before such statement is filed under this paragraph, and of the monthly income of the debtor, that shows how income, expenditures, and monthly income are calculated.

(g)(1) A statement referred to in subsection (f)(4) shall disclose—

(A) the amount and sources of the income of the debtor;

(B) the identity of any person responsible with the debtor for the support of any dependent of the debtor; and

(C) the identity of any person who contributed, and the amount contributed, to the household in which the debtor resides.

(2) The tax returns, amendments, and statement of income and expenditures described in subsections (e)(2)(A) and (f) shall be available to the United States trustee (or the bankruptcy

administrator, if any), the trustee, and any party in interest for inspection and copying, subject to the requirements of section 315(c) of the Bankruptcy Abuse Prevention and Consumer Protection Act of 2005.

(h) If requested by the United States trustee or by the trustee, the debtor shall provide—

(1) a document that establishes the identity of the debtor, including a driver's license, passport, or other document that contains a photograph of the debtor; or

(2) such other personal identifying information relating to the debtor that establishes the identity of the debtor.

(i)(1) Subject to paragraphs (2) and (4) and notwithstanding section 707(a), if an individual debtor in a voluntary case under chapter 7 or 13 fails to file all of the information required under subsection (a)(1) within 45 days after the date of the filing of the petition, the case shall be automatically dismissed effective on the 46th day after the date of the filing of the petition.

(2) Subject to paragraph (4) and with respect to a case described in paragraph (1), any party in interest may request the court to enter an order dismissing the case. If requested, the court shall enter an order of dismissal not later than 7 days after such request.

(3) Subject to paragraph (4) and upon request of the debtor made within 45 days after the date of the filing of the petition described in paragraph (1), the court may allow the debtor an additional period of not to exceed 45 days to file the information required under subsection (a)(1) if the court finds justification for extending the period for the filing.

(4) Notwithstanding any other provision of this subsection, on the motion of the trustee filed before the expiration of the applicable period of time specified in paragraph (1), (2), or (3), and after notice and a hearing, the court may decline to dismiss the case if the court finds that the debtor attempted in good faith to file all the information required by subsection (a)(1)(B)(iv) and that the best interests of creditors would be served by administration of the case.

(j)(1) Notwithstanding any other provision of this title, if the debtor fails to file a tax return that becomes due after the commencement of the case or to properly obtain an extension of the due date for filing such return, the taxing authority may request that the court enter an order converting or dismissing the case.

(2) If the debtor does not file the required return or obtain the extension referred to in paragraph (1) within 90 days after a request is filed by the taxing authority under that paragraph, the court shall convert or dismiss the case, whichever is in the best interests of creditors and the estate.

(Pub.L. 95–598, Nov. 6, 1978, 92 Stat. 2586; Pub.L. 98–353, Title III, §§ 305, 452, July 10, 1984, 98 Stat. 352, 375; Pub.L. 99–554, Title II, § 283(h), Oct. 27, 1986, 100 Stat. 3117; Pub.L. 109–8, Title I, § 106(d), Title II, § 225(b), Title III, §§ 304(1), 305(2), 315(b), 316, Title IV, § 446(a), Title VI, § 603(c), Title VII, § 720, Apr. 20, 2005, 119 Stat. 38, 66, 78, 80, 89, 90, 92, 118, 123, 133; Pub.L. 111–16, § 2(5), (6), May 7, 2009, 123 Stat. 1607; Pub.L. 111–327, § 2(a)(16), Dec. 22, 2010, 124 Stat. 3559.)

HISTORICAL AND STATUTORY NOTES

References in Text

Section 3 of the Employee Retirement Income Security Act of 1974, referred to in subsec. (a)(7), is Pub.L. 93–406, Title I, § 3, Sept. 2, 1974, 88 Stat. 833, which is classified to 29 U.S.C.A. § 1002.

Section 530(b)(1) of the Internal Revenue Code of 1986, referred to in subsec. (c), is classified to 26 U.S.C.A. § 530(b)(1).

Section 529(b)(1) of such Code, referred to in subsec. (c), is classified to 26 U.S.C.A. § 529(b)(1).

Section 315(c) of the Bankruptcy Abuse Prevention and Consumer Protection Act of 2005, referred to in subsec. (g)(2), is Pub.L. 109–8, Title III, § 315(c), Apr. 20, 2005, 119 Stat. 91, which is set out as a note under this section.

Amendments

   2014 Amendments. Sebsec. (c). Pub.L. 113-295, § 104(c), inserted ", an interest in an account in a qualified ABLE program (as defined in section 529A(b) of such Code," after "Internal Revenue Code of 1986)".

   2010 Amendments. Subsec. (a)(2)(A). Pub.L. 111–327, § 2(a)(16)(A)(i), struck out "the debtor shall" following "such period fixes,", and inserted "and" after the semicolon at the end.

   Subsec. (a)(2)(B). Pub.L. 111–327, § 2(a)(16)(A)(ii), struck out "the debtor shall" following "30-day period fixes,", and struck out "and" following the semicolon at the end.

   Subsec. (a)(2)(C). Pub.L. 111–327, § 2(a)(16)(A)(iii), struck out the designator "(C)" and inserted except that".

   Subsec. (a)(3). Pub.L. 111–327, § 2(a)(16)(B), inserted "is" following "auditor".

   Subsec. (a)(4). Pub.L. 111–327, § 2(a)(16)(B), inserted "is" following "auditor".

   2009 Amendments. Subsec. (e)(3)(B). Pub.L. 111–16, § 2(5), struck out "5 days" and inserted "7 days".

   Subsec. (i)(2). Pub.L. 111–16, § 2(6), struck out "5 days" and inserted "7 days".

   2005 Amendments. Subsec. (a). Pub.L. 109–8, § 106(d)(1), inserted "**(a)**" before "The debtor shall—".

   Pub.L. 109–8, § 304(1)(C), added concluding provisions.

   Subsec. (a)(1). Pub.L. 109–8, § 315(b)(1), rewrote par. (1), which formerly read: **"(1)** file a list of creditors, and unless the court orders otherwise, a schedule of assets and liabilities, a schedule of current income and current expenditures, and a statement of the debtor's financial affairs;"

   Subsec. (a)(2). Pub.L. 109–8, § 305(2)(A), struck out "consumer" preceding "debts which are secured by".

   Subsec. (a)(2)(B). Pub.L. 109–8, § 305(2)(B)(i), struck out "forty-five days after the filing of a notice of intent under this section" and inserted "30 days after the first date set for the meeting of creditors under section 341(a)".

   Pub.L. 109–8, § 305(2)(B)(ii), struck out "forty-five day" and inserted "30-day".

   Subsec. (a)(2)(C). Pub.L. 109–8, § 305(2)(C), inserted ", except as provided in section 362(h)" before the semicolon.

   Subsec. (a)(3). Pub.L. 109–8, § 603(c), inserted "or an auditor serving under section 586(f) of title 28" after "serving in the case".

   Subsec. (a)(4). Pub.L. 109–8, § 304(1)(A), struck out ", and" at the end of par. (4) and inserted a semicolon.

   Pub.L. 109–8, § 603(c), inserted "or an auditor serving under section 586(f) of title 28" after "serving in the case".

   Subsec. (a)(5). Pub.L. 109–8, § 304(1)(B), struck out the period at the end of par. (5) and inserted "; and".

   Pub.L. 109–8, § 446(a)(1), struck "and" at the end of par. (5).

   Subsec. (a)(6). Pub.L. 109–8, § 304(1)(C), added par. (6).

   Pub.L. 109–8, § 446(a)(2), struck the period at the end of par. (6) and inserted "; and".

   Subsec. (a)(7). Pub.L. 109–8, § 446(a)(3), added par. (7).

   Subsec. (b). Pub.L. 109–8, § 106(d)(2), added subsec. (b).

   Subsec. (c). Pub.L. 109–8, § 225(b), added subsec. (c).

   Subsec. (d). Pub.L. 109–8, § 305(2)(D), added subsec. (d).

   Subsecs. (e) to (h). Pub.L. 109–8, § 315(b)(2), added subsecs. (e), (f), (g), and (h).

   Subsec. (i). Pub.L. 109–8, § 316, added subsec. (i).

Subsec. (j). Pub.L. 109-8, § 720, added subsec. (j).

1986 Amendments. Par. (4). Pub.L. 99-554 added provisions relating to granting of immunity under section 344 of this title.

1984 Amendments. Par. (1). Pub.L. 98-353, § 305(2), added "a schedule of current income and current expenditures," following "liabilities,".

Par. (2). Pub.L. 98-353, § 305(3), added par. (2). Former par. (2) was redesignated as (3).

Par. (3). Pub.L. 98-353, § 305(1), redesignated former par. (2) as (3). Former par. (3) was redesignated as (4).

Pub.L. 98-353, § 452, which directed the insertion of ", whether or not immunity is granted under section 344 of this title" after second reference to "estate" in par. (3) as redesignated above, could not be executed because such reference appeared in par. (4) rather than in par. (3). See 1986 Amendments note under this section relating to par. (4).

Par. (4). Pub.L. 98-353, § 305(1), redesignated former par. (3) as (4). Former par. (4) was redesignated as (5).

Par. (5). Pub.L. 98-353, § 305(1), redesignated former par. (4) as (5).

Confidentiality of Tax Information

Pub.L. 109-8, Title III, § 315(c), Apr. 20, 2005, 119 Stat. 91, provided that:

"**(1)** Not later than 180 days after the date of the enactment of this Act [Apr. 20, 2005], the Director of the Administrative Office of the United States Courts shall establish procedures for safeguarding the confidentiality of any tax information required to be provided under this section.

"**(2)** The procedures under paragraph (1) shall include restrictions on creditor access to tax information that is required to be provided under this section.

"**(3)** Not later than 540 days after the date of enactment of this Act [Apr. 20, 2005], the director of the administrative office of the United States courts shall prepare and submit to the President pro tempore of the Senate and the speaker of the House of Representatives a report that—

"**(A)** assesses the effectiveness of the procedures established under paragraph (1); and

"**(B)** If appropriate, includes proposed legislation to—

"**(i)** further protect the confidentiality of tax information; and

"**(ii)** provide penalties for the improper use by any person of the tax information required to be provided under this section."

[Amendments by Pub.L. 109-8 effective, except as otherwise provided, 180 days after April 20, 2005, and inapplicable with respect to cases commenced under Title 11 before the effective date, see Pub.L. 109-8, § 1501, set out as a note under 11 U.S.C.A. § 101.]

Providing Requested Tax Documents to the Court.

Pub.L. 109-8, Title XII, § 1228, Apr. 20, 2005, 119 Stat. 200, provided that:

"**(a) Chapter 7 cases.**—The court shall not grant a discharge in the case of an individual who is a debtor in a case under chapter 7 of title 11, United States Code [11 U.S.C.A. § 701 et seq.], unless requested tax documents have been provided to the court.

"**(b) Chapter 11 and chapter 13 cases.**—The court shall not confirm a plan of reorganization in the case of an individual under chapter 11 or 13 of title 11, United States Code [11 U.S.C.A. § 1101 et seq. or 1301 et seq.], unless requested tax documents have been filed with the court.

"**(c) Document retention.**—The court shall destroy documents submitted in support of a bankruptcy claim not sooner than 3 years after the date of the conclusion of a case filed by an individual under chapter 7, 11, or 13 of title 11, United States Code [11 U.S.C.A. § 701 et seq. or 1101 et seq., or 1301 et seq.]. In the event of a pending audit or enforcement action, the court may extend the time for destruction of such requested tax documents."

[Amendments by Pub.L. 109-8 effective, except as otherwise provided, 180 days after April 20, 2005, and inapplicable with respect to cases commenced under Title 11 before the effective date, see Pub.L. 109-8, § 1501, set out as a note under 11 U.S.C.A. § 101.]

| Title 11 | CREDITORS, THE DEBTOR, AND THE ESTATE | 11 § 522 |

CROSS REFERENCES

Conversion or dismissal of—

    Chapter 11 case, see 11 USCA § 1112.

    Chapter 13 case, see 11 USCA § 1307.

Debtor's statement of intention, see Official Bankr. Form 8, 11 USCA.

Dismissal of Chapter 7 case, see 11 USCA § 707.

Filing of list, schedule and statement by trustee, see 11 USCA § 1106.

Lists, schedules, statements and fees, see Fed.Rules Bankr.Proc. Form B 200, 11 USCA.

Order converting case, see Fed.Rules Bankr.Proc. Form B 221A et seq., 11 USCA.

Penalty for persons who negligently or fraudulently prepare bankruptcy petitions or failure to file bankruptcy papers, see 11 USCA § 110.

Proof of claim or interest deemed filed if scheduled, see 11 USCA § 1111.

Property scheduled but unadministered before close of case deemed abandoned, see 11 USCA § 554.

Trustee's duty to ensure performance of debtor's intention as specified in subsec. (2)(B) of this section, see 11 USCA § 704.

§ 522. Exemptions

(a) In this section—

    (1) "dependent" includes spouse, whether or not actually dependent; and

    (2) "value" means fair market value as of the date of the filing of the petition or, with respect to property that becomes property of the estate after such date, as of the date such property becomes property of the estate.

(b)(1) Notwithstanding section 541 of this title, an individual debtor may exempt from property of the estate the property listed in either paragraph (2) or, in the alternative, paragraph (3) of this subsection. In joint cases filed under section 302 of this title and individual cases filed under section 301 or 303 of this title by or against debtors who are husband and wife, and whose estates are ordered to be jointly administered under Rule 1015(b) of the Federal Rules of Bankruptcy Procedure, one debtor may not elect to exempt property listed in paragraph (2) and the other debtor elect to exempt property listed in paragraph (3) of this subsection. If the parties cannot agree on the alternative to be elected, they shall be deemed to elect paragraph (2), where such election is permitted under the law of the jurisdiction where the case is filed.

    (2) Property listed in this paragraph is property that is specified under subsection (d), unless the State law that is applicable to the debtor under paragraph (3)(A) specifically does not so authorize.

    (3) Property listed in this paragraph is—

        (A) subject to subsections (o) and (p), any property that is exempt under Federal law, other than subsection (d) of this section, or State or local law that is applicable on the date of the filing of the petition to the place in which the debtor's domicile has been located for the 730 days immediately preceding the date of the filing of the petition or if the debtor's domicile has not been located in a single State for such 730-day period, the place in which the debtor's domicile was located for 180 days immediately preceding the 730-day period or for a longer portion of such 180-day period than in any other place;

        (B) any interest in property in which the debtor had, immediately before the commencement of the case, an interest as a tenant by the entirety or joint tenant to the extent that such interest as a tenant by the entirety or joint tenant is exempt from process under applicable nonbankruptcy law; and

(C) retirement funds to the extent that those funds are in a fund or account that is exempt from taxation under section 401, 403, 408, 408A, 414, 457, or 501(a) of the Internal Revenue Code of 1986.

If the effect of the domiciliary requirement under subparagraph (A) is to render the debtor ineligible for any exemption, the debtor may elect to exempt property that is specified under subsection (d).

(4) For purposes of paragraph (3)(C) and subsection (d)(12), the following shall apply:

(A) If the retirement funds are in a retirement fund that has received a favorable determination under section 7805 of the Internal Revenue Code of 1986, and that determination is in effect as of the date of the filing of the petition in a case under this title, those funds shall be presumed to be exempt from the estate.

(B) If the retirement funds are in a retirement fund that has not received a favorable determination under such section 7805, those funds are exempt from the estate if the debtor demonstrates that—

(i) no prior determination to the contrary has been made by a court or the Internal Revenue Service; and

(ii)(I) the retirement fund is in substantial compliance with the applicable requirements of the Internal Revenue Code of 1986; or

(II) the retirement fund fails to be in substantial compliance with the applicable requirements of the Internal Revenue Code of 1986 and the debtor is not materially responsible for that failure.

(C) A direct transfer of retirement funds from 1 fund or account that is exempt from taxation under section 401, 403, 408, 408A, 414, 457, or 501(a) of the Internal Revenue Code of 1986, under section 401(a)(31) of the Internal Revenue Code of 1986, or otherwise, shall not cease to qualify for exemption under paragraph (3)(C) or subsection (d)(12) by reason of such direct transfer.

(D)(i) Any distribution that qualifies as an eligible rollover distribution within the meaning of section 402(c) of the Internal Revenue Code of 1986 or that is described in clause (ii) shall not cease to qualify for exemption under paragraph (3)(C) or subsection (d)(12) by reason of such distribution.

(ii) A distribution described in this clause is an amount that—

(I) has been distributed from a fund or account that is exempt from taxation under section 401, 403, 408, 408A, 414, 457, or 501(a) of the Internal Revenue Code of 1986; and

(II) to the extent allowed by law, is deposited in such a fund or account not later than 60 days after the distribution of such amount.

(c) Unless the case is dismissed, property exempted under this section is not liable during or after the case for any debt of the debtor that arose, or that is determined under section 502 of this title as if such debt had arisen, before the commencement of the case, except—

(1) a debt of a kind specified in paragraph (1) or (5) of section 523(a) (in which case, notwithstanding any provision of applicable nonbankruptcy law to the contrary, such property shall be liable for a debt of a kind specified in such paragraph);

(2) a debt secured by a lien that is—

(A)(i) not avoided under subsection (f) or (g) of this section or under section 544, 545, 547, 548, 549, or 724(a) of this title; and

(ii) not void under section 506(d) of this title; or

(B) a tax lien, notice of which is properly filed;

(3) a debt of a kind specified in section 523(a)(4) or 523(a)(6) of this title owed by an institution-affiliated party of an insured depository institution to a Federal depository

Title 11   CREDITORS, THE DEBTOR, AND THE ESTATE   **11 § 522**

institutions regulatory agency acting in its capacity as conservator, receiver, or liquidating agent for such institution; or

(4) a debt in connection with fraud in the obtaining or providing of any scholarship, grant, loan, tuition, discount, award, or other financial assistance for purposes of financing an education at an institution of higher education (as that term is defined in section 101 of the Higher Education Act of 1965 (20 U.S.C. 1001)).

(d) The following property may be exempted under subsection (b)(2) of this section:

(1) The debtor's aggregate interest, not to exceed $22,975[1] in value, in real property or personal property that the debtor or a dependent of the debtor uses as a residence, in a cooperative that owns property that the debtor or a dependent of the debtor uses as a residence, or in a burial plot for the debtor or a dependent of the debtor.

(2) The debtor's interest, not to exceed $3,675[1] in value, in one motor vehicle. *x2 = 7350*

(3) The debtor's interest, not to exceed $575[1] in value in any particular item or $12,250[1] in aggregate value, in household furnishings, household goods, wearing apparel, appliances, books, animals, crops, or musical instruments, that are held primarily for the personal, family, or household use of the debtor or a dependent of the debtor.

(4) The debtor's aggregate interest, not to exceed $1,550[1] in value, in jewelry held primarily for the personal, family, or household use of the debtor or a dependent of the debtor.

(5) The debtor's aggregate interest in any property, not to exceed in value $1,225[1] plus up to $11,500[1] of any unused amount of the exemption provided under paragraph (1) of this subsection.

(6) The debtor's aggregate interest, not to exceed $2,300[1] in value, in any implements, professional books, or tools, of the trade of the debtor or the trade of a dependent of the debtor.

(7) Any unmatured life insurance contract owned by the debtor, other than a credit life insurance contract.

(8) The debtor's aggregate interest, not to exceed in value $12,250[1] less any amount of property of the estate transferred in the manner specified in section 542(d) of this title, in any accrued dividend or interest under, or loan value of, any unmatured life insurance contract owned by the debtor under which the insured is the debtor or an individual of whom the debtor is a dependent.

(9) Professionally prescribed health aids for the debtor or a dependent of the debtor.

(10) The debtor's right to receive—

    (A) a social security benefit, unemployment compensation, or a local public assistance benefit;

    (B) a veterans' benefit;

    (C) a disability, illness, or unemployment benefit;

    (D) alimony, support, or separate maintenance, to the extent reasonably necessary for the support of the debtor and any dependent of the debtor;

    (E) a payment under a stock bonus, pension, profitsharing, annuity, or similar plan or contract on account of illness, disability, death, age, or length of service, to the extent reasonably necessary for the support of the debtor and any dependent of the debtor, unless—

        (i) such plan or contract was established by or under the auspices of an insider that employed the debtor at the time the debtor's rights under such plan or contract arose;

---

[1] Dollar amount as adjusted by the Judicial Conference of the United States. See Adjustment of Dollar Amounts notes set out under this section and 11 U.S.C.A. § 104.

(ii) such payment is on account of age or length of service; and

(iii) such plan or contract does not qualify under section 401(a), 403(a), 403(b), or 408 of the Internal Revenue Code of 1986.

(11) The debtor's right to receive, or property that is traceable to—

(A) an award under a crime victim's reparation law;

(B) a payment on account of the wrongful death of an individual of whom the debtor was a dependent, to the extent reasonably necessary for the support of the debtor and any dependent of the debtor;

(C) a payment under a life insurance contract that insured the life of an individual of whom the debtor was a dependent on the date of such individual's death, to the extent reasonably necessary for the support of the debtor and any dependent of the debtor;

(D) a payment, not to exceed $22,975,[1] on account of personal bodily injury, not including pain and suffering or compensation for actual pecuniary loss, of the debtor or an individual of whom the debtor is a dependent; or

(E) a payment in compensation of loss of future earnings of the debtor or an individual of whom the debtor is or was a dependent, to the extent reasonably necessary for the support of the debtor and any dependent of the debtor.

(12) Retirement funds to the extent that those funds are in a fund or account that is exempt from taxation under section 401, 403, 408, 408A, 414, 457, or 501(a) of the Internal Revenue Code of 1986.

(e) A waiver of an exemption executed in favor of a creditor that holds an unsecured claim against the debtor is unenforceable in a case under this title with respect to such claim against property that the debtor may exempt under subsection (b) of this section. A waiver by the debtor of a power under subsection (f) or (h) of this section to avoid a transfer, under subsection (g) or (i) of this section to exempt property, or under subsection (i) of this section to recover property or to preserve a transfer, is unenforceable in a case under this title.

(f)(1) Notwithstanding any waiver of exemptions but subject to paragraph (3), the debtor may avoid the fixing of a lien on an interest of the debtor in property to the extent that such lien impairs an exemption to which the debtor would have been entitled under subsection (b) of this section, if such lien is—

(A) a judicial lien, other than a judicial lien that secures a debt of a kind that is specified in section 523(a)(5); or

(B) a nonpossessory, nonpurchase-money security interest in any—

(i) household furnishings, household goods, wearing apparel, appliances, books, animals, crops, musical instruments, or jewelry that are held primarily for the personal, family, or household use of the debtor or a dependent of the debtor;

(ii) implements, professional books, or tools, of the trade of the debtor or the trade of a dependent of the debtor; or

(iii) professionally prescribed health aids for the debtor or a dependent of the debtor.

(2)(A) For the purposes of this subsection, a lien shall be considered to impair an exemption to the extent that the sum of—

(i) the lien;

(ii) all other liens on the property; and

---

[1] Dollar amount as adjusted by the Judicial Conference of the United States. See Adjustment of Dollar Amounts notes set out under this section and 11 U.S.C.A. § 104.

(iii) the amount of the exemption that the debtor could claim if there were no liens on the property;

exceeds the value that the debtor's interest in the property would have in the absence of any liens.

(B) In the case of a property subject to more than 1 lien, a lien that has been avoided shall not be considered in making the calculation under subparagraph (A) with respect to other liens.

(C) This paragraph shall not apply with respect to a judgment arising out of a mortgage foreclosure.

(3) In a case in which State law that is applicable to the debtor—

(A) permits a person to voluntarily waive a right to claim exemptions under subsection (d) or prohibits a debtor from claiming exemptions under subsection (d); and

(B) either permits the debtor to claim exemptions under State law without limitation in amount, except to the extent that the debtor has permitted the fixing of a consensual lien on any property or prohibits avoidance of a consensual lien on property otherwise eligible to be claimed as exempt property;

the debtor may not avoid the fixing of a lien on an interest of the debtor or a dependent of the debtor in property if the lien is a nonpossessory, nonpurchase-money security interest in implements, professional books, or tools of the trade of the debtor or a dependent of the debtor or farm animals or crops of the debtor or a dependent of the debtor to the extent the value of such implements, professional books, tools of the trade, animals, and crops exceeds $6,225[1].

(4)(A) Subject to subparagraph (B), for purposes of paragraph (1)(B), the term "household goods" means—

    (i) clothing;

    (ii) furniture;

    (iii) appliances;

    (iv) 1 radio;

    (v) 1 television;

    (vi) 1 VCR;

    (vii) linens;

    (viii) china;

    (ix) crockery;

    (x) kitchenware;

    (xi) educational materials and educational equipment primarily for the use of minor dependent children of the debtor;

    (xii) medical equipment and supplies;

    (xiii) furniture exclusively for the use of minor children, or elderly or disabled dependents of the debtor;

    (xiv) personal effects (including the toys and hobby equipment of minor dependent children and wedding rings) of the debtor and the dependents of the debtor; and

    (xv) 1 personal computer and related equipment.

(B) The term "household goods" does not include—

    (i) works of art (unless by or of the debtor, or any relative of the debtor);

---

[1] Dollar amount as adjusted by the Judicial Conference of the United States. See Adjustment of Dollar Amounts notes set out under this section and 11 U.S.C.A. § 104.

(ii) electronic entertainment equipment with a fair market value of more than $650[1] in the aggregate (except 1 television, 1 radio, and 1 VCR);

(iii) items acquired as antiques with a fair market value of more than $650[1] in the aggregate

(iv) jewelry with a fair market value of more than $650[1] in the aggregate (except wedding rings); and

(v) a computer (except as otherwise provided for in this section), motor vehicle (including a tractor or lawn tractor), boat, or a motorized recreational device, conveyance, vehicle, watercraft, or aircraft.

(g) Notwithstanding sections 550 and 551 of this title, the debtor may exempt under subsection (b) of this section property that the trustee recovers under section 510(c)(2), 542, 543, 550, 551, or 553 of this title, to the extent that the debtor could have exempted such property under subsection (b) of this section if such property had not been transferred, if—

(1)(A) such transfer was not a voluntary transfer of such property by the debtor; and

(B) the debtor did not conceal such property; or

(2) the debtor could have avoided such transfer under subsection (f)(1)(B) of this section.

(h) The debtor may avoid a transfer of property of the debtor or recover a setoff to the extent that the debtor could have exempted such property under subsection (g)(1) of this section if the trustee had avoided such transfer, if—

(1) such transfer is avoidable by the trustee under section 544, 545, 547, 548, 549, or 724(a) of this title or recoverable by the trustee under section 553 of this title; and

(2) the trustee does not attempt to avoid such transfer.

(i)(1) If the debtor avoids a transfer or recovers a setoff under subsection (f) or (h) of this section, the debtor may recover in the manner prescribed by, and subject to the limitations of, section 550 of this title, the same as if the trustee had avoided such transfer, and may exempt any property so recovered under subsection (b) of this section.

(2) Notwithstanding section 551 of this title, a transfer avoided under section 544, 545, 547, 548, 549, or 724(a) of this title, under subsection (f) or (h) of this section, or property recovered under section 553 of this title, may be preserved for the benefit of the debtor to the extent that the debtor may exempt such property under subsection (g) of this section or paragraph (1) of this subsection.

(j) Notwithstanding subsections (g) and (i) of this section, the debtor may exempt a particular kind of property under subsections (g) and (i) of this section only to the extent that the debtor has exempted less property in value of such kind than that to which the debtor is entitled under subsection (b) of this section.

(k) Property that the debtor exempts under this section is not liable for payment of any administrative expense except—

(1) the aliquot share of the costs and expenses of avoiding a transfer of property that the debtor exempts under subsection (g) of this section, or of recovery of such property, that is attributable to the value of the portion of such property exempted in relation to the value of the property recovered; and

(2) any costs and expenses of avoiding a transfer under subsection (f) or (h) of this section, or of recovery of property under subsection (i)(1) of this section, that the debtor has not paid.

(l) The debtor shall file a list of property that the debtor claims as exempt under subsection (b) of this section. If the debtor does not file such a list, a dependent of the debtor may file such a

---

[1] Dollar amount as adjusted by the Judicial Conference of the United States. See Adjustment of Dollar Amounts notes set out under this section and 11 U.S.C.A. § 104.

list, or may claim property as exempt from property of the estate on behalf of the debtor. Unless a party in interest objects, the property claimed as exempt on such list is exempt.

(m) Subject to the limitation in subsection (b), this section shall apply separately with respect to each debtor in a joint case.

(n) For assets in individual retirement accounts described in section 408 or 408A of the Internal Revenue Code of 1986, other than a simplified employee pension under section 408(k) of such Code or a simple retirement account under section 408(p) of such Code, the aggregate value of such assets exempted under this section, without regard to amounts attributable to rollover contributions under section 402(c), 402(e)(6), 403(a)(4), 403(a) (5), and 403(b)(8) of the Internal Revenue Code of 1986, and earnings thereon, shall not exceed $1,245,475[1] in a case filed by a debtor who is an individual, except that such amount may be increased if the interests of justice so require.

(o) For purposes of subsection (b)(3)(A), and notwithstanding subsection (a), the value of an interest in—

(1) real or personal property that the debtor or a dependent of the debtor uses as a residence;

(2) a cooperative that owns property that the debtor or a dependent of the debtor uses as a residence;

(3) a burial plot for the debtor or a dependent of the debtor; or

(4) real or personal property that the debtor or a dependent of the debtor claims as a homestead;

shall be reduced to the extent that such value is attributable to any portion of any property that the debtor disposed of in the 10-year period ending on the date of the filing of the petition with the intent to hinder, delay, or defraud a creditor and that the debtor could not exempt, or that portion that the debtor could not exempt, under subsection (b), if on such date the debtor had held the property so disposed of.

(p)(1) Except as provided in paragraph (2) of this subsection and sections 544 and 548, as a result of electing under subsection (b)(3)(A) to exempt property under State or local law, a debtor may not exempt any amount of interest that was acquired by the debtor during the 1215-day period preceding the date of the filing of the petition that exceeds in the aggregate $155,675[1] in value in—

(A) real or personal property that the debtor or a dependent of the debtor uses as a residence;

(B) a cooperative that owns property that the debtor or a dependent of the debtor uses as a residence;

(C) a burial plot for the debtor or a dependent of the debtor; or

(D) real or personal property that the debtor or dependent of the debtor claims as a homestead.

(2)(A) The limitation under paragraph (1) shall not apply to an exemption claimed under subsection (b)(3)(A) by a family farmer for the principal residence of such farmer.

(B) For purposes of paragraph (1), any amount of such interest does not include any interest transferred from a debtor's previous principal residence (which was acquired prior to the beginning of such 1215-day period) into the debtor's current principal residence, if the debtor's previous and current residences are located in the same State.

(q)(1) As a result of electing under subsection (b)(3)(A) to exempt property under State or local law, a debtor may not exempt any amount of an interest in property described in subparagraphs (A), (B), (C), and (D) of subsection (p)(1) which exceeds in the aggregate $155,675[1] if—

---

[1] Dollar amount as adjusted by the Judicial Conference of the United States. See Adjustment of Dollar Amounts notes set out under this section and 11 U.S.C.A. § 104.

(A) the court determines, after notice and a hearing, that the debtor has been convicted of a felony (as defined in section 3156 of title 18), which under the circumstances, demonstrates that the filing of the case was an abuse of the provisions of this title; or

(B) the debtor owes a debt arising from—

(i) any violation of the Federal securities laws (as defined in section 3(a)(47) of the Securities Exchange Act of 1934), any State securities laws, or any regulation or order issued under Federal securities laws or State securities laws;

(ii) fraud, deceit, or manipulation in a fiduciary capacity or in connection with the purchase or sale of any security registered under section 12 or 15(d) of the Securities Exchange Act of 1934 or under section 6 of the Securities Act of 1933;

(iii) any civil remedy under section 1964 of title 18; or

(iv) any criminal act, intentional tort, or willful or reckless misconduct that caused serious physical injury or death to another individual in the preceding 5 years.

(2) Paragraph (1) shall not apply to the extent the amount of an interest in property described in subparagraphs (A), (B), (C), and (D) of subsection (p)(1) is reasonably necessary for the support of the debtor and any dependent of the debtor.

(Pub.L. 95–598, Nov. 6, 1978, 92 Stat. 2586; Pub.L. 98–353, Title III, §§ 306, 453, July 10, 1984, 98 Stat. 353, 375; Pub.L. 99–554, Title II, § 283(i), Oct. 27, 1986, 100 Stat. 3117; Pub.L. 101–647, Title XXV, § 2522(b), Nov. 29, 1990, 104 Stat. 4866; Pub.L. 103–394, Title I, § 108(d), Title III, §§ 303, 304(d), 310, Title V, § 501(d)(12), Oct. 22, 1994, 108 Stat. 4112, 4132, 4133, 4137, 4145; Pub.L. 106–420, § 4, Nov. 1, 2000, 114 Stat. 1868; Pub.L. 109–8, Title II, §§ 216, 224(a), (e)(1), Title III, §§ 307, 308, 313(a), 322(a), Apr. 20, 2005, 119 Stat. 55, 62, 65, 81, 87, 96; Pub.L. 111–327, § 2(a)(17), Dec. 22, 2010, 124 Stat. 3559.)

HISTORICAL AND STATUTORY NOTES

References in Text

Section 401, 403, 408, 408A, 414, 457, or 501(a) of the Internal Revenue Code of 1986, referred to in subsecs. (b)(2)(C), (4)(C), (D)(ii)(I), (d)(12), is classified to 26 U.S.C.A. § 401, 403, 408, 408A, 414, 457, or 501(a).

Section 7805 of the Internal Revenue Code of 1986, referred to in subsec. (b)(4)(A), (B), is 26 U.S.C.A. § 7805.

The Internal Revenue Code of 1986, referred to in subsec. (b)(4)(B)(ii)(I), (II), is classified to Title 26 of the Code.

Section 402(c) of the Internal Revenue Code of 1986, referred to in subsec. (b)(4)(D)(i), is 26 U.S.C.A. § 402(c).

Section 401(a), 403(a), 403(b), or 408, of the Internal Revenue Code of 1986, referred to in subsec. (d)(10)(E)(iii), is classified to 26 U.S.C.A. § 401(a), 403(a), 403(b), or 408.

Section 408 or 408A of the Internal Revenue Code of 1986, referred to in subsec. (n), is classified to 26 U.S.C.A. § 408 or 408A.

Section 402(c), 402(e)(6), 403(a)(4), 403(a)(5), and 403(b)(8) of the Internal Revenue Code of 1986, referred to in subsec. (n), are classified to 26 U.S.C.A. §§ 402(c), 402(e)(6), 403(a)(4), 403(a)(5), and 403(b)(8).

Section 3(a)(47) of the Securities Exchange Act of 1934, referred to in subsec. (q)(1)(B)(i), is June 6, 1934, c. 404, Title I, § 3(a)(47), 48 Stat. 882, as amended, which is classified to 15 U.S.C.A. § 78c(a)(47).

Section 12 or 15(d) of the Securities Exchange Act of 1934, referred to in subsec. (q)(1)(B)(ii), is June 6, 1934, c. 404, Title I, § 12 or 15, 48 Stat. 892 or 895, as amended, which is classified to 15 U.S.C.A. § 78*l* or 15 U.S.C.A. § 78o.

Section 6 of the Securities Act of 1933, referred to in subsec. (q)(1)(B)(ii), is Act May 27, 1933, c. 38, Title I, § 6, 48 Stat. 78, which is classified to 15 U.S.C.A. § 77f.

Title 11   CREDITORS, THE DEBTOR, AND THE ESTATE   11 § 522

Amendments

2010 Amendments. Subsec. (b)(3)(A). Pub.L. 111–327, § 2(a)(17)(A), struck out "petition at" and inserted "petition to", and struck out "located at" and inserted "located in".

Subsec. (c)(1). Pub.L. 111–327, § 2(a)(17)(B), struck out "section 523(a)(5)" and inserted "such paragraph".

2005 Amendments. Subsec. (b). Pub.L. 109–8, § 224(a)(1), rewrote subsec. (b), which formerly read: "**(b)** Notwithstanding section 541 of this title, an individual debtor may exempt from property of the estate the property listed in either paragraph (1) or, in the alternative, paragraph (2) of this subsection. In joint cases filed under section 302 of this title and individual cases filed under section 301 or 303 of this title by or against debtors who are husband and wife, and whose estates are ordered to be jointly administered under Rule 1015(b) of the Federal Rules of Bankruptcy Procedure, one debtor may not elect to exempt property listed in paragraph (1) and the other debtor elect to exempt property listed in paragraph (2) of this subsection. If the parties cannot agree on the alternative to be elected, they shall be deemed to elect paragraph (1), where such election is permitted under the law of the jurisdiction where the case is filed. Such property is—

"**(1)** property that is specified under subsection (d) of this section, unless the State law that is applicable to the debtor under paragraph (2)(A) of this subsection specifically does not so authorize; or, in the alternative,

"**(2)(A)** any property that is exempt under Federal law, other than subsection (d) of this section, or State or local law that is applicable on the date of the filing of the petition at the place in which the debtor's domicile has been located for the 180 days immediately preceding the date of the filing of the petition, or for a longer portion of such 180-day period than in any other place; and

"**(B)** any interest in property in which the debtor had, immediately before the commencement of the case, an interest as a tenant by the entirety or joint tenant to the extent that such interest as a tenant by the entirety or joint tenant is exempt from process under applicable nonbankruptcy law."

Subsec. (b)(3). Pub.L. 109–8, § 307(2), added "If the effect of the domiciliary requirement under subparagraph (A) is to render the debtor ineligible for any exemption, the debtor may elect to exempt property that is specified under subsection (d)." to the end of par. (3).

Subsec. (b)(3)(A). Pub.L. 109–8, § 307(1)(A), struck out "180 days" and inserted "730 days".

Pub.L. 109–8, § 307(1)(B), struck out ", or for a longer portion of such 180-day period than in any other place" and inserted "or if the debtor's domicile has not been located at a single State for such 730-day period, the place in which the debtor's domicile was located for 180 days immediately preceding the 730-day period or for a longer portion of such 180-day period than in any other place".

Pub.L. 109–8, § 308(1), inserted "subject to subsections (o) and (p)," before "any property".

Subsec. (c)(1). Pub.L. 109–8, § 216(1), rewrote par. (1) which formerly read: "a debt of a kind specified in section 523(a)(1) or 523(a)(5) of this title;"

Subsec. (d). Pub.L. 109–8, § 224(a)(2)(A), in the matter preceding par. (1), substituted "subsection (b)(2)" for "subsection (b)(1)".

Subsec. (d)(12). Pub.L. 109–8, § 224(a)(2)(B), added par. (12).

Subsec. (f)(1)(A). Pub.L. 109–8, § 216(2), substituted "of a kind that is specified in section 523(a)(5); or" for "a debt—

"**(i)** to a spouse, former spouse, or child of the debtor, for alimony to, maintenance for, or support of such spouse or child, in connection with a separation agreement, divorce decree or other order of a court of record, determination made in accordance with State or territorial law by a governmental unit, or property settlement agreement; and

"**(ii)** to the extent that such debt—

"**(I)** is not assigned to another entity, voluntarily, by operation of law, or otherwise; and

"**(II)** includes a liability designated as alimony, maintenance, or support, unless such liability is actually in the nature of alimony, maintenance or support.; or"

Subsec. (f)(4). Pub.L. 109–8, § 313(a), added par. (4).

Subsec. (g)(2). Pub.L. 109–8, § 216(3), substituted "subsection (f)(1)(B)" for "subsection (f)(2)".

Subsec. (n). Pub.L. 109–8, § 224(e)(1), added subsec. (n).

Subsec. (o). Pub.L. 109–8, § 308(2), added subsec. (o).

Subsec. (p). Pub.L. 109–8, § 322(a), added subsec. (p).

Subsec. (q). Pub.L. 109–8, § 322(a), added subsec. (q).

2000 Amendments. Subsec. (c). Pub.L. 106–420, § 4, struck out "or" at the end of par. (2), substituted "; or" for the period at the end of par. (3), and added par. (4).

1994 Amendments. Subsec. (b). Pub.L. 103–394, § 501(d)(12)(A), substituted "Federal Rules of Bankruptcy Procedure" for "Bankruptcy Rules".

Subsec. (d)(1). Pub.L. 103–394, § 108(d)(1), increased the debtor's aggregate interest exemption from $7,500 to $15,000.

Subsec. (d)(2). Pub.L. 103–394, § 108(d)(2), increased the exemption for the debtor's interest in one motor vehicle from $1,200 to $2,400.

Subsec. (d)(3). Pub.L. 103–394, § 108(d)(3), substituted "The debtor's interest, not to exceed $400 in value in any particular item or $8,000 in aggregate value," for "The debtor's interest, not to exceed $200 in value in any particular item or $4,000 in aggregate value,".

Subsec. (d)(4). Pub.L. 103–394, § 108(d)(4), increased the exemption for the debtor's aggregate interest in jewelry from $500 to $1,000.

Subsec. (d)(5). Pub.L. 103–394, § 108(d)(5), substituted "aggregate interest in any property, not to exceed in value $800 plus up to $7,500" for "aggregate interest in any property, not to exceed in value $400 plus up to $3,750".

Subsec. (d)(6). Pub.L. 103–394, § 108(d)(6), increased the exemption for the debtor's aggregate interest in any implements, professional books or tools, of the trade from $750 to $1,500.

Subsec. (d)(8). Pub.L. 103–394, § 108 (d)(7), increased the debtor's aggregate interest exemption from $4,000 to $8,000.

Subsec. (d)(10)(E)(iii). Pub.L. 103–394, § 501(d)(12)(B)(i), substituted "Internal Revenue Code of 1986" for "Internal Revenue Code of 1954 (26 U.S.C. 401(a), 403(a), 403(b), 408, or 409)"..

Subsec. (d)(11)(D). Pub.L. 103–394, § 108(d)(8), increased the exemption for the debtor's right to receive, or property that is traceable to, a payment on account of personal bodily injury from $7,500 to $15,000.

Subsec. (f)(1)(A). Pub.L. 103–394, § 304(d), added provisions excluding a judicial lien that secures to a specified extent a debt in connection with a separation agreement, divorce decree, or property settlement agreement.

Subsec. (f)(1). Pub.L. 103–394, § 303(1)–(3), designated existing text in entirety as par. (1), redesignated former pars. (1) and (2) as par. (1), subpars. (A) and (B) and former par. (2), subpars. (A) to (C) as par. (1), subpar. (B), cls. (i) to (iii).

Pub.L. 103–394, § 310(1), inserted "but subject to paragraph (3)" after "waiver of exemptions".

Subsec. (f)(2). Pub.L. 103–394, § 303(1)(B), (4), added par. (2) and redesignated former par. (2) as par. (1), subpar. (B).

Subsec. (f)(3). Pub.L. 103–394, § 310(2), added par. (3).

1990 Amendments. Subsec. (c)(3). Pub.L. 101–647 added par. (3).

1986 Amendments. Subsec. (h)(1). Pub.L. 99–554, § 283(i)(1), substituted "553 of this title" for "553 of this tittle".

Subsec. (i)(2). Pub.L. 99–554, § 283(i)(2), substituted "(g) of this section" for "(g) of his section".

1984 Amendments. Subsec. (a)(2). Pub.L. 98–353, § 453(a), added "or, with respect to property that becomes property of an estate after such date, as of the date such property becomes property of the estate" following "petition".

Subsec. (b). Pub.L. 98–353, § 306(a), added provision that in joint cases filed under section 302 of this title and individual cases filed under section 301 or 303 of this title by or against debtors who are husband and wife, and whose estates are ordered to be jointly administered under Rule 1015(b) of the Bankruptcy Rules, one debtor may not elect to exempt property listed in paragraph (1) and the other debtor elect to exempt property listed in paragraph (2) of this subsection, but that if the parties cannot agree on the alternative to be elected, they shall be deemed to elect paragraph (1), where such election is permitted under the law of the jurisdiction where the case is filed.

Subsec. (c). Pub.L. 98–353, § 453(b), substituted "Unless the case is dismissed, property exempted under this section is not liable during or after the case for any debt of the debtor that arose, or that is determined under section 502 of this title as if such debt had arisen, before the commencement of the case, except—

"(1) a debt of a kind specified in section 523(a)(1) or 523(a)(5) of this title; or

"(2) a debt secured by a lien that is—

"(A)(i) not avoided under subsection (f) or (g) of this section or under section 544, 545, 547, 548, 549, or 724(a) of this title; and

"(ii) not void under section 506(d) of this title; or

"(B) a tax lien, notice of which is properly filed." for "Unless the case is dismissed, property exempted under this section is not liable during or after the case for any debt of the debtor that arose, or that is determined under section 502 of this title as if such claim had arisen before the commencement of the case, except—

"(1) a debt of a kind specified in section 523(a)(1) or section 523(a)(5) of this title; or

"(2) a lien that is—

"(A) not avoided under section 544, 545, 547, 548, 549, or 724(a) of this title;

"(B) not voided under section 506(d) of this title; or

"(C)(i) a tax lien, notice of which is properly filed; and

"(ii) avoided under section 545(2) of this title.".

Subsec. (d)(3). Pub.L. 98–353, § 306(b), added "or $4,000 in aggregate value" following "item".

Subsec. (d)(5). Pub.L. 98–353, § 306(c), substituted "The debtor's aggregate interest in any property, not to exceed in value $400 plus up to $3,750 of any unused amount of the exemption provided under paragraph (1) of this subsection" for "The debtor's aggregate interest, not to exceed in value $400 plus any unused amount of the exemption provided under paragraph (1) of this subsection, in any property".

Subsec. (e). Pub.L. 98–353, § 453(c), substituted "an exemption" for "exemptions".

Subsec. (m). Pub.L. 98–353, § 306(d), substituted "Subject to the limitation in subsection (b), this section shall apply separately with respect to each debtor in a joint case" for "This section shall apply separately with respect to each debtor in a joint case".

Adjustment of Dollar Amounts

For adjustment of dollar amounts specified in subsecs. (d)(1) to (6), (8), (11)(D), (f)(3), (4)(B), (n), (p)(1), (q)(1) of this section by the Judicial Conference of the United States, see note set out under 11 U.S.C.A. § 104 of this title.

CROSS REFERENCES

Allowance of claims or interests, see 11 USCA § 502.

Automatic preservation of avoided transfer, see 11 USCA § 551.

Effect of dismissal, see 11 USCA § 349.

Election to terminate debtor's taxable year for purposes of Internal Revenue Code not available to debtor with no assets other than property treated as exempt under this section, see 26 USCA § 1398.

Exempt property as including property treated as exempt under this section for purposes of Federal Debt Collection Act, see 28 USCA § 3014.

11 § 523   BANKRUPTCY CODE   Title 11

Insolvent as meaning financial condition wherein entity's debts are greater than entity's property exclusive of property that may be exempted under this section, see 11 USCA § 101.

Involuntary cases and future adjustments, see 11 USCA § 104.

Penalty for persons who negligently or fraudulently prepare bankruptcy petitions and exempt funds, see 11 USCA § 110.

Postpetition effect of security interest, see 11 USCA § 552.

Property claimed as exempt, see Official Bankr. Form 6, 11 USCA.

Property exempt under this section not subject to enforcement of withdrawal liability for purposes of Employee Retirement Income Security Act Program, see 29 USCA § 1405.

Provisions in plan for use, sale or lease of exempt property, see 11 USCA § 1123.

Redemption, see 11 USCA § 722.

Reduction in basis not allowed for property exempt under this section for purposes of Internal Revenue Code, see 26 USCA § 1017.

Turnover of property to estate, see 11 USCA § 542.

§ 523. Exceptions to discharge

(a) A discharge under section 727, 1141, 1228(a), 1228(b), or 1328(b) of this title does not discharge an individual debtor from any debt—

(1) for a tax or a customs duty—

(A) of the kind and for the periods specified in section 507(a)(3) or 507(a)(8) of this title, whether or not a claim for such tax was filed or allowed;

(B) with respect to which a return, or equivalent report or notice, if required—

(i) was not filed or given; or

(ii) was filed or given after the date on which such return, report, or notice was last due, under applicable law or under any extension, and after two years before the date of the filing of the petition; or

(C) with respect to which the debtor made a fraudulent return or willfully attempted in any manner to evade or defeat such tax;

(2) for money, property, services, or an extension, renewal, or refinancing of credit, to the extent obtained by—

(A) false pretenses, a false representation, or actual fraud, other than a statement respecting the debtor's or an insider's financial condition;

(B) use of a statement in writing—

(i) that is materially false;

(ii) respecting the debtor's or an insider's financial condition;

(iii) on which the creditor to whom the debtor is liable for such money, property, services, or credit reasonably relied; and

(iv) that the debtor caused to be made or published with intent to deceive; or

(C)(i) for purposes of subparagraph (A)—

(I) consumer debts owed to a single creditor and aggregating more than $650[1] for luxury goods or services incurred by an individual debtor on or within 90

---

[1] Dollar amount as adjusted by the Judicial Conference of the United States. See Adjustment of Dollar Amounts notes set out under this section and 11 U.S.C.A. § 104.

days before the order for relief under this title are presumed to be nondischargeable; and

(II) cash advances aggregating more than $925[1] that are extensions of consumer credit under an open end credit plan obtained by an individual debtor on or within 70 days before the order for relief under this title, are presumed to be nondischargeable; and

(ii) for purposes of this subparagraph—

(I) the terms "consumer", "credit", and "open end credit plan" have the same meanings as in section 103 of the Truth in Lending Act; and

(II) the term "luxury goods or services" does not include goods or services reasonably necessary for the support or maintenance of the debtor or a dependent of the debtor;

(3) neither listed nor scheduled under section 521(a)(1) of this title, with the name, if known to the debtor, of the creditor to whom such debt is owed, in time to permit—

(A) if such debt is not of a kind specified in paragraph (2), (4), or (6) of this subsection, timely filing of a proof of claim, unless such creditor had notice or actual knowledge of the case in time for such timely filing; or

(B) if such debt is of a kind specified in paragraph (2), (4), or (6) of this subsection, timely filing of a proof of claim and timely request for a determination of dischargeability of such debt under one of such paragraphs, unless such creditor had notice or actual knowledge of the case in time for such timely filing and request;

(4) for fraud or defalcation while acting in a fiduciary capacity, embezzlement, or larceny;

(5) for a domestic support obligation;

(6) for willful and malicious injury by the debtor to another entity or to the property of another entity;

(7) to the extent such debt is for a fine, penalty, or forfeiture payable to and for the benefit of a governmental unit, and is not compensation for actual pecuniary loss, other than a tax penalty—

(A) relating to a tax of a kind not specified in paragraph (1) of this subsection; or

(B) imposed with respect to a transaction or event that occurred before three years before the date of the filing of the petition;

(8) unless excepting such debt from discharge under this paragraph would impose an undue hardship on the debtor and the debtor's dependents, for—

(A)(i) an educational benefit overpayment or loan made, insured, or guaranteed by a governmental unit, or made under any program funded in whole or in part by a governmental unit or nonprofit institution; or

(ii) an obligation to repay funds received as an educational benefit, scholarship, or stipend; or

(B) any other educational loan that is a qualified education loan, as defined in section 221(d)(1) of the Internal Revenue Code of 1986, incurred by a debtor who is an individual;

(9) for death or personal injury caused by the debtor's operation of a motor vehicle, vessel, or aircraft if such operation was unlawful because the debtor was intoxicated from using alcohol, a drug, or another substance;

---

[1] Dollar amount as adjusted by the Judicial Conference of the United States. See Adjustment of Dollar Amounts notes set out under this section and 11 U.S.C.A. § 104.

(10) that was or could have been listed or scheduled by the debtor in a prior case concerning the debtor under this title or under the Bankruptcy Act in which the debtor waived discharge, or was denied a discharge under section 727(a)(2), (3), (4), (5), (6), or (7) of this title, or under section 14c(1), (2), (3), (4), (6), or (7) of such Act;

(11) provided in any final judgment, unreviewable order, or consent order or decree entered in any court of the United States or of any State, issued by a Federal depository institutions regulatory agency, or contained in any settlement agreement entered into by the debtor, arising from any act of fraud or defalcation while acting in a fiduciary capacity committed with respect to any depository institution or insured credit union;

(12) for malicious or reckless failure to fulfill any commitment by the debtor to a Federal depository institutions regulatory agency to maintain the capital of an insured depository institution, except that this paragraph shall not extend any such commitment which would otherwise be terminated due to any act of such agency;

(13) for any payment of an order of restitution issued under title 18, United States Code;

(14) incurred to pay a tax to the United States that would be nondischargeable pursuant to paragraph (1);

(14A) incurred to pay a tax to a governmental unit, other than the United States, that would be nondischargeable under paragraph (1);

(14B) incurred to pay fines or penalties imposed under Federal election law;

(15) to a spouse, former spouse, or child of the debtor and not of the kind described in paragraph (5) that is incurred by the debtor in the course of a divorce or separation or in connection with a separation agreement, divorce decree or other order of a court of record, or a determination made in accordance with State or territorial law by a governmental unit;

(16) for a fee or assessment that becomes due and payable after the order for relief to a membership association with respect to the debtor's interest in a unit that has condominium ownership, in a share of a cooperative corporation, or a lot in a homeowners association, for as long as the debtor or the trustee has a legal, equitable, or possessory ownership interest in such unit, such corporation, or such lot, but nothing in this paragraph shall except from discharge the debt of a debtor for a membership association fee or assessment for a period arising before entry of the order for relief in a pending or subsequent bankruptcy case;

(17) for a fee imposed on a prisoner by any court for the filing of a case, motion, complaint, or appeal, or for other costs and expenses assessed with respect to such filing, regardless of an assertion of poverty by the debtor under subsection (b) or (f)(2) of section 1915 of title 28 (or a similar non-Federal law), or the debtor's status as a prisoner, as defined in section 1915(h) of title 28 (or a similar non-Federal law);

(18) owed to a pension, profit-sharing, stock bonus, or other plan established under section 401, 403, 408, 408A, 414, 457, or 501(c) of the Internal Revenue Code of 1986, under—

    (A) a loan permitted under section 408(b)(1) of the Employee Retirement Income Security Act of 1974, or subject to section 72(p) of the Internal Revenue Code of 1986; or

    (B) a loan from a thrift savings plan permitted under subchapter III of chapter 84 of title 5, that satisfies the requirements of section 8433(g) of such title;

but nothing in this paragraph may be construed to provide that any loan made under a governmental plan under section 414(d), or a contract or account under section 403(b), of the Internal Revenue Code of 1986 constitutes a claim or a debt under this title; or

    (19) that—

        (A) is for—

            (i) the violation of any of the Federal securities laws (as that term is defined in section 3(a)(47) of the Securities Exchange Act of 1934), any of the State securities laws, or any regulation or order issued under such Federal or State securities laws; or

Title 11　　　CREDITORS, THE DEBTOR, AND THE ESTATE　　　11 § 523

(ii) common law fraud, deceit, or manipulation in connection with the purchase or sale of any security; and

(B) results, before, on, or after the date on which the petition was filed, from—

(i) any judgment, order, consent order, or decree entered in any Federal or State judicial or administrative proceeding;

(ii) any settlement agreement entered into by the debtor; or

(iii) any court or administrative order for any damages, fine, penalty, citation, restitutionary payment, disgorgement payment, attorney fee, cost, or other payment owed by the debtor.

For purposes of this subsection, the term "return" means a return that satisfies the requirements of applicable nonbankruptcy law (including applicable filing requirements). Such term includes a return prepared pursuant to section 6020(a) of the Internal Revenue Code of 1986, or similar State or local law, or a written stipulation to a judgment or a final order entered by a nonbankruptcy tribunal, but does not include a return made pursuant to section 6020(b) of the Internal Revenue Code of 1986, or a similar State or local law.

(b) Notwithstanding subsection (a) of this section, a debt that was excepted from discharge under subsection (a)(1), (a)(3), or (a)(8) of this section, under section 17a(1), 17a(3), or 17a(5) of the Bankruptcy Act, under section 439A of the Higher Education Act of 1965, or under section 733(g) of the Public Health Service Act in a prior case concerning the debtor under this title, or under the Bankruptcy Act, is dischargeable in a case under this title unless, by the terms of subsection (a) of this section, such debt is not dischargeable in the case under this title.

(c)(1) Except as provided in subsection (a)(3)(B) of this section, the debtor shall be discharged from a debt of a kind specified in paragraph (2), (4), or (6) of subsection (a) of this section, unless, on request of the creditor to whom such debt is owed, and after notice and a hearing, the court determines such debt to be excepted from discharge under paragraph (2), (4), or (6), as the case may be, of subsection (a) of this section.

(2) Paragraph (1) shall not apply in the case of a Federal depository institutions regulatory agency seeking, in its capacity as conservator, receiver, or liquidating agent for an insured depository institution, to recover a debt described in subsection (a)(2), (a)(4), (a)(6), or (a)(11) owed to such institution by an institution-affiliated party unless the receiver, conservator, or liquidating agent was appointed in time to reasonably comply, or for a Federal depository institutions regulatory agency acting in its corporate capacity as a successor to such receiver, conservator, or liquidating agent to reasonably comply, with subsection (a)(3)(B) as a creditor of such institution-affiliated party with respect to such debt.

(d) If a creditor requests a determination of dischargeability of a consumer debt under subsection (a)(2) of this section, and such debt is discharged, the court shall grant judgment in favor of the debtor for the costs of, and a reasonable attorney's fee for, the proceeding if the court finds that the position of the creditor was not substantially justified, except that the court shall not award such costs and fees if special circumstances would make the award unjust.

(e) Any institution-affiliated party of an insured depository institution shall be considered to be acting in a fiduciary capacity with respect to the purposes of subsection (a)(4) or (11).

(Pub.L. 95–598, Nov. 6, 1978, 92 Stat. 2590; Pub.L. 96–56, § 3, Aug. 14, 1979, 93 Stat. 387; Pub.L. 97–35, Title XXIII, § 2334(b), Aug. 13, 1981, 95 Stat. 863; Pub.L. 98–353, Title III, §§ 307, 371, 454, July 10, 1984, 98 Stat. 353, 364, 375; Pub.L. 99–554, Title II, §§ 257(n), 281, 283(j), Oct. 27, 1986, 100 Stat. 3115 to 3117; Pub.L. 101–581, § 2(a), Nov. 15, 1990, 104 Stat. 2865; Pub.L. 101–647, Title XXV, § 2522(a), Title XXXI, § 3102(a), Title XXXVI, § 3621, Nov. 29, 1990, 104 Stat. 4865, 4916, 4964; Pub.L. 103–322, Title XXXII, § 320934, Sept. 13, 1994, 108 Stat. 2135; Pub.L. 103–394, Title II, § 221, Title III, §§ 304(e), (h)(3), 306, 309, Title V, § 501(d)(13), Oct. 22, 1994, 108 Stat. 4129, 4133 to 4135, 4137, 4145; Pub.L. 104–134, Title I, § 101[(a)][Title VIII, § 804(b)], Apr. 26, 1996, 110 Stat. 1321–74; renumbered Title I Pub.L. 104–140, § 1(a), May 2, 1996, 110 Stat. 1327; amended Pub.L. 104–193, Title III, § 374(a), Aug. 22, 1996, 110 Stat. 2255; Pub.L. 105–244, Title IX, § 971(a), Oct. 7, 1998, 112 Stat. 1837; Pub.L. 107–204, Title VIII, § 803, July 30, 2002, 116 Stat. 801; Pub.L. 109–8, Title II, §§ 215, 220, 224(c), Title III, §§ 301, 310, 314(a), Title IV, § 412, Title VII, § 714, Title XII, §§ 1209, 1235, Title XIV, § 1404(a), Title XV, § 1502(a)(2), Apr.

20, 2005, 119 Stat. 54, 59, 64, 75, 84, 88, 107, 128, 194, 204, 215, 216; Pub.L. 111–327, § 2(a)(18), Dec. 22, 2010, 124 Stat. 3559.)

HISTORICAL AND STATUTORY NOTES

References in Text

Section 6020(a) of the Internal Revenue Code of 1986, referred to in subsec. (a), is classified to 26 U.S.C.A. § 6020(a).

Section 6020(b) of the Internal Revenue Code of 1986, referred to in subsec. (a), is classified to 26 U.S.C.A. § 6020(b).

The Consumer Credit Protection Act, referred to in subsec. (a)(2)(C), is Pub.L. 90–321, May 29, 1968, 82 Stat. 146, as amended, which is classified principally to chapter 41 (section 1601 et seq.) of Title 15, Commerce and Trade. For complete classification of this Act to the Code, see Short Title note set out under section 1601 of Title 15 and Tables.

Section 103 of the Truth in Lending Act, referred to in subsec. (a)(2)(C)(ii)(I), is Pub.L. 90–321, Title I, § 103, May 29, 1968, 82 Stat. 147, as amended, which is classified to 15 U.S.C.A. § 1602.

The Social Security Act, referred to in subsec. (a)(5)(A), (18)(B), is Act Aug. 14, 1935, c. 531, 49 Stat. 620, as amended. Section 408(a)(3) of that Act is classified to section 608(a)(3) of Title 42, The Public Health and Welfare. Part D of Title IV of such Act is classified generally to part D (section 651 et seq.) of subchapter IV of chapter 7 of Title 42. For complete classification of this Act to the Code, see section 1305 of Title 42 and Tables.

Section 221(d)(1) of the Internal Revenue Code of 1986, referred to in subsec. (a)(8)(B), is classified to 26 U.S.C.A. § 221(d)(1).

The Bankruptcy Act, referred to in subsecs. (a)(10) and (b), is Act July 1, 1898, c. 541, 30 Stat. 544, as amended, which was classified generally to former Title 11. Sections 14c and 17a of the Bankruptcy Act were classified to sections 32(c) and 35(a) of former Title 11.

Section 401, 403, 408, 408A, 414, 457, or 501(c) of the Internal Revenue Code of 1986, referred to in subsec. (a)(18), is classified to 26 U.S.C.A. § 401, 403, 408, 408A, 414, 457, or 501(c).

Section 408(b)(1) of the Employee Retirement Income Security Act of 1974, referred to in subsec. (a)(18)(A), is Pub.L. 93–406, Title I, § 408(b)(1), Sept. 2, 1974, 88 Stat. 883, as amended, which is classified to 29 U.S.C.A. § 1108(b)(1).

Section 72(p) of the Internal Revenue Code of 1986, referred to in subsec. (a)(18)(A), is classified to 26 U.S.C.A. § 72(p).

Subchapter III of chapter 84 of title 5, referred to in subsec. (a)(18)(B), is 5 U.S.C.A. § 8431 et seq.

Section 414(d) or section 403(b) of the Internal Revenue Code, referred to in the undesignated paragraph following subsec. (a)(18), is classified to 26 U.S.C.A. § 414(d) or 26 U.S.C.A. § 403(b).

Section 3(a)(47) of the Securities Exchange Act of 1934, referred to in subsec. (a)(19)(A)(i), is section 3(a)(47) of Act June 6, 1934, c. 404, Title I, 48 Stat. 882, as amended, which is classified to 15 U.S.C.A. § 78c(a)(47).

Section 439A of the Higher Education Act of 1965, referred to in subsec. (b), is section 439A of Pub.L. 89–329, Title IV, as added Pub.L. 94–482, Title I, § 127(a), Oct. 12, 1976, 90 Stat. 2141, which was classified to section 1087–3 of Title 20, Education, and was repealed by Pub.L. 95–598, Title III, § 317, Nov. 6, 1978, 92 Stat. 2678.

Section 733 of the Public Health Service Act, referred to in subsec. (b), is section 733 of Act July 1, 1944, c. 373, Title VII as added Oct. 12, 1976, Pub.L. 94–484, Title IV, § 401(b)(3), 90 Stat. 2262, which was classified to section 294f of Title 42, The Public Health and Welfare, and which was repealed by Pub.L. 95–598, Title III, § 327, Nov. 6, 1978, 92 Stat. 2679. A subsec. (g), containing similar provisions, was added to section 733 by Pub.L. 97–35, Title XXVII, § 2730, Aug. 13, 1981, 95 Stat. 919. Section 733 was subsequently omitted in the general revision of subchapter V of chapter 6A of Title 42 by Pub.L. 102–408, Title I, § 102, Oct. 13, 1992, 106 Stat. 1992.

Codifications

Amendment by section 215(3) of Pub.L. 109–8, directing the amendment of par. (15) as added by Public Law 103–394, was executed by amending par. (15) of subsec. (a), as the probable intent of Congress.

Amendment by section 304(e) of Pub.L. 103–394, directing the addition of par. (15), was executed by adding par. (15) to subsec. (a), as the probable intent of Congress.

Pub.L. 101–581 and Pub.L. 101–647, § 3102(a), made identical amendments to subsec. (a)(9) of this section. See 1990 Amendments note set out under this section.

Amendment by section 283(j)(1) of Pub.L. 99–554, which redesignated the second par. (9) of subsec. (a) as (10), has been executed by redesignating as (10), par. (9) as enacted by Pub.L. 95–598 as the probable intent of Congress in view of amendment by section 371(2) of Pub.L. 98–353, which directed the addition of par. (9), as presently set out, to follow par. (8).

Amendments

2010 Amendments. Subsec. (a)(2)(C)(ii)(II). Pub.L. 111–327, § 2(a)(18)(A), struck out the period at the end and inserted a semicolon.

Subsec. (a)(3). Pub.L. 111–327, § 2(a)(18)(B), struck out "521(1)" and inserted "521(a)(1)".

2005 Amendments. Subsec. (a). Pub.L. 109–8, § 714(2), added "For purposes of this subsection, the term 'return' means a return that satisfies the requirements of applicable nonbankruptcy law (including applicable filing requirements). Such term includes a return prepared pursuant to section 6020(a) of the Internal Revenue Code of 1986, or similar State or local law, or a written stipulation to a judgment or a final order entered by a nonbankruptcy tribunal, but does not include a return made pursuant to section 6020(b) of the Internal Revenue Code of 1986, or a similar State or local law." at the end of subsec. (a).

Subsec. (a)(1)(A). Pub.L. 109–8, § 1502(a)(2), struck out "507(a)(2)" and inserted "507(a)(3)".

Subsec. (a)(1)(B). Pub.L. 109–8, § 714(1)(A), in the matter preceding cl. (i), inserted "or equivalent report or notice," after "a return,".

Subsec. (a)(1)(B)(i). Pub.L. 109–8, § 714(1)(B), inserted "or given" after "filed".

Subsec. (a)(1)(B)(ii). Pub.L. 109–8, § 714(1)(C)(i), inserted "or given" after "filed".

Pub.L. 109–8, § 714(1)(C)(ii), inserted ", report, or notice" after "return".

Subsec. (a)(2)(C). Pub.L. 109–8, § 310, rewrote subpar. (C), which formerly read: "for purposes of subparagraph (A) of this paragraph, consumer debts owed to a single creditor and aggregating more than $1,225 for 'luxury goods or services' incurred by an individual debtor on or within 60 days before the order for relief under this title, or cash advances aggregating more than $1,225 that are extensions of consumer credit under an open end credit plan obtained by an individual debtor on or within 60 days before the order for relief under this title, are presumed to be nondischargeable; 'luxury goods or services' do not include goods or services reasonably acquired for the support or maintenance of the debtor or a dependent of the debtor; an extension of consumer credit under an open end credit plan is to be defined for purposes of this subparagraph as it is defined in the Consumer Credit Protection Act;".

Subsec. (a)(5). Pub.L. 109–8, § 215(1)(A), rewrote par. (5), which formerly read:

"(5) to a spouse, former spouse, or child of the debtor, for alimony to, maintenance for, or support of such spouse or child, in connection with a separation agreement, divorce decree or other order of a court of record, determination made in accordance with State or territorial law by a governmental unit, or property settlement agreement, but not to the extent that—

"(A) such debt is assigned to another entity, voluntarily, by operation of law, or otherwise (other than debts assigned pursuant to section 408(a)(3) of the Social Security Act, or any such debt which has been assigned to the Federal Government or to a State or any political subdivision of such State); or

"(B) such debt includes a liability designated as alimony, maintenance, or support, unless such liability is actually in the nature of alimony, maintenance, or support;"

Subsec. (a)(8). Pub.L. 109–8, § 220, rewrote par. (8), which formerly read: "for an educational benefit overpayment or loan made, insured or guaranteed by a governmental unit, or made under any program funded in whole or in part by a governmental unit or nonprofit institution, or for an obligation to repay funds received as an educational benefit, scholarship or stipend, unless excepting such debt from discharge under this paragraph will impose an undue hardship on the debtor and the debtor's dependents;"

Subsec. (a)(9). Pub.L. 109–8, § 1209(2), struck out "motor vehicle" and inserted "motor vehicle, vessel, or aircraft".

Subsec. (a)(14A). Pub.L. 109–8, § 314(a), added par. (14A).

Subsec. (a)(14B). Pub.L. 109–8, § 1235, added par. (14B).

Subsec. (a)(15). Pub.L. 109–8, § 215(3), inserted "to a spouse, former spouse, or child of the debtor and" before "not of the kind", inserted "or" after "court of record,", and substituted a semicolon for "unless—

"(A) the debtor does not have the ability to pay such debt from income or property of the debtor not reasonably necessary to be expended for the maintenance or support of the debtor or a dependent of the debtor and, if the debtor is engaged in a business, for the payment of expenditures necessary for the continuation, preservation, and operation of such business; or

"(B) discharging such debt would result in a benefit to the debtor that outweighs the detrimental consequences to a spouse, former spouse, or child of the debtor;"

Pub.L. 109–8, § 1209(1), transferred paragraph (15), as added by Pub.L. 103–394, § 304(e), so as to insert such paragraph after subsection (a)(14A), as added by Pub.L. 109–8, § 314(a).

Subsec. (a)(16). Pub.L. 109–8, § 412, rewrote par. (16), which formerly read:

"(16) for a fee or assessment that becomes due and payable after the order for relief to a membership association with respect to the debtor's interest in a dwelling unit that has condominium ownership or in a housing corporation, but only if such fee or assessment is payable for a period during which—

"(A) the debtor physically occupied a dwelling unit in the condominium or cooperative project; or

"(B) the debtor rented the dwelling unit to a tenant and received payments from the tenant for such period,

"but nothing in this paragraph shall except from discharge the debt of a debtor for a membership association fee or assessment for a period arising before entry of the order for relief in a pending or subsequent bankruptcy case;"

Subsec. (a)(17). Pub.L. 109–8, § 301(1), struck out "by a court" and inserted "on a prisoner by any court".

Pub.L. 109–8, § 301(2), struck out "section 1915(b) or (f)" and inserted "subsection (b) or (f)(2) of section 1915".

Pub.L. 109–8, § 301(3), inserted "(or a similar non-Federal law)" after "title 28" each place it appears.

Subsec. (a)(18). Pub.L. 109–8, § 215(1)(B), struck out par. (18), which formerly read:

"(18) owed under State law to a State or municipality that is—

"(A) in the nature of support, and

"(B) enforceable under part D of title IV of the Social Security Act (42 U.S.C. 601 et seq.); or"

Pub.L. 109–8, § 224(c), inserted par. (18).

Subsec. (a)(19)(B). Pub.L. 109–8, § 1404(a), inserted ", before, on, or after the date on which the petition was filed," after "results".

Subsec. (c)(1). Pub.L. 109–8, § 215(2), substituted "or (6)" for "(6), or (15)" in two places.

Subsec. (e). Pub.L. 109–8, § 1209(3), struck out "a insured" and inserted "an insured".

2002 Amendments. Subsec. (a)(17). Pub.L. 107–204, § 803(1), struck out "or" at the end.

Subsec. (a)(18). Pub.L. 107–204, § 803(2), substituted "; or" for the period at the end.

Subsec. (a)(19). Pub.L. 107–204, § 803(3), added par. (19).

1998 Amendments. Subsec. (a)(8). Pub.L. 105–244, § 971(a), rewrote par. (8), which formerly read:

"**(8)** for an educational benefit overpayment or loan made, insured or guaranteed by a governmental unit, or made under any program funded in whole or in part by a governmental unit or nonprofit institution, or for an obligation to repay funds received as an educational benefit, scholarship or stipend, unless—

"**(A)** such loan, benefit, scholarship, or stipend overpayment first became due more than 7 years (exclusive of any applicable suspension of the repayment period) before the date of the filing of the petition; or

"**(B)** excepting such debt from discharge under this paragraph will impose an undue hardship on the debtor and the debtor's dependents;".

1996 Amendments. Subsec. (a)(5). Pub.L. 104–193, § 374(a)(4), substituted "section 408(a)(3)" for "section 402(a)(26)".

Subsec. (a)(17). Pub.L. 104–134, § 101[(a)][§ 804(b)], added par. (17).

Subsec. (a)(18). Pub.L. 104–193, § 374(a)(1) to (3), added par. (18).

1994 Amendments. Subsec. (a)(1)(A). Pub.L. 103–394, § 304(h)(3), substituted "507(a)(8)" for "507(a)(7)".

Subsec. (a)(2)(C). Pub.L. 103–394, § 306, substituted "$1,000 for 'luxury goods or services'" for "$500 for 'luxury goods or services'", "incurred by an individual debtor on or within 60 days" for "incurred by an individual debtor on or within forty days", and "obtained by an individual debtor on or within 60 days" for "obtained by an individual debtor on or within twenty days".

Pub.L. 103–394, § 501(d)(13)(A)(ii), struck out "(15 U.S.C. 1601 et seq.)" after "Consumer Credit Protection Act".

Subsec. (a)(13). Pub.L. 103–322, § 320934, added par. (13).

Subsec. (a)(14). Pub.L. 103–394, § 221, added par. (14).

Subsec. (a)(15). Pub.L. 103–394, § 304(e), added par. (15). See Codifications note under this section.

Subsec. (a)(16). Pub.L. 103–394, § 309, added par. (16).

Subsec. (a). Pub.L. 103–394, § 501(d)(13)(A)(i), struck out second comma following "1141".

Subsec. (b). Pub.L. 103–394, § 501(d)(13)(B), struck out "(20 U.S.C. 1087–3)" following "the Higher Education Act of 1965", and "(42 U.S.C. 294f)" following "the Public Health Service Act".

Subsec. (c)(1). Pub.L. 103–394, § 304(e)(2), substituted "(6), or (15)" for "or (6)" wherever appearing.

Subsec. (e). Pub.L. 103–394, § 501(d)(13)(C), substituted "insured depository institution" for "depository institution or insured credit union".

1990 Amendments. Subsec. (a)(8). Pub.L. 101–647, § 3621(1), in introductory provisions substituted "for an educational benefit overpayment or loan made" for "for an educational loan made" and inserted preceding "unless" the phrase "or for an obligation to repay funds received as an educational benefit, scholarship or stipend,".

Subsec. (a)(8)(A). Pub.L. 101–647, § 3621(2), substituted "such loan, benefit, scholarship, or stipend overpayment first became due more than 7 years" for "such loan first became due before five years".

Subsec. (a)(9). Pub.L. 101–581 and Pub.L. 101–647, § 3102(a), made identical amendments, substituting "for death or personal injury caused by the debtor's operation of a motor vehicle if such operation was unlawful because the debtor was intoxicated from using alcohol, a drug, or another substance; 01" for "to any entity, to the extent that such debt arises from a judgment or consent decree entered in a court of record against the debtor wherein liability was incurred by such debtor as a result of the debtor's operation of a motor vehicle while legally intoxicated under the laws or regulations of any jurisdiction within the United States or its territories wherein such motor vehicle was operated and within which such liability was incurred; 01".

Subsec. (a)(11), (12). Pub.L. 101–647, § 2522(a)(1), added pars. (11) and (12).

Subsec. (c)(1). Pub.L. 101–647, § 2522(a)(3)(A), designated existing provision as par. (1).

Subsec. (c)(2). Pub.L. 101–647, § 2522(a)(3)(B), added par. (2).

Subsec. (e). Pub.L. 101–647, § 2522(a)(2), added subsec. (e).

1986 Amendments. Subsec. (a). Pub.L. 99–554, § 257(n), added reference to section 1228(a) and (b) of this title.

Subsec. (a)(1)(A). Pub.L. 99–554, § 283(j)(1)(A), substituted "(7)" for "(6)".

Subsec. (a)(5). Pub.L. 99–554, § 281, inserted ", determination made in accordance with State or territorial law by a governmental unit," following "record", and substituted "decree" for "decree,".

Subsec. (a)(10). Pub.L. 99–554, § 283(j)(1)(B), redesignated par. (9), as added by Pub.L. 95–598, as par. (10). See Codifications note set out under this section.

Subsec. (b). Pub.L. 99–554, § 283(j)(2), substituted "Service" for "Services".

1984 Amendments. Subsec. (a)(2). Pub.L. 98–353, § 454(a)(1)(A), in provisions preceding subpar. (A), struck out "obtaining" following "for".

Pub.L. 98–353, § 454(a)(1)(B), in provisions preceding subpar. (A), substituted "refinancing of credit, to the extent obtained" for "refinance of credit,".

Subsec. (a)(2)(A). Pub.L. 98–353, § 307(a)(1), struck out "or" at the end of subpar. (A).

Subsec. (a)(2)(B). Pub.L. 98–353, § 307(a)(2), added "or" at the end of subpar. (B).

Subsec. (a)(2)(B)(iii). Pub.L. 98–353, § 454(a)(1)(A), struck out "obtaining" preceding "such".

Subsec. (a)(2)(C). Pub.L. 98–353, § 307(a)(3), added subpar. (C).

Subsec. (a)(5). Pub.L. 98–353, § 454(b)(1), added "or other order of a court of record" following "divorce decree," in provisions preceding subpar. (A).

Subsec. (a)(5)(A). Pub.L. 98–353, § 454(b)(2), added ", or any such debt which has been assigned to the Federal Government or to a State or any political subdivision of such State" following "Social Security Act".

Subsec. (a)(8). Pub.L. 98–353, § 454(a)(2), struck out "of higher education" following "a nonprofit institution of".

Pub.L. 98–353, § 371(1), struck out "or" at the end of par. (8).

Subsec. (a)(9). Pub.L. 98–353, § 371(2), added par. (9), relating to debts incurred by persons driving while intoxicated.

Subsec. (c). Pub.L. 98–353, § 454(c), added "of a kind" following "debt".

Subsec. (d). Pub.L. 98–353, § 307(b), substituted "the court shall grant judgment in favor of the debtor for the costs of, and a reasonable attorney's fee for, the proceeding if the court finds that the position of the creditor was not substantially justified, except that the court shall not award such costs and fees if special circumstances would make the award unjust" for "the court shall grant judgment against such creditor and in favor of the debtor for the costs of, and a reasonable attorney's fee for, the proceeding to determine dischargeability, unless such granting of judgment would be clearly inequitable.".

1981 Amendments. Subsec. (a)(5)(A). Pub.L. 97–35 substituted "law, or otherwise (other than debts assigned pursuant to section 402(a)(26) of the Social Security Act);" for "law, or otherwise;".

1979 Amendments. Subsec. (a)(8). Pub.L. 96–56, § 3(1), in the introductory provisions, substituted "for an educational loan made, insured, or guaranteed by a governmental unit, or made under any program funded in whole or in part by a governmental unit or a nonprofit institution of higher education" for "to a governmental unit, or a nonprofit institution of higher education, for an educational loan".

Subsec. (a)(8)(A). Pub.L. 96–56, § 3(2), inserted "(exclusive of any applicable suspension of the repayment period)" following "before five years".

Adjustment of Dollar Amounts

For adjustment of dollar amounts specified in this section by the Judicial Conference of the United States, see note set out under 11 U.S.C.A. § 104 of this title.

Title 11 CREDITORS, THE DEBTOR, AND THE ESTATE 11 § 524

CROSS REFERENCES

Disallowance of claim to extent claim is for unmatured debt and excepted from discharge as debt for alimony, maintenance or support, see 11 USCA § 502.

Discharge of debtor—

    Generally, see Official Bankr. Form 18, 11 USCA.

    Chapter 7 cases, see 11 USCA § 727.

    Chapter 12 cases, see 11 USCA § 1228.

    Chapter 13 cases, see 11 USCA § 1328.

Effect of confirmation, see 11 USCA § 1141.

Extent of priorities for unsecured claims of governmental units, see 11 USCA § 507.

Involuntary cases and future adjustments, see 11 USCA § 104.

Notice of filing, creditors and dates, see Official Bankr. Form 9, 11 USCA.

§ 524. Effect of discharge

(a) A discharge in a case under this title—

(1) voids any judgment at any time obtained, to the extent that such judgment is a determination of the personal liability of the debtor with respect to any debt discharged under section 727, 944, 1141, 1228, or 1328 of this title, whether or not discharge of such debt is waived;

(2) operates as an injunction against the commencement or continuation of an action, the employment of process, or an act, to collect, recover or offset any such debt as a personal liability of the debtor, whether or not discharge of such debt is waived; and

(3) operates as an injunction against the commencement or continuation of an action, the employment of process, or an act, to collect or recover from, or offset against, property of the debtor of the kind specified in section 541(a)(2) of this title that is acquired after the commencement of the case, on account of any allowable community claim, except a community claim that is excepted from discharge under section 523, 1228(a)(1), or 1328(a)(1), or that would be so excepted, determined in accordance with the provisions of sections 523(c) and 523(d) of this title, in a case concerning the debtor's spouse commenced on the date of the filing of the petition in the case concerning the debtor, whether or not discharge of the debt based on such community claim is waived.

(b) Subsection (a)(3) of this section does not apply if—

(1)(A) the debtor's spouse is a debtor in a case under this title, or a bankrupt or a debtor in a case under the Bankruptcy Act, commenced within six years of the date of the filing of the petition in the case concerning the debtor; and

(B) the court does not grant the debtor's spouse a discharge in such case concerning the debtor's spouse; or

(2)(A) the court would not grant the debtor's spouse a discharge in a case under chapter 7 of this title concerning such spouse commenced on the date of the filing of the petition in the case concerning the debtor; and

(B) a determination that the court would not so grant such discharge is made by the bankruptcy court within the time and in the manner provided for a determination under section 727 of this title of whether a debtor is granted a discharge.

(c) An agreement between a holder of a claim and the debtor, the consideration for which, in whole or in part, is based on a debt that is dischargeable in a case under this title is enforceable only to any extent enforceable under applicable nonbankruptcy law, whether or not discharge of such debt is waived, only if—

(1) such agreement was made before the granting of the discharge under section 727, 1141, 1228, or 1328 of this title;

(2) the debtor received the disclosures described in subsection (k) at or before the time at which the debtor signed the agreement;

(3) such agreement has been filed with the court and, if applicable, accompanied by a declaration or an affidavit of the attorney that represented the debtor during the course of negotiating an agreement under this subsection, which states that—

(A) such agreement represents a fully informed and voluntary agreement by the debtor;

(B) such agreement does not impose an undue hardship on the debtor or a dependent of the debtor; and

(C) the attorney fully advised the debtor of the legal effect and consequences of—

(i) an agreement of the kind specified in this subsection; and

(ii) any default under such an agreement;

(4) the debtor has not rescinded such agreement at any time prior to discharge or within sixty days after such agreement is filed with the court, whichever occurs later, by giving notice of rescission to the holder of such claim;

(5) the provisions of subsection (d) of this section have been complied with; and

(6)(A) in a case concerning an individual who was not represented by an attorney during the course of negotiating an agreement under this subsection, the court approves such agreement as—

(i) not imposing an undue hardship on the debtor or a dependent of the debtor; and

(ii) in the best interest of the debtor.

(B) Subparagraph (A) shall not apply to the extent that such debt is a consumer debt secured by real property.

(d) In a case concerning an individual, when the court has determined whether to grant or not to grant a discharge under section 727, 1141, 1228, or 1328 of this title, the court may hold a hearing at which the debtor shall appear in person. At any such hearing, the court shall inform the debtor that a discharge has been granted or the reason why a discharge has not been granted. If a discharge has been granted and if the debtor desires to make an agreement of the kind specified in subsection (c) of this section and was not represented by an attorney during the course of negotiating such agreement, then the court shall hold a hearing at which the debtor shall appear in person and at such hearing the court shall—

(1) inform the debtor—

(A) that such an agreement is not required under this title, under nonbankruptcy law, or under any agreement not made in accordance with the provisions of subsection (c) of this section; and

(B) of the legal effect and consequences of—

(i) an agreement of the kind specified in subsection (c) of this section; and

(ii) a default under such an agreement; and

(2) determine whether the agreement that the debtor desires to make complies with the requirements of subsection (c)(6) of this section, if the consideration for such agreement is based in whole or in part on a consumer debt that is not secured by real property of the debtor.

(e) Except as provided in subsection (a)(3) of this section, discharge of a debt of the debtor does not affect the liability of any other entity on, or the property of any other entity for, such debt.

(f) Nothing contained in subsection (c) or (d) of this section prevents a debtor from voluntarily repaying any debt.

(g)(1)(A) After notice and hearing, a court that enters an order confirming a plan of reorganization under chapter 11 may issue, in connection with such order, an injunction in accordance with this subsection to supplement the injunctive effect of a discharge under this section.

(B) An injunction may be issued under subparagraph (A) to enjoin entities from taking legal action for the purpose of directly or indirectly collecting, recovering, or receiving payment or recovery with respect to any claim or demand that, under a plan of reorganization, is to be paid in whole or in part by a trust described in paragraph (2)(B)(i), except such legal actions as are expressly allowed by the injunction, the confirmation order, or the plan of reorganization.

(2)(A) Subject to subsection (h), if the requirements of subparagraph (B) are met at the time an injunction described in paragraph (1) is entered, then after entry of such injunction, any proceeding that involves the validity, application, construction, or modification of such injunction, or of this subsection with respect to such injunction, may be commenced only in the district court in which such injunction was entered, and such court shall have exclusive jurisdiction over any such proceeding without regard to the amount in controversy.

(B) The requirements of this subparagraph are that—

(i) the injunction is to be implemented in connection with a trust that, pursuant to the plan of reorganization—

(I) is to assume the liabilities of a debtor which at the time of entry of the order for relief has been named as a defendant in personal injury, wrongful death, or property-damage actions seeking recovery for damages allegedly caused by the presence of, or exposure to, asbestos or asbestos-containing products;

(II) is to be funded in whole or in part by the securities of 1 or more debtors involved in such plan and by the obligation of such debtor or debtors to make future payments, including dividends;

(III) is to own, or by the exercise of rights granted under such plan would be entitled to own if specified contingencies occur, a majority of the voting shares of—

(aa) each such debtor;

(bb) the parent corporation of each such debtor; or

(cc) a subsidiary of each such debtor that is also a debtor; and

(IV) is to use its assets or income to pay claims and demands; and

(ii) subject to subsection (h), the court determines that—

(I) the debtor is likely to be subject to substantial future demands for payment arising out of the same or similar conduct or events that gave rise to the claims that are addressed by the injunction;

(II) the actual amounts, numbers, and timing of such future demands cannot be determined;

(III) pursuit of such demands outside the procedures prescribed by such plan is likely to threaten the plan's purpose to deal equitably with claims and future demands;

(IV) as part of the process of seeking confirmation of such plan—

(aa) the terms of the injunction proposed to be issued under paragraph (1)(A), including any provisions barring actions against third parties pursuant to paragraph (4)(A), are set out in such plan and in any disclosure statement supporting the plan; and

(bb) a separate class or classes of the claimants whose claims are to be addressed by a trust described in clause (i) is established and votes, by at least 75 percent of those voting, in favor of the plan; and

(V) subject to subsection (h), pursuant to court orders or otherwise, the trust will operate through mechanisms such as structured, periodic, or supplemental payments, pro rata distributions, matrices, or periodic review of estimates of the numbers and values of present claims and future demands, or other comparable mechanisms, that provide reasonable assurance that the trust will value, and be in a financial position to pay, present claims and future demands that involve similar claims in substantially the same manner.

(3)(A) If the requirements of paragraph (2)(B) are met and the order confirming the plan of reorganization was issued or affirmed by the district court that has jurisdiction over the reorganization case, then after the time for appeal of the order that issues or affirms the plan—

(i) the injunction shall be valid and enforceable and may not be revoked or modified by any court except through appeal in accordance with paragraph (6);

(ii) no entity that pursuant to such plan or thereafter becomes a direct or indirect transferee of, or successor to any assets of, a debtor or trust that is the subject of the injunction shall be liable with respect to any claim or demand made against such entity by reason of its becoming such a transferee or successor; and

(iii) no entity that pursuant to such plan or thereafter makes a loan to such a debtor or trust or to such a successor or transferee shall, by reason of making the loan, be liable with respect to any claim or demand made against such entity, nor shall any pledge of assets made in connection with such a loan be upset or impaired for that reason;

(B) Subparagraph (A) shall not be construed to—

(i) imply that an entity described in subparagraph (A)(ii) or (iii) would, if this paragraph were not applicable, necessarily be liable to any entity by reason of any of the acts described in subparagraph (A);

(ii) relieve any such entity of the duty to comply with, or of liability under, any Federal or State law regarding the making of a fraudulent conveyance in a transaction described in subparagraph (A)(ii) or (iii); or

(iii) relieve a debtor of the debtor's obligation to comply with the terms of the plan of reorganization, or affect the power of the court to exercise its authority under sections 1141 and 1142 to compel the debtor to do so.

(4)(A)(i) Subject to subparagraph (B), an injunction described in paragraph (1) shall be valid and enforceable against all entities that it addresses.

(ii) Notwithstanding the provisions of section 524(e), such an injunction may bar any action directed against a third party who is identifiable from the terms of such injunction (by name or as part of an identifiable group) and is alleged to be directly or indirectly liable for the conduct of, claims against, or demands on the debtor to the extent such alleged liability of such third party arises by reason of—

(I) the third party's ownership of a financial interest in the debtor, a past or present affiliate of the debtor, or a predecessor in interest of the debtor;

(II) the third party's involvement in the management of the debtor or a predecessor in interest of the debtor, or service as an officer, director or employee of the debtor or a related party;

(III) the third party's provision of insurance to the debtor or a related party; or

(IV) the third party's involvement in a transaction changing the corporate structure, or in a loan or other financial transaction affecting the financial condition, of the debtor or a related party, including but not limited to—

(aa) involvement in providing financing (debt or equity), or advice to an entity involved in such a transaction; or

(bb) acquiring or selling a financial interest in an entity as part of such a transaction.

(iii) As used in this subparagraph, the term "related party" means—

(I) a past or present affiliate of the debtor;

(II) a predecessor in interest of the debtor; or

(III) any entity that owned a financial interest in—

(aa) the debtor;

(bb) a past or present affiliate of the debtor; or

(cc) a predecessor in interest of the debtor.

(B) Subject to subsection (h), if, under a plan of reorganization, a kind of demand described in such plan is to be paid in whole or in part by a trust described in paragraph (2)(B)(i) in connection with which an injunction described in paragraph (1) is to be implemented, then such injunction shall be valid and enforceable with respect to a demand of such kind made, after such plan is confirmed, against the debtor or debtors involved, or against a third party described in subparagraph (A)(ii), if—

(i) as part of the proceedings leading to issuance of such injunction, the court appoints a legal representative for the purpose of protecting the rights of persons that might subsequently assert demands of such kind, and

(ii) the court determines, before entering the order confirming such plan, that identifying such debtor or debtors, or such third party (by name or as part of an identifiable group), in such injunction with respect to such demands for purposes of this subparagraph is fair and equitable with respect to the persons that might subsequently assert such demands, in light of the benefits provided, or to be provided, to such trust on behalf of such debtor or debtors or such third party.

(5) In this subsection, the term "demand" means a demand for payment, present or future, that—

(A) was not a claim during the proceedings leading to the confirmation of a plan of reorganization;

(B) arises out of the same or similar conduct or events that gave rise to the claims addressed by the injunction issued under paragraph (1); and

(C) pursuant to the plan, is to be paid by a trust described in paragraph (2)(B)(i).

(6) Paragraph (3)(A)(i) does not bar an action taken by or at the direction of an appellate court on appeal of an injunction issued under paragraph (1) or of the order of confirmation that relates to the injunction.

(7) This subsection does not affect the operation of section 1144 or the power of the district court to refer a proceeding under section 157 of title 28 or any reference of a proceeding made prior to the date of the enactment of this subsection.

(h) **Application to existing injunctions.**—For purposes of subsection (g)—

(1) subject to paragraph (2), if an injunction of the kind described in subsection (g)(1)(B) was issued before the date of the enactment of this Act, as part of a plan of reorganization confirmed by an order entered before such date, then the injunction shall be considered to meet the requirements of subsection (g)(2)(B) for purposes of subsection (g)(2)(A), and to satisfy subsection (g)(4)(A)(ii), if—

(A) the court determined at the time the plan was confirmed that the plan was fair and equitable in accordance with the requirements of section 1129(b);

(B) as part of the proceedings leading to issuance of such injunction and confirmation of such plan, the court had appointed a legal representative for the purpose of protecting the rights of persons that might subsequently assert demands described in subsection (g)(4)(B) with respect to such plan; and

(C) such legal representative did not object to confirmation of such plan or issuance of such injunction; and

(2) for purposes of paragraph (1), if a trust described in subsection (g)(2)(B)(i) is subject to a court order on the date of the enactment of this Act staying such trust from settling or paying further claims—

(A) the requirements of subsection (g)(2)(B)(ii)(V) shall not apply with respect to such trust until such stay is lifted or dissolved; and

(B) if such trust meets such requirements on the date such stay is lifted or dissolved, such trust shall be considered to have met such requirements continuously from the date of the enactment of this Act.

(i) The willful failure of a creditor to credit payments received under a plan confirmed under this title, unless the order confirming the plan is revoked, the plan is in default, or the creditor has not received payments required to be made under the plan in the manner required by the plan (including crediting the amounts required under the plan), shall constitute a violation of an injunction under subsection (a)(2) if the act of the creditor to collect and failure to credit payments in the manner required by the plan caused material injury to the debtor.

(j) Subsection (a)(2) does not operate as an injunction against an act by a creditor that is the holder of a secured claim, if—

(1) such creditor retains a security interest in real property that is the principal residence of the debtor;

(2) such act is in the ordinary course of business between the creditor and the debtor; and

(3) such act is limited to seeking or obtaining periodic payments associated with a valid security interest in lieu of pursuit of in rem relief to enforce the lien.

(k)(1) The disclosures required under subsection (c)(2) shall consist of the disclosure statement described in paragraph (3), completed as required in that paragraph, together with the agreement specified in subsection (c), statement, declaration, motion and order described, respectively, in paragraphs (4) through (8), and shall be the only disclosures required in connection with entering into such agreement.

(2) Disclosures made under paragraph (1) shall be made clearly and conspicuously and in writing. The terms "Amount Reaffirmed" and "Annual Percentage Rate" shall be disclosed more conspicuously than other terms, data or information provided in connection with this disclosure, except that the phrases "Before agreeing to reaffirm a debt, review these important disclosures" and "Summary of Reaffirmation Agreement" may be equally conspicuous. Disclosures may be made in a different order and may use terminology different from that set forth in paragraphs (2) through (8), except that the terms "Amount Reaffirmed" and "Annual Percentage Rate" must be used where indicated.

(3) The disclosure statement required under this paragraph shall consist of the following:

(A) The statement: "Part A: Before agreeing to reaffirm a debt, review these important disclosures:";

(B) Under the heading "Summary of Reaffirmation Agreement", the statement: "This Summary is made pursuant to the requirements of the Bankruptcy Code";

(C) The "Amount Reaffirmed", using that term, which shall be—

(i) the total amount of debt that the debtor agrees to reaffirm by entering into an agreement of the kind specified in subsection (c), and

(ii) the total of any fees and costs accrued as of the date of the disclosure statement, related to such total amount.

(D) In conjunction with the disclosure of the "Amount Reaffirmed", the statements—

(i) "The amount of debt you have agreed to reaffirm"; and

(ii) "Your credit agreement may obligate you to pay additional amounts which may come due after the date of this disclosure. Consult your " 'credit agreement.".

(E) The "Annual Percentage Rate", using that term, which shall be disclosed as—

(i) if, at the time the petition is filed, the debt is an extension of credit under an open end credit plan, as the terms "credit" and "open end credit plan" are defined in section 103 of the Truth in Lending Act, then—

(I) the annual percentage rate determined under paragraphs (5) and (6) of section 127(b) of the Truth in Lending Act, as applicable, as disclosed to the debtor in the most recent periodic statement prior to entering into an agreement of the kind specified in subsection (c) or, if no such periodic statement has been given to the debtor during the prior 6 months, the annual percentage rate as it would have been so disclosed at the time the disclosure statement is given to the debtor, or to the extent this annual percentage rate is not readily available or not applicable, then

(II) the simple interest rate applicable to the amount reaffirmed as of the date the disclosure statement is given to the debtor, or if different simple interest rates apply to different balances, the simple interest rate applicable to each such balance, identifying the amount of each such balance included in the amount reaffirmed, or

(III) if the entity making the disclosure elects, to disclose the annual percentage rate under subclause (I) and the simple interest rate under subclause (II); or

(ii) if, at the time the petition is filed, the debt is an extension of credit other than under an open end credit plan, as the terms "credit" and "open end credit plan" are defined in section 103 of the Truth in Lending Act, then—

(I) the annual percentage rate under section 128(a)(4) of the Truth in Lending Act, as disclosed to the debtor in the most recent disclosure statement given to the debtor prior to the entering into an agreement of the kind specified in subsection (c) with respect to the debt, or, if no such disclosure statement was given to the debtor, the annual percentage rate as it would have been so disclosed at the time the disclosure statement is given to the debtor, or to the extent this annual percentage rate is not readily available or not applicable, then

(II) the simple interest rate applicable to the amount reaffirmed as of the date the disclosure statement is given to the debtor, or if different simple interest rates apply to different balances, the simple interest rate applicable to each such balance, identifying the amount of such balance included in the amount reaffirmed, or

(III) if the entity making the disclosure elects, to disclose the annual percentage rate under (I) and the simple interest rate under (II).

(F) If the underlying debt transaction was disclosed as a variable rate transaction on the most recent disclosure given under the Truth in Lending Act, by stating "The interest rate on your loan may be a variable interest rate which changes from time to time, so that the annual percentage rate disclosed here may be higher or lower."

(G) If the debt is secured by a security interest which has not been waived in whole or in part or determined to be void by a final order of the court at the time of the disclosure, by disclosing that a security interest or lien in goods or property is asserted over some or all of the debts the debtor is reaffirming and listing the items and their original purchase price that are subject to the asserted security interest, or if not a purchase-money security interest then listing by items or types and the original amount of the loan.

(H) At the election of the creditor, a statement of the repayment schedule using 1 or a combination of the following—

    (i) by making the statement: "Your first payment in the amount of $___ is due on ___ but the future payment amount may be different. Consult your reaffirmation agreement or credit agreement, as applicable.", and stating the amount of the first payment and the due date of that payment in the places provided;

    (ii) by making the statement: "Your payment schedule will be:", and describing the repayment schedule with the number, amount, and due dates or period of payments scheduled to repay the debts reaffirmed to the extent then known by the disclosing party; or

    (iii) by describing the debtor's repayment obligations with reasonable specificity to the extent then known by the disclosing party.

(I) The following statement: "Note: When this disclosure refers to what a creditor 'may' do, it does not use the word 'may' to give the creditor specific permission. The word 'may' is used to tell you what might occur if the law permits the creditor to take the action. If you have questions about your reaffirming a debt or what the law requires, consult with the attorney who helped you negotiate this agreement reaffirming a debt. If you don't have an attorney helping you, the judge will explain the effect of your reaffirming a debt when the hearing on the reaffirmation agreement is held.".

(J)(i) The following additional statements:

"Reaffirming a debt is a serious financial decision. The law requires you to take certain steps to make sure the decision is in your best interest. If these steps are not completed, the reaffirmation agreement is not effective, even though you have signed it.

"1. Read the disclosures in this Part A carefully. Consider the decision to reaffirm carefully. Then, if you want to reaffirm, sign the reaffirmation agreement in Part B (or you may use a separate agreement you and your creditor agree on).

"2. Complete and sign Part D and be sure you can afford to make the payments you are agreeing to make and have received a copy of the disclosure statement and a completed and signed reaffirmation agreement.

"3. If you were represented by an attorney during the negotiation of your reaffirmation agreement, the attorney must have signed the certification in Part C.

"4. If you were not represented by an attorney during the negotiation of your reaffirmation agreement, you must have completed and signed Part E.

"5. The original of this disclosure must be filed with the court by you or your creditor. If a separate reaffirmation agreement (other than the one in Part B) has been signed, it must be attached.

"6. If you were represented by an attorney during the negotiation of your reaffirmation agreement, your reaffirmation agreement becomes effective upon filing with the court unless the reaffirmation is presumed to be an undue hardship as explained in Part D.

"7. If you were not represented by an attorney during the negotiation of your reaffirmation agreement, it will not be effective unless the court approves it. The court will notify you of the hearing on your reaffirmation agreement. You must attend this hearing in bankruptcy court where the judge will review your reaffirmation agreement. The bankruptcy court must approve your reaffirmation agreement as consistent with your best interests, except that no court approval is required if your reaffirmation agreement is for a consumer debt secured by a mortgage, deed of trust, security deed, or other lien on your real property, like your home.

"Your right to rescind (cancel) your reaffirmation agreement. You may rescind (cancel) your reaffirmation agreement at any time before the bankruptcy court enters a discharge order, or before the expiration of the 60-day period that begins on the date your reaffirmation agreement is filed with the court, whichever occurs later. To rescind (cancel) your reaffirmation agreement, you must notify the creditor that your reaffirmation agreement is rescinded (or canceled).

"What are your obligations if you reaffirm the debt? A reaffirmed debt remains your personal legal obligation. It is not discharged in your bankruptcy case. That means that if you default on your reaffirmed debt after your bankruptcy case is over, your creditor may be able to take your property or your wages. Otherwise, your obligations will be determined by the reaffirmation agreement which may have changed the terms of the original agreement. For example, if you are reaffirming an open end credit agreement, the creditor may be permitted by that agreement or applicable law to change the terms of that agreement in the future under certain conditions.

"Are you required to enter into a reaffirmation agreement by any law? No, you are not required to reaffirm a debt by any law. Only agree to reaffirm a debt if it is in your best interest. Be sure you can afford the payments you agree to make.

"What if your creditor has a security interest or lien? Your bankruptcy discharge does not eliminate any lien on your property. A 'lien' is often referred to as a security interest, deed of trust, mortgage or security deed. Even if you do not reaffirm and your personal liability on the debt is discharged, because of the lien your creditor may still have the right to take the property securing the lien if you do not pay the debt or default on it. If the lien is on an item of personal property that is exempt under your State's law or that the trustee has abandoned, you may be able to redeem the item rather than reaffirm the debt. To redeem, you must make a single payment to the creditor equal to the amount of the allowed secured claim, as agreed by the parties or determined by the court.".

(ii) In the case of a reaffirmation under subsection (m)(2), numbered paragraph 6 in the disclosures required by clause (i) of this subparagraph shall read as follows:

"6. If you were represented by an attorney during the negotiation of your reaffirmation agreement, your reaffirmation agreement becomes effective upon filing with the court.".

(4) The form of such agreement required under this paragraph shall consist of the following:

"Part B: Reaffirmation Agreement. I (we) agree to reaffirm the debts arising under the credit agreement described below.

"Brief description of credit agreement:

"Description of any changes to the credit agreement made as part of this reaffirmation agreement:

"Signature: Date:

"Borrower:

"Co-borrower, if also reaffirming these debts:

"Accepted by creditor:

"Date of creditor acceptance:".

(5) The declaration shall consist of the following:

(A) The following certification:

"Part C: Certification by Debtor's Attorney (If Any).

"I hereby certify that (1) this agreement represents a fully informed and voluntary agreement by the debtor; (2) this agreement does not impose an undue hardship on the debtor or any dependent of the debtor; and (3) I have fully advised the debtor of the legal effect and consequences of this agreement and any default under this agreement.

"Signature of Debtor's Attorney: Date:".

(B) If a presumption of undue hardship has been established with respect to such agreement, such certification shall state that, in the opinion of the attorney, the debtor is able to make the payment.

(C) In the case of a reaffirmation agreement under subsection (m)(2), subparagraph (B) is not applicable.

(6)(A) The statement in support of such agreement, which the debtor shall sign and date prior to filing with the court, shall consist of the following:

"Part D: Debtor's Statement in Support of Reaffirmation Agreement.

"1. I believe this reaffirmation agreement will not impose an undue hardship on my dependents or me. I can afford to make the payments on the reaffirmed debt because my monthly income (take home pay plus any other income received) is $___, and my actual current monthly expenses including monthly payments on post-bankruptcy debt and other reaffirmation agreements total $___, leaving $___ to make the required payments on this reaffirmed debt. I understand that if my income less my monthly expenses does not leave enough to make the payments, this reaffirmation agreement is presumed to be an undue hardship on me and must be reviewed by the court. However, this presumption may be overcome if I explain to the satisfaction of the court how I can afford to make the payments here: ___.

"2. I received a copy of the Reaffirmation Disclosure Statement in Part A and a completed and signed reaffirmation agreement.".

(B) Where the debtor is represented by an attorney and is reaffirming a debt owed to a creditor defined in section 19(b)(1)(A)(iv) of the Federal Reserve Act, the statement of support of the reaffirmation agreement, which the debtor shall sign and date prior to filing with the court, shall consist of the following:

"I believe this reaffirmation agreement is in my financial interest. I can afford to make the payments on the reaffirmed debt. I received a copy of the Reaffirmation Disclosure Statement in Part A and a completed and signed reaffirmation agreement.".

(7) The motion that may be used if approval of such agreement by the court is required in order for it to be effective, shall be signed and dated by the movant and shall consist of the following:

"Part E: Motion for Court Approval (To be completed only if the debtor is not represented by an attorney.). I (we), the debtor(s), affirm the following to be true and correct:

"I am not represented by an attorney in connection with this reaffirmation agreement.

"I believe this reaffirmation agreement is in my best interest based on the income and expenses I have disclosed in my Statement in Support of this reaffirmation agreement, and because (provide any additional relevant reasons the court should consider):

"Therefore, I ask the court for an order approving this reaffirmation agreement."

(8) The court order, which may be used to approve such agreement, shall consist of the following:

"Court Order: The court grants the debtor's motion and approves the reaffirmation agreement described above.".

(l) Notwithstanding any other provision of this title the following shall apply:

(1) A creditor may accept payments from a debtor before and after the filing of an agreement of the kind specified in subsection (c) with the court.

(2) A creditor may accept payments from a debtor under such agreement that the creditor believes in good faith to be effective.

(3) The requirements of subsections (c)(2) and (k) shall be satisfied if disclosures required under those subsections are given in good faith.

(m)(1) Until 60 days after an agreement of the kind specified in subsection (c) is filed with the court (or such additional period as the court, after notice and a hearing and for cause, orders before the expiration of such period), it shall be presumed that such agreement is an undue hardship on the debtor if the debtor's monthly income less the debtor's monthly expenses as shown on the debtor's completed and signed statement in support of such agreement required under subsection (k)(6)(A) is less than the scheduled payments on the reaffirmed debt. This presumption shall be reviewed by the court. The presumption may be rebutted in writing by the debtor if the statement includes an explanation that identifies additional sources of funds to make the payments as agreed upon under the terms of such agreement. If the presumption is not rebutted to the satisfaction of the court, the court may disapprove such agreement. No agreement shall be disapproved without notice and a hearing to the debtor and creditor, and such hearing shall be concluded before the entry of the debtor's discharge.

(2) This subsection does not apply to reaffirmation agreements where the creditor is a credit union, as defined in section 19(b)(1)(A)(iv) of the Federal Reserve Act.

(Pub.L. 95–598, Nov. 6, 1978, 92 Stat. 2592; Pub.L. 98–353, Title III, §§ 308, 455, July 10, 1984, 98 Stat. 354, 376; Pub.L. 99–554, Title II, §§ 257(o), 282, 283(k), Oct. 27, 1986, 100 Stat. 3115–3117; Pub.L. 103–394, Title I, §§ 103, 111(a), Title V, § 501(d)(14), Oct. 22, 1994, 108 Stat. 4108, 4113, 4145; Pub.L. 109–8, Title II, §§ 202, 203(a), Title XII, § 1210, Apr. 20, 2005, 119 Stat. 43, 194; Pub.L. 111–327, § 2(a)(19), Dec. 22, 2010, 124 Stat. 3559.)

HISTORICAL AND STATUTORY NOTES

References in Text

The Bankruptcy Act, referred to in subsec. (b)(1), is Act July 1, 1898, c. 541, 30 Stat. 544, as amended, which was classified generally to former Title 11.

The date of enactment of this subsection, referred to in subsec. (g), is the date of enactment of section 111(a) of Pub.L. 103–394, which enacted subsec. (g) of this section and which was approved Oct. 22, 1994.

The date of enactment of this Act, referred to in subsec. (h), probably means the date of enactment of Pub.L. 103–394, known as the Bankruptcy Reform Act of 1994, which was approved Oct. 22, 1994.

Section 103 of the Truth in Lending Act, referred to in subsec. (k)(3)(E)(i), (ii), is Pub.L. 90–321, Title I, § 103, May 29, 1968, 82 Stat. 147, as amended, which is classified to 15 U.S.C.A. § 1602.

Section 127(b) of the Truth in Lending Act, referred to in subsec. (k)(3)(E)(i)(I), is Pub.L. 90–321, Title I, § 127(b), May 29, 1968, 82 Stat. 153, as amended, which is classified to 15 U.S.C.A. § 1637(b).

Section 128(a)(4) of the Truth in Lending Act, referred to in subsec. (k)(3)(E)(ii)(I), is Pub.L. 90–321, Title I, § 128(a)(4), May 29, 1968, 82 Stat. 155, as amended, which is classified to 15 U.S.C.A. § 1638(a)(4).

The Truth in Lending Act, referred to in subsec. (k)(3)(F), is Title I of Pub.L. 90–321, May 29, 1968, 82 Stat. 146, as amended, also known as TILA, which is classified principally to subchapter I of chapter 41 of Title 15, 15 U.S.C.A. § 1601 et seq. For complete classification, see Short Title note set out under 15 U.S.C.A. § 1601 and Tables.

Section 19(b)(1)(A)(iv) of the Federal Reserve Act, referred to in subsecs. (k)(6)(B), (m)(2), is Act Dec. 23, 1913, c. 6, § 19(b)(1)(A)(iv), 38 Stat. 270, as amended, which is classified to 12 U.S.C.A. § 461(b)(1)(A)(iv).

Amendments

2010 Amendments. Subsec. (k)(3)(J)(i). Pub.L. 111–327, § 2(a)(19)(A), in the undesignated last paragraph, struck out "security property if" and inserted "property securing the lien if", struck out "current value of the security property" and inserted "amount of the allowed secured claim", and inserted "must" following "redeem, you".

Subsec. (k)(5)(B). Pub.L. 111–327, § 2(a)(19)(B), struck "that" and inserted "that,".

2005 Amendments. Subsec. (a)(3). Pub.L. 109–8, § 1210, struck out "section 523, 1228(a)(1), or 1328(a)(1) of this title, or that" and inserted "section 523, 1228(a)(1), or 1328(a)(1), or that". See 1994 and 1986 Amendments notes under this section.

Subsec. (c)(2). Pub.L. 109–8, § 203(a)(1), rewrote par. (2), which formerly read: "**(A)** such agreement contains a clear and conspicuous statement which advises the debtor that the agreement may be rescinded at any time prior to discharge or within sixty days after such agreement is filed with the court, whichever occurs later, by giving notice of rescission to the holder of such claim; and

"(B) such agreement contains a clear and conspicuous statement which advises the debtor that such agreement is not required under this title, under nonbankruptcy law, or under any agreement not in accordance with the provisions of this subsection;"

Subsec. (i). Pub.L. 109–8, § 202, added subsec. (i).

Subsec. (j). Pub.L. 109–8, § 202, added subsec. (j).

Subsec. (k). Pub.L. 109–8, § 203(a)(2), added subsec. (k).

Subsec. (l). Pub.L. 109–8, § 203(a)(2), added subsec. (k).

Subsec. (m). Pub.L. 109–8, § 203(a)(2), added subsec. (m).

1994 Amendments. Subsec. (a)(3). Pub.L. 103–394, § 501(d)(14)(A), substituted "1328(a)(1)" for "1328(c)(1)". See 1986 and 2005 Amendments notes under this section.

Subsec. (c)(2). Pub.L. 103–394, § 103(a)(1), designated existing provisions as subpar. (A) and added subpar. (B).

Subsec. (c)(3). Pub.L. 103–394, § 103(a)(2), added subpar. (C) and made conforming technical changes to subpars. (A) and (B).

Subsec. (c)(4). Pub.L. 103–394, § 501(d)(14)(B), substituted "rescission" for "recission".

Subsec. (d)(1)(B)(ii). Pub.L. 103–394, § 501(d)(14)(C), inserted "and" following the semicolon.

Subsec. (d). Pub.L. 103–465, § 103(b), in opening par. inserted "and was not represented by an attorney during the course of negotiating such agreement" after "this section".

Subsecs. (g), (h). Pub.L. 103–394, § 111(a), added subsecs. (g) and (h).

1986 Amendments. Subsec. (a)(1). Pub.L. 99–554, § 257(o)(1), added reference to section 1228 of this title.

Subsec. (a)(3). Pub.L. 99–554, § 257(o)(2), which directed the substitution of ", 1228(a)(1), or 1328(a)(1)" for "or 1328(a)(1)" was executed by substituting ", 1228(a)(1), or 1328(c)(1)" for "or 1328(c)(1)" as the probable intent of Congress. See 1994 and 2005 Amendments notes under this section.

Subsec. (c)(1). Pub.L. 99–554, § 257(o)(1), added reference to section 1228 of this title.

Subsec. (d). Pub.L. 99–554, § 257(o)(1), added reference to section 1228 of this title.

Pub.L. 99–554, § 282, substituted "may hold" for "shall hold" and "At any" for "At", and added provisions relating to required appearance by the debtor in person at required hearing held by the court.

Subsec. (d)(2). Pub.L. 99–554, § 283(k), substituted "section" for "subsection" following "subsection (c)(6) of this".

1984 Amendments. Subsec. (a)(2). Pub.L. 98–353, § 308(a), struck out "or from property of the debtor," before "whether or not discharge of such debt is waived".

Pub.L. 98–353, § 455, substituted "an act" for "any act".

Subsec. (a)(3). Pub.L. 98–353, § 455, substituted "an act" for "any act".

Subsec. (c)(2). Pub.L. 98–353, § 308(b)(1), (3), added par. (2). Former par. (2), which had related to situations where the debtor had not rescinded the agreement within 30 days after the agreement became enforceable, was struck out.

Subsec. (c)(3). Pub.L. 98–353, § 308(b)(3), added par. (3). Former par. (3) was redesignated as (5).

Subsec. (c)(4). Pub.L. 98–353, § 308(b)(3), added par. (4). Former par. (4) was redesignated as (6).

Subsec. (c)(5). Pub.L. 98–353, § 308(b)(2), redesignated par. (3) as (5).

Subsec. (c)(6). Pub.L. 98–353, § 308(b)(2), redesignated former par. (4) as (6).

Pub.L. 98–353, § 308(b)(4), struck out provisions relating to court approval of such agreements as are entered into in good faith and are in settlement of litigation under section 523 of this title or provide for redemption under section 722 of this title.

Subsec. (d)(2). Pub.L. 98–353, § 308(c), substituted "subsection (c)(6)" for "subsection (c)(4)".

Title 11   CREDITORS, THE DEBTOR, AND THE ESTATE   11 § 525

Subsec. (f). Pub.L. 98–353, § 308(d), added subsec. (f).

Rule of Construction

Section 111(b) of Pub.L. 103–394 provided that: "Nothing in subsection (a), or in the amendments made by subsection (a) [enacting subsecs. (g) and (h) of this section], shall be construed to modify, impair, or supersede any other authority the court has to issue injunctions in connection with an order confirming a plan of reorganization."

CROSS REFERENCES

Applicability of subsec. (a)(1), (2) of this section in Chapter 9 cases, see 11 USCA § 901.

Cancellation of indebtedness from discharged farm loans, see 12 USCA § 1150.

Extension of time generally, see 11 USCA § 108.

Meetings of creditors and equity security holders reaffirming a debt, see 11 USCA § 341.

§ 525. Protection against discriminatory treatment

(a) Except as provided in the Perishable Agricultural Commodities Act, 1930, the Packers and Stockyards Act, 1921, and section 1 of the Act entitled "An Act making appropriations for the Department of Agriculture for the fiscal year ending June 30, 1944, and for other purposes," approved July 12, 1943, a governmental unit may not deny, revoke, suspend, or refuse to renew a license, permit, charter, franchise, or other similar grant to, condition such a grant to, discriminate with respect to such a grant against, deny employment to, terminate the employment of, or discriminate with respect to employment against, a person that is or has been a debtor under this title or a bankrupt or a debtor under the Bankruptcy Act, or another person with whom such bankrupt or debtor has been associated, solely because such bankrupt or debtor is or has been a debtor under this title or a bankrupt or debtor under the Bankruptcy Act, has been insolvent before the commencement of the case under this title, or during the case but before the debtor is granted or denied a discharge, or has not paid a debt that is dischargeable in the case under this title or that was discharged under the Bankruptcy Act.

(b) No private employer may terminate the employment of, or discriminate with respect to employment against, an individual who is or has been a debtor under this title, a debtor or bankrupt under the Bankruptcy Act, or an individual associated with such debtor or bankrupt, solely because such debtor or bankrupt—

    (1) is or has been a debtor under this title or a debtor or bankrupt under the Bankruptcy Act;

    (2) has been insolvent before the commencement of a case under this title or during the case but before the grant or denial of a discharge; or

    (3) has not paid a debt that is dischargeable in a case under this title or that was discharged under the Bankruptcy Act.

(c)(1) A governmental unit that operates a student grant or loan program and a person engaged in a business that includes the making of loans guaranteed or insured under a student loan program may not deny a student grant, loan, loan guarantee, or loan insurance to a person that is or has been a debtor under this title or a bankrupt or debtor under the Bankruptcy Act, or another person with whom the debtor or bankrupt has been associated, because the debtor or bankrupt is or has been a debtor under this title or a bankrupt or debtor under the Bankruptcy Act, has been insolvent before the commencement of a case under this title or during the pendency of the case but before the debtor is granted or denied a discharge, or has not paid a debt that is dischargeable in the case under this title or that was discharged under the Bankruptcy Act.

(2) In this section, "student loan program" means any program operated under title IV of the Higher Education Act of 1965 or a similar program operated under State or local law.

(Pub.L. 95–598, Nov. 6, 1978, 92 Stat. 2593; Pub.L. 98–353, Title III, § 309, July 10, 1984, 98 Stat. 354; Pub.L. 103–394, Title III, § 313, Title V, § 501(d)(15), Oct. 22, 1994, 108 Stat. 4140, 4145; Pub.L. 109–8, Title XII, § 1211, Apr. 20, 2005, 119 Stat. 194.)

HISTORICAL AND STATUTORY NOTES

References in Text

The Perishable Agricultural Commodities Act, 1930, referred to in subsec. (a), is Act June 10, 1930, c. 436, 46 Stat. 531, as amended, which is classified principally to chapter 20A (section 499a et seq.) of Title 7, Agriculture. For complete classification of this Act to the Code, see section 499a of Title 7 and Tables.

The Packers and Stockyards Act, 1921, referred to in subsec. (a), is Act Aug. 15, 1921, c. 64, 42 Stat. 159, which is classified principally to chapter 9 (section 181 et seq.) of Title 7, Agriculture. For complete classification of this Act to the Code, see section 181 of Title 7 and Tables.

Section 1 of an Act entitled "An Act making appropriations for the Department of Agriculture for the fiscal year ending June 30, 1944, and for other purposes," approved July 12, 1943, referred to in subsec. (a), is section 1 of Act July 12, 1943, c. 215, 57 Stat. 422, which is classified to section 204 of Title 7, Agriculture.

The Bankruptcy Act, referred to in subsecs. (a), (b), and (c)(1), is Act July 1, 1898, c. 541, 30 Stat. 544, as amended, which was classified generally to former Title 11.

The Higher Education Act of 1965, referred to in subsec. (c)(2), is Pub.L. 89–329, Nov. 8, 1965, 79 Stat. 1219, as amended. Title IV of the Act is classified generally to subchapter IV of chapter 28 of Title 20, 20 U.S.C.A. § 1070 et seq., and part C of subchapter I of chapter 34 of Title 42, 42 U.S.C.A. § 2751 et seq. For complete classification, see Short Title note set out under 20 U.S.C.A. § 1001 and Tables.

Amendments

2005 Amendments. Subsec. (c)(1). Pub.L. 109–8, § 1211(1), inserted "student" before "grant, loan".

Subsec. (c)(2). Pub.L. 109–8, § 1211(2), struck out "the program operated under part B, D, or E of" and inserted "any program operated under".

1994 Amendments. Subsec. (a). Pub.L. 103–394, § 501(d)(15), struck out "(7 U.S.C. 499a-499s)" following "the Perishable Agricultural Commodities Act, 1930", "(7 U.S.C. 181–229)" following "the Packers and Stockyards Act, 1921", and "(57 Stat. 422; 7 U.S.C. 204)" following "approved July 12, 1943".

Subsec. (c). Pub.L. 103–394, § 313, added subsec. (c).

1984 Amendments. Subsec. (a). Pub.L. 98–353, § 309(1), designated existing provisions as subsec. (a).

Pub.L. 98–353, § 309(2), added "the" before "Perishable".

Subsec. (b). Pub.L. 98–353, § 309(3), added subsec. (b).

CROSS REFERENCES

Reporting of obsolete information prohibited, see 15 USCA § 1681c.

§ 526. Restrictions on debt relief agencies

(a) A debt relief agency shall not—

(1) fail to perform any service that such agency informed an assisted person or prospective assisted person it would provide in connection with a case or proceeding under this title;

(2) make any statement, or counsel or advise any assisted person or prospective assisted person to make a statement in a document filed in a case or proceeding under this title, that is untrue or misleading, or that upon the exercise of reasonable care, should have been known by such agency to be untrue or misleading;

(3) misrepresent to any assisted person or prospective assisted person, directly or indirectly, affirmatively or by material omission, with respect to—

(A) the services that such agency will provide to such person; or

(B) the benefits and risks that may result if such person becomes a debtor in a case under this title; or

(4) advise an assisted person or prospective assisted person to incur more debt in contemplation of such person filing a case under this title or to pay an attorney or bankruptcy petition preparer a fee or charge for services performed as part of preparing for or representing a debtor in a case under this title.

(b) Any waiver by any assisted person of any protection or right provided under this section shall not be enforceable against the debtor by any Federal or State court or any other person, but may be enforced against a debt relief agency.

(c)(1) Any contract for bankruptcy assistance between a debt relief agency and an assisted person that does not comply with the material requirements of this section, section 527, or section 528 shall be void and may not be enforced by any Federal or State court or by any other person, other than such assisted person.

(2) Any debt relief agency shall be liable to an assisted person in the amount of any fees or charges in connection with providing bankruptcy assistance to such person that such debt relief agency has received, for actual damages, and for reasonable attorneys' fees and costs if such agency is found, after notice and a hearing, to have—

(A) intentionally or negligently failed to comply with any provision of this section, section 527, or section 528 with respect to a case or proceeding under this title for such assisted person;

(B) provided bankruptcy assistance to an assisted person in a case or proceeding under this title that is dismissed or converted to a case under another chapter of this title because of such agency's intentional or negligent failure to file any required document including those specified in section 521; or

(C) intentionally or negligently disregarded the material requirements of this title or the Federal Rules of Bankruptcy Procedure applicable to such agency.

(3) In addition to such other remedies as are provided under State law, whenever the chief law enforcement officer of a State, or an official or agency designated by a State, has reason to believe that any person has violated or is violating this section, the State—

(A) may bring an action to enjoin such violation;

(B) may bring an action on behalf of its residents to recover the actual damages of assisted persons arising from such violation, including any liability under paragraph (2); and

(C) in the case of any successful action under subparagraph (A) or (B), shall be awarded the costs of the action and reasonable attorneys' fees as determined by the court.

(4) The district courts of the United States for districts located in the State shall have concurrent jurisdiction of any action under subparagraph (A) or (B) of paragraph (3).

(5) Notwithstanding any other provision of Federal law and in addition to any other remedy provided under Federal or State law, if the court, on its own motion or on the motion of the United States trustee or the debtor, finds that a person intentionally violated this section, or engaged in a clear and consistent pattern or practice of violating this section, the court may—

(A) enjoin the violation of such section; or

(B) impose an appropriate civil penalty against such person.

(d) No provision of this section, section 527, or section 528 shall—

(1) annul, alter, affect, or exempt any person subject to such sections from complying with any law of any State except to the extent that such law is inconsistent with those sections, and then only to the extent of the inconsistency; or

(2) be deemed to limit or curtail the authority or ability—

(A) of a State or subdivision or instrumentality thereof, to determine and enforce qualifications for the practice of law under the laws of that State; or

(B) of a Federal court to determine and enforce the qualifications for the practice of law before that court.

(Added Pub.L. 109–8, Title II, § 227(a), Apr. 20, 2005, 119 Stat. 67; amended Pub.L. 111–327, § 2(a)(20), Dec. 22, 2010, 124 Stat. 3560.)

HISTORICAL AND STATUTORY NOTES

Amendments

2010 Amendments. Subsec. (a)(2). Pub.L. 111–327, § 2(a)(20)(A), struck out "untrue and" and inserted "untrue or".

Subsec. (a)(4). Pub.L. 111–327, § 2(a)(20)(B), inserted "a" following "preparer".

§ 527. Disclosures

(a) A debt relief agency providing bankruptcy assistance to an assisted person shall provide—

(1) the written notice required under section 342(b)(1); and

(2) to the extent not covered in the written notice described in paragraph (1), and not later than 3 business days after the first date on which a debt relief agency first offers to provide any bankruptcy assistance services to an assisted person, a clear and conspicuous written notice advising assisted persons that—

(A) all information that the assisted person is required to provide with a petition and thereafter during a case under this title is required to be complete, accurate, and truthful;

(B) all assets and all liabilities are required to be completely and accurately disclosed in the documents filed to commence the case, and the replacement value of each asset as defined in section 506 must be stated in those documents where requested after reasonable inquiry to establish such value;

(C) current monthly income, the amounts specified in section 707(b)(2), and, in a case under chapter 13 of this title, disposable income (determined in accordance with section 707(b)(2)), are required to be stated after reasonable inquiry; and

(D) information that an assisted person provides during their case may be audited pursuant to this title, and that failure to provide such information may result in dismissal of the case under this title or other sanction, including a criminal sanction.

(b) A debt relief agency providing bankruptcy assistance to an assisted person shall provide each assisted person at the same time as the notices required under subsection (a)(1) the following statement, to the extent applicable, or one substantially similar. The statement shall be clear and conspicuous and shall be in a single document separate from other documents or notices provided to the assisted person:

"IMPORTANT INFORMATION ABOUT BANKRUPTCY ASSISTANCE SERVICES FROM AN ATTORNEY OR BANKRUPTCY PETITION PREPARER.

"If you decide to seek bankruptcy relief, you can represent yourself, you can hire an attorney to represent you, or you can get help in some localities from a bankruptcy petition preparer who is not an attorney. THE LAW REQUIRES AN ATTORNEY OR BANKRUPTCY PETITION PREPARER

TO GIVE YOU A WRITTEN CONTRACT SPECIFYING WHAT THE ATTORNEY OR BANKRUPTCY PETITION PREPARER WILL DO FOR YOU AND HOW MUCH IT WILL COST. Ask to see the contract before you hire anyone.

"The following information helps you understand what must be done in a routine bankruptcy case to help you evaluate how much service you need. Although bankruptcy can be complex, many cases are routine.

"Before filing a bankruptcy case, either you or your attorney should analyze your eligibility for different forms of debt relief available under the Bankruptcy Code and which form of relief is most likely to be beneficial for you. Be sure you understand the relief you can obtain and its limitations. To file a bankruptcy case, documents called a Petition, Schedules, and Statement of Financial Affairs, and in some cases a Statement of Intention, need to be prepared correctly and filed with the bankruptcy court. You will have to pay a filing fee to the bankruptcy court. Once your case starts, you will have to attend the required first meeting of creditors where you may be questioned by a court official called a 'trustee' and by creditors.

"If you choose to file a chapter 7 case, you may be asked by a creditor to reaffirm a debt. You may want help deciding whether to do so. A creditor is not permitted to coerce you into reaffirming your debts.

"If you choose to file a chapter 13 case in which you repay your creditors what you can afford over 3 to 5 years, you may also want help with preparing your chapter 13 plan and with the confirmation hearing on your plan which will be before a bankruptcy judge.

"If you select another type of relief under the Bankruptcy Code other than chapter 7 or chapter 13, you will want to find out what should be done from someone familiar with that type of relief.

"Your bankruptcy case may also involve litigation. You are generally permitted to represent yourself in litigation in bankruptcy court, but only attorneys, not bankruptcy petition preparers, can give you legal advice.".

(c) Except to the extent the debt relief agency provides the required information itself after reasonably diligent inquiry of the assisted person or others so as to obtain such information reasonably accurately for inclusion on the petition, schedules or statement of financial affairs, a debt relief agency providing bankruptcy assistance to an assisted person, to the extent permitted by nonbankruptcy law, shall provide each assisted person at the time required for the notice required under subsection (a)(1) reasonably sufficient information (which shall be provided in a clear and conspicuous writing) to the assisted person on how to provide all the information the assisted person is required to provide under this title pursuant to section 521, including—

    (1) how to value assets at replacement value, determine current monthly income, the amounts specified in section 707(b)(2) and, in a chapter 13 case, how to determine disposable income in accordance with section 707(b)(2) and related calculations;

    (2) how to complete the list of creditors, including how to determine what amount is owed and what address for the creditor should be shown; and

    (3) how to determine what property is exempt and how to value exempt property at replacement value as defined in section 506.

(d) A debt relief agency shall maintain a copy of the notices required under subsection (a) of this section for 2 years after the date on which the notice is given the assisted person.

(Added Pub.L. 109–8, Title II, § 228(a), Apr. 20, 2005, 119 Stat. 69; amended Pub.L. 111–327, § 2(a)(21), Dec. 22, 2010, 124 Stat. 3560.)

HISTORICAL AND STATUTORY NOTES

Amendments

2010 Amendments. Subsec. (b). Pub.L. 111–327, § 2(a)(21), in the fourth paragraph of undesignated matter, struck out "Schedules and Statement of Financial Affairs, as well as in some cases a Statement of Intention" and inserted "Schedules, and Statement of Financial Affairs, and in some cases a Statement of Intention,".

§ 528. Requirements for debt relief agencies

(a) A debt relief agency shall—

(1) not later than 5 business days after the first date on which such agency provides any bankruptcy assistance services to an assisted person, but prior to such assisted person's petition under this title being filed, execute a written contract with such assisted person that explains clearly and conspicuously—

(A) the services such agency will provide to such assisted person; and

(B) the fees or charges for such services, and the terms of payment;

(2) provide the assisted person with a copy of the fully executed and completed contract;

(3) clearly and conspicuously disclose in any advertisement of bankruptcy assistance services or of the benefits of bankruptcy directed to the general public (whether in general media, seminars or specific mailings, telephonic or electronic messages, or otherwise) that the services or benefits are with respect to bankruptcy relief under this title; and

(4) clearly and conspicuously use the following statement in such advertisement: "We are a debt relief agency. We help people file for bankruptcy relief under the Bankruptcy Code." or a substantially similar statement.

(b)(1) An advertisement of bankruptcy assistance services or of the benefits of bankruptcy directed to the general public includes—

(A) descriptions of bankruptcy assistance in connection with a chapter 13 plan whether or not chapter 13 is specifically mentioned in such advertisement; and

(B) statements such as "federally supervised repayment plan" or "Federal debt restructuring help" or other similar statements that could lead a reasonable consumer to believe that debt counseling was being offered when in fact the services were directed to providing bankruptcy assistance with a chapter 13 plan or other form of bankruptcy relief under this title.

(2) An advertisement, directed to the general public, indicating that the debt relief agency provides assistance with respect to credit defaults, mortgage foreclosures, eviction proceedings, excessive debt, debt collection pressure, or inability to pay any consumer debt shall—

(A) disclose clearly and conspicuously in such advertisement that the assistance may involve bankruptcy relief under this title; and

(B) include the following statement: "We are a debt relief agency. We help people file for bankruptcy relief under the Bankruptcy Code." or a substantially similar statement.

(Added Pub.L. 109–8, Title II, § 229(a), Apr. 20, 2005, 119 Stat. 71.)

SUBCHAPTER III—THE ESTATE

§ 541. Property of the estate

(a) The commencement of a case under section 301, 302, or 303 of this title creates an estate. Such estate is comprised of all the following property, wherever located and by whomever held:

(1) Except as provided in subsections (b) and (c)(2) of this section, all legal or equitable interests of the debtor in property as of the commencement of the case.

(2) All interests of the debtor and the debtor's spouse in community property as of the commencement of the case that is—

(A) under the sole, equal, or joint management and control of the debtor; or

(B) liable for an allowable claim against the debtor, or for both an allowable claim against the debtor and an allowable claim against the debtor's spouse, to the extent that such interest is so liable.

(3) Any interest in property that the trustee recovers under section 329(b), 363(n), 543, 550, 553, or 723 of this title.

(4) Any interest in property preserved for the benefit of or ordered transferred to the estate under section 510(c) or 551 of this title.

(5) Any interest in property that would have been property of the estate if such interest had been an interest of the debtor on the date of the filing of the petition, and that the debtor acquires or becomes entitled to acquire within 180 days after such date—

(A) by bequest, devise, or inheritance;

(B) as a result of a property settlement agreement with the debtor's spouse, or of an interlocutory or final divorce decree; or

(C) as a beneficiary of a life insurance policy or of a death benefit plan.

(6) Proceeds, product, offspring, rents, or profits of or from property of the estate, except such as are earnings from services performed by an individual debtor after the commencement of the case.

(7) Any interest in property that the estate acquires after the commencement of the case.

(b) Property of the estate does not include—

(1) any power that the debtor may exercise solely for the benefit of an entity other than the debtor;

(2) any interest of the debtor as a lessee under a lease of nonresidential real property that has terminated at the expiration of the stated term of such lease before the commencement of the case under this title, and ceases to include any interest of the debtor as a lessee under a lease of nonresidential real property that has terminated at the expiration of the stated term of such lease during the case;

(3) any eligibility of the debtor to participate in programs authorized under the Higher Education Act of 1965 (20 U.S.C. 1001 et seq.; 42 U.S.C. 2751 et seq.), or any accreditation status or State licensure of the debtor as an educational institution;

(4) any interest of the debtor in liquid or gaseous hydrocarbons to the extent that—

(A)(i) the debtor has transferred or has agreed to transfer such interest pursuant to a farmout agreement or any written agreement directly related to a farmout agreement; and

(ii) but for the operation of this paragraph, the estate could include the interest referred to in clause (i) only by virtue of section 365 or 544(a)(3) of this title; or

(B)(i) the debtor has transferred such interest pursuant to a written conveyance of a production payment to an entity that does not participate in the operation of the property from which such production payment is transferred; and

(ii) but for the operation of this paragraph, the estate could include the interest referred to in clause (i) only by virtue of section 365 or 542 of this title;

(5) funds placed in an education individual retirement account (as defined in section 530(b)(1) of the Internal Revenue Code of 1986) not later than 365 days before the date of the filing of the petition in a case under this title, but—

(A) only if the designated beneficiary of such account was a child, stepchild, grandchild, or stepgrandchild of the debtor for the taxable year for which funds were placed in such account;

(B) only to the extent that such funds—

(i) are not pledged or promised to any entity in connection with any extension of credit; and

(ii) are not excess contributions (as described in section 4973(e) of the Internal Revenue Code of 1986); and

(C) in the case of funds placed in all such accounts having the same designated beneficiary not earlier than 720 days nor later than 365 days before such date, only so much of such funds as does not exceed $6,225[1];

(6) funds used to purchase a tuition credit or certificate or contributed to an account in accordance with section 529(b)(1)(A) of the Internal Revenue Code of 1986 under a qualified State tuition program (as defined in section 529(b)(1) of such Code) not later than 365 days before the date of the filing of the petition in a case under this title, but—

(A) only if the designated beneficiary of the amounts paid or contributed to such tuition program was a child, stepchild, grandchild, or stepgrandchild of the debtor for the taxable year for which funds were paid or contributed;

(B) with respect to the aggregate amount paid or contributed to such program having the same designated beneficiary, only so much of such amount as does not exceed the total contributions permitted under section 529(b)(6) of such Code with respect to such beneficiary, as adjusted beginning on the date of the filing of the petition in a case under this title by the annual increase or decrease (rounded to the nearest tenth of 1 percent) in the education expenditure category of the Consumer Price Index prepared by the Department of Labor; and

(C) in the case of funds paid or contributed to such program having the same designated beneficiary not earlier than 720 days nor later than 365 days before such date, only so much of such funds as does not exceed $6,225[1];

(7) any amount—

(A) withheld by an employer from the wages of employees for payment as contributions—

(i) to—

(I) an employee benefit plan that is subject to title I of the Employee Retirement Income Security Act of 1974 or under an employee benefit plan which is a governmental plan under section 414(d) of the Internal Revenue Code of 1986;

(II) a deferred compensation plan under section 457 of the Internal Revenue Code of 1986; or

(III) a tax-deferred annuity under section 403(b) of the Internal Revenue Code of 1986;

except that such amount under this subparagraph shall not constitute disposable income as defined in section 1325(b)(2); or

(ii) to a health insurance plan regulated by State law whether or not subject to such title; or

(B) received by an employer from employees for payment as contributions—

(i) to—

(I) an employee benefit plan that is subject to title I of the Employee Retirement Income Security Act of 1974 or under an employee benefit plan which is a governmental plan under section 414(d) of the Internal Revenue Code of 1986;

(II) a deferred compensation plan under section 457 of the Internal Revenue Code of 1986; or

---

[1] Dollar amount as adjusted by the Judicial Conference of the United States. See Adjustment of Dollar Amounts notes set out under this section and 11 U.S.C.A. § 104.

(III) a tax-deferred annuity under section 403(b) of the Internal Revenue Code of 1986;

except that such amount under this subparagraph shall not constitute disposable income, as defined in section 1325(b)(2); or

(ii) to a health insurance plan regulated by State law whether or not subject to such title;

(8) subject to subchapter III of chapter 5, any interest of the debtor in property where the debtor pledged or sold tangible personal property (other than securities or written or printed evidences of indebtedness or title) as collateral for a loan or advance of money given by a person licensed under law to make such loans or advances, where—

(A) the tangible personal property is in the possession of the pledgee or transferee;

(B) the debtor has no obligation to repay the money, redeem the collateral, or buy back the property at a stipulated price; and

(C) neither the debtor nor the trustee have exercised any right to redeem provided under the contract or State law, in a timely manner as provided under State law and section 108(b);

(9) any interest in cash or cash equivalents that constitute proceeds of a sale by the debtor of a money order that is made—

(A) on or after the date that is 14 days prior to the date on which the petition is filed; and

(B) under an agreement with a money order issuer that prohibits the commingling of such proceeds with property of the debtor (notwithstanding that, contrary to the agreement, the proceeds may have been commingled with property of the debtor),

unless the money order issuer had not taken action, prior to the filing of the petition, to require compliance with the prohibition.

Paragraph (4) shall not be construed to exclude from the estate any consideration the debtor retains, receives, or is entitled to receive for transferring an interest in liquid or gaseous hydrocarbons pursuant to a farmout agreement; or

(10) funds placed in an account of a qualified ABLE program (as defined in section 529A(b) of the Internal Revenue Code of 1986) not later than 365 days before the date of the filing of the petition in a case under this title, but—

(A) only if the designated beneficiary of such account was a child, stepchild, grandchild, or stepgrandchild of the debtor for the taxable year for which funds were placed in such account;

(B) only to the extent that such funds—

(i) are not pledged or promised to any entity in connection with any extension of credit; and

(ii) are not excess contributions (as described in section 4973(h) of the Internal Revenue Code of 1986); and

(C) in the case of funds placed in all such accounts having the same designated beneficiary not earlier than 720 days nor later than 365 days before such date, only so much of such funds as does not exceed $6,225.

(c)(1) Except as provided in paragraph (2) of this subsection, an interest of the debtor in property becomes property of the estate under subsection (a)(1), (a)(2), or (a)(5) of this section notwithstanding any provision in an agreement, transfer instrument, or applicable nonbankruptcy law—

(A) that restricts or conditions transfer of such interest by the debtor; or

(B) that is conditioned on the insolvency or financial condition of the debtor, on the commencement of a case under this title, or on the appointment of or taking possession by a trustee in a case under this title or a custodian before such commencement, and that effects or gives an option to effect a forfeiture, modification, or termination of the debtor's interest in property.

(2) A restriction on the transfer of a beneficial interest of the debtor in a trust that is enforceable under applicable nonbankruptcy law is enforceable in a case under this title.

(d) Property in which the debtor holds, as of the commencement of the case, only legal title and not an equitable interest, such as a mortgage secured by real property, or an interest in such a mortgage, sold by the debtor but as to which the debtor retains legal title to service or supervise the servicing of such mortgage or interest, becomes property of the estate under subsection (a)(1) or (2) of this section only to the extent of the debtor's legal title to such property, but not to the extent of any equitable interest in such property that the debtor does not hold.

(e) In determining whether any of the relationships specified in paragraph (5)(A) or (6)(A) of subsection (b) exists, a legally adopted child of an individual (and a child who is a member of an individual's household, if placed with such individual by an authorized placement agency for legal adoption by such individual), or a foster child of an individual (if such child has as the child's principal place of abode the home of the debtor and is a member of the debtor's household) shall be treated as a child of such individual by blood.

(f) Notwithstanding any other provision of this title, property that is held by a debtor that is a corporation described in section 501(c)(3) of the Internal Revenue Code of 1986 and exempt from tax under section 501(a) of such Code may be transferred to an entity that is not such a corporation, but only under the same conditions as would apply if the debtor had not filed a case under this title.

(Pub.L. 95–598, Nov. 6, 1978, 92 Stat. 2594; Pub.L. 98–353, Title III, §§ 363(a), 456, July 10, 1984, 98 Stat. 363, 376; Pub.L. 101–508, Title III, § 3007(a)(2), Nov. 5, 1990, 104 Stat. 1388–28; Pub.L. 102–486, Title XXX, § 3017(b), Oct. 24, 1992, 106 Stat. 3130; Pub.L. 103–394, Title II, §§ 208(b), 223, Oct. 22, 1994, 108 Stat. 4124, 4129; Pub.L. 109–8, Title II, § 225(a), Title III, § 323, Title XII, §§ 1212, 1221(c), 1230, Apr. 20, 2005, 119 Stat. 65, 97, 194, 196, 201; Pub.L. 111–327, § 2(a)(22), Dec. 22, 2010, 124 Stat. 3560.)

HISTORICAL AND STATUTORY NOTES

References in Text

The Higher Education Act of 1965, referred to in subsec. (b)(3), is Pub.L. 89–329, Nov. 8, 1965, 79 Stat. 1219, as amended, which is classified principally to chapter 28 (§ 1001 et seq.) of Title 20, Education. For complete classification of this Act to the Code, see Short Title note set out under section 1001 of Title 20 and Tables.

Section 530(b)(1) of the Internal Revenue Code of 1986, referred to in subsec. (b)(5), is classified to 26 U.S.C.A. § 530(b)(1).

Section 4973(e) of the Internal Revenue Code of 1986, referred to in subsec. (b)(5)(B)(ii), is classified to 26 U.S.C.A. § 4973(e).

"Section 529(b)(1) of such Code" and "section 529(b)(6) of such Code", referred to in subsec. (b)(6), are classified to 26 U.S.C.A. § 529(b)(1) and to 26 U.S.C.A. § 529(b)(6), respectively.

Title I of the Employee Retirement Income Security Act of 1974, referred to in subsec. (b)(7)(A)(i)(I), (B)(i)(I), means Pub.L. 93–406, Title I, Sept. 2, 1974, 88 Stat. 829, which principally enacted subchapter I of chapter 18 of Title 29, 29 U.S.C.A. § 1001 et seq.; see Tables for complete classification.

Section 414(d) of the Internal Revenue Code of 1986, referred to in subsec. (b)(7)(A)(i)(I), (B)(i)(I), is 26 U.S.C.A. § 414(d).

Section 457 of the Internal Revenue Code of 1986, referred to in subsec. (b)(7)(A)(i)(II), (B)(i)(II), is 26 U.S.C.A. § 457.

Section 403(b) of the Internal Revenue Code of 1986, referred to in subsec. (b)(7)(A)(i)(III), (B)(i)(III), is 26 U.S.C.A. § 403(b).

Codifications

Section 223(2) of Pub.L. 103–394, directing that subsec. (b)(4) of this section be amended by striking out the period at the end and inserting "; or", was executed by inserting "or" following the semicolon at the end of subsec. (b)(4)(B)(ii) of this section, as added by section 208(b)(3) of Pub.L. 103–394, as the probable intent of Congress.

Amendments

2014 Amendments. Subsec. (b)(10). Pub.L. 113–295, § 104(a), struck our "or" at the end of par. (b)(8), inserted a semicolon and the word "or" at the end of par. (b)(9), and inserted new par. (10).

2010 Amendments. Subsec. (b)(6)(B). Pub.L. 111–327, § 2(a)(22), struck out "section 529(b)(7)" and inserted "section 529(b)(6)".

2005 Amendments. Subsec. (b)(4). Pub.L. 109–8, § 225(a)(1)(A), struck out "or" at the end of par. (4).

Subsec. (b)(4)(B)(ii). Pub.L.109–8, § 1212, inserted "365 or" before "542".

Subsec. (b)(5). Pub.L. 109–8, § 225(a)(1)(B), (C), inserted new par. (5) and redesignated former par. (5) as par. (9).

Subsec. (b)(6). Pub.L. 109–8, § 225(a)(1)(C), inserted new par. (6).

Subsec. (b)(7). Pub.L. 109–8, § 323, added par. (7).

Subsec. (b)(8). Pub.L.109–8, § 1230, added par. (8).

Subsec. (b)(9). Pub.L. 109–8, § 225(a)(1)(B), redesignated former par. (5) as par. (9).

Subsec. (e). Pub.L. 109–8, § 225(a)(2), added subsec. (e).

Subsec. (f). Pub.L.109–8, § 1221(c), added subsec. (f).

1994 Amendments. Subsec. (b)(4). Pub.L. 103–394, § 208(b), added subpar. (B) and redesignated former subpar. (A) as subpar. (A), cl. (i) and former subpar. (B) as subpar. (A), cl. (ii) and as so redesignated substituted "the interest referred to in clause (i)" for "such interest".

Subsec. (b)(4)(B). Pub.L. 103–394, § 208(b)(3), added subpar. (B).

Subsec. (b)(5). Pub.L. 103–394, § 223, added par. (5).

1992 Amendments. Subsec. (b). Pub.L. 102–486, § 3017(b), added par. (4) and closing sentence.

1990 Amendments. Subsec. (b)(3). Pub.L. 101–508, § 3007(a)(2), added par. (3).

1984 Amendments. Subsec. (a). Pub.L. 98–353, § 456(a)(1), (2), struck out "under" following "under" and added "and by whomever held" after "located".

Subsec. (a)(3). Pub.L. 98–353, § 456(a)(3), added "329(b), 363(n)," after "section".

Subsec. (a)(5). Pub.L. 98–353, § 456(a)(4), substituted "Any" for "An".

Subsec. (a)(6). Pub.L. 98–353, § 456(a)(5), substituted "or profits" for "and profits".

Subsec. (b). Pub.L. 98–353, § 363(a), substituted "Property of the estate does not include—

"(1) any power that the debtor may exercise solely for the benefit of an entity other than the debtor; or

"(2) any interest of the debtor as a lessee under a lease of nonresidential real property that has terminated at the expiration of the stated term of such lease before the commencement of the case under this title, and ceases to include any interest of the debtor as a lessee under a lease of nonresidential real property that has terminated at the expiration of the stated term of such lease during the case."

for

"Property of the estate does not include any power that the debtor may only exercise solely for the benefit of an entity other than the debtor.".

Subsec. (c)(1). Pub.L. 98–353, § 456(b)(1), added "in an agreement, transfer instrument, or applicable nonbankruptcy law" after "provision" in matter preceding subpar. (A).

Subsec. (c)(1)(B). Pub.L. 98–353, § 456(b)(2), substituted "taking" for "the taking" and added "before such commencement" after "custodian".

Subsec. (d). Pub.L. 98–353, § 456(c), added "(1) or (2)" after "(a)".

Subsec. (e). Pub.L. 98–353, § 456(d), struck out subsec. (e), which read "The estate shall have the benefit of any defense available to the debtor as against an entity other than the estate, including statutes of limitation, statutes of frauds, usury, and other personal defenses. A waiver of any such defense by the debtor after the commencement of the case does not bind the estate."

CROSS REFERENCES

Community claim defined, see 11 USCA § 101.

Distribution of property of estate, see 11 USCA § 726.

Effect of discharge, see 11 USCA § 524.

Executory contracts and unexpired leases, see 11 USCA § 365.

Exemptions, see 11 USCA § 522.

Ownership of copyright, see 17 USCA § 201.

Property of estate in—

    Chapter 13 cases, see 11 USCA § 1306.

    Chapter 12 cases, see 11 USCA § 1207.

Special tax provisions concerning estates of partners and partnerships, see 11 USCA § 728.

Trustee considered consignee of merchandise consigned to deceased or insolvent persons, see 19 USCA § 1485.

Venue of action brought under this title by trustee as statutory successor under this section to debtor, see 28 USCA § 1409.

§ 542. Turnover of property to the estate

(a) Except as provided in subsection (c) or (d) of this section, an entity, other than a custodian, in possession, custody, or control, during the case, of property that the trustee may use, sell, or lease under section 363 of this title, or that the debtor may exempt under section 522 of this title, shall deliver to the trustee, and account for, such property or the value of such property, unless such property is of inconsequential value or benefit to the estate.

(b) Except as provided in subsection (c) or (d) of this section, an entity that owes a debt that is property of the estate and that is matured, payable on demand, or payable on order, shall pay such debt to, or on the order of, the trustee, except to the extent that such debt may be offset under section 553 of this title against a claim against the debtor.

(c) Except as provided in section 362(a)(7) of this title, an entity that has neither actual notice nor actual knowledge of the commencement of the case concerning the debtor may transfer property of the estate, or pay a debt owing to the debtor, in good faith and other than in the manner specified in subsection (d) of this section, to an entity other than the trustee, with the same effect as to the entity making such transfer or payment as if the case under this title concerning the debtor had not been commenced.

(d) A life insurance company may transfer property of the estate or property of the debtor to such company in good faith, with the same effect with respect to such company as if the case under this title concerning the debtor had not been commenced, if such transfer is to pay a premium or to carry out a nonforfeiture insurance option, and is required to be made automatically, under a life insurance contract with such company that was entered into before the date of the filing of the petition and that is property of the estate.

(e) Subject to any applicable privilege, after notice and a hearing, the court may order an attorney, accountant, or other person that holds recorded information, including books, documents, records, and papers, relating to the debtor's property or financial affairs, to turn over or disclose such recorded information to the trustee.

(Pub.L. 95–598, Nov. 6, 1978, 92 Stat. 2595; Pub.L. 98–353, Title III, § 457, July 10, 1984, 98 Stat. 376; Pub.L. 103–394, Title V, § 501(d)(16), Oct. 22, 1994, 108 Stat. 4146.)

HISTORICAL AND STATUTORY NOTES

Amendments

1994 Amendments. Subsec. (e). Pub.L. 103–394, § 501(d)(16), substituted "to turn over" for "to to turn over".

1984 Amendments. Subsec. (e). Pub.L. 98–353 added "to turn over or" before "disclose".

CROSS REFERENCES

Assignability or accrual to third persons of farm loan agreements respecting credits or principal and interest, see 42 USCA § 1473.

Concealment of assets, see 18 USCA § 152.

Disallowance of claims of entity from which property is recoverable, see 11 USCA § 502.

Effect of dismissal, see 11 USCA § 349.

Exemptions, see 11 USCA § 522.

§ 543. Turnover of property by a custodian

(a) A custodian with knowledge of the commencement of a case under this title concerning the debtor may not make any disbursement from, or take any action in the administration of, property of the debtor, proceeds, product, offspring, rents, or profits of such property, or property of the estate, in the possession, custody, or control of such custodian, except such action as is necessary to preserve such property.

(b) A custodian shall—

(1) deliver to the trustee any property of the debtor held by or transferred to such custodian, or proceeds, product, offspring, rents, or profits of such property, that is in such custodian's possession, custody, or control on the date that such custodian acquires knowledge of the commencement of the case; and

(2) file an accounting of any property of the debtor, or proceeds, product, offspring, rents, or profits of such property, that, at any time, came into the possession, custody, or control of such custodian.

(c) The court, after notice and a hearing, shall—

(1) protect all entities to which a custodian has become obligated with respect to such property or proceeds, product, offspring, rents, or profits of such property;

(2) provide for the payment of reasonable compensation for services rendered and costs and expenses incurred by such custodian; and

(3) surcharge such custodian, other than an assignee for the benefit of the debtor's creditors that was appointed or took possession more than 120 days before the date of the filing of the petition, for any improper or excessive disbursement, other than a disbursement that has been made in accordance with applicable law or that has been approved, after notice and a hearing, by a court of competent jurisdiction before the commencement of the case under this title.

(d) After notice and hearing, the bankruptcy court—

(1) may excuse compliance with subsection (a), (b), or (c) of this section if the interests of creditors and, if the debtor is not insolvent, of equity security holders would be better served by permitting a custodian to continue in possession, custody, or control of such property, and

(2) shall excuse compliance with subsections (a) and (b)(1) of this section if the custodian is an assignee for the benefit of the debtor's creditors that was appointed or took possession more than 120 days before the date of the filing of the petition, unless compliance with such subsections is necessary to prevent fraud or injustice.

(Pub.L. 95–598, Nov. 6, 1978, 92 Stat. 2595; Pub.L. 98–353, Title III, § 458, July 10, 1984, 98 Stat. 376; Pub.L. 103–394, Title V, § 501(d)(17), Oct. 22, 1994, 108 Stat. 4146.)

HISTORICAL AND STATUTORY NOTES

Amendments

1994 Amendments. Subsec. (d)(1). Pub.L. 103–394, § 501(d)(17), struck out comma following "section".

1984 Amendments. Subsec. (a). Pub.L. 98–353, § 458(a), added ", product, offspring, rents, or profits" after "proceeds".

Subsec. (b)(1). Pub.L. 98–353, § 458(b)(1), added "held by" after "debtor", and ", product, offspring, rents, or profits" after "proceeds".

Subsec. (b)(2). Pub.L. 98–353, § 458(b)(2), added ", product, offspring, rents, or profits" after "proceeds".

Subsec. (c)(1). Pub.L. 98–353, § 458(c)(1), added "or proceeds, product, offspring, rents, or profits of such property" after "property".

Subsec. (c)(3). Pub.L. 98–353, § 458(c)(2), added "that has been" before "approved".

Subsec. (d)(1). Pub.L. 98–353, § 458(d), designated existing provisions as par. (1).

Subsec. (d)(2). Pub.L. 98–353, § 458(d), added par. (2).

CROSS REFERENCES

Administrative expenses of superseded custodians, see 11 USCA § 503.

Concealment of assets, see 18 USCA § 152.

Disallowance of claim of entity from which property is recoverable, see 11 USCA § 502.

Effect of dismissal, see 11 USCA § 349.

Order of payment on claims for expenses of superseded custodians, see 11 USCA § 726.

Property recoverable by trustee as exempt, see 11 USCA § 522.

§ 544. Trustee as lien creditor and as successor to certain creditors and purchasers

(a) The trustee shall have, as of the commencement of the case, and without regard to any knowledge of the trustee or of any creditor, the rights and powers of, or may avoid any transfer of property of the debtor or any obligation incurred by the debtor that is voidable by—

(1) a creditor that extends credit to the debtor at the time of the commencement of the case, and that obtains, at such time and with respect to such credit, a judicial lien on all property on which a creditor on a simple contract could have obtained such a judicial lien, whether or not such a creditor exists;

(2) a creditor that extends credit to the debtor at the time of the commencement of the case, and obtains, at such time and with respect to such credit, an execution against the debtor that is returned unsatisfied at such time, whether or not such a creditor exists; or

(3) a bona fide purchaser of real property, other than fixtures, from the debtor, against whom applicable law permits such transfer to be perfected, that obtains the status of a bona fide purchaser and has perfected such transfer at the time of the commencement of the case, whether or not such a purchaser exists.

(b)(1) Except as provided in paragraph (2), the trustee may avoid any transfer of an interest of the debtor in property or any obligation incurred by the debtor that is voidable under applicable law by a creditor holding an unsecured claim that is allowable under section 502 of this title or that is not allowable only under section 502(e) of this title.

(2) Paragraph (1) shall not apply to a transfer of a charitable contribution (as that term is defined in section 548(d)(3)) that is not covered under section 548(a)(1)(B), by reason of section 548(a)(2). Any claim by any person to recover a transferred contribution described in the preceding sentence under Federal or State law in a Federal or State court shall be preempted by the commencement of the case.

(Pub.L. 95–598, Nov. 6, 1978, 92 Stat. 2596; Pub.L. 98–353, Title III, § 459, July 10, 1984, 98 Stat. 377; Pub.L. 105–183, § 3(b), June 19, 1998, 112 Stat. 518.)

HISTORICAL AND STATUTORY NOTES

Amendments

1998 Amendments. Subsec. (b)(1). Pub.L. 105–183, § 3(b)(1), struck out "(b) The trustee" and inserted "(b)(1) Except as provided in paragraph (2), the trustee".

Subsec. (b)(2). Pub.L. 105–183, § 3(b)(2), added par. (2).

1984 Amendments. Subsec. (a)(1). Pub.L. 98–353, § 459(1), added "such" after "obtained".

Subsec. (a)(2). Pub.L. 98–353, § 459(2), substituted "; or" for "; and".

Subsec. (a)(3). Pub.L. 98–353, § 459(3), added ", other than fixtures," after "property"; and "and has perfected such transfer" after "purchaser" the second place it appeared.

Rule of Construction

Pub.L. 105–183, § 6, June 19, 1998, 112 Stat. 519, provided that: "Nothing in the amendments made by this Act [amending this section and sections 546, 548, 707, and 1325 of this title and enacting this note and provisions set out as notes under this section and section 101 of this title] is intended to limit the applicability of the Religious Freedom Restoration Act of 1993 (42 U.S.C. 2002bb et seq.)."

CROSS REFERENCES

Applicability of this section in Chapter nine cases, see 11 USCA § 901.

Appointment of trustee upon debtor's refusal to pursue cause of action under this section, see 11 USCA § 926.

Commencement of involuntary cases by transferees of voidable transfer, see 11 USCA § 303.

Disallowance of claims of entity that is transferee of avoidable transfer, see 11 USCA § 502.

Effect of dismissal, see 11 USCA § 349.

Exemptions, see 11 USCA § 522.

Recovery of voidable transfers in investor protection liquidation proceedings, see 15 USCA § 78fff–2.

Venue of action brought under this title by trustee as statutory successor under this section to creditors, see 28 USCA § 1409.

Voidable transfers in—

    Commodity broker liquidation cases, see 11 USCA § 764.

    Stockbroker liquidation proceedings, see 11 USCA § 749.

§ 545. Statutory liens

The trustee may avoid the fixing of a statutory lien on property of the debtor to the extent that such lien—

    (1) first becomes effective against the debtor—

(A) when a case under this title concerning the debtor is commenced;

(B) when an insolvency proceeding other than under this title concerning the debtor is commenced;

(C) when a custodian is appointed or authorized to take or takes possession;

(D) when the debtor becomes insolvent;

(E) when the debtor's financial condition fails to meet a specified standard; or

(F) at the time of an execution against property of the debtor levied at the instance of an entity other than the holder of such statutory lien;

(2) is not perfected or enforceable at the time of the commencement of the case against a bona fide purchaser that purchases such property at the time of the commencement of the case, whether or not such a purchaser exists, except in any case in which a purchaser is a purchaser described in section 6323 of the Internal Revenue Code of 1986, or in any other similar provision of State or local law;

(3) is for rent; or

(4) is a lien of distress for rent.

(Pub.L. 95–598, Nov. 6, 1978, 92 Stat. 2597; Pub.L. 98–353, Title III, § 460, July 10, 1984, 98 Stat. 377; Pub.L. 109–8, Title VII, § 711, Apr. 20, 2005, 119 Stat. 127.)

HISTORICAL AND STATUTORY NOTES

References in Text

Section 6323 of the Internal Revenue Code of 1986, referred to in par. (2), is classified to 26 U.S.C.A. § 6323.

Amendments

2005 Amendments. Par. (2). Pub.L. 109–8, § 711, inserted ", except in any case in which a purchaser is a purchaser described in section 6323 of the Internal Revenue Code of 1986, or in any other similar provision of State or local law" before the semicolon at the end.

1984 Amendments. Par. (1)(A). Pub.L. 98–353, § 460(1), struck out "is" following "is".

Par. (1)(C). Pub.L. 98–353, § 460(2), substituted "appointed or authorized to take" for "apponted".

Par. (2). Pub.L. 98–353, § 460(3), substituted "at the time of the commencement of the case" for "on the date of the filing of the petition" wherever appearing.

CROSS REFERENCES

Applicability of this section in Chapter nine cases, see 11 USCA § 901.

Appointment of trustee upon debtor's refusal to pursue cause of action under this section, see 11 USCA § 926.

Commencement of involuntary cases by transferees of voidable transfers, see 11 USCA § 303.

Disallowance of claims of entity that is a transferee of an avoidable transfer, see 11 USCA § 502.

Effect of dismissal, see 11 USCA § 349.

Exemptions, see 11 USCA § 522.

Recovery of voidable transfers in investor protection liquidation proceedings, see 15 USCA § 78fff–2.

Voidable transfers in—

Commodity broker liquidation cases, see 11 USCA § 764.

Stockbroker liquidation cases, see 11 USCA § 749.

§ 546. Limitations on avoiding powers

(a) An action or proceeding under section 544, 545, 547, 548, or 553 of this title may not be commenced after the earlier of—

(1) the later of—

(A) 2 years after the entry of the order for relief; or

(B) 1 year after the appointment or election of the first trustee under section 702, 1104, 1163, 1202, or 1302 of this title if such appointment or such election occurs before the expiration of the period specified in subparagraph (A); or

(2) the time the case is closed or dismissed.

(b)(1) The rights and powers of a trustee under sections 544, 545, and 549 of this title are subject to any generally applicable law that—

(A) permits perfection of an interest in property to be effective against an entity that acquires rights in such property before the date of perfection; or

(B) provides for the maintenance or continuation of perfection of an interest in property to be effective against an entity that acquires rights in such property before the date on which action is taken to effect such maintenance or continuation.

(2) If—

(A) a law described in paragraph (1) requires seizure of such property or commencement of an action to accomplish such perfection, or maintenance or continuation of perfection of an interest in property; and

(B) such property has not been seized or such an action has not been commenced before the date of the filing of the petition;

such interest in such property shall be perfected, or perfection of such interest shall be maintained or continued, by giving notice within the time fixed by such law for such seizure or such commencement.

(c)(1) Except as provided in subsection (d) of this section and in section 507(c), and subject to the prior rights of a holder of a security interest in such goods or the proceeds thereof, the rights and powers of the trustee under sections 544(a), 545, 547, and 549 are subject to the right of a seller of goods that has sold goods to the debtor, in the ordinary course of such seller's business, to reclaim such goods if the debtor has received such goods while insolvent, within 45 days before the date of the commencement of a case under this title, but such seller may not reclaim such goods unless such seller demands in writing reclamation of such goods—

(A) not later than 45 days after the date of receipt of such goods by the debtor; or

(B) not later than 20 days after the date of commencement of the case, if the 45-day period expires after the commencement of the case.

(2) If a seller of goods fails to provide notice in the manner described in paragraph (1), the seller still may assert the rights contained in section 503(b)(9).

(d) In the case of a seller who is a producer of grain sold to a grain storage facility, owned or operated by the debtor, in the ordinary course of such seller's business (as such terms are defined in section 557 of this title) or in the case of a United States fisherman who has caught fish sold to a fish processing facility owned or operated by the debtor in the ordinary course of such fisherman's business, the rights and powers of the trustee under sections 544(a), 545, 547, and 549 of this title are subject to any statutory or common law right of such producer or fisherman to reclaim such grain or fish if the debtor has received such grain or fish while insolvent, but—

(1) such producer or fisherman may not reclaim any grain or fish unless such producer or fisherman demands, in writing, reclamation of such grain or fish before ten days after receipt thereof by the debtor; and

(2) the court may deny reclamation to such a producer or fisherman with a right of reclamation that has made such a demand only if the court secures such claim by a lien.

(e) Notwithstanding sections 544, 545, 547, 548(a)(1)(B), and 548(b) of this title, the trustee may not avoid a transfer that is a margin payment, as defined in section 101, 741, or 761 of this title, or settlement payment, as defined in section 101 or 741 of this title, made by or to (or for the benefit of) a commodity broker, forward contract merchant, stockbroker, financial institution, financial participant, or securities clearing agency, or that is a transfer made by or to (or for the benefit of) a commodity broker, forward contract merchant, stockbroker, financial institution, financial participant, or securities clearing agency, in connection with a securities contract, as defined in section 741(7), commodity contract, as defined in section 761(4), or forward contract, that is made before the commencement of the case, except under section 548(a)(1)(A) of this title.

(f) Notwithstanding sections 544, 545, 547, 548(a)(1)(B), and 548(b) of this title, the trustee may not avoid a transfer made by or to (or for the benefit of) a repo participant or financial participant, in connection with a repurchase agreement and that is made before the commencement of the case, except under section 548(a)(1)(A) of this title.

(g) Notwithstanding sections 544, 545, 547, 548(a)(1)(B) and 548(b) of this title, the trustee may not avoid a transfer, made by or to (or for the benefit of) a swap participant or financial participant, under or in connection with any swap agreement and that is made before the commencement of the case, except under section 548(a)(1)(A) of this title.

(h) Notwithstanding the rights and powers of a trustee under sections 544(a), 545, 547, 549, and 553, if the court determines on a motion by the trustee made not later than 120 days after the date of the order for relief in a case under chapter 11 of this title and after notice and a hearing, that a return is in the best interests of the estate, the debtor, with the consent of a creditor and subject to the prior rights of holders of security interests in such goods or the proceeds of such goods, may return goods shipped to the debtor by the creditor before the commencement of the case, and the creditor may offset the purchase price of such goods against any claim of the creditor against the debtor that arose before the commencement of the case.

(i)(1) Notwithstanding paragraphs (2) and (3) of section 545, the trustee may not avoid a warehouseman's lien for storage, transportation, or other costs incidental to the storage and handling of goods.

(2) The prohibition under paragraph (1) shall be applied in a manner consistent with any State statute applicable to such lien that is similar to section 7–209 of the Uniform Commercial Code, as in effect on the date of enactment of the Bankruptcy Abuse Prevention and Consumer Protection Act of 2005, or any successor to such section 7–209.

(j) Notwithstanding sections 544, 545, 547, 548(a)(1)(B), and 548(b) the trustee may not avoid a transfer made by or to (or for the benefit of) a master netting agreement participant under or in connection with any master netting agreement or any individual contract covered thereby that is made before the commencement of the case, except under section 548(a)(1)(A) and except to the extent that the trustee could otherwise avoid such a transfer made under an individual contract covered by such master netting agreement.

(Pub.L. 95–598, Nov. 6, 1978, 92 Stat. 2597; Pub.L. 97–222, § 4, July 27, 1982, 96 Stat. 236; Pub.L. 98–353, Title III, §§ 351, 393, 461, July 10, 1984, 98 Stat. 358, 365, 377; Pub.L. 99–554, Title II, §§ 257(d), 283(*l*), Oct. 27, 1986, 100 Stat. 3114, 3117; Pub.L. 101–311, Title I, § 103, Title II, § 203, June 25, 1990, 104 Stat. 268, 269; Pub.L. 103–394, Title II, §§ 204(b), 209, 216, 222(a), Title V, § 501(b)(4), Oct. 22, 1994, 108 Stat. 4122, 4125, 4126, 4129, 4142; Pub.L. 105–183, § 3(c), June 19, 1998, 112 Stat. 518; Pub.L. 109–8, Title IV, § 406, Title IX, §§ 907(e), (o)(2), (3), Title XII, § 1227(a), Apr. 20, 2005, 119 Stat. 105, 177, 182, 199; Pub.L. 109–390, § 5(b), Dec. 12, 2006, 120 Stat. 2697.)

HISTORICAL AND STATUTORY NOTES

References in Text

The date of enactment of the Bankruptcy Abuse Prevention and Consumer Protection Act of 2005, referred to in subsec. (i)(2), is April 20, 2005, the approval date of Pub.L. 109–8, 119 Stat. 23.

Codifications

The amendment by Pub.L. 105–183, § 3(c)(3), to subsec. (g) of this section was executed to the first subsec. (g) of this section as the probable intent of Congress since the phrases being amended, "section 548(a)(1)" and "548(a)(2)", appeared only in the first subsec. (g).

Amendments

2006 Amendments. Subsec. (e). Pub.L. 109–390, § 5(b)(1)(A), inserted "(or for the benefit of)" before "a commodity broker".

Pub.L. 109–390, § 5(b)(1)(B), inserted "or that is a transfer made by or to (or for the benefit of) a commodity broker, forward contract merchant, stockbroker, financial institution, financial participant, or securities clearing agency, in connection with a securities contract, as defined in section 741(7), commodity contract, as defined in section 761(4), or forward contract," after "securities clearing agency,".

Subsec. (f). Pub.L. 109–390, § 5(b)(2)(A), struck out "that is a margin payment, as defined in section 741 or 761 of this title, or settlement payment, as defined in section 741 of this title," following "may not avoid a transfer".

Pub.L. 109–390, § 5(b)(2)(B), inserted "(or for the benefit of)" before "a repo participant".

Subsec. (g). Pub.L. 109–390, § 5(b)(3), inserted "(or for the benefit of)" before "a swap participant".

Subsec. (j). Pub.L. 109–390, § 5(b)(4), inserted "(or for the benefit of)" after "made by or to".

2005 Amendments. Subsec. (c). Pub.L. 109–8, § 1227(a), rewrote subsec. (c), which formerly read:

"(c) Except as provided in subsection (d) of this section, the rights and powers of a trustee under sections 544(a), 545, 547, and 549 of this title are subject to any statutory or common-law right of a seller of goods that has sold goods to the debtor, in the ordinary course of such seller's business, to reclaim such goods if the debtor has received such goods while insolvent, but—

"(1) such a seller may not reclaim any such goods unless such seller demands in writing reclamation of such goods—

"(A) before 10 days after receipt of such goods by the debtor; or

"(B) if such 10-day period expires after the commencement of the case, before 20 days after receipt of such goods by the debtor; and

"(2) the court may deny reclamation to a seller with such a right of reclamation that has made such a demand only if the court—

"(A) grants the claim of such a seller priority as a claim of a kind specified in section 503(b) of this title; or

"(B) secures such claim by a lien."

Subsec. (e). Pub.L. 109–8, § 907(o)(3), inserted "financial participant," after "financial institution,".

Subsec. (f). Pub.L. 109–8, § 907(o)(2), inserted "or financial participant" after "repo participant" each place such term appeared.

Subsec. (g). Pub.L. 109–8, § 406(1), redesignated the second subsec. (g), as added by Pub.L. 103–394, § 222(a), relating to returns of goods, as subsec. (h).

Pub.L. 109–8, § 907(e)(1), in subsec. (g) as added by Pub.L. 101–311, § 103, struck out "under a swap agreement" after "may not avoid a transfer", struck out "in connection with a swap agreement" and inserted "under or in connection with any swap agreement", and inserted "or financial participant" after "swap participant".

Subsec. (h). Pub.L. 109–8, § 406(1), (2), redesignated the second subsec. (g), as added by Pub.L. 103–394, § 222(a), as subsec. (h), and as so redesignated, inserted "and subject to the prior rights of holders of security interests in such goods or the proceeds of such goods" after "consent of a creditor".

Subsec. (i). Pub.L. 109–8, § 406(3), added subsec. (i).

Subsec. (j). Pub.L. 109–8, § 907(e)(2), added subsec. (j).

1998 Amendments. Subsec. (e). Pub.L. 105–183, § 3(c)(1), struck out "548(a)(2)" and inserted "548(a)(1)(B)" and struck out "548(a)(1)" and inserted "548(a)(1)(A)".

Subsec. (f). Pub.L. 105–183, § 3(c)(2), struck out "548(a)(2)" and inserted "548(a)(1)(B)" and struck out "548(a)(1)" and inserted "548(a)(1)(A)".

Subsec. (g). Pub.L. 105–183, § 3(c)(3), struck out "section 548(a)(1)" each place it appeared and inserted "section 548(a)(1)(A)" and struck out "548(a)(2)" and inserted "548(a)(1)(B)".

1994 Amendments. Subsec. (a)(1). Pub.L. 103–394, § 216, completely revised par. (1). Prior to revision, par. (1) read as follows:

"two years after the appointment of a trustee under section 702, 1104, 1163, 1302, or 1202 of this title; or".

Subsec. (b). Pub.L. 103–394, § 204(b), completely revised subsec. (b). Prior to revision, subsec. (b) read as follows:

"The rights and powers of a trustee under sections 544, 545, and 549 of this title are subject to any generally applicable law that permits perfection of an interest in property to be effective against an entity that acquires rights in such property before the date of such perfection. If such law requires seizure of such property or commencement of an action to accomplish such perfection, and such property has not been seized or such action has not been commenced before the date of the filing of the petition, such interest in such property shall be perfected by notice within the time fixed by such law for such seizure or commencement."

Subsec. (c)(1). Pub.L. 103–394, § 209, redesignated existing text as opening cl. and subpar. (A) and added subpar. (B).

Subsec. (e). Pub.L. 103–394, § 501(b)(4)(A), substituted "section 101, 741, or 761" for "section 101(34), 741(5), or 761(15)", and "section 101 or 741" for "section 101(35) or 741(8)".

Subsec. (f). Pub.L. 103–394, § 501(b)(4)(B), substituted "section 741 or 761" for "section 741(5) or 761(15)", and "section 741" for "section 741(8)".

Subsec. (g). Pub.L. 103–394, § 222(a), added subsec. (g), relating to return of goods.

1990 Amendments. Subsec. (e). Pub.L. 101–311, § 203, added provisions referring to sections 101(34) and 101(35) of this title.

Subsec. (g). Pub.L. 101–311, § 103, added subsec. (g), relating to swap agreements.

1986 Amendments. Subsec. (a)(1). Pub.L. 99–554, § 257(d), added reference to section 1202 of this title.

Subsec. (e). Pub.L. 99–554, § 283*(1)*, substituted "stockbroker," for "stockbroker".

1984 Amendments. Subsec. (a)(1). Pub.L. 98–353, § 461(a), substituted "or" for "and" following the semicolon at the end.

Subsec. (b). Pub.L. 98–353, § 461(b), substituted "a trustee under sections 544, 545, and" for "the trustee under sections 544, 545, or".

Subsec. (c). Pub.L. 98–353, § 351(1), substituted "Except as provided in subsection (d) of this section, the" for "The".

Pub.L. 98–353, § 461(c)(1)–(4), substituted "a trustee" for "the trustee", struck out "right" before "or common-law", added "of goods that has sold goods to the debtor" after "seller", and struck out "of goods to the debtor" after "business,".

Subsec. (c)(2). Pub.L. 98–353, § 461(c)(5)(A), added "the" after "if".

Subsec. (c)(2)(A). Pub.L. 98–353, § 461(c)(5)(B), substituted "a claim of a kind specified in section 503(b) of this title" for "an administrative expense".

Subsec. (d). Pub.L. 98–353, § 351(3), added subsec. (d). Former subsec. (d) was redesignated as (e).

Subsec. (e). Pub.L. 98–353, § 351(2), redesignated former subsec. (d) as (e).

Pub.L. 98–353, § 461(d), added "financial institution" after "stockbroker".

Subsec. (f). Pub.L. 98–353, § 393, added subsec. (f).

1982 Amendments. Subsec. (d). Pub.L. 97–222 added subsec. (d).

Title 11   CREDITORS, THE DEBTOR, AND THE ESTATE   11 § 547

Rule of Construction

Amendments made by Pub.L. 105–183 not intended to limit the applicability of the Religious Freedom Restoration Act of 1993 (42 U.S.C. 2002bb et seq.), see Pub.L. 105–183, § 6, June 19, 1998, 112 Stat. 519, set out as a note under section 544 of this title.

CROSS REFERENCES

Applicability of this section in Chapter nine cases, see 11 USCA § 901.

Automatic stay, see 11 USCA § 362.

Concealment of debtor's assets deemed continuing offense, see 18 USCA § 3284.

§ 547. Preferences

(a) In this section—

    (1) "inventory" means personal property leased or furnished, held for sale or lease, or to be furnished under a contract for service, raw materials, work in process, or materials used or consumed in a business, including farm products such as crops or livestock, held for sale or lease;

    (2) "new value" means money or money's worth in goods, services, or new credit, or release by a transferee of property previously transferred to such transferee in a transaction that is neither void nor voidable by the debtor or the trustee under any applicable law, including proceeds of such property, but does not include an obligation substituted for an existing obligation;

    (3) "receivable" means right to payment, whether or not such right has been earned by performance; and

    (4) a debt for a tax is incurred on the day when such tax is last payable without penalty, including any extension.

(b) Except as provided in subsections (c) and (i) of this section, the trustee may avoid any transfer of an interest of the debtor in property—

    (1) to or for the benefit of a creditor;

    (2) for or on account of an antecedent debt owed by the debtor before such transfer was made;

    (3) made while the debtor was insolvent;

    (4) made—

        (A) on or within 90 days before the date of the filing of the petition; or

        (B) between ninety days and one year before the date of the filing of the petition, if such creditor at the time of such transfer was an insider; and

    (5) that enables such creditor to receive more than such creditor would receive if—

        (A) the case were a case under chapter 7 of this title;

        (B) the transfer had not been made; and

        (C) such creditor received payment of such debt to the extent provided by the provisions of this title.

(c) The trustee may not avoid under this section a transfer—

    (1) to the extent that such transfer was—

        (A) intended by the debtor and the creditor to or for whose benefit such transfer was made to be a contemporaneous exchange for new value given to the debtor; and

        (B) in fact a substantially contemporaneous exchange;

(2) to the extent that such transfer was in payment of a debt incurred by the debtor in the ordinary course of business or financial affairs of the debtor and the transferee, and such transfer was—

    (A) made in the ordinary course of business or financial affairs of the debtor and the transferee; or

    (B) made according to ordinary business terms;

(3) that creates a security interest in property acquired by the debtor—

    (A) to the extent such security interest secures new value that was—

        (i) given at or after the signing of a security agreement that contains a description of such property as collateral;

        (ii) given by or on behalf of the secured party under such agreement;

        (iii) given to enable the debtor to acquire such property; and

        (iv) in fact used by the debtor to acquire such property; and

    (B) that is perfected on or before 30 days after the debtor receives possession of such property;

(4) to or for the benefit of a creditor, to the extent that, after such transfer, such creditor gave new value to or for the benefit of the debtor—

    (A) not secured by an otherwise unavoidable security interest; and

    (B) on account of which new value the debtor did not make an otherwise unavoidable transfer to or for the benefit of such creditor;

(5) that creates a perfected security interest in inventory or a receivable or the proceeds of either, except to the extent that the aggregate of all such transfers to the transferee caused a reduction, as of the date of the filing of the petition and to the prejudice of other creditors holding unsecured claims, of any amount by which the debt secured by such security interest exceeded the value of all security interests for such debt on the later of—

    (A)(i) with respect to a transfer to which subsection (b)(4)(A) of this section applies, 90 days before the date of the filing of the petition; or

        (ii) with respect to a transfer to which subsection (b)(4)(B) of this section applies, one year before the date of the filing of the petition; or

    (B) the date on which new value was first given under the security agreement creating such security interest;

(6) that is the fixing of a statutory lien that is not avoidable under section 545 of this title;

(7) to the extent such transfer was a bona fide payment of a debt for a domestic support obligation;

(8) if, in a case filed by an individual debtor whose debts are primarily consumer debts, the aggregate value of all property that constitutes or is affected by such transfer is less than $600; or

(9) if, in a case filed by a debtor whose debts are not primarily consumer debts, the aggregate value of all property that constitutes or is affected by such transfer is less than $6,225[1].

(d) The trustee may avoid a transfer of an interest in property of the debtor transferred to or for the benefit of a surety to secure reimbursement of such a surety that furnished a bond or other obligation to dissolve a judicial lien that would have been avoidable by the trustee under subsection

---

[1] Dollar amount as adjusted by the Judicial Conference of the United States. See Adjustment of Dollar Amounts notes set out under this section and 11 U.S.C.A. § 104.

Title 11   CREDITORS, THE DEBTOR, AND THE ESTATE   **11 § 547**

(b) of this section. The liability of such surety under such bond or obligation shall be discharged to the extent of the value of such property recovered by the trustee or the amount paid to the trustee.

(e)(1) For the purposes of this section—

(A) a transfer of real property other than fixtures, but including the interest of a seller or purchaser under a contract for the sale of real property, is perfected when a bona fide purchaser of such property from the debtor against whom applicable law permits such transfer to be perfected cannot acquire an interest that is superior to the interest of the transferee; and

(B) a transfer of a fixture or property other than real property is perfected when a creditor on a simple contract cannot acquire a judicial lien that is superior to the interest of the transferee.

(2) For the purposes of this section, except as provided in paragraph (3) of this subsection, a transfer is made—

(A) at the time such transfer takes effect between the transferor and the transferee, if such transfer is perfected at, or within 30 days after, such time, except as provided in subsection (c)(3)(B);

(B) at the time such transfer is perfected, if such transfer is perfected after such 30 days; or

(C) immediately before the date of the filing of the petition, if such transfer is not perfected at the later of—

(i) the commencement of the case; or

(ii) 30 days after such transfer takes effect between the transferor and the transferee.

(3) For the purposes of this section, a transfer is not made until the debtor has acquired rights in the property transferred.

(f) For the purposes of this section, the debtor is presumed to have been insolvent on and during the 90 days immediately preceding the date of the filing of the petition.

(g) For the purposes of this section, the trustee has the burden of proving the avoidability of a transfer under subsection (b) of this section, and the creditor or party in interest against whom recovery or avoidance is sought has the burden of proving the nonavoidability of a transfer under subsection (c) of this section.

(h) The trustee may not avoid a transfer if such transfer was made as a part of an alternative repayment schedule between the debtor and any creditor of the debtor created by an approved nonprofit budget and credit counseling agency.

(i) If the trustee avoids under subsection (b) a transfer made between 90 days and 1 year before the date of the filing of the petition, by the debtor to an entity that is not an insider for the benefit of a creditor that is an insider, such transfer shall be considered to be avoided under this section only with respect to the creditor that is an insider.

(Pub.L. 95–598, Nov. 6, 1978, 92 Stat. 2597; Pub.L. 98–353, Title III, §§ 310, 462, July 10, 1984, 98 Stat. 355, 377; Pub.L. 99–554, Title II, § 283(m), Oct. 27, 1986, 100 Stat. 3117; Pub.L. 103–394, Title II, § 203, Title III, § 304(f), Oct. 22, 1994, 108 Stat. 4121, 4133; Pub.L. 109–8, Title II, §§ 201(b), 217, Title IV, §§ 403, 409, Title XII, § 1213(a), 1222, Apr. 20, 2005, 119 Stat. 42, 55, 104, 106, 194, 196).)

HISTORICAL AND STATUTORY NOTES

Amendments

2005 Amendments. Subsec. (b). Pub.L.109–8, § 1213(a)(1), struck out "subsection (c)" and inserted "subsections (c) and (i)" in introductory provisions.

Subsec. (c)(2). Pub.L. 109–8, § 409(1), rewrote par. (2), which formerly read:

"(2) to the extent that such transfer was—

"(A) in payment of a debt incurred by the debtor in the ordinary course of business or financial affairs of the debtor and the transferee;

"(B) made in the ordinary course of business or financial affairs of the debtor and the transferee; and

"(C) made according to ordinary business terms;"

Subsec. (c)(3)(B). Pub.L.109–8, § 1222, struck out "20" and inserted "30".

Subsec. (c)(7). Pub.L. 109–8, § 217, rewrote par. (7) which formerly read:

"(7) to the extent such transfer was a bona fide payment of a debt to a spouse, former spouse, or child of the debtor, for alimony to, maintenance for, or support of such spouse or child, in connection with a separation agreement, divorce decree or other order of a court of record, determination made in accordance with State or territorial law by a governmental unit, or property settlement agreement, but not to the extent that such debt—

"(A) is assigned to another entity, voluntarily, by operation of law, or otherwise; or

"(B) includes a liability designated as alimony, maintenance, or support, unless such liability is actually in the nature of alimony, maintenance or support; or"

Subsec. (c)(8). Pub.L. 109–8, § 409(2), struck the period at the end and inserted "; or".

Subsec. (c)(9). Pub.L. 109–8, § 409(3), added par. (9).

Subsec. (e)(2)(A). Pub.L. 109–8, § 403, struck "10" prior to "days" and inserted "30".

Subsec. (e)(2)(B). Pub.L. 109–8, § 403, struck "10" prior to "days" and inserted "30".

Subsec. (e)(2)(C)(ii). Pub.L. 109–8, § 403, struck "10" prior to "days" and inserted "30".

Subsec. (h). Pub.L. 109–8, § 201(b), added subsec. (h).

Subsec. (i). Pub.L.109–8, § 1213(a)(2), added subsec. (i).

1994 Amendments. Subsec. (c)(3)(B). Pub.L. 103–394, § 203(1), substituted "20 days" for "10 days".

Subsec. (c)(7), (8). Pub.L. 103–394, § 304(f), added par. (7). Former par. (7) redesignated (8).

Subsec. (e)(2)(A). Pub.L. 103–394, § 203(2), inserted reference to subsec. (c)(3)(B).

1986 Amendments. Subsec. (b)(4)(B). Pub.L. 99–554 inserted "and" following the semicolon.

1984 Amendments. Subsec. (a)(2). Pub.L. 98–353, § 462(a)(1), added "including proceeds of such property," after "law,".

Subsec. (a)(4). Pub.L. 98–353, § 462(a)(2), struck out ", without penalty" after "any extension" and added "without penalty" after "payable".

Subsec. (b). Pub.L. 98–353, § 462(b)(1), substituted "of an interest of the debtor in property" for "of property of the debtor" in provisions preceding par. (1).

Subsec. (b)(4)(B). Pub.L. 98–353, § 462(b)(2), substituted "between ninety days and one year before the date of the filing of the petition, if such creditor at the time of such transfer was an insider;" for "between 90 days and one year before the date of the filing of the petition, if such creditor, at the time of such transfer—

"(i) was an insider; and

"(ii) had reasonable cause to believe the debtor was insolvent at the time of such transfer; and".

Subsec. (c)(2)(A). Pub.L. 98–353, § 462(d)(1), added "by the debtor" after "incurred".

Subsec. (c)(2)(B). Pub.L. 98–353, § 462(c), struck out subpar. (B), which read "made not later than 45 days after such debt was incurred;". Former subpar. (C) was redesignated as (B).

Subsec. (c)(2)(C). Pub.L. 98–353, § 462(c), redesignated former subpar. (D) as (C). Former subpar. (C) was redesignated as (B).

Subsec. (c)(2)(D). Pub.L. 98–353, § 462(c), redesignated former subpar. (D) as (C).

Subsec. (c)(3). Pub.L. 98–353, § 462(d)(2), substituted "that creates" for "of".

Subsec. (c)(3)(B). Pub.L. 98–353, § 462(d)(3), added "on or" after "perfected" and substituted "the debtor receives possession of such property" for "such security interest attaches".

Subsec. (c)(5). Pub.L. 98–353, § 462(d)(4), substituted "that creates" for "of" at the beginning of par. (5), and "all security interests" for "all security interest".

Subsec. (c)(5)(A)(ii). Pub.L. 98–353, § 462(d)(5), substituted "or" for "and".

Subsec. (c)(5)(B). Pub.L. 98–353, § 310(1), struck out "or" following "interest;".

Subsec. (c)(6). Pub.L. 98–353, § 310(2), substituted "; or" for the period at the end of par. (6).

Subsec. (c)(7). Pub.L. 98–353, § 310(3), added par. (7).

Subsec. (d). Pub.L. 98–353, § 462(e), substituted "The" for "A" before "trustee may avoid", added "an interest in" after "transfer of", added "to or for the benefit of a surety" after "transferred", and added "such" after "reimbursement of".

Subsec. (e)(2)(C)(i). Pub.L. 98–353, § 462(f), substituted "or" for "and".

Subsec. (g). Pub.L. 98–353, § 462(g), added subsec. (g).

Adjustment of Dollar Amounts

For adjustment of dollar amounts specified in subsec. (c)(9) of this section by the Judicial Conference of the United States, see note set out under 11 U.S.C.A. § 104.

CROSS REFERENCES

Applicability of this section in Chapter nine cases, see 11 USCA § 901.

Appointment of trustee upon debtor's refusal to pursue cause of action under this section, see 11 USCA § 926.

Automatic stay, see 11 USCA § 362.

Commencement of involuntary cases by transferees of voidable transfers, see 11 USCA § 303.

Disallowance of claims of entity that is transferee of avoidable transfer, see 11 USCA § 502.

Effect of dismissal, see 11 USCA § 349.

Exemptions, see 11 USCA § 522.

Persons who may be debtors in Chapter nine case, see 11 USCA § 109.

Recovery of voidable transfers in investor protection liquidation proceedings, see 15 USCA § 78fff–2.

Transfers to defeat cases under this title, see 18 USCA § 152.

Voidable transfers in—

    Commodity broker liquidation cases, see 11 USCA § 764.

    Stockbroker liquidation cases, see 11 USCA § 749.

§ 548. Fraudulent transfers and obligations

(a)(1) The trustee may avoid any transfer (including any transfer to or for the benefit of an insider under an employment contract) of an interest of the debtor in property, or any obligation (including any obligation to or for the benefit of an insider under an employment contract) incurred by the debtor, that was made or incurred on or within 2 years before the date of the filing of the petition, if the debtor voluntarily or involuntarily—

    (A) made such transfer or incurred such obligation with actual intent to hinder, delay, or defraud any entity to which the debtor was or became, on or after the date that such transfer was made or such obligation was incurred, indebted; or

    (B)(i) received less than a reasonably equivalent value in exchange for such transfer or obligation; and

(ii)(I) was insolvent on the date that such transfer was made or such obligation was incurred, or became insolvent as a result of such transfer or obligation;

(II) was engaged in business or a transaction, or was about to engage in business or a transaction, for which any property remaining with the debtor was an unreasonably small capital;

(III) intended to incur, or believed that the debtor would incur, debts that would be beyond the debtor's ability to pay as such debts matured; or

(IV) made such transfer to or for the benefit of an insider, or incurred such obligation to or for the benefit of an insider, under an employment contract and not in the ordinary course of business.

(2) A transfer of a charitable contribution to a qualified religious or charitable entity or organization shall not be considered to be a transfer covered under paragraph (1)(B) in any case in which—

(A) the amount of that contribution does not exceed 15 percent of the gross annual income of the debtor for the year in which the transfer of the contribution is made; or

(B) the contribution made by a debtor exceeded the percentage amount of gross annual income specified in subparagraph (A), if the transfer was consistent with the practices of the debtor in making charitable contributions.

(b) The trustee of a partnership debtor may avoid any transfer of an interest of the debtor in property, or any obligation incurred by the debtor, that was made or incurred on or within 2 years before the date of the filing of the petition, to a general partner in the debtor, if the debtor was insolvent on the date such transfer was made or such obligation was incurred, or became insolvent as a result of such transfer or obligation.

(c) Except to the extent that a transfer or obligation voidable under this section is voidable under section 544, 545, or 547 of this title, a transferee or obligee of such a transfer or obligation that takes for value and in good faith has a lien on or may retain any interest transferred or may enforce any obligation incurred, as the case may be, to the extent that such transferee or obligee gave value to the debtor in exchange for such transfer or obligation.

(d)(1) For the purposes of this section, a transfer is made when such transfer is so perfected that a bona fide purchaser from the debtor against whom applicable law permits such transfer to be perfected cannot acquire an interest in the property transferred that is superior to the interest in such property of the transferee, but if such transfer is not so perfected before the commencement of the case, such transfer is made immediately before the date of the filing of the petition.

(2) In this section—

(A) "value" means property, or satisfaction or securing of a present or antecedent debt of the debtor, but does not include an unperformed promise to furnish support to the debtor or to a relative of the debtor;

(B) a commodity broker, forward contract merchant, stockbroker, financial institution, financial participant, or securities clearing agency that receives a margin payment, as defined in section 101, 741, or 761 of this title, or settlement payment, as defined in section 101 or 741 of this title, takes for value to the extent of such payment;

(C) a repo participant or financial participant that receives a margin payment, as defined in section 741 or 761 of this title, or settlement payment, as defined in section 741 of this title, in connection with a repurchase agreement, takes for value to the extent of such payment;

(D) a swap participant or financial participant that receives a transfer in connection with a swap agreement takes for value to the extent of such transfer; and

(E) a master netting agreement participant that receives a transfer in connection with a master netting agreement or any individual contract covered thereby takes for value to the extent of such transfer, except that, with respect to a transfer under any individual contract covered thereby, to the extent that such master netting agreement participant otherwise did not take (or is otherwise not deemed to have taken) such transfer for value.

(3) In this section, the term "charitable contribution" means a charitable contribution, as that term is defined in section 170(c) of the Internal Revenue Code of 1986, if that contribution—

(A) is made by a natural person; and

(B) consists of—

(i) a financial instrument (as that term is defined in section 731(c)(2)(C) of the Internal Revenue Code of 1986); or

(ii) cash.

(4) In this section, the term "qualified religious or charitable entity or organization" means—

(A) an entity described in section 170(c)(1) of the Internal Revenue Code of 1986; or

(B) an entity or organization described in section 170(c)(2) of the Internal Revenue Code of 1986.

(e)(1) In addition to any transfer that the trustee may otherwise avoid, the trustee may avoid any transfer of an interest of the debtor in property that was made on or within 10 years before the date of the filing of the petition, if—

(A) such transfer was made to a self-settled trust or similar device;

(B) such transfer was by the debtor;

(C) the debtor is a beneficiary of such trust or similar device; and

(D) the debtor made such transfer with actual intent to hinder, delay, or defraud any entity to which the debtor was or became, on or after the date that such transfer was made, indebted.

(2) For the purposes of this subsection, a transfer includes a transfer made in anticipation of any money judgment, settlement, civil penalty, equitable order, or criminal fine incurred by, or which the debtor believed would be incurred by—

(A) any violation of the securities laws (as defined in section 3(a)(47) of the Securities Exchange Act of 1934 (15 U.S.C. 78c(a)(47))), any State securities laws, or any regulation or order issued under Federal securities laws or State securities laws; or

(B) fraud, deceit, or manipulation in a fiduciary capacity or in connection with the purchase or sale of any security registered under section 12 or 15(d) of the Securities Exchange Act of 1934 (15 U.S.C. 78l and 78o(d)) or under section 6 of the Securities Act of 1933 (15 U.S.C. 77f).

(Pub.L. 95–598, Nov. 6, 1978, 92 Stat. 2600; Pub.L. 97–222, § 5, July 27, 1982, 96 Stat. 236; Pub.L. 98–353, Title III, §§ 394, 463, July 10, 1984, 98 Stat. 365, 378; Pub.L. 99–554, Title II, § 283(n), Oct. 27, 1986, 100 Stat. 3117; Pub.L. 101–311, Title I, § 104, Title II, § 204, June 25, 1990, 104 Stat. 268, 269; Pub.L. 103–394, Title V, § 501(b)(5), Oct. 22, 1994, 108 Stat. 4142; Pub.L. 105–183, §§ 2, 3(a), June 19, 1998, 112 Stat. 517; Pub.L. 109–8, Title IX, § 907(f), (o)(4) to (6), Title XIV, § 1402, Apr. 20, 2005, 119 Stat. 177, 182, 214.)

HISTORICAL AND STATUTORY NOTES

References in Text

The Internal Revenue Code of 1986, referred to in subsec. (d)(3) and (4), is classified generally to Title 26.

Section 3(a)(47) of the Securities Exchange Act of 1934, referred to in subsec. (e)(2)(A), is June 6, 1934, c. 404, Title I, § 3(a)(47), 48 Stat. 882, as amended, which is classified to 15 U.S.C.A. § 78c(a)(47).

Section 12 of the Securities Exchange Act of 1934, referred to in subsec. (e)(2)(B), is June 6, 1934, c. 404, Title I, § 12, 48 Stat. 892, as amended, which is classified to 15 U.S.C.A. § 78l.

Section 15(d) of the Securities Exchange Act of 1934, referred to in subsec. (e)(2)(B), is June 6, 1934, c. 404, Title I, § 15(d), 48 Stat. 895, as amended, which is classified to 15 U.S.C.A. § 78o.

Section 6 of the Securities Act of 1933, referred to in subsec. (e)(2)(B), is Act May 27, 1933, c. 38, Title I, § 6, 48 Stat. 78, as amended, which is classified to 15 U.S.C.A. § 77f.

Amendments

2005 Amendments. Subsec. (a). Pub.L. 109–8, § 1402(1), (2), struck out "one year" and inserted "2 years", and inserted "(including any transfer to or for the benefit of an insider under an employment contract)" after "avoid any transfer", and "(including any obligation to or for the benefit of an insider under an employment contract)" after "or any obligation".

Subsec. (a)(1)(B)(ii)(II) to (IV). Pub.L. 109–8, § 1402(3), struck out "or" at the end of subcl. (II), struck out the period at the end of subcl. (III) and inserted "; or", and added subcl. (IV).

Subsec. (b). Pub.L. 109–8, § 1402(1), struck out "one year" and inserted "2 years".

Subsec. (d)(2)(B). Pub.L. 109–8, § 907(o)(4), inserted "financial participant," after "financial institution,".

Subsec. (d)(2)(C). Pub.L. 109–8, § 907(f)(1), struck out "and" at the end of subpar. (C).

Pub.L. 109–8, § 907(o)(5), inserted "or financial participant" after "repo participant".

Subsec. (d)(2)(D). Pub.L. 109–8, § 907(f)(2), substituted "; and" for the period at the end of subpar. (D).

Pub.L. 109–8, § 907(o)(6), inserted "or financial participant" after "swap participant".

Subsec. (d)(2)(E). Pub.L. 109–8, § 907(f)(3), added subpar. (E).

Subsec. (e). Pub.L. 109–8, § 1402(4), added subsec. (e).

1998 Amendments. Subsec. (a)(1). Pub.L. 105–183, § 3(a)(1), inserted "(1)" after "(a)".

Subsec. (a)(1)(A). Pub.L. 105–183, § 3(a)(2), struck out "(1) made" and inserted "(A) made".

Subsec. (a)(1)(B)(i). Pub.L. 105–183, § 3(a)(3), struck out "(2)(A)" and inserted "(B)(i)".

Subsec. (a)(1)(B)(ii)(I). Pub.L. 105–183, § 3(a)(4), struck out "(B)(i)" and inserted "(ii)(I)".

Subsec. (a)(1)(B)(ii)(II). Pub.L. 105–183, § 3(a)(5), struck out "(ii) was" and inserted "(II) was".

Subsec. (a)(1)(B)(ii)(III). Pub.L. 105–183, § 3(a)(6), struck out "(iii)" and inserted "(III)".

Subsec. (a)(2). Pub.L. 105–183, § 3(a)(7), added par. (2).

Subsec. (d). Pub.L. 105–183, § 2, added pars. (3) and (4).

1994 Amendments. Subsec. (d)(2)(B). Pub.L. 103–394, § 501(b)(5)(A), substituted "section 101, 741, or 761" for "section 101(34), 741(5), or 761(15)", and "section 101 or 741" for "section 101(35) or 741(8)".

Subsec. (d)(2)(C). Pub.L. 103–394, § 501(b)(5)(B), substituted "section 741 or 761" for "section 741(5) or 761(15)", and "section 741" for "section 741(8)".

1990 Amendments. Subsec. (d)(2)(B). Pub.L. 101–311, § 204, added provisions referring to sections 101(34) and 101(35) of this title.

Subsec. (d)(2)(D). Pub.L. 101–311, § 104, added subpar. (D).

1986 Amendments. Subsec. (d)(2)(B). Pub.L. 99–554 substituted ", financial institution" for "financial institution,".

1984 Amendments. Subsec. (a). Pub.L. 98–353, § 463(a)(1), substituted "if the debtor voluntarily or involuntarily" for "if the debtor" in provisions preceding par. (1).

Subsec. (a)(1). Pub.L. 98–353, § 463(a)(2), substituted "was made" for "occurred".

Subsec. (a)(2)(B)(ii). Pub.L. 98–353, § 463(a)(3), added "or a transaction" after "engaged in business".

Subsec. (c). Pub.L. 98–353, § 463(b)(1), added "or may retain" after "lien on" and struck out ", may retain any lien transferred," before "or may enforce any obligation incurred".

Subsec. (d)(1). Pub.L. 98–353, § 463(c)(1), substituted "is so" for "becomes so far", "applicable law permits such transfer to be" for "such transfer could have been", and "is made" for "occurs".

Subsec. (d)(2)(B). Pub.L. 98–353, § 463(c)(2), added "financial institution," after "stockbroker".

Subsec. (d)(2)(C). Pub.L. 98–353, § 394; added subpar. (C).

1982 Amendments. Subsec. (d)(2)(B). Pub.L. 97–222 substituted "a commodity broker, forward contract merchant, stockbroker, or securities clearing agency that receives a margin payment, as defined in section 741(5) or 761(15) of this title, or settlement payment, as defined in section 741(8) of this title, takes for value to the extent of such payment" for "a commodity broker or forward contract merchant that receives a margin payment, as defined in section 761(15) of this title, takes for value".

CROSS REFERENCES

Applicability of this section in Chapter nine cases, see 11 USCA § 901.

Appointment of trustee upon debtor's refusal to pursue cause of action under this section, see 11 USCA § 926.

Commencement of involuntary cases by transferees of voidable transfers, see 11 USCA § 303.

Disallowance of claims of entity that is transferee of avoidable transfer, see 11 USCA § 502.

Effect of dismissal, see 11 USCA § 349.

Exemptions, see 11 USCA § 522.

Inappropriate transfers included in determining net worth of employer, see 29 USCA § 1362.

Recovery of voidable transfers in investor protection liquidation proceedings, see 15 USCA § 78fff–2.

Transfers to defeat cases under this title, see 18 USCA § 152.

Voidable transfers in—

Commodity broker liquidation cases, see 11 USCA § 764.

Stockbroker liquidation cases, see 11 USCA § 749.

§ 549. Postpetition transactions

(a) Except as provided in subsection (b) or (c) of this section, the trustee may avoid a transfer of property of the estate—

(1) that occurs after the commencement of the case; and

(2)(A) that is authorized only under section 303(f) or 542(c) of this title; or

(B) that is not authorized under this title or by the court.

(b) In an involuntary case, the trustee may not avoid under subsection (a) of this section a transfer made after the commencement of such case but before the order for relief to the extent any value, including services, but not including satisfaction or securing of a debt that arose before the commencement of the case, is given after the commencement of the case in exchange for such transfer, notwithstanding any notice or knowledge of the case that the transferee has.

(c) The trustee may not avoid under subsection (a) of this section a transfer of an interest in real property to a good faith purchaser without knowledge of the commencement of the case and for present fair equivalent value unless a copy or notice of the petition was filed, where a transfer of an interest in such real property may be recorded to perfect such transfer, before such transfer is so perfected that a bona fide purchaser of such real property, against whom applicable law permits such transfer to be perfected, could not acquire an interest that is superior to such interest of such good faith purchaser. A good faith purchaser without knowledge of the commencement of the case and for less than present fair equivalent value has a lien on the property transferred to the extent of any present value given, unless a copy or notice of the petition was so filed before such transfer was so perfected.

(d) An action or proceeding under this section may not be commenced after the earlier of—

(1) two years after the date of the transfer sought to be avoided; or

(2) the time the case is closed or dismissed.

(Pub.L. 95–598, Nov. 6, 1978, 92 Stat. 2601; Pub.L. 98–353, Title III, § 464, July 10, 1984, 98 Stat. 379; Pub.L. 99–554, Title II, § 283(o), Oct. 27, 1986, 100 Stat. 3117; Pub.L. 103–394, Title V, § 501(d)(18), Oct. 22, 1994, 108 Stat. 4146; Pub.L. 109–8, Title XII, § 1214, Apr. 20, 2005, 119 Stat. 195.)

HISTORICAL AND STATUTORY NOTES

Amendments

2005 Amendments. Subsec. (c). Pub.L.109–8, § 1214, inserted "an interest in" after "transfer of" each place it appeared, struck out "such property" and inserted "such real property" following "a bona fide purchaser of", and struck out "the interest" and inserted "such interest".

1994 Amendments. Subsec. (b). Pub.L. 103–394, § 501(d)(18), inserted "the trustee may not avoid under subsection (a) of this section" following "In an involuntary case,".

1986 Amendments. Subsec. (b). Pub.L. 99–554 substituted "made" for "that occurs", and "to the extent" for "is valid against the trustee to the extent of", and inserted "is" preceding "given".

1984 Amendments. Subsec. (a). Pub.L. 98–353, § 464(a)(1), (2), substituted "(b) or (c)" for "(b) and (c)" in provisions preceding par. (1) and inserted "only" between "authorized" and "under" in par. (2)(A). In the original of Pub.L. 98–353, subsec. (a)(2) of section 464 thereof ended with a period but was followed by pars. (3), (4), and (5). Such pars. (3), (4), and (5) purported to amend subsec. (a) of this section in ways not susceptible of execution. In a predecessor bill [S. 445], these pars. (3), (4), and (5) formed a part of a subsec. (b) of section 361 thereof which amended subsec. (b) of this section. Such subsec. (b) of section 361 of S. 445 was not carried into Pub.L. 98–353, § 464.

Subsec. (c). Pub.L. 98–353, § 464(c), substituted "The trustee may not avoid under subsection (a) of this section a transfer of real property to a good faith purchaser without knowledge of the commencement of the case and for present fair equivalent value unless a copy or notice of the petition was filed, where a transfer of such real property may be recorded to perfect such transfer, before such transfer is so perfected that a bona fide purchaser of such property, against whom applicable law permits such transfer to be perfected, could not acquire an interest that is superior to the interest of such good faith purchaser. A good faith purchaser without knowledge of the commencement of the case and for less than present fair equivalent value has a lien on the property transferred to the extent of any present value given, unless a copy or notice of the petition was so filed before such transfer was so perfected." for "The trustee may not avoid under subsection (a) of this section a transfer, to a good faith purchaser without knowledge of the commencement of the case and for present fair equivalent value or to a purchaser at a judicial sale, of real property located other than in the county in which the case is commenced, unless a copy of the petition was filed in the office where conveyances of real property in such county are recorded before such transfer was so far perfected that a bona fide purchaser of such property against whom applicable law permits such transfer to be perfected cannot acquire an interest that is superior to the interest of such good faith or judicial sale purchaser. A good faith purchaser, without knowledge of the commencement of the case and for less than present fair equivalent value, of real property located other than in the county in which the case is commenced, under a transfer that the trustee may avoid under this section, has a lien on the property transferred to the extent of any present value given, unless a copy of the petition was so filed before such transfer was so perfected.".

Subsec. (d)(1). Pub.L. 98–353, § 464(d), substituted "or" for "and".

CROSS REFERENCES

Applicability of subsecs. (a), (c) and (d) of this section in Chapter 9 cases, see 11 USCA § 901.

Appointment of trustee upon debtor's refusal to pursue cause of action under this section, see 11 USCA § 926.

Commencement of involuntary cases by transferees of voidable transfers, see 11 USCA § 303.

Disallowance of claims of entity that is transferee of avoidable transfer, see 11 USCA § 502.

Effect of dismissal, see 11 USCA § 349.

Exemptions, see 11 USCA § 522.

Title 11 CREDITORS, THE DEBTOR, AND THE ESTATE **11 § 550**

Inappropriate transfers included in determining net worth of employer, see 29 USCA § 1362.

Recovery of voidable transfers in investor liquidation proceedings, see 15 USCA § 78fff–2.

Voidable transfers in—

> Commodity broker liquidation cases, see 11 USCA § 764.
>
> Stockbroker liquidation cases, see 11 USCA § 749.

§ 550. Liability of transferee of avoided transfer

(a) Except as otherwise provided in this section, to the extent that a transfer is avoided under section 544, 545, 547, 548, 549, 553(b), or 724(a) of this title, the trustee may recover, for the benefit of the estate, the property transferred, or, if the court so orders, the value of such property, from—

> (1) the initial transferee of such transfer or the entity for whose benefit such transfer was made; or
>
> (2) any immediate or mediate transferee of such initial transferee.

(b) The trustee may not recover under section[1] (a)(2) of this section from—

> (1) a transferee that takes for value, including satisfaction or securing of a present or antecedent debt, in good faith, and without knowledge of the voidability of the transfer avoided; or
>
> (2) any immediate or mediate good faith transferee of such transferee.

(c) If a transfer made between 90 days and one year before the filing of the petition—

> (1) is avoided under section 547(b) of this title; and
>
> (2) was made for the benefit of a creditor that at the time of such transfer was an insider;

the trustee may not recover under subsection (a) from a transferee that is not an insider.

(d) The trustee is entitled to only a single satisfaction under subsection (a) of this section.

(e)(1) A good faith transferee from whom the trustee may recover under subsection (a) of this section has a lien on the property recovered to secure the lesser of—

> (A) the cost, to such transferee, of any improvement made after the transfer, less the amount of any profit realized by or accruing to such transferee from such property; and
>
> (B) any increase in the value of such property as a result of such improvement, of the property transferred.

(2) In this subsection, "improvement" includes—

> (A) physical additions or changes to the property transferred;
>
> (B) repairs to such property;
>
> (C) payment of any tax on such property;
>
> (D) payment of any debt secured by a lien on such property that is superior or equal to the rights of the trustee; and
>
> (E) preservation of such property.

(f) An action or proceeding under this section may not be commenced after the earlier of—

> (1) one year after the avoidance of the transfer on account of which recovery under this section is sought; or

---

[1] So in original. Probably should be "subsection".

(2) the time the case is closed or dismissed.

(Pub.L. 95–598, Nov. 6, 1978, 92 Stat. 2601; Pub.L. 98–353, Title III, § 465, July 10, 1984, 98 Stat. 379; Pub.L. 103–394, Title II, § 202, Oct. 22, 1994, 108 Stat. 4121.)

HISTORICAL AND STATUTORY NOTES

Amendments

1994 Amendments. Subsecs. (c) to (f). Pub.L. 103–394, § 202, added subsec. (c) and redesignated former subsecs. (c) through (e) as (d) through (f), respectively.

1984 Amendments. Subsec. (a). Pub.L. 98–353, § 465(a), substituted "549, 553(b), or 724(a) of this title" for "549, or 724(a) of this title".

Subsec. (d)(1)(A). Pub.L. 98–353, § 465(b)(1), added "or accruing to" after "by".

Subsec. (d)(1)(B). Pub.L. 98–353, § 465(b)(2), substituted "the value of such property" for "value".

Subsec. (d)(2)(D). Pub.L. 98–353, § 465(b)(3), substituted "payment of any debt secured by a lien on such property that is superior or equal to the rights of the trustee; and" for "payment of any debt secured by a lien on such property."

Subsec. (d)(2)(E). Pub.L. 98–353, § 465(b)(3), (4), struck out subpar. (E) which read "discharge of any lien against such property that is superior or equal to the rights of the trustee; and" and redesignated former subpar. (F) as (E).

Subsec. (d)(2)(F). Pub.L. 98–353, § 465(b)(4), redesignated former subpar. (F) as (E).

Subsec. (e)(1). Pub.L. 98–353, § 465(c), substituted "or" for "and".

CROSS REFERENCES

Allowance of claims or interests, see 11 USCA § 502.

Applicability of this section in Chapter 9 cases, see 11 USCA § 901.

Appointment of trustee upon debtor's refusal to pursue cause of action under this section, see 11 USCA § 926.

Effect of dismissal, see 11 USCA § 349.

Exemptions, see 11 USCA § 522.

§ 551. Automatic preservation of avoided transfer

Any transfer avoided under section 522, 544, 545, 547, 548, 549, or 724(a) of this title, or any lien void under section 506(d) of this title, is preserved for the benefit of the estate but only with respect to property of the estate.

(Pub.L. 95–598, Nov. 6, 1978, 92 Stat. 2602.)

CROSS REFERENCES

Applicability of this section in Chapter 9 cases, see 11 USCA § 901.

Effect of dismissal, see 11 USCA § 349.

Exemptions, see 11 USCA § 522.

§ 552. Postpetition effect of security interest

(a) Except as provided in subsection (b) of this section, property acquired by the estate or by the debtor after the commencement of the case is not subject to any lien resulting from any security agreement entered into by the debtor before the commencement of the case.

(b)(1) Except as provided in sections 363, 506(c), 522, 544, 545, 547, and 548 of this title, if the debtor and an entity entered into a security agreement before the commencement of the case and if the security interest created by such security agreement extends to property of the debtor acquired before the commencement of the case and to proceeds, products, offspring, or profits of such property, then such security interest extends to such proceeds, products, offspring, or profits acquired by the estate after the commencement of the case to the extent provided by such security agreement and by applicable nonbankruptcy law, except to any extent that the court, after notice and a hearing and based on the equities of the case, orders otherwise.

(2) Except as provided in sections 363, 506(c), 522, 544, 545, 547, and 548 of this title, and notwithstanding section 546(b) of this title, if the debtor and an entity entered into a security agreement before the commencement of the case and if the security interest created by such security agreement extends to property of the debtor acquired before the commencement of the case and to amounts paid as rents of such property or the fees, charges, accounts, or other payments for the use or occupancy of rooms and other public facilities in hotels, motels, or other lodging properties, then such security interest extends to such rents and such fees, charges, accounts, or other payments acquired by the estate after the commencement of the case to the extent provided in such security agreement, except to any extent that the court, after notice and a hearing and based on the equities of the case, orders otherwise.

(Pub.L. 95–598, Nov. 6, 1978, 92 Stat. 2602; Pub.L. 98–353, Title III, § 466, July 10, 1984, 98 Stat. 380; Pub.L. 103–394, Title II, § 214(a), Oct. 22, 1994, 108 Stat. 4126; Pub.L. 109–8, Title XII, § 1204(2), Apr. 20, 2005, 119 Stat. 194.)

HISTORICAL AND STATUTORY NOTES

Amendments

2005 Amendments. Subsec. (b)(1). Pub.L. 109–8, § 1204(2), struck out "product" each place it appeared and inserted "products".

1994 Amendments. Subsec. (b). Pub.L. 103–394, § 214(a), designated existing provisions as par. (1) and as so designated, struck out "rents" before ", or profits" wherever appearing, and added par. (2).

1984 Amendments. Subsec. (b). Pub.L. 98–353, § 466, added "522," after "506(c),", substituted "an entity entered" for "a secured party enter", and substituted "except to any extent" for "except to the extent".

CROSS REFERENCES

Applicability of this section in Chapter 9 cases, see 11 USCA § 901.

"Cash collateral" as including proceeds, products, offspring, rents or profits of property subject to security interest as provided in this section, see 11 USCA § 363.

Special revenues acquired by debtor after commencement of Chapter 9 case subject to security interest, see 11 USCA § 928.

§ 553. Setoff

(a) Except as otherwise provided in this section and in sections 362 and 363 of this title, this title does not affect any right of a creditor to offset a mutual debt owing by such creditor to the debtor that arose before the commencement of the case under this title against a claim of such creditor against the debtor that arose before the commencement of the case, except to the extent that—

    (1) the claim of such creditor against the debtor is disallowed;

    (2) such claim was transferred, by an entity other than the debtor, to such creditor—

        (A) after the commencement of the case; or

        (B)(i) after 90 days before the date of the filing of the petition; and

        (ii) while the debtor was insolvent (except for a setoff of a kind described in section 362(b)(6), 362(b)(7), 362(b)(17), 362(b)(27), 555, 556, 559, 560, or 561); or

(3) the debt owed to the debtor by such creditor was incurred by such creditor—

    (A) after 90 days before the date of the filing of the petition;

    (B) while the debtor was insolvent; and

    (C) for the purpose of obtaining a right of setoff against the debtor (except for a setoff of a kind described in section 362(b)(6), 362(b)(7), 362(b)(17), 362(b)(27), 555, 556, 559, 560, or 561).

(b)(1) Except with respect to a setoff of a kind described in section 362(b)(6), 362(b)(7), 362(b)(17), 362(b)(27), 555, 556, 559, 560, 561, 365(h), 546(h), or 365(i)(2) of this title, if a creditor offsets a mutual debt owing to the debtor against a claim against the debtor on or within 90 days before the date of the filing of the petition, then the trustee may recover from such creditor the amount so offset to the extent that any insufficiency on the date of such setoff is less than the insufficiency on the later of—

    (A) 90 days before the date of the filing of the petition; and

    (B) the first date during the 90 days immediately preceding the date of the filing of the petition on which there is an insufficiency.

(2) In this subsection, "insufficiency" means amount, if any, by which a claim against the debtor exceeds a mutual debt owing to the debtor by the holder of such claim.

(c) For the purposes of this section, the debtor is presumed to have been insolvent on and during the 90 days immediately preceding the date of the filing of the petition.

(Pub.L. 95–598, Nov. 6, 1978, 92 Stat. 2602; Pub.L. 98–353, Title III, §§ 395, 467, July 10, 1984, 98 Stat. 365, 380; Pub.L. 101–311, Title I, § 105, June 25, 1990, 104 Stat. 268; Pub.L. 103–394, Title II, §§ 205(b), 222(b), Title V, § 501(d)(19), Oct. 22, 1994, 108 Stat. 4123, 4129, 4146; Pub.L. 109–8, Title IX, § 907(n), Apr. 20, 2005, 119 Stat. 181.)

HISTORICAL AND STATUTORY NOTES

Amendments

2005 Amendments. Subsec. (a)(2)(B)(ii). Pub.L. 109–8, § 907(n)(1), inserted before the semicolon the following: "(except for a setoff of a kind described in section 362(b)(6), 362(b)(7), 362(b)(17), 362(b)(27), 555, 556, 559, 560, or 561)".

Subsec. (a)(3)(C). Pub.L. 109–8, § 907(n)(2), inserted before the period the following: "(except for a setoff of a kind described in section 362(b)(6), 362(b)(7), 362(b)(17), 362(b)(27), 555, 556, 559, 560, or 561)".

Subsec. (b)(1). Pub.L. 109–8, § 907(n)(3), substituted "362(b)(17), 362(b)(27), 555, 556, 559, 560, 561," for "362(b)(14)," in introductory provisions.

1994 Amendments. Subsec. (a)(1). Pub.L. 103–394, § 501(d)(19)(A), struck out "other than under section 502(b)(3) of this title" after "is disallowed".

Subsec. (b)(1). Pub.L. 103–394, § 205(b), substituted "365(h)" for "365(h)(2)".

Pub.L. 103–394, § 222(b), inserted "546(h)," after "365(h),".

Pub.L. 103–394, § 501(d)(19)(B), substituted "362(b)(14)," for "362(b)(14),,".

1990 Amendments. Subsec. (b)(1). Pub.L. 101–311 added reference to section 362(b)(14) of this title.

1984 Amendments. Subsec. (b)(1). Pub.L. 98–353, § 395, added ", 362(b)(7)" after "362(b)(6)".

Pub.L. 98–353, § 467, substituted ", 365(h)(2), or 365(i)(2)" for "or 365(h)(1)".

CROSS REFERENCES

Allowance of claims or interests, see 11 USCA § 502.

Applicability of this section in Chapter 9 cases, see 11 USCA § 901.

Determination of secured status, see 11 USCA § 506.

Effect of dismissal, see 11 USCA § 349.

Recovered property as exempt, see 11 USCA § 522.

Stay of pending actions in investor protection liquidation proceedings, see 15 USCA § 78eee.

§ 554. Abandonment of property of the estate

(a) After notice and a hearing, the trustee may abandon any property of the estate that is burdensome to the estate or that is of inconsequential value and benefit to the estate.

(b) On request of a party in interest and after notice and a hearing, the court may order the trustee to abandon any property of the estate that is burdensome to the estate or that is of inconsequential value and benefit to the estate.

(c) Unless the court orders otherwise, any property scheduled under section 521(a)(1) of this title not otherwise administered at the time of the closing of a case is abandoned to the debtor and administered for purposes of section 350 of this title.

(d) Unless the court orders otherwise, property of the estate that is not abandoned under this section and that is not administered in the case remains property of the estate.

(Pub.L. 95–598, Nov. 6, 1978, 92 Stat. 2603; Pub.L. 98–353, Title III, § 468, July 10, 1984, 98 Stat. 380; Pub.L. 99–554, Title II, § 283(p), Oct. 27, 1986, 100 Stat. 3118; Pub.L. 111–327, § 2(a)(23), Dec. 22, 2010, 124 Stat. 3560.)

HISTORICAL AND STATUTORY NOTES

Amendments

2010 Amendments. Subsec. (c). Pub.L. 111–327, § 2(a)(23), struck out "521(1)" and inserted "521(a)(1)".

1986 Amendments. Subsec. (c). Pub.L. 99–554 substituted "521(1)" for "521(a)(1)".

1984 Amendments. Subsec. (a). Pub.L. 98–353, § 468(a), added "and benefit" after "value".

Subsec. (b). Pub.L. 98–353, § 468(a), added "and benefit" after "value".

Subsec. (c). Pub.L. 98–353, § 468(b), substituted "Unless the court orders otherwise, any property scheduled under section 521(a)(1) of this title not otherwise administered at the time of the closing of a case is abandoned to the debtor and administered for purposes of section 350 of this title." for "Unless the court orders otherwise, any property that is scheduled under section 521(1) of this title and that is not administered before a case is closed under section 350 of this title is deemed abandoned.".

Subsec. (d). Pub.L. 98–353, § 468(c), struck out "section (a) or (b) of" after "not abandoned under".

CROSS REFERENCES

Grain storage facility bankruptcies, expedited determinations, see 11 USCA § 557.

Redemption, see 11 USCA § 722.

§ 555. Contractual right to liquidate, terminate, or accelerate a securities contract

The exercise of a contractual right of a stockbroker, financial institution, financial participant, or securities clearing agency to cause the liquidation, termination, or acceleration of a securities contract, as defined in section 741 of this title, because of a condition of the kind specified in section 365(e)(1) of this title shall not be stayed, avoided, or otherwise limited by operation of any provision of this title or by order of a court or administrative agency in any proceeding under this title unless such order is authorized under the provisions of the Securities Investor Protection Act of 1970 or any statute administered by the Securities and Exchange Commission. As used in this section, the term "contractual right" includes a right set forth in a rule or bylaw of a derivatives clearing organization (as defined in the Commodity Exchange Act), a multilateral clearing organization (as defined in the Federal Deposit Insurance Corporation Improvement Act of 1991), a national securities exchange, a national securities association, a securities clearing agency, a contract market designated under the Commodity Exchange Act, a derivatives transaction execution facility registered under the Commodity Exchange Act, or a board of trade (as defined in the Commodity Exchange Act), or in a resolution of the governing board thereof, and a right, whether or not in writing, arising under common law, under law merchant, or by reason of normal business practice.

(Added Pub.L. 97–222, § 6(a), July 27, 1982, 96 Stat. 236; amended Pub.L. 98–353, Title III, § 469, July 10, 1984, 98 Stat. 380; Pub.L. 103–394, Title V, § 501(b)(6), (d)(20), Oct. 22, 1994, 108 Stat. 4143, 4146; Pub.L. 109–8, Title IX, § 907(g), (o)(7), Apr. 20, 2005, 119 Stat. 177, 182.)

HISTORICAL AND STATUTORY NOTES

References in Text

The Securities Investor Protection Act of 1970, referred to in text, is Pub.L. 91–598, Dec. 30, 1970, 84 Stat. 1636, as amended, which is classified generally to chapter 2B–1 (section 78aaa et seq.) of Title 15, Commerce and Trade. For complete classification of this Act to the Code, see section 78aaa of Title 15 and Tables.

The Commodity Exchange Act, referred to in text, is Act Sept. 21, 1922, c. 369, 42 Stat. 998, as amended, which is classified principally to chapter 1 of Title 7, 7 U.S.C.A. § 1 et seq. For complete classification, see Short Title set out as 7 U.S.C.A. § 1 and Tables.

The Federal Deposit Insurance Corporation Improvement Act of 1991, referred to in text, is Pub.L. 102–242, Dec. 19, 1991, 105 Stat. 2236. See Tables for classification.

Amendments

2005 Amendments. Heading. Pub.L. 109–8, § 907(g)(1), rewrote the section heading, which formerly read: "**Contractual right to liquidate a securities contract**".

Pub.L. 109–8, § 907(g)(2), substituted "liquidation, termination, or acceleration" for "liquidation" in the first sentence.

Pub.L. 109–8, § 907(o)(7)(A), inserted "financial participant," after "financial institution,".

Pub.L. 109–8, § 907(o)(7)(B), rewrote the second sentence, substituting "As used in this section, the term 'contractual right' includes a right set forth in a rule or bylaw of a derivatives clearing organization (as defined in the Commodity Exchange Act), a multilateral clearing organization (as defined in the Federal Deposit Insurance Corporation Improvement Act of 1991), a national securities exchange, a national securities association, a securities clearing agency, a contract market designated under the Commodity Exchange Act, a derivatives transaction execution facility registered under the Commodity Exchange Act, or a board of trade (as defined in the Commodity Exchange Act), or in a resolution of the governing board thereof, and a right, whether or not in writing, arising under common law, under law merchant, or by reason of normal business practice." for "As used in this section, the term 'contractual right' includes a right set forth in a rule or bylaw of a national securities exchange, a national securities association, or a securities clearing agency."

1994 Amendments. Pub.L. 103–394, § 501(b)(6), substituted "section 741 of this title" for "section 741(7)".

Pub.L. 103–394, § 501(d)(20), struck out "(15 U.S.C. 78aaa et seq.)" after "Securities Investor Protection Act of 1970".

1984 Amendments. Pub.L. 98–353 added ", financial institution," after "stockbroker".

§ 556. Contractual right to liquidate, terminate, or accelerate a commodities contract or forward contract

The contractual right of a commodity broker, financial participant, or forward contract merchant to cause the liquidation, termination, or acceleration of a commodity contract, as defined in section 761 of this title, or forward contract because of a condition of the kind specified in section 365(e)(1) of this title, and the right to a variation or maintenance margin payment received from a trustee with respect to open commodity contracts or forward contracts, shall not be stayed, avoided, or otherwise limited by operation of any provision of this title or by the order of a court in any proceeding under this title. As used in this section, the term "contractual right" includes a right set forth in a rule or bylaw of a derivatives clearing organization (as defined in the Commodity Exchange Act), a multilateral clearing organization (as defined in the Federal Deposit Insurance Corporation Improvement Act of 1991), a national securities exchange, a national securities association, a securities clearing agency, a contract market designated under the Commodity Exchange Act, a derivatives transaction execution facility registered under the Commodity Exchange Act, or a board of trade (as defined in the Commodity Exchange Act) or in a resolution of the governing board thereof and a right, whether or not evidenced in writing, arising under common law, under law merchant or by reason of normal business practice.

(Added Pub.L. 97–222, § 6(a), July 27, 1982, 96 Stat. 236; amended Pub.L. 101–311, Title II, § 205, June 25, 1990, 104 Stat. 270; Pub.L. 103–394, Title V, § 501(b)(7), Oct. 22, 1994, 108 Stat. 4143; Pub.L. 109–8, Title IX, § 907(h), (o)(8), Apr. 20, 2005, 119 Stat. 178, 182.)

HISTORICAL AND STATUTORY NOTES

References in Text

The Commodity Exchange Act, referred to in text, is Act Sept. 21, 1922, c. 369, 42 Stat. 998, as amended, which is classified principally to chapter 1 of Title 7, 7 U.S.C.A. § 1. For complete classification, see Short Title set out as 7 U.S.C.A. § 1 and Tables.

The Federal Deposit Insurance Corporation Improvement Act of 1991, referred to in text, is Pub.L. 102–242, Dec. 19, 1991, 105 Stat. 2236. See Tables for classification.

Amendments

2005 Amendments. Pub.L. 109–8, (h)(1), rewrote the section heading, which formerly read: "Contractual right to liquidate a commodities contract or forward contract".

Pub.L. 109–8, § 907(h)(2), in the first sentence, substituted "liquidation, termination, or acceleration" for "liquidation".

Pub.L. 109–8, § 907(o)(8), in the first sentence, inserted ", financial participant," after "commodity broker".

Pub.L. 109–8, § 907(h)(3), in the second sentence, substituted "As used in this section, the term 'contractual right' includes a right set forth in a rule or bylaw of a derivatives clearing organization (as defined in the Commodity Exchange Act), a multilateral clearing organization (as defined in the Federal Deposit Insurance Corporation Improvement Act of 1991), a national securities exchange, a national securities association, a securities clearing agency, a contract market designated under the Commodity Exchange Act, a derivatives transaction execution facility registered under the Commodity Exchange Act, or a board of trade (as defined in the Commodity Exchange Act) or in a resolution of the governing board thereof and a right," for "As used in this section, the term 'contractual right' includes a right set forth in a rule or bylaw of a clearing organization or contract market or in a resolution of the governing board thereof and a right,".

1994 Amendments. Pub.L. 103–394, § 501(b)(7), substituted "section 761 of this title" for "section 761(4)".

1990 Amendments. Pub.L. 101–311 added provisions relating to rights arising under common law, law merchant, or normal business practice.

§ 557. Expedited determination of interests in, and abandonment or other disposition of grain assets

(a) This section applies only in a case concerning a debtor that owns or operates a grain storage facility and only with respect to grain and the proceeds of grain. This section does not affect the application of any other section of this title to property other than grain and proceeds of grain.

(b) In this section—

(1) "grain" means wheat, corn, flaxseed, grain sorghum, barley, oats, rye, soybeans, other dry edible beans, or rice;

(2) "grain storage facility" means a site or physical structure regularly used to store grain for producers, or to store grain acquired from producers for resale; and

(3) "producer" means an entity which engages in the growing of grain.

(c)(1) Notwithstanding sections 362, 363, 365, and 554 of this title, on the court's own motion the court may, and on the request of the trustee or an entity that claims an interest in grain or the proceeds of grain the court shall, expedite the procedures for the determination of interests in and the disposition of grain and the proceeds of grain, by shortening to the greatest extent feasible such time periods as are otherwise applicable for such procedures and by establishing, by order, a timetable having a duration of not to exceed 120 days for the completion of the applicable procedure specified in subsection (d) of this section. Such time periods and such timetable may be modified by the court, for cause, in accordance with subsection (f) of this section.

(2) The court shall determine the extent to which such time periods shall be shortened, based upon—

(A) any need of an entity claiming an interest in such grain or the proceeds of grain for a prompt determination of such interest;

(B) any need of such entity for a prompt disposition of such grain;

(C) the market for such grain;

(D) the conditions under which such grain is stored;

(E) the costs of continued storage or disposition of such grain;

(F) the orderly administration of the estate;

(G) the appropriate opportunity for an entity to assert an interest in such grain; and

(H) such other considerations as are relevant to the need to expedite such procedures in the case.

(d) The procedures that may be expedited under subsection (c) of this section include—

(1) the filing of and response to—

(A) a claim of ownership;

(B) a proof of claim;

(C) a request for abandonment;

(D) a request for relief from the stay of action against property under section 362(a) of this title;

(E) a request for determination of secured status;

(F) a request for determination of whether such grain or the proceeds of grain—

(i) is property of the estate;

(ii) must be turned over to the estate; or

(iii) may be used, sold, or leased; and

(G) any other request for determination of an interest in such grain or the proceeds of grain;

(2) the disposition of such grain or the proceeds of grain, before or after determination of interests in such grain or the proceeds of grain, by way of—

(A) sale of such grain;

(B) abandonment;

(C) distribution; or

(D) such other method as is equitable in the case;

(3) subject to sections 701, 702, 703, 1104, 1202, and 1302 of this title, the appointment of a trustee or examiner and the retention and compensation of any professional person required to assist with respect to matters relevant to the determination of interests in or disposition of such grain or the proceeds of grain; and

(4) the determination of any dispute concerning a matter specified in paragraph (1), (2), or (3) of this subsection.

(e)(1) Any governmental unit that has regulatory jurisdiction over the operation or liquidation of the debtor or the debtor's business shall be given notice of any request made or order entered under subsection (c) of this section.

(2) Any such governmental unit may raise, and may appear and be heard on, any issue relating to grain or the proceeds of grain in a case in which a request is made, or an order is entered, under subsection (c) of this section.

(3) The trustee shall consult with such governmental unit before taking any action relating to the disposition of grain in the possession, custody, or control of the debtor or the estate.

(f) The court may extend the period for final disposition of grain or the proceeds of grain under this section beyond 120 days if the court finds that—

(1) the interests of justice so require in light of the complexity of the case; and

(2) the interests of those claimants entitled to distribution of grain or the proceeds of grain will not be materially injured by such additional delay.

(g) Unless an order establishing an expedited procedure under subsection (c) of this section, or determining any interest in or approving any disposition of grain or the proceeds of grain, is stayed pending appeal—

(1) the reversal or modification of such order on appeal does not affect the validity of any procedure, determination, or disposition that occurs before such reversal or modification, whether or not any entity knew of the pendency of the appeal; and

(2) neither the court nor the trustee may delay, due to the appeal of such order, any proceeding in the case in which such order is issued.

(h)(1) The trustee may recover from grain and the proceeds of grain the reasonable and necessary costs and expenses allowable under section 503(b) of this title attributable to preserving or disposing of grain or the proceeds of grain, but may not recover from such grain or the proceeds of grain any other costs or expenses.

(2) Notwithstanding section 326(a) of this title, the dollar amounts of money specified in such section include the value, as of the date of disposition, of any grain that the trustee distributes in kind.

(i) In all cases where the quantity of a specific type of grain held by a debtor operating a grain storage facility exceeds ten thousand bushels, such grain shall be sold by the trustee and the assets thereof distributed in accordance with the provisions of this section.

(Added Pub.L. 98–353, Title III, § 352(a), July 10, 1984, 98 Stat. 359; amended Pub.L. 99–554, Title II, § 257(p), Oct. 27, 1986, 100 Stat. 3115.)

HISTORICAL AND STATUTORY NOTES

Amendments

1986 Amendments. Subsec. (d)(3). Pub.L. 99–554 added reference to section 1202 of this title.

CROSS REFERENCES

Applicability of this section in Chapter nine cases, see 11 USCA § 901.

Priorities, see 11 USCA § 507.

Rights and powers of trustee subject to right of seller who is "producer" of "grain" sold to "grain storage facility" owned or operated by debtor, as such terms are defined under this section, see 11 USCA § 546.

§ 558. Defenses of the estate

The estate shall have the benefit of any defense available to the debtor as against any entity other than the estate, including statutes of limitation, statutes of frauds, usury, and other personal defenses. A waiver of any such defense by the debtor after the commencement of the case does not bind the estate.

(Added Pub.L. 98–353, Title III, § 470(a), July 10, 1984, 98 Stat. 380.)

§ 559. Contractual right to liquidate, terminate, or accelerate a repurchase agreement

The exercise of a contractual right of a repo participant or financial participant to cause the liquidation, termination, or acceleration of a repurchase agreement because of a condition of the kind specified in section 365(e)(1) of this title shall not be stayed, avoided, or otherwise limited by operation of any provision of this title or by order of a court or administrative agency in any proceeding under this title, unless, where the debtor is a stockbroker or securities clearing agency, such order is authorized under the provisions of the Securities Investor Protection Act of 1970 or any statute administered by the Securities and Exchange Commission. In the event that a repo participant or financial participant liquidates one or more repurchase agreements with a debtor and under the terms of one or more such agreements has agreed to deliver assets subject to repurchase agreements to the debtor, any excess of the market prices received on liquidation of such assets (or if any such assets are not disposed of on the date of liquidation of such repurchase agreements, at the prices available at the time of liquidation of such repurchase agreements from a generally recognized source or the most recent closing bid quotation from such a source) over the sum of the stated repurchase prices and all expenses in connection with the liquidation of such repurchase agreements shall be deemed property of the estate, subject to the available rights of setoff. As used in this section, the term "contractual right" includes a right set forth in a rule or bylaw of a derivatives clearing organization (as defined in the Commodity Exchange Act), a multilateral clearing organization (as defined in the Federal Deposit Insurance Corporation Improvement Act of 1991), a national securities exchange, a national securities association, a securities clearing agency, a contract market designated under the Commodity Exchange Act, a derivatives transaction execution facility registered under the Commodity Exchange Act, or a board of trade (as defined in the Commodity Exchange Act) or in a resolution of the governing board thereof and a right, whether or not evidenced in writing, arising under common law, under law merchant or by reason of normal business practice.

(Added Pub.L. 98–353, Title III, § 396(a), July 10, 1984, 98 Stat. 366; amended Pub.L. 103–394, Title V, § 501(d)(21), Oct. 22, 1994, 108 Stat. 4146; Pub.L. 109–8, Title IX, § 907(i), (o)(9), Apr. 20, 2005, 119 Stat. 178, 182.)

HISTORICAL AND STATUTORY NOTES

References in Text

The Securities Investor Protection Act of 1970, referred to in text, is Pub. L. 91–598, Dec. 30, 1970, 84 Stat. 1636, as amended, which is classified generally to chapter 2B–1 (section 78aaa et seq.) of Title 15, Commerce and Trade. For complete classification of this Act to the Code, see section 78aaa of Title 15 and Tables.

The Commodity Exchange Act, referred to in text, is Act Sept. 21, 1922, c. 369, 42 Stat. 998, as amended, which is classified principally to chapter 1 of Title 7, 7 U.S.C.A. § 1. For complete classification, see Short Title set out as 7 U.S.C.A. § 1 and Tables.

The Federal Deposit Insurance Corporation Improvement Act of 1991, referred to in text, is Pub.L. 102–242, Dec. 19, 1991, 105 Stat. 2236. See Tables for classification.

Amendments

2005 Amendments. Pub.L. 109–8, § 907(i)(1), rewrote the section heading, which formerly read: "Contractual right to liquidate a repurchase agreement".

Pub.L. 109–8, § 907(i)(2), in the first sentence, substituted "liquidation, termination, or acceleration" for "liquidation".

Pub.L. 109–8, § 907(i)(3), in the third sentence, substituted "As used in this section, the term 'contractual right' includes a right set forth in a rule or bylaw of a derivatives clearing organization (as defined in the Commodity Exchange Act), a multilateral clearing organization (as defined in the Federal Deposit Insurance Corporation Improvement Act of 1991), a national securities exchange, a national securities association, a securities clearing agency, a contract market designated under the Commodity Exchange Act, a derivatives transaction execution facility registered under the Commodity Exchange Act, or a board of trade (as defined in the Commodity Exchange Act) or in a resolution of the governing board thereof and a right," for "As used in this section, the term 'contractual right' includes a right set forth in a rule or bylaw, applicable to each party to the repurchase agreement, of a national securities exchange, a national securities association, or a securities clearing agency, and a right,".

Pub.L. 109–8, § 907(o)(9), inserted "or financial participant" after "repo participant" each place such term appeared.

1994 Amendments. Pub.L. 103–394, § 501(d)(21), struck out "(15 U.S.C. 78aaa et seq.)" following "the Securities Investor Protection Act of 1970".

§ 560. Contractual right to liquidate, terminate, or accelerate a swap agreement

The exercise of any contractual right of any swap participant or financial participant to cause the liquidation, termination, or acceleration of one or more swap agreements because of a condition of the kind specified in section 365(e)(1) of this title or to offset or net out any termination values or payment amounts arising under or in connection with the termination, liquidation, or acceleration of one or more swap agreements shall not be stayed, avoided, or otherwise limited by operation of any provision of this title or by order of a court or administrative agency in any proceeding under this title. As used in this section, the term "contractual right" includes a right set forth in a rule or bylaw of a derivatives clearing organization (as defined in the Commodity Exchange Act), a multilateral clearing organization (as defined in the Federal Deposit Insurance Corporation Improvement Act of 1991), a national securities exchange, a national securities association, a securities clearing agency, a contract market designated under the Commodity Exchange Act, a derivatives transaction execution facility registered under the Commodity Exchange Act, or a board of trade (as defined in the Commodity Exchange Act) or in a resolution of the governing board thereof and a right, whether or not evidenced in writing, arising under common law, under law merchant, or by reason of normal business practice.

(Added Pub.L. 101–311, Title I, § 106(a), June 25, 1990, 104 Stat. 268; amended Pub.L. 109–8, Title IX, § 907(j), (o)(10), Apr. 20, 2005, 119 Stat. 178, 182.)

HISTORICAL AND STATUTORY NOTES

References in Text

The Commodity Exchange Act, referred to in text, is Act Sept. 21, 1922, c. 369, 42 Stat. 998, as amended, which is classified principally to chapter 1 of Title 7, 7 U.S.C.A. § 1. For complete classification, see Short Title set out as 7 U.S.C.A. § 1 and Tables.

The Federal Deposit Insurance Corporation Improvement Act of 1991, referred to in text, is Pub.L. 102–242, Dec. 19, 1991, 105 Stat. 2236. See Tables for classification.

Amendments

2005 Amendments. Pub.L. 109–8, § 907(j)(1), rewrote the section heading, which formerly read: "Contractual right to terminate a swap agreement".

Pub.L. 109–8, § 907(j)(2), (3), in the first sentence, substituted "liquidation, termination, or acceleration of one or more swap agreements" for "termination of a swap agreement", and substituted "in connection with the termination, liquidation, or acceleration of one or more swap agreements" for "in connection with any swap agreement".

Pub.L. 109–8, § 907(o)(10), in the first sentence, inserted "or financial participant" after "swap participant".

Pub.L. 109–8, (j)(4), in the second sentence, substituted "As used in this section, the term 'contractual right' includes a right set forth in a rule or bylaw of a derivatives clearing organization (as defined in the Commodity Exchange Act), a multilateral clearing organization (as defined in the Federal Deposit Insurance Corporation Improvement Act of 1991), a national securities exchange, a national securities association, a securities clearing agency, a contract market designated under the Commodity Exchange Act, a derivatives transaction execution facility registered under the Commodity Exchange Act, or a board of trade (as defined in the Commodity Exchange Act) or in a resolution of the governing board thereof and a right," for "As used in this section, the term 'contractual right' includes a right, ".

§ 561. Contractual right to terminate, liquidate, accelerate, or offset under a master netting agreement and across contracts; proceedings under chapter 15

(a) Subject to subsection (b), the exercise of any contractual right, because of a condition of the kind specified in section 365(e)(1), to cause the termination, liquidation, or acceleration of or to offset or net termination values, payment amounts, or other transfer obligations arising under or in connection with one or more (or the termination, liquidation, or acceleration of one or more)—

(1) securities contracts, as defined in section 741(7);

(2) commodity contracts, as defined in section 761(4);

(3) forward contracts;

(4) repurchase agreements;

(5) swap agreements; or

(6) master netting agreements,

shall not be stayed, avoided, or otherwise limited by operation of any provision of this title or by any order of a court or administrative agency in any proceeding under this title.

(b)(1) A party may exercise a contractual right described in subsection (a) to terminate, liquidate, or accelerate only to the extent that such party could exercise such a right under section 555, 556, 559, or 560 for each individual contract covered by the master netting agreement in issue.

(2) If a debtor is a commodity broker subject to subchapter IV of chapter 7—

(A) a party may not net or offset an obligation to the debtor arising under, or in connection with, a commodity contract traded on or subject to the rules of a contract market designated under the Commodity Exchange Act or a derivatives transaction execution facility registered under the Commodity Exchange Act against any claim arising under, or in connection with, other instruments, contracts, or agreements listed in subsection (a) except to the extent that the party has positive net equity in the commodity accounts at the debtor, as calculated under such subchapter; and

(B) another commodity broker may not net or offset an obligation to the debtor arising under, or in connection with, a commodity contract entered into or held on behalf of a customer of the debtor and traded on or subject to the rules of a contract market designated under the Commodity Exchange Act or a derivatives transaction execution facility registered under the Commodity Exchange Act against any claim arising under, or in connection with, other instruments, contracts, or agreements listed in subsection (a).

(3) No provision of subparagraph (A) or (B) of paragraph (2) shall prohibit the offset of claims and obligations that arise under—

(A) a cross-margining agreement or similar arrangement that has been approved by the Commodity Futures Trading Commission or submitted to the Commodity Futures Trading

Commission under paragraph (1) or (2) of section 5c(c) of the Commodity Exchange Act and has not been abrogated or rendered ineffective by the Commodity Futures Trading Commission; or

(B) any other netting agreement between a clearing organization (as defined in section 761) and another entity that has been approved by the Commodity Futures Trading Commission.

(c) As used in this section, the term "contractual right" includes a right set forth in a rule or bylaw of a derivatives clearing organization (as defined in the Commodity Exchange Act), a multilateral clearing organization (as defined in the Federal Deposit Insurance Corporation Improvement Act of 1991), a national securities exchange, a national securities association, a securities clearing agency, a contract market designated under the Commodity Exchange Act, a derivatives transaction execution facility registered under the Commodity Exchange Act, or a board of trade (as defined in the Commodity Exchange Act) or in a resolution of the governing board thereof, and a right, whether or not evidenced in writing, arising under common law, under law merchant, or by reason of normal business practice.

(d) Any provisions of this title relating to securities contracts, commodity contracts, forward contracts, repurchase agreements, swap agreements, or master netting agreements shall apply in a case under chapter 15, so that enforcement of contractual provisions of such contracts and agreements in accordance with their terms will not be stayed or otherwise limited by operation of any provision of this title or by order of a court in any case under this title, and to limit avoidance powers to the same extent as in a proceeding under chapter 7 or 11 of this title (such enforcement not to be limited based on the presence or absence of assets of the debtor in the United States).

(Added Pub.L. 109–8, Title IX, § 907(k)(1), Apr. 20, 2005, 119 Stat. 179.)

HISTORICAL AND STATUTORY NOTES

References in Text

The Commodity Exchange Act, referred to in subsecs. (b)(2)(A) and (c), is Act Sept. 21, 1922, c. 369, 42 Stat. 998, as amended, which is classified principally to chapter 1 of Title 7, 7 U.S.C.A. § 1 et seq. For complete classification, see Short Title set out as 7 U.S.C.A. § 1 and Tables.

Section 5c(c) of the Commodity Exchange Act, referred to in subsec. (b)(2)(A), is Act Sept. 21, 1922, c. 369, § 5c, as added and amended Dec. 21, 2000, Pub.L. 106–554, § 1(a)(5) [Title I, § 113, Title II, § 251(h)], 114 Stat. 2763, 2763A-399, 2763a–444, which is classified to 7 U.S.C.A. § 7a–2.

The Federal Deposit Insurance Corporation Improvement Act of 1991, referred to in subsec. (c), is Pub.L. 102–242, Dec. 19, 1991, 105 Stat. 2236. See Tables for classification.

§ 562. Timing of damage measurement in connection with swap agreements, securities contracts, forward contracts, commodity contracts, repurchase agreements, and master netting agreements

(a) If the trustee rejects a swap agreement, securities contract (as defined in section 741), forward contract, commodity contract (as defined in section 761), repurchase agreement, or master netting agreement pursuant to section 365(a), or if a forward contract merchant, stockbroker, financial institution, securities clearing agency, repo participant, financial participant, master netting agreement participant, or swap participant liquidates, terminates, or accelerates such contract or agreement, damages shall be measured as of the earlier of—

(1) the date of such rejection; or

(2) the date or dates of such liquidation, termination, or acceleration.

(b) If there are not any commercially reasonable determinants of value as of any date referred to in paragraph (1) or (2) of subsection (a), damages shall be measured as of the earliest subsequent date or dates on which there are commercially reasonable determinants of value.

(c) For the purposes of subsection (b), if damages are not measured as of the date or dates of rejection, liquidation, termination, or acceleration, and the forward contract merchant, stockbroker, financial institution, securities clearing agency, repo participant, financial participant, master netting agreement participant, or swap participant or the trustee objects to the timing of the measurement of damages—

    (1) the trustee, in the case of an objection by a forward contract merchant, stockbroker, financial institution, securities clearing agency, repo participant, financial participant, master netting agreement participant, or swap participant; or

    (2) the forward contract merchant, stockbroker, financial institution, securities clearing agency, repo participant, financial participant, master netting agreement participant, or swap participant, in the case of an objection by the trustee,

has the burden of proving that there were no commercially reasonable determinants of value as of such date or dates.

(Added Pub.L. 109–8, Title IX, § 910(a)(1), Apr. 20, 2005, 119 Stat. 184.)

CHAPTER 7—LIQUIDATION

SUBCHAPTER I—OFFICERS AND ADMINISTRATION

Sec.
701. Interim trustee.
702. Election of trustee.
703. Successor trustee.
704. Duties of trustee.
705. Creditors' committee.
706. Conversion.
707. Dismissal of a case or conversion to a case under chapter 11 or 13.

SUBCHAPTER II—COLLECTION, LIQUIDATION, AND DISTRIBUTION OF THE ESTATE

721. Authorization to operate business.
722. Redemption.
723. Rights of partnership trustee against general partners.
724. Treatment of certain liens.
725. Disposition of certain property.
726. Distribution of property of the estate.
727. Discharge.
[728. Repealed.]

SUBCHAPTER III—STOCKBROKER LIQUIDATION

741. Definitions for this subchapter.
742. Effect of section 362 of this title in this subchapter.
743. Notice.
744. Executory contracts.
745. Treatment of accounts.
746. Extent of customer claims.
747. Subordination of certain customer claims.
748. Reduction of securities to money.
749. Voidable transfers.
750. Distribution of securities.
751. Customer name securities.
752. Customer property.
753. Stockbroker liquidation and forward contract merchants, commodity brokers, stockbrokers, financial institutions, financial participants, securities clearing agencies, swap participants, repo participants, and master netting agreement participants.

SUBCHAPTER IV—COMMODITY BROKER LIQUIDATION

761. Definitions for this subchapter.
762. Notice to the Commission and right to be heard.
763. Treatment of accounts.
764. Voidable transfers.
765. Customer instructions.
766. Treatment of customer property.
767. Commodity broker liquidation and forward contract merchants, commodity brokers, stockbrokers, financial institutions, financial participants, securities clearing agencies, swap participants, repo participants, and master netting agreement participants.

SUBCHAPTER V—CLEARING BANK LIQUIDATION

781. Definitions.
782. Selection of trustee.
783. Additional powers of trustee.
784. Right to be heard.

HISTORICAL AND STATUTORY NOTES

Amendments

2005 Amendments. Pub.L. 109–8, Title I, § 102(k), Apr. 20, 2005, 119 Stat. 35, rewrote item 707, which formerly read: "Sec. 707. Dismissal.".

BANKRUPTCY CODE — Title 11

Pub.L. 109–8, Title VII, § 719(b)(2), Apr. 20, 2005, 119 Stat. 133, struck out item 728, which formerly read: "728. Special tax provisions.".

Pub.L. 109–8, Title IX, § 907(p)(2), Apr. 20, 2005, 119 Stat. 182, added items 753 and 767.

2000 Amendments. Pub.L. 106–554, § 1(a)(5) [Title I, § 112(d)], Dec. 21, 2000, 114 Stat. 2763, 2763A–396, added items relating to subchapter V and sections 781 to 784 of this title.

1984 Amendments. Pub.L. 98–353, Title III, § 471, July 10, 1984, 98 Stat. 380, substituted "Successor" for "Succesor" in item 703.

CROSS REFERENCES

Amount received for claim through liquidation under this chapter as standard for confirmation requirement in—

    Chapter eleven cases, see 11 USCA § 1129.

    Chapter thirteen cases, see 11 USCA § 1325.

    Chapter twelve cases, see 11 USCA § 1225.

Amount received for claim through liquidation under this chapter as standard for discharge requirement in—

    Chapter thirteen cases, see 11 USCA § 1328.

    Chapter twelve cases, see 11 USCA § 1228.

Applicability of income tax provisions to cases under this chapter, see 26 USCA § 1398.

Certain provisions respecting commodity brokers under this chapter, see 7 USCA § 24.

Chapters 1, 3 and 5 of this title applicable in case under this chapter, see 11 USCA § 103.

Commencement of involuntary cases, see 11 USCA § 303.

Conversion to this chapter from—

    Chapter eleven, see 11 USCA § 1112.

    Chapter thirteen, see 11 USCA § 1307.

    Chapter twelve, see 11 USCA § 1208.

Debtor's duty under this chapter to file statement of intentions with respect to schedule of assets and liabilities, see 11 USCA § 521.

Denial of discharge under this chapter as affecting operation of injunction, see 11 USCA § 524.

Determination of net worth of person subject to liability for termination of single-employer plans includes improper transfers of assets in cases under this chapter, see 29 USCA § 1362.

Distribution of certain proceeds and property under this chapter as requirement for confirmation of plan, see 11 USCA § 1173.

Duration of automatic stay in case concerning an individual under this chapter, see 11 USCA § 362.

Duties of trustee in investor protection liquidation proceedings same as under this chapter, see 15 USCA § 78fff–1.

Duties of United States trustees, see 28 USCA § 586.

Effect of confirmation, see 11 USCA § 1141.

Effect of distribution other than under this title, see 11 USCA § 508.

Eligibility to serve as trustee, see 11 USCA § 321.

Employment of professional persons, see 11 USCA § 327.

Executory contracts and unexpired leases, see 11 USCA § 365.

Filing fees, see 28 USCA § 1930.

Limitation on compensation of trustee, see 11 USCA § 326.

Liquidation in railroad reorganization case as if under this chapter, see 11 USCA § 1174.

Meetings of creditors and equity security holders and oral examination of debtor, see 11 USCA § 341.

Objection to allowance of claims by creditor of partner in partnership that is debtor under this chapter, see 11 USCA § 502.

Payment of trustee from filing fee, see 11 USCA § 330.

Persons required to make returns of income under this chapter, see 26 USCA § 6012.

Persons who may be debtors under this chapter, see 11 USCA § 109.

Property of estate in cases converted to this chapter from—

> Chapter thirteen, see 11 USCA § 1306.
>
> Chapter twelve, see 11 USCA § 1207.

Recommendation by trustee of conversion from chapter 11 to this chapter, see 11 USCA § 1106.

Special tax provisions, see 11 USCA § 346.

Stay of action against codebtor in cases converted to this chapter from—

> Chapter thirteen, see 11 USCA § 1301.
>
> Chapter twelve, see 11 USCA § 1201.

Transfers enabling creditor to receive more than under this chapter, see 11 USCA § 547.

Treatment of debtor's estate in cases under this chapter as taxpayer for certain income tax purposes, see 26 USCA § 108.

Unclaimed property, see 11 USCA § 347.

SUBCHAPTER I—OFFICERS AND ADMINISTRATION

CROSS REFERENCES

Applicability of this subchapter in investor protection liquidation proceedings, see 15 USCA § 78fff.

Subchapter applicable only in case under this chapter, see 11 USCA § 103.

§ 701. Interim trustee

(a)(1) Promptly after the order for relief under this chapter, the United States trustee shall appoint one disinterested person that is a member of the panel of private trustees established under section 586(a)(1) of title 28 or that is serving as trustee in the case immediately before the order for relief under this chapter to serve as interim trustee in the case.

(2) If none of the members of such panel is willing to serve as interim trustee in the case, then the United States trustee may serve as interim trustee in the case.

(b) The service of an interim trustee under this section terminates when a trustee elected or designated under section 702 of this title to serve as trustee in the case qualifies under section 322 of this title.

(c) An interim trustee serving under this section is a trustee in a case under this title.

(Pub.L. 95–598, Nov. 6, 1978, 92 Stat. 2604; Pub.L. 99–554, Title II, § 215, Oct. 27, 1986, 100 Stat. 3100.)

HISTORICAL AND STATUTORY NOTES

Amendments

1986 Amendments. Subsec. (a). Pub.L. 99–554, § 215, designated existing provisions as par. (1), and, in par. (1) as so designated, substituted "the United States trustee shall appoint" for "the court shall appoint", "586(a)(1)" for "604(f)", and "that is serving" for "that was serving", and added par. (2).

CROSS REFERENCES

Appointment of interim trustee after commencement of involuntary case, see 11 USCA § 303.

Effect of conversion, see 11 USCA § 348.

Grain storage facility bankruptcies, expedited appointment of trustee, see 11 USCA § 557.

Qualification of trustee, see 11 USCA § 322.

§ 702. Election of trustee

(a) A creditor may vote for a candidate for trustee only if such creditor—

(1) holds an allowable, undisputed, fixed, liquidated, unsecured claim of a kind entitled to distribution under section 726(a)(2), 726(a)(3), 726(a)(4), 752(a), 766(h), or 766(i) of this title;

(2) does not have an interest materially adverse, other than an equity interest that is not substantial in relation to such creditor's interest as a creditor, to the interest of creditors entitled to such distribution; and

(3) is not an insider.

(b) At the meeting of creditors held under section 341 of this title, creditors may elect one person to serve as trustee in the case if election of a trustee is requested by creditors that may vote under subsection (a) of this section, and that hold at least 20 percent in amount of the claims specified in subsection (a)(1) of this section that are held by creditors that may vote under subsection (a) of this section.

(c) A candidate for trustee is elected trustee if—

(1) creditors holding at least 20 percent in amount of the claims of a kind specified in subsection (a)(1) of this section that are held by creditors that may vote under subsection (a) of this section vote; and

(2) such candidate receives the votes of creditors holding a majority in amount of claims specified in subsection (a)(1) of this section that are held by creditors that vote for a trustee.

(d) If a trustee is not elected under this section, then the interim trustee shall serve as trustee in the case.

(Pub.L. 95–598, Nov. 6, 1978, 92 Stat. 2604; Pub.L. 97–222, § 7, July 27, 1982, 96 Stat. 237; Pub.L. 98–353, Title III, § 472, July 10, 1984, 98 Stat. 380.)

HISTORICAL AND STATUTORY NOTES

Amendments

1984 Amendments. Subsec. (b). Pub.L. 98–353, § 472(a), inserted "held" after "meeting of creditors".

Subsec. (c)(1). Pub.L. 98–353, § 472(b)(1), inserted "of a kind" after "claims".

Subsec. (c)(2). Pub.L. 98–353, § 472(b)(2), substituted "for a trustee" for "for trustee".

Subsec. (d). Pub.L. 98–353, § 472(c), substituted "this section" for "subsection (c) of this section".

1982 Amendments. Subsec. (a)(1). Pub.L. 97–222 substituted "726(a)(4), 752(a), 766(h), or 766(i)" for "or 726(a)(4)".

CROSS REFERENCES

Grain storage facility bankruptcies, expedited appointment of trustee, see 11 USCA § 557.

Qualification of trustee, see 11 USCA § 322.

Time for bringing action, see 11 USCA § 546.

§ 703. Successor trustee

(a) If a trustee dies or resigns during a case, fails to qualify under section 322 of this title, or is removed under section 324 of this title, creditors may elect, in the manner specified in section 702 of this title, a person to fill the vacancy in the office of trustee.

(b) Pending election of a trustee under subsection (a) of this section, if necessary to preserve or prevent loss to the estate, the United States trustee may appoint an interim trustee in the manner specified in section 701(a).

(c) If creditors do not elect a successor trustee under subsection (a) of this section or if a trustee is needed in a case reopened under section 350 of this title, then the United States trustee—

(1) shall appoint one disinterested person that is a member of the panel of private trustees established under section 586(a)(1) of title 28 to serve as trustee in the case; or

(2) may, if none of the disinterested members of such panel is willing to serve as trustee, serve as trustee in the case.

(Pub.L. 95–598, Nov. 6, 1978, 92 Stat. 2605; Pub.L. 98–353, Title III, § 473, July 10, 1984, 98 Stat. 381; Pub.L. 99–554, Title II, § 216, Oct. 27, 1986, 100 Stat. 3100.)

HISTORICAL AND STATUTORY NOTES

Amendments

1986 Amendments. Subsec. (b). Pub.L. 99–554, § 216, substituted "the United States trustee may appoint" for "the court may appoint" and "manner specified in section 701(a)" for "manner and subject to the provisions of section 701 of this title".

Subsec. (c). Pub.L. 99–554, § 216, substituted "this section or" for "this section, or", "then the United States trustee" for "then the court", designated part of existing provisions as par. (1), and, in par. (1) as so designated, substituted "586(a)(1)" for "604(f)", "in the case; or" for "in the case.", and added par. (2).

1984 Amendments. Subsec. (b). Pub.L. 98–353 substituted "and subject to the provisions of section 701 of this title" for "specified in section 701(a) of this title. Sections 701(b) and 701(c) of this title apply to such interim trustee".

CROSS REFERENCES

Effect of vacancy in office of trustee, see 11 USCA § 325.

Grain storage facility bankruptcies, expedited appointment of trustee, see 11 USCA § 557.

Qualification of trustee, see 11 USCA § 322.

§ 704. Duties of trustee

(a) The trustee shall—

(1) collect and reduce to money the property of the estate for which such trustee serves, and close such estate as expeditiously as is compatible with the best interests of parties in interest;

(2) be accountable for all property received;

(3) ensure that the debtor shall perform his intention as specified in section 521(a)(2)(B) of this title;

(4) investigate the financial affairs of the debtor;

(5) if a purpose would be served, examine proofs of claims and object to the allowance of any claim that is improper;

(6) if advisable, oppose the discharge of the debtor;

(7) unless the court orders otherwise, furnish such information concerning the estate and the estate's administration as is requested by a party in interest;

(8) if the business of the debtor is authorized to be operated, file with the court, with the United States trustee, and with any governmental unit charged with responsibility for collection or determination of any tax arising out of such operation, periodic reports and summaries of the operation of such business, including a statement of receipts and disbursements, and such other information as the United States trustee or the court requires;

(9) make a final report and file a final account of the administration of the estate with the court and with the United States trustee;

(10) if with respect to the debtor there is a claim for a domestic support obligation, provide the applicable notice specified in subsection (c);

(11) if, at the time of the commencement of the case, the debtor (or any entity designated by the debtor) served as the administrator (as defined in section 3 of the Employee Retirement Income Security Act of 1974) of an employee benefit plan, continue to perform the obligations required of the administrator; and

(12) use all reasonable and best efforts to transfer patients from a health care business that is in the process of being closed to an appropriate health care business that—

(A) is in the vicinity of the health care business that is closing;

(B) provides the patient with services that are substantially similar to those provided by the health care business that is in the process of being closed; and

(C) maintains a reasonable quality of care.

(b)(1) With respect to a debtor who is an individual in a case under this chapter—

(A) the United States trustee (or the bankruptcy administrator, if any) shall review all materials filed by the debtor and, not later than 10 days after the date of the first meeting of creditors, file with the court a statement as to whether the debtor's case would be presumed to be an abuse under section 707(b); and

(B) not later than 7 days after receiving a statement under subparagraph (A), the court shall provide a copy of the statement to all creditors.

(2) The United States trustee (or bankruptcy administrator, if any) shall, not later than 30 days after the date of filing a statement under paragraph (1), either file a motion to dismiss or convert under section 707(b) or file a statement setting forth the reasons the United States trustee (or the bankruptcy administrator, if any) does not consider such a motion to be appropriate, if the United States trustee (or the bankruptcy administrator, if any) determines that the debtor's case should be presumed to be an abuse under section 707(b) and the product of the debtor's current monthly income, multiplied by 12 is not less than—

(A) in the case of a debtor in a household of 1 person, the median family income of the applicable State for 1 earner; or

(B) in the case of a debtor in a household of 2 or more individuals, the highest median family income of the applicable State for a family of the same number or fewer individuals.

(c)(1) In a case described in subsection (a)(10) to which subsection (a)(10) applies, the trustee shall—

(A)(i) provide written notice to the holder of the claim described in subsection (a)(10) of such claim and of the right of such holder to use the services of the State child support enforcement agency established under sections 464 and 466 of the Social Security Act for the State in which such holder resides, for assistance in collecting child support during and after the case under this title;

(ii) include in the notice provided under clause (i) the address and telephone number of such State child support enforcement agency; and

(iii) include in the notice provided under clause (i) an explanation of the rights of such holder to payment of such claim under this chapter;

(B)(i) provide written notice to such State child support enforcement agency of such claim; and

(ii) include in the notice provided under clause (i) the name, address, and telephone number of such holder; and

(C) at such time as the debtor is granted a discharge under section 727, provide written notice to such holder and to such State child support enforcement agency of—

(i) the granting of the discharge;

(ii) the last recent known address of the debtor;

(iii) the last recent known name and address of the debtor's employer; and

(iv) the name of each creditor that holds a claim that—

(I) is not discharged under paragraph (2), (4), or (14A) of section 523(a); or

(II) was reaffirmed by the debtor under section 524(c).

(2)(A) The holder of a claim described in subsection (a)(10) or the State child support enforcement agency of the State in which such holder resides may request from a creditor described in paragraph (1)(C)(iv) the last known address of the debtor.

(B) Notwithstanding any other provision of law, a creditor that makes a disclosure of a last known address of a debtor in connection with a request made under subparagraph (A) shall not be liable by reason of making such disclosure.

(Pub.L. 95–598, Nov. 6, 1978, 92 Stat. 2605; Pub.L. 98–353, Title III, §§ 311(a), 474, July 10, 1984, 98 Stat. 355, 381; Pub.L. 99–554, Title II, § 217, Oct. 27, 1986, 100 Stat. 3100; Pub.L. 109–8, Title I, § 102(c), Title II, § 219(a), Title IV, § 446(b), Title XI, § 1105(a), Apr. 20, 2005, 119 Stat. 32, 55, 118, 192; Pub.L. 111–16, § 2(7), May 7, 2009, 123 Stat. 1607; Pub.L. 111–327, § 2(a)(24), Dec. 22, 2010, 124 Stat. 3560.)

HISTORICAL AND STATUTORY NOTES

References in Text

Section 3 of the Employee Retirement Income Security Act of 1974, referred to in subsec. (a)(11), is Pub.L. 93–406, Title I, § 3, Sept. 2, 1974, 88 Stat. 833, which is classified to 29 U.S.C.A. § 1002.

Section 464 of the Social Security Act, referred to in subsec. (c)(1)(A)(i), is Act Aug. 14, 1935, c. 531, Title IV, § 464, as added Aug. 13, 1981, Pub.L. 97–35, Title XXIII, § 2331(a), 95 Stat. 860, and amended, which is classified to 42 U.S.C.A. § 664.

Section 466 of the Social Security Act, referred to in subsec. (c)(1)(A)(i), is Act Aug. 14, 1935, c. 531, Title IV, § 466, as added Aug. 16, 1984, Pub.L. 98–378, § 3(b), 98 Stat. 1306, and amended, which is classified to 42 U.S.C.A. § 666.

Amendments

2010 Amendments. Subsec. (a)(3). Pub.L. 111–327, § 2(a)(24), struck out "521(2)(B)" and inserted "521(a)(2)(B)".

2009 Amendments. Subsec. (b)(1)(B). Pub.L. 111–16, § 2(7), struck out "5 days" and inserted "7 days".

2005 Amendments. Subsec. (a). Pub.L. 109–8, § 102(c)(1), inserted "(a)" before "The trustee shall—".

Subsec. (a)(8). Pub.L. 109–8, § 219(a)(1)(A), struck out 'and' at the end of par. (8).

Subsec. (a)(9). Pub.L. 109–8, § 219(a)(1)(B), substituted a semicolon for the period at the end of par. (9).

Subsec. (a)(10). Pub.L. 109–8, § 219(a)(1)(C), added par. (10).

Pub.L. 109–8, § 446(b)(1), struck "and" at the end of par. (10).

Subsec. (a)(11). Pub.L. 109–8, § 446(b)(2), added par. (11).

Subsec. (a)(12). Pub.L. 109–8, § 1105(a), added par. (12).

Subsec. (b). Pub.L. 109–8, § 102(c)(2), inserted subsec. (b).

Subsec. (c). Pub.L. 109–8, § 219(a)(2), added subsec. (c).

1986 Amendments. Par. (8). Pub.L. 99–554, § 217(1), substituted "with the court, with the United States trustee, and with" for "with the court and with" and "information as the United States trustee or the court" for "information as the court".

Par. (9). Pub.L. 99–554, § 217(2), substituted "with the court and with the United States trustee." for "with the court.".

1984 Amendments. Par. (1). Pub.L. 98–353, § 474, substituted "close such estate" for "close up such estate".

Par. (3). Pub.L. 98–353, § 311(a)(2), added par. (3). Former par. (3) was redesignated as (4).

Pars. (4) to (9). Pub.L. 98–353, § 311(a)(1), redesignated pars. (3) to (8) as (4) to (9), respectively.

CROSS REFERENCES

Duties of trustee in—

    Chapter eleven cases, see 11 USCA § 1106.

    Chapter thirteen cases, see 11 USCA § 1302.

    Chapter twelve cases, see 11 USCA § 1202.

    Multiemployer plan termination proceedings, see 29 USCA § 1342.

Filing of reports and summaries by debtor engaged in business, see 11 USCA § 1304.

Powers and duties of trustee in investor protection liquidation proceedings, see 15 USCA § 78fff–1.

§ 705. Creditors' committee

(a) At the meeting under section 341(a) of this title, creditors that may vote for a trustee under section 702(a) of this title may elect a committee of not fewer than three, and not more than eleven, creditors, each of whom holds an allowable unsecured claim of a kind entitled to distribution under section 726(a)(2) of this title.

(b) A committee elected under subsection (a) of this section may consult with the trustee or the United States trustee in connection with the administration of the estate, make recommendations to the trustee or the United States trustee respecting the performance of the trustee's duties, and submit to the court or the United States trustee any question affecting the administration of the estate.

(Pub.L. 95–598, Nov. 6, 1978, 92 Stat. 2605; Pub.L. 99–554, Title II, § 218, Oct. 27, 1986, 100 Stat. 3100.)

HISTORICAL AND STATUTORY NOTES

Amendments

1986 Amendments. Subsec. (b). Pub.L. 99–554, § 218, substituted "with the trustee or the United States trustee in connection" for "with the trustee in connection", "to the trustee or the United States trustee respecting" for "to the trustee respecting", and "to the court or the United States trustee any question" for "to the court any question".

CROSS REFERENCES

Appointment of creditors' and equity security holders' committees in chapter 11 cases, see 11 USCA § 1102.

Powers and duties of committees in chapter 11 cases, see 11 USCA § 1103.

§ 706. Conversion

(a) The debtor may convert a case under this chapter to a case under chapter 11, 12, or 13 of this title at any time, if the case has not been converted under section 1112, 1208, or 1307 of this title. Any waiver of the right to convert a case under this subsection is unenforceable.

(b) On request of a party in interest and after notice and a hearing, the court may convert a case under this chapter to a case under chapter 11 of this title at any time.

(c) The court may not convert a case under this chapter to a case under chapter 12 or 13 of this title unless the debtor requests or consents to such conversion.

(d) Notwithstanding any other provision of this section, a case may not be converted to a case under another chapter of this title unless the debtor may be a debtor under such chapter.

(Pub.L. 95–598, Nov. 6, 1978, 92 Stat. 2606; Pub.L. 99–554, Title II, § 257(q), Oct. 27, 1986, 100 Stat. 3115; Pub.L. 103–394, Title V, § 501(d)(22), Oct. 22, 1994, 108 Stat. 4146; Pub.L. 109–8, Title I, § 101, Apr. 20, 2005, 119 Stat. 27.)

HISTORICAL AND STATUTORY NOTES

Amendments

2005 Amendments. Subsec. (c). Pub.L. 109–8, § 101, inserted "or consents to" after "requests".

1994 Amendments. Subsec. (a). Pub.L. 103–394, § 501(d)(22), substituted "1208, or 1307" for "1307, or 1208".

1986 Amendments. Subsec. (a). Pub.L. 99–554, § 257(q)(1), added references to chapter 12 and section 1208 of this title.

Subsec. (c). Pub.L. 99–554, § 257(q)(2), added reference to chapter 12.

CROSS REFERENCES

Conversion or dismissal of—

    Chapter eleven cases, see 11 USCA § 1112.

    Chapter thirteen cases, see 11 USCA § 1307.

    Chapter twelve cases, see 11 USCA § 1208.

Effect of conversion, see 11 USCA § 348.

Termination of debtor's taxable period in—

    Chapter eleven cases, see 11 USCA § 1146.

    Chapter twelve cases, see 11 USCA § 1231.

§ 707. Dismissal of a case or conversion to a case under chapter 11 or 13

(a) The court may dismiss a case under this chapter only after notice and a hearing and only for cause, including—

    (1) unreasonable delay by the debtor that is prejudicial to creditors;

    (2) nonpayment of any fees or charges required under chapter 123 of title 28; and

    (3) failure of the debtor in a voluntary case to file, within fifteen days or such additional time as the court may allow after the filing of the petition commencing such case, the information required by paragraph (1) of section 521(a), but only on a motion by the United States trustee.

(b)(1) After notice and a hearing, the court, on its own motion or on a motion by the United States trustee, trustee (or bankruptcy administrator, if any), or any party in interest, may dismiss a case filed by an individual debtor under this chapter whose debts are primarily consumer debts, or, with the debtor's consent, convert such a case to a case under chapter 11 or 13 of this title, if it finds that the granting of relief would be an abuse of the provisions of this chapter. In making a determination whether to dismiss a case under this section, the court may not take into consideration whether a debtor has made, or continues to make, charitable contributions (that meet the definition of "charitable contribution" under section 548(d)(3)) to any qualified religious or charitable entity or organization (as that term is defined in section 548(d)(4)).

(2)(A)(i) In considering under paragraph (1) whether the granting of relief would be an abuse of the provisions of this chapter, the court shall presume abuse exists if the debtor's current monthly income reduced by the amounts determined under clauses (ii), (iii), and (iv), and multiplied by 60 is not less than the lesser of—

(I) 25 percent of the debtor's nonpriority unsecured claims in the case, or $7,475[1], whichever is greater; or

(II) $12,475[1].

(ii)(I) The debtor's monthly expenses shall be the debtor's applicable monthly expense amounts specified under the National Standards and Local Standards, and the debtor's actual monthly expenses for the categories specified as Other Necessary Expenses issued by the Internal Revenue Service for the area in which the debtor resides, as in effect on the date of the order for relief, for the debtor, the dependents of the debtor, and the spouse of the debtor in a joint case, if the spouse is not otherwise a dependent. Such expenses shall include reasonably necessary health insurance, disability insurance, and health savings account expenses for the debtor, the spouse of the debtor, or the dependents of the debtor. Notwithstanding any other provision of this clause, the monthly expenses of the debtor shall not include any payments for debts. In addition, the debtor's monthly expenses shall include the debtor's reasonably necessary expenses incurred to maintain the safety of the debtor and the family of the debtor from family violence as identified under section 302 of the Family Violence Prevention and Services Act, or other applicable Federal law. The expenses included in the debtor's monthly expenses described in the preceding sentence shall be kept confidential by the court. In addition, if it is demonstrated that it is reasonable and necessary, the debtor's monthly expenses may also include an additional allowance for food and clothing of up to 5 percent of the food and clothing categories as specified by the National Standards issued by the Internal Revenue Service.

(II) In addition, the debtor's monthly expenses may include, if applicable, the continuation of actual expenses paid by the debtor that are reasonable and necessary for care and support of an elderly, chronically ill, or disabled household member or member of the debtor's immediate family (including parents, grandparents, siblings, children, and grandchildren of the debtor, the dependents of the debtor, and the spouse of the debtor in a joint case who is not a dependent) and who is unable to pay for such reasonable and necessary expenses. Such monthly expenses may include, if applicable, contributions to an account of a qualified ABLE program to the extent such contributions are not excess contributions (as described in section 4973(h) of the Internal Revenue Code of 1986) and if the designated beneficiary of such account is a child, stepchild, grandchild, or stepgrandchild of the debtor.

(III) In addition, for a debtor eligible for chapter 13, the debtor's monthly expenses may include the actual administrative expenses of administering a chapter 13 plan for the district in which the debtor resides, up to an amount of 10 percent of the projected plan payments, as determined under schedules issued by the Executive Office for United States Trustees.

(IV) In addition, the debtor's monthly expenses may include the actual expenses for each dependent child less than 18 years of age, not to exceed $1,875[1] per year per child, to attend a private or public elementary or secondary school if the debtor provides documentation of such expenses and a detailed explanation of why such expenses are reasonable and necessary, and why such expenses are not already accounted for in the National Standards, Local Standards, or Other Necessary Expenses referred to in subclause (I).

---

[1] Dollar amount as adjusted by the Judicial Conference of the United States. See Adjustment of Dollar Amounts notes set out under this section and 11 U.S.C.A. § 104.

(V) In addition, the debtor's monthly expenses may include an allowance for housing and utilities, in excess of the allowance specified by the Local Standards for housing and utilities issued by the Internal Revenue Service, based on the actual expenses for home energy costs if the debtor provides documentation of such actual expenses and demonstrates that such actual expenses are reasonable and necessary.

(iii) The debtor's average monthly payments on account of secured debts shall be calculated as the sum of—

(I) the total of all amounts scheduled as contractually due to secured creditors in each month of the 60 months following the date of the filing of the petition; and

(II) any additional payments to secured creditors necessary for the debtor, in filing a plan under chapter 13 of this title, to maintain possession of the debtor's primary residence, motor vehicle, or other property necessary for the support of the debtor and the debtor's dependents, that serves as collateral for secured debts;

divided by 60.

(iv) The debtor's expenses for payment of all priority claims (including priority child support and alimony claims) shall be calculated as the total amount of debts entitled to priority, divided by 60.

(B)(i) In any proceeding brought under this subsection, the presumption of abuse may only be rebutted by demonstrating special circumstances, such as a serious medical condition or a call or order to active duty in the Armed Forces, to the extent such special circumstances that justify additional expenses or adjustments of current monthly income for which there is no reasonable alternative.

(ii) In order to establish special circumstances, the debtor shall be required to itemize each additional expense or adjustment of income and to provide—

(I) documentation for such expense or adjustment to income; and

(II) a detailed explanation of the special circumstances that make such expenses or adjustment to income necessary and reasonable.

(iii) The debtor shall attest under oath to the accuracy of any information provided to demonstrate that additional expenses or adjustments to income are required.

(iv) The presumption of abuse may only be rebutted if the additional expenses or adjustments to income referred to in clause (i) cause the product of the debtor's current monthly income reduced by the amounts determined under clauses (ii), (iii), and (iv) of subparagraph (A) when multiplied by 60 to be less than the lesser of—

(I) 25 percent of the debtor's nonpriority unsecured claims, or $7,475[1], whichever is greater; or

(II) $12,475[1].

(C) As part of the schedule of current income and expenditures required under section 521, the debtor shall include a statement of the debtor's current monthly income, and the calculations that determine whether a presumption arises under subparagraph (A)(i), that show how each such amount is calculated.

(D) Subparagraphs (A) through (C) shall not apply, and the court may not dismiss or convert a case based on any form of means testing—

(i) if the debtor is a disabled veteran (as defined in section 3741(1) of title 38), and the indebtedness occurred primarily during a period during which he or she was—

(I) on active duty (as defined in section 101(d)(1) of title 10); or

---

[1] Dollar amount as adjusted by the Judicial Conference of the United States. See Adjustment of Dollar Amounts notes set out under this section and 11 U.S.C.A. § 104.

(II) performing a homeland defense activity (as defined in section 901(1) of title 32); or

(ii) with respect to the debtor, while the debtor is—

(I) on, and during the 540-day period beginning immediately after the debtor is released from, a period of active duty (as defined in section 101(d)(1) of title 10) of not less than 90 days; or

(II) performing, and during the 540-day period beginning immediately after the debtor is no longer performing, a homeland defense activity (as defined in section 901(1) of title 32) performed for a period of not less than 90 days;

if after September 11, 2001, the debtor while a member of a reserve component of the Armed Forces or a member of the National Guard, was called to such active duty or performed such homeland defense activity.

(3) In considering under paragraph (1) whether the granting of relief would be an abuse of the provisions of this chapter in a case in which the presumption in paragraph (2)(A)(i) does not arise or is rebutted, the court shall consider—

(A) whether the debtor filed the petition in bad faith; or

(B) the totality of the circumstances (including whether the debtor seeks to reject a personal services contract and the financial need for such rejection as sought by the debtor) of the debtor's financial situation demonstrates abuse.

(4)(A) The court, on its own initiative or on the motion of a party in interest, in accordance with the procedures described in rule 9011 of the Federal Rules of Bankruptcy Procedure, may order the attorney for the debtor to reimburse the trustee for all reasonable costs in prosecuting a motion filed under section 707(b), including reasonable attorneys' fees, if—

(i) a trustee files a motion for dismissal or conversion under this subsection; and

(ii) the court—

(I) grants such motion; and

(II) finds that the action of the attorney for the debtor in filing a case under this chapter violated rule 9011 of the Federal Rules of Bankruptcy Procedure.

(B) If the court finds that the attorney for the debtor violated rule 9011 of the Federal Rules of Bankruptcy Procedure, the court, on its own initiative or on the motion of a party in interest, in accordance with such procedures, may order—

(i) the assessment of an appropriate civil penalty against the attorney for the debtor; and

(ii) the payment of such civil penalty to the trustee, the United States trustee (or the bankruptcy administrator, if any).

(C) The signature of an attorney on a petition, pleading, or written motion shall constitute a certification that the attorney has—

(i) performed a reasonable investigation into the circumstances that gave rise to the petition, pleading, or written motion; and

(ii) determined that the petition, pleading, or written motion—

(I) is well grounded in fact; and

(II) is warranted by existing law or a good faith argument for the extension, modification, or reversal of existing law and does not constitute an abuse under paragraph (1).

(D) The signature of an attorney on the petition shall constitute a certification that the attorney has no knowledge after an inquiry that the information in the schedules filed with such petition is incorrect.

(5)(A) Except as provided in subparagraph (B) and subject to paragraph (6), the court, on its own initiative or on the motion of a party in interest, in accordance with the procedures described in rule 9011 of the Federal Rules of Bankruptcy Procedure, may award a debtor all reasonable costs (including reasonable attorneys' fees) in contesting a motion filed by a party in interest (other than a trustee or United States trustee (or bankruptcy administrator, if any)) under this subsection if—

(i) the court does not grant the motion; and

(ii) the court finds that—

(I) the position of the party that filed the motion violated rule 9011 of the Federal Rules of Bankruptcy Procedure; or

(II) the attorney (if any) who filed the motion did not comply with the requirements of clauses (i) and (ii) of paragraph (4)(C), and the motion was made solely for the purpose of coercing a debtor into waiving a right guaranteed to the debtor under this title.

(B) A small business that has a claim of an aggregate amount less than $1,250[1] shall not be subject to subparagraph (A)(ii)(I).

(C) For purposes of this paragraph—

(i) the term "small business" means an unincorporated business, partnership, corporation, association, or organization that—

(I) has fewer than 25 full-time employees as determined on the date on which the motion is filed; and

(II) is engaged in commercial or business activity; and

(ii) the number of employees of a wholly owned subsidiary of a corporation includes the employees of—

(I) a parent corporation; and

(II) any other subsidiary corporation of the parent corporation.

(6) Only the judge or United States trustee (or bankruptcy administrator, if any) may file a motion under section 707(b), if the current monthly income of the debtor, or in a joint case, the debtor and the debtor's spouse, as of the date of the order for relief, when multiplied by 12, is equal to or less than—

(A) in the case of a debtor in a household of 1 person, the median family income of the applicable State for 1 earner;

(B) in the case of a debtor in a household of 2, 3, or 4 individuals, the highest median family income of the applicable State for a family of the same number or fewer individuals; or

(C) in the case of a debtor in a household exceeding 4 individuals, the highest median family income of the applicable State for a family of 4 or fewer individuals, plus $675[1] per month for each individual in excess of 4.

(7)(A) No judge, United States trustee (or bankruptcy administrator, if any), trustee, or other party in interest may file a motion under paragraph (2) if the current monthly income of the debtor, including a veteran (as that term is defined in section 101 of title 38), and the debtor's spouse combined, as of the date of the order for relief when multiplied by 12, is equal to or less than—

(i) in the case of a debtor in a household of 1 person, the median family income of the applicable State for 1 earner;

(ii) in the case of a debtor in a household of 2, 3, or 4 individuals, the highest median family income of the applicable State for a family of the same number or fewer individuals; or

---

[1] Dollar amount as adjusted by the Judicial Conference of the United States. See Adjustment of Dollar Amounts notes set out under this section and 11 U.S.C.A. § 104.

(iii) in the case of a debtor in a household exceeding 4 individuals, the highest median family income of the applicable State for a family of 4 or fewer individuals, plus $675[1] per month for each individual in excess of 4.

(B) In a case that is not a joint case, current monthly income of the debtor's spouse shall not be considered for purposes of subparagraph (A) if—

(i)(I) the debtor and the debtor's spouse are separated under applicable nonbankruptcy law; or

(II) the debtor and the debtor's spouse are living separate and apart, other than for the purpose of evading subparagraph (A); and

(ii) the debtor files a statement under penalty of perjury—

(I) specifying that the debtor meets the requirement of subclause (I) or (II) of clause (i); and

(II) disclosing the aggregate, or best estimate of the aggregate, amount of any cash or money payments received from the debtor's spouse attributed to the debtor's current monthly income.

(c)(1) In this subsection—

(A) the term "crime of violence" has the meaning given such term in section 16 of title 18; and

(B) the term "drug trafficking crime" has the meaning given such term in section 924(c)(2) of title 18.

(2) Except as provided in paragraph (3), after notice and a hearing, the court, on a motion by the victim of a crime of violence or a drug trafficking crime, may when it is in the best interest of the victim dismiss a voluntary case filed under this chapter by a debtor who is an individual if such individual was convicted of such crime.

(3) The court may not dismiss a case under paragraph (2) if the debtor establishes by a preponderance of the evidence that the filing of a case under this chapter is necessary to satisfy a claim for a domestic support obligation.

(Pub.L. 95–598, Nov. 6, 1978, 92 Stat. 2606; Pub.L. 98–353, Title III, §§ 312, 475, July 10, 1984, 98 Stat. 355, 381; Pub.L. 99–554, Title II, § 219, Oct. 27, 1986, 100 Stat. 3100; Pub.L. 105–183, § 4(b), June 19, 1998, 112 Stat. 518; Pub.L. 109–8, Title I, § 102(a), (f), Apr. 20, 2005, 119 Stat. 27, 33; Pub.L. 110–438, § 2, Oct. 20, 2008, 122 Stat. 5000; Pub.L. 111–320, Title II, § 202(a), Dec. 20, 2010, 124 Stat. 3509; Pub.L. 111–327, § 2(a)(25), Dec. 22, 2010, 124 Stat. 3560.)

HISTORICAL AND STATUTORY NOTES

References in Text

The Family Violence Prevention and Services Act, referred to in subsec. (b)(2)(A)(ii)(I), is Pub.L. 98–457, Title III, § 301 et seq., as revised by Pub.L. 111–320, § 201, Dec. 20, 2010, 124 Stat. 3484, which is classified principally to chapter 110 of Title 42, 42 U.S.C.A. § 10401 et seq. Section 302 of the Act is classified to 42 U.S.C.A. § 10402.

Amendments

2014 Amendments. Subsec. (b)(2)(A)(ii)(II). Pub.L. 113-295, § 104(b), inserted at the end, "Such monthly expenses may include, if applicable, contributions to an account of a qualified ABLE program to the extent such contributions are not excess contributions (as described in section 4973(h) of the Internal Revenue Code of 1986) and if the designated beneficiary of such account is a child, stepchild, grandchild, or stepgrandchild of the debtor.".

2010 Amendments. Subsec. (a)(3). Pub.L. 111–327, § 2(a)(25)(A), struck out "521" and inserted "521(a)".

---

[1] Dollar amount as adjusted by the Judicial Conference of the United States. See Adjustment of Dollar Amounts notes set out under this section and 11 U.S.C.A. § 104.

Subsec. (b)(2)(A)(ii)(I). Pub.L. 111–320, § 202(a), struck out "section 309 of the Family Violence Prevention and Services Act" and inserted "section 302 of the Family Violence Prevention and Services Act".

Subsec. (b)(2)(A)(iii)(I). Pub.L. 111–327, § 2(a)(25)(B)(i), inserted "of the filing" following " date".

Subsec. (b)(3). Pub.L. 111–327, § 2(a)(25)(B)(ii), struck out "subparagraph (A)(i) of such paragraph" and inserted "paragraph (2)(A)(i)".

2008 Amendments. Subsec. (b)(2)(D). Pub.L. 110–438, § 2, rewrote subpar. (D), which formerly read:

"**(D)** Subparagraphs (A) through (C) shall not apply, and the court may not dismiss or convert a case based on any form of means testing, if the debtor is a disabled veteran (as defined in section 3741(1) of title 38), and the indebtedness occurred primarily during a period during which he or she was—

"**(i)** on active duty (as defined in section 101(d)(1) of title 10); or

"**(ii)** performing a homeland defense activity (as defined in section 901(1) of title 32)."

2005 Amendments. Heading. Pub.L. 109–8, § 102(a)(1), struck the existing section heading, which formerly read: " **§ 707. Dismissal**", and inserted " **§ 707. Dismissal of a case or conversion to a case under chapter 11 or 13**".

Subsec. (b). Pub.L. 109–8, § 102(a)(2), rewrote subsec. (b), which formerly read:

"**(b)** After notice and a hearing, the court, on its own motion or on a motion by the United States trustee, but not at the request or suggestion of any party in interest, may dismiss a case filed by an individual debtor under this chapter whose debts are primarily consumer debts if it finds that the granting of relief would be a substantial abuse of the provisions of this chapter. There shall be a presumption in favor of granting the relief requested by the debtor. In making a determination whether to dismiss a case under this section, the court may not take into consideration whether a debtor has made, or continues to make, charitable contributions (that meet the definition of 'charitable contribution' under section 548(d)(3)) to any qualified religious or charitable entity or organization (as that term is defined in section 548(d)(4))."

Subsec. (c). Pub.L. 109–8, § 102(f), added subsec. (c).

1998 Amendments. Subsec. (b). Pub.L. 105–183, § 4(b), added at the end "In making a determination whether to dismiss a case under this section, the court may not take into consideration whether a debtor has made, or continues to make, charitable contributions (that meet the definition of 'charitable contribution' under section 548(d)(3)) to any qualified religious or charitable entity or organization (as that term is defined in section 548(d)(4)).".

1986 Amendments. Subsec. (a)(3). Pub.L. 99–554, § 219(a), added par. (3).

Subsec. (b). Pub.L. 99–554, § 219(b), substituted "motion or on a motion by the United States trustee, but not" for "motion and not".

1984 Amendments. Subsec. (a). Pub.L. 98–353, § 312(1), designated existing provisions as subsec. (a).

Subsec. (a)(1). Pub.L. 98–353, § 475, substituted "or" for "and".

Subsec. (a)(2). Pub.L. 98–353, § 475, substituted "or" for "and".

Subsec. (b). Pub.L. 98–353, § 312(2), added subsec. (b).

Adjustment of Dollar Amounts

For adjustment of dollar amounts specified in this section by the Judicial Conference of the United States, see note set out under 11 U.S.C.A. § 104.

Schedules of Reasonable and Necessary Expenses

Pub.L. 109–8, Title I, § 107, Apr. 20, 2005, 119 Stat. 42, provided that: "For purposes of section 707(b) of title 11, United States Code [subsec. (b) of this section], as amended by this Act [Bankruptcy Abuse Prevention and Consumer Protection Act of 2005, Pub.L. 109–8, April 20, 2005, 119 Stat. 23, see Tables for classification], the Director of the Executive Office for United States Trustees shall, not later than 180 days after the date of enactment of this Act [April 20, 2005], issue schedules of reasonable and necessary administrative expenses of administering a chapter 13 plan [chapter 13 of this title is 11 U.S.C.A. § 1301 et seq.] for each judicial district of the United States."

CROSS REFERENCES

Conversion or dismissal of—

    Chapter eleven cases, see 11 USCA § 1112.

    Chapter thirteen cases, see 11 USCA § 1307.

Crime victims' rights, rights afforded and best efforts to accord rights, procedures to promote compliance, see 18 U.S.C.A. § 3771.

Dismissal of Chapter nine cases, see 11 USCA § 930.

Effect of dismissal, see 11 USCA § 349.

SUBCHAPTER II—COLLECTION, LIQUIDATION, AND DISTRIBUTION OF THE ESTATE

CROSS REFERENCES

Applicability of this subchapter in investor protection liquidation proceedings, see 15 USCA § 78fff.

Subchapter applicable only in case under this chapter, see 11 USCA § 103.

§ 721. Authorization to operate business

The court may authorize the trustee to operate the business of the debtor for a limited period, if such operation is in the best interest of the estate and consistent with the orderly liquidation of the estate.

(Pub.L. 95–598, Nov. 6, 1978, 92 Stat. 2606.)

CROSS REFERENCES

Authorization to operate business in Chapter eleven cases, see 11 USCA § 1108.

Debtor engaged in business in Chapter thirteen cases, see 11 USCA § 1304.

Executory contracts and unexpired leases, see 11 USCA § 365.

Executory contracts in stockbroker liquidation cases, see 11 USCA § 744.

Obtaining credit, see 11 USCA § 364.

Retention or replacement of professional persons, see 11 USCA § 327.

Treatment of accounts in—

    Commodity broker liquidation cases, see 11 USCA § 763.

    Stockbroker liquidation cases, see 11 USCA § 745.

Use, sale or lease of property, see 11 USCA § 363.

Utility service, see 11 USCA § 366.

§ 722. Redemption

An individual debtor may, whether or not the debtor has waived the right to redeem under this section, redeem tangible personal property intended primarily for personal, family, or household use, from a lien securing a dischargeable consumer debt, if such property is exempted under section 522 of this title or has been abandoned under section 554 of this title, by paying the holder of such lien the amount of the allowed secured claim of such holder that is secured by such lien in full at the time of redemption.

(Pub.L. 95–598, Nov. 6, 1978, 92 Stat. 2606; Pub.L. 109–8, Title III, § 304(2), Apr. 20, 2005, 119 Stat. 79.)

HISTORICAL AND STATUTORY NOTES

Amendments

2005 Amendments. Pub.L. 109–8, § 304(2), inserted "in full at the time of redemption" before the period at the end of the section.

§ 723. Rights of partnership trustee against general partners

(a) If there is a deficiency of property of the estate to pay in full all claims which are allowed in a case under this chapter concerning a partnership and with respect to which a general partner of the partnership is personally liable, the trustee shall have a claim against such general partner to the extent that under applicable nonbankruptcy law such general partner is personally liable for such deficiency.

(b) To the extent practicable, the trustee shall first seek recovery of such deficiency from any general partner in such partnership that is not a debtor in a case under this title. Pending determination of such deficiency, the court may order any such partner to provide the estate with indemnity for, or assurance of payment of, any deficiency recoverable from such partner, or not to dispose of property.

(c) The trustee has a claim against the estate of each general partner in such partnership that is a debtor in a case under this title for the full amount of all claims of creditors allowed in the case concerning such partnership. Notwithstanding section 502 of this title, there shall not be allowed in such partner's case a claim against such partner on which both such partner and such partnership are liable, except to any extent that such claim is secured only by property of such partner and not by property of such partnership. The claim of the trustee under this subsection is entitled to distribution in such partner's case under section 726(a) of this title the same as any other claim of a kind specified in such section.

(d) If the aggregate that the trustee recovers from the estates of general partners under subsection (c) of this section is greater than any deficiency not recovered under subsection (b) of this section, the court, after notice and a hearing, shall determine an equitable distribution of the surplus so recovered, and the trustee shall distribute such surplus to the estates of the general partners in such partnership according to such determination.

(Pub.L. 95–598, Nov. 6, 1978, 92 Stat. 2606; Pub.L. 98–353, Title III, § 476, July 10, 1984, 98 Stat. 381; Pub.L. 103–394, Title II, § 212, Oct. 22, 1994, 108 Stat. 4125; Pub.L. 111–327, § 2(a)(26), Dec. 22, 2010, 124 Stat. 3560.)

HISTORICAL AND STATUTORY NOTES

References in Text

Section 728(a), (b) of this title, referred to in subsec. (b), is subsecs. (a) and (b) of 11 U.S.C.A. § 728, which was repealed by Pub.L. 109–8, Title VII, § 719(b)(1), Apr. 20, 2005, 119 Stat. 133.

Amendments

2010 Amendments. Subsec. (c). Pub.L. 111–327, § 2(a)(26), struck out "Notwithstanding section 728(c) of this title, the" and inserted "The" preceding "trustee has a claim".

1994 Amendments. Subsec. (a). Pub.L. 103–394, § 212, substituted provisions directing that trustee shall have a claim against general partner to the extent that under applicable nonbankruptcy law general partner is personally liable for deficiency, for provisions directing that trustee shall have a claim for full amount of deficiency.

1984 Amendments. Subsec. (a). Pub.L. 98–353, § 476, substituted provisions that the trustee shall have a claim for the full amount of the deficiency against a general partner who is personally liable with respect to claims concerning partnerships which are allowed in a case under this chapter, for provisions that each general partner in the partnership would be liable to the trustee for the full amount of such deficiency.

Subsec. (c). Pub.L. 98–353, § 476(b), substituted "such partner's case" for "such case" wherever appearing, "by property of such partnership" for "be property of such partnership", and "a kind specified in such section" for "the kind specified in such section".

CROSS REFERENCES

Property of estate, see 11 USCA § 541.

§ 724. Treatment of certain liens

(a) The trustee may avoid a lien that secures a claim of a kind specified in section 726(a)(4) of this title.

(b) Property in which the estate has an interest and that is subject to a lien that is not avoidable under this title (other than to the extent that there is a properly perfected unavoidable tax lien arising in connection with an ad valorem tax on real or personal property of the estate) and that secures an allowed claim for a tax, or proceeds of such property, shall be distributed—

(1) first, to any holder of an allowed claim secured by a lien on such property that is not avoidable under this title and that is senior to such tax lien;

(2) second, to any holder of a claim of a kind specified in section 507(a)(1)(C) or 507(a)(2) (except that such expenses under each such section, other than claims for wages, salaries, or commissions that arise after the date of the filing of the petition, shall be limited to expenses incurred under this chapter and shall not include expenses incurred under chapter 11 of this title), 507(a)(1)(A), 507(a)(1)(B), 507(a)(3), 507(a)(4), 507(a)(5), 507(a)(6), or 507(a)(7) of this title, to the extent of the amount of such allowed tax claim that is secured by such tax lien;

(3) third, to the holder of such tax lien, to any extent that such holder's allowed tax claim that is secured by such tax lien exceeds any amount distributed under paragraph (2) of this subsection;

(4) fourth, to any holder of an allowed claim secured by a lien on such property that is not avoidable under this title and that is junior to such tax lien;

(5) fifth, to the holder of such tax lien, to the extent that such holder's allowed claim secured by such tax lien is not paid under paragraph (3) of this subsection; and

(6) sixth, to the estate.

(c) If more than one holder of a claim is entitled to distribution under a particular paragraph of subsection (b) of this section, distribution to such holders under such paragraph shall be in the same order as distribution to such holders would have been other than under this section.

(d) A statutory lien the priority of which is determined in the same manner as the priority of a tax lien under section 6323 of the Internal Revenue Code of 1986 shall be treated under subsection (b) of this section the same as if such lien were a tax lien.

(e) Before subordinating a tax lien on real or personal property of the estate, the trustee shall—

(1) exhaust the unencumbered assets of the estate; and

(2) in a manner consistent with section 506(c), recover from property securing an allowed secured claim the reasonable, necessary costs and expenses of preserving or disposing of such property.

(f) Notwithstanding the exclusion of ad valorem tax liens under this section and subject to the requirements of subsection (e), the following may be paid from property of the estate which secures a tax lien, or the proceeds of such property:

(1) Claims for wages, salaries, and commissions that are entitled to priority under section 507(a)(4).

(2) Claims for contributions to an employee benefit plan entitled to priority under section 507(a)(5).

(Pub.L. 95–598, Nov. 6, 1978, 92 Stat. 2607; Pub.L. 98–353, Title III, § 477, July 10, 1984, 98 Stat. 381; Pub.L. 99–554, Title II, § 283(r), Oct. 27, 1986, 100 Stat. 3118; Pub.L. 103–394, Title III, § 304(h)(4), Title V, § 501(d)(23), Oct. 22, 1994, 108 Stat. 4134, 4146; Pub.L. 109–8, Title VII, § 701(a), Apr. 20, 2005, 119 Stat. 124; Pub.L. 111–327, § 2(a)(27), Dec. 22, 2010, 124 Stat. 3560.)

HISTORICAL AND STATUTORY NOTES

References in Text

Section 6323 of the Internal Revenue Code of 1986, referred to in subsec. (d), is classified to section 6323 of Title 26, Internal Revenue Code.

Amendments

2010 Amendments. Subsec. (b)(2). Pub.L. 111–327, § 2(a)(27), struck out "507(a)(1)" and inserted "507(a)(1)(C) or 507(a)(2)", inserted "under each such section" following "such expenses", struck out "chapter 7 of this title" and inserted "this chapter", and struck out "507(a)(2)," and inserted "507(a)(1)(A), 507(a)(1)(B),".

2005 Amendments. Subsec. (b). Pub.L. 109–8, § 701(a)(1), in the matter preceding par. (1), inserted "(other than to the extent that there is a properly perfected unavoidable tax lien arising in connection with an ad valorem tax on real or personal property of the estate)" after "under this title".

Subsec. (b)(2). Pub.L. 109–8, § 701(a)(2), inserted "except that such expenses, other than claims for wages, salaries, or commissions that arise after the date of the filing of the petition, shall be limited to expenses incurred under chapter 7 of this title and shall not include expenses incurred under chapter 11 of this title)" after "507(a)(1)".

Subsec. (e). Pub.L. 109–8, § 701(a)(3), added subsec. (e).

Subsec. (f). Pub.L. 109–8, § 701(a)(3), added subsec. (f).

1994 Amendments. Subsec. (b)(2). Pub.L. 103–394, § 304(h)(4), substituted "507(a)(6), or 507(a)(7)" for "or 507(a)(6)".

Subsec. (d). Pub.L. 103–394, § 501(d)(23), substituted "Internal Revenue Code of 1986" for "Internal Revenue Code of 1954 (26 U.S.C. 6323)".

1986 Amendments. Subsec. (b)(2). Pub.L. 99–554 added reference to section 507(a)(6) of this title.

1984 Amendments. Subsec. (b). Pub.L. 98–353, § 477(a)(1), substituted "a tax" for "taxes" in provisions preceding par. (1).

Subsec. (b)(2). Pub.L. 98–353, § 477(a)(2), substituted "any holder of a claim of a kind specified" for "claims specified", "section 507(a)(1)" for "sections 507(a)(1)", and "or 507(a)(5) of this title" for "and 507(a)(5) of this title".

Subsec. (b)(3). Pub.L. 98–353, § 477(a)(3), substituted "allowed tax claim" for "allowed claim".

Subsec. (c). Pub.L. 98–353, § 477(b), substituted "holder of a claim is entitled" for "creditor is entitled" and "holders" for "creditors" wherever appearing.

Subsec. (d). Pub.L. 98–353, § 477(c), substituted "the priority of which" for "whose priority" and "the same as if such lien were a tax lien" for "the same as a tax lien".

CROSS REFERENCES

Automatic preservation of avoided transfer, see 11 USCA § 551.

Commencement of involuntary cases by transferees of voidable transfers, see 11 USCA § 303.

Disallowance of claims of entity that is transferee of avoidable transfer, see 11 USCA § 502.

Effect of dismissal, see 11 USCA § 349.

Exemptions, see 11 USCA § 522.

Liability of transferee of avoided transfer, see 11 USCA § 550.

Recovery of voidable transfers in investor protection liquidation proceedings, see 15 USCA § 78fff–2.

Voidable transfers in commodity broker liquidation cases, see 11 USCA § 764.

§ 725. Disposition of certain property

After the commencement of a case under this chapter, but before final distribution of property of the estate under section 726 of this title, the trustee, after notice and a hearing, shall dispose of any property in which an entity other than the estate has an interest, such as a lien, and that has not been disposed of under another section of this title.

(Pub.L. 95–598, Nov. 6, 1978, 92 Stat. 2607; Pub.L. 98–353, Title III, § 478, July 10, 1984, 98 Stat. 381.)

HISTORICAL AND STATUTORY NOTES

Amendments

1984 Amendments. Pub.L. 98–353 substituted "distribution of property of the estate" for "distribution".

§ 726. Distribution of property of the estate

(a) Except as provided in section 510 of this title, property of the estate shall be distributed—

(1) first, in payment of claims of the kind specified in, and in the order specified in, section 507 of this title, proof of which is timely filed under section 501 of this title or tardily filed on or before the earlier of—

(A) the date that is 10 days after the mailing to creditors of the summary of the trustee's final report; or

(B) the date on which the trustee commences final distribution under this section;

(2) second, in payment of any allowed unsecured claim, other than a claim of a kind specified in paragraph (1), (3), or (4) of this subsection, proof of which is—

(A) timely filed under section 501(a) of this title;

(B) timely filed under section 501(b) or 501(c) of this title; or

(C) tardily filed under section 501(a) of this title, if—

(i) the creditor that holds such claim did not have notice or actual knowledge of the case in time for timely filing of a proof of such claim under section 501(a) of this title; and

(ii) proof of such claim is filed in time to permit payment of such claim;

(3) third, in payment of any allowed unsecured claim proof of which is tardily filed under section 501(a) of this title, other than a claim of the kind specified in paragraph (2)(C) of this subsection;

(4) fourth, in payment of any allowed claim, whether secured or unsecured, for any fine, penalty, or forfeiture, or for multiple, exemplary, or punitive damages, arising before the earlier of the order for relief or the appointment of a trustee, to the extent that such fine, penalty, forfeiture, or damages are not compensation for actual pecuniary loss suffered by the holder of such claim;

(5) fifth, in payment of interest at the legal rate from the date of the filing of the petition, on any claim paid under paragraph (1), (2), (3), or (4) of this subsection; and

(6) sixth, to the debtor.

(b) Payment on claims of a kind specified in paragraph (1), (2), (3), (4), (5), (6), (7), (8), (9), or (10) of section 507(a) of this title, or in paragraph (2), (3), (4), or (5) of subsection (a) of this section, shall be made pro rata among claims of the kind specified in each such particular paragraph, except that in a case that has been converted to this chapter under section 1112, 1208, or 1307 of this title, a claim allowed under section 503(b) of this title incurred under this chapter after such conversion has priority over a claim allowed under section 503(b) of this title incurred under any other chapter of this title or under this chapter before such conversion and over any expenses of a custodian superseded under section 543 of this title.

(c) Notwithstanding subsections (a) and (b) of this section, if there is property of the kind specified in section 541(a)(2) of this title, or proceeds of such property, in the estate, such property or proceeds shall be segregated from other property of the estate, and such property or proceeds and other property of the estate shall be distributed as follows:

(1) Claims allowed under section 503 of this title shall be paid either from property of the kind specified in section 541(a)(2) of this title, or from other property of the estate, as the interest of justice requires.

(2) Allowed claims, other than claims allowed under section 503 of this title, shall be paid in the order specified in subsection (a) of this section, and, with respect to claims of a kind specified in a particular paragraph of section 507 of this title or subsection (a) of this section, in the following order and manner:

(A) First, community claims against the debtor or the debtor's spouse shall be paid from property of the kind specified in section 541(a)(2) of this title, except to the extent that such property is solely liable for debts of the debtor.

(B) Second, to the extent that community claims against the debtor are not paid under subparagraph (A) of this paragraph, such community claims shall be paid from property of the kind specified in section 541(a)(2) of this title that is solely liable for debts of the debtor.

(C) Third, to the extent that all claims against the debtor including community claims against the debtor are not paid under subparagraph (A) or (B) of this paragraph such claims shall be paid from property of the estate other than property of the kind specified in section 541(a)(2) of this title.

(D) Fourth, to the extent that community claims against the debtor or the debtor's spouse are not paid under subparagraph (A), (B), or (C) of this paragraph, such claims shall be paid from all remaining property of the estate.

(Pub.L. 95–598, Nov. 6, 1978, 92 Stat. 2608; Pub.L. 98–353, Title III, § 479, July 10, 1984, 98 Stat. 381; Pub.L. 99–554, Title II, §§ 257(r), 283(s), Oct. 27, 1986, 100 Stat. 3115, 3118; Pub.L. 103–394, Title II, § 213(b), Title III, § 304(h)(5), Title V, § 501(d)(24), Oct. 22, 1994, 108 Stat. 4126, 4134, 4146; Pub.L. 109–8, Title VII, § 713, Title XII, § 1215, Apr. 20, 2005, 119 Stat. 128, 195; Pub.L. 111–327, § 2(a)(28), Dec. 22, 2010, 124 Stat. 3560.)

HISTORICAL AND STATUTORY NOTES

Amendments

2010 Amendments. Subsec. (b). Pub.L. 111–327, § 2(a)(28), struck out "or (8)" and inserted "(8), (9), or (10)".

2005 Amendments. Subsec. (a)(1). Pub.L. 109–8, § 713, struck out "before the date on which the trustee commences distribution under this section;" and inserted "on or before the earlier of—".

Subsec. (a)(1)(A). Pub.L. 109–8, § 713, added subpar. (A).

Subsec. (a)(1)(B). Pub.L. 109–8, § 713, added subpar. (B).

Subsec. (b). Pub.L. 109–8, § 1215, struck out "1009," preceding "1112, 1208, or 1307 of this title".

1994 Amendments. Subsec. (a)(1). Pub.L. 103–394, § 213(b), added provisions relating to proof timely filed or tardily filed.

Subsec. (b). Pub.L. 103–394, § 304(h)(5), substituted ", (7), or (8)" for "or (7)".

Pub.L. 103–394, § 501(d)(24), substituted "chapter under section 1009, 1112," for "chapter under section 1112".

1986 Amendments. Subsec. (b). Pub.L. 99–554, § 257(r), added reference to section 1208 of this title.

Pub.L. 99–554, § 283(s), added reference to par. (7) of section 507(a) of this title.

1984 Amendments. Subsec. (b). Pub.L. 98–353, § 479(a), substituted "each such particular paragraph" for "a particular paragraph", "a claim allowed under section 503(b) of this title" for "administrative expenses" wherever appearing, and "has priority over" for "have priority over".

Subsec. (c)(1). Pub.L. 98–353, § 479(b)(1), substituted "Claims allowed under section 503 of this title" for "Administrative expenses".

Subsec. (c)(2). Pub.L. 98–353, § 479(b)(2), substituted "Allowed claims, other than claims allowed under section 503 of this title," for "Claims other than for administrative expenses".

CROSS REFERENCES

Customer property, distribution in—

    Commodity broker liquidation cases, see 11 USCA § 766.

    Stockbroker liquidation cases, see 11 USCA § 752.

Distribution in Chapter eleven cases, see 11 USCA § 1143.

Distribution of securities in stockbroker liquidation cases, see 11 USCA § 750.

Election of creditors holding certain claims entitled to distribution to creditors' committee, see 11 USCA § 705.

Election of trustee by creditors holding claims entitled to distribution, see 11 USCA § 702.

Impairment of claims and interests and objection to claims filed untimely, see 11 USCA § 502.

Ownership of copyright, see 17 USCA § 201.

Payment stopped on checks remaining unpaid 90 days after final distribution, see 11 USCA § 347.

Priorities of distribution in investor liquidation proceedings, see 15 USCA § 78fff.

Student Loan Marketing Association of the Robert T. Stafford Student Loan Program deemed person within meaning of this title for purposes of distribution of its property pursuant to this section, see 20 USCA § 1087–2.

§ 727. Discharge

(a) The court shall grant the debtor a discharge, unless—

    (1) the debtor is not an individual;

    (2) the debtor, with intent to hinder, delay, or defraud a creditor or an officer of the estate charged with custody of property under this title, has transferred, removed, destroyed, mutilated, or concealed, or has permitted to be transferred, removed, destroyed, mutilated, or concealed—

        (A) property of the debtor, within one year before the date of the filing of the petition; or

        (B) property of the estate, after the date of the filing of the petition;

    (3) the debtor has concealed, destroyed, mutilated, falsified, or failed to keep or preserve any recorded information, including books, documents, records, and papers, from which the debtor's financial condition or business transactions might be ascertained, unless such act or failure to act was justified under all of the circumstances of the case;

    (4) the debtor knowingly and fraudulently, in or in connection with the case—

        (A) made a false oath or account;

        (B) presented or used a false claim;

(C) gave, offered, received, or attempted to obtain money, property, or advantage, or a promise of money, property, or advantage, for acting or forbearing to act; or

(D) withheld from an officer of the estate entitled to possession under this title, any recorded information, including books, documents, records, and papers, relating to the debtor's property or financial affairs;

(5) the debtor has failed to explain satisfactorily, before determination of denial of discharge under this paragraph, any loss of assets or deficiency of assets to meet the debtor's liabilities;

(6) the debtor has refused, in the case—

(A) to obey any lawful order of the court, other than an order to respond to a material question or to testify;

(B) on the ground of privilege against self-incrimination, to respond to a material question approved by the court or to testify, after the debtor has been granted immunity with respect to the matter concerning which such privilege was invoked; or

(C) on a ground other than the properly invoked privilege against self-incrimination, to respond to a material question approved by the court or to testify;

(7) the debtor has committed any act specified in paragraph (2), (3), (4), (5), or (6) of this subsection, on or within one year before the date of the filing of the petition, or during the case, in connection with another case, under this title or under the Bankruptcy Act, concerning an insider;

(8) the debtor has been granted a discharge under this section, under section 1141 of this title, or under section 14, 371, or 476 of the Bankruptcy Act, in a case commenced within 8 years before the date of the filing of the petition;

(9) the debtor has been granted a discharge under section 1228 or 1328 of this title, or under section 660 or 661 of the Bankruptcy Act, in a case commenced within six years before the date of the filing of the petition, unless payments under the plan in such case totaled at least—

(A) 100 percent of the allowed unsecured claims in such case; or

(B)(i) 70 percent of such claims; and

(ii) the plan was proposed by the debtor in good faith, and was the debtor's best effort;

(10) the court approves a written waiver of discharge executed by the debtor after the order for relief under this chapter;

(11) after filing the petition, the debtor failed to complete an instructional course concerning personal financial management described in section 111, except that this paragraph shall not apply with respect to a debtor who is a person described in section 109(h)(4) or who resides in a district for which the United States trustee (or the bankruptcy administrator, if any) determines that the approved instructional courses are not adequate to service the additional individuals who would otherwise be required to complete such instructional courses under this section (The United States trustee (or the bankruptcy administrator, if any) who makes a determination described in this paragraph shall review such determination not later than 1 year after the date of such determination, and not less frequently than annually thereafter.); or

(12) the court after notice and a hearing held not more than 10 days before the date of the entry of the order granting the discharge finds that there is reasonable cause to believe that—

(A) section 522(q)(1) may be applicable to the debtor; and

(B) there is pending any proceeding in which the debtor may be found guilty of a felony of the kind described in section 522(q)(1)(A) or liable for a debt of the kind described in section 522(q)(1)(B).

(b) Except as provided in section 523 of this title, a discharge under subsection (a) of this section discharges the debtor from all debts that arose before the date of the order for relief under this chapter, and any liability on a claim that is determined under section 502 of this title as if such claim had arisen before the commencement of the case, whether or not a proof of claim based on any such debt or liability is filed under section 501 of this title, and whether or not a claim based on any such debt or liability is allowed under section 502 of this title.

(c)(1) The trustee, a creditor, or the United States trustee may object to the granting of a discharge under subsection (a) of this section.

(2) On request of a party in interest, the court may order the trustee to examine the acts and conduct of the debtor to determine whether a ground exists for denial of discharge.

(d) On request of the trustee, a creditor, or the United States trustee, and after notice and a hearing, the court shall revoke a discharge granted under subsection (a) of this section if—

(1) such discharge was obtained through the fraud of the debtor, and the requesting party did not know of such fraud until after the granting of such discharge;

(2) the debtor acquired property that is property of the estate, or became entitled to acquire property that would be property of the estate, and knowingly and fraudulently failed to report the acquisition of or entitlement to such property, or to deliver or surrender such property to the trustee;

(3) the debtor committed an act specified in subsection (a)(6) of this section; or

(4) the debtor has failed to explain satisfactorily—

(A) a material misstatement in an audit referred to in section 586(f) of title 28; or

(B) a failure to make available for inspection all necessary accounts, papers, documents, financial records, files, and all other papers, things, or property belonging to the debtor that are requested for an audit referred to in section 586(f) of title 28.

(e) The trustee, a creditor, or the United States trustee may request a revocation of a discharge—

(1) under subsection (d)(1) of this section within one year after such discharge is granted; or

(2) under subsection (d)(2) or (d)(3) of this section before the later of—

(A) one year after the granting of such discharge; and

(B) the date the case is closed.

(Pub.L. 95–598, Nov. 6, 1978, 92 Stat. 2609; Pub.L. 98–353, Title III, § 480, July 10, 1984, 98 Stat. 382; Pub.L. 99–554, Title II, §§ 220, 257(s), Oct. 27, 1986, 100 Stat. 3101, 3116; Pub.L. 109–8, Title I, § 106(b), Title III, §§ 312(1), 330(a), Title VI, § 603(d), Apr. 20, 2005, 119 Stat. 38, 86, 101, 123.)

HISTORICAL AND STATUTORY NOTES

References in Text

The Bankruptcy Act, referred to in subsec. (a)(7), is Act July 1, 1898, c. 541, 30 Stat. 544, as amended, which was classified generally to former Title 11, prior to repeal of such Act by Pub.L. 95–598, Title IV, § 401(a), Nov. 6, 1978, 92 Stat. 2692.

Sections 14, 371, and 476 of the Bankruptcy Act, referred to in subsec. (a)(8), are section 14 of Act July 1, 1898, c. 541, 30 Stat. 550, and sections 371 and 476 of Act July 1, 1898, c. 541, as added June 22, 1938, c. 575, § 1, 52 Stat. 912, 924, which were classified to sections 32, 771, and 876 of former Title 11, respectively.

Sections 660 and 661 of the Bankruptcy Act, referred to in subsec. (a)(9), are sections 660 and 661 of Act July 1, 1898, c. 541, as added June 22, 1938, c. 575, § 1, 52 Stat. 935, 936, which were classified, respectively, to sections 1060 and 1061 of former Title 11.

Amendments

2005 Amendments. Subsec. (a)(8). Pub.L. 109–8, § 312(1), struck out "six" and inserted "8".

Subsec. (a)(9). Pub.L. 109–8, § 106(b)(1), struck "or" at the end of the paragraph.

Subsec. (a)(10). Pub.L. 109–8, § 106(b)(2), struck the period and inserted "; or" at the end of the paragraph.

Pub.L. 109–8, § 330(a)(1), struck out "or" at the end of par. (10).

Subsec. (a)(11). Pub.L. 109–8, § 106(b)(3), added par. (11).

Pub.L. 109–8, § 330(a)(2), struck out the period at the end of par. (11) and inserted "; or".

Subsec. (a)(12). Pub.L. 109–8, § 330(a)(3), added par. (12).

Subsec. (d)(2). Pub.L. 109–8, § 603(d)(1), struck "or" at the end of the paragraph.

Subsec. (d)(3). Pub.L. 109–8, § 603(d)(2), struck the period at the end of paragraph (3) and inserted "; or".

Subsec. (d)(4). Pub.L. 109–8, § 603(d)(3), added par. (4).

1986 Amendments. Subsec. (a)(9). Pub.L. 99–554, § 257(s), added reference to section 1228 of this title.

Subsec. (c)(1). Pub.L. 99–554, § 220, substituted "The trustee, a creditor, or the United States trustee may object" for "The trustee or a creditor may object".

Subsec. (d). Pub.L. 99–554, § 220, substituted ", a creditor, or the United States trustee," for "or a creditor," in provisions preceding par. (1).

Subsec. (d)(2). Pub.L. 99–554, § 220, substituted "acquisition of or entitlement to such property" for "acquisition of, or entitlement to, such property".

Subsec. (e). Pub.L. 99–554, § 220, substituted "The trustee, a creditor, or the United States trustee may" for "The trustee or a creditor may" in provisions preceding par. (1).

Subsec. (e)(1). Pub.L. 99–554, § 220, substituted "section within" for "section, within" and "discharge is granted" for "discharge was granted".

Subsec. (e)(2). Pub.L. 99–554, § 220, substituted "section before" for "section, before" in provisions preceding subpar. (A).

Subsec. (e)(2)(A). Pub.L. 99–554, § 220, substituted "discharge; and" for "discharge; or".

1984 Amendments. Subsec. (a)(6)(C). Pub.L. 98–353, § 480(a)(1), substituted "properly" for "property".

Subsec. (a)(7). Pub.L. 98–353, § 480(a)(2), inserted ", under this title or under the Bankruptcy Act," after "another case".

Subsec. (a)(8). Pub.L. 98–353, § 480(a)(3), substituted "371," for "371".

Subsec. (c)(1). Pub.L. 98–353, § 480(b), substituted "to the granting of a discharge" for "to discharge".

Subsec. (e)(2)(A). Pub.L. 98–353, § 480(c), substituted "or" for "and".

CROSS REFERENCES

Cancellation of indebtedness from discharged farm loans, see 12 USCA § 1150.

Concealment of assets; false oaths and claims, see 18 USCA § 152.

Confirmation of plan as affecting discharge in—

    Chapter eleven cases, see 11 USCA § 1141.

    Chapter nine cases, see 11 USCA § 944.

Discharge in Chapter thirteen cases, see 11 USCA § 1328.

Duty of trustee to oppose discharge, see 11 USCA § 704.

Effect of—

    Conversion, see 11 USCA § 348.

    Discharge, see 11 USCA § 524.

Exceptions to discharge, see 11 USCA § 523.

Nondischargeability of capital improvement loans for multifamily housing projects in proceedings under this section, see 12 USCA § 1715z–1a.

[§ 728. Repealed. Pub.L. 109–8, Title VII, § 719(b)(1), Apr. 20, 2005, 119 Stat. 133]

SUBCHAPTER III—STOCKBROKER LIQUIDATION

CROSS REFERENCES

Subchapter applicable only in case under chapter concerning stockholder, see 11 USCA § 103.

§ 741. Definitions for this subchapter

In this subchapter—

  (1) "Commission" means Securities and Exchange Commission;

  (2) "customer" includes—

    (A) entity with whom a person deals as principal or agent and that has a claim against such person on account of a security received, acquired, or held by such person in the ordinary course of such person's business as a stockbroker, from or for the securities account or accounts of such entity—

      (i) for safekeeping;

      (ii) with a view to sale;

      (iii) to cover a consummated sale;

      (iv) pursuant to a purchase;

      (v) as collateral under a security agreement; or

      (vi) for the purpose of effecting registration of transfer; and

    (B) entity that has a claim against a person arising out of—

      (i) a sale or conversion of a security received, acquired, or held as specified in subparagraph (A) of this paragraph; or

      (ii) a deposit of cash, a security, or other property with such person for the purpose of purchasing or selling a security;

  (3) "customer name security" means security—

    (A) held for the account of a customer on the date of the filing of the petition by or on behalf of the debtor;

    (B) registered in such customer's name on such date or in the process of being so registered under instructions from the debtor; and

    (C) not in a form transferable by delivery on such date;

  (4) "customer property" means cash, security, or other property, and proceeds of such cash, security, or property, received, acquired, or held by or for the account of the debtor, from or for the securities account of a customer—

(A) including—

(i) property that was unlawfully converted from and that is the lawful property of the estate;

(ii) a security held as property of the debtor to the extent such security is necessary to meet a net equity claim of a customer based on a security of the same class and series of an issuer;

(iii) resources provided through the use or realization of a customer's debit cash balance or a debit item includible in the Formula for Determination of Reserve Requirement for Brokers and Dealers as promulgated by the Commission under the Securities Exchange Act of 1934; and

(iv) other property of the debtor that any applicable law, rule, or regulation requires to be set aside or held for the benefit of a customer, unless including such property as customer property would not significantly increase customer property; but

(B) not including—

(i) a customer name security delivered to or reclaimed by a customer under section 751 of this title; or

(ii) property to the extent that a customer does not have a claim against the debtor based on such property;

(5) "margin payment" means payment or deposit of cash, a security, or other property, that is commonly known to the securities trade as original margin, initial margin, maintenance margin, or variation margin, or as a mark-to-market payment, or that secures an obligation of a participant in a securities clearing agency;

(6) "net equity" means, with respect to all accounts of a customer that such customer has in the same capacity—

(A)(i) aggregate dollar balance that would remain in such accounts after the liquidation, by sale or purchase, at the time of the filing of the petition, of all securities positions in all such accounts, except any customer name securities of such customer; minus

(ii) any claim of the debtor against such customer in such capacity that would have been owing immediately after such liquidation; plus

(B) any payment by such customer to the trustee, within 60 days after notice under section 342 of this title, of any business related claim of the debtor against such customer in such capacity;

(7) "securities contract"—

(A) means—

(i) a contract for the purchase, sale, or loan of a security, a certificate of deposit, a mortgage loan, any interest in a mortgage loan, a group or index of securities, certificates of deposit, or mortgage loans or interests therein (including an interest therein or based on the value thereof), or option on any of the foregoing, including an option to purchase or sell any such security, certificate of deposit, mortgage loan, interest, group or index, or option, and including any repurchase or reverse repurchase transaction on any such security, certificate of deposit, mortgage loan, interest, group or index, or option (whether or not such repurchase or reverse repurchase transaction is a "repurchase agreement", as defined in section 101);

(ii) any option entered into on a national securities exchange relating to foreign currencies;

(iii) the guarantee (including by novation) by or to any securities clearing agency of a settlement of cash, securities, certificates of deposit, mortgage loans or interests therein, group or index of securities, or mortgage loans or interests therein (including any interest therein or based on the value thereof), or option on any of the foregoing, including an option to purchase or sell any such security, certificate of deposit, mortgage loan, interest, group or index, or option (whether or not such settlement is in connection with any agreement or transaction referred to in clauses (i) through (xi));

(iv) any margin loan;

(v) any extension of credit for the clearance or settlement of securities transactions;

(vi) any loan transaction coupled with a securities collar transaction, any prepaid forward securities transaction, or any total return swap transaction coupled with a securities sale transaction;

(vii) any other agreement or transaction that is similar to an agreement or transaction referred to in this subparagraph;

(viii) any combination of the agreements or transactions referred to in this subparagraph;

(ix) any option to enter into any agreement or transaction referred to in this subparagraph;

(x) a master agreement that provides for an agreement or transaction referred to in clause (i), (ii), (iii), (iv), (v), (vi), (vii), (viii), or (ix), together with all supplements to any such master agreement, without regard to whether the master agreement provides for an agreement or transaction that is not a securities contract under this subparagraph, except that such master agreement shall be considered to be a securities contract under this subparagraph only with respect to each agreement or transaction under such master agreement that is referred to in clause (i), (ii), (iii), (iv), (v), (vi), (vii), (viii), or (ix); or

(xi) any security agreement or arrangement or other credit enhancement related to any agreement or transaction referred to in this subparagraph, including any guarantee or reimbursement obligation by or to a stockbroker, securities clearing agency, financial institution, or financial participant in connection with any agreement or transaction referred to in this subparagraph, but not to exceed the damages in connection with any such agreement or transaction, measured in accordance with section 562; and

(B) does not include any purchase, sale, or repurchase obligation under a participation in a commercial mortgage loan;

(8) "settlement payment" means a preliminary settlement payment, a partial settlement payment, an interim settlement payment, a settlement payment on account, a final settlement payment, or any other similar payment commonly used in the securities trade; and

(9) "SIPC" means Securities Investor Protection Corporation.

(Pub.L. 95–598, Nov. 6, 1978, 92 Stat. 2611; Pub.L. 97–222, § 8, July 27, 1982, 96 Stat. 237; Pub.L. 98–353, Title III, § 482, July 10, 1984, 98 Stat. 382; Pub.L. 103–394, Title V, § 501(d)(25), Oct. 22, 1994, 108 Stat. 4146; Pub.L. 109–8, Title IX, § 907(a)(2), Apr. 20, 2005, 119 Stat. 173; Pub.L. 109–390, § 5(a)(3), Dec. 12, 2006, 120 Stat. 2697)

HISTORICAL AND STATUTORY NOTES

References in Text

The Securities Exchange Act of 1934, referred to in par. (4)(A)(iii), is Act June 6, 1934, c. 404, 48 Stat. 881, as amended, which is classified principally to chapter 2B (section 78a et seq.) of Title 15, Commerce and Trade. For complete classification of this Act to the Code, see section 78l of Title 15 and Tables.

Amendments

2006 Amendments. Par. (7)(A)(i). Pub.L. 109–390, § 5(a)(3)(A)(i), struck out "mortgage loan, or" following "a certificate of deposit, a" and inserted "mortgage loan,".

Pub.L. 109–390, § 5(a)(3)(A)(ii), inserted before the semicolon "(whether or not such repurchase or reverse repurchase transaction is a 'repurchase agreement', as defined in section 101)".

Par. (7)(A)(iii). Pub.L. 109–390, § 5(a)(3)(B)(i), inserted "(including by novation)" after "the guarantee".

Pub.L. 109–390, § 2(a)(3)(B)(ii), inserted before the semicolon "(whether or not such settlement is in connection with any agreement or transaction referred to in clauses (i) through (xi))".

Par. (7)(A)(v). Pub.L. 109–390, § 5(a)(3)(D), (E), redesignated former cl. (v) as (vii) and added a new cl. (v).

Par. (7)(A)(vi). Pub.L. 109–390, § 5(a)(3)(D), (E), redesignated former cl. (vi) as (viii) and added a new cl. (vi).

Par. (7)(A)(vii). Pub.L. 109–390, § 5(a)(3)(D), redesignated former cl. (v) as (vii). Former cl. (vii) redesignated (ix).

Par. (7)(A)(viii). Pub.L. 109–390, § 5(a)(3)(C), struck out "or (vii)" each place it appeared and inserted "(vii), (viii), or (ix)" in cl. (viii) before redesignation as cl. (x).

Pub.L. 109–390, § 5(a)(3)(D), redesignated former cl. (vi) as (viii). Former cl. (viii) redesignated (x).

Par. (7)(A)(ix). Pub.L. 109–390, § 5(a)(3)(D), redesignated former cl. (vii) as (ix). Former cl. (ix) redesignated (xi).

Par. (7)(A)(x). Pub.L. 109–390, § 5(a)(3)(D), redesignated former cl. (viii) as (x).

Par. (7)(A)(xi). Pub.L. 109–390, § 5(a)(3)(D), redesignated former cl. (ix) as (xi).

2005 Amendments. Par. (7). Pub.L. 109–8, § 907(a)(2), rewrote par. (7), which formerly read: " 'securities contract' means contract for the purchase, sale, or loan of a security, including an option for the purchase or sale of a security, certificate of deposit, or group or index of securities (including any interest therein or based on the value thereof), or any option entered into on a national securities exchange relating to foreign currencies, or the guarantee of any settlement of cash or securities by or to a securities clearing agency;".

1994 Amendments. Par. (4)(A)(iii). Pub.L. 103–394, § 501(d)(25), struck out "(15 U.S.C. 78a et seq.)" following "the Securities Exchange Act of 1934".

1984 Amendments. Par. (2)(A). Pub.L. 98–353, § 482(1), substituted "with whom a person deals" for "with whom the debtor deals", "that has a claim" for "that holds a claim", "against such person" for "against the debtor", "held by such person" for "held by the debtor", and "such person's business as a stockbroker," for "business as a stockbroker".

Par. (2)(B). Pub.L. 98–353, § 482(2)(A), (B), substituted "has a claim" for "holds a claim" and "against a person" for "against the debtor" in provisions preceding cl. (i).

Par. (2)(B)(ii). Pub.L. 98–353, § 482(2)(C), substituted "such person" for "the debtor".

Par. (4)(A)(i). Pub.L. 98–353, § 482(3), substituted "from and that is the lawful" for "and that is".

Par. (6)(A)(i). Pub.L. 98–353, § 482(4), substituted "petition," for "petition" and "except any customer name" for "except customer name".

Par. (7). Pub.L. 98–353, § 482(5), added provisions relating to options for the purchase or sale of certificates of deposit, or a group or index of securities (including any interest therein or based on the value thereof), or any option entered into on a national securities exchange relating to foreign currencies.

Par. (8). Pub.L. 98–353, § 482(6), substituted "settlement payment on account, a final settlement payment," for "settlement payment on account,".

1982 Amendments. Par. (4). Pub.L. 97–222, § 8(1), struck out "at any time" following "security, or property," in the provisions preceding subpar. (A), and inserted "of a customer" after "claim" in subpar. (A)(ii).

Par. (5). Pub.L. 97–222, § 8(3), added par. (5). Former par. (5) was redesignated (6).

Par. (6). Pub.L. 97–222, § 8(2), (4), redesignated former par. (5) as (6) and as so redesignated, in the provisions preceding subpar. (A), substituted "all accounts of a customer that such customer has" for "the aggregate of all of a customer's accounts that such customer holds", in subpar. (A)(2) inserted "in such capacity", and in subpar. (B) inserted "in such capacity". Former par. (6) was redesignated (9).

Pars. (7), (8). Pub.L. 97–222, § 8(5), added pars. (7) and (8).

Par. (9). Pub.L. 97–222, § 8(2), (6), redesignated former par. (6) as (9) and in par. (9), as so redesignated substituted "Securities" for "Security".

CROSS REFERENCES

Certain persons acting as agent or custodian for customer in connection with "securities contract" as defined under this section considered a financial institution for purposes of this title, see 11 USCA § 101.

Contractual right to liquidate "securities contract" as defined under this section not stayed, avoided or limited by operation of any provision of this title, see 11 USCA § 555.

"Customer" defined under this section as determining who is a stockbroker for purposes of this title, see 11 USCA § 101.

Definitions applicable in—

Chapter eleven cases, see 11 USCA § 1101.

Chapter nine cases, see 11 USCA § 902.

Commodity broker liquidation cases, see 11 USCA § 761.

Railroad reorganization cases, see 11 USCA § 1162.

Limitation on power of trustee to avoid transfer of "margin payment" and "settlement payment" as defined under this section, see 11 USCA § 546.

Receipt of "margin payment" or "settlement payment" as defined under this section is taking for value for purposes of avoidance of fraudulent transfers and obligations, see 11 USCA § 548.

"Securities contract" as defined under this section as having same meaning for purposes of—

Federal credit union insurance, see 12 USCA § 1787.

Federal deposit insurance corporation, see 12 USCA § 1821.

Setoff of mutual debt in connection with "securities contract", "margin payment" or "settlement payment", not stayed by filing of petitions for voluntary cases, joint cases or involuntary cases or protective decrees in investor protection liquidation proceedings, see 11 USCA § 362.

§ 742. Effect of section 362 of this title in this subchapter

Notwithstanding section 362 of this title, SIPC may file an application for a protective decree under the Securities Investor Protection Act of 1970. The filing of such application stays all proceedings in the case under this title unless and until such application is dismissed. If SIPC completes the liquidation of the debtor, then the court shall dismiss the case.

(Pub.L. 95–598, Nov. 6, 1978, 92 Stat. 2613; Pub.L. 97–222, § 9, July 27, 1982, 96 Stat. 237; Pub.L. 103–394, Title V, § 501(d)(26), Oct. 22, 1994, 108 Stat. 4146.)

HISTORICAL AND STATUTORY NOTES

References in Text

The Securities Investor Protection Act of 1970, referred to in text, is Pub.L. 91–598, Dec. 30, 1970, 84 Stat. 1636, as amended, which is classified generally to chapter 2B–1 (section 78aaa et seq.) of Title 15, Commerce and Trade. For complete classification of this Act to the Code, see section 78aaa of Title 15 and Tables.

Amendments

1994 Amendments. Pub.L. 103–394, § 501(d)(26), struck out "(15 U.S.C. 78aaa et seq.)" following "the Securities Investor Protection Act of 1970".

1982 Amendments. Pub.L. 97–222 substituted "title" for "chapter" following "all proceedings in the case under this".

CROSS REFERENCES

Automatic stay of enforcement of claims against debtor in Chapter 9 cases, see 11 USCA § 922.

Effect of dismissal, see 11 USCA § 349.

Stay of action against codebtor in Chapter 13 cases, see 11 USCA § 1301.

§ 743. Notice

The clerk shall give the notice required by section 342 of this title to SIPC and to the Commission.

(Pub.L. 95–598, Nov. 6, 1978, 92 Stat. 2613; Pub.L. 99–554, Title II, § 283(t), Oct. 27, 1986, 100 Stat. 3118; Pub.L. 103–394, Title V, § 501(d)(27), Oct. 22, 1994, 108 Stat. 4146.)

HISTORICAL AND STATUTORY NOTES

Codifications

Pub.L. 99–554, Title II, § 283(t), Oct. 27, 1986, 100 Stat. 3118, provided that this section be amended by striking out "(d)", which amendment was incapable of execution in view of present language of text.

Amendments

1994 Amendments. Pub.L. 103–394, § 501(d)(27), substituted "section 342" for "section 342(a)".

CROSS REFERENCES

Notice in Chapter nine cases, see 11 USCA § 923.

Notice to the Commodity Futures Trading Commission, see 11 USCA § 762.

§ 744. Executory contracts

Notwithstanding section 365(d) (1) of this title, the trustee shall assume or reject, under section 365 of this title, any executory contract of the debtor for the purchase or sale of a security in the ordinary course of the debtor's business, within a reasonable time after the date of the order for relief, but not to exceed 30 days. If the trustee does not assume such a contract within such time, such contract is rejected.

(Pub.L. 95–598, Nov. 6, 1978, 92 Stat. 2613; Pub.L. 97–222, § 10, July 27, 1982, 96 Stat. 238.)

HISTORICAL AND STATUTORY NOTES

Amendments

1982 Amendments. Pub.L. 97–222 inserted "but" following "relief,".

CROSS REFERENCES

Effect of rejection of lease of railroad line, see 11 USCA § 1169.

§ 745. Treatment of accounts

(a) Accounts held by the debtor for a particular customer in separate capacities shall be treated as accounts of separate customers.

(b) If a stockbroker or a bank holds a customer net equity claim against the debtor that arose out of a transaction for a customer of such stockbroker or bank, each such customer of such stockbroker or bank shall be treated as a separate customer of the debtor.

(c) Each trustee's account specified as such on the debtor's books, and supported by a trust deed filed with, and qualified as such by, the Internal Revenue Service, and under the Internal Revenue Code of 1986, shall be treated as a separate customer account for each beneficiary under such trustee account.

(Pub.L. 95–598, Nov. 6, 1978, 92 Stat. 2613; Pub.L. 97–222, § 11, July 27, 1982, 96 Stat. 238; Pub.L. 98–353, Title III, § 483, July 10, 1984, 98 Stat. 383; Pub.L. 103–394, Title V, § 501(d)(28), Oct. 22, 1994, 108 Stat. 4146.)

HISTORICAL AND STATUTORY NOTES

References in Text

The Internal Revenue Code of 1986, referred to in subsec. (c), is classified to Title 26, Internal Revenue Code.

Amendments

1994 Amendments. Subsec. (d). Pub.L. 103–394, § 501(d)(28), substituted "Internal Revenue Code of 1986" for "Internal Revenue Code of 1954 (26 U.S.C. 1 et seq.)".

1984 Amendments. Subsec. (a). Pub.L. 98–353 inserted "the debtor for" after "by".

1982 Amendments. Subsec. (c). Pub.L. 97–222 substituted "Each" for "A".

CROSS REFERENCES

Stockbroker defined, see 11 USCA § 101.

Treatment of accounts in commodity broker liquidation cases, see 11 USCA § 763.

§ 746. Extent of customer claims

(a) If, after the date of the filing of the petition, an entity enters into a transaction with the debtor, in a manner that would have made such entity a customer had such transaction occurred before the date of the filing of the petition, and such transaction was entered into by such entity in good faith and before the qualification under section 322 of this title of a trustee, such entity shall be deemed a customer, and the date of such transaction shall be deemed to be the date of the filing of the petition for the purpose of determining such entity's net equity.

(b) An entity does not have a claim as a customer to the extent that such entity transferred to the debtor cash or a security that, by contract, agreement, understanding, or operation of law, is—

  (1) part of the capital of the debtor; or

  (2) subordinated to the claims of any or all creditors.

(Pub.L. 95–598, Nov. 6, 1978, 92 Stat. 2613; Pub.L. 97–222, § 12, July 27, 1982, 96 Stat. 238.)

HISTORICAL AND STATUTORY NOTES

Amendments

1982 Amendments. Pub.L. 97–222, § 12(c), substituted "claims" for "claim" in section catchline.

Subsec. (a). Pub.L. 97–222, § 12(a), substituted "enters into" for "effects, with respect to cash or a security,", struck out "with respect to such cash or security" wherever appearing, and substituted "the date of the filing of the petition" for "such date", and "entered into" for "effected".

Subsec. (b). Pub.L. 97–222, § 12(b), substituted "transferred to the debtor" for "has a claim for" in the provisions preceding par. (1), and struck out "is" in par. (2).

CROSS REFERENCES

Allowance of claims or interests, see 11 USCA § 502.

§ 747. Subordination of certain customer claims

Except as provided in section 510 of this title, unless all other customer net equity claims have been paid in full, the trustee may not pay in full or pay in part, directly or indirectly, any net equity claim of a customer that was, on the date the transaction giving rise to such claim occurred—

    (1) an insider;

    (2) a beneficial owner of at least five percent of any class of equity securities of the debtor, other than—

        (A) nonconvertible stock having fixed preferential dividend and liquidation rights; or

        (B) interests of limited partners in a limited partnership;

    (3) a limited partner with a participation of at least five percent in the net assets or net profits of the debtor; or

    (4) an entity that, directly or indirectly, through agreement or otherwise, exercised or had the power to exercise control over the management or policies of the debtor.

(Pub.L. 95–598, Nov. 6, 1978, 92 Stat. 2613; Pub.L. 97–222, § 13, July 27, 1982, 96 Stat. 238.)

HISTORICAL AND STATUTORY NOTES

Amendments

1982 Amendments. Pub.L. 97–222 substituted "the transaction giving rise to such claim occurred" for "such claim arose" in provisions preceding par. (1).

CROSS REFERENCES

Insider defined, see 11 USCA § 101.

§ 748. Reduction of securities to money

As soon as practicable after the date of the order for relief, the trustee shall reduce to money, consistent with good market practice, all securities held as property of the estate, except for customer name securities delivered or reclaimed under section 751 of this title.

(Pub.L. 95–598, Nov. 6, 1978, 92 Stat. 2614.)

CROSS REFERENCES

Reduction of certain securities and property to money in commodity broker liquidation cases, see 11 USCA § 766.

§ 749. Voidable transfers

(a) Except as otherwise provided in this section, any transfer of property that, but for such transfer, would have been customer property, may be avoided by the trustee, and such property shall be treated as customer property, if and to the extent that the trustee avoids such transfer under section 544, 545, 547, 548, or 549 of this title. For the purpose of such sections, the property so transferred shall be deemed to have been property of the debtor and, if such transfer was made to a customer or for a customer's benefit, such customer shall be deemed, for the purposes of this section, to have been a creditor.

(b) Notwithstanding sections 544, 545, 547, 548, and 549 of this title, the trustee may not avoid a transfer made before seven days after the order for relief if such transfer is approved by the Commission by rule or order, either before or after such transfer, and if such transfer is—

(1) a transfer of a securities contract entered into or carried by or through the debtor on behalf of a customer, and of any cash, security, or other property margining or securing such securities contract; or

(2) the liquidation of a securities contract entered into or carried by or through the debtor on behalf of a customer.

(Pub.L. 95–598, Nov. 6, 1978, 92 Stat. 2614; Pub.L. 97–222, § 14, July 27, 1982, 96 Stat. 238; Pub.L. 111–16, § 2(8), May 7, 2009, 123 Stat. 1607.)

HISTORICAL AND STATUTORY NOTES

Amendments

2009 Amendments. Subsec. (b). Pub.L. 111–16, § 2(8), struck out "five days" and inserted "seven days".

1982 Amendments. Pub.L. 97–222 substituted "(a) Except as otherwise provided in this section, any" for "Any", and "but" for "except", inserted "such property", substituted "or 549" for "549, or 724(a)", and added subsec. (b).

CROSS REFERENCES

Voidable transfers in commodity broker liquidation cases, see 11 USCA § 764.

§ 750. Distribution of securities

The trustee may not distribute a security except under section 751 of this title.

(Pub.L. 95–598, Nov. 6, 1978, 92 Stat. 2614.)

CROSS REFERENCES

Distribution in Chapter eleven cases, see 11 USCA § 1143.

Distribution of property of estate, see 11 USCA § 726.

§ 751. Customer name securities

The trustee shall deliver any customer name security to or on behalf of the customer entitled to such security, unless such customer has a negative net equity. With the approval of the trustee, a customer may reclaim a customer name security after payment to the trustee, within such period as the trustee allows, of any claim of the debtor against such customer to the extent that such customer will not have a negative net equity after such payment.

(Pub.L. 95–598, Nov. 6, 1978, 92 Stat. 2614.)

§ 752. Customer property

(a) The trustee shall distribute customer property ratably to customers on the basis and to the extent of such customers' allowed net equity claims and in priority to all other claims, except claims of the kind specified in section 507(a)(2) of this title that are attributable to the administration of such customer property.

(b)(1) The trustee shall distribute customer property in excess of that distributed under subsection (a) of this section in accordance with section 726 of this title.

(2) Except as provided in section 510 of this title, if a customer is not paid the full amount of such customer's allowed net equity claim from customer property, the unpaid portion of such claim is a claim entitled to distribution under section 726 of this title.

(c) Any cash or security remaining after the liquidation of a security interest created under a security agreement made by the debtor, excluding property excluded under section 741(4)(B) of this title, shall be apportioned between the general estate and customer property in the same proportion as the general estate of the debtor and customer property were subject to such security interest.

(Pub.L. 95–598, Nov. 6, 1978, 92 Stat. 2614; Pub.L. 97–222, § 15, July 27, 1982, 96 Stat. 238; Pub.L. 98–353, Title III, § 484, July 10, 1984, 98 Stat. 383; Pub.L. 109–8, Title XV, § 1502(a)(3), Apr. 20, 2005, 119 Stat. 216.)

HISTORICAL AND STATUTORY NOTES

Codifications

Amendment by section 484(a)(3) of Pub.L. 98–353, directing that subsec. (a) of this section be amended by inserting "such" before "customer property", has been executed by inserting "such" before "customer property" following "the administration of" as the probable intent of Congress.

Amendments

2005 Amendments. Subsec. (a). Pub.L. 109–8, § 1502(a)(3), struck out "507(a)(1)" and inserted "507(a)(2)".

1984 Amendments. Subsec. (a). Pub.L. 98–353, § 484(a), substituted "customers' allowed" for "customers allowed", "except claims of the kind" for "except claims", and "the administration of such customer property" for "the administration of customer property". See Codifications note set out under this section.

Subsec. (b)(2). Pub.L. 98–353, § 484(b), substituted "section 726 of this title" for "section 726(a) of this title".

1982 Amendments. Subsec. (c). Pub.L. 97–222 substituted "Any cash or security remaining after the liquidation of a security interest created under a security agreement made by the debtor, excluding property excluded under section 741(4)(B) of this title, shall be apportioned between the general estate and customer property in the same proportion as the general estate of the debtor and customer property were subject to such security interest" for "Subject to section 741(4)(B) of this title, any cash or security remaining after the liquidation of a security interest created under a security agreement made by the debtor shall be apportioned between the general estate and customer property in the proportion that the general property of the debtor and the cash or securities of customers were subject to such security interest".

CROSS REFERENCES

Distribution in Chapter eleven cases, see 11 USCA § 1143.

Distribution of—

    Customer property in commodity broker liquidation cases, see 11 USCA § 766.

    Property of the estate, see 11 USCA § 726.

Election of trustee by creditors holding claims entitled to distribution, see 11 USCA § 702.

Priorities, see 11 USCA § 507.

§ 753. Stockbroker liquidation and forward contract merchants, commodity brokers, stockbrokers, financial institutions, financial participants, securities clearing agencies, swap participants, repo participants, and master netting agreement participants

Notwithstanding any other provision of this title, the exercise of rights by a forward contract merchant, commodity broker, stockbroker, financial institution, financial participant, securities clearing agency, swap participant, repo participant, or master netting agreement participant under this title shall not affect the priority of any unsecured claim it may have after the exercise of such rights.

(Added Pub.L. 109–8, Title IX, § 907(m), Apr. 20, 2005, 119 Stat. 181.)

SUBCHAPTER IV—COMMODITY BROKER LIQUIDATION

CROSS REFERENCES

Certain terms defined under this section as having same meaning for purposes of Commodity Exchange Act, see 7 USCA § 24.

Powers and duties of trustee in investor liquidation proceedings, see 15 USCA § 78fff–1.

Subchapter generally applicable only in case under chapter concerning commodity broker, see 11 USCA § 103.

§ 761. Definitions for this subchapter

In this subchapter—

(1) "Act" means Commodity Exchange Act;

(2) "clearing organization" means a derivatives clearing organization registered under the Act;

(3) "Commission" means Commodity Futures Trading Commission;

(4) "commodity contract" means—

(A) with respect to a futures commission merchant, contract for the purchase or sale of a commodity for future delivery on, or subject to the rules of, a contract market or board of trade;

(B) with respect to a foreign futures commission merchant, foreign future;

(C) with respect to a leverage transaction merchant, leverage transaction;

(D) with respect to a clearing organization, contract for the purchase or sale of a commodity for future delivery on, or subject to the rules of, a contract market or board of trade that is cleared by such clearing organization, or commodity option traded on, or subject to the rules of, a contract market or board of trade that is cleared by such clearing organization;

(E) with respect to a commodity options dealer, commodity option;

(F)(i) any other contract, option, agreement, or transaction that is similar to a contract, option, agreement, or transaction referred to in this paragraph; and

(ii) with respect to a futures commission merchant or a clearing organization, any other contract, option, agreement, or transaction, in each case, that is cleared by a clearing organization;

(G) any combination of the agreements or transactions referred to in this paragraph;

(H) any option to enter into an agreement or transaction referred to in this paragraph;

(I) a master agreement that provides for an agreement or transaction referred to in subparagraph (A), (B), (C), (D), (E), (F), (G), or (H), together with all supplements to such master agreement, without regard to whether the master agreement provides for an agreement or transaction that is not a commodity contract under this paragraph, except that the master agreement shall be considered to be a commodity contract under this paragraph only with respect to each agreement or transaction under the master agreement that is referred to in subparagraph (A), (B), (C), (D), (E), (F), (G), or (H); or

(J) any security agreement or arrangement or other credit enhancement related to any agreement or transaction referred to in this paragraph, including any guarantee or reimbursement obligation by or to a commodity broker or financial participant in connection with any agreement or transaction referred to in this paragraph, but not to exceed the damages in connection with any such agreement or transaction, measured in accordance with section 562;

(5) "commodity option" means agreement or transaction subject to regulation under section 4c(b) of the Act;

(6) "commodity options dealer" means person that extends credit to, or that accepts cash, a security, or other property from, a customer of such person for the purchase or sale of an interest in a commodity option;

(7) "contract market" means a registered entity;

(8) "contract of sale", "commodity", "derivatives clearing organization", "future delivery", "board of trade", "registered entity", and "futures commission merchant" have the meanings assigned to those terms in the Act;

(9) "customer" means—

(A) with respect to a futures commission merchant—

(i) entity for or with whom such futures commission merchant deals and that holds a claim against such futures commission merchant on account of a commodity contract made, received, acquired, or held by or through such futures commission merchant in the ordinary course of such futures commission merchant's business as a futures commission merchant from or for a commodity contract account of such entity; or

(ii) entity that holds a claim against such futures commission merchant arising out of—

(I) the making, liquidation, or change in the value of a commodity contract of a kind specified in clause (i) of this subparagraph;

(II) a deposit or payment of cash, a security, or other property with such futures commission merchant for the purpose of making or margining such a commodity contract; or

(III) the making or taking of delivery on such a commodity contract;

(B) with respect to a foreign futures commission merchant—

(i) entity for or with whom such foreign futures commission merchant deals and that holds a claim against such foreign futures commission merchant on account of a commodity contract made, received, acquired, or held by or through such foreign futures commission merchant in the ordinary course of such foreign futures commission merchant's business as a foreign futures commission merchant from or for the foreign futures account of such entity; or

(ii) entity that holds a claim against such foreign futures commission merchant arising out of—

(I) the making, liquidation, or change in value of a commodity contract of a kind specified in clause (i) of this subparagraph;

(II) a deposit or payment of cash, a security, or other property with such foreign futures commission merchant for the purpose of making or margining such a commodity contract; or

(III) the making or taking of delivery on such a commodity contract;

(C) with respect to a leverage transaction merchant—

(i) entity for or with whom such leverage transaction merchant deals and that holds a claim against such leverage transaction merchant on account of a commodity contract engaged in by or with such leverage transaction merchant in the ordinary course of such leverage transaction merchant's business as a leverage transaction merchant from or for the leverage account of such entity; or

(ii) entity that holds a claim against such leverage transaction merchant arising out of—

(I) the making, liquidation, or change in value of a commodity contract of a kind specified in clause (i) of this subparagraph;

(II) a deposit or payment of cash, a security, or other property with such leverage transaction merchant for the purpose of entering into or margining such a commodity contract; or

(III) the making or taking of delivery on such a commodity contract;

(D) with respect to a clearing organization, clearing member of such clearing organization with whom such clearing organization deals and that holds a claim against such clearing organization on account of cash, a security, or other property received by such clearing organization to margin, guarantee, or secure a commodity contract in such clearing member's proprietary account or customers' account; or

(E) with respect to a commodity options dealer—

(i) entity for or with whom such commodity options dealer deals and that holds a claim on account of a commodity contract made, received, acquired, or held by or through such commodity options dealer in the ordinary course of such commodity options dealer's business as a commodity options dealer from or for the commodity options account of such entity; or

(ii) entity that holds a claim against such commodity options dealer arising out of—

(I) the making of, liquidation of, exercise of, or a change in value of, a commodity contract of a kind specified in clause (i) of this subparagraph; or

(II) a deposit or payment of cash, a security, or other property with such commodity options dealer for the purpose of making, exercising, or margining such a commodity contract;

(10) "customer property" means cash, a security, or other property, or proceeds of such cash, security, or property, received, acquired, or held by or for the account of the debtor, from or for the account of a customer—

(A) including—

(i) property received, acquired, or held to margin, guarantee, secure, purchase, or sell a commodity contract;

(ii) profits or contractual or other rights accruing to a customer as a result of a commodity contract;

(iii) an open commodity contract;

(iv) specifically identifiable customer property;

(v) warehouse receipt or other document held by the debtor evidencing ownership of or title to property to be delivered to fulfill a commodity contract from or for the account of a customer;

(vi) cash, a security, or other property received by the debtor as payment for a commodity to be delivered to fulfill a commodity contract from or for the account of a customer;

(vii) a security held as property of the debtor to the extent such security is necessary to meet a net equity claim based on a security of the same class and series of an issuer;

(viii) property that was unlawfully converted from and that is the lawful property of the estate; and

(ix) other property of the debtor that any applicable law, rule, or regulation requires to be set aside or held for the benefit of a customer, unless including such property as customer property would not significantly increase customer property; but

(B) not including property to the extent that a customer does not have a claim against the debtor based on such property;

(11) "foreign future" means contract for the purchase or sale of a commodity for future delivery on, or subject to the rules of, a board of trade outside the United States;

(12) "foreign futures commission merchant" means entity engaged in soliciting or accepting orders for the purchase or sale of a foreign future or that, in connection with such a solicitation or acceptance, accepts cash, a security, or other property, or extends credit to margin, guarantee, or secure any trade or contract that results from such a solicitation or acceptance;

(13) "leverage transaction" means agreement that is subject to regulation under section 19 of the Commodity Exchange Act, and that is commonly known to the commodities trade as a margin account, margin contract, leverage account, or leverage contract;

(14) "leverage transaction merchant" means person in the business of engaging in leverage transactions;

(15) "margin payment" means payment or deposit of cash, a security, or other property, that is commonly known to the commodities trade as original margin, initial margin, maintenance margin, or variation margin, including mark-to-market payments, settlement payments, variation payments, daily settlement payments, and final settlement payments made as adjustments to settlement prices;

(16) "member property" means customer property received, acquired, or held by or for the account of a debtor that is a clearing organization, from or for the proprietary account of a customer that is a clearing member of the debtor; and

(17) "net equity" means, subject to such rules and regulations as the Commission promulgates under the Act, with respect to the aggregate of all of a customer's accounts that such customer has in the same capacity—

(A) the balance remaining in such customer's accounts immediately after—

(i) all commodity contracts of such customer have been transferred, liquidated, or become identified for delivery; and

(ii) all obligations of such customer in such capacity to the debtor have been offset; plus

(B) the value, as of the date of return under section 766 of this title, of any specifically identifiable customer property actually returned to such customer before the date specified in subparagraph (A) of this paragraph; plus

(C) the value, as of the date of transfer, of—

(i) any commodity contract to which such customer is entitled that is transferred to another person under section 766 of this title; and

(ii) any cash, security, or other property of such customer transferred to such other person under section 766 of this title to margin or secure such transferred commodity contract.

(Pub.L. 95–598, Nov. 6, 1978, 92 Stat. 2615; Pub.L. 97–222, § 16, July 27, 1982, 96 Stat. 238; Pub.L. 98–353, Title III, § 485, July 10, 1984, 98 Stat. 383; Pub.L. 103–394, Title V, § 501(d)(29), Oct. 22, 1994, 108 Stat. 4146; Pub.L. 106–554, § 1(a)(5) [Title I, § 112(c)(6)], Dec. 21, 2000, 114 Stat. 2763, 2763A–395; Pub.L. 109–8, Title IX, § 907(a)(3), Apr. 20, 2005, 119 Stat. 174; Pub.L. 111–203, Title VII, § 724(b), July 21, 2010, 124 Stat. 1684.)

Effective Date of 2010 Amendment

Unless otherwise provided, amendment by subtitle A (Secs. 711–754) of Title VII of Pub.L. 111–203, effective on the later of 360 days after July 21, 2010, or, to the extent a provision of subtitle A requires a rulemaking, not less than 60 days after publication of the final rule or regulation implementing such provision of subtitle A, see 2010 Amendment notes and 2010 Effective and Applicability Provisions notes set out under this section.

HISTORICAL AND STATUTORY NOTES

References in Text

The Commodity Exchange Act or the Act, referred to in pars. (1), (8), and (17), is Act Sept. 21, 1922, c. 369, 42 Stat. 998, as amended, which is classified generally to chapter 1 (section 1 et seq.) of Title 7, Agriculture. For complete classification of this Act to the Code, see section 1 of Title 7 and Tables.

Section 4c of the Commodity Exchange Act, referred to in par. (5), is section 4c of Act Sept. 21, 1922, c. 369, as added June 15, 1936, c. 545, § 5, 49 Stat. 1494, which is classified to section 6c of Title 7, Agriculture.

Section 19 of the Commodity Exchange Act, referred to in par. (13), is section 19 of Act Sept. 21, 1922, c. 369, as added Sept. 30, 1978, Pub.L. 95–405, § 23, 92 Stat. 876, which is classified to section 23 of Title 7.

Amendments

2010 Amendments. Par. (4)(F). Pub.L. 111–203, § 724(b)(1), rewrote subpar. (F), which formerly read: **"(F)** any other agreement or transaction that is similar to an agreement or transaction referred to in this paragraph;".

Par. (9)(A)(i). Pub.L. 111–203, § 724(b)(2), struck out "the commodity futures account" and inserting "a commodity contract account".

2005 Amendments. Par. (4)(D). Pub.L. 109–8, § 907(a)(3)(A), struck out "or" at the end of subpar. (D).

Par. (4)(F) to (J). Pub.L. 109–8, § 907(a)(3)(B), added subpars. (F) to (J).

2000 Amendments. Par. (2). Pub.L. 106–554, § 1(a)(5) [Title I, § 112(c)(6)(A)], revised par. (2). Prior to amendment, par. (2) read as follows:

"(2) 'clearing organization' means organization that clears commodity contracts made on, or subject to the rules of, a contract market or board of trade;".

Par. (7). Pub.L. 106–554, § 1(a)(5) [Title I, § 112(c)(6)(B)], revised par. (7). Prior to amendment, par. (7) read as follows:

"(7) 'contract market' means board of trade designated as a contract market by the Commission under the Act;".

Par. (8). Pub.L. 106–554, § 1(a)(5) [Title I, § 112(c)(6)(C)], revised par. (8). Prior to amendment, par. (8) read as follows:

"(8) 'contract of sale', 'commodity', 'future delivery', 'board of trade', and 'futures commission merchant' have the meanings assigned to those terms in the Act;".

1994 Amendments. Par. (1). Pub.L. 103–394, § 501(d)(29)(A), struck out "(7 U.S.C. 1 et seq.)" following "Commodity Exchange Act".

Par. (5). Pub.L. 103–394, § 501(d)(29)(B), struck out "(7 U.S.C. 6c(b))" following "section 4c(b) of the Act".

Par. (13). Pub.L. 103–394, § 501(d)(29)(C), struck out "(7 U.S.C. 23)" following "the Commodity Exchange Act".

1984 Amendments. Par. (10)(A)(viii). Pub.L. 98–353 substituted "from and that is the lawful property of the estate" for "and that is property of the estate".

1982 Amendments. Par. (2). Pub.L. 97–222, § 16(1), inserted "made" following "commodity contracts".

Par. (4). Pub.L. 97–222, § 16(2), substituted "with respect to" for "if the debtor is" wherever appearing, and substituted "cleared by such clearing organization, or commodity option traded on, or subject to the rules of, a contract market or board of trade that is cleared by such clearing organization" for "cleared by the debtor" in subpar. (D).

Par. (9). Pub.L. 97–222, § 16(3), substituted "with respect to" for "if the debtor is" wherever appearing, in subpar. (A) substituted "such futures commission merchant" for "the debtor" wherever appearing and "such futures commission merchant's" for "the debtor's", in subpar. (B) substituted "such foreign futures commission merchant" for "the debtor" wherever appearing and "such foreign futures commission merchant's" for "the debtor's", in subpar. (C) substituted "such leverage transaction merchant" for "the debtor" wherever appearing and "such leverage transaction merchant's" for "the debtor's", inserted "or" after the semicolon in cl. (i), and substituted "holds" for "hold" in cl. (ii), in subpar. (D) substituted "such clearing organization" for "the debtor" wherever appearing, and in subpar. (E) substituted "such commodity options dealer" for "the debtor" wherever appearing and "such commodity options dealer's" for "the debtor's".

Par. (10). Pub.L. 97–222, § 16(4), struck out "at any time" following "security, or property," in the provisions preceding subpar. (A).

Par. (12). Pub.L. 97–222, § 16(5), inserted a comma after "property" and struck out the comma after "credit".

Par. (13). Pub.L. 97–222, § 16(6), substituted "section 19 of the Commodity Exchange Act (7 U.S.C. 23)" for "section 217 of the Commodity Futures Trading Commission Act of 1974 (7 U.S.C. 15a)".

Par. (14). Pub.L. 97–222, § 16(7), struck out "that is engaged" following "means person".

Par. (15). Pub.L. 97–222, § 16(8), substituted "mark-to-market payments, settlement payments, variation payments, daily settlement payments, and final settlement payments made as adjustments to settlement prices" for "a daily variation settlement payment".

Par. (16). Pub.L. 97–222, § 16(9), struck out "at any time" following "customer property".

Par. (17). Pub.L. 97–222, § 16(10), in the provisions preceding subpar. (A) substituted "has" for "holds", in subpar. (A) inserted "the" after "(A)" in provisions preceding cl. (i), and "in such capacity" after "customer" in cl. (ii).

CROSS REFERENCES

Certain terms having same meanings as under this section, see 7 USCA § 24.

Commodity broker defined, see 11 USCA § 101.

"Commodity contract" defined under this section as having same meaning for purposes of Federal deposit insurance corporation, see 12 USCA § 1821.

Contractual right to liquidate "commodity contract" as defined under this section not stayed, avoided or limited by operation of any provision of this title, see 11 USCA § 556.

Definitions applicable in—

    Chapter eleven cases, see 11 USCA § 1101.

    Chapter nine cases, see 11 USCA § 902.

    Railroad reorganization cases, see 11 USCA § 1162.

    Stockbroker liquidation cases, see 11 USCA § 741.

Limitation on power of trustee to avoid transfer of "margin payment" as defined in this section, see 11 USCA § 546.

Reception of margin payments by commodity brokers or forward contract merchants as taking for value, see 11 USCA § 548.

Setoff of mutual debt in connection with "commodity contracts" or "margin payment" not stayed by filing of petitions for voluntary cases, joint cases or involuntary cases or protective decrees in investor protection liquidation proceedings, see 11 USCA § 362.

§ 762. Notice to the Commission and right to be heard

(a) The clerk shall give the notice required by section 342 of this title to the Commission.

(b) The Commission may raise and may appear and be heard on any issue in a case under this chapter.

(Pub.L. 95–598, Nov. 6, 1978, 92 Stat. 2618.)

CROSS REFERENCES

Notice in—

Chapter nine cases, see 11 USCA § 923.

Stockbroker liquidation proceedings, see 11 USCA § 743.

§ 763. Treatment of accounts

(a) Accounts held by the debtor for a particular customer in separate capacities shall be treated as accounts of separate customers.

(b) A member of a clearing organization shall be deemed to hold such member's proprietary account in a separate capacity from such member's customers' account.

(c) The net equity in a customer's account may not be offset against the net equity in the account of any other customer.

(Pub.L. 95–598, Nov. 6, 1978, 92 Stat. 2618; Pub.L. 98–353, Title III, § 486, July 10, 1984, 98 Stat. 383.)

HISTORICAL AND STATUTORY NOTES

Amendments

1984 Amendments. Subsec. (a). Pub.L. 98–353 substituted "by the debtor for" for "by" and "treated as" for "deemed to be".

CROSS REFERENCES

Treatment of accounts in stockbroker liquidation cases, see 11 USCA § 745.

§ 764. Voidable transfers

(a) Except as otherwise provided in this section, any transfer by the debtor of property that, but for such transfer, would have been customer property, may be avoided by the trustee, and such property shall be treated as customer property, if and to the extent that the trustee avoids such transfer under section 544, 545, 547, 548, 549, or 724(a) of this title. For the purpose of such sections, the property so transferred shall be deemed to have been property of the debtor, and, if such transfer was made to a customer or for a customer's benefit, such customer shall be deemed, for the purposes of this section, to have been a creditor.

(b) Notwithstanding sections 544, 545, 547, 548, 549, and 724(a) of this title, the trustee may not avoid a transfer made before seven days after the order for relief, if such transfer is approved by the Commission by rule or order, either before or after such transfer, and if such transfer is—

(1) a transfer of a commodity contract entered into or carried by or through the debtor on behalf of a customer, and of any cash, securities, or other property margining or securing such commodity contract; or

(2) the liquidation of a commodity contract entered into or carried by or through the debtor on behalf of a customer.

(Pub.L. 95–598, Nov. 6, 1978, 92 Stat. 2618; Pub.L. 97–222, § 17, July 27, 1982, 96 Stat. 240; Pub.L. 98–353, Title III, § 487, July 10, 1984, 98 Stat. 383; Pub.L. 111–16, § 2(9), May 7, 2009, 123 Stat. 1607.)

HISTORICAL AND STATUTORY NOTES

Amendments

2009 Amendments. Subsec. (b). Pub.L. 111–16, § 2(9), struck out "five days" and inserted "seven days".

1984 Amendments. Subsec. (a). Pub.L. 98–353 substituted "any transfer by the debtor" for "any transfer".

1982 Amendments. Subsec. (a). Pub.L. 97–222, § 17(a), substituted "but" for "except", inserted "such property" after "trustee, and", and substituted "shall be" for "is" wherever appearing.

Subsec. (b). Pub.L. 97–222, § 17(b), substituted "order for relief" for "date of the filing of the petition".

Subsec. (c). Pub.L. 97–222, § 17(c), struck out subsec. (c) which had provided that the trustee could not avoid a transfer that was a margin payment to or deposit with a commodity broker or forward contract merchant or was a settlement payment made by a clearing organization and that occurred before the commencement of the case.

CROSS REFERENCES

Voidable transfers in stockbroker liquidation cases, see 11 USCA § 749.

§ 765. Customer instructions

(a) The notice required by section 342 of this title to customers shall instruct each customer—

(1) to file a proof of such customer's claim promptly, and to specify in such claim any specifically identifiable security, property, or commodity contract; and

(2) to instruct the trustee of such customer's desired disposition, including transfer under section 766 of this title or liquidation, of any commodity contract specifically identified to such customer.

(b) The trustee shall comply, to the extent practicable, with any instruction received from a customer regarding such customer's desired disposition of any commodity contract specifically identified to such customer. If the trustee has transferred, under section 766 of this title, such a commodity contract, the trustee shall transmit any such instruction to the commodity broker to whom such commodity contract was so transferred.

(Pub.L. 95–598, Nov. 6, 1978, 92 Stat. 2619; Pub.L. 97–222, § 18, July 27, 1982, 96 Stat. 240; Pub.L. 98–353, Title III, § 488, July 10, 1984, 98 Stat. 383.)

HISTORICAL AND STATUTORY NOTES

Amendments

1984 Amendments. Subsec. (a). Pub.L. 98–353 substituted "notice required by" for "notice under".

1982 Amendments. Subsec. (b). Pub.L. 97–222 substituted "commodity contract" for "commitment".

CROSS REFERENCES

Executory contracts and unexpired leases, see 11 USCA § 365.

§ 766. Treatment of customer property

(a) The trustee shall answer all margin calls with respect to a specifically identifiable commodity contract of a customer until such time as the trustee returns or transfers such commodity contract, but the trustee may not make a margin payment that has the effect of a distribution to such customer of more than that to which such customer is entitled under subsection (h) or (i) of this section.

(b) The trustee shall prevent any open commodity contract from remaining open after the last day of trading in such commodity contract, or into the first day on which notice of intent to deliver on such commodity contract may be tendered, whichever occurs first. With respect to any commodity contract that has remained open after the last day of trading in such commodity contract or with respect to which delivery must be made or accepted under the rules of the contract market on which such commodity contract was made, the trustee may operate the business of the debtor for the purpose of—

(1) accepting or making tender of notice of intent to deliver the physical commodity underlying such commodity contract;

(2) facilitating delivery of such commodity; or

(3) disposing of such commodity if a party to such commodity contract defaults.

(c) The trustee shall return promptly to a customer any specifically identifiable security, property, or commodity contract to which such customer is entitled, or shall transfer, on such customer's behalf, such security, property, or commodity contract to a commodity broker that is not a debtor under this title, subject to such rules or regulations as the Commission may prescribe, to the extent that the value of such security, property, or commodity contract does not exceed the amount to which such customer would be entitled under subsection (h) or (i) of this section if such security, property, or commodity contract were not returned or transferred under this subsection.

(d) If the value of a specifically identifiable security, property, or commodity contract exceeds the amount to which the customer of the debtor is entitled under subsection (h) or (i) of this section, then such customer to whom such security, property, or commodity contract is specifically identified may deposit cash with the trustee equal to the difference between the value of such security, property, or commodity contract and such amount, and the trustee then shall—

(1) return promptly such security, property, or commodity contract to such customer; or

(2) transfer, on such customer's behalf, such security, property, or commodity contract to a commodity broker that is not a debtor under this title, subject to such rules or regulations as the Commission may prescribe.

(e) Subject to subsection (b) of this section, the trustee shall liquidate any commodity contract that—

(1) is identified to a particular customer and with respect to which such customer has not timely instructed the trustee as to the desired disposition of such commodity contract;

(2) cannot be transferred under subsection (c) of this section; or

(3) cannot be identified to a particular customer.

(f) As soon as practicable after the commencement of the case, the trustee shall reduce to money, consistent with good market practice, all securities and other property, other than commodity contracts, held as property of the estate, except for specifically identifiable securities or property distributable under subsection (h) or (i) of this section.

(g) The trustee may not distribute a security or other property except under subsection (h) or (i) of this section.

(h) Except as provided in subsection (b) of this section, the trustee shall distribute customer property ratably to customers on the basis and to the extent of such customers' allowed net equity claims, and in priority to all other claims, except claims of a kind specified in section 507(a)(2) of this title that are attributable to the administration of customer property. Such distribution shall be in the form of—

(1) cash;

(2) the return or transfer, under subsection (c) or (d) of this section, of specifically identifiable customer securities, property, or commodity contracts; or

(3) payment of margin calls under subsection (a) of this section.

Notwithstanding any other provision of this subsection, a customer net equity claim based on a proprietary account, as defined by Commission rule, regulation, or order, may not be paid either in whole or in part, directly or indirectly, out of customer property unless all other customer net equity claims have been paid in full.

(i) If the debtor is a clearing organization, the trustee shall distribute—

(1) customer property, other than member property, ratably to customers on the basis and to the extent of such customers' allowed net equity claims based on such customers' accounts other than proprietary accounts, and in priority to all other claims, except claims of a kind specified in section 507(a)(2) of this title that are attributable to the administration of such customer property; and

(2) member property ratably to customers on the basis and to the extent of such customers' allowed net equity claims based on such customers' proprietary accounts, and in priority to all other claims, except claims of a kind specified in section 507(a)(2) of this title that are attributable to the administration of member property or customer property.

(j)(1) The trustee shall distribute customer property in excess of that distributed under subsection (h) or (i) of this section in accordance with section 726 of this title.

(2) Except as provided in section 510 of this title, if a customer is not paid the full amount of such customer's allowed net equity claim from customer property, the unpaid portion of such claim is a claim entitled to distribution under section 726 of this title.

(Pub.L. 95–598, Nov. 6, 1978, 92 Stat. 2619; Pub.L. 97–222, § 19, July 27, 1982, 96 Stat. 240; Pub.L. 98–353, Title III, § 489, July 10, 1984, 98 Stat. 383; Pub.L. 109–8, Title XV, § 1502(a)(4), Apr. 20, 2005, 119 Stat. 216.)

HISTORICAL AND STATUTORY NOTES

Amendments

2005 Amendments. Subsec. (h). Pub.L. 109–8, § 1502(a)(4)(A), struck out "507(a)(1)" and inserted "507(a)(2)".

Subsec. (i). Pub.L. 109–8, § 1502(a)(4)(B), struck out "507(a)(1)" each place it appeared and inserted "507(a)(2)".

1984 Amendments. Subsec. (j)(2). Pub.L. 98–353 substituted "section 726 of this title" for "section 726(a) of this title".

1982 Amendments. Subsec. (a). Pub.L. 97–222, § 19(a), inserted "to such customer" after "distribution".

Subsec. (b). Pub.L. 97–222, § 19(b), struck out "that is being actively traded as of the date of the filing of the petition" after "any open commodity contract" and inserted "the" after "rules of".

Subsec. (d). Pub.L. 97–222, § 19(c), substituted "the amount to which the customer of the debtor is entitled under subsection (h) or (i) of this section, then such" for "such amount, then the" and "the trustee then shall" for "the trustee shall".

Subsec. (h). Pub.L. 97–222, § 19(d), added provision that notwithstanding any other provision of this subsection, a customer net equity claim based on a proprietary account, as defined by Commission rule, regulation, or order, may not be paid either in whole or in part, directly or indirectly, out of customer property unless all other customer net equity claims have been paid in full.

CROSS REFERENCES

Distribution in Chapter eleven cases, see 11 USCA § 1143.

Distribution of—

Customer property in stockbroker liquidation cases, see 11 USCA § 752.

Property of estate, see 11 USCA § 726.

Election of trustee by creditors holding claims entitled to distribution, see 11 USCA § 702.

Executory contracts and unexpired leases, see 11 USCA § 365.

Provisions relating to transferability of customer property and commodity contracts, see 7 USCA § 24.

§ 767. Commodity broker liquidation and forward contract merchants, commodity brokers, stockbrokers, financial institutions, financial participants, securities clearing agencies, swap participants, repo participants, and master netting agreement participants

Notwithstanding any other provision of this title, the exercise of rights by a forward contract merchant, commodity broker, stockbroker, financial institution, financial participant, securities clearing agency, swap participant, repo participant, or master netting agreement participant under this title shall not affect the priority of any unsecured claim it may have after the exercise of such rights.

(Added Pub.L. 109–8, Title IX, § 907(l), Apr. 20, 2005, 119 Stat. 181.)

SUBCHAPTER V—CLEARING BANK LIQUIDATION

HISTORICAL AND STATUTORY NOTES

Amendments

2000 Amendments. Pub.L. 106–554, § 1(a)(5) [Title I, § 112(c)(5)(B)], Dec. 21, 2000, 114 Stat. 2763, 2763A–394, added subchapter heading.

§ 781. Definitions

For purposes of this subchapter, the following definitions shall apply:

(1) **Board.**—The term "Board" means the Board of Governors of the Federal Reserve System.

(2) **Depository institution.**—The term "depository institution" has the same meaning as in section 3 of the Federal Deposit Insurance Act.

(3) **Clearing bank.**—The term "clearing bank" means an uninsured State member bank, or a corporation organized under section 25A of the Federal Reserve Act, which operates, or operates as, a multilateral clearing organization pursuant to section 409 of the Federal Deposit Insurance Corporation Improvement Act of 1991.

(Added Pub.L. 106–554, § 1(a)(5) [Title I, § 112(c)(5)(B)], Dec. 21, 2000, 114 Stat. 2763, 2763A–394.)

HISTORICAL AND STATUTORY NOTES

References in Text

Section 3 of the Federal Deposit Insurance Act, referred to in par. (2), is Act Sept. 21, 1950, c. 967, § 2[3], 64 Stat. 873, which is classified to 12 U.S.C.A. § 1813.

Section 25A of the Federal Reserve Act, referred to in par. (3), is Dec. 23, 1913, c. 6, § 25A, formerly § 25(a), as added Dec. 24, 1919, c. 18, 41 Stat. 378, as amended, which is classified to subchapter II of chapter 6 of Title 12, 12 U.S.C.A. § 611 et seq.

Section 409 of the Federal Deposit Insurance Corporation Improvement Act of 1991, referred to in par. (3), is Pub.L. 102–242, Title IV, § 409, as added by Pub.L. 106–554, § 1(a)(5) [Title I, § 112(a)(3)], Dec. 21, 2000, 114 Stat. 2763, 2763A–392, which is classified as 12 U.S.C.A. § 4422.

§ 782. Selection of trustee

(a) **In general.**—

(1) **Appointment.**—Notwithstanding any other provision of this title, the conservator or receiver who files the petition shall be the trustee under this chapter, unless the Board designates an alternative trustee.

(2) **Successor.**—The Board may designate a successor trustee if required.

(b) **Authority of trustee.**—Whenever the Board appoints or designates a trustee, chapter 3 and sections 704 and 705 of this title shall apply to the Board in the same way and to the same extent that they apply to a United States trustee.

(Added Pub.L. 106–554, § 1(a)(5) [Title I, § 112(c)(5)(B)], Dec. 21, 2000, 114 Stat. 2763, 2763A–394.)

§ 783. Additional powers of trustee

(a) **Distribution of property not of the estate.**—The trustee under this subchapter has power to distribute property not of the estate, including distributions to customers that are mandated by subchapters III and IV of this chapter.

(b) **Disposition of institution.**—The trustee under this subchapter may, after notice and a hearing—

(1) sell the clearing bank to a depository institution or consortium of depository institutions (which consortium may agree on the allocation of the clearing bank among the consortium);

(2) merge the clearing bank with a depository institution;

(3) transfer contracts to the same extent as could a receiver for a depository institution under paragraphs (9) and (10) of section 11(e) of the Federal Deposit Insurance Act;

(4) transfer assets or liabilities to a depository institution; and

(5) transfer assets and liabilities to a bridge depository institution as provided in paragraphs (1), (3)(A), (5), and (6) of section 11(n) of the Federal Deposit Insurance Act, paragraphs (9) through (13) of such section, and subparagraphs (A) through (H) and subparagraph (K) of paragraph (4) of such section 11(n), except that—

(A) the bridge depository institution to which such assets or liabilities are transferred shall be treated as a clearing bank for the purpose of this subsection; and

(B) any references in any such provision of law to the Federal Deposit Insurance Corporation shall be construed to be references to the appointing agency and that references to deposit insurance shall be omitted.

(c) **Certain transfers included.**—Any reference in this section to transfers of liabilities includes a ratable transfer of liabilities within a priority class.

(Added Pub.L. 106–554, § 1(a)(5) [Title I, § 112(c)(5)(B)], Dec. 21, 2000, 114 Stat. 2763, 2763A–395; amended Pub.L. 110–289, Div. A, Title VI, § 1604(b)(3), July 30, 2008, 122 Stat. 2829.)

HISTORICAL AND STATUTORY NOTES

References in Text

Subchapters III and IV of this chapter, referred to in subsec. (a), are 11 U.S.C.A. §§ 741 et seq. and 761 et seq.

Paragraphs (9) and (10) of section 11(e) of the Federal Deposit Insurance Act, referred to in subsec. (b)(3), are classified to 12 U.S.C.A. § 1821(e)(9), (10).

Paragraphs (1), (3)(A), (5), and (6) of section 11(n) of the Federal Deposit Insurance Act, paragraphs (9) through (13) of such section, and subparagraphs (A) through (H) and subparagraph (K) of paragraph

(4) of such section 11(n), referred to in subsec. (b)(5), are classified to 12 U.S.C.A. § 1821(n)(1), (3)(A), (5), (6), and (4)(A) to (K).

Codifications

Amendment by Pub.L. 110–289, § 1604(b)(3), which directed striking out "bridge bank" and inserting "bridge depository institution", was executed to both locations where the term appeared in subsec. (b)(5), as the probable intent of Congress. See 2008 Amendments note set out under this section.

Amendments

2008 Amendments. Subsec. (b)(5). Pub.L. 110–289, Div. A, Title VI, § 1604(b)(3), struck out "bridge bank" and inserted "bridge depository institution" in two locations. See Codifications note set out under this section.

§ 784. Right to be heard

The Board or a Federal reserve bank (in the case of a clearing bank that is a member of that bank) may raise and may appear and be heard on any issue in a case under this subchapter.

(Added Pub.L. 106–554, § 1(a)(5) [Title I, § 112(c)(5)(B)], Dec. 21, 2000, 114 Stat. 2763, 2763A–395.)

CHAPTER 9—ADJUSTMENT OF DEBTS OF A MUNICIPALITY

SUBCHAPTER I—GENERAL PROVISIONS

Sec.
901. Applicability of other sections of this title.
902. Definitions for this chapter.
903. Reservation of State power to control municipalities.
904. Limitation on jurisdiction and powers of court.

SUBCHAPTER II—ADMINISTRATION

921. Petition and proceedings relating to petition.
922. Automatic stay of enforcement of claims against the debtor.
923. Notice.
924. List of creditors.
925. Effect of list of claims.
926. Avoiding powers.
927. Limitation on recourse.
928. Post petition effect of security interest.
929. Municipal leases.
930. Dismissal.

SUBCHAPTER III—THE PLAN

941. Filing of plan.
942. Modification of plan.
943. Confirmation.
944. Effect of confirmation.
945. Continuing jurisdiction and closing of the case.
946. Effect of exchange of securities before the date of the filing of the petition.

HISTORICAL AND STATUTORY NOTES

Amendments

1988 Amendments. Pub.L. 100–597, § 11, Nov. 3, 1988, 102 Stat. 3030, added items 927 to 929 and redesignated as 930 former item 927.

SUBCHAPTER I—GENERAL PROVISIONS

CROSS REFERENCES

Allowance of administrative expenses of substantial contributors in cases under this chapter, see 11 USCA § 503.

Chapter one of this title and this chapter solely applicable in cases under this chapter except as provided in § 901 of this title, see 11 USCA § 103.

Claims arising from rejection of executory contracts or unexpired leases under this chapter's plans, see 11 USCA § 502.

Definitions applicable in this title, see 11 USCA § 101.

Duration of automatic stay, see 11 USCA § 362.

Entities which may be debtors under this chapter, see 11 USCA § 109.

Executory contracts and unexpired leases, see 11 USCA § 365.

Filing fees, see 28 USCA § 1930.

Unclaimed property, see 11 USCA § 347.

§ 901. Applicability of other sections of this title

(a) Sections 301, 333, 344, 347(b), 349, 350(b) 351,,[1] 361, 362, 364(c), 364(d), 364(e), 364(f), 365, 366, 501, 502, 503, 504, 506, 507(a)(2), 509, 510, 524(a)(1), 524(a)(2), 544, 545, 546, 547, 548, 549(a), 549(c), 549(d), 550, 551, 552, 553, 555, 556, 557, 559, 560, 561, 562, 1102, 1103, 1109, 1111(b), 1122, 1123(a)(1), 1123(a)(2), 1123(a)(3), 1123(a)(4), 1123(a)(5), 1123(b), 1123(d), 1124, 1125, 1126(a), 1126(b), 1126(c), 1126(e), 1126(f), 1126(g), 1127(d), 1128, 1129(a)(2), 1129(a)(3), 1129(a)(6), 1129(a)(8), 1129(a)(10), 1129(b)(1), 1129(b)(2)(A), 1129(b)(2)(B), 1142(b), 1143, 1144, and 1145 of this title apply in a case under this chapter.

(b) A term used in a section of this title made applicable in a case under this chapter by subsection (a) of this section or section 103(e) of this title has the meaning defined for such term for the purpose of such applicable section, unless such term is otherwise defined in section 902 of this title.

(c) A section made applicable in a case under this chapter by subsection (a) of this section that is operative if the business of the debtor is authorized to be operated is operative in a case under this chapter.

(Pub.L. 95–598, Nov. 6, 1978, 92 Stat. 2621; Pub.L. 98–353, Title III, §§ 353, 490, July 10, 1984, 98 Stat. 361, 383; Pub.L. 100–597, § 3, Nov. 3, 1988, 102 Stat. 3028; Pub.L. 109–8, Title V, § 502, Title XII, § 1216, Title XV, § 1502(a)(5), Apr. 20, 2005, 119 Stat. 118, 195, 216; Pub.L. 111–327, § 2(a)(29), Dec. 22, 2010, 124 Stat. 3560.)

HISTORICAL AND STATUTORY NOTES

References in Text

Section 103(e) of this title, referred to in subsec. (b), was redesignated subsec. (f) and a new subsec. (e) was added by Pub.L. 106–554, § 1(a)(5) [Title I, § 112(c)(5)(A)], Dec. 21, 2000, 114 Stat. 2763, 2763A–394.

Amendments

2010 Amendments. Subsec. (a). Pub.L. 111–327, § 2(a)(29), inserted "333," following "301,", and inserted "351," following "350(b)".

2005 Amendments. Subsec. (a). Pub.L. 109–8, § 502, inserted "555, 556," after "553," and inserted "559, 560, 561, 562," after "557,".

Pub.L.109–8, § 1216, inserted "1123(d)," after "1123(b),".

Pub.L. 109–8, § 1502(a)(5), struck out "507(a)(1)" and inserted "507(a)(2)".

1988 Amendments. Subsec. (a). Pub.L. 100–597 inserted reference to section "1129(a)(6)," after "1129(a)(3),".

1984 Amendments. Subsec. (a). Pub.L. 98–353, § 353, added "557," after "553".

Pub.L. 98–353, § 490, substituted "1111(b)," for "1111(b)" preceding "1122".

CROSS REFERENCES

Chapters one and nine of this title solely applicable in cases under Chapter nine except as provided in this section, see 11 USCA § 103.

Confirmation in Chapter nine cases upon compliance with provisions of this title made applicable by this section, see 11 USCA § 943.

§ 902. Definitions for this chapter

In this chapter—

(1) "property of the estate", when used in a section that is made applicable in a case under this chapter by section 103(e) or 901 of this title, means property of the debtor;

---

[1] So in original. The second comma should probably follow "350(b)".

(2) "special revenues" means—

(A) receipts derived from the ownership, operation, or disposition of projects or systems of the debtor that are primarily used or intended to be used primarily to provide transportation, utility, or other services, including the proceeds of borrowings to finance the projects or systems;

(B) special excise taxes imposed on particular activities or transactions;

(C) incremental tax receipts from the benefited area in the case of tax-increment financing;

(D) other revenues or receipts derived from particular functions of the debtor, whether or not the debtor has other functions; or

(E) taxes specifically levied to finance one or more projects or systems, excluding receipts from general property, sales, or income taxes (other than tax-increment financing) levied to finance the general purposes of the debtor;

(3) "special tax payer" means record owner or holder of legal or equitable title to real property against which a special assessment or special tax has been levied the proceeds of which are the sole source of payment of an obligation issued by the debtor to defray the cost of an improvement relating to such real property;

(4) "special tax payer affected by the plan" means special tax payer with respect to whose real property the plan proposes to increase the proportion of special assessments or special taxes referred to in paragraph (2) of this section assessed against such real property; and

(5) "trustee", when used in a section that is made applicable in a case under this chapter by section 103(e) or 901 of this title, means debtor, except as provided in section 926 of this title.

(Pub.L. 95–598, Nov. 6, 1978, 92 Stat. 2622; Pub.L. 98–353, Title III, § 491, July 10, 1984, 98 Stat. 383; Pub.L. 100–597, § 4, Nov. 3, 1988, 102 Stat. 3028.)

HISTORICAL AND STATUTORY NOTES

References in Text

Section 103(e) of this title, referred to in pars. (1) and (5), was redesignated section 103(f) and a new section 103(e) was added by Pub.L. 106–554, § 1(a)(5) [Title I, § 112(c)(5)(A)], Dec. 21, 2000, 114 Stat. 2763, 2763A–394.

Amendments

1988 Amendments. Par. (2). Pub.L. 100–597, § 4(1), (2), redesignated former par. (2) as (3) and added par. (2).

Pars. (3) to (5). Pub.L. 100–597, § 4(1), redesignated former pars. (2) to (4) as (3) to (5), respectively.

1984 Amendments. Par. (2). Pub.L. 98–353 substituted "legal or equitable title to real property against which a special assessment or special tax has been levied" for "title, legal or equitable, to real property against which has been levied a special assessment or special tax".

CROSS REFERENCES

Definitions applicable in—

Cases under this title, see 11 USCA § 101.

Chapter eleven cases, see 11 USCA § 1101.

Commodity broker liquidation cases, see 11 USCA § 761.

Railroad reorganization cases, see 11 USCA § 1162.

Stockbroker liquidation cases, see 11 USCA § 741.

§ 903. Reservation of State power to control municipalities

This chapter does not limit or impair the power of a State to control, by legislation or otherwise, a municipality of or in such State in the exercise of the political or governmental powers of such municipality, including expenditures for such exercise, but—

   (1) a State law prescribing a method of composition of indebtedness of such municipality may not bind any creditor that does not consent to such composition; and

   (2) a judgment entered under such a law may not bind a creditor that does not consent to such composition.

(Pub.L. 95–598, Nov. 6, 1978, 92 Stat. 2622; Pub.L. 98–353, Title III, § 492, July 10, 1984, 98 Stat. 383.)

HISTORICAL AND STATUTORY NOTES

Amendments

1984 Amendments. Par. (2). Pub.L. 98–353 struck out "to" preceding "that does not consent".

CROSS REFERENCES

Authorization by state to be debtor under this chapter, see 11 USCA § 109.

§ 904. Limitation on jurisdiction and powers of court

Notwithstanding any power of the court, unless the debtor consents or the plan so provides, the court may not, by any stay, order, or decree, in the case or otherwise, interfere with—

   (1) any of the political or governmental powers of the debtor;

   (2) any of the property or revenues of the debtor; or

   (3) the debtor's use or enjoyment of any income-producing property.

(Pub.L. 95–598, Nov. 6, 1978, 92 Stat. 2622.)

CROSS REFERENCES

Power of court, see 11 USCA § 105.

SUBCHAPTER II—ADMINISTRATION

HISTORICAL AND STATUTORY NOTES

Amendments

1984 Amendments. Pub.L. 98–353, Title III, § 493, July 10, 1984, 98 Stat. 383, corrected a typographical error in the original by substituting "SUBCHAPTER" for "SUBCHAPER" in the subchapter heading.

§ 921. Petition and proceedings relating to petition

(a) Notwithstanding sections 109(d) and 301 of this title, a case under this chapter concerning an unincorporated tax or special assessment district that does not have such district's own officials is commenced by the filing under section 301 of this title of a petition under this chapter by such district's governing authority or the board or body having authority to levy taxes or assessments to meet the obligations of such district.

(b) The chief judge of the court of appeals for the circuit embracing the district in which the case is commenced shall designate the bankruptcy judge to conduct the case.

(c) After any objection to the petition, the court, after notice and a hearing, may dismiss the petition if the debtor did not file the petition in good faith or if the petition does not meet the requirements of this title.

(d) If the petition is not dismissed under subsection (c) of this section, the court shall order relief under this chapter notwithstanding section 301(b).

(e) The court may not, on account of an appeal from an order for relief, delay any proceeding under this chapter in the case in which the appeal is being taken; nor shall any court order a stay of such proceeding pending such appeal. The reversal on appeal of a finding of jurisdiction does not affect the validity of any debt incurred that is authorized by the court under section 364(c) or 364(d) of this title.

(Pub.L. 95–598, Nov. 6, 1978, 92 Stat. 2622; Pub.L. 98–353, Title III, § 494, July 10, 1984, 98 Stat. 383; Pub.L. 109–8, Title V, § 501(a), Apr. 20, 2005, 119 Stat. 118.)

HISTORICAL AND STATUTORY NOTES

Amendments

2005 Amendments. Subsec. (d). Pub.L. 109–8, § 501(a), inserted "notwithstanding section 301(b)" before the period at the end.

1984 Amendments. Subsec. (a). Pub.L. 98–353, § 494(c), substituted "109(d)" for "109(c)".

Subsec. (c). Pub.L. 98–353, § 494(a)(1), substituted "any" for "an".

Pub.L. 98–353, § 494(a)(2), substituted "petition if the debtor did not file the petition in good faith" for "petition, if the debtor did not file the petition in good faith,".

Subsec. (d). Pub.L. 98–353, § 494(b), (d), redesignated former subsec. (e) as (d), and in subsec. (d), as so redesignated, substituted a reference to "subsection (c)" for a reference to "subsection (d)". Prior to such redesignation and amendment, no former subsec. (d) had been enacted.

Subsec. (e). Pub.L. 98–353, § 494(b), redesignated former subsec. (f) as (e). Former subsec. (e) was redesignated as (d).

Subsec. (f). Pub.L. 98–353, § 494(b), redesignated former subsec. (f) as (e).

§ 922. Automatic stay of enforcement of claims against the debtor

(a) A petition filed under this chapter operates as a stay, in addition to the stay provided by section 362 of this title, applicable to all entities, of—

> **(1)** the commencement or continuation, including the issuance or employment of process, of a judicial, administrative, or other action or proceeding against an officer or inhabitant of the debtor that seeks to enforce a claim against the debtor; and
>
> **(2)** the enforcement of a lien on or arising out of taxes or assessments owed to the debtor.

(b) Subsections (c), (d), (e), (f), and (g) of section 362 of this title apply to a stay under subsection (a) of this section the same as such subsections apply to a stay under section 362(a) of this title.

(c) If the debtor provides, under section 362, 364, or 922 of this title, adequate protection of the interest of the holder of a claim secured by a lien on property of the debtor and if, notwithstanding such protection such creditor has a claim arising from the stay of action against such property under section 362 or 922 of this title or from the granting of a lien under section 364(d) of this title, then such claim shall be allowable as an administrative expense under section 503(b) of this title.

(d) Notwithstanding section 362 of this title and subsection (a) of this section, a petition filed under this chapter does not operate as a stay of application of pledged special revenues in a manner consistent with section 927 of this title to payment of indebtedness secured by such revenues.

(Pub.L. 95–598, Nov. 6, 1978, 92 Stat. 2623; Pub.L. 98–353, Title III, § 495, July 10, 1984, 98 Stat. 384; Pub.L. 100–597, § 5, Nov. 3, 1988, 102 Stat. 3029.)

HISTORICAL AND STATUTORY NOTES

Amendments

1988 Amendments. Subsecs. (c), (d). Pub.L. 100–597 added subsecs. (c) and (d).

1984 Amendments. Subsec. (a)(1). Pub.L. 98–353, § 495(1), substituted "a judicial" for "judicial".

Pub.L. 98–353, § 495(2), substituted "action or proceeding" for "proceeding".

CROSS REFERENCES

Effect of § 362 of this title in stockbroker liquidation cases, see 11 USCA § 742.

Extension of time generally, see 11 USCA § 108.

Stay of action against codebtor in—
> Chapter thirteen cases, see 11 USCA § 1301.
> Chapter twelve cases, see 11 USCA § 1201.

§ 923. Notice

There shall be given notice of the commencement of a case under this chapter, notice of an order for relief under this chapter, and notice of the dismissal of a case under this chapter. Such notice shall also be published at least once a week for three successive weeks in at least one newspaper of general circulation published within the district in which the case is commenced, and in such other newspaper having a general circulation among bond dealers and bondholders as the court designates.

(Pub.L. 95–598, Nov. 6, 1978, 92 Stat. 2623.)

CROSS REFERENCES

Notice in—
> Commodity broker liquidation cases, see 11 USCA § 762.
> Stockbroker liquidation cases, see 11 USCA § 743.

Notice of order for relief, see 11 USCA § 342.

§ 924. List of creditors

The debtor shall file a list of creditors.

(Pub.L. 95–598, Nov. 6, 1978, 92 Stat. 2623.)

CROSS REFERENCES

Duty of—
> Debtor to file list of creditors, see 11 USCA § 521.
> Trustee to file list of creditors in Chapter 11 cases, see 11 USCA § 1106.

§ 925. Effect of list of claims

A proof of claim is deemed filed under section 501 of this title for any claim that appears in the list filed under section 924 of this title, except a claim that is listed as disputed, contingent, or unliquidated.

(Pub.L. 95–598, Nov. 6, 1978, 92 Stat. 2623.)

§ 926. Avoiding powers

(a) If the debtor refuses to pursue a cause of action under section 544, 545, 547, 548, 549(a), or 550 of this title, then on request of a creditor, the court may appoint a trustee to pursue such cause of action.

(b) A transfer of property of the debtor to or for the benefit of any holder of a bond or note, on account of such bond or note, may not be avoided under section 547 of this title.

(Pub.L. 95–598, Nov. 6, 1978, 92 Stat. 2623; Pub.L. 100–597, § 6, Nov. 3, 1988, 102 Stat. 3029.)

HISTORICAL AND STATUTORY NOTES

Amendments

1988 Amendments. Subsec. (a). Pub.L. 100–597, § 6(1), designated existing provision as subsec. (a).

Subsec. (b). Pub.L. 100–597, § 6(2), added subsec. (b).

CROSS REFERENCES

Appointment of trustee in—

Chapter eleven cases, see 11 USCA § 1104.

Chapter thirteen cases, see 11 USCA § 1302.

Railroad reorganization cases, see 11 USCA § 1163.

Trustee defined when used in sections made applicable to cases under this chapter, see 11 USCA § 902.

§ 927. Limitation on recourse

The holder of a claim payable solely from special revenues of the debtor under applicable nonbankruptcy law shall not be treated as having recourse against the debtor on account of such claim pursuant to section 1111(b) of this title.

(Added Pub.L. 100–597, § 7(2), Nov. 3, 1988, 102 Stat. 3029.)

HISTORICAL AND STATUTORY NOTES

Prior Provisions

A prior section 927, Pub.L. 95–598, Nov. 6, 1978, 92 Stat. 2623, as amended, relating to dismissal of cases under this chapter, was renumbered 930 by Pub.L. 100–597.

§ 928. Post petition effect of security interest

(a) Notwithstanding section 552(a) of this title and subject to subsection (b) of this section, special revenues acquired by the debtor after the commencement of the case shall remain subject to any lien resulting from any security agreement entered into by the debtor before the commencement of the case.

(b) Any such lien on special revenues, other than municipal betterment assessments, derived from a project or system shall be subject to the necessary operating expenses of such project or system, as the case may be.

(Added Pub.L. 100–597, § 8, Nov. 3, 1988, 102 Stat. 3029.)

§ 929. Municipal leases

A lease to a municipality shall not be treated as an executory contract or unexpired lease for the purposes of section 365 or 502(b)(6) of this title solely by reason of its being subject to termination in the event the debtor fails to appropriate rent.

(Added Pub.L. 100–597, § 9, Nov. 3, 1988, 102 Stat. 3030.)

§ 930. Dismissal

(a) After notice and a hearing, the court may dismiss a case under this chapter for cause, including—

    (1) want of prosecution;

    (2) unreasonable delay by the debtor that is prejudicial to creditors;

    (3) failure to propose a plan within the time fixed under section 941 of this title;

    (4) if a plan is not accepted within any time fixed by the court;

    (5) denial of confirmation of a plan under section 943(b) of this title and denial of additional time for filing another plan or a modification of a plan; or

    (6) if the court has retained jurisdiction after confirmation of a plan—

        (A) material default by the debtor with respect to a term of such plan; or

        (B) termination of such plan by reason of the occurrence of a condition specified in such plan.

(b) The court shall dismiss a case under this chapter if confirmation of a plan under this chapter is refused.

(Pub.L. 95–598, Nov. 6, 1978, 92 Stat. 2623, § 927; Pub.L. 98–353, Title III, § 496, July 10, 1984, 98 Stat. 384; renumbered § 930, Pub.L. 100–597, § 7(1), Nov. 3, 1988, 102 Stat. 3029.)

HISTORICAL AND STATUTORY NOTES

Amendments

1984 Amendments. Subsec. (b). Pub.L. 98–353 substituted "confirmation of a plan under this chapter" for "confirmation".

CROSS REFERENCES

Conversion or dismissal of—

    Chapter eleven cases, see 11 USCA § 1112.

    Chapter thirteen cases, see 11 USCA § 1307.

Dismissal of Chapter seven cases, see 11 USCA § 707.

Effect of dismissal, see 11 USCA § 349.

SUBCHAPTER III—THE PLAN

§ 941. Filing of plan

The debtor shall file a plan for the adjustment of the debtor's debts. If such a plan is not filed with the petition, the debtor shall file such a plan at such later time as the court fixes.

(Pub.L. 95–598, Nov. 6, 1978, 92 Stat. 2624.)

Title 11   DEBTS OF A MUNICIPALITY   11 § 942

CROSS REFERENCES

Dismissal for failure to timely propose plan, see 11 USCA § 930.

Filing of plan in Chapter thirteen cases, see 11 USCA § 1321.

Who may file a plan in Chapter eleven cases, see 11 USCA § 1121.

§ 942. Modification of plan

The debtor may modify the plan at any time before confirmation, but may not modify the plan so that the plan as modified fails to meet the requirements of this chapter. After the debtor files a modification, the plan as modified becomes the plan.

(Pub.L. 95–598, Nov. 6, 1978, 92 Stat. 2624.)

CROSS REFERENCES

Modification of plan after confirmation in—

    Chapter thirteen cases, see 11 USCA § 1329.

    Chapter twelve cases, see 11 USCA § 1229.

Modification of plan before confirmation in—

    Chapter thirteen cases, see 11 USCA § 1323.

    Chapter twelve cases, see 11 USCA § 1223.

Modification of plan in Chapter eleven cases, see 11 USCA § 1127.

§ 943. Confirmation

(a) A special tax payer may object to confirmation of a plan.

(b) The court shall confirm the plan if—

    (1) the plan complies with the provisions of this title made applicable by sections 103(e) and 901 of this title;

    (2) the plan complies with the provisions of this chapter;

    (3) all amounts to be paid by the debtor or by any person for services or expenses in the case or incident to the plan have been fully disclosed and are reasonable;

    (4) the debtor is not prohibited by law from taking any action necessary to carry out the plan;

    (5) except to the extent that the holder of a particular claim has agreed to a different treatment of such claim, the plan provides that on the effective date of the plan each holder of a claim of a kind specified in section 507(a)(2) of this title will receive on account of such claim cash equal to the allowed amount of such claim;

    (6) any regulatory or electoral approval necessary under applicable nonbankruptcy law in order to carry out any provision of the plan has been obtained, or such provision is expressly conditioned on such approval; and

    (7) the plan is in the best interests of creditors and is feasible.

(Pub.L. 95–598, Nov. 6, 1978, 92 Stat. 2624; Pub.L. 98–353, Title III, § 497, July 10, 1984, 98 Stat. 384; Pub.L. 100–597, § 10, Nov. 3, 1988, 102 Stat. 3030; Pub.L. 109–8, Title XV, § 1502(a)(6), Apr. 20, 2005, 119 Stat. 216.)

HISTORICAL AND STATUTORY NOTES

References in Text

Section 103(e) of this title, referred to in subsec. (b), was redesignated subsec. (f) and a new subsec. (e) was added by Pub.L. 106–554, § 1(a)(5) [Title I, § 112(c)(5)(A)], Dec. 21, 2000, 114 Stat. 2763, 2763A–394.

Amendments

2005 Amendments. Subsec. (b)(5). Pub.L. 109–8, § 1502(a)(6), struck out "507(a)(1)" and inserted "507(a)(2)".

1988 Amendments. Subsec. (b)(5)–(7). Pub.L. 100–597, § 10(1)–(3), struck out "and" at the end of par. (5); added par. (6); and redesignated former par. (6) as (7).

1984 Amendments. Subsec. (b)(4). Pub.L. 98–353, § 497(1), struck out "to be taken" following "necessary".

Subsec. (b)(5). Pub.L. 98–353, § 497(2), substituted provisions requiring the plan to provide payment of cash in an amount equal to the allowed amount of a claim except to the extent that the holder of a particular claim has agreed to different treatment of such claim, for provisions which required the plan to provide for payment of property of a value equal to the allowed amount of such claim except to the extent that the holder of a particular claim has waived such payment on such claim.

CROSS REFERENCES

Confirmation hearing in—

    Chapter eleven cases, see 11 USCA § 1128.

    Chapter thirteen cases, see 11 USCA § 1324.

    Chapter twelve cases, see 11 USCA § 1224.

Confirmation of plan in—

    Chapter eleven cases, see 11 USCA § 1129.

    Chapter thirteen cases, see 11 USCA § 1325.

    Chapter twelve cases, see 11 USCA § 1225.

    Railroad reorganization cases, see 11 USCA § 1173.

Dismissal for denial of confirmation of plan, see 11 USCA § 930.

Unclaimed property, see 11 USCA § 347.

§ 944. Effect of confirmation

(a) The provisions of a confirmed plan bind the debtor and any creditor, whether or not—

    (1) a proof of such creditor's claim is filed or deemed filed under section 501 of this title;

    (2) such claim is allowed under section 502 of this title; or

    (3) such creditor has accepted the plan.

(b) Except as provided in subsection (c) of this section, the debtor is discharged from all debts as of the time when—

    (1) the plan is confirmed;

    (2) the debtor deposits any consideration to be distributed under the plan with a disbursing agent appointed by the court; and

    (3) the court has determined—

        (A) that any security so deposited will constitute, after distribution, a valid legal obligation of the debtor; and

(B) that any provision made to pay or secure payment of such obligation is valid.

(c) The debtor is not discharged under subsection (b) of this section from any debt—

(1) excepted from discharge by the plan or order confirming the plan; or

(2) owed to an entity that, before confirmation of the plan, had neither notice nor actual knowledge of the case.

(Pub.L. 95–598, Nov. 6, 1978, 92 Stat. 2624.)

CROSS REFERENCES

Discharge in—

Chapter seven cases, see 11 USCA § 727.

Chapter thirteen cases, see 11 USCA § 1328.

Chapter twelve cases, see 11 USCA § 1228.

Effect of confirmation in—

Chapter eleven cases, see 11 USCA § 1141.

Chapter thirteen cases, see 11 USCA § 1327.

Chapter twelve cases, see 11 USCA § 1227.

Effect of discharge, see 11 USCA § 524.

Exceptions to discharge, see 11 USCA § 523.

§ 945. Continuing jurisdiction and closing of the case

(a) The court may retain jurisdiction over the case for such period of time as is necessary for the successful implementation of the plan.

(b) Except as provided in subsection (a) of this section, the court shall close the case when administration of the case has been completed.

(Pub.L. 95–598, Nov. 6, 1978, 92 Stat. 2625; Pub.L. 98–353, Title III, § 498, July 10, 1984, 98 Stat. 384.)

HISTORICAL AND STATUTORY NOTES

Amendments

1984 Amendments. Subsec. (a). Pub.L. 98–353 substituted "implementation" for "execution".

CROSS REFERENCES

Closing and reopening cases, see 11 USCA § 350.

§ 946. Effect of exchange of securities before the date of the filing of the petition

The exchange of a new security under the plan for a claim covered by the plan, whether such exchange occurred before or after the date of the filing of the petition, does not limit or impair the effectiveness of the plan or of any provision of this chapter. The amount and number specified in section 1126(c) of this title include the amount and number of claims formerly held by a creditor that has participated in any such exchange.

(Pub.L. 95–598, Nov. 6, 1978, 92 Stat. 2625.)

CHAPTER 11—REORGANIZATION

SUBCHAPTER I—OFFICERS AND ADMINISTRATION

Sec.
1101. Definitions for this chapter.
1102. Creditors' and equity security holders' committees.
1103. Powers and duties of committees.
1104. Appointment of trustee or examiner.
1105. Termination of trustee's appointment.
1106. Duties of trustee and examiner.
1107. Rights, powers, and duties of debtor in possession.
1108. Authorization to operate business.
1109. Right to be heard.
1110. Aircraft equipment and vessels.
1111. Claims and interests.
1112. Conversion or dismissal.
1113. Rejection of collective bargaining agreements.
1114. Payment of insurance benefits to retired employees.
1115. Property of the estate.
1116. Duties of trustee or debtor in possession in small business cases.

SUBCHAPTER II—THE PLAN

1121. Who may file a plan.
1122. Classification of claims or interests.
1123. Contents of plan.
1124. Impairment of claims or interests.
1125. Postpetition disclosure and solicitation.
1126. Acceptance of plan.
1127. Modification of plan.
1128. Confirmation hearing.
1129. Confirmation of plan.

SUBCHAPTER III—POSTCONFIRMATION MATTERS

1141. Effect of confirmation.
1142. Implementation of plan.
1143. Distribution.
1144. Revocation of an order of confirmation.
1145. Exemption from securities laws.
1146. Special tax provisions.

SUBCHAPTER IV—RAILROAD REORGANIZATION

1161. Inapplicability of other sections.
1162. Definition.
1163. Appointment of trustee.
1164. Right to be heard.
1165. Protection of the public interest.
1166. Effect of subtitle IV of title 49 and of Federal, State, or local regulations.
1167. Collective bargaining agreements.
1168. Rolling stock equipment.
1169. Effect of rejection of lease of railroad line.
1170. Abandonment of railroad line.
1171. Priority claims.
1172. Contents of plan.
1173. Confirmation of plan.
1174. Liquidation.

HISTORICAL AND STATUTORY NOTES

Amendments

2005 Amendments. Pub.L. 109–8, Title III, § 321(a)(2), Apr. 20, 2005, 119 Stat. 95, added item 1115.

Pub.L. 109–8, Title IV, § 436(b), Apr. 20, 2005, 119 Stat. 113, added item 1116.

1988 Amendments. Pub.L. 100–334, § 2(c), June 16, 1988, 102 Stat. 613, added item 1114.

1984 Amendments. Pub.L. 98–353, Title III, § 514(b), July 10, 1984, 98 Stat. 387 substituted "Implementation" for "Execution" in item 1142.

Pub.L. 98–353, Title III, § 541(b), July 10, 1984, 98 Stat. 391 added item 1113.

1983 Amendments. Pub.L. 97–449, § 5(a)(1), Jan. 12, 1983, 96 Stat. 2442, substituted "subtitle IV of title 49" for "Interstate Commerce Act" in item 1166.

CROSS REFERENCES

Allowance of administrative expenses of substantial contributors to cases under this chapter, see 11 USCA § 503.

Applicability of income tax provisions to cases under this chapter, see 26 USCA § 1398.

Chapters one, three, and five of this title applicable in cases under this chapter except as provided in § 1161 of this title, see 11 USCA § 103.

Claims arising from rejection under chapter plans of executory contracts or unexpired leases, see 11 USCA § 502.

Commencement of involuntary cases, see 11 USCA § 303.

Conversion to this chapter from—

    Chapter seven, see 11 USCA § 706.

    Chapter thirteen, see 11 USCA § 1307.

Core proceedings, see 28 USCA § 157.

Distress termination of single-employer plans in cases under this chapter, see 29 USCA § 1341.

Duration of automatic stay, see 11 USCA § 362.

Duties of United States trustees, see 28 USCA § 586.

Employment of professional persons, see 11 USCA § 327.

Establishment, operation and termination of Bankruptcy Appellate Panel Service and undue delay or increased costs, see 28 USCA § 158.

Executory contracts and unexpired leases, see 11 USCA § 365.

Filing fees, see 28 USCA § 1930.

Jurisdiction of courts in termination proceedings of employer plans brought by Pension Benefit Guaranty Corporation same as jurisdiction of courts in cases under this chapter, see 29 USCA § 1342.

Limitation on compensation of trustee, see 11 USCA § 326.

Persons required to make returns of income under this chapter, see 26 USCA § 6012.

Persons who may be debtors under this chapter, see 11 USCA § 109.

Powers of Courts to set date to file disclosure, see 11 USCA § 105.

Property of estate in cases converted from Chapter 13, see 11 USCA § 1306.

Provisions concerning reorganization plan of investment companies not to affect or derogate from powers of courts with reference to reorganizations under this title, see 15 USCA § 80a–25.

Return of excessive attorney compensation if transferred property was to be paid by debtor under plan under this chapter, see 11 USCA § 329.

Rights and powers of debtor in Chapter twelve case not encompassing certain duties of trustee serving in case under this chapter, see 11 USCA § 1203.

Special tax provisions, see 11 USCA § 346.

Stay of action against Chapter thirteen codebtor in cases converted to this chapter, see 11 USCA § 1301.

Supplemental injunctions and notice and hearings, see 11 USCA § 524.

Treatment of debtor's estate in cases under this chapter as taxpayer for certain income tax purposes, see 26 USCA § 108.

Unclaimed property, see 11 USCA § 347.

Use, sale or lease of property under plan under this chapter, see 11 USCA § 363.

SUBCHAPTER I—OFFICERS AND ADMINISTRATION

CROSS REFERENCES

Subchapter applicable only in case under this chapter except as provided in § 901 of this title, see 11 USCA § 103.

§ 1101. Definitions for this chapter

In this chapter—

(1) "debtor in possession" means debtor except when a person that has qualified under section 322 of this title is serving as trustee in the case;

(2) "substantial consummation" means—

(A) transfer of all or substantially all of the property proposed by the plan to be transferred;

(B) assumption by the debtor or by the successor to the debtor under the plan of the business or of the management of all or substantially all of the property dealt with by the plan; and

(C) commencement of distribution under the plan.

(Pub.L. 95–598, Nov. 6, 1978, 92 Stat. 2626.)

CROSS REFERENCES

Definitions applicable in—

Cases under this title, see 11 USCA § 101.

Chapter nine cases, see 11 USCA § 902.

Commodity broker liquidation cases, see 11 USCA § 761.

Railroad reorganization cases, see 11 USCA § 1162.

Stockbroker liquidation cases, see 11 USCA § 741.

§ 1102. Creditors' and equity security holders' committees

(a)(1) Except as provided in paragraph (3), as soon as practicable after the order for relief under chapter 11 of this title, the United States trustee shall appoint a committee of creditors holding unsecured claims and may appoint additional committees of creditors or of equity security holders as the United States trustee deems appropriate.

(2) On request of a party in interest, the court may order the appointment of additional committees of creditors or of equity security holders if necessary to assure adequate representation of creditors or of equity security holders. The United States trustee shall appoint any such committee.

(3) On request of a party in interest in a case in which the debtor is a small business debtor and for cause, the court may order that a committee of creditors not be appointed.

(4) On request of a party in interest and after notice and a hearing, the court may order the United States trustee to change the membership of a committee appointed under this subsection, if

the court determines that the change is necessary to ensure adequate representation of creditors or equity security holders. The court may order the United States trustee to increase the number of members of a committee to include a creditor that is a small business concern (as described in section 3(a)(1) of the Small Business Act), if the court determines that the creditor holds claims (of the kind represented by the committee) the aggregate amount of which, in comparison to the annual gross revenue of that creditor, is disproportionately large.

(b)(1) A committee of creditors appointed under subsection (a) of this section shall ordinarily consist of the persons, willing to serve, that hold the seven largest claims against the debtor of the kinds represented on such committee, or of the members of a committee organized by creditors before the commencement of the case under this chapter, if such committee was fairly chosen and is representative of the different kinds of claims to be represented.

(2) A committee of equity security holders appointed under subsection (a)(2) of this section shall ordinarily consist of the persons, willing to serve, that hold the seven largest amounts of equity securities of the debtor of the kinds represented on such committee.

(3) A committee appointed under subsection (a) shall—

   (A) provide access to information for creditors who—

   (i) hold claims of the kind represented by that committee; and

   (ii) are not appointed to the committee;

   (B) solicit and receive comments from the creditors described in subparagraph (A); and

   (C) be subject to a court order that compels any additional report or disclosure to be made to the creditors described in subparagraph (A).

(Pub.L. 95–598, Nov. 6, 1978, 92 Stat. 2626; Pub.L. 98–353, Title III, § 499, July 10, 1984, 98 Stat. 384; Pub.L. 99–554, Title II, § 221, Oct. 27, 1986, 100 Stat. 3101; Pub.L. 103–394, Title II, § 217(b), Oct. 22, 1994, 108 Stat. 4127; Pub.L. 109–8, Title IV, §§ 405, 432(b), Apr. 20, 2005, 119 Stat. 105, 110.)

HISTORICAL AND STATUTORY NOTES

References in Text

Section 3(a)(1) of the Small Business Act, referred to in subsec. (a)(4), is section 3(a)(1) of Pub.L. 85–536 § 2[3], July 18, 1958, 72 Stat. 384, as amended, which is classified to 15 U.S.C.A. § 632(a)(1). For complete classification, see Short Title note under 15 U.S.C.A. § 631 and Tables.

Amendments

2005 Amendments. Subsec. (a)(3). Pub.L. 109–8, § 432(b), inserted "debtor" after "small business".

Subsec. (a)(4). Pub.L. 109–8, § 405(a), added par. (4).

Subsec. (b)(3). Pub.L. 109–8, § 405(b), added par. (3).

1994 Amendments. Subsec. (a)(1). Pub.L. 103–394, § 217(b)(1), inserted reference to par. (3).

Subsec. (a)(3). Pub.L. 103–394, § 217(b)(2), added par. (3).

1986 Amendments. Subsec. (a)(1). Pub.L. 99–554, § 221(1), substituted "under chapter 11 of this title, the United States trustee shall appoint" for "under this chapter, the court shall appoint" and added "and may appoint additional committees of creditors or of equity security holders as the United States trustee deems appropriate" following "unsecured claims".

Subsec. (a)(2). Pub.L. 99–554, § 221(1), substituted "The United States trustee shall appoint" for "The court shall appoint".

Subsec. (c). Pub.L. 99–554, § 221(2), struck out subsec. (c) which read as follows: "On request of a party in interest and after notice and a hearing, the court may change the membership or the size of a committee appointed under subsection (a) of this section if the membership of such committee is not representative of the different kinds of claims or interests to be represented.".

1984 Amendments. Subsec. (b)(1). Pub.L. 98–353 substituted "commencement of the case" for "order for relief".

CROSS REFERENCES

Allowance of creditor committee expenses, see 11 USCA § 503.

Applicability of this section in Chapter nine cases, see 11 USCA § 901.

Creditors' committees in Chapter seven cases, see 11 USCA § 705.

Disallowance of administrative expenses for creditors' and equity security holders' committees, see 11 USCA § 503.

Effect of conversion, see 11 USCA § 348.

Inapplicability of subsec. (a)(1) of this section to railroad reorganization cases, see 11 USCA § 1161.

Limitation on compensation of professional persons, see 11 USCA § 328.

"Person" defined for purposes of this section, see 11 USCA § 101.

§ 1103. Powers and duties of committees

(a) At a scheduled meeting of a committee appointed under section 1102 of this title, at which a majority of the members of such committee are present, and with the court's approval, such committee may select and authorize the employment by such committee of one or more attorneys, accountants, or other agents, to represent or perform services for such committee.

(b) An attorney or accountant employed to represent a committee appointed under section 1102 of this title may not, while employed by such committee, represent any other entity having an adverse interest in connection with the case. Representation of one or more creditors of the same class as represented by the committee shall not per se constitute the representation of an adverse interest.

(c) A committee appointed under section 1102 of this title may—

(1) consult with the trustee or debtor in possession concerning the administration of the case;

(2) investigate the acts, conduct, assets, liabilities, and financial condition of the debtor, the operation of the debtor's business and the desirability of the continuance of such business, and any other matter relevant to the case or to the formulation of a plan;

(3) participate in the formulation of a plan, advise those represented by such committee of such committee's determinations as to any plan formulated, and collect and file with the court acceptances or rejections of a plan;

(4) request the appointment of a trustee or examiner under section 1104 of this title; and

(5) perform such other services as are in the interest of those represented.

(d) As soon as practicable after the appointment of a committee under section 1102 of this title, the trustee shall meet with such committee to transact such business as may be necessary and proper.

(Pub.L. 95–598, Nov. 6, 1978, 92 Stat. 2627; Pub.L. 98–353, Title III, §§ 324, 500, July 10, 1984, 98 Stat. 358, 384.)

HISTORICAL AND STATUTORY NOTES

Amendments

1984 Amendments. Subsec. (b). Pub.L. 98–353, § 324, substituted "An attorney or accountant" for "A person".

Pub.L. 98–353, § 500(a)(1), substituted "entity having an adverse interest" for "entity".

Pub.L. 98–353, § 500(a)(2), added provision that representation of one or more creditors of the same class as represented by the committee shall not per se constitute the representation of an adverse interest.

Subsec. (c)(3). Pub.L. 98–353, § 500(b)(1)(A), substituted "determinations" for "recommendations".

Pub.L. 98–353, § 500(b)(1)(B), substituted "acceptances or rejections" for "acceptances".

Subsec. (c)(4). Pub.L. 98–353, § 500(b)(2), struck out ", if a trustee or examiner, as the case may be, has not previously been appointed under this chapter in the case" following "section 1104 of this title".

CROSS REFERENCES

Applicability of this section in Chapter nine cases, see 11 USCA § 901.

Compensation of officers, see 11 USCA § 330.

Creditors' committees in Chapter seven cases, see 11 USCA § 705.

Interim compensation for professional persons, see 11 USCA § 331.

Limitation on compensation of professional persons, see 11 USCA § 328.

§ 1104. Appointment of trustee or examiner

(a) At any time after the commencement of the case but before confirmation of a plan, on request of a party in interest or the United States trustee, and after notice and a hearing, the court shall order the appointment of a trustee—

(1) for cause, including fraud, dishonesty, incompetence, or gross mismanagement of the affairs of the debtor by current management, either before or after the commencement of the case, or similar cause, but not including the number of holders of securities of the debtor or the amount of assets or liabilities of the debtor; or

(2) if such appointment is in the interests of creditors, any equity security holders, and other interests of the estate, without regard to the number of holders of securities of the debtor or the amount of assets or liabilities of the debtor.

[(3) Repealed. Pub.L. 111–327, § 2(a)(30)(A)(iii), Dec. 22, 2010, 124 Stat. 3560]

(b)(1) Except as provided in section 1163 of this title, on the request of a party in interest made not later than 30 days after the court orders the appointment of a trustee under subsection (a), the United States trustee shall convene a meeting of creditors for the purpose of electing one disinterested person to serve as trustee in the case. The election of a trustee shall be conducted in the manner provided in subsections (a), (b), and (c) of section 702 of this title.

(2)(A) If an eligible, disinterested trustee is elected at a meeting of creditors under paragraph (1), the United States trustee shall file a report certifying that election.

(B) Upon the filing of a report under subparagraph (A)—

(i) the trustee elected under paragraph (1) shall be considered to have been selected and appointed for purposes of this section; and

(ii) the service of any trustee appointed under subsection (a) shall terminate.

(C) The court shall resolve any dispute arising out of an election described in subparagraph (A).

(c) If the court does not order the appointment of a trustee under this section, then at any time before the confirmation of a plan, on request of a party in interest or the United States trustee, and after notice and a hearing, the court shall order the appointment of an examiner to conduct such an investigation of the debtor as is appropriate, including an investigation of any allegations of fraud, dishonesty, incompetence, misconduct, mismanagement, or irregularity in the management of the affairs of the debtor of or by current or former management of the debtor, if—

(1) such appointment is in the interests of creditors, any equity security holders, and other interests of the estate; or

(2) the debtor's fixed, liquidated, unsecured debts, other than debts for goods, services, or taxes, or owing to an insider, exceed $5,000,000.

(d) If the court orders the appointment of a trustee or an examiner, if a trustee or an examiner dies or resigns during the case or is removed under section 324 of this title, or if a trustee fails to qualify under section 322 of this title, then the United States trustee, after consultation with parties in interest, shall appoint, subject to the court's approval, one disinterested person other than the United States trustee to serve as trustee or examiner, as the case may be, in the case.

(e) The United States trustee shall move for the appointment of a trustee under subsection (a) if there are reasonable grounds to suspect that current members of the governing body of the debtor, the debtor's chief executive or chief financial officer, or members of the governing body who selected the debtor's chief executive or chief financial officer, participated in actual fraud, dishonesty, or criminal conduct in the management of the debtor or the debtor's public financial reporting.

(Pub.L. 95–598, Nov. 6, 1978, 92 Stat. 2627; Pub.L. 99–554, Title II, § 222, Oct. 27, 1986, 100 Stat. 3102; Pub.L. 103–394, Title II, § 211(a), Title V, § 501(d)(30), Oct. 22, 1994, 108 Stat. 4125, 4146; Pub.L. 109–8, Title IV, §§ 416, 442(b), Title XIV, § 1405, Apr. 20, 2005, 119 Stat. 107, 116, 215; Pub.L. 111–327, § 2(a)(30), Dec. 22, 2010, 124 Stat. 3560.)

HISTORICAL AND STATUTORY NOTES

Amendments

2010 Amendments. Subsec. (a)(1). Pub.L. 111–327, § 2(a)(30)(A)(i), inserted "or" following the semicolon at the end.

Subsec. (a)(2). Pub.L. 111–327, § 2(a)(30)(A)(ii), struck out "; or" at the end and inserted a period.

Subsec. (a)(3). Pub.L. 111–327, § 2(a)(30)(A)(iii), struck out par. (3), which formerly read: "**(3)** if grounds exist to convert or dismiss the case under section 1112, but the court determines that the appointment of a trustee or an examiner is in the best interests of creditors and the estate."

Subsec. (b)(2)(B)(ii). Pub.L. 111–327, § 2(a)(30)(B), struck out "subsection (d)" and inserted "subsection (a)".

2005 Amendments. Subsec. (a)(1). Pub.L. 109–8, § 442(b)(1), struck "or" at the end of par. (1).

Subsec. (a)(2). Pub.L. 109–8, § 442(b)(2), struck the period at the end of par. (2) and inserted "; or".

Subsec. (a)(3). Pub.L. 109–8, § 442(b)(3), added par. (3).

Subsec. (b), (b)(1). Pub.L. 109–8, § 416(1), inserted "**(1)**" after "**(b)**".

Subsec. (b)(2). Pub.L. 109–8, § 416(2), added par. (2).

Subsec. (e). Pub.L. 109–8, § 1405, added subsec. (e).

1994 Amendments. Subsec. (b). Pub.L. 103–394, § 211(a), added subsec. (b) and redesignated former subsec. (b) as (c).

Subsec. (c). Pub.L. 103–394, § 211(a)(1), redesignated former subsec. (b) as (c) and former subsec. (c) as (d).

Subsec. (d). Pub.L. 103–394, § 211(a)(1), redesignated former subsec. (c) as (d).

Pub.L. 103–394, § 501(d)(30), substituted "parties in interest," for "parties in interest".

1986 Amendments. Subsec. (a). Pub.L. 99–554, § 222(1), added "or the United States trustee" following "party in interest".

Subsec. (b). Pub.L. 99–554, § 222(2), added "or the United States trustee" following "party in interest".

Subsec. (c). Pub.L. 99–554, § 222(3), substituted "the United States trustee after consultation with parties in interest shall appoint, subject to the court's approval, one disinterested person other than the United States trustee to serve" for "the court shall appoint one disinterested person to serve".

CROSS REFERENCES

Appointment of Secretary of Transportation as sole trustee, see 46 USCA § 50305.

Appointment of trustee in—

Chapter thirteen cases, see 11 USCA § 1302.

Chapter twelve cases, see 11 USCA § 1202.

Railroad reorganization cases, see 11 USCA § 1163.

Election of trustee in Chapter seven cases, see 11 USCA § 702.

Grain storage facility bankruptcies, expedited appointment of trustee or examiner, see 11 USCA § 557.

Inapplicability of this section to railroad reorganization cases, see 11 USCA § 1161.

Qualification of trustee, see 11 USCA § 322.

Time for bringing action, see 11 USCA § 546.

§ 1105. Termination of trustee's appointment

At any time before confirmation of a plan, on request of a party in interest or the United States trustee, and after notice and a hearing, the court may terminate the trustee's appointment and restore the debtor to possession and management of the property of the estate and of the operation of the debtor's business.

(Pub.L. 95–598, Nov. 6, 1978, 92 Stat. 2628; Pub.L. 98–353, Title III, § 501, July 10, 1984, 98 Stat. 384; Pub.L. 99–554, Title II, § 223, Oct. 27, 1986, 100 Stat. 3102.)

HISTORICAL AND STATUTORY NOTES

Amendments

1986 Amendments. Pub.L. 99–554, § 223, added "or the United States trustee" following "party in interest".

1984 Amendments. Pub.L. 98–353 substituted "estate and of the" for "estate, and".

CROSS REFERENCES

Effect of vacancy in office of trustee, see 11 USCA § 325.

Inapplicability of this section to railroad reorganization cases, see 11 USCA § 1161.

Removal of trustee, see 11 USCA § 324.

§ 1106. Duties of trustee and examiner

(a) A trustee shall—

(1) perform the duties of the trustee, as specified in paragraphs (2), (5), (7), (8), (9), (10), (11), and (12) of section 704(a);

(2) if the debtor has not done so, file the list, schedule, and statement required under section 521(a)(1) of this title;

(3) except to the extent that the court orders otherwise, investigate the acts, conduct, assets, liabilities, and financial condition of the debtor, the operation of the debtor's business and the desirability of the continuance of such business, and any other matter relevant to the case or to the formulation of a plan;

(4) as soon as practicable—

(A) file a statement of any investigation conducted under paragraph (3) of this subsection, including any fact ascertained pertaining to fraud, dishonesty, incompetence, misconduct, mismanagement, or irregularity in the management of the affairs of the debtor, or to a cause of action available to the estate; and

(B) transmit a copy or a summary of any such statement to any creditors' committee or equity security holders' committee, to any indenture trustee, and to such other entity as the court designates;

(5) as soon as practicable, file a plan under section 1121 of this title, file a report of why the trustee will not file a plan, or recommend conversion of the case to a case under chapter 7, 12, or 13 of this title or dismissal of the case;

(6) for any year for which the debtor has not filed a tax return required by law, furnish, without personal liability, such information as may be required by the governmental unit with which such tax return was to be filed, in light of the condition of the debtor's books and records and the availability of such information;

(7) after confirmation of a plan, file such reports as are necessary or as the court orders; and

(8) if with respect to the debtor there is a claim for a domestic support obligation, provide the applicable notice specified in subsection (c).

(b) An examiner appointed under section 1104(d) of this title shall perform the duties specified in paragraphs (3) and (4) of subsection (a) of this section, and, except to the extent that the court orders otherwise, any other duties of the trustee that the court orders the debtor in possession not to perform.

(c)(1) In a case described in subsection (a)(8) to which subsection (a)(8) applies, the trustee shall—

(A)(i) provide written notice to the holder of the claim described in subsection (a)(8) of such claim and of the right of such holder to use the services of the State child support enforcement agency established under sections 464 and 466 of the Social Security Act for the State in which such holder resides, for assistance in collecting child support during and after the case under this title; and

(ii) include in the notice required by clause (i) the address and telephone number of such State child support enforcement agency;

(B)(i) provide written notice to such State child support enforcement agency of such claim; and

(ii) include in the notice required by clause (i) the name, address, and telephone number of such holder; and

(C) at such time as the debtor is granted a discharge under section 1141, provide written notice to such holder and to such State child support enforcement agency of—

(i) the granting of the discharge;

(ii) the last recent known address of the debtor;

(iii) the last recent known name and address of the debtor's employer; and

(iv) the name of each creditor that holds a claim that—

(I) is not discharged under paragraph (2), (4), or (14A) of section 523(a); or

(II) was reaffirmed by the debtor under section 524(c).

(2)(A) The holder of a claim described in subsection (a)(8) or the State child enforcement support agency of the State in which such holder resides may request from a creditor described in paragraph (1)(C)(iv) the last known address of the debtor.

(B) Notwithstanding any other provision of law, a creditor that makes a disclosure of a last known address of a debtor in connection with a request made under subparagraph (A) shall not be liable by reason of making such disclosure.

(Pub.L. 95–598, Nov. 6, 1978, 92 Stat. 2628; Pub.L. 98–353, Title III, §§ 311(b)(1), 502, July 10, 1984, 98 Stat. 355, 384; Pub.L. 99–554, Title II, § 257(c), Oct. 27, 1986, 100 Stat. 3114; Pub.L. 103–394, Title II,

§ 211(b), Oct. 22, 1994, 108 Stat. 4125; Pub.L. 109–8, Title II, § 219(b), Title IV, § 446(c), Title XI, § 1105(b), Apr. 20, 2005, 119 Stat. 56, 118, 192; Pub.L. 111–327, § 2(a)(31), Dec. 22, 2010, 124 Stat. 3560.)

HISTORICAL AND STATUTORY NOTES

References in Text

Section 464 of the Social Security Act, referred to in subsec. (c)(1)(A)(i), is Act Aug. 14, 1935, c. 531, Title IV, § 464, as added Aug. 13, 1981, Pub.L. 97–35, Title XXIII, § 2331(a), 95 Stat. 860, and amended, which is classified to 42 U.S.C.A. § 664.

Section 466 of the Social Security Act, referred to in subsec. (c)(1)(A)(i), is Act Aug. 14, 1935, c. 531, Title IV, § 466, as added Aug. 16, 1984, Pub.L. 98–378, § 3(b), 98 Stat. 1306, and amended, which is classified to 42 U.S.C.A. § 666.

Amendments

2010 Amendments. Subsec. (a)(1). Pub.L. 111–327, § 2(a)(31)(A), struck out "704" and inserted "704(a)".

Subsec. (a)(2). Pub.L. 111–327, § 2(a)(31)(B), struck out "521(1)" and inserted "521(a)(1)".

2005 Amendments. Subsec. (a)(1). Pub.L. 109–8, § 446(c), rewrote par. (1), which formerly read:

"**(1)** perform the duties of a trustee specified in sections 704(2), 704(5), 704(7), 704(8), and 704(9) of this title;"

Pub.L. 109–8, § 1105(b), struck out "and (11)" and inserted "(11), and (12)".

Subsec. (a)(6). Pub.L. 109–8, § 219(b)(1)(A), struck out "and" at the end of par. (6).

Subsec. (a)(7). Pub.L. 109–8, § 219(b)(1)(B), substituted "; and" for the period at the end of par. (7).

Subsec. (a)(8). Pub.L. 109–8, § 219(b)(1)(C), added par. (8).

Subsec. (c). Pub.L. 109–8, § 219(b)(2), added subsec. (c).

1994 Amendments. Subsec. (b). Pub.L. 103–394, § 211(b), substituted "An examiner appointed under section 1104(d)" for "An examiner appointed under section 1104(c)".

1986 Amendments. Subsec. (a)(5). Pub.L. 99–554, § 257(c), added reference to chapter 12.

1984 Amendments. Subsec. (a)(1). Pub.L. 98–353, § 311(b)(1), substituted "704(5), 704(7), 704(8), and 704(9)" for "704(4), 704(6), 704(7) and 704(8)".

Subsec. (b). Pub.L. 98–353, § 502, inserted ", except to the extent that the court orders otherwise," before "any other".

Payment of Certain Benefits to Retired Former Employees

Pub.L. 99–500, § 101(b) [Title VI, § 608], Oct. 18, 1986, 100 Stat. 1783–39, 1783–74, and Pub.L. 99–591, § 101(b) [Title VI, § 608], Oct. 30, 1986, 100 Stat. 3341–74, as amended by Pub.L. 100–41, May 15, 1987, 101 Stat. 309; Pub.L. 100–99, Aug. 18, 1987, 101 Stat. 716; Pub.L. 100–334, § 3(a), June 16, 1988, 102 Stat. 613, provided that:

"**(a)(1)** Subject to paragraphs (2), (3), (4), and (5), and notwithstanding title 11 of the United States Code [this title], the trustee shall pay benefits to retired former employees under a plan, fund, or program maintained or established by the debtor prior to filing a petition (through the purchase of insurance or otherwise) for the purpose of providing medical, surgical, or hospital care benefits, or benefits in the event of sickness, accident, disability, or death.

"**(2)** The level of benefits required to be paid by this subsection may be modified prior to confirmation of a plan under section 1129 of such title [section 1129 of this title] if—

"**(A)** the trustee and an authorized representative of the former employees with respect to whom such benefits are payable agree to the modification of such benefit payments; or

"**(B)** the court finds that a modification proposed by the trustee meets the standards of section 1113(b)(1)(A) of such title [section 1113(b)(1)(A) of this title] and the balance of the equities clearly favors the modification.

If such benefits are covered by a collective bargaining agreement, the authorized representative shall be the labor organization that is signatory to such collective bargaining agreement unless there is a conflict of interest.

"(3) The trustee shall pay benefits in accordance with this subsection until—

"(A) the dismissal of the case involved; or

"(B) the effective date of a plan confirmed under section 1129 of such title which provides for the continued payment after confirmation of the plan of all such benefits at the level established under paragraph (2) of this subsection, at any time prior to the confirmation of the plan, for the duration of the period the debtor (as defined in such title) has obligated itself to provide such benefits.

"(4) No such benefits paid between the filing of a petition in a case covered by this section and the time a plan confirmed under section 1129 of such title with respect to such case becomes effective shall be deducted or offset from the amount allowed as claims for any benefits which remain unpaid, or from the amount to be paid under the plan with respect to such claims for unpaid benefits, whether such claims for unpaid benefits are based upon or arise from a right to future benefits or from any benefit not paid as a result of modifications allowed pursuant to this section.

"(5) No claim for benefits covered by this section shall be limited by section 502(b)(7) of such title [section 502(b)(7) of this title].

"(b)(1) Notwithstanding any provision of title 11 of the United States Code [this title], the trustee shall pay an allowable claim of any person for a benefit paid—

"(A) before the filing of the petition under title 11 of the United States Code; and

"(B) directly or indirectly to a retired former employee under a plan, fund, or program described in subsection (a)(1);

if, as determined by the court, such person is entitled to recover from such employee, or any provider of health care to such employee, directly or indirectly, the amount of such benefit for which such person receives no payment from the debtor.

"(2) For purposes of paragraph (1), the term 'provider of health care' means a person who—

"(A) is the direct provider of health care (including a physician, dentist, nurse, podiatrist, optometrist, physician assistant, or ancillary personnel employed under the supervision of a physician); or

"(B) administers a facility or institution (including a hospital, alcohol and drug abuse treatment facility, outpatient facility, or health maintenance organization) in which health care is provided.

"(c) This section is effective with respect to cases commenced under chapter 11, of title 11, United States Code [this chapter], in which a plan for reorganization has not been confirmed by the court and in which any such benefit is still being paid on October 2, 1986, and in cases that become subject to chapter 11, title 11, United States Code, after October 2, 1986 and before the date of the enactment of the Retiree Benefits Bankruptcy Protection Act of 1988 [June 16, 1988].

"(d) This section shall not apply during any period in which a case is subject to chapter 7, title 11, United States Code [11 U.S.C.A. § 701 et seq.]."

Similar provisions were contained in Pub.L. 99–656, § 2, Nov. 14, 1986, 100 Stat. 3668, as amended by Pub.L. 100–41, May 15, 1987, 101 Stat. 309; Pub.L. 100–99, Aug. 18, 1987, 101 Stat. 716, and were repealed by Pub.L. 100–334, § 3(b), June 16, 1988, 102 Stat. 614.

CROSS REFERENCES

Duties of trustees in—

Chapter thirteen cases, see 11 USCA § 1302.

Chapter twelve cases, see 11 USCA § 1202.

Powers and duties of trustee in investor protection liquidation proceedings, see 15 USCA § 78fff–1.

Rights and powers of debtor in Chapter twelve case not encompassing duties specified in subsec. (a)(3) and (4) of this section, see 11 USCA § 1203.

§ 1107. Rights, powers, and duties of debtor in possession

(a) Subject to any limitations on a trustee serving in a case under this chapter, and to such limitations or conditions as the court prescribes, a debtor in possession shall have all the rights, other than the right to compensation under section 330 of this title, and powers, and shall perform all the functions and duties, except the duties specified in sections 1106(a)(2), (3), and (4) of this title, of a trustee serving in a case under this chapter.

(b) Notwithstanding section 327(a) of this title, a person is not disqualified for employment under section 327 of this title by a debtor in possession solely because of such person's employment by or representation of the debtor before the commencement of the case.

(Pub.L. 95–598, Nov. 6, 1978, 92 Stat. 2628; Pub.L. 98–353, Title III, § 503, July 10, 1984, 98 Stat. 384.)

HISTORICAL AND STATUTORY NOTES

Amendments

1984 Amendments. Subsec. (a). Pub.L. 98–353 substituted "on a trustee serving in a case" for "on a trustee" preceding "under this chapter".

CROSS REFERENCES

Debtor engaged in business in Chapter thirteen cases, see 11 USCA § 1304.

Debtor's duties, see 11 USCA § 521.

Inapplicability of this section in railroad reorganization cases, see 11 USCA § 1161.

Limitation on compensation of professional persons, see 11 USCA § 328.

Rights and powers of debtor in—

    Chapter thirteen cases, see 11 USCA § 1303.

    Chapter twelve cases, see 11 USCA § 1203.

§ 1108. Authorization to operate business

Unless the court, on request of a party in interest and after notice and a hearing, orders otherwise, the trustee may operate the debtor's business.

(Pub.L. 95–598, Nov. 6, 1978, 92 Stat. 2629; Pub.L. 98–353, Title III, § 504, July 10, 1984, 98 Stat. 384.)

HISTORICAL AND STATUTORY NOTES

Amendments

1984 Amendments. Pub.L. 98–353 inserted ", on request of a party in interest and after notice and a hearing," after "court".

CROSS REFERENCES

Authorization to operate business in Chapter seven cases, see 11 USCA § 721.

Executory contracts and unexpired leases, see 11 USCA § 365.

Executory contracts in stockbroker liquidation cases, see 11 USCA § 744.

Obtaining credit, see 11 USCA § 364.

Retention or replacement of professional persons, see 11 USCA § 327.

Treatment of accounts in—

Commodity broker liquidation cases, see 11 USCA § 763.

Stockbroker liquidation cases, see 11 USCA § 745.

Use, sale or lease of property, see 11 USCA § 363.

Utility service, see 11 USCA § 366.

§ 1109. Right to be heard

(a) The Securities and Exchange Commission may raise and may appear and be heard on any issue in a case under this chapter, but the Securities and Exchange Commission may not appeal from any judgment, order, or decree entered in the case.

(b) A party in interest, including the debtor, the trustee, a creditors' committee, an equity security holders' committee, a creditor, an equity security holder, or any indenture trustee, may raise and may appear and be heard on any issue in a case under this chapter.

(Pub.L. 95–598, Nov. 6, 1978, 92 Stat. 2629.)

CROSS REFERENCES

Applicability of this section in Chapter 9 cases, see 11 USCA § 901.

Right of Commodity Futures Trading Commission to be heard in commodity broker liquidation cases, see 11 USCA § 762.

Right of Interstate Commerce Commission, Department of Transportation, and State or local regulatory commission to be heard in railroad reorganization, see 11 USCA § 1164.

§ 1110. Aircraft equipment and vessels

(a)(1) Except as provided in paragraph (2) and subject to subsection (b), the right of a secured party with a security interest in equipment described in paragraph (3), or of a lessor or conditional vendor of such equipment, to take possession of such equipment in compliance with a security agreement, lease, or conditional sale contract, and to enforce any of its other rights or remedies, under such security agreement, lease, or conditional sale contract, to sell, lease, or otherwise retain or dispose of such equipment, is not limited or otherwise affected by any other provision of this title or by any power of the court.

(2) The right to take possession and to enforce the other rights and remedies described in paragraph (1) shall be subject to section 362 if—

(A) before the date that is 60 days after the date of the order for relief under this chapter, the trustee, subject to the approval of the court, agrees to perform all obligations of the debtor under such security agreement, lease, or conditional sale contract; and

(B) any default, other than a default of a kind specified in section 365(b)(2), under such security agreement, lease, or conditional sale contract—

(i) that occurs before the date of the order is cured before the expiration of such 60-day period;

(ii) that occurs after the date of the order and before the expiration of such 60-day period is cured before the later of—

(I) the date that is 30 days after the date of the default; or

(II) the expiration of such 60-day period; and

(iii) that occurs on or after the expiration of such 60-day period is cured in compliance with the terms of such security agreement, lease, or conditional sale contract, if a cure is permitted under that agreement, lease, or contract.

(3) The equipment described in this paragraph—

(A) is—

(i) an aircraft, aircraft engine, propeller, appliance, or spare part (as defined in section 40102 of title 49) that is subject to a security interest granted by, leased to, or conditionally sold to a debtor that, at the time such transaction is entered into, holds an air carrier operating certificate issued pursuant to chapter 447 of title 49 for aircraft capable of carrying 10 or more individuals or 6,000 pounds or more of cargo; or

(ii) a vessel documented under chapter 121 of title 46 that is subject to a security interest granted by, leased to, or conditionally sold to a debtor that is a water carrier that, at the time such transaction is entered into, holds a certificate of public convenience and necessity or permit issued by the Department of Transportation; and

(B) includes all records and documents relating to such equipment that are required, under the terms of the security agreement, lease, or conditional sale contract, to be surrendered or returned by the debtor in connection with the surrender or return of such equipment.

(4) Paragraph (1) applies to a secured party, lessor, or conditional vendor acting in its own behalf or acting as trustee or otherwise in behalf of another party.

(b) The trustee and the secured party, lessor, or conditional vendor whose right to take possession is protected under subsection (a) may agree, subject to the approval of the court, to extend the 60-day period specified in subsection (a)(1).

(c)(1) In any case under this chapter, the trustee shall immediately surrender and return to a secured party, lessor, or conditional vendor, described in subsection (a)(1), equipment described in subsection (a)(3), if at any time after the date of the order for relief under this chapter such secured party, lessor, or conditional vendor is entitled pursuant to subsection (a)(1) to take possession of such equipment and makes a written demand for such possession to the trustee.

(2) At such time as the trustee is required under paragraph (1) to surrender and return equipment described in subsection (a)(3), any lease of such equipment, and any security agreement or conditional sale contract relating to such equipment, if such security agreement or conditional sale contract is an executory contract, shall be deemed rejected.

(d) With respect to equipment first placed in service on or before October 22, 1994, for purposes of this section—

(1) the term 'lease' includes any written agreement with respect to which the lessor and the debtor, as lessee, have expressed in the agreement or in a substantially contemporaneous writing that the agreement is to be treated as a lease for Federal income tax purposes; and

(2) the term "security interest" means a purchase-money equipment security interest.

(Pub.L. 95–598, Nov. 6, 1978, 92 Stat. 2629; Pub.L. 103–272, § 5(c), July 5, 1994, 108 Stat. 1373; Pub.L. 103–394, Title II, § 201(a), Oct. 22, 1994, 108 Stat. 4119; Pub.L. 106–181, Title VII, § 744(b), Apr. 5, 2000, 114 Stat. 177; Pub.L. 109–304, § 17(b)(2), Oct. 6, 2006, 120 Stat. 1707.)

HISTORICAL AND STATUTORY NOTES

References in Text

Chapter 447 of Title 49, referred to in subsec. (a)(3)(A)(i), is classified to 49 U.S.C.A. § 44701 et seq.

Chapter 121 of this title, referred to in subsec. (a)(3)(A)(ii), is Documentation of Vessels, 46 U.S.C.A. § 12101 et seq.

Amendments

2006 Amendments. Subsec. (a)(3)(A)(ii). Pub.L. 109–304, § 17(b)(2), struck out "documented vessel (as defined in section 30101(1) of title 46)" and inserted "vessel documented under chapter 121 of title 46".

2000 Amendments. Pub.L. 106–181, Title VII, § 744(b), rewrote the section, which read:

"**(a)(1)** The right of a secured party with a security interest in equipment described in paragraph (2) or of a lessor or conditional vendor of such equipment to take possession of such equipment in compliance with a security agreement, lease, or conditional sale contract is not affected by section 362, 363, or 1129 or by any power of the court to enjoin the taking of possession unless—

"(A) before the date that is 60 days after the date of the order for relief under this chapter, the trustee, subject to the court's approval, agrees to perform all obligations of the debtor that become due on or after the date of the order under such security agreement, lease, or conditional sale contract; and

"(B) any default, other than a default of a kind specified in section 365(b)(2), under such security agreement, lease, or conditional sale contract—

"(i) that occurs before the date of the order is cured before the expiration of such 60-day period; and

"(ii) that occurs after the date of the order is cured before the later of—

"(I) the date that is 30 days after the date of the default; or

"(II) the expiration of such 60-day period.

"(2) Equipment is described in this paragraph if it is—

"(A) an aircraft, aircraft engine, propeller, appliance, or spare part (as defined in section 40102 of title 49) that is subject to a security interest granted by, leased to, or conditionally sold to a debtor that is a citizen of the United States (as defined in section 40102 of title 49) holding an air carrier operating certificate issued by the Secretary of Transportation pursuant to chapter 447 of title 49 for aircraft capable of carrying 10 or more individuals or 6,000 pounds or more of cargo; or

"(B) a documented vessel (as defined in section 30101(1) of title 46) that is subject to a security interest granted by, leased to, or conditionally sold to a debtor that is a water carrier that holds a certificate of public convenience and necessity or permit issued by the Interstate Commerce Commission.

"(3) Paragraph (1) applies to a secured party, lessor, or conditional vendor acting in its own behalf or acting as trustee or otherwise in behalf of another party.

"(b) The trustee and the secured party, lessor, or conditional vendor whose right to take possession is protected under subsection (a) may agree, subject to the court's approval, to extend the 60-day period specified in subsection (a)(1).

"(c) With respect to equipment first placed in service on or prior to the date of enactment of this subsection, for purposes of this section—

"(1) the term 'lease' includes any written agreement with respect to which the lessor and the debtor, as lessee, have expressed in the agreement or in a substantially contemporaneous writing that the agreement is to be treated as a lease for Federal income tax purposes; and

"(2) the term 'security interest' means a purchase-money equipment security interest."

1994 Amendments. Subsec. (a). Pub.L. 103–272, § 5(c), substituted "section 40102(a) of title 49" for "section 101 of the Federal Aviation Act of 1958 (49 U.S.C. 1301)", "section 30101 of title 46" for "subsection B(4) of the Ship Mortgage Act, 1920 (46 U.S.C. 911(4))", and "Secretary of Transportation" for "Civil Aeronautics Board".

Pub.L. 103–394, § 201(a), in subsec. (a) designated existing text as par. (1), as so designated, substituted provisions directing that the right to take possession of certain equipment is not affected by section 362, 363, or 1129, for provisions directing that the right to take possession of certain equipment is not affected by section 362 or 363 of this title, redesignated former pars. (1) and (2) as par. (1), subpars. (A) and (B), respectively, and added pars. (2) and (3) and subsecs. (c) and (d).

Aircraft Equipment Settlement Leases Act of 1993

Pub.L. 103–7, Mar. 17, 1993, 107 Stat. 36, provided:

"Section 1. Short Title.

"This Act [this note] may be cited as the 'Aircraft Equipment Settlement Leases Act of 1993'.

"**Sec. 2. Treatment of Aircraft Equipment Settlement Leases with the Pension Benefit Guaranty Corporation.**

"In the case of any settlement of liability under title IV of the Employee Retirement Income Security Act of 1974 [29 U.S.C.A. § 1301 et seq.], entered into by the Pension Benefit Guaranty Corporation and one or more other parties, if—

"**(1)** such settlement was entered into before, on, or after the date of the enactment of this Act [Mar. 17, 1993],

"**(2)** at least one party to such settlement was a debtor under title 11 of the United States Code [this title], and

"**(3)** an agreement that is entered into as part of such settlement provides that such agreement is to be treated as a lease,

then such agreement shall be treated as a lease for purposes of section 1110 of such title 11 [this section]."

Termination of Civil Aeronautics Board and Transfer of Certain Functions

All functions, powers, and duties of the Civil Aeronautics Board were terminated or transferred by section 1551 of Title 49, Appendix, Transportation, effective in part on Dec. 31, 1981, in part on Jan. 1, 1983, and in part on Jan. 1, 1985.

CROSS REFERENCES

Effect of conversion, see 11 USCA § 348.

Rights of certain secured parties in rolling stock equipment, see 11 USCA § 1168.

§ 1111. Claims and interests

(a) A proof of claim or interest is deemed filed under section 501 of this title for any claim or interest that appears in the schedules filed under section 521(a)(1) or 1106(a)(2) of this title, except a claim or interest that is scheduled as disputed, contingent, or unliquidated.

(b)(1)(A) A claim secured by a lien on property of the estate shall be allowed or disallowed under section 502 of this title the same as if the holder of such claim had recourse against the debtor on account of such claim, whether or not such holder has such recourse, unless—

(i) the class of which such claim is a part elects, by at least two-thirds in amount and more than half in number of allowed claims of such class, application of paragraph (2) of this subsection; or

(ii) such holder does not have such recourse and such property is sold under section 363 of this title or is to be sold under the plan.

(B) A class of claims may not elect application of paragraph (2) of this subsection if—

(i) the interest on account of such claims of the holders of such claims in such property is of inconsequential value; or

(ii) the holder of a claim of such class has recourse against the debtor on account of such claim and such property is sold under section 363 of this title or is to be sold under the plan.

(2) If such an election is made, then notwithstanding section 506(a) of this title, such claim is a secured claim to the extent that such claim is allowed.

(Pub.L. 95–598, Nov. 6, 1978, 92 Stat. 2630; Pub.L. 111–327, § 2(a)(32), Dec. 22, 2010, 124 Stat. 3561.)

HISTORICAL AND STATUTORY NOTES

Amendments

2010 Amendments. Subsec. (a). Pub.L. 111–327, § 2(a)(32), struck out "521(1)" and inserted "521(a)(1)".

CROSS REFERENCES

Applicability of subsec. (b) of this section in Chapter nine cases, see 11 USCA § 901.

Effect of list of claims in Chapter nine cases, see 11 USCA § 925.

Election as affecting confirmation of plan, see 11 USCA § 1129.

Filing and allowance of postpetition claims in Chapter thirteen cases, see 11 USCA § 1305.

Limitation on recourse of claim payable solely from special revenues of debtor, see 11 USCA § 927.

§ 1112. Conversion or dismissal

(a) The debtor may convert a case under this chapter to a case under chapter 7 of this title unless—

   (1) the debtor is not a debtor in possession;

   (2) the case originally was commenced as an involuntary case under this chapter; or

   (3) the case was converted to a case under this chapter other than on the debtor's request.

(b)(1) Except as provided in paragraph (2) and subsection (c), on request of a party in interest, and after notice and a hearing, the court shall convert a case under this chapter to a case under chapter 7 or dismiss a case under this chapter, whichever is in the best interests of creditors and the estate, for cause unless the court determines that the appointment under section 1104(a) of a trustee or an examiner is in the best interests of creditors and the estate.

   (2) The court may not convert a case under this chapter to a case under chapter 7 or dismiss a case under this chapter if the court finds and specifically identifies unusual circumstances establishing that converting or dismissing the case is not in the best interests of creditors and the estate, and the debtor or any other party in interest establishes that—

   (A) there is a reasonable likelihood that a plan will be confirmed within the timeframes established in sections 1121(e) and 1129(e) of this title, or if such sections do not apply, within a reasonable period of time; and

   (B) the grounds for converting or dismissing the case include an act or omission of the debtor other than under paragraph (4)(A)—

      (i) for which there exists a reasonable justification for the act or omission; and

      (ii) that will be cured within a reasonable period of time fixed by the court.

   (3) The court shall commence the hearing on a motion under this subsection not later than 30 days after filing of the motion, and shall decide the motion not later than 15 days after commencement of such hearing, unless the movant expressly consents to a continuance for a specific period of time or compelling circumstances prevent the court from meeting the time limits established by this paragraph.

   (4) For purposes of this subsection, the term 'cause' includes—

   (A) substantial or continuing loss to or diminution of the estate and the absence of a reasonable likelihood of rehabilitation;

   (B) gross mismanagement of the estate;

   (C) failure to maintain appropriate insurance that poses a risk to the estate or to the public;

   (D) unauthorized use of cash collateral substantially harmful to 1 or more creditors;

   (E) failure to comply with an order of the court;

   (F) unexcused failure to satisfy timely any filing or reporting requirement established by this title or by any rule applicable to a case under this chapter;

(G) failure to attend the meeting of creditors convened under section 341(a) or an examination ordered under rule 2004 of the Federal Rules of Bankruptcy Procedure without good cause shown by the debtor;

(H) failure timely to provide information or attend meetings reasonably requested by the United States trustee (or the bankruptcy administrator, if any);

(I) failure timely to pay taxes owed after the date of the order for relief or to file tax returns due after the date of the order for relief;

(J) failure to file a disclosure statement, or to file or confirm a plan, within the time fixed by this title or by order of the court;

(K) failure to pay any fees or charges required under chapter 123 of title 28;

(L) revocation of an order of confirmation under section 1144;

(M) inability to effectuate substantial consummation of a confirmed plan;

(N) material default by the debtor with respect to a confirmed plan;

(O) termination of a confirmed plan by reason of the occurrence of a condition specified in the plan; and

(P) failure of the debtor to pay any domestic support obligation that first becomes payable after the date of the filing of the petition.

(c) The court may not convert a case under this chapter to a case under chapter 7 of this title if the debtor is a farmer or a corporation that is not a moneyed, business, or commercial corporation, unless the debtor requests such conversion.

(d) The court may convert a case under this chapter to a case under chapter 12 or 13 of this title only if—

(1) the debtor requests such conversion;

(2) the debtor has not been discharged under section 1141(d) of this title; and

(3) if the debtor requests conversion to chapter 12 of this title, such conversion is equitable.

(e) Except as provided in subsections (c) and (f), the court, on request of the United States trustee, may convert a case under this chapter to a case under chapter 7 of this title or may dismiss a case under this chapter, whichever is in the best interest of creditors and the estate if the debtor in a voluntary case fails to file, within fifteen days after the filing of the petition commencing such case or such additional time as the court may allow, the information required by paragraph (1) of section 521(a), including a list containing the names and addresses of the holders of the twenty largest unsecured claims (or of all unsecured claims if there are fewer than twenty unsecured claims), and the approximate dollar amounts of each of such claims.

(f) Notwithstanding any other provision of this section, a case may not be converted to a case under another chapter of this title unless the debtor may be a debtor under such chapter.

(Pub.L. 95–598, Nov. 6, 1978, 92 Stat. 2630; Pub.L. 98–353, Title III, § 505, July 10, 1984, 98 Stat. 384; Pub.L. 99–554, Title II, §§ 224, 256, Oct. 27, 1986, 100 Stat. 3102, 3114; Pub.L. 103–394, Title II, § 217(c), Oct. 22, 1994, 108 Stat. 4127; Pub.L. 109–8, Title IV, § 442(a), Apr. 20, 2005, 119 Stat. 115; Pub.L. 111–327, § 2(a)(33), Dec. 22, 2010, 124 Stat. 3561.)

HISTORICAL AND STATUTORY NOTES

References in Text

Chapter 123 of title 28, referred to in subsec. (b)(4)(K), is 28 U.S.C.A. § 1911 et seq.

Amendments

2010 Amendments. Subsec. (b)(1). Pub.L. 111–327, § 2(a)(33)(A)(i), rewrote par. (1), which formerly read: "**(1)** Except as provided in paragraph (2) of this subsection, subsection (c) of this section, and section 1104(a)(3), on request of a party in interest, and after notice and a hearing, absent unusual circumstances specifically identified by the court that establish that the requested conversion or dismissal is not in the best interests of creditors and the estate, the court shall convert a case under this chapter to a case under chapter 7 or dismiss a case under this chapter, whichever is in the best interests of creditors and the estate, if the movant establishes cause."

Subsec. (b)(2). Pub.L. 111–327, § 2(a)(33)(A)(ii)(I), rewrote the matter preceding subpar. (A), which formerly read: "**(2)** The relief provided in paragraph (1) shall not be granted absent unusual circumstances specifically identified by the court that establish that such relief is not in the best interests of creditors and the estate, if the debtor or another party in interest objects and establishes that—".

Subsec. (b)(2)(B). Pub.L. 111–327, § 2(a)(33)(A)(ii)(II), struck out "granting such relief" and inserted "converting or dismissing the case".

Subsec. (e). Pub.L. 111–327, § 2(a)(33)(B), struck out "521" and inserted "521(a)".

2005 Amendments. Subsec. (b). Pub.L. 109–8, § 442(a), rewrote subsec. (b), which formerly read:

"**(b)** Except as provided in subsection (c) of this section, on request of a party in interest or the United States trustee or bankruptcy administrator, and after notice and a hearing, the court may convert a case under this chapter to a case under chapter 7 of this title or may dismiss a case under this chapter, whichever is in the best interest of creditors and the estate, for cause, including-

"**(1)** continuing loss to or diminution of the estate and absence of a reasonable likelihood of rehabilitation;

"**(2)** inability to effectuate a plan;

"**(3)** unreasonable delay by the debtor that is prejudicial to creditors;

"**(4)** failure to propose a plan under section 1121 of this title within any time fixed by the court;

"**(5)** denial of confirmation of every proposed plan and denial of a request made for additional time for filing another plan or a modification of a plan;

"**(6)** revocation of an order of confirmation under section 1144 of this title, and denial of confirmation of another plan or a modified plan under section 1129 of this title;

"**(7)** inability to effectuate substantial consummation of a confirmed plan;

"**(8)** material default by the debtor with respect to a confirmed plan;

"**(9)** termination of a plan by reason of the occurrence of a condition specified in the plan;

"**(10)** nonpayment of any fees or charges required under chapter 123 of title 28."

1994 Amendments. Subsec. (b). Pub.L. 103–394, § 217(c), added provisions authorizing the court to convert or dismiss a case on request of bankruptcy administrator.

1986 Amendments. Subsec. (b). Pub.L. 99–554, § 224(1)(A), added "or the United States trustee" following "party in interest".

Subsec. (b)(10). Pub.L. 99–554, § 224(1)(B)–(D), added par. (10).

Subsec. (d). Pub.L. 99–554, § 256(1), added reference to chapter 12.

Subsec. (d)(3). Pub.L. 99–554, § 256(2)–(4), added par. (3).

Subsec. (e). Pub.L. 99–554, § 224(3), added subsec. (e). Former subsec. (e) was redesignated (f).

Subsec. (f). Pub.L. 99–554, § 224(2), redesignated former subsec. (e) as (f).

1984 Amendments. Subsec. (a)(2). Pub.L. 98–353, § 505(a)(1), substituted "originally was commenced as an involuntary case under this chapter" for "is an involuntary case originally commenced under this chapter".

Subsec. (a)(3). Pub.L. 98–353, § 505(a)(2), substituted "other than on" for "on other than".

Subsec. (b)(5). Pub.L. 98–353, § 505(b)(1), added "a request made for" before "additional".

Subsec. (b)(8). Pub.L. 98–353, § 505(b)(2), substituted "or" for "and".

CROSS REFERENCES

Conversion of—

    Chapter seven cases, see 11 USCA § 706.

    Chapter thirteen cases, see 11 USCA § 1307.

    Chapter twelve cases, see 11 USCA § 1208.

Dismissal of—

    Chapter nine cases, see 11 USCA § 930.

    Chapter seven cases, see 11 USCA § 707.

Distribution of property of estate converted to Chapter seven, see 11 USCA § 726.

Effect of conversion, see 11 USCA § 348.

Effect of dismissal, see 11 USCA § 349.

Executory contracts and unexpired leases, see 11 USCA § 365.

Liquidation of estate in railroad reorganization cases, see 11 USCA § 1174.

Termination of debtor's taxable period for cases converted to Chapter seven, see 11 USCA § 728.

§ 1113. Rejection of collective bargaining agreements

    (a) The debtor in possession, or the trustee if one has been appointed under the provisions of this chapter, other than a trustee in a case covered by subchapter IV of this chapter and by title I of the Railway Labor Act, may assume or reject a collective bargaining agreement only in accordance with the provisions of this section.

    (b)(1) Subsequent to filing a petition and prior to filing an application seeking rejection of a collective bargaining agreement, the debtor in possession or trustee (hereinafter in this section "trustee" shall include a debtor in possession), shall—

        (A) make a proposal to the authorized representative of the employees covered by such agreement, based on the most complete and reliable information available at the time of such proposal, which provides for those necessary modifications in the employees benefits and protections that are necessary to permit the reorganization of the debtor and assures that all creditors, the debtor and all of the affected parties are treated fairly and equitably; and

        (B) provide, subject to subsection (d)(3), the representative of the employees with such relevant information as is necessary to evaluate the proposal.

    (2) During the period beginning on the date of the making of a proposal provided for in paragraph (1) and ending on the date of the hearing provided for in subsection (d)(1), the trustee shall meet, at reasonable times, with the authorized representative to confer in good faith in attempting to reach mutually satisfactory modifications of such agreement.

    (c) The court shall approve an application for rejection of a collective bargaining agreement only if the court finds that—

        (1) the trustee has, prior to the hearing, made a proposal that fulfills the requirements of subsection (b)(1);

        (2) the authorized representative of the employees has refused to accept such proposal without good cause; and

        (3) the balance of the equities clearly favors rejection of such agreement.

    (d)(1) Upon the filing of an application for rejection the court shall schedule a hearing to be held not later than fourteen days after the date of the filing of such application. All interested parties may appear and be heard at such hearing. Adequate notice shall be provided to such parties at least ten days before the date of such hearing. The court may extend the time for the commencement of such hearing for a period not exceeding seven days where the circumstances of the case, and the interests of justice require such extension, or for additional periods of time to which the trustee and representative agree.

(2) The court shall rule on such application for rejection within thirty days after the date of the commencement of the hearing. In the interests of justice, the court may extend such time for ruling for such additional period as the trustee and the employees' representative may agree to. If the court does not rule on such application within thirty days after the date of the commencement of the hearing, or within such additional time as the trustee and the employees' representative may agree to, the trustee may terminate or alter any provisions of the collective bargaining agreement pending the ruling of the court on such application.

(3) The court may enter such protective orders, consistent with the need of the authorized representative of the employee to evaluate the trustee's proposal and the application for rejection, as may be necessary to prevent disclosure of information provided to such representative where such disclosure could compromise the position of the debtor with respect to its competitors in the industry in which it is engaged.

(e) If during a period when the collective bargaining agreement continues in effect, and if essential to the continuation of the debtor's business, or in order to avoid irreparable damage to the estate, the court, after notice and a hearing, may authorize the trustee to implement interim changes in the terms, conditions, wages, benefits, or work rules provided by a collective bargaining agreement. Any hearing under this paragraph shall be scheduled in accordance with the needs of the trustee. The implementation of such interim changes shall not render the application for rejection moot.

(f) No provision of this title shall be construed to permit a trustee to unilaterally terminate or alter any provisions of a collective bargaining agreement prior to compliance with the provisions of this section.

(Added Pub.L. 98–353, Title III, § 541(a), July 10, 1984, 98 Stat. 390.)

HISTORICAL AND STATUTORY NOTES

References in Text

The Railway Labor Act, referred to in subsec. (a), is Act May 20, 1926, c. 347, 44 Stat. 577, as amended. Title I of the Railway Labor Act is classified principally to subchapter I (section 151 et seq.) of chapter 8 of Title 45, Railroads. For complete classification of this Act to the Code, see section 151 of Title 45 and Tables.

§ 1114. Payment of insurance benefits to retired employees

(a) For purposes of this section, the term "retiree benefits" means payments to any entity or person for the purpose of providing or reimbursing payments for retired employees and their spouses and dependents, for medical, surgical, or hospital care benefits, or benefits in the event of sickness, accident, disability, or death under any plan, fund, or program (through the purchase of insurance or otherwise) maintained or established in whole or in part by the debtor prior to filing a petition commencing a case under this title.

(b)(1) For purposes of this section, the term "authorized representative" means the authorized representative designated pursuant to subsection (c) for persons receiving any retiree benefits covered by a collective bargaining agreement or subsection (d) in the case of persons receiving retiree benefits not covered by such an agreement.

(2) Committees of retired employees appointed by the court pursuant to this section shall have the same rights, powers, and duties as committees appointed under sections 1102 and 1103 of this title for the purpose of carrying out the purposes of sections 1114 and 1129(a)(13) and, as permitted by the court, shall have the power to enforce the rights of persons under this title as they relate to retiree benefits.

(c)(1) A labor organization shall be, for purposes of this section, the authorized representative of those persons receiving any retiree benefits covered by any collective bargaining agreement to which that labor organization is signatory, unless (A) such labor organization elects not to serve as the authorized representative of such persons, or (B) the court, upon a motion by any party in interest, after notice and hearing, determines that different representation of such persons is appropriate.

(2) In cases where the labor organization referred to in paragraph (1) elects not to serve as the authorized representative of those persons receiving any retiree benefits covered by any collective bargaining agreement to which that labor organization is signatory, or in cases where the court, pursuant to paragraph (1) finds different representation of such persons appropriate, the court, upon a motion by any party in interest, and after notice and a hearing, shall appoint a committee of retired employees if the debtor seeks to modify or not pay the retiree benefits or if the court otherwise determines that it is appropriate, from among such persons, to serve as the authorized representative of such persons under this section.

(d) The court, upon a motion by any party in interest, and after notice and a hearing, shall order the appointment of a committee of retired employees if the debtor seeks to modify or not pay the retiree benefits or if the court otherwise determines that it is appropriate, to serve as the authorized representative, under this section, of those persons receiving any retiree benefits not covered by a collective bargaining agreement. The United States trustee shall appoint any such committee.

(e)(1) Notwithstanding any other provision of this title, the debtor in possession, or the trustee if one has been appointed under the provisions of this chapter (hereinafter in this section "trustee" shall include a debtor in possession), shall timely pay and shall not modify any retiree benefits, except that—

(A) the court, on motion of the trustee or authorized representative, and after notice and a hearing, may order modification of such payments, pursuant to the provisions of subsections (g) and (h) of this section, or

(B) the trustee and the authorized representative of the recipients of those benefits may agree to modification of such payments,

after which such benefits as modified shall continue to be paid by the trustee.

(2) Any payment for retiree benefits required to be made before a plan confirmed under section 1129 of this title is effective has the status of an allowed administrative expense as provided in section 503 of this title.

(f)(1) Subsequent to filing a petition and prior to filing an application seeking modification of the retiree benefits, the trustee shall—

(A) make a proposal to the authorized representative of the retirees, based on the most complete and reliable information available at the time of such proposal, which provides for those necessary modifications in the retiree benefits that are necessary to permit the reorganization of the debtor and assures that all creditors, the debtor and all of the affected parties are treated fairly and equitably; and

(B) provide, subject to subsection (k)(3), the representative of the retirees with such relevant information as is necessary to evaluate the proposal.

(2) During the period beginning on the date of the making of a proposal provided for in paragraph (1), and ending on the date of the hearing provided for in subsection (k)(1), the trustee shall meet, at reasonable times, with the authorized representative to confer in good faith in attempting to reach mutually satisfactory modifications of such retiree benefits.

(g) The court shall enter an order providing for modification in the payment of retiree benefits if the court finds that—

(1) the trustee has, prior to the hearing, made a proposal that fulfills the requirements of subsection (f);

(2) the authorized representative of the retirees has refused to accept such proposal without good cause; and

(3) such modification is necessary to permit the reorganization of the debtor and assures that all creditors, the debtor, and all of the affected parties are treated fairly and equitably, and is clearly favored by the balance of the equities;

except that in no case shall the court enter an order providing for such modification which provides for a modification to a level lower than that proposed by the trustee in the proposal found by the court to have complied with the requirements of this subsection and subsection (f): *Provided, however,* That at any time after an order is entered providing for modification in the payment of retiree benefits, or at any time after an agreement modifying such benefits is made between the trustee and the authorized representative of the recipients of such benefits, the authorized representative may apply to the court for an order increasing those benefits which order shall be granted if the increase in retiree benefits sought is consistent with the standard set forth in paragraph (3): *Provided further,* That neither the trustee nor the authorized representative is precluded from making more than one motion for a modification order governed by this subsection.

(h)(1) Prior to a court issuing a final order under subsection (g) of this section, if essential to the continuation of the debtor's business, or in order to avoid irreparable damage to the estate, the court, after notice and a hearing, may authorize the trustee to implement interim modifications in retiree benefits.

(2) Any hearing under this subsection shall be scheduled in accordance with the needs of the trustee.

(3) The implementation of such interim changes does not render the motion for modification moot.

(i) No retiree benefits paid between the filing of the petition and the time a plan confirmed under section 1129 of this title becomes effective shall be deducted or offset from the amounts allowed as claims for any benefits which remain unpaid, or from the amounts to be paid under the plan with respect to such claims for unpaid benefits, whether such claims for unpaid benefits are based upon or arise from a right to future unpaid benefits or from any benefits not paid as a result of modifications allowed pursuant to this section.

(j) No claim for retiree benefits shall be limited by section 502(b)(7) of this title.

(k)(1) Upon the filing of an application for modifying retiree benefits, the court shall schedule a hearing to be held not later than fourteen days after the date of the filing of such application. All interested parties may appear and be heard at such hearing. Adequate notice shall be provided to such parties at least ten days before the date of such hearing. The court may extend the time for the commencement of such hearing for a period not exceeding seven days where the circumstances of the case, and the interests of justice require such extension, or for additional periods of time to which the trustee and the authorized representative agree.

(2) The court shall rule on such application for modification within ninety days after the date of the commencement of the hearing. In the interests of justice, the court may extend such time for ruling for such additional period as the trustee and the authorized representative may agree to. If the court does not rule on such application within ninety days after the date of the commencement of the hearing, or within such additional time as the trustee and the authorized representative may agree to, the trustee may implement the proposed modifications pending the ruling of the court on such application.

(3) The court may enter such protective orders, consistent with the need of the authorized representative of the retirees to evaluate the trustee's proposal and the application for modification, as may be necessary to prevent disclosure of information provided to such representative where such disclosure could compromise the position of the debtor with respect to its competitors in the industry in which it is engaged.

(l) If the debtor, during the 180-day period ending on the date of the filing of the petition—

(1) modified retiree benefits; and

(2) was insolvent on the date such benefits were modified;

the court, on motion of a party in interest, and after notice and a hearing, shall issue an order reinstating as of the date the modification was made, such benefits as in effect immediately before such date unless the court finds that the balance of the equities clearly favors such modification.

(m) This section shall not apply to any retiree, or the spouse or dependents of such retiree, if such retiree's gross income for the twelve months preceding the filing of the bankruptcy petition equals or exceeds $250,000, unless such retiree can demonstrate to the satisfaction of the court that he is unable to obtain health, medical, life, and disability coverage for himself, his spouse, and his dependents who would otherwise be covered by the employer's insurance plan, comparable to the coverage provided by the employer on the day before the filing of a petition under this title.

(Added Pub.L. 100–334, § 2(a), June 16, 1988, 102 Stat. 610; amended Pub.L. 109–8, Title IV, § 447, Title XIV, § 1403, Apr. 20, 2005, 119 Stat. 118, 215.)

HISTORICAL AND STATUTORY NOTES

Amendments

2005 Amendments. Subsec. (d). Pub.L. 109–8, § 447, struck "appoint" and inserted "order the appointment of", and added at the end: "The United States trustee shall appoint any such committee.".

Subsec. (l). Pub.L. 109–8, § 1403, redesignated former subsec. (l) as subsec. (m), and added a new subsec. (l).

Subsec. (m). Pub.L. 109–8, § 1403(1), redesignated former subsec. (l) as subsec. (m).

Payment of Certain Benefits to Retired Former Employees

For payment of benefits by bankruptcy trustee to retired employees in enumerated circumstances with respect to cases commenced under this chapter in which a plan for reorganization had not been confirmed by the court and in which any such benefit was still being paid on October 2, 1986, and in cases that became subject to this chapter after October 2, 1986, and before June 16, 1988, see section 101(b) [title VI, § 608] of Pub.L. 99–500, and Pub.L. 99–591, as amended, set out as a note under section 1106 of this title.

CROSS REFERENCES

Confirmation of plan if plan provides for continuation of "retiree benefits" as defined under this section, see 11 USCA § 1129.

§ 1115. Property of the estate

(a) In a case in which the debtor is an individual, property of the estate includes, in addition to the property specified in section 541—

(1) all property of the kind specified in section 541 that the debtor acquires after the commencement of the case but before the case is closed, dismissed, or converted to a case under chapter 7, 12, or 13, whichever occurs first; and

(2) earnings from services performed by the debtor after the commencement of the case but before the case is closed, dismissed, or converted to a case under chapter 7, 12, or 13, whichever occurs first.

(b) Except as provided in section 1104 or a confirmed plan or order confirming a plan, the debtor shall remain in possession of all property of the estate.

(Added Pub.L. 109–8, Title III, § 321(a)(1), Apr. 20, 2005, 119 Stat. 94.)

HISTORICAL AND STATUTORY NOTES

References in Text

Chapter 7, 12, or 13, referred to in subsec. (a)(1), (2), is chapter 7, 12, or 13 of this title, 11 U.S.C.A. § 701 et seq., 11 U.S.C.A. § 1201 et seq., or 11 U.S.C.A. § 1301 et seq., respectively.

§ 1116. Duties of trustee or debtor in possession in small business cases

In a small business case, a trustee or the debtor in possession, in addition to the duties provided in this title and as otherwise required by law, shall—

(1) append to the voluntary petition or, in an involuntary case, file not later than 7 days after the date of the order for relief—

(A) its most recent balance sheet, statement of operations, cash-flow statement, and Federal income tax return; or

(B) a statement made under penalty of perjury that no balance sheet, statement of operations, or cash-flow statement has been prepared and no Federal tax return has been filed;

(2) attend, through its senior management personnel and counsel, meetings scheduled by the court or the United States trustee, including initial debtor interviews, scheduling conferences, and meetings of creditors convened under section 341 unless the court, after notice and a hearing, waives that requirement upon a finding of extraordinary and compelling circumstances;

(3) timely file all schedules and statements of financial affairs, unless the court, after notice and a hearing, grants an extension, which shall not extend such time period to a date later than 30 days after the date of the order for relief, absent extraordinary and compelling circumstances;

(4) file all postpetition financial and other reports required by the Federal Rules of Bankruptcy Procedure or by local rule of the district court;

(5) subject to section 363(c)(2), maintain insurance customary and appropriate to the industry;

(6)(A) timely file tax returns and other required government filings; and

(B) subject to section 363(c)(2), timely pay all taxes entitled to administrative expense priority except those being contested by appropriate proceedings being diligently prosecuted; and

(7) allow the United States trustee, or a designated representative of the United States trustee, to inspect the debtor's business premises, books, and records at reasonable times, after reasonable prior written notice, unless notice is waived by the debtor.

(Added Pub.L. 109–8, Title IV, § 436(a), Apr. 20, 2005, 119 Stat. 112.)

SUBCHAPTER II—THE PLAN

CROSS REFERENCES

Subchapter applicable only in case under this chapter except as provided in § 901 of this title, see 11 USCA § 103.

§ 1121. Who may file a plan

(a) The debtor may file a plan with a petition commencing a voluntary case, or at any time in a voluntary case or an involuntary case.

(b) Except as otherwise provided in this section, only the debtor may file a plan until after 120 days after the date of the order for relief under this chapter.

(c) Any party in interest, including the debtor, the trustee, a creditors' committee, an equity security holders' committee, a creditor, an equity security holder, or any indenture trustee, may file a plan if and only if—

(1) a trustee has been appointed under this chapter;

(2) the debtor has not filed a plan before 120 days after the date of the order for relief under this chapter; or

(3) the debtor has not filed a plan that has been accepted, before 180 days after the date of the order for relief under this chapter, by each class of claims or interests that is impaired under the plan.

(d)(1) Subject to paragraph (2), on request of a party in interest made within the respective periods specified in subsections (b) and (c) of this section and after notice and a hearing, the court may for cause reduce or increase the 120-day period or the 180-day period referred to in this section.

(2)(A) The 120-day period specified in paragraph (1) may not be extended beyond a date that is 18 months after the date of the order for relief under this chapter.

(B) The 180-day period specified in paragraph (1) may not be extended beyond a date that is 20 months after the date of the order for relief under this chapter.

(e) In a small business case—

(1) only the debtor may file a plan until after 180 days after the date of the order for relief, unless that period is—

(A) extended as provided by this subsection, after notice and a hearing; or

(B) the court, for cause, orders otherwise;

(2) the plan and a disclosure statement (if any) shall be filed not later than 300 days after the date of the order for relief; and

(3) the time periods specified in paragraphs (1) and (2), and the time fixed in section 1129(e) within which the plan shall be confirmed, may be extended only if—

(A) the debtor, after providing notice to parties in interest (including the United States trustee), demonstrates by a preponderance of the evidence that it is more likely than not that the court will confirm a plan within a reasonable period of time;

(B) a new deadline is imposed at the time the extension is granted; and

(C) the order extending time is signed before the existing deadline has expired.

(Pub.L. 95–598, Nov. 6, 1978, 92 Stat. 2631; Pub.L. 98–353, Title III, § 506, July 10, 1984, 98 Stat. 385; Pub.L. 99–554, Title II, § 283(u), Oct. 27, 1986, 100 Stat. 3118; Pub.L. 103–394, Title II, § 217(d), Oct. 22, 1994, 108 Stat. 4127; Pub.L. 109–8, Title IV, §§ 411, 437, Apr. 20, 2005, 119 Stat. 106, 113.)

HISTORICAL AND STATUTORY NOTES

Amendments

2005 Amendments. Subsec. (d), (d)(1). Pub.L. 109–8, § 411(1), struck "On" at the beginning of the subsection and inserted "(1) Subject to paragraph (2), on".

Subsec. (d)(2). Pub.L. 109–8, § 411(2), added par. (2).

Subsec. (e). Pub.L. 109–8, § 437, rewrote subsec. (e), which formerly read:

"(e) In a case in which the debtor is a small business and elects to be considered a small business—

"(1) only the debtor may file a plan until after 100 days after the date of the order for relief under this chapter;

"(2) all plans shall be filed within 160 days after the date of the order for relief; and

"(3) on request of a party in interest made within the respective periods specified in paragraphs (1) and (2) and after notice and a hearing, the court may—

"(A) reduce the 100-day period or the 160-day period specified in paragraph (1) or (2) for cause; and

"(B) increase the 100-day period specified in paragraph (1) if the debtor shows that the need for an increase is caused by circumstances for which the debtor should not be held accountable."

1994 Amendments. Subsec. (e). Pub.L. 103–394, § 217(d), added subsec. (e).

1986 Amendments. Subsec. (d). Pub.L. 99–554 added reference to subsection (b) of this section.

1984 Amendments. Subsec. (c)(3). Pub.L. 98–353, § 506(a), substituted "of claims or interests that is" for "the claims or interests of which are".

Subsec. (d). Pub.L. 98–353, § 506(b), added "made within the respective periods specified in subsection (c) of this section" following "interest".

CROSS REFERENCES

Effect of conversion, see 11 USCA § 348.

Failure to propose plan as cause for conversion or dismissal, see 11 USCA § 1112.

Filing of plan by trustee, see 11 USCA § 1106.

Filing of plan in—

    Chapter nine cases, see 11 USCA § 941.

    Chapter thirteen cases, see 11 USCA § 1321.

    Chapter twelve cases, see 11 USCA § 1221.

United States trustee not permitted to file plan, see 11 USCA § 307.

§ 1122. Classification of claims or interests

(a) Except as provided in subsection (b) of this section, a plan may place a claim or an interest in a particular class only if such claim or interest is substantially similar to the other claims or interests of such class.

(b) A plan may designate a separate class of claims consisting only of every unsecured claim that is less than or reduced to an amount that the court approves as reasonable and necessary for administrative convenience.

(Pub.L. 95–598, Nov. 6, 1978, 92 Stat. 2631.)

CROSS REFERENCES

Applicability of this section in Chapter 9 cases, see 11 USCA § 901.

Contents of plan filed in—

    Chapter thirteen cases, see 11 USCA § 1322.

    Chapter twelve cases, see 11 USCA § 1222.

Filing and allowance of postpetition claims in Chapter 13 cases, see 11 USCA § 1305.

Filing of proofs of claims or interests, see 11 USCA § 501.

§ 1123. Contents of plan

(a) Notwithstanding any otherwise applicable nonbankruptcy law, a plan shall—

    (1) designate, subject to section 1122 of this title, classes of claims, other than claims of a kind specified in section 507(a)(2), 507(a)(3), or 507(a)(8) of this title, and classes of interests;

    (2) specify any class of claims or interests that is not impaired under the plan;

    (3) specify the treatment of any class of claims or interests that is impaired under the plan;

    (4) provide the same treatment for each claim or interest of a particular class, unless the holder of a particular claim or interest agrees to a less favorable treatment of such particular claim or interest;

(5) provide adequate means for the plan's implementation, such as—

    (A) retention by the debtor of all or any part of the property of the estate;

    (B) transfer of all or any part of the property of the estate to one or more entities, whether organized before or after the confirmation of such plan;

    (C) merger or consolidation of the debtor with one or more persons;

    (D) sale of all or any part of the property of the estate, either subject to or free of any lien, or the distribution of all or any part of the property of the estate among those having an interest in such property of the estate;

    (E) satisfaction or modification of any lien;

    (F) cancellation or modification of any indenture or similar instrument;

    (G) curing or waiving of any default;

    (H) extension of a maturity date or a change in an interest rate or other term of outstanding securities;

    (I) amendment of the debtor's charter; or

    (J) issuance of securities of the debtor, or of any entity referred to in subparagraph (B) or (C) of this paragraph, for cash, for property, for existing securities, or in exchange for claims or interests, or for any other appropriate purpose;

(6) provide for the inclusion in the charter of the debtor, if the debtor is a corporation, or of any corporation referred to in paragraph (5)(B) or (5)(C) of this subsection, of a provision prohibiting the issuance of nonvoting equity securities, and providing, as to the several classes of securities possessing voting power, an appropriate distribution of such power among such classes, including, in the case of any class of equity securities having a preference over another class of equity securities with respect to dividends, adequate provisions for the election of directors representing such preferred class in the event of default in the payment of such dividends;

(7) contain only provisions that are consistent with the interests of creditors and equity security holders and with public policy with respect to the manner of selection of any officer, director, or trustee under the plan and any successor to such officer, director, or trustee; and

(8) in a case in which the debtor is an individual, provide for the payment to creditors under the plan of all or such portion of earnings from personal services performed by the debtor after the commencement of the case or other future income of the debtor as is necessary for the execution of the plan.

(b) Subject to subsection (a) of this section, a plan may—

    (1) impair or leave unimpaired any class of claims, secured or unsecured, or of interests;

    (2) subject to section 365 of this title, provide for the assumption, rejection, or assignment of any executory contract or unexpired lease of the debtor not previously rejected under such section;

    (3) provide for—

        (A) the settlement or adjustment of any claim or interest belonging to the debtor or to the estate; or

        (B) the retention and enforcement by the debtor, by the trustee, or by a representative of the estate appointed for such purpose, of any such claim or interest;

    (4) provide for the sale of all or substantially all of the property of the estate, and the distribution of the proceeds of such sale among holders of claims or interests;

    (5) modify the rights of holders of secured claims, other than a claim secured only by a security interest in real property that is the debtor's principal residence, or of holders of unsecured claims, or leave unaffected the rights of holders of any class of claims; and

(6) include any other appropriate provision not inconsistent with the applicable provisions of this title.

(c) In a case concerning an individual, a plan proposed by an entity other than the debtor may not provide for the use, sale, or lease of property exempted under section 522 of this title, unless the debtor consents to such use, sale, or lease.

(d) Notwithstanding subsection (a) of this section and sections 506(b), 1129(a)(7), and 1129(b) of this title, if it is proposed in a plan to cure a default the amount necessary to cure the default shall be determined in accordance with the underlying agreement and applicable nonbankruptcy law.

(Pub.L. 95–598, Nov. 6, 1978, 92 Stat. 2631; Pub.L. 98–353, Title III, § 507, July 10, 1984, 98 Stat. 385; Pub.L. 103–394, Title II, § 206, Title III, §§ 304(h)(6), 305(a), Title V, § 501(d)(31), Oct. 22, 1994, 108 Stat. 4123, 4134, 4146; Pub.L. 109–8, Title III, § 321(b), Title XV, § 1502(a)(7), Apr. 20, 2005, 119 Stat. 95, 216.)

HISTORICAL AND STATUTORY NOTES

Amendments

2005 Amendments. Subsec. (a)(1). Pub.L. 109–8, § 1502(a)(7), struck out "507(a)(1), 507(a)(2)" and inserted "507(a)(2), 507(a)(3)".

Subsec. (a)(6). Pub.L. 109–8, § 321(b)(1), struck out "and" at the end of par. (6).

Subsec. (a)(7). Pub.L. 109–8, § 321(b)(2), struck out the period at the end of par. (7) and inserted "; and".

Subsec. (a)(8). Pub.L. 109–8, § 321(b)(3), added par. (8).

1994 Amendments. Subsec. (a)(1). Pub.L. 103–394, § 304(h)(6), substituted "507(a)(8)" for "507(a)(7)".

Pub.L. 103–394, § 501(d)(31), which directed that a comma be inserted after "title" the last place it appears, required no change to text due to earlier amendment by section 507(a)(2)(B) of Pub.L. 98–353, which among other changes added a comma after "title" the last place it appears.

Subsec. (b)(5), (6). Pub.L. 103–394, § 206, added par. (5) and redesignated former par. (5) as (6).

Subsec. (d). Pub.L. 103–394, § 305(a), added subsec. (d).

1984 Amendments. Subsec. (a). Pub.L. 98–353, § 507(a)(1), in provisions preceding par. (1), substituted "Notwithstanding any otherwise applicable nonbankruptcy law, a" for "A".

Subsec. (a)(1). Pub.L. 98–353, § 507(a)(2)(A), added a comma after "classes of claims".

Pub.L. 98–353, § 507(a)(2)(B), substituted "507(a)(7) of this title," for "507(a)(6) of this title".

Subsec. (a)(3). Pub.L. 98–353, § 507(a)(3), struck out "shall" before "specify the treatment".

Subsec. (a)(5). Pub.L. 98–353, § 507(a)(4), substituted "implementation" for "execution".

Subsec. (a)(5)(G). Pub.L. 98–353, § 507(a)(5), added "of" after "waiving".

Subsec. (b)(2). Pub.L. 98–353, § 507(b)(1), substituted "rejection, or assignment" for "or rejection".

Pub.L. 98–353, § 507(b)(2) substituted "under such section" for "under section 365 of this title".

CROSS REFERENCES

Applicability of subsecs. (a)(1) to (5) and (b) of this section in Chapter 9 cases, see 11 USCA § 901.

Contents of plan filed in—

Chapter thirteen cases, see 11 USCA § 1322.

Chapter twelve cases, see 11 USCA § 1222.

Railroad reorganization cases, see 11 USCA § 1172.

§ 1124. Impairment of claims or interests

Except as provided in section 1123(a)(4) of this title, a class of claims or interests is impaired under a plan unless, with respect to each claim or interest of such class, the plan—

    (1) leaves unaltered the legal, equitable, and contractual rights to which such claim or interest entitles the holder of such claim or interest; or

    (2) notwithstanding any contractual provision or applicable law that entitles the holder of such claim or interest to demand or receive accelerated payment of such claim or interest after the occurrence of a default—

        (A) cures any such default that occurred before or after the commencement of the case under this title, other than a default of a kind specified in section 365(b)(2) of this title or of a kind that section 365(b)(2) expressly does not require to be cured;

        (B) reinstates the maturity of such claim or interest as such maturity existed before such default;

        (C) compensates the holder of such claim or interest for any damages incurred as a result of any reasonable reliance by such holder on such contractual provision or such applicable law;

        (D) if such claim or such interest arises from any failure to perform a nonmonetary obligation, other than a default arising from failure to operate a nonresidential real property lease subject to section 365(b)(1)(A), compensates the holder of such claim or such interest (other than the debtor or an insider) for any actual pecuniary loss incurred by such holder as a result of such failure; and

        (E) does not otherwise alter the legal, equitable, or contractual rights to which such claim or interest entitles the holder of such claim or interest.

(Pub.L. 95–598, Nov. 6, 1978, 92 Stat. 2633; Pub.L. 98–353, Title III, § 508, July 10, 1984, 98 Stat. 385; Pub.L. 103–394, Title II, § 213(d), Oct. 22, 1994, 108 Stat. 4126; Pub.L. 109–8, Title III, § 328(b), Apr. 20, 2005, 119 Stat. 100.)

HISTORICAL AND STATUTORY NOTES

Amendments

    2005 Amendments. Par. (2)(A). Pub.L. 109–8, § 328(b)(1), inserted "or of a kind that section 365(b)(2) expressly does not require to be cured" before the semicolon at the end.

    Par. (2)(C). Pub.L. 109–8, § 328(b)(2), struck out "and" at the end of subpar. (C).

    Par. (2)(D). Pub.L. 109–8, § 328(b)(3), (4), redesignated former subpar. (D) as subpar. (E), and inserted a new subpar. (D), respectively.

    Par. (2)(E). Pub.L. 109–8, § 328(b)(3), redesignated former subpar. (D) as subpar. (E).

    1994 Amendments. Par. (3). Pub.L. 103–394, § 213(d), struck out par. (3), which stated that a class of claims or interests is impaired under a plan unless the plan provides that on the plan's effective date, the holder of such claim or interest receives cash equal to certain amounts.

    1984 Amendments. Par. (2)(A). Pub.L. 98–353, § 508(1), substituted "cures any such default that occurred before or after the commencement of the case under this title, other than a default of a kind specified in section 365(b)(2) of this title;" for "cures any such default, other than a default of a kind specified in section 365(b)(2) of this title, that occurred before or after the commencement of the case under this title;".

    Par. (3)(B)(i). Pub.L. 98–353, § 508(2), substituted "or" for "and".

CROSS REFERENCES

Allowance of claims or interests, see 11 USCA § 502.

Applicability of this section in Chapter nine cases, see 11 USCA § 901.

Claims and interests generally, see 11 USCA § 1111.

Filing of proofs of claims or interests, see 11 USCA § 501.

§ 1125. Postpetition disclosure and solicitation

(a) In this section—

(1) "adequate information" means information of a kind, and in sufficient detail, as far as is reasonably practicable in light of the nature and history of the debtor and the condition of the debtor's books and records, including a discussion of the potential material Federal tax consequences of the plan to the debtor, any successor to the debtor, and a hypothetical investor typical of the holders of claims or interests in the case, that would enable such a hypothetical investor of the relevant class to make an informed judgment about the plan, but adequate information need not include such information about any other possible or proposed plan and in determining whether a disclosure statement provides adequate information, the court shall consider the complexity of the case, the benefit of additional information to creditors and other parties in interest, and the cost of providing additional information; and

(2) "investor typical of holders of claims or interests of the relevant class" means investor having—

(A) a claim or interest of the relevant class;

(B) such a relationship with the debtor as the holders of other claims or interests of such class generally have; and

(C) such ability to obtain such information from sources other than the disclosure required by this section as holders of claims or interests in such class generally have.

(b) An acceptance or rejection of a plan may not be solicited after the commencement of the case under this title from a holder of a claim or interest with respect to such claim or interest, unless, at the time of or before such solicitation, there is transmitted to such holder the plan or a summary of the plan, and a written disclosure statement approved, after notice and a hearing, by the court as containing adequate information. The court may approve a disclosure statement without a valuation of the debtor or an appraisal of the debtor's assets.

(c) The same disclosure statement shall be transmitted to each holder of a claim or interest of a particular class, but there may be transmitted different disclosure statements, differing in amount, detail, or kind of information, as between classes.

(d) Whether a disclosure statement required under subsection (b) of this section contains adequate information is not governed by any otherwise applicable nonbankruptcy law, rule, or regulation, but an agency or official whose duty is to administer or enforce such a law, rule, or regulation may be heard on the issue of whether a disclosure statement contains adequate information. Such an agency or official may not appeal from, or otherwise seek review of, an order approving a disclosure statement.

(e) A person that solicits acceptance or rejection of a plan, in good faith and in compliance with the applicable provisions of this title, or that participates, in good faith and in compliance with the applicable provisions of this title, in the offer, issuance, sale, or purchase of a security, offered or sold under the plan, of the debtor, of an affiliate participating in a joint plan with the debtor, or of a newly organized successor to the debtor under the plan, is not liable, on account of such solicitation or participation, for violation of any applicable law, rule, or regulation governing solicitation of acceptance or rejection of a plan or the offer, issuance, sale, or purchase of securities.

(f) Notwithstanding subsection (b), in a small business case—

(1) the court may determine that the plan itself provides adequate information and that a separate disclosure statement is not necessary;

(2) the court may approve a disclosure statement submitted on standard forms approved by the court or adopted under section 2075 of title 28; and

(3)(A) the court may conditionally approve a disclosure statement subject to final approval after notice and a hearing;

(B) acceptances and rejections of a plan may be solicited based on a conditionally approved disclosure statement if the debtor provides adequate information to each holder of a claim or interest that is solicited, but a conditionally approved disclosure statement shall be mailed not later than 25 days before the date of the hearing on confirmation of the plan; and

(C) the hearing on the disclosure statement may be combined with the hearing on confirmation of a plan.

(g) Notwithstanding subsection (b), an acceptance or rejection of the plan may be solicited from a holder of a claim or interest if such solicitation complies with applicable nonbankruptcy law and if such holder was solicited before the commencement of the case in a manner complying with applicable nonbankruptcy law.

(Pub.L. 95–598, Nov. 6, 1978, 92 Stat. 2633; Pub.L. 98–353, Title III, § 509, July 10, 1984, 98 Stat. 385; Pub.L. 103–394, Title II, § 217(e), Oct. 22, 1994, 108 Stat. 4127; Pub.L. 109–8, Title IV, §§ 408, 431, Title VII, § 717, Apr. 20, 2005, 119 Stat. 106, 109, 131.)

HISTORICAL AND STATUTORY NOTES

Amendments

2005 Amendments. Subsec. (a)(1). Pub.L. 109–8, § 431(1), inserted "and in determining whether a disclosure statement provides adequate information, the court shall consider the complexity of the case, the benefit of additional information to creditors and other parties in interest, and the cost of providing additional information" following "possible or proposed plan".

Pub.L. 109–8, § 717(1), inserted "including a discussion of the potential material Federal tax consequences of the plan to the debtor, any successor to the debtor, and a hypothetical investor typical of the holders of claims or interests in the case," after "records,".

Pub.L. 109–8, § 717(2), struck out "a hypothetical reasonable investor typical of holders of claims or interests" and inserted "such a hypothetical investor".

Subsec. (f). Pub.L. 109–8, § 431(2), rewrote subsec. (f), which formerly read:

"**(f)** Notwithstanding subsection (b), in a case in which the debtor has elected under section 1121(e) to be considered a small business—

"**(1)** the court may conditionally approve a disclosure statement subject to final approval after notice and a hearing;

"**(2)** acceptances and rejections of a plan may be solicited based on a conditionally approved disclosure statement as long as the debtor provides adequate information to each holder of a claim or interest that is solicited, but a conditionally approved disclosure statement shall be mailed at least 10 days prior to the date of the hearing on confirmation of the plan; and

"**(3)** a hearing on the disclosure statement may be combined with a hearing on confirmation of a plan."

Subsec. (g). Pub.L. 109–8, § 408, added subsec. (g).

1994 Amendments. Subsec. (f). Pub.L. 103–394, § 217(e), added subsec. (f).

1984 Amendments. Subsec. (a)(1). Pub.L. 98–353, § 509(a)(1), added ", but adequate information need not include such information about any other possible or proposed plan" after "plan".

Subsec. (a)(2)(B). Pub.L. 98–353, § 509(a)(2), added "the" after "with".

Subsec. (a)(2)(C). Pub.L. 98–353, § 509(a)(3), added "of" after "holders".

Subsec. (d). Pub.L. 98–353, § 509(b)(1), added "required under subsection (b) of this section" after "Whether a disclosure statement" the first place phase appears.

Pub.L. 98–353, § 509(b)(2), added ", or otherwise seek review of," after "appeal from".

Subsec. (e). Pub.L. 98–353, § 509(c)(1), added "acceptance or rejection of a plan" after "solicits".

Pub.L. 98–353, § 509(c)(2), added "solicitation of acceptance or rejection of a plan or" following "governing".

CROSS REFERENCES

Applicability of this section in Chapter nine cases, see 11 USCA § 901.

Duty of United States trustee to file comments with respect to plans and disclosure statements filed in connection with hearings under this section, see 28 USCA § 586.

Exemption from securities laws of certain transactions in which disclosure statements are provided, see 11 USCA § 1145.

§ 1126. Acceptance of plan

(a) The holder of a claim or interest allowed under section 502 of this title may accept or reject a plan. If the United States is a creditor or equity security holder, the Secretary of the Treasury may accept or reject the plan on behalf of the United States.

(b) For the purposes of subsections (c) and (d) of this section, a holder of a claim or interest that has accepted or rejected the plan before the commencement of the case under this title is deemed to have accepted or rejected such plan, as the case may be, if—

　(1) the solicitation of such acceptance or rejection was in compliance with any applicable nonbankruptcy law, rule, or regulation governing the adequacy of disclosure in connection with such solicitation; or

　(2) if there is not any such law, rule, or regulation, such acceptance or rejection was solicited after disclosure to such holder of adequate information, as defined in section 1125(a) of this title.

(c) A class of claims has accepted a plan if such plan has been accepted by creditors, other than any entity designated under subsection (e) of this section, that hold at least two-thirds in amount and more than one-half in number of the allowed claims of such class held by creditors, other than any entity designated under subsection (e) of this section, that have accepted or rejected such plan.

(d) A class of interests has accepted a plan if such plan has been accepted by holders of such interests, other than any entity designated under subsection (e) of this section, that hold at least two-thirds in amount of the allowed interests of such class held by holders of such interests, other than any entity designated under subsection (e) of this section, that have accepted or rejected such plan.

(e) On request of a party in interest, and after notice and a hearing, the court may designate any entity whose acceptance or rejection of such plan was not in good faith, or was not solicited or procured in good faith or in accordance with the provisions of this title.

(f) Notwithstanding any other provision of this section, a class that is not impaired under a plan, and each holder of a claim or interest of such class, are conclusively presumed to have accepted the plan, and solicitation of acceptances with respect to such class from the holders of claims or interests of such class is not required.

(g) Notwithstanding any other provision of this section, a class is deemed not to have accepted a plan if such plan provides that the claims or interests of such class do not entitle the holders of such claims or interests to receive or retain any property under the plan on account of such claims or interests.

(Pub.L. 95–598, Nov. 6, 1978, 92 Stat. 2634; Pub.L. 98–353, Title III, § 510, July 10, 1984, 98 Stat. 386.)

HISTORICAL AND STATUTORY NOTES

Amendments

1984 Amendments. Subsec. (b)(2). Pub.L. 98–353, § 510(a), substituted "1125(a)" for "1125(a)(1)".

Subsec. (d). Pub.L. 98–353, § 510(b), added a comma after "such interests".

Subsec. (f). Pub.L. 98–353, § 510(c)(1), substituted ", and each holder of a claim or interest of such class, are conclusively presumed" for "is deemed".

Pub.L. 98–353, § 510(c)(2), substituted "solicitation" for "solicititation".

Pub.L. 98–353, § 510(c)(3), substituted "interests" for "interest".

Subsec. (g). Pub.L. 98–353, § 510(d), substituted "receive or retain any property" for "any payment or compensation".

CROSS REFERENCES

Amount and number of claims within class as including claims formerly held by certain creditors, see 11 USCA § 946.

Applicability of subsecs. (a) to (c) and (e) to (g) of this section in Chapter nine cases, see 11 USCA § 901.

§ 1127. Modification of plan

(a) The proponent of a plan may modify such plan at any time before confirmation, but may not modify such plan so that such plan as modified fails to meet the requirements of sections 1122 and 1123 of this title. After the proponent of a plan files a modification of such plan with the court, the plan as modified becomes the plan.

(b) The proponent of a plan or the reorganized debtor may modify such plan at any time after confirmation of such plan and before substantial consummation of such plan, but may not modify such plan so that such plan as modified fails to meet the requirements of sections 1122 and 1123 of this title. Such plan as modified under this subsection becomes the plan only if circumstances warrant such modification and the court, after notice and a hearing, confirms such plan as modified, under section 1129 of this title.

(c) The proponent of a modification shall comply with section 1125 of this title with respect to the plan as modified.

(d) Any holder of a claim or interest that has accepted or rejected a plan is deemed to have accepted or rejected, as the case may be, such plan as modified, unless, within the time fixed by the court, such holder changes such holder's previous acceptance or rejection.

(e) If the debtor is an individual, the plan may be modified at any time after confirmation of the plan but before the completion of payments under the plan, whether or not the plan has been substantially consummated, upon request of the debtor, the trustee, the United States trustee, or the holder of an allowed unsecured claim, to—

  (1) increase or reduce the amount of payments on claims of a particular class provided for by the plan;

  (2) extend or reduce the time period for such payments; or

  (3) alter the amount of the distribution to a creditor whose claim is provided for by the plan to the extent necessary to take account of any payment of such claim made other than under the plan.

(f)(1) Sections 1121 through 1128 and the requirements of section 1129 apply to any modification under subsection (e).

(2) The plan, as modified, shall become the plan only after there has been disclosure under section 1125 as the court may direct, notice and a hearing, and such modification is approved.

(Pub.L. 95–598, Nov. 6, 1978, 92 Stat. 2635; Pub.L. 98–353, Title III, § 511, July 10, 1984, 98 Stat. 386; Pub.L. 109–8, Title III, § 321(e), Apr. 20, 2005, 119 Stat. 96; Pub.L. 111–327, § 2(a)(34), Dec. 22, 2010, 124 Stat. 3561.)

HISTORICAL AND STATUTORY NOTES

Amendments

2010 Amendments. Subsec. (f)(1). Pub.L. 111–327, § 2(a)(34), struck out "subsection (a)" and inserted "subsection (e)".

2005 Amendments. Subsec. (e). Pub.L. 109–8, § 321(e), added subsec. (e).

Subsec. (f). Pub.L. 109–8, § 321(e), added subsec. (f).

1984 Amendments. Subsec. (a). Pub.L. 98–353, § 511(a)(1), added "of a plan" after "After the proponent".

Pub.L. 98–353, § 511(a)(2), added "of such plan" after "modification".

Subsec. (b). Pub.L. 98–353, § 511(b), substituted "circumstances warrant such modification and the court, after notice and a hearing, confirms such plan as modified, under section 1129 of this title" for "the court, after notice and a hearing, confirms such plan, as modified, under section 1129 of this title, and circumstances warrant such modification".

CROSS REFERENCES

Applicability of subsec. (d) of this section in Chapter nine cases, see 11 USCA § 901.

Modification of plan after confirmation in—

    Chapter thirteen cases, see 11 USCA § 1329.

    Chapter twelve cases, see 11 USCA § 1229.

Modification of plan before confirmation in—

    Chapter thirteen cases, see 11 USCA § 1323.

    Chapter twelve cases, see 11 USCA § 1223.

Modification of plan in Chapter nine cases, see 11 USCA § 942.

§ 1128. Confirmation hearing

(a) After notice, the court shall hold a hearing on confirmation of a plan.

(b) A party in interest may object to confirmation of a plan.

(Pub.L. 95–598, Nov. 6, 1978, 92 Stat. 2635.)

CROSS REFERENCES

Applicability of this section in Chapter nine cases, see 11 USCA § 901.

Confirmation hearing in—

    Chapter thirteen cases, see 11 USCA § 1324.

    Chapter twelve cases, see 11 USCA § 1224.

Duty of United States trustee to file comments with respect to plans and disclosure statements filed in connection with hearings under this section, see 28 USCA § 586.

Right to be heard in cases under this chapter, see 11 USCA § 1109.

§ 1129. Confirmation of plan

(a) The court shall confirm a plan only if all of the following requirements are met:

    (1) The plan complies with the applicable provisions of this title.

    (2) The proponent of the plan complies with the applicable provisions of this title.

    (3) The plan has been proposed in good faith and not by any means forbidden by law.

    (4) Any payment made or to be made by the proponent, by the debtor, or by a person issuing securities or acquiring property under the plan, for services or for costs and expenses in or in connection with the case, or in connection with the plan and incident to the case, has been approved by, or is subject to the approval of, the court as reasonable.

(5)(A)(i) The proponent of the plan has disclosed the identity and affiliations of any individual proposed to serve, after confirmation of the plan, as a director, officer, or voting trustee of the debtor, an affiliate of the debtor participating in a joint plan with the debtor, or a successor to the debtor under the plan; and

(ii) the appointment to, or continuance in, such office of such individual, is consistent with the interests of creditors and equity security holders and with public policy; and

(B) the proponent of the plan has disclosed the identity of any insider that will be employed or retained by the reorganized debtor, and the nature of any compensation for such insider.

(6) Any governmental regulatory commission with jurisdiction, after confirmation of the plan, over the rates of the debtor has approved any rate change provided for in the plan, or such rate change is expressly conditioned on such approval.

(7) With respect to each impaired class of claims or interests—

(A) each holder of a claim or interest of such class—

(i) has accepted the plan; or

(ii) will receive or retain under the plan on account of such claim or interest property of a value, as of the effective date of the plan, that is not less than the amount that such holder would so receive or retain if the debtor were liquidated under chapter 7 of this title on such date; or

(B) if section 1111(b)(2) of this title applies to the claims of such class, each holder of a claim of such class will receive or retain under the plan on account of such claim property of a value, as of the effective date of the plan, that is not less than the value of such holder's interest in the estate's interest in the property that secures such claims.

(8) With respect to each class of claims or interests—

(A) such class has accepted the plan; or

(B) such class is not impaired under the plan.

(9) Except to the extent that the holder of a particular claim has agreed to a different treatment of such claim, the plan provides that—

(A) with respect to a claim of a kind specified in section 507(a)(2) or 507(a)(3) of this title, on the effective date of the plan, the holder of such claim will receive on account of such claim cash equal to the allowed amount of such claim;

(B) with respect to a class of claims of a kind specified in section 507(a)(1), 507(a)(4), 507(a)(5), 507(a)(6), or 507(a)(7) of this title, each holder of a claim of such class will receive—

(i) if such class has accepted the plan, deferred cash payments of a value, as of the effective date of the plan, equal to the allowed amount of such claim; or

(ii) if such class has not accepted the plan, cash on the effective date of the plan equal to the allowed amount of such claim;

(C) with respect to a claim of a kind specified in section 507(a)(8) of this title, the holder of such claim will receive on account of such claim regular installment payments in cash—

(i) of a total value, as of the effective date of the plan, equal to the allowed amount of such claim;

(ii) over a period ending not later than 5 years after the date of the order for relief under section 301, 302, or 303; and

(iii) in a manner not less favorable than the most favored nonpriority unsecured claim provided for by the plan (other than cash payments made to a class of creditors under section 1122(b)); and

(D) with respect to a secured claim which would otherwise meet the description of an unsecured claim of a governmental unit under section 507(a)(8), but for the secured status of that claim, the holder of that claim will receive on account of that claim, cash payments, in the same manner and over the same period, as prescribed in subparagraph (C).

(10) If a class of claims is impaired under the plan, at least one class of claims that is impaired under the plan has accepted the plan, determined without including any acceptance of the plan by any insider.

(11) Confirmation of the plan is not likely to be followed by the liquidation, or the need for further financial reorganization, of the debtor or any successor to the debtor under the plan, unless such liquidation or reorganization is proposed in the plan.

(12) All fees payable under section 1930 of title 28, as determined by the court at the hearing on confirmation of the plan, have been paid or the plan provides for the payment of all such fees on the effective date of the plan.

(13) The plan provides for the continuation after its effective date of payment of all retiree benefits, as that term is defined in section 1114 of this title, at the level established pursuant to subsection (e)(1)(B) or (g) of section 1114 of this title, at any time prior to confirmation of the plan, for the duration of the period the debtor has obligated itself to provide such benefits.

(14) If the debtor is required by a judicial or administrative order, or by statute, to pay a domestic support obligation, the debtor has paid all amounts payable under such order or such statute for such obligation that first become payable after the date of the filing of the petition.

(15) In a case in which the debtor is an individual and in which the holder of an allowed unsecured claim objects to the confirmation of the plan—

(A) the value, as of the effective date of the plan, of the property to be distributed under the plan on account of such claim is not less than the amount of such claim; or

(B) the value of the property to be distributed under the plan is not less than the projected disposable income of the debtor (as defined in section 1325(b)(2)) to be received during the 5-year period beginning on the date that the first payment is due under the plan, or during the period for which the plan provides payments, whichever is longer.

(16) All transfers of property under the plan shall be made in accordance with any applicable provisions of nonbankruptcy law that govern the transfer of property by a corporation or trust that is not a moneyed, business, or commercial corporation or trust.

(b)(1) Notwithstanding section 510(a) of this title, if all of the applicable requirements of subsection (a) of this section other than paragraph (8) are met with respect to a plan, the court, on request of the proponent of the plan, shall confirm the plan notwithstanding the requirements of such paragraph if the plan does not discriminate unfairly, and is fair and equitable, with respect to each class of claims or interests that is impaired under, and has not accepted, the plan.

(2) For the purpose of this subsection, the condition that a plan be fair and equitable with respect to a class includes the following requirements:

(A) With respect to a class of secured claims, the plan provides—

(i)(I) that the holders of such claims retain the liens securing such claims, whether the property subject to such liens is retained by the debtor or transferred to another entity, to the extent of the allowed amount of such claims; and

(II) that each holder of a claim of such class receive on account of such claim deferred cash payments totaling at least the allowed amount of such claim, of a value, as of the effective date of the plan, of at least the value of such holder's interest in the estate's interest in such property;

(ii) for the sale, subject to section 363(k) of this title, of any property that is subject to the liens securing such claims, free and clear of such liens, with such liens to attach to the proceeds of such sale, and the treatment of such liens on proceeds under clause (i) or (iii) of this subparagraph; or

      (iii) for the realization by such holders of the indubitable equivalent of such claims.

  (B) With respect to a class of unsecured claims—

      (i) the plan provides that each holder of a claim of such class receive or retain on account of such claim property of a value, as of the effective date of the plan, equal to the allowed amount of such claim; or

      (ii) the holder of any claim or interest that is junior to the claims of such class will not receive or retain under the plan on account of such junior claim or interest any property, except that in a case in which the debtor is an individual, the debtor may retain property included in the estate under section 1115, subject to the requirements of subsection (a)(14) of this section.

  (C) With respect to a class of interests—

      (i) the plan provides that each holder of an interest of such class receive or retain on account of such interest property of a value, as of the effective date of the plan, equal to the greatest of the allowed amount of any fixed liquidation preference to which such holder is entitled, any fixed redemption price to which such holder is entitled, or the value of such interest; or

      (ii) the holder of any interest that is junior to the interests of such class will not receive or retain under the plan on account of such junior interest any property.

(c) Notwithstanding subsections (a) and (b) of this section and except as provided in section 1127(b) of this title, the court may confirm only one plan, unless the order of confirmation in the case has been revoked under section 1144 of this title. If the requirements of subsections (a) and (b) of this section are met with respect to more than one plan, the court shall consider the preferences of creditors and equity security holders in determining which plan to confirm.

(d) Notwithstanding any other provision of this section, on request of a party in interest that is a governmental unit, the court may not confirm a plan if the principal purpose of the plan is the avoidance of taxes or the avoidance of the application of section 5 of the Securities Act of 1933. In any hearing under this subsection, the governmental unit has the burden of proof on the issue of avoidance.

(e) In a small business case, the court shall confirm a plan that complies with the applicable provisions of this title and that is filed in accordance with section 1121(e) not later than 45 days after the plan is filed unless the time for confirmation is extended in accordance with section 1121(e)(3).

(Pub.L. 95–598, Nov. 6, 1978, 92 Stat. 2635; Pub.L. 98–353, Title III, § 512, July 10, 1984, 98 Stat. 386; Pub.L. 99–554, Title II, §§ 225, 283(v), Oct. 27, 1986, 100 Stat. 3102, 3118; Pub.L. 100–334, § 2(b), June 16, 1988, 102 Stat. 613; Pub.L. 103–394, Title III, § 304(h)(7), Title V, § 501(d)(32), Oct. 22, 1994, 108 Stat. 4134, 4146; Pub.L. 109–8, Title II, § 213(1), Title III, § 321(c), Title IV, § 438, Title VII, § 710, Title XII, § 1221(b), Title XV, § 1502(a)(8), Apr. 20, 2005, 119 Stat. 52, 95, 113, 127, 196, 216; Pub.L. 111–327, § 2(a)(35), Dec. 22, 2010, 124 Stat. 3561.)

HISTORICAL AND STATUTORY NOTES

References in Text

    Section 5 of the Securities Act of 1933, referred to in subsec. (d), is section 5 of Act May 27, 1933, c. 38, Title I, 48 Stat. 77, which is classified to section 77e of Title 15, Commerce and Trade.

Amendments

    2010 Amendments. Subsec. (a)(16). Pub.L. 111–327, § 2(a)(35), struck out "of the plan" and inserted "under the plan".

2005 Amendments. Subsec. (a)(9). Pub.L. 109–8, § 1502(a)(8), struck out "507(a)(1) or 507(a)(2)" and inserted "507(a)(2) or 507(a)(3)" in subparagraph (A), and struck out "507(a)(3)" and inserted "507(a)(1)" in subparagraph (B).

Subsec. (a)(9)(B). Pub.L. 109–8, § 710(1), struck out "and" at the end of subpar. (B).

Subsec. (a)(9)(C). Pub.L. 109–8, § 710(2), struck out "deferred cash payments, over a period not exceeding six years after the date of assessment of such claim, of a value, as of the effective date of the plan, equal to the allowed amount of such claim." and inserted "regular installment payments in cash—"

Subsec. (a)(9)(C)(i). Pub.L. 109–8, § 710(2), added cl. (i).

Subsec. (a)(9)(C)(ii). Pub.L. 109–8, § 710(2), added cl. (ii).

Subsec. (a)(9)(C)(iii). Pub.L. 109–8, § 710(2), added cl. (iii).

Subsec. (a)(9)(D). Pub.L. 109–8, § 710(3), added subpar. (D).

Subsec. (a)(14). Pub.L. 109–8, § 213(1), added par. (14).

Subsec. (a)(15). Pub.L. 109–8, § 321(c)(1), added par. (15).

Subsec. (a)(16). Pub.L.109–8, § 1221(b), added subsec. (a)(16).

Subsec. (b)(2)(B)(ii). Pub.L. 109–8, § 321(c)(2), inserted ", except that in a case in which the debtor is an individual, the debtor may retain property included in the estate under section 1115, subject to the requirements of subsection (a)(14) of this section" before the period at the end of cl. (ii).

Subsec. (e). Pub.L. 109–8, § 438, added subsec. (e).

1994 Amendments. Subsec. (a)(4). Pub.L. 103–394, § 501(d)(32)(A)(i), substituted a period for a semicolon.

Subsec. (a)(9)(B). Pub.L. 103–394, § 304(h)(7)(i), inserted reference to section 507(a)(7) of this title.

Subsec. (a)(9)(C). Pub.L. 103–394, § 304(h)(7)(ii), substituted "507(a)(8)" for "507(a)(7)".

Subsec. (a)(12). Pub.L. 103–394, § 501(d)(32)(A)(ii), inserted "of title 28" following "section 1930".

Subsec. (d). Pub.L. 103–394, § 501(d)(32)(B), struck out "(15 U.S.C. 77e)" following "section 5 of the Securities Act of 1933".

1988 Amendments. Subsec. (a)(13). Pub.L. 100–334 added par. (13).

1986 Amendments. Subsec. (a)(7). Pub.L. 99–554, § 283(v)(1), substituted "to each" for "to of each".

Subsec. (a)(9)(B). Pub.L. 99–554, § 283(v)(2), added reference to section 507(a)(6) of this title.

Subsec. (a)(9)(C). Pub.L. 99–554, § 283(v)(3), substituted "507(a)(7)" for "507(a)(6)".

Subsec. (a)(12). Pub.L. 99–554, § 225, added par. (12).

1984 Amendments. Subsec. (a)(1). Pub.L. 98–353, § 512(a)(1), substituted "title" for "chapter".

Subsec. (a)(2). Pub.L. 98–353, § 512(a)(2), substituted "title" for "chapter".

Subsec. (a)(4). Pub.L. 98–353, § 512(a)(3), substituted "Any payment made or to be made by the proponent, by the debtor, or by a person issuing securities or acquiring property under the plan, for services or for costs and expenses in or in connection with the case, or in connection with the plan and incident to the case, has been approved by, or is subject to the approval of, the court as reasonable;" for "Any payment made or promised by the proponent, by the debtor, or by a person issuing securities or acquiring property under the plan, for services or for costs and expenses in, or in connection with, the case, or in connection with the plan and incident to the case, has been disclosed to the court; and (B)(i) any such payment made before confirmation of the plan is reasonable; or (ii) if such payment is to be fixed after confirmation of the plan, such payment is subject to the approval of the court as reasonable.".

Subsec. (a)(5)(A)(ii). Pub.L. 98–353, § 512(a)(4), substituted "; and" for the period at the end thereof.

Subsec. (a)(5)(B). Pub.L. 98–353, § 512(a)(5), substituted "the" for "The".

Subsec. (a)(6). Pub.L. 98–353, § 512(a)(6), added "governmental" after "Any".

Subsec. (a)(7). Pub.L. 98–353, § 512(a)(7)(A), substituted "of each impaired class of claims or interests" for "each class".

Subsec. (a)(7)(B). Pub.L. 98–353, § 512(a)(7)(B), substituted "holder's" for "creditor's".

Subsec. (a)(8). Pub.L. 98–353, § 512(a)(8), added "of claims or interests" after "each class".

Subsec. (a)(10). Pub.L. 98–353, § 512(a)(9), substituted "If a class of claims is impaired under the plan, at least one class of claims that is impaired under the plan has accepted the plan, determined without including any acceptance of the plan by any insider." for "At least one class of claims has accepted the plan, determined without including any acceptance of the plan by any insider holding a claim of such class.".

Subsec. (b)(2)(A)(i)(I). Pub.L. 98–353, § 512(b)(1), substituted "liens" for "lien" wherever appearing.

Subsec. (b)(2)(A)(ii). Pub.L. 98–353, § 512(b)(1), substituted "liens" for "lien" wherever appearing.

Subsec. (b)(2)(B)(ii). Pub.L. 98–353, § 512(b)(2), added "under the plan" after "retain".

Subsec. (b)(2)(C)(i). Pub.L. 98–353, § 512(b)(3)(A), substituted "interest" for "claim".

Pub.L. 98–353, § 512(b)(3)(B), substituted "or the value" for "and the value".

Subsec. (d). Pub.L. 98–353, § 512(c)(1), added "the application of" after "avoidance".

Pub.L. 98–353, § 512(c)(2), added provisions requiring that in any hearing under this subsection, the governmental unit has the burden of proof on the issue of avoidance.

CROSS REFERENCES

Applicability of subsecs. (a)(2), (3), (6), (8), (10) and (b)(1), (2)(A), (2)(B) of this section in Chapter nine cases, see 11 USCA § 901.

Confirmation of plan in—

    Chapter nine cases, see 11 USCA § 943.

    Chapter thirteen cases, see 11 USCA § 1325.

    Chapter twelve cases, see 11 USCA § 1225.

    Railroad reorganization cases, see 11 USCA § 1173.

Denial of confirmation of plan as cause for conversion or dismissal, see 11 USCA § 1112.

Effect of confirmation in cases under this chapter, see 11 USCA § 1141.

Inapplicability of subsecs. (a)(7) and (c) of this section in railroad reorganization cases, see 11 USCA § 1161.

Payment of insurance benefits to retired employees, see 11 USCA § 1114.

Revocation of order of confirmation in cases under this chapter, see 11 USCA § 1144.

Special tax provisions for certain dispositions of securities or instruments under confirmed plan, see 11 USCA § 1146.

Supplemental injunctions and plan fair and equitable, see 11 USCA § 524.

Unclaimed property, see 11 USCA § 347.

SUBCHAPTER III—POSTCONFIRMATION MATTERS

CROSS REFERENCES

Subchapter applicable only in case under this chapter except as provided in § 901 of this title, see 11 USCA § 103.

§ 1141. Effect of confirmation

    (a) Except as provided in subsections (d)(2) and (d)(3) of this section, the provisions of a confirmed plan bind the debtor, any entity issuing securities under the plan, any entity acquiring property under the plan, and any creditor, equity security holder, or general partner in the debtor, whether or not the claim or interest of such creditor, equity security holder, or general partner is impaired under the plan and whether or not such creditor, equity security holder, or general partner has accepted the plan.

(b) Except as otherwise provided in the plan or the order confirming the plan, the confirmation of a plan vests all of the property of the estate in the debtor.

(c) Except as provided in subsections (d)(2) and (d)(3) of this section and except as otherwise provided in the plan or in the order confirming the plan, after confirmation of a plan, the property dealt with by the plan is free and clear of all claims and interests of creditors, equity security holders, and of general partners in the debtor.

(d)(1) Except as otherwise provided in this subsection, in the plan, or in the order confirming the plan, the confirmation of a plan—

(A) discharges the debtor from any debt that arose before the date of such confirmation, and any debt of a kind specified in section 502(g), 502(h), or 502(i) of this title, whether or not—

(i) a proof of the claim based on such debt is filed or deemed filed under section 501 of this title;

(ii) such claim is allowed under section 502 of this title; or

(iii) the holder of such claim has accepted the plan; and

(B) terminates all rights and interests of equity security holders and general partners provided for by the plan.

(2) A discharge under this chapter does not discharge a debtor who is an individual from any debt excepted from discharge under section 523 of this title.

(3) The confirmation of a plan does not discharge a debtor if—

(A) the plan provides for the liquidation of all or substantially all of the property of the estate;

(B) the debtor does not engage in business after consummation of the plan; and

(C) the debtor would be denied a discharge under section 727(a) of this title if the case were a case under chapter 7 of this title.

(4) The court may approve a written waiver of discharge executed by the debtor after the order for relief under this chapter.

(5) In a case in which the debtor is an individual—

(A) unless after notice and a hearing the court orders otherwise for cause, confirmation of the plan does not discharge any debt provided for in the plan until the court grants a discharge on completion of all payments under the plan;

(B) at any time after the confirmation of the plan, and after notice and a hearing, the court may grant a discharge to the debtor who has not completed payments under the plan if—

(i) the value, as of the effective date of the plan, of property actually distributed under the plan on account of each allowed unsecured claim is not less than the amount that would have been paid on such claim if the estate of the debtor had been liquidated under chapter 7 on such date;

(ii) modification of the plan under section 1127 is not practicable; and

(iii) subparagraph (C) permits the court to grant a discharge; and

(C) the court may grant a discharge if, after notice and a hearing held not more than 10 days before the date of the entry of the order granting the discharge, the court finds that there is no reasonable cause to believe that—

(i) section 522(q)(1) may be applicable to the debtor; and

(ii) there is pending any proceeding in which the debtor may be found guilty of a felony of the kind described in section 522(q)(1)(A) or liable for a debt of the kind described in section 522(q)(1)(B);

and if the requirements of subparagraph (A) or (B) are met.

(6) Notwithstanding paragraph (1), the confirmation of a plan does not discharge a debtor that is a corporation from any debt—

(A) of a kind specified in paragraph (2)(A) or (2)(B) of section 523(a) that is owed to a domestic governmental unit, or owed to a person as the result of an action filed under subchapter III of chapter 37 of title 31 or any similar State statute; or

(B) for a tax or customs duty with respect to which the debtor—

(i) made a fraudulent return; or

(ii) willfully attempted in any manner to evade or to defeat such tax or such customs duty.

(Pub.L. 95–598, Nov. 6, 1978, 92 Stat. 2638; Pub.L. 98–353, Title III, § 513, July 10, 1984, 98 Stat. 387; Pub.L. 109–8, Title III, §§ 321(d), 330(b), Title VII, § 708, Apr. 20, 2005, 119 Stat. 95, 101, 126; Pub.L. 111–327, § 2(a)(36), Dec. 22, 2010, 124 Stat. 3561.)

HISTORICAL AND STATUTORY NOTES

References in Text

Subchapter III of chapter 37 of title 31, referred to in subsec. (d)(6)(A), is 31 U.S.C.A. § 3721 et seq.

Codifications

Amendment by Pub.L. 109–8, § 330(b), adding a new subparagraph (C) "at the end" of subsection (d) "as amended by section 321 [of Pub.L. 109–8, which added a new paragraph (5) to subsection (d) of this section]" was executed by adding the new subparagraph to the end of paragraph (5) of subsection (d), as the probable intent of Congress.

Amendments

2010 Amendments. Subsec. (d)(5)(B)(i). Pub.L. 111–327, § 2(a)(36)(A)(i), struck out "and" at the end following the semicolon.

Subsec. (d)(5)(B)(iii). Pub.L. 111–327, § 2(a)(36)(A)(ii)), added cl. (iii).

Subsec. (d)(5)(C). Pub.L. 111–327, § 2(a)(36)(B)(i), struck out "unless" and inserted "the court may grant a discharge if,".

Pub.L. 111–327, § 2(a)(36)(B)(iii), added the undesignated matter at the end following cl. (ii) reading, "and if the requirements of subparagraph (A) or (B) are met.".

Subsec. (d)(5)(C)(ii). Pub.L. 111–327, § 2(a)(36)(B)(ii), struck out the period at the end and inserted a semicolon.

2005 Amendments. Subsec. (d)(2). Pub.L. 109–8, § 321(d)(1), struck out "The confirmation of a plan does not discharge an individual debtor" and inserted "A discharge under this chapter does not discharge a debtor who is an individual".

Subsec. (d)(5). Pub.L. 109–8, § 321(d)(2), added par. (5).

Subsec. (d)(5)(C). Pub.L. 109–8, § 330(b), added subpar. (C). See Codifications note under this section.

Subsec. (d)(6). Pub.L. 109–8, § 708, added par. (6).

1984 Amendments. Subsec. (a). Pub.L. 98–353, § 513(a), substituted "any creditor, equity security holder, or general partner in" for "any creditor or equity security holder of, or general partner in,".

Subsec. (c). Pub.L. 98–353, § 513(b), substituted "Except as provided in subsections (d)(2) and (d)(3) of this section and except as otherwise provided in the plan or in the order confirming the plan, after confirmation of a plan, the property dealt with by the plan is free and clear of all claims and interests of creditors, equity security holders, and of general partners in the debtor." for "After confirmation of a plan, the property dealt with by the plan is free and clear of all claims and interests of creditors, of equity security holders, and of general partners in the debtor, except as otherwise provided in the plan or in the order confirming the plan.".

CROSS REFERENCES

Confirmation of plan filed under this chapter, see 11 USCA § 1129.

Discharge under Chapter seven, see 11 USCA § 727.

Effect of confirmation of plans filed in—

    Chapter nine cases, see 11 USCA § 944.

    Chapter thirteen cases, see 11 USCA § 1327.

    Chapter twelve cases, see 11 USCA § 1227.

Effect of conversion, see 11 USCA § 348.

Effect of discharge, see 11 USCA § 524.

Exceptions to discharge, see 11 USCA § 523.

Failure of discharge as cause for conversion, see 11 USCA § 1112.

Nondischargeability of capital improvement loans for multifamily housing projects in proceedings under this section, see 12 USCA § 1715z–1a.

Supplemental injunctions, debtor and plan of reorganization, see 11 USCA § 524.

§ 1142. Implementation of plan

(a) Notwithstanding any otherwise applicable nonbankruptcy law, rule, or regulation relating to financial condition, the debtor and any entity organized or to be organized for the purpose of carrying out the plan shall carry out the plan and shall comply with any orders of the court.

(b) The court may direct the debtor and any other necessary party to execute or deliver or to join in the execution or delivery of any instrument required to effect a transfer of property dealt with by a confirmed plan, and to perform any other act, including the satisfaction of any lien, that is necessary for the consummation of the plan.

(Pub.L. 95–598, Nov. 6, 1978, 92 Stat. 2639; Pub.L. 98–353, Title III, § 514(a), (c), (d), July 10, 1984, 98 Stat. 387.)

HISTORICAL AND STATUTORY NOTES

Amendments

1984 Amendments. Pub.L. 98–353, § 514(a), substituted "Implementation" for "Execution" in the section catchline.

Subsec. (a). Pub.L. 98–353, § 514(c), struck out the comma after "shall carry out the plan".

Subsec. (b). Pub.L. 98–353, § 514(d), added "a" following "by".

CROSS REFERENCES

Applicability of subsec. (b) of this section in Chapter nine cases, see 11 USCA § 901.

Supplemental injunctions, debtor and plan of reorganization, see 11 USCA § 524.

§ 1143. Distribution

If a plan requires presentment or surrender of a security or the performance of any other act as a condition to participation in distribution under the plan, such action shall be taken not later than five years after the date of the entry of the order of confirmation. Any entity that has not within such time presented or surrendered such entity's security or taken any such other action that the plan requires may not participate in distribution under the plan.

(Pub.L. 95–598, Nov. 6, 1978, 92 Stat. 2639.)

CROSS REFERENCES

Applicability of this section in Chapter nine cases, see 11 USCA § 901.

Distribution of property of estate in Chapter seven cases, see 11 USCA § 726.

Distribution of securities in stockbroker liquidation cases, see 11 USCA § 750.

Ownership of copyright, see 17 USCA § 201.

§ 1144. Revocation of an order of confirmation

On request of a party in interest at any time before 180 days after the date of the entry of the order of confirmation, and after notice and a hearing, the court may revoke such order if and only if such order was procured by fraud. An order under this section revoking an order of confirmation shall—

(1) contain such provisions as are necessary to protect any entity acquiring rights in good faith reliance on the order of confirmation; and

(2) revoke the discharge of the debtor.

(Pub.L. 95–598, Nov. 6, 1978, 92 Stat. 2639; Pub.L. 98–353, Title III, § 515, July 10, 1984, 98 Stat. 387.)

HISTORICAL AND STATUTORY NOTES

Amendments

1984 Amendments. Pub.L. 98–353 added "if and only" following "revoke such order".

CROSS REFERENCES

Applicability of this section in Chapter nine cases, see 11 USCA § 901.

Confirmation of one plan as affected by revocation, see 11 USCA § 1129.

Revocation of confirmation order as cause for conversion or dismissal, see 11 USCA § 1112.

Revocation of order of confirmation in—

Chapter thirteen cases, see 11 USCA § 1330.

Chapter twelve cases, see 11 USCA § 1230.

Supplemental injunctions, see 11 USCA § 524.

§ 1145. Exemption from securities laws

(a) Except with respect to an entity that is an underwriter as defined in subsection (b) of this section, section 5 of the Securities Act of 1933 and any State or local law requiring registration for offer or sale of a security or registration or licensing of an issuer of, underwriter of, or broker or dealer in, a security do not apply to—

(1) the offer or sale under a plan of a security of the debtor, of an affiliate participating in a joint plan with the debtor, or of a successor to the debtor under the plan—

(A) in exchange for a claim against, an interest in, or a claim for an administrative expense in the case concerning, the debtor or such affiliate; or

(B) principally in such exchange and partly for cash or property;

(2) the offer of a security through any warrant, option, right to subscribe, or conversion privilege that was sold in the manner specified in paragraph (1) of this subsection, or the sale of a security upon the exercise of such a warrant, option, right, or privilege;

(3) the offer or sale, other than under a plan, of a security of an issuer other than the debtor or an affiliate, if—

(A) such security was owned by the debtor on the date of the filing of the petition;

(B) the issuer of such security is—

(i) required to file reports under section 13 or 15(d) of the Securities Exchange Act of 1934; and

(ii) in compliance with the disclosure and reporting provision of such applicable section; and

(C) such offer or sale is of securities that do not exceed—

(i) during the two-year period immediately following the date of the filing of the petition, four percent of the securities of such class outstanding on such date; and

(ii) during any 180-day period following such two-year period, one percent of the securities outstanding at the beginning of such 180-day period; or

(4) a transaction by a stockbroker in a security that is executed after a transaction of a kind specified in paragraph (1) or (2) of this subsection in such security and before the expiration of 40 days after the first date on which such security was bona fide offered to the public by the issuer or by or through an underwriter, if such stockbroker provides, at the time of or before such transaction by such stockbroker, a disclosure statement approved under section 1125 of this title, and, if the court orders, information supplementing such disclosure statement.

(b)(1) Except as provided in paragraph (2) of this subsection and except with respect to ordinary trading transactions of an entity that is not an issuer, an entity is an underwriter under section 2(a)(11) of the Securities Act of 1933, if such entity—

(A) purchases a claim against, interest in, or claim for an administrative expense in the case concerning, the debtor, if such purchase is with a view to distribution of any security received or to be received in exchange for such a claim or interest;

(B) offers to sell securities offered or sold under the plan for the holders of such securities;

(C) offers to buy securities offered or sold under the plan from the holders of such securities, if such offer to buy is—

(i) with a view to distribution of such securities; and

(ii) under an agreement made in connection with the plan, with the consummation of the plan, or with the offer or sale of securities under the plan; or

(D) is an issuer, as used in such section 2(a)(11), with respect to such securities.

(2) An entity is not an underwriter under section 2(a)(11) of the Securities Act of 1933 or under paragraph (1) of this subsection with respect to an agreement that provides only for—

(A)(i) the matching or combining of fractional interests in securities offered or sold under the plan into whole interests; or

(ii) the purchase or sale of such fractional interests from or to entities receiving such fractional interests under the plan; or

(B) the purchase or sale for such entities of such fractional or whole interests as are necessary to adjust for any remaining fractional interests after such matching.

(3) An entity other than an entity of the kind specified in paragraph (1) of this subsection is not an underwriter under section 2(a)(11) of the Securities Act of 1933 with respect to any securities offered or sold to such entity in the manner specified in subsection (a)(1) of this section.

(c) An offer or sale of securities of the kind and in the manner specified under subsection (a)(1) of this section is deemed to be a public offering.

(d) The Trust Indenture Act of 1939 does not apply to a note issued under the plan that matures not later than one year after the effective date of the plan.

(Pub.L. 95–598, Nov. 6, 1978, 92 Stat. 2639; Pub.L. 98–353, Title III, § 516, July 10, 1984, 98 Stat. 387; Pub.L. 103–394, Title V, § 501(d)(33), Oct. 22, 1994, 108 Stat. 4146; Pub.L. 111–327, § 2(a)(37), Dec. 22, 2010, 124 Stat. 3561.)

HISTORICAL AND STATUTORY NOTES

References in Text

Section 5 of the Securities Act of 1933, referred to in subsec. (a), is section 5 of Act May 27, 1933, c. 38, Title I, 48 Stat. 77, which is classified to section 77e of Title 15, Commerce and Trade.

Section 13 or 15 of the Securities Exchange Act of 1934, referred to in subsec. (a)(3)(B)(i), are section 13 and 15 of Act June 6, 1934, c. 404, Title I, 48 Stat. 894, 895, which are classified to sections 78m and 78o, respectively, of Title 15.

Section 2(a)(11) of the Securities Act of 1933, referred to in subsec. (b), is subsec. (a)(11) of section 2 of Act May 27, 1933, c. 38, Title I, 48 Stat. 74, as amended, which is classified to 15 U.S.C.A. § 77b(a)(11).

The Trust Indenture Act of 1939, referred to in subsec. (d), is Title III of Act May 27, 1933, ch. 38, as added Aug. 3, 1939, ch. 411, 53 Stat. 1149, as amended, which is classified generally to subchapter III (section 77aaa et seq.) of chapter 2A of Title 15. For complete classification of this Act to the Code, see section 77aaa of Title 15 and Tables.

Amendments

2010 Amendments. Subsec. (b)(1). Pub.L. 111–327, § 2(a)(37), in the prefatory material preceding subpar. (A), struck out "2(11)" and inserted "2(a)(11)".

Subsec. (b)(1)(D). Pub.L. 111–327, § 2(a)(37), struck out "2(11)" and inserted "2(a)(11)".

Subsec. (b)(2). Pub.L. 111–327, § 2(a)(37), in the prefatory material preceding subpar. (A)(i), struck out "2(11)" and inserted "2(a)(11)".

Subsec. (b)(3). Pub.L. 111–327, § 2(a)(37), struck out "2(11)" and inserted "2(a)(11)".

1994 Amendments. Subsec. (a). Pub.L. 103–394, § 501(d)(33)(A)(i), (ii), substituted "do not apply to" for "does not apply to" and struck out "(15 U.S.C. 77e)" after "Securities Act of 1933".

Subsec. (a)(3)(B). Pub.L. 103–394, § 501(d)(33)(A)(iii), in cl. (i) struck out "(15 U.S.C. 78m or 78o(d))" after "Securities Exchange Act of 1934".

Subsec. (b)(1). Pub.L. 103–394, § 501(d)(33)(B), struck out "(15 U.S.C. 77b(11))" after "Securities Act of 1933".

Subsec. (d). Pub.L. 103–394, § 501(d)(33)(C), struck out "(15 U.S.C. 77aaa et seq.)" after "Trust Indenture Act of 1939".

1984 Amendments. Subsec. (a)(3)(B)(i). Pub.L. 98–353, § 516(a)(1), added "or 15(d)" following "13".

Pub.L. 98–353, § 516(a)(1), added "or 78o(d)" following "78m".

Subsec. (a)(3)(B)(ii). Pub.L. 98–353, § 516(a)(2), substituted "in compliance with the disclosure and reporting provision of such applicable section; and" for "in compliance with all applicable requirements for the continuance of trading in such security on the date of such offer or sale; and".

Subsec. (a)(4). Pub.L. 98–353, § 516(a)(3), substituted "by a stockbroker" for "by a stockholder" and "by such stockbroker" for "by such stockholder", respectively.

Subsec. (b)(1). Pub.L. 98–353, § 516(b)(1), added "and except with respect to ordinary trading transactions of an entity that is not an issuer" following "subsection".

Subsec. (b)(1)(C). Pub.L. 98–353, § 516(b)(2), substituted "from" for "for".

Subsec. (b)(2)(A)(i). Pub.L. 98–353, § 516(b)(3), substituted "or combining" for "combination".

Subsec. (b)(2)(A)(ii). Pub.L. 98–353, § 516(b)(4), substituted "from or to" for "among".

Subsec. (d). Pub.L. 98–353, § 516(c), struck out "commercial" preceding "note issued under the plan".

CROSS REFERENCES

Applicability of term "security" to offers or sales under § 364 of this title to underwriters, see 11 USCA § 364.

Applicability of this section in Chapter nine cases, see 11 USCA § 901.

Protection of securities customers, see 15 USCA § 78eee.

Racketeering activity defined as offense involving fraud in sale of securities in case under this title, see 18 USCA § 1961.

Securities exempted from Securities Act of 1933, see 15 USCA § 77c.

§ 1146. Special tax provisions

(a) The issuance, transfer, or exchange of a security, or the making or delivery of an instrument of transfer under a plan confirmed under section 1129 of this title, may not be taxed under any law imposing a stamp tax or similar tax.

(b) The court may authorize the proponent of a plan to request a determination, limited to questions of law, by a State or local governmental unit charged with responsibility for collection or determination of a tax on or measured by income, of the tax effects, under section 346 of this title and under the law imposing such tax, of the plan. In the event of an actual controversy, the court may declare such effects after the earlier of—

(1) the date on which such governmental unit responds to the request under this subsection; or

(2) 270 days after such request.

[(c) Redesignated (a)]

[(d) Redesignated (b)]

(Pub.L. 95–598, Nov. 6, 1978, 92 Stat. 2641; Pub.L. 98–353, Title III, § 517, July 10, 1984, 98 Stat. 388; Pub.L. 109–8, Title VII, § 719(b)(3), Apr. 20, 2005, 119 Stat. 133.)

HISTORICAL AND STATUTORY NOTES

Amendments

2005 Amendments. Subsec. (a). Pub.L. 109–8, § 719(b)(3), struck out former subsec. (a) and redesignated subsec. (c) as subsec. (a). Prior to striking, subsec. (a) read: **"(a)** For the purposes of any State or local law imposing a tax on or measured by income, the taxable period of a debtor that is an individual shall terminate on the date of the order for relief under this chapter, unless the case was converted under section 706 of this title."

Subsec. (b). Pub.L. 109–8, § 719(b)(3), struck out former subsec. (b) and redesignated subsec. (d) as subsec. (b). Prior to striking, subsec. (b) read: **"(b)** The trustee shall make a State or local tax return of income for the estate of an individual debtor in a case under this chapter for each taxable period after the order for relief under this chapter during which the case is pending."

Subsec. (c). Pub.L. 109–8, § 719(b)(3)(B), redesignated former subsec. (c) as subsec. (a).

Subsec. (d). Pub.L. 109–8, § 719(b)(3)(B), redesignated former subsec. (d) as subsec. (b).

1984 Amendments. Subsec. (c). Pub.L. 98–353, § 517(a), struck out "State or local" preceding "law imposing a stamp tax".

Subsec. (d)(1). Pub.L. 98–353, § 517(b), substituted "or" for "and".

CROSS REFERENCES

Declaratory judgments, see 28 USCA § 2201.

Determination of—

    Number of taxable periods during which debtor may use loss carryover or carryback, see 11 USCA § 346.

    Tax liability, see 11 USCA § 505.

Effect of conversion, see 11 USCA § 348.

Special tax provisions in Chapter 7 cases, see 11 USCA § 728.

SUBCHAPTER IV—RAILROAD REORGANIZATION

CROSS REFERENCES

"Carrier subject to liquidation" as meaning carrier subject to proceeding under this subchapter, see 45 USCA § 915.

Collective bargaining agreement, manner of assumption or rejection by trustee other than a trustee in a case covered by this subchapter, see 11 USCA § 1113.

Subchapter applicable only in cases under this chapter concerning railroad, see 11 USCA § 103.

Temporary operating approval granted to carrier subject to this subchapter as of January 14, 1983, see 45 USCA § 1017.

§ 1161. Inapplicability of other sections

Sections 341, 343, 1102(a)(1), 1104, 1105, 1107, 1129(a)(7), and 1129(c) of this title do not apply in a case concerning a railroad.

(Pub.L. 95–598, Nov. 6, 1978, 92 Stat. 2641.)

CROSS REFERENCES

Applicability of Chapters 1, 3, and 5 of this title to cases under Chapters 7, 11, or 13 of this title except as provided in this section, see 11 USCA § 103.

§ 1162. Definition

In this subchapter, "Board" means the "Surface Transportation Board".

(Added Pub.L. 104–88, Title III, § 302(1), Dec. 29, 1995, 109 Stat. 943.)

HISTORICAL AND STATUTORY NOTES

Prior Provisions

A prior section 1162, Pub.L. 95–598, Nov. 6, 1978, 92 Stat. 2641, defined the term "Commission" to mean the "Interstate Commerce Commission" for purposes of this subchapter and was repealed by Pub.L. 104–88, Title III, § 302(1), Dec. 29, 1995, 109 Stat. 943.

§ 1163. Appointment of trustee

As soon as practicable after the order for relief the Secretary of Transportation shall submit a list of five disinterested persons that are qualified and willing to serve as trustees in the case. The United States trustee shall appoint one of such persons to serve as trustee in the case.

(Pub.L. 95–598, Nov. 6, 1978, 92 Stat. 2641; Pub.L. 99–554, Title II, § 226, Oct. 27, 1986, 100 Stat. 3102.)

HISTORICAL AND STATUTORY NOTES

Amendments

1986 Amendments. Pub.L. 99–554, § 226, substituted "relief the Secretary" for "relief, the Secretary" and "The United States trustee shall appoint" for "The court shall appoint".

CROSS REFERENCES

Appointment of trustee in—

Cases under this chapter, see 11 USCA § 1104.

Chapter thirteen cases, see 11 USCA § 1302.

Chapter twelve cases, see 11 USCA § 1202.

Collective bargaining agreement, manner of assumption or rejection by trustee other than a trustee in a case covered by this subchapter, see 11 USCA § 1113.

Election of trustee in Chapter seven cases, see 11 USCA § 702.

Guarantees of certificates, see 45 USCA § 662.

Qualification of trustee, see 11 USCA § 322.

Time for bringing action, see 11 USCA § 546.

§ 1164. Right to be heard

The Board, the Department of Transportation, and any State or local commission having regulatory jurisdiction over the debtor may raise and may appear and be heard on any issue in a case under this chapter, but may not appeal from any judgment, order, or decree entered in the case.

(Pub.L. 95–598, Nov. 6, 1978, 92 Stat. 2641; Pub.L. 104–88, Title III, § 302(2), Dec. 29, 1995, 109 Stat. 943.)

HISTORICAL AND STATUTORY NOTES

Amendments

1995 Amendments. Pub.L. 104–88, § 302(2), substituted "Board" for "Commission".

CROSS REFERENCES

Right of Commodity Futures Trading Commission to be heard, see 11 USCA § 762.

Right of Securities and Exchange Commission and party in interest to be heard in case under this chapter, see 11 USCA § 1109.

§ 1165. Protection of the public interest

In applying sections 1166, 1167, 1169, 1170, 1171, 1172, 1173, and 1174 of this title, the court and the trustee shall consider the public interest in addition to the interests of the debtor, creditors, and equity security holders.

(Pub.L. 95–598, Nov. 6, 1978, 92 Stat. 2641.)

§ 1166. Effect of subtitle IV of title 49 and of Federal, State, or local regulations

Except with respect to abandonment under section 1170 of this title, or merger, modification of the financial structure of the debtor, or issuance or sale of securities under a plan, the trustee and the debtor are subject to the provisions of subtitle IV of title 49 that are applicable to railroads, and the trustee is subject to orders of any Federal, State, or local regulatory body to the same extent as the debtor would be if a petition commencing the case under this chapter had not been filed, but—

(1) any such order that would require the expenditure, or the incurring of an obligation for the expenditure, of money from the estate is not effective unless approved by the court; and

(2) the provisions of this chapter are subject to section 601(b) of the Regional Rail Reorganization Act of 1973.

(Pub.L. 95–598, Nov. 6, 1978, 92 Stat. 2642; Pub.L. 97–449, § 5(a)(2), Jan. 12, 1983, 96 Stat. 2442; Pub.L. 98–353, Title III, § 518, July 10, 1984, 98 Stat. 388; Pub.L. 103–394, Title V, § 501(d)(34), Oct. 22, 1994, 108 Stat. 4146.)

HISTORICAL AND STATUTORY NOTES

References in Text

Section 601(b) of Regional Rail Reorganization Act of 1973, referred to in par. (2), is section 601(b) of Pub.L. 93–236, Title VI, Jan. 2, 1974, 87 Stat. 1021, which is classified to section 791(b) of Title 45, Railroads.

Codifications

Pub.L. 98–353, Title III, § 518, July 10, 1984, 98 Stat. 388, substituted "subtitle IV of title 49" for "the Interstate Commerce Act (49 U.S.C. 1 et seq.)", which amendment was previously made by Pub.L. 97–449, thereby requiring no further change in text.

Amendments

1994 Amendments. Par. (2). Pub.L. 103–394, § 501(d)(34), struck out "(45 U.S.C. 791(b))" after "Regional Rail Reorganization Act of 1973".

1984 Amendments. Pub.L. 98–353, § 518, substituted "subtitle IV of title 49" for "the Interstate Commerce Act (49 U.S.C. 1 et seq.)". See Codifications note set out under this section.

1983 Amendments. Heading. Pub.L. 97–449, § 5(a)(2)(A), substituted "subtitle IV of title 49" for "Interstate Commerce Act".

Pub.L. 97–449, § 5(a)(2)(B), substituted "subtitle IV of title 49" for "the Interstate Commerce Act (49 U.S.C. § 1 et seq.)" following "subject to the provisions of" in text.

CROSS REFERENCES

Management and operation of property according to state law, see 28 USCA § 959.

§ 1167. Collective bargaining agreements

Notwithstanding section 365 of this title, neither the court nor the trustee may change the wages or working conditions of employees of the debtor established by a collective bargaining agreement that is subject to the Railway Labor Act except in accordance with section 6 of such Act.

(Pub.L. 95–598, Nov. 6, 1978, 92 Stat. 2642; Pub.L. 103–394, Title V, § 501(d)(35), Oct. 22, 1994, 108 Stat. 4146.)

HISTORICAL AND STATUTORY NOTES

References in Text

The Railway Labor Act, referred to in text, is Act May 20, 1926, c. 347, 44 Stat. 577, as amended, which is classified principally to chapter 8 (section 151 et seq.) of Title 45, Railroads. Section 6 of such Act is classified to section 156 of Title 15. For complete classification of this Act to the Code, see section 151 of Title 45 and Tables.

Amendments

1994 Amendments

Pub.L. 103–394, § 501(d)(35), struck out "(45 U.S.C. 151 et seq.)" after "Railway Labor Act" and "(45 U.S.C. 156)" after "section 6 of such Act".

CROSS REFERENCES

Authorization of trustee to operate business, see 11 USCA § 1108.

§ 1168. Rolling stock equipment

(a)(1) The right of a secured party with a security interest in or of a lessor or conditional vendor of equipment described in paragraph (2) to take possession of such equipment in compliance with an equipment security agreement, lease, or conditional sale contract, and to enforce any of its other rights or remedies under such security agreement, lease, or conditional sale contract, to sell, lease, or otherwise retain or dispose of such equipment, is not limited or otherwise affected by any other provision of this title or by any power of the court, except that right to take possession and enforce those other rights and remedies shall be subject to section 362, if—

(A) before the date that is 60 days after the date of commencement of a case under this chapter, the trustee, subject to the court's approval, agrees to perform all obligations of the debtor under such security agreement, lease, or conditional sale contract; and

(B) any default, other than a default of a kind described in section 365(b)(2), under such security agreement, lease, or conditional sale contract—

(i) that occurs before the date of commencement of the case and is an event of default therewith is cured before the expiration of such 60-day period;

(ii) that occurs or becomes an event of default after the date of commencement of the case and before the expiration of such 60-day period is cured before the later of—

(I) the date that is 30 days after the date of the default or event of the default; or

(II) the expiration of such 60-day period; and

(iii) that occurs on or after the expiration of such 60-day period is cured in accordance with the terms of such security agreement, lease, or conditional sale contract, if cure is permitted under that agreement, lease, or conditional sale contract.

(2) The equipment described in this paragraph—

(A) is rolling stock equipment or accessories used on rolling stock equipment, including superstructures or racks, that is subject to a security interest granted by, leased to, or conditionally sold to a debtor; and

(B) includes all records and documents relating to such equipment that are required, under the terms of the security agreement, lease, or conditional sale contract, that is to be surrendered or returned by the debtor in connection with the surrender or return of such equipment.

(3) Paragraph (1) applies to a secured party, lessor, or conditional vendor acting in its own behalf or acting as trustee or otherwise in behalf of another party.

(b) The trustee and the secured party, lessor, or conditional vendor whose right to take possession is protected under subsection (a) may agree, subject to the court's approval, to extend the 60-day period specified in subsection (a)(1).

(c)(1) In any case under this chapter, the trustee shall immediately surrender and return to a secured party, lessor, or conditional vendor, described in subsection (a)(1), equipment described in subsection (a)(2), if at any time after the date of commencement of the case under this chapter such secured party, lessor, or conditional vendor is entitled pursuant to subsection (a)(1) to take possession of such equipment and makes a written demand for such possession of the trustee.

(2) At such time as the trustee is required under paragraph (1) to surrender and return equipment described in subsection (a)(2), any lease of such equipment, and any security agreement or conditional sale contract relating to such equipment, if such security agreement or conditional sale contract is an executory contract, shall be deemed rejected.

(d) With respect to equipment first placed in service on or prior to October 22, 1994, for purposes of this section—

(1) the term "lease" includes any written agreement with respect to which the lessor and the debtor, as lessee, have expressed in the agreement or in a substantially contemporaneous writing that the agreement is to be treated as a lease for Federal income tax purposes; and

(2) the term "security interest" means a purchase-money equipment security interest.

(e) With respect to equipment first placed in service after October 22, 1994, for purposes of this section, the term "rolling stock equipment" includes rolling stock equipment that is substantially rebuilt and accessories used on such equipment.

(Pub.L. 95–598, Nov. 6, 1978, 92 Stat. 2642; Pub.L. 98–353, Title III, § 519, July 10, 1984, 98 Stat. 388; Pub.L. 103–394, Title II, § 201(b), Oct. 22, 1994, 108 Stat. 4120; Pub.L. 106–181, Title VII, § 744(a), Apr. 5, 2000, 114 Stat. 175.)

HISTORICAL AND STATUTORY NOTES

Amendments

2000 Amendments. Pub.L. 106–181, Title VII, § 744(a), rewrote the section, which read:

"**(a)(1)** The right of a secured party with a security interest in or of a lessor or conditional vendor of equipment described in paragraph (2) to take possession of such equipment in compliance with an equipment security agreement, lease, or conditional sale contract is not affected by section 362, 363, or 1129 or by any power of the court to enjoin the taking of possession, unless—

"**(A)** before the date that is 60 days after the date of commencement of a case under this chapter, the trustee, subject to the court's approval, agrees to perform all obligations of the debtor that become due on or after the date of commencement of the case under such security agreement, lease, or conditional sale contract; and

"**(B)** any default, other than a default of a kind described in section 365(b)(2), under such security agreement, lease, or conditional sale contract—

"**(i)** that occurs before the date of commencement of the case and is an event of default therewith is cured before the expiration of such 60-day period; and

"**(ii)** that occurs or becomes an event of default after the date of commencement of the case is cured before the later of—

"**(I)** the date that is 30 days after the date of the default or event of default; or

"**(II)** the expiration of such 60-day period.

"**(2)** Equipment is described in this paragraph if it is rolling stock equipment or accessories used on such equipment, including superstructures and racks, that is subject to a security interest granted by, leased to, or conditionally sold to the debtor.

"**(3)** Paragraph (1) applies to a secured party, lessor, or conditional vendor acting in its own behalf or acting as trustee or otherwise in behalf of another party.

"**(b)** The trustee and the secured party, lessor, or conditional vendor whose right to take possession is protected under subsection (a) may agree, subject to the court's approval, to extend the 60-day period specified in subsection (a)(1).

"**(c)** With respect to equipment first placed in service on or prior to the date of enactment of this subsection, for purposes of this section—

"**(1)** the term 'lease' includes any written agreement with respect to which the lessor and the debtor, as lessee, have expressed in the agreement or in a substantially contemporaneous writing that the agreement is to be treated as a lease for Federal income tax purposes; and

"**(2)** the term 'security interest' means a purchase-money equipment security interest.

"**(d)** With respect to equipment first placed in service after the date of enactment of this subsection, for purposes of this section, the term 'rolling stock equipment' includes rolling stock equipment that is substantially rebuilt and accessories used on such equipment."

1994 Amendments. Pub.L. 103–394, § 201(b), completely revised section, substituting provisions directing that the right to take possession of certain equipment is not affected by section 362, 363, or 1129, for provisions directing that the right to take possession of certain equipment is not affected by section 362 or 363 of this title.

1984 Amendments. Subsec. (b). Pub.L. 98–353 added a comma following "approval".

CROSS REFERENCES

Rights of certain secured parties in aircraft equipment and vessels, see 11 USCA § 1110.

§ 1169. Effect of rejection of lease of railroad line

(a) Except as provided in subsection (b) of this section, if a lease of a line of railroad under which the debtor is the lessee is rejected under section 365 of this title, and if the trustee, within such time as the court fixes, and with the court's approval, elects not to operate the leased line, the lessor under such lease, after such approval, shall operate the line.

(b) If operation of such line by such lessor is impracticable or contrary to the public interest, the court, on request of such lessor, and after notice and a hearing, shall order the trustee to continue operation of such line for the account of such lessor until abandonment is ordered under section 1170 of this title, or until such operation is otherwise lawfully terminated, whichever occurs first.

(c) During any such operation, such lessor is deemed a carrier subject to the provisions of subtitle IV of title 49 that are applicable to railroads.

(Pub.L. 95–598, Nov. 6, 1978, 92 Stat. 2643; Pub.L. 97–449, § 5(a)(3), Jan. 12, 1983, 96 Stat. 2442; Pub.L. 98–353, Title III, § 520, July 10, 1984, 98 Stat. 388.)

HISTORICAL AND STATUTORY NOTES

Codifications

Pub.L. 98–353, Title III, § 520, July 10, 1984, 98 Stat. 388, substituted "subtitle IV of title 49" for "the Interstate Commerce Act (49 U.S.C. 1 et seq.)", which amendment was previously made by Pub.L. 97–449, thereby requiring no further change in text.

Amendments

1984 Amendments. Pub.L. 98–353, § 520, substituted "subtitle IV of title 49" for "the Interstate Commerce Act (49 U.S.C. 1 et seq.)". See codifications note set out under this section.

1983 Amendments. Subsec. (c). Pub.L. 97–449 substituted "subtitle IV of title 49" for "the Interstate Commerce Act (49 U.S.C. 1 et seq.)" after "subject to the provisions of".

CROSS REFERENCES

Executory contracts in stockbroker liquidation cases, see 11 USCA § 744.

§ 1170. Abandonment of railroad line

(a) The court, after notice and a hearing, may authorize the abandonment of all or a portion of a railroad line if such abandonment is—

(1)(A) in the best interest of the estate; or

(B) essential to the formulation of a plan; and

(2) consistent with the public interest.

(b) If, except for the pendency of the case under this chapter, such abandonment would require approval by the Board under a law of the United States, the trustee shall initiate an appropriate application for such abandonment with the Board. The court may fix a time within which the Board shall report to the court on such application.

(c) After the court receives the report of the Board, or the expiration of the time fixed under subsection (b) of this section, whichever occurs first, the court may authorize such abandonment, after notice to the Board, the Secretary of Transportation, the trustee, any party in interest that has requested notice, any affected shipper or community, and any other entity prescribed by the court, and a hearing.

(d)(1) Enforcement of an order authorizing such abandonment shall be stayed until the time for taking an appeal has expired, or, if an appeal is timely taken, until such order has become final.

(2) If an order authorizing such abandonment is appealed, the court, on request of a party in interest, may authorize suspension of service on a line or a portion of a line pending the determination of such appeal, after notice to the Board, the Secretary of Transportation, the trustee, any party in interest that has requested notice, any affected shipper or community, and any other entity prescribed by the court, and a hearing. An appellant may not obtain a stay of the enforcement of an order authorizing such suspension by the giving of a supersedeas bond or otherwise, during the pendency of such appeal.

(e)(1) In authorizing any abandonment of a railroad line under this section, the court shall require the rail carrier to provide a fair arrangement at least as protective of the interests of employees as that established under section 11326(a) of title 49.

(2) Nothing in this subsection shall be deemed to affect the priorities or timing of payment of employee protection which might have existed in the absence of this subsection.

(Pub.L. 95–598, Nov. 6, 1978, 92 Stat. 2643; Pub.L. 96–448, Title II, § 227(a), Oct. 14, 1980, 94 Stat. 1931; Pub.L. 98–353, Title III, § 521, July 10, 1984, 98 Stat. 388; Pub.L. 104–88, Title III, § 302(2), Dec. 29, 1995, 109 Stat. 943; Pub.L. 109–8, Title XII, § 1217, Apr. 20, 2005, 119 Stat. 195.)

HISTORICAL AND STATUTORY NOTES

Amendments

2005 Amendments. Subsec. (e)(1). Pub.L.109–8, § 1217, struck out "section 11347" and inserted "section 11326(a)".

1995 Amendments. Subsec. (b). Pub.L. 104–88, § 302(2), substituted "Board" for "Commission".

Subsec. (c). Pub.L. 104–88, § 302(2), substituted "Board" for "Commission".

Subsec. (d)(2). Pub.L. 104–88, § 302(2), substituted "Board" for "Commission".

1984 Amendments. Subsec. (a). Pub.L. 98–353, § 521(a), added "of all or a portion" following "the abandonment".

Subsec. (c). Pub.L. 98–353, § 521(b), added a comma following "abandonment".

Subsec. (d)(2). Pub.L. 98–353, § 521(c)(1), substituted "such abandonment" for "the abandonment of a railroad line".

Pub.L. 98–353, § 521(c)(2), substituted "suspension" for "termination".

1980 Amendments. Subsec. (e). Pub.L. 96–448 added subsec. (e).

CROSS REFERENCES

Abandonment of lines of Milwaukee Railroad in cases pending under § 77 of Bankruptcy Act on November 4, 1979, see 45 USCA § 915.

Abandonment of lines of Milwaukee Railroad under this section, see 45 USCA § 904.

Abandonment of property of estate, see 11 USCA § 554.

§ 1171. Priority claims

(a) There shall be paid as an administrative expense any claim of an individual or of the personal representative of a deceased individual against the debtor or the estate, for personal injury to or death of such individual arising out of the operation of the debtor or the estate, whether such claim arose before or after the commencement of the case.

(b) Any unsecured claim against the debtor that would have been entitled to priority if a receiver in equity of the property of the debtor had been appointed by a Federal court on the date of the order for relief under this title shall be entitled to the same priority in the case under this chapter.

(Pub.L. 95–598, Nov. 6, 1978, 92 Stat. 2643; Pub.L. 98–353, Title III, § 522, July 10, 1984, 98 Stat. 388.)

HISTORICAL AND STATUTORY NOTES

Amendments

1984 Amendments. Subsec. (b). Pub.L. 98–353 substituted "the same" for "such".

CROSS REFERENCES

Allowance of administrative expenses, see 11 USCA § 503.

Priorities, see 11 USCA § 507.

§ 1172. Contents of plan

(a) In addition to the provisions required or permitted under section 1123 of this title, a plan—

(1) shall specify the extent to and the means by which the debtor's rail service is proposed to be continued, and the extent to which any of the debtor's rail service is proposed to be terminated; and

(2) may include a provision for—

(A) the transfer of any or all of the operating railroad lines of the debtor to another operating railroad; or

(B) abandonment of any railroad line in accordance with section 1170 of this title.

(b) If, except for the pendency of the case under this chapter, transfer of, or operation of or over, any of the debtor's rail lines by an entity other than the debtor or a successor to the debtor under the plan would require approval by the Board under a law of the United States, then a plan may not propose such a transfer or such operation unless the proponent of the plan initiates an appropriate application for such a transfer or such operation with the Board and, within such time as the court may fix, not exceeding 180 days, the Board, with or without a hearing, as the Board may determine, and with or without modification or condition, approves such application, or does not act on such application. Any action or order of the Board approving, modifying, conditioning, or disapproving such application is subject to review by the court only under sections 706(2)(A), 706(2)(B), 706(2)(C), and 706(2)(D) of title 5.

(c)(1) In approving an application under subsection (b) of this section, the Board shall require the rail carrier to provide a fair arrangement at least as protective of the interests of employees as that established under section 11326(a) of title 49.

(2) Nothing in this subsection shall be deemed to affect the priorities or timing of payment of employee protection which might have existed in the absence of this subsection.

(Pub.L. 95–598, Nov. 6, 1978, 92 Stat. 2644; Pub.L. 96–448, Title II, § 227(b), Oct. 14, 1980, 94 Stat. 1931; Pub.L. 104–88, Title III, § 302(2), Dec. 29, 1995, 109 Stat. 943; Pub.L. 109–8, Title XII, § 1218, Apr. 20, 2005, 119 Stat. 195.)

HISTORICAL AND STATUTORY NOTES

Amendments

2005 Amendments. Subsec. (c)(1). Pub.L.109–8, § 1218, struck out "section 11347" and inserted "section 11326(a)".

1995 Amendments. Subsec. (b). Pub.L. 104–88, § 302(2), substituted "Board" for "Commission".

Subsec. (c)(1). Pub.L. 104–88, § 302(2), substituted "Board" for "Commission".

1980 Amendments. Subsec. (c). Pub.L. 96–448 added subsec. (c).

CROSS REFERENCES

Contents of plan filed in—

    Chapter thirteen cases, see 11 USCA § 1322.

    Chapter twelve cases, see 11 USCA § 1222.

§ 1173. Confirmation of plan

(a) The court shall confirm a plan if—

    (1) the applicable requirements of section 1129 of this title have been met;

    (2) each creditor or equity security holder will receive or retain under the plan property of a value, as of the effective date of the plan, that is not less than the value of property that each such creditor or equity security holder would so receive or retain if all of the operating railroad lines of the debtor were sold, and the proceeds of such sale, and the other property of the estate, were distributed under chapter 7 of this title on such date;

    (3) in light of the debtor's past earnings and the probable prospective earnings of the reorganized debtor, there will be adequate coverage by such prospective earnings of any fixed charges, such as interest on debt, amortization of funded debt, and rent for leased railroads, provided for by the plan; and

    (4) the plan is consistent with the public interest.

(b) If the requirements of subsection (a) of this section are met with respect to more than one plan, the court shall confirm the plan that is most likely to maintain adequate rail service in the public interest.

(Pub.L. 95–598, Nov. 6, 1978, 92 Stat. 2644; Pub.L. 98–353, Title III, § 523, July 10, 1984, 98 Stat. 388.)

HISTORICAL AND STATUTORY NOTES

Amendments

    1984 Amendments. Subsec. (a)(4). Pub.L. 98–353 substituted "consistent" for "compatible".

CROSS REFERENCES

Confirmation of plan in—

    Chapter nine cases, see 11 USCA § 943.

    Chapter thirteen cases, see 11 USCA § 1325.

    Chapter twelve cases, see 11 USCA § 1225.

Effect of confirmation in cases under this chapter, see 11 USCA § 1141.

Nonrecognition of gain or loss for income tax purposes of exchanges of stock and securities in reorganizations confirmed under this section, see 26 USCA § 354.

Revocation of order of confirmation in cases under this chapter, see 11 USCA § 1144.

Unclaimed property, see 11 USCA § 347.

§ 1174. Liquidation

On request of a party in interest and after notice and a hearing, the court may, or, if a plan has not been confirmed under section 1173 of this title before five years after the date of the order for relief, the court shall, order the trustee to cease the debtor's operation and to collect and reduce to money all of the property of the estate in the same manner as if the case were a case under chapter 7 of this title.

(Pub.L. 95–598, Nov. 6, 1978, 92 Stat. 2644.)

CROSS REFERENCES

Conversion of—

    Chapter eleven cases, see 11 USCA § 1112.

    Chapter seven cases, see 11 USCA § 706.

    Chapter thirteen cases, see 11 USCA § 1307.

    Chapter twelve cases, see 11 USCA § 1208.

Dismissal of—

    Chapter nine cases, see 11 USCA § 930.

Chapter seven cases, see 11 USCA § 707.

CHAPTER 12—ADJUSTMENT OF DEBTS OF A FAMILY FARMER OR FISHERMAN WITH REGULAR ANNUAL INCOME

SUBCHAPTER I—OFFICERS, ADMINISTRATION, AND THE ESTATE

Sec.
1201. Stay of action against codebtor.
1202. Trustee.
1203. Rights and powers of debtor.
1204. Removal of debtor as debtor in possession.
1205. Adequate protection.
1206. Sales free of interests.
1207. Property of the estate.
1208. Conversion or dismissal.

SUBCHAPTER II—THE PLAN

1221. Filing of plan.
1222. Contents of plan.
1223. Modification of plan before confirmation.
1224. Confirmation hearing.
1225. Confirmation of plan.
1226. Payments.
1227. Effect of confirmation.
1228. Discharge.
1229. Modification of plan after confirmation.
1230. Revocation of an order of confirmation.
1231. Special tax provisions.

HISTORICAL AND STATUTORY NOTES

Amendments

2005 Amendments. Chapter Heading. Pub.L. 109–8, Title X, § 1007(c)(1), Apr. 20, 2005, 119 Stat. 188, inserted **"OR FISHERMAN"** after **"FAMILY FARMER"**.

Repeal and Reenactment of Chapter

Chapter 12 was originally a temporary measure and was set to sunset on October 1, 1993. Pub. L. 99–554, § 302(f). Pub. L. 103–65, § 1 extended the effective date of repeal to Oct. 1, 1998. Pub. L. 105–277, § 149(a), temporarily reenacted the chapter after it had sunset. Pub. L. 106–5, § 1(1), (2) extended the effective date of repeal to Oct. 1, 1999. Pub. L. 107–8, § 1 extended effective date of repeal to June 1, 2001. Pub. L. 107–17, § 1 extended the effective date of repeal to Oct. 1, 2001. Pub. L. 107–170, § 1 extended the effective date of repeal to June 1, 2002. Pub. L. 107–171, § 10814(a) extended the effective date of repeal to Jan. 1, 2003. Pub. L. 107–377, § 2(a) extended the effective date of repeal to July 1, 2003. Pub. L. 108–73, § 2(a) extended the effective date of repeal to Jan. 1, 2004. Pub. L. 108–369, § 2(a) extended effective date of repeal to July 1, 2005. Pub. L. 109–8, § 1001(a)(1), reenacted the chapter without providing for automatic repeal.

SUBCHAPTER I—OFFICERS, ADMINISTRATION, AND THE ESTATE

§ 1201. Stay of action against codebtor

(a) Except as provided in subsections (b) and (c) of this section, after the order for relief under this chapter, a creditor may not act, or commence or continue any civil action, to collect all or any part of a consumer debt of the debtor from any individual that is liable on such debt with the debtor, or that secured such debt, unless—

(1) such individual became liable on or secured such debt in the ordinary course of such individual's business; or

(2) the case is closed, dismissed, or converted to a case under chapter 7 of this title.

(b) A creditor may present a negotiable instrument, and may give notice of dishonor of such an instrument.

(c) On request of a party in interest and after notice and a hearing, the court shall grant relief from the stay provided by subsection (a) of this section with respect to a creditor, to the extent that—

  (1) as between the debtor and the individual protected under subsection (a) of this section, such individual received the consideration for the claim held by such creditor;

  (2) the plan filed by the debtor proposes not to pay such claim; or

  (3) such creditor's interest would be irreparably harmed by continuation of such stay.

(d) Twenty days after the filing of a request under subsection (c)(2) of this section for relief from the stay provided by subsection (a) of this section, such stay is terminated with respect to the party in interest making such request, unless the debtor or any individual that is liable on such debt with the debtor files and serves upon such party in interest a written objection to the taking of the proposed action.

(Added and amended Pub.L. 99–554, Title II, § 255, Title III, § 302(f), Oct. 27, 1986, 100 Stat. 3105, 3124; Pub.L. 103–65, § 1, Aug. 6, 1993, 107 Stat. 311; Pub.L. 105–277, Div. C, Title I, § 149(a), Oct. 21, 1998, 112 Stat. 2681–610; Pub.L. 106–5, § 1(1),(2), Mar. 30, 1999, 113 Stat. 9; Pub.L. 106–70, § 1, Oct. 9, 1999, 113 Stat. 1031; Pub.L. 107–8, § 1, May 11, 2001, 115 Stat. 10; Pub.L. 107–17, § 1, June 26, 2001, 115 Stat. 151; Pub.L. 107–170, § 1, May 7, 2002, 116 Stat. 133; Pub.L. 107–171, Title X, § 10814(a), May 13, 2002, 116 Stat. 532; Pub.L. 107–377, § 2(a), Dec. 19, 2002, 116 Stat. 3115; Pub.L. 108–73, § 2(a), Aug. 15, 2003, 117 Stat. 891; Pub.L. 108–369, § 2(a), Oct. 25, 2004, 118 Stat. 1749; Pub.L. 109–8, Title X, § 1001(a)(1), Apr. 20, 2005, 119 Stat. 185.)

CROSS REFERENCES

Automatic stay, see 11 USCA § 362.

Automatic stay of enforcement of claims against debtor in Chapter nine cases, see 11 USCA § 922.

Claims of codebtors, see 11 USCA § 509.

Effect of conversion, see 11 USCA § 348.

Effect of § 362 of this title in stockbroker liquidation cases, see 11 USCA § 742.

Extension of time generally, see 11 USCA § 108.

§ 1202. Trustee

(a) If the United States trustee has appointed an individual under section 586(b) of title 28 to serve as standing trustee in cases under this chapter and if such individual qualifies as a trustee under section 322 of this title, then such individual shall serve as trustee in any case filed under this chapter. Otherwise, the United States trustee shall appoint one disinterested person to serve as trustee in the case or the United States trustee may serve as trustee in the case if necessary.

(b) The trustee shall—

  (1) perform the duties specified in sections 704(a)(2), 704(a)(3), 704(a)(5), 704(a)(6), 704(a)(7), and 704(a)(9) of this title;

  (2) perform the duties specified in section 1106(a)(3) and 1106(a)(4) of this title if the court, for cause and on request of a party in interest, the trustee, or the United States trustee, so orders;

  (3) appear and be heard at any hearing that concerns—

    (A) the value of property subject to a lien;

    (B) confirmation of a plan;

    (C) modification of the plan after confirmation; or

    (D) the sale of property of the estate;

(4) ensure that the debtor commences making timely payments required by a confirmed plan;

(5) if the debtor ceases to be a debtor in possession, perform the duties specified in sections 704(a)(8), 1106(a)(1), 1106(a)(2), 1106(a)(6), 1106(a)(7), and 1203; and

(6) if with respect to the debtor there is a claim for a domestic support obligation, provide the applicable notice specified in subsection (c).

(c)(1) In a case described in subsection (b)(6) to which subsection (b)(6) applies, the trustee shall—

(A)(i) provide written notice to the holder of the claim described in subsection (b)(6) of such claim and of the right of such holder to use the services of the State child support enforcement agency established under sections 464 and 466 of the Social Security Act for the State in which such holder resides, for assistance in collecting child support during and after the case under this title; and

(ii) include in the notice provided under clause (i) the address and telephone number of such State child support enforcement agency;

(B)(i) provide written notice to such State child support enforcement agency of such claim; and

(ii) include in the notice provided under clause (i) the name, address, and telephone number of such holder; and

(C) at such time as the debtor is granted a discharge under section 1228, provide written notice to such holder and to such State child support enforcement agency of—

(i) the granting of the discharge;

(ii) the last recent known address of the debtor;

(iii) the last recent known name and address of the debtor's employer; and

(iv) the name of each creditor that holds a claim that—

(I) is not discharged under paragraph (2), (4), or (14A) of section 523(a); or

(II) was reaffirmed by the debtor under section 524(c).

(2)(A) The holder of a claim described in subsection (b)(6) or the State child support enforcement agency of the State in which such holder resides may request from a creditor described in paragraph (1)(C)(iv) the last known address of the debtor.

(B) Notwithstanding any other provision of law, a creditor that makes a disclosure of a last known address of a debtor in connection with a request made under subparagraph (A) shall not be liable by reason of making that disclosure.

(Added and amended Pub.L. 99–554, Title II, §§ 227, 255, Title III, § 302(f), Oct. 27, 1986, 100 Stat. 3103, 3106, 3124; Pub.L. 103–65, § 1, Aug. 6, 1993, 107 Stat. 311; Pub.L. 105–277, Div. C, Title I, § 149(a), Oct. 21, 1998, 112 Stat. 2681–610; Pub.L. 106–5, §§ 1(1), (2), Mar. 30, 1999, 113 Stat. 9; Pub.L. 106–70, § 1, Oct. 9, 1999, 113 Stat. 1031; Pub.L. 107–8, § 1, May 11, 2001, 115 Stat. 10; Pub.L. 107–17, § 1, June 26, 2001, 115 Stat. 151; Pub.L. 107–170, § 1, May 7, 2002, 116 Stat. 133; Pub.L. 107–171, Title X, § 10814(a), May 13, 2002, 116 Stat. 532; Pub.L. 107–377, § 2(a), Dec. 19, 2002, 116 Stat. 3115; Pub.L. 108–73, § 2(a), Aug. 15, 2003, 117 Stat. 891; Pub.L. 108–369, § 2(a), Oct. 25, 2004, 118 Stat. 1749; Pub.L. 109–8, Title II, § 219(c), Title X, § 1001(a)(1), Apr. 20, 2005, 119 Stat. 57, 185; Pub.L. 111–327, § 2(a)(38), Dec. 22, 2010, 124 Stat. 3561.)

HISTORICAL AND STATUTORY NOTES

References in Text

Section 464 of the Social Security Act, referred to in subsec. (c)(1)(A)(i), is Act Aug. 14, 1935, c. 531, Title IV, § 464, as added Aug. 13, 1981, Pub.L. 97–35, Title XXIII, § 2331(a), 95 Stat. 860, and amended, which is classified to 42 U.S.C.A. § 664.

Section 466 of the Social Security Act, referred to in subsec. (c)(1)(A)(i), is Act Aug. 14, 1935, c. 531, Title IV, § 466, as added Aug. 16, 1984, Pub.L. 98–378, § 3(b), 98 Stat. 1306, and amended, which is classified to 42 U.S.C.A. § 666.

Amendments

2010 Amendments. Subsec. (b)(1). Pub.L. 111–327, § 2(a)(38)(A), struck out "704(2), 704(3), 704(5), 704(6), 704(7), and 704(9)" and inserted "704(a)(2), 704(a)(3), 704(a)(5), 704(a)(6), 704(a)(7), and 704(a)(9)".

Subsec. (b)(5). Pub.L. 111–327, § 2(a)(38)(B), struck out "704(8)" and inserted "704(a)(8)".

2005 Amendments. Subsec. (b)(4). Pub.L. 109–8, § 219(c)(1)(A), struck out "and" at the end of par. (4).

Subsec. (b)(5). Pub.L. 109–8, § 219(c)(1)(B), substituted "; and" for the period at the end of par. (5).

Subsec. (b)(6). Pub.L. 109–8, § 219(c)(1)(C), added par. (6).

Subsec. (c). Pub.L. 109–8, § 219(c)(2), added subsec. (c).

1986 Amendments. Subsecs. (c) and (d). Pub.L. 99–554, § 227, struck out subsecs. (c) and (d) which read as follows:

"(c) If the number of cases under this chapter commenced in a particular judicial district so warrants, the court may appoint one or more individuals to serve as standing trustee for such district in cases under this chapter.

"(d)(1) A court that has appointed an individual under subsection (a) of this section to serve as standing trustee in cases under this chapter shall set for such individual—

"(A) a maximum annual compensation not to exceed the lowest annual rate of basic pay in effect for grade GS–16 of the General Schedule prescribed under section 5332 of title 5; and

"(B) a percentage fee not to exceed the sum of—

"(i) not to exceed ten percent of the payments made under the plan of such debtor, with respect to payments in an aggregate amount not to exceed $450,000; and

"(ii) three percent of payments made under the plan of such debtor, with respect to payments made after the aggregate amount of payments made under the plan exceeds $450,000;

based on such maximum annual compensation and the actual, necessary expenses incurred by such individual as standing trustee.

"(2) Such individual shall collect such percentage fee from all payments under plans in the cases under this chapter for which such individual serves as standing trustee. Such individual shall pay annually to the Treasury—

"(A) any amount by which the actual compensation received by such individual exceeds five percent of all such payments made under plans in cases under this chapter for which such individual serves as standing trustee; and

"(B) any amount by which the percentage fee fixed under paragraph (1)(B) of this subsection for all such cases exceeds—

"(i) such individual's actual compensation for such cases, as adjusted under subparagraph (A) of this paragraph; plus

"(ii) the actual, necessary expenses incurred by such individual as standing trustee in such cases.".

CROSS REFERENCES

Appointment of trustee in—

    Chapter eleven cases, see 11 USCA § 1104.

    Chapter thirteen cases, see 11 USCA § 1302.

    Railroad reorganization cases, see 11 USCA § 1163.

Compensation of officers, see 11 USCA § 330.

Election of trustee in Chapter seven case, see 11 USCA § 702.

Eligibility to serve as trustee, see 11 USCA § 321.

Grain storage facility bankruptcies, expedited appointment of trustee or examiner, see 11 USCA § 557.

Limitation on compensation of trustee, see 11 USCA § 326.

Qualification of trustee, see 11 USCA § 322.

Removal of trustee, see 11 USCA § 324.

Retention or replacement of professional persons, see 11 USCA § 327.

Role and capacity of trustee, see 11 USCA § 323.

Time of bringing action, see 11 USCA § 546.

Time of payment of percentage fee fixed for standing trustee, see 11 USCA § 1226.

§ 1203. Rights and powers of debtor

Subject to such limitations as the court may prescribe, a debtor in possession shall have all the rights, other than the right to compensation under section 330, and powers, and shall perform all the functions and duties, except the duties specified in paragraphs (3) and (4) of section 1106(a), of a trustee serving in a case under chapter 11, including operating the debtor's farm or commercial fishing operation.

(Added and amended Pub.L. 99–554, Title II, § 255, Title III, § 302(f), Oct. 27, 1986, 100 Stat. 3107, 3124; Pub.L. 103–65, § 1, Aug. 6, 1993, 107 Stat. 311; Pub.L. 105–277, Div. C, Title I, § 149(a), Oct. 21, 1998, 112 Stat. 2681–610; Pub.L. 106–5, § 1(1), (2), Mar. 30, 1999, 113 Stat. 9; Pub.L. 106–70, § 1, Oct. 9, 1999, 113 Stat. 1031; Pub.L. 107–8, § 1, May 11, 2001, 115 Stat. 10; Pub.L. 107–17, § 1, June 26, 2001, 115 Stat. 151; Pub.L. 107–170, § 1, May 7, 2002, 116 Stat. 133; Pub.L. 107–171, Title X, § 10814(a), May 13, 2002, 116 Stat. 532; Pub.L. 107–377, § 2(a), Dec. 19, 2002, 116 Stat. 3115; Pub.L. 108–73, § 2(a), Aug. 15, 2003, 117 Stat. 891; Pub.L. 108–369, § 2(a), Oct. 25, 2004, 118 Stat. 1749; Pub.L. 109–8, Title X, §§ 1001(a)(1), 1007(c)(2), Apr. 20, 2005, 119 Stat. 185, 188.)

HISTORICAL AND STATUTORY NOTES

Amendments

2005 Amendments.

Pub.L. 109–8, § 1007(c)(2), inserted "or commercial fishing operation" after "farm".

CROSS REFERENCES

Obtaining credit, see 11 USCA § 364.

Rights and powers of debtor in—

    Chapter eleven cases, see 11 USCA § 1107.

    Chapter thirteen cases, see 11 USCA § 1303.

Use, sale or lease of property, see 11 USCA § 363.

§ 1204. Removal of debtor as debtor in possession

(a) On request of a party in interest, and after notice and a hearing, the court shall order that the debtor shall not be a debtor in possession for cause, including fraud, dishonesty, incompetence, or gross mismanagement of the affairs of the debtor, either before or after the commencement of the case.

(b) On request of a party in interest, and after notice and a hearing, the court may reinstate the debtor in possession.

(Added and amended Pub.L. 99–554, Title II, § 255, Title III, § 302(f), Oct. 27, 1986, 100 Stat. 3107, 3124; Pub.L. 103–65, § 1, Aug. 6, 1993, 107 Stat. 311; Pub.L. 105–277, Div. C, Title I, § 149(a), Oct. 21, 1998, 112 Stat. 2681–610; Pub.L. 106–5, § 1(1), (2), Mar. 30, 1999, 113 Stat. 9; Pub.L. 106–70, § 1, Oct. 9, 1999, 113 Stat. 1031; Pub.L. 107–8, § 1, May 11, 2001, 115 Stat. 10; Pub.L. 107–17, § 1, June 26, 2001, 115 Stat. 151; Pub.L. 107–170, § 1, May 7, 2002, 116 Stat. 133; Pub.L. 107–171, Title X, § 10814(a), May 13, 2002, 116 Stat. 532; Pub.L. 107–377, § 2(a), Dec. 19, 2002, 116 Stat. 3115; Pub.L. 108–73, § 2(a), Aug. 15, 2003, 117 Stat. 891; Pub.L. 108–369, § 2(a), Oct. 25, 2004, 118 Stat. 1749; Pub.L. 109–8, Title X, § 1001(a)(1), Apr. 20, 2005, 119 Stat. 185.)

CROSS REFERENCES

Obtaining credit, see 11 USCA § 364.

Revocation of an order of confirmation, see 11 USCA § 1230.

Use, sale or lease of property, see 11 USCA § 363.

§ 1205. Adequate protection

(a) Section 361 does not apply in a case under this chapter.

(b) In a case under this chapter, when adequate protection is required under section 362, 363, or 364 of this title of an interest of an entity in property, such adequate protection may be provided by—

(1) requiring the trustee to make a cash payment or periodic cash payments to such entity, to the extent that the stay under section 362 of this title, use, sale, or lease under section 363 of this title, or any grant of a lien under section 364 of this title results in a decrease in the value of property securing a claim or of an entity's ownership interest in property;

(2) providing to such entity an additional or replacement lien to the extent that such stay, use, sale, lease, or grant results in a decrease in the value of property securing a claim or of an entity's ownership interest in property;

(3) paying to such entity for the use of farmland the reasonable rent customary in the community where the property is located, based upon the rental value, net income, and earning capacity of the property; or

(4) granting such other relief, other than entitling such entity to compensation allowable under section 503(b)(1) of this title as an administrative expense, as will adequately protect the value of property securing a claim or of such entity's ownership interest in property.

(Added and amended Pub.L. 99–554, Title II, § 255, Title III, § 302(f), Oct. 27, 1986, 100 Stat. 3107, 3124; Pub.L. 103–65, § 1, Aug. 6, 1993, 107 Stat. 311; Pub.L. 105–277, Div. C, Title I, § 149(a), Oct. 21, 1998, 112 Stat. 2681–610; Pub.L. 106–5, § 1(1), (2), Mar. 30, 1999, 113 Stat. 9; Pub.L. 106–70, § 1, Oct. 9, 1999, 113 Stat. 1031; Pub.L. 107–8, § 1, May 11, 2001, 115 Stat. 10; Pub.L. 107–17, § 1, June 26, 2001, 115 Stat. 151; Pub.L. 107–170, § 1, May 7, 2002, 116 Stat. 133; Pub.L. 107–171, Title X, § 10814(a), May 13, 2002, 116 Stat. 532; Pub.L. 107–377, § 2(a), Dec. 19, 2002, 116 Stat. 3115; Pub.L. 108–73, § 2(a), Aug. 15, 2003, 117 Stat. 891; Pub.L. 108–369, § 2(a), Oct. 25, 2004, 118 Stat. 1749; Pub.L. 109–8, Title X, § 1001(a)(1), Apr. 20, 2005, 119 Stat. 185.)

§ 1206. Sales free of interests

After notice and a hearing, in addition to the authorization contained in section 363(f), the trustee in a case under this chapter may sell property under section 363(b) and (c) free and clear of any interest in such property of an entity other than the estate if the property is farmland, farm equipment, or property used to carry out a commercial fishing operation (including a commercial fishing vessel), except that the proceeds of such sale shall be subject to such interest.

(Added and amended Pub.L. 99–554, Title II, § 255, Title III, § 302(f), Oct. 27, 1986, 100 Stat. 3108, 3124; Pub.L. 103–65, § 1, Aug. 6, 1993, 107 Stat. 311; Pub.L. 105–277, Div. C, Title I, § 149(a), Oct. 21, 1998,

112 Stat. 2681–610; Pub.L. 106–5, § 1(1), (2), Mar. 30, 1999, 113 Stat. 9; Pub.L. 106–70, § 1, Oct. 9, 1999, 113 Stat. 1031; Pub.L. 107–8, § 1, May 11, 2001, 115 Stat. 10; Pub.L. 107–17, § 1, June 26, 2001, 115 Stat. 151; Pub.L. 107–170, § 1, May 7, 2002, 116 Stat. 133; Pub.L. 107–171, Title X, § 10814(a), May 13, 2002, 116 Stat. 532; Pub.L. 107–377, § 2(a), Dec. 19, 2002, 116 Stat. 3115; Pub.L. 108–73, § 2(a), Aug. 15, 2003, 117 Stat. 891; Pub.L. 108–369, § 2(a), Oct. 25, 2004, 118 Stat. 1749; Pub.L. 109–8, Title X, §§ 1001(a)(1), 1007(c)(3), Apr. 20, 2005, 119 Stat. 185, 188.)

HISTORICAL AND STATUTORY NOTES

Amendments

2005 Amendments.

Pub.L. 109–8, § 1007(c)(3), struck out "if the property is farmland or farm equipment" and inserted "if the property is farmland, farm equipment, or property used to carry out a commercial fishing operation (including a commercial fishing vessel)".

§ 1207. Property of the estate

(a) Property of the estate includes, in addition to the property specified in section 541 of this title—

  (1) all property of the kind specified in such section that the debtor acquires after the commencement of the case but before the case is closed, dismissed, or converted to a case under chapter 7 of this title, whichever occurs first; and

  (2) earnings from services performed by the debtor after the commencement of the case but before the case is closed, dismissed, or converted to a case under chapter 7 of this title, whichever occurs first.

(b) Except as provided in section 1204, a confirmed plan, or an order confirming a plan, the debtor shall remain in possession of all property of the estate.

(Added and amended Pub.L. 99–554, Title II, § 255, Title III, § 302(f), Oct. 27, 1986, 100 Stat. 3108, 3124; Pub.L. 103–65, § 1, Aug. 6, 1993, 107 Stat. 311; Pub.L. 105–277, Div. C, Title I, § 149(a), Oct. 21, 1998, 112 Stat. 2681–610; Pub.L. 106–5, § 1(1), (2), Mar. 30, 1999, 113 Stat. 9; Pub.L. 106–70, § 1, Oct. 9, 1999, 113 Stat. 1031; Pub.L. 107–8, § 1, May 11, 2001, 115 Stat. 10; Pub.L. 107–17, § 1, June 26, 2001, 115 Stat. 151; Pub.L. 107–170, § 1, May 7, 2002, 116 Stat. 133; Pub.L. 107–171, Title X, § 10814(a), May 13, 2002, 116 Stat. 532; Pub.L. 107–377, § 2(a), Dec. 19, 2002, 116 Stat. 3115; Pub.L. 108–73, § 2(a), Aug. 15, 2003, 117 Stat. 891; Pub.L. 108–369, § 2(a), Oct. 25, 2004, 118 Stat. 1749; Pub.L. 109–8, Title X, § 1001(a)(1), Apr. 20, 2005, 119 Stat. 185.)

§ 1208. Conversion or dismissal

(a) The debtor may convert a case under this chapter to a case under chapter 7 of this title at any time. Any waiver of the right to convert under this subsection is unenforceable.

(b) On request of the debtor at any time, if the case has not been converted under section 706 or 1112 of this title, the court shall dismiss a case under this chapter. Any waiver of the right to dismiss under this subsection is unenforceable.

(c) On request of a party in interest, and after notice and a hearing, the court may dismiss a case under this chapter for cause, including—

  (1) unreasonable delay, or gross mismanagement, by the debtor that is prejudicial to creditors;

  (2) nonpayment of any fees and charges required under chapter 123 of title 28;

  (3) failure to file a plan timely under section 1221 of this title;

  (4) failure to commence making timely payments required by a confirmed plan;

(5) denial of confirmation of a plan under section 1225 of this title and denial of a request made for additional time for filing another plan or a modification of a plan;

(6) material default by the debtor with respect to a term of a confirmed plan;

(7) revocation of the order of confirmation under section 1230 of this title, and denial of confirmation of a modified plan under section 1229 of this title;

(8) termination of a confirmed plan by reason of the occurrence of a condition specified in the plan;

(9) continuing loss to or diminution of the estate and absence of a reasonable likelihood of rehabilitation; and

(10) failure of the debtor to pay any domestic support obligation that first becomes payable after the date of the filing of the petition.

(d) On request of a party in interest, and after notice and a hearing, the court may dismiss a case under this chapter or convert a case under this chapter to a case under chapter 7 of this title upon a showing that the debtor has committed fraud in connection with the case.

(e) Notwithstanding any other provision of this section, a case may not be converted to a case under another chapter of this title unless the debtor may be a debtor under such chapter.

(Added and amended Pub.L. 99–554, Title II, § 255, Title III, § 302(f), Oct. 27, 1986, 100 Stat. 3108, 3124; Pub.L. 103–65, § 1, Aug. 6, 1993, 107 Stat. 311; Pub.L. 105–277, Div. C, Title I, § 149(a), Oct. 21, 1998, 112 Stat. 2681–610; Pub.L. 106–5, § 1(1), (2), Mar. 30, 1999, 113 Stat. 9; Pub.L. 106–70, § 1, Oct. 9, 1999, 113 Stat. 1031; Pub.L. 107–8, § 1, May 11, 2001, 115 Stat. 10; Pub.L. 107–17, § 1, June 26, 2001, 115 Stat. 151; Pub.L. 107–170, § 1, May 7, 2002, 116 Stat. 133; Pub.L. 107–171, Title X, § 10814(a), May 13, 2002, 116 Stat. 532; Pub.L. 107–377, § 2(a), Dec. 19, 2002, 116 Stat. 3115; Pub.L. 108–73, § 2(a), Aug. 15, 2003, 117 Stat. 891; Pub.L. 108–369, § 2(a), Oct. 25, 2004, 118 Stat. 1749; Pub.L. 109–8, Title II, § 213(2), Title X, § 1001(a)(1), Apr. 20, 2005, 119 Stat. 52, 185.)

HISTORICAL AND STATUTORY NOTES

Amendments

2005 Amendments.

Subsec. (c)(8). Pub.L. 109–8, § 213(2)(A), struck out "or" at the end of par. (8).

Subsec. (c)(9). Pub.L. 109–8, § 213(2)(B), substituted "; and" for the period at the end of par. (9).

Subsec. (c)(10). Pub.L. 109–8, § 213(2)(C), added par. (10).

CROSS REFERENCES

Conversion from Chapter seven, see 11 USCA § 706.

Dismissal of Chapter thirteen cases where not converted under this section, see 11 USCA § 1307.

Distribution of property of estate converted to Chapter seven, see 11 USCA § 726.

Effect of—

    Conversion, see 11 USCA § 348.

    Dismissal, see 11 USCA § 349.

Executory contracts and unexpired leases, see 11 USCA § 365.

Liquidation of estate in railroad reorganization cases, see 11 USCA § 1174.

Termination of debtor's taxable period for cases converted to Chapter 7, see 11 USCA § 728.

SUBCHAPTER II—THE PLAN

§ 1221. Filing of plan

The debtor shall file a plan not later than 90 days after the order for relief under this chapter, except that the court may extend such period if the need for an extension is attributable to circumstances for which the debtor should not justly be held accountable.

(Added and amended Pub.L. 99–554, Title II, § 255, Title III, § 302(f), Oct. 27, 1986, 100 Stat. 3109, 3124; Pub.L. 103–65, §§ 1, 2, Aug. 6, 1993, 107 Stat. 311; Pub.L. 105–277, Div. C, Title I, § 149(a), Oct. 21, 1998, 112 Stat. 2681–610; Pub.L. 106–5, § 1(1), (2), Mar. 30, 1999, 113 Stat. 9; Pub.L. 106–70, § 1, Oct. 9, 1999, 113 Stat. 1031; Pub.L. 107–8, § 1, May 11, 2001, 115 Stat. 10; Pub.L. 107–17, § 1, June 26, 2001, 115 Stat. 151; Pub.L. 107–170, § 1, May 7, 2002, 116 Stat. 133; Pub.L. 107–171, Title X, § 10814(a), May 13, 2002, 116 Stat. 532; Pub.L. 107–377, § 2(a), Dec. 19, 2002, 116 Stat. 3115; Pub.L. 108–73, § 2(a), Aug. 15, 2003, 117 Stat. 891; Pub.L. 108–369, § 2(a), Oct. 25, 2004, 118 Stat. 1749; Pub.L. 109–8, Title X, § 1001(a)(1), Apr. 20, 2005, 119 Stat. 185.)

HISTORICAL AND STATUTORY NOTES

Amendments

1993 Amendments.

Pub.L. 103–65, § 2, substituted "the need for an extension is attributable to circumstances for which the debtor should not justly be held accountable" for "an extension is substantially justified".

CROSS REFERENCES

Conversion or dismissal for failure to timely file plan, see 11 USCA § 1208.

Effect of conversion, see 11 USCA § 348.

Filing of plan in—

    Chapter nine cases, see 11 USCA § 941.

    Chapter thirteen cases, see 11 USCA § 1321.

Who may file plan in Chapter eleven cases, see 11 USCA § 1121.

§ 1222. Contents of plan

(a) The plan shall—

(1) provide for the submission of all or such portion of future earnings or other future income of the debtor to the supervision and control of the trustee as is necessary for the execution of the plan;

(2) provide for the full payment, in deferred cash payments, of all claims entitled to priority under section 507, unless—

(A) the claim is a claim owed to a governmental unit that arises as a result of the sale, transfer, exchange, or other disposition of any farm asset used in the debtor's farming operation, in which case the claim shall be treated as an unsecured claim that is not entitled to priority under section 507, but the debt shall be treated in such manner only if the debtor receives a discharge; or

(B) the holder of a particular claim agrees to a different treatment of that claim;

(3) if the plan classifies claims and interests, provide the same treatment for each claim or interest within a particular class unless the holder of a particular claim or interest agrees to less favorable treatment; and

(4) notwithstanding any other provision of this section, a plan may provide for less than full payment of all amounts owed for a claim entitled to priority under section 507(a)(1)(B) only

if the plan provides that all of the debtor's projected disposable income for a 5-year period beginning on the date that the first payment is due under the plan will be applied to make payments under the plan.

(b) Subject to subsections (a) and (c) of this section, the plan may—

(1) designate a class or classes of unsecured claims, as provided in section 1122 of this title, but may not discriminate unfairly against any class so designated; however, such plan may treat claims for a consumer debt of the debtor if an individual is liable on such consumer debt with the debtor differently than other unsecured claims;

(2) modify the rights of holders of secured claims, or of holders of unsecured claims, or leave unaffected the rights of holders of any class of claims;

(3) provide for the curing or waiving of any default;

(4) provide for payments on any unsecured claim to be made concurrently with payments on any secured claim or any other unsecured claim;

(5) provide for the curing of any default within a reasonable time and maintenance of payments while the case is pending on any unsecured claim or secured claim on which the last payment is due after the date on which the final payment under the plan is due;

(6) subject to section 365 of this title, provide for the assumption, rejection, or assignment of any executory contract or unexpired lease of the debtor not previously rejected under such section;

(7) provide for the payment of all or part of a claim against the debtor from property of the estate or property of the debtor;

(8) provide for the sale of all or any part of the property of the estate or the distribution of all or any part of the property of the estate among those having an interest in such property;

(9) provide for payment of allowed secured claims consistent with section 1225(a)(5) of this title, over a period exceeding the period permitted under section 1222(c);

(10) provide for the vesting of property of the estate, on confirmation of the plan or at a later time, in the debtor or in any other entity;

(11) provide for the payment of interest accruing after the date of the filing of the petition on unsecured claims that are nondischargeable under section 1228(a), except that such interest may be paid only to the extent that the debtor has disposable income available to pay such interest after making provision for full payment of all allowed claims; and

(12) include any other appropriate provision not inconsistent with this title.

(c) Except as provided in subsections (b)(5) and (b)(9), the plan may not provide for payments over a period that is longer than three years unless the court for cause approves a longer period, but the court may not approve a period that is longer than five years.

(d) Notwithstanding subsection (b)(2) of this section and sections 506(b) and 1225(a)(5) of this title, if it is proposed in a plan to cure a default, the amount necessary to cure the default, shall be determined in accordance with the underlying agreement and applicable nonbankruptcy law.

(Added and amended Pub.L. 99–554, Title II, § 255, Title III, § 302(f), Oct. 27, 1986, 100 Stat. 3109, 3124; Pub.L. 103–65, § 1, Aug. 6, 1993, 107 Stat. 311; Pub.L. 103–394, Title III, § 305(b), Oct. 22, 1994, 108 Stat. 4134; Pub.L. 105–277, Div. C, Title I, § 149(a), Oct. 21, 1998, 112 Stat. 2681–610; Pub.L. 106–5, § 1(1), (2), Mar. 30, 1999, 113 Stat. 9; Pub.L. 106–70, § 1, Oct. 9, 1999, 113 Stat. 1031; Pub.L. 107–8, § 1, May 11, 2001, 115 Stat. 10; Pub.L. 107–17, § 1, June 26, 2001, 115 Stat. 151; Pub.L. 107–170, § 1, May 7, 2002, 116 Stat. 133; Pub.L. 107–171, Title X, § 10814(a), May 13, 2002 116 Stat. 532; Pub.L. 107–377, § 2(a), Dec. 19, 2002, 116 Stat. 3115; Pub.L. 108–73, § 2(a), Aug. 15, 2003, 117 Stat. 891; Pub.L. 108–369, § 2(a), Oct. 25, 2004, 118 Stat. 1749; Pub.L. 109–8, Title II, § 213(3), (4) Title X, §§ 1001(a)(1), 1003(a), Apr. 20, 2005, 119 Stat. 52, 185, 186.)

Title 11 DEBTS OF A FAMILY FARMER OR FISHERMAN **11 § 1223**

HISTORICAL AND STATUTORY NOTES

Amendments

2005 Amendments. Subsec. (a)(2). Pub.L. 109–8, § 213(3)(A), struck out "and" at the end of par. (2).

Pub.L. 109–8, § 1003(a), rewrote par. (2) which formerly read: **"(2)** provide for the full payment, in deferred cash payments, of all claims entitled to priority under section 507 of this title, unless the holder of a particular claim agrees to a different treatment of such claim; and".

Subsec. (a)(3). Pub.L. 109–8, § 213(3)(B), substituted "; and" for the period at the end of par. (3).

Subsec. (a)(4). Pub.L. 109–8, § 213(3)(C), added par. (4).

Subsec. (b)(10). Pub.L. 109–8, § 213(4)(A), struck out "and" at the end of par. (10).

Subsec. (b)(11), (12). Pub.L. 109–8, § 213(4)(B), (C), added a new par. (11) and renumbered former par. (11) as par. (12).

CROSS REFERENCES

Contents of plan filed in—

    Chapter eleven cases, see 11 USCA § 1123.

    Chapter thirteen cases, see 11 USCA § 1322.

    Railroad reorganization cases, see 11 USCA § 1172.

§ 1223. Modification of plan before confirmation

(a) The debtor may modify the plan at any time before confirmation, but may not modify the plan so that the plan as modified fails to meet the requirements of section 1222 of this title.

(b) After the debtor files a modification under this section, the plan as modified becomes the plan.

(c) Any holder of a secured claim that has accepted or rejected the plan is deemed to have accepted or rejected, as the case may be, the plan as modified, unless the modification provides for a change in the rights of such holder from what such rights were under the plan before modification, and such holder changes such holder's previous acceptance or rejection.

(Added and amended Pub.L. 99–554, Title II, § 255, Title III, § 302(f), Oct. 27, 1986, 100 Stat. 3110, 3124; Pub.L. 103–65, § 1, Aug. 6, 1993, 107 Stat. 311; Pub.L. 105–277, Div. C, Title I, § 149(a), Oct. 21, 1998, 112 Stat. 2681–610; Pub.L. 106–5, § 1(1), (2), Mar. 30, 1999, 113 Stat. 9; Pub.L. 106–70, § 1, Oct. 9, 1999, 113 Stat. 1031; Pub.L. 107–8, § 1, May 11, 2001, 115 Stat. 10; Pub.L. 107–17, § 1, June 26, 2001, 115 Stat. 151; Pub.L. 107–170, § 1, May 7, 2002, 116 Stat. 133; Pub.L. 107–171, Title X, § 10814(a), May 13, 2002, 116 Stat. 532; Pub.L. 107–377, § 2(a), Dec. 19, 2002, 116 Stat. 3115; Pub.L. 108–73, § 2(a), Aug. 15, 2003, 117 Stat. 891; Pub.L. 108–369, § 2(a), Oct. 25, 2004, 118 Stat. 1749; Pub.L. 109–8, Title X, § 1001(a)(1), Apr. 20, 2005, 119 Stat. 185.)

CROSS REFERENCES

Modification of plan filed in—

    Chapter eleven cases, see 11 USCA § 1127.

    Chapter nine cases, see 11 USCA § 942.

    Chapter thirteen cases, see 11 USCA § 1323.

§ 1224. Confirmation hearing

After expedited notice, the court shall hold a hearing on confirmation of the plan. A party in interest, the trustee, or the United States trustee may object to the confirmation of the plan. Except for cause, the hearing shall be concluded not later than 45 days after the filing of the plan.

(Added and amended Pub.L. 99–554, Title II, § 255, Title III, § 302(f), Oct. 27, 1986, 100 Stat. 3110, 3124; Pub.L. 103–65, § 1, Aug. 6, 1993, 107 Stat. 311; Pub.L. 105–277, Div. C, Title I, § 149(a), Oct. 21, 1998, 112 Stat. 2681–610; Pub.L. 106–5, § 1(1), (2), Mar. 30, 1999, 113 Stat. 9; Pub.L. 106–70, § 1, Oct. 9, 1999, 113 Stat. 1031; Pub.L. 107–8, § 1, May 11, 2001, 115 Stat. 10; Pub.L. 107–17, § 1, June 26, 2001, 115 Stat. 151; Pub.L. 107–170, § 1, May 7, 2002, 116 Stat. 133; Pub.L. 107–171, Title X, § 10814(a), May 13, 2002, 116 Stat. 532; Pub.L. 107–377, § 2(a), Dec. 19, 2002, 16 Stat. 3115; Pub.L. 108–73, § 2(a), Aug. 15, 2003, 117 Stat. 891; Pub.L. 108–369, § 2(a), Oct. 25, 2004, 118 Stat. 1749; Pub.L. 109–8, Title X, § 1001(a)(1), Apr. 20, 2005, 119 Stat. 185.)

CROSS REFERENCES

Confirmation hearing in—

    Chapter eleven cases, see 11 USCA § 1128.

    Chapter thirteen cases, see 11 USCA § 1324.

Duties of United States trustee, see 28 USCA § 586.

§ 1225. Confirmation of plan

(a) Except as provided in subsection (b), the court shall confirm a plan if—

    (1) the plan complies with the provisions of this chapter and with the other applicable provisions of this title;

    (2) any fee, charge, or amount required under chapter 123 of title 28, or by the plan, to be paid before confirmation, has been paid;

    (3) the plan has been proposed in good faith and not by any means forbidden by law;

    (4) the value, as of the effective date of the plan, of property to be distributed under the plan on account of each allowed unsecured claim is not less than the amount that would be paid on such claim if the estate of the debtor were liquidated under chapter 7 of this title on such date;

    (5) with respect to each allowed secured claim provided for by the plan—

        (A) the holder of such claim has accepted the plan;

        (B)(i) the plan provides that the holder of such claim retain the lien securing such claim; and

            (ii) the value, as of the effective date of the plan, of property to be distributed by the trustee or the debtor under the plan on account of such claim is not less than the allowed amount of such claim; or

        (C) the debtor surrenders the property securing such claim to such holder;

    (6) the debtor will be able to make all payments under the plan and to comply with the plan; and

    (7) the debtor has paid all amounts that are required to be paid under a domestic support obligation and that first become payable after the date of the filing of the petition if the debtor is required by a judicial or administrative order, or by statute, to pay such domestic support obligation.

(b)(1) If the trustee or the holder of an allowed unsecured claim objects to the confirmation of the plan, then the court may not approve the plan unless, as of the effective date of the plan—

    (A) the value of the property to be distributed under the plan on account of such claim is not less than the amount of such claim;

    (B) the plan provides that all of the debtor's projected disposable income to be received in the three-year period, or such longer period as the court may approve under section 1222(c), beginning on the date that the first payment is due under the plan will be applied to make payments under the plan; or

(C) the value of the property to be distributed under the plan in the 3-year period, or such longer period as the court may approve under section 1222(c), beginning on the date that the first distribution is due under the plan is not less than the debtor's projected disposable income for such period.

(2) For purposes of this subsection, "disposable income" means income which is received by the debtor and which is not reasonably necessary to be expended—

(A) for the maintenance or support of the debtor or a dependent of the debtor or for a domestic support obligation that first becomes payable after the date of the filing of the petition; or

(B) for the payment of expenditures necessary for the continuation, preservation, and operation of the debtor's business.

(c) After confirmation of a plan, the court may order any entity from whom the debtor receives income to pay all or any part of such income to the trustee.

(Added and amended Pub.L. 99–554, Title II, § 255, Title III, § 302(f), Oct. 27, 1986, 100 Stat. 3110, 3124; Pub.L. 103–65, § 1, Aug. 6, 1993, 107 Stat. 311; Pub.L. 105–277, Div. C, Title I, § 149(a), Oct. 21, 1998, 112 Stat. 2681–610; Pub.L. 106–5, § 1(1), (2), Mar. 30, 1999, 113 Stat. 9; Pub.L. 106–70, § 1, Oct. 9, 1999, 113 Stat. 1031; Pub.L. 107–8, § 1, May 11, 2001, 115 Stat. 10; Pub.L. 107–17, § 1, June 26, 2001, 115 Stat. 151; Pub.L. 107–170, § 1, May 7, 2002, 116 Stat. 133; Pub.L. 107–171, Title X, § 10814(a), May 13, 2002, 116 Stat. 532; Pub.L. 107–377, § 2(a), Dec. 19, 2002, 116 Stat. 3115; Pub.L. 108–73, § 2(a), Aug. 15, 2003, 117 Stat. 891; Pub.L. 108–369, § 2(a), Oct. 25, 2004, 118 Stat. 1749; Pub.L. 109–8, Title II, §§ 213(5), 218, Title X, §§ 1001(a)(1), 1006(a), Apr. 20, 2005, 119 Stat. 52, 55, 185, 187.)

HISTORICAL AND STATUTORY NOTES

Amendments

2005 Amendments. Subsec. (a)(5). Pub.L. 109–8, § 213(5)(A), struck out "and" at the end of par. (5).

Subsec. (a)(6). Pub.L. 109–8, § 213(5)(B), substituted "; and" for the period at the end of par. (6).

Subsec. (a)(7). Pub.L. 109–8, § 213(5)(C), added par. (7).

Subsec. (b)(1)(A). Pub.L. 109–8, § 1006(a)(1), struck out "or" at the end of subpar. (A).

Subsec. (b)(1)(B). Pub.L. 109–8, § 1006(a)(2), struck out the period at the end of subpar. (B) and inserted "; or".

Subsec. (b)(1)(C). Pub.L. 109–8, § 1006(a)(3), added subpar. (C).

Subsec. (b)(2)(A). Pub.L. 109–8, § 218, inserted "or for a domestic support obligation that first becomes payable after the date of the filing of the petition" after "dependent of the debtor".

CROSS REFERENCES

Confirmation of plan in—

    Chapter eleven cases, see 11 USCA § 1129.

    Chapter nine cases, see 11 USCA § 943.

    Chapter thirteen cases, see 11 USCA § 1325.

    Railroad reorganization cases, see 11 USCA § 1173.

Conversion or dismissal, see 11 USCA § 1208.

Unclaimed property, see 11 USCA § 347.

§ 1226. Payments

(a) Payments and funds received by the trustee shall be retained by the trustee until confirmation or denial of confirmation of a plan. If a plan is confirmed, the trustee shall distribute any such payment in accordance with the plan. If a plan is not confirmed, the trustee shall return any such payments to the debtor, after deducting—

    (1) any unpaid claim allowed under section 503(b) of this title; and

    (2) if a standing trustee is serving in the case, the percentage fee fixed for such standing trustee.

(b) Before or at the time of each payment to creditors under the plan, there shall be paid—

    (1) any unpaid claim of the kind specified in section 507(a)(2) of this title; and

    (2) if a standing trustee appointed under section 1202(c) of this title is serving in the case, the percentage fee fixed for such standing trustee under section 1202(d) of this title.

(c) Except as otherwise provided in the plan or in the order confirming the plan, the trustee shall make payments to creditors under the plan.

(Added and amended Pub.L. 99–554, Title II, § 255, Title III, § 302(f), Oct. 27, 1986, 100 Stat. 3111, 3124; Pub.L. 103–65, § 1, Aug. 6, 1993, 107 Stat. 311; Pub.L. 103–394, Title V, § 501(d)(36), Oct. 22, 1994, 108 Stat. 4147; Pub.L. 105–277, Div. C, Title I, § 149(a), Oct. 21, 1998, 112 Stat. 2681–610; Pub.L. 106–5, § 1(1), (2), Mar. 30, 1999, 113 Stat. 9; Pub.L. 106–70, § 1, Oct. 9, 1999, 113 Stat. 1031; Pub.L. 107–8, § 1, May 11, 2001, 115 Stat. 10; Pub.L. 107–17, § 1, June 26, 2001, 115 Stat. 151; Pub.L. 107–170, § 1, May 7, 2002, 116 Stat. 133; Pub.L. 107–171, Title X, § 10814(a), May 13, 2002, 116 Stat. 532; Pub.L. 107–377, § 2(a), Dec. 19, 2002, 116 Stat. 3115; Pub.L. 108–73, § 2(a), Aug. 15, 2003, 117 Stat. 891; Pub.L. 108–369, § 2(a), Oct. 25, 2004, 118 Stat. 1749; Pub.L. 109–8, Title X, § 1001(a)(1), Title XV, § 1502(a)(9), Apr. 20, 2005, 119 Stat. 185, 217.)

HISTORICAL AND STATUTORY NOTES

References in Text

Section 1202(c) and (d) of this title, referred to in subsec. (b)(2), were repealed by section 227 of Pub.L. 99–554, and provisions relating to appointment of and fixing percentage fees for standing trustees are contained in section 586(b) and (e) of Title 28, Judiciary and Judicial Procedure, as amended by section 113(b) and (c) of Pub.L. 99–554.

Amendments

    2005 Amendments.

Subsec. (b)(1). Pub.L. 109–8, § 1502(a)(9), struck out "507(a)(1)" and inserted "507(a)(2)".

    1994 Amendments. Subsec. (b)(2). Pub.L. 103–394, § 501(d)(36), substituted "1202(c)" for "1202(d)" and "1202(d)" for "1202(e)".

CROSS REFERENCES

Payment stopped on checks remaining unpaid 90 days after final distribution, see 11 USCA § 347.

Payments in Chapter thirteen cases, see 11 USCA § 1326.

§ 1227. Effect of confirmation

(a) Except as provided in section 1228(a) of this title, the provisions of a confirmed plan bind the debtor, each creditor, each equity security holder, and each general partner in the debtor, whether or not the claim of such creditor, such equity security holder, or such general partner in the debtor is provided for by the plan, and whether or not such creditor, such equity security holder, or such general partner in the debtor has objected to, has accepted, or has rejected the plan.

(b) Except as otherwise provided in the plan or the order confirming the plan, the confirmation of a plan vests all of the property of the estate in the debtor.

(c) Except as provided in section 1228(a) of this title and except as otherwise provided in the plan or in the order confirming the plan, the property vesting in the debtor under subsection (b) of this section is free and clear of any claim or interest of any creditor provided for by the plan.

(Added and amended Pub.L. 99–554, Title II, § 255, Title III, § 302(f), Oct. 27, 1986, 100 Stat. 3112, 3124; Pub.L. 103–65, § 1, Aug. 6, 1993, 107 Stat. 311; Pub.L. 105–277, Div. C, Title I, § 149(a), Oct. 21, 1998, 112 Stat. 2681–610; Pub.L. 106–5, § 1(1), (2), Mar. 30, 1999, 113 Stat. 9; Pub.L. 106–70, § 1, Oct. 9, 1999, 113 Stat. 1031; Pub.L. 107–8, § 1, May 11, 2001, 115 Stat. 10; Pub.L. 107–17, § 1, June 26, 2001, 115 Stat. 151; Pub.L. 107–170, § 1, May 7, 2002, 116 Stat. 133; Pub.L. 107–171, Title X, § 10814(a), May 13, 2002, 116 Stat. 532; Pub.L. 107–377, § 2(a), Dec. 19, 2002, 116 Stat. 3115; Pub.L. 108–73, § 2(a), Aug. 15, 2003, 117 Stat. 891; Pub.L. 108–369, § 2(a), Oct. 25, 2004, 118 Stat. 1749; Pub.L. 109–8, Title X, § 1001(a)(1), Apr. 20, 2005, 119 Stat. 185.)

CROSS REFERENCES

Effect of confirmation in—

    Chapter eleven cases, see 11 USCA § 1141.

    Chapter nine cases, see 11 USCA § 944.

    Chapter thirteen cases, see 11 USCA § 1327.

§ 1228. Discharge

  (a) Subject to subsection (d), as soon as practicable after completion by the debtor of all payments under the plan, and in the case of a debtor who is required by a judicial or administrative order, or by statute, to pay a domestic support obligation, after such debtor certifies that all amounts payable under such order or such statute that are due on or before the date of the certification (including amounts due before the petition was filed, but only to the extent provided for by the plan) have been paid, other than payments to holders of allowed claims provided for under section 1222(b)(5) or 1222(b)(9) of this title, unless the court approves a written waiver of discharge executed by the debtor after the order for relief under this chapter, the court shall grant the debtor a discharge of all debts provided for by the plan allowed under section 503 of this title or disallowed under section 502 of this title, except any debt—

    (1) provided for under section 1222(b)(5) or 1222(b)(9) of this title; or

    (2) of the kind specified in section 523(a) of this title.

  (b) Subject to subsection (d), at any time after the confirmation of the plan and after notice and a hearing, the court may grant a discharge to a debtor that has not completed payments under the plan only if—

    (1) the debtor's failure to complete such payments is due to circumstances for which the debtor should not justly be held accountable;

    (2) the value, as of the effective date of the plan, of property actually distributed under the plan on account of each allowed unsecured claim is not less than the amount that would have been paid on such claim if the estate of the debtor had been liquidated under chapter 7 of this title on such date; and

    (3) modification of the plan under section 1229 of this title is not practicable.

  (c) A discharge granted under subsection (b) of this section discharges the debtor from all unsecured debts provided for by the plan or disallowed under section 502 of this title, except any debt—

    (1) provided for under section 1222(b)(5) or 1222(b)(9) of this title; or

    (2) of a kind specified in section 523(a) of this title.

  (d) On request of a party in interest before one year after a discharge under this section is granted, and after notice and a hearing, the court may revoke such discharge only if—

    (1) such discharge was obtained by the debtor through fraud; and

    (2) the requesting party did not know of such fraud until after such discharge was granted.

(e) After the debtor is granted a discharge, the court shall terminate the services of any trustee serving in the case.

(f) The court may not grant a discharge under this chapter unless the court after notice and a hearing held not more than 10 days before the date of the entry of the order granting the discharge finds that there is no reasonable cause to believe that—

    (1) section 522(q)(1) may be applicable to the debtor; and

    (2) there is pending any proceeding in which the debtor may be found guilty of a felony of the kind described in section 522(q)(1)(A) or liable for a debt of the kind described in section 522(q)(1)(B).

(Added and amended Pub.L. 99–554, Title II, § 255, Title III, § 302(f), Oct. 27, 1986, 100 Stat. 3112, 3124; Pub.L. 103–65, § 1, Aug. 6, 1993, 107 Stat. 311; Pub.L. 105–277, Div. C, Title I, § 149(a), Oct. 21, 1998, 112 Stat. 2681–610; Pub.L. 106–5, § 1(1), (2), Mar. 30, 1999, 113 Stat. 9; Pub.L. 106–70, § 1, Oct. 9, 1999, 113 Stat. 1031; Pub.L. 106–518, Title II, § 208, Nov. 13, 2000, 114 Stat. 2415; Pub.L. 107–8, § 1, May 11, 2001, 115 Stat. 10; Pub.L. 107–17, § 1, June 26, 2001, 115 Stat. 151; Pub.L. 107–170, § 1, May 7, 2002, 116 Stat. 133; Pub.L. 107–171, Title X, § 10814(a), May 13, 2002, 116 Stat. 532; Pub.L. 107–377, § 2(a), Dec. 19, 2002, 116 Stat. 3115; Pub.L. 108–73, § 2(a), Aug. 15, 2003, 117 Stat. 891; Pub.L. 108–369, § 2(a), Oct. 25, 2004, 118 Stat. 1749; Pub.L. 109–8, Title II, § 213(6), Title III, § 330(c), Title X, § 1001(a)(1), Apr. 20, 2005, 119 Stat. 53, 101, 102, 185.)

HISTORICAL AND STATUTORY NOTES

Amendments

2005 Amendments. Subsec. (a). Pub.L. 109–8, § 213(6), in the matter preceding par. (1), inserted ", and in the case of a debtor who is required by a judicial or administrative order, or by statute, to pay a domestic support obligation, after such debtor certifies that all amounts payable under such order or such statute that are due on or before the date of the certification (including amounts due before the petition was filed, but only to the extent provided for by the plan) have been paid" after "completion by the debtor of all payments under the plan".

Pub.L. 109–8, § 330(c)(1), struck out "As" and inserted "Subject to subsection (d), as".

Subsec. (b). Pub.L. 109–8, § 330(c)(2), struck out "At" and inserted "Subject to subsection (d), at".

Subsec. (f). Pub.L. 109–8, § 330(c)(3), added subsec. (f).

2000 Amendments. Pub.L. 106–518, § 208, struck out "1222(b)(10)" each place it appeared and inserted "1222(b)(9)".

CROSS REFERENCES

Cancellation of indebtedness from discharged farm loans, see 12 USCA § 1150.

Discharge in—

    Chapter seven cases, see 11 USCA § 727.

    Chapter thirteen cases, see 11 USCA § 1328.

Effect of—

    Conversion, see 11 USCA § 348.

    Discharge, see 11 USCA § 524.

Exceptions to discharge, see 11 USCA § 523.

§ 1229. Modification of plan after confirmation

(a) At any time after confirmation of the plan but before the completion of payments under such plan, the plan may be modified, on request of the debtor, the trustee, or the holder of an allowed unsecured claim, to—

(1) increase or reduce the amount of payments on claims of a particular class provided for by the plan;

(2) extend or reduce the time for such payments; or

(3) alter the amount of the distribution to a creditor whose claim is provided for by the plan to the extent necessary to take account of any payment of such claim other than under the plan.

(b)(1) Sections 1222(a), 1222(b), and 1223(c) of this title and the requirements of section 1225(a) of this title apply to any modification under subsection (a) of this section.

(2) The plan as modified becomes the plan unless, after notice and a hearing, such modification is disapproved.

(c) A plan modified under this section may not provide for payments over a period that expires after three years after the time that the first payment under the original confirmed plan was due, unless the court, for cause, approves a longer period, but the court may not approve a period that expires after five years after such time.

(d) A plan may not be modified under this section—

(1) to increase the amount of any payment due before the plan as modified becomes the plan;

(2) by anyone except the debtor, based on an increase in the debtor's disposable income, to increase the amount of payments to unsecured creditors required for a particular month so that the aggregate of such payments exceeds the debtor's disposable income for such month; or

(3) in the last year of the plan by anyone except the debtor, to require payments that would leave the debtor with insufficient funds to carry on the farming operation after the plan is completed.

(Added and amended Pub.L. 99–554, Title II, § 255, Title III, § 302(f), Oct. 27, 1986, 100 Stat. 3113, 3124; Pub.L. 103–65, § 1, Aug. 6, 1993, 107 Stat. 311; Pub.L. 105–277, Div. C, Title I, § 149(a), Oct. 21, 1998, 112 Stat. 2681–610; Pub.L. 106–5, § 1(1), (2), Mar. 30, 1999, 113 Stat. 9; Pub.L. 106–70, § 1, Oct. 9, 1999, 113 Stat. 1031; Pub.L. 107–8, § 1, May 11, 2001, 115 Stat. 10; Pub.L. 107–17, § 1, June 26, 2001, 115 Stat. 151; Pub.L. 107–170, § 1, May 7, 2002, 116 Stat. 133; Pub.L. 107–171, Title X, § 10814(a), May 13, 2002, 116 Stat. 532; Pub.L. 107–377, § 2(a), Dec. 19, 2002, 116 Stat. 3115; Pub.L. 108–73, § 2(a), Aug. 15, 2003, 117 Stat. 891; Pub.L. 108–369, § 2(a), Oct. 25, 2004, 118 Stat. 1749; Pub.L. 109–8, Title X, §§ 1001(a)(1), 1006(b), Apr. 20, 2005, 199 Stat. 185, 187.)

HISTORICAL AND STATUTORY NOTES

Amendments

2005 Amendments. Subsec. (d). Pub.L. 109–8, § 1006(b), added subsec. (d).

CROSS REFERENCES

Conversion or dismissal upon denial of confirmation of modified plan, see 11 USCA § 1208.

Duties of United States trustee, see 28 USCA § 586.

Modification of plan in—

Chapter eleven cases, see 11 USCA § 1127.

Chapter nine cases, see 11 USCA § 942.

Chapter thirteen cases, see 11 USCA § 1329.

§ 1230. Revocation of an order of confirmation

(a) On request of a party in interest at any time within 180 days after the date of the entry of an order of confirmation under section 1225 of this title, and after notice and a hearing, the court may revoke such order if such order was procured by fraud.

(b) If the court revokes an order of confirmation under subsection (a) of this section, the court shall dispose of the case under section 1207 of this title, unless, within the time fixed by the court, the debtor proposes and the court confirms a modification of the plan under section 1229 of this title.

(Added and amended Pub.L. 99–554, Title II, § 255, Title III, § 302(f), Oct. 27, 1986, 100 Stat. 3113, 3124; Pub.L. 103–65, § 1, Aug. 6, 1993, 107 Stat. 311; Pub.L. 105–277, Div. C, Title I, § 149(a), Oct. 21, 1998, 112 Stat. 2681–610; Pub.L. 106–5, § 1(1), (2), Mar. 30, 1999, 113 Stat. 9; Pub.L. 106–70, § 1, Oct. 9, 1999, 113 Stat. 1031; Pub.L. 107–8, § 1, May 11, 2001, 115 Stat. 10; Pub.L. 107–17, § 1, June 26, 2001, 115 Stat. 151; Pub.L. 107–170, § 1, May 7, 2002, 116 Stat. 133; Pub.L. 107–171, Title X, § 10814(a), May 13, 2002, 116 Stat. 532; Pub.L. 107–377, § 2(a), Dec. 19, 2002, 116 Stat. 3115; Pub.L. 108–73, § 2(a), Aug. 15, 2003, 117 Stat. 891; Pub.L. 108–369, § 2(a), Oct. 25, 2004, 118 Stat. 1749; Pub.L. 109–8, Title X, § 1001(a)(1), Apr. 20, 2005, 119 Stat. 185.)

CROSS REFERENCES

Conversion or dismissal upon denial of confirmation of modified plan, see 11 USCA § 1208.

Revocation of order of confirmation in—

    Chapter eleven cases, see 11 USCA § 1144.

    Chapter thirteen cases, see 11 USCA § 1330.

§ 1231. Special tax provisions

(a) The issuance, transfer, or exchange of a security, or the making or delivery of an instrument of transfer under a plan confirmed under section 1225 of this title, may not be taxed under any law imposing a stamp tax or similar tax.

(b) The court may authorize the proponent of a plan to request a determination, limited to questions of law, by any governmental unit charged with responsibility for collection or determination of a tax on or measured by income, of the tax effects, under section 346 of this title and under the law imposing such tax, of the plan. In the event of an actual controversy, the court may declare such effects after the earlier of—

    (1) the date on which such governmental unit responds to the request under this subsection; or

    (2) 270 days after such request.

(c), (d) Redesignated (a), (b)

(Added and amended Pub.L. 99–554, Title II, § 255, Title III, § 302(f), Oct. 27, 1986, 100 Stat. 3113, 3124; Pub.L. 103–65, § 1, Aug. 6, 1993, 107 Stat. 311; Pub.L. 105–277, Div. C, Title I, § 149(a), Oct. 21, 1998, 112 Stat. 2681–610; Pub.L. 106–5, § 1(1), (2), Mar. 30, 1999, 113 Stat. 9; Pub.L. 106–70, § 1, Oct. 9, 1999, 113 Stat. 1031; Pub.L. 107–8, § 1, May 11, 2001, 115 Stat. 10; Pub.L. 107–17, § 1, June 26, 2001, 115 Stat. 151; Pub.L. 107–170, § 1, May 7, 2002, 116 Stat. 133; Pub.L. 107–171, Title X, § 10814(a), May 13, 2002, 116 Stat. 532; Pub.L. 107–377, § 2(a), Dec. 19, 2002, 116 Stat. 3115; Pub.L. 108–73, § 2(a), Aug. 15, 2003, 117 Stat. 891; Pub.L. 108–369, § 2(a), Oct. 25, 2004, 118 Stat. 1749; Pub.L. 109–8, Title VII, § 719(b)(4), Title X, §§ 1001(a)(1), 1003(b), Apr. 20, 2005, 119 Stat. 133, 185, 186.)

HISTORICAL AND STATUTORY NOTES

Amendments

2005 Amendments. Subsec. (a). Pub.L. 109–8, § 719(b)(4), struck out former subsec. (a) and redesignated subsec. (c) as subsec. (a). Prior to striking, subsec. (a) read: **"(a)** For the purpose of any State or local law imposing a tax on or measured by income, the taxable period of a debtor that is an individual shall terminate on the date of the order for relief under this chapter, unless the case was converted under section 706 of this title."

Subsec. (b). Pub.L. 109–8, § 719(b)(4), struck out former subsec. (b) and redesignated subsec. (d) as subsec. (b). Prior to striking, subsec. (b) read: **"(b)** The trustee shall make a State or local tax return of income for the estate of an individual debtor in a case under this chapter for each taxable period after the order for relief under this chapter during which the case is pending."

Pub.L. 109–8, § 1003(b), struck out "a State or local governmental unit" and inserted "any governmental unit" in subsec. (d) before redesignation as subsec. (b) by Pub.L. 109–8, § 719(b)(4)(B), such redesignation being effective 180 days after April 20, 2005.

Subsec. (c). Pub.L. 109–8, § 719(b)(4)(B), redesignated former subsec. (c) as subsec. (a).

Subsec. (d). Pub.L. 109–8, § 719(b)(4)(B), redesignated former subsec. (d) as subsec. (b).

CHAPTER 13—ADJUSTMENT OF DEBTS OF AN INDIVIDUAL WITH REGULAR INCOME

SUBCHAPTER I—OFFICERS, ADMINISTRATION, AND THE ESTATE

Sec.
1301. Stay of action against codebtor.
1302. Trustee.
1303. Rights and powers of debtor.
1304. Debtor engaged in business.
1305. Filing and allowance of postpetition claims.
1306. Property of the estate.
1307. Conversion or dismissal.
1308. Filing of prepetition tax returns.

SUBCHAPTER II—THE PLAN

1321. Filing of plan.
1322. Contents of plan.
1323. Modification of plan before confirmation.
1324. Confirmation hearing.
1325. Confirmation of plan.
1326. Payments.
1327. Effect of confirmation.
1328. Discharge.
1329. Modification of plan after confirmation.
1330. Revocation of an order of confirmation.

HISTORICAL AND STATUTORY NOTES

Amendments

2005 Amendments. Pub.L. 109–8, Title VII, § 716(b)(2), Apr. 20, 2005, 119 Stat. 130, added item 1308.

CROSS REFERENCES

Chapters 1, 3 and 5 of this title applicable in cases under this chapter, see 11 USCA § 103.

Claims arising from rejection of executory contracts or unexpired leases by plans under this chapter, see 11 USCA § 502.

Compensation of trustee, see 11 USCA § 330.

Conversion from—

    Chapter eleven, see 11 USCA § 1112.

    Chapter seven, see 11 USCA § 706.

    Chapter thirteen, see 11 USCA § 348.

Core proceedings, see 28 USCA § 157.

Duration of automatic stay, see 11 USCA § 362.

Eligibility to serve as trustee, see 11 USCA § 321.

Executory contracts and unexpired leases, see 11 USCA § 365.

Filing fees, see 28 USCA § 1930.

Inapplicability of restrictions on garnishment to orders of bankruptcy courts under this chapter, see 15 USCA § 1673.

"Individual with regular income" defined, see 11 USCA § 101.

Individuals who may be debtors under this chapter, see 11 USCA § 109.

Limitation on compensation of trustee, see 11 USCA § 326.

Recommendation by trustee of conversion from Chapter eleven to this chapter, see 11 USCA § 1106.

Return of excessive attorney compensation if transferred property was to be paid by debtor under plan under this chapter, see 11 USCA § 329.

Special tax provisions, see 11 USCA § 346.

Supervision of United States trustees' duties by Attorney General, see 28 USCA § 586.

Unclaimed property, see 11 USCA § 347.

Use, sale or lease of property under plan under this chapter, see 11 USCA § 363.

SUBCHAPTER I—OFFICERS, ADMINISTRATION, AND THE ESTATE

§ 1301. Stay of action against codebtor

(a) Except as provided in subsections (b) and (c) of this section, after the order for relief under this chapter, a creditor may not act, or commence or continue any civil action, to collect all or any part of a consumer debt of the debtor from any individual that is liable on such debt with the debtor, or that secured such debt, unless—

(1) such individual became liable on or secured such debt in the ordinary course of such individual's business; or

(2) the case is closed, dismissed, or converted to a case under chapter 7 or 11 of this title.

(b) A creditor may present a negotiable instrument, and may give notice of dishonor of such an instrument.

(c) On request of a party in interest and after notice and a hearing, the court shall grant relief from the stay provided by subsection (a) of this section with respect to a creditor, to the extent that—

(1) as between the debtor and the individual protected under subsection (a) of this section, such individual received the consideration for the claim held by such creditor;

(2) the plan filed by the debtor proposes not to pay such claim; or

(3) such creditor's interest would be irreparably harmed by continuation of such stay.

(d) Twenty days after the filing of a request under subsection (c)(2) of this section for relief from the stay provided by subsection (a) of this section, such stay is terminated with respect to the party in interest making such request, unless the debtor or any individual that is liable on such debt with the debtor files and serves upon such party in interest a written objection to the taking of the proposed action.

(Pub.L. 95–598, Nov. 6, 1978, 92 Stat. 2645; Pub.L. 98–353, Title III, §§ 313, 524, July 10, 1984, 98 Stat. 355, 388.)

HISTORICAL AND STATUTORY NOTES

Amendments

1984 Amendments. Subsec. (c)(3). Pub.L. 98–353, § 524, added "continuation of" after "by".

Subsec. (d). Pub.L. 98–353, § 313, added subsec. (d).

CROSS REFERENCES

Automatic stay, see 11 USCA § 362.

Automatic stay of enforcement of claims against debtor in Chapter nine cases, see 11 USCA § 922.

Claims of codebtors, see 11 USCA § 509.

Effect of conversion, see 11 USCA § 348.

Effect of § 362 of this title in stockbroker liquidation cases, see 11 USCA § 742.

Extension of time generally, see 11 USCA § 108.

§ 1302. Trustee

(a) If the United States trustee appoints an individual under section 586(b) of title 28 to serve as standing trustee in cases under this chapter and if such individual qualifies under section 322 of this title, then such individual shall serve as trustee in the case. Otherwise, the United States trustee shall appoint one disinterested person to serve as trustee in the case or the United States trustee may serve as a trustee in the case.

(b) The trustee shall—

(1) perform the duties specified in sections 704(a)(2), 704(a)(3), 704(a)(4), 704(a)(5), 704(a)(6), 704(a)(7), and 704(a)(9) of this title;

(2) appear and be heard at any hearing that concerns—

(A) the value of property subject to a lien;

(B) confirmation of a plan; or

(C) modification of the plan after confirmation;

(3) dispose of, under regulations issued by the Director of the Administrative Office of the United States Courts, moneys received or to be received in a case under chapter XIII of the Bankruptcy Act;

(4) advise, other than on legal matters, and assist the debtor in performance under the plan;

(5) ensure that the debtor commences making timely payments under section 1326 of this title; and

(6) if with respect to the debtor there is a claim for a domestic support obligation, provide the applicable notice specified in subsection (d).

(c) If the debtor is engaged in business, then in addition to the duties specified in subsection (b) of this section, the trustee shall perform the duties specified in sections 1106(a)(3) and 1106(a)(4) of this title.

(d)(1) In a case described in subsection (b)(6) to which subsection (b)(6) applies, the trustee shall—

(A)(i) provide written notice to the holder of the claim described in subsection (b)(6) of such claim and of the right of such holder to use the services of the State child support enforcement agency established under sections 464 and 466 of the Social Security Act for the State in which such holder resides, for assistance in collecting child support during and after the case under this title; and

(ii) include in the notice provided under clause (i) the address and telephone number of such State child support enforcement agency;

(B)(i) provide written notice to such State child support enforcement agency of such claim; and

(ii) include in the notice provided under clause (i) the name, address, and telephone number of such holder; and

(C) at such time as the debtor is granted a discharge under section 1328, provide written notice to such holder and to such State child support enforcement agency of—

(i) the granting of the discharge;

(ii) the last recent known address of the debtor;

(iii) the last recent known name and address of the debtor's employer; and

(iv) the name of each creditor that holds a claim that—

(I) is not discharged under paragraph (2) or (4) of section 523(a); or

(II) was reaffirmed by the debtor under section 524(c).

(2)(A) The holder of a claim described in subsection (b)(6) or the State child support enforcement agency of the State in which such holder resides may request from a creditor described in paragraph (1)(C)(iv) the last known address of the debtor.

(B) Notwithstanding any other provision of law, a creditor that makes a disclosure of a last known address of a debtor in connection with a request made under subparagraph (A) shall not be liable by reason of making that disclosure.

(Pub.L. 95–598, Nov. 6, 1978, 92 Stat. 2645; Pub.L. 98–353, Title III, §§ 314, 525, July 10, 1984, 98 Stat. 356, 388; Pub.L. 99–554, Title II, §§ 228, 283(w), Oct. 27, 1986, 100 Stat. 3103, 3118; Pub.L. 103–394, Title V, § 501(d)(37), Oct. 22, 1994, 108 Stat. 4147; Pub.L. 109–8, Title II, § 219(d), Apr. 20, 2005, 119 Stat. 58; Pub.L. 111–327, § 2(a)(39), Dec. 22, 2010, 124 Stat. 3561.)

HISTORICAL AND STATUTORY NOTES

References in Text

Chapter XIII of the Bankruptcy Act, referred to in subsec. (b)(3), is chapter XIII of Act July 1, 1898, c. 541, as added June 22, 1938, c. 575, § 1, 52 Stat. 930, which was classified to chapter 13 (section 1001 et seq.) of former Title 11.

Section 464 of the Social Security Act, referred to in subsec. (d)(1)(A)(i), is Act Aug. 14, 1935, c. 531, Title IV, § 464, as added Aug. 13, 1981, Pub.L. 97–35, Title XXIII, § 2331(a), 95 Stat. 860, and amended, which is classified to 42 U.S.C.A. § 664.

Section 466 of the Social Security Act, referred to in subsec. (d)(1)(A)(i), is Act Aug. 14, 1935, c. 531, Title IV, § 466, as added Aug. 16, 1984, Pub.L. 98–378, § 3(b), 98 Stat. 1306, and amended, which is classified to 42 U.S.C.A. § 666.

Amendments

2010 Amendments. Subsec. (b)(1). Pub.L. 111–327, § 2(a)(39), struck out "704(2), 704(3), 704(4), 704(5), 704(6), 704(7), and 704(9)" and inserted "704(a)(2), 704(a)(3), 704(a)(4), 704(a)(5), 704(a)(6), 704(a)(7), and 704(a)(9)".

2005 Amendments. Subsec. (b)(4). Pub.L. 109–8, § 219(d)(1)(A), struck out "and" at the end of par. (4).

Subsec. (b)(5). Pub.L. 109–8, § 219(d)(1)(B), substituted "; and" for the period at the end of par. (5).

Subsec. (b)(6). Pub.L. 109–8, § 219(d)(1)(C), added par. (6).

Subsec. (d). Pub.L. 109–8, § 219(d)(2), added subsec. (d).

1994 Amendments. Subsec. (b)(3). Pub.L. 103–394, § 501(d)(37), struck out "and" after "Bankruptcy Act;".

1986 Amendments. Subsec. (a). Pub.L. 99–554, § 228(1), substituted "If the United States trustee appoints" for "If the court has appointed", "section 586(b) of title 28" for "subsection (d) of this section", and "the United States trustee shall appoint one disinterested person to serve as trustee in the case or the United States trustee may serve as a trustee in the case" for "the court shall appoint a person to serve as trustee in the case".

Subsecs. (d) and (e). Pub.L. 99–554, § 228(2), struck out subsecs. (d) and (e) which read as follows:

"(d) If the number of cases under this chapter commenced in a particular judicial district so warrant, the court may appoint one or more individuals to serve as standing trustee for such district in cases under this chapter.

"(e)(1) A court that has appointed an individual under subsection (d) of this section to serve as standing trustee in cases under this chapter shall set for such individual—

"(A) a maximum annual compensation, not to exceed the lowest annual rate of basic pay in effect for grade GS–16 of the General Schedule prescribed under section 5332 of title 5; and

"**(B)** a percentage fee, not to exceed ten percent, based on such maximum annual compensation and the actual, necessary expenses incurred by such individual as standing trustee.

"**(2)** Such individual shall collect such percentage fee from all payments under plans in the cases under this chapter for which such individual serves as standing trustee. Such individual shall pay annually to the Treasury—

"**(A)** any amount by which the actual compensation received by such individual exceeds five percent of all such payments made under plans in cases under this chapter for which such individual serves as standing trustee; and

"**(B)** any amount by which the percentage fee fixed under paragraph (1)(B) of this subsection for all such cases exceeds—

"**(i)** such individual's actual compensation for such cases, as adjusted under subparagraph (A) of this paragraph; plus

"**(ii)** the actual, necessary expenses incurred by such individual as standing trustee in such cases.".

Pub.L. 99–554, § 283(w), which directed the amendment of subsec. (e)(1) by substituting "set for such individual" for "fix" could not be executed in view of the repeal of subsec. (e) by section 228(2) of Pub.L. 99–554.

1984 Amendments. Subsec. (b)(1). Pub.L. 98–353, § 314(1), substituted "perform the duties specified in sections 704(2), 704(3), 704(4), 704(5), 704(6), 704(7), and 704(9) of this title;" for "perform the duties specified in sections 704(2), 704(3), 704(4), 704(5), 704(6), and 704(8) of this title;".

Subsec. (b)(2). Pub.L. 98–353, § 314(2), struck out "and" at the end thereof.

Subsec. (b)(3). Pub.L. 98–353, § 525(a), added par. (3). Former par. (3) was redesignated as (4).

Pub.L. 98–353, § 314(3), substituted "; and" for the period at the end thereof.

Subsec. (b)(4). Pub.L. 98–353, § 525(a), redesignated former par. (3) as (4). Another par. (4), as added by Pub.L. 98–353, § 314(4), was redesignated par. (5).

Subsec. (b)(5). Pub.L. 98–353, § 314(4), added par. (5), originally enacted as par. (4) and subsequently redesignated.

Pub.L. 98–353, § 525(a), redesignated former par. (4) as (5).

Subsec. (e)(1). Pub.L. 98–353, § 525(b)(1), which directed the amendment of par. (4) by substituting "set for such individual" for "fix", was executed to par. (1) as the probable intent of Congress.

Subsec. (e)(1)(A). Pub.L. 98–353, § 525(b)(2), struck out "for such individual" after "a maximum annual compensation".

Subsec. (e)(2)(A). Pub.L. 98–353, § 525(b)(3)(A), substituted "received by" for "of".

Pub.L. 98–353, § 525(b)(3)(B), substituted "of all such payments made" for "upon all payments".

CROSS REFERENCES

Appointment of trustee in—

    Chapter eleven cases, see 11 USCA § 1104.

    Chapter twelve cases, see 11 USCA § 1202.

    Railroad reorganization cases, see 11 USCA § 1163.

Compensation of officers, see 11 USCA § 330.

Election of trustee, see 11 USCA § 702.

Eligibility to serve as trustee, see 11 USCA § 321.

Grain storage facility bankruptcies, expedited appointment of trustee or examiner, see 11 USCA § 557.

Limitation on compensation of trustee, see 11 USCA § 326.

Qualification of trustee, see 11 USCA § 322.

Removal of trustee, see 11 USCA § 324.

Role and capacity of trustee, see 11 USCA § 323.

Time of bringing action, see 11 USCA § 546.

§ 1303. Rights and powers of debtor

Subject to any limitations on a trustee under this chapter, the debtor shall have, exclusive of the trustee, the rights and powers of a trustee under sections 363(b), 363(d), 363(e), 363(f), and 363(l), of this title.

(Pub.L. 95–598, Nov. 6, 1978, 92 Stat. 2646.)

CROSS REFERENCES

Rights and powers of debtor in—
> Chapter eleven cases, see 11 USCA § 1107.
>
> Chapter twelve cases, see 11 USCA § 1203.

§ 1304. Debtor engaged in business

(a) A debtor that is self-employed and incurs trade credit in the production of income from such employment is engaged in business.

(b) Unless the court orders otherwise, a debtor engaged in business may operate the business of the debtor and, subject to any limitations on a trustee under sections 363(c) and 364 of this title and to such limitations or conditions as the court prescribes, shall have, exclusive of the trustee, the rights and powers of the trustee under such sections.

(c) A debtor engaged in business shall perform the duties of the trustee specified in section 704(a)(8) of this title.

(Pub.L. 95–598, Nov. 6, 1978, 92 Stat. 2646; Pub.L. 98–353, Title III, §§ 311(b)(2), 526, July 10, 1984, 98 Stat. 355, 389; Pub.L. 111–327, § 2(a)(40), Dec. 22, 2010, 124 Stat. 3562.)

HISTORICAL AND STATUTORY NOTES

Amendments

2010 Amendments. Subsec. (c). Pub.L. 111–327, § 2(a)(40), struck out "704(8)" and inserted "704(a)(8)".

1984 Amendments. Subsec. (b). Pub.L. 98–353, § 526, struck out the comma after "of the debtor".

Subsec. (c). Pub.L. 98–353, § 311(b)(2), substituted "section 704(8)" for "section 704(7)".

CROSS REFERENCES

Authorization of trustee to operate business in—
> Chapter eleven cases, see 11 USCA § 1108.
>
> Chapter seven cases, see 11 USCA § 721.

Obtaining credit, see 11 USCA § 364.

Rights, powers and duties of debtor in possession in Chapter 11 cases, see 11 USCA § 1107.

Use, sale or lease of property, see 11 USCA § 363.

§ 1305. Filing and allowance of postpetition claims

(a) A proof of claim may be filed by any entity that holds a claim against the debtor—

(1) for taxes that become payable to a governmental unit while the case is pending; or

(2) that is a consumer debt, that arises after the date of the order for relief under this chapter, and that is for property or services necessary for the debtor's performance under the plan.

(b) Except as provided in subsection (c) of this section, a claim filed under subsection (a) of this section shall be allowed or disallowed under section 502 of this title, but shall be determined as of the date such claim arises, and shall be allowed under section 502(a), 502(b), or 502(c) of this title, or disallowed under section 502(d) or 502(e) of this title, the same as if such claim had arisen before the date of the filing of the petition.

(c) A claim filed under subsection (a)(2) of this section shall be disallowed if the holder of such claim knew or should have known that prior approval by the trustee of the debtor's incurring the obligation was practicable and was not obtained.

(Pub.L. 95–598, Nov. 6, 1978, 92 Stat. 2647.)

CROSS REFERENCES

Allowance and filing of claims and interests in Chapter 11 cases, see 11 USCA § 1111.

Discharge of certain consumer debts, see 11 USCA § 1328.

Effect of conversion, see 11 USCA § 348.

Filing of proofs of claims or interests, see 11 USCA § 501.

Provisions in plans for payment of claims, see 11 USCA § 1322.

§ 1306. Property of the estate

(a) Property of the estate includes, in addition to the property specified in section 541 of this title—

(1) all property of the kind specified in such section that the debtor acquires after the commencement of the case but before the case is closed, dismissed, or converted to a case under chapter 7, 11, or 12 of this title, whichever occurs first; and

(2) earnings from services performed by the debtor after the commencement of the case but before the case is closed, dismissed, or converted to a case under chapter 7, 11, or 12 of this title, whichever occurs first.

(b) Except as provided in a confirmed plan or order confirming a plan, the debtor shall remain in possession of all property of the estate.

(Pub.L. 95–598, Nov. 6, 1978, 92 Stat. 2647; Pub.L. 99–554, Title II, § 257(u), Oct. 27, 1986, 100 Stat. 3116.)

HISTORICAL AND STATUTORY NOTES

Amendments

1986 Amendments. Subsec. (a)(1). Pub.L. 99–554, § 257(u)(1), added reference to chapter 12.

Subsec. (a)(2). Pub.L. 99–554, § 257(u)(2), added reference to chapter 12.

CROSS REFERENCES

Ownership of copyright, see 17 USCA § 201.

§ 1307. Conversion or dismissal

(a) The debtor may convert a case under this chapter to a case under chapter 7 of this title at any time. Any waiver of the right to convert under this subsection is unenforceable.

(b) On request of the debtor at any time, if the case has not been converted under section 706, 1112, or 1208 of this title, the court shall dismiss a case under this chapter. Any waiver of the right to dismiss under this subsection is unenforceable.

(c) Except as provided in subsection (f) of this section, on request of a party in interest or the United States trustee and after notice and a hearing, the court may convert a case under this chapter to a case under chapter 7 of this title, or may dismiss a case under this chapter, whichever is in the best interests of creditors and the estate, for cause, including—

(1) unreasonable delay by the debtor that is prejudicial to creditors;

(2) nonpayment of any fees and charges required under chapter 123 of title 28;

(3) failure to file a plan timely under section 1321 of this title;

(4) failure to commence making timely payments under section 1326 of this title;

(5) denial of confirmation of a plan under section 1325 of this title and denial of a request made for additional time for filing another plan or a modification of a plan;

(6) material default by the debtor with respect to a term of a confirmed plan;

(7) revocation of the order of confirmation under section 1330 of this title, and denial of confirmation of a modified plan under section 1329 of this title;

(8) termination of a confirmed plan by reason of the occurrence of a condition specified in the plan other than completion of payments under the plan;

(9) only on request of the United States trustee, failure of the debtor to file, within fifteen days, or such additional time as the court may allow, after the filing of the petition commencing such case, the information required by paragraph (1) of section 521(a);

(10) only on request of the United States trustee, failure to timely file the information required by paragraph (2) of section 521(a); or

(11) failure of the debtor to pay any domestic support obligation that first becomes payable after the date of the filing of the petition.

(d) Except as provided in subsection (f) of this section, at any time before the confirmation of a plan under section 1325 of this title, on request of a party in interest or the United States trustee and after notice and a hearing, the court may convert a case under this chapter to a case under chapter 11 or 12 of this title.

(e) Upon the failure of the debtor to file a tax return under section 1308, on request of a party in interest or the United States trustee and after notice and a hearing, the court shall dismiss a case or convert a case under this chapter to a case under chapter 7 of this title, whichever is in the best interest of the creditors and the estate.

(f) The court may not convert a case under this chapter to a case under chapter 7, 11, or 12 of this title if the debtor is a farmer, unless the debtor requests such conversion.

(g) Notwithstanding any other provision of this section, a case may not be converted to a case under another chapter of this title unless the debtor may be a debtor under such chapter.

(Pub.L. 95–598, Nov. 6, 1978, 92 Stat. 2647; Pub.L. 98–353, Title III, §§ 315, 527, July 10, 1984, 98 Stat. 356, 389; Pub.L. 99–554, Title II, §§ 229, 257(v), Oct. 27, 1986, 100 Stat. 3103, 3116; Pub.L. 109–8, Title II, § 213(7), Title VII, § 716(c), Apr. 20, 2005, 119 Stat. 53, 130; Pub.L. 111–327, § 2(a)(41), Dec. 22, 2010, 124 Stat. 3562.)

HISTORICAL AND STATUTORY NOTES

Amendments

2010 Amendments. Subsec. (c). Pub.L. 111–327, § 2(a)(41)(A)(i), struck out "subsection (e)" and inserted "subsection (f)".

Subsec. (c)(9). Pub.L. 111–327, § 2(a)(41)(A)(ii), struck out "521" and inserted "521(a)".

Subsec. (c)(10). Pub.L. 111–327, § 2(a)(41)(A)(iii), struck out "521" and inserted "521(a)".

Subsec. (d). Pub.L. 111–327, § 2(a)(41)(B), struck out "subsection (e)" and inserted "subsection (f)".

2005 Amendments. Subsec. (c)(9). Pub.L. 109–8, § 213(7)(A), struck out "or" at the end of par. (9).

Subsec. (c)(10). Pub.L. 109–8, § 213(7)(B), substituted "; or" for the period at the end of par. (10).

Subsec. (c)(11). Pub.L. 109–8, § 213(7)(C), added par. (11).

Subsec. (e). Pub.L. 109–8, § 716(c), redesignated subsec. (e) as subsec. (f) and inserted a new subsec. (e).

Subsec. (f). Pub.L. 109–8, § 716(c)(1), redesignated subsec. (e) as subsec. (f). Former subsec. (f) was redesignated subsec. (g).

Subsec. (g). Pub.L. 109–8, § 716(c)(1), redesignated subsec. (f) as subsec. (g).

1986 Amendments. Subsec. (b). Pub.L. 99–554, § 257(v)(1), added reference to section 1208 of this title.

Subsec. (c). Pub.L. 99–554, § 229(1)(A), added "or the United States trustee" following "party in interest" in provisions preceding par. (1).

Subsec. (c)(9), (10). Pub.L. 99–554, § 229(1)(B)–(D), added pars. (9) and (10).

Subsec. (d). Pub.L. 99–554, § 229(2), added "or the United States trustee" following "party in interest".

Pub.L. 99–554, § 257(v)(2), added reference to chapter 12.

Subsec. (e). Pub.L. 99–554, § 257(v)(3), added reference to chapter 12.

1984 Amendments. Subsec. (b). Pub.L. 98–353, § 527(a), added a comma after "time".

Subsec. (c)(4). Pub.L. 98–353, § 315(2), added par. (4). Former par. (4) was redesignated as (5).

Subsec. (c)(5). Pub.L. 98–353, § 315(1), redesignated former par. (4) as (5). Former par. (5) was redesignated as (6).

Pub.L. 98–353, § 527(b)(1), added "a request made for" before "additional".

Subsec. (c)(6). Pub.L. 98–353, § 315(1), redesignated former par. (5) as (6). Former par. (6) was redesignated as (7).

Subsec. (c)(7). Pub.L. 98–353, § 315(1), redesignated former par. (6) as (7). Former par. (7) was redesignated as (8).

Pub.L. 98–353, § 527(b)(2), substituted "; or" for "; and".

Subsec. (c)(8). Pub.L. 98–353, § 315(1), redesignated former par. (7) as (8).

Pub.L. 98–353, § 527(b)(3), added "other than completion of payments under the plan" after "in the plan".

CROSS REFERENCES

Conversion from Chapter seven, see 11 USCA § 706.

Conversion or dismissal upon revocation of order of confirmation, see 11 USCA § 1330.

Dismissal of—

    Chapter nine cases, see 11 USCA § 930.

    Chapter seven case, see 11 USCA § 707.

Distribution of property of estate converted to Chapter seven, see 11 USCA § 726.

Effect of—

    Conversion, see 11 USCA § 348.

    Dismissal, see 11 USCA § 349.

Executory contracts and unexpired leases, see 11 USCA § 365.

Liquidation of estate in railroad reorganization case, see 11 USCA § 1174.

§ 1308. Filing of prepetition tax returns

(a) Not later than the day before the date on which the meeting of the creditors is first scheduled to be held under section 341(a), if the debtor was required to file a tax return under applicable nonbankruptcy law, the debtor shall file with appropriate tax authorities all tax returns for all taxable periods ending during the 4-year period ending on the date of the filing of the petition.

(b)(1) Subject to paragraph (2), if the tax returns required by subsection (a) have not been filed by the date on which the meeting of creditors is first scheduled to be held under section 341(a), the trustee may hold open that meeting for a reasonable period of time to allow the debtor an additional period of time to file any unfiled returns, but such additional period of time shall not extend beyond—

    (A) for any return that is past due as of the date of the filing of the petition, the date that is 120 days after the date of that meeting; or

    (B) for any return that is not past due as of the date of the filing of the petition, the later of—

        (i) the date that is 120 days after the date of that meeting; or

        (ii) the date on which the return is due under the last automatic extension of time for filing that return to which the debtor is entitled, and for which request is timely made, in accordance with applicable nonbankruptcy law.

(2) After notice and a hearing, and order entered before the tolling of any applicable filing period determined under paragraph (1), if the debtor demonstrates by a preponderance of the evidence that the failure to file a return as required under paragraph (1) is attributable to circumstances beyond the control of the debtor, the court may extend the filing period established by the trustee under paragraph (1) for—

    (A) a period of not more than 30 days for returns described in paragraph (1)(A); and

    (B) a period not to extend after the applicable extended due date for a return described in paragraph (1)(B).

(c) For purposes of this section, the term "return" includes a return prepared pursuant to subsection (a) or (b) of section 6020 of the Internal Revenue Code of 1986, or a similar State or local law, or a written stipulation to a judgment or a final order entered by a nonbankruptcy tribunal.

(Added Pub.L. 109–8, Title VII, § 716(b)(1), Apr. 20, 2005, 119 Stat. 129; amended Pub.L. 111–327, § 2(a)(42), Dec. 22, 2010, 124 Stat. 3562.)

HISTORICAL AND STATUTORY NOTES

References in Text

Subsection (a) or (b) of section 6020 of the Internal Revenue Code of 1986, referred to in subsec. (c), is classified to 26 U.S.C.A. § 6020(a) or (b).

Amendments

2010 Amendments. Subsec. (b)(2). Pub.L. 111–327, § 2(a)(42)(C), in the matter preceding subpar. (A), struck out "this subsection" and inserted "paragraph (1)" in three places.

Subsec. (b)(2)(A). Pub.L. 111–327, § 2(a)(42)(A), struck out "paragraph (1)" and inserted "paragraph (1)(A)".

Subsec. (b)(2)(B). Pub.L. 111–327, § 2(a)(42)(B), struck out "paragraph (2)" and inserted "paragraph (1)(B)".

SUBCHAPTER II—THE PLAN

§ 1321. Filing of plan

The debtor shall file a plan.

(Pub.L. 95–598, Nov. 6, 1978, 92 Stat. 2648.)

CROSS REFERENCES

Conversion or dismissal for failure to timely file plan, see 11 USCA § 1307.

Filing of plan in—

Chapter nine cases, see 11 USCA § 941.

Chapter twelve cases, see 11 USCA § 1221.

Who may file plan in Chapter eleven cases, see 11 USCA § 1121.

§ 1322. Contents of plan

(a) The plan—

(1) shall provide for the submission of all or such portion of future earnings or other future income of the debtor to the supervision and control of the trustee as is necessary for the execution of the plan;

(2) shall provide for the full payment, in deferred cash payments, of all claims entitled to priority under section 507 of this title, unless the holder of a particular claim agrees to a different treatment of such claim;

(3) if the plan classifies claims, shall provide the same treatment for each claim within a particular class; and

(4) notwithstanding any other provision of this section, may provide for less than full payment of all amounts owed for a claim entitled to priority under section 507(a)(1)(B) only if the plan provides that all of the debtor's projected disposable income for a 5-year period beginning on the date that the first payment is due under the plan will be applied to make payments under the plan.

(b) Subject to subsections (a) and (c) of this section, the plan may—

(1) designate a class or classes of unsecured claims, as provided in section 1122 of this title, but may not discriminate unfairly against any class so designated; however, such plan may treat claims for a consumer debt of the debtor if an individual is liable on such consumer debt with the debtor differently than other unsecured claims;

(2) modify the rights of holders of secured claims, other than a claim secured only by a security interest in real property that is the debtor's principal residence, or of holders of unsecured claims, or leave unaffected the rights of holders of any class of claims;

(3) provide for the curing or waiving of any default;

(4) provide for payments on any unsecured claim to be made concurrently with payments on any secured claim or any other unsecured claim;

(5) notwithstanding paragraph (2) of this subsection, provide for the curing of any default within a reasonable time and maintenance of payments while the case is pending on

any unsecured claim or secured claim on which the last payment is due after the date on which the final payment under the plan is due;

  (6) provide for the payment of all or any part of any claim allowed under section 1305 of this title;

  (7) subject to section 365 of this title, provide for the assumption, rejection, or assignment of any executory contract or unexpired lease of the debtor not previously rejected under such section;

  (8) provide for the payment of all or part of a claim against the debtor from property of the estate or property of the debtor;

  (9) provide for the vesting of property of the estate, on confirmation of the plan or at a later time, in the debtor or in any other entity;

  (10) provide for the payment of interest accruing after the date of the filing of the petition on unsecured claims that are nondischargeable under section 1328(a), except that such interest may be paid only to the extent that the debtor has disposable income available to pay such interest after making provision for full payment of all allowed claims; and

  (11) include any other appropriate provision not inconsistent with this title.

(c) Notwithstanding subsection (b)(2) and applicable nonbankruptcy law—

  (1) a default with respect to, or that gave rise to, a lien on the debtor's principal residence may be cured under paragraph (3) or (5) of subsection (b) until such residence is sold at a foreclosure sale that is conducted in accordance with applicable nonbankruptcy law; and

  (2) in a case in which the last payment on the original payment schedule for a claim secured only by a security interest in real property that is the debtor's principal residence is due before the date on which the final payment under the plan is due, the plan may provide for the payment of the claim as modified pursuant to section 1325(a)(5) of this title.

(d)(1) If the current monthly income of the debtor and the debtor's spouse combined, when multiplied by 12, is not less than—

  (A) in the case of a debtor in a household of 1 person, the median family income of the applicable State for 1 earner;

  (B) in the case of a debtor in a household of 2, 3, or 4 individuals, the highest median family income of the applicable State for a family of the same number or fewer individuals; or

  (C) in the case of a debtor in a household exceeding 4 individuals, the highest median family income of the applicable State for a family of 4 or fewer individuals, plus $675[1] per month for each individual in excess of 4,

the plan may not provide for payments over a period that is longer than 5 years.

  (2) If the current monthly income of the debtor and the debtor's spouse combined, when multiplied by 12, is less than—

  (A) in the case of a debtor in a household of 1 person, the median family income of the applicable State for 1 earner;

  (B) in the case of a debtor in a household of 2, 3, or 4 individuals, the highest median family income of the applicable State for a family of the same number or fewer individuals; or

  (C) in the case of a debtor in a household exceeding 4 individuals, the highest median family income of the applicable State for a family of 4 or fewer individuals, plus $675[1] per month for each individual in excess of 4,

---

[1] Dollar amount as adjusted by the Judicial Conference of the United States. See Adjustment of Dollar Amounts notes set out under this section and 11 U.S.C.A. § 104.

the plan may not provide for payments over a period that is longer than 3 years, unless the court, for cause, approves a longer period, but the court may not approve a period that is longer than 5 years.

(e) Notwithstanding subsection (b)(2) of this section and sections 506(b) and 1325(a)(5) of this title, if it is proposed in a plan to cure a default, the amount necessary to cure the default, shall be determined in accordance with the underlying agreement and applicable nonbankruptcy law.

(f) A plan may not materially alter the terms of a loan described in section 362(b)(19) and any amounts required to repay such loan shall not constitute "disposable income" under section 1325.

(Pub.L. 95–598, Nov. 6, 1978, 92 Stat. 2648; Pub.L. 98–353, Title III, §§ 316, 528, July 10, 1984, 98 Stat. 356, 389; Pub.L. 103–394, Title III, §§ 301, 305(c), Oct. 22, 1994, 108 Stat. 4131, 4134; Pub.L. 109–8, Title II, §§ 213(8), (9), 224(d), Title III, § 318(1), Apr. 20, 2005, 119 Stat. 53, 65, 93; Pub.L. 111–327, § 2(a)(43), Dec. 22, 2010, 124 Stat. 3562.)

HISTORICAL AND STATUTORY NOTES

Amendments

2010 Amendments. Subsec. (a). Pub.L. 111–327, § 2(a)(43)(A), in the matter preceding par. (1), struck out "shall" following "The plan".

Subsec. (a)(1). Pub.L. 111–327, § 2(a)(43)(B), inserted "shall" following "(1)".

Subsec. (a)(2). Pub.L. 111–327, § 2(a)(43)(C), inserted "shall" following "(2)".

Subsec. (a)(3). Pub.L. 111–327, § 2(a)(43)(D), inserted "shall" following "claims,".

Subsec. (a)(4). Pub.L. 111–327, § 2(a)(43)(E), struck out "a plan" following "this section,".

2005 Amendments. Subsec. (a)(2). Pub.L. 109–8, § 213(8)(A), struck out "and" at the end of par. (2).

Subsec. (a)(3). Pub.L. 109–8, § 213(8)(B), substituted "; and" for the period at the end of par. (3).

Subsec. (a)(4). Pub.L. 109–8, § 213(8)(C), added par. (4).

Subsec. (b)(9). Pub.L. 109–8, § 213(9)(A), substituted a semicolon for "; and" at the end of par. (9).

Subsec. (b)(10), (11). Pub.L. 109–8, § 213(9)(B), (C), redesignated former par. (10) as par. (11) and added a new par. (10).

Subsec. (d). Pub.L. 109–8, § 318(1), rewrote subsec. (d), which formerly read: **"(d)** The plan may not provide for payments over a period that is longer than three years, unless the court, for cause, approves a longer period, but the court may not approve a period that is longer than five years."

Subsec. (f). Pub.L. 109–8, § 224(d), added subsec. (f).

1994 Amendments. Subsec. (c). Pub.L. 103–394, § 301, added subsec. (c). Former subsec. (c) redesignated (d).

Subsec. (d). Pub.L. 103–394, § 301(1), redesignated former subsec. (c) as (d).

Subsec. (e). Pub.L. 103–394, § 305(c), added subsec. (e).

1984 Amendments. Subsec. (a)(2). Pub.L. 98–353, § 528(a) added a comma after "payments".

Subsec. (b)(1). Pub.L. 98–353, § 316(1), substituted "designate a class or classes of unsecured claims, as provided in section 1122 of this title, but may not discriminate unfairly against any class so designated; however, such plan may treat claims for a consumer debt of the debtor if an individual is liable on such consumer debt with the debtor differently than other unsecured claims;" for "designate a class or classes of unsecured claims, as provided in section 1122 of this title, but may not discriminate unfairly against any class so designated;".

Subsec. (b)(2). Pub.L. 98–353, § 528(b)(1), added ", or leave unaffected the rights of the holders of any class of claims" following "unsecured claims".

Subsec. (b)(4). Pub.L. 98–353, § 528(b)(2), added "other" after "claim or any".

Subsec. (b)(7). Pub.L. 98–353, § 528(b)(3)(A), added "subject to section 365 of this title," before "provide".

Pub.L. 98–353, § 528(b)(3)(B), substituted ", rejection, or assignment" for "or rejection".

Pub.L. 98–353, § 528(b)(3)(C), substituted "under such section" for "under section 365 of this title".

Subsec. (b)(8). Pub.L. 98–353, § 528(b)(4), struck out "any" preceding "part of a claim".

Adjustment of Dollar Amounts

For adjustment of dollar amounts specified in subsec. (d)(1)(C), (2)(C) of this section by the Judicial Conference of the United States, see note set out under 11 U.S.C.A. § 104.

CROSS REFERENCES

Contents of plan filed in—

    Chapter eleven cases, see 11 USCA § 1123.

    Chapter twelve cases, see 11 USCA § 1222.

    Railroad reorganization cases, see 11 USCA § 1172.

§ 1323. Modification of plan before confirmation

(a) The debtor may modify the plan at any time before confirmation, but may not modify the plan so that the plan as modified fails to meet the requirements of section 1322 of this title.

(b) After the debtor files a modification under this section, the plan as modified becomes the plan.

(c) Any holder of a secured claim that has accepted or rejected the plan is deemed to have accepted or rejected, as the case may be, the plan as modified, unless the modification provides for a change in the rights of such holder from what such rights were under the plan before modification, and such holder changes such holder's previous acceptance or rejection.

(Pub.L. 95–598, Nov. 6, 1978, 92 Stat. 2649.)

CROSS REFERENCES

Modification of plan filed in—

    Chapter eleven cases, see 11 USCA § 1127.

    Chapter nine cases, see 11 USCA § 942.

    Chapter twelve cases, see 11 USCA § 1223.

§ 1324. Confirmation hearing

(a) Except as provided in subsection (b) and after notice, the court shall hold a hearing on confirmation of the plan. A party in interest may object to confirmation of the plan.

(b) The hearing on confirmation of the plan may be held not earlier than 20 days and not later than 45 days after the date of the meeting of creditors under section 341(a), unless the court determines that it would be in the best interests of the creditors and the estate to hold such hearing at an earlier date and there is no objection to such earlier date.

(Pub.L. 95–598, Nov. 6, 1978, 92 Stat. 2649; Pub.L. 98–353, Title III, § 529, July 10, 1984, 98 Stat. 389; Pub.L. 99–554, Title II, § 283(x), Oct. 27, 1986, 100 Stat. 3118; Pub.L. 109–8, Title III, § 317, Apr. 20, 2005, 119 Stat. 92.)

HISTORICAL AND STATUTORY NOTES

Amendments

2005 Amendments. Section. Pub.L. 109–8, § 317(1), struck out "After" and inserted "**(a)** Except as provided in subsection (b) and after".

Subsec. (b). Pub.L. 109–8, § 317(2), added subsec. (b).

1986 Amendments. Pub.L. 99–554 struck out "the" following "object to".

1984 Amendments. Pub.L. 98–353 struck out "the" preceding "confirmation of the plan".

CROSS REFERENCES

Confirmation hearing in—

　Chapter eleven cases, see 11 USCA § 1128.

　Chapter twelve cases, see 11 USCA § 1224.

Duties of United States trustee, see 28 USCA § 586.

§ 1325. Confirmation of plan

(a) Except as provided in subsection (b), the court shall confirm a plan if—

　(1) the plan complies with the provisions of this chapter and with the other applicable provisions of this title;

　(2) any fee, charge, or amount required under chapter 123 of title 28, or by the plan, to be paid before confirmation, has been paid;

　(3) the plan has been proposed in good faith and not by any means forbidden by law;

　(4) the value, as of the effective date of the plan, of property to be distributed under the plan on account of each allowed unsecured claim is not less than the amount that would be paid on such claim if the estate of the debtor were liquidated under chapter 7 of this title on such date;

　(5) with respect to each allowed secured claim provided for by the plan—

　　(A) the holder of such claim has accepted the plan;

　　(B)(i) the plan provides that—

　　　(I) the holder of such claim retain the lien securing such claim until the earlier of—

　　　　(aa) the payment of the underlying debt determined under nonbankruptcy law; or

　　　　(bb) discharge under section 1328; and

　　　(II) if the case under this chapter is dismissed or converted without completion of the plan, such lien shall also be retained by such holder to the extent recognized by applicable nonbankruptcy law;

　　(ii) the value, as of the effective date of the plan, of property to be distributed under the plan on account of such claim is not less than the allowed amount of such claim; and

　　(iii) if—

　　　(I) property to be distributed pursuant to this subsection is in the form of periodic payments, such payments shall be in equal monthly amounts; and

　　　(II) the holder of the claim is secured by personal property, the amount of such payments shall not be less than an amount sufficient to provide to the holder of such claim adequate protection during the period of the plan; or

　　(C) the debtor surrenders the property securing such claim to such holder;

　(6) the debtor will be able to make all payments under the plan and to comply with the plan;

　(7) the action of the debtor in filing the petition was in good faith;

(8) the debtor has paid all amounts that are required to be paid under a domestic support obligation and that first become payable after the date of the filing of the petition if the debtor is required by a judicial or administrative order, or by statute, to pay such domestic support obligation; and

(9) the debtor has filed all applicable Federal, State, and local tax returns as required by section 1308.

For purposes of paragraph (5), section 506 shall not apply to a claim described in that paragraph if the creditor has a purchase money security interest securing the debt that is the subject of the claim, the debt was incurred within the 910-day period preceding the date of the filing of the petition, and the collateral for that debt consists of a motor vehicle (as defined in section 30102 of title 49) acquired for the personal use of the debtor, or if collateral for that debt consists of any other thing of value, if the debt was incurred during the 1-year period preceding that filing.

(b)(1) If the trustee or the holder of an allowed unsecured claim objects to the confirmation of the plan, then the court may not approve the plan unless, as of the effective date of the plan—

(A) the value of the property to be distributed under the plan on account of such claim is not less than the amount of such claim; or

(B) the plan provides that all of the debtor's projected disposable income to be received in the applicable commitment period beginning on the date that the first payment is due under the plan will be applied to make payments to unsecured creditors under the plan.

(2) For purposes of this subsection, the term "disposable income" means current monthly income received by the debtor (other than child support payments, foster care payments, or disability payments for a dependent child made in accordance with applicable nonbankruptcy law to the extent reasonably necessary to be expended for such child) less amounts reasonably necessary to be expended—

(A)(i) for the maintenance or support of the debtor or a dependent of the debtor, or for a domestic support obligation, that first becomes payable after the date the petition is filed; and

(ii) for charitable contributions (that meet the definition of "charitable contribution" under section 548(d)(3)) to a qualified religious or charitable entity or organization (as defined in section 548(d)(4)) in an amount not to exceed 15 percent of gross income of the debtor for the year in which the contributions are made; and

(B) if the debtor is engaged in business, for the payment of expenditures necessary for the continuation, preservation, and operation of such business.

(3) Amounts reasonably necessary to be expended under paragraph (2), other than subparagraph (A)(ii) of paragraph (2), shall be determined in accordance with subparagraphs (A) and (B) of section 707(b)(2), if the debtor has current monthly income, when multiplied by 12, greater than—

(A) in the case of a debtor in a household of 1 person, the median family income of the applicable State for 1 earner;

(B) in the case of a debtor in a household of 2, 3, or 4 individuals, the highest median family income of the applicable State for a family of the same number or fewer individuals; or

(C) in the case of a debtor in a household exceeding 4 individuals, the highest median family income of the applicable State for a family of 4 or fewer individuals, plus $675[1] per month for each individual in excess of 4.

(4) For purposes of this subsection, the "applicable commitment period"—

(A) subject to subparagraph (B), shall be—

(i) 3 years; or

---

[1] Dollar amount as adjusted by the Judicial Conference of the United States. See Adjustment of Dollar Amounts notes set out under this section and 11 U.S.C.A. § 104.

(ii) not less than 5 years, if the current monthly income of the debtor and the debtor's spouse combined, when multiplied by 12, is not less than—

(I) in the case of a debtor in a household of 1 person, the median family income of the applicable State for 1 earner;

(II) in the case of a debtor in a household of 2, 3, or 4 individuals, the highest median family income of the applicable State for a family of the same number or fewer individuals; or

(III) in the case of a debtor in a household exceeding 4 individuals, the highest median family income of the applicable State for a family of 4 or fewer individuals, plus $675[1] per month for each individual in excess of 4; and

(B) may be less than 3 or 5 years, whichever is applicable under subparagraph (A), but only if the plan provides for payment in full of all allowed unsecured claims over a shorter period.

(c) After confirmation of a plan, the court may order any entity from whom the debtor receives income to pay all or any part of such income to the trustee.

(Pub.L. 95–598, Nov. 6, 1978, 92 Stat. 2649; Pub.L. 98–353, Title III, §§ 317, 530, July 10, 1984, 98 Stat. 356, 389; Pub.L. 99–554, Title II, § 283(y), Oct. 27, 1986, 100 Stat. 3118; Pub.L. 105–183, § 4(a), June 19, 1998, 112 Stat. 518; Pub.L. 109–8, Title I, § 102(g), (h), Title II, § 213(10), Title III, §§ 306(a), (b), 309(c)(1), 318(2), (3), Title VII, § 716(a), Apr. 20, 2005, 119 Stat. 33, 53, 80, 83, 93 129; Pub.L. 109–439, § 2, Dec. 20, 2006, 120 Stat. 3285; Pub.L. 111–327, § 2(a)(44), Dec. 22, 2010, 124 Stat. 3562.)

HISTORICAL AND STATUTORY NOTES

Amendments

2010 Amendments. Subsec. (a). Pub.L. 111–327, § 2(a)(44)(A), in the undesignated matter at the end, inserted "period" after "910-day".

Subsec. (b)(2)(A)(ii). Pub.L. 111–327, § 2(a)(44)(B), struck out "548(d)(3)" and inserted "548(d)(3))".

2006 Amendments. Subsec. (b)(3). Pub.L. 109–439, § 2, inserted ", other than subparagraph (A)(ii) of paragraph (2)," after "paragraph (2)".

2005 Amendments. Subsec. (a). Pub.L. 109–8, § 306(b), added "For purposes of paragraph (5), section 506 shall not apply to a claim described in that paragraph if the creditor has a purchase money security interest securing the debt that is the subject of the claim, the debt was incurred within the 910-day preceding the date of the filing of the petition, and the collateral for that debt consists of a motor vehicle (as defined in section 30102 of title 49) acquired for the personal use of the debtor, or if collateral for that debt consists of any other thing of value, if the debt was incurred during the 1-year period preceding that filing." to the end of subsec. (a).

Subsec. (a)(5). Pub.L. 109–8, § 102(g)(1), struck "and" at the end of par. (5).

Subsec. (a)(5)(B)(i). Pub.L. 109–8, § 306(a), rewrote cl. (i), which formerly read: "the plan provides that the holder of such claim retain the lien securing such claim; and".

Pub.L. 109–8, § 309(c)(1)(A), struck out "and" at the end of cl. (i).

Subsec. (a)(5)(B)(ii). Pub.L. 109–8, § 309(c)(1)(B), struck out "or" at the end of cl. (ii) and inserted "and".

Subsec. (a)(5)(B)(iii). Pub.L. 109–8, § 309(c)(1)(C), added cl. (iii).

Subsec. (a)(6). Pub.L. 109–8, § 102(g)(2), struck the period at the end of par. (6) and inserted a semicolon.

Subsec. (a)(7). Pub.L. 109–8, § 102(g)(3), added par. (7).

Subsec. (a)(8). Pub.L. 109–8, § 213(10), added par. (8).

---

[1] Dollar amount as adjusted by the Judicial Conference of the United States. See Adjustment of Dollar Amounts notes set out under this section and 11 U.S.C.A. § 104.

Subsec. (a)(9). Pub.L. 109–8, § 716(a), added par. (9).

Subsec. (b)(1)(B). Pub.L. 109–8, § 102(h)(1), inserted "to unsecured creditors" after "to make payments".

Pub.L. 109–8, § 318(2), struck out "three-year period" and inserted "applicable commitment period".

Subsec. (b)(2). Pub.L. 109–8, § 102(h)(2), rewrote par. (2), which formerly read:

"(2) For purposes of this subsection, 'disposable income' means income which is received by the debtor and which is not reasonably necessary to be expended—

"(A) for the maintenance or support of the debtor or a dependent of the debtor, including charitable contributions (that meet the definition of 'charitable contribution' under section 548(d)(3)) to a qualified religious or charitable entity or organization (as that term is defined in section 548(d)(4)) in an amount not to exceed 15 percent of the gross income of the debtor for the year in which the contributions are made; and

"(B) if the debtor is engaged in business, for the payment of expenditures necessary for the continuation, preservation, and operation of such business."

Subsec. (b)(3). Pub.L. 109–8, § 102(h)(2), added par. (3).

Subsec. (b)(4). Pub.L. 109–8, § 318(3), added par. (4).

1998 Amendments. Subsec. (b)(2)(A). Pub.L. 105–183, § 4(a), inserted before the semicolon ", including charitable contributions (that meet the definition of 'charitable contribution' under section 548(d)(3)) to a qualified religious or charitable entity or organization (as that term is defined in section 548(d)(4)) in an amount not to exceed 15 percent of the gross income of the debtor for the year in which the contributions are made".

1986 Amendments. Subsec. (b)(2)(A). Pub.L. 99–554 substituted "; and" for "; or".

1984 Amendments. Subsec. (a). Pub.L. 98–353, § 317(1), substituted "Except as provided in subsection (b), the" for "The".

Subsec. (a)(1). Pub.L. 98–353, § 530, added "the" before "other".

Subsec. (b). Pub.L. 98–353, § 317(3), added subsec. (b). Former subsec. (b) was redesignated as (c).

Subsec. (c). Pub.L. 98–353, § 317(2), redesignated former subsec. (b) as (c).

Adjustment of Dollar Amounts

For adjustment of dollar amounts specified in subsec. (b)(3) and (4) of this section by the Judicial Conference of the United States, see note set out under 11 U.S.C.A. § 104.

Rule of Construction

Amendments made by Pub.L. 105–183 not intended to limit the applicability of the Religious Freedom Restoration Act of 1993 (42 U.S.C. 2002bb et seq.), see Pub.L. 105–183, § 6, June 19, 1998, 112 Stat. 519, set out as a note under section 544 of this title.

CROSS REFERENCES

Confirmation of plan in—
- Chapter eleven cases, see 11 USCA § 1129.
- Chapter nine cases, see 11 USCA § 943.
- Chapter twelve cases, see 11 USCA § 1225.
- Railroad reorganization cases, see 11 USCA § 1173.

Conversion or dismissal, see 11 USCA § 1307.

§ 1326. Payments

(a)(1) Unless the court orders otherwise, the debtor shall commence making payments not later than 30 days after the date of the filing of the plan or the order for relief, whichever is earlier, in the amount—

    (A) proposed by the plan to the trustee;

    (B) scheduled in a lease of personal property directly to the lessor for that portion of the obligation that becomes due after the order for relief, reducing the payments under subparagraph (A) by the amount so paid and providing the trustee with evidence of such payment, including the amount and date of payment; and

    (C) that provides adequate protection directly to a creditor holding an allowed claim secured by personal property to the extent the claim is attributable to the purchase of such property by the debtor for that portion of the obligation that becomes due after the order for relief, reducing the payments under subparagraph (A) by the amount so paid and providing the trustee with evidence of such payment, including the amount and date of payment.

(2) A payment made under paragraph (1)(A) shall be retained by the trustee until confirmation or denial of confirmation. If a plan is confirmed, the trustee shall distribute any such payment in accordance with the plan as soon as is practicable. If a plan is not confirmed, the trustee shall return any such payments not previously paid and not yet due and owing to creditors pursuant to paragraph (3) to the debtor, after deducting any unpaid claim allowed under section 503(b).

(3) Subject to section 363, the court may, upon notice and a hearing, modify, increase, or reduce the payments required under this subsection pending confirmation of a plan.

(4) Not later than 60 days after the date of filing of a case under this chapter, a debtor retaining possession of personal property subject to a lease or securing a claim attributable in whole or in part to the purchase price of such property shall provide the lessor or secured creditor reasonable evidence of the maintenance of any required insurance coverage with respect to the use or ownership of such property and continue to do so for so long as the debtor retains possession of such property.

(b) Before or at the time of each payment to creditors under the plan, there shall be paid—

    (1) any unpaid claim of the kind specified in section 507(a)(2) of this title;

    (2) if a standing trustee appointed under section 586(b) of title 28 is serving in the case, the percentage fee fixed for such standing trustee under section 586(e)(1)(B) of title 28; and

    (3) if a chapter 7 trustee has been allowed compensation due to the conversion or dismissal of the debtor's prior case pursuant to section 707(b), and some portion of that compensation remains unpaid in a case converted to this chapter or in the case dismissed under section 707(b) and refiled under this chapter, the amount of any such unpaid compensation, which shall be paid monthly—

        (A) by prorating such amount over the remaining duration of the plan; and

        (B) by monthly payments not to exceed the greater of—

            (i) $25[1]; or

            (ii) the amount payable to unsecured nonpriority creditors, as provided by the plan, multiplied by 5 percent, and the result divided by the number of months in the plan.

(c) Except as otherwise provided in the plan or in the order confirming the plan, the trustee shall make payments to creditors under the plan.

(d) Notwithstanding any other provision of this title—

---

[1] Dollar amount as adjusted by the Judicial Conference of the United States. See Adjustment of Dollar Amounts notes set out under this section and 11 U.S.C.A. § 104.

(1) compensation referred to in subsection (b)(3) is payable and may be collected by the trustee under that paragraph, even if such amount has been discharged in a prior case under this title; and

(2) such compensation is payable in a case under this chapter only to the extent permitted by subsection (b)(3).

(Pub.L. 95–598, Nov. 6, 1978, 92 Stat. 2650; Pub.L. 98–353, Title III, §§ 318(a), 531, July 10, 1984, 98 Stat. 357, 389; Pub.L. 99–554, Title II, §§ 230, 283(z), Oct. 27, 1986, 100 Stat. 3103, 3118; Pub.L. 103–394, Title III, § 307, Oct. 22, 1994, 108 Stat. 4135; Pub.L. 109–8, Title III, § 309(c)(2), Title XII, § 1224, Title XV, § 1502(a)(10), Apr. 20, 2005, 119 Stat. 83, 199, 217.)

HISTORICAL AND STATUTORY NOTES

Amendments

2005 Amendments. Subsec. (a). Pub.L. 109–8, § 309(c)(2), rewrote subsec. (a), which formerly read:

"(a)(1) Unless the court orders otherwise, the debtor shall commence making the payments proposed by a plan within 30 days after the plan is filed.

"(2) A payment made under this subsection shall be retained by the trustee until confirmation or denial of confirmation of a plan. If a plan is confirmed, the trustee shall distribute any such payment in accordance with the plan as soon as practicable. If a plan is not confirmed, the trustee shall return any such payment to the debtor, after deducting any unpaid claim allowed under section 503(b) of this title."

Subsec. (b). Pub.L.109–8, § 1224(1), struck out "and" at the end of par. (1), struck out the period at the end of par. (2) and inserted "; and", and added par. (3).

Subsec. (b)(1). Pub.L. 109–8, § 1502(a)(10), struck out "507(a)(1)" and inserted "507(a)(2)".

Subsec. (d). Pub.L.109–8, § 1224(2), added subsec. (d).

1994 Amendments. Subsec. (a)(2). Pub.L. 103–394, § 307, added provisions directing trustee to distribute payment as soon as practicable.

1986 Amendments. Subsec. (a)(2). Pub.L. 99–554, 283(z), substituted "payment" for "payments" in last sentence.

Subsec. (b)(2). Pub.L. 99–554, § 230, substituted "586(b) of title 28" for "1302(d) of this title" and "586(e)(1)(B) of title 28" for "1302(e) of this title".

1984 Amendments. Subsec. (a). Pub.L. 98–353, § 318(a)(2), added subsec. (a). Former subsec. (a) was redesignated as (b).

Subsec. (b). Pub.L. 98–353, § 318(a)(1), redesignated former subsec. (a) as (b). Former subsec. (b) was redesignated as (c).

Subsec. (b)(2). Pub.L. 98–353, § 531, added "of this title" after "1302(d)".

Subsec. (c). Pub.L. 98–353, § 318(a)(1), redesignated former subsec. (b) as (c).

Adjustment of Dollar Amounts

For adjustment of dollar amounts specified in subsec. (b)(3)(B) of this section by the Judicial Conference of the United States, see note set out under 11 U.S.C.A. § 104.

CROSS REFERENCES

Conversion or dismissal for failure to commence making timely payments under this section, see 11 USCA § 1307.

Duty of trustee to ensure that debtor commences making timely payments under this section, see 11 USCA § 1302.

Payment stopped on checks remaining unpaid 90 days after final distribution, see 11 USCA § 347.

§ 1327. Effect of confirmation

(a) The provisions of a confirmed plan bind the debtor and each creditor, whether or not the claim of such creditor is provided for by the plan, and whether or not such creditor has objected to, has accepted, or has rejected the plan.

(b) Except as otherwise provided in the plan or the order confirming the plan, the confirmation of a plan vests all of the property of the estate in the debtor.

(c) Except as otherwise provided in the plan or in the order confirming the plan, the property vesting in the debtor under subsection (b) of this section is free and clear of any claim or interest of any creditor provided for by the plan.

(Pub.L. 95–598, Nov. 6, 1978, 92 Stat. 2650.)

CROSS REFERENCES

Effect of confirmation in—

    Chapter eleven cases, see 11 USCA § 1141.

    Chapter nine cases, see 11 USCA § 944.

    Chapter twelve cases, see 11 USCA § 1227.

§ 1328. Discharge

(a) Subject to subsection (d), as soon as practicable after completion by the debtor of all payments under the plan, and in the case of a debtor who is required by a judicial or administrative order, or by statute, to pay a domestic support obligation, after such debtor certifies that all amounts payable under such order or such statute that are due on or before the date of the certification (including amounts due before the petition was filed, but only to the extent provided for by the plan) have been paid, unless the court approves a written waiver of discharge executed by the debtor after the order for relief under this chapter, the court shall grant the debtor a discharge of all debts provided for by the plan or disallowed under section 502 of this title, except any debt—

    (1) provided for under section 1322(b)(5);

    (2) of the kind specified in section 507(a)(8)(C) or in paragraph (1)(B), (1)(C), (2), (3), (4), (5), (8), or (9) of section 523(a);

    (3) for restitution, or a criminal fine, included in a sentence on the debtor's conviction of a crime; or

    (4) for restitution, or damages, awarded in a civil action against the debtor as a result of willful or malicious injury by the debtor that caused personal injury to an individual or the death of an individual.

(b) Subject to subsection (d), at any time after the confirmation of the plan and after notice and a hearing, the court may grant a discharge to a debtor that has not completed payments under the plan only if—

    (1) the debtor's failure to complete such payments is due to circumstances for which the debtor should not justly be held accountable;

    (2) the value, as of the effective date of the plan, of property actually distributed under the plan on account of each allowed unsecured claim is not less than the amount that would have been paid on such claim if the estate of the debtor had been liquidated under chapter 7 of this title on such date; and

    (3) modification of the plan under section 1329 of this title is not practicable.

(c) A discharge granted under subsection (b) of this section discharges the debtor from all unsecured debts provided for by the plan or disallowed under section 502 of this title, except any debt—

(1) provided for under section 1322(b)(5) of this title; or

(2) of a kind specified in section 523(a) of this title.

(d) Notwithstanding any other provision of this section, a discharge granted under this section does not discharge the debtor from any debt based on an allowed claim filed under section 1305(a)(2) of this title if prior approval by the trustee of the debtor's incurring such debt was practicable and was not obtained.

(e) On request of a party in interest before one year after a discharge under this section is granted, and after notice and a hearing, the court may revoke such discharge only if—

(1) such discharge was obtained by the debtor through fraud; and

(2) the requesting party did not know of such fraud until after such discharge was granted.

(f) Notwithstanding subsections (a) and (b), the court shall not grant a discharge of all debts provided for in the plan or disallowed under section 502, if the debtor has received a discharge—

(1) in a case filed under chapter 7, 11, or 12 of this title during the 4-year period preceding the date of the order for relief under this chapter, or

(2) in a case filed under chapter 13 of this title during the 2-year period preceding the date of such order.

(g)(1) The court shall not grant a discharge under this section to a debtor unless after filing a petition the debtor has completed an instructional course concerning personal financial management described in section 111.

(2) Paragraph (1) shall not apply with respect to a debtor who is a person described in section 109(h)(4) or who resides in a district for which the United States trustee (or the bankruptcy administrator, if any) determines that the approved instructional courses are not adequate to service the additional individuals who would otherwise be required to complete such instructional course by reason of the requirements of paragraph (1).

(3) The United States trustee (or the bankruptcy administrator, if any) who makes a determination described in paragraph (2) shall review such determination not later than 1 year after the date of such determination, and not less frequently than annually thereafter.

(h) The court may not grant a discharge under this chapter unless the court after notice and a hearing held not more than 10 days before the date of the entry of the order granting the discharge finds that there is no reasonable cause to believe that—

(1) section 522(q)(1) may be applicable to the debtor; and

(2) there is pending any proceeding in which the debtor may be found guilty of a felony of the kind described in section 522(q)(1)(A) or liable for a debt of the kind described in section 522(q)(1)(B).

(Pub.L. 95–598, Nov. 6, 1978, 92 Stat. 2650; Pub.L. 98–353, Title III, § 532, July 10, 1984, 98 Stat. 389; Pub.L. 101–508, Title III, § 3007(b)(1), Nov. 5, 1990, 104 Stat. 1388–28; Pub.L. 101–581, §§ 2(b), 3, Nov. 15, 1990, 104 Stat. 2865; Pub.L. 101–647, Title XXXI, §§ 3102(b), 3103, Nov. 29, 1990, 104 Stat. 4916; Pub.L. 103–394, Title III, § 302, Title V, § 501(d)(38), Oct. 22, 1994, 108 Stat. 4132, 4147; Pub.L. 109–8, Title I, § 106(c), Title II, § 213(11), Title III, §§ 312(2), 314(b), 330(d), Title VII, § 707, Apr. 20, 2005, 119 Stat. 38, 53, 87, 88, 102, 126.)

HISTORICAL AND STATUTORY NOTES

Codifications

Pub.L. 101–581, §§ 2(b), 3(1) to (3) and Pub.L. 101–647, §§ 3102(b), 3103(1)–(3), contained identical amendments to subsec. (a)(2) and (a)(1)–(3) of this section.

Amendments by Pub.L. 101–581, § 2(b), and Pub.L. 101–647, § 3102(b), which both inserted "or 523(a)(9)" following "523(a)(5)", were incapable of literal execution in view of prior amendment by Pub.L.

101–508, which substituted "paragraph (5) or (8) of section 523(a)" for "section 523(a)(5)", thereby deleting language subsequently amended. See also 1990 Amendments note set out under this section.

Amendments

2005 Amendments. Subsec. (a). Pub.L. 109–8, § 213(11), inserted ", and in the case of a debtor who is required by a judicial or administrative order, or by statute, to pay a domestic support obligation, after such debtor certifies that all amounts payable under such order or such statute that are due on or before the date of the certification (including amounts due before the petition was filed, but only to the extent provided for by the plan) have been paid" after "completion by the debtor of all payments under the plan".

Pub.L. 109–8, § 330(d)(1), struck out "As" and inserted "Subject to subsection (d), as".

Pub.L. 109–8, § 314(b), struck out former pars. (1) through (3) of subsec. (a) and inserted new pars. (1) to (4). Prior to deletion, pars. (1) to (3) read:

"**(1)** provided for under section 1322(b)(5) of this title;

"**(2)** of the kind specified in paragraph (5), (8), or (9) of section 523(a) of this title; or

"**(3)** for restitution, or a criminal fine, included in a sentence on the debtor's conviction of a crime."

Subsec. (a)(2). Pub.L. 109–8, § 707, struck out "paragraph" and inserted "section 507(a)(8)(C) or in paragraph (1)(B), (1)(C),".

Subsec. (b). Pub.L. 109–8, § 330(d)(2), struck out "At" and inserted "Subject to subsection (d), at".

Subsec. (f). Pub.L. 109–8, § 312(2), added subsec. (f).

Subsec. (g). Pub.L. 109–8, § 106(c), added subsec. (g).

Subsec. (h). Pub.L. 109–8, § 330(d)(3), added subsec. (h).

1994 Amendments. Subsec. (a)(2). Pub.L. 103–394, § 501(d)(38)(A), substituted "(5), (8), or (9)" for "(5) or (8)".

Subsec. (a)(3). Pub.L. 103–394, § 302, added provisions excluding any debt for a criminal fine from the debts the court shall grant discharge of.

Pub.L. 103–394, § 501(d)(38)(B), struck out par. (3) as added by Pub.L. 101–647, § 3103(3), requiring no change in text. See 1990 Amendment notes set out under this section.

1990 Amendments. Subsec. (a)(1). Pub.L. 101–581, § 3(1), and Pub.L. 101–647, § 3103(1), made identical amendments striking "or" at end.

Subsec. (a)(2). Pub.L. 101–581, § 3(2), and Pub.L. 101–647, § 3103(2), made identical amendments substituting "; or" for period at end.

Pub.L. 101–581, § 2(b), and Pub.L. 101–647, § 3102(b), which directed identical insertions of "or 523(a)(9)" after "523(a)(5)", could not be executed because of a prior amendment by Pub.L. 101–508. See amendment note set out under this section.

Pub.L. 101–508, §§ 3007(b)(1), 3008, temporarily substituted "paragraph (5) or (8) of section 523(a)" for "section 523(a)(5)". See Effective and Applicability Provisions of 1990 Amendments note under this section.

Subsec. (a)(3). Pub.L. 101–581, § 3(3), and Pub.L. 101–647, § 3103(3), made identical amendments adding par. (3).

1984 Amendments. Subsec. (e)(1). Pub.L. 98–353, § 532(1), added "by the debtor" after "obtained".

Subsec. (e)(2). Pub.L. 98–353, § 532(2), substituted "the requesting party did not know of such fraud until" for "knowledge of such fraud came to the requesting party".

CROSS REFERENCES

Cancellation of indebtedness from discharged farm loans, see 12 USCA § 1150.

Discharge in—
    Chapter seven cases, see 11 USCA § 727.
    Chapter twelve cases, see 11 USCA § 1228.

Effect of, discharge, see 11 USCA § 524.

Exceptions to discharge, see 11 USCA § 523.

Nondischargeability of capital improvement loans for multifamily housing projects in proceedings under this section, see 12 USCA § 1715z–1a.

§ 1329. Modification of plan after confirmation

(a) At any time after confirmation of the plan but before the completion of payments under such plan, the plan may be modified, upon request of the debtor, the trustee, or the holder of an allowed unsecured claim, to—

(1) increase or reduce the amount of payments on claims of a particular class provided for by the plan;

(2) extend or reduce the time for such payments;

(3) alter the amount of the distribution to a creditor whose claim is provided for by the plan to the extent necessary to take account of any payment of such claim other than under the plan; or

(4) reduce amounts to be paid under the plan by the actual amount expended by the debtor to purchase health insurance for the debtor (and for any dependent of the debtor if such dependent does not otherwise have health insurance coverage) if the debtor documents the cost of such insurance and demonstrates that—

(A) such expenses are reasonable and necessary;

(B)(i) if the debtor previously paid for health insurance, the amount is not materially larger than the cost the debtor previously paid or the cost necessary to maintain the lapsed policy; or

(ii) if the debtor did not have health insurance, the amount is not materially larger than the reasonable cost that would be incurred by a debtor who purchases health insurance, who has similar income, expenses, age, and health status, and who lives in the same geographical location with the same number of dependents who do not otherwise have health insurance coverage; and

(C) the amount is not otherwise allowed for purposes of determining disposable income under section 1325(b) of this title;

and upon request of any party in interest, files proof that a health insurance policy was purchased.

(b)(1) Sections 1322(a), 1322(b), and 1323(c) of this title and the requirements of section 1325(a) of this title apply to any modification under subsection (a) of this section.

(2) The plan as modified becomes the plan unless, after notice and a hearing, such modification is disapproved.

(c) A plan modified under this section may not provide for payments over a period that expires after the applicable commitment period under section 1325(b)(1)(B) after the time that the first payment under the original confirmed plan was due, unless the court, for cause, approves a longer period, but the court may not approve a period that expires after five years after such time.

(Pub.L. 95–598, Nov. 6, 1978, 92 Stat. 2651; Pub.L. 98–353, Title III, §§ 319, 533, July 10, 1984, 98 Stat. 357, 389; Pub.L. 109–8, Title I, § 102(i), Title III, § 318(4), Apr. 20, 2005, 119 Stat. 34, 94.)

HISTORICAL AND STATUTORY NOTES

Amendments

2005 Amendments. Subsec. (a)(2). Pub.L. 109–8, § 102(i)(1), struck out "or" at the end.

Subsec. (a)(3). Pub.L. 109–8, § 102(i)(2), struck out the period and inserted "; or".

Subsec. (a)(4). Pub.L. 109–8, § 102(i)(3), added par. (4).

Subsec. (c). Pub.L. 109–8, § 318(4), struck out "three years" and inserted "the applicable commitment period under section 1325(b)(1)(B)".

1984 Amendments. Subsec. (a). Pub.L. 98–353, § 319, added provisions respecting requests by the debtor, the trustee, or the holder of an allowed unsecured claim for modification.

Pub.L. 98–353, § 533(1), added "of the plan" after "confirmation".

Pub.L. 98–353, § 533(2), substituted "such plan" for "a plan".

Subsec. (a)(3). Pub.L. 98–353, § 533(3), substituted "plan to" for "plan, to".

CROSS REFERENCES

Conversion or dismissal upon denial of confirmation of modified plan, see 11 USCA § 1307.

Duties of United States trustee, see 28 USCA § 586.

Modification of plan in—

    Chapter eleven cases, see 11 USCA § 1127.

    Chapter nine cases, see 11 USCA § 942.

    Chapter twelve cases, see 11 USCA § 1229.

§ 1330. Revocation of an order of confirmation

(a) On request of a party in interest at any time within 180 days after the date of the entry of an order of confirmation under section 1325 of this title, and after notice and a hearing, the court may revoke such order if such order was procured by fraud.

(b) If the court revokes an order of confirmation under subsection (a) of this section, the court shall dispose of the case under section 1307 of this title, unless, within the time fixed by the court, the debtor proposes and the court confirms a modification of the plan under section 1329 of this title.

(Pub.L. 95–598, Nov. 6, 1978, 92 Stat. 2651.)

CROSS REFERENCES

Conversion or dismissal upon revocation of order of confirmation, see 11 USCA § 1307.

Revocation of order of confirmation in—

    Chapter eleven cases, see 11 USCA § 1144.

    Chapter twelve cases, see 11 USCA § 1230.

CHAPTER 15—ANCILLARY AND OTHER CROSS-BORDER CASES

Sec.
1501. Purpose and scope of application.

SUBCHAPTER I—GENERAL PROVISIONS

1502. Definitions.
1503. International obligations of the United States.
1504. Commencement of ancillary case.
1505. Authorization to act in a foreign country.
1506. Public policy exception.
1507. Additional assistance.
1508. Interpretation.

SUBCHAPTER II—ACCESS OF FOREIGN REPRESENTATIVES AND CREDITORS TO THE COURT

1509. Right of direct access.
1510. Limited jurisdiction.
1511. Commencement of case under section 301 or 303[1].
1512. Participation of a foreign representative in a case under this title.
1513. Access of foreign creditors to a case under this title.
1514. Notification to foreign creditors concerning a case under this title.

SUBCHAPTER III—RECOGNITION OF A FOREIGN PROCEEDING AND RELIEF

1515. Application for recognition.
1516. Presumptions concerning recognition.
1517. Order granting recognition.
1518. Subsequent information.
1519. Relief that may be granted upon filing petition for recognition.
1520. Effects of recognition of a foreign main proceeding.
1521. Relief that may be granted upon recognition.
1522. Protection of creditors and other interested persons.
1523. Actions to avoid acts detrimental to creditors.
1524. Intervention by a foreign representative.

SUBCHAPTER IV—COOPERATION WITH FOREIGN COURTS AND FOREIGN REPRESENTATIVES

1525. Cooperation and direct communication between the court and foreign courts or foreign representatives.
1526. Cooperation and direct communication between the trustee and foreign courts or foreign representatives.
1527. Forms of cooperation.

SUBCHAPTER V—CONCURRENT PROCEEDINGS

1528. Commencement of a case under this title after recognition of a foreign main proceeding.
1529. Coordination of a case under this title and a foreign proceeding.
1530. Coordination of more than 1 foreign proceeding.
1531. Presumption of insolvency based on recognition of a foreign main proceeding.
1532. Rule of payment in concurrent proceedings.

HISTORICAL AND STATUTORY NOTES

Prior Provisions

A prior chapter 15, consisting of sections 1501 to 151326, related to a pilot program for a United States trustee system, prior to repeal by Pub.L. 99–554, Title II, § 231, Oct. 27, 1986, 100 Stat. 3103.

---

[1] So in original. Item does not conform to section catchline.

§ 1501. Purpose and scope of application

(a) The purpose of this chapter is to incorporate the Model Law on Cross-Border Insolvency so as to provide effective mechanisms for dealing with cases of cross-border insolvency with the objectives of—

(1) cooperation between—

(A) courts of the United States, United States trustees, trustees, examiners, debtors, and debtors in possession; and

(B) the courts and other competent authorities of foreign countries involved in cross-border insolvency cases;

(2) greater legal certainty for trade and investment;

(3) fair and efficient administration of cross-border insolvencies that protects the interests of all creditors, and other interested entities, including the debtor;

(4) protection and maximization of the value of the debtor's assets; and

(5) facilitation of the rescue of financially troubled businesses, thereby protecting investment and preserving employment.

(b) This chapter applies where—

(1) assistance is sought in the United States by a foreign court or a foreign representative in connection with a foreign proceeding;

(2) assistance is sought in a foreign country in connection with a case under this title;

(3) a foreign proceeding and a case under this title with respect to the same debtor are pending concurrently; or

(4) creditors or other interested persons in a foreign country have an interest in requesting the commencement of, or participating in, a case or proceeding under this title.

(c) This chapter does not apply to—

(1) a proceeding concerning an entity, other than a foreign insurance company, identified by exclusion in section 109(b);

(2) an individual, or to an individual and such individual's spouse, who have debts within the limits specified in section 109(e) and who are citizens of the United States or aliens lawfully admitted for permanent residence in the United States; or

(3) an entity subject to a proceeding under the Securities Investor Protection Act of 1970, a stockbroker subject to subchapter III of chapter 7 of this title, or a commodity broker subject to subchapter IV of chapter 7 of this title.

(d) The court may not grant relief under this chapter with respect to any deposit, escrow, trust fund, or other security required or permitted under any applicable State insurance law or regulation for the benefit of claim holders in the United States.

(Added Pub.L. 109–8, Title VIII, § 801(a), Apr. 20, 2005, 119 Stat. 135.)

HISTORICAL AND STATUTORY NOTES

References in Text

The Securities Investor Protection Act of 1970, referred to in subsec. (c)(3), is Pub.L. 91–598, Dec. 30, 1970, 84 Stat. 1636, also known as SIPA, which is classified principally to chapter 2B–1 of Title 15, 15 U.S.C.A. § 78aaa et seq.

Prior Provisions

Prior section 1501, Pub.L. 95–598, Title I, § 101, Nov. 6, 1978, 92 Stat. 2652, set forth applicability of chapter, which provided a pilot program for a United States trustee system, and was repealed by Pub.L.

99–554, Title II, § 231, Oct. 27, 1986, 100 Stat. 3103, effective 30 days after Oct. 27, 1986, except as otherwise provided for, see Pub.L. 99–554, § 302, set out as a note under 28 U.S.C.A. § 581.

SUBCHAPTER I—GENERAL PROVISIONS

§ 1502. Definitions

For the purposes of this chapter, the term—

  (1) "debtor" means an entity that is the subject of a foreign proceeding;

  (2) "establishment" means any place of operations where the debtor carries out a nontransitory economic activity;

  (3) "foreign court" means a judicial or other authority competent to control or supervise a foreign proceeding;

  (4) "foreign main proceeding" means a foreign proceeding pending in the country where the debtor has the center of its main interests;

  (5) "foreign nonmain proceeding" means a foreign proceeding, other than a foreign main proceeding, pending in a country where the debtor has an establishment;

  (6) "trustee" includes a trustee, a debtor in possession in a case under any chapter of this title, or a debtor under chapter 9 of this title;

  (7) "recognition" means the entry of an order granting recognition of a foreign main proceeding or foreign nonmain proceeding under this chapter; and

  (8) "within the territorial jurisdiction of the United States", when used with reference to property of a debtor, refers to tangible property located within the territory of the United States and intangible property deemed under applicable nonbankruptcy law to be located within that territory, including any property subject to attachment or garnishment that may properly be seized or garnished by an action in a Federal or State court in the United States.

(Added Pub.L. 109–8, Title VIII, § 801(a), Apr. 20, 2005, 119 Stat. 135.)

§ 1503. International obligations of the United States

To the extent that this chapter conflicts with an obligation of the United States arising out of any treaty or other form of agreement to which it is a party with one or more other countries, the requirements of the treaty or agreement prevail.

(Added Pub.L. 109–8, Title VIII, § 801(a), Apr. 20, 2005, 119 Stat. 136.)

§ 1504. Commencement of ancillary case

A case under this chapter is commenced by the filing of a petition for recognition of a foreign proceeding under section 1515.

(Added Pub.L. 109–8, Title VIII, § 801(a), Apr. 20, 2005, 119 Stat. 136.)

§ 1505. Authorization to act in a foreign country

A trustee or another entity (including an examiner) may be authorized by the court to act in a foreign country on behalf of an estate created under section 541. An entity authorized to act under this section may act in any way permitted by the applicable foreign law.

(Added Pub.L. 109–8, Title VIII, § 801(a), Apr. 20, 2005, 119 Stat. 136.)

§ 1506. Public policy exception

Nothing in this chapter prevents the court from refusing to take an action governed by this chapter if the action would be manifestly contrary to the public policy of the United States.

(Added Pub.L. 109–8, Title VIII, § 801(a), Apr. 20, 2005, 119 Stat. 136.)

§ 1507. Additional assistance

(a) Subject to the specific limitations stated elsewhere in this chapter the court, if recognition is granted, may provide additional assistance to a foreign representative under this title or under other laws of the United States.

(b) In determining whether to provide additional assistance under this title or under other laws of the United States, the court shall consider whether such additional assistance, consistent with the principles of comity, will reasonably assure—

(1) just treatment of all holders of claims against or interests in the debtor's property;

(2) protection of claim holders in the United States against prejudice and inconvenience in the processing of claims in such foreign proceeding;

(3) prevention of preferential or fraudulent dispositions of property of the debtor;

(4) distribution of proceeds of the debtor's property substantially in accordance with the order prescribed by this title; and

(5) if appropriate, the provision of an opportunity for a fresh start for the individual that such foreign proceeding concerns.

(Added Pub.L. 109–8, Title VIII, § 801(a), Apr. 20, 2005, 119 Stat. 136.)

§ 1508. Interpretation

In interpreting this chapter, the court shall consider its international origin, and the need to promote an application of this chapter that is consistent with the application of similar statutes adopted by foreign jurisdictions.

(Added Pub.L. 109–8, Title VIII, § 801(a), Apr. 20, 2005, 119 Stat. 137.)

SUBCHAPTER II—ACCESS OF FOREIGN REPRESENTATIVES AND CREDITORS TO THE COURT

§ 1509. Right of direct access

(a) A foreign representative may commence a case under section 1504 by filing directly with the court a petition for recognition of a foreign proceeding under section 1515.

(b) If the court grants recognition under section 1517, and subject to any limitations that the court may impose consistent with the policy of this chapter—

(1) the foreign representative has the capacity to sue and be sued in a court in the United States;

(2) the foreign representative may apply directly to a court in the United States for appropriate relief in that court; and

(3) a court in the United States shall grant comity or cooperation to the foreign representative.

(c) A request for comity or cooperation by a foreign representative in a court in the United States other than the court which granted recognition shall be accompanied by a certified copy of an order granting recognition under section 1517.

(d) If the court denies recognition under this chapter, the court may issue any appropriate order necessary to prevent the foreign representative from obtaining comity or cooperation from courts in the United States.

(e) Whether or not the court grants recognition, and subject to sections 306 and 1510, a foreign representative is subject to applicable nonbankruptcy law.

(f) Notwithstanding any other provision of this section, the failure of a foreign representative to commence a case or to obtain recognition under this chapter does not affect any right the foreign representative may have to sue in a court in the United States to collect or recover a claim which is the property of the debtor.

(Added Pub.L. 109–8, Title VIII, § 801(a), Apr. 20, 2005, 119 Stat. 137.)

§ 1510. Limited jurisdiction

The sole fact that a foreign representative files a petition under section 1515 does not subject the foreign representative to the jurisdiction of any court in the United States for any other purpose.

(Added Pub.L. 109–8, Title VIII, § 801(a), Apr. 20, 2005, 119 Stat. 138.)

§ 1511. Commencement of case under section 301, 302, or 303

(a) Upon recognition, a foreign representative may commence—

   (1) an involuntary case under section 303; or

   (2) a voluntary case under section 301 or 302, if the foreign proceeding is a foreign main proceeding.

(b) The petition commencing a case under subsection (a) must be accompanied by a certified copy of an order granting recognition. The court where the petition for recognition has been filed must be advised of the foreign representative's intent to commence a case under subsection (a) prior to such commencement.

(Added Pub.L. 109–8, Title VIII, § 801(a), Apr. 20, 2005, 119 Stat. 138; amended Pub.L. 111–327, § 2(a)(45), Dec. 22, 2010, 124 Stat. 3562.)

HISTORICAL AND STATUTORY NOTES

Amendments

2010 Amendments. Section heading. Pub.L. 111–327, § 2(a)(45), inserted ", 302," following "301".

§ 1512. Participation of a foreign representative in a case under this title

Upon recognition of a foreign proceeding, the foreign representative in the recognized proceeding is entitled to participate as a party in interest in a case regarding the debtor under this title.

(Added Pub.L. 109–8, Title VIII, § 801(a), Apr. 20, 2005, 119 Stat. 138.)

§ 1513. Access of foreign creditors to a case under this title

(a) Foreign creditors have the same rights regarding the commencement of, and participation in, a case under this title as domestic creditors.

(b)(1) Subsection (a) does not change or codify present law as to the priority of claims under section 507 or 726, except that the claim of a foreign creditor under those sections shall not be given a lower priority than that of general unsecured claims without priority solely because the holder of such claim is a foreign creditor.

(2)(A) Subsection (a) and paragraph (1) do not change or codify present law as to the allowability of foreign revenue claims or other foreign public law claims in a proceeding under this title.

(B) Allowance and priority as to a foreign tax claim or other foreign public law claim shall be governed by any applicable tax treaty of the United States, under the conditions and circumstances specified therein.

(Added Pub.L. 109–8, Title VIII, § 801(a), Apr. 20, 2005, 119 Stat. 138.)

§ 1514. Notification to foreign creditors concerning a case under this title

(a) Whenever in a case under this title notice is to be given to creditors generally or to any class or category of creditors, such notice shall also be given to the known creditors generally, or to creditors in the notified class or category, that do not have addresses in the United States. The court may order that appropriate steps be taken with a view to notifying any creditor whose address is not yet known.

(b) Such notification to creditors with foreign addresses described in subsection (a) shall be given individually, unless the court considers that, under the circumstances, some other form of notification would be more appropriate. No letter or other formality is required.

(c) When a notification of commencement of a case is to be given to foreign creditors, such notification shall—

(1) indicate the time period for filing proofs of claim and specify the place for filing such proofs of claim;

(2) indicate whether secured creditors need to file proofs of claim; and

(3) contain any other information required to be included in such notification to creditors under this title and the orders of the court.

(d) Any rule of procedure or order of the court as to notice or the filing of a proof of claim shall provide such additional time to creditors with foreign addresses as is reasonable under the circumstances.

(Added Pub.L. 109–8, Title VIII, § 801(a), Apr. 20, 2005, 119 Stat. 138.)

SUBCHAPTER III—RECOGNITION OF A FOREIGN PROCEEDING AND RELIEF

§ 1515. Application for recognition

(a) A foreign representative applies to the court for recognition of a foreign proceeding in which the foreign representative has been appointed by filing a petition for recognition.

(b) A petition for recognition shall be accompanied by—

(1) a certified copy of the decision commencing such foreign proceeding and appointing the foreign representative;

(2) a certificate from the foreign court affirming the existence of such foreign proceeding and of the appointment of the foreign representative; or

(3) in the absence of evidence referred to in paragraphs (1) and (2), any other evidence acceptable to the court of the existence of such foreign proceeding and of the appointment of the foreign representative.

(c) A petition for recognition shall also be accompanied by a statement identifying all foreign proceedings with respect to the debtor that are known to the foreign representative.

(d) The documents referred to in paragraphs (1) and (2) of subsection (b) shall be translated into English. The court may require a translation into English of additional documents.

(Added Pub.L. 109–8, Title VIII, § 801(a), Apr. 20, 2005, 119 Stat. 139.)

§ 1516. Presumptions concerning recognition

(a) If the decision or certificate referred to in section 1515(b) indicates that the foreign proceeding is a foreign proceeding and that the person or body is a foreign representative, the court is entitled to so presume.

(b) The court is entitled to presume that documents submitted in support of the petition for recognition are authentic, whether or not they have been legalized.

(c) In the absence of evidence to the contrary, the debtor's registered office, or habitual residence in the case of an individual, is presumed to be the center of the debtor's main interests.

(Added Pub.L. 109–8, Title VIII, § 801(a), Apr. 20, 2005, 119 Stat. 139.)

§ 1517. Order granting recognition

(a) Subject to section 1506, after notice and a hearing, an order recognizing a foreign proceeding shall be entered if—

  (1) such foreign proceeding for which recognition is sought is a foreign main proceeding or foreign nonmain proceeding within the meaning of section 1502;

  (2) the foreign representative applying for recognition is a person or body; and

  (3) the petition meets the requirements of section 1515.

(b) Such foreign proceeding shall be recognized—

  (1) as a foreign main proceeding if it is pending in the country where the debtor has the center of its main interests; or

  (2) as a foreign nonmain proceeding if the debtor has an establishment within the meaning of section 1502 in the foreign country where the proceeding is pending.

(c) A petition for recognition of a foreign proceeding shall be decided upon at the earliest possible time. Entry of an order recognizing a foreign proceeding constitutes recognition under this chapter.

(d) The provisions of this subchapter do not prevent modification or termination of recognition if it is shown that the grounds for granting it were fully or partially lacking or have ceased to exist, but in considering such action the court shall give due weight to possible prejudice to parties that have relied upon the order granting recognition. A case under this chapter may be closed in the manner prescribed under section 350.

(Added Pub.L. 109–8, Title VIII, § 801(a), Apr. 20, 2005, 119 Stat. 139.)

§ 1518. Subsequent information

From the time of filing the petition for recognition of a foreign proceeding, the foreign representative shall file with the court promptly a notice of change of status concerning—

  (1) any substantial change in the status of such foreign proceeding or the status of the foreign representative's appointment; and

  (2) any other foreign proceeding regarding the debtor that becomes known to the foreign representative.

(Added Pub.L. 109–8, Title VIII, § 801(a), Apr. 20, 2005, 119 Stat. 140.)

§ 1519. Relief that may be granted upon filing petition for recognition

(a) From the time of filing a petition for recognition until the court rules on the petition, the court may, at the request of the foreign representative, where relief is urgently needed to protect the assets of the debtor or the interests of the creditors, grant relief of a provisional nature, including—

(1) staying execution against the debtor's assets;

(2) entrusting the administration or realization of all or part of the debtor's assets located in the United States to the foreign representative or another person authorized by the court, including an examiner, in order to protect and preserve the value of assets that, by their nature or because of other circumstances, are perishable, susceptible to devaluation or otherwise in jeopardy; and

(3) any relief referred to in paragraph (3), (4), or (7) of section 1521(a).

(b) Unless extended under section 1521(a)(6), the relief granted under this section terminates when the petition for recognition is granted.

(c) It is a ground for denial of relief under this section that such relief would interfere with the administration of a foreign main proceeding.

(d) The court may not enjoin a police or regulatory act of a governmental unit, including a criminal action or proceeding, under this section.

(e) The standards, procedures, and limitations applicable to an injunction shall apply to relief under this section.

(f) The exercise of rights not subject to the stay arising under section 362(a) pursuant to paragraph (6), (7), (17), or (27) of section 362(b) or pursuant to section 362(o) shall not be stayed by any order of a court or administrative agency in any proceeding under this chapter.

(Added Pub.L. 109-8, Title VIII, § 801(a), Apr. 20, 2005, 119 Stat. 140; amended Pub.L. 111-327, § 2(a)(46), Dec. 22, 2010, 124 Stat. 3562.)

HISTORICAL AND STATUTORY NOTES

Amendments

2010 Amendments

Subsec. (f). Pub.L. 111-327, § 2(a)(46), struck out "362(n)" and inserted "362(o)".

§ 1520. Effects of recognition of a foreign main proceeding

(a) Upon recognition of a foreign proceeding that is a foreign main proceeding—

(1) sections 361 and 362 apply with respect to the debtor and the property of the debtor that is within the territorial jurisdiction of the United States;

(2) sections 363, 549, and 552 apply to a transfer of an interest of the debtor in property that is within the territorial jurisdiction of the United States to the same extent that the sections would apply to property of an estate;

(3) unless the court orders otherwise, the foreign representative may operate the debtor's business and may exercise the rights and powers of a trustee under and to the extent provided by sections 363 and 552; and

(4) section 552 applies to property of the debtor that is within the territorial jurisdiction of the United States.

(b) Subsection (a) does not affect the right to commence an individual action or proceeding in a foreign country to the extent necessary to preserve a claim against the debtor.

(c) Subsection (a) does not affect the right of a foreign representative or an entity to file a petition commencing a case under this title or the right of any party to file claims or take other proper actions in such a case.

(Added Pub.L. 109-8, Title VIII, § 801(a), Apr. 20, 2005, 119 Stat. 141.)

§ 1521. Relief that may be granted upon recognition

(a) Upon recognition of a foreign proceeding, whether main or nonmain, where necessary to effectuate the purpose of this chapter and to protect the assets of the debtor or the interests of the creditors, the court may, at the request of the foreign representative, grant any appropriate relief, including—

  (1) staying the commencement or continuation of an individual action or proceeding concerning the debtor's assets, rights, obligations or liabilities to the extent they have not been stayed under section 1520(a);

  (2) staying execution against the debtor's assets to the extent it has not been stayed under section 1520(a);

  (3) suspending the right to transfer, encumber or otherwise dispose of any assets of the debtor to the extent this right has not been suspended under section 1520(a);

  (4) providing for the examination of witnesses, the taking of evidence or the delivery of information concerning the debtor's assets, affairs, rights, obligations or liabilities;

  (5) entrusting the administration or realization of all or part of the debtor's assets within the territorial jurisdiction of the United States to the foreign representative or another person, including an examiner, authorized by the court;

  (6) extending relief granted under section 1519(a); and

  (7) granting any additional relief that may be available to a trustee, except for relief available under sections 522, 544, 545, 547, 548, 550, and 724(a).

(b) Upon recognition of a foreign proceeding, whether main or nonmain, the court may, at the request of the foreign representative, entrust the distribution of all or part of the debtor's assets located in the United States to the foreign representative or another person, including an examiner, authorized by the court, provided that the court is satisfied that the interests of creditors in the United States are sufficiently protected.

(c) In granting relief under this section to a representative of a foreign nonmain proceeding, the court must be satisfied that the relief relates to assets that, under the law of the United States, should be administered in the foreign nonmain proceeding or concerns information required in that proceeding.

(d) The court may not enjoin a police or regulatory act of a governmental unit, including a criminal action or proceeding, under this section.

(e) The standards, procedures, and limitations applicable to an injunction shall apply to relief under paragraphs (1), (2), (3), and (6) of subsection (a).

(f) The exercise of rights not subject to the stay arising under section 362(a) pursuant to paragraph (6), (7), (17), or (27) of section 362(b) or pursuant to section 362(o) shall not be stayed by any order of a court or administrative agency in any proceeding under this chapter.

(Added Pub.L. 109–8, Title VIII, § 801(a), Apr. 20, 2005, 119 Stat. 141; amended Pub.L. 111–327, § 2(a)(47), Dec. 22, 2010, 124 Stat. 3562.)

HISTORICAL AND STATUTORY NOTES

Amendments

  2010 Amendments. Subsec. (f). Pub.L. 111–327, § 2(a)(47), struck out "362(n)" and inserted "362(o)".

§ 1522. Protection of creditors and other interested persons

(a) The court may grant relief under section 1519 or 1521, or may modify or terminate relief under subsection (c), only if the interests of the creditors and other interested entities, including the debtor, are sufficiently protected.

(b) The court may subject relief granted under section 1519 or 1521, or the operation of the debtor's business under section 1520(a)(3), to conditions it considers appropriate, including the giving of security or the filing of a bond.

(c) The court may, at the request of the foreign representative or an entity affected by relief granted under section 1519 or 1521, or at its own motion, modify or terminate such relief.

(d) Section 1104(d) shall apply to the appointment of an examiner under this chapter. Any examiner shall comply with the qualification requirements imposed on a trustee by section 322.

(Added Pub.L. 109–8, Title VIII, § 801(a), Apr. 20, 2005, 119 Stat. 142.)

§ 1523. Actions to avoid acts detrimental to creditors

(a) Upon recognition of a foreign proceeding, the foreign representative has standing in a case concerning the debtor pending under another chapter of this title to initiate actions under sections 522, 544, 545, 547, 548, 550, 553, and 724(a).

(b) When a foreign proceeding is a foreign nonmain proceeding, the court must be satisfied that an action under subsection (a) relates to assets that, under United States law, should be administered in the foreign nonmain proceeding.

(Added Pub.L. 109–8, Title VIII, § 801(a), Apr. 20, 2005, 119 Stat. 142.)

§ 1524. Intervention by a foreign representative

Upon recognition of a foreign proceeding, the foreign representative may intervene in any proceedings in a State or Federal court in the United States in which the debtor is a party.

(Added Pub.L. 109–8, Title VIII, § 801(a), Apr. 20, 2005, 119 Stat. 142.)

SUBCHAPTER IV—COOPERATION WITH FOREIGN COURTS AND FOREIGN REPRESENTATIVES

§ 1525. Cooperation and direct communication between the court and foreign courts or foreign representatives

(a) Consistent with section 1501, the court shall cooperate to the maximum extent possible with a foreign court or a foreign representative, either directly or through the trustee.

(b) The court is entitled to communicate directly with, or to request information or assistance directly from, a foreign court or a foreign representative, subject to the rights of a party in interest to notice and participation.

(Added Pub.L. 109–8, Title VIII, § 801(a), Apr. 20, 2005, 119 Stat. 143.)

§ 1526. Cooperation and direct communication between the trustee and foreign courts or foreign representatives

(a) Consistent with section 1501, the trustee or other person, including an examiner, authorized by the court, shall, subject to the supervision of the court, cooperate to the maximum extent possible with a foreign court or a foreign representative.

(b) The trustee or other person, including an examiner, authorized by the court is entitled, subject to the supervision of the court, to communicate directly with a foreign court or a foreign representative.

(Added Pub.L. 109–8, Title VIII, § 801(a), Apr. 20, 2005, 119 Stat. 143.)

§ 1527. Forms of cooperation

Cooperation referred to in sections 1525 and 1526 may be implemented by any appropriate means, including—

    (1) appointment of a person or body, including an examiner, to act at the direction of the court;

    (2) communication of information by any means considered appropriate by the court;

    (3) coordination of the administration and supervision of the debtor's assets and affairs;

    (4) approval or implementation of agreements concerning the coordination of proceedings; and

    (5) coordination of concurrent proceedings regarding the same debtor.

(Added Pub.L. 109–8, Title VIII, § 801(a), Apr. 20, 2005, 119 Stat. 143.)

SUBCHAPTER V—CONCURRENT PROCEEDINGS

§ 1528. Commencement of a case under this title after recognition of a foreign main proceeding

After recognition of a foreign main proceeding, a case under another chapter of this title may be commenced only if the debtor has assets in the United States. The effects of such case shall be restricted to the assets of the debtor that are within the territorial jurisdiction of the United States and, to the extent necessary to implement cooperation and coordination under sections 1525, 1526, and 1527, to other assets of the debtor that are within the jurisdiction of the court under sections 541(a) of this title, and 1334(e) of title 28, to the extent that such other assets are not subject to the jurisdiction and control of a foreign proceeding that has been recognized under this chapter.

(Added Pub.L. 109–8, Title VIII, § 801(a), Apr. 20, 2005, 119 Stat. 143.)

§ 1529. Coordination of a case under this title and a foreign proceeding

If a foreign proceeding and a case under another chapter of this title are pending concurrently regarding the same debtor, the court shall seek cooperation and coordination under sections 1525, 1526, and 1527, and the following shall apply:

    (1) If the case in the United States is pending at the time the petition for recognition of such foreign proceeding is filed—

        (A) any relief granted under section 1519 or 1521 must be consistent with the relief granted in the case in the United States; and

        (B) section 1520 does not apply even if such foreign proceeding is recognized as a foreign main proceeding.

    (2) If a case in the United States under this title commences after recognition, or after the date of the filing of the petition for recognition, of such foreign proceeding—

        (A) any relief in effect under section 1519 or 1521 shall be reviewed by the court and shall be modified or terminated if inconsistent with the case in the United States; and

        (B) if such foreign proceeding is a foreign main proceeding, the stay and suspension referred to in section 1520(a) shall be modified or terminated if inconsistent with the relief granted in the case in the United States.

    (3) In granting, extending, or modifying relief granted to a representative of a foreign nonmain proceeding, the court must be satisfied that the relief relates to assets that, under the laws of the United States, should be administered in the foreign nonmain proceeding or concerns information required in that proceeding.

(4) In achieving cooperation and coordination under sections 1528 and 1529, the court may grant any of the relief authorized under section 305.

(Added Pub.L. 109-8, Title VIII, § 801(a), Apr. 20, 2005, 119 Stat. 144; amended Pub.L. 111-327, § 2(a)(48), Dec. 22, 2010, 124 Stat. 3562.)

HISTORICAL AND STATUTORY NOTES

Amendments

2010 Amendments. Par. (1). Pub.L. 111-327, § 2(a)(48), which directed amendment of par. (1) by inserting "is" after "States", was executed by making the insertion only in introductory provisions to reflect the probable intent of Congress.

§ 1530. Coordination of more than 1 foreign proceeding

In matters referred to in section 1501, with respect to more than 1 foreign proceeding regarding the debtor, the court shall seek cooperation and coordination under sections 1525, 1526, and 1527, and the following shall apply:

(1) Any relief granted under section 1519 or 1521 to a representative of a foreign nonmain proceeding after recognition of a foreign main proceeding must be consistent with the foreign main proceeding.

(2) If a foreign main proceeding is recognized after recognition, or after the filing of a petition for recognition, of a foreign nonmain proceeding, any relief in effect under section 1519 or 1521 shall be reviewed by the court and shall be modified or terminated if inconsistent with the foreign main proceeding.

(3) If, after recognition of a foreign nonmain proceeding, another foreign nonmain proceeding is recognized, the court shall grant, modify, or terminate relief for the purpose of facilitating coordination of the proceedings.

(Added Pub.L. 109-8, Title VIII, § 801(a), Apr. 20, 2005, 119 Stat. 144.)

§ 1531. Presumption of insolvency based on recognition of a foreign main proceeding

In the absence of evidence to the contrary, recognition of a foreign main proceeding is, for the purpose of commencing a proceeding under section 303, proof that the debtor is generally not paying its debts as such debts become due.

(Added Pub.L. 109-8, Title VIII, § 801(a), Apr. 20, 2005, 119 Stat. 144.)

§ 1532. Rule of payment in concurrent proceedings

Without prejudice to secured claims or rights in rem, a creditor who has received payment with respect to its claim in a foreign proceeding pursuant to a law relating to insolvency may not receive a payment for the same claim in a case under any other chapter of this title regarding the debtor, so long as the payment to other creditors of the same class is proportionately less than the payment the creditor has already received.

(Added Pub.L. 109-8, Title VIII, § 801(a), Apr. 20, 2005, 119 Stat. 145.)

[§§ 15101 to 151326. Repealed. Pub.L. 99-554, Title II, § 231, Oct. 27, 1986, 100 Stat. 3103]

HISTORICAL AND STATUTORY NOTES

Section 15101, Pub.L. 95-598, Nov. 6, 1978, 92 Stat. 2652, defined terms "entity" and "governmental unit".

Title 11 ANCILLARY AND OTHER CROSS-BORDER CASES **11 §§ 15101 to 151326**

Section 15102, Pub.L. 95–598, Nov. 6, 1978, 92 Stat. 2652, set forth rule of construction.

Section 15103, Pub.L. 95–598, Nov. 6, 1978, 92 Stat. 2652; Pub.L. 98–353, Title III, §§ 311(b)(3), 318(b), July 10, 1984, 98 Stat. 355, 357, set forth applicability of subchapters and sections.

Section 15303, Pub.L. 95–598, Nov. 6, 1978, 92 Stat. 2653, set forth provisions relating to involuntary cases.

Section 15321, Pub.L. 95–598, Nov. 6, 1978, 92 Stat. 2653, related to eligibility to serve as trustee.

Section 15322, Pub.L. 95–598, Nov. 6, 1978, 92 Stat. 2653, related to qualifications of trustees.

Section 15324, Pub.L. 95–598, Nov. 6, 1978, 92 Stat. 2653, related to removal of trustee or examiner.

Section 15326, Pub.L. 95–598, Nov. 6, 1978, 92 Stat. 2653, related to limitation on compensation of trustees.

Section 15330, Pub.L. 95–598, Nov. 6, 1978, 92 Stat. 2653, set forth compensation of officers.

Section 15343, Pub.L. 95–598, Nov. 6, 1978, 92 Stat. 2653, related to examination of the debtor.

Section 15345, Pub.L. 95–598, Nov. 6, 1978, 92 Stat. 2654; Pub.L. 97–258, § 3(c), Sept. 13, 1982, 96 Stat. 1064, related to money of estates.

Section 15701, Pub.L. 95–598, Nov. 6, 1978, 92 Stat. 2654, related to appointment, etc., of interim trustee.

Section 15703, Pub.L. 95–598, Nov. 6, 1978, 92 Stat. 2654, related to successor trustee.

Section 15704, Pub.L. 95–598, Nov. 6, 1978, 92 Stat. 2655, related to duties of trustees.

Section 15727, Pub.L. 95–598, Nov. 6, 1978, 92 Stat. 2655, set forth provisions relating to discharge under section 727(a) of this title.

Section 151102, Pub.L. 95–598, Nov. 6, 1978, 92 Stat. 2655, set forth provisions relating to creditors' and equity security holders' committees.

Section 151104, Pub.L. 95–598, Nov. 6, 1978, 92 Stat. 2655, related to appointment of trustee or examiner in reorganization matters.

Section 151105, Pub.L. 95–598, Nov. 6, 1978, 92 Stat. 2656, related to termination of trustee's appointment.

Section 151163, Pub.L. 95–598, Nov. 6, 1978, 92 Stat. 2656, related to appointment of trustee.

Section 151302, Pub.L. 95–598, Nov. 6, 1978, 92 Stat. 2656; Pub.L. 98–353, Title III, §§ 311(b)(4), 534, July 10, 1984, 98 Stat. 355, 390, related to functions of trustee with respect to adjustment of debts of an individual with regular income.

Section 151326, Pub.L. 95–598, Nov. 6, 1978, 92 Stat. 2657, set forth provisions relating to payments.

RELATED PROVISIONS OF U.S. CODE TITLES 18 AND 28

TITLE 18—CRIMES AND CRIMINAL PROCEDURE

CHAPTER 9—BANKRUPTCY

Sec.
151. Definition.
152. Concealment of assets; false oaths and claims; bribery.
153. Embezzlement against estate.
154. Adverse interest and conduct of officers.
155. Fee agreements in cases under title 11 and receiverships.
156. Knowing disregard of bankruptcy law or rule.
157. Bankruptcy fraud.
158. Designation of United States attorneys and agents of the Federal Bureau of Investigation to address abusive reaffirmations of debt and materially fraudulent statements in bankruptcy schedules.

CHAPTER 96—RACKETEER INFLUENCED AND CORRUPT ORGANIZATIONS

1961. Definitions.

CHAPTER 119—WIRE AND ELECTRONIC COMMUNICATIONS INTERCEPTION AND INTERCEPTION OF ORAL COMMUNICATIONS

2516. Authorization for interception of wire, oral, or electronic communications.

CHAPTER 203—ARREST AND COMMITMENT

3057. Bankruptcy investigations.

CHAPTER 213—LIMITATIONS

3284. Concealment of bankrupt's assets.

CHAPTER 601—IMMUNITY OF WITNESSES

6001. Definitions.

TITLE 28—JUDICIARY AND JUDICIAL PROCEDURE

PART I—ORGANIZATION OF COURTS

CHAPTER 6—BANKRUPTCY JUDGES

Sec.
151. Designation of bankruptcy courts.
152. Appointment of bankruptcy judges.
153. Salaries; character of service.
154. Division of business; chief judge.[1]
155. Temporary transfer of bankruptcy judges.
156. Staff; expenses.
157. Procedures.
158. Appeals.
159. Bankruptcy statistics.

CHAPTER 21—GENERAL PROVISIONS APPLICABLE TO COURTS AND JUDGES

455. Disqualification of justice, judge, or magistrate judge.

---

[1] So in original. Does not conform to section catchline.

RELATED PROVISIONS

PART II—DEPARTMENT OF JUSTICE

CHAPTER 39—UNITED STATES TRUSTEES

581.	United States trustees.
582.	Assistant United States trustees.
583.	Oath of office.
584.	Official stations.
585.	Vacancies.
586.	Duties; supervision by Attorney General.
587.	Salaries.
588.	Expenses.
589.	Staff and other employees.
589a.	United States Trustee System Fund.
589b.	Bankruptcy data.

PART III—COURT OFFICERS AND EMPLOYEES

CHAPTER 41—ADMINISTRATIVE OFFICE OF UNITED STATES COURTS

604.	Duties of Director generally.

CHAPTER 44—ALTERNATIVE DISPUTE RESOLUTION

651.	Authorization of alternative dispute resolution.
652.	Jurisdiction.
653.	Neutrals.
654.	Arbitration.
655.	Arbitrators.
656.	Subpoenas.
657.	Arbitration award and judgment.
658.	Compensation of arbitrators and neutrals.

CHAPTER 57—GENERAL PROVISIONS APPLICABLE TO COURT OFFICERS AND EMPLOYEES

959.	Trustees and receivers suable; management; State laws.

PART IV—JURISDICTION AND VENUE

CHAPTER 85—DISTRICT COURTS; JURISDICTION

1334.	Bankruptcy cases and proceedings.

CHAPTER 87—DISTRICT COURTS; VENUE

1408.	Venue of cases under title 11.
1409.	Venue of proceedings arising under title 11 or arising in or related to cases under title 11.
1410.	Venue of cases ancillary to foreign proceedings.
1411.	Jury trials.
1412.	Change of venue.
1413.	Venue of cases under chapter 5 of title 3.

CHAPTER 89—DISTRICT COURTS; REMOVAL OF CASES FROM STATE COURTS

1452.	Removal of claims related to bankruptcy cases.

PART V—PROCEDURE

CHAPTER 123—FEES AND COSTS

1930.	Bankruptcy fees.

[Miscellaneous Fee Schedule]

CHAPTER 131—RULES OF COURTS

2075.	Bankruptcy rules.

TITLE 18
CRIMES AND CRIMINAL PROCEDURES

CHAPTER 9—BANKRUPTCY

HISTORICAL AND STATUTORY NOTES

Amendments

2005 Amendments. Pub.L. 109–8, Title II, § 203(b)(2), Apr. 20, 2005, 119 Stat. 49, added item 158 "Designation of United States attorneys and agents of the Federal Bureau of Investigation to address abusive reaffirmations of debt and materially fraudulent statements in bankruptcy schedules.".

1994 Amendments. Section Analysis. Pub.L. 103–394, Title III, § 312(a)(2), Oct. 22, 1994, 108 Stat. 4140, substituted in item 153 "against estate" for "by trustee or officer", and added items 156 and 157.

1978 Amendments. Pub.L. 95–598, Title III, § 314(b)(2), (d)(3), (e)(3), (f)(3), Nov. 6, 1978, 92 Stat. 2677, substituted in item 151 "Definition" for "Definitions"; struck from item 153 ", receiver" following "trustee" and from item 154 "referees and other" preceding "officers"; and substituted in item 155 "cases under title 11 and receiverships" for "bankruptcy proceedings".

§ 151. Definition

As used in this chapter, the term "debtor" means a debtor concerning whom a petition has been filed under Title 11.

(June 25, 1948, c. 645, 62 Stat. 689; Nov. 6, 1978, Pub.L. 95–598, Title III, § 314(b)(1), 92 Stat. 2676; Sept. 13, 1994, Pub.L. 103–322, Title XXXIII, § 330008(5), 108 Stat. 2143.)

HISTORICAL AND STATUTORY NOTES

Amendments

1994 Amendments. Pub.L. 103–322, § 330008(5), substituted "means" for "mean".

1978 Amendments. Pub.L. 95–598 substituted "Definition" for "Definitions" in section catchline and definition of "debtor" as a debtor concerning whom a petition has been filed under title 11 for definition of "bankrupt" as a debtor by or against whom a petition has been filed under Title 11 and struck out definition of "bankruptcy" as including any proceeding arrangement, or plan pursuant to Title 11.

§ 152. Concealment of assets; false oaths and claims; bribery

A person who—

(1) knowingly and fraudulently conceals from a custodian, trustee, marshal, or other officer of the court charged with the control or custody of property, or, in connection with a case under title 11, from creditors or the United States Trustee, any property belonging to the estate of a debtor;

(2) knowingly and fraudulently makes a false oath or account in or in relation to any case under title 11;

(3) knowingly and fraudulently makes a false declaration, certificate, verification, or statement under penalty of perjury as permitted under section 1746 of title 28, in or in relation to any case under title 11;

(4) knowingly and fraudulently presents any false claim for proof against the estate of a debtor, or uses any such claim in any case under title 11, in a personal capacity or as or through an agent, proxy, or attorney;

(5) knowingly and fraudulently receives any material amount of property from a debtor after the filing of a case under title 11, with intent to defeat the provisions of title 11;

(6) knowingly and fraudulently gives, offers, receives, or attempts to obtain any money or property, remuneration, compensation, reward, advantage, or promise thereof for acting or forbearing to act in any case under title 11;

(7) in a personal capacity or as an agent or officer of any person or corporation, in contemplation of a case under title 11 by or against the person or any other person or corporation, or with intent to defeat the provisions of title 11, knowingly and fraudulently transfers or conceals any of his property or the property of such other person or corporation;

(8) after the filing of a case under title 11 or in contemplation thereof, knowingly and fraudulently conceals, destroys, mutilates, falsifies, or makes a false entry in any recorded information (including books, documents, records, and papers) relating to the property or financial affairs of a debtor; or

(9) after the filing of a case under title 11, knowingly and fraudulently withholds from a custodian, trustee, marshal, or other officer of the court or a United States Trustee entitled to its possession, any recorded information (including books, documents, records, and papers) relating to the property or financial affairs of a debtor,

shall be fined under this title, imprisoned not more than 5 years, or both.

(June 25, 1948, c. 645, 62 Stat. 689; June 12, 1960, Pub.L. 86–519, § 2, 74 Stat. 217; Sept. 2, 1960, Pub.L. 86–701, 74 Stat. 753; Oct. 18, 1976, Pub.L. 94–550, § 4, 90 Stat. 2535; Nov. 6, 1978, Pub.L. 95–598, Title III, § 314(a), (c), 92 Stat. 2676, 2677; Nov. 18, 1988, Pub.L. 100–690, Title VII, § 7017, 102 Stat. 4395; Sept. 13, 1994, Pub.L. 103–322, Title XXXIII, § 330016(1)(K), 108 Stat. 2147; Oct. 22, 1994, Pub.L. 103–394, Title III, § 312(a)(1)(A), 108 Stat. 4138; Oct. 11, 1996, Pub.L. 104–294, Title VI, § 601(a)(1), 110 Stat. 3498.)

HISTORICAL AND STATUTORY NOTES

Amendments

1996 Amendments. Pub.L. 104–294, § 601(a)(1), substituted "fined under this title" for "fined not more than $5,000".

1994 Amendments. Pub.L. 103–394, § 312(a)(1)(A), designated existing provisions as opening cl., pars. (1) to (9), and closing cl., and in pars. (1) and (9) as so designated added reference to United States Trustee.

Pub.L. 103–322, § 330016(1)(K), substituted "under this title" for "not more than $5,000" in tenth undesignated paragraph.

1988 Amendments. Pub.L. 100–690 substituted "penalty of perjury" for "penalty or perjury".

1978 Amendments. Pub.L. 95–598 substituted, wherever appearing, "debtor" for "bankrupt", "case under title 11" for "bankruptcy proceeding", and "provisions of title 11" for "bankruptcy law"; and substituted "a custodian" for "the receiver, custodian", wherever appearing, and "recorded information, including books, documents, records, and papers, relating to the property or financial affairs" for "document affecting or relating to the property or affairs".

1976 Amendments. Pub.L. 94–550 added paragraph covering the knowing and fraudulent making of a false declaration, certificate, verification, or statement under penalty of perjury as permitted under section 1746 of Title 28 or in relation to any bankruptcy proceeding.

1960 Amendments. Pub.L. 86–701 included fraudulent transfers and concealment of property by persons in their individual capacity, within sixth paragraph.

Pub.L. 86–519 deleted words "under oath" which followed "knowingly and fraudulently presents" in third paragraph.

CROSS REFERENCES

Bankruptcy investigations; duties of United States attorney, see 18 USCA § 3057.

Discharges, refusal to grant when offense committed under this section, see 11 USCA § 727.

Examination of bankrupt, evidence as inadmissible in criminal proceedings, see 11 USCA § 521.

Limitation of prosecutions, see 18 USCA §§ 3282 and 3284.

§ 153. Embezzlement against estate

(a) **Offense.**—A person described in subsection (b) who knowingly and fraudulently appropriates to the person's own use, embezzles, spends, or transfers any property or secretes or destroys any document belonging to the estate of a debtor shall be fined under this title, imprisoned not more than 5 years, or both.

(b) **Person to whom section applies.**—A person described in this subsection is one who has access to property or documents belonging to an estate by virtue of the person's participation in the administration of the estate as a trustee, custodian, marshal, attorney, or other officer of the court or as an agent, employee, or other person engaged by such an officer to perform a service with respect to the estate.

(June 25, 1948, c. 645, 62 Stat. 690; Nov. 6, 1978, Pub.L. 95–598, Title III, § 314(a)(1), (d)(1), (2), 92 Stat. 2676, 2677; Sept. 13, 1994, Pub.L. 103–322, Title XXXIII, § 330016(1)(K), 108 Stat. 2147; Oct. 22, 1994, Pub.L. 103–394, Title III, § 312(a)(1)(A), 108 Stat. 4139; Oct. 11, 1996, Pub.L. 104–294, Title VI, § 601(a)(1), 110 Stat. 3498.)

HISTORICAL AND STATUTORY NOTES

Amendments

1996 Amendments. Subsec. (a). Pub.L. 104–294, § 601(a)(1), substituted "fined under this title" for "fined not more than $5,000".

1994 Amendments. Pub.L. 103–394, § 312(a)(1)(A), completely revised section. Prior to revision, section read as follows:

" § 153. Embezzlement by trustee or officer

"Whoever knowingly and fraudulently appropriates to his own use, embezzles, spends, or transfers any property or secretes or destroys any document belonging to the estate of a debtor which came into his charge as trustee, custodian, marshal, or other officer of the court, shall be fined under this title or imprisoned not more than five years, or both."

Pub.L. 103–322, § 330016(1)(K), substituted "under this title" for "not more than $5,000" wherever appearing.

1978 Amendments. Pub.L. 95–598 deleted from heading ", receiver" following "trustee" and in text "receiver," preceding "custodian" and substituted "debtor" for "bankrupt".

CROSS REFERENCES

Debts of bankrupt created by fraud, embezzlement, misappropriation or defalcation while acting as an officer or in any fiduciary capacity as not affected by a discharge, see 11 USCA § 523.

Embezzlement by court officers, generally, see 18 USCA § 645.

§ 154. Adverse interest and conduct of officers

A person who, being a custodian, trustee, marshal, or other officer of the court—

(1) knowingly purchases, directly or indirectly, any property of the estate of which the person is such an officer in a case under title 11;

(2) knowingly refuses to permit a reasonable opportunity for the inspection by parties in interest of the documents and accounts relating to the affairs of estates in the person's charge by parties when directed by the court to do so; or

(3) knowingly refuses to permit a reasonable opportunity for the inspection by the United States Trustee of the documents and accounts relating to the affairs of an estate in the person's charge,

shall be fined under this title and shall forfeit the person's office, which shall thereupon become vacant.

(June 25, 1948, c. 645, 62 Stat. 690; Nov. 6, 1978, Pub.L. 95–598, Title III, § 314(a)(2), (e)(1), (2), 92 Stat. 2676, 2677; Sept. 13, 1994, Pub.L. 103–322, Title XXXIII, § 330016(1)(G), 108 Stat. 2147; Oct. 22, 1994, Pub.L. 103–394, Title III, § 312(a)(1)(A), 108 Stat. 4139; Oct. 11, 1996, Pub.L. 104–294, Title VI, § 601(a)(1), 110 Stat. 3498.)

HISTORICAL AND STATUTORY NOTES

Amendments

1996 Amendments. Pub.L. 104–294, § 601(a)(1), substituted "fined under this title" for "fined not more than $5,000".

1994 Amendments. Pub.L. 103–394, § 312(a)(1)(A), designated portion of existing text as pars. (1) and (2), added par. (3), and increased maximum fine from $500 to $5,000.

Pub.L. 103–322, § 330016(1)(G), substituted "under this title" for "not more than $500".

1978 Amendments. Pub.L. 95–598 struck out from section heading "referees and other" preceding "officers", initial par. "Whoever knowingly acts as a referee in a case in which he is directly or indirectly interested; or", and "referee, receiver," preceding "custodian" and substituted "case under title 11" for "bankruptcy proceeding".

§ 155. Fee agreements in cases under title 11 and receiverships

Whoever, being a party in interest, whether as a debtor, creditor, receiver, trustee or representative of any of them, or attorney for any such party in interest, in any receivership or case under title 11 in any United States court or under its supervision, knowingly and fraudulently enters into any agreement, express or implied, with another such party in interest or attorney for another such party in interest, for the purpose of fixing the fees or other compensation to be paid to any party in interest or to any attorney for any party in interest for services rendered in connection therewith, from the assets of the estate, shall be fined under this title or imprisoned not more than one year, or both.

(June 25, 1948, c. 645, 62 Stat. 690; May 24, 1949, c. 139, § 4, 63 Stat. 90; Nov. 6, 1978, Pub.L. 95–598, Title III, § 314(f)(1), (2) 92 Stat. 2677; Sept. 13, 1994, Pub.L. 103–322, Title XXXIII, § 330016(1)(K), 108 Stat. 2147.)

HISTORICAL AND STATUTORY NOTES

Amendments

1994 Amendments. Pub.L. 103–322, § 330016(1)(K), substituted "under this title" for "not more than $5,000" wherever appearing.

1978 Amendments. Pub.L. 95–598 substituted in the heading "cases under title 11 and receiverships" for "bankruptcy proceedings" and in the text "or cases under title 11" for ", bankruptcy or reorganization proceeding", inserted "knowingly and fraudulently" following "supervision,", and deleted penalty provision for a judge of a United States court to knowingly approve the payment of any fees or compensation that were fixed.

1949 Amendments. Act May 24, 1949, amended section to clarify it by inserting "or attorney for any such party in interest" in two places, and by inserting "in any United States court or under its supervision" in lieu of "in or under the supervision of any court of the United States."

§ 156. Knowing disregard of bankruptcy law or rule

(a) **Definitions.**—In this section—

(1) the term "bankruptcy petition preparer" means a person, other than the debtor's attorney or an employee of such an attorney, who prepares for compensation a document for filing; and

(2) the term "document for filing" means a petition or any other document prepared for filing by a debtor in a United States bankruptcy court or a United States district court in connection with a case under title 11.

(b) **Offense.**—If a bankruptcy case or related proceeding is dismissed because of a knowing attempt by a bankruptcy petition preparer in any manner to disregard the requirements of title 11, United States Code, or the Federal Rules of Bankruptcy Procedure, the bankruptcy petition preparer shall be fined under this title, imprisoned not more than 1 year, or both.

(Added Pub.L. 103–394, Title III, § 312(a)(1)(B), Oct. 22, 1994, 108 Stat. 4140; amended Pub.L. 109–8, Title XII, § 1220, Apr. 20, 2005, 119 Stat. 195.)

HISTORICAL AND STATUTORY NOTES

Amendments

2005 Amendments. Subsec. (a). Pub.L.109–8, § 1220, in the first undesignated paragraph, inserted "(1) the term" before "bankruptcy", and struck out the period at the end and inserted "; and"; and in the second undesignated paragraph, inserted "(2) the term" before "document", and struck out "this title" and inserted "title 11".

§ 157. Bankruptcy fraud

A person who, having devised or intending to devise a scheme or artifice to defraud and for the purpose of executing or concealing such a scheme or artifice or attempting to do so—

(1) files a petition under title 11, including a fraudulent involuntary petition under section 303 of such title;

(2) files a document in a proceeding under title 11; or

(3) makes a false or fraudulent representation, claim, or promise concerning or in relation to a proceeding under title 11, at any time before or after the filing of the petition, or in relation to a proceeding falsely asserted to be pending under such title,

shall be fined under this title, imprisoned not more than 5 years, or both.

(Added Pub.L. 103–394, Title III, § 312(a)(1)(B), Oct. 22, 1994, 108 Stat. 4140; amended Pub.L. 109–8, Title III, § 332(c), Apr. 20, 2005, 119 Stat. 103; Pub.L. 111–327, § 2(b), Dec. 22, 2010, 124 Stat. 3562.)

HISTORICAL AND STATUTORY NOTES

Amendments

2010 Amendments. Par. (1). Pub.L. 111–327, § 2(b)(1), struck out "bankruptcy" following "involuntary".

Par. (2). Pub.L. 111–327, § 2(b)(2), struck out ", including a fraudulent involuntary bankruptcy petition under section 303 of such title" following "title 11".

Par. (3). Pub.L. 111–327, § 2(b)(2), struck out ", including a fraudulent involuntary bankruptcy petition under section 303 of such title" following "title 11".

2005 Amendments. Pars. (1) to (3). Pub.L. 109–8, § 332(c), inserted ", including a fraudulent involuntary bankruptcy petition under section 303 of such title" after "title 11" wherever appearing, to reflect the probable intent of Congress.

§ 158. **Designation of United States attorneys and agents of the Federal Bureau of Investigation to address abusive reaffirmations of debt and materially fraudulent statements in bankruptcy schedules**

(a) **In general.**—The Attorney General of the United States shall designate the individuals described in subsection (b) to have primary responsibility in carrying out enforcement activities in addressing violations of section 152 or 157 relating to abusive reaffirmations of debt. In addition to addressing the violations referred to in the preceding sentence, the individuals described under subsection (b) shall address violations of section 152 or 157 relating to materially fraudulent statements in bankruptcy schedules that are intentionally false or intentionally misleading.

(b) **United States attorneys and agents of the Federal Bureau of Investigation.**—The individuals referred to in subsection (a) are—

(1) the United States attorney for each judicial district of the United States; and

(2) an agent of the Federal Bureau of Investigation for each field office of the Federal Bureau of Investigation.

(c) **Bankruptcy investigations.**—Each United States attorney designated under this section shall, in addition to any other responsibilities, have primary responsibility for carrying out the duties of a United States attorney under section 3057.

(d) **Bankruptcy procedures.**—The bankruptcy courts shall establish procedures for referring any case that may contain a materially fraudulent statement in a bankruptcy schedule to the individuals designated under this section.

(Added Pub.L. 109–8, Title II, § 203(b)(1), Apr. 20, 2005, 119 Stat. 49.)

CHAPTER 96—RACKETEER INFLUENCED AND CORRUPT ORGANIZATIONS

§ 1961. Definitions

As used in this chapter—

(1) "racketeering activity" means (A) any act or threat involving murder, kidnapping, gambling, arson, robbery, bribery, extortion, dealing in obscene matter, or dealing in a controlled substance or listed chemical (as defined in section 102 of the Controlled Substances Act), which is chargeable under State law and punishable by imprisonment for more than one year; (B) any act which is indictable under any of the following provisions of title 18, United States Code: Section 201 (relating to bribery), section 224 (relating to sports bribery), sections 471, 472, and 473 (relating to counterfeiting), section 659 (relating to theft from interstate shipment) if the act indictable under section 659 is felonious, section 664 (relating to embezzlement from pension and welfare funds), sections 891–894 (relating to extortionate credit transactions), section 1028 (relating to fraud and related activity in connection with identification documents), section 1029 (relating to fraud and related activity in connection with access devices), section 1084 (relating to the transmission of gambling information), section 1341 (relating to mail fraud), section 1343 (relating to wire fraud), section 1344 (relating to financial institution fraud), section 1351 (relating to fraud in foreign labor contracting), section 1425 (relating to the procurement of citizenship or nationalization unlawfully), section 1426 (relating to the reproduction of naturalization or citizenship papers), section 1427 (relating to the sale of naturalization or citizenship papers), sections 1461–1465 (relating to obscene matter), section 1503 (relating to obstruction of justice), section 1510 (relating to obstruction of criminal investigations), section 1511 (relating to the obstruction of State or local law enforcement), section 1512 (relating to tampering with a witness, victim, or an informant), section 1513 (relating to retaliating against a witness, victim, or an informant), section 1542 (relating to false statement in application and use of passport), section 1543 (relating to forgery or false use of passport), section 1544 (relating to misuse of passport), section 1546 (relating to fraud and misuse of visas, permits, and other documents), sections

1581–1592 (relating to peonage, slavery, and trafficking in persons).,[1] section 1951 (relating to interference with commerce, robbery, or extortion), section 1952 (relating to racketeering), section 1953 (relating to interstate transportation of wagering paraphernalia), section 1954 (relating to unlawful welfare fund payments), section 1955 (relating to the prohibition of illegal gambling businesses), section 1956 (relating to the laundering of monetary instruments), section 1957 (relating to engaging in monetary transactions in property derived from specified unlawful activity), section 1958 (relating to use of interstate commerce facilities in the commission of murder-for-hire), section 1960 (relating to illegal money transmitters), sections 2251, 2251A, 2252, and 2260 (relating to sexual exploitation of children), sections 2312 and 2313 (relating to interstate transportation of stolen motor vehicles), sections 2314 and 2315 (relating to interstate transportation of stolen property), section 2318 (relating to trafficking in counterfeit labels for phonorecords, computer programs or computer program documentation or packaging and copies of motion pictures or other audiovisual works), section 2319 (relating to criminal infringement of a copyright), section 2319A (relating to unauthorized fixation of and trafficking in sound recordings and music videos of live musical performances), section 2320 (relating to trafficking in goods or services bearing counterfeit marks), section 2321 (relating to trafficking in certain motor vehicles or motor vehicle parts), sections 2341–2346 (relating to trafficking in contraband cigarettes), sections 2421–24 (relating to white slave traffic), sections 175–178 (relating to biological weapons), sections 229–229F (relating to chemical weapons), section 831 (relating to nuclear materials), (C) any act which is indictable under title 29, United States Code, section 186 (dealing with restrictions on payments and loans to labor organizations) or section 501(c) (relating to embezzlement from union funds), (D) any offense involving fraud connected with a case under title 11 (except a case under section 157 of this title), fraud in the sale of securities, or the felonious manufacture, importation, receiving, concealment, buying, selling, or otherwise dealing in a controlled substance or listed chemical (as defined in section 102 of the Controlled Substances Act), punishable under any law of the United States, (E) any act which is indictable under the Currency and Foreign Transactions Reporting Act, (F) any act which is indictable under the Immigration and Nationality Act, section 274 (relating to bringing in and harboring certain aliens), section 277 (relating to aiding or assisting certain aliens to enter the United States), or section 278 (relating to importation of alien for immoral purpose) if the act indictable under such section of such Act was committed for the purpose of financial gain, or (G) any act that is indictable under any provision listed in section 2332b(g)(5)(B);

(2) "State" means any State of the United States, the District of Columbia, the Commonwealth of Puerto Rico, any territory or possession of the United States, any political subdivision, or any department, agency, or instrumentality thereof;

(3) "person" includes any individual or entity capable of holding a legal or beneficial interest in property;

(4) "enterprise" includes any individual, partnership, corporation, association, or other legal entity, and any union or group of individuals associated in fact although not a legal entity;

(5) "pattern of racketeering activity" requires at least two acts of racketeering activity, one of which occurred after the effective date of this chapter and the last of which occurred within ten years (excluding any period of imprisonment) after the commission of a prior act of racketeering activity;

(6) "unlawful debt" means a debt (A) incurred or contracted in gambling activity which was in violation of the law of the United States, a State or political subdivision thereof, or which is unenforceable under State or Federal law in whole or in part as to principal or interest because of the laws relating to usury, and (B) which was incurred in connection with the business of gambling in violation of the law of the United States, a State or political subdivision thereof, or the business of lending money or a thing of value at a rate usurious under State or Federal law, where the usurious rate is at least twice the enforceable rate;

---

[1] So in original.

(7) "racketeering investigator" means any attorney or investigator so designated by the Attorney General and charged with the duty of enforcing or carrying into effect this chapter;

(8) "racketeering investigation" means any inquiry conducted by any racketeering investigator for the purpose of ascertaining whether any person has been involved in any violation of this chapter or of any final order, judgment, or decree of any court of the United States, duly entered in any case or proceeding arising under this chapter;

(9) "documentary material" includes any book, paper, document, record, recording, or other material; and

(10) "Attorney General" includes the Attorney General of the United States, the Deputy Attorney General of the United States, the Associate Attorney General of the United States, any Assistant Attorney General of the United States, or any employee of the Department of Justice or any employee of any department or agency of the United States so designated by the Attorney General to carry out the powers conferred on the Attorney General by this chapter. Any department or agency so designated may use in investigations authorized by this chapter either the investigative provisions of this chapter or the investigative power of such department or agency otherwise conferred by law.

(Added Pub.L. 91–452, Title IX, § 901(a), Oct. 15, 1970, 84 Stat. 941; amended Pub.L. 95–575, § 3(c), Nov. 2, 1978, 92 Stat. 2465; Pub.L. 95–598, Title III, § 314(g), Nov. 6, 1978, 92 Stat. 2677; Pub.L. 98–473, Title II, §§ 901(g), 1020, Oct. 12, 1984, 98 Stat. 2136, 2143; Pub.L. 98–547, Title II, § 205, Oct. 25, 1984, 98 Stat. 2770; Pub.L. 99–570, Title XIII, § 1365(b), Oct. 27, 1986, 100 Stat. 3207–35; Pub.L. 99–646, § 50(a), Nov. 10, 1986, 100 Stat. 3605; Pub.L. 100–690, Title VII, §§ 7013, 7020(c), 7032, 7054, 7514, Nov. 18, 1988, 102 Stat. 4395, 4396, 4398, 4402, 4489; Pub.L. 101–73, Title IX, § 968, Aug. 9, 1989, 103 Stat. 506; Pub.L. 101–647, Title XXXV, § 3560, Nov. 29, 1990, 104 Stat. 4927; Pub.L. 103–322, Title IX, § 90104, Title XVI, § 160001(f), Title XXXIII, § 330021(1), Sept. 13, 1994, 108 Stat. 1987, 2037, 2150; Pub.L. 103–394, Title III, § 312(b), Oct. 22, 1994, 108 Stat. 4140; Pub.L. 104–132, Title IV, § 433, Apr. 24, 1996, 110 Stat. 1274; Pub.L. 104–153, § 3, July 2, 1996, 110 Stat. 1386; Pub.L. 104–208, Div. C, Title II, § 202, Sept. 30, 1996, 110 Stat. 3009–565; Pub.L. 104–294, Title VI, §§ 601(b)(3), (i)(3), 604(b)(6), Oct. 11, 1996, 110 Stat. 3499, 3501, 3506; Pub.L. 107–56, Title VIII, § 813, Oct. 26, 2001, 115 Stat. 382; Pub.L. 107–273, Div. B, Title IV, § 4005(f)(1), Nov. 2, 2002, 116 Stat. 1813; Pub.L. 108–193, § 5(b), Dec. 19, 2003, 117 Stat. 2879; Pub.L. 108–458, Title VI, § 6802(e), Dec. 17, 2004, 118 Stat. 3767; Pub.L. 109–164, Title I, § 103(c), Jan. 10, 2006, 119 Stat. 3563; Pub.L. 109–177, Title IV, § 403(a), Mar. 9, 2006, 120 Stat. 243; Pub.L. 113–4, Title XII, § 1211(a), Mar. 7, 2013, 127 Stat. 142.)

HISTORICAL AND STATUTORY NOTES

References in Text

Section 102 of the Controlled Substances Act, referred to in par. (1), is section 102 of Pub.L. 91–513, Title II, Oct. 27, 1970, 84 Stat. 1242, as amended, which is classified to section 802 of Title 21, Food and Drugs.

Sections 201, 224, 471, 472, 473, 659, 664, 891 to 894, 1028, 1029, 1084, 1341, 1343, 1344, 1461 to 1465, 1503, 1510, 1511, 1512, 1513, 1542, 1543, 1544, 1546, 1581 to 1591, 1951, 1952, 1953, 1954, 1955, 1956, 1957, 1958, 2251, 2252, 2312, 2313, 2314, 2315, 2321, 2341 to 2346, and 2421 to 2424 of title 18, United States Code, referred to in par. (1)(B), are sections 201, 224, 471, 472, 473, 659, 664, 891 to 894, 1028, 1029, 1084, 1341, 1343, 1344, 1461 to 1465, 1503, 1510, 1511, 1512, 1513, 1452, 1543, 1544, 1546, 1581 to 1591, 1951, 1952, 1953, 1954, 1955, 1956, 1957, 1958, 2251, 2252, 2312, 2313, 2314, 2315, 2321, 2341 to 2346, and 2421 to 2424 of this title, respectively.

The Currency and Foreign Transaction Reporting Act, as amended, referred to in par. (1)(E), was Pub.L. 91–508, Title II, Oct. 26, 1970, 84 Stat. 1118, which was classified generally to chapter 21 (section 1051 et seq.) of Title 31, Money and Finance prior to the revision of this title by Pub.L. 97–258, Sept. 12, 1982, 96 Stat. 995. For complete classification of this Act to the Code see section 5311 et seq. of revised Title 31 and Tables.

The Immigration and Nationality Act and such Act, referred to in par. (1)(F), is Act June 27, 1952, c. 477, 66 Stat. 163, as amended, which is classified principally to chapter 12 (section 1101 et seq.) of Title 8, Aliens and Nationality. Sections 274, 277 and 278 of such Act are classified to sections 1324, 1327 and 1328 of Title 8, respectively. For complete classification of this Act to the Code, see Tables.

The effective date of this chapter, referred to in par. (5), is Oct. 15, 1970.

Codifications

Section 5(b) of Pub.L. 108–193, which directed that paragraph (1)(A) of this section be amended by striking "sections 1581–1588 (relating to peonage and slavery)" and inserting "sections 1581–1591 (relating to peonage, slavery, and trafficking in persons)", was executed to paragraph (1)(B) of this section as the probable intent of Congress.

Amendments

2013 Amendments. Par. (1)(B). Pub.L. 113–4, § 1211(a), inserted "section 1351 (relating to fraud in foreign labor contracting)," preceding "section 1425".

2006 Amendments. Par. (1)(B). Pub.L. 109–177, § 403(a), inserted "section 1960 (relating to illegal money transmitters)," before "sections 2251".

Pub.L. 109–164, § 103(c), in par. (1)(B), struck out "1581–1591" and inserted "1581–1592".

2004 Amendments. Par. (1)(B). Pub.L. 108–458, § 6802(e), inserted "sections 175–178 (relating to biological weapons), sections 229–229F (relating to chemical weapons), section 831 (relating to nuclear materials)," before "(C) any act which is indictable under title 29".

2003 Amendments. Par. (1)(B). Pub.L. 108–193, § 5(b), struck out "sections 1581–1588 (relating to peonage and slavery)" and inserted "sections 1581–1591 (relating to peonage, slavery, and trafficking in persons)".

2002 Amendments. Par. (1). Pub.L. 107–273, § 4005(f)(1), amended the directory language of section 813(2) of Pub.L. 107–56, and thus required no change in text.

2001 Amendments. Par. (1). Pub.L. 107–56, § 813, substituted "(F)" for "or (F)" and inserted ", or (G) any act that is indictable under any provision listed in section 2332b(g)(5)(B)" after "committed for the purpose of financial gain".

1996 Amendments. Par. (1). Pub.L. 104–294, § 604(b)(6), amending Pub.L. 103–322, § 160001(f), substituted "sections 2251, 2251A, 2252, and 2258" for "sections 2251–2252".

Par. (1)(B). Pub.L. 104–294, § 601(i)(3), substituted "2252, and 2260" for "2252, and 2258".

Pub.L. 104–208, § 202, added provisions relating to sections 1425, 1426 and 1427 of this title, and struck out provisions relating to violations of sections 1028, 1542, 1543, 1544 and 1546 of this title committed for financial gain.

Pub.L. 104–153, § 3, inserted ", section 2318 (relating to trafficking in counterfeit labels for phonorecords, computer programs or computer program documentation or packaging and copies of motion pictures or other audiovisual works), section 2319 (relating to criminal infringement of a copyright), section 2319A (relating to unauthorized fixation of and trafficking in sound recordings and music videos of live musical performances), section 2320 (relating to trafficking in goods or services bearing counterfeit marks)" after "sections 2314 and 2315 (relating to interstate transportation of stolen property)".

Pub.L. 104–132, § 433, established certain alien smuggling-related crimes as Rico-predicate offenses.

Par. (1)(D). Pub.L. 104–294, § 601(b)(3), substituted "section 157 of this title" for "section 157 of that title".

1994 Amendments. Par. (1). Pub.L. 103–322, § 330021(1), substituted "kidnapping" for "kidnaping".

Pub.L. 103–322, § 90104, substituted "a controlled substance or listed chemical (as defined in section 102 of the Controlled Substances Act)" for "narcotic or other dangerous drugs" wherever appearing.

Pub.L. 103–322, § 160001(f), as amended Pub.L. 104–294, § 604(b)(6), substituted "sections 2251, 2251A, 2252, and 2258" for "sections 2251–2252".

Pub.L. 103–394, § 312(b), inserted "(except in cases under section 157 of that title)" after "offense involving fraud connected with a case under title 11".

1990 Amendments. Par. (1)(B). Pub.L. 101–647, § 3560(1), (2), substituted "relating to" for "relative to" in the parenthetical provision following "section 1029" and struck out "sections 2251 through 2252 (relating to sexual exploitation of children)," before ", section 1958".

1989 Amendments. Par. (1). Pub.L. 101–73 inserted "section 1344 (relating to financial institution fraud)," after "section 1343 (relating to wire fraud),".

1988 Amendments. Par. (1)(B). Pub.L. 100–690, § 7514, inserted "sections 2251 through 2252 (relating to sexual exploitation of children),".

Par. (1). Pub.L. 100–690, § 7032, substituted "section 2321" for "section 2320".

Pub.L. 100–690, § 7054, inserted ", section 1029 (relative to fraud and related activity in connection with access devices)" and ", section 1958 (relating to use of interstate commerce facilities in the commission of murder-for-hire), sections 2251–2252 (relating to sexual exploitation of children)".

Pub.L. 100–690, § 7013, made technical amendment to directory language of Pub.L. 99–646.

Par. (10). Pub.L. 100–690, § 7020(c), added "the Associate Attorney General of the United States," following "Deputy Attorney General of the United States,".

1986 Amendments. Par. (1). Pub.L. 99–646, as amended by Pub.L. 100–690, § 7013, inserted "section 1512 (relating to tampering with a witness, victim, or an informant), section 1513 (relating to retaliating against a witness, victim, or an informant)," after "obstruction of State of local law enforcement),".

Par. (1)(B). Pub.L. 99–570, § 1365(b), inserted "section 1956 (relating to the laundering of monetary instruments), section 1957 (relating to engaging in monetary transactions in property derived from specified unlawful activity)," after "section 1955 (relating to the prohibition of illegal gambling businesses),".

1984 Amendments. Par. (1). Pub.L. 98–473, § 901(g)(2), added ", or (E) any act which is indictable under the Currency and Foreign Transactions Reporting Act".

Par. (1)(A). Pub.L. 98–473, § 1020(1), added "dealing in obscene matter," after "extortion,".

Par. (1)(B). Pub.L. 98–473, § 1020(2), added "sections 1461–1465 (relating to obscene matter)," after "section 1343 (relating to wire fraud),".

Pub.L. 98–547, § 205(2), inserted reference to section 2320 (relating to trafficking in certain motor vehicles or motor vehicle parts).

Pub.L. 98–547, § 205(1), inserted reference to sections 2312 and 2313 (relating to interstate transportation of stolen motor vehicles).

1978 Amendments. Par. (1)(B). Pub.L. 95–575 inserted "sections 2341–2346 (relating to trafficking in contraband cigarettes)," following "sections 2314 and 2315 (relating to interstate transportation of stolen property),".

Par. (1) (D). Pub.L. 95–598 substituted "fraud connected with a case under title 11" for "bankruptcy fraud".

References to Coupons, Authorization Cards, or Access Devices under Food and Nutrition Act of 2008

References in any Federal, State, tribal, or local law to a "coupon", "authorization card", or other access device provided under the Food and Nutrition Act of 2008, 7 U.S.C.A. § 2011 et seq., considered to be a reference to a "benefit" provided under that Act, see Pub.L. 110–234, § 4115(d), and Pub.L. 110–246, § 4115(d), set out as a note under 7 U.S.C.A. § 2012.

Liberal Construction of Provisions; Supersedure of Federal or State Laws; Authority of Attorneys Representing United States

Section 904 of Pub.L. 91–452 provided that:

"(a) The provisions of this title [enacting this chapter and amending sections 1505, 2516, and 2517 of this title] shall be liberally construed to effectuate its remedial purposes.

"(b) Nothing in this title shall supersede any provision of Federal, State, or other law imposing criminal penalties or affording civil remedies in addition to those provided for in this title.

"(c) Nothing contained in this title shall impair the authority of any attorney representing the United States to—

"(1) lay before any grand jury impaneled by any district court of the United States any evidence concerning any alleged racketeering violation of law;

"(2) invoke the power of any such court to compel the production of any evidence before any such grand jury; or

"(3) institute any proceeding to enforce any order or process issued in execution of such power or to punish disobedience of any such order or process by any person."

CHAPTER 119—WIRE AND ELECTRONIC COMMUNICATIONS INTERCEPTION AND INTERCEPTION OF ORAL COMMUNICATIONS

§ 2516. Authorization for interception of wire, oral, or electronic communications

(1) The Attorney General, Deputy Attorney General, Associate Attorney General[1], or any Assistant Attorney General, any acting Assistant Attorney General, or any Deputy Assistant Attorney General or acting Deputy Assistant Attorney General in the Criminal Division or National Security Division specially designated by the Attorney General, may authorize an application to a Federal judge of competent jurisdiction for, and such judge may grant in conformity with section 2518 of this chapter an order authorizing or approving the interception of wire or oral communications by the Federal Bureau of Investigation, or a Federal agency having responsibility for the investigation of the offense as to which the application is made, when such interception may provide or has provided evidence of—

(a) any offense punishable by death or by imprisonment for more than one year under sections 2122 and 2274 through 2277 of title 42 of the United States Code (relating to the enforcement of the Atomic Energy Act of 1954), section 2284 of title 42 of the United States Code (relating to sabotage of nuclear facilities or fuel), or under the following chapters of this title: chapter 10 (relating to biological weapons)[2] chapter 37 (relating to espionage), chapter 55 (relating to kidnapping), chapter 90 (relating to protection of trade secrets), chapter 105 (relating to sabotage), chapter 115 (relating to treason), chapter 102 (relating to riots), chapter 65 (relating to malicious mischief), chapter 111 (relating to destruction of vessels), or chapter 81 (relating to piracy);

(b) a violation of section 186 or section 501(c) of title 29, United States Code (dealing with restrictions on payments and loans to labor organizations), or any offense which involves murder, kidnapping, robbery, or extortion, and which is punishable under this title;

(c) any offense which is punishable under the following sections of this title: section 37 (relating to violence at international airports), section 43 (relating to animal enterprise terrorism), section 81 (arson within special maritime and territorial jurisdiction), section 201 (bribery of public officials and witnesses), section 215 (relating to bribery of bank officials), section 224 (bribery in sporting contests), subsection (d), (e), (f), (g), (h), or (i) of section 844 (unlawful use of explosives), section 1032 (relating to concealment of assets), section 1084 (transmission of wagering information), section 751 (relating to escape), section 832 (relating to nuclear and weapons of mass destruction threats), section 842 (relating to explosive materials), section 930 (relating to possession of weapons in Federal facilities), section 1014 (relating to loans and credit applications generally; renewals and discounts), section 1114 (relating to officers and employees of the United States), section 1116 (relating to protection of foreign officials), sections 1503, 1512, and 1513 (influencing or injuring an officer, juror, or witness generally), section 1510 (obstruction of criminal investigations), section 1511 (obstruction of State or local law enforcement), section 1591 (sex trafficking of children by force, fraud, or coercion), section 1751 (Presidential and Presidential staff assassination, kidnapping, and assault), section 1951 (interference with commerce by threats or violence), section 1952 (interstate and foreign travel or transportation in aid of racketeering enterprises), section 1958 (relating to use of interstate commerce facilities in the commission of murder for hire), section 1959 (relating to violent crimes in aid of racketeering activity), section 1954 (offer, acceptance,

---

[1] See Codifications note set out under this section.
[2] So in original. A comma should probably appear.

or solicitation to influence operations of employee benefit plan), section 1955 (prohibition of business enterprises of gambling), section 1956 (laundering of monetary instruments), section 1957 (relating to engaging in monetary transactions in property derived from specified unlawful activity), section 659 (theft from interstate shipment), section 664 (embezzlement from pension and welfare funds), section 1343 (fraud by wire, radio, or television), section 1344 (relating to bank fraud), section 1992 (relating to terrorist attacks against mass transportation), sections 2251 and 2252 (sexual exploitation of children), section 2251A (selling or buying of children), section 2252A (relating to material constituting or containing child pornography), section 1466A (relating to child obscenity), section 2260 (production of sexually explicit depictions of a minor for importation into the United States), sections 2421, 2422, 2423, and 2425 (relating to transportation for illegal sexual activity and related crimes), sections 2312, 2313, 2314, and 2315 (interstate transportation of stolen property), section 2321 (relating to trafficking in certain motor vehicles or motor vehicle parts), section 2340A (relating to torture), section 1203 (relating to hostage taking), section 1029 (relating to fraud and related activity in connection with access devices), section 3146 (relating to penalty for failure to appear), section 3521(b)(3) (relating to witness relocation and assistance), section 32 (relating to destruction of aircraft or aircraft facilities), section 38 (relating to aircraft parts fraud), section 1963 (violations with respect to racketeer influenced and corrupt organizations), section 115 (relating to threatening or retaliating against a Federal official), section 1341 (relating to mail fraud), a felony violation of section 1030 (relating to computer fraud and abuse), section 351 (violations with respect to congressional, Cabinet, or Supreme Court assassinations, kidnapping, and assault), section 831 (relating to prohibited transactions involving nuclear materials), section 33 (relating to destruction of motor vehicles or motor vehicle facilities), section 175 (relating to biological weapons), section 175c (relating to variola virus), section 956 (conspiracy to harm persons or property overseas), section[3] a felony violation of section 1028 (relating to production of false identification documentation), section 1425 (relating to the procurement of citizenship or nationalization unlawfully), section 1426 (relating to the reproduction of naturalization or citizenship papers), section 1427 (relating to the sale of naturalization or citizenship papers), section 1541 (relating to passport issuance without authority), section 1542 (relating to false statements in passport applications), section 1543 (relating to forgery or false use of passports), section 1544 (relating to misuse of passports), or section 1546 (relating to fraud and misuse of visas, permits, and other documents), section 555 (relating to construction or use of international border tunnels);

(d) any offense involving counterfeiting punishable under section 471, 472, or 473 of this title;

(e) any offense involving fraud connected with a case under title 11 or the manufacture, importation, receiving, concealment, buying, selling, or otherwise dealing in narcotic drugs, marihuana, or other dangerous drugs, punishable under any law of the United States;

(f) any offense including extortionate credit transactions under sections 892, 893, or 894 of this title;

(g) a violation of section 5322 of title 31, United States Code (dealing with the reporting of currency transactions), or section 5324 of title 31, United States Code (relating to structuring transactions to evade reporting requirement prohibited);

(h) any felony violation of sections 2511 and 2512 (relating to interception and disclosure of certain communications and to certain intercepting devices) of this title;

(i) any felony violation of chapter 71 (relating to obscenity) of this title;

(j) any violation of section 60123(b) (relating to destruction of a natural gas pipeline), section 46502 (relating to aircraft piracy), the second sentence of section 46504 (relating to assault on a flight crew with dangerous weapon), or section 46505(b)(3) or (c) (relating to explosive or incendiary devices, or endangerment of human life, by means of weapons on aircraft) of title 49;

---

[3] So in original. The word "section" probably should not appear.

(k) any criminal violation of section 2778 of title 22 (relating to the Arms Export Control Act);

(l) the location of any fugitive from justice from an offense described in this section;

(m) a violation of section 274, 277, or 278 of the Immigration and Nationality Act (8 U.S.C. 1324, 1327, or 1328) (relating to the smuggling of aliens);

(n) any felony violation of sections 922 and 924 of title 18, United States Code (relating to firearms);

(o) any violation of section 5861 of the Internal Revenue Code of 1986 (relating to firearms);

(p) a felony violation of section 1028 (relating to production of false identification documents), section 1542 (relating to false statements in passport applications), section 1546 (relating to fraud and misuse of visas, permits, and other documents,[4] section 1028A (relating to aggravated identity theft))[5] of this title or a violation of section 274, 277, or 278 of the Immigration and Nationality Act (relating to the smuggling of aliens); or[6]

(q) any criminal violation of section 229 (relating to chemical weapons): or sections[7] 2332, 2332a, 2332b, 2332d, 2332f, 2332g, 2332h[8] 2339, 2339A, 2339B, 2339C, or 2339D of this title (relating to terrorism);

(r) any criminal violation of section 1 (relating to illegal restraints of trade or commerce), 2 (relating to illegal monopolizing of trade or commerce), or 3 (relating to illegal restraints of trade or commerce in territories or the District of Columbia) of the Sherman Act (15 U.S.C. 1, 2, 3);

(s) any violation of section 670 (relating to theft of medical products); or

(t) any conspiracy to commit any offense described in any subparagraph of this paragraph.

(2) The principal prosecuting attorney of any State, or the principal prosecuting attorney of any political subdivision thereof, if such attorney is authorized by a statute of that State to make application to a State court judge of competent jurisdiction for an order authorizing or approving the interception of wire, oral, or electronic communications, may apply to such judge for, and such judge may grant in conformity with section 2518 of this chapter and with the applicable State statute an order authorizing, or approving the interception of wire, oral, or electronic communications by investigative or law enforcement officers having responsibility for the investigation of the offense as to which the application is made, when such interception may provide or has provided evidence of the commission of the offense of murder, kidnapping, gambling, robbery, bribery, extortion, or dealing in narcotic drugs, marihuana or other dangerous drugs, or other crime dangerous to life, limb, or property, and punishable by imprisonment for more than one year, designated in any applicable State statute authorizing such interception, or any conspiracy to commit any of the foregoing offenses.

(3) Any attorney for the Government (as such term is defined for the purposes of the Federal Rules of Criminal Procedure) may authorize an application to a Federal judge of competent jurisdiction for, and such judge may grant, in conformity with section 2518 of this title, an order authorizing or approving the interception of electronic communications by an investigative or law enforcement officer having responsibility for the investigation of the offense as to which the application is made, when such interception may provide or has provided evidence of any Federal felony.

---

[4] So in original. Probably should read "other documents),".
[5] So in original. The second closing parenthesis probably should not appear.
[6] So in original. The word "or" probably should not appear.
[7] So in original. Probably should be "weapons) or section".
[8] So in original. A comma probably should appear.

18 § 2516 — RELATED PROVISIONS

(Added Pub.L. 90–351, Title III, § 802, June 19, 1968, 82 Stat. 216; amended Pub.L. 91–452, Title VIII, § 810, Title IX, § 902(a), Title XI, § 1103, Oct. 15, 1970, 84 Stat. 940, 947, 959; Pub.L. 91–644, Title IV, § 16, Jan. 2, 1971, 84 Stat. 1891; Pub.L. 95–598, Title III, § 314(h), Nov. 6, 1978, 92 Stat. 2677; Pub.L. 97–285, §§ 2(e), 4(e), Oct. 6, 1982, 96 Stat. 1220, 1221; Pub.L. 98–292, § 8, May 21, 1984, 98 Stat. 206; Pub.L. 98–473, Title II, § 1203(c), Oct. 12, 1984, 98 Stat. 2152; Pub.L. 99–508, Title I, §§ 101(c)(1)(A), 104, 105, Oct. 21, 1986, 100 Stat. 1851, 1855; Pub.L. 99–570, Title I, § 1365(c), Oct. 27, 1986, 100 Stat. 3207–35; Pub.L. 100–690, Title VI, § 6461, Title VII, §§ 7036, 7053(d), 7525, Nov. 18, 1988, 102 Stat. 4374, 4399, 4402, 4502; Pub.L. 101–298, § 3(b), May 22, 1990, 104 Stat. 203; Pub.L. 101–647, Title XXV, § 2531, Title XXXV, § 3568, Nov. 29, 1990, 104 Stat. 4879, 4928; Pub.L. 103–272, § 5(e)(11), July 5, 1994, 108 Stat. 1374; Pub.L. 103–322, Title XXXIII, §§ 330011(c)(1), (q)(1), (r), 330021(1), Sept. 13, 1994, 108 Stat. 2144, 2145, 2150; Pub.L. 103–414, Title II, § 208, Oct. 25, 1994, 108 Stat. 4292; Pub.L. 103–429, § 7(a)(4)(A), Oct. 31, 1994, 108 Stat. 4389; Pub.L. 104–132, Title IV, § 434, Apr. 24, 1996, 110 Stat. 1274; Pub.L. 104–208, Div. C, Title II, § 201, Sept. 30, 1996, 110 Stat. 3009–564; Pub.L. 104–287, § 6(a)(2), Oct. 11, 1996, 110 Stat. 3398; Pub.L. 104–294, Title I, § 102, Title VI, § 601(d), Oct. 11, 1996, 110 Stat. 3491, 3499; Pub.L. 105–318, § 6(b), Oct. 30, 1998, 112 Stat. 3011; Pub.L. 106–181, Title V, § 506(c)(2)(B), Apr. 5, 2000, 114 Stat. 139; Pub.L. 107–56, Title II, §§ 201, 202, Oct. 26, 2001, 115 Stat. 278; Pub.L. 107–197, Title III, § 301(a), June 25, 2002, 116 Stat. 728; Pub.L. 107–273, Div. B, Title IV, §§ 4002(c)(1), 4005(a)(1), Nov. 2, 2002, 116 Stat. 1808, 1812; Pub.L. 108–21, Title II, § 201, Apr. 30, 2003, 117 Stat. 659; Pub.L. 108–458, Title VI, § 6907, Dec. 17, 2004, 118 Stat. 3774; Pub.L. 109–162, Title XI, § 1171(b), Jan. 5, 2006, 119 Stat. 3123; Pub.L. 109–177, Title I, §§ 110(b)(3)(C), 113, Title V, § 506(a)(6), Mar. 9, 2006, 120 Stat. 208, 209, 248; Pub.L. 112–127, § 4, June 5, 2012, 126 Stat. 371; Pub.L. 112–186, § 5, Oct. 5, 2012, 126 Stat. 1429.)

HISTORICAL AND STATUTORY NOTES

References in Text

The Atomic Energy Act of 1954, referred to in par. (1)(a), is classified generally to 42 U.S.C.A. § 2011 et seq.

Chapters 10, 37, 55, 90, 105, 115, 102, 65, 111, and 81, referred to in par. (1)(a), are 18 U.S.C.A. §§ 175 et seq., 791 et seq., 1201 et seq., 1831 et seq., 2151 et seq., 2381 et seq., 2101 et seq., 1361 et seq., 2271 et seq., and 1651 et seq., respectively.

The Arms Export Control Act, referred to in par. (1)(k), is Pub.L. 90–629, Oct. 22, 1968, 82 Stat. 1320, as amended, which is classified generally to chapter 39 of Title 22, Foreign Relations and Intercourse (22 U.S.C.A. § 2751 et seq.). For complete classification of this Act to the Code, see Short Title note set out under 22 U.S.C.A. § 2751 and Tables.

Sections 274, 277, and 278 of the Immigration and Nationality Act, referred to in par. (1)(m) and (p), are sections 274, 277, and 278 of Act June 27, 1952, c. 477, 66 Stat. 163, as amended, which are classified to 8 U.S.C.A. §§ 1324, 1327, and 1328.

Sections 1, 2, or 3 of the Sherman Act, referred to in par. (1)(r), are sections 1, 2, or 3, of Act July 2, 1890, c. 647, 26 Stat. 209, also known as the Sherman Anti-Trust Act, which are classified to 15 U.S.C.A. § 1, 2, or 3.

Codifications

Pub.L. 98–473, § 1203(c)(4), which directed the amendment of the first par. of par. (1) by inserting "Deputy Attorney General, Associate Attorney General," after "Attorney General." was executed by making the insertion after the first reference to "Attorney General," to reflect the probable intent of Congress.

Section 102 of Pub.L. 104–294, which directed that par. (1)(c) of this section be amended by inserting "chapter 90 (relating to protection of trade secrets)," following "chapter 37 (relating to espionage),", could not be executed to text, as par. (1)(c) does not contain phrase "chapter 37 (relating to espionage),".

Amendment to par. (1)(c) by section 1365(c) of Pub.L. 99–570 was executed by inserting "section 1956 (laundering of monetary instruments), section 1957 (relating to engaging in monetary transactions in property derived from specified unlawful activity)," after "section 1955 (prohibition of business enterprises of gambling)," as the probable intent of Congress.

Amendment by section 601(d)(1) of Pub.L. 104–294, which directed that "or" be struck out after the semicolon in par. (1)(l), could not be executed in view of prior identical amendment by section 201(2) of Pub.L. 104–208.

Amendment by section 601(d)(2) of Pub.L. 104–294, which directed that "or" be substituted for "and" following the semicolon in par. (1)(n), could not be executed as the word "and" does not appear at the end of par. (1)(n). See also 2002 Amendments notes set out under this section.

Amendments

2012 Amendments. Par. (1)(r). Pub.L. 112–186, § 5(2), struck out "or" at the end.

Par. (1)(s). Pub.L. 112–186, § 5(1), (3), redesignated subsec. (s) as subsec. (t) and added a new subsec. (s).

Par. (1)(t). Pub.L. 112–186, § 5(1), redesignated former subsec. (s) as subsec. (t).

Par. (1)(c). Pub.L. 112–127, § 4, before the semicolon at the end, inserted ", section 555 (relating to construction or use of international border tunnels)".

2006 Amendments. Par. (1). Pub.L. 109–177, § 506(a)(6), inserted "or National Security Division" after "the Criminal Division".

Par. (1)(a). Pub.L. 109–177, § 113(a), inserted "chapter 10 (relating to biological weapons)" after "under the following chapters of this title:".

Par. (1)(c). Pub.L. 109–177, § 110(b)(3)(C), struck out "1992 (relating to wrecking trains),".

Pub.L. 109–177, § 113(b)(1), inserted "section 37 (relating to violence at international airports), section 43 (relating to animal enterprise terrorism)," after "the following sections of this title:".

Pub.L. 109–177, § 113(b)(2), inserted "section 832 (relating to nuclear and weapons of mass destruction threats), section 842 (relating to explosive materials), section 930 (relating to possession of weapons in Federal facilities)," after "section 751 (relating to escape),".

Pub.L. 109–177, § 113(b)(3), inserted "section 1114 (relating to officers and employees of the United States), section 1116 (relating to protection of foreign officials)," after "section 1014 (relating to loans and credit applications generally; renewals and discounts),".

Pub.L. 109–177, § 113(b)(4), inserted "section 1992 (relating to terrorist attacks against mass transportation)," after "section 1344 (relating to bank fraud),".

Pub.L. 109–177, § 113(b)(5), inserted "section 2340A (relating to torture)," after "section 2321 (relating to trafficking in certain motor vehicles or motor vehicle parts),".

Pub.L. 109–177, § 113(b)(6), inserted "section 81 (arson within special maritime and territorial jurisdiction)," before "section 201 (bribery of public officials and witnesses)".

Pub.L. 109–177, § 113(b)(7), inserted "section 956 (conspiracy to harm persons or property overseas)," after "section 175c (relating to variola virus)".

Par. (1)(g). Pub.L. 109–177, § 113(c), before the semicolon at the end, inserted ", or section 5324 of title 31, United States Code (relating to structuring transactions to evade reporting requirement prohibited)".

Par. (1)(j). Pub.L. 109–177, § 113(d), struck out "or" before "section 46502 (relating to aircraft piracy)" and inserted a comma after "section 60123(b) (relating to the destruction of a natural gas pipeline"; and inserted ", the second sentence of section 46504 (relating to assault on a flight crew with dangerous weapon), or section 46505(b)(3) or (c) (relating to explosive or incendiary devices, or endangerment of human life, by means of weapons on aircraft)" before "of title 49".

Par. (1)(p). Pub.L. 109–177, § 113(e), inserted ", section 1028A (relating to aggravated identity theft)" after "other documents".

Par. (1)(q). Pub.L. 109–162, § 1171(b), struck out the semicolon after "(relating to chemical weapons)" and substituted "section 2332" for "sections 2332".

Pub.L. 109–177, § 113(f), inserted "2339" after "2232h"; struck out "or" before "2339C"; and inserted ", or 2339D" after "2339C".

Pub.L. 109–177, § 113(g)(1), struck out "or" after the semicolon at the end.

Par. (1)(r). Pub.L. 109–177, § 113(g)(2), (3), redesignated former subpar. (r) as (s) and inserted a new subpar. (r).

Par. (1)(s). Pub.L. 109–177, § 113(g)(2), redesignated former subpar. (r) as subpar. (s).

2004 Amendments. Par. (1)(a). Pub.L. 108–458, § 6907(1), inserted "2122 and" following "sections".

Par. (1)(c). Pub.L. 108–458, § 6907(2), inserted "section 175c (relating to variola virus)," following "section 175 (relating to biological weapons),".

Par. (1)(q). Pub.L. 108–458, § 6907(3), inserted "2332g, 2332h," following "2332f,".

2003 Amendments. Par. (1)(a). Pub.L. 108–21, § 201(1), inserted "chapter 55 (relating to kidnapping)," after "chapter 37 (relating to espionage),".

Par. (1)(c). Pub.L. 108–21, § 201(2)(A), inserted "section 1591 (sex trafficking of children by force, fraud, or coercion)," after "section 1511 (obstruction of State or local law enforcement),".

Pub.L. 108–21, § 201(2)(B), inserted "section 2251A (selling or buying of children), section 2252A (relating to material constituting or containing child pornography), section 1466A (relating to child obscenity), section 2260 (production of sexually explicit depictions of a minor for importation into the United States), sections 2421, 2422, 2423, and 2425 (relating to transportation for illegal sexual activity and related crimes)," after "sections 2251 and 2252 (sexual exploitation of children),".

2002 Amendments. Par. (1)(n). Pub.L. 107–273, § 4002(c)(1), repealed section 601(d)(2) of Pub.L. 104–294, and thus required no change in text. See Codifications and 1996 Amendments notes set out under this section.

Par. (1)(q). Pub.L. 107–197, § 301(a), inserted "2332f," after "2332d," and substituted "2339B, or 2339C" for "or 2339B".

Pub.L. 107–273, § 4005(a)(1), adjusted the margins and thus required no change in text.

2001 Amendments. Par. (1)(c). Pub.L. 107–56, § 202, struck out "and section 1341 (relating to mail fraud)," and inserted "section 1341 (relating to mail fraud), a felony violation of section 1030 (relating to computer fraud and abuse),".

Par. (1)(p). Pub.L. 107–56, § 201(1), redesignated par. (1)(p) set out second as par. (1)(r).

Par. (1)(q). Pub.L. 107–56, § 201(2), added subpar. (q).

Par. (1)(r). Pub.L. 107–56, § 201(1), temporarily redesignated par. (1)(p) set out second as par. (1)(r). See Sunset Provisions note set out below.

2000 Amendments. Par. (1)(c). Pub.L. 106–181, § 506(c)(2)(B), inserted "section 38 (relating to aircraft parts fraud)," after "section 32 (relating to destruction of aircraft or aircraft facilities),".

1998 Amendments. Par. (1)(a). Pub.L. 105–318, § 6(b) inserted "chapter 90 (relating to protection of trade secrets)," following "to espionage),".

1996 Amendments. Par. (1)(c). Pub.L. 104–294, § 102, directed the insertion of "chapter 90 (relating to protection of trade secrets)," following "chapter 37 (relating to espionage),", which could not be executed to text. See Codification note set out under this section.

Pub.L. 104–208, § 201(1), added provisions relating to felony violation of section 1028, 1425, 1426, 1427, 1541, 1542, 1543, 1544 or 1546 of this title.

Par. (1)(j). Pub.L. 104–287, § 6(a)(2), amending Pub.L. 103–272, § 5(e)(11); Pub.L. 103–429, § 7(a)(4)(A), substituted "section 46502" for "46502".

Par. (1)(l). Pub.L. 104–294, § 601(d)(1), directed that "or" be struck out after the semicolon, which could not be executed to text. See Codifications note set out under this section.

Pub.L. 104–208, § 201(2), struck out "or" after the semicolon.

Par. (1)(m). Pub.L. 104–208, § 201(4), added par. (m). Former par. (m) redesignated (n).

Par. (1)(n). Pub.L. 104–294, § 601(d)(2), directed "or" be substituted for "and" following the semicolon, which could not be executed to text. See Codifications note set out under this section.

Pub.L. 104–208, § 201(3), redesignated former par. (m) as (n).

Par. (1)(o), (p). Pub.L. 104–208, § 201(3), redesignated former pars. (n) and (o) as (o) and (p) [set first], respectively.

Pub.L. 104–132, § 434, added par. (o) and redesignated former par. (o) as (p) [set second].

1994 Amendments. Par. (1). Pub.L. 103–414, § 208, inserted "or acting Deputy Assistant Attorney General" following "Deputy Assistant Attorney General".

Par. (1)(c). Pub.L. 103–322, § 330021(1), substituted "kidnapping" for "kidnaping" wherever appearing.

Par. (1)(j). Pub.L. 103–272, § 5(e)(11), as amended Pub.L. 103–429, § 7(a)(4)(A); Pub.L. 104–287, § 6(a)(2), substituted "section 60123(b) (relating to destruction of a natural gas pipeline) or section 46502 (relating to aircraft piracy) of title 49;" for "section 11(c)(2) of the Natural Gas Pipeline Safety Act of 1968 (relating to destruction of a natural gas pipeline) or subsection 902(i) or (n) of the Federal Aviation Act of 1958 (relating to aircraft piracy);".

1990 Amendments. Par. (1)(c). Pub.L. 101–647, § 2531(1)(A) to (E), inserted before the provisions as indicated: "section 215 (relating to bribery of bank officials)," before "section 224"; "section 1014 (relating to loans and credit applications generally; renewals and discounts)," before "sections 1503,"; "section 1032 (relating to concealment of assets)," before "section 1084"; "section 1344 (relating to bank fraud)," before "sections 2251 and 2252"; and struck "the section in chapter 65 relating to destruction of an energy facility," preceding "and section 1341 (relating to mail fraud)".

Pub.L. 101–298, § 3(b), as amended Pub.L. 103–322, § 330011(c)(1), inserted "section 175 (relating to biological weapons)," following "section 33 (relating to destruction of motor vehicles or motor vehicle facilities),".

Par. (1)(j). Pub.L. 101–647, § 2531(3), as amended Pub.L. 103–322, § 330011(r), substituted "any violation of section 11(c)(2) of the Natural Gas Pipeline Safety Act of 1968 (relating to destruction of a natural gas pipeline) or subsection (i) or (n) of section 902 of the Federal Aviation Act of 1958 (relating to aircraft piracy)" for "any violation of section 1679a(c)(2) (relating to destruction of a natural gas pipeline) or subsection (i) or (n) of section 1472 (relating to aircraft piracy) of title 49, of the United States Code". See Repeals note set out under this section.

Pub.L. 101–647, § 3568, which substituted "any violation of section 11(c)(2) of the Natural Gas Pipeline Safety Act of 1968 (relating to destruction of a natural gas pipeline) or section 902(i) or (n) of the Federal Aviation Act of 1958 (relating to aircraft piracy)" for "any violation of section 1679(c)(2) (relating to destruction of a natural gas pipeline) or subsection (i) or (n) of section 1472 (relating to aircraft piracy) of title 49, of the United States Code", was repealed by section 330011(q)(1) of Pub.L. 103–322. See Repeals note set out under this section.

Par. (1)(m), (n). Pub.L. 101–647, § 2531(2)(A)–(C), struck subpar. "(m) any conspiracy to commit any of the foregoing offenses."; struck from subpar. (m) relating to firearms) the word "and"; and substituted at the end of subpar. (n) "; and" for the period.

Par. (1)(o). Pub.L. 101–647, § 2531(2)(D), added subpar. (o).

1988 Amendments. Pub.L. 100–690, § 7036(a)(1), substituted "Associate Attorney General, or any" for "Associate Attorney General, any".

Par. (1)(a). Pub.L. 100–690, § 7036(c)(1), substituted "(relating to riots)," for "(relating to riots);".

Par. (1)(c). Pub.L. 100–690, § 7036(a)(2), struck out comma following "to mail fraud,", requiring no change in text.

Pub.L. 100–690, § 7036(b), substituted "section 2321" for "the second section 2320", and struck out "section 2252 or 2253 (sexual exploitation of children)," following "exploitation of children),".

Pub.L. 100–690, § 7053(d), substituted "1958" for "1952A", and "1959" for "1952B".

Par. (1)(i). Pub.L. 100–690, § 7525, added subpar. (i). Former subpar. (i) was redesignated (j).

Par. (1)(j). Pub.L. 100–690, § 7525, redesignated former subpar. (i) as (j). Former subpar. (j) was redesignated (k).

Pub.L. 100–690, § 7036(c)(2), struck out "or;" following "Export Control Act);".

Par. (1)(k). Pub.L. 100–690, § 7525, redesignated former subpar. (j) as (k). Former subpar. (k) was redesignated (l).

Pub.L. 100–690, § 7036(c)(3), substituted "section; or" for "section;".

Par. (1)(l). Pub.L. 100–690, § 7525, redesignated former subpar. (k) as (l). Former subpar. (l) was redesignated (m).

Par. (1)(m). Pub.L. 100–690, § 7525, redesignated former subpar. (l) as (m).

Par. (1)(m), (n). Pub.L. 100–690, § 6461, added subpars. (m) and (n).

1986 Amendments. Catchline. Pub.L. 99–508, § 101(c)(1)(A), substituted "wire, oral, or electronic communications" for "wire or oral communications".

Par. (1). Pub.L. 99–508, § 104, substituted "any Assistant Attorney General, any acting Assistant Attorney General, or any Deputy Assistant Attorney General in the Criminal Division specially designated for "or any Assistant Attorney General specially designated".

Par. (1)(a). Pub.L. 99–508, § 105(a)(5), added "section 2284 of title 42 of the United States Code (relating to sabotage of nuclear facilities or fuel)," following "Atomic Energy Act of 1954,", "chapter 65 (relating to malicious mischief), chapter 111 (relating to destruction of vessels), or chapter 81 (relating to piracy)" following "relating to riots)", and struck out "or" following "(relating to treason),".

Par. (1)(c). Pub.L. 99–570, § 1356(c), added references to section 1956 (laundering of monetary instruments) and section 1957 (relating to engaging in monetary transactions in property derived from specified unlawful activity). See Codification note set out under this section.

Pub.L. 99–508, § 105(a)(1), added "section 751 (relating to escape)," following "wagering information),", "the second section 2320 (relating to trafficking in certain motor vehicles or motor vehicle parts), section 1203 (relating to hostage taking), section 1029 (relating to fraud and related activity in connection with access devices), section 3146 (relating to penalty for failure to appear), section 3521(b)(3) (relating to witness relocation and assistance), section 32 (relating to destruction of aircraft or aircraft facilities)," following "stolen property),", "section 1952A (relating to use of interstate commerce facilities in the commission of murder for hire), section 1952B (relating to violent crimes in aid of racketeering activity)," following "racketeering enterprises),", ", section 115 (relating to threatening or retaliating against a Federal official), the section in chapter 65 relating to destruction of an energy facility, and section 1341 (relating to mail fraud)," following "corrupt organizations)", ", section 831 (relating to prohibited transactions involving nuclear materials), section 33 (relating to destruction of motor vehicles or motor vehicle facilities), or section 1992 (relating to wrecking trains)" following "Court assassinations, kidnaping, and assault)", and substituted "2312, 2313, 2314," for "2314" and "section 351" for "or section 351".

Par. (1)(h). Pub.L. 99–508, § 105(a)(3), added par. (h). Former par. (h) was redesignated (l).

Pars. (1)(i) to (k). Pub.L. 99–508, § 105(a)(3), added pars. (i) to (k).

Par. (1)(l). Pub.L. 99–508, § 105(a)(4), redesignated former par. (h) as (l).

Par. (2). Pub.L. 99–508, § 101(c)(1)(A), substituted "wire, oral, or electronic communications" for "wire or oral communications" wherever appearing in text.

Par. (3). Pub.L. 99–508, § 105(b), added par. (3).

1984 Amendments. Par. (1). Pub.L. 98–473, § 1203(c)(4), added "Deputy Attorney General, Associate Attorney General," after "Attorney General".

Par. (1)(c). Pub.L. 98–473, § 1203(c)(1), added "section 1343 (fraud by wire, radio, or television), section 2252 or 2253 (sexual exploitation of children)," after "section 664 (embezzlement from pension and welfare funds),".

Pub.L. 98–292 added "sections 2251 and 2252 (sexual exploitation of children)," after "section 664 (embezzlement from pension and welfare funds),".

Pub.L. 98–473, § 1203(c)(2), added references to sections 1512 and 1513 after "1503".

Par. (1)(g). Pub.L. 98–473, § 1203(c)(3), added par. (g). Former par. (g) was redesignated par. (h).

Par. (1)(h). Pub.L. 98–473, § 1203(c)(3), redesignated par. (g) as par. (h).

1982 Amendments. Par. (1)(c). Pub.L. 97–285, §§ 2(e), 4(e), substituted "(Presidential and Presidential staff assassination, kidnaping, and assault)" for "(Presidential assassinations, kidnaping, and assault)" following "section 1751" and substituted "(violations with respect to congressional, Cabinet, or Supreme Court assassinations, kidnaping, and assault)" for "(violations with respect to congressional assassination, kidnaping, and assault)" following "section 351".

1978 Amendments. Par. (1)(e). Pub.L. 95–598 substituted "fraud connected with a case under title 11" for "bankruptcy fraud".

1971 Amendments. Par. (1)(c). Pub.L. 91–644 added provision authorizing interception of communications with respect to section 351 offense (violations with respect to congressional assassination, kidnaping, and assault).

1970 Amendments. Par. (1)(c). Pub.L. 91–452 added provisions authorizing applicability to sections 844(d), (e), (f), (g), (h), or (i), 1511, 1955, and 1963 of this title.

CHAPTER 203—ARREST AND COMMITMENT

§ 3057. Bankruptcy investigations

(a) Any judge, receiver, or trustee having reasonable grounds for believing that any violation under chapter 9 of this title or other laws of the United States relating to insolvent debtors, receiverships or reorganization plans has been committed, or that an investigation should be had in connection therewith, shall report to the appropriate United States attorney all the facts and circumstances of the case, the names of the witnesses and the offense or offenses believed to have been committed. Where one of such officers has made such report, the others need not do so.

(b) The United States attorney thereupon shall inquire into the facts and report thereon to the judge, and if it appears probable that any such offense has been committed, shall without delay, present the matter to the grand jury, unless upon inquiry and examination he decides that the ends of public justice do not require investigation or prosecution, in which case he shall report the facts to the Attorney General for his direction.

(June 25, 1948, c. 645, 62 Stat. 818; May 24, 1949, c. 139, § 48, 63 Stat. 96; Nov. 6, 1978, Pub.L. 95–598, Title III, § 314(i), 92 Stat. 2677.)

HISTORICAL AND STATUTORY NOTES

Amendments

1978 Amendments. Subsec. (a). Pub.L. 95–598, § 314(i), substituted "judge" for "referee" and "violation under chapter 9 of this title" for "violations of the bankruptcy laws".

Subsec. (b). Pub.L. 95–598, § 314(i) (1), substituted "judge" for "referee".

1949 Amendments. Subsec. (a). Act May 24, 1949, substituted "or other laws of the United States" for "or laws".

CHAPTER 213—LIMITATIONS

§ 3284. Concealment of bankrupt's assets

The concealment of assets of a debtor in a case under title 11 shall be deemed to be a continuing offense until the debtor shall have been finally discharged or a discharge denied, and the period of limitations shall not begin to run until such final discharge or denial of discharge.

(June 25, 1948, c. 645, 62 Stat. 828; Nov. 6, 1978, Pub.L. 95–598, Title III, § 314(k), 92 Stat. 2678.)

HISTORICAL AND STATUTORY NOTES

Amendments

1978 Amendments. Pub.L. 95–598 substituted "debtor in a case under title 11" for "bankrupt or other debtor".

CROSS REFERENCES

Bankruptcy investigations, see 18 USCA § 3057.

Five year limitation on offenses relating to bankruptcy, see 18 USCA § 3282.

Offenses relating to bankruptcy, see 18 USCA § 151 et seq.

PART V—IMMUNITY OF WITNESSES

CHAPTER 601—IMMUNITY OF WITNESSES

§ 6001. Definitions

As used in this chapter—

(1) "agency of the United States" means any executive department as defined in section 101 of title 5, United States Code, a military department as defined in section 102 of title 5, United States Code, the Nuclear Regulatory Commission, the Board of Governors of the Federal Reserve System, the China Trade Act registrar appointed under 53 Stat. 1432 (15 U.S.C. sec. 143), the Commodity Futures Trading Commission, the Federal Communications Commission, the Federal Deposit Insurance Corporation, the Federal Maritime Commission, the Federal Power Commission, the Federal Trade Commission, the Surface Transportation Board, the National Labor Relations Board, the National Transportation Safety Board, the Railroad Retirement Board, an arbitration board established under 48 Stat. 1193 (45 U.S.C. sec. 157), the Securities and Exchange Commission, or a board established under 49 Stat. 31 (15 U.S.C. sec. 715d);

(2) "other information" includes any book, paper, document, record, recording, or other material;

(3) "proceeding before an agency of the United States" means any proceeding before such an agency with respect to which it is authorized to issue subpenas and to take testimony or receive other information from witnesses under oath; and

(4) "court of the United States" means any of the following courts: the Supreme Court of the United States, a United States court of appeals, a United States district court established under chapter 5, title 28, United States Code, a United States bankruptcy court established under chapter 6, title 28, United States Code, the District of Columbia Court of Appeals, the Superior Court of the District of Columbia, the District Court of Guam, the District Court of the Virgin Islands, the United States Court of Federal Claims, the Tax Court of the United States, the Court of International Trade, and the Court of Appeals for the Armed Forces.

(Added Pub.L. 91–452, Title II, § 201(a), Oct. 15, 1970, 84 Stat. 926; amended Pub.L. 95–405, § 25, Sept. 30, 1978, 92 Stat. 877; Pub.L. 95–598, Title III, § 314(l), Nov. 6, 1978, 92 Stat. 2678; Pub.L. 96–417, Title VI, § 601(1), Oct. 10, 1980, 94 Stat. 1744; Pub.L. 97–164, Title I, § 164(1), Apr. 2, 1982, 96 Stat. 50; Pub.L. 102–550, Title XV, § 1543, Oct. 28, 1992, 106 Stat. 4069; Pub.L. 102–572, Title IX, § 902(b)(1), Oct. 29, 1992, 106 Stat. 4519; Pub.L. 103–272, § 4(d), July 5, 1994, 108 Stat. 1361; Pub.L. 103–322, Title XXXIII, § 330013(2), (3), Sept. 13, 1994, 108 Stat. 2146; Pub.L. 103–337, Div. A, Title IX, § 924(d)(1)(B), Oct. 5, 1994, 108 Stat. 2832; Pub.L. 104–88, Title III, § 303(2), Dec. 29, 1995, 109 Stat. 943.)

HISTORICAL AND STATUTORY NOTES

Amendments

1995 Amendments. Par. (1). Pub.L. 104–88, § 303(2), substituted "Surface Transportation Board" for "Interstate Commerce Commission".

1994 Amendments. Pub.L. 103–322, § 330013(3), substituted "chapter" for "part" in the introductory text.

Par. (1). Pub.L. 103–272, § 4(d), deleted "the Civil Aeronautics Board" from list of U.S. agencies.

Pub.L. 103–322, § 330013(2), substituted "Nuclear Regulatory Commission" for "Atomic Energy Commission" and deleted "the Subversive Activities Control Board,".

Par. (4). Pub.L. 103–337, § 924(d)(1)(B), substituted "Court of Appeals for the Armed Forces" for "Court of Military Appeals".

1992 Amendments. Par. (1). Pub.L. 102–550, § 1543, added reference to the Board of Governors of the Federal Reserve System.

Par. (4). Pub.L. 102–572, § 902(b)(1), substituted "United States Court of Federal Claims" for "United States Claims Court".

1982 Amendments. Par. (4). Pub.L. 97–164 substituted "the United States Claims Court" for "the United States Court of Claims, the United States Court of Customs and Patent Appeals".

1980 Amendments. Par. (4). Pub.L. 96–417 redesignated the Customs Court as the Court of International Trade.

1978 Amendments. Par. (1). Pub.L. 95–405 inserted "the Commodity Futures Trading Commission," following "Civil Aeronautics Board,".

Par. (4). Pub.L. 95–598 inserted "a United States bankruptcy court established under chapter 6, title 28, United States Code," following "title 28, United States Code,".

TITLE 28
JUDICIARY AND JUDICIAL PROCEDURE

PART I—ORGANIZATION OF COURTS
CHAPTER 6—BANKRUPTCY JUDGES

HISTORICAL AND STATUTORY NOTES

Codifications

Chapter heading and section analysis of chapter 6, as added by Pub.L. 95–598, Title II, § 201(a), Nov. 6, 1978, 92 Stat. 2657, and amended Pub.L. 97–164, Title I, § 110(d), Apr. 2, 1982, 96 Stat. 29, effective June 28, 1984, pursuant to Pub.L. 95–598, Title IV, § 402(b), Nov. 6, 1978, 92 Stat. 2682, as amended by Pub.L. 98–249, § 1(a), Mar. 31, 1984, 98 Stat. 116; Pub.L. 98–271, § 1(a), Apr. 30, 1984, 98 Stat. 163; Pub.L. 98–299, § 1(a), May 25, 1984, 98 Stat. 214; Pub.L. 98–325, § 1(a), June 20, 1984, 98 Stat. 268, set out as a note preceding section 101 of Title 11, Bankruptcy, read as follows:

"CHAPTER 6—BANKRUPTCY COURTS"

Sec.

"151. Creation and composition of bankruptcy courts.

"152. Appointment of bankruptcy judges.

"153. Tenure and residence of bankruptcy judges.

"154. Salaries of bankruptcy judges.

"155. Chief judge; precedence of bankruptcy judges.

"156. Division of business among bankruptcy judges.

"157. Times of holding court.

"158. Accommodations at places for holding court.

"159. Vacant judgeship as affecting proceedings.

"160. Appellate panels."

Section 402(b) of Pub.L. 95–598 was amended by section 113 of Pub.L. 98–353 by substituting "shall not be effective" for "shall take effect on June 28, 1984", thereby eliminating the addition of the chapter heading and section analysis of chapter 6 by section 201(a) of Pub.L. 95–598, effective June 27, 1984, pursuant to section 122(c) of Pub.L. 98–353, set out as an Effective and Applicability Provisions note under section 151 of this title.

Section 121(a) of Pub.L. 98–353 directed that section 402(b) of Pub.L. 95–598 be amended by substituting "the date of enactment of the Bankruptcy Amendments and Federal Judgeship Act of 1984 [i.e. July 10, 1984]" for "June 28, 1984". This amendment was not executed in view of the prior amendment to section 402(b) of Pub.L. 95–598 by section 113 of Pub.L. 98–353.

Amendments

2005 Amendments. Pub.L. 109–8, Title VI, § 601(b), April 20, 2005, 119 Stat. 120, added item 159.

CROSS REFERENCES

Court of the United States defined as including bankruptcy court established under this chapter for purposes of immunity of witnesses, see 18 USCA § 6001.

Power of Bankruptcy Court, see 11 USCA § 105.

Recall of judges and magistrates, see 28 USCA § 375.

§ 151. Designation of bankruptcy courts

In each judicial district, the bankruptcy judges in regular active service shall constitute a unit of the district court to be known as the bankruptcy court for that district. Each bankruptcy judge, as a judicial officer of the district court, may exercise the authority conferred under this chapter with respect to any action, suit, or proceeding and may preside alone and hold a regular or special session of the court, except as otherwise provided by law or by rule or order of the district court.

(Added Pub.L. 98–353, Title I, § 104(a), July 10, 1984, 98 Stat. 336.)

HISTORICAL AND STATUTORY NOTES

Codifications

This section as added by Pub.L. 95–598, Title II, § 201(a), Nov. 6, 1978, 92 Stat. 2657, effective June 28, 1984, pursuant to Pub.L. 95–598, Title IV, § 402(b), Nov. 6, 1978, 92 Stat. 2682, as amended by Pub.L. 98–249, § 1(a), Mar. 31, 1984, 98 Stat. 116; Pub.L. 98–271, § 1(a), Apr. 30, 1984, 98 Stat. 163; Pub.L. 98–299, § 1(a), May 25, 1984, 98 Stat. 214; Pub.L. 98–325, § 1(a), June 20, 1984, 98 Stat. 268, set out as a note preceding section 101 of Title 11, Bankruptcy, read as follows:

§ 151. Creation and composition of bankruptcy courts

(a) There shall be in each judicial district, as an adjunct to the district court for such district, a bankruptcy court which shall be a court of record known as the United States Bankruptcy Court for the district.

(b) Each bankruptcy court shall consist of the bankruptcy judge or judges for the district in regular active service. Justices or judges designated and assigned shall be competent to sit as judges of the bankruptcy court.

(c) Except as otherwise provided by law, or rule or order of court, the judicial power of a bankruptcy court with respect to any action, suit or proceeding may be exercised by a single bankruptcy judge, who may preside alone and hold a regular or special session of court at the same time other sessions are held by other bankruptcy judges.

Section 402(b) of Pub.L. 95–598 was amended by section 113 of Pub.L. 98–353 by substituting "shall not be effective" for "shall take effect on June 28, 1984", thereby eliminating the addition of section 151 by section 201(a) of Pub.L. 95–598, effective June 27, 1984, pursuant to section 122(c) of Pub.L. 98–353, set out as an Effective and Applicability Provisions note under this section.

Section 121(a) of Pub.L. 98–353 directed that section 402(b) of Pub.L. 95–598 be amended by substituting "the date of enactment of the Bankruptcy Amendments and Federal Judgeship Act of 1984 [i.e. July 10, 1984]" for "June 28, 1984". This amendment was not executed in view of the prior amendment to section 402(b) of Pub.L. 95–598 by section 113 of Pub.L. 98–353.

§ 152. Appointment of bankruptcy judges

(a)(1) Each bankruptcy judge to be appointed for a judicial district, as provided in paragraph (2), shall be appointed by the court of appeals of the United States for the circuit in which such district is located. Such appointments shall be made after considering the recommendations of the Judicial Conference submitted pursuant to subsection (b). Each bankruptcy judge shall be appointed for a term of fourteen years, subject to the provisions of subsection (e). However, upon the expiration of the term, a bankruptcy judge may, with the approval of the judicial council of the circuit, continue to perform the duties of the office until the earlier of the date which is 180 days after the expiration of the term or the date of the appointment of a successor. Bankruptcy judges shall serve as judicial officers of the United States district court established under Article III of the Constitution.

(2) The bankruptcy judges appointed pursuant to this section shall be appointed for the several judicial districts as follows:

| Title 28 | U.S. CODE TITLES | 28 § 152 |

Districts	Judges
Alabama:	
Northern	5
Middle	2
Southern	2
Alaska	2
Arizona	7
Arkansas:	
Eastern and Western	3
California:	
Northern	9
Eastern	6
Central	21
Southern	4
Colorado	5
Connecticut	3
Delaware	1
District of Columbia	1
Florida:	
Northern	1
Middle	8
Southern	5
Georgia:	
Northern	8
Middle	3
Southern	2
Hawaii	1
Idaho	2
Illinois:	
Northern	10
Central	3
Southern	1
Indiana:	
Northern	3
Southern	4
Iowa:	
Northern	2
Southern	2
Kansas	4
Kentucky:	
Eastern	2
Western	3
Louisiana:	
Eastern	2
Middle	1
Western	3
Maine	2
Maryland	4
Massachusetts	5
Michigan:	
Eastern	4
Western	3
Minnesota	4
Mississippi:	
Northern	1
Southern	2
Missouri:	

Eastern	3
Western	3
Montana	1
Nebraska	2
Nevada	3
New Hampshire	1
New Jersey	8
New Mexico	2
New York:	
Northern	2
Southern	9
Eastern	6
Western	3
North Carolina:	
Eastern	2
Middle	2
Western	2
North Dakota	1
Ohio:	
Northern	8
Southern	7
Oklahoma:	
Northern	2
Eastern	1
Western	3
Oregon	5
Pennsylvania:	
Eastern	5
Middle	2
Western	4
Puerto Rico	2
Rhode Island	1
South Carolina	2
South Dakota	2
Tennessee:	
Eastern	3
Middle	3
Western	4
Texas:	
Northern	6
Eastern	2
Southern	6
Western	4
Utah	3
Vermont	1
Virginia:	
Eastern	5
Western	3
Washington:	
Eastern	2
Western	5
West Virginia:	
Northern	1
Southern	1
Wisconsin:	
Eastern	4
Western	2
Wyoming	1

(3) Whenever a majority of the judges of any court of appeals cannot agree upon the appointment of a bankruptcy judge, the chief judge of such court shall make such appointment.

(4) The judges of the district courts for the territories shall serve as the bankruptcy judges for such courts. The United States court of appeals for the circuit within which such a territorial district court is located may appoint bankruptcy judges under this chapter for such district if authorized to do so by the Congress of the United States under this section.

(b)(1) The Judicial Conference of the United States shall, from time to time, and after considering the recommendations submitted by the Director of the Administrative Office of the United States Courts after such Director has consulted with the judicial council of the circuit involved, determine the official duty stations of bankruptcy judges and places of holding court.

(2) The Judicial Conference shall, from time to time, submit recommendations to the Congress regarding the number of bankruptcy judges needed and the districts in which such judges are needed.

(3) Not later than December 31, 1994, and not later than the end of each 2-year period thereafter, the Judicial Conference of the United States shall conduct a comprehensive review of all judicial districts to assess the continuing need for the bankruptcy judges authorized by this section, and shall report to the Congress its findings and any recommendations for the elimination of any authorized position which can be eliminated when a vacancy exists by reason of resignation, retirement, removal, or death.

(c)(1) Each bankruptcy judge may hold court at such places within the judicial district, in addition to the official duty station of such judge, as the business of the court may require.

(2)(A) Bankruptcy judges may hold court at such places within the United States outside the judicial district as the nature of the business of the court may require, and upon such notice as the court orders, upon a finding by either the chief judge of the bankruptcy court (or, if the chief judge is unavailable, the most senior available bankruptcy judge) or by the judicial council of the circuit that, because of emergency conditions, no location within the district is reasonably available where the bankruptcy judges could hold court.

(B) Bankruptcy judges may transact any business at special sessions of court held outside the district pursuant to this paragraph that might be transacted at a regular session.

(C) If a bankruptcy court issues an order exercising its authority under subparagraph (A), the court—

(i) through the Administrative Office of the United States Courts, shall—

(I) send notice of such order, including the reasons for the issuance of such order, to the Committee on the Judiciary of the Senate and the Committee on the Judiciary of the House of Representatives; and

(II) not later than 180 days after the expiration of such court order submit a brief report to the Committee on the Judiciary of the Senate and the Committee on the Judiciary of the House of Representatives describing the impact of such order, including—

(aa) the reasons for the issuance of such order;

(bb) the duration of such order;

(cc) the impact of such order on litigants; and

(dd) the costs to the judiciary resulting from such order; and

(ii) shall provide reasonable notice to the United States Marshals Service before the commencement of any special session held pursuant to such order.

(d) With the approval of the Judicial Conference and of each of the judicial councils involved, a bankruptcy judge may be designated to serve in any district adjacent to or near the district for which such bankruptcy judge was appointed.

(e) A bankruptcy judge may be removed during the term for which such bankruptcy judge is appointed, only for incompetence, misconduct, neglect of duty, or physical or mental disability and only by the judicial council of the circuit in which the judge's official duty station is located. Removal may not occur unless a majority of all of the judges of such council concur in the order of removal. Before any order of removal may be entered, a full specification of charges shall be furnished to such bankruptcy judge who shall be accorded an opportunity to be heard on such charges.

(Added Pub.L. 98–353, Title I, § 104(a), July 10, 1984, 98 Stat. 336; amended Pub.L. 99–554, Title I, § 101, Oct. 27, 1986, 100 Stat. 3088; Pub.L. 100–587, Nov. 3, 1988, 102 Stat. 2982; Pub.L. 101–650, Title III, § 304, Dec. 1, 1990, 104 Stat. 5105; Pub.L. 102–361, §§ 2, 4, Aug. 26, 1992, 106 Stat. 965, 966; Pub.L. 109–8, Title XII, § 1223(d), Apr. 20, 2005, 119 Stat. 198; Pub.L. 109–63, § 2(c), Sept. 9, 2005, 119 Stat. 1994.)

HISTORICAL AND STATUTORY NOTES

Codifications

This section as added by Pub.L. 95–598, Title II, § 201(a), Nov. 6, 1978, 92 Stat. 2657, effective June 28, 1984, pursuant to Pub.L. 95–598, Title IV, § 402(b), Nov. 6, 1978, 92 Stat. 2682, as amended by Pub.L. 98–249, § 1(a), Mar. 31, 1984, 98 Stat. 116; Pub.L. 98–271, § 1(a), Apr. 30, 1984, 98 Stat. 163; Pub.L. 98–299, § 1(a), May 25, 1984, 98 Stat. 214; Pub.L. 98–325, § 1(a), June 20, 1984, 98 Stat. 268, set out as a note preceding section 101 of Title 11, Bankruptcy, read as follows:

" § 152. Appointment of bankruptcy judges

"The President shall appoint, by and with the advice and consent of the Senate, bankruptcy judges for the several judicial districts. In each instance, the President shall give due consideration to the recommended nominee or nominees of the Judicial Council of the Circuit within which an appointment is to be made."

Section 402(b) of Pub.L. 95–598 was amended by section 113 of Pub.L. 98–353 by substituting "shall not be effective" for "shall take effect on June 28, 1984", thereby eliminating the addition of section 152 by section 201(a) of Pub.L. 95–598, effective June 27, 1984, pursuant to section 122(c) of Pub.L. 98–353, set out as an Effective and Applicability Provisions note under 28 U.S.C.A. § 151.

Section 121(a) of Pub.L. 98–353 directed that section 402(b) of Pub.L. 95–598 be amended by substituting "the date of enactment of the Bankruptcy Amendments and Federal Judgeship Act of 1984 [i.e. July 10, 1984]" for "June 28, 1984". This amendment was not executed in view of the prior amendment to section 402(b) of Pub.L. 95–598 by section 113 of Pub.L. 98–353.

Amendments

2005 Amendments. Subsec. (a)(1). Pub.L. 109–8, § 1223(d)(1), rewrote the first sentence, substituting "Each bankruptcy judge to be appointed for a judicial district, as provided in paragraph (2), shall be appointed by the court of appeals of the United States for the circuit in which such district is located." for "The United States court of appeals for the circuit shall appoint bankruptcy judges for the judicial districts established in paragraph (2) in such numbers as are established in such paragraph."

Subsec. (a)(2). Pub.L. 109–8, § 1223(d)(2), in the item relating to the middle district of Georgia, substituted "3" for "2" and struck out the collective item relating to the number of judges for the middle and southern districts of Georgia, which had read: "Middle and Southern . . . . 1".

Subsec. (c)(1). Pub.L. 109–63, § 2(c)(1), redesignated the undesignated par. as par. (1).

Subsec. (c)(2). Pub.L. 109–63, § 2(c)(2), added par. (2).

1992 Amendments. Subsec. (a)(2). Pub.L. 102–361, § 2, amended par. (2) as follows:

(1) in the item relating to the district of Arizona by striking "5" and inserting "7";

(2) in the item relating to the central district of California by striking "19" and inserting "21";

(3) in the item relating to the district of Connecticut by striking "2" and inserting "3";

(4) in the item relating to the middle district of Florida by striking "4" and inserting "8";

(5) in the item relating to the southern district of Florida by striking "3" and inserting "5";

(6) in the item relating to the northern district of Georgia by striking "6" and inserting "8";

(7) in the item relating to Georgia by adding at the end the following:

"Middle and Southern .... 1";

(8) in the item relating to the district of Maryland by striking "3" and inserting "4";

(9) in the item relating to the district of Massachusetts by striking "4" and inserting "5";

(10) in the item relating to the district of New Jersey by striking "7" and inserting "8";

(11) in the item relating to the southern district of New York by striking "7" and inserting "9";

(12) in the item relating to the eastern district of Pennsylvania by striking "3" and inserting "5";

(13) in the item relating to the middle district of Tennessee by striking "2" and inserting "3";

(14) in the item relating to the western district of Tennessee by striking "3" and inserting "4";

(15) in the item relating to the northern district of Texas by striking "5" and inserting "6"; and

(16) in the item relating to the eastern district of Virginia by striking "4" and inserting "5".

Subsec. (b)(3). Pub.L. 102–361, § 4, added par. (3).

1990 Amendments. Subsec. (a)(1). Pub.L. 101–650 provided for extension of terms of office of bankruptcy judges until the earlier of 180 days after expiration of the term or appointment of a successor.

1988 Amendments. Subsec. (a)(2). Pub.L. 100–587 amended par. (2) as follows:

(1) in the item relating to the district of Alaska by striking "1" and inserting "2",

(2) in the item relating to the district of Colorado by striking "4" and inserting "5",

(3) in the item relating to the district of Kansas by striking "3" and inserting "4",

(4) in the item relating to the eastern district of Kentucky by striking "1" and inserting "2",

(5) in the item relating to the eastern district of Texas by striking "1" and inserting "2",

(6) in the item relating to the western district of Texas, by striking "3" and inserting "4", and

(7) in the item relating to the district of Arizona, by striking "4" and inserting "5".

1986 Amendments. Subsec. (a)(2). Pub.L. 99–554 amended subsec. (a)(2) as follows:

(1) in the item relating to the eastern district and the western district of Arkansas by striking out "2" and inserting in lieu thereof "3",

(2) in the item relating to the northern district of California by striking out "7" and inserting in lieu thereof "9",

(3) in the item relating to the eastern district of California by striking out "4" and inserting in lieu thereof "6",

(4) in the item relating to the central district of California by striking out "12" and inserting in lieu thereof "19",

(5) in the item relating to the southern district of California by striking out "3" and inserting in lieu thereof "4",

(6) in the item relating to the middle district of Florida by striking out "2" and inserting in lieu thereof "4",

(7) in the item relating to the northern district of Georgia by striking out "4" and inserting in lieu thereof "6",

(8) in the item relating to the southern district of Georgia by striking out "1" and inserting in lieu thereof "2",

(9) in the item relating to the district of Idaho by striking out "1" and inserting in lieu thereof "2",

(10) in the item relating to the northern district of Illinois by striking out "8" and inserting in lieu thereof "10",

(11) in the item relating to the central district of Illinois by striking out "2" and inserting in lieu thereof "3",

(12) in the item relating to the northern district of Indiana by striking out "2" and inserting in lieu thereof "3",

(13) in the item relating to the northern district of Iowa by striking out "1" and inserting in lieu thereof "2",

(14) in the item relating to the southern district of Iowa by striking out "1" and inserting in lieu thereof "2",

(15) in the item relating to the western district of Kentucky by striking out "2" and inserting in lieu thereof "3",

(16) in the item relating to the western district of Louisiana by striking out "2" and inserting in lieu thereof "3",

(17) in the item relating to the district of Maryland by striking out "2" and inserting in lieu thereof "3",

(18) in the item relating to the western district of Michigan by striking out "2" and inserting in lieu thereof "3",

(19) in the item relating to the district of Nebraska by striking out "1" and inserting in lieu thereof "2",

(20) in the item relating to the district of Nevada by striking out "2" and inserting in lieu thereof "3",

(21) in the item relating to the district of New Jersey by striking out "5" and inserting in lieu thereof "7",

(22) in the item relating to the western district of North Carolina by striking out "1" and inserting in lieu thereof "2",

(23) in the item relating to the northern district of Oklahoma by striking out "1" and inserting in lieu thereof "2",

(24) in the item relating to the western district of Oklahoma by striking out "2" and inserting in lieu thereof "3",

(25) in the item relating to the district of Oregon by striking out "4" and inserting in lieu thereof "5",

(26) in the item relating to the western district of Pennsylvania by striking out "3" and inserting in lieu thereof "4",

(27) in the item relating to the district of South Carolina by striking out "1" and inserting in lieu thereof "2",

(28) in the item relating to the district of South Dakota by striking out "1" and inserting in lieu thereof "2",

(29) in the item relating to the eastern district of Tennessee by striking out "2" and inserting in lieu thereof "3",

(30) in the item relating to the western district of Tennessee by striking out "2" and inserting in lieu thereof "3",

(31) in the item relating to the northern district of Texas by striking out "4" and inserting in lieu thereof "5",

(32) in the item relating to the southern district of Texas by striking out "3" and inserting in lieu thereof "6",

(33) in the item relating to the western district of Texas by striking out "2" and inserting in lieu thereof "3",

(34) in the item relating to the district of Utah by striking out "2" and inserting in lieu thereof "3",

(35) in the item relating to the eastern district of Virginia by striking out "3" and inserting in lieu thereof "4",

(36) in the item relating to the eastern district of Washington by striking out "1" and inserting in lieu thereof "2",

(37) in the item relating to the western district of Washington by striking out "4" and inserting in lieu thereof "5", and

(38) in the item relating to the eastern district of Wisconsin by striking out "3" and inserting in lieu thereof "4".

CROSS REFERENCES

Appeals, hearing of, see 28 USCA § 158.

Definition of Bankruptcy judge as including a judge appointed under this section for purposes of civil service retirement, see 5 USCA § 8331.

Removal of judges for disability to be in accordance with provisions of this section, see 28 USCA § 372.

Retirement of bankruptcy judges and magistrates, see 28 USCA § 377.

§ 153. Salaries; character of service

(a) Each bankruptcy judge shall serve on a full-time basis and shall receive as full compensation for his services, a salary at an annual rate that is equal to 92 percent of the salary of a judge of the district court of the United States as determined pursuant to section 135, to be paid at such times as the Judicial Conference of the United States determines.

(b) A bankruptcy judge may not engage in the practice of law and may not engage in any other practice, business, occupation, or employment inconsistent with the expeditious, proper, and impartial performance of such bankruptcy judge's duties as a judicial officer. The Conference may promulgate appropriate rules and regulations to implement this subsection.

(c) Each individual appointed under this chapter shall take the oath or affirmation prescribed by section 453 of this title before performing the duties of the office of bankruptcy judge.

(d) A bankruptcy judge appointed under this chapter shall be exempt from the provisions of subchapter I of chapter 63 of title 5.

(Added Pub.L. 98–353, Title I, § 104(a), July 10, 1984, 98 Stat. 338; amended Pub.L. 100–202, § 101(a) [Title IV, § 408(a)], Dec. 22, 1987, 101 Stat. 1329–26; Pub.L. 100–702, Title X, § 1003(a)(1), Nov. 19, 1988, 102 Stat. 4665.)

HISTORICAL AND STATUTORY NOTES

Codifications

This section as added by Pub.L. 95–598, Title II, § 201(a), Nov. 6, 1978, 92 Stat. 2657, effective June 28, 1984, pursuant to Pub.L. 95–598, Title IV, § 402(b), Nov. 6, 1978, 92 Stat. 2682, as amended by Pub.L. 98–249, § 1(a), Mar. 31, 1984, 98 Stat. 116; Pub.L. 98–271, § 1(a), Apr. 30, 1984, 98 Stat. 163; Pub.L. 98–299, § 1(a), May 25, 1984, 98 Stat. 214; Pub.L. 98–325, § 1(a), June 20, 1984, 98 Stat. 268, set out as a note preceding section 101 of Title 11, Bankruptcy, read as follows:

§ 153. Tenure and residence of bankruptcy judges

(a) Each bankruptcy judge shall hold office for a term of 14 years, but may continue to perform the duties of his office until his successor takes office, unless such office has been eliminated.

(b) Removal of a bankruptcy judge during the term for which he is appointed shall be only for incompetency, misconduct, neglect of duty, or physical or mental disability. Removal shall be by the judicial council of the circuit or circuits in which the bankruptcy judge serves, but removal may not occur unless a majority of all the judges of such circuit council or councils concur in the order of removal. Before any order of removal may be entered, a full specification of the charges shall be furnished to the bankruptcy judge, and he shall be accorded an opportunity to be heard on the charges. Any cause for removal of any bankruptcy judge coming to the knowledge of the Director of the Administrative Office of the United States Courts shall be reported by him to the chief judge of the circuit or circuits in which he serves, and a copy of the report shall at the same time be transmitted to the circuit council or councils and to the bankruptcy judge.

(c) Each bankruptcy judge shall reside in the district or one of the districts for which he is appointed, or within 20 miles of his official station.

(d) If the public interest and the nature of the business of a bankruptcy court require that a bankruptcy judge should maintain his abode at or near a particular part of the district the judicial council of the circuit may so declare and may make an appropriate order. If the bankruptcy judges of such a district are unable to agree as to which of them shall maintain his abode at or near the place or within the area specified in such an order the judicial council of the circuit may decide which of them shall do so.

Section 402(b) of Pub.L. 95–598 was amended by section 113 of Pub.L. 98–353 by substituting "shall not be effective" for "shall take effect on June 28, 1984", thereby eliminating the addition of section 153 by section 201(a) of Pub.L. 95–598, effective June 27, 1984, pursuant to section 122(c) of Pub.L. 98–353, set out as an Effective Date note under section 151 of this title.

Section 121(a) of Pub.L. 98–353 directed that section 402(b) of Pub.L. 95–598 be amended by substituting "the date of enactment of the Bankruptcy Amendments and Federal Judgeship Act of 1984 [i.e. July 10, 1984]" for "June 28, 1984". This amendment was not executed in view of the prior amendment to section 402(b) of Pub.L. 95–598 by section 113 of Pub.L. 98–353.

Amendments

1988 Amendments. Subsec. (d). Pub.L. 100–702 added subsec. (d).

1987 Amendments. Subsec. (a). Pub.L. 100–202 substituted salary at a rate equal to 92 percent of the salary of a district court judge as determined pursuant to section 135 of this title, for salary at a rate determined under section 225 of the Federal Salary Act of 1967 [2 U.S.C.A. § 351 et seq.] as adjusted by section 461 of this title.

§ 154. Division of businesses; chief judge

(a) Each bankruptcy court for a district having more than one bankruptcy judge shall by majority vote promulgate rules for the division of business among the bankruptcy judges to the extent that the division of business is not otherwise provided for by the rules of the district court.

(b) In each district court having more than one bankruptcy judge the district court shall designate one judge to serve as chief judge of such bankruptcy court. Whenever a majority of the judges of such district court cannot agree upon the designation as chief judge, the chief judge of such district court shall make such designation. The chief judge of the bankruptcy court shall ensure that the rules of the bankruptcy court and of the district court are observed and that the business of the bankruptcy court is handled effectively and expeditiously.

(Added Pub.L. 98–353, Title I, § 104(a), July 10, 1984, 98 Stat. 339.)

HISTORICAL AND STATUTORY NOTES

Codifications

This section as added by Pub.L. 95–598, Title II, § 201(a), Nov. 6, 1978, 92 Stat. 2657, effective June 28, 1984, pursuant to Pub.L. 95–598, Title IV, § 402(b), Nov. 6, 1978, 92 Stat. 2682, as amended by Pub.L. 98–249, § 1(a), Mar. 31, 1984, 98 Stat. 116; Pub.L. 98–271, § 1(a), Apr. 30, 1984, 98 Stat. 163; Pub.L. 98–299, § 1(a), May 25, 1984, 98 Stat. 214; Pub.L. 98–325, § 1(a), June 20, 1984, 98 Stat. 268, set out as a note preceding section 101 of Title 11, Bankruptcy, read as follows:

§ 154. Salaries of bankruptcy judges

Each judge of a bankruptcy court shall receive a salary at an annual rate of $50,000, subject to adjustment under section 225 of the Federal Salary Act of 1967 (2 U.S.C. 351–361), and section 461 of this title.

Section 402(b) of Pub.L. 95–598 was amended by section 113 of Pub.L. 98–353 by substituting "shall not be effective" for "shall take effect on June 28, 1984", thereby eliminating the addition of section 154 by section 201(a) of Pub.L. 95–598, effective June 27, 1984, pursuant to section 122(c) of Pub.L. 98–353, set out as an Effective Date note under section 151 of this title.

Section 121(a) of Pub.L. 98–353 directed that section 402(b) of Pub.L. 95–598 be amended by substituting "the date of enactment of the Bankruptcy Amendments and Federal Judgeship Act of 1984 [i.e. July 10, 1984]" for "June 28, 1984". This amendment was not executed in view of the prior amendment to section 402(b) of Pub.L. 95–598 by section 113 of Pub.L. 98–353.

§ 155. Temporary transfer of bankruptcy judges

(a) A bankruptcy judge may be transferred to serve temporarily as a bankruptcy judge in any judicial district other than the judicial district for which such bankruptcy judge was appointed upon the approval of the judicial council of each of the circuits involved.

(b) A bankruptcy judge who has retired may, upon consent, be recalled to serve as a bankruptcy judge in any judicial district by the judicial council of the circuit within which such district is located. Upon recall, a bankruptcy judge may receive a salary for such service in accordance with regulations promulgated by the Judicial Conference of the United States, subject to the restrictions on the payment of an annuity in section 377 of this title or in subchapter III of chapter 83, and chapter 84, of title 5 which are applicable to such judge.

(Added Pub.L. 98–353, Title I, § 104(a), July 10, 1984, 98 Stat. 339; amended Pub.L. 99–651, Title II, § 202(a), Nov. 14, 1986, 100 Stat. 3648; Pub.L. 100–659, § 4(a), Nov. 15, 1988, 102 Stat. 3918.)

HISTORICAL AND STATUTORY NOTES

Codifications

This section as added by Pub.L. 95–598, Title II, § 201(a), Nov. 6, 1978, 92 Stat. 2658, effective June 28, 1984, pursuant to Pub.L. 95–598, Title IV, § 402(b), Nov. 6, 1978, 92 Stat. 2682, as amended by Pub.L. 98–249, § 1(a), Mar. 31, 1984, 98 Stat. 116; Pub.L. 98–271, § 1(a), Apr. 30, 1984, 98 Stat. 163; Pub.L. 98–299, § 1(a), May 25, 1984, 98 Stat. 214; Pub.L. 98–325, § 1(a), June 20, 1984, 98 Stat. 268, set out as a note preceding section 101 of Title 11, Bankruptcy, read as follows:

§ 155. Chief judge; precedence of bankruptcy judges

(a) In each district having more than one judge the bankruptcy judge in regular active service who is senior in commission and under seventy years of age shall be the chief judge of the bankruptcy court. If all the bankruptcy judges in regular active service are 70 years of age or older the youngest shall act as chief judge until a judge has been appointed and qualified who is under 70 years of age, but a judge may not act as chief judge until he has served as a bankruptcy judge for one year.

(b) The chief judge shall have precedence and preside at any session which he attends.

Other bankruptcy judges shall have precedence and preside according to the seniority of their commissions. Judges whose commissions bear the same date shall have precedence according to seniority in age.

(c) A judge whose commission extends over more than one district shall be junior to all bankruptcy judges except in the district in which he resided at the time he entered upon the duties of his office.

(d) If a chief judge desires to be relieved of his duties as chief judge while retaining his active status as a bankruptcy judge, he may so certify to the chief judge of the court of appeals for the circuit in which the bankruptcy judge serves, and thereafter the bankruptcy judge in active service next in precedence and willing to serve shall be designated by the chief judge of the court of appeals as the chief judge of the bankruptcy court.

(e) If a chief judge is temporarily unable to perform his duties as such, they shall be performed by the bankruptcy judge in active service, present in the district and able and qualified to act, who is next in precedence.

(f) Service as a referee in bankruptcy or as a bankruptcy judge under the Bankruptcy Act shall be taken into account in the determination of seniority of commission under this section.

Section 402(b) of Pub.L. 95–598 was amended by section 113 of Pub.L. 98–353 by substituting "shall not be effective" for "shall take effect on June 28, 1984", thereby eliminating the addition of section 155 by section 201(a) of Pub.L. 95–598, effective June 27, 1984, pursuant to section 122(c) of Pub.L. 98–353, set out as an Effective Date note under section 151 of this title.

Section 121(a) of Pub.L. 98-353 directed that section 402(b) of Pub.L. 95-598 be amended by substituting "the date of enactment of the Bankruptcy Amendments and Federal Judgeship Act of 1984 [i.e. July 10, 1984]" for "June 28, 1984". This amendment was not executed in view of the prior amendment to section 402(b) of Pub.L. 95-598 by section 113 of Pub.L. 98-353.

Amendments

1988 Amendments. Subsec. (b). Pub.L. 100-659, § 4(a), inserted "section 377 of this title or in" after "annuity in" and "which are applicable to such judge" after "title 5", respectively.

1986 Amendments. Subsec. (b). Pub.L. 99-651, § 202(a), added reference to chapter 84 of Title 5.

CROSS REFERENCES

Recall of retired judges—

    Generally, see 28 USCA § 375.

    Actual abode deemed official station for purposes of residency, see 28 USCA § 374.

    Practicing attorney not eligible for recall, see 28 USCA § 377.

§ 156. Staff; expenses

(a) Each bankruptcy judge may appoint a secretary, a law clerk, and such additional assistants as the Director of the Administrative Office of the United States Courts determines to be necessary. A law clerk appointed under this section shall be exempt from the provisions of subchapter I of chapter 63 of title 5, unless specifically included by the appointing judge or by local rule of court.

(b) Upon certification to the judicial council of the circuit involved and to the Director of the Administrative Office of the United States Courts that the number of cases and proceedings pending within the jurisdiction under section 1334 of this title within a judicial district so warrants, the bankruptcy judges for such district may appoint an individual to serve as clerk of such bankruptcy court. The clerk may appoint, with the approval of such bankruptcy judges, and in such number as may be approved by the Director, necessary deputies, and may remove such deputies with the approval of such bankruptcy judges.

(c) Any court may utilize facilities or services, either on or off the court's premises, which pertain to the provision of notices, dockets, calendars, and other administrative information to parties in cases filed under the provisions of title 11, United States Code, where the costs of such facilities or services are paid for out of the assets of the estate and are not charged to the United States. The utilization of such facilities or services shall be subject to such conditions and limitations as the pertinent circuit council may prescribe.

(d) No office of the bankruptcy clerk of court may be consolidated with the district clerk of court office without the prior approval of the Judicial Conference and the Congress.

(e) In a judicial district where a bankruptcy clerk has been appointed pursuant to subsection (b), the bankruptcy clerk shall be the official custodian of the records and dockets of the bankruptcy court.

(f) For purposes of financial accountability in a district where a bankruptcy clerk has been certified, such clerk shall be accountable for and pay into the Treasury all fees, costs, and other monies collected by such clerk except uncollected fees not required by an Act of Congress to be prepaid. Such clerk shall make returns thereof to the Director of the Administrative Office of the United States Courts and the Director of the Executive Office For United States Trustees, under regulations prescribed by such Directors.

(Added Pub.L. 98-353, Title I, § 104(a), July 10, 1984, 98 Stat. 339; amended Pub.L. 99-554, Title I, §§ 103, 142, 144(a), Oct. 27, 1986, 100 Stat. 3090, 3096; Pub.L. 100-702, Title X, § 1003(a)(3), Nov. 19, 1988, 102 Stat. 4665.)

HISTORICAL AND STATUTORY NOTES

Codifications

This section as added by Pub.L. 95–598, Title II, § 201(a), Nov. 6, 1978, 92 Stat. 2659, effective June 28, 1984, pursuant to Pub.L. 95–598, Title IV, § 402(b), Nov. 6, 1978, 92 Stat. 2682, as amended by Pub.L. 98–249, § 1(a), Mar. 31, 1984, 98 Stat. 116; Pub.L. 98–271, § 1(a), Apr. 30, 1984, 98 Stat. 163; Pub.L. 98–299, § 1(a), May 25, 1984, 98 Stat. 214; Pub.L. 98–325, § 1(a), June 20, 1984, 98 Stat. 268, set out as a note preceding section 101 of Title 11, Bankruptcy, read as follows:

§ 156. Division of business among bankruptcy judges

The business of a bankruptcy court having more than one judge shall be divided among the judges as provided by the rules and orders of the court.

The chief judge of the bankruptcy court shall be responsible for the observance of such rules and orders, and shall divide the business and assign the cases so far as such rules and orders do not otherwise prescribe.

If the bankruptcy judges in any district are unable to agree upon the adoption of rules or orders for that purpose the judicial council of the circuit shall make the necessary orders.

Section 402(b) of Pub.L. 95–598 was amended by section 113 of Pub.L. 98–353 by substituting "shall not be effective" for "shall take effect on June 28, 1984", thereby eliminating the addition of section 156 by section 201(a) of Pub.L. 95–598, effective June 27, 1984, pursuant to section 122(c) of Pub.L. 98–353, set out as an Effective Date note under section 151 of this title.

Section 121(a) of Pub.L. 98–353 directed that section 402(b) of Pub.L. 95–598 be amended by substituting "the date of enactment of the Bankruptcy Amendments and Federal Judgeship Act of 1984 [i.e. July 10, 1984]" for "June 28, 1984". This amendment was not executed in view of the prior amendment to section 402(b) of Pub.L. 95–598 by section 113 of Pub.L. 98–353.

Amendments

1988 Amendments. Subsec. (a). Pub.L. 100–702 added provision that a law clerk appointed under this section be exempt from the provisions of subchapter I of chapter 63 of title 5, unless specifically included by the appointing judge or by local rule of court.

1986 Amendments. Subsec. (d). Pub.L. 99–554, § 103, added subsec. (d).

Subsec. (e). Pub.L. 99–554, § 142, added subsec. (e).

Subsec. (f). Pub.L. 99–554, § 144(a), added subsec. (f).

CROSS REFERENCES

Conversion fees in bankruptcy, see 28 USCA § 1930.

§ 157. Procedures

(a) Each district court may provide that any or all cases under title 11 and any or all proceedings arising under title 11 or arising in or related to a case under title 11 shall be referred to the bankruptcy judges for the district.

(b)(1) Bankruptcy judges may hear and determine all cases under title 11 and all core proceedings arising under title 11, or arising in a case under title 11, referred under subsection (a) of this section, and may enter appropriate orders and judgments, subject to review under section 158 of this title.

(2) Core proceedings include, but are not limited to—

(A) matters concerning the administration of the estate;

(B) allowance or disallowance of claims against the estate or exemptions from property of the estate, and estimation of claims or interests for the purposes of confirming a plan under chapter 11, 12, or 13 of title 11 but not the liquidation or estimation of contingent or unliquidated personal injury tort or wrongful death claims against the estate for purposes of distribution in a case under title 11;

(C) counterclaims by the estate against persons filing claims against the estate;

(D) orders in respect to obtaining credit;

(E) orders to turn over property of the estate;

(F) proceedings to determine, avoid, or recover preferences;

(G) motions to terminate, annul, or modify the automatic stay;

(H) proceedings to determine, avoid, or recover fraudulent conveyances;

(I) determinations as to the dischargeability of particular debts;

(J) objections to discharges;

(K) determinations of the validity, extent, or priority of liens;

(L) confirmations of plans;

(M) orders approving the use or lease of property, including the use of cash collateral;

(N) orders approving the sale of property other than property resulting from claims brought by the estate against persons who have not filed claims against the estate;

(O) other proceedings affecting the liquidation of the assets of the estate or the adjustment of the debtor-creditor or the equity security holder relationship, except personal injury tort or wrongful death claims; and

(P) recognition of foreign proceedings and other matters under chapter 15 of title 11.

(3) The bankruptcy judge shall determine, on the judge's own motion or on timely motion of a party, whether a proceeding is a core proceeding under this subsection or is a proceeding that is otherwise related to a case under title 11. A determination that a proceeding is not a core proceeding shall not be made solely on the basis that its resolution may be affected by State law.

(4) Non-core proceedings under section 157(b)(2)(B) of title 28, United States Code, shall not be subject to the mandatory abstention provisions of section 1334(c)(2).

(5) The district court shall order that personal injury tort and wrongful death claims shall be tried in the district court in which the bankruptcy case is pending, or in the district court in the district in which the claim arose, as determined by the district court in which the bankruptcy case is pending.

(c)(1) A bankruptcy judge may hear a proceeding that is not a core proceeding but that is otherwise related to a case under title 11. In such proceeding, the bankruptcy judge shall submit proposed findings of fact and conclusions of law to the district court, and any final order or judgment shall be entered by the district judge after considering the bankruptcy judge's proposed findings and conclusions and after reviewing de novo those matters to which any party has timely and specifically objected.

(2) Notwithstanding the provisions of paragraph (1) of this subsection, the district court, with the consent of all the parties to the proceeding, may refer a proceeding related to a case under title 11 to a bankruptcy judge to hear and determine and to enter appropriate orders and judgments, subject to review under section 158 of this title.

(d) The district court may withdraw, in whole or in part, any case or proceeding referred under this section, on its own motion or on timely motion of any party, for cause shown. The district court shall, on timely motion of a party, so withdraw a proceeding if the court determines that resolution of the proceeding requires consideration of both title 11 and other laws of the United States regulating organizations or activities affecting interstate commerce.

(e) If the right to a jury trial applies in a proceeding that may be heard under this section by a bankruptcy judge, the bankruptcy judge may conduct the jury trial if specially designated to exercise such jurisdiction by the district court and with the express consent of all the parties.

(Added Pub.L. 98–353, Title I, § 104(a), July 10, 1984, 98 Stat. 340; amended Pub.L. 99–554, Title I, §§ 143, 144(b), Oct. 27, 1986, 100 Stat. 3096; Pub.L. 103–394, Title I, § 112, Oct. 22, 1994, 108 Stat. 4117; Pub.L. 109–8, Title VIII, § 802(c)(1), Apr. 20, 2005, 119 Stat. 145.)

HISTORICAL AND STATUTORY NOTES

References in Text

Chapter 11, 12, or 13 of title 11, referred to in subsec. (b)(2)(B), is 11 U.S.C.A. § 1101 et seq., 11 U.S.C.A. § 1201 et seq., or 11 U.S.C.A. § 1301 et seq., respectively.

Chapter 15 of title 11, referred to in subsec. (b)(2)(P), is 11 U.S.C.A. § 1501 et seq.

Codifications

This section as added by Pub.L. 95–598, Title II, § 201(a), Nov. 6, 1978, 92 Stat. 2659, effective June 28, 1984, pursuant to Pub.L. 95–598, Title IV, § 402(b), Nov. 6, 1978, 92 Stat. 2682, as amended by Pub.L. 98–249, § 1(a), Mar. 31, 1984, 98 Stat. 116; Pub.L. 98–271, § 1(a), Apr. 30, 1984, 98 Stat. 163; Pub.L. 98–299, § 1(a), May 25, 1984, 98 Stat. 214; Pub.L. 98–325, § 1(a), June 20, 1984, 98 Stat. 268, set out as a note preceding section 101 of Title 11, Bankruptcy, read as follows:

" **§ 157. Times of holding court**

"(a) The bankruptcy court at each designated location shall be deemed to be in continuous session on all business days throughout the year.

"(b) Each bankruptcy court may establish by local rule or order schedules of court sessions at designated places of holding court other than the headquarters office of the court. Such schedules may be pretermitted by order of the court.

"(c) Bankruptcy court may be held at any place within the territory served, in any case, on order of the bankruptcy court, for the convenience of the parties, on such notice as the bankruptcy court orders."

Section 402(b) of Pub.L. 95–598 was amended by section 113 of Pub.L. 98–353 by substituting "shall not be effective" for "shall take effect on June 28, 1984", thereby eliminating the addition of section 157 by section 201(a) of Pub.L. 95–598, effective June 27, 1984, pursuant to section 122(c) of Pub.L. 98–353, set out as an Effective Date note under section 151 of this title.

Section 121(a) of Pub.L. 98–353 directed that section 402(b) of Pub.L. 95–598 be amended by substituting "the date of enactment of the Bankruptcy Amendments and Federal Judgeship Act of 1984 [i.e. July 10, 1984]" for "June 28, 1984". This amendment was not executed in view of the prior amendment to section 402(b) of Pub.L. 95–598 by section 113 of Pub.L. 98–353.

Amendments

2005 Amendments. Subsec. (b)(2)(N). Pub.L. 109–8, § 802(c)(1)(A), struck out "and" at the end of subpar. (N).

Subsec. (b)(2)(O). Pub.L. 109–8, § 802(c)(1)(B), struck out the period at the end and inserted "; and".

Subsec. (b)(2)(P). Pub.L. 109–8, § 802(c)(1)(C), added subpar. (P).

1994 Amendments. Subsec. (e). Pub.L. 103–394, § 112, added subsec. (e).

1986 Amendments. Subsec. (b)(2)(B). Pub.L. 99–554, § 143, added reference to chapter 12.

Pub.L. 99–554, § 144(b)(1), substituted "interests" for "interest".

Subsec. (b)(2)(G). Pub.L. 99–554, § 144(b)(2), substituted "annul," for "annul".

CROSS REFERENCES

Supplemental injunctions and power of district court to refer proceedings, see 11 USCA § 524.

§ 158. Appeals

(a) The district courts of the United States shall have jurisdiction to hear appeals[1]

    (1) from final judgments, orders, and decrees;

    (2) from interlocutory orders and decrees issued under section 1121(d) of title 11 increasing or reducing the time periods referred to in section 1121 of such title; and

    (3) with leave of the court, from other interlocutory orders and decrees;

and, with leave of the court, from interlocutory orders and decrees, of bankruptcy judges entered in cases and proceedings referred to the bankruptcy judges under section 157 of this title. An appeal under this subsection shall be taken only to the district court for the judicial district in which the bankruptcy judge is serving.

(b)(1) The judicial council of a circuit shall establish a bankruptcy appellate panel service composed of bankruptcy judges of the districts in the circuit who are appointed by the judicial council in accordance with paragraph (3), to hear and determine, with the consent of all the parties, appeals under subsection (a) unless the judicial council finds that—

    (A) there are insufficient judicial resources available in the circuit; or

    (B) establishment of such service would result in undue delay or increased cost to parties in cases under title 11.

Not later than 90 days after making the finding, the judicial council shall submit to the Judicial Conference of the United States a report containing the factual basis of such finding.

    (2)(A) A judicial council may reconsider, at any time, the finding described in paragraph (1).

    (B) On the request of a majority of the district judges in a circuit for which a bankruptcy appellate panel service is established under paragraph (1), made after the expiration of the 1-year period beginning on the date such service is established, the judicial council of the circuit shall determine whether a circumstance specified in subparagraph (A) or (B) of such paragraph exists.

    (C) On its own motion, after the expiration of the 3-year period beginning on the date a bankruptcy appellate panel service is established under paragraph (1), the judicial council of the circuit may determine whether a circumstance specified in subparagraph (A) or (B) of such paragraph exists.

    (D) If the judicial council finds that either of such circumstances exists, the judicial council may provide for the completion of the appeals then pending before such service and the orderly termination of such service.

    (3) Bankruptcy judges appointed under paragraph (1) shall be appointed and may be reappointed under such paragraph.

    (4) If authorized by the Judicial Conference of the United States, the judicial councils of 2 or more circuits may establish a joint bankruptcy appellate panel comprised of bankruptcy judges from the districts within the circuits for which such panel is established, to hear and determine, upon the consent of all the parties, appeals under subsection (a) of this section.

    (5) An appeal to be heard under this subsection shall be heard by a panel of 3 members of the bankruptcy appellate panel service, except that a member of such service may not hear an appeal originating in the district for which such member is appointed or designated under section 152 of this title.

    (6) Appeals may not be heard under this subsection by a panel of the bankruptcy appellate panel service unless the district judges for the district in which the appeals occur, by majority vote, have authorized such service to hear and determine appeals originating in such district.

---

[1] So in original.

(c)(1) Subject to subsections (b) and (d)(2), each appeal under subsection (a) shall be heard by a 3-judge panel of the bankruptcy appellate panel service established under subsection (b)(1) unless—

    (A) the appellant elects at the time of filing the appeal; or

    (B) any other party elects, not later than 30 days after service of notice of the appeal;

to have such appeal heard by the district court.

    (2) An appeal under subsections (a) and (b) of this section shall be taken in the same manner as appeals in civil proceedings generally are taken to the courts of appeals from the district courts and in the time provided by Rule 8002 of the Bankruptcy Rules.

(d)(1) The courts of appeals shall have jurisdiction of appeals from all final decisions, judgments, orders, and decrees entered under subsections (a) and (b) of this section.

(2)(A) The appropriate court of appeals shall have jurisdiction of appeals described in the first sentence of subsection (a) if the bankruptcy court, the district court, or the bankruptcy appellate panel involved, acting on its own motion or on the request of a party to the judgment, order, or decree described in such first sentence, or all the appellants and appellees (if any) acting jointly, certify that—

    (i) the judgment, order, or decree involves a question of law as to which there is no controlling decision of the court of appeals for the circuit or of the Supreme Court of the United States, or involves a matter of public importance;

    (ii) the judgment, order, or decree involves a question of law requiring resolution of conflicting decisions; or

    (iii) an immediate appeal from the judgment, order, or decree may materially advance the progress of the case or proceeding in which the appeal is taken;

and if the court of appeals authorizes the direct appeal of the judgment, order, or decree.

    (B) If the bankruptcy court, the district court, or the bankruptcy appellate panel—

    (i) on its own motion or on the request of a party, determines that a circumstance specified in clause (i), (ii), or (iii) of subparagraph (A) exists; or

    (ii) receives a request made by a majority of the appellants and a majority of appellees (if any) to make the certification described in subparagraph (A);

then the bankruptcy court, the district court, or the bankruptcy appellate panel shall make the certification described in subparagraph (A).

    (C) The parties may supplement the certification with a short statement of the basis for the certification.

    (D) An appeal under this paragraph does not stay any proceeding of the bankruptcy court, the district court, or the bankruptcy appellate panel from which the appeal is taken, unless the respective bankruptcy court, district court, or bankruptcy appellate panel, or the court of appeals in which the appeal is pending, issues a stay of such proceeding pending the appeal.

    (E) Any request under subparagraph (B) for certification shall be made not later than 60 days after the entry of the judgment, order, or decree.

(Added Pub.L. 98–353, Title I, § 104(a), July 10, 1984, 98 Stat. 341; amended Pub.L. 101–650, Title III, § 305, Dec. 1, 1990, 104 Stat. 5105; Pub.L. 103–394, Title I, §§ 102, 104(c), (d), Oct. 22, 1994, 108 Stat. 4108–4110; Pub.L. 109–8, Title XII, § 1233(a), Apr. 20, 2005, 119 Stat. 202; Pub.L. 111–327, § 2(c)(1), Dec. 22, 2010, 124 Stat. 3563.)

HISTORICAL AND STATUTORY NOTES

Codifications

Amendment by section 102 of Pub.L. 103–394, which directed amendment of subsec. (a) by striking "from" the first place it appeared and all that followed through "decrees," and making a substitution for such language, was executed by striking through "decrees," the first place it appeared, as the probable intent of Congress.

This section (section 158) and section 159 as added by Pub.L. 95–598, Title II, § 201(a), Nov. 6, 1978, 92 Stat. 2659, and section 160, as added by Pub.L. 95–598, Title II, § 201(a), Nov. 6, 1978, 92 Stat. 2659, and amended Pub.L. 97–164, Title I, § 110(d), Apr. 2, 1982, 96 Stat. 29, effective June 28, 1984, pursuant to Pub.L. 95–598, Title IV, § 402(b), Nov. 6, 1978, 92 Stat. 2682, as amended by Pub.L. 98–249, § 1(a), Mar. 31, 1984, 98 Stat. 116; Pub.L. 98–271, § 1(a), Apr. 30, 1984, 98 Stat. 163; Pub.L. 98–299, § 1(a), May 25, 1984, 98 Stat. 214; Pub.L. 98–325, § 1(a), June 20, 1984, 98 Stat. 268, set out as a note preceding section 101 of Title II, Bankruptcy, read as follows:

" § 158. Accommodations at places for holding court

"Court shall be held only at places where Federal quarters and accommodations are available, or suitable quarters and accommodations are furnished without cost to the United States. The foregoing restrictions shall not, however, preclude the Administrator of General Services, at the request of the Director of the Administrative Office of the United States Courts, from providing such court quarters and accommodations as the Administrator determines can appropriately be made available at places where court is authorized by law to be held, but only if such court quarters and accommodations have been approved as necessary by the judicial council of the appropriate circuit.

" § 159. Vacant judgeship as affecting proceedings

"When the office of a bankruptcy judge becomes vacant, all pending process, pleadings and proceedings shall, when necessary, be continued by the clerk until a judge is appointed or designated to hold such court.

" § 160. Appellate panels

"(a) If the circuit council of a circuit orders application of this section to a district within such circuit, the chief judge of each circuit shall designate panels of three bankruptcy judges to hear appeals from judgments, orders, and decrees of the bankruptcy court of the United States for such district. Except as provided in section 293(b) of this title, a panel shall be composed only of bankruptcy judges for districts located in the circuit in which the appeal arises. The chief judge shall designate a sufficient number of such panels so that appeals may be heard and disposed of expeditiously.

"(b) A panel designated under subsection (a) of this section may not hear an appeal from a judgment, order, or decree entered by a member of the panel.

"(c) When hearing an appeal, a panel designated under subsection (a) of this section shall sit at a place convenient to the parties to the appeal."

Section 402(b) of Pub.L. 95–598 was amended by section 113 of Pub.L. 98–353 by substituting "shall not be effective" for "shall take effect on June 28, 1984", thereby eliminating the additions of sections 158 to 160 by section 201(a) of Pub.L. 95–598, effective June 27, 1984, pursuant to section 122(c) of Pub.L. 98–353, set out as an Effective Date note under section 151 of this title.

Section 121(a) of Pub.L. 98–353 directed that section 402(b) of Pub.L. 95–598 be amended by substituting "the date of enactment of the Bankruptcy Amendments and Federal Judgeship Act of 1984 [i.e. July 10, 1984]" for "June 28, 1984". This amendment was not executed in view of the prior amendment to section 402(b) of Pub.L. 95–598 by section 113 of Pub.L. 98–353.

Amendments

2010 Amendments. Subsec. (d)(2)(D). Pub.L. 111–327, § 2(c)(1), struck out "appeal in" and inserted "appeal is".

2005 Amendments. Subsec. (c)(1). Pub.L.109–8, § 1233(a)(1), struck out "Subject to subsection (b)," and inserted "Subject to subsections (b) and (d)(2),".

Subsec. (d). Pub.L.109–8, § 1233(a)(2), inserted "(1)" after "(d)", and added paragraph (2).

1994 Amendments. Subsec. (a). Pub.L. 103–394, § 102, designated existing provision "from final judgments, orders, and decrees," following "jurisdiction to hear appeals" as par. (1), and added pars. (2) and (3).

Subsec. (b). Pub.L. 103–465, § 104(c), added pars. (1), (2), (3), (5), and (6), redesignated former par. (2) as (4), and struck out former pars. (1), (3), and (4), which authorized establishment of bankruptcy appellate panel without conditions, prohibited referral of appeal to panel unless authorized by majority vote of district judges, and provided that panel shall consist of 3 bankruptcy judges.

Subsec. (c). Pub.L. 103–465, § 104(d), designated existing text as par. (2) and added par. (1).

1990 Amendments. Subsec. (b)(2). Pub.L. 101–650, § 305(2), added par. (2). Former par. (2) redesignated (3).

Subsec. (b)(3), (4). Pub.L. 101–650, § 305(1), redesignated former pars. (2) and (3) as (3) and (4), respectively.

Procedural Rules

Pub.L. 109–8, Title XII, § 1233(b), Apr. 20, 2005, 119 Stat. 203, provided that:

"**(1) Temporary application.**—A provision of this subsection shall apply to appeals under section 158(d)(2) of title 28, United States Code, until a rule of practice and procedure relating to such provision and such appeals is promulgated or amended under chapter 131 of such title [28 U.S.C.A. § 2071 et seq.].

"**(2) Certification.**—A district court, a bankruptcy court, or a bankruptcy appellate panel may make a certification under section 158(d)(2) of title 28, United States Code, only with respect to matters pending in the respective bankruptcy court, district court, or bankruptcy appellate panel.

"**(3) Procedure.**—Subject to any other provision of this subsection, an appeal authorized by the court of appeals under section 158(d)(2)(A) of title 28, United States Code, shall be taken in the manner prescribed in subdivisions (a)(1), (b), (c), and (d) of rule 5 of the Federal Rules of Appellate Procedure. For purposes of subdivision (a)(1) of rule 5—

"**(A)** a reference in such subdivision to a district court shall be deemed to include a reference to a bankruptcy court and a bankruptcy appellate panel, as appropriate; and

"**(B)** a reference in such subdivision to the parties requesting permission to appeal to be served with the petition shall be deemed to include a reference to the parties to the judgment, order, or decree from which the appeal is taken.

"**(4) Filing of petition with attachment.**—A petition requesting permission to appeal, that is based on a certification made under subparagraph (A) or (B) of section 158(d)(2) shall—

"**(A)** be filed with the circuit clerk not later than 10 days after the certification is entered on the docket of the bankruptcy court, the district court, or the bankruptcy appellate panel from which the appeal is taken; and

"**(B)** have attached a copy of such certification.

"**(5) References in rule 5.**—For purposes of rule 5 of the Federal Rules of Appellate Procedure—

"**(A)** a reference in such rule to a district court shall be deemed to include a reference to a bankruptcy court and to a bankruptcy appellate panel; and

"**(B)** a reference in such rule to a district clerk shall be deemed to include a reference to a clerk of a bankruptcy court and to a clerk of a bankruptcy appellate panel.

"**(6) Application of rules.**—The Federal Rules of Appellate Procedure [set out in Title 28, Judiciary and Judicial Procedure] shall apply in the courts of appeals with respect to appeals authorized under section 158(d)(2)(A), to the extent relevant and as if such appeals were taken from final judgments, orders, or decrees of the district courts or bankruptcy appellate panels exercising appellate jurisdiction under subsection (a) or (b) of section 158 of title 28, United States Code."

[Except as otherwise provided, amendments by Pub.L. 109–8 effective 180 days after April 20, 2005, and inapplicable with respect to cases commenced under Title 11 before the effective date, see Pub.L. 109–8, § 1501, set out as a note under 11 U.S.C.A. § 101.]

CROSS REFERENCES

Orders and decisions not reviewable under this section—

Abstention from exercising jurisdiction generally, see 28 USCA § 1334.

Dismissal or suspension of bankruptcy case on abstention grounds, see 11 USCA § 305.

Remand orders, see 28 USCA § 1452.

§ 159. Bankruptcy statistics

(a) The clerk of the district court, or the clerk of the bankruptcy court if one is certified pursuant to section 156(b) of this title, shall collect statistics regarding debtors who are individuals with primarily consumer debts seeking relief under chapters 7, 11, and 13 of title 11. Those statistics shall be in a standardized format prescribed by the Director of the Administrative Office of the United States Courts (referred to in this section as the "Director").

(b) The Director shall—

   (1) compile the statistics referred to in subsection (a);

   (2) make the statistics available to the public; and

   (3) not later than July 1, 2008, and annually thereafter, prepare, and submit to Congress a report concerning the information collected under subsection (a) that contains an analysis of the information.

(c) The compilation required under subsection (b) shall—

   (1) be itemized, by chapter, with respect to title 11;

   (2) be presented in the aggregate and for each district; and

   (3) include information concerning—

      (A) the total assets and total liabilities of the debtors described in subsection (a), and in each category of assets and liabilities, as reported in the schedules prescribed pursuant to section 2075 of this title and filed by debtors;

      (B) the current monthly income, average income, and average expenses of debtors as reported on the schedules and statements that each such debtor files under sections 521 and 1322 of title 11;

      (C) the aggregate amount of debt discharged in cases filed during the reporting period, determined as the difference between the total amount of debt and obligations of a debtor reported on the schedules and the amount of such debt reported in categories which are predominantly nondischargeable;

      (D) the average period of time between the date of the filing of the petition and the closing of the case for cases closed during the reporting period;

      (E) for cases closed during the reporting period—

         (i) the number of cases in which a reaffirmation agreement was filed; and

         (ii)(I) the total number of reaffirmation agreements filed;

            (II) of those cases in which a reaffirmation agreement was filed, the number of cases in which the debtor was not represented by an attorney; and

            (III) of those cases in which a reaffirmation agreement was filed, the number of cases in which the reaffirmation agreement was approved by the court;

      (F) with respect to cases filed under chapter 13 of title 11, for the reporting period—

         (i)(I) the number of cases in which a final order was entered determining the value of property securing a claim in an amount less than the amount of the claim; and

            (II) the number of final orders entered determining the value of property securing a claim;

         (ii) the number of cases dismissed, the number of cases dismissed for failure to make payments under the plan, the number of cases refiled after dismissal, and the number of cases in which the plan was completed, separately itemized with respect to the number of modifications made before completion of the plan, if any; and

(iii) the number of cases in which the debtor filed another case during the 6-year period preceding the filing;

(G) the number of cases in which creditors were fined for misconduct and any amount of punitive damages awarded by the court for creditor misconduct; and

(H) the number of cases in which sanctions under rule 9011 of the Federal Rules of Bankruptcy Procedure were imposed against the debtor's attorney or damages awarded under such Rule.

(Added Pub.L. 109–8, Title VI, § 601(a), Apr. 20, 2005, 119 Stat. 119; amended Pub.L. 111–327, § 2(c)(2), Dec. 22, 2010, 124 Stat. 3563.)

HISTORICAL AND STATUTORY NOTES

Amendments

2010 Amendments. Subsec. (c)(3)(H). Pub.L. 111–327, § 2(c)(2), inserted "the" following "against".

CHAPTER 21—GENERAL PROVISIONS APPLICABLE TO COURTS AND JUDGES

§ 455. Disqualification of justice, judge, or magistrate judge

(a) Any justice, judge, or magistrate judge of the United States shall disqualify himself in any proceeding in which his impartiality might reasonably be questioned.

(b) He shall also disqualify himself in the following circumstances:

(1) Where he has a personal bias or prejudice concerning a party, or personal knowledge of disputed evidentiary facts concerning the proceeding;

(2) Where in private practice he served as lawyer in the matter in controversy, or a lawyer with whom he previously practiced law served during such association as a lawyer concerning the matter, or the judge or such lawyer has been a material witness concerning it;

(3) Where he has served in governmental employment and in such capacity participated as counsel, adviser or material witness concerning the proceeding or expressed an opinion concerning the merits of the particular case in controversy;

(4) He knows that he, individually or as a fiduciary, or his spouse or minor child residing in his household, has a financial interest in the subject matter in controversy or in a party to the proceeding, or any other interest that could be substantially affected by the outcome of the proceeding;

(5) He or his spouse, or a person within the third degree of relationship to either of them, or the spouse of such a person:

(i) Is a party to the proceeding, or an officer, director, or trustee of a party;

(ii) Is acting as a lawyer in the proceeding;

(iii) Is known by the judge to have an interest that could be substantially affected by the outcome of the proceeding;

(iv) Is to the judge's knowledge likely to be a material witness in the proceeding.

(c) A judge should inform himself about his personal and fiduciary financial interests, and make a reasonable effort to inform himself about the personal financial interests of his spouse and minor children residing in his household.

(d) For the purposes of this section the following words or phrases shall have the meaning indicated:

(1) "proceeding" includes pretrial, trial, appellate review, or other stages of litigation;

(2) the degree of relationship is calculated according to the civil law system;

(3) "fiduciary" includes such relationships as executor, administrator, trustee, and guardian;

(4) "financial interest" means ownership of a legal or equitable interest, however small, or a relationship as director, adviser, or other active participant in the affairs of a party, except that:

(i) Ownership in a mutual or common investment fund that holds securities is not a "financial interest" in such securities unless the judge participates in the management of the fund;

(ii) An office in an educational, religious, charitable, fraternal, or civic organization is not a "financial interest" in securities held by the organization;

(iii) The proprietary interest of a policyholder in a mutual insurance company, of a depositor in a mutual savings association, or a similar proprietary interest, is a "financial interest" in the organization only if the outcome of the proceeding could substantially affect the value of the interest;

(iv) Ownership of government securities is a "financial interest" in the issuer only if the outcome of the proceeding could substantially affect the value of the securities.

(e) No justice, judge, or magistrate judge shall accept from the parties to the proceeding a waiver of any ground for disqualification enumerated in subsection (b). Where the ground for disqualification arises only under subsection (a), waiver may be accepted provided it is preceded by a full disclosure on the record of the basis for disqualification.

(f) Notwithstanding the preceding provisions of this section, if any justice, judge, magistrate judge, or bankruptcy judge to whom a matter has been assigned would be disqualified, after substantial judicial time has been devoted to the matter, because of the appearance or discovery, after the matter was assigned to him or her, that he or she individually or as a fiduciary, or his or her spouse or minor child residing in his or her household, has a financial interest in a party (other than an interest that could be substantially affected by the outcome), disqualification is not required if the justice, judge, magistrate judge, bankruptcy judge, spouse or minor child, as the case may be, divests himself or herself of the interest that provides the grounds for the disqualification.

(June 25, 1948, c. 646, 62 Stat. 908; Dec. 5, 1974, Pub.L. 93–512, § 1, 88 Stat. 1609; Nov. 6, 1978, Pub.L. 95–598, Title II, § 214(a), (b), 92 Stat. 2661; Nov. 19, 1988, Pub.L. 100–702, Title X, § 1007, 102 Stat. 4667; Dec. 1, 1990, Pub.L. 101–650, Title III, § 321, 104 Stat. 5117.)

HISTORICAL AND STATUTORY NOTES

Amendments

1988 Amendments. Subsec. (f). Pub.L. 100–702 added subsec. (f).

1978 Amendments. Pub.L. 95–598 struck out references to referees in bankruptcy in the section catchline and in subsecs. (a) and (e).

1974 Amendments. Pub.L. 93–512 substituted "Disqualification of justice, judge, magistrate, or referee in bankruptcy" for "Interest of justice or judge" in section catchline, reorganized structure of provisions, and expanded applicability to include magistrates and referees in bankruptcy and grounds for which disqualification may be based, and added provisions relating to waiver of disqualification.

CROSS REFERENCES

Application to other courts, see 28 USCA § 460.

Arbitrators subject to disqualification rules under this section, see 28 USCA § 656.

Bias or prejudice of judge, see 28 USCA § 144.

Disqualification of trial judge to hear appeal, see 28 USCA § 47.

United States Court of Veterans affairs, judges and proceedings of subject to this section, see 38 USCA § 7264.

PART II—DEPARTMENT OF JUSTICE

CHAPTER 39—UNITED STATES TRUSTEES

HISTORICAL AND STATUTORY NOTES

Amendments

2005 Amendments. Pub.L. 109–8, Title VI, § 602(b), Apr. 20, 2005, 119 Stat. 122, added item 589b "Bankruptcy data.".

1986 Amendments. Pub.L. 99–554, Title I, § 115(b), Oct. 27, 1986, 100 Stat. 3095, added item 589a.

§ 581. United States trustees

(a) The Attorney General shall appoint one United States trustee for each of the following regions composed of Federal judicial districts (without regard to section 451):

(1) The judicial districts established for the States of Maine, Massachusetts, New Hampshire, and Rhode Island.

(2) The judicial districts established for the States of Connecticut, New York, and Vermont.

(3) The judicial districts established for the States of Delaware, New Jersey, and Pennsylvania.

(4) The judicial districts established for the States of Maryland, North Carolina, South Carolina, Virginia, and West Virginia and for the District of Columbia.

(5) The judicial districts established for the States of Louisiana and Mississippi.

(6) The Northern District of Texas and the Eastern District of Texas.

(7) The Southern District of Texas and the Western District of Texas.

(8) The judicial districts established for the States of Kentucky and Tennessee.

(9) The judicial districts established for the States of Michigan and Ohio.

(10) The Central District of Illinois and the Southern District of Illinois; and the judicial districts established for the State of Indiana.

(11) The Northern District of Illinois; and the judicial districts established for the State of Wisconsin.

(12) The judicial districts established for the States of Minnesota, Iowa, North Dakota, and South Dakota.

(13) The judicial districts established for the States of Arkansas, Nebraska, and Missouri.

(14) The District of Arizona.

(15) The Southern District of California; and the judicial districts established for the State of Hawaii, and for Guam and the Commonwealth of the Northern Mariana Islands.

(16) The Central District of California.

(17) The Eastern District of California and the Northern District of California; and the judicial district established for the State of Nevada.

(18) The judicial districts established for the States of Alaska, Idaho (exclusive of Yellowstone National Park), Montana (exclusive of Yellowstone National Park), Oregon, and Washington.

(19) The judicial districts established for the States of Colorado, Utah, and Wyoming (including those portions of Yellowstone National Park situated in the States of Montana and Idaho).

(20) he judicial districts established for the States of Kansas, New Mexico, and Oklahoma.

(21) The judicial districts established for the States of Alabama, Florida, and Georgia and for the Commonwealth of Puerto Rico and the Virgin Islands of the United States.

(b) Each United States trustee shall be appointed for a term of five years. On the expiration of his term, a United States trustee shall continue to perform the duties of his office until his successor is appointed and qualifies.

(c) Each United States trustee is subject to removal by the Attorney General.

(Added Pub.L. 95–598, Title II, § 224(a), Nov. 6, 1978, 92 Stat. 2662; amended Pub.L. 99–554, Title I, § 111(a) to (c), Oct. 27, 1986, 100 Stat. 3090, 3091.)

HISTORICAL AND STATUTORY NOTES

Codifications

Section 408(c) of Pub.L. 95–598, as amended, which provided for the repeal of this section and the deletion of any references to United States Trustees in this title at a prospective date, was repealed by section 307(b) of Pub.L. 99–554. See note set out preceding this section.

Amendments

1986 Amendments. Subsec. (a). Pub.L. 99–554, § 111(a), substituted in provision preceding par. (1) "regions composed of Federal judicial districts (without regard to section 451)" for "districts or groups of districts".

Subsec. (a)(1). Pub.L. 99–554, § 111(a), substituted "The judicial districts established for the States of Maine, Massachusetts, New Hampshire, and Rhode Island" for "District of Maine, District of New Hampshire, District of Massachusetts, and District of Rhode Island".

Subsec. (a)(2). Pub.L. 99–554, § 111(a), substituted "The judicial districts established for the States of Connecticut, New York, and Vermont" for "Southern District of New York".

Subsec. (a)(3). Pub.L. 99–554, § 111(a), substituted "The judicial districts established for the States of Delaware, New Jersey, and Pennsylvania" for "District of Delaware and District of New Jersey".

Subsec. (a)(4). Pub.L. 99–554, § 111(a), substituted "The judicial districts established for the States of Maryland, North Carolina, South Carolina, Virginia, and West Virginia and for the District of Columbia" for "Eastern District of Virginia and District of District of Columbia".

Subsec. (a)(5). Pub.L. 99–554, § 111(a), substituted "The judicial districts established for the States of Louisiana and Mississippi" for "Northern District of Alabama".

Subsec. (a)(6). Pub.L. 99–554, § 111(a), substituted "The Northern District of Texas and the Eastern District of Texas" for "Northern District of Texas".

Subsec. (a)(7). Pub.L. 99–554, § 111(a), substituted "The Southern District of Texas and the Western District of Texas" for "Northern District of Illinois".

Subsec. (a)(8). Pub.L. 99–554, § 111(a), substituted "The judicial districts established for the States of Kentucky and Tennessee" for "District of Minnesota, District of North Dakota, District of South Dakota".

Subsec. (a)(9). Pub.L. 99–554, § 111(a), substituted "The judicial districts established for the States of Michigan and Ohio" for "Central District of California".

Subsec. (a)(10). Pub.L. 99–554, § 111(a), substituted "The Central District of Illinois and the Southern District of Illinois; and the judicial districts established for the State of Indiana" for "District of Colorado and District of Kansas".

Subsec. (a)(11) to (21). Pub.L. 99–554, § 111(a), added pars. (11) to (21).

Subsec. (b). Pub.L. 99–554, § 111(b), substituted "five years" for "seven years" and "office" for "Office".

Subsec. (c). Pub.L. 99–554, § 111(c), struck out "for cause" after "removal".

CROSS REFERENCES

Appointment of acting United States trustee by Attorney General to serve until vacancy is filled by appointment under this section, see 28 USCA § 585.

§ 582. Assistant United States trustees

(a) The Attorney General may appoint one or more assistant United States trustees in any region when the public interest so requires.

(b) Each assistant United States trustee is subject to removal by the Attorney General.

(Added Pub.L. 95–598, Title II, § 224(a), Nov. 6, 1978, 92 Stat. 2663; amended Pub.L. 99–554, Title I, § 111(d), Oct. 27, 1986, 100 Stat. 3091.)

HISTORICAL AND STATUTORY NOTES

Codifications

Section 408(c) of Pub.L. 95–598, as amended, which provided for the repeal of this section and the deletion of any references to United States Trustees in this title at a prospective date, was repealed by section 307(b) of Pub.L. 99–554. See note set out preceding section 581 of this title.

Amendments

1986 Amendments. Subsec. (a). Pub.L. 99–554, § 111(d)(1), substituted "region" for "district".

Subsec. (b). Pub.L. 99–554, § 111(d)(2), struck out "for cause" after "removal".

Appointment of United States Trustees by Attorney General

Appointment of United States Trustees by the Attorney General of individuals otherwise qualified, serving as estate administrators under Title 11, Bankruptcy, before effective date of Pub.L. 99–554, see section 309 of Pub.L. 99–554, as amended; set out as a note under section 581 of this title.

§ 583. Oath of office

Each United States trustee and assistant United States trustee, before taking office, shall take an oath to execute faithfully his duties.

(Added Pub.L. 95–598, Title II, § 224(a), Nov. 6, 1978, 92 Stat. 2663.)

HISTORICAL AND STATUTORY NOTES

Codifications

Section 408(c) of Pub.L. 95–598, as amended, which provided for the repeal of this section and the deletion of any references to United States Trustees in this title at a prospective date, was repealed by section 307(b) of Pub.L. 99–554. See note set out preceding section 581 of this title.

§ 584. Official stations

The Attorney General may determine the official stations of the United States trustees and assistant United States trustees within the regions for which they were appointed.

(Added Pub.L. 95–598, Title II, § 224(a), Nov. 6, 1978, 92 Stat. 2663; amended Pub.L. 99–554, Title I, § 144(d), Oct. 27, 1986, 100 Stat. 3096.)

HISTORICAL AND STATUTORY NOTES

Codifications

Section 408(c) of Pub.L. 95–598, as amended, which provided for the repeal of this section and the deletion of any references to United States Trustees in this title at a prospective date, was repealed by section 307(b) of Pub.L. 99–554. See note set out preceding section 581 of this title.

Amendments

1986 Amendments. Pub.L. 99–554 substituted "regions" for "districts".

§ 585. Vacancies

(a) The Attorney General may appoint an acting United States trustee for a region in which the office of the United States trustee is vacant. The individual so appointed may serve until the date on which the vacancy is filled by appointment under section 581 of this title or by designation under subsection (b) of this section.

(b) The Attorney General may designate a United States trustee to serve in not more than two regions for such time as the public interest requires.

(Added Pub.L. 95–598, Title II, § 224(a), Nov. 6, 1978, 92 Stat. 2663; amended Pub.L. 99–554, Title I, § 112, Oct. 27, 1986, 100 Stat. 3091.)

HISTORICAL AND STATUTORY NOTES

Codifications

Section 408(c) of Pub.L. 95–598, as amended, which provided for the repeal of this section and the deletion of any references to United States Trustees in this title at a prospective date, was repealed by section 307(b) of Pub.L. 99–554. See note set out preceding section 581 of this title.

Amendments

1986 Amendments. Subsec. (a). Pub.L. 99–554, § 112, designated existing provision as subsec. (a), and in subsec. (a) as so designated, substituted "for a region" for "for a district", struck out ", or may designate a United States trustee for another judicial district for another judicial district to serve as trustee for the district in which such vacancy exists" after "is vacant", "or designated" after "so appointed", and "the earlier of 90 days after such appointment or designation, as the case may be, or" after "serve until" and inserted "or by designation under subsection (b) of this section" after "581 of this title".

Subsec. (b). Pub.L. 99–554, § 112, added subsec. (b).

§ 586. Duties; supervision by Attorney General

(a) Each United States trustee, within the region for which such United States trustee is appointed, shall—

    (1) establish, maintain, and supervise a panel of private trustees that are eligible and available to serve as trustees in cases under chapter 7 of title 11;

    (2) serve as and perform the duties of a trustee in a case under title 11 when required under title 11 to serve as trustee in such a case;

    (3) supervise the administration of cases and trustees in cases under chapter 7, 11, 12, 13, or 15 of title 11 by, whenever the United States trustee considers it to be appropriate—

        (A)(i) reviewing, in accordance with procedural guidelines adopted by the Executive Office of the United States Trustee (which guidelines shall be applied uniformly by the United States trustee except when circumstances warrant different treatment), applications filed for compensation and reimbursement under section 330 of title 11; and

(ii) filing with the court comments with respect to such application and, if the United States Trustee considers it to be appropriate, objections to such application;

(B) monitoring plans and disclosure statements filed in cases under chapter 11 of title 11 and filing with the court, in connection with hearings under sections 1125 and 1128 of such title, comments with respect to such plans and disclosure statements;

(C) monitoring plans filed under chapters 12 and 13 of title 11 and filing with the court, in connection with hearings under sections 1224, 1229, 1324, and 1329 of such title, comments with respect to such plans;

(D) taking such action as the United States trustee deems to be appropriate to ensure that all reports, schedules, and fees required to be filed under title 11 and this title by the debtor are properly and timely filed;

(E) monitoring creditors' committees appointed under title 11;

(F) notifying the appropriate United States attorney of matters which relate to the occurrence of any action which may constitute a crime under the laws of the United States and, on the request of the United States attorney, assisting the United States attorney in carrying out prosecutions based on such action;

(G) monitoring the progress of cases under title 11 and taking such actions as the United States trustee deems to be appropriate to prevent undue delay in such progress;

(H) in small business cases (as defined in section 101 of title 11), performing the additional duties specified in title 11 pertaining to such cases; and

(I) monitoring applications filed under section 327 of title 11 and, whenever the United States trustee deems it to be appropriate, filing with the court comments with respect to the approval of such applications;

(4) deposit or invest under section 345 of title 11 money received as trustee in cases under title 11;

(5) perform the duties prescribed for the United States trustee under title 11 and this title, and such duties consistent with title 11 and this title as the Attorney General may prescribe;

(6) make such reports as the Attorney General directs, including the results of audits performed under section 603(a) of the Bankruptcy Abuse Prevention and Consumer Protection Act of 2005;

(7) in each of such small business cases—

(A) conduct an initial debtor interview as soon as practicable after the date of the order for relief but before the first meeting scheduled under section 341(a) of title 11, at which time the United States trustee shall—

(i) begin to investigate the debtor's viability;

(ii) inquire about the debtor's business plan;

(iii) explain the debtor's obligations to file monthly operating reports and other required reports;

(iv) attempt to develop an agreed scheduling order; and

(v) inform the debtor of other obligations;

(B) if determined to be appropriate and advisable, visit the appropriate business premises of the debtor, ascertain the state of the debtor's books and records, and verify that the debtor has filed its tax returns; and

(C) review and monitor diligently the debtor's activities, to determine as promptly as possible whether the debtor will be unable to confirm a plan; and

(8) in any case in which the United States trustee finds material grounds for any relief under section 1112 of title 11, apply promptly after making that finding to the court for relief.

(b) If the number of cases under chapter 12 or 13 of title 11 commenced in a particular region so warrants, the United States trustee for such region may, subject to the approval of the Attorney General, appoint one or more individuals to serve as standing trustee, or designate one or more assistant United States trustees to serve in cases under such chapter. The United States trustee for such region shall supervise any such individual appointed as standing trustee in the performance of the duties of standing trustee.

(c) Each United States trustee shall be under the general supervision of the Attorney General, who shall provide general coordination and assistance to the United States trustees.

(d)(1) The Attorney General shall prescribe by rule qualifications for membership on the panels established by United States trustees under paragraph (a)(1) of this section, and qualifications for appointment under subsection (b) of this section to serve as standing trustee in cases under chapter 12 or 13 of title 11. The Attorney General may not require that an individual be an attorney in order to qualify for appointment under subsection (b) of this section to serve as standing trustee in cases under chapter 12 or 13 of title 11.

(2) A trustee whose appointment under subsection (a)(1) or under subsection (b) is terminated or who ceases to be assigned to cases filed under title 11, United States Code, may obtain judicial review of the final agency decision by commencing an action in the district court of the United States for the district for which the panel to which the trustee is appointed under subsection (a)(1), or in the district court of the United States for the district in which the trustee is appointed under subsection (b) resides, after first exhausting all available administrative remedies, which if the trustee so elects, shall also include an administrative hearing on the record. Unless the trustee elects to have an administrative hearing on the record, the trustee shall be deemed to have exhausted all administrative remedies for purposes of this paragraph if the agency fails to make a final agency decision within 90 days after the trustee requests administrative remedies. The Attorney General shall prescribe procedures to implement this paragraph. The decision of the agency shall be affirmed by the district court unless it is unreasonable and without cause based on the administrative record before the agency.

(e)(1) The Attorney General, after consultation with a United States trustee that has appointed an individual under subsection (b) of this section to serve as standing trustee in cases under chapter 12 or 13 of title 11, shall fix—

(A) a maximum annual compensation for such individual consisting of—

(i) an amount not to exceed the highest annual rate of basic pay in effect for level V of the Executive Schedule; and

(ii) the cash value of employment benefits comparable to the employment benefits provided by the United States to individuals who are employed by the United States at the same rate of basic pay to perform similar services during the same period of time; and

(B) a percentage fee not to exceed—

(i) in the case of a debtor who is not a family farmer, ten percent; or

(ii) in the case of a debtor who is a family farmer, the sum of—

(I) not to exceed ten percent of the payments made under the plan of such debtor, with respect to payments in an aggregate amount not to exceed $450,000; and

(II) three percent of payments made under the plan of such debtor, with respect to payments made after the aggregate amount of payments made under the plan exceeds $450,000;

based on such maximum annual compensation and the actual, necessary expenses incurred by such individual as standing trustee.

(2) Such individual shall collect such percentage fee from all payments received by such individual under plans in the cases under chapter 12 or 13 of title 11 for which such individual serves as standing trustee. Such individual shall pay to the United States trustee, and the United States trustee shall deposit in the United States Trustee System Fund—

(A) any amount by which the actual compensation of such individual exceeds 5 per centum upon all payments received under plans in cases under chapter 12 or 13 of title 11 for which such individual serves as standing trustee; and

(B) any amount by which the percentage for all such cases exceeds—

(i) such individual's actual compensation for such cases, as adjusted under subparagraph (A) of paragraph (1); plus

(ii) the actual, necessary expenses incurred by such individual as standing trustee in such cases. Subject to the approval of the Attorney General, any or all of the interest earned from the deposit of payments under plans by such individual may be utilized to pay actual, necessary expenses without regard to the percentage limitation contained in subparagraph (d)(1)(B) of this section.

(3) After first exhausting all available administrative remedies, an individual appointed under subsection (b) may obtain judicial review of final agency action to deny a claim of actual, necessary expenses under this subsection by commencing an action in the district court of the United States for the district where the individual resides. The decision of the agency shall be affirmed by the district court unless it is unreasonable and without cause based upon the administrative record before the agency.

(4) The Attorney General shall prescribe procedures to implement this subsection.

(f)(1) The United States trustee for each district is authorized to contract with auditors to perform audits in cases designated by the United States trustee, in accordance with the procedures established under section 603(a) of the Bankruptcy Abuse Prevention and Consumer Protection Act of 2005.

(2)(A) The report of each audit referred to in paragraph (1) shall be filed with the court and transmitted to the United States trustee. Each report shall clearly and conspicuously specify any material misstatement of income or expenditures or of assets identified by the person performing the audit. In any case in which a material misstatement of income or expenditures or of assets has been reported, the clerk of the district court (or the clerk of the bankruptcy court if one is certified under section 156(b) of this title) shall give notice of the misstatement to the creditors in the case.

(B) If a material misstatement of income or expenditures or of assets is reported, the United States trustee shall—

(i) report the material misstatement, if appropriate, to the United States Attorney pursuant to section 3057 of title 18; and

(ii) if advisable, take appropriate action, including but not limited to commencing an adversary proceeding to revoke the debtor's discharge pursuant to section 727(d) of title 11.

(Added Pub.L. 95–598, Title II, § 224(a), Nov. 6, 1978, 92 Stat. 2663; amended Pub.L. 99–554, Title I, § 113, Oct. 27, 1986, 100 Stat. 3091; Pub.L. 101–509, Title V, § 529 [Title I, § 110(a)], Nov. 5, 1990, 104 Stat. 1427, 1452; Pub.L. 103–394, Title II, § 224(a), Title V, § 502, Oct. 22, 1994, 108 Stat. 4130, 4147; Pub.L. 109–8, Title IV, § 439, Title VI, § 603(b), Title VIII, § 802(c)(3), Title XII, § 1231, Apr. 20, 2005, 119 Stat. 113, 122, 146, 201; Pub.L. 111–327, § 2(c)(3), Dec. 22, 2010, 124 Stat. 3563.)

HISTORICAL AND STATUTORY NOTES

References in Text

Chapter 12 or 13 of title 11, referred to in text, is 11 U.S.C.A. § 1201 et seq. or 11 U.S.C.A. § 1301 et seq., respectively.

Chapter 7, 11, 12, 13, or 15 of title 11, referred to in subsec. (a)(3), is 11 U.S.C.A. § 701 et seq., 11 U.S.C.A. § 1101 et seq., 11 U.S.C.A. § 1201 et seq., 11 U.S.C.A. § 1301 et seq., or 11 U.S.C.A. § 1501 et seq., respectively.

Level V of the Executive Schedule, referred to in subsec. (e)(1)(A)(i), is set out in section 5316 of Title 5, Government Organization and Employees.

Section 603(a) of the Bankruptcy Abuse Prevention and Consumer Protection Act of 2005, referred to in subsecs. (a)(6) and (f)(1), is Pub.L. 109–8, Title VII, § 603(a), Apr. 20, 2005, 119 Stat. 122, which is set out as a note under this section.

Codifications

Section 408(c) of Pub.L. 95–598, as amended, which provided for the repeal of this section and the deletion of any references to United States Trustees in this title at a prospective date, was repealed by section 307(b) of Pub.L. 99–554. See note set out preceding section 581 of this title.

Amendments

2010 Amendments. Subsec. (a)(3)(A)(ii). Pub.L. 111–327, § 2(c)(3)(A), struck out the period at the end and inserted a semicolon.

Subsec. (a)(7)(C). Pub.L. 111–327, § 2(c)(3)(B), struck out "identify" and inserted "determine".

Subsec. (a)(8). Pub.L. 111–327, § 2(c)(3)(C), struck out "the United States trustee shall" following "title 11,".

2005 Amendments. Subsec. (a)(3). Pub.L. 109–8, § 802(c)(3), in the matter preceding subpar. (A), struck out "or 13" and inserted "13, or 15".

Subsec. (a)(3)(G). Pub.L. 109–8, § 439(1)(A), struck out "and" at the end of subpar. (G).

Subsec. (a)(3)(H). Pub.L. 109–8, § 439(1)(B), (C), redesignated former subpar. (H) as (I), and inserted a new subpar. (H).

Subsec. (a)(3)(I). Pub.L. 109–8, § 439(1)(B), redesignated former subpar. (H) as (I).

Subsec. (a)(5). Pub.L. 109–8, § 439(2), struck out "and" at the end of par. (5).

Subsec. (a)(6). Pub.L. 109–8, § 439(3), struck out the period at the end of par. (6) and inserted a semicolon.

Pub.L. 109–8, § 603(b)(1), rewrote par. (6), which formerly read: "make such reports as the Attorney General directs;".

Subsec. (a)(7). Pub.L. 109–8, § 439(4), added par. (7).

Subsec. (a)(8). Pub.L. 109–8, § 439(4), added par. (8).

Subsec. (d). Pub.L.109–8, § 1231(a), inserted "(1)" after "(d)" and added paragraph (2).

Subsec. (e)(3), (4). Pub.L.109–8, § 1231(b), added pars. (3) and (4).

Subsec. (f). Pub.L. 109–8, § 603(b)(2), added subsec. (f).

1994 Amendments. Subsec. (a)(3)(A). Pub.L. 103–394, § 224(a), completely revised subpar. (A). Prior to revision, subpar. (A) read as follows:

"monitoring applications for compensation and reimbursement filed under section 330 of title 11 and, whenever the United States trustee deems it to be appropriate, filing with the court comments with respect to any of such applications;"

Subsec. (a)(3). Pub.L. 103–394, § 502, inserted "12," after "11,".

1990 Amendments. Subsec. (e)(1)(A). Pub.L. 101–509 substituted designated provisions setting maximum amount as amount not to exceed highest level V annual rate and cash value of employment benefits, for undesignated provisions setting such amount as annual rate for step 1 of grade GS–16 of the General Schedule.

1986 Amendments. Subsec. (a). Pub.L. 99–554, § 113(a)(1), substituted in provision preceding par. (1) "the region for which such United States trustee is appointed" for "his district".

Subsec. (a)(3). Pub.L. 99–554, § 113(a)(2), substituted "title 11 by, whenever the United States trustee considers it to be appropriate—" for "title 11;" and added subpars. (A) to (H).

Subsec. (a)(5). Pub.L. 99–554, § 113(a)(3), inserted "and this title, and such duties consistent with title 11 and this title as the Attorney General may prescribe" after "title 11".

Subsec. (b). Pub.L. 99–554, § 113(b), substituted "under chapter 12 or 13 of title 11 commenced in a particular region so warrants, the United States trustee for such region" for "under chapter 13 of title 11 commenced in a particular judicial district so warrant, the United States trustee for such district", "trustees to serve in cases" for "trustee, in cases" and "for such region shall" for "for such district shall".

Subsec. (d). Pub.L. 99–554, § 113(c), substituted "paragraph (a)(1) of this section" for "subsection (a)(1) of this section" and substituted "chapter 12 or 13" for "chapter 13" in two places.

Subsec. (e)(1). Pub.L. 99–554, § 113(c), substituted in provision preceding subpar. (A) "chapter 12 or 13" for "chapter 13", in subpar. (A) "annual rate of basic pay in effect for step 1 of grade" for "lowest annual rate of basic pay in effect for grade" and in subpar. (B) provision specifying the percentage fee in the case of a debtor who is not a family farmer and in the case of a debtor who is a family farmer for provision specifying the percentage fee without such a distinction.

Subsec. (e)(2). Pub.L. 99–554, § 113(c), substituted in provision preceding subpar. (A) "from all payments received by such individual under plans" for "from all payments under plans", "chapter 12 or 13" for "chapter 13" and "deposit in the United States Trustee System Fund" for "pay to the Treasury", in subpar. (A) substituted "5 per centum" for "five percent" and "received under plans in cases under chapter 12 or 13" for "under plans in cases under chapter 13", and in subpar. (B) substituted "individual's" for "individual" and "subparagraph (A) of paragraph (i)" for "subparagraph (A) of this paragraph", in cl. (i) and, in cl. (ii), inserted provision that, subject to the approval of the Attorney General, any and all of the interest earned from the deposit of payments under plans by such individual be utilized to pay actual, necessary expenses without regard to the percentage limitation contained in subpar. (d)(1)(B) of this section.

CROSS REFERENCES

Appointment of disinterested person from panel of private trustees established under this section to serve as—

Interim trustee, see 11 USCA § 701.

Successor trustee, see 11 USCA § 703.

Appointment of standing trustee to serve in cases under—

Chapter thirteen of Bankruptcy, see 11 USCA § 1302.

Chapter twelve of Bankruptcy, see 11 USCA § 1202.

Compensation for services or reimbursement of expenses not allowable for standing trustee appointed under this section, see 11 USCA § 326.

Payments to standing trustee; percentage fee fixed under this section, see 11 USCA § 1326.

§ 587. Salaries

Subject to sections 5315 through 5317 of title 5, the Attorney General shall fix the annual salaries of United States trustees and assistant United States trustees at rates of compensation not in excess of the rate of basic compensation provided for Executive Level IV of the Executive Schedule set forth in section 5315 of title 5, United States Code.

(Added Pub.L. 95–598, Title II, § 224(a), Nov. 6, 1978, 92 Stat. 2664; amended Pub.L. 99–554, Title I, § 114(a), Oct. 27, 1986, 100 Stat. 3093.)

HISTORICAL AND STATUTORY NOTES

Codifications

Section 408(c) of Pub.L. 95–598, as amended, which provided for the repeal of this section and the deletion of any references to United States Trustees in this title at a prospective date, was repealed by section 307(b) of Pub.L. 99–554. See note set out preceding section 581 of this title.

Amendments

1986 Amendments. Pub.L. 99–554 substituted "Subject to sections 5315 through 5317 of title 5, the" for "The" and "in excess of the rate of basic compensation provided for Executive Level IV of the

Executive Schedule set forth in section 5315 of title 5, United States Code" for "to exceed the lowest annual rate of basic pay in effect for grade GS–16 of the General Schedule prescribed under section 5332 of title 5".

§ 588. Expenses

Necessary office expenses of the United States trustee shall be allowed when authorized by the Attorney General.

(Added Pub.L. 95–598, Title II, § 224(a), Nov. 6, 1978, 92 Stat. 2664.)

HISTORICAL AND STATUTORY NOTES

Codifications

Section 408(c) of Pub.L. 95–598, as amended, which provided for the repeal of this section and the deletion of any references to United States Trustees in this title at a prospective date, was repealed by section 307(b) of Pub.L. 99–554. See note set out preceding section 581 of this title.

§ 589. Staff and other employees

The United States trustee may employ staff and other employees on approval of the Attorney General.

(Added Pub.L. 95–598, Title II, § 224(a), Nov. 6, 1978, 92 Stat. 2664.)

HISTORICAL AND STATUTORY NOTES

Codifications

Section 408(c) of Pub.L. 95–598, as amended, which provided for the repeal of this section and the deletion of any references to United States Trustees in this title at a prospective date, was repealed by section 307(b) of Pub.L. 99–554. See note set out preceding section 581 of this title.

§ 589a. United States Trustee System Fund

(a) There is hereby established in the Treasury of the United States a special fund to be known as the "United States Trustee System Fund" (hereinafter in this section referred to as the "Fund"). Monies in the Fund shall be available to the Attorney General without fiscal year limitation in such amounts as may be specified in appropriations Acts for the following purposes in connection with the operations of United States trustees—

    (1) salaries and related employee benefits;

    (2) travel and transportation;

    (3) rental of space;

    (4) communication, utilities, and miscellaneous computer charges;

    (5) security investigations and audits;

    (6) supplies, books, and other materials for legal research;

    (7) furniture and equipment;

    (8) miscellaneous services, including those obtained by contract; and

    (9) printing.

(b) For the purpose of recovering the cost of services of the United States Trustee System, there shall be deposited as offsetting collections to the appropriation "United States Trustee System Fund", to remain available until expended, the following—

    (1)(A) 40.46 percent of the fees collected under section 1930(a)(1)(A); and

(B) 28.33 percent of the fees collected under section 1930(a)(1)(B);

(2) 48.89 percent of the fees collected under section 1930(a)(3) of this title;

(3) one-half of the fees collected under section 1930(a)(4) of this title;

(4) one-half of the fees collected under section 1930(a)(5) of this title;

(5) 100 percent of the fees collected under section 1930(a)(6) of this title;

(6) three-fourths of the fees collected under the last sentence of section 1930(a) of this title;

(7) the compensation of trustees received under section 330(d) of title 11 by the clerks of the bankruptcy courts;

(8) excess fees collected under section 586(e)(2) of this title;

(9) interest earned on Fund investment; and

(10) fines imposed under section 110(l) of title 11, United States Code.

(c) Amounts in the Fund which are not currently needed for the purposes specified in subsection (a) shall be kept on deposit or invested in obligations of, or guaranteed by, the United States.

(d) The Attorney General shall transmit to the Congress, not later than 120 days after the end of each fiscal year, a detailed report on the amounts deposited in the Fund and a description of expenditures made under this section.

(e) There are authorized to be appropriated to the Fund for any fiscal year such sums as may be necessary to supplement amounts deposited under subsection (b) for the purposes specified in subsection (a).

(Added Pub.L. 99–554, Title I, § 115(a), Oct. 27, 1986, 100 Stat. 3094; amended Pub.L. 101–162, Title IV, § 406(c), Nov. 21, 1989, 103 Stat. 1016; Pub.L. 102–140, Title I, § 111(b), (c), Oct. 28, 1991, 105 Stat. 795; Pub.L. 103–121, Title I, § 111(a)(2), (b)(2), (3), Oct. 27, 1993, 107 Stat. 1164; Pub.L. 104–91, Title I, § 101(a), Jan. 6, 1996, 110 Stat. 11, as amended Pub.L. 104–99, Title II, § 211, Jan. 26, 1996, 110 Stat. 37; Pub.L. 104–208, Div. A, Title I, § 101(a) [Title I, § 109(b)], Sept. 30, 1996, 110 Stat. 3009–18; Pub.L. 106–113, Div. B, § 1000(a)(1) [Title I, § 113], Nov. 29, 1999, 113 Stat. 1535, 1501A–6, 1501A–20; Pub.L. 109–8, Title III, § 325(b), Apr. 20, 2005, 119 Stat. 99; Pub.L. 109–13, Div. A, Title VI, § 6058(a), May 11, 2005, 119 Stat. 297; Pub.L. 110–161, Div. B, Title II, § 212(a), Dec. 26, 2007, 121 Stat. 1914; Pub.L. 112–121, § 3(b), May 25, 2012, 126 Stat. 348.)

HISTORICAL AND STATUTORY NOTES

Codifications

Section 101(a) of Pub.L. 104–91, as amended by section 211 of Pub.L. 104–99, provided in part that section 111(b) and (c) of the General Provisions for the Department of Justice in Title I of the Departments of Commerce, Justice, and State, the Judiciary, and Related Agencies Appropriations Act, 1996 (H.R. 2076) as passed by the House of Representatives on Dec. 6, 1995, was enacted into permanent law. Such section 111(b) and (c) of H.R. 2076 amended subsecs. (b) and (f) of this section. See 1996 Amendments notes set out under this section.

Amendments

2012 Amendments. Subsec. (b)(2). Pub.L. 112–121, § 3(b), struck out "55" and inserted "48.89".

2007 Amendments. Subsec. (b)(8). Pub.L. 110–161, Div. B, § 212(a)(1), struck out "and".

Subsec. (b)(9). Pub.L. 110–161, Div. B, § 212(a)(2), struck out the period and inserted "; and".

Subsec. (b)(10). Pub.L. 110–161, Div. B, § 212(a)(3), added par. (10).

2005 Amendments. Subsec. (b)(1). Pub.L. 109–8, § 325(b)(1), as amended by Pub.L. 109–13, § 6058(a), added par. (1) and struck out former par. (1), which read as follows: "27.42 percent of the fees collected under section 1930(a)(1) of this title;".

Subsec. (b)(2). Pub.L. 109–8, § 325(b)(2), as amended by Pub.L. 109–13, § 6058(a), substituted "55 percent" for "one-half".

Subsec. (b)(4). Amendment by Pub.L. 109–8, § 325(b)(3), which struck out "one-half" and inserted "100 percent", was omitted in the amendment of Pub.L. 109–8, § 325 by Pub.L. 109–13, § 6058(a); thus, the language of subsec. (b)(4) reverted to "100 percent" after that amendment.

1999 Amendments. Subsec. (b)(1). Pub.L. 106–113 [§ 113] substituted "27.42 percent" for "23.08 percent".

Subsec. (b)(9). Pub.L. 106–113 [Title I] added par. (9).

1996 Amendments. Subsec. (b). Pub.L. 104–208, § 101(a) [§ 109(b)], substituted provisions requiring amounts to be deposited as offsetting collections to the appropriation "United States Trustee System Fund" for the purpose of recovering the cost of services of the United States Trustee System for provisions requiring amounts to be deposited in the Fund.

Subsec. (b)(2). Pub.L. 104–208, § 101(a) [§ 109(b)], increased the percentage of fees to be deposited under § 1930(a)(3) from 37.5% to 50%.

Subsec. (b)(5). Pub.L. 104–208, § 101(a) [§ 109(b)], increased the fees collected under § 1930(a)(6) from 60% until a reorganization plan is confirmed to 100%.

Pub.L. 104–91, § 101(a), as amended by Pub.L. 104–99, § 211, inserted provisions relating to confirmation of reorganization plan. See Codifications note set out under this section.

Subsec. (b)(8). Pub.L. 104–208, § 101(a) [§ 109(b)], added par. (8).

Subsec. (c). Pub.L. 104–208, § 101(a) [§ 109(b)], struck out par. (1) designation, struck out reference to the exception provided in par. (2), and struck out par. (2), which required the Secretary of the Treasury on each Nov. 1, to transfer certain Fund amounts exceeding 110% into the general fund of the Treasury.

Subsec. (d). Pub.L. 104–208, § 101(a) [§ 109(b)], struck out par. (1) designation, and struck out par. (2), which required the Secretary in certain instances to include in the report a recommendation regarding the manner in which fees payable under § 1930(a) of title 28 may be modified to cause the annual amount deposited to more closely approximate the annual amount expended.

Subsec. (f). Pub.L. 104–208, § 101(a) [§ 109(b)], struck out subsec. (f), which required 12.5% of fees collected under § 1930(a)(3), 40% of fees collected under § 1930(a)(6) until a reorganization plan is confirmed, and 100% of the fees collected under § 1930(a)(6) after the reorganization plan is confirmed, to be deposited to the Fund as offsetting collections.

Subsec. (f)(2). Pub.L. 104–91, § 101(a), as amended Pub.L. 104–99, § 211, inserted provisions relating to confirmation of reorganization plan. See Codifications note set out under this section.

Subsec. (f)(3). Pub.L. 104–91, § 101(a), as amended Pub.L. 104–99, § 211, added par. (3). See Codifications note set out under this section.

1993 Amendments. Subsec. (b)(1). Pub.L. 103–121, § 111(a)(2), substituted "23.08 per centum" for "one-fourth".

Subsec. (b)(2). Pub.L. 103–121, § 111(b)(2), substituted "37.5 per centum" for "50 per centum".

Subsec. (f)(1). Pub.L. 103–121, § 111(b)(3), substituted "12.5 per centum" for "16.7 per centum".

1991 Amendments. Subsec. (b)(2). Pub.L. 102–140, § 111(b)(1), substituted "50 per centum" for "three-fifths".

Subsec. (b)(5). Pub.L. 102–140, § 111(b)(2), substituted "60 per centum" for "all".

Subsec. (f). Pub.L. 102–140, § 111(c), added subsec. (f).

1989 Amendments. Subsec. (b)(1). Pub.L. 101–162, § 406(c), substituted "one-fourth" for "one-third".

CROSS REFERENCES

Compensation of Bankruptcy trustee to be deposited by clerk of bankruptcy court into Fund established by this section, see 11 USCA § 330.

§ 589b. Bankruptcy data

  (a) **Rules.**—The Attorney General shall, within a reasonable time after the effective date of this section, issue rules requiring uniform forms for (and from time to time thereafter to appropriately modify and approve)—

  (1) final reports by trustees in cases under chapters 7, 12, and 13 of title 11; and

  (2) periodic reports by debtors in possession or trustees in cases under chapter 11 of title 11.

  (b) **Reports.**—Each report referred to in subsection (a) shall be designed (and the requirements as to place and manner of filing shall be established) so as to facilitate compilation of data and maximum possible access of the public, both by physical inspection at one or more central filing locations, and by electronic access through the Internet or other appropriate media.

  (c) **Required information.**—The information required to be filed in the reports referred to in subsection (b) shall be that which is in the best interests of debtors and creditors, and in the public interest in reasonable and adequate information to evaluate the efficiency and practicality of the Federal bankruptcy system. In issuing rules proposing the forms referred to in subsection (a), the Attorney General shall strike the best achievable practical balance between—

  (1) the reasonable needs of the public for information about the operational results of the Federal bankruptcy system;

  (2) economy, simplicity, and lack of undue burden on persons with a duty to file reports; and

  (3) appropriate privacy concerns and safeguards.

  (d) **Final reports.**—The uniform forms for final reports required under subsection (a) for use by trustees under chapters 7, 12, and 13 of title 11 shall, in addition to such other matters as are required by law or as the Attorney General in the discretion of the Attorney General shall propose, include with respect to a case under such title—

  (1) information about the length of time the case was pending;

  (2) assets abandoned;

  (3) assets exempted;

  (4) receipts and disbursements of the estate;

  (5) expenses of administration, including for use under section 707(b), actual costs of administering cases under chapter 13 of title 11;

  (6) claims asserted;

  (7) claims allowed; and

  (8) distributions to claimants and claims discharged without payment,

in each case by appropriate category and, in cases under chapters 12 and 13 of title 11, date of confirmation of the plan, each modification thereto, and defaults by the debtor in performance under the plan.

  (e) **Periodic reports.**—The uniform forms for periodic reports required under subsection (a) for use by trustees or debtors in possession under chapter 11 of title 11 shall, in addition to such other matters as are required by law or as the Attorney General in the discretion of the Attorney General shall propose, include—

  (1) information about the industry classification, published by the Department of Commerce, for the businesses conducted by the debtor;

  (2) length of time the case has been pending;

  (3) number of full-time employees as of the date of the order for relief and at the end of each reporting period since the case was filed;

(4) cash receipts, cash disbursements and profitability of the debtor for the most recent period and cumulatively since the date of the order for relief;

(5) compliance with title 11, whether or not tax returns and tax payments since the date of the order for relief have been timely filed and made;

(6) all professional fees approved by the court in the case for the most recent period and cumulatively since the date of the order for relief (separately reported, for the professional fees incurred by or on behalf of the debtor, between those that would have been incurred absent a bankruptcy case and those not); and

(7) plans of reorganization filed and confirmed and, with respect thereto, by class, the recoveries of the holders, expressed in aggregate dollar values and, in the case of claims, as a percentage of total claims of the class allowed.

(Added Pub.L. 109–8, Title VI, § 602(a), Apr. 20, 2005, 119 Stat. 120.)

HISTORICAL AND STATUTORY NOTES

References in Text

The effective date of this section, referred to in subsec. (a), means 180 days after April 20, 2005. See Pub.L. 109–8, § 1501, set out as an Effective and Applicability Provisions note for 2005 Acts under 11 U.S.C.A. § 101.

Chapters 7, 12, and 13 of title 11, referred to in subsecs. (a)(1) and (d), are 11 U.S.C.A. § 701 et seq., 11 U.S.C.A. § 1201 et seq., and 11 U.S.C.A. § 1301 et seq., respectively.

Chapter 11 of title 11, referred to in subsecs. (a)(2) and (e), is 11 U.S.C.A. § 1101 et seq.

PART III—COURT OFFICERS AND EMPLOYEES

CHAPTER 41—ADMINISTRATIVE OFFICE OF UNITED STATES COURTS

§ 604. Duties of Director generally

(a) The Director shall be the administrative officer of the courts, and under the supervision and direction of the Judicial Conference of the United States, shall:

(1) Supervise all administrative matters relating to the offices of clerks and other clerical and administrative personnel of the courts;

(2) Examine the state of the dockets of the courts; secure information as to the courts' need of assistance; prepare and transmit semiannually to the chief judges of the circuits, statistical data and reports as to the business of the courts;

(3) Submit to the annual meeting of the Judicial Conference of the United States, at least two weeks prior thereto, a report of the activities of the Administrative Office and the state of the business of the courts, together with the statistical data submitted to the chief judges of the circuits under paragraph (a)(2) of this section, and the Director's recommendations, which report, data and recommendations shall be public documents.

(4) Submit to Congress and the Attorney General copies of the report, data and recommendations required by paragraph (a)(3) of this section;

(5) Fix the compensation of clerks of court, deputies, librarians, criers, messengers, law clerks, secretaries, stenographers, clerical assistants, and other employees of the courts whose compensation is not otherwise fixed by law, and, notwithstanding any other provision of law, pay on behalf of Justices and judges of the United States appointed to hold office during good behavior, United States magistrate judges, bankruptcy judges appointed under chapter 6 of this title, judges of the District Court of Guam, judges of the District Court for the Northern Mariana Islands, judges of the District Court of the Virgin Islands, bankruptcy judges and

magistrate judges retired under section 377 of this title, and judges retired under section 373 of this title, who are,[1] aged 65 or over, any increases in the cost of Federal Employees' Group Life Insurance imposed after April 24, 1999, including any expenses generated by such payments, as authorized by the Judicial Conference of the United States;

(6) Determine and pay necessary office expenses of courts, judges, and those court officials whose expenses are by law allowable, and the lawful fees of United States magistrate judges;

(7) Regulate and pay annuities to widows and surviving dependent children of justices and judges of the United States, judges of the United States Court of Federal Claims, bankruptcy judges, United States magistrate judges, Directors of the Federal Judicial Center, and Directors of the Administrative Office, and necessary travel and subsistence expenses incurred by judges, court officers and employees, and officers and employees of the Administrative Office, and the Federal Judicial Center, while absent from their official stations on official business, without regard to the per diem allowances and amounts for reimbursement of actual and necessary expenses established by the Administrator of General Services under section 5702 of title 5, except that the reimbursement of subsistence expenses may not exceed that authorized by the Director for judges of the United States under section 456 of this title;

(8) Disburse appropriations and other funds for the maintenance and operation of the courts;

(9) Establish pretrial services pursuant to section 3152 of title 18, United States Code;

(10) (A) Purchase, exchange, transfer, distribute, and assign the custody of lawbooks, equipment, supplies, and other personal property for the judicial branch of Government (except the Supreme Court unless otherwise provided pursuant to paragraph (17)); (B) provide or make available readily to each court appropriate equipment for the interpretation of proceedings in accordance with section 1828 of this title; and (C) enter into and perform contracts and other transactions upon such terms as the Director may deem appropriate as may be necessary to the conduct of the work of the judicial branch of Government (except the Supreme Court unless otherwise provided pursuant to paragraph (17)), and contracts for nonpersonal services providing pretrial services, agencies for the interpretation of proceedings, and for the provision of special interpretation services pursuant to section 1828 of this title may be awarded without regard to section 6101(b) to (d) of title 41;

(11) Audit vouchers and accounts of the courts, the Federal Judicial Center, the offices providing pretrial services, and their clerical and administrative personnel;

(12) Provide accommodations for the courts, the Federal Judicial Center, the offices providing pretrial services and their clerical and administrative personnel;

(13) Lay before Congress, annually, statistical tables that will accurately reflect the business transacted by the several bankruptcy courts, and all other pertinent data relating to such courts;

(14) Pursuant to section 1827 of this title, establish a program for the certification and utilization of interpreters in courts of the United States;

(15) Pursuant to section 1828 of this title, establish a program for the provision of special interpretation services in courts of the United States;

(16)(A) In those districts where the Director considers it advisable based on the need for interpreters, authorize the full-time or part-time employment by the court of certified interpreters; (B) where the Director considers it advisable based on the need for interpreters, appoint certified interpreters on a full-time or part-time basis, for services in various courts when he determines that such appointments will result in the economical provision of interpretation services; and (C) pay out of moneys appropriated for the judiciary interpreters'

---

[1] So in original. The comma probably should not appear.

salaries, fees, and expenses, and other costs which may accrue in accordance with the provisions of sections 1827 and 1828 of this title;

(17) In the Director's discretion, (A) accept and utilize voluntary and uncompensated (gratuitous) services, including services as authorized by section 3102(b) of title 5, United States Code; and (B) accept, hold, administer, and utilize gifts and bequests of personal property for the purpose of aiding or facilitating the work of the judicial branch of Government, but gifts or bequests of money shall be covered into the Treasury;

(18) Establish procedures and mechanisms within the judicial branch for processing fines, restitution, forfeitures of bail bonds or collateral, and assessments;

(19) Regulate and pay annuities to bankruptcy judges and United States magistrate judges in accordance with section 377 of this title and paragraphs (1)(B) and (2) of section 2(c) of the Retirement and Survivors' Annuities for Bankruptcy Judges and Magistrates Act of 1988;

(20) Periodically compile—

  (A) the rules which are prescribed under section 2071 of this title by courts other than the Supreme Court;

  (B) the rules which are prescribed under section 358 of this title; and

  (C) the orders which are required to be publicly available under section 360(b) of this title;

so as to provide a current record of such rules and orders;

(21) Establish a program of incentive awards for employees of the judicial branch of the United States Government, other than any judge who is entitled to hold office during good behavior;

(22) Receive and expend, either directly or by transfer to the United States Marshals Service or other Government agency, funds appropriated for the procurement, installation, and maintenance of security equipment and protective services for the United States Courts in courtrooms and adjacent areas, including building ingress/egress control, inspection of packages, directed security patrols, and other similar activities;

(23) Regulate and pay annuities to judges of the United States Court of Federal Claims in accordance with section 178 of this title; and

(24) Perform such other duties as may be assigned to him by the Supreme Court or the Judicial Conference of the United States.

(b) The clerical and administrative personnel of the courts shall comply with all requests by the Director for information or statistical data as to the state of court dockets.

(c) Inspection of court dockets outside the continental United States may be made through United States officials residing within the jurisdiction where the inspection is made.

(d) The Director, under the supervision and direction of the conference, shall:

  (1) supervise all administrative matters relating to the offices of the United States magistrate judges;

  (2) gather, compile, and evaluate all statistical and other information required for the performance of his duties and the duties of the conference with respect to such officers;

  (3) lay before Congress annually statistical tables and other information which will accurately reflect the business which has come before the various United States magistrate judges, including (A) the number of matters in which the parties consented to the exercise of jurisdiction by a magistrate judge, (B) the number of appeals taken pursuant to the decisions of magistrate judges and the disposition of such appeals, and (C) the professional background and qualifications of individuals appointed under section 631 of this title to serve as magistrate judges;

(4) prepare and distribute a manual, with annual supplements and periodic revisions, for the use of such officers, which shall set forth their powers and duties, describe all categories of proceedings that may arise before them, and contain such other information as may be required to enable them to discharge their powers and duties promptly, effectively, and impartially.

(e) The Director may promulgate appropriate rules and regulations approved by the conference and not inconsistent with any provision of law, to assist him in the performance of the duties conferred upon him by subsection (d) of this section. Magistrate judges shall keep such records and make such reports as are specified in such rules and regulations.

(f) The Director may make, promulgate, issue, rescind, and amend rules and regulations (including regulations prescribing standards of conduct for Administrative Office employees) as may be necessary to carry out the Director's functions, powers, duties, and authority. The Director may publish in the Federal Register such rules, regulations, and notices for the judicial branch of Government as the Director determines to be of public interest; and the Director of the Federal Register hereby is authorized to accept and shall publish such materials.

(g)(1) When authorized to exchange personal property, the Director may exchange or sell similar items and may apply the exchange allowance or proceeds of sale in such cases in whole or in part payment for the property acquired, but any transaction carried out under the authority of this subsection shall be evidenced in writing.

(2) The Director hereby is authorized to enter into contracts for public utility services and related terminal equipment for periods not exceeding ten years.

(3)(A) In order to promote the recycling and reuse of recyclable materials, the Director may provide for the sale or disposal of recyclable scrap materials from paper products and other consumable office supplies held by an entity within the judicial branch.

(B) The sale or disposal of recyclable materials under subparagraph (A) shall be consistent with the procedures provided in sections 541–555 of title 40 for the sale of surplus property.

(C) Proceeds from the sale of recyclable materials under subparagraph (A) shall be deposited as offsetting collections to the fund established under section 1931 of this title and shall remain available until expended to reimburse any appropriations for the operation and maintenance of the judicial branch.

(4) The Director is hereby authorized:

(A) to enter into contracts for the acquisition of severable services for a period that begins in one fiscal year and ends in the next fiscal year to the same extent as the head of an executive agency under the authority of section 253*l* of Title 41, United States Code;

(B) to enter into contracts for multiple years for the acquisition of property and services to the same extent as executive agencies under the authority of section 254c of Title 41, United States Code; and

(C) to make advance, partial, progress or other payments under contracts for property or services to the same extent as executive agencies under the authority of section 255 of title 41, United States Code.

(h)(1) The Director shall, out of funds appropriated for the operation and maintenance of the courts, provide facilities and pay necessary expenses incurred by the judicial councils of the circuits and the Judicial Conference under chapter 16 of this title, including mileage allowance and witness fees, at the same rate as provided in section 1821 of this title. Administrative and professional assistance from the Administrative Office of the United States Courts may be requested by each judicial council and the Judicial Conference for purposes of discharging their duties under chapter 16 of this title.

(2) The Director of the Administrative Office of the United States Courts shall include in his annual report filed with the Congress under this section a summary of the number of complaints filed with each judicial council under chapter 16 of this title, indicating the general nature of such complaints and the disposition of those complaints in which action has been taken.

(June 25, 1948, c. 646, 62 Stat. 914; Aug. 3, 1956, c. 944, § 3, 70 Stat. 1026; Dec. 20, 1967, Pub.L. 90–219, Title II, § 203, 81 Stat. 669; Oct. 17, 1968, Pub.L. 90–578, Title II, § 201, Title IV, § 402(b)(2), 82 Stat. 1114, 1118; Aug. 22, 1972, Pub.L. 92–397, § 4, 86 Stat. 580; Jan. 3, 1975, Pub.L. 93–619, Title II, § 204, 88 Stat. 2089; Oct. 28, 1978, Pub.L. 95–539, §§ 3, 4, 92 Stat. 2043; Nov. 6, 1978, Pub.L. 95–598, Title II, § 225, 92 Stat. 2664; Oct. 10, 1979, Pub.L. 96–82, § 5, 93 Stat. 645; Oct. 15, 1980, Pub.L. 96–458, § 5, 94 Stat. 2040; Dec. 12, 1980, Pub.L. 96–523, § 1(c)(1), 94 Stat. 3040; Sept. 27, 1982, Pub.L. 97–267, § 7, 96 Stat. 1139; Oct. 27, 1986, Pub.L. 99–554, Title I, § 116, 100 Stat. 3095; Dec. 11, 1987, Pub.L. 100–185, § 2, 101 Stat. 1279; Nov. 15, 1988, Pub.L. 100–659, § 6(a), 102 Stat. 3918; Nov. 19, 1988, Pub.L. 100–702, Title IV, § 402(a), Title X, §§ 1008, 1010, 1011, 1020(a)(2), 102 Stat. 4650, 4667, 4668, 4671; Oct. 30, 1990, Pub.L. 101–474, § 5(r), 104 Stat. 1101; Nov. 29, 1990, Pub.L. 101–647, Title XXV, § 2548, 104 Stat. 4888; Dec. 1, 1990, Pub.L. 101–650, Title III, §§ 306(e)(1), 321, 325(c)(1), 104 Stat. 5111, 5117, 5121; Oct. 29, 1992, Pub.L. 102–572, Title V, § 503, Title IX, § 902(b)(1), 106 Stat. 4513, 4516; Nov. 29, 1999, Pub.L. 106–113, § 1000(a)(1) [Title III, § 305], 113 Stat. 1535, 1501A–37; Nov. 13, 2000, Pub.L. 106–518, Title II, § 204, Title III, § 304(d), 114 Stat. 2414, 2418; Aug. 21, 2002, Pub.L. 107–217, § 3(g)(1), 116 Stat. 1299; Nov. 2, 2002, Pub.L. 107–273, Div. C, Title I, § 11043(e), 116 Stat. 1855; Nov. 30, 2005, Pub.L. 109–115, Div. A, Title IV, § 407(a), 119 Stat. 2470; Jan. 7, 2008, Pub.L. 110–177, Title V, § 502(a), 121 Stat. 2542; Mar. 11, 2009, Pub.L. 111–8, Div. D, Title III, § 307(a), 123 Stat. 648; Jan. 4, 2011, Pub.L. 111–350, § 5(g)(2), 124 Stat. 3848.)

HISTORICAL AND STATUTORY NOTES

References in Text

Chapter 6 of this title, referred to in subsec. (a)(5), is chapter 6 of part I of this title, which is classified to 28 U.S.C.A. § 151 et seq.

Section 2(c) of the Retirement and Survivors' Annuities for Bankruptcy Judges and Magistrates Act of 1988, referred to in subsec. (a)(19), is section 2(c) of Pub.L. 100–659, Nov. 15, 1988, 102 Stat. 3916, which is set out as a note under section 377 of this title.

Section 253*l* of Title 41, United States Code, referred to in subsec. (g)(4)(A), probably means section 303L of Act June 30, 1949, c. 288, which was classified to section 253*l* of former Title 41, Public Contracts, and was repealed and restated as section 3902 of Title 41, Public Contracts, by Pub.L. 111–350, §§ 3, 7(b), Jan. 4, 2011, 124 Stat. 3677, 3855.

Section 254c of Title 41, United States Code, referred to in subsec. (g)(4)(B), probably means section 304B of Act June 30, 1949, c. 288, which was classified to section 254c of former Title 41, Public Contracts, and was repealed and restated as section 3903 of Title 41, Public Contracts, by Pub.L. 111–350, §§ 3, 7(b), Jan. 4, 2011, 124 Stat. 3677, 3855.

Section 255 of Title 41, referred to in subsec. (g)(4)(C), probably means section 305 of Act June 30, 1949, c. 288, which was classified to section 255 of former Title 41, Public Contracts, and was repealed and restated as chapter 45 (§ 4501 et seq.) of Title 41, Public Contracts, by Pub. L. 111–350, §§ 3, 7(b), Jan. 4, 2011, 124 Stat. 3677, 3855.

Codifications

Pub.L. 101–650, § 306(e)(1)(A), directing amendment of Pub.L. 100–702, § 402(1), probably intended amendment of section 402(a)(1) of Pub.L. 100–702, which provided for redesignation of subsec. (a)(19) to be subsec. (a)(23) of this section, redesignated as subsec. (a)(24) by Pub.L. 101–650, § 306(e)(1)(B)(ii).

Amendment by Pub.L. 109–115, Div. A, § 407(a), which directed that this section is amended by adding "section (4) at the end of section '(g)' " was executed by adding par. (4) to the end of subsec. (g), as the probable intent of Congress.

Amendments

2011 Amendments. Subsec. (a)(10)(C). Pub.L. 111–350, § 5(g)(2), struck out "section 3709 of the Revised Statutes of the United States (41 U.S.C. 5)" and inserted "section 6101(b) to (d) of title 41".

2009 Amendments. Subsec. (a)(5). Pub.L. 111–8, Div. D, § 307(a), following "hold office during good behavior", struck out "magistrate judges appointed under section 631 of this title," and inserted ", United States magistrate judges, bankruptcy judges appointed under chapter 6 of this title, judges of the District Court of Guam, judges of the District Court for the Northern Mariana Islands, judges of the District Court of the Virgin Islands, bankruptcy judges and magistrate judges retired under section 377 of this title, and judges retired under section 373 of this title, who are".

2008 Amendments. Subsec. (a)(5). Pub.L. 110–177, § 502(a), inserted "magistrate judges appointed under section 631 of this title," following "hold office during good behavior".

2005 Amendments. Subsec. (g)(4). Pub.L. 109–115, § 407(a), added par. (4).

2002 Amendments. Subsec. (a)(20)(B). Pub.L. 107–273, § 11043(e)(1)(A), substituted "section 358 of this title" for "section 372(c)(11) of this title".

Subsec. (a)(20)(C). Pub.L. 107–273, § 11043(e)(1)(B), substituted "section 360(b) of this title" for "section 372(c)(15) of this title".

Subsec. (g)(3)(B). Pub.L. 107–217, § 3(g)(1), struck out "section 203 of the Federal Property and Administrative Services Act of 1949 (40 U.S.C. 484)" and substituted "sections 541–555 of title 40".

Subsec. (h)(1). Pub.L. 107–273, § 11043(e)(2)(A), substituted "chapter 16 of this title" for "section 372 of this title" wherever appearing.

Subsec. (h)(2). Pub.L. 107–273, § 11043(e)(2)(B), substituted "chapter 16 of this title" for "section 372(c) of this title".

2000 Amendments. Subsec. (a)(8). Pub.L. 106–518, § 304(d), rewrote par. (8), which formerly read: "Disburse, directly or through the several United States marshals, moneys appropriated for the maintenance and operation of the courts;".

Subsec. (a)(24). Pub.L. 106–518, § 204, struck out the second par. (24), which formerly read: "Lay before Congress, annually, statistical tables that will accurately reflect the business imposed on the Federal courts by the savings and loan crisis."

1999 Amendments. Subsec. (a)(5). Pub.L. 106–113 [§ 305] inserted provisions regarding payment on behalf of Justices and judges of the United States appointed to hold office during good behavior, aged 65 or over, any increases in the cost of Federal Employees' Group Life Insurance imposed after April 24, 1999, including expenses.

1992 Amendments. Subsec. (a)(7), (23), Pub.L. 102–572, § 902(b)(1), substituted "United States Court of Federal Claims" for "United States Claims Court".

Subsec. (g)(3). Pub.L. 102–572, § 503, added par. (3).

1990 Amendments. Subsec. (a)(7). Pub.L. 101–650, § 325(c)(1), amended Pub.L. 100–702, § 1011, resulting in the substitution of ", except that" for ": *Provided,* That" in par. (7), and deleted directory language which would have required substitution of a comma for a semicolon at the end of par. (7) as it existed prior to amendment by Pub.L. 100–702. See 1988 Amendments note under this section.

Pub.L. 101–650, § 306(e)(1)(B)(i), inserted "judges of the United States Claims Court," preceding "bankruptcy judges".

Subsec. (a)(19). Pub.L. 101–474, § 5(r), and Pub.L. 101–650, § 306(e)(1)(A), identically amended Pub.L. 100–702, § 402(a)(1), redesignating par. (19) as (23). See 1988 Amendments note under this section.

Subsec. (a)(23). Pub.L. 101–650, § 306(e)(1)(B)(iii), added par. (23). Former par. (23) redesignated (24).

Pub.L. 101–474, § 5(r), and Pub.L. 101–650, § 306(e)(1)(A), identically amended Pub.L. 100–702, § 402(a)(1), redesignating par. (19) as (23). See 1988 Amendments note under this section.

Subsec. (a)(24). Pub.L. 101–650, § 306(e)(1)(B)(ii), redesignated par. (23), relating to performance of other duties, as (24).

Pub.L. 101–647 added par. (24) relating to statistical tables.

1988 Amendments. Subsec. (a)(2). Pub.L. 100–702, § 1020(a)(2), substituted "semiannually" for "quarterly".

Subsec. (a)(7). Pub.L. 100–702, § 1011, which directed substitution of a comma for a semicolon at the end of par. (7) and added thereafter "without regard to the per diem allowances and amounts for reimbursement of actual and necessary expenses established by the Administrator of General Services under section 5702 of title 5: *Provided,* That the reimbursement of subsistence expenses may not exceed that authorized by the Director for judges of the United States under section 456 of this title;", was executed by inserting said provisions following the comma at the end of par. (7), as the probable intent of Congress.

Pub.L. 100–659, § 6(a)(1), inserted after "United States," the words "bankruptcy judges, United States magistrates,".

Subsec. (a)(14) to (17). Pub.L. 100–702, § 1008(1), redesignated second par. (14) relating to the provision of special interpretation services in courts of the United States, through par. (17) as pars. (15) through (18), respectively.

Subsec. (a)(18). Pub.L. 100–702, § 1008(1), redesignated par. (17) as (18). Former par. (18), as added by Pub.L. 100–659, redesignated (19).

Pub.L. 100–659, § 6(a)(3), added par. (18). Former par. (18) redesignated (19).

Subsec. (a)(19). Pub.L. 100–702, § 1008(1), redesignated par. (19), as added by Pub.L. 100–702, § 402(a)(2), as (20).

Pub.L. 100–702, § 402(a), which directed the redesignation of par. (18) as (23) and the addition of par. (19) was executed by redesignating par. (19), relating to performance of other duties, as (23) and adding par. (19), relating to compilation of rules and orders, to reflect the probable intent of Congress.

Pub.L. 100–659, § 6(a)(2), redesignated par. (18), relating to performance of other duties, as (19).

Subsec. (a)(20). Pub.L. 100–702, § 1008(1), redesignated par. (19), as added by Pub.L. 100–702, § 402(a)(2), as par. (20).

Subsec. (a)(21). Pub.L. 100–702, § 1008(2), added par. (21).

Subsec. (a)(22). Pub.L. 100–702, § 1010, added par. (22).

Subsec. (a)(23). Pub.L. 100–702, § 402(a)(1), redesignated par. (19), relating to performance of other duties, as (23).

1987 Amendments. Subsec. (a)(17), (18). Pub.L. 100–185, § 2, added par. (17) and redesignated former par. (17) as (18).

1986 Amendments. Subsec. (f). Pub.L. 99–554 struck out subsec. (f) as added by section 225(b) of Pub.L. 95–598, which related to the Director naming qualified persons to membership on the panel of trustees, their number, qualifications, removal, etc.

1982 Amendments. Subsec. (a)(9). Pub.L. Pub.L. 97–267, § 7(1), struck out "agencies" following "pretrial services".

Subsec. (a)(10). Pub.L. 97–267, § 7(2), substituted "providing pretrial services" for "for pretrial services agencies".

Subsec. (a)(11), (12). Pub.L. 97–267, § 7(3), (4), substituted "offices providing pretrial services" for "pretrial service agencies" in par. (11), and "offices providing pretrial services" for "pretrial services agencies" in par. (12), respectively.

1980 Amendments. Subsec. (a)(16)(A). Pub.L. 96–523 added "(b)" following "3102".

Subsec. (h). Pub.L. 96–458 added subsec. (h).

1979 Amendments. Subsec. (d)(3). Pub.L. 96–82 added cls. (A), (B), and (C).

1978 Amendments. Subsec. (a)(10). Pub.L. 95–539, § 3(a), expanded the duties of the Director to include providing or making available equipment for interpretation of proceedings in accordance with section 1828 of this title and to include entering into and performing contracts necessary to the conduct of the work of the judicial branch and exempted from the provisions of section 5 of Title 41 contracts for nonpersonal services for pretrial agencies, for interpretation of proceedings, and for special interpretation services pursuant to section 1828 of this title.

Subsec. (a)(13), (14). Pub.L. 95–598, § 225(a), added par. (13), relating to annual statistical tables reflecting the business of the several bankruptcy courts and redesignated former par. (13), relating to provision of special interpretation services in courts of the United States, as (14).

Subsec. (a)(13) to (16). Pub.L. 95–539, § 3(b), (c), added pars. (13) to (16). Former par. (13) redesignated (17).

Subsec. (a)(17). Pub.L. 95–539, § 3(b), redesignated former par. (13) as (17).

Subsec. (f). Pub.L. 95–598, § 225(b), added subsec. (f), relating to the naming of qualified persons to membership on the panel of trustees.

Subsecs. (f), (g). Pub.L. 95–539, § 4, added subsecs. (f) and (g).

1975 Amendments. Subsec. (a)(9). Pub.L. 93–619 added par. (9). Former par. (9) redesignated (10).

Subsec. (a)(10). Pub.L. 93–619 redesignated former par. (9) as (10), and in par. (10) as so redesignated, substituted "the offices of the United States magistrates and commissioners, and the offices of pretrial services agencies" for "and the Administrative Office and the offices of the United States magistrates". Former par. (10) redesignated (11).

Subsec. (a)(11). Pub.L. 93–619 redesignated former par. (10) as par. (11), and in par. (11), as so redesignated, added reference to pretrial service agencies. Former par. (11) redesignated (12).

Subsec. (a)(12). Pub.L. 93–619 redesignated former par. (11) as (12), and in par. (12) as so redesignated, added reference to pretrial service agencies. Former par. (12) redesignated (13).

Subsec. (a)(13). Pub.L. 93–619 redesignated former par. (12) as (13).

1972 Amendments. Subsec. (a)(7). Pub.L. Pub.L. 92–397 substituted "children of justices and judges of the United States" for "children of judges".

1968 Amendments. Subsec. (a)(9). Pub.L. 90–578, § 201(a), substituted "United States magistrates" for "United States Commissioners".

Subsecs. (d), (e). Pub.L. 90–578, § 201(b), added subsecs. (d) and (e).

1967 Amendments. Subsec. (a)(7). Pub.L. 90–219, § 203(a), inserted ", Directors of the Federal Judicial Center, and Directors of the Administrative Office," following "judges" and "and the Federal Judicial Center," following "Administrative Office".

Subsec. (a)(9). Pub.L. 90–219, § 203(b), inserted ", the Federal Judicial Center," following "courts."

Subsec. (a)(10). Pub.L. 90–219, § 203(c), inserted ", the Federal Judicial Center," following "courts."

Subsec. (a)(11). Pub.L. 90–219, § 203(c), inserted ", the Federal Judicial Center," following "courts".

1956 Amendments. Subsec. (a)(7). Act Aug. 3, 1956, inserted "annuities to widows and surviving dependent children of judges and" following "Regulate and pay".

CROSS REFERENCES

Actual abode of recalled judge or magistrate deemed official station for purposes of this section, see 28 USCA § 374.

Annual report to Judicial Conference under this section to include administration and operation pretrial services for previous year, see 18 USCA § 3155.

Classification and general schedule pay rates, see 5 USCA §§ 5101 et seq. and 5331 et seq.

Duties of Supreme Court Marshal, see 28 USCA § 672.

Expenses of judges and United States attorneys, see 28 USCA §§ 456, 460, 549, and 566.

Juror travel allowance not to exceed maximum rate per mile that Director prescribes pursuant to this section, see 28 USCA § 1871.

Notification to Attorney General of receipt of payment of unpaid fines, see 18 USCA § 3612.

Office expenses of clerks of court, see 28 USCA § 961.

Overtime pay, see 5 USCA § 5541 et seq.

Specification by Director in payment of fine as provided under this section, see 18 USCA § 3611.

Supreme Court officers and employees; compensation and disbursement, see 28 USCA § 671 et seq.

CHAPTER 44—ALTERNATIVE DISPUTE RESOLUTION

HISTORICAL AND STATUTORY NOTES

Amendments

1998 Amendments. Chapter heading and analysis. Pub.L. 105–315, § 12(b)(1), Oct. 30, 1998, 112 Stat. 2898, rewrote the chapter heading and analysis, which formerly read:

"CHAPTER 44—ARBITRATION

"Sec.

"651.	Authorization of arbitration.
"652.	Jurisdiction.
"653.	Powers of arbitrator; arbitration hearing.
"654.	Arbitration award and judgment.
"655.	Trial de novo.
"656.	Certification of arbitrators.
"657.	Compensation of arbitrators.
"658.	District courts that may authorize arbitration."

§ 651. Authorization of alternative dispute resolution

(a) **Definition.**—For purposes of this chapter, an alternative dispute resolution process includes any process or procedure, other than an adjudication by a presiding judge, in which a neutral third party participates to assist in the resolution of issues in controversy, through processes such as early neutral evaluation, mediation, minitrial, and arbitration as provided in sections 654 through 658.

(b) **Authority.**—Each United States district court shall authorize, by local rule adopted under section 2071(a), the use of alternative dispute resolution processes in all civil actions, including adversary proceedings in bankruptcy, in accordance with this chapter, except that the use of arbitration may be authorized only as provided in section 654. Each United States district court shall devise and implement its own alternative dispute resolution program, by local rule adopted under section 2071(a), to encourage and promote the use of alternative dispute resolution in its district.

(c) **Existing alternative dispute resolution programs.**—In those courts where an alternative dispute resolution program is in place on the date of the enactment of the Alternative Dispute Resolution Act of 1998, the court shall examine the effectiveness of that program and adopt such improvements to the program as are consistent with the provisions and purposes of this chapter [28 U.S.C.A. § 651 et seq.].

(d) **Administration of alternative dispute resolution programs.**—Each United States district court shall designate an employee, or a judicial officer, who is knowledgeable in alternative dispute resolution practices and processes to implement, administer, oversee, and evaluate the court's alternative dispute resolution program. Such person may also be responsible for recruiting, screening, and training attorneys to serve as neutrals and arbitrators in the court's alternative dispute resolution program.

(e) **Title 9 not affected.**—This chapter [28 U.S.C.A. § 651 et seq.] shall not affect title 9, United States Code.

(f) **Program support.**—The Federal Judicial Center and the Administrative Office of the United States Courts are authorized to assist the district courts in the establishment and improvement of alternative dispute resolution programs by identifying particular practices employed in successful programs and providing additional assistance as needed and appropriate.

(Added Pub.L. 100–702, Title IX, § 901(a), Nov. 19, 1988, 102 Stat. 4659; amended Pub.L. 105–315, § 3, Oct. 30, 1998, 112 Stat. 2993.)

HISTORICAL AND STATUTORY NOTES

References in Text

The enactment of the Alternative Dispute Resolution Act of 1998, referred to in subsec. (c), is the enactment of Pub.L. 105–315, 112 Stat. 2993, which was approved Oct. 30, 1998.

Amendments

1998 Amendments. Pub.L. 105–315, § 3, rewrote the section, which formerly read:

" **§ 651. Authorization of arbitration**

"**(a) Authority of Certain District Courts.**—Each United States district court described in section 658 may authorize by local rule the use of arbitration in any civil action, including an adversary proceeding in bankruptcy. A district court described in section 658(1) may refer any such action to arbitration as set forth in section 652(a). A district court described in section 658(2) may refer only such actions to arbitration as are set forth in section 652(a)(1)(A).

"**(b) Title 9 Not Affected.**—This chapter shall not affect title 9."

§ 652. Jurisdiction

(a) **Consideration of alternative dispute resolution in appropriate cases.**—Notwithstanding any provision of law to the contrary and except as provided in subsections (b) and (c), each district court shall, by local rule adopted under section 2071(a), require that litigants in all civil cases consider the use of an alternative dispute resolution process at an appropriate stage in the litigation. Each district court shall provide litigants in all civil cases with at least one alternative dispute resolution process, including, but not limited to, mediation, early neutral evaluation, minitrial, and arbitration as authorized in sections 654 through 658. Any district court that elects to require the use of alternative dispute resolution in certain cases may do so only with respect to mediation, early neutral evaluation, and, if the parties consent, arbitration.

(b) **Actions exempted from consideration of alternative dispute resolution.**—Each district court may exempt from the requirements of this section specific cases or categories of cases in which use of alternative dispute resolution would not be appropriate. In defining these exemptions, each district court shall consult with members of the bar, including the United States Attorney for that district.

(c) **Authority of the Attorney General.**—Nothing in this section shall alter or conflict with the authority of the Attorney General to conduct litigation on behalf of the United States, with the authority of any Federal agency authorized to conduct litigation in the United States courts, or with any delegation of litigation authority by the Attorney General.

(d) **Confidentiality provisions.**—Until such time as rules are adopted under chapter 131 of this title [28 U.S.C.A. § 2071 et seq.] providing for the confidentiality of alternative dispute resolution processes under this chapter [28 U.S.C.A. § 651 et seq.], each district court shall, by local rule adopted under section 2071(a), provide for the confidentiality of the alternative dispute resolution processes and to prohibit disclosure of confidential dispute resolution communications.

(Added Pub.L. 100–702, Title IX, § 901(a), Nov. 19, 1988, 102 Stat. 4659; amended Pub.L. 105–315, § 4, Oct. 30, 1998, 112 Stat. 2994.)

HISTORICAL AND STATUTORY NOTES

Amendments

1998 Amendments. Pub.L. 105–258, § 4, rewrote the section, which formerly read:

" **§ 652. Jurisdiction**

"**(a) Actions That May Be Referred to Arbitration.—(1)** Notwithstanding any provision of law to the contrary and except as provided in subsections (b) and (c) of this section, and section 901(c) of the

Judicial Improvements and Access to Justice Act, a district court that authorizes arbitration under section 651 may—

"**(A)** allow the referral to arbitration of any civil action (including any adversary proceeding in bankruptcy) pending before it if the parties consent to arbitration, and

"**(B)** require the referral to arbitration of any civil action pending before it if the relief sought consists only of money damages not in excess of $100,000 or such lesser amount as the district court may set, exclusive of interest and costs.

"**(2)** For purposes of paragraph (1)(B), a district court may presume damages are not in excess of $100,000 unless counsel certifies that damages exceed such amount.

"**(b) Actions That May Not Be Referred Without Consent of Parties.**—Referral to arbitration under subsection (a)(1)(B) may not be made—

"**(1)** of an action based on an alleged violation of a right secured by the Constitution of the United States, or

"**(2)** if jurisdiction is based in whole or in part on section 1343 of this title.

"**(c) Exceptions From Arbitration.**—Each district court shall establish by local rule procedures for exempting, sua sponte or on motion of a party, any case from arbitration in which the objectives of arbitration would not be realized—

"**(1)** because the case involves complex or novel legal issues,

"**(2)** because legal issues predominate over factual issues, or

"**(3)** for other good cause.

"**(d) Safeguards in Consent Cases.**—In any civil action in which arbitration by consent is allowed under subsection (a)(1)(A), the district court shall by local rule establish procedures to ensure that—

"**(1)** consent to arbitration is freely and knowingly obtained, and

"**(2)** no party or attorney is prejudiced for refusing to participate in arbitration."

§ 653. Neutrals

(a) **Panel of neutrals.**—Each district court that authorizes the use of alternative dispute resolution processes shall adopt appropriate processes for making neutrals available for use by the parties for each category of process offered. Each district court shall promulgate its own procedures and criteria for the selection of neutrals on its panels.

(b) **Qualifications and training.**—Each person serving as a neutral in an alternative dispute resolution process should be qualified and trained to serve as a neutral in the appropriate alternative dispute resolution process. For this purpose, the district court may use, among others, magistrate judges who have been trained to serve as neutrals in alternative dispute resolution processes, professional neutrals from the private sector, and persons who have been trained to serve as neutrals in alternative dispute resolution processes. Until such time as rules are adopted under chapter 131 of this title [28 U.S.C.A. § 2071 et seq.] relating to the disqualification of neutrals, each district court shall issue rules under section 2071(a) relating to the disqualification of neutrals (including, where appropriate, disqualification under section 455 of this title, other applicable law, and professional responsibility standards).

(Added Pub.L. 100–702, Title IX, § 901(a), Nov. 19, 1988, 102 Stat. 4660; amended Pub.L. 105–315, § 5, Oct. 30, 1998, 112 Stat. 2995.)

HISTORICAL AND STATUTORY NOTES

Amendments

1998 Amendments. Pub.L. 105–315, § 5, rewrote the section, which formerly read:

" § 653. Powers of arbitrator; arbitration hearing

"**(a) Powers.**—An arbitrator to whom an action is referred under section 652 shall have, within the judicial district of the district court which referred the action to arbitration, the power—

"**(1)** to conduct arbitration hearings,

"**(2)** to administer oaths and affirmations, and

"**(3)** to make awards.

"**(b) Time for Beginning Arbitration Hearing.**—An arbitration hearing under this chapter shall begin within a time period specified by the district court, but in no event later than 180 days after the filing of an answer, except that the arbitration proceeding shall not, in the absence of the consent of the parties, commence until 30 days after the disposition by the district court of any motion to dismiss the complaint, motion for judgment on the pleadings, motion to join necessary parties, or motion for summary judgment, if the motion was filed during a time period specified by the district court. The 180-day and 30-day periods specified in the preceding sentence may be modified by the court for good cause shown.

"**(c) Subpoenas.**—Rule 45 of the Federal Rules of Civil Procedure (relating to subpoenas) applies to subpoenas for the attendance of witnesses and the production of documentary evidence at an arbitration hearing under this chapter."

§ 654. Arbitration

(a) Referral of actions to arbitration.—Notwithstanding any provision of law to the contrary and except as provided in subsections (a), (b), and (c) of section 652 and subsection (d) of this section, a district court may allow the referral to arbitration of any civil action (including any adversary proceeding in bankruptcy) pending before it when the parties consent, except that referral to arbitration may not be made where—

(1) the action is based on an alleged violation of a right secured by the Constitution of the United States;

(2) jurisdiction is based in whole or in part on section 1343 of this title; or

(3) the relief sought consists of money damages in an amount greater than $150,000.

(b) Safeguards in consent cases.—Until such time as rules are adopted under chapter 131 of this title relating to procedures described in this subsection, the district court shall, by local rule adopted under section 2071(a), establish procedures to ensure that any civil action in which arbitration by consent is allowed under subsection (a)—

(1) consent to arbitration is freely and knowingly obtained; and

(2) no party or attorney is prejudiced for refusing to participate in arbitration.

(c) Presumptions.—For purposes of subsection (a)(3), a district court may presume damages are not in excess of $150,000 unless counsel certifies that damages exceed such amount.

(d) Existing programs.—Nothing in this chapter is deemed to affect any program in which arbitration is conducted pursuant to section[1] title IX of the Judicial Improvements and Access to Justice Act (Public Law 100–702), as amended by section 1 of Public Law 105–53.

(Added Pub.L. 100–702, Title IX, § 901(a), Nov. 19, 1988, 102 Stat. 4660; amended Pub.L. 105–315, § 6, Oct. 30, 1998, 112 Stat. 2995.)

HISTORICAL AND STATUTORY NOTES

References in Text

Title IX of the Judicial Improvements and Access to Justice Act, referred to in subsec. (d), is Pub.L. 100–702, Title IX, Nov. 19, 1988, 102 Stat. 4663. See Codifications note under this section.

---

[1] So in original. The word "section" probably should not appear.

Codifications

Section title IX of the Judicial Improvements and Access to Justice Act, referred to in subsec. (d), probably should read section 905 of title IX of the Judicial Improvements and Access to Justice Act, which is Pub.L. 100–702, Title IX, § 905, Nov. 19, 1988, 102 Stat. 4663, set out as a note under section 651 of this title.

Amendments

1998 Amendments. Pub.L. 105–315, § 6, rewrote the section, which formerly read:

" **§ 654. Arbitration award and judgment**

"**(a) Filing and Effect of Arbitration Award.**—An arbitration award made by an arbitrator under this chapter, along with proof of service of such award on the other party by the prevailing party or by the plaintiff, shall, promptly after the arbitration hearing is concluded, be filed with the clerk of the district court that referred the case to arbitration. Such award shall be entered as the judgment of the court after the time has expired for requesting a trial de novo under section 655. The judgment so entered shall be subject to the same provisions of law and shall have the same force and effect as a judgment of the court in a civil action, except that the judgment shall not be subject to review in any other court by appeal or otherwise.

"**(b) Sealing of Arbitration Award.**—The district court shall provide by local rule that the contents of any arbitration award made under this chapter shall not be made known to any judge who might be assigned to the case—

"**(1)** except as necessary for the court to determine whether to assess costs or attorney fees under section 655,

"**(2)** until the district court has entered final judgment in the action or the action has been otherwise terminated, or

"**(3)** except for purposes of preparing the report required by section 903(b) of the Judicial Improvements and Access to Justice Act.

"**(c) Taxation of Costs.**—The district court may by rule allow for the inclusion of costs as provided in section 1920 of this title as a part of the arbitration award."

§ 655. Arbitrators

(a) Powers of arbitrators.—An arbitrator to whom an action is referred under section 654 shall have the power, within the judicial district of the district court which referred the action to arbitration—

(1) to conduct arbitration hearings;

(2) to administer oaths and affirmations; and

(3) to make awards.

(b) Standards for certification.—Each district court that authorizes arbitration shall establish standards for the certification of arbitrators and shall certify arbitrators to perform services in accordance with such standards and this chapter. The standards shall include provisions requiring that any arbitrator—

(1) shall take the oath or affirmation described in section 453; and

(2) shall be subject to the disqualification rules under section 455.

(c) Immunity.—All individuals serving as arbitrators in an alternative dispute resolution program under this chapter are performing quasi-judicial functions and are entitled to the immunities and protections that the law accords to persons serving in such capacity.

(Added Pub.L. 100–702, Title IX, § 901(a), Nov. 19, 1988, 102 Stat. 4661; amended Pub.L. 105–315, § 7, Oct. 30, 1998, 112 Stat. 2996.)

Title 28 U.S. CODE TITLES 28 § 656

HISTORICAL AND STATUTORY NOTES

Amendments

1998 Amendments. Pub.L. 105–315, § 7, rewrote the section, which formerly read:

"**§ 655. Trial de novo**

"**(a) Time for Demand.**—Within 30 days after the filing of an arbitration award with a district court under section 654, any party may file a written demand for a trial de novo in the district court.

"**(b) Restoration to Court Docket.**—Upon a demand for a trial de novo, the action shall be restored to the docket of the court and treated for all purposes as if it had not been referred to arbitration. In such a case, any right of trial by jury that a party otherwise would have had, as well as any place on the court calendar which is no later than that which a party otherwise would have had, are preserved.

"**(c) Limitation on Admission of Evidence.**—The court shall not admit at the trial de novo any evidence that there has been an arbitration proceeding, the nature or amount of any award, or any other matter concerning the conduct of the arbitration proceeding, unless—

"**(1)** the evidence would otherwise be admissible in the court under the Federal Rules of Evidence, or

"**(2)** the parties have otherwise stipulated.

"**(d) Taxation of Arbitrator Fees as Cost.**—**(1)(A)** A district court may provide by rule that, in any trial de novo under this section, arbitrator fees paid under section 657 may be taxed as costs against the party demanding the trial de novo.

"**(B)** Such rule may provide that a party demanding a trial de novo under subsection (a), other than the United States or its agencies or officers, shall deposit a sum equal to such arbitrator fees as advanced payment of such costs, unless the party is permitted to proceed in forma pauperis.

"**(2)** Arbitrator fees shall not be taxed as costs under paragraph (1)(A), and any sum deposited under paragraph (1)(B) shall be returned to the party demanding the trial de novo, if—

"**(A)** the party demanding the trial de novo obtains a final judgment more favorable than the arbitration award, or

"**(B)** the court determines that the demand for the trial de novo was made for good cause.

"**(3)** Any arbitrator fees taxed as costs under paragraph (1)(A), and any sum deposited under paragraph (1)(B) that is not returned to the party demanding the trial de novo, shall be paid to the Treasury of the United States.

"**(4)** Any rule under this subsection shall provide that no penalty for demanding a trial de novo, other than that provided in this subsection, shall be assessed by the court.

"**(e) Assessment of Costs and Attorney Fees.**—In any trial de novo demanded under subsection (a) in which arbitration was done by consent of the parties, a district court may assess costs, as provided in section 1920 of this title, and reasonable attorney fees against the party demanding the trial de novo if—

"**(1)** such party fails to obtain a judgment, exclusive of interest and costs, in the court which is substantially more favorable to such party than the arbitration award, and

"**(2)** the court determines that the party's conduct in seeking a trial de novo was in bad faith."

§ 656. Subpoenas

Rule 45 of the Federal Rules of Civil Procedure (relating to subpoenas) applies to subpoenas for the attendance of witnesses and the production of documentary evidence at an arbitration hearing under this chapter.

(Added Pub.L. 100–702, Title IX, § 901(a), Nov. 19, 1988, 102 Stat. 4662; amended Pub.L. 105–315, § 8, Oct. 30, 1998, 112 Stat. 2996.)

HISTORICAL AND STATUTORY NOTES

Amendments

1998 Amendments. Pub.L. 105–315, § 8, rewrote the section, which formerly read:

"**§ 656. Certification of arbitrators**

"(a) **Standards for Certification.**—Each district court listed in section 658 shall establish standards for the certification of arbitrators and shall certify arbitrators to perform services in accordance with such standards and this chapter. The standards shall include provisions requiring that any arbitrator—

"(1) shall take the oath or affirmation described in section 453, and

"(2) shall be subject to the disqualification rules of section 455.

"(b) **Treatment of Arbitrator as Independent Contractor and Special Government Employee.**—An arbitrator is an independent contractor and is subject to the provisions of sections 201 through 211 of title 18 to the same extent as such provisions apply to a special Government employee of the executive branch. A person may not be barred from the practice of law because such person is an arbitrator."

§ 657. Arbitration award and judgment

(a) **Filing and effect of arbitration award.**—An arbitration award made by an arbitrator under this chapter, along with proof of service of such award on the other party by the prevailing party or by the plaintiff, shall be filed promptly after the arbitration hearing is concluded with the clerk of the district court that referred the case to arbitration. Such award shall be entered as the judgment of the court after the time has expired for requesting a trial de novo. The judgment so entered shall be subject to the same provisions of law and shall have the same force and effect as a judgment of the court in a civil action, except that the judgment shall not be subject to review in any other court by appeal or otherwise.

(b) **Sealing of arbitration award.**—The district court shall provide, by local rule adopted under section 2071(a), that the contents of any arbitration award made under this chapter shall not be made known to any judge who might be assigned to the case until the district court has entered final judgment in the action or the action has otherwise terminated.

(c) **Trial de novo of arbitration awards.**—

(1) **Time for filing demand.**—Within 30 days after the filing of an arbitration award with a district court under subsection (a), any party may file a written demand for a trial de novo in the district court.

(2) **Action restored to court docket.**—Upon a demand for a trial de novo, the action shall be restored to the docket of the court and treated for all purposes as if it had not been referred to arbitration.

(3) **Exclusion of evidence of arbitration.**—The court shall not admit at the trial de novo any evidence that there has been an arbitration proceeding, the nature or amount of any award, or any other matter concerning the conduct of the arbitration proceeding, unless—

(A) the evidence would otherwise be admissible in the court under the Federal Rules of Evidence; or

(B) the parties have otherwise stipulated.

(Added Pub.L. 100–702, Title IX, § 901(a), Nov. 19, 1988, 102 Stat. 4662; amended Pub.L. 105–315, § 9, Oct. 30, 1998, 112 Stat. 2997.)

HISTORICAL AND STATUTORY NOTES

Amendments

1998 Amendments. Pub.L. 105–315, § 9, rewrote the section, which formerly read:

" § 657. Compensation of arbitrators

"(a) Compensation.—The district court may, subject to limits set by the Judicial Conference of the United States, establish and pay the amount of compensation, if any, that each arbitrator shall receive for services rendered in each case.

"(b) Transportation Allowances.—Under regulations prescribed by the Director of the Administrative Office of the United States Courts, a district court may reimburse arbitrators for actual transportation expenses necessarily incurred in the performance of duties under this chapter."

§ 658. Compensation of arbitrators and neutrals

(a) Compensation.—The district court shall, subject to regulations approved by the Judicial Conference of the United States, establish the amount of compensation, if any, that each arbitrator or neutral shall receive for services rendered in each case under this chapter.

(b) Transportation allowances.—Under regulations prescribed by the Director of the Administrative Office of the United States Courts, a district court may reimburse arbitrators and other neutrals for actual transportation expenses necessarily incurred in the performance of duties under this chapter.

(Added Pub.L. 100–702, Title IX, § 901(a), Nov. 19, 1988, 102 Stat. 4662; amended Pub.L. 105–315, § 10, Oct. 30, 1998, 112 Stat. 2997.)

HISTORICAL AND STATUTORY NOTES

Amendments

1998 Amendments. Pub.L. 105–315, § 10, rewrote the section, which formerly read:

" § 658. District courts that may authorize arbitration

"The district courts for the following judicial districts may authorize the use of arbitration under this chapter:

"(1) Northern District of California, Middle District of Florida, Western District of Michigan, Western District of Missouri, District of New Jersey, Eastern District of New York, Middle District of North Carolina, Western District of Oklahoma, Eastern District of Pennsylvania, and Western District of Texas.

"(2) Ten additional judicial districts, which shall be approved by the Judicial Conference of the United States. The Judicial Conference shall give notice of the 10 districts approved under this paragraph to the Federal Judicial Center and to the public."

CHAPTER 57—GENERAL PROVISIONS APPLICABLE TO COURT OFFICERS AND EMPLOYEES

§ 959. Trustees and receivers suable; management; State laws

(a) Trustees, receivers or managers of any property, including debtors in possession, may be sued, without leave of the court appointing them, with respect to any of their acts or transactions in carrying on business connected with such property. Such actions shall be subject to the general equity power of such court so far as the same may be necessary to the ends of justice, but this shall not deprive a litigant of his right to trial by jury.

(b) Except as provided in section 1166 of title 11, a trustee, receiver or manager appointed in any cause pending in any court of the United States, including a debtor in possession, shall manage and operate the property in his possession as such trustee, receiver or manager according to the requirements of the valid laws of the State in which such property is situated, in the same manner that the owner or possessor thereof would be bound to do if in possession thereof.

(June 25, 1948, c. 646, 62 Stat. 926; Nov. 6, 1978, Pub.L. 95–598, Title II, § 235, 92 Stat. 2667.)

HISTORICAL AND STATUTORY NOTES

Amendments

1978 Amendments. Subsec. (b). Pub.L. 95–598 substituted "Except as provided in section 1166 of title 11, a trustee" for "A trustee".

CROSS REFERENCES

Capacity to sue or be sued, see Fed.Rules Civ.Proc. Rule 17, 28 USCA.

Mismanagement of property by receiver, criminal penalty, see 18 USCA § 1911.

Process and orders affecting property in different districts, see 28 USCA § 1692.

Receivers of property in different districts; jurisdiction, see 28 USCA § 754.

PART IV—JURISDICTION AND VENUE

CHAPTER 85—DISTRICT COURTS; JURISDICTION

§ 1334. Bankruptcy cases and proceedings

(a) Except as provided in subsection (b) of this section, the district courts shall have original and exclusive jurisdiction of all cases under title 11.

(b) Except as provided in subsection (e)(2), and notwithstanding any Act of Congress that confers exclusive jurisdiction on a court or courts other than the district courts, the district courts shall have original but not exclusive jurisdiction of all civil proceedings arising under title 11, or arising in or related to cases under title 11.

(c)(1) Except with respect to a case under chapter 15 of title 11, nothing in this section prevents a district court in the interest of justice, or in the interest of comity with State courts or respect for State law, from abstaining from hearing a particular proceeding arising under title 11 or arising in or related to a case under title 11.

(2) Upon timely motion of a party in a proceeding based upon a State law claim or State law cause of action, related to a case under title 11 but not arising under title 11 or arising in a case under title 11, with respect to which an action could not have been commenced in a court of the United States absent jurisdiction under this section, the district court shall abstain from hearing such proceeding if an action is commenced, and can be timely adjudicated, in a State forum of appropriate jurisdiction.

(d) Any decision to abstain or not to abstain made under subsection (c) (other than a decision not to abstain in a proceeding described in subsection (c)(2)) is not reviewable by appeal or otherwise by the court of appeals under section 158(d), 1291, or 1292 of this title or by the Supreme Court of the United States under section 1254 of this title. Subsection (c) and this subsection shall not be construed to limit the applicability of the stay provided for by section 362 of title 11, United States Code, as such section applies to an action affecting the property of the estate in bankruptcy.

(e) The district court in which a case under title 11 is commenced or is pending shall have exclusive jurisdiction—

(1) of all the property, wherever located, of the debtor as of the commencement of such case, and of property of the estate; and

(2) over all claims or causes of action that involve construction of section 327 of title 11, United States Code, or rules relating to disclosure requirements under section 327.

(June 25, 1948, c. 646, 62 Stat. 931; Nov. 6, 1978, Pub.L. 95–598, Title II, § 238(a), 92 Stat. 2667; July 10, 1984, Pub.L. 98–353, Title I, § 101(a), 98 Stat. 333; Oct. 27, 1986, Pub.L. 99–554, Title I, § 144(e), 100 Stat. 3096; Dec. 1, 1990, Pub.L. 101–650, Title III, § 309(b), 104 Stat. 5113; Oct. 22, 1994, Pub.L. 103–394, Title I, § 104(b), 108 Stat. 4109; Apr. 20, 2005, Pub.L. 109–8, Title III, § 324(a), Title VIII, § 802(c)(2), Title XII, § 1219, 119 Stat. 98, 145, 195.)

HISTORICAL AND STATUTORY NOTES

References in Text

Chapter 15 of title 11, referred to in subsec. (c), is 11 U.S.C.A. § 1501 et seq.

Codifications

This section was amended by Pub.L. 95–598, Title II, § 238(a), Nov. 6, 1978, 92 Stat. 2668, effective June 28, 1984, pursuant to Pub.L. 95–598, Title IV, § 402(b), Nov. 6, 1978, 92 Stat. 2682, as amended by Pub.L. 98–249, § 1(a), Mar. 31, 1984, 98 Stat. 116; Pub.L. 98–271, § 1(a), Apr. 30, 1984, 98 Stat. 163; Pub.L. 98–299, § 1(a), May 25, 1984, 98 Stat. 214; Pub.L. 98–325, § 1(a), June 20, 1984, 98 Stat. 268, set out as an Effective and Applicability Provisions note preceding section 101 of Title 11, Bankruptcy, to read as follows:

" **§ 1334. Bankruptcy appeals**

"**(a)** The district courts for districts for which panels have not been ordered appointed under section 160 of this title shall have jurisdiction of appeals from all final judgments, orders, and decrees of bankruptcy courts.

"**(b)** The district courts for such districts shall have jurisdiction of appeals from interlocutory orders and decrees of bankruptcy courts, but only by leave of the district court to which the appeal is taken.

"**(c)** A district court may not refer an appeal under that section to a magistrate or to a special master."

Section 402(b) of Pub.L. 95–598 was amended by section 113 of Pub.L. 98–353 by substituting "shall not be effective" for "shall take effect on June 28, 1984", thereby eliminating the amendment by section 238(a) of Pub.L. 95–598, effective June 27, 1984, pursuant to section 122(c) of Pub.L. 98–353, set out as an Effective and Applicability Provisions note under 28 U.S.C.A. § 151.

Section 121(a) of Pub.L. 98–353 directed that section 402(b) of Pub.L. 95–598 be amended by substituting "the date of enactment of the Bankruptcy Amendments and Federal Judgeship Act of 1984 [i.e. July 10, 1984]" for "June 28, 1984". This amendment was not executed in view of the prior amendment to section 402(b) of Pub.L. 95–598 by section 113 of Pub.L. 98–353.

Amendments

2005 Amendments. Subsec. (b). Pub.L. 109–8, § 324(a)(1), struck out "Notwithstanding" and inserted "Except as provided in subsection (e)(2), and notwithstanding".

Subsec. (c)(1). Pub.L. 109–8, § 802(c)(2), struck out "Nothing in" and inserted "Except with respect to a case under chapter 15 of title 11, nothing in".

Subsec. (d). Pub.L. 109–8, § 1219, struck out "made under this subsection" and inserted "made under subsection (c)", and substituted "Subsection (c) and this subsection" for "This subsection".

Subsec. (e). Pub.L. 109–8, § 324(a)(2), rewrote subsec. (e), which formerly read: "The district court in which a case under title 11 is commenced or is pending shall have exclusive jurisdiction of all of the property, wherever located, of the debtor as of the commencement of such case, and of property of the estate."

1994 Amendments. Subsecs. (c) to (e). Pub.L. 103–465, § 104(b), redesignated portion of existing subsec. (c)(2) as (d) and as so redesignated, inserted "(other than a decision not to abstain in a proceeding described in subsection (c)(2))" after "under this subsection", and redesignated former subsec. (d) as (e).

1990 Amendments. Subsec. (c)(2). Pub.L. 101–650 declared abstention determinations, including determination not to abstain, in bankruptcy cases and proceedings nonreviewable by the court of appeals or by the Supreme Court.

1986 Amendments. Subsec. (d). Pub.L. 99–554 substituted "and of property of the estate" for "and of the estate".

1984 Amendments. Catchline. Pub.L. 98–353 substituted "cases" for "matters".

Subsec. (a). Pub.L. 98–353 designated existing provision as subsec. (a), and in subsec. (a) as so designated, substituted "Except as provided in subsection (b) of this section, the district" for "The district" and "original and exclusive jurisdiction of all cases under title 11" for "original jurisdiction, exclusive of the courts of the States, of all matters and proceedings in bankruptcy".

Subsecs. (b) to (d). Pub.L. 98–353 added subsecs. (b) to (d).

1978 Amendments. Pub.L. 95–598 directed the general amendment of section to relate to bankruptcy appeals, which amendment did not become effective pursuant to section 402(b) of Pub.L. 95–598, as amended, set out as an Effective and Applicability Provisions note preceding section 101 of Title 11, Bankruptcy. Sec. Codifications note set out under this section.

CROSS REFERENCES

Appointment of clerk for bankruptcy court where warranted by number of cases and proceedings pending, see 28 USCA § 156.

Non-core proceedings not subject to mandatory abstention provisions, see 28 USCA § 157.

Removal of claims related to bankruptcy cases, see 28 USCA § 1452.

Venue, see 28 USCA §§ 1408 and 1409.

CHAPTER 87—DISTRICT COURTS; VENUE

§ 1408. Venue of cases under title 11

Except as provided in section 1410 of this title, a case under title 11 may be commenced in the district court for the district—

(1) in which the domicile, residence, principal place of business in the United States, or principal assets in the United States, of the person or entity that is the subject of such case have been located for the one hundred and eighty days immediately preceding such commencement, or for a longer portion of such one-hundred-and-eighty-day period than the domicile, residence, or principal place of business, in the United States, or principal assets in the United States, of such person were located in any other district; or

(2) in which there is pending a case under title 11 concerning such person's affiliate, general partner, or partnership.

(Added Pub.L. 98–353, Title I, § 102(a), July 10, 1984, 98 Stat. 334.)

HISTORICAL AND STATUTORY NOTES

Prior Provisions

A prior section 1408, added by Pub.L. 95–598, Title II, § 240(a), Nov. 6, 1978, 92 Stat. 2668, which related to bankruptcy appeals, did not become effective pursuant to section 402(b) of Pub.L. 95–598, as amended, set out as an Effective and Applicability Provisions note preceding section 101 of Title 11, Bankruptcy.

§ 1409. Venue of proceedings arising under title 11 or arising in or related to cases under title 11

(a) Except as otherwise provided in subsections (b) and (d), a proceeding arising under title 11 or arising in or related to a case under title 11 may be commenced in the district court in which such case is pending.

(b) Except as provided in subsection (d) of this section, a trustee in a case under title 11 may commence a proceeding arising in or related to such case to recover a money judgment of or property worth less than $1,250[1] or a consumer debt of less than $18,675[1], or a debt (excluding a consumer debt) against a noninsider of less than $12,475[1], only in the district court for the district in which the defendant resides.

(c) Except as provided in subsection (b) of this section, a trustee in a case under title 11 may commence a proceeding arising in or related to such case as statutory successor to the debtor or creditors under section 541 or 544(b) of title 11 in the district court for the district where the State or Federal court sits in which, under applicable nonbankruptcy venue provisions, the debtor or creditors, as the case may be, may have commenced an action on which such proceeding is based if the case under title 11 had not been commenced.

(d) A trustee may commence a proceeding arising under title 11 or arising in or related to a case under title 11 based on a claim arising after the commencement of such case from the operation of the business of the debtor only in the district court for the district where a State or Federal court sits in which, under applicable nonbankruptcy venue provisions, an action on such claim may have been brought.

(e) A proceeding arising under title 11 or arising in or related to a case under title 11, based on a claim arising after the commencement of such case from the operation of the business of the debtor, may be commenced against the representative of the estate in such case in the district court for the district where the State or Federal court sits in which the party commencing such proceeding may, under applicable nonbankruptcy venue provisions, have brought an action on such claim, or in the district court in which such case is pending.

(Added Pub.L. 98–353, Title I, § 102(a), July 10, 1984, 98 Stat. 334; amended Pub.L. 109–8, Title IV, § 410, Apr. 20, 2005, 119 Stat. 106.)

HISTORICAL AND STATUTORY NOTES

Adjustment of Dollar Amounts

For adjustment of dollar amounts specified in subsec. (b) of this section by the Judicial Conference of the United States, see note set out under 11 U.S.C.A. § 104.

§ 1410. Venue of cases ancillary to foreign proceedings

A case under chapter 15 of title 11 may be commenced in the district court of the United States for the district—

(1) in which the debtor has its principal place of business or principal assets in the United States;

(2) if the debtor does not have a place of business or assets in the United States, in which there is pending against the debtor an action or proceeding in a Federal or State court; or

(3) in a case other than those specified in paragraph (1) or (2), in which venue will be consistent with the interests of justice and the convenience of the parties, having regard to the relief sought by the foreign representative.

(Added Pub.L. 98–353, Title I, § 102(a), July 10, 1984, 98 Stat. 335; amended Pub.L. 109–8, Title VIII, § 802(c)(4), Apr. 20, 2005, 119 Stat. 146.)

HISTORICAL AND STATUTORY NOTES

Amendments

2005 Amendments. Pub.L. 109–8, § 802(c)(4), rewrote the text of the section, which formerly read:

---

[1] Dollar amount as adjusted by the Judicial Conference of the United States. See Adjustment of Dollar Amounts notes set out under this section and 11 U.S.C.A. § 104.

" § 1410. Venue of cases ancillary to foreign proceedings

"(a) A case under section 304 of title 11 to enjoin the commencement or continuation of an action or proceeding in a State or Federal court, or the enforcement of a judgment, may be commenced only in the district court for the district where the State or Federal court sits in which is pending the action or proceeding against which the injunction is sought.

"(b) A case under section 304 of title 11 to enjoin the enforcement of a lien against a property, or to require the turnover of property of an estate, may be commenced only in the district court for the district in which such property is found.

"(c) A case under section 304 of title 11, other than a case specified in subsection (a) or (b) of this section, may be commenced only in the district court for the district in which is located the principal place of business in the United States, or the principal assets in the United States, of the estate that is the subject of such case."

CROSS REFERENCES

Commencement of bankruptcy cases in district courts having venue except as provided by this section, see 28 USCA § 1408.

§ 1411. Jury trials

(a) Except as provided in subsection (b) of this section, this chapter and title 11 do not affect any right to trial by jury that an individual has under applicable nonbankruptcy law with regard to a personal injury or wrongful death tort claim.

(b) The district court may order the issues arising under section 303 of title 11 to be tried without a jury.

(Added Pub.L. 98–353, Title I, § 102(a), July 10, 1984, 98 Stat. 335.)

§ 1412. Change of venue

A district court may transfer a case or proceeding under title 11 to a district court for another district, in the interest of justice or for the convenience of the parties.

(Added Pub.L. 98–353, Title I, § 102(a), July 10, 1984, 98 Stat. 335.)

§ 1413. Venue of cases under chapter 5 of title 3

Notwithstanding the preceding provisions of this chapter, a civil action under section 1346(g) may be brought in the United States district court for the district in which the employee is employed or in the United States District Court for the District of Columbia.

(Added Pub.L. 104–331, § 3(b)(2)(A), Oct. 26, 1996, 110 Stat. 4069.)

HISTORICAL AND STATUTORY NOTES

Codifications

Amendment by Pub.L. 104–331, § 3(b)(2)(A), which directed the addition of this section to the end of chapter 37 of this title, was executed by adding this section to the end of this chapter, as the probable intent of Congress.

CHAPTER 89—DISTRICT COURTS; REMOVAL OF CASES FROM STATE COURTS

§ 1452. Removal of claims related to bankruptcy cases

(a) A party may remove any claim or cause of action in a civil action other than a proceeding before the United States Tax Court or a civil action by a governmental unit to enforce such governmental unit's police or regulatory power, to the district court for the district where such civil action is pending, if such district court has jurisdiction of such claim or cause of action under section 1334 of this title.

(b) The court to which such claim or cause of action is removed may remand such claim or cause of action on any equitable ground. An order entered under this subsection remanding a claim or cause of action, or a decision to not remand, is not reviewable by appeal or otherwise by the court of appeals under section 158(d), 1291, or 1292 of this title or by the Supreme Court of the United States under section 1254 of this title.

(Added Pub.L. 98–353, Title I, § 103(a), July 10, 1984, 98 Stat. 335; amended Pub.L. 101–650, Title III, § 309(c), Dec. 1, 1990, 104 Stat. 5113.)

HISTORICAL AND STATUTORY NOTES

Amendments

1990 Amendments. Subsec. (b). Pub.L. 101–650 declared remand determinations nonreviewable by the court of appeals or by the Supreme Court.

CHAPTER 123—FEES AND COSTS

§ 1930. Bankruptcy fees

(a) The parties commencing a case under title 11 shall pay to the clerk of the district court or the clerk of the bankruptcy court, if one has been certified pursuant to section 156(b) of this title, the following filing fees:

    (1) For a case commenced under—

        (A) chapter 7 of title 11, $245, and

        (B) chapter 13 of title 11, $235.

    (2) For a case commenced under chapter 9 of title 11, equal to the fee specified in paragraph (3) for filing a case under chapter 11 of title 11. The amount by which the fee payable under this paragraph exceeds $300 shall be deposited in the fund established under section 1931 of this title.

    (3) For a case commenced under chapter 11 of title 11 that does not concern a railroad, as defined in section 101 of title 11, $1,167.

    (4) For a case commenced under chapter 11 of title 11 concerning a railroad, as so defined, $1,000.

    (5) For a case commenced under chapter 12 of title 11, $200.

    (6) In addition to the filing fee paid to the clerk, a quarterly fee shall be paid to the United States trustee, for deposit in the Treasury, in each case under chapter 11 of title 11 for each quarter (including any fraction thereof) until the case is converted or dismissed, whichever occurs first. The fee shall be $325 for each quarter in which disbursements total less than $15,000; $650 for each quarter in which disbursements total $15,000 or more but less than $75,000; $975 for each quarter in which disbursements total $75,000 or more but less than $150,000; $1,625 for each quarter in which disbursements total $150,000 or more but less

than $225,000; $1,950 for each quarter in which disbursements total $225,000 or more but less than $300,000; $4,875 for each quarter in which disbursements total $300,000 or more but less than $1,000,000; $6,500 for each quarter in which disbursements total $1,000,000 or more but less than $2,000,000; $9,750 for each quarter in which disbursements total $2,000,000 or more but less than $3,000,000; $10,400 for each quarter in which disbursements total $3,000,000 or more but less than $5,000,000; $13,000 for each quarter in which disbursements total $5,000,000 or more but less than $15,000,000; $20,000 for each quarter in which disbursements total $15,000,000 or more but less than $30,000,000; $30,000 for each quarter in which disbursements total more than $30,000,000. The fee shall be payable on the last day of the calendar month following the calendar quarter for which the fee is owed.

(7) In districts that are not part of a United States trustee region as defined in section 581 of this title, the Judicial Conference of the United States may require the debtor in a case under chapter 11 of title 11 to pay fees equal to those imposed by paragraph (6) of this subsection. Such fees shall be deposited as offsetting receipts to the fund established under section 1931 of this title and shall remain available until expended.

An individual commencing a voluntary case or a joint case under title 11 may pay such fee in installments. For converting, on request of the debtor, a case under chapter 7, or 13 of title 11, to a case under chapter 11 of title 11, the debtor shall pay to the clerk of the district court or the clerk of the bankruptcy court, if one has been certified pursuant to section 156(b) of this title, a fee of the amount equal to the difference between the fee specified in paragraph (3) and the fee specified in paragraph (1).

(b) The Judicial Conference of the United States may prescribe additional fees in cases under title 11 of the same kind as the Judicial Conference prescribes under section 1914(b) of this title.

(c) Upon the filing of any separate or joint notice of appeal or application for appeal or upon the receipt of any order allowing, or notice of the allowance of, an appeal or a writ of certiorari $5 shall be paid to the clerk of the court, by the appellant or petitioner.

(d) Whenever any case or proceeding is dismissed in any bankruptcy court for want of jurisdiction, such court may order the payment of just costs.

(e) The clerk of the court may collect only the fees prescribed under this section.

(f)(1) Under the procedures prescribed by the Judicial Conference of the United States, the district court or the bankruptcy court may waive the filing fee in a case under chapter 7 of title 11 for an individual if the court determines that such individual has income less than 150 percent of the income official poverty line (as defined by the Office of Management and Budget, and revised annually in accordance with section 673(2) of the Omnibus Budget Reconciliation Act of 1981) applicable to a family of the size involved and is unable to pay that fee in installments. For purposes of this paragraph, the term "filing fee" means the filing fee required by subsection (a), or any other fee prescribed by the Judicial Conference under subsections (b) and (c) that is payable to the clerk upon the commencement of a case under chapter 7.

(2) The district court or the bankruptcy court may waive for such debtors other fees prescribed under subsections (b) and (c).

(3) This subsection does not restrict the district court or the bankruptcy court from waiving, in accordance with Judicial Conference policy, fees prescribed under this section for other debtors and creditors.

(Added Pub.L. 95–598, Title II, § 246(a), Nov. 6, 1978, 92 Stat. 2671; amended Pub.L. 98–353, Title I, § 111(a), (b), July 10, 1984, 98 Stat. 342; Pub.L. 99–500, Title I, § 101(b) [Title IV, § 407(b)], Oct. 18, 1986, 100 Stat. 1783–64; Pub.L. 99–554, Title I, §§ 117, 144(f), Oct. 27, 1986, 100 Stat. 3095, 3097; Pub.L. 99–591, Title I, § 101(b) [Title IV, § 407(b)], Oct. 30, 1986, 100 Stat. 3341–64; Pub.L. 101–162, Title IV, § 406(a), Nov. 21, 1989, 103 Stat. 1016; Pub.L. 102–140, Title I, § 111(a), Oct. 28, 1991, 105 Stat. 795; Pub.L. 103–121, Title I, § 111(a)(1), (b)(1), Oct. 27, 1993, 107 Stat. 1164; Pub.L. 104–91, Title I, § 101(a), Jan. 6, 1996, 110 Stat. 11; Pub.L. 104–99, Title II, § 211, Jan. 26, 1996, 110 Stat. 37; Pub.L. 104–208, Div. A, Title I, § 101(a) [Title I, § 109(a)], Sept. 30, 1996, 110 Stat. 3009–18; Pub.L. 106–113, Div. B, § 1000(a)(1) [Title I, § 113], Nov. 29, 1999, 113 Stat. 1535, 1501A–20; Pub.L. 106–518, Title I, §§ 103 to 105, Nov. 13, 2000, 114 Stat. 2411; Pub.L. 109–8, Title III, § 325(a), Title IV, § 418, Apr. 20, 2005, 119

Stat. 98, 108; Pub.L. 109–13, Div. A, Title VI, § 6058(a), May 11, 2005, 119 Stat. 297; Pub.L. 109–171, Title X, § 10101(a), Feb. 8, 2006, 120 Stat. 184; Pub.L. 110–161, Div. B, Title II, § 213(a), Dec. 26, 2007, 121 Stat. 1914; Pub.L. 112–121, § 3(a), May 25, 2012, 126 Stat. 348.)

JUDICIAL CONFERENCE SCHEDULE OF FEES

Bankruptcy Court Miscellaneous Fee Schedule (28 U.S.C. § 1930)

(Effective June 1, 2014)

The fees included in the Bankruptcy Court Miscellaneous Fee Schedule are to be charged for services provided by the bankruptcy courts.

- The United States should not be charged fees under this schedule, with the exception of those specifically prescribed in Items 1, 3 and 5 when the information requested is available through remote electronic access.

- Federal agencies or programs that are funded from judiciary appropriations (agencies, organizations, and individuals providing services authorized by the Criminal Justice Act, 18 U.S.C. § 3006A, and bankruptcy administrators) should not be charged any fees under this schedule.

(1) For reproducing any document, $.50 per page. This fee applies to services rendered on behalf of the United States if the document requested is available through electronic access.

(2) For certification of any document, $11.

For exemplification of any document, $21.

(3) For reproduction of an audio recording of a court proceeding, $30. This fee applies to services rendered on behalf of the United States if the recording is available electronically.

(4) For filing an amendment to the debtor's schedules of creditors, lists of creditors, or mailing list, $30, except:

- The bankruptcy judge may, for good cause, waive the charge in any case.

- This fee must not be charged if—

    o the amendment is to change the address of a creditor or an attorney for a creditor listed on the schedules; or

    o the amendment is to add the name and address of an attorney for a creditor listed on the schedules.

(5) For conducting a search of the bankruptcy court records, $30 per name or item searched. This fee applies to services rendered on behalf of the United States if the information requested is available through electronic access.

(6) For filing a complaint, $350, except:

- If the trustee or debtor-in-possession files the complaint, the fee must be paid only by the estate, to the extent there is an estate.

- This fee must not be charged if—

    - the debtor is the plaintiff; or

    - a child support creditor or representative files the complaint and submits the form required by § 304(g) of the Bankruptcy Reform Act of 1994.

(7) For filing any document that is not related to a pending case or proceeding, $46.

(8) Administrative fee:

- For filing a petition under Chapter 7, 12, or 13, $75.

- For filing a petition under Chapter 9, 11, or 15, $550.

- When a motion to divide a joint case under Chapter 7, 12, or 13 is filed, $75.

- When a motion to divide a joint case under Chapter 11 is filed, $550.

(9) For payment to trustees pursuant to 11 U.S.C. § 330(b)(2), a $15 fee applies in the following circumstances:

- For filing a petition under Chapter 7.
- For filing a motion to reopen a Chapter 7 case.
- For filing a motion to divide a joint Chapter 7 case.
- For filing a motion to convert a case to a Chapter 7 case.
- For filing a notice of conversion to a Chapter 7 case.

(10) In addition to any fees imposed under Item 9, above, the following fees must be collected:

- For filing a motion to convert a Chapter 12 case to a Chapter 7 case or a notice of conversion pursuant to 11 U.S.C. § 1208(a), $45.
- For filing a motion to convert a Chapter 13 case to a Chapter 7 case or a notice of conversion pursuant to 11 U.S.C. § 1307(a), $10.

The fee amounts in this item are derived from the fees prescribed in 28 U.S.C. § 1930(a).

If the trustee files the motion to convert, the fee is payable only from the estate that exists prior to conversion.

If the filing fee for the chapter to which the case is requested to be converted is less than the fee paid at the commencement of the case, no refund may be provided.

(11) For filing a motion to reopen, the following fees apply:

- For filing a motion to reopen a Chapter 7 case, $245.
- For filing a motion to reopen a Chapter 9 case, $1167.
- For filing a motion to reopen a Chapter 11 case, $1167.
- For filing a motion to reopen a Chapter 12 case, $200.
- For filing a motion to reopen a Chapter 13 case, $235.
- For filing a motion to reopen a Chapter 15 case, $1167.

The fee amounts in this item are derived from the fees prescribed in 28 U.S.C. § 1930(a).

The reopening fee must be charged when a case has been closed without a discharge being entered.

The court may waive this fee under appropriate circumstances or may defer payment of the fee from trustees pending discovery of additional assets. If payment is deferred, the fee should be waived if no additional assets are discovered.

The reopening fee must not be charged in the following situations:

- to permit a party to file a complaint to obtain a determination under Rule 4007(b); or
- when a debtor files a motion to reopen a case based upon an alleged violation of the terms of the discharge under 11 U.S.C. § 524; or
- when the reopening is to correct an administrative error.

(12) For retrieval of one box of records from a Federal Records Center, National Archives, or other storage location removed from the place of business of the court, $64. For retrievals involving multiple boxes, $39 for each additional box.

(13) For a check paid into the court which is returned for lack of funds, $53.

(14) For filing an appeal or cross appeal from a judgment, order, or decree, $293.

This fee is collected in addition to the statutory fee of $5 that is collected under 28 U.S.C. § 1930 (c) when a notice of appeal is filed.

Parties filing a joint notice of appeal should pay only one fee.

If a trustee or debtor-in-possession is the appellant, the fee must be paid only by the estate, to the extent there is an estate.

Upon notice from the court of appeals that a direct appeal or direct cross-appeal has been authorized, an additional fee of $157 must be collected.

(15) For filing a case under Chapter 15 of the Bankruptcy Code, $1167.

This fee is derived from and equal to the fee prescribed in 28 U.S.C. § 1930(a)(3) for filing a case commenced under Chapter 11 of Title 11.

(16) The court may charge and collect fees commensurate with the cost of providing copies of the local rules of court. The court may also distribute copies of the local rules without charge.

(17) The clerk shall assess a charge for the handling of registry funds deposited with the court, to be assessed from interest earnings and in accordance with the detailed fee schedule issued by the Director of the Administrative Office of the United States Courts.

For management of registry funds invested through the Court Registry Investment System, a fee at a rate of 2.5 basis points shall be assessed from interest earnings.

(18) For a motion filed by the debtor to divide a joint case filed under 11 U.S.C. § 302, the following fees apply:

- For filing a motion to divide a joint Chapter 7 case, $245.
- For filing a motion to divide a joint Chapter 11 case, $1167.
- For filing a motion to divide a joint Chapter 12 case, $200.
- For filing a motion to divide a joint Chapter 13 case, $235.

These fees are derived from and equal to the filing fees prescribed in 28 U.S.C. § 1930(a).

(19) For filing the following motions, $176:

- To terminate, annul, modify or condition the automatic stay;
- To compel abandonment of property of the estate pursuant to Rule 6007(b) of the Federal Rules of Bankruptcy Procedure; or
- To withdraw the reference of a case or proceeding under 28 U.S.C. § 157(d).

This fee must not be collected in the following situations:

- For a motion for relief from the co-debtor stay;
- For a stipulation for court approval of an agreement for relief from a stay; or
- For a motion filed by a child support creditor or its representative, if the form required by § 304(g) of the Bankruptcy Reform Act of 1994 is filed.

(20) For filing a transfer of claim, $25 per claim transferred.

Electronic Public Access Fee Schedule (Eff. 4/1/2013)

(Issued in Accordance with 28 U.S.C. §§ 1913, 1914, 1926, 1930, 1932)

The fees included in the Electronic Public Access Fee Schedule are to be charged for providing electronic public access to court records.

Fees for Public Access to Court Electronic Records (PACER)

(1) Except as provided below, for electronic access to any case document, docket sheet, or case-specific report via PACER: $0.10 per page, not to exceed the fee for thirty pages.

(2) For electronic access to transcripts and non-case specific reports via PACER (such as reports obtained from the PACER Case Locator or docket activity reports): $0.10 per page.

(3) For electronic access to an audio file of a court hearing via PACER: $2.40 per audio file.

Fees for Courthouse Electronic Access

(4) For printing copies of any record or document accessed electronically at a public terminal in a courthouse: $0.10 per page.

PACER Service Center Fees

(5) For every search of court records conducted by the PACER Service Center, $30 per name or item searched.

(6) For the PACER Service Center to reproduce on paper any record pertaining to a PACER account, if this information is remotely available through electronic access: $0.50 per page.

(7) For a check paid to the PACER Service Center returned for lack of funds: $53.

Free Access and Exemptions

(8) Automatic Fee Exemptions:

- No fee is owed for electronic access to court data or audio files via PACER until an account holder accrues charges of more than $15.00 in a quarterly billing cycle.

- Parties in a case (including pro se litigants) and attorneys of record receive one free electronic copy, via the notice of electronic filing or notice of docket activity, of all documents filed electronically, if receipt is required by law or directed by the filer.

- No fee is charged for access to judicial opinions.

- No fee is charged for viewing case information or documents at courthouse public access terminals.

(9) Discretionary Fee Exemptions:

- Courts may exempt certain persons or classes of persons from payment of the user access fee. Examples of individuals and groups that a court may consider exempting include: indigents, bankruptcy case trustees, pro bono attorneys, pro bono alternative dispute resolution neutrals, Section 501(c)(3) not-for-profit organizations, and individual researchers associated with educational institutions. Courts should not, however, exempt individuals or groups that have the ability to pay the statutorily established access fee. Examples of individuals and groups that a court should not exempt include: local, state or federal government agencies, members of the media, privately paid attorneys or others who have the ability to pay the fee.

- In considering granting an exemption, courts must find:

   o That those seeking an exemption have demonstrated that an exemption is necessary in order to avoid unreasonable burdens and to promote public access to information.

   o That individual researchers requesting an exemption have shown that the defined research project is intended for scholarly research, that it is limited in scope, and that it is not intended for redistribution on the internet or for commercial purposes.

- If the court grants an exemption:

   o The user receiving the exemption must agree not to sell the data obtained as a result, and must not transfer any data obtained as the result of a fee exemption, unless expressly authorized by the court.

   o The exemption should be granted for a definite period of time, should be limited in scope, and may be revoked at the discretion of the court granting the exemption.

- Courts may provide local court information at no cost (e.g., local rules, court forms, news items, court calendars, and other information) to benefit the public.

Applicability to the United States and State and Local Governments

(10) Unless otherwise authorized by the Judicial Conference, these fees must be charged to the United States, except to federal agencies or programs that are funded from judiciary appropriations (including, but not limited to, agencies, organizations, and individuals providing services authorized by the Criminal Justice Act [18 U.S.C. § 3006A], and bankruptcy administrators).

(11) The fee for printing copies of any record or document accessed electronically at a public terminal ($0.10 per page) described in (4) above does not apply to services rendered on behalf of the United States if the record requested is not remotely available through electronic access.

(12) The fee for local, state, and federal government entities, shall be $0.08 per page until April 1, 2015, after which time, the fee shall be $0.10 per page.

Judicial Conference Policy Notes

The Electronic Public Access (EPA) fee and its exemptions are directly related to the requirement that the judiciary charge user-based fees for the development and maintenance of electronic public access services. The fee schedule provides examples of users that may not be able to afford reasonable user fees (such as indigents, bankruptcy case trustees, individual researchers associated with educational institutions, 501(c)(3) not-for-profit organizations, and court-appointed pro bono attorneys), but requires those seeking an exemption to demonstrate that an exemption is limited in scope and is necessary in order to avoid an unreasonable burden. In addition, the fee schedule includes examples of other entities that courts should not exempt from the fee (such as local, state or federal government agencies, members of the media, and attorneys). The goal is to provide courts with guidance in evaluating a requestor's ability to pay the fee.

Judicial Conference policy also limits exemptions in other ways. First, it requires exempted users to agree not to sell the data they receive through an exemption (unless expressly authorized by the court). This prohibition is not intended to bar a quote or reference to information received as a result of a fee exemption in a scholarly or other similar work. Second, it permits courts to grant exemptions for a definite period of time, to limit the scope of the exemptions, and to revoke exemptions. Third, it cautions that exemptions should be granted as the exception, not the rule, and prohibits courts from exempting all users from EPA fees.

HISTORICAL AND STATUTORY NOTES

References in Text

Chapter 7, 11, 12, or 13 of title 11, referred to in text, is 11 U.S.C.A. § 701 et seq., 11 U.S.C.A. § 1101 et seq., 11 U.S.C.A. § 1201 et seq., or 11 U.S.C.A. § 1301 et seq., respectively.

Section 673(2) of the Omnibus Budget Reconciliation Act of 1981, referred to in subsec. (f)(1), is Pub.L. 97–35, Title VI, § 673(2), Aug. 13, 1981, as added Pub.L. 105–285, Title II, § 201, Oct. 27, 1998, 112 Stat. 2729, which is classified to 42 U.S.C.A. § 9902(2).

Codifications

Pub.L. 99–591 is a corrected version of Pub.L. 99–500.

The Chapter 11 filing fee will not change from its current amount of $1,000. It appears that Congress intended to increase chapter 11 filing fees from $1,000 to $2,750. However, there is a drafting error in the language of the Deficit Reduction Act of 2005 which references the incorrect statutory subsection [Pub.L. 109–171, Title X, § 10101(a)(2), Feb. 8, 2006, 120 Stat. 184]. Thus, the chapter 11 fee, at this time, is unaltered. See 2006 Amendments note set out under this section.

Section 101(a) of Pub.L. 104–91, as amended by section 211 of Pub.L. 104–99, provided in part that section 111(a) of the General Provisions for the Department of Justice in Title I of the Departments of Commerce, Justice, and State, the Judiciary, and Related Agencies Appropriations Act, 1996 (H.R. 2076) as passed by the House of Representatives on Dec. 6, 1995, was enacted into permanent law. Such section 111(a) of H.R. 2076 amended subsec. (a)(6) of this section. See 1996 Amendments note set out under this section.

Amendments

2012 Amendments. Subsec. (a)(3). Pub.L. 112–121, § 3(a), struck out "$1,000" and inserted "$1,167".

2007 Amendments. Subsec. (a)(6). Pub.L. 110–161, Div. B, § 213(a), struck out "The fee shall be $250 for each quarter in which disbursements total less than $15,000; $500 for each quarter in which disbursements total $15,000 or more but less than $75,000; $750 for each quarter in which disbursements total $75,000 or more but less than $150,000; $1,250 for each quarter in which disbursements total $150,000 or more but less than $225,000; $1,500 for each quarter in which disbursements total $225,000 or more but less than $300,000; $3,750 for each quarter in which disbursements total $300,000 or more but less than $1,000,000; $5,000 for each quarter in which disbursements total $1,000,000 or more but less than $2,000,000; $7,500 for each quarter in which disbursements total $2,000,000 or more but less than $3,000,000; $8,000 for each quarter in which disbursements total $3,000,000 or more but less than $5,000,000; $10,000 for each quarter in which disbursements total $5,000,000 or more. The fee shall be payable on the last day of the calendar month following the calendar quarter for which the fee is owed." and inserted "The fee shall be $325 for each quarter in which disbursements total less than $15,000; $650 for each quarter in which disbursements total $15,000 or more but less than $75,000; $975 for each quarter in which disbursements total $75,000 or more but less than $150,000; $1,625 for each quarter in which disbursements total $150,000 or more but less than $225,000; $1,950 for each quarter in which disbursements total $225,000 or more but less than $300,000; $4,875 for each quarter in which disbursements total $300,000 or more but less than $1,000,000; $6,500 for each quarter in which disbursements total $1,000,000 or more but less than $2,000,000; $9,750 for each quarter in which disbursements total $2,000,000 or more but less than $3,000,000; $10,400 for each quarter in which disbursements total $3,000,000 or more but less than $5,000,000; $13,000 for each quarter in which disbursements total $5,000,000 or more but less than $15,000,000; $20,000 for each quarter in which disbursements total $15,000,000 or more but less than $30,000,000; $30,000 for each quarter in which disbursements total more than $30,000,000. The fee shall be payable on the last day of the calendar month following the calendar quarter for which the fee is owed.".

2006 Amendments. Subsec. (a)(1)(A). Pub.L. 109–171, § 10101(a)(1)(A), struck out "$220" and inserted "$245".

Subsec. (a)(1)(B). Pub.L. 109–171, § 10101(a)(1)(B), struck out "$150" and inserted "$235".

Subsec. (a)(2). Pub.L. 109–171, § 10101(a)(2), which purported to strike out "$1,000" and insert "$2,750", in par. (2), was incapable of execution. See Codifications note set out under this section.

2005 Amendments. Subsec. (a)(1). Pub.L. 109–8, § 325(a)(1), as amended by Pub.L. 109–13, § 6058(a), added par. (1) and struck out former par. (1), which read as follows: "For a case commenced under chapter 7 or 13 of title 11, $155."

Pub.L. 109–8, § 325(a)(2), in subsec. (a)(3), struck out "$800" and inserted "$1000".

Subsec. (a)(3). Pub.L. 109–8, Sec. 325(a)(2), as amended by Pub.L. 109–13, § 6058(a), substituted "$1,000" for "$800".

Subsec. (f). Pub.L. 109–8, § 418(2), added subsec. (f).

2000 Amendments. Subsec. (a). Pub.L. 106–518, § 104, in the undesignated portion at the end, struck out "$400" and inserted "the amount equal to the difference between the fee specified in paragraph (3) and the fee specified in paragraph (1)".

Subsec. (a)(2). Pub.L. 106–518, § 103, struck out "$300" and inserted "equal to the fee specified in paragraph (3) for filing a case under chapter 11 of title 11. The amount by which the fee payable under this paragraph exceeds $300 shall be deposited in the fund established under section 1931 of this title".

Subsec. (a)(7). Pub.L. 106–518, § 105, added par. (7).

1999 Amendments. Subsec. (a)(1). Pub.L. 106–113, § 1000(a)(1) [§ 113] struck out "$130" and inserted "$155".

1996 Amendments. Subsec. (a)(3). Pub.L. 104–208, § 101(a) [§ 109(a)], inserted a dollar sign preceding "800".

Subsec. (a)(6). Pub.L. 104–208, § 101(a) [§ 109(a)], substituted provisions setting quarterly fees at $500 for disbursements between $15,000 and $75,000, $750 for those between $75,000 and $150,000, $1,250 for those between $150,000 and $225,000, $1,500 for those between $225,000 and $300,000, $3,750 for those between $300,000 and $1,000,000, $5,000 for those between $1,000,000 and $2,000,000, $7,500 for those between $2,000,000 and $3,000,000, $8,000 for those between $3,000,000 and $5,000,000, and $10,000 for those over $5,000,000 for provisions setting quarterly fees at $500 for disbursements between $15,000 and $150,000, $1,250 for those between $150,000 and $300,000, $3,750 for those between $300,000 and $3,000,000, and $5,000 for those over $3,000,000.

Pub.L. 104–91, § 101(a), as amended Pub.L. 104–99, § 211, struck out "a plan is confirmed or" preceding "the case is converted". See Codifications note set out under this section.

1993 Amendments. Subsec. (a)(1). Pub.L. 103–121, § 111(a)(1), increased filing fee for chapter 7 or 13 cases from $120 to $130.

Subsec. (a)(3). Pub.L. 103–121, § 111(a)(1), increased filing fee for chapter 11 cases from $600 to $800.

1991 Amendments. Subsec. (a)(3). Pub.L. 102–140, § 111(a)(1), substituted "$600" for "$500".

Subsec. (a)(6). Pub.L. 102–140, § 111(a)(2), substituted "$250" for "$150", "$500" for "$300", "$1,250" for "$750", "$3,750" for "$2,250", and "$5,000" for "$3,000".

1989 Amendments. Subsec. (a)(1). Pub.L. 101–162, § 406(a), substituted "$120" for "$90".

1986 Amendments. Subsec. (a). Pub.L. 99–554, § 117(5), in provision following numbered pars., inserted provision that for conversion, on request of the debtor, of a case under chapter 7 or 13 of title 11 to a case under chapter 11 of title 11, the debtor pay to the clerk of the court a fee of $400.

Pub.L. 99–554, § 144(f), substituted "of the district court or the clerk of the bankruptcy court, if one has been certified pursuant to section 156(b) of this title" for "of the court" wherever appearing.

Subsec. (a)(1). Pub.L. 99–500 and Pub.L. 99–591, and Pub.L. 99–554, § 117(1), amended par. (1) identically, substituting "$90" for "$60".

Subsec. (a)(3). Pub.L. 99–554, § 117(2), substituted "$500" for "$200".

Subsec. (a)(4). Pub.L. 99–554, § 117(3), substituted "$1,000" for "$500".

Subsec. (a)(5), (6). Pub.L. 99–554, § 117(4), added pars. (5) and (6).

1984 Amendments. Catchline. Pub.L. 98–353, § 111(b), substituted "fees" for "courts".

Subsecs. (a), (c), (e). Pub.L. 98–353, § 111(a), substituted "clerk of the court" for "clerk of the bankruptcy court".

Miscellaneous Fees

Section 406(a) of Pub.L. 101–162 provided in part that: "Pursuant to section 1930(b) of title 28 [subsec. (b) of this section] the Judicial Conference of the United States shall prescribe a fee of $60 on motions seeking relief from the automatic stay under 11 U.S.C. section 362(b) [section 362(b) of Title 11, Bankruptcy] and motions to compel abandonment of property of the estate. The fees established pursuant to the preceding two sentences shall take effect 30 days after the enactment of this Act [Nov. 21, 1989]."

Accrual and Payment of Quarterly Fees in Chapter 11 Cases After Jan. 27, 1996; Confirmation Status of Plans

Section 101(a) of Pub.L. 104–91, as amended Pub.L. 104–99, Title II, § 211, Jan. 26, 1996, 110 Stat. 37; Pub.L. 104–208, Div. A, Title I, § 101(a) [Title I, § 109(d)], Sept. 30, 1996, 110 Stat. 3009–19, provided, in part: "That, notwithstanding any other provision of law, the fees under 28 U.S.C. 1930(a)(6) [subsec. (a)(6) of this section] shall accrue and be payable from and after January 27, 1996, in all cases (including, without limitation, any cases pending as of that date), regardless of confirmation status of their plans."

Collection and Disposition of Fees in Bankruptcy Cases

Section 404(a) of Pub. L. 101–162 provided that: "For fiscal year 1990 and hereafter, such fees as shall be collected for the preparation and mailing of notices in bankruptcy cases as prescribed by the Judicial Conference of the United States pursuant to 28 U.S.C. 1930(b) [subsec. (b) of this section] shall be deposited to the 'Courts of Appeals, District Courts, and Other Judicial Services, Salaries and Expenses' appropriation to be used for salaries and other expenses incurred in providing these services."

Court Fees for Electronic Access to Information

Judicial Conference to prescribe reasonable fees for collection by courts under this section for access to information available through automatic data processing equipment and fees to be deposited in Judiciary Automation Fund, see section 303 of Pub.L. 102–140, set out as a note under section 1913 of this title.

Issuance of Notices to Creditors and Other Interested Parties

Section 403 of Pub.L. 101–162 provided that: "Notwithstanding any other provision of law, for fiscal year 1990 and hereafter, (a) The Administrative Office of the United States Courts, or any other agency or instrumentality of the United States, is prohibited from restricting solely to staff of the Clerks of the United States Bankruptcy Courts the issuance of notices to creditors and other interested parties. (b) The Administrative Office shall permit and encourage the preparation and mailing of such notices to be performed by or at the expense of the debtors, trustees or such other interested parties as the Court may direct and approve. (c) The Director of the Administrative Office of the United States Courts shall make appropriate provisions for the use of and accounting for any postage required pursuant to such directives."

Report on Bankruptcy Fees

Section 111(d) of Pub.L. 103–121 provided that:

"**(1) Report required.**—Not later than March 31, 1998, the Judicial Conference of the United States shall submit to the Committees on the Judiciary of the House of Representatives and the Senate, a report relating to the bankruptcy fee system and the impact of such system on various participants in bankruptcy cases.

"(2) **Contents of report.**—Such report shall include—

"(A)(i) an estimate of the costs and benefits that would result from waiving bankruptcy fees payable by debtors who are individuals, and

"(ii) recommendations regarding various revenue sources to offset the net cost of waiving such fees; and

"(B)(i) an evaluation of the effects that would result in cases under chapters 11 and 13 of title 11, United States Code [sections 1101 et seq. and 1301 et seq., respectively, of Title 11, Bankruptcy], from using a graduated bankruptcy fee system based on assets, liabilities, or both of the debtor, and

"(ii) recommendations regarding various methods to implement such a graduated bankruptcy fee system.

"(3) **Waiver of fees in selected districts.**—For purposes of carrying out paragraphs (1) and (2), the Judicial Conference of the United States shall carry out in not more than six judicial districts, throughout the 3-year period beginning on October 1, 1994, a program under which fees payable under section 1930 of title 28, United States Code [this section], may be waived in cases under chapter 7 of title 11, United States Code [section 701 et seq. of Title 11], for debtors who are individuals unable to pay such fees in installments.

"(4) **Study of graduated fee system.**—For purposes of carrying out paragraphs (1) and (2), the Judicial Conference of the United States shall carry out, in not fewer than six judicial districts, a study to estimate the results that would occur in cases under chapters 11 and 13 of title 11, United States Code [sections 1101 et seq. and 1301 et seq., respectively, of Title 11], if filing fees payable under section 1930 of title 28, United States Code [this section], were paid on a graduated scale based on assets, liabilities, or both of the debtor."

CROSS REFERENCES

Confirmation of reorganization plan contingent on payment of fees, see 11 USCA § 1129.

Recommendation for adjustment of dollar amounts of fees, see 11 USCA § 104.

United States Trustee System Fund, depositing of bankruptcy fees into Fund, see 28 USCA § 589a.

CHAPTER 131—RULES OF COURTS

§ 2075. Bankruptcy rules

The Supreme Court shall have the power to prescribe by general rules, the forms of process, writs, pleadings, and motions, and the practice and procedure in cases under title 11.

Such rules shall not abridge, enlarge, or modify any substantive right.

The Supreme Court shall transmit to Congress not later than May 1 of the year in which a rule prescribed under this section is to become effective a copy of the proposed rule. The rule shall take effect no earlier than December 1 of the year in which it is transmitted to Congress unless otherwise provided by law.

The bankruptcy rules promulgated under this section shall prescribe a form for the statement required under section 707(b)(2)(C) of title 11 and may provide general rules on the content of such statement.

(Added Pub.L. 88–623, § 1, Oct. 3, 1964, 78 Stat. 1001; amended Pub.L. 95–598, Title II, § 247, Nov. 6, 1978, 92 Stat. 2672; Pub.L. 103–394, Title I, § 104(f), Oct. 22, 1994, 108 Stat. 4110; Pub.L. 109–8, Title XII, § 1232, Apr. 20, 2005, 119 Stat. 202.)

HISTORICAL AND STATUTORY NOTES

Amendments

2005 Amendments. Pub.L.109–8, § 1232, inserted at the end the following new undesignated paragraph: "The bankruptcy rules promulgated under this section shall prescribe a form for the statement required under section 707(b)(2)(C) of title 11 and may provide general rules on the content of such statement."

1994 Amendments. Pub.L. 103–394, § 104(f), added the third undesignated paragraph and struck out the former third undesignated paragraph which read as follows: "Such rules shall not take effect until they have been reported to Congress by the Chief Justice at or after the beginning of a regular session thereof but not later than the first day of May and until the expiration of ninety days after they have been thus reported."

1978 Amendments. Pub.L. 95–598 substituted "in cases under title 11" for "under the Bankruptcy Act" and struck out provisions directing that all laws in conflict with bankruptcy rules be of no further force or effect after such rules have taken effect.

Additional Rulemaking Power

Pub.L. 95–598, Title IV, § 410, Nov. 6, 1978, 92 Stat. 2687, provided that: "The Supreme Court may issue such additional rules of procedure, consistent with Acts of Congress, as may be necessary for the orderly transfer of functions and records and the orderly transition to the new bankruptcy court system created by this Act [see Tables for complete classification of Pub.L. 95–598]."

Applicability of Rules to Cases Under Title 11

Pub.L. 95–598, Title IV, § 405(d), Nov. 6, 1978, 92 Stat. 2685, provided that: "The rules prescribed under section 2075 of title 28 of the United States Code and in effect on September 30, 1979, shall apply to cases under title 11, to the extent not inconsistent with the amendments made by this Act, or with this Act [see Tables for complete classification of Pub.L. 95–598], until such rules are repealed or superseded by rules prescribed and effective under such section, as amended by section 248 of this Act."

Rules Promulgated by Supreme Court

Pub.L. 98–353, Title III, § 320, July 10, 1984, 98 Stat. 357, provided that: "The Supreme Court shall prescribe general rules implementing the practice and procedure to be followed under section 707(b) of title 11, United States Code [section 707(b) of Title 11, Bankruptcy]. Section 2075 of title 28, United States Code [this section], shall apply with respect to the general rules prescribed under this section."

BANKRUPTCY RULES

Last Amended December 1, 2014

Part		Rule
I.	Commencement of Case: Proceedings Relating to Petition and Order for Relief	1002
II.	Officers and Administration; Notices; Meetings; Examinations; Elections; Attorneys and Accountants	2001
III.	Claims and Distribution to Creditors and Equity Interest Holders; Plans	3001
IV.	The Debtor: Duties and Benefits	4001
V.	Bankruptcy Courts and Clerks	5001
VI.	Collection and Liquidation of the Estate	6001
VII.	Adversary Proceedings	7001
VIII.	Appeals to District Court or Bankruptcy Appellate Panel	8001
IX.	General Provisions	9001
X.	United States Trustees [Abrogated]	X–1001

Rule 1001. Scope of Rules and Forms; Short Title

The Bankruptcy Rules and Forms govern procedure in cases under title 11 of the United States Code. The rules shall be cited as the Federal Rules of Bankruptcy Procedure and the forms as the Official Bankruptcy Forms. These rules shall be construed to secure the just, speedy, and inexpensive determination of every case and proceeding.

(As amended Mar. 30, 1987, eff. Aug. 1, 1987; Apr. 30, 1991, eff. Aug. 1, 1991.)

ADVISORY COMMITTEE NOTES

Section 247 of Public Law 95–598, 92 Stat. 2549 amended 28 U.S.C. § 2075 by omitting the last sentence. The effect of the amendment is to require that procedural rules promulgated pursuant to 28 U.S.C. § 2075 be consistent with the bankruptcy statute, both titles 11 and 28 U.S.C. Thus, although Rule 1001 sets forth the scope of the bankruptcy rules and forms, any procedural matters contained in title 11 or 28 U.S.C. with respect to cases filed under 11 U.S.C. would control. See 1 Collier, Bankruptcy ¶3.04[2][c] (15th ed. 1980).

28 U.S.C. § 151 establishes a United States Bankruptcy Court in each district as an adjunct to the district court. This provision does not, however, become effective until April 1, 1984. Public Law 95–598, § 402(b). From October 1, 1979 through March 31, 1984, the courts of bankruptcy as defined in § 1(10) of the Bankruptcy Act [former § 1(10) of this title], and created in § 2a of that Act [former § 11(a) of this title], continue to be the courts of bankruptcy. Public Law 95–598, § 404(a). From their effective date these rules and forms are to be applicable in cases filed under chapters 7, 9, 11 and 13 of title 11 regardless of whether the court is established by the Bankruptcy Act or by 28 U.S.C. § 151. Rule 9001 contains a broad and general definition of "bankruptcy court," "court" and "United States Bankruptcy Court" for this purpose.

"Bankruptcy Code" or "Code" as used in these rules means title 11 of the United States Code, the codification of the bankruptcy law. Public Law 95–598, § 101. See Rule 9001.

"Bankruptcy Act" as used in the notes to these rules means the Bankruptcy Act of 1898 as amended which was repealed by § 401(a) of Public Law 95–598.

These rules apply to all cases filed under the Code except as otherwise specifically stated.

The final sentence of the rule is derived from former Bankruptcy Rule 903. The objective of "expeditious and economical administration" of cases under the Code has frequently been recognized by the courts to be "a chief purpose of the bankruptcy laws." See Katchen v. Landy, 382 U.S. 323, 328 (1966); Bailey v. Glover, 88 U.S. (21 Wall.) 342, 346–47 (1874); Ex parte Christy, 44 U.S. (3 How.) 292, 312–14, 320–22 (1845). The rule also incorporates the wholesome mandate of the last sentence of Rule 1 of the Federal Rules of Civil Procedure. 2 Moore, Federal Practice ¶1.13 (2d ed. 1980); 4 Wright & Miller, Federal Practice and Procedure—Civil § 1029 (1969).

1987 Amendments

Title I of the Bankruptcy Amendments and Federal Judgeship Act of 1984, Pub.L. No. 98–353, 98 Stat. 333 (hereinafter the 1984 amendments), created a new bankruptcy judicial system in which the role of the district court was substantially increased. 28 U.S.C. § 1334 confers on the United States district courts original and exclusive jurisdiction over all cases under title 11 of the United States Code and original but not exclusive jurisdiction over civil proceedings arising under title 11 and civil proceedings arising in or related to a case under title 11.

Pursuant to 28 U.S.C. § 157(a) the district court may but need not refer cases and proceedings within the district court's jurisdiction to the bankruptcy judges for the district. Judgments or orders of the bankruptcy judges entered pursuant to 28 U.S.C. § 157(b)(1) and (c)(2) are subject to appellate review by the district courts or bankruptcy appellate panels under 28 U.S.C. § 158(a).

Rule 81(a)(1) F.R.Civ.P. provides that the civil rules do not apply to proceedings in bankruptcy, except as they may be made applicable by rules promulgated by the Supreme Court, *e.g.*, Part VII of these rules. This amended Bankruptcy Rule 1001 makes the Bankruptcy Rules applicable to cases and proceedings under title 11, whether before the district judges or the bankruptcy judges of the district.

1991 Amendments

The citation to these rules is amended to conform to the citation form of the Federal Rules of Civil Procedure, Federal Rules of Appellate Procedure, and Federal Rules of Criminal Procedure.

CROSS REFERENCES

Promulgation of bankruptcy rules by Supreme Court, see 28 USCA § 2075.

Scope of rules, see Federal Rules of Appellate Procedure Rule 1, 28 USCA.

Applicability of rules, see Fed.Rules Civ.Proc. Rule 81, 28 USCA.

Scope of rules, see Fed.Rules Civ.Proc. Rule 1, 28 USCA.

Applicability of rules, see Fed.Rules Evid. Rule 1101, 28 USCA.

Scope of rules, see Fed.Rules Evid. Rule 101, 28 USCA.

PART I—COMMENCEMENT OF CASE: PROCEEDINGS RELATING TO PETITION AND ORDER FOR RELIEF

Rule 1002. Commencement of Case

(a) Petition

A petition commencing a case under the Code shall be filed with the clerk.

(b) Transmission to United States trustee

The clerk shall forthwith transmit to the United States trustee a copy of the petition filed pursuant to subdivision (a) of this rule.

(As amended Mar. 30, 1987, eff. Aug. 1, 1987; Apr. 30, 1991, eff. Aug. 1, 1991.)

ADVISORY COMMITTEE NOTES

Under §§ 301–303 of the Code, a voluntary or involuntary case is commenced by filing a petition with the bankruptcy court. The voluntary petition may request relief under chapter 7, 9, 11, or 13 whereas an involuntary petition may be filed under only chapter 7 or 11. Section 109 of the Code specifies the types of debtors for whom the different forms of relief are available and § 303(a) indicates the persons against whom involuntary petitions may be filed.

The rule in subdivision (a) is in harmony with the Code in that it requires the filing to be with the bankruptcy court.

The number of copies of the petition to be filed is specified in this rule but a local rule may require additional copies. This rule provides for filing sufficient copies for the court's files and for the trustee in a chapter 7 or 13 case.

Official Form No. 1 may be used to seek relief voluntarily under any of the chapters. Only the original need be signed and verified, but the copies must be conformed to the original. See Rules 1008 and 9011(c). As provided in § 362(a) of the Code, the filing of a petition acts as a stay of certain acts and proceedings against the debtor, property of the debtor, and property of the estate.

1987 Amendments

Rules 1002(a), governing a voluntary petition, 1003(a), governing an involuntary petition, and 1003(e), governing a petition in a case ancillary to a foreign proceedings, are combined into this Rule 1002. If a bankruptcy clerk has been appointed for the district, the petition is filed with the bankruptcy clerk. Otherwise, the petition is filed with the clerk of the district court.

The elimination of the reference to the Official Forms of the petition is not intended to change the practice. Rule 9009 provides that the Official Forms "shall be observed and used" in cases and proceedings under the Code.

Subdivision (b) which provided for the distribution of copies of the petition to agencies of the United States has been deleted. Some of these agencies no longer wish to receive copies of the petition, while others not included in subdivision (b) have now requested copies. The Director of the Administrative Office will determine on an ongoing basis which government agencies will be provided a copy of the petition.

The number of copies of a petition that must be filed is a matter for local rule.

1991 Amendments

Subdivision (b) is derived from Rule X–1002(a). The duties of the United States trustee pursuant to the Code and 28 U.S.C. § 586(a) require that the United States trustee be apprised of the commencement of every case under chapters 7, 11, 12 and 13 and this is most easily accomplished by providing that office with a copy of the petition. Although 28 U.S.C. § 586(a) does not give the United States trustee an administrative role in chapter 9 cases, § 1102 of the Code requires the United States trustee to appoint committees and that section is applicable in chapter 9 cases pursuant to § 901(a). It is therefore appropriate that the United States trustee receive a copy of every chapter 9 petition.

Notwithstanding subdivision (b), pursuant to Rule 5005(b)(3), the clerk is not required to transmit a copy of the petition to the United States trustee if the United States trustee requests that it not be transmitted. Many rules require the clerk to transmit a certain document to the United States trustee, but Rule 5005(b)(3) relieves the clerk of that duty under this or any other rule if the United States trustee requests that such document not be transmitted.

CROSS REFERENCES

Commencement of voluntary cases, see 11 USCA § 301.

Debtors for whom relief available, see 11 USCA § 109.

Joint cases, see 11 USCA § 302.

Number of copies—

    Involuntary petition, see Fed.Rules Bankr.Proc. Rule 1003, 11 USCA.

    Schedules, statements, and lists, see Fed.Rules Bankr.Proc. Rule 1007, 11 USCA.

Signing and verification of petitions, see Fed.Rules Bankr.Proc. Rules 1008 and 9011, 11 USCA.

Stay of acts and proceedings against debtor and estate property, see 11 USCA § 362.

Rule 1003. Involuntary Petition

(a) Transferor or transferee of claim

A transferor or transferee of a claim shall annex to the original and each copy of the petition a copy of all documents evidencing the transfer, whether transferred unconditionally, for security, or otherwise, and a signed statement that the claim was not transferred for the purpose of commencing the case and setting forth the consideration for and terms of the transfer. An entity that has transferred or acquired a claim for the purpose of commencing a case for liquidation under chapter 7 or for reorganization under chapter 11 shall not be a qualified petitioner.

(b) Joinder of petitioners after filing

If the answer to an involuntary petition filed by fewer than three creditors avers the existence of 12 or more creditors, the debtor shall file with the answer a list of all creditors with their addresses, a brief statement of the nature of their claims, and the amounts thereof. If it appears that there are 12 or more creditors as provided in § 303(b) of the Code, the court shall afford a reasonable opportunity for other creditors to join in the petition before a hearing is held thereon.

(As amended Mar. 30, 1987, eff. Aug. 1, 1987.)

ADVISORY COMMITTEE NOTES

Subdivision (a). Official Form No. 11 (Involuntary Case: Creditors' Petition), is prescribed for use by petitioning creditors to have a debtor's assets liquidated under chapter 7 of the Code or the business reorganized under chapter 11. It contains the required allegations as specified in § 303(b) of the Code. Official Form 12 is prescribed for use by fewer than all the general partners to obtain relief for the partnership as governed by § 303(b)(3) of the Code and Rule 1004(b).

Although the number of copies to be filed is specified in Rule 1002, a local rule may require additional copies.

Only the original need be signed and verified, but the copies must be conformed to the original. See Rules 1008 and 9011(c). The petition must be filed with the bankruptcy court. This provision implements § 303(b) which provides that an involuntary case is commenced by filing the petition with the court.

As provided in § 362 of the Code, the filing of the petition acts as a stay of certain acts and proceedings against the debtor, the debtor's property and property of the estate.

Subdivision (c) retains the explicitness of former Bankruptcy Rule 104(d) that a transfer of a claim for the purpose of commencing a case under the Code is a ground for disqualification of a party to the transfer as a petitioner.

Section 303(b) "is not intended to overrule Bankruptcy Rule 104(d), which places certain restrictions on the transfer of claims for the purpose of commencing an involuntary case." House Report No. 95–595, 95th Cong., 1st Sess. (1977) 322; Senate Report No. 95–989, 95th Cong., 2d Sess. (1978) 33.

COMMENCEMENT OF CASE   Rule 1004

The subdivision requires disclosure of any transfer of the petitioner's claim as well as a transfer to the petitioner and applies to transfers for security as well as unconditional transfers. Cf. In re 69th & Crandon Bldg. Corp., 97 F.2d 392, 395 (7th Cir.), cert. denied, 305 U.S. 629 (1938), recognizing the right of a creditor to sign a bankruptcy petition notwithstanding a prior assignment of his claim for the purpose of security. This rule does not, however, qualify the requirement of § 303(b)(1) that a petitioning creditor must have a claim not contingent as to liability.

Subdivision (d). Section 303(c) of the Code permits a creditor to join in the petition at any time before the case is dismissed or relief is ordered. While this rule does not require the court to give all creditors notice of the petition, the list of creditors filed by the debtor affords a petitioner the information needed to enable him to give notice for the purpose of obtaining the co-petitioners required to make the petition sufficient. After a reasonable opportunity has been afforded other creditors to join in an involuntary petition, the hearing on the petition should be held without further delay.

Subdivision (e). This subdivision implements § 304. A petition for relief under § 304 may only be filed by a foreign representative who is defined in § 101(20) generally as a representative of an estate in a foreign proceeding. The term "foreign proceeding" is defined in § 101(19).

Section 304(b) permits a petition filed thereunder to be contested by a party in interest. Subdivision (e)(2) therefore requires that the summons and petition be served on any person against whom the relief permitted by § 304(b) is sought as well as on any other party the court may direct.

The rules applicable to the procedure when an involuntary petition is filed are made applicable generally when a case ancillary to a foreign proceeding is commenced. These rules include Rule 1010 with respect to issuance and service of a summons, Rule 1011 concerning responsive pleadings and motions, and Rule 1018 which makes various rules in Part VII applicable in proceedings on contested petitions.

The venue for a case ancillary to a foreign proceeding is provided in 28 U.S.C. § 1474.

1987 Amendments

The subject matter of subdivisions (a), (b), and (e) has been incorporated in Rules 1002, 1010, 1011, and 1018.

CROSS REFERENCES

Case ancillary to foreign proceeding—

    Commencement of and contested petitions, see 11 USCA § 304.

    Foreign proceeding and foreign representative defined, see 11 USCA § 101.

Debtors for whom relief available, see 11 USCA § 109.

Number of copies—

    Voluntary petition, see Fed.Rules Bankr.Proc. Rule 1002, 11 USCA.

Requisite allegations and joinder of parties, see 11 USCA § 303.

Signing and verification of petitions, see Fed.Rules Bankr.Proc. Rules 1008 and 9011, 11 USCA.

Stay of acts and proceedings against debtor and estate property, see 11 USCA § 362.

Rule 1004. Involuntary Petition Against a Partnership

After filing of an involuntary petition under § 303(b)(3) of the Code, (1) the petitioning partners or other petitioners shall promptly send to or serve on each general partner who is not a petitioner a copy of the petition; and (2) the clerk shall promptly issue a summons for service on each general partner who is not a petitioner. Rule 1010 applies to the form and service of the summons.

(As amended Apr. 29, 2002, eff. Dec. 1, 2002.)

ADVISORY COMMITTEE NOTES

This rule is adapted from former Bankruptcy Rule 105 and complements §§ 301 and 303(b)(3) of the Code.

Subdivision (a) specifies that while all general partners must consent to the filing of a voluntary petition, it is not necessary that they all execute the petition. It may be executed and filed on behalf of the partnership by fewer than all.

Subdivision (b) implements § 303(b)(3) of the Code which provides that an involuntary petition may be filed by fewer than all the general partners or, when all the general partners are debtors, by a general partner, trustee of the partner or creditors of the partnership. Rule 1010, which governs service of a petition and summons in an involuntary case, specifies the time and mode of service on the partnership. When a petition is filed against a partnership under § 303(b)(3), this rule requires an additional service on the nonfiling general partners. It is the purpose of this subdivision to protect the interests of the nonpetitioning partners and the partnership.

2002 Amendments

Section 303(b)(3)(A) of the Code provides that fewer than all of the general partners in a partnership may commence an involuntary case against the partnership. There is no counterpart provision in the Code setting out the manner in which a partnership commences a voluntary case. The Supreme Court has held in the corporate context that applicable nonbankruptcy law determines whether authority exists for a particular debtor to commence a bankruptcy case. *See Price v. Gurney*, 324 U.S. 100 (1945). The lower courts have followed this rule in the partnership context as well. *See, e.g., Jolly v. Pittore*, 170 B.R. 793 (S.D.N.Y. 1994); *Union Planters National Bank v. Hunters Horn Associates*, 158 B.R. 729 (Bankr. M.D. Tenn. 1993); *In re Channel 64 Joint Venture*, 61 B.R. 255 (Bankr. S.D. Oh. 1986). Rule 1004(a) could be construed as requiring the consent of all of the general partners to the filing of a voluntary petition, even if fewer than all of the general partners would have the authority under applicable nonbankruptcy law to commence a bankruptcy case for the partnership. Since this is a matter of substantive law beyond the scope of these rules, Rule 1004(a) is deleted as is the designation of subdivision (b).

The rule is retitled to reflect that it applies only to involuntary petitions filed against partnerships.

CROSS REFERENCES

Commencement of—

    Involuntary cases, see 11 USCA § 303.

    Voluntary cases, see 11 USCA § 301.

Contested petition by general partners, see Fed.Rules Bankr.Proc. Rule 1011, 11 USCA.

No change in status for purposes of state or local income tax law, see 11 USCA § 346.

Person defined to include partnership, see 11 USCA § 101.

Rule 1004.1. Petition for an Infant or Incompetent Person

If an infant or incompetent person has a representative, including a general guardian, committee, conservator, or similar fiduciary, the representative may file a voluntary petition on behalf of the infant or incompetent person. An infant or incompetent person who does not have a duly appointed representative may file a voluntary petition by next friend or guardian ad litem. The court shall appoint a guardian ad litem for an infant or incompetent person who is a debtor and is not otherwise represented or shall make any other order to protect the infant or incompetent debtor.

(Added Apr. 29, 2002, eff. Dec. 1, 2002.)

ADVISORY COMMITTEE NOTES
2002 Adoption

This rule is derived from Rule 17(c) F.R. Civ. P. It does not address the commencement of a case filed on behalf of a missing person. *See, e.g., In re King*, 234 B.R. 515 (Bankr. D.N.M. 1999).

Rule 1004.2. Petition in Chapter 15 Cases

(a) Designating center of main interests

A petition for recognition of a foreign proceeding under chapter 15 of the Code shall state the country where the debtor has its center of main interests. The petition shall also identify each country in which a foreign proceeding by, regarding, or against the debtor is pending.

(b) Challenging designation

The United States trustee or a party in interest may file a motion for a determination that the debtor's center of main interests is other than as stated in the petition for recognition commencing the chapter 15 case. Unless the court orders otherwise, the motion shall be filed no later than seven days before the date set for the hearing on the petition. The motion shall be transmitted to the United States trustee and served on the debtor, all persons or bodies authorized to administer foreign proceedings of the debtor, all entities against whom provisional relief is being sought under § 1519 of the Code, all parties to litigation pending in the United States in which the debtor was a party as of the time the petition was filed, and such other entities as the court may direct.

(Adopted Apr. 26, 2011, eff. Dec. 1, 2011.)

ADVISORY COMMITTEE NOTES

2011 Adoption

This rule is new. Subdivision (a) directs any entity that files a petition for recognition of a foreign proceeding under chapter 15 of the Code to state in the petition the center of the debtor's main interests. The petition must also list each country in which a foreign proceeding involving the debtor is pending. This information will assist the court and parties in interest in determining whether the foreign proceeding is a foreign main or nonmain proceeding.

Subdivision (b) sets a deadline of seven days before the date set for the hearing on the petition for recognition for filing a motion challenging the statement in the petition as to the country in which the debtor's center of main interests is located.

Rule 1005. Caption of Petition

The caption of a petition commencing a case under the Code shall contain the name of the court, the title of the case, and the docket number. The title of the case shall include the following information about the debtor: name, employer identification number, last four digits of the social-security number or individual debtor's taxpayer-identification number, any other federal taxpayer-identification number, and all other names used within eight years before filing the petition. If the petition is not filed by the debtor, it shall include all names used by the debtor which are known to the petitioners.

(As amended Mar. 30, 1987, eff. Aug. 1, 1987; Mar. 27, 2003, eff. Dec. 1, 2003; Apr. 23, 2008, eff. Dec. 1, 2008.)

ADVISORY COMMITTEE NOTES

The title of the case should include all names used by the debtor, such as trade names, former married names and maiden name. See also Official Form No. 1 and the Advisory Committee Note to that Form. Additional names of the debtor are also required to appear in the caption of each notice to creditors. See Rule 2002(m).

2003 Amendments

The rule is amended to implement the Judicial Conference policy to limit the disclosure of a party's social security number and similar identifiers. Under the rule, as amended, only the last four digits of the debtor's social security number need be disclosed. Publication of the employer identification number does not present the same identity theft or privacy protection issues. Therefore, the caption must include the full employer identification number.

Debtors must submit with the petition a statement setting out their social security numbers. This enables the clerk to include the full social security number on the notice of the section 341 meeting of creditors, but the statement itself is not submitted in the case or maintained in the case file.

2008 Amendments

The rule is amended to require the disclosure of all names used by the debtor in the past eight years. Section 727(a)(8) was amended in 2005 to extend the time between chapter 7 discharges from six to eight years, and the rule is amended to implement that change. The rule also is amended to require the disclosure of the last four digits of an individual debtor's taxpayer-identification number. This truncation of the number applies only to individual debtors. This is consistent with the requirements of Rule 9037.

CROSS REFERENCES

Conformance of captions of creditor notices with this rule, see Fed.Rules Bankr.Proc. Rule 2002, 11 USCA.

General requirements of form for petition, see Fed.Rules Bankr.Proc. Rule 9004, 11 USCA.

Rule 1006. Filing Fee

(a) General requirement

Every petition shall be accompanied by the filing fee except as provided in subdivisions (b) and (c) of this rule. For the purpose of this rule, "filing fee" means the filing fee prescribed by 28 U.S.C. § 1930(a)(1)–(a)(5) and any other fee prescribed by the Judicial Conference of the United States under 28 U.S.C. § 1930(b) that is payable to the clerk upon the commencement of a case under the Code.

(b) Payment of filing fee in installments

　(1) **Application to pay filing fee in installments**

　　A voluntary petition by an individual shall be accepted for filing if accompanied by the debtor's signed application, prepared as prescribed by the appropriate Official Form, stating that the debtor is unable to pay the filing fee except in installments.

　(2) **Action on application**

　　Prior to the meeting of creditors, the court may order the filing fee paid to the clerk or grant leave to pay in installments and fix the number, amount and dates of payment. The number of installments shall not exceed four, and the final installment shall be payable not later than 120 days after filing the petition. For cause shown, the court may extend the time of any installment, provided the last installment is paid not later than 180 days after filing the petition.

　(3) **Postponement of attorney's fees**

　　All installments of the filing fee must be paid in full before the debtor or chapter 13 trustee may make further payments to an attorney or any other person who renders services to the debtor in connection with the case.

(c) Waiver of filing fee

　A voluntary chapter 7 petition filed by an individual shall be accepted for filing if accompanied by the debtor's application requesting a waiver under 28 U.S.C. § 1930(f), prepared as prescribed by the appropriate Official Form.

(As amended Mar. 30, 1987, eff. Aug. 1, 1987; Apr. 23, 1996, eff. Dec. 1, 1996; Apr. 23, 2008, eff. Dec. 1, 2008.)

COMMENCEMENT OF CASE — Rule 1006

ADVISORY COMMITTEE NOTES

1983 Enactments

28 U.S.C. § 1930 specifies the filing fees for petitions under chapters 7, 9, 11 and 13 of the Code. It also permits the payment in installments by individual debtors.

Subdivision (b) is adapted from former Bankruptcy Rule 107. The administrative cost of installments in excess of four is disproportionate to the benefits conferred. Prolonging the period beyond 180 days after the commencement of the case causes undesirable delays in administration. Paragraph (2) accordingly continues the imposition of a maximum of four on the number of installments and retains the maximum period of installment payments allowable on an original application at 120 days. Only in extraordinary cases should it be necessary to give an applicant an extension beyond the four months. The requirement of paragraph (3) that filing fees be paid in full before the debtor may pay an attorney for services in connection with the case codifies the rule declared in In re Latham, 271 Fed. 538 (N.D.N.Y.1921), and In re Darr, 232 Fed. 415 (N.D.Cal.1916).

1987 Amendments

Subdivision (b)(3) is expanded to prohibit payments by the debtor or the chapter 13 trustee not only to attorneys but to any person who renders services to the debtor in connection with the case.

1996 Amendments

The Judicial Conference prescribes miscellaneous fees pursuant to 28 U.S.C. § 1930(b). In 1992, a $30 miscellaneous administrative fee was prescribed for all chapter 7 and chapter 13 cases. The Judicial Conference fee schedule was amended in 1993 to provide that an individual debtor may pay this fee in installments.

Subdivision (a) of this rule is amended to clarify that every petition must be accompanied by any fee prescribed under 28 U.S.C. § 1930(b) that is required to be paid when a petition is filed, as well as the filing fee prescribed by 28 U.S.C. § 1930(a). By defining "filing fee" to include Judicial Conference fees, the procedures set forth in subdivision (b) for paying the filing fee in installments will also apply with respect to any Judicial Conference fee required to be paid at the commencement of the case.

2008 Amendments

Subdivision (a) is amended to include a reference to new subdivision (c), which deals with fee waivers under 28 U.S.C. § 1930(f), which was added in 2005.

Subdivision (b)(1) is amended to delete the sentence requiring a disclosure that the debtor has not paid an attorney or other person in connection with the case. Inability to pay the filing fee in installments is one of the requirements for a fee waiver under the 2005 revisions to 28 U.S.C. § 1930(f). If the attorney payment prohibition were retained, payment of an attorney's fee would render many debtors ineligible for installment payments and thus enhance their eligibility for the fee waiver. The deletion of this prohibition from the rule, which was not statutorily required, ensures that debtors who have the financial ability to pay the fee in installments will do so rather than request a waiver.

Subdivision (b)(3) is amended in conformance with the changes to subdivision (b)(1) to reflect the 2005 amendments. The change is meant to clarify that subdivision (b)(3) refers to payments made after the debtor has filed the bankruptcy case and after the debtor has received permission to pay the fee in installments. Otherwise, the subdivision may conflict with the intent and effect of the amendments to subdivision (b)(1).

CROSS REFERENCES

District court; filing and miscellaneous fees; rules of court, see 28 USCA § 1914.

Enlargement of time for payment of filing fee installments permitted as limited under this rule, see Fed.Rules Bankr.Proc. Rule 9006, 11 USCA.

Specific amount of fee, see 28 USCA § 1930.

Rule 1007. Lists, Schedules, Statements, and Other Documents; Time Limits

(a) **Corporate ownership statement, list of creditors and equity security holders, and other lists**

   (1) **Voluntary case**

   In a voluntary case, the debtor shall file with the petition a list containing the name and address of each entity included or to be included on Schedules D, E, F, G, and H as prescribed by the Official Forms. If the debtor is a corporation, other than a governmental unit, the debtor shall file with the petition a corporate ownership statement containing the information described in Rule 7007.1. The debtor shall file a supplemental statement promptly upon any change in circumstances that renders the corporate ownership statement inaccurate.

   (2) **Involuntary case**

   In an involuntary case, the debtor shall file, within seven days after entry of the order for relief, a list containing the name and address of each entity included or to be included on Schedules D, E, F, G, and H as prescribed by the Official Forms.

   (3) **Equity security holders**

   In a chapter 11 reorganization case, unless the court orders otherwise, the debtor shall file within 14 days after entry of the order for relief a list of the debtor's equity security holders of each class showing the number and kind of interests registered in the name of each holder, and the last known address or place of business of each holder.

   (4) **Chapter 15 case**

   In addition to the documents required under § 1515 of the Code, a foreign representative filing a petition for recognition under chapter 15 shall file with the petition: (A) a corporate ownership statement containing the information described in Rule 7007.1; and (B) unless the court orders otherwise, a list containing the names and addresses of all persons or bodies authorized to administer foreign proceedings of the debtor, all parties to litigation pending in the United States in which the debtor is a party at the time of the filing of the petition, and all entities against whom provisional relief is being sought under § 1519 of the Code.

   (5) **Extension of time**

   Any extension of time for the filing of the lists required by this subdivision may be granted only on motion for cause shown and on notice to the United States trustee and to any trustee, committee elected under § 705 or appointed under § 1102 of the Code, or other party as the court may direct.

(b) **Schedules, statements, and other documents required**

   (1) Except in a chapter 9 municipality case, the debtor, unless the court orders otherwise, shall file the following schedules, statements, and other documents, prepared as prescribed by the appropriate Official Forms, if any:

   (A) schedules of assets and liabilities;

   (B) a schedule of current income and expenditures;

   (C) a schedule of executory contracts and unexpired leases;

   (D) a statement of financial affairs;

   (E) copies of all payment advices or other evidence of payment, if any, received by the debtor from an employer within 60 days before the filing of the petition, with redaction of all but the last four digits of the debtor's social-security number or individual taxpayer-identification number; and

   (F) a record of any interest that the debtor has in an account or program of the type specified in § 521(c) of the Code.

(2) An individual debtor in a chapter 7 case shall file a statement of intention as required by § 521(a) of the Code, prepared as prescribed by the appropriate Official Form. A copy of the statement of intention shall be served on the trustee and the creditors named in the statement on or before the filing of the statement.

(3) Unless the United States trustee has determined that the credit counseling requirement of § 109(h) does not apply in the district, an individual debtor must file a statement of compliance with the credit counseling requirement, prepared as prescribed by the appropriate Official Form which must include one of the following:

 (A) an attached certificate and debt repayment plan, if any, required by § 521(b);

 (B) a statement that the debtor has received the credit counseling briefing required by § 109(h)(1) but does not have the certificate required by § 521(b);

 (C) a certification under § 109(h)(3); or

 (D) a request for a determination by the court under § 109(h)(4).

(4) Unless § 707(b)(2)(D) applies, an individual debtor in a chapter 7 case shall file a statement of current monthly income prepared as prescribed by the appropriate Official Form, and, if the current monthly income exceeds the median family income for the applicable state and household size, the information, including calculations, required by § 707(b), prepared as prescribed by the appropriate Official Form.

(5) An individual debtor in a chapter 11 case shall file a statement of current monthly income, prepared as prescribed by the appropriate Official Form.

(6) A debtor in a chapter 13 case shall file a statement of current monthly income, prepared as prescribed by the appropriate Official Form, and, if the current monthly income exceeds the median family income for the applicable state and household size, a calculation of disposable income made in accordance with § 1325(b)(3), prepared as prescribed by the appropriate Official Form.

(7) Unless an approved provider of an instructional course concerning personal financial management has notified the court that a debtor has completed the course after filing the petition:

 (A) An individual debtor in a chapter 7 or chapter 13 case shall file a statement of completion of the course, prepared as prescribed by the appropriate Official Form; and

 (B) An individual debtor in a chapter 11 case shall file the statement if § 1141(d)(3) applies.

(8) If an individual debtor in a chapter 11, 12, or 13 case has claimed an exemption under § 522(b)(3)(A) in property of the kind described in § 522(p)(1) with a value in excess of the amount set out in § 522(q)(1), the debtor shall file a statement as to whether there is any proceeding pending in which the debtor may be found guilty of a felony of a kind described in § 522(q)(1)(A) or found liable for a debt of the kind described in § 522(q)(1)(B).

(c) Time limits

In a voluntary case, the schedules, statements, and other documents required by subdivision (b)(1), (4), (5), and (6) shall be filed with the petition or within 14 days thereafter, except as otherwise provided in subdivisions (d), (e), (f), and (h) of this rule. In an involuntary case, the schedules, statements, and other documents required by subdivision (b)(1) shall be filed by the debtor within 14 days after the entry of the order for relief. In a voluntary case, the documents required by paragraphs (A), (C), and (D) of subdivision (b)(3) shall be filed with the petition. Unless the court orders otherwise, a debtor who has filed a statement under subdivision (b)(3)(B), shall file the documents required by subdivision (b)(3)(A) within 14 days of the order for relief. In a chapter 7 case, the debtor shall file the statement required by subdivision (b)(7) within 60 days after the first date set for the meeting of creditors under § 341 of the Code, and in a chapter 11 or 13 case no later than the date when the last payment was made by the debtor as required by the plan or the filing of a motion for a discharge under § 1141(d)(5)(B) or § 1328(b) of the Code. The court may, at any time and in its discretion, enlarge the time to file the statement required by subdivision (b)(7). The debtor

Rule 1007   **BANKRUPTCY RULES**

shall file the statement required by subdivision (b)(8) no earlier than the date of the last payment made under the plan or the date of the filing of a motion for a discharge under §§[1] 1141(d)(5)(B), 1228(b), or 1328(b) of the Code. Lists, schedules, statements, and other documents filed prior to the conversion of a case to another chapter shall be deemed filed in the converted case unless the court directs otherwise. Except as provided in § 1116(3), any extension of time to file schedules, statements, and other documents required under this rule may be granted only on motion for cause shown and on notice to the United States trustee, any committee elected under § 705 or appointed under § 1102 of the Code, trustee, examiner, or other party as the court may direct. Notice of an extension shall be given to the United States trustee and to any committee, trustee, or other party as the court may direct.

(d) List of 20 largest creditors in chapter 9 municipality case or chapter 11 reorganization case

In addition to the list required by subdivision (a) of this rule, a debtor in a chapter 9 municipality case or a debtor in a voluntary chapter 11 reorganization case shall file with the petition a list containing the name, address and claim of the creditors that hold the 20 largest unsecured claims, excluding insiders, as prescribed by the appropriate Official Form. In an involuntary chapter 11 reorganization case, such list shall be filed by the debtor within 2 days after entry of the order for relief under § 303(h) of the Code.

(e) List in chapter 9 municipality cases

The list required by subdivision (a) of this rule shall be filed by the debtor in a chapter 9 municipality case within such time as the court shall fix. If a proposed plan requires a revision of assessments so that the proportion of special assessments or special taxes to be assessed against some real property will be different from the proportion in effect at the date the petition is filed, the debtor shall also file a list showing the name and address of each known holder of title, legal or equitable, to real property adversely affected. On motion for cause shown, the court may modify the requirements of this subdivision and subdivision (a) of this rule.

(f) Statement of social security number

An individual debtor shall submit a verified statement that sets out the debtor's social security number, or states that the debtor does not have a social security number. In a voluntary case, the debtor shall submit the statement with the petition. In an involuntary case, the debtor shall submit the statement within 14 days after the entry of the order for relief.

(g) Partnership and partners

The general partners of a debtor partnership shall prepare and file the list required under subdivision (a), the schedules of the assets and liabilities, schedule of current income and expenditures, schedule of executory contracts and unexpired leases, and statement of financial affairs of the partnership. The court may order any general partner to file a statement of personal assets and liabilities within such time as the court may fix.

(h) Interests acquired or arising after petition

If, as provided by § 541(a)(5) of the Code, the debtor acquires or becomes entitled to acquire any interest in property, the debtor shall within 14 days after the information comes to the debtor's knowledge or within such further time the court may allow, file a supplemental schedule in the chapter 7 liquidation case, chapter 11 reorganization case, chapter 12 family farmer's debt adjustment case, or chapter 13 individual debt adjustment case. If any of the property required to be reported under this subdivision is claimed by the debtor as exempt, the debtor shall claim the exemptions in the supplemental schedule. The duty to file a supplemental schedule in accordance with this subdivision continues notwithstanding the closing of the case, except that the schedule need not be filed in a chapter 11, chapter 12, or chapter 13 case with respect to property acquired after entry of the order confirming a chapter 11 plan or discharging the debtor in a chapter 12 or chapter 13 case.

---

[1] So in original. Probably should be only one section symbol.

COMMENCEMENT OF CASE Rule 1007

(i) Disclosure of list of security holders

After notice and hearing and for cause shown, the court may direct an entity other than the debtor or trustee to disclose any list of security holders of the debtor in its possession or under its control, indicating the name, address and security held by any of them. The entity possessing this list may be required either to produce the list or a true copy thereof, or permit inspection or copying, or otherwise disclose the information contained on the list.

(j) Impounding of lists

On motion of a party in interest and for cause shown the court may direct the impounding of the lists filed under this rule, and may refuse to permit inspection by any entity. The court may permit inspection or use of the lists, however, by any party in interest on terms prescribed by the court.

(k) Preparation of list, schedules, or statements on default of debtor

If a list, schedule, or statement, other than a statement of intention, is not prepared and filed as required by this rule, the court may order the trustee, a petitioning creditor, committee, or other party to prepare and file any of these papers within a time fixed by the court. The court may approve reimbursement of the cost incurred in complying with such an order as an administrative expense.

(l) Transmission to United States trustee

The clerk shall forthwith transmit to the United States trustee a copy of every list, schedule, and statement filed pursuant to subdivision (a)(1), (a)(2), (b), (d), or (h) of this rule.

(m) Infants and incompetent persons

If the debtor knows that a person on the list of creditors or schedules is an infant or incompetent person, the debtor also shall include the name, address, and legal relationship of any person upon whom process would be served in an adversary proceeding against the infant or incompetent person in accordance with Rule 7004(b)(2).

(As amended Mar. 30, 1987, eff. Aug. 1, 1987; Apr. 30, 1991, eff. Aug. 1, 1991; Apr. 23, 1996, eff. Dec. 1, 1996; Apr. 23, 2001, eff. Dec. 1, 2001; Mar. 27, 2003, eff. Dec. 1, 2003; Apr. 25, 2005, eff. Dec. 1, 2005; Apr. 23, 2008, eff. Dec. 1, 2008; Mar. 26, 2009, eff. Dec. 1, 2009; Apr. 28, 2010, eff. Dec. 1, 2010; Apr. 23, 2012, eff. Dec. 1, 2012; Apr. 16, 2013, eff. Dec. 1, 2013.)

ADVISORY COMMITTEE NOTES
1983 Enactments

This rule is an adaptation of former Rules 108, 8–106, 10–108 and 11–11. As specified in the rule, it is applicable in all types of cases filed under the Code.

Subdivision (a) requires at least a list of creditors with their names and addresses to be filed with the petition. This list is needed for notice of the meeting of creditors (Rule 2002) and notice of the order for relief (§ 342 of the Code). The list will also serve to meet the requirements of § 521(1) of the Code. Subdivision (a) recognizes that it may be impossible to file the schedules required by § 521(1) and subdivision (b) of the rule at the time the petition is filed but in order for the case to proceed expeditiously and efficiently it is necessary that the clerk have the names and addresses of creditors. It should be noted that subdivision (d) of the rule requires a special list of the 20 largest unsecured creditors in chapter 9 and 11 cases. That list is for the purpose of selecting a committee of unsecured creditors.

Subdivision (b) is derived from former Rule 11–11 and conforms with § 521. This subdivision indicates the forms to be used. The court may dispense with the filing of schedules and the statement of affairs pursuant to § 521.

Subdivisions (c) and (f) specify the time periods for filing the papers required by the rule as well as the number of copies. The provisions dealing with an involuntary case are derived from former Bankruptcy Rule 108. Under the Code, a chapter 11 case may be commenced by an involuntary petition (§ 303(a)), whereas under the Act [former Title 11], a Chapter XI [former § 1101 et seq. of this title] case could have been commenced only by a voluntary petition. A motion for an extension of time to file the schedules and statements is required to be made on notice to parties, as the court may direct, including a creditors' committee if one has been appointed under § 1102 of the Code and a trustee or examiner if one has been appointed pursuant to § 1104 of the Code. Although written notice is preferable, it is not required by the rule; in proper circumstances the notice may be by telephone or otherwise.

Subdivision (d) is new and requires that a list of the 20 largest unsecured creditors, excluding insiders as defined in § 101(25) of the Code, be filed with the petition. The court, pursuant to § 1102 of the Code, is required to appoint a committee of unsecured creditors as soon as practicable after the order for relief. That committee generally is to consist of the seven largest unsecured creditors who are willing to serve. The list should, as indicated on Official Form No. 9, specify the nature and amount of the claim. It is important for the court to be aware of the different types of claims existing in the case and this form should supply such information.

Subdivision (e) applies only in chapter 9 municipality cases. It gives greater discretion to the court to determine the time for filing a list of creditors and any other matter related to the list. A list of creditors must at some point be filed since one is required by § 924 of the Code. When the plan affects special assessments, the definitions in § 902(2) and (3) for "special tax payer" and "special tax payer affected by the plan" become relevant.

Subdivision (g) is derived from former Rules 108(c) and 11–11. Nondebtor general partners are liable to the partnership's trustee for any deficiency in the partnership's estate to pay creditors in full as provided by § 723 of the Code. Subdivision (g) authorizes the court to require a partner to file a statement of personal assets and liabilities to provide the trustee with the relevant information.

Subdivision (h) is derived from former Bankruptcy Rule 108(e) for chapter 7, 11 and 13 purposes. It implements the provisions in and language of § 541(a)(5) of the Code.

Subdivisions (i) and (j) are adapted from §§ 165 and 166 of the Act [former §§ 565 and 566 of this title] and former Rule 10–108(b) and (c) without change in substance. The term "party in interest" is not defined in the Code or the rules, but reference may be made to § 1109(b) of the Code. In the context of this subdivision, the term would include the debtor, the trustee, any indenture trustee, creditor, equity security holder or committee appointed pursuant to § 1102 of the Code.

Subdivision (k) is derived from former Rules 108(d) and 10–108(a).

1987 Amendments

Subdivisions (b), (c), and (g) are amended to provide for the filing of a schedule of current income and current expenditures and the individual debtor's statement of intention. These documents are required by the 1984 amendments to § 521 of the Code. Official Form No. 6A is prescribed for use by an individual debtor for filing a schedule of current income and current expenditures in a chapter 7 or chapter 11 case. Although a partnership or corporation is also required by § 521(1) to file a schedule of current income and current expenditures, no Official Form is prescribed therefor.

The time for filing the statement of intention is governed by § 521(2)(A). A copy of the statement of intention must be served on the trustee and the creditors named in the statement within the same time. The provisions of subdivision (c) governing the time for filing when a chapter 11 or chapter 13 case is converted to a chapter 7 case have been omitted from subdivision (c) as amended. Filing after conversion is now governed exclusively by Rule 1019.

Subdivision (f) has been abrogated. The number of copies of the documents required by this rule will be determined by local rule.

Subdivision (h) is amended to include a direct reference to § 541(a)(5).

Subdivision (k) provides that the court may not order an entity other than the debtor to prepare and file the statement of intention.

1991 Amendments

References to Official Form numbers and to the Chapter 13 Statement are deleted and subdivision (b) is amended in anticipation of future revision and renumbering of the Official Forms. The debtor in a chapter 12 or chapter 13 case shall file the list, schedules and statements required in subdivisions (a)(1), (b)(1), and (h). It is expected that the information currently provided in the Chapter 13 Statement will be included in the schedules and statements as revised not later than the effective date of these rule amendments.

Subdivisions (a)(4) and (c) are amended to provide the United States trustee with notice of any motion to extend the time for the filing of any lists, schedules, or statements. Such notice enables the

United States trustee to take appropriate steps to avoid undue delay in the administration of the case. See 28 U.S.C. § 586(a)(3)(G). Subdivisions (a)(4) and (c) are amended further to provide notice to committees elected under § 705 or appointed pursuant to § 1102 of the Code. Committees of retired employees appointed pursuant to § 1114 are not included.

The additions of references to unexpired leases in subdivisions (b)(1) and (g) indicate that the schedule requires the inclusion of unexpired leases as well as other executory contracts.

The words "with the court" in subdivisions (b)(1), (e), and (g) are deleted as unnecessary. See Rules 5005(a) and 9001(3).

Subdivision (l), which is derived from Rule X–1002(a), provides the United States trustee with the information required to perform certain administrative duties such as the appointment of a committee of unsecured creditors. In a chapter 7 case, the United States trustee should be aware of the debtor's intention with respect to collateral that secures a consumer debt so that the United States trustee may monitor the progress of the case. Pursuant to § 307 of the Code, the United States trustee has standing to raise, appear and be heard on issues and the lists, schedules and statements contain information that, when provided to the United States trustee, enable that office to participate effectively in the case. The United States trustee has standing to move to dismiss a chapter 7 or 13 case for failure to file timely the list, schedules or statement required by § 521(l) of the Code. See §§ 707(a)(3) and 1307(c)(9). It is therefore necessary for the United States trustee to receive notice of any extension of time to file such documents. Upon request, the United States trustee also may receive from the trustee or debtor in possession a list of equity security holders.

1996 Amendments

Subdivision (c) is amended to provide that schedules and statements filed prior to the conversion of a case to another chapter shall be deemed filed in the converted case, whether or not the case was a chapter 7 case prior to conversion. This amendment is in recognition of the 1991 amendments to the Official Forms that abrogated the Chapter 13 Statement and made the same forms for schedules and statements applicable in all cases.

This subdivision also contains a technical correction. The phrase "superseded case" creates the erroneous impression that conversion of a case results in a new case that is distinct from the original case. The effect of conversion of a case is governed by § 348 of the Code.

2001 Amendments

Subdivision (m) is added to enable the person required to mail notices under Rule 2002 to mail them to the appropriate guardian or other representative when the debtor knows that a creditor or other person listed is an infant or incompetent person.

The proper mailing address of the representative is determined in accordance with Rule 7004(b)(2), which requires mailing to the person's dwelling house or usual place of abode or at the place where the person regularly conducts a business or profession.

2003 Amendments

This rule is amended to require the debtor to file a corporate ownership statement setting out the information described in Rule 7007.1. Requiring debtors to file the statement provides the court with an opportunity to make judicial disqualification determinations at the outset of the case. This could reduce problems later in the case by preventing the initial assignment of the case to a judge who holds a financial interest in a parent company of the debtor or some other entity that holds a significant ownership interest in the debtor. Moreover, by including the disclosure statement filing requirement at the commencement of the case, the debtor does not have to make the same disclosure filing each time it is involved in an adversary proceeding throughout the case. The debtor also must file supplemental statements as changes in ownership might arise.

The rule is amended to add a requirement that a debtor submit a statement setting out the debtor's social security number. The addition is necessary because of the corresponding amendment to Rule 1005 which now provides that the caption of the petition includes only the final four digits of the debtor's social security number. The debtor submits the statement, but it is not filed, nor is it included in the case file. The statement provides the information necessary to include on the service copy of the notice required under Rule 2002(a)(1). It will also provide the information to facilitate the ability of creditors to search the court record by a search of a social security number already in the creditor's possession.

Rule 1007   BANKRUPTCY RULES

2005 Amendments

Notice to creditors and other parties in interest is essential to the operation of the bankruptcy system. Sending notice requires a convenient listing of the names and addresses of the entities to whom notice must be sent, and virtually all of the bankruptcy courts have adopted a local rule requiring the submission of a list of these entities with the petition and in a particular format. These lists are commonly called the "mailing matrix."

Given the universal adoption of these local rules, the need for such lists in all cases is apparent. Consequently, the rule is amended to require the debtor to submit such a list at the commencement of the case. This list may be amended when necessary. See Rule 1009(a).

The content of the list is described by reference to Schedules D through H of the Official Forms rather than by reference to creditors or persons holding claims. The cross reference to the Schedules as the source of the names for inclusion in the list ensures that persons such as codebtors or nondebtor parties to executory contracts and unexpired leases will receive appropriate notices in the case.

While this rule renders unnecessary, in part, local rules on the subject, this rule does not direct any particular format or form for the list to take. Local rules still may govern those particulars of the list.

Subdivision (c) is amended to reflect that subdivision (a)(1) no longer requires the debtor to file a schedule of liabilities with the petition in lieu of a list of creditors. The filing of the list is mandatory, and subdivision (b) of the rule requires the filing of schedules. Thus, subdivision (c) no longer needs to account for the possibility that the debtor can delay filing a schedule of liabilities when the petition is accompanied by a list of creditors. Subdivision (c) simply addresses the situation in which the debtor does not file schedules or statements with the petition, and the procedure for seeking an extension of time for filing.

Other changes are stylistic.

2008 Amendments

The title of this rule is expanded to refer to "documents" in conformity with the 2005 amendments to § 521 and related provisions of the Bankruptcy Code that include a wider range of documentary requirements.

Subdivision (a) is amended to require that any foreign representative filing a petition for recognition to commence a case under chapter 15, which was added to the Code in 2005, file a list of entities with whom the debtor is engaged in litigation in the United States. The foreign representative filing the petition for recognition must also list any entities against whom provisional relief is being sought as well as all persons or bodies authorized to administer foreign proceedings of the debtor. This should ensure that entities most interested in the case, or their representatives, will receive notice of the petition under Rule 2002(q).

Subdivision (a)(4) is amended to require the foreign representative who files a petition for recognition under chapter 15 to file the documents described in § 1515 of the Code as well as a corporate ownership statement. The subdivision is also amended to identify the foreign representative in language that more closely follows the text of the Code. Former subdivision (a)(4) is renumbered as subdivision (a)(5) and stylistic changes were made to the subdivision.

Subdivision (b)(1) addresses schedules, statements, and other documents that the debtor must file unless the court orders otherwise and other than in a case under chapter 9. This subdivision is amended to include documentary requirements added by the 2005 amendments to § 521 that apply to the same group of debtors and have the same time limits as the existing requirements of (b)(1). Consistent with the E-Government Act of 2002, Pub. L. No. 107–347, the payment advices should be redacted before they are filed.

Subdivision (b)(2) is amended to conform to the renumbering of the subsections of § 521.

Subdivisions (b)(3) through (b)(8) are new and implement the 2005 amendments to the Code. Subdivision (b)(3) provides for the filing of a document relating to the credit counseling requirement provided by the 2005 amendments to § 109 in the context of an Official Form that warns the debtor of the consequences of failing to comply with the credit counseling requirement.

Subdivision (b)(4) addresses the filing of information about current monthly income, as defined in § 101, for certain chapter 7 debtors and, if required, additional calculations of expenses required by the 2005 amendments to § 707(b).

Subdivision (b)(5) addresses the filing of information about current monthly income, as defined in § 101, for individual chapter 11 debtors. The 2005 amendments to § 1129(a)(15) condition plan confirmation for individual debtors on the commitment of disposable income, as defined in § 1325(b)(2), which is based on current monthly income.

Subdivision (b)(6) addresses the filing of information about current monthly income, as defined in § 101, for chapter 13 debtors and, if required, additional calculations of expenses. These changes are necessary because the 2005 amendments to § 1325 require that the determination of disposable income begin with current monthly income.

Subdivision (b)(7) reflects the 2005 amendments to §§ 727 and 1328 of the Code that condition the receipt of a discharge on the completion of a personal financial management course, with certain exceptions. Certain individual chapter 11 debtors may also be required to complete a personal financial management course under § 727(a)(11) as incorporated by § 1141(d)(3)(C). To evidence compliance with that requirement, the subdivision requires the debtor to file the appropriate Official Form certifying that the debtor has completed the personal financial management course.

Subdivision (b)(8) requires an individual debtor in a case under chapter 11, 12, or 13 to file a statement that there are no reasonable grounds to believe that the restrictions on a homestead exemption as set out in § 522(q) of the Code are applicable. Sections 1141(d)(5)(C), 1228(f), and 1328(h) each provide that the court shall not enter a discharge order unless it finds that there is no reasonable cause to believe that § 522(q) applies. Requiring the debtor to submit a statement to that effect in cases under chapters 11, 12, and 13 in which an exemption is claimed in excess of the amount allowed under § 522(q)(1) provides the court with a basis to conclude, in the absence of any contrary information, that § 522(q) does not apply. Creditors receive notice under Rule 2002(f)(11) of the time to request postponement of the entry of the discharge to permit an opportunity to challenge the debtor's assertions in the Rule 1007(b)(8) statement in appropriate cases.

Subdivision (c) is amended to include time limits for the filing requirements added to subdivision (b) due to the 2005 amendments to the Code, and to make conforming amendments. Separate time limits are provided for the documentation of credit counseling and for the statement of the completion of the financial management course. While most documents relating to credit counseling must be filed with the voluntary petition, the credit counseling certificate and debt repayment plan can be filed within 15 days of the filing of a voluntary petition if the debtor files a statement under subdivision (b)(3)(B) with the petition. Sections 727(a)(11), 1141(d)(3), and 1328(g) of the Code require individual debtors to complete a personal financial management course prior to the entry of a discharge. The amendment allows the court to enlarge the deadline for the debtor to file the statement of completion. Because no party is harmed by the enlargement, no specific restriction is placed on the court's discretion to enlarge the deadline, even after its expiration.

Subdivision (c) of the rule is also amended to recognize the limitation on the extension of time to file schedules and statements when the debtor is a small business debtor. Section 1116(3), added to the Code in 2005, establishes a specific standard for courts to apply in the event that the debtor in possession or the trustee seeks an extension for filing these forms for a period beyond 30 days after the order for relief.

2009 Amendments

The rule is amended to implement changes in connection with the amendment to Rule 9006(a) and the manner by which time is computed under the rules. Each deadline in the rule of fewer than 30 days is amended to substitute a deadline that is a multiple of seven days. Throughout the rules, deadlines are amended in the following manner:

- 5-day periods become 7-day periods
- 10-day periods become 14-day periods
- 15-day periods become 14-day periods
- 20-day periods become 21-day periods
- 25-day periods become 28-day periods

2010 Amendments

Subdivision (a)(2). Subdivision (a)(2) is amended to shorten the time for a debtor to file a list of the creditors included on the various schedules filed or to be filed in the case. This list provides the information necessary for the clerk to provide notice of the § 341 meeting of creditors in a timely manner.

Subdivision (c). Subdivision (c) is amended to provide additional time for individual debtors in chapter 7 to file the statement of completion of a course in personal financial management. This change is made in conjunction with an amendment to Rule 5009 requiring the clerk to provide notice to debtors of the consequences of not filing the statement in a timely manner.

2012 Amendments

Subdivision (c). In subdivision (c), the time limit for a debtor in an involuntary case to file the list required by subdivision (a)(2) is deleted as unnecessary. Subdivision (a)(2) provides that the list must be filed within seven days after the entry of the order for relief. The other change to subdivision (c) is stylistic.

Because this amendment is being made to conform to an amendment to Rule 1007(a)(2) that took effect on December 1, 2010, final approval is sought without publication.

2013 Amendments

Subdivision (b)(7) is amended to relieve an individual debtor of the obligation to file a statement of completion of a personal financial management course if the course provider notifies the court that the debtor has completed the course. Course providers approved under § 111 of the Code may be permitted to file this notification electronically with the court immediately upon the debtor's completion of the course. If the provider does not notify the court, the debtor must file the statement, prepared as prescribed by the appropriate Official Form, within the time period specified by subdivision (c).

CROSS REFERENCES

Committee of seven unsecured creditors appointed in reorganization case, see 11 USCA § 1102.

Compliance with this rule upon conversion to liquidation case, see Fed.Rules Bankr.Proc. Rule 1019, 11 USCA.

Duty of debtor to—

    Inform trustee as to property location and name and address of money and property obligors, see Fed.Rules Bankr.Proc. Rule 4002, 11 USCA.

    Prepare and file schedule and statement, see 11 USCA § 521.

Enlargement of time for filing list of twenty largest unsecured creditors not permitted, see Fed.Rules Bankr.Proc. Rule 9006, 11 USCA.

Filing of proof of interest by equity security holder obviated by list filed by debtor, see Fed.Rules Bankr.Proc. Rule 3003, 11 USCA.

Immunity from self-incrimination, see 11 USCA § 344.

Insider for purposes of list of 20 unsecured claims defined, see 11 USCA § 101.

List of exempt property to be filed—

    By dependent of debtor, see Fed.Rules Bankr.Proc. Rule 4003, 11 USCA.

    With schedule of assets, see Fed.Rules Bankr.Proc. Rule 4003, 11 USCA.

Motions; form and service, see Fed.Rules Bankr.Proc. Rule 9013, 11 USCA.

Notice required for—

    Creditors' meetings, see Fed.Rules Bankr.Proc. Rule 2002, 11 USCA.

    Order for relief, see 11 USCA § 342.

Rule 1008. Verification of Petitions and Accompanying Papers

All petitions, lists, schedules, statements and amendments thereto shall be verified or contain an unsworn declaration as provided in 28 U.S.C. § 1746.

(As amended Apr. 30, 1991, eff. Aug. 1, 1991.)

COMMENCEMENT OF CASE — Rule 1009

ADVISORY COMMITTEE NOTES

This rule retains the requirement under the Bankruptcy Act [former Title 11] and rules that petitions and accompanying papers must be verified. Only the original need be signed and verified, but the copies must be conformed to the original. See Rule 9011(c).

The verification may be replaced by an unsworn declaration as provided in 28 U.S.C. § 1746. See also, Official Form No. 1 and Advisory Committee Note.

1991 Amendments

The amendments to this rule are stylistic.

CROSS REFERENCES

Signing and verification of papers, see Fed.Rules Bankr.Proc. Rule 9011, 11 USCA.

Rule 1009. Amendments of Voluntary Petitions, Lists, Schedules and Statements

(a) General right to amend

A voluntary petition, list, schedule, or statement may be amended by the debtor as a matter of course at any time before the case is closed. The debtor shall give notice of the amendment to the trustee and to any entity affected thereby. On motion of a party in interest, after notice and a hearing, the court may order any voluntary petition, list, schedule, or statement to be amended and the clerk shall give notice of the amendment to entities designated by the court.

(b) Statement of intention

The statement of intention may be amended by the debtor at any time before the expiration of the period provided in § 521(a) of the Code. The debtor shall give notice of the amendment to the trustee and to any entity affected thereby.

(c) Statement of social security number

If a debtor becomes aware that the statement of social security number submitted under Rule 1007(f) is incorrect, the debtor shall promptly submit an amended verified statement setting forth the correct social security number. The debtor shall give notice of the amendment to all of the entities required to be included on the list filed under Rule 1007(a)(1) or (a)(2).

(d) Transmission to United States trustee

The clerk shall promptly transmit to the United States trustee a copy of every amendment filed or submitted under subdivision (a), (b), or (c) of this rule.

(As amended Mar. 30, 1987, eff. Aug. 1, 1987; Apr. 30, 1991, eff. Aug. 1, 1991; Apr. 12, 2006, eff. Dec. 1, 2006; Apr. 23, 2008, eff. Dec. 1, 2008.)

ADVISORY COMMITTEE NOTES

This rule continues the permissive approach adopted by former Bankruptcy Rule 110 to amendments of voluntary petitions and accompanying papers. Notice of any amendment is required to be given to the trustee. This is particularly important with respect to any amendment of the schedule of property affecting the debtor's claim of exemptions. Notice of any amendment of the schedule of liabilities is to be given to any creditor whose claim is changed or newly listed.

The rule does not continue the provision permitting the court to order an amendment on its own initiative. Absent a request in some form by a party in interest, the court should not be involved in administrative matters affecting the estate.

If a list or schedule is amended to include an additional creditor, the effect on the dischargeability of the creditor's claim is governed by the provisions of § 523(a)(3) of the Code.

1987 Amendments

Subdivision (a) is amended to require notice and a hearing in the event a party in interest other than the debtor seeks to amend. The number of copies of the amendment will be determined by local rule of court.

Subdivision (b) is added to treat amendments of the statement of intention separately from other amendments. The intention of the individual debtor must be performed within 45 days of the filing of the statement, unless the court extends the period. Subdivision (b) limits the time for amendment to the time for performance under § 521(2)(B) of the Code or any extension granted by the court.

1991 Amendments

The amendments to subdivision (a) are stylistic.

Subdivision (c) is derived from Rule X–1002(a) and is designed to provide the United States trustee with current information to enable that office to participate effectively in the case.

2006 Amendments

Subdivision (c). Rule 2002(a)(1) provides that the notice of the § 341 meeting of creditors include the debtor's social security number. It provides creditors with the full number while limiting publication of the social security number otherwise to the final four digits of the number to protect the debtor's identity from others who do not have the same need for that information. If, however, the social security number that the debtor submitted under Rule 1007(f) is incorrect, then the only notice to the entities contained on the list filed under Rule 1007(a)(1) or (a)(2) would be incorrect. This amendment adds a new subdivision (c) that directs the debtor to submit a verified amended statement of social security number and to give notice of the new statement to all entities in the case who received the notice containing the erroneous social security number.

Subdivision (d). Former subdivision (c) becomes subdivision (d) and is amended to include new subdivision (c) amendments in the list of documents that the clerk must transmit to the United States trustee.

Other amendments are stylistic.

2008 Amendments

Subdivision (b) is amended to conform to the 2005 amendments to § 521 of the Code.

CROSS REFERENCES

Dischargeability of debts added to list or schedule, see 11 USCA § 523.

Motions; form and service, see Fed.Rules Bankr.Proc. Rule 9013, 11 USCA.

Amended and supplemental pleadings, see Fed.Rules Civ.Proc. Rule 15, 28 USCA.

Rule 1010. Service of Involuntary Petition and Summons; Petition for Recognition of a Foreign Nonmain Proceeding

(a) Service of involuntary petition and summons; service of petition for recognition of foreign nonmain proceeding

On the filing of an involuntary petition or a petition for recognition of a foreign nonmain proceeding, the clerk shall forthwith issue a summons for service. When an involuntary petition is filed, service shall be made on the debtor. When a petition for recognition of a foreign nonmain proceeding is filed, service shall be made on the debtor, any entity against whom provisional relief is sought under § 1519 of the Code, and on any other party as the court may direct. The summons shall be served with a copy of the petition in the manner provided for service of a summons and complaint by Rule 7004(a) or (b). If service cannot be so made, the court may order that the summons and petition be served by mailing copies to the party's last known address, and by at least one publication in a manner and form directed by the court. The summons and petition may be served on the party anywhere. Rule 7004(e) and Rule 4(l) F.R.Civ.P. apply when service is made or attempted under this rule.

COMMENCEMENT OF CASE — Rule 1010

(b) Corporate ownership statement

Each petitioner that is a corporation shall file with the involuntary petition a corporate ownership statement containing the information described in Rule 7007.1.

(As amended Mar. 30, 1987, eff. Aug. 1, 1987; Apr. 30, 1991, eff. Aug. 1, 1991; Apr. 22, 1993, eff. Aug. 1, 1993; Apr. 11, 1997, eff. Dec. 1, 1997; Apr. 23, 2008, eff. Dec. 1, 2008.)

ADVISORY COMMITTEE NOTES

This rule provides the procedure for service of the involuntary petition and summons. It does not deal with service of a summons and complaint instituting an adversary proceeding pursuant to Part VII.

While this rule is similar to former Bankruptcy Rule 111, it substitutes the clerk of the bankruptcy court for the clerk of the district court as the person who is to issue the summons.

The modes of service prescribed by the rule are personal or by mail, when service can be effected in one of these ways in the United States. Such service is to be made in the manner prescribed in adversary proceedings by Rule 7004(a) and (b). If service must be made in a foreign country, the mode of service is one of that set forth in Rule 4(i) F.R.Civ.P.

When the method set out in Rule 7004(a) and (b) cannot be utilized, service by publication coupled with mailing to the last known address is authorized. Cf. Rule 7004(c). The court determines the form and manner of publication as provided in Rule 9007. The publication need not set out the petition or the order directing service by publication. In order to apprise the debtor fairly, however, the publication should include all the information required to be in the summons by Official Form No. 13 and a notice indicating how service is being effected and how a copy of the petition may be obtained.

There are no territorial limits on the service authorized by this rule, which continues the practice under the former rules and Act. There must, however, be a basis for jurisdiction pursuant to § 109(a) of the Code for the court to order relief. Venue provisions are set forth in 28 U.S.C. § 1472.

Subdivision (f) of Rule 7004 and subdivisions (g) and (h) of Rule 4 F.R.Civ.P. govern time and proof of service and amendment of process or of proof of service.

Rule 1004 provides for transmission to nonpetitioning partners of a petition filed against the partnership by fewer than all the general partners.

1987 Amendments

The rule has been broadened to include service of a petition commencing a case ancillary to a foreign proceeding, previously included in Rule 1003(e)(2).

1991 Amendments

Reference to the Official Form number is deleted in anticipation of future revision and renumbering of the Official Forms.

Rule 4(g) and (h) F.R.Civ.P. made applicable by this rule refers to Rule 4(g) and (h) F.R.Civ.P. in effect on January 1, 1990, notwithstanding any subsequent amendment thereto. See Rule 7004(g).

1993 Amendments

This rule is amended to delete the reference to the Official Form. The Official Form for the summons was abrogated in 1991. Other amendments are stylistic and make no substantive change.

1997 Amendments

The amendments to this rule are technical, are promulgated solely to conform to changes in subdivision designations in Rule 4, F.R.Civ.P., and in Rule 7004, and are not intended to effectuate any material change in substance.

In 1996, the letter designation of subdivision (f) of Rule 7004 (Summons; Time Limit for Service) was changed to subdivision (e). In 1993, the provisions of Rule 4, F.R.Civ.P., relating to proof of service contained in Rule 4(g) (Return) and Rule 4(h) (Amendments), were placed in the new subdivision (l) of Rule 4 (Proof of Service). The technical amendments to Rule 1010 are designed solely to conform to these new subdivision designations.

The 1996 amendments to Rule 7004 and the 1993 amendments to Rule 4, F.R.Civ.P., have not affected the availability of service by first class mail in accordance with Rule 7004(b) for the service of a summons and petition in an involuntary case commenced under § 303 or an ancillary case commenced under § 304 of the Code.

2008 Amendments

This rule is amended to implement the 2005 amendments to the Code, which repealed § 304 and replaced it with chapter 15 governing ancillary and other cross-border cases. Under chapter 15, a foreign representative commences a case by filing a petition for recognition of a pending foreign nonmain proceeding. The amendment requires service of the summons and petition on the debtor and any entity against whom the representative is seeking provisional relief. Until the court enters a recognition order under § 1517, no stay is in effect unless the court enters some form of provisional relief under § 1519. Thus, only those entities against whom specific provisional relief is sought need to be served. The court may, however, direct that service be made on additional entities as appropriate.

This rule does not apply to a petition for recognition of a foreign main proceeding.

The rule is also amended by renumbering the prior rule as subdivision (a) and adding a new subdivision (b) requiring any corporate creditor that files or joins an involuntary petition to file a corporate ownership statement.

CROSS REFERENCES

Applicability of this rule to—

> Involuntary case ancillary to foreign proceeding, see Fed.Rules Bankr.Proc. Rule 1003, 11 USCA.
>
> Involuntary partnership petitions, see Fed.Rules Bankr.Proc. Rule 1004, 11 USCA.

Form and manner of service by publication, see Fed.Rules Bankr.Proc. Rules 9007 and 9008, 11 USCA.

Jurisdictional basis for service, see 11 USCA § 109.

Process, see Fed.Rules Civ.Proc. Rule 4, 28 USCA.

Rule 1011. Responsive Pleading or Motion in Involuntary and Cross-Border Cases

(a) Who may contest petition

The debtor named in an involuntary petition, or a party in interest to a petition for recognition of a foreign proceeding, may contest the petition. In the case of a petition against a partnership under Rule 1004, a nonpetitioning general partner, or a person who is alleged to be a general partner but denies the allegation, may contest the petition.

(b) Defenses and objections; when presented

Defenses and objections to the petition shall be presented in the manner prescribed by Rule 12 F.R.Civ.P. and shall be filed and served within 21 days after service of the summons, except that if service is made by publication on a party or partner not residing or found within the state in which the court sits, the court shall prescribe the time for filing and serving the response.

(c) Effect of motion

Service of a motion under Rule 12(b) F.R.Civ.P. shall extend the time for filing and serving a responsive pleading as permitted by Rule 12(a) F.R.Civ.P.

(d) Claims against petitioners

A claim against a petitioning creditor may not be asserted in the answer except for the purpose of defeating the petition.

(e) Other pleadings

No other pleadings shall be permitted, except that the court may order a reply to an answer and prescribe the time for filing and service.

COMMENCEMENT OF CASE   Rule 1011

(f)   Corporate ownership statement

If the entity responding to the involuntary petition or the petition for recognition of a foreign proceeding is a corporation, the entity shall file with its first appearance, pleading, motion, response, or other request addressed to the court a corporate ownership statement containing the information described in Rule 7007.1.

(As amended Mar. 30, 1987, eff. Aug. 1, 1987; Apr. 26, 2004, eff. Dec. 1, 2004; Apr. 23, 2008, eff. Dec. 1, 2008; Mar. 26, 2009, eff. Dec. 1, 2009.)

ADVISORY COMMITTEE NOTES

This rule is derived from former Bankruptcy Rule 112. A petition filed by fewer than all the general partners under Rule 1004(b) to have an order for relief entered with respect to the partnership is referred to as a petition against the partnership because of the adversary character of the proceeding it commences. Cf. § 303(b)(3) of the Code; 2 Collier Bankruptcy ¶303.05[5][a] (15th ed.1981); id. ¶¶18.33[2], 18.46 (14th ed.1966). One who denies an allegation of membership in the firm is nevertheless recognized as a party entitled to contest a petition filed against a partnership under subdivision (b) of Rule 1004 in view of the possible consequences to him of an order for relief against the entity alleged to include him as a member. See § 723 of the Code; Francis v. McNeal, 228 U.S. 695 (1913); Manson v. Williams, 213 U.S. 453 (1909); Carter v. Whisler, 275 Fed. 743, 746–747 (8th Cir.1921). The rule preserves the features of the former Act and Rule 112 and the Code permitting no response by creditors to an involuntary petition or petition against a partnership under rule 1004(b).

Subdivision (b): Rule 12 F.R.Civ.P. has been looked to by the courts as prescribing the mode of making a defense or objection to a petition in bankruptcy. See Fada of New York, Inc. v. Organization Service Co., Inc., 125 F.2d 120 (2d Cir.1942); In the Matter of McDougald, 17 F.R.D. 2, 5 (W.D.Ark.1955); In the Matter of Miller, 6 Fed.Rules Serv. 12f.26, Case No. 1 (N.D.Ohio 1942); Tatum v. Acadian Production Corp. of La., 35 F.Supp. 40, 50 (E.D.La.1940); 2 Collier, supra ¶303.07 (15th ed.1981); 2 id. at 134–40 (14th ed.1966). As pointed out in the Note accompanying former Bankruptcy rule 915 an objection that a debtor is neither entitled to the benefits of the Code nor amenable to an involuntary petition goes to jurisdiction of the subject matter and may be made at any time consistent with Rule 12(h)(3) F.R.Civ.P. Nothing in this rule recognizes standing in a creditor or any other person not authorized to contest a petition to raise an objection that a person eligible to file a voluntary petition cannot be the subject of an order for relief on an involuntary petition. See Seligson & King, Jurisdiction and Venue in Bankruptcy, 36 Ref.J. 36, 38–40 (1962).

As Collier has pointed out with respect to the Bankruptcy Act, "the mechanics of the provisions in § 18a and b relating to time for appearance and pleading are unnecessarily confusing. It would seem, though, to be more straightforward to provide, as does Federal Rule 12(a), that the time to respond runs from the date of service rather than the date of issuance of process." 2 Collier, supra at 119. The time normally allowed for the service and filing of an answer or motion under Rule 1011 runs from the date of the issuance of the summons. Compare Rule 7012. Service of the summons and petition will ordinarily be made by mail under Rule 1010 and must be made within 10 days of the issuance of the summons under Rule 7004(e), which governs the time of service. When service is made by publication, the court should fix the time for service and filing of the response in the light of all the circumstances so as to afford a fair opportunity to the debtor to enter a defense or objection without unduly delaying the hearing on the petition. Cf. Rule 12(a) F.R.Civ.P.

Subdivision (c): Under subdivision (c), the timely service of a motion permitted by Rule 12(b), (e), (f), or (h) F.R.Civ.P. alters the time within which an answer must be filed. If the court denies a motion or postpones its disposition until trial on the merits, the answer must be served within 10 days after notice of the court's action. If the court grants a motion for a more definite statement, the answer may be served any time within 10 days after the service of the more definite statement.

Many of the rules governing adversary proceedings apply to proceedings on a contested petition unless the court otherwise directs as provided in Rule 1018. The specific provisions of this Rule 1011 or 7005, however, govern the filing of an answer or motion responsive to a petition. The rules of Part VII are adaptations of the corresponding Federal Rules of Civil Procedure, and the effect of Rule 1018 is thus to make the provisions of Civil Rules 5, 8, 9, 15, and 56, inter alia, generally applicable to the making of defenses and objections to the petition. Rule 1018 follows prior law and practice in this respect. See 2 Collier, Bankruptcy ¶¶18.39–18.41 (14th ed.1966).

Subdivision (d). This subdivision adopts the position taken in many cases that an affirmative judgment against a petitioning creditor cannot be sought by a counterclaim filed in an answer to an involuntary petition. See, e.g., Georgia Jewelers, Inc., v. Bulova Watch Co., 302 F.2d 362, 369–70 (5th Cir.1962); Associated Electronic Supply Co. of Omaha v. C.B.S. Electronic Sales Corp., 288 F.2d 683, 684–85 (8th Cir. 1961). The subdivision follows Harris v. Capehart-Farnsworth Corp., 225 F.2d 268 (8th Cir.1955), in permitting the debtor to challenge the standing of a petitioner by filing a counterclaim against him. It does not foreclose the court from rejecting a counterclaim that cannot be determined without unduly delaying the decision upon the petition. See In the Matter of Bichel Optical Laboratories, Inc., 299 F.Supp. 545 (D.Minn.1969).

Subdivision (e). This subdivision makes it clear that no reply needs to be made to an answer, including one asserting a counterclaim, unless the court orders otherwise.

1987 Amendments

The rule has been broadened to make applicable in ancillary cases the provisions concerning responsive pleadings to involuntary petitions.

2004 Amendments

The amendment to Rule 1004 that became effective on December 1, 2002, deleted former subdivision (a) of that rule leaving only the provisions relating to involuntary petitions against partnerships. The rule no longer includes subdivisions. Therefore, this technical amendment changes the reference to Rule 1004(b) to Rule 1004.

2008 Amendments

The rule is amended to reflect the 2005 amendments to the Code, which repealed § 304 and added chapter 15. Section 304 covered cases ancillary to foreign proceedings, while chapter 15 governs ancillary and other cross-border cases and introduces the concept of a petition for recognition of a foreign proceeding.

The rule is also amended in tandem with the amendment to Rule 1010 to require the parties responding to an involuntary petition and a petition for recognition of a foreign proceeding to file corporate ownership statements to assist the court in determining whether recusal is necessary.

2009 Amendments

The rule is amended to implement changes in connection with the amendment to Rule 9006(a) and the manner by which time is computed under the rules. The deadline in the rule is amended to substitute a deadline that is a multiple of seven days. Throughout the rules, deadlines are amended in the following manner:

- 5-day periods become 7-day periods
- 10-day periods become 14-day periods
- 15-day periods become 14-day periods
- 20-day periods become 21-day periods
- 25-day periods become 28-day periods

CROSS REFERENCES

Applicability of this rule to involuntary case ancillary to foreign proceeding, see Fed.Rules Bankr.Proc. Rule 1003, 11 USCA.

Entry of default upon failure to plead within time, see Fed.Rules Bankr.Proc. Rule 1013, 11 USCA.

Motions; form and service, see Fed.Rules Bankr.Proc. Rule 9013, 11 USCA.

Responsive pleadings, see 11 USCA § 303.

Pleadings—

Amended and supplemental, see Fed.Rules Civ.Proc. Rule 15, 28 USCA.

Capacity, fraud, and other special matters, see Fed.Rules Civ.Proc. Rule 9, 28 USCA.

General rules, see Fed.Rules Civ.Proc. Rule 8, 28 USCA.

COMMENCEMENT OF CASE — Rule 1012

Service and filing, see Fed.Rules Civ.Proc. Rule 5, 28 USCA.

Summary judgment, see Fed.Rules Civ.Proc. Rule 56, 28 USCA.

Rule 1012. [Abrogated Mar. 30, 1987, eff. Aug. 1, 1987]

ADVISORY COMMITTEE NOTES

This rule is abrogated. The discovery rules apply whenever an involuntary petition is contested. Rule 1018.

Rule 1013. Hearing and Disposition of Petition in Involuntary Cases

(a) Contested petition

The court shall determine the issues of a contested petition at the earliest practicable time and forthwith enter an order for relief, dismiss the petition, or enter any other appropriate order.

(b) Default

If no pleading or other defense to a petition is filed within the time provided by Rule 1011, the court, on the next day, or as soon thereafter as practicable, shall enter an order for the relief requested in the petition.

(c) [Abrogated]

(As amended Apr. 30, 1991, eff. Aug. 1, 1991; Apr. 22, 1993, eff. Aug. 1, 1993.)

ADVISORY COMMITTEE NOTES

This rule is adapted from former Bankruptcy Rule 115(a) and (c) and applies in chapter 7 and 11 cases. The right to trial by jury under § 19a of the Bankruptcy Act [former § 42(a) of this title] has been abrogated and the availability of a trial by jury is within the discretion of the bankruptcy judge pursuant to 28 U.S.C. § 1480(b). Rule 9015 governs the demand for a jury trial.

Subdivision (b) of Rule 1013 is derived from former Bankruptcy Rule 115(c) and § 18(e) of the Bankruptcy Act [former § 41(e) of this title]. If an order for relief is not entered on default, dismissal will ordinarily be appropriate but the court may postpone definitive action. See also Rule 9024 with respect to setting aside an order for relief on default for cause.

Subdivision (e) of former Bankruptcy Rule 115 has not been carried over because its provisions are covered by § 303(i) of the Code.

1991 Amendments

Reference to the Official Form number is deleted in anticipation of future revision and renumbering of the Official Forms.

1993 Amendments

Subdivision (c) is abrogated because the official form for the order for relief was abrogated in 1991. Other amendments are stylistic and make no substantive change.

CROSS REFERENCES

Costs, counsel fees, expenses and damages upon dismissal of petition, see 11 USCA § 303.

Power of court to render judgments, see 11 USCA § 105.

Setting aside default for cause, see Fed.Rules Bankr.Proc. Rule 9024, 11 USCA.

Instructions to jury; objection, see Fed.Rules Civ.Proc. Rule 51, 28 USCA.

Juries of less than twelve; majority verdict, see Fed.Rules Civ.Proc. Rule 48, 28 USCA.

Jurors, see Fed.Rules Civ.Proc. Rule 47, 28 USCA.

Jury trial of right, see Fed.Rules Civ.Proc. Rule 38, 28 USCA.

Motion for directed verdict and for judgment notwithstanding verdict, see Fed.Rules Civ.Proc. Rule 50, 28 USCA.

Special verdicts and interrogatories, see Fed.Rules Civ.Proc. Rule 49, 28 USCA.

Trial by jury or by court, see Fed.Rules Civ.Proc. Rule 39, 28 USCA.

Rule 1014. Dismissal and Change of Venue

(a) Dismissal and transfer of cases

(1) Cases filed in proper district

If a petition is filed in the proper district, the court, on the timely motion of a party in interest or on its own motion, and after hearing on notice to the petitioners, the United States trustee, and other entities as directed by the court, may transfer the case to any other district if the court determines that the transfer is in the interest of justice or for the convenience of the parties.

(2) Cases filed in improper district

If a petition is filed in an improper district, the court, on the timely motion of a party in interest or on its own motion, and after hearing on notice to the petitioners, the United States trustee, and other entities as directed by the court, may dismiss the case or transfer it to any other district if the court determines that transfer is in the interest of justice or for the convenience of the parties.

(b) Procedure when petitions involving the same debtor or related debtors are filed in different courts

If petitions commencing cases under the Code or seeking recognition under chapter 15 are filed in different districts by, regarding, or against (1) the same debtor, (2) a partnership and one or more of its general partners, (3) two or more general partners, or (4) a debtor and an affiliate, the court in the district in which the first-filed petition is pending may determine, in the interest of justice or for the convenience of the parties, the district or districts in which any of the cases should proceed. The court may so determine on motion and after a hearing, with notice to the following entities in the affected cases: the United States trustee, entities entitled to notice under Rule 2002(a), and other entities as the court directs. The court may order the parties to the later-filed cases not to proceed further until it makes the determination.

(As amended Mar. 30, 1987, eff. Aug. 1, 1987; Apr. 30, 1991, eff. Aug. 1, 1991; Apr. 30, 2007, eff. Dec. 1, 2007; Apr. 28, 2010, eff. Dec. 1, 2010; Apr. 25, 2014, eff. Dec. 1, 2014.)

ADVISORY COMMITTEE NOTES

This rule is derived from former Bankruptcy Rule 116 which contained venue as well as transfer provisions. Public Law 95–598, however, placed the venue provisions in 28 U.S.C. § 1472, and no purpose is served by repeating them in this rule. Transfer of cases is provided in 28 U.S.C. § 1475 but this rule adds the procedure for obtaining transfer. Pursuant to 28 U.S.C. § 1472, proper venue for cases filed under the Code is either the district of domicile, residence, principal place of business, or location of principal assets for 180 days or the longer portion thereof immediately preceding the petition. 28 U.S.C. § 1475 permits the court to transfer a case in the interest of justice and for the convenience of the parties. If the venue is improper, the court may retain or transfer the case in the interest of justice and for the convenience of the parties pursuant to 28 U.S.C. § 1477.

Subdivision (a) of the rule is derived from former Bankruptcy Rule 116(b). It implements 28 U.S.C. §§ 1475 and 1477 and clarifies the procedure to be followed in requesting and effecting transfer of a case. Subdivision (a) protects the parties against being subjected to a transfer except on a timely motion of a party in interest. If the transfer would result in fragmentation or duplication of administration, increase expense, or delay closing the estate, such a factor would bear on the timeliness of the motion as well as on the propriety of the transfer under the standards prescribed in subdivision (a). Subdivision (a) of the rule requires the interest of justice and the convenience of the parties to be the grounds of any transfer of a case or of the retention of a case filed in an improper district as does 28 U.S.C. § 1477. Cf. 28 U.S.C. § 1404(a) (district court may transfer any civil action "[f]or the convenience of parties and witnesses, in

COMMENCEMENT OF CASE   Rule 1014

the interest of justice"). It also expressly requires a hearing on notice to the petitioner or petitioners before the transfer of any case may be ordered. Under this rule, a motion by a party in interest is necessary. There is no provision for the court to act on its own initiative.

Subdivision (b) is derived from former Bankruptcy Rule 116(c). It authorizes the court in which the first petition is filed under the Code by or against a debtor to entertain a motion seeking a determination whether the case so commenced should continue or be transferred and consolidated or administered jointly with another case commenced by or against the same or related person in another court under a different chapter of the Code. Subdivision (b) is correlated with 28 U.S.C. § 1472 which authorizes petitioners to file cases involving a partnership and partners or affiliated debtors.

The reference in subdivision (b) to petitions filed "by" a partner or "by" any other of the persons mentioned is to be understood as referring to voluntary petitions. It is not the purpose of this subdivision to permit more than one case to be filed in the same court because a creditor signing an involuntary petition happens to be a partner, a partnership, or an affiliate of a debtor.

Transfers of adversary proceedings in cases under title 11 are governed by Rule 7087 and 28 U.S.C. § 1475.

1987 Amendments

Both paragraphs 1 and 2 of subdivision (a) are amended to conform to the standard for transfer in 28 U.S.C. § 1412. Formerly, 28 U.S.C. § 1477 authorized a court either to transfer or retain a case which had been commenced in a district where venue was improper. However, 28 U.S.C. § 1412, which supersedes 28 U.S.C. § 1477, authorizes only the transfer of a case. The rule is amended to delete the reference to retention of a case commenced in the improper district. Dismissal of a case commenced in the improper district as authorized by 28 U.S.C. § 1406 has been added to the rule. If a timely motion to dismiss for improper venue is not filed, the right to object to venue is waived.

The last sentence of the rule has been deleted as unnecessary.

1991 Amendments

Subdivision (b) is amended to provide that a motion for transfer of venue under this subdivision shall be filed in the district in which the first petition is pending. If the case commenced by the first petition has been transferred to another district prior to the filing of a motion to transfer a related case under this subdivision, the motion must be filed in the district to which the first petition had been transferred.

The other amendments to this rule are consistent with the responsibilities of the United States trustee in the supervision and administration of cases pursuant to 28 U.S.C. § 586(a)(3). The United States trustee may appear and be heard on issues relating to the transfer of the case or dismissal due to improper venue. See § 307 of the Code.

2007 Amendments

Courts have generally held that they have the authority to dismiss or transfer cases on their own motion. The amendment recognizes this authority and also provides that dismissal or transfer of the case may take place only after notice and a hearing.

Other amendments are stylistic.

2010 Amendments

Subdivision (b). Subdivision (b) of the rule is amended to provide that petitions for recognition of a foreign proceeding are included among those that are governed by the procedure for determining where cases should go forward when multiple petitions involving the same debtor are filed. The amendment adds a specific reference to chapter 15 petitions and also provides that the rule governs proceedings regarding a debtor as well as those that are filed by or against a debtor.

Other changes are stylistic.

2014 Amendments

Subdivision (b) provides a practical solution for resolving venue issues when related cases are filed in different districts. It designates the court in which the first-filed petition is pending as the decision maker if a party seeks a determination of where the related cases should proceed. Subdivision (b) is amended to clarify when proceedings in the subsequently filed cases are stayed. It requires an order of the court in which the first-filed petition is pending to stay proceedings in the related cases. Requiring a court order to trigger the stay will prevent the disruption of other cases unless there is a judicial determination that this subdivision of the rule applies and that a stay of related cases is needed while the court makes its venue determination.

Notice of the hearing must be given to all debtors, trustees, creditors, indenture trustees, and United States trustees in the affected cases, as well as any other entity that the court directs. Because the clerk of the court that makes the determination often may lack access to the names and addresses of entities in other cases, a court may order the moving party to provide notice.

The other changes to subdivision (b) are stylistic.

CROSS REFERENCES

Change of venue, see 28 USCA § 1404.

Motions; form and service, see Fed.Rules Bankr.Proc. Rule 9013, 11 USCA.

Transfer of adversary proceeding, see Fed.Rules Bankr.Proc. Rule 7087, 11 USCA.

Rule 1015. Consolidation or Joint Administration of Cases Pending in Same Court

(a) Cases involving same debtor

If two or more petitions by, regarding, or against the same debtor are pending in the same court, the court may order consolidation of the cases.

(b) Cases involving two or more related debtors

If a joint petition or two or more petitions are pending in the same court by or against (1) a husband and wife, or (2) a partnership and one or more of its general partners, or (3) two or more general partners, or (4) a debtor and an affiliate, the court may order a joint administration of the estates. Prior to entering an order the court shall give consideration to protecting creditors of different estates against potential conflicts of interest. An order directing joint administration of individual cases of a husband and wife shall, if one spouse has elected the exemptions under § 522(b)(2) of the Code and the other has elected the exemptions under § 522(b)(3), fix a reasonable time within which either may amend the election so that both shall have elected the same exemptions. The order shall notify the debtors that unless they elect the same exemptions within the time fixed by the court, they will be deemed to have elected the exemptions provided by § 522(b)(2).

(c) Expediting and protective orders

When an order for consolidation or joint administration of a joint case or two or more cases is entered pursuant to this rule, while protecting the rights of the parties under the Code, the court may enter orders as may tend to avoid unnecessary costs and delay.

(As amended Mar. 30, 1987, eff. Aug. 1, 1987; Apr. 23, 2008, eff. Dec. 1, 2008; Apr. 28, 2010, eff. Dec. 1, 2010.)

ADVISORY COMMITTEE NOTES

Subdivision (a) of this rule is derived from former Bankruptcy Rule 117(a). It applies to cases when the same debtor is named in both voluntary and involuntary petitions, when husband and wife have filed a joint petition pursuant to § 302 of the Code, and when two or more involuntary petitions are filed against the same debtor. It also applies when cases are pending in the same court by virtue of a transfer of one or more petitions from another court. Subdivision (c) allows the court discretion regarding the order of trial of issues raised by two or more involuntary petitions against the same debtor.

Subdivision (b) recognizes the propriety of joint administration of estates in certain kinds of cases. The election or appointment of one trustee for two or more jointly administered estates is authorized by Rule 2009. The authority of the court to order joint administration under subdivision (b) extends equally to the situation when the petitions are filed under different sections, e.g., when one petition is voluntary and the other involuntary, and when all of the petitions are filed under the same section of the Code.

Consolidation of cases implies a unitary administration of the estate and will ordinarily be indicated under the circumstances to which subdivision (a) applies. This rule does not deal with the consolidation of cases involving two or more separate debtors. Consolidation of the estates of separate debtors may sometimes be appropriate, as when the affairs of an individual and a corporation owned or controlled by that individual are so intermingled that the court cannot separate their assets and liabilities. Consolidation, as distinguished from joint administration, is neither authorized nor prohibited by this rule since the propriety of consolidation depends on substantive considerations and affects the substantive rights of the creditors of the different estates. For illustrations of the substantive consolidation of separate estates, see Sampsell v. Imperial Paper & Color Corp., 313 U.S. 215 [61 S.Ct. 904, 85 L.Ed. 1293] (1941). See also Chemical Bank N.Y. Trust Co. v. Kheel, 369 F.2d 845 (2d Cir. 1966); Seligson & Mandell, Multi-Debtor Petition—Consolidation of Debtors and Due Process of Law, 73 Com.L.J. 341 (1968); Kennedy, Insolvency and the Corporate Veil in the United States in Proceedings of the 8th International Symposium on Comparative Law 232, 248–55 (1971).

Joint administration as distinguished from consolidation may include combining the estates by using a single docket for the matters occurring in the administration, including the listing of filed claims, the combining of notices to creditors of the different estates, and the joint handling of other purely administrative matters that may aid in expediting the cases and rendering the process less costly.

Subdivision (c) is an adaptation of the provisions of Rule 42(a) F.R.Civ.P. for the purposes of administration of estates under this rule. The rule does not deal with filing fees when an order for the consolidation of cases or joint administration of estates is made.

A joint petition of husband and wife, requiring the payment of a single filing fee, is permitted by § 302 of the Code. Consolidation of such a case, however, rests in the discretion of the court; see § 302(b) of the Code.

1987 Amendments

The amendment to subdivision (b) implements the provisions of § 522(b) of the Code, as enacted by the 1984 amendments.

2008 Amendments

The rule is amended to conform to the change in the numbering of § 522(b) of the Code that was made as a part of the 2005 amendments. Former subsections (b)(1) and (b)(2) of § 522 were renumbered as subsections (b)(2) and (b)(3), respectively. The rule is amended to make the parallel change.

2010 Amendments

Subdivision (a). By amending subdivision (a) to include cases regarding the same debtor, the rule explicitly recognizes that the court's authority to consolidate cases when more than one petition is filed includes the authority to consolidate cases when one or more of the petitions is filed under chapter 15. This amendment is made in conjunction with the amendment to Rule 1014(b), which also governs petitions filed under chapter 15 regarding the same debtor as well as those filed by or against the debtor.

CROSS REFERENCES

Election of trustees in liquidation cases when joint administration ordered, see Fed.Rules Bankr.Proc. Rule 2009, 11 USCA.

Joint cases, see 11 USCA § 302.

Consolidation, see Fed.Rules Civ.Proc. Rule 42, 28 USCA.

Rule 1016. Death or Incompetency of Debtor

Death or incompetency of the debtor shall not abate a liquidation case under chapter 7 of the Code. In such event the estate shall be administered and the case concluded in the same manner, so far as possible, as though the death or incompetency had not occurred. If a reorganization, family farmer's debt adjustment, or individual's debt adjustment case is pending under chapter 11, chapter 12, or chapter 13, the case may be dismissed; or if further administration is possible and in the best interest of the parties, the case may proceed and be concluded in the same manner, so far as possible, as though the death or incompetency had not occurred.

(As amended Apr. 30, 1991, eff. Aug. 1, 1991.)

ADVISORY COMMITTEE NOTES

This rule is derived from former Rules 118 and 11–16. In a chapter 11 reorganization case or chapter 13 individual's debt adjustment case, the likelihood is that the case will be dismissed.

1991 Amendments

This rule is amended to conform to 25 F.R.Civ.P. and to include chapter 12 cases.

CROSS REFERENCES

Exemptions, see 11 USCA § 522.

Property of estate, see 11 USCA § 541.

Rule 1017. Dismissal or Conversion of Case; Suspension

(a) Voluntary dismissal; dismissal for want of prosecution or other cause

Except as provided in §§ 707(a)(3), 707(b), 1208(b), and 1307(b) of the Code, and in Rule 1017(b), (c), and (e), a case shall not be dismissed on motion of the petitioner, for want of prosecution or other cause, or by consent of the parties, before a hearing on notice as provided in Rule 2002. For the purpose of the notice, the debtor shall file a list of creditors with their addresses within the time fixed by the court unless the list was previously filed. If the debtor fails to file the list, the court may order the debtor or another entity to prepare and file it.

(b) Dismissal for failure to pay filing fee

(1) If any installment of the filing fee has not been paid, the court may, after a hearing on notice to the debtor and the trustee, dismiss the case.

(2) If the case is dismissed or closed without full payment of the filing fee, the installments collected shall be distributed in the same manner and proportions as if the filing fee had been paid in full.

(c) Dismissal of voluntary chapter 7 or chapter 13 case for failure to timely file list of creditors, schedules, and statement of financial affairs

The court may dismiss a voluntary chapter 7 or chapter 13 case under § 707(a)(3) or § 1307(c)(9) after a hearing on notice served by the United States trustee on the debtor, the trustee, and any other entities as the court directs.

(d) Suspension

The court shall not dismiss a case or suspend proceedings under § 305 before a hearing on notice as provided in Rule 2002(a).

(e) Dismissal of an individual debtor's chapter 7 case, or conversion to a case under chapter 11 or 13, for abuse

The court may dismiss or, with the debtor's consent, convert an individual debtor's case for abuse under § 707(b) only on motion and after a hearing on notice to the debtor, the trustee, the United States trustee, and any other entity as the court directs.

(1) Except as otherwise provided in § 704(b)(2), a motion to dismiss a case for abuse under § 707(b) or (c) may be filed only within 60 days after the first date set for the meeting of creditors under § 341(a), unless, on request filed before the time has expired, the court for cause extends the time for filing the motion to dismiss. The party filing the motion shall set forth in the motion all matters to be considered at the hearing. In addition, a motion to dismiss under § 707(b)(1) and (3) shall state with particularity the circumstances alleged to constitute abuse.

(2) If the hearing is set on the court's own motion, notice of the hearing shall be served on the debtor no later than 60 days after the first date set for the meeting of creditors under § 341(a). The notice shall set forth all matters to be considered by the court at the hearing.

COMMENCEMENT OF CASE   Rule 1017

(f) Procedure for dismissal, conversion, or suspension

(1) Rule 9014 governs a proceeding to dismiss or suspend a case, or to convert a case to another chapter, except under §§ 706(a), 1112(a), 1208(a) or (b), or 1307(a) or (b).

(2) Conversion or dismissal under §§ 706(a), 1112(a), 1208(b), or 1307(b) shall be on motion filed and served as required by Rule 9013.

(3) A chapter 12 or chapter 13 case shall be converted without court order when the debtor files a notice of conversion under §§ 1208(a) or 1307(a). The filing date of the notice becomes the date of the conversion order for the purposes of applying § 348(c) and Rule 1019. The clerk shall promptly transmit a copy of the notice to the United States trustee.

(As amended Mar. 30, 1987, eff. Aug. 1, 1987; Apr. 30, 1991, eff. Aug. 1, 1991; Apr. 22, 1993, eff. Aug. 1, 1993; Apr. 29, 1999, eff. Dec. 1, 1999; Apr. 17, 2000, eff. Dec. 1, 2000; Apr. 23, 2008, eff. Dec. 1, 2008.)

ADVISORY COMMITTEE NOTES

Subdivision (a) of this rule is derived from former Bankruptcy Rule 120(a). While the rule applies to voluntary and involuntary cases, the "consent of the parties" referred to is that of petitioning creditors and the debtor in an involuntary case. The last sentence recognizes that the court should not be confined to petitioning creditors in its choice of parties on whom to call for assistance in preparing the list of creditors when the debtor fails to do so. This subdivision implements §§ 303(j), 707, 1112 and 1307 of the Code by specifying the manner of and persons to whom notice shall be given and requiring the court to hold a hearing on the issue of dismissal.

Subdivision (b) is derived from former Bankruptcy Rule 120(b). A dismissal under this subdivision can occur only when the petition has been permitted to be filed pursuant to Rule 1006(b). The provision for notice in paragraph (3) is correlated with the provision in Rule 4006 when there is a waiver, denial, or revocation of a discharge. As pointed out in the Note accompanying Rule 4008, the purpose of notifying creditors of a debtor that no discharge has been granted is to correct their assumption to the contrary so that they can take appropriate steps to protect their claims.

Subdivision (c) is new and specifies the notice required for a hearing on dismissal or suspension pursuant to § 305 of the Code. The suspension to which this subdivision refers is that of the case; it does not concern abstention of the court in hearing an adversary proceeding pursuant to 28 U.S.C. § 1478(b).

Subdivision (d). Any proceeding, whether by a debtor or other party, to dismiss or convert a case under §§ 706, 707, 1112, or 1307 is commenced by a motion pursuant to Rule 9014.

1987 Amendments

Subdivision (d) is amended to provide that dismissal or conversion pursuant to §§ 706(a), 707(b), 1112(a), and 1307(b) is not automatically a contested matter under Rule 9014. Conversion or dismissal under these sections is initiated by the filing and serving of a motion as required by Rule 9013. No hearing is required on these motions unless the court directs.

Conversion of a chapter 13 case to a chapter 7 case as authorized by § 1307(a) is accomplished by the filing of a notice of conversion. The notice of conversion procedure is modeled on the voluntary dismissal provision of Rule 41(a)(1) F.R.Civ.P. Conversion occurs on the filing of the notice. No court order is required.

Subdivision (e) is new and provides the procedure to be followed when a court on its own motion has made a preliminary determination that an individual debtor's chapter 7 case may be dismissed pursuant to § 707(b) of the Code, which was added by the 1984 amendments. A debtor's failure to attend the hearing is not a ground for dismissal pursuant to § 707(b).

1991 Amendments

Subdivision (a) is amended to clarify that all entities required to receive notice under Rule 2002, including but not limited to creditors, are entitled to the 20 day notice of the hearing to dismiss the case. The United States trustee receives the notice pursuant to Rule 2002(k).

The word "petition" is changed to "case" in subdivisions (a), (b), and (c) to conform to §§ 707, 930, 1112, 1208, and 1307.

Subdivision (d) is amended to conform to § 348(c) of the Code which refers to the "conversion order."

Rule 1017   BANKRUPTCY RULES

Subdivisions (a) and (d) are amended to provide procedures for dismissal or conversion of a chapter 12 case. Procedures for dismissal or conversion under § 1208(a) and (b) are the same as the procedures for dismissal or conversion of a chapter 13 case under § 1307(a) and (b).

Subdivision (e) is amended to conform to the 1986 amendment to § 707(b) of the Code which permits the United States trustee to make a motion to dismiss a case for substantial abuse. The time limit for such a motion is added by this subdivision. In general, the facts that are the basis for a motion to dismiss under § 707(b) exist at the time the case is commenced and usually can be discovered early in the case by reviewing the debtor's schedules and examining the debtor at the meeting of creditors. Since dismissal for substantial abuse has the effect of denying the debtor a discharge in the chapter 7 case based on matters which may be discovered early, a motion to dismiss under § 707(b) is analogous to an objection to discharge pursuant to Rule 4004 and, therefore, should be required to be made within a specified time period. If matters relating to substantial abuse are not discovered within the time period specified in subdivision (e) because of the debtor's false testimony, refusal to obey a court order, fraudulent schedules or other fraud, and the debtor receives a discharge, the debtor's conduct may constitute the basis for revocation of the discharge under § 727(d) and (e) of the Code.

1993 Amendments

Subdivision (d) is amended to clarify that the date of the filing of a notice of conversion in a chapter 12 or chapter 13 case is treated as the date of the conversion order for the purpose of applying Rule 1019. Other amendments are stylistic and make no substantive change.

1999 Amendments

Subdivision (b)(3), which provides that notice of dismissal for failure to pay the filing fee shall be sent to all creditors within 30 days after the dismissal, is deleted as unnecessary. Rule 2002(f) provides for notice to creditors of the dismissal of a case.

Rule 2002(a) and this rule currently require notice to all creditors of a hearing on dismissal of a voluntary chapter 7 case for the debtor's failure to file a list of creditors, schedules, and statement of financial affairs within the time provided in § 707(a)(3) of the Code. A new subdivision (c) is added to provide that the United States trustee, who is the only entity with standing to file a motion to dismiss under § 707(a)(3) or § 1307(c)(9), is required to serve the motion on only the debtor, the trustee, and any other entities as the court directs. This amendment, and the amendment to Rule 2002, will have the effect of avoiding the expense of sending notices of the motion to all creditors in a chapter 7 case.

New subdivision (f) is the same as current subdivision (d), except that it provides that a motion to suspend all proceedings in a case or to dismiss a case for substantial abuse of chapter 7 under § 707(b) is governed by Rule 9014.

Other amendments to this rule are stylistic or for clarification.

2000 Amendments

This rule is amended to permit the court to grant a timely request filed by the United States trustee for an extension of time to file a motion to dismiss a chapter 7 case under § 707(b), whether the court rules on the request before or after the expiration of the 60-day period.

Reporter's Note on Text of Rule 1017(e). The above text of Rule 1017(e) is not based on the text of the rule in effect on this date. The above text embodies amendments that have been promulgated by the Supreme Court in April 1999 and, unless Congress acts with respect to the amendments, will become effective on December 1, 1999.

2008 Amendments

Subdivision (e) is amended to implement the 2005 amendments to § 707 of the Code. These statutory amendments permit conversion of a chapter 7 case to a case under chapter 11 or 13, change the basis for dismissal or conversion from "substantial abuse" to "abuse," authorize parties other than the United States trustee to bring motions under § 707(b) under certain circumstances, and add § 707(c) to create an explicit ground for dismissal based on the request of a victim of a crime of violence or drug trafficking. The conforming amendments to subdivision (e) preserve the time limits already in place for § 707(b) motions, except to the extent that § 704(b)(2) sets the deadline for the United States trustee to act. In contrast to the grounds for a motion to dismiss under § 707(b)(2), which are quite specific, the grounds under § 707(b)(1) and (3) are very general. Therefore, to enable the debtor to respond, subdivision (e) requires that motions to dismiss under § 707(b)(1) and (3) state with particularity the circumstances alleged to constitute abuse.

CROSS REFERENCES

Conversion of—

    Individual debt adjustment case, see 11 USCA § 1307.

    Liquidation case, see 11 USCA § 706.

    Reorganization case, see 11 USCA § 1112.

Dismissal of—

    Individual debt adjustment case, see 11 USCA § 1307.

    Involuntary petition, see 11 USCA § 303.

    Liquidation case, see 11 USCA § 707.

    Reorganization case, see 11 USCA § 1112.

Enlargement of thirty-day period for notice of dismissal for failure to pay filing fee not permitted, see Fed.Rules Bankr.Proc. Rule 9006, 11 USCA.

Motions; form and service, see Fed.Rules Bankr.Proc. Rule 9013, 11 USCA.

Rule 1018. Contested Involuntary Petitions; Contested Petitions Commencing Chapter 15 Cases; Proceedings to Vacate Order for Relief; Applicability of Rules in Part VII Governing Adversary Proceedings

Unless the court otherwise directs and except as otherwise prescribed in Part I of these rules, the following rules in Part VII apply to all proceedings contesting an involuntary petition or a chapter 15 petition for recognition, and to all proceedings to vacate an order for relief: Rules 7005, 7008–7010, 7015, 7016, 7024–7026, 7028–7037, 7052, 7054, 7056, and 7062. The court may direct that other rules in Part VII shall also apply. For the purposes of this rule a reference in the Part VII rules to adversary proceedings shall be read as a reference to proceedings contesting an involuntary petition or a chapter 15 petition for recognition, or proceedings to vacate an order for relief. Reference in the Federal Rules of Civil Procedure to the complaint shall be read as a reference to the petition.

(As amended Mar. 30, 1987, eff. Aug. 1, 1987; Apr. 28, 2010, eff. Dec. 1, 2010.)

ADVISORY COMMITTEE NOTES

The rules in Part VII to which this rule refers are adaptations of the Federal Rules of Civil Procedure for the purpose of governing the procedure in adversary proceedings in cases under the Code. See the Note accompanying Rule 7001 infra. Because of the special need for dispatch and expedition in the determination of the issues in an involuntary petition, see Acme Harvester Co. v. Beekman Lumber Co., 222 U.S. 300, 309 (1911), the objective of some of the Federal Rules of Civil Procedure and their adaptations in Part VII to facilitate the settlement of multiple controversies involving many persons in a single lawsuit is not compatible with the exigencies of bankruptcy administration. See United States F. & G. Co. v. Bray, 225 U.S. 205, 218 (1912). For that reason Rules 7013, 7014 and 7018–7023 will rarely be appropriate in a proceeding on a contested petition.

Certain terms used in the Federal Rules of Civil Procedure have altered meanings when they are made applicable in cases under the Code by these rules. See Rule 9002 infra. This Rule 1018 requires that the terms "adversary proceedings" when used in the rules in Part VII and "complaint" when used in the Federal Rules of Civil Procedure be given altered meanings when they are made applicable to proceedings relating to a contested petition or proceedings to vacate any order for relief. A motion to vacate an order for relief, whether or not made on a petition that was or could have been contested, is governed by the rules in Part VII referred to in this Rule 1018.

1987 Amendments

Rule 1018 is amended to include within its terms a petition commencing an ancillary case when it is contested. This provision was formerly included in Rule 1003(e)(4).

Although this rule does not contain an explicit authorization for the entry of an order for relief when a debtor refuses to cooperate in discovery relating to a contested involuntary petition, the court has ample power under Rule 37(b) F.R.Civ.P., as incorporated by Rule 7037, to enter an order for relief under appropriate circumstances. Rule 37(b) authorizes the court to enter judgment by default or an order that "facts shall be taken as established."

2010 Amendments

The rule is amended to reflect the enactment of chapter 15 of the Code in 2005. As to chapter 15 cases, the rule applies to contests over the petition for recognition and not to all matters that arise in the case. Thus, proceedings governed by § 1519(e) and § 1521(e) of the Code must comply with Rules 7001(7) and 7065, which provide that actions for injunctive relief are adversary proceedings governed by Part VII of the rules. The rule is also amended to clarify that it applies to contests over an involuntary petition, and not to matters merely "relating to" a contested involuntary petition. Matters that may arise in a chapter 15 case or an involuntary case, other than contests over the petition itself, are governed by the otherwise applicable rules.

Other changes are stylistic.

CROSS REFERENCES

Applicability of this rule to involuntary case ancillary to foreign proceeding, see Fed.Rules Bankr.Proc. Rule 1003, 11 USCA.

Effect of amendment of Federal Rules of Civil Procedure, see Fed.Rules Bankr.Proc. Rule 9032, 11 USCA.

Rule 1019. Conversion of a Chapter 11 Reorganization Case, Chapter 12 Family Farmer's Debt Adjustment Case, or Chapter 13 Individual's Debt Adjustment Case to a Chapter 7 Liquidation Case

When a chapter 11, chapter 12, or chapter 13 case has been converted or reconverted to a chapter 7 case:

(1) Filing of lists, inventories, schedules, statements

(A) Lists, inventories, schedules, and statements of financial affairs theretofore filed shall be deemed to be filed in the chapter 7 case, unless the court directs otherwise. If they have not been previously filed, the debtor shall comply with Rule 1007 as if an order for relief had been entered on an involuntary petition on the date of the entry of the order directing that the case continue under chapter 7.

(B) If a statement of intention is required, it shall be filed within 30 days after entry of the order of conversion or before the first date set for the meeting of creditors, whichever is earlier. The court may grant an extension of time for cause only on written motion filed, or oral request made during a hearing, before the time has expired. Notice of an extension shall be given to the United States trustee and to any committee, trustee, or other party as the court may direct.

(2) New filing periods

(A) A new time period for filing a motion under § 707(b) or (c), a claim, a complaint objecting to discharge, or a complaint to obtain a determination of dischargeability of any debt shall commence under Rules[1] 1017, 3002, 4004, or 4007, but a new time period shall not commence if a chapter 7 case had been converted to a chapter 11, 12, or 13 case and thereafter reconverted to a chapter 7 case and the time for filing a motion under § 707(b) or (c), a claim, a complaint objecting to discharge, or a complaint to obtain a determination of the dischargeability of any debt, or any extension thereof, expired in the original chapter 7 case.

---

[1] So in original. Probably should be "Rule".

(B) A new time period for filing an objection to a claim of exemptions shall commence under Rule 4003(b) after conversion of a case to chapter 7 unless:

    (i) the case was converted to chapter 7 more than one year after the entry of the first order confirming a plan under chapter 11, 12, or 13; or

    (ii) the case was previously pending in chapter 7 and the time to object to a claimed exemption had expired in the original chapter 7 case.

(3) Claims filed before conversion

All claims actually filed by a creditor before conversion of the case are deemed filed in the chapter 7 case.

(4) Turnover of records and property

After qualification of, or assumption of duties by the chapter 7 trustee, any debtor in possession or trustee previously acting in the chapter 11, 12, or 13 case shall, forthwith, unless otherwise ordered, turn over to the chapter 7 trustee all records and property of the estate in the possession or control of the debtor in possession or trustee.

(5) Filing final report and schedule of postpetition debts

    (a) Conversion of chapter 11 or chapter 12 case

Unless the court directs otherwise, if a chapter 11 or chapter 12 case is converted to chapter 7, the debtor in possession or, if the debtor is not a debtor in possession, the trustee serving at the time of conversion, shall:

    (i) not later than 14 days after conversion of the case, file a schedule of unpaid debts incurred after the filing of the petition and before conversion of the case, including the name and address of each holder of a claim; and

    (ii) not later than 30 days after conversion of the case, file and transmit to the United States trustee a final report and account;

    (B) Conversion of chapter 13 case

Unless the court directs otherwise, if a chapter 13 case is converted to chapter 7,

    (i) the debtor, not later than 14 days after conversion of the case, shall file a schedule of unpaid debts incurred after the filing of the petition and before conversion of the case, including the name and address of each holder of a claim; and

    (ii) the trustee, not later than 30 days after conversion of the case, shall file and transmit to the United States trustee a final report and account;

    (C) Conversion after confirmation of a plan

Unless the court orders otherwise, if a chapter 11, chapter 12, or chapter 13 case is converted to chapter 7 after confirmation of a plan, the debtor shall file:

    (i) a schedule of property not listed in the final report and account acquired after the filing of the petition but before conversion, except if the case is converted from chapter 13 to chapter 7 and § 348(f)(2) does not apply;

    (ii) a schedule of unpaid debts not listed in the final report and account incurred after confirmation but before the conversion; and

    (iii) a schedule of executory contracts and unexpired leases entered into or assumed after the filing of the petition but before conversion.

    (D) Transmission to United States trustee

The clerk shall forthwith transmit to the United States trustee a copy of every schedule filed pursuant to Rule 1019(5).

(6) Postpetition claims; preconversion administrative expenses; notice

A request for payment of an administrative expense incurred before conversion of the case is timely filed under § 503(a) of the Code if it is filed before conversion or a time fixed by the court. If the request is filed by a governmental unit, it is timely if it is filed before conversion or within the later of a time fixed by the court or 180 days after the date of the conversion. A claim of a kind specified in § 348(d) may be filed in accordance with Rules 3001(a)–(d) and 3002. Upon the filing of the schedule of unpaid debts incurred after commencement of the case and before conversion, the clerk, or some other person as the court may direct, shall give notice to those entities listed on the schedule of the time for filing a request for payment of an administrative expense and, unless a notice of insufficient assets to pay a dividend is mailed in accordance with Rule 2002(e), the time for filing a claim of a kind specified in § 348(d).

(7) [Abrogated]

(As amended Mar. 30, 1987, eff. Aug. 1, 1987; Apr. 30, 1991, eff. Aug. 1, 1991; Apr. 23, 1996, eff. Dec. 1, 1996; Apr. 11, 1997, eff. Dec. 1, 1997; Apr. 29, 1999, eff. Dec. 1, 1999; Apr. 23, 2008, eff. Dec. 1, 2008; Mar. 26, 2009, eff. Dec. 1, 2009; Apr. 28, 2010, eff. Dec. 1, 2010.)

ADVISORY COMMITTEE NOTES
1983 Enactments

This rule is derived from former Bankruptcy Rule 122 and implements § 348 of the Code. The rule applies to proceedings in a chapter 7 case following supersession of a case commenced under chapter 11 or 13, whether the latter was initiated by an original petition or was converted from a pending chapter 7 or another chapter case. The rule is not intended to invalidate any action taken in the superseded case before its conversion to chapter 7.

Paragraph (1). If requirements applicable in the superseded case respecting the filing of schedules of debts and property, or lists of creditors and inventory, and of statements of financial affairs have been complied with before the order directing conversion to liquidation, these documents will ordinarily provide all the information about the debts, property, financial affairs, and contracts of the debtor needed for the administration of the estate. If the information submitted in the superseded case is inadequate for the purposes of administration, however, the court may direct the preparation of further informational material and the manner and time of its submission pursuant to paragraph (1). If no schedules, lists, inventories, or statements were filed in the superseded case, this paragraph imposes the duty on the debtor to file schedules and a statement of affairs pursuant to Rule 1007 as if an involuntary petition had been filed on the date when the court directed the conversion of the case to a liquidation case.

Paragraphs (2) and (3). Paragraph (2) requires notice to be given to all creditors of the order of conversion. The notice is to be included in the notice of the meeting of creditors and Official Form No. 16 may be adapted for use. A meeting of creditors may have been held in the superseded case as required by § 341(a) of the Code but that would not dispense with the need to hold one in the ensuing liquidation case. Section 701(a) of the Code permits the court to appoint the trustee acting in the chapter 11 or 13 case as interim trustee in the chapter 7 case. Section 702(a) of the Code allows creditors to elect a trustee but only at the meeting of creditors held under § 341. The right to elect a trustee is not lost because the chapter 7 case follows a chapter 11 or 13 case. Thus a meeting of creditors is necessary. The date fixed for the meeting of creditors will control at least the time for filing claims pursuant to Rule 3002(c). That time will remain applicable in the ensuing chapter 7 case except as paragraph (3) provides, if that time had expired in an earlier chapter 7 case which was converted to the chapter 11 or 13 case, it is not revived in the subsequent chapter 7 case. The same is true if the time for filing a complaint objecting to discharge or to determine nondischargeability of a debt had expired. Paragraph (3), however, recognizes that such time may be extended by the court under Rule 4004 or 4007 on motion made within the original prescribed time.

Paragraph (4) renders it unnecessary to file anew claims that had been filed in the chapter 11 or 13 case before conversion to chapter 7.

Paragraph (5) contemplates that typically, after the court orders conversion of a chapter case to liquidation, a trustee under chapter 7 will forthwith take charge of the property of the estate and proceed expeditiously to liquidate it. The court may appoint the interim trustee in the chapter 7 case pursuant to § 701(a) of the Code. If creditors do not elect a trustee under § 702, the interim trustee becomes the trustee.

COMMENCEMENT OF CASE   Rule 1019

Paragraph (6) requires the trustee or debtor in possession acting in the chapter 11 or 13 case to file a final report and schedule of debts incurred in that case. This schedule will provide the information necessary for giving the notice required by paragraph (7) of the rule.

Paragraph (7) requires that claims that arose in the chapter 11 or 13 case be filed within 60 days after entry of the order converting the case to one under chapter 7. Claims not scheduled pursuant to paragraph (6) of the rule or arising from the rejection of an executory contract entered into during the chapter case may be filed within a time fixed by the court. Pursuant to § 348(c) of the Code, the conversion order is treated as the order for relief to fix the time for the trustee to assume or reject executory contracts under § 365(d).

Paragraph (8) permits the extension of the time for filing claims when claims are not timely filed but only with respect to any surplus that may remain in the estate. See also § 726(a)(2)(C) and (3) of the Code.

1987 Amendments

Paragraph (1) is amended to provide for the filing of a statement of intention in a case converted to chapter 7. Paragraph (1)(B) is added to provide for the filing of the statement of intention when a case is converted to chapter 7. The time for filing the statement of intention and for an extension of that time is governed by § 521(2)(A) of the Code. An extension of time for other required filings is governed by Rule 1007(c), which paragraph (1)(A) incorporates by reference. Because of the amendment to Rule 1007(c), the filing of new lists, schedules, and statements is now governed exclusively by Rule 1019(1).

Paragraph (3) of the rule is expanded to include the effect of conversion of a chapter 11 or 13 case to a chapter 7 case. On conversion of a case from chapter 11 or 13 to a chapter 7 case, parties have a new period within which to file claims or complaints relating to the granting of the discharge or the dischargeability of a debt. This amendment is consistent with the holding and reasoning of the court in *F & M Marquette Nat'l Bank v. Richards,* 780 F.2d 24 (8th Cir.1985).

Paragraph (4) is amended to deal directly with the status of claims which are properly listed on the schedules filed in a chapter 11 case and deemed filed pursuant to § 1111(a) of the Code. Section 1111(a) is only applicable to the chapter 11 case. On conversion of the chapter 11 case to a chapter 7 case, paragraph (4) governs the status of claims filed in the chapter 11 case. The Third Circuit properly construed paragraph (4) as applicable to claims deemed filed in the superseded chapter 11 case. *In re Crouthamel Potato Chip Co.,* 786 F.2d 141 (3d Cir.1986).

The amendment to paragraph (4) changes that result by providing that only claims that are actually filed in the chapter 11 case are treated as filed in the superseding chapter 7 case. When chapter 11 cases are converted to chapter 7 cases, difficulties in obtaining and verifying the debtors' records are common. It is unfair to the chapter 7 trustee and creditors to require that they be bound by schedules which may not be subject to verification.

Paragraph (6) is amended to place the obligation on the chapter 13 debtor to file a schedule of unpaid debts incurred during the superseded chapter 13 case.

1991 Amendments

This rule is amended to include conversion of a case from chapter 12 to chapter 7 and to implement the United States trustee system.

The amendments to paragraph (1)(A) are stylistic. Reference to the statement of executory contracts is deleted to conform to the amendment to Rule 1007(b)(1) which changes the statement to a schedule of executory contracts and unexpired leases.

Paragraph (1)(B) is amended to enable the United States trustee to monitor the progress of the case and to take appropriate action to enforce the debtor's obligation to perform the statement of intention in a timely manner.

Paragraph (2) is deleted because notice of conversion of the case is required by Rules 1017(d), 2002(f)(2), and 9022. The United States trustee, who supervises trustees pursuant to 28 U.S.C. § 586(a), may give notice of the conversion to the trustee in the superseded case.

Paragraph (6), renumbered as paragraph (5), is amended to reduce to 15 days the time for filing a schedule of postpetition debts and requires inclusion of the name and address of each creditor in connection with the postpetition debt. These changes will enable the clerk to send postpetition creditors a timely notice of the meeting of creditors held pursuant to § 341(a) of the Code. The amendments to this paragraph also provide the United States trustee with the final report and account of the superseded case, and with a copy of every schedule filed after conversion of the case. Conversion to chapter 7 terminates the service of the trustee in the superseded case pursuant to § 348(e) of the Code. Sections 704(a)(9), 1106(a)(1), 1107(a), 1202(b)(1), 1203 and 1302(b)(1) of the Code require the trustee or debtor in possession to file a final report and account with the court and the United States trustee. The words "with the court" are deleted as unnecessary. See Rules 5005(a) and 9001(3).

Paragraph (7), renumbered as paragraph (6), is amended to conform the time for filing postpetition claims to the time for filing prepetition claims pursuant to paragraph (3) (renumbered as paragraph (2)) of this rule and Rule 3002(c). This paragraph is also amended to eliminate the need for a court order to provide notice of the time for filing claims. It is anticipated that this notice will be given together with the notice of the meeting of creditors. It is amended further to avoid the need to fix a time for filing claims arising under § 365(d) if it is a no asset case upon conversion. If assets become available for distribution, the court may fix a time for filing such claims pursuant to Rule 3002(c)(4).

The additions of references to unexpired leases in paragraph (1)(A) and in paragraphs (6) and (7) (renumbered as paragraphs (5) and (6)) are technical amendments to clarify that unexpired leases are included as well as other executory contracts.

1996 Amendments

Subdivision (7) is abrogated to conform to the abrogation of Rule 3002(c)(6).

1997 Amendments

The amendments to subdivisions (3) and (5) are technical corrections and stylistic changes. The phrase "superseded case" is deleted because it creates the erroneous impression that conversion of a case results in a new case that is distinct from the original case. Similarly, the phrase "original petition" is deleted because it erroneously implies that there is a second petition with respect to a converted case. See § 348 of the Code.

1999 Amendments

Paragraph (1)(B) is amended to clarify that a motion for an extension of time to file a statement of intention must be made by written motion filed before the time expires, or by oral request made at a hearing before the time expires.

Subdivision (6) is amended to provide that a holder of an administrative expense claim incurred after the commencement of the case, but before conversion to chapter 7, is required to file a request for payment under § 503(a) within a time fixed by the court, rather than a proof of claim under § 501 and Rules 3001(a)-(d) and 3002. The 180-day period applicable to governmental units is intended to conform to § 502(b)(9) of the Code and Rule 3002(c)(1). It is unnecessary for the court to fix a time for filing requests for payment if it appears that there are not sufficient assets to pay preconversion administrative expenses. If a time for filing a request for payment of an administrative expense is fixed by the court, it may be enlarged as provided in Rule 9006(b). If an administrative expense claimant fails to timely file the request, it may be tardily filed under § 503(a) if permitted by the court for cause.

The final sentence of Rule 1019(6) is deleted because it is unnecessary in view of the other amendments to this paragraph. If a party has entered into a postpetition contract or lease with the trustee or debtor that constitutes an administrative expense, a timely request for payment must be filed in accordance with this paragraph and § 503(b) of the Code. The time for filing a proof of claim in connection with the rejection of any other executory contract or unexpired lease is governed by Rule 3002(c)(4).

The phrase "including the United States, any state, or any subdivision thereof" is deleted as unnecessary. Other amendments to this rule are stylistic.

2008 Amendments

Subdivision (2) is amended to include a new filing period for motions under § 707(b) and (c) of the Code when a case is converted to chapter 7. The establishment of a deadline for filing such motions is not intended to express a position as to whether such motions are permitted under the Code.

2009 Amendments

The rule is amended to implement changes in connection with the amendment to Rule 9006(a) and the manner by which time is computed under the rules. The deadlines in the rule are amended to substitute a deadline that is a multiple of seven days. Throughout the rules, deadlines are amended in the following manner:

- 5-day periods become 7-day periods
- 10-day periods become 14-day periods
- 15-day periods become 14-day periods
- 20-day periods become 21-day periods
- 25-day periods become 28-day periods

2010 Amendments

Subdivision (2). Subdivision (2) is redesignated as subdivision (2)(A), and a new subdivision (2)(B) is added to the rule. Subdivision (2)(B) provides that a new time period to object to a claim of exemption arises when a case is converted to chapter 7 from chapter 11, 12, or 13. The new time period does not arise, however, if the conversion occurs more than one year after the first order confirming a plan, even if the plan was subsequently modified. A new objection period also does not arise if the case was previously pending under chapter 7 and the objection period had expired in the prior chapter 7 case.

CROSS REFERENCES

Appointment of interim trustee, see Fed.Rules Bankr.Proc. Rule 2001, 11 USCA.

Election of trustee, see 11 USCA § 702.

Enlargement of twenty-day period for notice of order of conversion to liquidation case not permitted, see Fed.Rules Bankr.Proc. Rule 9006, 11 USCA.

Failure to effect plan or substantial consummation of confirmed plan, see 11 USCA § 1112.

Meeting of creditors or equity security holders, see Fed.Rules Bankr.Proc. Rule 2003, 11 USCA.

Rule 1020. Small Business Chapter 11 Reorganization Case

(a) Small business debtor designation

In a voluntary chapter 11 case, the debtor shall state in the petition whether the debtor is a small business debtor. In an involuntary chapter 11 case, the debtor shall file within 14 days after entry of the order for relief a statement as to whether the debtor is a small business debtor. Except as provided in subdivision (c), the status of the case as a small business case shall be in accordance with the debtor's statement under this subdivision, unless and until the court enters an order finding that the debtor's statement is incorrect.

(b) Objecting to designation

Except as provided in subdivision (c), the United States trustee or a party in interest may file an objection to the debtor's statement under subdivision (a) no later than 30 days after the conclusion of the meeting of creditors held under § 341(a) of the Code, or within 30 days after any amendment to the statement, whichever is later.

(c) Appointment of committee of unsecured creditors

If a committee of unsecured creditors has been appointed under § 1102(a)(1), the case shall proceed as a small business case only if, and from the time when, the court enters an order determining that the committee has not been sufficiently active and representative to provide effective oversight of the debtor and that the debtor satisfies all the other requirements for being a small business. A request for a determination under this subdivision may be filed by the United States trustee or a party in interest only within a reasonable time after the failure of the committee to be sufficiently active and representative. The debtor may file a request for a determination at any time as to whether the committee has been sufficiently active and representative.

(d) Procedure for objection or determination

Any objection or request for a determination under this rule shall be governed by Rule 9014 and served on: the debtor; the debtor's attorney; the United States trustee; the trustee; any committee appointed under § 1102 or its authorized agent, or, if no committee of unsecured creditors has been appointed under § 1102, the creditors included on the list filed under Rule 1007(d); and any other entity as the court directs.

(Added Apr. 11, 1997, eff. Dec. 1, 1997; amended Apr. 23, 2008, eff. Dec. 1, 2008; Mar. 26, 2009, eff. Dec. 1, 2009.)

ADVISORY COMMITTEE NOTES

1997 Amendments

This rule is designed to implement §§ 1121(e) and 1125(f), which were added to the Code by the Bankruptcy Reform Act of 1994.

2008 Amendments

Under the Code, as amended in 2005, there are no longer any provisions permitting or requiring a small business debtor to elect to be treated as a small business. Therefore, the election provisions in the rule are eliminated.

The 2005 amendments to the Code include several provisions relating to small business cases under chapter 11. Section 101 includes definitions of "small business debtor" and "small business case." The purpose of the new language in this rule is to provide a procedure for informing the parties, the United States trustee, and the court of whether the debtor is a small business debtor, and to provide procedures for resolving disputes regarding the proper characterization of the debtor. Because it is important to resolve such disputes early in the case, a time limit for objecting to the debtor's self-designation is imposed. Rule 9006(b)(1), which governs enlargement of time, is applicable to the time limits set forth in this rule.

An important factor in determining whether the debtor is a small business debtor is whether the United States trustee has appointed a committee of unsecured creditors under § 1102, and whether such a committee is sufficiently active and representative. Subdivision (c), relating to the appointment and activity of a committee of unsecured creditors, is designed to be consistent with the Code's definition of "small business debtor."

2009 Amendments

The rule is amended to implement changes in connection with the amendment to Rule 9006(a) and the manner by which time is computed under the rules. The deadline in the rule is amended to substitute a deadline that is a multiple of seven days. Throughout the rules, deadlines are amended in the following manner:

- 5-day periods become 7-day periods
- 10-day periods become 14-day periods
- 15-day periods become 14-day periods
- 20-day periods become 21-day periods
- 25-day periods become 28-day periods

Rule 1021. Health Care Business Case

(a) Health care business designation

Unless the court orders otherwise, if a petition in a case under Chapter 7, chapter 9, or chapter 11 states that the debtor is a health care business, the case shall proceed as a case in which the debtor is a health care business.

(b) Motion

The United States trustee or a party in interest may file a motion to determine whether the debtor is a health care business. The motion shall be transmitted to the United States trustee and served on: the debtor; the trustee; any committee elected under § 705 or appointed under § 1102 of the Code or its authorized agent, or, if the case is a chapter 9 municipality case or a chapter 11 reorganization case and no committee of unsecured creditors has been appointed under § 1102, the

COMMENCEMENT OF CASE Rule 1021

creditors included on the list filed under Rule 1007(d); and any other entity as the court directs. The motion shall be governed by Rule 9014.

(Added Apr. 23, 2008, eff. Dec. 1, 2008.)

ADVISORY COMMITTEE NOTES
2008 Adoption

Section 101(27A) of the Code, added by the 2005 amendments, defines a health care business. This rule provides procedures for designating the debtor as a health care business. The debtor in a voluntary case, or petitioning creditors in an involuntary case, make that designation by checking the appropriate box on the petition. The rule also provides procedures for resolving disputes regarding the status of the debtor as a health care business.

PART II—OFFICERS AND ADMINISTRATION; NOTICES; MEETINGS; EXAMINATIONS; ELECTIONS; ATTORNEYS AND ACCOUNTANTS

Rule
2001. Appointment of Interim Trustee Before Order for Relief in a Chapter 7 Liquidation Case.
2002. Notices to Creditors, Equity Security Holders, Administrators in Foreign Proceedings, Persons Against Whom Provisional Relief Is Sought in Ancillary and Other Cross-Border Cases, United States, and United States Trustee.
2003. Meeting of Creditors or Equity Security Holders.
2004. Examination.
2005. Apprehension and Removal of Debtor to Compel Attendance for Examination.
2006. Solicitation and Voting of Proxies in Chapter 7 Liquidation Cases.
2007. Review of Appointment of Creditors' Committee Organized Before Commencement of the Case.
2007.1. Appointment of Trustee or Examiner in a Chapter 11 Reorganization Case.
2007.2. Appointment of Patient Care Ombudsman in a Health Care Business Case.
2008. Notice to Trustee of Selection.
2009. Trustees for Estates When Joint Administration Ordered.
2010. Qualification by Trustee; Proceeding on Bond.
2011. Evidence of Debtor in Possession or Qualification of Trustee.
2012. Substitution of Trustee or Successor Trustee; Accounting.
2013. Public Record of Compensation Awarded to Trustees, Examiners, and Professionals.
2014. Employment of Professional Persons.
2015. Duty to Keep Records, Make Reports, and Give Notice of Case or Change of Status.
2015.1. Patient Care Ombudsman.
2015.2. Transfer of Patient in Health Care Business Case.
2015.3. Reports of Financial Information on Entities in Which a Chapter 11 Estate Holds a Controlling or Substantial Interest.
2016. Compensation for Services Rendered and Reimbursement of Expenses.
2017. Examination of Debtor's Transactions With Debtor's Attorney.
2018. Intervention; Right to Be Heard.
2019. Disclosure Regarding Creditors and Equity Security Holders in Chapter 9 and Chapter 11 Cases.
2020. Review of Acts by United States Trustee.

Rule 2001. Appointment of Interim Trustee Before Order for Relief in a Chapter 7 Liquidation Case

(a) Appointment

At any time following the commencement of an involuntary liquidation case and before an order for relief, the court on written motion of a party in interest may order the appointment of an interim trustee under § 303(g) of the Code. The motion shall set forth the necessity for the appointment and may be granted only after hearing on notice to the debtor, the petitioning creditors, the United States trustee, and other parties in interest as the court may designate.

(b) Bond of movant

An interim trustee may not be appointed under this rule unless the movant furnishes a bond in an amount approved by the court, conditioned to indemnify the debtor for costs, attorney's fee, expenses, and damages allowable under § 303(i) of the Code.

(c) Order of Appointment

The order directing the appointment of an interim trustee shall state the reason the appointment is necessary and shall specify the trustee's duties.

(d) Turnover and report

Following qualification of the trustee selected under § 702 of the Code, the interim trustee, unless otherwise ordered, shall (1) forthwith deliver to the trustee all the records and property of the estate in possession or subject to control of the interim trustee and, (2) within 30 days thereafter file a final report and account.

(As amended Mar. 30, 1987, eff. Aug. 1, 1987; Apr. 30, 1991, eff. Aug. 1, 1991.)

Rule 2002   BANKRUPTCY RULES

ADVISORY COMMITTEE NOTES

This rule is adapted from former Bankruptcy Rule 201. See also former Chapter X Rule 10–201. In conformity with title 11 of the United States Code, this rule substitutes "interim trustee" for "receiver." Subdivision (a) and (e) of Rule 201 are not included because the provisions contained therein are found in detail in § 303(g) of the Code, or they are inconsistent with § 701 of the Code. Similarly, the provisions in Rule 201(d) relating to a debtor's counterbond are not included because of their presence in § 303(g).

Subdivision (a) makes it clear that the court may not on its own motion order the appointment of an interim trustee before an order for relief is entered. Appointment may be ordered only on motion of a party in interest.

Subdivision (b) requires those seeking the appointment of an interim trustee to furnish a bond. The bond may be the same one required of petitioning creditors under § 303(e) of the Code to indemnify the debtor for damages allowed by the court under § 303(i).

Subdivision (c) requires that the order specify which duties enumerated in § 303(g) shall be performed by the interim trustee. Reference should be made to Rule 2015 for additional duties required of an interim trustee including keeping records and filing periodic reports with the court.

Subdivision (d) requires turnover of records and property to the trustee selected under § 702 of the Code, after qualification. That trustee may be the interim trustee who becomes the trustee because of the failure of creditors to elect one under § 702(d) or the trustee elected by creditors under § 702(b), (c).

1991 Amendments

This rule is amended to conform to § 303(g) of the Code which provides that the United States trustee appoints the interim trustee. See Rule X–1003. This rule does not apply to the exercise by the court of the power to act sua sponte pursuant to § 105(a) of the Code.

CROSS REFERENCES

Duty to keep and file records and reports, see Fed.Rules Bankr.Proc. Rule 2015, 11 USCA.

Interim trustee, see 11 USCA § 701.

Motions; form and service, see Fed.Rules Bankr.Proc. Rule 9013, 11 USCA.

Security; proceedings against sureties, see Fed.Rules Bankr.Proc. Rule 9025, 11 USCA.

Rule 2002. Notices to Creditors, Equity Security Holders, Administrators in Foreign Proceedings, Persons Against Whom Provisional Relief Is Sought in Ancillary and Other Cross-Border Cases, United States, and United States Trustee

(a) Twenty-one-day notices to parties in interest

Except as provided in subdivisions (h), (i), (l), (p), and (q) of this rule, the clerk, or some other person as the court may direct, shall give the debtor, the trustee, all creditors and indenture trustees at least 21 days' notice by mail of:

    (1) the meeting of creditors under § 341 or § 1104(b) of the Code, which notice, unless the court orders otherwise, shall include the debtor's employer identification number, social security number, and any other federal taxpayer identification number;

    (2) a proposed use, sale, or lease of property of the estate other than in the ordinary course of business, unless the court for cause shown shortens the time or directs another method of giving notice;

    (3) the hearing on approval of a compromise or settlement of a controversy other than approval of an agreement pursuant to Rule 4001(d), unless the court for cause shown directs that notice not be sent;

    (4) in a chapter 7 liquidation, a chapter 11 reorganization case, or a chapter 12 family farmer debt adjustment case, the hearing on the dismissal of the case or the conversion of the

OFFICERS AND ADMINISTRATION   Rule 2002

case to another chapter, unless the hearing is under § 707(a)(3) or § 707(b) or is on dismissal of the case for failure to pay the filing fee;

    (5) the time fixed to accept or reject a proposed modification of a plan;

    (6) a hearing on any entity's request for compensation or reimbursement of expenses if the request exceeds $1,000;

    (7) the time fixed for filing proofs of claims pursuant to Rule 3003(c); and

    (8) the time fixed for filing objections and the hearing to consider confirmation of a chapter 12 plan.

(b) Twenty-eight-day notices to parties in interest

Except as provided in subdivision (l) of this rule, the clerk, or some other person as the court may direct, shall give the debtor, the trustee, all creditors and indenture trustees not less than 28 days' notice by mail of the time fixed (1) for filing objections and the hearing to consider approval of a disclosure statement or, under § 1125(f), to make a final determination whether the plan provides adequate information so that a separate disclosure statement is not necessary; and (2) for filing objections and the hearing to consider confirmation of a chapter 9, chapter 11, or chapter 13 plan.

(c) Content of notice

    (1) Proposed Use, Sale, or Lease of Property

Subject to Rule 6004, the notice of a proposed use, sale, or lease of property required by subdivision (a)(2) of this rule shall include the time and place of any public sale, the terms and conditions of any private sale and the time fixed for filing objections. The notice of a proposed use, sale, or lease of property, including real estate, is sufficient if it generally describes the property. The notice of a proposed sale or lease of personally identifiable information under § 363(b)(1) of the Code shall state whether the sale is consistent with any policy prohibiting the transfer of the information.

    (2) Notice of hearing on compensation

The notice of a hearing on an application for compensation or reimbursement of expenses required by subdivision (a)(6) of this rule shall identify the applicant and the amounts requested.

    (3) Notice of hearing on confirmation when plan provides for an injunction

If a plan provides for an injunction against conduct not otherwise enjoined under the Code, the notice required under Rule 2002(b)(2) shall:

        (A) include in conspicuous language (bold, italic, or underlined text) a statement that the plan proposes an injunction;

        (B) describe briefly the nature of the injunction; and

        (C) identify the entities that would be subject to the injunction.

(d) Notice to equity security holders

In a chapter 11 reorganization case, unless otherwise ordered by the court, the clerk, or some other person as the court may direct, shall in the manner and form directed by the court give notice to all equity security holders of (1) the order for relief; (2) any meeting of equity security holders held pursuant to § 341 of the Code; (3) the hearing on the proposed sale of all or substantially all of the debtor's assets; (4) the hearing on the dismissal or conversion of a case to another chapter; (5) the time fixed for filing objections to and the hearing to consider approval of a disclosure statement; (6) the time fixed for filing objections to and the hearing to consider confirmation of a plan; and (7) the time fixed to accept or reject a proposed modification of a plan.

(e) Notice of no dividend

In a chapter 7 liquidation case, if it appears from the schedules that there are no assets from which a dividend can be paid, the notice of the meeting of creditors may include a statement to that

Rule 2002   BANKRUPTCY RULES

effect; that it is unnecessary to file claims; and that if sufficient assets become available for the payment of a dividend, further notice will be given for the filing of claims.

(f) Other notices

Except as provided in subdivision (l) of this rule, the clerk, or some other person as the court may direct, shall give the debtor, all creditors, and indenture trustees notice by mail of:

    (1) the order for relief;

    (2) the dismissal or the conversion of the case to another chapter, or the suspension of proceedings under § 305;

    (3) the time allowed for filing claims pursuant to Rule 3002;

    (4) the time fixed for filing a complaint objecting to the debtor's discharge pursuant to § 727 of the Code as provided in Rule 4004;

    (5) the time fixed for filing a complaint to determine the dischargeability of a debt pursuant to § 523 of the Code as provided in Rule 4007;

    (6) the waiver, denial, or revocation of a discharge as provided in Rule 4006;

    (7) entry of an order confirming a chapter 9, 11, or 12 plan;

    (8) a summary of the trustee's final report in a chapter 7 case if the net proceeds realized exceed $1,500;

    (9) a notice under Rule 5008 regarding the presumption of abuse;

    (10) a statement under § 704(b)(1) as to whether the debtor's case would be presumed to be an abuse under § 707(b); and

    (11) the time to request a delay in the entry of the discharge under §§ 1141(d)(5)(C), 1228(f), and 1328(h). Notice of the time fixed for accepting or rejecting a plan pursuant to Rule 3017(c) shall be given in accordance with Rule 3017(d).

(g) Addressing notices

    (1) Notices required to be mailed under Rule 2002 to a creditor, indenture trustee, or equity security holder shall be addressed as such entity or an authorized agent has directed in its last request filed in the particular case. For the purposes of this subdivision—

        (A) a proof of claim filed by a creditor or indenture trustee that designates a mailing address constitutes a filed request to mail notices to that address, unless a notice of no dividend has been given under Rule 2002(e) and a later notice of possible dividend under Rule 3002(c)(5) has not been given; and

        (B) a proof of interest filed by an equity security holder that designates a mailing address constitutes a filed request to mail notices to that address.

    (2) Except as provided in § 342(f) of the Code, if a creditor or indenture trustee has not filed a request designating a mailing address under Rule 2002(g)(1) or Rule 5003(e), the notices shall be mailed to the address shown on the list of creditors or schedule of liabilities, whichever is filed later. If an equity security holder has not filed a request designating a mailing address under Rule 2002(g)(1) or Rule 5003(e), the notices shall be mailed to the address shown on the list of equity security holders.

    (3) If a list or schedule filed under Rule 1007 includes the name and address of a legal representative of an infant or incompetent person, and a person other than that representative files a request or proof of claim designating a name and mailing address that differs from the name and address of the representative included in the list or schedule, unless the court orders otherwise, notices under Rule 2002 shall be mailed to the representative included in the list or schedules and to the name and address designated in the request or proof of claim.

    (4) Notwithstanding Rule 2002(g)(1)–(3), an entity and a notice provider may agree that when the notice provider is directed by the court to give a notice, the notice provider shall give the notice to the entity in the manner agreed to and at the address or addresses the entity supplies to the notice provider. That address is conclusively presumed to be a proper address for the notice. The notice provider's failure to use the supplied address does not invalidate any notice that is otherwise effective under applicable law.

(5) A creditor may treat a notice as not having been brought to the creditor's attention under § 342(g)(1) only if, prior to issuance of the notice, the creditor has filed a statement that designates the name and address of the person or organizational subdivision of the creditor responsible for receiving notices under the Code, and that describes the procedures established by the creditor to cause such notices to be delivered to the designated person or subdivision.

(h) Notices to creditors whose claims are filed

In a chapter 7 case, after 90 days following the first date set for the meeting of creditors under § 341 of the Code, the court may direct that all notices required by subdivision (a) of this rule be mailed only to the debtor, the trustee, all indenture trustees, creditors that hold claims for which proofs of claim have been filed, and creditors, if any, that are still permitted to file claims by reason of an extension granted pursuant to Rule 3002(c)(1) or (c)(2). In a case where notice of insufficient assets to pay a dividend has been given to creditors pursuant to subdivision (e) of this rule, after 90 days following the mailing of a notice of the time for filing claims pursuant to Rule 3002(c)(5), the court may direct that notices be mailed only to the entities specified in the preceding sentence.

(i) Notices to committees

Copies of all notices required to be mailed pursuant to this rule shall be mailed to the committees elected under § 705 or appointed under § 1102 of the Code or to their authorized agents. Notwithstanding the foregoing subdivisions, the court may order that notices required by subdivision (a)(2), (3) and (6) of this rule be transmitted to the United States trustee and be mailed only to the committees elected under § 705 or appointed under § 1102 of the Code or to their authorized agents and to the creditors and equity security holders who serve on the trustee or debtor in possession and file a request that all notices be mailed to them. A committee appointed under § 1114 shall receive copies of all notices required by subdivisions (a)(1), (a)(5), (b), (f)(2), and (f)(7), and such other notices as the court may direct.

(j) Notices to the United States

Copies of notices required to be mailed to all creditors under this rule shall be mailed (1) in a chapter 11 reorganization case, to the Securities and Exchange Commission at any place the Commission designates, if the Commission has filed either a notice of appearance in the case or a written request to receive notices; (2) in a commodity broker case, to the Commodity Futures Trading Commission at Washington, D.C.; (3) in a chapter 11 case, to the Internal Revenue Service at its address set out in the register maintained under Rule 5003(e) for the district in which the case is pending; (4) if the papers in the case disclose a debt to the United States other than for taxes, to the United States attorney for the district in which the case is pending and to the department, agency, or instrumentality of the United States through which the debtor became indebted; or (5) if the filed papers disclose a stock interest of the United States, to the Secretary of the Treasury at Washington, D.C.

(k) Notices to United States trustee

Unless the case is a chapter 9 municipality case or unless the United States trustee requests otherwise, the clerk, or some other person as the court may direct, shall transmit to the United States trustee notice of the matters described in subdivisions (a)(2), (a)(3), (a)(4), (a)(8), (b), (f)(1), (f)(2), (f)(4), (f)(6), (f)(7), (f)(8), and (q) of this rule and notice of hearings on all applications for compensation or reimbursement of expenses. Notices to the United States trustee shall be transmitted within the time prescribed in subdivision (a) or (b) of this rule. The United States trustee shall also receive notice of any other matter if such notice is requested by the United States trustee or ordered by the court. Nothing in these rules requires the clerk or any other person to transmit to the United States trustee any notice, schedule, report, application or other document in a case under the Securities Investor Protection Act, 15 U.S.C. § 78aaa et.[1] seq.

---

[1] So in original. Period probably should not appear.

Rule 2002   BANKRUPTCY RULES

(*l*) Notice by publication

The court may order notice by publication if it finds that notice by mail is impracticable or that it is desirable to supplement the notice.

(m) Orders designating matter of notices

The court may from time to time enter orders designating the matters in respect to which, the entity to whom, and the form and manner in which notices shall be sent except as otherwise provided by these rules.

(n) Caption

The caption of every notice given under this rule shall comply with Rule 1005. The caption of every notice required to be given by the debtor to a creditor shall include the information required to be in the notice by § 342(c) of the Code.

(o) Notice of order for relief in consumer case

In a voluntary case commenced by an individual debtor whose debts are primarily consumer debts, the clerk or some other person as the court may direct shall give the trustee and all creditors notice by mail of the order for relief within 21 days from the date thereof.

(p) Notice to a creditor with a foreign address

    (1) If, at the request of the United States trustee or a party in interest, or on its own initiative, the court finds that a notice mailed within the time prescribed by these rules would not be sufficient to give a creditor with a foreign address to which notices under these rules are mailed reasonable notice under the circumstances, the court may order that the notice be supplemented with notice by other means or that the time prescribed for the notice by mail be enlarged.

    (2) Unless the court for cause orders otherwise, a creditor with a foreign address to which notices under this rule are mailed shall be given at least 30 days' notice of the time fixed for filing a proof of claim under Rule 3002(c) or Rule 3003(c).

    (3) Unless the court for cause orders otherwise, the mailing address of a creditor with a foreign address shall be determined under Rule 2002(g).

(q) Notice of petition for recognition of foreign proceeding and of court's intention to communicate with foreign courts and foreign representatives

    (1) Notice of petition for recognition

The clerk, or some other person as the court may direct, shall forthwith give the debtor, all persons or bodies authorized to administer foreign proceedings of the debtor, all entities against whom provisional relief is being sought under § 1519 of the Code, all parties to litigation pending in the United States in which the debtor is a party at the time of the filing of the petition, and such other entities as the court may direct, at least 21 days' notice by mail of the hearing on the petition for recognition of a foreign proceeding. The notice shall state whether the petition seeks recognition as a foreign main proceeding or foreign nonmain proceeding.

    (2) Notice of court's intention to communicate with foreign courts and foreign representatives

The clerk, or some other person as the court may direct, shall give the debtor, all persons or bodies authorized to administer foreign proceedings of the debtor, all entities against whom provisional relief is being sought under § 1519 of the Code, all parties to litigation pending in the United States in which the debtor is a party at the time of the filing of the petition, and such other entities as the court may direct, notice by mail of the court's intention to communicate with a foreign court or foreign representative.

(As amended Pub.L. 98–91, § 2(a), Aug. 30, 1983, 97 Stat. 607; Pub.L. 98–353, Title III, § 321, July 10, 1984, 98 Stat. 357; Mar. 30, 1987, eff. Aug. 1, 1987; Apr. 30, 1991, eff. Aug. 1, 1991; Apr. 22, 1993, eff. Aug. 1, 1993; Apr. 23, 1996, eff. Dec. 1, 1996; Apr. 11, 1997, eff. Dec. 1, 1997; Apr. 29, 1999, eff. Dec. 1,

OFFICERS AND ADMINISTRATION — Rule 2002

1999; Apr. 17, 2000, eff. Dec. 1, 2000; Apr. 23, 2001, eff. Dec. 1, 2001; Mar. 27, 2003, eff. Dec. 1, 2003; Apr. 26, 2004, eff. Dec. 1, 2004; Apr. 25, 2005, eff. Dec. 1, 2005; Apr. 23, 2008, eff. Dec. 1, 2008; Mar. 26, 2009, eff. Dec. 1, 2009.)

ADVISORY COMMITTEE NOTES
1983 Enactments

Some of the notices required by this rule may be given either by the clerk or as the court may otherwise direct. For example, the court may order the trustee or debtor in possession to transmit one or more of the notices required by this rule, such as, notice of a proposed sale of property. See § 363(b) of the Code. When publication of notices is required or desirable, reference should be made to Rule 9008.

Notice of the order for relief is required to be given by § 342 of the Code and by subdivision (f)(1) of this rule. That notice may be combined with the notice of the meeting of creditors as indicated in Official Form No. 16, the notice and order of the meeting of creditors.

Subdivision (a) sets forth the requirement that 20 days notice be given of the significant events in a case under the Bankruptcy Code. The former Act and Rules provided a ten day notice in bankruptcy and Chapter XI [former § 701 et seq. of this title] cases, and a 20 day notice in a Chapter X [former § 501 et seq. of this title] case. This rule generally makes uniform the 20 day notice provision except that subdivision (b) contains a 25 day period for certain events in a chapter 9, 11, or 13 case. Generally, Rule 9006 permits reduction of time periods. Since notice by mail is complete on mailing, the requirement of subdivision (a) is satisfied if the notices are deposited in the mail at least 20 days before the event. See Rule 9006(e). The exceptions referred to in the introductory phrase include the modifications in the notice procedure permitted by subdivision (h) as to non-filing creditors, subdivision (i) as to cases where a committee is functioning, and subdivision (k) where compliance with subdivision (a) is impracticable.

The notice of a proposed sale affords creditors an opportunity to object to the sale and raise a dispute for the court's attention. Section 363(b) of the Code permits the trustee or debtor in possession to sell property, other than in the ordinary course of business, only after notice and hearing. If no objection is raised after notice, § 102(1) provides that there need not be an actual hearing. Thus, absent objection, there would be no court involvement with respect to a trustee's sale. Once an objection is raised, only the court may pass on it.

Prior to the Code the court could shorten the notice period for a proposed sale of property or dispense with notice. This subdivision (a), permits the 20 day period to be shortened in appropriate circumstances but the rule does not contain a provision allowing the court to dispense with notice. The rule is thus consistent with the Code, §§ 363(b) and 102(1)(A) of the Code. See 28 U.S.C. § 2075. It may be necessary, in certain circumstances, however, to use a method of notice other than mail. Subdivision (a)(2) vests the court with discretion, on cause shown, to order a different method. Reference should also be made to Rule 6004 which allows a different type of notice of proposed sales when the property is of little value.

Notice of the hearing on an application for compensation or reimbursement of expenses totalling $100 or less need not be given. In chapter 13 cases relatively small amounts are sometimes allowed for post-confirmation services and it would not serve a useful purpose to require advance notice.

Subdivision (b) is similar to subdivision (a) but lengthens the notice time to 25 days with respect to those events particularly significant in chapter 9, 11 and 13 cases. The additional time may be necessary to formulate objections to a disclosure statement or confirmation of a plan and preparation for the hearing on approval of the disclosure statement or confirmation. The disclosure statement and hearing thereon is only applicable in chapter 9 cases (§ 901(a) of the Code), and chapter 11 cases (§ 1125 of the Code).

Subdivision (c) specifies certain matters that should be included in the notice of a proposed sale of property and notice of the hearing on an application for allowances. Rule 6004 fixes the time within which parties in interest may file objections to a proposed sale of property.

Subdivision (d) relates exclusively to the notices given to equity security holders in chapter 11 cases. Under chapter 11, a plan may impair the interests of the debtor's shareholders or a plan may be a relatively simple restructuring of unsecured debt. In some cases, it is necessary that equity interest holders receive various notices and in other cases there is no purpose to be served. This subdivision indicates that the court is not mandated to order notices but rather that the matter should be treated with some flexibility. The court may decide whether notice is to be given and how it is to be given. Under § 341(b) of the Code, a meeting of equity security holders is not required in each case, only when it is ordered by the court. Thus subdivision (d)(2) requires notice only when the court orders a meeting.

Rule 2002   **BANKRUPTCY RULES**

In addition to the notices specified in this subdivision, there may be other events or matters arising in a case as to which equity security holders should receive notice. These are situations left to determination by the court.

Subdivision (e), authorizing a notice of the apparent insufficiency of assets for the payment of any dividend, is correlated with Rule 3002(c)(5), which provides for the issuance of an additional notice to creditors if the possibility of a payment later materializes.

Subdivision (f) provides for the transmission of other notices to which no time period applies. Clause (1) requires notice of the order for relief; this complements the mandate of § 342 of the Code requiring such notice as is appropriate of the order for relief. This notice may be combined with the notice of the meeting of creditors to avoid the necessity of more than one mailing. See Official Form No. 16, notice of meeting of creditors.

Subdivision (g) recognizes that an agent authorized to receive notices for a creditor may, without a court order, designate where notices to the creditor he represents should be addressed. Agent includes an officer of a corporation, an attorney at law, or an attorney in fact if the requisite authority has been given him. It should be noted that Official Forms Nos. 17 and 18 do not include an authorization of the holder of a power of attorney to receive notices for the creditor. Neither these forms nor this rule carries any implication that such an authorization may not be given in a power of attorney or that a request for notices to be addressed to both the creditor or his duly authorized agent may not be filed.

Subdivision (h). After the time for filing claims has expired in a chapter 7 case, creditors who have not filed their claims in accordance with Rule 3002(c) are not entitled to share in the estate except as they may come within the special provisions of § 726 of the Code or Rule 3002(c)(6). The elimination of notice to creditors who have no recognized stake in the estate may permit economies in time and expense. Reduction of the list of creditors to receive notices under this subdivision is discretionary. This subdivision does not apply to the notice of the meeting of creditors.

Subdivision (i) contains a list of matters of which notice may be given a creditors' committee or to its authorized agent in lieu of notice to the creditors. Such notice may serve every practical purpose of a notice to all the creditors and save delay and expense. In re Schulte-United, Inc., 59 F.2d 553, 561 (8th Cir.1932).

Subdivision (j). The premise for the requirement that the district director of internal revenue receive copies of notices that all creditors receive in a chapter 11 case is that every debtor is potentially a tax debtor of the United States. Notice to the district director alerts him to the possibility that a tax debtor's estate is about to be liquidated or reorganized and that the debtor may be discharged. When other indebtedness to the United States is indicated, the United States attorney is notified as the person in the best position to protect the interests of the government. In addition, the provision requires notice by mail to the head of any department, agency, or instrumentality of the United States through whose action the debtor became indebted to the United States. This rule is not intended to preclude a local rule from requiring a state or local tax authority to receive some or all of the notices to creditors under these rules.

Subdivision (k) specifies two kinds of situations in which notice by publication may be appropriate: (1) when notice by mail is impracticable; and (2) when notice by mail alone is less than adequate. Notice by mail may be impracticable when, for example, the debtor has disappeared or his records have been destroyed and the names and addresses of his creditors are unavailable, or when the number of creditors with nominal claims is very large and the estate to be distributed may be insufficient to defray the costs of issuing the notices. Supplementing notice by mail is also indicated when the debtor's records are incomplete or inaccurate and it is reasonable to believe that publication may reach some of the creditors who would otherwise be missed. Rule 9008 applies when the court directs notice by publication under this rule. Neither clause (2) of subdivision (a) nor subdivision (k) of this rule is concerned with the publication of advertisement to the general public of a sale of property of the estate at public auction under Rule 6004(b). See 3 Collier, Bankruptcy 522–23 (14th ed. 1971); 4B id. 1165–67 (1967); 2 id. ¶363.03 (15th ed. 1981).

Subdivision (m). Inclusion in notices to creditors of information as to other names used by the debtor as required by Rule 1005 will assist them in the preparation of their proofs of claim and in deciding whether to file a complaint objecting to the debtor's discharge. Additional names may be listed by the debtor on his statement of affairs when he did not file the petition. The mailing of notices should not be postponed to await a delayed filing of the statement of financial affairs.

OFFICERS AND ADMINISTRATION — Rule 2002

1987 Amendments

Subdivision (a) is amended to provide that notice of a hearing on an application for compensation must be given only when the amount requested is in excess of $500.

Subdivision (d). A new notice requirement is added as clause (3). When a proposed sale is of all or substantially all of the debtor's assets, it is appropriate that equity security holders be given notice of the proposed sale. The clauses of subdivision (d) are renumbered to accommodate this addition.

Subdivision (f). Clause (7) is eliminated. Mailing of a copy of the discharge order is governed by Rule 4004(g).

Subdivision (g) is amended to relieve the clerk of the duty to mail notices to the address shown in a proof of claim when a notice of no dividend has been given pursuant to Rule 2002. This amendment avoids the necessity of the clerk searching proofs of claim which are filed in no dividend cases to ascertain whether a different address is shown.

Subdivision (n) was enacted by § 321 of the 1984 amendments.

1991 Amendments

Subdivision (a)(3) is amended to exclude compromise or settlement agreements concerning adequate protection or which modify or terminate the automatic stay, provide for use of cash collateral, or create a senior or equal lien on collateral to obtain credit. Notice requirements relating to approval of such agreements are governed by Rule 4001(d).

Subdivision (a)(5) is amended to include a hearing on dismissal or conversion of a chapter 12 case. This subdivision does not apply when a hearing is not required. It is also amended to avoid the necessity of giving notice to all creditors of a hearing on the dismissal of a consumer debtor's case based on substantial abuse of chapter 7. Such hearings on dismissal under § 707(b) of the Code are governed by Rule 1017(e).

Subdivision (a)(9) is added to provide for notice of the time fixed for filing objections and the hearing to consider confirmation of a plan in a chapter 12 case. Section 1224 of the Code requires "expedited notice" of the confirmation hearing in a chapter 12 case and requires that the hearing be concluded not later than 45 days after the filing of the plan unless the time is extended for cause. This amendment establishes 20 days as the notice period. The court may shorten this time on its own motion or on motion of a party in interest. The notice includes both the date of the hearing and the date for filing objections, and must be accompanied by a copy of the plan or a summary of the plan in accordance with Rule 3015(d).

Subdivision (b) is amended to delete as unnecessary the references to subdivisions (h) and (i).

Subdivision (d) does not require notice to equity security holders in a chapter 12 case. The procedural burden of requiring such notice is outweighed by the likelihood that all equity security holders of a family farmer will be informed of the progress of the case without formal notice. Subdivision (d) is amended to recognize that the United States trustee may convene a meeting of equity security holders pursuant to § 341(b).

Subdivision (f)(2) is amended and subdivision (f)(4) is deleted to require notice of any conversion of the case, whether the conversion is by court order or is effectuated by the debtor filing a notice of conversion pursuant to §§ 1208(a) or 1307(a). Subdivision (f)(8), renumbered (f)(7), is amended to include entry of an order confirming a chapter 12 plan. Subdivision (f)(9) is amended to increase the amount to $1,500.

Subdivisions (g) and (j) are amended to delete the words "with the court" and subdivision (i) is amended to delete the words "with the clerk" because these phrases are unnecessary. See Rules 5005(a) and 9001(3).

Subdivision (i) is amended to require that the United States trustee receive notices required by subdivision (a)(2), (3) and (7) of this rule notwithstanding a court order limiting such notice to committees and to creditors and equity security holders who request such notices. Subdivision (i) is amended further to include committees elected pursuant to § 705 of the Code and to provide that committees of retired employees appointed in chapter 11 cases receive certain notices.

Subdivision (k) is derived from Rule X–1008. The administrative functions of the United States trustee pursuant to 28 U.S.C. § 586(a) and standing to be heard on issues under § 307 and other sections of the Code require that the United States trustee be informed of developments and issues in every case except chapter 9 cases. The rule omits those notices described in subdivision (a)(1) because a meeting of creditors is convened only by the United States trustee, and those notices described in subdivision (a)(4) (date fixed for filing claims against a surplus), subdivision (a)(6) (time fixed to accept or reject proposed modification of a plan), subdivision (a)(8) (time fixed for filing proofs of claims in chapter 11 cases), subdivision (f)(3) (time fixed for filing claims in chapter 7, 12, and 13 cases), and subdivision (f)(5) (time fixed for filing complaint to determine dischargeability of debt) because these notices do not relate to matters that generally involve the United States trustee. Nonetheless, the omission of these notices does not prevent the United States trustee from receiving such notices upon request. The United States trustee also receives notice of hearings on applications for compensation or reimbursement without regard to the $500 limitation contained in subdivision (a)(7) of this rule. This rule is intended to be flexible in that it permits the United States trustee in a particular judicial district to request notices in certain categories, and to request not to receive notices in other categories, when the practice in that district makes that desirable.

1993 Amendments

Subdivision (j) is amended to avoid the necessity of sending an additional notice to the Washington, D.C. address of the Securities and Exchange Commission if the Commission prefers to have notices sent only to a local office. This change also clarifies that notices required to be mailed pursuant to this rule must be sent to the Securities and Exchange Commission only if it has filed a notice of appearance or has filed a written request. Other amendments are stylistic and make no substantive change.

1996 Amendments

Paragraph (a)(4) is abrogated to conform to the abrogation of Rule 3002(c)(6). The remaining paragraphs of subdivision (a) are renumbered, and references to these paragraphs contained in other subdivisions of this rule are amended accordingly.

Paragraph (f)(8) is amended so that a summary of the trustee's final account, which is prepared after distribution of property, does not have to be mailed to the debtor, all creditors, and indenture trustees in a chapter 7 case. Parties are sufficiently protected by receiving a summary of the trustee's final report that informs parties of the proposed distribution of property.

Subdivision (h) is amended (1) to provide that an order under this subdivision may not be issued if a notice of no dividend is given pursuant to Rule 2002(e) and the time for filing claims has not expired as provided in Rule 3002(c)(5); (2) to clarify that notices required to be mailed by subdivision (a) to parties other than creditors must be mailed to those entities despite an order issued pursuant to subdivision (h); (3) to provide that if the court, pursuant to Rule 3002(c)(1) or 3002(c)(2), has granted an extension of time to file a proof of claim, the creditor for whom the extension has been granted must continue to receive notices despite an order issued pursuant to subdivision (h); and (4) to delete references to subdivision (a)(4) and Rule 3002(c)(6), which have been abrogated.

Other amendments to this rule are stylistic.

1997 Amendments

Paragraph (a)(1) is amended to include notice of a meeting of creditors convened under § 1104(b) of the Code for the purpose of electing a trustee in a chapter 11 case. The court for cause shown may order the 20-day period reduced pursuant to Rule 9006(c)(1).

Subdivision (n) is amended to conform to the 1994 amendment to § 342 of the Code. As provided in § 342(c), the failure of a notice given by the debtor to a creditor to contain the information required by § 342(c) does not invalidate the legal effect of the notice.

1999 Amendments

Paragraph (a)(4) is amended to conform to the amendments to Rule 1017. If the United States trustee files a motion to dismiss a case for the debtor's failure to file the list of creditors, schedules, or the statement of financial affairs within the time specified in § 707(a)(3), the amendments to this rule and to Rule 1017 eliminate the requirement that all creditors receive notice of the hearing.

Paragraph (a)(4) is amended further to conform to Rule 1017(b), which requires that notice of the hearing on dismissal of a case for failure to pay the filing fee be served on only the debtor and the trustee.

Paragraph (f)(2) is amended to provide for notice of the suspension of proceedings under § 305.

OFFICERS AND ADMINISTRATION — Rule 2002

2000 Amendments

Paragraph(a)(6) is amended to increase the dollar amount from $500 to $1,000. The amount was last amended in 1987, when it was changed from $100 to $500. The amendment also clarifies that the notice is required only if a particular entity is requesting more than $1,000 as compensation or reimbursement of expenses. If several professionals are requesting compensation or reimbursement, and only one hearing will be held on all applications, notice under paragraph (a)(6) is required only with respect to the entities that have requested more than $1,000. If each applicant requests $1,000 or less, notice under paragraph (a)(6) is not required even though the aggregate amount of all applications to be considered at the hearing is more than $1,000.

If a particular entity had filed prior applications or had received compensation or reimbursement of expenses at an earlier time in the case, the amounts previously requested or awarded are not considered when determining whether the present application exceeds $1,000 for the purpose of applying this rule.

2001 Amendments

Subdivision (c)(3) is added to assure that parties given notice of a hearing to consider confirmation of a plan under subdivision (b) are given adequate notice of an injunction provided for in the plan if it would enjoin conduct that is not otherwise enjoined by operation of the Code. The validity and effect of any injunction provided for in a plan are substantive law matters that are beyond the scope of these rules.

The notice requirement of subdivision (c)(3) is not applicable to an injunction contained in a plan if it is substantially the same as an injunction provided under the Code. For example, if a plan contains an injunction against acts to collect a discharged debt from the debtor, Rule 2002(c)(3) would not apply because that conduct would be enjoined under § 524(a)(2) upon the debtor's discharge. But if a plan provides that creditors will be enjoined from asserting claims against persons who are not debtors in the case, the notice of the confirmation hearing must include the information required under Rule 2002(c)(3) because that conduct would not be enjoined by operation of the Code. See § 524(e).

The requirement that the notice identify the entities that would be subject to the injunction requires only reasonable identification under the circumstances. If the entities that would be subject to the injunction cannot be identified by name, the notice may describe them by class or category if reasonable under the circumstances. For example, it may be sufficient for the notice to identify the entities as "all creditors of the debtor" and for the notice to be published in a manner that satisfies due process requirements.

Subdivision (g) has been revised to clarify that where a creditor or indenture trustee files both a proof of claim which includes a mailing address and a separate request designating a mailing address, the last paper filed determines the proper address. The amendments also clarify that a request designating a mailing address is effective only with respect to a particular case.

Under Rule 2002(g), a duly filed proof of claim is considered a request designating a mailing address if a notice of no dividend has been given under Rule 2002(e), but has been superseded by a subsequent notice of possible dividend under Rule 3002(c)(5). A duly filed proof of interest is considered a request designating a mailing address of an equity security holder.

Rule 2002(g)(3) is added to assure that notices to an infant or incompetent person under this rule are mailed to the appropriate guardian or other legal representative. Under Rule 1007(m), if the debtor knows that a creditor is an infant or incompetent person, the debtor is required to include in the list and schedule of creditors the name and address of the person upon whom process would be served in an adversary proceeding in accordance with Rule 7004(b)(2). If the infant or incompetent person, or another person, files a request or proof of claim designating a different name and mailing address, the notices would have to be mailed to both names and addresses until the court resolved the issue as to the proper mailing address.

The other amendments to Rule 2002(g) are stylistic.

2003 Amendments

Subdivision (a)(1) of the rule is amended to direct the clerk or other person giving notice of the § 341 or § 1104(b) meeting of creditors to include the debtor's full social security number on the notice. Official Form 9, the form of the notice of the meeting of creditors that will become a part of the court's file in the case, will include only the last four digits of the debtor's social security number. This rule, however, directs the clerk to include the full social security number on the notice that is served on the creditors and other identified parties, unless the court orders otherwise in a particular case. This will enable creditors and other parties in interest who are in possession of the debtor's social security number to verify the debtor's identity and proceed accordingly. The filed Official Form 9, however, will not include the debtor's full social security number. This will prevent the full social security number from becoming a part of the court's file in the case, and the number will not be included in the court's electronic records. Creditors who already have the debtor's social security number will be able to verify the existence of a case under the debtor's social security number, but any person searching the electronic case files without the number will not be able to acquire the debtor's social security number.

2004 Amendments

The rule is amended to reflect that the structure of the Internal Revenue Service no longer includes a District Director. Thus, rather than sending notice to the District Director, the rule now requires that the notices be sent to the location designated by the Service and set out in the register of addresses maintained by the clerk under Rule 5003(e). The other change is stylistic.

2005 Amendments

A new paragraph (g)(4) is inserted in the rule. The new paragraph authorizes an entity and a notice provider to agree that the notice provider will give notices to the entity at the address or addresses set out in their agreement. Rule 9001(9) sets out the definition of a notice provider.

The business of many entities is national in scope, and technology currently exists to direct the transmission of notice (both electronically and in paper form) to those entities in an accurate and much more efficient manner than by sending individual notices to the same creditor by separate mailings. The rule authorizes an entity and a notice provider to determine the manner of the service as well as to set the address or addresses to which the notices must be sent. For example, they could agree that all notices sent by the notice provider to the entity must be sent to a single, nationwide electronic or postal address. They could also establish local or regional addresses to which notices would be sent in matters pending in specific districts. Since the entity and notice provider also can agree on the date of the commencement of service under the agreement, there is no need to set a date in the rule after which notices would have to be sent to the address or addresses that the entity establishes. Furthermore, since the entity supplies the address to the notice provider, use of that address is conclusively presumed to be proper. Nonetheless, if that address is not used, the notice still may be effective if the notice is otherwise effective under applicable law. This is the same treatment given under Rule 5003(e) to notices sent to governmental units at addresses other than those set out in that register of addresses.

The remaining subdivisions of Rule 2002(g) continue to govern the addressing of a notice that is not sent pursuant to an agreement described in Rule 2002(g)(4).

2008 Amendments

Subdivision (b) is amended to provide for 25 days' notice of the time for the court to make a final determination whether the plan in a small business case can serve as a disclosure statement. Conditional approval of a disclosure statement in a small business case is governed by Rule 3017.1 and does not require 25 days' notice. The court may consider this matter in a hearing combined with the confirmation hearing in a small business case.

Because of the requirements of Rule 6004(g), subdivision (c)(1) is amended to require that a trustee leasing or selling personally identifiable information under § 363(b)(1)(A) or (B) of the Code, as amended in 2005, include in the notice of the lease or sale transaction a statement as to whether the lease or sale is consistent with a policy prohibiting the transfer of the information.

Subdivisions (f)(9) and (10) are new. They reflect the 2005 amendments to §§ 342(d) and 704(b) of the Code. Section 342(d) requires the clerk to give notice to creditors shortly after the commencement of the case as to whether a presumption of abuse exists. Subdivision (f)(9) adds this notice to the list of notices that the clerk must give. Subdivision (f)(10) implements the amendment to § 704(b), which requires the court to provide a copy to all creditors of a statement by the United States trustee or bankruptcy administrator as to whether the debtor's case would be presumed to be an abuse under § 707(b) not later than five days after receiving it.

Subdivision (f)(11) is also added to provide notice to creditors of the debtor's filing of a statement in a chapter 11, 12, or 13 case that there is no reasonable cause to believe that § 522(q) applies in the case. This allows a creditor who disputes that assertion to request a delay of the entry of the discharge in the case.

OFFICERS AND ADMINISTRATION   Rule 2002

Subdivision (g)(2) of the rule is amended because the 2005 amendments to § 342(f) of the Code permit creditors in chapter 7 and 13 individual debtor cases to file a notice with any bankruptcy court of the address to which the creditor wishes all notices to be sent. The amendment to Rule 2002(g)(2) therefore only limits application of the subdivision when a creditor files a notice under § 342(f).

New subdivision (g)(5) implements § 342(g)(1) which was added to the Code in 2005. Section 342(g)(1) allows a creditor to treat a notice as not having been brought to the creditor's attention, and so potentially ineffective, until it is received by a person or organizational subdivision that the creditor has designated to receive notices under the Bankruptcy Code. Under that section, the creditor must have established reasonable procedures for such notices to be delivered to the designated person or subdivision. The rule provides that, in order to challenge a notice under § 342(g)(1), a creditor must have filed the name and address of the designated notice recipient, as well as a description of the procedures for directing notices to that recipient, prior to the time that the challenged notice was issued. The filing required by the rule may be made as part of a creditor's filing under § 342(f), which allows a creditor to file a notice of the address to be used by all bankruptcy courts or by particular bankruptcy courts to provide notice to the creditor in cases under chapters 7 and 13. Filing the name and address of the designated notice recipient and the procedures for directing notices to that recipient will reduce uncertainty as to the proper party for receiving notice and limit factual disputes as to whether a notice recipient has been designated and as to the nature of procedures adopted to direct notices to the recipient.

Subdivision (k) is amended to add notices given under subdivision (q) to the list of notices which must be served on the United States trustee.

Section 1514(d) of the Code, added by the 2005 amendments, requires that such additional time as is reasonable under the circumstances be given to creditors with foreign addresses with respect to notices and the filing of a proof of claim. Thus, subdivision (p)(1) is added to this rule to give the court flexibility to direct that notice by other means shall supplement notice by mail, or to enlarge the notice period, for creditors with foreign addresses. If cause exists, such as likely delays in the delivery of mailed notices in particular locations, the court may order that notice also be given by email, facsimile, or private courier. Alternatively, the court may enlarge the notice period for a creditor with a foreign address. It is expected that in most situations involving foreign creditors, fairness will not require any additional notice or extension of the notice period. This rule recognizes that the court has discretion to establish procedures to determine, on its own initiative, whether relief under subdivision (p) is appropriate, but that the court is not required to establish such procedures and may decide to act only on request of a party in interest.

Subdivision (p)(2) is added to the rule to grant creditors with a foreign address to which notices are mailed at least 30 days' notice of the time within which to file proofs of claims if notice is mailed to the foreign address, unless the court orders otherwise. If cause exists, such as likely delays in the delivery of notices in particular locations, the court may extend the notice period for creditors with foreign addresses. The court may also shorten the additional notice time if circumstances so warrant. For example, if the court in a chapter 11 case determines that supplementing the notice to a foreign creditor with notice by electronic means, such as email or facsimile, would give the creditor reasonable notice, the court may order that the creditor be given only 20 days' notice in accordance with Rule 2002(a)(7).

Subdivision (p)(3) is added to provide that the court may, for cause, override a creditor's designation of a foreign address under Rule 2002(g). For example, if a party in interest believes that a creditor has wrongfully designated a foreign address to obtain additional time when it has a significant presence in the United States, the party can ask the court to order that notices to that creditor be sent to an address other than the one designated by the foreign creditor.

Subdivision (q) is added to require that notice of the hearing on the petition for recognition of a foreign proceeding be given to the debtor, all administrators in foreign proceedings of the debtor, entities against whom provisional relief is sought, and entities with whom the debtor is engaged in litigation at the time of the commencement of the case. There is no need at this stage of the proceedings to provide notice to all creditors. If the foreign representative should take action to commence a case under another chapter of the Code, the rules governing those proceedings will operate to provide that notice is given to all creditors.

The rule also requires notice of the court's intention to communicate with a foreign court or foreign representative.

2009 Amendments

The rule is amended to implement changes in connection with the amendment to Rule 9006(a) and the manner by which time is computed under the rules. The deadlines in the rule are amended to

Rule 2003 BANKRUPTCY RULES

substitute a deadline that is a multiple of seven days. Throughout the rules, deadlines are amended in the following manner:

- 5-day periods become 7-day periods
- 10-day periods become 14-day periods
- 15-day periods become 14-day periods
- 20-day periods become 21-day periods
- 25-day periods become 28-day periods

CROSS REFERENCES

Form and manner of publication of notices, see Fed.Rules Bankr.Proc. Rule 9008, 11 USCA.

General requirements of form for creditors' notices, see Fed.Rules Bankr.Proc. Rule 9004, 11 USCA.

Hearing on disclosure statement in municipality debt adjustment and reorganization cases, see Fed.Rules Bankr.Proc. Rule 3017, 11 USCA.

Notice by mail complete on mailing, see Fed.Rules Bankr.Proc. Rule 9006, 11 USCA.

Notice of—

Dismissal for failure to pay filing fees, see Fed.Rules Bankr.Proc. Rule 1017, 11 USCA.

Dividend and of time to file proof of claim in liquidation case, see Fed.Rules Bankr.Proc. Rule 3002, 11 USCA.

Hearing on compromise or settlement to creditors, debtor, indenture trustees, and others designated by court, see Fed.Rules Bankr.Proc. Rule 9019, 11 USCA.

Hearing on confirmation of individual debt adjustment plan to include plan or summary, see Fed.Rules Bankr.Proc. Rule 3015, 11 USCA.

Hearing on dismissal of case, see Fed.Rules Bankr.Proc. Rule 1017, 11 USCA.

Order of conversion to liquidation case, see Fed.Rules Bankr.Proc. Rule 1019, 11 USCA.

Time extended to file claims against surplus in converted liquidation case, see Fed.Rules Bankr.Proc. Rule 1019, 11 USCA.

Time fixed for filing complaint objecting to discharge in reorganization case, see Fed.Rules Bankr.Proc. Rule case, see Fed.Rules Bankr.Proc. Rule 4004, 11 USCA.

Time fixed for filing complaint to determine debt's dischargeability, see Fed.Rules Bankr.Proc. Rule 4007, 11 USCA.

Use, sale, or lease of property other than in ordinary course, see Fed.Rules Bankr.Proc. Rule 6004, 11 USCA.

Waiver, denial, or revocation of discharge, see Fed.Rules Bankr.Proc. Rule 4006, 11 USCA.

Reduction in time periods generally, see Fed.Rules Bankr.Proc. Rule 9006, 11 USCA.

Reduction in twenty-day period for notice to file claims not permitted—

Against surplus in estate in liquidation case, see Fed.Rules Bankr.Proc. Rule 9006, 11 USCA.

In municipality debt adjustment or reorganization cases, see Fed.Rules Bankr.Proc. Rule 9006, 11 USCA.

Review by court on plan's confirmation after notice and hearing pursuant to, see Fed.Rules Bankr.Proc. Rule 3020, 11 USCA.

Rule 2003. Meeting of Creditors or Equity Security Holders

(a) Date and place

Except as otherwise provided in § 341(e) of the Code, in a chapter 7 liquidation or a chapter 11 reorganization case, the United States trustee shall call a meeting of creditors to be held no fewer than 21 and no more than 40 days after the order for relief. In a chapter 12 family farmer debt adjustment case, the United States trustee shall call a meeting of creditors to be held no fewer than 21 and no more than 35 days after the order for relief. In a chapter 13 individual's debt adjustment case, the United States trustee shall call a meeting of creditors to be held no fewer than 21 and no more than 50 days after the order for relief. If there is an appeal from or a motion to vacate the order for relief, or if there is a motion to dismiss the case, the United States trustee may set a later date for the meeting. The meeting may be held at a regular place for holding court or at any other place designated by the United States trustee within the district convenient for the parties in interest. If the United States trustee designates a place for the meeting which is not regularly staffed by the United States trustee or an assistant who may preside at the meeting, the meeting may be held not more than 60 days after the order for relief.

(b) Order of meeting

(1) Meeting of creditors

The United States trustee shall preside at the meeting of creditors. The business of the meeting shall include the examination of the debtor under oath and, in a chapter 7 liquidation case, may include the election of a creditors' committee and, if the case is not under subchapter V of chapter 7, the election of a trustee. The presiding officer shall have the authority to administer oaths.

(2) Meeting of equity security holders

If the United States trustee convenes a meeting of equity security holders pursuant to § 341(b) of the Code, the United States trustee shall fix a date for the meeting and shall preside.

(3) Right to vote

In a chapter 7 liquidation case, a creditor is entitled to vote at a meeting if, at or before the meeting, the creditor has filed a proof of claim or a writing setting forth facts evidencing a right to vote pursuant to § 702(a) of the Code unless objection is made to the claim or the proof of claim is insufficient on its face. A creditor of a partnership may file a proof of claim or writing evidencing a right to vote for the trustee for the estate of a general partner notwithstanding that a trustee for the estate of the partnership has previously qualified. In the event of an objection to the amount or allowability of a claim for the purpose of voting, unless the court orders otherwise, the United States trustee shall tabulate the votes for each alternative presented by the dispute and, if resolution of such dispute is necessary to determine the result of the election, the tabulations for each alternative shall be reported to the court.

(c) Record of meeting

Any examination under oath at the meeting of creditors held pursuant to § 341(a) of the Code shall be recorded verbatim by the United States trustee using electronic sound recording equipment or other means of recording, and such record shall be preserved by the United States trustee and available for public access until two years after the conclusion of the meeting of creditors. Upon request of any entity, the United States trustee shall certify and provide a copy or transcript of such recording at the entity's expense.

(d) Report of election and resolution of disputes in a chapter 7 case

(1) Report of undisputed election

In a chapter 7 case, if the election of a trustee or a member of a creditors' committee is not disputed, the United States trustee shall promptly file a report of the election, including the name and address of the person or entity elected and a statement that the election is undisputed.

(2) Disputed election

If the election is disputed, the United States trustee shall promptly file a report stating that the election is disputed, informing the court of the nature of the dispute, and listing the name and address of any candidate elected under any alternative presented by the dispute. No later than the date on which the report is filed, the United States trustee shall mail a copy of the report to any party in interest that has made a request to receive a copy of the report. Pending disposition by the court of a disputed election for trustee, the interim trustee shall continue in office. Unless a motion for the resolution of the dispute is filed no later than 14 days after the United States trustee files a report of a disputed election for trustee, the interim trustee shall serve as trustee in the case.

(e) Adjournment

The meeting may be adjourned from time to time by announcement at the meeting of the adjourned date and time. The presiding official shall promptly file a statement specifying the date and time to which the meeting is adjourned.

(f) Special meetings

The United States trustee may call a special meeting of creditors on request of a party in interest or on the United States trustee's own initiative.

(g) Final meeting

If the United States trustee calls a final meeting of creditors in a case in which the net proceeds realized exceed $1,500, the clerk shall mail a summary of the trustee's final account to the creditors with a notice of the meeting, together with a statement of the amount of the claims allowed. The trustee shall attend the final meeting and shall, if requested, report on the administration of the estate.

(As amended Mar. 30, 1987, eff. Aug. 1, 1987; Apr. 30, 1991, eff. Aug. 1, 1991; Apr. 22, 1993, eff. Aug. 1, 1993; Apr. 29, 1999, eff. Dec. 1, 1999; Mar. 27, 2003, eff. Dec. 1, 2003; Apr. 23, 2008, eff. Dec. 1, 2008; Mar. 26, 2009, eff. Dec. 1, 2009; Apr. 26, 2011, eff. Dec. 1, 2011.)

ADVISORY COMMITTEE NOTES

Section 341(a) of the Code requires a meeting of creditors in a chapter 7, 11 or 13 case, and § 341(b) permits the court to order a meeting of equity security holders. A major change from prior law, however, prohibits the judge from attending or presiding over the meeting. Section 341(c).

This rule does not apply either in a case for the reorganization of a railroad or for the adjustment of debts of a municipality. Sections 1161 and 901 render §§ 341 and 343 inapplicable in these types of cases. Section 341 sets the requirement for a meeting of creditors and § 343 provides for the examination of the debtor.

Subdivision (a). The meeting is to be held between 20 and 40 days after the date of the order for relief. In a voluntary case, the date of the order for relief is the date of the filing of the petition (§ 301 of the Code); in an involuntary case, it is the date of an actual order (§ 303(i) of the Code).

Subdivision (b) provides flexibility as to who will preside at the meeting of creditors. The court may designate a person to serve as presiding officer, such as the interim trustee appointed under § 701 of the Code. If the court does not designate anyone, the clerk will preside. In either case, creditors may elect a person of their own choosing. In any event, the clerk may remain to record the proceedings and take appearances. Use of the clerk is not contrary to the legislative policy of § 341(c). The judge remains insulated from any information coming forth at the meeting and any information obtained by the clerk must not be relayed to the judge.

Although the clerk may preside at the meeting, the clerk is not performing any kind of judicial role, nor should the clerk give any semblance of performing such a role. It would be pretentious for the clerk to ascend the bench, don a robe or be addressed as "your honor". The clerk should not appear to parties or others as any type of judicial officer.

In a chapter 11 case, if a committee of unsecured creditors has been appointed pursuant to § 1102(a)(1) of the Code and a chairman has been selected, the chairman will preside or a person, such as the attorney for the committee, may be designated to preside by the chairman.

Since the judge must fix the bond of the trustee but cannot be present at the meeting, the rule allows the creditors to recommend the amount of the bond. They should be able to obtain relevant information concerning the extent of assets of the debtor at the meeting.

Paragraph (1) authorizes the presiding officer to administer oaths. This is important because the debtor's examination must be under oath.

Paragraph (3) of subdivision (b) has application only in a chapter 7 case. That is the only type of case under the Code that permits election of a trustee or committee. In all other cases, no vote is taken at the meeting of creditors. If it is necessary for the court to make a determination with respect to a claim, the meeting may be adjourned until the objection or dispute is resolved.

The second sentence recognizes that partnership creditors may vote for a trustee of a partner's estate along with the separate creditors of the partner. Although § 723(c) gives the trustee of a partnership a claim against a partner's estate for the full amount of partnership creditors' claims allowed, the purpose and function of this provision are to simplify distribution and prevent double proof, not to disfranchise partnership creditors in electing a trustee of an estate against which they hold allowable claims.

Subdivision (c) requires minutes and a record of the meeting to be maintained by the presiding officer. A verbatim record must be made of the debtor's examination but the rule is flexible as to the means used to record the examination.

Subdivision (d) recognizes that the court must be informed immediately about the election or nonelection of a trustee in a chapter 7 case. Pursuant to Rule 2008, the clerk officially informs the trustee of his election or appointment and how he is to qualify. The presiding person has no authority to resolve a disputed election.

For purposes of expediency, the results of the election should be obtained for each alternative presented by the dispute and immediately reported to the court. Thus, when an interested party presents the dispute to the court, its prompt resolution by the court will determine the dispute and a new or adjourned meeting to conduct the election may be avoided. The clerk is not an interested party.

A creditors' committee may be elected only in a chapter 7 case. In chapter 11 cases, a creditors' committee is appointed pursuant to § 1102.

While a final meeting is not required, Rule 2002(f)(10) provides for the trustee's final account to be sent to creditors.

1987 Amendments

Subdivision (a). Many courts schedule meetings of creditors at various locations in the district. Because the clerk must schedule meetings at those locations, an additional 20 days for scheduling the meetings is provided under the amended rule.

1991 Amendments

The amendment to subdivision (a) relating to the calling of the meeting of creditors in a chapter 12 case is consistent with the expedited procedures of chapter 12. Subdivision (a) is also amended to clarify that the United States trustee does not call a meeting of creditors in a chapter 9 case. Pursuant to § 901(a) of the Code, § 341 is inapplicable in chapter 9 cases. The other amendments to subdivisions (a), (b)(1), and (b)(2) and the additions of subdivisions (f) and (g) are derived from Rule X–1006 and conform to the 1986 amendments to § 341 of the Code. The second sentence of subdivision (b)(3) is amended because Rule 2009(e) is abrogated. Although the United States trustee fixes the date for the meeting, the clerk of the bankruptcy court transmits the notice of the meeting unless the court orders otherwise, as prescribed in Rule 2002(a)(1).

Pursuant to § 702 and § 705 of the Code, creditors may elect a trustee and a committee in a chapter 7 case. Subdivision (b) of this rule provides that the United States trustee shall preside over any election that is held under those sections. The deletion of the last sentence of subdivision (b)(1) does not preclude creditors from recommending to the United States trustee the amount of the trustee's bond when a trustee is elected. Trustees and committees are not elected in chapter 11, 12, and 13 cases.

If an election is disputed, the United States trustee shall not resolve the dispute. For purposes of expediency, the United States trustee shall tabulate the results of the election for each alternative presented by the dispute. However, if the court finds that such tabulation is not feasible under the circumstances, the United States trustee need not tabulate the votes. If such tabulation is feasible and if the disputed vote or votes would affect the result of the election, the tabulations of votes for each alternative presented by the dispute shall be reported to the court. If a motion is made for resolution of the dispute in accordance with subdivision (d) of this rule, the court will determine the issue and another meeting to conduct the election may not be necessary.

Subdivisions (f) and (g) are derived from Rule X–1006(d) and (e), except that the amount is increased to $1,500 to conform to the amendment to Rule 2002(f).

1993 Amendments

Subdivision (a) is amended to extend by ten days the time for holding the meeting of creditors in a chapter 13 case. This extension will provide more flexibility for scheduling the meeting of creditors. Other amendments are stylistic and make no substantive change.

1999 Amendments

Subdivision (d) is amended to require the United States trustee to mail a copy of a report of a disputed election to any party in interest that has requested a copy of it. Also, if the election is for a trustee, the rule as amended will give a party in interest ten days from the filing of the report, rather than from the date of the meeting of creditors, to file a motion to resolve the dispute.

The substitution of "United States trustee" for "presiding officer" is stylistic. Section 341(a) of the Code provides that the United States trustee shall preside at the meeting of creditors. Other amendments are designed to conform to the style of Rule 2007.1(b)(3) regarding the election of a trustee in a chapter 11 case.

2003 Amendments

The rule is amended to reflect the enactment of subchapter V of chapter 7 of the Code governing multilateral clearing organization liquidations. Section 782 of the Code provides that the designation of a trustee or alternative trustee for the case is made by the Federal Reserve Board. Therefore, the meeting of creditors in those cases cannot include the election of a trustee.

2008 Amendments

If the debtor has solicited acceptances to a plan before commencement of the case, § 341(e), which was added to the Code by the 2005 amendments, authorizes the court, on request of a party in interest and after notice and a hearing, to order that a meeting of creditors not be convened. The rule is amended to recognize that a meeting of creditors might not be held in those cases.

2009 Amendments

The rule is amended to implement changes in connection with the amendment to Rule 9006(a) and the manner by which time is computed under the rules. The deadlines in the rule are amended to substitute a deadline that is a multiple of seven days. Throughout the rules, deadlines are amended in the following manner:

- 5-day periods become 7-day periods
- 10-day periods become 14-day periods
- 15-day periods become 14-day periods
- 20-day periods become 21-day periods
- 25-day periods become 28-day periods

2011 Amendments

Subdivision (e). Subdivision (e) is amended to require the presiding official to file a statement after the adjournment of a meeting of creditors or equity security holders designating the period of the adjournment. The presiding official is the United States trustee or the United States trustee's designee. This requirement will provide notice to parties in interest not present at the initial meeting of the date and time to which the meeting has been continued. An adjourned meeting is "held open" as permitted by § 1308(b)(1) of the Code. The filing of this statement will also discourage premature motions to dismiss or convert the case under § 1307(e).

CROSS REFERENCES

Affirmations, see Fed.Rules Bankr.Proc. Rule 9012, 11 USCA.

Election of creditors' committee in liquidation case, see 11 USCA § 705.

Eligibility to serve as and qualification of trustee, see 11 USCA §§ 321 and 322.

Enlargement of time not permitted—

Date of meeting of creditors, see Fed.Rules Bankr.Proc. Rule 9006, 11 USCA.

Motion for resolution of trustee election dispute, see Fed.Rules Bankr.Proc. Rule 9006, 11 USCA.

Holders of multiple proxies to file list of proxies to be voted, see Fed.Rules Bankr.Proc. Rule 2006, 11 USCA.

Inapplicability of this rule to—

Municipality debt adjustment case, see 11 USCA § 901.

Railroad reorganization case, see 11 USCA § 1161.

Interim trustee in liquidation case, see Fed.Rules Bankr.Proc. Rule 2001, 11 USCA, and 11 USCA § 701.

Motions; form and service, see Fed.Rules Bankr.Proc. Rule 9013, 11 USCA.

Reduction of twenty-day period for date of meeting of creditors not permitted, see Fed.Rules Bankr.Proc. Rule 9006, 11 USCA.

Selection and substitution of trustees, see Fed.Rules Bankr.Proc. Rules 2008 and 2012, 11 USCA.

Time for objections to property claimed to be exempt, see Fed.Rules Bankr.Proc. Rule 4003, 11 USCA.

Rule 2004. Examination

(a) Examination on motion

On motion of any party in interest, the court may order the examination of any entity.

(b) Scope of examination

The examination of an entity under this rule or of the debtor under § 343 of the Code may relate only to the acts, conduct, or property or to the liabilities and financial condition of the debtor, or to any matter which may affect the administration of the debtor's estate, or to the debtor's right to a discharge. In a family farmer's debt adjustment case under chapter 12, an individual's debt adjustment case under chapter 13, or a reorganization case under chapter 11 of the Code, other than for the reorganization of a railroad, the examination may also relate to the operation of any business and the desirability of its continuance, the source of any money or property acquired or to be acquired by the debtor for purposes of consummating a plan and the consideration given or offered therefor, and any other matter relevant to the case or to the formulation of a plan.

(c) Compelling attendance and production of documents

The attendance of an entity for examination and for the production of documents, whether the examination is to be conducted within or without the district in which the case is pending, may be compelled as provided in Rule 9016 for the attendance of a witness at a hearing or trial. As an officer of the court, an attorney may issue and sign a subpoena on behalf of the court for the district in which the examination is to be held if the attorney is admitted to practice in that court or in the court in which the case is pending.

(d) Time and place of examination of debtor

The court may for cause shown and on terms as it may impose order the debtor to be examined under this rule at any time or place it designates, whether within or without the district wherein the case is pending.

(e) Mileage

An entity other than a debtor shall not be required to attend as a witness unless lawful mileage and witness fee for one day's attendance shall be first tendered. If the debtor resides more than 100 miles from the place of examination when required to appear for an examination under this rule, the mileage allowed by law to a witness shall be tendered for any distance more than 100 miles from the debtor's residence at the date of the filing of the first petition commencing a case under the Code or the residence at the time the debtor is required to appear for the examination, whichever is the lesser.

(As amended Mar. 30, 1987, eff. Aug. 1, 1987; Apr. 30, 1991, eff. Aug. 1, 1991; Apr. 29, 2002, eff. Dec. 1, 2002.)

ADVISORY COMMITTEE NOTES

Subdivision (a) of this rule is derived from former Bankruptcy Rule 205(a). See generally 2 Collier, Bankruptcy ¶¶ 343.02, 343.08, 343.13 (15th ed. 1981). It specifies the manner of moving for an examination. The motion may be heard ex parte or it may be heard on notice.

Subdivision (b) is derived from former Bankruptcy Rules 205(d) and 11–26.

Subdivision (c) specifies the mode of compelling attendance of a witness or party for an examination and for the production of evidence under this rule. The subdivision is substantially declaratory of the practice that had developed under § 21a of the Act [former § 44(a) of this title]. See 2 Collier, supra ¶ 343.11.

This subdivision will be applicable for the most part to the examination of a person other than the debtor. The debtor is required to appear at the meeting of creditors for examination. The word "person" includes the debtor and this subdivision may be used if necessary to obtain the debtor's attendance for examination.

Subdivision (d) is derived from former Bankruptcy Rule 205(f) and is not a limitation on subdivision (c). Any person, including the debtor, served with a subpoena within the range of a subpoena must attend for examination pursuant to subdivision (c). Subdivision (d) applies only to the debtor and a subpoena need not be issued. There are no territorial limits on the service of an order on the debtor. See, e.g., In re Totem Lodge & Country Club, Inc., 134 F.Supp. 158 (S.D.N.Y.1955).

Subdivision (e) is derived from former Bankruptcy Rule 205(g). The lawful mileage and fee for attendance at a United States court as a witness are prescribed by 28 U.S.C. § 1821.

Definition of debtor. The word "debtor" as used in this rule includes the persons specified in the definition in Rule 9001(5).

Spousal privilege. The limitation on the spousal privilege formerly contained in § 21a of the Act [former § 44(a) of this title] is not carried over in the Code. For privileges generally, see Rule 501 of the Federal Rules of Evidence made applicable in cases under the Code by Rule 1101 thereof.

1991 Amendments

This rule is amended to allow the examination in a chapter 12 case to cover the same matters that may be covered in an examination in a chapter 11 or 13 case.

2002 Amendments

Subdivision (c) is amended to clarify that an examination ordered under Rule 2004(a) may be held outside the district in which the case is pending if the subpoena is issued by the court for the district in which the examination is to be held and is served in the manner provided in Rule 45 F.R.Civ.P., made applicable by Rule 9016.

The subdivision is amended further to clarify that, in addition to the procedures for the issuance of a subpoena set forth in Rule 45 F.R.Civ.P., an attorney may issue and sign a subpoena on behalf of the court for the district in which a Rule 2004 examination is to be held if the attorney is authorized to practice, even if admitted pro hac vice, either in the court in which the case is pending or in the court for the district in which the examination is to be held. This provision supplements the procedures for the issuance of a subpoena set forth in Rule 45(a)(3)(A) and (B) F.R.Civ.P. and is consistent with one of the purposes of the 1991 amendments to Rule 45, to ease the burdens of interdistrict law practice.

CROSS REFERENCES

Allowances and travel expenses of witnesses, see 28 USCA § 1821.

Apprehension and removal of debtor to compel attendance for examination, see Fed.Rules Bankr.Proc. Rule 2005, 11 USCA.

Debtor as corporation or partnership for purposes of this rule, see Fed.Rules Bankr.Proc. Rule 9001, 11 USCA.

Duty of bankrupt to—

    Attend hearing on right to discharge, see 11 USCA § 524.

    Submit to examination, see Fed.Rules Bankr.Proc. Rule 4002, 11 USCA.

Duty of trustee to investigate debtor—

    Individual debt adjustment case, see 11 USCA § 1302.

    Liquidation case, see 11 USCA § 704.

Examination of debtor concerning compensation agreements with attorney, see Fed.Rules Bankr.Proc. Rule 2017, 11 USCA.

Immunity from self-incrimination, see 11 USCA § 344.

Motions; form and service, see Fed.Rules Bankr.Proc. Rule 9013, 11 USCA.

Subpoena, see Fed.Rules Civ.Proc. Rule 45, 28 USCA.

Privileges, see Fed.Rules Evid. Rule 501, 28 USCA.

Rule 2005. Apprehension and Removal of Debtor to Compel Attendance for Examination

(a) Order to compel attendance for examination

On motion of any party in interest supported by an affidavit alleging (1) that the examination of the debtor is necessary for the proper administration of the estate and that there is reasonable cause to believe that the debtor is about to leave or has left the debtor's residence or principal place of business to avoid examination, or (2) that the debtor has evaded service of a subpoena or of an order to attend for examination, or (3) that the debtor has willfully disobeyed a subpoena or order to attend for examination, duly served, the court may issue to the marshal, or some other officer authorized by law, an order directing the officer to bring the debtor before the court without unnecessary delay. If, after hearing, the court finds the allegations to be true, the court shall thereupon cause the debtor to be examined forthwith. If necessary, the court shall fix conditions for further examination and for the debtor's obedience to all orders made in reference thereto.

(b) Removal

Whenever any order to bring the debtor before the court is issued under this rule and the debtor is found in a district other than that of the court issuing the order, the debtor may be taken into custody under the order and removed in accordance with the following rules:

    (1) If the debtor is taken into custody under the order at a place less than 100 miles from the place of issue of the order, the debtor shall be brought forthwith before the court that issued the order.

    (2) If the debtor is taken into custody under the order at a place 100 miles or more from the place of issue of the order, the debtor shall be brought without unnecessary delay before the nearest available United States magistrate judge, bankruptcy judge, or district judge. If, after hearing, the magistrate judge, bankruptcy judge, or district judge finds that an order has issued under this rule and that the person in custody is the debtor, or if the person in custody waives a hearing, the magistrate judge, bankruptcy judge, or district judge shall order removal, and the person in custody shall be released on conditions ensuring prompt appearance before the court that issued the order to compel the attendance.

(c) Conditions of release

In determining what conditions will reasonably assure attendance or obedience under subdivision (a) of this rule or appearance under subdivision (b) of this rule, the court shall be governed by the provisions and policies of title 18, U.S.C., § 3146(a) and (b).

Rule 2006   BANKRUPTCY RULES

(As amended Mar. 30, 1987, eff. Aug. 1, 1987; Apr. 22, 1993, eff. Aug. 1, 1993.)

ADVISORY COMMITTEE NOTES

This rule is derived from former Bankruptcy Rule 206. The rule requires the debtor to be examined as soon as possible if allegations of the movant for compulsory examination under this rule are found to be true after a hearing. Subdivision (b) includes in paragraphs (1) and (2) provisions adapted from subdivisions (a) and (b) of Rule 40 of the Federal Rules of Criminal Procedure, which governs the handling of a person arrested in one district on a warrant issued in another. Subdivision (c) incorporates by reference the features of subdivisions (a) and (b) of 18 U.S.C. § 3146, which prescribe standards, procedures and factors to be considered in determining conditions of release of accused persons in noncapital cases prior to trial. The word "debtor" as used in this rule includes the persons named in Rule 9001(5).

The affidavit required to be submitted in support of the motion may be subscribed by the unsworn declaration provided for in 28 U.S.C. § 1746.

1993 Amendments

Subdivision (b)(2) is amended to conform to § 321 of the Judicial Improvements Act of 1990, Pub. L. No. 101–650, which changed the title of "United States magistrate" to "United States magistrate judge." Other amendments are stylistic and make no substantive change.

Change of Name

United States magistrate appointed under section 631 of Title 28, Judiciary and Judicial Procedure, to be known as United States magistrate judge after Dec. 1, 1990, with any reference to United States magistrate or magistrate in Title 28, in any other Federal statute, etc., deemed a reference to United States magistrate judge appointed under section 631 of Title 28, see section 321 of Pub.L. 101–650, set out as a note under section 631 of Title 28.

CROSS REFERENCES

Debtor as corporation or partnership for purposes of this rule, see Fed.Rules Bankr.Proc. Rule 9001, 11 USCA.

Motions; form and service, see Fed.Rules Bankr.Proc. Rule 9013, 11 USCA.

Commitment to another district; removal, see Fed.Rules Cr.Proc. Rule 40, 18 USCA.

Rule 2006. Solicitation and Voting of Proxies in Chapter 7 Liquidation Cases

(a) Applicability

This rule applies only in a liquidation case pending under chapter 7 of the Code.

(b) Definitions

(1) Proxy

A proxy is a written power of attorney authorizing any entity to vote the claim or otherwise act as the owner's attorney in fact in connection with the administration of the estate.

(2) Solicitation of proxy

The solicitation of a proxy is any communication, other than one from an attorney to a regular client who owns a claim or from an attorney to the owner of a claim who has requested the attorney to represent the owner, by which a creditor is asked, directly or indirectly, to give a proxy after or in contemplation of the filing of a petition by or against the debtor.

(c) Authorized solicitation

(1) A proxy may be solicited only by (A) a creditor owning an allowable unsecured claim against the estate on the date of the filing of the petition; (B) a committee elected pursuant to § 705 of the Code; (C) a committee of creditors selected by a majority in number and amount of claims of creditors (i) whose claims are not contingent or unliquidated, (ii) who are not disqualified from

voting under § 702(a) of the Code and (iii) who were present or represented at a meeting of which all creditors having claims of over $500 or the 100 creditors having the largest claims had at least seven days' notice in writing and of which meeting written minutes were kept and are available reporting the names of the creditors present or represented and voting and the amounts of their claims; or (D) a bona fide trade or credit association, but such association may solicit only creditors who were its members or subscribers in good standing and had allowable unsecured claims on the date of the filing of the petition.

(2) A proxy may be solicited only in writing.

(d) Solicitation not authorized

This rule does not permit solicitation (1) in any interest other than that of general creditors; (2) by or on behalf of any custodian; (3) by the interim trustee or by or on behalf of any entity not qualified to vote under § 702(a) of the Code; (4) by or on behalf of an attorney at law; or (5) by or on behalf of a transferee of a claim for collection only.

(e) Data required from holders of multiple proxies

At any time before the voting commences at any meeting of creditors pursuant to § 341(a) of the Code, or at any other time as the court may direct, a holder of two or more proxies shall file and transmit to the United States trustee a verified list of the proxies to be voted and a verified statement of the pertinent facts and circumstances in connection with the execution and delivery of each proxy, including:

(1) a copy of the solicitation;

(2) identification of the solicitor, the forwarder, if the forwarder is neither the solicitor nor the owner of the claim, and the proxyholder, including their connections with the debtor and with each other. If the solicitor, forwarder, or proxyholder is an association, there shall also be included a statement that the creditors whose claims have been solicited and the creditors whose claims are to be voted were members or subscribers in good standing and had allowable unsecured claims on the date of the filing of the petition. If the solicitor, forwarder, or proxyholder is a committee of creditors, the statement shall also set forth the date and place the committee was organized, that the committee was organized in accordance with clause (B) or (C) of paragraph (c)(1) of this rule, the members of the committee, the amounts of their claims, when the claims were acquired, the amounts paid therefor, and the extent to which the claims of the committee members are secured or entitled to priority;

(3) a statement that no consideration has been paid or promised by the proxyholder for the proxy;

(4) a statement as to whether there is any agreement and, if so, the particulars thereof, between the proxyholder and any other entity for the payment of any consideration in connection with voting the proxy, or for the sharing of compensation with any entity, other than a member or regular associate of the proxyholder's law firm, which may be allowed the trustee or any entity for services rendered in the case, or for the employment of any person as attorney, accountant, appraiser, auctioneer, or other employee for the estate;

(5) if the proxy was solicited by an entity other than the proxyholder, or forwarded to the holder by an entity who is neither a solicitor of the proxy nor the owner of the claim, a statement signed and verified by the solicitor or forwarder that no consideration has been paid or promised for the proxy, and whether there is any agreement, and, if so, the particulars thereof, between the solicitor or forwarder and any other entity for the payment of any consideration in connection with voting the proxy, or for sharing compensation with any entity, other than a member or regular associate of the solicitor's or forwarder's law firm which may be allowed the trustee or any entity for services rendered in the case, or for the employment of any person as attorney, accountant, appraiser, auctioneer, or other employee for the estate;

(6) if the solicitor, forwarder, or proxyholder is a committee, a statement signed and verified by each member as to the amount and source of any consideration paid or to be paid to such member in connection with the case other than by way of dividend on the member's claim.

Rule 2006 BANKRUPTCY RULES

(f) Enforcement of restrictions on solicitation

On motion of any party in interest or on its own initiative, the court may determine whether there has been a failure to comply with the provisions of this rule or any other impropriety in connection with the solicitation or voting of a proxy. After notice and a hearing the court may reject any proxy for cause, vacate any order entered in consequence of the voting of any proxy which should have been rejected, or take any other appropriate action.

(As amended Mar. 30, 1987, eff. Aug. 1, 1987; Apr. 30, 1991, eff. Aug. 1, 1991; Mar. 26, 2009, eff. Dec. 1, 2009.)

ADVISORY COMMITTEE NOTES

This rule is a comprehensive regulation of solicitation and voting of proxies in liquidation cases. It is derived from former Bankruptcy Rule 208. The rule applies only in chapter 7 cases because no voting occurs, other than on a plan, in a chapter 11 case. Former Bankruptcy Rule 208 did not apply to solicitations of acceptances of plans.

Creditor control was a basic feature of the Act and is continued, in part, by the Code. Creditor democracy is perverted and the congressional objective frustrated, however, if control of administration falls into the hands of persons whose principal interest is not in what the estate can be made to yield to the unsecured creditors but in what it can yield to those involved in its administration or in other ulterior objectives.

Subdivision (b). The definition of proxy in the first paragraph of subdivision (b) is derived from former Bankruptcy Rule 208.

Subdivision (c). The purpose of the rule is to protect creditors against loss of control of administration of their debtors' estates to holders of proxies having interests that differ from those of the creditors. The rule does not prohibit solicitation but restricts it to those who were creditors at the commencement of the case or their freely and fairly selected representatives. The special role occupied by credit and trade associations is recognized in the last clause of subdivision (c)(1). On the assumption that members or subscribers may have affiliated with an association in part for the purpose of obtaining its services as a representative in liquidation proceedings, an established association is authorized to solicit its own members, or its regular customers or clients, who were creditors on the date of the filing of the petition. Although the association may not solicit nonmembers or nonsubscribers for proxies, it may sponsor a meeting of creditors at which a committee entitled to solicit proxies may be selected in accordance with clause (C) of subdivision (c)(1).

Under certain circumstances, the relationship of a creditor, creditors' committee, or association to the estate or the case may be such as to warrant rejection of any proxy solicited by such a person or group. Thus a person who is forbidden by the Code to vote his own claim should be equally disabled to solicit proxies from creditors. Solicitation by or on behalf of the debtor has been uniformly condemned, e.g., In re White, 15 F.2d 371 (9th Cir. 1926), as has solicitation on behalf of a preferred creditor, Matter of Law, 13 Am.B.R. 650 (S.D.Ill.1905). The prohibition on solicitation by a receiver or his attorney made explicit by General Order 39 has been collaterally supported by rulings rejecting proxies solicited by a receiver in equity, In re Western States Bldg.-Loan Ass'n, 54 F.2d 415 (S.D.Cal.1931), and by an assignee for the benefit of creditors, Lines v. Falstaff Brewing Co., 233 F.2d 927 (9th Cir. 1956).

Subdivision (d) prohibits solicitation by any person or group having a relationship described in the preceding paragraph. It also makes no exception for attorneys or transferees of claims for collection. The rule does not undertake to regulate communications between an attorney and his regular client or between an attorney and a creditor who has asked the attorney to represent him in a proceeding under the Code, but any other communication by an attorney or any other person or group requesting a proxy from the owner of a claim constitutes a regulated solicitation. Solicitation by an attorney of a proxy from a creditor who was not a client prior to the solicitation is objectionable not only as unethical conduct as recognized by such cases as In the Matter of Darland Company, 184 F.Supp. 760 (S.D.Iowa 1960) but also and more importantly because the practice carries a substantial risk that administration will fall into the hands of those whose interest is in obtaining fees from the estate rather than securing dividends for creditors. The same risk attaches to solicitation by the holder of a claim for collection only.

Subdivision (e). The regulation of solicitation and voting of proxies is achieved by the rule principally through the imposition of requirements of disclosure on the holders of two or more proxies. The disclosures must be made to the clerk before the meeting at which the proxies are to be voted to afford the clerk or a party in interest an opportunity to examine the circumstances accompanying the acquisition of the proxies in advance of any exercise of the proxies. In the light of the examination the clerk or a party in interest should bring to the attention of the judge any question that arises and the judge may permit the proxies that comply with the rule to be voted and reject those that do not unless the holders can effect or establish compliance in such manner as the court shall prescribe. The holders of single proxies are excused from the disclosure requirements because of the insubstantiality of the risk that such proxies have been solicited, or will be voted, in an interest other than that of general creditors.

Every holder of two or more proxies must include in the submission a verified statement that no consideration has been paid or promised for the proxy, either by the proxyholder or the solicitor or any forwarder of the proxy. Any payment or promise of consideration for a proxy would be conclusive evidence of a purpose to acquire control of the administration of an estate for an ulterior purpose. The holder of multiple proxies must also include in the submission a verified statement as to whether there is any agreement by the holder, the solicitor, or any forwarder of the proxy for the employment of any person in the administration of an estate or for the sharing of any compensation allowed in connection with the administration of the estate. The provisions requiring these statements implement the policy of the Code expressed in § 504 as well as the policy of this rule to deter the acquisition of proxies for the purpose of obtaining a share in the outlays for administration. Finally the facts as to any consideration moving or promised to any member of a committee which functions as a solicitor, forwarder, or proxyholder must be disclosed by the proxyholder. Such information would be of significance to the court in evaluating the purpose of the committee in obtaining, transmitting, or voting proxies.

Subdivision (f) has counterparts in the local rules referred to in the Advisory Committee's Note to former Bankruptcy Rule 208. Courts have been accorded a wide range of discretion in the handling of disputes involving proxies. Thus the referee was allowed to reject proxies and to proceed forthwith to hold a scheduled election at the same meeting. E.g., In re Portage Wholesale Co., 183 F.2d 959 (7th Cir. 1950); In re McGill, 106 Fed. 57 (6th Cir. 1901); In re Deena Woolen Mills, Inc., 114 F.Supp. 260, 273 (D.Me.1953); In re Finlay, 3 Am.B.R. 738 (S.D.N.Y.1900). The bankruptcy judge may postpone an election to permit a determination of issues presented by a dispute as to proxies and to afford those creditors whose proxies are rejected an opportunity to give new proxies or to attend an adjourned meeting to vote their own claims. Cf. In the Matter of Lenrick Sales, Inc., 369 F.2d 439, 442–43 (3d Cir.), cert. denied, 389 U.S. 822 (1967); In the Matter of Construction Supply Corp., 221 F.Supp. 124, 128 (E.D.Va.1963). This rule is not intended to restrict the scope of the court's discretion in the handling of disputes as to proxies.

1991 Amendments

This rule is amended to give the United States trustee information in connection with proxies so that the United States trustee may perform responsibilities as presiding officer at the § 341 meeting of creditors. See Rule 2003.

The words "with the clerk" are deleted as unnecessary. See Rules 5005(a) and 9001(3).

2009 Amendments

The rule is amended to implement changes in connection with the amendment to Rule 9006(a) and the manner by which time is computed under the rules. The deadline in the rule is amended to substitute a deadline that is a multiple of seven days. Throughout the rules, deadlines are amended in the following manner:

- 5-day periods become 7-day periods
- 10-day periods become 14-day periods
- 15-day periods become 14-day periods
- 20-day periods become 21-day periods
- 25-day periods become 28-day periods

CROSS REFERENCES

Committee of unsecured creditors selected before order for relief, solicitation pursuant to this rule, see Fed.Rules Bankr.Proc. Rule 2007, 11 USCA.

Motions; form and service, see Fed.Rules Bankr.Proc. Rule 9013, 11 USCA.

Signing and verification of papers, see Fed.Rules Bankr.Proc. Rule 9011, 11 USCA.

Rule 2007. Review of Appointment of Creditors' Committee Organized Before Commencement of the Case

(a) Motion to review appointment

If a committee appointed by the United States trustee pursuant to § 1102(a) of the Code consists of the members of a committee organized by creditors before the commencement of a chapter 9 or chapter 11 case, on motion of a party in interest and after a hearing on notice to the United States trustee and other entities as the court may direct, the court may determine whether the appointment of the committee satisfies the requirements of § 1102(b)(1) of the Code.

(b) Selection of members of committee

The court may find that a committee organized by unsecured creditors before the commencement of a chapter 9 or chapter 11 case was fairly chosen if:

(1) it was selected by a majority in number and amount of claims of unsecured creditors who may vote under § 702(a) of the Code and were present in person or represented at a meeting of which all creditors having unsecured claims of over $1,000 or the 100 unsecured creditors having the largest claims had at least seven days' notice in writing, and of which meeting written minutes reporting the names of the creditors present or represented and voting and the amounts of their claims were kept and are available for inspection;

(2) all proxies voted at the meeting for the elected committee were solicited pursuant to Rule 2006 and the lists and statements required by subdivision (e) thereof have been transmitted to the United States trustee; and

(3) the organization of the committee was in all other respects fair and proper.

(c) Failure to comply with requirements for appointment

After a hearing on notice pursuant to subdivision (a) of this rule, the court shall direct the United States trustee to vacate the appointment of the committee and may order other appropriate action if the court finds that such appointment failed to satisfy the requirements of § 1102(b)(1) of the Code.

(As amended Mar. 30, 1987, eff. Aug. 1, 1987; Apr. 30, 1991, eff. Aug. 1, 1991; Mar. 26, 2009, eff. Dec. 1, 2009.)

ADVISORY COMMITTEE NOTES

Section 1102(b)(1) of the Code permits the court to appoint as the unsecured creditors' committee, the committee that was selected by creditors before the order for relief. This provision recognizes the propriety of continuing a "prepetition" committee in an official capacity. Such a committee, however, must be found to have been fairly chosen and representative of the different kinds of claims to be represented.

Subdivision (a) does not necessarily require a hearing but does require a party in interest to bring to the court's attention the fact that a prepetition committee had been organized and should be appointed. An application would suffice for this purpose. Party in interest would include the committee, any member of the committee, or any of its agents acting for the committee. Whether or not notice of the application should be given to any other party is left to the discretion of the court.

Subdivision (b) implements § 1102(b)(1). The Code provision allows the court to appoint, as the official § 1102(a) committee, a "prepetition" committee if its members were fairly chosen and the committee is representative of the different kinds of claims. This subdivision of the rule indicates some of the factors the court may consider in determining whether the requirements of § 1102(b)(1) have been satisfied. In effect, the subdivision provides various factors which are similar to those set forth in Rule 2006 with respect to the solicitation and voting of proxies in a chapter 7 liquidation case.

1987 Amendments

The rule is amended to conform to the 1984 amendments to § 1102(b)(1) of the Code.

1991 Amendments

This rule is amended to conform to the 1986 amendments to § 1102(a). The United States trustee appoints committees pursuant to § 1102 in chapter 11 cases. Section 1102 is applicable in chapter 9 cases pursuant to § 901(a).

Although § 1102(b)(1) of the Code permits the United States trustee to appoint a prepetition committee as the statutory committee if its members were fairly chosen and it is representative of the different kinds of claims to be represented, the amendment to this rule provides a procedure for judicial review of the appointment. The factors that may be considered by the court in determining whether the committee was fairly chosen are not new. A finding that a prepetition committee has not been fairly chosen does not prohibit the appointment of some or all of its members to the creditors' committee. Although this rule deals only with judicial review of the appointment of prepetition committees, it does not preclude judicial review under Rule 2020 regarding the appointment of other committees.

2009 Amendments

The rule is amended to implement changes in connection with the amendment to Rule 9006(a) and the manner by which time is computed under the rules. The deadline in the rule is amended to substitute a deadline that is a multiple of seven days. Throughout the rules, deadlines are amended in the following manner:

- 5-day periods become 7-day periods
- 10-day periods become 14-day periods
- 15-day periods become 14-day periods
- 20-day periods become 21-day periods
- 25-day periods become 28-day periods

CROSS REFERENCES

Representation of creditors and equity security holders in municipality debt adjustment and reorganization cases, see Fed.Rules Bankr.Proc. Rule 2019, 11 USCA.

Rule 2007.1. Appointment of Trustee or Examiner in a Chapter 11 Reorganization Case

(a) Order to appoint trustee or examiner

In a chapter 11 reorganization case, a motion for an order to appoint a trustee or an examiner under § 1104(a) or § 1104(c) of the Code shall be made in accordance with Rule 9014.

(b) Election of trustee

(1) Request for an election

A request to convene a meeting of creditors for the purpose of electing a trustee in a chapter 11 reorganization case shall be filed and transmitted to the United States trustee in accordance with Rule 5005 within the time prescribed by § 1104(b) of the Code. Pending court approval of the person elected, any person appointed by the United States trustee under § 1104(d) and approved in accordance with subdivision (c) of this rule shall serve as trustee.

(2) Manner of election and notice

An election of a trustee under § 1104(b) of the Code shall be conducted in the manner provided in Rules 2003(b)(3) and 2006. Notice of the meeting of creditors convened under § 1104(b) shall be given as provided in Rule 2002. The United States trustee shall preside at the meeting. A proxy for the purpose of voting in the election may be solicited only by a committee of creditors appointed under § 1102 of the Code or by any other party entitled to solicit a proxy pursuant to Rule 2006.

(3) Report of election and resolution of disputes.

(a) Report of undisputed election

If no dispute arises out of the election, the United States trustee shall promptly file a report certifying the election, including the name and address of the person elected and a statement that the election is undisputed. The report shall be accompanied by a verified statement of the person elected setting forth that person's connections with the debtor, creditors, any other party in interest, their respective attorneys and accountants, the United States trustee, or any person employed in the office of the United States trustee.

(B) Dispute arising out of an election

If a dispute arises out of an election, the United States trustee shall promptly file a report stating that the election is disputed, informing the court of the nature of the dispute, and listing the name and address of any candidate elected under any alternative presented by the dispute. The report shall be accompanied by a verified statement by each candidate elected under each alternative presented by the dispute, setting forth the person's connections with the debtor, creditors, any other party in interest, their respective attorneys and accountants, the United States trustee, or any person employed in the office of the United States trustee. Not later than the date on which the report of the disputed election is filed, the United States trustee shall mail a copy of the report and each verified statement to any party in interest that has made a request to convene a meeting under § 1104(b) or to receive a copy of the report, and to any committee appointed under § 1102 of the Code.

(c) Approval of appointment

An order approving the appointment of a trustee or an examiner under § 1104(d) of the Code shall be made on application of the United States trustee. The application shall state the name of the person appointed and, to the best of the applicant's knowledge, all the person's connections with the debtor, creditors, any other parties in interest, their respective attorneys and accountants, the United States trustee, or persons employed in the office of the United States trustee. The application shall state the names of the parties in interest with whom the United States trustee consulted regarding the appointment. The application shall be accompanied by a verified statement of the person appointed setting forth the person's connections with the debtor, creditors, any other party in interest, their respective attorneys and accountants, the United States trustee, or any person employed in the office of the United States trustee.

(Added Apr. 30, 1991, eff. Aug. 1, 1991; amended Apr. 11, 1997, eff. Dec. 1, 1997; Apr. 23, 2008, eff. Dec. 1, 2008.)

ADVISORY COMMITTEE NOTES

1991 Adoption

This rule is added to implement the 1986 amendments to § 1104 of the Code regarding the appointment of a trustee or examiner in a chapter 11 case. A motion for an order to appoint a trustee or examiner is a contested matter. Although the court decides whether the appointment is warranted under the particular facts of the case, it is the United States trustee who makes the appointment pursuant to § 1104(c) of the Code. The appointment is subject to approval of the court, however, which may be obtained by application of the United States trustee. Section 1104(c) of the Code requires that the appointment be made after consultation with parties in interest and that the person appointed be disinterested.

The requirement that connections with the United States trustee or persons employed in the United States trustee's office be revealed is not intended to enlarge the definition of "disinterested person" in § 101(13) of the Code, to supersede executive regulations or other laws relating to appointments by United States trustees, or to otherwise restrict the United States trustee's discretion in making appointments. This information is required, however, in the interest of full disclosure and confidence in the appointment process and to give the court all information that may be relevant to the exercise of judicial discretion in approving the appointment of a trustee or examiner in a chapter 11 case.

1997 Amendments

This rule is amended to implement the 1994 amendments to § 1104 of the Code regarding the election of a trustee in a chapter 11 case.

Eligibility for voting in an election for a chapter 11 trustee is determined in accordance with Rule 2003(b)(3). Creditors whose claims are deemed filed under § 1111(a) are treated for voting purposes as creditors who have filed proofs of claim.

Proxies for the purpose of voting in the election may be solicited only by a creditors' committee appointed under § 1102 or by any other party entitled to solicit proxies pursuant to Rule 2006. Therefore, a trustee or examiner who has served in the case, or a committee of equity security holders appointed under § 1102, may not solicit proxies.

The procedures for reporting disputes to the court derive from similar provisions in Rule 2003(d) applicable to chapter 7 cases. An election may be disputed by a party in interest or by the United States trustee. For example, if the United States trustee believes that the person elected is ineligible to serve as trustee because the person is not "disinterested," the United States trustee should file a report disputing the election.

The word "only" is deleted from subdivision (b), redesignated as subdivision (c), to avoid any negative inference with respect to the availability of procedures for obtaining review of the United States trustee's acts or failure to act pursuant to Rule 2020.

2008 Amendments

Under § 1104(b)(2) of the Code, as amended in 2005, if an eligible, disinterested person is elected to serve as trustee in a chapter 11 case, the United States trustee is directed to file a report certifying the election. The person elected does not have to be appointed to the position. Rather, the filing of the report certifying the election itself constitutes the appointment. The section further provides that in the event of a dispute in the election of a trustee, the court must resolve the matter. The rule is amended to be consistent with § 1104(b)(2).

When the United States trustee files a report certifying the election of a trustee, the person elected must provide a verified statement, similar to the statement required of professional persons under Rule 2014, disclosing connections with parties in interest and certain other persons connected with the case. Although court approval of the person elected is not required, the disclosure of the person's connections will enable parties in interest to determine whether the person is disinterested.

Rule 2007.2. Appointment of Patient Care Ombudsman in a Health Care Business Case

(a) Order to appoint patient care ombudsman

In a chapter 7, chapter 9, or chapter 11 case in which the debtor is a health care business, the court shall order the appointment of a patient care ombudsman under § 333 of the Code, unless the court, on motion of the United States trustee or a party in interest filed no later than 21 days after the commencement of the case or within another time fixed by the court, finds that the appointment of a patient care ombudsman is not necessary under the specific circumstances of the case for the protection of patients.

(b) Motion for order to appoint ombudsman

If the court has found that the appointment of an ombudsman is not necessary, or has terminated the appointment, the court, on motion of the United States trustee or a party in interest, may order the appointment at a later time if it finds that the appointment has become necessary to protect patients.

(c) Notice of appointment

If a patient care ombudsman is appointed under § 333, the United States trustee shall promptly file a notice of the appointment, including the name and address of the person appointed. Unless the person appointed is a State Long-Term Care Ombudsman, the notice shall be accompanied by a verified statement of the person appointed setting forth the person's connections with the debtor, creditors, patients, any other party in interest, their respective attorneys and

Rule 2007.2

accountants, the United States trustee, and any person employed in the office of the United States trustee.

(d) Termination of appointment

On motion of the United States trustee or a party in interest, the court may terminate the appointment of a patient care ombudsman if the court finds that the appointment is not necessary to protect patients.

(e) Motion

A motion under this rule shall be governed by Rule 9014. The motion shall be transmitted to the United States trustee and served on: the debtor; the trustee; any committee elected under § 705 or appointed under § 1102 of the Code or its authorized agent, or, if the case is a chapter 9 municipality case or a chapter 11 reorganization case and no committee of unsecured creditors has been appointed under § 1102, on the creditors included on the list filed under Rule 1007(d); and such other entities as the court may direct.

(Added Apr. 23, 2008, eff. Dec. 1, 2008. As amended Mar. 26, 2009, eff. Dec. 1, 2009.)

ADVISORY COMMITTEE NOTES
2008 Adoption

Section 333 of the Code, added by the 2005 amendments, requires the court to order the appointment of a health care ombudsman within the first 30 days of a health care business case, unless the court finds that the appointment is not necessary for the protection of patients. The rule recognizes this requirement and provides a procedure by which a party may obtain a court order finding that the appointment of a patient care ombudsman is unnecessary. In the absence of a timely motion under subdivision (a) of this rule, the court will enter an order directing the United States trustee to appoint the ombudsman.

Subdivision (b) recognizes that, despite a previous order finding that a patient care ombudsman is not necessary, circumstances of the case may change or newly discovered evidence may demonstrate the necessity of an ombudsman to protect the interests of patients. In that event, a party may move the court for an order directing the appointment of an ombudsman.

When the appointment of a patient care ombudsman is ordered, the United States trustee is required to appoint a disinterested person to serve in that capacity. Court approval of the appointment is not required, but subdivision (c) requires the person appointed, if not a State Long-Term Care Ombudsman, to file a verified statement similar to the statement filed by professional persons under Rule 2014 so that parties in interest will have information relevant to disinterestedness. If a party believes that the person appointed is not disinterested, it may file a motion asking the court to find that the person is not eligible to serve.

Subdivision (d) permits parties in interest to move for the termination of the appointment of a patient care ombudsman. If the movant can show that there no longer is any need for the ombudsman, the court may order the termination of the appointment.

2009 Amendments

The rule is amended to implement changes in connection with the amendment to Rule 9006(a) and the manner by which time is computed under the rules. The deadline in the rule is amended to substitute a deadline that is a multiple of seven days. Throughout the rules, deadlines are amended in the following manner:

- 5-day periods become 7-day periods
- 10-day periods become 14-day periods
- 15-day periods become 14-day periods
- 20-day periods become 21-day periods
- 25-day periods become 28-day periods

Rule 2008. Notice to Trustee of Selection

The United States trustee shall immediately notify the person selected as trustee how to qualify and, if applicable, the amount of the trustee's bond. A trustee that has filed a blanket bond pursuant to Rule 2010 and has been selected as trustee in a chapter 7, chapter 12, or chapter 13 case that does not notify the court and the United States trustee in writing of rejection of the office within seven days after receipt of notice of selection shall be deemed to have accepted the office. Any other person selected as trustee shall notify the court and the United States trustee in writing of acceptance of the office within seven days after receipt of notice of selection or shall be deemed to have rejected the office.

(As amended Mar. 30, 1987, eff. Aug. 1, 1987; Apr. 30, 1991, eff. Aug. 1, 1991; Mar. 26, 2009, eff. Dec. 1, 2009.)

ADVISORY COMMITTEE NOTES

This rule is adapted from former Bankruptcy Rule 209(c). The remainder of that rule is inapplicable because its provisions are covered by §§ 701–703, 321 of the Code.

If the person selected as trustee accepts the office, he must qualify within five days after his selection, as required by § 322(a) of the Code.

In districts having a standing trustee for chapter 13 cases, a blanket acceptance of the appointment would be sufficient for compliance by the standing trustee with this rule.

1987 Amendments

The rule is amended to eliminate the need for a standing chapter 13 trustee or member of the panel of chapter 7 trustees to accept or reject an appointment.

1991 Amendments

The amendments to this rule relating to the United States trustee are derived from Rule X–1004(a) and conform to the 1986 amendments to the Code and 28 U.S.C. § 586 which provide that the United States trustee appoints and supervises trustees, and in a chapter 7 case presides over any election of a trustee. This rule applies when a trustee is either appointed or elected. This rule is also amended to provide for chapter 12 cases.

2009 Amendments

The rule is amended to implement changes in connection with the amendment to Rule 9006(a) and the manner by which time is computed under the rules. The deadline in the rule is amended to substitute a deadline that is a multiple of seven days. Throughout the rules, deadlines are amended in the following manner:

- 5-day periods become 7-day periods
- 10-day periods become 14-day periods
- 15-day periods become 14-day periods
- 20-day periods become 21-day periods
- 25-day periods become 28-day periods

CROSS REFERENCES

Appointment of trustees—
    Individual debt adjustment case, see 11 USCA § 1302.
    Railroad reorganization case, see 11 USCA § 1163.
    Reorganization case, see 11 USCA § 1104.
Bonds of trustees, see 11 USCA § 322.
Election of trustee in liquidation case, see 11 USCA § 702.
Eligibility to serve as trustee, see 11 USCA § 321.

Limited purpose of trustee appointed in municipality debt adjustment case, see 11 USCA § 926.

Representation of creditors and equity security holders in municipality debt adjustment and reorganization cases, see Fed.Rules Bankr.Proc. Rule 2019, 11 USCA.

Right of creditors to elect single trustee when joint administration ordered, see Fed.Rules Bankr.Proc. Rule 2009, 11 USCA.

Rule 2009. Trustees for Estates When Joint Administration Ordered

(a) Election of single trustee for estates being jointly administered

If the court orders a joint administration of two or more estates under Rule 1015(b), creditors may elect a single trustee for the estates being jointly administered, unless the case is under subchapter V of chapter 7 of the Code.

(b) Right of creditors to elect separate trustee

Notwithstanding entry of an order for joint administration under Rule 1015(b), the creditors of any debtor may elect a separate trustee for the estate of the debtor as provided in § 702 of the Code, unless the case is under subchapter V of chapter 7.

(c) Appointment of trustees for estates being jointly administered

(1) Chapter 7 liquidation cases

Except in a case governed by subchapter V of chapter 7, the United States trustee may appoint one or more interim trustees for estates being jointly administered in chapter 7 cases.

(2) Chapter 11 reorganization cases

If the appointment of a trustee is ordered, the United States trustee may appoint one or more trustees for estates being jointly administered in chapter 11 cases.

(3) Chapter 12 family farmer's debt adjustment cases

The United States trustee may appoint one or more trustees for estates being jointly administered in chapter 12 cases.

(4) Chapter 13 individual's debt adjustment cases

The United States trustee may appoint one or more trustees for estates being jointly administered in chapter 13 cases.

(d) Potential conflicts of interest

On a showing that creditors or equity security holders of the different estates will be prejudiced by conflicts of interest of a common trustee who has been elected or appointed, the court shall order the selection of separate trustees for estates being jointly administered.

(e) Separate accounts

The trustee or trustees of estates being jointly administered shall keep separate accounts of the property and distribution of each estate.

(As amended Mar. 30, 1987, eff. Aug. 1, 1987; Apr. 30, 1991, eff. Aug. 1, 1991; Mar. 27, 2003, eff. Dec. 1, 2003.)

ADVISORY COMMITTEE NOTES

This rule is applicable in chapter 7 cases and, in part, in chapter 11 and 13 cases. The provisions in subdivisions (a) and (b) concerning creditor election of a trustee apply only in a chapter 7 case because it is only pursuant to § 702 of the Code that creditors may elect a trustee. Subdivision (c) of the rule applies in chapter 11 and 13 as well as chapter 7 cases; pursuant to § 1104 of the Code, the court may order the appointment of a trustee on application of a party in interest and, pursuant to § 1163 of the Code, the court must appoint a trustee in a railroad reorganization case. Subdivision (c) should not be taken as an indication that more than one trustee may be appointed for a single debtor. Section 1104(c) permits only one trustee for each estate. In a chapter 13 case, if there is no standing trustee, the court is to appoint a person to serve as trustee pursuant to § 1302 of the Code. There is no provision for a trustee in a chapter 9 case, except for a very limited purpose; see § 926 of the Code.

This rule recognizes that economical and expeditious administration of two or more estates may be facilitated not only by the selection of a single trustee for a partnership and its partners, but by such selection whenever estates are being jointly administered pursuant to Rule 1015. See In the Matter of International Oil Co., 427 F.2d 186, 187 (2d Cir.1970). The rule is derived from former § 5c of the Act [former § 23(c) of this title] and former Bankruptcy Rule 210. The premise of § 5c of the Act was that notwithstanding the potentiality of conflict between the interests of the creditors of the partners and those of the creditors of the partnership, the conflict is not sufficiently serious or frequent in most cases to warrant the selection of separate trustees for the firm and the several partners. Even before the proviso was added to § 5c of the Act in 1938 to permit the creditors of a general partner to elect their separate trustee for his estate, it was held that the court had discretion to permit such an election or to make a separate appointment when a conflict of interest was recognized. In re Wood, 248 Fed. 246, 249–50 (6th Cir.), cert. denied, 247 U.S. 512 (1918); 4 Collier, Bankruptcy ¶723.04 (15th ed.1980). The rule retains in subdivision (e) the features of the practice respecting the selection of a trustee that was developed under § 5 of the Act [former § 23 of this title]. Subdivisions (a) and (c) permit the court to authorize election of a single trustee or to make a single appointment when joint administration of estates of other kinds of debtors is ordered, but subdivision (d) requires the court to make a preliminary evaluation of the risks of conflict of interest. If after the election or appointment of a common trustee a conflict of interest materializes, the court must take appropriate action to deal with it.

Subdivision (f) is derived from § 5e of the Act [former § 23(e) of this title] and former Bankruptcy Rule 210(f) and requires that the common trustee keep a separate account for each estate in all cases that are jointly administered.

1991 Amendments

One or more trustees may be appointed for estates being jointly administered in chapter 12 cases.

The amendments to this rule are derived from Rule X–1005 and are necessary because the United States trustee, rather than the court, has responsibility for appointing trustees pursuant to §§ 701, 1104, 1202, and 1302 of the Code.

If separate trustees are ordered for chapter 7 estates pursuant to subdivision (d), separate and successor trustees should be chosen as prescribed in § 703 of the Code. If the occasion for another election arises, the United States trustee should call a meeting of creditors for this purpose. An order to select separate trustees does not disqualify an appointed or elected trustee from serving for one of the estates.

Subdivision (e) is abrogated because the exercise of discretion by the United States trustee, who is in the Executive Branch, is not subject to advance restriction by rule of court. United States v. Cox, 342 F.2d 167 (5th Cir.1965), cert. denied, 365 U.S. 863 (1965); United States v. Frumento, 409 F.Supp. 136, 141 (E.D.Pa.), aff'd, 563 F.2d 1083 (3d Cir.1977), cert. denied, 434 U.S. 1072 (1977); see, Smith v. United States, 375 F.2d 243 (5th Cir.1967); House Report No. 95–595, 95th Cong., 1st Sess. 110 (1977). However, a trustee appointed by the United States trustee may be removed by the court for cause. See § 324 of the Code. Subdivision (d) of this rule, as amended, is consistent with § 324. Subdivision (f) is redesignated as subdivision (e).

2003 Amendments

The rule is amended to reflect the enactment of subchapter V of chapter 7 of the Code governing multilateral clearing organization liquidations. Section 782 of the Code provides that the designation of a trustee or alternative trustee for the case is made by the Federal Reserve Board. Therefore, neither the United States trustee nor the creditors can appoint or elect a trustee in these cases.

Other amendments are stylistic.

CROSS REFERENCES

Partnerships—

    Commencement of involuntary cases, see 11 USCA § 303.

    Person defined to include partnerships, see 11 USCA § 101.

Representation of creditors and equity security holders in municipality debt adjustment and reorganization cases, see Fed.Rules Bankr.Proc. Rule 2019, 11 USCA.

Rule 2010. Qualification by Trustee; Proceeding on Bond

(a) Blanket bond

The United States trustee may authorize a blanket bond in favor of the United States conditioned on the faithful performance of official duties by the trustee or trustees to cover (1) a person who qualifies as trustee in a number of cases, and (2) a number of trustees each of whom qualifies in a different case.

(b) Proceeding on bond

A proceeding on the trustee's bond may be brought by any party in interest in the name of the United States for the use of the entity injured by the breach of the condition.

(As amended Mar. 30, 1987, eff. Aug. 1, 1987; Apr. 30, 1991, eff. Aug. 1, 1991.)

ADVISORY COMMITTEE NOTES

Subdivisions (a) and (b). Subdivision (a) gives authority for approval by the court of a single bond to cover (1) a person who qualifies as trustee in a number of cases, and (2) a number of trustees each of whom qualifies in a different case. The cases need not be related in any way. Substantial economies can be effected if a single bond covering a number of different cases can be issued and approved at one time. When a blanket bond is filed, the trustee qualifies under subdivision (b) of the rule by filing an acceptance of the office.

Subdivision (c) prescribes the evidentiary effect of a certified copy of an order approving the trustee's bond given by a trustee under this rule or, when a blanket bond has been authorized, of a certified copy of acceptance. This rule supplements the Federal Rules of Evidence, which apply in bankruptcy cases. See Rule 1101 of the Federal Rules of Evidence. The order of approval should conform to Official Form No. 25. See, however, § 549(c) of the Code which provides only for the filing of the petition in the real estate records of serve as constructive notice of the pendency of the case. See also Rule 2011 which prescribes the evidentiary effect of a certificate that the debtor is a debtor in possession.

Subdivision (d) is derived from former Bankruptcy Rule 212(f). Reference should be made to § 322(a) and (d) of the Code which requires the bond to be filed with the bankruptcy court and places a two year limitation for the commencement of a proceeding on the bond. A bond filed under this rule should conform to Official Form No. 25. A proceeding on the bond of a trustee is governed by the rules in Part VII. See the Note accompanying Rule 7001. See also Rule 9025.

1987 Amendments

Subdivision (b) is deleted because of the amendment to Rule 2008.

1991 Amendments

This rule is amended to conform to the 1986 amendment of § 322 of the Code. The United States trustee determines the amount and sufficiency of the trustee's bond. The amendment to subdivision (a) is derived from Rule X–1004(b).

Subdivision (b) is abrogated because an order approving a bond is no longer necessary in view of the 1986 amendments to § 322 of the Code. Subdivision (c) is redesignated as subdivision (b).

CROSS REFERENCES

Proceeding on trustee's bond as exception to procedural rule of prosecution in name of real party in interest, see Fed.Rules Bankr.Proc. Rule 7017, 11 USCA.

Security; proceedings against sureties, see Fed.Rules Bankr.Proc. Rule 9025, 11 USCA.

Two-year limitations period on bond proceeding, see 11 USCA § 322.

Parties plaintiff and defendant; capacity, see Fed.Rules Civ.Proc. Rule 17, 28 USCA.

Security; proceedings against sureties, see Fed.Rules Civ.Proc. Rule 65.1, 28 USCA.

Rule 2011. Evidence of Debtor in Possession or Qualification of Trustee

(a) Whenever evidence is required that a debtor is a debtor in possession or that a trustee has qualified, the clerk may so certify and the certificate shall constitute conclusive evidence of that fact.

(b) If a person elected or appointed as trustee does not qualify within the time prescribed by § 322(a) of the Code, the clerk shall so notify the court and the United States trustee.

(As amended Apr. 30, 1991, eff. Aug. 1, 1991.)

ADVISORY COMMITTEE NOTES

This rule prescribes the evidentiary effect of a certificate issued by the clerk that the debtor is a debtor in possession. See Official Form No. 26. Only chapter 11 of the Code provides for a debtor in possession. See § 1107(a) of the Code. If, however, a trustee is appointed in the chapter 11 case, there will not be a debtor in possession. See §§ 1101(1), 1105 of the Code.

1991 Amendments

This rule is amended to provide a procedure for proving that a trustee has qualified in accordance with § 322 of the Code. *Subdivision (b)* is added so that the court and the United States trustee will be informed if the person selected as trustee pursuant to §§ 701, 702, 1104, 1202, 1302, or 1163 fails to qualify within the time prescribed in § 322(a).

CROSS REFERENCES

Debtor in possession for purposes of reorganization case defined as debtor except when trustee is serving, see 11 USCA § 1101.

Rule 2012. Substitution of Trustee or Successor Trustee; Accounting

(a) Trustee

If a trustee is appointed in a chapter 11 case or the debtor is removed as debtor in possession in a chapter 12 case, the trustee is substituted automatically for the debtor in possession as a party in any pending action, proceeding, or matter.

(b) Successor trustee

When a trustee dies, resigns, is removed, or otherwise ceases to hold office during the pendency of a case under the Code (1) the successor is automatically substituted as a party in any pending action, proceeding, or matter; and (2) the successor trustee shall prepare, file, and transmit to the United States trustee an accounting of the prior administration of the estate.

(As amended Mar. 30, 1987, eff. Aug. 1, 1987; Apr. 30, 1991, eff. Aug. 1, 1991.)

ADVISORY COMMITTEE NOTES

Paragraph (1) of this rule implements § 325 of the Code. It provides that a pending action or proceeding continues without abatement and that the trustee's successor is automatically substituted as a party whether it be another trustee or the debtor returned to possession, as such party.

Paragraph (2) places it within the responsibility of a successor trustee to file an accounting of the prior administration of the estate. If an accounting is impossible to obtain from the prior trustee because of death or lack of cooperation, prior reports submitted in the earlier administration may be updated.

1987 Amendments

Subdivision (a) is new. The subdivision provides for the substitution of a trustee appointed in a chapter 11 case for the debtor in possession in any pending litigation.

The original provisions of the rule are now in subdivision (b).

1991 Amendments

Subdivision (a) is amended to include any chapter 12 case in which the debtor is removed as debtor in possession pursuant to § 1204(a) of the Code.

Subdivision (b) is amended to require that the accounting of the prior administration which must be filed with the court is also transmitted to the United States trustee who is responsible for supervising the administration of cases and trustees. See 28 U.S.C. § 586(a)(3). Because a court order is not required for the appointment of a successor trustee, requiring the court to fix a time for filing the accounting is inefficient and unnecessary. The United States trustee has supervisory powers over trustees and may require the successor trustee to file the accounting within a certain time period. If the successor trustee fails to file the accounting within a reasonable time, the United States trustee or a party in interest may take appropriate steps including a request for an appropriate court order. See 28 U.S.C. § 586(a)(3)(G). The words "with the court" are deleted in subdivision (b)(2) as unnecessary. See Rules 5005(a) and 9001(3).

CROSS REFERENCES

Abatement of suit or proceeding upon death or removal of trustee, see 11 USCA § 325.

Election by creditors of successor trustee in liquidation case, see 11 USCA § 703.

Exception to procedural rule for substitution of parties, see Fed.Rules Bankr.Proc. Rule 7025, 11 USCA.

Power of court to remove trustee, see 11 USCA § 324.

Substitution of public officer on death or separation from office, see Fed.Rules Civ.Proc. Rule 25, 28 USCA.

Rule 2013. Public Record of Compensation Awarded to Trustees, Examiners, and Professionals

(a) Record to be kept

The clerk shall maintain a public record listing fees awarded by the court (1) to trustees and attorneys, accountants, appraisers, auctioneers and other professionals employed by trustees, and (2) to examiners. The record shall include the name and docket number of the case, the name of the individual or firm receiving the fee and the amount of the fee awarded. The record shall be maintained chronologically and shall be kept current and open to examination by the public without charge. "Trustees," as used in this rule, does not include debtors in possession.

(b) Summary of record

At the close of each annual period, the clerk shall prepare a summary of the public record by individual or firm name, to reflect total fees awarded during the preceding year. The summary shall be open to examination by the public without charge. The clerk shall transmit a copy of the summary to the United States trustee.

(As amended Mar. 30, 1987, eff. Aug. 1, 1987; Apr. 30, 1991, eff. Aug. 1, 1991.)

ADVISORY COMMITTEE NOTES

This rule is adapted from former Rule 213. The first sentence of that rule is omitted because of the provisions in 28 U.S.C. §§ 586 and 604(f) creating panels of private trustees.

The rule is not applicable to standing trustees serving in chapter 13 cases. See § 1302 of the Code.

A basic purpose of the rule is to prevent what Congress has defined as "cronyism." Appointment or employment, whether in a chapter 7 or 11 case, should not center among a small select group of individuals unless the circumstances are such that it would be warranted. The public record of appointments to be kept by the clerk will provide a means for monitoring the appointment process.

Subdivision (b) provides a convenient source for public review of fees paid from debtors' estates in the bankruptcy courts. Thus, public recognition of appointments, fairly distributed and based on professional qualifications and expertise, will be promoted and notions of improper favor dispelled. This rule is in keeping with the findings of the Congressional subcommittees as set forth in the House Report of the Committee on the Judiciary, No. 95–595, 95th Cong., 1st Sess. 89–99 (1977). These findings included the observations that there were frequent appointments of the same person, contacts developed between the bankruptcy bar and the courts, and an unusually close relationship between the bar and the judges developed over the years. A major purpose of the new statute is to dilute these practices and instill greater public confidence in the system. Rule 2013 implements that laudatory purpose.

1987 Amendments

In subdivisions (b) and (c) the word awarded is substituted for the word paid. While clerks do not know if fees are paid, they can determine what fees are awarded by the court.

1991 Amendments

Subdivision (a) is deleted. The matter contained in this subdivision is more properly left for regulation by the United States trustee. When appointing trustees and examiners and when monitoring applications for employment of auctioneers, appraisers and other professionals, the United States trustee should be sensitive to disproportionate or excessive fees received by any person.

Subdivision (b), redesignated as subdivision (a), is amended to reflect the fact that the United States trustee appoints examiners subject to court approval.

Subdivision (c), redesignated as subdivision (b), is amended to furnish the United States trustee with a copy of the annual summary which may assist that office in the performance of its responsibilities under 28 U.S.C. § 586 and the Code.

The rule is not applicable to standing trustees serving in chapter 12 cases. See § 1202 of the Code.

CROSS REFERENCES

Compensation of officers to reimburse actual and necessary services, see 11 USCA § 330.

Limitation on compensation of trustee, see 11 USCA § 326.

Rule 2014. Employment of Professional Persons

(a) Application for an order of employment

An order approving the employment of attorneys, accountants, appraisers, auctioneers, agents, or other professionals pursuant to § 327, § 1103, or § 1114 of the Code shall be made only on application of the trustee or committee. The application shall be filed and, unless the case is a chapter 9 municipality case, a copy of the application shall be transmitted by the applicant to the United States trustee. The application shall state the specific facts showing the necessity for the employment, the name of the person to be employed, the reasons for the selection, the professional services to be rendered, any proposed arrangement for compensation, and, to the best of the applicant's knowledge, all of the person's connections with the debtor, creditors, any other party in interest, their respective attorneys and accountants, the United States trustee, or any person employed in the office of the United States trustee. The application shall be accompanied by a verified statement of the person to be employed setting forth the person's connections with the debtor, creditors, any other party in interest, their respective attorneys and accountants, the United States trustee, or any person employed in the office of the United States trustee.

(b) Services rendered by member or associate of firm of attorneys or accountants

If, under the Code and this rule, a law partnership or corporation is employed as an attorney, or an accounting partnership or corporation is employed as an accountant, or if a named attorney or accountant is employed, any partner, member, or regular associate of the partnership, corporation or individual may act as attorney or accountant so employed, without further order of the court.

(As amended Mar. 30, 1987, eff. Aug. 1, 1987; Apr. 30, 1991, eff. Aug. 1, 1991.)

ADVISORY COMMITTEE NOTES

Subdivision (a) is adapted from the second sentence of former Bankruptcy Rule 215(a). The remainder of that rule is covered by § 327 of the Code.

Subdivision (b) is derived from former Bankruptcy Rule 215(f). The compensation provisions are set forth in § 504 of the Code.

1991 Amendments

This rule is amended to include retention of professionals by committees of retired employees pursuant to § 1114 of the Code.

The United States trustee monitors applications filed under § 327 of the Code and may file with the court comments with respect to the approval of such applications. See 28 U.S.C. § 586(a)(3)(H). The United States trustee also monitors creditors' committees in accordance with 28 U.S.C. § 586(a)(3)(E). The addition of the second sentence of subdivision (a) is designed to enable the United States trustee to perform these duties.

Subdivision (a) is also amended to require disclosure of the professional's connections with the United States trustee or persons employed in the United States trustee's office. This requirement is not intended to prohibit the employment of such persons in all cases or to enlarge the definition of "disinterested person" in § 101(13) of the Code. However, the court may consider a connection with the United States trustee's office as a factor when exercising its discretion. Also, this information should be revealed in the interest of full disclosure and confidence in the bankruptcy system, especially since the United States trustee monitors and may be heard on applications for compensation and reimbursement of professionals employed under this rule.

The United States trustee appoints committees pursuant to § 1102 of the Code which is applicable in chapter 9 cases under § 901. In the interest of full disclosure and confidence in the bankruptcy system, a connection between the United States trustee and a professional employed by the committee should be revealed in every case, including a chapter 9 case. However, since the United States trustee does not have any role in the employment of professionals in chapter 9 cases, it is not necessary in such cases to transmit to the United States trustee a copy of the application under subdivision (a) of this rule. See 28 U.S.C. § 586(a)(3)(H).

CROSS REFERENCES

Application for compensation or reimbursement, see Fed.Rules Bankr.Proc. Rule 2016, 11 USCA.

Compensation for services and reimbursement of costs, see 11 USCA § 503.

Compensation of professional persons—

    Actual, necessary services, see 11 USCA § 330.

    Limitation on, see 11 USCA § 328.

    Sharing of, see 11 USCA § 504.

Rule 2015. Duty to Keep Records, Make Reports, and Give Notice of Case or Change of Status

(a) Trustee or debtor in possession

A trustee or debtor in possession shall:

(1) in a chapter 7 liquidation case and, if the court directs, in a chapter 11 reorganization case file and transmit to the United States trustee a complete inventory of the property of the debtor within 30 days after qualifying as a trustee or debtor in possession, unless such an inventory has already been filed;

(2) keep a record of receipts and the disposition of money and property received;

(3) file the reports and summaries required by § 704(a)(8) of the Code, which shall include a statement, if payments are made to employees, of the amounts of deductions for all taxes required to be withheld or paid for and in behalf of employees and the place where these amounts are deposited;

(4) as soon as possible after the commencement of the case, give notice of the case to every entity known to be holding money or property subject to withdrawal or order of the debtor, including every bank, savings or building and loan association, public utility company,

and landlord with whom the debtor has a deposit, and to every insurance company which has issued a policy having a cash surrender value payable to the debtor, except that notice need not be given to any entity who has knowledge or has previously been notified of the case;

(5) in a chapter 11 reorganization case, on or before the last day of the month after each calendar quarter during which there is a duty to pay fees under 28 U.S.C. § 1930(a)(6), file and transmit to the United States trustee a statement of any disbursements made during that quarter and of any fees payable under 28 U.S.C. § 1930(a)(6) for that quarter; and

(6) in a chapter 11 small business case, unless the court, for cause, sets another reporting interval, file and transmit to the United States trustee for each calendar month after the order for relief, on the appropriate Official Form, the report required by § 308. If the order for relief is within the first 15 days of a calendar month, a report shall be filed for the portion of the month that follows the order for relief. If the order for relief is after the 15th day of a calendar month, the period for the remainder of the month shall be included in the report for the next calendar month. Each report shall be filed no later than 21 days after the last day of the calendar month following the month covered by the report. The obligation to file reports under this subparagraph terminates on the effective date of the plan, or conversion or dismissal of the case.

(b) Chapter 12 trustee and debtor in possession

In a chapter 12 family farmer's debt adjustment case, the debtor in possession shall perform the duties prescribed in clauses (2)–(4) of subdivision (a) of this rule and, if the court directs, shall file and transmit to the United States trustee a complete inventory of the property of the debtor within the time fixed by the court. If the debtor is removed as debtor in possession, the trustee shall perform the duties of the debtor in possession prescribed in this paragraph.

(c) Chapter 13 trustee and debtor

(1) Business cases

In a chapter 13 individual's debt adjustment case, when the debtor is engaged in business, the debtor shall perform the duties prescribed by clauses (2)-(4) of subdivision (a) of this rule and, if the court directs, shall file and transmit to the United States trustee a complete inventory of the property of the debtor within the time fixed by the court.

(2) Nonbusiness cases

In a chapter 13 individual's debt adjustment case, when the debtor is not engaged in business, the trustee shall perform the duties prescribed by clause (2) of subdivision (a) of this rule.

(d) Foreign representative

In a case in which the court has granted recognition of a foreign proceeding under chapter 15, the foreign representative shall file any notice required under § 1518 of the Code within 14 days after the date when the representative becomes aware of the subsequent information.

(e) Transmission of reports

In a chapter 11 case the court may direct that copies or summaries of annual reports and copies or summaries of other reports shall be mailed to the creditors, equity security holders, and indenture trustees. The court may also direct the publication of summaries of any such reports. A copy of every report or summary mailed or published pursuant to this subdivision shall be transmitted to the United States trustee.

(As amended Mar. 30, 1987, eff. Aug. 1, 1987; Apr. 30, 1991, eff. Aug. 1, 1991; Apr. 23, 1996, eff. Dec. 1, 1996; Apr. 29, 2002, eff. Dec. 1, 2002; Apr. 23, 2008, eff. Dec. 1, 2008; Mar. 26, 2009, eff. Dec. 1, 2009; Apr. 23, 2012, eff. Dec. 1, 2012.)

Rule 2015   BANKRUPTCY RULES

ADVISORY COMMITTEE NOTES

This rule combines the provisions found in former Rules 218, 10–208, 11–30 and 13–208 of the Rules of Bankruptcy Procedure. It specifies various duties which are in addition to those required by §§ 704, 1106, 1302 and 1304 of the Code.

In **subdivision (a)** the times permitted to be fixed by the court in clause (3) for the filing of reports and summaries may be fixed by local rule or order.

Subdivision (b). This subdivision prescribes duties on either the debtor or trustee in chapter 13 cases, depending on whether or not the debtor is engaged in business (§ 1304 of the Code). The duty of giving notice prescribed by subdivision (a)(4) is not included in a nonbusiness case because of its impracticability.

Subdivision (c) is derived from former Chapter X Rule 10–208(c) which, in turn, was derived from § 190 of the Act [former § 590 of this title]. The equity security holders to whom the reports should be sent are those of record at the time of transmittal of such reports.

1987 Amendments

Subdivision (a) is amended to add as a duty of the trustee or debtor in possession the filing of a notice of or a copy of the petition. The filing of such notice or a copy of the petition is essential to the protection of the estate from unauthorized post-petition conveyances of real property. Section 549(c) of the Code protects the title of a good faith purchaser for fair equivalent value unless the notice or copy of the petition is filed.

1991 Amendments

This rule is amended to provide the United States trustee with information needed to perform supervisory responsibilities in accordance with 28 U.S.C. § 586(a)(3) and to exercise the right to raise, appear and be heard on issues pursuant to § 307 of the Code.

Subdivision (a)(3) is amended to conform to the 1986 amendments to § 704(8) of the Code and the United States trustee system. It may not be necessary for the court to fix a time to file reports if the United States trustee requests that they be filed within a specified time and there is no dispute regarding such time.

Subdivision (a)(5) is deleted because the filing of a notice of or copy of the petition to protect real property against unauthorized postpetition transfers in a particular case is within the discretion of the trustee.

The new subdivision (a)(5) was added to enable the United States trustee, parties in interest, and the court to determine the appropriate quarterly fee required by 28 U.S.C. § 1930(a)(6). The requirements of subdivision (a)(5) should be satisfied whenever possible by including this information in other reports filed by the trustee or debtor in possession. Nonpayment of the fee may result in dismissal or conversion of the case pursuant to § 1112(b) of the Code.

Rule X–1007(b), which provides that the trustee or debtor in possession shall cooperate with the United States trustee by furnishing information that the United States trustee reasonably requires, is deleted as unnecessary. The deletion of Rule X–1007(b) should not be construed as a limitation of the powers of the United States trustee or of the duty of the trustee or debtor in possession to cooperate with the United States trustee in the performance of the statutory responsibilities of that office.

Subdivision (a)(6) is abrogated as unnecessary. See § 1106(a)(7) of the Code.

Subdivision (a)(7) is abrogated. The closing of a chapter 11 case is governed by Rule 3022.

New **subdivision (b),** which prescribes the duties of the debtor in possession and trustee in a chapter 12 case, does not prohibit additional reporting requirements pursuant to local rule or court order.

1996 Amendments

Subdivision (a)(1) provides that the trustee in a chapter 7 case and, if the court directs, the trustee or debtor in possession in a chapter 11 case, is required to file and transmit to the United States trustee a complete inventory of the debtor's property within 30 days after qualifying as trustee or debtor in possession, unless such an inventory has already been filed. Subdivisions (b) and (c) are amended to clarify that a debtor in possession and trustee in a chapter 12 case, and a debtor in possession in a chapter 13 case where the debtor is engaged in business, are not required to file and transmit to the United States trustee

OFFICERS AND ADMINISTRATION — Rule 2015.1

a complete inventory of the property of the debtor unless the court so directs. If the court so directs, the court also fixes the time limit for filing and transmitting the inventory.

2002 Amendments

Subdivision (a)(5) is amended to provide that the duty to file quarterly disbursement reports continues only so long as there is an obligation to make quarterly payments to the United States trustee under 28 U.S.C. § 1930(a)(6).

Other amendments are stylistic.

2008 Amendments

Subparagraph (a)(6) implements § 308 of the Code, added by the 2005 amendments. That section requires small business chapter 11 debtors to file periodic financial and operating reports, and the rule sets the time for filing those reports and requires the use of an Official Form for the report. The obligation to file reports under this rule does not relieve the trustee or debtor of any other obligations to provide information or documents to the United States trustee.

The rule also is amended to fix the time for the filing of notices under § 1518, added to the Code in 2005. Former subdivision (d) is renumbered as subdivision (e).

Other changes are stylistic.

2009 Amendments

The rule is amended to implement changes in connection with the amendment to Rule 9006(a) and the manner by which time is computed under the rules. The deadlines in the rule are amended to substitute a deadline that is a multiple of seven days. Throughout the rules, deadlines are amended in the following manner:

- 5-day periods become 7-day periods
- 10-day periods become 14-day periods
- 15-day periods become 14-day periods
- 20-day periods become 21-day periods
- 25-day periods become 28-day periods

2012 Amendments

Subdivision (a)(3). Subdivision (a)(3) is amended to correct the reference to § 704. The 2005 amendments to the Code expanded § 704 and created subsections within it. The provision that was previously § 704(8) became § 704(a)(8). The other change to (a)(3) is stylistic.

Final approval of this technical amendment is sought without publication.

CROSS REFERENCES

Duties of trustee—

    Individual debt adjustment case, see 11 USCA § 1302.

    Reorganization case, see 11 USCA § 1106.

Operation of business by debtor, see 11 USCA § 1304.

Public access to papers filed in case under this title, see 11 USCA § 107.

Rule 2015.1. Patient Care Ombudsman

(a) Reports

A patient care ombudsman, at least 14 days before making a report under § 333(b)(2) of the Code, shall give notice that the report will be made to the court, unless the court orders otherwise. The notice shall be transmitted to the United States trustee, posted conspicuously at the health care facility that is the subject of the report, and served on: the debtor; the trustee; all patients; and any committee elected under § 705 or appointed under § 1102 of the Code or its authorized agent, or, if

Rule 2015.2   BANKRUPTCY RULES

the case is a chapter 9 municipality case or a chapter 11 reorganization case and no committee of unsecured creditors has been appointed under § 1102, on the creditors included on the list filed under Rule 1007(d); and such other entities as the court may direct. The notice shall state the date and time when the report will be made, the manner in which the report will be made, and, if the report is in writing, the name, address, telephone number, email address, and website, if any, of the person from whom a copy of the report may be obtained at the debtor's expense.

(b) Authorization to review confidential patient records

A motion by a patient care ombudsman under § 333(c) to review confidential patient records shall be governed by Rule 9014, served on the patient and any family member or other contact person whose name and address have been given to the trustee or the debtor for the purpose of providing information regarding the patient's health care, and transmitted to the United States trustee subject to applicable nonbankruptcy law relating to patient privacy. Unless the court orders otherwise, a hearing on the motion may not be commenced earlier than 14 days after service of the motion.

(Added Apr. 23, 2008, eff. Dec. 1, 2008; amended Mar. 26, 2009, eff. Dec. 1, 2009.)

ADVISORY COMMITTEE NOTES
2008 Adoption

This rule is new and implements § 333 of the Code, added by the 2005 amendments. Subdivision (a) is designed to give parties in interest, including patients or their representatives, sufficient notice so that they will be able to review written reports or attend hearings at which reports are made. The rule permits a notice to relate to a single report or to periodic reports to be given during the case. For example, the ombudsman may give notice that reports will be made at specified intervals or dates during the case.

Subdivision (a) of the rule also requires that the notice be posted conspicuously at the health care facility in a place where it will be seen by patients and their families or others visiting the patients. This may require posting in common areas and patient rooms within the facility. Because health care facilities and the patients they serve can vary greatly, the locations of the posted notice should be tailored to the specific facility that is the subject of the report.

Subdivision (b) requires the ombudsman to notify the patient and the United States trustee that the ombudsman is seeking access to confidential patient records so that they will be able to appear and be heard on the matter. This procedure should assist the court in reaching its decision both as to access to the records and appropriate restrictions on that access to ensure continued confidentiality. Notices given under this rule are subject to the provisions of applicable federal and state law that relate to the protection of patients' privacy, such as the Health Insurance Portability and Accountability Act of 1996, Pub. L. No. 104–191 (HIPAA).

2009 Amendments

The rule is amended to implement changes in connection with the amendment to Rule 9006(a) and the manner by which time is computed under the rules. The deadlines in the rule are amended to substitute a deadline that is a multiple of seven days. Throughout the rules, deadlines are amended in the following manner:

- 5-day periods become 7-day periods
- 10-day periods become 14-day periods
- 15-day periods become 14-day periods
- 20-day periods become 21-day periods
- 25-day periods become 28-day periods

Rule 2015.2.   Transfer of Patient in Health Care Business Case

Unless the court orders otherwise, if the debtor is a health care business, the trustee may not transfer a patient to another health care business under § 704(a)(12) of the Code unless the trustee gives at least 14 days' notice of the transfer to the patient care ombudsman, if any, the patient, and any family member or other contact person whose name and address has been given to the trustee or the debtor for the purpose of providing information regarding the patient's health care. The notice is subject to applicable nonbankruptcy law relating to patient privacy.

(Added Apr. 23, 2008, eff. Dec. 1, 2008; amended Mar. 26, 2009, eff. Dec. 1, 2009.)

ADVISORY COMMITTEE NOTES

2008 Adoption

This rule is new. Section 704(a)(12), added to the Code by the 2005 amendments, authorizes the trustee to relocate patients when a health care business debtor's facility is in the process of being closed. The Code permits the trustee to take this action without the need for any court order, but the notice required by this rule will enable a patient care ombudsman appointed under § 333, or a patient who contends that the trustee's actions violate § 704(a)(12), to have those issues resolved before the patient is transferred.

This rule also permits the court to enter an order dispensing with or altering the notice requirement in proper circumstances. For example, a facility could be closed immediately, or very quickly, such that 10 days' notice would not be possible in some instances. In that event, the court may shorten the time required for notice.

Notices given under this rule are subject to the provisions of applicable federal and state law that relate to the protection of patients' privacy, such as the Health Insurance Portability and Accountability Act of 1996, Pub. L. No. 104–191 (HIPAA).

2009 Amendments

The rule is amended to implement changes in connection with the amendment to Rule 9006(a) and the manner by which time is computed under the rules. The deadline in the rule is amended to substitute a deadline that is a multiple of seven days. Throughout the rules, deadlines are amended in the following manner:

- 5-day periods become 7-day periods
- 10-day periods become 14-day periods
- 15-day periods become 14-day periods
- 20-day periods become 21-day periods
- 25-day periods become 28-day periods

Rule 2015.3. Reports of Financial Information on Entities in Which a Chapter 11 Estate Holds a Controlling or Substantial Interest

(a) Reporting requirement

In a chapter 11 case, the trustee or debtor in possession shall file periodic financial reports of the value, operations, and profitability of each entity that is not a publicly traded corporation or a debtor in a case under title 11, and in which the estate holds a substantial or controlling interest. The reports shall be prepared as prescribed by the appropriate Official Form, and shall be based upon the most recent information reasonably available to the trustee or debtor in possession.

(b) Time for filing; service

The first report required by this rule shall be filed no later than seven days before the first date set for the meeting of creditors under § 341 of the Code. Subsequent reports shall be filed no less frequently than every six months thereafter, until the effective date of a plan or the case is dismissed or converted. Copies of the report shall be served on the United States trustee, any committee appointed under § 1102 of the Code, and any other party in interest that has filed a request therefor.

(c) Presumption of substantial or controlling interest; judicial determination

For purposes of this rule, an entity of which the estate controls or owns at least a 20 percent interest, shall be presumed to be an entity in which the estate has a substantial or controlling interest. An entity in which the estate controls or owns less than a 20 percent interest shall be presumed not to be an entity in which the estate has a substantial or controlling interest. Upon motion, the entity, any holder of an interest therein, the United States trustee, or any other party in interest may seek to rebut either presumption, and the court shall, after notice and a hearing, determine whether the estate's interest in the entity is substantial or controlling.

(d) Modification of reporting requirement

The court may, after notice and a hearing, vary the reporting requirement established by subdivision (a) of this rule for cause, including that the trustee or debtor in possession is not able, after a good faith effort, to comply with those reporting requirements, or that the information required by subdivision (a) is publicly available.

(e) Notice and protective orders

No later than 14 days before filing the first report required by this rule, the trustee or debtor in possession shall send notice to the entity in which the estate has a substantial or controlling interest, and to all holders—known to the trustee or debtor in possession—of an interest in that entity, that the trustee or debtor in possession expects to file and serve financial information relating to the entity in accordance with this rule. The entity in which the estate has a substantial or controlling interest, or a person holding an interest in that entity, may request protection of the information under § 107 of the Code.

(f) Effect of request

Unless the court orders otherwise, the pendency of a request under subdivisions (c), (d), or (e) of this rule shall not alter or stay the requirements of subdivision (a).

(Added Apr. 23, 2008, eff. Dec. 1, 2008; amended Mar. 26, 2009, eff. Dec. 1, 2009.)

ADVISORY COMMITTEE NOTES

2008 Adoption

This rule implements § 419 of the Bankruptcy Abuse Prevention and Consumer Protection Act of 2005 ("BAPCPA"). Reports are to be made on the appropriate Official Form. While § 419 of BAPCPA places the obligation to report upon the "debtor," this rule extends the obligation to include cases in which a trustee has been appointed. The court can order that the reports not be filed in appropriate circumstances, such as when the information that would be included in these reports is already available to interested parties.

2009 Amendments

The rule is amended to implement changes in connection with the amendment to Rule 9006(a) and the manner by which time is computed under the rules. The deadline in the rule is amended to substitute a deadline that is a multiple of seven days. Throughout the rules, deadlines are amended in the following manner:

- 5-day periods become 7-day periods
- 10-day periods become 14-day periods
- 15-day periods become 14-day periods
- 20-day periods become 21-day periods
- 25-day periods become 28-day periods

Rule 2016. Compensation for Services Rendered and Reimbursement of Expenses

(a) Application for compensation or reimbursement

An entity seeking interim or final compensation for services, or reimbursement of necessary expenses, from the estate shall file an application setting forth a detailed statement of (1) the services rendered, time expended and expenses incurred, and (2) the amounts requested. An application for compensation shall include a statement as to what payments have theretofore been made or promised to the applicant for services rendered or to be rendered in any capacity whatsoever in connection with the case, the source of the compensation so paid or promised, whether any compensation previously received has been shared and whether an agreement or understanding exists between the applicant and any other entity for the sharing of compensation received or to be received for services rendered in or in connection with the case, and the particulars of any sharing of compensation or agreement or understanding therefor, except that details of any agreement by the applicant for the sharing of compensation as a member or regular associate of a firm of lawyers or accountants shall not be required. The requirements of this subdivision shall apply to an application for compensation for services rendered by an attorney or accountant even though the application is filed by a creditor or other entity. Unless the case is a chapter 9 municipality case, the applicant shall transmit to the United States trustee a copy of the application.

(b) Disclosure of compensation paid or promised to attorney for debtor

Every attorney for a debtor, whether or not the attorney applies for compensation, shall file and transmit to the United States trustee within 14 days after the order for relief, or at another time as the court may direct, the statement required by § 329 of the Code including whether the attorney has shared or agreed to share the compensation with any other entity. The statement shall include the particulars of any such sharing or agreement to share by the attorney, but the details of any agreement for the sharing of the compensation with a member or regular associate of the attorney's law firm shall not be required. A supplemental statement shall be filed and transmitted to the United States trustee within 14 days after any payment or agreement not previously disclosed.

(c) Disclosure of compensation paid or promised to bankruptcy petition preparer

Before a petition is filed, every bankruptcy petition preparer for a debtor shall deliver to the debtor, the declaration under penalty of perjury required by § 110(h)(2). The declaration shall disclose any fee, and the source of any fee, received from or on behalf of the debtor within 12 months of the filing of the case and all unpaid fees charged to the debtor. The declaration shall also describe the services performed and documents prepared or caused to be prepared by the bankruptcy petition preparer. The declaration shall be filed with the petition. The petition preparer shall file a supplemental statement within 14 days after any payment or agreement not previously disclosed.

(As amended Mar. 30, 1987, eff. Aug. 1, 1987; Apr. 30, 1991, eff. Aug. 1, 1991; Mar. 27, 2003, eff. Dec. 1, 2003; Mar. 26, 2009, eff. Dec. 1, 2009.)

ADVISORY COMMITTEE NOTES

This rule is derived from former Rule 219. Many of the former rule's requirements are, however, set forth in the Code. Section 329 requires disclosure by an attorney of transactions with the debtor, § 330 sets forth the bases for allowing compensation, and § 504 prohibits sharing of compensation. This rule implements those various provisions.

Subdivision (a) includes within its provisions a committee, member thereof, agent, attorney or accountant for the committee when compensation or reimbursement of expenses is sought from the estate.

Regular associate of a law firm is defined in Rule 9001(9) to include any attorney regularly employed by, associated with, or counsel to that law firm. Firm is defined in Rule 9001(6) to include a partnership or professional corporation.

1987 Amendments

Subdivision (a) is amended to change "person" to "entity." There are occasions in which a governmental unit may be entitled to file an application under this rule. The requirement that the application contain a "detailed statement of services rendered, time expended and expenses incurred" gives to the court authority to ensure that the application is both comprehensive and detailed. No amendments are made to delineate further the requirements of the application because the amount of detail to be furnished is a function of the nature of the services rendered and the complexity of the case.

Subdivision (b) is amended to require that the attorney for the debtor file the § 329 statement before the meeting of creditors. This will assist the parties in conducting the examination of the debtor. In addition, the amended rule requires the attorney to supplement the § 329 statement if an undisclosed payment is made to the attorney or a new or amended agreement is entered into by the debtor and the attorney.

1991 Amendments

Subdivision (a) is amended to enable the United States trustee to perform the duty to monitor applications for compensation and reimbursement filed under § 330 of the Code. See 28 U.S.C. § 586(a)(3)(A).

Subdivision (b) is amended to give the United States trustee the information needed to determine whether to request appropriate relief based on excessive fees under § 329(b) of the Code. See Rule 2017.

The words "with the court" are deleted in subdivisions (a) and (b) as unnecessary. See Rules 5005(a) and 9001(3).

2003 Amendments

This rule is amended by adding subdivision (c) to implement § 110(h)(1) of the Code.

2009 Amendments

The rule is amended to implement changes in connection with the amendment to Rule 9006(a) and the manner by which time is computed under the rules. The deadline in the rule is amended to substitute a deadline that is a multiple of seven days. Throughout the rules, deadlines are amended in the following manner:

- 5-day periods become 7-day periods
- 10-day periods become 14-day periods
- 15-day periods become 14-day periods
- 20-day periods become 21-day periods
- 25-day periods become 28-day periods

Subdivision (c) is amended to reflect the 2005 amendment to § 110(h)(1) of the Bankruptcy Code which now requires that the declaration be filed with the petition. The statute previously required that the petition preparer file the declaration within 10 days after the filing of the petition. The amendment to the rule also corrects the cross reference to § 110(h)(1), which was redesignated as subparagraph (h)(2) of § 110 by the 2005 amendment to the Code.

Other changes are stylistic.

CROSS REFERENCES

Compensation of professional persons—
  Actual, necessary services, see 11 USCA § 330.
  Limitation on, see 11 USCA § 328.
  Sharing of, see 11 USCA § 504.
Definition of—
  Firm to include partnership or professional corporation, see Fed.Rules Bankr.Proc. Rule 9001, 11 USCA.

Regular associate to mean attorney employed by, associated with, as counsel to firm or individual, see Fed.Rules Bankr.Proc. Rule 9001, 11 USCA.

Employment of professional persons, see Fed.Rules Bankr.Proc. Rule 2014, 11 USCA.

Rule 2017. Examination of Debtor's Transactions With Debtor's Attorney

(a) Payment or transfer to attorney before order for relief

On motion by any party in interest or on the court's own initiative, the court after notice and a hearing may determine whether any payment of money or any transfer of property by the debtor, made directly or indirectly and in contemplation of the filing of a petition under the Code by or against the debtor or before entry of the order for relief in an involuntary case, to an attorney for services rendered or to be rendered is excessive.

(b) Payment or transfer to attorney after order for relief

On motion by the debtor, the United States trustee, or on the court's own initiative, the court after notice and a hearing may determine whether any payment of money or any transfer of property, or any agreement therefor, by the debtor to an attorney after entry of an order for relief in a case under the Code is excessive, whether the payment or transfer is made or is to be made directly or indirectly, if the payment, transfer, or agreement therefor is for services in any way related to the case.

(As amended Mar. 30, 1987, eff. Aug. 1, 1987; Apr. 30, 1991, eff. Aug. 1, 1991.)

ADVISORY COMMITTEE NOTES

This rule is derived from § 60d of the Act [former § 96(d) of this title] and former Bankruptcy Rule 220 and implements § 329 of the Code. Information required to be disclosed by the attorney for a debtor by § 329 of the Code and by the debtor in his Statement of Financial Affairs (Item #15 of Form No. 7, Item #20 of Form No. 8) will assist the court in determining whether to proceed under this rule. Section 60d was enacted in recognition of "the temptation of a failing debtor to deal too liberally with his property in employing counsel to protect him in view of financial reverses and probable failure." In re Wood & Henderson, 210 U.S. 246, 253 (1908). This rule, like § 60d of the Act and § 329 of the Code, is premised on the need for and appropriateness of judicial scrutiny of arrangements between a debtor and his attorney to protect the creditors of the estate and the debtor against overreaching by an officer of the court who is in a peculiarly advantageous position to impose on both the creditors and his client. 2 Collier, Bankruptcy ¶329.02 (15th ed. 1980); MacLachlan, Bankruptcy 318 (1956). Rule 9014 applies to any contested matter arising under this rule.

This rule is not to be construed to permit post-petition payments or transfers which may be avoided under other provisions of the Code.

1991 Amendments

This rule is amended to include within subdivision (a) a payment or transfer of property by the debtor to an attorney after the filing of an involuntary petition but before the order for relief. Any party in interest should be able to make a motion for a determination of whether such payment or transfer is excessive because the funds or property transferred may be property of the estate.

The United States trustee supervises and monitors the administration of bankruptcy cases other than chapter 9 cases and pursuant to § 307 of the Code may raise, appear and be heard on issues relating to fees paid to the debtor's attorney. It is consistent with that role to expect the United States trustee to review statements filed under Rule 2016(b) and to file motions relating to excessive fees pursuant to § 329 of the Code.

CROSS REFERENCES

Court filing of compensation paid or agreed to be paid, see 11 USCA § 329.

Motions; form and service, see Fed.Rules Bankr.Proc. Rule 9013, 11 USCA.

Proceedings under this rule as nonadversarial proceedings, see Fed.Rules Bankr.Proc. Rule 7001, 11 USCA.

Process; service of summons, complaint, see Fed.Rules Bankr.Proc. Rule 7004, 11 USCA.

Rule 2018. Intervention; Right to Be Heard

(a) Permissive intervention

In a case under the Code, after hearing on such notice as the court directs and for cause shown, the court may permit any interested entity to intervene generally or with respect to any specified matter.

(b) Intervention by Attorney General of a State

In a chapter 7, 11, 12, or 13 case, the Attorney General of a State may appear and be heard on behalf of consumer creditors if the court determines the appearance is in the public interest, but the Attorney General may not appeal from any judgment, order, or decree in the case.

(c) Chapter 9 municipality case

The Secretary of the Treasury of the United States may, or if requested by the court shall, intervene in a chapter 9 case. Representatives of the state in which the debtor is located may intervene in a chapter 9 case with respect to matters specified by the court.

(d) Labor unions

In a chapter 9, 11, or 12 case, a labor union or employees' association, representative of employees of the debtor, shall have the right to be heard on the economic soundness of a plan affecting the interests of the employees. A labor union or employees' association which exercises its right to be heard under this subdivision shall not be entitled to appeal any judgment, order, or decree relating to the plan, unless otherwise permitted by law.

(e) Service on entities covered by this rule

The court may enter orders governing the service of notice and papers on entities permitted to intervene or be heard pursuant to this rule.

(As amended Mar. 30, 1987, eff. Aug. 1, 1987; Apr. 30, 1991, eff. Aug. 1, 1991.)

ADVISORY COMMITTEE NOTES

This rule is derived from former Rules 8–210, 9–15 and 10–210 and it implements §§ 1109 and 1164 of the Code.

Pursuant to § 1109 of the Code, parties in interest have a right to be heard and the Securities and Exchange Commission may raise and be heard on any issue but it may not take an appeal. That section is applicable in chapter 9 cases (§ 901 of the Code) and in chapter 11 cases, including cases under subchapter IV thereof for the reorganization of a railroad.

In a railroad reorganization case under subchapter IV of chapter 11, § 1164 also gives the right to be heard to the Interstate Commerce Commission, the Department of Transportation and any state or local regulatory commission with jurisdiction over the debtor, but these entities may not appeal.

This rule does not apply in adversary proceedings. For intervention in adversary proceedings, see Rule 7024. The rules do not provide any right of compensation to or reimbursement of expenses for intervenors or others covered by this rule. Section 503(b)(3)(D) and (4) is not applicable to the entities covered by this rule.

Subdivision (a) is derived from former Chapter VIII Rule 8–210 and former Chapter X Rule 10–210. It permits intervention of an entity (see § 101(14), (21) of the Code) not otherwise entitled to do so under the Code or this rule. Such a party seeking to intervene must show cause therefor.

Subdivision (b) specifically grants the appropriate state's attorney General the right to appear and be heard on behalf of consumer creditors when it is in the public interest. See House Rep. No. 95–595, 95th Cong., 1st Sess. (1977) 189. While "consumer creditor" is not defined in the Code or elsewhere, it would include the type of individual entitled to priority under § 507(a)(5) of the Code, that is, an individual who has deposited money for the purchase, lease or rental of property or the purchase of services for the personal, family, or household use of the individual. It would also include individuals who purchased or leased property for such purposes in connection with which there may exist claims for breach of warranty.

This subdivision does not grant the Attorney General the status of party in interest. In other contexts, the Attorney General will, of course, be a party in interest as for example, in representing a state in connection with a tax claim.

Subdivision (c) recognizes the possible interests of the Secretary of the Treasury or of the state of the debtor's locale when a municipality is the debtor. It is derived from former Chapter IX Rule 9–15 and § 85(d) of the Act [former § 405(d) of this title].

Subdivision (d) is derived from former Chapter X Rule 10–210 which, in turn, was derived from § 206 of the Act [former § 606 of this title]. Section 206 has no counter-part in the Code.

Subdivision (e) is derived from former Chapter VIII Rule 8–210(d). It gives the court flexibility in directing the type of future notices to be given intervenors.

1987 Amendments

Subdivision (d) is amended to make it clear that the prohibition against appeals by labor unions is limited only to their participation in connection with the hearings on the plan as provided in subdivision (d). If a labor union would otherwise have the right to file an appeal or to be a party to an appeal, this rule does not preclude the labor union from exercising that right.

1991 Amendments

Subdivisions (b) and (d) are amended to include chapter 12.

CROSS REFERENCES

Consumer debt defined as debt primarily for personal, family, or household purpose, see 11 USCA § 101.

Definitions for purposes of this rule of—

    Entity, see 11 USCA § 101.

    Governmental unit, see 11 USCA § 101.

    Person, see 11 USCA § 101.

Intervention of—

    Department of Transportation, see 11 USCA § 1164.

    Interstate Commerce Commission, see 11 USCA § 1164.

    Party in interest, see 11 USCA § 1109.

    Securities and Exchange Commission, see 11 USCA § 1109.

    State or local regulatory commission, see 11 USCA § 1164.

Intervention in adversary proceedings, see Fed.Rules Bankr.Proc. Rule 7024, 11 USCA.

Rule 2019. Disclosure Regarding Creditors and Equity Security Holders in Chapter 9 and Chapter 11 Cases

(a) Definitions

In this rule the following terms have the meanings indicated:

(1) "Disclosable economic interest" means any claim, interest, pledge, lien, option, participation, derivative instrument, or any other right or derivative right granting the holder an economic interest that is affected by the value, acquisition, or disposition of a claim or interest.

(2) "Represent" or "represents" means to take a position before the court or to solicit votes regarding the confirmation of a plan on behalf of another.

Rule 2019   **BANKRUPTCY RULES**

(b) Disclosure by groups, committees, and entities

    (1) In a chapter 9 or 11 case, a verified statement setting forth the information specified in subdivision (c) of this rule shall be filed by every group or committee that consists of or represents, and every entity that represents, multiple creditors or equity security holders that are (A) acting in concert to advance their common interests, and (B) not composed entirely of affiliates or insiders of one another.

    (2) Unless the court orders otherwise, an entity is not required to file the verified statement described in paragraph (1) of this subdivision solely because of its status as:

        (A) an indenture trustee;

        (B) an agent for one or more other entities under an agreement for the extension of credit;

        (C) a class action representative; or

        (D) a governmental unit that is not a person.

(c) Information required

The verified statement shall include:

    (1) the pertinent facts and circumstances concerning:

        (A) with respect to a group or committee, other than a committee appointed under § 1102 or § 1114 of the Code, the formation of the group or committee, including the name of each entity at whose instance the group or committee was formed or for whom the group or committee has agreed to act; or

        (B) with respect to an entity, the employment of the entity, including the name of each creditor or equity security holder at whose instance the employment was arranged;

    (2) if not disclosed under subdivision (c)(1), with respect to an entity, and with respect to each member of a group or committee:

        (A) name and address;

        (B) the nature and amount of each disclosable economic interest held in relation to the debtor as of the date the entity was employed or the group or committee was formed; and

        (C) with respect to each member of a group or committee that claims to represent any entity in addition to the members of the group or committee, other than a committee appointed under § 1102 or § 1114 of the Code, the date of acquisition by quarter and year of each disclosable economic interest, unless acquired more than one year before the petition was filed;

    (3) if not disclosed under subdivision (c)(1) or (c)(2), with respect to each creditor or equity security holder represented by an entity, group, or committee, other than a committee appointed under § 1102 or § 1114 of the Code:

        (A) name and address; and

        (B) the nature and amount of each disclosable economic interest held in relation to the debtor as of the date of the statement; and

    (4) a copy of the instrument, if any, authorizing the entity, group, or committee to act on behalf of creditors or equity security holders.

(d) Supplemental statements

If any fact disclosed in its most recently filed statement has changed materially, an entity, group, or committee shall file a verified supplemental statement whenever it takes a position before the court or solicits votes on the confirmation of a plan. The supplemental statement shall set forth the material changes in the facts required by subdivision (c) to be disclosed.

OFFICERS AND ADMINISTRATION — Rule 2019

(e) Determination of failure to comply; sanctions

(1) On motion of any party in interest, or on its own motion, the court may determine whether there has been a failure to comply with any provision of this rule.

(2) If the court finds such a failure to comply, it may:

(A) refuse to permit the entity, group, or committee to be heard or to intervene in the case;

(B) hold invalid any authority, acceptance, rejection, or objection given, procured, or received by the entity, group, or committee; or

(C) grant other appropriate relief.

(As amended Mar. 30, 1987, eff. Aug. 1, 1987; Apr. 30, 1991, eff. Aug. 1, 1991; Apr. 26, 2011, eff. Dec. 1, 2011.)

ADVISORY COMMITTEE NOTES

This rule is a comprehensive regulation of representation in chapter 9 municipality and in chapter 11 reorganization cases. It is derived from §§ 209 to 213 of the Act [former §§ 609 to 613 of this title] and former Chapter X Rule 10–211.

Subdivision (b) is derived from §§ 212, 213 of the Act [former §§ 612 and 613 of this title]. As used in clause (2), "other authorization" would include a power or warrant of attorney which are specifically mentioned in § 212 of the Act. This rule deals with representation provisions in mortgages, trust deeds, etc. to protect the beneficiaries from unfair practices and the like. It does not deal with the validation or invalidation of security interests generally. If immediate compliance is not possible, the court may permit a representative to be heard on a specific matter, but there is no implicit waiver of compliance on a permanent basis.

1991 Amendments

Subdivision (a) is amended to exclude from the requirements of this rule committees of retired employees appointed pursuant to § 1114 of the Code. The words "with the clerk" are deleted as unnecessary. See Rules 5005(a) and 9001(3).

2011 Amendments

The rule is substantially amended to expand the scope of its coverage and the content of its disclosure requirements. Stylistic and organizational changes are also made in order to provide greater clarity. Because the rule no longer applies only to representatives of creditors and equity security holders, the title of the rule has been changed to reflect its broadened focus on disclosure of financial information in chapter 9 and chapter 11 cases.

Subdivision (a). The content of subdivision (a) is new. It sets forth a definition of the term "disclosable economic interest," which is used in subdivisions (c)(2), (c)(3), (d), and (e). The definition of the term is intended to be sufficiently broad to cover any economic interest that could affect the legal and strategic positions a stakeholder takes in a chapter 9 or chapter 11 case. A disclosable economic interest extends beyond claims and interests owned by a stakeholder and includes, among other types of holdings, short positions, credit default swaps, and total return swaps.

The second definition is of "represent" or "represents." The definition provides that representation requires active participation in the case or in a proceeding on behalf of another entity—either by taking a position on a matter before the court or by soliciting votes on the confirmation of a plan. Thus, for example, an attorney who is retained and consulted by a creditor or equity security holder to monitor the case, but who does not advocate any position before the court or engage in solicitation activities on behalf of that client, does not represent the creditor or equity security holder for purposes of this rule.

Subdivision (b). Subdivision (b)(1) specifies who is covered by the rule's disclosure requirements. In addition to an entity, group, or committee that *represents* more than one creditor or equity security holder, the amendment extends the rule's coverage to groups or committees that *consist* of more than one creditor or equity security holder. The rule no longer excludes official committees, except as specifically indicated. The rule applies to a group of creditors or equity security holders that act in concert to advance common interests (except when the group consists exclusively of affiliates or insiders of one another), even if the group does not call itself a committee.

Subdivision (b)(2) excludes certain entities from the rule's coverage. Even though these entities may represent multiple creditors or equity security holders, they do so under formal legal arrangements of trust or contact law that preclude them from acting on the basis of conflicting economic interests. For example, an indenture trustee's responsibilities are defined by the indenture, and individual interests of bondholders would not affect the trustee's representation.

Subdivision (c). Subdivision (c) sets forth the information that must be included in a verified statement required to be filed under this rule. Subdivision (c)(1) continues to require disclosure concerning the employment of an entity or indenture trustee and the formation of a committee or group, other than an official committee, and the employment of an entity.

Subdivision (c)(2) specifies information that must be disclosed with respect to the entity and each member of the committee and group filing the statement. In the case of a committee or group, the information about the nature and amount of a disclosable economic interest must be specifically provided on a member-by-member basis, and not in the aggregate. The quarter and year in which each disclosable economic interest was acquired by each member of a committee or group (other than an official committee) that claims to represent others must also be specifically provided, except for a disclosable economic interest acquired more than a year before the filing of the petition. Although the rule no longer requires the disclosure of the precise date of acquisition or the amount paid for disclosable economic interests, nothing in this rule precludes either the discovery of that information or its disclosure when ordered by the court pursuant to authority outside this rule.

Subdivision (c)(3) specifies information that must be disclosed with respect to creditors or equity security holders that are represented by an entity, group, committee, or indenture trustee. This provision does not apply with respect to those represented by official committees. The information required to be disclosed under subdivision (c)(3) parallels that required to be disclosed under subdivision (c)(2)(A) and (B). The amendment also clarifies that under (c)(3) the nature and amount of each disclosable economic interest of represented creditors and shareholders must be stated as of the date of the verified statement.

Subdivision (c)(4) requires the attachment of any instrument authorizing the filer of the verified statement to act on behalf of creditors or equity security holders.

Subdivision (d). Subdivision (d) requires the filing of a supplemental statement at the time an entity, group, or committee takes a position before the court or solicits votes on a plan if there has been a material change in any of the information contained in its last filed statement. The supplemental verified statement must set forth the material changes that have occurred regarding the information required to be disclosed by subdivision (c) of this rule.

Subdivision (e). Subdivision (e) addresses the court's authority to determine whether there has been a violation of this rule and to impose a sanction for any violation. It no longer addresses the court's authority to determine violations of other applicable laws regulating the activities and personnel of an entity, group, or committee.

CROSS REFERENCES

Appointment of creditors' committee organized before order for relief, see Fed.Rules Bankr.Proc. Rule 2007, 11 USCA.

Motions; form and service, see Fed.Rules Bankr.Proc. Rule 9013, 11 USCA.

Trustees for estates when joint administration ordered, see Fed.Rules Bankr.Proc. Rule 2009, 11 USCA.

Rule 2020. Review of Acts by United States Trustee

A proceeding to contest any act or failure to act by the United States trustee is governed by Rule 9014.

(Added Apr. 30, 1991, eff. Aug. 1, 1991.)

ADVISORY COMMITTEE NOTES

The United States trustee performs administrative functions, such as the convening of the meeting of creditors and the appointment of trustees and committees. Most of the acts of the United States trustee are not controversial and will go unchallenged. However, the United States trustee is not a judicial officer and does not resolve disputes regarding the propriety of its own actions. This rule, which is new, provides a procedure for judicial review of the United States trustee's acts or failure to act in connection with the administration of the case. For example, if the United States trustee schedules a § 341 meeting to be held 90 days after the petition is filed, and a party in interest wishes to challenge the propriety of that act in view of § 341(a) of the Code and Rule 2003 which requires that the meeting be held not more than 40 days after the order for relief, this rule permits the party to do so by motion.

This rule provides for review of acts already committed by the United States trustee, but does not provide for advisory opinions in advance of the act. This rule is not intended to limit the discretion of the United States trustee, provided that the United States trustee's act is authorized by, and in compliance with, the Code, title 28, these rules, and other applicable law.

PART III—CLAIMS AND DISTRIBUTION TO CREDITORS AND EQUITY INTEREST HOLDERS; PLANS

Rule
3001. Proof of Claim.
3002. Filing Proof of Claim or Interest.
3002.1. Notice Relating to Claims Secured by Security Interest in the Debtor's Principal Residence.
3003. Filing Proof of Claim or Equity Security Interest in Chapter 9 Municipality or Chapter 11 Reorganization Cases.
3004. Filing of Claims by Debtor or Trustee.
3005. Filing of Claim, Acceptance, or Rejection by Guarantor, Surety, Indorser, or Other Codebtor.
3006. Withdrawal of Claim; Effect on Acceptance or Rejection of Plan.
3007. Objections to Claims.
3008. Reconsideration of Claims.
3009. Declaration and Payment of Dividends in a Chapter 7 Liquidation Case.
3010. Small Dividends and Payments in Chapter 7 Liquidation, Chapter 12 Family Farmer's Debt Adjustment, and Chapter 13 Individual's Debt Adjustment Cases.
3011. Unclaimed Funds in Chapter 7 Liquidation, Chapter 12 Family Farmer's Debt Adjustment, and Chapter 13 Individual's Debt Adjustment Cases.
3012. Valuation of Security.
3013. Classification of Claims and Interests.
3014. Election Under § 1111(b) by Secured Creditor in Chapter 9 Municipality or Chapter 11 Reorganization Case.
3015. Filing, Objection to Confirmation, and Modification of a Plan in a Chapter 12 Family Farmer's Debt Adjustment or a Chapter 13 Individual's Debt Adjustment Case.
3016. Filing of Plan and Disclosure Statement in a Chapter 9 Municipality or Chapter 11 Reorganization Case.
3017. Court Consideration of Disclosure Statement in a Chapter 9 Municipality or Chapter 11 Reorganization Case.
3017.1. Court Consideration of Disclosure Statement in a Small Business Case.
3018. Acceptance or Rejection of Plan in a Chapter 9 Municipality or a Chapter 11 Reorganization Case.
3019. Modification of Accepted Plan in a Chapter 9 Municipality or a Chapter 11 Reorganization Case.
3020. Deposit; Confirmation of Plan in a Chapter 9 Municipality or Chapter 11 Reorganization Case.
3021. Distribution Under Plan.
3022. Final Decree in Chapter 11 Reorganization Case.

Rule 3001. Proof of Claim

(a) Form and content

A proof of claim is a written statement setting forth a creditor's claim. A proof of claim shall conform substantially to the appropriate Official Form.

(b) Who may execute

A proof of claim shall be executed by the creditor or the creditor's authorized agent except as provided in Rules 3004 and 3005.

(c) Supporting information

(1) Claim based on a writing

Except for a claim governed by paragraph (3) of this subdivision, when a claim, or an interest in property of the debtor securing the claim, is based on a writing, a copy of the writing shall be filed with the proof of claim. If the writing has been lost or destroyed, a statement of the circumstances of the loss or destruction shall be filed with the claim.

(2) Additional requirements in an individual debtor case: sanctions for failure to comply

In a case in which the debtor is an individual:

(A) If, in addition to its principal amount, a claim includes interest, fees, expenses, or other charges incurred before the petition was filed, an itemized statement of the interest, fees, expenses, or charges shall be filed with the proof of claim.

Rule 3001   BANKRUPTCY RULES

    (B) If a security interest is claimed in the debtor's property, a statement of the amount necessary to cure any default as of the date of the petition shall be filed with the proof of claim.

    (C) If a security interest is claimed in property that is the debtor's principal residence, the attachment prescribed by the appropriate Official Form shall be filed with the proof of claim. If an escrow account has been established in connection with the claim, an escrow account statement prepared as of the date the petition was filed and in a form consistent with applicable nonbankruptcy law shall be filed with the attachment to the proof of claim.

    (D) If the holder of a claim fails to provide any information required by this subdivision (c), the court may, after notice and hearing, take either or both of the following actions:

        (i) preclude the holder from presenting the omitted information, in any form, as evidence in any contested matter or adversary proceeding in the case, unless the court determines that the failure was substantially justified or is harmless; or

        (ii) award other appropriate relief, including reasonable expenses and attorney's fees caused by the failure.

(3) Claim based on an open-end or revolving consumer credit agreement

    (A) When a claim is based on an open-end or revolving consumer credit agreement—except one for which a security interest is claimed in the debtor's real property—a statement shall be filed with the proof of claim, including all of the following information that applies to the account:

        (i) the name of the entity from whom the creditor purchased the account;

        (ii) the name of the entity to whom the debt was owed at the time of an account holder's last transaction on the account;

        (iii) the date of an account holder's last transaction;

        (iv) the date of the last payment on the account; and

        (v) the date on which the account was charged to profit and loss.

    (B) On written request by a party in interest, the holder of a claim based on an open-end or revolving consumer credit agreement shall, within 30 days after the request is sent, provide the requesting party a copy of the writing specified in paragraph (1) of this subdivision.

(d) Evidence of perfection of security interest

If a security interest in property of the debtor is claimed, the proof of claim shall be accompanied by evidence that the security interest has been perfected.

(e) Transferred claim

(1) Transfer of claim other than for security before proof filed

If a claim has been transferred other than for security before proof of the claim has been filed, the proof of claim may be filed only by the transferee or an indenture trustee.

(2) Transfer of claim other than for security after proof filed

If a claim other than one based on a publicly traded note, bond, or debenture has been transferred other than for security after the proof of claim has been filed, evidence of the transfer shall be filed by the transferee. The clerk shall immediately notify the alleged transferor by mail of the filing of the evidence of transfer and that objection thereto, if any, must be filed within 21 days of the mailing of the notice or within any additional time allowed by the court. If the alleged transferor files a timely objection and the court finds, after notice and a hearing, that the claim has been transferred other than for security, it shall enter an order substituting the transferee for the transferor. If a timely objection is not filed by the alleged transferor, the transferee shall be substituted for the transferor.

(3) Transfer of claim for security before proof filed

If a claim other than one based on a publicly traded note, bond, or debenture has been transferred for security before proof of the claim has been filed, the transferor or transferee or both may file a proof of claim for the full amount. The proof shall be supported by a statement setting forth the terms of the transfer. If either the transferor or the transferee files a proof of claim, the clerk shall immediately notify the other by mail of the right to join in the filed claim. If both transferor and transferee file proofs of the same claim, the proofs shall be consolidated. If the transferor or transferee does not file an agreement regarding its relative rights respecting voting of the claim, payment of dividends thereon, or participation in the administration of the estate, on motion by a party in interest and after notice and a hearing, the court shall enter such orders respecting these matters as may be appropriate.

(4) Transfer of claim for security after proof filed

If a claim other than one based on a publicly traded note, bond, or debenture has been transferred for security after the proof of claim has been filed, evidence of the terms of the transfer shall be filed by the transferee. The clerk shall immediately notify the alleged transferor by mail of the filing of the evidence of transfer and that objection thereto, if any, must be filed within 21 days of the mailing of the notice or within any additional time allowed by the court. If a timely objection is filed by the alleged transferor, the court, after notice and a hearing, shall determine whether the claim has been transferred for security. If the transferor or transferee does not file an agreement regarding its relative rights respecting voting of the claim, payment of dividends thereon, or participation in the administration of the estate, on motion by a party in interest and after notice and a hearing, the court shall enter such orders respecting these matters as may be appropriate.

(5) Service of objection or motion; notice of hearing

A copy of an objection filed pursuant to paragraph (2) or (4) or a motion filed pursuant to paragraph (3) or (4) of this subdivision together with a notice of a hearing shall be mailed or otherwise delivered to the transferor or transferee, whichever is appropriate, at least 30 days prior to the hearing.

(f) Evidentiary effect

A proof of claim executed and filed in accordance with these rules shall constitute prima facie evidence of the validity and amount of the claim.

(g)[1] To the extent not inconsistent with the United States Warehouse Act or applicable State law, a warehouse receipt, scale ticket, or similar document of the type routinely issued as evidence of title by a grain storage facility, as defined in section 557 of title 11, shall constitute prima facie evidence of the validity and amount of a claim of ownership of a quantity of grain.

(As amended Pub.L. 98–353, Title III, § 354, July 10, 1984, 98 Stat. 361; Apr. 30, 1991, eff. Aug. 1, 1991; Mar. 26, 2009, eff. Dec. 1, 2009; Apr. 26, 2011, eff. Dec. 1, 2011; Apr. 23, 2012, eff. Dec. 1, 2012.)

ADVISORY COMMITTEE NOTES

This rule is adapted from former Bankruptcy Rules 301 and 302. The Federal Rules of Evidence, made applicable to cases under the Code by Rule 1101, do not prescribe the evidentiary effect to be accorded particular documents. Subdivision (f) of this rule supplements the Federal Rules of Evidence as they apply to cases under the Code.

Subdivision (c). This subdivision is similar to former Bankruptcy Rule 302(c) and continues the requirement for the filing of any written security agreement and provides that the filing of a duplicate of a writing underlying a claim authenticates the claim with the same effect as the filing of the original writing. Cf. Rules 1001(4) and 1003 of F.R. of Evid. Subdivision (d) together with the requirement in the first sentence of subdivision (c) for the filing of any written security agreement, is designed to facilitate

---

[1] So in original. Subsec. (g) was enacted without a catchline.

Rule 3001 BANKRUPTCY RULES

the determination whether the claim is secured and properly perfected so as to be valid against the trustee.

Subdivision (d). "Satisfactory evidence" of perfection, which is to accompany the proof of claim, would include a duplicate of an instrument filed or recorded, a duplicate of a certificate of title when a security interest is perfected by notation on such a certificate, a statement that pledged property has been in possession of the secured party since a specified date, or a statement of the reasons why no action was necessary for perfection. The secured creditor may not be required to file a proof of claim under this rule if he is not seeking allowance of a claim for a deficiency. But see § 506(d) of the Code.

Subdivision (e). The rule recognizes the differences between an unconditional transfer of a claim and a transfer for the purpose of security and prescribes a procedure for dealing with the rights of the transferor and transferee when the transfer is for security. The rule clarifies the procedure to be followed when a transfer precedes or follows the filing of the petition. The interests of sound administration are served by requiring the post-petition transferee to file with the proof of claim a statement of the transferor acknowledging the transfer and the consideration for the transfer. Such a disclosure will assist the court in dealing with evils that may arise out of post-bankruptcy traffic in claims against an estate. Monroe v. Scofield, 135 F.2d 725 (10th Cir. 1943); In re Philadelphia & Western Ry., 64 F.Supp. 738 (E.D.Pa.1946); cf. In re Latham Lithographic Corp., 107 F.2d 749 (2d Cir. 1939). Both paragraphs (1) and (3) of this subdivision, which deal with a transfer before the filing of a proof of claim, recognize that the transferee may be unable to obtain the required statement from the transferor, but in that event a sound reason for such inability must accompany the proof of claim filed by the transferee.

Paragraphs (3) and (4) clarify the status of a claim transferred for the purpose of security. An assignee for security has been recognized as a rightful claimant in bankruptcy. Feder v. John Engelhorn & Sons, 202 F.2d 411 (2d Cir. 1953). An assignor's right to file a claim notwithstanding the assignment was sustained in In re R & L Engineering Co., 182 F.Supp. 317 (S.D.Cal.1960). Facilitation of the filing of proofs by both claimants as holders of interests in a single claim is consonant with equitable treatment of the parties and sound administration. See In re Latham Lithographic Corp., 107 F.2d 749 (2d Cir. 1939).

Paragraphs (2) and (4) of subdivision (e) deal with the transfer of a claim after proof has been filed. Evidence of the terms of the transfer required to be disclosed to the court will facilitate the court's determination of the appropriate order to be entered because of the transfer.

Paragraph (5) describes the procedure to be followed when an objection is made by the transferor to the transferee's filed evidence of transfer.

The United States Warehouse Act, referred to in subd. (g), is Part C of Act Aug. 11, 1916, c. 313, 39 Stat. 486, as amended, which is classified generally to chapter 10 (§ 241 et seq.) of Title 7, Agriculture. For complete classification of this Act to the Code, see section 241 of Title 7 and Tables.

1984 Amendments

Subdivision (g) was added by § 354 of the 1984 amendments.

Subd. (g). Pub.L. 98–353 added subd. (g).

1991 Amendments

Subdivision (a) is amended in anticipation of future revision and renumbering of the Official Forms.

Subdivision (e) is amended to limit the court's role to the adjudication of disputes regarding transfers of claims. If a claim has been transferred prior to the filing of a proof of claim, there is no need to state the consideration for the transfer or to submit other evidence of the transfer. If a claim has been transferred other than for security after a proof of claim has been filed, the transferee is substituted for the transferor in the absence of a timely objection by the alleged transferor. In that event, the clerk should note the transfer without the need for court approval. If a timely objection is filed, the court's role is to determine whether a transfer has been made that is enforceable under nonbankruptcy law. This rule is not intended either to encourage or discourage postpetition transfers of claims or to affect any remedies otherwise available under nonbankruptcy law to a transferor or transferee such as for misrepresentation in connection with the transfer of a claim. "After notice and a hearing" as used in subdivision (e) shall be construed in accordance with paragraph (5).

The words "with the clerk" in subdivision (e)(2) and (e)(4) are deleted as unnecessary. See Rules 5005(a) and 9001(3).

CLAIMS — Rule 3001

1984 Acts

Amendment by Pub.L. 98–353 effective with respect to cases filed 90 days after July 10, 1984, see section 553 of Pub.L. 98–353, set out as a note under section 101 of this title.

2009 Amendments

The rule is amended to implement changes in connection with the amendment to Rule 9006(a) and the manner by which time is computed under the rules. The deadlines in the rule are amended to substitute a deadline that is a multiple of seven days. Throughout the rules, deadlines are amended in the following manner:

- 5-day periods become 7-day periods
- 10-day periods become 14-day periods
- 15-day periods become 14-day periods
- 20-day periods become 21-day periods
- 25-day periods become 28-day periods

2011 Amendments

Subdivision (c). Subdivision (c) is amended to prescribe with greater specificity the supporting information required to accompany certain proofs of claim and, in cases in which the debtor is an individual, the consequences of failing to provide the required information.

Existing subdivision (c) is redesignated as (c)(1).

Subdivision (c)(2) is added to require additional information to accompany proofs of claim filed in cases in which the debtor is an individual. When the holder of a claim seeks to recover-in addition to the principal amount of a debt-interest, fees, expenses, or other charges, the proof of claim must be accompanied by a statement itemizing these additional amounts with sufficient specificity to make clear the basis for the claimed amount.

If a claim is secured by a security interest in the property of the debtor and the debtor defaulted on the claim prior to the filing of the petition, the proof of claim must be accompanied by a statement of the amount required to cure the prepetition default.

If the claim is secured by a security interest in the debtor's principal residence, the proof of claim must be accompanied by the attachment prescribed by the appropriate Official Form. In that attachment, the holder of the claim must provide the information required by subparagraphs (A) and (B) of this paragraph (2). In addition, if an escrow account has been established in connection with the claim, an escrow account statement showing the account balance, and any amount owed, as of the date the petition was filed must be submitted in accordance with subparagraph (C). The statement must be prepared in a form consistent with the requirements of nonbankruptcy law. *See, e.g.,* 12 U.S.C. § 2601 *et seq.* (Real Estate Settlement Procedure Act). Thus the holder of the claim may provide the escrow account statement using the same form it uses outside of bankruptcy for this purpose.

Subparagraph (D) of subdivision (c)(2) sets forth sanctions that the court may impose on a creditor in an individual debtor case that fails to provide information required by subdivision (c). Failure to provide the required information does not itself constitute a ground for disallowance of a claim. See § 502(b) of the Code. But when an objection to the allowance of a claim is made or other litigation arises concerning the status or treatment of a claim, if the holder of that claim has not complied with the requirements of this subdivision, the court may preclude it from presenting as evidence any of the omitted information, unless the failure to comply with this subdivision was substantially justified or harmless. The court retains discretion to allow an amendment to a proof of claim under appropriate circumstances or to impose a sanction different from or in addition to the preclusion of the introduction of evidence.

2012 Amendments

Subdivision (c). Subdivision (c) is amended in several respects. The former requirement in paragraph (1) to file an original or duplicate of a supporting document is amended to reflect the current practice of filing only copies. The proof of claim form instructs claimants not to file the original of a document because it may be destroyed by the clerk's office after scanning.

Subdivision (c) is further amended to add paragraph (3). Except with respect to claims secured by a security interest in the debtor's real property (such as a home equity line of credit), paragraph (3) specifies information that must be provided in support of a claim based on an open-end or revolving consumer credit agreement (such as an agreement underlying the issuance of a credit card). Because a claim of this type may have been sold one or more times prior to the debtor's bankruptcy, the debtor may not recognize the name of the person filing the proof of claim. Disclosure of the information required by paragraph (3) will assist the debtor in associating the claim with a known account. It will also provide a basis for assessing the timeliness of the claim. The date, if any, on which the account was charged to profit and loss ("charge-off" date) under subparagraph (A)(v) should be determined in accordance with applicable standards for the classification and account management of consumer credit. A proof of claim executed and filed in accordance with subparagraph (A), as well as the applicable provisions of subdivisions (a), (b), (c)(2), and (e), constitutes prima facie evidence of the validity and amount of the claim under subdivision (f).

To the extent that paragraph (3) applies to a claim, paragraph (1) of subdivision (c) is not applicable. A party in interest, however, may obtain the writing on which an open-end or revolving consumer credit claim is based by requesting in writing that documentation from the holder of the claim. The holder of the claim must provide the documentation within 30 days after the request is sent. The court, for cause, may extend or reduce that time period under Rule 9006.

CROSS REFERENCES

Filed claims or interests deemed allowed, see 11 USCA § 502.

Filing of proofs of claims or interests, see 11 USCA § 501.

Notice to claimants in converted liquidation case, see Fed.Rules Bankr.Proc. Rule 1019, 11 USCA.

Admissibility of duplicates, see Fed.Rules Evid. Rule 1003, 28 USCA.

Rule 3002. Filing Proof of Claim or Interest

(a) Necessity for filing

An unsecured creditor or an equity security holder must file a proof of claim or interest for the claim or interest to be allowed, except as provided in Rules 1019(3), 3003, 3004, and 3005.

(b) Place of filing

A proof of claim or interest shall be filed in accordance with Rule 5005.

(c) Time for filing

In a chapter 7 liquidation, chapter 12 family farmer's debt adjustment, or chapter 13 individual's debt adjustment case, a proof of claim is timely filed if it is filed not later than 90 days after the first date set for the meeting of creditors called under § 341(a) of the Code, except as follows:

(1) A proof of claim filed by a governmental unit, other than for a claim resulting from a tax return filed under § 1308, is timely filed if it is filed not later than 180 days after the date of the order for relief. A proof of claim filed by a governmental unit for a claim resulting from a tax return filed under § 1308 is timely filed if it is filed no later than 180 days after the date of the order for relief or 60 days after the date of the filing of the tax return. The court may, for cause, enlarge the time for a governmental unit to file a proof of claim only upon motion of the governmental unit made before expiration of the period for filing a timely proof of claim.

(2) In the interest of justice and if it will not unduly delay the administration of the case, the court may extend the time for filing a proof of claim by an infant or incompetent person or the representative of either.

(3) An unsecured claim which arises in favor of an entity or becomes allowable as a result of a judgment may be filed within 30 days after the judgment becomes final if the judgment is for the recovery of money or property from that entity or denies or avoids the entity's interest in property. If the judgment imposes a liability which is not satisfied, or a duty which is not performed within such period or such further time as the court may permit, the claim shall not be allowed.

(4) A claim arising from the rejection of an executory contract or unexpired lease of the debtor may be filed within such time as the court may direct.

(5) If notice of insufficient assets to pay a dividend was given to creditors under Rule 2002(e), and subsequently the trustee notifies the court that payment of a dividend appears possible, the clerk shall give at least 90 days' notice by mail to creditors of that fact and of the date by which proofs of claim must be filed.

(6) If notice of the time to file a proof of claim has been mailed to a creditor at a foreign address, on motion filed by the creditor before or after the expiration of the time, the court may extend the time by not more than 60 days if the court finds that the notice was insufficient under the circumstances to give the creditor a reasonable time to file a proof of claim.

(As amended Mar. 30, 1987, eff. Aug. 1, 1987; Apr. 30, 1991, eff. Aug. 1, 1991; Apr. 23, 1996, eff. Dec. 1, 1996; Apr. 23, 2008, eff. Dec. 1, 2008.)

ADVISORY COMMITTEE NOTES

Subdivision (a) of this rule is substantially a restatement of the general requirement that claims be proved and filed. The exceptions refer to Rule 3003 providing for the filing of claims in chapter 9 and 11 cases, and to Rules 3004 and 3005 authorizing claims to be filed by the debtor or trustee and the filing of a claim by a contingent creditor of the debtor.

A secured claim need not be filed or allowed under § 502 or § 506(d) unless a party in interest has requested a determination and allowance or disallowance under § 502.

Subdivision (c) is adapted from former Bankruptcy Rule 302(e) but changes the time limits on the filing of claims in chapter 7 and 13 cases from six months to 90 days after the first date set for the meeting of creditors. The special rule for early filing by a secured creditor in a chapter 13 case, in former Rule 13–302(e)(1) is not continued.

Although the claim of a secured creditor may have arisen before the petition, a judgment avoiding the security interest may not have been entered until after the time for filing claims has expired. Under Rule 3002(c)(3) the creditor who did not file a secured claim may nevertheless file an unsecured claim within the time prescribed. A judgment does not become final for the purpose of starting the 30 day period provided for by paragraph (3) until the time for appeal has expired or, if an appeal is taken, until the appeal has been disposed of. In re Tapp, 61 F.Supp. 594 (W.D.Ky.1945).

Paragraph (1) is derived from former Bankruptcy Rule 302(e). The governmental unit may move for an extension of the 90 day period. Pursuant to § 501(c) of the Code, if the government does not file its claim within the proper time period, the debtor or trustee may file on its behalf. An extension is not needed by the debtor or trustee because the right to file does not arise until the government's time has expired.

Paragraph (4) is derived from former chapter rules. See, e.g., Rule 11–33(a)(2)(B). In light of the reduced time it is necessary that a party with a claim arising from the rejection of an executory contract have sufficient time to file that claim. This clause allows the court to fix an appropriate time.

Paragraph (5) of subdivision (c) is correlated with the provision in Rule 2002(e) authorizing notification to creditors of estates from which no dividends are anticipated. The clause permits creditors who have refrained from filing claims after receiving notification to be given an opportunity to file when subsequent developments indicate the possibility of a dividend. The notice required by this clause must be given in the manner provided in Rule 2002. The information relating to the discovery of assets will usually be obtained by the clerk from the trustee's interim reports or special notification by the trustee.

Provision is made in Rule 2002(a) and (h) for notifying all creditors of the fixing of a time for filing claims against a surplus under paragraph (6). This paragraph does not deal with the distribution of the surplus. Reference must also be made to § 726(a)(2)(C) and (3) which permits distribution on late filed claims.

Paragraph (6) is only operative in a chapter 7 case. In chapter 13 cases, the plan itself provides the distribution to creditors which is not necessarily dependent on the size of the estate.

1987 Amendments

Subdivision (a) is amended by adding a reference to Rule 1019(4). Rule 1019(4) provides that claims actually filed by a creditor in a chapter 11 or 13 case shall be treated as filed in a superseding chapter 7 case. Claims deemed filed in a chapter 11 case pursuant to § 1111(a) of the Code are not considered as filed in a superseding chapter 7 case. The creditor must file a claim in the superseding chapter 7 case.

1991 Amendments

Subdivision (a) is amended to conform to the renumbering of subdivisions of Rule 1019. Subdivision (c) is amended to include chapter 12 cases. Subdivision (c)(4) is amended to clarify that it includes a claim arising from the rejection of an unexpired lease.

1996 Amendments

The amendments are designed to conform to §§ 502(b)(9) and 726(a) of the Code as amended by the Bankruptcy Reform Act of 1994.

The Reform Act amended § 726(a)(1) and added § 502(b)(9) to the Code to govern the effects of a tardily filed claim. Under § 502(b)(9), a tardily filed claim must be disallowed if an objection to the proof of claim is filed, except to the extent that a holder of a tardily filed claim is entitled to distribution under § 726(a)(1), (2), or (3).

The phrase "in accordance with this rule" is deleted from Rule 3002(a) to clarify that the effect of filing a proof of claim after the expiration of the time prescribed in Rule 3002(c) is governed by § 502(b)(9) of the Code, rather than by this rule.

Section 502(b)(9) of the Code provides that a claim of a governmental unit shall be timely filed if it is filed "before 180 days after the date of the order for relief" or such later time as the Bankruptcy Rules provide. To avoid any confusion as to whether a governmental unit's proof of claim is timely filed under § 502(b)(9) if it is filed on the 180th day after the order for relief, paragraph (1) of subdivision (c) provides that a governmental unit's claim is timely if it is filed not later than 180 days after the order for relief.

References to "the United States, a state, or subdivision thereof" in paragraph (1) of subdivision (c) are changed to "governmental unit" to avoid different treatment among foreign and domestic governments.

2008 Amendments

Subdivision (c)(1) is amended to reflect the addition of § 1308 to the Bankruptcy Code in 2005. This provision requires that chapter 13 debtors file tax returns during the pendency of the case, and imposes bankruptcy-related consequences if debtors fail to do so. Subdivision (c)(1) provides additional time for governmental units to file a proof of claim for tax obligations with respect to tax returns filed during the pendency of a chapter 13 case. The amendment also allows the governmental unit to move for additional time to file a proof of claim prior to expiration of the applicable filing period.

Subdivision (c)(5) of the rule is amended to set a new period for providing notice to creditors that they may file a proof of claim in a case in which they were previously informed that there was no need to file a claim. Under Rule 2002(e), if it appears that there will be no distribution to creditors, the creditors are notified of this fact and are informed that if assets are later discovered and a distribution is likely that a new notice will be given to the creditors. This second notice is prescribed by Rule 3002(c)(5). The rule is amended to direct the clerk to give at least 90 days' notice of the time within which creditors may file a proof of claim. Setting the deadline in this manner allows the notices being sent to creditors to be more accurate regarding the deadline than was possible under the prior rule. The rule previously began the 90 day notice period from the time of the mailing of the notice, a date that could vary and generally would not even be known to the creditor. Under the amended rule, the notice will identify a specific bar date for filing proofs of claim thereby being more helpful to the creditors.

Subdivision (c)(6) is added to give the court discretion to extend the time for filing a proof of claim for a creditor who received notice of the time to file the claim at a foreign address, if the court finds that the notice was not sufficient, under the particular circumstances, to give the foreign creditor a reasonable time to file a proof of claim. This amendment is designed to comply with § 1514(d), added to the Code by the 2005 amendments, and requires that the rules and orders of the court provide such additional time as is reasonable under the circumstances for foreign creditors to file claims in cases under all chapters of the Code.

Other changes are stylistic.

CLAIMS Rule 3002.1

CROSS REFERENCES

Filed claims or interests deemed allowed, see 11 USCA § 502.

Filing of—

    Claims by debtor or trustee, see Fed.Rules Bankr.Proc. Rule 3004, 11 USCA.

    Claims by guarantor, surety, indorser, or other codebtor, see Fed.Rules Bankr.Proc. Rule 3005, 11 USCA.

    Proofs of claims or interests, see 11 USCA § 501.

Filing proof of claim in liquidation or individual debt adjustment case, ninety-day period—

    Enlargement permitted as limited in this rule, see Fed.Rules Bankr.Proc. Rule 9006, 11 USCA.

    Reduction not permitted, see Fed.Rules Bankr.Proc. Rule 9006, 11 USCA.

Motions; form and service, see Fed.Rules Bankr.Proc. Rule 9013, 11 USCA.

Notice by mail of time allowed to file claims, see Fed.Rules Bankr.Proc. Rule 2002, 11 USCA.

Time extended to file claims against surplus—

    Converted liquidation case, see Fed.Rules Bankr.Proc. Rule 1019, 11 USCA.

    Notice to creditors in liquidation case, see Fed.Rules Bankr.Proc. Rule 2002, 11 USCA.

Twenty-day notice of time to file claims against surplus, see Fed.Rules Bankr.Proc. Rule 2002, 11 USCA.

Rule 3002.1. Notice Relating to Claims Secured by Security Interest in the Debtor's Principal Residence

(a) In General

This rule applies in a chapter 13 case to claims that are (1) secured by a security interest in the debtor's principal residence, and (2) provided for under § 1322(b)(5) of the Code in the debtor's plan.

(b) Notice of payment changes

The holder of the claim shall file and serve on the debtor, debtor's counsel, and the trustee a notice of any change in the payment amount, including any change that results from an interest rate or escrow account adjustment, no later than 21 days before a payment in the new amount is due.

(c) Notice of fees, expenses, and charges

The holder of the claim shall file and serve on the debtor, debtor's counsel, and the trustee a notice itemizing all fees, expenses, or charges (1) that were incurred in connection with the claim after the bankruptcy case was filed, and (2) that the holder asserts are recoverable against the debtor or against the debtor's principal residence. The notice shall be served within 180 days after the date on which the fees, expenses, or charges are incurred.

(d) Form and content

A notice filed and served under subdivision (b) or (c) of this rule shall be prepared as prescribed by the appropriate Official Form, and filed as a supplement to the holder's proof of claim. The notice is not subject to Rule 3001(f).

(e) Determination of fees, expenses, or charges

On motion of the debtor or trustee filed within one year after service of a notice under subdivision (c) of this rule, the court shall, after notice and hearing, determine whether payment of any claimed fee, expense, or charge is required by the underlying agreement and applicable nonbankruptcy law to cure a default or maintain payments in accordance with § 1322(b)(5) of the Code.

Rule 3002.1

(f) Notice of final cure payment

Within 30 days after the debtor completes all payments under the plan, the trustee shall file and serve on the holder of the claim, the debtor, and debtor's counsel a notice stating that the debtor has paid in full the amount required to cure any default on the claim. The notice shall also inform the holder of its obligation to file and serve a response under subdivision (g). If the debtor contends that final cure payment has been made and all plan payments have been completed, and the trustee does not timely file and serve the notice required by this subdivision, the debtor may file and serve the notice.

(g) Response to notice of final cure payment

Within 21 days after service of the notice under subdivision (f) of this rule, the holder shall file and serve on the debtor, debtor's counsel, and the trustee a statement indicating (1) whether it agrees that the debtor has paid in full the amount required to cure the default on the claim, and (2) whether the debtor is otherwise current on all payments consistent with § 1322(b)(5) of the Code. The statement shall itemize the required cure or postpetition amounts, if any, that the holder contends remain unpaid as of the date of the statement. The statement shall be filed as a supplement to the holder's proof of claim and is not subject to Rule 3001(f).

(h) Determination of final cure and payment

On motion of the debtor or trustee filed within 21 days after service of the statement under subdivision (g) of this rule, the court shall, after notice and hearing, determine whether the debtor has cured the default and paid all required postpetition amounts.

(i) Failure to notify

If the holder of a claim fails to provide any information as required by subdivision (b), (c), or (g) of this rule, the court may, after notice and hearing, take either or both of the following actions:

    (1) preclude the holder from presenting the omitted information, in any form, as evidence in any contested matter or adversary proceeding in the case, unless the court determines that the failure was substantially justified or is harmless; or

    (2) award other appropriate relief, including reasonable expenses and attorney's fees caused by the failure.

(Adopted Apr. 26, 2011, eff. Dec. 1, 2011.)

ADVISORY COMMITTEE NOTES
2011 Adoption

This rule is new. It is added to aid in the implementation of § 1322(b)(5), which permits a chapter 13 debtor to cure a default and maintain payments of a home mortgage over the course of the debtor's plan. It applies regardless of whether the trustee or the debtor is the disbursing agent for postpetition mortgage payments.

In order to be able to fulfill the obligations of § 1322(b)(5), a debtor and the trustee must be informed of the exact amount needed to cure any prepetition arrearage, *see* Rule 3001(c)(2), and the amount of the postpetition payment obligations. If the latter amount changes over time, due to the adjustment of the interest rate, escrow account adjustments, or the assessment of fees, expenses, or other charges, notice of any change in payment amount needs to be conveyed to the debtor and trustee. Timely notice of these changes will permit the debtor or trustee to challenge the validity of any such charges, if necessary, and to adjust postpetition mortgage payments to cover any properly claimed adjustment. Compliance with the notice provision of the rule should also eliminate any concern on the part of the holder of the claim that informing a debtor of a change in postpetition payment obligations might violate the automatic stay.

Subdivision (a). Subdivision (a) specifies that this rule applies only in a chapter 13 case to claims secured by a security interest in the debtor's principal residence.

Subdivision (b). Subdivision (b) requires the holder of a claim to notify the debtor, debtor's counsel, and the trustee of any postpetition change in the mortgage payment amount at least 21 days before the new payment amount is due.

Subdivision (c). Subdivision (c) requires an itemized notice to be given, within 180 days of incurrence, of any postpetition fees, expenses, or charges that the holder of the claim asserts are recoverable in connection with a claim secured by the debtor's principal residence. This amount might include, for example, inspection fees, late charges, or attorney's fees.

Subdivision (d). Subdivision (d) provides the method of giving the notice under subdivisions (b) and (c). In both instances, the holder of the claim must give notice of the change as prescribed by the appropriate Official Form. In addition to serving the debtor, debtor's counsel, and the trustee, the holder of the claim must also file the notice on the claims register in the case as a supplement to its proof of claim. Rule 300 I (f) does not apply to any notice given under subdivision (b) or (c), and therefore the notice will not constitute prima facie evidence of the validity and amount of the payment change or of the fee, expense, or charge.

Subdivision (e). Subdivision (e) permits the debtor or trustee, within a year after service of a notice under subdivision (c), to seek a determination by the court as to whether the fees, expenses, or charges set forth in the notice are required by the underlying agreement or applicable nonbankruptcy law to cure a default or maintain payments.

Subdivision (f). Subdivision (f) requires the trustee to issue a notice to the holder of the claim, the debtor, and the debtor's attorney within 30 days after completion of payments under the plan. The notice must (1) indicate that all amounts required to cure a default on a claim secured by the debtor's principal residence have been paid, and (2) direct the holder to comply with subdivision (g). If the trustee fails to file this notice within the required time, this subdivision also permits the debtor to file and serve the notice on the trustee and the holder of the claim.

Subdivision (g). Subdivision (g) governs the response of the holder of the claim to the trustee's or debtor's notice under subdivision (f). Within 21 days after service of notice of the final cure payment, the holder of the claim must file and serve a statement indicating whether the prepetition default has been fully cured and also whether the debtor is current on all payments in accordance with § 1322(b)(5) of the Code. If the holder of the claim contends that all cure payments have not been made or that the debtor is not current on other payments required by § 1322(b)(5), the response must itemize all amounts, other than regular future installment payments, that the holder contends are due.

Subdivision (h). Subdivision (h) provides a procedure for the judicial resolution of any disputes that may arise about payment of a claim secured by the debtor's principal residence. Within 21 days after the service of the statement under (g), the trustee or debtor may move for a determination by the court of whether any default has been cured and whether any other non-current obligations remain outstanding.

Subdivision (i). Subdivision (i) specifies sanctions that may be imposed if the holder of a claim fails to provide any of the information as required by subdivisions (b), (c), or (g).

If, after the chapter 13 debtor has completed payments under the plan and the case has been closed, the holder of a claim secured by the debtor's principal residence seeks to recover amounts that should have been but were not disclosed under this rule, the debtor may move to have the case reopened in order to seek sanctions against the holder of the claim under subdivision (i).

Rule 3003. Filing Proof of Claim or Equity Security Interest in Chapter 9 Municipality or Chapter 11 Reorganization Cases

(a) Applicability of rule

This rule applies in chapter 9 and 11 cases.

(b) Schedule of liabilities and list of equity security holders

   (1) Schedule of liabilities

The schedule of liabilities filed pursuant to § 521(1) of the Code shall constitute prima facie evidence of the validity and amount of the claims of creditors, unless they are scheduled as disputed, contingent, or unliquidated. It shall not be necessary for a creditor or equity security holder to file a proof of claim or interest except as provided in subdivision (c)(2) of this rule.

(2) List of equity security holders

The list of equity security holders filed pursuant to Rule 1007(a)(3) shall constitute prima facie evidence of the validity and amount of the equity security interests and it shall not be necessary for the holders of such interests to file a proof of interest.

(c) Filing of proof of claim

(1) Who may file

Any creditor or indenture trustee may file a proof of claim within the time prescribed by subdivision (c)(3) of this rule.

(2) Who must file

Any creditor or equity security holder whose claim or interest is not scheduled or scheduled as disputed, contingent, or unliquidated shall file a proof of claim or interest within the time prescribed by subdivision (c)(3) of this rule; any creditor who fails to do so shall not be treated as a creditor with respect to such claim for the purposes of voting and distribution.

(3) Time for filing

The court shall fix and for cause shown may extend the time within which proofs of claim or interest may be filed. Notwithstanding the expiration of such time, a proof of claim may be filed to the extent and under the conditions stated in Rule 3002(c)(2), (c)(3), (c)(4), and (c)(6).

(4) Effect of filing claim or interest

A proof of claim or interest executed and filed in accordance with this subdivision shall supersede any scheduling of that claim or interest pursuant to § 521(a)(1) of the Code.

(5) Filing by indenture trustee

An indenture trustee may file a claim on behalf of all known or unknown holders of securities issued pursuant to the trust instrument under which it is trustee.

(d) Proof of right to record status

For the purposes of Rules 3017, 3018 and 3021 and for receiving notices, an entity who is not the record holder of a security may file a statement setting forth facts which entitle that entity to be treated as the record holder. An objection to the statement may be filed by any party in interest.

(As amended Mar. 30, 1987, eff. Aug. 1, 1987; Apr. 30, 1991, eff. Aug. 1, 1991; Apr. 23, 2008, eff. Dec. 1, 2008.)

ADVISORY COMMITTEE NOTES

Subdivision (a). This rule applies only in chapter 9 and chapter 11 cases. It is adapted from former Chapter X Rule 10–401 and provides an exception to the requirement for filing proofs of claim and interest as expressed in §§ 925 and 1111(a) of the Code.

Subdivision (b). This general statement implements §§ 925 and 1111(a) of the Code.

Subdivision (c). This subdivision permits, in paragraph (1), the filing of a proof of claim but does not make it mandatory. Paragraph (2) requires, as does the Code, filing when a claim is scheduled as disputed, contingent, or unliquidated as to amount. It is the creditor's responsibility to determine if the claim is accurately listed. Notice of the provision of this rule is provided for in Official Form No. 16, the order for the meeting of creditors. In an appropriate case the court may order creditors whose claims are scheduled as disputed, contingent, or unliquidated be notified of that fact but the procedure is left to the discretion of the court.

Subdivision (d) is derived from former Chapter X Rule 10–401(f).

Except with respect to the need and time for filing claims, the other aspects concerning claims covered by Rules 3001 and 3002 are applicable in chapter 9 and 11 cases.

Holders of equity security interests need not file proofs of interest. Voting and distribution participation is dependent on ownership as disclosed by the appropriate records of a transfer agent or the corporate or other business records at the time prescribed in Rules 3017 and 3021.

1991 Amendments

Paragraph (3) of subdivision (c) is amended to permit the late filing of claims by infants or incompetent persons under the same circumstances that permit late filings in cases under chapter 7, 12, or 13. The amendment also provides sufficient time in which to file a claim that arises from a postpetition judgment against the claimant for the recovery of money or property or the avoidance of a lien. It also provides for purposes of clarification that upon rejection of an executory contract or unexpired lease, the court shall set a time for filing a claim arising therefrom despite prior expiration of the time set for filing proofs of claim.

The caption of paragraph (4) of subdivision (c) is amended to indicate that it applies to a proof of claim.

2008 Amendments

Subdivision (c)(3) is amended to implement § 1514(d) of the Code, which was added by the 2005 amendments. It makes the new Rule 3002(c)(6) applicable in chapter 9 and chapter 11 cases. This change was necessary so that creditors with foreign addresses be provided such additional time as is reasonable under the circumstances to file proofs of claims.

CROSS REFERENCES

Acceptance or rejection of municipality debt adjustment or reorganization plan by obligor filing creditor's claim, see Fed.Rules Bankr.Proc. Rule 3005, 11 USCA.

Distribution under confirmed plan to indenture trustee filing under this rule, see Fed.Rules Bankr.Proc. Rule 3021, 11 USCA.

Exception to filing requirement for—

    Municipality debt adjustment case, see 11 USCA § 925.

    Reorganization case, see 11 USCA § 1111.

Filing of claims by—

    Debtor or trustee, see Fed.Rules Bankr.Proc. Rule 3004, 11 USCA.

    Guarantor, surety, indorser, or other codebtor, see Fed.Rules Bankr.Proc. Rule 3005, 11 USCA.

Twenty-day notice of time fixed to file proof of claim, see Fed.Rules Bankr.Proc. Rule 2002, 11 USCA.

Rule 3004. Filing of Claims by Debtor or Trustee

If a creditor does not timely file a proof of claim under Rule 3002(c) or 3003(c), the debtor or trustee may file a proof of the claim within 30 days after the expiration of the time for filing claims prescribed by Rule 3002(c) or 3003(c), whichever is applicable. The clerk shall forthwith give notice of the filing to the creditor, the debtor and the trustee.

(As amended Mar. 30, 1987, eff. Aug. 1, 1987; Apr. 25, 2005, eff. Dec. 1, 2005.)

ADVISORY COMMITTEE NOTES

This rule is adapted from former Bankruptcy Rule 303 but conforms with the changes made by § 501(c) of the Code. Rule 303 permitted only the filing of tax and wage claims by the debtor. Section 501(c) of the Code, however, permits the filing by the debtor or trustee on behalf of any creditor.

It is the policy of the Code that debtors' estates should be administered for the benefit of creditors without regard to the dischargeability of their claims. After their estates have been closed, however, discharged debtors may find themselves saddled with liabilities, particularly for taxes, which remain unpaid because of the failure of creditors holding nondischargeable claims to file proofs of claim and receive distributions thereon. The result is that the debtor is deprived of an important benefit of the Code without any fault or omission on the debtor's part and without any objective of the Code being served thereby.

Section 501(c) of the Code authorizes a debtor or trustee to file a proof of claim for any holder of a claim. Although all claims may not be nondischargeable, it may be difficult to determine, in particular, whether tax claims survive discharge. See Plumb, Federal Tax Liens and Priorities in Bankruptcy, 43 Ref.J. 37, 43–44 (1969); 1 Collier, Bankruptcy ¶17.14 (14th ed. 1967); 3 id. ¶523.06 (15th ed. 1979). To eliminate the necessity of the resolution of this troublesome issue, the option accorded the debtor by the Code does not depend on the nondischargeability of the claim. No serious administrative problems and no unfairness to creditors seemed to develop from adoption of Rule 303, the forerunner to § 501(c). The authority to file is conditioned on the creditor's failure to file the proof of claim on or before the first date set for the meeting of creditors, which is the date a claim must ordinarily be filed in order to be voted in a chapter 7 case. Notice to the creditor is provided to enable him to file a proof of claim pursuant to Rule 3002, which proof, when filed, would supersede the proof filed by the debtor or trustee. Notice to the trustee would serve to alert the trustee to the special character of the proof and the possible need for supplementary evidence of the validity and amount of the claim. If the trustee does not qualify until after a proof of claim is filed by the debtor pursuant to this rule, he should be notified as soon as practicable thereafter.

To the extent the claim is allowed and dividends paid thereon, it will be reduced or perhaps paid in full. If the claim is also filed pursuant to Rule 3005, only one distribution thereon may be made. As expressly required by Rule 3005 and by the purpose of this rule such distribution must diminish the claim.

1987 Amendments

Under the rule as amended, the debtor or trustee in a chapter 7 or 13 case has 120 days from the first date set for the meeting of creditors to file a claim for the creditor. During the first 90 days of that period the creditor in a Chapter 7 or 13 case may file a claim as provided by Rule 3002(c). If the creditor fails to file a claim, the debtor or trustee shall have an additional 30 days thereafter to file the claim. A proof of claim filed by a creditor supersedes a claim filed by the debtor or trustee only if it is timely filed within the 90 days allowed under Rule 3002(c).

2005 Amendments

The rule is amended to conform to § 501(c) of the Code. Under that provision, the debtor or trustee may file proof of a claim if the creditor fails to do so in a timely fashion. The rule previously authorized the debtor and the trustee to file a claim as early as the day after the first date set for the meeting of creditors under § 341(a). Under the amended rule, the debtor and trustee must wait until the creditor's opportunity to file a claim has expired. Providing the debtor and the trustee with the opportunity to file a claim ensures that the claim will participate in any distribution in the case. This is particularly important for claims that are nondischargeable.

Since the debtor and trustee cannot file a proof of claim until after the creditor's time to file has expired, the rule no longer permits the creditor to file a proof of claim that will supersede the claim filed by the debtor or trustee. The rule leaves to the courts the issue of whether to permit subsequent amendment of such proof of claim.

Other changes are stylistic.

CROSS REFERENCES

Exception to execution of proof of claim by creditor or agent, see Fed.Rules Bankr.Proc. Rule 3001, 11 USCA.

Filing of claims by debtor or trustee, see 11 USCA § 501.

Rule 3005. Filing of Claim, Acceptance, or Rejection by Guarantor, Surety, Indorser, or Other Codebtor

(a) Filing of claim

If a creditor does not timely file a proof of claim under Rule 3002(c) or 3003(c), any entity that is or may be liable with the debtor to that creditor, or who has secured that creditor, may file a proof of the claim within 30 days after the expiration of the time for filing claims prescribed by Rule 3002(c) or Rule 3003(c) whichever is applicable. No distribution shall be made on the claim except on satisfactory proof that the original debt will be diminished by the amount of distribution.

(b) Filing of acceptance or rejection; substitution of creditor

An entity which has filed a claim pursuant to the first sentence of subdivision (a) of this rule may file an acceptance or rejection of a plan in the name of the creditor, if known, or if unknown, in the entity's own name but if the creditor files a proof of claim within the time permitted by Rule 3003(c) or files a notice prior to confirmation of a plan of the creditor's intention to act in the creditor's own behalf, the creditor shall be substituted for the obligor with respect to that claim.

(As amended Mar. 30, 1987, eff. Aug. 1, 1987; Apr. 30, 1991, eff. Aug. 1, 1991; Apr. 25, 2005, eff. Dec. 1, 2005.)

ADVISORY COMMITTEE NOTES

This rule is adapted from former Rules 304 and 10–402. Together with § 501(b) of the Code, the rule makes clear that anyone who may be liable on a debt of the debtor, including a surety, guarantor, indorser, or other codebtor, is authorized to file in the name of the creditor of the debtor.

Subdivision (a). Rule 3002(c) provides the time period for filing proofs of claim in chapter 7 and 13 cases; Rule 3003(c) provides the time, when necessary, for filing claims in a chapter 9 or 11 case.

Subdivision (b). This subdivision applies in chapter 9 and 11 cases as distinguished from chapter 7 cases. It permits voting for or against a plan by an obligor who files a claim in place of the creditor.

1991 Amendments

The words "with the court" in subdivision (b) are deleted as unnecessary. See Rules 5005(a) and 9001(3).

2005 Amendments

The rule is amended to delete the last sentence of subdivision (a). The sentence is unnecessary because if a creditor has filed a timely claim under Rule 3002 or 3003(c), the codebtor cannot file a proof of such claim. The codebtor, consistent with § 501(b) of the Code, may file a proof of such claim only after the creditor's time to file has expired. Therefore, the rule no longer permits the creditor to file a superseding claim. The rule leaves to the courts the issue of whether to permit subsequent amendment of the proof of claim.

The amendment conforms the rule to § 501(b) by deleting language providing that the codebtor files proof of the claim in the name of the creditor.

Other amendments are stylistic.

CROSS REFERENCES

Exception to execution of proof of claim by creditor or agent, see Fed.Rules Bankr.Proc. Rule 3001, 11 USCA.

Rule 3006. Withdrawal of Claim; Effect on Acceptance or Rejection of Plan

A creditor may withdraw a claim as of right by filing a notice of withdrawal, except as provided in this rule. If after a creditor has filed a proof of claim an objection is filed thereto or a complaint is filed against that creditor in an adversary proceeding, or the creditor has accepted or rejected the plan or otherwise has participated significantly in the case, the creditor may not withdraw the claim except on order of the court after a hearing on notice to the trustee or debtor in possession, and any creditors' committee elected pursuant to § 705(a) or appointed pursuant to § 1102 of the Code. The order of the court shall contain such terms and conditions as the court deems proper. Unless the court orders otherwise, an authorized withdrawal of a claim shall constitute withdrawal of any related acceptance or rejection of a plan.

(As amended Apr. 30, 1991, eff. Aug. 1, 1991.)

ADVISORY COMMITTEE NOTES

This rule is derived from former Rules 305 and 10–404.

Since 1938 is has generally been held that Rule 41 F.R.Civ.P. governs the withdrawal of a proof of claim. In re Empire Coal Sales Corp., 45 F.Supp. 974, 976 (S.C.N.Y.), aff'd sub nom. Kleid v. Ruthbell Coal Co., 131 F.2d 372, 373 (2d Cir.1942); Kelso v. MacLaren, 122 F.2d 867, 870 (8th Cir.1941); In re Hills, 35 F.Supp. 532, 533 (W.D.Wash.1940). Accordingly the cited cases held that after an objection has been filed a proof of claim may be withdrawn only subject to approval by the court. This constitutes a restriction of the right of withdrawal as recognized by some though by no means all of the cases antedating the promulgation of the Federal Rules of Civil Procedure. See 3 Collier, Bankruptcy ¶57.12 (14th ed. 1961); Note, 20 Bost.U.L.Rev. 121 (1940).

The filing of a claim does not commence an adversary proceeding but the filing of an objection to the claim initiates a contest that must be disposed of by the court. This rule recognizes the applicability of the considerations underlying Rule 41(a) F.R.Civ.P. to the withdrawal of a claim after it has been put in issue by an objection. Rule 41(a)(2) F.R.Civ.P. requires leave of court to obtain dismissal over the objection of a defendant who has pleaded a counterclaim prior to the service of the plaintiff's motion to dismiss. Although the applicability of this provision to the withdrawal of a claim was assumed in Conway v. Union Bank of Switzerland, 204 F.2d 603, 608 (2d Cir.1953), Kleid v. Ruthbell Coal Co., supra, Kelso v. MacLaren, supra, and In re Hills, supra, this rule vests discretion in the court to grant, deny, or condition the request of a creditor to withdraw, without regard to whether the trustee has filed a merely defensive objection or a complaint seeking an affirmative recovery of money or property from the creditor.

A number of pre-1938 cases sustained denial of a creditor's request to withdraw proof of claim on the ground of estoppel or election of remedies. 2 Remington, Bankruptcy 186 (Henderson ed. 1956); cf. 3 Collier, supra ¶57.12, at 201 (1964). Voting a claim for a trustee was an important factor in the denial of a request to withdraw in Standard Varnish Works v. Haydock, 143 Fed. 318, 319–20 (6th Cir.1906), and In re Cann, 47 F.2d 661, 662 (W.D.Pa.1931). And it has frequently been recognized that a creditor should not be allowed to withdraw a claim after accepting a dividend. In re Friedmann, 1 Am.B.R. 510, 512 (Ref., S.D.N.Y.1899); 3 Collier 205 (1964); cf. In re O'Gara Coal Co., 12 F.2d 426, 429 (7th Cir.), cert. denied, 271 U.S. 683 (1926). It was held in Industrial Credit Co. v. Hazen, 222 F.2d 225 (8th Cir.1955), however, that although a claimant had participated in the first meeting of creditors and in the examination of witnesses, the creditor was entitled under Rule 41(a)(1) F.R.Civ.P. to withdraw the claim as of right by filing a notice of withdrawal before the trustee filed an objection under § 57g of the Act. While this rule incorporates the post-1938 case law referred to in the first paragraph of this note, it rejects the inference drawn in the Hazen case that Rule 41(a) F.R.Civ.P. supersedes the pre-1938 case law that vests discretion in the court to deny or restrict withdrawal of a claim by a creditor on the ground of estoppel or election of remedies. While purely formal or technical participation in a case by a creditor who has filed a claim should not deprive the creditor of the right to withdraw the claim, a creditor who has accepted a dividend or who has voted in the election of a trustee or otherwise participated actively in proceedings in a case should be permitted to withdraw only with the approval of the court on terms it deems appropriate after notice to the trustee. 3 Collier 205–06 (1964).

1991 Amendments

This amendment is stylistic. Notice of the hearing need not be given to committees of equity security holders appointed pursuant to § 1102 or committees of retired employees appointed pursuant to § 1114 of the Code.

CROSS REFERENCES

Dismissal of actions, see Fed.Rules Civ.Proc. Rule 41, 28 USCA.

Rule 3007. Objections to Claims

(a) Objections to claims

An objection to the allowance of a claim shall be in writing and filed. A copy of the objection with notice of the hearing thereon shall be mailed or otherwise delivered to the claimant, the debtor or debtor in possession, and the trustee at least 30 days prior to the hearing.

(b) Demand for relief requiring an adversary proceeding

A party in interest shall not include a demand for relief of a kind specified in Rule 7001 in an objection to the allowance of a claim, but may include the objection in an adversary proceeding.

(c) Limitation on joinder of claims objections

Unless otherwise ordered by the court or permitted by subdivision (d), objections to more than one claim shall not be joined in a single objection.

(d) Omnibus objection

Subject to subdivision (e), objections to more than one claim may be joined in an omnibus objection if all the claims were filed by the same entity, or the objections are based solely on the grounds that the claims should be disallowed, in whole or in part, because:

    (1) they duplicate other claims;

    (2) they have been filed in the wrong case;

    (3) they have been amended by subsequently filed proofs of claim;

    (4) they were not timely filed;

    (5) they have been satisfied or released during the case in accordance with the Code, applicable rules, or a court order;

    (6) they were presented in a form that does not comply with applicable rules, and the objection states that the objector is unable to determine the validity of the claim because of the noncompliance;

    (7) they are interests, rather than claims; or

    (8) they assert priority in an amount that exceeds the maximum amount under § 507 of the Code.

(e) Requirements for omnibus objection

An omnibus objection shall:

    (1) state in a conspicuous place that claimants receiving the objection should locate their names and claims in the objection;

    (2) list claimants alphabetically, provide a cross-reference to claim numbers, and, if appropriate, list claimants by category of claims;

    (3) state the grounds of the objection to each claim and provide a cross-reference to the pages in the omnibus objection pertinent to the stated grounds;

    (4) state in the title the identity of the objector and the grounds for the objections;

    (5) be numbered consecutively with other omnibus objections filed by the same objector; and

    (6) contain objections to no more than 100 claims.

(f) Finality of objection

The finality of any order regarding a claim objection included in an omnibus objection shall be determined as though the claim had been subject to an individual objection.

(As amended Apr. 30, 1991, eff. Aug. 1, 1991; Apr. 30, 2007, eff. Dec. 1, 2007.)

ADVISORY COMMITTEE NOTES

This rule is derived from § 47a(8) of the Act [former § 75(a)(8) of this title] and former Bankruptcy Rule 306. It prescribes the manner in which an objection to a claim shall be made and notice of the hearing thereon given to the claimant. The requirement of a writing does not apply to an objection to the allowance of a claim for the purpose of voting for a trustee or creditors' committee in a chapter 7 case. See Rule 2003.

The contested matter initiated by an objection to a claim is governed by rule 9014, unless a counterclaim by the trustee is joined with the objection to the claim. The filing of a counterclaim ordinarily commences an adversary proceeding subject to the rules in Part VII.

While the debtor's other creditors may make objections to the allowance of a claim, the demands of orderly and expeditious administration have led to a recognition that the right to object is generally exercised by the trustee. Pursuant to § 502(a) of the Code, however, any party in interest may object to a claim. But under § 704 the trustee, if any purpose would be served thereby, has the duty to examine proofs of claim and object to improper claims.

By virtue of the automatic allowance of a claim not objected to, a dividend may be paid on a claim which may thereafter be disallowed on objection made pursuant to this rule. The amount of the dividend paid before the disallowance in such event would be recoverable by the trustee in an adversary proceeding.

1991 Amendments

The words "with the court" are deleted as unnecessary. See Rules 5005(a) and 9001(3).

2007 Amendments

The rule is amended in a number of ways. First, the amendment prohibits a party in interest from including in a claim objection a request for relief that requires an adversary proceeding. A party in interest may, however, include an objection to the allowance of a claim in an adversary proceeding. Unlike a contested matter, an adversary proceeding requires the service of a summons and complaint, which puts the defendant on notice of the potential for an affirmative recovery. Permitting the plaintiff in the adversary proceeding to include an objection to a claim would not unfairly surprise the defendant as might be the case if the action were brought as a contested matter that included an action to obtain relief of a kind specified in Rule 7001.

The rule as amended does not require that a party include an objection to the allowance of a claim in an adversary proceeding. If a claim objection is filed separately from a related adversary proceeding, the court may consolidate the objection with the adversary proceeding under Rule 7042.

The rule also is amended to authorize the filing of a pleading that joins objections to more than one claim. Such filings present a significant opportunity for the efficient administration of large cases, but the rule includes restrictions on the use of these omnibus objections to ensure the protection of the due process rights of the claimants.

Unless the court orders otherwise, objections to more than one claim may be joined in a single pleading only if all of the claims were filed by the same entity, or if the objections are based solely on the grounds set out in subdivision (d) of the rule. Objections of the type listed in subdivision (d) often can be resolved without material factual or legal disputes. Objections to multiple claims permitted under the rule must comply with the procedural requirements set forth in subdivision (e). Among those requirements is the requirement in subdivision (e)(5) that these omnibus objections be consecutively numbered. Since these objections may not join more than 100 objections in any one omnibus objection, there may be a need for several omnibus objections to be filed in a particular case. Consecutive numbering of each omnibus objection and the identification of the objector in the title of the objection is essential to keep track of the objections on the court's docket. For example, the objections could be titled Debtor in Possession's First Omnibus Objection to Claims, Debtor in Possession's Second Omnibus Objection to Claims, Creditors' Committee's First Omnibus Objection to Claims, and so on. Titling the objections in this manner should avoid confusion and aid in tracking the objections on the docket.

Subdivision (f) provides that an order resolving an objection to any particular claim is treated, for purposes of finality, as if the claim had been the subject of an individual objection. A party seeking to appeal any such order is neither required, nor permitted, to await the court's resolution of all other joined objections. The rule permits the joinder of objections for convenience, and that convenience should not impede timely review of a court's decision with respect to each claim. Whether the court's action as to a particular objection is final, and the consequences of that finality, are not addressed by this amendment. Moreover, use of an omnibus objection generally does not preclude the objecting party from raising a subsequent objection to the claim on other grounds. See Restatement (Second) of Judgments § 26(1)(d) (1982) (generally applicable rule barring multiple actions based on same transaction or series of transactions is overridden when a statutory scheme permits splitting of claims).

CROSS REFERENCES

Allowance of claims or interests after objection, see 11 USCA § 502.

Contested matters, see Fed.Rules Bankr.Proc. Rule 9014, 11 USCA.

Duty of trustee to examine proofs of claims and to object to improper claims—

    Individual debt adjustment case, see 11 USCA § 1302.

    Liquidation case, see 11 USCA § 704.

    Reorganization case, see 11 USCA § 1106.

Objection to claim for purpose of voting for trustee or creditors' committee in liquidation case, see Fed.Rules Bankr.Proc. Rule 2003, 11 USCA.

Rule 3008. Reconsideration of Claims

A party in interest may move for reconsideration of an order allowing or disallowing a claim against the estate. The court after a hearing on notice shall enter an appropriate order.

ADVISORY COMMITTEE NOTES

Section 502(j) of the Code deals only with the reconsideration of allowed claims as did former § 57k of the Act [former § 93(k) of this title] and General Order 21(b). It had sometimes been held that a referee had no jurisdiction to reconsider a disallowed claim, or the amount or priority of an allowed claim, at the instance of the claimant. See, e.g., In re Gouse, 7 F.Supp. 106 (M.D.Pa.1934); In re Tomlinson & Dye, Inc., 3 F.Supp. 800 (N.D.Okla.1933). This view disregarded § 2a(2) of the Act [former § 11(a)(2) of this title] and the "ancient and elementary power" of a referee as a court to reconsider orders. In re Pottasch Bros. Co., Inc., 79 F.2d 613, 616 (2d Cir.1935); Castaner v. Mora, 234 F.2d 710 (1st Cir.1956). This rule recognizes, as did former Bankruptcy Rule 307, the power of the court to reconsider an order of disallowance on appropriate motion.

Reconsideration of a claim that has been previously allowed or disallowed after objection is discretionary with the court. The right to seek reconsideration of an allowed claim, like the right to object to its allowance, is generally exercised by the trustee if one has qualified and is performing the duties of that office with reasonable diligence and fidelity. A request for reconsideration of a disallowance would, on the other hand, ordinarily come from the claimant.

A proof of claim executed and filed in accordance with the rules in this Part III is prima facie evidence of the validity and the amount of the claim notwithstanding a motion for reconsideration of an order of allowance. Failure to respond does not constitute an admission, though it may be deemed a consent to a reconsideration. In re Goble Boat Co., 190 Fed. 92 (N.D.N.Y.1911). The court may decline to reconsider an order of allowance or disallowance without notice to any adverse party and without affording any hearing to the movant. If a motion to reconsider is granted, notice and hearing must be afforded to parties in interest before the previous action in the claim taken in respect to the claim may be vacated or modified. After reconsideration, the court may allow or disallow the claim, increase or decrease the amount of a prior allowance, accord the claim a priority different from that originally assigned it, or enter any other appropriate order.

The rule expands § 502(j) which provides for reconsideration of an allowance only before the case is closed. Authorities have disagreed as to whether reconsideration may be had after a case has been reopened. Compare 3 Collier, Bankruptcy ¶57.23[4] (14th ed. 1964), see generally 3 id. ¶502.10 (15th ed. 1979), with 2 Remington, Bankruptcy 498 (Henderson ed. 1956). If a case is reopened as provided in § 350(b) of the Code, reconsideration of the allowance or disallowance of a claim may be sought and granted in accordance with this rule.

CROSS REFERENCES

Closing and reopening cases, see 11 USCA § 350.

Exception to procedural rule on new trials and amendment of judgments, see Fed.Rules Bankr.Proc. Rule 9023, 11 USCA.

Motions; form and service, see Fed.Rules Bankr.Proc. Rule 9013, 11 USCA.

Reconsideration of claim prior to closing of case, see 11 USCA § 502.

Rule 3009. Declaration and Payment of Dividends in a Chapter 7 Liquidation Case

In a chapter 7 case, dividends to creditors shall be paid as promptly as practicable. Dividend checks shall be made payable to and mailed to each creditor whose claim has been allowed, unless a power of attorney authorizing another entity to receive dividends has been executed and filed in accordance with Rule 9010. In that event, dividend checks shall be made payable to the creditor and to the other entity and shall be mailed to the other entity.

(As amended Mar. 30, 1987, eff. Aug. 1, 1987; Apr. 22, 1993, eff. Aug. 1, 1993.)

ADVISORY COMMITTEE NOTES

This rule is derived from former Rules 308 and 11–35(a). The preparation of records showing dividends declared and to whom payable is subject to prescription by the Director of the Administrative Office pursuant to Rule 5003(e). The rule governs distributions to creditors having priority as well as to general unsecured creditors. Notwithstanding the detailed statutory provisions regulating the declaration of dividends, a necessarily wide discretion over this matter has been recognized to reside in the court. See 3A Collier, Bankruptcy ¶65.03 (14th ed. 1975): 1 Proceedings of Seminar for Newly Appointed Referees in Bankruptcy 173 (1964). Although the rule leaves to the discretion of the court the amount and the times of dividend payments, it recognizes the creditors' right to as prompt payment as practicable.

The second and third sentences of the rule make explicit the method of payment of dividends and afford protection of the interests of the creditor and the holder of a power of attorney authorized to receive payment.

The rule does not permit variance at local option. This represents a marked change from former Bankruptcy Rule 308.

1993 Amendments

This rule is amended to delete the requirement that the court approve the amounts and times of distributions in chapter 7 cases. This change recognizes the role of the United States trustee in supervising trustees. Other amendments are stylistic and make no substantive change.

CROSS REFERENCES

Dividend records kept by clerk, see Fed.Rules Bankr.Proc. Rule 5003, 11 USCA.

Unclaimed dividends, see 11 USCA § 347.

Rule 3010. Small Dividends and Payments in Chapter 7 Liquidation, Chapter 12 Family Farmer's Debt Adjustment, and Chapter 13 Individual's Debt Adjustment Cases

(a) Chapter 7 cases

In a chapter 7 case no dividend in an amount less than $5 shall be distributed by the trustee to any creditor unless authorized by local rule or order of the court. Any dividend not distributed to a creditor shall be treated in the same manner as unclaimed funds as provided in § 347 of the Code.

(b) Chapter 12 and chapter 13 cases

In a chapter 12 or chapter 13 case no payment in an amount less than $15 shall be distributed by the trustee to any creditor unless authorized by local rule or order of the court. Funds not distributed because of this subdivision shall accumulate and shall be paid whenever the accumulation aggregates $15. Any funds remaining shall be distributed with the final payment.

(As amended Mar. 30, 1987, eff. Aug. 1, 1987; Apr. 30, 1991, eff. Aug. 1, 1991.)

ADVISORY COMMITTEE NOTES

This rule permits a court to eliminate the disproportionate expense and inconvenience incurred by the issuance of a dividend check of less than $5 (or $15 in a chapter 13 case). Creditors are more irritated than pleased to receive such small dividends, but the money is held subject to their specific request as are unclaimed dividends under § 347(a) of the Code. When the trustee deposits undistributed dividends pursuant to a direction in accordance with this rule the trustee should file with the clerk a list of the names and addresses, so far as known, of the persons entitled to the money so deposited and the respective amounts payable to them pursuant to Rule 3011. In a chapter 13 case, the small dividend will accumulate and will be payable at the latest, with the final dividend. Local rule or order may change the practice permitted in this rule and, in that connection, the order may be incorporated in the order confirming a chapter 13 plan.

1991 Amendments

Subdivision (b) is amended to include chapter 12 cases.

Rule 3011. Unclaimed Funds in Chapter 7 Liquidation, Chapter 12 Family Farmer's Debt Adjustment, and Chapter 13 Individual's Debt Adjustment Cases

The trustee shall file a list of all known names and addresses of the entities and the amounts which they are entitled to be paid from remaining property of the estate that is paid into court pursuant to § 347(a) of the Code.

(As amended Mar. 30, 1987, eff. Aug. 1, 1987; Apr. 30, 1991, eff. Aug. 1, 1991.)

ADVISORY COMMITTEE NOTES

This rule is derived from former Bankruptcy Rule 310. The operative provisions of that rule, however, are contained in § 347(a) of the Code, requiring the trustee to stop payment of checks remaining unpaid 90 days after distribution. The rule adds the requirement of filing a list of the names and addresses of the persons entitled to these dividends. This rule applies in a chapter 7 or 13 case but not in a chapter 9 or 11 case. The latter cases are governed by § 347(b) of the Code which provides for unclaimed distributions to be returned to the debtor or other entity acquiring the assets of the debtor.

1991 Amendments

The title of this rule is amended to include chapter 12 cases. The words "with the clerk" are deleted as unnecessary. See Rules 5005(a) and 9001(3).

CROSS REFERENCES

Treatment of small dividends as unclaimed funds, see Fed.Rules Bankr.Proc. Rule 3010, 11 USCA.

Rule 3012. Valuation of Security

The court may determine the value of a claim secured by a lien on property in which the estate has an interest on motion of any party in interest and after a hearing on notice to the holder of the secured claim and any other entity as the court may direct.

(As amended Mar. 30, 1987, eff. Aug. 1, 1987.)

ADVISORY COMMITTEE NOTES

Pursuant to § 506(a) of the Code, secured claims are to be valued and allowed as secured to the extent of the value of the collateral and unsecured, to the extent it is enforceable, for the excess over such value. The valuation of secured claims may become important in different contexts, *e.g.*, to determine the issue of adequate protection under § 361, impairment under § 1124, or treatment of the claim in a plan pursuant to § 1129(b) of the Code. This rule permits the issue to be raised on motion by a party in interest. The secured creditor is entitled to notice of the hearing on the motion and the court may direct that others in the case also receive such notice.

Rule 3013   BANKRUPTCY RULES

An adversary proceeding is commenced when the validity, priority, or extent of a lien is at issue as prescribed by Rule 7001. That proceeding is relevant to the basis of the lien itself while valuation under Rule 3012 would be for the purposes indicated above.

CROSS REFERENCES

Definition of—

    Lien, see 11 USCA § 101.

    Security, see 11 USCA § 101.

    Security interest, see 11 USCA § 101.

Determination of secured status, see 11 USCA § 506.

Motions; form and service, see Fed.Rules Bankr.Proc. Rule 9013, 11 USCA.

Rule 3013. Classification of Claims and Interests

For the purposes of the plan and its acceptance, the court may, on motion after hearing on notice as the court may direct, determine classes of creditors and equity security holders pursuant to §§ 1122, 1222(b)(1), and 1322(b)(1) of the Code.

(As amended Apr. 30, 1991, eff. Aug. 1, 1991.)

ADVISORY COMMITTEE NOTES

Sections 1122 and 1322(b)(1) set the standards for classifying claims and interests but provide that such classification is accomplished in the plan. This rule does not change the standards; rather it recognizes that it may be desirable or necessary to establish proper classification before a plan can be formulated. It provides for a court hearing on such notice as the court may direct.

1991 Amendments

This rule is amended to include chapter 12 cases.

CROSS REFERENCES

Motions; form and service, see Fed.Rules Bankr.Proc. Rule 9013, 11 USCA.

Rule 3014. Election Under § 1111(b) by Secured Creditor in Chapter 9 Municipality or Chapter 11 Reorganization Case

An election of application of § 1111(b)(2) of the Code by a class of secured creditors in a chapter 9 or 11 case may be made at any time prior to the conclusion of the hearing on the disclosure statement or within such later time as the court may fix. If the disclosure statement is conditionally approved pursuant to Rule 3017.1, and a final hearing on the disclosure statement is not held, the election of application of § 1111(b)(2) may be made not later than the date fixed pursuant to Rule 3017.1(a)(2) or another date the court may fix. The election shall be in writing and signed unless made at the hearing on the disclosure statement. The election, if made by the majorities required by § 1111(b)(1)(A)(i), shall be binding on all members of the class with respect to the plan.

(As amended Apr. 11, 1997, eff. Dec. 1, 1997.)

ADVISORY COMMITTEE NOTES

Pursuant to § 1111(b)(1) of the Code, a nonrecourse secured loan is converted, automatically, into a recourse loan thereby entitling the creditor to an unsecured deficiency claim if the value of the collateral is less than the debt. The class, however, may retain the loan as a nonrecourse loan by electing application of § 1111(b)(2) by the majorities stated in § 1111(b)(1)(A)(i). That section does not specify any time periods for making the election.

Rule 3014 provides that if no agreement is negotiated, the election of § 1111(b)(2) of the Code may be made at any time prior to conclusion of the hearing on the disclosure statement. Once the hearing has been concluded, it would be too late for a secured creditor class to demand different treatment unless the court has fixed a later time. This would be the case if, for example, a public class of secured creditors should have an approved disclosure statement prior to electing under § 1111(b).

Generally it is important that the proponent of a plan ascertain the position of the secured creditor class before a plan is proposed. The secured creditor class must know the prospects of its treatment under the plan before it can intelligently determine its rights under § 1111(b). The rule recognizes that there may be negotiations between the proponent of the plan and the secured creditor leading to a representation of desired treatment under § 1111(b). If that treatment is approved by the requisite majorities of the class and culminates in a written, signed statement filed with the court, that statement becomes binding and the class may not thereafter demand different treatment under § 1111(b) with respect to that plan. The proponent of the plan is thus enabled to seek approval of the disclosure statement and transmit the plan for voting in anticipation of confirmation. Only if that plan is not confirmed may the class of secured creditors thereafter change its prior election.

While this rule and the Code refer to a class of secured creditors it should be noted that ordinarily each secured creditor is in a separate and distinct class. In that event, the secured creditor has the sole power to determine application of § 1111(b) with respect to that claim.

1997 Amendments

This amendment provides a deadline for electing application of § 1111(b)(2) in a small business case in which a conditionally approved disclosure statement is finally approved without a hearing.

CROSS REFERENCES

Hearing on disclosure statement, see Fed.Rules Bankr.Proc. Rule 3017, 11 USCA.

Reduction of time for election pursuant to § 1111(b) not permitted, see Fed.Rules Bankr.Proc. Rule 9006, 11 USCA.

Rule 3015. Filing, Objection to Confirmation, and Modification of a Plan in a Chapter 12 Family Farmer's Debt Adjustment or a Chapter 13 Individual's Debt Adjustment Case

(a) Chapter 12 plan

The debtor may file a chapter 12 plan with the petition. If a plan is not filed with the petition, it shall be filed within the time prescribed by § 1221 of the Code.

(b) Chapter 13 plan

The debtor may file a chapter 13 plan with the petition. If a plan is not filed with the petition, it shall be filed within 14 days thereafter, and such time may not be further extended except for cause shown and on notice as the court may direct. If a case is converted to chapter 13, a plan shall be filed within 14 days thereafter, and such time may not be further extended except for cause shown and on notice as the court may direct.

(c) Dating

Every proposed plan and any modification thereof shall be dated.

(d) Notice and copies

The plan or a summary of the plan shall be included with each notice of the hearing on confirmation mailed pursuant to Rule 2002. If required by the court, the debtor shall furnish a sufficient number of copies to enable the clerk to include a copy of the plan with the notice of the hearing.

(e) Transmission to United States trustee

The clerk shall forthwith transmit to the United States trustee a copy of the plan and any modification thereof filed pursuant to subdivision (a) or (b) of this rule.

Rule 3015   BANKRUPTCY RULES

(f) Objection to confirmation; determination of good faith in the absence of an objection

An objection to confirmation of a plan shall be filed and served on the debtor, the trustee, and any other entity designated by the court, and shall be transmitted to the United States trustee, before confirmation of the plan. An objection to confirmation is governed by Rule 9014. If no objection is timely filed, the court may determine that the plan has been proposed in good faith and not by any means forbidden by law without receiving evidence on such issues.

(g) Modification of plan after confirmation

A request to modify a plan pursuant to § 1229 or § 1329 of the Code shall identify the proponent and shall be filed together with the proposed modification. The clerk, or some other person as the court may direct, shall give the debtor, the trustee, and all creditors not less than 21 days' notice by mail of the time fixed for filing objections and, if an objection is filed, the hearing to consider the proposed modification, unless the court orders otherwise with respect to creditors who are not affected by the proposed modification. A copy of the notice shall be transmitted to the United States trustee. A copy of the proposed modification, or a summary thereof, shall be included with the notice. If required by the court, the proponent shall furnish a sufficient number of copies of the proposed modification, or a summary thereof, to enable the clerk to include a copy with each notice. Any objection to the proposed modification shall be filed and served on the debtor, the trustee, and any other entity designated by the court, and shall be transmitted to the United States trustee. An objection to a proposed modification is governed by Rule 9014.

(As amended Apr. 30, 1991, eff. Aug. 1, 1991; Apr. 22, 1993, eff. Aug. 1, 1993; Mar. 26, 2009, eff. Dec. 1, 2009.)

ADVISORY COMMITTEE NOTES

Section 1321 provides only that the "debtor shall file a plan." No time periods are specified, nor is any other detail provided. The rule requires a chapter 13 plan to be filed either with the petition or within 15 days thereafter. The court may, for cause, extend the time. The rule permits a summary of the plan to be transmitted with the notice of the hearing on confirmation. The court may, however, require the plan itself to be transmitted and the debtor to supply enough copies for this purpose. In the former rules under Chapter XIII [former § 1001 et seq. of this title] the plan would accompany the notice of the first meeting of creditors. It is more important for the plan or a summary of its terms to be sent with the notice of the confirmation hearing. At that hearing objections to the plan will be heard by the court.

1991 Amendments

This rule is amended to include chapter 12 plans. Section 1221 of the Code requires the debtor to file a chapter 12 plan not later than 90 days after the order for relief, except that the court may extend the period if an extension is "substantially justified."

Subdivision (e) enables the United States trustee to monitor chapter 12 and chapter 13 plans pursuant to 28 U.S.C. § 586(a)(3)(C).

1993 Amendments

Subdivision (b) is amended to provide a time limit for filing a plan after a case has been converted to chapter 13. The substitution of "may" for "shall" is stylistic and makes no substantive change.

Subdivision (d) is amended to clarify that the plan or a summary of the plan must be included with each notice of the confirmation hearing in a chapter 12 case pursuant to Rule 2002(a).

Subdivision (f) is added to expand the scope of the rule to govern objections to confirmation in chapter 12 and chapter 13 cases. The subdivision also is amended to include a provision that permits the court, in the absence of an objection, to determine that the plan has been proposed in good faith and not by any means forbidden by law without the need to receive evidence on these issues. These matters are now governed by Rule 3020.

Subdivision (g) is added to provide a procedure for post-confirmation modification of chapter 12 and chapter 13 plans. These procedures are designed to be similar to the procedures for confirmation of plans. However, if no objection is filed with respect to a proposed modification of a plan after confirmation, the court is not required to hold a hearing. *See* § 1229(b)(2) and § 1329(b)(2) which provide that the plan as modified becomes the plan unless, after notice and a hearing, such modification is disapproved. *See*

§ 102(1). The notice of the time fixed for filing objections to the proposed modification should set a date for a hearing to be held in the event that an objection is filed.

Amendments to the title of this rule are stylistic and make no substantive change.

2009 Amendments

The rule is amended to implement changes in connection with the amendment to Rule 9006(a) and the manner by which time is computed under the rules. The deadlines in the rule are amended to substitute a deadline that is a multiple of seven days. Throughout the rules, deadlines are amended in the following manner:

- 5-day periods become 7-day periods
- 10-day periods become 14-day periods
- 15-day periods become 14-day periods
- 20-day periods become 21-day periods
- 25-day periods become 28-day periods

CROSS REFERENCES

Acceptance or rejection of plans, see Fed.Rules Bankr.Proc. Rule 3018, 11 USCA.

Deposit; confirmation of plan, see Fed.Rules Bankr.Proc. Rule 3020, 11 USCA.

Reduction of time for filing plan not permitted, see Fed.Rules Bankr.Proc. Rule 9006, 11 USCA.

Rule 3016. Filing of Plan and Disclosure Statement in a Chapter 9 Municipality or Chapter 11 Reorganization Case

(a) Identification of plan

Every proposed plan and any modification thereof shall be dated and, in a chapter 11 case, identified with the name of the entity or entities submitting or filing it.

(b) Disclosure statement

In a chapter 9 or 11 case, a disclosure statement under § 1125 of the Code or evidence showing compliance with § 1126(b) shall be filed with the plan or within a time fixed by the court, unless the plan is intended to provide adequate information under § 1125(f)(1). If the plan is intended to provide adequate information under § 1125(f)(1), it shall be so designated and Rule 3017.1 shall apply as if the plan is a disclosure statement.

(c) Injunction under a plan

If a plan provides for an injunction against conduct not otherwise enjoined under the Code, the plan and disclosure statement shall describe in specific and conspicuous language (bold, italic, or underlined text) all acts to be enjoined and identify the entities that would be subject to the injunction.

(d) Standard form small business disclosure statement and plan

In a small business case, the court may approve a disclosure statement and may confirm a plan that conform substantially to the appropriate Official Forms or other standard forms approved by the court.

(As amended Mar. 30, 1987, eff. Aug. 1, 1987; Apr. 30, 1991, eff. Aug. 1, 1991; Apr. 23, 1996, eff. Dec. 1, 1996; Apr. 23, 2001, eff. Dec. 1, 2001; Apr. 23, 2008, eff. Dec. 1, 2008.)

ADVISORY COMMITTEE NOTES

This rule implements the Code provisions concerning the filing of plans in chapters 9 and 11.

Chapter 9 Cases. Section 941 provides that the debtor may file a plan with the petition or thereafter but within a time fixed by the court. A rule, therefore, is unnecessary to specify the time for filing chapter 9 plans.

Chapter 11 Nonrailroad Cases. Section 1121 contains detailed provisions with respect to who may file a chapter 11 plan and, in part, the time period. Section 1121(a) permits a debtor to file a plan with the petition or at any time during the case. Section 1121(b) and (c) grants exclusive periods of 120 days and 180 days for the debtor to file and obtain acceptance of a plan. Failure to take advantage of these periods or the appointment of a trustee would permit other parties in interest to file a plan. These statutory provisions are not repeated in the rules.

Chapter 11 Railroad Cases. Pursuant to subchapter IV of chapter 11, § 1121 of the Code is applicable in railroad cases; see §§ 1161, 103(g). A trustee, however, is to be appointed in every case; thus, pursuant to § 1121(c), any party in interest may file a plan. See discussion of subdivision (a) of this rule, infra.

Subdivision (a). Section 1121(c), while permitting parties in interest a limited right to file plans, does not provide any time limitation. This subdivision sets as the deadline, the conclusion of the hearing on the disclosure statement. The court may, however, grant additional time. It is derived from former Chapter X Rule 10–301(c)(2) which used, as the cut-off time, the conclusion of the hearing on approval of a plan. As indicated, supra, § 1121(a) permits a debtor to file a plan at any time during the chapter 11 case. Under § 1121(c), parties other than a debtor may file a plan only after a trustee is appointed or the debtor's exclusive time expires.

Subdivision (b) requires plans to be properly identified.

Subdivision (c). This provision is new. In chapter 9 and 11 cases (including railroad reorganization cases) postpetition solicitation of votes on a plan requires transmittal of a disclosure statement, the contents of which have been approved by the court. See § 1125 of the Code. A prepetition solicitation must either have been in conformity with applicable nonbankruptcy law or, if none, the disclosure must have been of adequate information as set forth in § 1125 of the Code. See § 1126(b). Subdivision (c) of this rule provides the time for filing the disclosure statement or evidence of compliance with § 1126(b) which ordinarily will be with the plan but the court may allow a later time or the court may, pursuant to the last sentence, fix a time certain. Rule 3017 deals with the hearing on the disclosure statement. The disclosure statement, pursuant to § 1125 is to contain adequate information. "Adequate information" is defined in § 1125(a) as information that would permit a reasonable creditor or equity security holder to make an informed judgment on the plan.

1991 Amendments

Subdivision (a) is amended to enlarge the time for filing competing plans. A party in interest may not file a plan without leave of court only if an order approving a disclosure statement relating to another plan has been entered and a decision on confirmation of the plan has not been entered. This subdivision does not fix a deadline beyond which a debtor may not file a plan.

1996 Amendments

Section 1121(c) gives a party in interest the right to file a chapter 11 plan after expiration of the period when only the debtor may file a plan. Under § 1121(d), the exclusive period in which only the debtor may file a plan may be extended, but only if a party in interest so requests and the court, after notice and a hearing, finds cause for an extension. Subdivision (a) is abrogated because it could have the effect of extending the debtor's exclusive period for filing a plan without satisfying the requirements of § 1121(d). The abrogation of subdivision (a) does not affect the court's discretion with respect to the scheduling of hearings on the approval of disclosure statements when more than one plan has been filed.

The amendment to subdivision (c), redesignated as subdivision (b), is stylistic.

2001 Amendments

Subdivision (c) is added to assure that entities whose conduct would be enjoined under a plan, rather than by operation of the Code, are given adequate notice of the proposed injunction. The validity and effect of any injunction are substantive law matters that are beyond the scope of these rules.

Specific and conspicuous language is not necessary if the injunction contained in the plan is substantially the same as an injunction provided under the Code. For example, if a plan contains an injunction against acts to collect a discharged debt from the debtor, Rule 3016(c) would not apply because that conduct would be enjoined nonetheless under § 524(a)(2). But if a plan provides that creditors will be permanently enjoined from asserting claims against persons who are not debtors in the case, the plan and disclosure statement must highlight the injunctive language and comply with the requirements of Rule 3016(c). *See* § 524(e).

The requirement in this rule that the plan and disclosure statement identify the entities that would be subject to the injunction requires reasonable identification under the circumstances. If the entities that would be subject to the injunction cannot be identified by name, the plan and disclosure statement may describe them by class or category. For example, it may be sufficient to identify the subjects of the injunction as "all creditors of the debtor."

2008 Amendments

Subdivision (b) is amended to recognize that, in 2005, § 1125(f)(1) was added to the Code to provide that the plan proponent in a small business case need not file a disclosure statement if the plan itself includes adequate information and the court finds that a separate disclosure statement is unnecessary. If the plan is intended to provide adequate information in a small business case, it may be conditionally approved as a disclosure statement under Rule 3017.1 and is subject to all other rules applicable to disclosure statements in small business cases.

Subdivision (d) is added to the rule to implement § 433 of the Bankruptcy Abuse Prevention and Consumer Protection Act of 2005 which requires the promulgation of Official Forms for plans and disclosure statements in small business cases. Section 1125(f)(2) of the Code provides that the court may approve a disclosure statement submitted on the appropriate Official Form or on a standard form approved by the court. The rule takes no position on whether a court may require a local standard form disclosure statement or plan of reorganization in lieu of the Official Forms.

Other amendments are stylistic.

CROSS REFERENCES

Filing of municipality debt adjustment plan, see 11 USCA § 941.

Hearing on disclosure statement, see Fed.Rules Bankr.Proc. Rule 3017, 11 USCA.

Rule 3017. Court Consideration of Disclosure Statement in a Chapter 9 Municipality or Chapter 11 Reorganization Case

(a) Hearing on disclosure statement and objections

Except as provided in Rule 3017.1, after a disclosure statement is filed in accordance with Rule 3016(b), the court shall hold a hearing on at least 28 days' notice to the debtor, creditors, equity security holders and other parties in interest as provided in Rule 2002 to consider the disclosure statement and any objections or modifications thereto. The plan and the disclosure statement shall be mailed with the notice of the hearing only to the debtor, any trustee or committee appointed under the Code, the Securities and Exchange Commission and any party in interest who requests in writing a copy of the statement or plan. Objections to the disclosure statement shall be filed and served on the debtor, the trustee, any committee appointed under the Code, and any other entity designated by the court, at any time before the disclosure statement is approved or by an earlier date as the court may fix. In a chapter 11 reorganization case, every notice, plan, disclosure statement, and objection required to be served or mailed pursuant to this subdivision shall be transmitted to the United States trustee within the time provided in this subdivision.

(b) Determination on disclosure statement

Following the hearing the court shall determine whether the disclosure statement should be approved.

(c) Dates fixed for voting on plan and confirmation

On or before approval of the disclosure statement, the court shall fix a time within which the holders of claims and interests may accept or reject the plan and may fix a date for the hearing on confirmation.

Rule 3017   BANKRUPTCY RULES

(d) Transmission and notice to United States trustee, creditors and equity security holders

Upon approval of a disclosure statement,[1]—except to the extent that the court orders otherwise with respect to one or more unimpaired classes of creditors or equity security holders—the debtor in possession, trustee, proponent of the plan, or clerk as the court orders shall mail to all creditors and equity security holders, and in a chapter 11 reorganization case shall transmit to the United States trustee,

    (1) the plan or a court-approved summary of the plan;

    (2) the disclosure statement approved by the court;

    (3) notice of the time within which acceptances and rejections of the plan may be filed; and

    (4) any other information as the court may direct, including any court opinion approving the disclosure statement or a court-approved summary of the opinion.

In addition, notice of the time fixed for filing objections and the hearing on confirmation shall be mailed to all creditors and equity security holders in accordance with Rule 2002(b), and a form of ballot conforming to the appropriate Official Form shall be mailed to creditors and equity security holders entitled to vote on the plan. If the court opinion is not transmitted or only a summary of the plan is transmitted, the court opinion or the plan shall be provided on request of a party in interest at the plan proponent's expense. If the court orders that the disclosure statement and the plan or a summary of the plan shall not be mailed to any unimpaired class, notice that the class is designated in the plan as unimpaired and notice of the name and address of the person from whom the plan or summary of the plan and disclosure statement may be obtained upon request and at the plan proponent's expense, shall be mailed to members of the unimpaired class together with the notice of the time fixed for filing objections to and the hearing on confirmation. For the purposes of this subdivision, creditors and equity security holders shall include holders of stock, bonds, debentures, notes, and other securities of record on the date the order approving the disclosure statement is entered or another date fixed by the court, for cause, after notice and a hearing.

(e) Transmission to beneficial holders of securities

At the hearing held pursuant to subdivision (a) of this rule, the court shall consider the procedures for transmitting the documents and information required by subdivision (d) of this rule to beneficial holders of stock, bonds, debentures, notes, and other securities, determine the adequacy of the procedures, and enter any orders the court deems appropriate.

(f) Notice and transmission of documents to entities subject to an injunction under a plan

If a plan provides for an injunction against conduct not otherwise enjoined under the Code and an entity that would be subject to the injunction is not a creditor or equity security holder, at the hearing held under Rule 3017(a), the court shall consider procedures for providing the entity with:

    (1) at least 28 days' notice of the time fixed for filing objections and the hearing on confirmation of the plan containing the information described in Rule 2002(c)(3); and

    (2) to the extent feasible, a copy of the plan and disclosure statement.

(As amended Mar. 30, 1987, eff. Aug. 1, 1987; Apr. 30, 1991, eff. Aug. 1, 1991; Apr. 11, 1997, eff. Dec. 1, 1997; Apr. 23, 2001, eff. Dec. 1, 2001; Mar. 26, 2009, eff. Dec. 1, 2009.)

ADVISORY COMMITTEE NOTES

This rule is adapted from former Rule 10–303 which dealt with the approval of a Chapter X plan by the court. There is no requirement for plan approval in a chapter 9 or 11 case under the Code but there is the requirement that a disclosure statement containing adequate financial information be approved by the court after notice and a hearing before votes on a plan are solicited. Section 1125(b) of the Code is

---

[1] So in original. The comma probably shoult not appear.

made applicable in chapter 9 cases by § 901(a). It is also applicable in railroad reorganization cases under subchapter IV of chapter 11; see § 1161 of the Code.

Subdivision (a) of this rule provides for the hearing on the disclosure statement. Thus, a hearing would be required in all cases; whether it may be ex parte would depend on the circumstances of the case, but a mere absence of objections would not eliminate the need for a hearing; see § 102(1) of the Code.

No provision similar to former Rule 10–303(f) is included. That subdivision together with former Rule 10–304 prohibited solicitation of votes until after entry of an order approving the plan. Section 1125(b) of the Code explicitly provides that votes on a plan may not be solicited until a disclosure statement approved by the court is transmitted. Pursuant to the change in rulemaking power, a comparable provision in this rule is unnecessary. 28 U.S.C. § 2075.

Copies of the disclosure statement and plan need not be mailed with the notice of the hearing or otherwise transmitted prior to the hearing except with respect to the parties explicitly set forth in the subdivision.

It should be noted that, by construction, the singular includes the plural. Therefore, the phrase "plan or plans" or "disclosure statement or statements" has not been used although the possibility of multiple plans and statements is recognized.

Subdivision (d) permits the court to require a party other than the clerk of the bankruptcy court to bear the responsibility for transmitting the notices and documents specified in the rule when votes on the plan are solicited. Ordinarily the person responsible for such mailing will be the proponent of the plan. In rare cases the clerk may be directed to mail these documents, particularly when the trustee would have the responsibility but there is insufficient money in the estate to enable the trustee to perform this task.

1987 Amendments

Subdivision (d). Section 1125(c) of the Code requires that the entire approved disclosure statement be provided in connection with voting on a plan. The court is authorized by § 1125(c) to approve different disclosure statements for different classes. Although the rule does not permit the mailing of a summary of the disclosure statement in place of the approved disclosure statement, the court may approve a summary of the disclosure statement to be mailed with the complete disclosure statement to those voting on the plan.

1991 Amendments

This rule is amended to enable the United States trustee to monitor and comment with regard to chapter 11 disclosure statements and plans. The United States trustee does not perform these functions in a chapter 9 municipal debt adjustment case. See 28 U.S.C. § 586(a)(3)(B).

Subdivision (d) is amended to give the court the discretion to direct that one or more unimpaired classes shall not receive disclosure statements, plans, or summaries of plans. Members of unimpaired classes are not entitled to vote on the plan. Although disclosure statements enable members of unimpaired classes to make informed judgments as to whether to object to confirmation because of lack of feasibility or other grounds, in an unusual case the court may direct that disclosure statements shall not be sent to such classes if to do so would not be feasible considering the size of the unimpaired classes and the expense of printing and mailing. In any event, all creditors are entitled to notice of the time fixed for filing objections and notice of the hearing to consider confirmation of the plan pursuant to Rule 2002(b) and the requirement of such notice may not be excused with respect to unimpaired classes. The amendment to subdivision (d) also ensures that the members of unimpaired classes who do not receive such documents will have sufficient information so that they may request these documents in advance of the hearing on confirmation. The amendment to subdivision (d) is not intended to give the court the discretion to dispense with the mailing of the plan and disclosure statement to governmental units holding claims entitled to priority under § 507(a)(7) because they may not be classified. See § 1123(a)(1).

The words "with the court" in subdivision (a) are deleted as unnecessary. See Rules 5005(a) and 9001(3). Reference to the Official Form number in subdivision (d) is deleted in anticipation of future revision and renumbering of the Official Forms.

Subdivision (e) is designed to ensure that appropriate measures are taken for the plan, disclosure statement, ballot and other materials which are required to be transmitted to creditors and equity security holders under this rule to reach the beneficial holders of securities held in nominee name. Such measures may include orders directing the trustee or debtor in possession to reimburse the nominees out of the funds of the estate for the expenses incurred by them in distributing materials to beneficial holders.

In most cases, the plan proponent will not know the identities of the beneficial holders and therefore it will be necessary to rely on the nominal holders of the securities to distribute the plan materials to the beneficial owners.

1997 Amendments

Subdivision (a) is amended to provide that it does not apply to the extent provided in new Rule 3017.1, which applies in small business cases.

Subdivision (d) is amended to provide flexibility in fixing the record date for the purpose of determining the holders of securities who are entitled to receive documents pursuant to this subdivision. For example, if there may be a delay between the oral announcement of the judge's order approving the disclosure statement and entry of the order on the court docket, the court may fix the date on which the judge orally approves the disclosure statement as the record date so that the parties may expedite preparation of the lists necessary to facilitate the distribution of the plan, disclosure statement, ballots, and other related documents.

The court may set a record date pursuant to subdivision (d) only after notice and a hearing as provided in § 102(1) of the Code. Notice of a request for an order fixing the record date may be included in the notice of the hearing to consider approval of the disclosure statement mailed pursuant to Rule 2002(b).

If the court fixes a record date pursuant to subdivision (d) with respect to the holders of securities, and the holders are impaired by the plan, the judge also should order that the same record date applies for the purpose of determining eligibility for voting pursuant to Rule 3018(a).

Other amendments to this rule are stylistic.

2001 Amendments

Subdivision (f) is added to assure that entities whose conduct would be enjoined under a plan, rather than by operation of the Code, and who will not receive the documents listed in subdivision (d) because they are neither creditors nor equity security holders, are provided with adequate notice of the proposed injunction. It does not address any substantive law issues relating to the validity or effect of any injunction provided under a plan, or any due process or other constitutional issues relating to notice. These issues are beyond the scope of these rules and are left for judicial determination.

This rule recognizes the need for adequate notice to subjects of an injunction, but that reasonable flexibility under the circumstances may be required. If a known and identifiable entity would be subject to the injunction, and the notice, plan, and disclosure statement could be mailed to that entity, the court should require that they be mailed at the same time that the plan, disclosure statement and related documents are mailed to creditors under Rule 3017(d). If mailing notices and other documents is not feasible because the entities subject to the injunction are described in the plan and disclosure statement by class or category and they cannot be identified individually by name and address, the court may require that notice under Rule 3017(f)(1) be published.

2009 Amendments

The rule is amended to implement changes in connection with the amendment to Rule 9006(a) and the manner by which time is computed under the rules. The deadlines in the rule are amended to substitute a deadline that is a multiple of seven days. Throughout the rules, deadlines are amended in the following manner:

- 5-day periods become 7-day periods
- 10-day periods become 14-day periods
- 15-day periods become 14-day periods
- 20-day periods become 21-day periods
- 25-day periods become 28-day periods

CROSS REFERENCES

Acceptance or rejection of plan—

Eligible persons, see Fed.Rules Bankr.Proc. Rule 3018, 11 USCA.

Preference among more than one plan, see Fed.Rules Bankr.Proc. Rule 3018, 11 USCA.

Disclosure statement—

> Different statements as between different classes of claims, see 11 USCA § 1125.
>
> Right to be heard on adequacy of information, see 11 USCA § 1125.
>
> Solicitation of plan's acceptance, see 11 USCA § 1125.

Notice of—

> Time fixed for plan's acceptance or rejection in accord with this rule, see Fed.Rules Bankr.Proc. Rule 2002, 11 USCA.

Proof of right to record status filed by security holder, see Fed.Rules Bankr.Proc. Rule 3003, 11 USCA.

Rule 3017.1. Court Consideration of Disclosure Statement in a Small Business Case

(a) Conditional approval of disclosure statement

In a small business case, the court may, on application of the plan proponent or on its own initiative, conditionally approve a disclosure statement filed in accordance with Rule 3016. On or before conditional approval of the disclosure statement, the court shall:

> (1) fix a time within which the holders of claims and interests may accept or reject the plan;
>
> (2) fix a time for filing objections to the disclosure statement;
>
> (3) fix a date for the hearing on final approval of the disclosure statement to be held if a timely objection is filed; and
>
> (4) fix a date for the hearing on confirmation.

(b) Application of Rule 3017

Rule 3017(a), (b), (c), and (e) do not apply to a conditionally approved disclosure statement. Rule 3017(d) applies to a conditionally approved disclosure statement, except that conditional approval is considered approval of the disclosure statement for the purpose of applying Rule 3017(d).

(c) Final approval

> **(1) Notice**
>
> Notice of the time fixed for filing objections and the hearing to consider final approval of the disclosure statement shall be given in accordance with Rule 2002 and may be combined with notice of the hearing on confirmation of the plan.
>
> **(2) Objections**
>
> Objections to the disclosure statement shall be filed, transmitted to the United States trustee, and served on the debtor, the trustee, any committee appointed under the Code and any other entity designated by the court at any time before final approval of the disclosure statement or by an earlier date as the court may fix.
>
> **(3) Hearing**
>
> If a timely objection to the disclosure statement is filed, the court shall hold a hearing to consider final approval before or combined with the hearing on confirmation of the plan.

(Added Apr. 11, 1997, eff. Dec. 1, 1997; amended Apr. 23, 2008, eff. Dec. 1, 2008.)

ADVISORY COMMITTEE NOTES

1997 Amendment

This rule is added to implement § 1125(f), which was added to the Code by the Bankruptcy Reform Act of 1994.

The procedures for electing to be considered a small business are set forth in Rule 1020. If the debtor is a small business and has elected to be considered a small business, § 1125(f) permits the court to conditionally approve a disclosure statement subject to final approval after notice and a hearing. If a disclosure statement is conditionally approved, and no timely objection to the disclosure statement is filed, it is not necessary for the court to hold a hearing on final approval.

2008 Amendments

Section 101 of the Code, as amended in 2005, defines a "small business case" and "small business debtor," and eliminates any need to elect that status. Therefore, the reference in the rule to an election is deleted.

As provided in the amendment to Rule 3016(b), a plan intended to provide adequate information in a small business case under § 1125(f)(1) may be conditionally approved and is otherwise treated as a disclosure statement under this rule.

Rule 3018. Acceptance or Rejection of Plan in a Chapter 9 Municipality or a Chapter 11 Reorganization Case

(a) Entities entitled to accept or reject plan; time for acceptance or rejection

A plan may be accepted or rejected in accordance with § 1126 of the Code within the time fixed by the court pursuant to Rule 3017. Subject to subdivision (b) of this rule, an equity security holder or creditor whose claim is based on a security of record shall not be entitled to accept or reject a plan unless the equity security holder or creditor is the holder of record of the security on the date the order approving the disclosure statement is entered or on another date fixed by the court, for cause, after notice and a hearing. For cause shown, the court after notice and hearing may permit a creditor or equity security holder to change or withdraw an acceptance or rejection. Notwithstanding objection to a claim or interest, the court after notice and hearing may temporarily allow the claim or interest in an amount which the court deems proper for the purpose of accepting or rejecting a plan.

(b) Acceptances or rejections obtained before petition

An equity security holder or creditor whose claim is based on a security of record who accepted or rejected the plan before the commencement of the case shall not be deemed to have accepted or rejected the plan pursuant to § 1126(b) of the Code unless the equity security holder or creditor was the holder of record of the security on the date specified in the solicitation of such acceptance or rejection for the purposes of such solicitation. A holder of a claim or interest who has accepted or rejected a plan before the commencement of the case under the Code shall not be deemed to have accepted or rejected the plan if the court finds after notice and hearing that the plan was not transmitted to substantially all creditors and equity security holders of the same class, that an unreasonably short time was prescribed for such creditors and equity security holders to accept or reject the plan, or that the solicitation was not in compliance with § 1126(b) of the Code.

(c) Form of acceptance or rejection

An acceptance or rejection shall be in writing, identify the plan or plans accepted or rejected, be signed by the creditor or equity security holder or an authorized agent, and conform to the appropriate Official Form. If more than one plan is transmitted pursuant to Rule 3017, an acceptance or rejection may be filed by each creditor or equity security holder for any number of plans transmitted and if acceptances are filed for more than one plan, the creditor or equity security holder may indicate a preference or preferences among the plans so accepted.

(d) Acceptance or rejection by partially secured creditor

A creditor whose claim has been allowed in part as a secured claim and in part as an unsecured claim shall be entitled to accept or reject a plan in both capacities.

(As amended Mar. 30, 1987, eff. Aug. 1, 1987; Apr. 30, 1991, eff. Aug. 1, 1991; Apr. 22, 1993, eff. Aug. 1, 1993; Apr. 11, 1997, eff. Dec. 1, 1997.)

ADVISORY COMMITTEE NOTES

This rule applies in chapter 9, 11 and 13 cases under the Code. The references in the rule to equity security holders will not, however, be relevant in chapter 9 or 13 cases. The rule will be of little utility in a chapter 13 case because only secured creditors may be requested to vote on a plan; unsecured creditors are not entitled to vote; see § 1325(a)(4), (5) of the Code.

Subdivision (a) is derived from former Rule 10–305(a). It substitutes, in a reorganization case, entry of the order approving the disclosure statement for the order approving a plan in conformity with the differences between Chapter X [former § 501 et seq. of this title] and chapter 11. In keeping with the underlying theory, it continues to recognize that the lapse of time between the filing of the petition and entry of such order will normally be significant and, during that interim, bonds and equity interests can change ownership.

Subdivision (b) recognizes the former Chapter XI [former § 701 et seq. of this title] practice permitting a plan and acceptances to be filed with the petition, as does § 1126(b) of the Code. However, because a plan under chapter 11 may affect shareholder interests, there should be reference to a record date of ownership. In this instance the appropriate record date is that used in the prepetition solicitation materials because it is those acceptances or rejections which are being submitted to the court.

While § 1126(c), (d), and (e) prohibits use of an acceptance or rejection not procured in good faith, the added provision in subdivision (b) of the rule is somewhat more detailed. It would prohibit use of prepetition acceptances or rejections when some but not all impaired creditors or equity security holders are solicited or when they are not given a reasonable opportunity to submit their acceptances or rejections. This provision together with § 1126(e) gives the court the power to nullify abusive solicitation procedures.

Subdivision (c). It is possible that multiple plans may be before the court for confirmation. Pursuant to § 1129(c) of the Code, the court may confirm only one plan but is required to consider the preferences expressed by those accepting the plans in determining which one to confirm.

Subdivisions (d) and (e) of former Rule 10–305 are not continued since comparable provisions are contained in the statute; see § 1126(c), (d), (e).

It should be noted that while the singular "plan" is used throughout, by construction the plural is included; see § 102(7).

1991 Amendments

Subdivisions (a) and (b) are amended to delete provisions that duplicate § 1126 of the Code. An entity who is not a record holder of a security, but who claims that it is entitled to be treated as a record holder, may file a statement pursuant to Rule 3003(d).

Subdivision (a) is amended further to allow the court to permit a creditor or equity security holder to change or withdraw an acceptance or rejection for cause shown whether or not the time fixed for voting has expired.

Subdivision (b) is also amended to give effect to a prepetition acceptance or rejection if solicitation requirements were satisfied with respect to substantially all members of the same class, instead of requiring proper solicitation with respect to substantially all members of all classes.

Subdivision (c) is amended to delete the Official Form number in anticipation of future revision and renumbering of the Official Forms.

1993 Amendments

The title of this rule is amended to indicate that it applies only in a chapter 9 or a chapter 11 case. The amendment of the word "Plans" to "Plan" is stylistic.

1997 Amendments

Subdivision (a) is amended to provide flexibility in fixing the record date for the purpose of determining the holders of securities who are entitled to vote on the plan. For example, if there may be a delay between the oral announcement of the judge's decision approving the disclosure statement and entry of the order on the court docket, the court may fix the date on which the judge orally approves the disclosure statement as the record date for voting purposes so that the parties may expedite preparation of the lists necessary to facilitate the distribution of the plan, disclosure statement, ballots, and other related documents in connection with the solicitation of votes.

The court may set a record date pursuant to subdivision (a) only after notice and a hearing as provided in § 102(1) of the Code. Notice of a request for an order fixing the record date may be included in the notice of the hearing to consider approval of the disclosure statement mailed pursuant to Rule 2002(b).

If the court fixes the record date for voting purposes, the judge also should order that the same record date shall apply for the purpose of distributing the documents required to be distributed pursuant to Rule 3017(d).

CROSS REFERENCES

Acceptance of altered or modified plan, see 11 USCA § 1127.

Disqualification of votes on acceptance in absence of good faith, see 11 USCA § 1126.

Filing of plan in—

    Individual debt adjustment case, see Fed.Rules Bankr.Proc. Rule 3015, 11 USCA.

    Municipality debt adjustment and reorganization cases, with disclosure statement, see Fed.Rules Bankr.Proc. Rule 3016, 11 USCA.

Proof of right to record status filed by security holder, see Fed.Rules Bankr.Proc. Rule 3003, 11 USCA.

Rule 3019. Modification of Accepted Plan in a Chapter 9 Municipality or a Chapter 11 Reorganization Case

(a) Modification of plan before confirmation

In a chapter 9 or chapter 11 case, after a plan has been accepted and before its confirmation, the proponent may file a modification of the plan. If the court finds after hearing on notice to the trustee, any committee appointed under the Code, and any other entity designated by the court that the proposed modification does not adversely change the treatment of the claim of any creditor or the interest of any equity security holder who has not accepted in writing the modification, it shall be deemed accepted by all creditors and equity security holders who have previously accepted the plan.

(b) Modification of plan after confirmation in individual debtor case

If the debtor is an individual, a request to modify the plan under § 1127(e) of the Code is governed by Rule 9014. The request shall identify the proponent and shall be filed together with the proposed modification. The clerk, or some other person as the court may direct, shall give the debtor, the trustee, and all creditors not less than 21 days' notice by mail of the time fixed to file objections and, if an objection is filed, the hearing to consider the proposed modification, unless the court orders otherwise with respect to creditors who are not affected by the proposed modification. A copy of the notice shall be transmitted to the United States trustee, together with a copy of the proposed modification. Any objection to the proposed modification shall be filed and served on the debtor, the proponent of the modification, the trustee, and any other entity designated by the court, and shall be transmitted to the United States trustee.

(As amended Mar. 30, 1987, eff. Aug. 1, 1987; Apr. 22, 1993, eff. Aug. 1, 1993; Apr. 23, 2008, eff. Dec. 1, 2008; Mar. 26, 2009, eff. Dec. 1, 2009.)

CLAIMS — Rule 3020

ADVISORY COMMITTEE NOTES

This rule implements §§ 942, 1127 and 1323 of the Code. For example, § 1127 provides for modification before and after confirmation but does not deal with the minor modifications that do not adversely change any rights. The rule makes clear that a modification may be made, after acceptance of the plan without submission to creditors and equity security holders if their interests are not affected. To come within this rule, the modification should be one that does not change the rights of a creditor or equity security holder as fixed in the plan before modification.

1993 Amendments

This rule is amended to limit its application to chapter 9 and chapter 11 cases. Modification of plans after confirmation in chapter 12 and chapter 13 cases is governed by Rule 3015. The addition of the comma in the second sentence is stylistic and makes no substantive change.

2008 Amendments

The 2005 amendments to § 1127 of the Code provide for modification of a confirmed plan in an individual debtor chapter 11 case. Therefore, the rule is amended to establish the procedure for filing and objecting to a proposed modification of a confirmed plan.

2009 Amendments

The rule is amended to implement changes in connection with the amendment to Rule 9006(a) and the manner by which time is computed under the rules. The deadline in the rule is amended to substitute a deadline that is a multiple of seven days. Throughout the rules, deadlines are amended in the following manner:

- 5-day periods become 7-day periods
- 10-day periods become 14-day periods
- 15-day periods become 14-day periods
- 20-day periods become 21-day periods
- 25-day periods become 28-day periods

CROSS REFERENCES

Acceptance or rejection of plans, see Fed.Rules Bankr.Proc. Rule 3018, 11 USCA.

Modification of plan in—

    Individual debt adjustment case, see 11 USCA § 1323.

    Municipality debt adjustment case, see 11 USCA § 942.

    Reorganization case, see 11 USCA § 1127.

Rule 3020. Deposit; Confirmation of Plan in a Chapter 9 Municipality or Chapter 11 Reorganization Case

(a) Deposit

In a chapter 11 case, prior to entry of the order confirming the plan, the court may order the deposit with the trustee or debtor in possession of the consideration required by the plan to be distributed on confirmation. Any money deposited shall be kept in a special account established for the exclusive purpose of making the distribution.

(b) Objection to and hearing on confirmation in a Chapter 9 or Chapter 11 case

    (1) Objection

An objection to confirmation of the plan shall be filed and served on the debtor, the trustee, the proponent of the plan, any committee appointed under the Code, and any other entity designated by the court, within a time fixed by the court. Unless the case is a chapter 9 municipality case, a copy of every objection to confirmation shall be transmitted by the

Rule 3020   BANKRUPTCY RULES

objecting party to the United States trustee within the time fixed for filing objections. An objection to confirmation is governed by Rule 9014.

(2) Hearing

The court shall rule on confirmation of the plan after notice and hearing as provided in Rule 2002. If no objection is timely filed, the court may determine that the plan has been proposed in good faith and not by any means forbidden by law without receiving evidence on such issues.

(c) Order of confirmation

(1) The order of confirmation shall conform to the appropriate Official Form. If the plan provides for an injunction against conduct not otherwise enjoined under the Code, the order of confirmation shall (1) describe in reasonable detail all acts enjoined; (2) be specific in its terms regarding the injunction; and (3) identify the entities subject to the injunction.

(2) Notice of entry of the order of confirmation shall be mailed promptly to the debtor, the trustee, creditors, equity security holders, other parties in interest, and, if known, to any identified entity subject to an injunction provided for in the plan against conduct not otherwise enjoined under the Code.

(3) Except in a chapter 9 municipality case, notice of entry of the order of confirmation shall be transmitted to the United States trustee as provided in Rule 2002(k).

(d) Retained power

Notwithstanding the entry of the order of confirmation, the court may issue any other order necessary to administer the estate.

(e) Stay of confirmation order

An order confirming a plan is stayed until the expiration of 14 days after the entry of the order, unless the court orders otherwise.

(As amended Mar. 30, 1987, eff. Aug. 1, 1987; Apr. 30, 1991, eff. Aug. 1, 1991; Apr. 22, 1993, eff. Aug. 1, 1993; Apr. 29, 1999, eff. Dec. 1, 1999; Apr. 23, 2001, eff. Dec. 1, 2001; Mar. 26, 2009, eff. Dec. 1, 2009.)

ADVISORY COMMITTEE NOTES

This rule is adapted from former Rules 10–307, 11–38, and 13–213. It applies to cases filed under chapters 9, 11 and 13. Certain subdivisions of the earlier rules have not been included, such as, a subdivision revesting title in the debtor because § 541 of the Code does not transfer title out of the debtor as did § 70a of the Bankruptcy Act [former § 110(a) of this title]; see also §§ 1141(b), 1327(b). Subdivision (b) of former Rule 13–213 is not included because its provisions are contained in the statute; see §§ 1322, 1325(b), 105.

Subdivision (a) gives discretion to the court to require in chapter 11 cases the deposit of any consideration to be distributed on confirmation. If money is to be distributed, it is to be deposited in a special account to assure that it will not be used for any other purpose. The Code is silent in chapter 11 with respect to the need to make a deposit or the person with whom any deposit is to be to made. Consequently, there is no statutory authority for any person to act in a capacity similar to the disbursing agent under former Chapter XI [former § 701 et seq. of this title] practice. This rule provides that only the debtor in possession or trustee should be appointed as the recipient of the deposit. Any consideration other than money, e.g., notes or stock may be given directly to the debtor in possession or trustee and need not be left in any kind of special account. In chapter 9 cases, § 944(b) provides for deposit with a disbursing agent appointed by the court of any consideration to be distributed under the plan.

Subdivision (d) clarifies the authority of the court to conclude matters pending before it prior to confirmation and to continue to administer the estate as necessary, e.g., resolving objections to claims.

1991 Amendments

The United States trustee monitors chapter 11, chapter 12, and chapter 13 plans and has standing to be heard regarding confirmation of a plan. See 28 U.S.C. § 586(a)(3). The amendments to subdivisions (b)(1) and (c) of this rule facilitate that role of the United States trustee. Subdivision (b)(1) is also amended to require service on the proponent of the plan of objections to confirmation. The words "with the court" in subdivision (b)(1) are deleted as unnecessary. See Rules 5005(a) and 9001(3).

In a chapter 12 case, the court is required to conduct and conclude the hearing on confirmation of the plan within the time prescribed in § 1224 of the Code.

Subdivision (c) is also amended to require that the confirmation order be mailed to the trustee. Reference to the Official Form number is deleted in anticipation of future revision and renumbering of the Official Forms.

1993 Amendments

This rule is amended to limit its application to chapter 9 and chapter 11 cases. The procedures relating to confirmation of plans in chapter 12 and chapter 13 cases are provided in rule 3015. Other amendments are stylistic and make no substantive change.

1999 Amendments

Subdivision (e) is added to provide sufficient time for a party to request a stay pending appeal of an order confirming a plan under chapter 9 or chapter 11 of the Code before the plan is implemented and an appeal becomes moot. Unless the court orders otherwise, any transfer of assets, issuance of securities, and cash distributions provided for in the plan may not be made before the expiration of the 10-day period. The stay of the confirmation order under subdivision (e) does not affect the time for filing a notice of appeal from the confirmation order in accordance with Rule 8002.

The court may, in its discretion, order that Rule 3020(e) is not applicable so that the plan may be implemented and distributions may be made immediately. Alternatively, the court may order that the stay under Rule 3020(e) is for a fixed period less than 10 days.

2001 Amendments

Subdivision (c) is amended to provide notice to an entity subject to an injunction provided for in a plan against conduct not otherwise enjoined by operation of the Code. This requirement is not applicable to an injunction contained in a plan if it is substantially the same as an injunction provided under the Code. The validity and effect of any injunction provided for in a plan are substantive law matters that are beyond the scope of these rules.

The requirement that the order of confirmation identify the entities subject to the injunction requires only reasonable identification under the circumstances. If the entities that would be subject to the injunction cannot be identified by name, the order may describe them by class or category if reasonable under the circumstances. For example, it may be sufficient to identify the entities as "all creditors of the debtor."

2009 Amendments

The rule is amended to implement changes in connection with the amendment to Rule 9006(a) and the manner by which time is computed under the rules. The deadline in the rule is amended to substitute a deadline that is a multiple of seven days. Throughout the rules, deadlines are amended in the following manner:

- 5-day periods become 7-day periods
- 10-day periods become 14-day periods
- 15-day periods become 14-day periods
- 20-day periods become 21-day periods
- 25-day periods become 28-day periods

CROSS REFERENCES

Modification of accepted plan before confirmation, see Fed.Rules Bankr.Proc. Rule 3019, 11 USCA.

Rule 3021. Distribution Under Plan

Except as provided in Rule 3020(e), after a plan is confirmed, distribution shall be made to creditors whose claims have been allowed, to interest holders whose interests have not been disallowed, and to indenture trustees who have filed claims under Rule 3003(c)(5) that have been allowed. For purposes of this rule, creditors include holders of bonds, debentures, notes, and other debt securities, and interest holders include the holders of stock and other equity securities, of record at the time of commencement of distribution, unless a different time is fixed by the plan or the order confirming the plan.

(As amended Apr. 11, 1997, eff. Dec. 1, 1997; Apr. 29, 1999, eff. Dec. 1, 1999.)

ADVISORY COMMITTEE NOTES

This rule is derived from former Chapter X Rule 10–405(a). Subdivision (b) of that rule is covered by § 1143 of the Code.

1997 Amendments

This rule is amended to provide flexibility in fixing the record date for the purpose of making distributions to holders of securities of record. In a large case, it may be impractical for the debtor to determine the holders of record with respect to publicly held securities and also to make distributions to those holders at the same time. Under this amendment, the plan or the order confirming the plan may fix a record date for distributions that is earlier than the date on which distributions commence.

This rule also is amended to treat holders of bonds, debentures, notes, and other debt securities the same as any other creditors by providing that they shall receive a distribution only if their claims have been allowed. Finally, the amendments clarify that distributions are to be made to all interest holders—not only those that are within the definition of "equity security holders" under § 101 of the Code—whose interests have not been disallowed.

1999 Amendments

This amendment is to conform to the amendments to Rule 3020 regarding the ten-day stay of an order confirming a plan in a chapter 9 or chapter 11 case. The other amendments are stylistic.

CROSS REFERENCES

Disposition of unclaimed property, see 11 USCA § 347.

Power of court to require transfers of property, see 11 USCA § 1142.

Proof of right to record status filed by security holder, see Fed.Rules Bankr.Proc. Rule 3003, 11 USCA.

Time for surrender of security or performance of required act under reorganization plan, see 11 USCA § 1143.

Rule 3022. Final Decree in Chapter 11 Reorganization Case

After an estate is fully administered in a chapter 11 reorganization case, the court, on its own motion or on motion of a party in interest, shall enter a final decree closing the case.

(As amended Mar. 30, 1987, eff. Aug. 1, 1987; Apr. 30, 1991, eff. Aug. 1, 1991.)

ADVISORY COMMITTEE NOTES

Section 350 of the Code requires the court to close the case after the estate is fully administered and the trustee has been discharged. Section 1143 places a five year limitation on the surrender of securities when required for participation under a plan but this provision should not delay entry of the final decree.

1991 Amendments

Entry of a final decree closing a chapter 11 case should not be delayed solely because the payments required by the plan have not been completed. Factors that the court should consider in determining whether the estate has been fully administered include (1) whether the order confirming the plan has become final, (2) whether deposits required by the plan have been distributed, (3) whether the property proposed by the plan to be transferred has been transferred, (4) whether the debtor or the successor of the debtor under the plan has assumed the business or the management of the property dealt with by the plan, (5) whether payments under the plan have commenced, and (6) whether all motions, contested matters, and adversary proceedings have been finally resolved.

The court should not keep the case open only because of the possibility that the court's jurisdiction may be invoked in the future. A final decree closing the case after the estate is fully administered does not deprive the court of jurisdiction to enforce or interpret its own orders and does not prevent the court from reopening the case for cause pursuant to § 350(b) of the Code. For example, on motion of a party in interest, the court may reopen the case to revoke an order of confirmation procured by fraud under § 1144 of the Code. If the plan or confirmation order provides that the case shall remain open until a certain date or event because of the likelihood that the court's jurisdiction may be required for specific purposes prior thereto, the case should remain open until that date or event.

CROSS REFERENCES

Close of case after trustee's discharge, see 11 USCA § 350.

Surrender of security or performance of required act under reorganization plan, denial of distribution, see 11 USCA § 1143.

PART IV—THE DEBTOR: DUTIES AND BENEFITS

Rule 4001. Relief From Automatic Stay; Prohibiting or Conditioning the Use, Sale, or Lease of Property; Use of Cash Collateral; Obtaining Credit; Agreements

(a) **Relief from stay; prohibiting or conditioning the use, sale, or lease of property**

    (1) **Motion**

    A motion for relief from an automatic stay provided by the Code or a motion to prohibit or condition the use, sale, or lease of property pursuant to § 363(e) shall be made in accordance with Rule 9014 and shall be served on any committee elected pursuant to § 705 or appointed pursuant to § 1102 of the Code or its authorized agent, or, if the case is a chapter 9 municipality case or a chapter 11 reorganization case and no committee of unsecured creditors has been appointed pursuant to § 1102, on the creditors included on the list filed pursuant to Rule 1007(d), and on such other entities as the court may direct.

    (2) **Ex parte relief**

    Relief from a stay under § 362(a) or a request to prohibit or condition the use, sale, or lease of property pursuant to § 363(e) may be granted without prior notice only if (A) it clearly appears from specific facts shown by affidavit or by a verified motion that immediate and irreparable injury, loss, or damage will result to the movant before the adverse party or the attorney for the adverse party can be heard in opposition, and (B) the movant's attorney certifies to the court in writing the efforts, if any, which have been made to give notice and the reasons why notice should not be required. The party obtaining relief under this subdivision and § 362(f) or § 363(e) shall immediately give oral notice thereof to the trustee or debtor in possession and to the debtor and forthwith mail or otherwise transmit to such adverse party or parties a copy of the order granting relief. On two days notice to the party who obtained relief from the stay without notice or on shorter notice to that party as the court may prescribe, the adverse party may appear and move reinstatement of the stay or reconsideration of the order prohibiting or conditioning the use, sale, or lease of property. In that event, the court shall proceed expeditiously to hear and determine the motion.

    (3) **Stay of order**

    An order granting a motion for relief from an automatic stay made in accordance with Rule 4001(a)(1) is stayed until the expiration of 14 days after the entry of the order, unless the court orders otherwise.

(b) **Use of cash collateral**

    (1) **Motion; service**

        (A) **Motion**

        A motion for authority to use cash collateral shall be made in accordance with Rule 9014 and shall be accompanied by a proposed form of order.

        (B) **Contents**

        The motion shall consist of or (if the motion is more than five pages in length) begin with a concise statement of the relief requested, not to exceed five pages, that lists or summarizes, and sets out the location within the relevant documents of, all material provisions, including:

            (i) the name of each entity with an interest in the cash collateral;

            (ii) the purposes for the use of the cash collateral;

            (iii) the material terms, including duration, of the use of the cash collateral; and

            (iv) any liens, cash payments, or other adequate protection that will be provided to each entity with an interest in the cash collateral or, if no additional adequate protection is proposed, an explanation of why each entity's interest is adequately protected.

(C) Service

The motion shall be served on: (1) any entity with an interest in the cash collateral; (2) any committee elected under § 705 or appointed under § 1102 of the Code, or its authorized agent, or, if the case is a chapter 9 municipality case or a chapter 11 reorganization case and no committee of unsecured creditors has been appointed under § 1102, the creditors included on the list filed under Rule 1007(d); and (3) any other entity that the court directs.

(2) Hearing

The court may commence a final hearing on a motion for authorization to use cash collateral no earlier than 14 days after service of the motion. If the motion so requests, the court may conduct a preliminary hearing before such 14-day period expires, but the court may authorize the use of only that amount of cash collateral as is necessary to avoid immediate and irreparable harm to the estate pending a final hearing.

(3) Notice

Notice of hearing pursuant to this subdivision shall be given to the parties on whom service of the motion is required by paragraph (1) of this subdivision and to such other entities as the court may direct.

(c) Obtaining credit

(1) Motion; service

(A) Motion

A motion for authority to obtain credit shall be made in accordance with Rule 9014 and shall be accompanied by a copy of the credit agreement and a proposed form of order.

(B) Contents

The motion shall consist of or (if the motion is more than five pages in length) begin with a concise statement of the relief requested, not to exceed five pages, that lists or summarizes, and sets out the location within the relevant documents of, all material provisions of the proposed credit agreement and form of order, including interest rate, maturity, events of default, liens, borrowing limits, and borrowing conditions. If the proposed credit agreement or form of order includes any of the provisions listed below, the concise statement shall also: briefly list or summarize each one; identify its specific location in the proposed agreement and form of order; and identify any such provision that is proposed to remain in effect if interim approval is granted, but final relief is denied, as provided under Rule 4001(c)(2). In addition, the motion shall describe the nature and extent of each provision listed below:

(i) a grant of priority or a lien on property of the estate under § 364(c) or (d);

(ii) the providing of adequate protection or priority for a claim that arose before the commencement of the case, including the granting of a lien on property of the estate to secure the claim, or the use of property of the estate or credit obtained under § 364 to make cash payments on account of the claim;

(iii) a determination of the validity, enforceability, priority, or amount of a claim that arose before the commencement of the case, or of any lien securing the claim;

(iv) a waiver or modification of Code provisions or applicable rules relating to the automatic stay;

(v) a waiver or modification of any entity's authority or right to file a plan, seek an extension of time in which the debtor has the exclusive right to file a plan, request the use of cash collateral under § 363(c), or request authority to obtain credit under § 364;

(vi) the establishment of deadlines for filing a plan of reorganization, for approval of a disclosure statement, for a hearing on confirmation, or for entry of a confirmation order;

(vii) a waiver or modification of the applicability of nonbankruptcy law relating to the perfection of a lien on property of the estate, or on the foreclosure or other enforcement of the lien;

(viii) a release, waiver, or limitation on any claim or other cause of action belonging to the estate or the trustee, including any modification of the statute of limitations or other deadline to commence an action;

(ix) the indemnification of any entity;

(x) a release, waiver, or limitation of any right under § 506(c); or

(xi) the granting of a lien on any claim or cause of action arising under §§[1] 544, 545, 547, 548, 549, 553(b), 723(a), or 724(a).

(C) Service

The motion shall be served on: (1) any committee elected under § 705 or appointed under § 1102 of the Code, or its authorized agent, or, if the case is a chapter 9 municipality case or a chapter 11 reorganization case and no committee of unsecured creditors has been appointed under § 1102, on the creditors included on the list filed under Rule 1007(d); and (2) on any other entity that the court directs.

(2) Hearing

The court may commence a final hearing on a motion for authority to obtain credit no earlier than 14 days after service of the motion. If the motion so requests, the court may conduct a hearing before such 14-day period expires, but the court may authorize the obtaining of credit only to the extent necessary to avoid immediate and irreparable harm to the estate pending a final hearing.

(3) Notice

Notice of hearing pursuant to this subdivision shall be given to the parties on whom service of the motion is required by paragraph (1) of this subdivision and to such other entities as the court may direct.

(d) Agreement relating to relief from the automatic stay, prohibiting or conditioning the use, sale, or lease of property, providing adequate protection, use of cash collateral, and obtaining credit

(1) Motion; service

(A) Motion

A motion for approval of any of the following shall be accompanied by a copy of the agreement and a proposed form of order:

(i) an agreement to provide adequate protection;

(ii) an agreement to prohibit or condition the use, sale, or lease of property;

(iii) an agreement to modify or terminate the stay provided for in § 362;

(iv) an agreement to use cash collateral; or

(v) an agreement between the debtor and an entity that has a lien or interest in property of the estate pursuant to which the entity consents to the creation of a lien senior or equal to the entity's lien or interest in such property.

---

[1] So in original. Probably should be only one section symbol.

(B) Contents

The motion shall consist of or (if the motion is more than five pages in length) begin with a concise statement of the relief requested, not to exceed five pages, that lists or summarizes, and sets out the location within the relevant documents of, all material provisions of the agreement. In addition, the concise statement shall briefly list or summarize, and identify the specific location of, each provision in the proposed form of order, agreement, or other document of the type listed in subdivision (c)(1)(B). The motion shall also describe the nature and extent of each such provision.

(C) Service

The motion shall be served on: (1) any committee elected under § 705 or appointed under § 1102 of the Code, or its authorized agent, or, if the case is a chapter 9 municipality case or a chapter 11 reorganization case and no committee of unsecured creditors has been appointed under § 1102, on the creditors included on the list filed under Rule 1007(d); and (2) on any other entity the court directs.

(2) Objection

Notice of the motion and the time within which objections may be filed and served on the debtor in possession or trustee shall be mailed to the parties on whom service is required by paragraph (1) of this subdivision and to such other entities as the court may direct. Unless the court fixes a different time, objections may be filed within 14 days of the mailing of the notice.

(3) Disposition; hearing

If no objection is filed, the court may enter an order approving or disapproving the agreement without conducting a hearing. If an objection is filed or if the court determines a hearing is appropriate, the court shall hold a hearing on no less than seven days' notice to the objector, the movant, the parties on whom service is required by paragraph (1) of this subdivision and such other entities as the court may direct.

(4) Agreement in settlement of motion

The court may direct that the procedures prescribed in paragraphs (1), (2), and (3) of this subdivision shall not apply and the agreement may be approved without further notice if the court determines that a motion made pursuant to subdivisions (a), (b), or (c) of this rule was sufficient to afford reasonable notice of the material provisions of the agreement and opportunity for a hearing.

(As amended Mar. 30, 1987, eff. Aug. 1, 1987; Apr. 30, 1991, eff. Aug. 1, 1991; Apr. 29, 1999, eff. Dec. 1, 1999; Apr. 30, 2007, eff. Dec. 1, 2007; Mar. 26, 2009, eff. Dec. 1, 2009; Apr. 28, 2010, eff. Dec. 1, 2010.)

ADVISORY COMMITTEE NOTES

This rule implements § 362 of the Code which sets forth provisions regarding the automatic stay that arises on the filing of a petition. That section and this rule are applicable in chapter 7, 9, 11 and 13 cases. It also implements § 363(c)(2) concerning use of cash collateral.

Subdivision (a) transforms with respect to the automatic stay what was an adversary proceeding under the former rules to motion practice. The Code provides automatic stays in several sections, e.g., §§ 362(a), 1301(a), and in § 362(d) provides some grounds for relief from the stay. This rule specifies that the pleading seeking relief is by means of a motion. Thus the time period in Rule 7012 to answer a complaint would not be applicable and shorter periods may be fixed. Section 362(e) requires the preliminary hearing to be concluded within 30 days of its inception, rendering ordinary complaint and answer practice inappropriate.

This subdivision also makes clear that a motion under Rule 9014 is the proper procedure for a debtor to seek court permission to use cash collateral. See § 363(c)(2). Pursuant to Rule 5005, the motion should be filed in the court in which the case is pending. The court or local rule may specify the persons to be served with the motion for relief from the stay; see Rule 9013.

Subdivision (b) of the rule fills a procedural void left by § 362. Pursuant to § 362(e), the automatic stay is terminated 30 days after a motion for relief is made unless the court continues the stay as a result of a final hearing or, pending final hearing, after a preliminary hearing. If a preliminary hearing is held, § 362(e) requires the final hearing to be commenced within 30 days after the preliminary hearing. Although the expressed legislative intent is to require expeditious resolution of a secured party's motion for relief, § 362 is silent as to the time within which the final hearing must be concluded. Subdivision (b) imposes a 30 day deadline on the court to resolve the dispute.

At the final hearing, the stay is to be terminated, modified, annulled, or conditioned for cause, which includes, inter alia, lack of adequate protection; § 362(d). The burden of proving adequate protection is on the party opposing relief from the stay; § 362(g)(2). Adequate protection is exemplified in § 361.

Subdivision (c) implements § 362(f) which permits ex parte relief from the stay when there will be irreparable damage. This subdivision sets forth the procedure to be followed when relief is sought under § 362(f). It is derived from former Bankruptcy Rule 601(d).

1987 Amendments

The scope of this rule is expanded and the former subdivisions (a), (b) and (c) are now combined in subdivision (a). The new subdivision (a)(2) is amended to conform to the 1984 amendments to § 362(e) of the Code.

Subdivision (b) deals explicitly with the procedures which follow after a motion to use cash collateral is made and served. Filing shall be pursuant to Rule 5005. Service of the motion may be made by any method authorized by Rule 7004 and, if service is by mail, service is complete on mailing. Rule 9006(e). Under subdivision (b)(2), the court may commence a final hearing on the motion within 15 days of service. Rule 9006(f) does not extend this 15 day period when service of the motion is by mail because the party served is not required to act within the 15 day period. In addition to service of the motion, notice of the hearing must be given. Rule 9007 authorizes the court to direct the form and manner of giving notice that is appropriate to the circumstances.

Section 363(c)(3) authorizes the court to conduct a preliminary hearing and to authorize the use of cash collateral "if there is a reasonable likelihood that the trustee will prevail at a final hearing." Subdivision (b)(2) of the rule permits a preliminary hearing to be held earlier than 15 days after service. Any order authorizing the use of cash collateral shall be limited to the amount necessary to protect the estate until a final hearing is held.

The objective of subdivision (b) is to accommodate both the immediate need of the debtor and the interest of the secured creditor in the cash collateral. The time for holding the final hearing may be enlarged beyond the 15 days prescribed when required by the circumstances.

The motion for authority to use cash collateral shall include (1) the amount of cash collateral sought to be used; (2) the name and address of each entity having an interest in the cash collateral; (3) the name and address of the entity in control or having possession of the cash collateral; (4) the facts demonstrating the need to use the cash collateral; and (5) the nature of the protection to be provided those having an interest in the cash collateral. If a preliminary hearing is requested, the motion shall also include the amount of cash collateral sought to be used pending final hearing and the protection to be provided.

Notice of the preliminary and final hearings may be combined. This rule does not limit the authority of the court under § 363(c)(2)(B) and § 102(1).

Subdivision (c) is new. The service, hearing, and notice requirements are similar to those imposed by subdivision (b). The motion to obtain credit shall include the amount and type of the credit to be extended, the name and address of the lender, the terms of the agreement, the need to obtain the credit, and the efforts made to obtain credit from other sources. If the motion is to obtain credit pursuant to § 364(c) or (d), the motion shall describe the collateral, if any, and the protection for any existing interest in the collateral which may be affected by the proposed agreement.

Subdivision (d) is new. In the event the 15 day period for filing objections to the approval of an agreement of the parties described in this subdivision is too long, the parties either may move for a reduction of the period under Rule 9006(c)(1) or proceed under subdivision (b) or (c), if applicable. Rule 9006(c)(1) requires that cause be shown for the reduction of the period in which to object. In applying this criterion the court may consider the option of proceeding under subdivision (b) or (c) and grant a preliminary hearing and relief pending final hearing.

Rule 4001 BANKRUPTCY RULES

1991 Amendments

Subdivision (a) is expanded to include a request to prohibit or condition the use, sale, or lease of property as is necessary to provide adequate protection of a property interest pursuant to § 363(e) of the Code.

Notice of the motion for relief from the automatic stay or to prohibit or condition the use, sale, or lease of property must be served on the entities entitled to receive notice of a motion to approve an agreement pursuant to subdivision (d). If the movant and the adverse party agree to settle the motion and the terms of the agreement do not materially differ from the terms set forth in the movant's motion papers, the court may approve the agreement without further notice pursuant to subdivision (d)(4).

Subdivision (a)(2) is deleted as unnecessary because of § 362(e) of the Code.

Subdivisions (b)(1), (c)(1), and (d)(1) are amended to require service on committees that are elected in chapter 7 cases. Service on committees of retired employees appointed under § 1114 of the Code is not required. These subdivisions are amended further to clarify that, in the absence of a creditors' committee, service on the creditors included on the list filed pursuant to Rule 1007(d) is required only in chapter 9 and chapter 11 cases. The other amendments to subdivision (d)(1) are for consistency of style and are not substantive.

Subdivision (d)(4) is added to avoid the necessity of further notice and delay for the approval of an agreement in settlement of a motion for relief from an automatic stay, to prohibit or condition the use, sale, or lease of property, for use of cash collateral, or for authority to obtain credit if the entities entitled to notice have already received sufficient notice of the scope of the proposed agreement in the motion papers and have had an opportunity to be heard. For example, if a trustee makes a motion to use cash collateral and proposes in the original motion papers to provide adequate protection of the interest of the secured party by granting a lien on certain equipment, and the secured creditor subsequently agrees to terms that are within the scope of those proposed in the motion, the court may enter an order approving the agreement without further notice if the entities that received the original motion papers have had a reasonable opportunity to object to the granting of the motion to use cash collateral.

If the motion papers served under subdivision (a), (b), or (c) do not afford notice sufficient to inform the recipients of the material provisions of the proposed agreement and opportunity for a hearing, approval of the settlement agreement may not be obtained unless the procedural requirements of subdivision (d)(1), (d)(2), and (d)(3) are satisfied. If the 15 day period for filing objections to the approval of the settlement agreement is too long under the particular circumstances of the case, the court may shorten the time for cause under Rule 9006(c)(1).

1999 Amendments

Paragraph (a)(3) is added to provide sufficient time for a party to request a stay pending appeal of an order granting relief from an automatic stay before the order is enforced or implemented. The stay under paragraph (a)(3) is not applicable to orders granted ex parte in accordance with Rule 4001(a)(2).

The stay of the order does not affect the time for filing a notice of appeal in accordance with Rule 8002. While the enforcement and implementation of an order granting relief from the automatic stay is temporarily stayed under paragraph (a)(3), the automatic stay continues to protect the debtor, and the moving party may not foreclose on collateral or take any other steps that would violate the automatic stay.

The court may, in its discretion, order that Rule 4001(a)(3) is not applicable so that the prevailing party may immediately enforce and implement the order granting relief from the automatic stay. Alternatively, the court may order that the stay under Rule 4001(a)(3) is for a fixed period less than 10 days.

2007 Amendments

The rule is amended to require that parties seeking authority to use cash collateral, to obtain credit, and to obtain approval of agreements to provide adequate protection, modify or terminate the stay, or to grant a senior or equal lien on property, submit with those requests a proposed order granting the relief, and that they provide more extensive notice to interested parties of a number of specified terms. The motion must either not exceed five pages in length, or, if it is longer, begin with a concise statement of five pages or less, that summarizes or lists the material provisions and which will assist the court and interested parties in understanding the nature of the relief requested. The concise statement must also set out the location within the documents of the summarized or listed provisions. The parties to agreements and lending offers frequently have concise summaries of their transactions that contain a list of the material provisions of the agreements, even if the agreements themselves are very lengthy. A similar summary should allow the court and interested parties to understand the relief requested.

In addition to the concise statement, the rule requires that motions under subdivisions (c) and (d) state whether the movant is seeking approval of any of the provisions listed in subdivision (c)(1)(B), and where those provisions are located in the documents. The rule is intended to enhance the ability of the court and interested parties to find and evaluate those provisions.

The rule also provides that any motion for authority to obtain credit must identify any provision listed in subdivision (c)(1)(B)(i)-(xi) that is proposed to remain effective if the court grants the motion on an interim basis under Rule 4001 (c)(2), but later denies final relief.

Other amendments are stylistic.

2009 Amendments

The rule is amended to implement changes in connection with the amendment to Rule 9006(a) and the manner by which time is computed under the rules. The deadlines in the rule are amended to substitute a deadline that is a multiple of seven days. Throughout the rules, deadlines are amended in the following manner:

- 5-day periods become 7-day periods
- 10-day periods become 14-day periods
- 15-day periods become 14-day periods
- 20-day periods become 21-day periods
- 25-day periods become 28-day periods

2010 Amendments

Subdivision (d). Subdivision (d) is amended to implement changes in connection with the 2009 amendment to Rule 9006(a) and the manner by which time is computed under the rules. The deadlines in subdivision (d)(2) and (d)(3) are amended to substitute deadlines that are multiples of seven days. Throughout the rules, deadlines have been amended in the following manner:

- 5 day periods become 7 day periods
- 10 day periods become 14 day periods
- 15 day periods become 14 day periods
- 20 day periods become 21 day periods
- 25 day periods become 28 day periods

CROSS REFERENCES

Enlargement of thirty-day period after which stay will expire following commencement of final hearing not permitted, see Fed.Rules Bankr.Proc. Rule 9006, 11 USCA.

Extension of time for trustee to redeem debtor's property, see 11 USCA § 108.

Methods for providing adequate protection, see 11 USCA § 361.

Motions—

For relief from stay filed with court in which case is pending, see Fed.Rules Bankr.Proc. Rule 5005, 11 USCA.

Form and service, see Fed.Rules Bankr.Proc. Rule 9013, 11 USCA.

Signing and verification of papers, see Fed.Rules Bankr.Proc. Rule 9011, 11 USCA.

Stay of actions on claims against, codebtor in individual debt adjustment case, see 11 USCA § 1301.

Rule 4002. Duties of Debtor

(a) In general

In addition to performing other duties prescribed by the Code and rules, the debtor shall:

(1) attend and submit to an examination at the times ordered by the court;

(2) attend the hearing on a complaint objecting to discharge and testify, if called as a witness;

(3) inform the trustee immediately in writing as to the location of real property in which the debtor has an interest and the name and address of every person holding money or property subject to the debtor's withdrawal or order if a schedule of property has not yet been filed pursuant to Rule 1007;

(4) cooperate with the trustee in the preparation of an inventory, the examination of proofs of claim, and the administration of the estate; and

(5) file a statement of any change of the debtor's address.

(b) Individual debtor's duty to provide documentation

(1) **Personal identification**

Every individual debtor shall bring to the meeting of creditors under § 341:

(A) a picture identification issued by a governmental unit, or other personal identifying information that establishes the debtor's identity; and

(B) evidence of social-security number(s), or a written statement that such documentation does not exist.

(2) **Financial information**

Every individual debtor shall bring to the meeting of creditors under § 341, and make available to the trustee, the following documents or copies of them, or provide a written statement that the documentation does not exist or is not in the debtor's possession:

(A) evidence of current income such as the most recent payment advice;

(B) unless the trustee or the United States trustee instructs otherwise, statements for each of the debtor's depository and investment accounts, including checking, savings, and money market accounts, mutual funds and brokerage accounts for the time period that includes the date of the filing of the petition; and

(C) documentation of monthly expenses claimed by the debtor if required by § 707(b)(2)(A) or (B).

(3) **Tax return**

At least 7 days before the first date set for the meeting of creditors under § 341, the debtor shall provide to the trustee a copy of the debtor's federal income tax return for the most recent tax year ending immediately before the commencement of the case and for which a return was filed, including any attachments, or a transcript of the tax return, or provide a written statement that the documentation does not exist.

(4) **Tax returns provided to creditors**

If a creditor, at least 14 days before the first date set for the meeting of creditors under § 341, requests a copy of the debtor's tax return that is to be provided to the trustee under subdivision (b)(3), the debtor, at least 7 days before the first date set for the meeting of creditors under § 341, shall provide to the requesting creditor a copy of the return, including any attachments, or a transcript of the tax return, or provide a written statement that the documentation does not exist.

DEBTOR: DUTIES AND BENEFITS — Rule 4002

(5) Confidentiality of tax information

The debtor's obligation to provide tax returns under Rule 4002(b)(3) and (b)(4) is subject to procedures for safeguarding the confidentiality of tax information established by the Director of the Administrative Office of the United States Courts.

(As amended Mar. 30, 1987, eff. Aug. 1, 1987; Apr. 23, 2008, eff. Dec. 1, 2008; Mar. 26, 2009, eff. Dec. 1, 2009.)

Advisory Committee Notes

This rule should be read together with §§ 343 and 521 of the Code and Rule 1007, all of which impose duties on the debtor. Clause (3) of this rule implements the provisions of Rule 2015(a).

1987 Amendments

New clause (5) of the rule imposes on the debtor the duty to advise the clerk of any change of the debtor's address.

2008 Amendments

This rule is amended to implement § 521(a)(1)(B)(iv) and (e)(2), added to the Code by the 2005 amendments. These Code amendments expressly require the debtor to file with the court, or provide to the trustee, specific documents. The amendments to the rule implement these obligations and establish a time frame for creditors to make requests for a copy of the debtor's Federal income tax return. The rule also requires the debtor to provide documentation in support of claimed expenses under § 707(b)(2)(A) and (B).

Subdivision (b) of the rule is also amended to require the debtor to cooperate with the trustee by providing materials and documents necessary to assist the trustee in the performance of the trustee's duties. Nothing in the rule, however, is intended to limit or restrict the debtor's duties under § 521, or to limit the access of the Attorney General to any information provided by the debtor in the case. Subdivision (b)(2) does not require that the debtor create documents or obtain documents from third parties; rather, the debtor's obligation is to bring to the meeting of creditors under § 341 the documents which the debtor possesses. Under subdivision (b)(2)(B), the trustee or the United States trustee can instruct debtors that they need not provide the documents described in that subdivision. Under subdivisions (b)(3) and (b)(4), the debtor must obtain and provide copies of tax returns or tax transcripts to the appropriate person, unless no such documents exist. Any written statement that the debtor provides indicating either that documents do not exist or are not in the debtor's possession must be verified or contain an unsworn declaration as required under Rule 1008.

Because the amendment implements the debtor's duty to cooperate with the trustee, the materials provided to the trustee would not be made available to any other party in interest at the § 341 meeting of creditors other than the Attorney General. Some of the documents may contain otherwise private information that should not be disseminated. For example, pay stubs and financial account statements might include the social-security numbers of the debtor and the debtor's spouse and dependents, as well as the names of the debtor's children. The debtor should redact all but the last four digits of all social-security numbers and the names of any minors when they appear in these documents. This type of information would not usually be needed by creditors and others who may be attending the meeting. If a creditor perceives a need to review specific documents or other evidence, the creditor may proceed under Rule 2004.

Tax information produced under this rule is subject to procedures for safeguarding confidentiality established by the Director of the Administrative Office of the United States Courts.

2009 Amendments

The rule is amended to implement changes in connection with the amendment to Rule 9006(a) and the manner by which time is computed under the rules. The deadline in the rule is amended to substitute a deadline that is a multiple of seven days. Throughout the rules, deadlines are amended in the following manner:

- 5-day periods become 7-day periods
- 10-day periods become 14-day periods
- 15-day periods become 14-day periods

- 20-day periods become 21-day periods
- 25-day periods become 28-day periods

CROSS REFERENCES

Debtor's duties to—

Appear at meeting of creditors, see 11 USCA § 343.

File list of creditors and assets, cooperate with trustee, and appear at discharge hearing, see 11 USCA § 521.

File lists, schedules, and statements, see Fed.Rules Bankr.Proc. Rule 1007, 11 USCA.

Keep records, make reports, and give notice, see Fed.Rules Bankr.Proc. Rule 2015, 11 USCA.

Immunity from self-incrimination, see 11 USCA § 344.

Rule 4003. Exemptions

(a) Claim of exemptions

A debtor shall list the property claimed as exempt under § 522 of the Code on the schedule of assets required to be filed by Rule 1007. If the debtor fails to claim exemptions or file the schedule within the time specified in Rule 1007, a dependent of the debtor may file the list within 30 days thereafter.

(b) Objecting to a claim of exemptions

(1) Except as provided in paragraphs (2) and (3), a party in interest may file an objection to the list of property claimed as exempt within 30 days after the meeting of creditors held under § 341(a) is concluded or within 30 days after any amendment to the list or supplemental schedules is filed, whichever is later. The court may, for cause, extend the time for filing objections if, before the time to object expires, a party in interest files a request for an extension.

(2) The trustee may file an objection to a claim of exemption at any time prior to one year after the closing of the case if the debtor fraudulently asserted the claim of exemption. The trustee shall deliver or mail the objection to the debtor and the debtor's attorney, and to any person filing the list of exempt property and that person's attorney.

(3) An objection to a claim of exemption based on § 522(q) shall be filed before the closing of the case. If an exemption is first claimed after a case is reopened, an objection shall be filed before the reopened case is closed.

(4) A copy of any objection shall be delivered or mailed to the trustee, the debtor and the debtor's attorney, and the person filing the list and that person's attorney.

(c) Burden of proof

In any hearing under this rule, the objecting party has the burden of proving that the exemptions are not properly claimed. After hearing on notice, the court shall determine the issues presented by the objections.

(d) Avoidance by debtor of transfers of exempt property

A proceeding by the debtor to avoid a lien or other transfer of property exempt under § 522(f) of the Code shall be by motion in accordance with Rule 9014. Notwithstanding the provisions of subdivision (b), a creditor may object to a motion filed under § 522(f) by challenging the validity of the exemption asserted to be impaired by the lien.

(As amended Mar. 30, 1987, eff. Aug. 1, 1987; Apr. 30, 1991, eff. Aug. 1, 1991; Apr. 17, 2000, eff. Dec. 1, 2000; Apr. 23, 2008, eff. Dec. 1, 2008.)

DEBTOR: DUTIES AND BENEFITS Rule 4003

ADVISORY COMMITTEE NOTES

This rule is derived from § 522(l) of the Code and, in part, former Bankruptcy Rule 403. The Code changes the thrust of that rule by making it the burden of the debtor to list his exemptions and the burden of parties in interest to raise objections in the absence of which "the property claimed as exempt on such list is exempt;" § 522(l).

Subdivision (a). While § 522(l) refers to a list of property claimed as exempt, the rule incorporates such a list as part of Official Form No. 6, the schedule of the debtor's assets, rather than requiring a separate list and filing. Rule 1007, to which subdivision (a) refers, requires that schedule to be filed within 15 days after the order for relief, unless the court extends the time.

Section 522(l) also provides that a dependent of the debtor may file the list if the debtor fails to do so. Subdivision (a) of the rule allows such filing from the expiration of the debtor's time until 30 days thereafter. Dependent is defined in § 522(a)(1).

Subdivision (d) provides that a proceeding by the debtor, permitted by § 522(f) of the Code, is a contested matter rather than the more formal adversary proceeding. Proceedings within the scope of this subdivision are distinguished from proceedings brought by the trustee to avoid transfers. The latter are classified as adversary proceedings by Rule 7001.

1991 Amendments

Subdivision (b) is amended to facilitate the filing of objections to exemptions claimed on a supplemental schedule filed under Rule 1007(h).

2000 Amendments

This rule is amended to permit the court to grant a timely request for an extension of time to file objections to the list of claimed exemptions, whether the court rules on the request before or after the expiration of the 30-day period. The purpose of this amendment is to avoid the harshness of the present rule which has been construed to deprive a bankruptcy court of jurisdiction to grant a timely request for an extension if it has failed to rule on the request within the 30-day period. See *In re Laurain*, 113 F.3d 595 (6th Cir. 1997); *Matter of Stoulig*, 45 F.3d 957 (5th Cir. 1995); *In re Brayshaw*, 912 F.2d 1255 (10th Cir. 1990). The amendments clarify that the extension may be granted only for cause. The amendments also conform the rule to § 522(l) of the Code by recognizing that any party in interest may file an objection or request for an extension of time under this rule. Other amendments are stylistic.

2008 Amendments

Subdivision (b) is rewritten to include four paragraphs.

Subdivision (b)(2) is added to the rule to permit the trustee to object to an exemption at any time up to one year after the closing of the case if the debtor fraudulently claimed the exemption. Extending the deadline for trustees to object to an exemption when the exemption claim has been fraudulently made will permit the court to review and, in proper circumstances, deny improperly claimed exemptions, thereby protecting the legitimate interests of creditors and the bankruptcy estate. However, similar to the deadline set in § 727(e) of the Code for revoking a discharge which was fraudulently obtained, an objection to an exemption that was fraudulently claimed must be filed within one year after the closing of the case. Subdivision (b)(2) extends the objection deadline only for trustees.

Subdivision (b)(3) is added to the rule to reflect the addition of subsection (q) to § 522 of the Code by the 2005 Act. Section 522(q) imposes a $136,875 limit on a state homestead exemption if the debtor has been convicted of a felony or owes a debt arising from certain causes of action. Other revised provisions of the Code, such as § 727(a)(12) and § 1328(h), suggest that the court may consider issues relating to § 522(q) late in the case, and the 30-day period for objections would not be appropriate for this provision.

Subdivision (d) is amended to clarify that a creditor with a lien on property that the debtor is attempting to avoid on the grounds that the lien impairs an exemption may raise in defense to the lien avoidance action any objection to the debtor's claimed exemption. The right to object is limited to an objection to the exemption of the property subject to the lien and for purposes of the lien avoidance action only. The creditor may not object to other exemption claims made by the debtor. Those objections, if any, are governed by Rule 4003(b).

Other changes are stylistic.

Rule 4004

BANKRUPTCY RULES

CROSS REFERENCES

Automatic preservation of avoided property transfers for benefit of estate, see 11 USCA § 551.

Enlargement of thirty-day period for filing objections to property claimed as exempt permitted as limited in this rule, see Fed.Rules Bankr.Proc. Rule 9006, 11 USCA.

Motions; form and service, see Fed.Rules Bankr.Proc. Rule 9013, 11 USCA.

Proceedings to avoid transfers of exempt property as nonadversarial proceedings, see Fed.Rules Bankr.Proc. Rule 7001, 11 USCA.

Reduction of time to claim property as exempt by dependent not permitted, see Fed.Rules Bankr.Proc. Rule 9006, 11 USCA.

Right of debtor's redemption of personal property from lien securing dischargeable consumer debt, see 11 USCA § 722.

Rule 4004. Grant or Denial of Discharge

(a) Time for objecting to discharge; notice of time fixed

In a chapter 7 case, a complaint, or a motion under § 727(a)(8) or (a)(9) of the Code, objecting to the debtor's discharge shall be filed no later than 60 days after the first date set for the meeting of creditors under § 341(a). In a chapter 11 case, the complaint shall be filed no later than the first date set for the hearing on confirmation. In a chapter 13 case, a motion objecting to the debtor's discharge under § 1328(f) shall be filed no later than 60 days after the first date set for the meeting of creditors under § 341(a). At least 28 days' notice of the time so fixed shall be given to the United States trustee and all creditors as provided in Rule 2002(f) and (k) and to the trustee and the trustee's attorney.

(b) Extension of Time

(1) On motion of any party in interest, after notice and hearing, the court may for cause extend the time to object to discharge. Except as provided in subdivision (b)(2), the motion shall be filed before the time has expired.

(2) A motion to extend the time to object to discharge may be filed after the time for objection has expired and before discharge is granted if (A) the objection is based on facts that, if learned after the discharge, would provide a basis for revocation under § 727(d) of the Code, and (B) the movant did not have knowledge of those facts in time to permit an objection. The motion shall be filed promptly after the movant discovers the facts on which the objection is based.

(c) Grant of discharge

(1) In a chapter 7 case, on expiration of the times fixed for objecting to discharge and for filing a motion to dismiss the case under Rule 1017(e), the court shall forthwith grant the discharge, except that the court shall not grant the discharge if:

(A) the debtor is not an individual;

(B) a complaint, or a motion under § 727(a)(8) or (a)(9), objecting to the discharge has been filed and not decided in the debtor's favor;

(C) the debtor has filed a waiver under § 727(a)(10);

(D) a motion to dismiss the case under § 707 is pending;

(E) a motion to extend the time for filing a complaint objecting to the discharge is pending;

(F) a motion to extend the time for filing a motion to dismiss the case under Rule 1017(e)(1) is pending;

(G) the debtor has not paid in full the filing fee prescribed by 28 U.S.C. § 1930(a) and any other fee prescribed by the Judicial Conference of the United States under 28

DEBTOR: DUTIES AND BENEFITS Rule 4004

U.S.C. § 1930(b) that is payable to the clerk upon the commencement of a case under the Code, unless the court has waived the fees under 28 U.S.C. § 1930(f);

    (H) the debtor has not filed with the court a statement of completion of a course concerning personal financial management if required by Rule 1007(b)(7);

    (I) a motion to delay or postpone discharge under § 727(a)(12) is pending;

    (J) a motion to enlarge the time to file a reaffirmation agreement under Rule 4008(a) is pending;

    (K) a presumption is in effect under § 524(m) that a reaffirmation agreement is an undue hardship and the court has not concluded a hearing on the presumption; or

    (L) a motion is pending to delay discharge because the debtor has not filed with the court all tax documents required to be filed under § 521(f).

    (2) Notwithstanding Rule 4004(c)(1), on motion of the debtor, the court may defer the entry of an order granting a discharge for 30 days and, on motion within that period, the court may defer entry of the order to a date certain.

    (3) If the debtor is required to file a statement under Rule 1007(b)(8), the court shall not grant a discharge earlier than 30 days after the statement is filed.

    (4) In a chapter 11 case in which the debtor is an individual, or a chapter 13 case, the court shall not grant a discharge if the debtor has not filed any statement required by Rule 1007(b)(7).

(d) Applicability of rules in Part VII and Rule 9014

An objection to discharge is governed by Part VII of these rules, except that an objection to discharge under §§[1] 727(a)(8), (a)(9), or 1328(f) is commenced by motion and governed by Rule 9014.

(e) Order of discharge

An order of discharge shall conform to the appropriate Official Form.

(f) Registration in other districts

An order of discharge that has become final may be registered in any other district by filing a certified copy of the order in the office of the clerk of that district. When so registered the order of discharge shall have the same effect as an order of the court of the district where registered.

(g) Notice of discharge

The clerk shall promptly mail a copy of the final order of discharge to those specified in subdivision (a) of this rule.

(As amended Mar. 30, 1987, eff. Aug. 1, 1987; Apr. 30, 1991, eff. Aug. 1, 1991; Apr. 23, 1996, eff. Dec. 1, 1996; Apr. 29, 1999, eff. Dec. 1, 1999; Apr. 17, 2000, eff. Dec. 1, 2000; Apr. 29, 2002, eff. Dec. 1, 2002; Apr. 23, 2008, eff. Dec. 1, 2008; Mar. 26, 2009, eff. Dec. 1, 2009; Apr. 28, 2010, eff. Dec. 1, 2010; Apr. 26, 2011, eff. Dec. 1, 2011; Apr. 16, 2013, eff. Dec. 1, 2013.)

ADVISORY COMMITTEE NOTES

This rule is adapted from former Bankruptcy Rule 404.

Subdivisions (a) and (b) of this rule prescribe the procedure for determining whether a discharge will be granted pursuant to § 727 of the Code. The time fixed by subdivision (a) may be enlarged as provided in subdivision (b).

The notice referred to in subdivision (a) is required to be given by mail and addressed to creditors as provided in Rule 2002.

An extension granted on a motion pursuant to subdivision (b) of the rule would ordinarily benefit only the movant, but its scope and effect would depend on the terms of the extension.

---

[1] So in original. Probably should be only one section symbol.

Subdivision (c). If a complaint objecting to discharge is filed, the court's grant or denial of the discharge will be entered at the conclusion of the proceeding as a judgment in accordance with Rule 9021. The inclusion of the clause in subdivision (c) qualifying the duty of the court to grant a discharge when a waiver has been filed is in accord with the construction of the Code. 4 Collier, Bankruptcy ¶727.12 (15th ed. 1979).

The last sentence of subdivision (c) takes cognizance of § 524(c) of the Code which authorizes a debtor to enter into enforceable reaffirmation agreements only prior to entry of the order of discharge. Immediate entry of that order after expiration of the time fixed for filing complaints objecting to discharge may render it more difficult for a debtor to settle pending litigation to determine the dischargeability of a debt and execute a reaffirmation agreement as part of a settlement.

Subdivision (d). An objection to discharge is required to be made by a complaint, which initiates an adversary proceeding as provided in Rule 7003. Pursuant to Rule 5005, the complaint should be filed in the court in which the case is pending.

Subdivision (e). Official Form No. 27 to which subdivision (e) refers, includes notice of the effects of a discharge specified in § 524(a) of the Code.

Subdivision (f). Registration may facilitate the enforcement of the order of discharge in a district other than that in which it was entered. See 2 Moore's Federal Practice ¶1.04[2] (2d ed. 1967). Because of the nationwide service of process authorized by Rule 7004, however, registration of the order of discharge is not necessary under these rules to enable a discharged debtor to obtain relief against a creditor proceeding anywhere in the United States in disregard of the injunctive provisions of the order of discharge.

Subdivision (g). Notice of discharge should be mailed promptly after the order becomes final so that creditors may be informed of entry of the order and of its injunctive provisions. Rule 2002 specifies the manner of the notice and persons to whom the notice is to be given.

1991 Amendments

This rule is amended to conform to § 727(c) which gives the United States trustee the right to object to discharge. This amendment is derived from Rule X–1008(a)(1) and is consistent with Rule 2002. The amendment to subdivision (c) is to prevent a timely motion to dismiss a chapter 7 case for substantial abuse from becoming moot merely because a discharge order has been entered. Reference to the Official Form number in subdivision (e) is deleted in anticipation of future revision and renumbering of the Official Forms.

1996 Amendments

Subsection (c) is amended to delay entry of the order of discharge if a motion pursuant to Rule 4004(b) to extend the time for filing a complaint objecting to discharge is pending. Also, this subdivision is amended to delay entry of the discharge order if the debtor has not paid in full the filing fee and the administrative fee required to be paid upon the commencement of the case. If the debtor is authorized to pay the fees in installments in accordance with Rule 1006, the discharge order will not be entered until the final installment has been paid.

The other amendments to this rule are stylistic.

1999 Amendments

Subdivision (a) is amended to clarify that, in a chapter 7 case, the deadline for filing a complaint objecting to discharge under § 727(a) is 60 days after the first date set for the meeting of creditors, whether or not the meeting is held on that date. The time for filing the complaint is not affected by any delay in the commencement or conclusion of the meeting of creditors. This amendment does not affect the right of any party in interest to file a motion for an extension of time to file a complaint objecting to discharge in accordance with Rule 4004(b).

The substitution of the word "filed" for "made" in subdivision (b) is intended to avoid confusion regarding the time when a motion is "made" for the purpose of applying these rules. *See, e.g., In re Coggin*, 30 F.3d 1443 (11th Cir. 1994). As amended, this rule requires that a motion for an extension of time for filing a complaint objecting to discharge be *filed* before the time has expired.

Other amendments to this rule are stylistic.

DEBTOR: DUTIES AND BENEFITS — Rule 4004

2000 Amendments

Subdivision (c) is amended so that a discharge will not be granted while a motion requesting an extension of time to file a motion to dismiss the case under § 707(b) is pending. Other amendments are stylistic.

2002 Amendments

Subdivision (c)(1)(D) is amended to provide that the filing of a motion to dismiss under § 707 of the Bankruptcy Code postpones the entry of the discharge. Under the present version of the rule, only motions to dismiss brought under § 707(b) cause the postponement of the discharge. This amendment would change the result in cases such as *In re Tanenbaum*, 210 B.R. 182 (Bankr. D. Colo. 1997).

2008 Amendments

Subdivision (c)(1)(G) is amended to reflect the fee waiver provision in 28 U.S.C. § 1930, added by the 2005 amendments.

Subdivision (c)(1)(H) is new. It reflects the 2005 addition to the Code of §§ 727(a)(11) and 1328(g), which require that individual debtors complete a course in personal financial management as a condition to the entry of a discharge. Including this requirement in the rule helps prevent the inadvertent entry of a discharge when the debtor has not complied with this requirement. If a debtor fails to file the required statement regarding a personal financial management course, the clerk will close the bankruptcy case without the entry of a discharge.

Subdivision (c)(1)(I) is new. It reflects the 2005 addition to the Code of § 727(a)(12). This provision is linked to § 522(q). Section 522(q) limits the availability of the homestead exemption for individuals who have been convicted of a felony or who owe a debt arising from certain causes of action within a particular time frame. The existence of reasonable cause to believe that § 522(q) may be applicable to the debtor constitutes grounds for withholding the discharge.

Subdivision (c)(1)(J) is new. It accommodates the deadline for filing a reaffirmation agreement established by Rule 4008(a).

Subdivision (c)(1)(K) is new. It reflects the 2005 revisions to § 524 of the Code that alter the requirements for approval of reaffirmation agreements. Section 524(m) sets forth circumstances under which a reaffirmation agreement is presumed to be an undue hardship. This triggers an obligation to review the presumption and may require notice and a hearing. Subdivision (c)(1)(J) has been added to prevent the discharge from being entered until the court approves or disapproves the reaffirmation agreement in accordance with § 524(m).

Subdivision (c)(1)(L) is new. It implements § 1228(a) of Public Law Number 109–8, an uncodified provision of the Bankruptcy Abuse Prevention and Consumer Protection Act of 2005, which prohibits entry of a discharge unless required tax documents have been provided to the court.

Subdivision (c)(3) is new. It postpones the entry of the discharge of an individual debtor in a case under chapter 11, 12, or 13 if there is a question as to the applicability of § 522(q) of the Code. The postponement provides an opportunity for a creditor to file a motion to limit the debtor's exemption under that provision.

Other changes are stylistic.

2009 Amendments

The rule is amended to implement changes in connection with the amendment to Rule 9006(a) and the manner by which time is computed under the rules. The deadline in the rule is amended to substitute a deadline that is a multiple of seven days. Throughout the rules, deadlines are amended in the following manner:

- 5-day periods become 7-day periods
- 10-day periods become 14-day periods
- 15-day periods become 14-day periods
- 20-day periods become 21-day periods
- 25-day periods become 28-day periods

2010 Amendments

Subdivision (a). Subdivision (a) is amended to include a deadline for filing a motion objecting to a debtor's discharge under §§ 727(a)(8), (a)(9), or 1328(f) of the Code. These sections establish time limits on the issuance of discharges in successive bankruptcy cases by the same debtor.

Subdivision (c). Subdivision (c)(1) is amended because a corresponding amendment to subdivision (d) directs certain objections to discharge to be brought by motion rather than by complaint. Subparagraph (c)(1)(B) directs the court not to grant a discharge if a motion or complaint objecting to discharge has been filed unless the objection has been decided in the debtor's favor.

Subdivision (c)(4) is new. It directs the court in chapter 11 and 13 cases to withhold the entry of the discharge if an individual debtor has not filed a statement of completion of a course concerning personal financial management as required by Rule 1007(b)(7).

Subdivision (d). Subdivision (d) is amended to direct that objections to discharge under §§ 727(a)(8), (a)(9), and 1328(f) be commenced by motion rather than by complaint. Objections under the specified provisions are contested matters governed by Rule 9014. The title of the subdivision is also amended to reflect this change.

2011 Amendments

Subdivision (b). Subdivision (b) is amended to allow a party, under certain specified circumstances, to seek an extension of time to object to discharge after the time for filing has expired. This amendment addresses the situation in which there is a gap between the expiration of the time for objecting to discharge and the entry of the discharge order. If, during that period, a party discovers facts that would provide grounds for revocation of discharge, it may not be able to seek revocation under § 727(d) of the Code because the facts would have been known prior to the granting of the discharge. Furthermore, during that period the debtor may commit an act that provides a basis for both denial and revocation of the discharge. In those situations, subdivision (b)(2) allows a party to file a motion for an extension of time to object to discharge based on those facts so long as they were not known to the party before expiration of the deadline for objecting. The motion must be filed promptly after discovery of those facts.

2013 Amendments

Subdivision (c)(1) is amended in several respects. The introductory language of paragraph (1) is revised to emphasize that the listed circumstances do not just relieve the court of the obligation to enter the discharge promptly but that they prevent the court from entering a discharge.

Subdivision (c)(1)(H) is amended to reflect the simultaneous amendment of Rule 1007(b)(7). The amendment of the latter rule relieves a debtor of the obligation to file a statement of completion of a course concerning personal financial management if the course provider notifies the court directly that the debtor has completed the course. Subparagraph (H) now requires postponement of the discharge when a debtor fails to file a statement of course completion only if the debtor has an obligation to file the statement.

Subdivision (c)(1)(K) is amended to make clear that the prohibition on entering a discharge due to a presumption of undue hardship under § 524(m) of the Code ceases when the presumption expires or the court concludes a hearing on the presumption.

Because this amendment is being made to conform to a simultaneous amendment of Rule 1007(b)(7) and is otherwise technical in nature, final approval is sought without publication.

CROSS REFERENCES

Discharge—

    Effect of, see 11 USCA § 524.

    Exceptions to, see 11 USCA § 523.

    Filing complaint to object to discharge, sixty-day period—

        Enlargement permitted as limited in this rule, see Fed.Rules Bankr.Proc. Rule 9006, 11 USCA.

        Reduction not permitted, see Fed.Rules Bankr.Proc. Rule 9006, 11 USCA.

DEBTOR: DUTIES AND BENEFITS   Rule 4005

Motions; form and service, see Fed.Rules Bankr.Proc. Rule 9013, 11 USCA.

Notice by mail—

    Order of discharge, see Fed.Rules Bankr.Proc. Rule 2002, 11 USCA.

    Time fixed to file complaint objecting to discharge, see Fed.Rules Bankr.Proc. Rule 2002, 11 USCA.

Time for filing complaint in reconverted liquidation case revived or extended as under this rule, see Fed.Rules Bankr.Proc. Rule 1019, 11 USCA.

Transfer of claim before or after proof of claim filed, see Fed.Rules Bankr.Proc. Rule 3001, 11 USCA.

Rule 4005. Burden of Proof in Objecting to Discharge

At the trial on a complaint objecting to a discharge, the plaintiff has the burden of proving the objection.

(As amended Mar. 30, 1987, eff. Aug. 1, 1987.)

ADVISORY COMMITTEE NOTES

This rule does not address the burden of going forward with the evidence. Subject to the allocation by the rule of the initial burden of producing evidence and the ultimate burden of persuasion, the rule leaves to the courts the formulation of rules governing the shift of the burden of going forward with the evidence in the light of considerations such as the difficulty of proving the nonexistence of a fact and of establishing a fact as to which the evidence is likely to be more accessible to the debtor than to the objector. See, e.g., In re Haggerty, 165 F.2d 977, 979–80 (2d Cir. 1948); Federal Provision Co. v. Ershowsky, 94 F.2d 574, 575 (2d Cir.1938); In re Riceputo, 41 F.Supp. 926, 927–28 (E.D.N.Y. 1941).

Rule 4006. Notice of No Discharge

If an order is entered: denying a discharge; revoking a discharge; approving a waiver of discharge; or, in the case of an individual debtor, closing the case without the entry of a discharge, the clerk shall promptly notify all parties in interest in the manner provided by Rule 2002.

(As amended Mar. 30, 1987, eff. Aug. 1, 1987; Apr. 23, 2008, eff. Dec. 1, 2008.)

ADVISORY COMMITTEE NOTES

The suspension by § 108(c) of the Code of the statute of limitations affecting any debt of a debtor terminates within 30 days after the debtor is denied a discharge or otherwise loses his right to a discharge. If, however, a debtor's failure to receive a discharge does not come to the attention of his creditors until after the statutes of limitations have run, the debtor obtains substantially the same benefits from his bankruptcy as a debtor who is discharged.

This rule requires the clerk to notify creditors if a debtor fails to obtain a discharge because a waiver of discharge was filed under § 727(a)(10) or as a result of an order denying or revoking the discharge under § 727(a) or (d).

2008 Amendments

This amendment was necessary because the 2005 amendments to the Code require that individual debtors in a chapter 7 or 13 case complete a course in personal financial management as a condition to the entry of a discharge. If the debtor fails to complete the course, the case may be closed and no discharge will be entered. Reopening the case is governed by § 350 and Rule 5010. The rule is amended to provide notice to parties in interest, including the debtor, that no discharge was entered.

CROSS REFERENCES

Notice by mail, see Fed.Rules Bankr.Proc. Rule 2002, 11 USCA.

Suspension of statute of limitations on debts of debtor, see 11 USCA § 108.

Rule 4007. Determination of Dischargeability of a Debt

(a) Persons entitled to file complaint

A debtor or any creditor may file a complaint to obtain a determination of the dischargeability of any debt.

(b) Time for commencing proceeding other than under § 523(c) of the Code

A complaint other than under § 523(c) may be filed at any time. A case may be reopened without payment of an additional filing fee for the purpose of filing a complaint to obtain a determination under this rule.

(c) Time for filing complaint under § 523(c) in a chapter 7 liquidation, chapter 11 reorganization, chapter 12 family farmer's debt adjustment case, or chapter 13 individual's debt adjustment case; notice of time fixed

Except as otherwise provided in subdivision (d), a complaint to determine the dischargeability of a debt under § 523(c) shall be filed no later than 60 days after the first date set for the meeting of creditors under § 341(a). The court shall give all creditors no less than 30 days' notice of the time so fixed in the manner provided in Rule 2002. On motion of a party in interest, after hearing on notice, the court may for cause extend the time fixed under this subdivision. The motion shall be filed before the time has expired.

(d) Time for filing complaint under § 523(a)(6) in a chapter 13 individual's debt adjustment case; notice of time fixed

On motion by a debtor for a discharge under § 1328(b), the court shall enter an order fixing the time to file a complaint to determine the dischargeability of any debt under § 523(a)(6) and shall give no less than 30 days' notice of the time fixed to all creditors in the manner provided in Rule 2002. On motion of any party in interest, after hearing on notice, the court may for cause extend the time fixed under this subdivision. The motion shall be filed before the time has expired.

(e) Applicability of Rules in Part VII

A proceeding commenced by a complaint filed under this rule is governed by Part VII of these rules.

(As amended Mar. 30, 1987, eff. Aug. 1, 1987; Apr. 30, 1991, eff. Aug. 1, 1991; Apr. 29, 1999, eff. Dec. 1, 1999; Apr. 23, 2008, eff. Dec. 1, 2008.)

ADVISORY COMMITTEE NOTES

This rule prescribes the procedure to be followed when a party requests the court to determine dischargeability of a debt pursuant to § 523 of the Code.

Although a complaint that comes within § 523(c) must ordinarily be filed before determining whether the debtor will be discharged, the court need not determine the issues presented by the complaint filed under this rule until the question of discharge has been determined under Rule 4004. A complaint filed under this rule initiates an adversary proceeding as provided in Rule 7003.

Subdivision (b) does not contain a time limit for filing a complaint to determine the dischargeability of a type of debt listed as nondischargeable under § 523(a)(1), (3), (5), (7), (8), or (9). Jurisdiction over this issue on these debts is held concurrently by the bankruptcy court and any appropriate nonbankruptcy forum.

Subdivision (c) differs from subdivision (b) by imposing a deadline for filing complaints to determine the issue of dischargeability of debts set out in § 523(a)(2), (4) or (6) of the Code. The bankruptcy court has exclusive jurisdiction to determine dischargeability of these debts. If a complaint is not timely filed, the debt is discharged. See § 523(c).

Subdivision (e). The complaint required by this subdivision should be filed in the court in which the case is pending pursuant to Rule 5005.

DEBTOR: DUTIES AND BENEFITS — Rule 4008

1991 Amendments

Subdivision (a) is amended to delete the words "with the court" as unnecessary. See Rules 5005(a) and 9001(3).

Subdivision (c) is amended to apply in chapter 12 cases the same time period that applies in chapter 7 and 11 cases for filing a complaint under § 523(c) of the Code to determine dischargeability of certain debts. Under § 1228(a) of the Code, a chapter 12 discharge does not discharge the debts specified in § 523(a) of the Code.

1999 Amendments

Subdivision (c) is amended to clarify that the deadline for filing a complaint to determine the dischargeability of a debt under § 523(c) of the Code is 60 days after the first date set for the meeting of creditors, whether or not the meeting is held on that date. The time for filing the complaint is not affected by any delay in the commencement or conclusion of the meeting of creditors. This amendment does not affect the right of any party in interest to file a motion for an extension of time to file a complaint to determine the dischargeability of a debt in accordance with this rule.

The substitution of the word "filed" for "made" in the final sentences of subdivisions (c) and (d) is intended to avoid confusion regarding the time when a motion is "made" for the purpose of applying these rules. *See, e.g., In re Coggin*, 30 F.3d 1443 (11th Cir. 1994). As amended, these subdivisions require that a motion for an extension of time be *filed* before the time has expired.

The other amendments to this rule are stylistic.

2008 Amendments

Subdivision (c) is amended because of the 2005 amendments to § 1328(a) of the Code. This revision expands the exceptions to discharge upon completion of a chapter 13 plan. Subdivision (c) extends to chapter 13 the same time limits applicable to other chapters of the Code with respect to the two exceptions to discharge that have been added to § 1328(a) and that are within § 523(c).

The amendment to subdivision (d) reflects the 2005 amendments to § 1328(a) that expands the exceptions to discharge upon completion of a chapter 13 plan, including two out of three of the provisions that fall within § 523(c). However, the 2005 revisions to § 1328(a) do not include a reference to § 523(a)(6), which is the third provision to which § 523(c) refers. Thus, subdivision (d) is now limited to that provision.

CROSS REFERENCES

Costs and attorney fees to consumer debtor upon discharge of debt, see 11 USCA § 523.

Effect of dismissal on dischargeability of debt, see 11 USCA § 349.

Filing complaint to determine dischargeability of debt, sixty-day period—

> Enlargement permitted as limited in this rule, see Fed.Rules Bankr.Proc. Rule 9006, 11 USCA.

> Reduction not permitted, see Fed.Rules Bankr.Proc. Rule 9006, 11 USCA.

> Motions; form and service, see Fed.Rules Bankr.Proc. Rule 9013, 11 USCA.

> Notice by mail of time fixed to file complaint, see Fed.Rules Bankr.Proc. Rule 2002, 11 USCA.

Time for filing complaint in reconverted liquidation case revived or extended as under this rule, see Fed.Rules Bankr.Proc. Rule 1019, 11 USCA.

Rule 4008. Filing of Reaffirmation Agreement; Statement in Support of Reaffirmation Agreement

(a) Filing of reaffirmation agreement

A reaffirmation agreement shall be filed no later than 60 days after the first date set for the meeting of creditors under § 341(a) of the Code. The reaffirmation agreement shall be accompanied by a cover sheet, prepared as prescribed by the appropriate Official Form. The court may, at any time and in its discretion, enlarge the time to file a reaffirmation agreement.

(b) Statement in support of reaffirmation agreement

Rule 4008

The debtor's statement required under § 524(k)(6)(A) of the Code shall be accompanied by a statement of the total income and expenses stated on schedules I and J. If there is a difference between the total income and expenses stated on those schedules and the statement required under § 524(k)(6)(A), the statement required by this subdivision shall include an explanation of the difference.

(As amended Apr. 30, 1991, eff. Aug. 1, 1991; Apr. 23, 2008, eff. Dec. 1, 2008; Mar. 26, 2009, eff. Dec. 1, 2009.)

ADVISORY COMMITTEE NOTES

Section 524(d) of the Code requires the court to hold a hearing to inform an individual debtor concerning the granting or denial of discharge and the law applicable to reaffirmation agreements.

The notice of the § 524(d) hearing may be combined with the notice of the meeting of creditors or entered as a separate order.

The expression "not more than" contained in the first sentence of the rule is for the explicit purpose of requiring the hearing to occur within that time period and cannot be extended.

1991 Amendments

This rule is changed to conform to § 524(d) of the Code as amended in 1986. A hearing under § 524(d) is not mandatory unless the debtor desires to enter into a reaffirmation agreement.

2008 Amendments

This rule is amended to establish a deadline for filing reaffirmation agreements. The Code sets out a number of prerequisites to the enforceability of reaffirmation agreements. Among those requirements, § 524(k)(6)(A) provides that each reaffirmation agreement must be accompanied by a statement indicating the debtor's ability to make the payments called for by the agreement. In the event that this statement reflects an insufficient income to allow payment of the reaffirmed debt, § 524(m) provides that a presumption of undue hardship arises, allowing the court to disapprove the reaffirmation agreement, but only after a hearing conducted prior to the entry of discharge. Rule 4004(c)(1)(K) accommodates this provision by delaying the entry of discharge where a presumption of undue hardship arises. However, in order for that rule to be effective, the reaffirmation agreement itself must be filed before the entry of discharge. Under Rule 4004(c)(1) discharge is to be entered promptly after the expiration of the time for filing a complaint objecting to discharge, which, under Rule 4004(a), is 60 days after the first date set for the meeting of creditors under § 341(a). Accordingly, that date is set as the deadline for filing a reaffirmation agreement.

Any party may file the agreement with the court. Thus, whichever party has a greater incentive to enforce the agreement usually will file it. In the event that the parties are unable to file a reaffirmation agreement in a timely fashion, the rule grants the court broad discretion to permit a late filing. A corresponding change to Rule 4004(c)(1)(J) accommodates such an extension by providing for a delay in the entry of discharge during the pendency of a motion to extend the time for filing a reaffirmation agreement.

Rule 4008 is also amended by deleting provisions regarding the timing of any reaffirmation and discharge hearing. As noted above, § 524(m) itself requires that hearings on undue hardship be conducted prior to the entry of discharge. In other respects, including hearings to approve reaffirmation agreements of unrepresented debtors under § 524(c)(6), the rule leaves discretion to the court to set the hearing at a time appropriate for the particular circumstances presented in the case and consistent with the scheduling needs of the parties.

2009 Amendments

Subdivision (a) of the rule is amended to require that the entity filing the reaffirmation agreement with the court also include Official Form 27, the Reaffirmation Agreement Cover Sheet. The form includes information necessary for the court to determine whether the proposed reaffirmation agreement is presumed to be an undue hardship for the debtor under § 524(m) of the Code.

CROSS REFERENCES

Confirmation of reorganization plan, see Fed.Rules Bankr.Proc. Rule 3020, 11 USCA.

Motions; form and service, see Fed.Rules Bankr.Proc. Rule 9013, 11 USCA.

PART V—BANKRUPTCY COURTS AND CLERKS

Rule
5001. Courts and Clerks' Offices.
5002. Restrictions on Appointments.
5003. Records Kept by the Clerk.
5004. Disqualification.
5005. Filing and Transmittal of Papers.
5006. Certification of Copies of Papers.
5007. Record of Proceedings and Transcripts.
5008. Notice Regarding Presumption of Abuse in Chapter 7 Cases of Individual Debtors.
5009. Closing Chapter 7 Liquidation, Chapter 12 Family Farmer's Debt Adjustment, Chapter 13 Individual's Debt Adjustment, and Chapter 15 Ancillary and Cross-Border Cases.
5010. Reopening Cases.
5011. Withdrawal and Abstention From Hearing a Proceeding.
5012. Agreements Concerning Coordination of Proceedings in Chapter 15 Cases.

Rule 5001. Courts and Clerks' Offices

(a) Courts always open

The courts shall be deemed always open for the purpose of filing any pleading or other proper paper, issuing and returning process, and filing, making, or entering motions, orders and rules.

(b) Trials and hearings; orders in chambers

All trials and hearings shall be conducted in open court and so far as convenient in a regular court room. Except as otherwise provided in 28 U.S.C. § 152(c), all other acts or proceedings may be done or conducted by a judge in chambers and at any place either within or without the district; but no hearing, other than one ex parte, shall be conducted outside the district without the consent of all parties affected thereby.

(c) Clerk's office

The clerk's office with the clerk or a deputy in attendance shall be open during business hours on all days except Saturdays, Sundays and the legal holidays listed in Rule 9006(a).

(As amended Mar. 30, 1987, eff. Aug. 1, 1987; Apr. 30, 1991, eff. Aug. 1, 1991; Apr. 23, 2008, eff. Dec. 1, 2008.)

ADVISORY COMMITTEE NOTES

This rule is adapted from subdivisions (a), (b) and (c) of Rule 77 F.R.Civ.P.

1987 Amendments

Rule 9001, as amended, defines court to mean the bankruptcy judge or district judge before whom a case or proceeding is pending. Clerk means the bankruptcy clerk, if one has been appointed for the district; if a bankruptcy clerk has not been appointed, clerk means clerk of the district court.

1991 Amendments

Subdivision (c) is amended to refer to Rule 9006(a) for a list of legal holidays. Reference to F.R.Civ.P. is not necessary for this purpose.

2008 Amendments

The rule is amended to permit bankruptcy judges to hold hearings outside of the district in which the case is pending to the extent that the circumstances lead to the authorization of the court to take such action under the 2005 amendment to 28 U.S.C. § 152(c). Under that provision, bankruptcy judges may hold court outside of their districts in emergency situations and when the business of the court otherwise so requires. This amendment to the rule is intended to implement the legislation.

CROSS REFERENCES

Legal holiday defined, see Fed.Rules Bankr.Proc. Rule 9006, 11 USCA.

Rule 5002. Restrictions on Appointments

(a) Approval of appointment of relatives prohibited

The appointment of an individual as a trustee or examiner pursuant to § 1104 of the Code shall not be approved by the court if the individual is a relative of the bankruptcy judge approving the appointment or the United States trustee in the region in which the case is pending. The employment of an individual as attorney, accountant, appraiser, auctioneer, or other professional person pursuant to §§ 327, 1103, or 1114 shall not be approved by the court if the individual is a relative of the bankruptcy judge approving the employment. The employment of an individual as attorney, accountant, appraiser, auctioneer, or other professional person pursuant to §§ 327, 1103, or 1114 may be approved by the court if the individual is a relative of the United States trustee in the region in which the case is pending, unless the court finds that the relationship with the United States trustee renders the employment improper under the circumstances of the case. Whenever under this subdivision an individual may not be approved for appointment or employment, the individual's firm, partnership, corporation, or any other form of business association or relationship, and all members, associates and professional employees thereof also may not be approved for appointment or employment.

(b) Judicial determination that approval of appointment or employment is improper

A bankruptcy judge may not approve the appointment of a person as a trustee or examiner pursuant to § 1104 of the Code or approve the employment of a person as an attorney, accountant, appraiser, auctioneer, or other professional person pursuant to §§ 327, 1103, or 1114 of the Code if that person is or has been so connected with such judge or the United States trustee as to render the appointment or employment improper.

(As amended Apr. 29, 1985, eff. Aug. 1, 1985; Apr. 30, 1991, eff. Aug. 1, 1991.)

ADVISORY COMMITTEE NOTES

This rule is adapted from former Bankruptcy Rule 505(a). The scope of the prohibition on appointment or employment is expanded to include an examiner appointed under § 1104 of the Code and attorneys and other professional persons whose employment must be approved by the court under § 327 or § 1103.

The rule supplements two statutory provisions. Under 18 U.S.C. § 1910, it is a criminal offense for a judge to appoint a relative as a trustee and, under 28 U.S.C. § 458, a person may not be "appointed to or employed in any office or duty in any court" if he is a relative of any judge of that court. The rule prohibits the appointment or employment of a relative of a bankruptcy judge in a case pending before that bankruptcy judge or before other bankruptcy judges sitting within the district.

A relative is defined in § 101(34) of the Code to be an "individual related by affinity or consanguinity within the third degree as determined by the common law, or individual in a step or adoptive relationship within such third degree." Persons within the third degree under the common law system are as follows: first degree—parents, brothers and sisters, and children; second degree—grandparents, uncles and aunts, first cousins, nephews and nieces, and grandchildren; third degree—great grandparents, great uncles and aunts, first cousins once removed, second cousins, grand nephews and nieces, great grandchildren. Rule 9001 incorporates the definitions of § 101 of the Code.

In order for the policy of this rule to be meaningfully implemented, it is necessary to extend the prohibition against appointment or employment to the firm or other business association of the ineligible person and to those affiliated with the firm or business association. "Firm" is defined in Rule 9001 to include a professional partnership or corporation of attorneys or accountants. All other types of business and professional associations and relationships are covered by this rule.

1985 Amendments

The amended rule is divided into two subdivisions. Subdivision (a) applies to relatives of bankruptcy judges and subdivision (b) applies to persons who are or have been connected with bankruptcy judges. Subdivision (a) permits no judicial discretion; subdivision (b) allows judicial discretion. In both subdivisions of the amended rule "bankruptcy judge" has been substituted for "judge." The amended rule makes clear that it only applies to relatives of, or persons connected with, the bankruptcy judge. *See In re Hilltop Sand and Gravel, Inc.*, 35 B.R. 412 (N.D.Ohio 1983).

Subd. (a). The original rule prohibited all bankruptcy judges in a district from appointing or approving the employment of (i) a relative of any bankruptcy judge serving in the district, (ii) the firm or business association of any ineligible relative and (iii) any member or professional employee of the firm or business association of an ineligible relative. In addition, the definition of relative, the third degree relationship under the common law, is quite broad. The restriction on the employment opportunities of relatives of bankruptcy judges was magnified by the fact that many law and accounting firms have practices and offices spanning the nation.

Relatives are not eligible for appointment or employment when the bankruptcy judge to whom they are related makes the appointment or approves the employment. Canon 3(b)(4) of the Code of Judicial Conduct, which provides that the judge "shall exercise his power of appointment only on the basis of merit, avoiding nepotism and favoritism," should guide a bankruptcy judge when a relative of a judge of the same bankruptcy court is considered for appointment or employment.

Subd. (b), derived from clause (2) of the original rule, makes a person ineligible for appointment or employment if the person is so connected with a bankruptcy judge making the appointment or approving the employment as to render the appointment or approval of employment improper. The caption and text of the subdivision emphasize that application of the connection test is committed to the sound discretion of the bankruptcy judge who is to make the appointment or approve the employment. All relevant circumstances are to be taken into account by the court. The most important of those circumstances include: the nature and duration of the connection with the bankruptcy judge; whether the connection still exists, and, if not, when it was terminated; and the type of appointment or employment. These and other considerations must be carefully evaluated by the bankruptcy judge.

The policy underlying subdivision (b) is essentially the same as the policy embodied in the Code of Judicial Conduct. Canon 2 of the Code of Judicial Conduct instructs a judge to avoid impropriety and the appearance of impropriety, and Canon 3(b)(4) provides that the judge "should exercise his power of appointment only on the basis of merit, avoiding nepotism and favoritism." Subdivision (b) alerts the potential appointee or employee and party seeking approval of employment to consider the possible relevance or impact of subdivision (b) and indicates to them that appropriate disclosure must be made to the bankruptcy court before accepting appointment or employment. The information required may be made a part of the application for approval of employment. See Rule 2014(a).

Subdivision (b) departs from the former rule in an important respect: a firm or business association is not prohibited from appointment or employment merely because an individual member or employee of the firm or business association is ineligible under subdivision (b).

The emphasis given to the bankruptcy court's judicial discretion in applying subdivision (b) and the absence of a *per se* extension of ineligibility to the firm or business association or any ineligible individual complement the amendments to subdivision (a). The change is intended to moderate the prior limitation on the employment opportunities of attorneys, accountants and other professional persons who are or who have been connected in some way with the bankruptcy judge. For example, in all but the most unusual situations service as a law clerk to a bankruptcy judge is not the type of connection which alone precludes appointment or employment. Even if a bankruptcy judge determines that it is improper to appoint or approve the employment of a former law clerk in the period immediately after completion of the former law clerk's service with the judge, the firm which employs the former law clerk will, absent other circumstances, be eligible for employment. In each instance all the facts must be considered by the bankruptcy judge.

Subdivision (b) applies to persons connected with a bankruptcy judge. "Person" is defined in § 101 of the Bankruptcy Code to include an "individual, partnership and corporation." A partnership or corporation may be appointed or employed to serve in a bankruptcy case. If a bankruptcy judge is connected in some way with a partnership or corporation, it is necessary for the court to determine whether the appointment or employment of that partnership or corporation is proper.

The amended rule does not regulate professional relationships which do not require approval of a bankruptcy judge. Disqualification of the bankruptcy judge pursuant to 28 U.S.C. § 455 may, however, be appropriate. Under Rule 5004(a), a bankruptcy judge may find that disqualification from only some aspect of the case, rather than the entire case, is necessary. A situation may also arise in which the disqualifying circumstance only comes to light after services have been performed. Rule 5004(b) provides that if compensation from the estate is sought for these services, the bankruptcy judge is disqualified from awarding compensation.

Rule 5003   BANKRUPTCY RULES

1991 Amendments

The 1986 amendments to the Code provide that the United States trustee shall appoint trustees in chapter 7, chapter 12, and chapter 13 cases without the necessity of court approval. This rule is not intended to apply to the appointment of trustees in those cases because it would be inappropriate for a court rule to restrict in advance the exercise of discretion by the executive branch. See COMMITTEE NOTE to Rule 2009.

In chapter 11 cases, a trustee or examiner is appointed by the United States trustee after consultation with parties in interest and subject to court approval. Subdivision (a), as amended, prohibits the approval of the appointment of an individual as a trustee or examiner if the person is a relative of the United States trustee making the appointment or the bankruptcy judge approving the appointment.

The United States trustee neither appoints nor approves the employment of professional persons employed pursuant to §§ 327, 1103, or 1114 of the Code. Therefore, subdivision (a) is not a prohibition against judicial approval of employment of a professional person who is a relative of the United States trustee. However, the United States trustee monitors applications for compensation and reimbursement of expenses and may raise, appear and be heard on issues in the case. Employment of relatives of the United States trustee may be approved unless the court finds, after considering the relationship and the particular circumstances of the case, that the relationship would cause the employment to be improper. As used in this rule, "improper" includes the appearance of impropriety.

United States trustee is defined to include a designee or assistant United States trustee. See Rule 9001. Therefore, subdivision (a) is applicable if the person appointed as trustee or examiner or the professional to be employed is a relative of a designee of the United States trustee or any assistant United States trustee in the region in which the case is pending.

This rule is not exclusive of other laws or rules regulating ethical conduct. See, e.g., 28 CFR § 45.735–5.

CROSS REFERENCES

Appointment of trustee or examiner, see 11 USCA § 1104.

Definition of relative, see 11 USCA § 101.

Nepotism in appointment of receiver or trustee, see 18 USCA § 1910.

Relative of justice or judge ineligible to appointment, see 28 USCA § 458.

Rule 5003. Records Kept by the Clerk

(a) Bankruptcy dockets

The clerk shall keep a docket in each case under the Code and shall enter thereon each judgment, order, and activity in that case as prescribed by the Director of the Administrative Office of the United States Courts. The entry of a judgment or order in a docket shall show the date the entry is made.

(b) Claims register

The clerk shall keep in a claims register a list of claims filed in a case when it appears that there will be a distribution to unsecured creditors.

(c) Judgments and orders

The clerk shall keep, in the form and manner as the Director of the Administrative Office of the United States Courts may prescribe, a correct copy of every final judgment or order affecting title to or lien on real property or for the recovery of money or property, and any other order which the court may direct to be kept. On request of the prevailing party, a correct copy of every judgment or order affecting title to or lien upon real or personal property or for the recovery of money or property shall be kept and indexed with the civil judgments of the district court.

(d) Index of cases; certificate of search

The clerk shall keep indices of all cases and adversary proceedings as prescribed by the Director of the Administrative Office of the United States Courts. On request, the clerk shall make a search of any index and papers in the clerk's custody and certify whether a case or proceeding has been filed in or transferred to the court or if a discharge has been entered in its records.

(e) Register of mailing addresses of federal and state governmental units and certain taxing authorities

The United States or the state or territory in which the court is located may file a statement designating its mailing address. The United States, state, territory, or local governmental unit responsible for collecting taxes within the district in which the case is pending may also file a statement designating an address for service of requests under § 505(b) of the Code, and the designation shall describe where further information concerning additional requirements for filing such requests may be found. The clerk shall keep, in the form and manner as the Director of the Administrative Office of the United States Courts may prescribe, a register that includes the mailing addresses designated under the first sentence of this subdivision, and a separate register of the addresses designated for the service of requests under § 505(b) of the Code. The clerk is not required to include in any single register more than one mailing address for each department, agency, or instrumentality of the United States or the state or territory. If more than one address for a department, agency, or instrumentality is included in the register, the clerk shall also include information that would enable a user of the register to determine the circumstances when each address is applicable, and mailing notice to only one applicable address is sufficient to provide effective notice. The clerk shall update the register annually, effective January 2 of each year. The mailing address in the register is conclusively presumed to be a proper address for the governmental unit, but the failure to use that mailing address does not invalidate any notice that is otherwise effective under applicable law.

(f) Other books and records of the clerk

The clerk shall keep any other books and records required by the Director of the Administrative Office of the United States Courts.

(As amended Mar. 30, 1987, eff. Aug. 1, 1987; Apr. 17, 2000, Dec. 1, 2000; Apr. 23, 2008, eff. Dec. 1, 2008.)

ADVISORY COMMITTEE NOTES

This rule consolidates former Bankruptcy Rules 504 and 507. The record-keeping duties of the referee under former Bankruptcy Rule 504 are transferred to the clerk. Subdivisions (a), (c), (d) and (e) are similar to subdivisions (a)–(d) of Rule 79 F.R.Civ.P.

Subdivision (b) requires that filed claims be listed on a claims register only when there may be a distribution to unsecured creditors. Compilation of the list for no asset or nominal asset cases would serve no purpose.

Rule 2013 requires the clerk to maintain a public record of fees paid from the estate and an annual summary thereof.

Former Bankruptcy Rules 507(d) and 508, which made materials in the clerk's office and files available to the public, are not necessary because § 107 of the Code guarantees public access to files and dockets of cases under the Code.

1987 Amendments

Subdivision (a) has been made more specific.

Subdivision (c) is amended to require that on the request of the prevailing party the clerk of the district court shall keep and index bankruptcy judgments and orders affecting title to or lien upon real or personal property or for the recovery of money or property with the civil judgments of the district court. This requirement is derived from former Rule 9021(b). The Director of the Administrative Office will provide guidance to the bankruptcy and district court clerks regarding appropriate paperwork and retention procedures.

2000 Amendments

Subdivision (e) is added to provide a source where debtors, their attorneys, and other parties may go to determine whether the United States or the state or territory in which the court is located has filed a statement designating a mailing address for notice purposes. By using the address in the register—which must be available to the public—the sender is assured that the mailing address is proper. But the use of

Rule 5004   BANKRUPTCY RULES

an address that differs from the address included in the register does not invalidate the notice if it is otherwise effective under applicable law.

The register may include a separate mailing address for each department, agency, or instrumentality of the United States or the state or territory. This rule does not require that addresses of municipalities or other local governmental units be included in the register, but the clerk may include them.

Although it is important for the register to be kept current, debtors, their attorneys, and other parties should be able to rely on mailing addresses listed in the register without the need to continuously inquire as to new or amended addresses. Therefore, the clerk must update the register, but only once each year.

To avoid unnecessary cost and burden on the clerk and to keep the register a reasonable length, the clerk is not required to include more than one mailing address for a particular agency, department, or instrumentality of the United States or the state or territory. But if more than one address is included, the clerk is required to include information so that a person using the register could determine when each address should be used. In any event, the inclusion of more than one address for a particular department, agency, or instrumentality does not impose on a person sending a notice the duty to send it to more than one address.

2008 Amendments

The rule is amended to implement § 505(b)(1) of the Code added by the 2005 amendments, which allows a taxing authority to designate an address to use for the service of requests under that subsection. Under the amendment, the clerk is directed to maintain a separate register for mailing addresses of governmental units solely for the service of requests under § 505(b). This register is in addition to the register of addresses of governmental units already maintained by the clerk. The clerk is required to keep only one address for a governmental unit in each register.

CROSS REFERENCES

Books and records kept by Clerk and entries therein, see Fed.Rules Civ.Proc. Rule 79, 28 USCA.

Judgment effective when entered as provided in this rule, see Fed.Rules Bankr.Proc. Rule 9021, 11 USCA.

Public access to case dockets, see 11 USCA § 107.

Public record of estate fees to be kept by clerk, see Fed.Rules Bankr.Proc. Rule 2013, 11 USCA.

Rule 5004. Disqualification

(a) Disqualification of judge

A bankruptcy judge shall be governed by 28 U.S.C. § 455, and disqualified from presiding over the proceeding or contested matter in which the disqualifying circumstances[1] arises or, if appropriate, shall be disqualified from presiding over the case.

(b) Disqualification of judge from allowing compensation

A bankruptcy judge shall be disqualified from allowing compensation to a person who is a relative of the bankruptcy judge or with whom the judge is so connected as to render it improper for the judge to authorize such compensation.

(As amended Apr. 29, 1985, eff. Aug. 1, 1985; Mar. 30, 1987, eff. Aug. 1, 1987.)

ADVISORY COMMITTEE NOTES

Subdivision (a). Disqualification of a bankruptcy judge is governed by 28 U.S.C. § 455. That section provides that the judge "shall disqualify himself in any proceeding in which his impartiality might reasonably be questioned" or under certain other circumstances. In a case under the Code it is possible that the disqualifying circumstance will be isolated to an adversary proceeding or contested matter. The

---

[1] So in original. Probably should be "circumstance".

rule makes it clear that when the disqualifying circumstance is limited in that way the judge need only disqualify himself from presiding over that adversary proceeding or contested matter.

It is possible, however, that even if the disqualifying circumstance arises in connection with an adversary proceeding, the effect will be so pervasive that disqualification from presiding over the case is appropriate. This distinction is consistent with the definition of "proceeding" in 28 U.S.C. § 455(d)(1).

Subdivision (b) precludes a bankruptcy judge from allowing compensation from the estate to a relative or other person closely associated with the judge. The subdivision applies where the judge has not appointed or approved the employment of the person requesting compensation. Perhaps the most frequent application of the subdivision will be in the allowance of administrative expenses under § 503(b)(3) to (5) of the Code. For example, if an attorney or accountant is retained by an indenture trustee who thereafter makes a substantial contribution in a chapter 11 case, the attorney or accountant may seek compensation under § 503(b)(4). If the attorney or accountant is a relative of or associated with the bankruptcy judge, the judge may not allow compensation to the attorney or accountant. Section 101(34) defines relative and Rule 9001 incorporates the definitions of the Code. See the Advisory Committee's Note to Rule 5002.

1987 Amendments

The rule is amended to be gender neutral. The bankruptcy judge before whom the matter is pending determines whether disqualification is required.

1985 Amendments

Subdivision (a) was affected by the Bankruptcy Amendments and Federal Judgeship Act of 1984, P.L. 98–353, 98 Stat. 333. The 1978 Bankruptcy Reform Act, P.L. 95–598, included bankruptcy judges in the definition of United States judges in 28 U.S.C. § 451 and they were therefore subject to the provisions of 28 U.S.C. § 455. This was to become effective on April 1, 1984, P.L. 95–598, § 404(b). Section 113 of P.L. 98–353, however, appears to have rendered the amendment to 28 U.S.C. § 451 ineffective. Subdivision (a) of the rule retains the substance and intent of the earlier draft by making bankruptcy judges subject to 28 U.S.C. § 455.

The word "associated" in subdivision (b) has been changed to "connected" in order to conform with Rule 5002(b).

CROSS REFERENCES

Definition of relative, see 11 USCA § 101.

Prohibited appointments, see Fed.Rules Bankr.Proc. Rule 5002, 11 USCA.

Rule 5005. Filing and Transmittal of Papers

(a) Filing

(1) Place of filing

The lists, schedules, statements, proofs of claim or interest, complaints, motions, applications, objections and other papers required to be filed by these rules, except as provided in 28 U.S.C. § 1409, shall be filed with the clerk in the district where the case under the Code is pending. The judge of that court may permit the papers to be filed with the judge, in which event the filing date shall be noted thereon, and they shall be forthwith transmitted to the clerk. The clerk shall not refuse to accept for filing any petition or other paper presented for the purpose of filing solely because it is not presented in proper form as required by these rules or any local rules or practices.

(2) Filing by electronic means

A court may by local rule permit or require documents to be filed, signed, or verified by electronic means that are consistent with technical standards, if any, that the Judicial Conference of the United States establishes. A local rule may require filing by electronic means only if reasonable exceptions are allowed. A document filed by electronic means in compliance with a local rule constitutes a written paper for the purpose of applying these rules, the Federal Rules of Civil Procedure made applicable by these rules, and § 107 of the Code.

Rule 5005   BANKRUPTCY RULES

(b) Transmittal to the United States trustee

(1) The complaints, motions, applications, objections and other papers required to be transmitted to the United States trustee by these rules shall be mailed or delivered to an office of the United States trustee, or to another place designated by the United States trustee, in the district where the case under the Code is pending.

(2) The entity, other than the clerk, transmitting a paper to the United States trustee shall promptly file as proof of such transmittal a verified statement identifying the paper and stating the date on which it was transmitted to the United States trustee.

(3) Nothing in these rules shall require the clerk to transmit any paper to the United States trustee if the United States trustee requests in writing that the paper not be transmitted.

(c) Error in filing or transmittal

A paper intended to be filed with the clerk but erroneously delivered to the United States trustee, the trustee, the attorney for the trustee, a bankruptcy judge, a district judge, the clerk of the bankruptcy appellate panel, or the clerk of the district court shall, after the date of its receipt has been noted thereon, be transmitted forthwith to the clerk of the bankruptcy court. A paper intended to be transmitted to the United States trustee but erroneously delivered to the clerk, the trustee, the attorney for the trustee, a bankruptcy judge, a district judge, the clerk of the bankruptcy appellate panel, or the clerk of the district court shall, after the date of its receipt has been noted thereon, be transmitted forthwith to the United States trustee. In the interest of justice, the court may order that a paper erroneously delivered shall be deemed filed with the clerk or transmitted to the United States trustee as of the date of its original delivery.

(As amended Mar. 30, 1987, eff. Aug. 1, 1987; Apr. 30, 1991, eff. Aug. 1, 1991; Apr. 22, 1993, eff. Aug. 1, 1993; Apr. 23, 1996, eff. Dec. 1, 1996; Apr. 12, 2006, eff. Dec. 1, 2006.)

ADVISORY COMMITTEE NOTES

Subdivision (a) is an adaptation of Rule 5(e) F.R.Civ.P. §§ 301–304 of the Code and Rules 1002 and 1003 require that cases under the Code be commenced by filing a petition "with the bankruptcy court." Other sections of the Code and other rules refer to or contemplate filing but there is no specific reference to filing with the bankruptcy court. For example, § 501 of the Code requires filing of proofs of claim and Rule 3016(c) requires the filing of a disclosure statement. This subdivision applies to all situations in which filing is required. Except when filing in another district is authorized by 28 U.S.C. § 1473, all papers, including complaints commencing adversary proceedings, must be filed in the court where the case under the Code is pending.

Subdivision (b) is the same as former Bankruptcy Rule 509(c).

1987 Amendments

Subdivision (a) is amended to conform with the 1984 amendments.

1991 Amendments

Subdivision (b)(1) is flexible in that it permits the United States trustee to designate a place or places for receiving papers within the district in which the case is pending. Transmittal of papers to the United States trustee may be accomplished by mail or delivery, including delivery by courier, and the technical requirements for service of process are not applicable. Although papers relating to a proceeding commenced in another district pursuant to 28 U.S.C. § 1409 must be filed with the clerk in that district, the papers required to be transmitted to the United States trustee must be mailed or delivered to the United States trustee in the district in which the case under the Code is pending. The United States trustee in the district in which the case is pending monitors the progress of the case and should be informed of all developments in the case wherever the developments take place.

Subdivision (b)(2) requires that proof of transmittal to the United States trustee be filed with the clerk. If papers are served on the United States trustee by mail or otherwise, the filing of proof of service would satisfy the requirements of this subdivision. This requirement enables the court to assure that papers are actually transmitted to the United States trustee in compliance with the rules. When the rules require that a paper be transmitted to the United States trustee and proof of transmittal has not been filed with the clerk, the court should not schedule a hearing or should take other appropriate action to assure that the paper is transmitted to the United States trustee. The filing of the verified statement with the clerk also enables other parties in interest to determine whether a paper has been transmitted to the United States trustee.

Subdivision (b)(3) is designed to relieve the clerk of any obligation under these rules to transmit any paper to the United States trustee if the United States trustee does not wish to receive it.

Subdivision (c) is amended to include the erroneous delivery of papers intended to be transmitted to the United States trustee.

1993 Amendments

Subdivision (a) is amended to conform to the 1991 amendment to Rule 5(e) F.R.Civ.P. It is not a suitable role for the office of the clerk to refuse to accept for filing papers not conforming to requirements of form imposed by these rules or by local rules or practices. The enforcement of these rules and local rules is a role for a judge. This amendment does not require the clerk to accept for filing papers sent to the clerk's office by facsimile transmission.

1996 Amendments

The rule is amended to permit, but not require, courts to adopt local rules that allow filing, signing, or verifying of documents by electronic means. However, such local rules must be consistent with technical standards, if any, promulgated by the Judicial Conference of the United States.

An important benefit to be derived by permitting filing by electronic means is that the extensive volume of paper received and maintained as records in the clerk's office will be reduced substantially. With the receipt of electronic data transmissions by computer, the clerk may maintain records electronically without the need to reproduce them in tangible paper form.

Judicial Conference standards governing the technological aspects of electronic filing will result in uniformity among judicial districts to accommodate an increasingly national bar. By delegating to the Judicial Conference the establishment and future amendment of national standards for electronic filing, the Supreme Court and Congress will be relieved of the burden of reviewing and promulgating detailed rules dealing with complex technological standards. Another reason for leaving to the Judicial Conference the formulation of technological standards for electronic filing is that advances in computer technology occur often, and changes in the technological standards may have to be implemented more frequently than would be feasible by rule amendment under the Rules Enabling Act process.

It is anticipated that standards established by the Judicial Conference will govern technical specifications for electronic data transmission, such as requirements relating to the formatting of data, speed of transmission, means to transmit copies of supporting documentation, and security of communication procedures. In addition, before procedures for electronic filing are implemented, standards must be established to assure the proper maintenance and integrity of the record and to provide appropriate access and retrieval mechanisms. These matters will be governed by local rules until system-wide standards are adopted by the Judicial Conference.

Rule 9009 requires that the Official Forms shall be observed and used "with alterations as may be appropriate." Compliance with local rules and any Judicial Conference standards with respect to the formatting or presentation of electronically transmitted data, to the extent that they do not conform to the Official Forms, would be an appropriate alteration within the meaning of Rule 9009.

These rules require that certain documents be in writing. For example, Rule 3001 states that a proof of claim is a "written statement." Similarly, Rule 3007 provides that an objection to a claim "shall be in writing." Pursuant to the new subdivision (a)(2), any requirement under these rules that a paper be written may be satisfied by filing the document by electronic means, notwithstanding the fact that the clerk neither receives nor prints a paper reproduction of the electronic data.

Section 107(a) of the Code provides that a "paper" filed in a case is a public record open to examination by an entity at reasonable times without charge, except as provided in § 107(b). The amendment to subdivision (a)(2) provides that an electronically filed document is to be treated as such a public record.

Although under subdivision (a)(2) electronically filed documents may be treated as written papers or as signed or verified writings, it is important to emphasize that such treatment is only for the purpose of applying these rules. In addition, local rules and Judicial Conference standards regarding verification must satisfy the requirements of 28 U.S.C. § 1746.

2006 Amendments

Subdivision (a). Amended Rule 5005(a)(2) acknowledges that many courts have required electronic filing by means of a standing order, procedures manual, or local rule. These local practices reflect the advantages that courts and most litigants realize from electronic filings. Courts requiring electronic filing must make reasonable exceptions for persons for whom electronic filing of documents constitutes an unreasonable denial of access to the courts. Experience with the rule will facilitate convergence on uniform exceptions in an amended Rule 5005(a)(2).

Subdivision (c). The rule is amended to include the clerk of the bankruptcy appellate panel among the list of persons required to transmit to the proper person erroneously filed or transmitted papers. The amendment is necessary because the bankruptcy appellate panels were not in existence at the time of the original promulgation of the rule. The amendment also inserts the district judge on the list of persons required to transmit papers intended for the United States trustee but erroneously sent to another person. The district judge is included in the list of persons who must transmit papers to the clerk of the bankruptcy court in the first part of the rule, and there is no reason to exclude the district judge from the list of persons who must transmit erroneously filed papers to the United States trustee.

CROSS REFERENCES

Filing of pleadings and other papers with court, see Fed.Rules Civ.Proc. Rule 5, 28 USCA.

Rule 5006. Certification of Copies of Papers

The clerk shall issue a certified copy of the record of any proceeding in a case under the Code or of any paper filed with the clerk on payment of any prescribed fee.

(As amended Apr. 30, 1991, eff. Aug. 1, 1991.)

ADVISORY COMMITTEE NOTES

Fees for certification and copying are fixed by the Judicial Conference under 28 U.S.C. § 1930(b).

Rule 1101 F.R.Evid. makes the Federal Rules of Evidence applicable to cases under the Code. Rule 1005 F.R.Evid. allows the contents of an official record or of a paper filed with the court to be proved by a duly certified copy. A copy certified and issued in accordance with Rule 5006 is accorded authenticity by Rule 902(4) F.R.Evid.

CROSS REFERENCES

Public records, see Fed.Rules Evid. Rule 1005, 28 USCA.

Rule 5007. Record of Proceedings and Transcripts

(a) Filing of record or transcript

The reporter or operator of a recording device shall certify the original notes of testimony, tape recording, or other original record of the proceeding and promptly file them with the clerk. The person preparing any transcript shall promptly file a certified copy.

(b) Transcript fees

The fees for copies of transcripts shall be charged at rates prescribed by the Judicial Conference of the United States. No fee may be charged for the certified copy filed with the clerk.

(c) Admissibility of record in evidence

A certified sound recording or a transcript of a proceeding shall be admissible as prima facie evidence to establish the record.

(As amended Mar. 30, 1987, eff. Aug. 1, 1987; Apr. 30, 1991, eff. Aug. 1, 1991.)

ADVISORY COMMITTEE NOTES

This rule supplements 28 U.S.C. § 773. A record of proceedings before the bankruptcy judge is to be made whenever practicable. By whatever means the record is made, subdivision (a) requires that the preparer of the record certify and file the original notes, tape recording, or other form of sound recording of the proceedings. Similarly, if a transcript is requested, the preparer is to file a certified copy with the clerk.

Subdivision (b) is derived from 28 U.S.C. § 753(f).

Subdivision (c) is derived from former Bankruptcy Rule 511(c). This subdivision extends to a sound recording the same evidentiary status as a transcript under 28 U.S.C. § 773(b).

1991 Amendments

The words "with the clerk" in the final sentence of subdivision (a) are deleted as unnecessary. See Rules 5005(a) and 9001(3).

CROSS REFERENCES

Reporters, see 28 USCA § 753.

Stenographer; stenographic report or transcript as evidence, see Fed.Rules Civ.Proc. Rule 80, 28 USCA.

Rule 5008. Notice Regarding Presumption of Abuse in Chapter 7 Cases of Individual Debtors

If a presumption of abuse has arisen under § 707(b) in a chapter 7 case of an individual with primarily consumer debts, the clerk shall within 10 days after the date of the filing of the petition notify creditors of the presumption of abuse in accordance with Rule 2002. If the debtor has not filed a statement indicating whether a presumption of abuse has arisen, the clerk shall within 10 days after the date of the filing of the petition notify creditors that the debtor has not filed the statement and that further notice will be given if a later filed statement indicates that a presumption of abuse has arisen. If a debtor later files a statement indicating that a presumption of abuse has arisen, the clerk shall notify creditors of the presumption of abuse as promptly as practicable.

(Added Apr. 23, 2008, eff. Dec. 1, 2008.)

ADVISORY COMMITTEE NOTES

2008 Amendments

This rule is new. The 2005 amendments to § 342 of the Code require that clerks give written notice to all creditors not later than 10 days after the date of the filing of the petition that a presumption of abuse has arisen under § 707(b). A statement filed by the debtor will be the source of the clerk's information about the presumption of abuse. This rule enables the clerk to meet its obligation to send the notice within the statutory time period set forth in § 342. In the event that the court receives the debtor's statement after the clerk has sent the first notice, and the debtor's statement indicates a presumption of abuse, the rule requires that the clerk send a second notice.

Rule 5009. Closing Chapter 7 Liquidation, Chapter 12 Family Farmer's Debt Adjustment, Chapter 13 Individual's Debt Adjustment, and Chapter 15 Ancillary and Cross-Border Cases

(a) **Cases under chapters 7, 12, and 13**

If in a chapter 7, chapter 12, or chapter 13 case the trustee has filed a final report and final account and has certified that the estate has been fully administered, and if within 30 days no objection has been filed by the United States trustee or a party in interest, there shall be a presumption that the estate has been fully administered.

Rule 5009 — BANKRUPTCY RULES

(b) Notice of failure to file Rule 1007(b)(7) statement

If an individual debtor in a chapter 7 or 13 case is required to file a statement under Rule 1007(b)(7) and fails to do so within 45 days after the first date set for the meeting of creditors under § 341(a) of the Code, the clerk shall promptly notify the debtor that the case will be closed without entry of a discharge unless the required statement is filed within the applicable time limit under Rule 1007(c).

(c) Cases under chapter 15

A foreign representative in a proceeding recognized under § 1517 of the Code shall file a final report when the purpose of the representative's appearance in the court is completed. The report shall describe the nature and results of the representative's activities in the court. The foreign representative shall transmit the report to the United States trustee, and give notice of its filing to the debtor, all persons or bodies authorized to administer foreign proceedings of the debtor, all parties to litigation pending in the United States in which the debtor was a party at the time of the filing of the petition, and such other entities as the court may direct. The foreign representative shall file a certificate with the court that notice has been given. If no objection has been filed by the United States trustee or a party in interest within 30 days after the certificate is filed, there shall be a presumption that the case has been fully administered.

(As amended Apr. 30, 1991, eff. Aug. 1, 1991; Apr. 28, 2010, eff. Dec. 1, 2010; Apr. 16, 2013, eff. Dec. 1, 2013.)

ADVISORY COMMITTEE NOTES

This rule is the same as § 350(a) of the Code. An estate may be closed even though the period allowed by Rule 3002(c) for filing claims has not expired. The closing of a case may be expedited when a notice of no dividends is given under Rule 2002(e). Dismissal of a case for want of prosecution or failure to pay filing fees is governed by Rule 1017.

1991 Amendments

The final report and account of the trustee is required to be filed with the court and the United States trustee under §§ 704(9), 1202(b)(1), and 1302(b)(1) of the Code. This amendment facilitates the United States trustee's performance of statutory duties to supervise trustees and administer cases under chapters 7, 12, and 13 pursuant to 28 U.S.C. § 586. In the absence of a timely objection by the United States trustee or a party in interest, the court may discharge the trustee and close the case pursuant to § 350(a) without the need to review the final report and account or to determine the merits of the trustee's certification that the estate has been fully administered.

Rule 3022 governs the closing of chapter 11 cases.

2010 Amendments

Subdivisions (a) and (b). The rule is amended to redesignate the former rule as subdivision (a) and to add new subdivisions (b) and (c) to the rule, Subdivision (b) requires the clerk to provide notice to an individual debtor in a chapter 7 or 13 case that the case may be closed without the entry of a discharge due to the failure of the debtor to file a timely statement of completion of a personal financial management course. The purpose of the notice is to provide the debtor with an opportunity to complete the course and file the appropriate document prior to the filing deadline. Timely filing of the document avoids the need for a motion to extend the time retroactively. It also avoids the potential for closing the case without discharge, and the possible need to pay an additional fee in connection with reopening. Timely filing also benefits the clerk's office by reducing the number of instances in which cases must be reopened.

Subdivision (c). Subdivision (c) requires a foreign representative in a chapter 15 case to file a final report setting out the foreign representative's actions and results obtained in the United States court. It also requires the foreign representative to give notice of the filing of the report, and provides interested parties with 30 days to object to the report after the foreign representative has certified that notice has been given. In the absence of a timely objection, a presumption arises that the case is fully administered, and the case may be closed.

COURTS AND CLERKS   Rule 5010

2013 Amendments

Subdivision (b) is amended to conform to the amendment of Rule 1007(b)(7). Rule 1007(b)(7) relieves an individual debtor of the obligation to file a statement of completion of a personal financial management course if the course provider notifies the court that the debtor has completed the course. The clerk's duty under subdivision (b) to notify the debtor of the possible closure of the case without discharge if the statement is not timely filed therefore applies only if the course provider has not already notified the court of the debtor's completion of the course.

CROSS REFERENCES

Debtor to succeed to any tax attributes of estate, see 11 USCA § 346.

Dismissal of case; suspension, see Fed.Rules Bankr.Proc. Rule 1017, 11 USCA.

Final decree, see Fed.Rules Bankr.Proc. Rule 3022, 11 USCA.

Postpetition transfers of estate property not avoidable by trustee after case closed, see 11 USCA § 549.

Scheduled property not administered before case closed deemed abandoned, see 11 USCA § 554.

Rule 5010. Reopening Cases

A case may be reopened on motion of the debtor or other party in interest pursuant to § 350(b) of the Code. In a chapter 7, 12, or 13 case a trustee shall not be appointed by the United States trustee unless the court determines that a trustee is necessary to protect the interests of creditors and the debtor or to insure efficient administration of the case.

(As amended Mar. 30, 1987, eff. Aug. 1, 1987; Apr. 30, 1991, eff. Aug. 1, 1991.)

ADVISORY COMMITTEE NOTES

Section 350(b) of the Code provides: "A case may be reopened in the court in which such case was closed to administer assets, to accord relief to the debtor, or for other cause."

Rule 9024, which incorporates Rule 60 F.R.Civ.P., exempts motions to reopen cases under the Code from the one year limitation of Rule 60(b).

Although a case has been closed the court may sometimes act without reopening the case. Under Rule 9024, clerical errors in judgments, orders, or other parts of the record or errors therein caused by oversight or omission may be corrected. A judgment determined to be non-dischargeable pursuant to Rule 4007 may be enforced after a case is closed by a writ of execution obtained pursuant to Rule 7069.

1987 Amendments

In order to avoid unnecessary cost and delay, the rule is amended to permit reopening of a case without the appointment of a trustee when the services of a trustee are not needed.

1991 Amendments

This rule is amended to conform to the 1986 amendments to the Code that give the United States trustee the duty to appoint trustees in chapter 7, 12 and 13 cases. See §§ 701, 702(d), 1202(a), and 1302(a) of the Code. In most reopened cases, a trustee is not needed because there are no assets to be administered. Therefore, in the interest of judicial economy, this rule is amended so that a motion will not be necessary unless the United States trustee or a party in interest seeks the appointment of a trustee in the reopened case.

CROSS REFERENCES

Motions; form and service, see Fed.Rules Bankr.Proc. Rule 9013, 11 USCA.

Relief from judgment or order, see Fed.Rules Bankr.Proc. Rule 9024, 11 USCA.

Rule 5011. Withdrawal and Abstention From Hearing a Proceeding

(a) Withdrawal

A motion for withdrawal of a case or proceeding shall be heard by a district judge.

(b) Abstention from hearing a proceeding

A motion for abstention pursuant to 28 U.S.C. § 1334(c) shall be governed by Rule 9014 and shall be served on the parties to the proceeding.

(c) Effect of filing of motion for withdrawal or abstention

The filing of a motion for withdrawal of a case or proceeding or for abstention pursuant to 28 U.S.C. § 1334(c) shall not stay the administration of the case or any proceeding therein before the bankruptcy judge except that the bankruptcy judge may stay, on such terms and conditions as are proper, proceedings pending disposition of the motion. A motion for a stay ordinarily shall be presented first to the bankruptcy judge. A motion for a stay or relief from a stay filed in the district court shall state why it has not been presented to or obtained from the bankruptcy judge. Relief granted by the district judge shall be on such terms and conditions as the judge deems proper.

(Added Mar. 30, 1987, eff. Aug. 1, 1987 and amended Apr. 30, 1991, eff. Aug. 1, 1991.)

ADVISORY COMMITTEE NOTES

Motions for withdrawal pursuant to 28 U.S.C. § 157(d) or abstention pursuant to 28 U.S.C. § 1334(c), like all other motions, are to be filed with the clerk as required by Rule 5005(a). If a bankruptcy clerk has been appointed for the district, all motions are filed with the bankruptcy clerk. The method for forwarding withdrawal motions to the district court will be established by administrative procedures.

Subdivision (a). Section 157(d) permits the district court to order withdrawal on its own motion or the motion of a party. Subdivision (a) of this rule makes it clear that the bankruptcy judge will not conduct hearings on a withdrawal motion. The withdrawal decision is committed exclusively to the district court.

Subdivision (b). A decision to abstain under 28 U.S.C. § 1334(c) is not appealable. The district court is vested originally with jurisdiction and the decision to relinquish that jurisdiction must ultimately be a matter for the district court. The bankruptcy judge ordinarily will be in the best position to evaluate the grounds asserted for abstention. This subdivision (b) provides that the initial hearing on the motion is before the bankruptcy judge. The procedure for review of the report and recommendation are governed by Rule 9033.

This rule does not apply to motions under § 305 of the Code for abstention from hearing a case. Judicial decisions will determine the scope of the bankruptcy judge's authority under § 305.

Subdivision (c). Unless the court so orders, proceedings are not stayed when motions are filed for withdrawal or for abstention from hearing a proceeding. Because of the district court's authority over cases and proceedings, the subdivision authorizes the district court to order a stay or modify a stay ordered by the bankruptcy judge.

1991 Amendments

Subdivision (b) is amended to delete the restriction that limits the role of the bankruptcy court to the filing of a report and recommendation for disposition of a motion for abstention under 28 U.S.C. § 1334(c)(2). This amendment is consistent with § 309(b) of the Judicial Improvements Act of 1990 which amended § 1334(c)(2) so that it allows an appeal to the district court of a bankruptcy court's order determining an abstention motion. This subdivision is also amended to clarify that the motion is a contested matter governed by Rule 9014 and that it must be served on all parties to the proceeding with is the subject of the motion.

Rule 5012. Agreements Concerning Coordination of Proceedings in Chapter 15 Cases

Approval of an agreement under § 1527(4) of the Code shall be sought by motion. The movant shall attach to the motion a copy of the proposed agreement or protocol and, unless the court directs otherwise, give at least 30 days' notice of any hearing on the motion by transmitting the motion to the United States trustee, and serving it on the debtor, all persons or bodies authorized to administer foreign proceedings of the debtor, all entities against whom provisional relief is being sought under § 1519, all parties to litigation pending in the United States in which the debtor was a party at the time of the filing of the petition, and such other entities as the court may direct.

(Added Apr. 28, 2010, eff. Dec. 1, 2010.)

ADVISORY COMMITTEE NOTES
2010 Adoption

This rule is new. In chapter 15 cases, any party in interest may seek approval of an agreement, frequently referred to as a "protocol," that will assist with the conduct of the case. Because the needs of the courts and the parties may vary greatly from case to case, the rule does not attempt to limit the form or scope of a protocol. Rather, the rule simply requires that approval of a particular protocol be sought by motion, and designates the persons entitled to notice of the hearing on the motion. These agreements, or protocols, drafted entirely by parties in interest in the case, are intended to provide valuable assistance to the court in the management of the case. Interested parties may find guidelines published by organizations, such as the American Law Institute and the International Insolvency Institute, helpful in crafting agreements or protocols to apply in a particular case.

PART VI—COLLECTION AND LIQUIDATION OF THE ESTATE

Rule
6001. Burden of Proof as to Validity of Postpetition Transfer.
6002. Accounting by Prior Custodian of Property of the Estate.
6003. Interim and Final Relief Immediately Following the Commencement of the Case—Applications for Employment; Motions for Use, Sale, or Lease of Property; and Motions for Assumption or Assignment of Executory Contracts.
6004. Use, Sale, or Lease of Property.
6005. Appraisers and Auctioneers.
6006. Assumption, Rejection or Assignment of an Executory Contract or Unexpired Lease.
6007. Abandonment or Disposition of Property.
6008. Redemption of Property From Lien or Sale.
6009. Prosecution and Defense of Proceedings by Trustee or Debtor in Possession.
6010. Proceeding to Avoid Indemnifying Lien or Transfer to Surety.
6011. Disposal of Patient Records in Health Care Business Case.

Rule 6001. Burden of Proof as to Validity of Postpetition Transfer

Any entity asserting the validity of a transfer under § 549 of the Code shall have the burden of proof.

ADVISORY COMMITTEE NOTES

This rule is derived from former Bankruptcy Rule 603. The Act contained, in § 70d [former § 110(d) of this title], a provision placing the burden of proof on the same person as did Rule 603. The Code does not contain any directive with respect to the burden of proof. This omission, in all probability, resulted from the intention to leave matters affecting evidence to these rules. See H.Rep. No. 95–595, 95th Cong. 1st Sess. (1977) 293.

Rule 6002. Accounting by Prior Custodian of Property of the Estate

(a) Accounting required

Any custodian required by the Code to deliver property in the custodian's possession or control to the trustee shall promptly file and transmit to the United States trustee a report and account with respect to the property of the estate and the administration thereof.

(b) Examination of administration

On the filing and transmittal of the report and account required by subdivision (a) of this rule and after an examination has been made into the superseded administration, after notice and a hearing, the court shall determine the propriety of the administration, including the reasonableness of all disbursements.

(As amended Mar. 30, 1987, eff. Aug. 1, 1987; Apr. 30, 1991, eff. Aug. 1, 1991; Apr. 22, 1993, eff. Aug. 1, 1993.)

ADVISORY COMMITTEE NOTES

"Custodian" is defined in § 101(10) of the Code. The definition includes a trustee or receiver appointed in proceedings not under the Code, as well as an assignee for the benefit of creditors.

This rule prescribes the procedure to be followed by a custodian who under § 543 of the Code is required to deliver property to the trustee and to account for its disposition. The examination under subdivision (b) may be initiated (1) on the motion of the custodian required to account under subdivision (a) for an approval of his account and discharge thereon, (2) on the motion of, or the filing of an objection to the custodian's account by, the trustee or any other party in interest, or (3) on the court's own initiative. Rule 9014 applies to any contested matter arising under this rule.

Section 543(d) is similar to an abstention provision. It grants the bankruptcy court discretion to permit the custodian to remain in possession and control of the property. In that event, the custodian is excused from complying with § 543(a)(c) and thus would not be required to turn over the property to the trustee. When there is no duty to turn over to the trustee, Rule 6002 would not be applicable.

Rule 6003 BANKRUPTCY RULES

1991 Amendments

This rule is amended to enable the United States trustee to review, object to, or to otherwise be heard regarding the custodian's report and accounting. See §§ 307 and 543 of the Code.

1993 Amendments

Subdivision (b) is amended to conform to the language of § 102(1) of the Code.

CROSS REFERENCES

Accountability of prior custodians for estate property, see 11 USCA § 543.

Definition of custodian, see 11 USCA § 101.

Proceedings under this rule as nonadversarial proceedings, see Fed.Rules Bankr.Proc. Rule 7001, 11 USCA.

Property of estate, see 11 USCA § 541.

Rule 6003. Interim and Final Relief Immediately Following the Commencement of the Case—Applications for Employment; Motions for Use, Sale, or Lease of Property; and Motions for Assumption or Assignment of Executory Contracts

Except to the extent that relief is necessary to avoid immediate and irreparable harm, the court shall not, within 21 days after the filing of the petition, issue an order granting the following:

(a) an application under Rule 2014;

(b) a motion to use, sell, lease, or otherwise incur an obligation regarding property of the estate, including a motion to pay all or part of a claim that arose before the filing of the petition, but not a motion under Rule 4001; or

(c) a motion to assume or assign an executory contract or unexpired lease in accordance with § 365.

(Added Apr. 30, 2007, eff. Dec. 1, 2007; amended Mar. 26, 2009, eff. Dec. 1, 2009; Apr. 26, 2011, eff. Dec. 1, 2011.)

ADVISORY COMMITTEE NOTES

2007 Adoption

There can be a flurry of activity during the first days of a bankruptcy case. This activity frequently takes place prior to the formation of a creditors' committee, and it also can include substantial amounts of materials for the court and parties in interest to review and evaluate. This rule is intended to alleviate some of the time pressures present at the start of a case so that full and close consideration can be given to matters that may have a fundamental impact on the case.

The rule provides that the court cannot grant relief on applications for the employment of professional persons, motions for the use, sale, or lease of property of the estate other than such a motion under Rule 4001, and motions to assume or assign executory contracts and unexpired leases for the first 20 days of the case, unless granting relief is necessary to avoid immediate and irreparable harm. This standard is taken from Rule 4001(b)(2) and (c)(2), and decisions under those provisions should provide guidance for the application of this provision.

This rule does not govern motions and applications made more than 20 days after the filing of the petition.

2009 Amendments

The rule is amended to implement changes in connection with the amendment to Rule 9006(a) and the manner by which time is computed under the rules. The deadline in the rule is amended to substitute a deadline that is a multiple of seven days. Throughout the rules, deadlines are amended in the following manner:

COLLECTION AND LIQUIDATION OF THE ESTATE — Rule 6004

- 5-day periods become 7-day periods
- 10-day periods become 14-day periods
- 15-day periods become 14-day periods
- 20-day periods become 21-day periods
- 25-day periods become 28-day periods

2011 Amendments

The rule is amended to clarify that it limits the timing of the entry of certain orders, but does not prevent the court from providing an effective date for such an order that may relate back to the time of the filing of the application or motion, or to some other date. For example, while the rule prohibits, absent immediate and irreparable harm, the court from authorizing the employment of counsel during the first 21 days of a case, it does not prevent the court from providing in an order entered after expiration of the 21-day period that the relief requested in the motion or application is effective as of a date earlier than the issuance of the order. Nor does it prohibit the filing of an application or motion for relief prior to expiration of the 21-day period. Nothing in the rule prevents a professional from representing the trustee or a debtor in possession pending the approval of an application for the approval of the employment under Rule 2014.

The amendment also clarifies that the scope of the rule is limited to granting the specifically identified relief set out in the subdivisions of the rule. Deleting "regarding" from the rule clarifies that the rule does not prohibit the court from entering orders in the first 21 days of the case that may relate to the motions and applications set out in (a), (b), and (c); it is only prohibited from granting the relief requested by those motions or applications. For example, in the first 21 days of the case, the court could grant the relief requested in a motion to establish bidding procedures for the sale of property of the estate, but it could not, absent immediate and irreparable harm, grant a motion to approve the sale of property.

Rule 6004. Use, Sale, or Lease of Property

(a) Notice of proposed use, sale, or lease of property

Notice of a proposed use, sale, or lease of property, other than cash collateral, not in the ordinary course of business shall be given pursuant to Rule 2002(a)(2), (c)(1), (i), and (k) and, if applicable, in accordance with § 363(b)(2) of the Code.

(b) Objection to proposal

Except as provided in subdivisions (c) and (d) of this rule, an objection to a proposed use, sale, or lease of property shall be filed and served not less than seven days before the date set for the proposed action or within the time fixed by the court. An objection to the proposed use, sale, or lease of property is governed by Rule 9014.

(c) Sale free and clear of liens and other interests

A motion for authority to sell property free and clear of liens or other interests shall be made in accordance with Rule 9014 and shall be served on the parties who have liens or other interests in the property to be sold. The notice required by subdivision (a) of this rule shall include the date of the hearing on the motion and the time within which objections may be filed and served on the debtor in possession or trustee.

(d) Sale of property under $2,500

Notwithstanding subdivision (a) of this rule, when all of the nonexempt property of the estate has an aggregate gross value less than $2,500, it shall be sufficient to give a general notice of intent to sell such property other than in the ordinary course of business to all creditors, indenture trustees, committees appointed or elected pursuant to the Code, the United States trustee and other persons as the court may direct. An objection to any such sale may be filed and served by a party in interest within 14 days of the mailing of the notice, or within the time fixed by the court. An objection is governed by Rule 9014.

(e) Hearing

If a timely objection is made pursuant to subdivision (b) or (d) of this rule, the date of the hearing thereon may be set in the notice given pursuant to subdivision (a) of this rule.

(f) Conduct of sale not in the ordinary course of business

(1) Public or private sale

All sales not in the ordinary course of business may be by private sale or by public auction. Unless it is impracticable, an itemized statement of the property sold, the name of each purchaser, and the price received for each item or lot or for the property as a whole if sold in bulk shall be filed on completion of a sale. If the property is sold by an auctioneer, the auctioneer shall file the statement, transmit a copy thereof to the United States trustee, and furnish a copy to the trustee, debtor in possession, or chapter 13 debtor. If the property is not sold by an auctioneer, the trustee, debtor in possession, or chapter 13 debtor shall file the statement and transmit a copy thereof to the United States trustee.

(2) Execution of instruments

After a sale in accordance with this rule the debtor, the trustee, or debtor in possession, as the case may be, shall execute any instrument necessary or ordered by the court to effectuate the transfer to the purchaser.

(g) Sale of personally identifiable information

(1) Motion

A motion for authority to sell or lease personally identifiable information under § 363(b)(1)(B) shall include a request for an order directing the United States trustee to appoint a consumer privacy ombudsman under § 332. Rule 9014 governs the motion which shall be served on: any committee elected under § 705 or appointed under § 1102 of the Code, or if the case is a chapter 11 reorganization case and no committee of unsecured creditors has been appointed under § 1102, on the creditors included on the list of creditors filed under Rule 1007(d); and on such other entities as the court may direct. The motion shall be transmitted to the United States trustee.

(2) Appointment

If a consumer privacy ombudsman is appointed under § 332, no later than seven days before the hearing on the motion under § 363(b)(1)(B), the United States trustee shall file a notice of the appointment, including the name and address of the person appointed. The United States trustee's notice shall be accompanied by a verified statement of the person appointed setting forth the person's connections with the debtor, creditors, any other party in interest, their respective attorneys and accountants, the United States trustee, or any person employed in the office of the United States trustee.

(h) Stay of order authorizing use, sale, or lease of property

An order authorizing the use, sale, or lease of property other than cash collateral is stayed until the expiration of 14 days after entry of the order, unless the court orders otherwise.

(As amended Mar. 30, 1987, eff. Aug. 1, 1987; Apr. 30, 1991, eff. Aug. 1, 1991; Apr. 29, 1999, eff. Dec. 1, 1999; Apr. 23, 2008, eff. Dec. 1, 2008; Mar. 26, 2009, eff. Dec. 1, 2009.)

ADVISORY COMMITTEE NOTES

Subdivisions (a) and (b). Pursuant to § 363(b) of the Code, a trustee or debtor in possession may use, sell, or lease property other than in the ordinary course of business only after notice and hearing. Rule 2002(a), (c) and (i) specifies the time when notice of sale is to be given, the contents of the notice and the persons to whom notice is to be given of sales of property. Subdivision (a) makes those provisions applicable as well to notices for proposed use and lease of property.

The Code does not provide the time within which parties may file objections to a proposed sale. Subdivision (b) of the rule requires the objection to be in writing and filed not less than five days before the proposed action is to take place. The objection should also be served within that time on the person who is proposing to take the action which would be either the trustee or debtor in possession. This time

COLLECTION AND LIQUIDATION OF THE ESTATE Rule 6004

period is subject to change by the court. In some instances there is a need to conduct a sale in a short period of time and the court is given discretion to tailor the requirements to the circumstances.

Subdivision (c). In some situations a notice of sale for different pieces of property to all persons specified in Rule 2002(a) may be uneconomic and inefficient. This is particularly true in some chapter 7 liquidation cases when there is property of relatively little value which must be sold by the trustee. Subdivision (c) allows a general notice of intent to sell when the aggregate value of the estate's property is less than $2,500. The gross value is the value of the property without regard to the amount of any debt secured by a lien on the property. It is not necessary to give a detailed notice specifying the time and place of a particular sale. Thus, the requirements of Rule 2002(c) need not be met. If this method of providing notice of sales is used, the subdivision specifies that parties in interest may serve and file objections to the proposed sale of any property within the class and the time for service and filing is fixed at not later than 15 days after mailing the notice. The court may fix a different time. Subdivision (c) would have little utility in chapter 11 cases. Pursuant to Rule 2002(i), the court can limit notices of sale to the creditors' committee appointed under § 1102 of the Code and the same burdens present in a small chapter 7 case would not exist.

Subdivision (d). If a timely objection is filed, a hearing is required with respect to the use, sale, or lease of property. Subdivision (d) renders the filing of an objection tantamount to requesting a hearing so as to require a hearing pursuant to §§ 363(b) and 102(1)(B)(i).

Subdivision (e) is derived in part from former Bankruptcy Rule 606(b) but does not carry forward the requirement of that rule that court approval be obtained for sales of property. Pursuant to § 363(b) court approval is not required unless timely objection is made to the proposed sale. The itemized statement or information required by the subdivision is not necessary when it would be impracticable to prepare it or set forth the information. For example, a liquidation sale of retail goods although not in the ordinary course of business may be on a daily ongoing basis and only summaries may be available.

The duty imposed by paragraph (2) does not affect the power of the bankruptcy court to order third persons to execute instruments transferring property purchased at a sale under this subdivision. See, e.g., In re Rosenberg, 138 F.2d 409 (7th Cir. 1943).

1987 Amendments

Subdivision (a) is amended to conform to the 1984 amendments to § 363(b)(2) of the Code.

Subdivision (b) is amended to provide that an objection to a proposed use, sale, or lease of property creates a contested matter governed by Rule 9014. A similar amendment is made to subdivision (d), which was formerly subdivision (c).

Subdivision (c) is new. Section 363(f) provides that sales free and clear of liens or other interests are only permitted if one of the five statutory requirements is satisfied. Rule 9013 requires that a motion state with particularity the grounds relied upon by the movant. A motion for approval of a sale free and clear of liens or other interests is subject to Rule 9014, service must be made on the parties holding liens or other interests in the property, and notice of the hearing on the motion and the time for filing objections must be included in the notice given under subdivision (a).

1991 Amendments

This rule is amended to provide notice to the United States trustee of a proposed use, sale or lease of property not in the ordinary course of business. See Rule 2002(k). Subdivision (f)(1) is amended to enable the United States trustee to monitor the progress of the case in accordance with 28 U.S.C. § 586(a)(3)(G).

The words "with the clerk" in subdivision (f)(1) are deleted as unnecessary. See Rules 5005(a) and 9001(3).

1999 Amendments

Subdivision (g) is added to provide sufficient time for a party to request a stay pending appeal of an order authorizing the use, sale, or lease of property under § 363(b) of the Code before the order is implemented. It does not affect the time for filing a notice of appeal in accordance with Rule 8002.

Rule 6004(g) does not apply to orders regarding the use of cash collateral and does not affect the trustee's right to use, sell, or lease property without a court order to the extent permitted under § 363 of the Code.

The court may, in its discretion, order that Rule 6004(g) is not applicable so that the property may be used, sold, or leased immediately in accordance with the order entered by the court. Alternatively, the court may order that the stay under Rule 6004(g) is for a fixed period less than 10 days.

2008 Amendments

The rule is amended by inserting a new subdivision (g) to implement §§ 332 and 363(b)(1)(B) of the Code, added by the 2005 amendments. This rule governs the proposed transfer of personally identifiable information in a manner inconsistent with any policy covering the transfer of the information. Rule 2002(c)(1) requires the seller to state in the notice of the sale or lease whether the transfer is consistent with and policy governing the transfer of the information.

Under § 332 of the Code, the consumer privacy ombudsman must be appointed at least five days prior to the hearing on a sale or lease of personally identifiable information. In an appropriate case, the consumer privacy ombudsman may seek a continuance of the hearing on the proposed sale to perform the tasks required of the ombudsman by § 332 of the Code.

Former subdivision (g) is redesignated as subdivision (h).

2009 Amendments

The rule is amended to implement changes in connection with the amendment to Rule 9006(a) and the manner by which time is computed under the rules. The deadlines in the rule are amended to substitute a deadline that is a multiple of seven days. Throughout the rules, deadlines are amended in the following manner:

- 5-day periods become 7-day periods
- 10-day periods become 14-day periods
- 15-day periods become 14-day periods
- 20-day periods become 21-day periods
- 25-day periods become 28-day periods

CROSS REFERENCES

Appraisers and auctioneers, see Fed.Rules Bankr.Proc. Rule 6005, 11 USCA.

Authorization to operate debtor's business—

Individual debt adjustment case, see 11 USCA § 1304.

Liquidation case, see 11 USCA § 721.

Reorganization case, see 11 USCA § 1108.

Twenty-day notice of property disposition to include certain information, see Fed.Rules Bankr.Proc. Rule 2002, 11 USCA.

Rule 6005. Appraisers and Auctioneers

The order of the court approving the employment of an appraiser or auctioneer shall fix the amount or rate of compensation. No officer or employee of the Judicial Branch of the United States or the United States Department of Justice shall be eligible to act as appraiser or auctioneer. No residence or licensing requirement shall disqualify an appraiser or auctioneer from employment.

(As amended Mar. 30, 1987, eff. Aug. 1, 1987; Apr. 30, 1991, eff. Aug. 1, 1991.)

ADVISORY COMMITTEE NOTES

This rule is derived from former Bankruptcy Rule 606(c) and implements § 327 of the Code. Pursuant to § 327, the trustee or debtor in possession may employ one or more appraisers or auctioneers, subject to court approval. This rule requires the court order approving such employment to fix the amount or rate of compensation. The second sentence of the former rule is retained to continue to safeguard against imputations of favoritism which detract from public confidence in bankruptcy administration. The final sentence is to guard against imposition of parochial requirements not warranted by any consideration having to do with sound bankruptcy administration.

Reference should also be made to Rule 2013(a) regarding the limitation on employment of appraisers and auctioneers, and Rule 2014(a) regarding the application for appointment of an appraiser or auctioneer.

CROSS REFERENCES

Employment—

Application for, see Fed.Rules Bankr.Proc. Rule 2014, 11 USCA.

Limitation on appointment, see Fed.Rules Bankr.Proc. Rule 2013, 11 USCA.

Professional persons, see 11 USCA § 327.

Sharing of compensation prohibited, see 11 USCA § 504.

Rule 6006. Assumption, Rejection or Assignment of an Executory Contract or Unexpired Lease

(a) Proceeding to assume, reject, or assign

A proceeding to assume, reject, or assign an executory contract or unexpired lease, other than as part of a plan, is governed by Rule 9014.

(b) Proceeding to require trustee to act

A proceeding by a party to an executory contract or unexpired lease in a chapter 9 municipality case, chapter 11 reorganization case, chapter 12 family farmer's debt adjustment case, or chapter 13 individual's debt adjustment case, to require the trustee, debtor in possession, or debtor to determine whether to assume or reject the contract or lease is governed by Rule 9014.

(c) Notice

Notice of a motion made pursuant to subdivision (a) or (b) of this rule shall be given to the other party to the contract or lease, to other parties in interest as the court may direct, and, except in a chapter 9 municipality case, to the United States trustee.

(d) Stay of order authorizing assignment

An order authorizing the trustee to assign an executory contract or unexpired lease under § 365(f) is stayed until the expiration of 14 days after the entry of the order, unless the court orders otherwise.

(e) Limitations

The trustee shall not seek authority to assume or assign multiple executory contracts or unexpired leases in one motion unless: (1) all executory contracts or unexpired leases to be assumed or assigned are between the same parties or are to be assigned to the same assignee; (2) the trustee seeks to assume, but not assign to more than one assignee, unexpired leases of real property; or (3) the court otherwise authorizes the motion to be filed. Subject to subdivision (f), the trustee may join requests for authority to reject multiple executory contracts or unexpired leases in one motion.

(f) Omnibus Motions

A motion to reject or, if permitted under subdivision (e), a motion to assume or assign multiple executory contracts or unexpired leases that are not between the same parties shall:

(1) state in a conspicuous place that parties receiving the omnibus motion should locate their names and their contracts or leases listed in the motion;

(2) list parties alphabetically and identify the corresponding contract or lease;

(3) specify the terms, including the curing of defaults, for each requested assumption or assignment;

Rule 6006   BANKRUPTCY RULES

(4) specify the terms, including the identity of each assignee and the adequate assurance of future performance by each assignee, for each requested assignment;

(5) be numbered consecutively with other omnibus motions to assume, assign, or reject executory contracts or unexpired leases; and

(6) be limited to no more than 100 executory contracts or unexpired leases.

(g) Finality of Determination

The finality of any order respecting an executory contract or unexpired lease included in an omnibus motion shall be determined as though such contract or lease had been the subject of a separate motion.

(As amended Mar. 30, 1987, eff. Aug. 1, 1987; Apr. 30, 1991, eff. Aug. 1, 1991; Apr. 22, 1993, eff. Aug. 1, 1993; Apr. 29, 1999, eff. Dec. 1, 1999; Apr. 30, 2007, eff. Dec. 1, 2007; Mar. 26, 2009, eff. Dec. 1, 2009.)

ADVISORY COMMITTEE NOTES

Section 365(a) of the Code requires court approval for the assumption or rejection of an executory contract by the trustee or debtor in possession. The trustee or debtor in possession may also assign an executory contract, § 365(f)(1), but must first assume the contract, § 365(f)(2). Rule 6006 provides a procedure for obtaining court approval. It does not apply to the automatic rejection of contracts which are not assumed in chapter 7 liquidation cases within 60 days after the order for relief, or to the assumption or rejection of contracts in a plan pursuant to § 1123(b)(2) or § 1322(b)(7).

Subdivision (a) by referring to Rule 9014 requires a motion to be brought for the assumption, rejection, or assignment of an executory contract. Normally, the motion will be brought by the trustee, debtor in possession or debtor in a chapter 9 or chapter 13 case. The authorization to assume a contract and to assign it may be sought in a single motion and determined by a single order.

Subdivision (b) makes applicable the same motion procedure when the other party to the contract seeks to require the chapter officer to take some action. Section 365(d)(2) recognizes that this procedure is available to these contractual parties. This provision of the Code and subdivision of the rule apply only in chapter 9, 11 and 13 cases. A motion is not necessary in chapter 7 cases because in those cases a contract is deemed rejected if the trustee does not timely assume it.

Subdivision (c) provides for the court to set a hearing on a motion made under subdivision (a) or (b). The other party to the contract should be given appropriate notice of the hearing and the court may order that other parties in interest, such as a creditors' committee, also be given notice.

1987 Amendments

Subdivisions (a) and (b) are amended to conform to the 1984 amendment to § 365 of the Code, which governs assumption or rejection of time share interests.

Section 1113, governing collective bargaining agreements, was added to the Code in 1984. It sets out requirements that must be met before a collective bargaining agreement may be rejected. The application to reject a collective bargaining agreement referred to in § 1113 shall be made by motion. The motion to reject creates a contested matter under Rule 9014, and service is made pursuant to Rule 7004 on the representative of the employees. The time periods set forth in § 1113(d) govern the scheduling of the hearing and disposition of a motion to reject the agreement.

1991 Amendments

References to time share interests are deleted as unnecessary. Time share interests are within the scope of this rule to the extent that they are governed by § 365 of the Code.

Subdivision (b) is amended to include chapter 12 cases.

Subdivision (c) is amended to enable the United States trustee to appear and be heard on the issues relating to the assumption or rejection of executory contracts and unexpired leases. See §§ 307, 365, and 1113 of the Code.

1993 Amendments

This rule is amended to delete the requirement for an actual hearing when no request for a hearing is made. See rule 9014.

1999 Amendments

Subdivision (d) is added to provide sufficient time for a party to request a stay pending appeal of an order authorizing the assignment of an executory contract or unexpired lease under § 365(f) of the Code before the assignment is consummated. The stay under subdivision (d) does not affect the time for filing a notice of appeal in accordance with Rule 8002.

The court may, in its discretion, order that Rule 6006(d) is not applicable so that the executory contract or unexpired lease may be assigned immediately in accordance with the order entered by the court. Alternatively, the court may order that the stay under Rule 6006(d) is for a fixed period less than 10 days.

2007 Amendments

The rule is amended to authorize the use of omnibus motions to reject multiple executory contracts and unexpired leases. In some cases there may be numerous executory contracts and unexpired leases, and this rule permits the combining of up to one hundred of these contracts and leases in a single motion to initiate the contested matter.

The rule also is amended to authorize the use of a single motion to assume or assign executory contracts and unexpired leases (i) when such contracts and leases are with a single nondebtor party, (ii) when such contracts and leases are being assigned to the same assignee, (iii) when the trustee proposes to assume, but not assign to more than one assignee, real property leases, or (iv) the court authorizes the filing of a joint motion to assume or to assume and assign executory contracts and unexpired leases under other circumstances that are not specifically recognized in the rule.

An omnibus motion to assume, assign, or reject multiple executory contracts and unexpired leases must comply with the procedural requirements set forth in subdivision (f) of the rule, unless the court orders otherwise. These requirements are intended to ensure that the nondebtor parties to the contracts and leases receive effective notice of the motion. Among those requirements is the requirement in subdivision (f)(5) that these motions be consecutively numbered (e.g., Debtor in Possession's First Omnibus Motion for Authority to Assume Executory Contracts and Unexpired Leases, Debtor in Possession's Second Omnibus Motion for Authority to Assume Executory Contracts and Unexpired Leases, etc.). There may be a need for several of these motions in a particular case. Numbering the motions consecutively is essential to keep track of these motions on the court's docket and should avoid confusion that might otherwise result from similar or identically-titled motions.

Subdivision (g) of the rule provides that the finality of any order respecting an executory contract or unexpired lease included in an omnibus motion shall be determined as though such contract or lease had been the subject of a separate motion. A party seeking to appeal any such order is neither required, nor permitted, to await the court's resolution of all other contracts or leases included in the omnibus motion to obtain appellate review of the order. The rule permits the listing of multiple contracts or leases for convenience, and that convenience should not impede timely review of the court's decision with respect to each contract or lease.

2009 Amendments

The rule is amended to implement changes in connection with the amendment to Rule 9006(a) and the manner by which time is computed under the rules. The deadline in the rule is amended to substitute a deadline that is a multiple of seven days. Throughout the rules, deadlines are amended in the following manner:

- 5-day periods become 7-day periods
- 10-day periods become 14-day periods
- 15-day periods become 14-day periods
- 20-day periods become 21-day periods
- 25-day periods become 28-day periods

CROSS REFERENCES

Assumption or rejection of executory contracts by trustee, see 11 USCA § 365.

Commodity contracts—

    Compliance by trustee with customer's instructions, see 11 USCA § 765.

Rule 6007 BANKRUPTCY RULES

Definition of, see 11 USCA § 761.

Treatment of customer property, see 11 USCA § 766.

Motions; form and service, see Fed.Rules Bankr.Proc. Rule 9013, 11 USCA.

Provisions in plan for assumption or rejection of certain executory contracts or unexpired leases, see 11 USCA §§ 1123 and 1322.

Rule 6007. Abandonment or Disposition of Property

(a) Notice of proposed abandonment or disposition; objections; hearing

Unless otherwise directed by the court, the trustee or debtor in possession shall give notice of a proposed abandonment or disposition of property to the United States trustee, all creditors, indenture trustees, and committees elected pursuant to § 705 or appointed pursuant to § 1102 of the Code. A party in interest may file and serve an objection within 14 days of the mailing of the notice, or within the time fixed by the court. If a timely objection is made, the court shall set a hearing on notice to the United States trustee and to other entities as the court may direct.

(b) Motion by party in interest

A party in interest may file and serve a motion requiring the trustee or debtor in possession to abandon property of the estate.

(c) [Abrogated]

(As amended Mar. 30, 1987, eff. Aug. 1, 1987; Apr. 30, 1991, eff. Aug. 1, 1991; Apr. 22, 1993, eff. Aug. 1, 1993; Mar. 26, 2009, eff. Dec. 1, 2009.)

ADVISORY COMMITTEE NOTES

Sections 554 and 725 of the Code permit and require abandonment and disposition of property of the estate. Pursuant to § 554, the trustee may abandon property but only after notice and hearing. This section is applicable in chapter 7, 11 and 13 cases. Section 725 requires the trustee to dispose of property in which someone other than the estate has an interest, prior to final distribution. It applies only in chapter 7 cases. Notice and hearing are also required conditions. Section 102(1) provides that "notice and hearing" is construed to mean appropriate notice and an opportunity for a hearing. Neither § 554 nor § 725 specify to whom the notices are to be sent. This rule does not apply to § 554(c). Pursuant to that subsection, property is deemed abandoned if it is not administered. A hearing is not required by the statute.

Subdivision (a) requires the notices to be sent to all creditors, indenture trustees, and committees elected under § 705 or appointed under § 1102 of the Code. This may appear burdensome, expensive and inefficient but the subdivision is in keeping with the Code's requirement for notice and the Code's intent to remove the bankruptcy judge from undisputed matters. The burden, expense and inefficiency can be alleviated in large measure by incorporating the notice into or together with the notice of the meeting of creditors so that separate notices would not be required.

Subdivision (b) implements § 554(b) which specifies that a party in interest may request an order that the trustee abandon property. The rule specifies that the request be by motion and, pursuant to the Code, lists the parties who should receive notice.

Subdivision (c) requires a hearing when an objection under subdivision (a) is filed or a motion under subdivision (b) is made. Filing of an objection is sufficient to require a hearing; a separate or joined request for a hearing is unnecessary since the objection itself is tantamount to such a request.

1991 Amendments

This rule is amended to conform to the 1986 amendments to 28 U.S.C. § 586(a) and to the Code. The United States trustee monitors the progress of the case and has standing to raise, appear and be heard on the issues relating to the abandonment or other disposition of property. See §§ 307 and 554 of the Code. Committees of retired employees appointed under § 1114 are not entitled to notice under subdivision (a) of this rule.

COLLECTION AND LIQUIDATION OF THE ESTATE   Rule 6008

1993 Amendments

This rule is amended to clarify that when a motion is made pursuant to subdivision (b), a hearing is not required if a hearing is not requested or if there is no opposition to the motion. *See* Rule 9014. Other amendments are stylistic and make no substantive change.

2009 Amendments

The rule is amended to implement changes in connection with the amendment to Rule 9006(a) and the manner by which time is computed under the rules. The deadline in the rule is amended to substitute a deadline that is a multiple of seven days. Throughout the rules, deadlines are amended in the following manner:

- 5-day periods become 7-day periods
- 10-day periods become 14-day periods
- 15-day periods become 14-day periods
- 20-day periods become 21-day periods
- 25-day periods become 28-day periods

CROSS REFERENCES

Abandonment of property burdensome or of little value to estate, see 11 USCA § 554.

Abandonment of railroad line—

    Authorization by court, see 11 USCA § 1170.

    Provision of plan, see 11 USCA § 1172.

Disposition of property with lien in liquidation case, see 11 USCA § 725.

Motions; form and service, see Fed.Rules Bankr.Proc. Rule 9013, 11 USCA.

Rule 6008. Redemption of Property From Lien or Sale

On motion by the debtor, trustee, or debtor in possession and after hearing on notice as the court may direct, the court may authorize the redemption of property from a lien or from a sale to enforce a lien in accordance with applicable law.

ADVISORY COMMITTEE NOTES

This rule is derived from former Bankruptcy Rule 609. No provision in the Code addresses the trustee's right of redemption. Ordinarily the secured creditor should be given notice of the trustee's motion so that any objection may be raised to the proposed redemption.

The rule applies also to a debtor exercising a right of redemption pursuant to § 722. A proceeding under that section is governed by Rule 9014.

CROSS REFERENCES

Motions; form and service, see Fed.Rules Bankr.Proc. Rule 9013, 11 USCA.

Tangible personal property—

    Enforceability of agreement between holder of claim and debtor having consideration based on dischargeable debt, see 11 USCA § 524.

    Redemption of exempt or abandoned property from lien securing dischargeable consumer debt, see 11 USCA § 722.

Rule 6009. Prosecution and Defense of Proceedings by Trustee or Debtor in Possession

With or without court approval, the trustee or debtor in possession may prosecute or may enter an appearance and defend any pending action or proceeding by or against the debtor, or commence and prosecute any action or proceeding in behalf of the estate before any tribunal.

ADVISORY COMMITTEE NOTES

This rule is derived from former Bankruptcy Rule 610.

CROSS REFERENCES

Suspension of statutes of limitations, see 11 USCA § 108.

Voluntary or involuntary petition filed to operate as automatic stay on other proceedings, see 11 USCA § 362.

Rule 6010. Proceeding to Avoid Indemnifying Lien or Transfer to Surety

If a lien voidable under § 547 of the Code has been dissolved by the furnishing of a bond or other obligation and the surety thereon has been indemnified by the transfer of, or the creation of a lien upon, nonexempt property of the debtor, the surety shall be joined as a defendant in any proceeding to avoid the indemnifying transfer or lien. Such proceeding is governed by the rules in Part VII.

(As amended Apr. 30, 1991, eff. Aug. 1, 1991.)

ADVISORY COMMITTEE NOTES

This rule is derived from former Bankruptcy Rule 612.

1991 Amendments

This rule is amended to conform to § 550(a) of the Code which provides that the trustee may recover the property transferred in a voidable transfer. The value of the property may be recovered in lieu of the property itself only if the court so orders.

CROSS REFERENCES

Motions; form and service, see Fed.Rules Bankr.Proc. Rule 9013, 11 USCA.

Rule 6011. Disposal of Patient Records in Health Care Business Case

(a) Notice by publication under § 351(1)(A)

A notice regarding the claiming or disposing of patient records under § 351(1)(A) shall not identify any patient by name or other identifying information, but shall:

(1) identify with particularity the health care facility whose patient records the trustee proposes to destroy;

(2) state the name, address, telephone number, email address, and website, if any, of a person from whom information about the patient records may be obtained;

(3) state how to claim the patient records; and

(4) state the date by which patient records must be claimed, and that if they are not so claimed the records will be destroyed.

(b) Notice by mail under § 351(1)(B)

Subject to applicable nonbankruptcy law relating to patient privacy, a notice regarding the claiming or disposing of patient records under § 351(1)(B) shall, in addition to including the

COLLECTION AND LIQUIDATION OF THE ESTATE — Rule 6011

information in subdivision (a), direct that a patient's family member or other representative who receives the notice inform the patient of the notice. Any notice under this subdivision shall be mailed to the patient and any family member or other contact person whose name and address have been given to the trustee or the debtor for the purpose of providing information regarding the patient's health care, to the Attorney General of the State where the health care facility is located, and to any insurance company known to have provided health care insurance to the patient.

(c) Proof of compliance with notice requirement

Unless the court orders the trustee to file proof of compliance with § 351(1)(B) under seal, the trustee shall not file, but shall maintain, the proof of compliance for a reasonable time.

(d) Report of destruction of records

The trustee shall file, no later than 30 days after the destruction of patient records under § 351(3), a report certifying that the unclaimed records have been destroyed and explaining the method used to effect the destruction. The report shall not identify any patient by name or other identifying information.

(Added Apr. 23, 2008, eff. Dec. 1, 2008.)

ADVISORY COMMITTEE NOTES
2008 Adoption

This rule is new. It implements § 351(1), which was added to the Code by the 2005 amendments. That provision requires the trustee to notify patients that their patient records will be destroyed if they remain unclaimed for one year after the publication of a notice in an appropriate newspaper. The Code provision also requires that individualized notice be sent to each patient and to the patient's family member or other contact person.

The variety of health care businesses and the range of current and former patients present the need for flexibility in the creation and publication of the notices that will be given. Nevertheless, there are some matters that must be included in any notice being given to patients, their family members, and contact persons to ensure that sufficient information is provided to these persons regarding the trustee's intent to dispose of patient records. Subdivision (a) of this rule lists the minimum requirements for notices given under § 351(1)(A), and subdivision (b) governs the form of notices under § 351(1)(B). Notices given under this rule are subject to provisions under applicable federal and state law that relate to the protection of patients' privacy, such as the Health Insurance Portability and Accountability Act of 1996, Pub. L. No. 104–191 (HIPAA).

Subdivision (c) directs the trustee to maintain proof of compliance with § 351(1)(B), but because the proof of compliance may contain patient names that should or must remain confidential, it prohibits filing the proof of compliance unless the court orders the trustee to file it under seal.

Subdivision (d) requires the trustee to file a report with the court regarding the destruction of patient records. This certification is intended to ensure that the trustee properly completed the destruction process. However, because the report will be filed with the court and ordinarily will be available to the public under § 107, the names, addresses, and other identifying information of patients are not to be included in the report to protect patient privacy.

PART VII—ADVERSARY PROCEEDINGS

Rule

7001.	Scope of Rules of Part VII.
7002.	References to Federal Rules of Civil Procedure.
7003.	Commencement of Adversary Proceeding.
7004.	Process; Service of Summons, Complaint.
7005.	Service and Filing of Pleadings and Other Papers.
7007.	Pleadings Allowed.
7007.1.	Corporate Ownership Statement.
7008.	General Rules of Pleading.
7009.	Pleading Special Matters.
7010.	Form of Pleadings.
7012.	Defenses and Objections—When and How Presented—By Pleading or Motion—Motion for Judgment on the Pleadings.
7013.	Counterclaim and Cross-Claim.
7014.	Third-Party Practice.
7015.	Amended and Supplemental Pleadings.
7016.	Pre-Trial Procedure; Formulating Issues.
7017.	Parties Plaintiff and Defendant; Capacity.
7018.	Joinder of Claims and Remedies.
7019.	Joinder of Persons Needed for Just Determination.
7020.	Permissive Joinder of Parties.
7021.	Misjoinder and Non-Joinder of Parties.
7022.	Interpleader.
7023.	Class Proceedings.
7023.1.	Derivative Actions.
7023.2.	Adversary Proceedings Relating to Unincorporated Associations.
7024.	Intervention.
7025.	Substitution of Parties.
7026.	General Provisions Governing Discovery.
7027.	Depositions Before Adversary Proceedings or Pending Appeal.
7028.	Persons Before Whom Depositions May Be Taken.
7029.	Stipulations Regarding Discovery Procedure.
7030.	Depositions Upon Oral Examination.
7031.	Deposition Upon Written Questions.
7032.	Use of Depositions in Adversary Proceedings.
7033.	Interrogatories to Parties.
7034.	Production of Documents and Things and Entry Upon Land for Inspection and Other Purposes.
7035.	Physical and Mental Examination of Persons.
7036.	Requests for Admission.
7037.	Failure to Make Discovery: Sanctions.
7040.	Assignment of Cases for Trial.
7041.	Dismissal of Adversary Proceedings.
7042.	Consolidation of Adversary Proceedings; Separate Trials.
7052.	Findings by the Court.
7054.	Judgments; Costs.
7055.	Default.
7056.	Summary Judgment.
7058.	Entering Judgment in Adversary Proceeding.
7062.	Stay of Proceedings to Enforce a Judgment.
7064.	Seizure of Person or Property.
7065.	Injunctions.
7067.	Deposit in Court.
7068.	Offer of Judgment.
7069.	Execution.
7070.	Judgment for Specific Acts; Vesting Title.
7071.	Process in Behalf of and Against Persons Not Parties.
7087.	Transfer of Adversary Proceeding.

Rule 7001. Scope of Rules of Part VII

An adversary proceeding is governed by the rules of this Part VII. The following are adversary proceedings:

(1) a proceeding to recover money or property, other than a proceeding to compel the debtor to deliver property to the trustee, or a proceeding under § 554(b) or § 725 of the Code, Rule 2017, or Rule 6002;

(2) a proceeding to determine the validity, priority, or extent of a lien or other interest in property, other than a proceeding under Rule 4003(d);

(3) a proceeding to obtain approval under § 363(h) for the sale of both the interest of the estate and of a co-owner in property;

(4) a proceeding to object to or revoke a discharge, other than an objection to discharge under §§[1] 727(a)(8), (a)(9), or 1328(f);

(5) a proceeding to revoke an order of confirmation of a chapter 11, chapter 12, or chapter 13 plan;

(6) a proceeding to determine the dischargeability of a debt;

(7) a proceeding to obtain an injunction or other equitable relief, except when a chapter 9, chapter 11, chapter 12, or chapter 13 plan provides for the relief;

(8) a proceeding to subordinate any allowed claim or interest, except when a chapter 9, chapter 11, chapter 12, or chapter 13 plan provides for subordination;

(9) a proceeding to obtain a declaratory judgment relating to any of the foregoing; or

(10) a proceeding to determine a claim or cause of action removed under 28 U.S.C. § 1452.

(As amended Mar. 30, 1987, eff. Aug. 1, 1987; Apr. 30, 1991, eff. Aug. 1, 1991; Apr. 29, 1999, eff. Dec. 1, 1999; Apr. 28, 2010, eff. Dec. 1, 2010.)

ADVISORY COMMITTEE NOTES

The rules in Part VII govern the procedural aspects of litigation involving the matters referred to in this Rule 7001. Under Rule 9014 some of the Part VII rules also apply to contested matters.

These Part VII rules are based on the premise that to the extent possible practice before the bankruptcy courts and the district courts should be the same. These rules either incorporate or are adaptations of most of the Federal Rules of Civil Procedure. Although the Part VII rules of the former Bankruptcy Rules also relied heavily on the F.R.Civ.P., the former Part VII rules departed from the civil practice in two significant ways: a trial or pretrial conference had to be scheduled as soon as the adversary proceeding was filed and pleadings had to be filed within periods shorter than those established by the F.R.Civ.P. These departures from the civil practice have been eliminated.

The content and numbering of these Part VII rules correlate to the content and numbering of the F.R.Civ.P. Most, but not all, of the F.R.Civ.P. have a comparable Part VII rule. When there is no Part VII rule with a number corresponding to a particular F.R.Civ.P., Parts V and IX of these rules must be consulted to determine if one of the rules in those parts deals with the subject. The list below indicates the F.R.Civ.P., or subdivision thereof, covered by a rule in either Part V or Part IX.

F.R.Civ.P.	Rule in Part V or IX
6	9006
7(b)	9013
10(a)	9004(b)
11	9011

---

[1] So in original. Probably should be only one section symbol.

ADVERSARY PROCEEDINGS — Rule 7001

F.R.Civ.P.	Rule in Part V or IX
38, 39	9015(a)–(e)
47–51	9015(f)
43, 44, 44.1	9017
45	9016
58	9021
59	9023
60	9024
61	9005
63	9028
77(a), (b), (c)	5001
77(d)	9022(d)
79(a)–(d)	5003
81(c)	9027
83	9029
92	9030

Proceedings to which the rules in Part VII apply directly include those brought to avoid transfers by the debtor under §§ 544, 545, 547, 548 and 549 of the Code; subject to important exceptions, proceedings to recover money or property; proceedings on bonds under Rules 5008(d) and 9025; proceedings under Rule 4004 to determine whether a discharge in a chapter 7 or 11 case should be denied because of an objection grounded on § 727 and proceedings in a chapter 7 or 13 case to revoke a discharge as provided in §§ 727(d) or 1328(e); and proceedings initiated pursuant to § 523(c) of the Code to determine the dischargeability of a particular debt. Those proceedings were classified as adversary proceedings under former Bankruptcy Rule 701.

Also included as adversary proceedings are proceedings to revoke an order of confirmation of a plan in a chapter 11 or 13 case as provided in §§ 1144 and 1330, to subordinate under § 510(c), other than as part of a plan, an allowed claim or interest, and to sell under § 363(h) both the interest of the estate and a co-owner in property.

Declaratory judgments with respect to the subject matter of the various adversary proceedings are also adversary proceedings.

Any claim or cause of action removed to a bankruptcy court pursuant to 28 U.S.C. § 1478 is also an adversary proceeding.

Unlike former Bankruptcy Rule 701, requests for relief from an automatic stay do not commence an adversary proceeding. Section 362(e) of the Code and Rule 4001 establish an expedited schedule for judicial disposition of requests for relief from the automatic stay. The formalities of the adversary proceeding process and the time for serving pleadings are not well suited to the expedited schedule. The motion practice prescribed in Rule 4001 is best suited to such requests because the court has the flexibility to fix hearing dates and other deadlines appropriate to the particular situation.

Clause (1) contains important exceptions. A person with an interest in property in the possession of the trustee or debtor in possession may seek to recover or reclaim that property under § 554(b) or § 725 of the Code. Since many attempts to recover or reclaim property under these two sections do not generate disputes, application of the formalities of the Part VII Rules is not appropriate. Also excluded from adversary proceedings is litigation arising from an examination under Rule 2017 of a debtor's payments of money or transfers of property to an attorney representing the debtor in a case under the Code or an examination of a superseded administration under Rule 6002.

Exemptions and objections thereto are governed by Rule 4003. Filing of proofs of claim and the allowances thereof are governed by Rules 3001–3005, and objections to claims are governed by Rule 3007.

Rule 7002   BANKRUPTCY RULES

When an objection to a claim is joined with a demand for relief of the kind specified in this Rule 7001, the matter becomes an adversary proceeding. See Rule 3007.

1987 Amendment

Another exception is added to clause (1). A trustee may proceed by motion to recover property from the debtor.

1991 Amendment

Clauses (5) and (8) are amended to include chapter 12 plans.

1999 Amendments

This rule is amended to recognize that an adversary proceeding is not necessary to obtain injunctive or other equitable relief that is provided for in a plan under circumstances in which substantive law permits the relief. Other amendments are stylistic.

2010 Amendments

Paragraph (4) of the rule is amended to create an exception for objections to discharge under §§ 727(a)(8), (a)(9), and 1328(f) of the Code. Because objections to discharge on these grounds typically present issues more easily resolved than other objections to discharge, the more formal procedures applicable to adversary proceedings, such as commencement by a complaint, are not required. Instead, objections on these three grounds are governed by Rule 4004(d). In an appropriate case, however, Rule 9014(c) allows the court to order that additional provisions of Part VII of the rules apply to these matters.

CROSS REFERENCES

Adversarial nature of proceeding—

    Avoidance of indemnifying lien or transfer to surety, see Fed.Rules Bankr.Proc. Rule 6010, 11 USCA.

    Commenced by complaint objecting to discharge, see Fed.Rules Bankr.Proc. Rule 4004, 11 USCA.

    Commenced by complaint to obtain determination of debt's dischargeability, see Fed.Rules Bankr.Proc. Rule 4007, 11 USCA.

    Joinder of objection to claim with demand for relief, see Fed.Rules Bankr.Proc. Rule 3007, 11 USCA.

    Liability of sureties on bond or stipulation or other undertaking, see Fed.Rules Bankr.Proc. Rule 9025, 11 USCA.

Applicability of rules of this part to removed claim or cause of action, see Fed.Rules Bankr.Proc. Rule 9027, 11 USCA.

Contested matters, applicability of and notice to parties of applicability of rules of this part, see Fed.Rules Bankr.Proc. Rule 9014, 11 USCA.

Effect of amendment of Federal Rules of Civil Procedure, see Fed.Rules Bankr.Proc. Rule 9032, 11 USCA.

Meanings of words in Federal Rules of Civil Procedure when applicable, see Fed.Rules Bankr.Proc. Rule 9002, 11 USCA.

Rule 7002. References to Federal Rules of Civil Procedure

Whenever a Federal Rule of Civil Procedure applicable to adversary proceedings makes reference to another Federal Rule of Civil Procedure, the reference shall be read as a reference to the Federal Rule of Civil Procedure as modified in this Part VII.

ADVISORY COMMITTEE NOTES

Rules 5, 12, 13, 14, 25, 27, 30, 41 and 52 F.R.Civ.P. are made applicable to adversary proceedings by Part VII. Each of those rules contains a cross reference to another Federal Rule; however, the Part VII

ADVERSARY PROCEEDINGS

rule which incorporates the cross-referenced Federal Rule modifies the Federal Rule in some way. Under this Rule 7002 the cross reference is to the Federal Rule as modified by Part VII. For example, Rule 5 F.R.Civ.P., which is made applicable to adversary proceedings by Rule 7005, contains a reference to Rule 4 F.R.Civ.P. Under this Rule 7002, the cross reference is to Rule 4 F.R.Civ.P. as modified by Rule 7004.

Rules 7, 10, 12, 13, 14, 19, 22, 23.2, 24–37, 41, 45, 49, 50, 52, 55, 59, 60, 62 F.R.Civ.P. are made applicable to adversary proceedings by Part VII or generally to cases under the Code by Part IX. Each of those Federal Rules contains a cross reference to another Federal Rule which is not modified by the Part VII or Part IX rule which makes the cross-referenced Federal Rule applicable. Since the cross-referenced rule is not modified by a Part VII rule this Rule 7002 does not apply.

Rule 7003. Commencement of Adversary Proceeding

Rule 3 F.R.Civ.P. applies in adversary proceedings.

ADVISORY COMMITTEE NOTES

Rule 5005(a) requires that a complaint commencing an adversary proceeding be filed with the court in which the case under the Code is pending unless 28 U.S.C. § 1473 authorizes the filing of the complaint in another district.

CROSS REFERENCES

Complaint filed with court in which case is pending, see Fed.Rules Bankr.Proc. Rule 5005, 11 USCA.

Rule 7004. Process; Service of Summons, Complaint

(a) Summons; service; proof of service

(1) Except as provided in Rule 7004(a)(2), Rule 4(a), (b), (c)(1), (d)(1), (e)–(j), (l), and (m) F.R.Civ.P. applies in adversary proceedings. Personal service under Rule 4(e)–(j) F.R.Civ.P. may be made by any person at least 18 years of age who is not a party, and the summons may be delivered by the clerk to any such person.

(2) The clerk may sign, seal, and issue a summons electronically by putting an "s/" before the clerk's name and including the court's seal on the summons.

(b) Service by first class mail

Except as provided in subdivision (h), in addition to the methods of service authorized by Rule 4(e)–(j) F.R.Civ.P., service may be made within the United States by first class mail postage prepaid as follows:

(1) Upon an individual other than an infant or incompetent, by mailing a copy of the summons and complaint to the individual's dwelling house or usual place of abode or to the place where the individual regularly conducts a business or profession.

(2) Upon an infant or an incompetent person, by mailing a copy of the summons and complaint to the person upon whom process is prescribed to be served by the law of the state in which service is made when an action is brought against such a defendant in the courts of general jurisdiction of that state. The summons and complaint in that case shall be addressed to the person required to be served at that person's dwelling house or usual place of abode or at the place where the person regularly conducts a business or profession.

(3) Upon a domestic or foreign corporation or upon a partnership or other unincorporated association, by mailing a copy of the summons and complaint to the attention of an officer, a managing or general agent, or to any other agent authorized by appointment or by law to receive service of process and, if the agent is one authorized by statute to receive service and the statute so requires, by also mailing a copy to the defendant.

(4) Upon the United States, by mailing a copy of the summons and complaint addressed to the civil process clerk at the office of the United States attorney for the district in which the action is brought and by mailing a copy of the summons and complaint to the Attorney General

of the United States at Washington, District of Columbia, and in any action attacking the validity of an order of an officer or an agency of the United States not made a party, by also mailing a copy of the summons and complaint to that officer or agency. The court shall allow a reasonable time for service pursuant to this subdivision for the purpose of curing the failure to mail a copy of the summons and complaint to multiple officers, agencies, or corporations of the United States if the plaintiff has mailed a copy of the summons and complaint either to the civil process clerk at the office of the United States attorney or to the Attorney General of the United States.

(5) Upon any officer or agency of the United States, by mailing a copy of the summons and complaint to the United States as prescribed in paragraph (4) of this subdivision and also to the officer or agency. If the agency is a corporation, the mailing shall be as prescribed in paragraph (3) of this subdivision of this rule. The court shall allow a reasonable time for service pursuant to this subdivision for the purpose of curing the failure to mail a copy of the summons and complaint to multiple officers, agencies, or corporations of the United States if the plaintiff has mailed a copy of the summons and complaint either to the civil process clerk at the office of the United States attorney or to the Attorney General of the United States. If the United States trustee is the trustee in the case and service is made upon the United States trustee solely as trustee, service may be made as prescribed in paragraph (10) of this subdivision of this rule.

(6) Upon a state or municipal corporation or other governmental organization thereof subject to suit, by mailing a copy of the summons and complaint to the person or office upon whom process is prescribed to be served by the law of the state in which service is made when an action is brought against such a defendant in the courts of general jurisdiction of that state, or in the absence of the designation of any such person or office by state law, then to the chief executive officer thereof.

(7) Upon a defendant of any class referred to in paragraph (1) or (3) of this subdivision of this rule, it is also sufficient if a copy of the summons and complaint is mailed to the entity upon whom service is prescribed to be served by any statute of the United States or by the law of the state in which service is made when an action is brought against such a defendant in the court of general jurisdiction of that state.

(8) Upon any defendant, it is also sufficient if a copy of the summons and complaint is mailed to an agent of such defendant authorized by appointment or by law to receive service of process, at the agent's dwelling house or usual place of abode or at the place where the agent regularly carries on a business or profession and, if the authorization so requires, by mailing also a copy of the summons and complaint to the defendant as provided in this subdivision.

(9) Upon the debtor, after a petition has been filed by or served upon the debtor and until the case is dismissed or closed, by mailing a copy of the summons and complaint to the debtor at the address shown in the petition or to such other address as the debtor may designate in a filed writing.

(10) Upon the United States trustee, when the United States trustee is the trustee in the case and service is made upon the United States trustee solely as trustee, by mailing a copy of the summons and complaint to an office of the United States trustee or another place designated by the United States trustee in the district where the case under the Code is pending.

(c) Service by publication

If a party to an adversary proceeding to determine or protect rights in property in the custody of the court cannot be served as provided in Rule 4(e)-(j) F.R.Civ.P. or subdivision (b) of this rule, the court may order the summons and complaint to be served by mailing copies thereof by first class mail, postage prepaid, to the party's last known address, and by at least one publication in such manner and form as the court may direct.

(d) Nationwide service of process

The summons and complaint and all other process except a subpoena may be served anywhere in the United States.

ADVERSARY PROCEEDINGS — Rule 7004

(e) Summons: time limit for service within the United States

Service made under Rule 4(e), (g), (h)(1), (i), or (j)(2) F.R.Civ.P. shall be by delivery of the summons and complaint within 7 days after the summons is issued. If service is by any authorized form of mail, the summons and complaint shall be deposited in the mail within 7 days after the summons is issued. If a summons is not timely delivered or mailed, another summons shall be issued and served. This subdivision does not apply to service in a foreign country.

(f) Personal jurisdiction

If the exercise of jurisdiction is consistent with the Constitution and laws of the United States, serving a summons or filing a waiver of service in accordance with this rule or the subdivisions of Rule 4 F.R.Civ.P. made applicable by these rules is effective to establish personal jurisdiction over the person of any defendant with respect to a case under the Code or a civil proceeding arising under the Code, or arising in or related to a case under the Code.

(g) Service on debtor's attorney

If the debtor is represented by an attorney, whenever service is made upon the debtor under this Rule, service shall also be made upon the debtor's attorney by any means authorized under Rule 5(b) F.R.Civ.P.

(h) Service of process on an insured depository institution

Service on an insured depository institution (as defined in section 3 of the Federal Deposit Insurance Act) in a contested matter or adversary proceeding shall be made by certified mail addressed to an officer of the institution unless—

(1) the institution has appeared by its attorney, in which case the attorney shall be served by first class mail;

(2) the court orders otherwise after service upon the institution by certified mail of notice of an application to permit service on the institution by first class mail sent to an officer of the institution designated by the institution; or

(3) the institution has waived in writing its entitlement to service by certified mail by designating an officer to receive service.

(As amended Mar. 30, 1987, eff. Aug. 1, 1987; Apr. 30, 1991, eff. Aug. 1, 1991; Oct. 22, 1994, Pub.L. 103–394, Title I, § 114, 108 Stat. 4118; Apr. 23, 1996, eff. Dec. 1, 1996; Apr. 29, 1999, eff. Dec. 1, 1999; Apr. 25, 2005, eff. Dec. 1, 2005; Apr. 12, 2006, eff. Dec. 1, 2006; Mar. 26, 2009, eff. Dec. 1, 2009; Apr. 25, 2014, eff. Dec. 1, 2014.)

ADVISORY COMMITTEE NOTES

Subdivision (a) of the rule, by incorporation of Rule 4(a), (b), (d), (e) and (g)–(i) F.R.Civ.P., governs the mechanics of issuance of a summons and its form, the manner of service on parties and their representatives, and service in foreign countries.

Subdivision (b), which is the same as former Rule 704(c), authorizes service of process by first class mail postage prepaid. This rule retains the modes of service contained in former Bankruptcy Rule 704. The former practice, in effect since 1976, has proven satisfactory.

Subdivision (c) is derived from former Bankruptcy Rule 704(d)(2).

Subdivision (d). Nationwide service of process is authorized by subdivision (d).

Subdivision (e) authorizes service by delivery on individuals and corporations in foreign countries if the party to be served is the debtor or any person required to perform the duties of the debtor and certain other persons, the adversary proceeding involves property in the custody of the bankruptcy court, or if federal or state law authorizes such service in a foreign country.

Subdivision (f). The requirement of former Bankruptcy Rule 704 that the summons be served within 10 days is carried over into these rules by subdivision (f).

Rule 7004 — BANKRUPTCY RULES

1987 Amendment

Subdivision (a) is amended to make Rule 4(j) F.R.Civ.P. applicable to service of the summons. If service is not completed within 120 days of the filing of the complaint, the complaint may be dismissed.

Technical amendments are made to subdivisions (a), (b), (e), and (f) to conform to recent amendments to Rule 4 F.R.Civ.P.

1991 Amendment

The United States trustee may serve as trustee in a case pursuant to 28 U.S.C. § 586(a)(2) and §§ 701(a)(2), 1202(a), and 1302(a) of the Code. This rule is amended to avoid the necessity of mailing copies of a summons and complaint or other pleadings to the Attorney General and to the United States attorney when service on the United States trustee is required only because the United States trustee is acting as a case trustee. For example, a proceeding commenced by a creditor to dismiss a case for unreasonable delay under § 707(a) is governed by Rule 9014 which requires service on the trustee pursuant to the requirements of Rule 7004 for the service of a summons and complaint. The Attorney General and the United States attorney would have no interest in receiving a copy of the motion to dismiss. Mailing to the office of the United States trustee when acting as the case trustee is sufficient in such cases.

The words "with the court" in subdivision (b)(9) are deleted as unnecessary. See Rules 5005(a) and 9001(3).

The new paragraph (10) of subdivision (b) does not affect requirements for service of process on the United States trustee when sued or otherwise a party to a litigation unrelated to its capacity as a trustee. If a proceeding is commenced against the United States trustee which is unrelated to the United States trustee's role as trustee, the requirements of paragraph (5) of subdivision (b) of this rule would apply.

Subdivision (g) is added in anticipation of substantial amendment to, and restructuring of subdivisions of, Rule 4 F.R.Civ.P. Any amendment to Rule 4 will not affect service in bankruptcy cases and proceedings until further amendment to the Bankruptcy Rules. On January 1, 1990, Rule 4 F.R.Civ.P. read as follows:

Rule 4 F.R.Civ.P.

PROCESS

(a) **Summons: issuance.** Upon the filing of the complaint the clerk shall forthwith issue a summons and deliver the summons of the plaintiff or the plaintiff's attorney, who shall be responsible for prompt service of the summons and a copy of the complaint. Upon request of the plaintiff separate or additional summons shall issue against any defendants.

(b) **Same: form.** The summons shall be signed by the clerk, be under the seal of the court, contain the name of the court and the names of the parties, be directed to the defendant, state the name and address of the plaintiff's attorney, if any, otherwise the plaintiff's address, and the time within which these rules require the defendant to appear and defend, and shall notify the defendant that in case of the defendant's failure to do so judgment by default will be rendered against the defendant for the relief demanded in the complaint. When, under Rule 4(e), service is made pursuant to a statute or rule of court of a state, the summons, or notice, or order in lieu of summons shall correspond as nearly as may be to that required by the statute or rule.

(c) **Service**

    (1) [Not applicable.]

    (2)(A) [Not applicable.]

    (B) [Not applicable.]

    (C) A summons and complaint may be served upon a defendant of any class referred to in paragraph (1) or (3) of subdivision (d) of this rule—

        (i) pursuant to the law of the State in which the district court held for the service of summons or other like process upon such defendant in an action brought in the courts of general jurisdiction of that State, or

        (ii) [Not applicable.]

    (D) [Not applicable.]

(E) [Not applicable.]

(3) [Not applicable.]

(d) Summons and complaint: person to be served. The summons and complaint shall be served together. The plaintiff shall furnish the person making service with such copies as are necessary. Service shall be made as follows:

(1) Upon an individual other than an infant or an incompetent person, by delivering a copy of the summons and of the complaint to the individual personally or by leaving copies thereof at the individual's dwelling house or usual place of abode with some person of suitable age and discretion then residing therein or by delivering a copy of the summons and of the complaint to an agent authorized by appointment or by law to receive service of process.

(2) Upon an infant or an incompetent person, by serving the summons and complaint in the manner prescribed by the law of the state in which the service is made for the service of summons or other like process upon any such defendant in an action brought in the courts of general jurisdiction of that state.

(3) Upon a domestic or foreign corporation or upon a partnership or other unincorporated association which the subject to suit under a common name, by delivering a copy of the summons and of the complaint to an officer, a managing or general agent, or to any other agent authorized by appointment or by law to receive service of process and, if the agent is one authorized by statute to receive service and the statute so requires, by also mailing a copy to the defendant.

(4) Upon the United States, by delivering a copy of the summons and of the complaint to the United States attorney for the district in which the action is brought or to an assistant United States attorney or clerical employee designated by the United States attorney in a writing filed with the clerk of the court and by sending a copy of the summons and of the complaint by registered or certified mail to the Attorney General of the United States at Washington, District of Columbia, and in any action attacking the validity of an order of an officer or agency of the United States not made a party, by also sending a copy of the summons and of the complaint by registered or certified mail to such officer or agency.

(5) Upon an officer or agency of the United States, by serving the United States and by sending a copy of the summons and of the complaint by registered or certified mail to such officer or agency. If the agency is a corporation the copy shall be delivered as provided in paragraph (3) of this subdivision of this rule.

(6) Upon a state or municipal corporation or other governmental organization thereof subject to suit, by delivering a copy of the summons and of the complaint to the chief executive officer thereof or by serving the summons and complaint in the manner prescribed by the law of that state for the service of summons or other like process upon any such defendant.

(e) Summons: service upon party not inhabitant of or found within state. Whenever a statute of the United States or an order of court thereunder provides for service of a summons, or of a notice, or of an order in lieu of summons upon a party not an inhabitant of or found within the state in which the district court is held, service may be made under the circumstances and in the manner prescribed by the statute or order, or, if there is no provision therein prescribing the manner of service, in a manner stated in this rule. Whenever a statute or rule of court of the state in which the district court is held provides (1) for service of a summons, or of a notice, or of an order in lieu of summons upon a party not an inhabitant of or found within the state, or (2) for service upon or notice to such a party to appear and respond or defend in an action by reason of the attachment or garnishment or similar seizure of the party's property located within the state, service may in either case be made under the circumstances and in the manner prescribed in the statute or rule.

(f) [Not applicable.]

(g) Return. The person serving the process shall make proof of service thereof to the court promptly and in any event within the time during which the person served must respond to the process. If service is made by a person other than a United States marshal or deputy United States marshal, such person shall make affidavit thereof. If service is made under subdivision (c)(2)(C)(ii) of this rule, return shall be made by the sender's filing with the court the acknowledgement received pursuant to such subdivision. Failure to make proof of service does not affect the validity of the service.

(h) Amendment. At any time in its discretion and upon such terms as it deems just, the court may allow any process or proof of service thereof to be amended, unless it clearly appears that material prejudice would result to the substantial rights of the party against whom the process issued.

(i) Alternative provisions for service in a foreign country.

(1) Manner. When the federal or state law referred to in subdivision (e) of this rule authorizes service upon a party not an inhabitant of or found within the state in which the district court is held, and service is to be effected upon the party in a foreign country, it is also sufficient if service of the summons and complaint is made: (A) in the manner prescribed by the law of the foreign country for service in that country in an action in any of its courts of general jurisdiction; or (B) as directed by the foreign authority in response to a letter rogatory, when service in either case is reasonably calculated to give actual notice; or (C) upon an individual, by delivery to the individual personally, and upon a corporation or partnership or association, by delivery to an officer, a managing or general agent; or (D) by any form of mail, requiring a signed receipt, to be addressed and dispatched by the clerk of the court to the party to be served; or (E) above may be made by any person who is not a party and is not less than 18 years of age or who is designated by order of the district court or by the foreign court. On request, the clerk shall deliver the summons to the plaintiff for transmission to the person or the foreign court or officer who will make the service.

(2) Return. Proof of service may be made as prescribed by subdivision (g) of this rule, or by the law of the foreign country, or by order of the court. When service is made pursuant to subparagraph (1)(D) of this subdivision, proof of service shall include a receipt signed by the addressee or other evidence of delivery to the addressee satisfactory to the court.

(j) Summons: time limit for service. If a service of the summons and complaint is not made upon a defendant within 120 days after the filing of the complaint and the party on whose behalf such service was required cannot show good cause why such service was not made within that period, the action shall be dismissed as to that defendant without prejudice upon the court's own initiative with notice to such party or upon motion. This subdivision shall not apply to service in a foreign country pursuant to subdivision (i) of this rule.

1996 Amendments

The purpose of these amendments is to conform the rule to the 1993 revisions of Rule 4 F.R.Civ.P. and to make stylistic improvements. Rule 7004, as amended, continues to provide for service by first class mail as an alternative to the methods of personal service provided in Rule 4 F.R.Civ.P., except as provided in the new subdivision (h).

Rule 4(d)(2) F.R.Civ.P. provides a procedure by which the plaintiff may request by first class mail that the defendant waive service of the summons. This procedure is not applicable in adversary proceedings because it is not necessary in view of the availability of service by mail pursuant to Rule 7004(b). However, if a written waiver of service of a summons is made in an adversary proceeding, Rule 4(d)(1) F.R.Civ.P. applies so that the defendant does not thereby waive any objection to the venue or the jurisdiction of the court over the person of the defendant.

Subdivisions (b)(4) and (b)(5) are amended to conform to the 1993 amendments to Rule 4(i)(3) F.R.Civ.P., which protect the plaintiff from the hazard of losing a substantive right because of failure to comply with the requirements of multiple service when the United States or an officer, agency, or corporation of the United States is a defendant. These subdivisions also are amended to require that the summons and complaint be addressed to the civil process clerk at the office of the United States attorney.

Subdivision (e), which has governed service in a foreign country, is abrogated and Rule 4(f) and (h)(2) F.R.Civ.P., as substantially revised in 1993, are made applicable in adversary proceedings.

The new subdivision (f) is consistent with the 1993 amendments to F.R.Civ.P. 4(k)(2). It clarifies that service or filing a waiver of service in accordance with this rule or the applicable subdivisions of F.R.Civ.P. 4 is sufficient to establish personal jurisdiction over the defendant. See the committee note to the 1993 amendments to Rule 4 F.R.Civ.P.

Subdivision (g) is abrogated. This subdivision was promulgated in 1991 so that anticipated revisions to Rule 4 F.R.Civ.P. would not affect service of process in adversary proceedings until further amendment to Rule 7004.

Subdivision (h) and the first phrase of subdivision (b) were added by § 114 of the Bankruptcy Reform Act of 1994, Pub.L. No. 103–394, 108 Stat. 4106.

ADVERSARY PROCEEDINGS   Rule 7004

1999 Amendments

Subdivision (e) is amended so that the ten-day time limit for service of a summons does not apply if the summons is served in a foreign country.

2005 Amendments

This amendment specifically authorizes the clerk to issue a summons electronically. In some bankruptcy cases the trustee or debtor in possession may commence hundreds of adversary proceedings simultaneously, and permitting the electronic signing and sealing of the summonses for those proceedings increases the efficiency of the clerk's office without any negative impact on any party. The rule only authorizes electronic issuance of the summons. It does not address the service requirements for the summons. Those requirements are set out elsewhere in Rule 7004, and nothing in Rule 7004(a)(2) should be construed as authorizing electronic service of a summons.

2006 Amendments

Under current Rule 7004, an entity may serve a summons and complaint upon the debtor by personal service or by mail. If the entity chooses to serve the debtor by mail, it must also serve a copy of the summons and complaint on the debtor's attorney by mail. If the entity effects personal service on the debtor, there is no requirement that the debtor's attorney also be served.

Subdivision (b)(9). The rule is amended to delete the reference in subdivision (b)(9) to the debtor's address as set forth in the statement of financial affairs. In 1991, the Official Form of the statement of financial affairs was revised and no longer includes a question regarding the debtor's current residence. Since that time, Official Form 1, the petition, has required the debtor to list both the debtor's residence and mailing address. Therefore, the subdivision is amended to delete the statement of financial affairs as a document that might contain an address at which the debtor can be served.

Subdivision (g). The rule is amended to require service on the debtor's attorney whenever the debtor is served with a summons and complaint. The amendment makes this change by deleting that portion of Rule 7004(b)(9) that requires service on the debtor's attorney when the debtor is served by mail, and relocates the obligation to serve the debtor's attorney into new subdivision (g). Service on the debtor's attorney is not limited to mail service, but may be accomplished by any means permitted under Rule 5(b) F.R.Civ.P.

2009 Amendments

The rule is amended to implement changes in connection with the amendment to Rule 9006(a) and the manner by which time is computed under the rules. The deadlines in the rule are amended to substitute a deadline that is a multiple of seven days. Throughout the rules, deadlines are amended in the following manner:

- 5-day periods become 7-day periods
- 10-day periods become 14-day periods
- 15-day periods become 14-day periods
- 20-day periods become 21-day periods
- 25-day periods become 28-day periods

2014 Amendment

Subdivision (e) is amended to alter the period of time during which service of the summons and complaint must be made. The amendment reduces that period from fourteen days to seven days after issuance of the summons. Because Rule 7012 provides that the defendant's time to answer the complaint is calculated from the date the summons is issued, a lengthy delay between issuance and service of the summons may unduly shorten the defendant's time to respond. The amendment is therefore intended to encourage prompt service after issuance of a summons. If service of the summons within any seven-day period is impracticable, a court retains the discretion to enlarge that period of time under Rule 9006(b).

CROSS REFERENCES

Contested matters, request for relief by motion served in manner provided in this rule, see Fed.Rules Bankr.Proc. Rule 9014, 11 USCA.

Form of pleadings, see Fed.Rules Bankr.Proc. Rule 7010, 11 USCA.

Service of—

    Motion for substitution of parties, see Fed.Rules Bankr.Proc. Rule 7025, 11 USCA.

    Notice of depositions before adversary proceedings or pending appeal, see Fed.Rules Bankr.Proc. Rule 7027, 11 USCA.

    Pleadings and other papers, see Fed.Rules Bankr.Proc. Rule 7005, 11 USCA.

Summons and involuntary petition—

    Manner of service, see Fed.Rules Bankr.Proc. Rule 1010, 11 USCA.

    Time limitations, see Fed.Rules Bankr.Proc. Rule 1010, 11 USCA.

Rule 7005. Service and Filing of Pleadings and Other Papers

Rule 5 F.R.Civ.P. applies in adversary proceedings.

ADVISORY COMMITTEE NOTES

Rule 5 F.R.Civ.P. refers to Rule 4 F.R.Civ.P. Pursuant to Rule 7002 this reference is to Rule 4 F.R.Civ.P. as incorporated and modified by Rule 7004.

CROSS REFERENCES

Applicability of this rule in proceedings on contested involuntary petition and to vacate order for relief, see Fed.Rules Bankr.Proc. Rule 1018, 11 USCA.

Form of pleadings, see Fed.Rules Bankr.Proc. Rule 7010, 11 USCA.

Service of—

    Motion for substitution, see Fed.Rules Bankr.Proc. Rule 7025, 11 USCA.

    Motion to intervene, see Fed.Rules Bankr. Proc. Rule 7024, 11 USCA.

    Notice of judgment or order, see Fed.Rules Bankr.Proc. Rule 9022, 11 USCA.

    Requests for depositions and discovery, see Fed.Rules Bankr.Proc. Rule 7027 et seq., 11 USCA.

Rule 7007. Pleadings Allowed

Rule 7 F.R.Civ.P. applies in adversary proceedings.

CROSS REFERENCES

Amended and supplemental pleadings, see Fed.Rules Bankr.Proc. Rule 7015, 11 USCA.

Counterclaim and cross-claim, see Fed.Rules Bankr.Proc. Rule 7013, 11 USCA.

Form of pleadings, see Fed.Rules Bankr.Proc. Rule 7010, 11 USCA.

Service and filing of pleadings and other papers, see Fed.Rules Bankr.Proc. Rule 7005, 11 USCA.

Third-party practice, see Fed.Rules Bankr.Proc. Rule 7014, 11 USCA.

Rule 7007.1. Corporate Ownership Statement

(a) Required disclosure

Any corporation that is a party to an adversary proceeding, other than the debtor or a governmental unit, shall file two copies of a statement that identifies any corporation, other than a governmental unit, that directly or indirectly owns 10% or more of any class of the corporation's equity interests, or states that there are no entities to report under this subdivision.

(b) Time for Filing

A party shall file the statement required under Rule 7007.1(a) with its first appearance, pleading, motion, response, or other request addressed to the court. A party shall file a supplemental statement promptly upon any change in circumstances that this rule requires the party to identify or disclose.

(Added Mar. 27, 2003, eff. Dec. 1, 2003. As amended Apr. 30, 2007, eff. Dec. 1, 2007.)

ADVISORY COMMITTEE NOTES
2003 Adoption

This rule is derived from Rule 26.1 of the Federal Rules of Appellate Procedure. The information that parties shall supply will support properly informed disqualification decisions in situations that call for automatic disqualification under Canon 3C(1)(c) of the Code of Conduct for United States Judges. This rule does not cover all of the circumstances that may call for disqualification under the subjective financial interest standard of Canon 3C, and does not deal at all with other circumstances that may call for disqualification. Nevertheless, the required disclosures are calculated to reach the majority of circumstances that are likely to call for disqualification under Canon 3C(1)(c).

The rule directs nongovernmental corporate parties to list those corporations that hold significant ownership interests in them. This includes listing membership interests in limited liability companies and similar entities that fall under the definition of a corporation in Bankruptcy Code § 101.

Under subdivision (b), parties must file the statement with the first document that they file in any adversary proceeding. The rule also requires parties and other persons to file supplemental statements promptly whenever changed circumstances require disclosure of new or additional information.

The rule does not prohibit the adoption of local rules requiring disclosures beyond those called for in Rule 7007.1.

2007 Amendments

The rule is amended to clarify that a party must file a corporate ownership statement with its initial paper filed with the court in an adversary proceeding. The party's initial filing may be a document that is not a "pleading" as defined in Rule 7 F. R. Civ. P., which is made applicable in adversary proceedings by Rule 7007. The amendment also brings Rule 7007.1 more closely in line with Rule 7.1 F. R. Civ. P.

Rule 7008. General Rules of Pleading

Rule 8 F.R.Civ.P. applies in adversary proceedings. The allegation of jurisdiction required by Rule 8(a) shall also contain a reference to the name, number, and chapter of the case under the Code to which the adversary proceeding relates and to the district and division where the case under the Code is pending. In an adversary proceeding before a bankruptcy judge, the complaint, counterclaim, cross-claim, or third-party complaint shall contain a statement that the proceeding is core or non-core and, if non-core, that the pleader does or does not consent to entry of final orders or judgment by the bankruptcy judge.

(As amended Mar. 30, 1987, eff. Aug. 1, 1987; Apr. 25, 2014, eff. Dec. 1, 2014.).)

ADVISORY COMMITTEE NOTES
1987 Amendment

Proceedings before a bankruptcy judge are either core or non-core. 28 U.S.C. § 157. A bankruptcy judge may enter a final order or judgment in a core proceeding. In a non-core proceeding, absent consent of the parties, the bankruptcy judge may not enter a final order or judgment but may only submit proposed findings of fact and conclusions of law to the district judge who will enter the final order or judgment. 28 U.S.C. § 157(c)(1). The amendment to subdivision (a) of this rule requires an allegation as to whether a proceeding is core or non-core. A party who alleges that the proceeding is non-core shall state whether the party does or does not consent to the entry of a final order or judgment by the bankruptcy judge. Failure to include the statement of consent does not constitute consent. Only express consent in the pleadings or otherwise is effective to authorize entry of a final order or judgment by the bankruptcy judge in a non-core proceeding. Amendments to Rule 7012 require that the defendant admit or deny the allegation as to whether the proceeding is core or non-core.

2014 Amendments

Former subdivision (a) is amended to remove the requirement that the pleader state whether the proceeding is core or non-core and to require in all proceedings that the pleader state whether the party does or does not consent to the entry of final orders or judgment by the bankruptcy court. Some proceedings that satisfy the statutory definition of core proceedings, 28 U.S.C. § 157(b)(2), may remain beyond the constitutional power of a bankruptcy judge to adjudicate finally. The amended rule calls for the pleader to make a statement regarding consent, whether or not a proceeding is termed non-core. Rule 7012(b) has been amended to require a similar statement in a responsive pleading. The bankruptcy judge will then determine the appropriate course of proceedings under Rule 7016.

The rule is also amended to delete subdivision (b), which required a request for attorney's fees always to be pleaded as a claim in an allowed pleading. That requirement, which differed from the practice under the Federal Rules of Civil Procedure, had the potential to serve as a trap for the unwary.

The procedures for seeking an award of attorney's fees are now set out in Rule 7054(b)(2), which makes applicable most of the provisions of Rule 54(d)(2) F.R.Civ.P. As specified by Rule 54(d)(2)(A) and (B) F.R.Civ.P., a claim for attorney's fees must be made by a motion filed no later than 14 days after entry of the judgment unless the governing substantive law requires those fees to be proved at trial as an element of damages. When fees are an element of damages, such as when the terms of a contract provide for the recovery of fees incurred prior to the instant adversary proceeding, the general pleading requirements of this rule still apply.

CROSS REFERENCES

Amended and supplemental pleadings, see Fed.Rules Bankr.Proc. Rule 7015, 11 USCA.

Applicability of this rule in proceedings on contested involuntary petition and to vacate order for relief, see Fed.Rules Bankr.Proc. Rule 1018, 11 USCA.

Defenses and objections, see Fed.Rules Bankr.Proc. Rule 7012, 11 USCA.

Joinder of claims and remedies, see Fed.Rules Bankr.Proc. Rule 7013, 11 USCA.

Rule 7009. Pleading Special Matters

Rule 9 F.R.Civ.P. applies in adversary proceedings.

CROSS REFERENCES

Applicability of this rule in proceedings on contested involuntary petition and to vacate order for relief, see Fed.Rules Bankr.Proc. Rule 1018, 11 USCA.

Parties plaintiff and defendant; capacity, see Fed.Rules Bankr.Proc. Rule 7017, 11 USCA.

Pleading affirmative defenses, see Fed.Rules Bankr.Proc. Rule 7008, 11 USCA.

Rule 7010. Form of Pleadings

Rule 10 F.R.Civ.P. applies in adversary proceedings, except that the caption of each pleading in such a proceeding shall conform substantially to the appropriate Official Form.

(As amended Apr. 30, 1991, eff. Aug. 1, 1991.)

ADVISORY COMMITTEE NOTES

1991 Amendment

Reference to the Official Form number is deleted in anticipation of future revision and renumbering of the Official Forms.

ADVERSARY PROCEEDINGS Rule 7012

CROSS REFERENCES

Applicability of this rule in proceedings on contested involuntary petition and to vacate order for relief, see Fed.Rules Bankr.Proc. Rule 1018, 11 USCA.

General requirements of form for adversarial pleading or paper, see Fed.Rules Bankr.Proc. Rule 9004, 11 USCA.

Rule 7012. Defenses and Objections—When and How Presented—By Pleading or Motion—Motion for Judgment on the Pleadings

(a) When presented

If a complaint is duly served, the defendant shall serve an answer within 30 days after the issuance of the summons, except when a different time is prescribed by the court. The court shall prescribe the time for service of the answer when service of a complaint is made by publication or upon a party in a foreign country. A party served with a pleading stating a cross-claim shall serve an answer thereto within 21 days after service. The plaintiff shall serve a reply to a counterclaim in the answer within 21 days after service of the answer or, if a reply is ordered by the court, within 21 days after service of the order, unless the order otherwise directs. The United States or an officer or agency thereof shall serve an answer to a complaint within 35 days after the issuance of the summons, and shall serve an answer to a cross-claim, or a reply to a counterclaim, within 35 days after service upon the United States attorney of the pleading in which the claim is asserted. The service of a motion permitted under this rule alters these periods of time as follows, unless a different time is fixed by order of the court: (1) if the court denies the motion or postpones its disposition until the trial on the merits, the responsive pleading shall be served within 14 days after notice of the court's action; (2) if the court grants a motion for a more definite statement, the responsive pleading shall be served within 14 days after the service of a more definite statement.

(b) Applicability of Rule 12(b)–(i) F.R.Civ.P.

Rule 12(b)–(i) F.R.Civ.P. applies in adversary proceedings. A responsive pleading shall admit or deny an allegation that the proceeding is core or non-core. If the response is that the proceeding is non-core, it shall include a statement that the party does or does not consent to entry of final orders or judgment by the bankruptcy judge. In non-core proceedings final orders and judgments shall not be entered on the bankruptcy judge's order except with the express consent of the parties.

(As amended Mar. 30, 1987, eff. Aug. 1, 1987; Apr. 23, 2008, eff. Dec. 1, 2008; Mar. 26, 2009, eff. Dec. 1, 2009.)

ADVISORY COMMITTEE NOTES

Subdivision (a) continues the practice of former Bankruptcy Rule 712(a) by requiring that the answer to a complaint be filed within 30 days after the issuance of the summons. Under Rule 7004(f), the summons must be served within 10 days of issuance. The other pleading periods in adversary proceedings are the same as those in civil actions before the district courts, except that the United States is allowed 35 rather than 60 days to respond.

Rule 12(b)(7) and (h)(2) F.R.Civ.P. refers to Rule 19 F.R.Civ.P. Pursuant to Rule 7002 these references are to Rule 19 F.R.Civ.P. as incorporated and modified by Rule 7019.

1987 Amendment

The amendment to subdivision (b) requires a response to the allegation that the proceeding is core or non-core. A final order of judgment may not be entered in a non-core proceeding heard by a bankruptcy judge unless all parties expressly consent. 28 U.S.C. § 157(c).

2008 Amendments

The rule is amended to conform to the changes made to the Federal Rules of Civil Procedure through the restyling of those rules effective on December 1, 2007.

2009 Amendments

The rule is amended to implement changes in connection with the amendment to Rule 9006(a) and the manner by which time is computed under the rules. The deadlines in the rule are amended to substitute a deadline that is a multiple of seven days. Throughout the rules, deadlines are amended in the following manner:

- 5-day periods become 7-day periods
- 10-day periods become 14-day periods
- 15-day periods become 14-day periods
- 20-day periods become 21-day periods
- 25-day periods become 28-day periods

CROSS REFERENCES

Averments of defense in separate statements, see Fed.Rules Bankr.Proc. Rule 7010, 11 USCA.

Counterclaim and cross-claim, see Fed.Rules Bankr.Proc. Rule 7013, 11 USCA.

Defenses of third-party defendant, see Fed.Rules Bankr.Proc. Rule 7014, 11 USCA.

Pleadings allowed, see Fed.Rules Bankr.Proc. Rule 7007, 11 USCA.

Removed actions, see Fed.Rules Bankr.Proc. Rule 9027, 11 USCA.

Waiver of sovereign immunity, see 11 USCA § 106.

Rule 7013. Counterclaim and Cross-Claim

Rule 13 F.R.Civ.P. applies in adversary proceedings, except that a party sued by a trustee or debtor in possession need not state as a counterclaim any claim that the party has against the debtor, the debtor's property, or the estate, unless the claim arose after the entry of an order for relief. A trustee or debtor in possession who fails to plead a counterclaim through oversight, inadvertence, or excusable neglect, or when justice so requires, may by leave of court amend the pleading, or commence a new adversary proceeding or separate action.

(As amended Mar. 30, 1987, eff. Aug. 1, 1987.)

ADVISORY COMMITTEE NOTES

Rule 13(h) F.R.Civ.P. refers to Rule 19 F.R.Civ.P. Pursuant to Rule 7002 this reference is to Rule 19 F.R.Civ.P. as incorporated and modified by Rule 7019.

CROSS REFERENCES

Amended and supplemental pleadings, see Fed.Rules Bankr.Proc. Rule 7015, 11 USCA.

Counterclaims and cross-claims of third-party defendant, see Fed.Rules Bankr.Proc. Rule 7014, 11 USCA.

Default judgment against counterclaimants and cross-claimants, see Fed.Rules Bankr.Proc. Rule 7055, 11 USCA.

Dismissal of counterclaims and cross-claims, see Fed.Rules Bankr.Proc. Rule 7041, 11 USCA.

Separate trial of counterclaims and cross-claims, see Fed.Rules Bankr.Proc. Rule 7042, 11 USCA.

Rule 7014. Third-Party Practice

Rule 14 F.R.Civ.P. applies in adversary proceedings.

ADVERSARY PROCEEDINGS Rule 7015

ADVISORY COMMITTEE NOTES

This rule does not purport to deal with questions of jurisdiction. The scope of the jurisdictional grant under 28 U.S.C. § 1471 and whether the doctrines of pendent or ancillary jurisdiction are applicable to adversary proceedings will be determined by the courts.

Rule 14 F.R.Civ.P. refers to Rules 12 and 13 F.R.Civ.P. Pursuant to Rule 7002 those references are to Rules 12 and 13 as incorporated and modified by Rules 7012 and 7013.

CROSS REFERENCES

Default judgment against third-party plaintiff, see Fed.Rules Bankr.Proc. Rule 7055, 11 USCA.

Joinder of claims, see Fed.Rules Bankr.Proc. Rule 7018, 11 USCA.

Requisites of pleading, see Fed.Rules Bankr.Proc. Rule 7008, 11 USCA.

Separate trial of third-party claim, see Fed.Rules Bankr.Proc. Rule 7042, 11 USCA.

Rule 7015. Amended and Supplemental Pleadings

Rule 15 F.R.Civ.P. applies in adversary proceedings.

CROSS REFERENCES

Amendments to pleadings considered at pre-trial conference, see Fed.Rules Bankr.Proc. Rule 7016, 11 USCA.

Applicability of this rule in proceedings on contested involuntary petition and to vacate order for relief, see Fed.Rules Bankr.Proc. Rule 1018, 11 USCA.

Substitution of parties, see Fed.Rules Bankr.Proc. Rule 7025, 11 USCA.

Rule 7016. Pre-Trial Procedure; Formulating Issues

Rule 16 F.R.Civ.P. applies in adversary proceedings.

CROSS REFERENCES

Amended and supplemental pleadings, see Fed.Rules Bankr.Proc. Rule 7015, 11 USCA.

Applicability of this rule in proceedings on contested involuntary petition and to vacate order for relief, see Fed.Rules Bankr.Proc. Rule 1018, 11 USCA.

Preliminary hearing before trial to determine merit of defenses, see Fed.Rules Bankr.Proc. Rule 7012, 11 USCA.

Rule 7017. Parties Plaintiff and Defendant; Capacity

Rule 17 F.R.Civ.P. applies in adversary proceedings, except as provided in Rule 2010(b).

(As amended Apr. 30, 1991, eff. Aug. 1, 1991.)

ADVISORY COMMITTEE NOTES

Rules 2010(d) and 5008(d), which implement §§ 322 and 345 of the Code, authorize a party in interest to prosecute a claim on the bond of a trustee or depository in the name of the United States.

1991 Amendment

Reference to Rule 5008(d) is deleted because of the abrogation of Rule 5008.

CROSS REFERENCES

Bond requirement for deposit or investment by trustee of estate money, see 11 USCA § 345.

Filing by trustee of bond in favor of United States as qualification to serve, see 11 USCA § 322.

Service upon infants or incompetent persons of—

> Notice of application for depositions before adversary proceedings or pending appeal, see Fed.Rules Bankr.Proc. Rule 7027, 11 USCA.
>
> Summons and complaint, see Fed.Rules Bankr.Proc. Rule 7004, 11 USCA.

Rule 7018. Joinder of Claims and Remedies

Rule 18 F.R.Civ.P. applies in adversary proceedings.

CROSS REFERENCES

Joinder of parties—

> Misjoinder and non-joinder, see Fed.Rules Bankr.Proc. Rule 7021, 11 USCA.
>
> Permissive joinder, see Fed.Rules Bankr.Proc. Rule 7020, 11 USCA.
>
> Persons needed for just determination, see Fed.Rules Bankr.Proc. Rule 7019, 11 USCA.

Rule 7019. Joinder of Persons Needed for Just Determination

Rule 19 F.R.Civ.P. applies in adversary proceedings, except that (1) if an entity joined as a party raises the defense that the court lacks jurisdiction over the subject matter and the defense is sustained, the court shall dismiss such entity from the adversary proceeding and (2) if an entity joined as a party properly and timely raises the defense of improper venue, the court shall determine, as provided in 28 U.S.C. § 1412, whether that part of the proceeding involving the joined party shall be transferred to another district, or whether the entire adversary proceeding shall be transferred to another district.

(As amended Mar. 30, 1987, eff. Aug. 1, 1987.)

ADVISORY COMMITTEE NOTES

This rule addresses a situation different from that encountered by the district court when its jurisdiction is based on diversity of citizenship under 28 U.S.C. § 1332. Joining of a party whose citizenship is the same as that of an adversary destroys the district court's jurisdiction over the entire civil action but under 28 U.S.C. § 1471 the attempted joinder of such a person would not affect the bankruptcy court's jurisdiction over the original adversary proceeding.

1987 Amendment

The rule is amended to delete the reference to retention of the adversary proceeding if venue is improper. See 28 U.S.C. § 1412.

CROSS REFERENCES

Additional parties for determination of counterclaim or cross-claim, see Fed.Rules Bankr.Proc. Rule 7013, 11 USCA.

Exception to procedural rule on transfer by court of adversary proceeding, see Fed.Rules Bankr.Proc. Rule 7087, 11 USCA.

Parties—

> Permissive joinder, see Fed.Rules Bankr.Proc. Rule 7020, 11 USCA.
>
> Substitution of, see Fed.Rules Bankr.Proc. Rule 7025, 11 USCA.

Rule 7020. Permissive Joinder of Parties

Rule 20 F.R.Civ.P. applies in adversary proceedings.

ADVERSARY PROCEEDINGS

CROSS REFERENCES

Additional parties for determination of counterclaim or cross-claim, see Fed.Rules Bankr.Proc. Rule 7013, 11 USCA.

Parties—

Joinder of persons needed for just determination, see Fed.Rules Bankr.Proc. Rule 7019, 11 USCA.

Substitution of, see Fed.Rules Bankr.Proc. Rule 7025, 11 USCA.

Rule 7021. Misjoinder and Non-Joinder of Parties

Rule 21 F.R.Civ.P. applies in adversary proceedings.

CROSS REFERENCES

Applicability of this rule in contested matters not otherwise provided for, see Fed.Rules Bankr.Proc. Rule 9014, 11 USCA.

Judgment on counterclaim or cross-claim rendered in separate trials, see Fed.Rules Bankr.Proc. Rule 7013, 11 USCA.

Separate trials—

In furtherance of convenience or to avoid prejudice, see Fed.Rules Bankr.Proc. Rule 7042, 11 USCA.

Of parties joined permissively, see Fed.Rules Bankr.Proc. Rule 7020, 11 USCA.

Rule 7022. Interpleader

Rule 22(a) F.R.Civ.P. applies in adversary proceedings. This rule supplements—and does not limit—the joinder of parties allowed by Rule 7020.

(As amended Apr. 23, 2008, eff. Dec. 1, 2008.)

ADVISORY COMMITTEE NOTES

2008 Amendments

The rule is amended to conform to the changes made to the Federal Rules of Civil Procedure through the restyling of those rules effective on December 1, 2007.

CROSS REFERENCES

Preliminary injunction in interpleader actions, see Fed.Rules Bankr.Proc. Rule 7065, 11 USCA.

Rule 7023. Class Proceedings

Rule 23 F.R.Civ.P. applies in adversary proceedings.

CROSS REFERENCES

Exception of class actions from procedural rule of necessary joinder of parties, see Fed.Rules Bankr.Proc. Rule 7019, 11 USCA.

Rule 7023.1. Derivative Actions

Rule 23.1 F.R.Civ.P. applies in adversary proceedings.

(As amended Apr. 23, 2008, eff. Dec. 1, 2008.)

ADVISORY COMMITTEE NOTES
2008 Amendments

The rule is amended to conform to the changes made to the Federal Rules of Civil Procedure through the restyling of those rules effective on December 1, 2007.

CROSS REFERENCES

Actions relating to unincorporated associations, see Fed.Rules Bankr.Proc. Rule 7023.1, 11 USCA.

Rule 7023.2. Adversary Proceedings Relating to Unincorporated Associations

Rule 23.2 F.R.Civ.P. applies in adversary proceedings.

CROSS REFERENCES

Capacity of unincorporated association to sue or be sued, see Fed.Rules Bankr.Proc. Rule 7017, 11 USCA.

Derivative actions by shareholders, see Fed.Rules Bankr.Proc. Rule 7023.1, 11 USCA.

Rule 7024. Intervention

Rule 24 F.R.Civ.P. applies in adversary proceedings.

ADVISORY COMMITTEE NOTES

A person may seek to intervene in the case under the Code or in an adversary proceeding relating to the case under the Code. Intervention in a case under the Code is governed by Rule 2018 and intervention in an adversary proceeding is governed by this rule. Intervention in a case and intervention in an adversary proceeding must be sought separately.

CROSS REFERENCES

Applicability of this rule in proceedings on contested involuntary petition and to vacate order for relief, see Fed.Rules Bankr.Proc. Rule 1018, 11 USCA.

Intervention in case under this title, see Fed.Rules Bankr.Proc. Rule 2018, 11 USCA.

Rule 7025. Substitution of Parties

Subject to the provisions of Rule 2012, Rule 25 F.R.Civ.P. applies in adversary proceedings.

ADVISORY COMMITTEE NOTES

Rule 25 F.R.Civ.P. refers to Rule 4 F.R.Civ.P. Pursuant to Rule 7002 that reference is to Rule 4 as incorporated and modified by Rule 7004.

CROSS REFERENCES

Applicability of this rule in—

    Contested matters not otherwise provided for, see Fed.Rules Bankr.Proc. Rule 9014, 11 USCA.

    Proceedings on contested involuntary petition and to vacate order for relief, see Fed.Rules Bankr.Proc. Rule 1018, 11 USCA.

Right to use depositions previously taken, see Fed.Rules Bankr.Proc. Rule 7026, 11 USCA.

Rule 7026. General Provisions Governing Discovery

Rule 26 F.R.Civ.P. applies in adversary proceedings.

CROSS REFERENCES

Applicability of this rule in—

    Contested matters not otherwise provided for, see Fed.Rules Bankr.Proc. Rule 9014, 11 USCA.

    Proceedings on contested involuntary petition and to vacate order for relief, see Fed.Rules Bankr.Proc. Rule 1018, 11 USCA.

Failure to make discovery; sanctions, see Fed.Rules Bankr.Proc. Rule 7037, 11 USCA.

Subpoena for taking depositions; place of examination, see Fed.Rules Bankr.Proc. Rule 9016, 11 USCA.

Rule 7027. Depositions Before Adversary Proceedings or Pending Appeal

Rule 27 F.R.Civ.P. applies to adversary proceedings.

ADVISORY COMMITTEE NOTES

Rule 27(a)(2) F.R.Civ.P. refers to Rule 4 F.R.Civ.P. Pursuant to Rule 7002 the reference is to Rule 4 F.R.Civ.P. as incorporated and modified by Rule 7004.

CROSS REFERENCES

Applicability of this rule in contested matters not otherwise provided for, see Fed.Rules Bankr.Proc. Rule 9014, 11 USCA.

Rule 7028. Persons Before Whom Depositions May Be Taken

Rule 28 F.R.Civ.P. applies in adversary proceedings.

CROSS REFERENCES

Affirmations, see Fed.Rules Bankr.Proc. Rule 9012, 11 USCA.

Applicability of this rule in—

    Contested matters not otherwise provided for, see Fed.Rules Bankr.Proc. Rule 9014, 11 USCA.

    Proceedings on contested involuntary petition and to vacate order for relief, see Fed.Rules Bankr.Proc. Rule 1018, 11 USCA.

Rule 7029. Stipulations Regarding Discovery Procedure

Rule 29 F.R.Civ.P. applies in adversary proceedings.

CROSS REFERENCES

Applicability of this rule in—

    Contested matters not otherwise provided for, see Fed.Rules Bankr.Proc. Rule 9014, 11 USCA.

    Proceedings on contested involuntary petition and to vacate order for relief, see Fed.Rules Bankr.Proc. Rule 1018, 11 USCA.

Rule 7030. Depositions Upon Oral Examination

Rule 30 F.R.Civ.P. applies in adversary proceedings.

ADVISORY COMMITTEE NOTES

Rule 30 F.R.Civ.P. refers to Rule 4 F.R.Civ.P. Pursuant to Rule 7002 that reference is a reference to Rule 4 F.R.Civ.P. as incorporated and modified by Rule 7004.

CROSS REFERENCES

Applicability of this rule in—

    Contested matters not otherwise provided for, see Fed.Rules Bankr.Proc. Rule 9014, 11 USCA.

    Proceedings on contested involuntary petition and to vacate order for relief, see Fed.Rules Bankr.Proc. Rule 1018, 11 USCA.

Failure to make discovery; sanctions, see Fed.Rules Bankr.Proc. Rule 7037, 11 USCA.

Subpoena for taking depositions; place of examination, see Fed.Rules Bankr.Proc. Rule 9016, 11 USCA.

Rule 7031. Deposition Upon Written Questions

Rule 31 F.R.Civ.P. applies in adversary proceedings.

CROSS REFERENCES

Applicability of this rule in—

    Contested matters not otherwise provided for, see Fed.Rules Bankr.Proc. Rule 9014, 11 USCA.

    Proceedings on contested involuntary petition and to vacate order for relief, see Fed.Rules Bankr.Proc. Rule 1018, 11 USCA.

Failure to make discovery; sanctions, see Fed.Rules Bankr.Proc. Rule 7037, 11 USCA.

Rule 7032. Use of Depositions in Adversary Proceedings

Rule 32 F.R.Civ.P. applies in adversary proceedings.

CROSS REFERENCES

Applicability of this rule in—

    Contested matters not otherwise provided for, see Fed.Rules Bankr.Proc. Rule 9014, 11 USCA.

    Proceedings on contested involuntary petition and to vacate order for relief, see Fed.Rules Bankr.Proc. Rule 1018, 11 USCA.

Rule 7033. Interrogatories to Parties

Rule 33 F.R.Civ.P. applies in adversary proceedings.

CROSS REFERENCES

Applicability of this rule in—

    Contested matters not otherwise provided for, see Fed.Rules Bankr.Proc. Rule 9014, 11 USCA.

    Proceedings on contested involuntary petition and to vacate order for relief, see Fed.Rules Bankr.Proc. Rule 1018, 11 USCA.

Failure to make discovery; sanctions, see Fed.Rules Bankr.Proc. Rule 7037, 11 USCA.

Rule 7034. Production of Documents and Things and Entry Upon Land for Inspection and Other Purposes

Rule 34 F.R.Civ.P. applies in adversary proceedings.

CROSS REFERENCES

Applicability of this rule in—

    Contested matters not otherwise provided for, see Fed.Rules Bankr.Proc. Rule 9014, 11 USCA.

    Proceedings on contested involuntary petition and to vacate order for relief, see Fed.Rules Bankr.Proc. Rule 1018, 11 USCA.

Failure to make discovery; sanctions, see Fed.Rules Bankr.Proc. Rule 7037, 11 USCA.

Subpoena for production of documentary evidence, see Fed.Rules Bankr.Proc. Rule 9016, 11 USCA.

Rule 7035. Physical and Mental Examination of Persons

Rule 35 F.R.Civ.P. applies in adversary proceedings.

CROSS REFERENCES

Applicability of this rule in—

    Contested matters not otherwise provided for, see Fed.Rules Bankr.Proc. Rule 9014, 11 USCA.

    Proceedings on contested involuntary petition and to vacate order for relief, see Fed.Rules Bankr.Proc. Rule 1018, 11 USCA.

Failure to make discovery; sanctions, see Fed.Rules Bankr.Proc. Rule 7037, 11 USCA.

Rule 7036. Requests for Admission

Rule 36 F.R.Civ.P. applies in adversary proceedings.

CROSS REFERENCES

Applicability of this rule in—

    Contested matters not otherwise provided for, see Fed.Rules Bankr.Proc. Rule 9014, 11 USCA.

    Proceedings on contested involuntary petition and to vacate order for relief, see Fed.Rules Bankr.Proc. Rule 1018, 11 USCA.

Pre-trial conference to obtain admissions of facts and documents, see Fed.Rules Bankr.Proc. Rule 7016, 11 USCA.

Rule 7037. Failure to Make Discovery: Sanctions

Rule 37 F.R.Civ.P. applies in adversary proceedings.

CROSS REFERENCES

Applicability of this rule in—

    Contested matters not otherwise provided for, see Fed.Rules Bankr.Proc. Rule 9014, 11 USCA.

    Proceedings on contested involuntary petition and to vacate order for relief, see Fed.Rules Bankr.Proc. Rule 1018, 11 USCA.

Rule 7040. Assignment of Cases for Trial

Rule 40 F.R.Civ.P. applies in adversary proceedings.

CROSS REFERENCES

Local bankruptcy rules on practice and procedure not inconsistent with these rules, see Fed.Rules Bankr.Proc. Rule 9029, 11 USCA.

Rule 7041. Dismissal of Adversary Proceedings

Rule 41 F.R.Civ.P. applies in adversary proceedings, except that a complaint objecting to the debtor's discharge shall not be dismissed at the plaintiff's instance without notice to the trustee, the United States trustee, and such other persons as the court may direct, and only on order of the court containing terms and conditions which the court deems proper.

(As amended Apr. 30, 1991, eff. Aug. 1, 1991.)

ADVISORY COMMITTEE NOTES

Dismissal of a complaint objecting to a discharge raises special concerns because the plaintiff may have been induced to dismiss by an advantage given or promised by the debtor or someone acting in his interest. Some courts by local rule or order have required the debtor and his attorney or the plaintiff to file an affidavit that nothing has been promised to the plaintiff in consideration of the withdrawal of the objection. By specifically authorizing the court to impose conditions in the order of dismissal this rule permits the continuation of this salutary practice.

Rule 41 F.R.Civ.P. refers to Rule 19 F.R.Civ.P. Pursuant to Rule 7002 that reference is to Rule 19 F.R.Civ.P. as incorporated and modified by Rule 7019.

1991 Amendment

The United States trustee has standing to object to the debtor's discharge pursuant to § 727(c) and may have refrained from commencing an adversary proceeding objecting to discharge within the time limits provided in Rule 4004 only because another party commenced such a proceeding. The United States trustee may oppose dismissal of the original proceeding.

The rule is also amended to clarify that the court may direct that other persons receive notice of a plaintiff's motion to dismiss a complaint objecting to discharge.

CROSS REFERENCES

Applicability of this rule in contested matters not otherwise provided for, see Fed.Rules Bankr.Proc. Rule 9014, 11 USCA.

Findings by court necessary when judgment rendered on merits of motion to dismiss after trial on facts, see Fed.Rules Bankr.Proc. Rule 7052, 11 USCA.

Sanction for failure to attend deposition, to answer interrogatories, or to respond to inspection request, see Fed.Rules Bankr.Proc. Rule 7037, 11 USCA.

Rule 7042. Consolidation of Adversary Proceedings; Separate Trials

Rule 42 F.R.Civ.P. applies in adversary proceedings.

CROSS REFERENCES

Applicability of this rule in contested matters not otherwise provided for, see Fed.Rules Bankr.Proc. Rule 9014, 11 USCA.

Separate trials—

> Joinder of party against whom no claim exists, see Fed.Rules Bankr.Proc. Rule 7020, 11 USCA.
>
> Separate judgments rendered on counterclaim or cross-claim, see Fed.Rules Bankr.Proc. Rule 7013, 11 USCA.

Rule 7052. Findings by the Court

Rule 52 F.R.Civ.P. applies in adversary proceedings, except that any motion under subdivision (b) of that rule for amended or additional findings shall be filed no later than 14 days after entry of judgment. In these proceedings, the reference in Rule 52 F.R.Civ.P. to the entry of judgment under Rule 58 F.R.Civ.P. shall be read as a reference to the entry of a judgment or order under Rule 5003(a).

(As amended Mar. 26, 2009, eff. Dec. 1, 2009.)

ADVISORY COMMITTEE NOTES

Rule 52(a) F.R.Civ.P. refers to Rule 12 F.R.Civ.P. Pursuant to Rule 7002 this reference is to Rule 12 F.R.Civ.P. as incorporated and modified by Rule 7012.

2009 Amendments

The rule is amended to clarify that the reference in Rule 52 F. R. Civ. P. to Rule 58 F. R. Civ. P. and its provisions is construed as a reference to the entry of a judgment or order under Rule 5003(a).

The rule is amended by limiting the time for filing post judgment motions for amended or additional findings. In 2009, Rule 52 F. R. Civ. P. was amended to extend the deadline for filing those post judgment motions to no later than 28 days after entry of the judgment. That deadline corresponds to the 30-day deadline for filing a notice of appeal in a civil case under Rule 4(a)(1)(A) F. R. App. P. In a bankruptcy case, the deadline for filing a notice of appeal is 14 days. Therefore, the 28-day deadline for filing a motion for amended or additional findings would effectively override the notice of appeal deadline under Rule 8002(a) but for this amendment.

CROSS REFERENCES

Amendment of findings—

On motion for new trial, see Fed.Rules Bankr.Proc. Rule 9023, 11 USCA.

Stay of proceedings to enforce judgment pending disposition of motion to amend, see Fed.Rules Bankr.Proc. Rule 7062, 11 USCA.

Applicability of this rule in—

Contested matters not otherwise provided for, see Fed.Rules Bankr.Proc. Rule 9014, 11 USCA.

Proceedings on contested involuntary petition and to vacate order for relief, see Fed.Rules Bankr.Proc. Rule 1018, 11 USCA.

Effect of motion to amend or to add fact findings on time for appeal, see Fed.Rules Bankr.Proc. Rule 8002, 11 USCA.

Enlargement of ten-day period for motion to amend findings of court not permitted, see Fed.Rules Bankr.Proc. Rule 9006, 11 USCA.

Rule 7054. Judgments; Costs

(a) Judgments

Rule 54(a)–(c) F.R.Civ.P. applies in adversary proceedings.

(b) Costs; Attorney's Fees

(1) Costs Other Than Attorney's Fees. The court may allow costs to the prevailing party except when a statute of the United States or these rules otherwise provides. Costs against the United States, its officers and agencies shall be imposed only to the extent permitted by law. Costs may be taxed by the clerk on 14 days' notice; on motion served within seven days thereafter, the action of the clerk may be reviewed by the court.

Rule 7054   BANKRUPTCY RULES

    (2) **Attorney's Fees.**

        (A) Rule 54(d)(2)(A)-(C) and (E) F.R.Civ.P. applies in adversary proceedings except for the reference in Rule 54(d)(2)(C) to Rule 78.

        (B) By local rule, the court may establish special procedures to resolve fee-related issues without extensive evidentiary hearings.

(As amended Apr. 23, 2012, eff. Dec. 1, 2012; Apr. 25, 2014, eff. Dec. 1, 2014.)

ADVISORY COMMITTEE NOTES
2012 Amendments

Subdivision (b). Subdivision (b) is amended to provide more time for a party to respond to the prevailing party's bill of costs. The former rule's provision of one day's notice was unrealistically short. The change to 14 days conforms to the change made to Civil Rule 54(d). Extension from five to seven days of the time for serving a motion for court review of the clerk's action implements changes in connection with the December 1, 2009, amendment to Rule 9006(a) and the manner by which time is computed under the rules. Throughout the rules, deadlines have been amended in the following manner:

- 5-day periods became 7-day periods.
- 10-day periods became 14-day periods.
- 15-day periods became 14-day periods.
- 20-day periods became 21-day periods.
- 25-day periods became 28-day periods.

2014 Amendments

Subdivision (b) is amended to prescribe the procedure for seeking an award of attorney's fees and related nontaxable expenses in adversary proceedings. It does so by adding new paragraph (2) that incorporates most of the provisions of Rule 54(d)(2) F.R.Civ.P. The title of subdivision (b) is amended to reflect the new content, and the previously existing provision governing costs is renumbered as paragraph (1) and re-titled.

As provided in Rule 54(d)(2)(A), new subsection (b)(2) does not apply to fees recoverable as an element of damages, as when sought under the terms of a contract providing for the recovery of fees incurred prior to the instant adversary proceeding. Such fees typically are required to be claimed in a pleading.

Rule 54(d)(2)(D) F.R.Civ.P. does not apply in adversary proceedings insofar as it authorizes the referral of fee matters to a master or a magistrate judge. The use of masters is not authorized in bankruptcy cases, see Rule 9031, and 28 U.S.C. § 636 does not authorize a magistrate judge to exercise jurisdiction upon referral by a bankruptcy judge. The remaining provision of

Rule 54(d)(2)(D) is expressed in subdivision (b)(2)(B) of this rule. Rule 54(d)(2)(C) refers to Rule 78 F.R.Civ.P., which is not applicable in adversary proceedings. Accordingly, that reference is not incorporated by this rule.

CROSS REFERENCES

Amendment or alteration—

    Stay of proceedings pending disposition of motion for, see Fed.Rules Bankr.Proc. Rule 7062, 11 USCA.

    Time for service of motion, see Fed.Rules Bankr.Proc. Rule 9023, 11 USCA.

Applicability of this rule in—

    Contested matters not otherwise provided for, see Fed.Rules Bankr.Proc. Rule 9014, 11 USCA.

    Proceedings on contested involuntary petition and to vacate order for relief, see Fed.Rules Bankr.Proc. Rule 1018, 11 USCA.

Entry of judgment, district court record of judgment, see Fed.Rules Bankr.Proc. Rule 9021, 11 USCA.

Relief from judgment or order, see Fed.Rules Bankr.Proc. Rule 9024, 11 USCA.

Rule 7055. Default

Rule 55 F.R.Civ.P. applies in adversary proceedings.

CROSS REFERENCES

Applicability of this rule in contested matters not otherwise provided for, see Fed.Rules Bankr.Proc. Rule 9014, 11 USCA.

Demand for judgment, see Fed.Rules Bankr.Proc. Rule 7054, 11 USCA.

Rule 7056. Summary Judgment

Rule 56 F.R.Civ.P. applies in adversary proceedings, except that any motion for summary judgment must be made at least 30 days before the initial date set for an evidentiary hearing on any issue for which summary judgment is sought, unless a different time is set by local rule or the court orders otherwise.

(As amended Apr. 23, 2012, eff. Dec. 1, 2012.)

ADVISORY COMMITTEE NOTES

2012 Amendments

The only exception to complete adoption of Rule 56 F.R.Civ.P. involves the default deadline for filing a summary judgment motion. Rule 56(c)(1)(A) makes the default deadline 30 days after the close of all discovery. Because in bankruptcy cases hearings can occur shortly after the close of discovery, a default deadline based on the scheduled hearing date, rather than the close of discovery, is adopted. As with Rule 56(c)(1), the deadline can be altered either by local rule or court order.

CROSS REFERENCES

Applicability of this rule in—

 Contested matters, not otherwise provided for, see Fed.Rules Bankr.Proc. Rule 9014, 11 USCA.

 Proceedings on contested involuntary petition and to vacate order for relief, see Fed.Rules Bankr.Proc. Rule 1018, 11 USCA.

Rule 7058. Entering Judgment in Adversary Proceeding

Rule 58 F.R.Civ.P. applies in adversary proceedings. In these proceedings, the reference in Rule 58 F.R.Civ.P. to the civil docket shall be read as a reference to the docket maintained by the clerk under Rule 5003(a).

(Added Mar. 26, 2009, eff. Dec. 1, 2009.)

ADVISORY COMMITTEE NOTES

2009 Adoption

This rule makes Rule 58 F.R.Civ.P. applicable in adversary proceedings and is added in connection with the amendments to Rule 9021.

Rule 7062. Stay of Proceedings to Enforce a Judgment

Rule 62 F.R.Civ.P. applies in adversary proceedings.

(As amended Apr. 30, 1991, eff. Aug. 1, 1991; Apr. 29, 1999, eff. Dec. 1, 1999.)

Rule 7064 BANKRUPTCY RULES

ADVISORY COMMITTEE NOTES

The additional exceptions set forth in this rule make applicable to those matters the consequences contained in Rule 62(c) and (d) with respect to orders in actions for injunctions.

1991 Amendment

This rule is amended to include as additional exceptions to Rule 62(a) an order granting relief from the automatic stay of actions against codebtors provided by § 1201 of the Code, the sale or lease of property of the estate under § 363, and the assumption or assignment of an executory contract under § 365.

1999 Amendments

The additional exceptions to Rule 62(a) consist of orders that are issued in contested matters. These exceptions are deleted from this rule because of the amendment to Rule 9014 that renders this rule inapplicable in contested matters unless the court orders otherwise. See also the amendments to Rules 3020, 3021, 4001, 6004, and 6006 that delay the implementation of certain types of orders for a period of ten days unless the court otherwise directs.

CROSS REFERENCES

Applicability of this rule in—

> Contested matters not otherwise provided for, see Fed.Rules Bankr.Proc. Rule 9014, 11 USCA.

> Proceedings on contested involuntary petition and to vacate order for relief, see Fed.Rules Bankr.Proc. Rule 1018, 11 USCA.

Effect of entry of judgment on availability of relief under this rule, see Fed.Rules Bankr.Proc. Rule 9021, 11 USCA.

Power of court to suspend or to order continuation of other proceedings pending appeal, see Fed.Rules Bankr.Proc. Rule 8005, 11 USCA.

Security; proceedings against sureties, see Fed.Rules Bankr.Proc. Rule 9025, 11 USCA.

Stay of new proceedings until payment of costs of previously dismissed action, see Fed.Rules Bankr.Proc. Rule 7041, 11 USCA.

Rule 7064. Seizure of Person or Property

Rule 64 F.R.Civ.P. applies in adversary proceedings.

CROSS REFERENCES

Applicability of this rule in contested matters not otherwise provided for, see Fed.Rules Bankr.Proc. Rule 9014, 11 USCA.

Writ of attachment or sequestration issued against property ordered by judgment to be conveyed, see Fed.Rules Bankr.Proc. Rule 7070, 11 USCA.

Rule 7065. Injunctions

Rule 65 F.R.Civ.P. applies in adversary proceedings, except that a temporary restraining order or preliminary injunction may be issued on application of a debtor, trustee, or debtor in possession without compliance with Rule 65(c).

CROSS REFERENCES

Injunction pending appeal of interlocutory or final judgment concerning injunction, see Fed.Rules Bankr.Proc. Rule 7062, 11 USCA.

Security; proceedings against sureties, see Fed.Rules Bankr.Proc. Rule 9025, 11 USCA.

Signing and verification of papers, see Fed.Rules Bankr.Proc. Rule 9011, 11 USCA.

Rule 7067. Deposit in Court

Rule 67 F.R.Civ.P. applies in adversary proceedings.

Rule 7068. Offer of Judgment

Rule 68 F.R.Civ.P. applies in adversary proceedings.

Rule 7069. Execution

Rule 69 F.R.Civ.P. applies in adversary proceedings.

CROSS REFERENCES

Applicability of this rule in contested matters not otherwise provided for, see Fed.Rules Bankr.Proc. Rule 9014, 11 USCA.

Effect of entry of judgment on availability of process to enforce judgment, see Fed.Rules Bankr.Proc. Rule 9021, 11 USCA.

Writ of execution to enforce judgment to deliver possession of property, see Fed.Rules Bankr.Proc. Rule 7070, 11 USCA.

Rule 7070. Judgment for Specific Acts; Vesting Title

Rule 70 F.R.Civ.P. applies in adversary proceedings and the court may enter a judgment divesting the title of any party and vesting title in others whenever the real or personal property involved is within the jurisdiction of the court.

(As amended Mar. 30, 1987, eff. Aug. 1, 1987.)

ADVISORY COMMITTEE NOTES

1987 Amendment

The reference to court is used in the amendment because the district court may preside over an adversary proceeding.

CROSS REFERENCES

Effect of entry of judgment on availability of relief under this rule, see Fed.Rules Bankr.Proc. Rule 9021, 11 USCA.

Rule 7071. Process in Behalf of and Against Persons Not Parties

Rule 71 F.R.Civ.P. applies in adversary proceedings.

CROSS REFERENCES

Applicability of this rule in contested matters not otherwise provided for, see Fed.Rules Bankr.Proc. Rule 9014, 11 USCA.

Rule 7087. Transfer of Adversary Proceeding

On motion and after a hearing, the court may transfer an adversary proceeding or any part thereof to another district pursuant to 28 U.S.C. § 1412, except as provided in Rule 7019(2).

(As amended Mar. 30, 1987, eff. Aug. 1, 1987.)

Rule 7087

ADVISORY COMMITTEE NOTES

1987 Amendment

The reference to the venue section of title 28 is amended to conform to the 1984 amendments to title 28.

PART VIII—APPEALS TO DISTRICT COURT OR BANKRUPTCY APPELLATE PANEL

Rule
8001. Scope of Part VIII Rules; Definition of "BAP"; Method of Transmission.
8002. Time for Filing Notice of Appeal.
8003. Appeal as of Right—How Taken; Docketing the Appeal.
8004. Appeal by Leave—How Taken; Docketing the Appeal.
8005. Election to Have an Appeal Heard by the District Court Instead of the BAP.
8006. Certifying a Direct Appeal to the Court of Appeals.
8007. Stay Pending Appeal; Bonds; Suspension of Proceedings.
8008. Indicative Rulings.
8009. Record on Appeal; Sealed Documents.
8010. Completing and Transmitting the Record.
8011. Filing and Service; Signature.
8012. Corporate Disclosure Statement.
8013. Motions; Intervention.
8014. Briefs.
8015. Form and Length of Briefs; Form of Appendices and Other Papers.
8016. Cross-Appeals.
8017. Brief of an Amicus Curiae.
8018. Serving and Filing Briefs; Appendices.
8019. Oral Argument.
8020. Frivolous Appeal and Other Misconduct.
8021. Costs.
8023. Voluntary Dismissal.
8024. Clerk's Duties on Disposition of the Appeal.
8025. Stay of a District Court or BAP Judgment.
8026. Rules by Circuit Councils and District Courts; Procedure When There is No Controlling Law.
8027. Notice of a Mediation Procedure.
8028. Suspension of Rules in Part VIII.

Rule 8001. Scope of Part VIII Rules; Definition of "BAP"; Method of Transmission

(a) General Scope

These Part VIII rules govern the procedure in a United States district court and a bankruptcy appellate panel on appeal from a judgment, order, or decree of a bankruptcy court. They also govern certain procedures on appeal to a United States court of appeals under 28 U.S.C. §158(d).

(b) Definition of "BAP"

"BAP" means a bankruptcy appellate panel established by a circuit's judicial council and authorized to hear appeals from a bankruptcy court under 28 U.S.C. § 158.

(c) Method of Transmitting Documents

A document must be sent electronically under these Part VIII rules, unless it is being sent by or to an individual who is not represented by counsel or the court's governing rules permit or require mailing or other means of delivery.

(Added Apr. 25, 2014, eff. Dec. 1, 2014.)

2014 Amendments

These Part VIII rules apply to appeals under 28 U.S.C. § 158(a) from bankruptcy courts to district courts and BAPs. The Federal Rules of Appellate Procedure generally govern bankruptcy appeals to courts of appeals.

Eight of the Part VIII rules do, however, relate to appeals to courts of appeals. Rule 8004(e) provides that the authorization by a court of appeals of a direct appeal of a bankruptcy court's interlocutory order or decree constitutes a grant of leave to appeal. Rule 8006 governs the procedure for certification under 28 U.S.C. § 158(d)(2) of a direct appeal from a judgment, order, or decree of a bankruptcy court to a court of appeals. Rule 8007 addresses stays pending a direct appeal to a court of appeals. Rule 8008 authorizes a bankruptcy court to issue an indicative ruling while an appeal is pending in a court of appeals. Rules 8009 and 8010 govern the record on appeal in a direct appeal to a court of appeals. Rule 8025 governs the granting of a stay of a district court or BAP judgment pending an appeal to the court of appeals. And Rule

8028 authorizes the court of appeals to suspend applicable Part VIII rules in a particular case, subject to certain enumerated exceptions.

These rules take account of the evolving technology in the federal courts for the electronic filing, storage, and transmission of documents. Except as applied to pro se parties, the Part VIII rules require documents to be sent electronically, unless applicable court rules or orders expressly require or permit another means of sending a particular document.

Rule 8002. Time for Filing Notice of Appeal

(a) **In General.**

(1) **Fourteen-Day Period**

Except as provided in subdivisions (b) and (c), a notice of appeal must be filed with the bankruptcy clerk within 14 days after entry of the judgment, order, or decree being appealed.

(2) **Filing Before the Entry of Judgment**

A notice of appeal filed after the bankruptcy court announces a decision or order—but before entry of the judgment, order, or decree—is treated as filed on the date of and after the entry.

(3) **Multiple Appeals**

If one party files a timely notice of appeal, any other party may file a notice of appeal within 14 days after the date when the first notice was filed, or within the time otherwise allowed by this rule, whichever period ends later.

(4) **Mistaken Filing in Another Court**

If a notice of appeal is mistakenly filed in a district court, BAP, or court of appeals, the clerk of that court must state on the notice the date on which it was received and transmit it to the bankruptcy clerk. The notice of appeal is then considered filed in the bankruptcy court on the date so stated.

(b) **Effect of a Motion on the Time to Appeal.**

(1) **In General**

If a party timely files in the bankruptcy court any of the following motions, the time to file an appeal runs for all parties from the entry of the order disposing of the last such remaining motion:

(A) to amend or make additional findings under Rule 7052, whether or not granting the motion would alter the judgment;

(B) to alter or amend the judgment under Rule 9023;

(C) for a new trial under Rule 9023; or

(D) for relief under Rule 9024 if the motion is filed within 14 days after the judgment is entered.

(2) **Filing an Appeal Before the Motion is Decided**

If a party files a notice of appeal after the court announces or enters a judgment, order, or decree—but before it disposes of any motion listed in subdivision (b)(1)—the notice becomes effective when the order disposing of the last such remaining motion is entered.

(3) **Appealing the Ruling on the Motion**

If a party intends to challenge an order disposing of any motion listed in subdivision (b)(1)—or the alteration or amendment of a judgment, order, or decree upon the motion—the party must file a notice of appeal or an amended notice of appeal. The notice or amended notice must comply with Rule 8003 or 8004 and be filed within the time prescribed by this rule, measured from the entry of the order disposing of the last such remaining motion.

APPEALS   Rule 8002

(4) **No Additional Fee**

No additional fee is required to file an amended notice of appeal.

(c) **Appeal by an Inmate Confined in an Institution**

(1) **In General**

If an inmate confined in an institution files a notice of appeal from a judgment, order, or decree of a bankruptcy court, the notice is timely if it is deposited in the institution's internal mail system on or before the last day for filing. If the institution has a system designed for legal mail, the inmate must use that system to receive the benefit of this rule. Timely filing may be shown by a declaration in compliance with 28 U.S.C. §1746 or by a notarized statement, either of which must set forth the date of deposit and state that first-class postage has been prepaid.

(2) **Multiple Appeals**

If an inmate files under this subdivision the first notice of appeal, the 14-day period provided in subdivision (a)(3) for another party to file a notice of appeal runs from the date when the bankruptcy clerk dockets the first notice.

(d) **Extending the Time to Appeal**

(1) **When the Time May be Extended**

Except as provided in subdivision (d)(2), the bankruptcy court may extend the time to file a notice of appeal upon a party's motion that is filed:

(A) within the time prescribed by this rule; or

(B) within 21 days after that time, if the party shows excusable neglect.

(2) **When the Time May Not be Extended**

The bankruptcy court may not extend the time to file a notice of appeal if the judgment, order, or decree appealed from:

(A) grants relief from an automatic stay under § 362, 922, 1201, or 1301 of the Code;

(B) authorizes the sale or lease of property or the use of cash collateral under §363 of the Code;

(C) authorizes the obtaining of credit under § 364 of the Code;

(D) authorizes the assumption or assignment of an executory contract or unexpired lease under § 365 of the Code;

(E) approves a disclosure statement under § 1125 of the Code; or

(F) confirms a plan under § 943, 1129, 1225, or 1325 of the Code.

(3) **Time Limits on an Extension**

No extension of time may exceed 21 days after the time prescribed by this rule, or 14 days after the order granting the motion to extend time is entered, whichever is later.

(Added Apr. 25, 2014, eff. Dec. 1, 2014.)

2014 Amendments

This rule is derived from former Rule 8002 and Fed. R. App. P. 4(a) and (c). With the exception of subdivision (c), the changes to the former rule are stylistic. The rule retains the former rule's 14-day time period for filing a notice of appeal, as opposed to the longer periods permitted for appeals in civil cases under Fed. R. App. P. 4(a).

Subdivision (a) continues to allow any other party to file a notice of appeal within 14 days after the first notice of appeal is filed, or thereafter to the extent otherwise authorized by this rule. Subdivision (a) also retains provisions of the former rule that prescribe the date the notice of appeal is deemed filed if the appellant files it prematurely or in the wrong court.

Subdivision (b), like former Rule 8002(b) and Fed. R. App. P. 4(a), tolls the time for filing a notice of appeal when certain postjudgment motions are filed, and it prescribes the effective date of a notice of appeal that is filed before the court disposes of all of the specified motions. As under the former rule, a party that wants to appeal the court's disposition of the motion or the alteration or amendment of a judgment, order, or decree in response to such a motion must file a notice of appeal or, if it has already filed one, an amended notice of appeal.

Although Rule 8003(a)(3)(C) requires a notice of appeal to be accompanied by the required fee, no additional fee is required for the filing of an amended notice of appeal.

Subdivision (c) mirrors the provisions of Fed. R. App. P. 4(c)(1) and (2), which specify timing rules for a notice of appeal filed by an inmate confined in an institution.

Subdivision (d) continues to allow the court to grant an extension of time to file a notice of appeal, except with respect to certain specified judgments, orders, and decrees.

Rule 8003. Appeal as of Right—How Taken; Docketing the Appeal

(a) **Filing the Notice of Appeal**

(1) **In General**

An appeal from a judgment, order, or decree of a bankruptcy court to a district court or BAP under 28 U.S.C. § 158(a)(1) or (a)(2) may be taken only by filing a notice of appeal with the bankruptcy clerk within the time allowed by Rule 8002.

(2) **Effect of Not Taking Other Steps**

An appellant's failure to take any step other than the timely filing of a notice of appeal does not affect the validity of the appeal, but is ground only for the district court or BAP to act as it considers appropriate, including dismissing the appeal.

(3) **Contents**

The notice of appeal must:

(A) conform substantially to the appropriate Official Form;

(B) be accompanied by the judgment, order, or decree, or the part of it, being appealed; and

(C) be accompanied by the prescribed fee.

(4) **Additional Copies**

If requested to do so, the appellant must furnish the bankruptcy clerk with enough copies of the notice to enable the clerk to comply with subdivision (c).

(b) **Joint or Consolidated Appeals.**

(1) **Joint Notice of Appeal**

When two or more parties are entitled to appeal from a judgment, order, or decree of a bankruptcy court and their interests make joinder practicable, they may file a joint notice of appeal. They may then proceed on appeal as a single appellant.

(2) **Consolidating Appeals**

When parties have separately filed timely notices of appeal, the district court or BAP may join or consolidate the appeals.

(c) **Serving the Notice of Appeal.**

(1) **Serving Parties and Transmitting to the United States Trustee**

The bankruptcy clerk must serve the notice of appeal on counsel of record for each party to the appeal, excluding the appellant, and transmit it to the United States trustee. If a party is proceeding pro se, the clerk must send the notice of appeal to the party's last known address. The clerk must note, on each copy, the date when the notice of appeal was filed.

(2) Effect of Failing to Serve or Transmit Notice

The bankruptcy clerk's failure to serve notice on a party or transmit notice to the United States trustee does not affect the validity of the appeal.

(3) Noting Service on the Docket

The clerk must note on the docket the names of the parties served and the date and method of the service.

(d) Transmitting the Notice of Appeal to the District Court or BAP; Docketing the Appeal.

(1) Transmitting the Notice

The bankruptcy clerk must promptly transmit the notice of appeal to the BAP clerk if a BAP has been established for appeals from that district and the appellant has not elected to have the district court hear the appeal. Otherwise, the bankruptcy clerk must promptly transmit the notice to the district clerk.

(2) Docketing in the District Court or BAP

Upon receiving the notice of appeal, the district or BAP clerk must docket the appeal under the title of the bankruptcy case and the title of any adversary proceeding, and must identify the appellant, adding the appellant's name if necessary.

(Added Apr. 25, 2014, eff. Dec. 1, 2014.)

2014 Amendments

This rule is derived from several former Bankruptcy Rule and Appellate Rule provisions. It addresses appeals as of right, joint and consolidated appeals, service of the notice of appeal, and the timing of the docketing of an appeal in the district court or BAP.

Subdivision (a) incorporates, with stylistic changes, much of the content of former Rule 8001(a) regarding the taking of an appeal as of right under 28 U.S.C. § 158(a)(1) or (2). The rule now requires that the judgment, order, or decree being appealed be attached to the notice of appeal.

Subdivision (b), which is an adaptation of Fed. R. App. P. 3(b), permits the filing of a joint notice of appeal by multiple appellants that have sufficiently similar interests that their joinder is practicable. It also allows the district court or BAP to consolidate appeals taken separately by two or more parties.

Subdivision (c) is derived from former Rule 8004 and Fed. R. App. P. 3(d). Under Rule 8001(c), the former rule's requirement that service of the notice of appeal be accomplished by mailing is generally modified to require that the bankruptcy clerk serve counsel by electronic means. Service on pro se parties must be made by sending the notice to the address most recently provided to the court.

Subdivision (d) modifies the provision of former Rule 8007(b), which delayed the docketing of an appeal by the district court or BAP until the record was complete and the bankruptcy clerk transmitted it. The new provision, adapted from Fed. R. App. P. 3(d) and 12(a), requires the bankruptcy clerk to promptly transmit the notice of appeal to the clerk of the district court or BAP. Upon receipt of the notice of appeal, the district or BAP clerk must docket the appeal. Under this procedure, motions filed in the district court or BAP prior to completion and transmission of the record can generally be placed on the docket of an already pending appeal.

Rule 8004. Appeal by Leave—How Taken; Docketing the Appeal

(a) Notice of Appeal and Motion for Leave to Appeal

To appeal from an interlocutory order or decree of a bankruptcy court under 28 U.S.C. § 158(a)(3), a party must file with the bankruptcy clerk a notice of appeal as prescribed by Rule 8003(a). The notice must:

(1) be filed within the time allowed by Rule 8002;

(2) be accompanied by a motion for leave to appeal prepared in accordance with subdivision (b); and

Rule 8004   BANKRUPTCY RULES

    (3) unless served electronically using the court's transmission equipment, include proof of service in accordance with Rule 8011(d).

(b) Contents of the Motion; Response

    (1) Contents

    A motion for leave to appeal under 28 U.S.C. §158(a)(3) must include the following:

        (A) the facts necessary to understand the question presented;

        (B) the question itself;

        (C) the relief sought;

        (D) the reasons why leave to appeal should be granted; and

        (E) a copy of the interlocutory order or decree and any related opinion or memorandum.

    (2) Response

    A party may file with the district or BAP clerk a response in opposition or a cross-motion within 14 days after the motion is served.

(c) Transmitting the Notice of Appeal and the Motion; Docketing the Appeal; Determining the Motion

    (1) Transmitting to the District Court or BAP

    The bankruptcy clerk must promptly transmit the notice of appeal and the motion for leave to the BAP clerk if a BAP has been established for appeals from that district and the appellant has not elected to have the district court hear the appeal. Otherwise, the bankruptcy clerk must promptly transmit the notice and motion to the district clerk.

    (2) Docketing in the District Court or BAP

    Upon receiving the notice and motion, the district or BAP clerk must docket the appeal under the title of the bankruptcy case and the title of any adversary proceeding, and must identify the appellant, adding the appellant's name if necessary.

    (3) Oral Argument Not Required

    The motion and any response or cross-motion are submitted without oral argument unless the district court or BAP orders otherwise.

(d) Failure to File a Motion With a Notice of Appeal

If an appellant timely files a notice of appeal under this rule but does not include a motion for leave, the district court or BAP may order the appellant to file a motion for leave, or treat the notice of appeal as a motion for leave and either grant or deny it. If the court orders that a motion for leave be filed, the appellant must do so within 14 days after the order is entered, unless the order provides otherwise.

(e) Direct Appeal to a Court of Appeals

If leave to appeal an interlocutory order or decree is required under 28 U.S.C. § 158(a)(3), an authorization of a direct appeal by the court of appeals under 28 U.S.C. § 158(d)(2) satisfies the requirement.

(Added Apr. 25, 2014, eff. Dec. 1, 2014.)

2014 Amendments

This rule is derived from former Rules 8001(b) and 8003 and Fed. R. App. P. 5. It retains the practice for interlocutory bankruptcy appeals of requiring a notice of appeal to be filed along with a motion for leave to appeal. Like current Rule 8003, it alters the timing of the docketing of the appeal in the district court or BAP.

Subdivision (a) requires a party seeking leave to appeal under 28 U.S.C. § 158(a)(3) to file with the bankruptcy clerk both a notice of appeal and a motion for leave to appeal.

Subdivision (b) prescribes the contents of the motion, retaining the requirements of former Rule 8003(a). It also continues to allow another party to file a cross-motion or response to the appellant's motion. Because of the prompt docketing of the appeal under the current rule, the cross-motion or response must be filed in the district court or BAP, rather than in the bankruptcy court as the former rule required.

Subdivision (c) requires the bankruptcy clerk to transmit promptly to the district court or BAP the notice of appeal and the motion for leave to appeal. Upon receipt of the notice and the motion, the district or BAP clerk must docket the appeal. Unless the district court or BAP orders otherwise, no oral argument will be held on the motion.

Subdivision (d) retains the provisions of former Rule 8003(c). It provides that if the appellant timely files a notice of appeal, but fails to file a motion for leave to appeal, the court can either direct that a motion be filed or treat the notice of appeal as the motion and either grant or deny leave.

Subdivision (e), like former Rule 8003(d), treats the authorization of a direct appeal by the court of appeals as a grant of leave to appeal under 28 U.S.C. § 158(a)(3) if the district court or BAP has not already granted leave. Thus, a separate order granting leave to appeal is not required. If the court of appeals grants permission to appeal, the record must be assembled and transmitted in accordance with Rules 8009 and 8010.

Rule 8005. Election to Have an Appeal Heard by the District Court Instead of the BAP

(a) Filing of a Statement of Election

To elect to have an appeal heard by the district court, a party must:

(1) file a statement of election that conforms substantially to the appropriate Official Form; and

(2) do so within the time prescribed by 28 U.S.C. § 158(c)(1).

(b) Transmitting the Documents Related to the Appeal

Upon receiving an appellant's timely statement of election, the bankruptcy clerk must transmit to the district clerk all documents related to the appeal. Upon receiving a timely statement of election by a party other than the appellant, the BAP clerk must transmit to the district clerk all documents related to the appeal and notify the bankruptcy clerk of the transmission.

(c) Determining the Validity of an Election

A party seeking a determination of the validity of an election must file a motion in the court where the appeal is then pending. The motion must be filed within 14 days after the statement of election is filed.

(d) Motion for Leave Without a Notice of Appeal—Effect on the Timing of an Election

If an appellant moves for leave to appeal under Rule 8004 but fails to file a separate notice of appeal with the motion, the motion must be treated as a notice of appeal for purposes of determining the timeliness of a statement of election.

(Added Apr. 25, 2014, eff. Dec. 1, 2014.)

2014 Amendments

This rule, which implements 28 U.S.C. § 158(c)(1), is derived from former Rule 8001(e). It applies only in districts in which an appeal to a BAP is authorized.

As the former rule required, **subdivision (a)** provides that an appellant that elects to have a district court, rather than a BAP, hear its appeal must file with the bankruptcy clerk a statement of election when it files its notice of appeal. The statement must conform substantially to the appropriate Official Form. For appellants, that statement is included in the Notice of Appeal Official Form. If a BAP has been established for appeals from the bankruptcy court and the appellant does not file a timely statement of election, any other party that elects to have the district court hear the appeal must file a statement of election with the BAP clerk no later than 30 days after service of the notice of appeal.

Subdivision (b) requires the bankruptcy clerk to transmit all appeal documents to the district clerk if the appellant files a timely statement of election. If the appellant does not make that election, the bankruptcy clerk must transmit those documents to the BAP clerk. Upon a timely election by any other party, the BAP clerk must promptly transmit the appeal documents to the district clerk and notify the bankruptcy clerk that the appeal has been transferred.

Subdivision (c) provides a new procedure for the resolution of disputes regarding the validity of an election. A motion seeking the determination of the validity of an election must be filed no later than 14 days after the statement of election is filed. Nothing in this rule prevents a court from determining the validity of an election on its own motion.

Subdivision (d) provides that, in the case of an appeal by leave, if the appellant files a motion for leave to appeal but fails to file a notice of appeal, the filing and service of the motion will be treated for timing purposes under this rule as the filing and service of the notice of appeal.

Rule 8006. Certifying a Direct Appeal to the Court of Appeals

(a) Effective Date of a Certification

A certification of a judgment, order, or decree of a bankruptcy court for direct review in a court of appeals under 28 U.S.C. § 158(d)(2) is effective when:

(1) the certification has been filed;

(2) a timely appeal has been taken under Rule 8003 or 8004; and

(3) the notice of appeal has become effective under Rule 8002.

(b) Filing The Certification

The certification must be filed with the clerk of the court where the matter is pending. For purposes of this rule, a matter remains pending in the bankruptcy court for 30 days after the effective date under Rule 8002 of the first notice of appeal from the judgment, order, or decree for which direct review is sought. A matter is pending in the district court or BAP thereafter.

(c) Joint Certification By All Appellants And Appellees

A joint certification by all the appellants and appellees under 28 U.S.C. § 158(d)(2)(A) must be made by using the appropriate Official Form. The parties may supplement the certification with a short statement of the basis for the certification, which may include the information listed in subdivision (f)(2).

(d) The Court That May Make the Certification

Only the court where the matter is pending, as provided in subdivision (b), may certify a direct review on request of parties or on its own motion.

(e) Certification on the Court's Own Motion.

(1) **How Accomplished**

A certification on the court's own motion must be set forth in a separate document. The clerk of the certifying court must serve it on the parties to the appeal in the manner required for service of a notice of appeal under Rule 8003(c)(1). The certification must be accompanied by an opinion or memorandum that contains the information required by subdivision (f)(2)(A)–(D).

(2) **Supplemental Statement by a Party**

Within 14 days after the court's certification, a party may file with the clerk of the certifying court a short supplemental statement regarding the merits of certification.

(f) Certification by the Court on Request

(1) **How Requested**

A request by a party for certification that a circumstance specified in 28 U.S.C. §158(d)(2)(A)(i)–(iii) applies—or a request by a majority of the appellants and a majority of the appellees—must be filed with the clerk of the court where the matter is pending within 60 days after the entry of the judgment, order, or decree.

(2) Service and Contents

The request must be served on all parties to the appeal in the manner required for service of a notice of appeal under Rule 8003(c)(1), and it must include the following:

 (A) the facts necessary to understand the question presented;

 (B) the question itself;

 (C) the relief sought;

 (D) the reasons why the direct appeal should be allowed, including which circumstance specified in 28 U.S.C. §158(d)(2)(A)(i)–(iii) applies; and

 (E) a copy of the judgment, order, or decree and any related opinion or memorandum.

(3) Time to File a Response or a Cross-Request

A party may file a response to the request within 14 days after the request is served, or such other time as the court where the matter is pending allows. A party may file a cross-request for certification within 14 days after the request is served, or within 60 days after the entry of the judgment, order, or decree, whichever occurs first.

(4) Oral Argument Not Required

The request, cross-request, and any response are submitted without oral argument unless the court where the matter is pending orders otherwise.

(5) Form and Service of the Certification

If the court certifies a direct appeal in response to the request, it must do so in a separate document. The certification must be served on the parties to the appeal in the manner required for service of a notice of appeal under Rule 8003(c)(1).

(g) Proceeding in the Court of Appeals Following a Certification

Within 30 days after the date the certification becomes effective under subdivision (a), a request for permission to take a direct appeal to the court of appeals must be filed with the circuit clerk in accordance with Fed. R. App. P. 6(c).

(Added Apr. 25, 2014, eff. Dec. 1, 2014.)

2014 Amendments

This rule is derived from former Rule 8001(f), and it provides the procedures for the certification of a direct appeal of a judgment, order, or decree of a bankruptcy court to the court of appeals under 28 U.S.C. § 158(d)(2). Once a case has been certified in the bankruptcy court, the district court, or the BAP for direct appeal and a request for permission to appeal has been timely filed with the circuit clerk, the Federal Rules of Appellate Procedure govern further proceedings in the court of appeals.

Subdivision (a), like the former rule, requires that an appeal be properly taken—now under Rule 8003 or 8004—before a certification for direct review in the court of appeals takes effect. This rule requires the timely filing of a notice of appeal under Rule 8002 and accounts for the delayed effectiveness of a notice of appeal under the circumstances specified in that rule. Ordinarily, a notice of appeal is effective when it is filed in the bankruptcy court. Rule 8002, however, delays the effectiveness of a notice of appeal when (1) it is filed after the announcement of a decision or order but prior to the entry of the judgment, order, or decree; or (2) it is filed after the announcement or entry of a judgment, order, or decree but before the bankruptcy court disposes of certain post-judgment motions.

When the bankruptcy court enters an interlocutory order or decree that is appealable under 28 U.S.C. § 158(a)(3), certification for direct review in the court of appeals may take effect before the district court or BAP grants leave to appeal. The certification is effective when the actions specified in subdivision (a) have occurred. Rule 8004(e) provides that if the court of appeals grants permission to take a direct appeal before leave to appeal an interlocutory ruling has been granted, the authorization by the court of appeals is treated as the granting of leave to appeal.

Rule 8007   **BANKRUPTCY RULES**

Subdivision (b) provides that a certification must be filed in the court where the matter is pending, as determined by this subdivision. This provision modifies the former rule. Because of the prompt docketing of appeals in the district court or BAP under Rules 8003 and 8004, a matter is deemed—for purposes of this rule only—to remain pending in the bankruptcy court for 30 days after the effective date of the notice of appeal. This provision will in appropriate cases give the bankruptcy judge, who will be familiar with the matter being appealed, an opportunity to decide whether certification for direct review is appropriate. Similarly, subdivision (d) provides that only the court where the matter is then pending according to subdivision (b) may make a certification on its own motion or on the request of one or more parties.

Section 158(d)(2) provides three different ways in which an appeal may be certified for direct review. Implementing these options, the rule provides in subdivision (c) for the joint certification by all appellants and appellees; in subdivision (e) for the bankruptcy court's, district court's, or BAP's certification on its own motion; and in subdivision (f) for the bankruptcy court's, district court's, or BAP's certification on request of a party or a majority of appellants and a majority of appellees.

Subdivision (g) requires that, once a certification for direct review is made, a request to the court of appeals for permission to take a direct appeal to that court must be filed with the clerk of the court of appeals no later than 30 days after the effective date of the certification. Federal Rule of Appellate Procedure 6(c), which incorporates all of Fed. R. App. P. 5 except subdivision (a)(3), prescribes the procedure for requesting the permission of the court of appeals and governs proceedings that take place thereafter in that court.

Rule 8007. Stay Pending Appeal; Bonds; Suspension of Proceedings

(a) **Initial Motion in the Bankruptcy Court**

    (1) **In General**

        Ordinarily, a party must move first in the bankruptcy court for the following relief:

        (A) a stay of a judgment, order, or decree of the bankruptcy court pending appeal;

        (B) the approval of a supersedeas bond;

        (C) an order suspending, modifying, restoring, or granting an injunction while an appeal is pending; or

        (D) the suspension or continuation of proceedings in a case or other relief permitted by subdivision (e).

    (2) **Time to File**

        The motion may be made either before or after the notice of appeal is filed.

(b) **Motion in the District Court, the BAP, or The Court of Appeals on Direct Appeal**

    (1) **Request for Relief**

        A motion for the relief specified in subdivision (a)(1)—or to vacate or modify a bankruptcy court's order granting such relief—may be made in the court where the appeal is pending.

    (2) **Showing or Statement Required**

        The motion must:

        (A) show that moving first in the bankruptcy court would be impracticable; or

        (B) if a motion was made in the bankruptcy court, either state that the court has not yet ruled on the motion, or state that the court has ruled and set out any reasons given for the ruling.

    (3) **Additional Content**

        The motion must also include:

        (A) the reasons for granting the relief requested and the facts relied upon;

        (B) affidavits or other sworn statements supporting facts subject to dispute; and

(C) relevant parts of the record.

(4) Serving Notice

The movant must give reasonable notice of the motion to all parties.

(c) Filing a Bond or Other Security

The district court, BAP, or court of appeals may condition relief on filing a bond or other appropriate security with the bankruptcy court.

(d) Bond for a Trustee or the United States

The court may require a trustee to file a bond or other appropriate security when the trustee appeals. A bond or other security is not required when an appeal is taken by the United States, its officer, or its agency or by direction of any department of the federal government.

(e) Continuation of Proceedings in the Bankruptcy Court

Despite Rule 7062 and subject to the authority of the district court, BAP, or court of appeals, the bankruptcy court may:

(1) suspend or order the continuation of other proceedings in the case; or

(2) issue any other appropriate orders during the pendency of an appeal to protect the rights of all parties in interest.

(Added Apr. 25, 2014, eff. Dec. 1, 2014.)

2014 Amendments

This rule is derived from former Rule 8005 and Fed. R. App. P. 8. It now applies to direct appeals in courts of appeals.

Subdivision (a), like the former rule, requires a party ordinarily to seek relief pending an appeal in the bankruptcy court. Subdivision (a)(1) expands the list of relief enumerated in Fed. R. App. P. 8(a)(1) to reflect bankruptcy practice. It includes the suspension or continuation of other proceedings in the bankruptcy case, as authorized by subdivision (e). Subdivision (a)(2) clarifies that a motion for a stay pending appeal, approval of a supersedeas bond, or any other relief specified in paragraph (1) may be made in the bankruptcy court before or after the filing of a notice of appeal.

Subdivision (b) authorizes a party to seek the relief specified in (a)(1), or the vacation or modification of the granting of such relief, by means of a motion filed in the court where the appeal is pending—district court, BAP, or the court of appeals on direct appeal. Accordingly, a notice of appeal need not be filed with respect to a bankruptcy court's order granting or denying such a motion. The motion for relief in the district court, BAP, or court of appeals must state why it was impracticable to seek relief initially in the bankruptcy court, if a motion was not filed there, or why the bankruptcy court denied the relief sought.

Subdivisions (c) and **(d)** retain the provisions of the former rule that permit the district court or BAP—and now the court of appeals—to condition the granting of relief on the posting of a bond by the appellant, except when that party is a federal government entity. Rule 9025 governs proceedings against sureties.

Subdivision (e) retains the provision of the former rule that authorizes the bankruptcy court to decide whether to suspend or allow the continuation of other proceedings in the bankruptcy case while the matter for which a stay has been sought is pending on appeal.

Rule 8008. Indicative Rulings

(a) Relief Pending Appeal

If a party files a timely motion in the bankruptcy court for relief that the court lacks authority to grant because of an appeal that has been docketed and is pending, the bankruptcy court may:

(1) defer considering the motion;

(2) deny the motion; or

Rule 8009   BANKRUPTCY RULES

(3) state that the court would grant the motion if the court where the appeal is pending remands for that purpose, or state that the motion raises a substantial issue.

(b) Notice to the Court Where the Appeal Is Pending

The movant must promptly notify the clerk of the court where the appeal is pending if the bankruptcy court states that it would grant the motion or that the motion raises a substantial issue.

(c) Remand After An Indicative Ruling

If the bankruptcy court states that it would grant the motion or that the motion raises a substantial issue, the district court or BAP may remand for further proceedings, but it retains jurisdiction unless it expressly dismisses the appeal. If the district court or BAP remands but retains jurisdiction, the parties must promptly notify the clerk of that court when the bankruptcy court has decided the motion on remand.

(Added Apr. 25, 2014, eff. Dec. 1, 2014.)

2014 Amendments

This rule is an adaptation of F.R.Civ.P. 62.1 and Fed. R. App. P. 12.1. It provides a procedure for the issuance of an indicative ruling when a bankruptcy court determines that, because of a pending appeal, the court lacks jurisdiction to grant a request for relief that the court concludes is meritorious or raises a substantial issue. The rule does not attempt to define the circumstances in which an appeal limits or defeats the bankruptcy court's authority to act in the face of a pending appeal. In contrast, Rule 8002(b) identifies motions that, if filed within the relevant time limit, suspend the effect of a notice of appeal filed before the last such motion is resolved. In those circumstances, the bankruptcy court has authority to resolve the motion without resorting to the indicative ruling procedure.

Subdivision (b) requires the movant to notify the court where an appeal is pending if the bankruptcy court states that it would grant the motion or that it raises a substantial issue. This provision applies to appeals pending in the district court, the BAP, or the court of appeals.

Federal Rules of Appellate Procedure 6 and 12.1 govern the procedure in the court of appeals following notification of the bankruptcy court's indicative ruling.

Subdivision (c) of this rule governs the procedure in the district court or BAP upon notification that the bankruptcy court has issued an indicative ruling. The district court or BAP may remand to the bankruptcy court for a ruling on the motion for relief. The district court or BAP may also remand all proceedings, thereby terminating the initial appeal, if it expressly states that it is dismissing the appeal. It should do so, however, only when the appellant has stated clearly its intention to abandon the appeal. Otherwise, the district court or BAP may remand for the purpose of ruling on the motion, while retaining jurisdiction to proceed with the appeal after the bankruptcy court rules, provided that the appeal is not then moot and a party wishes to proceed.

Rule 8009. Record on Appeal; Sealed Documents

(a) Designating the Record on Appeal; Statement of the Issues.

(1) **Appellant.**

(A) The appellant must file with the bankruptcy clerk and serve on the appellee a designation of the items to be included in the record on appeal and a statement of the issues to be presented.

(B) The appellant must file and serve the designation and statement within 14 days after:

(i) the appellant's notice of appeal as of right becomes effective under Rule 8002; or

(ii) an order granting leave to appeal is entered. A designation and statement served prematurely must be treated as served on the first day on which filing is timely.

(2) Appellee and Cross-Appellant

Within 14 days after being served, the appellee may file with the bankruptcy clerk and serve on the appellant a designation of additional items to be included in the record. An appellee who files a cross-appeal must file and serve a designation of additional items to be included in the record and a statement of the issues to be presented on the cross-appeal.

(3) Cross-Appellee

Within 14 days after service of the cross-appellant's designation and statement, a cross-appellee may file with the bankruptcy clerk and serve on the cross-appellant a designation of additional items to be included in the record.

(4) Record on Appeal

The record on appeal must include the following:

- docket entries kept by the bankruptcy clerk;
- items designated by the parties;
- the notice of appeal;
- the judgment, order, or decree being appealed;
- any order granting leave to appeal;
- any certification required for a direct appeal to the court of appeals;
  - any opinion, findings of fact, and conclusions of law relating to the issues on appeal, including transcripts of all oral rulings;
- any transcript ordered under subdivision (b);
- any statement required by subdivision (c); and
- any additional items from the record that the court where the appeal is pending orders.

(5) Copies for the Bankruptcy Clerk

If paper copies are needed, a party filing a designation of items must provide a copy of any of those items that the bankruptcy clerk requests. If the party fails to do so, the bankruptcy clerk must prepare the copy at the party's expense.

(b) Transcript of Proceedings.

(1) Appellant's Duty to Order

Within the time period prescribed by subdivision (a)(1), the appellant must:

(A) order in writing from the reporter, as defined in Rule 8010(a)(1), a transcript of such parts of the proceedings not already on file as the appellant considers necessary for the appeal, and file a copy of the order with the bankruptcy clerk; or

(B) file with the bankruptcy clerk a certificate stating that the appellant is not ordering a transcript.

(2) Cross-Appellant's Duty to Order

Within 14 days after the appellant files a copy of the transcript order or a certificate of not ordering a transcript, the appellee as cross-appellant must:

(A) order in writing from the reporter, as defined in Rule 8010(a)(1), a transcript of such additional parts of the proceedings as the cross-appellant considers necessary for the appeal, and file a copy of the order with the bankruptcy clerk; or

(B) file with the bankruptcy clerk a certificate stating that the cross-appellant is not ordering a transcript.

Rule 8009   BANKRUPTCY RULES

(3) Appellee's or Cross-Appellee's Right to Order

Within 14 days after the appellant or cross-appellant files a copy of a transcript order or certificate of not ordering a transcript, the appellee or cross-appellee may order in writing from the reporter a transcript of such additional parts of the proceedings as the appellee or cross-appellee considers necessary for the appeal. A copy of the order must be filed with the bankruptcy clerk.

(4) Payment

At the time of ordering, a party must make satisfactory arrangements with the reporter for paying the cost of the transcript.

(5) Unsupported Finding or Conclusion

If the appellant intends to argue on appeal that a finding or conclusion is unsupported by the evidence or is contrary to the evidence, the appellant must include in the record a transcript of all relevant testimony and copies of all relevant exhibits.

(c) Statement of the Evidence When a Transcript Is Unavailable

If a transcript of a hearing or trial is unavailable, the appellant may prepare a statement of the evidence or proceedings from the best available means, including the appellant's recollection. The statement must be filed within the time prescribed by subdivision (a)(1) and served on the appellee, who may serve objections or proposed amendments within 14 days after being served. The statement and any objections or proposed amendments must then be submitted to the bankruptcy court for settlement and approval. As settled and approved, the statement must be included by the bankruptcy clerk in the record on appeal.

(d) Agreed Statement as the Record on Appeal

Instead of the record on appeal as defined in subdivision (a), the parties may prepare, sign, and submit to the bankruptcy court a statement of the case showing how the issues presented by the appeal arose and were decided in the bankruptcy court. The statement must set forth only those facts alleged and proved or sought to be proved that are essential to the court's resolution of the issues. If the statement is accurate, it—together with any additions that the bankruptcy court may consider necessary to a full presentation of the issues on appeal—must be approved by the bankruptcy court and must then be certified to the court where the appeal is pending as the record on appeal. The bankruptcy clerk must then transmit it to the clerk of that court within the time provided by Rule 8010. A copy of the agreed statement may be filed in place of the appendix required by Rule 8018(b) or, in the case of a direct appeal to the court of appeals, by Fed. R. App. P. 30.

(e) Correcting or Modifying the Record.

    (1) *Submitting to the Bankruptcy Court*

If any difference arises about whether the record accurately discloses what occurred in the bankruptcy court, the difference must be submitted to and settled by the bankruptcy court and the record conformed accordingly. If an item has been improperly designated as part of the record on appeal, a party may move to strike that item.

    (2) *Correcting in Other Ways*

If anything material to either party is omitted from or misstated in the record by error or accident, the omission or misstatement may be corrected, and a supplemental record may be certified and transmitted:

        (A) on stipulation of the parties;

        (B) by the bankruptcy court before or after the record has been forwarded; or

        (C) by the court where the appeal is pending.

    (3) *Remaining Questions*

All other questions as to the form and content of the record must be presented to the court where the appeal is pending.

(f) Sealed Documents

A document placed under seal by the bankruptcy court may be designated as part of the record on appeal. In doing so, a party must identify it without revealing confidential or secret information, but the bankruptcy clerk must not transmit it to the clerk of the court where the appeal is pending as part of the record. Instead, a party must file a motion with the court where the appeal is pending to accept the document under seal. If the motion is granted, the movant must notify the bankruptcy court of the ruling, and the bankruptcy clerk must promptly transmit the sealed document to the clerk of the court where the appeal is pending.

(g) Other Necessary Actions

All parties to an appeal must take any other action necessary to enable the bankruptcy clerk to assemble and transmit the record.

(Added Apr. 25, 2014, eff. Dec. 1, 2014.)

2014 Amendments

This rule is derived from former Rule 8006 and Fed. R. App. P. 10 and 11(a). The provisions of this rule and Rule 8010 are applicable to appeals taken directly to a court of appeals under 28 U.S.C. § 158(d)(2), as well as to appeals to a district court or BAP. See Fed. R. App. P. 6(c)(2)(A) and (B).

The rule retains the practice of former Rule 8006 of requiring the parties to designate items to be included in the record on appeal. In this respect, the bankruptcy rule differs from the appellate rule. Among other things, Fed. R. App. P. 10(a) provides that the record on appeal consists of all the documents and exhibits filed in the case. This requirement would often be unworkable in a bankruptcy context because thousands of items might have been filed in the overall bankruptcy case.

Subdivision (a) provides the time period for an appellant to file a designation of items to be included in the record on appeal and a statement of the issues to be presented. It then provides for the designation of additional items by the appellee, cross-appellant, and cross-appellee, as well as for the cross-appellant's statement of the issues to be presented in its appeal. Subdivision (a)(4) prescribes the content of the record on appeal. Ordinarily, the bankruptcy clerk will not need to have paper copies of the designated items because the clerk will either transmit them to the appellate court electronically or otherwise make them available electronically. If the bankruptcy clerk requires a paper copy of some or all of the items designated as part of the record, the clerk may request the party that designated the item to provide the necessary copies, and the party must comply with the request or bear the cost of the clerk's copying.

Subdivision (b) governs the process for ordering a complete or partial transcript of the bankruptcy court proceedings. In situations in which a transcript is unavailable, subdivision (c) allows for the parties' preparation of a statement of the evidence or proceedings, which must be approved by the bankruptcy court.

Subdivision (d) adopts the practice of Fed. R. App. P. 10(d) of permitting the parties to agree on a statement of the case in place of the record on appeal. The statement must show how the issues on appeal arose and were decided in the bankruptcy court. It must be approved by the bankruptcy court in order to be certified as the record on appeal.

Subdivision (e), modeled on Fed. R. App. P. 10(e), provides a procedure for correcting the record on appeal if an item is improperly designated, omitted, or misstated.

Subdivision (f) is a new provision that governs the handling of any document that remains sealed by the bankruptcy court and that a party wants to include in the record on appeal. The party must request the court where the appeal is pending to accept the document under seal, and that motion must be granted before the bankruptcy clerk may transmit the sealed document to the district, BAP, or circuit clerk.

Subdivision (g) requires the parties' cooperation with the bankruptcy clerk in assembling and transmitting the record. It retains the requirement of former Rule 8006, which was adapted from Fed. R. App. P. 11(a).

Rule 8010   BANKRUPTCY RULES

Rule 8010. Completing and Transmitting the Record

(a) **Reporter's Duties.**

(1) **Proceedings Recorded Without a Reporter Present**

If proceedings were recorded without a reporter being present, the person or service selected under bankruptcy court procedures to transcribe the recording is the reporter for purposes of this rule.

(2) **Preparing and Filing the Transcript**

The reporter must prepare and file a transcript as follows:

(A) Upon receiving an order for a transcript in accordance with Rule 8009(b), the reporter must file in the bankruptcy court an acknowledgment of the request that shows when it was received, and when the reporter expects to have the transcript completed.

(B) After completing the transcript, the reporter must file it with the bankruptcy clerk, who will notify the district, BAP, or circuit clerk of its filing.

(C) If the transcript cannot be completed within 30 days after receiving the order, the reporter must request an extension of time from the bankruptcy clerk. The clerk must enter on the docket and notify the parties whether the extension is granted.

(D) If the reporter does not file the transcript on time, the bankruptcy clerk must notify the bankruptcy judge.

(b) **Clerk's Duties.**

(1) **Transmitting the Record—In General**

Subject to Rule 8009(f) and subdivision (b)(5) of this rule, when the record is complete, the bankruptcy clerk must transmit to the clerk of the court where the appeal is pending either the record or a notice that the record is available electronically.

(2) **Multiple Appeals**

If there are multiple appeals from a judgment, order, or decree, the bankruptcy clerk must transmit a single record.

(3) **Receiving the Record**

Upon receiving the record or notice that it is available electronically, the district, BAP, or circuit clerk must enter that information on the docket and promptly notify all parties to the appeal.

(4) **If Paper Copies Are Ordered**

If the court where the appeal is pending directs that paper copies of the record be provided, the clerk of that court must so notify the appellant. If the appellant fails to provide them, the bankruptcy clerk must prepare them at the appellant's expense.

(5) **When Leave to Appeal is Requested**

Subject to subdivision (c), if a motion for leave to appeal has been filed under Rule 8004, the bankruptcy clerk must prepare and transmit the record only after the district court, BAP, or court of appeals grants leave.

(c) **Record for a Preliminary Motion in the District Court, BAP, or Court of Appeals**

This subdivision (c) applies if, before the record is transmitted, a party moves in the district court, BAP, or court of appeals for any of the following relief:

- leave to appeal;
- dismissal;
- stay pending appeal;
- approval of a supersedeas bond, or additional security on a bond or undertaking on appeal;

or
- any other intermediate order.

The bankruptcy clerk must then transmit to the clerk of the court where the relief is sought any parts of the record designated by a party to the appeal or a notice that those parts are available electronically.

(Added Apr. 25, 2014, eff. Dec. 1, 2014.)

2014 Amendments

This rule is derived from former Rule 8007 and Fed. R. App. P. 11. It applies to an appeal taken directly to a court of appeals under 28 U.S.C. § 158(d)(2), as well as to an appeal to a district court or BAP.

Subdivision (a) generally retains the procedure of former Rule 8007(a) regarding the reporter's duty to prepare and file a transcript if a party requests one. It clarifies that the person or service that transcribes the recording of a proceeding is considered the reporter under this rule if the proceeding is recorded without a reporter being present in the courtroom. It also makes clear that the reporter must file with the bankruptcy court the acknowledgment of the request for a transcript and statement of the expected completion date, the completed transcript, and any request for an extension of time beyond 30 days for completion of the transcript.

Subdivision (b) requires the bankruptcy clerk to transmit the record to the district, BAP or circuit clerk when the record is complete and, in the case of appeals under 28 U.S.C. § 158(a)(3), leave to appeal has been granted. This transmission will be made electronically, either by sending the record itself or sending notice that the record can be accessed electronically. The court where the appeal is pending may, however, require that a paper copy of some or all of the record be furnished, in which case the clerk of that court will direct the appellant to provide the copies. If the appellant does not do so, the bankruptcy clerk must prepare the copies at the appellant's expense.

In a change from former Rule 8007(b), subdivision (b) of this rule no longer directs the clerk of the appellate court to docket the appeal upon receipt of the record from the bankruptcy clerk. Instead, under Rules 8003(d) and 8004(c) and Fed. R. App. P. 12(a), the district, BAP, or circuit clerk dockets the appeal upon receipt of the notice of appeal or, in the case of appeals under 28 U.S.C. § 158(a)(3), the notice of appeal and the motion for leave to appeal. Accordingly, by the time the district, BAP, or circuit clerk receives the record, the appeal will already be docketed in that court. The clerk of the appellate court must indicate on the docket and give notice to the parties to the appeal when the transmission of the record is received. Under Rule 8018(a) and Fed. R. App. P. 31, the briefing schedule is generally based on that date.

Subdivision (c) is derived from former Rule 8007(c) and Fed. R. App. P. 11(g). It provides for the transmission of parts of the record that the parties designate for consideration by the district court, BAP, or court of appeals in ruling on specified preliminary motions filed prior to the preparation and transmission of the record on appeal.

Rule 8011. Filing and Service; Signature

(a) Filing

(1) With the Clerk

A document required or permitted to be filed in a district court or BAP must be filed with the clerk of that court.

(2) Method and Timeliness

(A) In General

Filing may be accomplished by transmission to the clerk of the district court or BAP. Except as provided in subdivision (a)(2)(B) and (C), filing is timely only if the clerk receives the document within the time fixed for filing.

(B) Brief or Appendix

A brief or appendix is also timely filed if, on or before the last day for filing, it is:

Rule 8011   BANKRUPTCY RULES

>> (i) mailed to the clerk by first-class mail—or other class of mail that is at least as expeditious—postage prepaid, if the district court's or BAP's procedures permit or require a brief or appendix to be filed by mailing; or

>> (ii) dispatched to a third-party commercial carrier for delivery within 3 days to the clerk, if the court's procedures so permit or require.

> **(C) Inmate Filing**

> A document filed by an inmate confined in an institution is timely if deposited in the institution's internal mailing system on or before the last day for filing. If the institution has a system designed for legal mail, the inmate must use that system to receive the benefit of this rule. Timely filing may be shown by a declaration in compliance with 28 U.S.C. § 1746 or by a notarized statement, either of which must set forth the date of deposit and state that first-class postage has been prepaid.

> **(D) Copies**

> If a document is filed electronically, no paper copy is required. If a document is filed by mail or delivery to the district court or BAP, no additional copies are required. But the district court or BAP may require by local rule or by order in a particular case the filing or furnishing of a specified number of paper copies.

(3) Clerk's Refusal of Documents.

The court's clerk must not refuse to accept for filing any document transmitted for that purpose solely because it is not presented in proper form as required by these rules or by any local rule or practice.

(b) Service of All Documents Required

Unless a rule requires service by the clerk, a party must, at or before the time of the filing of a document, serve it on the other parties to the appeal. Service on a party represented by counsel must be made on the party's counsel.

(c) Manner of Service

(1) Methods

Service must be made electronically, unless it is being made by or on an individual who is not represented by counsel or the court's governing rules permit or require service by mail or other means of delivery. Service may be made by or on an unrepresented party by any of the following methods:

> (A) personal delivery;

> (B) mail; or

> (C) third-party commercial carrier for delivery within 3 days.

(2) When Service is Complete

Service by electronic means is complete on transmission, unless the party making service receives notice that the document was not transmitted successfully. Service by mail or by commercial carrier is complete on mailing or delivery to the carrier.

(d) Proof of Service.

(1) What is Required

A document presented for filing must contain either:

> (A) an acknowledgment of service by the person served; or

> (B) proof of service consisting of a statement by the person who made service certifying:

>> (i) the date and manner of service;

>> (ii) the names of the persons served; and

(iii) the mail or electronic address, the fax number, or the address of the place of delivery, as appropriate for the manner of service, for each person served.

(2) Delayed Proof

The district or BAP clerk may permit documents to be filed without acknowledgment or proof of service, but must require the acknowledgment or proof to be filed promptly thereafter.

(3) Brief or Appendix

When a brief or appendix is filed, the proof of service must also state the date and manner by which it was filed.

(e) Signature

Every document filed electronically must include the electronic signature of the person filing it or, if the person is represented, the electronic signature of counsel. The electronic signature must be provided by electronic means that are consistent with any technical standards that the Judicial Conference of the United States establishes. Every document filed in paper form must be signed by the person filing the document or, if the person is represented, by counsel.

(Added Apr. 25, 2014, eff. Dec. 1, 2014.)

2014 Amendments

This rule is derived from former Rule 8008 and Fed. R. App. P. 25. It adopts some of the additional details of the appellate rule, and it provides greater recognition of the possibility of electronic filing and service.

Subdivision (a) governs the filing of documents in the district court or BAP. Consistent with other provisions of these Part VIII rules, subdivision (a)(2) requires electronic filing of documents, including briefs and appendices, unless the district court's or BAP's procedures permit or require other methods of delivery to the court. An electronic filing is timely if it is received by the district or BAP clerk within the time fixed for filing. No additional copies need to be submitted when documents are filed electronically, by mail, or by delivery unless the district court or BAP requires them.

Subdivision (a)(3) provides that the district or BAP clerk may not refuse to accept a document for filing solely because its form does not comply with these rules or any local rule or practice. The district court or BAP may, however, direct the correction of any deficiency in any document that does not conform to the requirements of these rules or applicable local rules, and may prescribe such other relief as the court deems appropriate.

Subdivisions (b) and **(c)** address the service of documents in the district court or BAP. Except for documents that the district or BAP clerk must serve, a party that makes a filing must serve copies of the document on the other parties to the appeal. Service on represented parties must be made on counsel. Subdivision (c) expresses the general requirement under these Part VIII rules that documents be sent electronically. See Rule 8001(c). Local court rules, however, may provide for other means of service, and subdivision (c) specifies non-electronic methods of service by or on an unrepresented party. Electronic service is complete upon transmission, unless the party making service receives notice that the transmission did not reach the person intended to be served in a readable form.

Subdivision (d) retains the former rule's provisions regarding proof of service of a document filed in the district court or BAP. In addition, it provides that a certificate of service must state the mail or electronic address or fax number to which service was made.

Subdivision (e) is a new provision that requires an electronic signature of counsel or an unrepresented filer for documents that are filed electronically in the district court or BAP. A local rule may specify a method of providing an electronic signature that is consistent with any standards established by the Judicial Conference of the United States. Paper copies of documents filed in the district court or BAP must bear an actual signature of counsel or the filer. By requiring a signature, subdivision (e) ensures that a readily identifiable attorney or party takes responsibility for every document that is filed.

Rule 8012. Corporate Disclosure Statement

(a) Who Must File

Any nongovernmental corporate party appearing in the district court or BAP must file a statement that identifies any parent corporation and any publicly held corporation that owns 10% or more of its stock or states that there is no such corporation.

(b) Time to File; Supplemental Filing

A party must file the statement with its principal brief or upon filing a motion, response, petition, or answer in the district court or BAP, whichever occurs first, unless a local rule requires earlier filing. Even if the statement has already been filed, the party's principal brief must include a statement before the table of contents. A party must supplement its statement whenever the required information changes.

(Added Apr. 25, 2014, eff. Dec. 1, 2014.)

2014 Amendments

This rule is derived from Fed. R. App. P. 26.1. It requires the filing of corporate disclosure statements and supplemental statements in order to assist district court and BAP judges in determining whether they should recuse themselves. Rule 9001 makes the definitions in § 101 of the Code applicable to these rules. Under § 101(9) the word "corporation" includes a limited liability company, limited liability partnership, business trust, and certain other entities that are not designated under applicable law as corporations.

If filed separately from a brief, motion, response, petition, or answer, the statement must be filed and served in accordance with Rule 8011. Under Rule 8015(a)(7)(B)(iii), the corporate disclosure statement is not included in calculating applicable word-count limitations.

Rule 8013. Motions; Intervention

(a) Contents of a Motion; Response; Reply

(1) Request for Relief

A request for an order or other relief is made by filing a motion with the district or BAP clerk, with proof of service on the other parties to the appeal.

(2) Contents of a Motion

(A) Grounds and the Relief Sought

A motion must state with particularity the grounds for the motion, the relief sought, and the legal argument necessary to support it.

(B) Motion to Expedite an Appeal

A motion to expedite an appeal must explain what justifies considering the appeal ahead of other matters. If the district court or BAP grants the motion, it may accelerate the time to transmit the record, the deadline for filing briefs and other documents, oral argument, and the resolution of the appeal. A motion to expedite an appeal may be filed as an emergency motion under subdivision (d).

(C) Accompanying Documents

(i) Any affidavit or other document necessary to support a motion must be served and filed with the motion.

(ii) An affidavit must contain only factual information, not legal argument.

(iii) A motion seeking substantive relief must include a copy of the bankruptcy court's judgment, order, or decree, and any accompanying opinion as a separate exhibit.

(D) Documents Barred or Not Required

(i) A separate brief supporting or responding to a motion must not be filed.

APPEALS Rule 8013

   (ii) Unless the court orders otherwise, a notice of motion or a proposed order is not required.

(3) Response and Reply; Time to File

Unless the district court or BAP orders otherwise,

   (A) any party to the appeal may file a response to the motion within 7 days after service of the motion; and

   (B) the movant may file a reply to a response within 7 days after service of the response, but may only address matters raised in the response.

(b) Disposition of a Motion for a Procedural Order

The district court or BAP may rule on a motion for a procedural order— including a motion under Rule 9006(b) or (c)—at any time without awaiting a response. A party adversely affected by the ruling may move to reconsider, vacate, or modify it within 7 days after the procedural order is served.

(c) Oral Argument

A motion will be decided without oral argument unless the district court or BAP orders otherwise.

(d) Emergency Motion

(1) Noting the Emergency

When a movant requests expedited action on a motion because irreparable harm would occur during the time needed to consider a response, the movant must insert the word "Emergency" before the title of the motion.

(2) Contents of the Motion

The emergency motion must

   (A) be accompanied by an affidavit setting out the nature of the emergency;

   (B) state whether all grounds for it were submitted to the bankruptcy court and, if not, why the motion should not be remanded for the bankruptcy court to consider;

   (C) include the e-mail addresses, office addresses, and telephone numbers of moving counsel and, when known, of opposing counsel and any unrepresented parties to the appeal; and

   (D) be served as prescribed by Rule 8011.

(3) Notifying Opposing Parties

Before filing an emergency motion, the movant must make every practicable effort to notify opposing counsel and any unrepresented parties in time for them to respond. The affidavit accompanying the emergency motion must state when and how notice was given or state why giving it was impracticable.

(e) Power of a Single BAP Judge to Entertain a Motion

(1) Single Judge's Authority

A BAP judge may act alone on any motion, but may not dismiss or otherwise determine an appeal, deny a motion for leave to appeal, or deny a motion for a stay pending appeal if denial would make the appeal moot.

(2) Reviewing a Single Judge's Action

The BAP may review a single judge's action, either on its own motion or on a party's motion.

Rule 8013   BANKRUPTCY RULES

(f) Form of Documents; Page Limits; Number of Copies

(1) Format of a Paper Document

Rule 27(d)(1) Fed. R. App. P. applies in the district court or BAP to a paper version of a motion, response, or reply.

(2) Format of an Electronically Filed Document

A motion, response, or reply filed electronically must comply with the requirements for a paper version regarding covers, line spacing, margins, typeface, and type style. It must also comply with the page limits under paragraph (3).

(3) Page Limits

Unless the district court or BAP orders otherwise:

(A) a motion or a response to a motion must not exceed 20 pages, exclusive of the corporate disclosure statement and accompanying documents authorized by subdivision (a)(2)(C); and

(B) a reply to a response must not exceed 10 pages.

(4) Paper Copies

Paper copies must be provided only if required by local rule or by an order in a particular case.

(g) Intervening in an Appeal

Unless a statute provides otherwise, an entity that seeks to intervene in an appeal pending in the district court or BAP must move for leave to intervene and serve a copy of the motion on the parties to the appeal. The motion or other notice of intervention authorized by statute must be filed within 30 days after the appeal is docketed. It must concisely state the movant's interest, the grounds for intervention, whether intervention was sought in the bankruptcy court, why intervention is being sought at this stage of the proceeding, and why participating as an amicus curiae would not be adequate.

(Added Apr. 25, 2014, eff. Dec. 1, 2014.)

2014 Amendments

This rule is derived from former Rule 8011 and Fed. R. App. P. 15(d) and 27. It adopts many of the provisions of the appellate rules that specify the form and page limits of motions and accompanying documents, while also adjusting those requirements for electronic filing. In addition, it prescribes the procedure for seeking to intervene in the district court or BAP.

Subdivision (a) retains much of the content of former Rule 8011(a) regarding the contents of a motion, response, and reply. It also specifies the documents that may accompany a motion. Unlike the former rule, which allowed the filing of separate briefs supporting a motion, subdivision (a) now adopts the practice of Fed. R. App. P. 27(a) of prohibiting the filing of briefs supporting or responding to a motion. The motion or response itself must include the party's legal arguments.

Subdivision (a)(2)(B) clarifies the procedure for seeking to expedite an appeal. A motion under this provision seeks to expedite the time for the disposition of the appeal as a whole, whereas an emergency motion—which is addressed by subdivision (d)—typically involves an urgent request for relief short of disposing of the entire appeal (for example, an emergency request for a stay pending appeal to prevent imminent mootness). In appropriate cases—such as when there is an urgent need to resolve the appeal quickly to prevent harm—a party may file a motion to expedite the appeal as an emergency motion.

Subdivision (b) retains the substance of former Rule 8011 (b). It authorizes the district court or BAP to act on a motion for a procedural order without awaiting a response to the motion. It specifies that a party seeking reconsideration, vacation, or modification of the order must file a motion within 7 days after service of the order.

Subdivision (c) continues the practice of former Rule 8011(c) and Fed. R. App. P. 27(e) of dispensing with oral argument of motions in the district court or BAP unless the court orders otherwise.

Subdivision (d), which carries forward the content of former Rule 8011(d), governs emergency motions that the district court or BAP may rule on without awaiting a response when necessary to prevent irreparable harm. A party seeking expedited action on a motion in the district court or BAP must explain the nature of the emergency, whether all grounds in support of the motion were first presented to the bankruptcy court, and, if not, why the district court or BAP should not remand for reconsideration. The moving party must also explain the steps taken to notify opposing counsel and any unrepresented parties in advance of filing the emergency motion and, if they were not notified, why it was impracticable to do so.

Subdivision (e), like former Rule 8011(e) and similar to Fed. R. App. P. 27(c), authorizes a single BAP judge to rule on certain motions. This authority, however, does not extend to issuing rulings that would dispose of the appeal. For that reason, the rule now prohibits a single BAP judge from denying a motion for a stay pending appeal when the effect of that ruling would be to require dismissal of the appeal as moot. A ruling by a single judge is subject to review by the BAP.

Subdivision (f) incorporates by reference the formatting and appearance requirements of Fed. R. App. P. 27(d)(1). When paper versions of the listed documents are filed, they must comply with the requirements of the specified rules regarding reproduction, covers, binding, appearance, and format. When these documents are filed electronically, they must comply with the relevant requirements of the specified rules regarding covers and format. Subdivision (f) also specifies page limits for motions, responses, and replies, which is a matter that former Rule 8011 did not address.

Subdivision (g) clarifies the procedure for seeking to intervene in a proceeding that has been appealed. It is based on Fed. R. App. P. 15(d), but it also requires the moving party to explain why intervention is being sought at the appellate stage. The former Part VIII rules did not address intervention.

Rule 8014. Briefs

(a) Appellant's Brief

The appellant's brief must contain the following under appropriate headings and in the order indicated:

(1) a corporate disclosure statement, if required by Rule 8012;

(2) a table of contents, with page references;

(3) a table of authorities—cases (alphabetically arranged), statutes, and other authorities—with references to the pages of the brief where they are cited;

(4) a jurisdictional statement, including:

(A) the basis for the bankruptcy court's subject-matter jurisdiction, with citations to applicable statutory provisions and stating relevant facts establishing jurisdiction;

(B) the basis for the district court's or BAP's jurisdiction, with citations to applicable statutory provisions and stating relevant facts establishing jurisdiction;

(C) the filing dates establishing the timeliness of the appeal; and

(D) an assertion that the appeal is from a final judgment, order, or decree, or information establishing the district court's or BAP's jurisdiction on another basis;

(5) a statement of the issues presented and, for each one, a concise statement of the applicable standard of appellate review;

(6) a concise statement of the case setting out the facts relevant to the issues submitted for review, describing the relevant procedural history, and identifying the rulings presented for review, with appropriate references to the record;

(7) a summary of the argument, which must contain a succinct, clear, and accurate statement of the arguments made in the body of the brief, and which must not merely repeat the argument headings;

(8) the argument, which must contain the appellant's contentions and the reasons for them, with citations to the authorities and parts of the record on which the appellant relies;

Rule 8014　　BANKRUPTCY RULES

　　(9)　a short conclusion stating the precise relief sought; and

　　(10)　the certificate of compliance, if required by Rule 8015(a)(7) or (b).

(b) Appellee's Brief

The appellee's brief must conform to the requirements of subdivision (a)(1)–(8) and (10), except that none of the following need appear unless the appellee is dissatisfied with the appellant's statement:

　　(1)　the jurisdictional statement;

　　(2)　the statement of the issues and the applicable standard of appellate review; and

　　(3)　the statement of the case.

(c) Reply Brief

The appellant may file a brief in reply to the appellee's brief. A reply brief must comply with the requirements of subdivision (a)(2)–(3).

(d) Statutes, Rules, Regulations, or Similar Authority

If the court's determination of the issues presented requires the study of the Code or other statutes, rules, regulations, or similar authority, the relevant parts must be set out in the brief or in an addendum.

(e) Briefs in a Case Involving Multiple Appellants or Appellees

In a case involving more than one appellant or appellee, including consolidated cases, any number of appellants or appellees may join in a brief, and any party may adopt by reference a part of another's brief. Parties may also join in reply briefs.

(f) Citation of Supplemental Authorities

If pertinent and significant authorities come to a party's attention after the party's brief has been filed—or after oral argument but before a decision— a party may promptly advise the district or BAP clerk by a signed submission setting forth the citations. The submission, which must be served on the other parties to the appeal, must state the reasons for the supplemental citations, referring either to the pertinent page of a brief or to a point argued orally. The body of the submission must not exceed 350 words. Any response must be made within 7 days after the party is served, unless the court orders otherwise, and must be similarly limited.

(Added Apr. 25, 2014, eff. Dec. 1, 2014.)

2014 Amendments

This rule is derived from former Rule 8010(a) and (b) and Fed. R. App. P. 28. Adopting much of the content of Rule 28, it provides greater detail than former Rule 8010 contained regarding appellate briefs.

Subdivision (a) prescribes the content and structure of the appellant's brief. It largely follows former Rule 8010(a)(1), but, to ensure national uniformity, it eliminates the provision authorizing a district court or BAP to alter these requirements. Subdivision (a)(1) provides that when Rule 8012 requires an appellant to file a corporate disclosure statement, it must be placed at the beginning of the appellant's brief. Subdivision (a)(10) is new. It implements the requirement under Rule 8015(a)(7)(C) and (b) for the filing of a certificate of compliance with the limit on the number of words or lines allowed to be in a brief.

Subdivision (b) carries forward the provisions of former Rule 8010(a)(2).

Subdivision (c) is derived from Fed. R. App. P. 28(c). It authorizes an appellant to file a reply brief, which will generally complete the briefing process.

Subdivision (d) is similar to former Rule 8010(b), but it is reworded to reflect the likelihood that briefs will generally be filed electronically rather than in paper form.

Subdivision (e) mirrors Fed. R. App. P. 28(i). It authorizes multiple appellants or appellees to join in a single brief. It also allows a party to incorporate by reference portions of another party's brief.

Subdivision (f) adopts the procedures of Fed. R. App. P. 28(j) with respect to the filing of supplemental authorities with the district court or BAP after a brief has been filed or after oral argument. Unlike the appellate rule, it specifies a period of 7 days for filing a response to a submission of supplemental authorities. The supplemental submission and response must comply with the signature requirements of Rule 8011(e).

Rule 8015. Form and Length of Briefs; Form of Appendices and Other Papers

(a) Paper Copies of a Brief

If a paper copy of a brief may or must be filed, the following provisions apply:

(1) Reproduction

(A) A brief may be reproduced by any process that yields a clear black image on light paper. The paper must be opaque and unglazed. Only one side of the paper may be used.

(B) Text must be reproduced with a clarity that equals or exceeds the output of a laser printer.

(C) Photographs, illustrations, and tables may be reproduced by any method that results in a good copy of the original. A glossy finish is acceptable if the original is glossy.

(2) Cover

The front cover of a brief must contain:

(A) the number of the case centered at the top;

(B) the name of the court;

(C) the title of the case as prescribed by Rule 8003(d)(2) or 8004(c)(2);

(D) the nature of the proceeding and the name of the court below;

(E) the title of the brief, identifying the party or parties for whom the brief is filed; and

(F) the name, office address, telephone number, and e-mail address of counsel representing the party for whom the brief is filed.

(3) Binding

The brief must be bound in any manner that is secure, does not obscure the text, and permits the brief to lie reasonably flat when open.

(4) Paper Size, Line Spacing, and Margins

The brief must be on $8^1/_2$-by-11 inch paper. The text must be double-spaced, but quotations more than two lines long may be indented and single-spaced. Headings and footnotes may be single-spaced. Margins must be at least one inch on all four sides. Page numbers may be placed in the margins, but no text may appear there.

(5) Typeface

Either a proportionally spaced or monospaced face may be used.

(A) A proportionally spaced face must include serifs, but sans-serif type may be used in headings and captions. A proportionally spaced face must be 14-point or larger.

(B) A monospaced face may not contain more than $10^1/_2$ characters per inch.

(6) Type Styles

A brief must be set in plain, roman style, although italics or boldface may be used for emphasis. Case names must be italicized or underlined.

(7) Length

(A) Page limitation

A principal brief must not exceed 30 pages, or a reply brief 15 pages, unless it complies with (B) and (C).

(B) Type-volume limitation

(i) A principal brief is acceptable if:

- it contains no more than 14,000 words; or
- it uses a monospaced face and contains no more than 1,300 lines of text.

(ii) A reply brief is acceptable if it contains no more than half of the type volume specified in item (i).

(iii) Headings, footnotes, and quotations count toward the word and line limitations. The corporate disclosure statement, table of contents, table of citations, statement with respect to oral argument, any addendum containing statutes, rules, or regulations, and any certificates of counsel do not count toward the limitation.

(C) Certificate of Compliance

(i) A brief submitted under subdivision (a)(7)(B) must include a certificate signed by the attorney, or an unrepresented party, that the brief complies with the type-volume limitation. The person preparing the certificate may rely on the word or line count of the word-processing system used to prepare the brief. The certificate must state either:

- the number of words in the brief; or
- the number of lines of monospaced type in the brief.

(ii) The certification requirement is satisfied by a certificate of compliance that conforms substantially to the appropriate Official Form.

(b) Electronically Filed Briefs

A brief filed electronically must comply with subdivision (a), except for (a)(1), (a)(3), and the paper requirement of (a)(4).

(c) Paper Copies of Appendices

A paper copy of an appendix must comply with subdivision (a)(1), (2), (3), and (4), with the following exceptions:

(1) An appendix may include a legible photocopy of any document found in the record or of a printed decision.

(2) When necessary to facilitate inclusion of odd-sized documents such as technical drawings, an appendix may be a size other than 8½-by-11 inches, and need not lie reasonably flat when opened.

(d) Electronically Filed Appendices

An appendix filed electronically must comply with subdivision (a)(2) and (4), except for the paper requirement of (a)(4).

(e) Other Documents

(1) Motion

Rule 8013(f) governs the form of a motion, response, or reply.

(2) Paper Copies of Other Documents

A paper copy of any other document, other than a submission under Rule 8014(f), must comply with subdivision (a), with the following exceptions:

(A) A cover is not necessary if the caption and signature page together contain the information required by subdivision (a)(2).

(B) Subdivision (a)(7) does not apply.

(3) Other Documents Filed Electronically

Any other document filed electronically, other than a submission under Rule 8014(f), must comply with the appearance requirements of paragraph (2).

(f) Local Variation

A district court or BAP must accept documents that comply with the applicable requirements of this rule. By local rule, a district court or BAP may accept documents that do not meet all of the requirements of this rule.

(Added Apr. 25, 2014, eff. Dec. 1, 2014.)

2014 Amendments

This rule is derived primarily from Fed. R. App. P. 32. Former Rule 8010(c) prescribed page limits for principal briefs and reply briefs. Those limits are now addressed by subdivision (a)(7) of this rule. In addition, the rule incorporates most of the detail of Fed. R. App. P. 32 regarding the appearance and format of briefs, appendices, and other documents, along with new provisions that apply when those documents are filed electronically.

Subdivision (a) prescribes the form requirements for briefs that are filed in paper form. It incorporates Fed. R. App. P. 32(a), except it does not include color requirements for brief covers, it requires the cover of a brief to include counsel's email address, and cross-references to the appropriate bankruptcy rules are substituted for references to the Federal Rules of Appellate Procedure.

Subdivision (a)(7) decreases the length of briefs, as measured by the number of pages, that was permitted by former Rule 8010(c). Page limits are reduced from 50 to 30 pages for a principal brief and from 25 to 15 for a reply brief in order to achieve consistency with Fed. R. App. P. 32(a)(7). But as permitted by the appellate rule, subdivision (a)(7) also permits the limits on the length of a brief to be measured by a word or line count, as an alternative to a page limit. Basing the calculation of brief length on either of the type-volume methods specified in subdivision (a)(7)(B) will result in briefs that may exceed the designated page limits in (a)(7)(A) and that may be approximately as long as allowed by the prior page limits.

Subdivision (b) adapts for briefs that are electronically filed subdivision (a)'s form requirements. With the use of electronic filing, the method of reproduction, method of binding, and use of paper become irrelevant. But information required on the cover, formatting requirements, and limits on brief length remain the same.

Subdivisions (c) and **(d)** prescribe the form requirements for appendices. Subdivision (c), applicable to paper appendices, is derived from Fed. R. App. P. 32(b), and subdivision (d) adapts those requirements for electronically filed appendices.

Subdivision (e), which is based on Fed. R. App. P. 32(c), addresses the form required for documents—in paper form or electronically filed—that these rules do not otherwise cover.

Subdivision (f), like Fed. R. App. P. 32(e), provides assurance to lawyers and parties that compliance with this rule's form requirements will allow a brief or other document to be accepted by any district court or BAP. A court may, however, by local rule or, under Rule 8028 by order in a particular case, choose to accept briefs and documents that do not comply with all of this rule's requirements. The decision whether to accept a brief that appears not to be in compliance with the rules must be made by the court. Under Rule 8011(a)(3), the clerk may not refuse to accept a document for filing solely because it is not presented in proper form as required by these rules or any local rule or practice.

Under Rule 8011(e), the party filing the document or, if represented, its counsel must sign all briefs and other submissions. If the document is filed electronically, an electronic signature must be provided in accordance with Rule 8011(e).

Rule 8016. Cross-Appeals

(a) Applicability

This rule applies to a case in which a cross-appeal is filed. Rules 8014(a)–(c), 8015(a)(7)(A)–(B), and 8018(a)(1)–(3) do not apply to such a case, except as otherwise provided in this rule.

Rule 8016

(b) Designation of Appellant

The party who files a notice of appeal first is the appellant for purposes of this rule and Rule 8018(a)(4) and (b) and Rule 8019. If notices are filed on the same day, the plaintiff, petitioner, applicant, or movant in the proceeding below is the appellant. These designations may be modified by the parties' agreement or by court order.

(c) Briefs. In a case involving a cross-appeal:

(1) Appellant's Principal Brief

The appellant must file a principal brief in the appeal. That brief must comply with Rule 8014(a).

(2) Appellee's Principal and Response Brief

The appellee must file a principal brief in the cross-appeal and must, in the same brief, respond to the principal brief in the appeal. That brief must comply with Rule 8014(a), except that the brief need not include a statement of the case unless the appellee is dissatisfied with the appellant's statement.

(3) Appellant's Response and Reply Brief

The appellant must file a brief that responds to the principal brief in the cross-appeal and may, in the same brief, reply to the response in the appeal. That brief must comply with Rule 8014(a)(2)–(8) and (10), except that none of the following need appear unless the appellant is dissatisfied with the appellee's statement in the cross-appeal:

    (A) the jurisdictional statement;

    (B) the statement of the issues and the applicable standard of appellate review; and

    (C) the statement of the case.

(4) Appellee's Reply Brief

The appellee may file a brief in reply to the response in the cross-appeal. That brief must comply with Rule 8014(a)(2)–(3) and (10) and must be limited to the issues presented by the cross-appeal.

(d) Length

(1) Page Limitation

Unless it complies with paragraphs (2) and (3), the appellant's principal brief must not exceed 30 pages; the appellee's principal and response brief, 35 pages; the appellant's response and reply brief, 30 pages; and the appellee's reply brief, 15 pages.

(2) Type-Volume Limitation

    (A) The appellant's principal brief or the appellant's response and reply brief is acceptable if:

        (i) it contains no more than 14,000 words; or

        (ii) it uses a monospaced face and contains no more than 1,300 lines of text.

    (B) The appellee's principal and response brief is acceptable if:

        (i) it contains no more than 16,500 words; or

        (ii) it uses a monospaced face and contains no more than 1,500 lines of text.

    (C) The appellee's reply brief is acceptable if it contains no more than half of the type volume specified in subparagraph (A).

    (D) Headings, footnotes, and quotations count toward the word and line limitations. The corporate disclosure statement, table of contents, table of citations, statement with respect to oral argument, any addendum containing statutes, rules, or regulations, and any certificates of counsel do not count toward the limitation.

(3) Certificate of Compliance

A brief submitted either electronically or in paper form under paragraph (2) must comply with Rule 8015(a)(7)(C).

(e) Time to Serve and File a Brief

Briefs must be served and filed as follows, unless the district court or BAP by order in a particular case excuses the filing of briefs or specifies different time limits:

(1) the appellant's principal brief, within 30 days after the docketing of notice that the record has been transmitted or is available electronically;

(2) the appellee's principal and response brief, within 30 days after the appellant's principal brief is served;

(3) the appellant's response and reply brief, within 30 days after the appellee's principal and response brief is served; and

(4) the appellee's reply brief, within 14 days after the appellant's response and reply brief is served, but at least 7 days before scheduled argument unless the district court or BAP, for good cause, allows a later filing.

(Added Apr. 25, 2014, eff. Dec. 1, 2014.)

2014 Amendments

This rule is derived from Fed. R. App. P. 28.1. It governs the timing, content, length, filing, and service of briefs in bankruptcy appeals in which there is a cross-appeal. The former Part VIII rules did not separately address the topic of cross-appeals.

Subdivision (b) prescribes which party is designated the appellant when there is a cross-appeal. Generally, the first to file a notice of appeal will be the appellant.

Subdivision (c) specifies the briefs that the appellant and the appellee may file. Because of the dual role of the parties to the appeal and cross-appeal, each party is permitted to file a principal brief and a response to the opposing party's brief, as well as a reply brief. For the appellee, the principal brief in the cross-appeal and the response in the appeal are combined into a single brief. The appellant, on the other hand, initially files a principal brief in the appeal and later files a response to the appellee's principal brief in the cross-appeal, along with a reply brief in the appeal. The final brief that may be filed is the appellee's reply brief in the cross-appeal.

Subdivision (d), which prescribes page limits for briefs, is adopted from Fed. R. App. P. 28.1(e). It applies to briefs that are filed electronically, as well as to those filed in paper form. Like Rule 8015(a)(7), it imposes limits measured by either the number of pages or the number of words or lines of text.

Subdivision (e) governs the time for filing briefs in cases in which there is a cross-appeal. It adapts the provisions of Fed. R. App. P. 28.1(f)

Rule 8017. Brief of an Amicus Curiae

(a) When Permitted

The United States or its officer or agency or a state may file an amicus-curiae brief without the consent of the parties or leave of court. Any other amicus curiae may file a brief only by leave of court or if the brief states that all parties have consented to its filing. On its own motion, and with notice to all parties to an appeal, the district court or BAP may request a brief by an amicus curiae.

(b) Motion for Leave to File

The motion must be accompanied by the proposed brief and state:

(1) the movant's interest; and

(2) the reason why an amicus brief is desirable and why the matters asserted are relevant to the disposition of the appeal.

(c) Contents and Form

An amicus brief must comply with Rule 8015. In addition to the requirements of Rule 8015, the cover must identify the party or parties supported and indicate whether the brief supports affirmance or reversal. If an amicus curiae is a corporation, the brief must include a disclosure statement like that required of parties by Rule 8012. An amicus brief need not comply with Rule 8014, but must include the following:

(1) a table of contents, with page references;

(2) a table of authorities—cases (alphabetically arranged), statutes, and other authorities—with references to the pages of the brief where they are cited;

(3) a concise statement of the identity of the amicus curiae, its interest in the case, and the source of its authority to file;

(4) unless the amicus curiae is one listed in the first sentence of subdivision (a), a statement that indicates whether:

(A) a party's counsel authored the brief in whole or in part;

(B) a party or a party's counsel contributed money that was intended to fund preparing or submitting the brief; and

(C) a person—other than the amicus curiae, its members, or its counsel—contributed money that was intended to fund preparing or submitting the brief and, if so, identifies each such person;

(5) an argument, which may be preceded by a summary and need not include a statement of the applicable standard of review; and

(6) a certificate of compliance, if required by Rule 8015(a)(7)(C) or 8015(b).

(d) Length

Except by the district court's or BAP's permission, an amicus brief must be no more than one-half the maximum length authorized by these rules for a party's principal brief. If the court grants a party permission to file a longer brief, that extension does not affect the length of an amicus brief.

(e) Time for Filing

An amicus curiae must file its brief, accompanied by a motion for filing when necessary, no later than 7 days after the principal brief of the party being supported is filed. An amicus curiae that does not support either party must file its brief no later than 7 days after the appellant's principal brief is filed. The district court or BAP may grant leave for later filing, specifying the time within which an opposing party may answer.

(f) Reply Brief

Except by the district court's or BAP's permission, an amicus curiae may not file a reply brief.

(g) Oral Argument

An amicus curiae may participate in oral argument only with the district court's or BAP's permission.

(Added Apr. 25, 2014, eff. Dec. 1, 2014.)

2014 Amendments

This rule is derived from Fed. R. App. P. 29. The former Part VIII rules did not address the participation by an amicus curiae in a bankruptcy appeal.

Subdivision (a) adopts the provisions of Fed. R. App. P. 29(a). In addition, it authorizes the district court or BAP on its own motion—with notice to the parties—to request the filing of a brief by an amicus curiae.

Subdivisions (b)–(g) adopt Fed. R. App. P. 29(b)–(g).

Rule 8018. Serving and Filing Briefs; Appendices

(a) Time to Serve and File a Brief

The following rules apply unless the district court or BAP by order in a particular case excuses the filing of briefs or specifies different time limits:

(1) The appellant must serve and file a brief within 30 days after the docketing of notice that the record has been transmitted or is available electronically.

(2) The appellee must serve and file a brief within 30 days after service of the appellant's brief.

(3) The appellant may serve and file a reply brief within 14 days after service of the appellee's brief, but a reply brief must be filed at least 7 days before scheduled argument unless the district court or BAP, for good cause, allows a later filing.

(4) If an appellant fails to file a brief on time or within an extended time authorized by the district court or BAP, an appellee may move to dismiss the appeal—or the district court or BAP, after notice, may dismiss the appeal on its own motion. An appellee who fails to file a brief will not be heard at oral argument unless the district court or BAP grants permission.

(b) Duty to Serve and File an Appendix to the Brief

(1) Appellant

Subject to subdivision (e) and Rule 8009(d), the appellant must serve and file with its principal brief excerpts of the record as an appendix. It must contain the following:

(A) the relevant entries in the bankruptcy docket;

(B) the complaint and answer, or other equivalent filings;

(C) the judgment, order, or decree from which the appeal is taken;

(D) any other orders, pleadings, jury instructions, findings, conclusions, or opinions relevant to the appeal;

(E) the notice of appeal; and

(F) any relevant transcript or portion of it.

(2) Appellee

The appellee may also serve and file with its brief an appendix that contains material required to be included by the appellant or relevant to the appeal or cross-appeal, but omitted by the appellant.

(3) Cross-Appellee

The appellant as cross-appellee may also serve and file with its response an appendix that contains material relevant to matters raised initially by the principal brief in the cross-appeal, but omitted by the cross-appellant.

(c) Format of the Appendix

The appendix must begin with a table of contents identifying the page at which each part begins. The relevant docket entries must follow the table of contents. Other parts of the record must follow chronologically. When pages from the transcript of proceedings are placed in the appendix, the transcript page numbers must be shown in brackets immediately before the included pages. Omissions in the text of documents or of the transcript must be indicated by asterisks. Immaterial formal matters (captions, subscriptions, acknowledgments, and the like) should be omitted.

(d) Exhibits

Exhibits designated for inclusion in the appendix may be reproduced in a separate volume or volumes, suitably indexed.

(e) Appeal on the Original Record Without an Appendix

The district court or BAP may, either by rule for all cases or classes of cases or by order in a particular case, dispense with the appendix and permit an appeal to proceed on the original record, with the submission of any relevant parts of the record that the district court or BAP orders the parties to file.

(Added Apr. 25, 2014, eff. Dec. 1, 2014.)

2014 Amendments

This rule is derived from former Rule 8009 and Fed. R. App. P. 30 and 31. Like former Rule 8009, it addresses the timing of serving and filing briefs and appendices, as well as the content and format of appendices. Rule 8011 governs the methods of filing and serving briefs and appendices.

The rule retains the bankruptcy practice of permitting the appellee to file its own appendix, rather than requiring the appellant to include in its appendix matters designated by the appellee. Rule 8016 governs the timing of serving and filing briefs when a cross-appeal is taken. This rule's provisions about appendices apply to all appeals, including cross-appeals.

Subdivision (a) retains former Rule 8009's provision that allows the district court or BAP to dispense with briefing or to provide different time periods than this rule specifies. It increases some of the time periods for filing briefs from the periods prescribed by the former rule, while still retaining shorter time periods than some provided by Fed. R. App. P. 31(a). The time for filing the appellant's brief is increased from 14 to 30 days after the docketing of the notice of the transmission of the record or notice of the availability of the record. That triggering event is equivalent to docketing the appeal under former Rule 8007. Appellate Rule 31(a)(1), by contrast, provides the appellant 40 days after the record is filed to file its brief. The shorter time period for bankruptcy appeals reflects the frequent need for greater expedition in the resolution of bankruptcy appeals, while still providing the appellant more time to prepare its brief than the former rule provided.

Subdivision (a)(2) similarly expands the time period for filing the appellee's brief from 14 to 30 days after the service of the appellant's brief. This period is the same as F.R.App. 31(a)(1) provides.

Subdivision (a)(3) retains the 14-day time period for filing a reply brief that the former rule prescribed, but it qualifies that period to ensure that the final brief is filed at least 7 days before oral argument.

If a district court or BAP has a mediation procedure for bankruptcy appeals, that procedure could affect when briefs must be filed. See Rule 8027.

Subdivision (a)(4) is new. Based on Fed. R. App. P. 31(c), it provides for actions that may be taken—dismissal of the appeal or denial of participation in oral argument—if the appellant or appellee fails to file its brief.

Subdivisions (b) and **(c)** govern the content and format of the appendix to a brief. Subdivision (b) is similar to former Rule 8009(b), and subdivision (c) is derived from Fed. R. App. P. 30(d).

Subdivision (d), which addresses the inclusion of exhibits in the appendix, is derived from Fed. R. App. P. 30(e).

Rule 8019. Oral Argument

(a) Party's Statement

Any party may file, or a district court or BAP may require, a statement explaining why oral argument should, or need not, be permitted.

(b) Presumption of Oral Argument and Exceptions

Oral argument must be allowed in every case unless the district judge—or all the BAP judges assigned to hear the appeal—examine the briefs and record and determine that oral argument is unnecessary because

    (1) the appeal is frivolous;

    (2) the dispositive issue or issues have been authoritatively decided; or

APPEALS Rule 8019

(3) the facts and legal arguments are adequately presented in the briefs and record, and the decisional process would not be significantly aided by oral argument.

(c) Notice of Argument; Postponement

The district court or BAP must advise all parties of the date, time, and place for oral argument, and the time allowed for each side. A motion to postpone the argument or to allow longer argument must be filed reasonably in advance of the hearing date.

(d) Order and Contents of Argument

The appellant opens and concludes the argument. Counsel must not read at length from briefs, the record, or authorities.

(e) Cross-Appeals and Separate Appeals

If there is a cross-appeal, Rule 8016(b) determines which party is the appellant and which is the appellee for the purposes of oral argument. Unless the district court or BAP directs otherwise, a cross-appeal or separate appeal must be argued when the initial appeal is argued. Separate parties should avoid duplicative argument.

(f) Nonappearance of a Party

If the appellee fails to appear for argument, the district court or BAP may hear the appellant's argument. If the appellant fails to appear for argument, the district court or BAP may hear the appellee's argument. If neither party appears, the case will be decided on the briefs unless the district court or BAP orders otherwise.

(g) Submission on Briefs

The parties may agree to submit a case for decision on the briefs, but the district court or BAP may direct that the case be argued.

(h) Use of Physical Exhibits at Argument; Removal

Counsel intending to use physical exhibits other than documents at the argument must arrange to place them in the courtroom on the day of the argument before the court convenes. After the argument, counsel must remove the exhibits from the courtroom unless the district court or BAP directs otherwise. The clerk may destroy or dispose of the exhibits if counsel does not reclaim them within a reasonable time after the clerk gives notice to remove them.

(Added Apr. 25, 2014, eff. Dec. 1, 2014.)

2014 Amendments

This rule generally retains the provisions of former Rule 8012 and adds much of the additional detail of Fed. R. App. P. 34. By incorporating the more detailed provisions of the appellate rule, Rule 8019 promotes national uniformity regarding oral argument in bankruptcy appeals.

Subdivision (a), like Fed. R. App. P. 34(a)(1), now allows a party to submit a statement explaining why oral argument is or is not needed. It also authorizes a court to require this statement. Former Rule 8012 only authorized statements explaining why oral argument should be allowed.

Subdivision (b) retains the reasons set forth in former Rule 8012 for the district court or BAP to conclude that oral argument is not needed.

The remainder of this rule adopts the provisions of Fed. R. App. P. 34(b)–(g), with one exception. Rather than requiring the district court or BAP to hear appellant's argument if the appellee does not appear, subdivision (f) authorizes the district court or BAP to go forward with the argument in the appellee's absence. Should the court decide, however, to postpone the oral argument in that situation, it would be authorized to do so.

Rule 8020. Frivolous Appeal and Other Misconduct

(a) Frivolous Appeal—Damages and Costs

If the district court or BAP determines that an appeal is frivolous, it may, after a separately filed motion or notice from the court and reasonable opportunity to respond, award just damages and single or double costs to the appellee.

(b) Other Misconduct

The district court or BAP may discipline or sanction an attorney or party appearing before it for other misconduct, including failure to comply with any court order. First, however, the court must afford the attorney or party reasonable notice, an opportunity to show cause to the contrary, and, if requested, a hearing.

(Added Apr. 25, 2014, eff. Dec. 1, 2014.)

2014 Amendments

This rule is derived from former Rule 8020 and Fed. R. App. P. 38 and 46(c). Subdivision (a) permits an award of damages and costs to an appellee for a frivolous appeal. Subdivision (b) permits the district court or BAP to impose on parties as well as their counsel sanctions for misconduct other than taking a frivolous appeal. Failure to comply with a court order, for which sanctions may be imposed, may include a failure to comply with a local court rule.

Rule 8021. Costs

(a) Against Whom Assessed

The following rules apply unless the law provides or the district court or BAP orders otherwise:

(1) if an appeal is dismissed, costs are taxed against the appellant, unless the parties agree otherwise;

(2) if a judgment, order, or decree is affirmed, costs are taxed against the appellant;

(3) if a judgment, order, or decree is reversed, costs are taxed against the appellee;

(4) if a judgment, order, or decree is affirmed or reversed in part, modified, or vacated, costs are taxed only as the district court or BAP orders.

(b) Costs for and Against the United States

Costs for or against the United States, its agency, or its officer may be assessed under subdivision (a) only if authorized by law.

(c) Costs on Appeal Taxable in the Bankruptcy Court

The following costs on appeal are taxable in the bankruptcy court for the benefit of the party entitled to costs under this rule:

(1) the production of any required copies of a brief, appendix, exhibit, or the record;

(2) the preparation and transmission of the record;

(3) the reporter's transcript, if needed to determine the appeal;

(4) premiums paid for a supersedeas bond or other bonds to preserve rights pending appeal; and

(5) the fee for filing the notice of appeal.

(d) Bill of Costs; Objections

A party who wants costs taxed must, within 14 days after entry of judgment on appeal, file with the bankruptcy clerk, with proof of service, an itemized and verified bill of costs. Objections must be filed within 14 days after service of the bill of costs, unless the bankruptcy court extends the time.

(Added Apr. 25, 2014, eff. Dec. 1, 2014.)

2014 Amendments

This rule is derived from former Rule 8014 and Fed. R. App. P. 39. It retains the former rule's authorization for taxing appellate costs against the losing party and its specification of the costs that may be taxed. The rule also incorporates some of the additional details regarding the taxing of costs contained in Fed. R. App. P. 39. Consistent with former Rule 8014, the bankruptcy clerk has the responsibility for taxing all costs. Subdivision (b), derived from Fed. R. App. P. 39(b), clarifies that additional authority is required for the taxation of costs by or against federal governmental parties.

Rule 8022. Motion for Rehearing

(a) Time to File; Contents; Response; Action by the District Court or BAP if Granted

(1) Time

Unless the time is shortened or extended by order or local rule, any motion for rehearing by the district court or BAP must be filed within 14 days after entry of judgment on appeal.

(2) Contents

The motion must state with particularity each point of law or fact that the movant believes the district court or BAP has overlooked or misapprehended and must argue in support of the motion. Oral argument is not permitted.

(3) Response

Unless the district court or BAP requests, no response to a motion for rehearing is permitted. But ordinarily, rehearing will not be granted in the absence of such a request.

(4) Action by the District Court or BAP

If a motion for rehearing is granted, the district court or BAP may do any of the following:

(A) make a final disposition of the appeal without re-argument;

(B) restore the case to the calendar for reargument or re-submission; or

(C) issue any other appropriate order.

(b) Form of the Motion; Length

The motion must comply in form with Rule 8013(f)(1) and (2). Copies must be served and filed as provided by Rule 8011. Unless the district court or BAP orders otherwise, a motion for rehearing must not exceed 15 pages.

(Added Apr. 25, 2014, eff. Dec. 1, 2014.)

2014 Amendments

This rule is derived from former Rule 8015 and Fed. R. App. P. 40. It deletes the provision of former Rule 8015 regarding the time for appeal to the court of appeals because the matter is addressed by Fed. R. App. P. 6(b)(2)(A).

Rule 8023. Voluntary Dismissal

The clerk of the district court or BAP must dismiss an appeal if the parties file a signed dismissal agreement specifying how costs are to be paid and pay any fees that are due. An appeal may be dismissed on the appellant's motion on terms agreed to by the parties or fixed by the district court or BAP.

(Added Apr. 25, 2014, eff. Dec. 1, 2014.)

2014 Amendments

This rule is derived from former Rule 8001(c) and Fed. R. App. P. 42. The provision of the former rule regarding dismissal of appeals in the bankruptcy court prior to docketing of the appeal has been deleted. Now that docketing occurs promptly after a notice of appeal is filed, see Rules 8003(d) and 8004(c), an appeal likely will not be voluntarily dismissed before docketing.

The rule retains the provision of the former rule that the district or BAP clerk must dismiss an appeal upon the parties' agreement. District courts and BAPs continue to have discretion to dismiss an appeal on an appellant's motion. Nothing in the rule prohibits a district court or BAP from dismissing an appeal for other reasons authorized by law, such as the failure to prosecute an appeal.

Rule 8024. Clerk's Duties on Disposition of the Appeal

(a) Judgment on Appeal

The district or BAP clerk must prepare, sign, and enter the judgment after receiving the court's opinion or, if there is no opinion, as the court instructs. Noting the judgment on the docket constitutes entry of judgment.

(b) Notice of a Judgment

Immediately upon the entry of a judgment, the district or BAP clerk must:

(1) transmit a notice of the entry to each party to the appeal, to the United States trustee, and to the bankruptcy clerk, together with a copy of any opinion; and

(2) note the date of the transmission on the docket.

(c) Returning Physical Items

If any physical items were transmitted as the record on appeal, they must be returned to the bankruptcy clerk on disposition of the appeal.

(Added Apr. 25, 2014, eff. Dec. 1, 2014.)

2014 Amendments

This rule is derived from former Rule 8016, which was adapted from Fed. R. App. P. 36 and 45(c) and (d). The rule is reworded to reflect that only items in the record that are physically, as opposed to electronically, transmitted to the district court or BAP need to be returned to the bankruptcy clerk. Other changes to the former rule are stylistic.

Rule 8025. Stay of a District Court or BAP Judgment

(a) Automatic Stay of Judgment on Appeal

Unless the district court or BAP orders otherwise, its judgment is stayed for 14 days after entry.

(b) Stay Pending Appeal to the Court of Appeals

(1) **In General**

On a party's motion and notice to all other parties to the appeal, the district court or BAP may stay its judgment pending an appeal to the court of appeals.

(2) **Time Limit**

The stay must not exceed 30 days after the judgment is entered, except for cause shown.

(3) **Stay Continued**

If, before a stay expires, the party who obtained the stay appeals to the court of appeals, the stay continues until final disposition by the court of appeals.

(4) **Bond or Other Security**

A bond or other security may be required as a condition for granting or continuing a stay of the judgment. A bond or other security may be required if a trustee obtains a stay, but not if a stay is obtained by the United States or its officer or agency or at the direction of any department of the United States government.

APPEALS — Rule 8026

(c) Automatic Stay of an Order, Judgment, or Decree of a Bankruptcy Court

If the district court or BAP enters a judgment affirming an order, judgment, or decree of the bankruptcy court, a stay of the district court's or BAP's judgment automatically stays the bankruptcy court's order, judgment, or decree for the duration of the appellate stay.

(d) Power of a Court of Appeals Not Limited

This rule does not limit the power of a court of appeals or any of its judges to do the following:

(1) stay a judgment pending appeal;

(2) stay proceedings while an appeal is pending;

(3) suspend, modify, restore, vacate, or grant a stay or an injunction while an appeal is pending; or

(4) issue any order appropriate to preserve the status quo or the effectiveness of any judgment to be entered.

(Added Apr. 25, 2014, eff. Dec. 1, 2014.)

2014 Amendments

This rule is derived from former Rule 8017. Most of the changes to the former rule are stylistic. Subdivision (c) is new. It provides that if a district court or BAP affirms the bankruptcy court ruling and the appellate judgment is stayed, the bankruptcy court's order, judgment, or decree that is affirmed on appeal is automatically stayed to the same extent as the stay of the appellate judgment.

Rule 8026. Rules by Circuit Councils and District Courts; Procedure When There is No Controlling Law

(a) Local Rules by Circuit Councils and District Courts

(1) Adopting Local Rules

A circuit council that has authorized a BAP under 28 U.S.C. § 158(b) may make and amend rules governing the practice and procedure on appeal from a judgment, order, or decree of a bankruptcy court to the BAP. A district court may make and amend rules governing the practice and procedure on appeal from a judgment, order, or decree of a bankruptcy court to the district court. Local rules must be consistent with, but not duplicative of, Acts of Congress and these Part VIII rules. Rule 83 F.R.Civ.P. governs the procedure for making and amending rules to govern appeals.

(2) Numbering

Local rules must conform to any uniform numbering system prescribed by the Judicial Conference of the United States.

(3) Limitation on Imposing Requirements of Form

A local rule imposing a requirement of form must not be enforced in a way that causes a party to lose any right because of a nonwillful failure to comply.

(b) Procedure When There Is No Controlling Law

(1) In General

A district court or BAP may regulate practice in any manner consistent with federal law, applicable federal rules, the Official Forms, and local rules.

(2) Limitation on Sanctions

No sanction or other disadvantage may be imposed for noncompliance with any requirement not in federal law, applicable federal rules, the Official Forms, or local rules unless the alleged violator has been furnished in the particular case with actual notice of the requirement.

(Added Apr. 25, 2014, eff. Dec. 1, 2014.)

Rule 8027

2014 Amendments

This rule is derived from former Rule 8018. The changes to the former rule are stylistic.

Rule 8027. Notice of a Mediation Procedure

If the district court or BAP has a mediation procedure applicable to bankruptcy appeals, the clerk must notify the parties promptly after docketing the appeal of:

(a) the requirements of the mediation procedure; and

(b) any effect the mediation procedure has on the time to file briefs.

(Added Apr. 25, 2014, eff. Dec. 1, 2014.)

2014 Amendments

This rule is new. It requires the district or BAP clerk to advise the parties promptly after an appeal is docketed of any court mediation procedure that is applicable to bankruptcy appeals. The notice must state what the mediation requirements are and how the procedure affects the time for filing briefs.

Rule 8028. Suspension of Rules in Part VIII

In the interest of expediting decision or for other cause in a particular case, the district court or BAP, or where appropriate the court of appeals, may suspend the requirements or provisions of the rules in Part VIII, except Rules 8001, 8002, 8003, 8004, 8005, 8006, 8007, 8012, 8020, 8024, 8025, 8026, and 8028.

(Added Apr. 25, 2014, eff. Dec. 1, 2014.)

2014 Amendments

This rule is derived from former Rule 8019 and Fed. R. App. P. 2. To promote uniformity of practice and compliance with statutory authority, the rule includes a more extensive list of requirements that may not be suspended than either the former rule or the Federal Rules of Appellate Procedure provide. Rules governing the following matters may not be suspended:

- scope of the rules; definition of "BAP"; method of transmission;
- time for filing a notice of appeal;
- taking an appeal as of right;
- taking an appeal by leave;
- election to have an appeal heard by a district court instead of a BAP;
- certification of direct appeal to a court of appeals;
- stay pending appeal;
- corporate disclosure statement;
- sanctions for frivolous appeals and other misconduct;
- clerk's duties on disposition of an appeal;
- stay of a district court's or BAP's judgment;
- local rules; and
- suspension of the Part VIII rules.

PART IX—GENERAL PROVISIONS

Rule
9001.	General Definitions.
9002.	Meanings of Words in the Federal Rules of Civil Procedure When Applicable to Cases Under the Code.
9003.	Prohibition of Ex Parte Contacts.
9004.	General Requirements of Form.
9005.	Harmless Error.
9005.1.	Constitutional Challenge to a Statute—Notice, Certification, and Intervention.
9006.	Computing and Extending Time.
9007.	General Authority to Regulate Notices.
9008.	Service or Notice by Publication.
9009.	Forms.
9010.	Representation and Appearances; Powers of Attorney.
9011.	Signing of Papers; Representations to the Court; Sanctions; Verification and Copies of Papers.
9012.	Oaths and Affirmations.
9013.	Motions: Form and Service.
9014.	Contested Matters.
9015.	Jury Trials.
9016.	Subpoena.
9017.	Evidence.
9018.	Secret, Confidential, Scandalous, or Defamatory Matter.
9019.	Compromise and Arbitration.
9020.	Contempt Proceedings.
9021.	Entry of Judgment.
9022.	Notice of Judgment or Order.
9023.	New Trials; Amendment of Judgments.
9024.	Relief From Judgment or Order.
9025.	Security: Proceedings Against Sureties.
9026.	Exceptions Unnecessary.
9027.	Removal.
9028.	Disability of a Judge.
9029.	Local Bankruptcy Rules; Procedure When There Is No Controlling Law.
9030.	Jurisdiction and Venue Unaffected.
9031.	Masters Not Authorized.
9032.	Effect of Amendment of Federal Rules of Civil Procedure.
9033.	Review of Proposed Findings of Fact and Conclusions of Law in Non-Core Proceedings.
9034.	Transmittal of Pleadings, Motion Papers, Objections, and Other Papers to the United States Trustee.
9035.	Applicability of Rules in Judicial Districts in Alabama and North Carolina.
9036.	Notice by Electronic Transmission.
9037.	Privacy Protection for Filings Made With the Court.

Rule 9001. General Definitions

The definitions of words and phrases in §§ 101, 902, 1101, and 1502 of the Code, and the rules of construction in § 102, govern their use in these rules. In addition, the following words and phrases used in these rules have the meanings indicated:

(1) "Bankruptcy clerk" means a clerk appointed pursuant to 28 U.S.C. § 156(b).

(2) "Bankruptcy Code" or "Code" means title 11 of the United States Code.

(3) "Clerk" means bankruptcy clerk, if one has been appointed, otherwise clerk of the district court.

(4) "Court" or "judge" means the judicial officer before whom a case or proceeding is pending.

(5) "Debtor." When any act is required by these rules to be performed by a debtor or when it is necessary to compel attendance of a debtor for examination and the debtor is not a natural person: (A) if the debtor is a corporation, "debtor" includes, if designated by the court, any or all of its officers, members of its board of directors or trustees or of a similar controlling body, a controlling stockholder or member, or any other person in control; (B) if the debtor is a partnership, "debtor" includes any or all of its general partners or, if designated by the court, any other person in control.

(6) "Firm" includes a partnership or professional corporation of attorneys or accountants.

(7) "Judgment" means any appealable order.

(8) "Mail" means first class, postage prepaid.

(9) "Notice provider" means any entity approved by the Administrative Office of the United States Courts to give notice to creditors under Rule 2002(g)(4).

(10) "Regular associate" means any attorney regularly employed by, associated with, or counsel to an individual or firm.

(11) "Trustee" includes a debtor in possession in a chapter 11 case.

(12) "United States trustee" includes an assistant United States trustee and any designee of the United States trustee.

(As amended Mar. 30, 1987, eff. Aug. 1, 1987; Apr. 30, 1991, eff. Aug. 1, 1991; Apr. 25, 2005, eff. Dec. 1, 2005; Apr. 28, 2010, eff. Dec. 1, 2010.)

ADVISORY COMMITTEE NOTES

1987 Amendment

The terms "bankruptcy clerk" and "clerk" have been defined to reflect that unless otherwise stated, for the purpose of these rules, the terms are meant to identify the court officer for the bankruptcy records. If a bankruptcy clerk is appointed, all filings are made with the bankruptcy clerk. If one has not been appointed, all filings are with the clerk of the district court. Rule 5005.

The rule is also amended to include a definition of "court or judge." Since a case or proceeding may be before a bankruptcy judge or a judge of the district court, "court or judge" is defined to mean the judicial officer before whom the case or proceeding is pending.

1991 Amendment

Section 582 of title 28 provides that the Attorney General may appoint one or more assistant United States trustees in any region when the public interest so requires. This rule is amended to clarify that an assistant United States trustee, as well as any designee of the United States trustee, is included within the meaning of "United States trustee" in the rules.

2005 Amendments

The rule is amended to add the definition of a notice provider and to renumber the final three definitions in the rule. A notice provider is an entity approved by the Administrative Office of the United States Courts to enter into agreements with entities to give notice to those entities in the form and manner agreed to by those parties. The new definition supports the amendment to Rule 2002(g)(4) that authorizes a notice provider to give notices under Rule 2002.

Many entities conduct business on a national scale and receive vast numbers of notices in bankruptcy cases throughout the country. Those entities can agree with a notice provider to receive their notices in a form and at an address or addresses that the creditor and notice provider agree upon. There are processes currently in use that provide substantial assurance that notices are not misdirected. Any notice provider would have to demonstrate to the Administrative Office of the United States Courts that it could provide the service in a manner that ensures the proper delivery of notice to creditors. Once the Administrative Office of the United States Courts approves the notice provider to enter into agreements with creditors, the notice provider and other entities can establish the relationship that will govern the delivery of notices in cases as provided in Rule 2002(g)(4).

2010 Amendments

The rule is amended to add § 1502 of the Code to the list of definitional provisions that are applicable to the Rules. That section was added to the Code by the 2005 amendments.

CROSS REFERENCES

Clerk defined, see Fed.Rules Bankr.Proc. Rule 9002, 11 USCA.

Judgment defined, see Fed.Rules Bankr.Proc. Rules 7054 and 9002, 11 USCA.

Rule 9002. Meanings of Words in the Federal Rules of Civil Procedure When Applicable to Cases Under the Code

The following words and phrases used in the Federal Rules of Civil Procedure made applicable to cases under the Code by these rules have the meanings indicated unless they are inconsistent with the context:

(1) "Action" or "civil action" means an adversary proceeding or, when appropriate, a contested petition, or proceedings to vacate an order for relief or to determine any other contested matter.

(2) "Appeal" means an appeal as provided by 28 U.S.C. § 158.

(3) "Clerk" or "clerk of the district court" means the court officer responsible for the bankruptcy records in the district.

(4) "District court," "trial court," "court," "district judge," or "judge" means bankruptcy judge if the case or proceeding is pending before a bankruptcy judge.

(5) "Judgment" includes any order appealable to an appellate court.

(As amended Mar. 30, 1987, eff. Aug. 1, 1987; Apr. 22, 1993, eff. Aug. 1, 1993.)

ADVISORY COMMITTEE NOTES
1993 Amendments

This rule is revised to include the words "district judge" in anticipation of amendments to the Federal Rules of Civil Procedure.

CROSS REFERENCES

Contested matters, see Fed.Rules Bankr.Proc. Rule 9014, 11 USCA.

Judgment defined, see Fed.Rules Civ.Proc. Rule 54, 28 USCA.

One form of action, see Fed.Rules Civ.Proc. Rule 2, 28 USCA.

Procedural rules which govern adversary proceedings, see Fed.Rules Bankr.Proc. Rule 7001 et seq., 11 USCA.

Rule 9003. Prohibition of Ex Parte Contacts

(a) General prohibition

Except as otherwise permitted by applicable law, any examiner, any party in interest, and any attorney, accountant, or employee of a party in interest shall refrain from ex parte meetings and communications with the court concerning matters affecting a particular case or proceeding.

(b) United States trustee

Except as otherwise permitted by applicable law, the United States trustee and assistants to and employees or agents of the United States trustee shall refrain from ex parte meetings and communications with the court concerning matters affecting a particular case or proceeding. This rule does not preclude communications with the court to discuss general problems of administration and improvement of bankruptcy administration, including the operation of the United States trustee system.

(As amended Mar. 30, 1987, eff. Aug. 1, 1987; Apr. 30, 1991, eff. Aug. 1, 1991.)

ADVISORY COMMITTEE NOTES

This rule regulates the actions of parties in interest and their attorneys or others employed by parties in interest. This regulation of the conduct of parties in interest and their representative is designed to insure that the bankruptcy system operates fairly and that no appearance of unfairness is created. See H.Rep. No. 95–595, 95th Cong., 1st Sess. 95 et seq. (1977).

This rule is not a substitute for or limitation of any applicable canon of professional responsibility or judicial conduct. See, e.g., Canon 7, EC7–35, Disciplinary Rule 7–110(B) of the Code of Professional Responsibility: "Generally, in adversary proceedings a lawyer should not communicate with a judge relative to a matter pending before, or which is to be brought before, a tribunal over which he presides in circumstances which might have the effect or give the appearance of granting undue advantage to one party;" and Canon 3A(4) of the Code of Judicial Conduct: "A judge should . . . neither initiate nor consider ex parte or other communications concerning a pending or impending proceeding."

1987 Amendments

This rule is amended to apply to both the bankruptcy judges and the district judges of the district.

1991 Amendments

Subdivision (a) is amended to extend to examiners the prohibition on ex parte meetings and communications with the court.

Subdivision (b) is derived from Rule X–1010.

CROSS REFERENCES

Disqualification of judge, see Fed.Rules Bankr.Proc. Rule 5004, 11 USCA.

Rule 9004. General Requirements of Form

(a) Legibility; abbreviations

All petitions, pleadings, schedules and other papers shall be clearly legible. Abbreviations in common use in the English language may be used.

(b) Caption

Each paper filed shall contain a caption setting forth the name of the court, the title of the case, the bankruptcy docket number, and a brief designation of the character of the paper.

ADVISORY COMMITTEE NOTES

Subdivision (b). Additional requirements applicable to the caption for a petition are found in Rule 1005, to the caption for notices to creditors in Rule 2002(m), and to the caption for a pleading or other paper filed in an adversary proceeding in Rule 7010. Failure to comply with this or any other rule imposing a merely formal requirement does not ordinarily result in the loss of rights. See Rule 9005.

Rule 9005. Harmless Error

Rule 61 F.R.Civ.P. applies in cases under the Code. When appropriate, the court may order the correction of any error or defect or the cure of any omission which does not affect substantial rights.

Rule 9005.1. Constitutional Challenge to a Statute—Notice, Certification, and Intervention

Rule 5.1 F.R.Civ.P. applies in cases under the Code.

(Added Apr. 30, 2007, eff. Dec. 1, 2007.)

ADVISORY COMMITTEE NOTES

2007 Adoption

The rule is added to adopt the new rule added to the Federal Rules of Civil Procedure. The new Civil Rule replaces Rule 24(c) F. R. Civ. P., so the cross reference to Civil Rule 24 contained in Rule 7024 is no longer sufficient to bring the provisions of new Civil Rule 5.1 into adversary proceedings. This rule also makes Civil Rule 5.1 applicable to all contested matters and other proceedings within the bankruptcy case.

GENERAL PROVISIONS — Rule 9006

Rule 9006. Computing and Extending Time; Time for Motion Papers

(a) Computing time

The following rules apply in computing any time period specified in these rules, in the Federal Rules of Civil Procedure, in any local rule or court order, or in any statute that does not specify a method of computing time.

(1) Period stated in days or a longer unit

When the period is stated in days or a longer unit of time:

(A) exclude the day of the event that triggers the period;

(B) count every day, including intermediate Saturdays, Sundays, and legal holidays; and

(C) include the last day of the period, but if the last day is a Saturday, Sunday, or legal holiday, the period continues to run until the end of the next day that is not a Saturday, Sunday, or legal holiday.

(2) Period stated in hours

When the period is stated in hours:

(A) begin counting immediately on the occurrence of the event that triggers the period;

(B) count every hour, including hours during intermediate Saturdays, Sundays, and legal holidays; and

(C) if the period would end on a Saturday, Sunday, or legal holiday, then continue the period until the same time on the next day that is not a Saturday, Sunday, or legal holiday.

(3) Inaccessibility of clerk's office

Unless the court orders otherwise, if the clerk's office is inaccessible:

(A) on the last day for filing under Rule 9006(a)(1), then the time for filing is extended to the first accessible day that is not a Saturday, Sunday, or legal holiday; or

(B) during the last hour for filing under Rule 9006(a)(2), then the time for filing is extended to the same time on the first accessible day that is not a Saturday, Sunday, or legal holiday.

(4) "Last day" defined

Unless a different time is set by a statute, local rule, or order in the case, the last day ends:

(A) for electronic filing, at midnight in the court's time zone; and

(B) for filing by other means, when the clerk's office is scheduled to close.

(5) "Next day" defined

The "next day" is determined by continuing to count forward when the period is measured after an event and backward when measured before an event.

(6) "Legal holiday" defined

"Legal holiday" means:

(A) the day set aside by statute for observing New Year's Day, Martin Luther King Jr.'s Birthday, Washington's Birthday, Memorial Day, Independence Day, Labor Day, Columbus Day, Veterans' Day, Thanksgiving Day, or Christmas Day;

(B) any day declared a holiday by the President or Congress; and

(C) for periods that are measured after an event, any other day declared a holiday by the state where the district court is located. (In this rule, "state" includes the District of Columbia and any United States commonwealth or territory.)

(b) Enlargement

(1) In general

Except as provided in paragraphs (2) and (3) of this subdivision, when an act is required or allowed to be done at or within a specified period by these rules or by a notice given thereunder or by order of court, the court for cause shown may at any time in its discretion (1) with or without motion or notice order the period enlarged if the request therefor is made before the expiration of the period originally prescribed or as extended by a previous order or (2) on motion made after the expiration of the specified period permit the act to be done where the failure to act was the result of excusable neglect.

(2) Enlargement not permitted

The court may not enlarge the time for taking action under Rules 1007(d), 2003(a) and (d), 7052, 9023, and 9024.

(3) Enlargement governed by other rules

The court may enlarge the time for taking action under Rules 1006(b)(2), 1017(e), 3002(c), 4003(b), 4004(a), 4007(c), 4008(a), 8002, and 9033, only to the extent and under the conditions stated in those rules. In addition, the court may enlarge the time to file the statement required under Rule 1007(b)(7), and to file schedules and statements in a small business case under § 1116(3) of the Code, only to the extent and under the conditions stated in Rule 1007(c).

(c) Reduction

(1) In general

Except as provided in paragraph (2) of this subdivision, when an act is required or allowed to be done at or within a specified time by these rules or by a notice given thereunder or by order of court, the court for cause shown may in its discretion with or without motion or notice order the period reduced.

(2) Reduction not permitted

The court may not reduce the time for taking action under Rules 2002(a)(7), 2003(a), 3002(c), 3014, 3015, 4001(b)(2), (c)(2), 4003(a), 4004(a), 4007(c), 4008(a), 8002, and 9033(b). In addition, the court may not reduce the time under Rule 1007(c) to file the statement required by Rule 1007(b)(7).

(d) Motions papers

A written motion, other than one which may be heard ex parte, and notice of any hearing shall be served not later than seven days before the time specified for such hearing, unless a different period is fixed by these rules or by order of the court. Such an order may for cause shown be made on ex parte application. When a motion is supported by affidavit, the affidavit shall be served with the motion. Except as otherwise provided in Rule 9023, any written response shall be served not later than one day before the hearing, unless the court permits otherwise.

(e) Time of service

Service of process and service of any paper other than process or of notice by mail is complete on mailing.

(f) Additional time after service by mail or under Rule 5(b)(2)(D), (E), or (F) F.R.Civ.P.

When there is a right or requirement to act or undertake some proceedings within a prescribed period after service and that service is by mail or under Rule 5(b)(2)(D), (E), or (F) F.R.Civ.P., three days are added after the prescribed period would otherwise expire under Rule 9006(a).

GENERAL PROVISIONS Rule 9006

(g) Grain storage facility cases

This rule shall not limit the court's authority under § 557 of the Code to enter orders governing procedures in cases in which the debtor is an owner or operator of a grain storage facility.

(As amended Mar. 30, 1987, eff. Aug. 1, 1987; Apr. 25, 1989, eff. Aug. 1, 1989; Apr. 30, 1991, eff. Aug. 1, 1991; Apr. 23, 1996, eff. Dec. 1, 1996; Apr. 29, 1999, eff. Dec. 1, 1999; Apr. 23, 2001, eff. Dec. 1, 2001; Apr. 25, 2005, eff. Dec. 1, 2005; Apr. 23, 2008, eff. Dec. 1, 2008; Mar. 26, 2009, eff. Dec. 1, 2009; Apr. 16, 2013, eff. Dec. 1, 2013.)

ADVISORY COMMITTEE NOTES

Subdivision (a). This rule is an adaptation of Rule 6 F.R.Civ.P. It governs the time for acts to be done and proceedings to be had in cases under the Code and any litigation arising therein.

Subdivision (b) is patterned after Rule 6(b) F.R.Civ.P. and Rule 26(b) F.R.App.P.

Paragraph (1) of this subdivision confers on the court discretion generally to authorize extensions of time for doing acts required or allowed by these rules or orders of court. The exceptions to this general authority to extend the time are contained in paragraphs (2) and (3).

In the interest of prompt administration of bankruptcy cases certain time periods may not be extended. Paragraph (2) lists the rules which establish time periods which may not be extended: Rule 1007(d), time for filing a list of 20 largest creditors; Rule 1017(b)(3), 30 day period for sending notice of dismissal for failure to pay the filing fee; Rule 1019(2), 20 day period for notice of conversion to a chapter 7 case; Rule 2003(a), meeting of creditors not more than 40 days after order for relief; Rule 2003(d), 10 days for filing a motion for resolution of an election dispute; Rule 3014, time for the § 1111(b)(2) election; Rule 4001(b), expiration of stay 30 days following the commencement of final hearing; Rule 7052(b), 10 day period to move to amend findings of fact; Rule 9015(f), 20 day period to move for judgment notwithstanding the verdict; Rule 9023, 10 day period to move for a new trial; and Rule 9024, time to move for relief from judgment.

Many rules which establish a time for doing an act also contain a specific authorization and standard for granting an extension of time and, in some cases, limit the length of an extension. In some instances it would be inconsistent with the objective of the rule and sound administration of the case to permit extension under Rule 9006(b)(1), but with respect to the other rules it is appropriate that the power to extend time be supplemented by Rule 9006(b)(1). Unless a rule which contains a specific authorization to extend time is listed in paragraph (3) of this subdivision, an extension of the time may be granted under paragraph (1) of this subdivision. If a rule is included in paragraph (3) an extension may not be granted under paragraph (1). The following rules are listed in paragraph (3): Rule 1006(b)(2), time for paying the filing fee in installments; Rule 3002(c), 90 day period for filing a claim in a chapter 7 or 13 case; Rule 4003(b), 30 days for filing objections to a claim of exemptions; Rule 4004(a), 60 day period to object to a discharge; Rule 4007(b), 60 day period to file a dischargeability complaint; and Rule 8002, 10 days for filing a notice of appeal.

Subdivision (c). Paragraph (1) of this subdivision authorizes the reduction of the time periods established by these rules or an order of the court. Excluded from this general authority are the time periods established by the rules referred to in paragraph (2) of the subdivision: Rule 2002(a) and (b), 20 day and 25 day notices of certain hearings and actions in the case; Rule 2003(a), meeting of creditors to be not less than 20 days after the order for relief; Rule 3002(c), 90 days for filing a claim in a chapter 7 or 13 case; Rule 3014, time for § 1111(b)(2) election; Rule 3015, 10 day period after filing of petition to file a chapter 13 plan; Rule 4003(a), 15 days for a dependent to claim exemptions; Rule 4004(a), 60 day period to object to a discharge; Rule 4007(c), 60 day period to file a dischargeability complaint; and Rule 8002, 10 days for filing a notice of appeal. Reduction of the time periods fixed in the rules referred to in this subdivision would be inconsistent with the purposes of those rules and would cause harmful uncertainty.

[The Advisory Committee Note for subd. (c) above states that Rule 2002(a) and (b) are excluded from the general authority for the reduction of time periods while the text of subd. (c)(2) specifies that only Rule 2002(a)(4) and (a)(8) are excluded.]

Subdivision (d) is derived from Rule 6(d) F.R.Civ.P. The reference is to Rule 9023 instead of to Rule 59(c) F.R.Civ.P. because Rule 9023 incorporates Rule 59 F.R.Civ.P. but excepts therefrom motions to reconsider orders allowing and disallowing claims.

Subdivision (f) is new and is the same as Rule 6(e) F.R.Civ.P.

Rule 9006   BANKRUPTCY RULES

1987 Amendment

Subdivision (a) is amended to conform to the 1984 amendments to Rule 6 F.R.Civ.P.

Subdivision (b). The reference to Rule 4001(b) in paragraph (3) is deleted because of the amendments made to Rule 4001. Rule 9033, which is new, contains specific provisions governing the extension of time to file objections to proposed findings of fact and conclusions of law. Rule 9033 is added to the rules referred to in paragraph (3).

Subdivision (c). Rule 4001(b)(2) and (c)(2) provide that a final hearing on a motion to use cash collateral or a motion for authority to obtain credit may be held no earlier than 15 days after the filing of the motion. These two rules are added to paragraph (2) to make it clear that the 15 day period may not be reduced. Rule 9033 is also added to paragraph (2).

Subdivision (g) is new. Under § 557 of the Code, as enacted by the 1984 amendments, the court is directed to expedite grain storage facility cases. This subdivision makes it clear this rule does not limit the court's authority under § 557.

The original Advisory Committee Note to this rule included the 25 day notice period of Rule 2002(b) as a time period which may not be reduced under Rule 9006(C)(2). This was an error.

1989 Amendment

Prior to 1987, subdivision (a) provided that intermediate weekends and legal holidays would not be counted in the computation of a time period if the prescribed or allowed time was less than 7 days. This rule was amended in 1987 to conform to Fed. R. Civ. P. 6(a) which provides for the exclusion of intermediate weekends and legal holidays if the time prescribed or allowed is less than 11 days. An undesirable result of the 1987 amendment was that 10-day time periods prescribed in the interest of prompt administration of bankruptcy cases were extended to at least 14 calendar days.

As a result of the present amendment, 10-day time periods prescribed or allowed will no longer be extended to at least 14 calendar days because of intermediate weekends and legal holidays.

1991 Amendment

As a result of the 1989 amendment to this rule, the method of computing time under subdivision (a) is not the same as the method of computing time under Rule 6(a) F.R.Civ.P. Subdivision (a) is amended to provide that it governs the computation of time periods prescribed by the Federal Rules of Civil Procedure when the Bankruptcy Rules make a civil rule applicable to a bankruptcy case or proceeding.

Subdivision (b)(2) is amended because of the deletion of Rule 1019(2). Reference to Rule 9015(f) is deleted because of the abrogation of Rule 9015 in 1987.

Subdivision (b)(3) is amended to limit the enlargement of time regarding dismissal of a chapter 7 case for substantial abuse in accordance with Rule 1017(e).

1996 Amendment

Subdivision (c)(2) is amended to conform to the abrogation of Rule 2002(a)(4) and the renumbering of Rule 2002(a)(8) to Rule 2002(a)(7).

1999 Amendments

Rule 9006(b)(2) is amended to conform to the abrogation of Rule 1017(b)(3).

2001 Amendments

Rule 5(b) F.R.Civ.P., which is made applicable in adversary proceedings by Rule 7005, is being restyled and amended to authorize service by electronic means—or any other means not otherwise authorized under Rule 5(b)—if consent is obtained from the person served. The amendment to Rule 9006(f) is intended to extend the three-day "mail rule" to service under Rule 5(b)(2)(D), including service by electronic means. The three-day rule also will apply to service under Rule 5(b)(2)(C) F.R.Civ.P. when the person served has no known address and the paper is served by leaving a copy with the clerk of the court.

2005 Amendments

Rule 9006(f) is amended, consistent with a corresponding amendment to Rule 6(e) of the F.R. Civ. P, to clarify the method of counting the number of days to respond after service either by mail or under Civil Rule 5(b)(2)(C) or (D). Three days are added after the prescribed period expires. If, before the application of Rule 9006(f), the prescribed period is less than 8 days, intervening Saturdays, Sundays, and legal holidays are excluded from the calculation under Rule 9006(a). Some illustrations may be helpful.

Under existing Rule 9006(a), assuming that there are no legal holidays and that a response is due in seven days, if a paper is filed on a Monday, the seven day response period commences on Tuesday and concludes on Wednesday of the next week. Adding three days to the end of the period would extend it to Saturday, but because the response period ends on a weekend, the response day would be the following Monday, two weeks after the filing of the initial paper. If the paper is filed on a Tuesday, the seven-day response period would end on the following Thursday, and the response time would also be the following Monday. If the paper is mailed on a Wednesday, the initial seven-day period would expire nine days later on a Friday, but the response would again be due on the following Monday because of Rule 9006(f). If the paper is mailed on a Thursday, however, the seven day period ends on Monday, eleven days after the mailing of the service because of the exclusion of the two intervening Saturdays and Sundays. The response is due three days later on the following Thursday. If the paper is mailed on a Friday, the seven day period would conclude on a Tuesday, and the response is due three days later on a Friday.

No other change in the system of counting time is intended.

Other changes are stylistic.

2008 Amendments

Subdivision (b)(3) is amended to implement § 1116(3) of the Code, as amended by the 2005 amendments, which places specific limits on the extension of time for filing schedules and statements of financial affairs in a small business case.

Subdivisions (b)(3) and (c)(2) are amended to provide that enlargement or reduction of the time to file the statement of completion of a personal financial management course required by Rule 1007(b)(7) are governed by Rule 1007(c). Likewise, the amendments to subdivisions (b)(3) and (c)(2) recognize that the enlargement of time to file a reaffirmation agreement is governed by Rule 4008(a), and that reduction of the time provided under that rule is not permitted.

Other amendments are stylistic.

2009 Amendments

Subdivision (a). Subdivision (a) has been amended to simplify and clarify the provisions that describe how deadlines are computed. Subdivision (a) governs the computation of any time period found in a Federal Rule of Bankruptcy Procedure, a Federal Rule of Civil Procedure, a statute, a local rule, or a court order. In accordance with Bankruptcy Rule 9029(a), a local rule may not direct that a deadline be computed in a manner inconsistent with subdivision (a).

The time-computation provisions of subdivision (a) apply only when a time period must be computed. They do not apply when a fixed time to act is set. The amendments thus carry forward the approach taken in *Violette v. P.A. Days, Inc.*, 427 F.3d 1015, 1016 (6th Cir. 2005) (holding that Civil Rule 6(a) "does not apply to situations where the court has established a specific calendar day as a deadline"), and reject the contrary holding of *In re American Healthcare Management, Inc.*, 900 F.2d 827, 832 (5th Cir. 1990) (holding that Bankruptcy Rule 9006(a) governs treatment of date-certain deadline set by court order). If, for example, the date for filing is "no later than November 1, 2007," subdivision (a) does not govern. But if a filing is required to be made "within 10 days" or "within 72 hours," subdivision (a) describes how that deadline is computed.

Subdivision (a) does not apply when computing a time period set by a statute if the statute specifies a method of computing time. *See, e.g.*, 11 U.S.C. § 527(a)(2) (debt relief agencies must provide a written notice to an assisted person "not later than 3 business days" after providing bankruptcy assistance services).

Subdivision (a)(1). New subdivision (a)(1) addresses the computation of time periods that are stated in days. It also applies to time periods that are stated in weeks, months, or years. *See, e.g.*, Federal Rule of Civil Procedure 60(c)(1) made applicable to bankruptcy cases under Rule 9024. Subdivision (a)(1)(B)'s directive to "count every day" is relevant only if the period is stated in days (not weeks, months, or years).

Under former Rule 9006(a), a period of eight days or more was computed differently than a period of less than eight days. Intermediate Saturdays, Sundays, and legal holidays were included in computing the longer periods, but excluded in computing the shorter periods. Former Rule 9006(a) thus made computing deadlines unnecessarily complicated and led to counterintuitive results.

Rule 9006   BANKRUPTCY RULES

Under new subdivision (a)(1), all deadlines stated in days (no matter the length) are computed in the same way. The day of the event that triggers the deadline is not counted. All other days—including intermediate Saturdays, Sundays, and legal holidays—are counted, with only one exception: If the period ends on a Saturday, Sunday, or legal holiday, then the deadline falls on the next day that is not a Saturday, Sunday, or legal holiday. An illustration is provided below in the discussion of subdivision (a)(5). Subdivision (a)(3) addresses filing deadlines that expire on a day when the clerk's office is inaccessible.

Where subdivision (a) formerly referred to the "act, event, or default" that triggers the deadline, new subdivision (a) refers simply to the "event" that triggers the deadline; this change in terminology is adopted for brevity and simplicity, and is not intended to change meaning.

Periods previously expressed as less than eight days will be shortened as a practical matter by the decision to count intermediate Saturdays, Sundays, and legal holidays in computing all periods. Many of those periods have been lengthened to compensate for the change. *See, e.g.*, Rules 2008 (trustee's duty to notify court of acceptance of the appointment within five days is extended to seven days); 6004(b) (time for filing and service of objection to proposed use, sale or lease of property extended from five days prior to the hearing to seven days prior to the hearing); and 9006(d) (time for giving notice of a hearing extended from five days prior to the hearing to seven days).

Most of the 10-day periods were adjusted to meet the change in computation method by setting 14 days as the new period. *See, e.g.*, Rules 1007(h) (10-day period to file supplemental schedule for property debtor becomes entitled to acquire after the commencement of the case is extended to 14 days); 3020(e) (10-day stay of order confirming a chapter 11 plan extended to 14 days); 8002(a) (10-day period in which to file notice of appeal extended to 14 days). A 14-day period also has the advantage that the final day falls on the same day of the week as the event that triggered the period—the 14th day after a Monday, for example, is a Monday. This advantage of using week-long periods led to adopting seven-day periods to replace some of the periods set at less than 10 days, 21-day periods to replace 20-day periods, and 28-day periods to replace 25-day periods. Thirty-day and longer periods, however, were generally retained without change.

Subdivision (a)(2). New subdivision (a)(2) addresses the computation of time periods that are stated in hours. No such deadline currently appears in the Federal Rules of Bankruptcy Procedure. But some statutes contain deadlines stated in hours, as do some court orders issued in expedited proceedings.

Under subdivision (a)(2), a deadline stated in hours starts to run immediately on the occurrence of the event that triggers the deadline. The deadline generally ends when the time expires. If, however, the time period expires at a specific time (say, 2:17 p.m.) on a Saturday, Sunday, or legal holiday, then the deadline is extended to the same time (2:17 p.m.) on the next day that is not a Saturday, Sunday, or legal holiday. Periods stated in hours are not to be "rounded up" to the next whole hour. Subdivision (a)(3) addresses situations when the clerk's office is inaccessible during the last hour before a filing deadline expires.

Subdivision (a)(2)(B) directs that every hour be counted. Thus, for example, a 72-hour period that commences at 10:23 a.m. on Friday, November 2, 2007, will run until 9:23 a.m. on Monday, November 5; the discrepancy in start and end times in this example results from the intervening shift from daylight saving time to standard time.

Subdivision (a)(3). When determining the last day of a filing period stated in days or a longer unit of time, a day on which the clerk's office is not accessible because of the weather or another reason is treated like a Saturday, Sunday, or legal holiday. When determining the end of a filing period stated in hours, if the clerk's office is inaccessible during the last hour of the filing period computed under subdivision (a)(2) then the period is extended to the same time on the next day that is not a weekend, holiday, or day when the clerk's office is inaccessible.

Subdivision (a)(3)'s extensions apply "[u]nless the court orders otherwise." In some circumstances, the court might not wish a period of inaccessibility to trigger a full 24-hour extension; in those instances, the court can specify a briefer extension.

The text of the rule no longer refers to "weather or other conditions" as the reason for the inaccessibility of the clerk's office. The reference to "weather" was deleted from the text to underscore that inaccessibility can occur for reasons unrelated to weather, such as an outage of the electronic filing system. Weather can still be a reason for inaccessibility of the clerk's office. The rule does not attempt to define inaccessibility. Rather, the concept will continue to develop through caselaw. *See, e.g.*, William G. Phelps, *When Is Office of Clerk of Court Inaccessible Due to Weather or Other Conditions for Purpose of*

Computing Time Period for Filing Papers under Rule 6(a) of Federal Rules of Civil Procedure, 135 A.L.R. Fed. 259 (1996) (collecting cases). In addition, many local provisions address inaccessibility for purposes of electronic filing. *See, e.g.*, D. Kan. Rule 5.4.11 ("A Filing User whose filing is made untimely as the result of a technical failure may seek appropriate relief from the court.").

Subdivision (a)(4). New subdivision (a)(4) defines the end of the last day of a period for purposes of subdivision (a)(1). Subdivision (a)(4) does not apply in computing periods stated in hours under subdivision (a)(2), and does not apply if a different time is set by a statute, local rule, or order in the case. A local rule may provide, for example, that papers filed in a drop box after the normal hours of the clerk's office are filed as of the day that is date-stamped on the papers by a device in the drop box.

28 U.S.C. § 452 provides that "[a]ll courts of the United States shall be deemed always open for the purpose of filing proper papers, issuing and returning process, and making motions and orders." A corresponding provision exists in Rule 5001(a). Some courts have held that these provisions permit an after-hours filing by handing the papers to an appropriate official. *See, e.g., Casalduc v. Diaz*, 117 F.2d 915, 917 (1st Cir. 1941). Subdivision (a)(4) does not address the effect of the statute on the question of after-hours filing; instead, the rule is designed to deal with filings in the ordinary course without regard to Section 452.

Subdivision (a)(5). New subdivision (a)(5) defines the "next" day for purposes of subdivisions (a)(1)(C) and (a)(2)(C). The Federal Rules of Bankruptcy Procedure contain both forward-looking time periods and backward-looking time periods. A forward-looking time period requires something to be done within a period of time *after* an event. *See, e.g.*, Rules 1007(c) (the schedules, statements, and other documents shall be filed by the debtor within 14 days of the entry of the order for relief"); 1019(5)(B)(ii) ("the trustee, not later than 30 days after conversion of the case, shall file and transmit to the United States trustee a final report and account"); and 7012(a) ("If a complaint is duly served, the defendant shall serve an answer within 30 days after the issuance of the summons, except when a different time is prescribed by the court.").

A backward-looking time period requires something to be done within a period of time *before* an event. *See, e.g.*, Rules 6004(b) ("an objection to a proposed use, sale, or lease of property shall be filed and served not less than seven days before the date set for the proposed action"); 9006(d) ("A written motion, other than one which may be heard ex parte, and notice of any hearing shall be served not later than seven days before the time specified for such hearing"). In determining what is the "next" day for purposes of subdivisions (a)(1)(C) and (a)(2)(C), one should continue counting in the same direction—that is, forward when computing a forward-looking period and backward when computing a backward-looking period. If, for example, a filing is due within 10 days *after* an event, and the tenth day falls on Saturday, September 1, 2007, then the filing is due on Tuesday, September 4, 2007 (Monday, September 3, is Labor Day). But if a filing is due 10 days *before* an event, and the tenth day falls on Saturday, September 1, then the filing is due on Friday, August 31.

Subdivision (a)(6). New subdivision (a)(6) defines "legal holiday" for purposes of the Federal Rules of Bankruptcy Procedure, including the time-computation provisions of subdivision (a). Subdivision (a)(6) continues to include within the definition of "legal holiday" days that are declared a holiday by the President or Congress.

For forward-counted periods—*i.e.*, periods that are measured after an event—subdivision (a)(6)(C) includes certain state holidays within the definition of legal holidays, and defines the term "state"—for purposes of subdivision (a)(6)—to include the District of Columbia and any commonwealth or territory of the United States. Thus, for purposes of subdivision (a)(6)'s definition of "legal holiday," "state" includes the District of Columbia, Guam, American Samoa, the U.S. Virgin Islands, the Commonwealth of Puerto Rico, and the Commonwealth of the Northern Mariana Islands.

However, state legal holidays are not recognized in computing backward-counted periods. For both forward- and backward-counted periods, the rule thus protects those who may be unsure of the effect of state holidays. For forward-counted deadlines, treating state holidays the same as federal holidays extends the deadline. Thus, someone who thought that the federal courts might be closed on a state holiday would be safeguarded against an inadvertent late filing. In contrast, for backward-counted deadlines, not giving state holidays the treatment of federal holidays allows filing on the state holiday itself rather than the day before. Take, for example, Monday, April 21, 2008 (Patriot's Day, a legal holiday in the relevant state). If a filing is due 14 days after an event, and the fourteenth day is April 21, then the filing is due on Tuesday, April 22 because Monday, April 21 counts as a legal holiday. But if a filing is due 14 days before an event, and the fourteenth day is April 21, the filing is due on Monday, April 21; the fact that April 21 is a state holiday does not make April 21 a legal holiday for purposes of computing this backward-counted deadline. But note that if the clerk's office is inaccessible on Monday, April 21, then subdivision (a)(3) extends the April 21 filing deadline forward to the next accessible day that is not a Saturday, Sunday or legal holiday—no earlier than Tuesday, April 22.

The rule is amended [this Committee note relates to subdivision (d)] to implement changes in connection with the amendment to Rule 9006(a) and the manner by which time is computed under the rules. The deadline in the rule is amended to substitute a deadline that is a multiple of seven days. Throughout the rules, deadlines are amended in the following manner:

- 5-day periods become 7-day periods
- 10-day periods become 14-day periods
- 15-day periods become 14-day periods
- 20-day periods become 21-day periods
- 25-day periods become 28-day periods

Subdivision (f) is amended to conform to the changes made to Rule 5(b)(2) of the Federal Rules of Civil Procedure as a part of the Civil Rules Restyling Project. As a part of that project, subparagraphs (b)(2)(C) and (D) of that rule were rewritten as subparagraphs (b)(2)(D), (E), and (F). The cross reference to those rules contained in subdivision (f) of this rule is corrected by this amendment.

2013 Amendments

The title of this rule is amended to draw attention to the fact that it prescribes time limits for the service of motion papers. These time periods apply unless another Bankruptcy Rule or a court order, including a local rule, prescribes different time periods. Rules 9013 and 9014 should also be consulted regarding motion practice. Rule 9013 governs the form of motions and the parties who must be served. Rule 9014 prescribes the procedures applicable to contested matters, including the method of serving motions commencing contested matters and subsequent papers. Subdivision (d) is amended to apply to any written response to a motion, rather than just to opposing affidavits. The caption of the subdivision is amended to reflect this change. Other changes are stylistic.

CROSS REFERENCES

Completion of service by mail upon mailing, see Fed.Rules Civ.Proc. Rule 5, 28 USCA.

Computation and extension of time, see Federal Rules of Appellate Procedure Rule 26, 28 USCA.

Motions—

Form and service, see Fed.Rules Bankr.Proc. Rule 9013, 11 USCA.

On appeal to district court or bankruptcy appellate panel acted upon without hearing at any time, see Fed.Rules Bankr.Proc. Rule 8011, 11 USCA.

Time, see Fed.Rules Civ.Proc. Rule 6, 28 USCA.

Rule 9007. General Authority to Regulate Notices

When notice is to be given under these rules, the court shall designate, if not otherwise specified herein, the time within which, the entities to whom, and the form and manner in which the notice shall be given. When feasible, the court may order any notices under these rules to be combined.

(As amended Mar. 30, 1987, eff. Aug. 1, 1987.)

CROSS REFERENCES

Construction of phrase "after notice and a hearing", see 11 USCA § 102.

Notice as is appropriate of order for relief, see 11 USCA § 342.

Rule 9008. Service or Notice by Publication

Whenever these rules require or authorize service or notice by publication, the court shall, to the extent not otherwise specified in these rules, determine the form and manner thereof, including the newspaper or other medium to be used and the number of publications.

CROSS REFERENCES

Construction of phrase "after notice and a hearing", see 11 USCA § 102.

Notice as is appropriate of order for relief, see 11 USCA § 342.

Rule 9009. Forms

Except as otherwise provided in Rule 3016(d), the Official Forms prescribed by the Judicial Conference of the United States shall be observed and used with alterations as may be appropriate. Forms may be combined and their contents rearranged to permit economies in their use. The Director of the Administrative Office of the United States Courts may issue additional forms for use under the Code. The forms shall be construed to be consistent with these rules and the Code.

(As amended Apr. 30, 1991, eff. Aug. 1, 1991; Apr. 23, 2008, eff. Dec. 1, 2008.)

ADVISORY COMMITTEE NOTES

The rule continues the obligatory character of the Official Forms in the interest of facilitating the processing of the paperwork of bankruptcy administration, but provides that Official Forms will be prescribed by the Judicial Conference of the United States. The Supreme Court and the Congress will thus be relieved of the burden of considering the large number of complex forms used in bankruptcy practice. The use of the Official Forms has generally been held subject to a "rule of substantial compliance" and some of these rules, for example Rule 1002, specifically state that the filed document need only "conform substantially" to the Official Form. See also Rule 9005. The second sentence recognizes the propriety of combining and rearranging Official Forms to take advantage of technological developments and resulting economies.

The Director of the Administrative Office is authorized to issue additional forms for the guidance of the bar.

1991 Amendment

Rule 9029 is amended to clarify that local court rules may not prohibit or limit the use of the Official Forms.

2008 Amendments

The rule is amended to provide that a plan proponent in a small business chapter 11 case need not use an Official Form of a plan of reorganization and disclosure statement. The use of those forms is optional, and under Rule 3016(d) the proponent may submit a plan and disclosure statement in those cases that does not conform to the Official Forms.

CROSS REFERENCES

Correction of harmless errors or cure of harmless omissions, see Fed.Rules Bankr.Proc. Rule 9005, 11 USCA.

Rule 9010. Representation and Appearances; Powers of Attorney

(a) Authority to act personally or by attorney

A debtor, creditor, equity security holder, indenture trustee, committee or other party may (1) appear in a case under the Code and act either in the entity's own behalf or by an attorney authorized to practice in the court, and (2) perform any act not constituting the practice of law, by an authorized agent, attorney in fact, or proxy.

Rule 9011   BANKRUPTCY RULES

(b) Notice of appearance

An attorney appearing for a party in a case under the Code shall file a notice of appearance with the attorney's name, office address and telephone number, unless the attorney's appearance is otherwise noted in the record.

(c) Power of attorney

The authority of any agent, attorney in fact, or proxy to represent a creditor for any purpose other than the execution and filing of a proof of claim or the acceptance or rejection of a plan shall be evidenced by a power of attorney conforming substantially to the appropriate Official Form. The execution of any such power of attorney shall be acknowledged before one of the officers enumerated in 28 U.S.C. § 459, § 953, Rule 9012, or a person authorized to administer oaths under the laws of the state where the oath is administered.

(As amended Mar. 30, 1987, eff. Aug. 1, 1987; Apr. 30, 1991, eff. Aug. 1, 1991.)

ADVISORY COMMITTEE NOTES

This rule is substantially the same as former Bankruptcy Rule 910 and does not purport to change prior holdings prohibiting a corporation from appearing pro se. See In re Las Colinas Development Corp., 585 F.2d 7 (1st Cir.1978).

1987 Amendment

Subdivision (c) is amended to include a reference to Rule 9012 which is amended to authorize a bankruptcy judge or clerk to administer oaths.

1991 Amendment

References to Official Form numbers in subdivision (c) are deleted in anticipation of future revision and renumbering of the Official Forms.

CROSS REFERENCES

Ex parte relief from automatic stay, see Fed.Rules Bankr.Proc. Rule 4001, 11 USCA.

Payment of dividends to persons authorized to receive them by power of attorney executed and filed in accordance with this rule, see Fed.Rules Bankr.Proc. Rule 3009, 11 USCA.

Rule 9011. Signing of Papers; Representations to the Court; Sanctions; Verification and Copies of Papers

(a) Signing of papers

Every petition, pleading, written motion, and other paper, except a list, schedule, or statement, or amendments thereto, shall be signed by at least one attorney of record in the attorney's individual name. A party who is not represented by an attorney shall sign all papers. Each paper shall state the signer's address and telephone number, if any. An unsigned paper shall be stricken unless omission of the signature is corrected promptly after being called to the attention of the attorney or party.

(b) Representations to the court

By presenting to the court (whether by signing, filing, submitting, or later advocating) a petition, pleading, written motion, or other paper, an attorney or unrepresented party is certifying that to the best of the person's knowledge, information, and belief, formed after an inquiry reasonable under the circumstances,[1]—

>   (1) it is not being presented for any improper purpose, such as to harass or to cause unnecessary delay or needless increase in the cost of litigation;

---

[1] So in original. The comma probably should not appear.

(2) the claims, defenses, and other legal contentions therein are warranted by existing law or by a nonfrivolous argument for the extension, modification, or reversal of existing law or the establishment of new law;

(3) the allegations and other factual contentions have evidentiary support or, if specifically so identified, are likely to have evidentiary support after a reasonable opportunity for further investigation or discovery; and

(4) the denials of factual contentions are warranted on the evidence or, if specifically so identified, are reasonably based on a lack of information or belief.

(c) Sanctions

If, after notice and a reasonable opportunity to respond, the court determines that subdivision (b) has been violated, the court may, subject to the conditions stated below, impose an appropriate sanction upon the attorneys, law firms, or parties that have violated subdivision (b) or are responsible for the violation.

(1) How initiated

(A) By motion

A motion for sanctions under this rule shall be made separately from other motions or requests and shall describe the specific conduct alleged to violate subdivision (b). It shall be served as provided in Rule 7004. The motion for sanctions may not be filed with or presented to the court unless, within 21 days after service of the motion (or such other period as the court may prescribe), the challenged paper, claim, defense, contention, allegation, or denial is not withdrawn or appropriately corrected, except that this limitation shall not apply if the conduct alleged is the filing of a petition in violation of subdivision (b). If warranted, the court may award to the party prevailing on the motion the reasonable expenses and attorney's fees incurred in presenting or opposing the motion. Absent exceptional circumstances, a law firm shall be held jointly responsible for violations committed by its partners, associates, and employees.

(B) On court's initiative

On its own initiative, the court may enter an order describing the specific conduct that appears to violate subdivision (b) and directing an attorney, law firm, or party to show cause why it has not violated subdivision (b) with respect thereto.

(2) Nature of sanction; limitations

A sanction imposed for violation of this rule shall be limited to what is sufficient to deter repetition of such conduct or comparable conduct by others similarly situated. Subject to the limitations in subparagraphs (A) and (B), the sanction may consist of, or include, directives of a nonmonetary nature, an order to pay a penalty into court, or, if imposed on motion and warranted for effective deterrence, an order directing payment to the movant of some or all of the reasonable attorneys' fees and other expenses incurred as a direct result of the violation.

(A) Monetary sanctions may not be awarded against a represented party for a violation of subdivision (b)(2).

(B) Monetary sanctions may not be awarded on the court's initiative unless the court issues its order to show cause before a voluntary dismissal or settlement of the claims made by or against the party which is, or whose attorneys are, to be sanctioned.

(3) Order

When imposing sanctions, the court shall describe the conduct determined to constitute a violation of this rule and explain the basis for the sanction imposed.

(d) Inapplicability to discovery

Subdivisions (a) through (c) of this rule do not apply to disclosures and discovery requests, responses, objections, and motions that are subject to the provisions of Rules 7026 through 7037.

Rule 9011   BANKRUPTCY RULES

(e) Verification

Except as otherwise specifically provided by these rules, papers filed in a case under the Code need not be verified. Whenever verification is required by these rules, an unsworn declaration as provided in 28 U.S.C. § 1746 satisfies the requirement of verification.

(f) Copies of signed or verified papers

When these rules require copies of a signed or verified paper, it shall suffice if the original is signed or verified and the copies are conformed to the original.

(As amended Mar. 30, 1987, eff. Aug. 1, 1987; Apr. 30, 1991, eff. Aug. 1, 1991; Apr. 11, 1997, eff. Dec. 1, 1997.)

ADVISORY COMMITTEE NOTES

Subdivision (a). Excepted from the papers which an attorney for a debtor must sign are lists, schedules, statements of financial affairs, statements of executory contracts, Chapter 13 Statements and amendments thereto. Rule 1008 requires that these documents be verified by the debtor. Although the petition must also be verified, counsel for the debtor must sign the petition. See Official Form No. 1. An unrepresented party must sign all papers.

The last sentence of this subdivision authorizes a broad range of sanctions.

The word "document" is used in this subdivision to refer to all papers which the attorney or party is required to sign.

Subdivision (b) extends to all papers filed in cases under the Code the policy of minimizing reliance on the formalities of verification which is reflected in the third sentence of Rule 11 F.R.Civ.P. The second sentence of subdivision (b) permits the substitution of an unsworn declaration for the verification. See 28 U.S.C. § 1746. Rules requiring verification or an affidavit are as follows: Rule 1008, petitions, schedules, statements of financial affairs, Chapter 13 Statements and amendments; Rule 2006(e), list of multiple proxies and statement of facts and circumstances regarding their acquisition; Rule 4001(c), motion for ex parte relief from stay; Rule 7065, incorporating Rule 65(b) F.R.Civ.P. governing issuance of temporary restraining order; Rule 8011(d), affidavit in support of emergency motion on appeal.

1987 Amendment

The statement of intention of the debtor under § 521(2) of the Code is added to the documents which counsel is not required to sign.

1991 Amendment

Subdivision (a) is amended to conform to Rule 11 F.R.Civ.P. where appropriate, but also to clarify that it applies to the unnecessary delay or needless increase in the cost of the administration of the case. Deletion of the references to specific statements that are excluded from the scope of this subdivision is stylistic. As used in subdivision (a) of this rule, "statement" is limited to the statement of financial affairs and the statement of intention required to be filed under Rule 1007. Deletion of the reference to the Chapter 13 Statement is consistent with the amendment to Rule 1007(b).

1997 Amendment

This rule is amended to conform to the 1993 changes to F.R.Civ.P. 11. For an explanation of these amendments, see the advisory committee note to the 1993 amendments to F.R.Civ.P. 11.

The "safe harbor" provision contained in subdivision (c)(1)(A), which prohibits the filing of a motion for sanctions unless the challenged paper is not withdrawn or corrected within a prescribed time after service of the motion, does not apply if the challenged paper is a petition. The filing of a petition has immediate serious consequences, including the imposition of the automatic stay under § 362 of the Code, which may not be avoided by the subsequent withdrawal of the petition. In addition, a petition for relief under chapter 7 or chapter 11 may not be withdrawn unless the court orders dismissal of the case for cause after notice and a hearing.

GENERAL PROVISIONS Rule 9012

CROSS REFERENCES

Affidavit in support of—

    Complaint seeking temporary restraining order, see Fed.Rules Bankr.Proc. Rule 7065, 11 USCA.

    Emergency motion on appeal, see Fed.Rules Bankr.Proc. Rule 8011, 11 USCA.

    Motion for ex parte relief from stay, see Fed.Rules Bankr.Proc. Rule 4001, 11 USCA.

Verification of—

    Complaint seeking temporary restraining order, see Fed.Rules Bankr.Proc. Rule 7065, 11 USCA.

    List of multiple proxies and acquisition statement, see Fed.Rules Bankr.Proc. Rule 2006, 11 USCA.

    Motions for ex parte relief from stay, see Fed.Rules Bankr.Proc. Rule 4001, 11 USCA.

    Petitions and accompanying papers, see Fed.Rules Bankr.Proc. Rule 1008, 11 USCA.

Pleadings allowed; form of motions, see Fed.Rules Civ.Proc. Rule 7, 28 USCA.

Signing of pleadings, see Fed.Rules Civ.Proc. Rule 11, 28 USCA.

Statements in pleadings subject to obligations set forth in rule 11, see Fed.Rules Civ.Proc. Rule 8, 28 USCA.

Rule 9012. Oaths and Affirmations

(a) Persons authorized to administer oaths

The following persons may administer oaths and affirmations and take acknowledgments: a bankruptcy judge, clerk, deputy clerk, United States trustee, officer authorized to administer oaths in proceedings before the courts of the United States or under the laws of the state where the oath is to be taken, or a diplomatic or consular officer of the United States in any foreign country.

(b) Affirmation in lieu of oath

When in a case under the Code an oath is required to be taken, a solemn affirmation may be accepted in lieu thereof.

(As amended Mar. 30, 1987, eff. Aug. 1, 1987; Apr. 30, 1991, eff. Aug. 1, 1991.)

ADVISORY COMMITTEE NOTES

This rule is derived from Rule 43(d) F.R.Civ.P.

The provisions of former Bankruptcy Rule 912(a) relating to who may administer oaths have been deleted as unnecessary. Bankruptcy judges and the clerks and deputy clerks of bankruptcy courts are authorized by statute to administer oaths and affirmations and to take acknowledgments. 28 U.S.C. §§ 459, 953. A person designated to preside at the meeting of creditors has authority under Rule 2003(b)(1) to administer the oath. Administration of the oath at a deposition is governed by Rule 7028.

1987 Amendment

Subdivision (a) has been added to the rule to authorize bankruptcy judges and clerks to administer oaths.

1991 Amendment

This rule is amended to conform to the 1986 amendment to § 343 which provides that the United States trustee may administer the oath to the debtor at the § 341 meeting. This rule also allows the United States trustee to administer oaths and affirmations and to take acknowledgments in other situations. This amendment also affects Rule 9010(c) relating to the acknowledgment of a power of attorney. The words "United States trustee" include a designee of the United States trustee pursuant to Rule 9001 and § 102(9) of the Code.

CROSS REFERENCES

Acknowledgment of power of attorney, see Fed.Rules Bankr.Proc. Rule 9010, 11 USCA.

Administration of oaths and acknowledgments by—

    Clerks of court, see 28 USCA § 953.

    Justices or judges, see 28 USCA § 459.

Affirmation in lieu of oath, see Fed.Rules Civ.Proc. Rule 43, 28 USCA.

Oath defined to include affirmation, see 1 USCA § 1.

Oath or affirmation of witnesses, see Fed.Rules Evid. Rule 603, 28 USCA.

Rule 9013. Motions: Form and Service

A request for an order, except when an application is authorized by the rules, shall be by written motion, unless made during a hearing. The motion shall state with particularity the grounds therefor, and shall set forth the relief or order sought. Every written motion, other than one which may be considered ex parte, shall be served by the moving party within the time determined under Rule 9006(d). The moving party shall serve the motion on:

  (a) the trustee or debtor in possession and on those entities specified by these rules; or

  (b) the entities the court directs if these rules do not require service or specify the entities to be served.

(As amended Mar. 30, 1987, eff. Aug. 1, 1987; Apr. 16, 2013, eff. Dec. 1, 2013.)

ADVISORY COMMITTEE NOTES

This rule is derived from Rule 5(a) and Rule 7(b)(1) F.R.Civ.P. Except when an application is specifically authorized by these rules, for example an application under Rule 2014 for approval of the employment of a professional, all requests for court action must be made by motion.

2013 Amendments

A cross-reference to Rule 9006(d) is added to this rule to call attention to the time limits for the service of motions, supporting affidavits, and written responses to motions. Rule 9006(d) prescribes time limits that apply unless other limits are fixed by these rules, a court order, or a local rule. The other changes are stylistic.

Rule 9014. Contested Matters

  (a) Motion. In a contested matter not otherwise governed by these rules, relief shall be requested by motion, and reasonable notice and opportunity for hearing shall be afforded the party against whom relief is sought. No response is required under this rule unless the court directs otherwise.

  (b) Service. The motion shall be served in the manner provided for service of a summons and complaint by Rule 7004 and within the time determined under Rule 9006(d). Any written response to the motion shall be served within the time determined under Rule 9006(d). Any paper served after the motion shall be served in the manner provided by Rule 5(b) F. R. Civ. P.

  (c) Application of Part VII rules. Except as otherwise provided in this rule, and unless the court directs otherwise, the following rules shall apply: 7009, 7017, 7021, 7025, 7026, 7028–7037, 7041, 7042, 7052, 7054–7056, 7064, 7069, and 7071. The following subdivisions of Fed. R. Civ. P. 26, as incorporated by Rule 7026, shall not apply in a contested matter unless the court directs otherwise: 26(a)(1) (mandatory disclosure), 26(a)(2) (disclosures regarding expert testimony) and 26(a)(3) (additional pre-trial disclosure), and 26(f) (mandatory meeting before scheduling conference/ discovery plan). An entity that desires to perpetuate testimony may proceed in the same manner as provided in Rule 7027 for the taking of a deposition before an adversary proceeding. The court may at any stage in a particular matter direct that one or more of the other rules in Part VII shall apply.

GENERAL PROVISIONS — Rule 9014

The court shall give the parties notice of any order issued under this paragraph to afford them a reasonable opportunity to comply with the procedures prescribed by the order.

(d) Testimony of witnesses. Testimony of witnesses with respect to disputed material factual issues shall be taken in the same manner as testimony in an adversary proceeding.

(e) Attendance of witnesses. The court shall provide procedures that enable parties to ascertain at a reasonable time before any scheduled hearing whether the hearing will be an evidentiary hearing at which witnesses may testify.

(As amended Mar. 30, 1987, eff. Aug. 1, 1987; Apr. 29, 1999, eff. Dec. 1, 1999; Apr. 29, 2002, eff. Dec. 1, 2002; Apr. 26, 2004, eff. Dec. 1, 2004; Apr. 16, 2013, eff. Dec. 1, 2013.)

ADVISORY COMMITTEE NOTES

Rules 1017(d), 3020(b)(1), 4001(a), 4003(d), and 6006(a), which govern respectively dismissal or conversion of a case, objections to confirmation of a plan, relief from the automatic stay and the use of cash collateral, avoidance of a lien under § 522(f) of the Code, and the assumption or rejection of executory contracts or unexpired leases, specifically provide that litigation under those rules shall be as provided in Rule 9014. This rule also governs litigation in other contested matters.

Whenever there is an actual dispute, other than an adversary proceeding, before the bankruptcy court, the litigation to resolve that dispute is a contested matter. For example, the filing of an objection to a proof of claim, to a claim of exemption, or to a disclosure statement creates a dispute which is a contested matter. Even when an objection is not formally required, there may be a dispute. If a party in interest opposes the amount of compensation sought by a professional, there is a dispute which is a contested matter.

When the rules of Part VII are applicable to a contested matter, reference in the Part VII rules to adversary proceedings is to be read as a reference to a contested matter. See Rule 9002(1).

1999 Amendments

This rule is amended to delete Rule 7062 from the list of Part VII rules that automatically apply in a contested matter.

Rule 7062 provides that Rule 62 F.R.Civ.P., which governs stays of proceedings to enforce a judgment, is applicable in adversary proceedings. The provisions of Rule 62, including the ten-day automatic stay of the enforcement of a judgment provided by Rule 62(a) and the stay as a matter of right by posting a supersedeas bond provided in Rule 62(d), are not appropriate for most orders granting or denying motions governed by Rule 9014.

Although Rule 7062 will not apply automatically in contested matters, the amended rule permits the court, in its discretion, to order that Rule 7062 apply in a particular matter, and Rule 8005 gives the court discretion to issue a stay or any other appropriate order during the pendency of an appeal on such terms as will protect the rights of all parties in interest. In addition, amendments to Rules 3020, 4001, 6004, and 6006 automatically stay certain types of orders for a period of ten days, unless the court orders otherwise.

2002 Amendments

The list of Part VII rules that are applicable in a contested matter is extended to include Rule 7009 on pleading special matters, and Rule 7017 on real parties in interest, infants and incompetent persons, and capacity. The discovery rules made applicable in adversary proceedings apply in contested matters unless the court directs otherwise.

Subdivision (b) is amended to permit parties to serve papers, other than the original motion, in the manner provided in Rule 5(b) F.R. Civ.P. When the court requires a response to the motion, this amendment will permit service of the response in the same manner as an answer is served in an adversary proceeding.

Subdivision (d) is added to clarify that if the motion cannot be decided without resolving a disputed material issue of fact, an evidentiary hearing must be held at which testimony of witnesses is taken in the same manner as testimony is taken in an adversary proceeding or at a trial in a district court civil case. Rule 43(a), rather than Rule 43(e), F.R. Civ.P. would govern the evidentiary hearing on the factual dispute. Under Rule 9017, the Federal Rules of Evidence also apply in a contested matter. Nothing in the rule prohibits a court from resolving any matter that is submitted on affidavits by agreement of the parties.

Subdivision (e). Local procedures for hearings and other court appearances in a contested matter vary from district to district. In some bankruptcy courts, an evidentiary hearing at which witnesses may testify usually is held at the first court appearance in the contested matter. In other courts, it is customary for the court to delay the evidentiary hearing on disputed factual issues until some time after the initial hearing date. In order to avoid unnecessary expense and inconvenience, it is important for attorneys to know whether they should bring witnesses to a court appearance. The purpose of the final sentence of this rule is to require that the court provide a mechanism that will enable attorneys to know at a reasonable time before a scheduled hearing whether it will be necessary for witnesses to appear in court on that particular date.

Other amendments to this rule are stylistic.

2004 Amendments

The rule is amended to provide that the mandatory disclosure requirements of Fed. R. Civ. P. 26, as incorporated by Rule 7026, do not apply in contested matters. The typically short time between the commencement and resolution of most contested matters makes the mandatory disclosure provisions of Rule 26 ineffective. Nevertheless, the court may by local rule or by order in a particular case provide that these provisions of the rule apply in a contested matter.

2013 Amendments

A cross-reference to Rule 9006(d) is added to subdivision (b) to call attention to the time limits for the service of motions, supporting affidavits, and written responses to motions. Rule 9006(d) prescribes time limits that apply unless other limits are fixed by these rules, a court order, or a local rule.

CROSS REFERENCES

Contested matters—

> Assumption, rejection, or assignment of executory contract or unexpired lease, or proceeding to require trustee to act, see Fed.Rules Bankr.Proc. Rule 6006, 11 USCA.
>
> Avoidance by debtor of transfers of exempt property, see Fed.Rules Bankr.Proc. Rule 4003, 11 USCA.
>
> Dismissal or conversion to another chapter, see Fed.Rules Bankr.Proc. Rule 1017, 11 USCA.
>
> Objection to confirmation of plan, see Fed.Rules Bankr.Proc. Rule 3020, 11 USCA.
>
> Relief from automatic stay, see Fed.Rules Bankr.Proc. Rule 4001, 11 USCA.
>
> Request for use of cash collateral, see Fed.Rules Bankr.Proc. Rule 4001, 11 USCA.

Effect of amendment of Federal Rules of Civil Procedure, see Fed.Rules Bankr.Proc. Rule 9032, 11 USCA.

Meanings of words in Federal Rules of Civil Procedure when applicable, see Fed.Rules Bankr.Proc. Rule 9002, 11 USCA.

Motions; form and service, see Fed.Rules Bankr.Proc. Rule 9013, 11 USCA.

Rule 9015. Jury Trials

(a) Applicability of certain Federal Rules of Civil Procedure

Rules 38, 39, 47–49, and 51, F.R.Civ.P., and Rule 81(c) F.R.Civ.P. insofar as it applies to jury trials, apply in cases and proceedings, except that a demand made under Rule 38(b) F.R.Civ.P. shall be filed in accordance with Rule 5005.

(b) Consent to have trial conducted by bankruptcy judge

If the right to a jury trial applies, a timely demand has been filed pursuant to Rule 38(b) F.R.Civ.P., and the bankruptcy judge has been specially designated to conduct the jury trial, the parties may consent to have a jury trial conducted by a bankruptcy judge under 28 U.S.C. § 157(e) by jointly or separately filing a statement of consent within any applicable time limits specified by local rule.

(c) Applicability of Rule 50 F.R.Civ.P.

Rule 50 F.R.Civ.P. applies in cases and proceedings, except that any renewed motion for judgment or request for a new trial shall be filed no later than 14 days after the entry of judgment.

(Added Apr. 11, 1997, eff. Dec. 1, 1997; amended Mar. 26, 2009, eff. Dec. 1, 2009.)

ADVISORY COMMITTEE NOTES
1987 Abrogation

Former section 1480 of title 28 preserved a right to trial by jury in any case or proceeding under title 11 in which jury trial was provided by statute. Rule 9015 provided the procedure for jury trials in bankruptcy courts. Section 1480 was repealed. Section 1411 added by the 1984 amendments affords a jury trial only for personal injury or wrongful death claims, which 28 U.S.C. § 157(b)(5) requires be tried in the district court. Nevertheless, Rule 9015 has been cited as conferring a right to jury trial in other matters before bankruptcy judges. In light of the clear mandate of 28 U.S.C. § 2075 that the "rules shall not abridge, enlarge, or modify any substantive right," Rule 9015 is abrogated. In the event the courts of appeals or the Supreme Court define a right to jury trial in any bankruptcy matters, a local rule in substantially the form of Rule 9015 can be adopted pending amendment of these rules.

1997 Amendment

This rule provides procedures relating to jury trials. This rule is not intended to expand or create any right to trial by jury where such right does not otherwise exist.

2009 Amendments

The rule is amended by deleting Rule 50 F.R.Civ.P. from the list in subdivision (a) of rules made applicable in cases and proceedings. However, subdivision (c) is added to make Rule 50 applicable in cases and proceedings, but it limits the time for filing certain post judgment motions to 14 days after the entry of judgment. The amendment is necessary because Rule 50 F.R.Civ.P. was amended in 2009 to extend the deadline for the filing of these post judgment motions to 28 days. That deadline corresponds to the 30-day deadline for filing a notice of appeal in a civil case under Rule 4(a)(1)(A) F. R. App. P. In a bankruptcy case, the deadline for filing a notice of appeal is 14 days. Therefore, the 28-day deadline for filing these post judgment motions would effectively override the notice of appeal deadline under Rule 8002(a) but for this amendment.

Other amendments are stylistic.

Rule 9016. Subpoena

Rule 45 F.R.Civ.P. applies in cases under the Code.

(As amended Mar. 30, 1987, eff. Aug. 1, 1987.)

ADVISORY COMMITTEE NOTES

Although Rule 7004(d) authorizes nationwide service of process, Rule 45 F.R.Civ.P. limits the subpoena power to the judicial district and places outside the district which are within 100 miles of the place of trial or hearing.

CROSS REFERENCES

Compelling attendance of witnesses by use of subpoena—

> Deposition upon oral examination, see Fed.Rules Bankr.Proc. Rule 7030, 11 USCA.
>
> Deposition upon written questions, see Fed.Rules Bankr.Proc. Rule 7031, 11 USCA.

Examination of debtor—

> Apprehension and removal of debtor to compel attendance, see Fed.Rules Bankr.Proc. Rule 2005, 11 USCA.
>
> Compelling attendance for examination and production of documentary evidence, see Fed.Rules Bankr.Proc. Rule 2004, 11 USCA.

Rule 9017. Evidence

The Federal Rules of Evidence and Rules 43, 44 and 44.1 F.R.Civ.P. apply in cases under the Code.

ADVISORY COMMITTEE NOTES

Sections 251 and 252 of Public Law 95–598, amended Rule 1101 of the Federal Rules of Evidence to provide that the Federal Rules of Evidence apply in bankruptcy courts and to any case or proceeding under the Code. Rules 43, 44 and 44.1 of the F.R.Civ.P., which supplement the Federal Rules of Evidence, are by this rule made applicable to cases under the Code.

Examples of bankruptcy rules containing matters of an evidentiary nature are: Rule 2011, evidence of debtor retained in possession; Rule 3001(f), proof of claim constitutes prima facie evidence of the amount and validity of a claim; and Rule 5007(c), sound recording of court proceedings constitutes the record of the proceedings.

CROSS REFERENCES

Applicability of rules to proceedings and cases under this title, see Fed.Rules Evid. Rule 1101, 28 USCA.

Rule 9018. Secret, Confidential, Scandalous, or Defamatory Matter

On motion or on its own initiative, with or without notice, the court may make any order which justice requires (1) to protect the estate or any entity in respect of a trade secret or other confidential research, development, or commercial information, (2) to protect any entity against scandalous or defamatory matter contained in any paper filed in a case under the Code, or (3) to protect governmental matters that are made confidential by statute or regulation. If an order is entered under this rule without notice, any entity affected thereby may move to vacate or modify the order, and after a hearing on notice the court shall determine the motion.

(As amended Mar. 30, 1987, eff. Aug. 1, 1987.)

ADVISORY COMMITTEE NOTES

This rule provides the procedure for invoking the court's power under § 107 of the Code.

CROSS REFERENCES

Motion to strike scandalous matter, see Fed.Rules Civ.Proc. Rule 12, 28 USCA.

Motions; form and service, see Fed.Rules Bankr.Proc. Rule 9013, 11 USCA.

Protective orders, see Fed.Rules Civ.Proc. Rule 26, 28 USCA.

Rule 9019. Compromise and Arbitration

(a) Compromise

On motion by the trustee and after notice and a hearing, the court may approve a compromise or settlement. Notice shall be given to creditors, the United States trustee, the debtor, and indenture trustees as provided in Rule 2002 and to any other entity as the court may direct.

(b) Authority to compromise or settle controversies within classes

After a hearing on such notice as the court may direct, the court may fix a class or classes of controversies and authorize the trustee to compromise or settle controversies within such class or classes without further hearing or notice.

(c) Arbitration

On stipulation of the parties to any controversy affecting the estate the court may authorize the matter to be submitted to final and binding arbitration.

GENERAL PROVISIONS — Rule 9020

(As amended Mar. 30, 1987, eff. Aug. 1, 1987; Apr. 30, 1991, eff. Aug. 1, 1991; Apr. 22, 1993, eff. Aug. 1, 1993.)

ADVISORY COMMITTEE NOTES

Subdivisions (a) and (c) of this rule are essentially the same as the provisions of former Bankruptcy Rule 919 and subdivision (b) is the same as former Rule 8–514(b), which was applicable to railroad reorganizations. Subdivision (b) permits the court to deal efficiently with a case in which there may be a large number of settlements.

1991 Amendment

This rule is amended to enable the United States trustee to object or otherwise be heard in connection with a proposed compromise or settlement and otherwise to monitor the progress of the case.

1993 Amendments

Subdivision (a) is amended to conform to the language of § 102(1) of the Code. Other amendments are stylistic and make no substantive change.

CROSS REFERENCES

Motions; form and service, see Fed.Rules Bankr.Proc. Rule 9013, 11 USCA.

Rule 9020. Contempt Proceedings

Rule 9014 governs a motion for an order of contempt made by the United States trustee or a party in interest.

(As amended Mar. 30, 1987, eff. Aug. 1, 1987; Apr. 30, 1991, eff. Aug. 1, 1991; Apr. 23, 2001, eff. Dec. 1, 2001.)

ADVISORY COMMITTEE NOTES

Section 1481 of Title 28 provides that a bankruptcy court "may not _ _ _ punish a criminal contempt not committed in the presence of the judge of the court or warranting a punishment of imprisonment." Rule 9020 does not enlarge the power of bankruptcy courts.

Subdivision (a) is adapted from former Bankruptcy Rule 920 and Rule 42 F.R.Crim.P. Paragraph (1) of the subdivision permits summary imposition of punishment for contempt if the conduct is in the presence of the court and is of such nature that the conduct "obstruct[s] the administration of justice." See 18 U.S.C. § 401(a). Cases interpreting Rule 42(a) F.R.Crim.P. have held that when criminal contempt is in question summary disposition should be the exception: summary disposition should be reserved for situations where it is necessary to protect the judicial institution. 3 Wright, Federal Practice & Procedure—Criminal § 707 (1969). Those cases are equally pertinent to the application of this rule and, therefore, contemptuous conduct in the presence of the judge may often be punished only after the notice and hearing requirements of subdivision (b) are satisfied.

If the bankruptcy court concludes it is without power to punish or to impose the proper punishment for conduct which constitutes contempt, subdivision (a)(3) authorizes the bankruptcy court to certify the matter to the district court.

Subdivision (b) makes clear that when a person has a constitutional or statutory right to a jury trial in a criminal contempt matter this rule in no way affects that right. See Frank v. United States, 395 U.S. 147 (1969).

The Federal Rules of Civil Procedure do not specifically provide the procedure for the imposition of civil contempt sanctions. The decisional law governing the procedure for imposition of civil sanctions by the district courts will be equally applicable to the bankruptcy courts.

1987 Amendment

The United States Bankruptcy Courts, as constituted under the Bankruptcy Reform Act of 1978, were courts of law, equity, and admiralty with an inherent contempt power, but former 28 U.S.C. § 1481 restricted the criminal contempt power of bankruptcy judges. Under the 1984 amendments, bankruptcy judges are judicial officers of the district court, 28 U.S.C. §§ 151, 152(a)(1). There are no decisions by the

Rule 9020   **BANKRUPTCY RULES**

courts of appeals concerning the authority of bankruptcy judges to punish for either civil or criminal contempt under the 1984 amendments. This rule, as amended, recognizes that bankruptcy judges may not have the power to punish for contempt.

Sound judicial administration requires that the initial determination of whether contempt has been committed should be made by the bankruptcy judge. If timely objections are not filed to the bankruptcy judge's order, the order has the same force and effect as an order of the district court. If objections are filed within 10 days of service of the order, the district court conducts a de novo review pursuant to Rule 9033 and any order of contempt is entered by the district court on completion of the court's review of the bankruptcy judge's order.

1991 Amendments

The words "with the clerk" in subdivision (c) are deleted as unnecessary. See Rules 5005(a) and 9001(3).

2001 Amendments

The amendments to this rule cover a motion for an order of contempt filed by the United States trustee or a party in interest. This rule, as amended, does not address a contempt proceeding initiated by the court sua sponte.

Whether the court is acting on motion under this rule or is acting sua sponte, these amendments are not intended to extend, limit, or otherwise affect either the contempt power of a bankruptcy judge or the role of the district judge regarding contempt orders. Issues relating to the contempt power of bankruptcy judges are substantive and are left to statutory and judicial development, rather than procedural rules.

This rule, as amended in 1987, delayed for ten days from service the effectiveness of a bankruptcy judge's order of contempt and rendered the order subject to de novo review by the district court. These limitations on contempt orders were added to the rule in response to the Bankruptcy Amendments and Federal Judgeship Act of 1984, Pub. L. No. 98–353, 98 Stat. 333, which provides that bankruptcy judges are judicial officers of the district court, but does not specifically mention contempt power. See 28 U.S.C. § 151. As explained in the committee note to the 1987 amendments to this rule, no decisions of the courts of appeals existed concerning the authority of a bankruptcy judge to punish for either civil or criminal contempt under the 1984 Act and, therefore, the rule as amended in 1987 "recognizes that bankruptcy judges may not have the power to punish for contempt." Committee Note to 1987 Amendments to Rule 9020.

Since 1987, several courts of appeals have held that bankruptcy judges have the power to issue civil contempt orders. *See, e.g., Matter of Terrebonne Fuel and Lube, Inc.*, 108 F.3d 609 (5th Cir. 1997); *In re Rainbow Magazine, Inc.*, 77 F.3d 278 (9th Cir. 1996). Several courts have distinguished between a bankruptcy judge's civil contempt power and criminal contempt power. *See, e.g., Matter of Terrebonne Fuel and Lube, Inc.*, 108 F.3d at 613, n. 3 ("[a]lthough we find that bankruptcy judge's [sic] can find a party in civil contempt, we must point out that bankruptcy courts lack the power to hold persons in criminal contempt."). For other decisions regarding criminal contempt power, *see, e.g., In re Ragar*, 3 F.3d 1174 (8th Cir. 1993); *Matter of Hipp, Inc.*, 895 F.2d 1503 (5th Cir. 1990). To the extent that Rule 9020, as amended in 1987, delayed the effectiveness of civil contempt orders and required de novo review by the district court, the rule may have been unnecessarily restrictive in view of judicial decisions recognizing that bankruptcy judges have the power to hold parties in civil contempt.

Subdivision (d), which provides that the rule shall not be construed to impair the right to trial by jury, is deleted as unnecessary and is not intended to deprive any party of the right to a jury trial when it otherwise exists.

CROSS REFERENCES

Contempts, see 18 USCA §§ 401 et seq. and 3691 et seq.

Criminal contempt, see Fed.Rules Cr.Proc. Rule 42, 18 USCA.

Power of court to punish persons for contempts, see 11 USCA § 105.

Rule 9021. Entry of Judgment

A judgment or order is effective when entered under Rule 5003.

(As amended Mar. 30, 1987, eff. Aug. 1, 1987; Mar. 26, 2009, eff. Dec. 1, 2009.)

ADVISORY COMMITTEE NOTES

Subdivision (a). This rule is derived from Rule 58 F.R.Civ.P. The requirement that a judgment entered in an adversary proceeding or contested matter be set forth on a separate document is to eliminate uncertainty as to whether an opinion or memorandum of the court is a judgment. There is no sound reason to require that every order in a case under the Code be evidenced by a separate document.

Subdivision (b) establishes a procedure for entering a judgment of a bankruptcy court for the recovery of money or property in an index of judgments kept by the clerk of the district court. It clarifies the availability of the same remedies for the enforcement of a bankruptcy court judgment as those provided for the enforcement of a district court judgment. See 28 U.S.C. §§ 1961–63. When indexed in accordance with subdivision (b) of this rule a judgment of the bankruptcy court may be found by anyone searching for liens of record in the judgment records of the district court. Certification of a copy of the judgment to the clerk of the district court provides a basis for registration of the judgment pursuant to 28 U.S.C. § 1963 in any other district. When so registered, the judgment may be enforced by issuance of execution and orders for supplementary proceedings that may be served anywhere within the state where the registering court sits. See 7 Moore, Federal Practice 2409–11 (2d ed. 1971). The procedures available in the district court are not exclusive, however, and the holder of a judgment entered by the bankruptcy court may use the remedies under Rules 7069 and 7070 even if the judgment is indexed by the clerk of the district court.

Subdivision (c) makes it clear that when a district court hears a matter reserved to it by 28 U.S.C. §§ 1471, 1481, its judgments are entered in the district court's civil docket and in the docket of the bankruptcy court. When the district court acts as an appellate court, Rule 8016(a) governs the entry of judgments on appeal.

1987 Amendment

Former subdivision (a) was derived from Rule 58 F.R.Civ.P. As amended, Rule 9021 adopts Rule 58. The reference in Rule 58 to Rule 79(a) F.R.Civ.P. is to be read as a reference to Rule 5003.

2009 Amendments

The rule is amended in connection with the amendment that adds Rule 7058. The entry of judgment in adversary proceedings is governed by Rule 7058, and the entry of a judgment or order in all other proceedings is governed by this rule.

CROSS REFERENCES

Entry of judgment, see Fed.Rules Civ.Proc. Rule 58, 28 USCA.

Entry of judgment on appeal, see Fed.Rules Bankr.Proc. Rule 8016, 11 USCA.

Findings by court, see Fed.Rules Bankr.Proc. Rule 7052, 11 USCA.

Judgments rendered by district court—

    Effect as lien on local property, see 28 USCA § 1962.

    Interest allowed on money judgment, see 28 USCA § 1961.

    Registration of final judgments in other districts, see 28 USCA § 1963.

Rule 9022. Notice of Judgment or Order

(a) Judgment or order of bankruptcy judge

Immediately on the entry of a judgment or order the clerk shall serve a notice of entry in the manner provided in Rule 5(b) F.R.Civ.P. on the contesting parties and on other entities as the court directs. Unless the case is a chapter 9 municipality case, the clerk shall forthwith transmit to the United States trustee a copy of the judgment or order. Service of the notice shall be noted in the docket. Lack of notice of the entry does not affect the time to appeal or relieve or authorize the court to relieve a party for failure to appeal within the time allowed, except as permitted in Rule 8002.

(b) Judgment or order of district judge

Notice of a judgment or order entered by a district judge is governed by Rule 77(d) F.R.Civ.P. Unless the case is a chapter 9 municipality case, the clerk shall forthwith transmit to the United States trustee a copy of a judgment or order entered by a district judge.

(As amended Mar. 30, 1987, eff. Aug. 1, 1987; Apr. 30, 1991, eff. Aug. 1, 1991; Apr. 23, 2001, eff. Dec. 1, 2001.)

ADVISORY COMMITTEE NOTES

Subdivision (a) of this rule is an adaptation of Rule 77(d) F.R.Civ.P.

Subdivision (b) complements Rule 9021(b). When a district court acts as an appellate court, Rule 8016(b) requires the clerk to give notice of the judgment on appeal.

1991 Amendments

This rule is amended to enable the United States trustee to be informed of all developments in the case so that administrative and supervisory functions provided in 28 U.S.C. § 586(a) may be performed.

2001 Amendments

Rule 5(b) F.R.Civ.P., which is made applicable in adversary proceedings by Rule 7005, is being restyled and amended to authorize service by electronic means—or any other means not otherwise authorized under Rule 5(b)—if consent is obtained from the person served. The amendment to Rule 9022(a) authorizes the clerk to serve notice of entry of a judgment or order by electronic means if the person served consents, or to use any other means of service authorized under Rule 5(b), including service by mail. This amendment conforms to the amendments made to Rule 77(d) F.R. Civ. P.

CROSS REFERENCES

Entry of judgment; district court record of judgment, see Fed.Rules Bankr.Proc. Rule 9021, 11 USCA.

Notice of judgment on appeal, see Fed.Rules Bankr.Proc. Rule 8016, 11 USCA.

Rule 9023. New Trials; Amendment of Judgments

Except as provided in this rule and Rule 3008, Rule 59 F.R.Civ.P. applies in cases under the Code. A motion for a new trial or to alter or amend a judgment shall be filed, and a court may on its own order a new trial, no later than 14 days after entry of judgment. In some circumstances, Rule 8008 governs post-judgment motion practice after an appeal has been docketed and is pending.

(As amended Mar. 26, 2009, eff. Dec. 1, 2009; Apr. 25, 2014, eff. Dec. 1, 2014.)

ADVISORY COMMITTEE NOTES

Rule 59 F.R.Civ.P. regulates motions for a new trial and amendment of judgment. Those motions must be served within 10 days of the entry of judgment. No similar time limit is contained in Rule 3008 which governs reconsideration of claims.

2009 Amendments

The rule is amended to limit to 14 days the time for a party to file a post judgment motion for a new trial and for the court to order sua sponte a new trial. In 2009, Rule 59 F.R.Civ.P. was amended to extend the deadline for these actions to 28 days after the entry of judgment. That deadline corresponds to the 30-day deadline for filing a notice of appeal in a civil case under Rule 4(a)(1)(A) F. R. App. P. In a bankruptcy case, however, the deadline for filing a notice of appeal is 14 days. Therefore, the 28-day deadline for filing a motion for a new trial or a motion to alter or amend a judgment would effectively override the notice of appeal deadline under Rule 8002(a) but for this amendment.

2014 Amendments

This rule is amended to include a cross-reference to Rule 8008. That rule governs the issuance of an indicative ruling when relief is sought that the court lacks authority to grant because of an appeal that has been docketed and is pending.

CROSS REFERENCES

Amendment of findings by court, see Fed.Rules Bankr.Proc. Rule 7052, 11 USCA.

Effect of motion under this rule on time for appeal, see Fed.Rules Bankr.Proc. Rule 8002, 11 USCA.

Enlargement of ten-day period for motion for new trial not permitted, see Fed.Rules Bankr.Proc. Rule 9006, 11 USCA.

Time for service of opposing affidavits to motion for new trial, see Fed.Rules Bankr.Proc. Rule 9006, 11 USCA.

Rule 9024. Relief From Judgment or Order

Rule 60 F.R.Civ.P. applies in cases under the Code except that (1) a motion to reopen a case under the Code or for the reconsideration of an order allowing or disallowing a claim against the estate entered without a contest is not subject to the one year limitation prescribed in Rule 60(c), (2) a complaint to revoke a discharge in a chapter 7 liquidation case may be filed only within the time allowed by § 727(e) of the Code, and (3) a complaint to revoke an order confirming a plan may be filed only within the time allowed by § 1144, § 1230, or § 1330. In some circumstances, Rule 8008 governs post-judgment motion practice after an appeal has been docketed and is pending.

(As amended Apr. 30, 1991, eff. Aug. 1, 1991; Apr. 23, 2008, eff. Dec. 1, 2008; Apr. 25, 2014, eff. Dec. 1, 2014.)

ADVISORY COMMITTEE NOTES

Motions to reopen cases are governed by Rule 5010. Reconsideration of orders allowing and disallowing claims is governed by Rule 3008. For the purpose of this rule all orders of the bankruptcy court are subject to Rule 60 F.R.Civ.P.

Pursuant to § 727(e) of the Code a complaint to revoke a discharge must be filed within one year of the entry of the discharge or, when certain grounds of revocation are asserted, the later of one year after the entry of the discharge or the date the case is closed. Under § 1144 and § 1330 of the Code a party must file a complaint to revoke an order confirming a chapter 11 or 13 plan within 180 days of its entry. Clauses (2) and (3) of this rule make it clear that the time periods established by §§ 727(e), 1144 and 1330 of the Code may not be circumvented by the invocation of F.R.Civ.P. 60(b).

1991 Amendment

Clause (3) is amended to include a reference to § 1230 of the Code which contains time limitations relating to revocation of confirmation of a chapter 12 plan. The time periods prescribed by § 1230 may not be circumvented by the invocation of F.R.Civ.P. 60(b).

2008 Amendments

The rule is amended to conform to the changes made to the Federal Rules of Civil Procedure through the restyling of those rules effective on December 1, 2007.

2014 Amendments

This rule is amended to include a cross-reference to Rule 8008. That rule governs the issuance of an indicative ruling when relief is sought that the court lacks authority to grant because of an appeal that has been docketed and is pending.

CROSS REFERENCES

Enlargement of time for motion for relief from judgment or order not permitted, see Fed.Rules Bankr.Proc. Rule 9006, 11 USCA.

Motions; form and service, see Fed.Rules Bankr.Proc. Rule 9013, 11 USCA.

Rule 9025   **BANKRUPTCY RULES**

Reconsideration of allowance or disallowance of claims, see Fed.Rules Bankr.Proc. Rule 3008, 11 USCA.

Reopening cases, see Fed.Rules Bankr.Proc. Rule 5010, 11 USCA.

Revocation of discharges under individual debt adjustment plan, see 11 USCA § 1328.

Setting aside judgment by default, see Fed.Rules Bankr.Proc. Rule 7055, 11 USCA.

Rule 9025. Security: Proceedings Against Sureties

Whenever the Code or these rules require or permit the giving of security by a party, and security is given in the form of a bond or stipulation or other undertaking with one or more sureties, each surety submits to the jurisdiction of the court, and liability may be determined in an adversary proceeding governed by the rules in Part VII.

ADVISORY COMMITTEE NOTES

This rule is an adaptation of Rule 65.1 F.R.Civ.P. and applies to any surety on a bond given pursuant to § 303(e) of the Code, Rules 2001, 2010, 5008, 7062, 7065, 8005, or any other rule authorizing the giving of such security.

CROSS REFERENCES

Bonds—

    Deposit or investment by trustee of money of estates, see 11 USCA § 345.

    Indemnification bond in involuntary cases, see 11 USCA § 303.

    Qualification to serve as trustee, see 11 USCA § 322.

Enforcement of bond or undertaking on injunction against surety, see Fed.Rules Bankr.Proc. Rule 7065, 11 USCA.

Security; proceedings against sureties, see Fed.Rules Civ.Proc. Rule 65.1, 28 USCA.

Security defined, see 11 USCA § 101.

Rule 9026. Exceptions Unnecessary

Rule 46 F.R.Civ.P. applies in cases under the Code.

Rule 9027. Removal

(a) **Notice of removal**

    (1) **Where filed; form and content**

        A notice of removal shall be filed with the clerk for the district and division within which is located the state or federal court where the civil action is pending. The notice shall be signed pursuant to Rule 9011 and contain a short and plain statement of the facts which entitle the party filing the notice to remove, contain a statement that upon removal of the claim or cause of action the proceeding is core or non-core and, if non-core, that the party filing the notice does or does not consent to entry of final orders or judgment by the bankruptcy judge, and be accompanied by a copy of all process and pleadings.

    (2) **Time for filing; civil action initiated before commencement of the case under the code**

        If the claim or cause of action in a civil action is pending when a case under the Code is commenced, a notice of removal may be filed only within the longest of (A) 90 days after the order for relief in the case under the Code, (B) 30 days after entry of an order terminating a stay, if the claim or cause of action in a civil action has been stayed under § 362 of the Code, or

(C) 30 days after a trustee qualifies in a chapter 11 reorganization case but not later than 180 days after the order for relief.

(3) Time for filing; civil action initiated after commencement of the case under the Code

If a claim or cause of action is asserted in another court after the commencement of a case under the Code, a notice of removal may be filed with the clerk only within the shorter of (A) 30 days after receipt, through service or otherwise, of a copy of the initial pleading setting forth the claim or cause of action sought to be removed, or (B) 30 days after receipt of the summons if the initial pleading has been filed with the court but not served with the summons.

(b) Notice

Promptly after filing the notice of removal, the party filing the notice shall serve a copy of it on all parties to the removed claim or cause of action.

(c) Filing in non-bankruptcy court

Promptly after filing the notice of removal, the party filing the notice shall file a copy of it with the clerk of the court from which the claim or cause of action is removed. Removal of the claim or cause of action is effected on such filing of a copy of the notice of removal. The parties shall proceed no further in that court unless and until the claim or cause of action is remanded.

(d) Remand

A motion for remand of the removed claim or cause of action shall be governed by Rule 9014 and served on the parties to the removed claim or cause of action.

(e) Procedure after removal

(1) After removal of a claim or cause of action to a district court the district court or, if the case under the Code has been referred to a bankruptcy judge of the district, the bankruptcy judge, may issue all necessary orders and process to bring before it all proper parties whether served by process issued by the court from which the claim or cause of action was removed or otherwise.

(2) The district court or, if the case under the Code has been referred to a bankruptcy judge of the district, the bankruptcy judge, may require the party filing the notice of removal to file with the clerk copies of all records and proceedings relating to the claim or cause of action in the court from which the claim or cause of action was removed.

(3) Any party who has filed a pleading in connection with the removed claim or cause of action, other than the party filing the notice of removal, shall file a statement admitting or denying any allegation in the notice of removal that upon removal of the claim or cause of action the proceeding is core or non-core. If the statement alleges that the proceeding is non-core, it shall state that the party does or does not consent to entry of final orders or judgment by the bankruptcy judge. A statement required by this paragraph shall be signed pursuant to Rule 9011 and shall be filed not later than 14 days after the filing of the notice of removal. Any party who files a statement pursuant to this paragraph shall mail a copy to every other party to the removed claim or cause of action.

(f) Process after removal

If one or more of the defendants has not been served with process, the service has not been perfected prior to removal, or the process served proves to be defective, such process or service may be completed or new process issued pursuant to Part VII of these rules. This subdivision shall not deprive any defendant on whom process is served after removal of the defendant's right to move to remand the case.

(g) Applicability of Part VII

The rules of Part VII apply to a claim or cause of action removed to a district court from a federal or state court and govern procedure after removal. Repleading is not necessary unless the court so orders. In a removed action in which the defendant has not answered, the defendant shall answer or present the other defenses or objections available under the rules of Part VII within 21

Rule 9027   **BANKRUPTCY RULES**

days following the receipt through service or otherwise of a copy of the initial pleading setting forth the claim for relief on which the action or proceeding is based, or within 21 days following the service of summons on such initial pleading, or within seven days following the filing of the notice of removal, whichever period is longest.

(h) Record supplied

When a party is entitled to copies of the records and proceedings in any civil action or proceeding in a federal or a state court, to be used in the removed civil action or proceeding, and the clerk of the federal or state court, on demand accompanied by payment or tender of the lawful fees, fails to deliver certified copies, the court may, on affidavit reciting the facts, direct such record to be supplied by affidavit or otherwise. Thereupon the proceedings, trial and judgment may be had in the court, and all process awarded, as if certified copies had been filed.

(i) Attachment or sequestration; securities

When a claim or cause of action is removed to a district court, any attachment or sequestration of property in the court from which the claim or cause of action was removed shall hold the property to answer the final judgment or decree in the same manner as the property would have been held to answer final judgment or decree had it been rendered by the court from which the claim or cause of action was removed. All bonds, undertakings, or security given by either party to the claim or cause of action prior to its removal shall remain valid and effectual notwithstanding such removal. All injunctions issued, orders entered and other proceedings had prior to removal shall remain in full force and effect until dissolved or modified by the court.

(As amended Mar. 30, 1987, eff. Aug. 1, 1987; Apr. 30, 1991, eff. Aug. 1, 1991; Apr. 29, 2002, eff. Dec. 1, 2002; Mar. 26, 2009, eff. Dec. 1, 2009.)

ADVISORY COMMITTEE NOTES

Under 28 U.S.C. § 1478(a) "any claim or cause of action in a civil action, other than a proceeding before the United States Tax Court or a civil action by a Government unit to enforce [a] . . . regulatory or police power" may be removed "if the bankruptcy courts have jurisdiction over such claim or cause of action." This rule specifies how removal is accomplished, the procedure thereafter, and the procedure to request remand of the removed claim or cause of action. If the claim or cause of action which is removed to the bankruptcy court is subject to the automatic stay of § 362 of the Code, the litigation may not proceed in the bankruptcy court until relief from the stay is granted.

The subdivisions of this rule conform substantially to 28 U.S.C. §§ 1446–1450 and Rule 81(a) F.R.Civ.P. pertaining to removal to the district courts.

Subdivision (a)(1) is derived from 28 U.S.C. § 1446(a).

Subdivisions (a)(2) and (a)(3) are derived from paragraphs one and two of 28 U.S.C. § 1446(b). Timely exercise of the right to remove is as important in bankruptcy cases as in removals from a state court to a district court.

Subdivision (a)(2) governs the situation in which there is litigation pending and a party to the litigation becomes a debtor under the Code. Frequently, removal would be of little utility in such cases because the pending litigation will be stayed by § 362(a) on commencement of the case under the Code. As long as the stay remains in effect there is no reason to impose a time limit for removal to the bankruptcy court and, therefore, clause (B) of subdivision (a)(2) provides that a removal application may be filed within 30 days of entry of an order terminating the stay. Parties to stayed litigation will not be required to act immediately on commencement of a case under the Code to protect their right to remove. If the pending litigation is not stayed by § 362(a) of the Code, the removal application must ordinarily be filed within 90 days of the order for relief. Clause (C) contains an alternative period for a chapter 11 case. If a trustee is appointed, the removal application may be filed within 30 days of the trustee's qualification, provided that the removal application is filed not more than 180 days after the order for relief.

The removal application must be filed within the longest of the three possible periods. For example, in a chapter 11 case if the 90 day period expires but a trustee is appointed shortly thereafter, the removal application may be filed within 30 days of the trustee's qualification but not later than 180 days after the order for relief. Nevertheless, if the claim or cause of action in the civil action is stayed under § 362, the application may be filed after the 180 day period expires, provided the application is filed within 30 days of an order terminating the stay.

Subdivision (a)(3) applies to the situation in which the case under the Code is pending when the removable claim or cause of action is asserted in a civil action initiated in other than the bankruptcy court. The time for filing the application for removal begins to run on receipt of the first pleading containing the removable claim or cause of action. Only litigation not stayed by the code or by court order may properly be initiated after the case under the Code is commenced. See e.g., § 362(a).

Subdivision (b). With one exception, this subdivision is the same as 28 U.S.C. § 1446(d). The exemption from the bond requirement is enlarged to include a trustee or debtor in possession. Complete exemption from the bond requirement for removal is appropriate because of the limited resources which may be available at the beginning of a case and the small probability that an action will be improperly removed.

Recovery on the bond is permitted only when the removal was improper. If the removal is proper but the bankruptcy court orders the action remanded on equitable grounds, 28 U.S.C. § 1478(b), there is no recovery on the bond.

Subdivisions (c) and (d) are patterned on 28 U.S.C. § 1446(e).

Subdivision (e). There is no provision in the Federal Rules of Civil Procedure for seeking remand. The first sentence of this subdivision requires that a request for remand be by motion and that the moving party serve all other parties; however, no hearing is required. In recognition of the intrusion of the removal practice on the state and federal courts from which claims or causes of action are removed, the subdivision directs the bankruptcy court to decide remand motions as soon as practicable. The last sentence of this subdivision is derived from 28 U.S.C. § 1446(c).

Subdivisions (f) and (g), with appropriate changes to conform them to the bankruptcy context, are the same as 28 U.S.C. § 1447(a) and (b) and 28 U.S.C. § 1448, respectively.

Subdivisions (h) and (i) are taken from Rule 81(c) F.R.Civ.P.

Subdivisions (j) and (k) are derived from 28 U.S.C. § 1449 and § 1450, respectively.

Remand orders of bankruptcy judges are not appealable. 28 U.S.C. § 1478(b).

This rule does not deal with the question whether a single plaintiff or defendant may remove a claim or cause of action if there are two or more plaintiffs or defendants. See 28 U.S.C. § 1478.

1987 Amendment

Section 1452 of title 28, with certain exceptions, provides for removal of claims or causes of action in civil actions pending in state or federal courts when the claim or cause of action is within the jurisdiction conferred by 28 U.S.C. § 1334. An order granting or denying a motion for remand is not appealable. 28 U.S.C. § 1452(b). Under subdivision (e), as amended, the district court must enter the order on the remand motion; however, the bankruptcy judge conducts the initial hearing on the motion and files a report and recommendation. The parties may file objections. Review of the report and recommendation is pursuant to Rule 9033.

Subdivision (f) has been amended to provide that if there has been a referral pursuant to 28 U.S.C. § 157(a) the bankruptcy judge will preside over the removed civil action.

Subdivision (i) has been abrogated consistent with the abrogation of Rule 9015.

1991 Amendment

The abrogation of subdivision (b) is consistent with the repeal of 28 U.S.C. § 1446(d). The changes substituting the notice of removal for the application for removal conform to the 1988 amendments to 28 U.S.C. § 1446.

Rules 7008(a) and 7012(b) were amended in 1987 to require parties to allege in pleadings whether a proceeding is core or non-core and, if non-core, whether the parties consent to the entry of final orders or judgment by the bankruptcy judge. Subdivision (a)(1) is amended and subdivision (f)(3) is added to require parties to a removed claim or cause of action to make the same allegations. The party filing the notice of removal must include the allegation in the notice and the other parties who have filed pleadings must respond to the allegation in a separate statement filed within 10 days after removal. However, if a party to the removed claim or cause of action has not filed a pleading prior to removal, there is no need to file a separate statement under subdivision (f)(3) because the allegation must be included in the responsive pleading filed pursuant to Rule 7012(b).

Subdivision (e), redesignated as subdivision (d), is amended to delete the restriction that limits the role of the bankruptcy court to the filing of a report and recommendation for disposition of a motion for remand under 28 U.S.C. § 1452(b). This amendment is consistent with § 309(c) of the Judicial Improvements Act of 1990, which amended § 1452(b) so that it allows an appeal to the district court of a bankruptcy court's order determining a motion for remand. This subdivision is also amended to clarify that the motion is a contested matter governed by Rule 9014. The words "filed with the clerk" are deleted as unnecessary. See Rules 5005(a) and 9001(3).

2002 Amendments

Subdivision (a)(3) is amended to clarify that if a claim or cause of action is initiated after the commencement of a bankruptcy case, the time limits for filing a notice of removal of the claim or cause of action apply whether the case is still pending or has been suspended, dismissed, or closed.

2009 Amendments

The rule is amended to implement changes in connection with the amendment to Rule 9006(a) and the manner by which time is computed under the rules. The deadlines in the rule are amended to substitute a deadline that is a multiple of seven days. Throughout the rules, deadlines are amended in the following manner:

- 5-day periods become 7-day periods
- 10-day periods become 14-day periods
- 15-day periods become 14-day periods
- 20-day periods become 21-day periods
- 25-day periods become 28-day periods

CROSS REFERENCES

Removed actions, see Fed.Rules Civ.Proc. Rule 81, 28 USCA.

Removal of actions, see 28 USCA §§ 1446 to 1450.

Rule 9028. Disability of a Judge

Rule 63 F.R.Civ.P. applies in cases under the Code.

(As amended Mar. 30, 1987, eff. Aug. 1, 1987.)

ADVISORY COMMITTEE NOTES

This rule is an adaptation of Rule 63 F.R.Civ.P.

1987 Amendment

Rule 9028 has been changed to adopt the procedures contained in Rule 63 of the Federal Rules of Civil Procedure for substituting a judge in the event of disability.

CROSS REFERENCES

Disability of judge, see Fed.Rules Civ.Proc. Rule 63, 28 USCA.

Rule 9029. Local Bankruptcy Rules; Procedure When There Is No Controlling Law

(a) Local bankruptcy rules

(1) Each district court acting by a majority of its district judges may make and amend rules governing practice and procedure in all cases and proceedings within the district court's bankruptcy jurisdiction which are consistent with—but not duplicative of—Acts of Congress and these rules and which do not prohibit or limit the use of the Official Forms. Rule 83 F.R.Civ.P. governs the procedure for making local rules. A district court may authorize the

bankruptcy judges of the district, subject to any limitation or condition it may prescribe and the requirements of 83 F.R.Civ.P., to make and amend rules of practice and procedure which are consistent with—but not duplicative of—Acts of Congress and these rules and which do not prohibit or limit the use of the Official Forms. Local rules shall conform to any uniform numbering system prescribed by the Judicial Conference of the United States.

(2) A local rule imposing a requirement of form shall not be enforced in a manner that causes a party to lose rights because of a nonwillful failure to comply with the requirement.

(b) Procedure when there is no controlling law. A judge may regulate practice in any manner consistent with federal law, these rules, Official Forms, and local rules of the district. No sanction or other disadvantage may be imposed for noncompliance with any requirement not in federal law, federal rules, Official Forms, or the local rules of the district unless the alleged violator has been furnished in the particular case with actual notice of the requirement.

(As amended Mar. 30, 1987, eff. Aug. 1, 1987; Apr. 30, 1991, eff. Aug. 1, 1991; Apr. 27, 1995, eff. Dec. 1, 1995.)

ADVISORY COMMITTEE NOTES

This rule is an adaptation of Rule 83 F.R.Civ.P. and Rule 57(a) F.R.Crim.P. Under this rule bankruptcy courts may make local rules which govern practice before those courts. Circuit councils and district courts are authorized by Rule 8018 to make local rules governing appellate practice.

1987 Amendment

Rule 9029 is amended to authorize the district court to promulgate local rules governing bankruptcy practice. This rule, as amended, permits the district court to authorize the bankruptcy judges to promulgate or recommend local rules for adoption by the district court.

Effective August 1, 1985, Rule 83 F.R.Civ.P., governing adoption of local rules, was amended to achieve greater participation by the bar, scholars, and the public in the rule making process; to authorize the judicial council to abrogate local rules; and to make certain that single-judge standing orders are not inconsistent with these rules or local rules. Rule 9029 has been amended to incorporate Rule 83. The term "court" in the last sentence of the rule includes the judges of the district court and the bankruptcy judges of the district. Rule 9001(4).

1991 Amendments

This rule is amended to make it clear that the Official Forms must be accepted in every bankruptcy court.

1995 Amendments

Subdivision (a). This rule is amended to reflect the requirement that local rules be consistent not only with applicable national rules but also with Acts of Congress. The amendment also states that local rules should not repeat applicable national rules and Acts of Congress.

The amendment also requires that the numbering of local rules conform with any uniform numbering system that may be prescribed by the Judicial Conference. Lack of uniform numbering might create unnecessary traps for counsel and litigants. A uniform numbering system would make it easier for an increasingly national bar and for litigants to locate a local rule that applies to a particular procedural issue.

Paragraph (2) of subdivision (a) is new. Its aim is to protect against loss of rights in the enforcement of local rules relating to matters of form. For example, a party should not be deprived of a right to a jury trial because its attorney, unaware of—or forgetting—a local rule directing that jury demands be noted in the caption of the case, includes a jury demand only in the body of the pleading. The proscription of paragraph (2) is narrowly drawn—covering only violations that are not willful and only those involving local rules directed to matters of form. It does not limit the court's power to impose substantive penalties upon a party if it or its attorney stubbornly or repeatedly violates a local rule, even one involving merely a matter of form. Nor does it affect the court's power to enforce local rules that involve more than mere matters of form—for example, a local rule requiring that a party demand a jury trial within a specified time period to avoid waiver of the right to a trial by jury.

Subdivision (b). This rule provides flexibility to the court in regulating practice when there is no controlling law. Specifically, it permits the court to regulate practice in any manner consistent with federal law, with rules adopted under 28 U.S.C. § 2075, with Official Forms, and with the district's local rules.

This rule recognizes that courts rely on multiple directives to control practice. Some courts regulate practice through the published Federal Rules and the local rules of the court. Some courts also have used internal operating procedures, standing orders, and other internal directives. Although such directives continue to be authorized, they can lead to problems. Counsel or litigants may be unaware of various directives. In addition, the sheer volume of directives may impose an unreasonable barrier. For example, it may be difficult to obtain copies of the directives. Finally, counsel or litigants may be unfairly sanctioned for failing to comply with a directive. For these reasons, the amendment to this rule disapproves imposing any sanction or other disadvantage on a person for noncompliance with such an internal directive, unless the alleged violator has been furnished in a particular case with actual notice of the requirement.

There should be no adverse consequence to a party or attorney for violating special requirements relating to practice before a particular judge unless the party or attorney has actual notice of those requirements. Furnishing litigants with a copy outlining the judge's practices—or attaching instructions to a notice setting a case for conference or trial—would suffice to give actual notice, as would an order in a case specifically adopting by reference a judge's standing order and indicating how copies can be obtained.

CROSS REFERENCES

Local rules to govern appellate practice, see Fed.Rules Bankr.Proc. Rule 8018, 11 USCA.

Rules by district courts, see Fed.Rules Civ.Proc. Rule 83, 28 USCA.

Rules by district courts, see Fed.Rules Cr.Proc. Rule 57, 18 USCA.

Rule 9030. Jurisdiction and Venue Unaffected

These rules shall not be construed to extend or limit the jurisdiction of the courts or the venue of any matters therein.

(As amended Mar. 30, 1987, eff. Aug. 1, 1987.)

ADVISORY COMMITTEE NOTES

The rule is an adaptation of Rule 82 F.R.Civ.P.

CROSS REFERENCES

Jurisdiction and venue unaffected, see Fed.Rules Civ.Proc. Rule 82, 28 USCA.

Power of Supreme Court to prescribe bankruptcy rules, see 28 USCA § 2075.

Rule 9031. Masters Not Authorized

Rule 53 F.R.Civ.P. does not apply in cases under the Code.

ADVISORY COMMITTEE NOTES

This rule precludes the appointment of masters in cases and proceedings under the Code.

Rule 9032. Effect of Amendment of Federal Rules of Civil Procedure

The Federal Rules of Civil Procedure which are incorporated by reference and made applicable by these rules shall be the Federal Rules of Civil Procedure in effect on the effective date of these rules and as thereafter amended, unless otherwise provided by such amendment or by these rules.

(As amended Apr. 30, 1991, eff. Aug. 1, 1991.)

ADVISORY COMMITTEE NOTES
1991 Amendment

This rule is amended to provide flexibility so that the Bankruptcy Rules may provide that subsequent amendments to a Federal Rule of Civil Procedure made applicable by these rules are not effective with regard to Bankruptcy Code cases or proceedings. For example, in view of the anticipated amendments to, and restructuring of, Rule 4 F.R.Civ.P., Rule 7004(g) will prevent such changes from affecting Bankruptcy Code cases until the Advisory Committee on Bankruptcy Rules has an opportunity to consider such amendments and to make appropriate recommendations for incorporating such amendments into the Bankruptcy Rules.

Rule 9033. Review of Proposed Findings of Fact and Conclusions of Law in Non-Core Proceedings

(a) Service

In non-core proceedings heard pursuant to 28 U.S.C. § 157(c)(1), the bankruptcy judge shall file proposed findings of fact and conclusions of law. The clerk shall serve forthwith copies on all parties by mail and note the date of mailing on the docket.

(b) Objections: time for filing

Within 14 days after being served with a copy of the proposed findings of fact and conclusions of law a party may serve and file with the clerk written objections which identify the specific proposed findings or conclusions objected to and state the grounds for such objection. A party may respond to another party's objections within 14 days after being served with a copy thereof. A party objecting to the bankruptcy judge's proposed findings or conclusions shall arrange promptly for the transcription of the record, or such portions of it as all parties may agree upon or the bankruptcy judge deems sufficient, unless the district judge otherwise directs.

(c) Extension of time

The bankruptcy judge may for cause extend the time for filing objections by any party for a period not to exceed 21 days from the expiration of the time otherwise prescribed by this rule. A request to extend the time for filing objections must be made before the time for filing objections has expired, except that a request made no more than 21 days after the expiration of the time for filing objections may be granted upon a showing of excusable neglect.

(d) Standard of review

The district judge shall make a de novo review upon the record or, after additional evidence, of any portion of the bankruptcy judge's findings of fact or conclusions of law to which specific written objection has been made in accordance with this rule. The district judge may accept, reject, or modify the proposed findings of fact or conclusions of law, receive further evidence, or recommit the matter to the bankruptcy judge with instructions.

(Added Mar. 30, 1987, eff. Aug. 1, 1987; amended Mar. 26, 2009, eff. Dec. 1, 2009.)

ADVISORY COMMITTEE NOTES

Section 157(c)(1) of title 28 requires a bankruptcy judge to submit proposed findings of fact and conclusions of law to the district court when the bankruptcy judge has heard a non-core proceeding. This rule, which is modeled on Rule 72 F.R.Civ.P., provides the procedure for objecting to, and for review by, the district court of specific findings and conclusions.

Subdivision (a) requires the clerk to serve a copy of the proposed findings and conclusions on the parties. The bankruptcy clerk, or the district court clerk if there is no bankruptcy clerk in the district, shall serve a copy of the proposed findings and conclusions on all parties.

Subdivision (b) is derived from Rule 72(b) F.R.Civ.P. which governs objections to a recommended disposition by a magistrate.

Subdivision (c) is similar to Rule 8002(c) of the Bankruptcy Rules and provides for granting of extensions of time to file objections to proposed findings and conclusions.

Rule 9034 BANKRUPTCY RULES

Subdivision (d) adopts the de novo review provisions of Rule 72(b) F.R.Civ.P.

2009 Amendments

The rule is amended to implement changes in connection with the amendment to Rule 9006(a) and the manner by which time is computed under the rules. The deadlines in the rule are amended to substitute a deadline that is a multiple of seven days. Throughout the rules, deadlines are amended in the following manner:

- 5-day periods become 7-day periods
- 10-day periods become 14-day periods
- 15-day periods become 14-day periods
- 20-day periods become 21-day periods
- 25-day periods become 28-day periods

Rule 9034. Transmittal of Pleadings, Motion Papers, Objections, and Other Papers to the United States Trustee

Unless the United States trustee requests otherwise or the case is a chapter 9 municipality case, any entity that files a pleading, motion, objection, or similar paper relating to any of the following matters shall transmit a copy thereof to the United States trustee within the time required by these rules for service of the paper:

    (a) a proposed use, sale, or lease of property of the estate other than in the ordinary course of business;

    (b) the approval of a compromise or settlement of a controversy;

    (c) the dismissal or conversion of a case to another chapter;

    (d) the employment of professional persons;

    (e) an application for compensation or reimbursement of expenses;

    (f) a motion for, or approval of an agreement relating to, the use of cash collateral or authority to obtain credit;

    (g) the appointment of a trustee or examiner in a chapter 11 reorganization case;

    (h) the approval of a disclosure statement;

    (i) the confirmation of a plan;

    (j) an objection to, or waiver or revocation of, the debtor's discharge;

    (k) any other matter in which the United States trustee requests copies of filed papers or the court orders copies transmitted to the United States trustee.

(Added Apr. 30, 1991, eff. Aug. 1, 1991.)

ADVISORY COMMITTEE NOTES

Section 307 of the Code gives the United States trustee the right to appear and be heard on issues in cases and proceedings under the Code. This rule is intended to keep the United States trustee informed of certain developments and disputes in which the United States may wish to be heard. This rule, which derives from Rule X–1008, also enables the United States trustee to monitor the progress of the case in accordance with 28 U.S.C. § 586(a). The requirement to transmit copies of certain pleadings, motion papers and other documents is intended to be flexible in that the United States trustee in a particular judicial district may request copies of papers in certain categories, and may request not to receive copies of documents in other categories, when the practice in that district makes that desirable. When the rules require that a paper be served on particular parties, the time period in which service is required is also applicable to transmittal to the United States trustee.

Although other rules require that certain notices be transmitted to the United States trustee, this rule goes further in that it requires the transmittal to the United States trustee of other papers filed in connection with these matters. This rule is not an exhaustive list of the matters of which the United States trustee may be entitled to receive notice.

Rule 9035. Applicability of Rules in Judicial Districts in Alabama and North Carolina

In any case under the Code that is filed in or transferred to a district in the State of Alabama or the State of North Carolina and in which a United States trustee is not authorized to act, these rules apply to the extent that they are not inconsistent with any federal statute effective in the case.

(Added Apr. 30, 1991, eff. Aug. 1, 1991; amended Apr. 11, 1997, eff. Dec. 1, 1997.)

ADVISORY COMMITTEE NOTES

Section 302(d)(3) of the Bankruptcy Judges, United States Trustees, and Family Farmer Bankruptcy Act of 1986 provides that amendments to the Code relating to United States trustees and quarterly fees required under 28 U.S.C. § 1930(a)(6) do not become effective in any judicial district in the States of Alabama and North Carolina until the district elects to be included in the United States trustee system, or October 1, 1992, whichever occurs first, unless Congress extends the deadline. If the United States trustee system becomes effective in these districts, the transition provisions in the 1986 Act will govern the application of the United States trustee amendments to cases that are pending at that time. See § 302(d)(3)(F). The statute, and not the bankruptcy court, determines whether a United States trustee is authorized to act in a particular case.

Section 302(d)(3)(I) of the 1986 Act authorizes the Judicial Conference of the United States to promulgate regulations governing the appointment of bankruptcy administrators to supervise the administration of estates and trustees in cases in the districts in Alabama and North Carolina until the provisions of the Act relating to the United States trustee take effect in these districts. Pursuant to this authority, in September 1987, the Judicial Conference promulgated regulations governing the selection and appointment of bankruptcy administrators and regulations governing the establishment, duties, and functions of bankruptcy administrators. Guidelines relating to the bankruptcy administrator program have been prescribed by the Director of the Administrative Office of the United States Courts.

Many of these rules were amended to implement the United States trustee system in accordance with the 1986 Act. Since the provisions of the 1986 Act relating to the United States trustee system are not effective in cases in Alabama and North Carolina in which a bankruptcy administrator is serving, rules referring to United States trustees are at least partially inconsistent with the provisions of the Bankruptcy Code and title 28 of the United States Code effective in such cases.

In determining the applicability of these rules in cases in Alabama and North Carolina in which a United States trustee is not authorized to act, the following guidelines should be followed:

(1) The following rules do not apply because they are inconsistent with the provisions of the Code or title 28 in these cases: 1002(b), 1007(1), 1009(c), 2002(k), 2007.1(b), 2015(a)(6), 2020, 3015(b), 5005(b), 7004(b)(10), 9003(b), and 9034.

(2) The following rules are partially inconsistent with the provisions of the Code effective in these cases and, therefore, are applicable with the following modifications:

(a) **Rule 2001(a) and (c)**—The court, rather than the United States trustee, appoints the interim trustee.

(b) **Rule 2003**—The duties of the United States trustee relating to the meeting of creditors or equity security holders are performed by the officer determined in accordance with regulations of the Judicial Conference, guidelines of the Director of the Administrative Office, local rules or court orders.

(c) **Rule 2007**—The court, rather than the United States trustee, appoints committees in chapter 9 and chapter 11 cases.

(d) **Rule 2008**—The bankruptcy administrator, rather than the United States trustee, informs the trustee of how to qualify.

(e) **Rule 2009(c) and (d)**—The court, rather than the United States trustee, appoints interim trustees in chapter 7 cases and trustees in chapter 11, 12 and 13 cases.

(f) Rule 2010—The court, rather than the United States trustee, determines the amount and sufficiency of the trustee's bond.

(g) Rule 5010—The court, rather than the United States trustee, appoints the trustee when a case is reopened.

(3) All other rules are applicable because they are consistent with the provisions of the Code and title 28 effective in these cases, except that any reference to the United States trustee is not applicable and should be disregarded.

Many of the amendments to the rules are designed to give the United States trustee, a member of the Executive Branch, notice of certain developments and copies of petitions, schedules, pleadings, and other papers. In contrast, the bankruptcy administrator is an officer in the Judicial Branch and matters relating to notice of developments and access to documents filed in the clerk's office are governed by regulations of the Judicial Conference of the United States, guidelines of the Administrative Office of the United States Courts, local rules, and court orders. Also, requirements for disclosure of connections with the bankruptcy administrator in applications for employment of professional persons, restrictions on appointments of relatives of bankruptcy administrators, effects of erroneously filing papers with the bankruptcy administrator, and other matters not covered by these rules may be governed by regulations of the Judicial Conference, guidelines of the Director of the Administrative Office, local rules, and court orders.

This rule will cease to have effect if a United States trustee is authorized in every case in the districts in Alabama and North Carolina.

1997 Amendment

Certain statutes that are not codified in title 11 or title 28 of the United States Code, such as § 105 of the Bankruptcy Reform Act of 1994, Pub.L. 103–394, 108 Stat. 4106, relate to bankruptcy administrators in the judicial districts of North Carolina and Alabama. This amendment makes it clear that the Bankruptcy Rules do not apply to the extent that they are inconsistent with these federal statutes.

Rule 9036. Notice by Electronic Transmission

Whenever the clerk or some other person as directed by the court is required to send notice by mail and the entity entitled to receive the notice requests in writing that, instead of notice by mail, all or part of the information required to be contained in the notice be sent by a specified type of electronic transmission, the court may direct the clerk or other person to send the information by such electronic transmission. Notice by electronic means is complete on transmission.

(Added Apr. 22, 1993, eff. Aug. 1, 1993; amended Apr. 25, 2005, eff. Dec. 1, 2005.)

ADVISORY COMMITTEE NOTES
1993 Amendments

This rule is added to provide flexibility for banks, credit card companies, taxing authorities, and other entities that ordinarily receive notices by mail in a large volume of bankruptcy cases, to arrange to receive by electronic transmission all or part of the information required to be contained in such notices.

The use of electronic technology instead of mail to send information to creditors and interested parties will be more convenient and less costly for the sender and the receiver. For example, a bank that receives by mail, at different locations, notices of meetings of creditors pursuant to Rule 2002(a) in thousands of cases each year may prefer to receive only the vital information ordinarily contained in such notices by electronic transmission to one computer terminal.

The specific means of transmission must be compatible with technology available to the sender and the receiver. Therefore, electronic transmission of notices is permitted only upon request of the entity entitled to receive the notice, specifying the type of electronic transmission, and only if approved by the court.

Electronic transmission pursuant to the rule completes the notice requirements. The creditor or interested party is not thereafter entitled to receive the relevant notice by mail.

2005 Amendments

The rule is amended to delete the requirement that the sender of an electronic notice must obtain electronic confirmation that the notice was received. The amendment provides that notice is complete upon transmission. When the rule was first promulgated, confirmation of receipt of electronic notices was commonplace. In the current electronic environment, very few internet service providers offer the confirmation of receipt service. Consequently, compliance with the rule may be impossible, and the rule could discourage the use of electronic noticing.

Confidence in the delivery of email text messages now rivals or exceeds confidence in the delivery of printed materials. Therefore, there is no need for confirmation of receipt of electronic messages just as there is no such requirement for paper notices.

Rule 9037. Privacy Protection for Filings Made With the Court

(a) Redacted filings

Unless the court orders otherwise, in an electronic or paper filing made with the court that contains an individual's social-security number, taxpayer-identification number, or birth date, the name of an individual, other than the debtor, known to be and identified as a minor, or a financial-account number, a party or nonparty making the filing may include only:

(1) the last four digits of the social-security number and taxpayer-identification number;

(2) the year of the individual's birth;

(3) the minor's initials; and

(4) the last four digits of the financial-account number.

(b) Exemptions from the redaction requirement

The redaction requirement does not apply to the following:

(1) a financial-account number that identifies the property allegedly subject to forfeiture in a forfeiture proceeding;

(2) the record of an administrative or agency proceeding unless filed with a proof of claim;

(3) the official record of a state-court proceeding;

(4) the record of a court or tribunal, if that record was not subject to the redaction requirement when originally filed;

(5) a filing covered by subdivision (c) of this rule; and

(6) a filing that is subject to § 110 of the Code.

(c) Filings made under seal

The court may order that a filing be made under seal without redaction. The court may later unseal the filing or order the entity that made the filing to file a redacted version for the public record.

(d) Protective orders

For cause, the court may by order in a case under the Code:

(1) require redaction of additional information; or

(2) limit or prohibit a nonparty's remote electronic access to a document filed with the court.

(e) Option for additional unredacted filing under seal

An entity making a redacted filing may also file an unredacted copy under seal. The court must retain the unredacted copy as part of the record.

(f) Option for filing a reference list

A filing that contains redacted information may be filed together with a reference list that identifies each item of redacted information and specifies an appropriate identifier that uniquely corresponds to each item listed. The list must be filed under seal and may be amended as of right. Any reference in the case to a listed identifier will be construed to refer to the corresponding item of information.

(g) Waiver of protection of identifiers

An entity waives the protection of subdivision (a) as to the entity's own information by filing it without redaction and not under seal.

(Added Apr. 30, 2007, eff. Dec. 1, 2007.)

ADVISORY COMMITTEE NOTES
2007 Adoption

The rule is adopted in compliance with section 205(c)(3) of the E-Government Act of 2002, Public Law No. 107–347. Section 205(c)(3) requires the Supreme Court to prescribe rules "to protect privacy and security concerns relating to electronic filing of documents and the public availability . . . of documents filed electronically." The rule goes further than the E-Government Act in regulating paper filings even when they are not converted to electronic form, but the number of filings that remain in paper form is certain to diminish over time. Most districts scan paper filings into the electronic case file, where they become available to the public in the same way as documents initially filed in electronic form. It is electronic availability, not the form of the initial filing, that raises the privacy and security concerns addressed in the E-Government Act.

The rule is derived from and implements the policy adopted by the Judicial Conference in September 2001 to address the privacy concerns resulting from public access to electronic case files. *See* http://www.privacy.uscourts.gov/Policy.htm. The Judicial Conference policy is that documents in case files generally should be made available electronically to the same extent they are available at the courthouse, provided that certain "personal data identifiers" are not included in the public file.

While providing for the public filing of some information, such as the last four digits of an account number, the rule does not intend to establish a presumption that this information never could or should be protected. For example, it may well be necessary in individual cases to prevent remote access by nonparties to any part of an account number or social-security number. It may also be necessary to protect information not covered by the redaction requirement—such as driver's license numbers and alien registration numbers—in a particular case. In such cases, protection may be sought under subdivision (c) or (d). Moreover, the rule does not affect the protection available under other rules, such as Rules 16 and 26(c) of the Federal Rules of Civil Procedure, or under other sources of protective authority.

Any personal information not otherwise protected by sealing or redaction will be made available over the internet. Counsel should therefore notify clients of this fact so that an informed decision may be made on what information is to be included in a document filed with the court.

An individual debtor's full social-security number or taxpayer-identification number is included on the notice of the § 341 meeting of creditors sent to creditors. Of course, that is not filed with the court, see Rule 1007(f) (the debtor "submits" this information), and the copy of the notice that is filed with the court does not include the full social-security number or taxpayer-identification number. Thus, since the full social-security number or taxpayer-identification number is not filed with the court, it is not available to a person searching that record.

The clerk is not required to review documents filed with the court for compliance with this rule. As subdivision (a) recognizes, the responsibility to redact filings rests with counsel, parties, and others who make filings with the court.

Subdivision (d) recognizes the court's inherent authority to issue a protective order to prevent remote access to private or sensitive information and to require redaction of material in addition to that which would be redacted under subdivision (a) of the rule. These orders may be issued whenever necessary either by the court on its own motion, or on motion of a party in interest.

Subdivision (e) allows an entity that makes a redacted filing to file an unredacted document under seal. This provision is derived from section 205(c)(3)(iv) of the E-Government Act. Subdivision (f) allows the option to file a reference list of redacted information. This provision is derived from section 205(c)(3)(v) of the E-Government Act, as amended in 2004.

In accordance with the E-Government Act, subdivision (f) of the rule refers to "redacted" information. The term "redacted" is intended to govern a filing that is prepared with abbreviated identifiers in the first instance, as well as a filing in which a personal identifier is edited after its preparation.

Subdivision (g) allows an entity to waive the protections of the rule as to that entity's own information by filing it in unredacted form. An entity may elect to waive the protection if, for example, it is determined that the costs of redaction outweigh the benefits to privacy. As to financial account numbers, the instructions to Schedules E and F of Official Form 6 note that the debtor may elect to include the complete account number on those schedules rather than limit the number to the final four digits. Including the complete number would operate as a waiver by the debtor under subdivision (g) as to the full information that the debtor set out on those schedules. The waiver operates only to the extent of the information that the entity filed without redaction. If an entity files an unredacted identifier by mistake, it may seek relief from the court.

Trial exhibits are subject to the redaction requirements of Rule 9037 to the extent they are filed with the court. Trial exhibits that are not initially filed with the court must be redacted in accordance with this rule if and when they are filed as part of an appeal or for other reasons.

PART X—UNITED STATES TRUSTEES [ABROGATED]

[Rules X–1001 to X–1010. Abrogated Apr. 30, 1991, eff. Aug. 1, 1991]

OFFICIAL FORMS

Form
1.	Voluntary Petition.
2.	Declaration Under Penalty of Perjury on Behalf of a Corporation or Partnership.
3A.	Application and Order to Pay Filing Fee in Installments.
3B.	Application for Waiver of the Chapter 7 Filing Fee for Individuals Who Cannot Pay the Filing Fee in Full or in Installments.
4.	List of Creditors Holding 20 Largest Unsecured Claims.
5.	Involuntary Petition.
6.	Schedules.
7.	Statement of Financial Affairs.
8.	Individual Debtor's Statement of Intention.
9.	Notice of Commencement of Case Under the Bankruptcy Code, Meeting of Creditors, and Deadlines.
10.	Proof of Claim.
[11.	Omitted. See Form 5.].
11A.	General Power of Attorney.
11B.	Special Power of Attorney.
12.	Order and Notice for Hearing on Disclosure Statement.
13.	Order Approving Disclosure Statement and Fixing Time for Filing Acceptances or Rejections of Plan, Combined with Notice Thereof.
14.	Class [ ] Ballot for Accepting or Rejecting Plan of Reorganization.
15.	Order Confirming Plan.
16A.	Caption (Full).
16B.	Caption (Short Title).
16C.	Caption of Complaint in Adversary Proceeding Filed by a Debtor [Abrogated].
16D.	Caption for Use in Adversary Proceeding.
17.	Notice of Appeal Under 28 U.S.C. § 158(a) or (b) From a Judgment, Order, or Decree of a Bankruptcy Judge.
18.	Discharge of Debtor in a Chapter 7 Case.
19.	Declaration and Signature of Non-Attorney Bankruptcy Petition Preparer.
20A.	Notice of Motion or Objection.
20B.	Notice of Objection to Claim.
21.	Statement of Social-Security Number or Individual Taxpayer-Identification Number (ITIN).
22.	Statement of Current Monthly Income.
23.	Debtor's Certification of Completion of Postpetition Instructional Course Concerning Personal Financial Management.
24.	Certification to Court of Appeals by all Parties.
25A.	Plan of Reorganization in Small Business Case Under Chapter 11.
25B.	Disclosure Statement in Small Business Case Under Chapter 11.
25C.	Small Business Monthly Operating Report.
26.	Periodic Report Regarding Value, Operations and Profitability of Entities in Which the Debtor's Estate Holds a Substantial or Controlling Interest.
27.	Reaffirmation Agreement Cover Sheet.

INTRODUCTION AND GENERAL INSTRUCTIONS

Rule 9009 of the Federal Rules of Bankruptcy Procedure states that the Official Forms prescribed by the Judicial Conference of the United States "shall be observed and used." The Official Forms, accordingly, are obligatory in character.

Rule 9009 expressly permits the user of the Official Forms to make such "alterations as may be appropriate," and the use of the Official Forms has been held to be subject to a "rule of substantial compliance." Some rules, for example Fed.R.Bankr.P. 3001(a), specifically state that the filed document need only "conform substantially" to the Official Form. A document for which an Official Form is prescribed generally will meet the standard of substantial compliance if the document contains the complete substance, that is, all of the information required by the Official Form.

Rule 9009 also expressly permits the contents of Official Forms to be rearranged, and the format of the Official Forms traditionally has been quite flexible. The forms of the voluntary petition, the schedules, and the statement of financial affairs are printed and sold by private publishers. Design features such as type face, type size, layout, and side and top margins were not prescribed by the Judicial Conference, but rather left to the professional judgment of each publisher.

OFFICIAL FORMS

A great deal of variation, accordingly, has developed. Some publishers also add forms that are not official but which have been drafted by the publisher. A form for a chapter 13 plan, for example, frequently is included with commercially printed packages of forms for filing cases under chapter 13, although there is no Official Form for this purpose. The variety of formats has accelerated since the introduction of computer software for generating the petitions, schedules, and statements of affairs. It is the policy of the Judicial Conference that such diversity is desirable and should be encouraged.

The sheer volume of bankruptcy cases, however, has compelled the Judicial Conference, for the first time, to prescribe the format of certain Official Forms. In particular, the format of Form 1, the Voluntary Petition, now is prescribed. This format is designed to assist the clerk of the bankruptcy court to enter the case in the court's computer database and ensures that all required information is available to both the clerk and the United States trustee at the inception of the case. The rule of substantial compliance continues to apply, however. Accordingly, publishers may vary the size and style of the type and may alter the size and shape of the boxes on the form, within the bounds of that rule.

The Official Forms of the petitions, schedules, and statement of financial affairs, (Forms 1, 5, 6, and 7), are to be printed on one side of the paper only. Each page is to be pre-punched with two holes at the top, and sufficient top margin allowed so that neither caption nor text is destroyed or obscured. Compliance with these standards will facilitate both the securing of the papers in the case file and review of the file by the public.

Although Rule 9009 permits alteration, for most of the Official Forms, alteration will be appropriate only in rare circumstances. The special forms for chapter 11 cases, on the other hand, seldom will be used without alterations. Forms 12 through 15, while legally sufficient in any chapter 11 case, are intended by the Judicial Conference, and most often will be used, as a framework for drafting a document specially tailored to the particular case. These alterations generally will take the form of additions to the prescribed elements.

Rule 9009 provides for a balance of prescribed substance, to which full adherence is expected in all but the most unusual cases, and flexible formatting, under which requirements are kept to the minimum necessary for proper operation of the courts and the bankruptcy system. While Rule 9009 recognizes the overall need for flexibility, Rule 9029 makes it clear that the Official Forms must be accepted in every bankruptcy court.

Under Rule 9029, courts may not reject documents presented for filing in novel or unfamiliar formats if those documents contain the substance prescribed by the Official Form and meet the requirements for one-sided printing, pre-punched holes, and adequate top margins. Nor are courts authorized to impose local forms which vary in substance from the Official Forms or reject papers presented for filing on Official Forms on the basis that the proffered documents differ from a locally preferred version.

Special Instructions for Computer-Generated Forms

In Form 1, the Voluntary Petition, if a box contains multiple choices, a computer-generated petition that shows only the choice made is acceptable for filing. All sections of the petition must be shown and completed, however, unless instructions on the Official Form of the petition state that the box is applicable only to cases filed under a chapter other than the one selected by the debtor. If the debtor has no information to provide for a particular box, for example if the debtor has no prior bankruptcies to report, a computer-generated petition should so indicate by stating "None."

Form 6, the Schedules, on which the debtor reports all of the debtor's assets and liabilities, has been prescribed in a columnar format. Columns help to organize the information which the debtor is required to report and should be used when the printed schedules are completed on a typewriter. In a computerized law office, however, the organizational structure of the schedules can be built into the computer program, and a rigid columnar format may be a hindrance rather than a help. Schedules generated by computer which provide all of the information requested by the prescribed form are fully acceptable, regardless of the format of the printed page. The information must be appropriately labeled, however. In Schedule B, for example, all of the categories of personal property must be printed on the filed document together with the debtor's response to each. The space occupied by each category may be expanded, however, so that attachments are not needed. Instructions provided on the printed forms can simply be built into the computer program; they need not be reprinted on the filed document.

Form 7, the Statement of Financial Affairs, contains a series of questions which direct the debtor to answer by furnishing information. If the answer to a question is "None," or the question is not applicable,

OFFICIAL FORMS

an affirmative statement to that effect is required. To assure that the trustee and the creditors can review the debtor's statement properly, the complete text of each question must be printed on the filed document.

Form 9, the Notice of Filing under the Bankruptcy Code, Meeting of Creditors, and Fixing of Dates, will be prepared by the clerk of the bankruptcy court in most cases. The form is designed for use with automated printing and mailing equipment. Two free lines, which do not appear on the printed blank form, have been programmed into the form. Courts may use this space to add local information, such as directions for obtaining copies of the debtor's schedules.

CONVERSION TABLE FOR OFFICIAL BANKRUPTCY FORMS

Former Official Form Number

Form No. 1.   Voluntary Petition
[Revised; see new Official Form 1.]

Form No. 2.   Application and Order to Pay Filing Fee in Installments
[Renumbered; see new Official Form 3.]

Form No. 3.   Order for Payment of Filing Fee in Installments
[Abrogated and combined with Form No. 2; see new Official Form 3.]

Form No. 4.   Unsworn Declaration under Penalty of Perjury on Behalf of a Corporation or Partnership
[Renumbered; see new Official Form 2.]

Form No. 5.   Certificate of Commencement of Case
[Abrogated.]

Form No. 6.   Schedules of Assets and Liabilities
[Revised; see new Official Form 6.]

Form No. 6A.   Schedule of Current Income and Current Expenditures for Individual Debtor
[Revised; see new Official Form 6, Schedules I and J.]

Form No. 7.   Statement of Financial Affairs for Debtor Not Engaged in Business
[Revised and combined with former Form No. 8; see new Official Form 7.]

Form No. 8.   Statement of Financial Affairs for Debtor Engaged in Business
[Revised and combined with former Form No. 7; see new Official Form 7.]

Form No. 8A.   Chapter 7 Individual Debtor's Statement of Intention
[Renumbered; see new Official Form 8.]

Form No. 9.   List of Creditors Holding 20 Largest Unsecured Claims
[Renumbered; see new Official Form 4.]

Form No. 10.   Chapter 13 Statement
[Abrogated; see new Official Forms 6, 7, and 8.]

Form No. 11.   Involuntary Case: Creditors' Petition
[Revised, combined with former Form No. 12, and renumbered; see new Official Form 5.]

OFFICIAL FORMS

Form No. 12. Involuntary Case Against Partnership; Partner's Petition
[Abrogated and combined with former Form No. 11; see new Official Form 5.]

Form No. 13. Summons to Debtor
[Abrogated.]

Form No. 14. Order for Relief
[Abrogated.]

Form No. 15. Appointment of Committee of Unsecured Creditors in Chapter 9 Municipality or Chapter 11 Reorganization Case
[Abrogated.]

Form No. 16. Order for Meeting of Creditors and Related Orders, Combined with Notice Thereof and of Automatic Stay
[Revised and renumbered; see new Official Form 9.]

Form No. 17. General Power of Attorney
[Renumbered; see new Official Form 11A.]

Form No. 18. Special Power of Attorney
[Renumbered; see new Official Form No. 11B.]

Form No. 19. Proof of Claim
[Revised and renumbered; see new Official Form 10.]

Form No. 20. Proof of Claim for Wages, Salary, or Commissions
[Abrogated and combined with former Form No. 19; see new Official Form 10.]

Form No. 21. Proof of Multiple Claims for Wages, Salary, or Commissions
[Abrogated and combined with former Form No. 19; see new Official Form No. 10.]

Form No. 22. Order Appointing Interim Trustee and Fixing Amount of Bond
[Abrogated.]

Form No. 23. Order Approving Election of Trustee and Fixing Amount of Bond
[Abrogated.]

Form No. 24. Notice to Trustee of Selection and of Time Fixed for Filing a Complaint Objecting to Discharge of Debtor
[Abrogated.]

Form No. 25. Bond and Order Approving Bond of Trustee
[Abrogated.]

Form No. 26. Certificate of Retention of Debtor in Possession
[Abrogated.]

Form No. 27. Discharge of Debtor

OFFICIAL FORMS

[Renumbered; see new Official Form 18.]

Form No. 28.   Order and Notice for Hearing on Disclosure Statement

[Renumbered; see new Official Form 12.]

Form No. 29.   Order Approving Disclosure Statement and Fixing Time for Filing Acceptances or Rejections of Plan, Combined with Notice Thereof

[Renumbered; see new Official Form 13.]

Form No. 30.   Ballot for Accepting or Rejecting Plan

[Renumbered; see new Official Form 14.]

Form No. 31.   Order Confirming Plan

[Renumbered; see new Official Form 15.]

Form No. 32.   Notice of Filing Final Account

[Abrogated.]

Form No. 33.   Final Decree

[Abrogated.]

Form No. 34.   Caption of Adversary Proceedings

[Renumbered; see new Official Form No. 16C.]

Form No. 35.   Notice of Appeal to a District Court or Bankruptcy Appellate Panel from a Judgment of a Bankruptcy Court Entered in an Adversary Proceeding

[Revised and renumbered; see new Official Form 17.]

NOTE CONCERNING CONTINUED AVAILABILITY OF CERTAIN ABROGATED FORMS

Forms No. 5, 13, 14, 26, 32 and 33, although abrogated as Official Forms, continue to be available as procedural forms issued by the Director of the Administrative Office of the United States Courts. Members of the bar and the public may consult the Bankruptcy Forms Manual, which is available in the clerk's office at every bankruptcy court location. The contents of the Bankruptcy Forms Manual may be copied without restriction, subject to any applicable copy fee charged by the clerk.

Forms No. 15, 22, 23, 24 and 25, also abrogated as Official Forms, pertain to functions now performed by the United States trustee. Any forms deemed necessary for carrying out those functions will be issued by the Department of Justice.

Form 1

OFFICIAL FORMS

Form 1. Voluntary Petition

B1 (Official Form 1) (04/13)	
UNITED STATES BANKRUPTCY COURT	**VOLUNTARY PETITION**

Name of Debtor (if individual, enter Last, First, Middle):	Name of Joint Debtor (Spouse) (Last, First, Middle):
All Other Names used by the Debtor in the last 8 years (include married, maiden, and trade names):	All Other Names used by the Joint Debtor in the last 8 years (include married, maiden, and trade names):
Last four digits of Soc. Sec. or Individual-Taxpayer I.D. (ITIN)/Complete EIN (if more than one, state all):	Last four digits of Soc. Sec. or Individual-Taxpayer I.D. (ITIN)/Complete EIN (if more than one, state all):
Street Address of Debtor (No. and Street, City, and State): ZIP CODE	Street Address of Joint Debtor (No. and Street, City, and State): ZIP CODE
County of Residence or of the Principal Place of Business:	County of Residence or of the Principal Place of Business:
Mailing Address of Debtor (if different from street address): ZIP CODE	Mailing Address of Joint Debtor (if different from street address): ZIP CODE
Location of Principal Assets of Business Debtor (if different from street address above): ZIP CODE	

Type of Debtor (Form of Organization) (Check one box.)	Nature of Business (Check one box.)	Chapter of Bankruptcy Code Under Which the Petition is Filed (Check one box.)
☐ Individual (includes Joint Debtors) *See Exhibit D on page 2 of this form.* ☐ Corporation (includes LLC and LLP) ☐ Partnership ☐ Other (If debtor is not one of the above entities, check this box and state type of entity below.)	☐ Health Care Business ☐ Single Asset Real Estate as defined in 11 U.S.C. § 101(51B) ☐ Railroad ☐ Stockbroker ☐ Commodity Broker ☐ Clearing Bank ☐ Other	☐ Chapter 7 ☐ Chapter 15 Petition for Recognition of a Foreign Main Proceeding ☐ Chapter 9 ☐ Chapter 11 ☐ Chapter 12 ☐ Chapter 15 Petition for Recognition of a Foreign Nonmain Proceeding ☐ Chapter 13
Chapter 15 Debtors Country of debtor's center of main interests: Each country in which a foreign proceeding by, regarding, or against debtor is pending:	**Tax-Exempt Entity** (Check box, if applicable.) ☐ Debtor is a tax-exempt organization under title 26 of the United States Code (the Internal Revenue Code).	**Nature of Debts** (Check one box.) ☐ Debts are primarily consumer debts, defined in 11 U.S.C. § 101(8) as "incurred by an individual primarily for a personal, family, or household purpose." ☐ Debts are primarily business debts.

Filing Fee (Check one box.)	Chapter 11 Debtors
☐ Full Filing Fee attached. ☐ Filing Fee to be paid in installments (applicable to individuals only). Must attach signed application for the court's consideration certifying that the debtor is unable to pay fee except in installments. Rule 1006(b). See Official Form 3A. ☐ Filing Fee waiver requested (applicable to chapter 7 individuals only). Must attach signed application for the court's consideration. See Official Form 3B.	**Check one box:** ☐ Debtor is a small business debtor as defined in 11 U.S.C. § 101(51D). ☐ Debtor is not a small business debtor as defined in 11 U.S.C. § 101(51D). **Check if:** ☐ Debtor's aggregate noncontingent liquidated debts (excluding debts owed to insiders or affiliates) are less than $2,490,925 *(amount subject to adjustment on 4/01/16 and every three years thereafter)*. - **Check all applicable boxes:** ☐ A plan is being filed with this petition. ☐ Acceptances of the plan were solicited prepetition from one or more classes of creditors, in accordance with 11 U.S.C. § 1126(b).

Statistical/Administrative Information	THIS SPACE IS FOR COURT USE ONLY
☐ Debtor estimates that funds will be available for distribution to unsecured creditors. ☐ Debtor estimates that, after any exempt property is excluded and administrative expenses paid, there will be no funds available for distribution to unsecured creditors.	

Estimated Number of Creditors
☐ 1-49	☐ 50-99	☐ 100-199	☐ 200-999	☐ 1,000-5,000	☐ 5,001-10,000	☐ 10,001-25,000	☐ 25,001-50,000	☐ 50,001-100,000	☐ Over 100,000

Estimated Assets
☐ $0 to $50,000	☐ $50,001 to $100,000	☐ $100,001 to $500,000	☐ $500,001 to $1 million	☐ $1,000,001 to $10 million	☐ $10,000,001 to $50 million	☐ $50,000,001 to $100 million	☐ $100,000,001 to $500 million	☐ $500,000,001 to $1 billion	☐ More than $1 billion

Estimated Liabilities
☐ $0 to $50,000	☐ $50,001 to $100,000	☐ $100,001 to $500,000	☐ $500,001 to $1 million	☐ $1,000,001 to $10 million	☐ $10,000,001 to $50 million	☐ $50,000,001 to $100 million	☐ $100,000,001 to $500 million	☐ $500,000,001 to $1 billion	☐ More than $1 billion

OFFICIAL FORMS Form 1

B1 (Official Form 1) (04/13) — Page 2

Voluntary Petition *(This page must be completed and filed in every case.)*	Name of Debtor(s):	
All Prior Bankruptcy Cases Filed Within Last 8 Years (If more than two, attach additional sheet.)		
Location Where Filed:	Case Number:	Date Filed:
Location Where Filed:	Case Number:	Date Filed:
Pending Bankruptcy Case Filed by any Spouse, Partner, or Affiliate of this Debtor (If more than one, attach additional sheet.)		
Name of Debtor:	Case Number:	Date Filed:
District:	Relationship:	Judge:

Exhibit A
(To be completed if debtor is required to file periodic reports (e.g., forms 10K and 10Q) with the Securities and Exchange Commission pursuant to Section 13 or 15(d) of the Securities Exchange Act of 1934 and is requesting relief under chapter 11.)

☐ Exhibit A is attached and made a part of this petition.

Exhibit B
(To be completed if debtor is an individual whose debts are primarily consumer debts.)

I, the attorney for the petitioner named in the foregoing petition, declare that I have informed the petitioner that [he or she] may proceed under chapter 7, 11, 12, or 13 of title 11, United States Code, and have explained the relief available under each such chapter. I further certify that I have delivered to the debtor the notice required by 11 U.S.C. § 342(b).

X _____
   Signature of Attorney for Debtor(s)   (Date)

Exhibit C
Does the debtor own or have possession of any property that poses or is alleged to pose a threat of imminent and identifiable harm to public health or safety?

☐ Yes, and Exhibit C is attached and made a part of this petition.

☐ No.

Exhibit D
(To be completed by every individual debtor. If a joint petition is filed, each spouse must complete and attach a separate Exhibit D.)

☐ Exhibit D, completed and signed by the debtor, is attached and made a part of this petition.

If this is a joint petition:

☐ Exhibit D, also completed and signed by the joint debtor, is attached and made a part of this petition.

Information Regarding the Debtor - Venue
(Check any applicable box.)

☐ Debtor has been domiciled or has had a residence, principal place of business, or principal assets in this District for 180 days immediately preceding the date of this petition or for a longer part of such 180 days than in any other District.

☐ There is a bankruptcy case concerning debtor's affiliate, general partner, or partnership pending in this District.

☐ Debtor is a debtor in a foreign proceeding and has its principal place of business or principal assets in the United States in this District, or has no principal place of business or assets in the United States but is a defendant in an action or proceeding [in a federal or state court] in this District, or the interests of the parties will be served in regard to the relief sought in this District.

Certification by a Debtor Who Resides as a Tenant of Residential Property
(Check all applicable boxes.)

☐ Landlord has a judgment against the debtor for possession of debtor's residence. (If box checked, complete the following.)

_____
(Name of landlord that obtained judgment)

_____
(Address of landlord)

☐ Debtor claims that under applicable nonbankruptcy law, there are circumstances under which the debtor would be permitted to cure the entire monetary default that gave rise to the judgment for possession, after the judgment for possession was entered, and

☐ Debtor has included with this petition the deposit with the court of any rent that would become due during the 30-day period after the filing of the petition.

☐ Debtor certifies that he/she has served the Landlord with this certification. (11 U.S.C. § 362(l)).

Form 1   OFFICIAL FORMS

B1 (Official Form 1) (04/13)   Page 3

Voluntary Petition *(This page must be completed and filed in every case.)*	Name of Debtor(s):

Signatures

Signature(s) of Debtor(s) (Individual/Joint)	Signature of a Foreign Representative

I declare under penalty of perjury that the information provided in this petition is true and correct.
[If petitioner is an individual whose debts are primarily consumer debts and has chosen to file under chapter 7] I am aware that I may proceed under chapter 7, 11, 12 or 13 of title 11, United States Code, understand the relief available under each such chapter, and choose to proceed under chapter 7.
[If no attorney represents me and no bankruptcy petition preparer signs the petition] I have obtained and read the notice required by 11 U.S.C. § 342(b).
 	
I request relief in accordance with the chapter of title 11, United States Code, specified in this petition.
 	
X _____
    Signature of Debtor
 	
X _____
    Signature of Joint Debtor
 	
_____
Telephone Number (if not represented by attorney)
 	
_____
Date
	I declare under penalty of perjury that the information provided in this petition is true and correct, that I am the foreign representative of a debtor in a foreign proceeding, and that I am authorized to file this petition.
	
	(Check only one box.)
	
	☐ I request relief in accordance with chapter 15 of title 11, United States Code. Certified copies of the documents required by 11 U.S.C. § 1515 are attached.
	
	☐ Pursuant to 11 U.S.C. § 1511, I request relief in accordance with the chapter of title 11 specified in this petition. A certified copy of the order granting recognition of the foreign main proceeding is attached.
	
	X _____
	    (Signature of Foreign Representative)
	
	_____
	(Printed Name of Foreign Representative)
	
	_____
	Date

Signature of Attorney*	Signature of Non-Attorney Bankruptcy Petition Preparer

X _____
    Signature of Attorney for Debtor(s)
 	
_____
Printed Name of Attorney for Debtor(s)
 	
_____
Firm Name
 	
_____
Address
 	
_____
Telephone Number
 	
_____
Date
 	
*In a case in which § 707(b)(4)(D) applies, this signature also constitutes a certification that the attorney has no knowledge after an inquiry that the information in the schedules is incorrect.
	I declare under penalty of perjury that: (1) I am a bankruptcy petition preparer as defined in 11 U.S.C. § 110; (2) I prepared this document for compensation and have provided the debtor with a copy of this document and the notices and information required under 11 U.S.C. §§ 110(b), 110(h), and 342(b); and, (3) if rules or guidelines have been promulgated pursuant to 11 U.S.C. § 110(h) setting a maximum fee for services chargeable by bankruptcy petition preparers, I have given the debtor notice of the maximum amount before preparing any document for filing for a debtor or accepting any fee from the debtor, as required in that section. Official Form 19 is attached.
	
	_____
	Printed Name and title, if any, of Bankruptcy Petition Preparer
	
	_____
	Social-Security number (If the bankruptcy petition preparer is not an individual, state the Social-Security number of the officer, principal, responsible person or partner of the bankruptcy petition preparer.) (Required by 11 U.S.C. § 110.)
	
	_____
	Address
	
	X _____
	    Signature
	
	_____
	Date
	
	Signature of bankruptcy petition preparer or officer, principal, responsible person, or partner whose Social-Security number is provided above.
	
	Names and Social-Security numbers of all other individuals who prepared or assisted in preparing this document unless the bankruptcy petition preparer is not an individual.
	
	If more than one person prepared this document, attach additional sheets conforming to the appropriate official form for each person.
	
	A bankruptcy petition preparer's failure to comply with the provisions of title 11 and the Federal Rules of Bankruptcy Procedure may result in fines or imprisonment or both. 11 U.S.C. § 110; 18 U.S.C. § 156.

Signature of Debtor (Corporation/Partnership)	
I declare under penalty of perjury that the information provided in this petition is true and correct, and that I have been authorized to file this petition on behalf of the debtor. The debtor requests the relief in accordance with the chapter of title 11, United States Code, specified in this petition. X _____ Signature of Authorized Individual _____ Printed Name of Authorized Individual _____ Title of Authorized Individual _____ Date	

(Added Aug. 1, 1991; amended Mar. 16, 1993; Mar. 1995; Oct. 1, 1997; Dec. 1, 2001; Dec. 1, 2002; Dec. 1, 2003; Aug. 11, 2005, eff. Oct. 17, 2005; Oct. 12, 2006; Apr. 1, 2007; Dec. 1, 2007; Jan., 2008; Dec. 1, 2008; Dec. 2009; Apr. 1, 2010; Dec. 1, 2011; Apr. 1, 2013.)

OFFICIAL FORMS — Form 1

ADVISORY COMMITTEE NOTES

1991 Enactment

Form 1, the Voluntary Petition, is to be used to commence a voluntary case under chapter 7, 11, 12, or 13 of the Bankruptcy Code. A chapter 9 petition requires other allegations, (see § 109(c) of the Code), but this form may be adapted for such use. The form also may be adapted for use in filing a petition ancillary to a foreign proceeding under § 304 of the Code.

The form departs from the traditional format of a captioned pleading. All of the elements of the caption prescribed in Rule 1005 have been retained. Their placement on the page, however, has been changed to make the form compatible with electronic data processing by the clerk. The form of the caption of the case for use in other documents, formerly incorporated in Official Form No. 1, has been made a separate Form 16A.

All names used by the debtor, including trade names, names used in doing business, married names, and maiden names should be furnished in the spaces provided. If there is not sufficient room for all such names on the form itself, the list should be continued on an additional sheet attached to the petition. A complete list will enable creditors to identify the debtor properly when they receive notices and orders.

Redesign of this form into a box format also is intended to provide the court, the United States trustee, and other interested parties with as much information as possible during the 15-day period provided by Rule 1007(c), when schedules and statements may not have been filed. The box format separates into categories the data provided by the debtor, and enables the form to be used by all voluntary debtors in all chapters.

For the first time, the form requires both a street address and any separate mailing address, as well as any separate addresses used by a joint debtor. Disclosure of prior bankruptcies is new to the petition but formerly was required in the statement of financial affairs; its inclusion in the petition is intended to alert the trustee to cases in which an objection to discharge pursuant to § 727(a)(8) or (a)(9) or a motion to dismiss under § 109(g) may be appropriate. The information about pending related cases, also new to the petition, signals the clerk to assign the case to the judge to whom any related case has been assigned.

Rule 1008 requires all petitions to be verified or contain an unsworn declaration as provided in 28 U.S.C. § 1746. The unsworn declaration on page two of the petition conforms with 28 U.S.C. § 1746, which permits the declaration to be made in the manner indicated with the same force and effect as a sworn statement. The form may be adapted for use outside the United States by adding the words "under the laws of the United States" after the word "perjury."

Exhibit "A," to be attached to the petition of a corporate debtor, is for the purpose of supplying the Securities and Exchange Commission with information it needs at the beginning stages of a chapter 11 case in order to determine how actively to monitor the proceedings. Exhibit "B" was added by § 322 of Pub.L. No. 98–353, the Bankruptcy Amendments and Federal Judgeship Act of 1984. The references to chapters 11 and 12 of the Code found in Exhibit "B" and its related allegations were added by § 283(aa) of the 1986 amendments, (Pub.L. No. 99–554). This exhibit has been included in the form of the petition.

The form effects a merger of the petition and the bankruptcy cover sheet to assist the clerk in providing the statistical information required by the Director of the Administrative Office of the United States Courts pursuant to the Congressional reporting mandates of 28 U.S.C. § 604. The Director is authorized to change the particulars of the statistical portion of the form as needed in the performance of these statutory duties.

1993 Amendment

The form has been amended to require a debtor not represented by an attorney to provide a telephone number so that court personnel, the trustee, other parties in the case, and their attorneys can contact the debtor concerning matters in the case.

1995 Amendment

The form is amended to provide space for signing by a "bankruptcy petition preparer," as required under section 110 of the Code, which was added by the Bankruptcy Reform Act of 1994. In addition to signing, a bankruptcy petition preparer is required by section 110 to disclose the information requested. All signatories of Form 1 are requested to provide the clerk's office with a telephone number.

A chapter 11 debtor that qualifies as a "small business" under section 101 of the Code, as amended by the 1994 Act, may elect special, expedited treatment under amendments made to chapter 11 by the

Form 1   OFFICIAL FORMS

1994 Act. The court may order that a creditors committee not be appointed in a small business case. Accordingly, the first page of the petition is amended to require a small business filing under chapter 11 to identify itself. The petition also is amended to offer a small business chapter 11 debtor an opportunity to exercise its right to elect to be considered a small business at the commencement of the case.

Several clarifying and technical amendments also have been made to indicate that a debtor is to check only one box with respect to "Type of Debtor" and "Nature of Debt," to clarify the intent that the individual signing on behalf of a corporation or partnership is authorized to file the petition, and to require a debtor to represent that it is eligible for relief under the chapter of title 11 specified in the petition.

1997 Amendment

The form has been substantially amended to simplify its format and make the form easier to complete correctly. The Latin phrase "In re" has been deleted as unnecessary. The amount of information requested in the boxes labeled "Type of Debtor" and "Nature of Debt" has been reduced, and the reporting by a corporation of whether it is a publicly held entity has been moved to Exhibit "A" of the petition. The box labeled "Representation by Attorney" has been deleted; the information it contained is requested in the signature boxes on the second page of the form.

In the statistical information section, the labels on the ranges of estimated assets and liabilities have been rewritten to improve the accuracy of reporting. The asset/liability range of $10 million to $100 million has been divided into two categories to promote better statistical reporting of business cases. Requests for information in chapter 11 and chapter 12 cases concerning the number of the debtor's employees and equity security holders have been deleted.

The second page of the form has been simplified so that a debtor need only sign the petition once. The request for information concerning the filing of a plan has been deleted.

Exhibit "A" has been simplified. In addition, the category of chapter 11 debtors required to file Exhibit "A" is modified to include a corporation, partnership, or other entity, but only if the debtor has issued publicly-traded equity securities or debt instruments. Most small corporations will not be required to file Exhibit "A."

2001 Amendment

The form has been amended to require the debtor to disclose whether the debtor owns or has possession of any property that poses or is alleged to pose a threat of imminent and identifiable harm to public health or safety. If any such property exists, the debtor must complete and attach Exhibit "C" describing the property, its location, and the potential danger it poses. Exhibit "C" will alert the United States trustee and any person selected as trustee that immediate precautionary action may be necessary.

2002 Amendment

The form has been amended to provide a checkbox for designating a clearing bank case filed under subchapter V of chapter 7 of the Code enacted by § 112 of Pub. L. No. 106–554 (December 21, 2000).

2003 Amendment

The form is amended to require the debtor to disclose only the last four digits of the debtor's social security number to afford greater privacy to the individual debtor, whose bankruptcy case records may be available on the Internet. Pursuant to § 110(c) of the Bankruptcy Code, the certification by a non-attorney bankruptcy petition preparer requires a petition preparer to provide the full social security number of the individual who actually prepares the document.

2005 Amendment

The form is amended to implement amendments to the Bankruptcy Code contained in the Bankruptcy Abuse Prevention and Consumer Protection Act of 2005, Pub. L. No. 109–8, 119 Stat. 23 (April 20, 2005). The period for which the debtor must provide all names used and information about any prior bankruptcy cases is now eight years to match the required time between the granting of discharges to the same debtor in § 727(a)(8) of the Code as amended in 2005. The box indicating the debtor's selection of a chapter under which to file the case has been amended to delete "Sec. 304—Case ancillary to foreign proceeding" and replace it with "Chapter 15 Petition for Recognition of a Foreign Main Proceeding" and "Chapter 15 Petition for Recognition of a Foreign Nonmain Proceeding" reflecting the 2005 repeal of § 304 and enactment of chapter 15 of the Code. A statement of venue to be used in a chapter 15 case also has been added.

OFFICIAL FORMS — Form 1

The section of the form labeled "Type of Debtor" has been revised and subtitled "Form of Organization." This section is revised to make it clear that a limited liability corporation ("LLC") and limited liability partnership ("LLP") should identify itself as a "corporation." A new section titled "Nature of Business" has been created that includes both existing check boxes that identify certain types of debtors for which the Bankruptcy Code provides special treatment, such as stockbrokers and railroads, and a new checkbox for a "health care business" for which the 2005 amendments to the Code include specific requirements. This section of the form also contains checkboxes for single asset real estate debtors and nonprofit organizations which will be used by trustees and creditors and by the Director of the Administrative Office of the United States Courts in preparing statistical reports and analyses. The statistical section of the form also is amended to provide more detail concerning the number of creditors in a case. A check box also has been added for a debtor to indicate that the debtor is applying for a waiver of the filing fee, to implement the 2005 enactment of 28 U.S.C. § 1930(f) authorizing the bankruptcy court to waive the filing fee in certain circumstances.

Although the 2005 Act eliminated an eligible debtor's option to elect to be treated as a "small business" in a chapter 11 case, new provisions for such debtors added to the Code in 2005 make it desirable to identify eligible debtors at the outset of the case. Accordingly, the section of the form labeled "Chapter 11 Small Business" has been revised and renamed "Chapter 11 Debtors" for this purpose. Chapter 11 debtors that meet the definition of "small business debtor" in § 101 of the Code are directed to identify themselves in this section of the form. In addition, chapter 11 debtors whose aggregate noncontingent debts owed to non-insiders or affiliates are less than $2 million are directed to identify themselves in this section.

A space is provided for individuals to certify that they have received budget and credit counseling prior to filing, as required by § 109(h) which was added to the Code in 2005, or to request a waiver of the requirement. Space also is provided for a debtor who is a tenant of residential real property to state whether the debtor's landlord has a judgment against the debtor for possession of the premises, whether under applicable nonbankruptcy law the debtor would be permitted to cure the monetary default, and whether the debtor has made the appropriate deposit with the court. This addition to the form implements § 362(l) which was added to the Code in 2005.

The signature sections and the declaration under penalty of perjury by an individual debtor concerning the notice received about bankruptcy relief, the declaration under penalty of perjury by a bankruptcy petition preparer, and the declaration and certification by an attorney all are amended to include new material mandated by the 2005 Act. A signature section also is provided for a representative of a foreign proceeding.

2006 Amendment

Page one of the form is amended in several ways to assist the courts in evaluating their workload and fulfilling the statistical reporting requirements of 28 U.S.C. § 159. Section 159 was enacted as part of the Bankruptcy Abuse Prevention and Consumer Protection Act of 2005 (BAPCPA), Pub.L. No. 109–8 and takes effect October 17, 2006. Accordingly, in the section of the form labeled "Nature of Business," the instruction is amended to specify that only one box should be checked and only if the debtor is any of the entities listed. The "nonprofit" choice is separated into a discrete section and the language amended to the more precise "tax-exempt."

In addition, the section labeled "Type of Debtor" is amended to include, below the checkbox for "Individual or Joint," a direction to "See Exhibit D on page 2 of this form." Exhibit D replaces the certification concerning prepetition credit counseling and is described below. The section labeled "Nature of Debts" is amended to state the statutory definition of a "consumer debt" and to modify both the consumer and business categories by adding the word "primarily" to both make it clearer to individual debtors that "business" may be the more appropriate choice if personal debts have been incurred to finance a business venture.

In the section labeled "Chapter 11 Debtors," the language concerning whether the debtor owes less than $2 million is re-styled for clarity. This section also is augmented to provide the court with notice when a case if [sic] filed as a "pre-packaged" chapter 11 reorganization case. Two checkboxes are offered, using language adapted from § 1126(b) of the Code. Lastly, the information requested concerning estimated assets and liabilities is abbreviated, with the number of ranges reduced and the scope of each range amended. Statistical reports now will be derived from actual dollar amounts of assets and liabilities as shown on the debtor's schedules. The information on the petition, accordingly, is for case management and public information purposes only.

Form 1   OFFICIAL FORMS

Exhibit D replaces the section formerly labeled "Certification Concerning Debt Counseling by Individual/Joint Debtor(s)." Early cases decided under the 2005 amendments to the Bankruptcy Code indicate that individual debtors may not be aware of the requirement to obtain prepetition credit counseling, the few and very narrow exceptions to that requirement, or the potentially dire consequences to their efforts to obtain bankruptcy relief if they fail to complete the requirement. Accordingly, page 2 of the petition instructs individual debtors to attach a completed Exhibit D and makes it clear that each spouse in a joint case must complete and attach a separate Exhibit D. Exhibit D itself includes a warning about the requirement to obtain counseling and the consequences of failing to fulfill this requirement. It further provides checkboxes and instructions concerning the additional documents that are required in particular circumstances, in order to minimize the number of cases which the court must dismiss for ineligibility.

2005–2007 Amendments

(The 2005–2007 Committee Note incorporates Committee Notes previously published in 2005 and 2006.)

The form is amended to implement amendments to the Bankruptcy Code contained in the Bankruptcy Abuse Prevention and Consumer Protection Act of 2005, Pub. L. No. 109–8, 119 Stat. 23 (April 20, 2005)("BAPCPA"). The period for which the debtor must provide all names used and information about any prior bankruptcy cases is now eight years to match the required time between the granting of discharges to the same debtor in § 727(a)(8) of the Code as amended in 2005. In conformity with Rule 9037, the debtor is directed to provide only the last four digits of any individual's tax-identification number.

The box indicating the debtor's selection of a chapter under which to file the case is amended to delete "Sec. 304—Case ancillary to foreign proceeding" and replace it with "Chapter 15 Petition for Recognition of a Foreign Main Proceeding" and "Chapter 15 Petition for Recognition of a Foreign Nonmain Proceeding" reflecting the 2005 repeal of § 304 and enactment of chapter 15 of the Code. A statement of venue to be used in a chapter 15 case also is added on page 2 of the form.

The section labeled "Type of Debtor" is amended to include, below the checkbox for "Individual or Joint," a direction to "See Exhibit D on page 2 of this form." This addition alerts individual debtors that Exhibit D on page 2 of the form applies to them. Exhibit D, more fully described below, addresses the prepetition credit counseling requirements added to the Code by BAPCPA. The subtitle, "Form of Organization," is added, and this section also is revised to make clear that a limited liability corporation ("LLC") or limited liability partnership ("LLP") should identify itself as a "corporation."

The form also is amended in several ways to assist the courts in evaluating their workload and fulfilling the statistical reporting requirements of 28 U.S.C. § 159, enacted as part of BAPCPA. Accordingly, a new section of the form labeled "Nature of Business," is added that contains both existing checkboxes that identify certain types of debtors for which the Bankruptcy Code provides special treatment, such as stockbrokers and railroads, and a new checkbox for a "health care business" for which the 2005 amendments to the Code include specific requirements. This section of the form also contains a checkbox for single asset real estate debtors, so they can be identified at the time of filing. All other businesses will mark the checkbox labeled "Other." Another new section titled "Tax-Exempt Entity" contains a checkbox to be used by qualified organizations. The Judicial Conference of the United States and the Administrative Office of the United States Courts will use this information in preparing statistical reports and analyses for Congress.

A checkbox also is added for an individual debtor to indicate that the debtor is applying for a waiver of the filing fee, to implement the 2005 enactment of 28 U.S.C. § 1930(f) authorizing the bankruptcy court to waive the filing fee in certain circumstances. The description directs the debtor to the Official Form for the application that must be filed for the court's consideration.

The section labeled "Nature of Debts" is amended to state the statutory definition of a "consumer debt" and to modify both the consumer and business categories by adding the word "primarily" to both choices to make it clearer to individual debtors that "business" may be the appropriate choice if personal debts have been incurred to finance a business venture.

Although the 2005 Act eliminated from the Code any option to elect to be treated as a "small business" in a chapter 11 case, new provisions for "small business" debtors added by BAPCPA make it desirable to identify eligible debtors at the outset of the case. Accordingly, the section of the form labeled "Chapter 11 Small Business" is revised and renamed "Chapter 11 Debtors" for this purpose. Chapter 11 debtors that meet the definition of "small business debtor" in § 101 of the Code are directed to identify themselves in this section of the form. Chapter 11 debtors whose aggregate noncontingent debts owed to non-insiders or affiliates are less than $2,190,000 are directed to identify themselves in this section. A third part of this section attempts to identify chapter 11 cases that are filed as pre-packaged cases, using criteria taken from § 1126(b) of the Code. Identifying "pre-packs" at filing will assist judges and court staff to manage these cases appropriately.

The statistical information concerning the number of creditors and estimated assets and liabilities is revised to provide more detail.

BAPCPA also added a new § 109(h) to the Code. To implement this provision, a section labeled "Exhibit D" is inserted on page 2 of the form, and a separate Exhibit D is added. These additions will enable individual debtors to certify that they have received budget and credit counseling prior to filing, as required by § 109(h), or request a temporary waiver of, or exemption from, the requirement, if they meet the statutory requirements for such relief. Exhibit D includes directions to attach required documentation or, if the debtor requests a temporary waiver or an exemption, a motion for a determination by the court. Exhibit D also states the requirement that all individual debtors must obtain a briefing from an approved credit counseling agency before filing a bankruptcy case, unless one of the very limited exceptions applies, and further states the consequences that may be faced by any debtor who fails to comply.

Space is provided on page 2 for a debtor who is a tenant of residential real property to certify whether the debtor's landlord has a judgment against the debtor for possession of the premises, whether under applicable nonbankruptcy law the debtor would be permitted to cure the monetary default, and whether the debtor has made the appropriate deposit with the court. This addition to the form implements § 362(l) which was added to the Code in 2005. And a box is provided that allows the debtor to certify that s/he has served the landlord with the certification as required by § 362(l)(1).

The signature sections and the declaration under penalty of perjury by an individual debtor concerning the notice received about bankruptcy relief, the declaration under penalty of perjury by a bankruptcy petition preparer, and the attorney signature box are amended to include new material mandated by the 2005 Act. The attorney signature box is also amended to remind the attorney that in a case in which § 707(b)(4)(D) applies, that the signature constitutes a certification that the attorney has no knowledge after an inquiry that the information in the schedules filed with the petition is incorrect. A signature section is also provided for a representative of a foreign proceeding.

2008 Amendment

Paragraph 3 of Exhibit D is amended to delete any reference to a requirement that a debtor file a motion with the court to obtain an order approving a request for the postponement of the debtor's obligation to obtain a credit counseling briefing prior to the commencement of the case. The paragraph immediately following numbered paragraph 3 is also amended to reflect the deletion of the need for a separate motion beyond the completion of the certification itself. That paragraph continues to warn the debtor that the case may be dismissed if the court does not find that a postponement is warranted. It also advises the debtor that, even if the court concludes that postponement of the obligation is appropriate, the debtor still must complete the briefing within the time allowed under the Code.

2011 Amendment

The form is amended to implement Rule 1004.2. Subdivision (a) of that rule requires a chapter 15 petition to state the country of the debtor's center of main interests and to identify each country in which a foreign proceeding by, regarding, or against the debtor is pending. A box is added to the first page of the form for this purpose. Minor stylistic changes are also made.

Form 2   **OFFICIAL FORMS**

Form 2. Declaration Under Penalty of Perjury on Behalf of a Corporation or Partnership

Official Form 2
6/90

**DECLARATION UNDER PENALTY OF PERJURY
ON BEHALF OF A CORPORATION OR PARTNERSHIP**

I, [the president *or* other officer *or* an authorized agent of the corporation] [*or* a member *or* an authorized agent of the partnership] named as the debtor in this case, declare under penalty of perjury that I have read the foregoing [list *or* schedule *or* amendment *or* other document (describe)] and that it is true and correct to the best of my information and belief.

Date _____

Signature _____

_____
(Print Name and Title)

(Added Aug. 1, 1991.)

ADVISORY COMMITTEE NOTES

This form is derived from former Official Form No. 4.

Rule 1008 requires that all petitions, lists, schedules, statements, and amendments thereto be verified or contain an unsworn declaration conforming with 28 U.S.C. § 1746. This form or adaptations of the form have been incorporated into the official forms of the petitions, schedules, and statement of financial affairs. See Official Forms 1, 5, 6, and 7. The form has been amended for use in connection with other papers required by these rules to be verified or contain an unsworn declaration.

OFFICIAL FORMS   Form 3A

Form 3A.   Application and Order to Pay Filing Fee in Installments

---

Fill in this information to identify your case:

Debtor 1 _____ _____ _____
          First Name   Middle Name   Last Name

Debtor 2 _____ _____ _____
(Spouse, if filing) First Name   Middle Name   Last Name

United States Bankruptcy Court for the: _____ District of _____

Case number _____
(if known)

☐ Check if this is an amended filing

Official Form B 3A

Application for Individuals to Pay the Filing Fee in Installments   12/13

Be as complete and accurate as possible. If two married people are filing together, both are equally responsible for supplying correct information.

Part 1: Specify Your Proposed Payment Timetable

1. Which chapter of the Bankruptcy Code are you choosing to file under?

   ☐ Chapter 7 .... Fee: $306
   ☐ Chapter 11 .... Fee: $1,213
   ☐ Chapter 12 .... Fee: $246
   ☐ Chapter 13 .... Fee: $281

2. You may apply to pay the filing fee in up to four installments. Fill in the amounts you propose to pay and the dates you plan to pay them. Be sure all dates are business days. Then add the payments you propose to pay.

   You must propose to pay the entire fee no later than 120 days after you file this bankruptcy case. If the court approves your application, the court will set your final payment timetable.

   You propose to pay...

   $ _____   ☐ With the filing of the petition
                  ☐ On or before this date .... _____
                                                    MM / DD / YYYY

   $ _____   On or before this date .... _____
                                                    MM / DD / YYYY

   $ _____   On or before this date .... _____
                                                    MM / DD / YYYY

   + $ _____ On or before this date .... _____
                                                    MM / DD / YYYY

   Total $ _____   ◀ Your total must equal the entire fee for the chapter you checked in line 1.

Part 2: Sign Below

By signing here, you state that you are unable to pay the full filing fee at once, that you want to pay the fee in installments, and that you understand that:

- You must pay your entire filing fee before you make any more payments or transfer any more property to an attorney, bankruptcy petition preparer, or anyone else for services in connection with your bankruptcy case.

- You must pay the entire fee no later than 120 days after you first file for bankruptcy, unless the court later extends your deadline. Your debts will not be discharged until your entire fee is paid.

- If you do not make any payment when it is due, your bankruptcy case may be dismissed, and your rights in other bankruptcy proceedings may be affected.

X _____   X _____   X _____
  Signature of Debtor 1   Signature of Debtor 2   Your attorney's name and signature, if you used one

Date _____   Date _____   Date _____
     MM / DD / YYYY   MM / DD / YYYY   MM / DD / YYYY

Official Form B 3A   Application for Individuals to Pay the Filing Fee in Installments

Form 3A OFFICIAL FORMS

Fill in this information to identify the case:

Debtor 1 _____ _____ _____
         First Name   Middle Name   Last Name

Debtor 2 _____ _____ _____
(Spouse, if filing) First Name Middle Name Last Name

United States Bankruptcy Court for the: _____ District of _____

Case number (if known): _____

☐ Chapter 7
☐ Chapter 11
☐ Chapter 12
☐ Chapter 13

Order Approving Payment of Filing Fee in Installments

After considering the *Application for Individuals to Pay the Filing Fee in Installments* (Official Form B 3A), the court orders that:

[ ] The debtor(s) may pay the filing fee in installments on the terms proposed in the application.

[ ] The debtor(s) must pay the filing fee according to the following terms:

You must pay...	On or before this date...
$_____	_____ Month / day / year
$_____	_____ Month / day / year
$_____	_____ Month / day / year
+ $_____	_____ Month / day / year

Total $_____

Until the filing fee is paid in full, the debtor(s) must not make any additional payment or transfer any additional property to an attorney or to anyone else for services in connection with this case.

_____   By the court: _____
Month / day / year   United States Bankruptcy Judge

(Added Aug. 1, 1991, and amended Mar. 1995; Oct. 1, 1997; Dec. 1, 2003; Aug. 11, 2005, eff. Oct. 17, 2005; Dec. 1, 2007; Dec. 2013; Dec. 1, 2014.)

ADVISORY COMMITTEE NOTES

This form is derived from former Official Form No. 2.

A statement that the applicant is unable to pay the filing fee except in installments has been added as required by Rule 1006(b).

1995 Amendment

This form is a "document for filing" that may be prepared by a "bankruptcy petition preparer" as defined in 11 U.S.C. § 110, which was added to the Code by the Bankruptcy Reform Act of 1994;

accordingly, a signature line is provided for such preparer. In addition to signing, a bankruptcy petition preparer is required by section 110 to disclose the information requested. A signature line for a debtor's attorney also is added, as required by Rule 9011.

1997 Amendment

The form has been reorganized and the paragraphs numbered. The debtor's certification concerning payment for services in the case has been placed ahead of the statement of proposed terms for installment payment of court fees. Acknowledgment by the debtor of the potential consequences of failure to pay any installment when due has been added. (See 11 U.S.C. § 707(a)(2).) The language of the form also has been changed to conform to Rule 1006 and to clarify that a debtor is not disqualified from paying the filing fee in installments because the debtor has paid money to a bankruptcy petition preparer.

2003 Amendment

Pursuant to § 110(c) of the Bankruptcy Code, the certification by a non-attorney bankruptcy petition preparer requires a petition preparer to provide the full Social Security number of the individual who actually prepares the document pursuant to § 110(c) of the Code.

2005 Amendment

The form is amended to direct the debtor to state that, until the filing fee is paid in full, the debtor will not make any additional payment or transfer any additional property to an attorney or any other person for services in connection with the case. The declaration and certification by a non-attorney bankruptcy petition preparer in the form are amended to include material mandated by § 110 of the Code as amended by the Bankruptcy Abuse Prevention and Consumer Protection Act of 2005, Pub. L. No. 109–8, 119 Stat. 23 (April 20, 2005). The certification by a non-attorney bankruptcy petition preparer is re-named a declaration and also is revised to include material mandated by § 110 of the Code as amended in 2005. The order is amended to provide space for the court to set forth a payment schedule other than the one proposed by the debtor.

2005–2007 Amendments

(The 2005–2007 Committee Note incorporates the Committee Note previously published in 2005.)

The form is amended to direct the debtor to state that, until the filing fee is paid in full, the debtor will not make any additional payment or transfer any additional property to an attorney or any other person for services in connection with the case. The declaration and certification by a non-attorney bankruptcy petition preparer in the form are amended to include material mandated by § 110 of the Code as amended by the Bankruptcy Abuse Prevention and Consumer Protection Act of 2005, Pub. L. No. 109–8, 119 Stat. 23 (April 20, 2005). The certification by a non-attorney bankruptcy petition preparer is re-named a declaration and also is revised to include material mandated by § 110 of the Code as amended in 2005. The order is amended to provide space for the court to set forth a payment schedule other than the one proposed by the debtor.

2013 Amendment

This form, which applies only in cases of individual debtors, has been revised as part of the Forms Modernization Project, making the form easier to read and, as a result, likely to generate more complete and accurate responses. Also, the declaration and signature section for a non-attorney bankruptcy petition preparer (BPP) has been removed as unnecessary. The same declaration, required under 11 U.S.C. § 110, is contained in Official Form 19. That form must be completed and signed by the BPP, and filed with each document for filing prepared by a BPP.

2014 Amendment

The amounts of the bankruptcy filing fees for various chapters listed on page one of the form were removed from the form. The correct fee amounts are listed on Director's Forms 200 and 201A where they can be updated as necessary without having to go through the official form amendment process.

Form 3B   **OFFICIAL FORMS**

Form 3B.   Application to Have the Chapter 7 Filing Fee Waived

Fill in this information to identify your case:

Debtor 1 _____
        First Name   Middle Name   Last Name

Debtor 2 _____
(Spouse, if filing) First Name Middle Name   Last Name

United States Bankruptcy Court for the: _____ District of _____

Case number _____
(if known)

☐ Check if this is an amended filing

Official Form B 3B

Application to Have the Chapter 7 Filing Fee Waived   12/13

Be as complete and accurate as possible. If two married people are filing together, both are equally responsible for supplying correct information. If more space is needed, attach a separate sheet to this form. On the top of any additional pages, write your name and case number (if known).

Part 1:   Tell the Court About Your Family and Your Family's Income

1. What is the size of your family?
   Your family includes you, your spouse, and any dependents listed on *Schedule J: Current Expenditures of Individual Debtor(s)* (Official Form B 6J).

   Check all that apply:
   ☐ You
   ☐ Your spouse
   ☐ Your dependents _____ How many dependents? _____ Total number of people

2. Fill in your family's average monthly income.

   Include your spouse's income if your spouse is living with you, even if your spouse is not filing.

   Do not include your spouse's income if you are separated and your spouse is not filing with you.

   Add your income and your spouse's income. Include the value (if known) of any non-cash governmental assistance that you receive, such as food stamps (benefits under the Supplemental Nutrition Assistance Program) or housing subsidies.

   If you have already filled out *Schedule I: Your Income*, see line 10 of that schedule.

   That person's average monthly net income (take-home pay)

   You .... $_____
   Your spouse ... + $_____
   Subtotal .... $_____

   Subtract any non-cash governmental assistance that you included above. − $_____

   Your family's average monthly net income   Total .... $_____

3. Do you receive non-cash governmental assistance?
   ☐ No
   ☐ Yes. Describe .... Type of assistance _____

4. Do you expect your family's average monthly net income to increase or decrease by more than 10% during the next 6 months?
   ☐ No
   ☐ Yes. Explain .... _____

5. Tell the court why you are unable to pay the filing fee in installments within 120 days. If you have some additional circumstances that cause you to not be able to pay your filing fee in installments, explain them. _____

Official Form B 3B   Application to Have the Chapter 7 Filing Fee Waived   page 1

806

OFFICIAL FORMS   **Form 3B**

Debtor 1 _____ Case number (if known) _____
       First Name   Middle Name   Last Name

Part 2: Tell the Court About Your Monthly Expenses

6. Estimate your average monthly expenses.
Include amounts paid by any government assistance that you reported on line 2. $_____

If you have already filled out *Schedule J, Your Expenses*, copy line 22 from that form.

7. Do these expenses cover anyone who is not included in your family as reported in line 1?
☐ No
☐ Yes. Identify who _____

8. Does anyone other than you regularly pay any of these expenses?
If you have already filled out *Schedule I: Your Income*, copy the total from line 11.
☐ No
☐ Yes. How much do you regularly receive as contributions? $_____ monthly

9. Do you expect your average monthly expenses to increase or decrease by more than 10% during the next 6 months?
☐ No
☐ Yes. Explain _____

Part 3: Tell the Court About Your Property

If you have already filled out *Schedule A: Real Property (Official Form B 6A)* and *Schedule B: Personal Property (Official Form B 6B)*, attach copies to this application and go to Part 4.

10. How much cash do you have?
Examples: Money you have in your wallet, in your home, and on hand when you file this application
Cash: $_____

11. Bank accounts and other deposits of money?
Examples: Checking, savings, money market, or other financial accounts; certificates of deposit; shares in banks, credit unions, brokerage houses, and other similar institutions. If you have more than one account with the same institution, list each. Do not include 401(k) and IRA accounts.

	Institution name:	Amount:
Checking account:	_____	$_____
Savings account:	_____	$_____
Other financial accounts:	_____	$_____
Other financial accounts:	_____	$_____

12. Your home? (if you own it outright or are purchasing it)
Examples: House, condominium, manufactured home, or mobile home
Number Street _____
City _____ State ____ ZIP Code ____
Current value: $_____
Amount you owe on mortgage and liens: $_____

13. Other real estate?
Number Street _____
City _____ State ____ ZIP Code ____
Current value: $_____
Amount you owe on mortgage and liens: $_____

14. The vehicles you own?
Examples: Cars, vans, trucks, sports utility vehicles, motorcycles, tractors, boats
Make: _____
Model: _____
Year: _____
Mileage _____
Current value: $_____
Amount you owe on liens: $_____

Make: _____
Model: _____
Year: _____
Mileage _____
Current value: $_____
Amount you owe on liens: $_____

Official Form B 3B   Application to Have the Chapter 7 Filing Fee Waived   page 2

Form 3B OFFICIAL FORMS

Debtor 1 _____ _____ _____   **Case number** *(if known)* _____
First Name   Middle Name   Last Name

15. Other assets?
Do not include household items and clothing.

Describe the other assets:
_____

Current value: $_____
Amount you owe on liens: $_____

16. Money or property due you?
Examples: Tax refunds, past due or lump sum alimony, spousal support, child support, maintenance, divorce or property settlements, Social Security benefits, Workers' compensation, personal injury recovery

Who owes you the money or property?
_____
_____

How much is owed?
$_____
$_____

Do you believe you will likely receive payment in the next 180 days?
☐ No
☐ Yes. Explain:
_____

Part 4: Answer These Additional Questions

17. Have you paid anyone for services for this case, including filling out this application, the bankruptcy filing package, or the schedules?

☐ No
☐ Yes. Whom did you pay? *Check all that apply:*
  ☐ An attorney
  ☐ A bankruptcy petition preparer, paralegal, or typing service
  ☐ Someone else _____

How much did you pay?
$_____

18. Have you promised to pay or do you expect to pay someone for services for your bankruptcy case?

☐ No
☐ Yes. Whom do you expect to pay? *Check all that apply:*
  ☐ An attorney
  ☐ A bankruptcy petition preparer, paralegal, or typing service
  ☐ Someone else _____

How much do you expect to pay?
$_____

19. Has anyone paid someone on your behalf for services for this case?

☐ No
☐ Yes. Who was paid on your behalf? *Check all that apply:*
  ☐ An attorney
  ☐ A bankruptcy petition preparer, paralegal, or typing service
  ☐ Someone else _____

Who paid? *Check all that apply:*
  ☐ Parent
  ☐ Brother or sister
  ☐ Friend
  ☐ Pastor or clergy
  ☐ Someone else _____

How much did someone else pay?
$_____

20. Have you filed for bankruptcy within the last 8 years?

☐ No
☐ Yes. District _____ When __/__/____ Case number _____
District _____ When __/__/____ Case number _____
District _____ When __/__/____ Case number _____

Part 5: Sign Below

By signing here under penalty of perjury, I declare that I cannot afford to pay the filing fee either in full or in installments. I also declare that the information I provided in this application is true and correct.

✗ _____
Signature of Debtor 1

Date __/__/____
MM / DD / YYYY

✗ _____
Signature of Debtor 2

Date __/__/____
MM / DD / YYYY

Official Form B 3B   Application to Have the Chapter 7 Filing Fee Waived   page 3

OFFICIAL FORMS   Form 3B

Fill in this information to identify the case:

Debtor 1 _____ _____ _____
         First Name   Middle Name   Last Name

Debtor 2 _____ _____ _____
(Spouse, if filing) First Name Middle Name Last Name

United States Bankruptcy Court for the: _____ District of _____

Case number _____
(if known)

Order on the Application to Have the Chapter 7 Filing Fee Waived

After considering the debtor's *Application to Have the Chapter 7 Filing Fee Waived* (Official Form B 3B), the court orders that the application is:

[ ] **Granted.** However, the court may order the debtor to pay the fee in the future if developments in administering the bankruptcy case show that the waiver was unwarranted.

[ ] **Denied.** The debtor must pay the $306 filing fee according to the following terms:

You must pay...	On or before this date...
$_____	_____ Month / day / year
$_____	_____ Month / day / year
$_____	_____ Month / day / year
+ $_____	_____ Month / day / year
Total $_____	

If the debtor would like to propose a different payment timetable, the debtor must file a motion promptly with a payment proposal. The debtor may use *Application for Individuals to Pay the Filing Fee in Installments* (Official Form B 3A) for this purpose. The court will consider it.

The debtor must pay the entire filing fee before making any more payments or transferring any more property to an attorney, bankruptcy petition preparer, or anyone else in connection with the bankruptcy case. The debtor must also pay the entire filing fee to receive a discharge. If the debtor does not make any payment when it is due, the bankruptcy case may be dismissed and the debtor's rights in future bankruptcy cases may be affected.

[ ] **Scheduled for hearing.**

A hearing to consider the debtor's application will be held

on _____ at _____ AM / PM at _____.
   Month / day / year   Address of courthouse

If the debtor does not appear at this hearing, the court may deny the application.

_____   By the court: _____
Month / day / year   United States Bankruptcy Judge

(Added Aug. 11, 2005, eff. Oct. 17, 2005. Amended Apr. 9, 2006; Dec. 1, 2007; Nov. 2011; Dec. 2013; Dec. 1, 2014.)

Form 3B   OFFICIAL FORMS

ADVISORY COMMITTEE NOTES

2005 Amendment

This form is new. 28 U.S.C. § 1930(f), enacted as part of the Bankruptcy Abuse and Consumer Protection Act of 2005, Pub. L. No. 109–8, 119 Stat. 23 (April 20, 2005), provides that "under procedures prescribed by the Judicial Conference of the United States, the district court or the bankruptcy court may waive the filing fee in a case under chapter 7 of title 11 for an individual if the court determines that such individual has income less than 150 percent of the income official poverty line . . . applicable to a family of the size involved and is unable to pay that fee in installments." To implement this provision, Interim Rule 1006 adds a new subdivision (c). Official Form 3B is the form referenced in that subdivision, and is to be used by individual chapter 7 debtors when applying for a waiver of the filing fee. A corresponding standard order also is included.

2005–2007 Amendments

(The 2005–2007 Committee Note incorporates the Committee Note previously published in 2005.)

This form is new. 28 U.S.C. § 1930(f), enacted as part of the Bankruptcy Abuse and Consumer Protection Act of 2005, Pub. L. No. 109–8, 119 Stat. 23 (April 20, 2005), provides that "under procedures prescribed by the Judicial Conference of the United States, the district court or the bankruptcy court may waive the filing fee in a case under chapter 7 of title 11 for an individual if the court determines that such individual has income less than 150 percent of the income official poverty line . . . applicable to a family of the size involved and is unable to pay that fee in installments." To implement this provision, Fed. R. Bankr. P.1006 adds a new subdivision (c). Official Form 3B is the form referenced in that subdivision, and is to be used by individual chapter 7 debtors when applying for a waiver of the filing fee. A corresponding standard order also is included.

2013 Amendment

This form, which applies only in cases of individual debtors, has been revised as part of the Forms Modernization Project, making the form easier to read and, as a result, likely to generate more complete and accurate responses. Additionally, in calculating the income that determines the debtor's initial eligibility for a fee waiver, line 2 of the form now directs the debtor to exclude non-cash governmental assistance, such as food stamps and housing subsidies. However, because non-cash governmental assistance may be relevant in evaluating the additional requirement that the debtor be unable to pay the filing fee, the nature of any such assistance is to be reported separately on line 3. Also, the declaration and signature section for a non-attorney bankruptcy petition preparer (BPP) has been removed as unnecessary. The same declaration, required under 11 U.S.C. § 110, is contained in Official Form 19. That form must be completed and signed by the BPP, and filed with each document for filing prepared by a BPP.

2014 Amendment

The amount of the chapter 7 filing fee is no longer preprinted on the blank order attached to the form. If the request for a fee waiver is denied, and if the court instead orders payment by installments, the court or clerk will prepare the order with the correct fee amount.

OFFICIAL FORMS								Form 4

Form 4. List of Creditors Holding 20 Largest Unsecured Claims

B 4 (Official Form 4) (12/07)

UNITED STATES BANKRUPTCY COURT

In re _____,   Case No. _____
				Debtor
							Chapter _____

LIST OF CREDITORS HOLDING 20 LARGEST UNSECURED CLAIMS

Following is the list of the debtor's creditors holding the 20 largest unsecured claims. The list is prepared in accordance with Fed. R. Bankr. P. 1007(d) for filing in this chapter 11 [or chapter 9] case. The list does not include (1) persons who come within the definition of "insider" set forth in 11 U.S.C. § 101, or (2) secured creditors unless the value of the collateral is such that the unsecured deficiency places the creditor among the holders of the 20 largest unsecured claims. If a minor child is one of the creditors holding the 20 largest unsecured claims, state the child's initials and the name and address of the child's parent or guardian, such as "A.B., a minor child, by John Doe, guardian." Do not disclose the child's name. See, 11 U.S.C. §112 and Fed. R. Bankr. P. 1007(m).

(1)	(2)	(3)	(4)	(5)
Name of creditor and complete mailing address, including zip code	Name, telephone number and complete mailing address, including zip code, of employee, agent, or department of creditor familiar with claim who may be contacted	Nature of claim (trade debt, bank loan, government contract, etc.)	Indicate if claim is contingent, unliquidated, disputed or subject to setoff	Amount of claim [if secured also state value of security]

Date: _____

_____
Debtor

[Declaration as in Form 2]

(Added Aug. 1, 1991; amended Mar. 16, 1993; Aug. 11, 2005, eff. Oct. 17, 2005; Dec. 1, 2007.)

ADVISORY COMMITTEE NOTES
1991 Enactment

This form is derived from former Official Form No. 9.

In conformity with Rule 1007(d) and in recognition of the notice function served by this list under Rule 4001, governmental units must be listed if they are among the creditors holding the 20 largest claims.

Rule 1008 requires all lists to be verified or contain an unsworn declaration conforming with 28 U.S.C. § 1746.

1993 Amendment

The form has been amended to delete reference to the specific subsection of 11 U.S.C. § 101 in connection with the definition of the term "insider." Section 101 of the Bankruptcy Code contains

Form 4   **OFFICIAL FORMS**

numerous definitions, and statutory amendments from time to time have resulted in the renumbering of many of its subsections. The more general reference will avoid the necessity to amend the form further in the event of future amendments to § 101.

2005 Amendment

The form is amended to direct that the name of any minor child not be disclosed. The amendment implements § 112 of the Code, which was added by the Bankruptcy Abuse Prevention and Consumer Protection Act of 2005, Pub. L. No. 109–8, 119 Stat. 23 (April 20, 2005).

2005–2007 Amendments

(The 2005–2007 Committee Note incorporates Committee Notes previously published in 2005.)

The form is amended to direct that the name of any minor child not be disclosed. The amendment implements § 112 of the Code, which was added by the Bankruptcy Abuse Prevention and Consumer Protection Act of 2005, Pub. L. No. 109–8, 119 Stat. 23 (April 20, 2005). In addition, the form is amended to add to the reference to Rule 1007(m) a direction to include for noticing purposes the name, address, and legal relationship to the child of "a person described" in that rule. Rule 1007(m) requires the person named to be someone on whom process would be served in an adversary proceeding against the child.

OFFICIAL FORMS   Form 5

Form 5. Involuntary Petition

B 5 (Official Form 5) (12/07)

UNITED STATES BANKRUPTCY COURT	INVOLUNTARY PETITION

IN RE (Name of Debtor – If Individual: Last, First, Middle)	ALL OTHER NAMES used by debtor in the last 8 years (Include married, maiden, and trade names.)

Last four digits of Social-Security or other Individual's Tax-I.D. No./Complete EIN (If more than one, state all.):

STREET ADDRESS OF DEBTOR (No. and street, city, state, and zip code)	MAILING ADDRESS OF DEBTOR (If different from street address)
COUNTY OF RESIDENCE OR PRINCIPAL PLACE OF BUSINESS ZIP CODE	ZIP CODE

LOCATION OF PRINCIPAL ASSETS OF BUSINESS DEBTOR (If different from previously listed addresses)

CHAPTER OF BANKRUPTCY CODE UNDER WHICH PETITION IS FILED
  ☐ Chapter 7   ☐ Chapter 11

INFORMATION REGARDING DEBTOR (Check applicable boxes)

Nature of Debts (Check one box.)	Type of Debtor (Form of Organization)	Nature of Business (Check one box.)
Petitioners believe: ☐ Debts are primarily consumer debts ☐ Debts are primarily business debts	☐ Individual (Includes Joint Debtor) ☐ Corporation (Includes LLC and LLP) ☐ Partnership ☐ Other (If debtor is not one of the above entities, check this box and state type of entity below.) _____	☐ Health Care Business ☐ Single Asset Real Estate as defined in 11 U.S.C. § 101(51)(B) ☐ Railroad ☐ Stockbroker ☐ Commodity Broker ☐ Clearing Bank ☐ Other

VENUE	FILING FEE (Check one box)
☐ Debtor has been domiciled or has had a residence, principal place of business, or principal assets in the District for 180 days immediately preceding the date of this petition or for a longer part of such 180 days than in any other District. ☐ A bankruptcy case concerning debtor's affiliate, general partner or partnership is pending in this District.	☐ Full Filing Fee attached ☐ Petitioner is a child support creditor or its representative, and the form specified in § 304(g) of the Bankruptcy Reform Act of 1994 is attached. *[If a child support creditor or its representative is a petitioner, and if the petitioner files the form specified in § 304(g) of the Bankruptcy Reform Act of 1994, no fee is required.]*

PENDING BANKRUPTCY CASE FILED BY OR AGAINST ANY PARTNER OR AFFILIATE OF THIS DEBTOR (Report information for any additional cases on attached sheets.)

Name of Debtor	Case Number	Date
Relationship	District	Judge

ALLEGATIONS (Check applicable boxes)	COURT USE ONLY

1. ☐ Petitioner(s) are eligible to file this petition pursuant to 11 U.S.C. § 303 (b).
2. ☐ The debtor is a person against whom an order for relief may be entered under title 11 of the United States Code.
3.a. ☐ The debtor is generally not paying such debtor's debts as they become due, unless such debts are the subject of a bona fide dispute as to liability or amount;
    or
  b. ☐ Within 120 days preceding the filing of this petition, a custodian, other than a trustee receiver, or agent appointed or authorized to take charge of less than substantially all of the property of the debtor for the purpose of enforcing a lien against such property, was appointed or took possession.

Form 5   **OFFICIAL FORMS**

B 5 (Official Form 5) (12/07) – Page 2   Name of Debtor _____

Case No. _____

TRANSFER OF CLAIM
☐ Check this box if there has been a transfer of any claim against the debtor by or to any petitioner. Attach all documents that evidence the transfer and any statements that are required under Bankruptcy Rule 1003(a).

REQUEST FOR RELIEF
Petitioner(s) request that an order for relief be entered against the debtor under the chapter of title 11, United States Code, specified in this petition. If any petitioner is a foreign representative appointed in a foreign proceeding, a certified copy of the order of the court granting recognition is attached.

Petitioner(s) declare under penalty of perjury that the foregoing is true and correct according to the best of their knowledge, information, and belief.

x_____	x_____
Signature of Petitioner or Representative (State title)	Signature of Attorney Date
Name of Petitioner Date Signed	Name of Attorney Firm (If any)
Name & Mailing Address of Individual Signing in Representative Capacity	Address
	Telephone No.

x_____	x_____
Signature of Petitioner or Representative (State title)	Signature of Attorney Date
Name of Petitioner Date Signed	Name of Attorney Firm (If any)
Name & Mailing Address of Individual Signing in Representative Capacity	Address
	Telephone No.

x_____	x_____
Signature of Petitioner or Representative (State title)	Signature of Attorney Date
Name of Petitioner Date Signed	Name of Attorney Firm (If any)
Name & Mailing Address of Individual Signing in Representative Capacity	Address
	Telephone No.

PETITIONING CREDITORS

Name and Address of Petitioner	Nature of Claim	Amount of Claim
Name and Address of Petitioner	Nature of Claim	Amount of Claim
Name and Address of Petitioner	Nature of Claim	Amount of Claim

Note: If there are more than three petitioners, attach additional sheets with the statement under penalty of perjury, each petitioner's signature under the statement and the name of attorney and petitioning creditor information in the format above.   Total Amount of Petitioners' Claims

_____ continuation sheets attached

(Added Aug. 1, 1991; and amended Dec. 1, 2002; Dec. 1, 2003; Aug. 11, 2005, eff. Oct. 17, 2005; Oct. 12 2006; Dec. 1, 2007.)

ADVISORY COMMITTEE NOTES

1991 Amendment

This form has been redesigned in a box format similar to that of Form 1. See Advisory Committee Note to Form 1.

OFFICIAL FORMS Form 5

The allegations required under § 303 are grouped together, and a separate section has been provided for additional allegations based upon the prohibitions and requirements set forth in Rule 1003(a) concerning transfer of claims by petitioning creditors. Petitioners may wish to supplement the allegations set forth in the form with a further statement of facts. Additional information concerning any allegation can be requested by the debtor as part of the discovery process.

Each petitioning creditor, by signing on the line provided, signs both the petition and the unsworn declaration which 28 U.S.C. § 1746 permits instead of verification. The addresses as well as the names of individuals signing the petition in a representative capacity are required, together with disclosure of which petitioner is represented by each signatory.

This form is intended to be used in every involuntary case, including that of a partnership. The separate form for a petition by a partner has been abrogated. Pursuant to § 303(b)(3)(A) of the Code, a petition by fewer than all of the general partners seeking an order for relief with respect to the partnership is treated as an involuntary petition. Such a petition is adversarial in character because not all of the partners are joining in the petition.

Section 303(b)(3)(B) permits a petition against the partnership if relief has been ordered under the Code with respect to all of the general partners. In that event, the petition may be filed by a general partner, a trustee of a general partner's estate, or a creditor of the partnership. This form may be adapted for use in that type of case.

28 U.S.C. § 1408(1) specifies the proper venue alternatives for all persons, including partnerships, as domicile, residence, principal place of business, or location of principal assets. Venue also may be based on a pending case commenced by an affiliate, general partner, or partnership pursuant to 28 U.S.C. § 1408(2). Both options are set forth in the block labeled "Venue."

28 U.S.C. § 1746 permits the unsworn declaration instead of a verification. See Committee Note to Form 2.

1992 Amendment

The form has been amended to require the dating of signatures.

2002 Amendment

The form is amended to give notice that no filing fee is required if a child support creditor or its representative is a petitioner, and if the petitioner also files a form detailing the child support debt, its status, and other characteristics, as specified in § 304(g) of the Bankruptcy Reform Act of 1994, Pub. L. No. 103–394, 108 Stat. 4106 (Oct. 22, 1994).

2003 Amendment

The form is amended to require the petitioner to disclose the debtor's employer identification number, if any, and only the last four digits of the debtor's social security number to afford greater privacy to the individual debtor, whose bankruptcy case records may be available on the Internet. The form also is amended to delete the request for information concerning the "Type of Business," as this data no longer is collected for statistical purposes.

2005 Amendment

The form has been amended to delete statistical information no longer required and to add "as to liability or amount" to the language concerning debts that are the subject of a bona fide dispute, in conformity with § 303 of the Code as amended by the Bankruptcy Abuse Prevention and Consumer Protection Act of 2005, Pub. L. No. 109–8, 119 Stat. 23 (April 20, 2005). The petitioning creditors must now provide, to the extent known to them, all other names used by the debtor during the 8 years, rather than 6 years, before the filing of the petition. A new check box is provided for the petitioning creditors to identify the debtor that is a "health care business" as defined in § 101 of the Code, thereby alerting the court and the United States trustee of the necessity under § 333 to appoint an ombudsman to represent the interests of the patients of the health care business. These amendments also implement the 2005 amendments to the Code. A new checkbox also is provided for a "clearing bank," which may become a debtor upon the filing of a petition at the direction of the Board of Governors of the Federal Reserve System; this addition conforms to an amendment to § 109(b)(2) of the Code which was enacted in 2000.

2006 Amendment

The section of the form labeled "Information Regarding Debtor" is amended to facilitate, to the extent available in an involuntary case, the collection of the same statistical information that is requested

Form 5   **OFFICIAL FORMS**

in a voluntary case. Accordingly, information about whether the debtor is an individual, a corporation, or some other type of entity is separated from the checklist of types of debtors, such as health care businesses and railroads, concerning which the Code provides for specialized treatment.

2005–2007 Amendments

(The 2005–2007 Committee Note incorporates Committee Notes previously published in 2005 and 2006.)

The form has been amended to delete statistical information about the debtor that no longer is required, and to substitute checkboxes similar to those on the voluntary petition form. The form also is amended to add "as to liability or amount" to the language concerning debts that are the subject of a bona fide dispute, in conformity with § 303 of the Code as amended by the Bankruptcy Abuse Prevention and Consumer Protection Act of 2005, Pub. L. No. 109–8, 119 Stat. 23 (April 20, 2005). The petitioning creditors must now provide, to the extent known to them, all other names used by the debtor during the 8 years, rather than 6 years, before the filing of the petition. In conformity with Rule 9037, the petitioning creditors are directed to provide only the last four digits of any individual's tax-identification number. A new checkbox is provided for the petitioning creditors to identify the debtor that is a "health care business" as defined in § 101 of the Code, thereby alerting the court and the United States trustee of the necessity under § 333 of the Code to appoint an ombudsman to represent the interests of the patients of the health care business. These amendments also implement the 2005 amendments to the Code. A new checkbox also is provided for a "clearing bank," which may become a debtor upon the filing of a petition at the direction of the Board of Governors of the Federal Reserve System; this addition conforms to an amendment to § 109(b)(2) of the Code, which was enacted in 2000.

OFFICIAL FORMS — Form B6

Form 6. Schedules

Form B6

B6 Cover (Form 6 Cover) (12/07)

FORM 6. SCHEDULES

Summary of Schedules
Statistical Summary of Certain Liabilities and Related Data (28 U.S.C. § 159)

Schedule A - Real Property
Schedule B - Personal Property
Schedule C - Property Claimed as Exempt
Schedule D - Creditors Holding Secured Claims
Schedule E - Creditors Holding Unsecured Priority Claims
Schedule F - Creditors Holding Unsecured Nonpriority Claims
Schedule G - Executory Contracts and Unexpired Leases
Schedule H - Codebtors
Schedule I - Current Income of Individual Debtor(s)
Schedule J - Current Expenditures of Individual Debtors(s)

Unsworn Declaration Under Penalty of Perjury

GENERAL INSTRUCTIONS: The first page of the debtor's schedules and the first page of any amendments thereto must contain a caption as in Form 16B. Subsequent pages should be identified with the debtor's name and case number. If the schedules are filed with the petition, the case number should be left blank.

Schedules D, E, and F have been designed for the listing of each claim only once. Even when a claim is secured only in part or entitled to priority only in part, it still should be listed only once. A claim which is secured in whole or in part should be listed on Schedule D only, and a claim which is entitled to priority in whole or in part should be listed on Schedule E only. Do not list the same claim twice. If a creditor has more than one claim, such as claims arising from separate transactions, each claim should be scheduled separately.

Review the specific instructions for each schedule before completing the schedule.

Form B6   OFFICIAL FORMS

B 6 Summary (Official Form 6 - Summary) (12/14)

UNITED STATES BANKRUPTCY COURT

In re _____,   Case No. _____
                Debtor
                                                    Chapter _____

SUMMARY OF SCHEDULES

Indicate as to each schedule whether that schedule is attached and state the number of pages in each. Report the totals from Schedules A, B, D, E, F, I, and J in the boxes provided. Add the amounts from Schedules A and B to determine the total amount of the debtor's assets. Add the amounts of all claims from Schedules D, E, and F to determine the total amount of the debtor's liabilities. Individual debtors also must complete the "Statistical Summary of Certain Liabilities and Related Data" if they file a case under chapter 7, 11, or 13.

NAME OF SCHEDULE	ATTACHED (YES/NO)	NO. OF SHEETS	ASSETS	LIABILITIES	OTHER
A - Real Property			$		
B - Personal Property			$		
C - Property Claimed as Exempt					
D - Creditors Holding Secured Claims				$	
E - Creditors Holding Unsecured Priority Claims (Total of Claims on Schedule E)				$	
F - Creditors Holding Unsecured Nonpriority Claims				$	
G - Executory Contracts and Unexpired Leases					
H - Codebtors					
I - Current Income of Individual Debtor(s)					$
J - Current Expenditures of Individual Debtors(s)					$
TOTAL			$	$	

OFFICIAL FORMS   Form B6

B 6 Summary (Official Form 6 - Summary) (12/14)

UNITED STATES BANKRUPTCY COURT

In re _____,   Case No. _____
            Debtor
                                                   Chapter _____

SUMMARY OF SCHEDULES

Indicate as to each schedule whether that schedule is attached and state the number of pages in each. Report the totals from Schedules A, B, D, E, F, I, and J in the boxes provided. Add the amounts from Schedules A and B to determine the total amount of the debtor's assets. Add the amounts of all claims from Schedules D, E, and F to determine the total amount of the debtor's liabilities. Individual debtors also must complete the "Statistical Summary of Certain Liabilities and Related Data" if they file a case under chapter 7, 11, or 13.

NAME OF SCHEDULE	ATTACHED (YES/NO)	NO. OF SHEETS	ASSETS	LIABILITIES	OTHER
A - Real Property			$		
B - Personal Property			$		
C - Property Claimed as Exempt					
D - Creditors Holding Secured Claims				$	
E - Creditors Holding Unsecured Priority Claims (Total of Claims on Schedule E)				$	
F - Creditors Holding Unsecured Nonpriority Claims				$	
G - Executory Contracts and Unexpired Leases					
H - Codebtors					
I - Current Income of Individual Debtor(s)					$
J - Current Expenditures of Individual Debtors(s)					$
TOTAL			$	$	

Form B6   **OFFICIAL FORMS**

B 6 Summary (Official Form 6 - Summary) (12/14)

UNITED STATES BANKRUPTCY COURT

In re _____,   Case No. _____
            Debtor
                                          Chapter _____

STATISTICAL SUMMARY OF CERTAIN LIABILITIES AND RELATED DATA (28 U.S.C. § 159)

If you are an individual debtor whose debts are primarily consumer debts, as defined in § 101(8) of the Bankruptcy Code (11 U.S.C. § 101(8)), filing a case under chapter 7, 11 or 13, you must report all information requested below.

☐ Check this box if you are an individual debtor whose debts are NOT primarily consumer debts. You are not required to report any information here.

This information is for statistical purposes only under 28 U.S.C. § 159.

Summarize the following types of liabilities, as reported in the Schedules, and total them.

Type of Liability	Amount
Domestic Support Obligations (from Schedule E)	$
Taxes and Certain Other Debts Owed to Governmental Units (from Schedule E)	$
Claims for Death or Personal Injury While Debtor Was Intoxicated (from Schedule E) (whether disputed or undisputed)	$
Student Loan Obligations (from Schedule F)	$
Domestic Support, Separation Agreement, and Divorce Decree Obligations Not Reported on Schedule E	$
Obligations to Pension or Profit-Sharing, and Other Similar Obligations (from Schedule F)	$
TOTAL	$

State the following:

Average Income (from Schedule I, Line 12)	$
Average Expenses (from Schedule J, Line 22)	$
Current Monthly Income (from Form 22A-1 Line 11; **OR**, Form 22B Line 14; **OR**, Form 22C-1 Line 14)	$

State the following:

1. Total from Schedule D, "UNSECURED PORTION, IF ANY" column		$
2. Total from Schedule E, "AMOUNT ENTITLED TO PRIORITY" column.	$	
3. Total from Schedule E, "AMOUNT NOT ENTITLED TO PRIORITY, IF ANY" column		$
4. Total from Schedule F		$
5. Total of non-priority unsecured debt (sum of 1, 3, and 4)		$

OFFICIAL FORMS   Form B6A

Form B6A

B6A (Official Form 6A) (12/07)

In re _____,   Case No. _____
       Debtor   (If known)

SCHEDULE A - REAL PROPERTY

Except as directed below, list all real property in which the debtor has any legal, equitable, or future interest, including all property owned as a co-tenant, community property, or in which the debtor has a life estate. Include any property in which the debtor holds rights and powers exercisable for the debtor's own benefit. If the debtor is married, state whether the husband, wife, both, or the marital community own the property by placing an "H," "W," "J," or "C" in the column labeled "Husband, Wife, Joint, or Community." If the debtor holds no interest in real property, write "None" under "Description and Location of Property."

Do not include interests in executory contracts and unexpired leases on this schedule. List them in Schedule G - Executory Contracts and Unexpired Leases.

If an entity claims to have a lien or hold a secured interest in any property, state the amount of the secured claim. See Schedule D. If no entity claims to hold a secured interest in the property, write "None" in the column labeled "Amount of Secured Claim."

If the debtor is an individual or if a joint petition is filed, state the amount of any exemption claimed in the property only in Schedule C - Property Claimed as Exempt.

DESCRIPTION AND LOCATION OF PROPERTY	NATURE OF DEBTOR'S INTEREST IN PROPERTY	HUSBAND, WIFE, JOINT, OR COMMUNITY	CURRENT VALUE OF DEBTOR'S INTEREST IN PROPERTY, WITHOUT DEDUCTING ANY SECURED CLAIM OR EXEMPTION	AMOUNT OF SECURED CLAIM

Total▶ _____

(Report also on Summary of Schedules.)

Form B6B

Form B6B

OFFICIAL FORMS

B 6B (Official Form 6B) (12/07)

In re _____,   Case No. _____
            Debtor   (If known)

SCHEDULE B - PERSONAL PROPERTY

Except as directed below, list all personal property of the debtor of whatever kind. If the debtor has no property in one or more of the categories, place an "x" in the appropriate position in the column labeled "None." If additional space is needed in any category, attach a separate sheet properly identified with the case name, case number, and the number of the category. If the debtor is married, state whether the husband, wife, both, or the marital community own the property by placing an "H," "W," "J," or "C" in the column labeled "Husband, Wife, Joint, or Community." If the debtor is an individual or a joint petition is filed, state the amount of any exemptions claimed only in Schedule C - Property Claimed as Exempt.

Do not list interests in executory contracts and unexpired leases on this schedule. List them in Schedule G - Executory Contracts and Unexpired Leases.

If the property is being held for the debtor by someone else, state that person's name and address under "Description and Location of Property." If the property is being held for a minor child, simply state the child's initials and the name and address of the child's parent or guardian, such as "A.B., a minor child, by John Doe, guardian." Do not disclose the child's name. See, 11 U.S.C. §112 and Fed. R. Bankr. P. 1007(m).

TYPE OF PROPERTY	N O N E	DESCRIPTION AND LOCATION OF PROPERTY	HUSBAND, WIFE, JOINT, OR COMMUNITY	CURRENT VALUE OF DEBTOR'S INTEREST IN PROPERTY, WITHOUT DEDUCTING ANY SECURED CLAIM OR EXEMPTION
1. Cash on hand.				
2. Checking, savings or other financial accounts, certificates of deposit or shares in banks, savings and loan, thrift, building and loan, and homestead associations, or credit unions, brokerage houses, or cooperatives.				
3. Security deposits with public utilities, telephone companies, landlords, and others.				
4. Household goods and furnishings, including audio, video, and computer equipment.				
5. Books; pictures and other art objects; antiques; stamp, coin, record, tape, compact disc, and other collections or collectibles.				
6. Wearing apparel.				
7. Furs and jewelry.				
8. Firearms and sports, photographic, and other hobby equipment.				
9. Interests in insurance policies. Name insurance company of each policy and itemize surrender or refund value of each.				
10. Annuities. Itemize and name each issuer.				
11. Interests in an education IRA as defined in 26 U.S.C. § 530(b)(1) or under a qualified State tuition plan as defined in 26 U.S.C. § 529(b)(1). Give particulars. (File separately the record(s) of any such interest(s). 11 U.S.C. § 521(c).)				

OFFICIAL FORMS　　　　　　　　　　　　　　　　　　　　Form B6B

B 6B (Official Form 6B) (12/07) -- Cont.

In re _____,　　　Case No. _____
　　　　　　　Debtor　　　　　　　　　　　　　　　　　　　　(If known)

SCHEDULE B - PERSONAL PROPERTY
(Continuation Sheet)

TYPE OF PROPERTY	N O N E	DESCRIPTION AND LOCATION OF PROPERTY	HUSBAND, WIFE, JOINT, OR COMMUNITY	CURRENT VALUE OF DEBTOR'S INTEREST IN PROPERTY, WITHOUT DEDUCTING ANY SECURED CLAIM OR EXEMPTION
12. Interests in IRA, ERISA, Keogh, or other pension or profit sharing plans. Give particulars.				
13. Stock and interests in incorporated and unincorporated businesses. Itemize.				
14. Interests in partnerships or joint ventures. Itemize.				
15. Government and corporate bonds and other negotiable and non-negotiable instruments.				
16. Accounts receivable.				
17. Alimony, maintenance, support, and property settlements to which the debtor is or may be entitled. Give particulars.				
18. Other liquidated debts owed to debtor including tax refunds. Give particulars.				
19. Equitable or future interests, life estates, and rights or powers exercisable for the benefit of the debtor other than those listed in Schedule A – Real Property.				
20. Contingent and noncontingent interests in estate of a decedent, death benefit plan, life insurance policy, or trust.				
21. Other contingent and unliquidated claims of every nature, including tax refunds, counterclaims of the debtor, and rights to setoff claims. Give estimated value of each.				

823

Form B6B   OFFICIAL FORMS

B 6B (Official Form 6B) (12/07) -- Cont.

In re _____,   Case No. _____
              Debtor   (If known)

SCHEDULE B - PERSONAL PROPERTY
(Continuation Sheet)

TYPE OF PROPERTY	NONE	DESCRIPTION AND LOCATION OF PROPERTY	HUSBAND, WIFE, JOINT, OR COMMUNITY	CURRENT VALUE OF DEBTOR'S INTEREST IN PROPERTY, WITHOUT DEDUCTING ANY SECURED CLAIM OR EXEMPTION
22. Patents, copyrights, and other intellectual property. Give particulars.				
23. Licenses, franchises, and other general intangibles. Give particulars.				
24. Customer lists or other compilations containing personally identifiable information (as defined in 11 U.S.C. § 101(41A)) provided to the debtor by individuals in connection with obtaining a product or service from the debtor primarily for personal, family, or household purposes.				
25. Automobiles, trucks, trailers, and other vehicles and accessories.				
26. Boats, motors, and accessories.				
27. Aircraft and accessories.				
28. Office equipment, furnishings, and supplies.				
29. Machinery, fixtures, equipment, and supplies used in business.				
30. Inventory.				
31. Animals.				
32. Crops - growing or harvested. Give particulars.				
33. Farming equipment and implements.				
34. Farm supplies, chemicals, and feed.				
35. Other personal property of any kind not already listed. Itemize.				

_____ continuation sheets attached   Total▶ $ _____
(Include amounts from any continuation sheets attached. Report total also on Summary of Schedules.)

OFFICIAL FORMS   Form B6C

Form B6C

B 6C (Official Form 6C) (04/10)

In re _____ ,   Case No. _____
               Debtor   *(If known)*

SCHEDULE C - PROPERTY CLAIMED AS EXEMPT

Debtor claims the exemptions to which debtor is entitled under: ☐ Check if debtor claims a homestead exemption that exceeds
(Check one box) $146,450.*
☐ 11 U.S.C. § 522(b)(2)
☐ 11 U.S.C. § 522(b)(3)

DESCRIPTION OF PROPERTY	SPECIFY LAW PROVIDING EACH EXEMPTION	VALUE OF CLAIMED EXEMPTION	CURRENT VALUE OF PROPERTY WITHOUT DEDUCTING EXEMPTION

* *Amount subject to adjustment on 4/1/13, and every three years thereafter with respect to cases commenced on or after the date of adjustment.*

Form B6D

Form B6D

OFFICIAL FORMS

B 6D (Official Form 6D) (12/07)

In re _____, Case No. _____
　　　　　Debtor　　　　　　　　　　　　　　　　　(If known)

SCHEDULE D - CREDITORS HOLDING SECURED CLAIMS

　　　　State the name, mailing address, including zip code, and last four digits of any account number of all entities holding claims secured by property of the debtor as of the date of filing of the petition. The complete account number of any account the debtor has with the creditor is useful to the trustee and the creditor and may be provided if the debtor chooses to do so. List creditors holding all types of secured interests such as judgment liens, garnishments, statutory liens, mortgages, deeds of trust, and other security interests.
　　　　List creditors in alphabetical order to the extent practicable. If a minor child is the creditor, state the child's initials and the name and address of the child's parent or guardian, such as "A.B., a minor child, by John Doe, guardian." Do not disclose the child's name. See, 11 U.S.C. §112 and Fed. R. Bankr. P. 1007(m). If all secured creditors will not fit on this page, use the continuation sheet provided.
　　　　If any entity other than a spouse in a joint case may be jointly liable on a claim, place an "X" in the column labeled "Codebtor," include the entity on the appropriate schedule of creditors, and complete Schedule H – Codebtors. If a joint petition is filed, state whether the husband, wife, both of them, or the marital community may be liable on each claim by placing an "H," "W," "J," or "C" in the column labeled "Husband, Wife, Joint, or Community."
　　　　If the claim is contingent, place an "X" in the column labeled "Contingent." If the claim is unliquidated, place an "X" in the column labeled "Unliquidated." If the claim is disputed, place an "X" in the column labeled "Disputed." (You may need to place an "X" in more than one of these three columns.)
　　　　Total the columns labeled "Amount of Claim Without Deducting Value of Collateral" and "Unsecured Portion, if Any" in the boxes labeled "Total(s)" on the last sheet of the completed schedule. Report the total from the column labeled "Amount of Claim Without Deducting Value of Collateral" also on the Summary of Schedules and, if the debtor is an individual with primarily consumer debts, report the total from the column labeled "Unsecured Portion, if Any" on the Statistical Summary of Certain Liabilities and Related Data.

☐　Check this box if debtor has no creditors holding secured claims to report on this Schedule D.

CREDITOR'S NAME AND MAILING ADDRESS INCLUDING ZIP CODE AND AN ACCOUNT NUMBER (See Instructions Above.)	CODEBTOR	HUSBAND, WIFE, JOINT, OR COMMUNITY	DATE CLAIM WAS INCURRED, NATURE OF LIEN, AND DESCRIPTION AND VALUE OF PROPERTY SUBJECT TO LIEN	CONTINGENT	UNLIQUIDATED	DISPUTED	AMOUNT OF CLAIM WITHOUT DEDUCTING VALUE OF COLLATERAL	UNSECURED PORTION, IF ANY
ACCOUNT NO.								
			VALUE $					
ACCOUNT NO.								
			VALUE $					
ACCOUNT NO.								
			VALUE $					
_____ continuation sheets attached			Subtotal ▶ (Total of this page)				$	$
			Total ▶ (Use only on last page)				$	$
							(Report also on Summary of Schedules.)	(If applicable, report also on Statistical Summary of Certain Liabilities and Related Data.)

OFFICIAL FORMS Form B6D

B 6D (Official Form 6D) (12/07) – Cont.

In re _____, Case No. _____
                Debtor   (if known)

SCHEDULE D - CREDITORS HOLDING SECURED CLAIMS
(Continuation Sheet)

CREDITOR'S NAME AND MAILING ADDRESS INCLUDING ZIP CODE AND AN ACCOUNT NUMBER (See Instructions Above.)	CODEBTOR	HUSBAND, WIFE, JOINT, OR COMMUNITY	DATE CLAIM WAS INCURRED, NATURE OF LIEN, AND DESCRIPTION AND VALUE OF PROPERTY SUBJECT TO LIEN	CONTINGENT	UNLIQUIDATED	DISPUTED	AMOUNT OF CLAIM WITHOUT DEDUCTING VALUE OF COLLATERAL	UNSECURED PORTION, IF ANY
ACCOUNT NO.			VALUE $					
ACCOUNT NO.			VALUE $					
ACCOUNT NO.			VALUE $					
ACCOUNT NO.			VALUE $					
ACCOUNT NO.			VALUE $					

Sheet no.____ of ____ continuation sheets attached to Schedule of Creditors Holding Secured Claims

Subtotal (s) ▶ (Total(s) of this page) $ _____ $ _____

Total(s) ▶ (Use only on last page) $ _____ $ _____

(Report also on Summary of Schedules.)   (If applicable, report also on Statistical Summary of Certain Liabilities and Related Data.)

Form B6E OFFICIAL FORMS

Form B6E

B 6E (Official Form 6E) (04/10)

In re _____, Case No._____
           Debtor   (if known)

SCHEDULE E - CREDITORS HOLDING UNSECURED PRIORITY CLAIMS

A complete list of claims entitled to priority, listed separately by type of priority, is to be set forth on the sheets provided. Only holders of unsecured claims entitled to priority should be listed in this schedule. In the boxes provided on the attached sheets, state the name, mailing address, including zip code, and last four digits of the account number, if any, of all entities holding priority claims against the debtor or the property of the debtor, as of the date of the filing of the petition. Use a separate continuation sheet for each type of priority and label each with the type of priority.

The complete account number of any account the debtor has with the creditor is useful to the trustee and the creditor and may be provided if the debtor chooses to do so. If a minor child is a creditor, state the child's initials and the name and address of the child's parent or guardian, such as "A.B., a minor child, by John Doe, guardian." Do not disclose the child's name. See, 11 U.S.C. §112 and Fed. R. Bankr. P. 1007(m).

If any entity other than a spouse in a joint case may be jointly liable on a claim, place an "X" in the column labeled "Codebtor," include the entity on the appropriate schedule of creditors, and complete Schedule H-Codebtors. If a joint petition is filed, state whether the husband, wife, both of them, or the marital community may be liable on each claim by placing an "H," "W," "J," or "C" in the column labeled "Husband, Wife, Joint, or Community." If the claim is contingent, place an "X" in the column labeled "Contingent." If the claim is unliquidated, place an "X" in the column labeled "Unliquidated." If the claim is disputed, place an "X" in the column labeled "Disputed." (You may need to place an "X" in more than one of these three columns.)

Report the total of claims listed on each sheet in the box labeled "Subtotals" on each sheet. Report the total of all claims listed on this Schedule E in the box labeled "Total" on the last sheet of the completed schedule. Report this total also on the Summary of Schedules.

Report the total of amounts entitled to priority listed on each sheet in the box labeled "Subtotals" on each sheet. Report the total of all amounts entitled to priority listed on this Schedule E in the box labeled "Totals" on the last sheet of the completed schedule. Individual debtors with primarily consumer debts report this total also on the Statistical Summary of Certain Liabilities and Related Data.

Report the total of amounts not entitled to priority listed on each sheet in the box labeled "Subtotals" on each sheet. Report the total of all amounts not entitled to priority listed on this Schedule E in the box labeled "Totals" on the last sheet of the completed schedule. Individual debtors with primarily consumer debts report this total also on the Statistical Summary of Certain Liabilities and Related Data.

☐ Check this box if debtor has no creditors holding unsecured priority claims to report on this Schedule E.

TYPES OF PRIORITY CLAIMS (Check the appropriate box(es) below if claims in that category are listed on the attached sheets.)

☐ **Domestic Support Obligations**

Claims for domestic support that are owed to or recoverable by a spouse, former spouse, or child of the debtor, or the parent, legal guardian, or responsible relative of such a child, or a governmental unit to whom such a domestic support claim has been assigned to the extent provided in 11 U.S.C. § 507(a)(1).

☐ **Extensions of credit in an involuntary case**

Claims arising in the ordinary course of the debtor's business or financial affairs after the commencement of the case but before the earlier of the appointment of a trustee or the order for relief. 11 U.S.C. § 507(a)(3).

☐ **Wages, salaries, and commissions**

Wages, salaries, and commissions, including vacation, severance, and sick leave pay owing to employees and commissions owing to qualifying independent sales representatives up to $11,725* per person earned within 180 days immediately preceding the filing of the original petition, or the cessation of business, whichever occurred first, to the extent provided in 11 U.S.C. § 507(a)(4).

☐ **Contributions to employee benefit plans**

Money owed to employee benefit plans for services rendered within 180 days immediately preceding the filing of the original petition, or the cessation of business, whichever occurred first, to the extent provided in 11 U.S.C. § 507(a)(5).

* Amount subject to adjustment on 4/01/13, and every three years thereafter with respect to cases commenced on or after the date of adjustment.

OFFICIAL FORMS   **Form B6E**

B 6E (Official Form 6E) (04/10) – Cont.

In re _____ , Case No. _____
             Debtor   (if known)

☐ **Certain farmers and fishermen**

Claims of certain farmers and fishermen, up to $5,775* per farmer or fisherman, against the debtor, as provided in 11 U.S.C. § 507(a)(6).

☐ **Deposits by individuals**

Claims of individuals up to $2,600* for deposits for the purchase, lease, or rental of property or services for personal, family, or household use, that were not delivered or provided. 11 U.S.C. § 507(a)(7).

☐ **Taxes and Certain Other Debts Owed to Governmental Units**

Taxes, customs duties, and penalties owing to federal, state, and local governmental units as set forth in 11 U.S.C. § 507(a)(8).

☐ **Commitments to Maintain the Capital of an Insured Depository Institution**

Claims based on commitments to the FDIC, RTC, Director of the Office of Thrift Supervision, Comptroller of the Currency, or Board of Governors of the Federal Reserve System, or their predecessors or successors, to maintain the capital of an insured depository institution. 11 U.S.C. § 507 (a)(9).

☐ **Claims for Death or Personal Injury While Debtor Was Intoxicated**

Claims for death or personal injury resulting from the operation of a motor vehicle or vessel while the debtor was intoxicated from using alcohol, a drug, or another substance. 11 U.S.C. § 507(a)(10).

* *Amounts are subject to adjustment on 4/01/13, and every three years thereafter with respect to cases commenced on or after the date of adjustment.*

_____ continuation sheets attached

Form B6E   **OFFICIAL FORMS**

B 6E (Official Form 6E) (04/10) – Cont.

In re _____ , Case No. _____
          Debtor   (if known)

SCHEDULE E - CREDITORS HOLDING UNSECURED PRIORITY CLAIMS
(Continuation Sheet)

Type of Priority for Claims Listed on This Sheet _____

CREDITOR'S NAME, MAILING ADDRESS INCLUDING ZIP CODE, AND ACCOUNT NUMBER (*See instructions above.*)	CODEBTOR	HUSBAND, WIFE, JOINT, OR COMMUNITY	DATE CLAIM WAS INCURRED AND CONSIDERATION FOR CLAIM	CONTINGENT	UNLIQUIDATED	DISPUTED	AMOUNT OF CLAIM	AMOUNT ENTITLED TO PRIORITY	AMOUNT NOT ENTITLED TO PRIORITY, IF ANY
Account No.									
Account No.									
Account No.									
Account No.									

Sheet no. ___ of ___ continuation sheets attached to Schedule of Creditors Holding Priority Claims

Subtotals▶ (Totals of this page) $ _____ $ _____

Total▶ (Use only on last page of the completed Schedule E. Report also on the Summary of Schedules.) $ _____

Totals▶ (Use only on last page of the completed Schedule E. If applicable, report also on the Statistical Summary of Certain Liabilities and Related Data.) $ _____ $ _____

OFFICIAL FORMS   **Form B6F**

Form B6F

B 6F (Official Form 6F) (12/07)

In re _____,   Case No. _____
         Debtor   (if known)

SCHEDULE F - CREDITORS HOLDING UNSECURED NONPRIORITY CLAIMS

State the name, mailing address, including zip code, and last four digits of any account number, of all entities holding unsecured claims without priority against the debtor or the property of the debtor, as of the date of filing of the petition. The complete account number of any account the debtor has with the creditor is useful to the trustee and the creditor and may be provided if the debtor chooses to do so. If a minor child is a creditor, state the child's initials and the name and address of the child's parent or guardian, such as "A.B., a minor child, by John Doe, guardian." Do not disclose the child's name. See, 11 U.S.C. §112 and Fed. R. Bankr. P. 1007(m). Do not include claims listed in Schedules D and E. If all creditors will not fit on this page, use the continuation sheet provided.

If any entity other than a spouse in a joint case may be jointly liable on a claim, place an "X" in the column labeled "Codebtor," include the entity on the appropriate schedule of creditors, and complete Schedule H - Codebtors. If a joint petition is filed, state whether the husband, wife, both of them, or the marital community may be liable on each claim by placing an "H," "W," "J," or "C" in the column labeled "Husband, Wife, Joint, or Community."

If the claim is contingent, place an "X" in the column labeled "Contingent." If the claim is unliquidated, place an "X" in the column labeled "Unliquidated." If the claim is disputed, place an "X" in the column labeled "Disputed." (You may need to place an "X" in more than one of these three columns.)

Report the total of all claims listed on this schedule in the box labeled "Total" on the last sheet of the completed schedule. Report this total also on the Summary of Schedules and, if the debtor is an individual with primarily consumer debts, report this total also on the Statistical Summary of Certain Liabilities and Related Data..

☐ Check this box if debtor has no creditors holding unsecured claims to report on this Schedule F.

CREDITOR'S NAME, MAILING ADDRESS INCLUDING ZIP CODE, AND ACCOUNT NUMBER (See instructions above.)	CODEBTOR	HUSBAND, WIFE, JOINT, OR COMMUNITY	DATE CLAIM WAS INCURRED AND CONSIDERATION FOR CLAIM. IF CLAIM IS SUBJECT TO SETOFF, SO STATE.	CONTINGENT	UNLIQUIDATED	DISPUTED	AMOUNT OF CLAIM
ACCOUNT NO.							
ACCOUNT NO.							
ACCOUNT NO.							
ACCOUNT NO.							
						Subtotal ➤	$
_____ continuation sheets attached			Total ➤ (Use only on last page of the completed Schedule F.) (Report also on Summary of Schedules and, if applicable, on the Statistical Summary of Certain Liabilities and Related Data.)				$

Form B6F   **OFFICIAL FORMS**

B 6F (Official Form 6F) (12/07) - Cont.

In re _____, Case No. _____
      Debtor   (if known)

SCHEDULE F - CREDITORS HOLDING UNSECURED NONPRIORITY CLAIMS
(Continuation Sheet)

CREDITOR'S NAME, MAILING ADDRESS INCLUDING ZIP CODE, AND ACCOUNT NUMBER (See instructions above.)	CODEBTOR	HUSBAND, WIFE, JOINT, OR COMMUNITY	DATE CLAIM WAS INCURRED AND CONSIDERATION FOR CLAIM. IF CLAIM IS SUBJECT TO SETOFF, SO STATE.	CONTINGENT	UNLIQUIDATED	DISPUTED	AMOUNT OF CLAIM
ACCOUNT NO.							
ACCOUNT NO.							
ACCOUNT NO.							
ACCOUNT NO.							
ACCOUNT NO.							

Sheet no. ____ of ____ continuation sheets attached to Schedule of Creditors Holding Unsecured Nonpriority Claims

Subtotal➤ $

Total➤ $
(Use only on last page of the completed Schedule F.)
(Report also on Summary of Schedules and, if applicable on the Statistical Summary of Certain Liabilities and Related Data.)

OFFICIAL FORMS   Form B6G

Form B6G

B 6G (Official Form 6G) (12/07)

In re _____, Case No._____
           Debtor   (if known)

SCHEDULE G - EXECUTORY CONTRACTS AND UNEXPIRED LEASES

Describe all executory contracts of any nature and all unexpired leases of real or personal property. Include any timeshare interests. State nature of debtor's interest in contract, i.e., "Purchaser," "Agent," etc. State whether debtor is the lessor or lessee of a lease. Provide the names and complete mailing addresses of all other parties to each lease or contract described. If a minor child is a party to one of the leases or contracts, state the child's initials and the name and address of the child's parent or guardian, such as "A.B., a minor child, by John Doe, guardian." Do not disclose the child's name. See, 11 U.S.C. §112 and Fed. R. Bankr. P. 1007(m).

☐ Check this box if debtor has no executory contracts or unexpired leases.

NAME AND MAILING ADDRESS, INCLUDING ZIP CODE, OF OTHER PARTIES TO LEASE OR CONTRACT.	DESCRIPTION OF CONTRACT OR LEASE AND NATURE OF DEBTOR'S INTEREST. STATE WHETHER LEASE IS FOR NONRESIDENTIAL REAL PROPERTY. STATE CONTRACT NUMBER OF ANY GOVERNMENT CONTRACT.

Form B6H

Form B6H

OFFICIAL FORMS

B 6H (Official Form 6H) (12/07)

In re _____,   Case No. _____
         Debtor   (if known)

SCHEDULE H - CODEBTORS

Provide the information requested concerning any person or entity, other than a spouse in a joint case, that is also liable on any debts listed by the debtor in the schedules of creditors. Include all guarantors and co-signers. If the debtor resides or resided in a community property state, commonwealth, or territory (including Alaska, Arizona, California, Idaho, Louisiana, Nevada, New Mexico, Puerto Rico, Texas, Washington, or Wisconsin) within the eight-year period immediately preceding the commencement of the case, identify the name of the debtor's spouse and of any former spouse who resides or resided with the debtor in the community property state, commonwealth, or territory. Include all names used by the nondebtor spouse during the eight years immediately preceding the commencement of this case. If a minor child is a codebtor or a creditor, state the child's initials and the name and address of the child's parent or guardian, such as "A.B., a minor child, by John Doe, guardian." Do not disclose the child's name. See, 11 U.S.C. §112 and Fed. R. Bankr. P. 1007(m).

☐ Check this box if debtor has no codebtors.

NAME AND ADDRESS OF CODEBTOR	NAME AND ADDRESS OF CREDITOR

OFFICIAL FORMS   Form B6I

Form B6I

Fill in this information to identify your case:

Debtor 1 _____ _____ _____
    First Name   Middle Name   Last Name

Debtor 2 _____ _____ _____
(Spouse, if filing) First Name   Middle Name   Last Name

United States Bankruptcy Court for the: _____ District of _____

Case number _____
(If known)

Check if this is:
☐ An amended filing
☐ A supplement showing post-petition chapter 13 income as of the following date:
_____
MM / DD / YYYY

Official Form B 6I

Schedule I: Your Income

12/13

Be as complete and accurate as possible. If two married people are filing together (Debtor 1 and Debtor 2), both are equally responsible for supplying correct information. If you are married and not filing jointly, and your spouse is living with you, include information about your spouse. If you are separated and your spouse is not filing with you, do not include information about your spouse. If more space is needed, attach a separate sheet to this form. On the top of any additional pages, write your name and case number (if known). Answer every question.

Part 1: Describe Employment

1. Fill in your employment information.

   If you have more than one job, attach a separate page with information about additional employers.

   Include part-time, seasonal, or self-employed work.

   Occupation may include student or homemaker, if it applies.

	Debtor 1	Debtor 2 or non-filing spouse
Employment status	☐ Employed ☐ Not employed	☐ Employed ☐ Not employed
Occupation	_____	_____
Employer's name	_____	_____
Employer's address	_____ Number Street _____ _____ City State ZIP Code	_____ Number Street _____ _____ City State ZIP Code
How long employed there?	_____	_____

Part 2: Give Details About Monthly Income

Estimate monthly income as of the date you file this form. If you have nothing to report for any line, write $0 in the space. Include your non-filing spouse unless you are separated.

If you or your non-filing spouse have more than one employer, combine the information for all employers for that person on the lines below. If you need more space, attach a separate sheet to this form.

		For Debtor 1	For Debtor 2 or non-filing spouse
2. List monthly gross wages, salary, and commissions (before all payroll deductions). If not paid monthly, calculate what the monthly wage would be.	2.	$_____	$_____
3. Estimate and list monthly overtime pay.	3.	+ $_____	+ $_____
4. Calculate gross income. Add line 2 + line 3.	4.	$_____	$_____

Official Form B 6I   Schedule I: Your Income   page 1

Form B6I OFFICIAL FORMS

Debtor 1 _____ _____ _____   Case number (if known) _____
First Name   Middle Name   Last Name

	For Debtor 1	For Debtor 2 or non-filing spouse
Copy line 4 here .... → 4.	$_____	$_____

5. List all payroll deductions:

5a. Tax, Medicare, and Social Security deductions	5a.	$_____	$_____
5b. Mandatory contributions for retirement plans	5b.	$_____	$_____
5c. Voluntary contributions for retirement plans	5c.	$_____	$_____
5d. Required repayments of retirement fund loans	5d.	$_____	$_____
5e. Insurance	5e.	$_____	$_____
5f. Domestic support obligations	5f.	$_____	$_____
5g. Union dues	5g.	$_____	$_____
5h. Other deductions. Specify: _____	5h.	+$_____	+$_____

6. **Add the payroll deductions.** Add lines 5a + 5b + 5c + 5d + 5e +5f + 5g +5h.   6. $_____ $_____

7. **Calculate total monthly take-home pay.** Subtract line 6 from line 4.   7. $_____ $_____

8. List all other income regularly received:

   8a. **Net income from rental property and from operating a business, profession, or farm**
   Attach a statement for each property and business showing gross receipts, ordinary and necessary business expenses, and the total monthly net income.   8a. $_____ $_____

   8b. **Interest and dividends**   8b. $_____ $_____

   8c. **Family support payments that you, a non-filing spouse, or a dependent regularly receive**
   Include alimony, spousal support, child support, maintenance, divorce settlement, and property settlement.   8c. $_____ $_____

   8d. **Unemployment compensation**   8d. $_____ $_____

   8e. **Social Security**   8e. $_____ $_____

   8f. **Other government assistance that you regularly receive**
   Include cash assistance and the value (if known) of any non-cash assistance that you receive, such as food stamps (benefits under the Supplemental Nutrition Assistance Program) or housing subsidies.
   Specify: _____   8f. $_____ $_____

   8g. **Pension or retirement income**   8g. $_____ $_____

   8h. **Other monthly income.** Specify: _____   8h.   +$_____   +$_____

9. **Add all other income.** Add lines 8a + 8b + 8c + 8d + 8e + 8f +8g + 8h.   9. $_____ $_____

10. **Calculate monthly income.** Add line 7 + line 9.
    Add the entries in line 10 for Debtor 1 and Debtor 2 or non-filing spouse.   10. $_____ + $_____ = $_____

11. State all other regular contributions to the expenses that you list in *Schedule J*.
    Include contributions from an unmarried partner, members of your household, your dependents, your roommates, and other friends or relatives.
    Do not include any amounts already included in lines 2-10 or amounts that are not available to pay expenses listed in *Schedule J*.
    Specify: _____   11.   +$_____

12. Add the amount in the last column of line 10 to the amount in line 11. The result is the combined monthly income.
    Write that amount on the *Summary of Schedules* and *Statistical Summary of Certain Liabilities and Related Data*, if it applies   12. $_____
    Combined monthly income

13. Do you expect an increase or decrease within the year after you file this form?
    ☐ No.
    ☐ Yes. Explain: _____

Official Form B 6I   Schedule I: Your Income   page 2

OFFICIAL FORMS   Form B6J

Form B6J

Debtor 1 _____   Case number (if known) _____
         First Name   Middle Name   Last Name

		For Debtor 1	For Debtor 2 or non-filing spouse
Copy line 4 here .... →	4.	$_____	$_____

5. List all payroll deductions:

5a. Tax, Medicare, and Social Security deductions	5a.	$_____	$_____
5b. Mandatory contributions for retirement plans	5b.	$_____	$_____
5c. Voluntary contributions for retirement plans	5c.	$_____	$_____
5d. Required repayments of retirement fund loans	5d.	$_____	$_____
5e. Insurance	5e.	$_____	$_____
5f. Domestic support obligations	5f.	$_____	$_____
5g. Union dues	5g.	$_____	$_____
5h. Other deductions. Specify: _____	5h. +	$_____	+ $_____

6. **Add the payroll deductions.** Add lines 5a + 5b + 5c + 5d + 5e + 5f + 5g + 5h.   6. $_____ $_____

7. **Calculate total monthly take-home pay.** Subtract line 6 from line 4.   7. $_____ $_____

8. List all other income regularly received:

   8a. **Net income from rental property and from operating a business, profession, or farm**
       Attach a statement for each property and business showing gross receipts, ordinary and necessary business expenses, and the total monthly net income.   8a. $_____ $_____

   8b. **Interest and dividends**   8b. $_____ $_____

   8c. **Family support payments that you, a non-filing spouse, or a dependent regularly receive**
       Include alimony, spousal support, child support, maintenance, divorce settlement, and property settlement.   8c. $_____ $_____

   8d. **Unemployment compensation**   8d. $_____ $_____

   8e. **Social Security**   8e. $_____ $_____

   8f. **Other government assistance that you regularly receive**
       Include cash assistance and the value (if known) of any non-cash assistance that you receive, such as food stamps (benefits under the Supplemental Nutrition Assistance Program) or housing subsidies.
       Specify: _____   8f. $_____ $_____

   8g. **Pension or retirement income**   8g. $_____ $_____

   8h. **Other monthly income.** Specify: _____   8h. + $_____   + $_____

9. **Add all other income.** Add lines 8a + 8b + 8c + 8d + 8e + 8f + 8g + 8h.   9. $_____ $_____

10. **Calculate monthly income.** Add line 7 + line 9.
    Add the entries in line 10 for Debtor 1 and Debtor 2 or non-filing spouse.   10. $_____ + $_____ = $_____

11. State all other regular contributions to the expenses that you list in *Schedule J*.
    Include contributions from an unmarried partner, members of your household, your dependents, your roommates, and other friends or relatives.
    Do not include any amounts already included in lines 2-10 or amounts that are not available to pay expenses listed in *Schedule J*.
    Specify: _____   11. + $_____

12. Add the amount in the last column of line 10 to the amount in line 11. The result is the combined monthly income.
    Write that amount on the *Summary of Schedules* and *Statistical Summary of Certain Liabilities and Related Data*, if it applies   12. $_____
    Combined monthly income

13. **Do you expect an increase or decrease within the year after you file this form?**
    ☐ No.
    ☐ Yes. Explain: _____

Official Form B 6I   Schedule I: Your Income   page 2

837

Form B6J   OFFICIAL FORMS

Debtor 1 _____   Case number (if known) _____
         First Name Middle Name Last Name

                                                              Your expenses

5. Additional mortgage payments for your residence, such as home equity loans   5. $_____

6. Utilities:
    6a. Electricity, heat, natural gas   6a. $_____
    6b. Water, sewer, garbage collection   6b. $_____
    6c. Telephone, cell phone, Internet, satellite, and cable services   6c. $_____
    6d. Other. Specify: _____   6d. $_____

7. Food and housekeeping supplies   7. $_____
8. Childcare and children's education costs   8. $_____
9. Clothing, laundry, and dry cleaning   9. $_____
10. Personal care products and services   10. $_____
11. Medical and dental expenses   11. $_____
12. Transportation. Include gas, maintenance, bus or train fare.
    Do not include car payments.   12. $_____
13. Entertainment, clubs, recreation, newspapers, magazines, and books   13. $_____
14. Charitable contributions and religious donations   14. $_____

15. Insurance.
    Do not include insurance deducted from your pay or included in lines 4 or 20.
    15a. Life insurance   15a. $_____
    15b. Health insurance   15b. $_____
    15c. Vehicle insurance   15c. $_____
    15d. Other insurance. Specify: _____   15d. $_____

16. Taxes. Do not include taxes deducted from your pay or included in lines 4 or 20.
    Specify: _____   16. $_____

17. Installment or lease payments:
    17a. Car payments for Vehicle 1   17a. $_____
    17b. Car payments for Vehicle 2   17b. $_____
    17c. Other. Specify: _____   17c. $_____
    17d. Other. Specify: _____   17d. $_____

18. Your payments of alimony, maintenance, and support that you did not report as deducted
    from your pay on line 5, Schedule I, Your Income (Official Form B 6I).   18. $_____

19. Other payments you make to support others who do not live with you.
    Specify: _____   19. $_____

20. Other real property expenses not included in lines 4 or 5 of this form or on Schedule I: Your Income.
    20a. Mortgages on other property   20a. $_____
    20b. Real estate taxes   20b. $_____
    20c. Property, homeowner's, or renter's insurance   20c. $_____
    20d. Maintenance, repair, and upkeep expenses   20d. $_____
    20e. Homeowner's association or condominium dues   20e. $_____

Official Form B 6J   Schedule J: Your Expenses   page 2

OFFICIAL FORMS   **Form B6J**

Debtor 1 _____ Case number (if known) _____
         First Name   Middle Name   Last Name

21. **Other**. Specify: _____   21.   **+**$_____

22. **Your monthly expenses.** Add lines 4 through 21.
    The result is your monthly expenses.   22. $_____

23. **Calculate your monthly net income.**

    23a. Copy line 12 (*your combined monthly income*) from *Schedule I*.   23a. $_____

    23b. Copy your monthly expenses from line 22 above.   23b.   **−**$_____

    23c. Subtract your monthly expenses from your monthly income.
    The result is your *monthly net income*.   23c. $_____

24. **Do you expect an increase or decrease in your expenses within the year after you file this form?**

    For example, do you expect to finish paying for your car loan within the year or do you expect your mortgage payment to increase or decrease because of a modification to the terms of your mortgage?

    ☐ No.
    ☐ Yes.   Explain here:

Form 6　　　　　　　　　　　OFFICIAL FORMS

Form 6

B6 Declaration (Official Form 6 - Declaration) (12/07)

In re _____,　　　　Case No. _____
　　　　　　Debtor　　　　　　　　　　　　　　　　　　(if known)

DECLARATION CONCERNING DEBTOR'S SCHEDULES

DECLARATION UNDER PENALTY OF PERJURY BY INDIVIDUAL DEBTOR

I declare under penalty of perjury that I have read the foregoing summary and schedules, consisting of ____ sheets, and that they are true and correct to the best of my knowledge, information, and belief.

Date _____　　　　Signature: _____
　　　　　　　　　　　　　　　　　　　　　　　　　　　　　Debtor

Date _____　　　　Signature: _____
　　　　　　　　　　　　　　　　　　　　　　　　　　(Joint Debtor, if any)

　　　　　　　　　　　　　　　[If joint case, both spouses must sign.]

DECLARATION AND SIGNATURE OF NON-ATTORNEY BANKRUPTCY PETITION PREPARER (See 11 U.S.C. § 110)

I declare under penalty of perjury that: (1) I am a bankruptcy petition preparer as defined in 11 U.S.C. § 110; (2) I prepared this document for compensation and have provided the debtor with a copy of this document and the notices and information required under 11 U.S.C. §§ 110(b), 110(h) and 342(b); and, (3) if rules or guidelines have been promulgated pursuant to 11 U.S.C. § 110(h) setting a maximum fee for services chargeable by bankruptcy petition preparers, I have given the debtor notice of the maximum amount before preparing any document for filing for a debtor or accepting any fee from the debtor, as required by that section.

Printed or Typed Name and Title, if any,　　　　Social Security No.
of Bankruptcy Petition Preparer　　　　　　　　(Required by 11 U.S.C. § 110.)

If the bankruptcy petition preparer is not an individual, state the name, title (if any), address, and social security number of the officer, principal, responsible person, or partner who signs this document.

_____
_____
Address

X _____　　　　_____
Signature of Bankruptcy Petition Preparer　　　　Date

Names and Social Security numbers of all other individuals who prepared or assisted in preparing this document, unless the bankruptcy petition preparer is not an individual:

If more than one person prepared this document, attach additional signed sheets conforming to the appropriate Official Form for each person.

A bankruptcy petition preparer's failure to comply with the provisions of title 11 and the Federal Rules of Bankruptcy Procedure may result in fines or imprisonment or both. 11 U.S.C. § 110; 18 U.S.C. § 156.

DECLARATION UNDER PENALTY OF PERJURY ON BEHALF OF A CORPORATION OR PARTNERSHIP

I, the _____ [the president or other officer or an authorized agent of the corporation or a member or an authorized agent of the partnership] of the _____ [corporation or partnership] named as debtor in this case, declare under penalty of perjury that I have read the foregoing summary and schedules, consisting of ____ sheets (*Total shown on summary page plus 1*), and that they are true and correct to the best of my knowledge, information, and belief.

Date _____

　　　　　　　　　　　　　　Signature: _____

　　　　　　　　　　　　　　[Print or type name of individual signing on behalf of debtor.]

[An individual signing on behalf of a partnership or corporation must indicate position or relationship to debtor.]

Penalty for making a false statement or concealing property: Fine of up to $500,000 or imprisonment for up to 5 years or both. 18 U.S.C. §§ 152 and 3571.

(Added Aug. 1, 1991; amended Mar. 16, 1993; Mar. 1995; Oct. 1, 1997; Apr. 1, 1998; Dec. 1, 2003; April 1, 2004; Apr. 25, 2005, eff. Dec. 1, 2005; Aug. 11, 2005, eff. Oct. 17, 2005; Oct. 11, 2006; Apr. 1, 2007; Dec. 2007; Apr. 1, 2010; April 1, 2013; Dec. 2013; Dec. 1, 2014.)

OFFICIAL FORMS   Form 6

ADVISORY COMMITTEE NOTES
1991 Enactment

These schedules shall be used to comply with § 521(1) of the Code and Rule 1007(b). Schedules A, B, D, E, and F constitute the schedule of assets and liabilities. Schedules I and J constitute a schedule of current income and current expenditures for individual and joint debtors. Two new schedules have been created, Schedule G—Executory Contracts and Unexpired Leases, and Schedule H—Codebtors.

The order of the schedules has been arranged with the summary sheet in front and with the schedules of assets appearing first, followed by the schedules of liabilities. This structure corresponds to the customary pattern by which trustees and creditors review these documents and to the format of the accounting profession for balance sheets.

The schedules require a complete listing of assets and liabilities but leave many of the details to investigation by the trustee. Instructions in the former schedules to provide details concerning "written instruments" relating to the debtor's property or debts have been deleted. Section 521(3) of the Code requires the debtor to cooperate with the trustee, who can administer the estate more effectively by requesting any documents from the debtor rather than relying on descriptions in the schedules which may prove to be inaccurate.

Leasehold interests in both real and personal property are to be reported in Schedule G—Executory Contracts and Unexpired Leases. This information should not be repeated in the schedules of assets.

Generally in these schedules, a creditor's claim will be listed only once, even if the claim is secured only in part, or is entitled only in part to priority under § 507(a) of the Code, with the remainder of the claim to be treated as a general unsecured claim. For example, a partially secured creditor whose claim is reported in Schedule D—Creditors Holding Secured Claims will be listed together with the value of the property securing the claim and a notation of the amount of any unsecured portion of the claim. Information concerning the unsecured portion should not be repeated in Schedule F—Creditors Holding Nonpriority Unsecured Claims. Any resulting overstatement of the amounts owed on secured and priority claims as reported on the summary sheet is offset by a corresponding understatement of the amount owed on unsecured claims.

If a debtor has no property or no creditors in a particular category, an affirmative statement to that effect is required. Married debtors should indicate whether property is jointly or separately owned and whether spouses are jointly or separately liable for debts, using the columns provided in the schedules.

Former "Schedule B–3. Property not otherwise scheduled," has been deleted and its two questions moved. Schedule B—Personal Property now includes at item 33, "Other personal property of any kind not already listed." The only other question on former Schedule B–3 concerned assignments for the benefit of creditors; it has been moved to the Statement of Financial Affairs.

Schedule A—Real Property. Instructions at the top of the form indicate the scope of the interests in property to be reported on the schedule. Leasehold interests of the debtor are not reported here but on the Schedule of Executory Contracts and Unexpired Leases. The trustee will request copies of deeds or other instruments necessary to the administration of the estate.

Schedule B—Personal Property. This schedule is to be used for reporting all of the debtor's interests in personal property except leases and executory contracts, which are to be listed on the Schedule of Executory Contracts and Unexpired Leases. Several new categories of property have been added to the schedule, *i.e.*, aircraft, and interests in IRA, ERISA, Keogh, or other pension or profit-sharing plans. To minimize the potential for concealment of assets, the debtor must declare whether the debtor has any property in each category on the schedule. The trustee can request copies of any documents concerning the debtor's property necessary to the administration of the estate.

Schedule C—Property Claimed as Exempt. The form of the schedule has been modified to eliminate duplication of information provided elsewhere. The location of property, for example, which formerly was required here, is disclosed in the schedules of real and personal property. The requirement that the debtor state the present use of the property also has been eliminated as best left to inquiry by the trustee. Exemptions in some states are granted by constitutional provisions; accordingly, the requirement that the debtor state the "statute" creating an exemption has been changed to request a statement of the relevant "law."

This schedule adds a new requirement that the debtor state the market value of the property in addition to the amount claimed as exempt.

Form 6 OFFICIAL FORMS

Schedule D—Creditors Holding Secured Claims. Schedules D, E, and F have been redesigned with address boxes sized to match the number of characters which can be accommodated on the computerized noticing systems used by the courts. The size also closely approximates that of standard mailing labels. Space is designated at the top of the box for the debtor's account number with the creditor. The design of the form is intended to reduce the volume of misdirected creditor mail.

The form requires the debtor to state affirmatively that a claim is disputed, unliquidated, or contingent. The existence of any type of codebtor is to be disclosed, but details are to be provided in Schedule H, as they are not needed here. Duplication of information also has been kept to a minimum by deleting requests that the debtor indicate on this schedule whether a debt has been reduced to judgment and the date on which a creditor repossessed any collateral. Requests for details concerning negotiable instruments and the consideration for a claim, formerly part of the schedule, are left to the trustee's inquiries.

Schedule E—Creditors Holding Unsecured Priority Claims. The schedule lists all of the types of claims entitled to priority and requires the debtor to indicate the existence of claims in each category. Continuation sheets are provided. The type of priority claim is to be noted at the top of the continuation sheet, and each type must be reported on a separate sheet. This schedule also requires the debtor to indicate the existence of any codebtors. As in Schedule D—Creditors Holding Secured Claims, requests for information concerning judgments and negotiable instruments have been deleted.

Schedule F—Creditors Holding Unsecured Nonpriority Claims. This schedule has been revised generally in conformity with the other schedules of creditors. If a claim is subject to setoff, the debtor is required to so state.

Schedule G—Executory Contracts and Unexpired Leases. Rule 1007(b) requires the debtor to file a schedule of executory contracts and unexpired leases, unless the court orders otherwise. All unexpired leases of either real or personal property are to be reported on this schedule. The schedule also requires the debtor to disclose specific information to assist the trustee in identifying leases which must be assumed within 60 days after the order for relief or be deemed rejected under § 365(d) of the Code.

Schedule H—Schedule of Codebtors. This schedule is designed to provide the trustee and creditors with information about codebtors of all types other than spouses in joint cases. The completed schedule provides information concerning non-debtor parties, such as guarantors and non-debtor spouses having an interest in property as tenants by the entirety. In chapter 12 and chapter 13 cases, the completed schedule also indicates those persons who may be entitled to certain protections from creditor action under §§ 1201 and 1301 of the Code.

Schedule I—Schedule of Current Income of Individual Debtor(s) and Schedule J—Schedule of Current Expenditures of Individual Debtor(s). Former Official Form No. 6A has been divided into a schedule of current income and a separate schedule of current expenditures. The language is substantially the same as in former Official Form No. 6A. In light of the abrogation of Official Form No. 10, the Chapter 13 Statement, style changes have been made so that these schedules can be used by individual and joint debtors in all chapters.

1993 Amendment

Schedule E (Creditors Holding Unsecured Priority Claims) has been changed to conform to the statutory amendment that added subsection (a)(8) to § 507 of the Code. Pub.L. No. 101–647, (Crime Control Act of 1990), added the new subsection, which had the effect of creating an eighth priority for claims of certain governmental units based on commitments to maintain the capital of an insured depository institution.

1995 Amendment

Schedule E—Creditors Holding Unsecured Priority Claims is amended to add the new seventh priority afforded to debts for alimony, maintenance, or support of a spouse, former spouse, or child of the debtor by the Bankruptcy Reform Act of 1994. Statutory references are amended to conform to the paragraph numbers of section 507(a) of the Code as renumbered by the 1994 Act. Schedule E also is amended to add commissions owed to certain independent sales representatives and to raise the maximum dollar amounts for certain priorities in accordance with amendments made by the 1994 Act to section 507(a) of the Code. The 1994 Act also amended section 104 of the Code to provide for future adjustment of the maximum dollar amounts specified in section 507(a) to be made by administrative action at three-year intervals to reflect changes in the consumer price index. Schedule E is amended to

OFFICIAL FORMS   Form 6

give notice that these dollar amounts are subject to change without formal amendment to the official form.

The Schedules are a "document for filing" that may be prepared by a "bankruptcy petition preparer" as defined in 11 U.S.C. § 110, which was added to the Code by the 1994 Act; accordingly, a signature line for such preparer is added. In addition to signing, a bankruptcy petition preparer is required by section 110 to disclose the information requested.

1997 Amendment

The form is amended to add to the column labels a reference to community liability for claims. The amendment is technical and corrects an editorial oversight.

2003 Amendment

The instructions to Schedule D (Creditors Holding Secured Claims), Schedule E (Creditors Holding Unsecured Priority Claims), and Schedule F (Creditors Holding Unsecured Nonpriority Claims) are amended to inform the debtor that the debtor must list the last four digits of any account number with the listed creditor, and that the debtor may, in its discretion, include the entire account number in the schedules. Schedule I (Current Income of Individual Debtor(s)) is amended to provide greater privacy to minors and other dependents of the debtor by deleting the requirement that the debtor disclose their names. Pursuant to § 110(c) of the Bankruptcy Code, the certification by a non-attorney bankruptcy petition preparer requires a petition preparer to provide the full Social Security number of the individual who actually prepares the document.

2005 Amendment

The forms of the Schedules of Assets and Liabilities are amended to implement the provisions of the Bankruptcy Abuse Prevention and Consumer Protection Act of 2005, Pub. L. No. 109–8, 119 Stat. 23, (April 20, 2005). An amendment that directs the debtor to avoid disclosing the name of any minor child occurs in several of the schedules in conformity with § 112 which was added to the Code in 2005. Section 112 provides for the debtor to provide the name of any minor child confidentially to the court, should the trustee need the information to evaluate properly the information filed by the debtor.

The "Statistical Summary of Certain Liabilities" is added to collect information needed to prepare statistical reports required under 28 U.S.C. § 159, which was enacted as part of the 2005 Act.

Schedules A, B, C, and D are amended to delete the word "market" from the columns in which the debtor reports the value of various kinds of property. Amendments to § 506 of the Code enacted in 2005 specify that "replacement value" must be used in connection with certain property. The schedules no longer specify "market" value and permit the debtor to choose the appropriate one, whether that be replacement, market, or some other value. Valuation of property, generally, is the subject of extensive provisions in the Code, and the deletion of the word "market" from the determinations of value to be made by the debtor on the schedules is intended to remove any inference about choice of valuation standard. This deletion simply indicates that the form takes no position on which Code provision or valuation standard may be applicable in any instance.

The following paragraphs describe changes that are specific to each schedule.

Schedule B—Personal Property is amended to require the debtor to list any interests in an education IRA, as § 541(b)(5), added to the Code in 2005, makes special provision for them. The schedule also is amended to require the debtor to disclose the existence of any customer lists or other compilations containing personally identifiable information provided by an individual to the debtor in connection with obtaining a product or service from the debtor for personal, family, or household purposes. This amendment implements § 332, which was added to the Code in 2005.

Schedule C—Property Claimed as Exempt is amended to delete descriptive information concerning the length of domicile required for the debtor to qualify to claim certain exemptions. Any summary of the amendments enacted in 2005 to § 522 of the Code concerning these requirements might inadvertently cause the debtor to lose important rights. Accordingly, the form now directs the debtor to indicate whether exemptions are being claimed under § 522(b)(2) or § 522(b)(3) and whether the debtor claims a homestead exemption that exceeds $125,000.

Schedule E—Creditors Holding Unsecured Priority Claims is amended to implement the changes in priority to which a claim may be entitled under 11 U.S.C. § 507 as amended by the 2005 Act and to add the new priority included in the Reform Act for claims for death or personal injury while the debtor was

Form 6   **OFFICIAL FORMS**

intoxicated. "Subtotal" and "Total" boxes have been added to the column labeled "Amount Entitled to Priority" to assist the individual debtor to complete the Means Test form.

Schedule G—Executory Contracts and Unexpired Leases is amended by deleting the note to the debtor advising that parties listed on this schedule may not receive notice of the filing of the bankruptcy case unless they also are listed on one of the schedules of liabilities. The better practice is for all parties to transactions with the debtor to receive notice of the filing of the case, and an amendment to Rule 1007 requiring the debtor to provide a mailing list that includes these parties is scheduled to take effect December 1, 2005.

Schedule H—Codebtors is amended to add specifics about community property jurisdictions in connection with the requirement to provide the name of any spouse of a debtor who resides or resided in a community property jurisdiction. This amendment also mirrors amendments made in 1997 to Official Form 7, the Statement of Financial Affairs, and will assure that these codebtors receive notice of the filing of the bankruptcy case. The form also is amended to extend from six years to eight years the time period for which this information is reported pursuant to the 2005 amendments to § 727(a)(8) of the Code.

Schedule I—Current Income of Individual Debtor(s) is amended to require the income of a nondebtor spouse to be reported in cases filed under chapters 7 and 11. Line numbers have been added to assist the debtor in calculating and reporting totals. A new subtotal line for income from sources other than as an employee and a new "total monthly income" line provide for this form to be used in conjunction with Schedule J to satisfy the requirements of § 521(a)(1)(B)(v), which was added to the Code in 2005. The form also has been revised to provide the statement concerning any anticipated increase or decrease in income required in § 521(a)(1)(B)(vi), which also was added to the Code in 2005.

Schedule J—Current Expenditures of Individual Debtor(s). A direction has been added to require the debtor to report any increase or decrease in expenses anticipated to occur within the year following the filing of the document, as required by § 521(a)(1)(B)(vi), which was added to the Code in 2005. The form also is amended to provide, in conjunction with Schedule I, a statement of monthly net income, itemized to show how the amount is calculated, as required by § 522(a)(1)(B)(v), which was added to the Code in 2005.

Declaration Concerning Debtor's Schedules. The declaration by a non-attorney bankruptcy petition preparer is amended to include material mandated by § 110 of the Code as amended in 2005.

2006 Amendment

In order to comply fully with the statistical reporting requirements of 28 U.S.C. § 159, which was enacted as part of the 2005 Act and takes effect in October 2006, the "Statistical Summary of Certain Liabilities" is renamed "Statistical Summary of Certain Liabilities and Related Data," and additional information is required to be stated there. Collecting in one place the bulk of the information to be used in the reports required under 28 U.S.C. § 159 will assist the courts and the Director of the Administrative Office of the United States Courts to fulfill their statutory responsibilities.

Schedule D is amended to provide for creating a total of any unsecured amounts (amounts that exceed the value of the collateral) owed to creditors holding secured claims, and for stating this amount on the Statistical Summary of Certain Liabilities and Related Data.

Schedule E is amended to provide for creating totals of the amounts entitled to priority and of any amounts that exceed the statutory limits on certain priorities and to direct the debtor to report these amounts on the Statistical Summary of Certain Liabilities and Related Data. Schedule F is amended to direct the debtor to report the total of this schedule both on the Summary of Schedules and on the Statistical Summary of Certain Liabilities.

The statistical reports required under 28 U.S.C. § 159 must include "the current monthly income, average income, and average expenses" of individual debtors with primarily consumer debts as reported on the schedules filed by those debtors. Accordingly, Schedules I and J, on which debtors already are directed to report average income and average expenses are amended to label the totals arrived at by completing the schedules as " average monthly income" and "average monthly expenses." These amendments make no substantive changes, simply conforming the terminology on these schedules to that used in § 159.

The amount of the debtor's current monthly income, which also is required by § 159, is derived from Official Forms 22A, 22B, or 22C, depending on the chapter under which the debtor files. This amount is included on the Statistical Summary of Certain Liabilities and Related Data as a convenience to make reports under § 159 easier to compile.

OFFICIAL FORMS   Form 6

    The declaration Concerning Debtor's Schedules is amended in the section designated for signing and verifying by an individual or joint debtor. The amendment accommodates the requirement that individual debtors must complete both the Summary of Schedules and the Statistical Summary of Certain Liabilities and Related Data by directing the debtor to state number of pages being verified as the number of sheets in the completed schedules "plus 2."

2005–2007 Amendments

    (The 2005–2007 Committee Note incorporates Committee Notes previously published in 2005 and 2006.)

    The forms of the Schedules of Assets and Liabilities are amended to implement the provisions of the Bankruptcy Abuse Prevention and Consumer Protection Act of 2005, Pub. L. No. 109–8, 119 Stat. 23, (April 20, 2005) ("BAPCPA"). An amendment that directs the debtor to avoid disclosing the name and address of any minor child occurs in Schedules B, D, E, F, G, and H in conformity with § 112 which was added to the Code in 2005. Section 112 provides for the debtor to furnish the name of any minor child confidentially to the court, should the trustee need the information to evaluate properly the information filed by the debtor. In addition, those schedules are amended to add to the reference to Rule 1007(m), with respect to a minor child, a direction to include for noticing purposes the name, address, and legal relationship to the child of "a person described" in that rule. Rule 1007(m) requires the person named to be someone on whom process would be served in an adversary proceeding against the child.

    The "Statistical Summary of Certain Liabilities and Related Data" is added to collect from individual debtors with primarily consumer debts the information needed to prepare statistical reports required under 28 U.S.C. § 159, which was enacted as part of BAPCPA. Collecting the bulk of the information to be used in these statistical reports in the Summary of Schedules and the statistical summary will assist the courts and the Director of the Administrative Office to fulfill their statutory responsibilities. Schedules D and E are amended to provide additional totals and, together with Schedule F, to direct debtors who must complete the statistical summary to report total amounts there. Similarly, Schedules I and J are amended to conform their terminology to that used in 28 U.S.C. § 159 and direct debtors who must complete the statistical summary to report the specified amounts there.

    Schedules A, B, C, and D are amended to delete the word "market" from the columns in which the debtor reports the value of various kinds of property. Amendments to § 506 of the Code enacted in 2005 specify that "replacement value" must be used in connection with certain property. The schedules no longer specify "market" value and permit the debtor to choose the appropriate one, whether that be replacement, market, or some other value. Valuation of property, generally, is the subject of extensive provisions in the Code, and the deletion of the word "market" from the determinations of value to be made by the debtor on the schedules is intended to remove any inference about choice of valuation standard. This deletion simply indicates that the form takes no position on which Code provision or valuation standard may be applicable in any particular instance.

    The following paragraphs describe changes that are specific to each schedule:

    Schedule B—Personal Property is amended to require the debtor to list any interests in an education IRA, because § 541(b)(5), added to the Code in 2005, makes special provision for them. The schedule is also amended to require the debtor to disclose the existence of any customer lists or other compilations containing personally identifiable information provided by an individual to the debtor in connection with obtaining a product or service from the debtor for personal, family, or household purposes. This amendment implements § 332, which was added to the Code by BAPCPA in 2005.

    Schedule C—Property claimed as Exempt is amended to delete descriptive information concerning the length of domicile required for the debtor to qualify to claim certain exemptions. Any summary of the BAPCPA amendments to § 522 of the Code concerning these requirements might inadvertently cause the debtor to lose important rights. Accordingly, the form now directs the debtor to indicate whether exemptions are being claimed under § 522(b)(2) or § 522(b)(3) and whether the debtor claims a homestead exemption that exceeds $136,875.

    Schedule D—Creditors Holding Secured Claims is amended to provide for creating a total of any unsecured amounts (amounts that exceed the value of the collateral) owed to creditors holding secured claims. In addition to facilitating statistical reporting, providing a breakdown of the amounts owed to creditors listed on this schedule will assist the individual debtor in completing the means test calculation under § 707(b)(2)(A)(i) of the Code.

Form 6   **OFFICIAL FORMS**

Schedule E—Creditors Holding Unsecured Priority Claims is amended to implement the changes in priority to which a claim may be entitled under 11 U.S.C. § 507 as amended by BAPCPA and to add the new priority included in the 2005 Act for claims for death or personal injury while the debtor was intoxicated. "Subtotal" and "Total" boxes have been added to the columns labeled "Amount Entitled to Priority" and "Amount Not Entitled to Priority" for statistical reporting purposes and to assist the individual debtor in completing the means test calculation under § 707(b)(2)(A)(i) of the Code.

Schedule H—Codebtors is amended to add specifics about community property jurisdictions in connection with the requirement to provide the name of any spouse of a debtor who resides or resided in a community property jurisdiction. This amendment also mirrors amendments made in 1997 to Official Form 7, the Statement of Financial Affairs, and will assure that these codebtors receive notice of the filing of the bankruptcy case. The form also is amended to extend from six years to eight years the time period for which this information is reported pursuant to the 2005 amendments to § 727(a)(8) of the Code.

Schedule I—Current Income of Individual Debtor(s) is amended to make it clear that "every" married debtor must provide income information for both spouses, unless the spouses are separated and a joint petition is not filed. The description of the income to be reported is revised to clarify that the purpose of this schedule is to obtain information about actual income on the date the bankruptcy case is filed and which a debtor reasonably expects in the future in contrast to the debtor's "current monthly income" as defined in § 101(10A) and reported on Form 22A, 22B, or 22C. And a statement included at the top of the form also explains that the income calculated this form may be different than the current monthly income. Line numbers have been added to assist the debtor in calculating and reporting totals. A new subtotal line for income from sources other than as an employee and a new "average monthly income" line will enable this form to be used in conjunction with Schedule J to satisfy the requirements of § 521(a)(1)(B)(v), which was added to the Code by BAPCPA. New statistical reporting requirements in 28 U.S.C. § 159 also require "average monthly income." In addition, the form is revised to provide the statement concerning any anticipated increase or decrease in income required in § 521(a)(1)(B)(vi), also added to the Code in 2005.

Schedule J—Current Expenditures of Individual Debtor(s). In conjunction with amendments to Schedule I, the form is amended to provide for reporting the debtor's actual "average monthly expenses," as required by 28 U.S.C. § 159 and a statement of monthly net income, itemized to show how the amount is calculated, as required by § 522(a)(1)(B)(v), which was added to the Code by BAPCPA in 2005. In addition, line numbers have been inserted and the description of expenses revised to make it clear than the purpose of this schedule is to obtain information about a debtor's actual and reasonably foreseeable expenses on the date the bankruptcy case is filed. And a statement similar to the statement at the top of Schedule I explains that the expenses calculated on the form may differ from the expenses calculated on Forms 22A or 22C. A direction has been added to require the debtor to report any increase or decrease in expenses anticipated to occur within the year following the filing of the document, as required by § 521(a)(1)(B)(vi), which also was added to the Code in 2005.

Declaration Concerning Debtor's Schedules. The declaration by individual or joint debtors is amended to require the debtor to merely state the total number of pages being verified. The declaration and signature of any non-attorney bankruptcy petition preparer is amended to include material mandated by § 110 of the Code as amended in 2005.

2013 Amendment

Schedule I: Your Income (Official Form 6I) and Schedule J: Your Expenses (Official Form 6J), which apply only in cases of individual debtors, have been revised as part of the Forms Modernization Project, making the forms easier to read and, as a result, likely to generate more complete and accurate responses.

Revised Schedules I and J seek to obtain a full picture of the debtor's economic situation—to the extent that debtor receives income or has expenses. The revised forms are intended to avoid the situation that frequently happens with the current forms where debtor lives with and pools assets with other people and the household provides support to dependents who may not be related by blood or marriage to the debtor.

The amendments seek to avoid the situation where the expenses listed on Schedule J are for the entire household, but the income listed on Schedule I is only for the debtor. Line 11 on revised Schedule I now includes contributions made by someone else to the expenses on Schedule J, and the debtor is instructed to include contributions from an unmarried partner, members of the debtor's household, dependents, roommates, and other friends or relatives.

As revised, the initial Schedule J will provide estimated expenses at the beginning of the case and the debtor will so indicate in Part 2 of the form.

OFFICIAL FORMS Form 6

In drafting the form it became apparent that at least some courts are using Schedules I and J in analyzing proposed chapter 13 plans and potential modification of those plans or when a debtor's financial circumstances change. To avoid a lack of clarity on the form regarding the date to be used in computing expenses, and in order to allow Schedule J to continue to serve the plan feasibility function, the revised form may also be used as a supplement to the initial filing if the debtor checks the appropriate box in the caption and indicates the pertinent post-filing date of the estimate.

New lines 1, 2, and 3 on revised Schedule J request information about the debtor's household. Line 1 requires joint debtors who maintain separate households to file separate Schedule J forms. A check box has been added to the caption to identify such filings. Line 2 requires information about each dependent who lives with the debtor and each dependent who lives separately. In order to allow a full understanding of the debtor's expenses, Line 3 requires debtors to state whether their expenses include the expenses of persons other than themselves and their dependents. In addition, new line 23 on the form includes a calculation of the debtor's monthly net income.

Summary of Schedules (Official Form 6 Summary), is updated on page 2 to reflect new line number references to Schedules I and J for Average Income and Average Expenses.

2014 Amendment

Summary of Schedules (Official Forms 6 Summary), is updated on page 2 to give line number references to the amended means-test forms (Official Forms 22A-1, 22B, and 22C-1) for Current Monthly Income.

Form 7   **OFFICIAL FORMS**

Form 7. Statement of Financial Affairs

B 7 (Official Form 7) (04/10)

UNITED STATES BANKRUPTCY COURT

In re: _____,   Case No. _____
             Debtor   (if known)

STATEMENT OF FINANCIAL AFFAIRS

       This statement is to be completed by every debtor. Spouses filing a joint petition may file a single statement on which the information for both spouses is combined. If the case is filed under chapter 12 or chapter 13, a married debtor must furnish information for both spouses whether or not a joint petition is filed, unless the spouses are separated and a joint petition is not filed. An individual debtor engaged in business as a sole proprietor, partner, family farmer, or self-employed professional, should provide the information requested on this statement concerning all such activities as well as the individual's personal affairs. To indicate payments, transfers and the like to minor children, state the child's initials and the name and address of the child's parent or guardian, such as "A.B., a minor child, by John Doe, guardian." Do not disclose the child's name. See, 11 U.S.C. §112 and Fed. R. Bankr. P. 1007(m).

       Questions 1 - 18 are to be completed by all debtors. Debtors that are or have been in business, as defined below, also must complete Questions 19 - 25. **If the answer to an applicable question is "None," mark the box labeled "None."** If additional space is needed for the answer to any question, use and attach a separate sheet properly identified with the case name, case number (if known), and the number of the question.

DEFINITIONS

       "In business." A debtor is "in business" for the purpose of this form if the debtor is a corporation or partnership. An individual debtor is "in business" for the purpose of this form if the debtor is or has been, within six years immediately preceding the filing of this bankruptcy case, any of the following: an officer, director, managing executive, or owner of 5 percent or more of the voting or equity securities of a corporation; a partner, other than a limited partner, of a partnership; a sole proprietor or self-employed full-time or part-time. An individual debtor also may be "in business" for the purpose of this form if the debtor engages in a trade, business, or other activity, other than as an employee, to supplement income from the debtor's primary employment.

       "Insider." The term "insider" includes but is not limited to: relatives of the debtor; general partners of the debtor and their relatives; corporations of which the debtor is an officer, director, or person in control; officers, directors, and any owner of 5 percent or more of the voting or equity securities of a corporate debtor and their relatives; affiliates of the debtor and insiders of such affiliates; any managing agent of the debtor. 11 U.S.C. § 101.

---

1. **Income from employment or operation of business**

None   State the gross amount of income the debtor has received from employment, trade, or profession, or from operation of
☐   the debtor's business, including part-time activities either as an employee or in independent trade or business, from the beginning of this calendar year to the date this case was commenced. State also the gross amounts received during the **two years** immediately preceding this calendar year. (A debtor that maintains, or has maintained, financial records on the basis of a fiscal rather than a calendar year may report fiscal year income. Identify the beginning and ending dates of the debtor's fiscal year.) If a joint petition is filed, state income for each spouse separately. (Married debtors filing under chapter 12 or chapter 13 must state income of both spouses whether or not a joint petition is filed, unless the spouses are separated and a joint petition is not filed.)

                 AMOUNT   SOURCE

OFFICIAL FORMS — Form 7

2. Income other than from employment or operation of business

None ☐ State the amount of income received by the debtor other than from employment, trade, profession, operation of the debtor's business during the **two years** immediately preceding the commencement of this case. Give particulars. If a joint petition is filed, state income for each spouse separately. (Married debtors filing under chapter 12 or chapter 13 must state income for each spouse whether or not a joint petition is filed, unless the spouses are separated and a joint petition is not filed.)

AMOUNT   SOURCE

3. Payments to creditors

Complete a. or b., as appropriate, and c.

None ☐ a. *Individual or joint debtor(s) with primarily consumer debts:* List all payments on loans, installment purchases of goods or services, and other debts to any creditor made within **90 days** immediately preceding the commencement of this case unless the aggregate value of all property that constitutes or is affected by such transfer is less than $600. Indicate with an asterisk (*) any payments that were made to a creditor on account of a domestic support obligation or as part of an alternative repayment schedule under a plan by an approved nonprofit budgeting and credit counseling agency. (Married debtors filing under chapter 12 or chapter 13 must include payments by either or both spouses whether or not a joint petition is filed, unless the spouses are separated and a joint petition is not filed.)

NAME AND ADDRESS OF CREDITOR	DATES OF PAYMENTS	AMOUNT PAID	AMOUNT STILL OWING

None ☐ b. *Debtor whose debts are not primarily consumer debts:* List each payment or other transfer to any creditor made within **90 days** immediately preceding the commencement of the case unless the aggregate value of all property that constitutes or is affected by such transfer is less than $5,850*. If the debtor is an individual, indicate with an asterisk (*) any payments that were made to a creditor on account of a domestic support obligation or as part of an alternative repayment schedule under a plan by an approved nonprofit budgeting and credit counseling agency. (Married debtors filing under chapter 12 or chapter 13 must include payments and other transfers by either or both spouses whether or not a joint petition is filed, unless the spouses are separated and a joint petition is not filed.)

NAME AND ADDRESS OF CREDITOR	DATES OF PAYMENTS/ TRANSFERS	AMOUNT PAID OR VALUE OF TRANSFERS	AMOUNT STILL OWING

---

*Amount subject to adjustment on 4/01/13, and every three years thereafter with respect to cases commenced on or after the date of adjustment.

Form 7 OFFICIAL FORMS

None ☐   c. *All debtors*: List all payments made within **one year** immediately preceding the commencement of this case to or for the benefit of creditors who are or were insiders. (Married debtors filing under chapter 12 or chapter 13 must include payments by either or both spouses whether or not a joint petition is filed, unless the spouses are separated and a joint petition is not filed.)

NAME AND ADDRESS OF CREDITOR AND RELATIONSHIP TO DEBTOR	DATE OF PAYMENT	AMOUNT PAID	AMOUNT STILL OWING

4. Suits and administrative proceedings, executions, garnishments and attachments

None ☐   a. List all suits and administrative proceedings to which the debtor is or was a party within **one year** immediately preceding the filing of this bankruptcy case. (Married debtors filing under chapter 12 or chapter 13 must include information concerning either or both spouses whether or not a joint petition is filed, unless the spouses are separated and a joint petition is not filed.)

CAPTION OF SUIT AND CASE NUMBER	NATURE OF PROCEEDING	COURT OR AGENCY AND LOCATION	STATUS OR DISPOSITION

None ☐   b. Describe all property that has been attached, garnished or seized under any legal or equitable process within **one year** immediately preceding the commencement of this case. (Married debtors filing under chapter 12 or chapter 13 must include information concerning property of either or both spouses whether or not a joint petition is filed, unless the spouses are separated and a joint petition is not filed.)

NAME AND ADDRESS OF PERSON FOR WHOSE BENEFIT PROPERTY WAS SEIZED	DATE OF SEIZURE	DESCRIPTION AND VALUE OF PROPERTY

5. Repossessions, foreclosures and returns

None ☐   List all property that has been repossessed by a creditor, sold at a foreclosure sale, transferred through a deed in lieu of foreclosure or returned to the seller, within **one year** immediately preceding the commencement of this case. (Married debtors filing under chapter 12 or chapter 13 must include information concerning property of either or both spouses whether or not a joint petition is filed, unless the spouses are separated and a joint petition is not filed.)

NAME AND ADDRESS OF CREDITOR OR SELLER	DATE OF REPOSSESSION, FORECLOSURE SALE, TRANSFER OR RETURN	DESCRIPTION AND VALUE OF PROPERTY

OFFICIAL FORMS   **Form 7**

4

6. **Assignments and receiverships**

☐ None

a. Describe any assignment of property for the benefit of creditors made within **120 days** immediately preceding the commencement of this case. (Married debtors filing under chapter 12 or chapter 13 must include any assignment by either or both spouses whether or not a joint petition is filed, unless the spouses are separated and a joint petition is not filed.)

NAME AND ADDRESS OF ASSIGNEE	DATE OF ASSIGNMENT	TERMS OF ASSIGNMENT OR SETTLEMENT

☐ None

b. List all property which has been in the hands of a custodian, receiver, or court-appointed official within **one year** immediately preceding the commencement of this case. (Married debtors filing under chapter 12 or chapter 13 must include information concerning property of either or both spouses whether or not a joint petition is filed, unless the spouses are separated and a joint petition is not filed.)

NAME AND ADDRESS OF CUSTODIAN	NAME AND LOCATION OF COURT CASE TITLE & NUMBER	DATE OF ORDER	DESCRIPTION AND VALUE OF PROPERTY

7. **Gifts**

☐ None

List all gifts or charitable contributions made within **one year** immediately preceding the commencement of this case except ordinary and usual gifts to family members aggregating less than $200 in value per individual family member and charitable contributions aggregating less than $100 per recipient. (Married debtors filing under chapter 12 or chapter 13 must include gifts or contributions by either or both spouses whether or not a joint petition is filed, unless the spouses are separated and a joint petition is not filed.)

NAME AND ADDRESS OF PERSON OR ORGANIZATION	RELATIONSHIP TO DEBTOR, IF ANY	DATE OF GIFT	DESCRIPTION AND VALUE OF GIFT

8. **Losses**

☐ None

List all losses from fire, theft, other casualty or gambling within **one year** immediately preceding the commencement of this case **or since the commencement of this case**. (Married debtors filing under chapter 12 or chapter 13 must include losses by either or both spouses whether or not a joint petition is filed, unless the spouses are separated and a joint petition is not filed.)

DESCRIPTION AND VALUE OF PROPERTY	DESCRIPTION OF CIRCUMSTANCES AND, IF LOSS WAS COVERED IN WHOLE OR IN PART BY INSURANCE, GIVE PARTICULARS	DATE OF LOSS

Form 7 OFFICIAL FORMS

9. **Payments related to debt counseling or bankruptcy**

☐ None

List all payments made or property transferred by or on behalf of the debtor to any persons, including attorneys, for consultation concerning debt consolidation, relief under the bankruptcy law or preparation of a petition in bankruptcy within **one year** immediately preceding the commencement of this case.

NAME AND ADDRESS OF PAYEE	DATE OF PAYMENT, NAME OF PAYER IF OTHER THAN DEBTOR	AMOUNT OF MONEY OR DESCRIPTION AND VALUE OF PROPERTY

10. **Other transfers**

☐ None

a. List all other property, other than property transferred in the ordinary course of the business or financial affairs of the debtor, transferred either absolutely or as security within **two years** immediately preceding the commencement of this case. (Married debtors filing under chapter 12 or chapter 13 must include transfers by either or both spouses whether or not a joint petition is filed, unless the spouses are separated and a joint petition is not filed.)

NAME AND ADDRESS OF TRANSFEREE, RELATIONSHIP TO DEBTOR	DATE	DESCRIBE PROPERTY TRANSFERRED AND VALUE RECEIVED

☐ None

b. List all property transferred by the debtor within **ten years** immediately preceding the commencement of this case to a self-settled trust or similar device of which the debtor is a beneficiary.

NAME OF TRUST OR OTHER DEVICE	DATE(S) OF TRANSFER(S)	AMOUNT OF MONEY OR DESCRIPTION AND VALUE OF PROPERTY OR DEBTOR'S INTEREST IN PROPERTY

11. **Closed financial accounts**

☐ None

List all financial accounts and instruments held in the name of the debtor or for the benefit of the debtor which were closed, sold, or otherwise transferred within **one year** immediately preceding the commencement of this case. Include checking, savings, or other financial accounts, certificates of deposit, or other instruments; shares and share accounts held in banks, credit unions, pension funds, cooperatives, associations, brokerage houses and other financial institutions. (Married debtors filing under chapter 12 or chapter 13 must include information concerning accounts or instruments held by or for either or both spouses whether or not a joint petition is filed, unless the spouses are separated and a joint petition is not filed.)

NAME AND ADDRESS OF INSTITUTION	TYPE OF ACCOUNT, LAST FOUR DIGITS OF ACCOUNT NUMBER, AND AMOUNT OF FINAL BALANCE	AMOUNT AND DATE OF SALE OR CLOSING

OFFICIAL FORMS — Form 7

12. Safe deposit boxes

None ☐ List each safe deposit or other box or depository in which the debtor has or had securities, cash, or other valuables within **one year** immediately preceding the commencement of this case. (Married debtors filing under chapter 12 or chapter 13 must include boxes or depositories of either or both spouses whether or not a joint petition is filed, unless the spouses are separated and a joint petition is not filed.)

NAME AND ADDRESS OF BANK OR OTHER DEPOSITORY	NAMES AND ADDRESSES OF THOSE WITH ACCESS TO BOX OR DEPOSITORY	DESCRIPTION OF CONTENTS	DATE OF TRANSFER OR SURRENDER, IF ANY

13. Setoffs

None ☐ List all setoffs made by any creditor, including a bank, against a debt or deposit of the debtor within **90 days** preceding the commencement of this case. (Married debtors filing under chapter 12 or chapter 13 must include information concerning either or both spouses whether or not a joint petition is filed, unless the spouses are separated and a joint petition is not filed.)

NAME AND ADDRESS OF CREDITOR	DATE OF SETOFF	AMOUNT OF SETOFF

14. Property held for another person

None ☐ List all property owned by another person that the debtor holds or controls.

NAME AND ADDRESS OF OWNER	DESCRIPTION AND VALUE OF PROPERTY	LOCATION OF PROPERTY

15. Prior address of debtor

None ☐ If debtor has moved within **three years** immediately preceding the commencement of this case, list all premises which the debtor occupied during that period and vacated prior to the commencement of this case. If a joint petition is filed, report also any separate address of either spouse.

ADDRESS	NAME USED	DATES OF OCCUPANCY

Form 7   OFFICIAL FORMS

16. Spouses and Former Spouses

None ☐   If the debtor resides or resided in a community property state, commonwealth, or territory (including Alaska, Arizona, California, Idaho, Louisiana, Nevada, New Mexico, Puerto Rico, Texas, Washington, or Wisconsin) within **eight years** immediately preceding the commencement of the case, identify the name of the debtor's spouse and of any former spouse who resides or resided with the debtor in the community property state.

NAME

17. Environmental Information.

For the purpose of this question, the following definitions apply:

"Environmental Law" means any federal, state, or local statute or regulation regulating pollution, contamination, releases of hazardous or toxic substances, wastes or material into the air, land, soil, surface water, groundwater, or other medium, including, but not limited to, statutes or regulations regulating the cleanup of these substances, wastes, or material.

"Site" means any location, facility, or property as defined under any Environmental Law, whether or not presently or formerly owned or operated by the debtor, including, but not limited to, disposal sites.

"Hazardous Material" means anything defined as a hazardous waste, hazardous substance, toxic substance, hazardous material, pollutant, or contaminant or similar term under an Environmental Law.

None ☐   a. List the name and address of every site for which the debtor has received notice in writing by a governmental unit that it may be liable or potentially liable under or in violation of an Environmental Law. Indicate the governmental unit, the date of the notice, and, if known, the Environmental Law:

SITE NAME AND ADDRESS	NAME AND ADDRESS OF GOVERNMENTAL UNIT	DATE OF NOTICE	ENVIRONMENTAL LAW

None ☐   b. List the name and address of every site for which the debtor provided notice to a governmental unit of a release of Hazardous Material. Indicate the governmental unit to which the notice was sent and the date of the notice.

SITE NAME AND ADDRESS	NAME AND ADDRESS OF GOVERNMENTAL UNIT	DATE OF NOTICE	ENVIRONMENTAL LAW

None ☐   c. List all judicial or administrative proceedings, including settlements or orders, under any Environmental Law with respect to which the debtor is or was a party. Indicate the name and address of the governmental unit that is or was a party to the proceeding, and the docket number.

NAME AND ADDRESS OF GOVERNMENTAL UNIT	DOCKET NUMBER	STATUS OR DISPOSITION

18. Nature, location and name of business

None ☐   a. *If the debtor is an individual*, list the names, addresses, taxpayer-identification numbers, nature of the businesses, and beginning and ending dates of all businesses in which the debtor was an officer, director, partner, or managing

OFFICIAL FORMS

Form 7

executive of a corporation, partner in a partnership, sole proprietor, or was self-employed in a trade, profession, or other activity either full- or part-time within **six years** immediately preceding the commencement of this case, or in which the debtor owned 5 percent or more of the voting or equity securities within **six years** immediately preceding the commencement of this case.

If the debtor is a partnership, list the names, addresses, taxpayer-identification numbers, nature of the businesses, and beginning and ending dates of all businesses in which the debtor was a partner or owned 5 percent or more of the voting or equity securities, within **six years** immediately preceding the commencement of this case.

If the debtor is a corporation, list the names, addresses, taxpayer-identification numbers, nature of the businesses, and beginning and ending dates of all businesses in which the debtor was a partner or owned 5 percent or more of the voting or equity securities within **six years** immediately preceding the commencement of this case.

NAME	LAST FOUR DIGITS OF SOCIAL-SECURITY OR OTHER INDIVIDUAL TAXPAYER-I.D. NO. (ITIN)/ COMPLETE EIN	ADDRESS	NATURE OF BUSINESS	BEGINNING AND ENDING DATES

None ☐   b. Identify any business listed in response to subdivision a., above, that is "single asset real estate" as defined in 11 U.S.C. § 101.

NAME   ADDRESS

The following questions are to be completed by every debtor that is a corporation or partnership and by any individual debtor who is or has been, within **six years** immediately preceding the commencement of this case, any of the following: an officer, director, managing executive, or owner of more than 5 percent of the voting or equity securities of a corporation; a partner, other than a limited partner, of a partnership, a sole proprietor, or self-employed in a trade, profession, or other activity, either full- or part-time.

*(An individual or joint debtor should complete this portion of the statement **only** if the debtor is or has been in business, as defined above, within six years immediately preceding the commencement of this case. A debtor who has not been in business within those six years should go directly to the signature page.)*

---

19. Books, records and financial statements

None ☐   a. List all bookkeepers and accountants who within **two years** immediately preceding the filing of this bankruptcy case kept or supervised the keeping of books of account and records of the debtor.

NAME AND ADDRESS   DATES SERVICES RENDERED

None ☐   b. List all firms or individuals who within **two years** immediately preceding the filing of this bankruptcy case have audited the books of account and records, or prepared a financial statement of the debtor.

NAME   ADDRESS   DATES SERVICES RENDERED

Form 7
OFFICIAL FORMS

☐ None   c. List all firms or individuals who at the time of the commencement of this case were in possession of the books of account and records of the debtor. If any of the books of account and records are not available, explain.

       NAME   ADDRESS

☐ None   d. List all financial institutions, creditors and other parties, including mercantile and trade agencies, to whom a financial statement was issued by the debtor within **two years** immediately preceding the commencement of this case.

       NAME AND ADDRESS   DATE ISSUED

---

20. Inventories

☐ None   a. List the dates of the last two inventories taken of your property, the name of the person who supervised the taking of each inventory, and the dollar amount and basis of each inventory.

                                                                   DOLLAR AMOUNT
                                                                   OF INVENTORY
       DATE OF INVENTORY   INVENTORY SUPERVISOR   (Specify cost, market or other basis)

☐ None   b. List the name and address of the person having possession of the records of each of the inventories reported in a., above.

                                                           NAME AND ADDRESSES
                                                           OF CUSTODIAN
       DATE OF INVENTORY   OF INVENTORY RECORDS

---

21. Current Partners, Officers, Directors and Shareholders

☐ None   a. If the debtor is a partnership, list the nature and percentage of partnership interest of each member of the partnership.

       NAME AND ADDRESS   NATURE OF INTEREST   PERCENTAGE OF INTEREST

☐ None   b. If the debtor is a corporation, list all officers and directors of the corporation, and each stockholder who directly or indirectly owns, controls, or holds 5 percent or more of the voting or equity securities of the corporation.

                                                                       NATURE AND PERCENTAGE
       NAME AND ADDRESS   TITLE   OF STOCK OWNERSHIP

OFFICIAL FORMS   **Form 7**

22. Former partners, officers, directors and shareholders

None ☐   a.   If the debtor is a partnership, list each member who withdrew from the partnership within **one year** immediately preceding the commencement of this case.

NAME	ADDRESS	DATE OF WITHDRAWAL

None ☐   b.   If the debtor is a corporation, list all officers or directors whose relationship with the corporation terminated within **one year** immediately preceding the commencement of this case.

NAME AND ADDRESS	TITLE	DATE OF TERMINATION

23. Withdrawals from a partnership or distributions by a corporation

None ☐   If the debtor is a partnership or corporation, list all withdrawals or distributions credited or given to an insider, including compensation in any form, bonuses, loans, stock redemptions, options exercised and any other perquisite during **one year** immediately preceding the commencement of this case.

NAME & ADDRESS OF RECIPIENT, RELATIONSHIP TO DEBTOR	DATE AND PURPOSE OF WITHDRAWAL	AMOUNT OF MONEY OR DESCRIPTION AND VALUE OF PROPERTY

24. Tax Consolidation Group.

None ☐   If the debtor is a corporation, list the name and federal taxpayer-identification number of the parent corporation of any consolidated group for tax purposes of which the debtor has been a member at any time within **six years** immediately preceding the commencement of the case.

NAME OF PARENT CORPORATION	TAXPAYER-IDENTIFICATION NUMBER (EIN)

25. Pension Funds.

None ☐   If the debtor is not an individual, list the name and federal taxpayer-identification number of any pension fund to which the debtor, as an employer, has been responsible for contributing at any time within **six years** immediately preceding the commencement of the case.

NAME OF PENSION FUND	TAXPAYER-IDENTIFICATION NUMBER (EIN)

* * * * * *

Form 7 OFFICIAL FORMS

11

[If completed by an individual or individual and spouse]

I declare under penalty of perjury that I have read the answers contained in the foregoing statement of financial affairs and any attachments thereto and that they are true and correct.

Date _____   Signature of Debtor _____

Date _____   Signature of Joint Debtor (if any) _____

[If completed on behalf of a partnership or corporation]

I declare under penalty of perjury that I have read the answers contained in the foregoing statement of financial affairs and any attachments thereto and that they are true and correct to the best of my knowledge, information and belief.

Date _____   Signature _____

Print Name and Title _____

[An individual signing on behalf of a partnership or corporation must indicate position or relationship to debtor.]

___ continuation sheets attached

Penalty for making a false statement: Fine of up to $500,000 or imprisonment for up to 5 years, or both. 18 U.S.C. §§ 152 and 3571

DECLARATION AND SIGNATURE OF NON-ATTORNEY BANKRUPTCY PETITION PREPARER (See 11 U.S.C. § 110)

I declare under penalty of perjury that: (1) I am a bankruptcy petition preparer as defined in 11 U.S.C. § 110; (2) I prepared this document for compensation and have provided the debtor with a copy of this document and the notices and information required under 11 U.S.C. §§ 110(b), 110(h), and 342(b); and, (3) if rules or guidelines have been promulgated pursuant to 11 U.S.C. § 110(h) setting a maximum fee for services chargeable by bankruptcy petition preparers, I have given the debtor notice of the maximum amount before preparing any document for filing for a debtor or accepting any fee from the debtor, as required by that section.

Printed or Typed Name and Title, if any, of Bankruptcy Petition Preparer   Social-Security No. (Required by 11 U.S.C. § 110.)

If the bankruptcy petition preparer is not an individual, state the name, title (if any), address, and social-security number of the officer, principal, responsible person, or partner who signs this document.

Address

Signature of Bankruptcy Petition Preparer   Date

Names and Social-Security numbers of all other individuals who prepared or assisted in preparing this document unless the bankruptcy petition preparer is not an individual:

If more than one person prepared this document, attach additional signed sheets conforming to the appropriate Official Form for each person

A bankruptcy petition preparer's failure to comply with the provisions of title 11 and the Federal Rules of Bankruptcy Procedure may result in fines or imprisonment or both. 18 U.S.C. § 156.

(Added Aug. 1, 1991; amended Mar. 16, 1993; Mar. 1995; Sept. 2000; Dec. 1, 2003; Aug. 11, 2005, eff. Oct. 17, 2005; Apr. 1, 2007; Apr. 1, 2010; Dec. 1, 2012; Apr. 1, 2013.)

OFFICIAL FORMS　　　　　　　　　　　　　　　　　　　　　　Form 7

ADVISORY COMMITTEE NOTES

1991 Enactment

This form consolidates questions from former Official Forms No. 7, No. 8, and No. 10. This form is to be completed by all debtors. An individual debtor engaged in business as a sole proprietor, partner, family farmer, or self-employed professional should provide the information requested on this statement concerning all such activities as well as the individual's personal affairs.

The Chapter 13 Statement, former Official Form No. 10, has been abrogated. Chapter 13 debtors are to complete this statement and the schedules prescribed in Official Form 6.

All questions have been converted to affirmative directions to furnish information, and each question must be answered. If the answer is "none," or the question is not applicable, the debtor is required to so state by marking the box labeled "None" provided at each question.

See Committee Note to Form 2 for a discussion of the unsworn declaration at the end of this form.

1993 Amendment

The form has been amended in two ways. In the second paragraph of the instructions, the third sentence has been deleted to clarify that only a debtor that is or had been in business as defined in the form should answer Questions 16–21. In addition, administrative proceedings have been added to the types of legal actions to be disclosed in Question 4.a.

1995 Amendment

This form is a "document for filing" that may be prepared by a "bankruptcy petition preparer" as defined in 11 U.S.C. § 110, which was added to the Code by the Bankruptcy Reform Act of 1994; accordingly, a signature line for such preparer is added. In addition to signing, a bankruptcy petition preparer is required by section 110 to disclose the information requested.

2000 Amendment

The form has been amended to provide more information to taxing authorities, pension fund supervisors, and governmental units charged with environmental protection and regulation. Four new questions have been added to the form, covering community property owned by a debtor and the debtor's non-filing spouse or former spouse (Question 16), environmental information (Question 17), any consolidated tax group of a corporate debtor (Question 24), and the debtor's contributions to any employee pension fund (Question 25). In addition, every debtor will be required to state on the form whether the debtor has been in business within six years before filing the petition and, if so, must answer the remaining questions on the form (Questions 19–25). This is an enlargement of the two-year period previously specified. One reason for the longer "reach back" period is that business debtors often owe taxes that have been owed for more than two years. Another is that some of the questions already addressed to business debtors request information for the six-year period before the commencement of the case. Application of a six-year period to this section of the form will assure disclosure of all relevant information.

2003 Amendment

Pursuant to § 110(c) of the Bankruptcy Code, the certification by a non-attorney bankruptcy petition preparer requires a petition preparer to provide the full Social Security number of the individual who actually prepares the document.

2005 Amendment

The form is amended in several ways to reflect changes in the Bankruptcy Code made by the Bankruptcy Abuse Prevention and Consumer Protection Act of 2005, Pub. L. No. 109–8, 119 Stat. 23 (April 20, 2005). A new sentence in the introduction advises the debtor not to disclose the name and address of any minor child.

The definition of "in business" is amended in the introductory section and in Question 1 and Question 18 to clarify that various part-time activities can result in the debtor being "in business" for purposes of the form.

Question 1 is amended to specify that, in addition to the income from the debtor's primary employment, the debtor must include income from part-time activities either as an employee or from self-employment. The debtor now also will report the source of all income from employment or operation of

Form 7 OFFICIAL FORMS

a business, even if there is only one source, in order to assist the trustee in reviewing the pay stubs, etc., filed by the debtor in the case.

Question 3 is amended to accommodate amendments to § 547(c) of the Code enacted in 2005 which exempt from recovery by the trustee payments by a debtor for a domestic support obligation or as part of an alternative repayment schedule negotiated by an approved nonprofit budgeting and credit counseling agency. In addition, Question 3 now requires a debtor with primarily non-consumer debts to report only those transfers that aggregate more than $5,000 to any creditor in the 90-day period prior to the filing of the petition, as a result of the addition of § 547(c)(9) to the Code in 2005.

In Question 10, the extension of the reachback period for transfers from one year to two years reflects the 2005 amendment to § 548(a)(1) of the Code to permit a trustee to avoid a fraudulent transfer made by the debtor within two years of the date of the filing of the petition. Question 10 also is amended to implement new § 548(e) added to the Code in 2005 to require the debtor to disclose all transfers to any self-settled asset protection trust within the ten years before the filing of the petition.

Question 15 is amended to extend from two years to three years the prepetition time period for which the debtor must disclose the addresses of all premises occupied by the debtor. This information will assist the trustee, the United States trustee, and the court to ascertain whether any homestead exemption asserted by the debtor is properly claimed under § 522(v)(3)(A) as amended, and §§ 522(p) and (q) as added to the Code in 2005.

The form also is amended to extend from six years to eight years the period before the filing of the petition concerning which the debtor is required to disclose the name of the debtor's spouse or of any former spouse who resides or resided with the debtor in a community property state. In addition, the certification by a non-attorney bankruptcy petition preparer is renamed a "declaration" and is amended to include material mandated by 11 U.S.C. § 110 as amended by the 2005 Act.

2005–2007 Amendments

(The 2005–2007 Committee Note incorporates the Committee Note previously published in 2005.)

The form is amended in several ways to reflect changes in the Bankruptcy Code made by the Bankruptcy Abuse Prevention and Consumer Protection Act of 2005, Pub. L. No. 109–8, 119 Stat. 23 (April 20, 2005). A new sentence in the introduction advises the debtor not to disclose the name and address of any minor child in conformity with § 112, which was added to the Code by the 2005 Act. In addition, the form is amended to add to the reference to Rule 1007(m) with respect to a minor child a direction to include for noticing purposes the name, address, and legal relationship to the child of "a person described" in that rule. Rule 1007(m) requires the person named to be someone on whom process would be served in an adversary proceeding against the child.

The definition of "in business" is amended in the introductory section and in Question 1 and Question 18 to clarify that various part-time activities can result in the debtor being "in business" for purposes of the form.

Question 1 is amended to specify that, in addition to the income from the debtor's primary employment, the debtor must include income from part-time activities either as an employee or from self-employment. The debtor now also will report the source of all income from employment or operation of a business, even if there is only one source, in order to assist the trustee in reviewing the pay stubs, etc., filed by the debtor in the case.

Question 3 is amended to accommodate amendments to § 547(c) of the Code enacted in 2005 which exempt from recovery by the trustee payments by a debtor for a domestic support obligation or as part of an alternative repayment schedule negotiated by an approved nonprofit budgeting and credit counseling agency. In addition, Question 3 now requires a debtor with primarily non-consumer debts to report only those transfers that aggregate more than $5,475 to any creditor in the 90-day period prior to the filing of the petition, as a result of the addition of § 547(c)(9) to the Code in 2005. In addition, the language of the question is revised for clarity.

In Question 10, the extension of the reach-back period for transfers from one year to two years reflects the 2005 amendment to § 548(a)(1) of the Code to permit a trustee to avoid a fraudulent transfer made by the debtor within two years before the date of the filing of the petition. Question 10 also is amended to implement new § 548(e) added to the Code in 2005 to require the debtor to disclose all transfers to any self-settled asset protection trust within the ten years before the filing of the petition.

OFFICIAL FORMS — Form 7

Question 15 is amended to extend from two years to three years the prepetition time period for which the debtor must disclose the addresses of all premises occupied by the debtor. This information will assist the trustee, the United States trustee, and the court to ascertain whether any homestead exemption asserted by the debtor is properly claimed under § 522(b)(3)(A) as amended, and §§ 522(p) and (q) as added to the Code in 2005.

The form also is amended to extend from six years to eight years the period before the filing of the petition concerning which the debtor is required to disclose the name of the debtor's spouse or of any former spouse who resides or resided with the debtor in a community property state. In addition, the certification by a non-attorney bankruptcy petition preparer is renamed a "declaration" and is amended to include material mandated by 11 U.S.C. § 110 as amended by the 2005 Act.

2012 Amendment

The definition of "insider" is amended to conform to the statutory definition of the term. See 11 U.S.C. § 101(31). Under the Code definition, ownership of 5% or more of the voting shares of a corporate debtor does not automatically make the owner an insider of the corporation. And in order to be an affiliate of the debtor and an insider on that basis, ownership or control of at least 20% of the outstanding voting securities of the debtor is required. 11 U.S.C. § 101(2). The phrase "any owner of 5% or more of the voting or equity securities" is therefore deleted. Because § 101(31) provides that a person in control of a debtor corporation is an insider, that term is substituted for the deleted phrase.

Form 8   OFFICIAL FORMS

Form 8. Individual Debtor's Statement of Intention

B 8 (Official Form 8) (12/08)

UNITED STATES BANKRUPTCY COURT

In re _____,   Case No. _____
         Debtor   Chapter 7

CHAPTER 7 INDIVIDUAL DEBTOR'S STATEMENT OF INTENTION

PART A – Debts secured by property of the estate. *(Part A must be fully completed for EACH debt which is secured by property of the estate. Attach additional pages if necessary.)*

Property No. 1

Creditor's Name:	**Describe Property Securing Debt:**

Property will be *(check one)*:
    ☐ Surrendered   ☐ Retained

If retaining the property, I intend to *(check at least one)*:
    ☐ Redeem the property
    ☐ Reaffirm the debt
    ☐ Other. Explain _____ (for example, avoid lien using 11 U.S.C. § 522(f)).

Property is *(check one)*:
    ☐ Claimed as exempt   ☐ Not claimed as exempt

Property No. 2 *(if necessary)*

Creditor's Name:	**Describe Property Securing Debt:**

Property will be *(check one)*:
    ☐ Surrendered   ☐ Retained

If retaining the property, I intend to *(check at least one)*:
    ☐ Redeem the property
    ☐ Reaffirm the debt
    ☐ Other. Explain _____ (for example, avoid lien using 11 U.S.C. § 522(f)).

Property is *(check one)*:
    ☐ Claimed as exempt   ☐ Not claimed as exempt

OFFICIAL FORMS Form 8

B 8 (Official Form 8) (12/08) Page 2

PART B – Personal property subject to unexpired leases. *(All three columns of Part B must be completed for each unexpired lease. Attach additional pages if necessary.)*

Property No. 1		
Lessor's Name:	**Describe Leased Property:**	Lease will be Assumed pursuant to 11 U.S.C. § 365(p)(2): ❏ YES ❏ NO

Property No. 2 *(if necessary)*		
Lessor's Name:	**Describe Leased Property:**	Lease will be Assumed pursuant to 11 U.S.C. § 365(p)(2): ❏ YES ❏ NO

Property No. 3 *(if necessary)*		
Lessor's Name:	**Describe Leased Property:**	Lease will be Assumed pursuant to 11 U.S.C. § 365(p)(2): ❏ YES ❏ NO

_____ continuation sheets attached *(if any)*

I declare under penalty of perjury that the above indicates my intention as to any property of my estate securing a debt and/or personal property subject to an unexpired lease.

Date: _____   _____
                                 Signature of Debtor

                                 _____
                                 Signature of Joint Debtor

Form 8   **OFFICIAL FORMS**

B 8 (Official Form 8) (12/08)   Page 3

CHAPTER 7 INDIVIDUAL DEBTOR'S STATEMENT OF INTENTION
(Continuation Sheet)

PART A - Continuation

Property No.	
Creditor's Name:	**Describe Property Securing Debt:**

Property will be *(check one)*:
    ❏ Surrendered   ❏ Retained

If retaining the property, I intend to *(check at least one)*:
    ❏ Redeem the property
    ❏ Reaffirm the debt
    ❏ Other. Explain _____ (for example, avoid lien using 11 U.S.C. § 522(f)).

Property is *(check one)*:
    ❏ Claimed as exempt   ❏ Not claimed as exempt

PART B - Continuation

Property No.		
Lessor's Name:	**Describe Leased Property:**	Lease will be Assumed pursuant to 11 U.S.C. § 365(p)(2): ❏ YES ❏ NO

Property No.		
Lessor's Name:	**Describe Leased Property:**	Lease will be Assumed pursuant to 11 U.S.C. § 365(p)(2): ❏ YES ❏ NO

(Added Aug. 1, 1991; and amended Mar. 1995; Oct. 1, 1997; Dec. 1, 2003; Aug. 11, 2005, eff. Oct. 17, 2005; Dec. 1, 2008.)

ADVISORY COMMITTEE NOTES

    This form is derived from former Official Form No. 8A. Rule 1007(b)(2) requires the debtor to serve a copy of this statement on the trustee and all creditors named in the statement. In a joint case, if the property and debts of both debtors are the same, the form may be adapted for joint use. If joint debtors have separate debts, however, each debtor must use a separate form.

1995 Amendment

    This form is a "document for filing" that may be prepared by a "bankruptcy petition preparer" as defined in 11 U.S.C. § 110, which was added to the Code by the Bankruptcy Reform Act of 1994;

OFFICIAL FORMS   Form 8

accordingly, a signature line for such preparer is added. In addition to signing, a bankruptcy petition preparer is required by section 110 to disclose the information requested.

1997 Amendment

The form is amended to conform more closely to the language of the Bankruptcy Code. The amendments also make clear that the form is not intended to take a position regarding whether the options stated on the form are the only choices available to the debtor. Compare *Lowry Federal Credit Union v. West*, 882 F.2d 1543 (10th Cir. 1989), with *In re Taylor*, 3 F.3d 1512 (11th Cir. 1993).

2003 Amendment

Pursuant to § 110(c) of the Bankruptcy Code, the certification by a non-attorney bankruptcy petition preparer requires a petition preparer to provide the full Social Security number of the individual who actually prepares the document.

2005 Amendment

The form is amended to conform to § 521(a)(6), which was added to the Code by the Bankruptcy Abuse Prevention and Consumer Protection Act of 2005, Pub. L. No. 109–8, 119 Stat. 23 (April 20, 2005), by adding a section covering personal property subject to an unexpired lease and an option labeled "lease will be assumed pursuant to 11 U.S.C. § 362(h)(1)(A)" to the choices a debtor may make. The certification by a non-attorney bankruptcy petition preparer in the form is renamed a "declaration" and is amended to include material mandated by the 2005 amendments to § 110 of the Code.

2008 Amendment

The form is amended to conform to § 362(h), which was added to the Code, and § 521(a)(2), which was amended, by the Bankruptcy Abuse Prevention and Consumer Protection Act of 2005, Pub. L. No. 109–8, 119 Stat. 23 (April 20, 2005), by expanding the questions directed to the debtor regarding leased personal property and property subject to security interests. The form is also amended and reformatted to require the debtor to complete a series of statements describing the property and setting out what actions the debtor intends to take for each listed asset. The amended form is intended to elicit more complete information about the debtor's intentions with regard to property subject to security interests and personal property leases than has been obtained under the current version of the form.

In addition, the form is amended to specify that the debtor's signature is a declaration under penalty of perjury, as required by Rule 1008, and to provide space for the co-debtor's signature. A continuation page has been provided for use if necessary. The Declaration of Non-Attorney Bankruptcy Petition Preparer has been deleted from the form as duplicative of Form 19, Declaration and Signature of Non-Attorney Bankruptcy Petition Preparer. Form 19 contains both the petition preparer's declaration and signature and the notice the petition preparer is required to give to the debtor under § 110 of the Code.

Form 9   OFFICIAL FORMS

Form 9. Notice of Commencement of Case Under the Bankruptcy Code, Meeting of Creditors, and Deadlines

Form B9A

B9A (Official Form 9A) (Chapter 7 Individual or Joint Debtor No Asset Case) (12/12)

UNITED STATES BANKRUPTCY COURT _____ District of _____

Notice of
Chapter 7 Bankruptcy Case, Meeting of Creditors, & Deadlines

[A chapter 7 bankruptcy case concerning the debtor(s) listed below was filed on _____ (date).]
or [A bankruptcy case concerning the debtor(s) listed below was originally filed under chapter _____ on _____ (date) and was converted to a case under chapter 7 on _____ (date).]

You may be a creditor of the debtor. **This notice lists important deadlines.** You may want to consult an attorney to protect your rights. All documents filed in the case may be inspected at the bankruptcy clerk's office at the address listed below. NOTE: The staff of the bankruptcy clerk's office cannot give legal advice.

Creditors -- Do not file this notice in connection with any proof of claim you submit to the court.
See Reverse Side for Important Explanations.

Debtor(s) (name(s) and address):	Case Number:
	Last four digits of Social-Security or Individual Taxpayer-ID (ITIN) No(s)./Complete EIN:
All other names used by the Debtor(s) in the last 8 years (include married, maiden, and trade names):	Bankruptcy Trustee (name and address):
Attorney for Debtor(s) (name and address):	
Telephone number:	Telephone number:

Meeting of Creditors

Date: / /   Time: ( ) A. M.   Location:
                           ( ) P. M.

Presumption of Abuse under 11 U.S.C. § 707(b)
See "Presumption of Abuse" on the reverse side.

Depending on the documents filed with the petition, one of the following statements will appear.

       The presumption of abuse does not arise.
           Or
       The presumption of abuse arises.
           Or
       Insufficient information has been filed to date to permit the clerk to make any determination concerning the presumption of abuse. If more complete information, when filed, shows that the presumption has arisen, creditors will be notified.

Deadlines:
Papers must be *received* by the bankruptcy clerk's office by the following deadlines:
Deadline to Object to Debtor's Discharge or to Challenge Dischargeability of Certain Debts:

Deadline to Object to Exemptions:
Thirty (30) days after the *conclusion* of the meeting of creditors.

Creditors May Not Take Certain Actions:
In most instances, the filing of the bankruptcy case automatically stays certain collection and other actions against the debtor and the debtor's property. Under certain circumstances, the stay may be limited to 30 days or not exist at all, although the debtor can request the court to extend or impose a stay. If you attempt to collect a debt or take other action in violation of the Bankruptcy Code, you may be penalized. Consult a lawyer to determine your rights in this case.

Please Do Not File a Proof of Claim Unless You Receive a Notice To Do So.

Creditor with a Foreign Address:
A creditor to whom this notice is sent at a foreign address should read the information under "Do Not File a Proof of Claim at This Time" on the reverse side.

Address of the Bankruptcy Clerk's Office:	For the Court:
	Clerk of the Bankruptcy Court:
Telephone number:	
Hours Open:	Date:

866

OFFICIAL FORMS

Form B9A

EXPLANATIONS B9A (Official Form 9A) (12/12)

Filing of Chapter 7 Bankruptcy Case	A bankruptcy case under Chapter 7 of the Bankruptcy Code (title 11, United States Code) has been filed in this court by or against the debtor(s) listed on the front side, and an order for relief has been entered.
Legal Advice	The staff of the bankruptcy clerk's office cannot give legal advice. Consult a lawyer to determine your rights in this case.
Creditors Generally May Not Take Certain Actions	Prohibited collection actions are listed in Bankruptcy Code § 362. Common examples of prohibited actions include contacting the debtor by telephone, mail, or otherwise to demand repayment; taking actions to collect money or obtain property from the debtor; repossessing the debtor's property; starting or continuing lawsuits or foreclosures; and garnishing or deducting from the debtor's wages. Under certain circumstances, the stay may be limited to 30 days or not exist at all, although the debtor can request the court to extend or impose a stay.
Presumption of Abuse	If the presumption of abuse arises, creditors may have the right to file a motion to dismiss the case under § 707(b) of the Bankruptcy Code. The debtor may rebut the presumption by showing special circumstances.
Meeting of Creditors	A meeting of creditors is scheduled for the date, time, and location listed on the front side. *The debtor (both spouses in a joint case) must be present at the meeting to be questioned under oath by the trustee and by creditors.* Creditors are welcome to attend, but are not required to do so. The meeting may be continued and concluded at a later date specified in a notice filed with the court.
Do Not File a Proof of Claim at This Time	There does not appear to be any property available to the trustee to pay creditors. *You therefore should not file a proof of claim at this time.* If it later appears that assets are available to pay creditors, you will be sent another notice telling you that you may file a proof of claim, and telling you the deadline for filing your proof of claim. If this notice is mailed to a creditor at a foreign address, the creditor may file a motion requesting the court to extend the deadline. *Do not include this notice with any filing you make with the court.*
Discharge of Debts	The debtor is seeking a discharge of most debts, which may include your debt. A discharge means that you may never try to collect the debt from the debtor. If you believe that the debtor is not entitled to receive a discharge under Bankruptcy Code § 727(a) *or* that a debt owed to you is not dischargeable under Bankruptcy Code § 523(a)(2), (4), or (6), you must file a complaint -- or a motion if you assert the discharge should be denied under § 727(a)(8) or (a)(9) -- in the bankruptcy clerk's office by the "Deadline to Object to Debtor's Discharge or to Challenge the Dischargeability of Certain Debts" listed on the front of this form. The bankruptcy clerk's office must receive the complaint or motion and any required filing fee by that deadline.
Exempt Property	The debtor is permitted by law to keep certain property as exempt. Exempt property will not be sold and distributed to creditors. The debtor must file a list of all property claimed as exempt. You may inspect that list at the bankruptcy clerk's office. If you believe that an exemption claimed by the debtor is not authorized by law, you may file an objection to that exemption. The bankruptcy clerk's office must receive the objections by the "Deadline to Object to Exemptions" listed on the front side.
Bankruptcy Clerk's Office	Any paper that you file in this bankruptcy case should be filed at the bankruptcy clerk's office at the address listed on the front side. You may inspect all papers filed, including the list of the debtor's property and debts and the list of the property claimed as exempt, at the bankruptcy clerk's office.
Creditor with a Foreign Address	Consult a lawyer familiar with United States bankruptcy law if you have any questions regarding your rights in this case.

Refer To Other Side For Important Deadlines and Notices

Form B9B

OFFICIAL FORMS

Form B9B

B9B (Official Form 9B) (Chapter 7 Corporation/Partnership No Asset Case) (12/12)

UNITED STATES BANKRUPTCY COURT	District of

Notice of
Chapter 7 Bankruptcy Case, Meeting of Creditors, & Deadlines

[A chapter 7 bankruptcy case concerning the debtor(s) listed below was filed on _____ (date).]
or [A bankruptcy case concerning the debtor(s) listed below was originally filed under chapter ____ on _____ (date) and was converted to a case under chapter 7 on _____ (date).]

You may be a creditor of the debtor. **This notice lists important deadlines.** You may want to consult an attorney to protect your rights. All documents filed in the case may be inspected at the bankruptcy clerk's office at the address listed below. NOTE: The staff of the bankruptcy clerk's office cannot give legal advice.

**Creditors -- Do not file this notice in connection with any proof of claim you submit to the court.
See Reverse Side for Important Explanations.**

Debtor(s) (name(s) and address):	Case Number:
	Last four digits of Social-Security or Individual Taxpayer-ID (ITIN) No(s)./Complete EIN:
All other names used by the debtor(s) in the last 8 years (include trade names):	Bankruptcy Trustee (name and address):
Attorney for Debtor(s) (name and address):	
Telephone number:	Telephone number:

Meeting of Creditors

Date: / / Time: ( ) A. M. Location:
               ( ) P. M.

Creditors May Not Take Certain Actions:

In most instances, the filing of the bankruptcy case automatically stays certain collection and other actions against the debtor and the debtor's property. Under certain circumstances, the stay may be limited to 30 days or not exist at all, although the debtor can request the court to extend or impose a stay. If you attempt to collect a debt or take other action in violation of the Bankruptcy Code, you may be penalized. Consult a lawyer to determine your rights in this case.

Please Do Not File a Proof of Claim Unless You Receive a Notice To Do So.

Creditor with a Foreign Address:

A creditor to whom this notice is sent at a foreign address should read the information under "Do Not File a Proof of Claim at This Time" on the reverse side.

Address of the Bankruptcy Clerk's Office:	For the Court:
	Clerk of the Bankruptcy Court:
Telephone number:	
Hours Open:	Date:

OFFICIAL FORMS   **Form B9B**

EXPLANATIONS   B9B (Official Form 9B) (12/12)

Filing of Chapter 7 Bankruptcy Case	A bankruptcy case under Chapter 7 of the Bankruptcy Code (title 11, United States Code) has been filed in this court by or against the debtor(s) listed on the front side, and an order for relief has been entered.
Legal Advice	The staff of the bankruptcy clerk's office cannot give legal advice. Consult a lawyer to determine your rights in this case.
Creditors Generally May Not Take Certain Actions	Prohibited collection actions are listed in Bankruptcy Code § 362. Common examples of prohibited actions include contacting the debtor by telephone, mail, or otherwise to demand repayment; taking actions to collect money or obtain property from the debtor; repossessing the debtor's property; and starting or continuing lawsuits or foreclosures. Under certain circumstances, the stay may be limited to 30 days or not exist at all, although the debtor can request the court to extend or impose a stay.
Meeting of Creditors	A meeting of creditors is scheduled for the date, time, and location listed on the front side. *The debtor's representative must be present at the meeting to be questioned under oath by the trustee and by creditors.* Creditors are welcome to attend, but are not required to do so. The meeting may be continued and concluded at a later date specified in a notice filed with the court.
Do Not File a Proof of Claim at This Time	There does not appear to be any property available to the trustee to pay creditors. *You therefore should not file a proof of claim at this time.* If it later appears that assets are available to pay creditors, you will be sent another notice telling you that you may file a proof of claim, and telling you the deadline for filing your proof of claim. If this notice is mailed to a creditor at a foreign address, the creditor may file a motion requesting the court to extend the deadline. *Do not include this notice with any filing you make with the court.*
Bankruptcy Clerk's Office	Any paper that you file in this bankruptcy case should be filed at the bankruptcy clerk's office at the address listed on the front side. You may inspect all papers filed, including the list of the debtor's property and debts and the list of the property claimed as exempt, at the bankruptcy clerk's office.
Creditor with a Foreign Address	Consult a lawyer familiar with United States bankruptcy law if you have any questions regarding your rights in this case.

Refer To Other Side For Important Deadlines and Notices

Form B9C   **OFFICIAL FORMS**

Form B9C

B9C (Official Form 9C) (Chapter 7 Individual or Joint Debtor Asset Case) (12/12)

UNITED STATES BANKRUPTCY COURT _____ District of _____

Notice of
Chapter 7 Bankruptcy Case, Meeting of Creditors, & Deadlines

[A chapter 7 bankruptcy case concerning the debtor(s) listed below was filed on _____(date).]
or [A bankruptcy case concerning the debtor(s) listed below was originally filed under chapter_____ on
_____(date) and was converted to a case under chapter 7 on _____(date).]

You may be a creditor of the debtor. **This notice lists important deadlines.** You may want to consult an attorney to protect your rights. All documents filed in the case may be inspected at the bankruptcy clerk's office at the address listed below. NOTE: The staff of the bankruptcy clerk's office cannot give legal advice.

Creditors -- Do not file this notice in connection with any proof of claim you submit to the court.
See Reverse Side for Important Explanations.

Debtor(s) (name(s) and address):	Case Number:
	Last four digits of Social-Security or Individual Taxpayer-ID (ITIN) No(s)./Complete EIN:
All other names used by the Debtor(s) in the last 8 years (include married, maiden, and trade names):	Bankruptcy Trustee (name and address):
Attorney for Debtor(s) (name and address):	
Telephone number:	Telephone number:

Meeting of Creditors
Date: / /   Time: ( ) A. M.   Location:
                          ( ) P. M.

Presumption of Abuse under 11 U.S.C. § 707(b)
See "Presumption of Abuse" on the reverse side.

Depending on the documents filed with the petition, one of the following statements will appear.
    The presumption of abuse does not arise.
        Or
    The presumption of abuse arises.
        Or
    Insufficient information has been filed to date to permit the clerk to make any determination concerning the presumption of abuse. If more complete information, when filed, shows that the presumption has arisen, creditors will be notified.

Deadlines:
Papers must be *received* by the bankruptcy clerk's office by the following deadlines:

Deadline to File a Proof of Claim:
For all creditors (except a governmental unit):   For a governmental unit:
Creditor with a Foreign Address:
A creditor to whom this notice is sent at a foreign address should read the information under "Claims" on the reverse side.

Deadline to Object to Debtor's Discharge or to Challenge Dischargeability of Certain Debts:

Deadline to Object to Exemptions:
Thirty (30) days after the *conclusion* of the meeting of creditors.

Creditors May Not Take Certain Actions:
In most instances, the filing of the bankruptcy case automatically stays certain collection and other actions against the debtor and the debtor's property. Under certain circumstances, the stay may be limited to 30 days or not exist at all, although the debtor can request the court to extend or impose a stay. If you attempt to collect a debt or take other action in violation of the Bankruptcy Code, you may be penalized. Consult a lawyer to determine your rights in this case.

Address of the Bankruptcy Clerk's Office:	For the Court:
	Clerk of the Bankruptcy Court:
Telephone number:	
Hours Open:	Date:

OFFICIAL FORMS

Form B9C

EXPLANATIONS B9C (Official Form 9C) (12/12)

Filing of Chapter 7 Bankruptcy Case	A bankruptcy case under Chapter 7 of the Bankruptcy Code (title 11, United States Code) has been filed in this court by or against the debtor(s) listed on the front side, and an order for relief has been entered.
Legal Advice	The staff of the bankruptcy clerk's office cannot give legal advice. Consult a lawyer to determine your rights in this case.
Creditors Generally May Not Take Certain Actions	Prohibited collection actions are listed in Bankruptcy Code § 362. Common examples of prohibited actions include contacting the debtor by telephone, mail, or otherwise to demand repayment; taking actions to collect money or obtain property from the debtor; repossessing the debtor's property; starting or continuing lawsuits or foreclosures; and garnishing or deducting from the debtor's wages. Under certain circumstances, the stay may be limited to 30 days or not exist at all, although the debtor can request the court to extend or impose a stay.
Meeting of Creditors	A meeting of creditors is scheduled for the date, time, and location listed on the front side. *The debtor (both spouses in a joint case) must be present at the meeting to be questioned under oath by the trustee and by creditors.* Creditors are welcome to attend, but are not required to do so. The meeting may be continued and concluded at a later date specified in a notice filed with the court.
Claims	A Proof of Claim is a signed statement describing a creditor's claim. If a Proof of Claim form is not included with this notice, you can obtain one at any bankruptcy clerk's office. A secured creditor retains rights in its collateral regardless of whether that creditor files a Proof of Claim. If you do not file a Proof of Claim by the "Deadline to File a Proof of Claim" listed on the front side, you might not be paid any money on your claim from other assets in the bankruptcy case. To be paid, you must file a Proof of Claim even if your claim is listed in the schedules filed by the debtor. Filing a Proof of Claim submits the creditor to the jurisdiction of the bankruptcy court, with consequences a lawyer can explain. For example, a secured creditor who files a Proof of Claim may surrender important nonmonetary rights, including the right to a jury trial. **Filing Deadline for a Creditor with a Foreign Address:** The deadlines for filing claims set forth on the front of this notice apply to all creditors. If this notice has been mailed to a creditor at a foreign address, the creditor may file a motion requesting the court to extend the deadline. *Do not include this notice with any filing you make with the court.*
Discharge of Debts	The debtor is seeking a discharge of most debts, which may include your debt. A discharge means that you may never try to collect the debt from the debtor. If you believe that the debtor is not entitled to receive a discharge under Bankruptcy Code § 727(a) *or* that a debt owed to you is not dischargeable under Bankruptcy Code § 523(a)(2), (4), or (6), you must file a complaint -- or a motion if you assert the discharge should be denied under § 727(a)(8) or (a)(9) -- in the bankruptcy clerk's office by the "Deadline to Object to Debtor's Discharge or to Challenge the Dischargeability of Certain Debts" listed on the front of this form. The bankruptcy clerk's office must receive the complaint or motion and any required filing fee by that deadline.
Exempt Property	The debtor is permitted by law to keep certain property as exempt. Exempt property will not be sold and distributed to creditors. The debtor must file a list of all property claimed as exempt. You may inspect that list at the bankruptcy clerk's office. If you believe that an exemption claimed by the debtor is not authorized by law, you may file an objection to that exemption. The bankruptcy clerk's office must receive the objections by the "Deadline to Object to Exemptions" listed on the front side.
Presumption of Abuse	If the presumption of abuse arises, creditors may have the right to file a motion to dismiss the case under § 707(b) of the Bankruptcy Code. The debtor may rebut the presumption by showing special circumstances.
Bankruptcy Clerk's Office	Any paper that you file in this bankruptcy case should be filed at the bankruptcy clerk's office at the address listed on the front side. You may inspect all papers filed, including the list of the debtor's property and debts and the list of the property claimed as exempt, at the bankruptcy clerk's office.
Liquidation of the Debtor's Property and Payment of Creditors' Claims	The bankruptcy trustee listed on the front of this notice will collect and sell the debtor's property that is not exempt. If the trustee can collect enough money, creditors may be paid some or all of the debts owed to them, in the order specified by the Bankruptcy Code. To make sure you receive any share of that money, you must file a Proof of Claim, as described above.
Creditor with a Foreign Address	Consult a lawyer familiar with United States bankruptcy law if you have any questions regarding your rights in this case.

Refer To Other Side For Important Deadlines and Notices

Form B9D

OFFICIAL FORMS

Form B9D

B9D (Official Form 9D) (Chapter 7 Corporation/Partnership Asset Case) (12/12)

UNITED STATES BANKRUPTCY COURT_____ District of _____

Notice of
Chapter 7 Bankruptcy Case, Meeting of Creditors, & Deadlines

[A chapter 7 bankruptcy case concerning the debtor(s) listed below was filed on _____ (date).]
or [A bankruptcy case concerning the debtor(s) listed below was originally filed under chapter _____ on _____ (date) and was converted to a case under chapter 7 on _____ (date).]

You may be a creditor of the debtor. **This notice lists important deadlines.** You may want to consult an attorney to protect your rights. All documents filed in the case may be inspected at the bankruptcy clerk's office at the address listed below. NOTE: The staff of the bankruptcy clerk's office cannot give legal advice.

**Creditors -- Do not file this notice in connection with any proof of claim you submit to the court.
See Reverse Side for Important Explanations.**

Debtor(s) (name(s) and address):	Case Number:
	Last four digits of Social-Security or Individual Taxpayer-ID (ITIN) No(s)./Complete EIN:
All other names used by the Debtor(s) in the last 8 years (include trade names):	Bankruptcy Trustee (name and address):
Attorney for Debtor(s) (name and address):	
Telephone number:	Telephone number:

Meeting of Creditors

Date: / /   Time: ( ) A. M.   Location:
                              ( ) P. M.

Deadline to File a Proof of Claim

Papers must be *received* by the bankruptcy clerk's office by the following deadlines:

For all creditors (except a governmental unit):   For a governmental unit:

Creditor with a Foreign Address:
A creditor to whom this notice is sent at a foreign address should read the information under "Claims" on the reverse side.

Creditors May Not Take Certain Actions:

In most instances, the filing of the bankruptcy case automatically stays certain collection and other actions against the debtor and the debtor's property. Under certain circumstances, the stay may be limited to 30 days or not exist at all, although the debtor can request the court to extend or impose a stay. If you attempt to collect a debt or take other action in violation of the Bankruptcy Code, you may be penalized. Consult a lawyer to determine your rights in this case.

Address of the Bankruptcy Clerk's Office:	For the Court:
	Clerk of the Bankruptcy Court:
Telephone number:	
Hours Open:	Date:

OFFICIAL FORMS   Form B9D

EXPLANATIONS   B9D (Official Form 9D) (12/12)

Filing of Chapter 7 Bankruptcy Case	A bankruptcy case under Chapter 7 of the Bankruptcy Code (title 11, United States Code) has been filed in this court by or against the debtor(s) listed on the front side, and an order for relief has been entered.
Legal Advice	The staff of the bankruptcy clerk's office cannot give legal advice. Consult a lawyer to determine your rights in this case.
Creditors Generally May Not Take Certain Actions	Prohibited collection actions are listed in Bankruptcy Code § 362. Common examples of prohibited actions include contacting the debtor by telephone, mail, or otherwise to demand repayment; taking actions to collect money or obtain property from the debtor; repossessing the debtor's property; and starting or continuing lawsuits or foreclosures. Under certain circumstances, the stay may be limited to 30 days or not exist at all, although the debtor can request the court to extend or impose a stay.
Meeting of Creditors	A meeting of creditors is scheduled for the date, time, and location listed on the front side. *The debtor's representative must be present at the meeting to be questioned under oath by the trustee and by creditors.* Creditors are welcome to attend, but are not required to do so. The meeting may be continued and concluded at a later date specified in a notice filed with the court.
Claims	A Proof of Claim is a signed statement describing a creditor's claim. If a Proof of Claim form is not included with this notice, you can obtain one at any bankruptcy clerk's office. A secured creditor retains rights in its collateral regardless of whether that creditor files a Proof of Claim. If you do not file a Proof of Claim by the "Deadline to File a Proof of Claim" listed on the front side, you might not be paid any money on your claim from other assets in the bankruptcy case. To be paid, you must file a Proof of Claim even if your claim is listed in the schedules filed by the debtor. Filing a Proof of Claim submits the creditor to the jurisdiction of the bankruptcy court, with consequences a lawyer can explain. For example, a secured creditor who files a Proof of Claim may surrender important nonmonetary rights, including the right to a jury trial. **Filing Deadline for a Creditor with a Foreign Address:** The deadlines for filing claims set forth on the front of this notice apply to all creditors. If this notice has been mailed to a creditor at a foreign address, the creditor may file a motion requesting the court to extend the deadline. *Do not include this notice with any filing you make with the court.*
Liquidation of the Debtor's Property and Payment of Creditors' Claims	The bankruptcy trustee listed on the front of this notice will collect and sell the debtor's property that is not exempt. If the trustee can collect enough money, creditors may be paid some or all of the debts owed to them, in the order specified by the Bankruptcy Code. To make sure you receive any share of that money, you must file a Proof of Claim, as described above.
Bankruptcy Clerk's Office	Any paper that you file in this bankruptcy case should be filed at the bankruptcy clerk's office at the address listed on the front side. You may inspect all papers filed, including the list of the debtor's property and debts and the list of the property claimed as exempt, at the bankruptcy clerk's office.
Creditor with a Foreign Address	Consult a lawyer familiar with United States bankruptcy law if you have any questions regarding your rights in this case.

Refer To Other Side For Important Deadlines and Notices

Form B9E OFFICIAL FORMS

Form B9E

B9E (Official Form 9E) (Chapter 11 Individual or Joint Debtor Case) (12/12)

UNITED STATES BANKRUPTCY COURT _____ District of _____

Notice of
Chapter 11 Bankruptcy Case, Meeting of Creditors, & Deadlines

[A chapter 11 bankruptcy case concerning the debtor(s) listed below was filed on _____ (date).]
or [A bankruptcy case concerning the debtor(s) listed below was originally filed under chapter _____ on _____ (date) and was converted to a case under chapter 11 on _____ (date).]

You may be a creditor of the debtor. **This notice lists important deadlines.** You may want to consult an attorney to protect your rights. All documents filed in the case may be inspected at the bankruptcy clerk's office at the address listed below.
NOTE: The staff of the bankruptcy clerk's office cannot give legal advice

Creditors -- Do not file this notice in connection with any proof of claim you submit to the court.
See Reverse Side for Important Explanations.

Debtor(s) (name(s) and address):	Case Number:
	Last four digits of Social-Security or Individual Taxpayer-ID (ITIN) No(s)./Complete EIN:
All other names used by the Debtor(s) in the last 8 years (include married, maiden, and trade names):	Attorney for Debtor(s) (name and address): Telephone number:

Meeting of Creditors

Date: / /   Time: ( ) A.M.   Location:
                ( ) P.M.

Deadlines:
Papers must be *received* by the bankruptcy clerk's office by the following deadlines:

Deadline to File a Proof of Claim:
Notice of deadline will be sent at a later time.

Creditor with a Foreign Address:
A creditor to whom this notice is sent at a foreign address should read the information under "Claims" on the reverse side.

Deadline to File a Complaint to Determine Dischargeability of Certain Debts:

Deadline to File a Complaint Objecting to Discharge of the Debtor:

First date set for hearing on confirmation of plan
Notice of that date will be sent at a later time.

Deadline to Object to Exemptions:
Thirty (30) days after the *conclusion* of the meeting of creditors.

Creditors May Not Take Certain Actions:
In most instances, the filing of the bankruptcy case automatically stays certain collection and other actions against the debtor and the debtor's property. Under certain circumstances, the stay may be limited to 30 days or not exist at all, although the debtor can request the court to extend or impose a stay. If you attempt to collect a debt or take other action in violation of the Bankruptcy Code, you may be penalized. Consult a lawyer to determine your rights in this case.

Address of the Bankruptcy Clerk's Office:	For the Court:
	Clerk of the Bankruptcy Court:
Telephone number:	
Hours Open:	Date:

OFFICIAL FORMS

Form B9E

EXPLANATIONS   B9E (Official Form 9E) (12/12)

Filing of Chapter 11 Bankruptcy Case	A bankruptcy case under Chapter 11 of the Bankruptcy Code (title 11, United States Code) has been filed in this court by or against the debtor(s) listed on the front side, and an order for relief has been entered. Chapter 11 allows a debtor to reorganize or liquidate pursuant to a plan. A plan is not effective unless confirmed by the court. You may be sent a copy of the plan and a disclosure statement telling you about the plan, and you might have the opportunity to vote on the plan. You will be sent notice of the date of the confirmation hearing, and you may object to confirmation of the plan and attend the confirmation hearing. Unless a trustee is serving, the debtor will remain in possession of the debtor's property and may continue to operate any business.
Legal Advice	The staff of the bankruptcy clerk's office cannot give legal advice. Consult a lawyer to determine your rights in this case.
Creditors Generally May Not Take Certain Actions	Prohibited collection actions are listed in Bankruptcy Code § 362. Common examples of prohibited actions include contacting the debtor by telephone, mail, or otherwise to demand repayment; taking actions to collect money or obtain property from the debtor; repossessing the debtor's property; starting or continuing lawsuits or foreclosures; and garnishing or deducting from the debtor's wages. Under certain circumstances, the stay may be limited to 30 days or not exist at all, although the debtor can request the court to extend or impose a stay.
Meeting of Creditors	A meeting of creditors is scheduled for the date, time, and location listed on the front side. *The debtor (both spouses in a joint case) must be present at the meeting to be questioned under oath by the trustee and by creditors.* Creditors are welcome to attend, but are not required to do so. The meeting may be continued and concluded at a later date specified in a notice filed with the court. The court, after notice and a hearing, may order that the United States trustee not convene the meeting if the debtor has filed a plan for which the debtor solicited acceptances before filing the case.
Claims	A Proof of Claim is a signed statement describing a creditor's claim. If a Proof of Claim form is not included with this notice, you can obtain one at any bankruptcy clerk's office. You may look at the schedules that have been or will be filed at the bankruptcy clerk's office. If your claim is scheduled and is *not* listed as disputed, contingent, or unliquidated, it will be allowed in the amount scheduled unless you filed a Proof of Claim or you are sent further notice about the claim. Whether or not your claim is scheduled, you are permitted to file a Proof of Claim. If your claim is not listed at all *or* if your claim is listed as disputed, contingent, or unliquidated, then you must file a Proof of Claim or you might not be paid any money on your claim and may be unable to vote on a plan. The court has not yet set a deadline to file a Proof of Claim. If a deadline is set, you will be sent another notice. A secured creditor retains rights in its collateral regardless of whether that creditor files a Proof of Claim. Filing a Proof of Claim submits the creditor to the jurisdiction of the bankruptcy court, with consequences a lawyer can explain. For example, a secured creditor who files a Proof of Claim may surrender important nonmonetary rights, including the right to a jury trial. **Filing Deadline for a Creditor with a Foreign Address:** The deadline for filing claims will be set in a later court order and will apply to all creditors unless the order provides otherwise. If notice of the order setting the deadline is sent to a creditor at a foreign address, the creditor may file a motion requesting the court to extend the deadline. *Do not include this notice with any filing you make with the court.*
Discharge of Debts	Confirmation of a chapter 11 plan may result in a discharge of debts, which may include all or part of your debt. *See* Bankruptcy Code § 1141 (d). Unless the court orders otherwise, however, the discharge will not be effective until completion of all payments under the plan. A discharge means that you may never try to collect the debt from the debtor except as provided in the plan. If you believe that a debt owed to you is not dischargeable under Bankruptcy Code § 523 (a) (2), (4), or (6), you must start a lawsuit by filing a complaint in the bankruptcy clerk's office by the "Deadline to File a Complaint to Determine Dischargeability of Certain Debts" listed on the front side. The bankruptcy clerk's office must receive the complaint and any required filing fee by that Deadline. If you believe that the debtor is not entitled to receive a discharge under Bankruptcy Code § 1141 (d) (3), you must file a complaint with the required filing fee in the bankruptcy clerk's office not later than the first date set for the hearing on confirmation of the plan. You will be sent another notice informing you of that date.
Exempt Property	The debtor is permitted by law to keep certain property as exempt. Exempt property will not be sold and distributed to creditors, even if the debtor's case is converted to chapter 7. The debtor must file a list of property claimed as exempt. You may inspect that list at the bankruptcy clerk's office. If you believe that an exemption claimed by the debtor is not authorized by law, you may file an objection to that exemption. The bankruptcy clerk's office must receive the objection by the "Deadline to Object to Exemptions" listed on the front side.
Bankruptcy Clerk's Office	Any paper that you file in this bankruptcy case should be filed at the bankruptcy clerk's office at the address listed on the front side. You may inspect all papers filed, including the list of the debtor's property and debts and the list of the property claimed as exempt, at the bankruptcy clerk's office.
Creditor with a Foreign Address	Consult a lawyer familiar with United States bankruptcy law if you have any questions regarding your rights in this case.

Refer To Other Side For Important Deadlines and Notices

Form B9E ALT   OFFICIAL FORMS

Form B9E ALT

B9E ALT (Official Form 9E ALT) (Chapter 11 Individual or Joint Debtor Case) (12/12)

UNITED STATES BANKRUPTCY COURT _____ District of _____

Notice of
Chapter 11 Bankruptcy Case, Meeting of Creditors, & Deadlines

[A chapter 11 bankruptcy case concerning the debtor(s) listed below was filed on _____ (date).]
or [A bankruptcy case concerning the debtor(s) listed below was originally filed under chapter _____ on _____ (date) and was converted to a case under chapter 11 on _____ (date).]

You may be a creditor of the debtor. **This notice lists important deadlines.** You may want to consult an attorney to protect your rights. All documents filed in the case may be inspected at the bankruptcy clerk's office at the address listed below.
NOTE: The staff of the bankruptcy clerk's office cannot give legal advice.

Creditors -- Do not file this notice in connection with any proof of claim you submit to the court.
See Reverse Side for Important Explanations.

Debtor(s) (name(s) and address):	Case Number:
	Last four digits of Social-Security or Individual Taxpayer-ID (ITIN) No(s)./Complete EIN:
All other names used by the Debtor(s) in the last 8 years (include married, maiden, and trade names)	Attorney for Debtor(s) (name and address):
	Telephone number:

Meeting of Creditors

Date: / /   Time: ( ) A.M.   Location:
                         ( ) P.M.

Deadlines:

Papers must be *received* by the bankruptcy clerk's office by the following deadlines:
Deadline to File a Proof of Claim:

For all creditors (except a governmental unit):   For a governmental unit:

Creditor with a Foreign Address:
A creditor to whom this notice is sent at a foreign address should read the information under "Claims" on the reverse side.

Deadline to File a Complaint to Determine Dischargeability of Certain Debts:

Deadline to File a Complaint Objecting to Discharge of the Debtor:

First date set for hearing on confirmation of plan
Notice of that date will be sent at a later time.

Deadline to Object to Exemptions:
Thirty (30) days after the *conclusion* of the meeting of creditors.

Creditors May Not Take Certain Actions:
In most instances, the filing of the bankruptcy case automatically stays certain collection and other actions against the debtor and the debtor's property. Under certain circumstances, the stay may be limited to 30 days or not exist at all, although the debtor can request the court to extend or impose a stay. If you attempt to collect a debt or take other action in violation of the Bankruptcy Code, you may be penalized. Consult a lawyer to determine your rights in this case.

Address of the Bankruptcy Clerk's Office:	For the Court:
	Clerk of the Bankruptcy Court:
Telephone number:	
Hours Open:	Date:

OFFICIAL FORMS

Form B9E ALT

EXPLANATIONS   B9E ALT (Official Form 9E ALT) (12/12)

Filing of Chapter 11 Bankruptcy Case	A bankruptcy case under Chapter 11 of the Bankruptcy Code (title 11, United States Code) has been filed in this court by or against the debtor(s) listed on the front side, and an order for relief has been entered. Chapter 11 allows a debtor to reorganize or liquidate pursuant to a plan. A plan is not effective unless confirmed by the court. You may be sent a copy of the plan and a disclosure statement telling you about the plan, and you might have the opportunity to vote on the plan. You will be sent notice of the date of the confirmation hearing, and you may object to confirmation of the plan and attend the confirmation hearing. Unless a trustee is serving, the debtor will remain in possession of the debtor's property and may continue to operate any business.
Legal Advice	The staff of the bankruptcy clerk's office cannot give legal advice. Consult a lawyer to determine your rights in this case.
Creditors Generally May Not Take Certain Actions	Prohibited collection actions are listed in Bankruptcy Code § 362. Common examples of prohibited actions include contacting the debtor by telephone, mail, or otherwise to demand repayment; taking actions to collect money or obtain property from the debtor; repossessing the debtor's property; starting or continuing lawsuits or foreclosures; and garnishing or deducting from the debtor's wages. Under certain circumstances, the stay may be limited to 30 days or not exist at all, although the debtor can request the court to extend or impose a stay.
Meeting of Creditors	A meeting of creditors is scheduled for the date, time, and location listed on the front side. *The debtor (both spouses in a joint case) must be present at the meeting to be questioned under oath by the trustee and by creditors.* Creditors are welcome to attend, but are not required to do so. The meeting may be continued and concluded at a later date specified in a notice filed with the court. The court, after notice and a hearing, may order that the United States trustee not convene the meeting if the debtor has filed a plan for which the debtor solicited acceptances before filing the case.
Claims	A Proof of Claim is a signed statement describing a creditor's claim. If a Proof of Claim form is not included with this notice, you can obtain one at any bankruptcy clerk's office. You may look at the schedules that have been or will be filed at the bankruptcy clerk's office. If your claim is scheduled and is *not* listed as disputed, contingent, or unliquidated, it will be allowed in the amount scheduled unless you filed a Proof of Claim or you are sent further notice about the claim. Whether or not your claim is scheduled, you are permitted to file a Proof of Claim. If your claim is not listed at all *or* if your claim is listed as disputed, contingent, or unliquidated, then you must file a Proof of Claim by the "Deadline to File a Proof of Claim" listed on the front side or you might not be paid any money on your claim and may be unable to vote on a plan. A secured creditor retains rights in its collateral regardless of whether that creditor files a Proof of Claim. Filing a Proof of Claim submits the creditor to the jurisdiction of the bankruptcy court, with consequences a lawyer can explain. For example, a secured creditor who files a Proof of Claim may surrender important nonmonetary rights, including the right to a jury trial. **Filing Deadline for a Creditor with a Foreign Address:** The deadlines for filing claims set forth on the front of this notice apply to all creditors. If this notice has been mailed to a creditor at a foreign address, the creditor may file a motion requesting the court to extend the deadline. *Do not include this notice with any filing you make with the court.*
Discharge of Debts	Confirmation of a chapter 11 plan may result in a discharge of debts, which may include all or part of your debt. *See* Bankruptcy Code § 1141 (d). Unless the court orders otherwise, however, the discharge will not be effective until completion of all payments under the plan. A discharge means that you may never try to collect the debt from the debtor except as provided in the plan. If you believe that a debt owed to you is not dischargeable under Bankruptcy Code § 523 (a) (2), (4), or (6), you must start a lawsuit by filing a complaint in the bankruptcy clerk's office by the "Deadline to File a Complaint to Determine Dischargeability of Certain Debts" listed on the front side. The bankruptcy clerk's office must receive the complaint and any required filing fee by that Deadline. If you believe that the debtor is not entitled to receive a discharge under Bankruptcy Code § 1141 (d) (3), you must file a complaint with the required filing fee in the bankruptcy clerk's office not later than the first date set for the hearing on confirmation of the plan. You will be sent another notice informing you of that date.
Exempt Property	The debtor is permitted by law to keep certain property as exempt. Exempt property will not be sold and distributed to creditors, even if the debtor's case is converted to chapter 7. The debtor must file a list of property claimed as exempt. You may inspect that list at the bankruptcy clerk's office. If you believe that an exemption claimed by the debtor is not authorized by law, you may file an objection to that exemption. The bankruptcy clerk's office must receive the objection by the "Deadline to Object to Exemptions" listed on the front side.
Bankruptcy Clerk's Office	Any paper that you file in this bankruptcy case should be filed at the bankruptcy clerk's office at the address listed on the front side. You may inspect all papers filed, including the list of the debtor's property and debts and the list of the property claimed as exempt, at the bankruptcy clerk's office.
Creditor with a Foreign Address	Consult a lawyer familiar with United States bankruptcy law if you have any questions regarding your rights in this case.

Refer To Other Side For Important Deadlines and Notices

Form B9F OFFICIAL FORMS

Form B9F

B9F (Official Form 9F) (Chapter 11 Corporation/Partnership Case) (12/12)

UNITED STATES BANKRUPTCY COURT _____ District of _____

Notice of
Chapter 11 Bankruptcy Case, Meeting of Creditors, & Deadlines

[A chapter 11 bankruptcy case concerning the debtor(s) listed below was filed on _____ (date).]
or [A bankruptcy case concerning the debtor(s) listed below was originally filed under chapter _____ on _____ (date) and was converted to a case under chapter 11 on _____ (date).]

You may be a creditor of the debtor. **This notice lists important deadlines.** You may want to consult an attorney to protect your rights. All documents filed in the case may be inspected at the bankruptcy clerk's office at the address listed below.
NOTE: The staff of the bankruptcy clerk's office cannot give legal advice.

Creditors -- Do not file this notice in connection with any proof of claim you submit to the court.
See Reverse Side for Important Explanations.

Debtor(s) (name(s) and address):	Case Number:
	Last four digits of Social-Security or Individual Taxpayer-ID (ITIN) No(s)./Complete EIN:
All other names used by the Debtor(s) in the last 8 years (include trade names):	Attorney for Debtor(s) (name and address): Telephone number:

Meeting of Creditors

Date: / /   Time: ( ) A.M. Location:
                  ( ) P.M.

Deadline to File a Proof of Claim

Proof of Claim must be *received* by the bankruptcy clerk's office by the following deadline:

Notice of deadline will be sent at a later time.

Creditor with a Foreign Address:
A creditor to whom this notice is sent at a foreign address should read the information under "Claims" on the reverse side.

Deadline to File a Complaint to Determine Dischargeability of Certain Debts:

Creditors May Not Take Certain Actions:
In most instances, the filing of the bankruptcy case automatically stays certain collection and other actions against the debtor and the debtor's property. Under certain circumstances, the stay may be limited to 30 days or not exist at all, although the debtor can request the court to extend or impose a stay. If you attempt to collect a debt or take other action in violation of the Bankruptcy Code, you may be penalized. Consult a lawyer to determine your rights in this case.

Address of the Bankruptcy Clerk's Office: Telephone number:	**For the Court:** Clerk of the Bankruptcy Court:
Hours Open:	Date:

OFFICIAL FORMS   **Form B9F**

EXPLANATIONS   B9F (Official Form 9F) (12/12)

Filing of Chapter 11 Bankruptcy Case	A bankruptcy case under Chapter 11 of the Bankruptcy Code (title 11, United States Code) has been filed in this court by or against the debtor(s) listed on the front side, and an order for relief has been entered. Chapter 11 allows a debtor to reorganize or liquidate pursuant to a plan. A plan is not effective unless confirmed by the court. You may be sent a copy of the plan and a disclosure statement telling you about the plan, and you might have the opportunity to vote on the plan. You will be sent notice of the date of the confirmation hearing, and you may object to confirmation of the plan and attend the confirmation hearing. Unless a trustee is serving, the debtor will remain in possession of the debtor's property and may continue to operate any business.
Legal Advice	The staff of the bankruptcy clerk's office cannot give legal advice. Consult a lawyer to determine your rights in this case.
Creditors Generally May Not Take Certain Actions	Prohibited collection actions are listed in Bankruptcy Code § 362. Common examples of prohibited actions include contacting the debtor by telephone, mail, or otherwise to demand repayment; taking actions to collect money or obtain property from the debtor; repossessing the debtor's property; and starting or continuing lawsuits or foreclosures. Under certain circumstances, the stay may be limited to 30 days or not exist at all, although the debtor can request the court to extend or impose a stay.
Meeting of Creditors	A meeting of creditors is scheduled for the date, time, and location listed on the front side. *The debtor's representative must be present at the meeting to be questioned under oath by the trustee and by creditors.* Creditors are welcome to attend, but are not required to do so. The meeting may be continued and concluded at a later date specified in a notice filed with the court. The court, after notice and a hearing, may order that the United States trustee not convene the meeting if the debtor has filed a plan for which the debtor solicited acceptances before filing the case.
Claims	A Proof of Claim is a signed statement describing a creditor's claim. If a Proof of Claim form is not included with this notice, you can obtain one at any bankruptcy clerk's office. You may look at the schedules that have been or will be filed at the bankruptcy clerk's office. If your claim is scheduled and is *not* listed as disputed, contingent, or unliquidated, it will be allowed in the amount scheduled unless you filed a Proof of Claim or you are sent further notice about the claim. Whether or not your claim is scheduled, you are permitted to file a Proof of Claim. If your claim is not listed at all *or* if your claim is listed as disputed, contingent, or unliquidated, then you must file a Proof of Claim or you might not be paid any money on your claim and may be unable to vote on a plan. The court has not yet set a deadline to file a Proof of Claim. If a deadline is set, you will be sent another notice. A secured creditor retains rights in its collateral regardless of whether that creditor files a Proof of Claim. Filing a Proof of Claim submits the creditor to the jurisdiction of the bankruptcy court, with consequences a lawyer can explain. For example, a secured creditor who files a Proof of Claim may surrender important nonmonetary rights, including the right to a jury trial. **Filing Deadline for a Creditor with a Foreign Address:** The deadline for filing claims will be set in a later court order and will apply to all creditors unless the order provides otherwise. If notice of the order setting the deadline is sent to a creditor at a foreign address, the creditor may file a motion requesting the court to extend the deadline. *Do not include this notice with any filing you make with the court.*
Discharge of Debts	Confirmation of a chapter 11 plan may result in a discharge of debts, which may include all or part of your debt. *See* Bankruptcy Code § 1141 (d). A discharge means that you may never try to collect the debt from the debtor, except as provided in the plan. If you believe that a debt owed to you is not dischargeable under Bankruptcy Code § 1141 (d) (6) (A), you must start a lawsuit by filing a complaint in the bankruptcy clerk's office by the "Deadline to File a Complaint to Determine Dischargeability of Certain Debts" listed on the front side. The bankruptcy clerk's office must receive the complaint and any required filing fee by that deadline.
Bankruptcy Clerk's Office	Any paper that you file in this bankruptcy case should be filed at the bankruptcy clerk's office at the address listed on the front side. You may inspect all papers filed, including the list of the debtor's property and debts and the list of the property claimed as exempt, at the bankruptcy clerk's office.
Creditor with a Foreign Address	Consult a lawyer familiar with United States bankruptcy law if you have any questions regarding your rights in this case.

Refer To Other Side For Important Deadlines and Notices

Form B9F ALT   OFFICIAL FORMS

Form B9F ALT

B9F ALT (Official Form 9F ALT) (Chapter 11 Corporation/Partnership Case) (12/12)

UNITED STATES BANKRUPTCY COURT _____ District of _____

Notice of
Chapter 11 Bankruptcy Case, Meeting of Creditors, & Deadlines

[A chapter 11 bankruptcy case concerning the debtor(s) listed below was filed on _____ (date).]
or [A bankruptcy case concerning the debtor(s) listed below was originally filed under chapter ____ on _____ (date) and was converted to a case under chapter 11 on _____ (date).]

You may be a creditor of the debtor. **This notice lists important deadlines.** You may want to consult an attorney to protect your rights. All documents filed in the case may be inspected at the bankruptcy clerk's office at the address listed below.
NOTE: The staff of the bankruptcy clerk's office cannot give legal advice.

Creditors -- Do not file this notice in connection with any proof of claim you submit to the court.
See Reverse Side for Important Explanations.

Debtor(s) (name(s) and address):	Case Number:
	Last four digits of Social-Security or Individual Taxpayer-ID (ITIN) No(s)./Complete EIN:
All other names used by the Debtor(s) in the last 8 years (include trade names):	Attorney for Debtor(s) (name and address): Telephone number:

Meeting of Creditors

Date: / /   Time: ( ) A.M.   Location:
                      ( ) P.M.

Deadline to File a Proof of Claim

Proof of Claim must be *received* by the bankruptcy clerk's office by the following deadline:

For all creditors (except a governmental unit):   For a governmental unit:

Creditor with a Foreign Address:
A creditor to whom this notice is sent at a foreign address should read the information under "Claims" on the reverse side.

Deadline to File a Complaint to Determine Dischargeability of Certain Debts:

Creditors May Not Take Certain Actions:
In most instances, the filing of the bankruptcy case automatically stays certain collection and other actions against the debtor and the debtor's property. Under certain circumstances, the stay may be limited to 30 days or not exist at all, although the debtor can request the court to extend or impose a stay. If you attempt to collect a debt or take other action in violation of the Bankruptcy Code, you may be penalized. Consult a lawyer to determine your rights in this case.

Address of the Bankruptcy Clerk's Office:	For the Court:
	Clerk of the Bankruptcy Court:
Telephone number:	
Hours Open:	Date:

OFFICIAL FORMS   **Form B9F ALT**

EXPLANATIONS   B9F ALT (Official Form 9F ALT) (12/12)

Filing of Chapter 11 Bankruptcy Case	A bankruptcy case under Chapter 11 of the Bankruptcy Code (title 11, United States Code) has been filed in this court by or against the debtor(s) listed on the front side, and an order for relief has been entered. Chapter 11 allows a debtor to reorganize or liquidate pursuant to a plan. A plan is not effective unless confirmed by the court. You may be sent a copy of the plan and a disclosure statement telling you about the plan, and you might have the opportunity to vote on the plan. You will be sent notice of the date of the confirmation hearing, and you may object to confirmation of the plan and attend the confirmation hearing. Unless a trustee is serving, the debtor will remain in possession of the debtor's property and may continue to operate any business.
Legal Advice	The staff of the bankruptcy clerk's office cannot give legal advice. Consult a lawyer to determine your rights in this case.
Creditors Generally May Not Take Certain Actions	Prohibited collection actions are listed in Bankruptcy Code § 362. Common examples of prohibited actions include contacting the debtor by telephone, mail, or otherwise to demand repayment; taking actions to collect money or obtain property from the debtor; repossessing the debtor's property; and starting or continuing lawsuits or foreclosures. Under certain circumstances, the stay may be limited to 30 days or not exist at all, although the debtor can request the court to extend or impose a stay.
Meeting of Creditors	A meeting of creditors is scheduled for the date, time, and location listed on the front side. *The debtor's representative must be present at the meeting to be questioned under oath by the trustee and by creditors.* Creditors are welcome to attend, but are not required to do so. The meeting may be continued and concluded at a later date specified in a notice filed with the court. The court, after notice and a hearing, may order that the United States trustee not convene the meeting if the debtor has filed a plan for which the debtor solicited acceptances before filing the case.
Claims	A Proof of Claim is a signed statement describing a creditor's claim. If a Proof of Claim form is not included with this notice, you can obtain one at any bankruptcy clerk's office. You may look at the schedules that have been or will be filed at the bankruptcy clerk's office. If your claim is scheduled and is *not* listed as disputed, contingent, or unliquidated, it will be allowed in the amount scheduled unless you filed a Proof of Claim or you are sent further notice about the claim. Whether or not your claim is scheduled, you are permitted to file a Proof of Claim. If your claim is not listed at all *or* if your claim is listed as disputed, contingent, or unliquidated, then you must file a Proof of Claim by the "Deadline to File Proof of Claim" listed on the front side, or you might not be paid any money on your claim and may be unable to vote on a plan. A secured creditor retains rights in its collateral regardless of whether that creditor files a Proof of Claim. Filing a Proof of Claim submits the creditor to the jurisdiction of the bankruptcy court, with consequences a lawyer can explain. For example, a secured creditor who files a Proof of Claim may surrender important nonmonetary rights, including the right to a jury trial. **Filing Deadline for a Creditor with a Foreign Address:** The deadlines for filing claims set forth on the front of this notice apply to all creditors. If this notice has been mailed to a creditor at a foreign address, the creditor may file a motion requesting the court to extend the deadline. *Do not include this notice with any filing you make with the court.*
Discharge of Debts	Confirmation of a chapter 11 plan may result in a discharge of debts, which may include all or part of your debt. *See* Bankruptcy Code § 1141 (d). A discharge means that you may never try to collect the debt from the debtor, except as provided in the plan. If you believe that a debt owed to you is not dischargeable under Bankruptcy Code § 1141 (d) (6) (A), you must start a lawsuit by filing a complaint in the bankruptcy clerk's office by the "Deadline to File a Complaint to Determine Dischargeability of Certain Debts" listed on the front side. The bankruptcy clerk's office must receive the complaint and any required filing fee by that deadline.
Bankruptcy Clerk's Office	Any paper that you file in this bankruptcy case should be filed at the bankruptcy clerk's office at the address listed on the front side. You may inspect all papers filed, including the list of the debtor's property and debts and the list of the property claimed as exempt, at the bankruptcy clerk's office.
Creditor with a Foreign Address	Consult a lawyer familiar with United States bankruptcy law if you have any questions regarding your rights in this case.

Refer To Other Side For Important Deadlines and Notices

Form B9G OFFICIAL FORMS

Form B9G

B9G (Official Form 9G) (Chapter 12 Individual or Joint Debtor Family Farmer or Family Fisherman) (12/12)

UNITED STATES BANKRUPTCY COURT_____ District of_____

Notice of
Chapter 12 Bankruptcy Case, Meeting of Creditors, & Deadlines

[The debtor(s) listed below filed a chapter 12 bankruptcy case on_____(date).]
or [A bankruptcy case concerning the debtor(s) listed below was originally filed under chapter_____ on _____(date) and was converted to a case under chapter 12 on_____(date).]

You may be a creditor of the debtor. **This notice lists important deadlines.** You may want to consult an attorney to protect your rights. All documents filed in the case may be inspected at the bankruptcy clerk's office at the address listed below.
NOTE: The staff of the bankruptcy clerk's office cannot give legal advice.

Creditors -- Do not file this notice in connection with any proof of claim you submit to the court.
See Reverse Side for Important Explanations.

Debtor(s) (name(s) and address):	Case Number:
	Last four digits of Social-Security or Individual Taxpayer-ID (ITIN) No(s)./Complete EIN:
All other names used by the Debtor(s) in the last 8 years (include married, maiden, and trade names):	Bankruptcy Trustee (name and address):
Attorney for Debtor(s) (name and address):	
Telephone number:	Telephone number:

Meeting of Creditors
Date: / /   Time: ( ) A.M.   Location:
                    ( ) P.M.

Deadlines:
Papers must be *received* by the bankruptcy clerk's office by the following deadlines:

Deadline to File a Proof of Claim:

For all creditors(except a governmental unit):   For a governmental unit:

Creditor with a Foreign Address:
A creditor to whom this notice is sent at a foreign address should read the information under "Claims" on the reverse side.

Deadline to File a Complaint to Determine Dischargeability of Certain Debts:

Deadline to Object to Exemptions:
Thirty (30) days after the *conclusion* of the meeting of creditors.

Filing of Plan, Hearing on Confirmation of Plan
[The debtor has filed a plan. The plan or a summary of the plan is enclosed. The hearing on confirmation will be held:
Date:_____ Time:_____ Location:_____]
or [The debtor has filed a plan. The plan or a summary of the plan and notice of confirmation hearing will be sent separately.]
or [The debtor has not filed a plan as of this date. You will be sent separate notice of the hearing on confirmation of the plan.]

Creditors May Not Take Certain Actions:
In most instances, the filing of the bankruptcy case automatically stays certain collection and other actions against the debtor, the debtor's property, and certain codebtors. Under certain circumstances, the stay may be limited to 30 days or not exist at all, although the debtor can request the court to extend or impose a stay. If you attempt to collect a debt or take other action in violation of the Bankruptcy Code, you may be penalized. Consult a lawyer to determine your rights in this case.

Address of the Bankruptcy Clerk's Office:	For the Court:
	Clerk of the Bankruptcy Court:
Telephone number:	
Hours Open:	Date:

OFFICIAL FORMS   **Form B9G**

EXPLANATIONS   B9G (Official Form 9G) (12/12)

Filing of Chapter 12 Bankruptcy Case	A bankruptcy case under Chapter 12 of the Bankruptcy Code (title 11, United States Code) has been filed in this court by the debtor(s) listed on the front side, and an order for relief has been entered. Chapter 12 allows family farmers and family fishermen to adjust their debts pursuant to a plan. A plan is not effective unless confirmed by the court. You may object to confirmation of the plan and appear at the confirmation hearing. A copy or summary of the plan [is included with this notice] *or* [will be sent to you later], and [the confirmation hearing will be held on the date indicated on the front of this notice] *or* [you will be sent notice of the confirmation hearing]. The debtor will remain in possession of the debtor's property and may continue to operate the debtor's business unless the court orders otherwise.
Legal Advice	The staff of the bankruptcy clerk's office cannot give legal advice. Consult a lawyer to determine your rights in this case.
Creditors Generally May Not Take Certain Actions	Prohibited collection actions against the debtor and certain codebtors are listed in Bankruptcy Code § 362 and § 1201. Common examples of prohibited actions include contacting the debtor by telephone, mail, or otherwise to demand repayment; taking actions to collect money or obtain property from the debtor; repossessing the debtor's property; starting or continuing lawsuits or foreclosures; and garnishing or deducting from the debtor's wages. Under certain circumstances, the stay may be limited in duration or not exist at all, although the debtor may have the right to request the court to extend or impose a stay.
Meeting of Creditors	A meeting of creditors is scheduled for the date, time, and location listed on the front side. *The debtor (both spouses in a joint case) must be present at the meeting to be questioned under oath by the trustee and by creditors.* Creditors are welcome to attend, but are not required to do so. The meeting may be continued and concluded at a later date specified in a notice filed with the court.
Claims	A Proof of Claim is a signed statement describing a creditor's claim. If a Proof of Claim form is not included with this notice, you can obtain one at any bankruptcy clerk's office. A secured creditor retains rights in its collateral regardless of whether that creditor files a Proof of Claim. If you do not file a Proof of Claim by the "Deadline to File a Proof of Claim" listed on the front side, you might not be paid any money on your claim from other assets in the bankruptcy case. To be paid, you must file a Proof of Claim even if your claim is listed in the schedules filed by the debtor. Filing a Proof of Claim submits the creditor to the jurisdiction of the bankruptcy court, with consequences a lawyer can explain. For example, a secured creditor who files a Proof of Claim may surrender important nonmonetary rights, including the right to a jury trial. **Filing Deadline for a Creditor with a Foreign Address:** The deadlines for filing claims set forth on the front of this notice apply to all creditors. If this notice has been mailed to a creditor at a foreign address, the creditor may file a motion requesting the court to extend the deadline. *Do not include this notice with any filing you make with the court.*
Discharge of Debts	The debtor is seeking a discharge of most debts, which may include your debt. A discharge means that you may never try to collect the debt from the debtor. If you believe that a debt owed to you is not dischargeable under Bankruptcy Code § 523 (a) (2), (4), or (6), you must start a lawsuit by filing a complaint in the bankruptcy clerk's office by the "Deadline to File a Complaint to Determine Dischargeability of Certain Debts" listed on the front side. The bankruptcy clerk's office must receive the complaint and any required filing fee by that Deadline.
Exempt Property	The debtor is permitted by law to keep certain property as exempt. Exempt property will not be sold and distributed to creditors, even if the debtor's case is converted to chapter 7. The debtor must file a list of all property claimed as exempt. You may inspect that list at the bankruptcy clerk's office. If you believe that an exemption claimed by the debtor is not authorized by law, you may file an objection to that exemption. The bankruptcy clerk's office must receive the objection by the "Deadline to Object to Exemptions" listed on the front side.
Bankruptcy Clerk's Office	Any paper that you file in this bankruptcy case should be filed at the bankruptcy clerk's office at the address listed on the front side. You may inspect all papers filed, including the list of the debtor's property and debts and the list of the property claimed as exempt, at the bankruptcy clerk's office.
Creditor with a Foreign Address	Consult a lawyer familiar with United States bankruptcy law if you have any questions regarding your rights in this case.

Refer To Other Side For Important Deadlines and Notices

Form B9H

Form B9H

OFFICIAL FORMS

B9H (Official Form 9H) (Chapter 12 Corporation/Partnership Family Farmer or Family Fisherman) (12/12)

UNITED STATES BANKRUPTCY COURT_____ District of _____
Notice of **Chapter 12 Bankruptcy Case, Meeting of Creditors, & Deadlines**
[The debtor [corporation] *or* [partnership] listed below filed a chapter 12 bankruptcy case on _____ (date).] or [A bankruptcy case concerning the debtor [corporation] *or* [partnership] listed below was originally filed under chapter _____ on _____ (date) and was converted to a case under chapter 12 on _____ (date).] You may be a creditor of the debtor. **This notice lists important deadlines.** You may want to consult an attorney to protect your rights. All documents filed in the case may be inspected at the bankruptcy clerk's office at the address listed below. NOTE: The staff of the bankruptcy clerk's office cannot give legal advice. **Creditors -- Do not file this notice in connection with any proof of claim you submit to the court.** **See Reverse Side for Important Explanations.**

Debtor(s) (name(s) and address):	Case Number:
	Last four digits of Social-Security or Individual Taxpayer-ID (ITIN) No(s)./Complete EIN:
All other names used by the Debtor(s) in the last 8 years (include trade names):	Bankruptcy Trustee (name and address):
Attorney for Debtor(s) (name and address):	
Telephone number:	Telephone number:

Meeting of Creditors
Date: / /   Time: ( ) A. M.   Location: ( ) P. M.

Deadlines:
Papers must be *received* by the bankruptcy clerk's office by the following deadlines:

Deadline to File a Proof of Claim:

For all creditors (except a governmental unit):   For a governmental unit:

Creditor with a Foreign Address:
A creditor to whom this notice is sent at a foreign address should read the information under "Claims" on the reverse side.

Deadline to File a Complaint to Determine Dischargeability of Certain Debts:

Filing of Plan, Hearing on Confirmation of Plan

[The debtor has filed a plan. The plan or a summary of the plan is enclosed. The hearing on confirmation will be held:
Date:_____ Time:_____ Location:_____]
or [The debtor has filed a plan. The plan or a summary of the plan and notice of confirmation hearing will be sent separately.]
or [The debtor has not filed a plan as of this date. You will be sent separate notice of the hearing on confirmation of the plan.]

Creditors May Not Take Certain Actions:
In most instances, the filing of the bankruptcy case automatically stays certain collection and other actions against the debtor and the debtor's property. Under certain circumstances, the stay may be limited to 30 days or not exist at all, although the debtor can request the court to extend or impose a stay. If you attempt to collect a debt or take other action in violation of the Bankruptcy Code, you may be penalized. Consult a lawyer to determine your rights in this case.

Address of the Bankruptcy Clerk's Office:	**For the Court:**
	Clerk of the Bankruptcy Court:
Telephone number:	
Hours Open:	Date:

884

OFFICIAL FORMS Form B9H

EXPLANATIONS B9H (Official Form 9H) (12/12)

Filing of Chapter 12 Bankruptcy Case	A bankruptcy case under Chapter 12 of the Bankruptcy Code (title 11, United States Code) has been filed in this court by the debtor listed on the front side, and an order for relief has been entered. Chapter 12 allows family farmers and family fishermen to adjust their debts pursuant to a plan. A plan is not effective unless confirmed by the court. You may object to confirmation of the plan and appear at the confirmation hearing. A copy or summary of the plan [is included with this notice] *or* [will be sent to you later], and [the confirmation hearing will be held on the date indicated on the front of this notice] *or* [you will be sent notice of the confirmation hearing]. The debtor will remain in possession of the debtor's property and may continue to operate the debtor's business unless the court orders otherwise.
Legal Advice	The staff of the bankruptcy clerk's office cannot give legal advice. Consult a lawyer to determine your rights in this case.
Creditors Generally May Not Take Certain Actions	Prohibited collection actions against the debtor and certain codebtors are listed in Bankruptcy Code § 362 and § 1201. Common examples of prohibited actions include contacting the debtor by telephone, mail, or otherwise to demand repayment; taking actions to collect money or obtain property from the debtor; repossessing the debtor's property; and starting or continuing lawsuits or foreclosures. Under certain circumstances, the stay may be limited in duration or not exist at all, although the debtor may have the right to request the court to extend or impose a stay.
Meeting of Creditors	A meeting of creditors is scheduled for the date, time, and location listed on the front side. *The debtor's representative must be present at the meeting to be questioned under oath by the trustee and by creditors.* Creditors are welcome to attend, but are not required to do so. The meeting may be continued and concluded at a later date specified in a notice filed with the court.
Claims	A Proof of Claim is a signed statement describing a creditor's claim. If a Proof of Claim form is not included with this notice, you can obtain one at any bankruptcy clerk's office. A secured creditor retains rights in its collateral regardless of whether that creditor files a Proof of Claim. If you do not file a Proof of Claim by the "Deadline to File a Proof of Claim" listed on the front side, you might not be paid any money on your claim from other assets in the bankruptcy case. To be paid, you must file a Proof of Claim even if your claim is listed in the schedules filed by the debtor. Filing a Proof of Claim submits the creditor to the jurisdiction of the bankruptcy court, with consequences a lawyer can explain. For example, a secured creditor who files a Proof of Claim may surrender important nonmonetary rights, including the right to a jury trial. **Filing Deadline for a Creditor with a Foreign Address:** The deadlines for filing claims set forth on the front of this notice apply to all creditors. If this notice has been mailed to a creditor at a foreign address, the creditor may file a motion requesting the court to extend the deadline. *Do not include this notice with any filing you make with the court.*
Discharge of Debts	The debtor is seeking a discharge of most debts, which may include your debt. A discharge means that you may never try to collect the debt from the debtor. If you believe that a debt owed to you is not dischargeable under Bankruptcy Code § 523 (a) (2), (4), or (6), you must start a lawsuit by filing a complaint in the bankruptcy clerk's office by the "Deadline to File a Complaint to Determine Dischargeability of Certain Debts" listed on the front side. The bankruptcy clerk's office must receive the complaint and any required filing fee by that Deadline.
Bankruptcy Clerk's Office	Any paper that you file in this bankruptcy case should be filed at the bankruptcy clerk's office at the address listed on the front side. You may inspect all papers filed, including the list of the debtor's property and debts and the list of the property claimed as exempt, at the bankruptcy clerk's office.
Creditor with a Foreign Address	Consult a lawyer familiar with United States bankruptcy law if you have any questions regarding your rights in this case.

Refer To Other Side For Important Deadlines and Notices

Form B9I

Form B9I

OFFICIAL FORMS

B9I (Official Form 9I) (Chapter 13 Case) (12/12)

UNITED STATES BANKRUPTCY COURT_____ District of_____

Notice of
Chapter 13 Bankruptcy Case, Meeting of Creditors, & Deadlines

[The debtor(s) listed below filed a chapter 13 bankruptcy case on _____ (date).]
or [A bankruptcy case concerning the debtor(s) listed below was originally filed under chapter_____
on _____ (date) and was converted to a case under chapter 13 on_____(date).]

You may be a creditor of the debtor. **This notice lists important deadlines.** You may want to consult an attorney to protect your rights. All documents filed in the case may be inspected at the bankruptcy clerk's office at the address listed below.
NOTE: The staff of the bankruptcy clerk's office cannot give legal advice.

**Creditors -- Do not file this notice in connection with any proof of claim you submit to the court.
See Reverse Side for Important Explanations.**

Debtor(s) (name(s) and address):	Case Number:
	Last four digits of Social-Security or Individual Taxpayer-ID (ITIN) No(s)./Complete EIN:
All other names used by the Debtor(s) in the last 8 years (include married, maiden, and trade names):	Bankruptcy Trustee (name and address):
Attorney for Debtor(s) (name and address):	
Telephone number:	Telephone number:
Date: / / Time: ( ) A. M. ( ) P. M.	**Meeting of Creditors** Location:

Deadlines:
Papers must be *received* by the bankruptcy clerk's office by the following deadlines:
Deadline to File a Proof of Claim:
For all creditors (except a governmental unit):   For a governmental unit (except as otherwise provided in Fed. R. Bankr. P. 3002(c)(1)):

Creditor with a Foreign Address:
A creditor to whom this notice is sent at a foreign address should read the information under "Claims" on the reverse side.

Deadline to Object to Debtor's Discharge or to Challenge Dischargeability of Certain Debts:

Deadline to Object to Exemptions:
Thirty (30) days after the *conclusion* of the meeting of creditors.

Filing of Plan, Hearing on Confirmation of Plan
[The debtor has filed a plan. The plan or a summary of the plan is enclosed. The hearing on confirmation will be held:
Date: Time: Location:]
or [The debtor has filed a plan. The plan or a summary of the plan and notice of confirmation hearing will be sent separately.]
or [The debtor has not filed a plan as of this date. You will be sent separate notice of the hearing on confirmation of the plan.]

Creditors May Not Take Certain Actions:
In most instances, the filing of the bankruptcy case automatically stays certain collection and other actions against the debtor, the debtor's property, and certain codebtors. Under certain circumstances, the stay may be limited to 30 days or not exist at all, although the debtor can request the court to extend or impose a stay. If you attempt to collect a debt or take other action in violation of the Bankruptcy Code, you may be penalized. Consult a lawyer to determine your rights in this case.

Address of the Bankruptcy Clerk's Office:	**For the Court:**
	Clerk of the Bankruptcy Court:
Telephone number:	
Hours Open:	Date:

OFFICIAL FORMS — Form B9I

EXPLANATIONS   B9I (Official Form 9I) (12/12)

Filing of Chapter 13 Bankruptcy Case	A bankruptcy case under Chapter 13 of the Bankruptcy Code (title 11, United States Code) has been filed in this court by the debtor(s) listed on the front side, and an order for relief has been entered. Chapter 13 allows an individual with regular income and debts below a specified amount to adjust debts pursuant to a plan. A plan is not effective unless confirmed by the bankruptcy court. You may object to confirmation of the plan and appear at the confirmation hearing. A copy or summary of the plan [is included with this notice] *or* [will be sent to you later], and [the confirmation hearing will be held on the date indicated on the front of this notice] *or* [you will be sent notice of the confirmation hearing]. The debtor will remain in possession of the debtor's property and may continue to operate the debtor's business, if any, unless the court orders otherwise.
Legal Advice	The staff of the bankruptcy clerk's office cannot give legal advice. Consult a lawyer to determine your rights in this case.
Creditors Generally May Not Take Certain Actions	Prohibited collection actions against the debtor and certain codebtors are listed in Bankruptcy Code § 362 and § 1301. Common examples of prohibited actions include contacting the debtor by telephone, mail, or otherwise to demand repayment; taking actions to collect money or obtain property from the debtor; repossessing the debtor's property; starting or continuing lawsuits or foreclosures; and garnishing or deducting from the debtor's wages. Under certain circumstances, the stay may be limited to 30 days or not exist at all, although the debtor can request the court to exceed or impose a stay.
Meeting of Creditors	A meeting of creditors is scheduled for the date, time, and location listed on the front side. *The debtor (both spouses in a joint case) must be present at the meeting to be questioned under oath by the trustee and by creditors.* Creditors are welcome to attend, but are not required to do so. The meeting may be continued and concluded at a later date specified in a notice filed with the court.
Claims	A Proof of Claim is a signed statement describing a creditor's claim. If a Proof of Claim form is not included with this notice, you can obtain one at any bankruptcy clerk's office. A secured creditor retains rights in its collateral regardless of whether that creditor files a Proof of Claim. If you do not file a Proof of Claim by the "Deadline to File a Proof of Claim" listed on the front side, you might not be paid any money on your claim from other assets in the bankruptcy case. To be paid, you must file a Proof of Claim even if your claim is listed in the schedules filed by the debtor. Filing a Proof of Claim submits the creditor to the jurisdiction of the bankruptcy court, with consequences a lawyer can explain. For example, a secured creditor who files a Proof of Claim may surrender important nonmonetary rights, including the right to a jury trial. **Filing Deadline for a Creditor with a Foreign Address:** The deadlines for filing claims set forth on the front of this notice apply to all creditors. If this notice has been mailed to a creditor at a foreign address, the creditor may file a motion requesting the court to extend the deadline. *Do not include this notice with any filing you make with the court.*
Discharge of Debts	The debtor is seeking a discharge of most debts, which may include your debt. A discharge means that you may never try to collect the debt from the debtor. If you believe that the debtor is not entitled to a discharge under Bankruptcy Code § 1328(f), you must file a motion objecting to discharge in the bankruptcy clerk's office by the "Deadline to Object to Debtor's Discharge or to Challenge the Dischargeability of Certain Debts" listed on the front of this form. If you believe that a debt owed to you is not dischargeable under Bankruptcy Code § 523(a)(2) or (4), you must file a complaint in the bankruptcy clerk's office by the same deadline. The bankruptcy clerk's office must receive the motion or the complaint and any required filing fee by that deadline.
Exempt Property	The debtor is permitted by law to keep certain property as exempt. Exempt property will not be sold and distributed to creditors, even if the debtor's case is converted to chapter 7. The debtor must file a list of all property claimed as exempt. You may inspect that list at the bankruptcy clerk's office. If you believe that an exemption claimed by the debtor is not authorized by law, you may file an objection to that exemption. The bankruptcy clerk's office must receive the objection by the "Deadline to Object to Exemptions" listed on the front side.
Bankruptcy Clerk's Office	Any paper that you file in this bankruptcy case should be filed at the bankruptcy clerk's office at the address listed on the front side. You may inspect all papers filed, including the list of the debtor's property and debts and the list of the property claimed as exempt, at the bankruptcy clerk's office.
Creditor with a Foreign Address	Consult a lawyer familiar with United States bankruptcy law if you have any questions regarding your rights in this case.

Refer To Other Side For Important Deadlines and Notices

(Added Aug. 1, 1991; amended Mar. 16, 1993; Mar. 1995; Oct. 1, 1997; Dec. 1, 2003; Aug. 11, 2005, eff. Oct. 17, 2005; Oct. 2006; Dec. 1, 2007; Dec. 1, 2008; Dec. 1, 2010; Dec. 1, 2011; Dec. 1, 2012.)

Form B9I — OFFICIAL FORMS

ADVISORY COMMITTEE NOTES

1991 Enactment

The form has been redesigned to facilitate electronic generation of notice to creditors concerning the filing of the petition, the meeting of creditors, and important deadlines in the case. Adoption of a box format, with significant dates highlighted, is intended to assist creditors who may be unfamiliar with bankruptcy cases to understand the data provided. Nine variations of the form, designated 9A through 9I, have been created to meet the specialized notice requirements for chapters 7, 11, 12, and 13, asset and no-asset cases, and the various types of debtors.

1992 Amendment

Forms 9B, 9D, 9F, and 9H are amended to make a technical correction in the reference to Rule 9001(5). Form 9H also contains a technical correction deleting the reference to a complaint objecting to discharge of the debtor.

1993 Amendment

The title page of the form has been amended to conform to the headings used on Forms 9A–9I. Alternate versions of Form 9E and Form 9F have been added for the convenience of districts that routinely set a deadline for filing claims in a chapter 11 case. When a creditor receives the alternate form in a case, the box labeled "Filing Claims" will contain information about the bar date as follows: "Deadline for filing a claim: (date) ." If no deadline is set in a particular case, either the court will use Form 9E or Form 9F, as appropriate, or the alternate form will be used with the following sentence appearing in the box labeled "Filing Claims": "When the court sets a deadline for filing claims, creditors will be notified."

1995 Amendment

The form is amended to provide notice of the claims filing period provided to "a governmental unit" by section 502(b)(9) of the Code as amended by the Bankruptcy Reform Act of 1994. A court that routinely sets a deadline for filing proofs of claim at the outset of chapter 11 cases and, accordingly, uses Form 9E(Alt.) or Form 9F(Alt.) retains the option in any case in which no deadlines actually are set to substitute a message stating that creditors will be notified if the court fixes a deadline.

The form also is amended to add, in the paragraph labeled "Discharge of Debts," a reference to dischargeability actions under section 523(a)(15) of the Code, which was added by the 1994 Act.

1997 Amendment

Forms 9A, 9I (and the alternate versions of Forms 9E and 9F) have been amended, redesigned, and rewritten. Minor conforming changes have been made to respond to amendments made in the Bankruptcy Reform Act of 1994: the longer claims filing period for governmental units in section 502(b)(9) of the Code (see Forms 9C, 9D, 9E(Alt.), 9F(Alt.), 9G, 9H, and 9I); and a reference to dischargeability actions under section 523(a)(15) (see Forms 9A, 9C, 9E, and 9E(Alt.), 9G, and 9H). All of the forms have been substantially revised to make them easier to read and understand. The titles have been simplified. Recipients are told why they are receiving the notice. Explanations are provided on the back of the form and are set in larger type. Plain English is used. Deadlines are highlighted on the front of the form. Recipients are told that papers must be received by the bankruptcy clerk's office by the applicable deadline. The box for the trustee has been deleted from the chapter 11 notices (Forms 9E and 9F and the alternates). Various alternatives are set out in brackets in many of the forms, permitting each bankruptcy clerk's office to tailor the forms even more precisely to fit the needs of a particular case. The court may use blank spaces on the form to include additional information applicable to the particular district.

2003 Amendment

The form is amended to add to the information provided to creditors, the trustee and the United States trustee, all the names used by the debtor during the six years prior to the filing of the petition. The form includes the debtor's full employer identification number, if any, as well as the last four digits of the debtor's social security number. Rule 2002(a)(1) also is amended to direct the clerk to include the debtor's full social security number and employer identification number on the notices served on the United States trustee, the trustee, and creditors. This will enable creditors to identify the debtor accurately. The copy of Official Form 9 included in the case file, however, will show only the last four digits of the debtor's social security number. This should afford greater privacy to the individual debtor, whose bankruptcy case records may be available on the Internet.

OFFICIAL FORMS — Form B9I

2005 Amendment

The form is amended in a variety of ways to implement the provisions of the Bankruptcy Abuse Prevention and Consumer Protection Act of 2005, Pub. L. No. 109–8, 119 Stat. 23 (April 20, 2005). All versions of the form are amended to advise creditors to consult an attorney concerning what rights they may have in the specific case. All versions of the form are also amended to provide information about filing claims to creditors with foreign addresses and to advise those creditors to consult a lawyer familiar with United States bankruptcy law regarding any questions they may have about their rights in a particular case. These amendments implement § 1514, which was added to the Code in 2005.

Forms 9A and 9C are amended to include a box in which the clerk can notify creditors in a chapter 7 case filed by an individual with primarily consumer debts whether the presumption of abuse has arisen under § 707(b) of the Code as amended in 2005. Under § 342(d) of the Code, the clerk has a duty to notify creditors concerning the presumption within ten days of the filing of the petition. If cases in which the debtor does not file Official Form 22A with the petition, the forms provide for the clerk to state that insufficient information has been filed, and to inform creditors that if later-filed information indicates that the presumption arises, creditors will be sent another notice.

In cases involving serial filers (debtors who have filed more than one case within a specified period), the automatic stay provided by § 362(a) of the Code as amended in 2005 may not apply or may be limited in duration, unless the stay is extended or imposed by court order. The form contains a general statement alerting debtors to this possibility.

Section 1514, added to the Code in 2005, also requires that a secured creditor with a foreign address be advised whether the creditor is required to file a proof of claim, and Forms 9B, 9D, 9E, 9E (Alt.), 9F, 9F (Alt.), 9G, 9H, and 9I are amended to include general information addressing that question. Forms 9E, 9E (Alt.), 9F, and 9F (Alt.) also are amended to inform creditors that in a case in which the debtor has filed a plan for which it has solicited acceptances before filing the case, the court may, after notice and a hearing, order that the United States trustee not convene a meeting of creditors.

Forms 9E and 9E Alt. are amended to state that, unless the court orders otherwise, an individual chapter 11 debtor's discharge is not effective until completion of all payments under the plan, as provided in § 1141(d)(5) which was added to the Code in 2005. Forms 9F and 9F (Alt.) are amended to include a deadline to file a complaint to determine the dischargeability of a debt, in conformity with § 1141(d)(6) which was added to the Code in 2005.

Form 9I is amended to include a deadline to file a complaint to determine the dischargeability of certain debts. This amendment implements 2005 amendment to § 1328(a)(1) of the Code.

2006 Amendment

Forms 9G and 9H are amended to add "family fisherman" to the title and to the description of chapter 12. The 2005 amendments to the Code added a "family fisherman," as defined in § 101(19A), to the persons eligible to file a bankruptcy case under chapter 12. Form 9I is amended to provide general notice to parties in interest of the potential for a claim to be filed late in the case.

2005–2007 Amendments

(The 2005–2007 Committee Note incorporates Committee Notes previously published in 2005 and 2006.)

The form is amended in a variety of ways to implement the provisions of the Bankruptcy Abuse Prevention and Consumer Protection Act of 2005, Pub. L. No. 109–8, 119 Stat. 23 (April 20, 2005). All versions of the form are amended to advise creditors to consult an attorney concerning what rights they may have in the specific case. All versions of the form also are amended to provide to creditors with foreign addresses information about filing claims and to advise those creditors to consult a lawyer familiar with United States bankruptcy law regarding any questions they may have about their rights in a particular case. These amendments implement § 1514, which was added to the Code in 2005.

Forms 9A and 9C are amended to include a box in which the clerk can notify creditors in a chapter 7 case filed by an individual with primarily consumer debts if the presumption of abuse has arisen under § 707(b) of the Code as amended in 2005. Under § 342(d) of the Code, the clerk has a duty to notify creditors concerning the presumption within ten days of the filing of the petition. In cases in which the debtor does not file Official Form 22A with the petition, the forms provide for the clerk to state that insufficient information has been filed, and to inform creditors that if later-filed information indicates that the presumption arises, creditors will be sent another notice. Forms 9G and 9H are amended to add

Form B9I OFFICIAL FORMS

"family fishermen" to the notices used in chapter 12 cases, in conformity with the 2005 amendments to the Code extending the provisions of chapter 12 to family fishermen.

In cases involving serial filers (debtors who have filed more than one case within a specified period), the automatic stay provided by § 362(a) of the Code as amended in 2005 may not apply or may be limited in duration, unless the stay is extended or imposed by court order. The form contains a general statement alerting debtors to this possibility.

Section 1514, added to the Code in 2005, also requires that a secured creditor with a foreign address be advised whether the creditor is required to file a proof of claim, and Forms 9B, 9D, 9E, 9E (Alt.), 9F, 9F (Alt.), 9G, 9H, and 9I are amended to include general information addressing that question. Forms 9E, 9E (Alt.), 9F, and 9F (Alt.) also are amended to inform creditors that in a case in which the debtor has filed a plan for which it has solicited acceptances before filing the case, the court may, after notice and a hearing, order that the United States trustee not convene a meeting of creditors.

Forms 9E and 9E (Alt.) are amended to state that, unless the court orders otherwise, an individual chapter 11 debtor's discharge is not effective until completion of all payments under the plan, as provided in § 1141(d)(5) which was added to the Code in 2005. Forms 9F and 9F (Alt.) are amended to include a deadline to file a complaint to determine the dischargeability of a debt, in conformity with § 1141(d)(6), which also was added to the Code in 2005.

Form 9I is amended to include a deadline to file a complaint to determine the dischargeability of certain debts. This amendment implements a 2005 amendment to § 1328(a) of the Code.

In addition, all versions of the form are amended to provide to the public only the last four digits of any individual debtor's taxpayer-identification number. This amendment implements Rule 9037.

2010 Amendment

Forms 9A, 9C, and 9I are amended in the "Deadlines" section on the front and the "Discharge of Debts" section on the back. The changes conform to amendments to Bankruptcy Rules 4004 and 7001 that direct that certain objections to discharge be brought by motion rather than by complaint.

2011 Amendment

The form's explanation of the "Meeting of Creditors" is amended to take account of the amendment of Rule 2003(e). When a meeting of creditors is adjourned to another date, the rule requires the official presiding at the meeting to file a statement specifying the date and time to which the meeting is adjourned. The explanation on all versions of the form is amended to reflect that requirement. Stylistic changes to the form are also made.

2012 Amendment

All versions of the form have been updated on the first page and in the claims box on the explanation page to remind creditors that the form should not be included with or attached to any proof of claim or other filing in the case. Stylistic changes to the form are also made.

OFFICIAL FORMS Form 10

Form 10. Proof of Claim

B10 (Official Form 10) (04/13)

UNITED STATES BANKRUPTCY COURT		PROOF OF CLAIM
Name of Debtor:	Case Number:	

NOTE: *Do not use this form to make a claim for an administrative expense that arises after the bankruptcy filing. You may file a request for payment of an administrative expense according to 11 U.S.C. § 503.*

Name of Creditor (the person or other entity to whom the debtor owes money or property):

COURT USE ONLY

Name and address where notices should be sent:

☐ Check this box if this claim amends a previously filed claim.

Court Claim Number: _____
 (If known)

Telephone number: email:

Filed on: _____

Name and address where payment should be sent (if different from above):

☐ Check this box if you are aware that anyone else has filed a proof of claim relating to this claim. Attach copy of statement giving particulars.

Telephone number: email:

1. Amount of Claim as of Date Case Filed: $ _____

If all or part of the claim is secured, complete item 4.

If all or part of the claim is entitled to priority, complete item 5.

☐ Check this box if the claim includes interest or other charges in addition to the principal amount of the claim. Attach a statement that itemizes interest or charges.

2. Basis for Claim: _____
   (See instruction #2)

3. Last four digits of any number by which creditor identifies debtor:	3a. Debtor may have scheduled account as: _____ (See instruction #3a)	3b. Uniform Claim Identifier (optional): _____ (See instruction #3b)

4. Secured Claim (See instruction #4)
Check the appropriate box if the claim is secured by a lien on property or a right of setoff, attach required redacted documents, and provide the requested information.

Amount of arrearage and other charges, as of the time case was filed, included in secured claim, if any:

$ _____

Nature of property or right of setoff: ☐ Real Estate ☐ Motor Vehicle ☐ Other
Describe:

Basis for perfection: _____

Value of Property: $ _____

Amount of Secured Claim: $ _____

Annual Interest Rate _____ % ☐ Fixed or ☐ Variable
(when case was filed)

Amount Unsecured: $ _____

5. Amount of Claim Entitled to Priority under 11 U.S.C. § 507 (a). If any part of the claim falls into one of the following categories, check the box specifying the priority and state the amount.

☐ Domestic support obligations under 11 U.S.C. § 507 (a)(1)(A) or (a)(1)(B).

☐ Wages, salaries, or commissions (up to $12,475*) earned within 180 days before the case was filed or the debtor's business ceased, whichever is earlier – 11 U.S.C. § 507 (a)(4).

☐ Contributions to an employee benefit plan – 11 U.S.C. § 507 (a)(5).

Amount entitled to priority:

☐ Up to $2,775* of deposits toward purchase, lease, or rental of property or services for personal, family, or household use – 11 U.S.C. § 507 (a)(7).

☐ Taxes or penalties owed to governmental units – 11 U.S.C. § 507 (a)(8).

☐ Other – Specify applicable paragraph of 11 U.S.C. § 507 (a)(__).

$ _____

Amounts are subject to adjustment on 4/01/16 and every 3 years thereafter with respect to cases commenced on or after the date of adjustment.

6. Credits. The amount of all payments on this claim has been credited for the purpose of making this proof of claim. (See instruction #6)

Form 10   OFFICIAL FORMS

B10 (Official Form 10) (04/13)

7. Documents: Attached are **redacted** copies of any documents that support the claim, such as promissory notes, purchase orders, invoices, itemized statements of running accounts, contracts, judgments, mortgages, security agreements, or, in the case of a claim based on an open-end or revolving consumer credit agreement, a statement providing the information required by FRBP 3001(c)(3)(A). If the claim is secured, box 4 has been completed, and **redacted** copies of documents providing evidence of perfection of a security interest are attached. If the claim is secured by the debtor's principal residence, the Mortgage Proof of Claim Attachment is being filed with this claim. *(See instruction #7, and the definition of "redacted".)*

DO NOT SEND ORIGINAL DOCUMENTS. ATTACHED DOCUMENTS MAY BE DESTROYED AFTER SCANNING.

If the documents are not available, please explain:

8. Signature: (See instruction #8)

Check the appropriate box.

☐ I am the creditor.   ☐ I am the creditor's authorized agent.   ☐ I am the trustee, or the debtor, or their authorized agent. (See Bankruptcy Rule 3004.)   ☐ I am a guarantor, surety, indorser, or other codebtor. (See Bankruptcy Rule 3005.)

I declare under penalty of perjury that the information provided in this claim is true and correct to the best of my knowledge, information, and reasonable belief.

Print Name: _____
Title: _____
Company: _____
Address and telephone number (if different from notice address above): _____   (Signature)   (Date)

Telephone number: _____ email: _____

Penalty for presenting fraudulent claim: Fine of up to $500,000 or imprisonment for up to 5 years, or both. 18 U.S.C. §§ 152 and 3571.

INSTRUCTIONS FOR PROOF OF CLAIM FORM

The instructions and definitions below are general explanations of the law. In certain circumstances, such as bankruptcy cases not filed voluntarily by the debtor, exceptions to these general rules may apply.

Items to be completed in Proof of Claim form

Court, Name of Debtor, and Case Number:
Fill in the federal judicial district in which the bankruptcy case was filed (for example, Central District of California), the debtor's full name, and the case number. If the creditor received a notice of the case from the bankruptcy court, all of this information is at the top of the notice.

Creditor's Name and Address:
Fill in the name of the person or entity asserting a claim and the name and address of the person who should receive notices issued during the bankruptcy case. A separate space is provided for the payment address if it differs from the notice address. The creditor has a continuing obligation to keep the court informed of its current address. See Federal Rule of Bankruptcy Procedure (FRBP) 2002(g).

1. Amount of Claim as of Date Case Filed:
State the total amount owed to the creditor on the date of the bankruptcy filing. Follow the instructions concerning whether to complete items 4 and 5. Check the box if interest or other charges are included in the claim.

2. Basis for Claim:
State the type of debt or how it was incurred. Examples include goods sold, money loaned, services performed, personal injury/wrongful death, car loan, mortgage note, and credit card. If the claim is based on delivering health care goods or services, limit the disclosure of the goods or services so as to avoid embarrassment or the disclosure of confidential health care information. You may be required to provide additional disclosure if an interested party objects to the claim.

3. Last Four Digits of Any Number by Which Creditor Identifies Debtor:
State only the last four digits of the debtor's account or other number used by the creditor to identify the debtor.

3a. Debtor May Have Scheduled Account As:
Report a change in the creditor's name, a transferred claim, or any other information that clarifies a difference between this proof of claim and the claim as scheduled by the debtor.

3b. Uniform Claim Identifier:
If you use a uniform claim identifier, you may report it here. A uniform claim identifier is an optional 24-character identifier that certain large creditors use to facilitate electronic payment in chapter 13 cases.

4. Secured Claim:
Check whether the claim is fully or partially secured. Skip this section if the claim is entirely unsecured. (See Definitions.) If the claim is secured, check the box for the nature and value of property that secures the claim, attach copies of lien documentation, and state, as of the date of the bankruptcy filing, the annual interest rate (and whether it is fixed or variable), and the amount past due on the claim.

5. Amount of Claim Entitled to Priority Under 11 U.S.C. § 507 (a).
If any portion of the claim falls into any category shown, check the appropriate box(es) and state the amount entitled to priority. (See Definitions.) A claim may be partly priority and partly non-priority. For example, in some of the categories, the law limits the amount entitled to priority.

6. Credits:
An authorized signature on this proof of claim serves as an acknowledgment that when calculating the amount of the claim, the creditor gave the debtor credit for any payments received toward the debt.

7. Documents:
Attach redacted copies of any documents that show the debt exists and a lien secures the debt. You must also attach copies of documents that evidence perfection of any security interest and documents required by FRBP 3001(c) for claims based on an open-end or revolving consumer credit agreement or secured by a security interest in the debtor's principal residence. You may also attach a summary in addition to the documents themselves. FRBP 3001(c) and (d). If the claim is based on delivering health care goods or services, limit disclosing confidential health care information. Do not send original documents, as attachments may be destroyed after scanning.

8. Date and Signature:
The individual completing this proof of claim must sign and date it. FRBP 9011. If the claim is filed electronically, FRBP 5005(a)(2) authorizes courts to establish local rules specifying what constitutes a signature. If you sign this form, you declare under penalty of perjury that the information provided is true and correct to the best of your knowledge, information, and reasonable belief. Your signature is also a certification that the claim meets the requirements of FRBP 9011(b). Whether the claim is filed electronically or in person, if your name is on the signature line, you are responsible for the declaration. Print the name and title, if any, of the creditor or other person authorized to file this claim. State the filer's address and telephone number if it differs from the address given on the top of the form for purposes of receiving notices. If the claim is filed by an authorized agent, provide both the name of the individual filing the claim and the name of the agent. If the authorized agent is a servicer, identify the corporate servicer as the company. Criminal penalties apply for making a false statement on a proof of claim.

OFFICIAL FORMS — Form 10

DEFINITIONS

Debtor
A debtor is the person, corporation, or other entity that has filed a bankruptcy case.

Creditor
A creditor is a person, corporation, or other entity to whom debtor owes a debt that was incurred before the date of the bankruptcy filing. See 11 U.S.C. §101 (10).

Claim
A claim is the creditor's right to receive payment for a debt owed by the debtor on the date of the bankruptcy filing. See 11 U.S.C. §101 (5). A claim may be secured or unsecured.

Proof of Claim
A proof of claim is a form used by the creditor to indicate the amount of the debt owed by the debtor on the date of the bankruptcy filing. The creditor must file the form with the clerk of the same bankruptcy court in which the bankruptcy case was filed.

Secured Claim Under 11 U.S.C. § 506 (a)
A secured claim is one backed by a lien on property of the debtor. The claim is secured so long as the creditor has the right to be paid from the property prior to other creditors. The amount of the secured claim cannot exceed the value of the property. Any amount owed to the creditor in excess of the value of the property is an unsecured claim. Examples of liens on property include a mortgage on real estate or a security interest in a car. A lien may be voluntarily granted by a debtor or may be obtained through a court proceeding. In some states, a court judgment is a lien.

A claim also may be secured if the creditor owes the debtor money (has a right to setoff).

Unsecured Claim
An unsecured claim is one that does not meet the requirements of a secured claim. A claim may be partly unsecured if the amount of the claim exceeds the value of the property on which the creditor has a lien.

Claim Entitled to Priority Under 11 U.S.C. § 507 (a)
Priority claims are certain categories of unsecured claims that are paid from the available money or property in a bankruptcy case before other unsecured claims.

Redacted
A document has been redacted when the person filing it has masked, edited out, or otherwise deleted, certain information. A creditor must show only the last four digits of any social-security, individual's tax-identification, or financial-account number, only the initials of a minor's name, and only the year of any person's date of birth. If the claim is based on the delivery of health care goods or services, limit the disclosure of the goods or services so as to avoid embarrassment or the disclosure of confidential health care information.

Evidence of Perfection
Evidence of perfection may include a mortgage, lien, certificate of title, financing statement, or other document showing that the lien has been filed or recorded.

INFORMATION

Acknowledgment of Filing of Claim
To receive acknowledgment of your filing, you may either enclose a stamped self-addressed envelope and a copy of this proof of claim or you may access the court's PACER system (www.pacer.psc.uscourts.gov) for a small fee to view your filed proof of claim.

Offers to Purchase a Claim
Certain entities are in the business of purchasing claims for an amount less than the face value of the claims. One or more of these entities may contact the creditor and offer to purchase the claim. Some of the written communications from these entities may easily be confused with official court documentation or communications from the debtor. These entities do not represent the bankruptcy court or the debtor. The creditor has no obligation to sell its claim. However, if the creditor decides to sell its claim, any transfer of such claim is subject to FRBP 3001(e), any applicable provisions of the Bankruptcy Code (11 U.S.C. § 101 et seq.), and any applicable orders of the bankruptcy court.

(Added Aug. 1, 1991; amended Mar. 16, 1993; Mar. 1995; July, 1995; Oct. 1, 1997; Apr. 1, 1998; Dec. 1, 2003; April 1, 2004; Aug. 11, 2005, eff. Oct. 17, 2005; Apr. 1, 2007; Dec. 1, 2007; Dec. 1, 2008; Apr. 1, 2010; Dec. 1, 2011; Dec. 1, 2012; Apr. 1, 2013.)

ADVISORY COMMITTEE NOTES

1991 Enactment

This form replaces former Official Forms No. 19, No. 20, and No. 21. The box format and simplified language are intended to facilitate completion of the form.

The form directs the claimant to attach documents to support the claim or, if voluminous, a summary of such documents. These include any security agreement (if not included in the writing on which the claim is founded), and evidence of perfection of any security interest. See Committee Note to Rule 3001(d) concerning satisfactory evidence of perfection. If the claim includes prepetition interest or other charges such as attorney fees, a statement giving a detailed breakdown of the elements of the claim is required.

Rule 2002(g) requires the clerk to update the mailing list in the case by substituting the address provided by a creditor on a proof of claim, if that address is different from the one supplied by the debtor. The form contains checkboxes to assist the clerk in performing this duty. The form also alerts the trustee when the claim is an amendment to or replacement for an earlier claim.

1993 Amendment

The form has been amended to accommodate inclusion of the priority afforded in § 507(a)(8) of the Code, which was added by Pub.L. No. 101–647, (Crime Control Act of 1990), and to avoid the necessity of further amendment to the form if other priorities are added to § 507(a) in the future. In addition, sections 4 and 5 of the form have been amended to clarify that only prepetition arrearages and charges are to be included in the amount of the claim.

1995 Amendment

The form is amended to add the seventh priority granted by the Bankruptcy Reform Act of 1994 to debts for alimony, maintenance, or support of a spouse, former spouse, or child of the debtor. The form

Form 10 OFFICIAL FORMS

also amends the Code reference to the priority afforded to tax debts and the dollar maximums for the priorities granted to wages and customer deposits in conformity with amendments made by the 1994 Act to section 507(a) of the Code. The 1994 Act also amended section 104 of the Code to provide for future adjustment of the dollar amounts specified in section 507(a) to be made by administrative action at three-year intervals to reflect changes in the consumer price index. The form is amended to include notice that these dollar amounts are subject to change without formal amendment to the official form.

1997 Amendment

Numbered sections 4. and 5. of the form have been reformatted to eliminate redundant information and make it easier to complete the form correctly. A creditor will report the total amount of the claim first, and will report only that amount unless the claim is secured by collateral or entitled to a priority under § 507 of the Code.

Explanatory definitions and instructions for completing the form also have been added.

2003 Amendment

The form is amended to require a wage, salary, or other compensation creditor to disclose only the last four digits of the creditor's Social Security number to afford greater privacy to the creditor. A trustee can request the full information necessary for tax withholding and reporting at the time the trustee makes a distribution to creditors.

2005 Amendment

The form is amended to conform to changes in the priority afforded the claims of certain creditors in § 507(a) of the Code as amended by the Bankruptcy Abuse Prevention and Consumer Protection Act of 2005, Pub. L. No. 109–8, 119 Stat. 23 (April 20, 2005).

2005–2007 Amendments

(The 2005–2007 Committee Note incorporates Committee Notes previously published in 2005.)

The form is amended to conform to changes in the priority afforded the claims of certain creditors in § 507(a) of the Code as amended by the Bankruptcy Abuse Prevention and Consumer Protection Act of 2005, Pub. L. No. 109–8, 119 Stat. 23 (April 20, 2005).

In addition, the form and its instructions are amended in several respects based on the experiences of creditors and trustees in using it and on the technological changes that have occurred in the courts' processing of claims. A definition of the word "redacted" has been added in conformity with Rule 9037.

The creditor now has a space in which to provide a separate payment address if different from the creditor's address for receiving notices in the case. The checkboxes for indicating that the creditor's address provided on the proof of claim is a new address, and that the creditor never received any notices from the court in the case have been deleted. The computer systems now used by the courts make it unnecessary for a creditor to "flag" a new address or call attention to the fact that the creditor is making its first appearance in the case. In place of the deleted items is a new checkbox to be used when a debtor or a trustee files a proof of claim for a creditor; it will alert the clerk to send the notice required by Rule 3004. The box for indicating whether the claim replaces a previously filed claim also has been deleted as no longer necessary in light of the 2005 amendments to Rules 3004 and 3005. The creditor simply will amend the claim filed by the other party.

Requests for the creditor to state the date on which the debt was incurred and the date on which any court judgment concerning the debt was obtained have been deleted, based on reports from trustees that they rely on the documents supporting the claim for this information. The checkboxes for stating the basis for the creditor's claim have been replaced with a blank in which the creditor is to provide this information. Examples of the most common categories, based on the former checkboxes, can be found in the instructions on the form. The request to state the account number by which the creditor identifies the debtor has been moved to paragraph 3 of the form and has been revised to request only the last four digits of the number, in conformity with Rule 9037. In addition, a new paragraph 3a gives the creditor a place to notify the trustee and the court of any change in the creditor's name, or that the claim has been transferred, or to provide any other information to clarify a difference between the proof of claim and the creditor's claim as scheduled by the debtor.

The adjective "total" is deleted from the sections of the form where the creditor states the amount of the claim and the creditor now simply reports the amount of the claim. If the claim is a general unsecured claim, no further details are stated on the form, although a creditor still must attach a copy of any writing on which the claim is based, as required by Rule 3001(c), and must attach a statement itemizing any interest or other charges (in addition to the principal) that are included in the claim. If the claim or any part of it is secured or entitled to priority under § 507(a) of the Code, the creditor is directed to provide details in the appropriate sections of the form. The creditor now states the amount to be afforded priority only once, in the section of the form designated for describing the specific priority being asserted. The introductory language in the section where the creditor describes any priority to which it is entitled has been revised for clarity. The word "collateral" has been replaced with the less colloquial and more accurate phrase "lien on property" throughout the form.

Information about obtaining acknowledgment from the court of the filing of the proof of claim is revised and moved to a new section on the reverse side called "Information." This new section also alerts a creditor to the possibility that it may be approached about selling its claim, advises that the court has no role in any such solicitations, and states that a creditor is under no obligation to accept any offer to purchase its claim. A new instruction is added about signing a proof of claim. This instruction includes citations to Rules 9011 and 5005(a)(2) concerning signature requirements in an electronic filing environment.

Finally, all of the definitions and instructions on the reverse side of the form are amended generally to reflect the deletions, additions, and other changes made on page 1. These include a reminder to the creditor to keep the court informed of any changes in its address. The instructions now appear at the top of the page, and the text is revised both to reflect the substantive changes to the form and to improve the clarity and style of this explanatory material.

2008 Amendment

The form is amended at box seven on page one, and instructions two and seven on page two, to instruct the claimant that the information contained in or attached to a claim based on the delivery of health care goods or services should be limited so as to avoid embarrassment or the unnecessary disclosure of confidential information. The claimant is informed that additional disclosure may be required if the trustee or another party in interest objects to the claim.

Page two of the form is also amended to revise slightly the definitions of "creditor" and "claim" to conform more closely to the definitions of those terms in the Code.

2011 Amendment

The form is amended in several respects. A new section—3b—is added to allow the reporting of a uniform claim identifier. This identifier, consisting of 24 characters, is used by some creditors to facilitate automated receipt, distribution, and posting of payments made by means of electronic funds transfers by chapter 13 trustees. Creditors are not required to use a uniform claim identifier.

Language is added to section 4 to clarify that the annual interest rate that must be reported for a secured claim is the rate applicable at the time the bankruptcy case was filed. Checkboxes for indicating whether the interest rate is fixed or variable are also added.

Section 7 of the form is revised to clarify that, consistent with Rule 3001(c), writings supporting a claim or evidencing perfection of a security interest must be attached to the proof of claim. If the documents are not available, the filer must provide an explanation for their absence. The instructions for this section of the form explain that summaries of supporting documents may be attached only in addition to the documents themselves.

Section 8—the date and signature box—is revised to include a declaration that is intended to impress upon the filer the duty of care that must be exercised in filing a proof of claim. The individual who completes the form must sign it. By doing so, he or she declares under penalty of perjury that the information provided "is true and correct to the best of my knowledge, information and reasonable belief." That individual must also provide identifying information—name; title; company; and, if not already provided, mailing address, telephone number, and email address—and indicate by checking the appropriate box the basis on which he or she is filing the proof of claim (for example, as creditor or authorized agent for the creditor). Because a trustee or debtor that files a proof of claim under Rule 3004 will indicate that basis for filing here, the checkbox on the first page of the form for stating the filer's status as a trustee or debtor is deleted. When a servicing agent files a proof of claim on behalf of a creditor, the individual completing the form must sign it and must provide his or her own name, as well as the name of the company that is the servicing agent.

Amendments are made to the instructions that reflect the changes made to the form, and stylistic and formatting changes are made to the form and instructions. Spaces are added for providing email

Form 10 OFFICIAL FORMS

addresses in addition to other contact information in order to facilitate communication with the claimant. The provision of this additional information does not affect any requirements for serving or providing official notice to the claimant.

[Attachment A]. This form is new. It must be completed and attached to a proof of claim secured by a security interest in a debtor's principal residence. The form, which implements Rule 3001(c)(2), requires an itemization of prepetition interest, fees, expenses, and charges included in the claim amount, as well as a statement of the amount necessary to cure any default as of the petition date. If the mortgage installment payments include an escrow deposit, an escrow account statement must also be attached to the proof of claim, as required by Rule 3001(c)(2)(C).

[Supplement 1]. This form is new and applies in chapter 13 cases. It implements Rule 3002.1, which requires the holder of a claim secured by a security interest in the debtor's principal residence—or the holder's agent—to provide notice at least 21 days prior to a change in the amount of the ongoing mortgage installment payments. The form requires the holder of the claim to indicate the basis for the changed payment amount and when it will take effect. The notice must be filed as a supplement to the claim holder's proof of claim, and it must be served on the debtor, debtor's counsel, and the trustee.

The individual completing the form must sign and date it. By doing so, he or she declares under penalty of perjury that the information provided is true and correct to the best of that individual's knowledge, information, and reasonable belief. The signature is also a certification that the standards of Rule 9011(b) are satisfied.

[Supplement 2]. This form is new and applies in chapter 13 cases. It implements Rule 3002.1, which requires the holder of a claim secured by a security interest in the debtor's principal residence—or the holder's agent—to file a notice of all postpetition fees, expenses, and charges within 180 days after they are incurred. The notice must be filed as a supplement to the claim holder's proof of claim, and it must be served on the debtor, debtor's counsel, and the trustee.

The individual completing the form must sign and date it. By doing so, he or she declares under penalty of perjury that the information provided is true and correct to the best of that individual's knowledge, information, and reasonable belief. The signature is also a certification that the standards of Rule 9011(b) are satisfied.

2012 Amendment

Section 7 of the form is amended to remind filers of the need to attach documents required by Rule 3001(c) for claims based on an open-end or revolving consumer credit agreement or claims secured by a security interest in the debtor's principal residence.

Section 8 is revised to delete the direction that an authorized agent attach a power of attorney if one exists. Rule 9010(c) does not require that an agent's authority to file a proof of claim be evidenced by a power of attorney.

[Form 11. Omitted. See Form 5.]

Form 11A. General Power of Attorney

Official Form 11A
6/90

United States Bankruptcy Court

_____ District Of _____

In re _____,
      Debtor

Case No. _____

Chapter _____

GENERAL POWER OF ATTORNEY

To _____ of * _____, and
_____ of * _____.

    The undersigned claimant hereby authorizes you, or any one of you, as attorney in fact for the undersigned and with full power of substitution, to vote on any question that may be lawfully submitted to creditors of the debtor in the above-entitled case; [*if appropriate*] to vote for a trustee of the estate of the debtor and for a committee of creditors; to receive dividends; and in general to perform any act not constituting the practice of law for the undersigned in all matters arising in this case.

Dated: _____

Signed: _____

By _____

as _____

Address: _____
_____

[*If executed by an individual*] Acknowledged before me on _____.

[*If executed on behalf of a partnership*] Acknowledged before me on _____,
by _____, who says that he [*or* she] is a member of the partnership named above and is authorized to execute this power of attorney in its behalf.

[*If executed on behalf of a corporation*] Acknowledged before me on _____,
by _____, who says that he [*or* she] is _____ of the corporation named above and is authorized to execute this power of attorney in its behalf.

_____
_____
[*Official character.*]

* State mailing address.

(Added Aug. 1, 1991.)

ADVISORY COMMITTEE NOTES

This form previously was numbered Official Form No. 17.

Form 11B   **OFFICIAL FORMS**

Form 11B.   Special Power of Attorney

Official Form 11B
6/90

United States Bankruptcy Court

_____ District Of _____

In re _____,
       Debtor

Case No. _____

Chapter _____

SPECIAL POWER OF ATTORNEY

To _____ of * _____, and
_____ of * _____.

       The undersigned claimant hereby authorizes you, or any one of you, as attorney in fact for the undersigned [*if desired*: and with full power of substitution,] to attend the meeting of creditors of the debtor or any adjournment thereof, and to vote in my behalf on any question that may be lawfully submitted to creditors at such meeting or adjourned meeting, and for a trustee or trustees of the estate of the debtor.

Dated: _____

Signed: _____

By _____

as _____

Address: _____
_____

[*If executed by an individual*] Acknowledged before me on _____.

[*If executed on behalf of a partnership*] Acknowledged before me _____,
by _____, who says that he [*or* she] is a member of the partnership named above and is authorized to execute this power of attorney in its behalf.

[*If executed on behalf of a corporation*] Acknowledged before me on _____,
by _____, who says that he [*or* she] is _____ of the corporation named above and is authorized to execute this power of attorney in its behalf.

_____

[*Official character.*]

* State mailing address.

(Added Aug. 1, 1991.)

ADVISORY COMMITTEE NOTES

This form previously was numbered Official Form No. 18.

OFFICIAL FORMS Form 12

Form 12. Order and Notice for Hearing on Disclosure Statement

Official Form 12
(12/03)

Form 12. ORDER AND NOTICE FOR HEARING ON DISCLOSURE STATEMENT

[Caption as in Form 16A]

ORDER AND NOTICE FOR HEARING ON DISCLOSURE STATEMENT

To the debtor, its creditors, and other parties in interest:

A disclosure statement and a plan under chapter 11 [*or* chapter 9] of the Bankruptcy Code having been filed by _____ on _____,

IT IS ORDERED and notice is hereby given, that:

1. The hearing to consider the approval of the disclosure statement shall be held at: _____, on _____, at _____ o'clock __.m.

2. _____ is fixed as the last day for filing and serving in accordance with Fed. R. Bankr. P. 3017(a) written objections to the disclosure statement.

3. Within _____ days after entry of this order, the disclosure statement and plan shall be distributed in accordance with Fed. R. Bankr. P. 3017(a).

4. Requests for copies of the disclosure statement and plan shall be mailed to the debtor in possession [*or* trustee *or* debtor *or* _____] at * _____.

Dated: _____

BY THE COURT

_____
United States Bankruptcy Judge

* State mailing address

(Added Aug. 1, 1991; amended Dec. 2003.)

Form 12 OFFICIAL FORMS

ADVISORY COMMITTEE NOTES
1991 Enactment

This form previously was numbered Official Form No. 28. The form is related to Rule 3017(a). Section 1125 of the Code requires court approval of a disclosure statement before votes may be solicited for or against a plan in either chapter 11 reorganization or chapter 9 municipality cases.

Objections to the disclosure statement may be filed. Rule 3017(a) specifies that the court may fix a time for the filing of objections or they can be filed at any time prior to approval of the statement.

Rule 3017(a) also specifies the persons who are to receive copies of the statement and plan prior to the hearing. These documents will not be sent to all parties in interest because at this stage of the case it could be unnecessarily expensive and confusing. However, any party in interest may request copies. The request should be made in writing (Rule 3017(a)), and sent to the person mailing the statement and plan which, as the form indicates, would usually be the proponent of the plan.

This form may be adapted for use if more than one disclosure statement is to be considered by the court.

OFFICIAL FORMS — Form 13

Form 13. Order Approving Disclosure Statement and Fixing Time for Filing Acceptances or Rejections of Plan, Combined with Notice Thereof

Official Form 13
(12/03)

Form 13. ORDER APPROVING DISCLOSURE STATEMENT AND FIXING TIME FOR FILING ACCEPTANCES OR REJECTIONS OF PLAN, COMBINED WITH NOTICE THEREOF

[Caption as in Form 16A]

ORDER APPROVING DISCLOSURE STATEMENT AND FIXING TIME FOR FILING ACCEPTANCES OR REJECTIONS OF PLAN, COMBINED WITH NOTICE THEREOF

A disclosure statement under chapter 11 of the Bankruptcy Code having been filed by _____, on _____ [*if appropriate*, and by _____, on _____], referring to a plan under chapter 11 of the Code filed by _____, on _____ [*if appropriate*, and by _____, on _____ respectively] [*if appropriate*, as modified by a modification filed on _____]; and

It having been determined after hearing on notice that the disclosure statement [*or* statements] contain[s] adequate information:

IT IS ORDERED, and notice is hereby given, that:

A. The disclosure statement filed by _____ dated _____ [*if appropriate*, and by _____, dated _____ is [are] approved.

B. _____ is fixed as the last day for filing written acceptances or rejections of the plan [*or* plans] referred to above.

C. Within _____ days after the entry of this order, the plan [*or* plans] *or* a summary *or* summaries thereof approved by the court, [and [*if appropriate*] a summary approved by the court of its opinion, if any, dated _____, approving the disclosure statement [*or* statements]], the disclosure statement [*or* statements], and a ballot conforming to Official Form 14 shall be mailed to creditors, equity security holders, and other parties in interest, and shall be transmitted to the United States trustee, as provided in Fed. R. Bankr. P. 3017(d).

D. If acceptances are filed for more than one plan, preferences among the plans so accepted may be indicated.

E. [*If appropriate*] _____ is fixed for the hearing on confirmation of the plan [*or* plans].

F. [*If appropriate*] _____ is fixed as the last day for filing and serving pursuant to Fed. R. Bankr. P. 3020(b)(1) written objections to confirmation of the plan.

Dated: _____

BY THE COURT

_____
United States Bankruptcy Judge

[*If the court directs that a copy of the opinion should be transmitted in lieu of or in addition to the summary thereof, the appropriate change should be made in paragraph C of this order.*]

(Added Aug. 1, 1991; amended Dec. 2003.)

Form 14 OFFICIAL FORMS

ADVISORY COMMITTEE NOTES

1991 Enactment

This form is derived from former Official Form No. 29. The form may be adapted for use if more than one disclosure statement is approved by the court.

Form 14. Class [ ] Ballot for Accepting or Rejecting Plan of Reorganization

Official Form 14
(12/03)

Form 14. CLASS [ ] BALLOT FOR ACCEPTING OR REJECTING
PLAN OF REORGANIZATION

[Caption as in Form 16A]

CLASS [ ] BALLOT FOR ACCEPTING OR REJECTING
PLAN OF REORGANIZATION

[Proponent] filed a plan of reorganization dated *[Date]* (the "Plan") for the Debtor in this case. The Court has *[conditionally]* approved a disclosure statement with respect to the Plan (the "Disclosure Statement"). The Disclosure Statement provides information to assist you in deciding how to vote your ballot. If you do not have a Disclosure Statement, you may obtain a copy from *[name, address, telephone number and telecopy number of proponent/proponent's attorney.]* Court approval of the disclosure statement does not indicate approval of the Plan by the Court.

You should review the Disclosure Statement and the Plan before you vote. You may wish to seek legal advice concerning the Plan and your classification and treatment under the Plan. Your *[claim] [equity interest]* has been placed in class [ ] under the Plan. If you hold claims or equity interests in more than one class, you will receive a ballot for each class in which you are entitled to vote.

If your ballot is not received by *[name and address of proponent's attorney or other appropriate address]* on or before *[date]*, and such deadline is not extended, your vote will not count as either an acceptance or rejection of the Plan.

If the Plan is confirmed by the Bankruptcy Court it will be binding on you whether or not you vote.

ACCEPTANCE OR REJECTION OF THE PLAN

[At this point the ballot should provide for voting by the particular class of creditors or equity holders receiving the ballot using one of the following alternatives;]

[If the voter is the holder of a secured, priority, or unsecured nonpriority claim:]

The undersigned, the holder of a Class [ ] claim against the Debtor in the unpaid amount of Dollars ($)

[or, if the voter is the holder of a bond, debenture, or other debt security:]

The undersigned, the holder of a Class [ ] claim against the Debtor, consisting of Dollars ($) principal amount of *[describe bond, debenture, or other debt security]* of the Debtor (For purposes of this Ballot, it is not necessary and you should not adjust the principal amount for any accrued or unmatured interest.)

[or, if the voter is the holder of an equity interest:]

The undersigned, the holder of Class [ ] equity interest in the Debtor, consisting of _____ shares or other interests of *[describe equity interest]* in the Debtor

902

OFFICIAL FORMS   Form 14

Official Form 14 continued
(12/03)

[In each case, the following language should be included:]

    (Check one box only)

    [ ] ACCEPTS THE PLAN   [ ] REJECTS THE PLAN

Dated: _____

        Print or type name: _____

        Signature: _____

        Title (if corporation or partnership) _____

        Address: _____

                   _____

RETURN THIS BALLOT TO:

[Name and address of proponent's attorney or other appropriate address]

(Added Aug. 1, 1991; amended Oct. 1, 1997; Dec. 2003.)

ADVISORY COMMITTEE NOTES
1991 Enactment

    The form is derived from former Official Form No. 30. The form has been amended to facilitate the voting of a debtor's shares held in "street name." The form may be adapted to designate the class in which each ballot is to be tabulated. It is intended that a separate ballot will be provided for each class in which a holder may vote.

1997 Amendment

    The form has been substantially amended to simplify its format and make it easier to complete correctly.

    Directions or blanks for proponent to complete the text of the ballot are in italics and enclosed within brackets. A ballot should include only the applicable language from the alternatives shown on this form and should be adapted to the particular requirements of the case.

    If the plan provides for creditors in a class to have the right to reduce their claims so as to qualify for treatment given to creditors whose claims do not exceed a specified amount, the ballot should make provisions for the exercise of that right. See section 1122(b) of the Code.

    If debt or equity securities are held in the name of a broker/dealer or nominee, the ballot should require the furnishing of sufficient information to assure that duplicate ballots are not submitted and counted and that ballots submitted by a broker/dealer or nominee reflect the votes of the beneficial holders of such securities. See Rule 3017(e).

Form 15   **OFFICIAL FORMS**

In the event that more than one plan of reorganization is to be voted upon, the form of ballot will need to be adapted to permit holders of claims or equity interests (a) to accept or reject each plan being proposed, and (b) to indicate preferences among the competing plans. See section 1129(c) of the Code.

Form 15.   Order Confirming Plan

Form B15
(Rev. 12/01)

Form 15. ORDER CONFIRMING PLAN

[Caption as in Form 16A]

ORDER CONFIRMING PLAN

The plan under chapter 11 of the Bankruptcy Code filed by _____, on _____ *[if applicable,* as modified by a modification filed on _____,*]* or a summary thereof, having been transmitted to creditors and equity security holders; and

It having been determined after hearing on notice that the requirements for confirmation set forth in 11 U.S.C. § 1129(a) *[or, if appropriate,* 11 U.S.C. § 1129(b)*]* have been satisfied;

IT IS ORDERED that:

The plan filed by _____, on _____, *[If appropriate, include dates and any other pertinent details of modifications to the plan]* is confirmed. *[If the plan provides for an injunction against conduct not otherwise enjoined under the Code, include the information required by Rule 3020.]*

A copy of the confirmed plan is attached.

Dated: _____

                                                                    BY THE COURT

                                                            _____
                                                                 United States Bankruptcy Judge.

(Added Aug. 1, 1991; amended Dec. 1, 2001.)

ADVISORY COMMITTEE NOTES

This form is derived from former Official Form No. 31. The form has been simplified to avoid the necessity of repeating the statutory requirements of 11 U.S.C. § 1129(a). In the case of an individual chapter 11 debtor, Form 18 may be adapted for use together with this form.

OFFICIAL FORMS Form 16A

2001 Amendment

The form is amended to conform to the December 1, 2001, amendments to Rule 3020.

Form 16A. Caption (Full)

B16A (Official Form 16A) (12/07)

Form 16A. CAPTION (FULL)

United States Bankruptcy Court

_____ District Of _____

In re _____,)
 [Set forth here all names including married,)
 maiden, and trade names used by debtor within)
 last 8 years.])
             Debtor) Case No. _____
)
Address _____)
)
 _____) Chapter _____
)
Last four digits of Social-Security or Individual Tax-
Payer-Identification (ITIN) No(s).,(if any): _____)
)
Employer Tax-Identification (EIN) No(s).(if any): _____)
)

[Designation of Character of Paper]

(Added Aug. 1, 1991; and amended Mar. 1995; Dec. 1, 2003; Aug. 11, 2005, eff. Oct. 17, 2005; Dec. 1, 2007.)

ADVISORY COMMITTEE NOTES
1991 Enactment

This form has been transferred from former Official Form No. 1, which included the form of caption for the case. Rule 9004(b) requires a caption to set forth the title of the case. Rule 1005 provides that the title of the case shall include the debtor's name, all other names used by the debtor within six years before the commencement of the case, and the debtor's social security and tax identification numbers. This form of caption is prescribed for use on the petition, the notice of the meeting of creditors, the order of discharge, and the documents relating to a chapter 11 plan, (Official Forms 1, 9, 12, 13, 14, 15, and 18). See Rule 2002(m). In the petition, (Official Form 1), and the notice of the meeting of creditors, (Official Form 9), the information required by Rule 1005 appears in a block format. A notation of the chapter of the Bankruptcy Code under which the case is proceeding has been added to the form.

Form 16B OFFICIAL FORMS

1995 Amendment

The form is amended to provide for the debtor's address to appear in the caption in furtherance of the duty of the debtor to include this information on every notice given by the debtor. The Bankruptcy Reform Act of 1994 amended section 342 of the Code to add this requirement.

2003 Amendment

The form is amended to require disclosure of only the last four digits of the debtor's social security number to afford greater privacy to the individual debtor, whose bankruptcy case records may be available over the Internet.

2005 Amendment

The form is amended to require that the title of the case include all names used by the debtor within the last eight years in conformity with § 727(a)(8) as amended by the Bankruptcy Abuse Prevention and Consumer Protection Act of 2005, Pub. L. No. 109–8, 119 Stat. 23 (April 20, 2005), extending from six years to eight years the period during which a debtor is barred from receiving successive discharges.

2005–2007 Amendments

(The 2005–2007 Committee Note incorporates the Committee Note previously published in 2005.)

The form is amended to require that the title of the case include all names used by the debtor within the last eight years in conformity with § 727(a)(8) as amended by the Bankruptcy Abuse Prevention and Consumer Protection Act of 2005, Pub. L. No. 109–8, 119 Stat. 23 (April 20, 2005), extending from six years to eight years the period during which a debtor is barred from receiving successive discharges. In conformity with Rule 9037, the filer is directed to provide only the last four digits of any individual debtor's taxpayer-identification number.

Form 16B. Caption (Short Title)

Official Form 16B
12/94

FORM 16B. CAPTION (SHORT TITLE)

(May be used if 11 U.S.C. § 342(c) is not applicable)

United States Bankruptcy Court

_____ District Of _____

In re _____,
      Debtor

Case No. _____

Chapter _____

[Designation of Character of Paper]

(Added Aug. 1, 1991; and amended Mar. 1995.)

OFFICIAL FORMS   Form 16C

ADVISORY COMMITTEE NOTES

This form of caption is prescribed for general use in filing papers in a case under the Bankruptcy Code. Rule 9004(b) requires a caption to set forth the title of the case, and Rule 1005 specifies that the title must include all names used by the debtor within six years before the commencement of the case and the debtor's social security and tax identification numbers. This information is necessary in the petition, the notice of the meeting of creditors, the order of discharge, and the documents relating to the plan in a chapter 11 case. See Rule 2002(m) and Official Form 16A. In other notices, motions, applications, and papers filed in a case, however, a short title containing simply the name of the debtor or joint debtors may be used. Additional names, such as any under which the debtor has engaged in business, may be included in the short title as needed.

1995 Amendment

The title of this form is amended to specify that it can be used when section 342(c) of the Code, as added by the Bankruptcy Reform Act of 1994, is not applicable.

Form 16C. Caption of Complaint in Adversary Proceeding Filed by a Debtor [Abrogated]

ADVISORY COMMITTEE NOTES

This form previously was numbered Official Form No. 34. A notation of the chapter of the Bankruptcy Code under which the case is proceeding has been added to the form. Rule 7010 refers to this form as providing the caption of a pleading in an adversary proceeding.

1995 Amendment

The form is amended to conform to the amendments made to section 342 of the Code by the Bankruptcy Reform Act of 1994.

2003 Amendment

The form is abrogated. An amendment to Official Form 16A directs that only the last four digits of the debtor's Social Security number should appear in a caption. Section 342(c) of the Bankruptcy Code continues to require the debtor to provide a creditor with the debtor's name, address, and taxpayer identification number on any notice the debtor is required to give to the creditor. An individual debtor can fulfill this requirement by including the debtor's Social Security account number on only the creditor's copy of any notice or summons the debtor may serve on the creditor.

Form 16D   OFFICIAL FORMS

Form 16D.   **Caption for Use in Adversary Proceeding**

Official Form 16D
(12/04)

Form 16D. CAPTION FOR USE IN ADVERSARY PROCEEDING

United States Bankruptcy Court

_____ District Of _____

In re _____,   )
           Debtor   )   Case No._____
)
)   Chapter _____
_____,   )
           Plaintiff   )
)
)
)
_____,   )   Adv. Proc. No._____
           Defendant

COMPLAINT [*or* other Designation]

[If in a Notice of Appeal (see Form 17) or other notice filed and served by a debtor, this caption must be altered to include the debtor's address and Employer's Tax Identification Number(s) or last four digits of Social Security Number(s) as in Form 16A.]

(Added Mar. 1995; amended Dec. 1, 2004)

ADVISORY COMMITTEE NOTES
1995 Enactment

This form of caption may be used in an adversary proceeding when section 342(c) of the Code, as added by the Bankruptcy Reform Act of 1994, is not applicable.

2004 Amendment

The form is amended to reflect the 2003 abrogation of Form 16C. As a complaint initiating an adversary proceeding serves as a notice to the defendant of the filing of an action, a debtor filing an adversary proceeding must follow the notice requirements of § 342(c) of the Code. To protect individual privacy a debtor should use the defendant's copy of the summons to be served with the complaint to provide the information required by § 342(c) to any creditor named as a defendant.

OFFICIAL FORMS   Form 17A

Form 17A.   Notice of Appeal Under 28 U.S.C. § 158(a) or (b) From a Judgment, Order, or Decree of a Bankruptcy Judge

Official Form 17A (12/14)

[Caption as in Form 16A, 16B, or 16D, as appropriate]

NOTICE OF APPEAL AND STATEMENT OF ELECTION

Part 1: Identify the appellant(s)

1. Name(s) of appellant(s): _____

2. Position of appellant(s) in the adversary proceeding or bankruptcy case that is the subject of this appeal:

   For appeals in an adversary proceeding.
   ☐ Plaintiff
   ☐ Defendant
   ☐ Other (describe) _____

   For appeals in a bankruptcy case and not in an adversary proceeding.
   ☐ Debtor
   ☐ Creditor
   ☐ Trustee
   ☐ Other (describe) _____

Part 2: Identify the subject of this appeal

1. Describe the judgment, order, or decree appealed from: _____

2. State the date on which the judgment, order, or decree was entered: _____

Part 3: Identify the other parties to the appeal

List the names of all parties to the judgment, order, or decree appealed from and the names, addresses, and telephone numbers of their attorneys (attach additional pages if necessary):

1. Party: _____   Attorney: _____
                                        _____
                                        _____
                                        _____

2. Party: _____   Attorney: _____
                                        _____
                                        _____
                                        _____

Form 17A   OFFICIAL FORMS

Official Form 17A (12/14)

Part 4: Optional election to have appeal heard by District Court (applicable only in certain districts)

If a Bankruptcy Appellate Panel is available in this judicial district, the Bankruptcy Appellate Panel will hear this appeal unless, pursuant to 28 U.S.C. § 158(c)(1), a party elects to have the appeal heard by the United States District Court. If an appellant filing this notice wishes to have the appeal heard by the United States District Court, check below. Do not check the box if the appellant wishes the Bankruptcy Appellate Panel to hear the appeal.

❑ Appellant(s) elect to have the appeal heard by the United States District Court rather than by the Bankruptcy Appellate Panel.

Part 5: Sign below

_____   Date: _____
Signature of attorney for appellant(s) (or appellant(s)
if not represented by an attorney)

Name, address, and telephone number of attorney
(or appellant(s) if not represented by an attorney):
_____
_____
_____

Fee waiver notice: If appellant is a child support creditor or its representative and appellant has filed the form specified in § 304(g) of the Bankruptcy Reform Act of 1994, no fee is required.

910

Form 17B

Official Form 17B (12/14)

[Caption as in Form 16A, 16B, or 16D, as appropriate]

OPTIONAL APPELLEE STATEMENT OF ELECTION TO PROCEED IN DISTRICT COURT

This form should be filed only if all of the following are true:

- this appeal is pending in a district served by a Bankruptcy Appellate Panel,
- the appellant(s) did not elect in the Notice of Appeal to proceed in the District Court rather than in the Bankruptcy Appellate Panel,
- no other appellee has filed a statement of election to proceed in the district court, and
- you elect to proceed in the District Court.

Part 1: Identify the appellee(s) electing to proceed in the District Court

1. Name(s) of appellee(s):
   _____

2. Position of appellee(s) in the adversary proceeding or bankruptcy case that is the subject of this appeal:

   For appeals in an adversary proceeding.
   ☐ Plaintiff
   ☐ Defendant
   ☐ Other (describe) _____

   For appeals in a bankruptcy case and not in an adversary proceeding.
   ☐ Debtor
   ☐ Creditor
   ☐ Trustee
   ☐ Other (describe) _____

Part 2: Election to have this appeal heard by the District Court (applicable only in certain districts)

I (we) elect to have the appeal heard by the United States District Court rather than by the Bankruptcy Appellate Panel.

Part 3: Sign below

_____   Date: _____
Signature of attorney for appellee(s) (or appellee(s)
if not represented by an attorney)

Name, address, and telephone number of attorney
(or appellee(s) if not represented by an attorney):
_____
_____

Form 17C   OFFICIAL FORMS

Form 17C

Official Form 17C (12/14)

[This certification must be appended to your brief if the length of your brief is calculated by maximum number of words or lines of text rather than number of pages.]

Certificate of Compliance With Rule 8015(a)(7)(B) or 8016(d)(2)

This brief complies with the type-volume limitation of Rule 8015(a)(7)(B) or 8016(d)(2) because:

❏ this brief contains [*state the number of*] words, excluding the parts of the brief exempted by Rule 8015(a)(7)(B)(iii) or 8016(d)(2)(D), or

❏ this brief uses a monospaced typeface having no more than 10½ characters per inch and contains [*state the number of*] lines of text, excluding the parts of the brief exempted by Rule 8015(a)(7)(B)(iii) or 8016(d)(2)(D).

_____   Date: _____
Signature

Print name of person signing certificate of compliance:
_____

(Added Aug. 1, 1991; and amended Mar. 1995; Oct. 1, 1997; Dec. 1, 2002; Dec. 1, 2004; Dec. 1, 2014.)

ADVISORY COMMITTEE NOTES

This form is derived from former Official Form No. 35. The form has been amended to indicate that a final order may be entered other than in an adversary proceeding.

1995 Amendment

The form is amended to reflect the amendments to 28 U.S.C. § 158 concerning bankruptcy appellate panels made by the Bankruptcy Reform Act of 1994. Section 158(d) requires an appellant who elects to appeal to a district court rather than a bankruptcy appellate panel to do so "at the time of filing the appeal."

The 1994 Act also amended 28 U.S.C. § 158(a) to permit immediate appeal of interlocutory orders increasing or reducing a chapter 11 debtor's exclusive period to file a plan under section 1121 of the Code. The form is amended to provide appropriate flexibility.

1997 Amendment

The form has been amended to conform to Rule 8001(a), which requires the notice to contain the names of all parties to the judgment, order, or decree appealed from and the names, addresses, and telephone numbers of their respective attorneys. A party filing a notice of appeal pro se should provide equivalent information.

2002 Amendment

The form is amended to give notice that no filing fee is required if a child support creditor or its representative is the appellant, and if the child support creditor or its representative files a form detailing the child support debt, its status, and other characteristics, as specified in § 304(g) of the Bankruptcy Reform Act of 1994, Pub. L. No. 103–396, 108 Stat. 4106 (Oct. 22, 1994).

OFFICIAL FORMS — Form 17C

2004 Amendment

The form is amended to reflect the 2003 abrogation of Form 16C.

2014 Amendment

Form 17A] is amended and renumbered. It is amended to add to the Notice of Appeal an optional Statement of Election to have the appeal heard by the district court rather than by the bankruptcy appellate panel. Current Rule 8005(a) eliminates the requirement, imposed by former Rule 8001(e), that a separate document be used in making an election to have an appeal heard by the district court rather than the bankruptcy appellate panel. It instead requires a statement that conforms substantially to the Official Form for such an election. Form 17A effectuates Rule 8005(a)'s requirement for election by an appellant by combining the notice of appeal and statement of election. It thereby facilitates compliance with the statutory requirement that an appellant wishing to make an election do so at the time of filing the appeal. 28 U.S.C. § 158(c)(1)(A).

The statement of election in Part 4 is applicable only in districts for which appeals to a bankruptcy appellate panel have been authorized. If an appeal is being taken from a bankruptcy court located in a circuit that does not have a bankruptcy appellate panel or in a district that has not authorized appeals to be heard by the circuit's bankruptcy appellate panel, the appellant should not complete Part 4.

When a bankruptcy appellate panel is available to hear an appeal, completion of Part 4 is optional. An appellant that wants its appeal heard by the bankruptcy appellate panel should not complete this part.

The form is renumbered as Official Form 17A because a new companion form—Optional Appellee Statement of Election to Proceed in the District Court—is designated as Official Form 17B, and another bankruptcy appellate form— Certificate of Compliance with Rule 8015(a)(7)(B) or 8016(d)(2)—is designated as Official Form 17C.

The fixed caption has been deleted because the short title caption on the current form is not appropriate if the debtor is the appellant or if the appeal is in an adversary proceeding. See 11 U.S.C. § 342(c); Rule 7008; Rule 9004(b). The form should be captioned as in Official Form 16A, Caption (Full); Official Form 16B, Caption (Short Title); or Official Form 16D, Caption for Use in Adversary proceeding, as appropriate.

[Form 17B] is new. It is the Official Form for an appellee to state its election to have an appeal heard by the district court rather than by the bankruptcy appellate panel. If an appellee desires to make that election and the appellant or another appellee has not already done so, the appellee must file a statement that conforms substantially to this form within 30 days of service of the Notice of Appeal. 28 U.S.C. § 158(c)(1)(B).

The form is applicable only in districts for which appeals to a bankruptcy appellate panel have been authorized. If an appeal is being taken from a bankruptcy court located in a circuit that does not have a bankruptcy appellate panel or in a district that has not authorized appeals to be heard by the circuit's bankruptcy appellate panel, the appellee should not complete this form.

When a bankruptcy appellate panel is available to hear an appeal, completion of the form is optional. An appellee that wants its appeal heard by the bankruptcy appellate panel should not complete this form.

The form should be captioned as in Official Form 16A, Caption (Full); Official Form 16B, Caption (Short Title); or Official Form 16D, Caption for Use in Adversary proceeding, as appropriate. See 11 U.S.C. § 342(c); Rule 7008; Rule 9004(b).

[Form 17C] is new. When the length of a brief is calculated by the maximum number of words or lines of text rather than by number of pages, Rules 8015(a)(7)(C) and 8016(d)(3) require an attorney or unrepresented party to certify that the brief complies with the applicable type-volume limitation. Completion of this form satisfies that certification requirement. This form is not needed if the brief meets the applicable page limitation under Rule 8015(a)(7)(A) or 8016(d)(1).

The form does not include a caption because it is included in the brief.

Form 18   OFFICIAL FORMS

Form 18.   Discharge of Debtor in a Chapter 7 Case

B18 (Official Form 18) (12/07)

United States Bankruptcy Court

_____ District Of _____

In re _____,
[Set forth here all names including married, maiden, and trade names used by debtor within last 8 years.]
                    Debtor   ) Case No. _____
)
Address _____   )
)
        _____   ) Chapter 7
)
Last four digits of Social-Security or other Individual Taxpayer-
Identification No(s)(if any).: _____
Employer Tax-Identification No(s).(EIN) [if any]: _____

DISCHARGE OF DEBTOR

It appearing that the debtor is entitled to a discharge, IT IS ORDERED: The debtor is granted a discharge under section 727 of title 11, United States Code, (the Bankruptcy Code).

Dated: _____

                                        BY THE COURT

                                        _____
                                        United States Bankruptcy Judge

SEE THE BACK OF THIS ORDER FOR IMPORTANT INFORMATION.

OFFICIAL FORMS Form 18

B18 (Official Form 18) (12/07) - Cont.

EXPLANATION OF BANKRUPTCY DISCHARGE
IN A CHAPTER 7 CASE

This court order grants a discharge to the person named as the debtor. It is not a dismissal of the case and it does not determine how much money, if any, the trustee will pay to creditors.

Collection of Discharged Debts Prohibited

The discharge prohibits any attempt to collect from the debtor a debt that has been discharged. For example, a creditor is not permitted to contact a debtor by mail, phone, or otherwise, to file or continue a lawsuit, to attach wages or other property, or to take any other action to collect a discharged debt from the debtor. *[In a case involving community property:* There are also special rules that protect certain community property owned by the debtor's spouse, even if that spouse did not file a bankruptcy case.] A creditor who violates this order can be required to pay damages and attorney's fees to the debtor.

However, a creditor may have the right to enforce a valid lien, such as a mortgage or security interest, against the debtor's property after the bankruptcy, if that lien was not avoided or eliminated in the bankruptcy case. Also, a debtor may voluntarily pay any debt that has been discharged.

Debts that are Discharged

The chapter 7 discharge order eliminates a debtor's legal obligation to pay a debt that is discharged. Most, but not all, types of debts are discharged if the debt existed on the date the bankruptcy case was filed. (If this case was begun under a different chapter of the Bankruptcy Code and converted to chapter 7, the discharge applies to debts owed when the bankruptcy case was converted.)

Debts that are Not Discharged.

Some of the common types of debts which are <u>not</u> discharged in a chapter 7 bankruptcy case are:

a. Debts for most taxes;

b. Debts incurred to pay nondischargeable taxes;

c. Debts that are domestic support obligations;

d. Debts for most student loans;

e. Debts for most fines, penalties, forfeitures, or criminal restitution obligations;

f. Debts for personal injuries or death caused by the debtor's operation of a motor vehicle, vessel, or aircraft while intoxicated;

g. Some debts which were not properly listed by the debtor;

h. Debts that the bankruptcy court specifically has decided or will decide in this bankruptcy case are not discharged;

i. Debts for which the debtor has given up the discharge protections by signing a reaffirmation agreement in compliance with the Bankruptcy Code requirements for reaffirmation of debts; and

j. Debts owed to certain pension, profit sharing, stock bonus, other retirement plans, or to the Thrift Savings Plan for federal employees for certain types of loans from these plans.

This information is only a general summary of the bankruptcy discharge. There are exceptions to these general rules. Because the law is complicated, you may want to consult an attorney to determine the exact effect of the discharge in this case.

(Added Aug. 1, 1991; and amended Mar. 1995; Oct. 1, 1997; Aug. 11, 2005, eff. Oct. 17, 2005; Dec. 1, 2007.)

Form 18   **OFFICIAL FORMS**

ADVISORY COMMITTEE NOTES

1991 Enactment

This form previously was numbered Official Form No. 27. The form has been revised to accommodate cases commenced by the filing of either a voluntary or an involuntary petition.

1995 Amendment

The form is amended to include debts described in section 523(a)(15) of the Code, which was added by the Bankruptcy Reform Act of 1994, in the list of debts discharged unless determined by the court to be nondischargeable.

1997 Amendment

The discharge order has been simplified by deleting paragraphs which had detailed some, but not all, of the effects of the discharge. These paragraphs have been replaced with a plain English explanation of the discharge. This explanation is to be printed on the reverse of the order, to increase understanding of the bankruptcy discharge among creditors and debtors. The bracketed sentence in the second paragraph should be included when the case involves community property.

2005 Amendment

The form is amended to require that the title of the case include all names used by the debtor within the eight years prior to the filing of the petition in the case in conformity with § 727(a)(8) as amended by the Bankruptcy Abuse Prevention and Consumer Protection Act of 2005, Pub. L. No. 109–8, 119 Stat. 23 (April 20, 2005), extending from six years to eight years the period during which a debtor is barred from receiving successive discharges. The explanation part of the form is amended to include additional types of debts that are not discharged under § 523(a) as amended in 2005 and to revise certain terminology in conformity with provisions of the 2005 Act.

2005–2007 Amendments

(The 2005–2007 Committee Note incorporates the Committee Note previously published in 2005.)

The form is amended to require that the title of the case include all names used by the debtor within the eight years prior to the filing of the petition in the case in conformity with § 727(a)(8) as amended by the Bankruptcy Abuse Prevention and Consumer Protection Act of 2005, Pub. L. No. 109–8, 119 Stat. 23 (April 20, 2005), extending from six years to eight years the period during which a debtor is barred from receiving successive discharges. The explanation part of the form is amended to include additional types of debts that are not discharged under § 523(a), as amended in 2005, and to revise certain terminology in conformity with provisions of the 2005 Act. In conformity with Rule 9037 and Official Form 16A, the caption also is amended to provide only the last four digits of any individual debtor's taxpayer-identification number.

OFFICIAL FORMS   Form 19

Form 19.   Declaration and Signature of Non-Attorney Bankruptcy Petition Preparer

B19 (Official Form 19) (12/07)

United States Bankruptcy Court

In re _____,   Case No. _____
         Debtor
         Chapter _____

DECLARATION AND SIGNATURE OF NON-ATTORNEY BANKRUPTCY PETITION PREPARER (See 11 U.S.C. § 110)

I declare under penalty of perjury that: (1) I am a bankruptcy petition preparer as defined in 11 U.S.C. § 110; (2) I prepared the accompanying document(s) listed below for compensation and have provided the debtor with a copy of the document(s) and the attached notice as required by 11 U.S.C. §§ 110(b), 110(h), and 342(b); and (3) if rules or guidelines have been promulgated pursuant to 11 U.S.C. § 110(h) setting a maximum fee for services chargeable by bankruptcy petition preparers, I have given the debtor notice of the maximum amount before preparing any document for filing for a debtor or accepting any fee from the debtor, as required by that section.

Accompanying documents: Printed or Typed Name and Title, if any, of Bankruptcy Petition Preparer:
_____
_____   _____
_____   Social-Security No. of Bankruptcy Petition
_____   Preparer (Required by 11 U.S.C. § 110):
_____
         _____

If the bankruptcy petition preparer is not an individual, state the name, title (if any), address, and social-security number of the officer, principal, responsible person, or partner who signs this document.

_____
Address
X_____
Signature of Bankruptcy Petition Preparer   Date

Names and social-security numbers of all other individuals who prepared or assisted in preparing this document, unless the bankruptcy petition preparer is not an individual:

If more than one person prepared this document, attach additional signed sheets conforming to the appropriate Official Form for each person.

A bankruptcy petition preparer's failure to comply with the provisions of title 11 and the Federal Rules of Bankruptcy Procedure may result in fines or imprisonment or both. 11 U.S.C. § 110; 18 U.S.C. § 156.

Form 19 OFFICIAL FORMS

B19 (Official Form 19) (12/07) - Cont. 2

NOTICE TO DEBTOR BY NON-ATTORNEY BANKRUPTCY PETITION PREPARER
[Must be filed with any document(s) prepared by a bankruptcy petition preparer.]

I am a bankruptcy petition preparer. I am not an attorney and may not practice law or give legal advice. Before preparing any document for filing as defined in § 110(a)(2) of the Bankruptcy Code or accepting any fees, I am required by law to provide you with this notice concerning bankruptcy petition preparers. Under the law, § 110 of the Bankruptcy Code (11 U.S.C. § 110), I am forbidden to offer you any legal advice, including advice about any of the following:

- whether to file a petition under the Bankruptcy Code (11 U.S.C. § 101 et seq.);
- whether commencing a case under chapter 7, 11, 12, or 13 is appropriate;
- whether your debts will be eliminated or discharged in a case under the Bankruptcy Code;
- whether you will be able to retain your home, car, or other property after commencing a case under the Bankruptcy Code;
- the tax consequences of a case brought under the Bankruptcy Code;
- the dischargeability of tax claims;
- whether you may or should promise to repay debts to a creditor or enter into a reaffirmation agreement with a creditor to reaffirm a debt;
- how to characterize the nature of your interests in property or your debts; or
- bankruptcy procedures and rights.

[The notice may provide additional examples of legal advice that a bankruptcy petition preparer is not authorized to give.]

In addition, under 11 U.S.C. § 110(h), the Supreme Court or the Judicial Conference of the United States may promulgate rules or guidelines setting a maximum allowable fee chargeable by a bankruptcy petition preparer. As required by law, I have notified you of this maximum allowable fee, if any, before preparing any document for filing or accepting any fee from you.

_____   _____
Signature of Debtor   Date   Joint Debtor (if any)   Date

[In a joint case, both spouses must sign.]

(Added Mar. 1995; and amended Dec. 1, 2003; Aug. 11, 2005, eff. Oct. 17, 2005; Dec. 1, 2007.)

ADVISORY COMMITTEE NOTES
1995 Amendment

This form is new. The Bankruptcy Reform Act of 1994 requires a "bankruptcy petition preparer," as defined in 11 U.S.C. § 110, to sign any "document for filing" that the bankruptcy petition preparer prepares for compensation on behalf of a debtor, to disclose on the document certain information, and to provide the debtor with a copy of the document. This form or adaptations of this form have been incorporated into the official forms of the voluntary petition, the schedules, the statement of financial affairs, and other official forms that typically would be prepared for a debtor by a bankruptcy petition preparer. This form is to be used in connection with any other document that a bankruptcy petition preparer prepares for filing by a debtor in a bankruptcy case.

2003 Amendment

Pursuant to § 110(c) of the Bankruptcy Code, the certification by a non-attorney bankruptcy petition preparer requires a petition preparer to provide the full Social Security number of the individual who actually prepares the document.

2005 Amendment

The certification by a non-attorney bankruptcy petition preparer in this form is renamed a "declaration" and is amended to include material mandated by amendments to § 110 of the Code in the Bankruptcy Abuse Prevention and Consumer Protection Act of 2005, Pub. L. No. 109–8, 119 Stat. 23 (April 20, 2005).

OFFICIAL FORMS   Form 19

2005–2007 Amendments

(The 2005–2007 Committee Note incorporates the Committee Notes to Forms 19A and 19B previously published in 2005.)

This form is new. It is derived from form 19B and replaces forms 19A and 19B (which forms are abrogated). The form contains the notice a bankruptcy petition preparer is required to give to a debtor under § 110 of the Code as amended by the Bankruptcy Abuse Prevention and Consumer Protection Act of 2005, Pub. L. No. 109–8, 119 Stat. 23 (April 20, 2005), and the bankruptcy petition preparer's signed declaration (also required by § 110 of the Code) that the notice was given to the debtor.

The notice states, in language mandated in the 2005 Act, that the bankruptcy petition preparer is not an attorney and must not give legal advice. The notice also includes examples of advice a bankruptcy petition preparer may not give that are taken from § 110(e)(2) of the Code.

Although space is provided in the declaration to list multiple documents prepared for a single filing, a new form 19 must be completed and accompany subsequent filings. For example, one form 19 listing all forms prepared by the bankruptcy petition preparer would be filed with the debtor's petition package. Another form 19 would be required if the debtor files amended schedules later in the case that were prepared by the bankruptcy petition preparer.

The form must be signed by the debtor and the bankruptcy petition preparer where indicated, and must be filed with each document for filing prepared by the bankruptcy petition preparer.

Form 20A OFFICIAL FORMS

Form 20A. Notice of Motion or Objection

B20A (Official Form 20A) (Notice of Motion or Objection) (12/10)

United States Bankruptcy Court
_____ District of _____

In re)
[Set forth here all names including married, maiden, and)
trade names used by debtor within last 8 years.])
)
                    Debtor) Case No. _____
)
Address _____)
_____)
) Chapter _____
Last four digits of Social Security or Individual Tax-payer Identification)
(ITIN) No(s).,(if any): _____)
)
Employer's Tax Identification (EIN) No(s).(if any): _____)
)

NOTICE OF [MOTION TO] [OBJECTION TO]

_____ has filed papers with the court to [relief sought in motion or objection].

Your rights may be affected. You should read these papers carefully and discuss them with your attorney, if you have one in this bankruptcy case. (If you do not have an attorney, you may wish to consult one.)

If you do not want the court to [relief sought in motion or objection], or if you want the court to consider your views on the [motion] [objection], then on or before (date) , you or your attorney must:

[File with the court a written request for a hearing {or, if the court requires a written response, an answer, explaining your position} at:

    {address of the bankruptcy clerk's office}

If you mail your {request}{response} to the court for filing, you must mail it early enough so the court will **receive** it on or before the date stated above.

You must also mail a copy to:

    {movant's attorney's name and address}

    {names and addresses of others to be served}]

[Attend the hearing scheduled to be held on (date) , (year) , at ____ a.m./p.m. in Courtroom____, United States Bankruptcy Court, {address}.]

[Other steps required to oppose a motion or objection under local rule or court order.]

If you or your attorney do not take these steps, the court may decide that you do not oppose the relief sought in the motion or objection and may enter an order granting that relief.

Date: _____ Signature: _____
                                          Name:
                                          Address

OFFICIAL FORMS Form 20A

(Added Oct. 1, 1997; amended Dec. 2003; Dec. 1, 2010.)

ADVISORY COMMITTEE NOTES

1997 Enactment

These forms are new. They are intended to provide uniform, plain English explanations to parties regarding what they must do to respond in certain contested matters which occur frequently in bankruptcy cases. Such explanations have been given better in some courts than in others. The forms are intended to make bankruptcy proceedings more fair, equitable, and efficient, by aiding parties, who sometimes do not have counsel, in understanding the applicable rules. It is hoped that use of these forms also will decrease the number of inquiries to bankruptcy clerks' offices.

These notices will be sent by the movant unless local rules provide for some other entity to give notice.

These forms are not intended to dictate the specific procedures to be used by different bankruptcy courts. The forms contain optional language that can be used or adapted, depending on local procedures. Similarly, the signature line will be adapted to identify the actual sender of the notice in each circumstance. All adaptations of the form should carry out the intent to give notice of applicable procedures in easily understood language.

2010 Amendment

The form is amended to require that the title of the case include all names used by the debtor within the last eight years. This change conforms to the 2005 amendment of § 727(a)(8), which extended from six years to eight years the period during which a debtor is barred from receiving successive discharges. In conformity with Rule 9037, the filer is directed to provide only the last four digits of any individual debtor's taxpayer-identification number.

Form 20B   OFFICIAL FORMS

Form 20B.   Notice of Objection to Claim

B20B (Official Form 20B) (Notice of Objection to Claim) (12/10)

United States Bankruptcy Court
_____ District of _____

In re   )
    [Set forth here all names including married, maiden, and   )
    trade names used by debtor within last 8 years.]   )
)
                                   Debtor   )   Case No. _____
)
Address _____   )
)
_____   )
)   Chapter _____
Last four digits of Social Security or Individual Tax-payer Identification)
(ITIN) No(s).,(if any): _____   )
)
)
Employer's Tax Identification (EIN) No(s).(if any): _____   )
_____   )

NOTICE OF OBJECTION TO CLAIM

_____ has filed an objection to your claim in this bankruptcy case.

Your claim may be reduced, modified, or eliminated. You should read these papers carefully and discuss them with your attorney, if you have one.

    If you do not want the court to eliminate or change your claim, then on or before (date) , you or your lawyer must:

        {If required by local rule or court order.}

    [File with the court a written response to the objection, explaining your position, at:

        {address of the bankruptcy clerk's office}

If you mail your response to the court for filing, you must mail it early enough so that the court will **receive** it on or before the date stated above.

You must also mail a copy to:

{objector's attorney's name and address}

{names and addresses of others to be served}]

    Attend the hearing on the objection, scheduled to be held on (date) , (year) , at ___ a.m./p.m. in Courtroom____, United States Bankruptcy Court, {address}.

    If you or your attorney do not take these steps, the court may decide that you do not oppose the objection to your claim.

Date: _____   Signature: _____
                                         Name:
                                         Address

(Added Oct. 1, 1997; amended Dec. 2003; Dec. 1, 2010.)

OFFICIAL FORMS   Form 20B

ADVISORY COMMITTEE NOTES

1997 Enactment

These forms are new. They are intended to provide uniform, plain English explanations to parties regarding what they must do to respond in certain contested matters which occur frequently in bankruptcy cases. Such explanations have been given better in some courts than in others. The forms are intended to make bankruptcy proceedings more fair, equitable, and efficient, by aiding parties, who sometimes do not have counsel, in understanding the applicable rules. It is hoped that use of these forms also will decrease the number of inquiries to bankruptcy clerks' offices.

These notices will be sent by the movant unless local rules provide for some other entity to give notice.

These forms are not intended to dictate the specific procedures to be used by different bankruptcy courts. The forms contain optional language that can be used or adapted, depending on local procedures. Similarly, the signature line will be adapted to identify the actual sender of the notice in each circumstance. All adaptations of the form should carry out the intent to give notice of applicable procedures in easily understood language.

2010 Amendment

The form is amended to require that the title of the case include all names used by the debtor within the last eight years. This change conforms to the 2005 amendment of § 727(a)(8), which extended from six years to eight years the period during which a debtor is barred from receiving successive discharges. In conformity with Rule 9037, the filer is directed to provide only the last four digits of any individual debtor's taxpayer-identification number.

Form 21   **OFFICIAL FORMS**

Form 21. Statement of Social-Security Number or Individual Taxpayer-Identification Number (ITIN)

B21 (Official Form 21) (12/12)

UNITED STATES BANKRUPTCY COURT

In re _____ ,
      [Set forth here all names including married, maiden,
      and trade names used by debtor within last 8 years]

                              Debtor   Case No. _____

Address _____

           _____   Chapter _____

Last four digits of Social-Security or Individual Taxpayer-
Identification (ITIN) No(s).,(if any):
_____

Employer Tax-Identification (EIN) No(s).(if any):
_____

STATEMENT OF SOCIAL-SECURITY NUMBER(S)
(or other Individual Taxpayer-Identification Number(s) (ITIN(s)))*

1. Name of Debtor (Last, First, Middle): _____
(Check the appropriate box and, if applicable, provide the required information.)

    ☐ Debtor has a Social-Security Number and it is: _____
        (If more than one, state all.)
    ☐ Debtor does not have a Social-Security Number but has an Individual Taxpayer-Identification Number (ITIN), and it is: _____
        (If more than one, state all.)
    ☐ Debtor does not have either a Social-Security Number or an Individual Taxpayer-Identification Number (ITIN).

2. Name of Joint Debtor (Last, First, Middle): _____
(Check the appropriate box and, if applicable, provide the required information.)

    ☐ Joint Debtor has a Social-Security Number and it is: _____
        (If more than one, state all.)
    ☐ Joint Debtor does not have a Social-Security Number but has an Individual Taxpayer-Identification Number (ITIN) and it is: _____
        (If more than one, state all.)
    ☐ Joint Debtor does not have either a Social-Security Number or an Individual Taxpayer-Identification Number (ITIN).

I declare under penalty of perjury that the foregoing is true and correct.

    X _____   _____
                    Signature of Debtor   Date

    X _____   _____
                  Signature of Joint Debtor   Date

_____

*Joint debtors must provide information for both spouses.
Penalty for making a false statement: Fine of up to $250,000 or up to 5 years imprisonment or both. 18 U.S.C. §§ 152 and 3571.

(Added Oct. 14, 2003, eff. Dec. 1, 2003; Dec. 1, 2007; Dec. 1, 2012.)

OFFICIAL FORMS

Form 21

ADVISORY COMMITTEE NOTES

2003 Enactment

The form implements Rule 1007(f), which requires a debtor to submit a statement under penalty of perjury setting out the debtor's Social Security number. The form is necessary because Rule 1005 provides that the caption of the petition includes only the final four digits of the debtor's Social Security number. The statement provides the information necessary for the clerk to include the debtor's full Social Security number on the notice of the meeting of creditors, as required under Rule 2002(a)(1). Creditors in a case, along with the trustee and United States trustee or bankruptcy administrator, will receive the full Social Security number on their copy of the notice of the meeting of creditors. The copy of that notice which goes into the court file will show only the last four digits of the number.

2007 Amendment

The form is amended to direct an individual debtor who does not have a social-security number but has another government-issued individual taxpayer-identification number to furnish that number to the court. In light of the new Rule 9037 which limits public disclosure to all but the last four digits of any individual taxpayer-identification number, the amendment to this form will ensure that the court and creditors can properly identify a debtor who does not have a social-security number.

2012 Amendment

The form is amended to remind debtors that, in accordance with Rule 1007(f), it should be submitted to the court, but not filed on the public docket. This rule protects an individual debtor's social-security number or taxpayer-identification number from becoming accessible to the public.

Form 22   OFFICIAL FORMS

Form 22.   Statement of Current Monthly Income

Form B22A1

Fill in this information to identify your case:

Debtor 1 _____ First Name _____ Middle Name _____ Last Name

Debtor 2 (Spouse, if filing) _____ First Name _____ Middle Name _____ Last Name

United States Bankruptcy Court for the _____ District of _____

Case number (if known) _____

Check one box only as directed in this form and in Form 22A-1Supp:

☐ 1. There is no presumption of abuse.

☐ 2. The calculation to determine if a presumption of abuse applies will be made under *Chapter 7 Means Test Calculation* (Official Form 22A–2).

☐ 3. The Means Test does not apply now because of qualified military service but it could apply later.

☐ Check if this is an amended filing

OFFICIAL FORM B 22A1

Chapter 7 Statement of Your Current Monthly Income   12/14

Be as complete and accurate as possible. If two married people are filing together, both are equally responsible for being accurate. If more space is needed, attach a separate sheet to this form. Include the line number to which the additional information applies. On the top of any additional pages, write your name and case number (if known). If you believe that you are exempted from a presumption of abuse because you do not have primarily consumer debts or because of qualifying military service, complete and file *Statement of Exemption from Presumption of Abuse Under § 707(b)(2)* (Official Form 22A-1Supp) with this form.

Part 1: Calculate Your Current Monthly Income

1. What is your marital and filing status? Check one only.

   ☐ Not married. Fill out Column A, lines 2-11.

   ☐ Married and your spouse is filing with you. Fill out both Columns A and B, lines 2-11.

   ☐ Married and your spouse is NOT filing with you. You and your spouse are:

        ☐ Living in the same household and are not legally separated. Fill out both Columns A and B, lines 2-11.

        ☐ Living separately or are legally separated. Fill out Column A, lines 2-11; do not fill out Column B. By checking this box, you declare under penalty of perjury that you and your spouse are legally separated under nonbankruptcy law that applies or that you and your spouse are living apart for reasons that do not include evading the Means Test requirements. 11 U.S.C. § 707(b)(7)(B).

   Fill in the average monthly income that you received from all sources, derived during the 6 full months before you file this bankruptcy case. 11 U.S.C. § 101(10A). For example, if you are filing on September 15, the 6-month period would be March 1 through August 31. If the amount of your monthly income varied during the 6 months, add the income for all 6 months and divide the total by 6. Fill in the result. Do not include any income amount more than once. For example, if both spouses own the same rental property, put the income from that property in one column only. If you have nothing to report for any line, write $0 in the space.

	Column A Debtor 1	Column B Debtor 2 or non-filing spouse
2. **Your gross wages, salary, tips, bonuses, overtime, and commissions** (before all payroll deductions).	$_____	$_____
3. **Alimony and maintenance payments.** Do not include payments from a spouse if Column B is filled in.	$_____	$_____
4. **All amounts from any source which are regularly paid for household expenses of you or your dependents, including child support.** Include regular contributions from an unmarried partner, members of your household, your dependents, parents, and roommates. Include regular contributions from a spouse only if Column B is not filled in. Do not include payments you listed on line 3.	$_____	$_____
5. **Net income from operating a business, profession, or farm**		
Gross receipts (before all deductions) $_____		
Ordinary and necessary operating expenses − $_____		
Net monthly income from a business, profession, or farm $_____ Copy here→	$_____	$_____
6. **Net income from rental and other real property**		
Gross receipts (before all deductions) $_____		
Ordinary and necessary operating expenses − $_____		
Net monthly income from rental or other real property $_____ Copy here→	$_____	$_____
7. **Interest, dividends, and royalties**	$_____	$_____

Official Form B 22A1   Chapter 7 Statement of Your Current Monthly Income   page 1

OFFICIAL FORMS   **Form B22A1**

Debtor 1 _____   Case number (if known) _____
       First Name   Middle Name   Last Name

	Column A Debtor 1	Column B Debtor 2 or non-filing spouse

8. **Unemployment compensation** $_____ $_____

    Do not enter the amount if you contend that the amount received was a benefit
    under the Social Security Act. Instead, list it here:........................ ↓

        For you .... $_____
        For your spouse .... $_____

9. **Pension or retirement income.** Do not include any amount received that was a $_____ $_____
    benefit under the Social Security Act.

10. **Income from all other sources not listed above.** Specify the source and amount.
    Do not include any benefits received under the Social Security Act or payments received
    as a victim of a war crime, a crime against humanity, or international or domestic
    terrorism. If necessary, list other sources on a separate page and put the total on line 10c.

    10a. _____ $_____ $_____
    10b. _____ $_____ $_____
    10c. Total amounts from separate pages, if any.   +$_____   +$_____

11. **Calculate your total current monthly income.** Add lines 2 through 10 for each $_____ + $_____ = $_____
    column. Then add the total for Column A to the total for Column B.   Total current monthly
                                                                                                                     income

---

Part 2: Determine Whether the Means Test Applies to You

12. **Calculate your current monthly income for the year.** Follow these steps:

    12a.   Copy your total current monthly income from line 11.................................. Copy line 11 here → 12a. $_____

           Multiply by 12 (the number of months in a year).   x 12

    12b.   The result is your annual income for this part of the form.   12b. $_____

13. **Calculate the median family income that applies to you.** Follow these steps:

    Fill in the state in which you live.   [_____]

    Fill in the number of people in your household.   [_____]

    Fill in the median family income for your state and size of household. .... 13. $_____
    To find a list of applicable median income amounts, go online using the link specified in the separate
    instructions for this form. This list may also be available at the bankruptcy clerk's office.

14. **How do the lines compare?**

    14a. ☐ Line 12b is less than or equal to line 13. On the top of page 1, check box 1, *There is no presumption of abuse.*
             Go to Part 3.

    14b. ☐ Line 12b is more than line 13. On the top of page 1, check box 2, *The presumption of abuse is determined by Form 22A-2.*
             Go to Part 3 and fill out Form 22A-2.

Part 3: Sign Below

By signing here, I declare under penalty of perjury that the information on this statement and in any attachments is true and correct.

✗ _____   ✗ _____
   Signature of Debtor 1   Signature of Debtor 2

Date _____   Date _____
    MM / DD / YYYY   MM / DD / YYYY

If you checked line 14a, do NOT fill out or file Form 22A-2.

If you checked line 14b, fill out Form 22A-2 and file it with this form.

[Reset]   [Save As...]   [Print]

Official Form B 22A1   Chapter 7 Statement of Your Current Monthly Income

Form B22A1   OFFICIAL FORMS

Fill in this information to identify your case:

Debtor 1 _____ _____ _____
         First Name   Middle Name   Last Name

Debtor 2 _____ _____ _____
(Spouse, if filing) First Name Middle Name   Last Name

United States Bankruptcy Court for the: _____ District of _____

Case number _____
(if known)

☐ Check if this is an amended filing

OFFICIAL FORM B 22A1 SUPP

Statement of Exemption from Presumption of Abuse Under § 707(b)(2)   12/14

File this supplement together with *Chapter 7 Statement of Your Current Monthly Income* (Official Form 22A-1), if you believe that you are exempted from a presumption of abuse. Be as complete and accurate as possible. If two married people are filing together, and any of the exclusions in this statement applies to only one of you, the other person should complete a separate Form 22A-1 if you believe that this is required by 11 U.S.C. § 707(b)(2)(C).

Part 1: Identify the Kind of Debts You Have

1. **Are your debts primarily consumer debts?** *Consumer debts* are defined in 11 U.S.C. § 101(8) as "incurred by an individual primarily for a personal, family, or household purpose." Make sure that your answer is consistent with the "Nature of Debts" box on page 1 of the *Voluntary Petition* (Official Form 1).

   ☐ No. Go to Form 22A-1; on the top of page 1 of that form, check box 1, *There is no presumption of abuse*, and sign Part 3. Then submit this supplement with the signed Form 22A-1.

   ☐ Yes. Go to Part 2.

Part 2: Determine Whether Military Service Provisions Apply to You

2. **Are you a disabled veteran** (as defined in 38 U.S.C. § 3741(1))?

   ☐ No. Go to line 3.

   ☐ Yes. Did you incur debts mostly while you were on active duty or while you were performing a homeland defense activity? 10 U.S.C. § 101(d)(1)); 32 U.S.C. § 901(1).

   ☐ No. Go to line 3.

   ☐ Yes. Go to Form 22A-1; on the top of page 1 of that form, check box 1, *There is no presumption of abuse*, and sign Part 3. Then submit this supplement with the signed Form 22A-1.

3. **Are you or have you been a Reservist or member of the National Guard?**

   ☐ No. Complete Form 22A-1. Do not submit this supplement.

   ☐ Yes. Were you called to active duty or did you perform a homeland defense activity? 10 U.S.C. § 101(d)(1); 32 U.S.C. § 901(1)

   ☐ No. Complete Form 22A-1. Do not submit this supplement.

   ☐ Yes. Check any one of the following categories that applies:

   ☐ I was called to active duty after September 11, 2001, for at least 90 days and remain on active duty.

   ☐ I was called to active duty after September 11, 2001, for at least 90 days and was released from active duty on _____, which is fewer than 540 days before I file this bankruptcy case.

   ☐ I am performing a homeland defense activity for at least 90 days.

   ☐ I performed a homeland defense activity for at least 90 days, ending on _____, which is fewer than 540 days before I file this bankruptcy case.

   If you checked one of the categories to the left, go to Form 22A-1. On the top of page 1 of Form 22A-1, check box 3, *The Means Test does not apply now*, and sign Part 3. Then submit this supplement with the signed Form 22A-1. You are not required to fill out the rest of Official Form 22A-1 during the exclusion period. The *exclusion period* means the time you are on active duty or are performing a homeland defense activity, and for 540 days afterward. 11 U.S.C. § 707(b)(2)(D)(ii).

   If your exclusion period ends before your case is closed, you may have to file an amended form later.

[Reset]   [Save As...]   [Print]

Official Form B 22A1 Supp   Statement of Exemption from Presumption of Abuse Under § 707(b)(2)   page 1

OFFICIAL FORMS   Form B22A2

Form B22A2

Fill in this information to identify your case:

Debtor 1 _____ _____ _____
         First Name   Middle Name   Last Name

Debtor 2 _____ _____ _____
(Spouse, if filing) First Name Middle Name   Last Name

United States Bankruptcy Court for the: _____ District of _____
                                                              (State)

Case number _____
(if known)

Check the appropriate box as directed in lines 40 or 42:

According to the calculations required by this Statement:

☐ 1. There is no presumption of abuse.

☐ 2. There is a presumption of abuse.

☐ Check if this is an amended filing

Official Form B 22A2

Chapter 7 Means Test Calculation

12/14

To fill out this form, you will need your completed copy of *Chapter 7 Statement of Your Current Monthly Income* (Official Form 22A-1).

Be as complete and accurate as possible. If two married people are filing together, both are equally responsible for being accurate. If more space is needed, attach a separate sheet to this form. Include the line number to which the additional information applies. On the top of any additional pages, write your name and case number (if known).

Part 1: Determine Your Adjusted Income

1. Copy your total current monthly income. .... Copy line 11 from Official Form 22A-1 here ➔ .... 1. $_____

2. Did you fill out Column B in Part 1 of Form 22A-1?
   ☐ No. Fill in $0 on line 3d.
   ☐ Yes. Is your spouse filing with you?
      ☐ No. Go to line 3.
      ☐ Yes. Fill in $0 on line 3d.

3. Adjust your current monthly income by subtracting any part of your spouse's income not used to pay for the household expenses of you or your dependents. Follow these steps:

   On line 11, Column B of Form 22A-1, was any amount of the income you reported for your spouse NOT regularly used for the household expenses of you or your dependents?

   ☐ No. Fill in 0 on line 3d.
   ☐ Yes. Fill in the information below:

State each purpose for which the income was used For example, the income is used to pay your spouse's tax debt or to support people other than you or your dependents	Fill in the amount you are subtracting from your spouse's income
3a. _____	$_____
3b. _____	$_____
3c. _____	+$_____
3d. **Total.** Add lines 3a, 3b, and 3c.	$_____ Copy total here ➔ ....3d. −$_____

4. **Adjust your current monthly income.** Subtract line 3d from line 1. $_____

Official Form B 22A2   Chapter 7 Means Test Calculation   page 1

Form B22A2   OFFICIAL FORMS

Debtor 1 _____ Case number *(if known)* _____
        First Name   Middle Name   Last Name

Part 2: Calculate Your Deductions from Your Income

The Internal Revenue Service (IRS) issues National and Local Standards for certain expense amounts. Use these amounts to answer the questions in lines 6-15. To find the IRS standards, go online using the link specified in the separate instructions for this form. This information may also be available at the bankruptcy clerk's office.

Deduct the expense amounts set out in lines 6-15 regardless of your actual expense. In later parts of the form, you will use some of your actual expenses if they are higher than the standards. Do not deduct any amounts that you subtracted from your spouse's income in line 3 and do not deduct any operating expenses that you subtracted from income in lines 5 and 6 of Form 22A-1.

If your expenses differ from month to month, enter the average expense.

Whenever this part of the form refers to *you*, it means both you and your spouse if Column B of Form 22A-1 is filled in.

5. **The number of people used in determining your deductions from income**

   Fill in the number of people who could be claimed as exemptions on your federal income tax return, plus the number of any additional dependents whom you support. This number may be different from the number of people in your household.

National Standards   You must use the IRS National Standards to answer the questions in lines 6-7.

6. **Food, clothing, and other items:** Using the number of people you entered in line 5 and the IRS National Standards, fill in the dollar amount for food, clothing, and other items. $_____

7. **Out-of-pocket health care allowance:** Using the number of people you entered in line 5 and the IRS National Standards, fill in the dollar amount for out-of-pocket health care. The number of people is split into two categories—people who are under 65 and people who are 65 or older—because older people have a higher IRS allowance for health care costs. If your actual expenses are higher than this IRS amount, you may deduct the additional amount on line 22.

   People who are under 65 years of age

   7a. Out-of-pocket health care allowance per person $_____

   7b. Number of people who are under 65   X_____

   7c. **Subtotal.** Multiply line 7a by line 7b. $_____   Copy line 7c here ➔ .... $_____

   People who are 65 years of age or older

   7d. Out-of-pocket health care allowance per person $_____

   7e. Number of people who are 65 or older   X_____

   7f. **Subtotal.** Multiply line 7d by line 7e. $_____   Copy line 7f here ➔ .... + $_____

   7g. **Total.** Add lines 7c and 7f... $_____   Copy total here ➔ 7g. $_____

Official Form B 22A2   Chapter 7 Means Test Calculation   page 2

OFFICIAL FORMS   Form B22A2

Debtor 1 _____   Case number (if known)_____
        First Name   Middle Name   Last Name

Local Standards   You must use the IRS Local Standards to answer the questions in lines 8-15.

Based on information from the IRS, the U.S. Trustee Program has divided the IRS Local Standard for housing for bankruptcy purposes into two parts:

- Housing and utilities – Insurance and operating expenses
- Housing and utilities – Mortgage or rent expenses

To answer the questions in lines 8-9, use the U.S. Trustee Program chart.

To find the chart, go online using the link specified in the separate instructions for this form. This chart may also be available at the bankruptcy clerk's office.

8. **Housing and utilities – Insurance and operating expenses:** Using the number of people you entered in line 5, fill in the dollar amount listed for your county for insurance and operating expenses. $_____

9. **Housing and utilities – Mortgage or rent expenses:**

   9a. Using the number of people you entered in line 5, fill in the dollar amount listed for your county for mortgage or rent expenses.   9a. $_____

   9b. Total average monthly payment for all mortgages and other debts secured by your home.

   To calculate the total average monthly payment, add all amounts that are contractually due to each secured creditor in the 60 months after you file for bankruptcy. Then divide by 60.

Name of the creditor	Average monthly payment
_____	$_____
_____	$_____
_____	+ $_____

   9b. Total average monthly payment $_____   Copy line 9b here ➔ – $_____   Repeat this amount on line 33a.

   9c. Net mortgage or rent expense.
   Subtract line 9b (*total average monthly payment*) from line 9a (*mortgage or rent expense*). If this amount is less than $0, enter $0.   9c. $_____   Copy line 9c here ➔ $_____

10. **If you claim that the U.S. Trustee Program's division of the IRS Local Standard for housing is incorrect and affects the calculation of your monthly expenses, fill in any additional amount you claim.** $_____

    Explain why: _____
    _____

11. **Local transportation expenses:** Check the number of vehicles for which you claim an ownership or operating expense.

    ☐ 0. Go to line 14.
    ☐ 1. Go to line 12.
    ☐ 2 or more. Go to line 12.

12. **Vehicle operation expense:** Using the IRS Local Standards and the number of vehicles for which you claim the operating expenses, fill in the *Operating Costs* that apply for your Census region or metropolitan statistical area. $_____

Official Form B 22A2   Chapter 7 Means Test Calculation   page 3

Form B22A2   OFFICIAL FORMS

Debtor 1 _____   Case number (if known) _____
         First Name   Middle Name   Last Name

13. **Vehicle ownership or lease expense:** Using the IRS Local Standards, calculate the net ownership or lease expense for each vehicle below. You may not claim the expense if you do not make any loan or lease payments on the vehicle. In addition, you may not claim the expense for more than two vehicles.

   Vehicle 1   Describe Vehicle 1: _____
   _____

   13a. Ownership or leasing costs using IRS Local Standard   13a. $_____

   13b. Average monthly payment for all debts secured by Vehicle 1.
        Do not include costs for leased vehicles.

        To calculate the average monthly payment here and on line 13e, add all amounts that are contractually due to each secured creditor in the 60 months after you filed for bankruptcy. Then divide by 60.

Name of each creditor for Vehicle 1	Average monthly payment
_____	$_____

   Copy 13b here ➔ − $_____   Repeat this amount on line 33b.

   13c. Net Vehicle 1 ownership or lease expense
        Subtract line 13b from line 13a. If this amount is less than $0, enter $0.   13c. $_____   Copy net Vehicle 1 expense here ..... ➔ $_____

   Vehicle 2   Describe Vehicle 2: _____
   _____

   13d. Ownership or leasing costs using IRS Local Standard   13d. $_____

   13e. Average monthly payment for all debts secured by Vehicle 2. Do not include costs for leased vehicles.

Name of each creditor for Vehicle 2	Average monthly payment
_____	$_____

   Copy 13e here ➔ − $_____   Repeat this amount on line 33c.

   13f. Net Vehicle 2 ownership or lease expense
        Subtract line 13e from 13d. If this amount is less than $0, enter $0.   13f. $_____   Copy net Vehicle 2 expense here ..... ➔ $_____

14. **Public transportation expense:** If you claimed 0 vehicles in line 11, using the IRS Local Standards, fill in the *Public Transportation* expense allowance regardless of whether you use public transportation. $_____

15. **Additional public transportation expense:** If you claimed 1 or more vehicles in line 11 and if you claim that you may also deduct a public transportation expense, you may fill in what you believe is the appropriate expense, but you may not claim more than the IRS Local Standard for *Public Transportation*. $_____

OFFICIAL FORMS   **Form B22A2**

Debtor 1 _____   Case number (if known) _____
         First Name   Middle Name   Last Name

Other Necessary Expenses   In addition to the expense deductions listed above, you are allowed your monthly expenses for the following IRS categories.

16. **Taxes:** The total monthly amount that you will actually owe for federal, state and local taxes, such as income taxes, self-employment taxes, social security taxes, and Medicare taxes. You may include the monthly amount withheld from your pay for these taxes. However, if you expect to receive a tax refund, you must divide the expected refund by 12 and subtract that number from the total monthly amount that is withheld to pay for taxes. $_____

 Do not include real estate, sales, or use taxes.

17. **Involuntary deductions:** The total monthly payroll deductions that your job requires, such as retirement contributions, union dues, and uniform costs. $_____

 Do not include amounts that are not required by your job, such as voluntary 401(k) contributions or payroll savings.

18. **Life insurance:** The total monthly premiums that you pay for your own term life insurance. If two married people are filing together, include payments that you make for your spouse's term life insurance. Do not include premiums for life insurance on your dependents, for a non-filing spouse's life insurance, or for any form of life insurance other than term. $_____

19. **Court-ordered payments:** The total monthly amount that you pay as required by the order of a court or administrative agency, such as spousal or child support payments. $_____

 Do not include payments on past due obligations for spousal or child support. You will list these obligations in line 35.

20. **Education:** The total monthly amount that you pay for education that is either required:
 - as a condition for your job, or
 - for your physically or mentally challenged dependent child if no public education is available for similar services. $_____

21. **Childcare:** The total monthly amount that you pay for childcare, such as babysitting, daycare, nursery, and preschool. $_____

 Do not include payments for any elementary or secondary school education.

22. **Additional health care expenses, excluding insurance costs:** The monthly amount that you pay for health care that is required for the health and welfare of you or your dependents and that is not reimbursed by insurance or paid by a health savings account. Include only the amount that is more than the total entered in line 7.
 Payments for health insurance or health savings accounts should be listed only in line 25. $_____

23. **Optional telephones and telephone services:** The total monthly amount that you pay for telecommunication services for you and your dependents, such as pagers, call waiting, caller identification, special long distance, or business cell phone service, to the extent necessary for your health and welfare or that of your dependents or for the production of income, if it is not reimbursed by your employer.   + $_____

 Do not include payments for basic home telephone, internet and cell phone service. Do not include self-employment expenses, such as those reported on line 5 of Official Form 22A-1, or any amount you previously deducted.

24. **Add all of the expenses allowed under the IRS expense allowances.** $_____
 Add lines 6 through 23.

Official Form B 22A2   Chapter 7 Means Test Calculation   page 5

Form B22A2   OFFICIAL FORMS

Debtor 1 _____   Case number (if known) _____
         First Name   Middle Name   Last Name

Additional Expense Deductions These are additional deductions allowed by the Means Test.
Note: Do not include any expense allowances listed in lines 6-24.

25. **Health insurance, disability insurance, and health savings account expenses.** The monthly expenses for health insurance, disability insurance, and health savings accounts that are reasonably necessary for yourself, your spouse, or your dependents.

Health insurance	$_____
Disability insurance	$_____
Health savings account	+ $_____
Total	$_____

    Copy total here ➔ .... $_____

    Do you actually spend this total amount?
    ☐ No. How much do you actually spend? $_____
    ☐ Yes

26. **Continued contributions to the care of household or family members.** The actual monthly expenses that you will continue to pay for the reasonable and necessary care and support of an elderly, chronically ill, or disabled member of your household or member of your immediate family who is unable to pay for such expenses. $_____

27. **Protection against family violence.** The reasonably necessary monthly expenses that you incur to maintain the safety of you and your family under the Family Violence Prevention and Services Act or other federal laws that apply. $_____

    By law, the court must keep the nature of these expenses confidential.

28. **Additional home energy costs.** Your home energy costs are included in your non-mortgage housing and utilities allowance on line 8.

    If you believe that you have home energy costs that are more than the home energy costs included in the non-mortgage housing and utilities allowance, then fill in the excess amount of home energy costs. $_____

    You must give your case trustee documentation of your actual expenses, and you must show that the additional amount claimed is reasonable and necessary.

29. **Education expenses for dependent children who are younger than 18.** The monthly expenses (not more than $156.25* per child) that you pay for your dependent children who are younger than 18 years old to attend a private or public elementary or secondary school. $_____

    You must give your case trustee documentation of your actual expenses, and you must explain why the amount claimed is reasonable and necessary and not already accounted for in lines 6-23.

    * Subject to adjustment on 4/01/16, and every 3 years after that for cases begun on or after the date of adjustment.

30. **Additional food and clothing expense.** The monthly amount by which your actual food and clothing expenses are higher than the combined food and clothing allowances in the IRS National Standards. That amount cannot be more than 5% of the food and clothing allowances in the IRS National Standards. $_____

    To find a chart showing the maximum additional allowance, go online using the link specified in the separate instructions for this form. This chart may also be available at the bankruptcy clerk's office.

    You must show that the additional amount claimed is reasonable and necessary.

31. **Continuing charitable contributions.** The amount that you will continue to contribute in the form of cash or financial instruments to a religious or charitable organization. 26 U.S.C. § 170(c)(1)-(2). $_____

32. **Add all of the additional expense deductions.** $_____
    Add lines 25 through 31.

Official Form B 22A2   Chapter 7 Means Test Calculation   page 6

OFFICIAL FORMS   Form B22A2

Debtor 1 _____   Case number (if known)_____
         First Name   Middle Name   Last Name

Deductions for Debt Payment

33. **For debts that are secured by an interest in property that you own, including home mortgages, vehicle loans, and other secured debt, fill in lines 33a through 33g.**

    To calculate the total average monthly payment, add all amounts that are contractually due to each secured creditor in the 60 months after you file for bankruptcy. Then divide by 60.

	Average monthly payment
Mortgages on your home:	
33a. Copy line 9b here .... →	$_____
Loans on your first two vehicles:	
33b. Copy line 13b here. .... →	$_____
33c. Copy line 13e here. .... →	$_____

Name of each creditor for other secured debt	Identify property that secures the debt	Does payment include taxes or insurance?	
33d. _____	_____	☐ No ☐ Yes	$_____
33e. _____	_____	☐ No ☐ Yes	$_____
33f. _____	_____	☐ No ☐ Yes	+ $_____

    33g. Total average monthly payment. Add lines 33a through 33f. .... $_____ Copy total here → $_____

34. **Are any debts that you listed in line 33 secured by your primary residence, a vehicle, or other property necessary for your support or the support of your dependents?**

    ☐ No. Go to line 35.
    ☐ Yes. State any amount that you must pay to a creditor, in addition to the payments listed in line 33, to keep possession of your property (called the *cure amount*). Next, divide by 60 and fill in the information below.

Name of the creditor	Identify property that secures the debt	Total cure amount		Monthly cure amount
_____	_____	$_____	÷ 60 =	$_____
_____	_____	$_____	÷ 60 =	$_____
_____	_____	$_____	÷ 60 =	+ $_____
		Total		$_____ Copy total here → $_____

35. **Do you owe any priority claims such as a priority tax, child support, or alimony — that are past due as of the filing date of your bankruptcy case? 11 U.S.C. § 507.**

    ☐ No. Go to line 36.
    ☐ Yes. Fill in the total amount of all of these priority claims. Do not include current or ongoing priority claims, such as those you listed in line 19.

    Total amount of all past-due priority claims .... $_____ ÷ 60 = $_____

Official Form B 22A2   Chapter 7 Means Test Calculation   page 7

Form B22A2   OFFICIAL FORMS

Debtor 1 _____   Case number (if known)_____
         First Name   Middle Name   Last Name

36. **Are you eligible to file a case under Chapter 13?** 11 U.S.C. § 109(e).
    For more information, go online using the link for *Bankruptcy Basics* specified in the separate instructions for this form. *Bankruptcy Basics* may also be available at the bankruptcy clerk's office.

    ☐ No. Go to line 37.
    ☐ Yes. Fill in the following information.

    Projected monthly plan payment if you were filing under Chapter 13 $_____

    Current multiplier for your district as stated on the list issued by the Administrative Office of the United States Courts (for districts in Alabama and North Carolina) or by the Executive Office for United States Trustees (for all other districts).   x _____

    To find a list of district multipliers that includes your district, go online using the link specified in the separate instructions for this form. This list may also be available at the bankruptcy clerk's office.

    Average monthly administrative expense if you were filing under Chapter 13 $_____   Copy total here ➔ $_____

37. **Add all of the deductions for debt payment.**
    Add lines 33g through 36. $_____

Total Deductions from Income

38. **Add all of the allowed deductions.**

    Copy line 24, *All of the expenses allowed under IRS expense allowances* .... $_____

    Copy line 32, *All of the additional expense deductions* .... $_____

    Copy line 37, *All of the deductions for debt payment* .... + $_____

    Total deductions $_____   Copy total here ➔ $_____

| Part 3: | Determine Whether There Is a Presumption of Abuse |

39. **Calculate monthly disposable income for 60 months**

    39a. Copy line 4, *adjusted current monthly income* ..... $_____

    39b. Copy line 38, *Total deductions* ....   – $_____

    39c. Monthly disposable income. 11 U.S.C. § 707(b)(2).
         Subtract line 39b from line 39a. $_____   Copy line 39c here ➔ $_____

         For the next 60 months (5 years) ....   x 60

    39d. **Total.** Multiply line 39c by 60. .... 39d. $_____   Copy line 39d here ➔ $_____

40. **Find out whether there is a presumption of abuse.** Check the box that applies:

    ☐ **The line 39d is less than $7,475*.** On the top of page 1 of this form, check box 1, *There is no presumption of abuse.* Go to Part 5.

    ☐ **The line 39d is more than $12,475*.** On the top of page 1 of this form, check box 2, *There is a presumption of abuse.* You may fill out Part 4 if you claim special circumstances. Then go to Part 5.

    ☐ **The line 39d is at least $7,475*, but not more than $12,475*.** Go to line 41.

    * Subject to adjustment on 4/01/16, and every 3 years after that for cases filed on or after the date of adjustment.

OFFICIAL FORMS   Form B22A2

Debtor 1 _____   Case number (if known)_____
         First Name   Middle Name   Last Name

41. 41a. **Fill in the amount of your total nonpriority unsecured debt.** If you filled out *A Summary of Your Assets and Liabilities and Certain Statistical Information Schedules* (Official Form 6), you may refer to line 5 on that form.   41a. $_____

                                                                                 x .25

    41b. **25% of your total nonpriority unsecured debt.** 11 U.S.C. § 707(b)(2)(A)(i)(I) $_____
         Multiply line 41a by 0.25.   Copy
                                                                                                 here → $_____

42. **Determine whether the income you have left over after subtracting all allowed deductions is enough to pay 25% of your unsecured, nonpriority debt.**
    Check the box that applies:

    ☐ **Line 39d is less than line 41b.** On the top of page 1 of this form, check box 1, *There is no presumption of abuse*. Go to Part 5.

    ☐ **Line 39d is equal to or more than line 41b.** On the top of page 1 of this form, check box 2, *There is a presumption of abuse*. You may fill out Part 4 if you claim special circumstances. Then go to Part 5.

Part 4: Give Details About Special Circumstances

43. **Do you have any special circumstances that justify additional expenses or adjustments of current monthly income for which there is no reasonable alternative?** 11 U.S.C. § 707(b)(2)(B).

    ☐ No. Go to Part 5.
    ☐ Yes. Fill in the following information. All figures should reflect your average monthly expense or income adjustment for each item. You may include expenses you listed in line 25.

    You must give a detailed explanation of the special circumstances that make the expenses or income adjustments necessary and reasonable. You must also give your case trustee documentation of your actual expenses or income adjustments.

Give a detailed explanation of the special circumstances	Average monthly expense or income adjustment
_____	$_____
_____	$_____
_____	$_____
_____	$_____

Part 5: Sign Below

By signing here, I declare under penalty of perjury that the information on this statement and in any attachments is true and correct.

✗ _____   ✗ _____
  Signature of Debtor 1   Signature of Debtor 2

  Date _____   Date _____
       MM / DD / YYYY   MM / DD / YYYY

Official Form B 22A2   Chapter 7 Means Test Calculation

Form B22B

Form B22B

OFFICIAL FORMS

Fill in this information to identify your case:

Debtor 1 _____ _____ _____
           First Name   Middle Name   Last Name

Debtor 2 _____ _____ _____
(Spouse, if filing) First Name Middle Name   Last Name

United States Bankruptcy Court for the: _____ District of _____

Case number _____
(If known)

☐ Check if this is an amended filing

Official Form B 22B

Chapter 11 Statement of Your Current Monthly Income   12/14

You must file this form if you are an individual and are filing for bankruptcy under Chapter 11. If more space is needed, attach a separate sheet to this form. Include the line number to which the additional information applies. On the top of any additional pages, write your name and case number (if known).

Part 1: Calculate Your Average Monthly Income

1. **What is your marital and filing status?** Check one only.

   ☐ Not married. Fill out Column A, lines 2-11.
   ☐ Married and your spouse is filing with you. Fill out both Columns A and B, lines 2-11.
   ☐ Married and your spouse is NOT filing with you. Fill out Column A, lines 2-11.

   Fill in the average monthly income that you received from all sources, derived during the 6 full months before you file this bankruptcy case. 11 U.S.C. § 101(10A). For example, if you are filing on September 15, the 6-month period would be March 1 through August 31. If the amount of your monthly income varied during the 6 months, add the income for all 6 months and divide the total by 6. Fill in the result.

   Do not include any income amount more than once. For example, if both spouses own the same rental property, put the income from that property in one column only. If you have nothing to report for any line, write $0 in the space.

	Column A Debtor 1	Column B Debtor 2

2. **Your gross wages, salary, tips, bonuses, overtime, and commissions** (before all payroll deductions). $_____ $_____

3. **Alimony and maintenance payments.** Do not include payments from a spouse if Column B is filled in. $_____ $_____

4. **All amounts from any source which are regularly paid for household expenses of you or your dependents, including child support.** Include regular contributions from an unmarried partner, members of your household, your dependents, parents, and roommates. Include regular contributions from a spouse only if Column B is not filled in. Do not include payments you listed on line 3. $_____ $_____

5. **Net income from operating a business, profession, or farm**

   Gross receipts (before all deductions) $_____
   Ordinary and necessary operating expenses   − $_____
   Net monthly income from a business, profession, or farm $_____ Copy here → $_____ $_____

6. **Net income from rental and other real property**

   Gross receipts (before all deductions) $_____
   Ordinary and necessary operating expenses   − $_____
   Net monthly income from rental or other real property $_____ Copy here → $_____ $_____

Official Form B 22B   Chapter 11 Statement of Your Current Monthly Income   page 1

OFFICIAL FORMS   Form B22B

Debtor 1 _____   Case number (if known) _____
         First Name   Middle Name   Last Name

	Column A Debtor 1	Column B Debtor 2
7. Interest, dividends, and royalties	$_____	$_____
8. Unemployment compensation	$_____	$_____

Do not enter the amount if you contend that the amount received was a benefit under the Social Security Act. Instead, list it here:.............................. ↓

    For you .... $_____

    For your spouse .... $_____

9. Pension or retirement income. Do not include any amount received that was a benefit under the Social Security Act. $_____ $_____

10. Income from all other sources not listed above. Specify the source and amount.

Do not include any benefits received under the Social Security Act or payments received as a victim of a war crime, a crime against humanity, or international or domestic terrorism. If necessary, list other sources on a separate page and put the total on line 10c.

  10a. _____ $_____ $_____

  10b. _____ $_____ $_____

  10c. Total amounts from separate pages, if any.   + $_____   + $_____

11. Calculate your total average monthly income.
Add lines 2 through 10 for each column.
Then add the total for Column A to the total for Column B. $_____ + $_____ = $_____

Total average monthly income

Part 2: Deduct any applicable marital adjustment

12. Copy your total average monthly income from line 11. $_____

13. Calculate the marital adjustment. Check one:

☐ You are not married. Fill in 0 in line 13d.

☐ You are married and your spouse is filing with you. Fill in 0 in line 13d.

☐ You are married and your spouse is not filing with you.
Fill in the amount of the income listed in line 11, Column B, that was NOT regularly paid for the household expenses of you or your dependents, such as payment of the spouse's tax liability or the spouse's support of someone other than you or your dependents.

In lines 13a-c, specify the basis for excluding this income and the amount of income devoted to each purpose. If necessary, list additional adjustments on a separate page.

If this adjustment does not apply, enter 0 on line 13d.

  13a. _____ $_____

  13b. _____ $_____

  13c. _____   + $_____

  13d. Total.. $_____   Copy here. → 13d. – $_____

14. Your current monthly income. Subtract line 13d from line 12.   14. $_____

Official Form B 22B   Chapter 11 Statement of Your Current Monthly Income   page 2

Form B22B   OFFICIAL FORMS

Debtor 1 _____   Case number (if known) _____
          First Name   Middle Name   Last Name

Part 3: Sign Below

By signing here, under penalty of perjury I declare that the information on this statement and in any attachments is true and correct.

✗ _____   ✗ _____
Signature of Debtor 1   Signature of Debtor 2

Date _____   Date _____
     MM / DD / YYYY   MM / DD / YYYY

[Reset]   [Save As...]   [Print]

Official Form B 22B   Chapter 11 Statement of Your Current Monthly Income   page 3

OFFICIAL FORMS   Form B22C1

Form B22C1

Fill in this information to identify your case:

Debtor 1 _____ _____ _____
         First Name   Middle Name   Last Name

Debtor 2 _____ _____ _____
(Spouse, if filing) First Name Middle Name Last Name

United States Bankruptcy Court for the: _____ District of _____

Case number _____
(If known)

Check as directed in lines 17 and 21:

According to the calculations required by this Statement:

☐ 1. Disposable income is not determined under 11 U.S.C. § 1325(b)(3).

☐ 2. Disposable income is determined under 11 U.S.C. § 1325(b)(3).

☐ 3. The commitment period is 3 years.
☐ 4. The commitment period is 5 years.

☐ Check if this is an amended filing

Official Form B 22C1

Chapter 13 Statement of Your Current Monthly Income and Calculation of Commitment Period   12/14

Be as complete and accurate as possible. If two married people are filing together, both are equally responsible for being accurate. If more space is needed, attach a separate sheet to this form. Include the line number to which the additional information applies. On the top of any additional pages, write your name and case number (if known).

Part 1: Calculate Your Average Monthly Income

1. **What is your marital and filing status?** Check one only.
   ☐ Not married. Fill out Column A, lines 2-11.
   ☐ Married. Fill out both Columns A and B, lines 2-11.

   Fill in the average monthly income that you received from all sources, derived during the 6 full months before you file this bankruptcy case. 11 U.S.C. § 101(10A). For example, if you are filing on September 15, the 6-month period would be March 1 through August 31. If the amount of your monthly income varied during the 6 months, add the income for all 6 months and divide the total by 6. Fill in the result. Do not include any income amount more than once. For example, if both spouses own the same rental property, put the income from that property in one column only. If you have nothing to report for any line, write $0 in the space.

	Column A Debtor 1	Column B Debtor 2 or non-filing spouse
2. **Your gross wages, salary, tips, bonuses, overtime, and commissions** (before all payroll deductions).	$_____	$_____
3. **Alimony and maintenance payments.** Do not include payments from a spouse if Column B is filled in.	$_____	$_____
4. **All amounts from any source which are regularly paid for household expenses of you or your dependents, including child support.** Include regular contributions from an unmarried partner, members of your household, your dependents, parents, and roommates. Include regular contributions from a spouse only if Column B is not filled in. Do not include payments you listed on line 3.	$_____	$_____
5. **Net income from operating a business, profession, or farm**		
Gross receipts (before all deductions) $_____		
Ordinary and necessary operating expenses −$_____		
Net monthly income from a business, profession, or farm $_____ Copy here ➔	$_____	$_____
6. **Net income from rental and other real property**		
Gross receipts (before all deductions) $_____		
Ordinary and necessary operating expenses −$_____		
Net monthly income from rental or other real property $_____ Copy here ➔	$_____	$_____

Form B22C1   OFFICIAL FORMS

Debtor 1 _____   Case number (if known)_____
         First Name   Middle Name   Last Name

	Column A Debtor 1	Column B Debtor 2 or non-filing spouse
7. Interest, dividends, and royalties	$_____	$_____
8. Unemployment compensation	$_____	$_____

Do not enter the amount if you contend that the amount received was a benefit under the Social Security Act. Instead, list it here: ....↓

For you .... $_____
For your spouse .... $_____

9. **Pension or retirement income.** Do not include any amount received that was a benefit under the Social Security Act. $_____ $_____

10. **Income from all other sources not listed above.** Specify the source and amount. Do not include any benefits received under the Social Security Act or payments received as a victim of a war crime, a crime against humanity, or international or domestic terrorism. If necessary, list other sources on a separate page and put the total on line 10c.

    10a. _____ $_____ $_____
    10b. _____ $_____ $_____
    10c. Total amounts from separate pages, if any.   + $_____   + $_____

11. **Calculate your total average monthly income.** Add lines 2 through 10 for each column. Then add the total for Column A to the total for Column B. $_____ + $_____ = $_____
                                                                                                          Total average monthly income

Part 2: Determine How to Measure Your Deductions from Income

12. Copy your total average monthly income from line 11. .... $_____

13. **Calculate the marital adjustment.** Check one:

    ☐ You are not married. Fill in 0 in line 13d.
    ☐ You are married and your spouse is filing with you. Fill in 0 in line 13d.
    ☐ You are married and your spouse is not filing with you.
       Fill in the amount of the income listed in line 11, Column B, that was NOT regularly paid for the household expenses of you or your dependents, such as payment of the spouse's tax liability or the spouse's support of someone other than you or your dependents.

       In lines 13a-c, specify the basis for excluding this income and the amount of income devoted to each purpose. If necessary, list additional adjustments on a separate page.

       If this adjustment does not apply, enter 0 on line 13d.

    13a. _____ $_____
    13b. _____ $_____
    13c. _____   + $_____
    13d. Total... $_____   Copy here. ➔ 13d.   — _____

14. **Your current monthly income.** Subtract line 13d from line 12.   14. $_____

15. **Calculate your current monthly income for the year.** Follow these steps:

    15a. Copy line 14 here ➔ .... 15a. $_____
         Multiply line 15a by 12 (the number of months in a year).   x 12
    15b. The result is your current monthly income for the year for this part of the form. 15b. $_____

Official Form B 22C1   Chapter 13 Statement of Your Current Monthly Income and Calculation of Commitment Period   page 2

OFFICIAL FORMS Form B22C1

Debtor 1 _____ Case number (if known)_____
         First Name Middle Name Last Name

16. Calculate the median family income that applies to you. Follow these steps:

    16a. Fill in the state in which you live. _____

    16b. Fill in the number of people in your household. _____

    16c. Fill in the median family income for your state and size of household. .... 16c. $_____
         To find a list of applicable median income amounts, go online using the link specified in the separate
         instructions for this form. This list may also be available at the bankruptcy clerk's office.

17. How do the lines compare?

    17a. ☐ Line 15b is less than or equal to line 16c. On the top of page 1 of this form, check box 1, *Disposable income is not determined under 11 U.S.C. § 1325(b)(3)*. **Go to Part 3.** Do NOT fill out *Calculation of Disposable Income* (Official Form 22C–2).

    17b. ☐ Line 15b is more than line 16c. On the top of page 1 of this form, check box 2, *Disposable income is determined under 11 U.S.C. § 1325(b)(3)*. **Go to Part 3 and fill out Calculation of Disposable Income (Official Form 22C–2).** On line 39 of that form, copy your current monthly income from line 14 above.

Part 3:   Calculate Your Commitment Period Under 11 U.S.C. §1325(b)(4)

18. Copy your total average monthly income from line 11. .... 18. $_____

19. **Deduct the marital adjustment if it applies.** If you are married, your spouse is not filing with you, and you contend that calculating the commitment period under 11 U.S.C. § 1325(b)(4) allows you to deduct part of your spouse's income, copy the amount from line 13d.

    If the marital adjustment does not apply, fill in 0 on line 19a.   19a. – $_____

    Subtract line 19a from line 18.   19b. $_____

20. Calculate your current monthly income for the year. Follow these steps:

    20a. Copy line 19b. .... 20a. $_____

         Multiply by 12 (the number of months in a year).   x 12

    20b. The result is your current monthly income for the year for this part of the form.   20b. $_____

    20c. Copy the median family income for your state and size of household from line 16c. .... $_____

21. How do the lines compare?

    ☐ Line 20b is less than line 20c. Unless otherwise ordered by the court, on the top of page 1 of this form, check box 3, *The commitment period is 3 years.* Go to Part 4.

    ☐ Line 20b is more than or equal to line 20c. Unless otherwise ordered by the court, on the top of page 1 of this form, check box 4, *The commitment period is 5 years.* Go to Part 4.

Part 4:   Sign Below

By signing here, under penalty of perjury I declare that the information on this statement and in any attachments is true and correct.

✗ _____   ✗ _____
   Signature of Debtor 1   Signature of Debtor 2

   Date _____   Date _____
        MM / DD / YYYY   MM / DD / YYYY

If you checked 17a, do NOT fill out or file Form 22C–2.

If you checked 17b, fill out Form 22C–2 and file it with this form. On line 39 of that form, copy your current monthly income from line 14 above.

[Reset]   [Save As...]   [Print]

Official Form B 22C1   Chapter 13 Statement of Your Current Monthly Income and Calculation of Commitment Period   page 3

Form B22C2   OFFICIAL FORMS

Form B22C2

Fill in this information to identify your case:

Debtor 1 _____ _____ _____
         First Name   Middle Name   Last Name

Debtor 2 _____ _____ _____
(Spouse, if filing) First Name Middle Name Last Name

United States Bankruptcy Court for the: _____ District of _____

Case number _____
(If known)

☐ Check if this is an amended filing

Official Form B 22C2

Chapter 13 Calculation of Your Disposable Income   12/14

To fill out this form, you will need your completed copy of *Chapter 13 Statement of Your Current Monthly Income and Calculation of Commitment Period* (Official Form 22C–1).

Be as complete and accurate as possible. If two married people are filing together, both are equally responsible for being accurate. If more space is needed, attach a separate sheet to this form. Include the line number to which the additional information applies. On the top of any additional pages, write your name and case number (if known).

Part 1: Calculate Your Deductions from Your Income

The Internal Revenue Service (IRS) issues National and Local Standards for certain expense amounts. Use these amounts to answer the questions in lines 6-15. To find the IRS standards, go online using the link specified in the separate instructions for this form. This information may also be available at the bankruptcy clerk's office.

Deduct the expense amounts set out in lines 6-15 regardless of your actual expense. In later parts of the form, you will use some of your actual expenses if they are higher than the standards. Do not include any operating expenses that you subtracted from income in lines 5 and 6 of Form 22C–1, and do not deduct any amounts that you subtracted from your spouse's income in line 13 of Form 22C–1.

If your expenses differ from month to month, enter the average expense.

Note: Line numbers 1-4 are not used in this form. These numbers apply to information required by a similar form used in chapter 7 cases.

5. **The number of people used in determining your deductions from income**
   Fill in the number of people who could be claimed as exemptions on your federal income tax return, plus the number of any additional dependents whom you support. This number may be different from the number of people in your household.

National Standards   You must use the IRS National Standards to answer the questions in lines 6-7.

6. **Food, clothing, and other items:** Using the number of people you entered in line 5 and the IRS National Standards, fill in the dollar amount for food, clothing, and other items. $_____

7. **Out-of-pocket health care allowance:** Using the number of people you entered in line 5 and the IRS National Standards, fill in the dollar amount for out-of-pocket health care. The number of people is split into two categories—people who are under 65 and people who are 65 or older—because older people have a higher IRS allowance for health care costs. If your actual expenses are higher than this IRS amount, you may deduct the additional amount on line 22.

Official Form B 22C2   Chapter 13 Calculation of Your Disposable Income   page 1

OFFICIAL FORMS   Form B22C2

Debtor 1 _____   Case number (if known) _____
         First Name   Middle Name   Last Name

People who are under 65 years of age

7a. Out-of-pocket health care allowance per person $_____
7b. Number of people who are under 65   X _____
7c. Subtotal. Multiply line 7a by line 7b. $_____   Copy line 7c here ➔ $_____

People who are 65 years of age or older

7d. Out-of-pocket health care allowance per person $_____
7e. Number of people who are 65 or older   X _____
7f. Subtotal. Multiply line 7d by line 7e. $_____   Copy line 7f here ➔ + $_____

7g. **Total.** Add lines 7c and 7f. .... $_____   Copy total here ➔ ....7g. $_____

Local Standards   You must use the IRS Local Standards to answer the questions in lines 8-15.

Based on information from the IRS, the U.S. Trustee Program has divided the IRS Local Standard for housing for bankruptcy purposes into two parts:

- Housing and utilities – Insurance and operating expenses

- Housing and utilities – Mortgage or rent expenses

To answer the questions in lines 8-9, use the U.S. Trustee Program chart. To find the chart, go online using the link specified in the separate instructions for this form. This chart may also be available at the bankruptcy clerk's office.

8. **Housing and utilities – Insurance and operating expenses:** Using the number of people you entered in line 5, fill in the dollar amount listed for your county for insurance and operating expenses. $_____

9. **Housing and utilities – Mortgage or rent expenses:**

   9a. Using the number of people you entered in line 5, fill in the dollar amount listed for your county for mortgage or rent expenses. $_____

   9b. Total average monthly payment for all mortgages and other debts secured by your home.

   To calculate the total average monthly payment, add all amounts that are contractually due to each secured creditor in the 60 months after you file for bankruptcy. Next divide by 60.

Name of the creditor	Average monthly payment
_____	$_____
_____	$_____
_____	+ $_____

   9b. Total average monthly payment .... $_____   Copy line 9b here ➔   – $_____   Repeat this amount on line 33a.

   9c. Net mortgage or rent expense.
   Subtract line 9b (*total average monthly payment*) from line 9a (*mortgage or rent expense*). If this number is less than $0, enter $0. $_____   Copy 9c here ➔ $_____

10. If you claim that the U.S. Trustee Program's division of the IRS Local Standard for housing is incorrect and affects the calculation of your monthly expenses, fill in any additional amount you claim. $_____
    Explain why: _____
    _____

Official Form B 22C2   Chapter 13 Calculation of Your Disposable Income   page 2

Form B22C2   OFFICIAL FORMS

Debtor 1 _____ Case number (if known)_____
       First Name   Middle Name   Last Name

11. **Local transportation expenses:** Check the number of vehicles for which you claim an ownership or operating expense.
    - ☐ 0. Go to line 14.
    - ☐ 1. Go to line 12.
    - ☐ 2 or more. Go to line 12.

12. **Vehicle operation expense:** Using the IRS Local Standards and the number of vehicles for which you claim the operating expenses, fill in the *Operating Costs* that apply for your Census region or metropolitan statistical area. $_____

13. **Vehicle ownership or lease expense:** Using the IRS Local Standards, calculate the net ownership or lease expense for each vehicle below. You may not claim the expense if you do not make any loan or lease payments on the vehicle. In addition, you may not claim the expense for more than two vehicles.

    Vehicle 1   Describe Vehicle 1: _____

    13a. Ownership or leasing costs using IRS Local Standard   13a. $_____

    13b. Average monthly payment for all debts secured by Vehicle 1.
    Do not include costs for leased vehicles.

    To calculate the average monthly payment here and on line 13e, add all amounts that are contractually due to each secured creditor in the 60 months after you file for bankruptcy. Then divide by 60.

Name of each creditor for Vehicle 1	Average monthly payment
_____	$_____

    Copy 13b here ➔ − $_____   Repeat this amount on line 33b.

    13c. Net Vehicle 1 ownership or lease expense
    Subtract line 13b from line 13a. If this number is less than $0, enter $0.   13c. $_____   Copy net Vehicle 1 expense here ➔ $_____

    Vehicle 2   Describe Vehicle 2: _____

    13d. Ownership or leasing costs using IRS Local Standard   13d. $_____

    13e. Average monthly payment for all debts secured by Vehicle 2.
    Do not include costs for leased vehicles.

Name of each creditor for Vehicle 2	Average monthly payment
_____	$_____

    Copy here ➔ − $_____   Repeat this amount on line 33c.

    13f. Net Vehicle 2 ownership or lease expense
    Subtract line 13e from 13d. If this number is less than $0, enter $0.   13f. $_____   Copy net Vehicle 2 expense here ➔ $_____

14. **Public transportation expense:** If you claimed 0 vehicles in line 11, using the IRS Local Standards, fill in the *Public Transportation* expense allowance regardless of whether you use public transportation. $_____

15. **Additional public transportation expense:** If you claimed 1 or more vehicles in line 11 and if you claim that you may also deduct a public transportation expense, you may fill in what you believe is the appropriate expense, but you may not claim more than the IRS Local Standard for *Public Transportation*. $_____

Official Form B 22C2   Chapter 13 Calculation of Your Disposable Income   page 3

OFFICIAL FORMS   **Form B22C2**

Debtor 1 _____   Case number (if known) _____
         First Name   Middle Name   Last Name

Other Necessary Expenses   In addition to the expense deductions listed above, you are allowed your monthly expenses for the following IRS categories.

16. **Taxes:** The total monthly amount that you actually pay for federal, state and local taxes, such as income taxes, self-employment taxes, social security taxes, and Medicare taxes. You may include the monthly amount withheld from your pay for these taxes. However, if you expect to receive a tax refund, you must divide the expected refund by 12 and subtract that number from the total monthly amount that is withheld to pay for taxes. $_____

 Do not include real estate, sales, or use taxes.

17. **Involuntary deductions:** The total monthly payroll deductions that your job requires, such as retirement contributions, union dues, and uniform costs.

 Do not include amounts that are not required by your job, such as voluntary 401(k) contributions or payroll savings. $_____

18. **Life insurance:** The total monthly premiums that you pay for your own term life insurance. If two married people are filing together, include payments that you make for your spouse's term life insurance.

 Do not include premiums for life insurance on your dependents, for a non-filing spouse's life insurance, or for any form of life insurance other than term. $_____

19. **Court-ordered payments:** The total monthly amount that you pay as required by the order of a court or administrative agency, such as spousal or child support payments. $_____

 Do not include payments on past due obligations for spousal or child support. You will list these obligations in line 35.

20. **Education:** The total monthly amount that you pay for education that is either required:
 - as a condition for your job, or
 - for your physically or mentally challenged dependent child if no public education is available for similar services. $_____

21. **Childcare:** The total monthly amount that you pay for childcare, such as babysitting, daycare, nursery, and preschool.
 Do not include payments for any elementary or secondary school education. $_____

22. **Additional health care expenses, excluding insurance costs:** The monthly amount that you pay for health care that is required for the health and welfare of you or your dependents and that is not reimbursed by insurance or paid by a health savings account. Include only the amount that is more than the total entered in line 7. $_____

 Payments for health insurance or health savings accounts should be listed only in line 25.

23. **Optional telephones and telephone services:** The total monthly amount that you pay for telecommunication services for you and your dependents, such as pagers, call waiting, caller identification, special long distance, or business cell phone service, to the extent necessary for your health and welfare or that of your dependents or for the production of income, if it is not reimbursed by your employer.   + $_____

 Do not include payments for basic home telephone, internet or cell phone service. Do not include self-employment expenses, such as those reported on line 5 of Form 22C-1, or any amount you previously deducted.

24. **Add all of the expenses allowed under the IRS expense allowances.**
 Add lines 6 through 23. $_____

Additional Expense Deductions   These are additional deductions allowed by the Means Test.
Note: Do not include any expense allowances listed in lines 6-24.

25. **Health insurance, disability insurance, and health savings account expenses.** The monthly expenses for health insurance, disability insurance, and health savings accounts that are reasonably necessary for yourself, your spouse, or your dependents.

Health insurance	$_____
Disability insurance	$_____
Health savings account	+ $_____
Total	$_____ Copy total here ➔ $_____

 Do you actually spend this total amount?
 ☐ No. How much do you actually spend? $_____
 ☐ Yes

26. **Continuing contributions to the care of household or family members.** The actual monthly expenses that you will continue to pay for the reasonable and necessary care and support of an elderly, chronically ill, or disabled member of your household or member of your immediate family who is unable to pay for such expenses. $_____

27. **Protection against family violence.** The reasonably necessary monthly expenses that you incur to maintain the safety of you and your family under the Family Violence Prevention and Services Act or other federal laws that apply. $_____

 By law, the court must keep the nature of these expenses confidential.

Official Form B 22C2   Chapter 13 Calculation of Your Disposable Income   page 4

Form B22C2   OFFICIAL FORMS

Debtor 1 _____   Case number (if known)_____
         First Name   Middle Name   Last Name

28. **Additional home energy costs.** Your home energy costs are included in your non-mortgage housing and utilities allowance on line 8.

   If you believe that you have home energy costs that are more than the home energy costs included in the non-mortgage housing and utilities allowance, then fill in the excess amount of home energy costs. $_____

   You must give your case trustee documentation of your actual expenses, and you must show that the additional amount claimed is reasonable and necessary.

29. **Education expenses for dependent children who are younger than 18.** The monthly expenses (not more than $156.25* per child) that you pay for your dependent children who are younger than 18 years old to attend a private or public elementary or secondary school. $_____

   You must give your case trustee documentation of your actual expenses, and you must explain why the amount claimed is reasonable and necessary and not already accounted for in lines 6-23.

   * Subject to adjustment on 4/01/16, and every 3 years after that for cases begun on or after the date of adjustment.

30. **Additional food and clothing expense.** The monthly amount by which your actual food and clothing expenses are higher than the combined food and clothing allowances in the IRS National Standards. That amount cannot be more than 5% of the food and clothing allowances in the IRS National Standards. $_____

   To find a chart showing the maximum additional allowance, go online using the link specified in the separate instructions for this form. This chart may also be available at the bankruptcy clerk's office.

   You must show that the additional amount claimed is reasonable and necessary.

31. **Continuing charitable contributions.** The amount that you will continue to contribute in the form of cash or financial instruments to a religious or charitable organization. 11 U.S.C. § 548(d)3 and (4).   + _____

   Do not include any amount more than 15% of your gross monthly income.

32. **Add all of the additional expense deductions.** $_____
    Add lines 25 through 31.

Deductions for Debt Payment

33. For debts that are secured by an interest in property that you own, including home mortgages, vehicle loans, and other secured debt, fill in lines 33a through 33g.

   To calculate the total average monthly payment, add all amounts that are contractually due to each secured creditor in the 60 months after you file for bankruptcy. Then divide by 60.

	Average monthly payment
Mortgages on your home	
33a. Copy line 9b here... →	$_____
Loans on your first two vehicles	
33b. Copy line 13b here... →	$_____
33c. Copy line 13e here... →	$_____

Name of each creditor for other secured debt	Identify property that secures the debt	Does payment include taxes or insurance?	
33d. _____	_____	☐ No ☐ Yes	$_____
33e. _____	_____	☐ No ☐ Yes	$_____
33f. _____	_____	☐ No ☐ Yes	+ $_____

   33g. Total average monthly payment. Add lines 33a through 33f. .... $_____   Copy total here → $_____

Official Form B 22C2   Chapter 13 Calculation of Your Disposable Income   page 5

OFFICIAL FORMS Form B22C2

Debtor 1 _____ Case number (if known) _____
         First Name   Middle Name   Last Name

34. **Are any debts that you listed in line 33 secured by your primary residence, a vehicle, or other property necessary for your support or the support of your dependents?**

   ☐ No. Go to line 35.
   ☐ Yes. State any amount that you must pay to a creditor, in addition to the payments listed in line 33, to keep possession of your property (called the *cure amount*). Next, divide by 60 and fill in the information below.

Name of the creditor	Identify property that secures the debt	Total cure amount		Monthly cure amount
_____	_____	$_____	÷ 60 =	$_____
_____	_____	$_____	÷ 60 =	$_____
_____	_____	$_____	÷ 60 = +	$_____
		Total	$_____	Copy total here ➔ $_____

35. **Do you owe any priority claims—such as a priority tax, child support, or alimony—that are past due as of the filing date of your bankruptcy case? 11 U.S.C. § 507.**

   ☐ No. Go to line 36.
   ☐ Yes. Fill in the total amount of all of these priority claims. Do not include current or ongoing priority claims, such as those you listed in line 19.

   Total amount of all past-due priority claims. .... $_____ ÷ 60 = $_____

36. **Projected monthly Chapter 13 plan payment** .... $_____

   Current multiplier for your district as stated on the list issued by the Administrative Office of the United States Courts (for districts in Alabama and North Carolina) or by the Executive Office for United States Trustees (for all other districts).

   To find a list of district multipliers that includes your district, go online using the link specified in the separate instructions for this form. This list may also be available at the bankruptcy clerk's office.

   x _____

   Average monthly administrative expense $_____ Copy total here ➔ $_____

37. **Add all of the deductions for debt payment. Add lines 33g through 36.** $_____

Total Deductions from Income

38. **Add all of the allowed deductions.**

   Copy line 24, *All of the expenses allowed under IRS expense allowances* .... $_____

   Copy line 32, *All of the additional expense deductions* .... $_____

   Copy line 37, *All of the deductions for debt payment* .... + $_____

   Total deductions $_____ Copy total here ➔ $_____

Official Form B 22C2   Chapter 13 Calculation of Your Disposable Income   page 6

Form B22C2   OFFICIAL FORMS

Debtor 1 _____ _____ _____ Case number (if known) _____
         First Name   Middle Name   Last Name

Part 2: Determine Your Disposable Income Under 11 U.S.C. § 1325(b)(2)

39. **Copy your total current monthly income** from line 14 of Form 22C-1, *Chapter 13 Statement of Your Current Monthly Income and Calculation of Commitment Period.* .... $ _____

40. **Fill in any reasonably necessary income you receive for support for dependent children.** The monthly average of any child support payments, foster care payments, or disability payments for a dependent child, reported in Part I of Form 22C-1, that you received in accordance with applicable nonbankruptcy law to the extent reasonably necessary to be expended for such child. $ _____

41. **Fill in all qualified retirement deductions.** The monthly total of all amounts that your employer withheld from wages as contributions for qualified retirement plans, as specified in 11 U.S.C. § 541(b)(7) plus all required repayments of loans from retirement plans, as specified in 11 U.S.C. § 362(b)(19). $ _____

42. **Total of all deductions allowed under 11 U.S.C. § 707(b)(2)(A).** Copy line 38 here .... → $ _____

43. **Deduction for special circumstances.** If special circumstances justify additional expenses and you have no reasonable alternative, describe the special circumstances and their expenses. You must give your case trustee a detailed explanation of the special circumstances and documentation for the expenses.

Describe the special circumstances	Amount of expense
43a. _____	$ _____
43b. _____	$ _____
43c. _____	+ $ _____
43d. **Total.** Add lines 43a through 43c.............	$ _____ Copy 43d here → + $ _____

44. **Total adjustments.** Add lines 40 through 43d. .... → $ _____   Copy total here → − $ _____

45. **Calculate your monthly disposable income under § 1325(b)(2).** Subtract line 44 from line 39. $ _____

Part 3: Change in Income or Expenses

46. **Change in income or expenses.** If the income in Form 22C-1 or the expenses you reported in this form have changed or are virtually certain to change after the date you filed your bankruptcy petition and during the time your case will be open, fill in the information below. For example, if the wages reported increased after you filed your petition, check 22C-1 in the first column, enter line 2 in the second column, explain why the wages increased, fill in when the increase occurred, and fill in the amount of the increase.

Form	Line	Reason for change	Date of change	Increase or decrease?	Amount of change
☐ 22C–1 ☐ 22C–2	____	_____	_____	☐ Increase ☐ Decrease	$ _____
☐ 22C–1 ☐ 22C–2	____	_____	_____	☐ Increase ☐ Decrease	$ _____
☐ 22C–1 ☐ 22C–2	____	_____	_____	☐ Increase ☐ Decrease	$ _____
☐ 22C–1 ☐ 22C–2	____	_____	_____	☐ Increase ☐ Decrease	$ _____

Official Form B 22C2   Chapter 13 Calculation of Your Disposable Income   page 7

OFFICIAL FORMS — Form B22C2

Debtor 1 _____ Case number *(if known)* _____
    First Name   Middle Name   Last Name

Part 4: Sign Below

By signing here, under penalty of perjury you declare that the information on this statement and in any attachments is true and correct.

✗ _____ ✗ _____
  Signature of Debtor 1   Signature of Debtor 2

Date _____ Date _____
  MM / DD / YYYY   MM / DD / YYYY

[Reset]   [Save As...]   [Print]

Official Form B 22C2   Chapter 13 Calculation of Your Disposable Income   page 8

(Added Aug. 11, 2005, eff. Oct. 17, 2005 and amended Apr. 1, 2007; Jan., 2008; Nov. 18, 2008, eff. Dec. 19, 2008; Apr. 1, 2010; Dec. 1, 2010; Apr. 1, 2013; Dec. 1, 2014.)

Form B22C2   OFFICIAL FORMS

ADVISORY COMMITTEE NOTES

2005 Amendment

A. Overview

Among the changes introduced by the Bankruptcy Abuse Prevention and Consumer Protection Act of 2005 are interlocking provisions defining "current monthly income" and establishing a means test to determine whether relief under Chapter 7 should be presumed abusive. Current monthly income ("CMI") is defined in § 101(10A) of the Code, and the means test is set out in § 707(b)(2). These provisions have a variety of applications. In Chapter 7, if the debtor's CMI exceeds a defined level the debtor is subject to the means test, and § 707(b)(2)(C) specifically requires debtors to file a statement of CMI and calculations to determine the applicability of the means test presumption. In Chapters 11 and 13, CMI provides the starting point for determining the disposable income that must be contributed to payment of unsecured creditors. Moreover, Chapter 13 debtors with CMI above defined levels are required by § 1325(b)(3) to complete the means test in order to determine the amount of their monthly disposable income, and pursuant to § 1325(b)(4), the level of CMI determines the "applicable commitment period" over which projected disposable income must be paid to unsecured creditors.

To provide for the reporting and calculation of CMI and for the completion of the means test where required, three separate official forms have been created—one for Chapter 7, one for Chapter 11, and one for Chapter 13. This note first describes the calculation of CMI that is common to all three of the forms, next describes the means test as set out in the Chapter 7 and 13 forms, and finally addresses particular issues that are unique to each of the separate forms.

B. Calculation of CMI

Although Chapters 7, 11, and 13 use CMI for different purposes, the basic computation is the same in each. As defined in § 101(10A), CMI is the monthly average of certain income that the debtor (and in a joint case, the debtor's spouse) received in the six calendar months before the bankruptcy filing. The definition includes in this average (1) income from all sources, whether or not taxable, and (2) any amount paid by an entity other than the debtor (or the debtor's spouse in a joint case) on a regular basis for the household expenses of the debtor, the debtor's dependents, and (in a joint case) the debtor's spouse if not otherwise a dependent. At the same time, the definition excludes from the averaged income "benefits received under the Social Security Act" and certain payments to victims of terrorism, war crimes, and crimes against humanity.

Each of the forms provides for reporting income items constituting CMI. The items are reported in a set of entry lines—Part II of the Chapter 7 form and Part I of the forms for Chapter 11 and Chapter 13—that include separate columns for reporting income of the debtor and of the debtor's spouse. The first of these entry lines includes a set of instructions and check boxes indicating when the "debtor's spouse" column must be completed. The instructions also direct the required averaging of reported income.

The subsequent entry lines specify several common types of income and are followed by a "catch-all" line for other income. The specific entry lines address (a) gross wages; (b) business income; (c) rental income; (d) interest, dividends, and royalties; (e) pension and retirement income; (f) regular contributions to the debtor's household expenses; and (g) unemployment compensation. Gross wages (before taxes) are required to be entered. Consistent with usage in the Internal Revenue Manual and the American Community Survey of the Census Bureau, business and rental income is defined as gross receipts less ordinary and necessary expenses. Unemployment compensation is given special treatment. Because the federal government provides funding for state unemployment compensation under the Social Security Act, there may be a dispute about whether unemployment compensation is a "benefit received under the Social Security Act." The forms take no position on the merits of this argument, but give debtors the option of reporting unemployment compensation separately from the CMI calculation. This separate reporting allows parties in interest to determine the materiality of an exclusion of unemployment compensation and to challenge it. The forms provide for totaling the income lines.

C. The means test: deductions from current monthly income (CMI)

The means test operates by deducting from CMI defined allowances for living expenses and payment of secured and priority debt, leaving disposable income presumptively available to pay unsecured non-priority debt. These deductions from CMI under are set out in § 707(b)(2)(A)(ii)–(iv). The forms for Chapter 7 and Chapter 13 have identical sections (Parts V and III, respectively) for calculating these deductions. The calculations are divided into subparts reflecting three different kinds of allowed deductions.

OFFICIAL FORMS — Form B22C2

1. **Deductions under IRS standards**

   Subpart A deals with deductions from CMI, set out in § 707(b)(2)(A)(ii), for "the debtor's applicable monthly expense amounts specified under the National Standards and Local Standards, and the debtor's actual monthly expenses for the categories specified as Other Necessary Expenses issued by the Internal Revenue Service for the area in which the debtor resides." The forms provide entry lines for each of the specified expense deductions under the IRS standards, and instructions on the entry lines identify the website of the U.S. Trustee Program, where the relevant IRS allowances can be found. As with all of the deductions in § 707(b)(2)(A)(ii), deductions under the IRS standards are subject to the proviso that they not include "any payments for debts."

   The IRS National Standards provide a single allowance for food, clothing, household supplies, personal care, and miscellany, depending on income and household size. The forms contain an entry line for the applicable allowance.

   The IRS Local Standards provide one set of deductions for housing and utilities and another set for transportation expenses, with different amounts for different areas of the country, depending on the size of the debtor's family and the number of the debtor's vehicles. Each of the amounts specified in the Local Standards are treated by the IRS as a cap on actual expenses, but because § 707(b)(2)(A)(ii) provides for deductions in the "amounts specified under the . . . Local Standards," the forms treat these amounts as allowed deductions. The forms again direct debtors to the website of the U.S. Trustee Program to obtain the appropriate allowances.

   The Local Standards for housing and utilities, as published by the IRS for its internal purposes, present single amounts covering all housing expenses; however, for bankruptcy purposes, the IRS has separated these amounts into a non-mortgage component and a mortgage/rent component. The non-mortgage component covers a variety of expenses involved in maintaining a residence, such as utilities, repairs and maintenance. The mortgage/rent component covers the cost of acquiring the residence. For homeowners with mortgages, the mortgage/rent component involves debt payment, since the cost of a mortgage is part of the allowance. Accordingly, the forms require debtors to deduct from the mortgage/rent component their average monthly mortgage payment (including required payments for taxes and insurance), up to the full amount of the IRS mortgage/rent component, and instruct debtors that this average monthly payment is the one reported on the separate line of the forms for deductions of secured debt under § 707(b)(2)(A)(iii). The forms allow debtors to challenge the appropriateness of this method of computing the Local Standards allowance for housing and utilities and to claim any additional housing allowance to which they contend they are entitled, but the forms require specification of the basis for such a contention.

   The IRS issues Local Standards for transportation in two components for its internal purposes as well as for bankruptcy: one component covers vehicle operation/public transportation expense and the other ownership/lease expense. The amount of the vehicle operation/public transportation allowance depends on the number of vehicles the debtor operates, with debtors who do not operate vehicles being given a public transportation allowance. The instruction for this line item makes it clear that every debtor is thus entitled to some transportation expense allowance. No debt payment is involved in this allowance. The ownership/lease component, on the other hand, may involve debt payment. Accordingly, the forms require debtors to reduce the allowance for ownership/lease expense by the average monthly loan payment amount (principal and interest), up to the full amount of the IRS ownership/lease expense amount. This average payment is as reported on the separate line of the forms for deductions of secured debt under § 707(b)(2)(A)(iii).

   The IRS does not set out specific dollar allowances for "Other Necessary Expenses." Rather, it specifies a number of categories for such expenses, and describes the nature of the expenses that may be deducted in each of these categories. Section 707(b)(2)(A)(ii) allows a deduction for the debtor's actual expenses in these specified categories, subject to its requirement that payment of debt not be included. Several of the IRS categories deal with debt repayment and so are not included in the forms. Several other categories deal with expense items that are more expansively addressed by specific statutory allowances. Subpart A sets out the remaining categories of "Other Necessary Expenses" in individual entry lines. Instructions in these entry lines reflect limitations imposed by the IRS and the need to avoid inclusion of items deducted elsewhere on the forms.

   Subpart A concludes with a subtotal of the deductions allowed under the IRS standards.

Form B22C2   OFFICIAL FORMS

2. Additional statutory expense deductions

In addition to the expense deductions allowed under the IRS standards, the means test makes provision—in subclauses (I), (II), (IV), and (V) of § 707(b)(2)(A)(ii)—for six special expense deductions. Each of these additional expense items is set out on a separate entry line in Subpart B, introduced by an instruction that there should not be double counting of any expense already included in the IRS deductions. Contributions to tax-exempt charities provide another statutory expense deduction. Section 1325(b)(2)(A)(ii) expressly allows a deduction from CMI for such contributions (up to 15% of the debtor's gross income), and § 707(b)(1) provides that in considering whether a Chapter 7 filing is an abuse, the court may not take into consideration "whether a debtor . . . continues to make [tax-exempt] charitable contributions." Accordingly, Subpart B also includes an entry line for charitable contributions. The subpart concludes with a subtotal of the additional statutory expense deductions.

3. Deductions for payment of debt

Subpart C of the forms deals with the means test's deductions from CMI for payment of secured and priority debt, as well as a deduction for administrative fees that would be incurred if the debtor paid debts through a Chapter 13 plan. In accord with § 707(b)(2)(A)(iii), the deduction for secured debt is divided into two entry lines—one for payments that are contractually due during the 60 months following the bankruptcy filing, the other for amounts needed to retain necessary collateral securing debts in default. In each situation, the instructions for the entry lines require dividing the total payment amount by 60, as the statute directs. Priority debt, deductible pursuant to § 707(b)(2)(A)(iv), is treated on a single entry line, also requiring division by 60. The defined deduction for the expenses of administering a Chapter 13 plan is allowed by § 707(b)(2)(A)(ii)(III) only for debtors eligible for Chapter 13. The forms treat this deduction in an entry line requiring the eligible debtor to state the amount of the prospective Chapter 13 plan payment and multiply that payment amount by the percentage fee established for the debtor's district by the Executive Office for United States Trustees. The forms refer debtors to the website of the U.S. Trustee Program to obtain this percentage fee. The subpart concludes with a subtotal of debt payment deductions.

4. Total deductions

Finally, the forms direct that the subtotals from Subparts A, B, and C be added together to arrive at the total of allowed deductions from CMI under the means test.

5. Additional claimed deductions

The forms do not provide for means test deductions from CMI for expenses in categories that are not specifically identified as "Other Necessary Expenses" in the Internal Revenue Manual. However, debtors may wish to claim expenses that do not fall within the categories listed as "Other Necessary Expenses" in the forms. Part VII of the Chapter 7 form and Part VI of the Chapter 13 form provide for such expenses to be identified and totaled. Although expenses listed in these sections are not deducted from CMI for purposes of the means test calculation, the listing provides a basis for debtors to assert that these expenses should be deducted from CMI under § 707(b)(2)(A)(ii)(I), and that the results of the forms' calculation, therefore, should be modified.

D. The chapter-specific forms

1. Chapter 7

The Chapter 7 form has several unique aspects. The form includes, in the upper right corner of the first page, a check box directing the debtor to state whether or not the calculations required by the form result in a presumption of abuse. The debtor is not bound by this statement and may argue, in response to a motion brought under § 707(b)(1), that there should be no presumption despite the calculations required by the form. The check box is intended to give clerks of court a conspicuous indication of the cases for which they are required to provide notice of a presumption of abuse pursuant to § 342(d).

Part I of the form implements the provision of § 707(b)(2)(D) that excludes certain disabled veterans from all means testing, making it unnecessary to compute the CMI of such veterans. Debtors who declare under penalty of perjury that they are disabled veterans within the statutory definition are directed to verify their declaration in Part VII, to check the "no presumption" box at the beginning of the form, and to disregard the remaining parts of the form.

Part II of the form is the computation of CMI. Section 707(b)(7) eliminates standing to assert the means test's presumption of abuse if the debtor's annualized CMI does not exceed a defined median state income. For this purpose, the statute directs that CMI of the debtor's spouse be combined with the debtor's CMI even if the debtor's spouse is not a joint debtor, unless the debtor declares under penalty of

OFFICIAL FORMS — Form B22C2

perjury that the spouses are legally separated or living separately other than for purposes of evading the means test. Accordingly, the calculation of CMI in Part II directs a computation of the CMI of the debtor's spouse not only in joint cases, but also in cases of married debtors who do not make the specified declaration, and the CMI of both spouses in these cases is combined for purposes of determining standing under § 707(b)(7).

Part III of the form provides for the comparison of the debtor's CMI to the applicable state median income for purposes of § 707(b)(7). It then directs debtors whose income does not exceed the applicable median to verify the form, to check the "no presumption" box at the beginning of the form, and not to complete the remaining parts of the form. Debtors whose CMI does exceed the applicable state median are required to complete the remaining parts of the form.

Part IV of the form provides for an adjustment to the CMI of a married debtor, not filing jointly, whose spouse's CMI was combined with the debtor's for purposes of determining standing to assert the means test presumption. The means test itself does not charge a married debtor in a non-joint case with the income of the non-filing spouse, but rather only with contributions made by that spouse to the household expenses of the debtor or the debtor's dependents, as provided in the definition of CMI in § 101(10A). Accordingly, Part IV calls for the combined CMI of Part II to be reduced by the amount of the non-filing spouse's income that was not contributed to the household expenses of the debtor or the debtor's dependents.

Part V of the form provides for a calculation of the means test's deductions from the debtor's CMI, as described above.

Part VI provides for a determination of whether the debtor's CMI, less the allowed deductions, gives rise to a presumption of abuse under § 707(b)(2)(A). Depending on the outcome of this determination, the debtor is directed to check the appropriate box at the beginning of the form and to sign the verification in Part VIII. Part VII allows the debtor to claim additional deductions, as discussed above.

2. Chapter 11

The Chapter 11 form is the simplest of the three, since the means-test deductions of § 707(b)(2) are not employed in determining the extent of an individual Chapter 11 debtor's disposable income. Section 1129(a)(15) requires payments of disposable income "as defined in section 1325(b)(2)," and that paragraph allows calculation of disposable income under judicially-determined standards, rather than pursuant to the means test deductions, specified for higher income Chapter 13 debtors by § 1325(b)(3). However, § 1325(b)(2) does require that CMI be used as the starting point in the judicial determination of disposable income, and so the Chapter 11 form requires this calculation (in Part I of the form), as described above, together with a verification (in Part II).

3. Chapter 13

Like the Chapter 7 form, the form for Chapter 13 debtors contains a number of special provisions. The upper right corner of the first page includes check boxes requiring the debtor to state whether, under the calculations required by the statement, the applicable commitment period under § 1325(b)(4) is three years or five years and whether the means test deductions are required by § 1325(b)(3) to be used in determining the debtor's disposable income. The check box is intended to inform standing trustees and other interested parties about these items, but does not prevent the debtor from arguing that the calculations required by the form do not accurately reflect the debtor's disposable income.

Part I of the form is a report of income to be used for determining CMI. Section 1325(b)(4) imposes a five-year applicable commitment period—rather than a three-year period—if the debtor's annualized CMI is not less than a defined median state income. For this purpose, as under § 707(b)(4), the CMI of the debtor's spouse is required by the statute to be combined with the debtor's CMI, and there is no exception for spouses who are legally separated or living separately. Accordingly, the report of income in Part I directs a combined reporting of the income of both spouses in all cases of married debtors.

Part II of the form computes the applicable commitment period by annualizing the income calculated in Part I and comparing it to the applicable state median. The form allows debtors to contend that the income of a non-filing spouse should not be treated as CMI and permits debtors to claim a deduction for any income of a non-filing spouse to the extent that this income was not contributed to the household expenses of the debtor or the debtor's dependents. The debtor is directed to check the appropriate box at the beginning of the form, stating the applicable commitment period.

Part III of the form compares the debtor's CMI to the applicable state median, allowing a determination of whether the means-test deductions must be used, pursuant to § 1325(b)(3), in calculating

Form B22C2   OFFICIAL FORMS

disposable income. For this purpose, since § 1325(b)(3) does not provide for including the income of the debtor's spouse, the form directs a deduction of the income of a non-filing spouse that is not contributed to the household expenses of the debtor or the debtor's dependents. Again, the debtor is directed to check the appropriate box at the beginning of the form, indicating whether the means test deductions are applicable. If so, the debtor is directed to complete the remainder of the form. If not, the debtor is directed to complete the verification in Part VII but not complete the other parts of the form.

Part IV provides for calculation of the means-test deductions provided in § 707(b)(2), described above, as incorporated by § 1325(b)(3) for debtors with CMI above the applicable state median.

Part V provides for three adjustments required by special provisions affecting disposable income in Chapter 13. First, § 1325(b)(2) itself excludes from the CMI used in determining disposable income certain "child support payments, foster care payments, [and] disability payments for a dependent child." Because payments of this kind are included in the definition of CMI in § 101(10A), a line entry for deduction of these payments is provided. Second, a line entry is provided for deduction of contributions by the debtor to certain retirement plans, listed in § 541(b)(7)(B), since that provision states that such contributions "shall not constitute disposable income, as defined in section 1325(b)." Third, the same line entry also allows a deduction from disposable income for payments on loans from retirement accounts that are excepted from the automatic stay by § 362(b)(19), since § 1322(f) provides that for a "loan described in section 362(b)(19) . . . any amounts required to repay such loan shall not constitute 'disposable income' under section 1325."

The Chapter 13 form does not provide a deduction from disposable income for the Chapter 13 debtor's anticipated attorney fees. There is no specific statutory allowance for such a deduction, and none appears necessary. Section 1325(b)(1)(B) requires that disposable income contributed to a Chapter 13 plan be used to pay "unsecured creditors." A debtor's attorney who has not taken a security interest in the debtor's property is an unsecured creditor who may be paid from disposable income.

Part VI of the form allows the debtor to claim additional deductions, as described above, and Part VII is the verification.

2006 Amendment

Forms 22A, Line 43, and Form 22C, Line 48, are amended to delete the phrase "in default" with respect to "Other payments on secured claims." A debtor may be required to make other payments to the creditor even when the debt is not in default, such as to retain collateral. Form 22C, Line 17, also is amended to require all chapter 13 debtors, including those whose income falls below the applicable median income, to determine their disposable income under § 1325(b)(3) of the Code by completing Part III of the form. Both forms contain stylistic amendments to conform the wording more closely to that used in the 2005 Act.

2005–2008 Amendment

(The 2005–2007 Committee Note incorporates Committee Notes previously published in 2005 and 2006.)

A. Overview

Among the changes introduced by the Bankruptcy Abuse Prevention and Consumer Protection Act of 2005 was a set of interlocking provisions defining "current monthly income" and establishing a means test to determine whether relief under Chapter 7 should be presumed abusive. Current monthly income ("CMI") is defined in § 101(10A) of the Code, and the means test is set out in § 707(b)(2). These provisions have a variety of applications. In Chapter 7, if the debtor's CMI exceeds a defined level the debtor is subject to the means test, and § 707(b)(2)(C) specifically requires debtors to file a statement of CMI and calculations to determine the applicability of the means test presumption. In Chapters 11 and 13, CMI provides the starting point for determining the disposable income that debtors may be required to pay to unsecured creditors. Moreover, Chapter 13 debtors with CMI above defined median income levels are required by § 1325(b)(3) to use the deductions from income prescribed by the means test in order to determine what part of their income is "disposable," and pursuant to § 1325(b)(4), the level of CMI determines the "applicable commitment period" over which projected disposable income must be paid to unsecured creditors.

To provide for the reporting and calculation of CMI and for the completion of the means test where required, three separate official forms have been created—one for Chapter 7, one for Chapter 11, and one for Chapter 13. This note first describes the calculation of CMI that is common to all three of the forms, next describes the means test deductions set out in the Chapter 7 and 13 forms, and finally addresses particular issues that are unique to each of the separate forms.

OFFICIAL FORMS   Form B22C2

B. Calculation of CMI

Although Chapters 7, 11, and 13 use CMI for different purposes, the basic computation is the same in each. As defined in § 101(10A), CMI is the monthly average of certain income that the debtor (and in a joint case, the debtor's spouse) received in the six calendar months before the bankruptcy filing. The definition includes in this average (1) income from all sources, whether or not taxable, and (2) any amount paid by an entity other than the debtor (or the debtor's spouse in a joint case) on a regular basis for the household expenses of the debtor, the debtor's dependents, and (in a joint case) the debtor's spouse if not otherwise a dependent. At the same time, the definition excludes from the averaged income "benefits received under the Social Security Act" and certain payments to victims of terrorism, war crimes, and crimes against humanity.

Each of the three forms provides for reporting income items constituting CMI. The items are reported in a set of entry lines—Part II of the form for Chapter 7 and Part I of the forms for Chapter 11 and Chapter 13—that include separate columns for reporting income of the debtor and of the debtor's spouse. The first of these entry lines includes a set of instructions and check boxes indicating when the "debtor's spouse" column must be completed. The instructions also direct the required averaging of reported income.

The subsequent entry lines for income reporting specify several common types of income and are followed by a "catch-all" line for other income. The entry lines address (a) gross wages; (b) business income; (c) rental income; (d) interest, dividends, and royalties; (e) pension and retirement income; (f) regular payments of the household expenses of the debtor or the debtor's dependents; (g) unemployment compensation, and (h) all other forms of income (the "catch-all" line).

Gross wages (before taxes) are required to be entered. However, consistent with usage in the Internal Revenue Manual and the American Community Survey of the Census Bureau, business and rental income are defined as gross receipts less ordinary and necessary expenses.

Unemployment compensation is given special treatment. Because the federal government provides funding for state unemployment compensation under the Social Security Act, there may be a dispute about whether unemployment compensation is a "benefit received under the Social Security Act." The forms take no position on the merits of this argument, but give debtors the option of reporting unemployment compensation separately from the CMI calculation. This separate reporting allows parties in interest to determine the materiality of an exclusion of unemployment compensation and to challenge it.

Alimony and child support are also given special treatment. Child support is not generally considered "income" to the recipient. See 26 U.S.C. § 71(c). Thus, child support is only part of CMI if it is paid on a regular basis for the household expenses of the debtor or the debtor's dependents. On the other hand, alimony and other forms of spousal support are considered income to the recipient, and thus are within CMI regardless of the regularity and use of the payments. To address this distinction, the instruction in the entry line for regular payments of household expenses directs that the entry include regular child support payments used for household expenses of the debtor or the debtor's dependents, and the instruction for the "catch-all" line directs inclusion of all spousal support payments that are not otherwise reported as spousal income.

The forms provide for totaling the income reporting lines.

C. The means test: deductions from current monthly income

The means test operates by deducting from CMI defined allowances for living expenses and payment of secured and priority debt, leaving disposable income presumptively available to pay unsecured non-priority debt. These deductions from CMI are set out in the Code at § 707(b)(2)(A)(ii)-(iv). The forms for Chapter 7 and Chapter 13 have similar sections (Parts V and IV, respectively) for calculating these deductions. The calculations are divided into subparts reflecting three different kinds of allowed deductions.

1. Deductions under IRS standards

Subpart A deals with deductions from CMI, set out in § 707(b)(2)(A)(ii), for "the debtor's applicable monthly expense amounts specified under the National Standards and Local Standards, and the debtor's actual monthly expenses for the categories specified as Other Necessary Expenses issued by the Internal Revenue Service for the area in which the debtor resides." The forms provide entry lines for each of the specified expense deductions under the IRS standards, and instructions on the entry lines identify the website of the U.S. Trustee Program, where the relevant IRS allowances can be found. As with all of the deductions in § 707(b)(2)(A)(ii), deductions under the IRS standards are subject to the proviso that they not include "any payments for debts."

National Standards. The IRS National Standards provide a single allowance for food, clothing, household supplies, personal care, and miscellany, depending on household size, which can be entered directly from a table supplied by the IRS. There is also a National Standard for out-of-pocket health care expenses, which provides two different per-person allowances, depending on age group: the allowance for persons 65 or older is greater than the allowance for those under 65. Accordingly, the forms direct debtors to compute the National Standard allowance for health care by first multiplying each of the two age-group allowances by the number of household members within that age group and then adding subtotals for the two age groups to obtain the total allowance.

Local Standards. The IRS Local Standards provide one set of deductions for housing and utilities and another set for transportation expenses, with different amounts for different areas of the country, depending on the size of the debtor's household and the number of the debtor's vehicles. Each of the amounts specified in the Local Standards are treated by the IRS as a cap on actual expenses, but because § 707(b)(2)(A)(ii) provides for deductions in the "amounts specified under the . . . Local Standards," the forms treat these amounts as allowed deductions.

The Local Standards for housing and utilities, as published by the IRS for its internal purposes, present single amounts covering all housing expenses; however, for bankruptcy purposes, the IRS has provided the Executive Office for United States Trustees with information allowing a division of these amounts into a non-mortgage component and a mortgage/rent component. The non-mortgage component covers a variety of expenses involved in maintaining a residence, such as utilities, repairs and maintenance. The mortgage/rent component covers the cost of acquiring the residence. The forms take no position on the question of whether the debtor must actually be making payments on a home in order to claim a mortgage/rent allowance. For homeowners with mortgages, the mortgage/rent allowance involves debt payment, since the cost of a mortgage is the basis for the allowance. Accordingly, the forms require debtors to deduct from the mortgage/rent allowance their average monthly mortgage payment, up to the full amount of the IRS mortgage/rent allowance, and instruct debtors that this average monthly payment is the one reported on the separate line of the forms for deductions of secured debt under § 707(b)(2)(a)(iii). The forms allow debtors to challenge the appropriateness of this method of computing the Local Standards allowance for housing and utilities and to claim any additional housing allowance to which they contend they are entitled, but the forms require specification of the basis for such a contention.

The IRS issues Local Standards for transportation in two components for its internal purposes as well as for bankruptcy: one component covers vehicle operation/public transportation expense and the other ownership/lease expense. The amount of the vehicle operation/public transportation allowance depends on the number of vehicles the debtor operates; debtors who do not operate vehicles are given a public transportation allowance, regardless of whether they actually use public transportation. It is not clear whether the public transportation allowance may also be claimed by debtors who do make use of public transportation but also operate vehicles. The forms permit debtors to claim both a public transportation and vehicle operating allowance, but take no position as to whether it is appropriate to claim both allowances. No debt payment is involved in the vehicle operation/public transportation component of the Local Standards for transportation.

The ownership/lease component, on the other hand, may involve debt payment. Accordingly, the forms require debtors to reduce the allowance for ownership/lease expense by the average monthly loan payment amount (principal and interest), up to the full amount of the IRS ownership/lease expense amount. This average payment is as reported on the separate line of the forms for deductions of secured debt under § 707(b)(2)(a)(iii). The forms take no position on the question of whether the debtor must actually be making payments on a vehicle in order to claim the ownership/lease allowance.

Other Necessary Expenses. The IRS does not set out specific dollar allowances for "Other Necessary Expenses." Rather, it specifies a number of categories for such expenses, and describes the nature of the expenses that may be deducted in each of these categories. Section 707(b)(2)(a)(ii) allows a deduction for the debtor's actual expenses in these specified categories, subject to its requirement that payment of debt not be included. Several of the IRS categories deal with debt repayment and so are not included in the forms. Several other categories deal with expense items that are more expansively addressed by specific statutory allowances. Subpart A sets out the remaining categories of "Other Necessary Expenses" in individual entry lines. Instructions in these entry lines reflect limitations imposed by the IRS and the need to avoid inclusion of items deducted elsewhere on the forms.

Subpart A concludes with a subtotal of the deductions allowed under the IRS standards.

OFFICIAL FORMS   **Form B22C2**

2. **Additional statutory expense deductions**

In addition to the expense deductions allowed under the IRS standards, the means test makes provision—in subclauses (I), (II), (IV), and (V) of § 707(b)(2)(A)(ii)—for six special expense deductions. Each of these additional expense items is set out on a separate entry line in Subpart B, introduced by an instruction that tracks the statutory language and provides that there should not be double counting of any expense already included in the IRS deductions.

One of these special expense deductions presents a problem of statutory construction. Section 707(b)(2)A)(ii)(I), after directing the calculation of the debtor's monthly expenses under the IRS standards, states, "Such expenses shall include reasonably necessary health insurance, disability insurance, and health saving account expenses...." There is no express statutory limitation to expenses actually incurred by the debtor, and so the provision appears to allow a reasonable "monthly expense" deduction for health and disability insurance or a health savings account even if the debtor does not make such payments, similar to the way in which the National Standards give an allowance for food, clothing and personal care expenses without regard to the debtor's actual expenditures. However, the statutory language might also be read as providing that the debtor's "Other Necessary Expenses" should include reasonable insurance and health savings account payments. Since "Other Necessary Expenses" are limited to actual expenditures, such a limitation could be implied here. The forms deal with this ambiguity by allowing the debtor to claim a deduction for reasonable insurance and health savings account expenses even if not made, but also require a statement of the amount actually expended in these categories, thus allowing a challenge by any party who believes that only actual expenditures are properly deductible.

Contributions to tax-exempt charities provide another statutory expense deduction. Section 707(b)(1) provides that in considering whether a Chapter 7 filing is an abuse, the court may not take into consideration "whether a debtor ... continues to make [tax-exempt] charitable contributions." Section 1325(b)(2)(A)(ii) expressly allows a deduction from CMI for such contributions that are "reasonably necessary" (up to 15% of the debtor's gross income), and the Religious Liberty and Charitable Donation Clarification Act of 2005 added language to § 1325(b)(3) to provide the same deduction for above-median income debtors whose disposable income is determined using means test deductions. Accordingly, Subpart B of both the Chapter 7 and Chapter 13 forms includes an entry line for charitable contributions, employing the different statutory deductions allowed in each context.

The Subpart B concludes with a subtotal of the additional statutory expense deductions.

3. **Deductions for payment of debt**

Subpart C deals with the means test's deductions from CMI for payment of secured and priority debt, as well as a deduction for administrative fees that would be incurred if the debtor paid debts through a Chapter 13 plan.

In accord with § 707(b)(2)(A)(iii), the deduction for secured debt is divided into two entry lines—one for payments that are contractually due during the 60 months following the bankruptcy filing, the other for amounts needed to retain necessary collateral securing debts in default. In each situation, the instructions for the entry lines require dividing the total payment amount by 60, as the statute directs. The forms recognize another ambiguity in this connection: "payments contractually due" might either be understood as limited to payments of principal and interest (payable to secured creditor) or, in the context of a mortgage with an escrow, might be understood as including payments of property taxes and insurance (ultimately paid to taxing bodies and insurers, but initially payable to the mortgagee). The forms require the debtor to specify whether the amount deducted includes taxes and insurance, allowing a party in interest to inquire into the deduction and raise an objection.

Priority debt, deductible pursuant to § 707(b)(2)(A)(iv), is treated on a single entry line, also requiring division by 60. The instruction for this line makes clear that only past due priority debt—not anticipated debts—should be included. Thus, future support or tax obligations, and future fees that might be payable to a Chapter 13 debtor's attorney, are not included.

The defined deduction for the expenses of administering a Chapter 13 plan is allowed by § 707(b)(2)(A)(ii)(III) only for debtors eligible for Chapter 13. The forms treat this deduction in an entry line requiring the eligible debtor to state the amount of the prospective Chapter 13 plan payment and multiply that payment amount by the percentage fee established for the debtor's district by the Executive Office for United States Trustees. The forms refer debtors to the website of the U.S. Trustee Program to obtain this percentage fee.

Form B22C2   **OFFICIAL FORMS**

The subpart concludes with a subtotal of debt payment deductions.

4. Total deductions

Finally, the forms direct that the subtotals from Subparts A, B, and C be added together to arrive at the total of allowed deductions from CMI under the means test.

5. Additional claimed deductions

The forms do not provide for means test deductions from CMI for expenses in categories that are not specifically identified as "Other Necessary Expenses" in the Internal Revenue Manual. However, debtors may wish to claim expenses that do not fall within the categories listed as "Other Necessary Expenses" in the forms. Part VII of the Chapter 7 form and Part VI of the Chapter 13 form provide for such expenses to be identified and totaled. Although expenses listed in these sections are not deducted from CMI for purposes of the means test calculation, the listing provides a basis for debtors to assert that these expenses should be deducted from CMI under § 707(b)(2)(A)(ii)(I), and that the results of the forms' calculation should therefore be modified.

D. The chapter-specific forms

1. Chapter 7

The Chapter 7 form has several unique aspects. The form includes, in the upper right corner of the first page, a check box directing the debtor to state whether or not the calculations required by the form result in a presumption of abuse. The debtor is not bound by this statement and may argue, in response to a motion brought under § 707(b)(1), that there should be no presumption despite the calculations required by the form. The check box is intended to give clerks of court a conspicuous indication of the cases for which they are required to provide notice of a presumption of abuse pursuant to § 342(d).

Part I implements the provision of § 707(b)(2)(D) that excludes certain disabled veterans from all means testing, making it unnecessary to compute the CMI of such veterans. Debtors who declare under penalty of perjury that they are disabled veterans within the statutory definition are directed to verify their declaration in Part VII, to check the "no presumption" box at the beginning of the form, and to disregard the remaining parts of the form.

Part I also provides an exclusion for debtors who do not have primarily consumer debts. These debtors are not subject to any of the provisions of § 707(b)—including the requirement of § 707(b)(2)(C) for filing a CMI statement—since § 707(b) applies, by its terms, only to "an individual debtor . . . whose debts are primarily consumer debts." However, a debtor may be found to have asserted non-consumer status incorrectly. Unless such a debtor has filed the CMI form within the 45 days after filing the case, the case could be subject to automatic dismissal under § 521(i). To avoid this possibility, debtors asserting principally non-consumer status may complete the appropriate portions of Part I, claim an exclusion from the balance of the form, and promptly file the form. If it is subsequently determined that the debtor does have primarily consumer debts, the form will have been filed within the deadline established by § 521(i), and can be amended to include the necessary CMI and means test information.

Part II computes CMI for purposes of the safe harbor of § 707(b)(7). Section 707(b)(7) prohibits a motion to dismiss based on the means test's presumption of abuse if the debtor's annualized CMI does not exceed a defined median state income. For this purpose, the statute directs that CMI of the debtor's spouse be combined with the debtor's CMI even if the debtor's spouse is not a joint debtor, unless the debtor declares under penalty of perjury that the spouses are legally separated or living separately other than for purposes of evading the means test. Accordingly, the calculation of CMI in Part II directs a computation of the CMI of the debtor's spouse not only in joint cases, but also in cases of married debtors who do not make the specified declaration, and the CMI of both spouses in these cases is combined for purposes of determining standing under § 707(b)(7).

Part III compares the debtor's CMI to the applicable state median income for purposes of § 707(b)(7). It then directs debtors whose income does not exceed the applicable median to verify the form, to check the "no presumption" box at the beginning of the form, and not to complete the remaining parts of the form. Debtors whose CMI does exceed the applicable state median are required to complete the remaining parts of the form.

Part IV adjusts the CMI of a married debtor, not filing jointly, whose spouse's CMI was combined with the debtor's in Part II. The means test itself does not charge a married debtor in a non-joint case with the income of the non-filing spouse, but only with payments regularly made by that spouse for the household expenses of the debtor or the debtor's dependents, as provided in the definition of CMI in

§ 101(10A). Accordingly, Part IV calls for the combined CMI of Part II to be reduced by the amount of the non-filing spouse's income that was not regularly paid for the household expenses of the debtor or the debtor's dependents. The form requires that the alternative uses of the spouse's income be specified.

Part V of the form provides for a calculation of the means test's deductions from the debtor's CMI, as described above in § C.

Part VI provides for a determination of whether the debtor's CMI, less the allowed deductions, gives rise to a presumption of abuse under § 707(b)(2)(A). Depending on the outcome of this determination, the debtor is directed to check the appropriate box at the beginning of the form and to sign the verification in Part VIII. Part VII allows the debtor to claim additional deductions, as discussed above in § C.5.

2. Chapter 11

The Chapter 11 form is the simplest of the three, since the means-test deductions of § 707(b)(2) are not employed in determining the extent of an individual Chapter 11 debtor's disposable income. Section 1129(a)(15) requires payments of disposable income "as defined in section 1325(b)(2)," and that paragraph allows calculation of disposable income under judicially-determined standards, rather than pursuant to the means test deductions, specified for higher income Chapter 13 debtors by § 1325(b)(3). However, § 1325(b)(2) does require that CMI be used as the starting point in the judicial determination of disposable income, and so the Chapter 11 form requires this calculation (in Part I of the form), as described above, together with a verification (in Part II).

3. Chapter 13

Like the Chapter 7 form, the form for Chapter 13 debtors contains a number of special provisions. The upper right corner of the first page includes check boxes requiring the debtor to state whether, under the calculations required by the statement, the applicable commitment period under § 1325(b)(4) is three years or five years and whether § 1325(b)(3) requires the means-test deductions to be used in determining the debtor's disposable income. The check box is intended to inform standing trustees and other interested parties about these items, but does not prevent the debtor from arguing that the calculations required by the form do not accurately reflect the debtor's disposable income.

Part I is a report of income to be used for determining CMI. In the absence of full payment of allowed unsecured claims, § 1325(b)(4) imposes a five-year applicable commitment period—rather than a three-year period—if the debtor's annualized CMI is not less than a defined median state income. For this purpose, as under § 707(b)(7), § 1325(b)(4) requires that the CMI of the debtor's spouse be combined with the debtor's CMI, but, unlike § 707(b)(7), no exception is made for spouses who are legally separated or living separately. Accordingly, the report of income in Part I directs a combined reporting of the income of both spouses in all cases of married debtors.

Part II computes the applicable commitment period by annualizing the income calculated in Part I and comparing it to the applicable state median. The form allows debtors to contend that the income of a non-filing spouse should not be treated as CMI and permits debtors to claim a deduction for any income of a non-filing spouse to the extent that this income was not regularly paid for the household expenses of the debtor or the debtor's dependents (with the alternative uses specified). The debtor is directed to check the appropriate box at the beginning of the form, stating the applicable commitment period. The check box does not prevent a debtor from proposing an applicable commitment period of less than three or five years in conjunction with a plan that pays all allowed unsecured claims in full.

Part III compares the debtor's CMI to the applicable state median, allowing a determination of whether the means-test deductions must be used, pursuant to § 1325(b)(3), in calculating disposable income. For this purpose, since § 1325(b)(3) does not provide for including the income of the debtor's spouse, the form directs a deduction of the income of a nonfiling spouse that was not contributed to the household expenses of the debtor or the debtor's dependents. Again, the debtor is directed to check the appropriate box at the beginning of the form, indicating whether the means test deductions are applicable. If so, the debtor is directed to complete the remainder of the form. If not, the debtor is directed to complete the verification in Part VII but not complete the other parts of the form.

Part IV provides for calculation of the means-test deductions provided in § 707(b)(2), described above in § C, as incorporated by § 1325(b)(3) for debtors with CMI above the applicable state median.

Part V provides for four adjustments required by special provisions affecting disposable income in Chapter 13. First, § 1325(b)(2) itself excludes from the CMI used in determining disposable income certain "child support payments, foster care payments, [and] disability payments for a dependent child." Because payments of this kind are included in the definition of CMI in § 101(10A), a line entry for deduction of

Form B22C2   **OFFICIAL FORMS**

these payments is provided. Second, a line entry is provided for deduction of contributions by the debtor to certain retirement plans, listed in § 541(b)(7)(B), since that provision states that such contributions "shall not constitute disposable income, as defined in section 1325(b)." Third, the same line entry also allows a deduction from disposable income for payments on loans from retirement accounts that are excepted from the automatic stay by § 362(b)(19), since § 1322(f) provides that for a "loan described in section 362(b)(19) . . . any amounts required to repay such loan shall not constitute 'disposable income' under section 1325." Finally, § 1325(b)(3) requires that deductions from income for above-median income debtors be determined not only in accordance with the means test deductions, set out in subparagraph (A) of § 707(b)(2), but also in accordance with subparagraph (B), which sets out the grounds for rebutting a presumption of abuse based on a demonstration of additional expenses justified by special circumstances. Part V includes an entry line for such additional expenses, with a warning that the debtor will be required (as provided by § 707(b)(2)(B)) to document the expenses and provide a detailed explanation of the special circumstances that make them reasonable and necessary.

The Chapter 13 form does not provide a deduction from disposable income for the Chapter 13 debtor's anticipated attorney fees. No specific statutory allowance for such a deduction exists, and none appears necessary. Section 1325(b)(1)(B) requires that disposable income contributed to a Chapter 13 plan be used to pay "unsecured creditors." A debtor's attorney who has not taken a security interest in the debtor's property is an unsecured creditor who may be paid from disposable income.

Part VI allows the debtor to declare expenses not allowed under the form without deducting them from CMI, as described above in § C.5.

2008 Amendment

The chapter 7 form is amended to implement the temporary exclusion from means testing created by the National Guard and Reservists Debt Relief Act of 2008. That law amended § 707(b)(2)(D) for a period of three years by adding a new subsection (ii) to provide a temporary exclusion from the application of the means test for certain members of the National Guard and reserve components of the Armed Forces. The new temporary exclusion would last for the period that the qualifying debtor is on active duty or is performing a homeland defense activity, and for 540 days thereafter.

Because the exclusion for Reservists and National Guard members applies only for a defined period of time, it may expire during the course of the chapter 7 case filed by a debtor initially entitled to the exclusion. For that reason, a new check box is added to the top of the form that states that the "presumption is temporarily inapplicable." A debtor who is entitled to claim the Reservists and National Guard exclusion at the commencement of the chapter 7 case may check that box.

The new exclusion applies only to a debtor who satisfies all of the requirements of § 707(b)(2)(D)(ii), and its expiration date depends on facts specific to each debtor. Therefore, in a joint case in which the exclusion in part 1C is claimed by either or both filers, each joint filer must complete a separate statement. If only one joint debtor qualifies for the exclusion in part IC, the other joint debtor must complete the form.

Part 1C is added to the form to allow qualifying debtors to claim the temporary exclusion under § 707(b)(2)(D)(ii). Debtors who declare under penalty of perjury that they satisfy all of the requirements of that provision are directed to verify their declaration in Part VIII and to check the "temporary presumption" box at the beginning of the form. They are not required to complete the remaining parts of the form for so long as the exclusion remains applicable.

A debtor who is or has been a Reservist or a National Guard member may qualify for the exclusion described in part 1C by being called to active duty service after September 11, 2001, for a period of at least 90 days, or while performing homeland defense activity for a period of at least 90 days. After the debtor has been released from active duty or has ceased performing homeland defense activity, the exclusion applies for a period of 540 days after the release date or cessation of homeland defense activity. Under those circumstances the debtor must state the date of release from active duty or the date on which the performance of homeland defense activity terminated.

If the Reservist and National Guard exclusion terminates during the course of a chapter 7 case— because of the expiration of the 540 day period following the release from active duty or the cessation of homeland defense activity—then the debtor may be required to complete the remaining parts of the form that are applicable to the debtor. If the exclusion terminates while a timely motion to dismiss under § 707(b)(2) may still be filed, Interim Rule 1007-I(n) requires that the debtor complete the remaining parts of the form no later than 14 days after the termination. If the obligation to complete the form arises in

OFFICIAL FORMS   Form B22C2

these circumstances and the debtor has not previously completed the form, the clerk is required to give the debtor notice of the obligation.

2010 Amendment

Form 22A, lines 19A, 19B, 20A, and 20B, and Form 22C, lines 24A, 24B, 25A, and 25B, are amended to delete the terms "household" and "household size" and to replace them with "number of persons" or "family size." Under § 707(b)(2)(A)(ii)(I) means test deductions for food, clothing, and other items and for health care are permitted to be taken in the amounts specified in the IRS National Standards. The IRS National Standards are based on numbers of persons, not household size. Similarly, the IRS Local Standards are based on family, not household, size. The IRS itself generally determines the applicable number of persons or family size for these purposes according to the number of dependents that the debtor claims for federal income tax purposes.

In order for Forms 22A and 22C to reflect more accurately the manner in which the specified National and Local Standards are applied by the IRS, the references to "household" and "household size" are deleted, and the substituted terms—"number of persons" and "family size"—are defined in terms of exemptions on the debtor's federal income tax return and other dependents.

Form 22A, line 8, Form 22B, line 7, and Form 22C, line 7, are amended to add an instruction that only one joint filer should report regular payments by another person for household expenses. Reporting of the figure by both spouses results in an erroneous double-counting of this source of income.

The introductory instruction to Part I of Form 22A is amended to direct debtors in joint cases to file separate forms if only one of the debtors is entitled to an exemption under Part I and the debtors believe that the filing of separate forms is required by § 707(b)(2)(C) of the Code. The language of § 707(b) is ambiguous about how the exclusions from means testing authorized by § 707(b)(1) (for debtors whose debts are not primarily consumer debts) and (b)(2)(D) (for certain disabled veterans, National Guard members, and Armed Forces reservists) are to be applied in joint cases. The form does not impose a particular interpretation of these provisions. It leaves up to joint debtors the initial determination of whether the exclusion of one spouse from means testing relieves the other spouse from the obligation to complete the form, and allows any dispute over this matter to be resolved by the courts.

2014 Amendment

Official Forms 22A-1, 22A-1Supp, 22A-2, 22C-1, and 22C-2 are new versions of the "means test" forms used by individuals in chapter 7 and 13, formerly Official Forms 22A and 22C. The original forms were substantially revised as part of the Forms Modernization Project. Official Form 22B, used by individuals in chapter 11, has also been revised as part of the project, which was designed so that the individuals completing the forms would do so more accurately and completely.

The revised versions of the means test forms present the relevant information in a format different from the original forms. For chapter 7, former Official Form 22A has been split into two forms: 22A-1 and 22A-2. The first form, Official Form 22A-1, *Chapter 7 Statement of Your Current Monthly Income*, is to be completed by all chapter 7 debtors. It calculates a debtor's current monthly income and compares that calculation to the median income for households of the same size in the debtor's state. The second form, Official Form 22A-2, *Chapter 7 Means Test Calculation*, is to be completed only by those chapter 7 debtors whose income is above the applicable state median. The prior version of Official Form 22A was introduced by several questions bearing on the applicability of the means test. Debtors who do not have primarily consumer debts, as well as certain members of the armed forces, are exempt from a presumption of abuse under the means test, and so are excused from completing the form. However, the great majority of individual debtors in chapter 7 do not fall within the exemptions. Accordingly, the exemptions from means testing have been placed in a separate supplement, Official Form 22A-1Supp, that will be filed only where applicable, making Form 22A present the relevant information more directly and in a manner consistent with the parallel chapter 13 form.

For chapter 13, there is a similar split of income and expense calculations. All chapter 13 debtors must complete Official Form 22C-1, *Chapter 13 Statement of Your Current Monthly Income and Calculation of Commitment Period*, which calculates current monthly income and the plan commitment period. Debtors only need to complete the second form, Official Form 22C-2, *Chapter13 Calculation of Your Disposable Income*, if their current monthly income exceeds the applicable median. Form 22C-2 calculates disposable income under 11 U.S.C. § 1325(b)(3), through a report of allowed expense deductions.

Form B22C2   **OFFICIAL FORMS**

Line 60 of former Official Form 22C has not been repeated in Official Form 22C-2. This line allowed debtors to list, but not deduct from income, "Other Necessary Expense" items that are not included within the categories specified by the Internal Revenue Service. Because debtors are separately allowed to list—and deduct—any expenses arising from special circumstances, former Line 60 was rarely used.

Form 22C-2 also reflects the Supreme Court's decision in *Hamilton v. Lanning*, 560 U.S. 505 (2010). Adopting a forward-looking approach, the Court held in Lanning that the calculation of a chapter 13 debtor's projected disposable income under § 1325(b) required consideration of changes to income or expenses reported elsewhere on former Official Form 22C that, at the time of plan confirmation, had occurred or were virtually certain to occur. Those changes could result in either an increased or decreased projected disposable income. Because only debtors whose annualized current monthly income exceeds the applicable median family income have their projected disposable income determined by the information provided on Official Form 22C-2, only these debtors are required to provide the information about changes to income and expenses on Official Form 22C-2. Part 3 of Official Form 22C-2 provides for the reporting of those changes.

In reporting changes to income a debtor must indicate whether the amounts reported in Official Form 22C-1—which are monthly averages of various types of income received during the six months prior to the filing of the bankruptcy case—have already changed or are virtually certain to change during the pendency of the case. For each change, the debtor must indicate the line of Official Form 22C-1 on which the amount to be changed was reported, the reason for the change, the date of its occurrence, whether the change is an increase or decrease of income, and the amount of the change. Similarly, in reporting changes to expenses, a debtor must list changes to the debtor's actual expenditures reported in Part 1 of Official Form 22C-2 that are virtually certain to occur while the case is pending. With respect to the deductible amounts reported in Part 1 that are determined by the IRS national and local standards, only changed amounts that result from changed circumstances in the debtor's life—such as the addition of a family member or the surrender of a vehicle—should be reported. For each change in expenses, the same information required to be provided for income changes must be reported.

Unlike former Official Forms 22A and 22C, Official Forms 22A-2 and 22C-2 permit, at line 23, the deduction of cell phone expenses necessary for the production of income if those expenses have not been reimbursed by the debtor's employer or deducted by the debtor in calculating net self-employment income. The same line also states that expenses for internet service may be deducted as a telecommunication services expense only if necessary for the production of income. Under IRS guidelines adopted in 2011, expenses for home internet service used for other purposes are included in the Local Standards for Housing and Utilities—Insurance and Operating Expenses. Also, Official Forms 22A-2 and 22C-2 now provide, at line 18, for deductions of the premiums paid by one jointly filing debtor on term life insurance policies of the other joint debtor as well as for premium payments on the debtor's own policies.

OFFICIAL FORMS Form 23

Form 23. Debtor's Certification of Completion of Postpetition Instructional Course Concerning Personal Financial Management

B 23 (Official Form 23) (12/13)

UNITED STATES BANKRUPTCY COURT

In re _____,   Case No. _____
            Debtor

                                         Chapter _____

DEBTOR'S CERTIFICATION OF COMPLETION OF POSTPETITION INSTRUCTIONAL COURSE CONCERNING PERSONAL FINANCIAL MANAGEMENT

This form should not be filed if an approved provider of a postpetition instructional course concerning personal financial management has already notified the court of the debtor's completion of the course. Otherwise, every individual debtor in a chapter 7 or a chapter 13 case or in a chapter 11 case in which § 1141(d)(3) applies must file this certification. If a joint petition is filed and this certification is required, each spouse must complete and file a separate certification. Complete one of the following statements and file by the deadline stated below:

☐ I, _____, the debtor in the above-styled case, hereby
      (Printed Name of Debtor)
certify that on _____ (Date), I completed an instructional course in personal financial management provided by _____, an approved personal financial
                    (Name of Provider)
management provider.

Certificate No. (if any): _____.

☐ I, _____, the debtor in the above-styled case, hereby
      (Printed Name of Debtor)
certify that no personal financial management course is required because of *[Check the appropriate box.]*:
    ☐ Incapacity or disability, as defined in 11 U.S.C. § 109(h);
    ☐ Active military duty in a military combat zone; or
    ☐ Residence in a district in which the United States trustee (or bankruptcy administrator) has determined that the approved instructional courses are not adequate at this time to serve the additional individuals who would otherwise be required to complete such courses.

Signature of Debtor: _____

Date: _____

Instructions: Use this form only to certify whether you completed a course in personal financial management and only if your course provider has not already notified the court of your completion of the course. (Fed. R. Bankr. P. 1007(b)(7).) Do NOT use this form to file the certificate given to you by your prepetition credit counseling provider and do NOT include with the petition when filing your case.

Filing Deadlines: In a chapter 7 case, file within 60 days of the first date set for the meeting of creditors under § 341 of the Bankruptcy Code. In a chapter 11 or 13 case, file no later than the last payment made by the debtor as required by the plan or the filing of a motion for a discharge under § 1141(d)(5)(B) or § 1328(b) of the Code. (See Fed. R. Bankr. P. 1007(c).)

(Added Aug. 11, 2005, eff. Oct. 17, 2005; amended Oct. 11, 2006; Dec. 1, 2007; Dec. 1, 2008; Dec. 1, 2009; Dec. 1, 2010; Dec. 2013.)

Form 23 — OFFICIAL FORMS

ADVISORY COMMITTEE NOTES

2005 Amendment

The form is new. Sections 727(a)(11) and 1328(g)(1), which were added to the Code by the Bankruptcy Abuse Prevention and Consumer Protection Act of 2005, Pub. L. No. 109–8, 119 Stat. 23 (April 20, 2005), require the debtor to complete an instructional course concerning personal financial management as a condition for receiving a discharge. The completed form, when filed by the debtor, will signal the clerk that this condition has been satisfied.

2006 Amendment

The form is amended to direct each individual debtor, including both spouses in a joint case, to file a separate certification and to provide the certificate number of the certificate of completion issued to the debtor by the approved personal financial management counselor. The form also is amended to include the deadlines for filing the certification in cases under chapters 7 and 13 and to instruct the debtor that the form is not to be used to file the certificate provided by the debtor's prepetition credit counselor.

2005–2007 Amendments

(The 2005–2007 Committee Note incorporates Committee Notes previously published in 2005 and 2006.)

The form was issued in 2005. Sections 727(a)(11), 1141(d)(3) and 1328(g)(1), which were added to the Code by the Bankruptcy Abuse Prevention and Consumer Protection Act of 2005, Pub. L. No. 109–8, 119 Stat. 23 (April 20, 2005), require individual debtors to complete an instructional course concerning personal financial management as a condition for receiving a discharge. The completed form will signal the clerk that this condition has been satisfied. Each individual debtor, including both spouses in a joint case, must file a separate certification and provide the certificate number of the certificate of completion issued to the debtor by the approved personal financial management counselor. Instructions are included that state the deadlines for filing the certification in chapter 7, chapter 11 in which § 1141(d)(3) applies, and chapter 13 cases, and remind the debtor that the form is not to be used for filing a certification of prepetition credit counseling.

2009 Amendment

The statement of the deadline for filing the form in a chapter 7 case is amended to conform to amended Rule 1007(c).

2010 Amendment

The statement of the deadline for filing the form in a chapter 7 case is amended to conform to amended Rule 1007(c).

2013 Amendment

The form is amended to reflect the amendment of Rule 1007(b)(7). As amended, that rule allows an approved provider of a personal financial management course to notify the court directly of the debtor's completion of the course. That notification relieves the debtor of the obligation to file this form.

OFFICIAL FORMS   Form 24

Form 24.   **Certification to Court of Appeals by all Parties**

B 24 (Official Form 24) (12/07)

[Caption as described in Fed. R. Bankr. P. 7010 or 9004(b), as applicable.]

CERTIFICATION TO COURT OF APPEALS
BY ALL PARTIES

A notice of appeal having been filed in the above-styled matter on _____ [Date], _____, _____, and _____, [Names of all the appellants and all the appellees, if any], who are all the appellants [and all the appellees] hereby certify to the court under 28 U.S.C. § 158(d)(2)(A) that a circumstance specified in 28 U.S.C. § 158(d)(2) exists as stated below.

Leave to appeal in this matter ☐ is ☐ is not required under 28 U.S.C. § 158(a).

[If from a final judgment, order, or decree] This certification arises in an appeal from a final judgment, order, or decree of the United States Bankruptcy Court for the _____ District of _____ entered on _____ [Date].

[If from an interlocutory order or decree] This certification arises in an appeal from an interlocutory order or decree, and the parties hereby request leave to appeal as required by 28 U.S.C. § 158(a).

[The certification shall contain one or more of the following statements, as is appropriate to the circumstances.]

The judgment, order, or decree involves a question of law as to which there is no controlling decision of the court of appeals for this circuit or of the Supreme Court of the United States, or involves a matter of public importance.

Or

The judgment, order, or decree involves a question of law requiring resolution of conflicting decisions.

Or

An immediate appeal from the judgment, order, or decree may materially advance the progress of the case or proceeding in which the appeal is taken.

Form 24   OFFICIAL FORMS

B 24 (Official Form 24) (12/07) - Cont.   Page 2

[The parties may include or attach the information specified in Rule 8001(f)(3)(C).]

Signed: *[If there are more than two signatories, all must sign and provide the information requested below. Attach additional signed sheets if needed.]*

Attorney for Appellant (or Appellant, if not represented by an attorney)	Attorney for Appellee (or Appellee if not represented by an attorney)
Printed Name of Signer	Printed Name of Signer
Address	Address
Telephone No.	Telephone No.
Date	Date

(Added Aug. 11, 2005, eff. Oct. 17, 2005; Dec. 1, 2007.)

ADVISORY COMMITTEE NOTES

2005 Amendment

This form is new. Rule 8001, as amended in 2005, requires that any certification of an appeal, bankruptcy court judgment, order, or decree directly to the United States Court of Appeals by all the appellants and appellees (if any) acting jointly be filed on this form.

2005–2007 Amendments

(The 2005–2007 Committee Note incorporates the Committee Note previously published in 2005.)

This form was issued in 2005. Rule 8001 requires that any certification of an appeal, bankruptcy court judgment, order, or decree directly to the United States Court of Appeals by all the appellants and appellees (if any) acting jointly be filed on this form.

OFFICIAL FORMS   Form 25A

Form 25A. Plan of Reorganization in Small Business Case Under Chapter 11

B25A (Official Form 25A) (12/11)

United States Bankruptcy Court
_____ District of _____

In re_____,   Case No._____
      Debtor

Small Business Case under Chapter 11

[NAME OF PROPONENT]'S PLAN OF REORGANIZATION, DATED [INSERT DATE]

ARTICLE I
SUMMARY

This Plan of Reorganization (the "Plan") under chapter 11 of the Bankruptcy Code (the "Code") proposes to pay creditors of [insert the name of the debtor] (the "Debtor") from [specify sources of payment, such as an infusion of capital, loan proceeds, sale of assets, cash flow from operations, or future income].

This Plan provides for _____ classes of secured claims; _____ classes of unsecured claims; and _____ classes of equity security holders. Unsecured creditors holding allowed claims will receive distributions, which the proponent of this Plan has valued at approximately __ cents on the dollar. This Plan also provides for the payment of administrative and priority claims [if payment is not in full on the effective date of this Plan with respect to any such claim (to the extent permitted by the Code or the claimant's agreement), identify such claim and briefly summarize the proposed treatment.]

All creditors and equity security holders should refer to Articles III through VI of this Plan for information regarding the precise treatment of their claim. A disclosure statement that provides more detailed information regarding this Plan and the rights of creditors and equity security holders has been circulated with this Plan. **Your rights may be affected. You should read these papers carefully and discuss them with your attorney, if you have one. (If you do not have an attorney, you may wish to consult one.)**

ARTICLE II
CLASSIFICATION OF CLAIMS AND INTERESTS

2.01   <u>Class 1</u>.   All allowed claims entitled to priority under § 507 of the Code (except administrative expense claims under § 507(a)(2), ["gap" period claims in an involuntary case under § 507(a)(3),] and priority tax claims under § 507(a)(8)).

2.02   <u>Class 2</u>.   The claim of _____, to the extent allowed as a secured claim under § 506 of the Code.

Form 25A   **OFFICIAL FORMS**

B25A (Official Form 25A) (12/11) - Cont.

[Add other classes of secured creditors, if any. Note: Section 1129(a)(9)(D) of the Code provides that a secured tax claim which would otherwise meet the description of a priority tax claim under § 507(a)(8) of the Code is to be paid in the same manner and over the same period as prescribed in § 507(a)(8).]

2.03   Class 3.   All unsecured claims allowed under § 502 of the Code.

[Add other classes of unsecured claims, if any.]

2.04   Class 4.   Equity interests of the Debtor. [If the Debtor is an individual, change this heading to "The interests of the individual Debtor in property of the estate."]

ARTICLE III
TREATMENT OF ADMINISTRATIVE EXPENSE CLAIMS, U.S. TRUSTEES FEES, AND PRIORITY TAX CLAIMS

3.01   Unclassified Claims. Under section §1123(a)(1), administrative expense claims, ["gap" period claims in an involuntary case allowed under § 502(f) of the Code,] and priority tax claims are not in classes.

3.02   Administrative Expense Claims. Each holder of an administrative expense claim allowed under § 503 of the Code [, and a "gap" claim in an involuntary case allowed under § 502(f) of the Code,] will be paid in full on the effective date of this Plan (as defined in Article VII), in cash, or upon such other terms as may be agreed upon by the holder of the claim and the Debtor.

3.03   Priority Tax Claims. Each holder of a priority tax claim will be paid [specify terms of treatment consistent with § 1129(a)(9)(C) of the Code].

3.04   United States Trustee Fees. All fees required to be paid by 28 U.S.C. §1930(a)(6) (U.S. Trustee Fees) will accrue and be timely paid until the case is closed, dismissed, or converted to another chapter of the Code. Any U.S. Trustee Fees owed on or before the effective date of this Plan will be paid on the effective date.

ARTICLE IV
TREATMENT OF CLAIMS AND INTERESTS UNDER THE PLAN

4.01   Claims and interests shall be treated as follows under this Plan:

OFFICIAL FORMS Form 25A

B25A (Official Form 25A) (12/11) - Cont.

Class	Impairment	Treatment
Class 1 - Priority Claims	[State whether impaired or unimpaired.]	[Insert treatment of priority claims in this Class, including the form, amount and timing of distribution, if any. For example: "Class 1 is unimpaired by this Plan, and each holder of a Class 1 Priority Claim will be paid in full, in cash, upon the later of the effective date of this Plan as defined in Article VII, or the date on which such claim is allowed by a final non-appealable order. Except: _____."]
Class 2 – Secured Claim of [Insert name of secured creditor.]	[State whether impaired or unimpaired.]	[Insert treatment of secured claim in this Class, including the form, amount and timing of distribution, if any.] [Add class[es] of secured claims if applicable]
Class 3 - General Unsecured Creditors	[State whether impaired or unimpaired.]	[Insert treatment of unsecured creditors in this Class, including the form, amount and timing of distribution, if any.] [Add administrative convenience class if applicable]
Class 4 - Equity Security Holders of the Debtor	[State whether impaired or unimpaired.]	[Insert treatment of equity security holders in this Class, including the form, amount and timing of distribution, if any.]

ARTICLE V
ALLOWANCE AND DISALLOWANCE OF CLAIMS

5.01 Disputed Claim. A disputed claim is a claim that has not been allowed or disallowed [by a final non-appealable order], and as to which either: (i) a proof of claim has been filed or deemed filed, and the Debtor or another party in interest has filed an objection; or (ii) no proof of claim has been filed, and the Debtor has scheduled such claim as disputed, contingent, or unliquidated.

5.02 Delay of Distribution on a Disputed Claim. No distribution will be made on account of a disputed claim unless such claim is allowed [by a final non-appealable order].

5.03 Settlement of Disputed Claims. The Debtor will have the power and authority to settle and compromise a disputed claim with court approval and compliance with Rule 9019 of the Federal Rules of Bankruptcy Procedure.

Form 25A OFFICIAL FORMS

B25A (Official Form 25A) (12/11) - Cont.

ARTICLE VI
PROVISIONS FOR EXECUTORY CONTRACTS AND UNEXPIRED LEASES

6.01 <u>Assumed Executory Contracts and Unexpired Leases</u>.

    (a) The Debtor assumes the following executory contracts and/or unexpired leases effective upon the [Insert "effective date of this Plan as provided in Article VII," "the date of the entry of the order confirming this Plan," or other applicable date]:

[List assumed executory contracts and/or unexpired leases.]

    (b) The Debtor will be conclusively deemed to have rejected all executory contracts and/or unexpired leases not expressly assumed under section 6.01(a) above, or before the date of the order confirming this Plan, upon the [Insert "effective date of this Plan," "the date of the entry of the order confirming this Plan," or other applicable date]. A proof of a claim arising from the rejection of an executory contract or unexpired lease under this section must be filed no later than _____ (__) days after the date of the order confirming this Plan.

ARTICLE VII
MEANS FOR IMPLEMENTATION OF THE PLAN

[Insert here provisions regarding how the plan will be implemented as required under §1123(a)(5) of the Code. For example, provisions may include those that set out how the plan will be funded, as well as who will be serving as directors, officers or voting trustees of the reorganized debtor.]

ARTICLE VIII
GENERAL PROVISIONS

8.01 <u>Definitions and Rules of Construction.</u> The definitions and rules of construction set forth in §§ 101 and 102 of the Code shall apply when terms defined or construed in the Code are used in this Plan, and they are supplemented by the following definitions: [Insert additional definitions if necessary].

8.02 <u>Effective Date of Plan</u>. The effective date of this Plan is the first business day following the date that is fourteen days after the entry of the order of confirmation. If, however, a stay of the confirmation order is in effect on that date, the effective date will be the first business day after the date on which the stay of the confirmation order expires or is otherwise terminated.

OFFICIAL FORMS Form 25A

B25A (Official Form 25A) (12/11) - Cont.   5

8.03 <u>Severability</u>. If any provision in this Plan is determined to be unenforceable, the determination will in no way limit or affect the enforceability and operative effect of any other provision of this Plan.

8.04 <u>Binding Effect</u>. The rights and obligations of any entity named or referred to in this Plan will be binding upon, and will inure to the benefit of the successors or assigns of such entity.

8.05 <u>Captions</u>. The headings contained in this Plan are for convenience of reference only and do not affect the meaning or interpretation of this Plan.

[8.06 <u>Controlling Effect</u>. Unless a rule of law or procedure is supplied by federal law (including the Code or the Federal Rules of Bankruptcy Procedure), the laws of the State of _____ govern this Plan and any agreements, documents, and instruments executed in connection with this Plan, except as otherwise provided in this Plan.]

[8.07 <u>Corporate Governance</u>. [If the Debtor is a corporation include provisions required by § 1123(a)(6) of the Code.]]

ARTICLE IX
DISCHARGE

[If the Debtor is not entitled to discharge under 11 U.S.C. § 1141(d)(3) change this heading to **"NO DISCHARGE OF DEBTOR."**]

9.01. **[Option 1 – If Debtor is an individual and § 1141(d)(3) is not applicable]**
<u>Discharge</u>. Confirmation of this Plan does not discharge any debt provided for in this Plan until the court grants a discharge on completion of all payments under this Plan, or as otherwise provided in § 1141(d)(5) of the Code. The Debtor will not be discharged from any debt excepted from discharge under § 523 of the Code, except as provided in Rule 4007(c) of the Federal Rules of Bankruptcy Procedure.

[Option 2 -- If the Debtor is a partnership and section 1141(d)(3) of the Code is not applicable]
<u>Discharge</u>. On the confirmation date of this Plan, the debtor will be discharged from any debt that arose before confirmation of this Plan, subject to the occurrence of the effective date, to the extent specified in § 1141(d)(1)(A) of the Code. The Debtor will not be discharged from any debt imposed by this Plan.

Form 25A   OFFICIAL FORMS

B25A (Official Form 25A) (12/11) - Cont.

[Option 3 -- If the Debtor is a corporation and § 1141(d)(3) is not applicable]

Discharge. On the confirmation date of this Plan, the debtor will be discharged from any debt that arose before confirmation of this Plan, subject to the occurrence of the effective date, to the extent specified in § 1141(d)(1)(A) of the Code, except that the Debtor will not be discharged of any debt: (i) imposed by this Plan; (ii) of a kind specified in § 1141(d)(6)(A) if a timely complaint was filed in accordance with Rule 4007(c) of the Federal Rules of Bankruptcy Procedure; or (iii) of a kind specified in § 1141(d)(6)(B).

[Option 4 -- If § 1141(d)(3) is applicable]

No Discharge. In accordance with § 1141(d)(3) of the Code, the Debtor will not receive any discharge of debt in this bankruptcy case.

ARTICLE X
OTHER PROVISIONS

[Insert other provisions, as applicable.]

Respectfully submitted,

By: _____
The Plan Proponent

By: _____
Attorney for the Plan Proponent

(Added Dec. 1, 2008, and amended Dec. 1, 2011.)

ADVISORY COMMITTEE NOTES
2008 Enactment

This form is new. It implements § 433 of the Bankruptcy Abuse Prevention and Consumer Protection Act of 2005, Pub. L. No. 109–8, 119 Stat. 23 (April 20, 2005). This form for a small business chapter 11 plan of reorganization may be used in cases where the debtor (whether an individual or an artificial entity) is a small business debtor under § 101(51D) of the Code. The form is intended to be used in conjunction with the small business chapter 11 disclosure statement form (Official Form 25B).

Because the type of debtor and the details of the proposed plan of reorganization may vary, the form is intended to provide an illustrative format, rather than a specific prescription for the language or content of a plan in any particular case. The form includes instructions and examples of the types of information needed to complete it.

2011 Amendment

Provision 8.02 of Article VIII of the form, which specifies the plan's effective date, is amended to reflect the change in the time periods of Rules 3020(e) and 8002(a) for a stay of the confirmation order and the filing of a notice of appeal. As of December 1, 2009, both time periods were increased from ten to fourteen days. The effective date of the plan will generally be the first business day after those time periods expire. Accordingly, the effective date of the plan is extended to the first business day following the date that is fourteen days after the entry of the order of confirmation. If, however, a stay of the confirmation order remains in effect on the specified effective date, the plan will instead go into effect on the first business day after the stay expires or is terminated, so long as the order of confirmation has not been vacated.

OFFICIAL FORMS   Form 25B

Form 25B. Disclosure Statement in Small Business Case Under Chapter 11

B25B (Official Form 25B) (12/08)

United States Bankruptcy Court
_____ District of _____

In re _____,   Case No. _____
      Debtor

Small Business Case under Chapter 11

[NAME OF PLAN PROPONENT]'S DISCLOSURE STATEMENT, DATED [INSERT DATE]

Table of Contents

[Insert when text is finalized]

B25B (Official Form 25B) (12/08) – Cont.

I. INTRODUCTION

This is the disclosure statement (the "Disclosure Statement") in the small business chapter 11 case of _____ (the "Debtor"). This Disclosure Statement contains information about the Debtor and describes the [insert name of plan] (the "Plan") filed by [the Debtor] on [insert date]. A full copy of the Plan is attached to this Disclosure Statement as Exhibit A. *Your rights may be affected. You should read the Plan and this Disclosure Statement carefully and discuss them with your attorney. If you do not have an attorney, you may wish to consult one.*

The proposed distributions under the Plan are discussed at pages ___ - ___ of this Disclosure Statement. [General unsecured creditors are classified in Class ___, and will receive a distribution of ___% of their allowed claims, to be distributed as follows _____.]

A. Purpose of This Document

This Disclosure Statement describes:

- The Debtor and significant events during the bankruptcy case,
- How the Plan proposes to treat claims or equity interests of the type you hold (*i.e.*, what you will receive on your claim or equity interest if the plan is confirmed),
- Who can vote on or object to the Plan.
- What factors the Bankruptcy Court (the "Court") will consider when deciding whether to confirm the Plan.
- Why [the Proponent] believes the Plan is feasible, and how the treatment of your claim or equity interest under the Plan compares to what you would receive on your claim or equity interest in liquidation, and
- The effect of confirmation of the Plan.

Be sure to read the Plan as well as the Disclosure Statement. This Disclosure Statement describes the Plan, but it is the Plan itself that will, if confirmed, establish your rights.

B. Deadlines for Voting and Objecting; Date of Plan Confirmation Hearing

The Court has not yet confirmed the Plan described in this Disclosure Statement. This section describes the procedures pursuant to which the Plan will or will not be confirmed.

    1. *Time and Place of the Hearing to [Finally Approve This Disclosure Statement and] Confirm the Plan*

The hearing at which the Court will determine whether to [finally approve this Disclosure Statement and] confirm the Plan will take place on [insert date], at [insert time], in Courtroom _____, at the [Insert Courthouse Name, and Full Court Address, City, State, Zip Code].

    2. *Deadline For Voting to Accept or Reject the Plan*

Form 25B   OFFICIAL FORMS

B25B (Official Form 25B) (12/08) – Cont.

If you are entitled to vote to accept or reject the plan, vote on the enclosed ballot and return the ballot in the enclosed envelope to [insert address]. See section IV.A. below for a discussion of voting eligibility requirements.

Your ballot must be received by [insert date] or it will not be counted.

    3.   *Deadline For Objecting to the [Adequacy of Disclosure and] Confirmation of the Plan*

Objections to [this Disclosure Statement or to] the confirmation of the Plan must be filed with the Court and served upon [insert entities] by [insert date].

    4.   *Identity of Person to Contact for More Information*

If you want additional information about the Plan, you should contact [insert name and address of representative of plan proponent].

   C.   **Disclaimer**

The Court has [conditionally] approved this Disclosure Statement as containing adequate information to enable parties affected by the Plan to make an informed judgment about its terms. The Court has not yet determined whether the Plan meets the legal requirements for confirmation, and the fact that the Court has approved this Disclosure Statement does not constitute an endorsement of the Plan by the Court, or a recommendation that it be accepted. [The Court's approval of this Disclosure Statement is subject to final approval at the hearing on confirmation of the Plan. Objections to the adequacy of this Disclosure Statement may be filed until _____.]

II. BACKGROUND

   A.   **Description and History of the Debtor's Business**

The Debtor is a [corporation, partnership, etc.]. Since [insert year operations commenced], the Debtor has been in the business of _____. [Describe the Debtor's business].

   B.   **Insiders of the Debtor**

[Insert a detailed list of the names of Debtor's insiders as defined in §101(31) of the United States Bankruptcy Code (the "Code") and their relationship to the Debtor. For each insider, list all compensation paid by the Debtor or its affiliates to that person or entity during the two years prior to the commencement of the Debtor's bankruptcy case, as well as compensation paid during the pendency of this chapter 11 case.]

   C.   **Management of the Debtor Before and During the Bankruptcy**

During the two years prior to the date on which the bankruptcy petition was filed, the officers, directors, managers or other persons in control of the Debtor (collectively the "Managers") were [List the Managers of the Debtor prior to the petition date].

OFFICIAL FORMS   Form 25B

B25B (Official Form 25B) (12/08) – Cont.   4

      The Managers of the Debtor during the Debtor's chapter 11 case have been: [List Managers of the Debtor during the Debtor's chapter 11 case.]

      After the effective date of the order confirming the Plan, the directors, officers, and voting trustees of the Debtor, any affiliate of the Debtor participating in a joint Plan with the Debtor, or successor of the Debtor under the Plan (collectively the "Post Confirmation Managers"), will be: [List Post Confirmation Managers of the Debtor.] The responsibilities and compensation of these Post Confirmation Managers are described in section ___ of this Disclosure Statement.

    D.   **Events Leading to Chapter 11 Filing**

[Describe the events that led to the commencement of the Debtor's bankruptcy case.]

    E.   **Significant Events During the Bankruptcy Case**

[Describe significant events during the Debtor's bankruptcy case:

- Describe any asset sales outside the ordinary course of business, debtor in possession financing, or cash collateral orders.
- Identify the professionals approved by the court.
- Describe any adversary proceedings that have been filed or other significant litigation that has occurred (including contested claim disallowance proceedings), and any other significant legal or administrative proceedings that are pending or have been pending during the case in a forum other than the Court.
- Describe any steps taken to improve operations and profitability of the Debtor.
- Describe other events as appropriate.]

    F.   **Projected Recovery of Avoidable Transfers [Choose the option that applies]**

[Option 1 – If the Debtor does not intend to pursue avoidance actions]

      The Debtor does not intend to pursue preference, fraudulent conveyance, or other avoidance actions.

[Option 2 – If the Debtor intends to pursue avoidance actions]

      The Debtor estimates that up to $_____ may be realized from the recovery of fraudulent, preferential or other avoidable transfers. While the results of litigation cannot be predicted with certainty and it is possible that other causes of action may be identified, the following is a summary of the preference, fraudulent conveyance and other avoidance actions filed or expected to be filed in this case:

Transaction	Defendant	Amount Claimed

[Option 3 – If the Debtor does not yet know whether it intends to pursue avoidance actions]

Form 25B   OFFICIAL FORMS

B25B (Official Form 25B) (12/08) – Cont.   5

The Debtor has not yet completed its investigation with regard to prepetition transactions. If you received a payment or other transfer within 90 days of the bankruptcy, or other transfer avoidable under the Code, the Debtor may seek to avoid such transfer.

G. **Claims Objections**

Except to the extent that a claim is already allowed pursuant to a final non-appealable order, the Debtor reserves the right to object to claims. Therefore, even if your claim is allowed for voting purposes, you may not be entitled to a distribution if an objection to your claim is later upheld. The procedures for resolving disputed claims are set forth in Article V of the Plan.

H. **Current and Historical Financial Conditions**

The identity and fair market value of the estate's assets are listed in Exhibit B. [Identify source and basis of valuation.]

The Debtor's most recent financial statements [if any] issued before bankruptcy, each of which was filed with the Court, are set forth in Exhibit C.

[The most recent post-petition operating report filed since the commencement of the Debtor's bankruptcy case are set forth in Exhibit D.] [A summary of the Debtor's periodic operating reports filed since the commencement of the Debtor's bankruptcy case is set forth in Exhibit D.]

III. **SUMMARY OF THE PLAN OF REORGANIZATION AND TREATMENT OF CLAIMS AND EQUITY INTERESTS**

A. **What is the Purpose of the Plan of Reorganization?**

As required by the Code, the Plan places claims and equity interests in various classes and describes the treatment each class will receive. The Plan also states whether each class of claims or equity interests is impaired or unimpaired. If the Plan is confirmed, your recovery will be limited to the amount provided by the Plan.

B. **Unclassified Claims**

Certain types of claims are automatically entitled to specific treatment under the Code. They are not considered impaired, and holders of such claims do not vote on the Plan. They may, however, object if, in their view, their treatment under the Plan does not comply with that required by the Code. As such, the Plan Proponent has *not* placed the following claims in any class:

1. *Administrative Expenses*

Administrative expenses are costs or expenses of administering the Debtor's chapter 11 case which are allowed under § 507(a)(2) of the Code. Administrative expenses also include the value of any goods sold to the Debtor in the ordinary course of business and received within 20 days before the date of the bankruptcy petition. The Code requires that all administrative expenses be paid on the effective date of the Plan, unless a particular claimant agrees to a different treatment.

OFFICIAL FORMS — Form 25B

B25B (Official Form 25B) (12/08) – Cont.

The following chart lists the Debtor's estimated administrative expenses, and their proposed treatment under the Plan:

Type	Estimated Amount Owed	Proposed Treatment
Expenses Arising in the Ordinary Course of Business After the Petition Date		Paid in full on the effective date of the Plan, or according to terms of obligation if later
The Value of Goods Received in the Ordinary Course of Business Within 20 Days Before the Petition Date		Paid in full on the effective date of the Plan, or according to terms of obligation if later
Professional Fees, as approved by the Court.		Paid in full on the effective date of the Plan, or according to separate written agreement, or according to court order if such fees have not been approved by the Court on the effective date of the Plan
Clerk's Office Fees		Paid in full on the effective date of the Plan
Other administrative expenses		Paid in full on the effective date of the Plan or according to separate written agreement
Office of the U.S. Trustee Fees		Paid in full on the effective date of the Plan
TOTAL		

2. *Priority Tax Claims*

Priority tax claims are unsecured income, employment, and other taxes described by § 507(a)(8) of the Code. Unless the holder of such a § 507(a)(8) priority tax claim agrees otherwise, it must receive the present value of such claim, in regular installments paid over a period not exceeding 5 years from the order of relief.

Form 25B OFFICIAL FORMS

B25B (Official Form 25B) (12/08) – Cont.

The following chart lists the Debtor's estimated § 507(a)(8) priority tax claims and their proposed treatment under the Plan:

Description (name and type of tax)	Estimated Amount Owed	Date of Assessment	Treatment
			Pmt interval = [Monthly] payment = Begin date = End date = Interest Rate % = Total Payout Amount = $
			Pmt interval = [Monthly] payment = Begin date = End date = Interest Rate % = Total Payout Amount = $

C. **Classes of Claims and Equity Interests**

The following are the classes set forth in the Plan, and the proposed treatment that they will receive under the Plan:

1. *Classes of Secured Claims*

Allowed Secured Claims are claims secured by property of the Debtor's bankruptcy estate (or that are subject to setoff) to the extent allowed as secured claims under § 506 of the Code. If the value of the collateral or setoffs securing the creditor's claim is less than the amount of the creditor's allowed claim, the deficiency will [be classified as a general unsecured claim].

OFFICIAL FORMS — Form 25B

B25B (Official Form 25B) (12/08) – Cont.

The following chart lists all classes containing Debtor's secured prepetition claims and their proposed treatment under the Plan:

Class #	Description	Insider? (Yes or No)	Impairment	Treatment
	Secured claim of: Name = Collateral description = Allowed Secured Amount = $_____ Priority of lien = Principal owed = $_____ Pre-pet. arrearage = $_____ Total claim = $_____		[State whether impaired or unimpaired]	[Monthly] Pmt = Pmts Begin = Pmts End = [Balloon pmt] = Interest rate % = Treatment of Lien = [Additional payment required to cure defaults] =
	Secured claim of: Name = Collateral description = Allowed Secured Amount = $_____ Priority of lien = Principal owed = $_____ Pre-pet. arrearage = $_____ Total claim = $_____		[State whether impaired or unimpaired]	Monthly Pmt = Pmts Begin = Pmts End = [Balloon pmt] = Interest rate % = Treatment of Lien = [Additional payment required to cure defaults] =

2. *Classes of Priority Unsecured Claims*

Certain priority claims that are referred to in §§ 507(a)(1), (4), (5), (6), and (7) of the Code are required to be placed in classes. The Code requires that each holder of such a claim receive cash on the effective date of the Plan equal to the allowed amount of such claim. However, a class of holders of such claims may vote to accept different treatment.

Form 25B   OFFICIAL FORMS

B25B (Official Form 25B) (12/08) – Cont.   9

The following chart lists all classes containing claims under §§ 507(a)(1), (4), (5), (6), and (a)(7) of the Code and their proposed treatment under the Plan:

Class #	Description	Impairment	Treatment
	Priority unsecured claim pursuant to Section [insert] Total amt of claims = $	[State whether impaired or unimpaired]	
	Priority unsecured claim pursuant to Section [insert] Total amt of claims = $	[State whether impaired or unimpaired]	

3. *Class[es] of General Unsecured Claims*

General unsecured claims are not secured by property of the estate and are not entitled to priority under § 507(a) of the Code. [Insert description of §1122(b) convenience class if applicable.]

The following chart identifies the Plan's proposed treatment of Class[es] __ through __, which contain general unsecured claims against the Debtor:

Class #	Description	Impairment	Treatment
	[1122(b) Convenience Class]	[State whether impaired or unimpaired]	[Insert proposed treatment, such as "Paid in full in cash on effective date of the Plan or when due under contract or applicable nonbankruptcy law"]
	General Unsecured Class	[State whether impaired or unimpaired]	Monthly Pmt = Pmts Begin = Pmts End = [Balloon pmt] = Interest rate % from [date] = Estimated percent of claim paid =

4. *Class[es] of Equity Interest Holders*

982

OFFICIAL FORMS — Form 25B

B25B (Official Form 25B) (12/08) – Cont.

Equity interest holders are parties who hold an ownership interest (*i.e.*, equity interest) in the Debtor. In a corporation, entities holding preferred or common stock are equity interest holders. In a partnership, equity interest holders include both general and limited partners. In a limited liability company ("LLC"), the equity interest holders are the members. Finally, with respect to an individual who is a debtor, the Debtor is the equity interest holder.

The following chart sets forth the Plan's proposed treatment of the class[es] of equity interest holders: [There may be more than one class of equity interests in, for example, a partnership case, or a case where the prepetition debtor had issued multiple classes of stock.]

Class #	Description	Impairment	Treatment
	Equity interest holders	[State whether impaired or unimpaired]	

D. **Means of Implementing the Plan**

 1. *Source of Payments*

Payments and distributions under the Plan will be funded by the following:

[Describe the source of funds for payments under the Plan.]

 2. *Post-confirmation Management*

The Post-Confirmation Managers of the Debtor, and their compensation, shall be as follows:

Name	Affiliations	Insider (yes or no)?	Position	Compensation

E. **Risk Factors**

The proposed Plan has the following risks:

[List all risk factors that might affect the Debtor's ability to make payments and other distributions required under the Plan.]

F. **Executory Contracts and Unexpired Leases**

Form 25B OFFICIAL FORMS

B25B (Official Form 25B) (12/08) – Cont. 11

The Plan, in Exhibit 5.1, lists all executory contracts and unexpired leases that the Debtor will assume under the Plan. Assumption means that the Debtor has elected to continue to perform the obligations under such contracts and unexpired leases, and to cure defaults of the type that must be cured under the Code, if any. Exhibit 5.1 also lists how the Debtor will cure and compensate the other party to such contract or lease for any such defaults.

If you object to the assumption of your unexpired lease or executory contract, the proposed cure of any defaults, or the adequacy of assurance of performance, you must file and serve your objection to the Plan within the deadline for objecting to the confirmation of the Plan, unless the Court has set an earlier time.

All executory contracts and unexpired leases that are not listed in Exhibit 5.1 will be rejected under the Plan. Consult your adviser or attorney for more specific information about particular contracts or leases.

If you object to the rejection of your contract or lease, you must file and serve your objection to the Plan within the deadline for objecting to the confirmation of the Plan.

[*The Deadline for Filing a Proof of Claim Based on a Claim Arising from the Rejection of a Lease or Contract Is* _____. Any claim based on the rejection of a contract or lease will be barred if the proof of claim is not timely filed, unless the Court orders otherwise.]

G. **Tax Consequences of Plan**

Creditors and Equity Interest Holders Concerned with How the Plan May Affect Their Tax Liability Should Consult with Their Own Accountants, Attorneys, And/Or Advisors.

The following are the anticipated tax consequences of the Plan: [List the following general consequences as a minimum: (1)Tax consequences to the Debtor of the Plan; (2) General tax consequences on creditors of any discharge, and the general tax consequences of receipt of plan consideration after confirmation.]

IV. **CONFIRMATION REQUIREMENTS AND PROCEDURES**

To be confirmable, the Plan must meet the requirements listed in §§ 1129(a) or (b) of the Code. These include the requirements that: the Plan must be proposed in good faith; at least one impaired class of claims must accept the plan, without counting votes of insiders; the Plan must distribute to each creditor and equity interest holder at least as much as the creditor or equity interest holder would receive in a chapter 7 liquidation case, unless the creditor or equity interest holder votes to accept the Plan; and the Plan must be feasible. These requirements are not the only requirements listed in § 1129, and they are not the only requirements for confirmation.

A. Who May Vote or Object

Any party in interest may object to the confirmation of the Plan if the party believes that the requirements for confirmation are not met.

Many parties in interest, however, are not entitled to vote to accept or reject the Plan. A creditor or equity interest holder has a right to vote for or against the Plan only if that creditor or equity interest holder has a claim or equity interest that is both (1) allowed or allowed for voting purposes and (2) impaired.

In this case, the Plan Proponent believes that classes _____ are impaired and that holders of claims in each of these classes are therefore entitled to vote to accept or reject the Plan. The Plan Proponent believes that classes _____ are unimpaired and that holders of claims in each of these classes, therefore, do not have the right to vote to accept or reject the Plan.

1. *What Is an Allowed Claim or an Allowed Equity Interest?*

Only a creditor or equity interest holder with an allowed claim or an allowed equity interest has the right to vote on the Plan. Generally, a claim or equity interest is allowed if either (1) the Debtor has scheduled the claim on the Debtor's schedules, unless the claim has been scheduled as disputed, contingent, or unliquidated, or (2) the creditor has filed a proof of claim or equity interest, unless an objection has been filed to such proof of claim or equity interest. When a claim or equity interest is not allowed, the creditor or equity interest holder holding the claim or equity interest cannot vote unless the Court, after notice and hearing, either overrules the objection or allows the claim or equity interest for voting purposes pursuant to Rule 3018(a) of the Federal Rules of Bankruptcy Procedure.

The deadline for filing a proof of claim in this case was _____.
[If applicable – The deadline for filing objections to claims is _____.]

2. *What Is an Impaired Claim or Impaired Equity Interest?*

As noted above, the holder of an allowed claim or equity interest has the right to vote only if it is in a class that is *impaired* under the Plan. As provided in § 1124 of the Code, a class is considered impaired if the Plan alters the legal, equitable, or contractual rights of the members of that class.

3. *Who is Not Entitled to Vote*

The holders of the following five types of claims and equity interests are *not* entitled to vote:
- holders of claims and equity interests that have been disallowed by an order of the Court;

- holders of other claims or equity interests that are not "allowed claims" or "allowed equity interests" (as discussed above), unless they have been "allowed" for voting purposes.

- holders of claims or equity interests in unimpaired classes;

Form 25B OFFICIAL FORMS

B25B (Official Form 25B) (12/08) – Cont.

- holders of claims entitled to priority pursuant to §§ 507(a)(2), (a)(3), and (a)(8) of the Code; and

- holders of claims or equity interests in classes that do not receive or retain any value under the Plan;

- administrative expenses.

Even If You Are Not Entitled to Vote on the Plan, You Have a Right to Object to the Confirmation of the Plan [and to the Adequacy of the Disclosure Statement].

    4.   *Who Can Vote in More Than One Class*

A creditor whose claim has been allowed in part as a secured claim and in part as an unsecured claim, or who otherwise hold claims in multiple classes, is entitled to accept or reject a Plan in each capacity, and should cast one ballot for each claim.

  B.   **Votes Necessary to Confirm the Plan**

If impaired classes exist, the Court cannot confirm the Plan unless (1) at least one impaired class of creditors has accepted the Plan without counting the votes of any insiders within that class, and (2) all impaired classes have voted to accept the Plan, unless the Plan is eligible to be confirmed by "cram down" on non-accepting classes, as discussed later in Section [B.2.].

    1.   *Votes Necessary for a Class to Accept the Plan*

A class of claims accepts the Plan if both of the following occur: (1) the holders of more than one-half (1/2) of the allowed claims in the class, who vote, cast their votes to accept the Plan, and (2) the holders of at least two-thirds (2/3) in dollar amount of the allowed claims in the class, who vote, cast their votes to accept the Plan.

A class of equity interests accepts the Plan if the holders of at least two-thirds (2/3) in amount of the allowed equity interests in the class, who vote, cast their votes to accept the Plan.

    2.   *Treatment of Nonaccepting Classes*

Even if one or more impaired classes reject the Plan, the Court may nonetheless confirm the Plan if the nonaccepting classes are treated in the manner prescribed by § 1129(b) of the Code. A plan that binds nonaccepting classes is commonly referred to as a "cram down" plan. The Code allows the Plan to bind nonaccepting classes of claims or equity interests if it meets all the requirements for consensual confirmation except the voting requirements of § 1129(a)(8) of the Code, does not "discriminate unfairly," and is "fair and equitable" toward each impaired class that has not voted to accept the Plan.

You should consult your own attorney if a "cramdown" confirmation will affect your claim or equity interest, as the variations on this general rule are numerous and complex.

OFFICIAL FORMS — Form 25B

B25B (Official Form 25B) (12/08) – Cont.

C. **Liquidation Analysis**

To confirm the Plan, the Court must find that all creditors and equity interest holders who do not accept the Plan will receive at least as much under the Plan as such claim and equity interest holders would receive in a chapter 7 liquidation. A liquidation analysis is attached to this Disclosure Statement as Exhibit E.

D. **Feasibility**

The Court must find that confirmation of the Plan is not likely to be followed by the liquidation, or the need for further financial reorganization, of the Debtor or any successor to the Debtor, unless such liquidation or reorganization is proposed in the Plan.

1. *Ability to Initially Fund Plan*

The Plan Proponent believes that the Debtor will have enough cash on hand on the effective date of the Plan to pay all the claims and expenses that are entitled to be paid on that date. Tables showing the amount of cash on hand on the effective date of the Plan, and the sources of that cash are attached to this disclosure statement as Exhibit F.

2. *Ability to Make Future Plan Payments And Operate Without Further Reorganization*

The Plan Proponent must also show that it will have enough cash over the life of the Plan to make the required Plan payments.

The Plan Proponent has provided projected financial information. Those projections are listed in Exhibit G.

The Plan Proponent's financial projections show that the Debtor will have an aggregate annual average cash flow, after paying operating expenses and post-confirmation taxes, of $__-__. The final Plan payment is expected to be paid on _____.

[Summarize the numerical projections, and highlight any assumptions that are not in accord with past experience. Explain why such assumptions should now be made.]

You Should Consult with Your Accountant or other Financial Advisor If You Have Any Questions Pertaining to These Projections.

V. **EFFECT OF CONFIRMATION OF PLAN**

A. **DISCHARGE OF DEBTOR** [If the Debtor is not entitled to discharge pursuant to 11 U.S.C. § 1141(d)(3) change this heading to "**NO DISCHARGE OF DEBTOR**."]

[**Option 1 – If Debtor is an individual and § 1141(d)(3) is not applicable**]

Form 25B OFFICIAL FORMS

B25B (Official Form 25B) (12/08) – Cont.

Discharge. Confirmation of the Plan does not discharge any debt provided for in the Plan until the court grants a discharge on completion of all payments under the Plan, or as otherwise provided in § 1141(d)(5) of the Code. Debtor will not be discharged from any debt excepted from discharge under § 523 of the Code, except as provided in Rule 4007(c) of the Federal Rules of Bankruptcy Procedure.

[Option 2 -- If the Debtor is a partnership and § 1141(d)(3) of the Code is not applicable]

Discharge. On the effective date of the Plan, the Debtor shall be discharged from any debt that arose before confirmation of the Plan, subject to the occurrence of the effective date, to the extent specified in § 1141(d)(1)(A) of the Code. However, the Debtor shall not be discharged from any debt imposed by the Plan. After the effective date of the Plan your claims against the Debtor will be limited to the debts imposed by the Plan.

[Option 3 -- If the Debtor is a corporation and § 1141(d)(3) is not applicable]

Discharge. On the effective date of the Plan, the Debtor shall be discharged from any debt that arose before confirmation of the Plan, subject to the occurrence of the effective date, to the extent specified in § 1141(d)(1)(A) of the Code, except that the Debtor shall not be discharged of any debt (i) imposed by the Plan, (ii) of a kind specified in § 1141(d)(6)(A) if a timely complaint was filed in accordance with Rule 4007(c) of the Federal Rules of Bankruptcy Procedure, or (iii) of a kind specified in § 1141(d)(6)(B). After the effective date of the Plan your claims against the Debtor will be limited to the debts described in clauses (i) through (iii) of the preceding sentence.

[Option 4 – If § 1141(d)(3) is applicable]

No Discharge. In accordance with § 1141(d)(3) of the Code, the Debtor will not receive any discharge of debt in this bankruptcy case.

B. **Modification of Plan**

The Plan Proponent may modify the Plan at any time before confirmation of the Plan. However, the Court may require a new disclosure statement and/or revoting on the Plan.

[If the Debtor is not an individual, add the following: "The Plan Proponent may also seek to modify the Plan at any time after confirmation only if (1) the Plan has not been substantially consummated *and* (2) the Court authorizes the proposed modifications after notice and a hearing."]

[If the Debtor is an individual, add the following: "Upon request of the Debtor, the United States trustee, or the holder of an allowed unsecured claim, the Plan may be modified at any time after confirmation of the Plan but before the completion of payments under the Plan, to (1) increase or reduce the amount of payments under the Plan on claims of a particular class, (2) extend or reduce the time period for such payments, or (3) alter the amount of distribution to a creditor whose claim is provided for by the Plan to the extent necessary to take account of any payment of the claim made other than under the Plan."]

C. **Final Decree**

OFFICIAL FORMS   Form 25B

B25B (Official Form 25B) (12/08) – Cont.   16

      Once the estate has been fully administered, as provided in Rule 3022 of the Federal Rules of Bankruptcy Procedure, the Plan Proponent, or such other party as the Court shall designate in the Plan Confirmation Order, shall file a motion with the Court to obtain a final decree to close the case. Alternatively, the Court may enter such a final decree on its own motion.

VI.   OTHER PLAN PROVISIONS

    [Insert other provisions here, as necessary and appropriate.]

_____
[Signature of the Plan Proponent]

_____
[Signature of the Attorney for the Plan Proponent]

B25B (Official Form 25B) (12/08) – Cont.   17

EXHIBITS

B25B (Official Form 25B) (12/08) – Cont.   18

Exhibit A – Copy of Proposed Plan of Reorganization

B25B (Official Form 25B) (12/08) – Cont.   19

Exhibit B – Identity and Value of Material Assets of Debtor

B25B (Official Form 25B) (12/08) – Cont.   20

Exhibit C – Prepetition Financial Statements
(to be taken from those filed with the court)

B25B (Official Form 25B) (12/08) – Cont.   21

Exhibit D – [Most Recently Filed Postpetition Operating Report][Summary of Postpetition Operating Reports]

Form 25B OFFICIAL FORMS

B25B (Official Form 25B) (12/08) – Cont. 22

Exhibit E – Liquidation Analysis

Plan Proponent's Estimated Liquidation Value of Assets

Assets
a. Cash on hand $
b. Accounts receivable $
c. Inventory $
d. Office furniture & equipment $
e. Machinery & equipment $
f. Automobiles $
g. Building & Land $
h. Customer list $
i. Investment property (such as stocks, bonds or other financial assets) $
j. Lawsuits or other claims against third-parties $
k. Other intangibles (such as avoiding powers actions) $

Total Assets at Liquidation Value $

Less:
Secured creditors' recoveries $
Less:
Chapter 7 trustee fees and expenses $
Less:
Chapter 11 administrative expenses $
Less:
Priority claims, excluding administrative expense claims $
[**Less:**
Debtor's claimed exemptions] $

(1) Balance for unsecured claims $

(2) Total dollar amount of unsecured claims $

Percentage of Claims Which Unsecured Creditors Would Receive Or Retain in a Chapter 7 Liquidation: $

Percentage of Claims Which Unsecured Creditors Will Receive or Retain under the Plan: ____% [Divide (1) by (2)]

____%

OFFICIAL FORMS　　　　　　　　　　　　　　　　Form 25B

B25B (Official Form 25B) (12/08) – Cont.

Exhibit F – Cash on hand on the effective date of the Plan

Cash on hand on effective date of the Plan:　　　　　　　　$

Less –

Amount of administrative expenses payable on effective date of the Plan	-
Amount of statutory costs and charges	-
Amount of cure payments for executory contracts	-
Other Plan Payments due on effective date of the Plan	-
Balance after paying these amounts...............	$

The sources of the cash Debtor will have on hand by the effective date of the Plan are estimated as follows:

$		Cash in Debtor's bank account now
+		Additional cash Debtor will accumulate from net earnings between now and effective date of the Plan [state the basis for such projections]
+		Borrowing [separately state terms of repayment]
+		Capital Contributions
+		Other
$		Total [This number should match "cash on hand" figure noted above

B25B (Official Form 25B) (12/08) – Cont.

Exhibit G – Projections of Cash Flow and Earnings for Post-Confirmation Period

(Added Dec. 1, 2008.)

ADVISORY COMMITTEE NOTES
2008 Enactment

　　This form is new. It implements § 433 of the Bankruptcy Abuse Prevention and Consumer Protection Act of 2005, Pub. L. No. 109–8, 119 Stat. 23 (April 20, 2005), which provides for an official form for a disclosure statement that may be used in cases where the debtor (whether an individual or an artificial entity) is a small business debtor under § 101(51D) of the Code. The form provides a format for disseminating information to parties in interest about the plan of reorganization in a small business debtor's chapter 11 case, so that a party can make a reasonably informed judgment whether to accept, reject, or object to a proposed plan of reorganization or liquidation.

　　The form is intended to be used in conjunction with the form small business chapter 11 plan (Official Form 25A). As required by § 433 of the 2005 Act, the form seeks to strike a practical balance between the reasonable needs of the courts, the United States trustee, creditors, and other parties in interest for reasonably complete information, on the one hand, and economy and simplicity for debtors, on the other. The form includes instructions and examples of the types of information needed to complete it.

Form 25B OFFICIAL FORMS

Because the relevant legal requirements for, and effect of, a plan's confirmation may vary depending on the nature of the debtor and the details of the proposed plan, this form is intended to provide an illustrative format for disclosure, rather than a specific prescription for the language or content of a particular disclosure statement. The form highlights the factual and legal disclosures required for adequate disclosure under § 1125 of the Code. The form is not intended to restrict a plan proponent from providing additional information where that would be useful. Plan proponents are encouraged to present material information in as clear a manner as possible, including, where feasible, by providing an accompanying executive summary, approved by the court, that highlights particular creditors' or interest holders' voting status and treatment under the plan.

Rule 3016 specifies the manner in which the disclosure statement is to be filed. Rule 3017 specifies the manner in which the court will consider it. Rule 3017.1 specifies special procedures for the court's conditional approval of a disclosure statement in a small business case.

OFFICIAL FORMS Form 25C

Form 25C. Small Business Monthly Operating Report

B 25C (Official Form 25C) (12/08)

UNITED STATES BANKRUPTCY COURT

In re _____,   Case No. _____
                Debtor
                                                  Small Business Case under Chapter 11

SMALL BUSINESS MONTHLY OPERATING REPORT

Month: _____   Date filed: _____

Line of Business: _____   NAISC Code: _____

IN ACCORDANCE WITH TITLE 28, SECTION 1746, OF THE UNITED STATES CODE, I DECLARE UNDER PENALTY OF PERJURY THAT I HAVE EXAMINED THE FOLLOWING SMALL BUSINESS MONTHLY OPERATING REPORT AND THE ACCOMPANYING ATTACHMENTS AND, TO THE BEST OF MY KNOWLEDGE, THESE DOCUMENTS ARE TRUE, CORRECT AND COMPLETE.

RESPONSIBLE PARTY:

_____
Original Signature of Responsible Party

_____
Printed Name of Responsible Party

Questionnaire: *(All questions to be answered on behalf of the debtor.)*   Yes   No

1. IS THE BUSINESS STILL OPERATING?   ☐   ☐
2. HAVE YOU PAID ALL YOUR BILLS ON TIME THIS MONTH?   ☐   ☐
3. DID YOU PAY YOUR EMPLOYEES ON TIME?   ☐   ☐
4. HAVE YOU DEPOSITED ALL THE RECEIPTS FOR YOUR BUSINESS INTO THE DIP ACCOUNT   ☐   ☐
   THIS MONTH?
5. HAVE YOU FILED ALL OF YOUR TAX RETURNS AND PAID ALL OF YOUR TAXES THIS   ☐   ☐
   MONTH
6. HAVE YOU TIMELY FILED ALL OTHER REQUIRED GOVERNMENT FILINGS?   ☐   ☐
7. HAVE YOU PAID ALL OF YOUR INSURANCE PREMIUMS THIS MONTH?   ☐   ☐
8. DO YOU PLAN TO CONTINUE TO OPERATE THE BUSINESS NEXT MONTH?   ☐   ☐
9. ARE YOU CURRENT ON YOUR QUARTERLY FEE PAYMENT TO THE U.S. TRUSTEE?   ☐   ☐
10. HAVE YOU PAID ANYTHING TO YOUR ATTORNEY OR OTHER PROFESSIONALS THIS   ☐   ☐
    MONTH?
11. DID YOU HAVE ANY UNUSUAL OR SIGNIFICANT UNANTICIPATED EXPENSES THIS   ☐   ☐
    MONTH?
12. HAS THE BUSINESS SOLD ANY GOODS OR PROVIDED SERVICES OR TRANSFERRED ANY   ☐   ☐
    ASSETS TO ANY BUSINESS RELATED TO THE DIP IN ANY WAY?
13. DO YOU HAVE ANY BANK ACCOUNTS OPEN OTHER THAN THE DIP ACCOUNT?   ☐   ☐

Form 25C   OFFICIAL FORMS

B 25C (Official Form 25C) (12/08)

14. HAVE YOU SOLD ANY ASSETS OTHER THAN INVENTORY THIS MONTH? ☐ ☐
15. DID ANY INSURANCE COMPANY CANCEL YOUR POLICY THIS MONTH? ☐ ☐
16. HAVE YOU BORROWED MONEY FROM ANYONE THIS MONTH? ☐ ☐
17. HAS ANYONE MADE AN INVESTMENT IN YOUR BUSINESS THIS MONTH? ☐ ☐
18. HAVE YOU PAID ANY BILLS YOU OWED BEFORE YOU FILED BANKRUPTCY? ☐ ☐

TAXES

DO YOU HAVE ANY PAST DUE TAX RETURNS OR PAST DUE POST-PETITION TAX OBLIGATIONS? ☐ ☐

IF YES, PLEASE PROVIDE A WRITTEN EXPLANATION INCLUDING WHEN SUCH RETURNS WILL BE FILED, OR WHEN SUCH PAYMENTS WILL BE MADE AND THE SOURCE OF THE FUNDS FOR THE PAYMENT.

(Exhibit A)

INCOME

PLEASE SEPARATELY LIST ALL OF THE INCOME YOU RECEIVED FOR THE MONTH. THE LIST SHOULD INCLUDE ALL INCOME FROM CASH AND CREDIT TRANSACTIONS. *(THE U.S. TRUSTEE MAY WAIVE THIS REQUIREMENT.)*

TOTAL INCOME $ _____

SUMMARY OF CASH ON HAND

Cash on Hand at Start of Month $ _____
Cash on Hand at End of Month $ _____

PLEASE PROVIDE THE TOTAL AMOUNT OF CASH CURRENTLY AVAILABLE TO YOU   TOTAL $ _____

(Exhibit B)

EXPENSES

PLEASE SEPARATELY LIST ALL EXPENSES PAID BY CASH OR BY CHECK FROM YOUR BANK ACCOUNTS THIS MONTH. INCLUDE THE DATE PAID, WHO WAS PAID THE MONEY, THE PURPOSE AND THE AMOUNT. *(THE U.S. TRUSTEE MAY WAIVE THIS REQUIREMENT.)*

TOTAL EXPENSES $ _____

(Exhibit C)

CASH PROFIT

INCOME FOR THE MONTH *(TOTAL FROM EXHIBIT B)* $ _____
EXPENSES FOR THE MONTH *(TOTAL FROM EXHIBIT C)* $ _____

(Subtract Line C from Line B)   **CASH PROFIT FOR THE MONTH** $ _____

OFFICIAL FORMS   Form 25C

B 25C (Official Form 25C) (12/08)

UNPAID BILLS

PLEASE ATTACH A LIST OF ALL DEBTS (INCLUDING TAXES) WHICH YOU HAVE INCURRED SINCE THE DATE YOU FILED BANKRUPTCY BUT HAVE NOT PAID. THE LIST MUST INCLUDE THE DATE THE DEBT WAS INCURRED, WHO IS OWED THE MONEY, THE PURPOSE OF THE DEBT AND WHEN THE DEBT IS DUE. *(THE U.S. TRUSTEE MAY WAIVE THIS REQUIREMENT.)*

TOTAL PAYABLES $ _____

(Exhibit D)

MONEY OWED TO YOU

PLEASE ATTACH A LIST OF ALL AMOUNTS OWED TO YOU BY YOUR CUSTOMERS FOR WORK YOU HAVE DONE OR THE MERCHANDISE YOU HAVE SOLD. YOU SHOULD INCLUDE WHO OWES YOU MONEY, HOW MUCH IS OWED AND WHEN IS PAYMENT DUE. *(THE U.S. TRUSTEE MAY WAIVE THIS REQUIREMENT.)*

TOTAL RECEIVABLES $ _____

(Exhibit E)

BANKING INFORMATION

PLEASE ATTACH A COPY OF YOUR LATEST BANK STATEMENT FOR EVERY ACCOUNT YOU HAVE AS OF THE DATE OF THIS FINANCIAL REPORT OR HAD DURING THE PERIOD COVERED BY THIS REPORT.

(Exhibit F)

EMPLOYEES

NUMBER OF EMPLOYEES WHEN THE CASE WAS FILED? _____

NUMBER OF EMPLOYEES AS OF THE DATE OF THIS MONTHLY REPORT? _____

PROFESSIONAL FEES

BANKRUPTCY RELATED:

PROFESSIONAL FEES RELATING TO THE BANKRUPTCY CASE PAID DURING THIS REPORTING PERIOD? $ _____

TOTAL PROFESSIONAL FEES RELATING TO THE BANKRUPTCY CASE PAID SINCE THE FILING OF THE CASE? $ _____

NON-BANKRUPTCY RELATED:

PROFESSIONAL FEES NOT RELATING TO THE BANKRUPTCY CASE PAID DURING THIS REPORTING PERIOD? $ _____

TOTAL PROFESSIONAL FEES NOT RELATING TO THE BANKRUPTCY CASE PAID SINCE THE FILING OF THE CASE? $ _____

Form 25C OFFICIAL FORMS

B 25C (Official Form 25C) (12/08)

PROJECTIONS

COMPARE YOUR ACTUAL INCOME AND EXPENSES TO THE PROJECTIONS FOR THE FIRST 180 DAYS OF YOUR CASE PROVIDED AT THE INITIAL DEBTOR INTERVIEW.

	Projected	Actual	Difference
INCOME	$	$	$
EXPENSES	$	$	$
CASH PROFIT	$	$	$

TOTAL PROJECTED INCOME FOR THE NEXT MONTH: $ _____

TOTAL PROJECTED EXPENSES FOR THE NEXT MONTH: $ _____

TOTAL PROJECTED CASH PROFIT FOR THE NEXT MONTH: $ _____

ADDITIONAL INFORMATION

PLEASE ATTACH ALL FINANCIAL REPORTS INCLUDING AN INCOME STATEMENT AND BALANCE SHEET WHICH YOU PREPARE INTERNALLY.

(Added Dec. 1, 2008.)

ADVISORY COMMITTEE NOTES
2008 Enactment

This form is new. It implements §§ 434 and 435 of the Bankruptcy Abuse Prevention and Consumer Protection Act of 2005, Pub. L. No. 109–8, 119 Stat. 23 (April 20, 2005), which provided for rules and an official form to assist small business debtors in chapter 11 cases to fulfill their responsibilities under § 308 of the Code, a provision added by the 2005 Act. The form directs the debtor to disclose the information required under § 308 and resembles those developed earlier by the United States trustees for use in supervising debtors in possession in chapter 11 cases.

OFFICIAL FORMS   Form 26

Form 26.   Periodic Report Regarding Value, Operations and Profitability of Entities in Which the Debtor's Estate Holds a Substantial or Controlling Interest

B26 (Official Form 26) (12/08)

United States Bankruptcy Court
_____ District of _____

In re_____,   Case No._____

       Debtor   Chapter 11

PERIODIC REPORT REGARDING VALUE, OPERATIONS AND PROFITABILITY OF ENTITIES IN WHICH THE ESTATE OF [NAME OF DEBTOR] HOLDS A SUBSTANTIAL OR CONTROLLING INTEREST

      This is the report as of _____ on the value, operations and profitability of those entities in which the estate holds a substantial or controlling interest, as required by Bankruptcy Rule 2015.3. The estate of [Name of Debtor] holds a substantial or controlling interest in the following entities:

Name of Entity	Interest of the Estate	Tab #

This periodic report (the "Periodic Report") contains separate reports ("Entity Reports") on the value, operations, and profitability of each entity listed above.

      Each Entity Report shall consist of three exhibits. Exhibit A contains a valuation estimate for the entity as of a date not more than two years prior to the date of this report. It also contains a description of the valuation method used. Exhibit B contains a balance sheet, a statement of income (loss), a statement of cash flows, and a statement of changes in shareholders' or partners' equity (deficit) for the period covered by the Entity Report, along with summarized footnotes. Exhibit C contains a description of the entity's business operations.

THIS REPORT MUST BE SIGNED BY A REPRESENTATIVE OF THE TRUSTEE OR DEBTOR IN POSSESSION.

The undersigned, having reviewed the above listing of entities in which the estate of [Debtor] holds a substantial or controlling interest, and being familiar with the Debtor's financial affairs, verifies under the penalty of perjury that the listing is complete, accurate and truthful to the best of his/her knowledge.

Form 26 OFFICIAL FORMS

B26 (Official Form 26) (12/08) – Cont. 2

Date: _____

_____
Signature of Authorized Individual

_____
Name of Authorized Individual

_____
Title of Authorized Individual

[If the Debtor is an individual or in a joint case]

Signature(s) of Debtor(s) (Individual/Joint)

_____
Signature of Debtor

_____
Signature of Joint Debtor

B26 (Official Form 26) (12/08) – Cont. 3

Exhibit A
Valuation Estimate for [Name of Entity]

[Provide a statement of the entity's value and the value of the estate's interest in the entity, including a description of the basis for the valuation, the date of the valuation and the valuation method used. This valuation must be no more than two years old. Indicate the source of this information.]

B26 (Official Form 26) (12/08) – Cont. 4

Exhibit B
Financial Statements for [Insert Name of Entity]

B26 (Official Form 26) (12/08) – Cont. 5

Exhibit B-1
Balance Sheet for [Name of Entity]
As of [date]

[Provide a balance sheet dated as of the end of the most recent six-month period of the current fiscal year and as of the end of the preceding fiscal year. Indicate the source of this information.]

B26 (Official Form 26) (12/08) – Cont.

Exhibit B-2
Statement of Income (Loss) for [Name of Entity]
Period ending [date]

[Provide a statement of income (loss) for the following periods:

    (i) For the initial report:
        a. the period between the end of the preceding fiscal year and the end of the most recent six-month period of the current fiscal year; and
        b. the prior fiscal year.
    (ii) For subsequent reports, since the closing date of the last report.

Indicate the source of this information.]

B26 (Official Form 26) (12/08) – Cont.

Exhibit B-3
Statement of Cash Flows for [Name of Entity]
For the period ending [date]

[Provide a statement of changes in cash flows for the following periods:

    (i) For the initial report:
        a. the period between the end of the preceding fiscal year and the end of the most recent six-month period of the current fiscal year; and
        b. the prior fiscal year.
    (ii) For subsequent reports, since the closing date of the last report.

Indicate the source of this information.]

B26 (Official Form 26) (12/08) – Cont.

Exhibit B-4
Statement of Changes in Shareholders'/Partners' Equity (Deficit) for [Name of Entity]
period ending [date]

[Provide a statement of changes in shareholders'/partners equity (deficit) for the following periods:

    (i) For the initial report:
        a. the period between the end of the preceding fiscal year and the end of the most recent six-month period of the current fiscal year; and
        b. the prior fiscal year.
    (ii) For subsequent reports, since the closing date of the last report.

Indicate the source of this information.]

Form 26 OFFICIAL FORMS

B26 (Official Form 26) (12/08) – Cont.

Exhibit C
Description of Operations for [name of entity]

[Describe the nature and extent of the estate's interest in the entity.

Describe the business conducted and intended to be conducted by the entity, focusing on the entity's dominant business segment(s). Indicate the source of this information.]

(Added Dec. 1, 2008.)

ADVISORY COMMITTEE NOTES
2008 Enactment

This form is new. It implements § 419 of the Bankruptcy Abuse Prevention and Consumer Protection Act of 2005, Pub. L. No. 109–8, 119 Stat. 23 (April 20, 2005), which requires a chapter 11 debtor to file periodic reports on the profitability of any entities in which the estate holds a substantial or controlling interest. The form is to be used when required by Bankruptcy Rule 2015.3, with such variations as may be approved by the court pursuant to subdivisions (d) and (e) of that rule. The form includes instructions and examples of the types of information needed to complete it.

OFFICIAL FORMS   Form 27

Form 27.   **Reaffirmation Agreement Cover Sheet**

B 27 (Official Form 27) (12/13)

UNITED STATES BANKRUPTCY COURT

In re _____,
             Debtor

Case No. _____
Chapter ____

REAFFIRMATION AGREEMENT COVER SHEET

This form must be completed in its entirety and filed, with the reaffirmation agreement attached, within the time set under Rule 4008. It may be filed by any party to the reaffirmation agreement.

1. Creditor's Name: _____

2. Amount of the debt subject to this reaffirmation agreement:
   $_____ on the date of bankruptcy $_____ to be paid under reaffirmation agreement

3. Annual percentage rate of interest: _____% prior to bankruptcy
   _____% under reaffirmation agreement (___ Fixed Rate ___ Adjustable Rate)

4. Repayment terms (if fixed rate): $_____ per month for _____ months

5. Collateral, if any, securing the debt: Current market value: $_____
   Description: _____

6. Does the creditor assert that the debt is nondischargeable? ___Yes ___No
(If yes, attach a declaration setting forth the nature of the debt and basis for the contention that the debt is nondischargeable.)

Debtor's Schedule I and J Entries	Debtor's Income and Expenses as Stated on Reaffirmation Agreement
7A. Total monthly income from $_____ Schedule I, line 12	7B. Monthly income from all $_____ sources after payroll deductions
8A. Total monthly expenses $_____ from Schedule J, line 22	8B. Monthly expenses $_____
9A. Total monthly payments on $_____ reaffirmed debts not listed on Schedule J	9B. Total monthly payments on $_____ reaffirmed debts not included in monthly expenses
	10B. Net monthly income $_____ (Subtract sum of lines 8B and 9B from line 7B. If total is less than zero, put the number in brackets.)

1001

Form 27   OFFICIAL FORMS

B27 (Official Form 27) (12/13)   Page 2

11. Explain with specificity any difference between the income amounts (7A and 7B):

12. Explain with specificity any difference between the expense amounts (8A and 8B):

If line 11 or 12 is completed, the undersigned debtor, and joint debtor if applicable, certifies that any explanation contained on those lines is true and correct.

_____   _____
Signature of Debtor (only required if   Signature of Joint Debtor (if applicable, and only
line 11 or 12 is completed)   required if line 11 or 12 is completed)

Other Information

☐ Check this box if the total on line 10B is less than zero. If that number is less than zero, a presumption of undue hardship arises (unless the creditor is a credit union) and you must explain with specificity the sources of funds available to the Debtor to make the monthly payments on the reaffirmed debt:

Was debtor represented by counsel during the course of negotiating this reaffirmation agreement?
_____ Yes   _____ No

If debtor was represented by counsel during the course of negotiating this reaffirmation agreement, has counsel executed a certification (affidavit or declaration) in support of the reaffirmation agreement?
_____ Yes   _____ No

FILER'S CERTIFICATION

I hereby certify that the attached agreement is a true and correct copy of the reaffirmation agreement between the parties identified on this Reaffirmation Agreement Cover Sheet.

_____
Signature

_____
Print/Type Name & Signer's Relation to Case

(Added Dec. 2009; amended Dec. 2013.)

ADVISORY COMMITTEE NOTES
2009 Enactment

This form is new. It gathers certain financial information, including information necessary for the court to determine whether a reaffirmation agreement creates a presumption of undue hardship under § 524(m) of the Code, and it allows the debtor to provide additional information that may rebut such a presumption.

To implement the requirements of Bankruptcy Rule 4008(b), the form also provides for a disclosure of any differences between the income and expenses reported on schedules I and J and the income and expenses reported in the debtor's statement in support of the reaffirmation agreement, together with an explanation of any such differences.

OFFICIAL FORMS — Form 27

Finally, the form requires a certification that the information supplied is true and correct.

2013 Amendment

Lines 7A and 8A of the form are updated to revise references to new line numbers on Schedules I and J for Total Monthly Income and Total Monthly Expenses.

RELATED UNIFORM LAWS

Uniform Voidable Transactions Act.

Uniform Fraudulent Transfer Act.

Uniform Commercial Code (Selected Sections).

UNIFORM VOIDABLE TRANSACTIONS ACT

(Formerly Uniform Fraudulent Transfer Act)

§ 1. Definitions

As used in this [Act]:

(1) "Affiliate" means:

    (i) a person that directly or indirectly owns, controls, or holds with power to vote, 20 percent or more of the outstanding voting securities of the debtor, other than a person that holds the securities:

        (A) as a fiduciary or agent without sole discretionary power to vote the securities; or

        (B) solely to secure a debt, if the person has not in fact exercised the power to vote;

    (ii) a corporation 20 percent or more of whose outstanding voting securities are directly or indirectly owned, controlled, or held with power to vote, by the debtor or a person that directly or indirectly owns, controls, or holds, with power to vote, 20 percent or more of the outstanding voting securities of the debtor, other than a person that holds the securities:

        (A) as a fiduciary or agent without sole discretionary power to vote the securities; or

        (B) solely to secure a debt, if the person has not in fact exercised the power to vote;

    (iii) a person whose business is operated by the debtor under a lease or other agreement, or a person substantially all of whose assets are controlled by the debtor; or

    (iv) a person that operates the debtor's business under a lease or other agreement or controls substantially all of the debtor's assets.

(2) "Asset" means property of a debtor, but the term does not include:

    (i) property to the extent it is encumbered by a valid lien;

    (ii) property to the extent it is generally exempt under nonbankruptcy law; or

    (iii) an interest in property held in tenancy by the entireties to the extent it is not subject to process by a creditor holding a claim against only one tenant.

(3) "Claim", except as used in "claim for relief", means a right to payment, whether or not the right is reduced to judgment, liquidated, unliquidated, fixed, contingent, matured, unmatured, disputed, undisputed, legal, equitable, secured, or unsecured.

(4) "Creditor" means a person that has a claim.

(5) "Debt" means liability on a claim.

(6) "Debtor" means a person that is liable on a claim.

(7) "Electronic" means relating to technology having electrical, digital, magnetic, wireless, optical, electromagnetic, or similar capabilities.

(8) "Insider" includes:

(i) if the debtor is an individual:

(A) a relative of the debtor or of a general partner of the debtor;

(B) a partnership in which the debtor is a general partner;

(C) a general partner in a partnership described in clause (B); or

(D) a corporation of which the debtor is a director, officer, or person in control;

(ii) if the debtor is a corporation:

(A) a director of the debtor;

(B) an officer of the debtor;

(C) a person in control of the debtor;

(D) a partnership in which the debtor is a general partner;

(E) a general partner in a partnership described in clause (D); or

(F) a relative of a general partner, director, officer, or person in control of the debtor;

(iii) if the debtor is a partnership:

(A) a general partner in the debtor;

(B) a relative of a general partner in, a general partner of, or a person in control of the debtor;

(C) another partnership in which the debtor is a general partner;

(D) a general partner in a partnership described in clause (C); or

(E) a person in control of the debtor;

(iv) an affiliate, or an insider of an affiliate as if the affiliate were the debtor; and

(v) a managing agent of the debtor.

(9) "Lien" means a charge against or an interest in property to secure payment of a debt or performance of an obligation, and includes a security interest created by agreement, a judicial lien obtained by legal or equitable process or proceedings, a common-law lien, or a statutory lien.

(10) "Organization" means a person other than an individual.

(11) "Person" means an individual, estate, business or nonprofit entity, public corporation, government or governmental subdivision, agency, or instrumentality, or other legal entity.

(12) "Property" means anything that may be the subject of ownership.

(13) "Record" means information that is inscribed on a tangible medium or that is stored in an electronic or other medium and is retrievable in perceivable form.

(14) "Relative" means an individual related by consanguinity within the third degree as determined by the common law, a spouse, or an individual related to a spouse within the third degree as so determined, and includes an individual in an adoptive relationship within the third degree.

(15) "Sign" means, with present intent to authenticate or adopt a record:

(i) to execute or adopt a tangible symbol; or

(ii) to attach to or logically associate with the record an electronic symbol, sound, or process.

(16) "Transfer" means every mode, direct or indirect, absolute or conditional, voluntary or involuntary, of disposing of or parting with an asset or an interest in an asset, and includes payment of money, release, lease, license, and creation of a lien or other encumbrance.

(17) "Valid lien" means a lien that is effective against the holder of a judicial lien subsequently obtained by legal or equitable process or proceedings.

§ 2. Insolvency

(a) A debtor is insolvent if, at a fair valuation, the sum of the debtor's debts is greater than the sum of the debtor's assets.

(b) A debtor that is generally not paying the debtor's debts as they become due other than as a result of a bona fide dispute is presumed to be insolvent. The presumption imposes on the party against which the presumption is directed the burden of proving that the nonexistence of insolvency is more probable than its existence.

(c) Assets under this section do not include property that has been transferred, concealed, or removed with intent to hinder, delay, or defraud creditors or that has been transferred in a manner making the transfer voidable under this [Act].

(d) Debts under this section do not include an obligation to the extent it is secured by a valid lien on property of the debtor not included as an asset.

§ 3. Value

(a) Value is given for a transfer or an obligation if, in exchange for the transfer or obligation, property is transferred or an antecedent debt is secured or satisfied, but value does not include an unperformed promise made otherwise than in the ordinary course of the promisor's business to furnish support to the debtor or another person.

(b) For the purposes of Section 4(a)(2) and Section 5, a person gives a reasonably equivalent value if the person acquires an interest of the debtor in an asset pursuant to a regularly conducted, noncollusive foreclosure sale or execution of a power of sale for the acquisition or disposition of the interest of the debtor upon default under a mortgage, deed of trust, or security agreement.

(c) A transfer is made for present value if the exchange between the debtor and the transferee is intended by them to be contemporaneous and is in fact substantially contemporaneous.

§ 4. Transfer or Obligation Voidable as to Present or Future Creditor

(a) A transfer made or obligation incurred by a debtor is voidable as to a creditor, whether the creditor's claim arose before or after the transfer was made or the obligation was incurred, if the debtor made the transfer or incurred the obligation:

(1) with actual intent to hinder, delay, or defraud any creditor of the debtor; or

(2) without receiving a reasonably equivalent value in exchange for the transfer or obligation, and the debtor:

(i) was engaged or was about to engage in a business or a transaction for which the remaining assets of the debtor were unreasonably small in relation to the business or transaction; or

(ii) intended to incur, or believed or reasonably should have believed that the debtor would incur, debts beyond the debtor's ability to pay as they became due.

(b) In determining actual intent under subsection (a)(1), consideration may be given, among other factors, to whether:

(1) the transfer or obligation was to an insider;

(2) the debtor retained possession or control of the property transferred after the transfer;

(3) the transfer or obligation was disclosed or concealed;

(4) before the transfer was made or obligation was incurred, the debtor had been sued or threatened with suit;

(5) the transfer was of substantially all the debtor's assets;

(6) the debtor absconded;

(7) the debtor removed or concealed assets;

(8) the value of the consideration received by the debtor was reasonably equivalent to the value of the asset transferred or the amount of the obligation incurred;

(9) the debtor was insolvent or became insolvent shortly after the transfer was made or the obligation was incurred;

(10) the transfer occurred shortly before or shortly after a substantial debt was incurred; and

(11) the debtor transferred the essential assets of the business to a lienor that transferred the assets to an insider of the debtor.

(c) A creditor making a claim for relief under subsection (a) has the burden of proving the elements of the claim for relief by a preponderance of the evidence.

§ 5. Transfer or Obligation Voidable as to Present Creditor

(a) A transfer made or obligation incurred by a debtor is voidable as to a creditor whose claim arose before the transfer was made or the obligation was incurred if the debtor made the transfer or incurred the obligation without receiving a reasonably equivalent value in exchange for the transfer or obligation and the debtor was insolvent at that time or the debtor became insolvent as a result of the transfer or obligation.

(b) A transfer made by a debtor is voidable as to a creditor whose claim arose before the transfer was made if the transfer was made to an insider for an antecedent debt, the debtor was insolvent at that time, and the insider had reasonable cause to believe that the debtor was insolvent.

(c) Subject to Section 2(b), a creditor making a claim for relief under subsection (a) or (b) has the burden of proving the elements of the claim for relief by a preponderance of the evidence.

§ 6. When Transfer is Made or Obligation is Incurred

For the purposes of this [Act]:

(1) a transfer is made:

(i) with respect to an asset that is real property other than a fixture, but including the interest of a seller or purchaser under a contract for the sale of the asset, when the transfer is so far perfected that a good-faith purchaser of the asset from the debtor against which applicable law permits the transfer to be perfected cannot acquire an interest in the asset that is superior to the interest of the transferee; and

(ii) with respect to an asset that is not real property or that is a fixture, when the transfer is so far perfected that a creditor on a simple contract cannot acquire a judicial lien otherwise than under this [Act] that is superior to the interest of the transferee;

(2) if applicable law permits the transfer to be perfected as provided in paragraph (1) and the transfer is not so perfected before the commencement of an action for relief under this [Act], the transfer is deemed made immediately before the commencement of the action;

(3) if applicable law does not permit the transfer to be perfected as provided in paragraph (1), the transfer is made when it becomes effective between the debtor and the transferee;

(4) a transfer is not made until the debtor has acquired rights in the asset transferred; and

(5) an obligation is incurred:

(i) if oral, when it becomes effective between the parties; or

(ii) if evidenced by a record, when the record signed by the obligor is delivered to or for the benefit of the obligee.

§ 7. Remedies of Creditor

(a) In an action for relief against a transfer or obligation under this [Act], a creditor, subject to the limitations in Section 8, may obtain:

(1) avoidance of the transfer or obligation to the extent necessary to satisfy the creditor's claim;

(2) an attachment or other provisional remedy against the asset transferred or other property of the transferee if available under applicable law; and

(3) subject to applicable principles of equity and in accordance with applicable rules of civil procedure:

(i) an injunction against further disposition by the debtor or a transferee, or both, of the asset transferred or of other property;

(ii) appointment of a receiver to take charge of the asset transferred or of other property of the transferee; or

(iii) any other relief the circumstances may require.

(b) If a creditor has obtained a judgment on a claim against the debtor, the creditor, if the court so orders, may levy execution on the asset transferred or its proceeds.

§ 8. Defenses, Liability, and Protection of Transferee or Obligee

(a) A transfer or obligation is not voidable under Section 4(a)(1) against a person that took in good faith and for a reasonably equivalent value given the debtor or against any subsequent transferee or obligee.

(b) To the extent a transfer is avoidable in an action by a creditor under Section 7(a)(1), the following rules apply:

(1) Except as otherwise provided in this section, the creditor may recover judgment for the value of the asset transferred, as adjusted under subsection (c), or the amount necessary to satisfy the creditor's claim, whichever is less. The judgment may be entered against:

(i) the first transferee of the asset or the person for whose benefit the transfer was made; or

(ii) an immediate or mediate transferee of the first transferee, other than:

(A) a good-faith transferee that took for value; or

(B) an immediate or mediate good-faith transferee of a person described in clause (A).

(2) Recovery pursuant to Section 7(a)(1) or (b) of or from the asset transferred or its proceeds, by levy or otherwise, is available only against a person described in paragraph (1)(i) or (ii).

(c) If the judgment under subsection (b) is based upon the value of the asset transferred, the judgment must be for an amount equal to the value of the asset at the time of the transfer, subject to adjustment as the equities may require.

(d) Notwithstanding voidability of a transfer or an obligation under this [Act], a good-faith transferee or obligee is entitled, to the extent of the value given the debtor for the transfer or obligation, to:

(1) a lien on or a right to retain an interest in the asset transferred;

(2) enforcement of an obligation incurred; or

(3) a reduction in the amount of the liability on the judgment.

(e) A transfer is not voidable under Section 4(a)(2) or Section 5 if the transfer results from:

(1) termination of a lease upon default by the debtor when the termination is pursuant to the lease and applicable law; or

(2) enforcement of a security interest in compliance with Article 9 of the Uniform Commercial Code, other than acceptance of collateral in full or partial satisfaction of the obligation it secures.

(f) A transfer is not voidable under Section 5(b):

(1) to the extent the insider gave new value to or for the benefit of the debtor after the transfer was made, except to the extent the new value was secured by a valid lien;

(2) if made in the ordinary course of business or financial affairs of the debtor and the insider; or

(3) if made pursuant to a good-faith effort to rehabilitate the debtor and the transfer secured present value given for that purpose as well as an antecedent debt of the debtor.

(g) The following rules determine the burden of proving matters referred to in this section:

(1) A party that seeks to invoke subsection (a), (d), (e), or (f) has the burden of proving the applicability of that subsection.

(2) Except as otherwise provided in paragraphs (3) and (4), the creditor has the burden of proving each applicable element of subsection (b) or (c).

(3) The transferee has the burden of proving the applicability to the transferee of subsection (b)(1)(ii)(A) or (B).

(4) A party that seeks adjustment under subsection (c) has the burden of proving the adjustment.

(h) The standard of proof required to establish matters referred to in this section is preponderance of the evidence.

§ 9. Extinguishment of Claim for Relief

A claim for relief with respect to a transfer or obligation under this [Act] is extinguished unless action is brought:

(a) under Section 4(a)(1), not later than four years after the transfer was made or the obligation was incurred or, if later, not later than one year after the transfer or obligation was or could reasonably have been discovered by the claimant;

(b) under Section 4(a)(2) or 5(a), not later than four years after the transfer was made or the obligation was incurred; or

(c) under Section 5(b), not later than one year after the transfer was made.

§ 10. Governing Law

(a) In this section, the following rules determine a debtor's location:

(1) A debtor who is an individual is located at the individual's principal residence.

(2) A debtor that is an organization and has only one place of business is located at its place of business.

(3) A debtor that is an organization and has more than one place of business is located at its chief executive office.

(b) A claim for relief in the nature of a claim for relief under this [Act] is governed by the local law of the jurisdiction in which the debtor is located when the transfer is made or the obligation is incurred.

§ 11. Application to Series Organization

(a) In this section:

(1) "Protected series" means an arrangement, however denominated, created by a series organization that, pursuant to the law under which the series organization is organized, has the characteristics set forth in paragraph (2).

(2) "Series organization" means an organization that, pursuant to the law under which it is organized, has the following characteristics:

(i) The organic record of the organization provides for creation by the organization of one or more protected series, however denominated, with respect to specified property of the organization, and for records to be maintained for each protected series that identify the property of or associated with the protected series.

(ii) Debt incurred or existing with respect to the activities of, or property of or associated with, a particular protected series is enforceable against the property of or associated with the protected series only, and not against the property of or associated with the organization or other protected series of the organization.

(iii) Debt incurred or existing with respect to the activities or property of the organization is enforceable against the property of the organization only, and not against the property of or associated with a protected series of the organization.

(b) A series organization and each protected series of the organization is a separate person for purposes of this [Act], even if for other purposes a protected series is not a person separate from the organization or other protected series of the organization.

Legislative Note: This section should be enacted even if the enacting jurisdiction does not itself have legislation enabling the creation of protected series. For example, in such an enacting jurisdiction this section will apply if a protected series of a series organization organized under the law of a different jurisdiction makes a transfer to another protected series of that organization and, under applicable choice of law rules, the voidability of the transfer is governed by the law of the enacting jurisdiction.

§ 12. Supplementary Provisions

Unless displaced by the provisions of this [Act], the principles of law and equity, including the law merchant and the law relating to principal and agent, estoppel, laches, fraud, misrepresentation, duress, coercion, mistake, insolvency, or other validating or invalidating cause, supplement its provisions.

§ 13. Uniformity of Application and Construction

This [Act] shall be applied and construed to effectuate its general purpose to make uniform the law with respect to the subject of this [Act] among states enacting it.

§ 14. Relation to Electronic Signatures in Global and National Commerce Act

This [Act] modifies, limits, or supersedes the Electronic Signatures in Global and National Commerce Act, 15 U.S.C. Section 7001 et seq., but does not modify, limit, or supersede Section 101(c) of that act, 15 U.S.C. Section 7001(c), or authorize electronic delivery of any of the notices described in Section 103(b) of that act, 15 U.S.C. Section 7003(b).

§ 15. Short Title

This [Act], which was formerly cited as the Uniform Fraudulent Transfer Act, may be cited as the Uniform Voidable Transactions Act.

§ 16. Repeals; Conforming Amendments

(a) . . . .

(b) . . . .

(c) . . . .

§ 16 UNIFORM VOIDABLE TRANSACTIONS ACT

Legislative Note: *The legislation enacting the 2014 amendments in a jurisdiction in which the act is already in force should provide as follows: (i) the amendments apply to a transfer made or obligation incurred on or after the effective date of the enacting legislation, (ii) the amendments do not apply to a transfer made or obligation incurred before the effective date of the enacting legislation, (iii) the amendments do not apply to a right of action that has accrued before the effective date of the enacting legislation, and (iv) for the foregoing purposes a transfer is made and an obligation is incurred at the time provided in Section 6 of the act. In addition, the enacting legislation should revise any reference to the act by its former title in other permanent legislation of the enacting jurisdiction.*

UNIFORM FRAUDULENT TRANSFER ACT*

See, also, Uniform Fraudulent Conveyance Act, to which this act is the successor.

Sec.
1. Definitions.
2. Insolvency.
3. Value.
4. Transfers Fraudulent as to Present and Future Creditors.
5. Transfers Fraudulent as to Present Creditors.
6. When Transfer is Made or Obligation is Incurred.
7. Remedies of Creditors.
8. Defenses, Liability, and Protection of Transferee.
9. Extinguishment of [Claim for Relief] [Cause of Action].
10. Supplementary Provisions.
11. Uniformity of Application and Construction.
12. Short Title.
13. Repeal.

§ 1. Definitions

As used in this [Act]:

(1) "Affiliate" means:

(i) a person who directly or indirectly owns, controls, or holds with power to vote, 20 percent or more of the outstanding voting securities of the debtor, other than a person who holds the securities,

(A) as a fiduciary or agent without sole discretionary power to vote the securities; or

(B) solely to secure a debt, if the person has not exercised the power to vote;

(ii) a corporation 20 percent or more of whose outstanding voting securities are directly or indirectly owned, controlled, or held with power to vote, by the debtor or a person who directly or indirectly owns, controls, or holds, with power to vote, 20 percent or more of the outstanding voting securities of the debtor, other than a person who holds the securities,

(A) as a fiduciary or agent without sole power to vote the securities; or

(B) solely to secure a debt, if the person has not in fact exercised the power to vote;

(iii) a person whose business is operated by the debtor under a lease or other agreement, or a person substantially all of whose assets are controlled by the debtor; or

(iv) a person who operates the debtor's business under a lease or other agreement or controls substantially all of the debtor's assets.

(2) "Asset" means property of a debtor, but the term does not include:

(i) property to the extent it is encumbered by a valid lien;

(ii) property to the extent it is generally exempt under nonbankruptcy law; or

(iii) an interest in property held in tenancy by the entireties to the extent it is not subject to process by a creditor holding a claim against only one tenant.

---

* Reproduced by permission of the National Conference of Commissioners on Uniform State Laws.

(3) "Claim" means a right to payment, whether or not the right is reduced to judgment, liquidated, unliquidated, fixed, contingent, matured, unmatured, disputed, undisputed, legal, equitable, secured, or unsecured.

(4) "Creditor" means a person who has a claim.

(5) "Debt" means liability on a claim.

(6) "Debtor" means a person who is liable on a claim.

(7) "Insider" includes:

    (i) if the debtor is an individual,

        (A) a relative of the debtor or of a general partner of the debtor;

        (B) a partnership in which the debtor is a general partner;

        (C) a general partner in a partnership described in clause (B); or

        (D) a corporation of which the debtor is a director, officer, or person in control;

    (ii) if the debtor is a corporation,

        (A) a director of the debtor;

        (B) an officer of the debtor;

        (C) a person in control of the debtor;

        (D) a partnership in which the debtor is a general partner;

        (E) a general partner in a partnership described in clause (D); or

        (F) a relative of a general partner, director, officer, or person in control of the debtor;

    (iii) if the debtor is a partnership,

        (A) a general partner in the debtor;

        (B) a relative of a general partner in, a general partner of, or a person in control of the debtor;

        (C) another partnership in which the debtor is a general partner;

        (D) a general partner in a partnership described in clause (C); or

        (E) a person in control of the debtor;

    (iv) an affiliate, or an insider of an affiliate as if the affiliate were the debtor; and

    (v) a managing agent of the debtor.

(8) "Lien" means a charge against or an interest in property to secure payment of a debt or performance of an obligation, and includes a security interest created by agreement, a judicial lien obtained by legal or equitable process or proceedings, a common-law lien, or a statutory lien.

(9) "Person" means an individual, partnership, corporation, association, organization, government or governmental subdivision or agency, business trust, estate, trust, or any other legal or commercial entity.

(10) "Property" means anything that may be the subject of ownership.

(11) "Relative" means an individual related by consanguinity within the third degree as determined by the common law, a spouse, or an individual related to a spouse within the third degree as so determined, and includes an individual in an adoptive relationship within the third degree.

(12) "Transfer" means every mode, direct or indirect, absolute or conditional, voluntary or involuntary, of disposing of or parting with an asset or an interest in an asset, and includes payment of money, release, lease, and creation of a lien or other encumbrance.

(13) "Valid lien" means a lien that is effective against the holder of a judicial lien subsequently obtained by legal or equitable process or proceedings.

§ 2. Insolvency

(a) A debtor is insolvent if the sum of the debtor's debts is greater than all of the debtor's assets at a fair valuation.

(b) A debtor who is generally not paying his [or her] debts as they become due is presumed to be insolvent.

(c) A partnership is insolvent under subsection (a) if the sum of the partnership's debts is greater than the aggregate, at a fair valuation, of all of the partnership's assets and the sum of the excess of the value of each general partner's nonpartnership assets over the partner's nonpartnership debts.

(d) Assets under this section do not include property that has been transferred, concealed, or removed with intent to hinder, delay, or defraud creditors or that has been transferred in a manner making the transfer voidable under this [Act].

(e) Debts under this section do not include an obligation to the extent it is secured by a valid lien on property of the debtor not included as an asset.

§ 3. Value

(a) Value is given for a transfer or an obligation if, in exchange for the transfer or obligation, property is transferred or an antecedent debt is secured or satisfied, but value does not include an unperformed promise made otherwise than in the ordinary course of the promisor's business to furnish support to the debtor or another person.

(b) For the purposes of Sections 4(a)(2) and 5, a person gives a reasonably equivalent value if the person acquires an interest of the debtor in an asset pursuant to a regularly conducted, noncollusive foreclosure sale or execution of a power of sale for the acquisition or disposition of the interest of the debtor upon default under a mortgage, deed of trust, or security agreement.

(c) A transfer is made for present value if the exchange between the debtor and the transferee is intended by them to be contemporaneous and is in fact substantially contemporaneous.

§ 4. Transfers Fraudulent as to Present and Future Creditors

(a) A transfer made or obligation incurred by a debtor is fraudulent as to a creditor, whether the creditor's claim arose before or after the transfer was made or the obligation was incurred, if the debtor made the transfer or incurred the obligation:

(1) with actual intent to hinder, delay, or defraud any creditor of the debtor; or

(2) without receiving a reasonably equivalent value in exchange for the transfer or obligation, and the debtor:

(i) was engaged or was about to engage in a business or a transaction for which the remaining assets of the debtor were unreasonably small in relation to the business or transaction; or

(ii) intended to incur, or believed or reasonably should have believed that he [or she] would incur, debts beyond his [or her] ability to pay as they became due.

(b) In determining actual intent under subsection (a)(1), consideration may be given, among other factors, to whether:

(1) the transfer or obligation was to an insider;

(2) the debtor retained possession or control of the property transferred after the transfer;

(3) the transfer or obligation was disclosed or concealed;

(4) before the transfer was made or obligation was incurred, the debtor had been sued or threatened with suit;

(5) the transfer was of substantially all the debtor's assets;

(6) the debtor absconded;

(7) the debtor removed or concealed assets;

(8) the value of the consideration received by the debtor was reasonably equivalent to the value of the asset transferred or the amount of the obligation incurred;

(9) the debtor was insolvent or became insolvent shortly after the transfer was made or the obligation was incurred;

(10) the transfer occurred shortly before or shortly after a substantial debt was incurred; and

(11) the debtor transferred the essential assets of the business to a lienor who transferred the assets to an insider of the debtor.

§ 5. Transfers Fraudulent as to Present Creditors

(a) A transfer made or obligation incurred by a debtor is fraudulent as to a creditor whose claim arose before the transfer was made or the obligation was incurred if the debtor made the transfer or incurred the obligation without receiving a reasonably equivalent value in exchange for the transfer or obligation and the debtor was insolvent at that time or the debtor became insolvent as a result of the transfer or obligation.

(b) A transfer made by a debtor is fraudulent as to a creditor whose claim arose before the transfer was made if the transfer was made to an insider for an antecedent debt, the debtor was insolvent at that time, and the insider had reasonable cause to believe that the debtor was insolvent.

§ 6. When Transfer is Made or Obligation is Incurred

For the purposes of this [Act]:

(1) a transfer is made:

(i) with respect to an asset that is real property other than a fixture, but including the interest of a seller or purchaser under a contract for the sale of the asset, when the transfer is so far perfected that a good-faith purchaser of the asset from the debtor against whom applicable law permits the transfer to be perfected cannot acquire an interest in the asset that is superior to the interest of the transferee; and

(ii) with respect to an asset that is not real property or that is a fixture, when the transfer is so far perfected that a creditor on a simple contract cannot acquire a judicial lien otherwise than under this [Act] that is superior to the interest of the transferee;

(2) if applicable law permits the transfer to be perfected as provided in paragraph (1) and the transfer is not so perfected before the commencement of an action for relief under this [Act], the transfer is deemed made immediately before the commencement of the action;

(3) if applicable law does not permit the transfer to be perfected as provided in paragraph (1), the transfer is made when it becomes effective between the debtor and the transferee;

(4) a transfer is not made until the debtor has acquired rights in the asset transferred;

(5) an obligation is incurred:

(i) if oral, when it becomes effective between the parties; or

(ii) if evidenced by a writing, when the writing executed by the obligor is delivered to or for the benefit of the obligee.

§ 7. Remedies of Creditors

(a) In an action for relief against a transfer or obligation under this [Act], a creditor, subject to the limitations in Section 8, may obtain:

(1) avoidance of the transfer or obligation to the extent necessary to satisfy the creditor's claim;

[(2) an attachment or other provisional remedy against the asset transferred or other property of the transferee in accordance with the procedure prescribed by [ ];]

(3) subject to applicable principles of equity and in accordance with applicable rules of civil procedure,

(i) an injunction against further disposition by the debtor or a transferee, or both, of the asset transferred or of other property;

(ii) appointment of a receiver to take charge of the asset transferred or of other property of the transferee; or

(iii) any other relief the circumstances may require.

(b) If a creditor has obtained a judgment on a claim against the debtor, the creditor, if the court so orders, may levy execution on the asset transferred or its proceeds.

§ 8. Defenses, Liability, and Protection of Transferee

(a) A transfer or obligation is not voidable under Section 4(a)(1) against a person who took in good faith and for a reasonably equivalent value or against any subsequent transferee or obligee.

(b) Except as otherwise provided in this section, to the extent a transfer is voidable in an action by a creditor under Section 7(a)(1), the creditor may recover judgment for the value of the asset transferred, as adjusted under subsection (c), or the amount necessary to satisfy the creditor's claim, whichever is less. The judgment may be entered against:

(1) the first transferee of the asset or the person for whose benefit the transfer was made; or

(2) any subsequent transferee other than a good faith transferee who took for value or from any subsequent transferee.

(c) If the judgment under subsection (b) is based upon the value of the asset transferred, the judgment must be for an amount equal to the value of the asset at the time of the transfer, subject to adjustment as the equities may require.

(d) Notwithstanding voidability of a transfer or an obligation under this [Act], a good-faith transferee or obligee is entitled, to the extent of the value given the debtor for the transfer or obligation, to

(1) a lien on or a right to retain any interest in the asset transferred;

(2) enforcement of any obligation incurred; or

(3) a reduction in the amount of the liability on the judgment.

(e) A transfer is not voidable under Section 4(a)(2) or Section 5 if the transfer results from:

(1) termination of a lease upon default by the debtor when the termination is pursuant to the lease and applicable law; or

(2) enforcement of a security interest in compliance with Article 9 of the Uniform Commercial Code.

(f) A transfer is not voidable under Section 5(b):

(1) to the extent the insider gave new value to or for the benefit of the debtor after the transfer was made unless the new value was secured by a valid lien;

(2) if made in the ordinary course of business or financial affairs of the debtor and the insider; or

(3) if made pursuant to a good-faith effort to rehabilitate the debtor and the transfer secured present value given for that purpose as well as an antecedent debt of the debtor.

§ 9. Extinguishment of [Claim for Relief] [Cause of Action]

A [claim for relief] [cause of action] with respect to a fraudulent transfer or obligation under this [Act] is extinguished unless action is brought:

(a) under Section 4(a)(1), within 4 years after the transfer was made or the obligation was incurred or, if later, within one year after the transfer or obligation was or could reasonably have been discovered by the claimant;

(b) under Section 4(a)(2) or 5(a), within 4 years after the transfer was made or the obligation was incurred; or

(c) under Section 5(b), within one year after the transfer was made or the obligation was incurred.

§ 10. Supplementary Provisions

Unless displaced by the provisions of this [Act], the principles of law and equity, including the law merchant and the law relating to principal and agent, estoppel, laches, fraud, misrepresentation, duress, coercion, mistake, insolvency, or other validating or invalidating cause, supplement its provisions.

§ 11. Uniformity of Application and Construction

This [Act] shall be applied and construed to effectuate its general purpose to make uniform the law with respect to the subject of this [Act] among states enacting it.

§ 12. Short Title

This [Act] may be cited as the Uniform Fraudulent Transfer Act.

§ 13. Repeal

The following acts and all other acts and parts of acts inconsistent herewith are hereby repealed:

UNIFORM COMMERCIAL CODE

Selected Sections

Reprinted by permission of the National Conference of Commissioners on Uniform State Laws

Article 1. General Provisions

The American Law Institute and National Conference of Commissioners on Uniform State Laws

Part 2. General Definitions And Principles Of Interpretation

§ 1–201. General Definitions

* * *

(b) Subject to definitions contained in other articles of [the Uniform Commercial Code] that apply to particular articles or parts thereof:

* * *

(3) "Agreement", as distinguished from "contract", means the bargain of the parties in fact, as found in their language or inferred from other circumstances, including course of performance, course of dealing, or usage of trade as provided in Section 1–303.

* * *

(9) "Buyer in ordinary course of business" means a person that buys goods in good faith, without knowledge that the sale violates the rights of another person in the goods, and in the ordinary course from a person, other than a pawnbroker, in the business of selling goods of that kind. * * *

* * *

(11) "Consumer" means an individual who enters into a transaction primarily for personal, family, or household purposes

* * *

(13) "Creditor" includes a general creditor, a secured creditor, a lien creditor, and any representative of creditors, including an assignee for the benefit of creditors, a trustee in bankruptcy, a receiver in equity, and an executor or administrator of an insolvent debtor's or assignor's estate.

* * *

(20) "Good faith," except as otherwise provided in Article 5, means honesty in fact and the observance of reasonable commercial standards of fair dealing.

* * *

(29) "Purchase" means taking by sale, lease, discount, negotiation, mortgage, pledge, lien, security interest, issue or reissue, gift, or any other voluntary transaction creating an interest in property.

(30) "Purchaser" means a person that takes by purchase.

(31) "Record" means information that is inscribed on a tangible medium or that is stored in an electronic or other medium and is retrievable in perceivable form.

* * *

(35) "Security interest" means an interest in personal property or fixtures which secures payment or performance of an obligation. "Security interest" includes any interest of a consignor and a buyer of accounts, chattel paper, a payment intangible, or a promissory note in a transaction that is subject to Article 9. "Security interest" does not include the special property interest of a buyer of goods on identification of those goods to a contract for sale under Section 2–401, but a buyer may also acquire a "security interest" by complying with Article 9. Except as otherwise provided in Section 2–505, the right of a seller or lessor of goods under Article 2 or 2A to retain or acquire possession of the goods is not a "security interest", but a seller or lessor may also acquire a "security interest" by complying with Article 9. The retention or reservation of title by a seller of goods notwithstanding shipment or delivery to the buyer under Section 2–401 is limited in effect to a reservation of a "security interest." Whether a transaction in the form of a lease creates a "security interest" is determined pursuant to Section 1–203.

* * *

(37) "Signed" includes using any symbol executed or adopted with present intention to adopt or accept a writing.

* * *

As amended in 2003.

Uniform Commercial Code

Article 2. Sales

Official Text

The American Law Institute and National Conference of Commissioners on Uniform State Laws

Part 7. Remedies

§ 2–702. Seller's Remedies On Discovery Of Buyer's Insolvency

(1) If the seller discovers that the buyer is insolvent, the seller may refuse delivery except for cash including payment for all goods theretofore delivered under the contract, and stop delivery under Section 2–705.

(2) If the seller discovers that the buyer has received goods on credit while insolvent, the seller may reclaim the goods upon demand made within a reasonable time after the buyer's receipt of the goods. Except as provided in this subsection, the seller may not base a right to reclaim goods on the buyer's fraudulent or innocent misrepresentation of solvency or of intent to pay.

(3) The seller's right to reclaim under subsection (2) is subject to the rights of a buyer in ordinary course of business or other good-faith purchaser for value under Section 2–403. Successful reclamation of goods excludes all other remedies with respect to them.

As amended in 2003.

Uniform Commercial Code

Article 9. Secured Transactions

The American Law Institute and National Conference of Commissioners on Uniform State Laws

Part 1. General Provisions

[Subpart 1. Short Title, Definitions, And General Concepts]

§ 9–102. Definitions And Index Of Definitions

(a) [Article 9 definitions.] In this article:

* * *

(3) "Account debtor" means a person obligated on an account, chattel paper, or general intangible. The term does not include persons obligated to pay a negotiable instrument, even if the instrument constitutes part of chattel paper.

* * *

(7) "Authenticate" means:

(A) to sign; or

(B) with present intent to adopt or accept a record, to attach to or logically associate with the record an electronic sound, symbol, or process.

* * *

(9) "Cash proceeds" means proceeds that are money, checks, deposit accounts, or the like.

* * *

(12) "Collateral" means the property subject to a security interest or agricultural lien. The term includes:

(A) proceeds to which a security interest attaches;

(B) accounts, chattel paper, payment intangibles, and promissory notes that have been sold; and

(C) goods that are the subject of a consignment.

(13) "Commercial tort claim" means a claim arising in tort with respect to which:

(A) the claimant is an organization; or

(B) the claimant is an individual and the claim:

(i) arose in the course of the claimant's business or profession; and

(ii) does not include damages arising out of personal injury to or the death of an individual.

* * *

(23) "Consumer goods" means goods that are used or bought for use primarily for personal, family, or household purposes.

* * *

(28) "Debtor" means:

(A) a person having an interest, other than a security interest or other lien, in the collateral, whether or not the person is an obligor;

(B) a seller of accounts, chattel paper, payment intangibles, or promissory notes; or

§ 9–102   UNIFORM COMMERCIAL CODE

      (C)   a consignee.

* * *

(33) "Equipment" means goods other than inventory, farm products, or consumer goods.

(34) "Farm products" means goods, other than standing timber, with respect to which the debtor is engaged in a farming operation and which are:

      (A)   crops grown, growing, or to be grown, including:

           (i)   crops produced on trees, vines, and bushes; and

           (ii)   aquatic goods produced in aquacultural operations;

      (B)   livestock, born or unborn, including aquatic goods produced in aquacultural operations;

      (C)   supplies used or produced in a farming operation; or

      (D)   products of crops or livestock in their unmanufactured states.

* * *

(44) "Goods" means all things that are movable when a security interest attaches. The term includes (i) fixtures, (ii) standing timber that is to be cut and removed under a conveyance or contract for sale, (iii) the unborn young of animals, (iv) crops grown, growing, or to be grown, even if the crops are produced on trees, vines, or bushes, and (v) manufactured homes. The term also includes a computer program embedded in goods and any supporting information provided in connection with a transaction relating to the program if (i) the program is associated with the goods in such a manner that it customarily is considered part of the goods, or (ii) by becoming the owner of the goods, a person acquires a right to use the program in connection with the goods. The term does not include a computer program embedded in goods that consist solely of the medium in which the program is embedded. The term also does not include accounts, chattel paper, commercial tort claims, deposit accounts, documents, general intangibles, instruments, investment property, letter-of-credit rights, letters of credit, money, or oil, gas, or other minerals before extraction.

* * *

(48) "Inventory" means goods, other than farm products, which:

      (A)   are leased by a person as lessor;

      (B)   are held by a person for sale or lease or to be furnished under a contract of service;

      (C)   are furnished by a person under a contract of service; or

      (D)   consist of raw materials, work in process, or materials used or consumed in a business.

(49) "Investment property" means a security, whether certificated or uncertificated, security entitlement, securities account, commodity contract, or commodity account.

* * *

(52) "Lien creditor" means:

      (A)   a creditor that has acquired a lien on the property involved by attachment, levy, or the like;

      (B)   an assignee for benefit of creditors from the time of assignment;

      (C)   a trustee in bankruptcy from the date of the filing of the petition; or

      (D)   a receiver in equity from the time of appointment.

* * *

(57) "New value" means (i) money, (ii) money's worth in property, services, or new credit, or (iii) release by a transferee of an interest in property previously transferred to the transferee. The term does not include an obligation substituted for another obligation.

* * *

(64) "Proceeds", except as used in Section 9–609(b), means the following property:

(A) whatever is acquired upon the sale, lease, license, exchange, or other disposition of collateral;

(B) whatever is collected on, or distributed on account of, collateral;

(C) rights arising out of collateral;

(D) to the extent of the value of collateral, claims arising out of the loss, nonconformity, or interference with the use of, defects or infringement of rights in, or damage to, the collateral; or

(E) to the extent of the value of collateral and to the extent payable to the debtor or the secured party, insurance payable by reason of the loss or nonconformity of, defects or infringement of rights in, or damage to, the collateral.

* * *

(70) "Record", except as used in "for record", "of record", "record or legal title", and "record owner", means information that is inscribed on a tangible medium or which is stored in an electronic or other medium and is retrievable in perceivable form.

* * *

(73) "Secured party" means:

(A) a person in whose favor a security interest is created or provided for under a security agreement, whether or not any obligation to be secured is outstanding;

(B) a person that holds an agricultural lien;

(C) a consignor;

(D) a person to which accounts, chattel paper, payment intangibles, or promissory notes have been sold;

(E) a trustee, indenture trustee, agent, collateral agent, or other representative in whose favor a security interest or agricultural lien is created or provided for; or

(F) a person that holds a security interest arising under Section 2–401, 2–505, 2–711(3), 2A–508(5), 4–210, or 5–118.

(74) "Security agreement" means an agreement that creates or provides for a security interest.

* * *

[Subpart 2. Applicability Of Article]

§ 9–109. Scope

(a) [General scope of article.] Except as otherwise provided in subsections (c) and (d), this article applies to:

(1) a transaction, regardless of its form, that creates a security interest in personal property or fixtures by contract;

(2) an agricultural lien;

(3) a sale of accounts, chattel paper, payment intangibles, or promissory notes;

(4) a consignment;

(5) a security interest arising under Section 2–401, 2–505, 2–711(3), or 2A–508(5), as provided in Section 9–110; and

(6) a security interest arising under Section 4–210 or 5–118.

§ 9–201

* * *

Part 2. Effectiveness Of Security Agreement; Attachment Of Security Interest; Rights Of Parties To Security Agreement

[Subpart 1. Effectiveness And Attachment]

§ 9–201. General Effectiveness Of Security Agreement

(a) [General effectiveness.] Except as otherwise provided in [the Uniform Commercial Code], a security agreement is effective according to its terms between the parties, against purchasers of the collateral, and against creditors.

* * *

§ 9–203. Attachment And Enforceability Of Security Interest; Proceeds; Supporting Obligations; Formal Requisites

(a) [Attachment.] A security interest attaches to collateral when it becomes enforceable against the debtor with respect to the collateral, unless an agreement expressly postpones the time of attachment.

(b) [Enforceability.] Except as otherwise provided in subsections (c) through (i), a security interest is enforceable against the debtor and third parties with respect to the collateral only if:

(1) value has been given;

(2) the debtor has rights in the collateral or the power to transfer rights in the collateral to a secured party; and

(3) one of the following conditions is met:

(A) the debtor has authenticated a security agreement that provides a description of the collateral and, if the security interest covers timber to be cut, a description of the land concerned;

(B) the collateral is not a certificated security and is in the possession of the secured party under Section 9–313 pursuant to the debtor's security agreement;

(C) the collateral is a certificated security in registered form and the security certificate has been delivered to the secured party under Section 8–301 pursuant to the debtor's security agreement; or

(D) the collateral is deposit accounts, electronic chattel paper, investment property, letter-of-credit rights, or electronic documents, and the secured party has control under Section 7–106, 9–104, 9–105, 9–106, or 9–107 pursuant to the debtor's security agreement.

* * *

§ 9–204. After-Acquired Property; Future Advances

(a) [After-acquired collateral.] Except as otherwise provided in subsection (b), a security agreement may create or provide for a security interest in after-acquired collateral.

(b) [When after-acquired property clause not effective.] A security interest does not attach under a term constituting an after-acquired property clause to:

(1) consumer goods, other than an accession when given as additional security, unless the debtor acquires rights in them within 10 days after the secured party gives value; or

(2) a commercial tort claim.

(c) [Future advances and other value.] A security agreement may provide that collateral secures, or that accounts, chattel paper, payment intangibles, or promissory notes are sold in connection with, future advances or other value, whether or not the advances or value are given pursuant to commitment.

Part 3. Perfection And Priority

[Subpart 1. Law Governing Perfection And Priority]

§ 9-301. Law Governing Perfection And Priority Of Security Interests

Except as otherwise provided in Sections 9-303 through 9-306, the following rules determine the law governing perfection, the effect of perfection or nonperfection, and the priority of a security interest in collateral:

(1) Except as otherwise provided in this section, while a debtor is located in a jurisdiction, the local law of that jurisdiction governs perfection, the effect of perfection or nonperfection, and the priority of a security interest in collateral.

(2) While collateral is located in a jurisdiction, the local law of that jurisdiction governs perfection, the effect of perfection or nonperfection, and the priority of a possessory security interest in that collateral.

* * *

§ 9-307. Location Of Debtor

(a) ["Place of business."] In this section, "place of business" means a place where a debtor conducts its affairs.

(b) [Debtor's location: general rules.] Except as otherwise provided in this section, the following rules determine a debtor's location:

(1) A debtor who is an individual is located at the individual's principal residence.

(2) A debtor that is an organization and has only one place of business is located at its place of business.

(3) A debtor that is an organization and has more than one place of business is located at its chief executive office.

* * *

[Subpart 2. Perfection]

§ 9-308. When Security Interest Or Agricultural Lien Is Perfected; Continuity Of Perfection

(a) [Perfection of security interest.] Except as otherwise provided in this section and Section 9-309, a security interest is perfected if it has attached and all of the applicable requirements for perfection in Sections 9-310 through 9-316 have been satisfied. A security interest is perfected when it attaches if the applicable requirements are satisfied before the security interest attaches.

* * *

§ 9-309. Security Interest Perfected Upon Attachment

The following security interests are perfected when they attach:

(1) a purchase-money security interest in consumer goods, except as otherwise provided in Section 9–311(b) with respect to consumer goods that are subject to a statute or treaty described in Section 9–311(a);

(2) an assignment of accounts or payment intangibles which does not by itself or in conjunction with other assignments to the same assignee transfer a significant part of the assignor's outstanding accounts or payment intangibles;

* * *

§ 9–310. When Filing Required To Perfect Security Interest Or Agricultural Lien; Security Interests And Agricultural Liens To Which Filing Provisions Do Not Apply

(a) [General rule: perfection by filing.] Except as otherwise provided in subsection (b) and Section 9–312(b), a financing statement must be filed to perfect all security interests and agricultural liens.

* * *

§ 9–313. When Possession By Or Delivery To Secured Party Perfects Security Interest Without Filing

(a) [Perfection by possession or delivery.] Except as otherwise provided in subsection (b), a secured party may perfect a security interest in tangible negotiable documents, goods, instruments, money, or tangible chattel paper by taking possession of the collateral. A secured party may perfect a security interest in certificated securities by taking delivery of the certificated securities under Section 8–301.

* * *

§ 9–315. Secured Party's Rights On Disposition Of Collateral And In Proceeds

(a) [Disposition of collateral: continuation of security interest or agricultural lien; proceeds.] Except as otherwise provided in this article and in Section 2–403(2):

(1) a security interest or agricultural lien continues in collateral notwithstanding sale, lease, license, exchange, or other disposition thereof unless the secured party authorized the disposition free of the security interest or agricultural lien; and

(2) a security interest attaches to any identifiable proceeds of collateral.

* * *

(c) [Perfection of security interest in proceeds.] A security interest in proceeds is a perfected security interest if the security interest in the original collateral was perfected.

(d) [Continuation of perfection.] A perfected security interest in proceeds becomes unperfected on the 21st day after the security interest attaches to the proceeds unless:

(1) the following conditions are satisfied:

(A) a filed financing statement covers the original collateral;

(B) the proceeds are collateral in which a security interest may be perfected by filing in the office in which the financing statement has been filed; and

(C) the proceeds are not acquired with cash proceeds;

(2) the proceeds are identifiable cash proceeds; or

(3) the security interest in the proceeds is perfected other than under subsection (c) when the security interest attaches to the proceeds or within 20 days thereafter.

(e) [When perfected security interest in proceeds becomes unperfected.] If a filed financing statement covers the original collateral, a security interest in proceeds which remains perfected under subsection (d)(1) becomes unperfected at the later of:

(1) when the effectiveness of the filed financing statement lapses under Section 9–515 or is terminated under Section 9–513; or

(2) the 21st day after the security interest attaches to the proceeds.

[Subpart 3. Priority]

§ 9–317. Interests That Take Priority Over Or Take Free Of Security Interest Or Agricultural Lien

(a) [Conflicting security interests and rights of lien creditors.] A security interest or agricultural lien is subordinate to the rights of:

(1) a person entitled to priority under Section 9–322; and

(2) except as otherwise provided in subsection (e), a person that becomes a lien creditor before the earlier of the time:

(A) the security interest or agricultural lien is perfected; or

(B) one of the conditions specified in Section 9–203(b)(3) is met and a financing statement covering the collateral is filed.

(b) [Buyers that receive delivery.] Except as otherwise provided in subsection (e), a buyer, other than a secured party, of tangible chattel paper, tangible documents, goods, instruments, or a certificated security takes free of a security interest or agricultural lien if the buyer gives value and receives delivery of the collateral without knowledge of the security interest or agricultural lien and before it is perfected.

* * *

(e) [Purchase-money security interest.] Except as otherwise provided in Sections 9–320 and 9–321, if a person files a financing statement with respect to a purchase-money security interest before or within 20 days after the debtor receives delivery of the collateral, the security interest takes priority over the rights of a buyer, lessee, or lien creditor which arise between the time the security interest attaches and the time of filing.

§ 9–320. Buyer Of Goods

(a) [Buyer in ordinary course of business.] Except as otherwise provided in subsection (e), a buyer in ordinary course of business, other than a person buying farm products from a person engaged in farming operations, takes free of a security interest created by the buyer's seller, even if the security interest is perfected and the buyer knows of its existence.

(b) [Buyer of consumer goods.] Except as otherwise provided in subsection (e), a buyer of goods from a person who used or bought the goods for use primarily for personal, family, or household purposes takes free of a security interest, even if perfected, if the buyer buys:

(1) without knowledge of the security interest;

(2) for value;

(3) primarily for the buyer's personal, family, or household purposes; and

(4) before the filing of a financing statement covering the goods.

* * *

(e) [Possessory security interest not affected.] Subsections (a) and (b) do not affect a security interest in goods in the possession of the secured party under Section 9–313.

§ 9–322. Priorities Among Conflicting Security Interests In And Agricultural Liens On Same Collateral

(a) [General priority rules.] Except as otherwise provided in this section, priority among conflicting security interests and agricultural liens in the same collateral is determined according to the following rules:

(1) Conflicting perfected security interests and agricultural liens rank according to priority in time of filing or perfection. Priority dates from the earlier of the time a filing covering the collateral is first made or the security interest or agricultural lien is first perfected, if there is no period thereafter when there is neither filing nor perfection.

(2) A perfected security interest or agricultural lien has priority over a conflicting unperfected security interest or agricultural lien.

(3) The first security interest or agricultural lien to attach or become effective has priority if conflicting security interests and agricultural liens are unperfected.

(b) [Time of perfection: proceeds and supporting obligations.] For the purposes of subsection (a)(1):

(1) the time of filing or perfection as to a security interest in collateral is also the time of filing or perfection as to a security interest in proceeds; and

(2) the time of filing or perfection as to a security interest in collateral supported by a supporting obligation is also the time of filing or perfection as to a security interest in the supporting obligation.

* * *

§ 9–323. Future Advances

* * *

(b) [Lien creditor.] Except as otherwise provided in subsection (c), a security interest is subordinate to the rights of a person that becomes a lien creditor to the extent that the security interest secures an advance made more than 45 days after the person becomes a lien creditor unless the advance is made:

(1) without knowledge of the lien; or

(2) pursuant to a commitment entered into without knowledge of the lien.

* * *

(d) [Buyer of goods.] Except as otherwise provided in subsection (e), a buyer of goods other than a buyer in ordinary course of business takes free of a security interest to the extent that it secures advances made after the earlier of:

(1) the time the secured party acquires knowledge of the buyer's purchase; or

(2) 45 days after the purchase.

(e) [Advances made pursuant to commitment: priority of buyer of goods.] Subsection (d) does not apply if the advance is made pursuant to a commitment entered into without knowledge of the buyer's purchase and before the expiration of the 45-day period.

* * *

§ 9–324. Priority Of Purchase-Money Security Interests

(a) [General rule: purchase-money priority.] Except as otherwise provided in subsection (g), a perfected purchase-money security interest in goods other than inventory or livestock has priority over a conflicting security interest in the same goods, and, except as otherwise provided in Section 9–327, a perfected security interest in its identifiable proceeds also has priority, if the purchase-money security interest is perfected when the debtor receives possession of the collateral or within 20 days thereafter.

(b) [Inventory purchase-money priority.] Subject to subsection (c) and except as otherwise provided in subsection (g), a perfected purchase-money security interest in inventory has priority over a conflicting security interest in the same inventory, has priority over a conflicting security interest in chattel paper or an instrument constituting proceeds of the inventory and in proceeds of the chattel paper, if so provided in Section 9–330, and, except as otherwise provided in Section 9–327, also has priority in identifiable cash proceeds of the inventory to the extent the identifiable cash proceeds are received on or before the delivery of the inventory to a buyer, if:

(1) the purchase-money security interest is perfected when the debtor receives possession of the inventory;

(2) the purchase-money secured party sends an authenticated notification to the holder of the conflicting security interest;

(3) the holder of the conflicting security interest receives the notification within five years before the debtor receives possession of the inventory; and

(4) the notification states that the person sending the notification has or expects to acquire a purchase-money security interest in inventory of the debtor and describes the inventory.

(c) [Holders of conflicting inventory security interests to be notified.] Subsections (b)(2) through (4) apply only if the holder of the conflicting security interest had filed a financing statement covering the same types of inventory:

(1) if the purchase-money security interest is perfected by filing, before the date of the filing; or

(2) if the purchase-money security interest is temporarily perfected without filing or possession under Section 9–312(f), before the beginning of the 20-day period thereunder.

* * *

(g) [Conflicting purchase-money security interests.] If more than one security interest qualifies for priority in the same collateral under subsection (a), (b), (d), or (f):

(1) a security interest securing an obligation incurred as all or part of the price of the collateral has priority over a security interest securing an obligation incurred for value given to enable the debtor to acquire rights in or the use of collateral; and

(2) in all other cases, Section 9–322(a) applies to the qualifying security interests.

§ 9–332. Transfer Of Money; Transfer Of Funds From Deposit Account

(a) [Transferee of money.] A transferee of money takes the money free of a security interest unless the transferee acts in collusion with the debtor in violating the rights of the secured party.

(b) [Transferee of funds from deposit account.] A transferee of funds from a deposit account takes the funds free of a security interest in the deposit account unless the transferee acts in collusion with the debtor in violating the rights of the secured party.

§ 9–333. Priority Of Certain Liens Arising By Operation Of Law

(a) ["Possessory lien."] In this section, "possessory lien" means an interest, other than a security interest or an agricultural lien:

(1) which secures payment or performance of an obligation for services or materials furnished with respect to goods by a person in the ordinary course of the person's business;

(2) which is created by statute or rule of law in favor of the person; and

§ 9–339   UNIFORM COMMERCIAL CODE

(3) whose effectiveness depends on the person's possession of the goods.

(b) [Priority of possessory lien.] A possessory lien on goods has priority over a security interest in the goods unless the lien is created by a statute that expressly provides otherwise.

§ 9–339. Priority Subject To Subordination

This article does not preclude subordination by agreement by a person entitled to priority.

[Subpart 4. Rights of Bank]

§ 9–340. Effectiveness Of Right Of Recoupment Or Set-Off Against Deposit Account

(a) [Exercise of recoupment or set-off.] Except as otherwise provided in subsection (c), a bank with which a deposit account is maintained may exercise any right of recoupment or set-off against a secured party that holds a security interest in the deposit account.

(b) [Recoupment or set-off not affected by security interest.] Except as otherwise provided in subsection (c), the application of this article to a security interest in a deposit account does not affect a right of recoupment or set-off of the secured party as to a deposit account maintained with the secured party.

(c) [When set-off ineffective.] The exercise by a bank of a set-off against a deposit account is ineffective against a secured party that holds a security interest in the deposit account which is perfected by control under Section 9–104(a)(3), if the set-off is based on a claim against the debtor.

Part 4. Rights Of Third Parties

§ 9–401. Alienability Of Debtor's Rights

(a) [Other law governs alienability; exceptions.] Except as otherwise provided in subsection (b) and Sections 9–406, 9–407, 9–408, and 9–409, whether a debtor's rights in collateral may be voluntarily or involuntarily transferred is governed by law other than this article.

(b) [Agreement does not prevent transfer.] An agreement between the debtor and secured party which prohibits a transfer of the debtor's rights in collateral or makes the transfer a default does not prevent the transfer from taking effect.

§ 9–407. Restrictions On Creation Or Enforcement Of Security Interest In Leasehold Interest Or In Lessor's Residual Interest

(a) Term restricting assignment generally ineffective.] Except as otherwise provided in subsection (b), a term in a lease agreement is ineffective to the extent that it:

(1) prohibits, restricts, or requires the consent of a party to the lease to the assignment or transfer of, or the creation, attachment, perfection, or enforcement of a security interest in an interest of a party under the lease contract or in the lessor's residual interest in the goods; or

(2) provides that the assignment or transfer or the creation, attachment, perfection, or enforcement of the security interest may give rise to a default, breach, right of recoupment, claim, defense, termination, right of termination, or remedy under the lease.

(b) [Effectiveness of certain terms.] Except as otherwise provided in Section 2A–303(7), a term described in subsection (a)(2) is effective to the extent that there is:

(1) a transfer by the lessee of the lessee's right of possession or use of the goods in violation of the term; or

(2) a delegation of a material performance of either party to the lease contract in violation of the term.

* * *

Part 5. Filing

[Subpart 1. Filing Office; Contents And Effectiveness Of Financing Statement]

§ 9–501. Filing Office

(a) [Filing offices.] Except as otherwise provided in subsection (b), if the local law of this State governs perfection of a security interest or agricultural lien, the office in which to file a financing statement to perfect the security interest or agricultural lien is:

(1) the office designated for the filing or recording of a record of a mortgage on the related real property, if:

(A) the collateral is as-extracted collateral or timber to be cut; or

(B) the financing statement is filed as a fixture filing and the collateral is goods that are or are to become fixtures; or

(2) the office of [ ] [or any office duly authorized by [ ]], in all other cases, including a case in which the collateral is goods that are or are to become fixtures and the financing statement is not filed as a fixture filing.

* * *

§ 9–502. Contents Of Financing Statement; Record Of Mortgage As Financing Statement; Time Of Filing Financing Statement

(a) [Sufficiency of financing statement.] Subject to subsection (b), a financing statement is sufficient only if it:

(1) provides the name of the debtor;

(2) provides the name of the secured party or a representative of the secured party; and

(3) indicates the collateral covered by the financing statement.

* * *

(d) [Filing before security agreement or attachment.] A financing statement may be filed before a security agreement is made or a security interest otherwise attaches.

§ 9–515. Duration And Effectiveness Of Financing Statement; Effect Of Lapsed Financing Statement

(a) [Five-year effectiveness.] Except as otherwise provided in subsections (b), (e), (f), and (g), a filed financing statement is effective for a period of five years after the date of filing.

* * *

(c) [Lapse and continuation of financing statement.] The effectiveness of a filed financing statement lapses on the expiration of the period of its effectiveness unless before the lapse a continuation statement is filed pursuant to subsection (d). Upon lapse, a financing statement ceases to be effective and any security interest or agricultural lien that was perfected by the financing statement becomes unperfected, unless the security interest is perfected otherwise. If the security interest or agricultural lien becomes unperfected upon lapse, it is deemed never to have been perfected as against a purchaser of the collateral for value.

§ 9-516   UNIFORM COMMERCIAL CODE

(d) [When continuation statement may be filed.] A continuation statement may be filed only within six months before the expiration of the five-year period specified in subsection (a) or the 30-year period specified in subsection (b), whichever is applicable.

(e) [Effect of filing continuation statement.] Except as otherwise provided in Section 9–510, upon timely filing of a continuation statement, the effectiveness of the initial financing statement continues for a period of five years commencing on the day on which the financing statement would have become ineffective in the absence of the filing. Upon the expiration of the five-year period, the financing statement lapses in the same manner as provided in subsection (c), unless, before the lapse, another continuation statement is filed pursuant to subsection (d). Succeeding continuation statements may be filed in the same manner to continue the effectiveness of the initial financing statement.

* * *

§ 9-516. What Constitutes Filing; Effectiveness Of Filing

(a) [What constitutes filing.] Except as otherwise provided in subsection (b), communication of a record to a filing office and tender of the filing fee or acceptance of the record by the filing office constitutes filing.

* * *

Part 6. Default

[Subpart 1. Default And Enforcement Of Security Interest]

§ 9-601. Rights After Default; Judicial Enforcement; Consignor Or Buyer Of Accounts, Chattel Paper, Payment Intangibles, Or Promissory Notes

(a) [Rights of secured party after default.] After default, a secured party has the rights provided in this part and, except as otherwise provided in Section 9–602, those provided by agreement of the parties. A secured party:

    (1) may reduce a claim to judgment, foreclose, or otherwise enforce the claim, security interest, or agricultural lien by any available judicial procedure; and

    (2) if the collateral is documents, may proceed either as to the documents or as to the goods they cover.

* * *

§ 9-607. Collection And Enforcement By Secured Party

(a) [Collection and enforcement generally.] If so agreed, and in any event after default, a secured party:

    (1) may notify an account debtor or other person obligated on collateral to make payment or otherwise render performance to or for the benefit of the secured party;

    (2) may take any proceeds to which the secured party is entitled under Section 9–315;

    (3) may enforce the obligations of an account debtor or other person obligated on collateral and exercise the rights of the debtor with respect to the obligation of the account debtor or other person obligated on collateral to make payment or otherwise render performance to the debtor, and with respect to any property that secures the obligations of the account debtor or other person obligated on the collateral;

(4) if it holds a security interest in a deposit account perfected by control under Section 9–104(a)(1), may apply the balance of the deposit account to the obligation secured by the deposit account; and

(5) if it holds a security interest in a deposit account perfected by control under Section 9–104(a)(2) or (3), may instruct the bank to pay the balance of the deposit account to or for the benefit of the secured party.

* * *

§ 9–609. Secured Party's Right To Take Possession After Default

(a) [Possession; rendering equipment unusable; disposition on debtor's premises.] After default, a secured party:

(1) may take possession of the collateral; and

(2) without removal, may render equipment unusable and dispose of collateral on a debtor's premises under Section 9–610.

(b) [Judicial and nonjudicial process.] A secured party may proceed under subsection (a):

(1) pursuant to judicial process; or

(2) without judicial process, if it proceeds without breach of the peace.

(c) [Assembly of collateral.] If so agreed, and in any event after default, a secured party may require the debtor to assemble the collateral and make it available to the secured party at a place to be designated by the secured party which is reasonably convenient to both parties.

§ 9–610. Disposition Of Collateral After Default

(a) [Disposition after default.] After default, a secured party may sell, lease, license, or otherwise dispose of any or all of the collateral in its present condition or following any commercially reasonable preparation or processing.

(b) [Commercially reasonable disposition.] Every aspect of a disposition of collateral, including the method, manner, time, place, and other terms, must be commercially reasonable. If commercially reasonable, a secured party may dispose of collateral by public or private proceedings, by one or more contracts, as a unit or in parcels, and at any time and place and on any terms.

* * *

§ 9–611. Notification Before Disposition Of Collateral

* * *

(b) [Notification of disposition required.] Except as otherwise provided in subsection (d), a secured party that disposes of collateral under Section 9–610 shall send to the persons specified in subsection (c) a reasonable authenticated notification of disposition.

(c) [Persons to be notified.] To comply with subsection (b), the secured party shall send an authenticated notification of disposition to:

(1) the debtor;

(2) any secondary obligor; and

(3) if the collateral is other than consumer goods:

(A) any other person from which the secured party has received, before the notification date, an authenticated notification of a claim of an interest in the collateral;

(B) any other secured party or lienholder that, 10 days before the notification date, held a security interest in or other lien on the collateral perfected by the filing of a financing statement that:

    (i) identified the collateral;

    (ii) was indexed under the debtor's name as of that date; and

    (iii) was filed in the office in which to file a financing statement against the debtor covering the collateral as of that date; and

(C) any other secured party that, 10 days before the notification date, held a security interest in the collateral perfected by compliance with a statute, regulation, or treaty described in Section 9–311(a).

* * *

§ 9–612. Timeliness Of Notification Before Disposition Of Collateral

(a) [Reasonable time is question of fact.] Except as otherwise provided in subsection (b), whether a notification is sent within a reasonable time is a question of fact.

(b) [10-day period sufficient in non-consumer transaction.] In a transaction other than a consumer transaction, a notification of disposition sent after default and 10 days or more before the earliest time of disposition set forth in the notification is sent within a reasonable time before the disposition.

§ 9–615. Application Of Proceeds Of Disposition; Liability For Deficiency And Right To Surplus

(a) [Application of proceeds.] A secured party shall apply or pay over for application the cash proceeds of disposition under Section 9–610 in the following order to:

(1) the reasonable expenses of retaking, holding, preparing for disposition, processing, and disposing, and, to the extent provided for by agreement and not prohibited by law, reasonable attorney's fees and legal expenses incurred by the secured party;

(2) the satisfaction of obligations secured by the security interest or agricultural lien under which the disposition is made;

(3) the satisfaction of obligations secured by any subordinate security interest in or other subordinate lien on the collateral if:

    (A) the secured party receives from the holder of the subordinate security interest or other lien an authenticated demand for proceeds before distribution of the proceeds is completed;

* * *

§ 9–620. Acceptance Of Collateral In Full Or Partial Satisfaction Of Obligation; Compulsory Disposition Of Collateral

(a) [Conditions to acceptance in satisfaction.] Except as otherwise provided in subsection (g), a secured party may accept collateral in full or partial satisfaction of the obligation it secures only if:

(1) the debtor consents to the acceptance under subsection (c);

(2) the secured party does not receive, within the time set forth in subsection (d), a notification of objection to the proposal authenticated by:

    (A) a person to which the secured party was required to send a proposal under Section 9–621; or

(B) any other person, other than the debtor, holding an interest in the collateral subordinate to the security interest that is the subject of the proposal;

(3) if the collateral is consumer goods, the collateral is not in the possession of the debtor when the debtor consents to the acceptance; and

(4) subsection (e) does not require the secured party to dispose of the collateral or the debtor waives the requirement pursuant to Section 9–624.

* * *

(e) [Mandatory disposition of consumer goods.] A secured party that has taken possession of collateral shall dispose of the collateral pursuant to Section 9–610 within the time specified in subsection (f) if:

(1) 60 percent of the cash price has been paid in the case of a purchase-money security interest in consumer goods; or

(2) 60 percent of the principal amount of the obligation secured has been paid in the case of a non-purchase-money security interest in consumer goods.

* * *

(g) [No partial satisfaction in consumer transaction.] In a consumer transaction, a secured party may not accept collateral in partial satisfaction of the obligation it secures.

§ 9–622. Effect Of Acceptance Of Collateral

(a) [Effect of acceptance.] A secured party's acceptance of collateral in full or partial satisfaction of the obligation it secures:

(1) discharges the obligation to the extent consented to by the debtor;

(2) transfers to the secured party all of a debtor's rights in the collateral;

(3) discharges the security interest or agricultural lien that is the subject of the debtor's consent and any subordinate security interest or other subordinate lien; and

(4) terminates any other subordinate interest.

(b) [Discharge of subordinate interest notwithstanding noncompliance.] A subordinate interest is discharged or terminated under subsection (a), even if the secured party fails to comply with this article.

§ 9–623. Right To Redeem Collateral

(a) [Persons that may redeem.] A debtor, any secondary obligor, or any other secured party or lienholder may redeem collateral.

(b) [Requirements for redemption.] To redeem collateral, a person shall tender:

(1) fulfillment of all obligations secured by the collateral; and

(2) the reasonable expenses and attorney's fees described in Section 9–615(a)(1).

(c) [When redemption may occur.] A redemption may occur at any time before a secured party:

(1) has collected collateral under Section 9–607;

(2) has disposed of collateral or entered into a contract for its disposition under Section 9–610; or

(3) has accepted collateral in full or partial satisfaction of the obligation it secures under Section 9–622.

[Subpart 2. Noncompliance With Article]

§ 9-625. Remedies For Secured Party's Failure To Comply With Article

* * *

(b) [Damages for noncompliance.] Subject to subsections (c), (d), and (f), a person is liable for damages in the amount of any loss caused by a failure to comply with this article. Loss caused by a failure to comply may include loss resulting from the debtor's inability to obtain, or increased costs of, alternative financing.

* * *

FEDERAL TAX LIEN STATUTES INTERNAL REVENUE CODE—

Selected Sections

Title 26, United States Code
Subtitle F. Procedure and Administration
Chapter 64. Collection
Subchapter C. Lien for Taxes
Part II. Liens

Sec.
6321. Lien for taxes.
6322. Period of lien.
6323. Validity and priority against certain persons.

§ 6321. Lien for taxes

If any person liable to pay any tax neglects or refuses to pay the same after demand, the amount (including any interest, additional amount, addition to tax, or assessable penalty, together with any costs that may accrue in addition thereto) shall be a lien in favor of the United States upon all property and rights to property, whether real or personal, belonging to such person.

(Aug. 16, 1954, c. 736, 68A Stat. 779.)

CROSS REFERENCES

Action to enforce lien or to subject property to payment of tax, see 26 USCA § 7403.

Liability of operators for repayments to Mine Safety and Health Fund, see 30 USCA § 934.

Lien for liability, Employee Retirement Income Security Program, see 29 USCA § 1368.

§ 6322. Period of lien

Unless another date is specifically fixed by law, the lien imposed by section 6321 shall arise at the time the assessment is made and shall continue until the liability for the amount so assessed (or a judgment against the taxpayer arising out of such liability) is satisfied or becomes unenforceable by reason of lapse of time.

(Aug. 16, 1954, c. 736, 68A Stat. 779; Nov. 2, 1966, Pub.L. 89–719, Title I, § 113(a), 80 Stat. 1146.)

HISTORICAL AND STATUTORY NOTES

Amendments

1966 Amendments. Pub.L. 89–719 inserted phrase "(or a judgment against the taxpayer arising out of such liability)."

§ 6323. Validity and priority against certain persons

(a) **Purchasers, holders of security interests, mechanic's lienors, and judgment lien creditors.**—The lien imposed by section 6321 shall not be valid as against any purchaser, holder of a security interest, mechanic's lienor, or judgment lien creditor until notice thereof which meets the requirements of subsection (f) has been filed by the Secretary.

(b) Protection for certain interests even though notice filed.—Even though notice of a lien imposed by section 6321 has been filed, such lien shall not be valid—

  (1) Securities.—With respect to a security (as defined in subsection (h)(4))—

   (A) as against a purchaser of such security who at the time of purchase did not have actual notice or knowledge of the existence of such lien; and

   (B) as against a holder of a security interest in such security who, at the time such interest came into existence, did not have actual notice or knowledge of the existence of such lien.

  (2) Motor vehicles.—With respect to a motor vehicle (as defined in subsection (h)(3)), as against a purchaser of such motor vehicle, if—

   (A) at the time of the purchase such purchaser did not have actual notice or knowledge of the existence of such lien, and

   (B) before the purchaser obtains such notice or knowledge, he has acquired possession of such motor vehicle and has not thereafter relinquished possession of such motor vehicle to the seller or his agent.

  (3) Personal property purchased at retail.—With respect to tangible personal property purchased at retail, as against a purchaser in the ordinary course of the seller's trade or business, unless at the time of such purchase such purchaser intends such purchase to (or knows such purchase will) hinder, evade, or defeat the collection of any tax under this title.

  (4) Personal property purchased in casual sale.—With respect to household goods, personal effects, or other tangible personal property described in section 6334(a) purchased (not for resale) in a casual sale for less than $1,000, as against the purchaser, but only if such purchaser does not have actual notice or knowledge (A) of the existence of such lien, or (B) that this sale is one of a series of sales.

  (5) Personal property subject to possessory lien.—With respect to tangible personal property subject to a lien under local law securing the reasonable price of the repair or improvement of such property, as against a holder of such a lien, if such holder is, and has been, continuously in possession of such property from the time such lien arose.

  (6) Real property tax and special assessment liens.—With respect to real property, as against a holder of a lien upon such property, if such lien is entitled under local law to priority over security interests in such property which are prior in time, and such lien secures payment of—

   (A) a tax of general application levied by any taxing authority based upon the value of such property;

   (B) a special assessment imposed directly upon such property by any taxing authority, if such assessment is imposed for the purpose of defraying the cost of any public improvement; or

   (C) charges for utilities or public services furnished to such property by the United States, a State or political subdivision thereof, or an instrumentality of any one or more of the foregoing.

  (7) Residential property subject to a mechanic's lien for certain repairs and improvements.—With respect to real property subject to a lien for repair or improvement of a personal residence (containing not more than four dwelling units) occupied by the owner of such residence, as against a mechanic's lienor, but only if the contract price on the contract with the owner is not more than $5,000.

  (8) Attorneys' liens.—With respect to a judgment or other amount in settlement of a claim or of a cause of action, as against an attorney who, under local law, holds a lien upon or a contract enforceable against such judgment or amount, to the extent of his reasonable compensation for obtaining such judgment or procuring such settlement, except that this paragraph shall not apply to any judgment or amount in settlement of a claim or of a cause of action against the United States to the extent that the United States offsets such judgment or amount against any liability of the taxpayer to the United States.

(9) Certain insurance contracts.—With respect to a life insurance, endowment, or annuity contract, as against the organization which is the insurer under such contract, at any time—

(A) before such organization had actual notice or knowledge of the existence of such lien;

(B) after such organization had such notice or knowledge, with respect to advances required to be made automatically to maintain such contract in force under an agreement entered into before such organization had such notice or knowledge; or

(C) after satisfaction of a levy pursuant to section 6332(b), unless and until the Secretary delivers to such organization a notice, executed after the date of such satisfaction, of the existence of such lien.

(10) Deposit-secured loans.—With respect to a savings deposit, share, or other account, with an institution described in section 581 or 591, to the extent of any loan made by such institution without actual notice or knowledge of the existence of such lien, as against such institution, if such loan is secured by such account.

(c) Protection for certain commercial transactions financing agreements, etc.—

(1) In general.—To the extent provided in this subsection, even though notice of a lien imposed by section 6321 has been filed, such lien shall not be valid with respect to a security interest which came into existence after tax lien filing but which—

(A) is in qualified property covered by the terms of a written agreement entered into before tax lien filing and constituting—

(i) a commercial transactions financing agreement,

(ii) a real property construction or improvement financing agreement, or

(iii) an obligatory disbursement agreement, and

(B) is protected under local law against a judgment lien arising, as of the time of tax lien filing, out of an unsecured obligation.

(2) Commercial transactions financing agreement.—For purposes of this subsection—

(A) Definition.—The term "commercial transactions financing agreement" means an agreement (entered into by a person in the course of his trade or business)—

(i) to make loans to the taxpayer to be secured by commercial financing security acquired by the taxpayer in the ordinary course of his trade or business, or

(ii) to purchase commercial financing security (other than inventory) acquired by the taxpayer in the ordinary course of his trade or business;

but such an agreement shall be treated as coming within the term only to the extent that such loan or purchase is made before the 46th day after the date of tax lien filing or (if earlier) before the lender or purchaser had actual notice or knowledge of such tax lien filing.

(B) Limitation on qualified property.—The term "qualified property", when used with respect to a commercial transactions financing agreement, includes only commercial financing security acquired by the taxpayer before the 46th day after the date of tax lien filing.

(C) **Commercial financing security defined.**—The term "commercial financing security" means (i) paper of a kind ordinarily arising in commercial transactions, (ii) accounts receivable, (iii) mortgages on real property, and (iv) inventory.

(D) **Purchaser treated as acquiring security interest.**—A person who satisfies subparagraph (A) by reason of clause (ii) thereof shall be treated as having acquired a security interest in commercial financing security.

(3) **Real property construction or improvement financing agreement.**—For purposes of this subsection—

(A) **Definition.**—The term "real property construction or improvement financing agreement" means an agreement to make cash disbursements to finance—

(i) the construction or improvement of real property,

(ii) a contract to construct or improve real property, or

(iii) the raising or harvesting of a farm crop or the raising of livestock or other animals.

For purposes of clause (iii), the furnishing of goods and services shall be treated as the disbursement of cash.

(B) **Limitation on qualified property.**—The term "qualified property", when used with respect to a real property construction or improvement financing agreement, includes only—

(i) in the case of subparagraph (A)(i), the real property with respect to which the construction or improvement has been or is to be made,

(ii) in the case of subparagraph (A)(ii), the proceeds of the contract described therein, and

(iii) in the case of subparagraph (A)(iii), property subject to the lien imposed by section 6321 at the time of tax lien filing and the crop or the livestock or other animals referred to in subparagraph (A)(iii).

(4) **Obligatory disbursement agreement.**—For purposes of this subsection—

(A) **Definition.**—The term "obligatory disbursement agreement" means an agreement (entered into by a person in the course of his trade or business) to make disbursements, but such an agreement shall be treated as coming within the term only to the extent of disbursements which are required to be made by reason of the intervention of the rights of a person other than the taxpayer.

(B) **Limitation on qualified property.**—The term "qualified property", when used with respect to an obligatory disbursement agreement, means property subject to the lien imposed by section 6321 at the time of tax lien filing and (to the extent that the acquisition is directly traceable to the disbursements referred to in subparagraph (A)) property acquired by the taxpayer after tax lien filing.

(C) **Special rules for surety agreements.**—Where the obligatory disbursement agreement is an agreement ensuring the performance of a contract between the taxpayer and another person—

(i) the term "qualified property" shall be treated as also including the proceeds of the contract the performance of which was ensured, and

(ii) if the contract the performance of which was ensured was a contract to construct or improve real property, to produce goods, or to furnish services, the term "qualified property" shall be treated as also including any tangible personal property used by the taxpayer in the performance of such ensured contract.

(d) **45-day period for making disbursements.**—Even though notice of a lien imposed by section 6321 has been filed, such lien shall not be valid with respect to a security interest which came into existence after tax lien filing by reason of disbursements made before the 46th day after the date of tax lien filing, or (if earlier) before the person making such disbursements had actual notice or knowledge of tax lien filing, but only if such security interest—

 (1) is in property (A) subject, at the time of tax lien filing, to the lien imposed by section 6321, and (B) covered by the terms of a written agreement entered into before tax lien filing, and

 (2) is protected under local law against a judgment lien arising, as of the time of tax lien filing, out of an unsecured obligation.

(e) Priority of interest and expenses.—If the lien imposed by section 6321 is not valid as against a lien or security interest, the priority of such lien or security interest shall extend to—

 (1) any interest or carrying charges upon the obligation secured,

 (2) the reasonable charges and expenses of an indenture trustee or agent holding the security interest for the benefit of the holder of the security interest,

 (3) the reasonable expenses, including reasonable compensation for attorneys, actually incurred in collecting or enforcing the obligation secured,

 (4) the reasonable costs of insuring, preserving, or repairing the property to which the lien or security interest relates,

 (5) the reasonable costs of insuring payment of the obligation secured, and

 (6) amounts paid to satisfy any lien on the property to which the lien or security interest relates, but only if the lien so satisfied is entitled to priority over the lien imposed by section 6321,

to the extent that, under local law, any such item has the same priority as the lien or security interest to which it relates.

(f) Place for filing notice; form.—

 (1) Place for filing.—The notice referred to in subsection (a) shall be filed—

  (A) Under State laws.—

   (i) Real property.—In the case of real property, in one office within the State (or the county, or other governmental subdivision), as designated by the laws of such State, in which the property subject to the lien is situated; and

   (ii) Personal property.—In the case of personal property, whether tangible or intangible, in one office within the State (or the county, or other governmental subdivision), as designated by the laws of such State, in which the property subject to the lien is situated, except that State law merely conforming to or reenacting Federal law establishing a national filing system does not constitute a second office for filing as designated by the laws of such State; or

  (B) With clerk of district court.—In the office of the clerk of the United States district court for the judicial district in which the property subject to the lien is situated, whenever the State has not by law designated one office which meets the requirements of subparagraph (A); or

  (C) With Recorder of Deeds of the District of Columbia.—In the office of the Recorder of Deeds of the District of Columbia, if the property subject to the lien is situated in the District of Columbia.

 (2) Situs of property subject to lien.—For purposes of paragraphs (1) and (4), property shall be deemed to be situated—

  (A) Real property.—In the case of real property, at its physical location; or

  (B) Personal property.—In the case of personal property, whether tangible or intangible, at the residence of the taxpayer at the time the notice of lien is filed.

For purposes of paragraph (2)(B), the residence of a corporation or partnership shall be deemed to be the place at which the principal executive office of the business is located, and the residence of a taxpayer whose residence is without the United States shall be deemed to be in the District of Columbia.

(3) **Form.**—The form and content of the notice referred to in subsection (a) shall be prescribed by the Secretary. Such notice shall be valid notwithstanding any other provision of law regarding the form or content of a notice of lien.

(4) **Indexing required with respect to certain real property.**—In the case of real property, if—

(A) under the laws of the State in which the real property is located, a deed is not valid as against a purchaser of the property who (at the time of purchase) does not have actual notice or knowledge of the existence of such deed unless the fact of filing of such deed has been entered and recorded in a public index at the place of filing in such a manner that a reasonable inspection of the index will reveal the existence of the deed, and

(B) there is maintained (at the applicable office under paragraph (1)) an adequate system for the public indexing of Federal tax liens,

then the notice of lien referred to in subsection (a) shall not be treated as meeting the filing requirements under paragraph (1) unless the fact of filing is entered and recorded in the index referred to in subparagraph (B) in such a manner that a reasonable inspection of the index will reveal the existence of the lien.

(5) **National filing systems.**—The filing of a notice of lien shall be governed solely by this title and shall not be subject to any other Federal law establishing a place or places for the filing of liens or encumbrances under a national filing system.

(g) **Refiling of notice.**—For purposes of this section—

(1) **General rule.**—Unless notice of lien is refiled in the manner prescribed in paragraph (2) during the required refiling period, such notice of lien shall be treated as filed on the date on which it is filed (in accordance with subsection (f)) after the expiration of such refiling period.

(2) **Place for filing.**—A notice of lien refiled during the required refiling period shall be effective only—

(A) if—

(i) such notice of lien is refiled in the office in which the prior notice of lien was filed, and

(ii) in the case of real property, the fact of refiling is entered and recorded in an index to the extent required by subsection (f)(4); and

(B) in any case in which, 90 days or more prior to the date of a refiling of notice of lien under subparagraph (A), the Secretary received written information (in the manner prescribed in regulations issued by the Secretary) concerning a change in the taxpayer's residence, if a notice of such lien is also filed in accordance with subsection (f) in the State in which such residence is located.

(3) **Required refiling period.**—In the case of any notice of lien, the term "required refiling period" means—

(A) the one-year period ending 30 days after the expiration of 10 years after the date of the assessment of the tax, and

(B) the one-year period ending with the expiration of 10 years after the close of the preceding required refiling period for such notice of lien.

(4) **Transitional rule.**—Notwithstanding paragraph (3), if the assessment of the tax was made before January 1, 1962, the first required refiling period shall be the calendar year 1967.

(h) **Definitions.**—For purposes of this section and section 6324—

(1) **Security interest.**—The term "security interest" means any interest in property acquired by contract for the purpose of securing payment or performance of an obligation or indemnifying against loss or liability. A security interest exists at any time (A) if, at such time, the property is in existence and the interest has become protected under local law against a subsequent judgment lien arising out of an unsecured obligation, and (B) to the extent that, at such time, the holder has parted with money or money's worth.

(2) **Mechanic's lienor.**—The term "mechanic's lienor" means any person who under local law has a lien on real property (or on the proceeds of a contract relating to real property) for services, labor, or materials furnished in connection with the construction or improvement of such property. For purposes of the preceding sentence, a person has a lien on the earliest date such lien becomes valid under local law against subsequent purchasers without actual notice, but not before he begins to furnish the services, labor, or materials.

(3) **Motor vehicle.**—The term "motor vehicle" means a self-propelled vehicle which is registered for highway use under the laws of any State or foreign country.

(4) **Security.**—The term "security" means any bond, debenture, note, or certificate or other evidence of indebtedness, issued by a corporation or a government or political subdivision thereof, with interest coupons or in registered form, share of stock, voting trust certificate, or any certificate of interest or participation in, certificate of deposit or receipt for, temporary or interim certificate for, or warrant or right to subscribe to or purchase, any of the foregoing; negotiable instrument; or money.

(5) **Tax lien filing.**—The term "tax lien filing" means the filing of notice (referred to in subsection (a)) of the lien imposed by section 6321.

(6) **Purchaser.**—The term "purchaser" means a person who, for adequate and full consideration in money or money's worth, acquires an interest (other than a lien or security interest) in property which is valid under local law against subsequent purchasers without actual notice. In applying the preceding sentence for purposes of subsection (a) of this section, and for purposes of section 6324—

(A) a lease of property,

(B) a written executory contract to purchase or lease property,

(C) an option to purchase or lease property or any interest therein, or

(D) an option to renew or extend a lease of property,

which is not a lien or security interest shall be treated as an interest in property.

(i) **Special rules.**—

(1) **Actual notice or knowledge.**—For purposes of this subchapter, an organization shall be deemed for purposes of a particular transaction to have actual notice or knowledge of any fact from the time such fact is brought to the attention of the individual conducting such transaction, and in any event from the time such fact would have been brought to such individual's attention if the organization had exercised due diligence. An organization exercises due diligence if it maintains reasonable routines for communicating significant information to the person conducting the transaction and there is reasonable compliance with the routine. Due diligence does not require an individual acting for the organization to communicate information unless such communication is part of his regular duties or unless he has reason to know of the transaction and that the transaction would be materially affected by the information.

(2) Subrogation.—Where, under local law, one person is subrogated to the rights of another with respect to a lien or interest, such person shall be subrogated to such rights for purposes of any lien imposed by section 6321 or 6324.

(3) Forfeitures.—For purposes of this subchapter, a forfeiture under local law of property seized by a law enforcement agency of a State, county, or other local governmental subdivision shall relate back to the time of seizure, except that this paragraph shall not apply to the extent that under local law the holder of an intervening claim or interest would have priority over the interest of the State, county, or other local governmental subdivision in the property.

(4) Cost-of-living adjustment.—In the case of notices of liens imposed by section 6321 which are filed in any calendar year after 1998, each of the dollar amounts under paragraph (4) or (7) of subsection (b) shall be increased by an amount equal to.—

(A) such dollar amount, multiplied by

(B) the cost-of-living adjustment determined under section 1(f)(3) for the calendar year, determined by substituting "calendar year 1996" for "calendar year 1992" in subparagraph (B) thereof.

If any amount as adjusted under the preceding sentence is not a multiple of $10, such amount shall be rounded to the nearest multiple of $10.

(j) Withdrawal of notice in certain circumstances.—

(1) In general.—The Secretary may withdraw a notice of a lien filed under this section and this chapter shall be applied as if the withdrawn notice had not been filed, if the Secretary determines that—

(A) the filing of such notice was premature or otherwise not in accordance with administrative procedures of the Secretary,

(B) the taxpayer has entered into an agreement under section 6159 to satisfy the tax liability for which the lien was imposed by means of installment payments, unless such agreement provides otherwise,

(C) the withdrawal of such notice will facilitate the collection of the tax liability, or

(D) with the consent of the taxpayer or the National Taxpayer Advocate, the withdrawal of such notice would be in the best interests of the taxpayer (as determined by the National Taxpayer Advocate) and the United States.

Any such withdrawal shall be made by filing notice at the same office as the withdrawn notice. A copy of such notice of withdrawal shall be provided to the taxpayer.

(2) Notice to credit agencies, etc.—Upon written request by the taxpayer with respect to whom a notice of a lien was withdrawn under paragraph (1), the Secretary shall promptly make reasonable efforts to notify credit reporting agencies, and any financial institution or creditor whose name and address is specified in such request, of the withdrawal of such notice. Any such request shall be in such form as the Secretary may prescribe.

(Aug. 16, 1954, c. 736, 68A Stat. 779; Feb. 26, 1964, Pub.L. 88–272, Title II, § 236(a), (c)(1), 78 Stat. 127, 128; July 5, 1966, Pub.L. 89–493, § 17(a), 80 Stat. 266; Nov. 2, 1966, Pub.L. 89–719, Title I, § 101(a), 80 Stat. 1125; Oct. 4, 1976, Pub.L. 94–455, Title XII, § 1202(h)(2), Title XIX, § 1906(b)(13)(A), Title XX, § 2008(c), 90 Stat. 1688, 1834, 1892; Nov. 6, 1978, Pub.L. 95–600, Title VII, § 702(q)(1), (2), 92 Stat. 2937, 2938; Oct. 22, 1986, Pub.L. 99–514, Title XV, § 1569(a), 100 Stat. 2764; Nov. 10, 1988, Pub.L. 100–647, Title I, § 1015(s)(1), 102 Stat. 3573; Nov. 5, 1990, Pub.L. 101–508, Title XI, §§ 11317(b), 11704(a)(26), 104 Stat. 1388–458, 1388–519; July 30, 1996, Pub.L. 104–168, Title V, § 501(a), 110 Stat. 1460; July 22, 1998, Pub.L. 105–206, Title I, §§ 1102(d)(1)(A), Title III, 3435(a), (b), 112 Stat. 704, 760, 761.)

HISTORICAL AND STATUTORY NOTES

Amendments

1998 Amendments. Subsec. (b)(4). Pub.L. 105–206, § 3435(a)(1)(A), substituted "$1,000" for "$250".

Subsec. (b)(7). Pub.L. 105–206, § 3435(a)(1)(B), substituted "$5,000" for "$1,000".

Subsec. (b)(10). Pub.L. 105–206, § 3435(b), substituted "Deposit-secured loans" for "Passbook loans" in the par. heading, struck out ", evidenced by a passbook," following "savings deposit, share, or other account" and substituted a period for "and if such institution has been continuously in possession of such passbook from the time the loan is made." following "secured by such account".

Subsec. (i)(4). Pub.L. 105–206, § 3435(a)(2), added par. (4).

Subsec. (j)(1)(D). Pub.L. 105–206, § 1102(d)(1)(A), substituted "National Taxpayer Advocate" for "Taxpayer Advocate" each place it appeared.

1996 Amendments. Subsec. (j). Pub.L. 104–168, § 501(a) added subsec. (j).

1990 Amendments. Subsec. (a). Pub.L. 101–508, § 11704(a)(26), substituted "Purchasers" for "Purchases" in the heading.

Subsec. (g). Pub.L. 101–508, § 11317(b), substituted "10 years" for "6 years" wherever appearing.

1988 Amendments. Subsec. (f)(1)(A)(ii). Pub.L. 100–647, § 1015(s)(1)(A), added provision that State law merely conforming to or reenacting Federal law establishing a national filing system does not constitute a second office for filing as designated by the laws of such State.

Subsec. (f)(5). Pub.L. 100–647, § 1015(s)(1)(B), added par. (5).

1986 Amendments. Subsec. (i)(3). Pub.L. 99–514 added par. (3).

1978 Amendments. Subsec. (f) (4). Pub.L. 95–600, § 702(q) (1), in par. heading substituted "Indexing required with respect to certain real property" for "Index" and in text added provisions relating to the validity of a deed, under the laws of the State in which the real property is located, as against a purchaser who does not have actual notice or knowledge of the existence of such deed and provisions relating to the maintenance of an adequate system for the public indexing of Federal tax liens.

Subsec. (g) (2) (A). Pub.L. 95–600, § 702(q) (2), inserted reference to real property.

1976 Amendments. Subsecs. (a), (b). Pub.L. 94–455, § 1906(b)(13)(A), struck out "or his delegate" following "Secretary" wherever appearing.

Subsec. (f) (2). Pub.L. 94–455, § 2008(c) (1) (B), inserted introductory reference to par. (4).

Subsec. (f) (3). Pub.L. 94–455, § 1906(b)(13)(A) struck out "or his delegate" following "Secretary".

Subsec. (f) (4). Pub.L. 94–455, § 2008(c) (1) (A), added par. (4).

Subsec. (g) (2) (A). Pub.L. 94–455, § 2008(c) (2), required the fact of refiling be entered and recorded in an index in accordance with subsec. (f) (4).

Subsec. (g)(2)(B). Pub.L. 94–455, § 1906(b)(13)(A), struck out "or his delegate" following "Secretary" wherever appearing.

Subsec. (i) (3). Pub.L. 94–455, § 1202(h) (2), struck out par. (3) which provided for special rule respecting disclosure of amount of outstanding lien.

1966 Amendments. Subsec. (a). Pub.L. 89–719 redesignated as the entire subsec. (a) that part of former subsec. (a) which preceded pars. (1)–(3) thereof, and, in subsec. (a) as so redesignated, substituted holder of a security interest, mechanic's lienor, and judgment lien creditor for mortgagee, pledgee, and judgment creditor, struck out reference to an exception provided in subsecs. (c) and (d), and inserted reference to the requirements of subsec. (f).

Subsec. (a)(3). Pub.L. 89–493 substituted the Recorder of Deeds of the District of Columbia for the clerk of the United States District Court for the District of Columbia.

Subsec. (b)(1). Pub.L. 89–719 redesignated provisions of former subsec. (c)(1) as subsec. (b)(1) and, in subsec. (b)(1) as so redesignated, substituted "holder of a security interest" for "mortgagee and pledgee" and purchaser of such security interest for purchaser of such security for any adequate and full consideration of money or money's worth.

Subsec. (b)(2). Pub.L. 89–719 redesignated provisions of former subsec. (d)(1) as subsec. (b)(2) and, in subsec. (b)(2) as so redesignated, substituted purchaser of such motor vehicle for purchaser of such motor vehicle for an adequate and full consideration in money or money's worth and substituted actual notice or knowledge for notice or knowledge.

Subsec. (b)(3)–(10). Pub.L. 89–719 added pars. (3)–(10).

Subsecs. (c)–(e). Pub.L. 89–719 added subsecs. (c)–(e).

Subsec. (f)(1). Pub.L. 89–719 redesignated provisions of former subsec. (a)(1)–(3) as subsec. (f)(1).

Subsec. (f)(2). Pub.L. 89–719 added par. (2).

Subsec. (f)(3). Pub.L. 89–719 redesignated provisions of former subsec. (b) as subsec. (f)(3) and, in subsec. (f)(3) as so redesignated, substituted provisions that the form and content of the notice be prescribed by the Secretary or his delegate for provisions limiting the effectiveness of the notice to situations in which the notice is in such form as would be valid if filed with the clerk of the United States district court when state or territory law fails to designate an office for the filing of notice.

Subsec. (g). Pub.L. 89–719 added subsec. (g).

Subsec. (h)(1), (2). Pub.L. 89–719 added pars. (1), (2).

Subsec. (h)(3). Pub.L. 89–719 redesignated provisions of former subsec. (d)(2) as subsec. (h)(3).

Subsec. (h)(4). Pub.L. 89–719 redesignated provisions of former subsec. (c)(2) as subsec. (h)(4).

Subsec. (h)(5), (6). Pub.L. 89–719 added pars. (5), (6).

Subsec. (i)(1), (2). Pub.L. 89–719 added subsec. (i)(1), (2).

Subsec. (i)(3). Pub.L. 89–719 redesignated the provisions of former subsec. (e) as subsec. (i)(3) and, in subsec. (i)(3) as so redesignated, substituted "regulations" for "rules and regulations".

1964 Amendments. Subsec. (a). Pub.L. 88–272, § 236(c)(1), substituted "subsections (c) and (d)" for "subsection (c)."

Subsec. (d). Pub.L. 88–272, § 236(a), added subsec. (d) and redesignated former subsec. (d) as (e).

Subsec. (e). Pub.L. 88–272, § 236(a), redesignated former subsec. (d) as (e).

CROSS REFERENCES

Hazardous substances releases, liability, see 42 USCA § 9607.

Liability of operators for repayments to Mine Safety and Health Fund, see 30 USCA § 934.

Treatment of certain liens in liquidation, see 11 USCA § 724.

Subsec. (b)(7). Pub.L. 105–206, § 3435(a)(1)(B), substituted "$5,000" for "$1,000".

Subsec. (b)(10). Pub.L. 105–206, § 3435(b), substituted "Deposit-secured loans" for "Passbook loans" in the par. heading, struck out ", evidenced by a passbook," following "savings deposit, share, or other account" and substituted a period for "and if such institution has been continuously in possession of such passbook from the time the loan is made." following "secured by such account".

Subsec. (i)(4). Pub.L. 105–206, § 3435(a)(2), added par. (4).

Subsec. (j)(1)(D). Pub.L. 105–206, § 1102(d)(1)(A), substituted "National Taxpayer Advocate" for "Taxpayer Advocate" each place it appeared.

1996 Amendments. Subsec. (j). Pub.L. 104–168, § 501(a) added subsec. (j).

1990 Amendments. Subsec. (a). Pub.L. 101–508, § 11704(a)(26), substituted "Purchasers" for "Purchases" in the heading.

Subsec. (g). Pub.L. 101–508, § 11317(b), substituted "10 years" for "6 years" wherever appearing.

1988 Amendments. Subsec. (f)(1)(A)(ii). Pub.L. 100–647, § 1015(s)(1)(A), added provision that State law merely conforming to or reenacting Federal law establishing a national filing system does not constitute a second office for filing as designated by the laws of such State.

Subsec. (f)(5). Pub.L. 100–647, § 1015(s)(1)(B), added par. (5).

1986 Amendments. Subsec. (i)(3). Pub.L. 99–514 added par. (3).

1978 Amendments. Subsec. (f) (4). Pub.L. 95–600, § 702(q) (1), in par. heading substituted "Indexing required with respect to certain real property" for "Index" and in text added provisions relating to the validity of a deed, under the laws of the State in which the real property is located, as against a purchaser who does not have actual notice or knowledge of the existence of such deed and provisions relating to the maintenance of an adequate system for the public indexing of Federal tax liens.

Subsec. (g) (2) (A). Pub.L. 95–600, § 702(q) (2), inserted reference to real property.

1976 Amendments. Subsecs. (a), (b). Pub.L. 94–455, § 1906(b)(13)(A), struck out "or his delegate" following "Secretary" wherever appearing.

Subsec. (f) (2). Pub.L. 94–455, § 2008(c) (1) (B), inserted introductory reference to par. (4).

Subsec. (f) (3). Pub.L. 94–455, § 1906(b)(13)(A) struck out "or his delegate" following "Secretary".

Subsec. (f) (4). Pub.L. 94–455, § 2008(c) (1) (A), added par. (4).

Subsec. (g) (2) (A). Pub.L. 94–455, § 2008(c) (2), required the fact of refiling be entered and recorded in an index in accordance with subsec. (f) (4).

Subsec. (g)(2)(B). Pub.L. 94–455, § 1906(b)(13)(A), struck out "or his delegate" following "Secretary" wherever appearing.

Subsec. (i) (3). Pub.L. 94–455, § 1202(h) (2), struck out par. (3) which provided for special rule respecting disclosure of amount of outstanding lien.

1966 Amendments. Subsec. (a). Pub.L. 89–719 redesignated as the entire subsec. (a) that part of former subsec. (a) which preceded pars. (1)–(3) thereof, and, in subsec. (a) as so redesignated, substituted holder of a security interest, mechanic's lienor, and judgment lien creditor for mortgagee, pledgee, and judgment creditor, struck out reference to an exception provided in subsecs. (c) and (d), and inserted reference to the requirements of subsec. (f).

Subsec. (a)(3). Pub.L. 89–493 substituted the Recorder of Deeds of the District of Columbia for the clerk of the United States District Court for the District of Columbia.

Subsec. (b)(1). Pub.L. 89–719 redesignated provisions of former subsec. (c)(1) as subsec. (b)(1) and, in subsec. (b)(1) as so redesignated, substituted "holder of a security interest" for "mortgagee and pledgee" and purchaser of such security interest for purchaser of such security for any adequate and full consideration of money or money's worth.

Subsec. (b)(2). Pub.L. 89–719 redesignated provisions of former subsec. (d)(1) as subsec. (b)(2) and, in subsec. (b)(2) as so redesignated, substituted purchaser of such motor vehicle for purchaser of such motor vehicle for an adequate and full consideration in money or money's worth and substituted actual notice or knowledge for notice or knowledge.

Subsec. (b)(3)–(10). Pub.L. 89–719 added pars. (3)–(10).

Subsecs. (c)–(e). Pub.L. 89–719 added subsecs. (c)–(e).

Subsec. (f)(1). Pub.L. 89–719 redesignated provisions of former subsec. (a)(1)–(3) as subsec. (f)(1).

Subsec. (f)(2). Pub.L. 89–719 added par. (2).

Subsec. (f)(3). Pub.L. 89–719 redesignated provisions of former subsec. (b) as subsec. (f)(3) and, in subsec. (f)(3) as so redesignated, substituted provisions that the form and content of the notice be prescribed by the Secretary or his delegate for provisions limiting the effectiveness of the notice to situations in which the notice is in such form as would be valid if filed with the clerk of the United States district court when state or territory law fails to designate an office for the filing of notice.

Subsec. (g). Pub.L. 89–719 added subsec. (g).

Subsec. (h)(1), (2). Pub.L. 89–719 added pars. (1), (2).

Subsec. (h)(3). Pub.L. 89–719 redesignated provisions of former subsec. (d)(2) as subsec. (h)(3).

Subsec. (h)(4). Pub.L. 89–719 redesignated provisions of former subsec. (c)(2) as subsec. (h)(4).

Subsec. (h)(5), (6). Pub.L. 89–719 added pars. (5), (6).

Subsec. (i)(1), (2). Pub.L. 89–719 added subsec. (i)(1), (2).

Subsec. (i)(3). Pub.L. 89–719 redesignated the provisions of former subsec. (e) as subsec. (i)(3) and, in subsec. (i)(3) as so redesignated, substituted "regulations" for "rules and regulations".

1964 Amendments. Subsec. (a). Pub.L. 88–272, § 236(c)(1), substituted "subsections (c) and (d)" for "subsection (c)."

Subsec. (d). Pub.L. 88–272, § 236(a), added subsec. (d) and redesignated former subsec. (d) as (e).

Subsec. (e). Pub.L. 88–272, § 236(a), redesignated former subsec. (d) as (e).

CROSS REFERENCES

Hazardous substances releases, liability, see 42 USCA § 9607.

Liability of operators for repayments to Mine Safety and Health Fund, see 30 USCA § 934.

Treatment of certain liens in liquidation, see 11 USCA § 724.

INDEX

International Trade Court, this index
Judges or Justices, this index
United States Magistrate Judges, this index

APPRAISAL AND APPRAISERS
Bankruptcy, this index

ARBITRATION
Arbitrators,
    Certificates and certification, 28 § 655
    Compensation and salaries, 28 § 658
    Disqualification, 28 § 655
    Privileges and immunities, 28 § 655
    Referrals, 28 § 655
Awards,
    Referrals, 28 §§ 655, 657
    Sealing, 28 § 657
Bankruptcy, this index
Certificates and certification, arbitrators, 28 § 655
Compensation and salaries, 28 § 658
Disqualification, arbitrators, 28 § 655
Dockets and docketing, new trial, 28 § 657
Hearings, referrals, 28 § 655
Judgments and decrees, 28 § 657
Neutrals, compensation and salaries, 28 § 658
New trial, 28 § 657
Oaths and affirmations, 28 § 655
Powers and duties, arbitrators, 28 § 655
Privileges and immunities, arbitrators, 28 § 655
Process, awards, 28 § 657
Production of books and papers, 28 § 656
Referrals, 28 §§ 654, 655
Sealing, awards, 28 § 657
Subpoenas, 28 § 656
Time, new trial, 28 § 657
Traveling expenses, 28 § 658
Trial de novo, 28 § 657

ARBITRATORS
Arbitration, this index

ARIZONA
Bankruptcy, judges or justices, appointments, 28 § 152
United States trustees, appointments, 28 § 581

ARKANSAS
Bankruptcy, judges or justices, appointments, 28 § 152
United States trustees, judicial districts, appointments, 28 § 581

ARMED FORCES
Application of law, bankruptcy, reserves, chapter 7 proceedings, 11 § 707 nt
Bankruptcy,
    Chapter 7 proceedings, abuse, 11 § 707
    Counseling services, exemptions, 11 § 109
    Reserves, chapter 7 proceedings, 11 § 707
Counseling services, bankruptcy, exemptions, 11 § 109
Reserves, bankruptcy, chapter 7 proceedings, 11 § 707

ARMED SERVICES
Armed Forces, generally, this index

ASSASSINATION
Congress, this index
Interception of wire, oral, or electronic communications, 18 § 2516
Justices of Supreme Court, 18 § 2516
President of the United States, this index
Vice President of the United States, this index

ASSAULT AND BATTERY
Cabinet departments, interception of wire, oral, or electronic communications, 18 § 2516
Congress, this index
Interception of wire, oral, or electronic communications, public officers and employees, 18 § 2516
Justices of Supreme Court, interception of wire, oral, or electronic communications, 18 § 2516
President of the United States, this index
Secretary of Agriculture, this index
Secretary of Commerce, this index
Secretary of Defense, this index
Secretary of Education, this index
Secretary of Energy, this index
Secretary of Housing and Urban Development, this index
Secretary of Labor, this index
Secretary of State, this index
Secretary of the Interior, this index
Secretary of the Treasury, this index
Secretary of Transportation, this index

ASSESSMENTS
Bankruptcy, this index

ASSIGNMENTS
Bankruptcy, this index

ASSIGNMENTS FOR BENEFIT OF CREDITORS
Custodians, property, 11 § 543

ASSISTED LIVING FACILITIES
Bankruptcy,
    Definitions, 11 § 101
    Ombudsman, 11 § 333
    Records and recordation, 11 § 351
Definitions, bankruptcy, 11 § 101
Ombudsman, bankruptcy, 11 § 333
Records and recordation, bankruptcy, 11 § 351

ASSOCIATIONS AND SOCIETIES
Cooperatives, generally, this index
Racketeering, generally, this index
Religious Organizations and Societies, generally, this index

ATHLETICS
Bribery and corruption, interception of wire, oral, or electronic communications, 18 § 2516

ATOMIC ENERGY
Crimes and offenses, interception of wire, oral, or electronic communications, 18 § 2516
Interception of wire, oral, or electronic communications, 18 § 2516

ATROPINE SULFATE
Controlled Substances, generally, this index

ATTORNEY FEES
Attorneys, this index

INDEX

ATTORNEY GENERAL
Assassination, interception of wire, oral, or electronic communications, 18 § 2516
Assault and battery, interception of wire, oral, or electronic communications, 18 § 2516
Bankruptcy, this index
Deputies, surveillance, 18 § 2516
Director, Administrative Office of U.S. Courts, reports, 28 § 604
Kidnapping, interception of wire, oral, or electronic communications, 18 § 2516

ATTORNEYS
Attorney General, generally, this index
Bankruptcy, this index
Fees,
    Bankruptcy, this index
    Judges or justices, discipline, 28 § 372
    Receivers and receivership, fraud, 18 § 155
    Title 11, fraud, 18 § 155
    United States magistrate judges, 28 § 372
Interception of Wire, Oral, or Electronic Communications, this index
Judges or justices, disqualification, 28 § 455
United States Tax Court, this index

AUCTIONS AND AUCTIONEERS
Bankruptcy, this index

AUDITS AND AUDITORS
Administrative Office of U.S. Courts, 28 § 604
Bankruptcy, this index
Judicial Center, 28 § 604

AUTOMATIC STAY
Bankruptcy, this index

AVIATION
Aircraft, generally, this index

AVOIDANCE
Bankruptcy, this index

AWARDS
Arbitration, this index
Incentive Pay or Awards, generally, this index

BACK PAY
Bankruptcy, 11 § 503

BAD FAITH
Bankruptcy, this index

BANKRUPTCY
    Generally, 11 § 101 et seq.; BKR 1001 et seq.
Abandonment, 11 § 347; BKR 3011, 6007
    Grain, 11 § 557
    Notice, 11 § 554
    Railroads, 11 § 1170
Abstention, 11 § 305; BKR 5011
    Comity, 28 § 1334
    Foreign representatives, appearances, 11 § 306
    Reciprocity, 28 § 1334
Abuse,
    Chapter 7 proceedings, post
    Homesteads, exemptions, 11 § 522
    Reaffirmation agreements, 18 § 158
Acceleration, contracts, 11 § 555 et seq.
Acceptances,
    Chapter 9 proceedings, BKR 3018
    Chapter 11 proceedings, post
    Plans and specifications, BKR 3005, 3006
Access, foreign countries, 11 § 1509 et seq.
Accountants, 11 § 503 et seq.; BKR 2014
    Appointments, BKR 5002
    Compensation and salaries, 11 § 504
        Administrative expenses, 11 § 503
        Priorities and preferences, 11 § 507
    Definitions, 11 § 101
Accounts and accounting,
    Coverdell education savings accounts, 11 §§ 521, 541
    Custodians, BKR 6002
    Disclosure, orders of court, 11 § 542
    Filing, 11 § 543
    Inspection and inspectors, 18 § 154
    Money, possession, 11 § 363
    Separate accounts, joint administration, BKR 2009
    Taxation, 11 § 346
    Trusts and trustees, post
    Turnovers, property, 11 § 542
Actions and proceedings, 11 § 108; BKR 6009
    Adversary proceedings, generally, post
    Alternative dispute resolution, 28 § 651 et seq.
    Automatic stay, generally, post
    Chapter 9 proceedings, post
    Community property, discharge, 11 § 524
    Compromise and settlement, generally, post
    Contracts, rejection, 11 § 365
    Core proceedings, 28 § 157
    Damages, generally, post
    Discharge, 11 § 524
    Dismissal and nonsuit, generally, post
    Ex parte proceedings, BKR 9003
    Expenses and expenditures, allowances, 11 § 503
    Foreign countries, generally, post
    Frivolous actions, generally, post
    Governmental units, 11 § 362; 28 § 1452
    Grain, 11 § 557
    Injunctions, generally, post
    Involuntary proceedings, generally, post
    Joint proceedings, generally, post
    Liens and incumbrances, generally, post
    Limitation of actions, generally, post
    Managers and management, 28 § 959
    Noncore proceedings,
        Abstention, 28 § 157
        Findings, BKR 9033
    Original jurisdiction, 28 § 1334
    Pending actions, generally, post
    Postpetition, generally, post
    References, generally, post
    Removal of cases or causes, generally, post
    Repurchase agreements, liquidation, 11 § 559
    Sales, avoidance, 11 § 363
    Securities, automatic stay, 11 § 362
    Stay of proceedings, generally, post
    Taxation,
        Automatic stay, 11 § 362
        Contests, 11 § 505
    Timeshares, rejection, 11 § 365
    Trusts and trustees, post
Actual notice, transfers, 11 § 542

INDEX

Addresses,
    Foreign countries, **11 § 1514**
    Governmental units, mail and mailing, **BKR 5003**
    Notice, **11 § 342; BKR 2002**
    Taxation, **11 § 505; BKR 5003**
Adjustments,
    Core proceedings, **28 § 157**
    Individual debtors. Chapter 13 proceedings, generally, post
    Money, **11 § 104**
    Municipal corporations. Chapter 9 proceedings, generally, post
Administration, **11 § 301 et seq.; 28 § 604**
    Chapter 13 proceedings, expenses and expenditures, schedules, **11 § 707 nt**
    Examinations and examiners, **BKR 6002**
    Exemptions, expenses and expenditures, **11 § 522**
    Expenses and expenditures,
        Assurance of payment, public utilities, **11 § 366**
        Chapter 13 proceedings, schedules, **11 § 707 nt**
        Conversion, payment, **BKR 1019**
        Exemptions, **11 § 522**
        Hearings, **11 § 503**
        Leases, **11 § 503**
        Taxation, **11 §§ 346, 503**
    Foreign countries, **11 § 1519 et seq.**
    Hearings, expenses and expenditures, **11 § 503**
    Leases, expenses and expenditures, **11 § 503**
    Notice, expenses and expenditures, **11 § 503**
    Payment, expenses and expenditures, **11 § 503**
    Presumptions, **BKR 5009**
    Reopening proceedings, **11 § 350**
    Taxation, expenses and expenditures, **11 §§ 346, 503**
    Transition, **28 § 151**
Administrative Office of United States Courts,
    Bankruptcy Division, compensation and salaries, **11 § 102**
    Judges or justices,
        Assistants, appointments, **28 § 156**
        Official stations, recommendations, **28 § 152**
    Returns, **28 § 156**
    Trusts and trustees, individual debtors, money, **11 § 1302**
Administrators,
    Appointments, **11 § 341 nt**
    Employee Retirement Income Security Program, **11 §§ 521, 704**
Admissions, **BKR 7036**
Advances, discharge, **11 § 523**
Adversary proceedings, **BKR 7001 et seq.**
    Application of rules, **BKR 7001**
    Applications, **BKR 1018**
    Captions, complaints, forms, **BKR Form 16D**
    Claims, withdrawal, **BKR 3006**
    Forms,
        Captions, complaints, **BKR Form 16D**
        Complaints, captions, **BKR Form 16D**
Adverse or pecuniary interest. Conflict of interest, generally, post

Advertisements, debt relief agencies, **11 § 528**
Affidavits, time, **BKR 9006**
Affiliates,
    Chapter 11 proceedings, venue, **28 § 1408**
    Definitions, **11 § 101**
Affirmations. Oaths and affirmations, generally, post
Agents and agencies,
    Committees, compensation and salaries, **11 § 504**
    Concealment, sentence and punishment, **18 § 152**
    Debt relief agencies, generally, post
Agreements. Contracts, generally, post
Agricultural Products, this index
Agriculture. Chapter 12 proceedings, generally, post
Aircraft,
    Discharge, **11 § 523**
    Security interest, **11 § 1110**
Alabama, **BKR 9035**
Alimony,
    Automatic stay, **11 § 362**
    Avoidance, **11 § 547**
    Chapter 11 proceedings, **11 § 1129**
    Chapter 12 proceedings, **11 §§ 1208, 1222 et seq.**
    Chapter 13 proceedings, **11 §§ 1307, 1322 et seq.**
    Collection, **11 § 362**
    Definitions, **11 § 101**
    Discharge, **11 § 523**
    Exemptions, **11 §§ 522, 523**
    Priorities and preferences, **11 § 507**
Allowances,
    Claims, post
    Compensation and salaries, generally, post
Alternative dispute resolution, **28 § 651 et seq.**
Alternative repayment schedule, avoidance, **11 § 547**
Amendments,
    Application of law, **11 § 101 nt**
    Federal Rules of Civil Procedure, **BKR 9032**
    Judgments and decrees, **BKR 9023**
    Lists, **BKR 1009**
    Pleadings, **BKR 7015**
Ancillary cases. Foreign countries, generally, post
Animals, **11 § 541**
    Custodians, transfers, **11 § 543**
    Exemptions, **11 § 522**
    Security interest, **11 § 363**
    Transfers, custodians, **11 § 543**
Annuities, exemptions, **11 § 522**
Answers, **BKR 7012**
    Petitions, claims, **BKR 1011**
Antecedent debt, avoidance, preferences, **11 § 547**
Anticramdown Law, chapter 13 proceedings, **11 § 1325**
Appeal and review, **BKR 8001 et seq.**
    Abstention, **11 § 305**
    Appendix, **BKR 8009, 8010**
    Bankruptcy appellate panels, generally, post
    Briefs, **BKR 8009, 8010**
    Certificates and certification, **BKR 8001; BKR Form 24**
    Chapter 9 proceedings, post
    Claims, removal, **28 § 1452**
    Clerks of court, **BKR 8016**

INDEX

Committees, organization, **BKR 2007**
Contempt, **BKR 9020**
Costs, **BKR 8014**
Credit, extensions, 11 § 364
Direct appeals, 28 § 158
Disposition, **BKR 8013**
Dockets and docketing, **BKR 8007**
Frivolous appeals, damages, **BKR 8020**
Grain, 11 § 557
Issue statement, **BKR 8006**
Jurisdiction, 28 §§ 158, 1334
Leave of court, **BKR 8003**
Local rules, **BKR 8018**
Motions,
    Emergencies, **BKR 8011**
    Rehearings, **BKR 8015**
Noncore proceedings, **BKR 9033**
Notice,
    Filing, fees, 28 § 1930
    Forms, **BKR Form 17**
    Service, **BKR 8004**
    Time, **BKR 8002**
Oral arguments, **BKR 8012**
Orders of court, 28 § 157
Records and recordation, **BKR 8006, 8007, 8016**
Rules, revocation or suspension, **BKR 8019**
Sales, modification, 11 § 363
Standards, **BKR 8013**
Statements, issues, **BKR 8006**
Stay of proceedings, **BKR 8005, 8017**
Transcripts, **BKR 8007**
Trusts and trustees, indebtedness, 11 § 364
Venue, 28 § 1408
Appearances, 11 § 521
    Chapter 11 proceedings, 11 §§ 1109, 1164
    Dismissal and nonsuit, 11 § 109
    Nonsuit, 11 § 109
    Notice, **BKR 9010**
    Parties, **BKR 9010**
    Railroads, 11 § 1164
Appellate panel. Bankruptcy appellate panels, generally, post
Appendix, appeal and review, briefs, **BKR 8009**
Appliances, exemptions, 11 § 522
Application of law, 11 § 102
    Amendments, 11 § 101 nt
    Armed Forces, reserves, chapter 7 proceedings, 11 § 707 nt
    Foreign countries, 11 § 1508
    Notice, 11 § 102
Applications, labor and employment, **BKR 6003**
Appointments,
    Consumer privacy ombudsman, **BKR 6004**
    Examinations and examiners, post
    Foreign countries, post
    Patient care ombudsman, 11 § 333; **BKR 2007.2**
    Trusts and trustees, post
    United States trustees, post
Appraisal and appraisers, 11 § 327; **BKR 2014, 6005**
    Appointments, **BKR 5002**
    Compensation and salaries,
        Records and recordation, **BKR 2013**
        Sharing, 11 § 504
    Records and recordation, compensation and salaries, **BKR 2013**

    Sharing, compensation and salaries, 11 § 504
Apprehension, examinations and examiners, **BKR 2005**
Arbitration, **BKR 9019**
    Reference, 28 § 654
Armed Forces, this index
Assessments,
    Claims, 11 § 502
    Payment, 11 § 505
Assignments, 11 § 365
    Contracts, 11 § 365; **BKR 6003**
    Leases, 11 § 365; **BKR 6006**
Assistance,
    Definitions, 11 § 101
    Foreign countries, 11 § 1507
Assistants,
    Judges or justices, appointments, 28 § 156
    United States trustees, post
Assisted Living Facilities, this index
Assumptions,
    Contracts, 11 § 365; **BKR 6003**
    Leases, **BKR 6006**
Assurance of payment, definitions, 11 § 366
Attachment, removal of cases or causes, **BKR 9027**
Attendance, examinations and examiners, **BKR 2005, 4002**
Attorney General,
    Audits and auditors, 28 § 586 nt
    Investigations, reports, 18 § 3057
Attorneys, 11 § 327 et seq.; **BKR 2014, 9010**
    Appointments, **BKR 5002**
    Automatic stay, fees, 11 § 362
    Cancellation, fees, 11 §§ 329, 541
    Chapter 7 proceedings, fees, 11 § 707
        Consumer debt, 11 § 523
    Chapter 13 proceedings, post
    Claims, 11 § 502
        Fees, **BKR 3001**
        Services, disallowance, 11 § 502
    Committees, 11 § 504
    Consumer debts, 11 § 523
    Corporations, reorganization, fees, 11 § 503
    Counseling services, fees, 11 § 111
    Debt relief agencies, fees, 11 § 526
    Definitions, 11 § 101
    Discharge, 11 § 524
    Disclosure, fees, **BKR 2016**
    Discretion of court, fees, 11 § 503
    Examinations and examiners, **BKR 2017**
    Excessive fees, 11 § 329; **BKR 2017**
    Expenses and expenditures, allowances, 11 § 503
    Fees, 11 § 329 et seq.
        Automatic stay, 11 § 362
        Cancellation, 11 §§ 329, 541
        Chapter 7 proceedings, 11 § 707
            Consumer debt, 11 § 523
        Chapter 13 proceedings, post
        Claims, **BKR 3001**
        Consumer debts, 11 § 523
        Corporations, reorganization, 11 § 503
        Counseling services, 11 § 111
        Debt relief agencies, 11 § 526
        Disclosure, **BKR 2016**
        Discretion of court, 11 § 503
        Excessive fees, 11 § 329; **BKR 2017**
        Fraud, 18 § 155
        Interim compensation, 11 § 331

INDEX

Involuntary proceedings, 11 §§ 303, 504
Petitions, 11 § 110
Pleading, BKR 7008
Priorities and preferences, 11 § 507
Professional services, 11 § 503
Records and recordation, BKR 2013
Recovery, 11 § 541
Sales, 11 § 363
Sharing, 11 § 504
Statements, 11 § 329
Subordination, BKR 1006
Financial statements and reports, 11 § 542
Fraud, fees, 18 § 155
Interim compensation, fees, 11 § 331
Involuntary proceedings, fees, 11 §§ 303, 504
Judges or justices, practice of law, 28 § 153
Labor and employment, 11 § 327 et seq.
Meetings, 11 § 341
Motions, fees, examinations and examiners, BKR 2017
Orders of court,
    Excessive compensation, 11 § 329
    Interim compensation, 11 § 331
Petitions, fees, 11 § 110
Pleading, fees, BKR 7008
Power of attorney, generally, post
Priorities and preferences, fees, 11 § 507
Professional associations, 11 § 504
Professional services, fees, 11 § 503
Public service attorney referral program, 11 § 504
Records and recordation, fees, BKR 2013
Recovery, fees, 11 § 541
Sales, fees, 11 § 363
Sharing, fees, 11 § 504
Signatures, chapter 7 proceedings, 11 § 707
Statements, fees, 11 § 329
Subordination, fees, BKR 1006
Trusts and trustees, post
United States attorneys, generally, post
Auctions and auctioneers, BKR 2014, 6005
    Appointments, BKR 5002
    Compensation and salaries, 11 § 504; BKR 2013
    Labor and employment, 11 § 327
Audits and auditors,
    Attorney General, 28 § 586 nt
    Automatic stay, political subdivisions, 11 § 362
    Chapter 7 proceedings, discharge, 11 § 727
    Judicial Conference of the United States, 28 § 586 nt
    Political subdivisions, automatic stay, 11 § 362
    United States trustees, 28 § 586
Automatic stay, 11 § 361; BKR 4001
    Alimony, 11 § 362
    Attorneys, fees, recovery, 11 § 362
    Bad faith, 11 § 362
    Chapter 9 proceedings, post
    Children and minors, 11 § 362
    Children born out of wedlock, 11 § 362
    Commodities, 11 § 362
    Consumer debt, 11 § 362
    Contracts, BKR 6006
    Damages, 11 § 362
    Divorce, 11 § 362
    Domestic violence, 11 § 362
    Evictions, 11 § 362
    Foreign countries, 11 § 1519 et seq.
    Forward contracts, 11 §§ 362, 553
    Good faith, 11 § 362
    Interest, 11 § 362
    Joint proceedings, post
    Landlord and tenant, 11 § 362
    Leases, post
    Liens and incumbrances, 11 § 362
    Master netting agreements, 11 § 362
    Medicare, 11 § 362
    Negotiable instruments, 11 § 362
    Notice, 11 § 362; BKR 4001
    Objections and exceptions, 11 § 362
    Pending actions, 11 § 109
    Presumptions, 11 § 362
    Real estate, 11 § 362
    Repurchase agreements, 11 § 362
    Retirement and pensions, 11 § 362
    Sales, 11 § 553; BKR 6004
    Securities, 11 §§ 362, 553
    Security interest, 11 § 362
    Set-off and counterclaim, 11 § 553
        Repurchase agreements, 11 § 362
    Support, 11 § 362
    Swap agreements, 11 § 362
    Taxation, post
    Termination, 11 § 362
    Unlawful detainer, 11 § 362
Avoidance, 11 §§ 541, 544 et seq.
    Alimony, 11 § 547
    Alternative repayment schedule, 11 § 547
    Antecedent debt, preferences, 11 § 547
    Automatic preservation, 11 §§ 541, 551
    Burden of proof, preferences, 11 § 547
    Chapter 9 proceedings, 11 §§ 109, 926
    Commodities, 11 §§ 546, 764
    Consumer debt, 11 § 547
    Damages, 11 §§ 501, 550
    Definitions, priorities and preferences, 11 § 547
    Evidence, priorities and preferences, 11 § 547
    Exemptions, 11 § 551; BKR 4003
        Transfers, 11 § 522
    Fraud, 11 § 548
    Insiders, 11 § 547
    Judicial liens, 11 §§ 544, 547
    Liens and incumbrances, 11 §§ 349, 522, 544 et seq.
        Indemnity, BKR 6010
    Limitation of actions, 11 §§ 546, 550
    Perfected security interest, 11 § 547
    Postpetition transactions, 11 § 549
    Preferences, 11 § 547
    Priorities and preferences, 11 § 547
    Real estate, good faith purchasers, 11 § 549
    Reinstatement, 11 § 349
    Repayment, alternative repayment schedule, 11 § 547
    Security interest, 11 §§ 522, 547
    Statutory liens, 11 § 545 et seq.
    Support, 11 § 547
    Tax liens, 11 §§ 522, 545
    Waiver, 11 § 522
Awards, Crime Victims Reparation Law, exemptions, 11 § 522
Back pay, 11 § 503

INDEX

Bad faith,
    Automatic stay, **11 § 362**
    Chapter 7 proceedings, **11 § 707**
    Chapter 13 proceedings, **11 § 348**
Ballots, reorganization, plans and specifications, forms, **BKR Form 14**
Bankruptcy Administrator, appointments, **11 § 341 nt**
Bankruptcy appellate panels, **28 § 158**
    Clerks of courts, powers and duties, **BKR 8016**
    Joint appellate panels, **28 § 158**
    Local rules, **BKR 8018**
Bankruptcy Division, Administrative Office of U.S. Courts, officers and employees, compensation and salaries, **11 § 102**
Banks and banking,
    Definitions, **11 § 101**
    Margin, transfers, **11 § 546**
    Qualifications, **11 § 109**
    Securities, liquidation, **11 § 555**
    Unsecured claims, priorities and preferences, **11 §§ 753, 767**
Barley, **11 § 557**
Beans, dry edible beans, **11 § 557**
Bias and prejudice, dismissal and nonsuit, **11 § 349**
Bifurcation of claims, chapter 13 proceedings, **11 § 1325**
Boards and commissions, National Bankruptcy Review Commission, **11 nt prec § 101**
Bodily injury, payments, exemptions, **11 § 522**
Bona fide purchasers, **11 § 544 et seq.**
    Perfection, **11 § 548**
    Preferences, real estate, **11 § 547**
    Real estate, **11 §§ 544, 547**
    Statutory liens, avoidance, **11 § 545**
Bonds (officers and fiduciaries), **BKR 9025**
    Claims, evidence, **BKR 3005**
    Deposits, money, **11 § 345**
    Involuntary proceedings, **11 § 303**
    Liens and incumbrances, **BKR 6010**
    Money, deposits, **11 § 345**
    Preferences, transfers, **11 § 547**
    Removal of cases or causes, **BKR 9027**
    Stay of proceedings, **BKR 8005**
    Transfers, preferences, **11 § 547**
    Trusts and trustees, post
    Voluntary proceedings, **11 § 303**
Bonus, retention bonuses, **11 § 503**
Books and papers, **BKR 5003**
    Certified copies, **BKR 5006**
    Concealment, crimes and offenses, **18 § 152**
    Disclosure, hearings, **11 § 542**
    Exemptions, **11 § 522**
    Filing, **BKR 5005**
    Inspection and inspectors, **11 § 107; 18 § 154**
    Liens and incumbrances, nonpossessory, **11 § 522**
    Surrender, **11 § 521**
    Trade, exemptions, **11 § 522**
Bribery and corruption, **18 § 152**
Briefs, appeal and review, **BKR 8009, 8010**
Brokers,
    Commodities, post
    Shares and shareholders, post
Building and loan associations, qualifications, **11 § 109**
Buildings, **28 § 156**
    Expenses and expenditures, **28 § 156**
    National Bankruptcy Review Commission, **11 nt prec § 101**
Burden of proof. Evidence, generally, post
Burial plot, exemptions, **11 § 522**
Business and commerce,
    Claims, ordinary course of business, **11 § 507**
    Crimes and offenses, **11 § 503**
    Foreign countries, post
    Goods, wares and merchandise, returns, **11 § 546**
    Health care businesses, generally, post
    Individual debtors, operating businesses, **11 § 1304**
    Information, public access, **11 § 107**
    Involuntary proceedings, **11 § 303**
    Liens and incumbrances, **11 § 522**
    Location, **11 § 109**
    Operating businesses, **11 § 363**
        Foreign countries, **11 §§ 1520, 1522**
        Individual debtors, **11 § 1304**
        Reorganization, **11 § 1108**
        Trusts and trustees, **11 § 303**
    Ordinary course of business, claims, **11 § 507**
    Place of business, generally, post
    Public access, information, **11 § 107**
    Reorganization, operating businesses, **11 § 1108**
    Returns, goods, wares and merchandise, **11 § 546**
    Small businesses, generally, post
    Taxation, deductions, **11 § 346**
    Trusts and trustees, **11 § 303**
Cancellation,
    Attorneys, fees, **11 §§ 329, 541**
    Reaffirmation agreements, **11 § 524**
Capacity, parties, **BKR 7017**
Captions,
    Forms, post
    Notice, **BKR 2002**
    Petitions, **BKR 1005**
Carrybacks, taxation, **11 § 346**
Carryovers, taxation, **11 § 346**
Cash. Money, generally, post
Cash collateral, definitions, **11 § 363**
Cause, definitions, **11 § 1112**
Certificates and certification,
    Appeal and review, **BKR 8001; BKR Form 24**
    Copies, **BKR 5006**
    Counseling services, **11 § 521**
    Financial management training curriculum, certification of completion, forms, **BKR Form 23**
    Foreign countries, **11 § 1515 et seq.**
    Forms, nonattorney petition preparers, **BKR Form 6**
    Nonattorney petition preparers, forms, **BKR Form 6**
    Professional personnel, compensation and salaries, **11 § 330**
    Records and recordation, searches and seizures, **BKR 5003**
    Residential rental housing, possession, **11 § 362**
Certified copies, **BKR 5006**
Certiorari, fees, receipts, **28 § 1930**
Chambers, orders of court, **BKR 5001**

INDEX

Changes,
    Statements, **BKR 4002**
    Venue, **28 § 1412; BKR 1014**
Chapter 7 proceedings, **11 § 701 et seq.**
    Abandonment,
        Consumer debt, liens and incumbrances, redemption, **11 § 722**
        Disposition, **BKR 3011**
    Abuse, **11 § 707**
        Notice, **11 § 342; BKR 5008**
        Trusts and trustees, **11 §§ 704, 707**
    Accounts and accounting, **11 § 704**
    Actions and proceedings, dismissal and nonsuit, **11 § 707**
    Addresses, notice, **11 § 342**
    Application of law, **11 § 103**
    Attorneys, fees, **11 § 707**
        Consumer debt, **11 § 523**
    Audits and auditors, discharge, **11 § 727**
    Bad faith, **11 § 707**
    Banks and banking, qualifications, **11 § 109**
    Building and loan associations, qualifications, **11 § 109**
    Business and commerce, reports, filing, **11 § 704**
    Chapter 11 proceedings, conversion, **11 § 707**
    Chapter 13 proceedings,
        Automatic stay, time, **11 § 362**
        Consumer debts, dismissal and nonsuit, **11 § 707**
    Charities, contributions, dismissal and nonsuit, **11 § 707**
    Claims,
        Amount, **11 § 702**
        Conversion, **BKR 1019**
        Time, **11 § 348**
        Distributions, payment, **11 § 726**
        Evidence,
            Examinations and examiners, **11 § 704**
            Filing, **BKR 3002**
        Fraud, discharge, revocation or suspension, **11 § 727**
        General partner, **11 § 723**
        Liens and incumbrances, avoidance, **11 § 724**
        Partnership,
            Allowances, objections and exceptions, **11 § 502**
            Deficiencies, damages, **11 § 723**
        Trusts and trustees, elections, **11 § 702**
        Unsecured claims,
            Distributions, elections, **11 § 705**
            Payment, **11 § 726**
    Clearing banks, **11 § 781 et seq.**
    Closings, **BKR 5009**
    Collection, **11 § 721 et seq.**
        Application of law, **11 § 103**
        Discharge, **11 § 727**
        Disposition, **11 § 725**
        Liens and incumbrances, **11 § 724**
        Money, **11 § 704**
        Partnership, rights, **11 § 723**
        Redemption, **11 § 722**
        Support, **11 § 704**
    Committees, elections, **11 §§ 703, 705**
    Complaints, discharge, **BKR 4004 et seq.**

Consumer debt,
    Costs, discharge, **11 § 523**
    Discharge, costs, **11 § 523**
    Liens and incumbrances, redemption, **11 § 722**
    Redemption, liens and incumbrances, **11 § 722**
Contracts, **11 § 555 et seq.**
    Objections and exceptions, **11 § 365**
Conversion, **11 § 348; BKR 1017, 1019**
    Chapter 11 proceedings, **11 § 706; 28 § 1930**
    Chapter 12 proceedings, **11 § 706**
    Chapter 13 proceedings, **11 §§ 706, 1301, 1307**
Cooperative banks, qualifications, **11 § 109**
Copies, **11 § 521**
Corporations, judicial districts, offices, **11 § 321**
Costs, **11 § 707**
Credit unions, qualifications, **11 § 109**
Crimes and offenses, dismissal and nonsuit, **11 § 707**
Customs duties, discharge, objections and exceptions, **11 § 523**
Damages,
    Claims, distribution, payment, **11 § 726**
    General partners, deficiencies, damages, **11 § 723**
    Liens and incumbrances, avoidance, **11 § 724**
Death, **BKR 1016**
    Trusts and trustees, successor trustees, **11 § 703**
Deficiencies, partnership, claims, damages, **11 § 723**
Definitions, **11 § 707**
Destruction of property, discharge, denial, **11 § 727**
Discharge, **11 § 727; BKR 4004**
    Driving while intoxicated, objections and exceptions, **11 § 523**
    Forms, **BKR Form 18**
    Good faith, **11 § 727**
    Opposition, **11 § 704**
Dismissal and nonsuit, **11 § 707**
    Abuse, **BKR 1017**
    Death, mental health, **BKR 1016**
    Schedules, **11 § 521**
Disposition, **11 § 725**
Distribution, **11 § 726**
    Application of law, **11 § 103**
    Final distribution, hearings, **11 § 725**
    Liens and incumbrances, treatment, **11 § 724**
Dividends, payment, **BKR 3009, 3010**
Divorce, discharge, objections and exceptions, **11 § 523**
Drugs and medicine, trafficking, dismissal and nonsuit, **11 § 707**
Education, loans, **11 § 523**
Elections,
    Meetings, **11 § 702**
    Proxies, **BKR 2006**
    Termination, trusts and trustees, **11 § 701**
    Trusts and trustees, termination, **11 § 701**

INDEX

Embezzlement, discharge, objections and exceptions, 11 § 523
Evidence,
    Abuse, 11 § 707
    Claims, filing, BKR 3002
    Filing, claims, BKR 3002
Examinations and examiners, claims, evidence, 11 § 704
Exemptions, consumer debt, liens and incumbrances, discharge, 11 § 722
Expenses and expenditures, payment, 11 § 726
    Dismissal and nonsuit, 11 § 707
Fees, filing, 28 § 1930
    Waiver, BKR 1006
        Forms, BKR Form 3B
Filing,
    Fees, 28 § 1930
        Waiver, BKR 1006
            Forms, BKR Form 3B
    Involuntary proceedings, 11 § 303
    Trusts and trustees, fees, 11 § 330
    Unsecured claims, 11 § 726
    Voluntary proceedings, dismissal and nonsuit, 11 § 707
Final account, 11 § 704
Financial management training curriculum, 11 § 727
Fines and penalties, 11 § 707
    Claims, distributions, 11 § 726
    Governmental unit, discharge, objections and exceptions, 11 § 523
Foreign banks, qualifications, 11 § 109
Forms,
    Filing, fees, waiver, BKR Form 3B
    Notice, BKR Form 9
    Statement of intention, individual debtors, BKR Form 8
Fraud,
    Claims, discharge, denial, 11 § 727
    Discharge, objections and exceptions, 11 § 523
General partners,
    Deficiencies, recovery, 11 § 723
    Distributions, payment, 11 § 508
Good faith,
    Claims, customers, 11 § 746
    Customers, claims, 11 § 746
    Discharge, 11 § 727
    Schedules, filing, 11 § 521
Health care businesses, BKR 1021
Hearings,
    Discharge, 11 § 523
    Dismissal and nonsuit, 11 § 707
    Distributions, 11 § 725
    Party in interest, conversion, 11 § 706
        Trusts and trustees, discharge, revocation or suspension, 11 § 727
Homestead associations, qualifications, 11 § 109
Indemnity, partnership, deficiencies, 11 § 723
Information, party in interest, 11 § 704
Insiders, trusts and trustees, elections, 11 § 702
Insurance, qualifications, 11 § 109

Interest, payment, time, 11 § 726
Inventories, BKR 2015
Investigations, 11 § 704
Involuntary proceedings, 11 § 303
Joint administration, appointments, BKR 2009
Judgments and decrees, consumer debts, discharge, costs, 11 § 523
Larceny, discharge, objections and exceptions, 11 § 523
Liens and incumbrances,
    Avoidance, 11 § 724
    Consumer debt, redemption, 11 § 722
    Discharge, objections and exceptions, 11 § 523
    Taxation, 11 § 724
Lists, discharge, objections and exceptions, 11 § 523
Lost property, discharge, revocation or suspension, 11 § 727
Meetings, BKR 2003
    Corporations, forms, BKR Form 9
    Elections, trusts and trustees, 11 § 702
    Individual debtors, forms, BKR Form 9
    Joint debtors, forms, BKR Form 9
    Partnership, forms, BKR Form 9
    Trusts and trustees, elections, 11 § 702
Mental health, BKR 1016
Money, fraud, discharge, objections and exceptions, 11 § 523
Motions,
    Discharge, objections and exceptions, time, BKR 4004
    Dismissal and nonsuit, abuse, BKR 1017
    Interim trustees, appointments, BKR 2001
    Proxies, BKR 2006
    Reopening, BKR 5010
National Guard, 11 § 707
No asset notice, BKR 2002
Notice, BKR 2002
    Abuse, 11 § 342; BKR 5008
    Addresses, 11 § 342
    Corporations, forms, BKR Form 9
    Debtors in possession, BKR 2015
    Discharge, BKR 4004
    Forms, BKR Form 9
    Individual debtors, forms, BKR Form 9
    Joint debtors, forms, BKR Form 9
    Partnership, forms, BKR Form 9
    Proxies, BKR 2006
    Support, 11 § 704
Oaths and affirmations, 11 § 707
    Discharge, fraud, 11 § 727
    Fraud, discharge, 11 § 727
Objections and exceptions, 11 § 523
    Claims, allowances, 11 § 704
    Closings, BKR 5009
    Discharge, 11 § 727
        Time, BKR 4004
Operation, businesses, 11 § 721
Panel, trusts and trustees, 28 § 586
    Appointments, 11 § 701
Parties,

INDEX

Audits and auditors, discharge, **11 § 727**
Conversion, hearings, **11 § 706**
Information, **11 § 704**
Involuntary proceedings, trusts and trustees, appointments, **11 § 303**
Partnership,
    Claims, objections and exceptions, **11 § 502**
    General partners,
        Deficiencies, damages, **11 § 723**
        Payment, **11 § 508**
Payment, dividends, **BKR 3009, 3010**
Pending actions, **11 § 727**
Petitions, involuntary proceedings, **11 § 303**
Political subdivisions, **11 § 523**
    Reports, taxation, **11 § 704**
    Taxation, reports, **11 § 704**
Powers and duties, trusts and trustees, **11 § 704**
Presumptions, **11 § 707**
    Abuse, **BKR 5008**
Prior bankruptcies, discharge, **11 § 727**
Priorities and preferences, **11 § 726**
    Liens and incumbrances, **11 § 724**
    Partnership, deficiencies, damages, **11 § 723**
    Unsecured claims, **11 §§ 753, 767**
Privileges and immunities, material questions, **11 § 727**
Proxies, **BKR 2006**
Railroads, reorganization, **11 § 1174**
Records and recordation, **BKR 2001**
    Concealment, **11 § 727**
    Debtors in possession, **BKR 2015**
Redemption, **11 § 722**
Referees, fees, **11 nt prec § 101**
Registration, discharge, **BKR 4004**
Reopening, **BKR 5010**
    Trusts and trustees, appointments, **11 § 703**
Reorganization, railroads, **11 § 1174**
Reports, **BKR 2001**
    Final, filing, **11 § 704**
Repurchase agreement, liquidation, contracts, **11 § 559**
Resignation, trusts and trustees, successor trustees, **11 § 703**
Revocation or suspension, discharge, **11 § 727**
Savings and loan association, qualifications, **11 § 109**
Savings banks, qualifications, **11 § 109**
Schedules, **11 § 523**
    Dismissal and nonsuit, **11 § 521**
Securities, contracts, **11 § 555**
Self-incrimination, **11 § 727**
Senior liens, **11 § 724**
Separation agreements, discharge, objections and exceptions, **11 § 523**
Solicitation, proxies, **BKR 2006**
Spouses,
    Alimony, maintenance, support, **11 § 523**
    Discharge, denial, **11 § 524**
Statements,
    Business and commerce, operation, filing, **11 § 704**
    Intention, **BKR 1007**

Successor trustees, qualifications, **11 §§ 322, 703**
Supervision, **28 § 586**
Supplemental schedules, **BKR 1007**
Support, **11 § 704**
Tangible, consumer debt, liens and incumbrances, redemption, **11 § 722**
Taxation, **11 § 346**
    Discharge, objections and exceptions, **11 § 523**
    Liens and incumbrances, **11 § 724**
    Tardy priority claims, **11 § 726**
Termination, **11 § 701**
Time,
    Abuse, notice, **BKR 5008**
    Discharge, **BKR 4007**
        Objections and exceptions, **BKR 4004**
    Trusts and trustees, discharge, revocation or suspension, **11 § 727**
Transfers,
    Avoidance, priorities and preferences, **11 § 547**
    Destruction of property, discharge, denial, **11 § 727**
Trusts and trustees,
    Abuse, **11 §§ 704, 707**
    Accounts and accounting, **11 § 704**
        Turnovers, delivery, **11 § 542**
    Application of law, **11 § 103**
    Appointments, successors, **11 § 703**
    Avoidance, liens and incumbrances, **11 § 724**
    Candidates, elections, **11 § 702**
    Committees,
        Consultants, **11 § 705**
        Trusts and trustees, elections, **11 § 702**
        Vacancies in office, elections, **11 § 703**
    Commodity brokers, contracts, objections and exceptions, **11 § 365**
    Compensation and salaries, payment, **11 § 330**
    Conversion, termination, **11 § 348**
    Credit, **11 § 364**
    Damages, general partners, deficiencies, **11 § 723**
    Death, successors, **11 § 703**
    Discharge, objections and exceptions, **11 § 704**
    Distribution, surplus property, **11 § 723**
    Elections, **11 § 702**
        Qualifications, **11 § 322**
    Eligibility, domicile and residence, **11 § 321**
    Filing, fees, payment, **11 § 330**
    Interim trustees, **11 § 701**
        Appointments, **11 § 703; BKR 2001**
            Qualifications, **11 § 322**
            Vacancies in office, **11 § 703**
    Investigations, **11 § 704**
    Objections and exceptions, discharge, **11 § 727**

INDEX

Partnership, deficiencies, damages, **11 § 723**
Powers and duties, **11 § 704**
Professional persons, labor and employment, **11 § 327**
Removal from office, successors, **11 § 703**
Resignation, successors, **11 § 703**
Successor trustee, United States trustee, appointments, **11 § 703**
Support, **11 § 704**
Termination, **11 § 701**
Vacancies in office, successors, **11 § 703**
Unclaimed property, disposition, **11 § 347; BKR 3011**
Unexpired leases, objections and exceptions, **11 § 365**
United States trustees, post
Vacating or setting aside, proxies, **BKR 2006**
Veterans, disabled veterans, **11 § 707**
Voluntary proceedings, dismissal and nonsuit, filing, **11 § 707**
Waiver,
    Consumer debt, liens and incumbrances, redemption, **11 § 722**
    Conversion, **11 § 706**
    Discharge, **11 § 524**
    Fees, filing, **28 § 1930; BKR 1006**
    Forms, **BKR Form 3B**
Chapter 9 proceedings, **11 § 901 et seq.**
    Acceptances, plans and specifications, **BKR 3018, 3019**
    Dismissal and nonsuit, **11 § 930**
    Actions and proceedings, **11 § 922**
        Avoidance, transfers, **11 § 926**
        Confirmation of plan, **11 § 943**
        Petitions, **11 § 921**
        Transfers, avoidance, **11 § 926**
    Administration, expenses and expenditures, **11 § 901**
    Appeal and review, **11 § 901**
        Stay of proceedings, **11 § 921**
    Application of law, **11 §§ 103, 901**
    Appointments, trusts and trustees, **11 § 926**
    Automatic stay, **11 § 901**
        Claims, **11 § 922**
        Confirmation of plan, **BKR 3020**
        Time, **11 § 362**
    Avoidance, transfers, **11 §§ 109, 901, 926**
    Best interest, confirmation of plan, **11 § 943**
    Bonds, dealers, notice, **11 § 923**
    Chief Judge, designation, **11 § 921**
    Claims,
        Automatic stay, petitions, enforcement, **11 § 922**
        Codebtor, **11 § 901**
        Confirmation of plan, **11 § 943**
        Evidence, filing, **BKR 3003**
        Exchanges, security, **11 § 946**
        Interests,
            Allowances, **11 § 901**
            Evidence, lists, filing, **11 § 925**
        Lists, **11 § 925**
    Closings, **11 § 945**
    Committees, **11 § 901**
        Allowances, **11 § 503**
        Organization, **BKR 2007**

        Priorities and preferences, **11 § 507**
    Community, **11 § 901**
    Compliance, confirmation of plan, **11 § 943**
    Confirmation of plan, **11 § 943; BKR 3020**
        Notice, **11 § 944**
    Contingent claim, lists, filing, **11 § 925**
    Contracts, qualifications, **11 § 109**
    Credit, **11 § 901**
    Damages, avoidance, **11 § 901**
    Debt adjustment plan, qualifications, **11 § 109**
    Definitions, **11 § 902**
        Application of law, **11 § 901**
        Representatives and representation, statements, **BKR 2019**
    Delay,
        Appeal and review, orders, **11 § 921**
        Unreasonable, dismissal and nonsuit, **11 § 930**
    Deposits, **BKR 3020**
    Discharge, **11 § 524**
        Confirmation of plan, **11 § 944**
        Judgments and decrees, **11 § 901**
    Disclosure,
        Confirmation of plan, expenses and expenditures, payment, **11 § 943**
        Forms, **BKR Form 12**
        Statements, **BKR 3017**
        Filing, **BKR 3016**
    Dismissal and nonsuit, **11 § 923**
        Application of law, **11 § 901**
        Notice, **11 §§ 923, 930**
        Petitions, objections and exceptions, **11 § 921**
    Disputes, lists, filing, **11 § 925**
    Elections, nonrecourse loans, **BKR 3014**
    Evidence,
        Claims, filing, **BKR 3003**
        Lists, **11 § 925**
    Exchanges, security, **11 § 946**
    Executory contracts, rejection, **11 § 365**
    Filing,
        Claims, **11 § 901**
            Automatic stay, **11 § 922**
            Evidence, **BKR 3003**
        Fees, payment, **28 § 1930**
        Plans and specifications, **11 § 941**
    Fraud, transfers, **11 §§ 901, 926**
    Good faith, **11 § 901**
        Confirmation of plan, **BKR 3020**
        Negotiations, **11 § 109**
        Petitions, **11 § 921**
    Health care businesses, **BKR 1021**
    Hearings, dismissal and nonsuit, **11 § 930**
    Injunctions,
        Discharge, **11 § 901**
        Plans and specifications, **BKR 3017**
    Insolvency, qualifications, **11 § 109**
    Intervention, **BKR 2018**
    Judges or justices, designation, **11 § 921**
    Judgments and decrees,
        Jurisdiction, **11 § 904**
        State laws, binding, consent, **11 § 903**
    Jurisdiction,
        Appeal and review, **11 § 921**
        Confirmation of plan, **11 § 930**
        Plans and specifications, **11 § 945**
    Leases, **11 §§ 901, 929**

INDEX

Assumption, 11 § 365
Liens and incumbrances,
    Claims, reorganization, 11 § 901
    Taxation, petitions, filing, 11 § 922
Lists,
    Claims, 11 § 925
    Filing, 11 §§ 521, 924
    Twenty largest creditors, BKR 1007
Material default, dismissal and nonsuit, 11 § 930
Modification, plans and specifications, 11 § 942; BKR 3019
Negotiations, qualifications, 11 § 109
Newspapers, notice, 11 § 923
Nonrecourse loans, elections, BKR 3014
Notice, 11 § 923
    Disclosure, statements, BKR 3017
    Dismissal and nonsuit, 11 § 930
Objections and exceptions,
    Confirmation of plan, 11 § 943; BKR 3020
    Disclosure, statements, BKR 3017
    Dismissal and nonsuit, 11 § 921
Orders of court,
    Appeal and review, delays, 11 § 921
    Confirmation of plan, BKR 3020
    Disclosure, statements, BKR 3017
    Jurisdiction, 11 § 904
    Notice, 11 § 923
Petitions, 11 § 921
    Automatic stay, filing, 11 § 922
    Time, filing, 11 § 941
Plans and specifications, 11 § 941 et seq.
    Acceptances, BKR 3018, 3019
    Closings, 11 § 945
    Confirmation of plan, 11 §§ 943, 944
        Dismissal and nonsuit, 11 § 930
    Core proceeding, 28 § 157
    Exchanges, security, 11 § 946
    Executory contracts, assumption, 11 § 501
    Filing, 11 § 941; BKR 3016
    Injunctions, BKR 3017
    Jurisdiction, 11 § 945
    Leases, unexpired leases, assumption, 11 § 501
    Modification, 11 § 942; BKR 3019
    Rejection, BKR 3018
Political subdivisions,
    Jurisdiction, 11 § 904
    Powers and duties, preservation, 11 § 903
Postpetition,
    Avoidance, transfers, 11 § 901
    Security interest, 11 § 928
Powers and duties, transfers, avoidance, 11 § 926
Preferences, 11 § 901
Preservation, States, powers and duties, 11 § 903
Priorities and preferences, 11 § 901
Process, automatic stay, 11 § 922
Prosecution, dismissal and nonsuit, 11 § 930
Publication, notice, 11 § 923
Qualifications, 11 § 109
Recourse, 11 § 927
Rejection, plans and specifications, BKR 3018

Reopening, 11 § 901
Reorganization, 11 §§ 103, 901
Representatives and representation, statements, BKR 2019
Retention, dismissal and nonsuit, jurisdiction, 11 § 930
Schedules, liabilities, BKR 3003
Securities,
    Exchanges, 11 § 946
    Money, disposition, 11 § 347
Security interest,
    Postpetition, 11 § 928
        Set-off and counterclaim, 11 § 901
    Set-off and counterclaim, postpetition, 11 § 901
Self-incrimination, 11 § 901
Service of process, automatic stay, 11 § 922
Spouses, definitions, 11 § 902
State laws, 11 §§ 109, 903
Statute of limitations, transfers, avoidance, 11 § 901
Statutory liens, 11 § 901
Stay of proceedings, 11 § 921
    Jurisdiction, 11 § 904
    Petitions, filing, 11 § 922
Subordination, 11 § 901
Taxation,
    Confirmation of plan, objections and exceptions, 11 § 943
    Petitions, 11 § 921
    Special taxpayer, definitions, 11 § 902
Termination, 11 § 930
Time, filing of plan, 11 § 941
Transfers, avoidance, 11 §§ 109, 926
Trusts and trustees, 11 § 901
    Appointments, 11 § 926
    Compensation and salaries, priorities and preferences, 11 § 507
    Contributions, 11 § 503
    Definitions, 11 § 902
Unliquidated claims, lists, filing, 11 § 925
Unreasonable delay, dismissal and nonsuit, 11 § 930
Utilities, 11 § 901
Waiver, discharge, 11 § 524
Want of prosecution, dismissal and nonsuit, 11 § 930
Chapter 11 proceedings, 11 § 1101 et seq.
    Abandonment, railroads, 11 § 1170
    Acceptances, 11 § 1126
        Forms, plans and specifications, BKR Forms 13, 14
        Plans and specifications, BKR 3018, 3019
    Administration, application of laws, 11 § 103
    Aircraft, machinery and equipment, 11 § 1110
    Alimony, 11 § 1129
    Appearance, 11 § 1109
        Railroads, 11 § 1164
    Application of laws,
        Administration, 11 § 103
        Railroads, 11 § 1161
    Automatic stay, 11 § 362
        Confirmation of plan, BKR 3020
    Cause, dismissal and nonsuit, 11 § 1112
    Chapter 7 proceedings, conversion, 11 § 707

INDEX

Claims, 11 § 1111
    Classification, 11 §§ 1122, 1123
    Evidence, filing, BKR 3003
    Impairment, 11 § 1124
    Railroads, priorities and preferences, 11 § 1171
Classification, claims, 11 §§ 1122, 1123
Collective bargaining agreements,
    Railroads, 11 § 1167
    Rejection, 11 § 1113
Committees, 11 §§ 1102, 1103; BKR 2007
Complaints, discharge, BKR 4004
Confirmation of plan, 11 §§ 1128, 1129; BKR 3020
    Dismissal and nonsuit, 11 § 1112
    Forms, objections and exceptions, BKR Form 13
    Orders of court, BKR Form 15
    Postconfirmation, 11 § 1141 et seq.
    Railroads, 11 § 1173
Consumer debts, 11 § 523
Controlling interest, financial statements and reports, BKR 2015.3; BKR Form 26
Conversion, 11 § 1112
    Eligibility, 11 § 706
    Individual debtors, 11 § 1301
    Liquidation, BKR 1019
Customs duties, discharge, objections and exceptions, 11 § 523
Debtors in possession, powers and duties, 11 § 1107
Default, 11 § 1123
    Dismissal and nonsuit, 11 § 1112
    Railroads, 11 § 1172
Definitions, 11 § 1101
    Fair and equitable, plans and specifications, 11 § 1129
    Property of the estate,
        Individual debtors, 11 § 1115
        Municipal debt adjustment, 11 § 902
    Railroads, 11 § 1162
    Representatives and representation, statements, BKR 2019
Delivery, plans and specifications, 11 § 1142
Deposits, BKR 3020
Discharge, 11 § 524; BKR 4004
    Confirmation of plan, 11 § 1141
Disclosure,
    Dismissal and nonsuit, 11 § 1112
    Forms, BKR Form 12 et seq.
    Objections and exceptions, statements, BKR 3017, 3017.1
    Orders of court, forms, BKR Form 12 et seq.
    Postpetition, 11 § 1125
    Small businesses, statements, 11 § 1125; BKR 3017.1
    Statements, BKR 3016 et seq.
    Taxation, 11 § 1125
Dismissal and nonsuit, 11 § 1112
Distribution, 11 § 1143
Divorce, discharge, objections and exceptions, 11 § 523
Elections,
    Ballots, plans and specifications, forms, BKR Form 14

Nonrecourse loans, BKR 3014
    Plans and specifications, ballots, forms, BKR Form 14
Embezzlement, fiduciaries, 11 § 523
Evidence, 11 § 1111
    Claims, filing, BKR 3003
Examinations and examiners,
    Appointments, 11 § 1104; BKR 2007.1
    Powers and duties, 11 § 1106
Exemptions, securities, 11 § 1145
Federal, State or local laws, railroads, 11 § 1166
Fees,
    Dismissal and nonsuit, 11 § 1112
    Fraud, 18 § 155
Filing, 11 § 1106
    Claims, evidence, BKR 3003
    Controlling interest, financial statements and reports, BKR 2015.3
    Dismissal and nonsuit, 11 § 1112
    Plans and specifications, BKR 3016
    Substantial or controlling interest, financial statements and reports, BKR 2015.3
Financial statements and reports, substantial or controlling interest, BKR 2015.3; BKR Form 26
Foreign countries, venue, 28 § 1408
Forms, BKR Form 9
    Small businesses, BKR Form 25 et seq.
    Substantial or controlling interest, financial statements and reports, BKR Form 26
Fraud,
    Fees, 18 § 155
    Taxation, discharge, 11 § 1141
    Trusts and trustees, 11 § 1104
Good faith,
    Collective bargaining, 11 § 1113
    Confirmation of plan, 11 §§ 1129, 1144; BKR 3020
    Plans and specifications, 11 § 1126
    Postpetition, solicitation, 11 § 1125
    Retirement and pensions, 11 § 1114
Health care businesses, BKR 1021
Hearings, confirmation of plan, 11 § 1128
Impairment, claims, 11 § 1124
Injunctions, plans and specifications, BKR 3017
Insurance,
    Dismissal and nonsuit, 11 § 1112
    Retirement and pensions, payment, 11 § 1114
Inventories, BKR 2015
Involuntary proceedings, 11 § 303
Joint administration, appointments, BKR 2009
Judgments and decrees, BKR 3022
Jurisdiction, 28 § 1334
Liquidation, railroads, 11 § 1174
Lists, BKR 1007
    Filing, 11 § 1106
Losses,
    Dismissal and nonsuit, 11 § 1112
    Nonmonetary obligations, 11 § 1124
Managers and management, 28 § 959

INDEX

Dismissal and nonsuit, 11 § 1112
Meetings, **BKR 2003; BKR Form 9**
    Dismissal and nonsuit, 11 § 1112
Modification, plans and specifications, 11 § 1127; **BKR 3019**
Motions, judgments and decrees, **BKR 3022**
Nonrecourse loans, elections, **BKR 3014**
Notice, **BKR 2002**
    Confirmation of plan, 11 § 1128
    Controlling interest, financial statements and reports, **BKR 2015.3**
    Corporations, forms, **BKR Form 9**
    Discharge, **BKR 4004**
    Disclosure, statements, **BKR 3017, 3017.1**
    Individual debtors, forms, **BKR Form 9**
    Joint debtors, forms, **BKR Form 9**
    Partnership, forms, **BKR Form 9**
    Substantial or controlling interest, financial statements and reports, **BKR 2015.3**
    Support, 11 § 1106
    Trusts and trustees, **BKR 2015**
Objections and exceptions,
    Confirmation of plan, 11 §§ 1128, 1129; **BKR 3020**
    Forms, **BKR Form 13**
    Discharge, time, **BKR 4004**
    Disclosure, statements, **BKR 3017, 3017.1**
    Forms, confirmation of plan, **BKR Form 13**
Operating businesses, 11 § 1108
Orders of court,
    Confirmation of plan, **BKR 3020**
    Disclosure, statements, **BKR 3017; BKR Form 12 et seq.**
    Dismissal and nonsuit, 11 § 1112
Parties, appearance, 11 § 1109
Payment,
    Personal services, plans and specifications, 11 § 1123
    Retirement and pensions, insurance, 11 § 1114
    Taxation, periodic payment, 11 § 1129
Pending actions, 11 § 1141
Plans and specifications, 11 § 1121 et seq.
    Acceptances, **BKR 3018, 3019**
    Filing, **BKR 3016**
    Forms, **BKR Form 13 et seq.**
    Injunctions, **BKR 3017**
    Modification, 11 § 1127; **BKR 3019**
    Orders of court, 11 § 1142
        Forms, **BKR Form 13 et seq.**
        Revocation or suspension, 11 § 1144
    Railroads, 11 § 1172
    Rejection, **BKR 3018**
    Revocation or suspension, 11 § 1144
Postconfirmation, 11 § 1141 et seq.
Postpetition, disclosure, 11 § 1125
Powers and duties,
    Committees, 11 § 1103
    Trusts and trustees, 11 § 1106
    United States trustees, 28 § 586

Presumptions, substantial or controlling interest, financial statements and reports, **BKR 2015.3**
Priorities and preferences, railroads, claims, 11 § 1171
Property of the estate,
    Individual debtors, definitions, 11 § 1115
    Municipal debt adjustment, definitions, 11 § 902
Protective orders, substantial or controlling interest, financial statements and reports, **BKR 2015.3**
Public interest, railroads, 11 § 1165
Qualifications, trusts and trustees, 11 §§ 322, 1163
Railroads, **11 § 1161 et seq.**
    Abandonment, 11 § 1170
    Appearance, 11 § 1164
    Application of laws, 11 § 1161
    Appointments, trusts and trustees, 11 § 1163
    Collective bargaining, 11 § 1167
    Confirmation of plan, 11 § 1173
    Default, 11 § 1172
    Definitions, 11 §§ 101, 1162
    Federal laws, 11 § 1166
    Leases, rejection, 11 § 1169
    Liquidation, 11 § 1174
        Qualifications, 11 § 109
    Plans and specifications, 11 § 1172
    Public interest, 11 § 1165
    Reorganization, default, 11 § 1172
    Rolling stock, 11 § 1168
    State or local laws, 11 § 1166
    Trusts and trustees, appointments, 11 § 1163
Records and recordation, debtors in possession, **BKR 2015**
Registration, discharge, **BKR 4004**
Rejection,
    Collective bargaining, 11 § 1113
    Forms, plans and specifications, **BKR Forms 13, 14**
    Plans and specifications, **BKR 3018**
        Forms, **BKR Forms 13, 14**
Reports,
    Confirmation of plan, 11 § 1106
    Dismissal and nonsuit, 11 § 1112
Representatives and representation, statements, **BKR 2019**
Retirement and pensions, insurance, payment, 11 § 1114
Revocation or suspension, confirmation of plan, orders of court, 11 § 1144
Rolling stock, railroads, 11 § 1168
Schedules,
    Filing, 11 §§ 523, 1106
    Liabilities, **BKR 3003**
Secretary of the Treasury, reorganization, 11 § 1126
Securities, exemptions, 11 § 1145
Ships and shipping, 11 § 1110
Small businesses,
    Disclosure, statements, 11 § 1125; **BKR 3016, 3017.1**
    Forms, **BKR Form 25 et seq.**
Solicitation, postpetition, 11 § 1125

INDEX

State or local laws, railroads, 11 § 1166
Substantial or controlling interest, financial statements and reports, **BKR 2015.3; BKR Form 26**
Supplemental schedules, **BKR 1007**
Support, 11 §§ 1106, 1129
    Dismissal and nonsuit, 11 § 1112
    Taxation, 11 §§ 346, 1146
        Disclosure, 11 § 1125
        Dismissal and nonsuit, 11 § 1112
        Fraud, discharge, 11 § 1141
        Periodic payment, 11 § 1129
Termination, trusts and trustees, appointments, 11 § 1105
Time,
    Controlling interest, financial statements and reports, **BKR 2015.3**
    Discharge, **BKR 4007**
        Objections and exceptions, **BKR 4004**
    Substantial or controlling interest, financial statements and reports, **BKR 2015.3**
Transportation Department, railroads, appearances, 11 § 1164
Trusts and trustees,
    Appearance, 11 § 1109
    Appointments, 11 §§ 1104, 1105; **BKR 2007.1**
    Fraud, 11 § 1104
    Powers and duties, 11 § 1106
    Qualifications, 11 §§ 322, 1163
    Railroads, appointments, 11 § 1163
    Substitution, **BKR 2012**
    Support, 11 § 1106
United States trustees, post
Venue, 28 §§ 1408, 1409
Chapter 12 proceedings, 11 § 1201 et seq.
    Abandonment, disposition, **BKR 3011**
    Actions and proceedings, stay of proceedings, 11 § 1201
    Alimony, 11 §§ 1208, 1222 et seq.
    Application of law, 11 §§ 103, 1205
    Attorneys, fees, 11 § 329
    Claims,
        Allowances, 28 § 157
        Evidence, filing, **BKR 3002**
    Closings, **BKR 5009**
    Codebtors, stay of proceedings, 11 § 1201
    Compensation and salaries, trusts and trustees, 11 § 330
    Confirmation of plan, 11 § 1223 et seq.
        Abandoned or unclaimed property, 11 § 347
        Revocation or suspension, 11 § 1230
    Contracts, assumption, 11 § 365
    Conversion, 11 §§ 348, 1208
        Chapter 7 proceedings, 11 § 706; **BKR 1019**
        Chapter 13 proceedings, 11 § 1307
    Corporations, trusts and trustees, 11 § 321
    Credit, 11 § 364
    Debtors in possession, 11 § 1207
        Powers and duties, 11 § 1203
        Removal, 11 § 1204
    Discharge, 11 §§ 524, 1228
        Objections and exceptions, 11 § 523

Dismissal and nonsuit, 11 § 1208
Dividends, payment, **BKR 3010**
Evidence, claims, filing, **BKR 3002**
Family Farmers Protection Act of 2002, 11 §§ 101 nt, 1201 et seq.
Fees, filing, 28 § 1930
Filing,
    Fees, 28 § 1930
    Plans and specifications, objections and exceptions, **BKR 3015**
    Pleading, demand, time, extensions, 11 § 108
Forms,
    Corporations, **BKR Form 9**
    Individual debtors, **BKR Form 9**
    Joint debtors, **BKR Form 9**
    Partnership, **BKR Form 9**
Good faith, confirmation of plan, 11 § 1225; **BKR 3015**
Interests, sales, notice, 11 § 1206
Inventories, **BKR 2015**
Involuntary proceedings, objections and exceptions, 11 § 303
Joint administration, appointments, **BKR 2009**
Leases, assumption, 11 § 365
Liquidation, conversion, 11 § 1208
Meetings, **BKR 2003; BKR Form 9**
Modification, plans and specifications, **BKR 3015**
Motions, reopening, **BKR 5010**
Negotiable instruments, dishonor, notice, 11 § 1201
Notice,
    Corporations, forms, **BKR Form 9**
    Debtors in possession, **BKR 2015**
    Family farmers, forms, **BKR Form 9**
    Individual debtors, forms, **BKR Form 9**
    Joint debtors, forms, **BKR Form 9**
    Modification, plans and specifications, **BKR 3015**
    Partnership, forms, **BKR Form 9**
    Plans and specifications, modification, **BKR 3015**
    Support, 11 § 1202
Objections and exceptions,
    Closings, **BKR 5009**
    Plans and specifications, **BKR 3015**
    Stay of proceedings, 11 § 1201
Parties, plans and specifications, objections and exceptions, 11 § 1224
Payment, 11 § 1226
    Dividends, **BKR 3010**
    Time, 11 §§ 1222, 1229
Pending actions, 11 § 1228
Plans and specifications, 11 § 1221 et seq.
    Applications, 11 § 1221 nt
    Conversion, 11 § 348
    Default, 11 § 1222
    Disapproval, modification, 11 § 1229
    Filing, 11 § 1221
    Good faith, confirmation of plan, 11 § 1225
    Hearings, confirmation of plan, 11 § 1224
    Modification, confirmation of plan, 11 § 1229

INDEX

Objections and exceptions, **BKR 3015**
    Discharge, **11 § 523**
    Parties, objections and exceptions, **11 § 1224**
    Revocation or suspension,
        Confirmation of plan, **11 § 1230**
        Discharge, **11 § 1228**
    Taxation, **11 § 1231**
    Time,
        Filing, **11 § 1221**
        Payment, **11 §§ 1222, 1229**
    Trusts and trustees, objections and exceptions, **11 § 1224**
    Unclaimed property, disposition, **11 § 347**
    Unsecured debts, discharge, objections and exceptions, **11 § 1228**
    Vested rights, confirmation of plan, **11 § 1227**
    Waiver, discharge, **11 § 524**
Powers and duties,
    Debtors in possession, **11 § 1203**
    Trusts and trustees, **11 § 1202**
Professional persons, labor and employment, **11 § 327**
Qualifications, trusts and trustees, **11 § 322**
Records and recordation, possession, **BKR 2015**
Reinstatement, debtors in possession, notice, **11 § 1204**
Removal, debtors in possession, **11 § 1204**
Reopening, **BKR 5010**
Sales, **11 § 1206**
Stay of proceedings, codebtor, **11 § 1201**
Supplemental schedules, **BKR 1007**
Support, **11 §§ 1202, 1208, 1222 et seq.**
Taxation, **11 §§ 346, 1231**
Termination, **11 § 1201**
Time, discharge, **BKR 4007**
Trusts and trustees,
    Compensation and salaries, limitation, **11 §§ 326, 330**
    Eligibility, **11 § 321**
    Extension, time, filing, **11 § 108**
    Powers and duties, **11 § 1202**
        Avoidance, **11 § 546**
    Professional services, labor and employment, **11 § 327**
    Qualifications, **11 § 322**
    Residential real property, **11 § 365**
    Substitution, **BKR 2012**
    Support, **11 § 1202**
Unclaimed funds, disposition, **BKR 3011**
United States trustees, post
Vested rights, **11 § 1227**
Waiver, conversion, **11 §§ 706, 1208**
Chapter 13 proceedings, **11 § 1301 et seq.**
    Abandonment, disposition, **BKR 3011**
    Acceptance, confirmation of plan, **11 § 1327**
    Accounts and accounting, **11 § 1302**
    Actions and proceedings, **11 § 1301**
    Addresses, notice, **11 § 342**
    Administrative expenses, schedules, **11 § 707 nt**
    Administrative Office of United States Courts, trusts and trustees, money, **11 § 1302**
    Agriculture, **11 § 1307**

Alimony, **11 §§ 1307, 1322 et seq.**
Allowances, postpetition, **11 § 1305**
Anticramdown Law, **11 § 1325**
Appearance, trusts and trustees, valuation, **11 § 1302**
Application of law, **11 § 103**
Assignments, **11 § 1322**
Assumption, contracts, **11 § 1322**
Attorneys,
    Contracts, cancellation, **11 § 329**
    Discharge, **11 § 523**
    Fees,
        Contracts, cancellation, **11 § 329**
        Discharge, **11 § 523**
        Security interest, domicile and residence, notice, **BKR 3002.1**
    Security interest, domicile and residence, notice, **BKR 3002.1**
Automatic stay, **11 § 362**
Bifurcation of claims, **11 § 1325**
Business and commerce, operating businesses, **11 § 1304**
Chapter 7 proceedings, ante
Claims, **11 § 348**
    Confirmation of plan, **11 § 1325**
    Disallowance, **11 § 1305**
    Evidence,
        Filing, **BKR 3002**
        Postpetition, **11 § 1305**
    Examinations and examiners, **11 § 1302**
    Postpetition, **11 § 1305**
    Priorities and preferences, payment, **11 § 1322**
    Secured claims, **11 §§ 348, 1323**
    Taxation, **11 § 1305**
Closings, **BKR 5009**
    Stay of proceedings, objections and exceptions, **11 § 1301**
Codebtors, stay of proceedings, **11 § 1301**
Committees, investigations, **11 § 1302**
Commodity brokers, qualifications, **11 § 109**
Compensation and salaries, **11 § 1306**
    Trusts and trustees, **11 §§ 326, 330**
Confirmation of plan, **11 § 1324 et seq.**
    Conversion, **11 § 1307**
    Hearings, **11 § 1302**
    Objections and exceptions, **11 § 1325**
    Revocation or suspension, **11 § 1330**
Consideration, claims, **11 § 1301**
Consumer debt, **11 § 1302**
    Claims, treatment, **11 § 1322**
    Discharge, judgments and decrees, costs, **11 § 523**
    Filing, **11 § 1305**
    Stay of proceedings, **11 § 1301**
    Transfers, **11 § 547**
Contracts, assumption, **11 § 1322**
Conversion, **11 § 348**
    Good faith, **11 § 348**
    Liquidation, **11 §§ 706, 1301; BKR 1019**
    Notice, **11 § 1307**
    Reorganization, **11 §§ 1301, 1307; 28 § 1930**
    Waiver, **11 § 1307**

INDEX

Conviction of crime, restitution, objections and exceptions, 11 § 1328
Copies, 11 § 521
Corporations, eligibility, 11 § 321
Costs, security interest, domicile and residence, notice, **BKR 3002.1**
Crimes and offenses, discharge, 11 § 1328
Customs duties, objections and exceptions, 11 § 523
Damages, discharge, 11 § 1328
Debtors in possession, 11 § 1306
Declarations, **BKR Form 6**
Default, plans and specifications, 11 § 1322
Discharge, 11 § 524
    Damages, 11 § 1328
    Objections and exceptions, 11 §§ 523, 1302
    Restitution, 11 § 1328
    Waiver, 11 § 1328
Dismissal and nonsuit, 11 § 1307; **BKR 1017**
    Consumer debt, stay of proceedings, objections and exceptions, 11 § 1301
    Schedules, 11 § 521
Disposal, money, hearings, 11 § 1302
Distributions, confirmation of plan, 11 § 1325
Dividends, payment, **BKR 3010**
Divorce, discharge, objections and exceptions, 11 § 523
Domicile and residence, security interest, notice, **BKR 3002.1**
Driving while intoxicated, damages, discharge, 11 § 523
Education, loans, objections and exceptions, 11 § 523
Embezzlement, fiduciaries, discharge, 11 § 523
Evidence, claims,
    Filing, **BKR 3002**
    Postpetition, 11 § 1305
Examinations and examiners, 11 § 1302
Expenses and expenditures, 11 § 1307
    Confirmation of plan, payment, 11 § 1325
Extensions, time, 11 § 108
Fees, attorneys, consumer debt, discharge, 11 § 523
Filing,
    Accounts and accounting, 11 § 1302
    Claims, postpetition, 11 § 1305
    Fees, payment, 28 § 1930
    Payment, fees, 28 § 1930
    Postpetition, claims, 11 § 1305
    Prepetition tax returns, 11 § 1308
Final report, 11 § 1302
Financial management training curriculum, 11 § 1328
Financial statements and reports, investigations, 11 § 1302
Fines and penalties, political subdivisions, objections and exceptions, 11 § 523
Forms,
    Mortgages, **BKR Form 10**
    Notice, **BKR Form 9**
Fraud, discharge, 11 § 1328
    Exemptions, 11 § 523
Future earnings, 11 § 1322
Good faith,

Confirmation of plan, 11 § 1325; **BKR 3015**
    Schedules, filing, 11 § 521
Hanging Law, 11 § 1325
Health insurance, 11 § 1329
Hearings,
    Confirmation of plan, 11 § 1324
    Conversion, 11 § 1307
    Discharge,
        Notice, 11 § 523
        Revocation or suspension, 11 § 1328
    Security interest, domicile and residence, notice, **BKR 3002.1**
    Stay of proceedings, 11 § 1301
    Trusts and trustees, appearance, 11 § 1302
Holders, unsecured claims, confirmation of plan, 11 § 1325
Husband and wife,
    Alimony, maintenance, support, 11 § 523
    Qualifications, 11 § 109
Information, 11 § 1302
Insurance, personal property, 11 § 1326
Inventories, **BKR 2015**
Investigations, financial statements and reports, 11 § 1302
Irreparable harm, consumer debt, 11 § 1301
Joint administration, appointments, **BKR 2009**
Judgments and decrees, consumer debt, discharge, fees, 11 § 523
Larceny, fiduciaries, discharge, 11 § 523
Leases, 11 § 1303
    Assumption, 11 § 1322
    Personal property, payment, 11 § 1326
Liens and incumbrances,
    Confirmation of plan, 11 § 1325
    Valuation, hearings, 11 § 1302
Limitation of actions, security interest, domicile and residence, notice, **BKR 3002.1**
Lists, filing, 11 § 523
Means test, 11 § 1325
Meetings, **BKR 2003**
    Forms, **BKR Form 9**
Modification, 11 § 1307
    Hearings, 11 § 1302
    Plans and specifications, 11 § 1322; **BKR 3015**
    Time, 11 §§ 1323, 1329
Money,
    Disposal, 11 § 1302
    Fraud, 11 § 523
Mortgages, forms, **BKR Form 10**
Motions,
    Discharge, **BKR 4007**
    Reopening, **BKR 5010**
    Security interest, domicile and residence, notice, **BKR 3002.1**
Negotiable instruments, dishonor, notice, 11 § 1301
Nonpayment, fees, 11 § 1307
Notice,
    Addresses, 11 § 342
    Domicile and residence, security interest, **BKR 3002.1**

INDEX

Forms, **BKR Form 9**
    Negotiable instruments, dishonor, **11 § 1301**
    Plans and specifications, objections and exceptions, **BKR 3015**
    Security interest, domicile and residence, **BKR 3002.1**
    Support, **11 § 1302**
    Trusts and trustees, **BKR 2015**
Objections and exceptions,
    Claims, **11 § 1302**
    Closings, **BKR 5009**
    Confirmation of plan, **11 §§ 1324, 1327**
    Discharge, **11 § 1302**
    Plans and specifications, **BKR 3015**
        Confirmation of plan, **11 §§ 1324, 1327**
Operating businesses, **11 § 1304**
Orders of court,
    Consumer debt, **11 § 1305**
    Conversion, **11 § 1307**
    Discharge, waiver, **11 § 1328**
    Stay of proceedings, **11 § 1301**
Parties,
    Confirmation of plan, objections and exceptions, **11 § 1324**
    Conversion, notice, **11 § 1307**
    Information, **11 § 1302**
    Stay of proceedings, notice, **11 § 1301**
Payment,
    Claims, **11 § 1326**
        Priorities and preferences, **11 § 1322**
    Confirmation of plan, **11 § 1325**
    Dividends, **BKR 3010**
    Priorities and preferences, claims, **11 § 1322**
    Time, **11 §§ 1302, 1322**
Pending actions, **11 § 1328**
Personal injuries, discharge, **11 § 1328**
Personal property, **11 § 1326**
Petitions, claims, postpetition, **11 § 1305**
Plans and specifications,
    Consumer debt, unsecured claims, **11 § 1322**
    Contracts, **11 § 501**
    Conversion, **11 § 1307**
    Core proceedings, **28 § 157**
    Discharge, **11 § 1328**
    Filing, **11 § 1321**
        Alternate plans, **11 § 1307**
        Claims, **11 § 1301**
        Modification, **11 § 1323**
        Objections and exceptions, **BKR 3015**
        Payment, **11 § 1326**
    Leases, **11 § 501**
    Liquidation, **11 § 1307**
    Modification, **11 §§ 1307, 1329**
        Time, **11 § 1323**
    Objections and exceptions, **BKR 3015**
    Payment, **11 § 1326**
        Time, **11 § 1302**
    Time,
        Conversion, **11 § 1307**
        Designated plans, **11 § 1322**
        Payment, **11 § 1302**

Vested rights, confirmation of plan, **11 § 1327**
Waiver, **11 § 1307**
    Discharge, **11 § 1328**
Political subdivisions,
    Education, loans, discharge, **11 § 523**
    Taxation, **11 § 1305**
Postpetition, claims, **11 § 1305**
Prepetition tax returns, **11 § 1308**
Principal residence, liens and incumbrances, **11 § 1322**
Priorities and preferences, claims, **11 § 1322**
Proof of claim, postpetition, **11 § 1305**
Property, **11 § 1306**
Records and recordation, **BKR 2015**
Referees, fees, **11 nt prec § 101**
Rejection,
    Contracts, **11 § 1322**
    Plans and specification, confirmation of plan, **11 § 1327**
    Secured claims, modification, **11 § 1323**
Reopening, **BKR 5010**
Reports, **11 § 1302**
Restitution,
    Conviction of crime, discharge, **11 § 1328**
    Objections and exceptions, **11 § 523**
Revocation or suspension,
    Confirmation of plan, **11 § 1307**
    Discharge, notice, **11 § 1328**
Sales, **11 § 1303**
Schedules,
    Administrative expenses, **11 § 707 nt**
    Dismissal and nonsuit, **11 § 521**
    Filing, **11 § 523**
Security interest, **11 § 109**
    Confirmation of plan, **11 § 1325**
    Domicile and residence, notice, **BKR 3002.1**
Self-employment, **11 § 1304**
Separation agreement, discharge, objections and exceptions, **11 § 523**
Statements, investigations, filing, **11 § 1302**
Stay of proceedings, **11 § 1301**
Stockbrokers, qualifications, **11 § 109**
Supplemental schedules, **BKR 1007**
Support, **11 §§ 1302, 1307, 1322 et seq.**
Taxation,
    Confirmation of plan, **11 § 1325**
    Discharge, **11 § 523**
    Dismissal and nonsuit, **11 § 1307**
    Postpetition claims, **11 § 1305**
    Prepetition returns, **11 § 1308**
Termination, **11 § 1307**
Tests, means test, **11 § 1325**
Time,
    Confirmation of plan, hearings, **11 § 1324**
    Conversion, **11 § 1307**
    Designated plans, **11 § 1322**
    Discharge, **BKR 4007**
    Payment, **11 § 1302**
    Security interest, domicile and residence, notice, **BKR 3002.1**
Timeshares, assumption, **11 § 1322**
Trusts and trustees, **11 § 1302**
    Appointments, qualifications, **11 §§ 322, 1302**

INDEX

Compensation and salaries, **11 § 330**
    Standing trustees, payments, **11 § 1326**
Confirmation of plan, **11 § 1325**
Conversion, termination, **11 § 348**
Credit, **11 § 364**
Eligibility, **11 § 321**
Fraud, **11 § 1302**
Investigations, **11 § 1302**
Objections and exceptions, confirmation of plan, **11 § 1325**
Payment, **11 § 1326**
Standing trustees,
    Compensation and salaries, **11 § 1326; 28 § 586**
    Service, **11 § 1302**
    Support, **11 § 1302**
    Time, payment, **11 § 1302**
Unclaimed property, disposition, **11 § 347**
Unexpired leases, assumption, **11 § 365**
United States trustees, post
Unsecured claims, objections and exceptions, **11 § 1325**
Unsecured debts, qualifications, **11 § 109**
Valuation, hearings, **11 § 1302**
Vested rights, **11 § 1327**
Waiver,
    Default, **11 § 1322**
    Discharge, **11 §§ 524, 1328**
    Dismissal and nonsuit, **11 § 1307**
Chapter 15 proceedings. Foreign countries, generally, post
Charities,
    Dismissal and nonsuit, **11 § 707**
    Fraud, **11 § 548**
    Transfers, **11 §§ 363, 541, 1129**
Charters, discrimination, **11 § 525**
Checks, trusts and trustees, disposition, **11 § 347**
Chemical and biological warfare and weapons, claims, **11 § 362**
Chief Judge. Judges or justices, post
Children and minors,
    Appointments, **BKR 5002**
    Automatic stay, **11 § 362**
    Consideration, **11 § 524**
    Discharge, objections and exceptions, **11 § 523**
    Disclosure, **11 § 112**
    Exemptions, **11 § 522**
    Petitions, **BKR 1004.1**
    Priorities and preferences, **11 §§ 507, 547**
    Process, **BKR 1007**
    Support, generally, post
Children born out of wedlock, automatic stay, **11 § 362**
Citation, **BKR 1001**
Civil Aeronautics Board, **11 § 1110**
Civil procedure, **BKR 7002**
Claims, **11 § 502; BKR 3001 et seq.**
    Abstention, **11 § 305**
    Acceptances, plans and specifications, **BKR 3005**
    Adversary proceedings, withdrawal, **BKR 3006**
    Allowances, **11 § 502 et seq.**
        Core proceeding, **28 § 157**
        Distributions, **11 § 508**
        Fines and penalties, damages, **11 § 522**
        Subordination, notice, **11 § 510**
Attorneys, ante
Automatic stay, **11 §§ 362, 501**
Bonds (officers and fiduciaries), evidence, **BKR 3005**
Breach of performance, **11 § 502**
Chapter 7 proceedings, ante
Chapter 9 proceedings, ante
Chapter 11 proceedings, ante
Chapter 13 proceedings, ante
Chemical and biological warfare and weapons, **11 § 362**
Classification, **BKR 3013**
Codebtors, **11 § 509; BKR 3005**
Collection, automatic stay, petitions, **11 § 362**
Commodities, **11 §§ 765, 766**
Community claim,
    Definitions, **11 § 101**
    Notice, **11 § 342**
Community property,
    Damages, **11 § 541**
    Discharge, **11 § 524**
Consumer credit protection, open end or revolving consumer credit agreements, **BKR 3001**
Contingent, estimates, **11 § 502**
Contracts, rejection, filing, **11 § 501**
Copies, objections and exceptions, **BKR 3007**
Costs, **BKR 3001**
Credit cards and plates, **BKR 3001**
Damages, **11 §§ 501, 502**
Definitions, **11 § 101**
Disallowance, **11 § 502**
    Liens and incumbrances, **11 § 506**
Elections, nonrecourse loans, **BKR 3014**
Employment contracts, termination, damages, **11 § 502**
Evidence, **BKR 3001 et seq.**
    Chapter 11 proceedings, **11 § 1111**
    Exemptions, **BKR 4003**
    Foreign countries, **BKR 3002**
    Forms, **BKR Form 10**
    Fraud, **18 § 152**
    Individual debtors, postpetition, **11 § 1305**
    Involuntary proceedings, **11 § 501**
    Time, extensions, **11 § 108**
    Unsecured claims, reduction, **11 § 502**
Exemptions, **BKR 4003**
Fees, **BKR 3001**
Filing, **BKR 5005**
    Delays, **11 § 502**
    Evidence, **11 § 501; BKR 3002 et seq.**
    Objections and exceptions, **BKR 3007**
Foreign countries, **11 § 1513; BKR 3002**
Forms, **BKR 3001; BKR Form 10**
    Notice, **BKR Form 20B**
    Secured claims, schedules, **BKR Form 6**
    Unsecured claims, schedules, **BKR Form 6**
Fraud, crimes and offenses, **18 § 152**
Frauds, statute of, **BKR 3001**
    Nonrecourse loans, elections, **BKR 3014**
Grain, **11 § 557**
Guarantors, evidence, **BKR 3005**
Indorsers, evidence, **BKR 3005**

INDEX

Insider, services, disallowance, **11 § 502**
Interest, **BKR 3001**
Involuntary proceedings, **11 §§ 303, 501**
    Ordinary course of business, filing, **11 § 501**
Leases, damages, termination, **11 § 502**
Liens and incumbrances,
    Valuation, **BKR 3012**
    Void, **11 § 506**
Location, **BKR 3002**
Mortgages, forms, **BKR Form 10**
Motions, post
Nonrecourse loans, elections, **BKR 3014**
Notice, **11 § 502; BKR 2002**
    Classification, **BKR 3013**
    Filing, **BKR 3004**
    Forms, **BKR Form 20B**
    Liens and incumbrances, valuation, **BKR 3012**
    Objections and exceptions, **BKR 3007**
    Reconsideration, **BKR 3008**
    Withdrawal, **BKR 3006**
Objections and exceptions, **BKR 3007**
    Discharge, **11 § 502**
    Exemptions, **BKR 4003**
Omnibus objections, **BKR 3007**
Open end credit plans, **BKR 3001**
Open end or revolving consumer credit agreements, **BKR 3001**
Orders of court, **11 § 348**
    Reconsideration, **BKR 3008**
    Withdrawal, **BKR 3006**
Partnership, general partner, **11 § 502**
Petitions, answer, **BKR 1011**
Plans and specifications, **BKR 3015 et seq.**
    Acceptances, rejection, **BKR 3005**
Predatory loans, **11 § 363**
Priorities and preferences, **11 §§ 507, 726**
Reaffirmation agreements, **11 § 524**
Reconsideration, **11 § 502; BKR 3008**
Recovery, allowances, **11 § 502**
Register, **BKR 5003**
Reimbursement,
    Damages, filing, **11 § 501**
    Disallowance, **11 § 502**
Rejection,
    Contracts, **11 § 501**
    Plans and specifications, **BKR 3005**
Removal, **28 § 1452**
Revolving consumer credit agreements, **BKR 3001**
Sales, **11 § 363**
Secured claims, **11 § 501 et seq.**
    Automatic stay, **11 § 362**
    Chapter 13 proceedings, **11 §§ 348, 1323**
    Contributions, **11 § 502**
    Evidence, **11 § 501**
    Fines and penalties, **11 § 522**
    Liens and incumbrances,
        Ordinary course of business, **11 § 546**
        Sales, **11 § 363**
    Ordinary course of business, liens and incumbrances, **11 § 546**
    Priorities and preferences, **11 § 507**
    Proof of claim, **11 § 501**
    Qualifications, **11 § 109**

    Sales, liens and incumbrances, **11 § 363**
    Schedules, forms, **BKR Form 6**
    Status, **11 § 506**
    Subordination, **11 § 541**
    Subrogation, **11 § 509**
Setoff and counterclaim, post
Signatures, **BKR 3001**
    Nonrecourse loans, elections, **BKR 3014**
Sovereign immunity, abrogation, governmental units, **11 § 106**
Subordination, **11 § 510**
Subrogation, **11 §§ 502, 507, 509**
Taxation, post
Time, **11 § 501 et seq.; BKR 3002 et seq.**
Transfers, **BKR 3001**
Trusts and trustees, post
Unclaimed funds, disposition, **BKR 3011**
Unsecured claims,
    Administration, expenses and expenditures, **11 § 364**
    Avoidance, **11 § 544**
    Employee benefit plans, priorities and preferences, **11 § 507**
    Evidence, reduction, **11 § 502**
    Exemptions, **11 § 522**
    Fish and game, sales, priorities and preferences, **11 § 507**
    Individual debtors, confirmation of plan, **11 §§ 1325, 1329**
    Involuntary proceedings, ordinary course of business,
        Discharge, **11 § 523**
        Priorities and preferences, **11 § 507**
    Liquidation, priorities and preferences, **11 §§ 753, 767**
    Objections and exceptions, notice, **11 § 502**
    Political subdivisions, taxation, priorities and preferences, **11 § 501**
    Priorities and preferences, **11 §§ 507, 753, 767**
    Qualifications, **11 § 109**
    Reduction, **11 § 502**
    Schedules, forms, **BKR Form 6**
Valuation, liens and incumbrances, **BKR 3012**
    Withdrawal, **BKR 3006**
Class actions, **BKR 7023**
Clearing banks, liquidation, **11 § 781 et seq.**
Clearing organizations. Commodities, post
Clerks of courts, **BKR 5001**
    Appointments, **28 § 156**
    Consumer debt, notice, **11 § 342**
    Fees, **28 § 1930**
    Fraud, notice, **28 § 586**
    Statistics, **28 § 159**
Closings, **11 § 350; BKR 5009**
    Abandonment, **11 § 554**
    Automatic stay, **11 § 362**
    Avoidance, **11 § 546**
    Foreign countries, **11 § 1517**
Clothing, exemptions, **11 § 522**
Codebtors,
    Claims, **11 § 509**
        Evidence, **BKR 3005**

INDEX

Demand, pleading, 11 § 108
Evidence, claims, BKR 3005
Pleading, demand, 11 § 108
Schedules, forms, BKR Form 6
Stay of proceedings, family farmers, 11 § 1201
Collection, BKR 6001 et seq.
Alimony, 11 § 362
Chapter 7 proceedings, ante
Liquidation, 11 § 103
Maintenance, 11 § 362
Support, post
Collective bargaining, chapter 11 proceedings,
Railroads, 11 § 1167
Rejection, 11 § 1113
Colleges and Universities, this index
Comity, abstention, 11 § 305; 28 § 1334
Commerce. Business and commerce, generally, ante
Commercial fishing operation, definitions, 11 § 101
Commercial fishing vessel, definitions, 11 § 101
Committees,
Appointments, appeal and review, BKR 2007
Chapter 9 proceedings, ante
Equity security holders, post
Notice, BKR 2002
Priorities and preference, actual and necessary expenses, 11 § 507
Professional persons, employment, 11 §§ 327, 328
Reimbursement, allowances, expenses, 11 § 503
Small businesses, 11 § 1102; BKR 1020
Commodities, 11 § 761 et seq.
Acceleration, contracts, 11 § 556
Accounts and accounting, 11 § 763
Appearance, Commodity Futures Trading Commission, 11 § 762
Automatic stay, 11 § 362
Avoidance, 11 §§ 546, 764
Board of Trade, definitions, 11 § 761
Brokers, 11 § 761 et seq.
Definitions, 11 § 101
Margin, transfers, 11 § 546
Setoff and counterclaim, margin, 11 § 362
Cash, setoff or counterclaim, 11 § 362
Claims, 11 §§ 765, 766
Clearing organizations, 11 § 766
Accounts and accounting, 11 § 763
Definitions, 11 § 761
Commodity Futures Trading Commission,
Appearance, 11 § 762
Avoidance, 11 § 764
Rules and regulations, 11 § 766
Compromise and settlement, fraud, 11 § 548
Contracts, 11 § 766
Acceleration, 11 § 556
Damages, 11 § 562
Liquidation, 11 § 556
Avoidance, 11 § 764
Margin, setoff or counterclaim, 11 § 362
Notice, instructions, 11 § 765
Termination, 11 § 556
Customers,
Accounts and accounting, 11 § 763
Definitions, 11 § 761
Notice, 11 § 765
Treatment, 11 § 766
Damages, contracts, 11 § 562
Definitions, 11 § 761
Distribution, 11 § 766
Evidence, filing, notice, 11 § 765
Forward contract merchant, setoff or counterclaim, 11 § 362
Futures contracts,
Automatic stay, setoff or counterclaim, 11 § 553
Setoff or counterclaim, 11 § 362
Instructions, customers, 11 § 765
Margin,
Definitions, 11 § 761
Setoff or counterclaim, 11 § 362
Master agreements, 11 § 761
Net equity,
Accounts and accounting, 11 § 763
Definitions, 11 § 761
Notice, 11 § 765
Commission, 11 § 762
Customers, instructions, 11 § 765
Options, automatic stay, setoff or counterclaim, 11 § 553
Options dealer, definitions, 11 § 761
Orders of court, avoidance, 11 § 764
Securities, 11 § 766
Setoff and counterclaim,
Margin, 11 § 362
Net equity, treatment, 11 § 763
Termination, contracts, 11 § 556
Transfers, 11 § 764 et seq.
Avoidance, 11 §§ 546, 764
Brokers, margin, 11 § 546
Notice, 11 § 765
Trusts and trustees, post
Unsecured claims, priorities and preferences, 11 §§ 753, 767
Voidable transfers, 11 § 764
Commodity Futures Trading Commission.
Commodities, ante
Communications,
Foreign countries, 11 § 1525 et seq.
Interception, orders of court, 18 § 2516
Community claim,
Definitions, 11 § 101
Notice, 11 § 342
Community property. Husband and wife, post
Compensation and salaries, 11 § 502 et seq.
Accountants, ante
Allowances, 11 § 503
Applications, BKR 2016
Chapter 13 proceedings, ante
Consumer privacy ombudsman, 11 § 330
Custodians, post
Denial, 11 § 328
Disclosure, petitions, preparers, BKR 2016
Employee benefit plans, contributions, priorities and preferences, 11 § 507
Employment contract, termination, disallowance, 11 § 502
Examinations and examiners, post
Exclusions, 11 § 541
Future earnings, losses, payment, exemptions, 11 § 522
Interim compensation, 11 § 331
Judges or justices, post

INDEX

Leases, default, **11 § 365**
Notice, **BKR 2002**
Patient care ombudsman, **11 § 330**
Petitions, preparers, **BKR 2016**
Priorities and preferences, **11 § 507**
Professional associations, **11 § 504**
Professional personnel, post
Public service attorney referral program, **11 § 504**
Retired judges, recall, **28 § 155**
Sharing, **11 § 504**
Trusts and trustees, post
Unemployment compensation, exemptions, **11 § 522**
United States trustees, post
Vacation, allowances, priorities and preferences, **11 § 507**
Complaints,
    Discharge, **BKR 4004 et seq.**
    Filing, **BKR 5005**
Compromise and settlement, **11 § 541; BKR 9019**
    Commodity brokers,
        Avoidance, **11 § 546**
        Fraud, valuation, **11 § 548**
    Definitions, **11 § 101**
    Discharge, objections and exceptions, **11 § 523**
    Exemptions, **11 § 522**
    Shares and shareholders,
        Definitions, **11 § 741**
        Stay of proceedings, **11 § 362**
Computers, exemptions, **11 § 522**
Concealment, **18 § 3284**
    Books and papers, **18 § 152**
    Perjury, sentence and punishment, **18 § 152**
    Recovery, exemptions, **11 § 522**
Concurrent proceedings, foreign countries, **11 § 1528 et seq.**
Condominiums, discharge, **11 § 523**
Conferences, **11 § 105**
    Judicial Conference of the United States, generally, post
Confidential or privileged information,
    Income tax, returns, **BKR 4002**
    Patient care ombudsman, **11 § 333; BKR 2015.1**
    Trade secrets, **11 § 107; BKR 9018**
Confirmation of plan,
    Chapter 9 proceedings, ante
    Chapter 11 proceedings, ante
    Chapter 12 proceedings, ante
    Chapter 13 proceedings, ante
    Conversion, **BKR 1019**
    Core proceedings, **28 § 157**
    Distribution, **BKR 3021**
    Small businesses, **11 § 1129**
Conflict of interest,
    Examinations and examiners, **BKR 5002**
    Joint administration, **BKR 2009**
    Judges or justices, post
    Labor and employment, objections and exceptions, **11 § 327**
    Professional personnel, **11 §§ 327, 328**
    Sentence and punishment, **18 § 154**
Conflict of laws, foreign countries, **11 § 1503**
Consent,
    Arbitration, alternative dispute resolution, referrals, **28 § 654**

Involuntary proceedings, dismissal and nonsuit, **11 § 303**
Sales, **11 § 363**
Consideration, claims, discharge, **11 § 524**
Consolidations and mergers, **BKR 1015, 7042**
    Joint proceedings, **11 § 302**
    Preliminary hearings, automatic stay, **11 § 362**
    Sales, notice, objections and exceptions, **11 § 363**
Constitution of the United States, challenges, statutes, **BKR 9005.1**
Construction, rules, **11 § 102**
Consumer credit protection, open end or revolving consumer credit agreements, claims, **BKR 3001**
Consumer debt,
    Attorneys, fees, **11 § 523**
    Automatic stay, **11 § 362**
    Avoidance, **11 § 547**
    Chapter 7 proceedings, ante
    Chapter 13 proceedings, ante
    Clerks of courts, notice, **11 § 342**
    Definitions, **11 § 101**
    Discharge, **11 § 523**
    Extensions, open end credit plan, discharge, **11 § 523**
    Fraud, notice, **11 § 342**
    Good faith, discharge, **11 § 523**
    Liquidation, dismissal and nonsuit, **11 § 707**
    Luxury goods or services, discharge, **11 § 523**
    Notice, **11 § 342; BKR 2002**
    Real estate,
        Discharge, exemptions, **11 § 524**
        Statements, **11 §§ 521, 704**
        Statements, discharge, exemptions, **11 §§ 521, 704**
    Reduction, unsecured claims, **11 § 502**
Consumer Price Index, adjustments, filing, **11 § 104**
Consumer privacy ombudsman, **11 § 332**
    Appointments, **BKR 6004**
    Compensation and salaries, **11 § 330**
    Salaries, **11 § 330**
Contempt, **BKR 9020**
Contests, **BKR 9014**
    Petitions, **BKR 1011, 1013**
    United States trustees, **BKR 2020**
Contracts, **BKR 6006**
    Acceleration, **11 § 555 et seq.**
    Assignments, **11 § 365; BKR 6003**
    Assumptions, **11 § 365; BKR 6003**
    Attorneys, fees, statements, filing, **11 § 329**
    Breach of performance, allowances, **11 § 502**
    Chapter 7 proceedings, ante
    Claims,
        Disallowance, **11 § 502**
        Fees, **11 § 506**
    Commodities, ante
    Compromise and settlement, generally, ante
    Consideration, **11 § 524**
    Death benefit plan, beneficiaries, **11 § 521**
    Debt relief agencies, **11 §§ 526, 528**
    Definitions,
        Commodities, **11 § 556**
        Master agreements, **11 § 561**
        Repurchase agreements, **11 § 559**
        Securities, **11 § 555**

INDEX

Swap agreements, 11 § 560
Exemptions, life insurance, 11 § 522
Forward contracts, generally, post
Illness, payment, exemptions, 11 § 522
Insurance, nonforfeitures, good faith, 11 § 542
Insured depository institutions, assumptions, 11 § 365
Intellectual property, licenses and permits, 11 § 365
Labor and employment, damages, 11 § 502
Leases, generally, post
Licenses and permits, intellectual property, 11 § 365
Life insurance, exemptions, 11 § 522
Liquidation, 11 § 555 et seq.
Master agreements, generally, post
Motions, BKR 4001
Reaffirmation agreements, generally, post
Rejections, 11 §§ 365, 502
Rent, generally, post
Repurchase agreements, generally, post
Sales, 11 § 363
    Avoidance, 11 §§ 363, 541
Schedules, forms, BKR Form 6
Security agreement, definitions, 11 § 101
Security interest, generally, post
Separation agreements, 11 §§ 522, 523
Shares and shareholders, post
Statutory contracts, rejection, evidence, 11 § 501
Subordination, 11 § 510
Swap agreements, generally, post
Timeshares, rejection, 11 § 365
Transfers,
    Life insurance, premiums, payment, exemptions, 11 § 522
    Real estate, priorities and preferences, 11 § 547
Trusts and trustees, post
Contributions,
    Damages, filing, 11 § 501
    Disallowance, 11 § 502
    Employee benefit plans, 11 § 541
        Priorities and preferences, 11 § 507
    Rescission, subordination, 11 § 510
Controlling interest, chapter 11 proceedings, financial statements and reports, BKR 2015.3; BKR Form 26
Conversion, 11 § 348; BKR 1017, 1019
    Chapter 7 proceedings, ante
    Chapter 11 proceedings, ante
    Chapter 12 proceedings, ante
    Chapter 13 proceedings, ante
    Waiver, rights, 11 § 706
Conveyances. Fraudulent conveyances, generally, post
Cooperation, foreign countries, 11 § 1525 et seq.
Cooperative banks, qualifications, 11 § 109
Cooperatives, residence, exemptions, 11 § 522
Coordination, foreign countries, 11 § 1529 et seq.
Coowners, sales, distributions, 11 § 363
Copies,
    Certificates and certification, BKR 5006
    Chapter 7 proceedings, 11 § 521
    Chapter 13 proceedings, 11 § 521
    Claims, objections and exceptions, BKR 3007
    Conversion, BKR 1019

Debt relief agencies, 11 §§ 527, 528
Fees, 11 § 521
Income tax, returns, BKR 4002
Partnership, petitions, BKR 1004
Payment, 11 § 521
Petitions, post
Reaffirmation agreements, 11 § 524
Schedules, BKR 1007
Core proceedings, 28 § 157
Corn, 11 § 557
Corporations,
    Bylaws, 11 § 321
    Chapter 7 proceedings, ante
    Chapter 11 proceedings, generally, ante
    Declarations, forms, BKR Forms 2, 6
    Definitions, 11 § 101
    Disclosure, title to property, BKR 1007, 7007.1
    Foreign countries, recognition petitions, ownership statements, BKR 1011
    Involuntary proceedings,
        Objections and exceptions, 11 § 303
        Ownership statements, BKR 1011
    Reorganization. Chapter 11 proceedings, generally, ante
    Statements, title to property, BKR 1007, 7007.1
    Taxation, 11 § 346
    Title to property, statements, BKR 1007, 7007.1
    Trusts and trustees, 11 § 321
Costs, BKR 7054
    Appeal and review, BKR 8014
    Chapter 7 proceedings, 11 § 707
    Chapter 13 proceedings, security interest, domicile and residence, notice, BKR 3002.1
    Claims, BKR 3001
    Consumer debt, discharge, 11 § 523
    Counseling services, 11 § 111
    Debt relief agencies, 11 § 526
    Dismissal and nonsuit, 28 § 1930
    Frivolous appeals, BKR 8020
    Political subdivisions, awards, 11 § 106
Councils. Judicial Council, generally, post
Counseling services, 11 § 109
    Certificates and certification, 11 § 521
    Financial management training curriculum, generally, post
    Notice, 11 §§ 111, 342
    Plans and specifications, 11 § 521
    Statement of compliance, BKR 1007
Counselors. Attorneys, generally, ante
Counterclaim. Setoff and counterclaim, post
Courtesy, trusts and trustees, sales, 11 § 363
Courts,
    Discretion of court, attorneys, fees, 11 § 503
    Emergencies, special sessions, 28 § 152
    Findings, BKR 7052
    Judges or justices, generally, post
    Jurisdiction, generally, post
    Leave of court, appeal and review, BKR 8003
    Location, 28 § 152
    Orders of court, generally, post
    Powers and duties, 11 § 105
Courts of appeals,
    Judges or justices, appointments, 28 § 152
    Jurisdiction, 28 § 158

INDEX

Cover sheet, reaffirmation agreements, forms, **BKR Form 27**
Coverdell education savings accounts, **11 §§ 521, 541**
Credit cards and plates, claims, **BKR 3001**
Credit (payment of indebtedness),
    Core proceedings, orders of court, **28 § 157**
    Counseling services, generally, ante
    Fraud, discharge, **11 § 523**
    Motions, **BKR 4001**
    Taxation, **11 § 503**
    Trusts and trustees, **11 § 364**
Credit unions, **11 § 109**
Crimes and offenses, **18 § 151 et seq.**
    Actions and proceedings, **11 § 362**
    Bribery and corruption, **18 § 152**
    Chapter 7 proceedings, dismissal and nonsuit, **11 § 707**
    Concealment, **18 § 152**
    Conflict of interest, **18 § 154**
    Definitions, **18 § 151**
    Embezzlement, **18 § 153**
    Expenses and expenditures, priorities and preferences, **11 § 507**
    Fees, **18 § 155**
    Fraud, generally, post
    Homesteads, exemptions, **11 § 522**
    Inspection and inspectors, **18 § 154**
    Oaths and affirmations, **18 § 152**
    Pending actions, statements, **BKR 1007**
    Preparers, **18 § 156**
    Priorities and preferences, expenses and expenditures, **11 § 507**
    Reaffirmation agreements, **18 § 158**
    Reports, **18 § 3057**
    Victims, awards, exemptions, **11 § 522**
Crockery, exemptions, **11 § 522**
Crops, exemptions, **11 § 522**
Cross border cases. Foreign countries, generally, post
Cross claims, **BKR 7013**
Currency. Money, generally, post
Current monthly income,
    Definitions, **11 § 707**
    Forms, current monthly income and means test calculation, **BKR Form 22**
    Statements, **BKR 1007**
Curriculum. Financial management training curriculum, generally, post
Custodians, **11 § 541**
    Accounts and accounting, **11 § 543**; **BKR 6002**
    Adverse or pecuniary interest, **18 § 154**
    Animals, transfers, **11 § 543**
    Assignments for benefit of creditors, **11 § 543**
    Compensation and salaries,
        Hearings, **11 § 543**
        Priorities and preferences, **11 § 507**
        Turnovers, allowances, **11 § 503**
    Conflict of interest, **18 § 154**
    Contracts, default, **11 § 365**
    Definitions, **11 § 101**
    Dismissal and nonsuit, reinstatement, **11 § 349**
    Embezzlement, **18 § 153**
    Inspection and inspectors, refusal, **18 § 154**
    Liens and incumbrances, possession, avoidance, **11 § 545**
    Motor vehicles, expenses and expenditures, objections and exceptions, **11 § 543**
    Turnovers, property, **11 §§ 503, 543**
Customers,
    Commodities, ante
    Shares and shareholders, post
Customs duties,
    Discharge, objections and exceptions, **11 § 523**
    Exemptions, **11 § 522**
Damages,
    Automatic stay, **11 § 362**
    Avoidance, transfers, **11 § 550**
    Chapter 7 proceedings, ante
    Chapter 13 proceedings, discharge, **11 § 1328**
    Claims, **11 §§ 501, 502**
    Commodities, contracts, **11 § 562**
    Contribution, **11 § 502**
    Counseling services, **11 § 111**
    Debt relief agencies, **11 § 526**
    Disallowance, **11 § 502**
    Driving while intoxicated, discharge, **11 § 523**
    Employment contracts, termination, **11 § 502**
    Exemptions, **11 § 522**
    Forward contracts, **11 § 562**
    Frivolous appeals, **BKR 8020**
    Involuntary proceedings, bad faith, petitions, **11 § 303**
    Leases, rejection, set-off and counterclaim, **11 § 365**
    Liens and incumbrances, avoidance, **11 §§ 550, 551**
    Master agreements, **11 § 562**
    Political subdivisions, awards, **11 § 106**
    Purchasers and purchasing, subordination, **11 § 510**
    Reimbursement, **11 § 502**
    Repurchase agreements, **11 § 562**
    Sales, **11 § 363**
    Securities, **11 § 562**
    Serial filers, **11 § 362**
    Swap agreements, **11 § 562**
    Taxation, post
    Time, **11 §§ 502, 562**
    Timeshares, rejection, setoff and counterclaim, **11 § 365**
Death, **BKR 1016**
    Benefit plans, **11 § 541**
    Trusts and trustees,
        Liquidation, **11 § 703**
        Successors, **BKR 2012**
    Wrongful death, generally, post
Debt relief agencies, **11 § 526 et seq.**
    Advertisements, **11 § 528**
    Attorneys, fees, **11 § 526**
    Contracts, **11 §§ 526, 528**
    Copies, **11 §§ 527, 528**
    Costs, **11 § 526**
    Damages, **11 § 526**
    Definitions, **11 § 101**
    Disclosure, **11 §§ 527, 528**
    Fees, **11 § 526**
    Fines and penalties, **11 § 526**
    Fraud, **11 § 526**
    Hearings, **11 § 526**
    Injunctions, **11 § 526**
    Jurisdiction, **11 § 526**

INDEX

Motions, fines and penalties, 11 § 526
Notice, 11 § 526 et seq.
Statements, 11 §§ 527, 528
Time,
    Contracts, 11 § 528
    Disclosure, 11 § 527
Waiver, 11 § 526
Debtors in possession,
    Actions and proceedings, 28 § 959; BKR 6009
    Chapter 11 proceedings, 11 § 1107
    Chapter 12 proceedings, ante
    Chapter 13 proceedings, 11 § 1306
    Defenses, BKR 6009
    Evidence, BKR 2011
    Individual debtors, 11 § 1306
    Notice, BKR 2015
    Records and recordation, BKR 2015
    Reorganization, 11 § 1107
    Reports, BKR 2015
    Small businesses, 11 § 1116
Debtor's monthly expenses, definitions, 11 § 707
Debtor's principal residence, definitions, 11 § 101
Deceit. Fraud, generally, post
Declarations,
    Corporations, forms, BKR Forms 2, 6
    Individual debtors, BKR Form 6
    Partnership, forms, BKR Forms 2, 6
    Petitions, preparers, 11 § 110
        Nonattorneys, BKR Forms 6, 19A
    Schedules, BKR Forms 2, 6
Decrees. Judgments and decrees, generally, post
Deductions, taxation, 11 § 346
Deeds and conveyances. Fraudulent conveyances, generally, post
Defamation, 11 § 107; BKR 9018
Default, BKR 1013
    Chapter 11 proceedings, ante
    Chapter 12 proceedings, 11 § 1222
    Chapter 13 proceedings, plans and specifications, 11 § 1322
    Contracts, 11 § 365
    Family farmers, 11 § 1222
    Individual debtors, plans and specifications, 11 § 1322
    Judgments and decrees, BKR 7055
    Railroads, reorganization, 11 § 1172
    Reorganization, 11 § 1123
        Railroads, 11 § 1172
    Security interest, 11 § 521
Defenses, 11 § 558; BKR 6009, 7012
    Petitions, BKR 1011
    Predatory loans, 11 § 363
    Usury, 11 § 558
Definitions, 11 § 101; BKR 9001, 9002
    Avoidance, priorities and preferences, 11 § 547
    Cause, 11 § 1112
    Chapter 7 proceedings, 11 § 707
    Chapter 9 proceedings, post
    Chapter 11 proceedings, ante
    Clearing banks, 11 § 781
    Contracts, ante
    Cooperation, foreign countries, 11 § 1527
    Counseling services, 11 § 109
    Foreign countries, post
    Fraud, transfers, 11 § 548
    Grain, 11 § 557

Household goods, exemptions, 11 § 522
Petitions, preparers, 11 § 110
Priorities and preferences, avoidance, 11 § 547
Profits, 11 § 308
Property of the estate, 11 §§ 902, 1115
Proxies, BKR 2006
Reaffirmation agreements, 11 § 524
Replacement value, 11 § 506
Returns,
    Discharge, 11 § 523
    Prepetition returns, 11 § 1308
Small businesses, 11 § 707
Swap agreements, post
Time, BKR 9006
Transfers, post
Trusts and trustees, post
Delivery, chapter 11 proceedings, plans and specifications, 11 § 1142
Demand,
    Definitions, discharge, 11 § 524
    Filing, 11 § 108
Depositions, BKR 7027 et seq.
Depository institutions, process, BKR 7004
Deposits, 11 § 345; BKR 7067
    Interest, 28 § 589a
    Investments, 11 § 345
    Leases, 11 § 365
    Public utilities, 11 § 366
    Unsecured claims, 11 § 507
Deputies, clerks, 28 § 156
Derivative actions, BKR 7023.1
Destruction,
    Health care businesses, patient records, BKR 6011
    Taxation, documents, 11 § 521 nt
    Trusts and trustees, health care businesses, records and recordation, 11 § 351
Devises, 11 § 541
Direct appeals, 28 § 158
Directors, Administrative Office of United States Courts, powers and duties, 28 § 604
Disability. Handicapped persons, generally, post
Disallowance, 11 § 502
Disbursements, 11 § 543
Discharge, 11 § 523 et seq.; BKR 4004 et seq.
    Aircraft, 11 § 523
    Alimony, 11 § 523
    Chapter 7 proceedings, ante
    Chapter 9 proceedings, ante
    Chapter 11 proceedings, ante
    Chapter 12 proceedings, ante
    Chapter 13 proceedings, ante
    Claims, disallowance, 11 § 502
    Community property, 11 § 524
    Consumer debt, discharge, costs, 11 § 523
    Contracts, consideration, 11 § 524
    Core proceedings, objections and exceptions, 28 § 157
    Customs duties, 11 § 523
    Damages, 11 § 524
    Discrimination, 11 § 525
    Dismissal and nonsuit, 11 § 349
    Driving while intoxicated, damages, 11 § 523
    Elections, fines and penalties, 11 § 523
    Evidence, objections and exceptions, BKR 4005

INDEX

Federally insured depository institutions, exceptions, **11 § 523**
Fines and penalties, political subdivisions, objections and exceptions, **11 § 523**
Forma pauperis proceedings, frivolous or malicious, **11 § 523**
Forms, chapter 7 proceedings, **BKR Form 18**
Fraud, **11 § 523**
Fraudulent conveyances, **11 § 524**
Good faith, **11 § 524**
Injunctions, **11 § 524**
Luxury goods or services, **11 § 523**
No discharge, notice, **BKR 4006**
Nonprofit institution, education, loans, **11 § 523**
Notice, **11 § 523**
   Revocation or suspension, **BKR 4006**
Objections and exceptions, **11 § 523**
   Evidence, **BKR 4005**
Open end credit plan, money, advances, **11 § 523**
Orders of court, **11 § 523**
Personal injuries, post
Political subdivisions, **11 § 523**
Pro se, **11 § 524**
Reaffirmation agreements, **11 § 524**
Repayment, voluntary, **11 § 524**
Restitution, **11 §§ 523, 1328**
Retirement and pensions, exemptions, **11 § 523**
Revocation or suspension, notice, **BKR 4006**
Ships and shipping, **11 § 523**
Statements, writing, fraud, **11 § 523**
Supplemental injunction, **11 § 524**
Support, **11 § 523**
Taxation, **11 § 523**
Time, **BKR 4007**
Trusts and trustees, bonds (officers and fiduciaries), **11 § 322**
Waiver, **BKR 4006**
Disclosure,
   Chapter 9 proceedings, ante
   Chapter 11 proceedings, ante
   Children and minors, **11 § 112**
   Compensation and salaries, ante
   Consumer privacy ombudsman, **11 § 332**
   Corporations, title to property, **BKR 7007.1**
   Counseling services, **11 § 111**
   Debt relief agencies, **11 §§ 527, 528**
   Definitions, chapter 9 proceedings, chapter 11 proceedings, representatives and representation, statements, **BKR 2019**
   Equity security holders, representatives and representation, statements, **BKR 2019**
   Forms, orders of court, **BKR Form 12 et seq.**
   Lists, **BKR 1007**
   Orders of court, forms, **BKR Form 12 et seq.**
   Reaffirmation agreements, **11 § 524**
   Representatives and representation, statements, **BKR 2019**
   Small businesses, post
   Social security, numbers and numbering, **11 § 342**
   Statements, **BKR Form 12 et seq.**
Discovery, **BKR 7026 et seq.**
Discrimination, **11 § 525**

Dishes, exemptions, **11 § 522**
Disinterested person, definitions, **11 § 101**
Dismissal and nonsuit, **11 § 349**; **BKR 1017, 7041**
   Abstention, **11 § 305**
   Automatic stay, **11 §§ 109, 362**
   Chapter 7 proceedings, ante
   Chapter 9 proceedings, ante
   Chapter 11 proceedings, **11 § 1112**
   Chapter 13 proceedings, ante
   Costs, **28 § 1930**
   Death, **BKR 1016**
   Exemptions, **11 § 522**
   Involuntary proceedings, **11 § 303**
   Mental health, **BKR 1016**
   Orders of court, **11 § 109**
   Petitions, **BKR 1013, 1014**
   Postpetition transfers, **11 § 549**
   Reinstatement, **11 § 349**
   Support, **11 § 1112**
   Taxation, post
   Voluntary, **11 § 109**; **BKR 8001**
Disposable income, definitions, **11 § 1325**
Disposition, **BKR 6007**
Dispute resolution, **28 § 651 et seq.**
Disqualification, judges or justices, **28 § 455**; **BKR 5004**
Disregard, Bankruptcy Law or Rule, fines and penalties, **18 § 156**
Distribution, **11 § 508**; **BKR 3021**
   Abandoned or unclaimed property, **11 § 347**
   Chapter 7 proceedings, ante
   Chapter 11 proceedings, **11 § 1143**
   Claims, subordination, **11 § 510**
   Examinations and examiners, **BKR 6002**
   Foreign countries, **11 § 1521**
   Retirement and pensions, exemptions, **11 § 522**
   Trusts and trustees, compensation and salaries, **11 § 330**
District of Columbia,
   Judges or justices, appointments, **28 § 152**
   Taxation, automatic stay, postpetition, **11 § 362**
Dividends,
   Chapter 7 proceedings,
     No dividends, notice, **BKR 2002**
     Payment, **BKR 3009**
   Payment, **BKR 3010**
Divorce,
   Alimony, generally, ante
   Automatic stay, **11 § 362**
   Discharge, **11 § 523**
   Exemptions, **11 § 522**
   Settlement agreements, **11 § 541**
Dockets and docketing, **BKR 5003**
   Access, **11 § 107**
   Appeal and review, **BKR 8007**
   Custodians, **28 § 156**
Documents. Books and papers, generally, ante
Dollar amounts, adjustments, **11 § 104**
Domestic violence, automatic stay, **11 § 362**
Domicile and residence, **11 § 109**
   Chapter 11 proceedings, **28 § 1408**
   Chapter 13 proceedings, security interest, notice, **BKR 3002.1**
   Definitions, **11 § 101**
   Exemptions, **11 § 522**

INDEX

Foreign countries, 11 § 1516
    Trusts and trustees, 11 § 321
Dower and curtesy, 11 § 363
Driving while intoxicated or under the influence.
    Motor vehicles, post
Drugs and medicine, trafficking, chapter 7
    proceedings, dismissal and nonsuit, 11 § 707
Dry edible beans, 11 § 557
Duties. Powers and duties, generally, post
Education,
    Coverdell education savings accounts, 11 §§ 521, 541
    Financial management training curriculum, generally, post
    Judges or justices, 11 § 101 nt
    Loans, exemptions, 11 § 523
    Materials, exemptions, 11 § 522
Elections,
    Chapter 7 proceedings, ante
    Chapter 11 proceedings, ante
    Discharge, fines and penalties, 11 § 523
    Exemptions, 11 § 522
    Fines and penalties, discharge, 11 § 523
    Meetings, BKR 2003
        Liquidation, 11 § 702
    Nonrecourse loans, BKR 3014
    Trusts and trustees, post
Electronic filing, BKR 5005
    Notice, BKR 9036
Electronic summons, BKR 7004
Eligibility, trusts and trustees, 11 § 321
Embezzlement, 11 § 523; 18 § 153
Emergencies,
    Appeal and review, motions, BKR 8011
    Courts, special sessions, 28 § 152
Employee Retirement Income Security Program,
    Administrators, 11 §§ 521, 704
    Contributions, 11 § 541
        Priorities and preferences, 11 § 507
    Priorities and preferences, contributions, 11 § 507
Employees. Officers and employees, generally, post
Employment. Labor and employment, generally, post
Entry, judgments and decrees, BKR 7058, 8016, 9021
Entry upon land, BKR 7034
    Small businesses, 11 § 1116
Equity,
    Automatic stay, 11 § 362
    Equity security holders, generally, post
Equity security holders, 11 § 501 et seq.
    Administrators, 11 § 341 nt
    Allowances, 11 § 502
    Classification, BKR 3013
    Committees,
        Compensation and salaries, professional persons, 11 §§ 328, 504
        Priorities and preferences, expenses and expenditures, 11 § 507
        Professional persons, compensation and salaries, 11 §§ 328, 504
    Core proceedings, 28 § 157
    Definitions, 11 § 101
    Evidence, filing, 11 § 501; BKR 3003
    Expenses and expenditures, priorities and preferences, 11 § 507
    Filing, evidence, 11 § 501; BKR 3003
    Lists, BKR 1007
    Meetings, 11 § 341
    Notice, BKR 2002
    Priorities and preferences, expenses and expenditures, 11 § 507
    Representatives and representation, statements, BKR 2019
    Statements, representatives and representation, BKR 2019
Error,
    Filing, BKR 5005
    Harmless error, BKR 9005
Evictions, automatic stay, 11 § 362
Evidence, BKR 9017
    Avoidance, preferences, 11 §§ 363, 547
    Chapter 7 proceedings, ante
    Chapter 13 proceedings, claims, postpetition, 11 § 1305
    Claims, ante
    Debtors in possession, BKR 2011
    Discharge, objections and exceptions, BKR 4005
    Exemptions, claims, BKR 4003
    Foreign countries, 11 § 1515 et seq.; BKR 3002
    Loans, 11 § 364
    Postpetition transfers, validation, BKR 6001
    Preferences, avoidance, 11 §§ 363, 547
    Presumptions, generally, post
    Priorities and preferences, avoidance, 11 §§ 363, 547
    Privileges and immunities, 11 § 344
    Sales, 11 § 363
    Self-incrimination, 11 § 344
    Transcripts, BKR 5007
    Trusts and trustees, post
Ex parte proceedings, BKR 9003
    Identity and identification, theft, 11 § 107
Examinations and examiners, 11 § 343; BKR 2004, 2005
    Administration, BKR 6002
    Administrative expenses, 11 § 503
    Administrators, 11 § 341 nt
    Appointments,
        Foreign countries, 11 § 1522
        Judges or justices, relatives, BKR 5002
        United States trustees, relatives, BKR 5002
    Attendance, BKR 4002
    Attorneys, BKR 2017
    Books and papers, 11 § 107
    Chapter 11 proceedings, ante
    Compensation and salaries, 11 § 330
        Administrative expenses, 11 § 503
        Interim compensation, 11 § 331
        Priorities and preferences, 11 § 507
        Records and recordation, BKR 2013
        Sharing, 11 § 504
    Conflict of interest, BKR 5002
    Conversion, 11 § 348
    Foreign countries, post
    Grain, 11 § 557
    Interim compensation, 11 § 331
    Labor and employment, 11 § 327
    Meetings, BKR 2003
    Political subdivisions, tax returns, 11 § 505

INDEX

Priorities and preferences, compensation and salaries, 11 § 507
Privileges and immunities, 11 § 344
Records and recordation, compensation and salaries, BKR 2013
Removal, 11 § 324
Self-incrimination, 11 § 344
Sharing, compensation and salaries, 11 § 504
Tax returns, governmental units, 11 § 505
Trusts and trustees, post
United States trustees, post
Exceptions. Objections and exceptions, generally, post
Exclusive jurisdiction, 28 § 1334
Execution, BKR 7069
    Avoidance, statutory liens, 11 § 545
    Railroads, reorganization, 11 § 1172
    Reorganization, railroads, 11 § 1172
    Statutory liens, avoidance, 11 § 545
    Trusts and trustees, 11 § 544
Executory contracts. Contracts, generally, ante
Exemptions, 11 § 522; BKR 4003
    Alimony, 11 §§ 522, 523
    Animals, 11 § 522
    Annuities, 11 § 522
    Appliances, 11 § 522
    Automatic preservation, avoided transfers, 11 § 551
    Avoidance, ante
    Books and papers, 11 § 522
    Burial plot, ante
    Chapter 11 proceedings, securities, 11 § 1145
    Clothing, 11 § 522
    Colleges and universities, financial assistance, fraud, 11 § 522
    Computers, 11 § 522
    Cooperatives, 11 § 522
    Counseling services, 11 § 109
    Crime Victims Reparation Law, 11 § 522
    Crockery, 11 § 522
    Crops, 11 § 522
    Dependents, 11 § 522
    Disability, 11 § 522
    Dishes, 11 § 522
    Domicile and residence, 11 § 522
    Elections, 11 § 522
    Filing, 11 § 522
    Fraud, 11 §§ 522, 523; BKR 4003
    Furniture, 11 § 522
    Future earnings, losses, 11 § 522
    Handicapped persons, benefits, 11 § 522
    Health aids, 11 § 522
    Homesteads, post
    Household goods, 11 § 522
    Hydrocarbons, 11 § 541
    Illnesses, benefits, 11 § 522
    Insured depository institutions, 11 § 522
    Jewelry, 11 § 522
    Joint proceedings, post
    Joint property, 11 § 522
    Kitchenware, 11 § 522
    Liens and incumbrances, 11 § 522; BKR 4003
    Life insurance, 11 § 522
    Linens, 11 § 522
    Lists, 11 § 522
    Livestock, 11 § 522
    Maintenance, 11 § 522
    Medical devices, 11 § 522
    Motions, avoidance, BKR 4003
    Motor vehicles, 11 § 522
    New markets venture capital companies, 11 § 109
    Objections and exceptions, 11 § 522
    Pensions, 11 § 522
    Personal effects, 11 § 522
    Personal injuries, 11 § 522
    Personal property, 11 § 522
    Privacy protection, BKR 9037
    Profit-sharing plans, 11 § 522
    Public assistance, 11 § 522
    Real estate, post
    Redemption, 11 § 541
    Retirement and pensions, 11 § 522
    Schedules, forms, BKR Form 6
    Scholarships, fraud, 11 § 522
    Securities, reorganization, 11 § 1145
    Security interest, 11 § 552
    Separate maintenance, 11 § 522
    Sickness, benefits, 11 § 522
    Social security, 11 § 522
    Stock bonus plans, 11 § 522
    Support, 11 § 522
    Television and radio, 11 § 522
    Tools of trade, 11 § 522
    Toys, 11 § 522
    Trade tools, 11 § 522
    Transfers, BKR 4003
        Avoidance, 11 §§ 522, 551
    Turnovers, property, 11 § 542
    Unemployment compensation, 11 § 522
    Veterans, benefits, 11 § 522
    Video cassette recorders, 11 § 522
    Waiver, 11 § 522
    Wrongful death, 11 § 522; 28 § 157
Expenses and expenditures, 28 § 604
    Administration, ante
    Automatic stay, 11 § 362
    Buildings, 28 § 156
    Claims, 11 § 506
    Community property, 11 § 363
    Consumer debts, discharge, 11 § 523
    Creditors, 11 § 503
    Custodians, 11 § 543
    Filing, 11 § 503
    Grain, 11 § 557
    Involuntary proceedings, post
    Mileage. Traveling expenses, generally, post
    Priorities and preferences, 11 § 507
    Professional persons, 11 § 328
    References, 11 § 102
    Reimbursement, generally, post
    Schedules, 11 § 521
        Forms, BKR Form 6
    Taxation, 11 § 503
    Traveling expenses, generally, post
    Trusts and trustees, post
    United States trustees, 28 §§ 586, 588
Extensions, 11 § 108; BKR 9006
    Appeal and review, BKR 8002
    Judicial liens, 11 § 544
    Leases, 11 § 365
    Taxation, 11 § 505
Facilities. Buildings, generally, ante
Family Farmers Protection Act of 2002, 11 §§ 101 nt, 1201 et seq.

INDEX

Family fisherman, definitions, **11 § 101**
Family fisherman with regular annual income, definitions, **11 § 101**
Farmers. Chapter 12 proceedings, generally, ante
Federal Bureau of Investigation, powers and duties, **18 § 158**
Federal depository institutions regulatory agency, definitions, **11 § 101**
Federal Rules of Civil Procedure, amendments, **BKR 9032**
Fees, **28 § 1930**
    Administrators, **28 § 1930**
    Attorneys, ante
    Chapter 7 proceedings, ante
    Chapter 11 proceedings, ante
    Claims, **BKR 3001**
    Copies, **11 § 521**
    Counseling services, **11 § 111**
    Debt relief agencies, **11 § 526**
    Filing, post
    Financial management training curriculum, **11 § 111**
    Fraud, **18 § 155**
    Judicial Conference of the United States, **28 § 1930**
    Petitions,
        Filing, **BKR 1006**
        Preparers, **11 § 110**
    Priorities and preferences, **11 § 507**
    Professional persons, **11 § 330**
    References, **11 nt prec § 101**
    Transcripts, **BKR 5007**
    Treasury of United States, post
    United States trustees, post
    Witnesses, post
Fiduciaries,
    Fraud, **11 § 523**
    Trusts and trustees, generally, post
Filing,
    Access, **11 § 107**
    Adversary proceedings, **BKR 7005**
    Appeal and review, **BKR 8008**
        Briefs, **BKR 8009**
    Assets, schedules, **11 § 521**
    Attorneys, fees, statements, **11 § 329**
    Books and papers, **BKR 5005**
    Briefs, appeal and review, **BKR 8009**
    Chapter 7 proceedings, ante
    Chapter 9 proceedings, ante
    Chapter 11 proceedings, ante
    Chapter 12 proceedings, ante
    Chapter 13 proceedings, ante
    Claims, ante
    Consumer debts, statements, **11 § 521**
    Custodians, accounts and accounting, **11 § 543**
    Delays, claims, **11 § 502**
    Error, **BKR 5005**
    Evidence, claims, **11 § 501**
    Exemptions, **11 § 522**
    Extension of time, **11 § 108**
    Fees, **28 § 1930**
        Dismissal and nonsuit, **BKR 1017**
        Installment payments, forms, **BKR Form 3A**
    Foreign countries, post
    Grain, **11 § 557**
    Liabilities, schedules, **11 § 521**
    Noncore proceedings, proposed findings, **BKR 9033**
    Partnership, petitions, **BKR 1004**
    Petitions, post
    Pleading, **11 § 108**
    Postpetition transactions, avoidance, **11 § 549**
    Privacy protection, **BKR 9037**
    Public access, **11 § 107**
    Reaffirmation agreements, **BKR 4008**
    Records and recordation, **BKR 5005, 5007**
    Redacted filings, **BKR 9037**
    Removal, **BKR 9027**
    Schedules, **11 § 521**
    Serial filers, **11 § 362**
    Signatures, **11 § 110**
    Stay of proceedings, termination, proposed actions, **11 § 1301**
    Taxation, returns, **11 § 346**
    Time, extension of time, **11 § 108**
    Trusts and trustees, bonds (officers and fiduciaries), **11 § 322**
    Voluntary proceedings, **11 §§ 301, 302**
Financial management training curriculum, **11 § 111**
    Certification of completion, forms, **BKR Form 23**
    Chapter 7 proceedings, **11 § 727**
    Chapter 13 proceedings, **11 § 1328**
    Forms, certification of completion, **BKR Form 23**
    Reports, **11 § 111 nt**
    Statement of course completion, **BKR 1007**
        Discharge, **BKR 4004**
    Tests, **11 § 111 nt**
Financial statements and reports, **BKR 1007**
    Chapter 11 proceedings, substantial or controlling interest, **BKR 2015.3; BKR Form 26**
    Filing, **11 § 521**
    Forms, **BKR Form 7**
    Small businesses, **11 §§ 308, 1116**
Findings, courts, **BKR 7052**
Fines and penalties, **BKR 9011**
    Administration, expenses and expenditures, **11 § 503**
    Bribery and corruption, **18 § 152**
    Chapter 7 proceedings, ante
    Chapter 13 proceedings, **11 § 1328**
    Concealment, assets, **18 § 152**
    Conflict of interest, **18 § 154**
    Debt relief agencies, **11 § 526**
    Discovery, **BKR 7037**
    Elections, discharge, **11 § 523**
    Embezzlement, **18 § 153**
    Equity security holders, representatives and representation, statements, **BKR 2019**
    Exemptions, **11 § 522**
    Fraud, generally, post
    Governmental units, **11 § 523**
    Liens and incumbrances, **11 §§ 522, 550 et seq.**
    Life insurance, **11 § 542**
    Petitions, preparers, **11 § 110**
    Priorities and preferences, **11 § 507**
    Representatives and representation, statements, **BKR 2019**
    Taxation, post

INDEX

Trusts and trustees, personal liability, **11 § 322**
Fish and game,
   Commercial fishing,
      Chapter 12 proceedings, generally, ante
      Definitions, **11 § 101**
   Definitions, **11 § 101**
   Family fishermen. Chapter 12 proceedings, generally, ante
   Processing facilities,
      Sales, **11 § 546**
         Unsecured claims, priorities and preferences, **11 § 507**
Flax and flaxseed, **11 § 557**
Foreign banks in the United States, **11 § 109**
Foreign countries, **11 § 1501 et seq.**
   Abstention, **11 § 305**
   Access, **11 § 1509 et seq.**
   Addresses, **11 § 1514**
   Administration, **11 § 1519 et seq.**
   Adversary proceedings, **BKR 1018**
   Appearances, **11 § 306**
   Application of law, **11 § 1508**
   Appointments, **11 § 1515**
      Examinations and examiners, **11 § 1522**
   Assistance, **11 § 1507**
   Automatic stay, **11 § 1519 et seq.**
   Business and commerce,
      Operating businesses, **11 §§ 1520, 1522**
      Venue, **28 § 1410**
   Certificates and certification, **11 § 1515 et seq.**
   Chapter 11 proceedings, venue, **28 § 1408**
   Claims, **11 § 1513; BKR 3002**
   Closings, **11 § 1517**
   Communications, **11 § 1525 et seq.**
   Concurrent proceedings, **11 § 1528 et seq.**
   Conflict of laws, **11 § 1503**
   Contests, petitions, **BKR 1011**
   Cooperation, **11 § 1525 et seq.**
   Coordination, **11 § 1529 et seq.**
   Core proceedings, **28 § 157**
   Corporations, recognition petitions, ownership statements, **BKR 1011**
   Definitions, **11 §§ 101, 1502**
      Cooperation, **11 § 1527**
   Distribution, **11 § 1521**
   Domicile and residence, **11 § 1516**
   Evidence, **11 § 1515 et seq.; BKR 3002**
   Examinations and examiners,
      Appointments, **11 § 1522**
      Powers and duties, **11 § 1505**
      Supervision, **11 § 1526**
   Fees, filing, **28 § 1930**
   Filing,
      Fees, **28 § 1930**
      Petitions, **11 §§ 1504, 1509 et seq.**
   Information, **11 § 1521**
   Injunctions, **11 §§ 1519, 1521**
   Intervention, **11 § 1524**
   Involuntary proceedings, **11 § 1511**
   Jurisdiction,
      Concurrent proceedings, **11 § 1528 et seq.**
      Representatives and representation, **11 §§ 306, 1510**
   Master agreements, **11 § 561**
   Modification, **11 §§ 1517, 1522**
      Concurrent proceedings, **11 § 1529**
   Motions, **BKR 1003**
      Pending actions, petitions, **BKR 1004.2**
   Multiple proceedings, **11 § 1530**
   Notice, **11 § 1514 et seq.; BKR 2002**
      Time, **BKR 2015**
   Operating businesses, **11 §§ 1520, 1522**
   Orders of court, **11 § 1509 et seq.**
   Parties, **11 § 1512**
   Payment, **11 § 1532**
   Pending actions, **11 § 1523**
      Abstention, **11 § 305**
      Concurrent proceedings, **11 § 1528 et seq.**
      Petitions, **BKR 1004.2**
      Venue, **28 § 1410**
   Petitions, **BKR 1003, 1004.2**
      Contests, **BKR 1011**
      Filing, **11 §§ 1504, 1509 et seq.**
      Recognition petitions, **11 § 1515 et seq.; BKR 1010 et seq.**
   Pleading, **BKR 1003**
   Presumptions, **11 § 1516**
      Concurrent proceedings, **11 § 1531**
   Public policy, **11 §§ 1501, 1506**
   Recognition petitions, **11 § 1515 et seq.; BKR 1010 et seq.**
   Representatives and representation, **11 § 1509 et seq.**
   Responsive pleadings, **BKR 1011**
   Revocation or suspension, **11 § 1520 et seq.**
   Security interest, **11 § 1520**
   Status, **11 § 1518**
   Stay of proceedings, **11 § 1519 et seq.**
   Summons, **BKR 1003**
   Supervision,
      Examinations and examiners, **11 § 1526**
      Trusts and trustees, **11 § 1526**
   Taxation, **11 § 1513**
   Termination, **11 §§ 1517, 1522**
      Concurrent proceedings, **11 § 1529**
   Time, notice, **BKR 2015**
   Transfers, **11 § 1520 et seq.**
   Trusts and trustees,
      Additional relief, **11 § 1521**
      Powers and duties, **11 § 1505**
      Supervision, **11 § 1526**
   United States trustees, post
   Venue, **28 § 1410**
      Chapter 11 proceedings, **28 § 1408**
   Voluntary proceedings, **11 § 1511**
   Witnesses, **11 § 1521**
Foreign insurance, **11 § 109**
Forfeitures, **11 § 363**
Forgiveness, taxation, **11 § 346**
Forma pauperis, frivolous actions, **11 § 523**
Forms, **BKR 9009; BKR Form 1 et seq.**
   Adversary proceedings, ante
   Ballots, reorganization, plans and specifications, **BKR Form 14**
   Captions,
      Adversary proceedings, complaints, **BKR Form 16D**
      Full captions, **BKR Form 16A**
      Short title, **BKR Form 16B**
   Certificates and certification, ante

INDEX

Chapter 7 proceedings, ante
Chapter 11 proceedings, ante
Chapter 12 proceedings, ante
Chapter 13 proceedings, ante
Claims, ante
Current monthly income and means test calculation, **BKR Form 22**
Declarations, **BKR Forms 2, 6**
Discharge, ante
Disclosure, ante
Evidence, claims, **BKR Form 10**
Fees, installments, **BKR Form 3A**
Filing, fees, installments, **BKR Form 3A**
Financial management training curriculum, certification of completion, **BKR Form 23**
Financial statements and reports, **BKR Form 7**
Full captions, **BKR Form 16A**
General power of attorney, **BKR Form 11A**
Income, post
Individual debtors, intentions, statements, **BKR Form 8**
Installments, fees, **BKR Form 3A**
Involuntary proceedings, post
Landlord and tenant, automatic stay, 11 § 362
Lists, unsecured claims, **BKR Form 4**
Mortgages, **BKR Form 10**
Motions, post
Nonattorney petition preparers,
    Declarations, **BKR Form 6**
    Notice, **BKR Form 19B**
Nonattorney preparers, declarations, **BKR Form 19A**
Notice, post
Orders of court, post
Petitions, post
Power of attorney,
    General power of attorney, **BKR Form 11A**
    Special power of attorney, **BKR Form 11B**
Proof of claim, **BKR Form 10**
Reaffirmation agreements, post
Schedules, post
Short titles, captions, **BKR Form 16B**
Small businesses, **BKR Form 25 et seq.**
Special power of attorney, **BKR Form 11B**
Statements, post
Statistics, 28 § 159
Unsecured claims, lists, **BKR Form 4**
Voluntary proceedings, petitions, **BKR Form 1**

Forward contracts,
    Acceleration, 11 § 556
    Automatic stay, 11 §§ 362, 553
    Damages, 11 § 562
    Definitions, 11 § 101
    Liquidation, 11 § 556
    Margin payments, 11 § 546
    Termination, 11 § 556
    Unsecured claims, priorities and preferences, 11 §§ 753, 767
Fraud, 18 § 152
    Attorneys, fees, 18 § 155
    Avoidance, transfers, trusts and trustees, 11 § 546 et seq.

Chapter 9 proceedings, transfers, 11 §§ 901, 926
Chapter 11 proceedings, ante
Chapter 13 proceedings, ante
Charities, 11 § 548
Clerks of courts, notice, 28 § 586
Concealment, 18 § 157
Consumer debt, notice, 11 § 342
Conveyances. Fraudulent conveyances, generally, post
Debt relief agencies, 11 § 526
Definitions, transfers, 11 § 548
Discharge, 11 §§ 523, 1328
Exemptions, 11 §§ 522, 523; **BKR 4003**
Fees, 18 § 155
Fiduciaries, 11 § 523
Homesteads, exemptions, 11 § 522
Insiders, transfers, 11 § 548
Interception of wire, oral, or electronic communications, 18 § 2516
Liability, transfers, avoidance, 11 § 550
Lien creditors, transfers, avoidance, 11 § 551
Limitation of actions, transfers, 11 § 546
Master netting agreements, 11 § 548
Partnership, transfers, avoidance, 11 § 548
Petitions, preparers, 11 § 110
Racketeer influenced and corrupt organizations, 18 § 1961
References, schedules, 18 § 158
Religious organizations and societies, 11 § 548
Repurchase agreements, 11 § 548
Schedules, 18 § 158
Securities,
    Discharge, 11 § 523
    Transfers, 11 § 548
Security interest, 11 § 552
Statute of frauds, 11 § 558
Tax returns, 11 §§ 505, 523
Transfers,
    Avoidance, trusts and trustees, 11 § 546 et seq.
    Chapter 9 proceedings, 11 §§ 901, 926
    Definitions, 11 § 548
    Exemptions, 11 § 522
    Fraudulent conveyances, generally, post
    Insiders, 11 § 548
    Liability, avoidance, 11 § 550
    Lien creditors, avoidance, 11 § 551
    Limitation of actions, 11 § 546
    Master netting agreements, 11 § 548
    Partnership, avoidance, 11 § 548
    Repurchase agreements, 11 § 548
    Security interest, 11 § 552
    Trusts and trustees, avoidance, 11 § 546 et seq.
Trusts and trustees, avoidance, 11 § 546 et seq.
United States trustees, reports, 28 § 586
Frauds, statute of, 11 § 558
    Claims, **BKR 3001**
    Nonrecourse loans, elections, **BKR 3014**
Fraudulent conveyances, 11 § 548
    Discharge, 11 § 524
    Judges or justices, 28 § 157
    Limitation of actions, 11 § 546
Frivolous actions,

INDEX

    Appeal and review, **BKR 8020**
    Forma pauperis, **11 § 523**
    Review, **BKR 8020**
Fuel, taxation, **11 § 501**
Furniture, exemptions, **11 § 522**
Future earnings, exemptions, **11 § 522**
General power of attorney, forms, **BKR Form 11A**
Gifts, **11 § 541**
    National Bankruptcy Review Commission, **11 nt prec § 101**
Good faith,
    Automatic stay, **11 § 362**
    Avoidance, damages, **11 § 550**
    Chapter 7 proceedings, ante
    Chapter 9 proceedings, ante
    Chapter 11 proceedings, ante
    Chapter 12 proceedings, confirmation of plan, **11 § 1225; BKR 3015**
    Chapter 13 proceedings, ante
    Consumer debt, discharge, **11 § 523**
    Discharge, **11 § 524**
    Leases, **11 § 363**
    Liens and incumbrances, **11 § 364**
    Loans, **11 § 364**
    Postpetition transactions, real estate, **11 § 549**
    Priorities and preferences, **11 § 364**
    Real estate, postpetition transactions, **11 § 549**
    Sales, **11 § 363**
    Small businesses, **11 § 362**
    Transfers, **11 §§ 542, 548**
    Turnovers, property, **11 § 542**
Goods, wares and merchandise, **11 § 546**
Grain, **11 § 557**
    Claims, evidence, **BKR 3001**
    Priorities and preferences, unsecured claims, **11 § 507**
    Storage, **11 § 546**
    Unsecured claims, priorities and preferences, **11 § 507**
Grand jury, investigations, **18 § 3057**
Grants, discrimination, **11 § 525**
Guaranty, claims, evidence, **BKR 3005**
Handicapped persons, **BKR 9028**
    Benefits, exemptions, **11 § 522**
    Exemptions, benefits, **11 § 522**
    Judges or justices, **28 § 152; BKR 9028**
Hanging Law, chapter 13 proceedings, **11 § 1325**
Hardship, reaffirmation agreements, **11 § 524**
Harmless error, **BKR 9005**
Health aids, exemptions, **11 § 522**
Health care businesses, **BKR 1021**
    Definitions, **11 § 101**
    Destruction, patient records, **BKR 6011**
    Notice, patient records, **BKR 6011**
    Patient care ombudsman, generally, post
    Records and recordation, patients, **BKR 6011**
    Reports, patient records, destruction, **BKR 6011**
    Transfers, patients, **BKR 2015.2**
Health insurance, chapter 13 proceedings, **11 § 1329**
Hearings, **28 § 157; BKR 5001**
    Abandonment, **11 § 554; BKR 6007**
    Abstention, **11 § 305**
    Administration, expenses and expenditures, **11 § 503**

    Appearance, **11 § 521**
    Automatic stay, **11 §§ 362, 506**
    Cash, collateral, **11 § 363**
    Chapter 7 proceedings, ante
    Chapter 11 proceedings, confirmation of plans, **11 § 1128**
    Chapter 13 proceedings, ante
    Clearing banks, liquidation, **11 § 784**
    Compensation and salaries, **11 §§ 330, 331**
    Consumer privacy ombudsman, **11 § 332**
    Debt relief agencies, **11 § 526**
    Discharge, **11 § 523**
    Financial statements and reports, **11 § 542**
    Interim compensation, **11 § 331**
    Involuntary proceedings, **11 § 303**
    Judges or justices, removal, **28 § 152**
    Leases, **BKR 6004**
    Liens and incumbrances, **11 § 364**
    Loans, **11 § 364**
    Objections and exceptions, claims, **11 § 502**
    Officers and employees, removal, **11 § 324**
    Panels, bankruptcy appellate panels, **28 § 158**
    Personally identifiable information, disposition, **11 §§ 332, 363**
    Plans and specifications, **11 § 506**
    Priorities and preferences, **11 § 363**
    Public utilities, deposits, **11 § 366**
    Reaffirmation agreements, **11 § 524**
    Rules of construction, **11 § 102**
    Sales, **BKR 6004**
    Subordination, claims, **11 § 510**
    Trusts and trustees, post
    Turnovers, custodians, **11 § 543**
Holidays, **BKR 5001**
Home Health Agencies, this index
Homestead associations, **11 § 109**
Homesteads, exemptions, **11 § 522**
Hospices, this index
Hospitals, this index
Hours of labor, offices, **BKR 5001**
Household goods, exemptions, **11 § 522**
Husband and wife,
    Alimony, generally, ante
    Avoidance, preferences, **11 § 547**
    Community property, **11 § 541**
        Discharge, **11 § 524**
        Sales, **11 § 363**
    Discharge, community property, **11 § 524**
    Divorce, generally, ante
    Exemptions, **11 § 522**
    Joint proceedings, **11 § 302**
    Maintenance. Alimony, generally, ante
    Preferences, avoidance, **11 § 547**
    Qualifications, **11 § 109**
    Sales, community property, **11 § 363**
    Settlement agreements, **11 § 541**
    Support. Alimony, generally, ante
Hydrocarbons, exemptions, **11 § 541**
Identity and identification,
    Notice, **11 § 342**
    Personally identifiable information, generally, post
    Petitions, preparers, **11 § 110**
    Social security, numbers and numbering, **BKR 4002**
    Theft, **11 § 107**
Illnesses, benefits, exemptions, **11 § 522**

INDEX

Immunities. Privileges and immunities, generally, post
Improvements, transfers, avoidance, liability, 11 § 550
Incidental property, definitions, 11 § 101
Income,
    Current monthly income, generally, ante
    Documentation, BKR 4002
    Forms,
        Current monthly income and means test calculation, BKR Form 22
        Schedules, BKR Form 6
    Schedules, 11 § 521
        Forms, BKR Form 6
Income tax,
    Confidential or privileged information, returns, BKR 4002
    Copies, returns, BKR 4002
    Returns, copies, BKR 4002
Incompetency. Mental health, generally, post
Incumbrances. Liens and incumbrances, generally, post
Indemnity,
    Involuntary proceedings, 11 § 303
    Liens and incumbrances, BKR 6010
Indenture trust and trustees,
    Compensation and salaries, priorities and preferences, 11 § 507
    Definitions, 11 § 101
    Examinations and examiners, 11 § 343
    Expenses and expenditures, priorities and preferences, 11 § 507
    Involuntary proceedings, 11 § 303
    Proof of claim, 11 § 501
Indexes, BKR 5003
Individual debtors. Chapter 13 proceedings, generally, ante
Indorsers, claims, evidence, BKR 3005 Industrial banks, 11 § 109
Information,
    Financial information, documentation, BKR 4002
    Foreign countries, 11 § 1521
    Personally identifiable information, generally, post
Inheritances, 11 § 541
Injunctions, BKR 7065
    Automatic stay, generally, ante
    Chapter 9 proceedings, plans and specifications, BKR 3017
    Chapter 11 proceedings, plans and specifications, BKR 3017
    Debt relief agencies, 11 § 526
    Discharge, 11 § 524
    Foreign countries, 11 §§ 1519, 1521
    Petitions, preparers, 11 § 110
    Plans and specifications, notice, BKR 2002
    Removal of cases or causes, BKR 9027
    Supplemental injunctions, 11 § 524
Injuries. Personal injuries, generally, post
Insiders,
    Avoidance, 11 § 547
    Definitions, 11 § 101
    Fraud, transfers, 11 § 548
    Involuntary proceedings, 11 § 303
    Services, claims, 11 § 502
    Subordination, claims, 11 § 747
Inspection and inspectors,
    Lists, BKR 1007
    Sentence and punishment, 18 § 154
Installments,
    Filing, fees, forms, BKR Form 3A
    Forms, filing, fees, BKR Form 3A
    Joint proceedings, 28 § 1930
    Petitions, fees, payment, BKR 1006
    Voluntary proceedings, 28 § 1930
Instructions, commodities, customers, 11 § 765
Instruments,
    Musical instruments, 11 § 522
    Negotiable instruments, 11 § 362
Insurance,
    Chapter 11 proceedings, ante
    Chapter 13 proceedings, personal property, 11 § 1326
    Life insurance, generally, post
    Liquidation, 11 § 109
    Small businesses, 11 § 1116
Insured depository institutions, service of process, BKR 7004
Intellectual property,
    Definitions, 11 § 101
    Licenses and permits, contracts, 11 § 365
Intent, fraudulent transfers, 11 § 548
Interception of wire, oral, or electronic communications, 18 § 2516
Interest, 11 § 541
    Automatic stay, 11 § 362
    Cash, collateral, 11 § 363
    Chapter 11 proceedings, railroads, 11 § 1165
    Claims, BKR 3001
    Deposits, 28 § 589a
    Grain, 11 § 557
    Hydrocarbons, 11 § 541
    Railroads, reorganization, 11 § 1165
    Reaffirmation agreements, 11 § 524
    Security interest, generally, post
    Taxation, 11 § 511
    Unmatured interest, 11 § 502
Interim compensation, 11 § 331
Interim trustees. Trusts and trustees, post
Interlocutory orders, 28 § 158
Intermediate Care Facilities, this index
Interpleader, BKR 7022
Interpreters, 11 § 1515
Interrogatories, BKR 7033
Interstate commerce, 28 § 157
Intervention, BKR 2018, 7024
    Foreign countries, 11 § 1524
Intoxication, driving while intoxicated, damages, discharge, 11 § 523
Inventories, BKR 2015
    Conversion, BKR 1019
    Preferences, 11 § 547
    Trusts and trustees, BKR 4002
Investigations, 18 § 3057
    United States attorneys, 18 § 3057
Investments, deposits, 11 § 345
Involuntary proceedings, 11 § 541; BKR 1010 et seq.
    Adversary proceedings, BKR 1018
    Attorneys, 11 § 504
    Automatic stay, 11 §§ 362, 553
    Avoidance, transfers, 11 § 303
    Contests, adversary proceedings, BKR 1018
    Corporations,
        Objections and exceptions, 11 § 303

INDEX

Ownership statements, **BKR 1011**
Evidence, claims, **11 § 501**
Exemptions, transfers, **11 § 522**
Expenses and expenditures,
    Allowances, **11 § 503**
    Priorities and preferences, **11 § 507**
Filing,
    Claims, **11 § 501**
    Petitions, **11 § 303**
Foreign countries, **11 § 1511**
Foreign representatives, **11 § 306**
Forms, petitions, **BKR Form 5**
Joinder, **11 § 303; BKR 1003**
Lists, **BKR 1007**
Orders of court,
    Claims, priorities and preferences, **11 § 507**
    Petitions, **11 § 303**
    Priorities and preferences, claims, **11 § 507**
Partnership, petitions, **BKR 1004**
Petitions, **BKR 1003, 1010 et seq.**
    Contests, **BKR 1013**
    Filing, **11 § 303**
    Forms, **BKR Form 5**
Priorities and preferences, **11 § 507**
Schedules, **BKR 1007**
Securities, automatic stay, **11 § 362**
Time, schedules, **BKR 1007**
Transfers,
    Avoidance, **11 § 303**
    Claims, **BKR 1003**
    Exemptions, **11 § 522**
    Validation, **11 § 549**
Unsecured claims, discharge, **11 § 523**
Validation, transfers, **11 § 549**
Irreparable injuries, automatic stay, **11 § 363**
Issues, statements, appeal and review, **BKR 8006**
Jewelry,
    Exemptions, **11 § 522**
    Liens and incumbrances, exemptions, **11 § 522**
Joinder,
    Claims, **BKR 7018**
    Involuntary proceedings, **11 § 303; BKR 1003**
    Liens and incumbrances, indemnity, **BKR 6010**
    Parties, **BKR 7019 et seq.**
Joint administration, **BKR 2009**
    Consolidations and mergers, **BKR 1015**
Joint appellate panels, **28 § 158**
Joint proceedings, **11 §§ 302, 541**
    Automatic stay, **11 § 362**
        Securities, exemptions, **11 § 362**
        Setoff and counterclaim, **11 § 553**
    Exemptions, **11 § 522**
        Automatic stay, securities, **11 § 362**
        Fees, filing, **28 § 1930**
        Filing, fees, **28 § 1930**
        Securities, automatic stay, **11 § 362**
    Fees, filing, exemptions, **28 § 1930**
    Filing, fees, exemptions, **28 § 1930**
    Securities, exemptions, automatic stay, **11 § 362**
    Setoff and counterclaim, automatic stay, **11 § 553**
Joint property, exemptions, **11 § 522**

Joint tenants, **11 § 363**
Judges or justices, **28 § 151 et seq.**
    Adjacent districts, **28 § 152**
    Annual leave, **28 § 153**
    Appeal and review, **28 § 158**
    Appellate panels, **28 § 158**
    Appointments, **11 § 105; 28 § 152**
    Chief Judge, **28 § 154**
        Court of appeals, **28 § 152**
    Compensation and salaries, **28 §§ 153, 604**
        Relatives, disqualification, **BKR 5004**
        Retired judges, **28 § 604**
        Recall, **28 § 155**
    Conflict of interest, **28 § 153**
        Disqualification, **BKR 5004**
    Core proceedings, **28 § 157**
    Disability, **BKR 9028**
    Discipline, **28 § 372**
    Disqualification, **28 § 455; BKR 5004**
    Education, **11 § 101 nt**
    Expenses and expenditures, **28 § 604**
    Fraudulent conveyances, **28 § 157**
    Handicapped persons, **BKR 9028**
    Law clerks, **28 § 156**
    Leave of absence, **28 § 153**
    Meetings, **11 § 341**
    Mental health, **28 § 152**
    Oaths and affirmations, **28 § 153**
    Official duty station, **28 § 152**
    Practice of law, **28 § 153**
    Puerto Rico, appointments, **28 § 152**
    Recall, **28 § 155**
    References, generally, post
    Relatives, compensation and salaries, disqualification, **BKR 5004**
    Removal from office, **28 § 372**
        Grounds, **28 § 152**
    Reports, **18 § 3057**
    Retirement and pensions, recall, **28 § 155**
    Secretaries, **28 § 156**
    Sick leave, **28 § 153**
    Staff, **28 § 156**
    Terms of office, **28 § 152**
    Territories, **28 § 152**
    Transfers, **28 § 155**
    Vacancies in office, **28 § 152**
Judgments and decrees, **28 § 157; BKR 7054 et seq.**
    Amendments, **BKR 9023**
    Automatic stay, **11 § 362**
    Chapter 11 proceedings, **BKR 3022**
    Consumer debts, discharge, **11 § 523**
    Discharge, **11 § 524**
    Dismissal and nonsuit, **11 § 349**
    Entry, **BKR 7058, 8016, 9021**
    Involuntary proceedings, dismissal and nonsuit, **11 § 303**
    Motions,
        Amendments, time, **BKR 9023**
        Time, **BKR 9015**
    Notice, **BKR 8016, 9022**
    Offers, **BKR 7068**
    Powers and duties, **11 § 105**
    Records and recordation, **BKR 5003**
    Relief, **BKR 9024**
    Summary judgment, **BKR 7056**
    Time, amendments, **BKR 9023**

INDEX

Judicial Conference of the United States, 28 § 152 et seq.
    Adjustments, 11 § 104
    Assessments, reports, 28 § 152
    Audits and auditors, 28 § 586 nt
    Compensation and salaries, retired judges, 28 § 155
    Fees, 28 § 1930
    Filing, fees, 28 § 1930
    Merger and consolidation, 28 § 156
    Payment, 28 § 153
    Reports, assessments, 28 § 152
    Retired judges, compensation and salaries, 28 § 155
Judicial Council,
    Appellate panels, 28 § 158
    Appointments, 28 § 156
    Joint appellate panels, 28 § 158
    Recall, 28 § 155
    Removal, judges or justices, 28 §§ 152, 372
    Reports, appellate panels, 28 § 158
Judicial districts,
    Trusts and trustees, 11 § 321
    United States trustees, appointments, 28 § 581
Judicial liens. Liens and incumbrances, post
Judicial review. Appeal and review, generally, ante
Jurisdiction, 28 § 1334; BKR 9030
    Abstention, 28 § 1334
    Appeal and review, 28 § 158
    Chapter 9 proceedings, ante
    Chapter 11 proceedings, 28 § 1334
    Debt relief agencies, 11 § 526
    Dismissal and nonsuit, 28 § 1930
    Foreign countries, ante
    Grain, 11 § 557
    Jury, 28 § 157
    Sureties and suretyship, BKR 9025
Jury, 28 § 157; BKR 9015
    Contempt, BKR 9020
    Personal injuries, 28 § 1411
    Wrongful death, 28 § 1411
Justices. Judges or justices, generally, ante
Kitchenware, exemptions, 11 § 522
Labor and employment,
    Applications, BKR 6003
    Attorneys, 11 § 327 et seq.
    Contracts, termination, damages, 11 § 502
    Discrimination, 11 § 525
    Priorities and preferences, taxation, 11 § 507
    Professional personnel, generally, post
    Taxation, priorities and preferences, 11 § 507
    Unemployment compensation, exemptions, 11 § 522
Labor organizations, intervention, BKR 2018
Landlord and tenant,
    Assignments, deposits, 11 § 365
    Automatic stay, 11 § 362
    Possession, certificates and certification, 11 § 362
Larceny,
    Discharge, exemptions, 11 § 523
    Fiduciaries, 11 § 523
    Identity and identification, 11 § 107
Law clerks, 28 § 156
Leases, 11 § 361 et seq.; BKR 6004, 6006
    Administration, expenses and expenditures, 11 § 503
    Assignments, 11 § 365
    Automatic stay, 11 § 362; BKR 6004, 6006
        Personal property, 11 § 365
    Chapter 9 proceedings, ante
    Chapter 13 proceedings, ante
    Consumer privacy ombudsman, 11 § 332
    Damages, termination, 11 § 502
    Default, 11 § 365
    Definitions, 11 § 365
    Good faith, 11 § 363
    Motions, BKR 4001, 6003
        Personally identifiable information, BKR 6004
    Municipalities, 11 § 929
    Nonresidential real property, 11 § 541
        Automatic stay, 11 § 362
    Notice, 11 § 363; BKR 2002, 4001, 6004 et seq.
        Personal property, 11 § 365
    Orders of court, 28 § 157
    Personal property, 11 § 365
        Chapter 13 proceedings, payment, 11 § 1326
    Personally identifiable information, 11 §§ 332, 363; BKR 6004
    Proof of claim, 11 § 501
    Railroads, 11 § 1169
    Rejection, 11 §§ 365, 502
    Sales, 11 § 363
    Schedules, forms, BKR Form 6
    Setoff and counterclaim, 11 § 553
    Termination, damages, 11 § 502
    Trusts and trustees, post
    Turnovers, 11 § 542
Leave of absence,
    Judges or justices, 28 § 153
    Law clerks, 28 § 156
Leave of court, appeal and review, BKR 8003
Letters of credit, 11 § 101
Leverage transactions, stay of proceedings, 11 § 553
Liability. Damages, generally, ante
Licenses and permits, discrimination, 11 § 525
Liens and incumbrances, 11 § 361 et seq.
    Automatic stay, 11 § 362
    Avoidance, ante
    Bona fide purchasers, 11 § 545
    Chapter 7 proceedings, ante
    Chapter 13 proceedings, ante
    Definitions, 11 § 101
    Exemptions, 11 § 522; BKR 4003
    Fines and penalties, 11 §§ 522, 550 et seq.
    Good faith, 11 § 364
    Goods, wares and merchandise, 11 § 546
    Household goods, 11 § 522
    Indemnity, BKR 6010
    Judicial liens, 11 § 522
        Avoidance, trusts and trustees, 11 §§ 544, 547
        Definitions, 11 § 101
        Trusts and trustees, avoidance, 11 §§ 544, 547
    Notice, 11 § 364
        Taxation, 11 § 522
    Operating businesses, 11 § 364
    Priorities and preferences, 11 §§ 364, 507
    Reaffirmation agreements, 11 § 524
    Redemption, BKR 6008

INDEX

Replacement liens, 11 § 361
Sales, 11 § 363; BKR 6004
Status, 11 § 506
Statutory liens, 11 § 545 et seq.
    Automatic preservation, 11 § 551
    Avoidance, 11 § 545 et seq.
    Definitions, 11 § 101
    Exemptions, 11 § 522
    Postpetition transactions, 11 § 552
Subordination, 11 § 510
Taxation, post
Trusts and trustees, post
Validation, 28 § 157
Valuation, 11 § 363; BKR 3012
Void liens, 11 §§ 506, 541, 551
Life insurance, 11 § 541
    Exemptions, payment, 11 § 522
    Good faith, transfers, 11 § 542
    Payment, exemptions, 11 § 522
    Transfers, good faith, 11 § 542
Limitation of actions,
    Avoidance, transfers, 11 §§ 546, 550
    Bonds (officers and fiduciaries), 11 § 322
    Chapter 13 proceedings, security interest, domicile and residence, notice, BKR 3002.1
    Defenses, 11 § 558
    Fraudulent conveyances, 11 § 546
    Postpetition, 11 § 549
    Preferences, 11 § 546
    Priorities and preferences, 11 § 546
    Revocation or suspension, 11 § 108
    Taxation, 11 § 346
    Transfers, avoidance, 11 §§ 546, 550
Limited appearance, foreign representatives, 11 § 306
Linens, exemptions, 11 § 522
Liquidations. Chapter 7 proceedings, generally, ante
Lists, BKR 1007
    Abandonment, disposition, BKR 3011
    Amendments, BKR 1009
    Chapter 9 proceedings, ante
    Chapter 11 proceedings, ante
    Conversion, BKR 1019
    Counseling services, 11 § 111
    Discharge, exemptions, 11 § 523
    Exemptions, discharge, 11 § 523
    Filing, 11 § 521
    Taxation, 11 § 505
    Unsecured claims, forms, BKR Form 4
    Verification, BKR 1008
Livestock and livestock products. Animals, generally, ante
Loans,
    Chapter 9 proceedings, nonrecourse loans, BKR 3014
    Chapter 11 proceedings, nonrecourse loans, BKR 3014
    Discharge, nonprofit institutions, 11 § 523
    Education, exemptions, 11 § 523
    Evidence, 11 § 364
    Good faith, 11 § 364
    Nonprofit institutions, discharge, 11 § 523
    Notice, BKR 4001
    Predatory loans, 11 § 363
    Securities, 11 § 364
    Usury, 11 § 558

Local rules, BKR 8018, 9029
Location,
    Business and commerce, 11 § 109
    Claims, BKR 3002
    Courts, 28 § 152
    Examinations and examiners, BKR 2004
    Meetings, BKR 2003
Long term care. Nursing Homes, this index
Losses,
    Chapter 11 proceedings, ante
    Evidence, 11 § 108
    Taxation, 11 § 346
Luxury goods or services, definitions, 11 § 523
Mail and mailing,
    Governmental units, addresses, BKR 5003
    Notice, BKR 2002
    Process, BKR 7004, 9006
    Service of process, BKR 7004, 9006
    Trusts and trustees, health care businesses, records and recordation, 11 § 351
Maintenance. Alimony, generally, ante
Managers and management,
    Actions and proceedings, 28 § 959
    Chapter 11 proceedings, ante
    Financial management training curriculum, generally, ante
Margins,
    Commodity brokers,
        Avoidance, transfers, 11 § 546
        Fraudulent transfers, 11 § 548
    Definitions, 11 § 101
    Repurchase agreements,
        Fraudulent transfers, 11 § 548
        Set-off and counterclaim, 11 §§ 362, 546
    Securities,
        Avoidance, transfers, 11 § 546
        Fraudulent transfers, 11 § 548
    Shares and shareholders, post
Mask work, definitions, 11 § 101
Master agreements,
    Acceleration, 11 § 561
    Automatic stay, 11 § 362
    Avoidance, 11 § 546
    Commodities, 11 § 761
    Damages, 11 § 562
    Definitions, 11 §§ 101, 561
    Foreign countries, 11 § 561
    Fraud, transfers, 11 § 548
    Liquidation, 11 § 561
    Offsets, 11 § 561
    Termination, 11 § 561
    Unsecured claims, priorities and preferences, 11 §§ 753, 767
Masters, BKR 9031
Means test, chapter 13 proceedings, 11 § 1325
Median family income, definitions, 11 § 101
Medical devices, exemptions, 11 § 522
Medicare, automatic stay, 11 § 362
Meetings, 11 § 341; BKR 2003
    Chapter 7 proceedings, ante
    Chapter 11 proceedings, ante
    Chapter 12 proceedings, BKR 2003; BKR Form 9
    Chapter 13 proceedings, ante
    Examinations and examiners, 11 § 343
    Small businesses, 11 § 1116
Mental health, BKR 1016

INDEX

    Counseling services, **11 § 109**
    Examinations and examiners, **BKR 7035**
    Judges or justices, **28 § 152**
    Petitions, **BKR 1004.1**
    Process, **BKR 1007**
Mergers. Consolidations and mergers, generally, ante
Mileage. Traveling expenses, generally, post
Minors. Children and minors, generally, ante
Misjoinder, parties, **BKR 7021**
Misrepresentation. Fraud, generally, ante
Modification,
    Chapter 9 proceedings, plans and specifications, **11 § 942; BKR 3019**
    Chapter 11 proceedings, plans and specifications, **11 § 1127; BKR 3019**
    Chapter 12 proceedings, plans and specifications, **BKR 3015**
    Chapter 13 proceedings, ante
    Foreign countries, ante
    Grain, **11 § 557**
Money, **BKR 4001**
    Adjustments, **11 § 104**
    Administration, **11 § 363**
    Allowances, **11 § 502**
    Definitions, **11 § 363**
    Deposits, generally, ante
    Discharge, fraud, **11 § 523**
    Fraud, discharge, **11 § 523**
    Investments, **11 § 345**
    Orders of court, **28 § 157**
    Satisfaction, **11 § 363**
    Set-off and counterclaim, **11 § 362**
    Trusts and trustees, **11 § 363**
    Unsecured claims, **11 § 507**
Money orders, **11 § 541**
Monopolies and combinations, notice, **11 § 363**
Mortgages, **11 § 541**
    Forms, **BKR Form 10**
    Secretary of HUD, **11 § 362**
Motions, **BKR 9013**
    Abandonment, **BKR 6007**
    Abstention, **BKR 5011**
    Appeal and review, ante
    Attorneys, fees, examinations and examiners, **BKR 2017**
    Chapter 7 proceedings, ante
    Chapter 11 proceedings, judgments and decrees, **BKR 3022**
    Chapter 13 proceedings, ante
    Claims,
        Classification, **BKR 3013**
        Liens and incumbrances, valuation, **BKR 3012**
    Committees, appointments, appeal and review, **BKR 2007**
    Core proceedings, **28 § 157**
    Debt relief agencies, fines and penalties, **11 § 526**
    Dismissal and nonsuit, **BKR 1017**
    Equity security holders, representatives and representation, disclosure, statements, **BKR 2019**
    Examinations and examiners, **BKR 2005**
    Exemptions, avoidance, **BKR 4003**
    Filing, **BKR 5005**
    Foreign countries, ante
    Forms, **28 § 2075**

    Notice, **BKR Form 20A**
    Grain, **11 § 557**
    Health care businesses, **BKR 1021**
    Involuntary proceedings, dismissal and nonsuit, **11 § 303**
    Judgments and decrees, ante
    Leases, ante
    Leave of court, appeal and review, **BKR 8003**
    Lists, impounding, **BKR 1007**
    New trial, time, **BKR 9015, 9023**
    Notice, forms, **BKR Form 20A**
    Patient care ombudsman, **BKR 2007.2**
    Petitions, preparers, fines and penalties, **11 § 110**
    Reaffirmation agreements, post
    Rehearings, **BKR 8015**
    Reopening, **BKR 5010**
    Representatives and representation, disclosure, statements, **BKR 2019**
    Sales, post
    Signatures, **BKR 9011**
    State laws, claims, abstention, **28 § 1334**
    Time, **BKR 9006**
        Judgments and decrees, **BKR 9015**
        Amendments, **BKR 9023**
        New trial, **BKR 9015, 9023**
    Trade secrets, **11 § 107**
    Trial, new trial, time, **BKR 9015, 9023**
    United States trustees, **BKR 9034**
    Venue, change of venue, **BKR 1014**
    Withdrawal, **28 § 157; BKR 5011**
Motor vehicles,
    Claims, driving while intoxicated or under the influence, priorities and preferences, **11 § 507**
    Damages, driving while intoxicated or under the influence, discharge, **11 § 523**
    Driving while intoxicated or under the influence,
        Claims, priorities and preferences, **11 § 507**
        Damages, discharge, **11 § 523**
        Discharge, damages, **11 § 523**
        Priorities and preferences, claims, **11 § 507**
    Exemptions, **11 § 522**
Multiple foreign proceedings, **11 § 1530**
Municipal corporations. Chapter 9 proceedings, generally, ante
Musical instruments, **11 § 522**
Names, **11 § 109 et seq.**
    Petitions, **BKR 1005**
National Bankruptcy Review Commission, **11 nt prec § 101**
National Guard, chapter 7 proceedings, **11 § 707**
National securities association, **11 § 555**
    Repurchase agreements, **11 § 559**
Negotiable instruments,
    Automatic stay, **11 § 362**
    Family farmers, dishonor, notice, **11 § 1201**
    Individual debtors, dishonor, notice, **11 § 1301**
    Municipalities, recourse, **11 § 927**
Net equity,
    Commodity brokers, **11 § 761**
    Stockbrokers, **11 § 741**
Netting agreements. Master agreements, generally, ante

INDEX

New markets venture capital companies, exemptions, 11 § 109
New trial. Trial, post
Newspapers, municipal debt adjustment, notice, 11 § 923
No asset notice, chapter 7 proceedings, **BKR 2002**
Nonattorney preparers. Petitions, post
Noncore proceedings,
    Abstention, 28 § 157
    Proposed findings, **BKR 9033**
Nonjoinder, parties, **BKR 7021**
Nonparties, process, **BKR 7071**
Nonprofit corporations, involuntary proceedings, 11 § 303
Nonprofit organizations or associations,
    Counseling services, generally, ante
    Discharge, loans, 11 § 523
    Loans, discharge, 11 § 523
Nonrecourse loans, elections, **BKR 3014**
Nonresidential real property, leases,
    Automatic stay, 11 § 362
    Termination, 11 § 541
Nonsuit. Dismissal and nonsuit, generally, ante
North Carolina, **BKR 9035**
Notice, **BKR 2002, 9007**
    Abandonment, 11 § 554; **BKR 6007**
    Abstention, 11 § 305
    Addresses, 11 § 342; **BKR 2002**
    Administration, expenses and expenditures, 11 § 503
        Payment, **BKR 1019**
    Appeal and review, ante
    Appearances, **BKR 9010**
    Application of law, 11 § 102
    Automatic stay, 11 § 362; **BKR 4001**
    Avoidance, transfers, 11 § 549
    Chapter 7 proceedings, ante
    Chapter 9 proceedings, ante
    Chapter 11 proceedings, ante
    Chapter 12 proceedings, ante
    Chapter 13 proceedings, ante
    Claims, ante
    Codebtors, claims, 11 § 509
    Commodities, ante
    Community claim holders, orders of court, 11 § 342
    Compensation and salaries, 11 § 330
    Compromise and settlement, **BKR 9019**
    Consumer debt, ante
    Consumer privacy ombudsman, 11 § 332
    Contempt, **BKR 9020**
    Contracts, **BKR 6006**
    Counseling services, 11 §§ 111, 342
    Courts, emergencies, special sessions, 28 § 152
    Debt relief agencies, 11 § 526 et seq.
    Discharge, 11 § 523
        Revocation or suspension, **BKR 4006**
    Disclosure, orders of court, 11 § 542
    Disposition, **BKR 6007**
    Electronic filing, **BKR 9036**
    Financial management training curriculum, 11 § 111
    Foreign countries, ante
    Forms,
        Appeal and review, **BKR Form 17**
        Chapter 13 proceedings, **BKR Form 9**
        Motions, **BKR Form 20A**
        Nonattorney petition preparers, **BKR Form 19B**
        Objections and exceptions, **BKR Forms 20A, 20B**
    Grain, 11 § 557
    Health care businesses, patient records, **BKR 6011**
    Identity and identification, numbers and numbering, 11 § 342
    Interim compensation, 11 § 331
    Interim trustees, involuntary proceedings, appointments, 11 § 303
    Intervention, **BKR 2018**
    Involuntary proceedings, dismissal and nonsuit, 11 § 303
    Judgments and decrees, ante
    Leases, ante
    Liens and incumbrances, 11 § 364
        Taxation, 11 § 522
    Loans, **BKR 4001**
    Money, collateral, **BKR 4001**
    Monopolies and combinations, 11 § 363
    Negotiable instruments, dishonor, 11 § 362
    Nonattorney petition preparers, **BKR Form 19B**
    Objections and exceptions, forms, **BKR Forms 20A, 20B**
    Orders of court,
        Community claim holders, 11 § 342
        Disclosure, 11 § 542
    Parties, post
    Patient care ombudsman, **BKR 2007.2**
        Reports, **BKR 2015.1**
    Perfection, security interest, avoidance, 11 § 546
    Personally identifiable information, disposition, 11 §§ 332, 363
    Petitions, preparers, 11 § 110
    Public utilities, deposits, 11 § 366
    Publication, **BKR 9008**
    Reaffirmation agreements, 11 § 524
    Removal from office,
        Examinations and examiners, 11 § 324
        Trusts and trustees, 11 § 324
    Removal of cases or causes, **BKR 9027**
    Sales, 11 § 363; **BKR 4001, 6004**
    Security interest, postpetition transactions, 11 § 552
    Statements, amendments, **BKR 1009**
    Subordination, 11 § 510
    Taxation, post
    Time, extension of time, 11 § 108
    Transfers, avoidance, 11 § 549
    Trusts and trustees, post
    Turnovers, 11 §§ 542, 543
    United States trustees, post
Numbers and numbering,
    Petitions, post
    Social security, post
Nursing Homes, this index
Oaths and affirmations, **BKR 9012**
    Administrators, 11 § 341 nt
    Chapter 7 proceedings, ante
    Examinations and examiners, 11 § 343
    Fraud, 18 § 152
        Liquidations, 11 § 727
    Judges or justices, 28 § 153
    Liquidations, fraud, 11 § 727

INDEX

Meetings, **BKR 2003**
Petition preparers, **11 § 110**
United States trustees, **11 § 343**
Oats, **11 § 557**
Objections and exceptions, **11 § 541; BKR 7012, 9026**
    Abandonment, **BKR 6007**
    Automatic stay, **11 § 362**
    Chapter 7 proceedings, ante
    Chapter 9 proceedings, ante
    Chapter 11 proceedings, ante
    Chapter 12 proceedings, ante
    Chapter 13 proceedings, ante
    Claims, ante
    Closings, **BKR 5009**
    Conflict of interest, **11 § 327**
    Discharge, **11 § 523**
        Evidence, **BKR 4005**
    Executory contracts, **11 § 365**
    Exemptions, **11 § 522**
    Filing, **BKR 5005**
    Forms, notice, **BKR Forms 20A, 20B**
    Leases, **BKR 6004**
    Motions, **BKR 4001**
    Noncore proceedings, proposed findings, **BKR 9033**
    Notice, forms, **BKR Forms 20A, 20B**
    Petitions, **BKR 1011**
    Professional persons, conflict of interest, **11 § 327**
    Sales, **BKR 6004**
    Small businesses, statements, reorganization, **BKR 1020**
    Stay of proceedings, **11 § 1301**
    United States trustees, **BKR 9034**
Offenses. Crimes and offenses, generally, ante
Offers, judgments and decrees, **BKR 7068**
Officers and employees, **11 §§ 105, 321 et seq.**
    Attorneys, generally, ante
    Contracts, termination, **11 § 502**
    Custodians, generally, ante
    Discrimination, **11 § 525**
    Examinations and examiners, generally, ante
    Paraprofessionals, **11 §§ 330, 507**
    Priorities and preferences, compensation and salaries, **11 § 507**
    Professional personnel, generally, post
    Termination, contracts, **11 § 502**
    Trusts and trustees, generally, post
    United States trustees, generally, post
Offices, **BKR 5001**
Official bankruptcy forms. Forms, generally, ante
Official stations, courts, judges or justices, **28 § 152**
Offsets, master agreements, **11 § 561**
Ombudsman,
    Consumer privacy ombudsman, generally, ante
    Patient care ombudsman, generally, post
Omnibus objections, claims, **BKR 3007**
Open end credit plans,
    Claims, **BKR 3001**
    Discharge, **11 § 523**
Open end or revolving consumer credit agreements, claims, **BKR 3001**
Operating businesses. Business and commerce, ante
Options,
    Automatic stay, **11 § 553**

Life insurance, **11 § 542**
Oral arguments, appeal and review, **BKR 8012**
Oral examinations, depositions, **BKR 7030**
Orders of court, **28 § 157**
    Adversary proceedings, **BKR 1018**
    Appraisal and appraisers, **BKR 6005**
    Attorneys,
        Excessive compensation, **11 § 329**
        Interim compensation, **11 § 331**
    Auctions and auctioneers, **BKR 6005**
    Chambers, **BKR 5001**
    Chapter 9 proceedings, ante
    Chapter 11 proceedings, ante
    Chapter 13 proceedings, ante
    Claims, ante
    Consolidations and mergers, **BKR 1015**
    Consumer debts, discharge, **11 § 523**
    Consumer privacy ombudsman, **11 § 332**
    Conversion, **11 § 348**
    Default, **BKR 1013**
    Discharge, **11 § 523**
    Disclosure, forms, **BKR Form 12 et seq.**
    Dismissal and nonsuit, **11 § 349**
    Examinations and examiners, **BKR 2004**
        Interim compensation, **11 § 331**
    Foreign countries, **11 § 1509 et seq.**
    Forms, disclosure, **BKR Form 12 et seq.**
    Grain, **11 § 557**
    Involuntary proceedings, ante
    Issuance, **11 § 105**
    Joint administration, husband and wife, exemptions, **11 § 522**
    Joint proceedings, **11 § 302**
    Jury, **28 § 1411**
    Notice, **11 § 542; BKR 2002, 9022**
    Obedience, **11 § 109**
    Open end credit plans, **11 § 523**
    Patient care ombudsman, **11 § 333**
    Petitions, fees, payment, **BKR 1006**
    Professional personnel, labor and employment, **BKR 2014**
    Professional persons, interim compensation, **11 § 331**
    Protective orders, generally, post
    Public utilities, **11 § 366**
    Purchases and purchasing, **11 § 363**
    Records and recordation, **11 § 542; BKR 5003**
    Relief, **BKR 9024**
    Repurchase agreements, **11 § 559**
    Sales, **11 § 363; 28 § 157**
    Security interest, **11 § 552**
    Sessions, **28 § 151**
    Shares and shareholders, post
    Taxation, **11 § 346**
    Time, extension of time, **11 § 108**
    Torts, **28 § 157**
    Trusts and trustees, interim compensation, **11 § 331**
    Vacating or setting aside, **BKR 1018**
    Voluntary proceedings, **11 § 301**
    Wiretapping, **18 § 2516**
Ordinary course of business, payment, priorities and preferences, **11 § 547**
Original jurisdiction, **28 § 1334**
Panel trustees, **28 § 586**
Panels. Bankruptcy appellate panels, generally, ante

INDEX

Papers. Books and papers, generally, ante
Paraprofessionals, labor and employment, 11 §§ 330, 507
Parties,
    Abandonment, 11 § 554
    Automatic stay, 11 § 362
    Avoidance, preferences, 11 § 547
    Books and papers, 11 § 107
    Chapter 7 proceedings, post
    Chapter 11 proceedings, 11 § 1109
    Chapter 12 proceedings, 11 § 1224
    Chapter 13 proceedings, ante
    Discharge, 11 § 1328
    Exemptions, lists, 11 § 522
    Foreign countries, 11 § 1512
    Involuntary proceedings, 11 § 303
    Lists, exemptions, 11 § 522
    Notice, BKR 2002
        Compensation and salaries, 11 § 330
    Preferences, avoidance, 11 § 547
    Public utilities, deposits, 11 § 366
    Real party in interest, BKR 7017
    Substitution, BKR 7025
Partnership,
    Chapter 7 proceedings, ante
    Chapter 11 proceedings, venue, 28 § 1408
    Claims, general partner, 11 § 541
    Compensation and salaries, 11 § 504
    Contests, petitions, BKR 1011
    Copies, petitions, BKR 1004
    Declarations, forms, BKR Forms 2, 6
    Definitions, 11 § 101
    Distributions, 11 § 508
    Filing, petitions, BKR 1004
    Fraudulent transfers, 11 § 548
    Involuntary proceedings, 11 § 303; BKR 1004
    Objections and exceptions, 11 § 502
    Petitions, BKR 1004
        Contests, BKR 1011
        Involuntary proceedings, 11 § 303
    Statements, BKR 1007
    Summons, BKR 1004
    Taxation, 11 § 346
    Venue, BKR 1014
Party in interest. Parties, generally, ante
Paternity, support, automatic stay, 11 § 362
Patient, definitions, 11 § 101
Patient care ombudsman, 11 § 333; BKR 2007.2
    Compensation and salaries, 11 § 330
    Confidential or privileged information, BKR 2015.1
    Notice, reports, BKR 2015.1
    Reports, notice, BKR 2015.1
    Salaries, 11 § 330
Patient records, definitions, 11 § 101
Payment,
    Chapter 7 proceedings, dividends, BKR 3009, 3010
    Chapter 11 proceedings, ante
    Chapter 12 proceedings, ante
    Chapter 13 proceedings, ante
    Claims, 11 § 502
    Codebtors, 11 § 509
    Compensation and salaries, generally, ante
    Confirmation of plan, 11 § 1326
    Copies, 11 § 521
    Distributions, 11 § 508

Dividends, BKR 3010
    Foreign countries, 11 § 1532
    Margins, generally, ante
    Matured debts, 11 § 542
    Ordinary course of business, priorities and preferences, 11 § 547
    Petitions, fees, BKR 1006
    Reconsidered claims, 11 § 502
    Repayment, generally, post
    Taxation, post
    Trusts and trustees, post
    Unconfirmed plans, 11 § 1326
Penalties. Fines and penalties, generally, ante
Pending actions, BKR 6009
    Chapter 7 proceedings, 11 § 727
    Chapter 11 proceedings, 11 § 1141
    Chapter 12 proceedings, 11 § 1228
    Chapter 13 proceedings, 11 § 1328
    Crimes and offenses, statements, BKR 1007
    Discharge, BKR 4004
    Foreign countries, ante
Pensions. Retirement and pensions, generally, post
Perfection, 11 § 546 et seq.
    Automatic stay, preferences, 11 § 362
    Postpetition, 11 § 549
    Preferences, 11 § 547
        Automatic stay, 11 § 362
    Real estate, bona fide purchasers, 11 §§ 544, 547
    Security interest, evidence, BKR 3001
Perjury, 18 § 152
    Declarations, BKR Forms 2, 6
Permissive joinder, BKR 7020
Personal defenses, 11 § 558
Personal effects, exemptions, 11 § 522
Personal injuries,
    Chapter 13 proceedings, discharge, 11 § 1328
    Discharge, 11 § 523
        Chapter 13 proceedings, 11 § 1328
    Jury, 28 § 1411
    Liquidation, exemptions, 28 § 157
    Payments, exemptions, 11 § 522
Personal jurisdiction, BKR 7004
Personal property,
    Chapter 13 proceedings, 11 § 1326
    Exemptions, 11 § 522
    Forms, schedules, BKR Form 6
    Leases, 11 § 365
        Chapter 13 proceedings, payment, 11 § 1326
    Possession, 11 § 521
    Schedules, forms, BKR Form 6
Personally identifiable information, BKR 4002
    Consumer privacy ombudsman, 11 § 332
        Compensation and salaries, 11 § 330
    Definitions, 11 § 101
    Leases, 11 §§ 332, 363; BKR 6004
    Sales, 11 §§ 332, 363; BKR 6004
    Theft, 11 § 107
    Trusts and trustees, disposition, 11 §§ 332, 363
Petitions, 11 § 541; BKR 1002 et seq.
    Amendments, BKR 1009
    Answers, claims, BKR 1011
    Attorneys, fees, filing, BKR 1006
    Avoidance, transfers, 11 § 547 et seq.
    Captions, BKR 1005
    Chapter 9 proceedings, ante

INDEX

Chapter 13 proceedings, ante
Children and minors, **BKR 1004.1**
Claims, answer, **BKR 1011**
Compensation and salaries, preparers, **BKR 2016**
Contests, **BKR 1011, 1013**
Conversion, 11 § 348
Copies,
    Amendments, **BKR 1009**
    Numbers and numbering, **BKR 1002, 1003**
Debt relief agencies, generally, ante
Declarations, preparers, 11 § 110
Defenses, **BKR 1011**
Definitions, preparers, 11 § 110
Dismissal and nonsuit, **BKR 1013, 1014**
Fees,
    Filing, **BKR 1006**
    Preparers, 11 § 110
Filing, 11 § 541; **BKR 1002, 5005**
    Automatic stay, 11 §§ 362, 553
    Avoidance, transfers, 11 § 547 et seq.
    Bad faith, dismissal and nonsuit, 11 § 303
    Bias and prejudice, 11 § 349
    Conversions, 11 § 348
    Definitions, repo participants, 11 § 101
    Fees, **BKR 1006**
    Fraudulent transfers, avoidance, 11 § 548
    Involuntary proceedings, automatic stay, 11 § 553
    Joint proceedings, automatic stay, 11 § 553
    Life insurance, 11 § 542
    Preferences, avoidance, 11 § 547
    Security interest, 11 § 552
    Setoff and counterclaim, 11 § 553
    Signatures, 11 § 110
    Single petitions, 11 § 302
    Transfers, avoidance, 11 § 547 et seq.
    Unmatured debts, disallowance, 11 § 502
    Voluntary proceedings, automatic stay, 11 § 553
Fines and penalties, preparers, 11 § 110
Foreign countries, ante
Forms, **BKR 9004**
    Nonattorney preparers,
        Declarations, **BKR Forms 6, 19A**
        Notice, **BKR Form 19B**
Fraud, preparers, 11 § 110
Identity and identification, preparers, 11 § 110
Injunctions, preparers, 11 § 110
Installments, fees, payment, **BKR 1006**
Involuntary proceedings, ante
Mental health, **BKR 1004.1**
Motions, preparers, fines and penalties, 11 § 110
Names, **BKR 1005**
Nonattorney preparers,
    Declarations, **BKR Forms 6, 19A**
    Notice, **BKR Form 19B**
Nonresidential real property, leases, 11 § 362
Notice, preparers, 11 § 110
    Nonattorneys, **BKR Form 19B**
Numbers and numbering,
    Copies, **BKR 1002, 1003**
    Social security, 11 § 110; **BKR 1005**
Objections and exceptions, **BKR 1011**
Orders of court, fees, payment, **BKR 1006**
Partnership, ante
Payment, fees, **BKR 1006**
Postpetition, generally, post
Preferences, avoidance, 11 § 547
Preparers, 11 § 110
    Compensation and salaries, **BKR 2016**
    Debt relief agencies, generally, ante
    Forms, nonattorney preparers,
        Declarations, **BKR Forms 6, 19A**
        Notice, **BKR Form 19B**
    Nonattorney preparers,
        Declarations, **BKR Forms 6, 19A**
        Notice, **BKR Form 19B**
Process, **BKR 1010**
Recognition petitions, foreign countries, 11 § 1515 et seq.; **BKR 1010 et seq.**
Signatures, **BKR 9011**
    Nonattorney petition preparers,
        Declarations, **BKR Forms 6, 19A**
        Notice, **BKR Form 19B**
    Preparers, 11 § 110
Social security, numbers and numbering, 11 § 110; **BKR 1005**
Summons, **BKR 1010**
    Contests, **BKR 1011**
TIN (taxpayer identification number), **BKR 1005**
Transfers, avoidance, 11 § 547 et seq.
Verification, **BKR 1008**
Voluntary proceedings, post
Physical examinations, **BKR 7035**
Place of business, 11 § 109
    Venue, 28 §§ 1408, 1410
Plans and specifications,
    Acceptances, **BKR 3005**
        Rejection, **BKR 3006**
    Chapter 9 proceedings, ante
    Chapter 11 proceedings, ante
    Chapter 12 proceedings, ante
    Chapter 13 proceedings, ante
    Confirmation of plan, generally, ante
    Counseling services, 11 § 521
    Examinations and examiners, **BKR 2004**
    Exemptions, 11 § 522
    Injunctions, notice, **BKR 2002**
    Rejection, **BKR 3005**
    Small businesses, 11 § 1121
    Timeshares, generally, post
Pleading,
    Adversary proceedings, **BKR 7005 et seq.**
    Filing, 11 § 108
    Foreign proceedings, **BKR 1003**
    Forms, 28 § 2075; **BKR 7010, 9004**
    Grain, responsive pleading, 11 § 557
    Representatives and representation, **BKR 9011**
    Responsive pleading, **BKR 1011**
        Grain, 11 § 557
    Signatures, **BKR 9011**
    Special matters, **BKR 7009**
    Supplemental pleadings, **BKR 7015**
    United States trustees, **BKR 9034**
    Verification, **BKR 9011**
Political subdivisions,

INDEX

Abrogation, sovereign immunity, 11 § 106
Actions and proceedings, 11 § 362; 28 § 1452
Addresses, mail and mailing, BKR 5003
Chapter 7 proceedings, ante
Chapter 9 proceedings, generally, ante
Definitions, 11 § 101
Discrimination, 11 § 525
Education, loans, discharge, 11 § 523
Fines and penalties, discharge, 11 § 523
Grain, 11 § 557
Judgments and decrees, stay of proceedings, 11 § 362
Mail and mailing, addresses, BKR 5003
Money, deposits, 11 § 345
Notice, taxation, 11 § 362
Priorities and preferences, 11 § 507
Process, 11 § 106
Qualifications, 11 § 109
Sovereign immunity, abrogation, 11 § 106
Stay of proceedings, 11 § 362
Taxation, generally, post
Possession,
    Automatic stay, 11 § 362
    Debtors in possession, generally, ante
    Personal property, 11 § 521
    Turnovers, property, 11 §§ 542, 543
Postpetition,
    Chapter 9 proceedings, ante
    Chapter 11 proceedings, 11 § 1125
    Chapter 13 proceedings, claims, 11 § 1305
    Conversion, BKR 1019
    Exemptions, 11 § 522
    Individual debtors, claims, 11 § 1305
    Limitation of actions, 11 § 549
    Reorganization, 11 § 1125
    Taxation, automatic stay, 11 § 362
    Transfers, post
Power of attorney, BKR 9010
    General power, forms, BKR Form 11A
    Special power, forms, BKR Form 11B
Powers and duties, 11 §§ 361 et seq., 521 et seq.; BKR 4001 et seq.
    Administrative Office of United States Courts, directors, 28 § 604
    Automatic stay, 11 § 362
    Chapter 9 proceedings, transfers, avoidance, 11 § 926
    Chapter 11 proceedings, ante
    Courts, 11 § 105
    Exemptions, 11 §§ 522, 541
    Trusts and trustees, post
    United States trustees, 11 § 307
Predatory loans, 11 § 363
Preferences. Priorities and preferences, generally, post
Prejudice, dismissal and nonsuit, 11 § 349
Preliminary hearing, automatic stay, 11 § 362
Preparers. Petitions, ante
Prepetition tax returns, 11 § 1308
Prepetition taxes, automatic stay, 11 § 362
Preservation, actual, expenses and expenditures, allowances, 11 § 503
President of the United States, Judicial Conference of the United States, 11 § 104
Presumptions,
    Administration, BKR 5009
    Automatic stay, 11 § 362
    Chapter 7 proceedings, ante

Chapter 11 proceedings, substantial or controlling interest, financial statements and reports, BKR 2015.3
Consumer debts, 11 § 707
Foreign countries, ante
Open end credit plans, 11 § 523
Preferences, 11 § 547
Reaffirmation agreements, 11 § 524
Pretrial procedure, BKR 7016
Prima facie evidence. Evidence, generally, ante
Priorities and preferences,
    Alimony, 11 § 507
    Automatic stay, 11 § 362
    Antecedent debt, 11 § 547
    Automatic preservation, 11 § 551
    Automatic stay, 11 § 362
    Avoidance, 11 § 547
    Chapter 7 proceedings, ante
    Child support, automatic stay, 11 § 362
    Claims, 11 §§ 507, 726
    Compensation and salaries, 11 § 507
    Definitions, 11 § 547
    Driving while intoxicated or under the influence, claims, 11 § 507
    Evidence, 11 § 547
    Exemptions, 11 § 522
    Good faith, 11 § 364
    Goods, wares and merchandise, 11 § 546
    Inventories, 11 § 547
    Liability, transferees, 11 § 550
    Liens and incumbrances, 11 §§ 364, 507
    Limitation of actions, 11 § 546
    Loans, 11 § 364
    Motor vehicles, driving while intoxicated or under the influence, claims, 11 § 507
    Ordinary course of business, payment, 11 § 547
    Prepetition transfers, 11 § 547
    Preservation, automatic preservation, 11 § 551
    Presumptions, 11 § 547
    Railroads, 11 § 1171
    Securities, post
    Security interest, 11 § 552
    Subrogation, 11 § 507
    Support, 11 § 507
    Taxation, post
    Time, 11 § 547
    Transfers, avoidance, 11 § 547
    Trusts and trustees, avoidance, 11 § 547
    Unsecured claims, 11 §§ 507, 753, 767
    Witnesses, fees, 11 § 507
Privacy, BKR 9037
    Consumer privacy ombudsman, generally, ante
Privileged information. Confidential or privileged information, generally, ante
Privileges and immunities, 11 §§ 344, 521
    Examinations and examiners, 11 § 344
    Support, post
    Witnesses, 18 § 6001
Procedures, 28 § 157
Proceedings. Actions and proceedings, generally, ante
Proceeds, 11 § 541
    Custodians, accounts and accounting, 11 § 543
    Grain, 11 § 557

INDEX

Security interest, **11 § 552**
Process, **11 § 105**
    Adversary proceedings, **BKR 7004, 7005**
    Appeal and review, **BKR 8004, 8008**
    Automatic stay, **11 § 362**
    Briefs, **BKR 8009**
    Children and minors, **BKR 1007**
    Community property, **11 § 524**
    Contempt, **BKR 9020**
    Governmental units, **11 § 106**
    Injunctions, **11 § 524**
    Intervention, **BKR 2018**
    Involuntary proceedings, petitions, **BKR 1010**
    Mail and mailing, **BKR 7004, 9006**
    Mentally ill persons, **BKR 1007**
    Motions, **BKR 9013**
    Noncore proceedings, **BKR 9033**
    Nonparties, **BKR 7071**
    Publication, **BKR 7004, 9008**
    Removal of cases or causes, **BKR 9027**
    Time, **BKR 7004**
Production of books and papers, **BKR 2004, 7034**
Professional associations, compensation and salaries, **11 § 504**
Professional personnel, **11 § 326 et seq.; BKR 2014**
    Accountants, **11 § 507**
    Administration, expenses and expenditures, reimbursement, **11 § 503**
    Certificates and certification, compensation and salaries, **11 § 330**
    Compensation and salaries, **11 §§ 328, 504**
        Certificates and certification, **11 § 330**
        Interim compensation, **11 § 331**
        Priorities and preferences, **11 § 507**
        Records and recordation, **BKR 2013**
        Sharing, **11 § 504**
    Conflict of interest, **11 §§ 327, 328**
    Disclosure, records and recordation, **11 § 542**
    Grain, **11 § 557**
    Interim compensation, **11 § 331**
    Priorities and preferences, compensation and salaries, **11 § 507**
    Records and recordation,
        Compensation and salaries, **BKR 2013**
        Disclosure, **11 § 542**
    Reimbursement, administration, expenses and expenditures, **11 § 503**
    Sharing, compensation and salaries, **11 § 504**
Profits, **11 § 541**
    Accounts and accounting, custodians, **11 § 543**
    Custodians, accounts and accounting, **11 § 543**
    Definitions, **11 § 308**
    Exemptions, profit-sharing plans, **11 § 522**
    Small businesses, **11 § 308**
Proof of claim, **BKR 3001 et seq.**
Property of the estate, definitions, **11 §§ 902, 1115**
Proposed findings, noncore proceedings, **BKR 9033**
Protective orders, **BKR 9018**
    Chapter 11 proceedings, substantial or controlling interest, financial statements and reports, **BKR 2015.3**
    Consolidations and mergers, **BKR 1015**
    Privacy protection, **BKR 9037**
    Securities, **11 § 742**
    Shares and shareholders, **11 § 742**
Proxies, chapter 7 proceedings, **BKR 2006**
Public access, books and papers, **11 § 107**
Public assistance, exemptions, **11 § 522**
Public policy, foreign countries, **11 §§ 1501, 1506**
Public service attorney referral program, **11 § 504**
Public utilities, deposits, **11 § 366**
Publication,
    Municipal debt adjustment, notice, **11 § 923**
    Notice, **BKR 2002**
    Process, **BKR 7004, 9008**
Puerto Rico, judges or justices, appointments, **28 § 152**
Punitive damages. Damages, generally, ante
Purchasers and purchasing,
    Bona fide purchasers, generally, ante
    Damages, transfers, **11 § 550**
    Definitions, **11 § 101**
    Limitation of actions, **11 § 546**
    Modification, **11 § 363**
    Real estate, postpetition, **11 § 549**
Qualifications, **11 § 109**
    Trusts and trustees, **11 § 322**
Racketeer influenced and corrupt organizations, fraud, **18 § 1961**
Railroads. Chapter 11 proceedings, ante
Reaffirmation agreements, **11 § 524**
    Abuse, **18 § 158**
    Cover sheet, forms, **BKR Form 27**
    Crimes and offenses, **18 § 158**
    Discharge, undue hardship, presumptions, **BKR 4004**
    Filing, **BKR 4008**
    Forms, cover sheet, **BKR Form 27**
    Motions, **11 § 524**
    Statements, **11 § 524; BKR 4008**
Real estate,
    Automatic stay, **11 § 362**
    Avoidance, postpetition, **11 § 549**
    Bona fide purchasers, **11 §§ 544, 547**
    Consumer debt, ante
    Exemptions, **11 § 522**
    Nonresidential real property, leases,
        Automatic stay, **11 § 362**
        Termination, **11 § 541**
    Postpetition, avoidance, **11 § 549**
    Schedules, forms, **BKR Form 6**
Real party in interest, **BKR 7017**
Recall, judges or justices, **28 § 155**
Receivable, definitions, **11 § 547**
Receivers and receivership, **28 § 959**
    Appointments, **11 § 105**
    Fees, **18 § 155**
    Goods, wares and merchandise, **11 § 546**
    Reports, **18 § 3057**
Reciprocity, abstention, **11 § 305; 28 § 1334**
Reclamation,
    Goods, wares and merchandise, **11 § 546**
    Shares and shareholders, **11 § 751**
Recognition petitions, foreign countries, **11 § 1515 et seq.; BKR 1010 et seq.**
Reconsideration, claims, **11 § 502; BKR 3008**
Records and recordation, **BKR 5003**
    Access, **11 § 107**
    Appeal and review, **BKR 8006, 8007, 8016**
    Assisted living facilities, **11 § 351**
    Certified copies, **BKR 5006**
    Chapter 7 proceedings, ante

INDEX

Chapter 11 proceedings, ante
    Compensation and salaries, **BKR 2013**
    Custodians, **28 § 156**
    Disclosure, **11 § 542**
    Filing, **BKR 5005, 5007**
    Health care businesses, patients, **BKR 6011**
    Home health agencies, **11 § 351**
    Hospices, **11 § 351**
    Hospitals, **11 § 351**
    Intermediate care facilities, **11 § 351**
    Long term care, facilities, **11 § 351**
    Meetings, **BKR 2003**
    Nursing homes, **11 § 351**
    Patient care ombudsman, **11 § 333**
    Real estate, transfers, avoidance, **11 § 549**
    Removal of cases or causes, **BKR 9027**
    Skilled nursing facilities, **11 § 351**
    Trusts and trustees, post
    Turnovers, **BKR 1019**
Recourse, municipalities, **11 § 927**
Recovery,
    Attorneys, fees, **11 § 541**
    Costs, trusts and trustees, **11 § 506**
    Liens and incumbrances, trusts and trustees, good faith, **11 § 550**
Redacted filings, **BKR 9037**
Redemption,
    Exemptions, **11 § 541**
    Liens and incumbrances, **BKR 6008**
    Liquidation, **11 § 722**
    Sales, **BKR 6008**
Reduction,
    Consumer debt, unsecured claims, **11 § 502**
    Homesteads, exemptions, fraud, **11 § 522**
Referees. References, generally, post
References, **28 § 157**
    Alternative dispute resolution, **28 § 654**
    Appellate panels, **28 § 158**
    Arbitration, **28 § 654**
    Assistants, **11 § 102**
    Chapter 11 proceedings, **28 § 157**
    Expenses and expenditures, **11 § 102**
    Fees, **11 nt prec § 101**
    Fraud, schedules, **18 § 158**
    Public service attorney referral program, **11 § 504**
    Salary and Expense Fund, **11 § 102; 11 nt prec § 101**
    Sessions, **28 § 151**
    Stay of proceedings, **11 § 362**
    Stenographers, **11 § 102**
    Supervision, **11 § 102**
Referrals. References, generally, ante
Refunds. Taxation, post
Regional Rail Reorganization, this index
Register, claims, **BKR 5003**
Rehearings, motions, **BKR 8015**
Reimbursement, **BKR 2016**
    Custodians, liens and incumbrances, avoidance, **11 § 349**
    Disallowance, **11 § 502**
    Evidence, **11 § 501**
    Officers and employees, **11 § 330**
    Professional persons, **11 § 330**
    Securities, rescission, **11 § 510**
Reinstatement, transfers, avoidance, **11 § 349**
Rejection,
    Chapter 11 proceedings, ante

Chapter 13 proceedings, ante
    Collective bargaining, agreements, **11 § 1113**
    Contracts, **11 § 365; BKR 6006**
    Executory contracts, **11 § 502**
    Leases, **11 §§ 365, 502; BKR 6006**
    Plans and specifications, **BKR 3005**
    Railroads, leases, **11 § 1169**
    Shares and shareholders, executory contracts, **11 § 744**
    Timeshares, **11 § 365**
    Trusts and trustees, **BKR 2008**
    Unexpired leases, **11 § 553**
Related party, definitions, **11 § 524**
Relatives,
    Definitions, **11 § 101**
    Judges or justices, compensation and salaries, disqualification, **BKR 5004**
Release, examinations and examiners, **BKR 2005**
Religious organizations and societies, fraud, **11 § 548**
Remand, **28 § 1452; BKR 9027**
Removal from office,
    Judges or justices, ante
    Trusts and trustees, post
Removal of cases or causes, **BKR 2005, 9027**
    Attachment, **BKR 9027**
    Bonds (officers and fiduciaries), **BKR 9027**
    Claims, **28 § 1452**
    Grounds, **28 § 152**
    Injunctions, **BKR 9027**
    Process, **BKR 9027**
    Records and recordation, **BKR 9027**
Rent, **11 § 541**
    Custodians, **11 § 543**
    Leases, generally, ante
    Liens and incumbrances, avoidance, **11 § 545**
    Security interest, **11 § 552**
Reopening, **BKR 5010**
Reorganization,
    Chapter 11 proceedings, generally, ante
    Chapter 12 proceedings, generally, ante
Repayment,
    Avoidance, alternative repayment schedule, **11 § 547**
    Discharge, ante
Replacement value, definitions, **11 § 506**
Repo participants. Repurchase agreements, generally, post
Reports,
    Chapter 7 proceedings, **BKR 2001**
    Chapter 11 proceedings, ante
    Crimes and offenses, **18 § 3057**
    Elections, **BKR 2003**
    Financial management training curriculum, **11 § 111 nt**
    Financial statements and reports, generally, ante
    Health care businesses, patient records, destruction, **BKR 6011**
    Individual debtors, **11 § 1302**
    National Bankruptcy Review Commission, **11 nt prec § 101**
    Patient care ombudsman, notice, **BKR 2015.1**
    Reorganization, confirmation of plan, **11 § 1106**
    Small businesses, monthly operating reports, **BKR Form 25**

INDEX

Statistics, 28 § 159
Trusts and trustees, post
United States trustees, post
Representatives and representation,
    Chapter 11 proceedings, venue, 28 § 1409
    Foreign countries, 11 § 1509 et seq.
    Parties, BKR 9010
    Pleading, BKR 9011
    Statements, BKR 2019
Repurchase agreements,
    Acceleration, 11 § 559
    Automatic stay, 11 § 362
    Avoidance, set-off and counterclaim, 11 § 546
    Damages, 11 § 562
    Definitions, 11 § 101
    Fraud, 11 § 548
    Liquidation, 11 § 559
    National securities association, 11 § 559
    Reverse repurchase agreements, 11 § 101
    Securities,
        Automatic stay, 11 § 362
        Liquidation, 11 § 559
    Set-off and counterclaim, 11 §§ 362, 546, 559
    Termination, 11 § 559
    Unsecured claims, priorities and preferences, 11 §§ 753, 767
Rescission, reaffirmation agreements, 11 § 524
Residence. Domicile and residence, generally, ante
Responsive pleading, BKR 1011
    Grain, 11 § 557
Restitution, discharge, 11 §§ 523, 1328
Retention, bonuses, 11 § 503
Retirement and pensions,
    Automatic stay, 11 § 362
    Chapter 11 proceedings, insurance, 11 § 1114
    Discharge, 11 § 523
    Education individual retirement accounts, 11 §§ 521, 541
    Employee Retirement Income Security Program, generally, ante
    Exemptions, 11 § 522
    Insurance, chapter 11 proceedings, 11 § 1114
    Judges or justices, ante
Returns,
    Attorneys, fees, cancellation, 11 §§ 329, 541
    Goods, wares and merchandise, 11 § 546
    Income tax, copies, BKR 4002
    Taxation, post
Reversal, orders of court, grain, 11 § 557
Reverse repurchase agreements, 11 § 101
Review. Appeal and review, generally, ante
Revocation or suspension, BKR 1017
    Abstention, 11 § 305
    Appeal and review, BKR 8019
    Foreign countries, 11 § 1520 et seq.
    Individual debtors, fraud, 11 § 1330
    Reorganization, confirmation of plan, 11 § 1144
    Taxation, 11 § 346
    Time, 11 § 108
    Trusts and trustees, 28 § 586
Revolving consumer credit agreements, claims, BKR 3001
Rice, 11 § 557
RICO, fraud, 18 § 1961
Rolling stock, railroads, 11 § 1168
Rye, 11 § 557

Salaries. Compensation and salaries, generally, ante
Sales, 11 § 361 et seq.; BKR 6004
    Administrative expenses, 11 § 503
    Automatic stay, 11 § 553; BKR 6004
    Chapter 13 proceedings, 11 § 1303
    Community property, 11 § 363
    Consumer privacy ombudsman, 11 § 332
    Contracts, ante
    Damages, 11 § 363
    Dower and curtesy, 11 § 363
    Good faith, 11 § 363
    Grain, 11 § 557
    Individual debtors, 11 § 1303
    Joint tenants, 11 § 363
    Liens and incumbrances, 11 § 363; BKR 6004
    Motions, BKR 4001, 6003
        Personally identifiable information, BKR 6004
    Notice, BKR 2002, 6004
    Orders of court, 11 § 363; 28 § 157
    Personally identifiable information, 11 §§ 332, 363; BKR 6004
    Proceeds, generally, ante
    Reclamation, 11 § 546
    Redemption, BKR 6008
    Taxation, 11 § 346
    Trusts and trustees, post
Satisfaction, money, 11 § 363
Savings and loan associations, 11 § 109
Savings banks, 11 § 109
Scandalous matters, 11 § 107; BKR 9018
Schedules, BKR 1007
    Abandonment, 11 § 554
    Amendments, BKR 1009
    Assets, filing, 11 § 521
    Chapter 7 proceedings, ante
    Chapter 9 proceedings, liabilities, BKR 3003
    Chapter 11 proceedings, ante
    Chapter 13 proceedings, ante
    Codebtors, forms, BKR Form 6
    Conversion, BKR 1019
    Declarations, BKR Forms 2, 6
    Discharge, 11 § 523
    Executory contracts, forms, BKR Form 6
    Exemptions, forms, BKR Form 6
    Expenses and expenditures, 11 § 521; BKR Form 6
    Filing, 11 § 521; BKR 5005
    Forms, BKR 9004
        Declarations, BKR Forms 2, 6
        Summaries, BKR Form 6
    Fraud, 18 § 158
    Income, ante
    Leases, forms, BKR Form 6
    Liabilities, filing, 11 § 521
    Personal property, forms, BKR Form 6
    Real estate, forms, BKR Form 6
    Secured claims, forms, BKR Form 6
    Small businesses, 11 § 1116
    Summaries, forms, BKR Form 6
    Supplemental schedules, BKR 1007
    Trusts and trustees, 11 § 704
    Unsecured claims, forms, BKR Form 6
    Verification, BKR 1008
Scholarships,
    Discharge, 11 § 523

INDEX

Fraud, exemptions, 11 § 522
Searches and seizures, BKR 7064
    Certificates and certification, records and recordation, BKR 5003
    Records and recordation, certificates and certification, BKR 5003
Secretaries, judges or justices, 28 § 156
Secretary of HUD, mortgages, foreclosure, stay of proceedings, 11 § 362
Secretary of the Treasury, reorganization, 11 § 1126
Secured claims. Claims, ante
Securities, 11 § 741 et seq.
    Acceleration, contracts, 11 § 555
    Automatic stay, 11 §§ 362, 553
    Chapter 7 proceedings, ante
    Chapter 9 proceedings, ante
    Chapter 11 proceedings, ante
    Compromise and settlement, 11 § 362
    Damages, 11 § 562
    Definitions, 11 §§ 101, 741
    Discharge, fraud, 11 § 523
    Dismissal and nonsuit, 11 § 349
    Equity security holders, generally, ante
    Exemptions, chapter 11 proceedings, 11 § 1145
    Fraud,
        Discharge, 11 § 523
        Transfers, 11 § 548
    Limitation of actions, transfers, 11 § 546
    Loans, 11 § 364
    Margins,
        Avoidance, transfers, 11 § 546
        Fraudulent transfers, 11 § 548
    Names, customers, 11 § 751
        Definitions, 11 § 741
    National securities association, 11 § 555
        Repurchase agreements, 11 § 559
    Notice, orders of court, 11 § 743
    Priorities and preferences, unsecured claims, 11 §§ 753, 767
    Protective orders, 11 § 742
    Repurchase agreements,
        Automatic stay, 11 § 362
        Liquidation, 11 § 559
    Rescission, 11 § 510
    Stay of proceedings, 11 § 555
    Subordination, 11 § 510
    Termination, contracts, 11 § 555
    Transfers,
        Fraud, 11 § 548
        Limitation of actions, 11 § 546
        Voidable transfers, 11 § 749
    Unsecured claims, priorities and preferences, 11 §§ 753, 767
    Voidable transfers, 11 § 749
Security interest,
    Aircraft, 11 § 1110
    Animals, 11 § 363
    Automatic stay, 11 § 362
    Avoidance, 11 §§ 522, 547
    Chapter 9 proceedings, ante
    Chapter 13 proceedings, ante
    Default, 11 § 521
    Definitions, 11 § 101
    Evidence, perfection, BKR 3001
    Foreign countries, 11 § 1520
    Postpetition, 11 § 552

Reaffirmation agreements, 11 § 524
Sales, BKR 6004
Seizures. Searches and seizures, generally, ante
Self-employment, 11 § 1304
Self-incrimination, 11 § 344
    Examinations and examiners, 11 § 344
    Liquidation, 11 § 727
Sellers, goods, wares and merchandise, reclamation, 11 § 546
Sentence and punishment, 18 § 152 et seq.
Separation agreements, 11 §§ 522, 523
Sequestration, removal of cases or causes, BKR 9027
Serial filers, 11 § 362
Service of process. Process, generally, ante
Services,
    Administration, expenses and expenditures, 11 § 503
    Compensation and salaries, exemptions, 11 § 541
Setoff and counterclaim, 11 § 553; BKR 7013
    Automatic stay, 11 § 362
    Avoidance, transfers, 11 §§ 522, 550
    Commodity contracts, margins, 11 § 362
    Definitions, 11 § 553
    Evidence, 11 § 501
    Governmental units, 11 § 106
    Hearings, 28 § 157
    Leases, 11 § 365
    Matured debts, 11 § 542
    Prepetition claims, 11 § 553
    Proof of claim, 11 § 501
    Repurchase agreements, 11 §§ 362, 546, 559
    Secured claims, 11 § 506
    Swap agreements, 11 § 553
    Taxation, refunds, 11 § 362
    Time shares, 11 § 365
    Transfers, avoidance, 11 §§ 522, 550
Settlement. Compromise and settlement, generally, ante
Severance pay. Compensation and salaries, generally, ante
Shares and shareholders, 11 § 741 et seq.
    Accounts and accounting, 11 § 745
    Assumptions, executory contracts, 11 § 744
    Automatic stay, 11 § 742
    Banks and banking, net equity claims, 11 § 745
    Bonus plans, exemptions, 11 § 522
    Brokers, 11 § 741 et seq.
        Contracts, liquidation, 11 § 555
        Definitions, 11 § 101
        Repurchase agreements, 11 § 559
        Transfers, limitation of actions, 11 § 546
    Compromise and settlement,
        Definitions, 11 § 741
        Stay of proceedings, 11 § 362
    Contracts,
        Definitions, 11 § 741
        Executory contracts, 11 § 744
        Liquidation, 11 §§ 555, 752
        Transfers, 11 § 746
    Customers,
        Capacity, 11 § 745
        Definitions, 11 § 741
        Net equity claims, 11 § 745
        Voidable transfers, 11 § 749

INDEX

Definitions, 11 § 741
Derivative actions, BKR 7023.1
Dismissal and nonsuit, 11 § 742
Distribution, 11 § 750
Executory contracts, 11 § 744
Fraudulent transfers, 11 § 548
Margins,
    Avoidance, transfers, 11 § 546
    Definitions, 11 § 741
    Fraudulent transfers, 11 § 548
Net equity, definitions, 11 § 741
Net equity claims, 11 § 745
Notice, orders of court, 11 § 743
Orders of court,
    Executory contracts, 11 § 744
    Notice, 11 § 743
    Voidable transfers, 11 § 749
Protective orders, 11 § 742
Qualifications, 11 § 109
Reclamation, 11 § 751
Rejection, executory contracts, 11 § 744
Repurchase agreements, liquidation, 11 § 559
Stay of proceedings, 11 §§ 362, 746, 747
Subordination, 11 §§ 746, 747
Transfers, voidable transfers, 11 § 749
Trusts and trustees, post
United States trustees, 28 § 586
Voidable transfers, 11 § 749
Ships and shipping,
    Automatic stay, 11 § 362
    Discharge, 11 § 523
    Reorganization, 11 § 1110
Short titles, BKR 1001
    Captions, forms, BKR Form 16B
Signatures,
    Attorneys, chapter 7 proceedings, 11 § 707
    Claims, BKR 3001
    Filing, 11 § 110
    Nonrecourse loans, elections, BKR 3014
    Petitions, ante
    Pleading, BKR 9011
Single asset real estate,
    Automatic stay, 11 § 362
    Definitions, 11 § 101
Single petition, joint proceedings, 11 § 302
Small business investment companies,
    qualifications, 11 § 109
Small businesses,
    Chapter 11 proceedings, ante
    Committees, 11 § 1102; BKR 1020
    Confirmation of plan, 11 § 1129
    Debtors in possession, 11 § 1116
    Definitions, 11 §§ 101, 707
    Disclosure,
        Forms, statements, BKR Form 25
        Statements, 11 § 1125; BKR 3016, 3017.1
            Forms, BKR Form 25
    Entry upon land, 11 § 1116
    Financial statements and reports, 11 §§ 308, 1116
    Forms, BKR Form 25 et seq.
    Good faith, 11 § 362
    Insurance, 11 § 1116
    Meetings, 11 § 1116
    Objections and exceptions, statements, reorganization, BKR 1020

Plans and specifications, 11 § 1121
    Profits, 11 § 308
    Reorganization, statements, BKR 1020
    Reports, monthly operating reports, BKR Form 25
    Schedules, 11 § 1116
    Statements,
        Disclosure, 11 § 1125; BKR 3016, 3017.1
        Reorganization, BKR 1020
    Taxation, returns, 11 §§ 308, 1116
    Trusts and trustees, 11 § 1116
    United States trustees, 28 § 586
Social security,
    Disclosure, numbers and numbering, 11 § 342
    Exemptions, 11 § 522
    Forms, numbers and numbering, statements, BKR Form 21
    Identity and identification, numbers and numbering, BKR 4002
    Numbers and numbering,
        Disclosure, 11 § 342
        Forms, statements, BKR Form 21
        Identity and identification, BKR 4002
        Petitions, 11 § 110; BKR 1005
        Protection, 11 § 342
        Statements, BKR 1007, 2002
            Forms, BKR Form 21
        Voluntary proceedings, amendments, BKR 1009
    Petitions, numbers and numbering, 11 § 110; BKR 1005
    Protection, numbers and numbering, 11 § 342
    Statements, numbers and numbering, BKR 1007, 2002
        Forms, BKR Form 21
    Voluntary proceedings, numbers and numbering, amendments, BKR 1009
Solicitation,
    Chapter 7 proceedings, proxies, BKR 2006
    Chapter 11 proceedings, postpetition, 11 § 1125
Sovereign immunity, abrogation, 11 § 106
Soybeans, 11 § 557
Special matters, pleading, BKR 7009
Special power of attorney, forms, BKR Form 11B
Special sessions, courts, emergencies, 28 § 152
Specific performance, BKR 7070
Spouses. Husband and wife, generally, ante
Standards, statutory liens, avoidance, 11 § 545
Standing trustees. United States trustees, post
Statements,
    Amendments, BKR 1009
    Changes, BKR 4002
    Consumer debts, security interest, 11 § 521
    Conversion, BKR 1019
    Corporations, title to property, BKR 1007, 7007.1
    Counseling services, statement of compliance, BKR 1007
    Current monthly income, BKR 1007
    Debt relief agencies, 11 §§ 527, 528
    Disclosure, BKR Form 12 et seq.
    Filing, BKR 5005

INDEX

Financial management training curriculum, statement of course completion, **BKR 1007**
    Discharge, **BKR 4004**
Financial statements and reports, generally, ante
Forms,
    Disclosure, **BKR Form 12 et seq.**
    Financial affairs statements, **BKR Form 7**
    Individual debtors, intentions, **BKR Form 8**
    Reorganization, **BKR Form 13**
Fraud, discharge, **11 § 523**
Individual debtors, intentions, forms, **BKR Form 8**
Intentions, reorganization, **BKR 1007**
Issues, appeal and review, **BKR 8006**
Partnership, **BKR 1007**
Reaffirmation agreements, **11 § 524; BKR 4008**
Representatives and representation, **BKR 2019**
Small businesses, ante
Verification, **BKR 1008**
States,
    Automatic stay, income tax, **11 § 362**
    Chapter 9 proceedings, **11 §§ 109, 903**
    Chapter 11 proceedings,
        Managers and management, **28 § 959**
        Railroads, **11 § 1166**
    Claims, **11 § 502**
    Core proceedings, **28 § 157**
    Exemptions, **11 § 522**
    Managers and management, chapter 11 proceedings, **28 § 959**
    Priorities and preferences, income tax, **11 § 507**
    Railroads, chapter 11 proceedings, **11 § 1166**
    Securities, sales, **11 § 364**
    Taxation, **11 § 346**
Statistics, **28 § 159**
    Liabilities, summaries, **BKR Form 6**
    Summaries, liabilities, **BKR Form 6**
Status,
    Conferences, **11 § 105**
    Foreign countries, **11 § 1518**
    Liens and incumbrances, **11 § 506**
Statute of frauds, **11 § 558**
Statute of limitations. Limitation of actions, generally, ante
Statutory liens. Liens and incumbrances, ante
Stay of proceedings, **11 § 362; BKR 7062**
    Annulment, **11 § 362**
    Appeal and review, **BKR 8005, 8017**
    Automatic stay, generally, ante
    Chapter 9 proceedings, ante
    Community property, discharge, **11 § 524**
    Core proceedings, **28 § 157**
    Discharge, **11 § 524**
    Foreign countries, **11 § 1519 et seq.**
    Grain, **11 § 557**
    Hearings, **11 § 362**
    Negotiable instruments, dishonor, **11 § 362**
    Notice, **11 § 362**
    Objections and exceptions, **11 § 1301**
    Paternity, support, **11 § 362**
    Petitions,
        Filing, **11 § 362**
        Preparers, **11 § 110**
    Preliminary hearings, **11 § 362**
    Real estate, **11 § 362**
    Repurchase agreements, liquidation, **11 § 559**
    Securities, **11 § 555**
    Shares and shareholders, **11 §§ 362, 746, 747**
    Supplemental injunctions, **11 § 524**
    Swap agreements, **11 § 560**
    Taxation, **11 § 505**
    Termination, **11 § 362**
    Time, **11 § 362**
    Venue, change of venue, **BKR 1014**
    Withdrawal, **BKR 5011**
Stipulations, discovery, **BKR 7029**
Stock and stockholders,
    Securities, generally, ante
    Shares and shareholders, generally, ante
Straight bankruptcy. Chapter 7 proceedings, generally, ante
Student loans, discrimination, **11 § 525**
Subordination, **11 § 510**
Subpoenas, **BKR 9016**
Subrogation, **11 § 509**
    Allowance of claim or interest, **11 § 502**
    Priorities and preferences, **11 § 507**
Substantial or controlling interest, chapter 11 proceedings, financial statements and reports, **BKR 2015.3; BKR Form 26**
Substitution, parties, **BKR 7025**
Successors. Trusts and trustees, post
Summaries, schedules, forms, **BKR Form 6**
Summary judgment, **BKR 7056**
Summons,
    Electronic summons, **BKR 7004**
    Foreign countries, **BKR 1003**
    Partnership, **BKR 1004**
    Petitions, **BKR 1010**
        Contests, **BKR 1011**
    Service, **BKR 7004, 7005**
Supersedeas. Stay of proceedings, generally, ante
Supervision, **28 § 586**
    Examinations and examiners, foreign countries, **11 § 1526**
    Trusts and trustees, foreign countries, **11 § 1526**
Supplemental injunctions, **11 § 524**
Supplemental pleadings, **BKR 7015**
Supplemental schedules, **BKR 1007**
Support,
    Alimony, generally, ante
    Automatic stay, **11 § 362**
    Avoidance, **11 § 547**
    Chapter 7 proceedings, **11 § 704**
    Chapter 11 proceedings, ante
    Chapter 12 proceedings, **11 §§ 1202, 1208, 1222 et seq.**
    Chapter 13 proceedings, **11 §§ 1302, 1307, 1322 et seq.**
    Collection,
        Automatic stay, **11 § 362**
        Chapter 7 proceedings, **11 § 704**
        Chapter 11 proceedings, **11 § 1106**
        Chapter 12 proceedings, **11 § 1202**
        Chapter 13 proceedings, **11 § 1302**
    Definitions, **11 § 101**
    Discharge, **11 § 523**

INDEX

Dismissal and nonsuit, 11 § 1112
Exemptions, 11 § 522
Priorities and preferences, 11 § 507
Privileges and immunities,
    Chapter 7 proceedings, 11 § 704
    Chapter 11 proceedings, 11 § 1106
    Chapter 12 proceedings, 11 § 1202
    Chapter 13 proceedings, 11 § 1302
Supreme Court, 28 § 2075
Surcharge, custodians, disbursements, 11 § 543
Sureties and surety bonds. Bonds (officers and fiduciaries), generally, ante
Suspension. Revocation or suspension, generally, ante
Swap agreements, 11 § 546
    Acceleration, 11 § 560
    Automatic stay, 11 § 362
    Cleared swaps, 11 § 761
    Damages, 11 § 562
    Definitions, 11 §§ 101, 560
    Fraud, 11 § 548
    Liquidation, 11 § 560
    Set-off and counterclaim, 11 § 553
    Termination, 11 § 560
    Unsecured claims, priorities and preferences, 11 §§ 753, 767
Taxation, 11 §§ 346, 505
    Accounts and accounting, 11 § 346
    Addresses, 11 § 505; BKR 5003
    Administrative expenses, 11 § 503
    Assessments, 11 § 502
    Automatic stay, 11 § 505
        Objections and exceptions, 11 § 362
        Prepetition taxes, 11 § 362
    Avoidance, liens and incumbrances, 11 §§ 522, 545
    Business and commerce, ante
    Carrybacks, 11 § 346
    Carryovers, 11 § 346
    Chapter 7 proceedings, ante
    Chapter 9 proceedings, ante
    Chapter 11 proceedings, ante
    Chapter 12 proceedings, 11 §§ 346, 1231
    Chapter 13 proceedings, ante
    Claims, 11 § 346
        Foreign countries, 11 § 1513
        Priorities and preferences, 11 §§ 501, 502
    Contests, 11 § 505
    Copies, returns, 11 § 521
    Corporations, 11 § 346
    Damages, discharge, 11 § 505
    Deductions, 11 § 346
    Destruction, documents, 11 § 521 nt
    Discharge, objections and exceptions, 11 § 523
    Dismissal and nonsuit, 11 § 346
        Returns, 11 § 521
    Evidence, priorities and preferences, 11 § 501
    Exemptions, 11 § 522
    Expenses and expenditures, 11 § 503
    Exports and imports, customs duties, priorities and preferences, 11 § 507
    Filing, returns, 11 § 346
    Fines and penalties, 11 § 505
        Priorities and preferences, 11 § 503
    Foreign countries, 11 § 1513
    Forgiveness, 11 § 346

Fraud, returns, 11 § 523
Fuel, 11 § 501
Gross receipts, priorities and preferences, 11 § 507
Individual debtors, 11 §§ 523, 1305
Interest, 11 § 511
Liens and incumbrances,
    Automatic stay, 11 § 362
    Avoidance, 11 §§ 522, 545
    Notice, avoidance, 11 § 522
Limitation of actions, 11 § 346
Lists, 11 § 505
Losses, 11 § 346
Notice, 11 § 362
    Liens and incumbrances, 11 § 522
    Requests, tax determinations, 11 § 505
    Stay of proceedings, 11 § 362
Orders of court, 11 § 346
Partnership, 11 § 346
Payment, 11 § 505
    Secured claims, 11 § 506
Prepetition returns, 11 § 1308
Prepetition taxes, automatic stay, 11 § 362
Priorities and preferences, 11 § 507
    Claims, 11 § 502
    Evidence, 11 § 501
    Foreign countries, 11 § 1513
Refunds, 11 § 505
    Set-off and counterclaim, 11 § 362
Returns,
    Copies, 11 § 521
    Discharge, 11 §§ 505, 523
    Dismissal and nonsuit, 11 § 521
    Filing, 11 § 346
    Prepetition returns, 11 § 1308
    Small businesses, 11 §§ 308, 1116
Revocation or suspension, 11 § 346
Sales, 11 § 346
Set-off and counterclaim, refunds, 11 § 362
Small businesses, returns, 11 §§ 308, 1116
States, 11 § 346
Time, claims, 11 § 502
Transfers, 11 § 346
Trusts and trustees, post
Unsecured claims, 11 § 523
Withholding, 11 § 346
Telecommunications, interception, orders, 18 § 2516
Television and radio, exemptions, 11 § 522
Tenants by the entirety, sales, 11 § 363
Tenants in common, sales, 11 § 363
Tentative carryback adjustment, taxation, priorities and preferences, 11 § 507
Term overriding royalty, definitions, 11 § 101
Termination,
    Air carriers, terminals, 11 § 365
    Automatic stay, 11 § 362
    Chapter 7 proceedings, 11 § 701
    Chapter 9 proceedings, 11 § 930
    Chapter 11 proceedings, ante
    Chapter 12 proceedings, 11 § 1201
    Chapter 13 proceedings, 11 § 1307
    Commodities, contracts, 11 § 556
    Foreign countries, ante
    Forward contracts, 11 § 556
    Master agreements, 11 § 561
    Nonresidential real property, leases, 11 § 541
    Patient care ombudsman, BKR 2007.2

INDEX

Repurchase agreements, **11 § 559**
Securities, contracts, **11 § 555**
Swap agreements, **11 § 560**
Trusts and trustees, **28 § 586**
Terms of office. Judges or justices, ante
Tests,
    Chapter 13 proceedings, means test, **11 § 1325**
    Financial management training curriculum, **11 § 111 nt**
Theft. Larceny, generally, ante
Third parties, **BKR 7014**
Time, **BKR 9006**
    Appeal and review, **BKR 8002**
    Avoidance, **11 § 546**
    Chapter 7 proceedings, ante
    Chapter 11 proceedings, ante
    Chapter 12 proceedings, discharge, **BKR 4007**
    Chapter 13 proceedings, ante
    Claims, **11 § 501 et seq.; BKR 3002 et seq.**
    Consolidations and mergers, orders of court, **BKR 1015**
    Consumer debts, schedules, **11 § 521**
    Corporations, title to property, statements, **BKR 7007.1**
    Courts, findings, **BKR 7052**
    Damages, **11 §§ 502, 562**
    Debt relief agencies,
        Contracts, **11 § 528**
        Disclosure, **11 § 527**
    Definitions, **BKR 9006**
    Discharge, **BKR 4007**
    Examinations and examiners, **BKR 2004**
    Extensions, generally, ante
    Findings, courts, **BKR 7052**
    Foreign countries, notice, **BKR 2015**
    Grain, **11 § 557**
    Judgments and decrees, amendments, **BKR 9023**
    Lists, schedules, **BKR 1007**
    Meetings, **BKR 2003**
    Motions, ante
    New trial, **BKR 9015, 9023**
    Offices, **BKR 5001**
    Open end or revolving consumer credit agreements, claims, **BKR 3001**
    Preferences, **11 § 547**
    Priorities and preferences, **11 § 547**
    Process, **BKR 7004**
    Reaffirmation agreements, **11 § 524**
    Sales, notice, **11 § 363**
    Summary judgment, **BKR 7056**
    Taxation, claims, **11 § 502**
    Venue, **28 § 1408**
Timeshares,
    Definitions, **11 § 101**
    Individual debt adjustment, **11 § 1322**
    Setoff and counterclaim, **11 § 365**
TIN (taxpayer identification number), petitions, **BKR 1005**
Title of act, **11 nt prec § 101**
Title to property, **11 § 541**
    Corporations, statements, **BKR 1007, 7007.1**
    Vested rights, **BKR 7070**
Tools, exemptions, **11 § 522**
Toys, exemptions, **11 § 522**
Trade secrets, **11 § 107; BKR 9018**

Training. Financial management training curriculum, generally, ante
Transcripts, **BKR 5007**
    Appeal and review, **BKR 8007**
    Review, **BKR 8007**
Transfers,
    Actual notice, **11 § 542**
    Adversary proceedings, **BKR 7087**
    Antecedent debt, avoidance, preferences, **11 § 547**
    Avoidance, generally, ante
    Bona fide purchasers, **11 § 548**
    Chapter 7 proceedings, ante
    Chapter 9 proceedings, avoidance, **11 §§ 109, 926**
    Charities, **11 §§ 363, 541, 1129**
    Claims, **BKR 3001**
    Commodities, ante
    Consumer debt, avoidance, **11 § 547**
    Damages, avoidance, **11 § 550**
    Definitions, **11 § 101**
        Avoidance, priorities and preferences, **11 § 547**
        Fraud, **11 § 548**
    Dismissal and nonsuit, **11 § 349**
    Distributions, **11 § 508**
    Evidence, claims, **BKR 3001**
    Exemptions, **BKR 4003**
        Avoidance, **11 §§ 501, 522**
    Foreign countries, **11 § 1520 et seq.**
    Fraud, ante
    Health care businesses, patients, **BKR 2015.2**
    Improvements, avoidance, liability, **11 § 550**
    Involuntary proceedings, ante
    Judges or justices, **28 § 155**
    Judicial liens, avoidance, **11 § 547**
    Liens and incumbrances, indemnity, **BKR 6010**
    Limitation of actions, avoidance, **11 §§ 546, 550**
    Notice, claims, evidence, **BKR 3001**
    Objections and exceptions, claims, evidence, **BKR 3001**
    Ordinary course of business, payments, avoidance, **11 § 547**
    Payment, avoidance, ordinary course of business, **11 § 547**
    Perfection, preferences, **11 § 547**
        Automatic stay, **11 § 362**
    Postpetition, **BKR 6001**
        Avoidance, **11 §§ 546, 549, 551**
    Preferences, avoidance, **11 § 547**
    Priorities and preferences, avoidance, **11 § 547**
    Real estate, bona fide purchasers, preferences, **11 § 547**
    Reconsideration, claims, **11 § 502**
    Reinstatement, avoidance, **11 § 349**
    Securities, ante
    Security interest, avoidance, **11 § 547**
    Set-off and counterclaim, **11 § 553**
    Taxation, **11 § 346**
    Time, preferences, **11 § 547**
    Trusts and trustees, post
    Validation, postpetition transfers, **BKR 6001**
    Waiver, avoidance, **11 § 522**

INDEX

Transportation Department, railroads, appearances, 11 § 1164
Traveling expenses, 11 § 503
    National Bankruptcy Review Commission, 11 nt prec § 101
    Witnesses, BKR 2004
Treasury of United States,
    Fees, 28 § 156
        Referees, 11 nt prec § 101
        Standing trustees, 28 § 586
    Referees, fees, 11 nt prec § 101
    Standing trustees, fees, 28 § 586
Treaties, 11 § 1503
Trial, BKR 5001
    Assignments, BKR 7040
    New trial, BKR 9023
        Time, BKR 9015
Trustees. Trusts and trustees, generally, post
Trusts and trustees, 11 § 321 et seq.; BKR 2007.1 et seq.
    Abandonment, 11 § 554
    Accounts and accounting, 11 § 327
        Compensation and salaries, 11 § 328
        Joint administration, BKR 2009
        Successors, BKR 2012
    Actions and proceedings, 11 § 323; 28 § 959; BKR 6009
        Vacancies in office, 11 § 325
    Administrative expenses, credit, 11 § 364
    Appeal and review, credit, 11 § 364
    Appointments,
        Judges or justices, relatives, BKR 5002
        Standing trustees, 28 § 586
        United States trustees, relatives, BKR 5002
    Attorneys,
        Cancellation, fees, 11 § 541
        Fees, sharing, 11 § 504
        Labor and employment, 11 § 327 et seq.
    Avoidance, generally, ante
    Beneficial interest, transfers, 11 § 541
    Bonds (officers and fiduciaries), 11 § 322; BKR 2008, 2010
        Chapter 7 proceedings, interim trustees, BKR 2001
        Involuntary proceedings, 11 § 303
    Business and commerce, sales, hearings, 11 § 363
    Cash collateral, definitions, administration, 11 § 363
    Chapter 7 proceedings, ante
    Chapter 9 proceedings, ante
    Chapter 11 proceedings, ante
    Chapter 12 proceedings, ante
    Chapter 13 proceedings, ante
    Checks, disposition, 11 § 347
    Claims,
        Business and commerce, venue, 28 § 1409
        Evidence, 11 § 108; BKR 3003, 3004
        Grain, 11 § 557
        Time, 11 § 501
    Clearing banks, liquidation, 11 § 781 et seq.
    Commodities, 11 § 766
        Customers, instructions, 11 § 765
        Open commodity contracts, statements, 11 § 766

    Transfers, void, 11 § 764
Community property, sales, 11 § 363
Compensation and salaries, 11 § 326
    Administrative expenses, allowances, 11 § 503
    Contracts, 11 § 365
    Priorities and preferences, payment, 11 § 507
    Records and recordation, BKR 2013
    Sharing, 11 § 504
Confirmation of plan, individual debt adjustment, objections and exceptions, 11 § 1325
Conflict of interest, BKR 5002
Consent, 11 § 363
Consumer debt, avoidance, transfers, 11 § 547
Contracts, BKR 6006
    Assumption, 11 § 364
        Sales, setoff and counterclaim, 11 § 553
    Performance, time, 11 § 365
Conversion, termination of service, 11 § 348
Cooperation, 11 § 521
Corporations, 11 § 321
Credit, 11 § 364
Custodians, appointments, 11 § 545
Damages, avoidance, transfers, 11 § 550
Death, successors, BKR 2012
Default, curing, time, 11 § 108
Defenses, BKR 6009
Definitions,
    Chapter 9 proceedings, 11 § 902
    Powers and duties, 11 § 323
Demand, filing, time, 11 § 108
Deposits, 11 § 345
Destruction, health care businesses, records and recordation, 11 § 351
Disclosure, records and recordation, hearings, 11 § 542
Elections, 11 § 702; BKR 2007.1
    Qualifications, 11 §§ 322, 702
    Reports, BKR 2003
Eligibility, 11 § 321
Embezzlement, 18 § 153
Evidence, 11 §§ 363, 364
    Avoidance, priorities and preferences, 11 § 547
    Claims, 11 § 108; BKR 3003, 3004
    Qualifications, BKR 2011
Examinations and examiners, 11 § 343
    Conduct, 11 § 341
    Conflict of interest, 11 § 327
Execution, 11 § 544
    Avoidance, 11 § 545
Exemptions, liens and incumbrances, 11 § 522
Expenses and expenditures,
    Claims, secured claims, recovery, 11 § 506
    Loans, 11 § 364
Extensions, actions and proceedings, 11 § 108
Fees, contracts, fraud, 18 § 155
Filing, claims, evidence, 11 § 108; BKR 3003, 3004
Fines and penalties, damages, 11 § 322
Fish and game, reclamation, 11 § 546

INDEX

Foreign countries, ante
Fraud, avoidance, 11 §§ 548, 550
Good faith, real estate, 11 § 549
Grain, 11 § 557
Hearings,
    Leases, 11 § 363
    Removal from office, 11 § 324
    Sales, 11 § 363
Indenture trust and trustees, generally, ante
Inspection and inspectors, records and recordation, 18 § 154
Interim trustees, 11 § 322
    Chapter 7 proceedings, appointments, BKR 2001
    Compensation and salaries, 11 § 331
    Involuntary proceedings, 11 § 303
Inventories, BKR 4002
Involuntary proceedings, transfers, validation, 11 § 549
Joint administration, BKR 2009
Labor and employment, powers and duties, 11 § 327
Leases, BKR 6006
    Powers and duties, 11 §§ 363, 365
    Setoff, 11 § 553
Liens and incumbrances, 11 § 544 et seq.
    Loans, 11 § 364
Loans, liens and incumbrances, 11 § 364
Losses, filing, time, 11 § 108
Mail and mailing, health care businesses, records and recordation, 11 § 351
Money, 11 § 363
    Judgments and decrees, venue, 28 § 1409
Multiple trustees, compensation and salaries, 11 § 326
Notice, BKR 2002, 2015
    Claims, filing, BKR 3004
    Elections, BKR 2007.1
    Health care businesses, records and recordation, 11 § 351
    Leases, 11 § 363
    Perfection, security interest, 11 § 546
    Removal from office, 11 § 324
    Sales, 11 § 363
    Selection, BKR 2008
    Taxation, returns, 11 § 505
    Time, extensions, 11 § 108
Objections and exceptions, confirmation of plan, individual debt adjustment, 11 § 1325
Partnership,
    Avoidance, fraud, 11 § 548
    Claims, 11 § 541
Payment, confirmation of plan, individual debt adjustment, 11 § 1326
Perfection,
    Automatic stay, 11 § 362
    Avoidance, 11 § 546
Personally identifiable information, disposition, 11 §§ 332, 363
Petitions, transmission, BKR 1002
Plans and specifications,
    Individual debt adjustment, 11 § 1326
    Modifications, 11 § 1329
Pleading, filing, extensions, 11 § 108
Possession, money, 11 § 363
Postpetition,
    Avoidance, 11 §§ 549, 550
    Security interest, 11 § 552
Powers and duties, 11 § 323
    Avoidance, 11 § 544 et seq.
    Fraud, transfers, avoidance, 11 § 548
    Labor and employment, 11 § 327
    Leases, 11 § 363
    Liens and incumbrances, avoidance, 11 § 545
    Limitation of actions, avoidance, 11 § 546
    Postpetition, avoidance, 11 §§ 549, 550
    Priorities and preferences, avoidance, 11 § 547
    Sales, 11 § 363
Priorities and preferences,
    Avoidance, damages, 11 § 550
    Claims, 11 § 507
Qualifications, 11 § 322
Records and recordation, BKR 2015
    Compensation and salaries, BKR 2013
    Health care businesses, 11 § 351
Recovery,
    Costs, 11 § 506
    Liens and incumbrances, good faith, 11 § 550
Rejection, BKR 2008
Removal from office,
    Hearings, 11 § 324
    Successors, BKR 2012
Rent, statutory liens, avoidance, 11 § 545
Reports, 18 § 3057; BKR 2015
    Elections, BKR 2007.1
Returns, taxation, 11 § 346
Revocation or suspension, 28 § 586
Sales,
    Avoidance, 11 §§ 363, 541
    Curtesy, 11 § 363
    Dower, 11 § 363
    Reclamation, 11 § 546
    Turnovers, property, 11 § 542
Schedules, 11 § 704
Security interest, postpetition transactions, 11 § 552
Shares and shareholders,
    Accounts and accounting, trust deeds, 11 § 745
    Contracts, 11 § 744
    Customers, 11 § 751
        Distribution, 11 § 752
    Distribution, 11 § 750
        Customers, 11 § 752
    Payment, net equity, subordination, 11 § 747
    Reduction, 11 § 748
Small businesses, 11 § 1116
Standing trustees. United States trustees, post
Statutory liens, avoidance, 11 §§ 545, 550
Statutory successors, 28 § 1409
Substitution, parties, BKR 2012
Successors, 11 § 544
    Avoidance, transfers, 11 § 544 et seq.
    Damages, avoidance, transfers, 11 § 550
    Discharge, taxation, 11 § 505
    Preservation, avoidance, transfers, 11 § 551

INDEX

Qualifications, 11 §§ 322, 703
Security interests, postpetition transactions, 11 § 552
Statutory successors, 28 § 1409
Substitution, 11 § 325; BKR 2012
Taxation, discharge, 11 § 505
Swap agreements, 11 § 546
Taxation, 11 § 505
Returns, 11 § 346
Termination, 28 § 586
Timeshares, rejection, setoff and counterclaim, 11 § 365
Transfers,
Avoidance, 11 § 544 et seq.
Patients, 11 § 704
Unclaimed property, disposition, 11 § 347
Undivided interest, sales, 11 § 363
United States trustees, generally, post
Utilities, 11 § 366
Vacancies in office, 11 § 325
Venue, 28 § 1409
Turnovers,
Property, 11 §§ 542, 543
Records and recordation, BKR 1019
Unclaimed property. Abandonment, generally, ante
Undercapitalization, avoidance, fraud, 11 § 548
Undertakings. Bonds (officers and fiduciaries), generally, ante
Underwriters, definitions, 11 § 364
Undivided interest in property, sales, 11 § 363
Unemployment compensation, exemptions, 11 § 522
Unenforceability, conversion, waiver, 11 § 706
Unincorporated associations, adversary proceedings, BKR 7023.2
United States attorneys,
Investigations, 18 § 3057
Reaffirmation agreements, abuse, 18 § 158
Schedules, fraud, 18 § 158
United States Marshals Service,
Conflict of interest, 18 § 154
Embezzlement, 18 § 153
United States Tax Court, this index
United States trustees, 28 § 581 et seq.
Abuse, chapter 7 proceedings, 11 §§ 704, 707
Applications, compensation and salaries, 28 § 586
Appointments, 28 § 581
Chapter 11 proceedings, committees, 11 §§ 1102, 1114
Consumer privacy ombudsman, 11 § 332
Standing trustees, 28 § 586
Appropriations, System Fund, 28 § 589a
Assistants,
Appointments, 28 § 582
Compensation and salaries, limitation, 28 § 587
Official stations, 28 § 584
Removal from office, 28 § 582
Audits and auditors, 28 § 586
Bonds(officers and fiduciaries), 11 § 322
Chapter 7 proceedings, 11 § 703 et seq.
Abuse, 11 §§ 704, 707
Appointments, successor trustees, 11 § 703
Committees, consultants, 11 § 705
Discharge, objections and exceptions, 11 § 727
Dismissal and nonsuit, 11 § 707
Interim trustee, appointments, BKR 2001

Motions, consumer debts, dismissal and nonsuit, 11 § 707
Objections and exceptions,
Conflict of interest, 11 § 327
Discharge, 11 § 727
Reports, filing, 11 § 704
Revocation or suspension, discharge, 11 § 727
Successor trustees, appointments, 11 § 703
Chapter 11 proceedings, 28 § 586
Appointments, committees, 11 §§ 1102, 1114
Committees, appointments, 11 §§ 1102, 1114
Chapter 12 proceedings,
Appointments, 11 § 1202
Compensation and salaries, 11 § 326; 28 § 586
Confirmation of plan, objections and exceptions, 11 § 1224
Chapter 13 proceedings, 11 § 1307
Appointments, individual debtors, 11 § 1302
Conversion, 11 § 1307
Powers and duties, 28 § 586
Compensation and salaries,
Assistants, 28 § 587
Officers and employees, notice, 11 § 330
Standing trustees, 28 § 586
Consumer privacy ombudsman, appointments, 11 § 332
Contests, BKR 2020
Costs, recovery, deposits, 28 § 589a
Counseling services, 11 § 111
Deposits, 28 § 586
Districts, regions, appointments, 28 § 581
Entities, 11 § 101
Ex parte contacts, BKR 9003
Examinations and examiners, 11 § 341
Oaths and affirmations, 11 § 343
Executive Office, Director, 28 § 156
Expenses and expenditures, 28 §§ 586, 588
Fees,
Percentage fee, 28 § 586
Quarterly fees, 28 § 1930
Filing, records and recordation, BKR 5005
Financial management training curriculum, 11 § 111
Foreign countries, 28 § 586
Motions, pending actions, petitions, BKR 1004.2
Fraud, reports, 28 § 586
Interest, deposits, System Fund, 28 § 589a
Involuntary proceedings, interim trustee, 11 § 303
Judicial districts, appointments, 28 § 581
Meetings, 11 § 341; BKR 2003
Moneys, deposits, 11 § 345
Notice, BKR 2002
Compensation and salaries, 11 § 330
Oaths and affirmations, 11 § 343; 28 § 583
Objections and exceptions, BKR 9034
Removal from office, 11 § 324
Officers and employees, 28 § 589
Official stations, 28 § 584
Panel trustees, 28 § 586
Powers and duties, 11 § 307; 28 § 581 et seq.
Private trustees, 28 § 586

INDEX

Professional persons, conflict of interest, objections and exceptions, **11 § 327**
Quarterly fees, payment, **28 § 1930**
Records and recordation, filing, **BKR 5005**
Regions, judicial districts, appointments, **28 § 581**
Removal from office, **28 § 581**
Reports, **28 § 586**
    System Fund, deposits, **28 § 589a**
Rules and regulations, **11 § 102**
Small businesses, **28 § 586**
Standing trustees, **11 § 307 nt**
    Qualifications, **28 § 586**
Supervision, standing trustees, **28 § 586**
System Fund,
    Compensation and salaries, **11 § 330**
    Investments, **28 § 589a**
Terms of office, **28 § 581**
Transmission, pleadings, **BKR 9034**
Treasury of United States,
    Quarterly fees, deposits, **28 § 1930**
    System Fund, **28 § 589a**
Vacancies in office, **28 § 585**
Voluntary proceedings, petitions, amendments, **BKR 1009**
Universities. Colleges and Universities, this index
Unlawful detainer, automatic stay, **11 § 362**
Unsecured claims. Claims, ante
Usury, defenses, **11 § 558**
Utilities, **11 § 366**
Vacancies in office,
    Judges or justices, **28 § 152**
    Trusts and trustees, **11 § 325**
Vacating or setting aside,
    Chapter 7 proceedings, proxies, **BKR 2006**
    Committees, appointments, **BKR 2007**
    Orders of court, **BKR 1018**
Vacation pay. Compensation and salaries, generally, ante
Validation,
    Liens and incumbrances, **28 § 157**
    Postpetition transfers, **BKR 6001**
    Taxation, **11 § 505**
Valuation,
    Definitions,
        Fraud, **11 §§ 542, 548**
        Powers and duties, **11 § 522**
    Liens and incumbrances, **11 § 363; BKR 3012**
Venue, **28 § 1408 et seq.; BKR 9030**
    Change of venue, **28 § 1412; BKR 1014**
    Chapter 11 proceedings, **28 §§ 1408, 1409**
    Foreign countries, ante
    Place of business, **28 §§ 1408, 1410**
Verification,
    Lists, **BKR 1008**
    Pleadings, **BKR 9011**
Vested rights,
    Family farmers, **11 § 1227**
    Individual debtors, **11 § 1327**
    Title to property, **BKR 7070**
Veterans,
    Benefits, exemptions, **11 § 522**
    Chapter 7 proceedings, disabled veterans, **11 § 707**
    Disabled veterans, chapter 7 proceedings, **11 § 707**
    Exemptions, benefits, **11 § 522**

Video cassette recorders, exemptions, **11 § 522**
Void liens, **11 §§ 506, 541, 551**
Voluntary proceedings, **11 §§ 301, 541**
    Automatic stay, **11 § 362**
        Setoff and counterclaim, **11 § 553**
    Dismissal and nonsuit, **BKR 8001**
    Fees, filing, payment, **28 § 1930**
    Foreign countries, **11 § 1511**
    Lists, **BKR 1007**
    Petitions, **11 § 301; BKR 1002**
        Amendments, **BKR 1009**
        Forms, **BKR Form 1**
    Repayment, **11 § 524**
    Schedules, **BKR 1007**
    Securities, automatic stay, **11 § 362**
    Time, schedules, **BKR 1007**
Wage earners bankruptcy. Chapter 13 proceedings, generally, ante
Waiver,
    Chapter 7 proceedings, ante
    Chapter 13 proceedings, ante
    Community claims, property, discharge, **11 § 524**
    Contracts, claims, **11 § 524**
    Conversion, **11 § 706**
    Counseling services, **11 § 109**
    Debt relief agencies, **11 § 526**
    Defenses, **11 § 558**
    Discharge, **11 § 524; BKR 4006**
    Dismissal and nonsuit, **11 § 1307**
    Exemptions, **11 § 522**
    Powers and duties, **11 §§ 522, 524**
    Privacy protection, **BKR 9037**
    Recovery, **11 § 522**
    Sovereign immunity, abrogation, **11 § 106**
    Transfers, avoidance, **11 § 522**
Warehouses and warehousemen, liens and incumbrances, avoidance, **11 § 546**
Warrants, automatic stay, setoff and counterclaim, **11 § 553**
Wearing apparel, exemptions, **11 § 522**
Wheat, **11 § 557**
Wife. Husband and wife, generally, ante
Willful or malicious injury, exceptions, **11 § 523**
Wiretapping, orders of court, **18 § 2516**
Withdrawal, **28 § 157; BKR 5011**
    Claims, **BKR 3006**
Withholding, taxation, **11 § 346**
Witnesses,
    Fees, **11 § 503**
        Priorities and preferences, **11 § 507**
    Foreign countries, **11 § 1521**
    Priorities and preferences, fees, **11 § 507**
    Privileges and immunities, **18 § 6001**
    Traveling expenses, **BKR 2004**
Writs, **28 § 2075**
Written questions, depositions, **BKR 7031**
Wrongful death,
    Exemptions, **11 § 522; 28 § 157**
    Jury, **28 § 1411**

BANKS AND BANKING
Bankruptcy, this index
Clearing banks, liquidation, **11 § 781 et seq.**
Financial assistance. Colleges and Universities, this index
Fraud, bankruptcy, **11 §§ 522, 523**

INDEX

BARBITAL
Controlled Substances, generally, this index

BARBITURIC ACID
Controlled Substances, generally, this index

BARLEY
Bankruptcy, 11 § 557
Commodity Exchanges, generally, this index

BATTERY
Assault and Battery, generally, this index

BEANS
Bankruptcy, dry edible beans, 11 § 557
Dry edible beans, bankruptcy, 11 § 557

BENZETHIDINE
Controlled Substances, generally, this index

BENZILATE
Controlled Substances, generally, this index

BENZYL CHLORIDE
Controlled Substances, generally, this index

BENZYL CYANIDE
Controlled Substances, generally, this index

BENZYLMORPHINE
Controlled Substances, generally, this index

BETACETYLMETHADOL
Controlled Substances, generally, this index

BETAMEPRODINE
Controlled Substances, generally, this index

BETAMETHADOL
Controlled Substances, generally, this index

BETAPRODINE
Controlled Substances, generally, this index

BEZITRAMIDE
Controlled Substances, generally, this index

BIAS AND PREJUDICE
Bankruptcy, dismissal and nonsuit, 11 § 349
Judges or justices, 28 § 455

BIOTERRORISM
Interception of wire, oral, or electronic communications, 18 § 2516

BOARDS AND COMMISSIONS
Bankruptcy, National Bankruptcy Review Commission, 11 nt prec § 101
Civil Aeronautics Board, generally, this index
Labor Disputes, this index
National Bankruptcy Review Commission, 11 nt prec § 101

BOARDS OF TRADE
Commodity Exchanges, this index

BONA FIDE PURCHASERS
Bankruptcy, this index

BONDS (OFFICERS AND FIDUCIARIES)
Bankruptcy, this index

BONUS
Bankruptcy, retention bonuses, 11 § 503

Shares and Shareholders, this index

BOOKS AND PAPERS
Bankruptcy, this index

BOUNDARIES
Mexico, this index

BRIBERY AND CORRUPTION
Athletics, this index
Bankruptcy, sentence and punishment, 18 § 152
Federal Officers and Employees, this index
Racketeering, generally, this index
Witnesses, this index

BUFOTENINE
Controlled Substances, generally, this index

BUGGING
Interception of Wire, Oral, or Electronic Communications, generally, this index

BUILDING AND LOAN CORPORATIONS OR ASSOCIATIONS
Bankruptcy, 11 § 109

BUILDINGS
Bankruptcy, this index
Intermediate Care Facilities, generally, this index

BUSINESS AND COMMERCE
Bankruptcy, this index
Boards of trade. Commodity Exchanges, this index
Commodity Exchanges, generally, this index
Interference, interception of wire, oral, or electronic communications, 18 § 2516
International Trade Court, generally, this index
Secretary of Commerce, generally, this index
Threats, interception of wire, oral, or electronic communications, 18 § 2516

BUTYL NITRITE
Controlled Substances, generally, this index

CAB
Civil Aeronautics Board, generally, this index

CABLES
Interception of Wire, Oral, or Electronic Communications, generally, this index

CABOOSES
Railroads, generally, this index

CALIFORNIA
Bankruptcy, judges or justices, appointments, 28 § 152
United States trustees, judicial districts, 28 § 581

CARRIERS
Aircraft, generally, this index
Planes. Aircraft, generally, this index
Railroads, generally, this index

CARRYING AWAY
Kidnapping, generally, this index

CARS
Railroads, generally, this index

CHAPTER 7 PROCEEDINGS
Bankruptcy, this index

1102

INDEX

CHAPTER 9 PROCEEDINGS
Bankruptcy, this index

CHAPTER 11 PROCEEDINGS
Bankruptcy, this index

CHAPTER 12 PROCEEDINGS
Bankruptcy, this index

CHAPTER 13 PROCEEDINGS
Bankruptcy, this index

CHARITIES
Bankruptcy, this index
Fraud, bankruptcy, 11 § 548
Judges or justices, disqualification, 28 § 455

CHECKS
Bankruptcy, trusts and trustees, disposition, 11 § 347

CHEMICAL AND BIOLOGICAL WARFARE AND WEAPONS
Bankruptcy, claims, 11 § 362
Claims, bankruptcy, 11 § 362

CHIEF JUDGE OR JUSTICE
Courts of Appeals, this index
International Trade Court, this index
Supreme Court, this index

CHILD
Children and Minors, generally, this index

CHILDREN AND MINORS
Bankruptcy, this index
Custody, bankruptcy, automatic stay, 11 § 362
Disqualification, judges or justices, 28 § 455
Interception of wire, oral, or electronic communications, sexual exploitation, 18 § 2516
Judges or justices, disqualification, 28 § 455
Sexual exploitation, interception of wire, oral, or electronic communications, 18 § 2516
Visitation, bankruptcy, automatic stay, 11 § 362

CHILDREN BORN OUT OF WEDLOCK
Bankruptcy, automatic stay, 11 § 362
Support, bankruptcy, relief from automatic stay, 11 § 362

CHINA TRADE ACT CORPORATIONS
Federal agencies, privileges and immunities, 18 § 6001
Privileges and immunities, Federal agencies, 18 § 6001

CHLORAL BETAINE
Controlled Substances, generally, this index

CHLORAL HYDRATE
Controlled Substances, generally, this index

CHORHEXADOL
Controlled Substances, generally, this index

CHRONIC DISEASES
Nursing Homes, generally, this index

CIGARETTES AND CIGARS
Racketeering, 18 § 1961
Trafficking, racketeering, 18 § 1961

CINCINNATI, OH
Court of Appeals for Sixth Circuit, generally, this index

CITIZENS AND CITIZENSHIP
Wiretap, interception, 18 § 2516

CIVIL AERONAUTICS BOARD
Bankruptcy, 11 § 1110
Privileges and immunities, witnesses, 18 § 6001
Witnesses, privileges and immunities, 18 § 6001

CIVIL AIRCRAFT
Aircraft, generally, this index

CIVIL SERVICE
Retirement and pensions. Judges or Justices, this index

CLAIMS
Bankruptcy, this index
Court of Federal Claims, generally, this index
District Courts, generally, this index

CLAIMS COURT
Court of Federal Claims, generally, this index

CLASSROOMS
Colleges and Universities, generally, this index

CLEARING BANKS
Banks and Banking, this index

CLERKS OF COURTS
Bankruptcy, this index
Compensation and salaries,
    Deputies, 28 § 604
    Director of Administrative Office of U.S. Courts, 28 § 604
Deputies, compensation and salaries, 28 § 604
Director of Administrative Office of U.S. Courts, supervision, 28 § 604
District courts. Clerks of District Courts, generally, this index
Incentive pay or awards, 28 § 604
Supervision, Director of Administrative Office of U.S. Courts, 28 § 604

CLERKS OF DISTRICT COURTS
Compensation and salaries, Director of Administrative Office of U.S. Courts, 28 § 604
Director of Administrative Office of U.S. Courts, compensation and salaries, 28 § 604
Incentive pay or awards, 28 § 604

CLONITAZENE
Controlled Substances, generally, this index

CLOTHING
Bankruptcy, exemptions, 11 § 522
Exemptions, bankruptcy, 11 § 522

CODEBTORS
Bankruptcy, this index

CODEINE
Controlled Substances, generally, this index

COLLECTIVE BARGAINING
Bankruptcy, this index

INDEX

COLLEGES AND UNIVERSITIES
Assistance,
    Loans, generally, post
    Scholarships, generally, this index
Bankruptcy,
    Financial assistance, fraud, exemptions, **11 § 522**
    Robert T. Stafford Federal Student Loan Program, **11 § 525**
Coverdell education savings accounts, bankruptcy, **11 §§ 521, 541**
Disqualification, judges or justices, **28 § 455**
Financial assistance,
    Bankruptcy, fraud, exemptions, **11 § 522**
    Fraud, bankruptcy, exemptions, **11 § 522**
    Loans, generally, post
    Scholarships, generally, this index
Fraud,
    Financial assistance, ante
    Loans, post
Income tax, tuition,
    Coverdell education savings accounts, bankruptcy, **11 §§ 521, 541**
    Education individual retirement accounts, bankruptcy, **11 §§ 521, 541**
    Individual retirement account, bankruptcy, **11 §§ 521, 541**
    Retirement accounts, bankruptcy, **11 §§ 521, 541**
Judges or justices, disqualification, **28 § 455**
Loans,
    Bankruptcy, fraud, exemptions, **11 § 522**
    Fraud, bankruptcy, exemptions, **11 § 522**
    Robert T. Stafford Federal Student Loan Program, bankruptcy, **11 § 525**
Robert T. Stafford Federal Student Loan Program.
    Loans, ante
Scholarships, generally, this index
Student loans. Loans, generally, ante
Tuition. Income tax, ante

COLORADO
Bankruptcy, judges or justices, appointments, **28 § 152**

COMMANDER-IN-CHIEF
President of the United States, generally, this index

COMMERCE DEPARTMENT
Secretary of Commerce, generally, this index

COMMERCE SECRETARY
Secretary of Commerce, generally, this index

COMMITTEES
Bankruptcy, this index

COMMODITIES
Bankruptcy, this index
Brokers, liquidation, **28 § 586**
Exchanges. Commodity Exchanges, generally, this index

COMMODITY EXCHANGES
Boards of trade, definitions, bankruptcy, **11 § 761**
Commodity Futures Trading Commission,
    Bankruptcy, this index
    Definitions, bankruptcy, **11 § 761**
    Privileges and immunities, witnesses, **18 § 6001 et seq.**
Witnesses, privileges and immunities, **18 § 6001 et seq.**

COMMODITY FUTURES
Commodity Exchanges, generally, this index

COMMODITY FUTURES TRADING COMMISSION
Commodity Exchanges, this index

COMMONWEALTH
Northern Mariana Islands, generally, this index

COMMUNICATIONS
Bankruptcy, this index
Interception of Wire, Oral, or Electronic Communications, generally, this index

COMPENSATION AND SALARIES
Arbitration, **28 § 658**
Bankruptcy, this index
Clerks of Courts, this index
Clerks of District Courts, this index
Court Criers, this index
Courts of Appeals, this index
District Judges, this index
Guam, this index
Incentive Pay or Awards, generally, this index
Judges or Justices, this index
Law Clerks, this index
Messengers, courts, **28 § 604**
Northern Mariana Islands, this index
Stenographers, this index
Subsistence, generally, this index
Supreme Court, this index
United States Magistrate Judges, this index
Virgin Islands, this index

COMPLAINTS
Court of Appeals for Sixth Circuit, this index

COMPROMISE AND SETTLEMENT
Bankruptcy, this index

COMPUTERS
Bankruptcy, this index
Fraud, interception of wire, oral, or electronic communications, **18 § 2516**
Interception of wire, oral, or electronic communications, **18 § 2516**

CONCURRENT PROCEEDINGS
Bankruptcy, foreign countries, **11 § 1528 et seq.**

CONDOMINIUMS
Bankruptcy, discharge, **11 § 523**

CONFERENCES
Bankruptcy, this index
Judicial Conference of the United States, generally, this index

CONFIDENTIAL OR PRIVILEGED INFORMATION
Alternative dispute resolution, **28 § 652**
Bankruptcy, this index
District courts, alternative dispute resolution, **28 § 652**

INDEX

CONFINEMENT
Kidnapping, generally, this index

CONFLICT OF INTEREST
Bankruptcy, this index
Judges or justices, disqualification, **28 § 455**
United States Magistrate Judges, this index

CONFLICT OF LAWS
Bankruptcy, foreign countries, **11 § 1503**

CONGRESS
Assassination, interception of wire, oral, or electronic communications, **18 § 2516**
Assault and battery, interception of wire, oral, or electronic communications, **18 § 2516**
Kidnapping, interception of wire, oral, or electronic communications, **18 § 2516**

CONNECTICUT
Bankruptcy, judges or justices, appointments, **28 § 152**
Judicial districts, United States trustees, appointments, **28 § 581**
United States trustees, judicial districts, appointments, **28 § 581**

CONSOLIDATIONS AND MERGERS
Bankruptcy, this index

CONSPIRACY
Interception of wire, oral, or electronic communications, **18 § 2516**

CONSUMER CREDIT PROTECTION
Bankruptcy, this index
Fraud. Credit Cards and Plates, this index
Interception of wire, oral, or electronic communications, **18 § 2516**

CONSUMER DEBT
Bankruptcy, this index

CONSUMER PRIVACY OMBUDSMAN
Bankruptcy, this index

CONTRACTS
Administrative Office of United States Courts, this index
Annuities, generally, this index
Bankruptcy, this index
Long term care. Nursing Homes, generally, this index
Nursing Homes, generally, this index

CONTRIBUTIONS
Bankruptcy, this index

CONTROLLED SUBSTANCES
Concealment, interception of wire, oral, or electronic communications, **18 § 2516**
Exports and imports, interception of wire, oral, or electronic communications, **18 § 2516**
Interception of wire, oral, or electronic communications, orders, **18 § 2516**
Investigations, racketeering **18 § 2516**
Manufacturers and manufacturing, interception of wire, oral, or electronic communications, **18 § 2516**
Marijuana, interception of wire, oral, or electronic communications, **18 § 2516**
Sales, interception of wire, oral, or electronic communications, **18 § 2516**

CONVERSION
Bankruptcy, this index

COOPERATIVE BANKS
Bankruptcy, **11 § 109**

COOPERATIVES
Bankruptcy, exemptions, **11 §§ 522, 523**
Exemptions, bankruptcy, **11 §§ 522, 523**

CORN
Bankruptcy, **11 § 557**
Commodity Exchanges, generally, this index

CORPORATIONS
Bankruptcy, this index
Banks and Banking, generally, this index
Railroads, generally, this index

COSTS
Bankruptcy, this index

COTTON
Commodity Exchanges, generally, this index

COUNSELING SERVICES
Armed Forces, this index
Bankruptcy, this index

COUNSELORS
Attorneys, generally, this index

COUNTERFEITING
Interception of wire, oral, or electronic communications, **18 § 2516**
Mail and Mailing, this index
Racketeering, **18 § 1961**

COURT CRIERS
Compensation and salaries, Director of Administrative Office of U.S. Courts, **28 § 604**
Director of Administrative Office of U.S. Courts, compensation and salaries, **28 § 604**

COURT OF APPEALS
Courts of Appeals, generally, this index

COURT OF APPEALS FOR FIRST CIRCUIT
Discipline, complaints, **28 § 372**

COURT OF APPEALS FOR SECOND CIRCUIT
Judges or justices, complaints, **28 § 372**

COURT OF APPEALS FOR THIRD CIRCUIT
Discipline, judges or justices, complaints, **28 § 372**

COURT OF APPEALS FOR FOURTH CIRCUIT
Judges or justices, complaints, **28 § 372**

COURT OF APPEALS FOR FIFTH CIRCUIT
Judges or justices, complaints, **28 § 372**

COURT OF APPEALS FOR SIXTH CIRCUIT
Complaints, judges or justices, **28 § 372**
Judges or justices,
    Complaints, **28 § 372**
    Disability, complaints, **28 § 372**

INDEX

Misconduct, 28 § 372

COURT OF APPEALS FOR SEVENTH CIRCUIT
Judges or justices, complaints, 28 § 372

COURT OF APPEALS FOR EIGHTH CIRCUIT
Judges or justices, discipline, 28 § 372

COURT OF APPEALS FOR NINTH CIRCUIT
Judges or justices, complaints, 28 § 372

COURT OF APPEALS FOR TENTH CIRCUIT
Judges or justices, complaints, 28 § 372

COURT OF APPEALS FOR ELEVENTH CIRCUIT
Judges or justices, complaints, 28 § 372

COURT OF APPEALS FOR THE ARMED FORCES
Privileges and immunities, witnesses, 18 § 6001 et seq.
Witnesses, privileges and immunities, 18 § 6001 et seq.

COURT OF APPEALS FOR THE DISTRICT OF COLUMBIA
Witnesses, privileges and immunities, 18 § 6001 et seq.

COURT OF CLAIMS
Court of Federal Claims, generally, this index

COURT OF FEDERAL CLAIMS
Administrative Office of United States Courts, annuities, 28 § 604
Appeal and review, judges, discipline, 28 § 372
Discipline, judges or justices, 28 § 372
Judges or justices,
    Complaints,
        Appeal and review, 28 § 372
        Discipline, 28 § 372
    Discipline, 28 § 372
    Retirement and pensions, annuities, payment, 28 § 604
Witnesses, privileges and immunities, 18 § 6001 et seq.

COURTHOUSES AND COURTROOMS
Administrative Office of United States Courts, generally, this index

COURTS
Accommodations, 28 § 604
Administrative Office of United States Courts, generally, this index
Attorneys, generally, this index
Audits and auditors, 28 § 604
Bankruptcy, this index
Calendars. Dockets and Docketing, generally, this index
Center. Judicial Center, generally, this index
Clerical assistants,
    Compensation and salaries, 28 § 604
    Salaries, 28 § 604
Clerks of Courts, generally, this index
Court of Appeals for Sixth Circuit, generally, this index
Court of Federal Claims, generally, this index
Courts of Appeals, generally, this index
District Courts, generally, this index
District Judges, generally, this index
Dockets and Docketing, generally, this index
Federal Judicial Center. Judicial Center, generally, this index
Incentive pay or awards, 28 § 604
Inspection and inspectors, overseas, dockets and docketing, 28 § 604
International Trade Court, generally, this index
Judges or Justices, generally, this index
Judicial Center, generally, this index
Judicial Conference of the United States, generally, this index
Jury, generally, this index
Law Clerks, generally, this index
Machinery and equipment, 28 § 604
Magistrates. United States Magistrate Judges, generally, this index
Marshals. United States Marshals Service, generally, this index
Messengers, compensation and salaries, 28 § 604
Office expenses, payment, 28 § 604
Officers and employees,
    Incentive pay or awards, 28 § 604
    United States Marshals Service, generally, this index
Records and recordation,
    Disqualification, judges or justices, 28 § 455
    Judges or justices, disqualification, 28 § 455
Secretaries, compensation and salaries, 28 § 604
Security, 28 § 604
Speedy trial. Trial, this index
Stenographers, compensation and salaries, 28 § 604
Supplies, 28 § 604
Supreme Court, generally, this index
Tax Court. United States Tax Court, generally, this index
United States courts of appeals. Courts of Appeals, generally, this index
United States Magistrate Judges, generally, this index
United States Marshals Service, generally, this index
United States Tax Court, generally, this index
Witnesses, generally, this index

COURTS OF APPEALS
Bankruptcy, this index
Chief Judge or Justice, disability, 28 § 372
Compensation and salaries,
    Law clerks, 28 § 604
    Secretaries, 28 § 604
Incentive pay or awards, 28 § 604
Judges or justices,
    Additional judges, 28 § 372
    Compensation and salaries, disability, 28 § 372
    Disability, 28 § 372
    Retirement and pensions, disability, 28 § 372
    Vacancies in office, 28 § 372
Officers and employees, incentive pay or awards, 28 § 604
Privileges and immunities, 18 § 6001 et seq.
Reports, Administrative Office of U.S. Courts, 28 § 604
Sixth Circuit. Court of Appeals for Sixth Circuit, generally, this index

INDEX

United States magistrate judges, **28 § 604**
Witnesses, privileges and immunities, **18 § 6001 et seq.**

COVERDELL EDUCATION SAVINGS ACCOUNTS
Bankruptcy, **11 §§ 521, 541**

CRACK (COCAINE)
Controlled Substances, generally, this index

CREDIT CARDS AND PLATES
Fraud, Secret Service, **18 § 2516**

CREDIT (PAYMENT OF INDEBTEDNESS)
Bankruptcy, this index
Usury, generally, this index

CREDIT UNIONS
Bankruptcy, **11 § 109**

CRIME VICTIMS
Interception of wire, oral, or electronic communications, **18 § 2516**
Restitution, generally, this index
Retaliation, interception of wire, oral, or electronic communications, **18 § 2516**
Tampering, interception of wire, oral, or electronic communications, **18 § 2516**

CRIMES AND OFFENSES
Aliens, this index
Assault and Battery, generally, this index
Atomic Energy, this index
Bankruptcy, this index
Battery. Assault and Battery, generally, this index
Crime Victims, generally, this index
Embezzlement, generally, this index
Explosives, this index
Immigration, this index
Interception of Wire, Oral, or Electronic Communications, generally, this index
Kidnapping, generally, this index
Misapplication of funds. Embezzlement, generally, this index
Motor Vehicles, this index
Pretrial services,
    Accommodations, **28 § 604**
    Administrative Office of United States Courts, Director, **28 § 604**
    Administrative personnel, **28 § 604**
    Judicial Conference of the United States, **28 § 604**
    Law books, **28 § 604**
    Supplies, **28 § 604**
    Vouchers, audits and auditing, **28 § 604**
Racketeering, generally, this index
Receivers and Receivership, this index
Restitution, generally, this index
Speedy trial. Trial, this index
Trial, generally, this index
Victims. Crime Victims, generally, this index
Witnesses, generally, this index

CRIMINAL CODE
Crimes and Offenses, generally, this index

CRIMINAL JUSTICE SYSTEM
Crimes and Offenses, generally, this index

CRIMINAL PROCEDURE
Crimes and Offenses, generally, this index

CRIMINAL SYNDICALISM
Racketeering, generally, this index

CROCKERY
Bankruptcy, exemptions, **11 § 522**

CURRENT MONTHLY INCOME
Bankruptcy, this index

CUSTODIANS
Bankruptcy, this index

CUSTODY
Children and minors, bankruptcy, automatic stay, **11 § 362**
Kidnapping, generally, this index

CYPRENORPHINE
Controlled Substances, generally, this index

DAMAGES
Bankruptcy, this index
District Courts, this index

DANGEROUS DRUGS
Controlled Substances, generally, this index

DEATH
Bankruptcy, this index
Hospices, generally, this index
International Trade Court, this index
Justices or judges, vacancies in office, **28 § 372**

DEBT RELIEF AGENCIES
Bankruptcy, this index

DEBTORS IN POSSESSION
Bankruptcy, this index

DEFAULT
Bankruptcy, this index
Railroads, this index

DEFENSE DEPARTMENT
Head of Department. Secretary of Defense, generally, this index

DEFENSE SECRETARY
Secretary of Defense, generally, this index

DEFINITIONS
Words and Phrases, generally, this index

DELAWARE
Bankruptcy, judges or justices, appointments, **28 § 152**
United States trustees of judicial districts, appointment, **28 § 581**

DEPENDENTS
Bankruptcy, exemptions, **11 § 522**

DEPOSITS
Bankruptcy, this index
Public utilities, bankruptcy, **11 § 366**

DESOMORPHINE
Controlled Substances, generally, this index

DEXTROMETHORPHAN
Controlled Substances, generally, this index

INDEX

DEXTROMORAMIDE
Controlled Substances, generally, this index

DEXTRORPHAN
Controlled Substances, generally, this index

DIAMPROMIDE
Controlled Substances, generally, this index

DIETHYLTHIAMBUTENE
Controlled Substances, generally, this index

DIETHYLTRYPTAMINE
Controlled Substances, generally, this index

DIGITAL SIGNALS
Interception of Wire, Oral, or Electronic Communications, generally, this index

DIHYDROCODEINE
Controlled Substances, generally, this index

DIHYDROCODEINONE
Controlled Substances, generally, this index

DIHYDROMORPHINE
Controlled Substances, generally, this index

DIMENOXADOL
Controlled Substances, generally, this index

DIMEPHEPTANOL
Controlled Substances, generally, this index

DIMETHYLTHIAMBUTENE
Controlled Substances, generally, this index

DIMETHYLTRYPTAMINE
Controlled Substances, generally, this index

DIOXAPHETYL BUTYRATE
Controlled Substances, generally, this index

DIPHENOXYLATE
Controlled Substances, generally, this index

DIPIPANONE
Controlled Substances, generally, this index

DISBURSING OFFICIALS, CLERKS, AND AGENTS
Administrative Office of U.S. Courts, 28 § 604

DISCIPLINE
Court of Appeals for First Circuit, this index
Court of Appeals for Third Circuit, this index
Court of Federal Claims, this index
International Trade Court, this index

DISCLOSURE
Bankruptcy, this index

DISCRIMINATION
Bankruptcy, 11 § 525
Student Loan Program, bankruptcy, 11 § 525

DISEASES
Drugs and Medicine, generally, this index

DISHES
Bankruptcy, exemptions, 11 § 522

DISMISSAL AND NONSUIT
Bankruptcy, this index

DISPUTE RESOLUTION
Alternative Dispute Resolution, generally, this index
Arbitration, generally, this index

DISTRICT COURTS
Alternative Dispute Resolution, generally, this index
Appeal and review. Courts of Appeals, generally, this index
Arbitration, referrals, 28 § 654
Bankruptcy, generally, this index
Clerks of District Courts, generally, this index
Damages, alternative dispute resolution, 28 § 654
Definitions, alternative dispute resolution, 28 § 651
District Judges, generally, this index
Exemptions, alternative dispute resolution, 28 § 652
Guam, this index
Judges. District Judges, generally, this index
Jurisdiction, alternative dispute resolution, 28 § 652
Neutrals, alternative dispute resolution, 28 § 653
Northern Mariana Islands, this index
Pretrial services. Crimes and Offenses, this index
Referrals, arbitration, 28 § 654
Security, 28 § 604
United States Magistrate Judges, generally, this index
Virgin Islands, this index
Witnesses, privileges and immunities, 18 § 6001 et seq.

DISTRICT JUDGES
Appointment, disability, 28 § 372
Certificates and certification, disability, 28 § 372
Compensation and salaries,
    Disability, 28 § 372
    Secretaries, 28 § 604
Discipline, 28 § 372
Handicapped persons,
    Appointments, 28 § 372
    Retirement and pensions, 28 § 372
Law clerks, compensation and salaries, 28 § 604
Precedence, disability, 28 § 372
Resignation, disability, 28 § 372
United States Magistrate Judges, generally, this index
Vacancies in office, 28 § 372

DISTRICT OF COLUMBIA
Bankruptcy, this index
United States trustees, judicial districts, 28 § 581

DISTRICTS
District Courts, generally, this index

DIVORCE
Bankruptcy, this index

DOCKETS AND DOCKETING
Administrative Office of U.S. Courts, information, 28 § 604
Arbitration, this index
Bankruptcy, this index
Examinations and examiners, 28 § 604
Information, Administrative Office of U.S. Courts, 28 § 604

INDEX

DOCUMENTARY EVIDENCE
Racketeer influenced and corrupt organizations, 18 § 1961

DOMESTIC VIOLENCE
Bankruptcy, automatic stay, 11 § 362

DOMICILE AND RESIDENCE
Bankruptcy, this index

DOMICILIARY CARE
Nursing Homes, generally, this index

DOWER AND CURTESY
Bankruptcy, sales, 11 § 363
Sales, bankruptcy, 11 § 363

DRUGS AND MEDICINE
Bankruptcy, trafficking, chapter 7 proceedings, dismissal and nonsuit, 11 § 707
Controlled Substances, generally, this index
Interception of wire, oral, or electronic communications, 18 § 2516
Racketeering, generally, this index
Trafficking, bankruptcy, chapter 7 proceedings, dismissal and nonsuit, 11 § 707

EAVESDROPPING
Interception of Wire, Oral, or Electronic Communications, generally, this index

EDUCATION
Bankruptcy, this index
Colleges and Universities, generally, this index
Coverdell education savings accounts, bankruptcy, 11 §§ 521, 541
Income Tax, this index
Scholarships, generally, this index
Secretary of Education, generally, this index

EDUCATION DEPARTMENT
Secretary of Education, generally, this index

EDUCATION INDIVIDUAL RETIREMENT ACCOUNTS
Bankruptcy, 11 §§ 521, 541

EDUCATION SECRETARY
Secretary of Education, generally, this index

EGGS AND EGG PRODUCTS
Commodity Exchanges, generally, this index

ELECTIONS
Bankruptcy, this index

ELECTRONIC FILING
Bankruptcy, this index

ELECTRONIC SURVEILLANCE
Interception of Wire, Oral, or Electronic Communications, generally, this index

EMBEZZLEMENT
Bankruptcy, 11 § 523; 18 § 153
Interception of wire, oral, or electronic communications, Pension and Welfare Fund, 18 § 2516

EMERGENCIES
Bankruptcy, this index

EMIGRATION
Immigration, generally, this index

EMPLOYEE RETIREMENT INCOME SECURITY PROGRAM
Bankruptcy, this index
Theft, 18 § 2516

ENERGY
Interception, wire and oral communications, 18 § 2516
Secretary of Energy, generally, this index

ENERGY DEPARTMENT
Head of Department. Secretary of Energy, generally, this index
Secretary of Energy, generally, this index

ENERGY SECRETARY
Secretary of Energy, generally, this index

ENGINE HOUSES
Railroads, generally, this index

ENTIRETIES, ESTATES BY
Bankruptcy, sales, 11 § 363

ENTRY UPON LAND
Bankruptcy, this index

EQUITY
Bankruptcy, this index
Receivers and receivership, 28 § 959
Trusts and trustees, 28 § 959

EQUITY SECURITY HOLDERS
Bankruptcy, this index

ERGONOVINE
Controlled Substances, generally, this index

ERGOTAMINE
Controlled Substances, generally, this index

ESCAPE
Interception of wire, oral, or electronic communications, 18 § 2516

ESPIONAGE
Interception of wire, oral, or electronic communications, 18 § 2516

ESTATE TAX
United States Tax Court, generally, this index

ETHCHLORVYNOL
Controlled Substances, generally, this index

ETHINAMATE
Controlled Substances, generally, this index

ETHYL ETHER
Controlled Substances, generally, this index

ETHYLMETHYLTHIAMBUTENE
Controlled Substances, generally, this index

ETHYLMORPHINE
Controlled Substances, generally, this index

ETONITAZENE
Controlled Substances, generally, this index

INDEX

ETORPHINE
Controlled Substances, generally, this index

ETOXERIDINE
Controlled Substances, generally, this index

EVICTIONS
Landlord and Tenant, this index

EVIDENCE
Bankruptcy, this index
Witnesses, generally, this index

EXAMINATIONS AND EXAMINERS
Bankruptcy, this index

EXECUTION
Bankruptcy, this index

EXECUTIVE DEPARTMENTS
Justice Department, generally, this index
President of the United States, generally, this index
Secretary of Agriculture, generally, this index
Secretary of Commerce, generally, this index
Secretary of Energy, generally, this index
Secretary of Housing and Urban Development, generally, this index
Secretary of Labor, generally, this index
Secretary of State, generally, this index
Secretary of the Interior, generally, this index
Secretary of the Treasury, generally, this index
Witnesses, privileges and immunities, 18 § 6001 et seq.

EXECUTIVE MANSION
White House, generally, this index

EXECUTIVE OFFICE
President of the United States, this index

EXECUTORS AND ADMINISTRATORS
Disqualification, judges or justices, 28 § 455
Judges or justices, disqualification, 28 § 455

EXEMPTIONS
Annuities, this index
Bankruptcy, this index
Clothing, this index
Cooperatives, this index
New markets venture capital companies, bankruptcy, 11 § 109

EXPENSES AND EXPENDITURES
Administrative Office of U.S. Courts, 28 § 604
Bankruptcy, this index
Court officers and employees, payment, Administrative Office of U.S. Courts, 28 § 604
Judges or Justices, this index
Subsistence, generally, this index
Traveling Expenses, generally, this index

EXPLOSIVES
Crimes and offenses, communications, interceptions, 18 § 2516
Interception of wire, oral, or electronic communications, 18 § 2516

EXPORTS AND IMPORTS
Controlled Substances, this index
Courts. International Trade Court, generally, this index
International Trade Court, generally, this index

EXTENDED CARE SERVICES
Nursing Homes, generally, this index

EXTORTION
Credit (payment of indebtedness), 18 § 2516
Interception of wire, oral, or electronic communications, credit (payment of indebtedness), 18 § 2516

FAMILY FARMERS PROTECTION ACT OF 2002
Generally, 11 §§ 101 nt, 1201 et seq.

FATHERS
Children and Minors, generally, this index

FEDERAL AGENCIES
Arbitration, generally, this index
Interception of wire, oral, or electronic communications, 18 § 2516
Officers and employees. Federal Officers and Employees, generally, this index
Privileges and immunities, witnesses, 18 § 6001 et seq.
Witnesses, privileges and immunities, 18 § 6001 et seq.

FEDERAL BUREAU OF INVESTIGATION
Bankruptcy, powers and duties, 18 § 158
Interception of wire, oral, or electronic communications, 18 § 2516

FEDERAL CLAIMS COURT
Court of Federal Claims, generally, this index

FEDERAL DEPOSIT INSURANCE CORPORATION
Privileges and immunities, witnesses, 18 § 6001 et seq.
Witnesses, privileges and immunities, 18 § 6001 et seq.

FEDERAL JUDICIAL CENTER
Judicial Center, generally, this index

FEDERAL MARITIME COMMISSION
Privileges and immunities, 18 § 6001 et seq.
Witnesses, privileges and immunities, 18 § 6001 et seq.

FEDERAL OFFICERS AND EMPLOYEES
Bribery and corruption, interception of wire, oral, or electronic communications, 18 § 2516
Disqualification, judges or justices, 28 § 455
Influence, injuries, interception of wire, electronic or oral communications, 18 § 2516
Interception of wire, oral, or electronic communications, 18 § 2516
Judges or justices, disqualification, 28 § 455
President of the United States, generally, this index
Secretary of Agriculture, generally, this index
Secretary of Commerce, generally, this index
Secretary of Education, generally, this index
Secretary of Health and Human Services, generally, this index
Secretary of Housing and Urban Development, generally, this index
Secretary of Labor, generally, this index

INDEX

Secretary of State, generally, this index
Secretary of Transportation, generally, this index
United States Marshals Service, generally, this index
Vice President of the United States, generally, this index

FEDERAL REGISTER
Administrative Office of United States Courts, rules and regulations, 28 § 604

FEDERAL TRADE COMMISSION
Witnesses, privileges and immunities, 18 § 6001 et seq.

FELONIES
Crimes and Offenses, generally, this index

FENTANYL
Controlled Substances, generally, this index

FIDUCIARIES
Bankruptcy, this index
Disqualification, judges or justices, 28 § 455
Judges or justices, disqualification, 28 § 455
Receivers and Receivership, generally, this index

FINANCIAL INSTITUTIONS
Banks and Banking, generally, this index

FINANCIAL MANAGEMENT TRAINING CURRICULUM
Bankruptcy, this index

FINANCIAL STATEMENTS AND REPORTS
Bankruptcy, this index

FINES AND PENALTIES
Bankruptcy, this index
Restitution, generally, this index

FISH AND GAME
Bankruptcy, this index
Commercial fishing. Bankruptcy, this index

FLAX AND FLAXSEED
Bankruptcy, 11 § 557
Commodity Exchanges, generally, this index

FLIGHTS
Aircraft, generally, this index

FLORIDA
Bankruptcy, judges or justices, appointments, 28 § 152
United States trustees, appointments, 28 § 581

FOREIGN AND INTERNATIONAL RELATIONS
Secretary of State, generally, this index

FOREIGN BANKS IN THE UNITED STATES
Bankruptcy, 11 § 109

FOREIGN COUNTRIES
Aliens, generally, this index
Bankruptcy, this index
Immigration, generally, this index
Mexico, generally, this index
Secretary of State, generally, this index

FOREIGN COURTS OR TRIBUNALS
Exports and imports. International Trade Court, generally, this index

FOREIGN INSURANCE
Bankruptcy, 11 § 109

FOREIGNERS
Aliens, generally, this index

FORFEITURES
Bankruptcy, 11 § 363

FORMULARIES
Drugs and Medicine, generally, this index

FORWARD CONTRACTS
Bankruptcy, this index

FOUNDATIONS
Scholarships, generally, this index

FRATERNAL ASSOCIATIONS AND SOCIETIES
Disqualification, judges or justices, 28 § 455
Judges or justices, disqualification, 28 § 455

FRAUD
Bankruptcy, this index
Banks and Banking, this index
Charities, this index
Colleges and Universities, this index
Computers, this index
Credit Cards and Plates, this index
Passports, this index
Racketeering, generally, this index
Receivers and Receivership, this index
Religious organizations and societies, bankruptcy, 11 § 548
Scholarships, this index
Secret Service, this index

FRAUDS, STATUTE OF
Bankruptcy, this index

FRAUDULENT CONVEYANCES
Bankruptcy, this index

FREE BASE (COCAINE)
Controlled Substances, generally, this index

FRIVOLOUS ACTIONS
Bankruptcy, this index

FUEL
Bankruptcy, taxation, 11 § 501
Taxation, bankruptcy, 11 § 501

FUNDS
Retirement and Pensions, this index
Scholarships, generally, this index

FURETHIDINE
Controlled Substances, generally, this index

FURNITURE
Bankruptcy, exemptions, 11 § 522

FUTURES (COMMODITIES)
Commodity Exchanges, generally, this index

GAMBLING
Interceptions, communications, 18 § 2516

INDEX

Racketeering, generally, this index
Syndicated gambling, crimes and offenses, **18 § 2516**

GEORGIA
Bankruptcy, judges or justices, appointments, **28 § 152**

GI
Armed Forces, generally, this index

GIFT TAX
United States Tax Court, generally, this index

GIFTS
Bankruptcy, this index
National Bankruptcy Review Commission, **11 nt prec § 101**

GLUTETHIMIDE
Controlled Substances, generally, this index

GOLD
Commodity Exchanges, generally, this index

GOOD FAITH
Bankruptcy, this index

GOODS, WARES AND MERCHANDISE
Bankruptcy, liens and incumbrances, **11 § 546**
Household Goods, generally, this index

GOVERNMENT EMPLOYEES
Federal Officers and Employees, generally, this index

GOVERNMENT OFFICERS AND EMPLOYEES
Federal Officers and Employees, generally, this index

GRAIN
Bankruptcy, this index
Commodity Exchanges, generally, this index
Futures. Commodity Exchanges, generally, this index

GRAND JURY
Bankruptcy, investigations, **18 § 3057**

GRANTS
Bankruptcy, discrimination, **11 § 525**

GUAM
Compensation and salaries,
    District courts, judges or justices, **28 § 604**
    Judges or justices, district courts, **28 § 604**
District courts,
    Compensation and salaries, judges or justices, **28 § 604**
    Judges or justices, compensation and salaries, **28 § 604**
    Witnesses, **18 § 6001 et seq.**
United States trustees of judicial districts, **28 § 581**

GUARDIAN AND WARD
Disqualification, judges or justices, **28 § 455**
Judges or justices, disqualification, **28 § 455**

HABIT FORMING DRUGS
Controlled Substances, generally, this index

HANDICAPPED PERSONS
Bankruptcy, this index
District Judges, this index
Intermediate Care Facilities, generally, this index
Judges or Justices, this index
Supreme Court, this index

HANGING LAW
Bankruptcy, chapter 13 proceedings, **11 § 1325**

HARDSHIP
Bankruptcy, reaffirmation agreements, **11 § 524**

HAWAII
Bankruptcy, judges or justices, appointments, **28 § 152**
United States, judicial district trustees, appointments, **28 § 581**

HEALTH AND HUMAN SERVICES DEPARTMENT
Head of Department. Secretary of Health and Human Services, generally, this index
Secretary of Health and Human Services, generally, this index

HEALTH AND HUMAN SERVICES SECRETARY
Secretary of Health and Human Services, generally, this index

HEALTH AND SANITATION
Controlled Substances, generally, this index

HEALTH CARE BUSINESSES
Bankruptcy, this index

HEALTH CARE FACILITIES AND SERVICES
Hospitals, generally, this index

HEALTH CARE PROVIDERS
Long term care. Nursing Homes, generally, this index
Nursing Homes, generally, this index

HEALTH INSURANCE
Bankruptcy, chapter 13 proceedings, **11 § 1329**
Long term care. Nursing Homes, generally, this index
Nursing Homes, generally, this index

HEARINGS
Arbitration, this index
Bankruptcy, this index

HIGH SCHOOLS OR SECONDARY SCHOOLS
Income tax, education individual retirement accounts, bankruptcy, **11 §§ 521, 541**

HIGHER EDUCATION
Colleges and Universities, generally, this index

HOG (PCP)
Controlled Substances, generally, this index

HOME CARE
Agents and agencies. Home Health Agencies, generally, this index

HOME HEALTH AGENCIES
Bankruptcy,
    Definitions, **11 § 101**
    Ombudsman, **11 § 333**

INDEX

Records and recordation, **11 § 351**
Definitions, bankruptcy, **11 § 101**
Ombudsman, bankruptcy, **11 § 333**
Records and recordation, bankruptcy, **11 § 351**

HOMES
Nursing Homes, generally, this index

HOMESTEAD ASSOCIATIONS
Bankruptcy, **11 § 109**

HOMESTEADS
Bankruptcy, this index

HOSPICES
Bankruptcy,
    Definitions, **11 § 101**
    Ombudsman, **11 § 333**
    Records and recordation, **11 § 351**
Definitions, bankruptcy, **11 § 101**
Ombudsman, bankruptcy, **11 § 333**
Records and recordation, bankruptcy, **11 § 351**

HOSPITALS
Bankruptcy,
    Definitions, **11 § 101**
    Ombudsman, **11 § 333**
    Records and recordation, **11 § 351**
Definitions, bankruptcy, **11 § 101**
Long term care. Nursing Homes, generally, this index
Nursing Homes, generally, this index
Ombudsman, bankruptcy, **11 § 333**
Records and recordation, bankruptcy, **11 § 351**

HOSTAGES
Interception of wire, oral, or electronic communications, **18 § 2516**

HOUSEHOLD GOODS
Bankruptcy, exemptions, **11 § 522**
Definitions, bankruptcy, exemptions, **11 § 522**
Exemptions, bankruptcy, **11 § 522**
Liens and incumbrances, bankruptcy, **11 § 522**

HOUSING
Assisted Living Facilities, generally, this index
Secretary of Housing and Urban Development, generally, this index

HOUSING AND URBAN DEVELOPMENT DEPARTMENT
Secretary of Housing and Urban Development, generally, this index

HUMAN TRAFFICKING
Trafficking, this index

HUSBAND AND WIFE
Bankruptcy, this index
Judges or justices, disqualification, **28 § 455**

HYDRIODIC ACID
Controlled Substances, generally, this index

HYDROMORPHINOL
Controlled Substances, generally, this index

HYDROXYPETHIDINE
Controlled Substances, generally, this index

IBOGAINE
Controlled Substances, generally, this index

IDAHO
Bankruptcy, judges or justices, appointments, **28 § 152**
United States trustees, judicial districts, **28 § 581**

IDENTITY AND IDENTIFICATION
Bankruptcy, this index
Personally identifiable information. Bankruptcy, this index
Theft, bankruptcy, **11 § 107**

ILLINOIS
Bankruptcy, judges or justices, appointments, **28 § 152**
United States trustees, judicial districts, **28 § 581**

IMMIGRATION
Crimes and offenses,
    Smuggling, **18 § 1961**
    Wiretapping, **18 § 2516**
Interception of wire, oral, or electronic communications, investigations, alien smuggling, **18 § 2516**
Investigations, smuggling, **18 § 2516**
Smuggling,
    RICO-predicate offenses, **18 § 1961**
    Wiretapping, **18 §§ 1961, 2516**
Wiretapping, **18 § 2516**

IMMUNITIES
Privileges and Immunities, generally, this index

INCENTIVE PAY OR AWARDS
Administrative Office of United States Courts, **28 § 604**
Clerks of courts, **28 § 604**
Clerks of district courts, **28 § 604**
Courts, **28 § 604**
Courts of appeals, **28 § 604**
Law clerks, **28 § 604**

INCOME
Bankruptcy, this index

INCOME TAX
Bankruptcy, this index
Colleges and Universities, this index
Coverdell education savings accounts, bankruptcy, **11 §§ 521, 541**
Education,
    Coverdell education savings accounts, bankruptcy, **11 §§ 521, 541**
    Individual retirement accounts, bankruptcy, **11 §§ 521, 541**
High Schools or Secondary Schools, this index
Individual retirement accounts,
    Coverdell education savings accounts, bankruptcy, **11 §§ 521, 541**
    Education, bankruptcy, **11 §§ 521, 541**
    Higher education, bankruptcy, **11 §§ 521, 541**
Schools and School Districts, this index
Tax Court. United States Tax Court, generally, this index
Tuition. Colleges and Universities, this index
United States Tax Court, generally, this index

INDEBTEDNESS
Bankruptcy, generally, this index

INDEX

Municipal corporations, chapter 9 proceedings. Bankruptcy, this index
Receivers and Receivership, generally, this index
Usury, generally, this index

INDEMNITY
Bankruptcy, this index

INDENTURE TRUST AND TRUSTEES
Bankruptcy, this index

INDEXES
Bankruptcy, this index

INDIANA
Bankruptcy, judges or justices, appointments, 28 § 152
United States trustees, judicial districts, appointments, 28 § 581

INDIVIDUAL RETIREMENT ACCOUNTS
Income Tax, this index

INFANTS
Children and Minors, generally, this index

INJUNCTIONS
Bankruptcy, this index

INSOLVENCY
Bankruptcy, generally, this index
Investigations, crimes and offenses, 18 § 3057

INSPECTION AND INSPECTORS
Bankruptcy, this index

INSTALLMENTS
Bankruptcy, this index

INSTITUTIONS OF HIGHER EDUCATION OR LEARNING
Colleges and Universities, generally, this index

INSTRUCTIONS
Bankruptcy, commodities, customers, 11 § 765

INSTRUMENTALITIES OF THE UNITED STATES
Federal Agencies, generally, this index

INSURANCE
Bankruptcy, this index
Judges or Justices, this index
Long term care. Nursing Homes, generally, this index
Nursing Homes, generally, this index

INTELLECTUAL PROPERTY
Bankruptcy, this index

INTERCEPTION OF WIRE, ORAL, OR ELECTRONIC COMMUNICATIONS
Aircraft, 18 § 2516
Aliens, smuggling, 18 § 2516
Atomic energy, 18 § 2516
Attorneys, Federal officers and employees, felonies, 18 § 2516
Authorization, 18 § 2516
Bioterrorism, 18 § 2516
Bribery and corruption, 18 § 2516
Bureau of Investigation, 18 § 2516
Business and commerce, interference, 18 § 2516
Cabinet departments, applications, 18 § 2516
Chemical and biological warfare and weapons, 18 § 2516
Children and minors, sexual exploitation, 18 § 2516
Citizens and citizenship, naturalization, 18 § 2516
Computers, 18 § 2516
Congress, applications, 18 § 2516
Conspiracy, 18 § 2516
Controlled substances, manufacturers and manufacturing, exports and imports, 18 § 2516
Counterfeiting, 18 § 2516
Credit, extortion, 18 § 2516
Currency, exports and imports, 18 § 2516
Employee benefit plans, investigations, 18 § 2516
Energy, facilities, 18 § 2516
Escape, 18 § 2516
Espionage, 18 § 2516
Explosives, 18 § 2516
Federal agencies, 18 § 2516
Federal Officers and Employees, this index
Fraud, 18 § 2516
Fugitives from justice, 18 § 2516
Gambling, 18 § 2516
Hostages, 18 § 2516
Immigration, smuggling, 18 § 2516
Labor and employment, 18 § 2516
Labor organizations, 18 § 2516
Mail and mailing, fraud, 18 § 2516
Malicious mischief, 18 § 2516
Marihuana, 18 § 2516
Mexico, border tunnels, 18 § 2516
Military assistance and sales, exports and imports, 18 § 2516
Money laundering, 18 § 2516
Motor vehicles, trafficking, 18 § 2516
Murder, hired killers, 18 § 2516
Narcotics, 18 § 2516
Natural gas, pipes and pipelines, 18 § 2516
Naturalization, 18 § 2516
Obscenity, 18 § 2516
Obstruction, 18 § 2516
Passports, forgery, 18 § 2516
Pension or Welfare Fund, 18 § 2516
Piracy, 18 § 2516
President of the United States, assassinations, 18 § 2516
Racketeer influenced and corrupt organizations, 18 § 2516
Railroads, 18 § 2516
Retaliation, 18 § 2516
Riots and mobs, 18 § 2516
Sabotage, 18 § 2516
Sexual exploitation, children and minors, 18 § 2516
Smallpox, 18 § 2516
Smuggling, aliens, 18 § 2516
Sports, bribery and corruption, 18 § 2516
Stolen property, interstate transportation, 18 § 2516
Supreme Court, applications, 18 § 2516
Syndicated gambling, 18 § 2516
Tampering, 18 § 2516
Television and radio, fraud, 18 § 2516
Terrorists and Terrorism, this index
Treason, 18 § 2516
Vessels, destruction, 18 § 2516
Visas, 18 § 2516
Witnesses, 18 § 2516

INDEX

INTEREST
Bankruptcy, this index
Usury, generally, this index

INTERIOR DEPARTMENT
Secretary of the Interior, generally, this index

INTERIOR SECRETARY
Secretary of the Interior, generally, this index

INTERLOCUTORY ORDERS
Bankruptcy, 28 § 158

INTERMEDIATE CARE FACILITIES
Bankruptcy,
    Definitions, 11 § 101
    Ombudsman, 11 § 333
    Records and recordation, 11 § 351
Definitions, bankruptcy, 11 § 101
Ombudsman, bankruptcy, 11 § 333
Records and recordation, bankruptcy, 11 § 351

INTERNAL REVENUE CODE
Income Tax, generally, this index

INTERNATIONAL TRADE COURT
Appeal and review, judges or justices, discipline, 28 § 372
Chief Judge or Justice, disability, 28 § 372
Death, judges or justices, 28 § 372
Discipline, judges or justices, 28 § 372
Judges or justices,
    Additional judges, 28 § 372
    Compensation and salaries, disability, 28 § 372
    Disability, 28 § 372
    Vacancies in office, 28 § 372
Resignation, judges or justices, 28 § 372
Retirement and pensions, judges or justices, disability, 28 § 372
Witnesses, privileges and immunities, 18 § 6001 et seq.

INTERPRETERS
Bankruptcy, 11 § 1515

INTERSTATE AND FOREIGN COMMERCE
Aircraft, destruction, 18 § 2516
Racketeering, 18 § 2516

INTERVENTION
Bankruptcy, this index

INVEIGLE AND INVEIGLING
Kidnapping, generally, this index

INVENTORIES
Bankruptcy, this index

INVESTIGATIONS
Aliens, this index
Bankruptcy, this index
Controlled Substances, this index
Immigration, this index
Interception of Wire, Oral, or Electronic Communications, generally, this index
Prostitutes and Prostitution, this index
Smuggling, aliens, interception of wire, oral, or electronic communications, 18 § 2516
United States Attorneys, this index

INVESTMENTS
Bankruptcy, this index

INVOLUNTARY BANKRUPTCY IMPROVEMENT ACT OF 2005
Generally, 11 §§ 101 nt, 303; 18 § 157

INVOLUNTARY PROCEEDINGS
Bankruptcy, this index

IOWA
Bankruptcy, judges or justices, appointments, 28 § 152
United States trustees, judicial districts, appointments, 28 § 581

ISLANDS
Northern Mariana Islands, generally, this index
Virgin Islands, generally, this index

ISOMETHADONE
Controlled Substances, generally, this index

ISONIPECAINE
Controlled Substances, generally, this index

JET AIRCRAFT
Aircraft, generally, this index

JEWELRY
Bankruptcy,
    Exemptions, 11 § 522
    Liens and incumbrances, exemptions, 11 § 522

JOINDER
Bankruptcy, this index

JOINT TENANTS
Bankruptcy, 11 § 363

JUDGES OR JUSTICES
Administrative Office of United States Courts, generally, this index
Adverse or pecuniary interest, disqualification, 28 § 455
Appeal and review, disqualification, 28 § 455
Appointments, disability, 28 § 372
Attorneys, this index
Bankruptcy, this index
Center. Judicial Center, generally, this index
Certificates and certification, disability, retirement and pensions, 28 § 372
Compensation and salaries,
    Life insurance, group premiums, 28 § 604
    Resignation, 28 § 372
Conflict of interest, disqualification, 28 § 455
Court of Appeals for Second Circuit, this index
Court of Appeals for Fourth Circuit, this index
Court of Appeals for Fifth Circuit, this index
Court of Appeals for Sixth Circuit, this index
Court of Appeals for Seventh Circuit, this index
Court of Appeals for Eighth Circuit, this index
Court of Appeals for Ninth Circuit, this index
Court of Appeals for Tenth Circuit, this index
Court of Appeals for Eleventh Circuit, this index
Court of Federal Claims, this index
Courts of Appeals, this index
Definitions, disqualification, 28 § 455
Degree of relationship, definitions, 28 § 455
Discipline, complaints, 28 § 372

INDEX

Disqualification, **28 § 455**
Expenses and expenditures, Director of
    Administrative Office of U.S. Courts, **28
    § 604**
Federal Judicial Center. Judicial Center, generally,
    this index
Federal Officers and Employees, this index
Fiduciary, definitions, **28 § 455**
Group insurance. Life insurance, post
Handicapped persons,
    Appointments, **28 § 372**
    Retirement and pensions, **28 § 372**
Insurance, group insurance, premiums,
    compensation and salaries, **28 § 604**
International Trade Court, this index
Judicial Center, generally, this index
Life insurance,
    Group insurance, premiums, compensation
        and salaries, **28 § 604**
    Premiums, group insurance, compensation
        and salaries, **28 § 604**
Magistrate judges. United States Magistrate
    Judges, generally, this index
Office expenses, Director of Administrative Office
    of U.S. Courts, **28 § 604**
President of the United States, disability, **28 § 372**
Proceeding, definitions, **28 § 455**
Recall, bankruptcy, **28 § 155**
Recusal, **28 § 455**
Relatives, disqualification, **28 § 455**
Retirement and pensions,
    Bankruptcy, this index
    Handicapped persons, **28 § 372**
    Substitutes, **28 § 372**
Secretaries,
    Bankruptcy, **28 § 156**
    Compensation and salaries, **28 § 604**
Subsistence, **28 § 604**
Substitutes, retirement and pensions, **28 § 372**
Traveling expenses, **28 § 604**
United States Magistrate Judges, generally, this
    index
Vacancies in office,
    Death, **28 § 372**
    Disability, **28 § 372**
Virgin Islands, this index
Waivers, disqualification, **28 § 455**
Witnesses, disqualification, **28 § 455**

JUDGMENTS AND DECREES
Arbitration, this index
Bankruptcy, this index

JUDICIAL CENTER
Accommodations, **28 § 604**
Audits and auditors, **28 § 604**
Director, **28 § 604**
Law books, **28 § 604**
Machinery and equipment, **28 § 604**
Subsistence, **28 § 604**
Supplies, **28 § 604**
Traveling expenses, **28 § 604**

JUDICIAL CONFERENCE OF THE UNITED STATES
Bankruptcy, this index
Director of Administrative Office of the U.S.
    Courts, **28 § 604**
Pretrial services, **28 § 604**

Supervision, Director of Administrative Office of
    the U.S. Courts, **28 § 604**
United States Magistrate Judges, this index

JUDICIAL COUNCIL
Bankruptcy, this index
Disability, retirement and pensions, **28 § 372**
Discipline, **28 § 372**

JUDICIAL DISTRICTS
Bankruptcy, this index
Connecticut, this index
New York, this index
South Dakota, this index

JURISDICTION
Bankruptcy, this index
District Courts, this index

JURY
Bankruptcy, this index
Influence, interception of wire, oral, or electronic
    communications, **18 § 2516**
Interception of wire, oral, or electronic
    communications, influence, **18 § 2516**
Receivers and receivership, **28 § 959**
Trusts and trustees, **28 § 959**

JUSTICE DEPARTMENT
Attorney General, generally, this index
Marshals. United States Marshals Service,
    generally, this index
Oaths and affirmations, United States trustees, **28
    § 583**
Trusts and trustees, United States trustees,
    bankruptcy, **28 § 581 et seq.**
United States Marshals Service, generally, this
    index
United States trustees,
    Bankruptcy, **28 § 581 et seq.**
    Oaths and affirmations, **28 § 583**

JUSTICES
Judges or Justices, generally, this index

KANSAS
Bankruptcy, judges or justices, appointments, **28
    § 152**
United States trustees, appointments, **28 § 581**

KENTUCKY
Bankruptcy, judges or justices, appointments, **28
    § 152**
United States trustees, judicial districts, **28 § 581**

KETOBEMIDONE
Controlled Substances, generally, this index

KIDNAPPING
Attorney General, this index
Cabinet departments, interception of wire, oral, or
    electronic communications, **18 § 2516**
Congress, this index
Interception of wire, oral, or electronic
    communications, President, Congress, **18
    § 2516**
Justices of Supreme Court, interception of wire,
    oral, or electronic communications, **18 § 2516**
President of the United States, this index
Racketeering, generally, this index
Secretary of Agriculture, this index

INDEX

Secretary of Housing and Urban Development, this index
Secretary of Labor, this index
Secretary of State, this index
Secretary of the Interior, this index
Secretary of the Treasury, this index
Vice President of the United States, this index

KITCHENWARE
Bankruptcy, exemptions, **11 § 522**

LABOR AND EMPLOYMENT
Bankruptcy, this index
Secretary of Labor, generally, this index

LABOR DEPARTMENT
Head of Department. Secretary of Labor, generally, this index
Secretary of Labor, generally, this index

LABOR DISPUTES
Boards and commissions, witnesses, privileges and immunities, **18 § 6001 et seq.**
Labor organizations, payment, loans, **18 § 2516**

LABOR ORGANIZATIONS
Labor Disputes, this index

LABOR SECRETARY
Secretary of Labor, generally, this index

LANDLORD AND TENANT
Bankruptcy, automatic stay, **11 § 362**
Evictions, bankruptcy, automatic stay, **11 § 362**
Unlawful detainer, bankruptcy, automatic stay, **11 § 362**

LARCENY
Bankruptcy, this index

LAW BOOKS
Director of Administrative Office of U.S. Courts, **28 § 604**
United States magistrate judges, **28 § 604**

LAW CLERKS
Bankruptcy, **28 § 156**
Compensation and salaries, incentive pay or awards, **28 § 604**
District Judges, this index
Incentive pay or awards, **28 § 604**

LAW ENFORCEMENT
Interception of Wire, Oral, or Electronic Communications, generally, this index

LAW ENFORCEMENT OFFICERS
United States Marshals Service, generally, this index

LAW LIBRARIES
Librarians, courts, compensation and salaries, **28 § 604**

LAWYERS
Attorneys, generally, this index

LEASES
Bankruptcy, this index

LEAVE OF COURT
Bankruptcy, this index
Trusts and trustees, **28 § 959**

LEGAL REPRESENTATIVES
Attorneys, generally, this index

LEGAL SERVICES
Attorneys, generally, this index

LETTERS OF CREDIT
Bankruptcy, **11 § 101**

LEVOMETHORPHAN
Controlled Substances, generally, this index

LEVOMORAMIDE
Controlled Substances, generally, this index

LEVOPHENACYLMORPHAN
Controlled Substances, generally, this index

LEVORPHANOL
Controlled Substances, generally, this index

LIBRARIANS
Law Libraries, this index

LICENSES AND PERMITS
Bankruptcy, discrimination, **11 § 525**

LIENS AND INCUMBRANCES
Bankruptcy, this index
Household Goods, this index
Warehouses and warehousemen, bankruptcy, avoidance, **11 § 546**

LIFE INSURANCE
Bankruptcy, this index
Group insurance. Judges or Justices, this index
Judges or Justices, this index

LIMITATION OF ACTIONS
Bankruptcy, this index

LINENS
Bankruptcy, exemptions, **11 § 522**

LISTS
Bankruptcy, this index

LOANS
Bankruptcy, this index
Colleges and Universities, this index
Interest. Usury, generally, this index
Usury, generally, this index

LONG TERM CARE
Nursing Homes, generally, this index

LOUISIANA
Bankruptcy, judges or justices, appointments, **28 § 152**
United States trustees, judicial districts, appointments, **28 § 581**

LYSERGIC ACID
Controlled Substances, generally, this index

LYSERGIC ACID AMIDE
Controlled Substances, generally, this index

MAGISTRATES
United States Magistrate Judges, generally, this index

MAIL AND MAILING
Bankruptcy, this index

INDEX

Counterfeiting, interception of wire, oral, or electronic communications, 18 § 2516
Interception of Wire, Oral, or Electronic Communications, this index

MAINE
United States trustees, judicial districts, appointments, 28 § 581

MALICIOUS MISCHIEF
Energy facilities, destruction, 18 § 2516
Interception of wire, oral, or electronic communications, 18 § 2516

MANAGERS AND MANAGEMENT
Bankruptcy, this index
Property, this index

MANUFACTURERS AND MANUFACTURING
Controlled Substances, this index

MARGINS
Bankruptcy, this index

MARIANA ISLANDS
Northern Mariana Islands, generally, this index

MARIJUANA
Controlled Substances, this index

MARKETS AND MARKETING
Commodity Exchanges, generally, this index

MARSHALS
United States Marshals Service, generally, this index

MARYLAND
Bankruptcy, judges or justices, appointments, 28 § 152
United States trustees, judicial districts, 28 § 581

MASSACHUSETTS
Bankruptcy, judges or justices, appointments, 28 § 152
United States trustees of judicial districts, appointment, 28 § 581

MASTER AGREEMENTS
Bankruptcy, this index

MEAL FEEDS
Commodity Exchanges, generally, this index

MEDIATION AND MEDIATORS
Alternative Dispute Resolution, generally, this index

MEDICAL CARE AND TREATMENT
Drugs and Medicine, generally, this index
Hospitals, generally, this index
Long term care. Nursing Homes, generally, this index
Nursing Homes, generally, this index

MEDICAL DEVICES
Bankruptcy, exemptions, 11 § 522

MEDICAL FACILITIES
Hospitals, generally, this index

MEDICARE
Bankruptcy, automatic stay, 11 § 362

MEDICINE
Drugs and Medicine, generally, this index

MENTAL HEALTH
Bankruptcy, this index

MEPROBAMATE
Controlled Substances, generally, this index

MESCALINE
Controlled Substances, generally, this index

MESSENGERS
Courts, compensation and salaries, 28 § 604

METAZOCINE
Controlled Substances, generally, this index

METHADONE
Controlled Substances, generally, this index

METHOHEXITAL
Controlled Substances, generally, this index

METHYLDESORPHINE
Controlled Substances, generally, this index

METHYLHYDROMORPHINE
Controlled Substances, generally, this index

METHYLPHENIDATE
Controlled Substances, generally, this index

METHYLPHENOBARBITAL
Controlled Substances, generally, this index

METHYPRYLON
Controlled Substances, generally, this index

MEXICO
Boundaries,
    Interception of wire, oral, or electronic communications, tunnels, 18 § 2516
    Tunnels, interception of wire, oral, or electronic communications, 18 § 2516
Interception of wire, oral, or electronic communications, border tunnels, 18 § 2516

MICHIGAN
Bankruptcy, judges or justices, appointments, 28 § 152
United States trustees, judicial districts, appointments, 28 § 581

MILEAGE
Traveling Expenses, generally, this index

MILITARY DEPARTMENTS
Privileges and immunities, witnesses, 18 § 6001 et seq.
Witnesses, privileges and immunities, 18 § 6001 et seq.

MILITARY FORCES
Armed Forces, generally, this index

MINITRIALS
Alternative Dispute Resolution, generally, this index

MINNESOTA
Bankruptcy, judges or justices, appointments, 28 § 152

INDEX

United States trustees, judicial districts, appointments, 28 § 581

MINORS
Children and Minors, generally, this index

MISDEMEANORS
Crimes and Offenses, generally, this index

MISSISSIPPI
Bankruptcy, judges or justices, appointments, 28 § 152
United States trustees, judicial districts, appointments, 28 § 581

MISSOURI
Bankruptcy, judges or justices, appointments, 28 § 152
United States trustees, judicial districts, 28 § 581

MONEY
Bankruptcy, this index
Embezzlement, generally, this index
Racketeering, generally, this index
Records and recordation, interception of wire, oral or electronic communications, 18 § 2516

MONEY LAUNDERING
Definitions, organized crime, 18 § 1961
Interception of wire, oral or electronic communications, 18 § 2516

MONTANA
Bankruptcy, judges or justices, appointments, 28 § 152
United States trustees, judicial districts, appointments, 28 § 581

MORAMIDE
Controlled Substances, generally, this index

MORPHERIDINE
Controlled Substances, generally, this index

MORPHINE
Controlled Substances, generally, this index

MORTGAGES
Bankruptcy, this index

MOTHERS
Children and Minors, generally, this index

MOTIONS
Bankruptcy, this index

MOTOR VEHICLES
Bankruptcy, this index
Crimes and offenses, attempts, interception of wire, oral, or electronic communications, 18 § 2516
Driving while intoxicated or under the influence. Bankruptcy, this index
Stolen property, interception of wire, oral, or electronic communications, 18 § 2516

MUNICIPAL CORPORATIONS
Chapter 9 proceedings. Bankruptcy, this index
Indebtedness, chapter 9 proceedings. Bankruptcy, this index

MURDER
Interception of wire, oral, or electronic communications, 18 § 2516

Internationally protected persons, interception of wire, oral, or electronic communications, 18 § 2516

MUSIC
Bankruptcy, liens and incumbrances, exemptions, 11 § 522

MUTUAL FUNDS
Judges or justices, disqualification, 28 § 455

MUTUAL INSURANCE
Judges or justices, disqualification, 28 § 455

MYROPHINE
Controlled Substances, generally, this index

N-ACETYLANTHRANILIC ACID
Controlled Substances, generally, this index

N-PHENYL-N-[1-(2-PHENYLETHYL)-4-PIPERIDINYL] PROPANAMIDE
Controlled Substances, generally, this index

NALORPHINE
Controlled Substances, generally, this index

NAMES
Bankruptcy, 11 § 109 et seq.
United States Bankruptcy Court, 28 § 151

NARCOTICS
Controlled Substances, generally, this index

NATIONAL BANKRUPTCY REVIEW COMMISSION ACT
Generally, 11 nt prec § 101

NATIONAL DEFENSE
Armed Forces, generally, this index
Secretary of Defense, generally, this index

NATIONAL GUARD
Bankruptcy, chapter 7 proceedings, 11 § 707

NATIONAL GUARD AND RESERVISTS DEBT RELIEF ACT OF 2008
Generally, 11 §§ 101 nt, 707, 707 nt

NATIONAL GUARD AND RESERVISTS DEBT RELIEF ACT OF 2011
Generally, 11 §§ 101 nt, 707 nt

NATIONAL NARCOTICS ACT OF 1984
Controlled Substances, generally, this index

NATIONAL SECURITIES ASSOCIATION
Securities, this index

NATIONAL TRANSPORTATION SAFETY BOARD
Privileges and immunities, witnesses, 18 § 6001 et seq.
Witnesses, privileges and immunities, 18 § 6001 et seq.

NATURAL RESOURCES
Secretary of Energy, generally, this index

NEBRASKA
Bankruptcy, judges or justices, appointments, 28 § 152
United States trustees, judicial districts, appointments, 28 § 581

INDEX

NEGOTIABLE INSTRUMENTS
Bankruptcy, this index
Racketeering, generally, this index

NET EQUITY
Bankruptcy, this index

NEUTRALITY
Alternative dispute resolution, 28 § 653

NEVADA
Bankruptcy, judges or justices, appointments, 28 § 152
United States trustees of judicial districts, appointment, 28 § 581

NEW HAMPSHIRE
Bankruptcy, judges or justices, appointments, 28 § 152
United States trustees, judicial districts, appointments, 28 § 581

NEW JERSEY
Bankruptcy, judges or justices, appointments, 28 § 152
United States trustees, judicial districts, appointment, 28 § 581

NEW MARKETS VENTURE CAPITAL COMPANIES
Bankruptcy, exemptions, 11 § 109
Exemptions, bankruptcy, 11 § 109

NEW MEXICO
Bankruptcy, judges or justices, appointments, 28 § 152
United States trustees, judicial districts, appointments, 28 § 581

NEW TRIAL
Arbitration, 28 § 657

NEW YORK
Bankruptcy, judges or justices, appointments, 28 § 152
Judicial districts, United States trustees, appointments, 28 § 581
United States trustees, judicial districts, appointments, 28 § 581

NEWSPAPERS
Bankruptcy, municipal debt adjustment, notice, 11 § 923

NICOCODEINE
Controlled Substances, generally, this index

NICOMORPHINE
Controlled Substances, generally, this index

NONCITIZENS
Aliens, generally, this index

NONPROFIT CORPORATIONS
Bankruptcy, involuntary proceedings, 11 § 303

NONPROFIT ORGANIZATIONS OR ASSOCIATIONS
Bankruptcy, this index

NONRESIDENTS
Aliens, generally, this index

NORACYMETHADOL
Controlled Substances, generally, this index

NORLEVORPHANOL
Controlled Substances, generally, this index

NORMETHADONE
Controlled Substances, generally, this index

NORMORPHINE
Controlled Substances, generally, this index

NORPIPANONE
Controlled Substances, generally, this index

NORPSEUDOEPHEDRINE
Controlled Substances, generally, this index

NORTH CAROLINA
Bankruptcy, judges or justices, appointments, 28 § 152
United States trustees, judicial districts, appointments, 28 § 581

NORTH DAKOTA
Bankruptcy, judges or justices, appointments, 28 § 152
United States trustees, judicial districts, appointments, 28 § 581

NORTHERN MARIANA ISLANDS
Compensation and salaries,
    District courts, judges or justices, 28 § 604
    Judges or justices, district courts, 28 § 604
District courts, judges or justices, compensation and salaries, 28 § 604
United States trustees of judicial districts, 28 § 581

NORTHERN MARIANAS, COMMONWEALTH OF
Northern Mariana Islands, generally, this index

NOTICE
Bankruptcy, this index

NURSING HOMES
Bankruptcy,
    Definitions, 11 § 101
    Ombudsman, 11 § 333
    Records and recordation, 11 § 351
Definitions, bankruptcy, 11 § 101
Ombudsman, bankruptcy, 11 § 333
Records and recordation, bankruptcy, 11 § 351

OATHS AND AFFIRMATIONS
Arbitration, 28 § 655
Bankruptcy, this index
United States trustees, 28 § 583

OATS
Bankruptcy, 11 § 557
Commodity Exchanges, generally, this index

OBJECTIONS AND EXCEPTIONS
Bankruptcy, this index

OBSCENITY
Racketeering, 18 § 1961
Wiretapping, 18 § 2516

OBSTRUCTING JUSTICE
Interception of wire, oral, or electronic communications, 18 § 2516

INDEX

OFFENSES
Crimes and Offenses, generally, this index

OFFICERS AND EMPLOYEES
Administrative Office of United States Courts, this index
Bankruptcy, this index
Courts, this index
Courts of Appeals, this index
Federal Officers and Employees, generally, this index
Judges or Justices, generally, this index
White House, this index

OFFICES
White House, generally, this index

OFFICIAL STATIONS
Bankruptcy, courts, judges or justices, 28 § 152

OHIO
Bankruptcy, judges or justices, appointments, 28 § 152
United States trustees of judicial districts, appointment, 28 § 581

OIL AND GAS
Secretary of Energy, generally, this index

OKLAHOMA
Bankruptcy, judges or justices, appointments, 28 § 152
United States trustees, judicial districts, appointments, 28 § 581

OMBUDSMAN
Consumer privacy ombudsman. Bankruptcy, this index
Long term care. Nursing Homes, this index
Nursing Homes, this index
Patient care ombudsman. Bankruptcy, this index

OPTIONS
Bankruptcy, this index

ORAL COMMUNICATIONS
Interception of Wire, Oral, or Electronic Communications, generally, this index

ORDERS OF COURT
Bankruptcy, this index
Protective orders. Bankruptcy, this index

OREGON
Bankruptcy, judges or justices, appointments, 28 § 152
United States trustees, judicial districts, appointments, 28 § 581

ORGANIZED CRIME
Racketeering, generally, this index

PANELS
Bankruptcy appellate panels. Bankruptcy, this index

PARALDEHYDE
Controlled Substances, generally, this index

PARAPROFESSIONALS
Bankruptcy, labor and employment, 11 §§ 330, 507

PARENT AND CHILD
Children and Minors, generally, this index

PARTIES
Bankruptcy, this index
Disqualification, judges or justices, 28 § 455
Judges or justices, disqualification, 28 § 455

PARTNERSHIP
Bankruptcy, this index
Racketeering, generally, this index

PASSPORTS
Fraud, wiretapping, investigations and investigators, 18 § 2516
Wiretapping, investigations and investigators, 18 § 2516

PATIENT CARE OMBUDSMAN
Bankruptcy, this index

PENAL CODE
Crimes and Offenses, generally, this index

PENAL LAWS
Crimes and Offenses, generally, this index

PENNSYLVANIA
Bankruptcy, judges or justices, appointments, 28 § 152
United States trustees, appointments, 28 § 581

PERFECTION
Bankruptcy, this index

PERJURY
Bankruptcy, this index

PERSONAL EFFECTS
Bankruptcy, exemptions, 11 § 522

PERSONAL INJURIES
Bankruptcy, this index

PERSONAL PROPERTY
Bankruptcy, this index

PERSONALLY IDENTIFIABLE INFORMATION
Bankruptcy, this index

PETHIDINE
Controlled Substances, generally, this index

PETIT JURY
Jury, generally, this index

PETITIONS
Bankruptcy, this index

PETRICHLORAL
Controlled Substances, generally, this index

PHENADOXONE
Controlled Substances, generally, this index

PHENAMPROMIDE
Controlled Substances, generally, this index

PHENAZOCINE
Controlled Substances, generally, this index

PHENMETRAZINE
Controlled Substances, generally, this index

INDEX

PHENOBARBITAL
Controlled Substances, generally, this index

PHENOMORPHAN
Controlled Substances, generally, this index

PHENOPERIDINE
Controlled Substances, generally, this index

PHENYLACETIC ACID
Controlled Substances, generally, this index

PHOLCODINE
Controlled Substances, generally, this index

PHRASES
Words and Phrases, generally, this index

PHYSICIANS AND SURGEONS
Drugs and Medicine, generally, this index

PIMINODINE
Controlled Substances, generally, this index

PIPRADROL
Controlled Substances, generally, this index

PIRACY
Interception of wire, oral, or electronic communications, 18 § 2516

PIRITRAMIDE
Controlled Substances, generally, this index

PLANES
Aircraft, generally, this index

PLANS AND SPECIFICATIONS
Bankruptcy, this index

PLATINUM
Commodity Exchanges, generally, this index

PLEADING
Bankruptcy, this index

POISONS
Controlled Substances, generally, this index

POLITICAL SUBDIVISIONS
Bankruptcy, this index

POSTSECONDARY EDUCATION AND SCHOOLS
Colleges and Universities, generally, this index

POWER OF ATTORNEY
Bankruptcy, this index

PRESIDENT OF THE UNITED STATES
Assassination, interception of wire, oral, or electronic communications, 18 § 2516
Assault and battery, interception of wire, oral, or electronic communications, 18 § 2516
Bankruptcy, this index
Domicile and residence. White House, generally, this index
Executive mansion. White House, generally, this index
Executive Office,
    Assassination, officers and employees, 18 § 2516
    Officers and employees, assassination, 18 § 2516
    Venue, officers and employees, 28 § 1413
Interception of Wire, Oral, or Electronic Communications, this index
Judges or Justices, this index
Kidnapping, interception of wire, oral, or electronic communications, 18 § 2516
Venue, Executive Office, officers and employees, 28 § 1413
White House, generally, this index

PRESUMPTIONS
Bankruptcy, this index

PRETRIAL SERVICES
Crimes and Offenses, this index

PRIORITIES AND PREFERENCES
Bankruptcy, this index

PRIVACY
Bankruptcy, this index
Consumer privacy ombudsman. Bankruptcy, this index

PRIVILEGES AND IMMUNITIES
Arbitrators, 28 § 655
Bankruptcy, this index
Federal Agencies, this index
Federal Deposit Insurance Corporation, this index
Federal Maritime Commission, 18 § 6001 et seq.
Military departments, witnesses, 18 § 6001 et seq.
Securities and Exchange Commission, this index
Witnesses, this index

PROCESS
Arbitration, this index
Bankruptcy, this index

PRODUCTION OF BOOKS AND PAPERS
Arbitration, 28 § 656

PROFESSIONAL PERSONNEL
Bankruptcy, this index

PROFESSIONS AND OCCUPATIONS
Attorneys, generally, this index
Receivers and Receivership, generally, this index

PROFIT-SHARING PLANS
Bankruptcy, 11 § 522

PROFITS
Bankruptcy, this index

PROHEPTAZINE
Controlled Substances, generally, this index

PROPELLERS
Aircraft, destruction, 18 § 2516

PROPERIDINE
Controlled Substances, generally, this index

PROPERTY
Bankruptcy, generally, this index
Managers and management, actions and proceedings, 28 § 959

PROSTITUTES AND PROSTITUTION
Interception of wire, oral, or electronic communications, 18 § 2516
Investigations, interception of wire, oral, or electronic communications, 18 § 2516

INDEX

PROTECTION OF FAMILY FARMERS ACT OF 2002
Generally, 11 §§ 101 nt, 1201 et seq.

PSILOCYBIN
Controlled Substances, generally, this index

PSILOCYN
Controlled Substances, generally, this index

PUBLIC EDUCATION
Colleges and Universities, generally, this index

PUBLIC OFFICERS AND EMPLOYEES
Federal Officers and Employees, generally, this index

PUBLIC RECORDS
Records and Recordation, generally, this index

PUBLIC UTILITIES
Bankruptcy, deposits, 11 § 366
Deposits, bankruptcy, 11 § 366

PUBLICATION
Bankruptcy, this index

PUERTO RICO
United States trustees of judicial districts, 28 § 581

PURCHASERS AND PURCHASING
Bankruptcy, this index

RACEMETHORPHAN
Controlled Substances, generally, this index

RACEMORAMIDE
Controlled Substances, generally, this index

RACEMORPHAN
Controlled Substances, generally, this index

RACKETEERING
Generally, 18 § 1961 et seq.
Attorney General, definitions, 18 § 1961
Bankruptcy, fraud, 18 § 1961
Cigarettes and cigars, 18 § 1961
Counterfeiting, 18 § 1961
Definitions, 18 § 1961
Documents, definitions, 18 § 1961
Interception of wire, oral, or electronic communications, 18 § 2516
Interstate and foreign commerce, interception of wire, oral, or electronic communications, 18 § 2516
Listed chemical, definitions, 18 § 1961
Motion pictures, counterfeiting, brands, marks and labels, trafficking, 18 § 1961
Music videos, counterfeiting, brands, marks and labels, trafficking, 18 § 1961
Obscenity, 18 § 1961
Pattern of racketeering activity, definitions, 18 § 1961
Person, definitions, 18 § 1961
Sound recordings, counterfeiting, brands, marks and labels, 18 § 1961
Terrorists and terrorism, 18 § 1961
Traffickers in persons, 18 § 1961

RAIL CARRIERS
Railroads, generally, this index

RAILROAD RETIREMENT BOARD
Witnesses, privileges and immunities, 18 § 6001 et seq.

RAILROADS
Default,
    Bankruptcy, reorganization, 11 § 1172
    Reorganization, bankruptcy, 11 § 1172
Interception of wire, oral, or electronic communications, 18 § 2516

RAILWAYS
Railroads, generally, this index

REAFFIRMATION AGREEMENTS
Bankruptcy, this index

REAL ESTATE
Bankruptcy, this index
Landlord and Tenant, generally, this index
Records and Recordation, generally, this index

RECALL
Bankruptcy, judges or justices, 28 § 155
Judges or Justices, this index

RECEIVERS AND RECEIVERSHIP
Bankruptcy, this index
Crimes and offenses, investigations, 18 § 3057
Fees, fraud, 18 § 155
Fraud,
    Compensation and salaries, 18 § 155
    Fees, 18 § 155
Investigations, crimes and offenses, 18 § 3057
Managers and management, 28 § 959

RECIPROCITY
Bankruptcy, abstention, 11 § 305; 28 § 1334

RECORDS AND RECORDATION
Assisted living facilities, bankruptcy, 11 § 351
Bankruptcy, this index
Courts, this index
Home health agencies, bankruptcy, 11 § 351
Hospices, bankruptcy, 11 § 351
Hospitals, bankruptcy, 11 § 351
Intermediate care facilities, bankruptcy, 11 § 351
Long term care, bankruptcy, 11 § 351
Money, this index
Nursing homes, bankruptcy, 11 § 351
Skilled nursing facilities, bankruptcy, 11 § 351
United States Magistrate Judges, this index

RECUSAL
Judges or Justices, this index
United States magistrate judges, 28 § 455

RECYCLING AND RESOURCE RECOVERY
Courts, 28 § 604

REDEMPTION
Bankruptcy, this index

REFEREES SALARY AND EXPENSE FUND ACT OF 1984
Generally, 11 nt prec § 101

REFERENCES
Bankruptcy, this index

REGIONAL RAIL REORGANIZATION
Bankruptcy, 11 § 1166

INDEX

RELATIVES
Judges or Justices, this index

RELIGION
Associations and societies. Religious Organizations and Societies, generally, this index
Corporations. Religious Organizations and Societies, generally, this index
Religious Organizations and Societies, generally, this index

RELIGIOUS LIBERTY AND CHARITABLE DONATION CLARIFICATION ACT OF 2006
Generally, 11 §§ 101 nt, 1325

RELIGIOUS ORGANIZATIONS AND SOCIETIES
Bankruptcy, fraud, 11 § 548
Disqualification, judges or justices, 28 § 455
Fraud, bankruptcy, 11 § 548
Judges or justices, disqualification, 28 § 455

REMAND
Bankruptcy, this index

REMOVAL OF CASES OR CAUSES
Bankruptcy, this index

RENT
Bankruptcy, this index

REPARATIONS
Restitution, generally, this index

REPORTS
Bankruptcy, this index
Courts of Appeals, this index

REPRESENTATIVES AND REPRESENTATION
Bankruptcy, this index
Congress, generally, this index

REPURCHASE AGREEMENTS
Bankruptcy, this index

RESERVES
Armed Forces, this index

RESIDENT ALIENS
Aliens, generally, this index

RESTITUTION
Administrative Office of U.S. Courts, Director, powers and duties, 28 § 604
Bankruptcy, discharge, 11 §§ 523, 1328

RETALIATION
Crime Victims, this index
Witnesses, this index

RETIREMENT AND PENSIONS
Annuities, generally, this index
Bankruptcy, this index
Funds,
    Embezzlement, interception of wire, oral, or electronic communications, 18 § 2516
    Interception of wire, oral, or electronic communications, embezzlement, 18 § 2516
Judges or Justices, this index

RETURNS
Bankruptcy, this index

RHODE ISLAND
Bankruptcy, judges or justices, appointments, 28 § 152
United States trustees of judicial districts, appointment, 28 § 581

RICE
Bankruptcy, 11 § 557
Commodity Exchanges, generally, this index

RICO
Racketeering, generally, this index

RICO ACT
Generally, 18 § 1961 et seq.
Racketeering, generally, this index

RIOTS AND MOBS
Interception of wire, oral, or electronic communications, 18 § 2516

ROBBERY
Interception of wire, oral, or electronic communications, 18 § 2516
Racketeering, generally, this index

RULES OF BANKRUPTCY
Bankruptcy, generally, this index

RULES OF COURT
Court of Appeals for Sixth Circuit, generally, this index

RYE
Bankruptcy, 11 § 557
Commodity Exchanges, generally, this index

SABOTAGE
Aircraft, this index
Planes. Aircraft, this index

SAINT CROIX
Virgin Islands, generally, this index

SAINT JOHN
Virgin Islands, generally, this index

SAINT THOMAS
Virgin Islands, generally, this index

SALES
Bankruptcy, this index
Commodity Exchanges, generally, this index
Controlled Substances, this index

SANATORIUMS
Hospitals, generally, this index

SAVINGS ACCOUNTS
Coverdell education savings accounts, bankruptcy, 11 §§ 521, 541

SAVINGS ASSOCIATIONS
Bankruptcy, liquidation, 11 § 109

SAVINGS BANKS AND INSTITUTIONS
Bankruptcy, 11 § 109

SCHOLARSHIPS
Bankruptcy,
    Discharge, 11 § 523

INDEX

Fraud, exemptions, **11 § 522**
Fraud, bankruptcy, exemptions, **11 § 522**

SCHOOLS AND SCHOOL DISTRICTS
Income tax, education individual retirement accounts, bankruptcy, **11 §§ 521, 541**
Postsecondary education and schools. Colleges and Universities, generally, this index

SEARCHES AND SEIZURES
Bankruptcy, this index
Interception of Wire, Oral, or Electronic Communications, generally, this index

SECRET SERVICE
Credit cards and plates, fraud, **18 § 2516**
Fraud, credit cards and plates, **18 § 2516**

SECRETARIES
Bankruptcy, judges or justices, **28 § 156**
Judges or Justices, this index

SECRETARY OF AGRICULTURE
Assassination, **18 § 2516**
Assault and battery, interception of wire, oral, or electronic communications, **18 § 2516**
Kidnapping, interception of wire, oral, or electronic communications, **18 § 2516**

SECRETARY OF COMMERCE
Assassination, **18 § 2516**
Assault and battery, interception of wire, oral, or electronic communications, **18 § 2516**
Kidnapping, interception of wire, oral, or electronic communications, **18 § 2516**

SECRETARY OF DEFENSE
Assassination, **18 § 2516**
Assault and battery, interception of wire, oral, or electronic communications, **18 § 2516**
Kidnapping, interception of wire, oral, or electronic communications, **18 § 2516**

SECRETARY OF EDUCATION
Assassination, **18 § 2516**
Assault and battery, interception of wire, oral, or electronic communications, **18 § 2516**
Kidnapping, interception of wire or oral communications, **18 § 2516**

SECRETARY OF ENERGY
Assassination, **18 § 2516**
Assault and battery, interception of wire, oral, or electronic communications, **18 § 2516**
Kidnapping, interception of wire, oral, or electronic communications, **18 § 2516**

SECRETARY OF HEALTH AND HUMAN SERVICES
Assassination, interception of wire, oral, or electronic communications, **18 § 2516**
Assault and battery, interception of wire, oral, or electronic communications, **18 § 2516**
Kidnapping, interception of wire, oral, or electronic communications, **18 § 2516**

SECRETARY OF HOUSING AND URBAN DEVELOPMENT
Assassination, **18 § 2516**
Assault and battery, interception of wire, oral, or electronic communications, **18 § 2516**

Bankruptcy, mortgage or deed of trust, **11 § 362**
Kidnapping, interception of wire, oral, or electronic communications, **18 § 2516**

SECRETARY OF LABOR
Assassinations, **18 § 2516**
Assault and battery, interception of wire, oral, or electronic communications, **18 § 2516**
Kidnapping, interception of wire, oral, or electronic communications, **18 § 2516**

SECRETARY OF STATE
Assassination, **18 § 2516**
Assault and battery, interception of wire, oral, or electronic communications, **18 § 2516**
Kidnapping, wiretapping, **18 § 2516**

SECRETARY OF THE INTERIOR
Assassination, **18 § 2516**
Assault and battery, interception of wire, oral, or electronic communications, **18 § 2516**
Kidnapping, interception of wire, oral, or electronic communications, **18 § 2516**

SECRETARY OF THE TREASURY
Assassination, **18 § 2516**
Assault and battery, interception of wire, oral, or electronic communications, **18 § 2516**
Bankruptcy, reorganization, **11 § 1126**
Kidnapping, interception of wire, oral, or electronic communications, **18 § 2516**

SECRETARY OF TRANSPORTATION
Assassination, **18 § 2516**
Assault and battery, interception of wire, oral, or electronic communications, **18 § 2516**
Kidnapping, interception of wire, oral, or electronic communications, **18 § 2516**

SECURITIES
Bankruptcy, this index
Equity security holders. Bankruptcy, this index
National securities association, bankruptcy, **11 § 555**
Repurchase agreements, **11 § 559**

SECURITIES AND EXCHANGE COMMISSION
Privileges and immunities, witnesses, **18 § 6001 et seq.**
Witnesses, privileges and immunities, **18 § 6001 et seq.**

SECURITY
United States Marshals Service, **28 § 604**

SECURITY INTEREST
Aircraft, this index
Bankruptcy, this index
Planes. Aircraft, this index

SELF-EMPLOYMENT
Bankruptcy, **11 § 1304**

SELF-INCRIMINATION
Bankruptcy, this index

SENATE
Judges or justices, disability, appointments, **28 § 372**

INDEX

SENTENCE AND PUNISHMENT
Bankruptcy, 18 § 152 et seq.
Restitution, generally, this index
Witnesses, this index

SETOFF AND COUNTERCLAIM
Bankruptcy, this index

SEXUAL EXPLOITATION
Children and Minors, this index

SHARES AND SHAREHOLDERS
Bankruptcy, this index
Bonus, bankruptcy, payment, 11 § 522

SHIPS AND SHIPPING
Bankruptcy, this index
Interception of wire, oral, or electronic communications, theft, 18 § 2516

SIGNATURES
Bankruptcy, this index

SILVER
Commodity Exchanges, generally, this index

SKILLED NURSING FACILITIES
Nursing Homes, generally, this index

SLAVERY
Human trafficking. Trafficking, this index
Trafficking, human trafficking. Trafficking, this index

SMALL BUSINESS INVESTMENT COMPANIES
Bankruptcy, liquidation, 11 § 109

SMALL BUSINESSES
Bankruptcy, this index

SMALLPOX
Interception of wire, oral, or electronic communications, 18 § 2516

SMUGGLING
Aliens, this index
Immigration, this index

SOCIAL SECURITY
Bankruptcy, this index

SOCIAL SERVICES
Secretary of Health and Human Services, generally, this index

SOLICITATION
Bankruptcy, this index

SORGHUMS
Bankruptcy, 11 § 557
Commodity Exchanges, generally, this index

SOUTH CAROLINA
Bankruptcy, judges or justices, appointments, 28 § 152
United States trustees, judicial districts, appointment, 28 § 581

SOUTH DAKOTA
Bankruptcy, judges or justices, appointments, 28 § 152
Judicial districts, United States trustees, 28 § 581

United States trustees, judicial districts, 28 § 581

SOVEREIGN IMMUNITY
Bankruptcy, abrogation, 11 § 106

SOYBEANS
Bankruptcy, 11 § 557

SPEEDY TRIAL
Trial, this index

STATE DEPARTMENT
Secretary of State, generally, this index

STATE LAWS
Gambling, crimes and offenses, interception of wire, oral, or electronic communications, 18 § 2516
Syndicated gambling, crimes and offenses, interception of wire, oral or electronic communications, 18 § 2516
Trusts and trustees, United States courts, 28 § 959

STATES
Bankruptcy, this index
Connecticut, generally, this index
Laws. State Laws, generally, this index
New York, generally, this index
South Dakota, generally, this index
Statutes. State Laws, generally, this index

STATISTICS
Bankruptcy, this index
Savings and loan associations, 28 § 604

STATUTES
State Laws, generally, this index

STAY OF PROCEEDINGS
Automatic stay. Bankruptcy, this index
Bankruptcy, this index

STENOGRAPHERS
Administrative Office of United States Courts, compensation and salaries, 28 § 604
Compensation and salaries, Administrative Office of United
States Courts, 28 § 604

STOLEN PROPERTY
Interception of wire, oral, or electronic communications, 18 § 2516
Motor Vehicles, this index
Racketeering, generally, this index
Transportation, interception of wire, oral, or electronic communications, 18 § 2516

STUDENTS
Colleges and Universities, generally, this index

SUBPOENAS
Arbitration, 28 § 656
Bankruptcy, this index

SUBROGATION
Bankruptcy, this index

SUBSISTENCE
Administrative Office of U.S. Courts, 28 § 604
Court officers and employees, 28 § 604
Judges or Justices, this index
Judicial Center, officers and employees, 28 § 604

INDEX

SUBSTANCE ABUSE
Controlled Substances, generally, this index

SULFONDIETHYLMETHANE
Controlled Substances, generally, this index

SULFONETHYLMETHANE
Controlled Substances, generally, this index

SULFONMETHANE
Controlled Substances, generally, this index

SUMMONS
Bankruptcy, this index

SUPPLIES
Courts, Administrative Office of United States Courts, 28 § 604

SUPPORT
Bankruptcy, this index
Children born out of wedlock, bankruptcy, relief from automatic stay, 11 § 362
Paternity, bankruptcy, relief from automatic stay, 11 § 362

SUPREME COURT
Bankruptcy, 28 § 2075
Chief Judge or Justice, handicapped persons, certificates and certification, 28 § 372
Compensation and salaries, Chief Judge or Justice, disability retirement, 28 § 372
Handicapped persons, retirement and pensions, 28 § 372
Justices,
    Assassination, interception of wire, oral, or electronic communications, 18 § 2516
    Handicapped persons, certificate of disability, 28 § 372
Witnesses, privileges and immunities, 18 § 6001 et seq.

SURCHARGE
Bankruptcy, custodians, 11 § 543

SURFACE TRANSPORTATION BOARD
Privileges and immunities, witnesses, 18 § 6001 et seq.
Witnesses, privileges and immunities, 18 § 6001 et seq.

SWAP AGREEMENTS
Bankruptcy, this index

SYNDICATED GAMBLING
Gambling, this index

TAX COURT
United States Tax Court, generally, this index

TAXATION
Bankruptcy, this index
Fuel, this index
Income Tax, generally, this index
United States Tax Court, generally, this index

TELECOMMUNICATIONS
Interception of Wire, Oral, or Electronic Communications, generally, this index
Wiretapping. Interception of Wire, Oral, or Electronic Communications, generally, this index

TELEVISION AND RADIO
Bankruptcy, this index
Interception of Wire, Oral, or Electronic Communications, this index

TENANTS
Landlord and Tenant, generally, this index

TENANTS IN COMMON
Bankruptcy, sales, 11 § 363

TENEMENTS
Landlord and Tenant, generally, this index

TENNESSEE
Bankruptcy, judges or justices, appointments, 28 § 152
United States trustees, judicial districts, appointment, 28 § 581

TERMINALLY ILL
Hospices, generally, this index

TERRITORIES
Guam, generally, this index
Northern Mariana Islands, generally, this index
Virgin Islands, generally, this index

TERRORISTS AND TERRORISM
Interception of wire, oral, or electronic communications, 18 § 2516
Racketeering, 18 § 1961

TESTS
Bankruptcy, this index

TETRAHYDROCANNABINOLS
Controlled Substances, generally, this index

TEXAS
Bankruptcy, judges or justices, appointments, 28 § 152
United States trustees, judicial districts, appointments, 28 § 581

THEBACON
Controlled Substances, generally, this index

THIRD PARTIES
Bankruptcy, this index

THREATS
Business and commerce, interference, 18 § 2516

TIMESHARES
Bankruptcy, this index

TIN (TAXPAYER IDENTIFICATION NUMBER)
Bankruptcy, this index

TITLE TO PROPERTY
Bankruptcy, this index

TOLUENE
Controlled Substances, generally, this index

TOYS
Bankruptcy, exemptions, 11 § 522

TRADE SECRETS
Bankruptcy, this index

INDEX

TRADEMARKS AND TRADE NAMES
Trafficking, interception of wire, oral, or electronic communications, 18 § 2516

TRAFFICKING
Cigarettes and Cigars, this index
Drugs and Medicine, this index
Human trafficking, racketeering, 18 § 1961
Racketeering, traffickers in persons, 18 § 1961
Trademarks and Trade Names, this index

TRAINS
Railroads, generally, this index

TRANSCRIPTS
Bankruptcy, this index

TRANSPORTATION
Aircraft, generally, this index
Expenses and expenditures. Traveling Expenses, generally, this index
Mass transportation. Railroads, generally, this index
Planes. Aircraft, generally, this index
Railroads, generally, this index
Secretary of Commerce, generally, this index
Secretary of Transportation, generally, this index
Stolen Property, this index

TRANSPORTATION DEPARTMENT
Bankruptcy, railroads, appearances, 11 § 1164
Secretary of Transportation, generally, this index

TRANSPORTATION SECRETARY
Secretary of Transportation, generally, this index

TRAVELING EXPENSES
Administrative Office of United States Courts, this index
Arbitration, 28 § 658
Bankruptcy, this index
Court officers and employees, 28 § 604
Judges or Justices, this index
Judicial Center, this index
National Bankruptcy Review Commission, 11 nt prec § 101

TREASON
Interception of wire, oral, or electronic communications, 18 § 2516

TREASURY DEPARTMENT
Secretary of the Treasury, generally, this index

TREASURY OF UNITED STATES
Bankruptcy, this index

TREASURY SECRETARY
Secretary of the Treasury, generally, this index

TREATIES
Bankruptcy, 11 § 1503

TRIAL
Bankruptcy, this index
Disqualification, judges or justices, 28 § 455
Judges or justices, disqualification, 28 § 455
Jury, generally, this index
Speedy trial, 28 § 604

TRIBUNALS
Courts, generally, this index

TRIMEPERIDINE
Controlled Substances, generally, this index

TRUST TERRITORY OF PACIFIC ISLANDS
Northern Mariana Islands, generally, this index

TRUSTS AND TRUSTEES
Bankruptcy, this index
Justice Department, United States trustees, bankruptcy, 28 § 581 et seq.
United States trustees. Bankruptcy, this index

TUNNELS
United States. Mexico, this index

UNEMPLOYMENT COMPENSATION
Bankruptcy, exemptions, 11 § 522

UNITED STATES
Agents and agencies. Federal Agencies, generally, this index
Boundaries,
    Mexico, this index
    Tunnels. Mexico, this index
Claims. Court of Federal Claims, generally, this index
Courts, generally, this index
Hawaii, this index
Marshals. United States Marshals Service, generally, this index
Officers and employees. Federal Officers and Employees, generally, this index
President of the United States, generally, this index
Tunnels. Mexico, this index

UNITED STATES ARMED FORCES
Armed Forces, generally, this index

UNITED STATES ATTORNEYS
Bankruptcy, this index
Investigations, bankruptcy, 18 § 3057

UNITED STATES COURT OF FEDERAL CLAIMS
Court of Federal Claims, generally, this index

UNITED STATES COURT OF INTERNATIONAL TRADE
International Trade Court, generally, this index

UNITED STATES COURTS OF APPEALS
Courts of Appeals, generally, this index

UNITED STATES DISTRICT COURTS
District Courts, generally, this index

UNITED STATES INSTRUMENTALITY
Federal Agencies, generally, this index

UNITED STATES JUDGES OR JUSTICES
Judges or Justices, generally, this index

UNITED STATES MAGISTRATE JUDGES
Appeal and review, disqualification, 28 § 455
Compensation and salaries, 28 § 604
Conflict of interest, 28 § 455
Courtrooms, 28 § 604
Definitions, disqualification, 28 § 455
Discipline, 28 § 372
Disqualification, 28 § 455
Judicial Conference of the United States,

INDEX

Evaluations, 28 § 604
Rules and regulations, 28 § 604
Law books, 28 § 604
Manuals, 28 § 604
Part-time Magistrate Judges, 28 § 604
Records and recordation, preservation, 28 § 604
Reports, 28 § 604
Security, courtrooms, 28 § 604
Statistics, 28 § 604
Supervision, 28 § 604
Supplies, 28 § 604
Waiver, disqualification, 28 § 455

UNITED STATES MARSHALS SERVICE
Administrative Office of U.S. Courts, disbursements, 28 § 604
Bankruptcy, this index
Disbursements, Administrative Office of U.S. Courts, 28 § 604
Security, 28 § 604

UNITED STATES OFFICERS AND EMPLOYEES
Federal Officers and Employees, generally, this index

UNITED STATES TAX COURT
Attorneys,
Bankruptcy, 28 § 1452
Debtors and creditors, automatic stay, petitions, 11 § 362
Bankruptcy,
Attorneys, 28 § 1452
Automatic stay, 11 § 362
Removal of cases or causes, 28 § 1452
Privileges and immunities, witnesses, 18 § 6001 et seq.
Removal of cases or causes, bankruptcy, 28 § 1452
Witnesses, privileges and immunities, 18 § 6001 et seq.

UNITED STATES TRUSTEES
Bankruptcy, this index

UNIVERSITIES
Colleges and Universities, generally, this index

UNLAWFUL DETAINER
Bankruptcy, automatic stay, 11 § 362

UNLAWFUL RESTRAINT
Kidnapping, generally, this index

USURY
Bankruptcy, defenses, 11 § 558
Defenses, bankruptcy, 11 § 558
Interception of wire, oral, or electronic communications, 18 § 2516

UTAH
Bankruptcy, judges or justices, appointments, 28 § 152
United States trustees, judicial districts, appointments, 28 § 581

VENUE
Bankruptcy, this index
President of the United States, this index

VERMONT
Bankruptcy, judges or justices, appointments, 28 § 152

VETERANS
Bankruptcy, this index
Benefits, bankruptcy, exemptions, 11 § 522

VICE PRESIDENT OF THE UNITED STATES
Assassination, interception of wire, oral, or electronic communications, 18 § 2516
Kidnapping, interception of wire, oral, or electronic communications, 18 § 2516
Officers and employees, interception of wire, oral, or electronic communications, 18 § 2516

VICTIMS
Crime Victims, generally, this index

VIDEO
Bankruptcy, exemptions, video cassette recorders, 11 § 522

VIRGIN ISLANDS
Compensation and salaries, district courts, judges or justices, 28 § 604
District courts,
Compensation and salaries, judges or justices, 28 § 604
Judges or justices, compensation and salaries, 28 § 604
Judges or justices, compensation and salaries, district courts, 28 § 604
United States trustees of judicial districts, 28 § 581
Witnesses, privileges and immunities, 18 § 6001 et seq.

VIRGINIA
Bankruptcy, judges or justices, appointments, 28 § 152

VISAS
Wiretapping, investigations and investigators, 18 § 2516

VOLUNTARY PROCEEDINGS
Bankruptcy, this index

WAREHOUSES AND WAREHOUSEMEN
Bankruptcy, liens and incumbrances, avoidance, 11 § 546
Liens and incumbrances, bankruptcy, avoidance, 11 § 546

WARRANTS
Bankruptcy, automatic stay, setoff and counterclaim, 11 § 553

WASHINGTON (STATE)
Bankruptcy, judges or justices, appointments, 28 § 152
United States trustees, judicial districts, appointments, 28 § 581

WEST VIRGINIA
Bankruptcy, judges or justices, appointments, 28 § 152

WHEAT
Bankruptcy, 11 § 557

INDEX

WHITE HOUSE
Officers and employees,
    Assassination, 18 § 2516
    Assault and battery, 18 § 2516
    Interception of wire, oral, or electronic communications, 18 § 2516
    Kidnapping, 18 § 2516

WIRETAP
Interception of Wire, Oral, or Electronic Communications, generally, this index

WISCONSIN
Bankruptcy, judges or justices, appointments, 28 § 152
United States trustees of judicial districts, appointment, 28 § 581

WITNESSES
Bankruptcy, this index
Bribery and corruption, interception of wire, oral, or electronic communications, 18 § 2516
Commodity Exchanges, this index
Court of Federal Claims, this index
District Courts, this index
Federal Agencies, this index
Federal Maritime Commission, this index
Federal Trade Commission, this index
Influencing, interception of wire, oral, or electronic communications, 18 § 2516
Injuring, interception of wire, oral, or electronic communications, 18 § 2516
Interception of wire, oral, or electronic communications, 18 § 2516
International Trade Court, this index
Judges or Justices, this index
Military Departments, this index
National Transportation Safety Board, this index
Privileges and immunities, 18 § 6001 et seq.
    Definitions, 18 § 6001
Retaliation, interception of wire, oral, or electronic communications, 18 § 2516
Securities and Exchange Commission, this index
Sentence and punishment, disclosure, relocation, 18 § 2516
Surface Transportation Board, this index
Tampering, interception of wire, oral, or electronic communications, 18 § 2516
United States Tax Court, this index
Virgin Islands, this index

WOOL
Commodity Exchanges, generally, this index

WORDS AND PHRASES
Accountant, bankruptcy, 11 § 101
Act, bankruptcy, commodity brokers, 11 § 761
Adequate information, bankruptcy, reorganization, postpetition, 11 § 1125
Affiliates, bankruptcy, 11 § 101
Agency of the United States, Federal Maritime Commission, witnesses, privileges and immunities, 18 § 6001
Alternative dispute resolution, district courts, 28 § 651
Amount reaffirmed, bankruptcy, reaffirmation agreements, 11 § 524
Annual percentage rate, bankruptcy, reaffirmation agreements, 11 § 524

Applicable commitment period, bankruptcy, individual debtors, confirmation of plan, 11 § 1325
Assisted living facility, bankruptcy, 11 § 101
Assisted person, bankruptcy, 11 § 101
Assurance of payment, public utilities, bankruptcy, 11 § 366
Attorney, bankruptcy, 11 § 101
Attorney General, racketeer influenced and corrupt organizations, 18 § 1961
Authorized representative, bankruptcy, reorganization, retirement and pensions, 11 § 1114
Avoidable preferences, bankruptcy, 11 § 547
Bankruptcy, patient, 11 § 101
Bankruptcy assistance, 11 § 101
Bankruptcy petition preparers, 11 § 110; 18 § 156
Board,
    Clearing banks, bankruptcy, liquidation, 11 § 781
    Railroads, bankruptcy, 11 § 1162
Board of Trade, bankruptcy, commodity brokers, 11 § 761
Cash collateral, bankruptcy, trusts and trustees, 11 § 363
Cause, bankruptcy, dismissal and nonsuit, 11 § 1112
Charitable contribution, bankruptcy, 11 § 548
Claim, bankruptcy, 11 § 101
Clearing bank, bankruptcy, liquidation, 11 § 781
Clearing organization, bankruptcy, commodity brokers, 11 § 761
Commercial fishing operation, bankruptcy, 11 § 101
Commercial fishing vessel, bankruptcy, 11 § 101
Commission, bankruptcy,
    Commodity brokers, 11 § 761
    Stockbrokers, 11 § 741
Commodity, bankruptcy, brokers, 11 § 751
Commodity broker, bankruptcy, 11 § 101
Commodity contracts, bankruptcy, commodity brokers, 11 § 761
Commodity option, bankruptcy, commodity brokers, 11 § 761
Commodity option dealer, bankruptcy, commodity brokers, 11 § 761
Community claim, bankruptcy, 11 § 101
Consumer debt, bankruptcy, 11 § 101
Contract market, bankruptcy, commodity brokers, 11 § 761
Contract of sale, bankruptcy, commodity brokers, 11 § 761
Contractual right, bankruptcy,
    Commodities, 11 § 556
    Master agreements, 11 § 561
    Repurchase agreements, 11 § 559
    Securities, 11 § 555
    Swap agreements, 11 § 560
Conveyances, bankruptcy, fraud, 11 § 548
Cooperation, bankruptcy, foreign countries, 11 § 1527
Core proceedings, bankruptcy, 28 § 157
Corporation, bankruptcy, 11 § 101
Court of the United States, witnesses, privileges and immunities, 18 § 6001
Creditor, bankruptcy, 11 § 101
Current monthly income, bankruptcy, dismissal and nonsuit, 11 § 707

INDEX

Custodian, bankruptcy, 11 § 101
Customer, bankruptcy,
    Commodity brokers, 11 § 761
    Stockbrokers, 11 § 741
Customer name securities, bankruptcy,
    stockbrokers, 11 § 741
Customer property, bankruptcy,
    Commodity brokers, 11 § 761
    Stockbrokers, 11 § 741
Debt, bankruptcy, 11 § 101
Debt relief agency, bankruptcy, 11 § 101
Debtor, bankruptcy, 11 § 101
    Crimes and offenses, 18 § 151
    Foreign countries, 11 § 1502
Debtor in possession, bankruptcy, reorganization, 11 § 1101
Debtor's monthly expenses, bankruptcy, dismissal and nonsuit, 11 § 707
Debtor's principal residence, bankruptcy, 11 § 101
Degree of relationship, judges or justices, disqualification, 28 § 455
Demand, bankruptcy discharge, 11 § 524
Dependent, bankruptcy, exemptions, 11 § 522
Depository institution, clearing banks, bankruptcy, liquidation, 11 § 781
Disability, bankruptcy, counseling services, 11 § 109
Disinterested person, bankruptcy, 11 § 101
Disposable income, bankruptcy,
    Family farmers, confirmation of plan, 11 § 1225
    Individual debtors, confirmation of plan, 11 § 1325
Distribution, bankruptcy, retirement and pensions, exemptions, 11 § 522
Document for filing, bankruptcy, 18 § 156
    Preparers, 11 § 110
Documentary material, racketeer influenced and corrupt organizations, 18 § 1961
Domestic support obligation, bankruptcy, 11 § 101
Enterprise, racketeer influenced and corrupt organizations, 18 § 1961
Entity, bankruptcy, 11 § 101
Equity securities, bankruptcy, 11 § 101
Equity security holder, bankruptcy, 11 § 101
Establishment, bankruptcy, foreign countries, 11 § 1502
Estate, bankruptcy, 11 § 101
Fair and equitable, bankruptcy, reorganization, plans and specifications, 11 § 1129
Family farmer, bankruptcy, 11 § 101
Family farmer with regular annual income, bankruptcy, 11 § 101
Family fisherman, bankruptcy, 11 § 101
Family fisherman with regular annual income, bankruptcy, 11 § 101
Farming operation, bankruptcy, 11 § 101
Farmout agreement, bankruptcy, 11 § 101
Federal depository institutions regulatory agency, bankruptcy, 11 § 101
Fiduciary, judges or justices, disqualification, 28 § 455
Financial institution, bankruptcy, 11 § 101
Financial interest, judges or justices, disqualification, 28 § 455
Foreign court, bankruptcy, 11 § 1502
Foreign future, bankruptcy, commodity brokers, 11 § 761

Foreign futures commission merchant, bankruptcy, commodity brokers, 11 § 761
Foreign main proceeding, bankruptcy, 11 § 1502
Foreign nonmain proceeding, bankruptcy, 11 § 1502
Foreign proceeding, bankruptcy, 11 § 101
Foreign representative, bankruptcy, 11 § 101
Forward contract, bankruptcy, 11 § 101
Forward contract merchant, bankruptcy, 11 § 101
Fraudulent transfers, bankruptcy, 11 § 548
Futures commission merchant, bankruptcy, commodity brokers, 11 § 761
Governmental unit, bankruptcy, 11 § 101
Grain, bankruptcy, 11 § 557
Health care business, bankruptcy, 11 § 101
Household goods, bankruptcy, exemptions, 11 § 522
Improvements, bankruptcy, transfers, avoidance, liability, 11 § 550
Incapacity, bankruptcy, counseling services, 11 § 109
Incidental property, bankruptcy, 11 § 101
Indenture, bankruptcy, 11 § 101
Indenture trustee, bankruptcy, 11 § 101
Individual with regular income, bankruptcy, 11 § 101
Insider, bankruptcy, 11 § 101
Insolvent, bankruptcy, 11 § 101
Institution affiliated party, bankruptcy, 11 § 101
Insufficiency, bankruptcy, set-off and counterclaim, 11 § 553
Insured credit union, bankruptcy, 11 § 101
Intellectual property, bankruptcy, 11 § 101
Inventory, bankruptcy, 11 § 547
Investor typical of holders of claims or interest of the relative class, bankruptcy, reorganization, postpetition, 11 § 1125
Judicial lien, bankruptcy, 11 § 101
Lease,
    Aircraft, bankruptcy, 11 § 1110
    Railroads, bankruptcy, reorganization, 11 § 1168
Legal advice, bankruptcy, petitions, preparers, 11 § 110
Lessee, bankruptcy, rejection, 11 § 365
Leverage transaction, bankruptcy, commodity brokers, 11 § 761
Leverage transaction merchant, bankruptcy, commodity brokers, 11 § 761
Lien, bankruptcy, 11 § 101
    Reaffirmation agreements, 11 § 524
Listed chemicals, RICO, 18 § 1961
Luxury goods or services, bankruptcy, discharge, 11 § 523
Margin payment, bankruptcy, 11 § 101
    Commodity brokers, 11 § 761
    Stockbrokers, 11 § 741
Mask work, bankruptcy, 11 § 101
Master netting agreement, bankruptcy, 11 § 101
Master netting agreement participant, bankruptcy, 11 § 101
May, bankruptcy, reaffirmation agreements, 11 § 524
Median family income, bankruptcy, 11 § 101
Member property, bankruptcy, commodity brokers, 11 § 761
Money laundering, racketeering influenced and corrupt organizations, 18 § 1961

INDEX

Municipality, bankruptcy, **11 § 101**
Net equity, bankruptcy,
    Commodity brokers, **11 § 761**
    Stockbrokers, **11 § 741**
New value, bankruptcy, preferences, **11 § 547**
Other information, witnesses, privileges and immunities, **18 § 6001**
Patient, bankruptcy, **11 § 101**
Patient records, bankruptcy, **11 § 101**
Pattern of racketeering activity, **18 § 1961**
Person,
    Bankruptcy, **11 § 101**
    Racketeer influenced and corrupt organizations, **18 § 1961**
Petition, bankruptcy, **11 § 101**
Preferences, bankruptcy, avoidance, **11 § 547**
Priorities and preferences, bankruptcy, avoidance, **11 § 547**
Proceeding, judges or justices, disqualification, **28 § 455**
Proceedings before an agency of the United States, witnesses, privileges and immunities, **18 § 6001**
Producer, grain, bankruptcy, **11 § 557**
Profitability, bankruptcy, **11 § 308**
Property of the estate, bankruptcy,
    Individual debtors, **11 § 1115**
    Municipal debt adjustment, **11 § 902**
Purchaser, bankruptcy, **11 § 101**
Qualified religious or charitable entity or organization, bankruptcy, **11 § 548**
Racketeering activity, **18 § 1961**
Racketeering investigators, **18 § 1961**
Railroad, bankruptcy, **11 § 101**
Receivable, bankruptcy, preferences, **11 § 547**
Recognition, bankruptcy, foreign countries, **11 § 1502**
Reduction payment, bankruptcy, **11 § 101**
Related party, bankruptcy, discharge, **11 § 524**
Relative, bankruptcy, **11 § 101**
Replacement value, bankruptcy, **11 § 506**
Repo participants, bankruptcy, **11 § 101**
Repurchase agreement, bankruptcy, **11 § 101**
Retiree benefits, bankruptcy, reorganization, **11 § 1114**
Returns, bankruptcy,
    Discharge, **11 § 523**
    Prepetition returns, **11 § 1308**
Rolling stock equipment, railroads, bankruptcy, **11 § 1168**
Secured party, railroads, bankruptcy, reorganization, **11 § 1168**
Securities, bankruptcy, **11 § 101**
Securities clearing agency, bankruptcy, **11 § 101**
Securities contract, bankruptcy, stockbrokers, **11 § 741**
Securities self regulatory organization, bankruptcy, **11 § 101**
Security agreement, bankruptcy, **11 § 101**
Security interest,
    Aircraft, bankruptcy, **11 § 1110**
    Bankruptcy, **11 § 101**
Settlement payment, bankruptcy, **11 § 101**
    Stockbrokers, **11 § 741**
Single asset real estate, bankruptcy, **11 § 101**

SIPC, BANKRUPTCY, STOCKBROKERS, 11 § 741
Small business, bankruptcy, chapter 7 proceedings, dismissal and nonsuit, **11 § 707**
Small business case, bankruptcy, **11 § 101**
Small business debtor, bankruptcy, **11 § 101**
Special taxpayer, bankruptcy, municipal debt adjustment, **11 § 902**
Spouse, bankruptcy, municipal debt adjustment, **11 § 902**
State,
    Bankruptcy, **11 § 101**
    Racketeering, **18 § 1961**
Statutory lien, bankruptcy, **11 § 101**
Stockbroker, bankruptcy, **11 § 101**
Student Loan Program, bankruptcy, **11 § 525**
Substantial consummation, bankruptcy, reorganization, **11 § 1101**
Swap agreement, bankruptcy, **11 § 101**
Swap participant, bankruptcy, **11 § 101**
Term overriding royalty, bankruptcy, **11 § 101**
Timeshare interest, bankruptcy, **11 § 101**
Timeshare plan, bankruptcy, **11 § 101**
Transfers, bankruptcy, **11 § 101**
    Fraud, **11 § 548**
    Preferences, avoidance, **11 § 547**
Trustees, bankruptcy,
    Foreign countries, **11 § 1502**
    Municipal debt adjustment, **11 § 902**
    Powers and duties, **11 § 323**
Underwriter, bankruptcy, reorganization, securities, exemptions, **11 § 1145**
Uninsured State member bank, bankruptcy, **11 § 101**
United States, bankruptcy, **11 § 101**
Unlawful debt, racketeer influenced and corrupt organizations, **18 § 1961**
Value, bankruptcy,
    Exemptions, **11 § 522**
    Fraud, **11 § 548**
Within the territorial jurisdiction of the United States, bankruptcy, **11 § 1502**

WRITS
Bankruptcy, this index

WRONGFUL DEATH
Bankruptcy, this index

WYOMING
Bankruptcy, judges or justices, appointments, **28 § 152**
United States trustees, judicial districts, **28 § 581**

YOUTH
Children and Minors, generally, this index